DATE DUE

PIERS PLOWMAN: THE THREE VERSIONS

General Editor

GEORGE KANE

PIERS PLOWMAN: THE B VERSION

WILL'S VISIONS OF PIERS PLOWMAN, DO-WELL, DO-BETTER AND DO-BEST

AN EDITION IN THE FORM OF TRINITY COLLEGE CAMBRIDGE MS B.15.17, CORRECTED AND RESTORED FROM THE KNOWN EVIDENCE, WITH VARIANT READINGS

BY

GEORGE KANE

AND

E. TALBOT DONALDSON

UNIVERSITY OF LONDON
THE ATHLONE PRESS
1975

Published by
THE ATHLONE PRESS
UNIVERSITY OF LONDON
at 4 *Gower Street London* WC1

Distributed by Tiptree Book Services Ltd
Tiptree, Essex

USA and Canada
Humanities Press Inc
New Jersey

ISBN 0 485 13502 7

Printed in Great Britain by
WESTERN PRINTING SERVICES LTD
Bristol

PREFACE

In the sense that we could go on reconsidering a number of its textual cruces indefinitely our edition is not finished. But in an undertaking of this kind a moment comes when the advantages of deferring publication have become slight, and we judge that we have reached it. We will therefore brave the possibility that we shall think of satisfactory answers to the unsolved problems as soon as the book is out. There are a number of formal practices and conventions of presentation in Apparatus and Introduction which we would now like to alter. Some of these we adopted as long as fifteen years ago, at those stages in the editing where they became practical necessities, and we could today with more experience improve them and thus shorten the book by a few pages. But because they have no bearing at all on the readings of the text or on the principles by which these were determined, and because recasting them would be a long slow job involving much risk of inaccuracy, we will not undertake it.

It is first our pleasure to make grateful acknowledgement of the financial support accorded to our work, that is of fellowships awarded by the John Simon Guggenheim Foundation and the American Council of Learned Societies (E.T.D.) and of grants in aid of research from the Leverhulme Trust and the Central Research Fund of the University of London (G.K.).

We have next to thank the Master and Fellows of Trinity College Cambridge for formal permission to publish the text of their *Piers Plowman* manuscript B.15.17, and in addition the Bodleian Library, the Syndics of Cambridge University Library, the British Library Board, the Provost and Fellows of Oriel College, the President and Fellows of Corpus Christi College Oxford, the Principal and Fellows of Newnham College, the Trustees of the Huntington Library, and the President and Court of Governors of Sion College, for permission to publish variant readings and other information from their *Piers Plowman* manuscripts.

We have incurred personal obligations to which we wish to give prominence. The first is to Mrs Annie M. Gregory, Miss Dorothy Rayner, and Mrs Polina Williams for typing our work at various stages. Its scale and the number of copies needed for a transatlantic collaboration made us heavily dependent on their help, for which we express our warmest thanks. Our particular debt is to Mrs Williams who with remarkable steadfastness and accuracy typed not only earlier drafts but the whole book in its final form, meanwhile saving us time and again from our own errors of haste and preoccupation. The second is to Miss Joan Gibbs of the Palæography Room of the University of London Library, whom we single out of an invariably helpful profession for the unusual generosity with which she gave both time and expert knowledge. The third is to our publishers, whose support over the years, both moral and practical, has gone far beyond what we could reasonably have expected. The fourth is to Ronald Waldron for his help with proofreading.

For professional help we are greatly in the debt of three palæographers, Professor T. J. Brown, Dr A. I. Doyle and Dr N. R. Ker. The old notion that simply by undertaking to edit a text a man becomes a palæographer has been discredited in our time with the growth in knowledge and understanding of vernacular manuscripts, and while we think we know how to use these we make no pretence to palæographic expertise; anything in our edition which might seem to suggest it we owe to the patient instruction of these three. Our particular obligation is to Dr Doyle, who read and checked our descriptions of manuscripts. We have made a point of indicating detailed obligations where he protected us against error or showed us something we had missed, but we wish also to make a general expression of gratitude for his most friendly and erudite help.

The amiable and long-suffering editor of the C version, Professor G. H. Russell, whom we have with unremitting mercilessness for years plagued with demands for information, has our special thanks for his good nature. Our references are to his provisional text as it stood in 1973 when we handed over copy. In the cases where we have invoked that text the implication must be that we judge his decisions there to have been correct. But it will be understood that we cannot hold him to them: it would be insufferable for our opinions to deprive him of the right to change his mind.

If convention did not seem to forbid it we would like to end our tale of debts and obligations by thanking each other. We have both found our collaboration over a quarter of a century invariably enjoyable and rewarding. Not that we have always agreed on all issues: far from it! But each of us, priding himself on being a reasonable man, has tended to give way in the face of the other's strongly held opinion—and as often as not has found himself its more active supporter in the end. We have liked to think, from the way we have so often reached the same conclusion by widely various processes, that our minds are complementary. In any event we are glad today that we have done this work together, which one of us first touched in 1939, and to which we set our hands jointly in 1950, knowing little then of what we were undertaking.

At some times it has seemed an almost insupportable burden to be endlessly sustained, at others an irresistible challenge. But looking back we have a sense of great privilege from having been engaged in the restoration of such a noble and splendid work of art. We hope that we may, at least in the taking of pains, have made ourselves equal to it.

G. K.
E. T. D.

CONTENTS

I

THE MANUSCRIPTS

The second version of *Piers Plowman* is known to have survived in the following copies.

Bm *Additional 10574*[1] *British Museum*

S. xiv/xv.[2] 91 vellum leaves containing *Piers Plowman* **C** Prologue 1–II 131, **A** II 90–212,[3] and **B** III 1–XX 354, followed by a paper supply (two leaves, the second blank) completing the poem in the hand of Dr Adam Clarke.[4] Collation $1–3^{12}4^{4}5–8^{12}9$ three (imperfect). Foliation modern 1–91. All catchwords and many signatures, of which there are two distinct systems, have survived cropping. The unusual fourth gathering of 2 bifolia is unmistakable.[5] The loss from the final gathering (now fols 89–91, signatured *a*, *b*, *c*) was early. Flyleaves and binding modern. Size[6] of page 25 × 17 cm, of frame 19.75 × 12.75 cm. Average of 40 lines per side.[7] 'Paragraphs' not spaced, but set off by red and blue or red or blue parasigns. Hand anglicana formata.[8] Ornamental pen-drawn capitals in red and/or blue at passus beginnings. Line initials touched with red; Latin and occasional English expressions in red or underlined in red. No running titles; marginal *nota*'s and subject pointers variously in English or Latin by main scribe. Corrections, by him and others, relatively sparse. Some sixteenth-century marginalia. On fol. 91b lower margin 'Brought from Kelsey xxvj° octob anno xxxiiij° Rhviij^{ui} *per* me Ion Thynne'.

[1] See Clarke, J. B. B., *Catalogue of Dr Clarke's MSS*, London, 1835, p. 60; Skeat, W. W., *The Vision of William concerning Piers the Plowman,... The 'Crowley' Text; or Text B*, EETS 38, London 1869 and repr., pp. xxvi, xxvii.

[2] We follow in this notation Ker, Neil, *Medieval Manuscripts in British Libraries, I, London*, Oxford, 1969, p. vii.

[3] In this area the most prominent difference between **A** and **B** confidently identfiable as authorial occurs in **B** II 174–6 and 209, 210; there Bm's text agrees with that of **A**. In particular Bm agrees with one **A** manuscript, H^2, in several eccentricities. E.g., like that copy, a conjoint **AC** manuscript, it reads a scribal expansion of **A** II 168. It agrees with H^2 in the reading for **A** II 190b, and like H^2 has a spurious line at this point. Bo (Bodley MS 814) and Cot (B.M.MS Cotton Caligula A XI) share this character. See below, pp. 2, 5.

[4] See Skeat, *B-Text*, p. xxvi, and *DNB*, iv, pp. 413, 414. The text of this supply agrees even in details of spelling (allowing for modernization of *þ* and *ȝ*) with that of Hm (Huntington Library MS 128: see below, pp. 9, 10.).

[5] It comprises ff. 37a–40b: 37a, 38a, 39a are signatured *cj*, *cij*, *ciij*, the last struck through; there is a catchword on 40b. It is notable that Bo also has this irregular feature.

[6] *Here and in all following descriptions measurements should be taken as approximate.*

[7] The page content of Bm and Bo (see n. 5 above) was apparently intended to correspond. There is a difference of a line one way or another from 2b to 11b, after which uniformity is maintained.

[8] We use the terminology of Parkes, M. B., *English Cursive Book Hands: 1250–1500*, Oxford, 1969. The hand of Bm occasionally varies, as for instance on fols 20b, 21a, 23b, 28b, 31b, 35a, but is probably that of a single scribe (A. I. Doyle).

Bo *Bodley 814*[9] *Bodleian Library S.C.2683*

S. xiv/xv. 94 leaves containing *Piers Plowman* **C** Prologue 1–II 131, **A** II 90–212 and **B** III 1–XX 386;[10] the last two blank. Collation iii + 1–3¹²4⁴5–8¹²9⁶ + iv.[11] Foliation ink early modern 1–93. Most catchwords and signatures intact.[12] Binding *s. xvi/xvii* board and leather, flyleaves paper.[13] Size of page 25 × 17 cm, of frame 19 × 13 cm. Average of 40 lines per side.[14] Alternate blue and red parasigns. Two distinct anglicana formata hands, the second covering the small fourth gathering (fols 37–40) and most of the last three (fols 65ff). Ornamental capitals like those of Bm. Latin in Hand I engrossed; throughout in red or underlined in red. No running titles. A few marginal *nota*'s and subject pointers, mainly in two sixteenth-century hands, in the earlier part. Some correction by the main scribe, more often within the text than marginal. On fol. 93a in one sixteenth-century hand the names 'John Thomas, London', 'John Thomas of Tichefilde', and 'Henrye theighte', and in another the name of an owner, 'thomas hobsun'.

C *Dd. 1. 17*[15] *Cambridge University Library*

S. *xiv/xv*. 420 vellum leaves with the following contents:[16] fol. 2a Higden, *Polychronicon*;[17] fol. 111a Geoffrey of Monmouth, *Historia Britonum*; fol. 121a 'Letter of Henry of Huntington to King Henry'; fol. 122b Jean Turpin, *De Vita Caroli Magni*; fol. 129a Martin Polonius, *Chronica*; fol. 159a 'A brief chronicle of the Kings of England'; fol. 160b Guido delle Colonne, *Historia Troiana*; fol. 203b 'Prophecy of John of Lignano'; fol. 204a Jaques de Vitri, *Historia Hierosolimitana*; fol. 231a Jacobus de Theramo, *Consolatio Peccatorum*; then[18] fol. 1a *Testamentum Patriarcharum*; fol. 6a a Latin prayer; fol. 6a a compilation of Henry of Huntington, Simeon of Durham and Florence of Worcester; fol. 38b Marco Polo, *De Statu et Consuetudinibus Orientalium Regionum*; fol. 56a Friar Hayton, *Flos ystoriarum terrae orientis*; fol. 71a *De Fide Saracenorum*; fol. 71a *Gesta Machometi*; fol.

[9] See Skeat, *B-Text*, pp. xxv, xxvi, and Madan, F. and H. Craster, *A Summary Catalogue of Western Manuscripts in the Bodleian Library*, ii pt 1 (1922), pp. 491, 492.

[10] The composite text of Bo agrees minutely with those of Bm (see above) and Cot (see below, p. 5). Bm and Bo are certainly from the same workshop, on this and other grounds. The relation of the three manuscripts is discussed below, pp. 40–42.

[11] Bo's collation resembles that of Bm even in the unusually small fourth gathering. Bo like Bm has signatures running *i–iij* here (fols 37–9), the third similarly cancelled; also a catchword on 40b.

[12] There is an additional signature system on the leaves written by the second hand (A. I. Doyle).

[13] The watermarks are of the hand-and-flower type represented by Briquet 11037, 11048, dated 1595, 1600.

[14] The correspondence of the page content of Bm and Bo is to be recalled: see n. 7 above.

[15] See Halliwell, J. O., *Manuscript Rarities of the University of Cambridge*, London, 1841, pp. 3, 4; *A Catalogue of the Manuscripts Preserved in the Library of the University of Cambridge*, i, Cambridge, 1856, pp. 15–26; Skeat, *B-Text*, pp. xxiii–xxv; Brunner, K., *The Seven Sages of Rome*, EETS 191, London, 1933, p. x; Bennett, J. W., *The Rediscovery of Sir John Mandeville*, New York, 1954, p. 289; Seymour, M. C., 'The English Manuscripts of *Mandeville's Travels*', *Edinburgh Bibliographical Society Transactions* iv, 5 (1966), pp. 179, 180.

[16] We have neither the competence nor the room to do justice to the contents of this manuscript, which await study by an expert in medieval historiography. Our list leans heavily on manuscript accounts most handsomely made available to us in the Cambridge University Library.

[17] Formerly bound as the last item: see *A Catalogue*, p. 26; and Taylor, J., *The Universal Chronicle of Ranulf Higden*, Oxford, 1966, pp. 122, 123.

[18] The manuscript is foliated as if in three parts: see below, n. 22.

74b William of Tripoli, *De Statu Saracenorum*; fol. 79a *Ortus et processus Mochometi*; fol. 83a Gildas, *De Excidio Britanniae*; then, fol. 1a the **B** version of *Piers Plowman*; fol. 31a 'Visiting the Sick' *incip.* 'my dere sone or doughter in god it semes þat thow hiest the fast' *explic.* 'in thy merciful handes I put it Amen Amen';[19] fol. 32b Mandeville, *Journey to the Holy Land*;[20] fol. 54a *The Seven Sages of Rome*;[21] fol. 63b Clement of Lanthony, *Concordia Evangelistarum.* Collation:[22] i + 1^{12} (lacks 1) $2–5^{12}6^{12}$ (lacks 7) $7,8^{12}$ 9^{12} (lacks 2–12) 10^{12} (lacks 1,2) 11^{12} 12^{12} (lacks 6,7) $13–21^{12}$ 22^{10} (lacks 10) 23 lost[23] 24^{12} 25^{12} (plus an insertion) $26–9^{12}$ 30^{12} (lacks 8–10) 31^{12} (lacks 10–12) $32–4^{12}$ 35^{12} (lacks 1) $36–8^{12}$ 39^{8} (lacks 4–8) + i. Flyleaves vellum. Various attempts at foliation, the only serviceable one top right recto in three series: I 1–66, 68–97, 111–37, 140–261; II 1–14, 14*, 15–79, 89–93; III 1–36, 38–87. Binding modern. Average size of page 44 × 30.5 cm. Text throughout in double columns. Average size of column frame in Latin texts 32.5 × 9 cm; in *Piers* and 'Visiting the Sick' 32.3 × 11.3 cm; in Mandeville 32.3 × 9.2 cm; in *Seven Sages* 32.5 × 6.5 cm. Number of lines per page of Latin text 66–74, of English 60 or 61, oftener the latter. Probably one scribe, writing a text-hand in the Latin contents and an anglicana formata in the English part (the incipits[24] and Latin quotations here in bastard anglicana); for the last item, in Latin, he reverts to the first hand. The *Piers* text not paragraphed but set off by alternate red and blue parasigns, as also in Mandeville and *Seven Sages*. Much rubrication in the Latin part; in the English one running heads, Latin elements, important words and proper names boxed in red. Blue and red pen-drawn capitals of uniform style but various size and elaboration throughout; decorated cartouches for catchwords throughout. Various running heads. On front flyleaf recto in a sixteenth-century hand a Latin table of contents. The names Robert Morrys or Roberte and Jane Staford or Stafford occur on fols 3rd ser. 34a,44b,63a, and 3rd ser. 96b respectively. The manuscript was no. 289 in the collection of Bishop Moore, presented by George I in 1715. Its connexion with Glastonbury has recently been authoritatively denied.[25]

[19] Horstmann, C., *Yorkshire Writers: Richard Rolle of Hampole*, ii, London, 1896, pp. 449, 450. Compare Wells, J. E., *A Manual of the Writings in Middle English: 1050–1400*, New Haven, 1926, p. 360.

[20] See Wells, *Manual*, pp. 433–7 and Bennett and Seymour, op. cit.

[21] *IMEV* 3187, and see Brunner, op. cit.

[22] This collation was made for us by Mr H. Pink of the Cambridge University Library in 1965 when the binding of the manuscript was about to be repaired. We are greatly obliged to him for his help in this as in many other matters. We have, however, modified his notation which followed the system of signatures adopted by Henry Bradshaw when preparing the manuscript for rebinding in 1862. Bradshaw treated it as if composed of three distinct volumes, but we can find no grounds for doing so; the indications of layout, handwriting, ornament and content are that it was meant to be a single great book, differentiated only in handwriting according to whether the local text was in Latin or English.

[23] There is evidence for this loss from signatures and from the table of contents.

[24] We have taken the liberty of extending the meaning of this term to include passus headings and explicits.

[25] Ker, N. R., *Medieval Libraries of Great Britain*, 2nd edn, London, 1964, p. 335. The language of the English texts in the manuscript supports his view. The northernisms were imposed by the scribe of C; this appears from their diminishing frequency as the poem goes on. Had he been eliminating them from an exemplar in a Northern dialect we would expect the opposite. 'The Glastonbury attribution presumably comes from the edition of Gildas by Josselyn, London, 1568, where the more recent of the two copies used is said to come from there, and must be this manuscript' (A. I. Doyle, who also draws our attention to Bromwich, J., 'The First Book Printed in Anglo-Saxon Types', *Transactions of the Cambridge Bibliographical Society*, iii (1959–63), pp. 273, 274).

C^2 *Ll. 4. 14*[26] *Cambridge University Library*

S. xv[1]. 160 folio paper[27] leaves containing the following items: 1. fols 1a–107a *Piers Plowman* **B**: 2. fols 107b–19b *Mum and the Sothsegger*, *IMEV* no. *6; 3. fols 127a–48b a prose treatise on arithmetic in English;[28] 4. fols 153a–6b a prose treatise *incip.* 'Here bigynneth the wyse boke of philosophie and astronomye' *explic.* 'blake cloþinge he loueth moste'; 5. fols 156b–9b a prose treatise *incip.* 'Here bigynneth the tretys of þe booke of phisonomye a nobile knowinge of nature' *explic.* 'An harde eere betokneth a man of good disposicioun of body A nasshe'; 6. fols 161a–3a a Latin verse table of the arguments of the Psalms *incip.* 'Hec sunt psalmorum sacra carmina dauiticorum' *explic.* 'Magnus et excelsus quod ab omnibus confiteatur terrigenis'; 7. fols 164a–7a sayings of the Latin fathers with translations into English verse, *IMEV* 4128; 8. fols 169b–70b glosses to words from *Piers Plowman*;[29] 9. fols 173a–4b 'A doctrine of Fisshing and foulyng', *IMEV* 71; 10. fol. 174b a quatrain of prayer, *IMEV* 1686. Collation iii + $1–8^{14} 9^{14}$ (lacks 8–13) $10^{16} 11^{10}$ (lacks 7–10) 12^{8} (lacks 8) 13^{12} (lacks 8, 11, 12) 14^{2} + ii.[30] Two foliations: one arabic, ink, top centre, 1–119, possibly by the sixteenth-century annotator and glossator (A. I. Doyle); the other modern pencil, top right, 1–119, 126–48, 153–9, 161–7, 169, 170, 173, 174, taking account of the losses. Binding modern. Size of leaf 28.5 × 21 cm, of frame of items 1 and 2, 20.5 × 12.75 cm, otherwise 22.5 × 15.75 cm. Item 9 in double columns. Lines per page in items 1 and 2, 32–6, most often 35; otherwise average 40. Several handwritings: items 1–5 in one small anglicana tending to currency, with some secretary forms; items 6 and 9 in a second with marked secretary influence; item 7 in a third; item 8 in mid-sixteenth-century secretary by the second annotator of the *Piers Plowman* text (A. I. Doyle). Pen-drawn ornamental initial capitals in items 1, 2, 4 and 5, one blue, others red; Latin underlined in red. Text not paragraphed or marked off. Occasional marginal subject heads in item 1 by main scribe; others in another hand and ink. On a front flyleaf, in a mid-fifteenth-century hand, 7 lines in praise of the Virgin *incip.* 'Salue sancta parens enixa puerpera regem' *explic.* 'Sola sine exemplo placuisti femina christo'.[31] On a slip bound in at front a mid-sixteenth-century memorandum refers to 'on knape fermer of whitchurche in the cunte of oxon'.

[26] See C.U.L., *Catalogue of Manuscripts*, iv, 1861, pp. 66–8; Skeat, *B-Text*, pp. xx, xxi; *C-Text*, pp. ciii-cv; Day, M. and R. Steele, ed., *Mum and the Sothsegger*, EETS 199, London, 1936, pp. x, xii, xiii. But C^2 is not 'a copy of the Oriel MS' as they imagined.

[27] Watermarks are *Mont*, Briquet 11684 (1394), on fols 126, 170, 174, *Balance* very like Briquet 2375, 2376 (1400–26) on fols 147, 164, and *Coutelas* (A. I. Doyle) like Briquet 5130 (1413) on fol. 30. The implication of these watermarks, as of the hand, is that the *Piers Plowman* text is late in the first half of the fifteenth century.

[28] See Steele, R., ed., *The Earliest Arithmetics in English*, EETS ES 118, London, 1922 for 1916, p. v.

[29] Printed by Skeat, *B-Text*, pp. 421–4.

[30] The collation was noted by Pink when the manuscript was rebound. He treated it as two, divided after the ninth gathering. The identity of hands 1–5 argues against this.

[31] Compare Walther, H., *Initia Carminum ac Versuum Medii Aevi Posterioris Latinorum*, Göttingen, 1959, p. 899 nos. 17155, 17150.

Cot *Cotton Caligula A XI*[32] *British Museum*

Cot is the second of three distinct vellum manuscripts or parts of manuscripts probably first bound together for Sir Robert Cotton:[33]

I 1. fol. 2a a sixteenth-century Latin table of contents of the volume; 2. fols 3a–168b the 'earlier recension' of Robert of Gloucester's Chronicle;[34] 3. fol. 169b 43 lines of Latin verse *incip.* 'Noctis sub silencium tempore brumali' *explic.* 'Celsaque pallacia turres quas fundasti'.[35]

II fols 170a–286a a mainly **B** text of *Piers Plowman* (see below).

III fols 287a–8b some 300 lines of Latin verse *incip.* 'Quid deceat monachum vel qualis debeat esse' *explic.* 'Quam male dilatum multum :::: negatum'.[36]

The Piers Plowman *Manuscript*[37]

*S. xv*¹. 113 leaves containing *Piers Plowman* **C** Prologue 1–II 131, **A** II 90–212 and **B** III 1–XX 386.[38] Collation probably eights throughout.[39] Three foliations: one ancient, by tens, verso top left, ending at 200; one ink (165–278) struck through; the most recent, 170–286, in pencil. Museum binders once inserted three vellum leaves, numbered 274–6; the text before and after is intact. Size of page 22 × 15.5 cm, of frame 14.5 × 12 cm. Average of 32 lines per side. Hand anglicana with mixture of secretary forms.[40] Initial capitals of passus blue with red pen-drawn ornament. Paragraphs not set off but marked with blue signs. Latin in red or underlined in red. A few corrections by the main scribe; many others, of both spelling and substance, as also subject guides and glosses, in various medieval and later hands perhaps including Selden's. There is a barely decipherable name, 'John Godere' or 'Godeve' on fol. 269a.[41]

[32] See *A Catalogue of Manuscripts in the Cottonian Library Deposited in the British Museum*, London, 1802, p. 45; Skeat, *B-Text*, p. xxvii; Wright, W. A., *The Metrical Chronicle of Robert of Gloucester*, London, 1887, pp. xl, xli; Hudson, Anne, *An Edition of Part of the Chronicle Attributed to Robert of Gloucester with a Study of the Original Language of the Poem*, unpublished Oxford D.Phil thesis, 1963, pp. 5–7; 'Robert of Gloucester and the Antiquaries, 1550–1800', *Notes & Queries*, ccxiv (1969), pp. 324, 328, 330.

[33] Cotton's hand occurs at the head of fols 3 and 287. The table of contents on fol. 2a is in the hand of Archbishop Parker's secretary (Hudson, Thesis, p. 6, quoting Neil Ker).

[34] This is the text used by Wright (see n. 32 above).

[35] Walther, *Initia*, p. 610 no. 11894.

[36] Walther, *Initia*, p. 821 no. 15778.

[37] Cot's dating is implicated with that of Bm and Bo (see above, pp. 1, n. 3, and below, 40ff.). Neil Ker noted its 'new type of hand', while adding that this was 'quite possible in the early fifteenth century'. With information that in all textual senses Cot is extremely close to Bm and Bo, probably distanced from them by at most one stage of copying, A. I. Doyle inclines to date it 1410–30. We cannot disagree but would wish to place it early in that period.

[38] This is the combination found in Bm and Bo.

[39] Cropping and successive rebindings have obscured the evidence. There survive a catchword on fol. 225, a signature (*j iiii*) on 237, signatures (*kj–iiij*) on 242–5, and a singleton (*Mj*) on 258. The indication is that the first 56 leaves, 170–225, were in 7 gatherings. Fol. 173 'is a cancel by the same hand' (A. I. Doyle).

[40] Slope and proportions are by no means uniform but the text is 'all by one hand' (A. I. Doyle).

[41] On fol. 286b, twice in distinct hands, occurs the opening of Surrey's 'A Goodly Ensample' (Padelford no. 13). The second is variant: 'When raginge Love withe extreme Payne moost krvle oon ple ther parte'.

Cr *Robert Crowley's Three Impressions of 1550*[42]

Collation is from the three following copies.

Cr[1] *British Museum C 71.c.29*

Title page: THE VISION / of Pierce Plowman, now / fyrste imprynted by Roberte / Crowley, dwellyng in Ely / rentes in Holburne. / Anno Domini, / 1505[43]
Cum priuilegio ad im- / primendum solum.
Colophon (fol. cxviib): Imprinted at London by Roberte / Crowley, dwellyng in Elye rentes / in Holburne. The yere of / our Lord. M. D. L.

Cr[2] *British Museum C 71.c.28*

Title page: The vision of / Pierce Plowman, nowe the seconde time imprinted / by Roberte Crowley dwellynge in Elye rentes in Holburne. / Whereunto are added certayne notes and cotations in the / mergyne, geuynge light to the Reader. And in the begynning / is set a briefe summe of all the principall matters spoken of in / the boke. And as the boke is deuided into twenty partes cal- / led Passus: so is the Summary diuided, for euery parte hys / summarie, rehearsynge the matters spoken of in eue- / rye parte, euen in suche order as they / stande there.
Imprinted at London by Roberte / Crowley, dwellyng in Elye rentes / in Holburne. The yere of / our Lord. M. D. L.
Cum priuilegio ad imprimendum / solum.
Colophon (fol. cxviib): as above Imprinted...solum.

Cr[3] *British Museum C 122.d.9*

Title page: The vision of / Pierce Plowman, nowe the seconde tyme imprinted / by Roberte Crowlye dwellynge in Elye rentes in Holburne / Whereunto are added certayne notes and cotations in the / mergyne, geuyng light to the Reader. And in the begynning / is set a brefe summe of all the principal matters spoken of in / the boke. And as the boke is deuided into twenty partes cal- / led Passus: so is the Summary diuided, for euery parte hys / summarie, rehearsynge the matters spoken of in eue- / ry parte. euen in suche order as they / stande there.

[42] On Crowley see especially Cowper, J. M., ed., *The Select Works of Robert Crowley*, EETS ES 15, 1872, and Illston, Olga, *A literary and bibliographical study of the work of Robert Crowley (1517–1588) printer, puritan and poet*, unpublished University of London M.A. thesis, 1953. The standard bibliographical references to his printing of *Piers Plowman* are Herbert, William, *Typographical Antiquities: or an Historical Account of the Origin and Progress of Printing...and a Register of Books*, ii, London, 1786, pp. 757ff.; Skeat, *B-Text*, pp. xxxi–xxxv, 387–426; Duff, E. G., W. W. Greg *et al.*, *Hand-List of English Printers 1501–1556*, iv, London, 1913, unpaginated; Pollard, A. W. and G. R. Redgrave, *A Short-Title Catalogue of Books Printed in England,...1475–1640*, London, 1926, items 19906, 19907, 19907a. For textual information concerning Crowley's printings of *Piers Plowman* we are indebted to the unpublished Yale University dissertation of Crawford, William R., *Robert Crowley's Editions of Piers Plowman: a Bibliographical and Textual Study*, 1957.

[43] This date is an obvious error. It has been corrected in ink in the British Museum copy.

Imprinted at London by Roberte / Crowley, dwellyng in Elye rentes / in Holburne, The yere of / our Lord, M.D.L,
Cum priuilegio ad imprimendum / solum.
Colophon (fol. cxviib): Imprynted / at London by Roberte Crowley, / dwellynge in Elye rentes in Hol- / burne. The yere of our Lorde. / M.D.L.
Cum priuilegio ad imprimendum / solum

The first impression of Crowley's edition represents the text of a lost manuscript,[44] in places arbitrarily emended by Crowley. The second impression was reset, and appears to offer a conflated text based on a new manuscript (also lost) under constant comparison with the text of the first impression.[45] The text of the third impression may incorporate 'correction' from yet another manuscript.

We find the sequence of impressions proposed by Skeat[46] to be supported by the evidence of textual variation and therefore the correct one. But we accept that the indication of textual evidence about this cannot be conclusive and must be subject to confirmation or rejection through expert bibliographical analysis. This has yet to be carried out and we do not have the skills to undertake it. Perhaps the availability of help from our collations will encourage some bibliographer to do so.

Meanwhile we are confident that our procedure, notwithstanding the complex bibliographical history of Crowley's edition and the relative abundance of copies of this, has ensured the inclusion and consideration of all significant Crowley variants of the text of the **B** version of *Piers Plowman.*

Our choice of British Museum copies for collation was, as must be obvious, for reasons of convenience. But conscious of the many differences between copies of the three impressions we also consulted those in the Yale University Library. The comparison proved of great bibliographical interest.[47] But it did not bring a single new reading of significance for the determination of originality to light.

[44] Its genetic affinity is exceptionally clear. See below, pp. 38ff., 42ff., 49ff.

[45] See below, p. 19, n. 13.

[46] *B-Text*, pp. xxxiv, xxv.

[47] Comparison reveals that the British Museum copy of Cr² has for its I-quire (VI 126–VII 144α) a variant state of the I-quire that appears in Cr¹ as witnessed both by British Museum C 71.c.29 and Yale University Library 550 and 550b (the variant quire also appears in Yale University 550c, which is made up of quires of both the first and second impressions). That this variant quire belongs properly to the first impression is shown by its running head 'The vision of / Pierce Ploughman' and by its seven marginal notes; the second and third impressions have the running head 'Passus sextus' (or 'septimus') and eighteen marginal notes. While agreeing with the Yale Cr² (550d) and with Cr³ in nineteen readings (VI 127, 154, 212, 217, 220, 248 (2), 266, 276, 289, 295, 306, 308, 309, 328; VII 30, 33 (2), 42), the I-quire of the British Museum Cr² agrees with Cr¹ against the Yale Cr² where the latter agrees with Cr³ in more than sixty readings: VI 143, 147, 160, 165, 167, 175, 182, 183, 184, 187, 192, 194, 198, 200, 215, 216 (3), 219 (2), 221 (*and... wolde*]), 223, 227, 231, 232, 233, 234 (2), 235, 239, 240, 241, 243, 250, 252 (2), 252α, 253, 254, 261, 265, 270, 277, 291 (2), 292, 295, 301, 306, 308, 310, 312, 324, 329, 330; VII 2 (2), 3, 13, 26, 34, 36. Only in VI 221 (*lene*]) does the Yale Cr² agree with both Cr¹ and the British Museum Cr² against Cr³. There are seven readings peculiar to British Museum Cr² in the I-quire (VI 204 (2), 216, 257, 276, 278; VII 23) and one peculiar to the Yale Cr² (VI 141: *dyngen*] *dinging*).

The D-quire of the British Museum copy of Cr³ (III 80–327) appears to have been borrowed from the Cr² printing, although the only substantive readings where this copy disagrees with the Yale Cr³ (550bb) are III 157 (*þikke*] *think*) and 224 (*Asken*] *asken aftir*). See Skeat, *B-Text*, p. xxxv, n. 1.

F *Corpus Christi College Oxford 201*[48]

S. xv^{1}. 93 vellum leaves containing the **B** version of *Piers Plowman*. Collation ii + 1^{10} (3 and 8 singles) 2^{10} (2 and 9 singles) 3^{10} (4 and 7 singles) 4^{10} (3 and 8 singles) 5^{10} (4 and 7 singles) 6^{8} (5 and 7 singles) 7^{10} (3 and 8 singles) 8^{8} (3 and 6 singles) 9^{10} (4 and 7 singles) 10^{10} (lacks 8–10). Foliation 1–93 pencil top right recto. Binding sixteenth-century vellum. Severely cropped; size of page 29.3 × 17.3 cm, of frame 24.3 × 11 cm. Average number of lines per page 43. Text not paragraphed. One rather current anglicana with Latin in text-hand or fere-textura by main scribe throughout. Illuminated capital with demi-vinet of late fourteenth-, or early fifteenth-century provincial, style at beginning (A. I. Doyle); subsequent passus initials pen-drawn, sometimes elaborately, at first green and red, later blue and red. Latin in red with green initial capitals. Line initials and names in text touched in red. Paragraph signs first alternately green and red, then from fol. 68b blue and red. Passus numbers in red roman top right recto, mainly on first pages of passus.[49] Some good corrections, mainly interlinear, by main scribe and others. Marginal crosses sometimes appear to signal notable passages rather than errors. Otherwise a few marginal *nota*'s and subject pointers. A variant *Wy*] *wykumbe* at V 203 may indicate provenance.

G *Gg. 4. 31*[50] *Cambridge University Library*

S. xvi^{1}. 106 quarto paper leaves[51] containing: 1. fols 1–101a the **B** version of *Piers Plowman*; 2. fols 101b–3a 'þe table of pyers plowman', outlining its content by passus; 3. fols 104a–5b 'A goodly preaer', *IMEV* 532. Collation i + 1^{12} (lacks 1) $2^{8}3^{16}4\text{–}8^{12}9^{12}$ (lacks 12) + i.[52] Foliation 1–101 top right recto ink by main scribe; where lost in cropping supplied in modern pencil, e.g., 95 (=94), 95–8, 100–6. Binding late seventeenth-century[53] leather. Very severely cropped with loss of text from side and head margins; size of page 24.9 × 17.5 cm. After fol. 1a only the left and head margins ruled, the former averaging 2.2 cm wide. Lines per page 33–45. Text not paragraphed or marked off. One fluent but untidy secretary hand throughout. Latin in red, more formalized but probably by same hand; passus initials crudely drawn in black ink, 'possibly by W.H., who initials a marginal note on fol. 69b, on 72b, and a reference thereto on fol. 103a' (A. I. Doyle). Good corrections by main scribe, especially of his own omissions. Many trifling spelling modernizations in a distinctive ink.[54] Some marginal subject heads in main hand and one other. In the Cambridge University Library by the late seventeenth century.

[48] See Coxe, H. O., *Catalogus Codicum MSS. Qui in Collegiis Aulisque Oxoniensibus Hodie Adservantur*, ii, Oxford, 1852, p. 80; Skeat, *B-Text*, pp. xxvii–xxx.

[49] These are highly idiosyncratic: see Skeat, *B-Text*, loc. cit. Once a sixteenth-century hand indicates a correct division.

[50] See C.U.L., *Catalogue of Manuscripts*, iii, 1858, p. 177; Skeat, *B-Text*, p. xxiii.

[51] Watermark of water-wheel with three (oak?) leaves; compare Briquet 13396 *Roue dentée* with multiple leaves (1514), and nearer, Heawood 4025 (1579) (A. I. Doyle).

[52] Noted by a Cambridge librarian when the binding was repaired in 1962.

[53] Watermarks in the flyleaves are of the general type Heawood 655, 661, 677 (1648–77) (Heawood, E., *Watermarks Mainly of the 17th and 18th Centuries*, Hilversum, 1950).

[54] We have not collated these.

H *Harley 3954 British Museum*

This manuscript is described in Volume I.[55] From the beginning (fol. 92a) to about V 127 its *Piers Plowman* text represents the **B** version.

Hm, Hm² *Huntington Library MS 128*[56]

S. xv in. 219 vellum leaves[57] containing the following items: 1. fols 1–94a *The Prick of Conscience*, East Midland recension, *IMEV* 3429; 2. fol. 95a *Piers Plowman* **B** III 50–72α, fols 96a,b *Piers Plowman* **B** II 209–III 49 (these fragments are Hm²);[58] 3. fols 97a–112b commentaries on the sequences for Sundays and feastdays according to Sarum use; 4. fols 113a–205a the **B** version of *Piers Plowman*; 5. fols 205a–216a *The Siege of Jerusalem, IMEV* 1583; 6. fols 216b–19a *How the Good Wife Taught her Daughter, IMEV* 671. Collation i + $1–26^8 27^6$ + one leaf 28^4 + i.[59] Three foliations: one, right head recto, including front flyleaf, 1–220; a second, lower right-hand margin recto, begins with fol. 1; a third runs 1–10, thereafter every fifth leaf, then 95–7, then correctly 112, 113, then every fifth leaf, 201, 219. Binding first half of sixteenth century. Pastedowns from an unidentified fifteenth-century theological text. Flyleaves vellum, contemporary. Size of page 24.75 × 17 cm, of frame 19.75 × 12.75 cm.[60] Various anglicana formata hands of which at least five, of fairly similar character but showing more or less secretary influence, appear in the copying and correction of the *Piers Plowman* content.[61] An average of 40 lines per side in the *Piers* texts. At the beginning of *Piers* a large initial capital in red and

[55] Viz. Kane, G., *Piers Plowman: The A Version*, London, 1960, pp. 7, 8. A. I. Doyle would however date the manuscript *S. xv.*¹. See his review of Vol. I in *English Studies*, xliii, 1962, p. 58.

[56] See *Catalogue of the Collection of Dr Adam Clarke*, p. 69; Madden, F., *How the Goode Wif thaught hir Doughter*, London, 1838, pp. iii, iv; Skeat, *B-Text*, pp. xxi–xxiii; *Catalogue of the Manuscripts at Ashburnham Place*, London, n.d., *Appendix* CXXX; Haselden, R. B., 'The Fragment of *Piers Plowman* in Ashburnham No. CXXX', *MP*, xxix (1932), pp. 391–4; Kölbing, E. and M. Day, *The Siege of Jerusalem*, EETS 188, London, 1932, pp. viii, ix; Chambers, R. W., 'The Manuscripts of *Piers Plowman* in the Huntington Library, and their Value for Fixing the Text of the Poem', *Huntington Library Bulletin* No. 8 (1935), pp. 14–18, 26, 27; de Ricci, S. and W. J. Wilson, *Census of Medieval and Renaissance Manuscripts in the United States and Canada*, New York, 1935, i, p. 54; Mustanoja, T. F., *The Good Wife Taught Her Daughter; The Good Wyfe Wold a Pylgremage; The Thewis of Good Women*, Helsinki, 1948, pp. 102, 103.

[57] *Prima facie* the volume appears composite. For instance the presence of a whole *Piers* text and a fragment of the same version within a single cover suggests that there was a historical division of items after fol. 97 at least; moreover the appearance and feel of the leaves containing item 3 are distinctive enough to suggest that these two putative gatherings had a distinct unbound history; meanwhile the transitions *Piers* ⟩ *Siege* and *Siege* ⟩ *Good Wife* occur within leaves. Thus fols 113–219 might seem a distinct book. But a general palæographic similarity between *The Prick of Conscience*, the *Piers* fragment, and the whole *Piers* text, suggests a common and contemporaneous origin for items 1, 2 and 4, and therefore also for 5 and 6. With item 3 (*Sequences*) there is more doubt: this apparently occupied two gatherings, the absence of which would not disturb the collation of the rest. Haselden's argument, op. cit., pp. 391ff., is to be noted.

[58] For the explanation of their presence see Haselden, op. cit., pp. 392–4.

[59] This collation was recorded by Huntington palæographers in the 1930s. The manuscript had on rebinding to be resewn irregularly because of broken folds. All catchwords and signatures are cropped away.

[60] The only item to differ in this respect is item 3, *Sequences*, which is in double columns.

[61] The hands of three text-writers and two correctors were identified by Capt. Haselden and Dr Schulz of the Huntington Library, in an exhaustive examination employing ultraviolet light and microscopy. There are corresponding, marked varieties of dialect and orthography. Even the *Piers* fragment Hm² is in several hands.

blue with pen decoration; passus initials smaller, blue with red. Passus numbers rubricated. Paragraphs not set off, but marked in alternate blue and red. The text was much altered in the workshop by erasure and overwriting,[62] but a major dislocation in the exemplar, affecting fols 156a–61b, where XI 425–XII 81 and XI 111–217 appear in each other's place[63] apparently escaped the correctors' notice.[64] A few marginal subject guides or *nota*'s. On the front endpaper two ascriptions of *Piers Plowman*, the second in John Bale's hand;[65] and in late fifteenth- or sixteenth-century hands the following names: 'Richard Richard'[66] (front flyleaf); 'Alleksander London' or 'Loudon' (fol. 101a); 'cysley' (fol. 144b); 'Betoun Brigges' (fol. 149a); 'Mavde' (fol. 153a); 'John sar*um*' (rear endpaper).[67] The manuscript was Ashburnham Appendix cxxx.

L *Laud Misc. 581*[68] *Bodleian Library S.C.987*

S. xv in. 93 vellum leaves of superior quality containing the **B** version of *Piers Plowman* on fols 1–91; fols 92, 93 blank. Collation i + $1–11^{8}12^{6}$ (lacks 6). Foliations: 1–93 ink, lower right recto, early modern; ditto pencil, upper right recto, modern. Binding ancient calf with Archbishop Laud's arms impressed in gilt front and back. Cropped but no damage to text; size of page 26.75 × 18.5 cm, of frame 22.6 × 12.5 cm. Ruled for 46–9 lines per page, generally 48. Text divided into paragraphs. One anglicana formata of uniform size throughout. Line initials spaced off. Passus initials pen-drawn red and blue. Incipits in red by several hands; Latin and catchwords boxed in red; paragraph signs blue. Marginal subject heads and *nota*'s by main scribe; some boxed in red; two by a rubricator; others, Latin and English, in sixteenth-century hands. Several interlinear glosses by main scribe. Variously corrected or marked for correction with marginal crosses, often in error. On fol. 1a a mid-sixteenth-century note 'Robart Langelande borne by malborne hilles', by one of the annotators. On fol. 92a 'liber Ricardi Johnson';[69] also the name 'T. Long of Dorchester' in seventeenth-century script; on fols 92a, 93a 'Ion Thynne' (compare above, p. 1); on fol. 93a 'Raffe Coppynger';[70] also the '*Memorandum* þat I

[62] More than 1000 changes affecting anything from a block of a dozen lines to a single letter were identified by Haselden and Schulz. The most frequent are removal or addition of final *e* and substitution of a preferred word- or spelling-form. Occasionally a large block of text was erased and recopied merely to allow supply of a line omitted at first copying (there is a particularly clear example of this on fol. 187a). The density of alteration of all kinds is remarkably sustained throughout the text. We record that which is material to the sense, or may have a bearing on originality.

[63] Thus on fol. 156a XI 109 is followed by XI 425. After 104 lines by Hm count, on fol. 157b XII 81 is followed by XI 218. After 206 lines, on fol. 160a XI 424 is followed by XI 111. After 101 lines, on fol. 161b XI 217 is followed by XII 82.

[64] The easiest explanation of the disorder is that in an antecedent copy a gathering of eight leaves (quaternion) with 25 or 26 lines to a side had its two outer bifolia misfolded, the inner two continuing correct. See Chambers, *Huntington Libr. Bull.*, p. 15, n. 3.

[65] These are discussed in Kane, G., *Piers Plowman: The Evidence for Authorship*, London, 1965, pp. 37–42.

[66] The same curious inscription occurs in Lincoln Cathedral Chapter Library MS 70, *Chronicle of Brut* (Woolley, R. W., *Catalogue of the Manuscripts of Lincoln Cathedral Chapter Library*, Oxford, 1927, p. 40).

[67] Very possibly John Jewel (A. I. Doyle). See *DNB*, x, pp. 815–17.

[68] See Skeat, *B-Text*, pp. vi–x; *Summary Catalogue*, ii, pt i, p. 41; Bennett, J. A. W., 'A New Collation of a *Piers Plowman* Manuscript', *Medium Ævum*, xvii (1948), p. 22 n. 2.

[69] See Doyle, A. I., 'Books Belonging to R. Johnson', *Notes & Queries*, cxcvii (1952), pp. 293, 294.

[70] *Ob.* 1551 (A. I. Doyle).

haue lente to Nicholas brigham[71] the pers ploughman which I borowed of Mr Le of Addyngton'.

M *Additional 35287*[72] *British Museum*

S. xv[1]. 104 vellum leaves of good quality containing the **B** version of *Piers Plowman.* Collation 1–13[8]. One modern pencil foliation throughout, 1–104. Size of page 30 × 19.5 cm; of frame most often approximately 21.5 × 14 cm. Ruled variously for 39–42, most often 41 lines per side. Text divided into paragraphs. Hand anglicana of widely various degrees of formality, proportion and manner.[73] Binding modern. Initial capitals of passus red; Latin red or boxed in red. No running titles, but on fol. 4a top right, in the hand of a marginal annotator, the heading 'primus passus', and so forth. A few marginal titles by the main scribe; many others, Latin or English, in various medieval and later hands. The text has been very extensively altered, mainly by erasure and overwriting, by more than two persons.[74] Some of the alterations are enlightened, many are substantial, but most are merely trifling.[75] On fol. 104b among fifteenth-century and later jottings which might reward expert and leisured study, a form of the quatrain *IMEV* 4202, and a monogram of the letters *D E N* with the date 1545.

O *Oriel College Oxford 79*[76]

The first of two distinct parts of manuscripts, one vellum, one paper, bound together in the eighteenth century.[77]

I 1. fol. 1a the last eight lines of a Latin poem: Et sine verborum sonitu fit doctor eorum *explic.* Hoc tibi det munus qui regnat trinus et unus; then in the same hand after space left for a rubric and with a headline title 2. fols 1a–88a the **B** version of *Piers Plowman*, imperfect; 3. fol. 88b a Latin quatrain (in textura) *incip.* Sunt tria vere que faciunt me dolere *explic.* Pro tercio flebo quia nescio quo remanebo;[78] 4. fol. 88b in another fifteenth-

[71] For Brigham see *DNB*, vi, pp. 330, 331, and Cargill, O., 'The Langland Myth', *PMLA*, l (1935), pp. 43–5.

[72] See Skeat, *B-Text*, pp. xv, xvi; *Catalogue of the Manuscripts at Ashburnham Place, Appendix* CXXIX; *A Catalogue of Additions to the Manuscripts in the British Museum in the Years 1894–1899*, London, 1901, p. 234. The manuscript was Ashburnham Appendix No. cxxix, and Lot 77 at Sotheby's, 1 March 1899.

[73] A. I. Doyle discounts the view that more than one scribe was concerned, pointing out that the formality and size vary within continuous passages, and the constituents of the writing are the same throughout. He fixes a point on fol. 42b where there is a change to a lower (medium) grade of script, but emphasizes the scribe's ability and finds him, on fols 19–23, writing a script like that of the Ellesmere MS.

[74] Two, and presumably the earliest, correctors seem to have been concerned in the actual production of the manuscript, from their notes *corr.* or *correc.*, in different inks and plummet. There are examples on fols 64b, 80b, 88b, for instance.

[75] They extend even to lengthening the tail of the letter *y*. We record all changes material to the sense or with a possible bearing on originality. We do not normally record such changes as erasure of final *e*, or of initial *ȝ* from *ȝif*; or *þ* > *th*; or *ȝ* > *y*; or *y* > *i* (as in *þi* > *thy*, *þei* > *they*); or *u* > *y* (as in *þuder* > *thyder*); or final *re* > *er*; or erasure of final *de*, *me*, *ne*, *te* (e.g. from *badde*, *somme*, *kynne*, *witte*); or erasure of final *n*. The density of alteration is, as commonly, not sustained, and diminishes in the latter part of the poem. For significant alteration see below, pp. 50, 51.

[76] See Coxe, *Catalogus*, i, 1852, pp. 27, 28; Skeat, *B-Text*, pp. xvi–xx.

[77] For the antiquary Joseph Ames; see *DNB*, i, p. 353. His name is impressed on both covers.

[78] Walther, *Initia*, p. 989 no. 18886.

century anglicana the Latin and Greek refrain of the Improperia with an English version (A. I. Doyle).

II 1. fol. 89a 16 Latin verses on the four complexions;[79] 2. fol. 89a a 'Bess Ballad' written as prose, *IMEV Supplement* 1589.5;[80] 3. fol. 89b a list of London wards and their ratings; 4. fols 89b–91a, 92a, b, a list of London churches; fols 93a–7a the Privilege of Westminster *incip.* bee thay ashamyd and afferdid that violyn oþer brekyn the priuileges of this holy Church in anything *explic.* many other confermed the said Chartre.[81] 6. fols 98a–109a *The Book of Courtesy, IMEV* 1919.

The Piers Plowman *Manuscript*

S. xv[1]. 88 vellum leaves principally containing *Piers Plowman* **B** Prologue 1–XVII 98, XVII 347–XIX 280 and XIX 359–XX 386. Collation xvi + 1^8 (lacks 1–4) 2–9^8 10^8 (lacks 5–7) 11^8 12^8 (lacks 1).[82] Two foliations, one pencil top right recto 1–88, another allowing for losses, [76]–[84], [86]–[92]. Cropped; size of page 21.5 × 15.7 cm, of frame 15.8 × 10.8 cm. Text continuous but paragraphs marked off. Average number of lines per page 39. *Piers* hand one small anglicana formata throughout. Passus initials in red; Latin underlined in red; initials of lines touched with red; catchwords boxed in black. Many marginal subject guides by main scribe, some rubricated. Some good corrections by him, and others in a second (fifteenth-century) hand; occasional marginal glosses by main scribe. On fol. 88b, legible by ultraviolet light, twice the name of a fifteenth-century owner, William Rogger; and in another hand a deeding of the manuscript by him to Roger Sambrok before John at Style and other witnesses.[83] Then in a new hand two Latin verses concluding 'Nomen scriptoris Johannes Mallyng Plenus Amoris', and twice in sixteenth-century italic the name 'W. Smethwik'.

R *Lansdowne 398* *British Museum*
Rawlinson Poetry 38[84] *Bodleian Library S.C.15563*

S. xv in. 105 vellum leaves ('the best matt-finished membrane': A. I. Doyle); four, the remnant of an original first gathering, are BM MS Lansdowne 398 fols 77–80.[85] Content *Piers Plowman* **B** Prologue 125–I 140, II 41–XVIII 410, XX 27–386. Collation 1^8 (in Lansdowne: lacks 1, 2, 7, 8); then (Rawlinson) i + 2–8^8 9^7 (4 a single) 10–13^8 14^8 (lost) 15^6 + i. Most catchwords and signatures survive. Rawlinson foliated modern pencil top right recto 1–101. Binding modern. The margins of the Lansdowne leaves and of Rawlinson fols 1–7 cut away for the vellum, with loss of text at side (serious on verso),

[79] Printed by Skeat, *B-Text*, p. xix. Walther, H., *Proverbia Sententiaeque Latinitatis Medii Aevi*, ii/2, Göttingen, 1964, p. 689 no. 13474.

[80] Robbins, R. and J. Cutler, *Supplement to the Index of Middle English Verse*, Lexington, 1965.

[81] A version of a text found in more than one form in Westminster Abbey manuscripts of the third quarter of the fifteenth century (A. I. Doyle).

[82] Then follow the 21 paper leaves of II and 15 flyleaves. Part II is all of the middle or second half of the century, but for the Bess ballad which is *s. xv/xvi*.

[83] It is possible to read in the deed the date 19 September 17 Henry VI.

[84] See Skeat, *B-Text*, pp. xi–xiii; *Summary Catalogue*, iii, 1895, p. 436.

[85] They were identified by Skeat: see *B-Text*, p. xi.

before the manuscript was first bound. Otherwise cropping not severe: size of page 28.8 × 20.7 cm, of frame 20.5 × 12.5 cm. Pages ruled for 36, later 37 and occasionally 38 lines: text paragraphed. One large bastard anglicana hand throughout. Line initials spaced off. Passus initials pen-drawn in blue and red or red; several flourished with grotesques; paragraph signs in earlier part variously, sometimes alternately, green or blue and red. Incipits in red; Latin boxed in red. A little correction in main hand; a few marginal subject-guides in others. Various names: the earliest *s.xv/xvi* fol. 101a 'William Butte' or 'Buttes' and 101b same hand 'Butte' or 'Buttes William'; in late sixteenth-century hands: fol. 2a 'Robart Bente you shalbe with vs at Budworthe and there to testyfy youre knowlegh in a mater'; fol. 3a 'John naylle'; fol. 47a 'david' (twice) and 'Rondull wyily'; fol. 84a 'John Sympson Smithe John'; fol. 101b 'John Walton', 'James Simpson', 'John Freman', 'Thomas', 'Bennett', 'Thomas Wryght'; on front flyleaf 'Suum cuique Tho. Hearne Sept. 29 1732'.[86] In Stow's hand (A. I. Doyle) on fol. 63a 'stratford', and in an early fifteenth-century hand on fols 63a and 64a (beside XIII 270 and 339) 'Chicestre Maior london' and 'sowter of sotwerk'.

W *Trinity College Cambridge B. 15. 17*[87]

S. xiv/xv. 147 vellum leaves of good quality containing: 1. fols 1a–130b the **B** version of *Piers Plowman*; 2. fols 131a–47a a prose treatise *incip.* In euery synful man or womman þat is bounden in dedly synne *explic.* þanke god and pray for me þe grace of Iesu crist be wiþ þee and kepe þee Amen;[88] 3. fols 147a,b *Crist made to man a fair present, IMEV* 611. Collation ii + 1–16^{8} 17^{2} 18^{8} 19 indeterminable (9 leaves) + ii.[89] Foliation modern pencil top right recto 1–147. Binding seventeenth-century leather, the arms of George Willmer[90] impressed and gilded front and rear. Irregularly cropped with occasional loss of text or marginalia. Size of page 28.7 × 19 cm, of frame 23 × 14 cm (*Piers*), 23.5 × 13.5 cm overall double columns (item 2). Ruled for 33–5 lines per page. The text of *Piers* divided into paragraphs with alternate blue and red signs. Text in one anglicana formata hand throughout;[91] elaborated ascenders in top lines; incipits and Latin engrossed in bastard anglicana by main scribe. On fol. 1a a handsome illuminated initial capital and vinet in late fourteenth-, or early fifteenth-century provincial, style, much rubbed and stained. Passus initials and some others pen-drawn in red and blue; incipits red; Latin boxed in red. A few marginal subject-heads, corrections and interlinear glosses by main scribe; some *nota*'s in another hand; some favourite lines singled out in fifteenth-century hand by 'a feyrse' (e.g. I 85 on fol. 6b). Among (fifteenth-century?) pen-trials on fols

86 Discussed by Cargill, 'The Langland Myth', pp. 53, 54.

87 See Skeat, *B-Text*, pp. xiii, xiv; James, M. R., *The Western Manuscripts in the Library of Trinity College, Cambridge*, i, Cambridge, 1900, pp. 480, 481; Greg, Sir Walter, *Facsimiles of Twelve Early English Manuscripts in the Library of Trinity College, Cambridge*, Oxford, 1913, pl. vii.

88 Identified for us by Peter Jolliffe as Rolle's *Form of Living*. See Wells, pp. 449, 450, and Allen, H. E., *Writings Ascribed to Richard Rolle*, London, 1927, pp. 256, 257.

89 This is from catchwords only.

90 He presented the manuscript to Trinity. Described by James as 'in the high commission a justice of the peace for Middlesex, and dying 1626 was buried at Westham in Essex' (op. cit., ii, 1901, p. 289).

91 It bears a strong resemblance to the hand of the Ellesmere manuscript, and while not by the Ellesmere scribe, is pretty certainly of the same school and period.

1a, 87a and last leaf the names 'bond John Rychard'. On fol. 77a beside XIII 266, 'stratford' in a hand 'very like John Stow's' (A. I. Doyle), as also '1350' on fol. 77b beside XIII 269.

Y *Yates-Thompson MS*[92] *Newnham College Cambridge*

S. xv^1. 109 vellum leaves of good quality containing: 1. fols 1a–104a the **B** version of *Piers Plowman*; 2. fols 104b–9b *The Lay Folks' Mass Book, IMEV* 3507; 3. fol. 109b a grace, *IMEV* 620. Collation ii + 1–13^8 14^5 (5 a single?) + ii. Foliation modern pencil top right recto 1–109. Binding (much repaired) and flyleaves eighteenth-century. Cropped with some loss of marginalia but most catchwords and signatures survive. Average size of page 29.5 × 18.25 cm, of frame 21.3 × 13 cm (*Piers*), 23.5 × 13.4 cm (items 2 and 3). Ruled for 39–47 lines per page, most often 40[93] (*Piers*) and 33 (items 2 and 3). Text of *Piers* divided into paragraphs, often incorrectly. *Piers* in two anglicana formata hands, the first with some secretary influence, varying in size in the second gathering and later.[94] Hand of items 2 and 3 more formal, larger and less expert. On fol. 1a an illuminated capital and vinet 'in the style of the first quarter of the fifteenth century' (A. I. Doyle); on fols 35a (*dowel*) 68b (*dobet*) and 98b (*dobest*) capitals with gilding; other passus initials pen-drawn in blue and red. Incipits and Latin in red; many nouns in text rubricated as subject-guides. Paragraph signs alternately blue and red. On fols 1a, 35a, 68b and 98b pen-drawings of an eagle with the letter *L* on its breast, on a patch of green. A few subject-guides and *nota*'s in main hand; a few corrections, some good, and one or two *nota*'s in another.

Rejected Manuscripts[95]

Huntington Library MS 114 (formerly Phillipps 8252)

This is a text produced by conflation of the three versions of *Piers Plowman*, sophisticated and with added spurious matter. Skeat's description of it as 'one of those MSS. which are

[92] See Skeat, *B-Text*, pp. xiv, xv.

[93] The second gathering is distinctive in being ruled for 43–7 lines per page, and in dry-point or brown lead later erased, whereas the others are ruled for 39 or 40 lines in ink.

[94] There is the familiar difficulty of deciding whether to identify one or two scribes.

[95] The editor of **A** takes the opportunity of mentioning in this category Bodleian Library MS 851 (S.C.3041) which he rightly dismissed as worthless for editorial use, but should have formally rejected in Vol. I. This is the manuscript called Z by Skeat (*C-Text*, pp. xxx–xxxiii).

Z is a conjoint manuscript. Its earlier part, to fol. 140b, is a conflated and sophisticated text resembling **A** more than **B** or **C**. There is no doubt that its origin was in the **A** tradition. It has also an unmistakable element of **C** version lines and a few lines and readings characteristic of **B**. That part of the text which is referable to **A** is much disordered and lacks many lines and passages. The passus are most often misdivided, apparently by guess. The text there contains many lines not relatable to any version, thus presumably spurious, and some of these occur at points of omission, as where the confessions of Envy and Avarice are reduced to 13 lines of which ten are peculiar to Z (see Skeat, op. cit., pp. xxxi, xxxii). In the later part, that is on fols 141ff. from Skeat's **C** XI 1 onward, it reads a good text of **C**.

The significant features of the first part are the extremely uneven quality of its text, which for short stretches can be quite good, the large amount of omission, the frequent disordering of lines, producing an imperfect or wholly inconsequent exposition, and the circumstance that some of the groups of 'new' lines occur where approximate multiples of 20 or 40 lines are wanting (i.e. the presumptive contents of sides or leaves). One possibility is that the early part of Z was copied

best avoided' is correct.[96] It is however not, as he apparently thought, a **C** copy, but a ruinously corrupted descendant of the **B** archetype, very heavily contaminated from **C** and to a lesser extent from **A**. Where there is no contamination the text is very corrupt by substitution, often at the expense of the metre, whether by rearrangement accompanying the contamination, or omission, or rewriting through miscomprehension. It has been twice examined throughout,[97] and has failed to produce one reading useful in editing **B**. Inclusion of its variants would more than double the size of the critical apparatus.

Sion College MS Arc. L.40 2/E (S)

This paper manuscript, copied c. 1550, was discovered by Neil Ker in 1966.[98] It is in pure descent from the **B** archetype, a member of the larger family of **B** manuscripts and of a particular subgroup.[99] We have rejected it because of the amount and character of its individual variation and because none of its readings helps with restoring the original text of the poem. Variation in S comprises not just the usual scribal substitutions, all quite typical, but also extensive arbitrary variation of a particular type. Some of this changes word-order, some is morphological, some is grammatical, a great deal is lexical. The latter ranges from effective substitution of a current for an obsolescent or obsolete term, or of a simplex for a compound or the reverse, through guesses of varying accuracy, to cases where blank ignorance leads to substitution of an unspecific 'dummy' or even simply to omission. This variation taken as a whole suggests powerfully that the copyist entertained no notion of fidelity to his exemplar, and also that his intention, deliberately and quite methodically effected,[100] was to modernize the language of the poem. As a result the manuscript contains some 2700 peculiar unoriginal variants (excluding simplex-compound variation and the innumerable substitutions for *ac*, *ne* and *ooþer*).

We collated S throughout but do not record the variation peculiar to it in our critical apparatus. Neither do we record the more than 2500 agreements of S with other manuscripts in recorded variation. The majority of these are merely products of coincident chronological variation;[101] none does more than reenforce the already abundant evidence for recovering the archetypal text of **B**.

S is, however, a representative of the **B** tradition, and we therefore include consideration of its 500 odd variational groupings in the classification of manuscripts.

from a text produced by someone acquainted with all versions of the poem, literate and able to write tolerable long lines, who was restoring from memory, and occasionally by sophistication, a physically defective copy, very imperfect, or in many places defaced, or both, of the **A** version. The other possibility is that the whole of the '**A**' component of the manuscript is merely a memorial reconstruction, the uneven quality of the text and the occasional coincidence of omission with sophistication being simply results of uneven recollection.

[96] *C-Text*, pp. xix, xx, n.

[97] By the **C** editor as well as by Kane. The former has published an account which illustrates the character of its *Piers Plowman* text: Russell, G. H. and Venetia Nathan, 'A *Piers Plowman* Manuscript in the Huntington Library', *Huntington Library Quarterly*, xxvi (1963), pp. 119–30. See also Chambers, 'Manuscripts of *Piers Plowman* in the Huntington Library', p. 18.

[98] It had previously escaped notice through being classified as '15th or 16th cent. English MS on paper, rhyming couplets'.

[99] See below, pp. 32ff.

[100] We have noticed some 50 instances where he let stand a Middle English word elsewhere usually eliminated.

[101] See the variational groups below, pp. 28, 32–4.

II

CLASSIFICATION OF THE MANUSCRIPTS

The copies of *Piers Plowman* described in the preceding section substantially agree in attesting a version[1] of the poem distinguished in shape, content, organization and particular readings from both the **A** version[2] and the **C** version.[3] It is divided into twenty-one parts, not twelve or thirteen like the **A** version, or twenty-three like the **C** version. It contains some 1400 lines of a distinctive character.[4] It lacks some

[1] Credit for identifying this belongs, as is the case with so many other *Piers Plowman* discoveries, to Skeat (*Parallel Extracts from Twenty-Nine Manuscripts of Piers Plowman, EETS* 17, London, 1866, pp. 1–12). His identification has only once been questioned: by Görnemann, G., *Zur Verfasserschaft und Entstehungsgeschichte von 'Piers the Plowman'*, Heidelberg, 1915. She maintained (p. 119) 'dass drei Versionen von *Piers Plowman* ursprünglich nicht vorhanden sind, sondern dass alle Hss. auf **ein** Urms. zurückgehen. Denn die von Skeat angenommenen, nach Inhalt und Form abgeschlossenen Versionen bestehen in Wirklichkeit nicht, der Unterschied zwischen den einzelnen Mss. ist ebenso gross wie der zwischen A, B und C.' Her arguments in support of this view were easily demolished by Krog, F., *Studien zu Chaucer und Langland*, Heidelberg, 1928, pp. 133–70.

[2] Defined in Vol. I, pp. 19–52.

[3] The **C** version is both distinctive and well attested, as will be shown in Vol. III of the present edition. Meanwhile it is definable as the form of *Piers Plowman* preserved in those manuscripts not of the **A** version, or under discussion here, or manifestly scribal in composition (for some otherwise respectable conjoint manuscripts see Donaldson below). The **C** manuscripts number eighteen and a fragment (recently discovered by Professor John Holloway); two other known primary copies, Bodley MS 851 and Huntington Library MS 114, appear from their isolation and the poor literary quality of their texts to be scribally created mixtures of several versions. (See above, pp. 14f.) There is a classified list of *Piers Plowman* manuscripts in Donaldson, E. T., *Piers Plowman: the C-Text and its Poet*, New Haven, 2nd edn. 1966, pp. 228–30. To this must now be added the Sion College manuscript of the **B** version discovered by Neil Ker (S) and the Holloway fragment.

[4] Prologue 50–2, 106, 115, 121–4, 128–31, 137, 139–45, 152, 159, 163, 164, 180, 189–92, 197, 207, 208, 223. I 116, 118, 120–3, 150, 151. II 13, 14, 31, 37, 38, 57, 97, 98, 174–6, 209, 210. III 234α–45, 332, 344–7, 351. IV 34, 40, 41, 125, 151, 153–6, 169, 170. V 36–8, 43, 52–5, 86, 88–92, 107, 116, 138–43, 162, 165–8, 235, 236, 242–6, 249, 254–9, 261, 264, 268, 272–3α, 277–81α, 286, 364, 365, 375, 378, 412, 418, 421, 486α,β, 546–8, 607, 608, 639–42. VI 36, 139–44, 147–51, 181, 182, 192, 194–6, 225–8, 316, 327, 328. VII 42, 43, 45, 46, 52α, 60α, 71, 74–7β, 79–87. VIII 52, 54–6, 130, 131. IX 15, 35–46, 60, 62–7, 71–94α, 98, 99, 100α–9, 115–20, 122, 128, 150–5, 193, 194, 210. X 22, 24, 25, 29, 31, 39–45, 92–105, 112–16α, 119, 197–9, 204α–11, 222, 223, 239, 241, 243–5, 246α–8, 250, 252, 257–97, 308, 330, 333, 335, 342–5, 351, 359, 359α, 360–7, 379, 401, 402, 413, 414, 434, 435, 437–47, 471–5, 481, 481α. XI 47–52, 64–70, 75–83, 86, 87, 94, 97, 99, 100, 155–7, 160–70, 174, 175, 177–83, 185, 187–9, 197–200, 211α–28, 230–2, 244, 246–8, 254, 265, 270–86α, 301, 302, 318–20, 322, 323, 325, 343, 358, 360–2, 378, 379, 383, 383α, 392–4, 396–401, 410, 421, 422, 433. XII 4–54α, 57, 57α, 58, 61–3, 65–7, 69, 69α, 71, 74–91, 93–8, 118, 119, 127, 147α, 165–8, 218–20, 222–4, 227, 228, 230–5, 244, 245, 247–61, 293–6. XIII 17, 24, 26, 31, 32, 34, 53–6, 67α, 72–3α, 108, 110, 111, 120–3, 128–36, 139–42, 148, 150–7, 160, 163α, 164, 166, 168, 171, 171α, 175, 178–97, 202–15, 225, 239, 241, 242, 244–8, 252, 253, 260–76, 284–90, 295, 297, 298, 300, 301, 305, 313–23, 331, 332, 342, 352–7, 359, 360, 368, 375–82, 389, 390, 399, 400, 402, 404–8, 414, 457–9. XIV 1–28, 30, 31, 33–7, 73–5, 78–100, 108, 124–30, 142–56, 168–95, 212α, 215α,

240 lines found in the **A** version,[5] and more than 1300 other lines found in the **C** version.[6] About 250 of its lines, mainly from Passus XIII, are differently located and applied in the **C** version.[7] Common possession of these broad features, together with innumerable less striking resemblances, creates a presumption that these copies represent a single manuscript[8] tradition: they are descendants of an exclusive common ancestor, differentiated from this and from one another entirely by the various effects of scribal transmission. The correctness of this presumption will now begin to appear from our account of their classification.

In presenting that account immediately after the description of the manuscripts we follow traditional editorial practice. But we do so only to observe a formality: classification of manuscripts is properly one of the last processes of editing. As originally conceived the investigation of the genetic history of a text had the specific object of providing its editor with a stemma to use in recension, that is the automatic elimination of unoriginal readings, and thus appeared a preliminary editorial operation. But actually if an attempt to classify manuscripts by recovering their genetic relation is to have any chance of producing accurate results it must observe two principles: that the evidence for genetic relation is agreement in *unoriginal* readings; and that to draw conclusions from any selection of such evidence (made on whatever grounds) is not just potentially but probably misleading.[9] Therefore classification of manuscripts cannot be safely undertaken until the whole text they contain is for practical purposes fixed.[10]

282–7, 307α, 308, 323–35. XV 1–14, 22, 58, 66–8, 73, 75, 81α–6, 89–91, 119–27, 134, 135, 138–43, 146–8, 150, 154, 155, 161, 164, 165, 170, 171, 175, 180, 184–6, 196, 198, 200–8, 211–16, 218, 241–3, 245, 246, 248–55, 257–78, 281–5, 295, 298, 299, 301–4, 312–17, 326–48, 355, 363, 368, 376, 390–2, 395, 409, 414–91α, 499, 500, 501–3α, 522, 525, 572, 574–81, 583, 584, 591, 594α, 598α–600, 605, 606. XVI 1–24, 25α, 26, 42, 46–50, 53–66, 69, 70, 73, 78, 86, 101, 103, 105–8, 110–12, 121, 124, 127, 130, 133–5α, 137, 138, 140–50, 155, 160–71, 174, 178, 179, 183, 184, 187, 189, 190, 200–3, 207–9, 211–18, 222–4, 227, 229, 234, 242α, 245, 246, 251. XVII 9, 39–45, 76–8, 84–6, 88–90, 92, 105–26, 136, 137, 153, 155–68, 173, 175, 192–4, 298. XVIII 6, 9, 139, 256, 301, 302, 306, 316α, 317α, 318α, 337, 344, 350–2, 354–7, 360, 360α, 391, 392.

[5] See Vol. I, pp. 21, 22.

[6] Many of these are cited in Skeat, W. W., *The Visions of William concerning Piers the Plowman*, *EETS* 54, London, 1873, pp. lxxxiv–xciv.

[7] The differences are illustrated in Skeat's *The Vision of William concerning Piers the Plowman in Three Parallel Texts*, I, Oxford, 1886.

[8] We beg leave, for economy of space, to extend the term 'manuscript' to Crowley's print which for our purposes represents a lost manuscript.

[9] See Vol. I, pp. 53–114.

[10] In this situation lodges the ultimate absurdity of recension as an editorial method: to employ it the editor must have a stemma; to draw the stemma he must first edit his text by other methods. If he has not done this efficiently his stemma will be inaccurate or obscure, and his results corre-

It was not, however, as a formality that we undertook our classification. For one thing we were obliged to test the accuracy of a published genealogy of the **B** manuscripts.[11] For another we believed (with justice, as it has turned out) that examination of the variational groups assumed by the manuscripts of our poem could not fail to be rewarding, notwithstanding our total scepticism about recension, and all genetic considerations apart. Whether or not the results of the process of classification supported earlier genetic conclusions, or even brought a new stemma to light, the operation would establish whether the **B** manuscripts were in fact descended from an exclusive common ancestor. It could not fail to illustrate the character of their tradition by indicating the extent of discernible corruption in its later stages, as well as of lateral transmission and coincident substitution; or to establish the status of individual manuscripts, especially whether any of these was a copy of another extant copy; or to improve our understanding of the transmission of Middle English texts in general; and it might possibly identify at least some genetic groups, from knowledge of which strength of manuscript support could be more accurately assessed.

Our method of classification was that employed in editing the **A** version. We first established a text at all possible points by comparison of variant readings, identifying or restoring the original reading from knowledge of typical scribal substitutions and on considerations of sense, alliteration and the poet's *usus scribendi*.[12] All agreements in substantive variation from this text, that is all agreements in certainly or presumably unoriginal readings affecting its sense, we treated as potential evidence of genetic relation. The variant groups formed by such agreements, whether in simple variation or in complex variation (if this could be confidently traced) we collected, analyzed and attempted to interpret.[13]

spondingly deficient; if he has been a successful editor he does not need a stemma, or recension, for his editing.

[11] Chick, E., *A Preliminary Investigation of the Pedigree of the B-Text MSS. of Piers Plowman*, unpublished University of London M.A. thesis, 1914; her conclusions were subsequently presented in Blackman, E., 'Notes on the B-Text MSS. of *Piers Plowman*', *JEGP*, xvii (1918), pp. 498–518.

[12] There is a full account of our editorial methods below, pp. 128ff.

[13] We made certain deliberate exclusions, of two kinds. First we ignored groups formed by agreement in several substantive variations unlikely to have genetic significance, or in variations of which the substantive character was open to question. Thus we did not collect groups formed by agreement in *Ac*] *But* or *Ac*] *And* or *Ac*] *om* because linguistic change made coincidence in these variations almost inevitable. For the same reason we ignored agreement in *lere*/*lerne* variation. We took no account of variation between *at* and *atte*, as possibly no more than orthographical in fifteenth-century manuscripts. Where from the context gender did not seem in doubt we ignored

We do not know of any other method of classification which would answer as well as this one to the circumstances of manuscript transmission;[14] nevertheless we must, before presenting our results, insist on its limitations. The first is human: because the method requires exercise of judgement at every stage, in the determinations of originality which afford its data, in the tracing of complex variation, and in the discrimination of variational and genetic groups, it implies successive possibilities of error. The second limitation is set by the almost always conflicting, often obscure quality of the evidence and the problem of interpretation by assessing relative probabilities that this poses.

The surviving manuscripts of the **B** tradition assume more than 1300 variational groups of which well more than 50 are markedly or relatively persistent. Even allowing for possible changes of exemplar these cannot all be genetic groups; some must be products of convergent variation, whether lateral transmission or coincident substitution. Our problem was to distinguish them.

Its nature and difficulty can be quickly shown by describing the procedure for making such distinctions. First, for reasons elsewhere set out,[15] we rejected the possibility of identifying any particular kinds of variants as necessarily produced by vertical transmission. This left us three criteria: relative persistence of agreement, distribution of agreement, and the congruency of variational groups presumed genetic. Each of these has its theoretical and practical limitations. With respect to persistence of agreement: there might seem to be a *prima facie* likelihood that manuscripts will agree in variation more often through common descent than through convergent variation. But that likelihood is manifestly not absolutely determinable; moreover it depends on two assumptions which are far from easy. The first is that the frequency of convergent variation is somehow limited. But for such limitation there is no evidence; indeed on the showing of our analysis it must have

she/heo/he variation as probably only linguistic. Agreements in variation in Latin lines we took into account at discretion. Second we reduced variant groups formed through visible correction by eliminating the corrected manuscripts, as evidently present by lateral transmission. The manuscripts most often concerned were M and Hm. For the same reason where the readings of the Crowley impressions differed we treated Cr[1] as the source of genetic information, and the readings of Cr[23] or Cr[2] and Cr[3] as deriving from 'correction'. (The source of most if not all of this 'correction' was a manuscript very similar to the group ancestor of OC[2].) Except for agreements of these two kinds, and for unintentional oversights, our analysis included all agreements in substantive variation.

[14] See Vol. I, pp. 53ff. for our reasons.

[15] See Vol. I, pp. 59–62, and below, p. 63.

occurred with extreme frequency. The second assumption is that all transmission is uniformly corrupt, that genetic relation will always be indicated by relatively abundant agreement in error. If this assumption is put in another form, that all the human agents of manuscript transmission were equally inefficient, its difficulty appears.[16] The same assumptions are necessary to the use of distribution of agreement as a criterion of genetic relation; this is made possible only by accepting the evidential force of persistent agreement, and by readiness to dismiss conflicting evidence as the product of convergent variation. It seems right to emphasize that our procedures contain arguments which could nullify them; but the hard fact is that there is no more satisfactory alternative. If there is to be a genetic analysis the assumptions must be made. As to the reliability of the further test of congruency,[17] this is necessarily contingent, since the effectiveness of its application must depend both on the correctness of all other genetic identifications than the one being tested and on the relatively complete recovery of the history of transmission.

Thus the best method of genetic analysis known to us is an indifferent one. It can reach conclusions only by assumptions of convenience; it demands recourse to explanations of change of exemplar, correction or conflation, and coincident substitution; it can be applied only flexibly, that is expeditiously. Its character and that of our particular problem are reflected in the limited and qualified results we present. Even to give an account of these is attended with difficulties, for while the whole classification is a single process, each part of which depends on every other one, to represent its logic it must be presented as a consecutive demonstration.

Our classification begins with variational groups of two manuscripts. Seventeen manuscripts can form 136 combinations; of this possible number more than 100 actually occur. We cite those supported by a dozen or more agreements.

[16] Thus in the case of two conflicting variational groups, XY agreeing in 100 readings, and XZ agreeing in 50, by identifying XY as the genetic group we reject the possibility that X and Z are the descendants of an exclusive common ancestor copied with unusual care which transmitted relatively few peculiar errors to its twin progeny, that Z preserved the text of this ancestor with relative purity, and that the XY agreements came about by convergent variation.

[17] For instance in the case of two variational groups WX (50 agreements) and XY (50 agreements), all other things being equal, if WX form an element of a persistent larger group UVWX and XY do not occur in any larger group, there seems a probability that WX is genetic and XY random.

Bm
BmBo 123[18]

Bo
BoCot 130
BmBo 123

C
YC 23
CF 21
GC 18

C^2
OC^2 330
GC^2 66
C^{2}F 22
C^{2}S 20

Cot
BoCot 130
CotF 18

Cr
CrS 215
CrF 83
CrG 47
HmCr 20
CrM 17
WCr 17
CrR 12

F
RF 504
FS 160
GF 142
FH 87
HmF 87
CrF 83
MF 36
WF 26
C^{2}F 22
CF 21
CotF 18

G
GF 142
GC^2 66
GS 65
CrG 47
GH 42
HmG 38
GC 18
GY 16
GR 14

H
FH 87
GH 42
HS 31
HmH 18

Hm
HmF 87
WHm 43
HmG 38
HmS 26
HmCr 20
HmH 18

L
LR 24
LM 12

M
MF 36
CrM 17
MS 13
LM 12

O
OC^2 330

R
RF 504
LR 24
GR 14
CrR 12

S
CrS 215
FS 160
GS 65
HS 31
HmS 26
C^{2}S 20
MS 13

W
WHm 43
WF 26
WCr 17

Y
YC 23
GY 16

The situation represented in this table disappoints any expectation that genetic pairs might stand out as strikingly persistent or at any rate unchallenged among the variational groups. The manuscript Bo

[18] These figures do not include agreement shown in the apparatus as of two manuscripts if the reading concerned also occurs in S. When in the following pages we cite the variants supporting any group we shall note those excluded because shared by S.

occurs in two groups of practically equal persistence, BmBo and BoCot; a very persistent group OC^2 appears to be challenged by GC^2 of marked persistence; Cr occurs in three groups of marked persistence; F, while a member of one of the most persistent of all the **B** manuscript variational groups, RF, also pairs notably with five other manuscripts, S, G, H, Hm and Cr; meanwhile the conflicting groups so formed are challenged in their turn not only by RF but also by GS, GC^2, GH, CrS and CrG. The evidence is limited as well as obscure: there is no indication that C or L or Y pairs genetically.

The survival of genetic pairs is not an invariable feature of manuscript traditions. From this consideration and from the conflict of evidence it might then seem conceivable that most if not all these variational groups were formed by convergent variation, that is conflation and coincident substitution, in indeterminable combinations. But there are indications that the variational groupings of these manuscripts in pairs are not all random: the quite striking persistence of three of them, OC^2, RF and CrS, and the circumstance that one constituent of two of these pairs appears infrequently in conflicting groups. These suggest the possibility that notwithstanding contradictory indications OC^2 and RF probably, and CrS possibly, are genetic groups.[19]

To accept this suggestion seems easiest in the case of OC^2, which, although less well supported than RF, is less often and less variously challenged. The following are the agreements of OC^2.

Prologue 25 preieres] *sg.* 32 men] *om.* 34 giltlees] not synles. 39 *addl. line after.* 42 þe] *om.* 44 as] þe. 52 to] *om.* 67 Molde] erþe; faste] wel f. 102 lefte] self. 109 impugnen] i. it. 184 route of] *om.* I 21 and] *om.* 31 *line om.* 38 nauȝt] þou n. 39 þe] a. 41 it] *om.* 42 beste] bettre. 47 Tho] to; hym] þat h. 57 For] And. 89 Dooþ] And. 104 þat] þe. 131 er] erst. 135 *line om.* 151 to] in. 155 þis] þe; taken] *om.* 170 wiþ] bi. 198 no] in. 206 er] erst; þise] þe trewe. II 5 he] sche. 40 sherewe] *om.* 54 That] And. 66 *line om.* 79 speche] felaw. 97 soupen] to s. 101 be] he be. 134 wit] witti. 153 þi wedded] *tp.* 215 with hym] *tp.* III 10 into] in. 20 Mede þanne] *tp.* 31 And] *om.* 58 sonnest] is s. 75 For] And. 82 poisone] punyschen. 98 That] þat is. 108 þe] þis. 127 she] *om.* 131 tikel] fikil. 146 youre] oure. 163 in] into. 164 in(1)] into. 192 ylasted] durid. 199 I] And I. 201 his] *om.* 210 mekely] myldelich. 221 men] mene. 281 wol] wolde. 284 tauȝte] t. it. 298 lordes] londis. 340 no] *om.* IV 30 hem] *om.* 178 bi þis] on a. 181 folk] *om.* V 8 on] of. 12 wiþ] *om.* 13 preued] *pres.* 30 He] And. 53 ouþer] ⁊ o.; ye] he. 60 and reherced] reherede. 82 lene] lere. 87 and] of. 117 I] And I; my] myn owne. 126 redily] rede I. 138 þe] *om.* 154 þan] or. 176 *line om.* 183 speche] sight. 249 hem] *om.* 282 in] of. 308

[19] A genetic relation for OC^2 and for RF was proposed by Mrs Blackman. See 'Notes on the B-Text MSS.', pp. 500, 501–3, 509, 517.

boþe] after. 338 vmwhile] oþerwhile. 364 so] þoo so. 421 in(2)] *om.* 423 yerne] sone. 430 vnkynde] vnhynde. 432 þer] if. 462 soore] *om.* 464 on] on þe. 469 I] *om.* 470 so] *om.* 471 feloun] schrewe. 496 þow] *om.* 498 al] *om.* 525 hym] *om.* 535 scrippe] s. wende. 568 þat] *om.* 583 to] do. 590 And] *om.* 617 grace] til g. 634 hym] alle. VI 16 wol] comaundeþ] biddiþ. 31 foweles] bestis. 33 þise] hise. 77 now] but. 81 it] ful. 85 Forþi] For. 125 for(2)] *om.* 127 youre] *om.* 137 whete] swete. 153 he] *om.* 159 þe(1)] *om.* 165 bettre] þe b. 167 was] nas. 195 his] her. 198 mesurable] resonable. 203 and] of. 219 false] fawti; men] man. 227 god] go. 299 it neȝed] *tp.* 312 heiȝliche] hye. VII 15 And] *om.* 23 his] her. 24 best liked] *tp.* 37 in(1)] into. 56 outen] *om.* 92 worþen] & w. 143 On] Or on. 179–86 *lines om.* 192 and] at. VIII 7 *line om.* 23 *line om.* 31 stonde] stumble. 78 þe] *om.* 96 boþe] hem b. 109 þe] þi. 119 we(2)] I. IX 41 lettre] *pl.* 51 As] And þat is as. 59 or] &. 64 deuel] deuelis. 108 hem] *om.* 128 wedded] ioyned. 144 a] & a. 164 seiþ crist] *om.* 186 Wreke] werke. X 27 holi] þe h. 28 gyueþ] good g. 51 games] myrþes. 75 is] been. 102 maad] *om.* 103 al] *om.* 110 wil] wiles] whyles. 116 torende] renten. 120 þis] his. 122 to] *om.* 184 lerned] kennede. 189 A] And. 230 heuene] þis world. 256 Ne] For. 341 it] *om.* 381 lif] seyntis. 383 it] *om.* 395 of] *om.* 399 meschief] m. is. 415 clause] cause. 435 wisedom] *pl.* 441 so] þere; for] as. 444 ben] *om.* 449 That clergie] Clergie þo] Clergie. 475 manye] *disloc.* XI 10 to] vnto. 91 it] *om.* 97 and] or. 210 And] For. 224 Boþe] But. 230 mannes] *pl.* 245 Ther] þat. 263 penaunce] pacience. 266 *line om.* 279 *addl. line after.* 313 crouneþ] *om.* 331 and] hadde. 340 And] *om.* 349 wriȝte] wyȝt. 358 breþyng] bredyng. 379 a(2)] of. 382 suffreþ] *pret.* 404 þer] her. XII 17 ynowe] *om.* 38 continue] contene. 40 þe] his. 60 lowe] þe l. 67 And] *om.* 69 ne] þe. 79 gretter in] *tp.* 106 enemy] *pl.* 129 and] *om.* 140 þis] his. 164 þo] þe. 183 auenture] a. he. 192 þow] ȝe. 240 þe(2)] *om.* 246 of] on. 252 repente] r. hym. XIII 56 priueliche] *om.* 58 tales] wordis. 84 Iuste] Iutte. 85 hym] me] men. 106 day] *om.* 107 han] *om.* 128 þat] *om.* 135 kan] knoweþ. 139 Thus] *om.* 154 And] In. 162 enemy] *pl.* 189 litel] ful l. 201 pak] bak. 214 preued] serued. 222 hym] h. þoo. 225 Al] And alle. 240 wiþ] *om.* 249 bocches myȝte] *tp.* 253 it] *om.* 264 hem] *om.* 321 yuel] y. wicked. 339 or] &. 360 And] And I. 362 worste] wors; a] *om.* 383 herde] *pres.* 390 a] *om.* 391 if] *om.* 410 mysdedes] dedis. 414 with hym] *om*; or] &. 416 Whan] And w. 418 þe] *om.* 459 it(2)] *om.* XIV 17 filþe] synnes. 21 it] *om.* 52 clyngest] chillist. 53 gyues] gomes. 86 bere] here. 89 surgiens] *sg.*; failleþ] *pret.* 100 and(2)] & þanne. 117 beestes] breddis / bidders. 145 riche] r. men. 163 men] *om.* 169 *ingrati*] vnkynde. 170 hem] vs. 201 be] *om.* 202 vs] þee. 243 a] *om.* 253 of] *om*; vntyled] vnhiled. 266 Hir] And. 275 quod he] *om.* 282 woot] it w. 285 spiritual] perpetuel. 290 kynges] *sg.* 295 he] *om.* 307 þat] *om.* 316 to] for. 330 lordshipe] larde. XV 12 a] &. 24 and] or. 31 I] *om.* 63 Putte] Pullede. 81 siluer] goodis. 121 forbeere] heer for. 122 *spurious line.* 124 botons] barres. 134 wiþ] þoruȝ. 144 By] Be þei (*twice*). 150 fauntelte] fauntee. 154 poore] þe p. 156 preiseþ] precheþ. 161 kenne] tellen. 162 neuere] *om.* 181 wel] *om.* 183 liggeþ] been. 184 liflode] *om.* 213 lolleris] losels. 229 and(1)] *om.* 232 he] *om.* 262 oure] *om.* 290 Poul] Anoþer p. 315 hadde] *pres.* 317 hadde] han. 326 þe] *om.* 348 is] been. 353 foule] ful. 355 it semeþ] I leue. 357 witty] *om.* 361 shepherdes] heerdis. 367 þe(2)] *om.* 375 Ne] Is. 421 Antony...dominyk] domynyk... antony. 433 It] *om.* 462 seiþ] *pret.* 465 And] *om.* 470 as] so. 510 That] And. 529 in] *om.* 586 on] *om.* XVI 32 and] of. 51 pureliche] puriliche. 57 longe] been þei l. 59 of(2)] of oo. 69 as] as a. 71 wole] wolde. 81 Ysaye] ysaac. 84 men] *om.* 87 it] he. 100 þe] þat.

138 hir] *om.* 160 in] i. þe. 165 deeþ] þe d. 171 *line om.* 182 myght] *om.* 187 of] of al. 202 *line om.* 224 holy] *om.* 245 foot] forþ. 257 he] h. þoo. 258 is] i. þis. 264 may] *om.* 266 som day] *om.* XVII 32 He] I; his] my. 33 it] þee. 81 lette] *om.* 83 hym] wiþ h. XVIII 389 trewe] been t.[20]

The question is how seriously this impressive list of agreements in variants of all kinds is challenged by the following agreements of GC².

Prologue 214 loue] the l. I 20 of] on. V 314 of] o. þe. 494 out] *om.* 630 a] *om.* VI 145 Nones] ones. X 67 þise] the. XI 260 on a] a(n). XIV 292 comaundement] *pl.* XV 430 heuedes] bedis. XVI 101 hir] hys. 207 oþeres] other. XVII 204 so] *om.* 210 leye] lyght. 213 beleue] leele b. 217 brenneþ] swellith. 220 shapte] gave. 277 and] of. 322 For to] *om.* XVIII 29 adoun] downe. 34 And] (and) to. 181 *line om.* 189 þat] *om.* 221 To] &; to] *om.* 249 þo] þer. 258 vnioynen...vnlouken] vnloken...vnbynden. 270 me] vs. 278 For] *om.* 285 þat] *twice.* 327 amendes] *sg.* 335 persone] likenesse. 349 here] *om.* 383 on] vpon. 394 acale] cold. XIX 11 it is] *tp.* 46 from] it f. 90 truþe] trewe. 186 þat] *om.* 200 to(2)] *om.* 213 þanne] tho. 236 to] *om.* 303 in(2)] in ony. 329 deuysede] anon d. 356 we vs] vs well. 367 Thanne] that. 376 penyes] pennaunce. 440 wroȝte al] *tp.* 444 and] or. 454 neuere] no. 475 borwe] *pret.* XX 3 at] in. 14 he] h. be. 36 lakkyng] lacke. 40 Ioye] *pl.* 98 pestilences] *sg.* 118 Weren] *om.* 181 a(1)] to a. 182 The] that was þe; it] *om.* 219 purses] gypsers. 251 lafte þei] *tp.* 253 kynde] k. wytt. 280 of] in. 298 pynne] vnpynne. 316 Conscience] confessyon. 340 seide] he s. 373 seigh] seithe.[21]

That these two groups are not actually in conflict appears from the respective distribution of agreements which support them. For where the OC² agreement falls off in the later passus (as is apparent even when O's defections in XVII 99–346 and XIX 281–358 are taken into account) the number of GC² agreements increases. If then we can accept that the dozen GC² agreements in Prologue–XVI[22] and the OC² agreement in XVIII are coincidental, the evidence of these two variational groups is that OC² had an exclusive common ancestor to some point in XVII,[23] and that thereafter C² derives from a different exemplar. Whether this exemplar was also the ancestor of G, and GC² a genetic pair in XVIII–XX, is not however immediately

[20] Variants in which OC² agree at I 53, III 76, VIII 73, XIII 358, XVI 237 also occur in S. These agreements are thus not evidence for a genetic group OC².

[21] Variants in which GC² agree at V 98, XV 467 also occur in S.

[22] Only one, at XV 430 is striking. But it could have occurred coincidentally on the suggestion of 426–8, esp. *bedemen*, 428.

[23] O is defective in XVII 99–346 and XIX 281–358; this and the fact that C² is the later manuscript might suggest that C² was copied from O to XVII 98, and thereafter from a complete manuscript. But the existence of some 30 unoriginal readings peculiar to O makes this seem unlikely. For if C² were a copy of O they would presuppose a corrector of C² more intelligent than the character of that manuscript otherwise leads one to expect.

indicated, for G also forms a variational group with F, established by some 140 agreements. This group will be considered in relation to the outstandingly persistent variational group RF.

The common characteristics of R and F have long been recognized, and a close relation between them accepted. Indeed the text which they preserve is in certain respects so distinctive as to have generated the opinion that it is an intermediate version of the poem, a stage in the revision from **A** to **B** or **B** to **C.** We shall presently show that this opinion was mistaken.[24] Meanwhile in the context of the genetic history of the **B** manuscripts the persistent agreements of RF in unoriginal readings must be set out, if only because their indication of a genetic relation between R and F is so seriously challenged. R and F agree in the following variations.[25]

Prologue 144 *line om.* 153 of] *om.* 171, 172 *lines om.* 216 til] er. 223 kynne] *om.* I 41 shendeþ] sueth. 44 holdeþ] kepeth. 78 me leelly] *tp.* 82 *line om.* 87 It] þat i. 88 who] He (þat). 103 And] Ne. 110 To] And. 133 and troneþ] for to / þat shal saue. 134 siȝte of] *om.* 138 kenne me] lerne. II 41 fikel] f. of. 51 lat] þat / at. 57 assembled] ensembled. 68 Thei] And. 83 Vnbuxome...bolde] bold & v. 85 cheste] gestes. 98 as] as a; hem] hym. 161 hem] hym; þis] þe. 228 with] to. 239 ek] also. III 8 gilt] *pl.* 19 cast...craft] crafte... cast. 33 ne] *om.* 51–62 *lines om with padding.* 63 of...house] to ȝow alle. 78 on(1)] vpon. 80 on] vpon. 82 For þei] And. 91 loue(1)] lord. 127 false] faire. 149b, 150a *om.* 155 youre] þe. 178 And] A. þat. 187 kyng] kniȝt. 205 blood] lond. 214 yonge men] ȝoumen. 219 biddynge] beggyng. 243 truþe] trewe. 258 a(1)] *om.* 265 his(1)] my. 310 spille] lese. 328 þat siȝte] þe s. þerof. 352 Mede] me. IV 26 Mede...erþe] on eerth m. þe mayde maketh. 40 Reson] *om.* 55 hewen] hennes. 92 Bettre] þat b. 156 þat] þe. 173 wiþ] *om*; loked] *pres.* 181 moost] alle. V 19 in] *om.* 40 spilleþ] he s. 70 alle] *om.* 73 þe Saterday] euery d. / on þe d. 76 shewe] schrewe / shryue. 111 haþ] h. on. 128 sory] euere s. 133 chaffare] ware. 141 abrood] *om.* 146 freres] *om.* 153 boþe] *om.* 178 at] wel a. 223 vsed] *pres.* 224 was] is. 251 lordes] l. quod heo / he. 255 as(2)] as þe. 266 nolde] wolde nouȝt. 277α Shal] For s. 312 Sire] and s. 315 dysshere] dissheres douȝter. 322 ben] to b. 385 slymy] slymed. 393 *add* quod he. 405 feble] seke. 406 haue] hadde. 420 and] or. 432 þe] *om.* 441 Repentestow] Repentest. 455 And...I(1)] what I nam / have take. 473 *line om.* 490 þe] þat. 495 in] þennes i. 504 ruþe] mercy. 519 bolle] bulle. 522 keyes] þe k. 540 hym] hem. 552 hewe] man / men; he] þei; haþ] haue. 566 of] of þi. 582 þow] ȝe. 596 for] *om.* 599 for] of. 611 forþ] *om.* 639 knowe þere] welcome. VI 39 hem] men. 48 cherles] clerkes / a clerk. 50 þi] *om.* 52 Hold] H. nauȝt. 83 olde] holde. 86–8 *misdivision and omission.* 89 me] *om.* 98 deye] *pret.* 113 To] & wente / ȝeed to. 155 with] on. 202 to] þo to. 217 *line om.* 218 Fortune] fals(hed). 231 þee] god. 246 wel] for. 250 þe] a. 270 þe] *om.* 286 plauntes] herbes. 302 nolde] wolde no; noȝt] *om.* 308 noȝt] *om.* 310, 311

[24] See below, pp. 63ff.

[25] R is defective in Prologue 1–124, I 141–II 40 and XVIII 411–XX 26.

misdivision and omissions. 322 faste] ful f. 323 water] wat / what. VII 19 noon *A*] no; graunte] nauȝt g. 21 by...and] ofte. 24 liked] *pres*. 25 wynnyng] *pl*. 32 som] *om*. 38 were] w. manye; murie] *om*; manye] þat. 40 *misdivision*. 42α *line om*. 49 Confortep] And c. 79 þe] *om*. 80 yeueþ] ȝift. 82 For] Forthi. 124 penaunce] *pl*. 129 he] or. 130 foweles] foles. 138 þe Abbesse] *om*. 161 cleyme] reue. 194 acountes] and a. 196 didest] *pres*. 204 while] þe w. VIII 4 was] were. 9 Maistres] And m. 12 contree] court; as] þer. 14–17 *lines om*. 66 louely] *om*. 77 to] hym to. 128 ben] *om*. IX 2 kynnes] maner. 11 sire] *om*. 20 and(2)] a. sire. 22 grete lordes] a g. lord. 23 lady] *om*. 31 hym moost] *tp*. 52 word] his w. 61 man] wiȝt. 67 he shoop] s. hem. 83 Ne] And. 88 Eyþer] þat ayther / ech; of hem] *om*; þat] hem. 98 drede] loue; dooþ þerfore] (for) to do. 103 siþþe] seche / swiche. 116b–19a *lines om*. 120 þe(1)] þere / here. 121 folk] f. and. 138 ywasshen] Iwasted. 161 swich] þat. 162 þe] þat. 163, 164 *lines om*. 165 crist] Ihesus. 169 *line om*. 173–5 *lines om with padding*. 182–8 *lines om*. 202–6 *lines om*. 209 werk] *pl*. X 14 on erþe] here. 20 to] and. 48 value] worth. 67 gorge] *pl*. 73 tyme] *om*. 76 is pride] *tp*. 87 And] Euere as he. 138 bolde] *om*. 150 For] And f. 165 clergie] cherche / crist. 170 speche] berynge. 179 mo] *om*. 188 sotile] sauȝtele. 192 þee likeþ] þow thenke. 223 to] for to; what is] *om*. 252 scripture] euaungelie(3). 256 merite] mercy. 279 now] no / not. 292 or to greue] *om*. 343 as nede techeþ] at pure / in gret n. 366 moþ] mote. 382 witnesseþ] telleth. 393 and] a. here. 397 men] man. 401 dide...oþere] and o.d. 420 On] For on / a. 431 *line om*. 464 konne] knowe. 474 hir] þe. 477 þe] *om*. 478 knowyng] kunnyng. XI 6 mette me þanne] me tydde to dreme. 37 poete] p. þo. 46–9 *lines om*. 84 lewte] l. þo. 108 if] *om*; knewe] knowe. 121 saufte] safly] saue. 125 reneye] receyue. 130 a reneyed] he renne(th). 138 al to] may al. 145 and(2)] of. 147 in] of. 158 ye] þe. 180 Who] For ho. 185 Iesu] is I. 211 for] here f. 221 alowaunce maad] alowed (þei both). 247 mennes] men. 257 folwe] wolde / welde. 270 folk] men. 280 *expanded*. 286 dide] *om*. 297 riche] *om*. 349 nys] is no. 371 tyme] *pl*. 399 Euery] vch. 424 þi] in þ.; to] efte to; suwe] sitte. 425 Shal] For s. 435 *add* by my soule. 436 no þyng] non / no man. 437 hym(2)...man] no m. loueth his felachipp. XII 11 pestilences] penaunce(s). 13, 13α *lines om*. 21 Seide] And s. 23 herde] *pres*. 30 and(2)] *om*. 34 while] þe w. 48 badenesse she] badd vse. 49 I may] *tp*. 69 wit þe] wit his / witys. 76 *line om*. 78 caractes...wroot] cristes c. 99 eiȝen] siȝte. 126 kepere] kynge / keye and k. 134 broȝt] bouȝte. 139–47α *lines om*. 148 þe] an. 153 Clerkes] And c. 169 *line om*. 178 coutereþ] kenneth. 183 *add* boþe. 186 *line om*. 187 to...sette] sette to scole. 194 *line om*. 203 Seint] *om*. 211 þef] *om*. 216 assoille] telle. 222 colours] *sg*. 228 to] þere to. 261 it] he. 268 Aristotle] For a. 269 logik] glosing / glose. 275 soules] *sg*. 287 þat] *om*. XIII 2 fey] fere / afeerd. 14–20 *lines om*. 41 eet] hadde; mete] *pl*. 45 wepe] many. 57 *ad te*] *om*. 76 They] Ac / But þei. 84 Iuste] Iusty. 86 preynte on] bad. 92 braun] b. ne. 93 penaunt] *pl*. 112 curteisly] ful c. 123 to(2)] *om*. 142 þow] to. 149 coueiteþ] desireth. 157 lat] and l.; deme if] se wher. 173 and] ne. 192 a] vch a / euery. 208 and] of. 209 Sarsens] and s. 220 of] and o.; þei(2)] *om*. 232 Iogele] iangele. 235 brynge] *pret*. 249 And] *om*. 256 þe(1)] no. 259 pureliche] priueliche. 301 on] *om*. 343 his] myn. 353 hir(1)] *om*. 372,373 *misdivision and omissions*. 382 me] *om*. 393 eschaunges] chaunges. XIV 12 neuere] nouȝt. 14 þoruȝ word] thouȝt. 29 no] þow n. 47 liflode it] þat l. 52 drye] drouȝthe. 53 gyues] feytour(es). 60 bettre] leuere. 98 Where] Ȝe w. 102 paciente] pacience and. 134 afore] tofore. 135 he(1)] *om*; he(2)] þei. 142 moore] huire. 143 hire] heuene. 152 rewfulliche] riȝtfullich. 155–9 *lines om*. 177 wynter tymes] wyntres tyme. 181 of] o. alle.

187 Confession...knowlichynge] knowlechyng...confession. 212 Richesse] (þe) riche. 213 preesseþ] precheth / procheþ. 239 if] þouȝ. 252,253 *lines om.* 263 lond] lorde. 301 is] is þe; helþe] hele. 312α *line om.* 319 lettred] lered. 326 seweþ] scheweth. XV 8 ne] and. 72 *line om.* 73 swich] *om.* 93 lawe] *pl.* 111 dongehill] dongoun. 121 baselardes...broches] broches / broode...baselardes. 122 and] or. 130 hadde] maked. 136 as] and. 156 oure saueour] god. 160 neded hym] *tp.* 162 a] *om.* 175 good] *pl.* 181 Aues] *sg.* 200 þe] *om.* 224 stille] so. 254α *line om.* 263 wel...man] euery m. may w. 278 of] o. þe. 282 tymes] *sg.* 283 adayes] on a d. 285 fond] fedde. 286 hym] in h. 293 soden] eeten. 294 lyued and] a. by. 297 many...yeres] amonges wilde bestes. 317 rule] ordre. 342 feeste] fede. 346 deliuereþ] is deliuered. 356 For] F. what. 371 þe element] clement. 387 suffiseþ] *sufficit.* 403,404 *lines om.* 405 enchauntede] chaunted / chawnteþ. 408 As] And. 418 Peeren] Peres. 421 and] or. 422 and] or. 423 almesse] fyndynge. 424 goode] lele. 427 brynge] hem b. 499 For] To; and] a. to. 502 me þynkeþ] it semeth. 504 and... bileueþ] to on persone to helpe. 505 In] On; greet] *om*; god] g. þei greden. 533–69 *lines om.* 572 techen] schewen. 580 ferme] for me / formed. 585 men] it hem. 594 deed...stank] stanke and d. 604 hir] ȝet h. XVI 4 trewely] treuthe. 17 Vnder] And v. 27,28 *mis-division and omissions.* 38 Thoruȝ] with. 48 whan] what. 51 pureliche] priueliche. 78 rogged] rused / rusched. 115 þe] þat. 152 of] þoruȝ. 158 to] and. 160 On] In. 176 noȝt] n. me / me n. 189 The...haþ] þat alle þe liȝt of / & þe lif. 192 knowe] *om.* 198 children] barnes. 199 and] a. alle. 209 þus] þat. 252 seiȝ] seyde; vs] hem. 254 For] And; þat] & þ. 264 *line om.* 270–3 *lines om with padding.* XVII 3 wiþ] þerewith. 7,8 *misdivision and om.* 10 þi lettres] þat lettre. 25 Ye] *om.* 39–49 *lines om.* 60 of] on. 67 hande] *pl.* 87 þat(1)] þe. 97 he] *om.* 98 passion] þe p. 106 take] taketh. 111 vnhardy...harlot] vnharlot / but an h. 115–26 *lines om.* 136 highte] bihiȝt. 141 foldynge] folden. 150 at] and. 154 hand] fust. 162 Inne] *om.* 173 and] or. 204 in] aȝeynes. 221–47 *lines om.* 249 tow] tacche. 257 *ingratus*] ingrat; kynde] kynne. 266 þat] & þ. 293 vs(1)] *om.* 300 now] nouȝt. 304 þoruȝ] to. 311 lyues] lyue. 316 power] per. 320 *line om.* 330 þe borre] cowȝhe. 333 ben þus] *tp.* 344 cause] resoun. XVIII 12 spakliche] spracliche. 41 Iewes] *om.* 50 rybaud] *pl.* 59 The] Til (þe). 62 depe] here. 69 þat] *om.* 83 stode] stede. 85 baar] þat b. 86 vnspered] opned. 93 for] hem f. 121 Whan] And w. 124 which] swich. 129 kynnes] kende. 147 I] *om.* 158 fordo] do. 180 *line om.* 183 my suster] *om.* 190 it] þow it. 199 *line om.* 203 preue] preie. 214 to(2)] and. 217 is ynogh] is nouȝte / it is. 219 murþe] ioye. 221 was] is. 234 wise of] men in. 245 louke] loke. 246 see] mone. 248 biquasshed] biquasche. 252,253 *lines om.* 256 of] o. a. 262α,263 *run together.* 270 it] hem. 277 he robbeþ] & robbe. 281 If] þat ȝif. 284 seuene] þis(e) s. 291 so] al so. 297 tyme] *om.* 303 I(1)] And I; leued] *pres.* 304 suffre] nauȝt s. 314 we haue] *tp.* 317 soone] *om.* 319 Dukes] *sg.* 321 brak] braste. 348 noȝt] neuere. 353 þoruȝ(1)] with; is] was. 355 þo] þing. 362 widder] grettere. 383 if] and. 395 se] s. his. 398 kynde] kyn. 409 sharpe] scharpest. XX 45 to(2)] or t. 65 were] we(e). 91 Confort] *om.* 97 after] a. hym. 102 leet] left. 132 bright] rede. 139 and] and a. 142 while] þe w. 151 kille] calle. 152 lepte aside] seith / seyde *occide.* 158 wo] *om.* 166 hym] *om.* 174 dryuen] to d.; Dyas] dayes. 202 me] my lif. 214 Conscience] *om.* 233 for] f. no. 238,239 *lines om.* 240 And] For. 242 þo] *om.* 283 penaunce] *pl.* 305 ben] were. 378 haþ] h. so.[26]

[26] Variants in which RF agree at V 215, XVI 25, 148 also occur in S.

This impressive body of evidence must powerfully suggest genetic relation. The obstacle to immediate acceptance of that indication is the number of conflicting variational groups in which F figures.[27] If RF are a genetic pair the many agreements supporting these latter groups can have been produced only by changes of exemplar or by convergent variation.

The most persistent of the conflicting groups is FS.

I 159 Forþi] þerfore. II 14 enuenymes] enemyes. 168 hire feet] foote. 198 lokeþ] will. III 30 hem(2)] hem to. 97 þise] *om.* 129 Is] þer is. 158 hire] she. 274 boþe] *om.* 301 a] *om.* 341 þat] on þe. IV 5 But] B. if. 30 þe] for þe. 42 And] *om.* 50 chekes] wille. 62 luft] wyght. 108 þe] *om.* 147 afeld donge] dunk to (the) feelde. 160 leten] helden. 182 commune] comonys. V 6 ferþer a foot] a foote furthere. 86 Ech a] euery. 356 smauȝte] smellid. 405 puttes] prisoun. 424 forsake] forswere. 484 to] into. 571 on ydel] in ydelnesse. VI 5 þis] þat. 6 teche] ȝow t. 99 yede] wente. 170 manaced] þrette. 233 tilie] wynne. 237 and bidde] *om.* 247 ech] euery. 277 þat] ⁊. 297 yerne] faste. VII 2 erþe] grownde. 42 konneþ] knowith. 84 biddeþ] beggiþ. 98 lyue] leede. 148 yede] wente. 175 Indulgences] all I. 177 vnderfongen] take(n). 187 renkes] all. VIII 21 siþes] tymes. 117 yeden] wentyn. 123 to(2)] *om.* IX 97 That] he þat; he] *om.* 172 Haue þei] *tp.* X 61 Is] þere ys. 96 hir] his. 140 þat] *om.* 266 and] if. 404 doon] do þei. 415 *culorum*] conclusioun; curatours] of c. 435 wonye] dwelle. XI 87 by(2)] *om.* 91 lif] man. 101 Þyng] A þ. 104 be] but be. 143 wite] knowe. 180 leneþ] beleveþ. 198 ben som] *tp.* 209 Forþi] þerfore. 269 riȝt] *om.* 284 for] *om.* 316 eiþer is] boþe been. 326 ech a] euery. 328 yeden] wentyn. 367 And] *om.* 377 þiself] þou. 421 Lakkedest] þou l. XII 2 ne] or. 11 with] *om.* 34 forþ] *om.* 99 a] *om.* 178 ech a] euery. 239 is] *om.* 297 riȝt] *om.* XIII 88 ech a] euery. 89 goþele] gowle. 99 seide] bad. 188 foryelde] forbeede. 222 he sholde] hym to. 261 commune] *pl.* 267 a litel] *om.* 299 gomes] men. 316 by þe two] on bothe. 357 it myȝte] *tp.* 386 leue me] *om.* 387 dedly...doon] do dedly synne. 458 þerof] *om.* XIV 19 beten... bouken] bowke...beete. 85 myȝte(2)] may. 188 manye siþes] ofte. 192 of...moste] muste ben of pouerte. 249 þan] or. 271 ech a] euery. 295 Wynneþ he] *tp.* XV 23 quod he] *om.* 39 coueitest to] wilt. 75 of(1)] *om.* 104 bifel...clerkes] clerkis sholde (be). 144 by] ⁊. 175 Coueiteþ he] *tp.* 189 þe] hise. 202 as] *om.* 203 And] But. 298 laundes] londe. 350 þat] þe. 373 is] þere is. 508 wonyen] dwell. 572 Tellen] To t. 595 Dide] he d. XVI 66 þe] me þe. 83 Bar] ⁊ b. 126 whoso] who. 131 þrowe] it þ. 183 one] selue. 223 forþ] *om.* XVII 94 heele] helthe. 183 in] of. 270 Ech a] Euery. 289 myȝte] may. 325 and] ⁊ it. 327 sighte] eyȝen. XVIII 7 me] y. 9 and penaunce] *om.* 30 in(1)] on. 75 goddes] crystis. 77 hond] *pl.* 264 Prynces] ȝee p. 310 vs] we. XIX 5 me mette] ẏ drempte. 42 bicomeþ] b. wel. 99 konne] knowe. 160 ech a] euery. 198 And] ⁊ þe. 201 to(2)] *om.* 369 were] ben. 372 nas] was. 416 comune] *pl.* 462 acounte] *pl.* 466,472,476 comune] *pl.* XX 7 to(3)] *om.* 19 ech] euery. 56 ech a] euery. 68 lewed] oþer. 131 garte] maden. 136 yede] wente. 162 ech] euery. 179 a...auaille] avayle a myte. 224 sixty] s. moo. 226 hise] *om.* 250 Wiþ] So. 263 ech a] euery. 293 to] tyl. 343 wynter] ȝeer(es).

[27] R is stable, like O in the group OC². It forms no other variational groups of remotely comparable persistence and appears in only one which requires notice: LR. See pp. 21, 37.

Next in order of persistence is GF.

Prologue 26 Al] *om.* 57 to] for t. 59 Prechynge] þat preyched. 60 Glosed] & g. 96 in] yn þe. I 1 bymeneþ] meneth. 18 of(1)] &. 38 *line om.* 74 were] was. 95 Riden] and r. 136 lewed] ye l. 171 þat(1)] the. II 3 þe(2)] *om.* 178 pryuees] peple. III 3 kan] know. 33 am] a. wel. 39 alle] *om.* 94 For] *om.* 264 hoteþ] þe h. 274 witnesseþ] telliþ. 347 han torned] torne. IV 119 Til] and. 182 wole] *om.* V 36 noȝt] *om.* 88 of] *om.* 107 for(2)] &. 131 gart] made. 168 þanne] *om.* 233 Repentaunce] he. 258 in] i. the. 263 Ne] and; hem] *om.* 273 That] tyll. 340 goþelen] gowle. 366 þerof] *om.* 398 as] þat. 412 yserued] well y. 417 in(2)] *om.* 422 and] or. 443 it] *om.* 462 And] *om.* 552 ne] *om.* 566 so] *om.* 586 aboute] all a. 620 That] the. 623 þe] þat. 632 Wite] wold. VI 31 foweles] *sg.* 46 here] *om.* 173 quod he] *om.* 196 to] *om.* 273 lord] our l. VII 34 myn] þe. 57 on] *om.* 122 quod Piers] *om.* 135 Haue þei] *tp.* 149 tyme] a t. 188 of] on. VIII 37 on] on thys. 82 his(1)] þe; or] of; land] hand(ys). 121 on] In. IX 49 ay] euer. 148 her] þer. X 4 seide] she s. 5 wisdomes] *sg.* 181 if] *om.* 238 lyf] *om.* 282 þat] *om.* 331 And] *om.* XI 24 ne] *om.* 36 þe] hys. 81 þe] *om.* 104 first] *om.* 139 oure] *om.* 145 my] hys. 152 my] *om.* 156 a] þe. 190 þat] *om.* 202 þere] *om.* 336 and] *om.* 351 how] of. 417 hadde] he h. 440 hym] *om.* XII 23 quod I] *om.* 49 of(1)] bothe o. 90 breþeren] *om.* 100 first] *om.* 130 toforn] before. 200 or] *om.* 213 þe] *om.* 225 ne(2)] *om.* 227 hir] hys. 240 And] *om.* 244 þe] *om.* 288 But] and. XIII 98 any] *om.* 99 þus] *om.* 118 precheþ] techeþ. 344 a(1)] *om.* XIV 58 Ne] *om.* 77 Weex] was. 80 vile] foule. 110 þe] *om.* 163 is] ytt i. 244 þe(2)] *om.* 283 of] to. 291 any(2)] the. 303 alle] *om.* XV 20 knowe] well Ik. 21 a] *om.* 100 right] *om.* 144 is] *pl.* 164 noȝt] no. 175 erþely] erly / yerly. 235 In] yn þe. 305 fierse] wylde. 336 þat] þem þ. 375 þat] *om.* 494 and] of. 503 so] *om.* XVI 45 som tyme] *om.* 222 crist] *om.* 236 male] *pl.* XVII 70 þat] *om.* XVIII 18 bymente] mente. 221 was] w. / ys &. 294 for] *om.* 302 For] f. þe. XIX 82 þe] thys. 101 so] *om.* 160 a] *om.* 168 dore] *pl.* 231 of] o. þe. 258 þe] *om.* 365 ben] b. of. 368 one] alone. 469 it haue] *tp.* XX 26 tyme] *pl.* 135 his] *om.* 226 arwes] a. with. 255 at(2)] yn. 272 and] *om.* 330 was] þat w.[28]

Another group in conflict with RF is FH,[29] established by the following agreements.

Prologue 4 Wente] & w. 23 pride] p. &. 31 þei] to. 42 fouȝten] & f. 46 pliȝten] pyghtyn. 62 þise] þe. 74 bonched] blessid. 78 Were] But w. 85 a] *om.* 88 in] to. 107 of(1)] *om.* 116 and(1)] & his. 124 clergially he] & c. 149 a(2)] þe. 163 leue] best. 176 þo] whanne. 180 hem] hemselue. 182 A] Thanne a. 185 þe] þat. 189 The] For. 197 by nyȝte] on nyghtis. 199 route of] *om.* 200 Nere] Ne were. 207 þei] he. 212 it] þey. 214 lippes] *sg.* 221 in] of. I 7 þis(2)] *om.* 40 For] &. 64 it] *om.* 66 Counseilled] And (he) c. 91 *line om.* 108 made] he m. 109 Tauȝte] & t. 115 a] þe. 118 on] vpon. 122 garte þe] made. 162 taxeþ] askeþ. 182 good] *pl.* 183 in(*both*)] of. 187 þe] *om.* II 29 þe] *om.* 40 worþ þis] shal be. 57 þis] þat. 59 As] Of. 90 werkes] werkynge(s); and(1)] *om*; and(2)]

[28] Variants in which GF agree at I 164, 186, III 269, V 427, 530, VI 106, 163, VII 70, VIII 12, 97, X 74, 230, XI 174, 353, XIII 215, 338, XIV 68, XV 277, XVII 184, XIX 263, XX 92 also occur in S.

[29] It is to be recalled that R is defective in Prol. 1–124 and I 141–II 40 and that collation of H ceases at V 127.

in. 100 to(1)] *om.* 110 Bette] & B. 111 Reynald] and r. 132 a] & a. 149 Tho] whan. 159 segges] men. III 32 þe] þo. 69–72 *lines om.* 78 Pillories] *sg.* 80 þis] *om.* 103 hire] *om.* 104 to] for t. 105 To] & t. 149 þise] *om.* 162 wel] but. 166 now] oure. 225 kynne] manere of. 236 þis] þus. 237 assoileþ] *pret.* 250 And] *om.* 264 þee] þou. 268 Widwes...wyues] Wyuys...wydewis; wommen] & w. 303 middel] *om.* IV 16 to ryde] *om.* 36 is...leaute] loue & l. is. 64 hym] *om.* 99 hym] *om.* 125 to] *om.* 136 ensamples] *sg.* 150 Al] *om.* 189 Erles] Lordes. V 15 pertliche] apertly. 20 hem] vs. 37 dide] seyde. 49 þy] *om.* 56 and] or. 63 lord] our l. 67 me(1)] *om.* 78 discryue] discryȝe. 79 a(2)] a long. 116 dedly] euere.[30]

Another persistent conflicting group is HmF; these manuscripts agree in the following readings.

Prologue 84 parisshe] paryschenes. 197 þer] *shifted.* I 114 þat] the. 165 a] *om.* II 26 to] on. 42 faire] fals. 90 As] *om.* 91 And] *om*; wiþ] in. 201,210,213 Falsnesse] fals. 218 Liȝtliche] Full l. III 26 to conforten] & confortid. 39 Falshede] fals. 112 þat] the. 132 þe] *om.* 186 famed] defamed. 191 into] in. 204 for] *om.* 223 to goode] of god. 283 soþes] here s. 307 if] *om.* 313 vse] it v. IV 60 to] for t. 180 lete] leue. V 139 and] a. on. 158 a] *om.* 173 to(2)] *om.* 204 marchaundise] of m. 209 a] my. 255 haþ] *om.* 274 þat] þo þ. 281, 284 it] *om.* 289 to(2)] *om.* 463 yet] *om.* 494 The] þat. 525 fro] *om.* 573 noȝt] þou n. 593 of(2)] and. VI 146 er] tyl on. VII 88 beggerie] beggers; in] on. 183 penaunce...preieres] prayers...penaunce. 195 þow...þi] ȝe...ȝour. 196 þow didest] ȝe dedyn / don. VIII 66 lerne] lystne. IX 55 þe] þat. 64 here] *om.* X 184 leuel] to l. 283 eiȝen] owe(n) e. 456 neuere] euere. XI 116 dispute] desputyd. 141 at] of. 306 so] *om.* XII 84 ende] nede. 135 but] *om.* 136 science] *pl.* XIII 22 to conforte] and conforted. 231 ne(2)] *om.* 382 swoor] y s. 394 me conforte] thyng c. me XIV 168 þi] *om.* 174 poore] þe p. XV 23 am I] *tp.* 106 to(2)] *om.* 329 spende] it s. 372 þe] þat is (þe). XVI 7 speche] *pl.* 9 Charite] of c. 12 whiderout] where. 55 þreve] þrowe. 73 and] ȝif. 173 and] *om.* XVII 6 is] i. þe. 66 so(2)] as. 202 as(2)] *om.* 281 manere] *om.* 295 so] *om.* 351 ne] *om.* XVIII 39 sharpe] ful s. 72 a croos] croyses. 188 þow art] *tp.* 265 þat] the. 288 sete] þou s. XIX 141 And] *om.* 282 ete] *pres.* 470 alle] ȝow a.[31]

Then there is the conflicting group CrF, almost as well attested.

Prologue 61 construwed] *pres.* 115,117,118,121 commune] *pl.* 126 lene] leue. I 138 Yet haue I] I h. 140 doted] dotest. II 101 þis] that. III 269 Moebles(*both*)] Mevable. 308 to(1)] into. 312 eche] euery. IV 31 from(2)] *om.* V 9 mette me] I sawe. 78 a] *om.* 90 and] if. 223 my wif] she. 255 pouere men] þe p. 256 myȝte] *om.* 289 restitue] restore. 344 wexed] wyped. 345 his] a. 355 Is] There i. 402 eche] euery. 406 of Souters] *om.* 429 man] *om.* 528 in(2)] and. 532 auȝt] not. VI 292 Al] And a. VII 19 wolde] wyll. 78 neuere] not. 82 mo] *om.* 95 moore] *om.* VIII 52 to(1)] two; yeresȝyue] *pl.* IX 41 þe] his. 106 tauernes] *sg.* X 58 þe] hyr. 292 to blame yow] y. t. b. 411 lene] leue. 447 þo he seide] *om.* XI 173 al] *om.* 179 hir] *om.* 180 leneþ] (be)leveþ. 204 made] *pres.* XII 69 forþ] *om.* 74 in auoutrye taken] t. i. a. 170 it] *om.* 189 verset] versicle. 207 to(2)] *om.* 214

[30] Variants in which FH agree at Prologue 73, 177, I 1, 68, II 221, IV 45 also occur in S.

[31] Variants in which HmF agree at II 136, 146, 211, III 293, 342. IV 105, XI 53, XVII 207, XVIII 349 also occur in S.

yald] gan yeld. XIII 9 in hir(2)] *om.* 54 ooþer] *om.* 68 huppen] *pret.* 86 be] *om.* 116 do] is (to) do. 236 hir] þe. 397 ne] *om.* 410 mysdedes] mysse / myssis. XIV 13 or] o. with. 196 on] *om.* 271 a] *om.* 299 folies] foles. XV 170 leneþ] (be)leviþ. 175 heueneriche] heuenlych. 299 beest] *pl.* 338 filled] *pres.* 380 decrees] degrees. XVI 26 And] *om.* 55 þouȝtes] *sg.* XVII 50 þus] *displaced.* 79 to] for. 85 þei] he. 159 þyng] *pl.* 202 as(1)] *om.* XVIII 65 hir(2)] þe. 313 leued] beleued. XIX 4 þo] *om.* 266 plow] p. and. 311 vices] v. to. 350 wiþ(2)] or w. XX 13 noon(1)] þat. 65 holye] h. men. 132 adoun] doun.[32]

When distribution of support for the above conflicting variational groups is examined the RF agreement appears not only the most persistent but also strikingly more persistent in any part of the poem than agreement of F with another manuscript. On that ground RF seems the likely genetic group, and change of exemplar in the tradition of F appears an unlikely explanation of its conflicting pairings. Further, because in the distribution of support for those pairings there is no striking unevenness it also seems improbable that there was change of exemplar toward F in the various manuscripts concerned. The likelihood is then that these groups were produced by convergent variation and are random.

There is no agreement between F and any of these manuscripts which could not be coincidental. Those few which may at first sight seem remarkable are readily explicable in terms which admit the possibility of convergent variation. Thus FS VII 187 *renkes*] *all* could have been produced by substitution of a more emphatic expression by F who knew what *renkes* means, and of a generalizing one by S who did not; GF II 178 *pryuees*] *peple* is very likely the product of memorial contamination from the **A** tradition; GF VIII 82 *land*] *hand(ys)* is probably a visual error induced by the preceding line. The one striking CrF reading, V 344 *wexed*] *wyped*, explains itself in terms of the context. Of the HmF readings X 456 *neuere*] *euere*, which might seem deliberate from its radical effect on the sense, is probably the mechanical result of ‹*n n*› adjacency in *wan neuere*; HmF XII 84 *ende*] *nede* probably occurred through unconscious metathesis induced by preceding *meschief*. In general the readings establishing these variational groups are very ordinary, and of familiar types. If they have any intrinsic interest at all it is in the number which reflect the differences, lexical or grammatical, between the English of the 1370's and that of the fifteenth

[32] Variants in which CrF agree at Prologue 155, I 167, III 230, V 149, 178, 180, 578, VI 241, VII 187, 201, VIII 39, IX 144, X 54, 89, 317, XI 185, 195, 214, 310, 368, XII 111, 200, XIV 82, 312, XV 344, XIX 21, 105, 373, 419, 480, XX 31 also occur in S.

century or even later. For instance, nearly half the agreements of the most persistent conflicting group FS are in chronological variants. This is relevant: the existence of such differences will have necessarily led to convergent variation.

The difficulty is not with allowing the possibility of coincident agreement in the single instance but in accepting that coincidence of variation should be so frequent.[33] There is, however, no reasonable alternative. Since it is unlikely that all the variational groups in the above instances were random it seems necessary to conclude that RF is the genetic group, whatever implications this may have about the frequency of coincident error.

The same conclusion seems necessary in the conflict RF⟩⟨FH. Here the particular difficulty is that the 80 odd agreements of FH occur in something less than one fifth of the poem;[34] their number thus might seem to suggest a relation almost as 'close' as that of RF.[35] But it is by definition impossible for both RF and FH to be genetic pairs in the same part of the poem; the speculation how often FH would agree if H contained a complete **B** text must be set against the fact of massive RF agreement throughout the poem wherever R exists; taken singly any FH agreements could be coincidental;[36] and the group RF handsomely passes the test of congruency.[37] The alternatives are to accept FH as a random group or to conclude that no conclusion is possible.

Next in order of persistence among the groups of two manuscripts is CrS, based on the following agreements.[38]

Prologue 75 rynges] both r. 122 ech] euery. 200 yow] vs. I 12 on] vpon. 24 mysese] disease. 28 by] wyth. 173 and(2)] þat. II 48 worþe] worke. 134 wit] my w. 153 wit]

[33] This is an unreal difficulty, as the late Sir Walter Greg observed: 'The easier it is to explain how an error arose, the less valid the assumption that it only arose once' (*The Calculus of Variants: An Essay in Textual Criticism*, Oxford, 1927, p. 20, n. 1). But contrast two assertions by Eleanor Hammond: 'Since, in spite of the general tendency to err, no two human characters are alike in detail, no two scribes will show identical errors if working independently. Persistent identity thus implies identity of origin', and 'unless two scribes are using the same original, it is highly unlikely that they will commit identical errors' (*Chaucer: A Bibliographical Manual*, New York, 1908, pp. 109, 107).

[34] Since H becomes an **A** text somewhere between V 100 and 150.

[35] Because of R's defectiveness at the beginning of the poem a numerical comparison of RF agreement in Prol.–V 100 with that of other groups in this area would simply be misleading.

[36] They comprise some 30 substitutions of approximate equivalents, some 20 relatively trivial additions, about 20 omissions, and a few changes of word order.

[37] See above, p. 20 and below, pp. 57ff.

[38] The readings supporting this group occur in all the Crowley impressions, or in Cr^1 only. Readings of Cr^2, Cr^3 or Cr^{23} are excluded as not reliable evidence for the text of Crowley's copy manuscript because of differentiating correction from other sources.

þe wits. 204 lacche] cache. III 55 a] *om.* 69 Forþi] Therfore. 85 on] all. 112 lord] God. 135 ne were] were not. 146 As] As maye. 309 Pykoise] pykeaxe. IV 63 afered] afraied. 98 to] for. 107 þe...be] be the bolder. 142 no] *om*; but] b. if. V 39α it] *om.* 66 *line om.* 72 *line om.* 92 þouȝ] if. 127 is sauacion] *tp.* 160 worþ] was. 176 Forþi] Therfore. 182 neuere] you n. 187 me] hym. 197 sholde noȝt wandre] had n. walkt. 284 Forþi] Therfore. 534 þe] that. 605 þee] to the. VI 48 in] in þe. 66 lese] glene. 85, 94 Forþi] Therefore. 110 Ech] Euery. 250 þe] *om.* VII 50 sheweþ] spekith. 84 Forþi] Therfore. 130 bisy] be b. VIII 75 yeer] *pl.* IX 49 his] our. 129 Caymes] C. kind. 130 seþ] Sem. 142 hulles] downes. 154 he] it. 158 Forþi] Therfore. 173 do hem] gone. 176 Forþi] Therfore. 202 lawe techeþ] lawes techen. X 9 margery] Margarite. 21 to...cleped] is oft cleped / callid to counsell. 34 Pilat] P. falsely. 97 ech] euery. 105 myȝtes] *sg.* 118 on] of. 135 now] ⁊. 143 grounde] erth. 170 Sympletee] simplicitie. 188 *line om.* 199 he lereþ] it lerneth. 210 Forþi] Therefor. 271 ouþer] or. 290 made] þat m. 328 hir] *om.* 376 Ech] Euery; but] b. if. 377 am] *om.* 383 lettrure] letter. 398, 403 forþi] therfore. 442 And] For. XI 41 bigile...wolt] but / onlesse þou wilt bigile the(self). 107 an heiȝ] vp. 212 neiþer] *om.* 229 Forþi] Therfore. 291 nedeþ] nede. 368 kynde] *pl.* 409 þynkeþ] think. 433 shrapeþ] shakeþ. XII 16 þee] *om.* 39 soule] soules. 92, 94, 97 Forþi] Therfore. 188 lif] both l. 193 yald] knew. 224 ouþer] and. XIII 26 louted] he l. 60 murþe] merye. 74 on] in. 125 one] onelye. 147 worþe] be. 151 lyne] *om.* 223 to...contree] whither. 281 And] A. is. 353 elde] age. 358 witnesse] wyghtes / weight. 360 awaited] *pres.*; þoruȝ] bi; to] he myght. 398 helpes] *sg.* XIV 47 But] And. 62 beestes] *sg.* 93 a] *om.* 100 Ther] That. 156 wye] man. 157 cloþyng] clothes. 201 Forþi] Therfore. 208 Ther] And. 211 softe] ofte him þat. 260 Forþi] Therfore. 282 is] is a. 309 Forþi] Therfore. 333 one] only. XV 14 I(1)] he; þe] *om.* 80 ye] they. 99 so] so of. 103 Forþi] Therfore. 122 hand] *pl.* 138 þanne] *om.* 165 ne(1)] *om.* 174 meschiefs] *sg.* 346 a] *om*; purgatorie] paine. 372 now] n. the. 385 afered] afrayed. 394 lord] god. 450 hise(1)] *om.* 561 þo] they. 598 pure] *om.* XVI 11 saulee] salue. 20 þe] *om.* 35 riȝt] euen. 87 how] if. 90 þanne] *om.* 191 for] to. 192 owene] *om.* 232 þe] *om.* 262 may] ther m.; vs] me. XVII 11 plukkede] pulled. 29 parcelles] p. ech. 34 to(2)] *om.* 47 lene] leue / beleue. 108 he(2)] him. 120 lettre] lore. 154 Thus] Than. 162 Wythin hem thre the wyde worlde (they) holden. 172 or] ⁊ to. 176 is] þat is. 214 That] And. 222 werchen...waken] waken...worken; wyntres] wynter. 238 wol forȝyue] forgeueth. 273 dayes] *sg.* 300 now] *om.* 325 bedde] head. 351 and(1)] if; lene] leue / beleue. 353 and] a. of. XVIII 89 aþynkeþ] forthinketh. 110 þis] the. 122 wonder] meruell. 150 myldely] mekelye. 201 Forþi] Therfore. 204 mowe] must; þe] *om.* 218 Forþi] Therfore. 224 now] *om.* 237 quod] saith. 248 biquasshed] toquassed. 249 helle] heuen. 286 seide] quod. 289 selue] name. 342 by] in. 366 deide] *pres.* XIX 36 þer noon] none therin. 83 Ruþe] Truthe. 99 it] *om.* 113 boþe] also. 136 Forþi] Therfore. 167 hir dore] the dores. 190 one] onelye. 225 Forþi] Therfore. 227 gaf] giue. 229 Some] To s. 241 *line om.* 307 present] *pl.* 361 alle] to a. 368 one] onely. 410 I] That. 439 a] the. 443 ouer] of. 445 blood] folke. 459 þis] the. XX 1 as] *om.* 46 nede(2)] nedes. 48 Forþi] Therfore. 49 *line om.* 70 aboute] a. where he yede / went. 93,94 er] their. 95 Elde] Age. 111 he] she. 151 oone] onely. 153 Heele] Health. 165, 167 Elde] age. 175 þe] *om.* 233 soules] *sg.* 262 Alle] For a. 268, 271 Forþi] Therfore. 273 heet] bad. 283 Alle] To a. 321 if] if that. 346 þe] *om.* 375 eft] out.

The strength of support for this group CrS necessarily suggests that it is genetic, but there are contrary indications. Two very persistent conflicting variational groups FS and CrF we have already shown.[39]

Another is GS based on the following agreements.

I 134 er] *om.* III 97 lordes] men. 119 For] *om.* 310 hym] þem. 312 dyngen] dyggen. IV 107 hewen] men. 113 no] *om*; to] for to. V 5 feyntise] feyntnes. 10 For] *om.* 84 yede] went. 134 myȝt] þe m. 142 han] had. 235 were] had byn. 416 lyues] *sg.* 447 þat] but. 499 Iohan...Lucas] luke...Iohan. 568 yow] ye. 604 and] off. 613 worstow] beest / art þou. VI 85 do] *om.* 266 for] *om.* 271 lete] leyue. 292 þo] then. VII 148 a myle] my. VIII 77 and] *om.* 115 But] *om.* IX 184 is] ys a. X 49 nouþe] nowe. 133 so] soeuer. XI 36 tyne] lose. 41 Ne] *om.* 79 is] *om.* 106 for(2)] not for. 251 self] hymselue. XII 3 wynter] *pl.* 13 þat] as. 61 þer] where. 135 com] comethe. 161 hir] *om.* 195 ben] *om.* 241 and] yff. XIII 136 þo] þen. 324 bak] *pl.* 337 on] to. 355 desiryng] desyre. 393 here] þer. 455 þo] þem. XIV 77 payn] foode. 240 hir] *om.* 323 þo] þen. XV 47 by] *om.* 77 foliliche] folysshlyche. 148 in(1)] *om.* 422 þe] *om.* 610 hem] þem by. XVI 67 now] *om.* 232 hiȝte] bad. XVII 114 þis ilke] by thys. 245 and] yff. XVIII 246 she] he. XIX 26 konne] knowest. 203 kynne] maner. XX 24 *Iusticie...fortitudinis*] *fortitudinis... Iustitie.* 78 comune] *pl.* 302 wel] full.

Yet another well supported conflicting variational group is CrG.

Prologue 64 haþ ben] was. 213 Pleteden] *pres.* I 105 kyngene kyng] kyng of kyngis. II 141 soure] sore. 189 seiȝ] *pres.* 223 wiped] *pres.* III 28 þi] we. 307 þe] *om.* 339 herte] well. IV 40 þo] the. V 279 han hanged] hang. 297 to(1)] t. the. 492 Aboute] At. 575 it] thei. 578 þi] the. 593 to] of. VI 190 dikeden] diggen. 229 wolde noȝt] nolde. 270 þe] his. 291 þee] my. IX 112 Confessours] *sg.* 115 werche] to w. X 213 gynful] gylful. 254, 364 þus] this. 383 on] *om.* XI 158 ye] *om.* 238 hise] these. XII 210 riȝt] *om.* 211 That] But. XIII 388 As] And. 421 Ye] The. XIV 15 flobre] slober(ed). XV 236 þe] *om.* 259 at] in. 317 and] *om.* 320 bifore] afore. 489 þus] this. 581 shul] *om.* XVI 79 adoun] downe. XVII 10 Lat] L. vs. 149 erþe] the e. XIX 174 þoledest] *pres.* XX 32 falle] faile. 50 pouerer] pore. 72 gyour] gydour. 294 her] ther. 343 wynter] *pl.*

CrS is the most persistent variational group in which either of its component manuscripts appears. Each member of this group however pairs with each of the two other manuscripts involved in the conflict, and all four manuscripts form persistent groups of two.[40] The variation in which respective groups agree is generally similar in character (again much of it is chronological variation), and distribution of agreement suggests no explanation of their conflict. Thus the situation epitomizes one aspect of the geneticist's problem. He must either throw up his

[39] See above, pp. 28 and 30f.

[40] We recall FS, GF and CrF, shown above on pp. 28, 29, 30f.

hands, or accept both the extreme frequency of coincident variation and the general probability that relative persistence of agreement will indicate the genetic relation. On that indication CrS are at this stage of the analysis to be considered a possible genetic pair.

From such provisional conclusions, that OC² are a genetic pair to XVII, that despite contrary indications RF and CrS are genetic pairs, and that if GF is a random group GC² may be genetic in XVIII–XX, we turn to two markedly persistent variational groups which claim attention because, notwithstanding the fact that they conflict, none of their three constituents forms a group of two of remotely comparable persistence with any other manuscript. These are BmBo and BoCot, and they represent another aspect of the problem.

The following are the agreements of BmBo.

V 353 grym] heuy. 543 suwed] feed. 579 euene] heuene. 589 Botrased] Bretaskid. 594 þe(1)] þo. 604 þe(3)] þat þ. VI 54 þe(1)] þo. 93 hym] hem. 102 mennes] *sg.* 183 flowen] folwen. 274 drynkes] drynkyngis. 296 axed] *pres.* 316 gruccheþ] *pret.* 317 corseþ] *pret.* VII 93 calleþ] *pret.* VIII 19, 20 *transposed.* 85 dooþ] do. IX 62 glubberes] clobberis. 151 þe(2)] of þe. X 163 þow wolt] þat wold. 172 þat] þan. 179 Aristotle] Aristole. 348 no] noȝt. 361 þi] þe. 396 vngracious] vngracyouns. XI 42 gan] he g. 64 oure] o. owen] ouren. 65 buried] buriel. 213 woot no man] n. m. not. 353 hem] hym. XII 51 renkes] men þenken. 148 To] Tho. 183 auenture] aduerture. XIII 3 amendynaunt] amendement. 4 þouȝt] þouȝ. 10 hem] hym. 32 sitte] sette. 243 prouendre] prouende. 253 I] *om.* 324 hem] hym. 340 word] *om.* 361 made] *pres.* 425 deyinge] doynge. XIV 26 þow] þo. 44, 65 bestes] *sg.* 78, 113 hem] hym. 156 double] doublid. 174 þi] þei. 245 but] b. a. 300 cristes] criste. XV 21 welcomeþ] welcome. 132 Executours] Sectorous. 224, 312, 320 hem] hym. 330 swiche] hym. 344 conformen] conforte. 356 þoruȝ] þough. 364 tiled] *pres.* 443 Engelond] Englong. 502 lightlier] liȝt(h)lokeþ. 504 parfitly] parfithi. 507 in(2)] *om.* 532 or] er. 559 An] And. 573, 595, 597 hem] hym. XVI 45 afore] tofore. 106, 127 hem] hym. 130 seide] *twice*; hem] hym. 186 Sothfastnesse] stefast. 196 ocupie] ocupiem. 235 circumscised] circumsidid. XVII 65 Dredfully] Dredful. 162, 167 hem] hym. 216 The] þer. 232 Mynut] mynuten. 254 þat þow] þan. 323 is] his. 356 awakede] *pres.* XVIII 4 eft] oft. 35 adoun] adon. 98 geten] genten. 136 be] is. 142 tale of] taile. 154 scorpion] scorpiom. 218 of his] *tp.* 227, 272 hem] hym. 292 gile] gele. 318 mayn] mani. 330 recorde] recor. 332 hem] hym. 399 nameliche] ma(n)liche; nedes] nede. XIX 25 com] *pres.* 51 hym] hem. 78 sonne] of s. 79 hir] erþe. 146 blissede] bisseful. 233 hem] hym. 250 lele] lee. 292 worldly] no. 344 worþ] wroþ. 448 remenaunt] renaunt. XX 13 noon(1)] ne; haþ] haþ ne. 58 hem] hym. 61 as(1)] also. 70 boldely] buldly. 74 foolis] foulis. 213 to] til. 258 hem(2)] hym. 262 bataille] *pl.* 267 oonliche] holiche. 278 god made] *tp.* 281 sholde] *pres.* 292 hem] hym. 344 þere] þ. þat. 348 opene] vppon.[41]

[41] Variants in which BmBo agree at V 375, XIX 452 also occur in S.

The following are the agreements of BoCot.

III 1 na mo] nomen. 19 and] a. 37 in] *om.* IV 143 *Nullum*] *multum.* 158 comendede] *pres.* V 175 and] *om.* 176 þo] *om.* 198 biknowe...here] knew...neuere. 264 þat] *twice.* 299 hym] *om.* 341 in] and more in. 399 Ne] For. 480 God] *om.* 499 And] To. 541 while] þer w. 552 hewe] hynen. 585 þe] *om.* 586 The] Þat. VI 30 myne] men. 162 þat] *om.* 177 after] tyme. 251 þat] *om.* 291 likeþ] *pret.* 325 foule wedres] foolis wordis. VII 7 mestier] mynysterye. 111 lynes] leues. VIII 32 stumbleþ] tumbleþ. 76 me telle] ywysse. 85 he] *om.* 108 be] þe. 119 we(1)] y. IX 57 hir(1)] *om.* 58 Inwit] wytt. 123 on] and. 169 ioyelees] geolous. 200 shul] soule shal. X 15 Or] Of; or] and of. 18 it be] he. 90 meneþ] meþ] semeþ. 149 As] And (as). 150 to] y. 198 feiþlees] feyles. 264 dobest] dobet. 394 so] *om.* 457 þe] *om.* 459 þe olde] yholde. 466 pastours] portours. XI 36 þe] *om.* 256 wise] wyes / weies. 413 Haddestow] Haddist. 432 nymeþ] nyme. XII 6 of] *om.* 79 Giltier] Gilty. 158 clerkes] clergie. 169 semeþ] comeþ. 195 That] þam. XIII 27 wel] *om.* 71 wol] wolde. 210 oon] oure. 330 ysherewed] in sherwid / in shrewid. 370 pynched] pikid. 387 noȝt þat] *tp.* XIV 23 moþe] moche. 53 gyues] synne. 71 be] *om.* 130 And] and his. 134 Hewen] þay. 176 þoruȝ] of. 240 hir] for. 243 nauele] name. 289 as] a. XV 40 as] *om.* 120 who] *om.* 127 it] *om.* 209 colour] colou. 217 murieste] merþe. 311 þat] þa / than. 316 þer] þe. 384 in] *om.* 530 curatours] creatouris. XVI 55 þreve] trewe. XVII 43 lerne] here. 50 vs] v. þus. 61 by] *om.* 104 and] as. 160 a] *om.* 170 shappere] chappere. 181 þe(2)] *om.* 223 blaseþ] *pret.* XVIII 40 Tho] to. 86 The] þat. 119 truþe] treuli. 131 wem] hemme. 136 fro] for. 137 þis(1)] þe. 146 hem] hym. 169 leue] le(i)gge. 252 For Iesus] fi gigas / figigat. 267 leue] loue. 299 trolled] tollid. 313 þi] þise. 327 soule] *pl.* XIX 53 called] *om.* 69 moore] *om.* 106 a] *om.* 112 louede] *pres.* 131 he] *om.* 134 his] *om.* 135 burdes] burges. 139 Iesus] *om.* 204 waggede] wegged. 242 sholde] shulle. 246 wissed] wissen / wissem. 316 þe] *om.* 400 ale(2)] alle. 451 For] *om.* 458 a(2)] *om.* XX 5 and] and a. 40 al] of. 51 I] a. 66 vsede] *pres.* 124 wynnen] wynnyng. 164 threw] drow / drw. 167 Elde] helpe. 182 men] of. 197 at] *om.* 210 he] I. 230 and] *om.* 232 neer] þere. 306 men] *om.*[42]

If neither of the above variational groups is random they must result from a genetic relation of some complexity. The notable features of the evidence are the almost equal persistence of the two groups, the general similarity of the variation in which they agree,[43] the presence of Bo in both, the rarity of agreement between Bm and Cot,[44] and the circum-

[42] Variants in which BoCot agree at X 39, XVI 230 also occur in S. Agreements of BoCot after XX 355 are not significant because Bm is thenceforward defective.

[43] BmBo's readings comprise some 50 substitutions more likely to be unconscious than deliberate, some 40 variants resulting from either miswriting or misreading of copy, a few omissions, a few minor additions, and a small number of changes of word order. Those of BoCot, while comprising more than 40 substitutions similar to those of BmBo, about 40 miswritings and misreadings, a few additions and a change of word order, include rather more careless omissions. There is a further difference: more than a dozen of BoCot's shared variants are smoothings of a corrupt original, whereas BmBo's shared variants include less than half as many smoothings. But these differences seem relatively insignificant in comparison with the general similarity of variation in the two groups.

[44] This occurs at IV 32 hem] hym. XVIII 70 be(1)] *om (by correction).* 350 myne] hem. XX 13 Ne] No. 251 lafte] loste.

stance already noted that none of these three manuscripts forms a variational group of any persistence with any other copy. The situation offers two immediate suggestions: that Bo shared an exclusive common ancestor alternately with Bm and Cot, and that the three manuscripts are themselves a genetic group. These two possibilities, which must be considered together, will be examined during the analysis of variational groups of three manuscripts.[45]

A summary of the results of our analysis to this point is now called for. First it has shown up four variational groups which may be genetic: OC² for Prologue–XVI, GC² for XVII–XX, RF and CrS for the whole poem; and it has indicated an unquestionable but indeterminate genetic relation between Bm, Bo and Cot. Second, if these presumptions are correct, and unless changes of exemplar which left no trace occurred, it has established the random character of most of the 23 variational groups of two manuscripts shown on our table but not so far considered. For if RF are a genetic pair then the groups CF, C²F, CotF, MF, WF, CrR, GR and LR are necessarily products of convergent variation; and the same must be true of CrM, C²S, HS, HmS and MS if the group CrS is genetic. Third it has shown the degree to which genetic analysis relies on relative persistence of agreement. For unless there is significant distribution of agreement, which we found in only one instance of conflict, or unless the character of the variants which form the substance of an agreement is so distinctive as to exclude the possibility of coincidence, which we nowhere found, there is simply no alternative to accepting the indication of markedly greater agreement in unoriginal readings. Whatever its theoretical limits as a criterion of genetic relation, to show its inapplicability in any given case seems difficult.[46] Fourth, it has demonstrated absolutely the extreme frequency of convergent, and particularly coincident variation in the transmission of *Piers Plowman*.[47] Fifth, in its findings about the genetic relations of

[45] See below, pp. 40ff.

[46] The criterion of persistence has an additional implication. We were forced to dismiss three well supported groups containing G as random: GF with 142 agreements, GS with 65, and CrG with 47. Having done this we would find difficulty in arguing that GH (42 agreements) or HmG (38) or GC (18) or GY (16) was a genetic group. Similarly if FH with 87 agreements is random, the case for HmH with 18 being genetic must seem poor.

[47] Because of its importance in determining editorial practice this merits attention. Not one of the identifications of possible genetic relation discussed above could be made without accepting this phenomenon. If we consider the least speculative of them, the group RF, whose genetic character can be established to the limit of proof possible in such matters (see below, pp. 61ff.), the errant partner F appears, even only in the groups of two manuscripts set out on our table, in well more than 600 random agreements. The logic of convergent variation is harsh: whether or

groups of two manuscripts our analysis has both positively supported and negatively qualified the older classification.[48]

The negative qualification is in two particulars. First, our analysis has failed to confirm the confident opinion that LM are a genetic group;[49] the evidence for this, weighed in full knowledge of variation in *Piers Plowman* manuscripts, seems very slight:

V 144 han] *possibly by correction* M; *om* L. 283α *quasi*] *om*. VI 9 þe(1)] *om*. 136 or(1)] and. 241 hym] *om*. VII 133 in] on. VIII 40 walkeþ] walweþ. 53 and] a. X 327α ⁊] *om*. XI 48 þou3te] ne þ. XII 148 þe] þat. XVI 145 self] *om*.

A number of these agreements actually depend on identification of an original M reading obscured by correction. It is, to be sure, just as possible that many other LM agreements obscured by correction of M may have been missed. But even so it would never occur to anyone with all the evidence before him to spy a genetic relation here.[50]

The second particular relates to earlier identification of WCr as a genetic pair.[51] That identification has proved incorrect. W and Cr may well have a more immediate common ancestor, but there is no evidence that their relation to this was exclusive. For one thing the majority of the readings in which W and Cr agree also occur in S.[52] For another, as will be recalled, Cr agrees very persistently with S.[53] For a third, W's most persistent variational grouping in a pair is actually with Hm.[54] WHm agree in the following readings.

I 70 bitrayed are] bitrayeþ he hem. III 36 melled] mened. V 17 segges...ye] þat ye s. 31 That] For. VI 124 ye] þe. VII 99 he(2)] þei. IX 103 spire] spicerie / spicere. XI 181 ech] e. a. 414 conceyued] contreued. XII 131 The] For. 192 speke] *pres*. XIII 328 mannes] *pl*. XV 82 þe(2)] þise. 223 eiþer] boþe. 605 grekes] Iewes. XVI 78 I] And I. XVII 22 He seiþ] Ye seien. 27 on] so. 135 faste] fully. 169 yfolden] yholden.

not any of our genetic identifications is accepted the variant groups of the **B** manuscripts proclaim its occurrence. These manuscripts are necessarily in some vertical genetic relation; where they form many variant groups in the nature of things only a few of these can be genetic. The rest—identified or not—must have originated in convergent variation.

[48] Blackman, 'Notes on the B-Text MSS.'; see the stemma on p. 517 for her classification of RF, OC² and the BmBoCot complex. She was aware of the GC² agreements (p. 509) although these are not shown in the stemma.

[49] Blackman, op. cit., pp. 500f and 517. Mrs Blackman, whose collation extended to just over a third of the text, was possibly misled by Skeat (*The Vision of William concerning Piers Plowman*, Part IV, EETS 81, London, 1885, p. 840). She may have missed the reservation in his suggestion.

[50] For further discussion of M see below, pp. 50, 51.

[51] Blackman, op. cit., pp. 505, 517.

[52] See below, p. 43.

[53] See above, pp. 32f. At this point, also, Cr's presumably random agreements with F (see above, pp. 30ff.) and G (see above, p. 34) are to be recalled.

[54] To which Mrs Blackman did not have access.

213 *line om.* 234 noon] *om.* XVIII 105 Ne] To. 159 dide] fordide. 204 wo] from wo. 209 wite] neuere w. 217 is ynogh] *tp.* 225 þat...of] and what is. 330 Al] And. 331 þei] he. 423 loue] *om.* XIX 124 was woxen] *tp.* 146 sholde risen] *tp.* 169 hise] þise. 184 synnes] *sg.* 186 kneweliche] *pret.* 215 dyuyde] ȝyue diuine. 290 was] w. he. 379 of þe] out of. 467 defende] fende / fonde. XX 114 laughynge] Ianglynge. 191 and...teeþ] a. my t. owt beet / þat out my t. he bette. 235 to] and.[55]

The above is certainly a more impressive list of agreements than the following, shared by WCr.

V 560 ye þat] if yow. VI 65 or] and. IX 147 forefadres] fadres. XI 349 nest] *pl.* XIV 212 letteþ] hym l. XV 133 This] That. 139 wiþ] myd. 156 saueour] lord. 411 lered] lyued þo; lewed] lyue. 414 Ac] *om.* XVI 159 pees] pays. 211 Might] Mighty. XVII 167 serelepes] serelopes. 244 wiþ] myd; in] in þe. XVIII 74 hir] þe. 313 þi] on þi. XX 255 at(2)] *om.*

But if on the ground of their more persistent agreement WHm are to be considered a genetic pair, and WCr to be dismissed as a random group, then so also must HmCr which agree in the following readings.

V 97 frendes] *sg.* 233 a] *om.* 253 noȝt] *om.* 434 sixty] sixe. VI 63 wol(1)] wolde. VII 33 hem] hym. VIII 12 costes] *sg.* 63 wilde] wyde. X 2 lene] leue / lef. 355 lele] lely. XI 177 leue] *om.* 397 shaft] schap. XII 39 þow] *om*; neuere] n. no. 200 þe(1)] *om.* XIII 96 be] by. XVI 22 on(2,3)] oon / one; top] crop. 26 abite] byte. XVII 117 forþ] fore. XVIII 274 hym] it. XX 306 men] hem.

This is by no means the whole extent of the conflict. Any genetic presumptions about WHm must further take into account the very persistent group HmF, a substantially attested group HmG, and even a group WF.[56]

It is then clearly easier to dismiss the proposal that WCr are a genetic group than to reach any conclusion at this stage about the

[55] Variants in which WHm agree at X 158, XIX 284, 448, XX 234 also occur in S.

[56] HmF agreements are shown above, p. 30.

HmG agree in the following readings. Prologue 185 sholde] schall. I 14 and] that. II 90 with] of. 96 in] on. 210 to(2)] *om.* III 6 of þis] vpon. 258 worþ] *om.* IV 107 þe] *om.* 146 in] *om.* V 85 or] and. 169 tyme] *pl.* 174 am] *om.* 280 þe] *om.* 382 Fryday] *pl.* 441 riȝt] *om.* 470 at] on. 482 hym] *om.* 491 for a] at þat. 596 man he] men hem. VII 2 þe] his. X 49 amonges...is] is amonge men. 112 gynneþ] *pret.* 163 þat] *om.* XI 72 for] *om.* 105 þow] *om.* XIV 87 he bileuede] *om.* 141 in...herberwyng] here yn ȝour berynge. 149 bigonne] b. to wurche/to worche b. 159 dureþ] endureþ. 196 on] yn. XV 457 þe] *om.* 580 goddes] god. XVII 44 bileue] to b. 132 alle] a. my. XVIII 33 And] & to. XIX 402 on] yn. XX 103 þat] *om.* 359 to] *om.*

WF, as the only other group of two of any persistence to include W, is a curiosity. It is based on the following readings.

I 50 ylike] was lik. 51 seen] s. it. II 57 was] were; man] men. III 154 fouleþ] defouleþ. V 416 Yet] And y. 480 make] to m. 568 þer] þerInne. VI 215 wombe] *pl.* 299 newe] & n. 331 if] *om.* X 90 meneþ] seiþ. XI 421 noȝt] þe n. XII 9 bidde] to b. 54 lesen] þei l. XIII 418 and(1)] of. XIV 185 be] to be. XV 36 spirit] a s. 45 hire] my. 62 science] *pl.* 307 fynde] fede. 308 brynge] sholde b. 418 to] to þe. XVI 205 Adam] A. was; Eue] And E. XVII 156 he] it. XIX 347 oure] *om.* XX 170 hadde] he h. (A variant in which WF agree at XI 196 also occurs in S.)

possible relation of W and Hm; it will also require some boldness, having discounted HmF's 80 odd agreements as random, to argue another genetic connexion for Hm on the grounds of some 40 agreements. Nevertheless from the indication of relatively persistent larger groups where W, Hm and Cr variously figure together, these manuscripts may be somehow related, and we shall return to them.

The variational groups of three formed by the **B** manuscripts number almost 200, but only a few are significant as absolutely or relatively persistent. These are BmBoCot, agreeing in more than 800 variants, CrMS agreeing in 77, WCrS agreeing in 57, YOC[2] agreeing in 33, and HmCrS agreeing in 24. Most of the remaining groups of any persistence contain one or the other element of the very persistent group RF and thus appear probably random.[57]

The quite exceptional persistence of BmBoCot, the most strongly attested variational group of the **B** tradition, supports the implication already present in the character of the two variant groups BmBo and BoCot that special circumstances operated in its formation. From considerations of space we do not set out the collected readings of BmBoCot; they are to be identified by the group sigil B in the critical apparatus. On grounds of persistence we must identify BmBoCot as a genetic group; there is, indeed, no alternative except to deny altogether the evidential value of persistent agreement. Its theoretical limitations can scarcely be held to apply in this instance.

The presumption of a genetic group BmBoCot accounts only to some extent for the character of the variational groups of two formed by its components. In a situation of this kind where three manuscripts known to have an exclusive common ancestor form two conflicting variational groups the evidence should, in theory, respond to one of three classic interpretations, all involving change of exemplar.

I. There were three exemplars: the exclusive common ancestor B and two of its three known descendants. Where the variational group BmBo occurs *Cot*[58] is a copy of B, and BmBo are copies of *Cot*; where

[57] OC²F agree in 37 variants, CrFS in 31, GFS in 22, LMR in 12, and LRF in 13. There is also CrGS agreeing in 20 variants. The random nature of these groups will seem confirmed at later stages of our analysis.

[58] By *Cot* we here signify ambiguously the actual surviving copy Cotton Caligula A XI or an intervening ancestor. Our experts have disagreed about the date of this manuscript. Neil Ker thinks it may be contemporary with Bm and Bo; A. I. Doyle judges it to be later than Bm and Bo, which from both handwriting and their physical resemblance are exactly contemporary. See above, pp. 1, 2 and 5.

the variational group BoCot occurs Bm is a copy of B and Bo*Cot* are copies of Bm.

II. Again there were three exemplars: B and two of its three known descendants. Where the variational group BmBo occurs Bm and *Cot* are copies of B and Bo is a copy of Bm, *or* Bo and *Cot* are copies of B and Bm is a copy of Bo; where the variational group BoCot occurs Bm and Bo are copies of B and *Cot* is a copy of Bo, *or* Bm and *Cot* are copies of B and Bo is a copy of *Cot*.

III. There were two exemplars: the necessarily posited exclusive common ancestor B and a hypothetical lost copy of this, B^1. Where the variational group BmBo occurs *Cot* is a copy of B and BmBo are copies of B^1; where the variational group BoCot occurs Bm is a copy of B and Bo*Cot* are copies of B^1.

In theory any of these three processes might have occurred in a situation where the manuscripts were copied in proximity. But none satisfactorily explains the evidence. The difficulty with I and II is the existence of unoriginal readings peculiar to each of the three surviving manuscripts, which seems to rule out the possibility of any having been the exemplar of one or both of the others.[59]

Thus III might seem the most acceptable explanation of the evidence. But there is still a further difficulty in adopting it, or for that matter either of the others. This arises from the distribution of the agreements in error which severally establish BmBo and BoCot as variational groups. Transfer of exemplar should leave evidence of some system of change, such as a least common denominator of a gathering or a bifolium or even a side. In this instance we cannot find one; except that evidence for BoCot begins with Passus III while there is none for BmBo until V, the agreements of the two groups seem to occur in no discernible pattern. For instance, between the BoCot agreements at V 541 and V 552 there is a BmBo agreement at V 543; between the BmBo agreements at XI 28 and XI 42 there is a BoCot agreement at XI 36. There are more than a dozen such instances where the first suggestion of the evidence is that an exemplar was used for less than a side of 30 lines.

There can be no doubt that the evidence has been to a large but

[59] This difficulty would be met in the case of Cot by a presumption, according with its probably more recent date, that its connexion with the group is distanced by an intervening ancestor. The individual errors of Cot could then be explained away as acquired during this intermediate stage of transmission.

indeterminable extent obscured by convergent variation such as is indicated at VIII 85, XVIII 136, XIX 139 and XX 13, where both variational groups occur in the same line. But it is only very rarely possible to penetrate the obscurity.[60] Further, we suppose that, however impracticable it seems to us, frequent and irregularly spaced change of exemplar may have occurred. The best proposal we can offer is that the classification of these manuscripts is [Bm(BoCot)] in III and IV, and thereafter alternately and variously [(BmBo)]Cot] and [Bm(BoCot)]. We do not see how to proceed further except by guesswork.

What is, however, quite clear, is that three manuscripts, Bm, Bo and Cot or its intermediate ancestor originated in close proximity. Of Bm and Bo this would in any case be certain from their physical resemblance;[61] there is also evidence of consultation.[62] Once, at XVII 116, all three record difficulty with an apparently illegible exemplar. Their scribes seem to have been under an injunction to copy slavishly rather than critically.[63] On such indications Bm, Bo and the intervening ancestor of Cot originated in the same strictly but not intelligently regulated workshop.

The next variational group of three manuscripts to be considered is CrMS, which agree in the following unoriginal readings.

XIV 192 þis] the. XVI 223 of] o. hem. 228 afterward] after. 231 if] whether. XVII 22 founded it] it found. 48 for] f. so. 52 ful] well. 65 þe] *om.* 66 þe] þis. 80 þee] it. 120 forþ with] for. 171 þe] that. 185 or] and. 236 be þei] all. 248 a] the. 250 al] *om.* 260 blowynge] brennyng. 271 þat(1)] your. 276 as] a. done. 283 so] þat. 308 peel] plee. 353 men] of. 354 hem] him. XVIII 72 Vpon...crist] Bisides C. apon a crosse. 143 and(2)] *om.* 158 deeþ] *om.* 214 se] *om.* 275 deueles] fendes. 285 lete] leaue. 296 he... aboute] he hath gone. 319 þise] the. 352 þoruȝ] by. 376 in] of. 382 Iuwise] els. 400 oure]

[60] For instance at V 541 BoCot vary from the corrupt group reading, indicating a classification [Bm(BoCot)], and at V 543 further variation by BmBo indicates [(BmBo) Cot]. This suggests that V 542 was a point of change of exemplar, and that BoCot's agreement at V 552 is coincident. But there is not enough identifiable further variation to enable solution of the puzzle; we have collected only six scattered instances for [(BmBo)Cot] and a dozen for [Bm(BoCot)].

[61] Their page contents generally correspond throughout the poem and their collation is identical. See above, pp. 1 and 2.

[62] This was not, however, necessarily intelligent. For instance, at XVI 32 Bm's correct reading is altered to the unoriginal group reading; at XVII 48 Bo's correct reading is made to conform to the unoriginal reading of Cot.

[63] *See for example the faithful reproduction of misspellings or miswritings*: at X 179 Aristole BmBo; XV 443 Englong BmBo; 502 liȝt(h)lokeþ BmBo; 504 parfithi BmBo; 552 deso depose BmBo Cot; XVI 186 stefast BmBo; 196 occupiem BmBo; 235 circumsidid BmBo; XVIII 98 genten BmBo; 252 fi gigas/figigat BoCot; XIX 250 lee BmBo; *the acceptance of incorrect abbreviations*: X 396 vngracyou*n*s BmBo; XII 183 adu*er*ture BmBo; XVII 232 mynute*n* BmBo; XVIII 35 adon BmBo; XIX 448 renaunt BmBo; *the acceptance of nonsense readings*: IV 143 *multum* BoCot; V 299 wiþ þat BoCot; XVI 241 inne BmBo; XVIII 103 it BmBo; XIX 112 loueþ BoCot.

this. XIX 1 awaked] walked. 18 name] heiȝe n.; god] *om.* 63 his] þe. 69 to(1)] for t. 73 of] o. thys. 87 siþþe...sooþliche] sothly...sithens. 115 tolde] sayde. 119 For] *om.* 122 þoruȝ] by. 154 hem] *om.* 163 al] *om.* 220 þee(2)] *om.* 240 And] *om.* 291 and] or. 307 preiere] *pl.* 351 queyntise] couetise. 376 penaunce] paines. 395 ben(2)] *om.* 456 faire... vices] foule vices as vertues (foule *over erasure* M). 473 at] of. 475 I may] *tp.* XX 44 fle] f. and; and(2)] *om.* 71 after] a. þe. 74 þo] *om*; ye] *om.* 101 knyghtes...kaysers] Kaysers... knightes. 103 stired] stode. 115 wiþ] w. a. 140 and cryde] *om.* 141 were] w. a. 152 lauȝte] caught. 155 sorwe] deþ. 162 at] of. 217 wiþ] was. 235 wol] *om.* 250 for] *om.* 265 wole] wolde. 271 Registre] *pl.* 278 to] *om.* 314 bi fer] he can. 334 are] is. 366 masse] *pl.* 370 wikked] *om.*

This group is challenged by WCrS, which agree in the following readings.

Prologue 77 þat] as. I 183 ne(2)] nor. III 222 of hem] after. IV 175 youre] *om.* V 9 tolde] of t. 598 þe(2)] þat þ. VI 200 into] vnto. VIII 48 þiselue wole] *tp.* IX 77 fader, moder] *pl.* 120 þe(1)] and in; is] *om.* X 27 lordes] *om.* 103 spille...spende] spende...spille. 222 þise tokenes] *sg.* 439 loue] *om.* XI 82 a] *om.* 182 pore] þe p. XII 188 saued] *pres.* XIII 105 Do] Is do. 134 knoweþ] mouþed. 178 þo] þow. 229 lordes] l. or. 240 wiþ] w. my. 282 so] noon so. 283 noon] *om.* 416 soule] *pl.* XIV 75 Ac] Therfore. 79 Diden] Thei d. 171 weet] w. hem greue. 204 Ribaudes] Ribaud he. 211 softe] ofte / manye tyme. 212 ofte] *om.* 241 a] *om.* 248 breke] b. and; it] *om.* 267 Muche] M. moore; þat maide] *om.* 268 Moore] *om.* 289 Or] For. 311 For] Therfore. 312 He] For he. 320 bisynesse] b. ladde. XV 15 for...loue] anoon. 65 so] s. he. 107 of vntrewe] but of trewe. 209 hym] *om.* 375 Ne] *om.* 397, 398 *misdivision.* 411 lered] lyued þo / then lyued. 432 Ac] For. 553 and(3)] by. 601 ȝit] *om.* XVI 86 þat] of þ. 87 happe] hitte. 204 taken ...man] out of man t. XVII 244 in] i. þe. XVIII 259 reuerensen] reuersen. 267 it] out. XIX 428 peple] þe world. XX 102 ne] and.

The presence of CrS[64] in both these well supported but conflicting groups directs attention to a third where they also figure, namely HmCrS, based on the following agreements.

Prologue 169 a] his. I 136 it(1)] on. III 245 a] here. V 39α is] *om.* 107 for(2)] and f. 518 ywounden] (y)boundyn. X 230 vpon] on. 282 eiȝen] *sg.* 455 of] *om.* XI 244 tyme] *pl.* 301 as] *om.* XII 9 preyeres] *sg.* 39 þow] *om.* 255 chiteryng] chatrynge. XIII 13 curatours] creatures. 18 ben] they b. 49 toforn] before. 51 dure] endure. 348 in] on. XIV 140 shulle] schulde. 277 on] yn. XVI 71 peeris] pere. 86 a pil] appul. XVII 291 it] *om.*

Between two of these variational groups the conflict is only apparent, and disappears when distribution of agreement is taken into account. more than 70 of the variants peculiar to CrMS occur in XVII–XX; This circumstance indicates that the agreements between CrS and M

[64] For the very persistent agreement of CrS see above, pp. 32, 33.

resulted from change of exemplar in an ancestor of M.[65] The existence of a group CrMS does not therefore question the genetic character of WCrS.

The situation respecting WCrS and HmCrS is more difficult. The *prima facie* indication of its greater persistence, that WCrS is genetic and that HmCrS is a random group, cannot be simply accepted. For the well supported group WHm (see above, pp. 38f.) has suggested a connexion which might somehow extend to WCrS and HmCrS; and in fact WHmCrS do form a relatively persistent group.[66] No conclusion about these four manuscripts is possible except in terms of that larger group, and we must therefore defer consideration of them.

The remaining variational groups of three manuscripts of any persistence are OC²F (37), YOC² (33), and GOC² (27). Of these we dismiss OC²F as random on the grounds of F's massive agreement with R, since if RF are a genetic pair it is impossible for F to be in a vertical genetic relation of three which excludes R. The following are the agreements of YOC².

Prologue 39 hyne] knaue. I 148 of] in. II 25 haþ] *pret.* III 36 melled] medled. IV 34 wiles] wily. 118 an heþyng] vnhende. V 113 liȝteþ...herte] myn h. askeþ. 234 ben] to b. VI 82 so] *om.* 207 And it] & yet they. 255 boþe] ben seke otherwhile. 289 tyme] t. come. 308, 309 *run together with omissions.* 308 Deyneþ...day] wolde ete no. 309 May] ne drynk no. VIII 68 mette] m. I. 83 tailende] taillyng. IX 144 ech] e. a. XI 6 mette] m. I. XIII 43 vnsauourly] vnsauorye. 359 for] it f. XIV 105 rede] *pret.*

[65] Since the agreements of CrS are distributed throughout the poem. Our explanation is neither extended nor seriously questioned by the variational groups CrM (Prologue 97 messe] *pl.* V 533 dwelleþ] wonyeth. VII 3 hym] *om.* X 191 þat] as. XIV 93 it] *om.* 255 hym] hem. XVII 91 his] & h. XVIII 58 þat] doth that. 362 to] *om.* XIX 77 knowelichede] *pres.* 326 watlede...walled] walled...watled. 415 pelure] *pl.* XX 14 sleighte] *pl.* 16 come] *pret.* 102 he] he ne. 105 swelted] *pres.* 334 are] is; oþere] another.) and MS (IV 42 gate] weye. V 276 so] *om.* VII 35 you dere] *tp.* X 210 durest] lyuest. XI 234 yede] wente. 297 lond] *pl.* XII 236 of(2)] *om.* XV 241 maken] þei m. 535 fro(2)] *om.* XVIII 48 to] for to. XIX 393, 407, 411 Cardinale] cardynales.) which we confidently dismiss as random.

The only other group of any persistence in which M figures is MF. I 48 þe] *om.* IV 64 and] he. V 44 shul] *om.* 116 herof] þereof. 149 þat] til. 182 neuere] it n. 195 wynter] ȝeer. 287 falshede] falsenesse. 293 a] *om.* 299 of] *om.* 400 if(2)] *om.* 536 er] til. 563 þynges] *sg.* 634 þe] *om.* VI 57 Perkyn] Piers. 66 Shal] He s. 310 if] *om.* VII 16 þe] *om.* 88 banneþ] blameþ. 109 þe] his. 130, 151 þe] *om.* VIII 8 bifel] fel. IX 179 wercheþ] w. ȝee. X 47 neuere] neyþur. 105 of(2)] *om.* 275 to] *om.* 472 Ye] *om.* XII 209 boþe] *om.* XIII 157 þis] þe. 239 of] on. 343 eiȝe] *pl.* XIV 119 Ioye] of I. 224 werkes] of w. XV 249 ne] *om.* 260 suffrede(1)] *pres.*

We used, before S came to light, to entertain the possibility that M, which shows signs of sixteenth-century handling and has visible modernizing spelling changes of a kind to suggest that it might have been prepared for a printer, might have had some direct connexion with Crowley's first impression. But now it seems clear from CrMS and from the poor support for CrM that the relation in XVIII–XX is between an ancestor of M and the exclusive common ancestor of CrS. The affiliation of M in Prologue–XVII is obscure: the MF agreements certainly fail to throw any light on it.

[66] See below, pp. 49–51.

130 And] A. ek. 298 synne] *pl.* XV 31 chepe] clepe. 80 I] I ne. 113 and were] without a. XVI 57 longe] l. þei ben / ben þei l. 71 erst] rapest. XVII 3 þe] it. 35 comseþ] bigynneth. XVIII 372 mennes] *sg.* XX 63 siþ...was] than...to be.[67]

The following are the agreements of GOC².

Prologue 22 with] In. II 4 to] for to. III 13 somme] comen / came. 245 a] *om.* IV 43 þei] he. 54 I] that I. VI 155 with] hym w. VIII 83 his(1)] *om.* IX 37 her] þer. XII 100 no] a. 270 no] þe. XIII 373 or] ⁊. XV 49 kouþe] konne. 104 bifel] fell. 392 god] g. to. 404 to] Into. 437 bihynde ben] *tp.* XVI 130 it] *om.* 135 of] *om.* 148 to(2)...is] ys to moche. 252 here] hym. XVII 49 wol] *om.* XIX 378 ernynge] rennyng. 440 wykke] ille. XX 55 sprynge, sprede] *pret.* 187 þe] thy. 192 gyued] gyede / guyded.

Neither YOC² nor GOC² is strikingly persistent, and the difference in strength of support is not very great. Nor does the respective distribution of agreements appear significant. It is however to be recalled that G has figured in variational groups of two with F, C², Cr, Hm and S (of which GC² may be genetic for part of the poem), whereas Y is a very stable manuscript. For this reason, unless both groups are random, YOC² seems the more probably genetic; that presumption will be supported by the test of congruency, and it then seems that GOC² is a random group created by convergent variation, and more specifically in view of the character of its agreements, by coincident substitution.

The indications of the analysis at the stage of examining groups of three manuscripts are thus various but useful. BmBoCot have an exclusive common ancestor; otherwise their genetic relation appears fluctuating and indeterminable. The presumed genetic character of CrS is confirmed by the test of congruency.[68] The obscurity of M's genetic position is partly clarified by indication that in XVII–XX its position is [(CrS)M] by change of its exemplar. A suggestion emerges that W, Hm, Cr and S may be genetically related in some complicated way. And the otherwise unaffiliated manuscript Y seems classifiable in [Y(OC²)] at least until the end of XVI.

[67] YOC²'s agreement at IV 54 is shared by S.

[68] There is further support of a similar character in the variational group CrFS (see above, p. 31, n. 32), as also in a group CrGS, supported by the following variants. I 56 it] *om.* II 38 shul] should. 166 feyntly] feetely. III 48 wel] *om.* IV 94 meken] meuen. V 338 vmwhile] somewhyle. 471 of] on. 503 merciable] merciful. VI 175 boþe] *om.* VII 6 holpen] helpe. 108 on] in. XI 14 þat] the. 57 for] *om.* 257 it] *om.* XII 162, 163 That] The. XIII 183 nouþe] nowe. XV 46 þinkeþ] thinke. XVII 10 þi] the. XIX 381 nouþe] now. These groups are respectively explicable as products of convergent variation, by F or by G and the exclusive common ancestor of CrS.

Among the more than 200 variational groups of four manuscripts three are relatively persistent: CBmBoCot established by more than 250 agreements, BmBoCotF by more than 80, and WHmCrS by some 60. CBmBoCot agree in the following readings.

III 154 foulep] folwep. 205 blood] kynne. 256 mesurable] resonable. 291 lowenesse] lewednesse. 292 on] of. 329 For] And. IV 33 *line om.* 57 *line om.* 58 for] f. a. 67 wan] whan(t). 70 by] my. 76 wit] witty. 125 to] þe. 136 as] *om.* 160 mansed] mased. 172 riȝtfully] reufulliche. V 27 hire] *om.* 119 lyue] loue. 126 and] haþ. 131 gart] grete. 134 wole] wolde. 142 wel] *om.* 158 hem Ioutes] hir wortes. 168 yuele] ille. 190 wiþ] boþe w. 198 coueitous] coueitise. 253 his] hir. 256 coueitise of] to haue. 260 neuere] *om.* 270 þee noȝt] *tp.* 276 þat I liȝe] this be nouȝt soþ. 280 hym] *om.* 335 sire] wel. 397 hem] h. alle. 399 synnes] *sg.* 421 *line om.* 430 ayeins] to. 435 tyme] *pl.* 486α–9 *lines om.* 497 þe] þow. 498 And] *om.* 508, 515 That] Til. 608 sires] eires. 613 as] as a. VI 3, 8 *lines om.* 14 so] *om.* 39 hem] *om.* 40 þi] þe. 82 *line om.* 90 leue] bileue. 219, 220 *lines om.* 221 hem(*both*)] *sg.* 235 seiȝ] se. 263 til] for. 275 Piers] Perkyn. 281 *line om.* 283 ybake] I take. 293, 294 *run together, with omissions.* 298 to peisen] *om.* 301 *line om.* 302 Wastour] *om.* 304–6 *run together, with omissions.* 306 and...selle] ale. 307–9 *lines om.* 324 swich] *om.* VII 27 *line om.* 130 þat are] we shul. 200 hele] hule. VIII 23 wel...yuele] *tp.* 83 *line om.* 94, 95 *run together, with omissions.* 106 bede] did. IX 11 And] As. 21 Sire] And. 56 *line om.* 57 hir(2)] his. 71 *line om.* 81 he] *om.* 91 vnkyndenesse] wikkednesse. 130 Saueour] lorde. 132, 133 *run together.* 132 wraþed...seide] s. for wrathe. 133 it] *om.* 164 I(1)] For I. 189 in vntyme] vnite. 190 boþe] *om.* 200 shul] soule. 202 to] *om.* 210 þoruȝ] with. X 89 hym] hem. 103 to(2)] and t. 127, 129 *run together, with omissions.* 204 And] A. also. 250 to] it t. 260 word] werke. 262 beryng] lernynge. 278 selue] *om.* 295 for] *om.* 349 wiþseye] reherce. 351 *line om.* 361 abouen] of; alle] al thyng] alle thynges. 369 *line om.* 375, 376 *run together, with omissions.* 437 Ther] Thay; witty] willy. 441 for] *om.* 444 leue...ben] b. fewe. 447 was] *om.* XI 33 brynge] brouȝt. 52 *line om.* 78 boþe beþ] hath ben. 87 ȝis] *om.* 147 in] *om.* 195 *line om.* 199 his] *om.* 256 þe] *om.* 290 tellep] til. 358, 371 *lines om.* 378 to] nouȝt to. 421 doone] doute. XII 18 is] *om.* 21 conforted] to conforte. 27 do] *om.* 33 þow(1)] he. 65 As] And. 104 lettrure] clergie. 107 clerkes] clergie. 136 science] sightes. 170 þe] that. 180 lente] leaut(e). 196 þeef hadde] *om.* 220 be] so. 228 þere] *om.* 240 proude] *om.* 258 And] *om.* XIII 10 he] *om.* 42 wel] *om.* 56 Bryng] And b.; pitaunce] *om.* 102 vs] v. al. 106 þanne] *om.* 132 dar] *om.* 172 a(1)] as. 174 enemys] *sg.* 184 to] ye to. 190 þe(2)] that. 201 þi] this. 232 *line om.* 236 preieþ] prechiþ. 264 *line om.* 299 to] the. 370 pynched] picched. 376 presentes] *sg.* 411 enioyneþ] *pret.* 414 is] or eche. 433 harlot] *pl.* XIV 4 bymolen] bifoule / defoule. 17 clawe] *om.* 23 bymolen] bynolnen. 45 þe] se (þe). 74 pryde] *om.* 85 *line om.* 91 synne] *pl.* 97 ne] *om.* 102 driȝte] sight. 121 wroþerhele] wo other wel. 141 herberwyng] hee / hyȝe beryng. 144 god] yow. 146 as] a. þe. 151 cote] Cite. 155 yseien] so y. 186 synne] som / somer. 206 poore] pouert(e). 246 goodes] soddes. 310 welle] wille. 320 A] *om.* XV 17 his] *om.* 111 is likned] *tp.* 152 lyued] *om.* 166 of(1)] as. 197 clerkes knowen] clergie knew. 200 wille] welle. 227 biheld I] biholde. 249 *line om.* 357 Weder] Whedir. 361 Shipmen] Chapmen; sheep] ship and shipmen. 373 newe] now. 391 lyue] leuen. 464 folwede] *pres.* 468 sustenep] *pret.* 585 And] Ac. 602 *line om.* XVI 26 piles] floures. 30 Thanne] That. 46 lettep] lacchiþ. 56–91 *lines om.* 104 hym]

h. a. 108 þe] of the. 132 *line om.* 169 I] and. 173 an] any. 186 Sothfastnesse] stedfast(nesse). 191 þre] ther. 238 þis] his. 242 Mercy] More. 256 *line om.* XVII 35 comseþ] bicometh. 53 Comynge] Com. 55 þe] *om.* 73 hym(2)] he. 112 þis day] *pl.* 120 telleþ] hem / hym t. 130 þre] this (is). 146 likeþ] liked / lydyd. 148–50 *lines om.* 177 þe wriþen] he wriþeþ þe. 191 clucche] clenche; to(2)] or. 193 of] and o. 231 þe] *om.* 266 a blynd] an vnkynde. 280 lif] þe l. 297 lakkiþ] hatiþ / hattes. 305 þer] the. 315 þat helpe] *om.* 346 so] *om.* XVIII 8 folk] *pl.* 41 temple] peple. 54 þat] *om.* 102 ye] *om.* 119 comely] manli / many. 162 sleight] sighte. 208 as] is as. 211 is] is ne wele. 221 it] *om.* 247 heuynesse] buxomnesse. 347 destruye] *pret.* 358 alle] a. other. 372 mennes] manere. 388–90 *lines om.* 395 hym] it. XIX 91 þo] *om.* 94, 95 *run together, with omissions.* 117 crist] chirche. 146 blissede] blisful. 159 lyues] lymes. 160 *copied twice.* 190 alle] *om.* 226 Antecrist] any cristyne. 240 figures] membres. 260 prowor] plowgh(t). 267 foure] f. grete. 273 an] and. 366 hem] he. 419 þis] the. XX 45 to(1)] (þat) it. 56 contree] Court. 107 cesse] se. 127 þei] hem. 276 alle] *om.* 285 And] To. 341 Pees] piers.[69]

Its extreme persistence alone would argue the genetic character of the variational group CBmBoCot, the agreements recording the legacy of a carelessly and imperceptively copied exclusive common ancestor to its descendants. This identification will be confirmed by the test of congruency; and it is not challenged by the relative distributions of agreement of CBmBoCot and BmBoCotF. Therefore BmBoCotF is in all probability a random group formed by convergent variation. Because of the importance of accepting this phenomenon in the editing of Middle English texts, we now cite the agreements of BmBoCotF as a final illustration of its effects.

III 9 hiȝte] hym h. 13 Gentilliche] Ful g. 24 a] hadde a. 25 leue] her l. IV 146 þow] he. V 350 and] and ouer / oþer. 395 and] a. of. 422 if] *om.* 447 is(1)] þer i. 493 fore] *om.* 511 Cride] & c. 568 in] into. VI 53 at] at thy. 64 To] On. 74 Truþe] For t. 78 whan] wel w. 106 acre] a. þer. VII 112 in] *om.* 141 As] A. a. 143 selden] ful s. VIII 40 wyndes] *sg.* IX 158 so] *om.* X 50 Lecherie] But l. 87 in] of. 158 of] on. 173 Seye] Telle. 175 to(1)] *om.* 202 as] *om.* 219 þer] þou þ. 435 of] *om.* 469 passen] p. þurgh. 471 inparfitly] in parfit lif. XI 213 woot no man] n. m. wot / not. 295 foond] fynde. XII 51 so] s. þat. 246 looþ] loþli. 263 riche] r. man. 272 hem] hym. XIII 221 þo] *om.* 267 longe] on l. 327 of] *om.* 360 awaited] waytid. 391 seruauntȝ] *sg.* XIV 12 by...it] kepen it by crist. 41 weet] þe w. 153 hire] *om.* 329 Swouned] he s. 333 Ne] *om.* XV 144 lered...lewed] *tp.* 227 beggeris] a begger. 277 ne(2)] þei. 330 as] þat. 331 ne] nede. 377 if] *om.* XVII 65 as] as a. 270 riche] r. man. 338 þenkeþ] hym / hym he þynkiþ. XVIII 34 legge] lede. 45 bi] on. 58 Pitousliche] Ful p. 67 til] into. 81 Maugree] & m. 84 of] of þe. 130 weex] she w. 149 patriark] and p. 195 Adam] and a. 274 is] it i. 369 vendage] vengeaunce. 394 hungry] on / and hungred. 429 goddes] cristis. XIX 27 kyng] k. and. 50 on] o. þe. 75 after] a. and. 79 Aungeles] an angel. 142 Killeden] And k.

[69] Variants in which CBmBoCot agree at IX 135, X 119, XI 409 also occur in S.

247 lawes] *sg.* 250 loue] to l. 263 chered] chere. 290 was] he w. 317 for to] *om.* 319 god] goddis. 405 by] b. þe. 431 at] boþe a. 441 þat] þo þ. 446 lawe(2)] *om.* XX 124 hiden] holden. 282 to(2)] *om.*[70]

In designating BmBoCotF a random group we propose that rather more than once in 100 lines scribal variation in the exclusive common ancestor of BmBoCot and in F or an immediate ancestor took the same form at the same point. No other conclusion seems logically possible; further, the convergent variation was, specifically, coincident. This phenomenon should not seem difficult in terms of Greg's axiom;[71] for the shared readings of BmBoCotF are readily explicable as typical scribal error. Almost half are more explicit substitutions; a few are easier or more emphatic; a dozen are carelessly substituted, approximately equivalent expressions; there are a few grammatical substitutions and changes of word order. The seven readings which do not obviously fall into these classes are slightly more complex but just as confidently explicable. XIX 263 *chered*] *chere* results from the scribal tendency to set up parallel constructions; XIX 319 *god Grace*] *goddis g.* is a misreading induced by the common collocation; the nonsense readings X 471 *inparfitly*] *in parfit lif*, XV 331 *ne*] *nede* and XVIII 369 *vendage*] *vengeaunce* are visual errors induced by unreflective awareness of the surrounding context; XX 124 *hiden*] *holden* was suggested by preceding *wynnen*; XVIII 34 *legge*] *lede* is an obvious approximate equivalent substituted through imperfect recollection of the copy. The character of the BmBoCotF readings, numerous as they are, conforms to the indication of relative persistence that it is a random group.

But the number of its agreements draws renewed attention to the rôle of chance in manuscript classification. In this particular case the evidence for the genetic group was copious enough to enable its identification. But suppose that, as is theoretically altogether possible, the characterizing exclusive common ancestor of CBmBoCot had been a carefully copied manuscript. It would have transmitted comparatively few peculiar errors to its descendants; the evidence of relatively greater persistence would have been wanting; and the likelihood of identifying the group as genetic, for that reason already small enough, would have been reduced to insignificance by the preponderance of the evidence for the random group BmBoCotF.

[70] Variants in which BmBoCotF agree at V 102, 553, X 211, XX 23 also occur in S.
[71] *Calculus*, p. 20, n. 1; already quoted above, p. 32, n. 33.

The third persistent group of four manuscripts is WHmCrS, which agree in the following readings.

Prologue 212 semed] bisemed. I 124 wonderwise] in w. II 40 to] vnto. 90 and(2)] a. in. IV 29 cheker] thescheker. 131 hym] it. 189 counseil comen] c. commune / comen c. VII 99 he...man] þei were men. VIII 100 ordeyned] han o. X 27 lordes] woordes / *om.* 28 moost gyueþ] *tp.* 62 hunsen] hunten. 213 is] so. 252α *line om.* 257 þi] þe. 402 was] were. 410 wrightes] wightes. 422 beknew on] bek(e)nede to. 444 liþere] oþere. XI 20 myrþes] my3te(s) / lordinges. 80 as] a. þise. 151 may] *om.* 185 For] And. 220 ne] or. 255 þe] þat. 259 þer] þerafter / yet after. 316 of] is. 333 at ones] al. a. XII 21 his] me (his). 47 bisette] to bileue. 78 For] And. 103 *line om.* 205 þe] *om.* 210 tilde] dwelte. XIII 36 a] þe. 39 of alle] and of. 50 drou3] brou3te. 73 goode ben] g. men. 96 þe] he. 134 knoweþ] moutheþ / mouþed. 155 is] as. 351 hadde] *om.* 354 his] þis. 394 tyme] while. 410 Is...men] He þat. 428 sermon] *pl.* XIV 23 myx] myst] cheeste. 124 þo] þe. 179 riche] richesse. 226 For] And. 289 Or] hor / For. 322 þus] þis. XV 8 seide] s. I. 15 for...loue] leue / anoon. 96 And] I. 152 I(2)] he. 374 *line om.* 550 þo] þe. XVI 43 cheste] þe c. XVIII 109 hir] of h. 300 slepynge] lepynge. XIX 78 sond] lond.

Although support for WHmCrS is not of an order comparable with that for CBmBoCot the group merits attention. It is relatively more persistent than any remaining group of four manuscripts; its component manuscripts have already notably associated themselves in smaller groups;[72] and there are no groups of four or more manuscripts which seriously conflict with it. The relative persistence of WHmCrS, WCrS and CrS at once suggests a genetic hypothesis ⟨Hm[W(CrS)]⟩. But distribution of agreement limits and qualifies this. First, except in the case of CrS the evidence is scanty in Prologue–X. Second, the agreements of WHmCrS and WCrS, though they occur in most passus, are relatively frequent only in X–XV; it is WHm, the next group of any of these four manuscripts in order of persistence, which receives particular support in XVII–XX where, meanwhile, WCrS agreement is sparse. Thus the evidence points to not one but two classifications for these manuscripts: in X–XV ⟨Hm[W(CrS)]⟩; and in XVII–XX [(WHm)(CrS)]. As always there are discrepant groups,[73]

[72] See above, pp. 38–40.

[73] These are HmCrS (see above, p. 43), WHmS (see above, p. 39, n. 55), HmCr (see above, p. 39), WCr (see above, p. 39), and three not yet cited: HmS (II 73 vnfoldeþ] *pret.* 219 tolugged] lugged. III 239 wiþ(2)] *om.* IV 105 er I] furst y woll. V 99 meyne(*both*)] man. 143 þan] that. 469 But] *om.* VI 190 dikeden] diggedyn. 306 Burgh] the b. VIII 53 wi3t] man. X 151 To] so þat 3e. XI 233 lome...ben] hath ofte b./hath b. ofte. 256 I] þat y. XII 4 haue] y h. 83 repenten] r. hem. XIII 139 *similar misdivision.* 355 colomy] comely. XIV 277 kenne] telle. XV 343 riche ben] *tp.* 563 possession] *pl.* XVI 157 worse] wurste. 195 for] (as) a. XVIII 124 a(2)] *om.* 406 lete] leue. XIX 326 his] *om.* XX 369 to(2)] *om.*); WS (IX 105 his] þis. 168 in] in hir. XI 100 were] be. XII 137 ne] and. XIII 383 In] On. XIV 161 gange] gone. XVII 244 merke]

but almost without exception[74] their agreements are in very commonplace, that is readily explicable variations easy to accept as coincidental. There is then a strong first presumption that WHmCrS are a genetic group from at least X onwards: these manuscripts are descended from two copies having an exclusive common ancestor, with a change of exemplar in the particular tradition of W at some point between XV 601 and XVII 22.[75]

The general presumption of a genetic group WHmCrS extends, in the absence of serious contrary evidence, to Prologue–IX. But here more detailed classification seems impossible. There is, to be sure, more support in these passus for WCrS than for WHm, but the number of agreements involved is very small. Moreover the indications of the two instances of analyzable complex variation by WHmCrS in Prologue–IX are conflicting.[76] The specific relationship of these manuscripts before Passus X seems not recoverable.

The infrequency of agreement in error between these presumably related manuscripts in Prologue–IX suggests that their exclusive common ancestor was there a faithfully copied text. By contrast the markedly greater number of such agreements in X–XV suggests the activity here of a second scribe who did not copy so faithfully. He might, indeed, have been the same who copied the exclusive common ancestor of WHm XVII–XX, which was also markedly less accurate in those passus than elsewhere. Taken together with the change of exemplar in W's tradition this evidence for two scribes working on a single text implies that the history of these manuscripts began with a period of copying in close proximity such as that of a workshop. That implication of the local proximity of lost ancestors is supported by the peculiar connexion of M with WHmCrS. It is not only that by change of exemplar M joins the tradition;[77] M is also at various points visibly

derke. XVIII 406 what(2)] whom. XIX 117 cleped and] *om.*); and WHmCr (II 135 lawe] it. VI 200 erd] yerd/yard. VII 194 bifore] tofore. VIII 131 this] thus. X 440 and] a. for. XI 300 at] at his. XIII 81 witterly] ful w. XV 331 ne] *om.* XIX 274 Cardynales] *sg.*). To these must also be added the eight discrepant agreements of WHm in XI–XV and the five of WCrS in XVII–XX.

[74] Only one, WHm XI 414 *conceyued*] *contreued*, where Cr reads *kend* and S has the original reading may seem notable. But this could be coincident visual error, possibly induced by recollection of *contreued* in X 182.

[75] A slight preponderance of WCrS over WHm agreements in XVI suggests that the change took place at the end of XVI.

[76] At IV 189, *counseil comen*] *counseil commune* WCrS; *comen conseil* Hm is evidence for 〈Hm[W(CrS)]〉; at IX 103 *spire*] *enspired* CrS, *spicerie* W; *spicere* Hm is evidence for [(WHm) (CrS)].

[77] See above, pp. 43, 44.

corrected to ancestral group readings of the genetic complex WHmCrS. For example a 'corrector' aligns M with WHmCrS at X 62, XIII 410, XIV 179, XV 8, 503 and XVIII 109, 300 (and with WHmCr at VI 200 where S is so modernized as to conceal the reading of its original); with WCrS at V 9, IX 120, XIII 178, 240, XIV 248, 289, 320, XV 411 and 553; with CrS at V 186, 187, IX 130, XIII 360, XVII 162, 176, 187, XVIII 122, XIX 36, and XX 273. To be sure all the readings adopted by M occur in Cr, with which M is also elsewhere aligned. But from the hands of the above alterations they were made well before 1550 and must therefore signify that the M 'corrector' had access, if not to Crowley's lost manuscript, then to several lost manuscripts in the WHmCrS tradition.[78] There is the further fact that Hm's contemporary 'corrector' twice aligns his text with W's, at XV 425 and XVII 178, and that a curious HmCr agreement in Prologue 1 occurs over erasure in Hm. All indications are that the connexion of WHmCrS was not only genetic but also somehow local.

Among the variational groups of four manuscripts there are then two probable genetic groups, [C(BmBoCot)] and WHmCrS, the latter not precisely definable in Prologue–IX, but probably ⟨Hm [W(CrS)]⟩ in X–XV.[79]

One genetic group of five manuscripts is created by changes of exemplar in W and M. It will be recalled that in XVII–XX M formed a group of three manuscripts with CrS as [(CrS)M]. That group extends the relationship of [(WHm)(CrS)] in XVII–XX to ⟨[WHm][(CrS)M]⟩.

The next variational group of marked persistence comprises seven manuscripts, YOC^{2}CBmBoCot; these agree in the following more than 70 readings.

III 209 a(2)] the. V 133 to(2)] *om.* 134 þoruȝ] by. 158 of] with. 168 hele] holde. 178 at] it at. 235 for] quod he. 255 pouere men] hem. 257 and] ⁊ of. 263 wel] *om.* 269 *spurious*

[78] From the indication of a marginal *deficit* on fol. 75b opposite XV 462, 463 a corrector of M knew of a manuscript which possessed XV 472–85, missing from the larger group. But there is no evidence that M was corrected to (RF).

[79] There is no support for the earlier notion that LMRF are a genetic group (Blackman, 'Notes on the B-Text MSS.', p. 517). The agreement of these manuscripts is simply not persistent enough to have evidential force. It occurs in the following readings. III 236 in] on. VI 8 þe] þere. 147 And] A. of my. 228 biloue] bilowe/loowe. VII 72 of] of þe. 75 *tua*(1)] *om.* VIII 91 to] into. XIII 222 he] hym he/hym. XV 200 What] þat. See Donaldson, E. T., 'MSS R and F in the B-Tradition of Piers Plowman', *Transactions of the Connecticut Academy of Arts and Sciences*, xxxix (1955) pp. 179–212.

line after.[80] 282 werche] do. 289 wite] wost. 295 oure lordes] his; lette] wite; *spurious line after.* 330 *spurious line after.* 334 raþest] rather. 366 þi] *om.* 394 it] *om.* 397 fourty] fifty. 415 wynter] yere. 436b, 437b *transposed.* 480 gonne] þat g. 538 bokes] *sg.* 540 suren] swere; hym(1)] *om.* 560 *spurious line after.* 587 And] *om.* 593 preieres] *sg.* 594 þat] *om.* 610 to] til. 629 any] the. 640 go] *om.* VI 45 And] *om.* 47α *spurious line after.* 48 at] & (in). 50 tales þow] loke thow t. 55 seide þe kny3t] the k. s. 57 And] *om.* 66 lese] lacche. 67 hym] *om.* 129 it(1)] this; þat ye seyn] *om.* 151 ri3t...of] no þinge in. 183 fere] f. therof. 189 wiþ(2)] *om.* 216 þe gomes] they. 237 he shal] *tp.* 258 ouer] to; grone] to g. 266 of] o. his. 288 dro3te lasteþ] weder is drye. 289 lamesse] herueste. 295 And profrede] To make; þis] a. 299 neer] *om.* 310 if it be] *om.* 313 *line om.* 319 þer...noon] wolde they nat. VII 11 li3tly] lighte. 31 foode...heuene] liflode. 45 a Iustice] Iustices. 59 for] f. his. 85 haþ to] may. 123 Ne] N. be; bisy be] bisily. 127 othere manye] *tp.* VIII 82 land] *pl.* X 446 on] of. XII 131 selkouþes] *sg.* 176 þe] thy. XIII 77 and] or. 190 þe(3)] ye. XV 7 wiþ] and w. 78 in(2)] and. 594 hym] he. XVI 182 and (1)] a. oon. XVII 19 deeþ] deet / dette. 31 synnes] *sg.* 85 to(1)] til. XVIII 11 on] and o. XIX 265 moost] þe m.

With YOC²CBmBoCot is to be considered the only persistent variational group of eight manuscripts, GYOC²CBmBoCot, which agree in the following more than 190 readings.

V 392 What] *om.* 533 wye] he. 572 þow] *om.* VI 50 tales] loke thow tales. 51 of(2)] *om.* 143 in(1)] *om.* 150 self] *om.* 167 wol I no3t] I nill. 200 erd] erthe / yerthe. 274 it] *om.* VIII 54 and] & also. 98 þat] the. 117 we] *om.* IX 42 bible] boke. 43 seide] *pres.* 93 a Iaper] Iapers. 97,98 *run together.* 99 He...hym] thow doest best yff þou withdrawe. 157 wedlokes] *sg.* 158 of...mariages] *om.* 184 likynge] lokyng. 207 to(2)] ys to. X 23 gestes] g. gretly. 34 þe] *om.* 90 manliche] moche. 95 Nou3t] Ac / And / And how n. 98 ne] &. 162 she] stodye. 191 neuere] no. 197 go me to] do hem. 201 He] &. 208 oure lord] god. 223 To] I. 252 scripture] euangelyst. 254 lewed] men. 257 helþe] sake. 263 be] *om.* 293 carpe] do. 309 is] ys a. 315 his(2)] hym (þe). 326 wiþ] &. 343 it] *om*; as...techeþ] as it nedeth / vs n. 399 hir] þe. 410 *line om.* 462 to(2)] In / on; men] to; ne] and (to). 473 konne] *om.* XI 5 wynkynge] wyndyng. 32 hir] it. 46 anoon] sone. 47 and a fifte] or fifty and / or. 49 leue me] *om*; þe leste] ne (no) luste. 74 my(2)] þe. 87 hem] *om.* 134 arerages] *sg.* 146 wilned] *pres.* 188 ei3en] *sg.* 210 of] if. 213 nei3] *om.* 233 hir] nys. 254 Boþe] b. In; and] & In. 264 a(1)] *om.* 302 knowen] knowing. 322 my] *om.* 341 ne(1)] *om.* 359 caukede] kakeled. 379 a(1)] *om.* 419 and] of. XII 16 makynges] mastryes. 34 boþe] here. 49 may] myght. 50 wolde shewe] can say. 92 þat þow] to. 102 þe] hys. 138 it] *om.* 143 ri3t(1)] *om.* 154 *spurious line after.* 159 se] s. ytt / 3it. 193 knewliched] knew / know. 201 a beggere] beggers. 227 it] *om.* 278 neiþer] no. XIII 6 my3te we euere] w.m. neuere. 15 his] *om.* 34 And] *om.* 43 ouer] euer. 48 mete] make. 53 he...vs] *om.* 57 hadde] come (þer)to. 79 he] men h. 95 a(2)] *om.* 120 in] at. 278 si3te] eyghe.

[80] In this variation, and at V 295, 330, 436, 437, 560, VI 47α and 313 YOC²CBmBoCot agree with the Huntington Library MS Hm 114 which we have rejected as useless for editing. See Chambers, 'Manuscripts of *Piers Plowman* in the Huntington Library', p. 18, and above, pp. 14, 15. This suggests that Hm 114 might be genetically related to the group. But the character of the manuscript would otherwise obscure the evidence for its genetic relation.

300 cofre] *pl.* 307 ye] þou. 316 half] *om.* 342 wisloker] bisiloker. 374 hir] my. XIV 2 selde clene] fowle. 3 hous] *om.* 4 wollen] wolden. 14 þoruȝ(2)] *om.* 21 to(1)] *om.* 56 in(2)] *om.* 87 in] *om.* 94 As] And. 97 neuere...is] is n. eft. 112 knoweþ] couthe. 191 so] *om.* 201 coueitous] coueyte. 244 it] *om.* 269 As] and. 277 kenne] seyn. 286 *animarum*] *a.* þe second. 295 wiþ(2)] *om.* 334 mercy faste] *tp.* XV 50 inparfit] vnparfytt. 66 grete] *om.* 71 Ye] *om.* 87 at] of. 124 or] ⁊. 130 þe...god] of witty g. the w. 160 neded] *pres.* 195 quod I] *om.* 200 What] where. 229 *spurious line after.* 253, 254 *transposed.* 271 in(1)] ⁊ yn. 314 wherby] mete þat. 316 o] any. 328 þise] þe. 371 element] *pl.* 376 in(2)] *om*; or] ⁊. 403 places] *sg.* 509 a] in (a). 555 shul ye] *tp.* 582 it] *om.* 583 was] is. 587 knewe] *pres.* 605 pharisees...Sarȝens] *tp.* XVI 126 mete] brede. 176 þat] þis. 180 buyrn] barn. 181 in] on. 185 propre] *om.* 186 of...is] ys off that syre. 210 *line om.* 212 if] it if. 214 resembleþ] resemblant / in semblaunt. 248 a] *om.* 264 no] ne n. XVII 47 lele] leles. 48 to] *om.* 348 That] *om.* 355 lyard he] harde. XVIII 2 As] ⁊ as. 9 rauȝte] taughte. 11 cam] gan. 24 *deus*] *est.* 35 forbete] for to bete. 36 muche] *om.* 83 or] ⁊. 109 þe] ⁊. 145 alofte] a. shall. 172 ner] neigh. 180 Thanne] *om.* 222 Auntred] graunted. 260 bileue] leue; *spurious line after.*[81] 280 *line om.* 295 *spurious line after.*[81] 363 hast] *om.* 385 Ther] where. XIX 3,4 *run together, with omissions.* 5 *line om.* 66 so] *om.* 121 of] *om.* 135 þo] þat / þan. 149 it] hym. 167 ybarred] isperred. 168 and(1)] *om.* 205 for þe] off þat. 218, 226 *run together omitting* 219–25. 227 gide] go. 238 thecche] hegge. 253 *line om.* 360 And] *om.* 458 for] with. 463 þei] to. XX 18 for] *om.* 95, 96 *lines om.* 182 confort] courte. 191 and...my] ⁊ bett me on þe. 236 siþen] sey(e)n. 256 sterres] preestes. 304 koude wel] w. kouthe. 345 lordes] lady(es); ladies] lordes.[82]

Taken together with GYOC^{2}CBmBoCot the earlier presented variational groups OC^2/GC^2, BmBoCot, YOC^2, CBmBoCot and YOC^{2}CBmBoCot might now seem to constitute as impressive a pattern of evidence as any geneticist could reasonably expect, a gradually unfolding history of these eight manuscripts. And indeed when distribution of agreement is taken into account a kind of scheme of their genesis can be proposed.

1. An exclusive common ancestor for (OC^2) and possibly for [Y(OC^2)] in Prologue–XVII.
2. An exclusive common ancestor for [C(BmBoCot)] from about III 150 to the end of IV.
3. Through change of exemplar by either 1 or 2, an exclusive common ancestor for ⟨[Y(OC^2)][C(BmBoCot)]⟩ in V–VII.
4. Through change of exemplar by either 3 or an ancestor of G, an

[81] These lines also occur in Huntington MS 114. See above, p. 52, n. 80, and Russell and Nathan, 'A *Piers Plowman* Manuscript in the Huntington Library', pp. 128, 129.

[82] Variants in which GYOC^{2}CBmBoCot agree at IX 25, XII 268, 271, XIV 44, XVII 81 also occur in S.

exclusive common ancestor for ⟨G[Y(OC^2)][C(BmBoCot)]⟩[83] from VIII–XVI.

5. Through change of exemplar an exclusive ancestor for (GC^2) in XVII or XVIII–XX so that the classification of 4 there becomes ⟨O.Y.[GC^2][C(BmBoCot)]⟩.

This reconstruction seems to us to have a very fair chance of being correct; it is certainly simpler than any other hypotheses by which the evidence might be explained. Nevertheless it is far from satisfactory. It requires assumptions that three exemplars were used and three changes of exemplar took place during the formation of the tradition. Even with those assumptions it is impossible to determine which exemplar eventually becomes that of GYOC^{2}CBmBoCot; in other words whether any surviving manuscript represents an unbroken tradition of descent. One of the genetic identifications, [Y(OC^2)], has had to be made on relatively slight attestation, and is principally indicated by the presence of Y in the group YOC^{2}CBmBoCot. The hypothesis stops short of explaining the inner relation of (BmBoCot); it leaves obscure the earlier history of G; and it fails to show how O, after ceasing to be a genetic twin of C^2, nevertheless continues, on the showing of the evidence, to derive from the exclusive common ancestor of GYOC^{2}C BmBoCot. To construct the hypothesis at all it has been necessary to dismiss as products of convergent variation a very large number of conflicting agreements, both between manuscripts within the group GYOC^{2}CBmBoCot and between members of that group and other manuscripts. Thus the results of a genetic analysis conducted in what might seem most favourable circumstances must be hedged about with severe qualifications, as partial and provisional only; and at their best useless to a recensionist.

There remains one markedly persistent variational group, WHmCr GYOC^{2}CBmBoCotLMS, established by the following agreements.

III 130 and(2)] in. 214 Thoruȝ] For; yerne] renne. 301 pees] a p. IV 103 myne] me. 118 an heþyng] an hyne / vnhende. 141 þoruȝ] for. V 15 pride] pure p. 183 speche]

[83] The evidence for this genetic group in XVII 99–346 and XIX 281–358, where O is defective, is the variational group GYC^{2}CBmBoCot, which there agrees in the following readings: XVII 125, 126 *as three lines, padded.* 128 enformed] *pres.* 141 as] *om.* 167 serelepes] sereples. 171 of] o. al. 188 *line om.* 221 as] a. a; gledes] glede ne. 319 rightwisnesse] ryghtfulnes. 326 and sekeþ] al aboute; slepe] lygge. 327 and] or. XIX 285 *line om.* 315 kynde] kyndly. 317 Grace] g. to Piers. 337 *line om.* (An agreement of GYC^{2}CBmBoCot at XVII 241 is shared by S.) Note however the agreements of this group in XIX 87, 191 and XX 103, 178 where O is not defective.

sight / riȝt / nyght. 196 lepe] haue lopen. 197 wandre] (haue) walked. 214 þe Spynnestere] Spynnesteres. 239 a...Iewes] and I. a lesson. 279 þe] þat. 312,313 *transposed.* 326 þe] þise. 358 to] hom / onto. 369 and...sydes] *om.* 407 of] at. 419 clausemele] clause wel. 494 it blente] was blent. 501 it] me. 545 he] truþe. 550 of hym] *om.* VI 30 bukkes] brokkes. 42 þow] ye. 45 man] men. 88 defende...fend] fro þe f. it d. 103 pote] foot; at] atwo. 105 þe] hise. 179 bileue] cesse] to c. 216 and] *om.* 273 mo] manye; þan] *om.* 310 yfryed] fryed ouþer ybake. VII 63 herte] *pl.* 94 þei] he / ȝe. 98 Tho] And þei. 106 vpon] on. 108 shal] wol. 140 liked] sholdest. VIII 57 þi] youre. 64 abide me made] brouȝte me aslepe. 77 me] me þat. 90 And] A. þus. IX 179 Wideweres] Wodewes. 181 ye] ye þe. 207 is dowel] *tp.* X 20 lette] l. wiþ. 78 þise pestilences] þe pestilence. 79, 80 *lines om.* 88 techeþ] telleþ / told (S). 131 þe Iew] to þe Iewes. 132 he wolde] þow woldest. 136 alle] boþe. 140 how] what / þat (S). 212 is] i. an. 222 to] *om.* 225 my wey] awey. 227 þe(2)...wif] Studie. 252 scripture] Euaungelist(es). 290 manly] safly. 297–308 *lines om.* 320 pure] *om.* 374 *line om.* 375 in(1)] hem in. 383 *add* quod I. 385 alle] a. hise. 386 *line om.* 397 herte] *pl.* 417–19 *lines om.* 429 dide] *om.* XI 5 til I weex] w. I. 7 For] That. 41 graiþly] gretly. 110 *line om.* 131, 132 *run together, with omissions.* 160–70 *lines om.* 197 *line om.* 198 Ac] *om.* 201 at] on. 205 þe(2)] holy. 209 children] breþeren. 264 Makeþ] For it m. 267 segge] man. 283 wise] parfite. 331 se boþe] b. biholde. 383–93 *lines om.* 398 wrouȝt] dide. 403 That] T. ne. 429–31 *run together, with omissions.* XII 23 here] *pret.* 55–7α *lines om.* 59 for] of. 66 a] and. 91 dide þe caractes] þe caractes d. 104 lereþ] ledeþ. 116–25α *lines om.* 151, 152 *lines om.* 219–20, 221–2 *transposed.* 230 Kynde] *om.* 285 Ac] For. 290 trewe] *om.* XIII 35 mettes] macches. 48 mete] macche/make. 51 lif] I lyue/leue. 80 and] he. 82 þis] þ. ilke. 86 preynte] wynked. 103 dobest] dowel. 104 drank after] took þe cuppe and d. 164–71α *lines om.* 228 and] to. 266 bake] *om.* 289 bold] badde. 292–8 *lines om.* 322 lakkynge] laughynge. 348 wel] w. in/on. 349 lef] wel. 360 wittes wyes] which wey. 390 conscience] herte. 399–408 *lines om.* 425 me] m. ful. 436–53 *lines om.* XIV 21 sonnen] sowen. 28 which is] with his. 183 *line om.* 189 pouke] pope. 204 þo Ribaudes] þat/þe Ribaud. 205 reuerences] *sg.* 217 Or] Arst. 228–38 *lines om.* 273 so...pouerte] and so to hise seintes. 274 I...yow] ye. 275 pacience] wiþ p. 294 poore] any p.; riȝt] *om.* 303 yliche] a leche. 312 þat] and. XV 100 Is þe] That aren. 106 auȝt] noȝt. 115 cloþes] c. also. 188 seche] speke / to enstruct (S). 193 Thanne] And t. 244–8 *lines om.* 303,304 *lines om.* 338 ful] *om.* 396 *line om.* 461 keperes] creperes / cropers. 472–85 *lines om.* 490α *line om.* 505 o] þe holy; grace] g. þei. 511–28 *lines om.* 529 Nauȝt to] That. 530 in] *om.* 532 Er] Er þat / þan / any; were] was. 573b–6a *run together with omissions.* 586 and] ȝit a. 588 And] *om.* 592 þei] men. 604 deuyneþ] ȝit / þei d. XVI 43 brewe] breke. 50 planke] plante. 93 tyme] fully. 119 þat] and. 121 Iesus] ich. 123 self] s. seiþ crist. 140 cene] maundee. 142 som] oon. 193 self] *om*; suffreþ hem] þei suffre. 211 in] *om.* 220 pure] *om.* 250 buyrn] barn. 262 wye] man. 275 What] And w. XVII 9 *line om.* 11 He plukkede] Than p. he. 33 brynge] bigynne. 59 aboute] a. hym / but hymselue. 71 *line om.* 76 þe] to þ. 94 vnder] on. 352 good] and g. XVIII 28 feiþ...þe] he þe foule; to deye] and deeþ. 76 þrowe] tyme. 87 Iesu] hym. 101 deeþ...yvenquisshed] his d....avenged. 157 vertu] venym. 262 A] How a. 266 helle] hem alle. 270 laȝar is] hym / he (S) likeþ. 275 þis lord] hym. 296 he...aboute] haþ he / he hath gon. 313, 314 *run together, with omissions.* 318 The] And. 343 clayme] c. it. 359 turne] t. ayein. 401 I] me. XX 27 body] of hem. 36 þat] of þ. 37 *line om.* 38 Philosophres] Wise men. 39 wel elengely] in wildernesse. 42 was he nedy] n. h. w. 55 made] *om.* 60 cam] forþ c. 62 gladdere] leuere. 67 gile] any while. 78 on] to. 87 Largeliche] That l. 93 Thanne] and þanne. 114 wiþ] w. a. 138 Meneuer Mantel] Mantel of M. 141 to fighte] a fightere. 191 wangteeþ] teeþ. 198 heo] she sooþly. 210 lakke] quod he/I l. 211 Weede...mete] Mete...weede. 218 passynge an hundred] mo þan a þousand. 221 was] *om.* 249 lakke] faille. 253 telle] teche. 256 hem] *om.* 260 take...wages] hem paie. 263 parisshe] place. 277 He] And yet he. 284 be] sholde be. 291 shul] wol. 326 lettre] *pl.* 342 any] som. 350 here so] so it.[84]

The absolute persistence of this larger group requires it to be identified as probably genetic from III onwards, where BmBoCot have become copies of the **B** version. Distribution of agreement supports this identification; it quickly becomes remarkably uniform, more so, actually, than we have so far allowed the evidence to indicate.

We did not, for instance, cite the following agreements of WHm CrGYOC²CBmBoCotLMS in XVIII 411–XX 26 where R is defective.

XVIII 424 carolden] dauncede. XIX 43 his(1)] *om.* 56–9 *lines om.* 60 yeueþ] *pret.* 73 riȝt] *om.* 75 sense] *om.* 94 Erþeliche] Thre yliche. 118 fauntekyn] faunt fyn. 130 and(1)] to here and. 145 frend] *pl.*; it] hym. 149 biknewe] b. it. 152 and...after] *om.* 153 yede] he y. 208 god] g. and. 216 hise] hir. 236,237 *run together, with omissions.* 273 aiþes] harewes. 274 Piers greynes] g. þe. 394 Or] That. 400 þat] for þ. 408 þow art] þei ben. 412 feþere] f. or an hennes. 422 Iewes] þe I. 426 Plowman] *om*; þe] ek wiþ his. 446 bereþ witnesse] þerof witnesseþ. 457 to] for t.

We made this exclusion because F by itself does not reliably indicate the text of (RF),[85] and therefore the exclusiveness of the WHmCr GYOC²CBmBoCotLMS agreements, upon which their force as evidence for genetic relation must depend, is here indeterminable. But it is altogether probable that many, if not the great majority of these instances actually record corruption peculiar to the larger group and indicate its genetic character in XVIII 411–XX 26.

Nor did we cite evidence from XVII 99–346 and XIX 281–358 where O is defective. But again there seems little doubt that the presumption of the genetic character of the larger group is strengthened by the agreements of WHmCrGYC²CBmBoCotLMS, both in XVII where R is represented and in XIX where it is defective. They are the following.

[84] At X 479, XIII 311, XVII 143, XX 119, 336, where WHmCrGYOC²CBmBoCotLM agree in unoriginal readings S agrees with RF by felicitous coincident variation. At other points like III 131, XIII 363, XV 116 where the reading of the larger group is scribal the alignment of S has been obscured by modernizing further variation.

[85] On the character of F see below, pp. 166–73.

XVII 105 an...is] Outlawes. 114α *line om.* 168 may an hand] myn hand may. 178 þe] alle þ. 179,181 *run together, with omissions.* 183 or] and. 198 he seide] me þynkeþ. 206 For] And. 293 semed] were. 303 so] s. wel. 306 be] þat is. 313, 314 *lines om.* 324 hire] fro h. 329 smerteþ] smyteþ (in). 330 þe borre] hoors. 340 ouȝte] ofte. XIX 283 meschief] muchel drynke. 284 scornere] s. ne scolde. 314,315 *misdivision.* 330 home] *om.* 334 *line om.* 343 sew] þere hadde ysowen.[86]

The strong showing of this body of evidence must be that from III onwards the manuscripts WHmCrGYOC²CBmBoCotLMS are a main genetic group with an exclusive common ancestor that contained a large number of distinctive unoriginal readings.

This group, which comes into existence with the accession of BmBoCot in III, then takes a place beside RF as a second main line of transmission in the **B** tradition. The fact that RF agreement begins with immediate persistence in the Prologue suggests by exclusion that the two lines exist from the beginning of the poem; the positive evidence for this is however relatively slight; the agreements of WHmCrGYOC² CLMS here are not comparably persistent and their evidential value is obscured by the defectiveness of R. They are the following.

Prologue 73 bulle] *pl.* 213 pounded] poundes. I 104 his] þe. 182 Of] *om.* II 5 on] vpon. 9 pureste on] fyneste vpon. 91 wenes] wedes.[87]

There are, however, no serious conflicting agreements, that is no persistent agreements in error between RF and one or more of WHm CrGYOC²CLMS in Prologue–II; there is then at least a good possibility that the relation suggested by WHmCrGYOC²CBm BoCotLMS begins with the Prologue.

In our opinion the indication of the evidence that there are two main families of **B** manuscripts, RF and WHmCrGYOC²CBmBoCot LMS must be accepted.[88] But we point out that (inevitably, as it will now seem) there is contrary evidence. This is of two kinds. The first is the existence of variational groups which conflict with the division into two putative families. Such conflict we are prepared to dismiss as the result of convergent variation; these groups must attract notice, but none is persistent enough, absolutely or relatively, to appear genetic in the face of the massive agreements of RF or WHmCrGYOC²CBm

[86] XVII 209 where WHmCrGYC²CBmBoCotLM agree is omitted by S.

[87] Where WHmCrGYOC²CLM agree at Prologue 37 and 44 S is defective.

[88] In this we differ from Mrs Blackman, who proposed a trifid stemma. See her 'Notes on the B-Text MSS.', pp. 517, 525.

BoCotLMS.[89] The reader who finds convergent variation a difficult explanation for their existence is invited to reflect on the character of any other. The second kind occurs when either R or F has the original reading and the other member of the pair agrees in error with the group reading of WHmCrGYOC²CBmBoCotLMS and sometimes with H as well, or with such of these manuscripts as are represented.[90] There are some 30 agreements in error between F and the represented manuscripts of the larger group; and almost 100 between R and that group.

We do not wish to seem to minimize the difficulty that these two classes of agreement create; nevertheless we discount them as not of genetic significance. First, because they are themselves in conflict they cannot both be evidence for a vertical genetic relation; therefore if either of the groups which they establish were treated as genetic the other would have to be explained away by arguments just as well applicable to the first. Second, although numerous they occur sporadically, and we do not find this a usual feature of agreements reflecting genetic groups. Third, they are very markedly less persistent than the agreements supporting the two putative families; this in the end is the deciding factor. For if they are taken to indicate that RF and WHmCrGYOC²CBmBoCotLMS are not genetic groups, it will be necessary to adopt some other explanation of the 500 odd agreements of the pair and the 200 odd of the fourteen; this would be very difficult.

We can see no reasonable alternative to accepting the groups RF

[89] One such group, LMRF, has already been noticed (see above, p. 51). Others, to illustrate further, are the following.
LMR: IV 23 twies] tweye. V 230 or] ne. 234 be] *om.* 407 neiȝebores] *sg.* 445 to] so to. IX 63 soules] *sg.* 158 of] for. XI 209 of] vp. XII 161 sikerer] siker. XIII 121 hem] hym. XV 63 Putte] Pulte. 453 be] is.
LRF: V 210 pak] bat. 350 þrumbled] trembled/tripplid. VI 328 multiplie] multiplied. X 249 made] he m. 453 and(1)] at. XII 176 Salmes] *sg.* XIII 73 ben] men b. XIV 1 hool] *om.* 239 cacche] wolde c. XV 36 *Spiritus*] and *S.* XVI 221 children] her c. XVII 164 is þer] *tp.* 167 þei] *om.*
WHmCrLMRFS: VI 23 I] by crist I. XI 2 sette] she/he s. XIII 96 leef] lyue/lyne. 132 dar] d. wel. 140 and (1)] a. wiþ. 145 werk, word] *pl.* 152 a bouste] aboute. 270 were] þere w. XIV 320 and] a. for. XV 116 and] a. youre. XVI 251 and] a. to. XVII 18 Whoso] And w. 171 Al] And a./as (S). XX 163 wex] was.

[90] This occurs, *where R's reading is correct or more correct*, at III 49, 67, V 113, 217, 271, 304, 320, 588, VI 76, 175, 325, VII 58, VIII 50, 119, IX 191, X 61, 227, 245, XI 8, 59, 134, 180, 185, 240, 436, XII 209, XIII 386, XV 18, 109, 531, XVI 136, XX 60, 221, 360, 363; and *where F's reading is correct or more correct*, at Prologue 150, 206, I 24, 43, 45, 73, 118, II 212, III 39, 42, 145, IV 7, 80, 106, 168, V 23, 32, 35, 78, 81, 105, 115, 118, 127, 411, 599, VI 37, 38, 39, 41, 56, 76, 95, 103, 150, 183, 206, 232, 253, 291, VII 10, 34, 117, VIII 24, 37, 42, 44, 49, 50, 57, 78, 80, 92, 97, 103, 105, 108, 109, 112–13, 118, 125, IX 23, 24, 33, 34, 40, 73, 137, X 138, 142, 143, 154, 228, 270, 311, 337, 424, XI 56, 84, 93, 94, 109, 342, 344, XIII 345, 393, XIV 22, 78, 131α, 190, 213, XVII 90, 144, XX 70, 109, 140, 366. In a few other instances R or F agrees coincidentally with S in the right reading.

and WHmCrGYOC²CBmBoCotLMS as genetic, probably in Prologue–II and certainly in III–XX. The implication of such acceptance is that the 30 odd agreements of F with the larger group in unoriginal readings, and the greater number of similar agreements of R have to be explained as products of convergent variation. In the case of the F agreements the character of the readings in question points specifically to coincident variation as the explanation.[91] With F's other very numerous random agreements in mind their number is not hard to accept. As for the agreements between R and WHmCrGYOC²CBmBoCotLMS in unoriginal readings, we have had to conclude that the convergent variation which produced these was specifically correction to original readings in the immediate tradition of F,[92] and that the unoriginal readings in question are archetypal errors.

The groups RF and WHmCrGYOC²CBmBoCotLMS have accounted for all the respectable manuscripts of the **B** version except H which represents that version to about V 127. The variational groupings of H are conflicting, and as genetic evidence, obscure. There is for instance a variational group RFH which might suggest a relation [(RF)H].

Prologue 202 me] myself. I 129 and] to. II 108 which] þis. 154 wiþ] thorȝ. III 100 Offices] *sg.* 140 þe trewe] trewthe. IV 104 crist] god. V 80 þe] his.

Such a relation many of the FH agreements where R is defective[93] might well further reflect. But H also agrees in unoriginal readings with the larger group, both before and after the accession of BmBoCot. Thus it appears in WHmCrGYOC²CLMHS.

Where R *is present*: Prologue 179 his] þe cattes. 185 hadde killed] kylled/killen. I 113 Til] But for. II 101 his] hir. 183 fobbes] Freres. 238 fere] drede.
Where R *is defective*: Prologue 22 þise] *om* (*line om* Hm; *defective* S). 48 Wenten] They w. (*defective* S). 103 most vertuous] þe beste. 122 lif] man. I 175 þe] yow.

And it appears in WHmCrGYOC²CBmBoCotLMHS.

III 63 ech] euery. 150 she] *om*. 162 he] she. 231 bi] wiþ. IV 94 meken] mengen/meue/medel. V 19 And] *om*; tail] *pl.* (*modernized* S). 29 fro] f. þe.

[91] See below, p. 168, n. 89 for an analysis of the variants in question.
[92] For our reasoning see below, pp. 166ff.
[93] See above, p. 29. There is also a variational group HS based on some 30 agreements. But it is to be dismissed as random on the grounds of the persistence of CrS and the congruency of this group in WHmCrS.

The position of H is further obscured by its agreements in error with all the manuscripts except R *or* F as in the following cases.

WHmCrGYOC²CBmBoCotLMFHS: III 49 þere] þerInne. 67 god] crist. V 113 his] mennes.
WHmCrGYOC²CLMRHS: Prologue 150 at] at his. 206 slen] do. I 24 That...is] And. 43 A] *om.* 45 whom] w. madame. 73 halsede] asked. 118 Lucifer] hym (*line om* C). II 212 feeres] felawes.
WHmCrGYOC²CBmBoCotLMRHS: III 39 fiftene] fifty. 42 clerkes...kny3tes] kny3tes...clerkes. 124 she] *om.* 145 She] And. IV 7 þat þow] þow/to. 80 wel] *om.* 106 awey] *om.* 168 also] *om.* V 70 þat] þis. 78 He was] And. 81 As] And as. 105 and] a. sholde. 113 it] þat. 115 I] And. 127 synne] *pl.*

H's agreements with the larger group are the more persistent; further, a more specific place for H in this group might seem to be indicated by the variational group GH, with the following agreements.

Prologue 34 leeue] trowe. 51 þat] *om.* 86 is] ys so. 111 of] of þat. 173 þe] *om.* 223 lybbynge] *om.* 229 of(1)] ꝛ. I 7 þis(1)] þe. 39 wolde] that w. 109 to] for to. 116 man] *pl.* 177 þat] *om.* 186 feet] dede. 187 as(1)] *om.* 196 ye] ꝛ. II 5 and] *om.* 28 a] the. 36 construeþ] *pret.* 71 Cyuylle...Symonye] symonye...cyuyll. 100 so] *om.* 159 shires] þe shyre. 193 and] yff. 218 þanne] thence. III 64 grauynge] wrytyng. 104 comseþ] gynneth/began. 135 of Shires] *om.* 136 lif] *pl.* 148 seleþ] sellen. 196 at] on. 337 lady] *om.* IV 39 or] ꝛ. 94 to] *om.* 110 þat] þe. 155 man] owen. 169 For] Full. 174 almoost hadde] had nyghe. V 10 bifore] ere. 66 fiers] frele. 77 as(1)] *om*; he] hym. 85 wiþ] *om.* 92 þou3] *om.* 123 aswage] swage.[94]

If this were all the evidence it might not unreasonably be interpreted, in terms of relative persistence of agreement, and by recourse to convergent variation, as signifying a genetic relation of H with the larger group, and specifically with G.[95] But there is a third, conflicting class of evidence: a number of agreements in error between all manuscripts except H, where H has the original reading. These agreements, which could indicate a relation ⟨H[(RF)(WHmCrGYOC²CBmBoCot LMS)]⟩, are as follows.

Agreements of WHmCrGYOC²CLMFS *in the absence of both* R *and* BmBoCot: Prologue 2 a shroud] shroudes (*defective* S). 59 þe wombe] hemselue (*defective* S). 76 helpe] kepe. I 186 feblere...nou3t] (ri3t) noþyng worþi.
Agreements of WHmCrGYOC²CLMRFS *before the accession of* BmBoCot; Prologue 224 dede] *pl.* I 11 may...bymeene] is þis to meene. 92 it(1)] þis. (*At* I 79 S *agrees with* H, *by modernization, against the other manuscripts.*)
Agreements of WHmCrGYOC²CBmBoCotLMRFS *in* III–V 127: III 48 stonden]

[94] Variants in which GH agree at II 121 and IV 6 also occur in S.
[95] It will be recalled that G's genetic position in Prologue–VII is obscure.

sitten (*modernized* S). 114 Thanne] And þanne. 198 meynee] men. 211 to (1) and t. (*line om* S). 226 Marchaundiȝe] Marchaunt3. IV 29 cheker] þe c. 47 Thanne] And þanne. 90 Amenden] so a. 145 on englissh] vnglosid. 190 henne] fro me. V 10 tolde] seide. 42 it] (it) on. 72 mysdede] *pl.* (*line om* Cr¹S). (At IV 47 *the correct reading* vp (*var.* forþ) *also occurs in* S.)

This situation to some extent resembles the one created by the presence of original readings in R or F. It differs in two circumstances: the evidence affords no criterion of strikingly greater persistence, such as existed in the case of the respective agreements of RF and WHmCr GYOC²CBmBoCotLMS; and it is not evidently or indeed at all explicable in terms of the character of H. Therefore, while we allow that H, where it is a **B** text, may belong to the larger group and have been distinguished in the above instances by correction, we cannot confidently exclude that its agreements with the larger group are fortuitous and that it represents, as long as it is a **B** text, a third line of transmission. The genetic position of H in the **B** tradition seems to us indeterminable.

With this typically inconclusive result our analysis ends. The evidence for conducting it was almost invariably conflicting; we could interpret it only by accepting several unverifiable assumptions. Having constant regard to the nature of these, and also to the essential artificiality of any assessment of probability possible to the textual critic, we have tried to be as little speculative as we could; it would have been easy to make much more elaborate proposals, but they would not have been useful and might not have been interesting. Those which we offer interpret the data as simply, and therefore it seems to us, as safely as possible; but we wish to emphasize that the specific information available about the genetic history of the **B** manuscripts is, at all stages remote or immediate, both hypothetical and incomplete. With these qualifications we now sum up our findings.

We identify two main genetic groups of **B** manuscripts, thus: [(RF)(WHmCrGYOC²CBmBoCotLMS)]. The evidence for the first of these begins to appear in the Prologue, for the other in III; nevertheless we think it likely that both lines of transmission exist from the beginning of the poem. One manuscript, H, we have not placed in either group because the evidence for its genetic relation is ambiguous: it may belong in the larger group or it may represent a third main line of descent.

Within the larger group we identify two changing sets of more particular relations.

First we find in V–VII a family ⟨[Y(OC^{2})][C(BmBoCot)]⟩; in VIII–XVII the same family augmented: ⟨G[Y(OC^{2})][C(BmBoCot)]⟩; then in XVIII–XX these manuscripts in a different relation ⟨O.Y.[GC^{2}][C(BmBoCot)]⟩. But we recall that the evidence for [Y(OC^{2})] is very slight and that the precise relation of (BmBoCot) is indeterminable.

Second we find in X–XV a family ⟨Hm[W(CrS)]⟩; and in XVII–XX the same manuscripts, with M, in an altered relation ⟨[WHm][(CrS)M]⟩. We also find some evidence in Prologue–IX for a genetic relation between WHmCrS in which CrS are a genetic pair but the classification of W and Hm is indeterminable.

About the remaining manuscripts we can make no proposals. The genetic relations of G in the early part of the poem, of M before XVII, and of L are obscure.[96]

Such scanty and heavily qualified results must seem a poor return for the laborious process of analysis. At best what we have been able to recover of the history of the surviving **B** manuscripts is an incomplete structure of possibilities, some more and some less likely than others. The **B** version of *Piers Plowman* would be the despair of a recensionist.

The general showing of the analysis is, however, more satisfying, and of direct editorial value. First it has demonstrated the homogeneity of the **B** tradition,[97] quite apart from our limited genetic findings. Consideration of the number and character of the conflicting variational groups has put it beyond doubt that the differentiations of one manu-

[96] To illustrate the difficulty of classifying the early part of G we recall the variational group GH (see above, p. 60). This would be congruent with a group WHmCrGH, agreeing in the following readings: Prologue 27 haue] h. (þer)after. 41 bely] *pl.* 69 wiþ] w. many; which after the accession of S appears as WHmCrGHS, agreeing in the following readings: Prologue 149 court] contree. I 147 *line om*; II 100 hym] *pl.* 137 wiþ] to. 156 þat] þe. III 101 fro] f. þe. 142 risshe] bene. 280 shewe] telle. 335 muche] moost. But it would not be congruent with WHmCrGS, established by the following agreements before VIII: Prologue 162 wenden] wenten. 163 leue] self. 170 *line om.* I 6 ben] b. alle. II 187 *line om.* III 99 þe] *om.* V 267 for...of] so god. 367 gome] grom. 606 sitte] *om.* VI 127 of] for. 147 cope] kepe. (An agreement of WHmCrGH at III 351 is not shared by S.) Which, if any, of these groups might be genetic it seems impossible to determine.

With respect to L, the possibility of a genetic group WHmCrLMS might seem suggested by the following agreements. VII 191 and] a. for. IX 98 dredeþ hym] *om.* X 252 scripture] Euaungelistes. XI 2 sette] she s. XIII 48 mette] macche. XIV 303 lewde] land. XV 78 in(2)] and into. XVI 11 to] for t. XVIII 180 Thanne] And. 242 witnesseþ] *pret.* (There are also agreements of WHmCrLM at V 552 and XI 49 where the reading of S's exemplar is obscured by modernization.) But this group is not persistent enough to warrant more than notice.

[97] We emphasize that this extends to H; the problem with this manuscript has not been whether its first part belongs in the **B** tradition, but what is its genetic classification.

script from another are not merely scribal but uniformly typical of scribes. The **B** manuscripts are distinguished not by the kind of error but by its frequency. Their similarities or differences are accidents of copying. Some are evidently more corrupt than others, but whether more or less corrupt they exhibit the same types of variation, and a 'good' manuscript will agree with a 'bad' one in any of these kinds. That homogeneity[98] of the tradition is our general authorization for editing a **B** version; but more particularly it implies that no manuscript is sacrosanct; no manuscript is demonstrably 'closer to' or 'more remote from' the original except with regard to the particular reading.

The second result of the analysis has been to establish the extreme frequency of convergent variation in the transmission of *Piers Plowman* manuscripts. This should no longer need to be argued; it is the only possible explanation of the many random agreements of these manuscripts. Whether this convergent variation was by conflation or coincident substitution is seldom conclusively determinable: there are several **B** manuscripts which show physical evidence of conflation (or 'correction'), and from this it is apparent that the matter of conflation may as easily be trifling as substantial.[99] Against that there are well more than 1000 variational groups of **B** manuscripts agreeing in less than 10 readings; these alone would be proof that coincident substitution frequently occurred. The distinction luckily is not material to editing. What is important is that this situation brings home to the editor the relative unimportance of strength of attestation as evidence of originality,[100] and directs his attention to the readings.

One further consideration arising out of the history of the subject will complete this section: the relation of the texts of the **B** version preserved in RF and WHmCrGYOC²CBmBoCotLMS. The text of RF contains about 175 lines not found in WHmCrGYOC²CBmBoCotLMS; and these latter manuscripts (with H where it is a **B** text) contain about 170 lines not found in RF. These differences have suggested some form of authorial differentiation: specifically, that RF might preserve an authorial form of the poem intermediate between **B** and **C**; or conversely that the text of WHmCrGYOC²CBmBoCot

[98] It will be further demonstrated. See below, pp. 78–82.

[99] This should finally dispose of any notion that it might be possible to identify from their character agreements likely to have originated in lateral transmission. Cp. Vol. I, pp. 56–60.

[100] The old maxim 'manuscripts must be weighed, not counted' should be revised to run 'readings should be weighed, not manuscripts counted'. But to the inexperienced in textual criticism an array of sigils after a variant is bound to seem impressive.

LMS might incorporate changes made by the poet.[101] At least two circumstances combined to encourage such opinions. First, an impression of uniformity of attestation in the **B** manuscripts, conveyed by Skeat's incomplete critical apparatus, encouraged an attitude of mind in which any marked variation, especially a variation from his printed text, was bound to appear striking. And second, the earlier, mistaken genetic location of RF with LM as [(LM)(RF)][102] made it difficult to account for differences between these pairs of manuscripts, or agreements of LM with WHmCrGYOC²CBmBoCot against RF, except by assuming some form of authorial intervention, or contamination. The main difficulty was with the lines and passages found in one family but not in the other; these tended to seem present by addition rather than absent by omission. But it is now clear that the difficulty was unreal.

Full collation of the **B** manuscripts has done away with any impression of their uniformity of attestation; they are frequently and strikingly corrupt. The genetic analysis has not only confirmed that no relation [(LM)(RF)] exists; it has also placed the differentiating characteristics of both RF and WHmCrGYOC²CBmBoCotLMS in respective settings of extensive variation. The unoriginal readings of the two families and of H are all of a piece, the effects of negative forces, relatively common instances of the deterioration which is axiomatically a result of manuscript copying. In this setting the omissions appear less striking; the presence of some 40 substantial omissions among 500 shared unoriginal readings seems more probable than otherwise.

But because the relation of these two families to one another, and thus in the **B** tradition, concerns the propriety of including in our text the matter distinctive of one or the other it is of fundamental importance; we cannot therefore stop short with general assertions. The conclusive indication that the differentiations of RF and WHmCrGYOC²CBmBoCotLMS are scribal is the possibility of identifying physical reasons for the absence of almost all the lines and passages. Each family descends from an exclusive common ancestor copied by a scribe liable

[101] See Skeat, *B-Text*, p. xii; Blackman, 'Some Notes on the B-MSS.', pp. 502, 3; Day, M., 'The Revisions of Piers Plowman', *MLR*, xxiii (1928), pp. 25–7; Chambers, R. W., 'Manuscripts of *Piers Plowman* in the Huntington Library', p. 12; Kane, G., 'Piers Plowman: Problems and Methods of Editing the B-Text', *MLR*, xliii (1948), pp. 23–5; Donaldson, E. T., *Piers Plowman: The C-Text and Its Poet*, pp. 249, 50; 'MSS R and F in the B-Tradition', p. 211. Both editors must admit to having earlier published opinions on this subject which they now disown.

[102] See above, p. 51, n. 79.

to small, unconscious inaccuracies.[103] And each scribe, from this identifiable characteristic as well as *a priori*, would commit larger errors of inadvertence. How these occurred will now be proposed.

It will be seen that the occasions of omission are very ordinary. Omissions are most frequent when the text encourages 'eyeskip' through homo- and homœoarchy, homo- and homœoteleuton; or from rubric to rubric; or where the expected completion of a predictable syntactical scheme is deferred by an intervening unit; or where the impetus of the progressing sense is such as to carry a reader briskly forward; or where the attraction of alliteration operates. That such circumstances caused verse paragraphs to be omitted as easily as single lines should not seem surprising; it is to be remembered that *Piers Plowman* falls into paragraphs, which were often so copied and signified. To see the paragraph only as a probable authorial addition is misleading, for it is also, as a unit of sense, particularly liable to be omitted. In addition, because the end of a paragraph afforded a natural point of pause for the scribe, the mere occurrence of similar or related words or notions at approximately corresponding points in two successive paragraphs could cause omission of one of these. A scribe might not be allowed or able to mark his point of resumption in his exemplar;[104] if tired or bored or distracted or in a hurry after an interruption he would try to find this by running his eye over the open pages before him without actually reading. He would then easily mistake a paragraph in which familiar words or notions in approximately recollected corresponding positions caught his eye for the one copied just before he broke off, and go on to the next for his beginning. A notable case of such omission occurs at XVII 221–47 where a large paragraph, possibly a whole side, omitted by RF, is studded with words and notions like those in the passage before it. But a scribe might just as easily omit the first of two paragraphs with such corresponding features. Paragraph omission corresponds to the accepted phenomenon of stanza omission, and occurred for similar reasons. Any of the

[103] A substantial proportion of the shared errors of each family are the results of unconscious scribal substitutions for familiar reasons: imperfect verbatim recall because the scribe had taken up too much copy; omission of intervening syntactical units; simple visual error; misreading through inducement by preceding or following context; subconscious attraction to preceding copy; anticipation of following copy; substitution of more common collocations; substitution of inferentially habitual expressions. There are some 60 such errors in the text of the exclusive common ancestor of WHmCrGYOC²CBmBoCotLMS, and considerably more in that of RF.

[104] If, for instance, it was a commissioned copy, or was privately owned and lent for copying.

circumstances which could cause omission of smaller line units might also cause omission of one or several paragraphs.

On these considerations the absence of lines and passages present in RF from WHmCrGYOC²CBmBoCotLMS is to be explained as the consequence of accidental omission from their exclusive common ancestor.

X 79,80: Homoarchy (*That* 78, 80).
X 297–308: Homœoteleuton (*al...*‸*nesse...herte* 296, *al...*‸*nesse...lerne* 308).
X 374: Homoarchy (*For* 374, 375: see apparatus); or rubricator's omission.
X 386: Omission of an intervening syntactical unit through progress of attention from *hym* 385 to *He* 387. Note accompanying insertion of *hise* 385.
X 417–19: Homœoarchy (*At...day* 417, *On...day* 420), and distraction by the need to leave room for a rubricated Latin line.
XI 110: Homœoarchy (*Þe...leue* 109, *The bileue* 110), and the implied suggestion of *louyen it* (see apparatus, 109) that the sense of the statement is complete.
XI 131b, 132a: Homoteleuton at the cæsura (*wiþ hym and* 131, 132).
XI 160–70: Resumption at a wrong point induced by *clerkes* 143, *men of holy chirche* 160; *helle* 144, *helle* 164; *loue and leautee* 145, *Loue and lewtee* 167; *loue and...lyuynge in truþe* 152, *loue and lyuyng in truþe* 162; *fro bitter peyne* 153, *out of pyne* 163; *bokes* 155, *book* 168; *Sarsen* 157, *sarsyn* 165; *lesson* 158, *lere* 170.
XI 197: Resumption at a wrong point induced by *riche men* 197, *ben...riche* 198.
XI 383–93: Homœoarchy (*Holy writ...wye wisseþ* followed by Latin 383, *wise...witty wroot...bible* followed by Latin 394).
XI 429b–31a: Homoteleuton at the cæsura (*þanne* 429, 431).
XII 55–7α: Homœoteleuton (*soule(s)* followed by Latin 54, 57).
XII 116–25α: Resumption at a wrong point induced by *Archa dei* 113, 119; *clerkes* 109, *clergie* 121; *cheste* 114, 125.
XII 151, 152: Resumption at a wrong point resulting from distraction by the rubric, or notional homœoteleuton (*solas* 150, *blisse* 152).
XIII 164–71α: Homœoteleuton (*þee...þow* 163, *þow...þei* 171, and rubrics at 163α, 171α).
XIII 292–8: Resumption at a wrong point induced by *louelokest to loken on* 294, *a lyoun on to loke* 301.
XIII 399–408: Resumption at a wrong point resulting from distraction by the rubric and by notional homœoteleuton (*grace...helpes* 398; *mercy amenden* 408).
XIII 436–53: Notional and verbal homœoarchy (*minstrales* 436, *fooles* 454; *loue...festes* 437, *louen* (see apparatus)*...feste* 455).
XIV 183: Homoarchy (*To...to...to* 182, 183) and similarity of syntax.
XIV 228–38: Resumption at a wrong point induced by homœoteleuton (*cheueþ* 227, ‸*chief* 238) and by internal correspondences (*And if* 230, 239; *For* 231, 241; *And* 232, 240; *And* 233, 244).
XV 244–8: Resumption at a wrong point induced by *amonges* 237, 244; *For* 238, 245; *matrimoyne* 241, *patrymoyne* 246.

XV 303, 304: Omission of an intervening syntactical unit through progress of attention from *yfed...foweles* 302 to *foode...foweles* 305; note also *beestes* 303, 305.
XV 396: Homœoteleuton (*bileueþ in oon god* 395, *on oon god bileueþ* 396).
XV 472–85: Resumption at a wrong point induced by *mene after* 459, *menyng after* 475; *Rude and vnresonable* 461, *rude...reson* 476; *feste* 462, *fedde* 463, *feden...and festen* 485; *foweles... whistlyng* 464, 479.
XV 490α: Rubricator's oversight.
XV 511–28: Homœoteleuton (*bere bisshopes names* 510, *bisshopes...bereþ þe name* 527, 528).
XV 573b–6a: Homœoteleuton (*foode and nedy folk to fynden* 573, *foode to gyue þere it nedeþ* 576).
XVII 9: Homœoteleuton (*ye mowe knowen* 9, *we myghte...knowe* 10).
XVII 71: Homoarchy (*And* 71, 72).
XVII 114α: Rubricator's oversight.
XVII 179b–81a: Homoteleuton at the cæsura (*fust* 179, 181).
XVII 313, 314: Omission through distraction by the corrupt copy preceding (*folwen*] *falsly*; *wille*] *lyues* 311).
XVIII 313b, 314a: Homœoteleuton at the cæsura (*lesynges* 313, *lesynge* 314).
XIX 56–9: Homoarchy (*And* 56, 60).
XIX 236b, 237a: Homœoteleuton at the cæsura (*laboure* 236, *labour* 237).
XIX 334: Omission of a delaying syntactical unit through attraction between *Piers* 333 and *Piers* 335.
XX 37: Distraction by *nedeþ* 36, *nede...nede...nedes* 37, *nedy* 38.

The absence from RF of lines and passages present in WHmCr GYOC²CBmBoCotLM(H)S is to be similarly accounted for.

Prologue 144: Omission of intervening syntactical unit induced by attraction between *vers of latyn* 143 and the rubric.
Prologue 171, 172: Homoarchy and homoteleuton (*And...we mowen* 170, 172).
I 82: Omission of intervening syntactical unit through attraction of *kenne me...to* 81 to *Teche me to* 83.
III 51–62: Verbal and notional homœoteleuton (*glaȝe...graue þere þi name* 49, *glaȝen... portraye who paied* 61, 62).[105]
III 149b, 50a: Omission of intervening syntactical units through movement of attention from *Bisshopes* 149 to *preestes* 150.[106]
V 473: Eyeskip (*his* 473, 474).
VI 217: Homoarchy (*And* 216, 217).
VI 311a: Alliterative attraction to *for* 311.
VII 42α: Rubricator's oversight.
VIII 14–17: Resumption at wrong point induced by *Where...dowel dwelleþ dooþ* 13, *dowel...wher...dwelle boþe* 17.
IX 116b–19a: Homoarchy (*And þus was wedlok ywroȝt* 116, 119).

[105] The deficiency, which would be obvious to an attentive reader, was subsequently made good from memory of **A** III 50–1.
[106] Padding and redivision took place in F: see apparatus.

IX 163, 164: Omission of a parenthetic sense-unit.
IX 169: The line was marginal in the archetype; compare its dislocation in the other family.
IX 173–5: Homœoarchy and homœoteleuton (*Haue þei...-twene* 172, *But þei...tyne* 175).[107]
IX 182–8: Homœoarchy (*maner...man* 182, *man and womman* 189).
IX 202–6: Homœoarchy (*Dowel...is* 202, *is dowel* 207).
X 431 Omission through subconscious suggestion of the parallelism *Or...Dauid þat, Or Poul...þat*, that 430, like 429, was a completed statement.
XI 46–9: Homoarchy[108] (*Coueitise of eiȝes* 46, 50); note also *likyng* in 45, 49.
XII 13, 13α: Homœoteleuton (rubrics at 12α, 13α).
XII 76: Homœoteleuton (*deþe* 75, *dede* 76).
XII 139–47α: Homœoteleuton (rubrics at 138α, 147α).
XII 169: Homœoteleuton (*it semeþ* 169, *it sheweþ* 170); note also *neuere...swymme* 168, *swymme...noȝt* 169.
XII 186: Notional correspondence amounting to homœoarchy (*Wo* 186, *Wel* 187), and distraction by the need to remember to leave space for a rubricated line.
XII 194: Homœoarchy (*grace of god* 192, *grace...of god* 194).
XIII 14–20: Resumption at a wrong point induced by multiple homoarchy (*And how þat* 6, 7, 12, 14; *And how* 11, 12, 16; *And* 8, 9, 19, 20).
XIII 372b, 373a: Omission of intervening syntactical units through attraction from *-bore* 372 to *or* 373.
XIV 155–9: Homoarchy (*Ac* 155, 160).
XIV 252, 253: Homœoarchy (*A...stuwes* 252, *A...suwe* 254).
XIV 312α: Rubricator's oversight.
XV 72: Homœoteleuton (*bileue* 72, (*bi*)*leuen* 73).
XV 254α: Rubricator's oversight.
XV 403, 404: Notional and verbal homœoteleuton (*his ere* 402, *þe clerkes ere* 405).
XV 533–69: Notional and verbal homœoteleuton (*Er cristendom were knowe þere or any cros honoured* 532, *That contrarien cristes lawes and cristendom dispise* 569). See also below, p. 178, n. 101.
XVI 27b, 28a: Homoteleuton at the cæsura (*wynd* 27, 28).
XVI 264: Omission of intervening syntactical unit through grammatical attraction between *may...no buyrn...brynge vs* 262, 263 and *Til* 265.
XVI 270–3: Homœoarchy (*Allas I* 270, *I* 274).[109]
XVII 39–49: Resumption at a wrong point induced by *Abraham* 28, 30, 44; *Thre persones* 29, *þre louely persones* 46; *lawe* 33, 35, 49; *Spes* 35, 48; *To bileeue and louye* 37, *to louye and lene* 47.
XVII 115–26: Resumption at a wrong point induced by *feiþ* 103, 115; *feiþ and his felawe* 103 (see apparatus); *suwen Feiþ & his felawe* 109, *Feiþ and folwen his felawes* 126; *feloun* 113, *folwen* 126.

[107] This loss was subsequently noticed, and spurious lines with some traces of the original wording supplied.

[108] The two lines following were later omitted in the tradition of F through a recurrence of this distraction: note *Coueitise of eiȝes* 52.

[109] The loss was subsequently noticed, and spurious lines supplied to bridge the gap in sense.

XVII 221–47: Resumption at a wrong point induced by *fader...sone* 202, *sire...sone* 224; *The holy goost* 203, 226; *fir flawmynge* 208; *flawmeþ...fir* 229; *And as wex...warm* 209, 235; *blase...brenneþ* 216; *brennen and blasen* 236; *þe weke* 216, 243; *holy goost...mercy* 218, *crist... mercy* 245; *oure lord* 220, *fader of heuene* 247.
XVII 320: Resumption at a wrong point induced by *restitucion* 319, *satisfaccion* 320.
XVIII 180: Homœoarchy (*I shal* 180, *Ihus* 181).
XVIII 199: Omission induced by connotational attraction (*fend* 198, *perpetuel peyne* 200, or by pseudogrammatical attraction (*wille* 198, *That* 200).
XVIII 252, 253: Omission induced by successive *And*'s (250, 251, 255).
XX 238, 239: Omission induced by *And siþen* 236, 240; *Lat hem* 237, 241; or by notional correspondence (*liflode...beggeris* 239, *beggeris...lyue...foode* 241).

From this examination it must, we believe, conclusively appear that the distinctiveness of WHmCrGYOC²CBmBoCotLM(H)S and RF with respect to content is a matter of loss rather than insertion of lines and passages. The absence of these from either group then constitutes an unoriginal reading of that group, and can thus evidence no more than that its component manuscripts share an exclusive common ancestor. Neither family is the 'closer' to the poet except where it has preserved original readings corrupted or lost in the other; the differences between the two families arose through the incidence of corruption in each; and in the end there is not much to choose between them. Both belong to the **B** tradition. Its homogeneity is confirmed, not called into question, by the variation in them.

III

THE ARCHETYPAL **B** MANUSCRIPT

The analysis of variational agreements will have shown that no manuscript of the **B** version uniformly preserves the text of the exclusive common ancestor of the seventeen **B** copies. Each departs from this in a greater or lesser number of readings. The text of that ancestor, the 'archetypal' **B** text, can generally be ascertained from the evidence afforded by the **B** manuscripts.[1] But its recovery is only the beginning of the restoration of the original text of the **B** version.

This is a consequence of the existence of the poem in three forms. That circumstance creates an intellectual compulsion to account for the differences between the forms; it requires them to be compared and their relationships to be examined. One conclusion of such comparison and examination is that the archetypal **B** text, as restorable from the evidence of the **B** manuscripts, was markedly corrupt, having already when it generated these manuscripts been distanced by scribal agency from the original text of the version. This is no new finding,[2] but its implications have proved vastly more extensive than was formerly believed. Because they are fundamental to our editing we must now discuss the situation at some length.

The similarities of content and the character of the differences between the three forms of *Piers Plowman* have made them seem not three distinct poems but three versions of a single poem. Two determinants therefore govern their comparison: the origin of the three versions, and their sequence. The first of these will not detain us: the combined showing of both external evidence and literary history, in the present state of knowledge, is that they are the work of a single author. The second is more problematic and requires a digression.

When a poem exists in several versions the order of their composition is ideally determinable by external evidence: in the present case none,

[1] Not, of course, by recension; other considerations apart the bifid stemma of the manuscripts, possibly throughout the poem and certainly after V, would preclude the use of that method.

[2] See especially Blackman, 'Notes on the B-Text MSS.', pp. 529, 530, and Chambers, R. W., and J. H. G. Grattan, 'The Text of "Piers Plowman" ', *MLR*, xxvi (1931), pp. 2–7.

to our knowledge, exists.[3] In such a situation the sequence of composition will for any critic appear to be that which best conforms to his *a priori* conception of the nature of poets' revisions, and so seems best to account for the similarities and differences between the versions. Thus the order of composition of the three versions of *Piers Plowman*, however conceived, must both appear obvious,[4] and be strictly hypothetical.

To us the sequence of composition proposed by Skeat and accepted by almost a consensus of *Piers Plowman* scholars[5] seems to afford the best hypothesis. Because of the importance of the sequence of composition in the comparison of versions and thus to our editing we now give reasons for that opinion.

First, the three forms of *Piers Plowman*, severally of substantive literary excellence, and established by independent manuscript traditions, fall *prima facie* into physical series. One form is by far the shortest. When the content of the three forms is compared this shortest one proves to contain

(i) material common to all three forms (*ABC*);
(ii) material shared with one other (*AB*);
(iii) a relatively small amount of distinctive material (*A*).

Moreover in this form there occur notions and subjects that are much more extensively developed or fully discussed in the other two forms. In the absence of other considerations a natural presumption that a poem under revision will grow in content, scope and meaning, rather than diminish, must make this seem the earliest form of *Piers Plowman*. Again with respect to content, of the two longer forms one appears distinctly closer to the shortest. This contains

(i) material common to all three forms (*ABC*);
(ii) material peculiar to itself and the shortest form (*AB*);

[3] Topical references have been identified in the several versions, and advanced as evidence of their dates. For a summary see Bloomfield, M. W., *Piers Plowman as a Fourteenth-Century Apocalypse*, New Brunswick (New Jersey), 1962, pp. 89, 90, 203. But the evidence of a topical reference is equivocal, since its absence admits of two explanations: the event to which it refers might indeed not yet have occurred at the time of composition; but reference to this might equally have been deleted during revision because it seemed no longer of interest or relevance. We must therefore allow H. Meroney's objection to the use of this class of evidence in establishing the sequence of versions ('The Life and Death of Longe Wille', *ELH*, xvii (1950), p. 20).

[4] Compare Skeat's assertions (*C-Text*, p. xiv): 'when we proceed to place the *three* texts side by side, it is at once apparent that the B-text is *intermediate* in form between the other two; so that the order of texts must either be A, B, C, or C, B, A; but the A-text so evidently comes *first*, that the C-text can only come *last*; and this settles the question.'

[5] It has only twice been challenged since the three forms of the poem were known; by Görnemann (see above, p. 16, n. 1), and by Meroney, 'The Life and Death of Longe Wille', pp. 1–35. The advocates of multiple authorship, we would note, accepted it without question.

(iii) material which, where this form generally corresponds to the shortest, appears as additional, some of this being peculiar to itself (*B*), and some common to itself and the third form (*BC*);

(iv) a long continuation, in part peculiar to itself (*B*), in part common to itself and the third form (*BC*).

The third form, finally, contains

(i) material common to all versions (*ABC*);

(ii) the bulk of the additions and of the continuation wanting in the shortest form (*BC*);

(iii) material peculiar to itself (*C*);

and correspondingly it lacks

(i) material peculiar to the shortest form (*A*);

(ii) material peculiar to the second form (*B*);

(iii) material common to those two forms (*AB*).

The implication of this situation must quite simply be that because in its major features **B** resembles **A** more than **C** does, and also resembles **C** more than **A** does, or in other words because its respective affinities with **A** and **C** are very substantially greater than those between **A** and **C**, it occupies the medial position. This physical sequence is a fact.[6]

Our second reason is a matter of judgement. We believe that the simplest and critically most satisfactory explanation of the literary aspect of the relation of the three versions is a hypothesis of authorial revision from the shortest to a longer form, and thus, since **B** is intermediate, from **A** to **B** and from **B** to **C**. The basis of our judgement is the general proposition that unless there are contrary indications any authorial version of a poem which both comprises a shorter version and extends its development is likely to be the subsequent one.[7] Contrary indications in the present case could only be literary. They would presumably take the form of crudities of conception and execution,

[6] It is not really a matter of dispute, and has only once been questioned, by Görnemann. Her remarkable assertion that there are 'viel nähere Beziehungen zwischen dem A- und C-Text, als zwischen A und B, und C und B' (*Zur Verfasserschaft*, p. 96) bears no relation to the data, literary or statistical, and need not be taken seriously.

[7] To represent this proposition in extreme form and without qualification as Meroney does ('The Life and Death of Longe Wille', p. 20: 'that short works universally precede long, as the lay the epic, betrays a notion of literary craftsmanship which, if not outmoded, is not unchallenged') fails to invalidate it; his analogy of lay and epic does not apply, and there are enough actual, particular instances where the general notion is correct. In the case of *Piers Plowman* it may be to the point that with a single material exception (H) scribal adaptations of the poem were from the shorter to the longer.

comparative poverty of imagination and banality of expression, in brief a manifest inferiority of the shorter version as poetry. If the **A** version exhibited such characteristics they would be reasons for considering it an abridgement by a scribe[8] or a redactor,[9] but we think that it does not. Recognizing that this critical judgement with its implications is the foundation of our argument for the antecedence of **A** we will assert that the **A** version has no literary qualities which would justify considering it the work of anyone but a major poet. We find in it the integral characteristics of a substantive work of art, a poem free, except for scribal damage, of the marks of debasement inevitably left by an inferior talent reducing that which itself it could not have created.[10]

Specifically the hypothesis of an order **A**>**B**>**C** explains the **A** version as the first authorial form of *Piers Plowman*, a poem either unfinished or hastily and perfunctorily brought to an unsatisfactory termination, promising development which it does not fulfil,[11] preserved in an independent manuscript tradition generated before any longer form of the poem existed.[12]

The hypothesis, further, from the literary point of view answers to our sense of probability as no other sequence of composition and revision could do, by enabling what we think the best explanation of the character of the three versions. It permits good and relatively simple explanations of **B** and **C**'s more extended development and impression of completeness; and makes it possible to account convincingly, as we believe, for the reviser's various omissions, reductions, rearrangements and additions. The expectations of treatment raised but disappointed in

[8] Görnemann, *Zur Verfasserschaft*, pp. 81, 82.

[9] Meroney, 'The Life and Death of Longe Wille', pp. 22, 23.

[10] We have not been able to identify any of the 'many differences between the texts [of **A** and **B** which] indicate that the writer of A has failed to comprehend the original', one of Meroney's grounds for denying the authorial character of **A** ('The Life and Death of Longe Wille', p. 23).

[11] The evidence for this assessment of the **A** version is of two kinds, textual and literary. The first is indicated in Kane, *Piers Plowman*: *The Evidence*, pp. 21, 22, 47, 48, n. 11, and p. 51. The second is more a matter of critical judgement and interpretation, based on the sense of unfulfilled expectation awakened generally by **A**'s relatively disproportionate treatment of *Visio* and *Vita*, and its abrupt, inconclusive-seeming termination, specifically by indications (at **A** IX 69, 104–6, 117, 118, XI 87–92, 179–81) that the poet intended to develop the subject of the Three Lives at length, and to carry the search for them to a successful conclusion rather than leave the Dreamer disappointed as he is in XI 258ff. To use Meroney's words, we find 'difficult a belief that the A-Version contains the entirety of its initial design' ('The Life and Death of Longe Wille', p. 21).

[12] The **A** tradition is defined in Vol. I, pp. 19–52; the **A** manuscripts descend from an exclusive common ancestor which contained a distinct form of the poem. As for its tradition being 'debased' (Meroney, 'Life and Death of Longe Wille', p. 19), this is true only in the sense of textual criticism that all manuscript traditions are debased by progressive scribal corruption during transmission.

A are fulfilled in **B**; the differences between **B** and **C** appear as differences between a first, completed poem and a more soberly reflective, but unfinished[13] revision of this. The hypothetical order **A**$\rangle$**B**$\rangle$**C** seems to reveal and relate to a gradual enlargement of imaginative conception and a progressive deepening and refinement of meaning such as the artistic quality of any of the three versions would lead us to expect of its poet.

To these reasons, which for the majority of scholars have seemed good and sufficient to establish Skeat's order of revision, we add a third. The detailed and more minute relationships of the texts of the three forms of the poem are most readily and reasonably explicable as phenomena of Middle English authorship, publication and transmission on the hypothesis that **B** is a textual descendant of **A** and **C** a textual descendant of **B**. The explanation thus afforded is not simple; if it were, this book would be shorter. But it presents itself to our judgement as the simplest one possible, the easiest and the most convincing in our experience of textual criticism. And indeed, if our exposition of these relationships is successful its acceptability may constitute the ultimate demonstration of the sequence of versions of *Piers Plowman*.[14] If that proves the case the hypothesis will have admirably fulfilled itself; the efficiency of its operation will constitute the demonstration of its correctness. But we would not anticipate judgement. Our situation is that the editing of *Piers Plowman* can proceed only on some hypothesis of the order of versions, and we have adopted the one which for our stated reasons seems to us best.

Given single authorship and a sequence of composition where **B** is the middle version its editors are placed in an unusual logical situation. For about a third of the poem, that is to the end of **B** X, there are many single lines, as well as passages of various length, where the three versions recognizably correspond and can be minutely compared at the textual level with respect to local expression and to technical form, without distraction by larger considerations of meaning and structure.

[13] See below, pp. 124, 125.

[14] Our demonstration must in any case dispose of Meroney's single valid objection to accepting the traditional sequence: 'while the B-Text is deemed a rewriting of A, no demonstration of this process has ever been carried out at the level of words and phrases; although each body of MSS has been subjected independently to the standard tests of higher criticism...no such methods, e.g. by a principle of *lectio durior*, have been applied in common to justify the claims of A's originality' ('The Life and Death of Longe Wille', p. 20). Most of Meroney's arguments are no more than iterations of *nay* and *yea*, but he was right to insist on the need for examining the bases of received opinions.

Because inaccurate copying axiomatically occurs at all stages in the transmission of manuscript texts all differences of reading revealed by such comparison are possible indications of unoriginality. Not all can be authorial; some must necessarily have been created by scribal variation in one or more of the archetypal traditions. Therefore determination of originality in any version[15] must include consideration in the first instance of all differences between versions and in the second particularly of those differences not evidently or probably resulting from authorial revision. In the editing of **B** this principle has special force because the archetypal text of **B** can be compared over so much of its length not only with the text of **A** or the text of **C** but also, where all versions correspond, with both, that is with two texts of itself preserved in distinct manuscript traditions. There are thus exceptional resources for assessing the quality of the **B** archetype.[16]

The comparison reveals many lines and passages which, while they recognizably correspond, nevertheless differ in such ways as to establish a likelihood of revision, whether progressive (**A**>**B**>**C**), or on first rewriting only (**A**>**BC**), or on second rewriting (**AB**>**C**). The determination of the likelihood is inevitably subjective; *a posteriori* because a purpose imputable to the author, as the whole poem reveals him, seems discernible behind the change; or aesthetic because the change seems of a kind which a poet rather than a scribe would make. In other words such differences suggest enlargements of imaginative conception, insights into new modes of development, altered senses of the poetic or doctrinal value of topics, or intensified homiletic purpose. But there are also many differences between the versions where, because these kinds of consideration are absent, authorial revision seems questionable or improbable. In this latter class all possible alignments occur: two of them, of **AB** against **C**, and of **BC** against **A**, predictable

[15] The editor of **A** now considers that he allowed insufficient weight to readings from other versions in his editing, and that his earlier view of the situation (Vol. I, p. 147, n. 1 and p. 157) was mistaken. The evidence set out in the present section constitutes the reason for his change of opinion.

[16] This situation approximates remarkably to the ideal editorial conditions for assessing the quality of an archetype envisaged by Paul Maas (*Textkritik*, 4. Auflage, Leipzig, 1960, p. 12): 'Wenn ein Archetypus...durch Zeugen, die einer älteren Spaltung entstammen, streckenweise zum Variantenträger oder gar zum codex descriptus degradiert wird, so sind die in diesen Strecken nachweisbaren Gattungen seiner Fehler auch in den Strecken zu vermuten, wo wir ihn nicht kontrollieren können. Hierin liegt der grosse Wert der Zitate, soweit diese einer älteren Spaltung entstammen.' Thus where unrevised **B** corresponds to **A** the **B** archetype is reduced to a *codex descriptus*; where **B** corresponds to unrevised **C** it appears in **C** as a *Zitat*; where the three versions correspond it has both characters.

from the presumptive sequence of revision; a third, of **AC** against **B**, *prima facie* surprising. Even more striking is the fact that in many of the latter instances the **B** manuscripts are unanimous, that is, the reading of their exclusive common ancestor, the archetypal **B** manuscript, is not in doubt.

These agreements between the texts of **A** and **C** against the archetypal text of **B** amount to a compelling assessment of the quality of this archetypal text; they are, in fact, the determinant circumstance in the editing of the **B** version of *Piers Plowman*. For if the texts of **A** and **C**, the earliest and latest versions of the poem, agree in a reading, their agreement sets up a presumption that no revision occurred at that point. And if there the archetypal text of **B**, the middle version, differs from that attested by **AC**, unless this text of **AC** is itself unoriginal the disagreement admits of only two explanations: that the archetypal text of **B** is corrupt; or that the poet, having first changed the reading of **A** to that of **B**, subsequently had second thoughts and in his third version returned to the reading of **A**.

In the abstract decision between these alternatives might well seem impossible, for there is nothing intrinsically improbable in either. Poets are known, from external evidence, to have gone back after a revision to the expression of their earlier choice, and there is no theoretical reason why Langland should not have done this. Equally, because the copying of manuscripts invariably implies textual corruption, the exclusive common ancestor of a manuscript tradition must necessarily contain scribal errors.[17] But the ambiguity of the situation disappears in practice. The choice between the alternatives is made by two considerations: the character of the **B** readings in question, and the number of instances of agreement of **AC** against **B**.

Taken together these considerations seem decisive. In those parts of *Piers Plowman* where the three versions can be minutely compared and there is no appearance of radical revision, there are almost 150 instances where the readings of the **A** and **C** versions agree against that of the **B** archetype. In all these instances the reading of the **B** archetype is manifestly corrupt, or appears inferior in verse technique, or gives inferior sense, or is otherwise explicable by reference to a known tendency of scribal variation. Compared with the shared reading of **A**

[17] This will be true even if it was an autograph, since authors make mistakes in copying their own work.

and **C** it seems of such a kind as the poet would not for any conceivable reason have preferred; or of such a kind that no reason for thinking it an authorial revision is apparent whereas an explanation of its presence through a familiar process of scribal agency can be offered; or of such a kind as the poet might occasionally have preferred, but which he would be unlikely to have preferred time and again whereas the repeated preference for such an alteration is a known characteristic of scribes. The choice is then between these possibilities. Either Langland, while revising from **A** to **B**, in a relatively large number of cases experienced remarkable lapses of taste, judgement, imaginative power, verbal resource or technical competence, in consequence of which he made changes for the worse of a kind to which, meanwhile, scribes were demonstrably prone; and subsequently, in his second revision, from **B** to **C**, with an unaccountably restored critical faculty he reverted to what he had first written. Or, during the early transmission of the **B** version, specifically between the generation of the **B** manuscript used in the **C** revision and the copying of the exclusive common ancestor of the surviving **B** manuscripts, the tradition of **B** suffered extensive, often serious corruption. Put in these terms the choice seems obvious.

Its conclusiveness depends on two propositions. The first is that when variant readings are compared it is possible to identify those which are scribal at least often enough to justify the process of editing. The second is that when a poem exists in several versions some or many of the differences between versions will be not just presumably but evidently authorial, that is of a kind readily imputable to an artist and explicable in terms of his changed or changing conception of his work. The first proposition is fundamental to textual criticism. The second is no more than a particular form of that article of faith by which all students of literature validate their preoccupation with it: that the intellective and critical processes, when applied to literary works of art, can produce accurate results. These two propositions would be hard to dispute in theory; the practicability of applying them is a matter of demonstration. So we pass to our evidence for the corruption of the archetypal text of the **B** version of *Piers Plowman*.

This evidence was obtained by comparing the unanimous or confidently reconstructable text of the exclusive common ancestor of the surviving **B** manuscripts with the text of the **A** version published in the first volume of this edition and a provisional text of the **C** version made available to us by its editor.[18] The lists are restricted to instances where the text of that exclusive common ancestor of the **B** manuscripts is not in doubt, that is where both **B** families are represented and where the manuscripts are either unanimous or differentiated only by analyzable further variation.[19] The readings are classified according to the arguments by which their unoriginality is identified. They have this in common, that if no possibility of authorial revision were involved in the explanation of their difference from the reading of **AC**, they would from their character in relation to this reading be unhesitatingly identified as scribal.

Our first list illustrates those differences between the archetypal text of **B** and the text of **AC** which are explicable as the result of mechanical error by a scribe in the archetypal **B** tradition.

Prologue 41 (of) breed ful **B**: bratful **A** (Prologue 41) **C** (Prologue 42). *Visual error.* I 88 Who(so) **B**: For who(so) **A** (I 86) **C** (I 84). *Failure of memory through preoccupation with difficult context.* I 91 ylik **B**: ek lyk **A** (I 89) also lyk **C** (I 87). *Omission through homoteleuton.* II 47 þi tonge **B**: þe from hem alle **A** (II 29) **C** (II 50). *Error of memory induced by following context.* II 89 And **B**: Wiþ **A** (II 61) **C** (II 96). *Failure of memory replaces the rhetorically insistent preposition with a conjunction.* II 180 Cartsadle **B**: let cartesadil **A** (II 141) **C** (II 193). *Omission of the second of two short words.* II 190 priked **B**: prikede forþ on **A** (II 151) **C** (II 204). *Omission through alliterative attraction.* II 201 faste Falsnesse **B**: falsnesse faste **A** (II 162) **C** (II 215). *The notion which seemed more important unconsciously promoted.* II 203 *copied after* 207 **B**: *after the equivalent of* 202 **A** (II 164) **C** (II 217). *The line, omitted by homoarchy, was inserted when the omission was noticed.* II 224 wiþ seles on Sondayes **B**: on sundais wiþ selis **A** (II 183) **C** (II 234). *Compare* II 201 *above.* II 231 helden **B**: wiþheld **A** (II 190) **C** (II 241). *Omission by alliterative attraction.* III 87 haþ bisouȝt/haþ she prayed **B**: heo besouȝte **A** (III 76) **C** (III 115). *Variation to the expected tense.* III 141 harm dide **B**: harmide **A** (III 130) **C** (III 179). *Visual or auditory error.* III 223, 224 *misdivided through unconscious resistance to a run-on line, followed by padding: cp.* **A** (III 211) *and* **C** (III 278). III 281 men noon **B**: me non **A** (III 259) **C** (III 434). *Anticipation of following copy.* III 289 hem/hem alle/al þe frape **B**: vs **A** (III 265) **C** (III 442). *Inducement of preceding line.* IV 184 Alle **B**: And alle **A** (IV 147) **C** (IV 178). *The conjunction omitted because* 184 *was read as an explication of* 183*b*. V 26 lete **B**: leue **A** (V 26) **C** (V 128). *Thoughtless substitution of a near-equivalent.* V 70 For **B**: Of **A** (V 53) **C** (VI 11). *Substitution induced by*

[18] Our **C** references are to the forthcoming volume in the present edition, not to Skeat. This is bound to be irritating, but it is unavoidable because the new **C** text will often differ substantially from Skeat's in its readings, which are necessary to our argument, though not always, and never extremely, in line numbering. The only pronounced difference is that Skeat's **C** Passus I becomes the Prologue in the new edition, which change requires an adjustment of subsequent passus numbers.

[19] A few instances where the archetypal **B** reading is unmistakably wrong and S alone of the **B** manuscripts has the reading presumed original must be noted. They occur at I 36, II 1, III 79, 180, IV 194. Otherwise, where its reading has not been obscured by modernization S is wrong with the **B** archetype.

careless misreading of the line. V 129 þus **B**: so **A** (V 106) **C** (VI 94). *Alliterative inducement of preceding* þat. V 211 presse **B**: pressour **A** (V 127) pressoures **C** (VI 219). *Loss of* -ur *suspension.* V 327 *not in* **B**: *see* **A** (V 176) **C** (VI 385). *Omission caused by preoccupation with the difficult sense.* V 337 *not in* **B**: *see* **A** (V 186) **C** (VI 395). *Omission by attraction between parallel successions of* and'*s in* 336, 338. V 462 wherof **B**: wherewith **A** (V 234) **C** (VI 316). *Thoughtless substitution of a near-equivalent.* V 532 corsaint **B**: corseint quaþ þei **A** (VI 20) **C** (VII 177). *Omission of a syntactically intervening unit.* V 588 kerneled wiþ **B**: kirnelis ben of **A** (VI 75) **C** (VII 235). *Attraction to following grammatical construction.* V 610 He **B**: For he **A** (VI 96) **C** (VII 261). *Unconscious simplification of grammar, the more remote causal relation replaced by paratactic modification.* VI 2 wolde **B**: miȝte **A** (VII 2) **C** (VII 308). *The force of* miȝte *missed through inattention.* VI 92 catel **B**: my catel **A** (VII 84) **C** (VIII 101). *Omission caused by alliterative attraction.* VI 197 þerof was Piers proud **B**: pieris was proud þerof **A** (VII 184) **C** (VIII 202: *see apparatus*). *Cp.* II 201 *above.* VI 200 þere **B**: þere euere **A** (VII 187) **C** (VIII 206). *Omission through homoteleuton.* VI 279 Til **B**: Er **A** (VII 263) **C** (VIII 301). *Substitution of a more habitual locution.* VII 148 a my/as y my/and my/my/many **B**: a myle **A** (VIII 130) **C** (IX 296). *Visual error.* VII 175 passed **B**: passiþ **A** (VIII 153) **C** (IX 319). *Attraction to tense of preceding verb.* VIII 74 who/what **B**: quaþ I who **A** (IX 65) **C** (X 72). *Eyeskip.* VIII 122 chere **B**: speche **A** (IX 112) **C** (X 118). *Inducement of the preceding details of physical appearance.* IX 124 *not in* **B**: *see* **A** (X 141) **C** (X 214). *Omitted through preoccupation with the rubric to come.* IX 171 arn **B**: arn manye **A** (X 192) **C** (X 273). *Omission by alliterative attraction.* IX 191 soule **B**: loue **A** (X 204) **C** (X 291). *Confusion of* l *and long* s, *on the suggestion of the common collocation.* IX 192 derne dede **B**: dede derne **A** (X 205) **C** (X 292). *Cp.* II 201 *above.* X 9 *noli* **B**: *Nolite* **A** (XI 9) **C** (XI 7). *Substitution of the singular induced by the number of the noun following.*

Many of the differences between the texts of **B** and **AC** are explicable in terms of the tendencies of variation exhibited by scribes copying *Piers Plowman.*[20] Thus a number of **B** readings produce a text grammatically, lexically, or in some way contextually easier than that of **AC**.

Prologue 76 þei/men/þe puple...hire **B**: ȝe...ȝoure **A** (Prologue 73) **C** (Prologue 74). II 10 wiþ **B**: in **A** (II 10) **C** (II 11). II 93 gaf **B**: *pres. t.* **A** (II 64) **C** (II 100). II 181 vs **B**: oure **A** (II 142) **C** (II 194). V 450 lette **B**: make **A** (V 222) **C** (VII 64). V 514 bankes/balkys **B**: baches **A** (VI 2) **C** (VII 159). V 555 shal wisse yow witterly þe wey to **B**: wile wisse ȝow wel riȝt to **A** (VI 42) **C** (VII 199). V 567 Til **B**: Forto **A** (VI 54) **C** (VII 214). VI 179 cesse **B**: beleue **A** (VII 164) **C** (VIII 176). VI 215 Abate **B**: abaue **A** (VII 201) **C** (VIII 225). VII 49 wiþouten coueitise of **B**: coueitiþ nouȝt his/here **A** (VIII 51) **C** (IX 48). VII 97 alle **B**: alle oþer **A** (VIII 79) many oþere **C** (IX 172). IX 190 bourde on bedde **B**: bedbourd **A** (X 203) **C** (X 290). X 37 loued **B**: louid or lete by/herfore **A** (XI 29) **C** (XI 32).

A particular manifestation of the scribal tendency to produce an easier text is variation which makes the expression of the sense more explicit.

[20] On these see Vol. I, pp. 126ff.

The following differences between the archetypal text of **B** and the text of **AC** are explicable in terms of variation resulting from that tendency.

Prologue 77 swiche/þo Losels **B:** loselis **A** (Prologue 74) lorelles **C** (Prologue 75). I 1 þis **B:** þe **A** (I 1) **C** (I 1). I 36 It is nouȝt al **B:** Al is not **A** (I 34) **C** (I 34). I 99 And dide **B:** Dide **A** (I 97) **C** (I 103). I 136 lettred men **B:** lettrid **A** (I 125) **C** (I 135). I 142 knowyng quod she **B:** knowyng **A** (I 130) **C** (I 141). II 198 wol loke **B:** lokis **A** (II 159) **C** (II 212). II 202 and lat **B:** let **A** (II 163) **C** (II 216). III 117 To wite what **B:** What **A** (III 106) **C** (III 154). III 147 For she **B:** She **A** (III 136) **C** (III 185). III 210 mede to men **B:** men mede **A** (III 197) **C** (III 266). III 284 it me tauȝte/me tauȝte it/me yt taughte **B:** me tauȝte **A** (III 260) **C** (III 437). IV 106 For loþe **B:** Leþe **A** (IV 93) **C** (IV 101). IV 136 ouþerwhile/somme tyme **B:** oþer **A** (IV 119) **C** (IV 133). V 34 And þanne/namely he **B:** He **A** (V 32) **C** (V 136). V 195 And in/He hadde on **B:** In **A** (V 111) **C** (VI 203). V 197 walke/haue walked **B:** wandre **A** (V 113) **C** (VI 205). V 211 And putte **B:** Putte **A** (V 127) **C** (VI 219). V 215 Ac/But/And þe **B:** Þe **A** (V 131) **C** (VI 223). V 303 Hastow (ouȝt) in þi purs **B:** Hast þou **A** (V 153) **C** (VI 358). V 309 prentices **B:** knaues **A** (V 160) **C** (VI 364). V 609 þat is a/he is a **B:** þat **A** (VI 95) **C** (VII 261). V 617 And neuere happily eft entre but grace þow haue **B:** And geten it aȝen þoruȝ grace ⁊/ac þoruȝ no gift ellis **A** (VI 103) **C** (VII 269). V 628 for any **B:** any **A** (VI 113) **C** (VII 281). VI 20 to werche **B:** werche **A** (VII 22) **C** (VIII 18). VI 25 That I **B:** I **A** (VII 27) **C** (VIII 24). VI 26 oþere labours do **B:** laboure **A** (VII 28) **C** (VIII 25). VI 34 Piers quod he **B:** piers **A** (VII 36) **C** (VIII 33). VI 94 Forþy/Therfore is he/he is **B:** He is **A** (VII 86) **C** (VIII 103). VI 156 Wiltow or **B:** Wilt þou **A** (VII 143) **C** (VIII 153). VI 179 hunger **B:** hym **A** (VII 164) **C** (VIII 176). VI 205 For meschief **B:** Meschief **A** (VII 191) **C** (VIII 211). VI 210 And now **B:** Now **A** (VII 196) **C** (VIII 219). VI 277 now hunger **B:** now **A** (VII 261) **C** (VIII 298). VI 289 And by **B:** Be **A** (VII 273) **C** (VIII 312). VI 291 And þanne **B:** Þanne **A** (VII 275) **C** (VIII 314). VII 7 ooþer **B:** maner **A** (VIII 7) **C** (IX 7). VII 24 That þei sholde **B:** And/That bad hem **A** (VIII 26) **C** (IX 28). VII 95 And siþþe/A sitthe/⁊ so **B:** And **A** (VIII 77) **C** (IX 170). VII 96 mysshapen peple **B:** mysshapen **A** (VIII 78) **C** (IX 171). VII 173 And al **B:** Al **A** (VIII 149) **C** (IX 317). VII 180 heuene **B:** Ioye **A** (VIII 158) **C** (IX 325). VIII 12 as/þere þei wente **B:** aboute **A** (IX 12) **C** (X 12). IX 17 al þe wacche **B:** hem alle **A** (X 16) **C** (X 143). IX 192 That ilke **B:** Þat **A** (X 205) **C** (X 292). IX 195 And þei þat **B:** Þat **A** (X 209) **C** (X 294). X 21 He þat **B:** Þat **A** (XI 21) **C** (XI 18). X 55 and taken **B:** take **A** (XI 41) **C** (XI 36). X 56 forþ a **B:** forþ **A** (XI 42) **C** (XI 37). X 159 And gladder **B:** Gladdere **A** (XI 111) **C** (XI 101).

A number of readings in the archetype of **B** which make its text more emphatic than that of **AC** are explicable as the result of scribal participation in the sense and feeling of the poem.

Prologue 45 sory sleuþe **B:** sleuþe **A** (Prologue 45) **C** (Prologue 46). III 113 soone **B:** ellys **A** (III 102) **C** (III 150). III 124 (bi)trayeþ/dysseyuyt **B:** teniþ **A** (III 113) **C** (III 161). III 132 ech(a)/euery knaue þat walkeþ/of towhne **B:** knaue/knaues ⁊ to alle **A**

(III 121) **C** (III 169). IV 109 he lyueþ **B:** I lyue **A** (IV 96) **C** (IV 104). V 190 eiȝen as a blynde hagge **B:** eiȝen **A** (V 109) **C** (VI 198). V 195 tawny tabard...Al totorn and baudy and ful of lys crepyng **B:** torn tabbard **A** (V 111) **C** (VI 203). V 216 whoso/who þat **B:** whanne I **A** (V 132) **C** (VI 224). V 225 al hire lif tyme **B:** elleuene wynter **A** (V 141) **C** (VI 233). V 470 Ne dampne **B:** Dampne **A** (V 244) **C** (VI 324). V 540 sikerly/sewrly **B:** siþþe **A** (VI 28) **C** (VII 185). VI 221 lawe of god/goddes lawe (so) techeþ **B:** lawe of kynde wolde **A** (VII 207) **C** (VIII 230). VI 272 for liflode is swete **B:** lest liflode hym/hem faile **A** (VII 256) **C** (VIII 293). VI 306 in Burgh is to selle **B:** breusteris sellen **A** (VII 290) **C** (VIII 328). VII 91 Manye **B:** Þei/*zero* **A** (VIII 73) **C** (IX 167). VII 111 leef **B:** lettre **A** (VIII 93) **C** (IX 284). IX 22 forsoþe **B:** alle **A** (X 21) **C** (X 148). X 174 (manye) bokes **B:** þe/a bible **A** (XI 126) **C** (XI 114). X 391 ydampned **B:** in helle **A** (XI 271) **C** (XI 218).

Some differences between the archetypal text of **B** and the text of **AC** are explicable as the results of deliberate substitution arising from mis-comprehension, stylistic preference, 'smoothing' after earlier variation, or an intention of censorship.

I 112 *not in* **B:** *cp.* **A** (I 110) **C** (I 107). *Suppression of the notion that Lucifer could be beautiful.* II 1 courbed **B:** knelide **A** (II 1) **C** (II 1). *Elimination of the jingle* kneled...knees. III 69 werkes **B:** wrytyng **A** (III 60) writynges **C** (III 73). *Elimination of a jingle* (writen 70). III 97 leodes/men **B:** lordis **A** (III 86) **C** (III 125). *Suppression of a subversive notion.* III 151 haue **B:** holde **A** (III 140) **C** (III 189). *Substitution of a more obviously apt term because the force of* holde, 'continue to keep, maintain', *was missed.* V 223 And yet **B:** Whanne **A** (V 139) **C** (VI 231). *Attempt to clarify the account of the fraud.* VI 59 my, 60 My(*all*), 61 myn(*both*) **B:** his, Hise(*all*), his(*both*) **A** (VII 54,55,56) **C** (VIII 58,59,60). *The reported action between two passages of direct speech is systematically assimilated to this.* VI 198 mete as he myȝte aforþe and mesurable hyre **B:** mete & monie as þei miȝte asserue **A** (VII 185) **C** (VIII 203). *The substitution refers to the seasonal variations in peasant diet, perhaps with* 280*ff. below in mind.* VI 313 waille **B:** warie **A** (VII 297) **C** (VIII 335). *Censorship.* IX 7 enuye hir hateþ **B:** to hire haþ enuye **A** (X 7) **C** (X 134). *A difficult original misunderstood and 'corrected'.* X 54 a tale ouþer tweye **B:** how two slowe þe þridde **A** (XI 40) **C** (XI 35). *Censorship.* X 72 founde **B:** founden vp **A** (XI 58) **C** (XI 52). *Omission of an adverb deemed superfluous because the sense of* founden vp, 'devised, invented', *was not perceived.* X 384 tauȝte **B:** made **A** (XI 265) **C** (XI 209). *A more obviously apt reading preferred because the sense* made, 'composed', *was missed.*

There are, finally, a number of differences between the archetypal text of **B** and the text of **AC**, variously explicable like those already set out, where in addition the line as **B** reads it appears inferior[21] with respect to verse technique.

[21] The indications, from thousands of verses where originality as it affects alliteration is not seriously in doubt, are that the poet's commonest alliterative pattern was *aa*/|*ax*; that he occasionally employed *aaa*//*xy* or *aaa*//*bb*; and that he did not write wholly English lines alliterating *aa*//*xa* or *ax*//*aa* or *xa*//*aa*, or *aa*//*bb*, or *xa*//*ay* or *ax*//*ay* or *aa*//*xy*. For a full discussion see below, pp. 131ff.

I 165 bigynneþ> *a a x y* **B**: comsiþ **A** (I 139) **C** (I 159). *Substitution of an easier term.* I 200 gospel> *a a x y* **B**: Euaungelie **A** (I 174) **C** (I 195). *Substitution of an easier term.* II 200 þyng> *a a x y* **B**: tresour **A** (II 161) **C** (II 214). *Substitution of a more inclusive, therefore emphatic term.* III 98 brenne> *a a b b* **B**: forbrenne **A** (III 87) **C** (III 126). *Unconscious substitution of the simplex through preoccupation with the sense.* III 222 teche children> *prose line* **B**: kenne clerkis **A** (III 209) **C** (III 277). *Substitution of an easier reading.* IV 86 And lete (hym)/⁊> *x a a y* **B**: He shal **A** (IV 73) he sholde **C** (IV 82) (*the line scans* shál séuen séen). *Substitution of a more explicit reading.* V 47 ruled> *a a x y* **B**: stewid **A** (V 39) **C** (V 145). *Substitution of a more emphatic and easier reading, possibly with deliberate elimination of the pun.* VII 106 þis erþe> *a a x y* **B**: þis pur erþe **A** (VIII 88) **C** (IX 185). *Omission of a word used in a difficult sense.* VIII 22 dooþ yuele> *a a x y* **B**: sertis **A** (IX 18) **C** (X 25). *Substitution of a more explicit statement.* VIII 30 boot waggyng> *a a x a* **B**: waggyng of þe boot **A** (IX 26) **C** (X 34). *Unconscious promotion of the notion appearing more important.* VIII 110 noon ooþer wise> *x a a y* **B**: oþere wise ⁊ ellis nouȝt **A** (IX 100) **C** (X 106). *Substitution of a more emphatic reading.* X 176 manye oþere lawes> *a a x a* **B**: al þe lawe aftir **A** (XI 128) **C** (XI 116). *Substitution of a more emphatic expression.* X 428 what womman dide> *a a b b b* **B**: who miȝte do **A** (XI 287) **C** (XI 261). *Substitution of a more explicit reading.*

The decision whether the above 140 odd instances of difference between the texts of **B** and **AC** are to be explained by reference to vacillating authorial revision or to scribal variation in the archetypal **B** tradition must, like most matters in textual criticism, be governed by assessment of relative probability. But with this qualification the direction of the evidence seems clear: the choice is one between possibility and a strong likelihood. An author may make an indeterminate number of scribal errors when copying his own work; a scribe will probably make a great many. Poets are known to have made ill-judged revisions which they later, with a recovered critical faculty, rejected in favour of what they had first written. Thus it is not impossible that Langland in the course of his greatest undertaking experienced frequent moments of singular artistic ineptness when by alterations such as in other situations are characteristic of scribal variation he weakened the meaning of his poem, relaxed its tension and power of engaging the mind, reduced its stylistic crispness to prolixity, diminished its directness and force, and spoiled its verse technique. But against this possibility there is the sure knowledge that such effects, amounting to a general deterioration of literary quality, are the common consequence of scribal variation. In this situation it seems to us right to reject the possibility of the erratic poet for the established certainty of the inaccurate copyist, and to recognize the agreements of **AC** against **B** as evidence of the corruption of the archetypal text of **B**.

Thus between them the text of **A**, in terms of which a **B** reading may be either an authorial revision or a scribal variation, and the text of **C** with its implications about the **C** reviser's **B** manuscript, afford a rigorous check upon the originality of readings in the exclusive common ancestor of the **B** manuscripts.[22] Even if there were impressive contrary indications the results of such a check could not be ignored. But contrary indications are not considerable. There are cases where comparison between the text of **A** and the presumably unrevised archetypal **B** text shows the **B** reading as the probable original of both versions, and somewhat more often, cases where comparison of the archetypal text of **B** with the presumably unrevised text of **C** indicates archetypal error in the **C** tradition. But in general both these comparisons forcefully bear out the conclusion of the first, that the **B** tradition was seriously corrupted at the archetypal stage.

Thus, first, where the **A** and **B** versions recognizably correspond, but **C** does not, and where radical revision did not manifestly take place, there are many differences between the text of **A** and the archetypal text of **B** which are either the consequence of inaccurate transmission in one of the two traditions or the products of minute authorial revision during the composition of **B**. In a number of such cases the indication is that the archetypal text of **A** is unoriginal.[23] In the rest the poor quality of the **B** reading awakens suspicion. Here again there are general considerations: that the author of **B** who had previously written **A**, and was on that showing a poet of a high order, would be likely most often to revise not casually or capriciously but for critically valid reasons; that meanwhile scribes as an agency for the multiplication of texts notoriously departed from their originals in various identifiable ways; and that the archetypal text of **B** otherwise appears, from comparison with the shared text of **A** and **C**, to be seriously corrupt. To these is added the particular consideration of the character of many differences between **A** and **B**; more than 300 of these are of such a kind that, if the possibility of revision were absent, they would confidently be explained as caused by scribal agency in the **B** tradition.

One or a few such differences might, it seems to us, be explicable as the products of ill-judged authorial revision, or of the poet himself falling into scribal error. But by the principle that a major artist's

[22] See above, p. 75, n. 16.

[23] For archetypal **A** errors see below, pp. 205, 210.

revision should imply general improvement, whereas scribal transmission demonstrably implies persistent corruption of identifiable, even predictable kinds, we rule out these explanations. For to impute such a long succession of inferior, elsewhere typically scribal readings to the revising poet of **B** would require us to accept that he experienced a frequently recurrent falling-off of taste, judgement, imagination and technical powers with respect to detail during the major creative process of composing a whole, fulfilled poem, and this at points where in his first version he had written adequately or more than adequately. Such repeated regression from the greater to the lesser during a sustained progression from the lesser to the greater seems to us a categorical unlikelihood. Therefore we account for the general prosification, loss of technical correctness, weakening or dilution of sense, and diminished tension produced by the **B** readings in question as the effects of scribal activity. The accumulation of instances where the **B** reading is intrinsically inferior to that of **A**, or is on comparison a typically scribal reading, argues that these **B** readings are scribal corruptions of an original common to **A** and **B** which was generally better preserved in the **A** manuscript tradition.[24] They are thus a further indication of the quality of the **B** archetype.

A number of differences between the text of **A** and the archetypal text of **B** are explicable as the results of mechanical error in the archetypal **B** tradition.

I 98, 99, 100–3 *transposed* **B**: *cp.* **A** I 96–101. *Eyeskip* (knyȝtes 98, 100) *with subsequent insertion of omitted matter.* II 6 hire **B**: hise **A** (II 6). *Grammatical attraction.* III 32 lette **B**: hym lette **A** (III 31). *Omission by alliterative attraction.* III 36 he melled/medled/mened þise wordes **B**: mekeliche he loutide **A** (III 35). *Memorial contamination with* 105 *below.* III 140 And **B**: Heo **A** (III 129). *Substitution of the conjunction induced by succession of instances.* III 233 wel werchen **B**: werchen wel **A** (III 220). *Subconscious promotion of the operative notion.* IV 23 he **B**: we **A** (IV 21). *Inducement of earlier pronoun.* IV 46 wel wisely a gret while **B**: a gret while wel wisly **A** (IV 33). *Transposition induced by the common collocation* '*wise words*'. V 94, 95 *not in* **B**: *cp.* **A** V 74, 75. *Omission caused by homoteleuton.* V 97 maad **B**: don **A** (V 77). *Substitution of an equivalent through failure of memory.* V 317 And **B**: Of **A** (V 166). *The meaning of* vpholderes *mistaken.* V 634 hem/hem alle/alle **B**: hym **A** (VI 119). *Inducement of the preceding context.* VI 16 for so **B**: for cold for so **A** (VII 15). *Eyeskip.* VI 44 Purgatorie it hatte **B**: þat purcatorie hattiþ **A** (VII 43). *Omission of* þat *by alliterative attraction, with smoothing.* VI 131 olde **B**: holde **A** (VII 123). *Visual*

[24] In some of these cases **C** shares what we find to be a corrupt archetypal **B** reading. These are discussed below, pp. 98ff.

error through inattention to sense. VI 249 þei wroȝte **B**: it alse **A** (VII 233). *Inducement of* wolde...wroȝte *in* 247 *above.* VI 266 lecherous **B**: a lecchour **A** (VII 250). *Inducement of following* likerous. VI 276, 277 *transposed* **B**: *cp.* **A** (VII 260, 261). 276 *first omitted because of the resemblance between* 275*b and* 276*a, then copied when the oversight was noticed.* VII 132 ensamples **B**: ensaumple **A** (VIII 114). *Attraction to surrounding plurals.* VII 134 *not in* **B**: *cp.* **A** (VIII 116). *Omission caused by preoccupation with the answer to the question in* 133, *or by* fynt hem (mete) 133, 135. VII 159 was...nempned **B**: nempne **A** (VIII 137). *Attraction to surrounding preterites.* VII 164 lower **B**: lesse **A** (VIII 142). *Substitution induced by* 162 *above.* VIII 36 his...þoruȝ **B**: þe manis...for **A** (IX 32). *Inducement of surrounding pronouns, and of alliteration* (þere *or* þanne) *respectively.* VIII 43 a day seuen siþes **B**: seuene siþes in þe day **A** (IX 39). *Imperfect recollection through advancement of the more important notion.* IX 127 Sem/Seem/seyn **B**: seþ **A** (X 157, *and cp. also* 153). *Visual error caused by* þ><y *confusion.* IX 133 makede man **B**: man makide **A** (X 164). *Inattentive substitution of prose order.* IX 142 dales **B**: dounes **A** (X 173). *Substitution of the more common collocation.* IX 160 wedded, 161 mariages **B**: maried, weddyng **A** (X 183, 184). *Transposition of terminal words through imperfect recollection.* X 19 contreue **B**: construe **A** (XI 19). *Visual error.* X 36 *not in* **B**: *see* **A** (XI 28). *Omission by homoteleuton* (techeþ 36, 37). X 47 Sholde **B**: Wolde **A** (XI 33). *Visual error or imperfect recollection.* X 49 murþe and mynstralcie **B**: Menstralsie & merþe **A** (XI 35). *Anticipation of the sequence of* 53 *below.* X 61 neer **B**: In **A** (XI 47). *Substitution by alliterative inducement.* X 107 clerkes **B**: clergie **A** (XI 65). *Inducement of* clerkes *in* 105 *above.* X 129 euere **B**: euere eft **A** (XI 82). *Omission caused by homoarchy.* X 203 whan hem nedeþ **B**: at here nede **A** (XI 152). *Substitution induced by preceding pronoun.* X 229 hem/hym **B**: hire **A** (XI 172). *Change of number induced by preceding context.* X 230 þe worlde **B**: heuene **A** (XI 173). *Unconscious substitution of a more usual expression.* X 234, 235 *not in* **B**: *cp.* **A** (XI 177, 178). *Eyeskip caused by* wittes...wif...studie *in* 233 *and* 235. X 354 an **B**: arn **A** (XI 237). *Visual error.*

A very large number of differences between the text of **A** and the archetypal text of **B** correspond to and are explicable in terms of scribal tendencies of variation. In the following instances the text of **B** has an easier reading.

Prologue 34 synnelees **B**: giltles **A** (Prologue 34). Prologue 36 Feynen **B**: Fonden **A** (Prologue 36). Prologue 214 And **B**: Ac **A** (Prologue 87). Prologue 217 bondemen **B**: bondage **A** (Prologue 96). I 25 þow driest **B**: þe driȝeþ **A** (I 25). I 195 bodies **B**: body **A** (I 169). II 116 mote þow haue **B**: on þi bokes **A** (II 80). II 134 also/bothe **B**: aftir **A** (II 98). II 135 yshewed **B**: yhandlit **A** (II 99). II 136 lawe **B**: Leaute **A** (II 100). III 42 torne/twyne/serue **B**: felle **A** (III 41). III 95 tolde hem **B**: tok hym **A** (III 84). III 97 is to mene **B**: amountiþ **A** (III 86). III 168 þei **B**: hem **A** (III 155). III 194 hyedest **B**: hastidest þe **A** (III 181). IV 14 ryt (riȝt) **B**: riȝt renneþ **A** (IV 14). IV 21 witty wordes **B**: wytful **A** (IV 19). IV 95 pure **B**: purid **A** (IV 82). V 76 *mea culpa* **B**: his cope **A** (V 59). V 114 for **B**: of **A** (V 94). V 299 And **B**: And heo **A** (V 149). V 554 he **B**: wy **A** (VI 41). V 625 And **B**: Ac **A** (VI 110). VI 103 pikstaf **B**: pyk **A** (VII 95). VI 190 dryue awey **B**: ditte out **A** (VII 176). VII 28 do boote to **B**: bynde **A** (VIII 30). VII 64 Haueþ **B**: Hadde **A** (VIII 66). VII 123 bely ioye **B**: belyue **A** (VIII

105). VII 127 Sauter seith **B**: sauter vs seiþ ⁊ **A** (VIII 109). VII 129 vs **B**: vs anoþer **A** (VIII 112). VII 133 feld **B**: firmament **A** (VIII 115). VII 146 in þe **B**: euene **A** (VIII 128). VII 198 ye **B**: þou **A** (VIII 176). VII 199 yow **B**: þe **A** (VIII 177). VIII 46 man...mannes **B**: þe...þi **A** (IX 42). IX 49 to **B**: ⁊ **A** (X 37). IX 178 togideres **B**: ysamme **A** (X 199). IX 208 þe mody **B**: mody **A** (X 217). X 70 oþere (kynnes) **B**: kete **A** (XI 56). X 137 lif **B**: leste degre **A** (XI 90). X 141 loke **B**: mele **A** (XI 94). X 155 Scripture is hir name **B**: þat scripture is nempnid **A** (XI 107). X 165 þerwiþ **B**: with hym **A** (XI 117). X 172 þynges **B**: wyttes **A** (XI 124). X 183 and compased **B**: I kende ferst **A** (XI 135). X 187 deuyne...þynkeþ **B**: deuynide...þouȝte **A** (XI 139). X 193 of loues kynne **B**: drawen of louis scole **A** (XI 145). X 202 bidde for **B**: blissen **A** (XI 151). X 216 makyng **B**: wittes **A** (XI 159). X 226 til **B**: er **A** (XI 169). X 349 repreue/reherce **B**: wiþsigge **A** (XI 232). X 356 any man **B**: an heiȝ **A** (XI 239). X 392 sholde **B**: shal **A** (XI 276). X 464 konnynge **B**: kete **A** (XI 308).

In the following instances the archetypal text of **B** is more explicit than the text of **A** and therefore probably differentiated from it by scribal agency.

Prologue 57 And shopen **B**: Shopen **A** (Prologue 54). Prologue 64 For siþ **B**: Siþen **A** (Prologue 61). Prologue 222 and Mynours **B**: mynours **A** (Prologue 101). I 48 Wheiþer **B**: Ȝif **A** (I 46). I 69 and lieþ **B**: leiȝeþ **A** (I 67). I 78 And to **B**: To **A** (I 76). I 105 But crist **B**: And crist **A** (I 103). I 107 And yaf **B**: Ȝaf **A** (I 105). II 3 þat **B**: þe **A** (II 3). II 74 And þus **B**: Þus **A** (II 56). II 120 And god **B**: God **A** (II 84). II 128 abiggen it **B**: abigge **A** (II 92). II 134 Forþi/Therefore wercheþ **B**: Werchiþ **A** (II 98). II 135 And ledeþ **B**: Lediþ **A** (II 99). II 160 bad hem alle **B**: alle **A** (II 124). II 163 fette forþ **B**: fette **A** (II 127). II 164 And sette **B**: Sette **A** (II 128). II 166 a Flaterere **B**: fair speche **A** (II 130). II 184 And þus Fals **B**: Fals **A** (II 145). II 201 And fettreþ **B**: Feteriþ **A** (II 162). II 227 That he sholde **B**: For to **A** (II 186). III 108 þat/þis **B**: þe **A** (III 97). III 165 For clergie **B**: Clergie **A** (III 152). III 234 þerof **B**: it **A** (III 221). III 246 anoþer **B**: a **A** (III 225). III 278 Saul þe **B**: þe **A** (III 256). III 290 as she is nouþe **B**: on erþe **A** (III 266). IV 22 And hange **B**: Hange **A** (IV 20). IV 44 ayeins **B**: in to **A** (IV 31). IV 101 And I **B**: I **A** (IV 88). IV 111 after **B**: boþe **A** (IV 98). IV 194 And I **B**: I **A** (IV 157). V 79 and a knyf **B**: a knyf **A** (V 62). V 101 And whan **B**: Whanne **A** (V 81). V 103 For he **B**: He **A** (V 83). V 105 And whan **B**: Whanne **A** (V 85). V 110 Auter þanne **B**: auter **A** (V 90). V 119 And þus **B**: Þus **A** (V 98). V 220 beste ale **B**: beste **A** (V 136). V 363 how wikkedly he lyuede **B**: of wykkidnesse ⁊ synne **A** (V 205). V 560 ȝif ȝe **B**: ȝe þat **A** (VI 47). V 565 he **B**: men **A** (VI 52). VI 16 And casteþ **B**: Caste **A** (VII 15). VI 19 mete and drynke **B**: þe mete **A** (VII 21). VI 33 kynȝt þanne **B**: kniȝt **A** (VII 35). VI 65 sowen er I wende **B**: any þing swynke **A** (VII 59). VI 90 a relees **B**: reles **A** (VII 82). VI 170 Piers **B**: hym **A** (VII 155). VI 219 fonde þow **B**: fond **A** (VII 205). VI 237 And þerfore he **B**: He **A** (VII 221). VI 239 That *Seruus*...chaffare **B**: *Seruus*...it vsen **A** (VII 223). VI 270 wiþ **B**: ⁊ **A** (VII 254). VI 276 For þis **B**: Þis **A** (VII 260). VI 277 þow wolt **B**: þi wille is **A** (VII 261). VI 298 Wiþ grene **B**: Grene **A** (VII 282). VI 304 But of **B**: But **A** (VII 288). VI 317 corseþ he...al his **B**: curse...alle þe **A** (VII 298). VII 17 And at **B**: At **A**

(VIII 19). VII 26 myseise folk **B:** myseise **A** (VIII 28). VII 27 And wikkede **B:** Wykkide **A** (VIII 29). VII 32 And sette **B:** Sette **A** (VIII 34). VII 52 and his soule **B:** sykirly **A** (VIII 54). VII 94 som/þe **B:** his **A** (VIII 76). VII 119 atweyne **B:** assondir **A** (VIII 101). VII 133 fynt hem mete **B:** fynt hem **A** (VIII 115). VII 138 quod Piers myn **B:** myn **A** (VIII 120). VII 163 And as **B:** As **A** (VIII 141). VII 177 And how dowel **B:** Dowel **A** (VIII 155). VIII 34 rauȝte to **B:** rauȝte **A** (IX 30). VIII 36 (And) þanne **B:** Þere **A** (IX 32). VIII 45 And þat **B:** Þat **A** (IX 41). VIII 77 Where þat...þat/hym to **B:** Where...to **A** (IX 68). VIII 89 heeld **B:** hadde **A** (IX 80). VIII 95 god yow **B:** god **A** (IX 85). VIII 109 And to **B:** And **A** (IX 99). IX 26 wit **B:** he **A** (X 27). IX 49 And þat is lif **B:** Lif **A** (X 37). IX 50 And þat/þis **B:** Þat **A** (X 38). IX 51 And is as **B:** As **A** (X 39). IX 52 And þat **B:** Þat **A** (X 40). IX 162 (of) tolde **B:** shewide **A** (X 185). IX 170 Many a **B:** Manye **A** (X 191). IX 198 þei cacche mowe **B:** þei mowe **A** (X 212). IX 207 drede god **B:** dreden **A** (X 216). X 3 wit me **B:** wyt **A** (XI 3). X 13 seye it **B:** say **A** (XI 13). X 140 dame Studie **B:** his wif **A** (XI 93). X 202 For he **B:** And **A** (XI 151). X 221 And founded **B:** Foundit **A** (XI 164). X 228 hem boþe **B:** boþe **A** (XI 171). X 341 (to) haue heuene **B:** in heuene **A** (XI 229). X 353 They mowen **B:** Mowe **A** (XI 236). X 356 þe heritage of **B:** eritage in **A** (XI 239). X 376 mysdedes...lette **B:** misdede...make **A** (XI 257).

In the following instances the archetypal text of **B** is more emphatic than the text of **A**, and the difference between them probably records scribal response to the sense and feeling of the poem in the archetypal **B** tradition.

I 103 siluer **B:** ȝeftis **A** (I 101). I 195 Manye...hem...hire **B:** Ȝe...ȝow...ȝour **A** (I 169). II 74 ful **B:** wel **A** (II 56). III 37 ful **B:** wel **A** (III 36). III 82 and **B:** wel **A** (III 71). III 102 wiþ sergeauntȝ manye **B:** seriauntis hire fette **A** (III 91). III 232 grаunteþ **B:** gyueþ **A** (III 219). III 250 gold **B:** giftes **A** (III 229). IV 102 þe kyng **B:** ȝe **A** (IV 89). IV 162 al þe halle **B:** soþnesse **A** (IV 138). V 98 ful **B:** wel **A** (V 78). V 103 do noon ooþer **B:** non harm don hym **A** (V 83). V 115 wel werse **B:** wers **A** (V 95). V 118 me soore **B:** myn herte **A** (V 97). V 120 body **B:** brest **A** (V 99). V 126 þe beste **B:** goode **A** (V 103). VI 23 by crist I wole assaye **B:** I wile conne eren **A** (VII 25). VI 44 ful **B:** wel **A** (VII 43). VI 108 faste **B:** ȝerne **A** (VII 100). VI 275 Poul/Peter **B:** pernel **A** (VII 259). VI 296 Al hunger eet **B:** Hungir eet þis **A** (VII 280). VII 17 þe heiȝe **B:** here **A** (VIII 19). VII 151 ful **B:** wel **A** (VIII 132). VII 198 of (alle) **B:** among **A** (VIII 176). VIII 85 riȝt þus **B:** þus **A** (IX 76). VIII 97 halie men fro helle **B:** holde men in good lif **A** (IX 87). IX 191 in parfit charite **B:** of lawe also **A** (X 204). X 69 I haue seiȝen it ofte **B:** seke it in *Memento* **A** (XI 55). X 166 likerouse **B:** longe **A** (XI 118). X 214 ful **B:** wel **A** (XI 157). X 350 by Peter and by Poul boþe **B:** be þe pistil þat petir is nempnid **A** (XI 233).

A substantial number of differences between the archetypal text of **B** and the text of **A** are explicable as the results of deliberate substitution arising from scribal miscomprehension, stylistic preference, 'smoothing' after earlier variation, or an intention of censorship.

Prologue 38 wol **B:** dar **A** (Prologue 38). *Failure to perceive the ironic disclaimer of* dar. I 60 yow **B:** þe **A** (I 58). *Stylistic preference for the formal plural.* I 152 also **B:** ek **A** (I 137). *Stylistic preference.* I 197 hem **B:** ȝow **A** (I 171). *Smoothing after substitution* in 195. II 152 certes sire **B:** certis **A** (II 116). *Embellishment of alliteration.* III 41 bedeman **B:** baudekyn **A** (III 40). *Censorship in the friar's favour; cp. variation in* 46 *below.* IV 64 pees **B:** his pes **A** (IV 50). *Omission of the possessive because the force of the objective genitive was missed.* IV 102 bettre **B:** more **A** (IV 89). *Elimination of a repetition.* IV 135 in þis moot **B:** to mote in þis **A** (IV 118). *Smoothing after anticipation of copy.* IV 162 heiȝe **B:** loude **A** (IV 138). *Alliterative smoothing.* IV 195 oure lyf lasteþ **B:** I lyue **A** (IV 158). *Objection to the repetition of* lyue. V 84 wryngynge (he yede) with **B:** wroþliche he wroþ **A** (V 67). *Elimination of the pun.* V 104 god woot my wille **B:** I wolde murdre hym for euere **A** (V 84). *Suppression of the violent statement.* V 214 oute **B:** softe **A** (V 130). *A general expression preferred to the technical one.* VI 16 comaundeþ/biddiþ **B:** wile **A** (VII 15). *Alliterative smoothing after omission of a stave.* VI 24 ye profre yow so faire **B:** þou profrist þe so lowe **A** (VII 26). *The statement is made more appropriate to a social superior.* VI 190 and dikeden **B:** drit & dung **A** (VII 176). *Genteel censorship.* VI 283 two loues **B:** a lof **A** (VII 267). *Scribal interest in food causes mitigation of Piers's poverty.* VI 298 poisone **B:** peysen **A** (VII 282). *The peasants' action is taken to be a hostile one.* VII 32 oþere **B:** skynes **A** (VIII 34). *Substitution of a more explicit term because the distinction between learning at books and learning a trade was missed.* VII 50 And sheweþ lawe for oure lordes loue as he it haþ ylerned **B:** Ac for oure lordis loue lawe for hym shewiþ **A** (VIII 52). *Padding after inadvertent prosification.* VII 130 worldes blisse **B:** bely ioye **A** (VIII 112). *Smoothing after anticipation of* bely ioye *in* 123. VII 178 And **B:** He **A** (VIII 156). *Smoothing after substitution in* 177. IX 179 þe same **B:** riȝt also **A** (X 200). *Smoothing after substitution in* 178. X 2 lere...liche boþe **B:** lich...louȝ chere **A** (XI 2). *Substitution for emphasis because the meaning of* lowe chere, *'unhealthy appearance', was not perceived.* X 110 wiles and wordes **B:** werk & wille **A** (XI 68). *An expression with more immediate, therefore easier application is preferred.* X 126 yow **B:** vs **A** (XI 79). *Smoothing to exclude the speaker from the petition because her intention of humility was not perceived.* X 156 techyng **B:** besekyng **A** (XI 108). *Substitution of a term more apparently appropriate to the speaker's earlier attitude.* X 214 two **B:** þre **A** (XI 157). *The scribe has miscounted.* X 448 *not in* **B,** 449 litel **B:** *cp.* **A** (XI 293), neuere (XI 294). *Omission of a difficult line and smoothing after omission.*

There are, finally, some differences between the archetypal text of **B** and the text of **A,** variously explicable like those already set out, where in addition the line, as **B** reads it, appears inferior with respect to verse technique.

III 71 dele〉 *a a b b* **B:** giue **A** (III 62). *Alliterative attraction to* doles. III 254 Taken hire Mede here as Mathew vs techeþ〉 *x a a y* **B:** Shal haue mede on þis molde þat mattheu haþ grauntid **A** (III 233). *Smoothing after* Shal haue] Taken *substitution induced by* taken Mede (253). V 2 matyns of þe day and þe masse〉 *x a a y* **B:** matynes & masse and to þe mete **A** (V 2). *The piety of the occasion is increased by excluding a mundane detail.* VI 137 He shal ete whete breed and drynke wiþ myselue〉 *a prose line* **B:** Þei shuln éte ás good as Í so me god helpe **A** (VII 131). *Substitution induced by the scribe's interest in food.* VI 138 goodnesse amendement hym sende> *a a x y* **B**: grace gare hem to arise **A** (VII 132). *Early substitution of an easier reading followed by smoothing.* VI 219 Or any manere false> *x a a y* **B**: Wiþ fuyr or wiþ false **A** (VII 205). *Substitution of an easier, general expression.* VI 223, 224 *as one line scanning a a b b* **B**: *cp.* **A** (VII 209, 210). *Compression and prosification through faulty recollection.* VI 242 And yaf þat Mnam to hym þat ten Mnames hadde> *x a a y* **B**: And ȝaf it hym in haste þat hadde ten before **A** (VII 226). *Substitution of a more explicit reading.* VI 243 wiþ þat he seide þat holy chirche it herde> *x y a a* **B**: siþen he seide his seruaunts it herde **A** (VII 227). *A more explicit reading.* VI 248 dikynge...deluynge> *a a x y* **B**: teching... telling **A** (VII 232). *Substitution of an easier reading.* VI 273 Þer aren mo morareres þan / For murþereris are manye> *a a x a* **B**: Þere arn mo liȝeris þan **A** (VII 257). *A more emphatic reading.* VII 160 dremels> *a a x y or a x a y* **B**: sweuene **A** (VIII 138). *Substitution induced by* 158 *above.* VII 181 oure bileue> *x a a y* **B**: a lef of oure beleue **A** (VIII 159). *Eyeskip.* VIII 69 wiȝt in world> *x a a a* **B**: driȝt in doute **A** (IX 60). *Substitution of an easier reading.* VIII 94 And suffreþ> *x a a y* **B**: Ȝe wise suffriþ **A** (IX 84). *Unconscious omission through inducement of preceding series of* And's. IX 32 spak> *a x a y* **B**: warþ **A** (X 33). *Unconscious substitution of the prose term or stylistic preference: cp. the archetypal scribe's use of* warp *in* V 362. IX 34 And made man likkest to hymself one> *a a x y* **B**: Saue man þat he made ymage to himselue **A** (X 35). *Substitution of an easier and more emphatic statement.* IX 123 yuel> *a x a y* **B**: cursid **A** (X 140). *Substitution of a more explicit reading.* X 109 man> *a a x y* **B**: wy **A** (XI 67). *Substitution of an easier reading.* X 189 *a x a y* **B**: *cp.* **A** (XI 141). *Substitution of an easier and more emphatic reading.* X 207 namely> *x a a y* **B**: souereynliche **A** (XI 249). *Substitution of an easier reading.* X 217, 218 *as one line*> *a a x y* **B**: *cp.* **A** (XI 160, 161). *Censorship.* X 353 þat> *a a x y* **B**: so **A** (XI 236). *Objection to repetition of* so.

In all these instances revealed when the archetypal text of the second version of *Piers Plowman* is compared with the text of the first, the later reading has the look of a typical scribal reflex of the earlier. One explanation of this situation is that the inferior **B** readings record a frequent succession of failures of attention or judgement by the poet, in consequence of which he copied his own work with striking inaccuracy, or spoiled his earlier economy of style by adopting more explicit statement, slackened the tension of his poem by substituting easier expressions, diminished its force by more insistent emphasis, weakened his meaning through miscomprehension of his own creation, and prosified his verses. These are however the common effects of scribal variation on poetic texts. This points to the alternative explanation: that the inferior **B** readings brought to light by comparison with **A** are further instances of the scribal corruption in the early stages of the **B** tradition which was indicated by comparison of **B** with **A** and **C** together. Once more the choice between possible authorial aberration and likely scribal corruption seems clear.

When the archetypal text of **B** is compared with the text of the final or **C** version similar differences with similar effects are to be observed. Thus for example there are instances where the reading of **B,** taken in context, might seem to have been derived from that of **C** by typical mechanical error.

III 322 Thanne **B:** þat **C** (III 475). *Visual error.* V 181 couþe **B:** couhede/cough **C** (VI 163). *Visual error.* V 289 whiche ne whom **B:** whom ne where **C** (VI 344). *Insertion of the ousted reading after noting the substitution.* V 329 (by) þe Southe/fram his sete **B:** they bisouhte **C** (VI 387). *Metathesis of* þei be-. X 320 charite/charge **B:** chartre **C** (V 166). *Visual error.* XI 5 wraþe **B:** warth **C** (XI 165). *Visual error.* XI 56 fecche/fette/sette **B:** festene **C** (XII 8). *Visual error.* XI 84 loked **B:** louhe **C** (XII 23). *Inducement of* Loke 83. XI 253 folwed/fulfylde **B:** alowede **C** (XII 140). *Visual error.* XI 338 riȝt þer **B:** they reste **C** (XIII 146). *Misreading through preoccupation with difficult context following.* XIII 95 frayel after **B:** forel of **C** (XV 102). XIII 330 men & cursed **B:** myn euencristene **C** (VI 75). *Miscomprehension induced by preceding context.* XIII 455 loued/louen **B:** lythed **C** (VII 115). *Substitution induced by* loued *in* 451 *above.* XV 76 mysspenden hir fyue wittes **B:** here fyue wittes myspenen **C** (XVI 235). *Substitution of prose order through imperfect recollection.* XV 98 bowes **B:** stokkes **C** (XVI 251). *Substitution induced by* bowes 97. XV 102 fruyt **B:** fruyt wexe **C** (XVI 255). *Omission caused by the succession of correlatives.* XVI 115 as **B:** ar **C** (XVIII 145). *Misreading through confusion of* r *and* s. XVII 184 they are/are þei **B:** thre is **C** (XIX 150). *Visual error.* XVII 211 *not in* **B:** *cp.* **C** (XIX 177). *Omission through inducement to complete the correlative construction begun in* 209. XVII 267 *not in* **B:** *cp.* **C** (XIX 234). *Omission induced by preoccupation with adjacent rubric.* XVII 296, 297 *as one line* **B:** *cp.* **C** (XIX 277, 278). *Omission through eyeskip,* Leue...loue. XVII 299 noȝt/not/now **B:** nouthe **C** (XIX 279). *Misreading or visual error.* XVIII 51 þe **B:** a **C** (XX 51). *Substitution of a more familiar use.* XVIII 95 hym ybounde **B:** the dede **C** (XX 98). *Anticipation of sense of* 97. XVIII 106 al **B:** as **C** (XX 109). *Visual error from tendency to emphasize.* XVIII 131 wem **B:** wommane wem **C** (XX 134). *Omission through homœoarchy.* XVIII 149 prophete **B:** parfit **C** (XX 152). *Misreading of a contraction.* XVIII 153 *not in* **B:** *cp.* **C** (XX 156). *Omission induced by* For venym 152, For of alle venymes 154. XVIII 161, 162 *as one line* **B:** *cp.* **C** (XX 164, 165). *Omission by eyeskip* (good 161, 162). XVIII 254 *not in* **B:** *cp.* **C** (XX 263). *Omission by homoarchy and homœoteleuton* (And...likeþ 254, And...lyue 255). XVIII 284 hundred **B:** thousand **C** (XX 309). *Misreading of numerals or imperfect recollection.* XVIII 315 a watre **B:** in helle **C** (XX 349). *Substitution of the commoner expression.* XIX 148 demede **B:** deuyned **C** (XXI 148). *Misreading occasioned by minims and nasal contraction.* XIX 271 folweþ **B:** folewede **C** (XXI 271). *Inducement of* -þ *preceding.* XIX 280 kepe **B:** kele **C** (XXI 280). *Visual error induced by* saue *following.* XIX 292 lesynges ne lyere **B:** lyare with lesynges **C** (XXI 292). *Anticipation of copy with smoothing by subsequently writing in the ousted word.* XIX 298 euere **B:** euene **C** (XXI 298). *Misreading induced by* hardy...euere *in* 290 *above.* XIX 429 sendeþ **B:** soudeth **C** (XXI 429). *Homœograph substituted for a difficult reading.* XIX 437 *not in* **B:** *cp.* **C** (XXI 437). *Omission caused by homoteleuton* (434, 437). XIX 453 if þei **B:** hit **C** (XXI 453). *Substitution induced by the grammar of* 451 *above.* XIX 477 konne **B:** þe comune **C** (XXI 477). *Misreading of* *contraction.* XX 67 hem **B**: here **C** (XXII 67). *Substitution induced by preceding* hem. XX 106 to **B**: tho **C** (XXII 106). *Substitution induced by* To 107.

Similarly in the following instances the archetypal reading of **B** has a scribal quality in being easier than the reading of **C**.

Prologue 166 awey renne **B**: here way roume **C** (Prologue 188). II 84 wraþe **B**: yre **C** (II 91). III 321 baron **B**: buyrne **C** (III 474). V 391 rored **B**: remede **C** (VII 7). XI 342 belwe **B**: bere **C** (XIII 150). XIII 80 to Pacience **B**: compacience **C** (XV 87). XIV 56 etynge **B**: ondynge **C** (XV 255). XIV 315 if **B**: thogh **C** (XVI 149). XV 193 seiþ wepynge **B**: wepynge **C** (XVI 336). XVIII 198 felawes/feerys **B**: flesch **C** (XX 203). XIX 97 gan to **B**: comsed **C** (XXI 97). XX 300 made **B**: ȝeuen **C** (XXII 300). XX 381 walken...lasteþ **B**: wenden...regneth (=renneþ) **C** (XXII 381).

In the following instances the archetypal reading of **B** is more explicit than that of the **C** text.

I 153 it was so heuy of hymself **B**: so heuy hit semede **C** (I 149). V 44 If ye lyuen **B**: Lyue (ȝe) **C** (V 142). V 151 ryden aboute **B**: ryde **C** (VI 126). V 479 and do **B**: do **C** (VII 121). V 480 Now god **B**: God **C** (VII 122). V 494 And þoruȝ þe **B**: The **C** (VII 134). VI 201 For I **B**: I **C** (VIII 207). IX 147 þei ferden/fared they **B**: ferden **C** (X 235). X 84 good hemselue **B**: godes **C** (XI 64). XI 203 and gentil **B**: gentel **C** (XII 111). XI 292 youre title...youre wages **B**: a title...wages **C** (XIII 106). XI 293 if þat ye ben worþi **B**: and enbaumed ȝoure fyngeres **C** (XIII 107). XI 412 certes quod I **B**: certes **C** (XIII 220). XII 178 hym fro **B**: fro **C** (XIV 118). XIII 427 and prechours **B**: precheours **C** (VII 87). XIV 57 lynnen cloþ ne wollen **B**: cloth **C** (XV 256). XVII 203 is as it were **B**: he is as **C** (XIX 169). XIX 164 for to **B**: to **C** (XXI 164). XIX 174 Thow deidest **B**: Deyedest **C** (XXI 174). XIX 197 to þe **B**: to **C** (XXI 197). XIX 335 and pride **B**: pryde **C** (XXI 335). XIX 357 And praye **B**: Preye **C** (XXI 357). XIX 362 For to **B**: To **C** (XXI 362). XX 87 hir **B**: the **C** (XXII 87). XX 228 or ellis **B**: or **C** (XXII 228). XX 313 þis **B**: the **C** (XXII 313). XX 337 kan do **B**: can **C** (XXII 337). XX 360 chaunge hem **B**: chaungen **C** (XXII 360). XX 375 and bad Clergie **B**: clergie **C** (XXII 375).

In the following instances the archetypal reading of **B** is more emphatic than that of the **C** text.

IV 37 of god one goose wynge **B**: of good fayth woet god the sothe **C** (IV 37). V 152 wikked folk **B**: folk **C** (VI 127). V 193 bondeman of his...bidraueled **B**: bondemannes... yshaue **C** (VI 201). V 483 al for **B**: for **C** (VII 125). VI 155 forpynede **B**: pyuische **C** (VIII 151). XI 371 and ofte **B**: me thouhte **C** (XIII 181). XIV 46 and loue as god **B**: As oure lord **C** (XV 244). XIV 255 his maister **B**: a mene **C** (XVI 95). XV 358 loore of Philosofres **B**: lodesterre(s) **C** (XVII 96). XVII 285 manye mo **B**: mo **C** (XIX 266). XVII 311 falsly al hire lyues **B**: folewen here owene will **C** (XIX 291). XVIII 40 pilour **B**: pelour **C** (XX 39). XVIII 46 I warante hym a wicche **B**: he can of wycchecrafte **C** (XX 46). XVIII 53 his deeþ yuel hise daies were ydone **B**: his deth to lette and his dayes lenghe **C** (XX 53). XVIII 119 ful comely **B**: comely **C** (XX 122). XIX 254 alle/togeddre as **B**: as **C** (XXI 254). XIX 308 power **B**: knowyng **C** (XXI 308). XX 25 ful **B**: wel **C** (XXII 25). XX 183 anoon after **B**: aftur **C** (XXII 183). XX 365 al **B**: hem **C** (XXII 365). XX 372 souerayneste **B**: souereyne **C** (XXII 372).

And in the following instances the archetypal reading of **B** might in its context seem to be a deliberate alteration of an original which was like the reading of the **C** text, arising from scribal miscomprehension, stylistic preference, 'smoothing' after earlier variation, or an intention of censorship.

I 4 a **B**: þe **C** (I 4). *Failure to identify the reference of the definite article.* III 334 That þei þat/they that/Þat þei/Of hem þat **B**: That **C** (III 486). *Padding after omission.* V 386 seide þe segge **B**: to be shryue **C** (VII 2). *Censorship of an outrageous notion.* XI 84 after **B**: on þe frere **C** (XII 23). *Smoothing after* louȝ] loked *earlier in line.* XI 239 ne by carpynge of tunge **B**: so caytifliche he ȝede **C** (XII 128). *Objection to the implication that Christ could act* caytifliche. XI 241 of speche **B**: vch man til oþer **C** (XII 130). *Extension of the substitution in the preceding line.* XI 242 apparaille vs noȝt (ouer) proudly **B**: pacient as pilgrimes **C** (XII 131). *Smoothing by restoring the notion of poor clothing ousted from* 239 *above.* XI 411 Of me what þyng it were **B**: What is dowel quod þat wyhte **C** (XIII 219). *Smoothing after substitution of an easier reading in* 410. XIII 41 þei **B**: he **C** (XV 46). *Smoothing after the corruption in* 40. XIV 58 *zero* **B**: ne deuel **C** (XV 257). *Omission (with redivision of* 57 *and* 58) *to smooth after augmentation of* 57. XV 382 also to **B**: assoile **C** (XVII 115). *Substitution of a homœograph for a hard reading.* XVIII 83 houed on hors **B**: houed þer **C** (XX 85). *Alliterative embellishment.* XVIII 97 mysdo a deed body **B**: bete a body ybounde **C** (XX 100). *Smoothing after anticipation of copy in* 95. XVIII 152 and that y preue by resoun **B**: þer feche y euydence **C** (XX 155). *Smoothing of copy which lacked line* 153. XVIII 179 haue **B**: synge **C** (XX 182). *Smoothing after earlier* merye] mercy *corruption.* XIX 301 for/fro **B**: thorw **C** (XXI 301). *Miscomprehension.* XX 127 preched to þe peple **B**: presed on þe pope **C** (XXII 127). *Censorship.* XX 130 kneled to **B**: knokked **C** (XXII 130). *Misguided 'improvement'.* XX 376 also Contricion for **B**: and baed contricioun to come **C** (XXII 376). *Smoothing after substitution in* 375.

There are, finally, more than 90 places in the poem where the reading of the archetypal **B** text, when compared with the text of **C**, seems scribal on two distinct considerations: because it could have been derived from the latter by one of the known processes of scribal variation, and because it creates an unalliterative or less normatively alliterative line than that in the **C** text.

Prologue 117 hemself⟩ *a a x y* **B**: here comunes **C** (Prologue 141). *Elimination of the pun.* Prologue 201 wille⟩ *a x a y* **B**: reik **C** (Prologue 216). *Substitution of easier reading.* II 27 riȝt as kynde askeþ⟩ *a a x y* **B**: as men of kynde carpeth **C** (II 27). *Substitution of a more emphatic reading.* II 43 þat she⟩ *a a x y* **B**: this lady **C** (II 46). *Mede is denied the title of respect.* III 292 truþe⟩ *a a x y* **B**: trewe men **C** (III 445). *Unconscious substitution induced by* truþe *in* 293. III 296 cloke/clooth> *a x a y* **B**: panelon **C** (III 449). *Substitution of an easier reading.* III 316 Ouerlede> *x a a y* **B**: Ouerkarke **C** (III 469). *An easier reading.* III 334 ȝiftes> *a a x y* **B**: ȝeftes taketh ȝeme **C** (III 486). *Omission of a syntactically intervening expression.* III 341 ooþer> *a x a y* **B**: luft **C** (III 493). *Unconscious substitution induced by a common collocation.* IV 38 *expanded for emphasis, producing a spurious unalliterating line,* 38 *and* 39 *misdivided* **B**: *cp.* **C** (IV 38, 39). V 176 likyng> *x a a y* **B**: luste lef me **C** (VI 158). *Omission of a syntactically intervening expression.* V 185 by cause þerof> *a x a y* **B**: ne thy wit **C** (VI 167). *Visual error* (þi wit] þer with) *followed by smoothing.* V 196 lepe/han lopen þe bettre> *a x a y* **B**: lepe y leue and y trowe **C** (VI 204). *Substitution of more explicit reading.* V 276 leueþ noȝt þis be sooþ> *a x a y* **B**: leueth þat y lye **C** (VI 301). *Suppression of the notion that Repentance could lie.* V 393 me list nouȝt to loke> *a a b b* **B**: y drede me sore **C** (VII 9). *Substitution of more emphatic reading.* V 496 after> *a x a y* **B**: þeraftur **C** (VII 136). *Inattentive omission.* V 508 Seintes in heuene> *a x a y* **B**: seyntes for synfol **C** (VII 153). *Unconscious substitution of a common collocation.* VI 123 and preide hym of grace> *a a x y* **B**: how þei myht nat worche **C** (VIII 130). *Substitution for dramatic emphasis.* IX 16 *Anima* þat lady is lad by his leryng> *x a a a* **B**: And by his leryng is lad þat ilke lady *Anima* **C** (X 142). *Substitution of prose order through imperfect recollection.* X 313 Manere> *a a b b* **B**: places **C** (V 159). *Substitution of a commoner expression.* X 399, 400 *as one line*> *a a b b* **B**: *cp.* **C** (XI 230). *Attraction to a grammatically related expression.* X 452, 453 *as three lines, the second and third unalliterative* **B**: *cp.* **C** (XI 277, 278). *Substitution of an easier and more explicit statement.* X 478 lewed men> *a x a y* **B**: lewede laborers **C** (XI 299). *Imperfect recollection.* XI 127 catel> *a a x y* **B**: chatel **C** (XII 62). *Thoughtless substitution of alternative form.* XI 205 *as two lines, the second a a x y with padding* **B**: *cp.* **C** (XII 113). *Redivision to keep within frame lines.* XI 233 ofte> *a a x y* **B**: lome **C** (XII 122). *Substitution of an easier reading.* XI 291 take> *a a x y* **B**: nyme **C** (XIII 105). *Substitution induced by* take *in* 290. XI 340 in euenynges also þe males ben fro femelles> *a a x y* **B**: femeles to femeles ferddede and drowe **C** (XIII 148). *Smoothing to suit the misunderstanding of* 339. XI 347, 348 *divided after* lerned, 348> *a x a y* **B**: *divided after* pye **C** (XIII 158, 159). *Unconscious resistance to separation of subject and object.* XI 356 hir makes> *a x a y* **B**: y toke kepe **C** (XIII 165). *Substitution of a more explicit reading.* XI 372, 373 *divided after* rebukede> 373 *a b b a*, 374 *a a b b* **B**: *cp.* **C** (XIII 182, 183). *Omission of* 372b *induced by* Reson, 372, 373, *followed by padding.* XI 374 of þee quod I> *a x a y* **B**: in my wit **C** (XIII 184). *Elimination of the pun on* wit. XI 408, 409 *prose or scanning a a x y* **B**: *cp.* **C** (XIII 216, 217). *Substitution of a more emphatic assertion.* XI 440 folwed hym after> *a a x y* **B**: reuerensed hym fayre **C** (XIII 246). *Substitution induced by inaccurate visualization of preceding line.* XI 441 preyde hym of his curteisie to telle me his name> *a prose line* **B**: yf his wille were A wolde his name telle **C** (XIII 247). *Smoothing accompanying substitution in* 440. XII 60 but amonges lowe> *a a x y* **B**: til gode wil gyne reyne **C** (XIV 24). *Substitution induced by sense of following line.* XII 204 Confessours ne wydewes> *a a x y* **B**: mylde weddewes **C** (XIV 143). *Substitution of a more emphatic statement.* XIII 8 folk> *x a a y* **B**: peple **C** (XV 10). *Unconscious substitution induced by* folk *in preceding line.* XIII 25 seiȝ> *x a a y* **B**: metten **C** (XV 29). *Substitution of an easier reading.* XIII 35 were> *a x a y* **B**: prestly was **C** (XV 40). *Omission by grammatical attraction.* XIII 47, 48 *as one line scanning a a b b* **B**: *cp.* **C** (XV 53, 54). *Omission from end of* 48 *caused by* mette/mete *confusion, followed by further omission and redivision to smooth.* XIII 85 To telle me> *x a a y* **B**: And apose hym **C** (XV 92). *Substitution of an easier and more explicit* *reading.* XIII 117 *omission and rearrangement*> *x a a a* **B**: *cp.* **C** (XV 125). *Prosification through imperfect recollection.* XIII 174 conformen> *x a a y* **B**: perfourme **C** (XV 172). *Substitution by alliterative inducement of* Kan *preceding.* XIII 254 *as two lines* scanning *a b b a, x a a y* **B**: *cp.* **C** (XV 224). *Redivision after additions made for emphasis.* XIII 325 tellen it watte> *a a x a* **B**: to watekyn he tolde it **C** (VI 70). *Adoption of prose order through imperfect recollection.* XIII 340 word> *a x a y* **B**: word ne gras **C** (VI 84). *Omission of syntactically intervening expression.* XIII 423 to do> *a a x a* **B**: in hope to do **C** (VII 83). *Omission through eyeskip* (to...to). XIV 260 may cleymen and asken> *a a x y* **B**: of puyr rihte may claymen **C** (XVI 100). *Substitution induced by* asken *in* 262 *below.* XIV 270 good> *a x a y* **B**: catel **C** (XVI 110). *Substitution through imperfect recollection.* XIV 301, 302 *as one line scanning a x a a* **B**: *cp.* **C** (XVI 137, 138). *Omission induced by* of...of 301, leche 302, yliche 303, *followed by smoothing.* XIV 307 bereþ...hardier> *x y a a* **B**: lede...lihtere **C** (XVI 142). *Substitution of easier reading, and of synonym induced by* hardy *in* 308 *below.* XIV 314 wel> *x a a y* **B**: sothly **C** (XVI 148). *Substitution of the colourless intensifier through failure of memory.* XV 70 men> *a a x y* **B**: folk **C** (XVI 231). *Thoughtless substitution caused by preoccupation with the sense.* XV 111 dongehill> *a a x y* **B**: lothly donghep **C** (XVI 266). *Omission induced by grammatical attraction.* XV 115 cloþes (also)> *a a x y* **B**: bele clothes **C** (XVI 270). *Elimination of a repetition.* XV 117 spekeþ> *a a x y* **B**: carpeth **C** (XVI 272). *Substitution of an easier reading.* XV 231 fern ago in Seint> *a x a y* **B**: fer and fele ȝer **C** (XVI 357). *Substitution of an easier and more explicit reading.* XV 237 In court amonges Iaperis> *a x a y* **B**: Amongus þe comune in Court **C** (XVI 363). *Deliberate alteration through misconception of the kind of court in question.* XVI 109 to goode turnede> *a a x y* **B**: clansed hem of synne **C** (XVIII 142). *Unconscious transposition* of 109b, 110b, *followed by smoothing.* XVI 158 at/and (þorgh)> *a a b b* **B**: to **C** (XVIII 175). *Substitution of a more usual expression.* XVI 267 legge> *x a a a* **B**: wagen **C** (XVIII 283). *Substitution induced by* ligge 268. XVII 54 chaced> *a a x y* **B**: Iaced **C** (XIX 52). *Substitution of a homœograph for a hard reading, or visual error.* XVII 80 *as divided from* 79> *a a x y* **B**: *cp.* **C** (XIX 77) for his medicyne. *Omission followed by redivision with padding.* XVII 82 to Ierusalemward þe riȝte wey to ryde> *a x a a* **B**: to ryde the rihte way to Ierusalem **C** (XIX 79). *Unconscious transposition of notions induced by* to...to. XVII 217 þe macche brenneþ> *a a x y* **B**: lith fuyr in þe mache **C** (XIX 183). *Substitution of an easier and more explicit reading.* XVIII 32 *scans a a x a* **B**: *cp.* **C** (XX 31). *Misdivision through imperfect recollection.* XVIII 82 *scans x y a a* **B**: *cp.* **C** (XX 84). *The line rewritten to exclude the notion that Longinus was a Jew.* XVIII 119 comely creature> *a a x y* **B**: comely creature and a clene **C** (XX 122). *Omission through movement of attention to the identity of the* creature. XVIII 155 helpe> *a a x y* **B**: amende **C** (XX 158). *Substitution of an easier and more explicit reading.* XVIII 160 as þoruȝ gile man was bigiled > *x a y a* **B**: as the gylour thorw gyle bigiled man **C** (XX 163). *Prosification through imperfect recollection.* XVIII 170 he> *x a a y* **B**: loue **C** (XX 173). *Stylistic objection to repetition of the noun.* XVIII 299 forþ> *x a a y* **B**: forth lyke a tydy man **C** (XX 332). *Omission to shorten an exceptionally long line.* XVIII 307 hiderward seillynge> *a a x a* **B**: sylinge hidward **C** (XX 341). *Unconscious change of word order to bring two commonly collocated words together.* XVIII 309 he> *a x a y* **B**: the fende **C** (XX 343). *Substitution of the pronoun induced by the rhyming monosyllables* we fle *preceding.* XVIII 401 Tho> *x a a y* **B**: Tho ledis **C** (XX 444). *Omission of an archaic term, or stylistic objection to the jingle* lede...ledes. XVIII 405 boldeste > *a a x y* **B**: leste **C** (XX 448). *Substitution of an easier reading.* XIX 101 hadde tyme to

> *a a b b* **B**: durste **C** (XXI 101). *An apparently pointless expression eliminated because the boldness of the comparison was missed.* XIX 154 bisouȝte> *a a x y* **B**: preyede **C** (XXI 154). *Stylistic objection to repeated use of a word.* XIX 243 telle it er it felle> *a a x y* **B**: be ywaer bifore **C** (XXI 243). *Substitution of a more explicit reading.* XIX 251 forbad hem alle debat þat noon were> *a a x y* **B**: no boest ne debaet be **C** (XXI 251). *Substitution of a more emphatic and explicit reading.* XIX 253 *as two lines, the second unalliterative* **B**: *cp.* **C** (XXI 253). *Expansion for emphasis.* XIX 303 he> *a a x y* **B**: the kyng **C** (XXI 303). *Objection to repeated use of the noun.* XIX 314 worþi> *x a a y* **B**: Forþy **C** (XXI 314). *Visual error followed by redivision.* XIX 343 *scans a a x y* **B**: *cp.* **C** (XXI 343). *Misdivision after* sedes *in resistance to separating verb and object, followed by omission of* sire *and padding.* XIX 369 *as two lines, one scanning a a x y, the other unmetrical* **B**: *cp.* **C** (XXI 369). *Insertion of more explicit and emphatic readings.* XX 19 for þurst deide> *a a x a* **B**: deye for furste **C** (XXII 19). *Unconscious promotion of the apparently more important notion.* XX 33α, 34 *as one line*> *a a b b* **B**: *cp.* **C** (XXII 33α, 34). *Misdivision and omission through distraction by the difficult meaning.* XX 54 Torned (it)> *a x a y* **B**: Turned hit tyd **C** (XXII 54). *Omission through auditory error.* XX 62, 63 *divided after* lyue, 63 *scanning a a x y* **B**: *cp.* **C** (XXII 62, 63). *Misdivision through inducement to complete the comparison.* XX 163 war> *a x a y* **B**: sley **C** (XXII 163). *Substitution by alliterative inducement.* XX 308 Piers> *a a x y* **B**: Peres pardon **C** (XXII 308). *Omission because the remote reference of* pardon *was not perceived.* XX 379 plastred hem so esily *unalliterative* **B**: doth men drynke dwale **C** (XXII 379). *Substitution of an easier reading.*

A circumstance which might hinder easy conclusions about the originality or unoriginality of these **B** readings is the anterior position of **B** in the sequence of revision; this might affect the assessment of probabilities. Since **C** is a revision of **B** a general superiority of **C** is *prima facie* likely, and it could be argued that such superiority extends to minutiae. Thus the better reading of **C** would be ascribable to effective authorial revision. But four distinct considerations diminish the force of such an argument.

The first is the axiom that corruption takes place at all stages in the transmission of texts. This implies both that not all differences between **B** and **C** can be authorial, and that some, specifically, must be the result of scribal variation in the **B** tradition. The second, which strengthens the first, is the presumptive corruptness of the archetypal **B** text, already clearly indicated by the comparison of **B** with **AC** and **A**. This implies that the corruption observable where **B** corresponds with **AC** or **A** was not confined to those areas but occurred also in the parts of the poem where **B** corresponds with **C**. The third is the character of the **B** readings in question: they are of the same types which in the other two textual situations were explicable as resulting from corruption of **B**. The fourth is their number. This is such as to raise the question whether our poet could conceivably so often have first written so ineptly that what he wrote on second attempt made his first effort look like a scribal variation from the second. From these considerations it seems to us that **B** readings inferior in certain familiar, classifiable ways to the corresponding readings of **C** are *a priori* imputable to scribes and not to the poet. We therefore conclude that in the instances cited above the **B** and **C** texts have a common original reading, preserved in the **C** tradition, which was corrupted during that stage of the archetypal **B** tradition subsequent to the generation of the **B** manuscript used in the revision of **C**. We take this to be a further demonstration of the quality of the **B** archetype.

It is now time to survey the whole body of evidence revealed by the three comparisons to which the archetypal text of **B** can be subjected. Its first striking feature is the similarity of **B** variation in the three situations of comparison. The second is the close resemblance of the **B** readings, both individually and as a body of textual evidence, to the demonstrably scribal variations in the post-archetypal tradition of **B**.[25] The third is their number: more than 600 in the more than 6000 lines where **B** corresponds with one or both of the other versions. Having regard to their character and number the effect of these variants on the **B** version as a poem constitutes a massive commentary either on the art of the **B** reviser or on the quality of transmission in the archetypal stage of the **B** tradition.

Because the assessment of this quality is the most fundamental operation in the editing of the **B** version we have been at pains to expose the evidence and our interpretation of it for judgement rather than to present firm conclusions. But now, since no further discussion except scrutiny of each individual instance (which considerations of space would forbid) seems possible, the point has been reached where we may appropriately state our own conclusion firmly: that the matter is not in any reasonable doubt. The instances which we have adduced, of difference between **B** and **AC**, and **B** and **A**, and **B** and **C**, are the effects of scribal variation in the archetypal tradition of **B**. The unanimity or general agreement with which the **B** manuscripts attest the readings of their exclusive common ancestor conceals a history in the archetypal **B** tradition of very extensive scribal substitution, in part

[25] These are conveniently illustrated by the demonstrations of variational groups in Section II above.

careless and unconscious, and if deliberate directed generally towards simplifying, or rendering more accessible the sense of the text—as scribes understood or misunderstood this—at the expense of compression, pregnancy, technical excellence, and in the end, of the poetry. This seems to us clear to the limit of certainty possible in textual criticism.

Our conclusion has two implications. The first is immediate and limited: the agreement of the **B** manuscripts in the 600 odd readings which we have identified as scribal and unoriginal finally demonstrates the unity of the **B** manuscript tradition.[26] The second is altogether more extensive: the strong presumption of the corruptness of the archetypal text of the **B** version of *Piers Plowman* is a main instrument for its editors.[27]

[26] See above, pp. 64ff.
[27] Its use as such is discussed at length below, pp. 128ff.

IV

THE C REVISER'S B MANUSCRIPT

Comparison of the archetypal text of the **B** version, that is the determinable text of the exclusive common ancestor of the surviving **B** manuscripts, with the corresponding texts of **AC** and **A** and **C** has revealed its corruption and accordingly its distance from original **B**. In particular, agreements of **AC** against **B** where the archetypal **B** reading appears as scribal, and differences between **B** and **C** with a similar indication, imply that the manuscript of the **B** version used by Langland for his revision to **C** preserved at many points original readings lost from the exclusive common ancestor of the surviving **B** manuscripts.[1]

But the same comparisons also establish that, notwithstanding its superior originality at those points, this **B** manuscript used by Langland for his second revision was a corrupt scribal copy. The evidence from which we draw this conclusion is bulky and of some complexity, and its interpretation touches issues not merely of textual criticism but also of the general circumstances of poetic revision in the fourteenth century and the particular methods and nature of Langland's revisions. Nevertheless the editorial importance of the conclusion is such as to require its demonstration by a full discussion. To this the present section is devoted.[2]

The first evidence that Langland used a scribal copy of the **B** version when revising to **C** consists of some 100 differences between the text of **A** and the text in which **BC** agree not manifestly created by authorial revision and possessing, on scrutiny, the appearance of differences between an original reading preserved in the **A** tradition and a scribal

[1] That circumstance, which might seem naturally presumable, is not a theoretically necessary one: while there is a primary likelihood that an author revising his own work will have used certainly the best text he could get, probably a better one than any which survives, and perhaps even *prima facie* his own original, it would also be conceivable, in theory, for the exclusive common ancestor of the surviving **B** manuscripts to have been that original. Therefore the contrary demonstration of the evidence which has emerged from comparison of the versions is of main importance.

[2] There is also some evidence that he used a scribal copy of **A** for his revision to **B**. See below, pp. 205, 210f.

reflex of this preserved in the traditions of **B** and **C**. In other words, while the **BC** readings encourage no plausible *a posteriori* inference about authorial motives for change, they fall readily into the types of scribal variation familiar from other textual situations.

To begin with a number of differences between **A** and **BC** are explicable as having originated in various mechanical errors.

Substitutions induced by the local context: V 527 In...in **BC** (VII 172): At...at **A** (VI 15). (in boþe 527, In...in 528). V 531 helþe **BC** (VII 175): hele **A** (VI 19). (tru-þe 532). V 596 hym **BC** (VII 244): he **A** (VI 83). (*accusative* yow *preceding*). VI 21 he kenneþ **BC** (VIII 19): þou kennist **A** (VII 23). (*third person in* 19, 20). VII 26 amende **BC** (IX 30): make **A** (VIII 28). (amende 27). X 147 loute **BC** (XI 85): knele **A** (XI 100). (louted 145). *Variations induced by more common collocations:* VII 151 Piers þe Plowman **BC** (IX 299): peris loue þe plouȝman **A** (VIII 132). VIII 40 wyndes and wedres **BC** (X 46): wyndis & watris **A** (IX 36). IX 142 dales and hulles **BC** (X 230): dounes & hilles **A** (X 173). *Transposition induced by the preceding context:* III 226 Marchaunt3/Marchandyse and Mede **BC** (III 281): Mede & marchaundise **A** (III 213). (Emperours... ȝiftes 213, 214; Pope...present3 215; Seruaunt3...Mede 217, 218; Beggeres...Mede 219; Mynstrales...Mede 220; *etc.*). *Memorial contamination or anticipation of copy:* V 625 seuene **BC** (VII 278): sistris **A** (VI 110). (seuene 627). *Visual error induced by the context:* VI 186 potful **BC** (VIII 182): potel **A** (VII 174). *Substitution induced by the alliteration of the line:* X 13 swiche **BC** (XI 11): þo **A** (XI 13). *Omission by eyeskip:* VIII 62, 63 *as one line with later padding* **BC** (X 61, 62): *cp.* **A** (IX 53, 54).

In the majority of cases, however, the **BC** readings represent themselves as scribal reflexes of corresponding readings in the **A** version by answering to the effects of the common scribal tendencies of variation.

The following **BC** readings are easier than the corresponding **A** readings in various ways.

Grammatically easier readings: III 99 houses...homes **BC** (III 127): hous...home **A** (III 88). V 47 stedes **BC** (V 145): stede **A** (V 39). V 445 synnes **BC** (VII 59): synne **A** (V 217). VI 122 legges **BC** (VIII 129): leg **A** (VII 114). VII 105 hertes **BC** (IX 184): herte **A** (VIII 87). *Plurals for distributive singulars.* V 621 hise **BC** (VII 273): hire **A** (VI 107). *Simple possessive for objective genitive.* X 151 Wiþ þat ye **BC** (XI 89): To **A** (XI 103). *Conditional clause for adverbial infinitive.*

Lexically easier readings: Prologue 31 chosen **BC** (Prologue 33): chosen hem to **A** (Prologue 31). I 63 wight **BC** (I 59): wy **A** (I 61). I 185 Iugged/iugeth **BC** (I 181): ioynide **A** (I 159). III 106 womman **BC** (III 134): wy **A** (III 95). IV 130 graue ne vngraue gold neiþer siluer **BC** (IV 127): grotis ne gold ygraue wiþ kynges coyn **A** (IV 113). IV 140 in **BC** (IV 137): at **A** (IV 123). V 200 wayte **BC** (VI 208): loke **A** (V 116). VI 33 comsed **BC** (VIII 32): conseyuede **A** (VII 35). IX 178 togideres **BC** (X 280): ysamme **A** (X 199).

Contextually easier readings: III 38 boþe **BC** (III 40): ichone **A** (III 37). III 84 Wiþ **BC** (III 83): Of **A** (III 73). VI 104 clense **BC** (VIII 65): close **A** (VII 96). VI 303 Inne were **BC** (VIII 325): in come **A** (VII 287). VI 318 greue **BC** (VIII 339): chaste **A** (VII 299). VII 189 ye **BC** (IX 334): þou **A** (VIII 167). X 161 quod I **BC** (XI 103): to hym **A** (XI 113).

Lexically and contextually easier readings: Prologue 42 Faiteden **BC** (Prologue 43): Flite þanne **A** (Prologue 42). Prologue 72 hise wordes **BC** (Prologue 70): his speche **A** (Prologue 69). V 70 hated **BC** (VI 11): had enuye **A** (V 53).

The following **BC** readings are more explicit than the corresponding readings of **A** by the presence of simple or modal conjunctions, demonstrative or possessive adjectives, expressed objects, or otherwise more specific language.

Prologue 22 And wonnen **BC** (Prologue 24): Wonne **A** (Prologue 22). I 80 And preide **BC** (I 77): Preiȝede **A** (I 78). I 89 And dooþ **BC** (I 85): Doþ **A** (I 87). I 198 And þat **BC** (I 193): Þat **A** (I 172). II 72 Thanne Symonye **BC** (II 74): Symonye **A** (II 54). II 134 Forþi wercheþ **BC** (II 150): Werchiþ **A** (II 98). II 160 And bad hem **BC** (II 176): And **A** (II 124). II 233 And for **BC** (II 243): For **A** (II 192). III 31 do callen **BC** (III 34): callen **A** (III 30). III 38 lewed men...lered men **BC** (III 40): lerid...lewide **A** (III 37). III 64 to alle **BC** (III 68): alle **A** (III 53). III 122 For she **BC** (III 159): She **A** (III 111). III 126 And lereþ **BC** (III 163): Leriþ **A** (III 115). III 131 For she **BC** (III 168): She **A** (III 120). III 136 For she **BC** (III 174): She **A** (III 125). III 140 and tieþ **BC** (III 178): teiȝeþ **A** (III 129). III 148 For (Sire) **BC** (III 186): Sire **A** (III 137). IV 57 and bereþ **BC** (IV 60): beriþ **A** (IV 44). IV 90 þat is mysdo **BC** (IV 86): þat mysdede **A** (IV 77). IV 145 þis **BC** (IV 142): it **A** (IV 128). V 9 And þanne **BC** (V 109): Þanne **A** (V 9). V 342 his...his **BC** (VI 400): þe...þe **A** (V 190). V 345 myȝte neiþer steppe ne stonde **BC** (VI 403): hadde no strengþe to stonde **A** (V 193). V 525 first **BC** (VII 170): faire **A** (VI 13). V 541 to sowe and to **BC** (VII 186): sowe and **A** (VI 29). V 578 And leue **BC** (VII 225): Leue **A** (VI 65). V 585 as cler **BC** (VII 232): cler **A** (VI 72). VI 30 breken doun **BC** (VIII 29): breken **A** (VII 32). VI 31 go/so/to affaite þi...wilde **BC** (VIII 30): fecche þe hom...þe **A** (VII 33). VI 94 his masse **BC** (VIII 103): mynde **A** (VII 86). VI 114 He sholde **BC** (VIII 121): Shulde **A** (VII 106). VI 153 And to **BC** (VIII 150): To **A** (VII 140). VI 167 and now **BC** (VIII 164): now **A** (VII 152). VI 173 þise wastours **BC** (VIII 170): wastours **A** (VII 158). VI 292 peple þo **BC** (VIII 315): peple **A** (VII 276). VII 6 to sette or to sowe **BC** (IX 6): to sowen **A** (VIII 6). VII 7 auaille **BC** (IX 7): helpen **A** (VIII 7). VII 59 hir motyng **BC** (IX 54): motyng **A** (VIII 60). VII 67 but if **BC** (IX 63): but **A** (VIII 69). VII 187 on þis **BC** (IX 332): on **A** (VIII 165). VII 192 purchace yow **BC** (IX 337): purchace **A** (VIII 170). VII 195 lawes **BC** (IX 340): lawe **A** (VIII 173). VII 196 And how **BC** (IX 341): What **A** (VIII 174). VII 202 oure meene **BC** (IX 347): mene **A** (VIII 180). VIII 41 oure **BC** (X 47): þe **A** (IX 37). VIII 75 þis seuen **BC** (X 73): seuen **A** (IX 66). VIII 86 and louelich **BC** (X 83): louelich **A** (IX 77). X 18 kemben **BC** (XI 15): don **A** (XI 18).

The following **BC** readings are variously more emphatic than the corresponding readings of **A**.

Prologue 26 ful **BC** (Prologue 28): wel **A** (Prologue 26). I 77 fulfille **BC** (I 74): werche **A** (I 75). II 193 Now by **BC** (II 207): Be **A** (II 154). III 124 ful **BC** (III 161); wel **A** (III 113). III 180 gabbe **BC** (III 226): leiȝe **A** (III 167). IV 183 ful **BC** (IV 177): wel **A** (IV 146). V 21 ful **BC** (V 123): wel **A** (V 21). V 612 bienfetes **BC** (VII 264): bienfait **A** (VI 98). V 623, 628 ful **BC** (VII 275, 281): wel **A** (VI 109, 113). VI 28 þis world struyeþ **BC** (VIII 27): wolde me destroye **A** (VII 30). VI 178 guttes **BC** (VIII 175): mawis **A** (VII 163). VI 209 ay as **BC** (VIII 218): aftir þat **A** (VII 195). VII 58 ful **BC** (IX 53): wel **A** (VIII 59). IX 26 þynges **BC** (X 152): bestis **A** (X 27). IX 199 serue **BC** (X 298): plesen **A** (X 213). X 17 kerse **BC** (XI 14): risshe **A** (XI 17).

A few **BC** readings appear, on comparison with the corresponding readings of **A**, as various other kinds of scribal substitution.

I 81, III 182, III 204 also **BC** (I 78, III 228, III 261): ek **A** (I 79, III 169, 191) *register personal preference for an exactly equivalent term.* II 139 And **BC** (II 155): For **A** (II 103) *records objection to successive causal clauses.* III 123 And **BC** (III 160): She **A** (III 112) *indicates resistance to the parataxis of* 122 *and* 123. IV 146 ye **BC** (IV 143): þou **A** (IV 129) *prefers the courteous second person plural to the preacher's unceremonious singular.* V 31 half (a) **BC** (V 133): a **A** (V 31) *and* V 199 Style **BC** (VI 207): nok **A** (V 115) *and* VIII 20α And seide sooþly *Sepcies* **BC** (X 21): *Sepcies* **A** (IX 17) *are alliterative embellishments.* V 321 Hakeneyman **BC** (VI 378): hostiler **A** (V 170) *is memorial contamination by* 310 *above.* VIII 23 And **BC** (X 27): Þat **A** (IX 19) *is smoothing after substitution in the preceding line.* VIII 77 knowe **BC** (X 75): wisse **A** (IX 68) *is smoothing after anticipation of* wisse *in* 76.

At this stage in the demonstration there would in theory be four possible explanations for the existence of archetypal **BC** agreements against **A** in readings not manifestly or evidently produced by authorial revision and also on other grounds possibly scribal.

The first would be that, notwithstanding the absence of *a posteriori* indications that these readings are revisions, they are actually authorial, and that the procedures by which we profess to identify revision, and to distinguish original from unoriginal readings, have here failed to be effective. Three related considerations apply: Langland's quality as a poet; the positively scribal character of the **BC** readings, in that their effect on the text is exactly like the visible damage done by scribes elsewhere; and the actual occurrence of more than half of them as scribal variants of original **A** readings in the post-archetypal tradition of **A**, that is in surviving **A** manuscripts.[3] These test the explanation in terms of an opposition between an unassessable possibility that the **BC** readings cited above are pointless or inept authorial revisions, and a probability established by their character that they are scribal substitutions. In other words the observable generation in one textual tradition of certain specific kinds of readings by the identifiable operation of known scribal tendencies establishes something like a near certainty that the same or similar readings in another tradition will have a similar origin. We therefore reject the possibility of authorial revision.

The second possible explanation of these **BC** agreements in readings of a scribal character would be that they exist because the poet, himself copying the **B** version as his own scribe, fell into such typical scribal variations and later let them stand when revising to **C** from the text of **B** which he had thus corrupted. This, while certainly not inconceivable, seems to be ruled out by a further class of **BC** agreements in readings manifestly inferior in sense to the corresponding readings of **A** and evincing such incomprehension of the latter that it would be hard to impute them to the poet. They are as follows.

III 158 þe lawe **BC** (III 194): lawe **A** (III 148). *The definite article destroys the personification.* V 129 megre **BC** (VI 94): mat **A** (V 106). *Envy's swollen condition (83 above) has been forgotten and that of Covetousness imputed to him.* V 213 webbe **BC** (VI 221): wynstere **A** (V 129). *The totally inappropriate term 'male weaver'*[4] *is a desperate substitution for an evidently very difficult term.*[5] V 220 lay in my bour or in my bedchambre **BC** (VI 228): in my bedchaumbre lay be þe wouȝ **A** (V 136). *Puzzlement over the details of the fraud expresses itself in a woolly attempt to visualize the setting.* VI 97 douȝtres **BC** (VIII 106): frendis **A** (VII 89). *This is a substitution to make the line alliterate by a scribe who missed the scansion* amóng mý mý, *in which the staves emphasize Piers's insistence that his wife should execute his testament in accordance with his particular wishes.*[6] VI 268 eris **BC** (VIII 289): armes **A** (VII 252). *A commoner and more apparently apt expression was substituted because the polysemy of the term 'Hunger's arms' was missed.* IX 172 hem bitwene **BC** (X 274): betwene **A** (X 193). *The adverbial meaning of* bitwene, *'at intervals, in the intervals', was missed and the pronoun inserted to emphasize that the* choppes *did not include a third party.* X 58 wiþ **BC** (XI 39):

[3] They occur at **A** Prologue 22, 26, 31, 42, 69. I 61, 78, 79, 87, 159. II 54, 103, 124, 154. III 30, 53, 88, 95, 111, 112, 113, 115, 129, 169, 191, 213. IV 44, 123, 128, 146. V 21, 31, 39, 116, 190, 217. VI 13, 19, 29, 72, 83, 98, 107, 109, 113. VII 32, 33, 35, 86, 96, 114, 140, 158, 174, 276, 287. VIII 6, 7, 59, 69, 87, 132, 167, 173, 174. IX 66, 77. X 199.

[4] We take issue with *NED* s.v. *Webbe* 2. The only instances there cited to support the sense 'female weaver' are the present one and another where *webster* occurs as a textual variant. Here is an example of the consequence of using corrupt texts for lexicographical purposes. Three scribes in the visible **B** tradition knew enough at any rate to correct its archetypal bad lexicography here.

[5] The evidence for its difficulty is the variation that it underwent in the **A** tradition.

[6] Unless *children* means specifically male as distinct from female offspring, which we certainly do not find to be lexically authorized, the reading *douȝtres* makes nonsense of the line.

in **A** (XI 44). *The appallingly graphic representation of blasphemy,* gnawen god in þe gorge, '*bite God persistently in the throat*', *was either missed or rejected as outrageous, and a more colourless expression substituted; but* gnawen wiþ þe gorge *is actually non-sense.*[7]

The third explanation is that, if the poet was not responsible for the **BC** agreements, either as an ineptly revising author, or as his own inefficient scribe, and the readings in question are unoriginal reflexes of original readings preserved in the **A** tradition, the **BC** agreements might have resulted from extensive, very early coincident variation in the two traditions, both **B** and **C** having originally read as **A** does. This possibility again could not be theoretically excluded. But it seems open to an objection of principle: to explain textual phenomena as random is (we believe) permissible only when there is no reasonable alternative, that is when other explanations in terms of established processes of cause and effect are not acceptable.[8] Therefore we would allow the 100 odd **BC** agreements cited above to be explained as coincidental only if they could not be accounted for in some other not merely possible but also likely way.

There is, finally, the fourth explanation: our identifications of originality in **A** and unoriginality in **BC** are correct; the **BC** readings were produced by scribal variation in the pre-archetypal **B** tradition, that is before the exclusive common ancestor of the surviving **B** manuscripts was copied; and they are present in the **C** archetype because Langland, when he revised **B** to **C**, used a scribal **B** manuscript where they occurred and let them stand, for whatever reason.

If decision between these last two explanations had to be made solely on the evidence so far presented it would not be easy. Coincident variation unquestionably occurred in the transmission at least of fourteenth-century Middle English texts, and our knowledge of the procedures of authorial revision during that period is neither abundant, nor indeed assured, since it is based principally on interpretations of cases like the present one. Thus a convincing assessment of relative probabilities might be hard to achieve. There is, however, a type of situation in which the relation of the readings of the three versions of

[7] *MED* is misled into glossing *gnawen* in this passage incorrectly (*gnauen* v. 3a) as 'disparage, carp at, slander, revile' by the more explicit scribal variant *in here* for *in þe*.

[8] It will be recalled that such a situation arose in the classification of the **B** manuscripts. There the choice of explanation to account for the existence of extensive conflicting variational groups was between coincident variation and absolutely prevalent lateral transmission; the latter alternative our observation did not allow us to accept.

Piers Plowman cannot be coincidental, and which seems to indicate unmistakably that Langland used a scribal **B** manuscript for his revision to **C**. The characteristics of this situation are: that a presumably original reading is preserved in the **A** tradition; that the archetypal **B** reading, on comparison with this, appears scribal; that the **C** reading is evidently a revision; that the **B** reading cannot derive from the reading of **C** but must derive from that of **A**; and that the **C** reading reflects not the putative original common to **A** and **B**, but **B**'s corrupt archetypal form of this.

For instance, in the archetypal **B** text I 98–103 are disordered, 98 and 99 being copied after 103. The scribal character of this sequence appears from comparison with the corresponding lines of **A** (I 96–101) which have superior sense: there the authority of David's example and the notion of constantly serving Truth are integral to the positive definition of *þe profession...þat apendeþ to kny3tes*; in **B** they follow it like an afterthought. The transposition will have occurred because early in the **B** archetypal tradition **B** I 98, 99 were first omitted through homoteleuton (*kny3tes* 98, 100) and then copied in as soon as the omission was remarked, or else copied from the margin into the wrong place. The **B** lines include another archetypal variation: substitution of more explicit *siluer* for original *yiftes* (103). The corresponding lines in **C** (I 94–103), although patently revised, reflect the dislocation of the archetypal **B** text; the revising poet smoothed the incorrect sequence in the scribal manuscript before him, incidentally letting the scribal reading *siluer* stand.

In I 191, where the archetypal **B** text read *Are none Auarouser þan hij whan þei ben auaunced*, the reading *Auarouser*,[9] compared with **A**'s *hardere* (I 165), appears from its clumsiness and more explicit character as a scribal variation induced by anticipation of *Auarice* in 197. **C** reads *Aren none hardore ne hungriore then men of holy chirche/Auerous and euel willed when þei ben avaunsed* (I 187, 188). The ousted reading has been firmly restored to its original position, but apparently from memory: for while the recasting of the line as two indicates the revising poet's dissatisfaction with what he found in the **B** manuscript before him, the presence of *Auerous* in **C** 188 is evidence that his **B** line had the scribal reading of the **B** archetype.

In I 195, 196 **B** archetypally read *Manye curatours kepen hem clene of*

[9] One late **B** manuscript reads *herder* by correction.

hire bodies/Thei ben acombred wiþ coueitise where **A**'s text (I 169, 170) makes an abrupt and forceful transition to the preacher's direct accusation, *ȝe curatours þat kepe ȝow clene of ȝour body* and continues in the second person. **B**'s variation is scribal: the archetypal substitution of the third person, probably inattentive and unconscious, was induced by the surrounding context, and the more emphatic *Manye curatours* of 195 specifically echoes *Manye Chapeleyns* of 190. This weakly repetitive line offended the **C** poet; his revision took the form of omitting it altogether. The scribal character of the **B** manuscript that was before him is indicated by his retention of archetypal **B**'s third person pronouns *thei* and *hem* (**C** I 191, 192).

In II 6 **B** archetypally read *Boþe Fals and Fauel and hire feeres manye* where **A** (II 6) reads *hise feris*. **B**'s plural is easier, for to identify the referent of *hise* calls for attention and reflection; in addition substitution of *hire* could have been subconsciously induced by the shape of the following word. **C**'s recasting of this line as two (II 6, 7) indicates his dissatisfaction with the form it took in his **B** manuscript. The expression *here maners* (**C** II 7), an unmistakable reflex of *hire feeres*, is evidence that the **B** manuscript which he was using here had the scribal reading of the **B** archetype.

In II 116 archetypal **B** makes Theology say in anger to Civil Law *now sorwe mote þow haue*, where **A** (II 80) reads *now sorewe on þi bokes*. As an easier, less pregnant expression, lacking the special aptness of **A**'s to the allegorical context, **B**'s reading is scribal, probably a parallelism in subconscious anticipation of 118b. The **C** reviser, generally uneasy with the line in his manuscript, redirected Theology's ill-wish to Simony (II 120); also sensible, though without accurate recollection, of a loss of meaning, he introduced an approximation to the meaning of *on þi bokes* by substituting in 122 for *wo þe betide* of **AB** *wo to al ȝoure consayle*. That his **B** manuscript had the archetypal error is indicated by the presence of *mot thow haue* in 120.

In II 227 archetypal **B** reads *That he sholde wonye with hem* where **A** (II 186) reads *For to wone wiþ hem*. From consideration of its easier grammar and greater explicitness **B**'s reading is not a revision but a variant substituted by an archetypal scribe. **C**'s form of the expression, *That lyare sholde wonye with hem* (II 237), indicates that the reviser's **B** manuscript contained the **B** archetype's scribal reading.

In III 36–46 the archetypal text of **B**, on comparison with **A**, is studded with unoriginal readings. Line 36, *he melled þise wordes* represents censorship of *mekeliche he loutide* (**A** III 35); in line 38, *lewed men and lered men*, the transposition reflects scribal promotion of the more sensational notion, and the twice-added noun is more explicit than **A**'s *lerid & lewide* (III 37); in line 41 *be þi bedeman and bere wel þi message* substitutes a censored and an easier reading respectively for *be þi baudekyn & bere wel þin arnede* (**A** III 40); line 42, *Conscience to torne* substitutes an explicit, more literal reading for the figurative *consience to felle* (**A** III 41); in line 46 *hire brocour als*[10] registers censorship of *hire baude aftir* (**A** III 45). The **C** reviser reduced **B** 36 and 37, tautologous after the archetypal substitution, to a single line, restoring something of the lost original sense in *myldeliche* (III 39). He was not satisfied with *bere wel þi message...Conscience to torne*, and rewrote **B** 41, 42, restoring the sense of *felle* in *brynge adoun Consience* (III 43). He rejected *hire brocour als*, replacing it with the lost expression of **B** 41, *bere wel here ernde* (**A** III 48). All these changes reflect not the putative **B** original but the archetypal text of **B** shown to be corrupt by comparison with **A**; two of its errors which the reviser let stand, *lewed men...lered men* (40) and *bedman* (43) preserve the archetypal **B** reading.

In III 98 the **B** archetype read *fir shal falle & brenne al to bloo askes* for original *& forbrenne at þe laste* (**A** III 87). The **B** reading records two distinct corruptions: unconscious omission of the prefix *for-* through connotational attraction (*fir* > *brenne*) with loss of a stave, and smoothing by substitution of a more emphatic and explicit, but actually less meaningful reading which incidentally produced a new but un-Langlandian alliteration *aabb*. The corresponding line in **C** (III 126) indicates that the reviser had a corrupt text before him: the stave word he restored, but he let *al to blew ayshes* stand.

In III 180 the **B** archetype read *Wel þow woost wernard but if þow wolt gabbe*; on comparison with **A** (III 167), *Wel þou wost consience but ȝif þou wilt leiȝe, wernard* and *gabbe* by their abusive emphasis, actually out of character since Meed is speaking more in sorrow than in anger (cp. 170 above), and because *wernard* embellishes the alliteration, appear as scribal substitutions. The text before the **C** reviser read like archetypal **B**: he rejected *wernard* for *weye* (a visual reflex of it) but *gabbe* he allowed to stand (III 226).

In IV 14, 15 the **B** archetype read *And ryt riȝt to Reson and rouneþ in*

[10] One late **B** manuscript has *baud* by correction.

his ere/And seide as þe kyng bad, where **A** (IV 14, 15) reads *And riȝt renneþ...as þe king sente*. From its easier meaning,[11] and the likelihood of inducement to substitution by *ryde* in line 7 above, *ryt riȝt* is a scribal variant of *riȝt renneþ*; similarly *bad*, as more explicit and incidentally unmetrical, glosses original *sente*. **C** IV 14 *rood forth* rejects the jingle of **B**; *sayde hym as þe kyng sayde* (15) repairs the alliteration made imperfect by *bad*. But **C**'s *rood* reflects the verb of the corrupt archetypal **B** text.

In the archetypal text of **B** IV 21 the saddle is to be kept on Suffer-till-I-see-my-time *wiþ witty wordes gerþes*, in **A** (IV 19) *wiþ wytful gerþis*. **B**'s variant here is a scribal substitution of an easier reading, additionally attractive as increasing the alliteration, for a manifestly difficult expression.[12] The **C** reviser rejects *witty wordes*. But from the character of his revision this stood in the text before him, for he reproduces the sense of the expression which he could not tolerate: *auyseth-þe-byfore* (IV 21) are in fact *witty wordes*.

In IV 102 archetypal **B** read *So þat þe kyng assente I kan seye no bettre*, where **A** (IV 89) reads *So þat ȝe assente I can sey no more*. Comparison indicates two unoriginal readings in the **B** line: *þe kyng* is a more explicit substitution by a scribe who forgot or failed to note that Peace is actually addressing the king (98 above); *bettre* is an elegant stylistic variation to eliminate repetition. **C**'s revision, a rearrangement and compression of **B** 101–3, was from a manuscript containing the unoriginal **B** substitution *kyng* for *ȝe*, which survives in **C** IV 98.

In V 76 the archetypal **B** text read, of Envy confessing, *carefully mea culpa he comsed to shewe*, where **A** reads *carfulliche his cope comsiþ he to shewe* (V 59). On consideration of the difficulty of *cope*,[13] the possibility of visual inducement to substitution by a form *coulpe/culpe*,[14] and the actual inappropriateness of *mea culpa* to the sense, the **B** reading is scribal. **C** reads *cryede mea culpa corsynge alle his enemyes* (VI 64); otherwise entirely recast, and with a new point, this revision nevertheless incorporates the archetypal substitution of **B**.

In VI 23 the **B** archetype read *Ac kenne me quod þe knyȝt and by crist I wole assaye* where **A** reads *& I wile conne eren* (VII 25). On comparison **B**'s variation is a scribal substitution occasioned by the difficulty of

[11] Vol. I, p. 439.
[12] The perplexities of **A** scribes over *wytful* are apparent from **A** variants; see Vol. I, p. 255.
[13] Vol. I, pp. 440, 441.
[14] See **A** variants, Vol. I, p. 276.

conne,[15] and maintaining the alliteration by repeating the oath of 21 above, but losing the implications of the pun in *teme* (22) which *conne* suggests. The **C** reviser's dissatisfaction with the line in his **B** manuscript appears from his having recast it as two (VIII 21, 22); that this line was in the corrupt form of the **B** archetype is indicated by the presence of *by Crist* and *assaye* in **C**'s revision.

In VI 65 the **B** archetype read *whoso helpeþ me to erie or sowe er I wende*, where **A** (VII 59) reads *or any þing swynke*. **B**'s variant, as a more explicit reading suggested by 63 above, is an archetypal scribe's substitution. The **C** reviser's manuscript contained the archetypal corruption: he would not have Piers helped with the sowing, which by now for him had symbolical value,[16] but he accepted the specification of a second task in the corrupt copy before him, and his particular choice was evidently induced by the shape of *wende* (>*wedy* **C** VIII 66).

In VI 108, 109 the **B** archetype read *Therwiþ was Perkyn apayed and preised hem faste/Oþere werkmen þer were þat wroȝten ful ȝerne*, where **A** (VII 100, 101) reads *preisid hem ȝerne...wrouȝte ful faste*. On the ground of the inferior sense of *preisen faste* this difference is not to be ascribed to authorial revision: it represents either scribal anticipation of copy followed by smoothing through insertion of the supplanted expression or simply the scribe's inaccurate recollection. C's revision replaced the objectionable *preised hem faste* with *payede wel hem here huyre* (VIII 115); but that the **B** lines before him had the corrupt reading of the archetype is evident from the survival of *wrouhten fol ȝerne* in the following **C** line.

In VI 116 the **B** archetype read *holpen ere his half acre* where **A** (VII 108) reads *þe half akir*. Unless the revising **B** poet specifically intended to attribute ownership of the land to Piers the archetypal **B** reading is not revision and must be explained as scribal substitution, either of a (mistakenly) more explicit term, or of one induced by the alliteration. **C** (VIII 123), reading *this half aker*, rejected the notion that the field is Piers's property, which would, of course, make nonsense of the allegory. Meanwhile the shape of the word he preferred indicates that the reading of the **B** manuscript before him was *his*.[17]

In the archetypal **B** text VI 223, 224 appear as a single line, *That nedy ben and nouȝty help hem wiþ þi goodes*, where **A** (VII 209, 210) has

[15] See Vol. I, pp. 446 and (for the difficulties of **A** scribes) 315.
[16] From **B** XIX 274ff., esp. 289, 297.
[17] The **B** manuscript W's variation to *þis* is coincidental. There is no evidence that W was corrected from a **C** manuscript.

two: *Þat nedy ben or nakid & nouȝt han to spende/Wiþ mete or wiþ mone let make hem fare þe betere.* **B**'s line does not alliterate; its first half contains an echo of **A** 209, and its second is a prose paraphrase of **A** 210. On these grounds **B**'s text is no revision but a scribal corruption of an original which read like **A**. In **C** (VIII 232, 233) there are two new lines; by the presence of *hem helpe* in the first they reflect not our presumptive original **B** but the corrupt archetypal form of the line.

In VI 296 the archetypal **B** text read *Al hunger eet in haste* where **A** (VII 280) reads *Hungir eet þis in haste.* As a more emphatic variation also found in several **A** manuscripts[18] **B**'s reading *Al* is a scribal substitution. In **C**, which reads *Hunger eet al* (VIII 318), the rhythmic stress again falls more significantly on the personification as in **A**; but the presence of *al* indicates that the reviser was correcting a line which had the archetypal **B** reading.

In VIII 22, 23 the **B** archetype read *And whoso synneþ I seide dooþ yuele as me þynkeþ/And dowel and do yuele mowe noȝt dwelle togideres*; **A** (IX 18, 19) reads *Ac whoso synneþ I seiȝe sertis me þinkiþ/Þat dowel & do euele* etc. **B**'s more explicit statement, markedly easier grammar, and less pregnant meaning identify the source of the difference as scribal substitution. **C** rewrote line 22 as two lines (X 25, 26); the presence in his revised form of three of **B**'s substitutions (*And* for *Ac* in 25, preterite *sayde* for the present, and *doth euele* in 26) indicates that he was working from a manuscript which contained the archetypal errors.

In VIII 85 the **B** archetype read *Dobet dooþ riȝt þus ac he dooþ muche moore* where **A** (IX 76) reads *Dobet þus doþ.* **B**'s reading is for a start more emphatic; in addition, because *riȝt þus* diminishes the stress on *dooþ*, it weakens the characteristic Langlandian *adnominatio.* On these grounds **B**'s reading is a scribal substitution. **C**'s equivalent, *Dobet doth al this* (X 82), reflecting the word order and word shape of **B**, indicates that his **B** manuscript contained the archetypal **B** variation.

In VIII 87 the **B** archetype read *And helpeþ alle men after þat hem nedeþ*, in contrast with **A** (IX 78) *Whiles he haþ ouȝt of his owene he helpiþ þere nede is.* The inferior doctrine of **B**'s line (compare VII 76ff) suggests an unoriginality confirmed in **C** (X 84) *And helpeth alle men of þat he may spare*, which returns to the sense of **A**. But the shape of **C**'s line indicates that this sense was reimposed on the archetypally corrupted **B** line.

[18] See apparatus, Vol. I, p. 343.

In IX 26, 27 the archetypal **B** text describes *Kynde* as *creatour of alle kynnes þynges/Fader and formour of al þat euere was maked*, where **A** (X 27, 28) reads *creatour of alle kenis bestis/...þe ferste of alle þing*. From the more emphatic expression and defective alliteration of **B**'s 27 the **B** variation is no revision but a scribal substitution of more inclusive and thus more emphatic *þynges* for *bestis*, with smoothing to avoid repetition. **C** eliminated the more emphatic *euere* of 27b, but his retention of *thynges* (X 152) and the shape of his revised 27b, *of al þat forth groweth* (X 153), indicate that he was working from the **B** archetype's scribal form of the line.

In IX 178, 179 the archetypal **B** text read *maidenes and maydenes macche yow togideres/Wideweres and Wodewes wercheþ þe same*; **A** (X 199, 200) reads *macche ȝow ysamme/...werchiþ riȝt also*. The difference is of scribal origin: **B**'s *togideres* is a gloss of the difficult word *ysamme*; in the next line *þe same* is a conscience-salving homœograph of the word just supplanted. **C** (X 280, 281) reads *marie ȝow togyderes/...weddeth (ȝow) ayþer oþer*. The reviser rejected *wercheþ þe same*, but the corrupt reading *togideres* of his scribal **B** manuscript he allowed to stand.

In X 19 the **B** archetype read *Whoso kan contreue deceites*, where **A** (XI 19) reads *Þat can construe deseites*. Of the two readings *construe*, 'construct'[19] is evidently much harder than *contreue*, 'contrive, devise', and the latter from its very common use with connotations of trickery[20] would naturally suggest itself as an easier alternative. From these considerations *contreue* appears as not a revision but a scribal substitution. The **C** reviser does not accept the **B** line, but rewrites, *Ho can caste and contreue* (XI 16). The presence of *Ho* and *contreue* in his revision reflects a line with the archetypal **B** reading.

In X 69 the **B** archetype read *I haue seiȝen it ofte* where **A** (XI 55) reads *seke it in Memento*. **B**'s variant here is a scribal substitution most probably occasioned by inability to read a contracted form of *Memento*. The **C** reviser firmly restored this word, but evidently from memory, for the verb in his version, *y say hit in memento* (XI 49) reflects the corruption of the **B** archetype.

In X 464 the **B** archetype read *þise konnynge clerkes þat konne manye bokes* where **A** (XI 308) reads *þise kete clerkis*. **B**'s variant, as a much easier term with diminished meaning, is a scribal substitution, which

19 *NED Construe* v., 1. *MED construen* v. 5b, 'settle quarrels' is quite wrong.

20 See *MED contreven* v. 4, 'plan with intent to deceive' for many instances.

will have been induced by following *konne*. The **C** reviser rewrites the line; his revised form, *clerkes most knowyng in konnyng* (XI 290) clearly indicates that he had before him one which read like that of the archetypal **B** text.

Some 100 instances have been presented where, on comparison with the **A** version, the archetypal reading of **B** appears as a scribal corruption of the **A** reading and the **C** version reads like **B**. In more than twenty others, where again on comparison with **A** the archetypal **B** reading appeared scribal, the corresponding **C** text, while evidently revised, reflects not a presumptive original **B** but the archetypal reading. Excluding the possibility that this situation was created by inept **A**⟩**B** revision, or by authorial scribal error, or by coincident variation in the early archetypal traditions of **B** and **C**, we interpret it as indicating that the **C** reviser used a corrupt scribal **B** manuscript.

We find that interpretation confirmed in yet other instances where, although the **A** version is not available for comparison, we confidently identify scribal corruption in the **B** tradition, and where either the unrevised **C** version has the presumedly corrupt **B** reading or a revised **C** version reflects a corrupt **B** reading and must derive from it. We cite first those instances where **C** is unrevised.

There are two lines where the unoriginality of the archetypal **B** reading, also found in **C**, is evident from the inferiority of the sense.

In XI 60 the archetypal **B** text read *Til I foryat youþe and yarn into Elde*. Here the suspicious element is *foryat*, for which no contextually appropriate meaning seems recorded.[21] The sense required by the context is either 'go from, forsake, leave', provided by *forgo* (*NED* s.v.4; *MED forgon*, v.1b) or 'lose, be deprived of' (MED *forgon* v.2). Therefore we conjecture *foryede*, assuming corruption by visual error. Like the archetypal **B** text **C** (XII 13) has an unoriginal reading *forȝet*.

In XVII 94 archetypal **B** read *May no medicyne vnder molde þe man to heele brynge* (*on molde* records sophisticating further variation by one genetic group). This is contextually not meaningful. The 'medicine' is to be Christ's redeeming blood, and thereafter the sacraments of confession and communion. The obvious original reading, restorable

[21] We cannot accept *MED*'s classification of this instance (*foryeten* v. 4c); the *Piers Plowman* quotation stands out like a sore thumb in the paragraph of examples.

on the suggestion of *vnder*, is *vnder mone*, 'sublunary, earthly, subject to decay', which we have adopted. The **C** text here (XIX 84) reproduces the corrupt reading of the **B** archetype.

A rather larger number of corrupt archetypal **B** lines which survive in **C** are identifiable as such from their metrical character. In some cases the corruption is readily accounted for and the original can be easily and confidently restored. In others, while the defective character of the line is clearly evident, it is possible only to conjecture.[22] For instance in I 160, *And a meene as þe Mair is bitwene þe kyng & þe commune*, scanning *aaxa*, there is every likelihood that the word order of the second half-line is unoriginal, recording either memorial contamination from Prologue 121 or substitution of a sequence corresponding to the difference of degree. The sense of the passage, identifying the interest of the intermediacy, from the lower to the higher, corresponds to the alliterative norm *aaax*, and thus points to an original *bitwene þe commune & þe kyng*. (**C** I 156 reads as does the **B** archetype.) But reconstruction is not always so easy. In V 173 the **B** archetype read *And doon me faste frydayes to breed and to watre*, scanning *aaxy*. Evidently a stave, whether on *f* or *d*, was lost from the second half-line. The context suggests that it was a term signifying food of poor quality. This, to be sure, our conjecture *þerf* supplies;[23] and if it was original the unobvious and therefore slightly difficult *f þ* alliteration might in several ways have led to its omission. We offer *þerf breed* because we do not know a more likely original. What we do assert confidently is that the line in archetypal **B** (and also in **C** at VI 155) is scribal in form. The element of doubt does not extend to the unoriginality of **B**.

The metrical deficiencies of these lines are of kinds which, in observable conditions, were created by scribal substitutions.[24] In addition to the two instances just discussed, where the **B** archetype has a line with inferior alliteration, which is therefore presumed scribal, and where the corresponding line in the **C** version is like that of the **B** archetype, there are the following.

B V 440:**C** VII 54 (*aaxy*); **B** IX 185:**C** X 286 (*axay* and *abba*); **B** IX 202:**C** X 301 (*axay*); **B** X 307:**C** V 154 (*aaxy*); **B** X 319:**C** V 165 (*aaxy*); **B** XI 14:**C** XI 173 (*abab*); **B** XII 101:**C** XIV 46 (*aaxa*); **B** XII 162:**C** XIV 106 (*xaay*); **B** XII 291:**C** XIV 213 (*aaxy* etc.); **B** XIV 226:**C** XVI 67 (*xaay*); **B** XIV 271:**C** XVI 111 (*xaay*); **B** XV

[22] Our position respecting conjectural emendation is described below, pp. 190ff.

[23] See the Vernon variant to **A** VII 266, Vol. I, p. 342 and *NED* s.v. *Tharf, a.*

[24] See below, pp. 131ff.

63:C XVI 225 (*aabb*); **B** XV 114:**C** XVI 269 (*xaaa*); **B** XV 492:**C** XVII 187 (*aaxa*); **B** XVI 33:**C** XVIII 37 (*aaxy* or *aabb*); **B** XVI 192:**C** XVIII 201 (*aaxa*); **B** XVII 33:**C** XIX 34 (*axay*); **B** XVII 227:**C** XIX 193 (*aaxa*); **B** XVII 247:**C** XIX 213 (*xaay* or *abab*); **B** XVII 282:**C** XIX 263 (*misdivision from preceding line*); **B** XVII 301:**C** XIX 281 (*aaxy*); **B** XVIII 180; **C** XX 183 (*xaay*); **B** XVIII 223: **C** XX 232 (*xaay*); **B** XVIII 239:**C** XX 248 (*aaxy*); **B** XVIII 295:**C** XX 325 (*aaxy*).[25]

The indication of the above instances of **BC** agreement in readings which can be identified as scribal without the assistance of the **A** version is repeated in the second type of situation, where **A** is again not available for comparison, but where for good editorial reasons the readings of the archetypal **B** text are identifiable as corruptions of originals which can be restored or conjectured with some confidence. In this situation **C** is revised, and the **C** revision has features which make it seem to derive not from the presumptive original **B** reading but from the presumedly corrupt archetypal reading of **B**. Clear instances of this kind are not numerous, but they are striking.[26]

In VI 162, 163 the **B** archetype read *For þo wasten and wynnen noȝt and þat ilke while Worþ neuere plentee among þe peple þe while my plowȝ liggeþ*. On several distinct grounds the text of these two lines is scribal: 162's unLanglandian scansion *aaxa*; the uncharacteristic (because not meaningful) repetition of *while*; the wordiness and pointless emphasis of 162b; the presence of a *w* alliteration at the beginning of 163; and the known resistance of scribes to run-on lines, all indicate a misdivision with padding. This is easily correctable: *þat ilke while* represents an original adverb of time, and the original line-division left the stave *Worþ* in 162 thus: *and* [*þo*] *worþ neuere*/ *Plentee*. The **C** reviser rejected the archetypal **B** form of the line, even to the extent of eliminating the second, presumably original *while*. But his revision, *For ther worth no plente quod Perus and þe plouh lygge* (VIII 160) preserves the misdivision of the archetypal text which was a feature of his **B** manuscript.

In VII 35 the **B** archetype read *no deuel shal yow dere ne fere yow in youre deying*. Here again the inferior alliterative pattern *aaxa* is suspect; the likelihood of substitution of an easier prose order and the added possibility of *dere* ⟨ *fere* attraction argue powerfully for an original which read *ne in youre deying fere yow*. **C**'s revision, *ne despeyre in ȝoure deynge* (IX 38) advances the stave in the second half line to its normative

[25] Our emendations of these lines are discussed below, pp. 206ff.

[26] For a discussion of restoration of the original **B** reading with the help of revised **C** see below, pp. 179ff.

position by substituting for *fere* a notion taken from **B** 36, which is then altogether omitted; but the revised line reflects the prose order of archetypal **B**.

In XI 301, 302 the archetypal **B** text read

> *He haþ moore bileue as I leue to lacche þoruȝ his croune*
> *Cure þan for konnyng or knowen for clene of berynge*
> *I haue wonder for why and wherfore þe bisshop*
> *Makeþ swiche preestes þat lewed men bitrayen.*

The topic of discussion is priests without either learning or patronage, who have only a tonsure and a worthless guarantee of support[27] to keep themselves with. In that context 301 is deficient in appropriate meaning, for it lacks an expected negative. The first half of line 302 makes no sense and the whole line fails to follow on from 301. The two lines are in fact untranslatable as they stand. We have little doubt that they are seriously corrupt, and that the original sense is recovered in our emendation. The source of the corruption is identifiable: scribal misreading of polysemous *bileue*, 'livelihood', as 'faith, credit', induced partly by the difficulty of the word and partly by original deferment of the comparative *moore* to 302. This misreading occasioned omission of a contextually necessary and therefore presumptively original negative in 301. The absence of that negative gave rise to further corruption: substitution of *haþ* for an original auxiliary of predication (again contextually indicated); and attraction of *moore* to the new verb from its original position at the beginning of 302. The third and fourth lines quoted above make sense; but one is tautologous and trite; the other is unmetrical. Together they prosily anticipate the powerful and contextually integral lines 311–14 below. On these grounds we identify them as spurious, stimulated by scribal participation in the speaker's criticism and satisfying an impulse to formulate this clearly.[28] In the **C** version 301 and 302 are absent: the implication is that the reviser omitted them because he found them corrupt beyond easy repair in his **B** manuscript. He also found there the two spurious lines following 302; this is clear from **C** XIII 115, 116 which correspond to them, both generally in reproaching lax bishops and particularly in the position of *lewede* (116), the same as that in the second spurious archetypal **B** line.

[27] See *NED* s.v. *Title* sb. 8.

[28] For a discussion of spurious lines in the **B** archetype see below, p. 193.

In XII 130 the **B** archetype read *Lyueris toforn vs vseden to marke.* The total absence of alliteration from this line indicates that it embodies at least two substitutions. Our restoration identifies a surviving stave in the second syllable of the emphatically placed *toforn,* and explains *Lyueris* and *vseden* as visual errors for *Dyuyneris* and *viseden,* the presumptive original having scanned *Dyuýneris tofórn víseden.* In **C** the line is rewritten as part of a larger revision: *And markede hit in here manere and mused þeron to knowe* (XIV 74); *mused* echoes *vseden* of the corrupt archetypal **B** reading.

In XII 146 the **B** archetype read *Ne in none beggers cote was þat barn born*; the alliteration, lacking one stave, indicates corruption. The easiest variation, and the likeliest to have produced this condition is substitution of *was* for original *nas* by a scribe who failed to perceive the exaggerated negative emphasis *Né nóne nás* required by the sarcastic context, perhaps through distraction by the secondary alliteration on *b*.[29] That the **C** poet disliked the line as he found it in his **B** manuscript appears from his having rewritten it on a new stave sound: *Ne in no cote ne Caytyfs hous crist was ybore* (XIV 90); the positive *was* in his revision reflects the archetypal **B** reading.

In XIII 106 the **B** archetype read *By þis day sire doctour quod I þanne be ye noȝt in dowel.* The alliterative pattern *aaxa* indicates that the second half-line acquired its archetypal form through scribal prosification of original *þanne in dowel be ye noȝt*.[30] The **C** poet rewrote the line as two (XV 114, 115): the position of *dowel* at the end of the second, reflecting its place in archetypal **B**, is evidence that he was working with a **B** copy which contained that corruption.

In XV 321 the **B** archetype read *Er þei amortisede to monkes or Chanons hir rentes,* with an alliterative pattern *aaxy* which points to scribal substitution in the second half-line. The obvious original reading is *monyales,* for which *Chanons* could readily have been substituted, unconsciously, by inducement of the common collocation (cp. X 324), or consciously, whether from the scribe's personal choice of unworthy recipients of benefactions, or even out of regard for the other sex. **C** repairs the damaged alliteration: *Ar they amorteysed eny more for monkes or for Chanouns* (XVII 55); but the presence of *Chanouns* in his

[29] This, as it should be noted, characteristically introduces the primary alliteration of the following line.

[30] For other instances of such prosifying damage see below, pp. 180, 194.

revision shows that he was working from a **B** manuscript with the corrupt archetypal reading.

In XV 504–69 the archetypal **B** text has another order than the one we print, lines 533–69 coming before 504–32. Our grounds for believing that this archetypal order is the result of an early scribal error, and that the original sequence was the one we have adopted are briefly: the inconsequence of the discourse in the archetypal text; its superior coherence as we have conjecturally rearranged it; and the existence of textual features to account for the presumed dislocation.[31] In the **C** version the corresponding passage has the same order as that of the **B** archetype: **C** XVII 193–250 are our XV 533–69, and **C** XVII 254–81 are our XV 504–32. The differences between the two versions[32] have the appearance of attempts to improve a defective sequence, as if the **C** reviser had experienced the same sense of inconsequence which first led us to suspect textual corruption. Our relevant point here is that in his **B** manuscript the order of these two passages was that of the **B** archetype, which we presume scribal.

In XVIII 71, finally, the **B** archetype read *Two þeues also þoled deeþ þat tyme,* with an alliterative pattern *xaaa* which must be scribal. The line is easily restored. The corruption took the form either of unconscious transposition of two notions through imperfect recollection, or of anticipation of copy followed by supply of an expression containing the ousted notion; the original, there seems little doubt, read *Two þeues þat tyme þoled deeþ also.* **C** reads *Two theues tho tholed deth þat tyme* (XX 73). The lost stave has been replaced, but the expression *þat tyme*, surviving in the position it occupied in the corrupt archetypal **B** text, indicates the scribal character of the **C** reviser's manuscript.

In this demonstration we have so far cited no evidence from **B** XIX and XX (**C** XXI, XXII). These passus are a special case: here there is no revision in **C**.[33] Notwithstanding that circumstance the **C** manuscripts in XXI and XXII maintain the same genetic relation as in the earlier, revised part of the poem; in that sense they are still '**C**' manuscripts. But now in the absence of revision they also represent a second, distinct and substantive tradition of the **B** version. This second tradition ultimately shares an exclusive common ancestor with the first: a manuscript in the archetypal **B** tradition earlier than the exclusive

[31] The argument is set out at length below, pp. 176ff.

[32] Discussed below, p. 177.

[33] On this see below, pp. 124, 125ff.

common ancestor of the surviving **B** manuscripts. Therefore in **C** XXI and XXII the **C** manuscript tradition represented by the archetype of the surviving **C** copies must reflect not only that ultimate exclusive common ancestor, but also the **C** reviser's **B** manuscript, the quality of the archetypal **B** tradition at the moment when the **C** reviser's **B** manuscript was generated, and its closeness to or remoteness from original **B** at that stage. Comparison of the archetypal texts of **B** and **C** in these passus reveals the presence in the **C** archetype of a number of unoriginal readings also found in **B**. It thus provides a further demonstration for all **C** that the reviser worked from a scribal **B** manuscript.

This evidence we now present, confining ourselves to clear instances of identifiable corruption where the agreement of the **B** and **C** archetypal readings is beyond doubt. There are for a start two lines where the poor quality of the meaning points unmistakably to scribal substitution.

In **B** XX 215 (**C** XXII 215) where the archetypes read *bisegede sooþly wiþ seuene grete geaunt3*, the adverb *sooþly* quite lacks contextual point. The veracity of the statement does not need support; the adverb should apply to the conduct of the siege. The scribal origin of *sooþly* is confirmed by the existence of a word which is both contextually and metrically apt and could by its relatively difficult use and partial synonymity have given rise to substitution of the archetypal reading: the presumed original *sikerly*, 'In a secure manner, firmly, fast' (*NED* s.v. *Sickerly* 5) has also a more immediate sense, 'certainly, assuredly', (s.v.2), which is reflected in *sooþly*.

In XX 236 (XXII 236) the archetypes read *chele and cheitiftee pouerte*. This is scribal from its grammar: the two words at the end of the line are nouns and cannot both be original.[34] The corruption is readily accounted for: the original read simply *chele and cheitiftee*, and *pouerte* derives from an early marginal gloss identifying the applicable sense of an ambiguous term, which was subsequently copied into the archetypal text.

The majority of unoriginal lines in these two passus draw attention to themselves by defective alliteration. Two which are certainly corrupt

[34] Nor can the adjective *chaitif/caitif* which occurs as a manuscript variant in both traditions. It is unlikely to have given rise to a variant *cheitiftee*, and is to be explained as coincident scribal smoothing of the archetype's grammatical anomaly.

we cannot confidently restore. One is XIX 240 (XXI 240), scanning *aaxy*, where from context the corruption is likely to have arisen through substitution of an easier reading. The other, XIX 442 (XXI 442), *xaay*, might have been corrupted through enthusiastic scribal participation in the sentiment it expresses.[35] In the case of the rest we identify the types of variation responsible for corruption with some confidence.

Two, XIX 60 (XXI 60), *xaaa*, and XIX 345 (XXI 345), *aaxa*, received their archetypal form through unconscious substitution of prose order. Two others, XIX 212 (XXI 212), and XIX 321[36] (XXI 321), *aabb* and *aaxy*, were evidently corrupted through substitution of a term of commoner collocation. In XIX 270 (XXI 270), *aaxa*, subconscious inducement to parallelism explains the unsatisfactory alliteration. In XIX 235 (XXI 235), *xaay*, a stave word appears to have been ousted by a synonymous but unalliterative variant from the preceding context. In XIX 368 (XXI 368), *aabb*, substitution induced by a closely preceding word destroyed the alliteration. In XX 354 (XXII 354), *aaxa*, the source of disturbance seems to have been dislocation through attraction to an assonant word (*hen-* ⟨ *en-*).

Substitution of an easier reading accounts for the inferior alliteration of seven other lines in the **B** and **C** archetypes of these passus. In XIX 229 (XXI 229) where at one stage the archetypes read *Some men he yaf wit*, scanning *xaay* or *xaaa*, *men/zero*[37] stands for original *wyes*. XIX 301 (XXI 301) scans *xaay*, lacking a stave on *s* or *sh* in the first half-line; this, originally, was very likely *Shal* in its unobvious and therefore difficult sense of necessity or inevitability (*NED* s.v. *Shall* 3). In XIX 316 (XXI 316), *aaxy*, the corruption was evidently in the first half-line;[38] the alliteration here can be restored by conjecturing substitution of *after* for original *to* with the less usual sense 'in accordance with' (*NED* s.v. *To* prep.20),[39] instanced in XVI 158 above. In XIX 409 (XXI 409) the alliteration is defective whether scanned on *m* (*aaxy*) or on *l* (*xaay*). From the sense the form of the second half-line is probably original; the scribal element in the first half-line is likely to be *man*, for which we conjecture original *lif*, with punning implications, rather

[35] These cruces are discussed below, pp. 207, 208.

[36] The lost original reading appears from XVIII 48.

[37] *men* was omitted at a later stage of archetypal **B** transmission, probably through inducement of preceding *Som-me* or *So-me*.

[38] From considerations of sense the second half-line must be original. Therefore, evidently, the original alliterative pattern was *aaa//xy*. For this see below, p. 138.

[39] For other uses of prepositions as staves see below, pp. 134, 135.

than *lede*.[40] In XX 307 (XXII 307) the original alliteration seems not at first identifiable; but it is unlikely to have been on *w*, since original *wikked werkes* is too easy and aptly emphatic to have generated corruption. A likelier source of substitution is *mysfetes* (cp. *mysfeet*, **B** XI 375), the line having originally scanned *aaaxy*, *Fór mysfétes þéi*. In XX 372 (XXII 372) the scansion *aaxa* indicates at least disturbance of original word order in the second half-line. As an evident stave word *synnes* must be original; moved to the normal stave position in a second half-line it reveals the probable original reading, *synnes of kynde*, with enough unexpressed relevance to be very difficult.

There remain in the last two passus five points of agreement between the archetypal texts of **B** and **C** in somewhat more complex unoriginal readings, the majority signalled by unsatisfactory alliteration. At XIX 302, 303 (XXI 302, 303) both archetypes set out these two lines as three, of which the middle one, composed of the padded end and beginning of two original lines, reads *Hem þat ben gilty And for to correcte*, without alliteration. The misdivision and this padding were a feature of the exclusive common ancestor of the two traditions, which the further variation in the **B** tradition does not obscure. At XIX 348 (XXI 348) both archetypes set out the line as two:

That Conscience shal noȝt knowe by contricion
Ne by Confession who is cristene or heþene.

Here unoriginality is indicated not merely by the metrical inadequacy of the second line but also, if we understand the allegory correctly, by the bad sense of the two. This agreement in unoriginality is explained by very early intrusion of a misguided gloss, *by contricion ne by Confession*, into the text, with consequent redivision. Similarly for XX 292 (XXII 292) both archetypes read two lines:

A parcel to preye for hem and make hem murye
Wiþ þe remenaunt þat oþere men biswonke.

Both the absence of a third stave from the first line, as of any alliteration at all from the pure prose of the second, and the echo of 289 in the pair, make it clear that the form of these lines cannot be original. The corruption will have begun with substitution of unalliterating *make hem mery*, by memorial contamination (cp. 289 above), for some word

[40] One **C** manuscript reads *leode*, probably as a metrical correction.

like our conjectured *pleye*; thereafter the now unduly long line would be divided and its second part padded.[41] At XX 325, 326 (XXII 325, 326) both archetypes divide the lines after *to curen* and pad out 326 with *he were* after *curatour*. This robs 326 of its first stave, the absence of which is evidence of unoriginality. The source of this corruption will have been the scribal tendency to complete the sense of an expression within the line.

Finally the **B** and **C** archetypes agree in unmistakable and complex scribal error at XIX 183–5 (XXI 183–5) where both read, of Christ's last action on earth, that he

> *...yaf Piers power and pardon he grauntede*
> *To alle maner men mercy and forȝifnesse*
> *Hym*[42] *myght men to assoille of alle manere synnes.*

The first indication of unoriginality is the impossible grammar of *Hym myght*; the next is deficiency of sense, in the failure of the second and third lines to follow on consecutively from the first. The only verb which can have governed *Hym* is *grauntede*; a further indication of unoriginality appears when on the strength of this *Hym* is detached from *myght*, and the force of *myght* as a noun is felt: the third line in the archetypal order manifestly should be the second, as has already been suggested by the grammatical cohesion of *grauntede hym*. And when this rearrangement is made a final sign of unoriginality reveals itself: *power* and *pardon*, since *myght* is now in apposition to *power*, are in the wrong order.[43] A part of the confirmation of these indications of corruption in the passage is the availability of explanations for the posited substitutions. Misdivision separating *grauntede hym* occurred while the lines were in their original order, probably by *h‸ym* > *my‸ght* attraction. Unconscious transposition of original 184 and 185 was induced by the analogous wording and sense of the lines. For the transposition of *pardon* and *power* two explanations are possible: memorial contamination from 188 below, or smoothing after the transposition of the second and third lines. These processes belong to the early phase of archetypal **B** transmission. The ruin they created was

[41] The **B** tradition's further variation, adding *þe residue and*, records a subsequent attempt to furnish the second line with at least some sort of alliteration, perhaps from recollection of V 459 or VI 100.

[42] One **C** family reads *And ȝaf hym*; this is relatively late scribal smoothing on the suggestion of 183.

[43] A single **C** manuscript has the right order, by felicitous variation from the archetype.

present in the exclusive common ancestor of the **B** and **C** manuscript traditions, and thus in the manuscript used by the **C** reviser, which is unmistakably revealed in these last two unrevised passus as a scribal copy.

In the above demonstration we interpreted five distinct classes of evidence. The first four were from the part of *Piers Plowman* where the **B** version has been revised, that is to the end of **B** XVIII: agreements between **B** and **C** in readings which, compared with those of **A**, appeared scribal; agreements between **B** and **C** in readings which on absolute editorial grounds appeared scribal; instances where archetypal **B** readings judged corrupt on comparison with **A** were reflected in revised **C**; and instances where **B** readings judged corrupt on absolute editorial grounds were reflected in revised **C**. The uniform indication of these four classes, that the **C** reviser used a scribal **B** manuscript, was confirmed in the fifth class, taken from the last two passus of the poem where there was no revision and where, aside from further variation, the **C** tradition of manuscripts must reproduce the **C** reviser's **B** copy; here again there were agreements of the archetypal **B** and **C** texts in scribal readings. The reiterative import of these numerous and various textual situations seems to us conclusive.

We did not come easily or quickly to this position; we were forced to it by the evidence. Undoubtedly the notion of the **C** reviser's 'extraordinarily good MS. of the B-text',[44] which figured in the authorship controversy, influenced our thinking.[45] There was, further, a biographical preconception that 'Langland is not likely to have had a clean copy of the poem in his possession', and also the authoritative opinion that it would have been easier for a fourteenth-century poet to revise in his 'foul papers' than in a fair copy of his poem.[46]

But these grounds for our reluctance turned out to be poor. It quickly became evident that the **C** reviser's **B** manuscript need not have been 'extraordinarily good' to be in many places of superior originality to the

[44] Chambers, R. W., and J. H. G. Grattan, 'The Text of "Piers Plowman" ', *MLR*, xxvi (1931), p. 11.

[45] Chambers and Grattan (op. cit., p. 37) had very cautiously qualified their position: 'It is no part of the theory of single authorship to assume that William Langland made his new texts necessarily from the original rough drafts of his earlier texts.' But for one of us, at one period, 'extraordinarily good' meant 'very near to the autograph' if not actually that autograph. (Kane, ' "Piers Plowman": Problems and Methods of Editing the B-Text', p. 9.)

[46] Bennett, H. S., 'The Production and Dissemination of Vernacular Manuscripts in the Fifteenth Century', *The Library*, fifth series, i (1947), pp. 177, 178.

archetype of the surviving **B** manuscripts. Instead of a probability of Langland having been so destitute that he could not afford a fair copy of his own poem, for which there is no evidence, we found a historical likelihood that if he did not have a place he had a patron or group of supporters.[47] And for the opinion that Langland would more easily have made changes on 'foul papers' than a fair copy we can discover no reason: it seems simply mistaken. For an author's own fair copy is at least as likely as not to have been unbound; thus there would be no necessary physical difficulty about rearranging its content. And its clean margins (probably handsomer than those in surviving manuscripts, which are most often cropped) would as any author knows not merely accommodate but actively invite additions and substitutions.

We came, finally, to realize that the question of Langland's methods of revision can be answered only absolutely and without regard to preconceptions in terms of the readings of the three versions of his poem, and further, without respect to other similar situations. The proposition that a fourteenth-century poet would make an imperfect scribal copy of his work the basis for a revision of it turns out to be no novelty and has been used to explain phenomena in the texts of works by Langland's near-contemporaries.[48] But we can see no precedent or authority in those instances: just as external evidence about fourteenth-century methods of revision is scarce and ambiguous,[49] so the data in

[47] See especially Tout, T. F., 'Literature and Learning in the English Civil Service in the Fourteenth Century', *Speculum*, iv (1929), pp. 381–2; Coulton, G. G., *Medieval Panorama*, Cambridge, 1938, pp. 580–1; also Bennett, H. S., 'The Author and His Public in the Fourteenth and Fifteenth Centuries', *Essays and Studies*, xxiii, Oxford, 1938, pp. 9–11; *Chaucer and the Fifteenth Century*, Oxford, 1948, p. 107. More specifically, Burrow, J., in 'The Audience of *Piers Plowman*', *Anglia*, lxxv (1957), pp. 373–84, has made the point that Langland's public was not of the market place or inn-yard; from its character his poem was directed to persons of education and therefore of some standing. This implies a patron or patrons, and the presumption is that one of these will have paid for making a necessarily postulated first, clean, scribal copy from which not only the manuscript tradition of **B** but also—all hypotheses apart—the tradition of **C** XXI and XXII must descend.

[48] Explicitly in Root, R. K., *The Book of Troilus and Criseyde*, Princeton, 1926, pp. lxxvi, lxxvii; Robinson, F. N., ed., *The Works of Geoffrey Chaucer*, 2nd edn, Cambridge, Mass., 1957, 'Textual Notes' to The Prologue to *The Legend of Good Women*, p. 913; Dempster G., 'Manly's Conception of the Early History of the *Canterbury Tales*', *PMLA*, lxi (1946), p. 380; and by implication in Macaulay, G. C., ed., *The English Works of John Gower*, i, EETS ES 81, London, 1900, pp. cxxx, cxxxi.

[49] We have been able to find very little. It seems that Higden entered his revisions of the *Polychronicon* in an autograph manuscript (Galbraith, V. H., 'An Autograph MS of Ranulph Higden's Polychronicon', *Huntington Library Quarterly*, xxiii (1959), pp. 1–18). De Deguileville, if he reports truthfully, had proposed to do the same with his *Pelerinage de Vie Humaine* (*The Pilgrimage of the Life of Man*, translated by John Lydgate, ed. Furnivall F. J., and K. B. Locock, EETS ES 77, 83, 92, London, 1899–1904, lines 218ff.). But Petrarch, although he seldom destroyed his rough papers, would sometimes revise in a scribal copy (Pasquali, G., *Storia della Tradizione e Critica del Testo*, 2nd edn, Florence, 1952, p. 439).

their cases appear slight or obscure or questionable by comparison with those in the manuscripts of the *Piers Plowman* versions.[50] The *Piers Plowman* problem is evidently *sui generis*, and whether Langland used an autograph or a scribal manuscript for his revisions is a matter to be determined entirely from the evidence of his own texts. Thus an interpretation of that evidence must stand or fall by its own quality.

We have faith in our conclusions, but we also recognize that our demonstration cannot, from the nature of the problem, amount to absolute proof. Its effectiveness depends generally on the enabling proposition of textual criticism, that it is possible in a sufficiently large number of cases to distinguish original from unoriginal readings, and more particularly on the degree to which we as editors have been successful in such distinction. It operates by assessments of probability to which no numerical criteria but only an editorial sense developed through experience can be applied. It is almost wholly empirical. These are qualifications that must be made, but having expressed them we will affirm that we can see no acceptable alternative to our conclusion, no better explanation for one class of the phenomena in a most intricate literary situation. As textual critics we have found it also the most illuminating.

The proposition that Langland used an extensively corrupted scribal copy of the **B** version for his revision to **C** raises three questions. First, what was the position of this manuscript in the **B** tradition? Second, how or why did Langland come to let so many corruptions stand in the manuscript he used for revision? Third, what in general was the character of his revision?

The first can be quickly answered. The **C** reviser's **B** manuscript represents an earlier stage in the archetypal tradition of **B** than does the exclusive common ancestor or archetype of the surviving **B** manuscripts;

[50] The several 'recensions' of *Confessio Amantis* are generally distinguished in comparatively small particulars (Macaulay, *English Works*, i, pp. cxxviiff.). The differences of content and arrangement between the 'forms' of *Troilus and Criseyde* are not very considerable (Root, pp. lxxiff.), and an old argument that they are of scribal origin (Brusendorff, A., *The Chaucer Tradition*, London, 1925, pp. 169ff.), which has never to our knowledge been dismissed, has great force. In the case of the Prologue to *The Legend of Good Women* where the scale of revision is considerable the order of versions is still problematic. As to the proposed author's variants in the manuscripts of *The Canterbury Tales* (for which see Manly, J. M., and E. Rickert, *The Text of the Canterbury Tales*, Chicago, 1940, ii, pp. 495ff., and Dempster, op. cit., pp. 384, 385, 396), the genuineness of a number of these has been questioned (Severs, J. B., 'Did Chaucer Revise the Clerk's Tale?', *Speculum*, xxi (1946), pp. 295–302; 'Author's Revision in Block C of the Canterbury Tales,' *Speculum*, xxix (1954), pp. 512–30); and it would not be hard to challenge others.

the latter is differentiated from it simply by further variation. Those unoriginal readings common to the archetypal texts of both **B** and **C**, and thus present in the **B** manuscript used by Langland for revision, were introduced in a first phase of transmission which ended with the copying of that manuscript. The additional unoriginal readings peculiar to the **B** archetype[51] were introduced in the second, subsequent phase which ended with the copying of that archetype, the exclusive common ancestor of the surviving **B** manuscripts. Thus the received opinion that the **C** reviser's **B** manuscript was a less corrupted copy than any that can be reconstructed from the evidence of the surviving **B** manuscripts is correct if correctly understood: for instance, in the more than 800 lines of the last two passus its text contained some twenty clearly identifiable unoriginal readings; the text of the exclusive common ancestor of the surviving **B** manuscripts embodies both these and more than 60 others acquired in the second phase of archetypal transmission. How many manuscript generations went to each phase seems not determinable, but there is some indication that copying in the first phase was professional.[52]

The answer to the next question, why Langland let stand so many of the unoriginal readings present in the scribal manuscript that he used for his second revision lies in the nature of that revision, as it appears from comparison of the texts of the two versions. As far as the present discussion is concerned[53] the most striking particular revealed by such comparison is the absence of revision from the last two passus of **C**.[54] This might conceivably signify that the poet was satisfied with these passus in their first form, but it seems more likely to us to indicate that

[51] See above, III, pp. 78ff.

[52] The variation in that phase gives the impression of being predominantly mechanical, or of answering to the common scribal tendencies of substitution; in the variation of the second phase deliberate, 'editorial' substitution, whether by sophistication and smoothing or by the addition of lines seems more noticeable.

[53] This volume is not the place for extended consideration of **B**>**C** revision, which is reserved for the editor of **C**. Meanwhile see Russell, G. H., 'The Salvation of the Heathen: the Exploration of a Theme in *Piers Plowman*', *Journal of the Warburg and Courtauld Institutes*, xxix (1966), pp. 102–4, and 'Some Aspects of the Process of Revision in *Piers Plowman*', in Hussey, S. S., ed., *Piers Plowman: Critical Approaches*, London, 1969, pp. 27–49.

[54] Between the archetypal texts of the two traditions in the more than 800 lines of these passus there are some 100 differences of substance. In every instance the difference lacks such qualities as would *a priori* suggest authorial revision; in all but a few the reading of one or the other version has the characteristics of a scribal substitution, and can be accounted for in terms of known variational patterns. Thus there are more than 50 differences where the reading of the archetypal **B** tradition looks like a scribal derivative of the reading of archetypal **C**; and more than 30 where the reverse is true. The residue comprises differences so slight and trifling that the editors have felt unable to identify originality with confidence. The absence of revision from these passus of **C** must not seem a matter of doubt.

his revision was not completed. For that conclusion there is support in the fact that a number of **C** revisions in other parts of the poem appear unfinished and imperfectly smoothed into the text.[55]

If on these indications Langland did not finish his revision of the poem it must appear that he also had not in any real sense 'finished with' revising **B** Prologue–XVIII when he broke off. For there is, further, no evidence that his revision was systematic, began with Prologue 1, and went forward passus by passus, and an intrinsic unlikelihood that it was so. The distribution of differences between the two versions suggests that he did not give equally close attention to all parts of Prologue–XVIII. At the same time he visibly reacted to many of the readings which we, for distinct modern editorial reasons, have identified as archetypally corrupt in **B**. The impression given is that when he did so this was not because he was æsthetically dissatisfied with what he believed he had earlier written but because he sensed that what lay before him was not as he had written it, was in an alien *usus scribendi*. We have already shown how some of his revisions of a corrupt expression contain traces of the actual corrupt reading to which he reacted.[56] If the meaning of a line in his **B** manuscript was inappropriate or inferior he would improve it;[57] if the alliteration of a line was defective through scribal substitution, rearrangement or misdivision he would rewrite and remetre it;[58] at a number of points he seems to have revised by simple cancellation;[59] occasionally it almost seems from the revised

[55] So Russell, 'Salvation of the Heathen', pp. 103, 104: 'the C revision was apparently left incomplete and...this incompleteness may be seen not only in the total absence of revision from the last two passus—which, after all, is capable of other explanations—but also in the shape in which lines and passages appear in the archetype of the surviving [C] manuscripts, a shape which, on occasions, does not suggest scribal corruption so much as authorial intention incompletely realized. This incompleteness may be revealed especially in lines that have the appearance of unfinished drafts and of passages transposed or altered but not adequately bedded down into their new contexts.' See also Russell, 'Some Aspects of the Process of Revision', *passim*.

[56] See above, pp. 104–11.

[57] See for example: **B** IV 162 (cp. **A** IV 138:**C** IV 157); **B** VI 298:**C** VIII 320; **B** XII 161:**C** XIV 105; **B** XIII 40:**C** XV 45; **B** XVI 157, 158:**C** XVIII 174, 175.

[58] See for example: **B** III 303:**C** III 457; **B** III 319:**C** III 472; **B** V 130:**C** VI 96; **B** V 414:**C** VII 29; **B** V 439:**C** VII 53; **B** VI 137:**C** VIII 144, 145; **B** VII 70, 71:**C** IX 66–8; **B** VIII 94:**C** X 91; **B** IX 27:**C** X 153; **B** X 432:**C** XI 268; **B** XI 149:**C** XII 84; **B** XI 437:**C** XIII 243; **B** XII 194:**C** XIV 133; **B** XIII 82:**C** XV 90; **B** XIII 106:**C** XV 114, 115; **B** XIV 62:**C** XV 260; **B** XV 224:**C** XVI 350; **B** XV 234:**C** XVI 360; **B** XV 295:**C** XVII 22; **B** XV 321:**C** XVII 55; **B** XV 324:**C** XVII 57, 58; **B** XVI 231:**C** XVIII 247, 248; **B** XVII 3:**C** XIX 3; **B** XVII 73:**C** XIX 72; **B** XVII 77:**C** XIX 76; **B** XVII 80:**C** XIX 77; **B** XVII 103:**C** XIX 93; **B** XVIII 2:**C** XX 2; **B** XVIII 113:**C** XX 116; **B** XVIII 374:**C** XX 416.

[59] For example, of unmetrical **B** lines: III 344–6, V 260, VI 138, IX 15, X 189, XV 164, XVII 90, 92; of dislocated lines or groups of lines: Prologue 189–92, XI 353, XIV 284–7, XVI 108–10, XVIII 6, 9, 316α, 317α, 318α; of lines corrupted to the point of meaninglessness: XI 301, 302; of a passage with only one corrupt line: XI 177–83 (corrupt in 182); of a longer, generally corrupt passage: XV 119–27.

form of a line as if he had been determined, when rewriting it, that it should not be as easily corrupted as the old one. We limit discussion to one example. At X 193 the **B** archetype reads *dobet and dobest ben of loues kynne*, unexceptionable allegory until compared with **A** (XI 145) *ben drawen of louis scole*, when it appears an easier reading. **C**'s correction *here doctour is dere loue* (XI 133) not only firmly restores **A**'s sense but suggests by the new wording an intention to reduce the possibility of further corruption.[60] The presence of an unacceptable expression or line or passage in his manuscript very often prompted him to fresh composition, such as rewriting the passage following or surrounding the corruption.[61] Even a spurious line could stimulate him;[62] indeed, 'where B is most corrupt C's revision is most heavy'.[63] All indications are that he revised or rewrote rather than restored his text, and the implication is strong that he did not have the means to do the latter.[64] It must clearly follow that he did not check or even very closely scrutinize the manuscript to be used for his revision before he began to revise;[65] but that those deficiencies in it which are corrected are the ones that caught the attention of an extraordinary sensibility;[66] that his revision was neither systematic nor thorough, was not necessarily consecutive, and was almost certainly never completed. This seems the required explanation of the survival of scribal readings from the **B** tradition in the **C** version of *Piers Plowman*. Whether Langland would ever have got round to removing them, and beyond that why he did not

[60] Other examples are **B** V 439:**C** VII 53; **B** VI 298:**C** VIII 320; **B** XII 161:**C** XIV 105; **B** XII 273:**C** XIV 195.

[61] We restrict ourselves to two examples of this common phenomenon. **B** VII 70, 71 are archetypally misdivided and 71 is unalliterative; at **C** IX 70ff there is inserted an extended treatment of the notion expressed in the corrupt **B** lines. **B** IX 69, 70 are archetypally run together with some loss of sense and a consequently different emphasis from that of the original; in **C** X 183ff an insertion develops the point more emphatically presented in corrupt **B**.

[62] Two such spurious lines following **B** XI 302 appear recast as unmistakably Langlandian verse at **C** XIII 115, 116.

[63] Russell, 'Salvation of the Heathen', p. 103.

[64] There are suggestions of restoration from memory, for example, where the sense of **B** is inferior or defective: **B** II 91:**C** II 98; **B** III 36–42:**C** III 39–49; **B** V 94, 95 (cp. **A** V 74, 75):**C** VI 69; **B** IX 27:**C** X 153; **B** XV 224:**C** XVI 350; **B** XVI 157, 158:**C** XVIII 174, 175; and where the alliteration of **B** is inferior or defective: **B** II 84:**C** II 91; **B** V 414:**C** VII 29; **B** VIII 112, 113: **C** X 108, 109; **B** XI 148, 149:**C** XII 83, 84; **B** XIV 62:**C** XV 260; **B** XV 237:**C** XVI 363; **B** XVII 297:**C** XIX 278. It would of course be quite impossible to establish any proof from examples of this kind.

[65] In this lack of a discipline which even the modern editor has to learn through hard experience Langland may not have been alone in his time. Dempster ('Manly's Conception of the Early History', pp. 380, 382) mentions the 'perfunctoriness' of Chaucer's 'proofreading of his scribes' copies' and refers to numerous 'indications that it was hasty and incomplete'.

[66] If there is need for proof of the common authorship of **B** and **C** evidence can be found in the extended demonstration of that sensibility afforded by the **C** revisions.

complete his revision must to some extent remain matters of speculation.[67] For the editors of both **B** and **C** the important consideration is that the uncompleted **C** version looks as if it had, so to speak, been seen through the scriptorium by a literary executor.

For the editors of **B** this has a particular force: the presumption that Langland used a scribal **B** manuscript when revising from **B** to **C**, and that the archetypal text of the **C** version embodies surviving unoriginal **B** readings, implies quite simply that agreement between the archetypal readings of the **B** and **C** manuscripts does not necessarily signify the originality of those readings.

[67] See, however, Kane, *Evidence for Authorship*, p. 33.

V

EDITING THE **B** VERSION

It must by now have appeared that the editing of the **B** version of *Piers Plowman*, if by editing is understood attempting to recover the original text of the poem, is no simple matter, and that the editors' methods are not so much indicated as dictated by the circumstances of its composition and transmission. The poem is the middle version of three, preserved in numerous manuscripts which abound in variation. In this situation the necessarily first editorial operation must be to recover the text of their exclusive common ancestor, the archetypal text of the surviving manuscripts. The second must of equal necessity be to compare that text with corresponding archetypal texts of **A** and **C**, the earlier and subsequent versions. The aim of these two operations is identical: to distinguish between authorial and scribal readings; they differ in that while the first is a matter of simple distinction since the question of revision does not arise in the visible tradition of **B**, in the second it is complex, involving discrimination between readings of which more than one may be authorial.

The findings of these two processes virtually prescribe a third, the absolute scrutiny of all readings however well attested. From comparison of variants in the visible **B** tradition it emerges that no single manuscript can have more authority than any other, since all are corrupted in similar ways and differ only in the degree of their identifiable corruption. Classification of the manuscripts further diminishes the already questionable authority of numerical support for readings both by its identification of a genetic group comprising as many as fourteen manuscripts, whose shared unoriginal readings result from a single history of substitution, and by its incidental demonstration of the necessarily extreme frequency of convergent variation. Comparison of the reconstructed archetypal text of **B** with those of **A** and **C**, whether in agreement or severally, reveals the occurrence of intensive scribal substitution in the archetypal tradition of **B**, in consequence of which many unoriginal **B** readings have unanimous or majority support.

Finally comparison of the text of **A** with that of **BC** brings to light a number of probably unoriginal readings present in the archetypes of both the **B** and **C** traditions, attested by all or most manuscripts of those two traditions. These findings combine to discredit manuscript authority: relative strength of attestation is altogether unreliable, and unanimous attestation even in several traditions by no means surely reliable evidence of originality.[1] Only the readings, ultimately, afford such evidence. This may be clear and positive, or obscure, or simply negative in proclaiming corruption, but it must be ultimately authoritative, and reliable if correctly interpreted.

These findings also determine our aim as editors. The archetype of the **B** manuscripts is exposed to scrutiny and control in five different textual situations. It can be variously compared with the text of **AC** or of **A** or of **C**, and also, when these comparisons have resulted in the presumptive delimitation of revision, often with a revised text of **C**. Finally where no corresponding text of **AC** or **A** or **C** exists it is subject to absolute scrutiny in terms of the results of the first four comparisons. In every case the indication is of massive corruption in the tradition from **B** original to archetype. With this knowledge continually brought home to us we are not able to view the conservative presentation of a reconstructed archetype of the surviving manuscripts as an 'edited' text otherwise than as a poor-spirited and slothful undertaking, of strictly limited value, moreover, with respect to recovery of the historical truth of the poem. The alternative has been to accept the logic of the situation, even if by doing so we seem to prefer foolhardiness to caution. In consequence our text is heavily emended, whether from the evidence of available **B** readings, or from that of other versions,[2] or conjecturally.

The means left to us, by which to confirm decisions about originality between variant readings in the **B** manuscripts, or to differentiate finally between authorial and scribal variations, or to assess absolutely the originality of unanimously or unambiguously attested archetypal readings are in fact those employed in the editing of the **A** version.[3]

[1] Compare Vol. I, p. 148: 'In practice unanimity of support must be accepted as establishing the strongest presumption of originality, unless the reading attested by all the manuscripts is patently unsatisfactory.' Full knowledge of variation in the **B** and **C** versions has brought home to the editor of **A** the force of the qualification which he there expressed.

[2] This is a more extended application of the reasoning set out in Vol. I, pp. 146f. The restrictions upon the use of evidence from other versions there expressed by the editor of **A** have not survived 'full knowledge of documents'.

[3] See Vol. I, pp. 115–46.

These criteria are essentially traditional, having been discovered during several centuries of editing classical texts, the *New Testament*, and the *Divine Comedy*,[4] and our own editing is radical only in the greater degree to which we have allowed their logical force. The editorial problems of the **B** version have shown us no cause for modifying them, only for extending their use. But since that extension is the main determinant of the character of our edition, which has little to offer anyone who will not accept it, we must necessarily illustrate our procedure.

The first is the *usus scribendi* of copyists, formed from the sum of *a priori* knowledge of the circumstances of manuscript transmission and of the common processes and characteristic effects of the axiomatic scribal debasement of texts.[5] The application of this criterion was not in general difficult. Mechanical error is easily recognizable; a more explicit or more emphatic or easier reading is not only identifiable as such but comes with experience to have a familiar, typically scribal quality; further variation to smooth a corruption in the exemplar is most often unmistakable.

The second is the *usus scribendi* of the poet, with respect to style, sense and versification. In its three particulars this is obviously more problematic.

To determine originality from the criterion of the relative or absolute appropriateness of readings to the poet's style is the obverse of identifying a scribal quality in them. Just as scribal variants tend to flat statement or crude overemphasis, diffuseness in denotation and loss of connotation, dilution of meaning and absence of tension, in general a bald, colourless and prosy expression, so the style of the poet is vigorous, nervous, flexible and relatively compressed, made distinctive by characteristic mannerisms and figures. The two styles differ in both poetic quality and the detail which determines this. Any editor of *Piers Plowman* who did not take this difference into account would make small progress in recovering its original text, and we for our part would not wish to deny that a sense of Langland's highly individual ways of writing has played

[4] See Vol. I, pp. 53, 54, n.3. To the list there may be added Hall, F. W., *A Companion to Classical Texts*, Oxford, 1913; Dain, A., *Les Manuscrits*, Paris, 1949; a second, enlarged edition of Pasquali's *Storia*, Florence, 1952; the separate issue of Maas's *Textkritik* (and more recently, 4. Auflage, Leipzig, 1960); Marichal, R., 'La Critique des Textes', in *L'Histoire et ses Méthodes, Encyclopédie de la Pléiade*, xi, Paris, 1961, pp. 1247–366; van Groningen, B. A., *Traité d'Histoire et de Critique des Textes Grecs*, Amsterdam, 1963.

[5] The reasoning by which the latter are established is set out in Vol. I, pp. 127, 128.

a major part in our editing of his poem. Granted that this sense is aesthetic, subjective,[6] and open to question in particular instances, we have found it indispensable.

To judge which of several readings is the most appropriate to the sense of the poem, both locally and in the large context, or whether a single available reading is absolutely so appropriate, requires two qualifications: familiarity with the content of the poem, and a historically correct understanding of its whole structure of meaning. The first we think we may reasonably claim to possess. The second we must at best hope to have approached not too remotely. Instances where the criterion of appropriate meaning is paramount vary extremely in difficulty, and we are sensible of a grave responsibility in that our decisions about the more difficult ones may affect future interpretative criticism. In principle this criterion may seem easy to apply: because it is presumable that the poet understood his own poem any reading repugnant to its meaning must have originated in scribal miscomprehension of this. In practice the matter is not so simple, for the reading in question is a component of the whole meaning of the poem and the editor can judge its appropriateness only in terms of his notion of that whole meaning to which, if original, it contributes. The possibility of error in such arbitration is formidable, we are well aware. But our alternatives have been to face and accept this editorial hazard or to refrain from editing.

By comparison the criterion of the appropriateness of readings to the poet's verse technique seems relatively simple to apply once that technique, specifically his alliterative practice,[7] has been determined. In attempting this we had little help from earlier studies of the Middle English alliterative long line,[8] and had finally to make our own analysis. Its results have been of crucial importance in determining originality and we must therefore discuss them here.

The evidence for our analysis is both positive and negative. There are thousands of lines in the poem where originality is either not

[6] See below, p. 213.

[7] This particularization is enforced by the nature of the verse system. Alliteration, considered in relation to the pause or cæsura of a line, appears to be its only determinable organic principle.

[8] Most concern themselves with the historical relation of this measure to Old English verse, but there are three which examine the alliteration of Middle English poems in some detail: Schipper, J., *A History of English Versification*, Oxford, 1910; Schumacher, L., *Studien über den Stabreim in der mittelenglischen Alliterationsdichtung*, Bonn, 1914; and Oakden, J. P., *Alliterative Poetry in Middle English: The Dialectal and Metrical Survey*, Manchester, 1930. Of these Schumacher allows for the possible effects of textual corruption on his conclusions.

seriously in question or else is confidently determinable; these presumably illustrate the alliterative principles which the poet set himself and observed in his verse. There are also a great many variant forms of lines for discrete reasons identifiable as corrupted, in which substitution has affected the alliteration of the identifiable or recoverable original; such lines instance a number of alliterative practices differing from the former, and because of their origin presumably not authorial. By means of these two classes of evidence it has been possible to determine how Langland almost certainly did and very probably did not employ alliteration. It appears that the system he followed, while in some particulars ingeniously expeditious, was far from libertarian, and that in general he was skilful and careful rather than inept or perfunctory in managing the alliteration of his lines. In the absence of any modern study of the alliterative systems of other fourteenth-century poets which takes the corruption of their texts into account it is not clear to what extent Langland's system is individual. But within broad limits it is consistent and unquestionably effective both in accentuating meaning and in conveying a sense of disciplined, subtly modulated progression.

A description of his system must begin by defining his understanding of alliteration. Some of his initial rhymes are commonplace. Such are exact alliteration of single consonant sounds or consonant groups; or of a single consonant sound with that of the first element of a consonant group; vocalic alliteration; and alliteration of a vowel with an aspirated vowel. Alliterating a single consonant sound with that of the second element of a consonant group, less evidently acceptable as authorial practice, is nevertheless instanced in a number of lines which otherwise are of unquestionable originality.[9] From similar evidence it also appears that the poet employed certain approximate rhymes. He was clearly satisfied to alliterate [s] with [ʃ][10] and [f] with [θ] and [ð].[11] He also,

[9] The following are examples: VII 74 stóries téchep bistówe; X 306 clóistre scóle skíles; X 309 scóle scórn clérk; XI 36 stóupe týme týne; XVII 40 twó stáues tó; XIX 201 *Spíritus páraclitus* Píers; XIX 455 *Spíritus prúdencie* péple; XX 31 *Spíritus prúdencie* póint; XX 115 prýuee spéche péyntede. They are cited by Schumacher (pp. 115–19) along with others from lines where we would scan differently.

[10] For example: Prologue 89 sígne shólden shrýuen; I 132 síker sóule shál; II 24 sóoþnesse só shé; III 190 sélf sóoþly shámedest; V 73 shólde Sáterday séuen; VII 66 súggestion sóoþ shápeþ; X 146 sígne shólde biséchen; XV 296 shólde séuen síggen; XV 442 sált shólde sáue: XVII 86 séiȝ sóiourned shóop. Compare Schumacher, pp. 94–104. In one single instance [s] appears to alliterate with [tʃ]: V 192 sídder chýn chýueled.

[11] For example: I 155 þís fóld fléssh; XI 54 confésse þée frére þí; XIV 33 þát faílle þýng; XVI 140 þúrsday bifóre þére; XVII 194 þóuȝ þómbe fýngres; XVII 337 þát fórȝyuen fórȝeten; XVIII 336 Fálsliche féttest þýng; XVIII 367 fáuȝt þúrsteþ fór; XVIII 382 Thére féloun þóle.

undoubtedly, rhymed orthographically indicated [f] with [v],[12] but this may have been an exact rhyme in his dialect.[13] By natural extension he also occasionally rhymed orthographically indicated [f] with both [v] and [θ] or [ð] in a single line.[14] There is one word, *who*, which he appears to have used for two rhymes, either with [w] or with [h] and vowels.[15] He did not, we find, rhyme [b] with [p], [d] with [t], [g] with [k], [dʒ] with [tʃ], [f] with [w], [s] with [θ]/[ð], or [j] with vowels.[16]

The next element of Langland's verse system to be considered is the relation of alliterating syllables to the presumed natural stress, both of words as parts of larger expressions, and of individual words. For establishing this the evidence is again those lines in the poem where originality is not otherwise seriously in question or is confidently determinable. The relation seems notable in three particulars.

The first is his occasional location of two staves in a single word. This occurs unmistakably at V 124 *Ne no Díapenidíon drýue it fro myn herte*; VII 159 *That Nábugodonósor némpneþ þise clerkes*; XI 207 *And after his résuréxcion Rédemptor was his name*; XV 357 *Wéderwíse shipmen and wítty clerkes also*; XIX 239 *To wynne wiþ hir líflóde bi lóore of his techynge*; and XX 299 *Of alle táletélleris and títeleris in ydel*. These lines are unexceptionable; all the words containing two staves are polysyllables or compounds of sufficient weight to receive two natural stresses. But identification of the practice is important because of its bearing on further analysis of the verse system.[17]

The second particular is more remarkable in itself: the use of a number of disyllabic or polysyllabic words to alliterate variously on one or another syllable. The following are examples.

[12] For example: II 77 vértue fáirnesse frée; V 397 auówes fóurty fóryete; V 405 vísited féble féttred; XIII 329 Auénge féle fréte; XIV 80 Véngeaunce fil víle; XV 463 fédde vényson fésaunt3; XVII 292 Véngeaunce véngeaunce fór3yue; XVIII 154 Fór vénymes fóulest; XIX 153 Vérray bifóre fórþ; XIX 456 fáire vértues víces. Compare Schumacher, pp. 62–8.

[13] Schumacher (p. 64) and Oakden (p. 163) indicate this possibility.

[14] This occurs, for instance, at I 23, Thát vésture fróm þée; V 409 Vígilies fástyng þíse; VI 144 þóru3 suffráunce véngeaunce.

[15] *Compare* X 443 whó wére wére; XI 347 wónder whóm whér; XV 120 whó wás wónder *and* X 388 Áristotle hé whó; XI 380 whó hé Í; XIX 277 whóso éte ýmagynen; XIX 290 whóso éte hárdy.

[16] Without exception the *Piers Plowman* lines cited by Schumacher as possible evidence of these alliterations (pp. 121–61) are either for discrete reasons suspect of corruption, or else otherwise scannable. To do Schumacher justice, he was aware of both possibilities and several times referred to them.

[17] There are two staves within a single word in III 100, X 48 *yéres3ýue(s)* and XIX 196 *dómesdáy*, where we identify an acceptable alliterative pattern *aaa//xy* (to be discussed below, p. 138), and in XIX 43 *cónquérour*, where the pattern is *aaa//bb* (see below, p. 138).

II 61 Fórgoers, 188 Forgóer; V 54 contrárieþ, XV 569 cóntrarien; V 296 bigýnneþ, XIII 346 bígynneþ; V 502 bíseche, X 146 biséchen; V 564 néȝebores, XIV 296 neighebóres; VI 144 suffráunce, XI 379 Súffraunce; VII 101 wómmen, XVII 21 wommén; VIII 56 dowél, IX 199 dówel; IX 18 Inwít, XIII 288 Ínwit; X 219 þérwiþ, XIX 481 þerwíþ; X 341 inpóssible, XVIII 419 ínpossible; XI 178 enemýes, XIII 143 énemy; XIII 32 Wélcome, XX 60 welcóme; XIII 346 býneþe, XVI 67 bynéþe; XIII 389 euencrísten, XVII 137 éuenecristene; XV 95 préesthode, XIX 332 preesthód; XV 283 áboute, XV 329 abóute; XV 320 bifóre, XX 184 bífore; XVII 110 mankýnde, XVIII 213 mánkynde; XVII 272 ýnkynde, 277 Vnkýnde; XX 53 Antecríst, 69 Ántecrist.

In some of these instances it is possible to discern a literary reason for the practice, a presumable design to give prominence to the meaning of one or another element of a compound: as in *Forgoer(s)* the respective notions of precedence and movement; in *þerwiþ* to the notions of demonstration or accompaniment; in *inpossible* and *vnkynde* to the negatory force of the prefix. In others, such as *neȝebores*, *dowel*, *Inwit*, *welcome*, *euencristen*, *mankynde*, *Antecrist*, the two elements are of equal weight and neither necessarily monopolizes the stress. Of prepositions like *byneþe*, *bifore*, *aboute*, it is conceivable that the fourteenth-century stress was not so firmly fixed as ours is today. But instances like *wommen* and *enemyes* remain to suggest that this variable treatment of stress was at least sometimes a convenient licence.[18] Be that as it may, this is an unquestionable feature of Langland's verse system.

The third particular is the use of 'little' words as staves, instanced in several hundred lines of the **B** version. Such use, which has been considered inferior practice,[19] must be accepted as a feature of Langland's verse system. This is a necessary conclusion unless the lines in question are corrupt, which our experience of editing affords no grounds for thinking, or unless they are—as far as the poet's care for technique went—unalliterative, the rhyming of the 'little' words being accidental, a possibility which their number and the ingenuity of his versification elsewhere discount.

Whether the use of such 'little' staves actually represents inferior

[18] The rhyme on the second syllable of *woman* in *The Manciple's Tale* line 219 and in *The Awntyrs Off Arthure* line 107 (ed. Gates, R. J., Philadelphia, 1969, p. 103) points to a variable stress in at least one of these words.

[19] See Skeat, W. W., 'An Essay on Alliterative Poetry', in Hales, J. W. and F. J. Furnivall, *Bishop Percy's Folio Manuscript*, iii, London, 1868, p. xvi: 'Occasional instances may be found where rime-letters begin *soft* syllables...; this, however, is decidedly bad, the fundamental principle of alliterative verse being this, that alliteration and heavy stress should always go together.' Oakden (pp. 178, 179) refers to the use of little words as staves as an 'extensive' liberty.

practice is material to editing, since it relates to the extent of the poet's concern for technical detail. In some cases it is evident that the 'little' staves are words on which the immediate sense confers importance and weight, and which were therefore presumably stressed by design; in others this is not so apparent.[20] Nevertheless we think it judicious to allow Langland the benefit of the doubt, since we have virtually no information about Middle English sentence intonation. How, for instance, did he read VI 47 *That he worþ worþier set and wiþ moore blisse*? We today would stress *moore* most heavily in the second half-line, but there is the fact that the alliteration appears to throw a stress on *wiþ*. It is a real possibility that linguistic change will have obscured many effects of his otherwise well instanced technical virtuosity. And this is exceptional: for example at XVI 147 and XIX 217 alliteration falls on infinitive signs; that might seem a little too expeditious, until it is observed that the unusual augmentation of stress in fact brings out the purposive sense in the two expressions concerned. Even in lines where all the staves are 'little' words the relation of rhythmic emphasis to meaning is often very skilful.[21] Langland's use of 'little' stave-words should not then necessarily imply that his attitude to alliteration was careless or perfunctory.

The number of staves which the poet considered requisite to the line in his verse system[22] is the next consideration. A historical presumption that this number was at least three is strengthened by the fact that the great majority of lines in the archetypal text of *Piers Plowman* have three staves.[23] The existence of some hundreds of four-stave and a few five-stave lines does not weaken it: the presence of the fourth or indeed the

[20] For instance we can sense the augmented weight in prepositional staves like III 235 wiþ, IV 77 myd, VII 67 but, X 156 after, *but not in* Prologue 22 with, IV 52 for, V 150 by, XI 116 wiþ, XIII 210 intil; in some staves on the verb *to be*, such as III 270 be, X 351 be, XII 25 were, XVII 236 be, XVIII 211 were, XVIII 419 is, *but not in* III 27 beþ, V 86 was, X 351 beþ, XIII 381 was, XIX 344 ben; in some 'little' adverbial staves such as II 24 so, VII 83 yet, XVI 48 forþ, *but not in* II 239, V 85, XI 234 whan; in the pronominal stave XVIII 247 he, *but not in* XVIII 69 we; in the possessive adjectival stave XIV 59 his *but not in* XVIII 183 my; in the verbal stave III 145 may, *but not in* XVII 346 may.

[21] For instance at I 108 scanning óuer hís hém; II 194 ór(I) ány híse; III 107 þów þó þów; V 132 hé Í Í; VIII 72 þów þó þát; VIII 131 þéi þré thís. 'Little' stave words occur in other alliterative poems. See Oakden, pp. 178, 179.

[22] By staves we understand those alliterating syllables or words in the two parts of a line which, by resisting the effect of the cæsura to divide it, set up the sensory tension peculiar to this kind of verse and are thus part of its structural principle. We distinguish this primary from secondary alliteration which, however functionally important it may be, is extraneous to the verse system and can have no rôle in editing. The specific restriction to Langland's form of the long line is called for by the variety of fourteenth- and fifteenth-century treatments of the measure.

[23] From Oakden's analyses (pp. 168, 169 and pp. 181ff.) this appears true of most fourteenth- and fifteenth-century alliterative verse.

fifth stave is often explicable as an accidental consequence of the vocabulary of the immediate topic, or as possibly intended for some special effect,[24] and thus seems not structural. It appears then that the normative number of staves in Langland's alliterative long line is three.

There are however some 350 lines in the archetypal text of the **B** version with less than three staves, some with only two alliterating syllables and some with no identifiable alliteration. Their incidence is hardly sufficient to challenge the identification of a norm of three staves; the question is rather whether they are scribal or whether their presence in the archetypal text is to be interpreted as evidence of the poet's sense of permissible licence.

The editorial implications of the answer are obvious. Moreover the question in itself epitomizes the typical predicament of the textual critic, faced with data of which an indeterminate number are by axiom false. There are editorial situations in which answering it would be impossible. In ours, luckily, because of the existence of three versions of the poem and of so many **B** manuscripts this is not so. The evidence affords practical confirmation of the theoretically necessary existence of false data, actually identifies and eliminates a proportion of these, and reveals their characteristics as a class.

Thus experience of editing the other versions dispels any uncertainty about the frequency of scribal damage to alliteration in the transmission of *Piers Plowman*.[25] Further, from the possibility of comparing the archetypal texts of the three versions it is clear that such damage specifically occurred in the archetypal tradition of **B**, and incidentally that almost a third of the **B** version's two-stave lines are scribal from considerations other than of versification.[26] Finally, because the number of surviving descendants of the archetypal **B** manuscript is relatively large there is abundant visible evidence of the effects of scribal transmission on the alliteration of this version, for these manuscripts contain some 800 substitutions affecting alliteration for which the explanations are editorial commonplaces,[27] and where direction of variation is not

[24] The latter explanation could apply in Prologue 50 or 208 or 227, or in III 320.

[25] See Vol. I, pp. 135, 136 for a list of almost 150 substitutions in the visible **A** tradition which deprive the lines where they occur of a stave.

[26] See above, pp. 81, 82, 88, 89, 92–5.

[27] They result from mechanical error including inadvertent omission; visual misreading of copy; miscomprehension of copy; misguided 'correction'; substitution of a dialect variant or a synonym or an easier reading or a more explicit reading or a more emphatic reading; and censorship. They occur in single manuscripts or variational or presumed genetic groups, and are variations from a surviving original.

in doubt. In these it is possible to identify alliterative patterns repeatedly created by scribal variation, in other words to establish the characteristics of the false data.

The majority of these substitutions deprive the lines where they occur of a stave.[28] In consequence there are some 330 lines of scribal form in the surviving **B** manuscripts which have the alliterative pattern *aa//xy*; some 200 others have a pattern *ax//ay*; about 180 more a pattern *xa//ay*; less frequently the lines of scribal form scan *aa//bb* or even *ab//ab*. These are precisely the alliterative patterns of the two-stave lines in the archetypal **B** text.[29] For that reason and because in the case of many of the latter we can discern other effects of familiar processes of corruption,[30] we conclude that these archetypal two-stave lines are certainly not, except negatively, evidence about the verse system of *Piers Plowman*, and indeed that their form is, with a few possible exceptions,[31] scribal.[32] The evidence is then that Langland conceived of his verse system as requiring at least three staves, and that he may have ignored this requirement only in certain special circumstances.[33]

From the fact that two of these three staves, in the great majority of lines, come before the cæsura,[34] it appears that the poet understood this distribution to be a principle of his verse, either with specific respect to the number of staves appropriate to a half-line, or generally in the sense that of a three-stave line the first half should normatively preponderate.[35] The evidence that he would form a line with staves in the reverse

[28] Others misplace a stave; these are also important and will be considered below (p. 138).

[29] They even occur in approximately similar proportions, *aa//xy* most often, *xa//ay* and *ax//ay* in that order less often but still a substantial number of times, and *aa//bb* and *ab//ab* occasionally.

[30] See for example below, pp. 147, 148.

[31] The exceptions are a number of lines containing a Latin element. Many lines containing Latin scan normatively, but there are others of which it is impossible to see how they could originally have had three staves; at the same time they have otherwise nothing about them to suggest unoriginality. Examples are III 339, VII 73, XII 189, XVI 46, XIX 276, XX 29.

[32] We include in this classification eight lines with unsatisfactory alliteration found in all three versions, six of a similar character in the archetypes of both **A** and **B**, and the 33 in the archetypes of both **B** and **C** discussed above (pp. 112, 113 and 118, 119). For these last we have already offered an explanation. The others we account for as having been already corrupt in the **A** manuscript used for revision to **B**. They will be considered below, pp. 205, 210.

[33] He would, *a fortiori*, not have written lines without discernible alliteration. We can therefore not accept Skeat's contrary opinion that 'A line wholly without alliteration was quite admissible *as a variation*' ('An Essay', p. xviii). For Oakden (p. 167) lines without alliteration are 'failures'.

[34] 'In English prosody: A pause or breathing-place about the middle of a metrical line, generally indicated by a pause in the sense.' *NED* s.v.2.

[35] In most four-stave lines the two halves are of 'equal' weight, but there are exceptions with the pattern *aaa//ax*, as for instance at Prologue 34, 67, VII 34, X 192.

proportion is very slight.[36] But there can be no doubt that he regarded a distribution of initial rhymes in which all three staves of a line came before its cæsura as permissible variation from the norm.[37] We have noted some 80 occurrences.[38] Of these rather more than half have the pattern *aaa*//*xy*;[39] the remainder, with secondary alliteration, a pattern *aaa*//*bb*.[40] It could be held that although in these patterns the first half-line preponderates as it does, for instance, in *aa*//*ax*, they seem to violate the definitive principle of the alliterative long line because their staves perform no linking function.[41] But this cannot be an editorial consideration. The lines which scan *aaa*//*xy* and *aaa*//*bb* are otherwise unexceptionable and it is necessary to admit these patterns as a feature of Langland's verse system.

It remains to consider the position of the stave in the second half-line. From the presumed norm *aa*//*ax*, fulfilled in several thousands of lines, this should be early rather than late, and the poet's sense of that requirement seems unmistakable from his inversions of word order in many second half-lines.[42] At the same time there is, from other lines where

[36] We have noted eight archetypal or original **B** lines with three staves where two follow the cæsura. Five of these we have treated as scribal: *xa*//*aa* lines at III 345, V 260, IX 110, XI 399, and an *ax*//*aa* line at XVII 103; three we have let stand as possibly original: *xa*//*aa* lines at XI 16, XII 290 and XV 1. About these latter we may have been mistaken. Both patterns occur in scribal forms of lines in surviving **B** manuscripts, *xa*//*aa* fourteen times and *ax*//*aa* nine times.

[37] There is, we appreciate, a subjective element in the reading of verse which may affect identification of the cæsural pause. In many of these lines, however, location of the cæsura cannot be a matter of doubt because their grammar, phrasing and sense make a pause seem impossible before some particular point, as in III 100 *Yiftes or yeresyeues*, IV 171 *The kyng callede Conscience*, XX 232 *Nede neghede þo neer*; instances of this kind establish the practice. We think it further evidenced in lines with several possible cæsural points, of which one divides the line with uncomfortable disproportion. Examples are: V 72 *To maken mercy for his mysdede bitwene god and hym*; X 343 *And Caton kenneþ vs to coueiten it nauȝt but as nede techeþ*; XI 154 *Lo ye lordes what leautee dide by an Emperour of Rome*; XIX 168 *Crist cam in and al closed boþe dore and ȝates.*

[38] Schumacher identified this pattern and observed that lines of its type occur fairly regularly throughout *Piers Plowman* (p. 25). That they are also to be found in other Middle English poems appears from his analyses (pp. 18ff.).

[39] Examples are: III 196 And bere hire bras at þi bak to Caleis to selle; V 455 And yet wole I yelde ayein if I so muche haue; IX 118 And siþenes by assent of hemself as þei two myȝte acorde; XVI 90 And þanne spak *spiritus sanctus* in Gabrielis mouþe; XIX 445 And fynt folk to fiȝte and cristen blood to spille.

[40] Examples are: Prologue 95 And somme seruen as seruauntȝ lordes and ladies; V 406 I haue leuere here an harlotrye or a Somer game of Souters; XI 39 If truþe wol witnesse it be wel do Fortune to folwe; XVII 172 The fyngres formen a ful hand to portreye or peynten; XIX 74 Aungeles out of heuene come knelynge and songe.

[41] Skeat ('An Essay', p. xvii) thought them 'a great blemish'. Oakden (p. 167) included the pattern *aaa*//*xy* among 'Types which are failures'.

[42] Examples are: Prologue 173 þe while hym pléye likeþ; 174 and his wéye shonye; III 325 fýnde men shul þe worste; IV 153 and léfte Reson manye; VII 87 of séintes lyues redyng; 91 þat þei wíþ dele; X 102 mén to eten Inne; XIII 339 or of Shórdych dame Emme; XIV 192 of póuerte be moste; XV 147 in mýnde haueþ; 209 knówe shaltow hym neuere; 284 þat he bý lyuede; 299 ne ooþer béest wilde; 542 whoso whý askeþ; XVII 223 þat cáught haþ fir and blaseþ; 258 ne hélpe may þee by reson; 271 þat gráce of ariseþ; 328 or wéte to slepe; XVIII 9 þe péple þat ofrauȝte; 78 kéne spere ygrounde; XIX 131 þat hým of grace askede; 322 for mankýnde on pyned.

originality seems not in question, evidence that he considered it permissible to make a final stave of the first syllable of a trisyllabic or polysyllabic final word.[43] He did not, however, it appears, allow himself the further licence of making the second-last or final syllable of a line his stave. There are 46 lines in the archetypal text of **B** where the stave has one of these positions, another two such in the archetypal text of **AB**, and eleven more in that of **BC**.[44] We conclude that the alliterative pattern of these lines is due to scribal agency from four considerations. The first is that eight of these 46 archetypal **B** lines appear scribal on comparison of their text with that of **AC** or **A** or **C**.[45] The second is that in the case of others, which are revised in **C**, a part of the poet's revision was firmly to set a third stave nearer the beginning of the second half-line, whatever other changes he made.[46] The third consideration is the frequency with which scribal substitutions having the effect *aa*//*ax*] *aa*//*xa* occurred in the transmission of *Piers Plowman* generally. In the visible **B** tradition variation by individual manuscripts or by variational or genetic groups produces *aa*//*xa* at least 18 times by substitution or omission, and at least 34 times by change of word order; we have also noted more than 50 instances of substitutions with similar effect in the visible **A** tradition and at least as many in that of **C**. The fourth consideration is the ease with which, by rearrangements less violent than many of the poet's own inversions noticed above, the second half-line can be given an alliterative pattern known to have been used by him.[47] On this showing the alliterative pattern *aa*//*xa*, where the third stave is a second-last or final syllable, is a scribal one and not a feature of Langland's verse system.

It will have emerged during the above account that establishment of the poet's verse technique is inseparable from the process of editing. A line is presumed not to be evidence for that technique because for one or more of various discrete editorial reasons it appears to be scribal; thereafter the occurrence of the verse pattern which it exemplifies is in

[43] Likely examples are: III 240 v́surie; IV 32 cóueitise; 178 déserued; V 436 vítailles; 526 Sépulcre; XIV 318 síknesse; XVI 78 rúfulliche; XVII 195 máleese; 267 mýschaunce; XVIII 156 déstruyeþ; 259 Résurexion; XIX 31 héndenesse; 329 déuysede; 397 *Iústicie*; 448 rémenaunt; XX 8 *témperancie*; 283 énioigne; 317 ýpocrisye.

[44] See respectively below, pp. 194ff., and above, pp. 112ff., for instances of these.

[45] See above, pp. 81, 82, 88, 89, 92–5.

[46] This occurs, for instance at IV 36 **C** IV 36; VII 35 **C** IX 38; XI 437 **C** XIII 243; XIII 325 **C** VI 70; XVIII 2 **C** XX 2; XVIII 54 **C** XX 54.

[47] This will appear from the editorial treatment of the archetypal **B** lines scanning *aa*//*xa*, which is discussed below, pp. 194ff.

other lines treated as evidence of scribal corruption. This reasoning which in the abstract may well appear precarious is safeguarded in the case of *Piers Plowman* by the existence of controlled situations where the effects of unmistakable scribal substitution on the versification can be observed. The textual circumstances of the tradition make it possible to define what, in this poem, constitutes technical competence; its editors are thus not merely able but virtually required to give effect to the presumption that such competence would be the first equipment of a major poet by assessing the appropriateness of readings to his verse system as they have identified it.

The validity of the criteria discussed above is not, we think, open to theoretical objection: if a poem like *Piers Plowman* is preserved in a tradition where manuscript authority at all stages is manifestly dubious there can be no other means of editing it than by scrutiny of its variant readings and forms in the terms we have set out. The acceptability of a text constructed by that means is, however, as we well appreciate, quite another matter. The difference is between theory and its application: that the logic of the first is good does not guarantee the efficiency of the other. Our text must then be assessed not generally but in its detail, by the quality of the arguments with which we support that detail and the appropriateness[48] of its readings. Therefore, and especially because we have accepted the full implications of the history of transmission that we exposed, and have not stopped short, after discriminating between available variants, with indicating likely points of unoriginality in the archetypal **B** text but have attempted to 'transcend the tradition',[49] we must now expose for scrutiny the means by which, in applying the editorial criteria discussed above, we have determined our text.

Considerations of space and the bulk of the material restrict us to selective demonstration. We have therefore taken pains to choose instances typical of the several textual situations, and to relate fulness of illustration to the character of the problems. Thus by limiting our examples in the simpler and easier cases (as well as by generally merely referring to analyses of variation already set out in preceding sections)

[48] We would emphasize this consideration. In editing there is beyond a certain point no question of absolute demonstration. An edited text is essentially a hypothesis (see below, p. 212). Its individual readings must be judged as elements of the hypothesis, in which naturally the poet's *usus scribendi* is a most important consideration.

[49] Hall, *A Companion*, p. 108.

we have allowed ourselves greater scope for discussion of the more complex textual issues, to say nothing of those where our readings have a speculative character and will thus seem most open to question.

The editorial criteria were applied in three processes theoretically distinct but by no means always practically separable: discrimination, that is identification of originality among surviving variants, reconstruction, that is restoration of original readings not actually preserved as such but indicated by surviving variation; and conjecture. The nature of their application varied with the situation of the particular line, that is according to whether it had or did not have a recognizable equivalent in one or both the other versions. Similarly the editorial objective varied: it might be identification of the archetypal **B** reading; or distinction between scribal and authorial variation, that is the delimitation of revision; or the absolute scrutiny of readings. Editing was further complicated by the interdependence of all final editorial decisions, which the earlier parts of this Introduction will already have shown. In these circumstances any demonstration, however organized, would inevitably appear a simplification. But we have concluded that one planned to illustrate the three editorial processes successively in the various textual situations will be the least misleading, for in exposing systematically the kinds of reasoning by which we have reached decisions it will most clearly show the character of our edition, and thus also the variable authority of our text.

We therefore begin by illustrating discrimination, that is identification of originality among available readings, in the situation where **B** has no recognizable equivalent in another version. Our examples are of cases where the resultant text is such as to raise no suspicion of error in the archetypal tradition.[50] This situation is the simplest of all: authorial revision is not in question; and presumptive identification of originality is effected by establishing direction of variation. Our methods and results can thus here be scrutinized without distracting considerations.

At its most elementary discrimination operates by eliminating variants created by unconscious mechanical error. Such variants are numerous but seldom problematic when exposed to comparison: they attract attention by their quality and the textual circumstances which

[50] For discussion of lines peculiar to **B** which are presumed archetypally corrupt see below, pp. 192ff.

can generate them are familiar.[51] For instance, at XVII 111, *vnhardy þat harlot*] *vnharlot*, an obvious nonsense variant, is explicable as caused by attraction to following copy; at IX 103 *sippe*] *seche* is a contextually meaningless variation that occurred through either *t/c* confusion in an exemplar reading *sethe(n)* or simply attraction to following *speche*; at XV 580 *ferme*] *for me*, also with poor sense,[52] was caused by *e/o* confusion; at X 279 *now*] *no*, impossible in the context, was induced by *noȝt* 278, 280. At IX 88 the shape of the line in the group ancestor of RF, *þat eyþer helpeþ ooþer of hem þat hym nedeþ*, is evidently corrupt; comparison shows it to have been caused by attraction to the second *of*+pronoun group. At XII 219–22 the order of the lines in one main genetic group is inconsequential: it is explicable as resulting from transposition induced by the presence of *And...of...of* in 219, 221. At X 113 where the variation *ye*] *þe* obviously arose through *þ/y* confusion the article might pass muster if unchallenged, but in the context the superior originality of *ye* is unmistakable; similarly at XIII 322 *lakkynge*] *laughynge* is explicable by the resemblance of *kk* and *w*; again if *laughynge* were a unique reading it would possibly be accepted, but comparison shows its inferior contextual appropriateness. Damage to the text through mechanical variation can also be extreme, when it takes the form of omission of lines or passages of text.[53] But its identification and repair from the evidence of visible variation are classic processes which do not, we believe, need further illustration here.

In the case of another type of probably unconscious variations discrimination is not quite so easy. This comprises readings where the effect of disagreement differs from that created by mechanical error

[51] See Vol. I, pp. 116–25 for extended discussion and illustration of these. The following few examples will be enough to show that variation in the **B** version is of the same character. Prologue 106 opene it] openet: *attraction to the* t *of* it to; I 122 stekie] stekþe: þ/y *confusion*: II 14 enuenymes] enemyes: *confusion over minims or loss of nasal suspension*; III 351 shewed] schede: *attraction to second* e; IV 155 mouþ] mony: *confusion of minims and* þ/y; V 38 bihoueþ] he houyth: *misreading of* b *for* h *induced by following* h; VI 226 yworþe] worche: c/t *confusion*; VII 79 walke] wawe: *confusion* of lk *and* w; VIII 52 yeme] seme: *attraction to* s *of* selue; IX 155 sestow] sistow: *attraction to* i *of* sire *preceding*; X 43 Lykne] kykne: *attraction to following copy*; XI 97 ech a lawe] lawe euere lawe: *diplography through attention to substitution* (ech] euery); XII 47 bisette] bileue: *confusion of long* s *and* l; XIII 55 derne] dernes: *attraction to* s *of* shrifte *following*; XIV 176 derþe] drighte: *attraction to* droghte *following, and subconscious suggestion of* '*dry*'; XV 91 likeþ] lokethe: *attraction to vowel of preceding* whoso; XVI 61 tid] stit: *attraction to* s *of preceding* as; XVII 162 wide] wyld: *attraction to* l *of following* world; XVIII 352 recouere] recorue: *metathesis through confusion over* er *contraction*.

[52] The sophistications *but an harlot*, *all swiche* and *formed* in F are to be noted as registering an editing scribe's sense of the unsatisfactory meaning of his copy.

[53] How we account for the serious cases of such omission has been shown at length above, pp. 66ff.

because the inferiority of one reading and therefore the superior originality of the other do not so readily appear from comparison: the difference between readings is thus too slight to invoke the criterion of style or sense. In such cases originality is, however, often indicated by the existence in text and context of circumstances which can, if one reading is presumed original, have caused the other to derive from it: that is which establish the likelier direction of variation. We illustrate this procedure first from minute variation which, as must be obvious, is the most difficult, and therefore an ideal model.

At IV 156 *þat freke* / *þe f.*, the demonstrative is more explicit and could therefore be unoriginal; on the other hand unconscious substitution of the article could have been induced by its frequent occurrence in the immediately preceding context. At XV 282 *sondry tymes as* / *s. tyme as*, both uses are lexicographically supported. The plural, as more explicit, could be scribal; equally the auditory similarity of the syllables -*es* and *as* could have caused unconscious assimilation of the first to the second. At XII 222 *colours so* / *colour so*, the plural is easier than the distributive singular and might thus be a scribal substitution; but loss of a final letter when it also begins the following word is a very common unconscious copying error. The arguments in these particular cases might seem perfectly balanced but for one consideration: that scribes were rather, in general, passive and inattentive than careful and active; this implies a greater likelihood of the mechanical variation. The following are examples of editorial decisions reached by similar reasoning.

XIII 123 *to*(2)] *om* caused by *to*...-*t* in *to any wiȝt* preceding; 301 *on*] *om* caused by last syllable of *lyoun* preceding; XII 23 *here*] *herde* assimilation to tense of following difficult and preoccupying line; XVII 106 *take*] *taketh* attraction to tense of *lotieþ* above it; IX 67 *he shoop*] *shoop hem* parallelism induced by preceding *forsaken hem*; X 265 *seest*] *semest* induced by *semest* (261, 263); XV 160 *neded hym*] *hym neded* promotion of the pronoun induced by iterative *he*, *his* (159); IX 83 *Ne*] *And* substitution induced by preoccupation with meaning of following *and*, 'if'; XV 342 *feeste*] *fede* induced by *fedeþ* (340); 423 *almesse*] *fyndynge* induced by *fynde* (425) and -*ynge* (424); 424 *goode*] *lele* induced by *lele* (423); XVI 4 *trewely*] *treuthe* induced by *ruþe* (5); 8 *pouere*] *pure* induced by *pure* preceding; 160 *On*] *In* induced by *in* following; XI 270 *folk seeþ*] *men s.* a more common collocation substituted; XIV 12 *neuere*] *nouȝt* induced by preoccupation with coming *þoruȝ word*] *þouȝt* sophistication (14); 142 *moore*] *huire* induced by attention to meaning of preceding *salarie*;[54] XII 49 *I may*] transposition induced by attraction of the alliteration; XVI 140 *cene*] *maundee* induced by alliterative suggestion of *made* preceding.

[54] The word may have been difficult; *NED* cites this occurrence as the earliest.

While the differences between variants in the above examples are hardly insignificant since all have implications for the style of the poem and some for Middle English grammar and lexicography, the actual character of the differences is not such as to afford clear evidence of originality.[55] Such evidence is, however, available when readings differ in ways which can be related to the scribal tendencies of variation, and thus are subject to the criterion of style. Discrimination by this means will be familiar from the editing of **A**;[56] we therefore illustrate it only briefly here.

The following selected examples illustrate variations where one reading can be identified as scribal because its existence is explicable by the operation of a scribal tendency of variation.

More explicit readings: V 165 eiþer] hir e.; 255 pedlere] þe p.; IX 120 þe] here/þere; X 223 to knowe] for to k.; 292 Thanne] And þ.; 361 alle] a. þyng; XI 180 Who] For ho; 185 Iesu] is I.; 225 cristene] c. men; 226 were] þat w.; 421 to doone] to be d.; XII 48 baddenesse] badd vse; 228 to] þere to; XIII 140 and (1)] a. wiþ; 270 were] þere w.; XV 175 good] godes; 278 foweles] of f.; 285 fond] fedde; 427 brynge] hem b.; XVI 142 som] oon.

Readings otherwise easier:[57] IV 40 *Forþi*] *Therfore*; V 116 *vndernymeþ*] *vndyrtake*; XII 295 *wye*] *wight* chronological variations. XVI 78 *rogged*] *rused* variation to an equivalent not regionally restricted. X 333 *ouerse*] *haue seen* variation to an unambiguous expression. X 402 *was*] *were*; XV 346 *deliuereþ*] *is deliuered* variations to easier grammar (in X 402 the formal plural *werkes* in its iterative sense with singular meaning[58] is difficult; in XV 346 the subject of *deliuereþ* is remote). XII 91 *dide þe caractes*] *þe c. dide*; XV 263 *wel may euery man*] *e. man may w.* variations to prose order. XV 121 *baselardes...broches*] *broches...baselardes* variation from chiasmus to parallelism with 122. III 243 *þe truþe*] *þe trewe* variation from abstract to concrete. X 474 *hir paternoster*] *þe p.*; XII 11 *poustees*] *poustee* variations to less pregnant expressions.

More emphatic readings: V 639 knowe þere] welcome; VI 228 lowe] lewed; VII 84 nede] grete n.; VIII 130 wolde] fayn w.; X 103 spille þat spende] spende þat spille; 209 god] g. hymself; 343 as nede techeþ] at pure/in gret n.; XII 261 as] riȝt as; XIII 131 knowe] k. wel; 132 dar] d. wel; 192 a] vch a.

Censorship: X 267 grymly] greuously.

Application of the criterion of style in cases like these is seldom problematic: the diffuseness and crude emphasis characteristic of the

[55] It is for instance not possible to be certain that the poet would not have used an infinitive without *to* in XIII 123, or that in XIII 301 *as a lyoun to loke* might not have meant 'like a lion in appearance'. As for XIV 12, decision between *neuere* and *nouȝt* without extraneous indication of the direction of variation would have been extremely hard: *neuere* is certainly the more emphatic variant, but it is also particularly apt to Haukyn's state of mind.

[56] Vol. I, pp. 128–45.

[57] A great many easier variants also affect the sense or alliteration and are thus doubly identifiable as scribal. See, for instance, below, pp. 147, 148.

[58] Mustanoja, T., *A Middle English Syntax*, i, Helsinki, 1960, p. 61.

copyist's *usus scribendi* are not usually hard to identify. But cruces do occur. For instance in XIV 1 Haukyn says either *I haue but oon hater* or *I haue but oon hool hater*; *hool* can have been inserted as a more explicit substitution or else omitted to emphasize his poverty. The possibilities seem balanced; the criterion of appropriate meaning could be applied only if the symbolic value of the cloak were quite precisely definable, which seems difficult; and the line scans vocalically with or without *hool*. Fortunately there is here outside evidence: at XIII 313 Conscience has referred to Haukyn's *beste cote*. On this indication of the poet's conception of his subject *hool* was original and was deliberately omitted for greater emphasis.

The obscurity of the symbolism here would make it impossible to judge whether the meaning of this line and of the Haukyn episode required *hool* or not. In many instances, however, variants differ both markedly enough and in such ways as to seem clearly more or less appropriate to the meaning of local and larger context. The differences range from that between sense and near nonsense to that between a possible and a better, because somehow demonstrably more appropriate (and therefore also a harder) meaning. Discrimination is not, however, simply by such difference: with the showing of the criterion of sense must go the possibility of accounting plausibly for the substitution of the variant presumed inferior.

Some substitutions appreciably affecting the meaning are evidently mechanical, others not determinably conscious or unconscious, and a few clearly deliberate. They appear to have been most often generated mechanically, or by unconscious misreading of copy through inattention or distraction, less often by conscious attempts to improve it. The following examples illustrate both their nature and variety and our grounds for identifying them as unoriginal.

VII 80 *yeueþ*] *ʒift*: the noun obscures the reference of preceding *he* and weakens the meaningful parallelism of 79–81; variation through misreading of an -*eth* suspension. XIV 21 *sonnen*] *sowen*: drying in the sun is a more appropriate action than needlework; visual error or confusion over minims. XIV 90 *ynliche*] *yliche*: reference to the *contritio cordis* which must accompany *shrift of mouþ* gives the more appropriate meaning: loss or oversight of *n* suspension. XV 418 *Peeren*] *Peres*: the noun in apposition is less appropriate to the movement of sense than the verb, which is also, because of its suppressed relative subject, more difficult: substitution induced by recurrent -*es* in 417. XVI 211 *Might is in matrimoyne*] *M. is m.*: only the one variant[59] makes sense in the exposition; mechanical

[59] *Mighty* WCr is a sophistication.

omission induced by the proximity of two homoarchic small words. XV 200 *What is þe wille*] *What is w.*: the article is essential for the required meaning of *wille*, 'the intention by which the morality of an action is judged'; cp. 200α; unconscious omission through distraction by the possible meanings and references of *wille*. XII 11 *pestilences*] *penaunce(s)*: the topical reference has appropriate meaning; unconscious substitution induced by the group *Pouerte or penaunce* in 9 above. XII 66 *a konnynge of heuene*] *and k. of h.*: the sense given by the conjunction, 'and learning (comes) from heaven', which interrupts and is irrelevant to the exposition of the preceding Latin, is less appropriate than that given by the article, 'a celestial ability', one further commendable (70) for the love of Christ *þat of Clergie is roote* (71); misreading induced by the *Of...comeþ* pattern in 66a, 67a. XIII 142 *so þow lere þe*] *so to l. (and)*: the imperative with subject-pronoun expressed for emphasis[60] gives a superior meaning to that of the infinitive construction expressing consequence; variation induced by attraction to following *to louye*. XV 499 *For cristene and vncristene*] *To c. and to v.*: Only the one variant makes good sense; unconscious substitution induced by *seide* 498, *seide to* 499. XIV 143 *hire*] *heuene*: the illustration expressed in 142, 143 requires the more material sense of *hire*; substitution induced by the notional patterns of 141 and the difficulty of 142. XVI 50 *planke*] *plante*: only one reading makes good sense; unconscious substitution induced by *feccheþ...floures* 45, *fruyt...fecche* 49, and the difficulty of the passage. X 366 *moþeeten be*] *mote eten ben*: the sense of the latter, 'which could be converted into money to buy food' is less pregnant than that which implies the infrequent use and thus the size of the rich man's wardrobe; visual error induced by the context of starvation. XI 421 *Lakkedest and losedest*] *L. a. lostest/losest*: the context requires a contrast between 'blame' and 'praise'; meanwhile that sense is hard because the predictable conjunction is *or*, not *and*; substitution induced by the contextual suggestion of 'loss' of Reason's favour and of further instruction. XIII 249 *And þat*] *That*: the conjunction is needed to separate the distinct notions of 248 and 249; unconscious omission through inducement to parallelism with the beginning of 248. XII 261 *as it wolde*] *as he w.*: by its more precise visualization the neuter pronoun, referring to the actual testamentary document and the physical act of witnessing it, gives greater force to the instance of betrayal of trust; substitution through inducement to parallelism by *his wille* 260. XIII 353 *of hir harlotrie*] *of harlotrie*: for the richer meaning created by the possessive compare the Wife of Bath's *Unto this day it dooth myn herte boote That I have had my world as in my tyme*; unconscious moralistic simplification. VIII 130 *man or no man*] *m. or womman*: the direction of the question to the sex of Do Well is not meaningful; variation induced by the common collocation. XIV 152 *rewfulliche*] *riȝtfullich*: lines 145 and 148 show that the appropriate notion is of compassion (how the *noȝt riche* have double hire appears from 153, 154); variation induced by the common collocation *riȝtfulliche libben*, or simply substitution of an easier reading. VII 79 *is þe trecherie*] *is t.*: the remote reference of the article to 68, 69 is necessary; omission through alliterative inducement. XV 461 *keperes*] *creperes/cropers*: 'cruppers', which could hardly apply to any wild animals except ponies, is a sophistication of *creperes*, where the *r* was induced by the alliteration. XI 378 *Amende þow*] *A. þow it*: the implication of the object that the Dreamer is being enjoined to reform the general state of affairs under discussion is not appropriate; cp. 377 *þiself hast noȝt to doone*, 'it is none of your concern'. He is to mend his own ways (*NED* s.v. *Amend* 1.c.) Variation through inattentive misreading. XIII

[60] Mustanoja, *Syntax*, pp. 475, 476

208 *and alle kynnes londes*] *of a. k. l.*: the conjunction, by relating the half-line to 209 and introducing this, supplies a transition to the theme of evangelism; by contrast to specify kings 'of all sorts of countries' adds nothing to the meaning. Inattentive misreading of the line as a grammatical unit, with smoothing by addition of conjunction in 209. XIII 121 *to leren hem*] *to l.*: the more pregnant expression with the plural object (the variant *hym* is a nonsense reflex of this) meaning 'so that he should teach them', is superior to 'in order to learn'; variation through inattentive substitution of an easier reading. XI 400 *moste wo polie*] *most wo poliep*: comparison of the amount of misery to be endured by various kinds of creatures is less appropriate in the context than implication of the Creator's prescience—'who would have to endure misery'; visual error or misreading induced by the tendency to increase emphasis. XIII 289 *bold*] *badde*: the one reading is at variance with the speaker's purpose: thoughtless substitution of a more emphatic expression. XIII 73 *greue...þat goode ben*] *greue...goode men*: the appropriate object of protection from offence is 'friars who are virtuous', not simply 'good men', who as a class are unlikely to be offended by criticism of friars; sophistication excluding the suggestion that there are virtuous friars, or simply substitution of an easier reading. XIV 189 *pouke*] *pope*: only one variant gives the sense required by the context (cp. 191): a preferred villain substituted.

The above examples will have illustrated the reasoning by which the criterion of appropriate meaning is applied. The authority of a text determined by it clearly lies in the accuracy with which greater appropriateness of meaning in and to the context is identified; our critical apparatus lays this open to examination.

Discrimination by the criterion of appropriateness of readings to the poet's verse technique operates by analogous reasoning. If among competing variants there is one which contributes to a presumably normative alliterative pattern it appears the likelier original; that appearance is confirmed if the other can be shown to have derived from it by established or likely processes of scribal variation. Here the determinant of authority is the degree of correctness to which the poet's verse technique has been identified.[61] The following are instances where originality seems indicated by this criterion.

X 439 *Wher for loue*] *Wherfore*⟩ *aaxy*: unconscious omission induced by misreading of *Wher*, 'Whether'. IX 98 *dredeþ hym*] *om*⟩ *axay*: omission induced by having copied the expression in 97. IV 40 *Reson*] *om*⟩ *xaay*: omission induced by attraction between modifier and its verb. V 141 *abrood*] *om*⟩ *xaay*: omission induced by attraction between the verb and the more sensational of its two modifiers. XV 338 *ful*] *om*⟩ *axay*: inattentive omission of a notion implicit in preceding *filled* through attraction to its complement. XIII 266 *bake*] *om*⟩ *xaay*: omission through distraction by the topical reference or, if *bake breed* means 'Hard-baked bread, biscuit', through failure to take in this added meaning. X 401 *dide and swiche oþere*] *and o.d.*⟩ *axay*: omission through unconscious variation toward

[61] See above, pp. 131–40.

easier prose order. XI 286 *dide*] *om*〉 *xaay*: omission through subconscious suggestion of the prose order, *þei dide hir deuoir*, that the verb had already been copied. XIV 14 *þoruȝ word*] *thouȝt*〉 *axay* or *aaxy*: visual error induced by subconscious amalgamation of *þo*(*ruȝ*) and (*si*)*ȝte* immediately above. XV 317 *rule*] *ordre*〉 *aaxy*: unconscious substitution of a near-equivalent aurally induced by preceding *youre*. XIII 205 *seide*] *quod*〉 *axay*: substitution of an exact equivalent induced by alliterative attraction to following *Conscience*. IX 89 *ne wol*] *nel*〉 *aaxy* or *xaaa* from *aaabb*:[62] inattentive substitution of an exact equivalent through preoccupation with the negative force of the line. IX 98 *dredeþ...drede*] *d....loue*〉 *axay*: substitution induced by *dredeþ...loue* in 97. X 222 *to*] *om*〉 *aaxy*: omission induced by preceding construction without preposition (*Tel Clergie*). XV 572 *techen*] *schewen*〉 *axay*: substitution through attraction to preceding copy (*shewe hym* 571). X 290 *manly*] *safly*〉 *axay*, or *aaxa* on another stave: substitution of an easier reading. XI 283 *wise*] *parfit*〉 *axay* or *aaxy*: substitution of a more emphatic reading. XIII 390 *conscience*] *herte*〉 *aabb*: sophistication; Conscience is not to appear in an unfavourable context.

These various examples of determining originality by discrimination will have shown what we understand by the authority of readings to which we earlier referred.[63] It remains to show from the textual situation where **B** has no recognizable equivalent in another version how we find such authority superior to that of majority manuscript support. This will appear from the following instances, of a similar character to those already set out, where the reading from its quality more probably original is attested by only one manuscript, or a single subgroup, or a few unrelated manuscripts, against the evidence of the rest.

XV 139 *meyne*] HmF; *men*: visual error; compare variation at V 99. V 37 *to*] CrC²; *so to*: substitution of a more explicit reading, perhaps induced by the alliteration. V 286 *þi bondes*] GF; *þi two b.*, XVI 147 *to knowe*] G; *how to k.*: more explicit readings. XI 278 *bidden*] GF; *b. good*: an easier reading; *bidden* used absolutely in the expression 'beg and bid' has the sense 'offer prayer for the almsgiver'. Prologue 152 *dedes*] OC²; *dredes*: the senses 'fear of fears' or 'fear of occasions of fear'[64] seem less appropriate and easier than 'fear of actions' with an accompanying pun on *dedes*, 'deaths'. The *r* of *drede* was subconsciously induced by the synonymic suggestion of *doute*. XI 217 *in comen*] *in come* G; *in commune*: the notion of the woman as an intruder, or at least unexpectedly present at the feast *in domo Pharisei* is necessary (compare Luke, vii, 45, *ex quo intrauit*). A visual error or misreading induced by preceding *commune*. XIII 331 *me loueþ*] WCr; *y loue*: the notion that the speaker's charity is ephemeral is inappropriate since from his report of himself he practises none: the contextual sense is superior when 331 and 332 are parallel. Substitution of the active voice induced by its recurrence in the preceding context. XIII 354 *his*] LR; *of h.*: the preposition is grammatically inappropriate; *his cote* must be subject of *Was* 355. Variation through attraction to preceding copy. XIV 171 *hem deere*] OC²; *be hem d.*: the

[62] For evidence that the poet used this pattern see above, p. 138.

[63] See above, pp. 128, 129.

[64] We do not consider that the meanings 'object or cause of fear', or 'danger, risk' (*NED* s.v. *Dread* sb. 2, *MED* s.v. *dred(e* 5) are lexically warranted by the respective examples offered.

sense 'be expensive for them', as less embracing than 'harm them', is inferior. Variation subconsciously induced by knowledge that food prices rise in times of scarcity, or simply to an easier reading. I 116 *myd*] W; *wyth* > *axay*: inattentive substitution of an unalliterating equivalent. VI 226 *þow*] LR; *om* > *aaxy*: omission of the rarely expressed imperative subject-pronoun induced by attraction between the imperative and its complementary infinitive. X 245 *propre*] R; *om* > *xaay*: omission through attraction between the two parts of the common collocation, or possibly because of difficulty with contraction or suspension.[65]

In this last group of examples identification of originality in a poorly attested reading includes the presumption that its survival in a single or a few manuscripts occurred by one of two processes: extensive convergent variation from the presumed original, or enlightened correction. Acceptance of these two possibilities is not, however, in any sense radical. The necessarily extreme frequency of the occurrence of convergent variation has already been shown at length.[66] For the occurrence of correction in some **B** manuscripts, which might on the present showing alone seem a purely speculative explanation, there is further strong evidence in textual situations where control from another version can be applied.[67] It is not, therefore, merely possible, but actually likely that the existence of majority or massive support for a variant of scribal character is the fortuitous result of coincident post-archetypal substitution; or, alternatively, that when a variant of intrinsically superior originality appears in certain manuscripts, it came to be there by correction of archetypal error. From these circumstances the strength of the authority of readings, as this is indicated by the editorial criteria, should be clear.

We pass now to illustrations from the textual situation where versions lineally correspond and the readings of **B** are exposed to comparison with those preserved in the manuscript traditions of the other versions.

Here discrimination is applied in the first instance to determine whether differences between the archetypal readings of the **B** tradition and those of **AC** or **A** or **C** were created by authorial revision or scribal variation. This minute delimitation of versions, which, we appreciate, is the most crucial operation in the whole editing of *Piers Plowman*, we

[65] We further discuss identification of originality in a uniquely attested variant below, pp. 165ff.

[66] In II above; see especially pp. 31, 32, 37, 38, 47, 63.

[67] See below, pp. 169–71.

have endeavoured to conduct with restraint, permitting ourselves to reach conclusions only in cases which seemed beyond serious doubt. For instance we accepted as authorial not only all large differences of structure or meaning, but also every smaller difference of meaning which did not seem explicable in terms of scribal imperception or evident stupidity, and every stylistic difference which might conceivably reflect an author's taste rather than a scribal tendency of variation. Where we could see so much as a possibility that the difference between **B** and another version might reflect some authorial intention we allowed this full force. Further we allowed the greater likelihood of finical and relatively insignificant revision in certain positions: for instance near the beginnings and ends of passus, as more exposed to the revising poet's attention; or in the vicinity of manifest revisions, especially insertions; or within heavily revised passages which the poet might himself have recopied in full and therefore more extensively altered in detail. We took particular account of the circumstance that the poet's revisions from **B** to **C** in the earlier part of the poem would be affected by his developing conception of his subject in the later part of **B**.[68] And we accepted the practical impossibility of editorial decision in many cases of trivial differences between the **B** and **C** versions where no motive for revision or unambiguous indication of direction of variation by scribes suggests itself. Such are most commonly simple differences between **B** and **C** of number, tense or word order, of prepositions with corresponding functions, of equally appropriate pronouns, of equally appropriate expressions with distinct meanings, of equally serviceable grammatical constructions, or of the presence or absence of a term where either circumstance would be explicable as a scribal variation.[69] They occur

[68] Major instances will quickly come to mind, such as the transference of detail from Haukyn's account of his spiritual state to the confessions of the Sins, and the amalgamation in **C** V of the traits and attributes progessively acquired by the Dreamer during the composition of **B**. This circumstance also bears on minor differences. For example at **B** I 146 Holychurch enjoins the Dreamer, *Loke þow suffre hym to seye and siþen lere it after*, while in **C** I 145 the second half-line reads *and so thow myht lerne*. The fact that the change can be related to **B** XI, especially 413ff., where the need to listen rather than dispute is enjoined, suggests that this difference is by authorial revision. The same is true of an altered Latin element of a line: at **B** III 328 it is prophesied that Saracens will sing *Gloria in excelsis*, at **C** III 481 their song is to be a clause from the Creed; the change relates to the theme of evangelism extensively developed in **B** XV, and specifically to 611 there.

[69] The following examples illustrate the most material differences of this type. Prol. 102 **C** Prol. 130 hiȝte/wolde; XI 350 **C** XIII 161 it were/me thynketh; XII 192 **C** XIV 131 speke/toldest; XII 205 **C** XIV 144 erþe/grounde; XII 209 **C** XIV 148 neiþer/no; XII 286 **C** XIV 208 þat/al; XIV 263 **C** XVI 103 and/in; XV 26 **C** XVI 186 is my name/y hatte; XVI 264 **C** XVIII 280 Out of/Fro; XVII 29 **C** XIX 30 in parcelles/parselmele; XVII 336 **C** XIX 316 it/he; XVIII 29 **C** XX 28 shal/wol; XVIII 145 **C** XX 148 þow/hit.

throughout the poem, but most often in its second half where **A** is not available as a control, and especially in passages where major revision is absent. Our positive findings, that is of instances where the text of **B** differs from that of other versions by scribal agency in the archetypal **B** tradition, together with the arguments in support, form the substance of Section III and we cannot repeat them here. We will, however, extend the illustration to include instances where the difference between a majority **B** reading and that of **AC** or **A** or **C** results from early corruption in the **B** tradition, but where because of the absence or vagrancy of one or more **B** manuscripts it is not possible to treat that corrupt reading as archetypal with entire confidence.

Here as elsewhere discrimination relies on two considerations: the inferiority of one reading with respect to style, sense or verse technique; and the possibility of accounting for its existence by established processes of substitution. Examples are arranged in accordance with the latter.

Thus when compared with the reading of **AC**, the majority (and possibly archetypal) reading of **B** appears scribal in the following cases.

Attraction to preceding copy: V 613 so[70]] **A** VI 99 **C** VII 265; þanne/*zero*. *Alliterative inducement:* VI 323 þoruȝ] **A** VII 304 **C** VIII 344; wiþ/sum. *A more explicit reading substituted:* Prologue 29 Coueiten] **A** Prologue 29 **C** Prologue 31; And/that c.; Prologue 48 Wenten] **A** Prologue 48 **C** Prologue 49; They/⁊ w.; I 188 Chastite] **A** I 162 **C** I 184; Forþi/þerfore/for c.; V 188 Thanne] **A** V 107 **C** VI 196; And þanne/Affter hym; VIII 70 lik] **A** IX 61 **C** X 68; and/mychil l.; IX 173 Though] **A** X 194 **C** X 275; And þouȝ. *An easier reading substituted:* V 514 baches] **A** VI 2 **C** VII 159; bankes/balkys. *A more emphatic reading substituted:* V 630 By] **A** VI 115 **C** VII 283; Now/A by; VI 88 defende it fro þe fende] **A** VII 80 **C** VIII 97; fro þe f. it defende/Ikeped it; X 431 Cristene] **A** XI 290 **C** XI 267; Muche c. *Smoothing after preceding transposition:* I 104 passeþ] **A** I 102 **C** I 98; passed.

Similarly when compared with the reading of **A** the majority reading of **B** appears scribal in the following.

Attraction to preceding copy: VI 301 þei] **A** VII 285; and/þan. *Alliterative inducement:* V 112 Thanne I wisshe] **A** V 92; I w. þanne/that/ofte. *A more explicit reading substituted:* I 49 he] **A** I 47; god/cryst; I 107 Yaf] **A** I 105; And y.; IV 15 sente] **A** IV 15; bad/seide⟩*axay*; V 72 hym] **A** V 55; his soule; V 348 to lacche wiþ] **A** V 196; for to l./cacche; V 515 late] **A** VI 3; l. was/it was l.; V 525 faire] **A** VI 13; first/*zero*; V 526 þe Sepulcre] **A** VI 14; oure lordes S./ synay hyȝe hilles; VI 58 þe wey] **A** VII 53; I wile/*zero*; VI 87

[70] The spelling of the presumed original is that of our text. Where two or more **B** variants are cited the first is the likelier archetypal reading, and the explanation of variation applies to this; other **B** variants are taken to be by further variation or by sophistication.

haþ deserued] **A** VII 79; haþ d. it/ys worthy; VI 167 now] **A** VII 152; and now/ne... now; VI 301 hym] **A** VII 285; hunger/he; VI 310 yfryed] **A** VII 294; fryed ouþer ybake; VI 312 But] **A** VII 296; But if/and but/And but if; VII 187 on erþe] **A** VIII 165; on þis e./heere; VIII 83 Trusty] **A** IX 74; And is t./& trewe; IX 145 þe] **A** X 176; þi/þis; X 5 wit quod she] **A** XI 5; q. s. to wit/ q.s. *An easier reading substituted:* II 183 iotten] **A** II 144; rennen/ȝede; IV 118 an heþyng] **A** IV 104; vnhende/an hyne/nauȝte/vanite; V 473 coupe] **A** V 247; gilt; V 621 hire] **A** VI 107; hise/the; VI 267 alonged] **A** VII 251; afyngred/alustyd; IX 27 þe first of alle þynges] **A** X 28; of al þat euere was maked/of alle þynge on erthe; X 128 hele] **A** XI 81; fynger/elbowe; X 352 as] **A** XI 235; amonges/ of. *A more emphatic reading substituted:* Prologue 37 hem liste] **A** Prologue 37; they schulde/ wolde; III 215 wiþ hise] **A** III 202; and alle/also; V 328 togideres] **A** V 177; in truþe/þat tyȝme; V 448 faste] **A** V 220; swiþe/on þe forhed; X 51 þise arn games nowadaies] **A** XI 37; þis murþe/glee þei louyeþ; X 339 yeris] **A** XI 227; heris; X 340 ne rentes] **A** XI 228; riȝt noȝt.

And when compared with the reading of **C** the majority reading of **B** appears scribal in the following.

Visual error: XVIII 100 remyng] **C** XX 103; rennyng/renegat. *Unconscious omission:* IX 182 man] **C** X 283; *zero* (*note* manere *preceding*); IX 185 and yeep] **C** X 286; *zero* (*eyeskip*); IX 203b, 204a] *cp.* **C** X 302, 303; *zero, with padding* (*homœoarchy*); XVII 237 noȝt] **C** XIX 203; *zero* (*attraction to stave word*). *Substitution induced by preceding copy:* III 62 who paied] **C** III 66; and paie; VIII 14 ye] **C** X 14; þei; XVI 273 we] **C** XVIII 289; he; XVIII 48 grene] **C** XX 48; kene/þat〉 *axay*; XVIII 106 by vsurie libben] **C** XX 109; vsurie vsen/ȝee v. shull vse. *Substitution induced by following copy:* XV 546 clerkes] **C** XVII 207; men. *Attraction to class of surrounding personal pronouns:* XVII 320 swich] **C** XIX 296; hym〉 *aaxy*. *Attraction between verb and adverb:* XIX 62 may be wel] **C** XXI 62; m. wel be/m. be. *Alliterative attraction:* XIII 174 Kan...parfournen] **C** XV 172; K...conformen/ confirme〉 *xaay*. *A more explicit reading substituted:* V 478 I] **C** VII 120; For I/&; XII 201 But] **C** XIV 140; But sete/& s.; XVII 330 þe borre] **C** XIX 310; hoors/cowȝhe〉 *aaxy*; XIX 15 crist] **C** XXI 15; c. quod I/he; XIX 153 yede] **C** XXI 153; he y; XIX 159 cride] **C** XXI 159; she/he c. *An easier reading substituted:* XI 121 saufte] **C** XII 56; saue/ safly; XIII 16 ech lif] **C** XV 19; bestes/briddes〉 *axay*; XV 548 Mynne] **C** XVII 209; Wite〉 *xaay*; XV 551 er come auȝt] **C** XVII 213; er〉 *aaxy*; XV 566 Charite] **C** XVII 230; Good〉 *xaay*; XIX 182 þouȝte] **C** XXI 182; tauȝte/took sone; XIX 205 for] **C** XXI 205; of〉 *axaa or axay*; XX 104 hir lemmans] **C** XXII 104; lemmans (of). *A more emphatic reading substituted:* XV 555 lese ye shul for euere] **C** XVII 217; for euere s. y. l.〉 *aaxa*; XIX 448 of] **C** XXI 448; of al. *Sophistication:* VI 189 to wedynge and mowynge] **C** VIII 186; wiþ spades and (wiþ) shoueles〉 *aabb* / to swynkyn abowtyn〉 *aaxy* (*sense adjusted to following line*): XIX 154 preide(2)] **C** XXI 154; bisouȝte〉 *aaxy* (*eliminating repetition*); XIX 363 in holynesse] **C** XXI 363; in vnite/strong (*eliminating jingle*).

As well as revealing the many certain or probable archetypal **B** errors discussed above and earlier in III, the editorial situation where **B** can be compared with the presumably unrevised text of **AC** or **A** or **C** brings to light hundreds of instances in which, while the **B** manuscripts disagree, a genetic or variational **B** group or even a single **B** manuscript agrees in its reading with the presumed original text of one or both the other versions.

While such agreement is necessarily significant, it can never mechanically decide originality among the **B** variants. This is still to be identified by the discrimination which has already suggested the improbability of revision. The first effect of the external support is to draw attention to a particular **B** variant; the second is to raise the question whether that variant is likely to have generated its rivals by known processes of corruption, and whether the editorial criteria show these to have the scribal quality which establishes direction of variation. Only on these considerations does the variant which external support has initially represented as authorial in another version appear also as the original reading of **B**. Moreover if the so indicated original reading of **B** is attested by a random group or a single **B** copy a reasonable explanation for such attestation must be possible.[71] Thus the ultimate authority is that of the variants.

This reasoning can be shown from the many points where the text of **A** or **C** is itself an edited text, the product of discrimination. There it often occurs that variation in **A** or **C** manuscripts resembles that of the **B** tradition. For instance where all versions are available the choice of originality can lie between two variants found in manuscripts of **A**, **B** and **C**, or between two variants found in the **A** and **B** manuscripts, of which only one occurs in **C**, or between two variants found in **B** and **C** manuscripts, of which only one occurs in **A**. At such points decisions about the originality of **B**, if independently made, would simply repeat decisions required in the case of one or both other versions. But unless authorial revision seems a possibility they cannot be independently made. The situation where the choice between readings of **B** is the same as that called for in another version shows discrimination in its real character, as a single determination of originality applicable to several versions and based on their joint evidence.

Thus the choice at V 208 **A** V 124 **C** VI 216 is between partially synonymous *list* and *liser* attested in manuscripts of all versions; at I 206 **A** I 180 **C** I 201 between *by siȝte of* attested in manuscripts of all versions and *by* attested in those of **A** and **B**; at IX 9 **A** X 9 **C** X 136

[71] This requirement we discuss below, pp. 164ff.

between partially synonymous *if* attested in manuscripts of all versions and *and* attested in those of **B** and **C**. In each case the nature of the variation makes revision seem an improbability; all versions are therefore presumed to have had the same original text. The distribution of support is evidently no indication of originality. If this is to be identified at all[72] it will be by means of the criteria which suggest direction of variation. Thus at V 208 substitution of *liser* can have been induced by attraction to following *lenger*, while the local text has no features to suggest the reverse; therefore *list* is presumed original. At I 206 *siȝte of* is essential if the second half-line is to alliterate; its unconscious omission could have been induced by preoccupation with the notion of authority present in *textes*. On these grounds the original text read *by siȝte of*. At IX 9 *and*, as ambiguous, might seem harder than *if*, and therefore the likelier to have been ousted. But the occurrence of *and* twice in the line with different values constitutes a pun, and the poet never plays on words except significantly, which would not here seem the case. Meanwhile *if*] *and* variation could have been induced by the presence of *And* at the head of the line; therefore *if* is the likelier original. Examples of discrimination in circumstances of these kinds are very numerous; we restrict ourselves to the following.

All versions are represented and rival **B** readings occur in manuscripts of one or both the others. *Unconscious omission, induced by alliterative attraction:* Prologue 22 **A** Prol. 22 **C** Prol. 24 þise] *om*; II 138 **A** II 102 **C** II 154 þe] *om*; *by homoarchy*: VI 95 **A** VII 87 **C** VIII 104 me] *om*; *by homoteleuton*: X 179 **A** XI 131 **C** XI 119 mo] *om*. *Visual error induced by preceding context:* V 325 **A** V 174 **C** VI 383 Tho] Two. *Attraction to preceding copy:* I 176 **A** I 150 **C** I 172 myȝty] myȝtful; II 228 **A** II 187 **C** II 238 wiþ] to. *Careless substitution through inattention to sense:* I 54 **A** I 52 **C** I 50 riȝtfully] ryȝtful. *A more explicit reading substituted:* I 85 **A** I 83 **C** I 81 tried] t. quod she; II 108 **A** II 72 **C** II 112 which] þis (>*axay or aaxa*); IV 58 **A** IV 45 **C** IV 61 Otes] of O.; IV 79 **A** IV 65 **C** IV 75 woot] it w.; IV 110 **A** IV 97 **C** IV 105 Somme] Som men; IV 131 **A** IV 114 **C** IV 128 who] whoso; IV 186 **A** IV 149 **C** IV 180 But] B. if; V 29 **A** V 29 **C** V 131 fro] f. þe; VII 34 **A** VIII 36 **C** IX 37 angel] Archangel. *An easier reading substituted:* I 73 **A** I 71 **C** I 70 halsede] asked; VI 127 **A** VII 119 **C** VIII 133 of] for. VIII 40 **A** IX 36 **C** X 46 walkeþ] walweþ.[73] *A more emphatic reading substituted:* V 128 **A** V 105 **C** VI 93 sory] euere s.; VII 65 **A** VIII 67 **C** IX 61 and] ne/nor; IX 4 **A** X 4 **C** X 131 wittily] witterly. *Sophistication:* II 238 **A** II 197 **C** II 254 fere] drede (*avoiding repetition*); VII 117 **A** VIII 99 **C** IX 290 and(2)] *om* (*rejecting apparent parallelism of the two parts of the line*).

[72] See below, pp. 162, 163 for the type of variation where this seems impossible.
[73] **A** should have been emended here.—*G.K.*

The **A** and **B** versions are represented and rival **B** readings occur in manuscripts of **A.** *Misreading of an orthographically difficult word:* II 185 **A** II 146 meynee] men. *Terminal transposition through failure of memory:* VI 109 **A** VII 100 faste] yerne. *Attraction to preceding copy:* V 108 **A** V 88 hym] *pl.*; VII 4 **A** VIII 4 euere] for e.; X 227 **A** XI 170 I] And. *Attraction to following copy:* III 293 **A** III 268 to] ayein. *Alliterative attraction:* III 5 **A** III 5 wol] shal; III 6 **A** III 6 world] moolde (>*aaxy*); VI 45 **A** VII 44 shalt] may/might. *A more explicit reading substituted:* I 59 **A** I 57 The] That; I 125 **A** I 114 somme(2)] and s.; II 113 **A** II 77 þe(3)] þis; II 122 **A** II 86 The] Thi; III 209 **A** III 196 a(1)] to a; VII 103 **A** VIII 85 myschief] *pl.*; VII 139 **A** VIII 121 after] afterward; X 138 **A** XI 91 I] For I; X 337 **A** XI 225 but] b. if; X 375 **A** XI 256 punysshe] p. hem; X 467 **A** XI 311 swiche] and s. *An easier reading substituted:* Prol. 224 **A** Prol. 102 dede] *pl.*; I 25 **A** I 25 it] *om*; II 9 **A** II 9 pureste] fyneste; II 140 **A** II 104 fals] þe f.; IV 142 **A** IV 125 made] make; VIII 125 **A** IX 115 To] And; X 167 **A** XI 119 hym] it. *A more emphatic reading substituted:* IV 31 **A** IV 28 seluen] for siluer; V 72 **A** V 55 mysdede] *pl.*; VI 76 **A** VII 68 holde] hote; VI 204 **A** VII 190 ille] ful i.; VI 269 **A** VII 253 hood] *pl.*; VII 139 **A** VIII 121 bettre] muche moore; X 311 **A** XI 211 rennere] Romere; X 338 **A** XI 226 auȝt] noȝt. *'Improvement' of alliteration:* I 8 **A** I 8 kepe] wilne; I 108 **A** I 106 meynee] meene m.[74] *Stylistic substitutions:* V 78 **A** V 61 He was] And (*repetition avoided*); VI 41 **A** VII 40 þee] yow (*the courteous plural preferred*); X 157 **A** XI 109 wel] it (*the jingle* do wel...dar wel *avoided:* > *aaxy*). *Sophistication:* IX 23 **A** X 22 sixe] fyue (*miscounting:* > *xaay*); IX 31 **A** X 32 shape] shafte (*censorship*).

The **B** and **C** versions are represented and rival **B** readings occur in manuscripts of **C.** *Unconscious omission, induced by the sensational topic:* XV 530 **C** XVII 279 in] *om*; *by attraction between opposites:* XIV 294 **C** XVI 129 riȝt] *om* (>*xaay*); *by attraction between verb and principal adverb:* XIX 73 **C** XXI 73 riȝt] *om* (>*axay*); *by attraction between imperative and emphatic adverb:* XI 103 **C** XII 37 þow] *om* (>*xaay*); *by adjacency of homonyms:* XX 350 **C** XXII 350 here(2)] *om*. *Auditory error:* XVII 340 **C** XIX 320 ouȝte] ofte. *Misreading of an unexpected adjective:* III 342 **C** III 494 felle] fele. *Careless substitution of exact equivalent:* XVIII 420 **C** XX 463 seyde] quod (>*aaxy*). *Substitution induced by preceding context:* Prol. 176 **C** Prol. 190 ybrouȝt] Ibouȝt (bugge 168 **C** 183). *Attraction to following copy:* XVII 183 **C** XIX 149 or] and; XIX 394 **C** XXI 394 Or] That. *Alliterative attraction:* XVIII 424 **C** XX 467 carolden] dauncede. *A more explicit reading substituted:* Prol. 150 **C** Prol. 168 at] at his; Prol. 175 **C** Prol. 189 þe] þis; V 182 **C** VI 164 repente] r. þee; XI 250 **C** XII 136 made] she m.; XVII 59 **C** XIX 58 aboute] a. hym; XVII 324 **C** XIX 304 fleeþ] f. fro; XIX 415 **C** XXI 415 and(1)] a. hir; XIX 422 **C** XXI 422 Iewes] þe I.; XIX 457 **C** XXI 457 to] for to; XX 36 **C** XXII 36 þat] of þ. *An easier reading substituted:* V 291 **C** VI 346 be] is (>*aaxy* or *aaxa*); XI 8 **C** XI 167 and loue] allone; XI 267 **C** XII 152 segge] man (>*aaxy*); XI 328 **C** XIII 136 make] *pl*; XIII 35 **C** XV 40 mettes] macches; XIII 51 **C** XV 57 lif] I lyue; XIII 103 **C** XV 110 dobest] dowel; XIV 198 **C** XVI 39 welle] wille; XV 532 **C** XVII 281 were] was; XVIII 101 **C** XX 104 yvenquisshed] avenged; XVIII 199 **C** XX 204 I] and; XIX 216 **C** XXI 216 kan hise] han hir (>*aaxy*); XIX 273 **C** XXI 273 aiþes] harewes; XX 60 **C** XXII 60 a] þat; XX 360 **C** XXII 360 And]

[74] This variant could also derive from copying an interlinear spelling correction into the text.

He; XX 363 **C** XXII 363 gropeþ] and g. *A more emphatic reading substituted:* XIX 249 **C** XXI 249 pacience] penaunce; XIX 412 **C** XXI 412 feþere] f. or an hennes. *Sophistication:* V 500 **C** VII 140 dou3tiest] dou3ty (*the scribe, missing the reference to Christ's passion, crucifixion and resurrexion, registers the view that all His deeds were equally 'doughty'*).

The above demonstrations will have shown how any authority possessed by the reading of another version derives entirely from the quality of that reading; the fact that the **A** or **C** variants in question most often[75] presented the same choice as those of **B** brings this out clearly. The same principle applies without qualification when the archetypal **A** or **C** reading which agrees with one of several **B** readings is unanimous or otherwise unmistakable. The fact that it is not subject to challenge within its own tradition is no immediate guarantee of its originality, for this signifies in the first instance only the necessarily fortuitous absence of variation in the post-archetypal tradition of the version concerned at that point. When therefore the **B** manuscripts disagree and the reading of a genetic or variational **B** group or a **B** manuscript happens also to be that of the archetypal **AC** or **A** or **C** text we apply discrimination as rigorously as in the case of variation among **B** manuscripts where the text of **B** is unique. Its effectiveness depends, naturally, on our perception as editors, but there is never any question of mechanically accepting external support as superior authority. As elsewhere we find originality in the reading which answers best to the sense or *usus scribendi* or verse technique of the poet while relating the other variation to conditions which would induce substitution or to the typical scribal effects of substitution.

This we now illustrate from examples where the manuscripts of **B** disagree and where one of the **B** readings which for distinct reasons appears original receives external support from the unanimously attested or otherwise unmistakable archetypal text of **AC** or **A** or **C**.

Attraction, to preceding copy: IX 24 **A** X 24 **C** X 150 kepe] saue (>*aabb*); *to following copy:* V 583 **A** VI 70 **C** VII 230 þow see] ye see (se-ye). *Substitution of a more explicit reading:* I 92 **A** I 90 **C** I 88 it(1)] þis; III 114 **A** III 103 **C** III 151 Thanne] And þ.; III 160 **A** III 149 **C** III 198 mote] m. hire/here; V 212 **A** V 128 **C** VI 220 tolled] hadde t.; V 638 **A** VI 123 **C** VII 291 so] by soo; VI 207 **A** VII 193 **C** VIII 216 for] quod Piers f.; VII 1 **A** VIII 1 **C** IX 1 sente] he s. *Substitution of an easier reading:* II 212 **A** II 171 **C** II 222 feeres] felawes; X 225 **A** XI 167 **C** XI 134 my wey] awey. *Substitution of a more*

[75] There are exceptions, when three versions are represented and only two vary similarly, among the examples on pp. 153 ff.

emphatic reading: IV 105 **A** IV 92 **C** IV 100 er I] erst wole I; V 15 **A** V 15 **C** V 117 pride] pure p.; VII 65 **A** VIII 67 **C** IX 61 beþ] ne b. *Sophistication:* III 48 **A** III 47 **C** III 51 stonden] sitten (*miscomprehension*); VIII 44 **A** IX 40 **C** X 43 helpeþ] kepeþ (*avoiding repetition*).

Unconscious variation to prose order: VIII 78 **A** IX 69 Dowel quod he] Dowel...þridde q. h. *Substitution induced by preceding copy:* VIII 42 **A** IX 38 false] frele (brotel 41).[76] *Substitution of a more explicit reading:* II 45 **A** II 27 There] And þ.; II 153 **A** II 117 wit] *pl.*; II 158 **A** II 122 Fals] Falsnesse; III 115 **A** III 104 clerkes] as c.; IV 111 **A** IV 98 to] for to; V 27 **A** V 27 nede] hire n.; VI 124 **A** VII 116 We] For we.; VI 183 **A** VII 171 fere] f. ther/herof; VI 232 **A** VII 216 geaunt] g. þe; VIII 90 **A** IX 81 And] A. þus; VIII 92 **A** IX 83 þe] to þe; X 421 **A** XI 280 þefte] wiþ þ. *Substitution of an easier reading:* VI 51 **A** VII 46 it be] þei ben. *Substitution of a more emphatic reading:* I 70 **A** I 68 bitrayed are] bitrayeþ he; IV 99 **A** IV 86 ofte] so o.; V 83 **A** V 66 bollen] tobollen; V 128 **A** V 105 sory] euere s.; VIII 57 **A** IX 48 conceyuen] c. alle; X 427 **A** XI 286 Wiþouten] W. any. *Sophistication:* Prol. 62 **A** Prol. 59 maistres] m. freres (*incorporation of interlinear gloss*); III 46 **A** III 45 baude] brocour (*censorship*); V 632 **A** VI 117 waferer] wafrestere (*anti-feminism*); VI 253 **A** VII 237 þee] yow (*courteous plural preferred*); X 424 **A** XI 283 Or] And or/er (*conjunction mistaken for temporal adverb*).

Unconscious omission of intervening syntactical element: XI 240 **C** XII 129 sooþliche] *om* (>*axay*). *Suspension misread:* Prol. 149 **C** Prol. 167 court] contree; X 256 **C** XI 157 merite] mercy. *Careless visual error:* XIII 410 **C** VII 70 Is whan men] hys woman; XX 310 **C** XXII 310 in þe sege] þe segge. *Variation by inducement to parallelism:* III 301 **C** III 454 pees] a p.; V 32 **C** V 134 He] And. *Substitution induced by alliterative attraction:* III 67 **C** III 71 god] crist; V 405 **C** VII 21 men(2)] folk; XI 436 **C** XIII 242 foule] soure; XIX 118 **C** XXI 118 fauntekyn] faunt fyn; XX 62 **C** XXII 62 gladdere] leuere. *Transposition induced by alliterative attraction:* XX 211 **C** XXII 211 Weede...mete] Mete...weede. *Attraction to preceding copy:* Prol. 179 **C** Prol. 193 his] þe cattes; X 88 **C** XI 68 techeþ] telleþ (deleþ 87); XI 20 **C** XI 179 myrþes] myȝtes; XI 102 **C** XII 36 To] And; XIII 96 **C** XV 103 leef] lif/lyue/lyne; XVII 154 **C** XIX 129 hand] fust; XVII 329 **C** XIX 309 smerteþ] smyteþ; XIX 77 **C** XXI 77 knowlichede] knowelichynge (askynge). *Attraction to following copy:* V 501 **C** VII 141 it] me (se- þe we); XII 99 **C** XIV 44 eiȝen] siȝte; XV 532 **C** XVII 281 Er] Er any; XVI 77 **C** XVIII 109 he] it. *Substitution induced by preceding context:* I 154 **C** I 150 selue] fille (yeten *misread as* '*eaten*'); XII 104 **C** XIV 49 lereþ] ledeþ (strete 103 *and the topic of blindness*); XIX 117 **C** XXI 117 oonly] holy. *Substitution of a more explicit reading:* V 393 **C** VII 9 day] d. quod he; V 504 **C** VII 149 soore] here s.; XI 109 **C** XII 43 louyen] l. it; XI 263 **C** XII 149 So] So is; XI 264 **C** XII 150 Makeþ] For it m.; XII 187 **C** XIV 126 hym to book sette] h.s. to scole (>*aabb*); XII 280 **C** XIV 202 to] for to; XIV 213 **C** XVI 54 bifore] b. þe riche; XX 27 **C** XXII 27 body] of hem (>*aaxy*); XX 60 **C** XXII 60 cam] forþ c.; XX 208 **C** XXII 208 leef] l. of; XX 210 **C** XXII 210 lelly] l. quod he; XX 253 **C** XXII 253 telle] teche; XX 277 **C** XXII 277 He] And yet he; XX 284 **C** XXII 284 be] sholde be. *Substitution of an easier reading:* V 239

[76] Here and in several other of these instances **C** has the **B** reading presumed unoriginal. Cp. above, pp. 99–103.

C VI 241 a lesson and of Iewes] and I. a lesson (>*aaxa*); VI 72 **C** VIII 73 faitour] þe f.; X 87 **C** XI 67 ledes] londes; X 397 **C** XI 228 herte] *pl.*; XV 100 **C** XVI 253 Is þe] That aren; XVII 144 **C** XIX 118 þe piþ of] purely; XVII 306 **C** XIX 286 be] þat is; XVIII 157 **C** XX 160 vertu] venym; XIX 130 **C** XXI 130 and dombe speke and herde] to here and d.s. he made; XX 38 **C** XXII 38 Philosophres] Wise men; XX 126 **C** XXII 126 suede] sente; XX 291 **C** XXII 291 shul] wol; XX 382 **C** XXII 382 myȝte] may. *Substitution of a more emphatic reading:* III 335 **C** III 487 muche] moost; VII 152 **C** IX 300 þe] al þe; XIV 294 **C** XVI 129 poore] any p.; XIX 179 **C** XXI 179 be] alle be; XIX 283 **C** XXI 283 meschief] muchel drynke; XIX 284 **C** XXI 284 scornere] s. ne scolde; XX 39 **C** XXII 39 wel elengely] in wildernesse; XX 191 **C** XXII 191 wangteeþ] teeþ. *Sophistication:* V 183 **C** VI 165 speche] siȝt (*the modification of the adverbial phrases mistaken*); XI 289 **C** XIII 103 lynnen ne wollen] w. ne l. (>*aaxa: elegant variation from* 282); XI 297 **C** XIII 111 riche] *zero* (*an apparently superfluous element omitted to shorten the line*); XI 331 **C** XIII 139 se boþe] b. biholde (*the meaning of* boþe, '*as well*', *missed*); XX 55 **C** XXII 55 made] *zero* (sprynge *and* sprede *mistaken for finite verbs*); XX 67 **C** XXII 67 gile] any while (*smoothing after* hir] hem *variation*); XX 260 **C** XXII 260 take hem wages] hem paie (>*axay: shortening a long line*); XX 336 **C** XXII 336 frere] segge (*embellishing alliteration*).

In contrast with the above instances where discrimination shows originality to lie with a **B** variant found also in manuscripts of another version there are others where it shows a **B** reading, whether unanimous or challenged within the **B** tradition, to be of superior originality to the reading or readings of another version and therefore the probable original of both. These instances again comprise all types of variation and degrees of interest and complexity; similarly the distribution of support is various: the **B** reading found original may be unanimous; or **B** variation may differ altogether from that of the other tradition; or the reading of the other tradition found unoriginal may also appear as a **B** variant.

For instance at III 76, 77 **A** III 65, 66 the archetypal **A** text reads *Meiris and maceris hij þat ben mene / Betwyn þe king & þe comunes to kepe þe lawis*; in all **B** manuscripts the lines are divided after 'between'. The scansion of the first line in **A**, *aaxa*, is characteristically scribal; **A**'s archetypal line division is explicable as produced by scribal resistance to the separation of close grammatical units. On these grounds the lines in both originals were divided as in the **B** manuscripts. At IV 77 **A** IV 63, which scans *Méde mýd mércy*, the alliteration of the archetypal **A** line is imperfect through inattentive substitution of *wiþ*, which also occurs as a variant in some **B** manuscripts. At VIII 64 **A** IX 55 where one genetic **B** group reads *abide me made* archetypal **A** has the prose order *made me abide*, against scanning *aaxa*. At X 393 **A** XI 277 a possibility that the second half-line is revised, which we have allowed, does not extend to the first: on grounds of its inappropriate sense the archetypal **A** form cannot have been original. The meaning required by the preceding context in both versions is that of the unanimous **B** reading, *That for hir werkes*, 'Who, despite their achievements'. Substitution of the *And* of archetypal **A** will have been induced by its occurrence at the head of the two preceding lines.

In addition to these evident errors the archetype of **A** contains others which it shares with **BC** or **B**,[77] but otherwise it seems to have been relatively uncorrupt.[78] This cannot be said of the archetypal **C** text: the occasions when the **B** tradition preserves an original reading common to **B** and **C** but lost from the **C** tradition are more numerous. To complete our illustration of the reasoning and results of discrimination we now discuss a selection of these.

For instance at XVIII 55, 56 **C** XX 55, 56 the archetypal **C** text, by misdivision and padding, has three lines: the pattern *xaay* of the first and the absence of alliteration from the second show this division to be a scribal variation from that unanimously attested in the **B** tradition. At VIII 7 **C** X 7 for **B**'s archetypal *þis leode* all **C** manuscripts read simply *this* or a smoothing further variation, their line scanning *xaay*: *leode* was evidently original, and archetypally lost in **C** through homoarchy. At XX 70 **C** XXII 70 *bar it bare*] *bar þe/þat baner; it bar* (>*xaay*), originality is identifiable from the superior meaning of *bare*, 'uncased', 'displayed as a sign of battle', as also from the likelihood of substitution or insertion of *banere* as an easier reading or alliterative repair and the inducement of homoarchy to omission. In both **B** and **C** manuscripts variation is free; the original survives in F, here in the absence of R possibly representing its group (RF).

The **C** archetype was otherwise variously corrupted by omission. At XIV 71 **C** XV 270 a variant form *neuere moore*] *neuere*, found in some **B** and all **C** manuscripts, lacks a third stave and scans *aaxy*. From considerations of verse technique *moore* was originally present in both versions; it will have been omitted either deliberately to shorten a long line or unconsciously through attraction between the more emphatic

[77] These are discussed below, pp. 210, 211.

[78] Various differences between its text as printed in Vol. I and that of **B** are in fact scribal and will disappear on more rigorously logical editing of **A**. Its editor is now embarrassed to recall his conservatism with respect to some of these.

element of a compound adverb and its verb. At XIX 75 **C** XXI 75 the variation is *offrede sense*] *offrede*. It is plain that reference to incense is called for here from 86 below, no less than from two scribes having worked the word *Rechels* or *Ensence* into the next line. The necessity of its original presence is confirmed by the possibility of explaining its loss: through the inducement to parallelism exercised by *knelynge and songe* just above. The original reading is preserved in two **B** manuscripts, one visibly corrected and the other probably representing a main genetic group.

The **C** archetype contains visual errors correctable from **B** evidence. At X 468 **C** XI 294 **C**'s banal and pointless alternative, *paradys oper heuene* is not even conceivably a revision of **B**'s *paleys of heuene* and must register either careless misreading or a guess at a partly illegible exemplar. At XI 339 **C** XIII 147 most **B** and all **C** manuscripts read *a/on/in/and morwenynge(s)* which, in the context of the seasonal mating of animals, is absurd: a single **B** manuscript reads *all mornynge*. Referring to the ancient notion *post coitum est omne animal triste*, this variant appears the probable original as both meaningful and by its difficulty likely to have generated a homœograph. At XVII 22 **C** XIX 23 **C**'s *(y)founde* is a visual error for the more meaningful *founded* (*NED* s.v. *Found* v.[1] 4.b) of some **B** manuscripts. At XIX 76 **C** XXI 76 most **B** and all **C** manuscripts read *wipouten mercy askynge*. In this context *mercy* in its primary senses is pointless, and the lexical evidence for taking it to mean 'thanks' is very poor.[79] One **B** manuscript reads *mercede*, the last three letters by correction, and a **B** subgroup [(CrS)M] reads *mede*, in M over erasure of more than four letters. Thus originality lies between *mede* and the rare, but Langlandian expression *mercede*. Since the latter could have generated a gloss *mede* and a homœograph *mercy* it is identified as original from likelihood of direction of variation. At XIX 478 **C** XXI 478 most **B** and all **C** manuscripts read *right wel and in*, unobjectionable in itself. This is challenged by *as right wyll &* in a single copy. The unspecific and uncritical emphasis of the majority reading shows it to be scribal. At XX 366 **C** XXII 366 most **B** and **C** manuscripts have the probably archetypal variant *my lady* by misreading of contracted *memoria*.

The **B** tradition preserves original readings where the **C** archetype

[79] The three *Piers Plowman* instances where the word has this sense are evidently social gallicisms and thus not analogous uses. See I 43, X 224 and XVII 88.

was corrupted by subconsciously induced faulty recollection. For instance at III 217 **C** III 273 for *we seeþ wel þe soþe* the **C** archetype reads *Mede they asken* (>*aaxy*) by attraction to the third line following; at XX 109 **C** XXII 109, like most **B** manuscripts, it varies *sone*] *þo* by inducement of *to* following or of *þo kynde* (106) or of *þo* (110). It has readings which on comparison with a **B** variant appear unoriginal as more explicit: XX 97 **C** XXII 97 *after*] *a. hym*; or easier: XVIII 76 **C** XX 78 *þrowe*] *tyme*; or more emphatic: III 283 **C** III 436 *soþes*] *soþest.*[80] From evidence in the **B** tradition it is occasionally even possible to identify sophistication in the text of archetypal **C** or, in the last two passus, in the ultimate common archetype of both traditions. Thus at XV 371 **C** XVII 107 where one main genetic **B** group reads *element(s)* the **C** archetype has *clymat*. Both terms, in medieval scientific senses, could pass muster in the context. But while no reason for substitution of *element* suggests itself there is one for the reverse in the alliteration of the line: scanning *cálcúled cóntrarie* this would be hard, as indeed is indicated by the **B** nonsense variant *clement* which records scribal preoccupation with it. Thus unless it is an authorial revision *clymat* originated in scribal 'improvement' of the alliteration. At XVIII 194 **C** XX 199 most **B** and most **C** manuscripts read *þe fruyt eten* (>*aaxy*); one **C** manuscript *tasted of þe fruyt*; one **B** manuscript *þe trees fruyt eten*. The variant *tasted of* etc. cannot have generated the corruption of the majority. On the other hand, while the insertion of a repetitive term is not typically scribal, its omission, because the point of the emphatic reiteration was missed, is a likely variation. On these considerations the original read *trees fruyt*, and the **C** variant *tasted* etc. is a skilful scribal emendation. At XIX 90 **C** XXI 90 the majority of **B** and **C** manuscripts read in the first half-line *and resoun to ryche gold*: one **B** and two **C** manuscripts respectively omit the line or its second half for identifiable physical reasons and may therefore be ignored; one **B** manuscript reads *For it shal turne tresoun*. The sense of the majority reading is unacceptable: at line 86 it was incense which signified reason. Moreover a line mentioning treason in connexion with kings could seem indiscreet to a scribe.[81] On these grounds the majority reading originated in scribal censorship.

[80] The superlative here might also have been induced by following *sonnest*, or by variation to an easier reading: the possible difficulty of *soþes* is indicated by a variant *soþ(e)* in **C** manuscripts.

[81] Cp. W's variant at V 49.

If further demonstration that our use of discrimination is not mechanical were needed this class of its results where the original common to more than one version is found in the **B** tradition would provide it. The same editorial reasoning that elsewhere showed the extreme corruption of the archetypal **B** text, or the frequent unanimous preservation of an original reading in another version where the **B** manuscripts vary, has here indicated that the archetypal **B** tradition was not uniformly more corrupt than those of **A** and **C**.

There are, finally, in the editorial situation where **B** can be compared with one or both the other versions and where revision seems improbable, cases where variation is not of such a kind as to enable confident discrimination. Here we have had to fall back on attestation as the only available indication of originality: our alternatives were to follow copy text, which might have created a false impression of revisional differences between versions, or to accept the indication of numerical probabilities of substitution, notwithstanding the many lost and irrecoverable circumstances which might have disturbed it. In some cases we found even this impossible;[82] in others there seemed to us a fair chance that its showing is correct.

The simplest cases are of equally acceptable variants. Thus at V 35 **A** V 33 **C** V 137 the variant **B** word orders *forwanye hem/hem forwanye* give no clue to direction of variation: we adopt that found in one **B** manuscript, F, all **A** manuscripts but one, and all **C**. At III 142 **A** III 131 **C** III 180 **B** variation is between contextually equivalent *risshe* and *bene*: we adopt *risshe* as overwhelmingly or unanimously attested in **A** and **C**. At V 205 **A** V 121 **C** VI 213 where **B** varies *ware/chaffare* we adopt the variant unanimously attested in **A** and **C**. At XX 249 **C** XXII 249 *lakke/faille* we adopt the **B** family reading unanimously attested in **C**.

We also allow attestation in another version to decide between rival **B** readings where indications of originality seem in balance. For instance at Prol. 185 **C** Prol. 199 *hadde killed/killed* and X 73 **A** XI 59 **C** XI 53 *pestilence tyme/pestilence* the fuller expression could be a more explicit substitution or an original element could have been omitted through distraction by the sensational adjacent notion. At III 327 **C** III 480 *torne/ to torne* and XI 129 **C** XII 64 *fro/so fro* the infinitive sign and the adverb could be more explicit substitutions or have been respectively

[82] See above, p. 150 and n. 69.

lost through homoarchy and homoteleuton. At V 48 **C** V 180 *his/the* and XVIII 87 **C** XX 89 *Iesu/hym* variation could have been either: › a more explicit reading or through attraction to the preceding contexts. At V 61 **A** V 44 **C** VI 2 *made/garte* the former variant is easier, but the latter is suspect because the poet tends to use northernisms mainly for alliteration, which is not the case here. At XIX 330 **C** XXI 330 *carie home/carie* the one variant is certainly more explicit, but if, by the presence of *home*, it has the allegorical sense 'bring mankind to salvation', it is also appreciably harder. At XVIII 389 **C** XX 431 *may/zero* and X 466 **C** XI 292 *pouere/opere* the expressions which might seem respectively more explicit and emphatic are also stave words. In each of these cases we have allowed the unanimous or overwhelming support of one or both the other versions to tip the balance of evidence.

There is, lastly, a type of crux where we have relied very heavily on attestation. For instance at XVI 193 **C** XVIII 202 *selue...suffreþ hem/zero...þei suffre* we find difficult the meaning of both variants, but particularly the first. While the former has more normative alliteration this alone would hardly justify its adoption when we cannot confidently translate it. It is however without question the archetypal **C** reading, and we therefore read it. At XVII 209 **C** XIX 175 the problem is lexical. Alliteration points to the originality of *warm* as a stave, unless the line scanned *as and hoot*, or unless the poet here gave *hot* the value [wɔt], which seems historically improbable. But the qualified sense of *warm*, 'affording or giving out a considerable degree of heat (less than that indicated by *hot*)' (*NED* s.v.1) seems not quite apt; if *warm* was original here its lexicography must be reviewed. It is however the archetypal reading of **C** and in our predicament we accept this attestation as the only means of decision.

From the above discussions it will have become clear how far we set the reliability of discrimination as a determinant of originality in various editorial situations above that of attestation. This therefore is the point to review the bases of our position. Experience has shown us the necessarily extreme frequency of convergent variation and how it can fortuitously produce even massive random agreement in support of an unoriginal variant. Any given piece of text contains a particular set of potential inducements to variation. It may of course notwithstanding their presence be repeatedly copied intact. But when it is corrupted the effect of such a particular set of inducements will be to produce variations corresponding typically to itself. And therefore if it is repeatedly corrupted that correspondence of variation to the conditions which induced this is likely to result in coincident substitution. From another viewpoint, when a strongly supported variant appears unoriginal on comparison simply the possibility of identifying direction of variation implied in that appearance is a measure of the likelihood of coincident substitution: the evidence on which we find a variant scribal is also a reason for expecting its independent occurrence on distinct occasions. From this it follows that the significance of numerical support for readings is both essentially obscure and potentially misleading. If readings are original agreement in support of them signifies no more than that the manuscripts where it occurs are there copies of the same work; if they are unoriginal it may indeed be the result of vertical transmission but it may also, almost as easily, result from coincident substitution or conflation. From this consideration relative strength of attestation is a secondary consideration in the determination of originality.

It will however also be clear that while the evidence of other versions is not applied to systematically voting down a **B** reading, the existence of such evidence affords the editors a great advantage by enlarging the scope of the essential activity of comparison. It is comparison with readings outside the tradition of the **B** manuscripts which enables accurate assessment of the quality of their archetype and its frequent correction, to say nothing of discrimination in those passages attested by only one main **B** group.[83] Comparison admittedly aggravates the editorial responsibility by thus demonstrating the necessity of conjecture, but it also defines this and reduces its speculative character by affording evidence of typical archetypal corruptions. Finally comparison substantiates the authority of readings by our editorial criteria intrinsically superior, but attested only in single **B** manuscripts. The appearance of many such readings in the tradition of another version not only shows these to be authorial variants rather than felicitous scribal improvements; it also suggests the probable originality of other uniquely attested readings of a similar character in those **B** passages where comparison is not possible.

[83] For example, where WHmCrGYOC²CBLMS omit, in X 303 **A** XI 209 **C** V 150, XII 125 **C** XIV 68, XIII 441 **C** VII 101, XIII 453 **C** VII 113, XV 523 **C** XVII 273; and where RF omit, in IX 182 **C** X 283, XIII 16 **C** XV 19, XV 546 **C** XVII 207, XVII 237 **C** XIX 203, XVIII 252, 253 **C** XX 261, 262.

It will already have appeared how often we identify originality in such readings. But as we indicated above[84] the validity of the identification must rest on the possibility of accounting for the presence of original readings in single manuscripts. This possibility we now discuss with particular reference to F (Corpus Christi College Oxford MS 201) as the manuscript most often in question.[85]

The sigil F stands in our apparatus as the sole **B** support, or the sole support, for well more than 100 emendations of various kinds. In the case of 30 of these, which occur where R the genetic twin of F is defective, F's reading is explicable as probably or possibly that of the main genetic group (RF).[86] The problem is to account for the large remainder.

This is easy in theory: there are three processes by which an original reading may be present in a single manuscript of a complex tradition like those of the *Piers Plowman* versions. It can have been restored by genuine correction; or fortuitously restored by felicitous scribal variation, in particular by skilful sophistication; or it can have been preserved by faithful vertical transmission and isolated by coincident substitution in the other manuscripts. Logically, then, the identification of originality in a uniquely attested reading presents no difficulty;

[84] pp. 153ff.

[85] There are also less numerous original readings uniquely attested by B, Cr, G, H, Hm, L, M, O, W, and Y. On the showing of the following discussion all or any of these may have been acquired by correction. There is also a possibility that where any two of these manuscripts agree in attesting an original reading the agreement may result from independent correction. It will be recalled that the actual copies Hm and M show abundant physical evidence of having been corrected. See above, pp. 10, 11.

[86] Most of the readings of F presumed original where R is absent are also those of one or both other versions. Classified by the presumed explanations of their loss these now follow. *Unconscious omissions*: XIX 43 **C** XXI 43 his (*attraction* conq- conq-); XIX 56–9 **C** XXI 56–9 (*homoarchy*); XIX 73 **C** XXI 73 riȝt *om* (> *axay*) (*attraction between verb and principal adverb*); XIX 152 **C** XXI 152 and...after (*om while leaving space for rubrication*); XIX 236b, 237a **C** XXI 236, 237 (*homoteleuton*); XIX 334 **C** XXI 334 *om* (*attraction* tilie><plow). *Unconscious substitutions variously induced*: XIX 94 **C** XXI 94 Erþeliche] Thre yliche (*by preceding context*); XIX 118 **C** XXI 118 fauntekyn] faunt fyn (*by preceding copy*); XIX 394 **C** XXI 394 Or] That (*by surrounding copy*). *More explicit substitutions*: XIX 130 **C** XXI 130 and dombe speke and herde] to here and dombe speke he made; XIX 145 **C** XXI 145 frend] *pl.*; XIX 208 **C** XXI 208 grace] and g.; XIX 336 **C** XXI 336 greuen] to g.; XIX 422 **C** XXI 422 Iewes] þe I.; XIX 446 **C** XXI 446 bereþ witnesse] þerof witnesseþ; XIX 457 **C** XXI 457 to] for to. *Easier substitutions*: Prol. 22 **A** Prol. 22 **C** Prol. 24 þise] *om*; XIX 273 **C** XXI 273 aiþes] harewes; XIX 283 **C** XXI 283 meschief] muchel drynke. *More emphatic substitutions*: XIX 284 **C** XXI 284 scornere] s. ne scolde; XIX 412 **C** XXI 412 feþere] f. or an hennes. *Sophistications*: XVIII 424 **C** XX 467 carolden] dauncede (*alliteration augmented*); XIX 274 **C** XXI 274 Piers] *om* (*the subject of* sew 275 *misconceived*); XIX 330 **C** XXI 330 home] *om* (*the allegorical force of* home *not perceived*). Two instances where R is defective and F's reading possesses superior originality to that of **C** (XIX 90 and XX 70) we have already discussed above (pp. 159, 161); two more (XIX 400 **C** XXI 400 þat] for/and þ. and XIX 408 **C** XXI 408 þow art] þei/we ben) belong with them. Finally there is a probably original unique F reading where R is defective in a line peculiar to **B**; Prol 122 lif] man > *aaxy*.

indeed in the abstract the availability of several explanations should be not an embarrassment but an advantage to the editor. In practice, however, he cannot rest on broad theory but must examine the relative likelihood of these processes in the particular instances.

Moreover he must do this without preconception. He may think correction an unacceptable explanation of the presence of original readings when variational differences are minute; or find felicitous sophistication, which could never be conclusively shown, unduly speculative; or be chary of invoking coincident substitution as too opportunistic a presumption. Nevertheless the fact of the original readings confronts him, and some one of these three processes must have been responsible for every situation where such a reading stands isolated in a single manuscript of a tradition. The possibility of establishing likelihoods will depend on the character of the manuscript generally, and the nature of the readings in particular. How this applies to F we shall now show.

This unusual manuscript which was formerly scorned[87] certainly does not recommend itself *prima facie* to an editor. In addition to some 700 archetypal errors of the **B** tradition, the 500 odd wrong readings which it shares with R, and hundreds more where it is in random agreements, it contains more than 1,000 individual unoriginal variants. Analysis of these reveals sustained and intensely interested scribal activity. Hundreds of substitutions making the text more explicit show close attention to its meaning; the relatively small number of more emphatic variants suggests judicious rather than indiscriminate enthusiasm. The infrequency of substitution of easier readings implies acquaintance with the vocabulary of alliterative poetry. Many variants look like sophistications of the sense of the exemplar, others of its style; others are evidently censorship; some hundreds more repair or augment alliteration. F's treatment of the texts of both archetypal **B** and the exclusive common ancestor it shares with R records the activity of an intelligent and critical scribe in its immediate tradition. It is thus, in the old sense, a thoroughly unreliable manuscript.

Nevertheless where R is represented F alone of the **B** manuscripts has about 100 readings by our criteria of intrinsic authority; and more than 70 of these are shown to be authorial by external support, that is

[87] Skeat, *B-Text*, p. xxx; Blackman, 'Some Notes on the B-Text MSS.', p. 502; Chambers, 'The Manuscripts of *Piers Plowman* in the Huntington Library', pp. 12, 13.

by their occurrence in **AC** or **A** or **C**. The question how F came by these latter readings which have an existence independent of the possibilities of sophistication in its immediate tradition can be answered only by examination of individual variants.

The evidence of the majority is ambiguous. Given that F's history includes heavy sophistication by at least one intelligent scribe, and that coincident variation was a frequent occurrence, their presence in F alone among the **B** manuscripts would be explicable by one of these two processes, quite apart from the possibility of its being the result of correction, also a known and demonstrable phenomenon.

To begin with there are readings presumed original and attested by no **B** manuscript except F in lines where F's text is otherwise corrupt or sophisticated, sometimes heavily. The suggestion is that F there acquired the original reading fortuitously as part of a larger variation; the alternative is that F was first corrected, then corrupted or sophisticated, and that the original reading restored by correction survived the damage. The following are instances of such readings, arranged according to the explanations offered for the unoriginal majority **B** variant.

Unconscious variation: V 115 **A** V 95 I] And, VI 103 **A** VII 95 putte] picche, XI 84 **C** XII 23 for] and (*attraction to preceding copy*); I 24 **A** I 24 That oþer is] And (*attraction to following copy*); III 124 **A** III 113 **C** III 161 she] *om* (*alliterative attraction*); VII 10 **A** VIII 10 Reme] *pl.* (*grammatical attraction*); VIII 27 **A** IX 23 **C** X 31 synneþ on þe day] on þe d. s. (*inducement of the Latin word order*). *More explicit substitutions:* V 105 **A** V 85 and] a. sholde; V 113 **A** V 93 it] þat; VI 183 **A** VII 171 fere] f. ther/herof; VII 34 **A** VIII 36 sende] s. yow; VII 203 **A** VIII 181 er] here er; VIII 39 **A** IX 35 þe] to þe; IX 190 **A** X 203 but] b. if. *More emphatic substitutions:* VIII 57 **A** IX 48 conceyuen] c. alle; IX 34 **A** X 35 self] s. one. *Sophistication:* V 70 **A** V 53 þat] þis (*miscomprehension*); XI 56 **C** XII 8 in] to (*smoothing after visual error*).

Fortuitous variation by F back to the original reading rather than detailed correction might also seem to account for a number of cases where the variational difference is minute. Such are the following.

Substitution induced by preceding copy: VIII 118 **A** IX 108 on] vpon (Dis-pu-tyng). *A more explicit substitution:* VIII 92 **A** IX 83 þe] to þe. *Easier substitutions:* VII 61 **A** VIII 63 by] wiþ; VIII 125 **A** IX 115 To] And. *Sophistications:* III 42 **A** III 41 clerkes and kny3tes] k. and c. (*to a seemlier order*); X 424 **A** XI 283 Or] And or/er (*miscomprehension*).

Each of the rejected readings in this last group either stands in a corresponding unrevised **C** line or is reflected in the revised line. All therefore, as corruptions from the first archetypal phase of the **B** tradi-tion, were also present in the exclusive common ancestor of RF. This is not necessarily true of another group of instances where **C** either reads correctly or is not concerned, and where it may be that F is the only **B** manuscript attesting a presumed original reading simply because R has coincidentally varied with WHmCrGYOC²CBmBoCot LM(H)S. This explanation rather than correction in F may seem indicated by a common characteristic of the group: the ease with which variation in each instance can be accounted for; that indication has great force.[88] We have accepted a similar one in the corresponding situation where F agrees in error with the larger group and R has original readings.[89] But there R's unsophisticated character created a presumption that its uniquely attested readings survive by vertical transmission; of F, which is hardly so innocent, this presumption is less easy. Nevertheless actual evidence of R varying coincidentally with the larger group survives. At I 45 **A** I 43 **C** I 43 both R and WHmCr GYOC²CLMH read *madame*, caught up from line 43; their variation appears post-archetypal and coincidental from the differing points of insertion. At I 73 **A** I 71 **C** I 70 *halsede*] *asked*, the form of R's variant *hasked* shows that it does not reproduce an archetypal **B** error but reflects a reading *halsede* of its group ancestor (RF). Both on these indications and from the principle that the possibility of explaining a variation easily implies a likelihood of its recurrence all or any of the following could be instances of F preserving an original reading by vertical transmission and R agreeing with the larger group by coincident variation.

Unconscious variations: I 43 **A** I 41 **C** I 41 A] *om* (*failure to supply initial capital*); IV 7 **A** IV 7 **C** IV 7 þat] *om* (*parallelism*); IV 80 **A** IV 66 knewen wel] knowe (knowe)⟨soþe *attraction*); IV 106 **A** IV 93 **C** IV 101 awey] *om*; VI 95 **A** VII 87 **C** VIII 104 me] *om*

[88] See above, pp. 32, n. 33, and 163, 164.

[89] See above, p. 58. F's agreements with the larger group are in the commonest sorts of variation. Ten are more explicit readings: III 49, 67; V 217, 320; IX 191; XII 209; XIII 386; XV 18; XX 360, 363. Thirteen are careless substitutions:- of a plural for a generic singular: V 304; of a plural for a singular through contextual inducement: V 113; VI 325; VII 58; of prose order: VI 175; VIII 119; of a grammatical smoothing after misreading: XVI 136; of a contextually suggested term: XX 60; of a term of common collocation: V 588; XI 180; of an alliterating near-equivalent: VI 76; XI 59; of a regional for a national notion: XV 531. Two are misreadings, one caused by minims: XI 8; the other induced by the context: VIII 50. Four are elementary sophistications: insertion of a word omitted from the preceding line: X 227; and smoothing of corrupt copy: X 61; XI 185, 436. All the variations by omission are easily explicable: one shortens an unusually long line: V 271; two eliminate interruption of a close grammatical relation: XI 134, 240; one simplifies a grammatically complex notion: XV 109; two are induced by the existence of a more common collocation of terms: X 245; XX 221.

(*homoarchy*); VII 179, 180 **A** VIII 157, 158 **C** IX 324, 325 *misdivision* (*grammatical attraction*); VIII 24 **A** IX 20 **C** X 28 at hoom] *om* (alwey)⟨amonges *attraction*); VIII 37 **A** IX 33 Riȝt] & (*preoccupation with* significatio). *Unconscious substitutions:* III 145 **A** III 134 **C** III 183 She] And (*inducement of preceding list of charges*); V 32 **C** V 134 He] And (*attraction to following grammar*); V 35 **A** V 33 **C** V 137 forwanye hem] *tp* (*influence of preceding rhythm*); VIII 78 **A** IX 69 quod he] *shifted* (⟩*prose order*); VIII 97 **A** IX 87 at] on (*attraction to following*); XI 342 **C** XIII 150 bole] *pl.* (*attraction to preceding*). *More explicit substitutions:* Prologue 150 **C** Prologue 168 at] at his; V 81 **A** V 64 As] And as; V 118 **A** V 97 And] For; V 629 **A** VI 114 **C** VII 282 gate] g. þere; VI 56 **A** VII 51 word] *pl.*; VI 206 **A** VII 192 of] of hire; VI 232 **A** VII 216 engendrour] þe e.; IX 137 **C** X 225 bideþ] b. ye; X 138 **A** XI 91 I] For I; X 143 **A** XI 96 kouþe] k. after; X 311 **A** XI 211 rennere] Romere; X 337 **A** XI 225 but] b. if; XI 109 **C** XII 43 louyen] l. it; XIV 213 **C** XVI 54 bifore] b. þe riche. *Easier substitutions:* X 228 **A** XI 171 his wif I] þe w. and; XIII 345 **C** VI 179 som] s. tyme; XIII 393 **C** VI 280 my] *om*. *More emphatic substitutions:* V 599 **A** VI 86 **C** VII 246 sory] ful s.; X 154 **A** XI 106 woukes] monþes. *Sophistications:* II 212 **A** II 171 **C** II 222 feeres] felawes (*eliminating a jingle*); V 78 **A** V 61 He was] And; VIII 44 **A** IX 40 **C** X 43 helpeþ] kepeþ (*eliminating repetition*); VII 117 **A** VIII 99 **C** IX 290 and(2)] *om* (*rejecting apparent parallelism between two parts of the line*).

In all the evidence so far examined fortuitous variation, whether by F toward the original or by R away from it, has seemed a likelihood. We do not find this of the remainder. There are first four instances with two characteristics in common: the corruption of the majority, probably archetypal **B** reading is of such a kind as to attract the notice of an attentive reader and thus invite correction; and the original or an approximation of it can be deduced from the context. Here two explanations of F uniquely attesting an original or less corrupt reading are possible: either skilful conjectural emendation, or correction (in one case obscured by later sophistication). At III 39 **A** III 38 *fiftene*] *fifty* is a thoughtlessly emphatic early archetypal substitution like the *four score* of one **A** manuscript. An editing scribe whose exemplar contained this variant might think Meed thus too old for a marriageable *mayde*; and the resemblance between *fifty* and *fiftene* could as naturally suggest the correction as it did the unoriginal variant. At VI 291 **A** VII 275 *þee*] *me* is unconscious archetypal variation induced by the tendency to parallelize (290 *I...my*) or by attraction to the person of the preceding pronoun. To anyone who noticed that *me* breaks off the allegory the required correction would be obvious. At VIII 42 **A** IX 38 *false*] *frele* the archetypal substitution was induced by *brotel* 41, or the frequent collocation of *frele* with *flessh* preceding, or the moral commonplace 'How frail is worldly welfare', or any combination of these. An intelligent scribe might notice the unaptness of *frele* to describe the world conceived of as one of the three sources of temptation; correction would be guided by its primary attribute in that conception (*wolde þee bitraye* I 39). At IX 23 **A** X 22 *sixe*] *fyue* (>*xaay*) is an early archetypal mis-correction through failure to include the father in the count of Anima's guardians. An exemplar reading *fyue* might seem faulty for that reason or because of its defective alliteration; again the appropriate correction would be easy. At XIII 326 **C** VI 71 *þat by watte he wiste*] *þ. he of walter w.* F; *þat watte w.* is an unconscious archetypal substitution induced by following *wille wiste*. The pointlessness of extending the reproach for backbiting from Haukyn to Watte might strike an attentive reader; and his experience of life could show him how to improve his copy. To account for the corruption original **B** must have read like **C**; the form of F's approximate variant and his other variations in the line suggest either scribal emendation or correction followed by sophistication.

The general character of F might make skilful conjectural emendation seem the likelier explanation of the above instances. There is, however, another small but important class of evidence to which this could hardly apply: that is situations where, while F has an original reading, the unoriginal majority **B** reading is archetypal,[90] and is not of such a kind as to have attracted scribal notice by its inappropriateness unless exposed to comparison; and there is no obvious guide to correction in the subject or the context. Thus at VI 37, 41 **A** VII 38, 40 *þee*] *yow*, and VI 38 **A** VII 39 *þow*] *ye* the archetypal variation registers a scribe's preference for the deferential plural which is apt enough, but also less meaningful than the preacher's singular with its implications about the status of Piers. At VI 45 **A** VII 44 *shalt*] *may* the inferior sense of the variation, unconsciously anticipating following copy, appears only from comparison with that of *shalt*, 'you are bound to', but there is no suggestion in the context or the topic that this ought to be the sense. At VI 76 **A** VII 68 *holde*] *hote* is an early archetypal substitution of a more emphatic reading unobjectionable in itself. Nothing in the context would suggest that 'required' rather than 'commanded' is a more appropriate meaning. At VI 253 **A** VII 237 *þee...þow*] *yow...ye* again a scribe has preferred the deferential plural, appropriately as it might seem. But the singular, implying that Piers knows Hunger

[90] This is shown by its presence in the manuscript used for revision to **C**.

intimately, is clearly more meaningful. The variational differences at these points are small but significant. Even though the scribe responsible for the character of F was exceptional in his interest and capabilities, it is not really conceivable that he should there so accurately have deduced the poet's purpose and restored its expression. The greater likelihood is that these readings are present in F by correction.

That likelihood is confirmed by F's attestation of a number of lines in near proximity not found in the other **B** manuscripts, namely VIII 49, 80, 103, 105 (**A** IX 45, 71, 93, 95), VIII 112b, 113a (**A** IX 102b, 103a **C** X 108b, 109a), and IX 33 (**A** X 34). On these considerations: that in this area most differences between **A** and **B** have a scribal character, **B** appearing corrupted rather than revised, while in **C** there are signs of the reviser's dissatisfaction with the text of **B** he was using;[91] that no motives for the exclusion of these lines by the **B** reviser suggest themselves to us; and that if they are presumed originally present in **B** as they stand in **A** their inadvertent scribal omission is explicable by familiar processes of corruption, we judge them to be original **B** lines restored by correction in F.

We do not seriously doubt that correction took place in the immediate tradition of F. Considered detail by detail the evidence is ambiguous. The greater part of it falls into four classes each of which can be plausibly accounted for by another explanation than correction. But the plausibility of each explanation as applied to the single class does not survive consideration of the whole body of evidence. To accept the sum of the explanations in their variety (leaving, meanwhile, some awkward cases not accounted for) seems less reasonable than to presume the occurrence of a single known and even likely phenomenon, which could account for all the evidence. Scribes did correct manuscripts and did sometimes hit upon superior texts for the purpose. Their corrections were anything but systematic: they variously removed trivial and serious errors as these caught their notice and interest. And they tended not to see the business through. The circumstance that the uniquely attested original readings in F have these characteristics points to correction as the explanation for at least the bulk of them. Their

[91] Thus **B** VIII 44–56 where we presume loss of original 49 are rewritten as **C** X 50–5. **B** VIII 80 which in the archetype is the ruin of two original lines appears in **C** in the corrupt **B** form with something of the lost sense of *meke of his mouþ milde of his speche* restored in new **C** X 79 *loueth his emcristene*. **B** VIII 102–6 where we presume loss of 103, 105, appear as a single **C** line, X 102. **B** IX 33–5 presumed corrupt by loss of 33 (and otherwise) are represented in the revision by a new passage, **C** X 158–70.

distribution in particular is to that effect: it suggests a critical comparison perceptive but not thorough, relatively close in VI–X and much diminished if not terminated after XIV.[92]

The correction was not, we believe, memorial but from a manuscript: this is implied by the minuteness of variational differences at many points and their unobtrusiveness at others,[93] as well as by the pattern of distribution, which is not random. The correction was a separate operation from the sophistication of the manuscript, which continues unabated to the end. That it was also anterior is apparent from the kind of error which it removed; little of this would be likely to stand out as requiring correction in a comparison of F's present text with a good **B** copy.[94] That text might indeed seem uncorrectable. Correction of F was, finally, from a manuscript of the **B** version and not severally from manuscripts of **A** and **C**: this is indicated by the superiority of a number of F's readings to those of the archetypal **C** tradition[95] and confirmed by F's possession of intrinsically more authoritative readings in that part of the poem, also, where **B**'s text is unique.

The presumption of correction of F must be understood to give that manuscript no 'authority' in the old sense of the term but to establish its character as a source of certain specific readings which, because both more appropriate by our editorial criteria, and capable of having generated less appropriate majority variants, are presumed original. We appreciate that adoption of such readings from F may seem the most radical element in the process of discrimination. Therefore an analysis of our reasons for doing so where the text of **B** is unique and F's reading is not shown authorial by external support seems an appropriate end to the illustration of discrimination.

The style of the majority reading is on comparison with that of the reading of F, *which could have generated it, scribal.* XI 93, 94 *misdivision.* XI 278 begge] goon and b.; XII 193 crist] c. on þe cros: *more explicit substitutions.* X 270 is] *om: grammatically easier.* XV 268 verred] verray: *lexically easier and more emphatic. The sense of the majority reading is inferior.* V 127 synne] *pl.: unconscious parallelizing.* XIV 22 kepe...werkes] *om: distraction by the rubric.* VI 39

[92] F has no unmistakable uniquely attested original readings in XVI or XVIII, only one in XV, one in XVII and four in XX. In XIX where R is defective F's character is obscure since its relation to their exclusive common ancestor is not there determinable. Thus for instance at XIX 463 F's original reading *tooken* (**C** XXI 463) could also be the (RF) group reading.

[93] See the class discussed on pp. 170, 171 above.

[94] Just as F's superior readings escaped the notice of earlier editors who compared its text with that of L: the sensational differences introduced by the sophisticator were an absolute distraction.

[95] See above, pp. 159 and 161. To these should be added XIV 223 C XVI 64 *ben*] *þey been* F; *aren* >*aaxy* and XX 109 **C** XXII 109 *sone*] F; *þo* >*axay*.

þow] ȝe: *the deferential plural preferred.* IX 40 and] if: *smoothing after* if] and *substitution in* 39. X 244 is] gost is: *the second half-line strengthened because the weight of* is, *deriving from its reference* (qui simul utroque procedit) *was missed.* XIV 190 We] He: *the necessary meaning misconceived.*

The versification of the majority reading is inferior. IV 168 also] *om*> *axay: loss of an 'unessential' term through preoccupation with the sensational topic.* IX 73 hem] *om* > *aaxa: parallelizing.* IX 194 þus] *om*> *aabb: failure to notice* f þ *alliteration.* XVII 90 þus] *om*> *aaxy: auditory assimilation to preceding* siþþe. V 411 moste] go >*aaxy*; XIV 78 mete] þat þei ete >*aaxy: more explicit substitutions.* Prol. 122 lif] man> *aaxy*; V 23 preche gan Reson] R. gan to p. >*aaxa*; XI 344 saue man allone] þat wiþ fole were >*aaxy: easier substitutions.* VI 150 a pitaunce biside] make hemself at ese>*aaxy: a more emphatic substitution.* Prol. 206 slen] doon >*aaxy: censorship.* I 118 Lucifer] *om: elimination of repetition.*

We next illustrate reconstruction, the second editorial process. This comprises all restorations of original **B** readings not actually preserved as such in any manuscript from the evidence of surviving variation. It is applied in various textual situations and circumstances. The crux which it most typically resolves is one where there is choice of variant readings, whether in the traditions of several versions or only in that of **B**, and where the **B** original cannot be identified in any surviving variant from either its intrinsic authority or its likelihood of having generated the others. In such a case it can happen that the joint evidence of the variants points to a hypothetical **B** reading which both could have generated all variants and would satisfy the criteria of style, sense and alliteration. But reconstruction can simply amount to restoring an alliterating dialect variant, or interpreting palæographic error or the effects of split variation or misdivision or disarrangement, large or small. It also is of course a classic process, distinctive in our use only because in taking account of several versions it may involve the delimitation of revision, and because we have found that even a revised **C** line can indicate the necessary or likely original form of its **B** equivalent. Our examples are again arranged according to the various textual situations.

Where all versions are represented and there appears to have been revision it is sometimes possible to reconstruct a hypothetical **B** reading of at least superior originality to the archetypal **B** text. For instance, at VII 30, 31 this text reads a single line, *Pouere peple and prisons fynden hem hir foode.* With respect to sense and alliteration (*aaabb*) this is unexceptionable. But the circumstance that in both **A** (VIII 32, 33) and **C** (IX 34, 35) its elements *Pouere* and *fynden* occur in separate lines suggests that original **B** also read two lines here. These were not identical either with the **A** lines, which cannot have generated the **B** variation, or with the **C** lines where there is further revision embracing our **B** 32. The presence in **C** 35 of *Fynde...for loue* echoing **A** 33 directs reconstruction of a hypothetical pair of original **B** lines derivable from **A** by revision and revisable to **C**. Their corruption will have been by unconscious parallelizing with the preceding four injunctions, each comprised in a single line. Similarly the archetypal line representing IX 68, 69, *Fooles þat fauten Inwit I fynde þat holy chirche* can be repaired. This line too has adequate alliteration and sense. But it stands for three lines in both **A** (X 64, 69, 70) and **C** (X 183–5); it lacks the distinction between two kinds of innocents, *fauntes* and *foles*, explicit in **A** and **C**, and its use of *fynde* (which suspiciously also occurs in the next line) is lexically difficult. On these indications it is a corruption of two original **B** lines, one expressing the distinction just noted (as in **C** 183), the other specifying the Church's obligation (as does **A** 69). The presumption then is that the original **B** reading was a revision of **A**, in its turn revised by **C** as part of a larger recasting. Omission and telescoping in the archetypal **B** tradition will have been induced by alliterative attraction.

In the textual situation where **B** can be compared with one other version it is **C** which commonly affords evidence for reconstruction. The relation between **A** and **B**, that is between an original and an authorially revised or an original and a scribally corrupted text is most often established by discrimination.[96] But where **C** is unrevised its variants are those of another **B** tradition; where **C** is revised its text is an authorial reflex of an intact or corrupted archetypal **B** text. In both circumstances the evidence can enable restoration of an original **B** reading that has not actually survived: whether from the additional variants of the second tradition or from indications in the revised **C** line.

Where **C** is unrevised, at XIX 238 **B** variation is *to dyke/dyche... thecche/presche/hegge*; that of **C** (XXI 238) *to theche/teche/take/diche... coke/loke*. On the showing of both traditions one of the two original verbs was *thecche*. As between *coke* and *dyke* the latter is scribal, being unambiguous and therefore easier or because if *coke* were misread 'cook' it might seem inappropriate in context and invite substitution. Of the

[96] A notable exception is IX 15, archetypally scanning *aaxy* or *axaa*. The lost stave *boldeþ* (*NED Bold* v. 2 and cp. III 199) is suggested by the reading of one **A** manuscript J (Vol. I, p. 49). J's variant represents lines lost from **A** early in its archetypal tradition.

two arrangements *coke...thecche* can have generated the archetypal **B** line by substitution and that of **C** by 'improvement' of alliteration (note the variant *teche*; actually the third stave is *to* (2)), whereas no reason for the reverse process suggests itself. We therefore reconstruct from the language of the **C** tradition and the arrangement of that of **B**. At XIX 479 **C** XXI 479 the two archetypes respectively read *Take þow mayst in reson* and *That thow haue thyn askyng*. The **B** reading both is unalliterative and could not have generated that of **C**. It will have been corrupted because of the difficulty of the original pun on *asken*; *Take* comes from 468 or 473 and *in reson* from 478. The **C** reading alliterates, but its grammar is not Langlandian, and how, if original, it could have generated the **B** variant is hard to see; as a variant it is explicable by inducement of **C** 476b. Our reconstruction restores the evidently original *askyng* in an expression that could have generated both variants. At XX 377 the **B** archetype read *He lyþ and dremeþ* (altered to *adreynt* in the group ancestor of BmBoCot and promptly recorrupted in Bo); that of **C** (XXII 377) *He lyeth adreint*. This is obviously 'split variation': each tradition has omitted one of an original pair of palæographically similar expressions.[97]

In the textual situation where archetypal **B** can be compared with revised **C** and a line or passage of **B** has features suggesting its corruptness the direction of the evidence can take several forms. The comparison can show that the features by which we identify corruption were already present in the **B** manuscript used for revision to **C**;[98] then it can appear that the reviser restored an original reading, perhaps from memory, or that he otherwise minimized the effects of a corrupt reading. Or the comparison can show that the features indicating corruption were acquired in the second phase of the archetypal **B** tradition; then **C**, although revised, can have preserved a lost original **B** reading, or it can suggest the necessarily or more likely original sense or form of **B**. Or simply the fact of revision, by implying the reviser's dissatisfaction with the **B** line before him, can confirm our doubts about its originality.

Very occasionally the original of an archetypal **B** reading inferior by

[97] Two other restorations, at XIX 229 and XIX 302, 303, where the reading of both archetypes is unoriginal but that of **B** has been further corrupted at a late archetypal stage are discussed above, pp. 118, 119.

[98] The evidence that Langland used a corrupt scribal copy of **B** for his last revision is set out in IV above, pp. 98ff.

the criterion of style can be restored by reference to the corresponding revised **C** line. This happens at III 302, archetypally *wonder glade*. Here the reduced emphasis of **C**'s equivalent (III 455) *so glade*, 'accordingly joyous', suggests that *wonder* was a very early scribal insertion for emphasis and that original **B** read simply *glade*.[99]

More often it is by the criterion of sense that the archetypal **B** reading appears unoriginal. Its inferiority can consist simply in the inconsequence of discourse, on a small or large scale. An example of the former is Prologue 189–97. The disjointed character of the text in the archetypal order 193–7, 189–92, jumbling two distinct arguments, and also the implication of the content of our 197 and 198, that they belong together, suggest scribal disarrangement. Another example is XVIII 6–9 where archetypally line 9, coming before 6–8, reverses the historical sequence of events: this order again could be scribal. In each case the corresponding part of **C** (Prologue 203ff. and XX 6, 7) lacks the lines which seem out of place in the archetypal **B** text. That circumstance, registering Langland's dissatisfaction with the **B** text before him, implies that it had the archetypal order which we suspect and further that this is scribal.[100] Since disarrangement is a classically explicable common corruption we accept this implication and reconstruct a likely original order of lines from the indications of the sense.

A much larger reconstruction is XV 504–69, a passage which in the archetypal **B** text is ordered 533–69, 504–32. The archetypal deficiency is here again inconsequence, taking the form of discourse interrupted for no apparent homiletic or dramatic purpose or effect, and with unsmoothed transitions, as follows. Lines 501–3α immediately preceding the suspect passage are the climax of a criticism of prelates for failing to evangelize the Saracens and Jews. In the archetype they are followed by (our 533–69) a contrast between the self-sacrifice of missionaries in past times which drew a general blessing, and the covetousness of the present clergy which is being punished and may even end in the disendowment of the Church. Then only (our 504–32) comes what would more naturally follow 501–3α, reinforcement of the criticism there expressed by the argument that conversion of Saracens and Jews would be easy since they are monotheists, and by reference to

[99] So indeed does one **B** manuscript, whether by enlightened correction or felicitous omission.

[100] Examples of his violently revising passages corrupt in the **B** archetype by cancellation are given above, p. 125, n. 59.

the examples of Christ and many martyred saints. Thus broken, and shifting its trend abruptly, the passage is both hard to follow and less forceful than the very simple rearrangement which we adopt has made it.

In **C** the general order of the corresponding passage is still that of archetypal **B**: **C** XVII 193–250 are our XV 533–69 and **C** XVII 254–81 our XV 504–32. But three revisions of detail relate to precisely the shortcomings we sense in the passage. First, within a larger insertion (**C** XVII 125–64), the poet has set three lines (156–8) which anticipate a notion, of the true and false intermediary, long deferred in the archetypal **B** order (504–7). Second, just before what we presume the point of dislocation he has introduced new XVII 232–48 as if to smooth an awkward transition. And third, he has postponed **B** XV 501–3α, the climax of the criticism which hangs fire in the archetypal order, to a point (**C** XVII 251) where now it is immediately followed by its supporting reasons (**C** XVII 254–81). Taken together these changes clearly show both his unease with the passage as it stood in his **B** manuscript and his insight into the nature of its deficiency.

If, as we believe, the archetypal **B** order is scribal, it is easily accounted for. The dislocation will have occurred through misfolding of the inner bifolium of a quire of the unbound exemplar after some of its content had been copied. This bifolium had 20 lines to a side, as follows:

496–513 / 514–32 // 533–51 / 552–69.

The scribe copied from it up to the Latin line 503α and then broke off. During the pause this bifolium, uppermost in his open, unbound copy, was disturbed. When replaced it was incorrectly refolded so that it now ran:

533–51 / 552–69 // 496–513 / 514–32.

Resuming work the scribe remembered that his place was on the first side of the middle fold of the uppermost quire. As this now lay he knew that he had not yet copied the first line and went ahead (possibly even encouraged by the presence in 533ff. of several themes which, from memory of 504–32, he was expecting). He copied two sides, to 569. Glancing at the third (496–513) he noticed the Latin *Querite et inuenietis* (503α), which he knew he had copied. He therefore did not copy 496–503α, but did copy 504–32; line 570, to which he then came, was on a new bifolium. If he signified his error by indicating the correct order whoever used his copy as an exemplar ignored or missed his signals.[101]

There would be nothing radical in our reconstruction so far: dislocation of matter followed by reproduction of the disordered text was a common occurrence,[102] and its correction by the criterion of sense is an editorial imperative.[103] The complicating circumstance is the existence of an alternative explanation for the deficiency of this **B** passage: the features which we take to be evidence of scribal disarrangement, and which Langland by perfunctory revision attempted to reduce, may have originated in his own bad composition. Indeed the fact that his revision did not take the form of restoring our presumptive original order might seem to support that possibility. We recognize the force of these considerations. But editorial decision must finally turn on assessment of relative likelihoods. Here the factors are: that Langland was not a uniformly careful and never a systematic reviser; that he evidently did not and possibly could not consult his original **B** manuscript; that however prone to digression he may have been he was not given to incoherent or otherwise feeble argument; that meanwhile scribal disarrangement of copy and the multiplication of texts corrupted by it were commonplace occurrences. On these grounds we identify early corruption by dislocation in the archetypal text of **B** XV 504–69

[101] The presumptive dislocation was distinct from and preceded omission of XV 511–28 by WHmCrGYOC²CBLMS and of XV 533–69 by RF, which are post-archetypal corruptions. The fact that RF's omission is of the matter presumed dislocated is not significant; there is no connexion between the events. RF's omission is typical of a scribe of their exclusive common ancestral tradition (see above, pp. 65f.), who often located his point of resumption by scanning the pages before him without actually reading, and would mistake it if in two adjacent paragraphs or passages similar or related words or notions in approximately similar positions caught his eye. So here (bearing in mind the archetypal order) the following will have induced omission: *isruþe* 533, 539, 508; *riche and Religious* 544, *pope and prelates* 509; *Fer fro kyth and fro kyn* 535, *in fele contrees* 520; *bisshopes* 554, 527; *holy kirke* 557, 526; *preesthode* 568, *curatours* 530; *cristes lawe* 569, *cristes loue* 531; *cristendom dispise* 569, *cristendom honoured* 532. The omission from the other group was evidently by homoteleuton (*bere(þ) name(s)* 510, 528).

[102] Instances in the **A** tradition of *Piers Plowman* are described in Vol. I, pp. 3, 4, 14, 16. There is also a **B** manuscript, Hm, with major dislocations going back at least to its exemplar, which escaped the notice of both the scribe who copied Hm and its corrector, or was too much for their powers of restoration (see above, p. 10). The identical disarrangements in both surviving texts of *The Romaunt of the Rose*, first identified by Tyrwhitt, are to be recalled (see Skeat, W. W., ed., *The Works of Geoffrey Chaucer and Others Being a Reproduction in Facsimile of the First Collected Edition*, etc., London, n.d., p. xxx, and Robinson, *Chaucer*, p. 928).

[103] The simplicity of the present instance must appear if one imagines *Piers Plowman* having survived only in the **A** version and only in manuscripts of the RU tradition or in D, or else in the **B** version uniquely preserved in a copy of Hm.

and emend by reconstruction as the criterion of sense and the suggestion of revised **C** direct.[104]

Other reconstructions indicated by the criterion of sense and guided by the corresponding, revised text of **C** are smaller but not necessarily simple, as we now show. At X 310 where the archetypal **B** text reads *gret loue and likyng for ech of hem loueþ ooþer* the pointlessness of the repetitive *loueþ* suggests corruption. **C**'s corresponding line (V 155) contains the notion of humility, *louhnesse*, which would be apt also in **B**. A further consideration that *ech loweþ hym to*] *ech of hem loueþ* would be a natural unconscious substitution induced by preceding copy supports the reconstruction. At XI 326 archetypal **B** reads *Thorugh ech a creature and kynde my creatour to louye, kynde* signifying the natural world which embraces all created beings. The sense of this passage is suspect because it accords badly with XII 226ff. where in reference to the present discussion *kynde* has the meaning *natura naturans*. **C**'s corresponding revised line (XIII 133) *To knowe by vch a creature kynde to louye* indicates the necessary original sense of **B** which we restore by excluding *and* as intrusive.[105] At XII 161, archetypally *hir noon sikerer*, the adjective seems unaptly general among a list of physical attributes, and its meaning is at variance with the sense of 164ff. In its place the corresponding revised **C** line (XIV 105) reads *heuegore*, indicating the necessary original sense of **B**. The actual original **B** reading is likely to have been *sadder*, partly synonymous with both *heuegore* and *sikerer*; the latter will have been unconsciously substituted by inducement of the general question of the relative safety of the swimmers. At XIII 18, reading archetypally *creatures þat crepen*, the category seems unduly limited in view of lines 15–17 before it. **C**'s revised reading (XV 20) *alle...þat walketh oþer crepeth* directs restoration of original **B**; the omission can have been simply by alliterative attraction. At XIII 40 (after various dishes, Austin, Ambrose, the evangelists, were set before the friar theologian) archetypal **B** reads that neither *þis maister ne his man* ate meat of any kind, but dined on more expensive foods. The passage is suspect because no companion has been mentioned; because it is not Langland's dramatic practice to introduce unfunctional personages;

[104] At this point we note that one **C** manuscript, M (B. M. Cotton Vespasian B XVI) transposes XVII 188–257 and 258–84β, that is to something like our rearrangement. We cannot, however, say whether M reads thus by sophistication or by good correction. On the manuscript see Skeat, *C-Text*, pp. xxxix, xl, and Chambers, 'The Manuscripts of *Piers Plowman* in the Huntington Library', p. 22.

[105] Compare a similar corruption at V 486.

and because declining to eat meat would be uncharacteristic of a glutton. The revised **C** line (XV 45), *of this mete þat mayster myhte nat wel shewe* ('chew'), points to the violent allegorical figure we have reconstructed as the original **B** reading. Its corruption will have been by revulsion, whether conscious or unconscious, from even the suggestion of cannibalism. At XIV 196 the sense of archetypal *al þat euere we writen* is impossible in view of what follows; from **C**'s equivalent (XVI 37), *al oure lyuynge here*, original **B** must have referred to more general activity. The rejected *writen* will have been caught up from 199 below. At XVI 157 the archetypal **B** reading *þe worse and* in Christ's curse upon Judas is meaningless, as scribal editing in the visible **B** tradition would confirm. The corresponding **C** line (XVIII 174) while radically revised nevertheless contains an expression *to þe worldes ende* from which the likely original **B** reading can be restored. This will have been corrupted by thoughtless augmentation of emphasis.

Of the archetypal **B** readings where corruption is indicated by the criterion of versification a number can be reconstructed from the evidence of the revised **C** equivalent.

In four instances where the **B** line is suspect because it has an alliterative pattern *aaxa*, first the fact that **C** is revised suggests both corruption early in the **B** tradition and the poet's dissatisfaction with the line in his **B** manuscript; and second, the form of the revision to the pattern *aaax*, identifying the object of his dissatisfaction, directs the restoration of the line. Thus at Prologue 103 archetypal **B** reads *þe beste of alle vértues*, and the revised line in **C** (Prologue 128) has a stave in the normative position. On this particular confirmation of the poet's verse practice we presume an original which by substitution of an easier reading could have generated the archetypal **B** line. Similarly, at VII 35, archetypally *fere yow in youre déying*, **C** IX 38 *déspeyre in ȝoure deynge*; at XI 437 *euery man hym shónyeþ*, **C** XIII 243 *vch man shóneth his companye*; and at XVIII 2 *of no wo récchep*, **C** XX 2 *récheth nat of sorwe*, the revision evinces an unmistakable wish to have a stave in the earlier position. In each of these cases the likely **B** original can be restored by simple rearrangement, on the presumption that it was early corrupted by prosification or manipulation of emphasis.

When the suspicious feature of the archetypal **B** line is its lack of a third stave reconstruction is sometimes possible because the corresponding, revised line of **C** suggests a word which could serve as that stave.

The aptness of such a word from **C** to the alliterative pattern of **B** implies the possibility that it was originally present there. If on that supposition its loss and the corrupt archetypal form of **B** are easy to account for, the possibility becomes a likelihood. In general such reconstruction is not complicated by other considerations; the issue is simply whether the determining assumption necessary in each case is acceptable: that the **C** reading apt to the alliteration of **B** has survived revision, or been restored from memory, or echoes the unrevised **B** line. The most problematic instance is at IV 158 where the archetypal **B** line *And wit acorded þerwiþ and comendede his wordes*, scanning either *aaxa* on [w] or *xaax* on [k], appears corrupt in one or the other half. There are two obvious emendations to a normative scansion: rearrangement to *and his wórdes comendede*, or reading *Kýnde wit acorded* on the suggestion of revised **C** (IV 152), where Natural Intelligence is one of Reason's supporters. The former emendation is less drastic but sense points to the latter because in this passus *wit* has been corrupt and venal. At the same time the fact that he has figured prominently there, together with the succession of *And*'s in the immediate context, will explain *Kynde*] *And* substitution. Another archetypal **B** line with dubious verse structure, whether two-stave or scanning *axaa* or *aaxa*, is XVII 7 *And whan it is enseled so I woot wel þe soþe*. The revised **C** line (XIX 9), with a stave *þerwíth* corresponding to **B**'s *so*, suggests that original **B** also alliterated on [w]. Because *þerwiþ*] *so* substitution could have been caused by attraction to the alliteration of preceding *enseled* or the form of following *soþe* or both in combination we accept the **C** reading as probably original for **B**. Twice the revised **C** line enables repair of archetypally defective alliteration by indicating the degree of emphasis intended by the poet and thus the lost stave word: at IV 36 (**C** IV 36) *hem likeþ*] *þei wol* (>*aaxy*), and V 404 (**C** VII 20) *pure*] *ful* (>*aaxy*). On that indication the stave was lost from both lines through scribal augmentation of emphasis. In V 414b, archetypally *and þanne vp gesse I shryue me* (>*aaxy*), a stave on [t] is clearly needed, and **C**'s *telle* (VII 29) recommends itself. Our reconstruction presumes a more explicit archetypal *telle*] *shryue me* substitution with rearrangement for greater emphasis. Other **B** lines for which we have found a third stave in the revised **C** equivalent are: VI 327 **C** VIII 350 where we presume *mone*] *sonne* variation by alliterative attraction; X 478 **C** XI 293 *laborers*] *men* (inducement of the commoner collocation); XIV 62 **C**

XV 261 *boþe*] *mowen* (alliterative attraction); X 470 **C** XI 295 *parfit*] *om* (homoarchy); XIV 253 **C** XVI 93 *noon haunt*] *no þyng* (an easier reading); and XVII 3 **C** XIX 3 *riȝt*] *om* (adjacency of similar small words).

The revised **C** line can indicate how archetypal **B** was corrupted and so point to its original form. Thus at V 369 **C** VI 427 from the reviser's elimination of *& holy dome* this appears an early scribal addition for greater emphasis; correspondingly the absence of *and his sydes* from one **B** family will be a post-archetypal omission to shorten the line. At XIV 307, archetypally *And euer þe lasse þat he bereþ þe hardier he is of herte*, the vocalic alliteration leaves *lasse*, the main notion in the first half-line, unstressed; and *hardier...of herte*, with sense not evidently appropriate, is further suspect because of the following *hardy...of herte*. If original **B** had contained the staves *lede* and *lihtere* of **C**'s revision (XVI 142), thus stressing *lasse* and also making good sense, *lede*] *bereþ* would be explicable as an easier substitution and *liȝter*] *hardier* as caught up from 308 once the control of alliteration was lost. At XVIII 54, scanning archetypally *xaya*, the corresponding **C** line (XX 54), whether slightly revised or itself archetypally corrupted, nevertheless directs restoration of **B** by indicating the lost stave and the original order of the second half-line. At V 151, 152, which the **B** archetype copies as three lines scanning *xaay*, *nil* and *xaay*, the revised **C** equivalent (VI 126, 127) confirms the originality of the redivision which produces normative alliteration.

Elsewhere the revised **C** equivalent enables more elaborate reconstruction. At V 374–7 (**C** VI 434, 435) the archetypal **B** text is suspect because *fastyng dayes* occurs in both 374 and 377; because the point of *dyned* in 376 is not clear; and because 377 has a scribal alliteration *aabb*. **C**'s revision, excluding 374, 375, and recasting 376, implies that they were already corrupt in his **B** manuscript; it also suggests a possibly original alliteration for 377. On these indications our reconstruction presumes *feeste*] *fastyng* substitution for greater emphasis in 374, *byed*] *dyned* misreading induced by *drynke* in 376, and smoothing in 377 from an original containing 'fed' and 'before' to copy in the ousted *byed* of 376. At X 399, 400 the **B** archetype reads a single line. The suggestion of its scribal alliteration *aabb* that it may be two original first half-lines run together is confirmed by **C** XI 230, which we take to be also the unrevised original **B** form of 399. We find the second half-line for 400 in **C** XI 224 which, from the echo (*lif lete* > *leuere*) which so often characterizes revised lines, is its equivalent. Corruption here, probably in the second archetypal phase, will have been by attraction between the complementary meanings of 399a and 400a. At XVI 108–10 we find the archetypal lines corrupt because we can see no significance in their repetition of *sike and synfulle boþe*, because the meaning of the second is imperfect, and because the third scans *aaxy*. **C**'s revised equivalent (XVIII 141, 142) is too compressed and simplified to show whether the lines in the revising poet's **B** text had the first two of these features, but it does indicate his intention to keep the physical and spiritual healing distinct, and that archetypal 110 is made of parts of two original lines. This evidence directs our rearrangement: the elements of lines are reassembled to separate the categories *sike* and *synfulle* and the defective alliteration is supplied from **C**. Corruption in the archetypal **B** tradition is explicable as caused first by eyeskip (*sike and* 108, 110), and then by an attempt to smooth the miscopying.[106]

We now illustrate reconstruction from **B** evidence alone, where **C** has no corresponding line, or where the corresponding line of **C** appears itself archetypally corrupt, or is evidently a revision of a corrupt **B** line, or is otherwise too radically revised any longer to relate in detail to **B**. In these circumstances it can happen that while the editorial criteria point to scribal damage in a **B** line, the necessary original of the corruption is evident from the variation.

Some reconstructions are very simple and obvious. An example is the restoration of alliterating dialect forms, as at V 439 which with its archetypal reading *ran* scans *xaay*, while the alliteration calls for unmetathesized *yarn*, used as a stave in XI 60 and there similarly corrupted in some manuscripts (note also *yerne*, XV 188). Another is elementary lexical reinterpretation, as at XII 74 where the variation *where she, were sche* and zero requires original *wher*, 'whether', which will have been corrupted by inducement of preceding *womman were*. At XVII 116 the meaningless archetypal reading *kennen out comune men*, with various smoothings registering scribal perplexity, is simply a

[106] Other examples of comparable reconstruction are XI 148, 149, **C** XII 83, 84; XI 353, 354 **C** XIII 167; XII 240–3 **C** XIV 172–6; XII 262, 263 **C** XIV 183, 184; XIV 47–50 **C** XV 246–9; XIV 124, 125 **C** XV 302; XV 378, 379 **C** XVII 113; XVII 296, 297 **C** XIX 277, 278; XVIII 316α–18α **C** XX 360, 361; also, discussed above (pp. 113ff.) in another connexion: VI 162, 163; XI 301, 302; XII 130, 146; XIII 106; XV 321; XVIII 71.

thoughtless misdivision of *k. outcomen men* (*NED* s.vv. *Ken* v.[1] 4, *Outcome* ppl.a.).

Correction of palæographic error belongs in this same class. Thus at XI 96, archetypally with the scribal pattern *aabb*, *segge* must represent original *legge*, with *l* misread as long *s* by inducement of the common collocation *segge soþe*. At XI 185 reconstruction begins with identifying direction of variation: the majority reading *hele* cannot have generated R's *euel* whereas the impossible sense of *euel* shows *hele* to be a scribal smoothing and *euel* to represent the corrupt archetypal reading. This, then, because the alliteration of the line is established by the prominence of *Ioye* and *Iesu*, appears a palæographic error for original *Iuel* (*NED* s.v. *Jewel* sb.3). At XX 219, where *pisseris* is suspect from its extreme lexical difficulty,[107] a probable correction *gypsers*, 'purses', in GC[2] points to a prosaic but more meaningful original which could, by misreading of contractions, have generated the probably archetypal majority reading.[108]

Reconstruction is also straightforward where post-archetypal variation is 'split' and the text, while imperfect in all copies, has distinct corruptions in two families or variational or genetic groups or manuscripts, and its uncorrupted features are thus complementary. For instance at IX 98 the line in both WHmCrLMS and RF fails to scan normatively; comparison indicates omission from the larger group (of a deliberately repetitive expression) and substitution in RF (induced by the preceding line). At X 473 variation in one subgroup is *koupe on þe boke*, with a scribal scansion *xaay*, in most other manuscripts *koupe or knewe*, suspect because tautologous. Neither variant is likely to have generated the other. The evidence suggests that their common original contained a verb both similar enough to *koupe* to give rise to the *or* in *or knewe* and capable of forming an appropriately meaningful group with *on þe boke*. We find this in *konne*, 'get to know, learn'. Where the text survives in only two copies, at XI 197 R preserves the form of the

[107] Skeat's suggestion (*The Vision of...Piers Plowman*, Part IV Section I, *EETS* 81, London 1877, p. 449) that *pisseris* is a 'cant term, or nickname' for soldiers or armed retainers is implausible. The Vulgate *mingentem ad parietem* (*Regum* III, 14.10 and 16.11) means specifically male as opposed to female, nothing more. In any event the Old Testament would be an unlikely source for Middle English cant terms.

[108] Our only adventurous palæographic reconstruction, at XII 130, has already been cited in another connexion (above, p. 115). The scribal features of that line are its lack of alliteration and the lexical oddity of *Lyueris*. The original alliteration of the line is suggested by *toforn*, which from its position might be a stave word; and the probable original of *Lyueris* is deduced from the following context with its implications of a special skill, but one not likely to save souls.

line but corrupts its sense by visual error, while F prosifies it; at XII 119 it is F which, though typically sophisticated, keeps the form and normative scansion, while R disturbs the original order.

The authority of a text produced by reconstruction varies necessarily from line to line, whether the determinant (our own limitations apart) is the amount of lexical information available, or the scale of the reconstruction, or its complexity.[109] The rationale is, however, constant: all variants are unsatisfactory by the editorial criteria, or if that is not the case, no variant appears likely to have generated the remainder, but from their joint indications it is possible to hypothesize an original which could both have generated them all and satisfies the criteria of style, sense and verse technique. We now illustrate the range of its application.

This begins with simple reconstructions which are almost automatic: V 399, archetypally *aaxy*, where F's *soþly*, itself too easy to have been corrupted, is a substitution for original *so þe I*[110] restored in the F tradition by correction; XI 180 where *oure lord* is not original because unlikely to have been corrupted, and *god* does not alliterate, but both variants could originate in unmodified *lord*; XIII 406 where original *worþ* is established by the sense of *wente* (an easier reading) and the shape of *wrathe* (unconscious substitution induced by preceding *dedlich synne*); XV 213 where *lyueþ* is established by the sense of unalliterating *is* (an easier reading) and the shape of contextually meaningless *loveþ* (misreading of a correction induced by the subject, charity); and XVI 161 where original *ynome* is evidenced by the pointless homœograph *his name* and a correction later corrupted by attraction to preceding copy.

Other reconstructions of comparable authority are more interesting. At XV 224 none of the variants can be original: the group readings *so* and *for* because they cannot conceivably have generated *til*, and *til* because it neither alliterates nor makes sense. These characteristics of *til* however establish direction of variation as *til*] *so*/*for* by smoothing to an alliterative and meaningful or simply a meaningful expression. They also indicate that any resemblance between *til* and the original will be of shape, not sense. The alliteration of the line points to *stille*.[111] Its indication is confirmed by the possibility of explaining loss of *s* from *yset stille* as induced by *t*⟩⟨*t* attraction. At XVI 136 the tense of

[109] This applies, of course, to all edited texts. See Vol. I, p. 165.

[110] Cp. Vol. I, p. 164.

[111] *NED* s.v. *Still* adv. 3, 'continually, invariably'.

R's variant *aren* makes this seem unoriginal; the majority variant *was*, which could pass muster with vocalic scansion, can in its turn scarcely have generated *aren*. Unless then the context induced substitution of a present tense in R, which we think unlikely, *aren* is a reflex of the original and *was* a further variation smoothing its grammar. The obvious original is *arne*, 'welled up' (cp. XIX 378 *ernynge*), confusedly preserved in R and coincidentally sophisticated in F and the larger group.

Some simple reconstructions are more problematic because, although direction of variation can be established to the extent that no surviving variant appears the original of all others, the presumption of the common original is not so obviously directed by the evidence. Thus at II 91 *wenyngis* (actions 'of thinking, supposing, expecting, etc.'), *wedes* and *wedynges* have no senses appropriate to the context of lechery, and for *wendys* there seems to be no lexical attestation. There is, however, a word resembling all variants in shape: *wenes* (*NED* s.v. *Ween* sb.2, 'expectation, hope') which could with a particular sexual application have generated severally *wedes* and *wenyngis*] *wedynges* as easier homœographs. At XIII 152 *I bere þerInne aboute/abounte/abewte* the first variant would make sense but appears unoriginal as too easy to have been generally corrupted; the second and third lack contextually appropriate meanings. If the original expression was not adverbial as in *aboute*, and did not specify the object carried, which is presently named, it presumably referred to the container. This suggests original *in a bouste* (*NED Boist* sb., 'box, casket'), both appropriate from its religious meaning *hostiarium* (*MED* s.v. *boist(e*, n. 1 (a)) and hard enough to be misread or to generate a homœograph. At XIV 141 the random type-variations *here beryng, heer beyng/dwellyng* and *hee/hiȝe beryng* point to a polysyllabic original with components resembling *here* and *beryng* in shape. If that original was *herberwyng*, 'lodging, accommodation', i.e. on the journey to the next life, it would have been hard enough to generate the misreadings and substitutions in the manuscripts.

Under that caveat about the variable authority of our text we now illustrate more elaborate reconstruction, beginning with instances confined to the single line. At V 419 *oon clause wel* seems easy, satisfactorily emphatic, and unlikely to have been corrupted; *it clause mel* lacks a referent for the pronoun. Both variants reflect original *clausemele*, corrupted in one family by anticipation of following copy, in the other to an easier and more emphatic reading. At XI 49 *if þe leste/list* is pointless since no one is being addressed; *ne (no) lust* is repetitious. Distribution of support suggests group variations here from a common original. This is identified from the spelling *leste* and the notion of degree in the preceding context. At XII 81 archetypal *The Clergie þat þere was* is both verbose and suspiciously like the text of 80 above it. F's variant, which we interpret as a correction followed by sophistica-tion (note F's passive verb) suggests the original; the expanded archetypal reading will be the result of attraction to preceding copy. At V 267 *of þyne bi my soule hele* appears corrupt from its lack of a stave; *so god my soule hele* etc. are further variations smoothing to the scribal pattern *aabb*. F's *so mote pyȝghne in helle* could be alliterative 'improvement'. But the circumstances that the original probably referred to the fate of the speaker's soul, that it contained a stave alliterating on [p], and that its character must have encouraged sub-stitution draw attention to the rhyme *pine:pyȝghne*. From this we infer an original likely to have been corrupted to the archetypal reading to avoid an unlucky reference.[112] At X 316 with the archetypal readings *axeth...tauȝte* the line is unalliterative unless lamely on vowels: F's emphatic *loþly* and *lythirly* appear as sophistications. But the variant *lackeþ* in Hm, a manuscript otherwise sometimes effectively corrected,[113] directs repair of the alliteration to a possibly original form. At XIV 28 comparison of the two readings *Haukyns wif...which is* (R) and *Haukyns wif...with his* (WHmCrGYOC²CBLM) indicates direction of varia-tion by showing *which is*] *with his* as smoothing further variation. R's reading is thus that of its group ancestor (RF) and of the archetype; F's *Haukyn...which is* a correction or an editing sophistication. From the poor sense of *wif* (why should her clothes be compared with those of heralds and harpers?) this is unoriginal; from its stave position it is not intrusive but reflects an original both meaningful and likely to generate *wif*. This must have been *wil*, corrupted through *l*>*f* misreading, per-haps induced by following *w-f*.

Reconstruction can also extend over several lines; notwithstanding this larger scale it is sometimes very simple. It can involve no more than redivision and the exclusion of padding, as at VII 70, 71 where the first stave of 71 was copied at the end of 70 through grammatical

112 Cp. Vol. I, p. 138.

113 See its readings at III 179, 302, IV 104, V 96, 291, 304, VII 4, X 375, XVIII 106, 194.

attraction and *þan þe* introduced to fill out 71; or at XV 267, 268 where misdivision similarly induced left archetypal 268 with only two staves, and *quod he* is subsequent padding.[114] It can restore a misplaced stave: at XIV 80, 81 (*abab*) the necessary first stave *So* of 81 was anticipated in the copying of 80; at XV 163, 164 (*axay* or *abab*), the damage consists of transposition of a pronoun and its following referent.[115] It can, by beginning with redivision to lines with normative patterns, which shows up prosification and padding, direct correction of the one and elimination of the other, as at XIII 138, 139. Or it can restore meaning by elementary repair, as at IX 39, 40, identifiable as corrupt from their poor sense (only one requisite for writing should be wanting) and partly corrected in F; here the corruption was obviously reciprocal *if*][*and* substitution.

Some reconstructions extending over several lines involve considerable rearrangement of the text. This can take the form of redisposition of half-lines. Thus at I 122, 123 the archetypal text appears corrupt because of the dubious lexicography of *stable* in 122[116] and the *xaay* alliteration of 123. Both deficiencies vanish when the half-lines are transposed and *gan*, as presumable smoothing, is excluded. Here archetypal miscopying is explicable by attraction to the prominent [st] alliteration. At VII 40, 46 both lines, scanning *aaxy*, are evidently corrupt. If archetypal 40b and 46b are exchanged the scansion becomes normative, from which fact there is a presumption that their position in the manuscripts is scribal. Dislocation is explicable as having originated in desire to increase the emphasis of 40. At XI 182, 184 the archetypal scansion *aaxy* of 182 and the echo indicate corruption; reconstruction is guided first by the appropriateness of *souereynly pore peple* to 184 and second by F's line 182, which appears to contain original sense obscured by chronological variation. Corruption here will have been by unconscious anticipation of following copy.

Other reconstructions by rearrangement are more radical. At V 260,

[114] Other applications of this particular process, at XIX 302, 303 and 348, are discussed above, p. 119.

[115] For more complex but (we think) authoritative reconstructions of this kind, at XI 301, 302 and XIX 184, 185 see above, pp. 114, 120, 121. Compare also XII 229, 230 where the first stave of 230, *Kynde*, having supplanted a near-synonym at the end of 229 by inducement of preceding copy at the archetypal stage, was nevertheless copied again at the head of 230, and only later smoothed out in the group ancestor of one family.

[116] See *NED* s.v. *Stable* v.[1] 6, where the meaning 'cease from action' is forced out of the present archetypal use: the clear meaning of the word is 'To come to a stand, become stable', which cannot apply to God.

261 the suspicious features of the archetypal text are the length of 260, its scansion *xaaa*, and the superfluousness of *on þis grounde* in 261. Reconstruction is directed by the presumption that this expression is padding, the alliterative congruence of *God lene þee neuere* in the second archetypal line, and the ease of rearranging what remains of 260 to *aaax*. Corruption will here have occurred by grammatical attraction between an opening adverb and the clause to which it belongs. At IX 42, 43 corruption is evidenced by the defective alliteration of archetypal 42, the identity of its Latin with 33α, and the anomaly of *There he seide Dixit.* This last feature suggests that *There he seide* is dislocated rather than intrusive; alliteration indicates its original position in 42. Its appropriateness there is confirmed if F's variant contains the original quotation (by correction, as may well be). At XIII 53–5 reconstruction extends to the reordering of archetypal lines. Here the evidence of corruption is the repetition of *he brouȝte vs* (smoothed by omission in one family) and the scansion *aaxy* of 55. The correct order of lines appears from the sense of *þanne...ooþer*, and the aptness of *in a dissh* as the first stave of 55. When the lines are rearranged on these suggestions the explanation of the corruption (eyeskip: *And...of* 53, 54) seems obvious.[117]

So that the authority of these reconstructions, irrespective of their scale and complexity, may be correctly assessed, we end our illustration of the process by reference to two instances where, while the unoriginality of the archetypal text is unmistakable, the ruined lines afford less clear evidence of their original. One is at XIV 7–9 where the archetypal scansions *axay*, *aaxy* and *axax* suggest both misdivision and the loss of two staves, but the evidence for the original form of these stops short with their alliteration: here we can be confident only that the original line division has been restored. The other is at XV 126, 127, archetypally one almost meaningless line. This would be an insoluble crux but for the variants of OC² (in 126b and 122b above),[118] and F's spurious line after 125 (*þat is betake to tauerne hows for ten schelyng plegge*) suggests how its component language might reflect meaningfully related notions appropriate to the discourse. With the help of this we think we may here have recovered the original sense.

[117] To these examples add the reconstruction of XIX 183–5, already discussed in another connexion (see above, pp. 120, 121).

[118] Even the origin of these variants is perplexing, for while the exclusive common ancestor of OC² is not evidently corrected, it is also free of sophistication.

Our third editorial process, conjecture, remains to be illustrated. This process consists in two operations: identifying as unoriginal unanimous or unmistakably archetypal readings of the manuscripts; and proposing in their place unattested, therefore entirely hypothetical readings as likely or possible originals. However arbitrary and high-handed conjectural editing may seem, it is in fact a classic editorial method of which the theoretical validity is not really open to question; it is rather to be seen as an obligatory part of the editorial function.[119] The element of doubt lies in the practicability of applying it. There are editorial circumstances in which the effectiveness of conjecture as a means of recovering historical truth must be severely limited by the inadequacy of information: as when a text is of indifferent literary quality, where the *usus scribendi* of author and copyist would be practically indistinguishable, or is uniquely preserved, where the quality of the tradition is indeterminable.

In the case of the **B** version of *Piers Plowman*, however, there is often abundant information for both operations of conjecture.[120] This information first establishes archetypal corruption as a fact: the medial position of **B** enables confident assessment of the quality of its archetype. For long passages two or even all three versions correspond: thus where unrevised **B** corresponds to **A** the **B** archetype is testable as a *codex descriptus*; where **B** corresponds to unrevised **C** the latter, as a quotation from an earlier, therefore axiomatically less corrupted phase in the archetypal **B** tradition, further tests the quality of the received **B** archetype; where all versions correspond and the text of **BC** is effectually a *codex descriptus* of **A**, the quality of even the earlier archetypal **B** phase is subject to control. The showing of these checks by comparison that the archetypal **B** text was very much corrupted establishes a presumption that its corruption extends also to those parts where it is unique.[121]

[119] See Maas, *Textkritik*, pp. 9–15, and especially his comment on p. 13: 'Dass die Konjekturalkritik eine Zeitlang grundsätzlich bekämpft wurde, sei als vorübergehende Verirrung der Forschung nur eben erwähnt.' Our point of view has been expressed by Kane, 'Conjectural Emendation', in Pearsall, D., and R. Waldron, ed., *Medieval Literature and Civilization: Studies in Memory of G. N. Garmonsway*, London, 1969, pp. 155–69.

[120] Our text actually instances the circumstances described by Maas as ideal for the operation of conjecture (*Textkritik*, pp. 11, 12).

[121] Compare Maas, *Textkritik*, p. 12: 'Wenn ein Archetypus (oder codex unicus) durch Zeugen, die einer älteren Spaltung entstammen, streckenweise zum Variantenträger oder gar zum codex descriptus degradiert wird, so sind die in diesen Strecken nachweisbaren Gattungen seiner Fehler auch in den Strecken zu vermuten, wo wir ihn nicht kontrollieren können. Hierin liegt der grosse Wert der Zitate, soweit diese einer älteren Spaltung entstammen.' That presumption could be rejected only on acceptance of two extremely difficult contingent assumptions, as follows:

A priori, then, the archetypal **B** text was corrupt throughout its length. Further, the specific corruptions revealed where that text is exposed to comparison, taken together with the numerous visible variations at the post-archetypal stage in the many copies of each version, afford an unusual wealth of data for classifying the variation to which the text of *Piers Plowman* was characteristically subject.[122] With such information it is possible to bring the general presumption of archetypal corruption in unique **B** passages to bear on its particular readings.[123]

For the second operation of conjecture, the hypothesis of the lost original reading, circumstances are also favourable. Because of the length of the poem and its preservation in so many copies there are countless opportunities at the stage of visible variation for comparison between readings strongly presumed original and readings evidently or almost certainly scribal. Because these fall into typical relationships it is possible not merely to discriminate between authorial and scribal *usus scribendi* but often also, when an archetypal reading has a scribal look, actually to deduce the authorial reading likely to have generated it. In particular, crucial situations tend to resemble one another or even to recur so often that they become familiar and the editorial action required proclaims itself. Undoubtedly this situation encourages an intuitive approach: the editors cannot help acquiring, from the wealth of stored impressions, a feeling (whether accurate or otherwise) for the turns of language and even of thought respectively characteristic of the poet and his scribes.

Notwithstanding these favourable circumstances the results of conjectural editing, but especially of conjectural emendation, will vary in the strength of their claim to acceptance. With respect to this the two operations are to be distinguished. How accurately we have conducted the first, that is identified corruption in the archetypal text of **B**, is determinable from the validity of our editorial criteria and the degree of skill with which we have applied them. Assurance here is obviously

whereas in the controllable parts of **B** the poet showed himself an excellent artist, while scribal damage to his text was extreme, where control is not possible (*i*) he often wrote ineptly, producing a text like that elsewhere created by scribal variation, and (*ii*) in these parts of the poem his text, ineptitudes and all, was faithfully transmitted. Editorial experience rejects these assumptions.

[122] See Vol. I, pp. 125ff. and the preceding sections of this Introduction.

[123] Compare Maas, *Textkritik*, p. 12: 'Anderseits kann es notwendig werden, alle Sonderfehler eines codex descriptus zu sammeln und zu gruppieren, um für die Fälle, wo derselbe Zeuge Variantenträger oder codex unicus ist, ein Urteil über seine zu vermutenden Sonderfehler zu gewinnen.' Sections III and IV above incorporate such collections and analyses.

independent of the possibility of conjecturing an emendation. The second operation, however, of proposing a lost and wholly unattested original, is by contrast purely speculative, and for speculation there is no intrinsic test except its plausibility.[124] In this, however, it resembles many other branches of literary study: conjectural emendation operates at least in part by the rationalization of affects; its quality depends on the accuracy of the affective data, and on the informed reasoning applied to them. Short, then, of external verification such as the discovery of an autograph, which would support or discredit our conjectural emendations, they are to be tested by one means only, reenactment of the textual criticism through which we arrived at them.

To us they have seemed variously obvious and easy, or likely, or possible restorations of original readings. We have given our readers all the information we possess to test our editing. Whether our conjectures find favour or not, however, we shall have served one main purpose of conjectural editing by cautioning against the uncritical acceptance of unanimous or evidently archetypal readings as necessarily original.[125] But we would like to hope that we have also more than just occasionally contrived to bring the poem back closer to its historical original than the scribes of its traditions left it.

Our illustration begins with conjecture in the editorial situation where the **B** line or passage is either unique or so differentiated by revision that neither **A** nor **C** is useful in editing it. Here, not surprisingly, conjecture is most often called for; here, also, its application is generally not complicated by the consideration in which archetypal phase the putative corruption occurred. Since the object of the illustration is to enable assessment of likelihoods we indicate our own opinion of these: we have divided our conjectures into three groups, those in which we have as much confidence as editorial experience allows, those which we judge at least likely restorations of a corrupted original, and those where, while we have no doubt of the archetypal corruption, we cannot rate our emendation higher than as possibly original.

In this textual situation a few readings appear unoriginal by the criterion of style. This criterion, where comparison of readings is not possible, can generally serve only to draw attention to scribal augmenta-

[124] Hence, we assume, the old notion that a conjectural emendation is validated by the acclaim of those competent to judge it, 'die Übereinstimmung aller Urteilsfähigen' (Maas, *Textkritik*, p. 12).

[125] On this point see Maas, *Textkritik*, p. 13, and Kane, 'Conjectural Emendation', pp. 161–3.

tions. On the showing of those parts of the archetypal **B** text exposed to comparison this must also, where it is unique, contain much spurious matter. But recognizing the degree of subjectivity involved we have made only a very few absolutely conjectural[126] exclusions of any size.[127] They are of archetypal lines after: V 39α, 54, 195, 234, 277α, 281, 556; VI 17, 182; VII 60; X 272, 303; XI 67, 302; XIV 33; XIX 252. They are characterized by prosiness and verbosity; none is material to the sense; only three conform to the poet's alliterative practices. They appear with their variants in the critical apparatus. All are explicable as induced by scribal response to the immediate context. Two are inserted for greater explicitness (after V 234 and 556); four are prompted by a Latin line and introduce or translate it (after V 39α, 54, 281, and VII 60); two increase emphasis (after V 195 and X 303[128]). The rest relate to scribal participation in the sense of a living text. Two register elementary interest in food (after VI 17, 182); three participate in criticism of the clergy (after X 272, XI 67 and 302); one relates the immediate discussion to a consideration earlier and subsequently expressed (after V 277α); and one is prompted by a Latin quotation earlier referred to (after XIV 33, echoing VII 130). On such grounds these lines seem merely larger instances of the kinds of corruption to which the archetypal tradition of **B** was generally subject, and we therefore judge them to be spurious.

In this textual situation there are five places where the criterion of sense shows the archetypal **B** text to be corrupt and the original can be confidently restored by conjecture. At VII 125 archetypal *slepe* must be unoriginal: the meaning developed in 122–4 and continued in the second half of 125 requires in its place an original verb denoting 'labour'. This should, moreover, be set in contrast with the stave *wepen*; it will therefore have been alliterating *werche* rather than *swynke* or *trauaille* or *laboure*. Its corruption by rhyming inducement of preceding *slepen* or by the suggestion of *lacrime...nocte* is easy to assume. At VIII 53 *And þat is*, destroying any consequence upon 52, was scribally

[126] We distinguish as not conjectural exclusions of archetypal readings scribally introduced to smooth otherwise manifest corruption, as of *þan he/nauȝtier* at VII 71 after misdivision, of *ouȝt* at XI 49 after misreading of *leste*, of *quod he* at XV 268 after substitution of an easier reading, and of whole lines introduced for smoothing as after XIX 369.

[127] There are also a very few exclusions of smaller archetypal expressions; an example is at XV 460 where *wilde* (1) was scribally induced by attraction to following copy.

[128] The passage where this line occurs is preserved only in RF; the line is therefore not certainly archetypal, for it may have intruded during the RF tradition.

introduced because *to* in 52 was mistaken for the numeral. At XIII 213 archetypal *fauntekyns and oober folk ylered* makes nonsense of the second category: *and* was scribally induced either by its preceding occurrence or by subconscious wavering between *and* and *ooþer* as the more appropriate conjunction. At XIV 23 archetypal *myst*, 'water vapour' is inappropriate as a substance unlikely to stain or spot (*bymolen*) Haukyn's coat; the original must have been *myx*, 'filth', for which *myst* is either a visual error or a homœograph induced by subconscious censorship. At XV 390 and 501 *Iewes* is suspect as both repetitious and creating an imbalance of categories with *Sarȝens*. Line 605, *Grekes*, directs our conjecture. This would have been hard for a copyist ignorant of the Eastern Church, and the commoner collocation would either prompt substitution or actually lead to unconscious misreading.

The criterion of the poet's verse technique shows many archetypal **B** readings to be unoriginal. A number of these are recognizable as the products of familiar processes of corruption; there the original can be confidently restored.

One such process is disarrangement of the second half-line, producing the scribal alliteration *aaxa*. We conjecture that this occurred at IX 157 and X 279 through subconscious promotion of an element in the half-line for emphasis; at X 329, XI 52, 70, XIII 82, 106, XV 123, 312 and 314 through variation to or toward easier, prose order; at XV 395 and XVI 202 through parallelizing with the preceding line; at XVII 155 by attraction to a preceding numeral; and at XVIII 342 by inducement of the position of *by...lawe* in 343. Restoration to *aaax* is by rearrangement, either simple or accompanied by minor adjustments (X 329 *þer...Inne* for *in which*, XI 70 *hym* for *hymself*, XIII 82 *þis* for *þis ilke*, XV 314 *wherby* for *þat...by*).

Scribal disarrangement can extend to the whole line. We consider this to have occurred in the following lines with archetypal alliterative patterns other than normative: at IX 110, XI 399, XII 24, 268 and XV 445 through variation to or toward easier prose order; and at XVII 103 through *feiþ*><*Spes* attraction. Here also we conjecture an original restorable by rearrangement (with minute adjustments at XI 399 and XII 268). Two lines scanning *xaay* (XI 53 and XVII 77), where variation to prose order was accompanied by loss of a stave, thus, *Haue...quod*] *And seide haue*, are just as confidently restorable.

A very common means of scribal damage to the versification was substitution of an unalliterating synonym for a stave-word. There are lines with defective alliteration where such a stave-word readily suggests itself. If, on presumption of its originality, variation to the actual, unsatisfactory archetypal reading seems easily explicable, we adopt it with confidence. Thus we conjecture unconscious variation: at III 241 *peple*] *men* (by inducement of a common collocation); at XII 6 *whiles*] *þo* (by attraction to following copy); and at X 252 *scripture*] *euaungelieȝ*, XIII 211 *seide*] *quod*, XVII 73 *barm*] *lappe*, XVIII 350 *maugree*] *ayeins* (by alliterative attraction). We conjecture substitution of more explicit readings at X 432 *swiche*] *hise*, XV 140 *nempneþ hym*] *seyen he was*; of lexically or contextually easier readings at Prologue 143 *comsed*] *gan*, II 36 *caccheþ*] *takeþ*, III 298 *ledeþ*] *ruleþ*, V 52 *loke*] *kepe*, 130 *biggyng*] *dwellyng*,[129] IX 101 *Tynynge*] *Lesynge*, XI 325 *forbisenes*] *ensamples*, XII 4 *mynne*] *þynke*, XIII 86 *preynte*] *wynked*, 375 *what body*] *whoso*, XIV 99 *Wye*] *Man*, XV 72 *lome*] *ofte tymes*, 243 *vndignely*] *vnworþily*, 353 *myd*] *wiþ*, XVI 66 *dyuyse*] *discryue*, and XVII 92 *segge*] *man*: and of a more emphatic reading at X 91 *wisse*] *rule*. We conjecture a stylistic substitution, to eliminate repetition, at VI 181 *Lat*] *Suffre*.

Alliteration was often damaged by substitution of a variant only approximately or partly synonymous. There are archetypal lines with defective alliteration which seem to have been so corrupted, that is lines where the ousted, alliterating original reading seems obvious and its corruption to the unsatisfactory received reading by a familiar process is easily presumed. Here also it is possible to emend conjecturally with confidence. Thus we presume unconscious variation: by attraction to preceding copy at III 345 *souȝte*] *loked on* (*loked* 341), XIII 253 *me þynkeþ*] *I bileue* (*le-che*), XVII 166 *fader*] *lord* (*bi-longeþ*); by attraction to following copy at X 278 *Thouȝ*] *If* (*it*), XIV 82 *we*] *oure*; by alliterative inducement at XV 84 *me þynkeþ*] *it semeþ* (*-sakeþ*), XVI 71 *erst*] *raþest* (*ripe*).[130] In two lines we conjecture unconscious omission of a grammatically superfluous but alliterating negative through preoccupation with the sense of the line: XII 146 *nas*] *was* and XIV 96 *nadde*] *hadde*. We believe that substitution of a more explicit reading

[129] Here conjecture includes the presumption that the substitution reproduces the contextually inappropriate alternative meaning of an ambiguous term: we understand *biggyng* to mean 'buying, engaging in trade'.

[130] An added factor in the corruption of our conjectured originals at X 278, XV 84, XVI 71 and XVII 166 would be unobvious original [ð]/[θ]: [f]/[v] or vocalic alliteration.

took place at XIV 78 *men*] *þei*, and of variously easier readings at X 257 *So*] *Thanne*, XV 451 *Enformed*[131]] *And seide*, and XVIII 378 *dureþ*] *is*.

Where variation in an archetypal line with defective alliteration was not evidently to a synonym or near synonym it is less often possible to propose a lost original with much assurance. There are, however, a few lines of this kind which we emend conjecturally with as much confidence as our editorial experience allows. At IX 93 *Iugged wiþ*] *wors þan* the stave-sound can only be [dʒ]; the lost sense and language are indicated by 87 above; the substitution was for greater emphasis. At XV 419 *þise*] *hise* the stave-sound must be [f]; our conjecture not merely seems the only possible means of providing a stave for the second half-line but also presumes an original doubly subject to corruption: by simple visual error, and because the unobvious alliteration would be missed. At XVIII 374 *best*] *euere* the original must have been an adverb completing *wherso* and alliterating on [b]; our conjecture is of the only possible reading which satisfies these requisites, one also liable to be ousted by the more common collocation.

Defective alliteration sometimes results from scribal omission. In two lines where this seems to have happened we conjecturally restore the lost stave with some confidence. At V 254 *for pure nede*] *mote nedes* the stave-sound was necessarily [p]; our conjecture of an original expression which scribes evidently found difficult in certain senses[132] is confidently offered.[133] At X 134 *for to*] *to* our conjecture recommends itself by its simplicity, by the contextually apt stress it throws on the demonstratives and the expression of purpose, and by the ease of explaining loss of *for*, either because [ð] [f] alliteration was missed, or through preoccupation with difficult vocabulary.

These examples of confident emendation by conjecture illustrate its reasoning: an archetypal reading is shown to be unoriginal by one of the editorial criteria; it has the appearance of resulting from a process of corruption such as can elsewhere actually be observed; by applying that process in reverse we bring to light a probable original.

[131] That is, 'Instructed'; compare III 241.

[132] For instance, an archetypal scribe omitted *pure* at V 404 (controlled by **C**) and VII 106 (controlled by **AC**). The word was also subject to post-archetypal corruption, for instance at XI 195 and 276.

[133] An alternative emendation, reading *peple* for *men*, with the alliteration *aaaxy*, seems ruled out by the shape and language of 255 following: in this examination of conscience question should be echoed by answer.

Clearly, then, the degree of confidence in conjectural emendation depends on the availability of information, that is on our familiarity with the relationship between the archetypal reading presumed corrupt and the hypothesized original. That confidence can be variously reduced. In some cases alternative possibilities of emendation suggest themselves; the choice between them increases the element of doubt. In others the limitation is lexical, as when the hypothetical reading which satisfies the editorial criteria and could have generated the suspect archetypal reading is an expression not elsewhere used or so used by Langland. Or a conjecture may rest on an interpretation of contextually required sense that could be questioned. The element of boldness in any conjecture which seriously affects the style or sense of a line must also reduce confidence. And of course conjecture involving actual addition to a line rather than substitution must seem especially adventurous.

It is from considerations like these that we present our second group of conjectures where the text of **B** is not subject to comparison with somewhat less confidence. This is not to say that we regard them as frivolous or unlikely to have hit the mark, but that they are more speculative than the former group. In all instances the primary indication of archetypal unoriginality is defective alliteration.

Four conjectured originals are of alliterating synonyms or equivalent expressions with particular contextual meanings lexically well established but not actually instanced in *Piers Plowman*. They are Prologue 159 *salue*[134]] *help*, V 167 *purueiede*] *ordeyned*[135], IX 79 *purchace*[136]] *haue*, and X 285 *barnes*[137]] *folk*. One more is of a word not found in the poem in any sense: X 330 *vngodly*] *han yuele*; and another, at XVIII 282 *driȝten*] *he*, of a word used by Langland but not preserved in the form[138] which we feel to be here required by the rhythm. In all these cases corruption is explicable by substitution of more explicit or variously easier readings.

Some conjectures affect the style of the line. This occurs at V 38

[134] See *NED* s.v. *Salve* sb.[1] 2 *fig.* 'a remedy (esp. for spiritual disease, sorrow and the like)'. The **B** line with this reading actually occurs as a later insertion in one **C** manuscript, P², but since we cannot account for its presence there we must treat our emendation as conjectural.

[135] Cr's reading *prouided* must be the work of the editor.

[136] For this sense compare Chaucer, *Troilus and Criseide*, II 713, *purchace hate*.

[137] See *MED* s.v. *barn* n. 3.

[138] The word occurs at XIII 268 as *driȝte*, and at XIV 102 where, however, its archetypal form is obscured by variation.

Lo] *That* and XII 40 *Lo*] *For* where we presume loss during rubrication: our adopted reading intensifies the predicatory tone; at XII 22 *so*] *as* where we would explain corruption by misreading of the original grammar our emendation alters the flow of the Dreamer's statement; and at XII 95 *by*] *oure* which we explain as variation to a more explicit reading our emendation gives the line a new emphasis.

Others change or extend the sense of the line. This occurs where we have presumed unconscious substitution at X 280 *wis*] *lered* (inducement of the common collocation), XII 89 *iugged*] *brouȝte* (inducement of *pouȝte* following), XV 394 *lord*] *persone* (inducement of the preceding numeral), XV 324 *bisette*] *ȝyueþ* (attraction to preceding copy); where we explain corruption as the result of scribal tendencies of substitution, at XVIII 391 *keuered*] *wasshen* (more explicit), III 319 *may*] *wole*, III 346 *trewe*] *good*, XV 201 *pure*] *ful*, XV 295 *meditacion*[139]] *deuocion*, XV 471 *menen...after*[140]] *doon* (easier readings), XI 422 *litel*] *no* (more emphatic); or where we conjecture substitution for stylistic preference at XI 432 *nede*] *doute*, to eliminate repetition[141].

There are, further, lines which we find unoriginal because of defective alliteration, where the corruption seems to result from omission and we identify the stave presumably lost by inference of what might there most readily have been omitted, thus actually inserting matter in the text. This kind of conjecture is bound to seem radical. It will be plausible only if the alliterating sound of the line has been correctly identified, and if from consideration of the expression supplied and the explanation offered for its loss omission seems the likeliest source of corruption.

In the following lines we conjecture loss of a stave for palæographic reasons. At X 327 *Bynymen that*] *That* the stave-sound must be [b]; the sense and grammar require a verb. Our conjecture[142] could have been archetypally omitted (as indecipherable) if written *Bĩimen* or *Binĩen*. At XI 81 *clene come*] *come*, archetypally *aabb*, the line lacks a stave on [k]; the likeliest of possible lost expressions seems our adopted *clene*, both apt to the sense and in danger of omission from *c-e co* resemblance. At XV 269 *Lo in*] *In* the archetypal alliteration *abab* is not normative: a stave on [l] was lost. Our conjectured original would

[139] This word in its special sense, 'private devotional exercise' (*NED* s.v. *Meditation* 2) seems both required by the context and more difficult than *deuocion*, 'devoutness'.

[140] For the model of this conjecture see 405 above and 475 below it.

[141] Compare Langland's extended play on *nede* in XX 4ff. and the omission of XX 37 by one genetic group.

[142] The word carries a stave on the prefix at III 314.

be subject to omission during rubrication. In other lines with defective alliteration omission subconsciously induced seems the likely explanation. At VI 148 *riȝt noȝt*] *noȝt* the cause could have been *shal*><*noȝt* attraction; at XV 234 *ledeþ wel*] *ledeþ* attraction between the two parts of the common collocation 'lead...life'; at XVI 231 *I feiþ*] *I* attraction between subject and predicate; at I 121 *ful nyne*] *nyne* distraction by the number; at XVIII 113 *Where out*[143]] *Out* distraction by the high allegory. At III 344 *mysferde*[144]] *ferde*, where only [m] can have been the stave-sound, simply end-of-passus fatigue would be a likely cause of omission. At XVIII 283 *siþen he*] *he* occurrence of an expression in two successive lines would be likely to cause its omission from one or the other. Sometimes defective alliteration is explicable by reference to the scribal tendencies of substitution. Thus at III 303 *myddel*] *þis* we conjecture omission of a difficult term followed by smoothing; at XIII 196 *purely for*] *for* omission of a word used in a sense found difficult by scribes; similarly at XV 422 *Boþe Beneit*] *Beneit* we explain loss of the missing stave through omission because of its difficult use.[145] In two cases alternative explanations for loss of the presumed original stave suggest themselves: at III 75 *god in þe gospel*] *þe gospel* omission could have been either simply unconscious abridgement or a deliberate correction, since it is Christ, not God who speaks; at XI 67 *At kirke*] *That* omission could have been to exclude a dialect form or merely to shorten an unusually long line.

The plausibility of a conjecturally emended line must be affected if it contains two speculative readings, even though singly they recommend themselves. Thus at IX 90, archetypally unalliterative, identifying an original stave in emphatic *shame* we presume *So*] *As* corruption induced by the suggestion of correlation in 89 (which actually refers to preceding matter) and accompanying or subsequent *shul*] *þat* smoothing. At XII 129 *by tastes of truþe*] *of tastes of truþe and of deceites* we presume both substitution through attraction to preceding copy and a more explicit scribal augmentation. At XV 138, identifying the original alliteration as vocalic, we conjecture both substitution of a more explicit reading *endeþ*] *deieþ* and variation to prose order in the second half-line.

In three lines, finally, the element of doubt is increased by the existence

143 For the model of this conjecture see XVIII 168.

144 For Langland's use of this verb see **C** X 162 *mysfare*.

145 That is its reference to more than two persons, and its adverbial force, 'likewise'.

of several possible original readings between which, inevitably, our choice must be to some degree subjective. At XIII 128 the stave-sound must be [d]; we conjecture *demeþ*, 'pronounces'[146] rather than *declareþ* or *deuyneþ*, as the most characteristic of the poet's style. At XIII 358 the line could be emended to scan either *mésures mét mýd* or *Thróuȝ fáls fáls*; we adopt the latter as creating the more meaningful emphasis. At XV 119 the obviously scribal element of the line is *men*; either of the two possible originals *wyes* and *ledes* would restore normative alliteration. We adopt *ledes* because a stave-sound [l] throws more emphasis on the most prominent notion of the line, the contrast between ignorance and information expressed in *lewed...latyn*.[147]

The conjectures in this second group, which we have represented as less confidently adopted, nevertheless recommend themselves to us as attributable to the poet, whereas the readings of the archetypal text have characteristics of scribal substitution. They are products of the same reasoning which led us to the conjectures in the first group, differentiated only by the amount of information available; here the way of inference back to the lost original has been less clearly marked, or more extended or complex.

From this same consideration of availability of information, or obversely, of the degree to which conjecture is speculative, we classify a third group as possible rather than likely or almost certain originals. Here also, as will be evident, the element of subjectivity has been the largest. Nevertheless these are not desperate guesses[148] but inferences made on good editorial grounds, albeit from minimal data or more than usually extensive. The propriety of admitting them to our text is open to assessment: all are clearly signalled; we draw attention to their hypothetical character; the apparatus contains full information about rejected readings; and our grounds for considering these unoriginal are shown. Even if none finds favour we shall have exercised one editorial function by emphatically drawing attention to suspect and, as we believe, corrupt archetypal readings.[149]

There are first two lines with defective alliteration where several possibilities of emendation suggest themselves and there is no unmistak-

[146] *NED* s.v. *Deem* v. 10.

[147] The emended line accords with a characteristically subtle Langlandian use of the verse line, in manipulating emphasis by two alliterations, one satisfying the structural principle (as here *léwed lédes látyn*), the other secondary (*wìste whàt*).

[148] We have refrained from these: see below, pp. 210, 211.

[149] Kane, 'Conjectural Emendation', pp. 162f.

able or strong indication at what point the line is corrupt. At IX 40 a part of the reconstruction is a conjecture *wiste to*] *koude*; we adopt this in preference to an alternative emendation *welde*] *hadde* only because its alliterative pattern *aaaxy* seems the more susceptible to corruption. At X 248 *man and his make*] *mankynde*, other possibilities would be, in the first half line *and wommán*[150] or *bi his myȝt*, or in the second half-line *alle manere beestes*; our choice is simply of the least violent emendation as one also liable to be corrupted for emphasis to the archetypal reading.

In one case the limiting factor was lack of indication of the original language. At VII 60, represented in the archetype by two lines with the unmistakable characteristics of scribal expansion, the necessary sense of the original half-line so corrupted seems clear enough, but the wording of our emendation which embodies this is partly speculative: we conjecture a compressed and difficult original thus liable to easier and more emphatic variation.

Elsewhere the limitation relates to the original sense. There are three lines where evidently a stave has been lost but the context affords no clear indication of its necessary meaning. Our conjectures here are directed by the sole consideration what original, in their position, might have most easily been corrupted: III 351 *teme*] *þat* to an easier[151] reading; X 373 *so*] *al* to a more emphatic reading; XV 307 *Riȝt so*] *As who(so) seiþ* to a more explicit reading. These conjectures scarcely affect the meaning of their lines; in another instance our adopted reading alters the archetypal sense by extending it: at XVI 121 where a stave on [tʃ] is wanting and we read *chidde*] *quod*, presuming scribal softening of an action that seemed inappropriate to the speaker.

In other lines conjecture affects the sense more radically: this occurs when corruption is indicated by the unsatisfactory meaning of the archetypal text but the context prescribes no obvious or necessarily original meaning. The only indication of originality can then be from consideration what readings, by their form or position, would most likely have generated the unsatisfactory archetypal text, while also producing appropriate sense. At XII 248 *taille is al of*] *tail(le) of alle is* the necessary meaning of the punning noun is either 'account, reckoning' or 'reversion' (*NED* s.v. *Tail* sb.² 4b or 3); thus *of alle* is

[150] For such alliteration see above, p. 134.

[151] The sense would be of *NED Theme* sb. 2, used ironically by Conscience as if Meed were a moral preceptor.

inappropriate. We conjecture *al of*, 'entirely of', as likely to have been unconsciously misread or misremembered through preoccupation with the preceding topic of peacocks' tails. At XV 313 *by goddes behestes*] *be goddes foweles and* where the archetypal line is meaningless in terms of the discussion before and after it and the alliteration is defective, we hypothesize two stages of substitution. The point of corruption is evidently *foweles*; what this replaces is not contextually indicated, but there is an associational link in the passage between *foweles* and *beestes*. If the text at one archetypal stage had read *beestes* this might easily have prompted scribal correction to *foweles*. In its turn *beestes*, so repugnant to the context that it could only be a homœograph or visual error, could well reflect an original *behestes*,[152] both apt to the context and alliterative. This we adopt, also excluding *and* as smoothing. At XV 361 *shipe*] *ship and sheep* the pointless tautology of the archetype suggests corruption; an original which could have given rise to the variation by natural misreading and amplification or by way of interlinear correction is our conjectured *shipe*, 'wages, reward', where *wiþ* acquires the meaning 'in return for, in consideration of'. At XVI 201 archetypal *hym likede and louede* is untranslatable and not obviously related to its very difficult context. Our conjecture *he*, which gives the line some meaning, rests on the likelihood that in this position between *hym* and *hym* an original nominative pronoun would very easily be omitted.

The scale of some conjectures places them in this group, not simply because being larger they must seem more daring, but because they embrace several contingent emendations; the interdependence of these naturally increases the hypothetical element. Thus at XII 194 *þat graiþ is hem euere*] *and he is euere redy* conjecture presumes three corruptions: substitution of easier *redy*, smoothing of the pronoun case, and variation to easier prose order. At XIII 139, tautologous and unusually long after the original division of 137 and 138 has been restored, our conjecture *lerede...lemman*] *tauȝte...lemman þat I louede* presumes both careless substitution of an unalliterating synonym and subsequent padding to restore alliteration. From our experience of scribal variation such multiple corruption is altogether probable; nevertheless to infer its occurrence simply from the character of an unsatisfactory archetypal reading is undeniably more speculative than identification and reversal of a single variation. This consideration applies *a fortiori* where con-

[152] One such would be *Ne soliciti sitis*, quoted at VII 131.

jecture is even more extensive than in these two cases, as will now be shown.

At XIV 7–9 all three lines are corrupt on the showing of their imperfect alliteration. The first step in restoring them is to identify the points of corruption. In line 7 from the importance of *losse* and *loþ* to the sense a stave on [l] is missing near the beginning. Line 8 also lacks a stave, but since *agulte* at the end of 7 alliterates with *god* and *good* lines 7 and 8 have been misdivided. Therefore also line 7 has lost matter at the end, and line 8 is probably padded. In line 9 from the importance of *shryuen* the stave-sound was [ʃ] or [s]. Therefore it lacks an early stave, and its latter half, scanning *xa*, is probably disordered. The second step is to recover lost matter. In line 7 from the context the lost [l] stave had to do with laundry; on the suggestion of *laued...Wiþ* it was a past participle also governed by *haþ ben* in 5; it was probably because of its shape liable to omission. Our conjecture *lapered*, with these features, seems an obvious possibility. At the end of 7 the sense requires an expression denoting change of heart; the only clue to its form is the inappropriate purposive *forto*. Our conjecture *forto me loþ were* recommends itself as highly likely to have generated *loþ for to*. In line 8 rearrangement of the second half to *ax* is easy, but for recovery of the missing first stave there is no guidance except the likelihood of its unconscious loss: our conjecture *siþþe* would be liable to omission by homœoarchy and homoteleuton.

At XIV 284–7 archetypal line 285 is unalliterative; the sense of its proposition of 'spiritual health to the body' is dubious, and it is unusually short. The archetypal order of lines 286 and 287 attracts notice by not conforming to the general manner of proceeding in this discussion where, otherwise, each part of the argument is closed by the particular element of the long quotation at 276 which it demonstrated: the notion of contrition as a comfort belongs with 282–5 and thus before *Ergo paupertas*. Conjectural restoration of 285, beginning with the suggestion of 283's *solace to þe soule*, embraces 284 by its indication that *and Ioye* of 284 was originally in 285 near *spiritual*; this further suggests archetypal corruption of an original where *is to þe body* completed 284 while *and Ioye* began 285. Presumption of that original order turns 284 into a meaningful expansion of 283a; it also supports the indication of the brevity of 285 that it was archetypally corrupted by omission. Our conjecture of *pacient pouere* as the lost matter is based on the possibility that this expressed the condition in which the spiritual benefit of poverty is effectual, which the context indicates (cp. 102, 218, 220, 260, 272, 317), and that it was in a form liable to omission by homœo-archy and homoteleuton. We complete this conjecture by reversing the archetypal order of 286 and 287.

Finally there are two adjacent pairs of lines which we emend partly by reconstruction and partly by conjecture. The first is XV 121, 122 which we find unoriginal from their style and verse technique: in both the correspondence between rhythmic stress and notional importance seems imperfect to the extent of being uncharacteristic of the poet. Thus in archetypal 121 the primary notion of substitution expressed in *for* receives no structural emphasis; in 122 the archetypal vocalic scansion, while technically unobjectionable, actually detracts from the emphasis on the important terms *bedes* and *book*. In 121 our adopted reading *forbeere*] *beere for*, presuming variation to an easier reading, creates a more meaningful scale of emphasis; in 122 where we presume *And beere*] *A peire* as smoothing after the preceding substitution the new alliteration throws *bedes* and *book* into emphatic prominence. At XV 126, 127 the question is not whether the scarcely meaningful and unduly long archetypal line is corrupt, for it is evidently the ruin of an original pair, but what was the sense and form of these. Here we presume that subconscious corruption through distraction by the topic, and facilitated by the two lines having the same alliteration, began with transposition of parts of them. We find the suggestion of an original apt to the context both in the ruinous archetypal line and in the readings of OC^2 there and in 122, which we explain as informed corrections displaced and obscured by sophistication. So much is inference, albeit on slight indication; *bokelees* in 127 is pure conjecture. The editing in these four lines is probably the most extremely hypothetical in the whole of our text. Nevertheless we judge that lines 121, 122 as we have restored them, with the play on *forbeere beere*, are more typical of the poet than their counterpart in the archetype; and it must be allowed that our emended text of 126, 127 has a better chance of being original than the archetypal text, since this latter is patently corrupt.

We pass now to conjectural emendation in the textual situation where two versions are represented. The rationale of conjecture here is unchanged; the circumstance that it complicates the larger issue by bringing to light agreements in unoriginality between several versions cannot logically affect it. Such agreements certainly call for explanation, but that requirement is a consequence, not a part, of the reasoning of conjecture. For agreements between versions are not primarily relevant to the question of originality; they become problematic only after they are identified as agreements in unoriginality. Then, to be sure, they form part of an argument from the quality of the received archetypes to the poet's methods of revision. The circumstance that a reading found scribal occurs in two archetypal traditions is an issue distinct from that of its originality: conjecture where two versions are represented consists as elsewhere in acceptance of the indication of the editorial criteria that an archetypal reading is scribal, followed by inference from its character and any other available evidence about the necessary or likely or possible sense and form of the original. Conjecture in this textual situation is distinguished only by the greater implication of its results, which here contribute to extending the whole editorial hypothesis.[153]

There are two lines where the archetypes of **A** and **B** agree in defective alliteration of an easily explicable sort, and it is possible to conjecture[154] the same lost original of both versions with assurance. They are IX 166 **A** X 187 *yolde*[155]] *olde*, corrupted by visual error or substitution of an easier reading or censorship, and X 109 **A** XI 67 *wiled*] *giled* corrupted by substitution of an easier reading.[156] These two archetypal agreements of **A** and **B** in unoriginality form part of the evidence for Langland's use of a scribal manuscript of **A** when revising that version.[157]

In the textual situation where **B** and **C** run parallel our conjectures are more numerous; correspondingly they also figure large in one class

[153] This is not, of course, to suggest that we ever undertake conjecture light-heartedly.

[154] We must here emphasize a distinction. Fourteen lines where the emended **B** text differs from the text of **A** in Vol. I are not conjectures, but instances of post-archetypal or archetypal corruption in the **A** tradition which its editor, had he not been deluded by the 'ideal' of conservative editing, could have restored from existing evidence. In four cases this is actual **A** manuscript readings: III 260 **A** III 239 *þat*] *þe*; IV 194 **A** IV 157 *graunte gladly*] *graunte*; V 210 **A** V 126 *Proched*] *Brochide*; VI 286 **A** VII 270 *plaunte coles*] *cole plauntes*. In two others the necessary original of **A** and **B** can be reconstructed from **A** evidence: I 112 **A** I 110 *of liȝt*] *of siȝt/to loken on*; and III 255 **A** III 234 *lowe lewede*] *lowe/lewede*. With these belong three lines where the text of **A** in Vol. I and the **BC** archetypes can all be corrected from **A** manuscript evidence: III 177 **A** III 164 **C** III 223 *most*]*gret*; V 191 **A** V 110 **C** VI 199 *lik*] *as*; V 534 **A** VI 22 **C** VII 179 *god glade me*] *me god helpe*. Last there are four lines where the **AB** archetypes have scribal readings while the **C** tradition preserves the original of all versions: III 229 **A** III 216 **C** III 285 *worþi me þynkeþ*] *worþi* etc., IV 91 **A** IV 78 **C** IV 87 *witnessede*] *seide*; V 9 **A** V 9 **C** V 109 *mette me*] *mette I/sauȝ I*; and VI 282 **A** VII 266 **C** VIII 304 *a cake of otes*] *an hauer cake*; and one where the **AC** archetypes can be corrected from **B** manuscript evidence: V 535 **A** VI 23 **C** VII 180 *ne*] *om.*

[155] See *NED* s.v. *Yolden, yold.* p. part. 2 for the sense.

[156] See Vol. I, p. 156.

[157] See also below, pp. 210f.

of the evidence that the **B** manuscript used by Langland when revising to **C** was scribal. Many of them we have already discussed and assessed in establishing that proposition and can only refer to here.[158] The remainder complete our illustration of the editorial process of conjectural emendation. Again we grade them by our assessment of their plausibility, while emphasizing that this relates not so much to the identification of unoriginality in the archetypes, which we regard as sure, as to the degree of speculation in the proposition of the lost original.

Our confident conjectural emendations are all at points where the archetypes of **B** and **C** have the same imperfect alliteration which in context appears the result of easy and familiar processes of substitution. Some of these are unconscious. The disturbance of word order at XI 14 **C** XI 173 where we conjecture *þat ooþer was ycalled*] *y. w. þ. o.*, could have been induced by the position of *called* in the line above. We conjecture unconscious substitutions as induced: at XVII 247 **C** XIX 213 *Fro*] *To* by expectation set up in the previous discourse; at XVII 301 **C** XIX 281 *crist*] *god* by *god*><*made* attraction; at XVIII 180 **C** XX 183 *Thanne*] *And* by preoccupation with the difficult or already corrupt preceding line; at XVIII 223 **C** XX 232 *se*] *wite* by alliterative attraction; at XVIII 295 **C** XX 325 *do*] *wol* by attraction to *god wol* in 293. We account for the misdivision of XVII 281, 282 **C** XIX 262, 263 as caused by attraction between verb and complement. In other lines variation appears to have been to an easier reading. We restore normative alliteration in three half-lines and two whole lines on the presumption that they were disarranged by variation to or toward easier prose order; they are XII 101 **C** XIV 46, XV 63 **C** XVI 225, XV 114 **C** XVI 269, XV 492 **C** XVII 187, XVI 192 **C** XVIII 201, respectively. In two lines where we conjecture an alliterative, near-synonymous original, XIV 271 **C** XVI 111 *preueþ*] *fareþ*, and XVI 33 **C** XVIII 37 *anoþer*] *som*, we presume substitution of an easier reading. In two others our conjecture presumes sophistication: at IX 202 **C** X 301 *dere*] *frend* to eliminate an unusual, possibly old-fashioned form of address,[159] and XVII 33 **C** XIX 34 *now*] *þanne* to smooth after tense confusion.

[158] See above, Section IV, pp. 112ff., 118ff. The conjectures in question are: I 160, V 173, XI 60, XIX 60, 212, 235, 270, 301, 316, 321, 345, 348, 368, 409, XX 215, 236, 292, 307, 325, 326, 354, 372.

[159] The model of this conjecture is VI 254; the expression is subject to variation there and in the corresponding **A** line, VII 238.

Next we offer four conjectures which we think likely to have recovered the original but must represent less confidently because some element of doubt in each makes it more speculative than any in the first group. In all the evidence of unoriginality is imperfect alliteration. At X 307 **C** V 154 *carpe*] *chide*, where corruption is explicable by sub-stitution of a reading both easier and more emphatic, our emendation is lexically adventurous.[160] At X 319 **C** V 165 *be þei purely*] *be hemself* where scribal difficulty with *pure* and *purely* in their isolative senses can account for the substitution we have introduced an additional word. At XIV 226 **C** XVI 67 *þe feblere is þe poore*] *þe p. is but feble*, explicable by substitution of an easier reading, we have radically altered the archetypal grammar. At XIX 240 **C** XXI 240 *figures*] *noumbres*, while we can establish from the association of these terms[161] that scribal substitution of one for the other is altogether probable, and the pre-sumed original alliteration would also, as unobvious, exercise no control, we must own that our understanding of the terms is at best imperfect.[162]

Five conjectural emendations of the archetypes of **B** and **C** we must grade as possible rather than likely or confident restorations because, resting on less information, they involve a larger speculative element. At V 440 **C** VII 54, archetypally with the scribal alliterative pattern *aabb*, while the original sense is unmistakable, the context offers no clue to the original language. Our conjecture *by cause of my*] *for my foule*, presuming substitution for greater emphasis, is simply of a spare expression of the necessary original sense which happens also to restore normative alliteration. At XVII 227 **C** XIX 193 where the archetypal scansion of the second half-line is unsatisfactory our conjecture *glede vnglade*] *glede/glade* includes a more than usually complex presumption of split variation.[163] At XVIII 239 **C** XX 248 *The oostes*] *Tho þat weren* our conjecture depends first on identification of the original stave-sound from the position and importance of *heuene* and second on

[160] See *NED* s.v. *Carp* v.[1] 5 and the note to this definition.

[161] The terms were partly synonymous in Middle English: for this see *NED* s. vv. *Figure* sb. 2 and *Number* sb. III 11 b. On the evidence of *NED* quotations under both heads they were also very commonly associated. See especially under *Figure* 19, 1425 *Craft of Nombrynge* I: *In þis craft ben vsid teen figurys.* To the dictionary's examples might be added Chaucer, *Book of the Duchess* 437ff.: *For by tho* [*ten*] *figures mowe al ken / Yf they be crafty, rekene and noumbre / And telle of every thing the noumbre.*

[162] That same difficulty with meaning, if shared by scribes, could have encouraged substitution.

[163] This is because treating W's *glade* as the vertically transmitted reading of a group ancestor implies the agreement of the remaining manuscripts by convergent variation.

rejection of the possible emendations *Hij*] *Tho* and *benten*] *token* in favour of one which, while from its shape likely to have generated *Tho*[164] and also suggested by the gospel narrative,[165] does involve adding a word to the text. At XIX 407 **C** XXI 407 where both archetypes at an early phase read *Conscience be þi comune fode* the variations *fode*] *fede*] *sede* in both traditions record the scribal perplexity created by Conscience being the speaker. For two reasons: that the line was difficult in this way, and that *comune fode* is not Langland's usual term for 'daily fare' we judge *fode* to be intrusive and conjecture original *comunes*, presuming *fode* to be an early gloss prompted by the difficult original meaning. Here the accuracy of our view of the poet's style and usage is the doubtful factor. At XIX 442 **C** XXI 442 it lies in the identification of original meaning and therefore of the point of corruption. The line lacks a stave on [p]; if *god* was original the line might have read *god haue pite on*, or *pardon*, or *make parfit* or *punisshe*, or even *preie god amende þe pope*. But from consideration of the identity of the speaker and the suggestion of 426ff. it seems to us more probable that Piers, *Emperour of al þe world* in an ideal universal Christendom, is the likelier agency invoked. While these indications are strong our decision nevertheless is arbitrary.

There remain a few conjectures of originals for **B** and **C** which need fuller discussion. Three, where the two archetypes have been differentiated by further variation, we offer with some confidence. At IX 185 **C** X 286 the **B** tradition in its latest archetypal phase lost *and yeep* through eyeskip (*and*>*and*). The survival of this expression in the **C** tradition however enables identification of the stave-sound, after which *yet kene*] *kene*, the omission having occurred in the first archetypal **B** phase, is an easy restoration. At XVIII 179 **C** XX 182 the archetypal **B** reading *mercy shul haue*, in itself unobjectionable, becomes difficult when read with *daunce þerto* in 180. **C**'s *Mercy shal synge* also makes poor sense because the speaker is replying to Righteousness, not Mercy. Original *merye shul synge* is suggested by *Ioye* of 181; the process of corruption was then at the first archetypal **B** phase *merye*] *mercy* misreading induced by the preceding story, followed in the second phase by *synge*] *haue* smoothing; **C**'s reading preserves the text at the first

[164] Especially if written *Thoost* with *es* suspension.

[165] Luke 2.13 *multitudo militiae celestis*; for M.E. use of *hoste* to translate this sense of *militia* see *NED* s.v. *Host* sb.[1] 3a, b.

phase. At XX 155 **C** XXII 155 the further variation was in the **C** tradition: **C**'s *sorwe*] *ȝowthe* is a scribal reminiscence of **C** XII 12 (**B** XI 60); the **B** tradition preserves the line as first corrupted. There the importance of *sorwe*, 'contrition', and *synne* indicates the original stave-sound; thereafter conjecture of *so*] *to* corruption by unconscious variation to the expected infinitive sign, and rearrangement of the presumably prosified second half-line to *ax* are easy.

There are, finally, two conjectural restorations, one complex and one simple, which are speculative because of the extent to which they severally depend on our reading of the contextually appropriate meaning. At XII 291 **C** XIV 213 from the manuscript evidence of both traditions their common archetypal reading was *And wheþer it worþ or noȝt worþ þe bileue is gret of treuþe.*[166] The sense of this line is to say the least obscure. There are, however, clues to the nature of its corruption: the recurrence of *worþ*, which might lead to omission by eyeskip, and the circumstance that the meaninglessness of the second half-line results from the position of *of treuþe*, which suggests dislocation. But inference from these clues depends on identification of the original meaning: we find this suggested in line 289 above, implying the possibility of attaining enlightenment, which would make *worþ*(1) significant as a verb.[167] Next the expression *is gret* suggests that *worþ*(2), in the archetypal text apparently a verb, actually reflects an original noun, 'value'. Finally the preceding context suggests that *of treuþe*, meaninglessly located in the archetype, was originally the complement of *worþ*(1). Our conjecture directed by these suggestions includes the presumption that *of treuþe* was first omitted by eyeskip, then restored by interlinear or marginal correction, and subsequently copied in at the wrong point. The plausibility of this intricate restoration must be judged by the appropriateness of its meaning, freely 'And the intrinsic value of faith is great, whether it actually comes to be faith in the true religion (cp. *if þer were he wolde amende*) or not'. At XV 16, 17 **C** XVI 167, 168 we find evidence of unoriginality in the contextually unsatisfactory sense of archetypal 16: *cristes creature...and cristene in many a place*, implying reference to unbaptized souls, seems an inappropriate conjunction in view of 18–22, 26 and 33ff. which

[166] The agreement of some **B** and **C** manuscripts in *noȝt worþ*] *worþ noȝt* is the result of coincident post-archetypal parallelizing induced by *Wheiþer*.

[167] With the sense 'comes to be'; see *NED* s.v. *Worth* v.[1] 3.

exclude this; conversely *Cristes creature* in archetypal 16a and *of his kyn a party* in 17b together express a high doctrinal concept that is elsewhere a main consideration of the poet (e.g. at V 481, 503). We interpret this situation as evidence that the archetypal positions of 16b and 17b are the results of scribal transposition, probably unconscious and induced by the distracting occurrence of *cristes* in 15, 16 and 17. Here the emendation is physically simple; but the relation of its plausibility to our interpretation of the necessary original meaning is absolute.

We hope now to have shown by our illustrations of conjectural emendation that it is not an exercise of purely subjective preference, but a real process of inference from available data for which, in effect, the other two editorial processes, of discrimination and reconstruction, were our training. Many of these conjectures were laboriously attained; such as began with intuitions we accepted only if we could rationalize them to our satisfaction. In grading their plausibility, a highly subjective operation, we have taken care to be severe. They will seem numerous in sum: actually they are a mere remnant of our first excited corrections generated by discovery of the extreme corruption of the **B** archetype.[168] No conjecture has survived which does not carry for us at least some degree of conviction; this can be read as an admission of subjectivity; we prefer to view it as evidence of self-criticism. The practical consequence is that in a number of places where the archetype appears corrupt our text is unemended.

At two points conjecture is simply not feasible. From considerations of sense a line is missing after Prologue 105, specifying those for whom the gates of heaven are shut or opened: the context affords no indication of its exact meaning or language beyond that it must have provided a reference for *hem* in 106. There is also, on the showing of **A** V 206 and **C** VI 422 a line missing after V 363, and on the showing of **A** VII 180 and **C** VIII 189, one missing after VI 192, but their precise meaning and the form of their language are lost.[169] In the others archetypal corruption is indicated by the criterion of verse technique. One occurs where the text of **B** is unique, at V 138. Six are **AB** lines where **C** has been revised: Prologue 11 **A** Prologue 11, I 18 **A** I 18, II 127 **A** II 91, III 10 **A** III 10, IV 59 **A** IV 46 and V 627 **A** VI 112. Seven occur in

[168] We might thus take comfort from Maas: 'nur die besten werden sich durchsetzen' (*Textkritik*, p. 13), but the final assessment of our work does not rest with ourselves.

[169] There is thus a limit to Maas's proposition, 'Kein Fehler ist so unmöglich, wie ein Text notwendig sein kann, selbst ein durch divinatio gefundener.' (*Textkritik*, p. 11.)

all versions: IV 12 **A** IV 12 **C** IV 12, V 14 **A** V 14 **C** V 116, V 320 **A** V 169 **C** VI 377, V 465 **A** V 237 **C** VI 319, V 557 **A** VI 44 **C** VII 201, V 626 **A** VI 111 **C** VII 279 and VII 190 **A** VIII 168 **C** IX 335.

In the case of two of these lines, although we believe them corrupt, we cannot wholly exclude the possibility of eccentric stress patterns: I 18 *wolléne* and V 627 *séuène*. Four others simply defeat our powers of confident speculation: Prologue 11, V 14, 465 and 557. In three our difficulty is lexicographical. At III 10, *aaxy*, the missing stave would be provided by a reading *mente*, presumably 'brought, conducted', found in one otherwise corrected **B** manuscript, but we cannot authenticate that sense of *menen* and can conjecture no alternative stave. II 127 and VII 190 are problematic because of the term *nameliche*: in one line it seems the obvious lost stave, in the other it seems not to alliterate; more information about it might enable us to emend the one line and scan the other.[170] In one line, IV 59, we cannot decide between alternatives, an original *And yet he* [*prétep*] *me pérto and* [*fórlip*] *my mayde* and, supposing absence of revision, **C**'s *manescheth me and myne* for *betep me perto*. In the remaining five we could propose emendations, but not to our own conviction.[171] These lines stand in our text, then, as corrupted by archetypal scribal error which we cannot correct or correct plausibly.[172]

The illustration of our editorial processes is at last complete; its length and burdensome detail, reflecting the evidence to which we applied them, are necessitated by the results to which they led. An edition variously radical in its preference for the authority of readings over manuscript attestation, in taking account of the readings of other versions, and in admitting reconstruction and conjecture must above all

[170] We suspect that *namelich* was subject to metathetic pronunciation, like modern *anemone* and *irrelevant*, and that the poet used it for both [n] and [m] alliteration, but our only evidence is *Piers Plowman* manuscript variation, *nameliche*] *manliche* at **B** XVIII 399 and **C** II 162, IX 335, and *man liche*] *namly* at **C** VII 123, which is not necessarily a linguistic variant.

[171] *For instance*: III 339 [That plesed hire herte was *omnia probate*]; IV 12 How [lered and lewed þow lernest þe peple]; V 138 [garte] þe Couentes Gardyner *or* Gardyner [garte]; V 320 [next] newe faire; V 626 wonder[wise] welcome. The difficulty is to explain how such easy originals would be lost without trace.

[172] The agreements in unoriginality between **A** and **B** where **C** is revised and between all versions are to be explained as early archetypal errors of the **A** tradition which escaped notice in respectively one or both revisions. They are thus incidentally evidence that Langland used a scribal **A** manuscript for revising to **B**. Other evidence to the same effect is the **AB** agreements in unoriginality at IX 166 and X 109 discussed above (p. 205), and at III 229, IV 91, V 9 and VI 282 where the errors were corrected during revision to **C**.

be open to its users. Therefore we have both given all the data embraced by our problem and set out at such length the means by which we either reached reasoned conclusions or rationalized intuitions.

The edition as a whole can be viewed as a theoretical structure, a complex hypothesis designed to account for a body of phenomena in the light of knowledge about the circumstances which generated them, that is, governed by a presumption of the quality of Langland's art and by established information about the effects of manuscript copying on the language, form and meaning of texts. Since it is a hypothesis of textual criticism it necessarily implies accounting for data of which an indeterminate number are false, that is identifying those which are manifestly true or manifestly false and applying their respective characteristics to the less obviously classifiable remainder. In this respect, and in the circumstance that every editorial consideration has seemed to bear on almost all others, that editorial decisions are most often contingent and so to speak of simultaneous implication, it involves what can be called circular reasoning. We have found no alternative to accepting this as a feature of editing, an element in the only rationale we know by which a complicated textual problem can be attempted. In any case our edition, as a hypothesis, continues subject to the classic test: whether it is the simplest that can be devised to account convincingly for the phenomena to which it applies. Like all hypotheses it is also essentially presumptive, that is subject to modification by the emergence of new data, or to replacement by a superior hypothesis.

The authority of our text is then, like that of all edited texts, in no sense absolute. It can however be judged from the information we have provided, first in particular terms of how perceptively we have, line by line and reading by reading, identified originality, and second, more generally, by whether in arguing from such identification to the question of revision we have correctly interpreted the detailed relations between the texts of the three versions of the poem. Its user should scrutinize our assumptions, check our affective responses against his own, and examine the logic of our inferences. He will find, as we have already taken pains to show, that our text is of varying authority; we would like to hope that he may also, from our editing in the simpler cases where authority seems strongest, acquire some confidence in our more venturesome reconstructions and conjectures.

The question whether the poem actually justifies the erection of such an elaborate and intricate structure of hypothesis we reject on two grounds. The first is that it cannot in any real sense be edited otherwise. Any editor who approached it with the intention of recovering its historical truth, that is its original language or where the evidence does not enable this at least its original sense, would quickly find himself in our position. The edition asserts its own character, as we found when, having undertaken it in relative ignorance of what was involved, we came to face the choice between accepting the implications of the evidence in their full force and giving up. The existence of revisions, the date and language of the poem, the nature of its effect on scribes, and its popularity between them shape the editorial problem. The second ground, these considerations apart, is that the **B** version in its character as the one form of *Piers Plowman* which at some moment in history its author might have considered finished would justify every effort toward the recovery of its original readings.

There remains the question whether we have not constructed an 'ideal text'. If this implies that a part of our editorial thinking was to measure the readings of manuscripts against our *idea* of how the poet would write we have certainly done so: we would not know how else to edit. In this we admit to subjectivity, but it seems to us that editorial subjectivity, correctly understood in the circumstances of this text, is not merely an inevitable factor but actually a valuable instrument. The data are abundant; the editor's subconscious mind cannot fail to store so many impressions from comparison between readings strongly presumed original and readings evidently or almost certainly scribal that he will at length acquire, as we hope we may have done, some accuracy of feeling for the turns of speech and even of thought respectively characteristic of the poet and his scribes. If the expression 'ideal text' is understood to imply a risk of improving the original poem we cannot take it very seriously: we are not poets, let alone fourteenth-century poets. The risk, in any event, would be small from two considerations: the extreme probability, demonstrable beyond reasonable doubt, that a bad reading in a manually transmitted text of a great poem is scribal, not authorial, which must limit the occasions of danger; and the fact that the excellence of Langland's poem, having survived the axiomatic deterioration of scribal transmission, must once have been even greater than the received copies now represent it to be.

Our basic manuscript, which provides the linguistic form of the edition, is W, Trinity College Cambridge MS B.15.17, one of the three whole, relatively good copies of the **B** version which might have served.[173] Of the other two Y (Newnham College Cambridge), markedly more corrupt and thus farthest of the three from the archetype, could be rejected out of hand. Thus the choice was between W and L (Laud Misc. 581) used by Skeat in his edition.

The ideal basic manuscript or copy-text[174] is the one which first provides the closest dialectal and chronological approximation to the poet's language, and then second, most accurately reflects his original in substantive readings. It is because the function of a copy- or basic text is to furnish the accidentals of an edition that the first requirement is primary: the least corrupt manuscript will not necessarily fulfil it best.[175]

In favour of L there would be the single consideration of its superior originality:[176] W has about 150 more group errors, and also more individual errors, than L. But W is recommended by two features probably connected with its being earlier than L:[177] the exceptional consistency of its spelling, and the conformity of its grammar with 'standard' late fourteenth-century usage as this is instanced in the best known manuscripts of Chaucer and Gower.

W's relatively larger number of errors seems proportionately insignificant[178] in terms of the very numerous corrections necessitated in any basic text by the corruption of the archetypal **B** text. The disadvantage it implies, of slightly increasing the number of diacritics in a text already studded with them, is wholly outweighed by the

[173] The majority of manuscripts are less serviceable because defective (O and R) or heavily corrected (M) or both internally disordered and corrected (Hm) or late and more than usually corrupt (C^2 and C) or heavily sophisticated (F) or very late (Cr and G) or only partial copies of **B** (Bm Bo Cot and H). The rejected manuscripts S, defective, very late and modernized, and Ht, a conflation, do not merit consideration.

[174] The authoritative discussion of this subject is by Greg, W. W., 'The Rationale of Copy-Text', *Studies in Bibliography*, iii (1950–1), pp. 19–36.

[175] Compare Greg, 'Rationale', p. 26: 'it may happen that in a critical edition the text rightly chosen as copy may not by any means be the one that supplies most substantive readings in cases of variation'; also Chambers ('The Manuscripts of *Piers Plowman* in the Huntington Library', p. 11): 'it is important to select as our basic manuscript one which is as free as possible from eccentricities of spelling and of grammar, even though in actual wording it may not be superior, or may even be a little inferior, to a rival manuscript.'

[176] This has long been recognized: see Skeat, *B-Text*, pp. viii, ix, xiv; Blackman, 'Notes on the B-Text MSS.', p. 529; Chambers, 'The Manuscripts of *Piers Plowman* in the Huntington Library', p. 12.

[177] On the dates of these manuscripts see above, pp. 10, 13.

[178] In this sense at least the view (Blackman, op. cit., p. 503) that W is only 'slightly inferior' to L is correct.

advantages of presenting that text in a well spelled and systematically grammatical form.[179]

For one thing W's consistent spelling and systematic grammar afford a clear model for the many readings that have to be introduced into the text by emendation.[180] For another, in default of any evidence about the original dialect of the poem,[181] or about Langland's capacity to spell and to write grammatically,[182] the form most appropriate for its presentation must be the one which will least distract or mislead its readers.[183] If that form also (the original linguistic form being irrecoverable) makes *Piers Plowman* more accessible to the reader this is no more than the poem deserves. Finally, all other considerations apart the linguistic form of W is chronologically nearer to the poet's usage than that of L.[184]

[179] Skeat (*B-text*, pp. xli–xlv), in comparing the grammar of L and W, and concentrating on a single largely irrelevant point, seriously underestimated the grammatical and orthographical untidiness of L. Citing Morris to the effect that the preterite third person of weak verbs such as *loven* should be *lovede*(*n*), he quite correctly observed that L and W both have many preterites ending simply in *-d*; but actually in late fourteenth-century English weak verbs whose preterites have more than two syllables before the *-d* were not necessarily inflected further, though *-e*(*n*) might be added, as often in Chaucer's verse, for syllabic increase. Meanwhile he omitted to consider the more essential points of grammar in which W is superior to L: distinction between the weak and the strong position of the adjective (*-e*/zero); between the preterite singular (first and third) of strong verbs and that of weak verbs with only one syllable before the preterite suffix (zero/*-e*); between the past participles of strong and weak verbs (*-e*(*n*)/zero); between adjectival *-lich* and adverbial *-liche*; and between nouns and adjectives with inherited final *-e* and those without it.

[180] Cp. Greg, 'Rationale', p. 30: 'editorial emendations should be made to conform to the habitual spelling of the copy-text.' Obviously, then, a copy text with consistent linguistic habits is preferable.

[181] We are aware that Langland's native dialect is unlikely to have been that of W. But then there is no evidence that he wrote *Piers Plowman* in that native dialect, any more than that he retained this in adulthood. His vocabulary draws on the common word-stock of Middle English alliterative poetry, which is generally supposed to be of Northern origin, but only sparingly; he uses both *ȝ* and *g*, *ch* and *k* dialect variants impartially for alliteration; and much of his language accords with London English of his time. It is possible that his literary English was adventitious, compromising between alliterative convenience and an aim of general intelligibility not always characteristic of alliterative poets.

[182] Skeat's unlucky notion that L might be an autograph (*B-Text* p. ix) led him to a false position about this. For instance, 'It has been objected, that the spelling [of L] is faulty; but is there any reason for supposing that Langland could or would have spelt better?' (*B-Text* p. x); and 'It is obvious that, if the author had small regard for grammar, then the MS. which is very correct in that respect, does in effect, in that same respect, represent him least.' (*B-Text*, p. xli). Though here Skeat proposed Langland's 'small regard for grammar' guardedly in a conditional clause the context shows that he considered it as a fact. There is, of course, no reason to suppose that Langland had not been taught to spell and to write grammatical English, and we have the evidence of his poem to show his understanding of how the language functioned.

[183] We have no doubt that the orthographical and grammatical untidiness of L (more correctly seen as either a feature of or the evidence for its lateness) has contributed to the notion that Langland was a disorganized thinker.

[184] From the way its orthography, grammar and even handwriting recall those of the Ellesmere and Hengwrt manuscripts of *The Canterbury Tales* W was probably the product of a London workshop. In adopting W as our basic text we do not, of course, propose that its careful

In transcribing W we have followed the practice of Volume I[185] as closely as the circumstances of the present version allow. The otherwise clear hand of W presented only one difficulty, to identify its capitalization of *a*, *m*, *s* and *w* confidently on all occasions; we may have made mistakes at this. With respect to suspensions and contractions W's intention is generally clear, and his uniform spelling directs their expansion. He rarely adds flourishes to terminal letters;[186] when they do occur we ignore them unless they are necessarily suspensions, not merely automatic or decorative.

As in Volume I we draw attention by square brackets to every substitution of another reading for that of the basic manuscript, every addition to its text, every rearrangement of its matter within the line, and every omission of a part of a word from it. When we admit a line or passage to the text from another source than W we not only indicate this by enclosing it in square brackets but further use these within the adopted line or passage to signal emendations of the kinds just specified. To indicate rearrangements of line order we use the half-brackets ⌈ and ⌋ at the beginning and end of the passage affected. Within that part again, we signal emendations of the kinds specified above by square brackets.

While we invariably record them in the apparatus we do not show by a diacritic exclusions of words or larger expressions or whole lines from the text of our basic manuscript W, whether individual or group or archetypal variants. Because of their large number the reason given for the same practice in **A**[187] applies here *a fortiori*. These exclusions occur at the following points where attention is not drawn to the apparatus by square brackets within the line; the asterisk signifies exclusion of a whole line or several lines.

Prologue 20, 39, 45, 48, 57, 64, 69, 80, 110, 148, 150, 177, 193, 205, 221, 222, 229. I 6, 16, 31, 45, 69, 78, 85, 89, 99, 107, 108, 124, 125, 126, 142, 174, 188, 199, 209. II 20, 72, 75, 88, 128, 152, 160, 164, 184, 191, 193, 202, 223, 233. III 31, 64, 101,

handling of final *-e* (the chief instrument of grammatical expression in late fourteenth-century Middle English) bears any necessary relation to Langland's spoken practice, e.g. that the phrase *þe gode man* had for him one more sounded syllable than *a good man*. Such grammatical manipulation of final *-e* may well have been purely formal. But if the phonetic value of final *-e* in *Piers Plowman* is ever determined this will be from manuscripts like W where the letter is seldom omitted when it has either ascertainable grammatical function or historical sanction, and seldom added when it has neither (the exception being the quasi-inflexional final *e* which scribes copying alliterative texts tended to affix to a noun at the end of a line).

[185] See pp. 166–70. [186] Compare Vol. I, pp. 166, 167. [187] Vol. I, p. 168.

112, 115, 118, 122, 126, 131, 136, 147, 158, 160, 165, 183, 209, 211, 235, 278, 284, 301, 302, 327, 350. IV 20, 22, 56, 58, 79, 99, 101, 104, 132, 137, 150, 186, 192. V 15, 27, 29, 34, 37, *39α, 42, *54, 67, 81, 87, 105, 107, 110, 117, 149, 151, 165, 169, 182, 190, 194, *195, 212, 217, 219, *234, 235, 251, *277α, *281, 286, 303, 305, 320, 324, 353, 358, 381, 387, 409, 416, 427, 458, 460, 470, 472, 478, 479, 483, 484, 486, 504, 515, 522, 536, 541, 552, *556, 559, 568, 570, 578, 585, 598, 627, 630, 631. VI 9, *17, 20, 25, 34, 49, 50, 53, 64, 84, 87, 90, 113, 114, 133, 145, 146, 153, 156, 157, 167, 173, *182, 183, 185, 201, 203, 204, 205, 206, 232, 247, 258, 262, 281, 285, 288, 290, 292, 299, 312, 319. VII 1, 4, 6, 27, 42, 59, 67, 71, 84, 96, 138, 152, 163, 173, 177, 187, 191, 192, 202, 203. VIII 20α, 31, 34, 39, 53, 70, 75, 82, 83, 86, 90, 92, 95. IX 51, 137, 138, 141, 149, 164, 168, 170, 175, 181, 201, 209. X 34, 55, 56, 84, 95, 118, 138, 150, 159, 160, 180, 212, 221, 244, *272, 281, 337, 375, 382, 383, 385, 406, 421, 424, 427, 431, 440, 441, 479. XI 2, 9, 58α, *67, 79, 80, 83, 109, 129, 130, 133, 150, 158, 160, 165, 203, 204α, 226, 255, 263, 264, 278, 300, 305, 326, 333, 357, 363, 378, 382, 396, 403, 410, 412, 420, 421. XII 9, 21, 42, 54, 82, 90, 133, 163, 178, 187, 193, 201, 209, 219, 226, 233, 249, 261, 262, 276, 280, 284. XIII 3, 44, 46, 54, 68, 81, 105, 113, 131, 132, 140, 159, 163α, 165, 167, 171α, 213, 222, 229, 240, 254, 270, 278, 300, 311, 334, 345, 366, 367, 372, 374, 382, 386, 425, 427, 430, 441. XIV 8, 32, *33, 57, 79, 80, 86, 118, 142, 146, 171, 185, 202, 213, 215, 275, 277, 283, 293, 316, 320. XV 8, 36, 38, 41, 65, 99, 157, 195, 198, 255, 275, 308, 329, 346, 366, 376, 401, 418, 429, 431α, 460, 513, 521, 522, 530α, 571, 581, 604, 610. XVI 9, 17, 22, 38, 73, 78, 123, 131, 147, 182, 205, 214, 219α, 245, 251, 275. XVII 18, 26, 42, 59, 76, 79, 89, 152α, 171, 176, 269, 272, 282, 300, 303, 324, 341α. XVIII 41, 123, 147, 204, 209, 262, 338, 343, 359, 414. XIX 64, 68, 89, 149, 159, 164, 173, 174, 179, 197, 208, 246, *252, 262, 335, 336, 348, 357, 362, 380, 399, 400, 412, 415, 422, 448, 457, 470. XX 10, 36, 64, 119, 125, 140, 170, 208, 210, 228, 236, 273, 277, 283, 290, 305, 320, 337, 355, 356, 363.

All emendations by addition and substitution, small or large, are made to conform to the spelling and grammar of W's scribe: the uniformity of his language in these particulars makes this not merely possible but actually requisite, even in details like emending *þ* to [*Th*] where redivision or exclusion promotes a word with initial *þ* to the beginning of a line.[188] Correspondingly we normalize W's 'false forms', that is the W scribe's few formal variants which are evidently departures from his usual practice through mechanical variation.[189]

The critical apparatus supporting our text records, as in Volume I, all substantive variation, that is all variation affecting or possibly affecting sense,[190] in all manuscripts of the **B** version known to us

[188] The scribe of W wrote *þ* only twice in that position, at XI 101 and 109, probably through neglect to adapt the spelling of his exemplar.

[189] For instance IV 183 *hertoo*, V 164 *hite*, 437 *boþ*, 592 *brugg*, XIII 459 *whasshen*, XX 136 *An*.

[190] Spurious lines occurring in single manuscripts or groups of manuscripts are collected in an appendix on pp. 221f.

except S and Ht.[191] It also records any formal variation, dialectal or orthographic, which might conceivably throw light on situations where originality is in question. We have thus presented every variant at all possibly relevant to the recovery of originality.

In this volume, however, from considerations of space and because linguistic variation in *Piers Plowman* manuscripts can no longer have any controversial significance, the critical apparatus records no formal variation, whether regional, chronological or merely orthographical, for its own sake. For instance, regional variations of the *ch/k* and *ȝ/g* type are included only when they affect the alliteration of a line. As a rule of thumb for authenticating a formal variant we have used *NED*; thus, if a variant form is shown there and we are quite confident that no question of a different meaning arises in the particular context we exclude it. Specifically we exclude consistently eccentric spellings such as Bm's *þo* for *þe*, C's *Th-* for *T*, and G's *saght* for *saw* when they are unambiguous, and Hm's *atte* for *at* when it cannot represent *at þe*.

We do, however, record formal variants about which we can be reasonably certain that they alter the syllabic value of the alliterative line. Thus while we do not normally cite purely formal variants with identical syllabic value of the types *abye/abigge, bitwene/bitwixe, flapten/flapped, go/goþ/gon, hiȝte/hatte,*[192] *lep/lepte, lore/lost, mo/more, moste/mote, pesen/peses, seldom/selden, seluen/selues,* or purely formal variants of fluctuating and thus indeterminate syllabic value of the types *amyd(de)/amyddes/amydst, auntre/aunter/auenture, corouned/crowned, elleuen/enleue, folwen/folowen, han/haue/hauen, knowen/known, kyn(ne)/kyn(ne)s, lip/liep, louyen/louen, may/mowe/mow(e)n, morwenyng(e)/mornyng(e), punyshe/punsche, put/pute/putte, togider/togid(e)r(e)s,* or the presence or absence of inflexional final *-e*, we do always cite variants with an additional final or initial syllable likely to have had phonetic value. Thus we always record the presence or absence of the inflexions *-eþ, -en, -es* (though we do not undertake to differentiate them unless there is possibility of grammatical difference), and the presence or absence of final *-d* or *-n* (as e.g. in *bake*] *baken/baked*, though again we may group these), and the presence or absence of the perfective prefix *y-*.

The apparatus does not record all erasures and alterations. To have

[191] For these copies see above, pp. 14, 15.

[192] These variant forms are without tense-definition in *Piers Plowman* manuscripts. See *NED* s.v. *Hight* v.[1], 'Forms'.

noted every self-correction by a main scribe, or every attention to which G, Hm and M were subjected by their 'correctors' would have swollen it unduly, in particular with irrelevant fifteenth- and sixteenth-century orthographical and grammatical preferences. We have therefore excluded alterations in these and other manuscripts which we consider unimportant. When however a cited variant reading in any manuscript is wholly or partly over an erasure or otherwise altered, when a line or group of lines in Hm is by a corrector over an erasure, when it is a correction affecting sense, however slightly, which aligns M with WHmCr, we record this. But we exclude such attentions as addition or removal of final *e*, alteration of initial *ȝ* to *y*, persistent correction of *gome* to *grome*, the systematic modernizations of G in another hand and ink, and alterations prompted by sectarian zeal.

In setting out the apparatus we follow the conventions described in Volume I,[193] with two modifications designed to save space. The first is to use, when this can be done without loss of clarity, an element of a compound word as the lemma. The second is to set up a double apparatus in certain situations: where a large part of a line is corrupt, as at IV 46 and V 260; where the whole form of the archetypal line is corrupt, as at XII 24 and 268; and where the archetypal variant is a spurious line, as at V 39α and 54. In such instances the second apparatus, enclosed in parentheses, records further variation from the larger, usually archetypal variant reading.

The order of citing sigils of manuscripts in support of any reading is WHmCr¹Cr²Cr³GYOC²CBmBoCotLMRFH, the sigil Cr without a superior number signifying agreement of the three Crowley impressions, and the sigil B agreement of the closely related copies BmBoCot. We depart from that order only in the situations specified in Volume I.[194] Indeed in the complex circumstances of editing the **B** version we have thought it important to exclude distraction by eccentric spellings or imposed dialect forms from consideration of the evidence for originality. At the same time it must be clear that, precisely because the apparatus does not include morphological variation unless this bears on determination of originality, support of several sigils for a variant reading signifies only substantive agreement between the manuscripts which they denote. The crucial situations in which collation is more minute will easily be identified.

193 On pp. 170–2.

194 On p. 171.

We have applied the practices followed in transcribing W to all the manuscripts. We have found it difficult to be systematic in expanding contractions and suspensions, especially terminal flourishes of fluctuating value,[195] and cannot hope to have succeeded in this. The same is true of reproducing capitals within the line, to which the practice of Volume I commits us. In transcribing the late copies Cr and G we have distinguished *þ* and *y* except where the possibility of their confusion has editorial significance.

We offer our text, then, as a restored **B** version of *Piers Plowman*, in the language of a London scribe of about 1400, whose consistent spelling and systematic grammar are to all appearances exceptional. The apparatus supporting that text contains all material evidence for determining its original form afforded by the known **B** manuscripts other than S and Ht. How we have interpreted that evidence, and the evidence of the **A** and **C** versions bearing on it, has been laid wholly open to scrutiny in the preceding pages of this Introduction. Whether we have carried out our task efficiently must be assessed by reenacting it.

[195] It has been impossible not to transcribe these arbitrarily, as a single case will show: in one manuscript (F) at X 107 both the terms *crabbed word* end in the 7 flourish.

APPENDIX

On page 193 above we specified lines in the archetypal **B** text which we judged to be unoriginal, that is not written by the poet. Those lines with their variants are to be found in the Critical Apparatus. There are also, in various collated manuscripts, and attested by one or several copies, lines or passages which we have judged to be unoriginal but which we merely refer to in the Apparatus. These we now set out, in two classes and within these by alphabetical order of sigils of attestation.

The first class is of contaminations, that is lines which come from other parts of *Piers Plowman* and are thus not strictly speaking spurious, that is scribally composed. From their small number the likelihood is that they are insertions from memory, like the one visible in M after V 414 where another hand has copied, in the paragraph-gap, the Latin from **B** IV 36α. They are the following.

Cr *after* III 30: *compare* **C** III 33
To begge hem benifices pluralities to haue
Cr[23] *after* Prologue 216: *compare* **A** Prologue 90–5
I sawe bishops bolde and bachilers of diuine
Become clarkes of accountes the kynge for to serue
Arckedeakens and deanes that dignities haue
To preache to the people and pore men to fede
Ben ilope to London by leaue of her bishop
And ben clarkes of the kinges benche the contrye to shend
F *after* Prologue 94: *compare* **A** Prologue 95
& summe be Clerkis of þe ky*n*gys bench þe cu*ntre* to shende
H *for* II 123: *compare* **A** II 86α, 87
For worthy is þe werkma*n* hys mede to haue
Dignus est operarius mercede sua &c
OC[2] *beside* XI 279: *compare* **B** VII 89
Non vidi iustum derelictum nec semen eius querens panem
RF *for* III 51–62: *compare* **A** III 50, 51
wist I þat quatȝ mede þere nys wyndow no wowȝ
þat I ne wolde make and amende it with of myne
And my name write openliche þerInne

The second class is of lines and passages which we judge to have been composed by scribes. Our grounds for identifying them as spurious are the ones set out in Volume I (p. 51). They are the following.

BmBoCot *after* XVII 178
and to strecche out þe synwes and weynes boþe

after XVIII 41
and seide he wolde felle adou*n* þe temple þat is so strong
Cr *for* V 168
Lest happeli thei had had no grace to hold harlatri in
For they are ticle of her tonges & must al secretes tel
Cr[23] *after* III 162 (*see also under* GYOC²CB *and* YOC²CB)
Bi good reso*n* þat is gret ruth reherse me*n* what he*m* liketh
F *after* Prologue 75
& þorghȝ þe seelis on þe selk syluer gret plente
wi*th* wheche his konkebyne at hom is klad ful klene
after Prologue 80
But þe p*er*sou*n* er þe preest ys cawse of þe gilte
after II 61
& manye oþ*er* myst*er* me*n* mo þan ben i*n* myȝnde
after III 10
& þe Clerk gan *con*forte hire for gret cony*n*ge he hadde
after V 43
& ell*es* will þe peple parle in ȝour*e* parshȝ abowhte
after V 111
þerfor*e* y brende bett*er*ly þ*at* my*n* brestboon ga*n* krake
after V 276
Or p*ra*ye þe of forgyfnesse or to doon yt for þy sowle
& ell*es* he shal have evil hap but he heendely wirche
his catel shal fally*n* hy*m* froo or ell*es* hise freendis goode
Or ell*es* his soule shal dry*n*ke sour*e* at o dayes tyme
after V 580
Bysyde is a fair*e* fyld fals flat*er*yng ys þe name
after VI 116
þ*at* þey filly*n* flat on þe floor so feyþfully þey swonke
after VII 75
God seyþ hy*m* in his gospel *nesciat sinistra quid faciat dextra*
before VIII 1
ANd wa*n*ne y awakid was y wondred wer*e* y wer*e*
Tyl þ*at* y beþowhte me what þy*n*g y dremede
after IX 32
& grene gres grew sone on grownde al abowhte
& trees wery*n* frawht wi*th* frut fayre vpon erthe
after X 25
& owt of our*e* Lord*es* lawe þ*at* leneþ hem þ*at* welthe
& þynke not who it oweþ þ*at* þei wasten heere
after X 246α
Non tres dij sed vnus est deus
for XI 5
& of myn wynkynge y awook & wondrede þa*n*ne
Of all þe dremes þ*at* y drempte so dau*n*gerous þei wer*e*

⁊ *tur*ned me on þe oþ*er* syde for to take my*n* eese
ANd as y lay ⁊ lookede vpon þe lau*n*de grene
I þouhte on þe Metelis hou m*er*veyl*ous* þei were
Tyl sodynly hevynesse on slepe brouht me þa*n*ne

for XI 320

⁊ þus y fel in þowhtis feele flappynge in my*n* herte
þ*at* all my*n* spiritys wery*n* sore stoned ⁊ þ*er*w*ith* y wakned
⁊ as manye ⁊ feele þowhtis felle flappynge in my*n* herte
All my*n* spirytis wery*n* stoned ⁊ þ*er*w*ith* y awaked
⁊ ful sore syʒhede þe syghte was so m*er*vylous
⁊ streyhte me ⁊ *tur*ned me ⁊ to myselue y seid
þis ys a mychil m*er*veyle what meny*n*ge it meneþ
⁊ in þis þowht still y lay a long tyme after
AS y lay ⁊ lokede forþ lowe vpon þe greene

after XIII 233

þerfore fewe rewarde me my re*n*te is þe lasse

after XIV 22

⁊ þey þou slyde or stu*m*ble sore soone vp þou ryʒse

after XV 51

⁊ held hymselue as gret as god swich g*ra*ce he hade

after XV 125

þ*at* is betake to tauerne hows for ten schelyng plegge

before XVI 1

AGeyn y gan to sleepe softe ⁊ my syʒde y gan to *tur*ne
⁊ anoon y seyʒ as y seyʒ erst ⁊ spak to hy*m* w*ith* mowþe

after XVI 44

þe stakys for to steppen oon been exseketouris trewþe

after XVI 167

⁊ for y hadde so soore yslept sory was y þanne
⁊ on þe dremy*n*ge y dre*m*pte eu*er*y doynge y þowhte
ANd whan y hadde longe ley*n* y lawhte to me herte

after XIX 18

For *In nomine iesu omne genu flectitur celestia terrestria ⁊ infernorum* (*but cp.* XIX 80α)

after XIX 252

⁊ he þ*at* is ʒoure althir drevel myghte mayster ben holden
If g*ra*ce wolde haue g*ra*ntyd hy*m* but þynk þou wel þ*er*after
If he leede weel his lyf his Ioyʒe shal encresen
And al þ*at* he swynkeþ harde heere to blysse it shal hy*m* *tur*ne

GYOC²CB *after* XII 154

⁊ goddys sonne þ*at* syttethe yn heyuen ⁊ shall saue vs all

after XV 229

⁊ clenlyche yclothed In cypres ⁊ In tartaryne

after XVIII 260 (*so also* Ht)

all þis I boke wytnecce ⁊ yett moche more

after XVIII 295 (so also Cr[23] *and* Ht)
owte off our pouste ⁊ leyden þem hence
H *after* Prologue 196
Wo to þe lond þer þe kyng is a chyld
Hm *after* XVIII 320
Attollite portas principes vestras ⁊ eleuamini porte eternales ⁊ introibit rex glorie ⁊c
OC[2] *beside* Prologue 39
Qui non laborat non manducet
after XV 559
hodie venenum est effusum in ecclesiam domini
after XVI 94
Annis quingentis decies rursumque ducentis vnus defuerat cum deus ortus erat
RF *after* V 277α
þere is no laborere wolde leue with he*m* þ*a*t knoweth peres þe plowma*n*
for IX 173–75
And for to go to du*n*mowe to fecche hom here bakon
And whan þei haue brouȝt it hom to whom is best to selle it
And þus þei lyuen in coueytise þe deuel and þei togyderes
for XVI 270–73
Allas thouȝte I þo þat is a longe abydynge
And sued hym for he softe ȝede
þat he toek vs as tit ac trewly to telle
Y *after* XV 148
Illarem datorem diligit deus
YOC[2]CB *after* V 269 (*so also* Cr[23] *and* Ht)
Or elles that I kouthe knowe it by any kynnes wise
after V 295 (*so also* Ht)
For he sholde help yow of oure lordes goode
after V 330 (*so also* Cr[23] *and* Ht)
For to trie this chaffare bitwixen hem three
after V 560 (*so also* Ht)
That I shal sey to yow and sette yow in the sothe
after VI 47α (*so also* Cr[23] (*after* 47) *and* Ht)
Thanne thow but thow do bet and lyue as thow shulde

WILL'S VISIONS OF PIERS PLOWMAN, DO-WELL, DO-BETTER AND DO-BEST

PROLOGUE

IN a somer seson whan softe was þe sonne *fol.* 1 a
I shoop me into [a] shrou[d] as I a sheep weere;
In habite as an heremite, vnholy of werkes,
Wente wide in þis world wondres to here.
Ac on a May morwenynge on Maluerne hilles
Me bifel a ferly, of Fairye me þoȝte.
I was wery forwandred and wente me to reste
Vnder a brood bank by a bourn[e] syde,
And as I lay and lenede and loked on þe watres
I slombred into a slepyng, it sweyed so murye.
Thanne gan I meten a merueillous sweuene,
That I was in a wildernesse, wiste I neuere where.
[Ac] as I biheeld into þe Eest, an heiȝ to þe sonne,
I seiȝ a tour on a toft trieliche ymaked,
A deep dale byneþe, a dongeon þerInne
Wiþ depe diches and derke and dredfulle of siȝte.
A fair feeld ful of folk fond I þer bitwene

1–12 *over erasure another ink* Hm.

1 a] *om* F. somer] someres HmG. softe] set HmCr.

2 into] In GYOC^{2}CLMH (to *above line* M). a shroud] a schroude H; shroudes WHm GYOC^{2}CLMF; shroubes Cr. a(2)] *om* F. sheep] schep H; shepe CrGYCL.

3 *line om* F. In] In an H. as] of HmH.

4 Wente] & wente FH; Wend Cr^1. þis] þe H.

5 Ac] But H; And CrGC^{2}CF; *erased* M. on(1)] *in* H. a] *om* F. morwenynge] mornyg H; morwe F.

6 Me bifel] Byfel me F. of] of a Cr^2; as F. Fairye] Fayre C^{2}C. me þoȝte] me bethouȝt C^2; In thoght G.

7 forwandred] of wandrynge CrFH. wente] *om* C^2.

8 Vnder] Vpon F. bourne] CrGFH; bournes WHmYOC^{2}CLM.

9 on] in YOC^{2}CL; vpon G. watres] water Cr; wawys F.

10 into] in YOC^{2}CLM. a] *om* F. it] *after cancelled* In G; & H. sweyed] sweyd G; swyȝed HmCrF; sweyued YOC^{2}CL; sweuenyd H. so] ful H.

11 Thanne] And þan H. meten] mete Y; to meten CrGOC^{2}CLMF; to mete H.

12 a] *om* Cr^{12}GOC^2. wiste I] I wyste Cr.

13 Ac] And WCMH (? *over erasure* M); *om* HmCrGYOC^{2}LF. as] *om* CF. in...to] on hey est onto H. into] to (in *added above line*) M. þe(1)] *om* F. to] vnto Hm.

14 seiȝ] sauȝt (see *above it another hand*) C^2. trieliche] triedliche O; trychlych Cr^3; ryaly H; rieliche (*erasure at beginning*) CM; rychely HmCr^{12}; reallecle (trikanlie *above it another hand*) C^2. ymaked] ytymbryd F.

15 A] & a F. byneþe] benethe it H.

16 diches] dykys HC. dredfulle] dreaful Cr^3. of] to F.

17 A] & a F. fond I] y fond F.

Of alle man*er*e of men, þe meene and þe riche,
Werchynge and wandrynge as þe world askeþ.
Some putten hem to plouȝ, pleiden ful selde,
In settynge and sowynge swonken ful harde;
Wonnen þat [þise] wastours w*ith* glotonye destruyeþ.
And so*m*me putten hem to pride, apparailed hem þ*er*after,
In contenaunce of cloþynge comen d[is]gised.
In preieres and penaunc[e] putten hem manye,
Al for loue of oure lord lyueden [wel] streyte
In hope [for] to haue heueneriche blisse. |
As Ancres and heremites þ*at* holden hem in hire selles, *fol.* 1 *b*
Coueiten noȝt in contree to [cairen] aboute
For no likerous liflode hire likame to plese.
And so*m*me chosen [hem to] chaffare; þei cheueden þe bettre,
As it semeþ to oure siȝt þ*at* swiche men þryueþ.
And so*m*me murþes to make as Mynstralles konne,
And geten gold w*ith* hire glee [gilt]lees, I leeue.

18 of] *om* Cr^{23}.

19 þe] this F.

20 putten] putte OCrYC^{2}CLMFH. hem] hemselue F; him C. to] GF; to þe WHmCrYOC^{2}CLMH. pleiden] pleyede OYC^{2}LM; ⁊ pleyede F; pleyid he*m* H; pleden Cr^{1}G. ful] *om* F. selde] selden CF.

21 In] ⁊ in F. settynge] syttyng H. and] and in HmGYCL. swonken] þey swonken F; swynken C; trauelyd H. harde] sore H.

22 *line om* Hm; *copied after line* 24 F. Wonnen] And wonnen WCrYOCLMF; And wo*n*nien C^{2}; and wynnen G; And wan H. þise] þese F; *om* WCrGYOC^{2}CLMH. w*ith*] In GOC^{2}. destruyeþ] dystroid H.

23 And] *om* G. putten] put CrFH. hem(1)] he H. apparailed] apparayleden HmOC^{2}; ⁊ ap*ar*ayled FH. hem(2)] *om* Cr.

24 contenaunce] co*n*tynances F. comen] þei come H; kemen fele F; commen Cr^{2}; commenly Cr^{13}. disgised] CrHmGYOC^{2}CLMFH; degised W.

25 preieres] preyere OC^{2}. and] and in YOC^{2}CLMF. penaunce] CrGYOC^{2}CLMH; penaunces WHmF. putten] put HF. hem] hemselue F; he*m* ful H.

26 *transposed with* 27 Cr. Al] And CrH; a *imperfect* C; *om* GF. for] OC^{2}CLM; for þe WHmCrGYFH. lyueden] leuyd H; þei lyvedyn F; lyuende C^{2}. wel] ful WHmCrGYOC^{2}CLMFH. streyte] harde Cr.

27 for] YOC^{2}CLM; *om* WHmCrGFH. haue] YOC^{2}CLM; haue after WHmCrG; haue þ*er*after H; have to hyre F.

28 As] ⁊ G. holden] holde FCrH; held G. hem] he*m*selue F. hire] *om* F.

29 Coueiten] And coueiten WCrGYOC^{2}CLM; ⁊ coueyte FH; that coueytyn Hm. contree] cu*n*tres F. cairen] cayren GOLMF; carien WHmCrYC^{2}H (en *over erasure* Hm); walken C. aboute] abouten M.

30 likame] careyn H; lykyng C^{2}.

31 And] *om* G. chosen] chose H; chesen CHmF. hem to chaffare] chaffare WHmCrGYOC^{2}CLMFH. þei] to FH. cheueden] cheued M; cheuen YGOCLF; chese H; schosyn C^{2}.

32 to] by Hm. þ*at*] *om* H. men] do Cr; *om* OC^{2}. þryueþ] schulde *over erasure* Hm.

33 *run together with* 34 F. somme] *om* Cr^{1}. make] maken Cr^{12}. as...konne] *om* F. as] s *erased* Hm. konne] konneth YHmCrOC^{2}LM; knaueth C; donne G.

34 And...glee] *om* F. geten] gete H. giltlees] synnelees WHmCrGYCLMFH; not synles OC^{2}. leeue] *over erasure* Hm; trowe GH.

Ac Iaperes and Iangeleres, Iudas children,
[Fonden] hem fantasies and fooles hem makeþ,
And han wit at wille to werken if [hem liste].
That Poul *pre*cheþ of hem I [dar] nat preue it here;
Qui loquitur turpiloquium is luciferes hyne.
Bidderes and beggeres faste aboute yede
[Til] hire bel[y] and hire bagg[e were bret]ful ycrammed;
[Flite þanne] for hire foode, fouȝten at þe ale.
In glotonye, god woot, go þei to bedde,
And risen [vp] wiþ ribaudie [as] Roberdes knaues;
Sleep and sleuþe seweþ hem euere.
Pilgrymes and Palm*er*es pliȝten hem togidere
For to seken Seint Iame and Seintes at Rome;
Wenten forþ in hire wey wiþ many wise tales,
And hadden leue to lyen al hire lif after.

35 Ac] butt GFH; As CrYOC^{2}CM (s *another ink* M). Iudas] ben Iudas F.
36 Fonden] Feynen WGL; Feyn CH; Fayneth Cr; þei feynen F; That feynen YOC^{2}M (þat *in margin another ink* M); feynede (de *over erasure*) Hm. hem(1)] he*m in* H. makeþ] made (de *over erasure*) Hm.
37 han] welden F. wit] FH; hire wit WHmCrGYOC^{2}CLM. at] at her OC^{2}H. to] *om* H. werken] werke HmCrGOC^{2}CLFH. if] what F. hem liste] þei wolde WH; they schulde HmCrGYCLMF; þei schulden OC^{2}.
38 That] what F. hem] *om* H. dar] wol W; wyll GFH; nel HmCr^{1}LM; nyl YCr^{23}OC^{2}C. nat] *om* G. it] *om* H.
39 *line om* F. *Qui*] HmCrGYOC^{2}CLMH; But *Qui* W. *loquitur turpiloquium*] *loquitur above line another hand and ink* M; *turpiloquium loquitur* YOC^{2}CL. is...hyne] *⁊c* Cr^{1}CL; *om* MH (*est seruus diaboli another hand and ink* M). is] *⁊c* Is Cr^{23}Y. hyne] knaue Cr^{23}YOC^{2} (*above it* hyne *another hand* C^{2}). *Here an additional Latin line in margin* OC^{2}; *see above*, p. 224.
40 Bidderes] Boþe bidderis F. aboute] abowty*n* F. yede] ȝedyn C^{2}O; wentyn F.
41 *line om* F. Til] Wiþ WHmCrGYOC^{2}CLMH. bely] YOC^{2}CLM; belies WHmCrGH. bagge] YLM; bagges WHmCrGOC^{2}CH. were bretful] bred ful H; of breed ful WHmCrGYOC^{2}CLM. ycrammed] ycramned C; cra*mm*ed HmCrGH.
42 Flite þanne] Faiteden WYOCLM; Faytode (ytode *over erasure*) Hm; Faytenden Cr; Faydend C^{2}; fast fayten G; ⁊ fele fayted F; Waytyng H. fouȝten] ⁊ fowtyn FH. þe] *om* OC^{2}.
43 In...woot] ⁊ god woot wit*h* glotenye F. woot] it woot HmYOC^{2}CLM. go þei] þey goon togydre F.
44 risen] ryse Cr. vp] FH; *om* WHmCrGYOC^{2}CLM. as] CrG; þo WHmYCLMFH; þe OC^{2}. Roberdes] robers C^{2}F; Rebertes Cr.
45 Sleep] ⁊ sleep F. sleuþe] sory sleuþe WHmCrGYOC^{2}CLMFH. seweþ] sheweth Cr^{12}GC; semyth H.
46 pliȝten] plyght Cr; plighted YLM; pliȝteden OC^{2}; pyghtyn F; pyth H; gedir C.
47 For] *om* YOC^{2}CLMF. seken] seke HmCrGYOC^{2}CLMH. at] in YOC^{2}CLMF; of H.
48 Wenten] ⁊ wenty*n* F; They wenten WHmOC^{2}M; They wente YCrGCLH. in] on F; *om* Cr. many] fele F.
49 hadden] had CrG. to] for to GYOC^{2}MF. lyen] lye CrGYOC^{2}CLMH. lif] lyuys G.

I sei3 so*m*me þ*at* seiden þei hadde ysou3t Seintes;
To ech a tale þ*at* þei tolde hire tonge was tempred to lye
Moore þan to seye sooþ, it semed bi hire speche.
Heremytes on an heep wit*h* hoked staues |
Wenten to walsyngham, and hire wenches after; *fol. 2 a*
Grete lobies and longe þat loþe were to swynke
Cloþed hem in copes to ben knowen from oþere;
Shopen hem heremytes hire ese to haue.
I fond þ*er*e Freres, alle þe foure ordres,
Prechynge þe peple for p*ro*fit of [þe wombe];
Glosed þe gospel as hem good liked;
For coueitise of copes construwed it as þei wolde.
Manye of þise maistre[s mowe] cloþen hem at likyng
For hire moneie and hire marchaundi3e marchen togideres.
Siþ charite haþ ben chapman and chief to shryue lordes
Manye ferlies han fallen in a fewe yeres.
But holy chirche and hij holde bettre togidres

50-4 *lines om* F.
50 I...so*m*me] So*m*me I say H. seiden] seyde HCr. þei] he H; þ*at* they G. hadde] hadden HmOC^{2}H. ysou3t] sou3t HmCrGC^{2}; sen H.
51 a] *om* HmH. þ*at*] *om* GH. tolde] tolden OC^{2}.
52 to] *om* OC^{2}. semed] semeth Hm.
54 Wenten] went CH.
55 Grete...longe] ⁊ grete longe lobyes F. lobies] bodyis H. loþe were] were loth H. were] weren OMF. swynke] swynky*n* H.
56 Cloþed] cloþeden HmOLM. knowen] knowe HmFH.
57 Shopen] And shopen WHmCrGYOC^{2}CLM; ⁊ shoop FH. hem] hem lyk F. hire...haue] to hauen her ese Hm. to] for to GF. haue] kacche F.
58 þ*er*e] ther the Cr^{1}; þ*er*e of þe F. alle] off alle MH (off *above line another ink* M). þe] *om* C^{2}.
59 Prechynge] prechyng (yng *over erasure another hand*) Hm; Preched YCrC^{2}CLH; Precheden OM; þ*at* preyched G; þ*at* precheden F. þe(1)] to the Cr. þe wombe] her wombys H; hemselue WHmYF; hemseluen OGC^{2}CLM; hemselues Cr.
60 Glosed] Gloseden O; ⁊ gloseden F; ⁊ glosen G. good] selue F. liked] lykythe G.
61 coueitise] couetous Cr. construwed] construeden O; construe Cr; þei co*n*stru*e* F. it] *om* GFH. þei] þem G. wolde] wolden OC^{2}; will F; lyked G.
62 Manye] Fele F. þise] þe FH. maistres] Mayst*ris* FG; maistres frers CYL; maistre freres WHmCrOC^{2}MH. mowe] GYC^{2}CLM; mowen HmO; may FH; might Cr; now W. cloþen] cloþe HmCrGFH. at] at her H.
63 hire(2)] *om* GYOC^{2}CLMF. marchaundi3e] marchaundises OYC^{2}; manchandises C. marchen] macchen Hm; mete H; meten *above, similar hand* C^{2}.
64 Siþ] For siþ WHmCrGYOC^{2}LMFH; For sythin C. haþ ben] was CrG; is F.
65 Manye] Fele F. fallen] Ifallen (I *inserted*) C^{2}; ben falle F. a] *om* CrH.
66 *line om* H. But] but yff G; ⁊ but F. and hij] and hir (*cancelled for* amend it and *another hand*) M. hij] they HmCr^{23}GOC^{2}F; I Cr^{1}. holde] holden HmY; hold not (not *another ink*) G. bettre] bittre Y.

The mooste meschief on Molde is mountynge [vp] faste.
Ther p*re*ched a p*ar*doner as he a preest were;
Brouȝte forþ a bulle wiþ Bisshopes seles,
And seide þ*at* hymself myȝte assoillen hem alle
Of falshede of fastynge [and] of Auowes ybroken.
Lewed men leued [hym] wel and liked hi[s speche];
Comen vp knelynge to kissen hi[s] bull[e].
He bonched hem w*ith* his breuet and blered hire eiȝen
And rauȝte w*ith* his Rageman rynges and broches.
Thus [ye] gyuen [youre] gold glotons to [helpe]
And leneþ it Losels [þat] leccherie haunten.
Were þe Bisshop yblessed and worþ boþe hise eris
His seel sholde noȝt be sent to deceyue þe peple.
It is noȝt by þe bisshop þ*at* þe boy p*re*cheþ;
[Ac] þe parisshe preest and þe p*ar*done*r* parten þe siluer

67 *line om* H. meschief] mychief L. Molde] erþe OC^2. vp] G; vp wel C^{2}O (wel *beneath, main hand* O); wel WHmCr YCLM (*cancelled for* vpwardes Fast *another hand* M); *om* F.
68 as...preest] a preest as he YM.
69 Brouȝte] ⁊ browhte F; Put H. wiþ] with YOC^{2}CLMF; wiþ many WHmCr GH.
70 assoillen] asoyle CCrF.
71 falshede] falsnes G; false oþis F. of(1)] and of Cr; ⁊ GF. fastynge] fastyngis F. and] HmCrGYOC^{2}CFH; *om* WLM. of (2)] fele F. Auowes] vowes CrYOC^{2}CLM. ybroken] broken HmCrGFH.
72 Lewed] ⁊ lewide F. leued] leueden O; belevid F; lykede HmH. hym] HmCr GYOC^{2}CLMH; he*m* F; it W. wel] *om* G. liked] likeden OF; leueden HmH. his speche] hise wordes WHmCrGYOC^2 CLMFH (*over erasure another hand* Hm).
73 Comen] Come C; ⁊ keme*n* FH. to] ⁊ F. kissen] kysse Cr; kessed F. his bulle] FH; hise bulles WHmCrGYOC^2 CLM.
74 *transposed with* 75 Hm. He] ⁊ he F. bonched] *cancelled for* blessid *another hand* M; bouchid Cr; blessid FH; touuchid C^2. blered] blessede Hm.
75 rauȝte] lawhte F. w*ith*] hym G. rynges] both ringes Cr. *Hereafter two spurious lines* F; *see above*, p. 222.
76 Thus] ⁊ þus F. ye] þei WHmCrGYO C^{2}CLM; me*n* F; þe puple H. gyuen] giue Cr; ȝyuen C^{2}H. youre] hire WHmCr YOC^{2}CLMFH; theym G. helpe] H; kepe WHmCrGYOC^{2}CLMF.
77 leneþ] leueth Cr^{12}; louen OC^2; beleven F. it] *above line another ink* M; it to Cr; on F; *om* OC^{2}CLH. Losels] swiche Losels WHmCrGYOC^{2}CLMH; þo loselis F. þat] that HmGYOC^{2}CLMFH; as WCr. haunten] hunteth Cr^2.
78 Were] But were H; But where F. Bisshop...and] blessynge bisshop F. yblessed] blessed HmCrH; ye blessed G. and] or GYMH. worþ...eris] wytty hy*m* one H. boþe hise] hise boþe O. eris] eryn F; heren *over erasure* Hm.
79 be] by Hm. sent] set H.
80 It] Ac it WHmYOLM; but ytt GFH; And it CrC^{2}C. is] *om* F. by] be FH; butt G. þat] þ*at* so F. þe boy] the both C; þei both G. *Hereafter a spurious line* F; *see above*, p. 222.
81 Ac] For WHmCrGYOC^{2}CLMFH. parisshe] *om* F. pardone*r*] partener H. parten] part Cr; shull dep*ar*ten F.

That þe [pouere peple] of þe parisshe sholde haue if þei ne
  were. |
P*er*sons and parisshe preestes pleyned hem to þe Bisshop *fol. 2 b*
That hire parissh[e] wer[e] pou*er*e siþ þe pestilence tyme,
To haue a licence and leue at London to dwelle,
[To] syngen for symonie for siluer is swete.
Bisshopes and Bachelers, boþe maistres and doctours,
That han cure vnder crist, and crownynge in tokene
And signe þ*at* þei sholden shryuen hire parisshens,
Prechen and praye for hem, and þe pou*er*e fede,
Liggen at Londou*n* in Lenten and ellis.
So*m*me s*er*uen þe kyng and his siluer tellen,
In Cheker and in Chauncelrie chalangen hise dettes
Of wardes and of wardemotes, weyues and streyves.
And so*m*me s*er*uen as s*er*uauntȝ lordes and ladies,
And in stede of Stywardes sitten and demen.

82 *line om* H. pouere...parisshe] p*ar*ycyoners G. pouere peple] pou*er*e poraille YOC^{2}M (poraile *over erasure of smaller word* M); pore me*n* F; poraille WHmCL; pouerty Cr. þei] thy Cr^2. ne were] *over erasure* M; nere CLF.
83 P*er*sons] Bothe p*er*sonys F. parisshe preestes] vikerys F; her priestes Cr. pleyned] pleyneden O; pleyny*n* H. hem] *om* F.
84 parisshe] p*ar*ysch HC; parisshes WCr GYOC^{2}LM; paryschenes HmF. were] HmCrGYC^{2}CLM; weren WO; where F; ha*n* be*n* H. þe] *om* C.
85 a] *om* FH. leue] a leue YCL. dwelle] dwellyn F.
86 To] Cr; And WHmGYOC^{2}CLMFH. syngen] synge CrC^{2}H. for(1)] MH (þere *above line another ink* M); þer for WHmCr GYOC^{2}CLF. for(2)] *om* G. is] ys so GH.
87 Bisshopes...maistres] Boþe Mayst*ri*s ⁊ Bisshopis ⁊ bacheleres F. Bachelers] bichilers Y.
88 crownynge] crounede(*final* e *erased*) M; Crownes C^2; a croune H; crowng C; konynge F. in] to FH. tokene] knowe F.
89 And] In H. signe] charge F. sholden] schulde CCrH; sholden at hom F. shryuen] shryue CrGH. parisshens] parisheneris C^{2}G; parishynges Cr.
90 Prechen] Preache Cr; ⁊ prechen F; P*re*sche he*m* H. praye] prayen MHmG. and(2)] ⁊ for G. pou*er*e] poore leene ⁊ F.
91 Liggen] Lye Cr; þei lyn H; and nowe they lyȝen Hm; ⁊ nowht lyȝn F; Liggand C. at] in YOCLMF. Lenten and] lente tyme or H.
92 So*m*me] ⁊ su*m*me F; sumtyme Hm. s*er*uen] s*er*ue HmH. his] þe H. siluer] money Hm. tellen] tell Cr^1.
93 In] In þe F. in] *in* þe F; *om* H. chalangen] chalange HCrC; to chalange F; Calengen C^2.
94 and of] ⁊ CrGYCLM; of HmOC^{2}H. wardemotes] wardenmotes C; warmottes Cr. weyues] of weyves HmCrOC^{2}FH. and(2)] of HmOC^2. streyves] strayes FH. *Here* F *adds a line like* **A** *Prologue* 95; *see above*, p. 221.
95 And] *om* G. s*er*uen] serue Cr^{1}H. as] of Hm. lordes] w*ith* lordys H; to lordes Cr. and] and to Cr.
96 And] *om* H. in] yn þe GF. of] os F. Stywardes] styward F. sitten] sitte Cr; þey Iuggyn F. demen] deme Cr^{1}H.

Hire messe & hire matyns and many of hire houres
Arn doon vndeuoutliche; drede is at þe laste
Lest crist in Consistorie acorse ful manye.
I p*ar*ceyued of þe power þat Peter hadde to kepe,
To bynden and vnbynden as þe book telleþ,
How he it lefte wiþ loue as oure lord hiȝte
Amonges foure v*er*tues, [most vertuous of alle],
That Cardinals ben called and closynge yates
There [crist is in] kyngdom, to close and to shette,
And to opene it to hem and heuene blisse shewe.
Ac of þe Cardinals at court þat kauȝte of þat name,
And power p*re*sumed in hem a pope to make
To han [þe] power þ*at* Peter hadde—impugnen I nelle—
For in loue and lettrure þe eleccion bilongeþ;
Forþi I kan & kan nauȝt of court speke moore. |
Thanne kam þ*er* a kyng; knyȝthod hym ladde; *fol.* 3 *a*
Might of þe co*m*munes made hym to regne.
And þanne cam kynde wit and clerkes he made
For to counseillen þe kyng and þe co*m*mune saue.

97 Hire] But here F. messe] messes MCr; mase F. &] ne F; *om* H. hire(1)] *om* F. and] ne F.
98 Be not salysbery hews her*e* Ordynal so tellyþ F. is at] it H.
99 *line om* F. in] *in* hys H. Consistorie] constorye GL; constry H. acorse] curse OC^2; accuse Hm.
100 of] on of H. þe] þat F.
101 bynden (*both*)] bynde YOC^{2}CLMFH. and] and to YOC^{2}CLM.
102 it lefte] lefte it MCrFH; it self OC^2. hiȝte] hy*m* hyghte F.
103 *line om* C. most vertuous] most v*er*tuous F; þe beste WHmCrYOC^{2}LMH; best G. alle] alle v*er*tues WHmCrGYO C^{2}LMH; hevene F.
104 called] cleped C^{2}OH. and closynge] to closen F. yates] hevene ȝatys F; þates Y.
105 *line om* H. crist is] YCrGOC^{2}CLMF; is crist W; cryst Hm. in] CrGYOC^{2}CLM; in his WHmF.
106 *line om* H. opene it] openet C^2. heuene] heuens Cr. shewe] hem shewe F.
107 Ac] but GH; And CrC^{2}CF. of(1)] *om* FH. þe] *om* Cr. at] at þe FHmCLM; of H. court] rome H. þat...þat] of þat couth þe H; of he*m* kawty*n* F. kauȝte] kauȝten HmOC^2. þat(2)] the Hm.
108 And] Ac O; For F. power...hem] p*re*sumyd i*n* he*m* wit*h* powyr H. p*re*sumed] p*re*sumeden O; p*re*sumeþ F. to] for to G.
109 þe] FH; þat WHmCrGYOC^{2}CLM. impugnen] Impugne OCrC^{2}FH. I] it I OC^2.
110 and] HmCr^{1}GYOC^{2}CLM; and in WCr^{23}FH. lettrure] letture Cr^1; lecture Cr^{23}. þe] *om* H. eleccion] lecciou*n* F.
111 *line om* Hm. &] & I OC^{2}H. kan nauȝt] nouȝt kan Y. of] of þe F; of þ*at* HG. speke] carpy*n* F.
112 hym] he F.
113 Might] & þe myght F. þe] hyse F; *om* H. made] maden F.
114 þanne] forþ F. kynde wit] knyth H. made] hadde F.
115 to] *om* C^2. counseillen] counceyle OHmCrGYC^{2}CLMFH. þe(2)] hise F. commune] communes CrF.

The kyng and kny3thod and clergie boþe
Casten þat þe co*m*mune sholde [hire communes] fynde.
The co*m*mune contreued of kynde wit craftes,
And for p*ro*fit of al þe peple Plowmen ordeyned
To tilie and to t*ra*uaille as trewe lif askeþ.
The kyng and þe co*m*mune and kynde wit þe þridde
Shopen lawe and leaute, ech [lif] to knowe his owene.
Thanne loked vp a lunatik, a leene þyng wiþalle,
And knelynge to þe kyng clergially he seide,
'Crist kepe þee, sire kyng, and þi kyngryche,
And lene þee lede þi lond so leaute þee louye,
And for þi ri3tful rulyng be rewarded in heuene'.
And siþen in þe Eyr an hei3 an Aungel of heuene
Lowed to speke in latyn, for lewed men ne koude
Iangle ne Iugge þat Iustifie hem sholde,
But suffren and s*er*uen; forþi seide þe Aungel,
'*Sum Rex, sum princeps; neutrum fortasse deinceps.*

116 The] ⁊ þe F. and(1)] ⁊ his FH; and the HmM. and(2)] and þe MFH. boþe] also F.
117 Casten] Cast H; þey casten F. co*m*mune] como*n*ys FCr^{23}; commous Cr^{1}. sholde] schulden OC^{2}. hire...fynde] fy3nde he*m*selue F. hire communes] hemself WHmYOC^{2}CLMH; hemselues Cr; theymselfen G. fynde] Fynde*n* C^{2}.
118 co*m*mune] commons CrF. contreued ...wit] be kynde wit cont*ri*ueden F. contreued] tho contreued Hm; co*n*streuyd H. of] wit*h* H. wit] of H.
119 for] for þe G. al] *om* HmGMFH. men] man YC. ordeyned] ordeyneden O; he ordeyned Y; þey made F.
120 tilie...t*ra*uaille] swynke ⁊ to tylye F. tilie] tilen (en *over erasure*) M. to] *om* YOC^{2}CL. trewe lif] trewe skyl F; trewth H.
121 The] þa*n*ne þe F. þe(1)] *om* F. co*m*mune] commons CrF. and(2)] *om* C. kynde wit] knyth wit*h* H.
122 Shopen] Schope C^{2}GCLMH; Shepe Y. and] be F; *om* C^{2}. ech] euery Cr. lif] lyf F; man WHmCrGYOC^{2}CLMH.
123 vp] *om* F. þyng] *om* H.
124–35 *over erasure another hand* Hm.
124 And knelynge] And knelyd H; he ga*n* knele F. clergially he] ⁊ clergyaly FH.
125 **Here R begins**; *see above*, p. 12. kepe þee] the kepe Y. þi] the G; þe þi (þe *cancelled*) O. kyngryche] kyngdom ryche F; knythys ryche H.
126 lene] leue Cr; leve F. þee(1)] þee to OYC^{2}M; þe so F. so] so þat (þat *by corrector*) M. leaute] lenty Cr^{3}. þee(2)] he þe H. louye] loueth Cr; leue H; alowe F.
127 be] þou be F; to be H. rewarded] reward H.
128 siþen in] ano*n* fram F. þe] *om* H. Eyr] heir R; hevene F. hei3] height CrG; erthe H. an...heuene] com dou*n* an angyl F. of] on C^{2}.
129 Lowed] loued C^{2}H; ⁊ lowhde F. to] dyd *altered from* to *main scribe* G; *om* F. speke] spak F. in] *om* H. men] *om* H. ne] to Y. koude] kouden OC^{2}; sholde F.
130 Iangle] Ianglyn F. ne] no*n* H. Iugge] Iuggen hym F; chyde H. þat] ne F. Iustifie] Iustice C^{2}M. hem sholde] hy*m* wit*h* mowþe F.
131 suffren] sufre C^{2}H. s*er*uen] s*er*ue H; seruy*n* softly F. forþi] þ*er*for H.
132 *Sum* (*both*)] *Cum* C^{2}. *neutrum*] *uenturum* Y.

O qui iura regis christi specialia regis,
Hoc quod agas melius, iustus es, esto pius!
Nudum ius a te vestiri vult pietate.
Qualia vis metere, talia grana sere.
Si ius nudatur nudo de iure metatur; |
Si seritur pietas de pietate metas.' *fol. 3 b*
Thanne greued hym a Goliardeis, a gloton of wordes,
And to þe Aungel an heiȝ answerde after:
'*Dum rex a regere dicatur nomen habere*
Nomen habet sine re nisi studet iura tenere.'
Thanne [comsed] al þe co*m*mune crye in vers of latyn
To þe kynges counseil, construe whoso wolde,
'*Precepta Regis sunt nobis vincula legis*'.
Wiþ þat ran þ*er* a route of Ratons at ones
And smale mees myd hem; mo þan a þousand
Comen to a counseil for þe co*m*mune p*ro*fit.
For a cat of a [court] cam whan hym liked
And ou*er*leep hem liȝtliche and lauȝte hem at wille
And pleide wiþ hem p*er*illousli and possed aboute.

133 *regis*(2)] *legis* F.
134 *quod*] *vt* HmG; *quo* Cr^{3}; *p* (*cancelled*) H. *melius*] mesius C^{2}. *es*] ⁊ H.
135 *Nudum*] *Non dum* H. *ius*] *vis* RF. *vestiri*] *vestire* RFH. *vult*] wlt R.
136 *talia*] *tali* H.
137 *ius*] *vis* RFH.
138 *seritur*] *seritur* pietur R.
139 greued hym] gronyd H. Goliardeis] golyard (*erasure at end*) Hm. a(2)] ⁊ a (a *above line*) H.
140 answerde] answered (d *over erasure*) HmM; he answerede F; answeres LR. after] soone F.
141–4 *in margin main hand* M.
141 *Dum*] *Cum* $YOC^{2}C$. *dicatur nomen*] *nomen dicatur* H.
142 *nisi studet*] *studeat nisi* HmG (*over erasure another hand* Hm).
143 Thanne] And þanne LCR. comsed...crye] cryeden alle þe como*n*ys F. comsed] gan $WHmCrGYOC^{2}CLRH$; biga*n* M. al] *om* H. þe] a R. co*m*mune] comunes $OCrC^{2}$. crye] to cry H. in...latyn] w*ith* o voys atonys F. vers] a vers R; verses Cr^{23}.
144 *line om* RF. kynges] ky*n*g ⁊ his M. wolde] wyl H.
145 *Precepta*] Precipta M. *sunt nobis*] *nobis sunt* H.
146 ran þ*er*] ran H; kemen F. at ones] manye F.
147 smale] Manye F. myd] wyth $HmCrGYOC^{2}CLMRFH$.
148 Comen] And comen $WHmCrGYOC^{2}LMRH$; And come C; ⁊ wenty*n* F. a] *om* HmCrH. þe] her $OC^{2}CLMR$; a H.
149 of] in F. a(2)] þe FH. court] $OCr^{23}YC^{2}CLRF$; contree $WHmCr^{1}GMH$ (*over erasure another ink* M). hym] hire F. liked] lyst*es* H.
150 liȝtliche] lytly H; lyghlyche G. lauȝte] caught Cr. hem...wille] þat hy*m* lykyth H. at] F; at his $WHmCrGYOC^{2}CLR$; atte his M.
151 *transposed with* 152 *but correct order indicated* H. pleide] pleyeþ F. hem p*er*illousli] vs ap*er*tly F. possed] possed he*m* $YOC^{2}CMRH$; posseþ vs F.

'For doute of diu*er*se d[e]des we dar noȝt wel loke,
And if we grucche of his gamen he wol greuen vs alle,
Cracchen vs or clawen vs, and in hise clouches holde
That vs loþeþ þe lif er he late vs passe.
Miȝte we wiþ any wit his wille wiþstonde
We myȝte be lordes o lofte and lyuen at oure ese.'
A Raton of renoun, moost renable of tonge,
Seide for a sou*er*eyn [salue] to [hem alle].
'I haue yseyen segges', quod he, 'in þe Cite of Londou*n*
Beren beiȝes ful briȝte abouten hire nekkes,
And so*m*me colers of crafty werk; vncoupled þei wen[d]en
Boþe in wareyne and in waast where hem [leue] like[þ];
And ouþ*er* while þei arn elliswhere, as I here telle.
Were þer a belle on hire beiȝe, by I*es*u, as me þynkeþ,
Men myȝte witen wher þei wente and [hire] wey r[oum]e. |
And riȝt so', quod þat Raton, 'Reson me sheweþ *fol.* 4 *a*

152 For...dedes] & for drede of deeþ F. dedes] OC^{2}; dredes WHmCrYCLMRH; drede (*the error noted*) G. dar] doren O; ne dore F. noȝt wel] nouthe C. loke] looken F.
153 And] but G. grucche] grucchen OC^{2}MR. of] at CrGY; *om* RF. gamen] game CrGH; gameȝ C^{2}; will F. wol] wel H; wolde Hm. greuen] greue HmGYOC^{2}CLRFH. alle] sore F.
154 Cracchen] cracche HmGYOC^{2}CLMRH; & cracche F; Scratchyng Cr. or] and HmCrYOC^{2}MF. clawen] clawe HmGYOC^{2}CLMRFH; clawyng Cr. clouches] cloche vs F; clawes Cr; clauwys vs H.
155 vs loþeþ] vs is loth H; we loþyn F; we loth Cr. þe] oure GFH. passe] passen F.
156 Miȝte] Myȝten OC^{2}; But myghte F. wiþ] be F. wit] wyth H. wille] wylle to Hm; wit C.
157 myȝte] myȝten OC^{2}M; weryn F. be] *om* F. lyuen] lyue Cr; leue*n* C^{2}C; leue H. at oure] at Cr^{23}; i*n* gret F.
158–95 *left margin cropped* R.
158 A] þa*n*ne a F. renable] resonable HmR.
159 for...salue] a resonable resou*n* & helplych F. salue] help WHmCrGYOC^{2}CLMRH. to] for H. hem alle] RF; hymselue WHmCrGYCLMH (*over erasure another hand* Hm); hymseluen OC^{2}.
160 yseyen] seyn HmCrGOC^{2}CH; herd of F. segges] segthis C.
161 Beren...briȝte] þat me*n* bery*n* bryghte byȝes F. Beren] Bere CrH; Weren C. abouten] aboute HmCrGYCH.
162 of] w*ith* G. werk] werkis C^{2}. wenden] YOC^{2}CLMR (*altered to* wenten M); wenten WG; wente HmCr; walke F; were H.
163 hem] hym Hm. leue] Cr^{23}YOCLM; lef R; leffee C^{2}; best FH; self WHmCr^{1}; selue G. likeþ] lyketh HmCr^{23}YOC^{2}CLRF; liked WCr^{1}GMH (d *over erasure* M).
164 ouþ*er* while] so*m*me tyme H. þei arn] *om* F. I here] weyȝes me F.
165–76 *over erasure another hand* Hm.
165 Were] where F. þer...beiȝe] here a beyȝe or a belle H. hire] hys G. beiȝe] biȝes YOC; bight Cr; breste C^{2}. I*es*u] Iesus RF; Iohn G. as] *om* H. þynkeþ] thynke C.
166 myȝte] myȝten OMF. witen] wite YHmCrGOCLRH. þei] he (*above line main hand*) H. wente] wenten OC^{2}. hire...roume] awey renne WHmCr^{23}GYOC^{2}CLMRFH; awayn ru*n*ne Cr^{1}.
167 And] *om* F. þat] the GOC^{2}F. Raton] rato G. Reson] as resou*n* F.

To bugge a belle of bras or of bri3t siluer
And knytten it on a coler for oure co*mm*une p*ro*fit
[And hangen it vpon þe cattes hals; þanne here we mowen]
Wher he ryt or rest or r[om]eþ to pleye;
And if hym list for to laike þanne loke we mowen
And peeren in his p*re*sence þe while hym pleye likeþ,
And if hym wraþeþ be war and his wey shonye.'
Al þ[e] route of Ratons to þis reson assented.
Ac þo þe belle was ybrou3t and on þe bei3e hanged
Ther ne was Raton in þe route, for al þe Reaume of F*ra*unce,
That dorste haue bounden þe belle aboute þe cattes nekke,
Ne hangen it aboute [his] hals al Engelond to wynne;
[Ac] helden hem vnhardy and hir counseil feble,
And leten hire labour lost and al hire longe studie.
A Mous þat muche good kouþe, as me [þo] þou3te,
Strook forþ sternely and stood bifore hem alle

168 To] It were best to F. bugge] bygen G. belle of bras] bras belle F. bri3t] shy3n F.
169 knytten] knytte OCrC^{2}FH. it] *above line another ink* M; *om* Cr^{23}GOC^{2}CL. a] his HmCr.
170 LCr^{23}YOC^{2}CMRFH; *line om* WHm Cr^{1}G. hangen] hange OC^{2}FH. vpon] on C^{2}H; aboute Cr^{23}F. þanne here] so here H; þ*at* here hy*m* F. mowen] mowe FH.
171 *line om* RF. Wher] Whether Cr; Where þ*at* Y. ryt] rydys H. rest] resteþ HmOC^2; rennys H. or(2)] & H. romeþ] rometh Y; renneþ WHmGOC^{2}CLM; run Cr; restyth H. to] or H.
172 *line om* RF. hym] hem Y; vs H. list] liste YOC^2; lyke HmH. for] *om* H. we] they G. mowen] myght Cr.
173 peeren] peer CCrH; apperen HmF. p*re*sence] absen*s*e F. þe] ther HmYOCL MR; *om* GH. hym] v*us* F.
174 hym] he CrGFH. wraþeþ] wratthe F; wrath Cr; wrath hym G; be wroth H. be] to be F. war] ywar YOCLR. his] *om* H. shonye] esshewe C^2; wende H.
175 Al] þanne alle F; and G. þe] RF; þis WHmCrGYOC^{2}CLMH. of] of þe R. reson] C^{2}HmGOMFH; reson þei WCrY CLR. assented] assenteden O.
176 Ac] butt GFH; And CrC^{2}C. þo] thogh G; whanne FH. ybrou3t] brought Cr^{1}G; Ibou3t OYC^{2}CLMRH; bought Cr^{23}F. and on] or H. bei3e] bight Cr. hanged] Ihanged R.
177 ne was] nas GM; ne was a Cr^1; nas no Hm; was no FH. in] GMH; in al WHm CrYOC^{2}CLR; of F. þe(1)] that HmFH; *om* R. al] *om* F.
178 haue] a HmF; *om* CrH. bounden] bounde OC^{2}F; ybounden YCL; Ibounde R; bynd CrH. þe(1)] þ*at* F. belle] bey3e HmM; bond F.
179 Ne...his] ne haue take the kat by the Hm. hangen] hange HCrF; hangid C^2. it] *above line another ink* M; *om* GL. his] RF; þe cattes WCrGYOC^{2}CLMH.
180 Ac] But F; and HmCrGYOC^{2}CLM; ::nd R; Alle W; þei H. helden] helde CrH; holden Hm. hem] he*m*selue FH; him Cr^2. hir] al here F.
181 leten] let CrH; al F. lost] Ilost R; was loost F. al] *om* YOC^{2}MF. longe studie] large costes F.
182 A] Tha*nn*e a FH. muche] mychil F. me] men Hm. þo] tho G; *om* WHmCr YOC^{2}CLMRFH. þou3te] thou3ten Hm.
183 sternely] sterly C^2; streyly (? streþly) H.

And to þe route of Ratons reherced þise wordes:
'Thou3 we [hadde] kille[d] þe cat yet sholde þ*er* come anoþ*er*
To c[r]acchen vs & al oure kynde þou3 we cropen vnder benches;
Forþi I counseille al þe co*m*mune to late þe cat worþe,
And be we neu*ere* [so] bolde þe belle hym to shewe.
⌈The while he cacceþ conynges he coueiteþ no3t [o]ure caroyne
But fedeþ hym al wiþ venyson, defame we hym neu*ere*;
For bettre is a litel los þan a long sorwe.
The ma3e among vs alle þei3 we mysse a sherewe,
For I herde my sire seyn, seuen yeer ypassed,
Ther þe cat is a kitou*n* þe court is ful elenge;
That witnesseþ holy writ, whoso wole it rede:
Ve terre vbi puer Rex est &c.
For may no renk þ*er* reste haue for Ratons by ny3te,⌋
[And] many m[a]nnes malt we mees wolde destruye, ⌋

184 route of] ratou*n* of H; *om* OC^{2}. reherced] he reersyd F.
185 hadde killed] haddy*n* kyllyd F; had Iculled R; kylled C^{2}; kulled CLM; killeden O; killen WHmG; kylle HYCr. þe] thys Cr; þat FH. sholde] schall HmG. þ*er*] *om* H.
186 To] & F; *cropped* R. cracchen] cracche OYCLR; cacchen WG; cacche HmCrC^{2}MFH (ca *over erasure* M). al] *om* F. þou3] whan F. cropen] crope RLM; crepe HmCrGYC; kroule F; carpe H. vnder benches] abowte F.
187 *line om* Cr^{23}. Forþi] þerfor H. I] by my F. al þe co*m*mune] 3ow alle H; *om* F. co*m*mune] co*m*mens Cr^{1}. late] soffre F. worþe] Iworthe R; aworthe F; wurche HmCr^{1}; werke H; pas G.
188 be we neu*ere*] no bacheler be F. we] *om* H. so] HmCrGYOC^{2}CLMRFH; *om* W. hym] *om* Hm.
189–92 *copied after* 197 WHmCrGYOC^{2}CLMRFH; *see above*, p. 176.
189 The] ther Hm; For FH. he...conynges] þe catt is ful fyllyd H. he(1)] the kat Hm. conynges] conies CrF. coueiteþ] coueyt H. oure] OHmCrGYC^{2}CLMRFH; youre W. caroyne] bowkys F.
190 fedeþ] fet YOLMR. al] *om* HmCrOC^{2}MFH.
191 For] but HmG. long] more H.
192 *line om* C. The] they G.
193 *line om* H. seyn] say CrG; seyn is WYOC^{2}LMRF; seyn it is Hm; say his C. yeer] yers G. ypassed] passed HmCrGC^{2}.
194 Ther] Where Cr; For þ*er* H. a] *om* F. kitou*n*] kylling Cr^{1}; kitling Cr^{23}. þe court] *om* G. ful] *om* F. elenge] elynge C; elyng LR; alange H; *glossed* aylynge *another hand* C^{2}.
195 witnesseþ] witnesse C; wytnessyd H. holy] woly G. writ] writinge Cr. it] I H.
196 *divided from* 197 *after* haue R. *puer Rex*] *rex puer* GH. *Rex est*] *est rex* HmOC^{2}R. *&c*] *om* HmCrRF. *Here* H *adds a spurious line*; *see above*, p. 224.
197 For] For ther Hm; There F. renk] reuke Cr; ma*n* H; thyng Hm. þ*er*] no R; *om* HmF. reste haue] haue reste F. for Ratons] for rattys F; *om* H. by ny3te] on nyghtis FH; bi nigh Cr^{2}. *Here* WHmCrGYOC^{2}CLMRFH *copy lines* 189–92.
198 And] For WHmCrGYOC^{2}CLMRFH. mannes] YC^{2}CLMRH; mennes WHmCrGOF. we] ell*es* we F. wolde] wolden HmO; will F.

And also ye route of Ratons rende mennes cloþes *fol. 4 b*
Nere þe cat of þ[e] court þ*at* kan yow ouerlepe;
For hadde ye rattes youre [raik] ye kouþe no3t rule yowselue.
I seye for me', quod þe Mous, 'I se so muchel after,
Shal neu*ere* þe cat ne þe kiton by my counseil be greued,
[Ne] carpynge of þis coler þat costed me neu*ere*;
And þou3 it costned me catel biknowen it I nolde
But suffren as hymself wolde to [slen þat] hym likeþ,
Coupled and vncoupled to cacche what þei mowe.
Forþi ech a wis wi3t I warne, wite wel his owene.'
What þis metels bymeneþ, ye men þ*at* ben murye,
Deuyne ye, for I ne dar, by deere god in heuene.
Yet houed þ*er* an hundred in howues of selk,
Sergeant3 it [s]emed þat s*er*ueden at þe barre,
Pleteden for penyes and pounde[d] þe lawe
[Ac] no3t for loue of oure lord vnlose hire lippes ones.

199 ye] ellis 3ee F; the HmCr^1GYOC^2CH. route of] *om* FH. rende] wolde renden F; rente Cr^1. mennes] mannes Y; renkes F. **200** Nere] Ne wer*e* FH; Ther Y. þe(1)] þat OYC^2CLR (at *erased* C). þe(2)] C^2Hm GRFH; þat WCrYOCLM. court] cu*n*tre H. yow ouer] among 3ow F. yow] vs Cr. **201** hadde] hadden O; *om* H. ye(*both*)] you Cr. ye(1)] þe Y. rattes] ratons GRFH. raik] wille WHmCrGYOC^2 CLMRFH. kouþe] couþen O. yow] yo G; your CrYC^2CLMRF; 3orw H. selue] selue*n* C^2. **202** for] it for R; þis for F. me] myself RFH. I(2)] ⁊ F. muchel] muche HmH. **203** neu*ere*] neither Cr. þe(1)] *om* HmGF. þe(2)] *om* HmGC^2F. kiton] kitling Cr. greued] blamyd H. **204** Ne] CrGYOC^2CLMRFH; ne no Hm; Thoru3 W. carpynge] carpe H. þis] his HmFH. coler] colore*s* G. þat] *om* F. costed] coste HmYCFH. neu*ere*] neuere aft*er* F. **205** it(1)] RGF; it hadde WHmCrYOC^2 CLMH. costned] costed HmMR; coste YCrGOC^2CLFH. catel] *om* G. biknowen it] be it aknowe H. biknowen] byknowe HmGOC^2CF. it(2)] *om* G. nolde] nylle F. **206** suffren] suffre HmCrGYOC^2LMRFH. hymself wolde] su*m*me oþere do F. wolde] wyll G; lykyth H. to...likeþ] ⁊ as he wold do H. slen þat] slen what F; doon as WCr; do as HmGYOC^2CLMR. **207** to] lo Cr^1; *om* H. þei] he FH. mowe] wille F. **208** *line om* H. Forþi] For R; ⁊ F. ech] euery F. a] *om* F. wi3t] man C^2R; Mows F. wite] to wacche F. his] hy*m* F; *om* C^2. owene] selue F. **209** þis] thise YOC^2. metels] metall G; mety*n*g H. bymeneþ] bement C^2; bymene R; meneþ F. ye] þe R. murye] her*e*Inne F. **210** Deuyne...dar] I ne dar dyvyne it 3ow F. for...dar] ne dar I nou3t R. ne dar] nout dar H; dare not Cr. in] of Cr^{23}H. **211** houed] howyt H; houeden O. howues] hownes Cr; hures Hm. of selk] on Molde F. **212** it] as it C; þey FH; theym G. semed] GYC^2CLMRH; semeden OF; bisemed WHmCr. þat] at R. s*er*ueden] seruede CMF; seruen CrGH. **213** Pleteden] Pletyd HC^2; Pleten CrG. penyes] þe peny F; peynes G. pounded] pownded F; pou*n*tyd H; poudres R; poundes WHmCrGYOC^2CLM. **214** Ac] And WHmCrGYOC^2CLMRFH. loue...lord] oure lordys love F. loue] the loue Cr^3GC^2. vnlose] vnlese LR; vnclosen Cr. lippes] lyppe FH.

Thow myȝtest bettre meete myst on Maluerne hilles
Than gete a mom of hire mouþ til moneie be shewed.
Barons and Burgeises and bond[age] als
I seiȝ in þis assemblee, as ye shul here after.
Baksteres and Brewesteres and Bochiers manye,
Wollen webbesters and weueres of lynnen,
Taillours, Tynkers and Tollers in Markettes,
Masons, Myn*ours* and many oþ*ere* craftes;
Of alle kynne lybbynge laborers lopen forþ so*m*me,
As dykeres and delueres þat doon hire ded[e] ille
And dryueþ forþ þe longe day wi*th* '*Dieu saue dame Emme*'.
Cokes and hire knaues cryden, 'hote pies, hote!
Goode gees and grys! go we dyne, go we!' |
Tau*er*ners [t]il hem tolden þe same: *fol. 5 a*
'Whit wyn of Oseye and wyn of Gascoigne,
Of þe Ryn and of þe Rochel þe roost to defie!'
[Al þis I seiȝ slepyng and seuene sythes more].

215 myȝtest] myghte CH. meete] meten F. myst] the myst HmCrYOC^{2}CLM; wi*th* þe myst H.
216 gete] gety*n* F. mom] worde Y. hire] hys G. til] but YOC^{2}CLMH; er F; her (h *erased*) R. be] were YCLM; hem by R. shewed] Ishe (*cropped*) R. *Here* Cr^{23} *add lines like* **A** *Prologue* 90–5; *see above*, p. 221.
217 *line om* F. Burgeises] burgeis Hm YOC^{2}CLMRH. bondage] bondemen WHmCrGYOC^{2}CLMRH. als] also Cr GOC^2.
218 assemblee] semele H. after] hereafter G.
219 Baksteres] Boþe Bakerys F. and(1)] *om* G. Brewesteres] brewers C^2; brukesters Cr^2.
220 Wollen] wolle LR; & also wolle F. webbesters] webberys H. weueres] webberys F.
221 Taillours] & Tayloures F. Tynkers] tynkers G; and Tynkers WHmCrYOC^2 CLMRFH. Tollers] tollere Hm. in] of FH. Markettes] Market F.
222 Masons] Masons and WHmCrGYOC^2 CLMRH; & Masonys & F. oþere] mo M.
223 kynne] man*er* of H; *om* RF. lybbynge] *om* GH. laborers] labores C. lopen] lepen Y; lope þ*ere* F; were þ*er* H. forþ] *om* H. somme] aft*er* C^2.

Prol. 224–I 20 *left margin cropped* R.
224 As] and Hm. dede] H; dedes WHm CrGYOC^{2}CLMRF. ille] all G.
225 dryueþ] dryue CrGCFH. þe longe] þe fayre F; þe dere L; þe H; here R. longe] *over erasure* M. day] dayes here R. *Dieu...Emme*] how trolly lolly H. *saue*] *vous saue* HmCr^{23}YOC^{2}CLMRF; *soit* G. *Emme*] enuye G.
226 Cokes...hire] þ*ere* wheren kene Cokys F. cryden] Cried C^2; cryen G. hote (*both*)] wott G.
227 Goode] Goode fatte F. gees...grys] gris and gees YCMRF; gris a gees L. grys] gryses G.
228 Tau*er*ners] & þe Tauernerys F. til] vntil WHmCrGYOC^{2}CLMRF; o H. tolden] HmOC^{2}H; tolde CrGYCLMR; tolledyn F; trewely tolden W.
229 Whit] wyth HmCr^1; wi*th* FH. wyn of Oseye] good fyȝn Maluesyn F. of(1)] & GH. and] or F. wyn(2)] F; reed wyn WHmCrGYOC^{2}CLMH; *om* R.
230 Of...Rochel] Or Rochel or Romeney F. and] *om* H. of] *om* GR. þe(2)] *om* O. defie] defyen GY.
231 LHmCrGOC^{2}CMRH; *line om* WYF. Al] *om* Cr. I seiȝ] I sagh G; seiȝ I LHmCr OC^{2}CMRH.

I

What þ[e] Mountaigne bymeneþ and þe m*er*ke dale
And þe feld ful of folk I shal yow faire shewe.
A louely lady of leere in lynnen ycloþed
Cam doun from [þe] Castel and called me faire,
And seide, 'sone, slepestow? sestow þis peple,
How bisie þei ben aboute þe ma3e?
The mooste partie of þis peple þat passeþ on þis erþe,
Haue þei worship in þis world þei [kepe] no bettre;
Of ooþ*er* heuene þan here holde þei no tale.'
I was afered of hire face þei3 she fair weere
And seide, 'm*er*cy, madame, what [may] þis [by]meene?'
'The tour on þe toft', quod she, 'truþe is þ*er*Inne,
And wolde þ*a*t ye wrou3te as his word techeþ.
For he is fader of feiþ, and formed yow alle
Boþe w*ith* fel and w*ith* face, and yaf yow fyue wittes
For to worshipe hym þ*er*wiþ while ye ben here.
And þ*er*fore he hi3te þe erþe to helpe yow echone

1 þe(1)] þis WHmCrGYOC^{2}CLMRFH. bymeneþ] meneth GF. þe(2)] þis H. merke] derke FH.
2 þe] þis H. yow faire] fair*e* 3ow F.
3 louely] love F. leere] lore H. ycloþed] clothed Cr^{1}GH.
4 doun] *om* F. þe] a WHmCrGYOC^{2}CLMRFH. called me] full callede me full (full(1) *cancelled*) Hm.
6 How] Ho H. bisie] bysely þ*a*t F. ben] YOC^{2}CLMRFH (alle *added* M); ben alle WHmCrG. aboute] abouten CLMRF.
7 mooste] moosti Y. partie] part CrGH. þis(1)] þe GH. passeþ] perychyd H. þis(2)] þe Y; *om* FH.
8 þei(1)] þe R. in] of C^2. þei kepe] kepe þei H. kepe] G; wilne WHmLR; wilnen YOCMF; wullen C^2; wil Cr.
9 þan] þa*n* is H. holde þei] they tell G. holde] holden OC^{2}R.
10 afered] afrayed Cr.
11 may...bymeene] may þis bemene H; is þis to meene WHmCrGYOC^{2}CLMRF.
12 The...she] Q*uo*d she In þe tour vpon þe toft F. on] vpon Cr; vp YOC^{2}CLMR. quod she] *om* Cr^3. is] it H.
13 And] he F. ye] me*n* F. wrou3te] wrou3ten HmYOC^{2}MH. techeþ] tellyþ F.
14 is] *om* O. and] that HmG; *om* YOC^{2}CLMR. formed] former of Cr. yow] hem F.
15 fel] flesch H. face] fel H. and(2)] he F.
16 worshipe] worchepy*n* H. þer] *om* GFH. while] þe while YCr^{23}OC^{2}CLMR; yea whyle Cr^1. ye] GCr^{1}OC^{2}FH; you Cr^{23}; þ*a*t ye WHmCLMR; þe ye Y.
17 *line om* Cr^3. And] ::::t R; *om* H. þer] her M. þe] þou þe H. helpe] hepe H.

Of wollene, of lynnen, of liflode at nede
In mesurable manere to make yow at ese;
And comaunded of his curteisie in commune þree þynges;
Are none nedfulle but þo; and nempne hem I þynke
And rekene hem by reson: reherce þow hem after.
That oon [is] vesture from [chele] þee to saue;
[That oþer is] mete at meel for mysese of þiselue; |
And drynke whan þ[ee] drie[þ], ac do [it] no3t out of
    reson *fol. 5 b*
That þow worþe þe wers whan þow werche sholdest.
For Lot, in hise lifdayes, for likynge of drynke,
Dide by hise dou3tres þat þe deuel liked;
Delited hym in drynke as þe deuel wolde,
And Leccherie hym lau3te, and lay by hem boþe;
And al he witte it wyn þat wikked dede:
Inebri[e]mus eum vino dormiamusque cum eo
    Vt seruare possimus de patre nostro semen.
Thoru3 wyn and þoru3 wommen þer was loth acombred,

18 of(1)] ⁊ GF. of(2)...at] o lifode atte C. of(2)] and of Cr; ⁊ F.
19 at] atte C.
20 And] he F. comaunded] Commauunde 3ou C^2. of] on GC^2.
21 Are] *om* F. nedfulle] needfullere F; nydfull (n *over erased* m) Hm. but] þan F. þo] thys G; thyo (y *cancelled*) C. and] *om* OC^2. nempne] neuene G; nemele H; named Cr^1.
22 *line om* H. rekene] rekened Cr^1. hem(1)] *om* F. reson] reyson ⁊ G; rewe Cr^1. þow] 3e HmCrOC^{2}MF (ye *above line main hand* M); *om* GY.
23 That oon] þe fyrste F. is] CrHmGYOC^{2}CLMFH; his (h *erased*) R; *om* W. vesture] clothinge C^2. chele] HmCrGYOLMRF; chelde C; cold WC^2; colod H. þee] þo H; *om* Cr.
24 That...is] þe toþir ys F; And WHmCrGYOC^{2}CLMRH. at] at þe RCLM; at þin H. mysese] disease Cr. of þi] to the F. selue] seluen HmG; *om* F.
25 And] þe þrydd ys F. þee drieþ] þow driest WHmCrGYOC^{2}CLMRFH. ac] but GFH; ⁊ CrC^{2}C. it] FGH; *om* WHmCrYOC^{2}CLMR. no3t] *om* F. out of reson] oft G. out of] to offte out of H; in F.
26 That] Lesse H. worþe] ne worth3 (? worch3) F; wroth Cr^2; wurche Hm; be H. whan...werche] worche when þow G. werche] swynk H.
27 lif] *om* Cr^3. for] þorgh3 F.
28 by] wyth Cr. liked] well lykede Hm; lyketh Cr^3; wolde C.
29 *line om* C. Delited] Delite Cr^2; For he delytyd F. hym] *om* Cr. *Here* H *copies lines* 31α *and* 31β.
30 lay] he lay F.
31 *line om* OC^2. witte] wyted GYH. it] LGRF; it þe WHmYCM; the CrH. þat] that foule Hm.
31α *copied after line* 29 H. *Inebriemus*] YOC^{2}CRH; *Inebriamus* WHmCrGLMF. *que*] *om* G. *eo*] *eo* ⁊*c* Y.
31β *possimus*] *possumus* GF. *semen*] *semen* ⁊*c* H.
32 Thoru3] For þorgh3 F. þoru3] *om* CrGFH. þer] þo H. loth] *om by rubricator* Y. acombred] encombred HmG.

And þ*er*e gat in glotonie gerles þ*at* were cherles.
Forþi dred delitable drynke and þow shalt do þe bettre;
Mesure is medicine þouȝ þow muchel yerne.
[Al is nouȝt] good to þe goost þat þe gut askeþ,
Ne liflode to þ[e] likame [þat leef is to þ[e] soule.
Lef nauȝt þi licame] for a liere hym techeþ,
That is þe wrecched world wolde þee bitraye.
For þe fend and þi flessh folwen togidere,
And that [shendeþ] þi soule; [set] it in þin herte.
And for þow sholdest ben ywar I wisse þee þe beste.'
'[A] madame, mercy', quod I, 'me likeþ wel youre wordes.
Ac þe moneie [on] þis molde þat men so faste holdeþ,
Tel me to whom þat tresour appendeþ.'
'Go to þe gospel', quod she, 'þat god seide hymseluen,
Tho þe poeple hym apposede wiþ a peny in þe temple

33 þ*er*e] there he HmYOC^{2}MH; *om* F. in] wi*th* gret F. gerles] barnes C. were] weren OF. cherles] karles C.

34 Forþi] Þ*er*for H. delitable] delectable CrGC^{2}H. and] *om* H.

35 *line om* H. Mesure] For Mesure F. medicine] medcyne L. þouȝ] al thow (thow *over erasure*) Hm. þow] you Cr; *om* G. muchel] moche HmGYOC^{2}LMR.

36 Al is nouȝt] It is nouȝt al WHmCr YOC^{2}CLMRFH; ytt ys not G. good] *om* Cr. to] for CrOC^{2}H. þe(*both*)] þi F. þe gut] guttis C. askeþ] ȝernyth H.

37 *line om* CrH; *run together with* 38 WHm CL. Ne] no G. þe(1)] the G; þi WHm YOC^{2}CLMRF. þat...soule] OGYC^{2}M RF (*over erasure* M); *om* WHmCL. to(2)] *om* R. þe(2)] GYM; þi OC^{2}RF (*altered from* þis C^2).

38 *line om* GF; *in margin main hand* M. Lef...licame] RCrYOC^{2}M; Loue nout þ*in* frele flesch H; *om* WHmCL. nauȝt] þou not OC^2. hym] it hym Hm.

39 That] For þat F; thys G. þe] a OC^2. wolde] that wold GH; he wolde F.

40 For] & FH. þe] thy (*corrected*) Y. þi] þe HCr. folwen] folwe H; folwen þe RCr YOC^{2}CLM; folwe þe F.

41 *line om* H. And...shendeþ] take thys In G. And that] þese thre F; This and that WHmCrYOC^{2}CLMR. shendeþ] seeþ WCr^{1}OM; sees C; seiþ C^{2}Cr^{23}; seest YL; sueth R; sewe F; sleth (l *over erasure*) Hm. þi] þe (e *over erasure*) M. soule] Y; soule and WHmCrGOC^{2}CLMR; sowle to F. set...herte] shende it þey casten F. set] sett G; setth C; seith WHmYOC^{2}LR; saith M; seeth Cr. it] *om* OC^2. þin] thi *over erasure* Hm.

42 And...ywar] Þ*er*fore be war H. ywar] war HmCrGC^{2}CMF. I wisse] for þ*in* sowle wyschyt H. wisse] wysshe FCr; vyse G. þee þe] þe YC^{2}CFH. beste] bettre OC^2.

43 A] F; *om* WHmCrGYOC^{2}CLMRH. madame mercy] Mercy madame H. youre] thy G.

44 Ac] butt GFH; And CrC^{2}C. on] HmF; of WCrYOC^{2}CLMRH; In G. molde] werld H. holdeþ] kepeth R; kepe F.

45 Tel] Telleth R; Tell ȝee F. me] *om* G to whom] F; to whom madame WHmCr GYOC^{2}CLM; madame to whom RH.

46 Go...she] Q*uo*d she go to þe gospel F. to] *om* Cr^{12}. seluen] selue RHmCrF.

47 Tho] whan FGCH; To OC^2. poeple] temple (*corrected to* people *another hand*) H. hym...peny] wi*th* a peny aposed hy*m* F. hym] þat hy*m* OC^2. in] of H.

[If] þei sholde [worshipe þerwiþ Cesar þe kyng].
And [he] asked of h[e]m of whom spak þe lettre,
And þe ymage [y]lik[e] þat þ*er*Inne stondeþ. |
"*Cesar*[*i*]*s*", þei seiden, "we seen wel echone." *fol. 6 a*
"*Reddite Cesari*", quod god, "þat *Cesari* bifalleþ,
Et que sunt dei deo or ellis ye don ille."
For riȝtfully reson sholde rule yow alle,
And kynde wit be wardeyn youre welþe to kepe
And tutour of youre tresor, and take it yow at nede;
For housbondrie and h[e] holden togidres.'
Thanne I frayned hire faire for hym þ*at* [hire] made,
'Th[e] dongeon in þe dale þ*at* dredful is of siȝte—
What may it [by]meene, madame, I [þee] biseche?'
'That is þe castel of care; whoso comþ þ*er*Inne
May banne þ*at* he born was to bodi or to soule.
TherInne wonyeþ a [wye] þ*at* wrong is yhote;

48 If] Wheiþ*er* WHmCrGYOC^{2}CLMR FH. þei sholde] xal þei H. sholde] schulden OC^{2}F. worshipe...kyng] woreshyp therw*ith* cesar the kyng G; worchepe w*ith* þat sesar þe kyng H; þerwiþ worshipe þe kyng Cesar WHmCr YOC^{2}CLMRF (þe] *om* MF).
49 he] god WHmCrGYOC^{2}CLMRH; cryst F. asked] *after cancelled* asketh G; asketh Cr. of(1)] þere F; *om* Cr. hem] HmCrGYOC^{2}CLMRFH; hym W. spak] speaketh Cr^{23}. lettre] lettrure Hm.
50–79 *left margin cropped* R.
50 ylike] CrYOC^{2}CL; ylyk HmR; also H; is ylik (is *above line main hand, e erased after* k) M; lyke þat G; was lik WF.
51 *Cesaris...*seiden] Alle þey seyden Cesar F. *Cesaris*] YOC^{2}LR; Cesares WHmCr^1 M; Cesars Cr^{23}; cesar GCH. seiden] seide YCrCLM. wel] well GH; it wel WF; hym wel HmYOC^{2}CLMR; her well Cr^1; here well Cr^{23}.
52 *as two lines divided after deo* H. *Reddite*] *Redde* Cr^{23}. *Cesari*(1)] *ergo que sunt sesaris sesari & sunt dei deo* ȝeld to sesar H. god] cryst F. *Cesari*(2)] cesar C; to Cesar Y; to hy*m* H. bifalleþ] to falleth F; belongeth CrG; longyth H.
53 *Et...deo*] And to god þ*at* longyth to hy*m* H. ye don] do ye G. ille] yuele OC^2.
54 riȝtfully] ryȝtfull HmCrGYOC^{2}CLM RFH.
55 wit] with C. welþe] welthys H; wele C. to] for to G. kepe] kype C.
56 and] to Y. take] taken RH. it] it nouȝt (nouȝt *cancelled*) Hm; *om* CrG.
57 For] And OC^2. housbondrie...he] he & husbondrye F. he] Cr^{23}H; heo R; hij WCr^{1}YCLM; hy Hm; þei OGC^2.
58 faire] *om* R. hire(2)] ROC^{2}CLMF (i *over erasure* M); me WHmCrGYH.
59 The] H; Of þe F; That WHmCr GYOC^{2}CLMR. in] & H. dredful is] ys so dirk F. of] to F; in M.
60 bymeene] bemene C^{2}Cr^{3}GFH; be to meene WHmCr^{12}YOCLMR. I...biseche] ȝee me telle F. þee] yow WHm CrGYOC^{2}LMRH; yow be C.
61 That] It F. þe] a RH. care] Care q*uod* she F. comþ] come H.
62 May] He may F. þat] *om* F. born] borne borne (e *of* (1) *erased*, (2) *cancelled*) Hm. or] & GOC^{2}H.
63 Ther] For þere F. wye] wight WHm CrGYOC^{2}CLMRFH. yhote] Ihotyd H; Ihite C^2.

Fader of falshede, [he] founded it hymselue.
Adam and Eue he egged to ille,
Counseilled Kaym to killen his broþ*er*,
Iudas he iaped wiþ Iewen siluer
And siþen on an Eller hanged hym [after].
He is lettere of loue, lieþ hem alle;
That trusten on his tresour bitraye[d are] sonnest.'
Thanne hadde I wonder in my wit what wo*m*man it weere
That swiche wise wordes of holy writ shewed,
And [halsede] hire on þe heiȝe name, er she þennes yede,
What she were witterly þat wissed me so faire.
'Holi chirche I am', quod she; 'þow ouȝtest me to knowe.
I vnderfeng þee first and þ[i] feiþ [þee] tauȝte.
[Thow] brouȝtest me borwes my biddyng to [werche],
To louen me leelly while þi lif dureþ.' |
Thanne I [kneled] on my knees and cried hire of g*ra*ce; *fol. 6 b*

64 Fader] He is fadir F. he] HmF; and WCrGYOC^{2}CLMRH. founded] foun*n*dour H. it] *om* FH. hym] hem Hm. selue] seluen CH.
65 Adam] For boþe Adam F. egged] eggyd he*m* F; co*n*ceylid C^{2}.
66–9 *lines om* Hm.
66 Counseilled] And conseld H; ⁊ he conseyled F. killen] kyll CrGY; slen H.
67 Iudas] ⁊ to Iudas F. Iewen] Iewes CrC^{2}R; þe Iewys FGH.
68 an] *om* C. Eller] hyldyr tre H; ellerne tre he F. hanged] to hangy*n* H. after] CrGYC^{2}CLMR; selue after (selue *cancelled*) O; selue WF; seluy*n* H.
69 is] ys a (a *above line same ink*) G. lettere] byttyr H. loue] loue and WCrGYOC^{2}CLMRFH. lieþ] lyethe to (to *above line same ink*) G; bylyȝeþ F.
70 That] þey þat F. trusten] truste CrF. on] in Cr. bitrayed are] bytrayed are GRF (ra *above line same ink* G); bitrayeþ he OCrYCLM; bitrayeth he*m* C^{2}; bitrayeþ he hem W; bytrayeth he hem alle (alle *cancelled*) Hm; he dysseyuyth he*m* H.
71 Thanne] That Cr^{1}. hadde] haddy H. in] of C^{2}. wo*m*man] wo*m*men C^{2}. it] sche HmRF.
72 shewed] me scheued C.
73 And] and y HmCrF. halsede] F; hasked R; asked WHmCrGYOC^{2}CLMH. on] in HmOC^{2}C; of H. þe] *om* H. heiȝe] height Cr. er] ers C. she] heo LMR. yede] wente F; passyd H.
74 she] he R. were] *in margin* H; was GF. witterly] wysely Cr.
75 Holi...she] Q*uo*d she y am holy chirche F. chirche] churce G. she] he R. ouȝtest] askyst H.
76 I] For F. feng] fonged GF. þi] þe thye G; þe WHmCrYC^{2}CLMRF; þee O; *om* H. þee] the HmFH; *om* WCrGYOC^{2}CLMR.
77 Thow] Thou CrGFH; and thu HmOC^{2}; And WYCLM; ::d R. brouȝtest] broust H. biddyng] biddings Cr. werche] fulfille WHmCrGYOC^{2}CLMRFH.
78 To] And to WHmCrGYOC^{2}CLMFH; ::d to R. louen] loue HmCrGYOC^{2}CLMRFH. me leelly] lely me RF. me] *om* CH. leelly] truely C^{2}; dernely H. while] wyle GH; whylys F; þe while WHmCr^{12}YOC^{2}CLMR; þat while Cr^{3}. þi] the CrY. dureþ] dured G; endureth Hm; lestyth (e *corrected from* y *main hand*) H.
79 I kneled] knelyd I H. kneled] courbed WCrGYOC^{2}LMR (*cancelled for* crouched *another hand* G); kurblyd dou*n* F; cowryd Hm; coureed C. my] *om* F. cried...g*ra*ce] g*ra*ce hyr besouth H.

Preide hire pitously [to] preye for my synnes;
And [ek] kenne me kyndely on crist to bileue,
That I my3te werchen his wille þat wro3te me to man.
'Teche me to no tresor, but tel me þis ilke,
How I may saue my soule þat Seint art yholden.'
'Whan alle tresors arn tried treuþe is þe beste;
I do it on *Deus caritas* to deme þe soþe.
It is as dereworþe a drury as deere god hymseluen.
[For] who is trewe of his tonge, telleþ noon ooþ*er*,
Dooþ þe werkes þ*er*wiþ and wilneþ no man ille,
He is a god by þe gospel, a grounde and o lofte,
And [ek] ylik to oure lord by Seint Lukes wordes.
The clerkes þat knowen [it] sholde kennen it aboute
For cristen and vncristen cleymeþ it echone.
Kynges and kny3tes sholde kepen it by reson,
Riden and rappen doun in Reaumes aboute,
And taken *transgressores* and tyen hem faste
Til treuþe hadde ytermyned hire trespas to þe ende.

80 Preide] And preide WHmCrGYOC^{2}CLMRFH. to] HmGRFH; *om* WCrYOC^{2}CLM.
81 ek] also WHmCrGYOC^{2}CLMRFH. kenne me] kende me L; *om* (*a corrector supplies*) M.
82 *line om* RF. werchen] worche OCrC^{2}H.
83 Teche] ⁊ teche F; To teche H. to] *om* H. tel] teche F. þis] þat H; þe F. ilke] soþe F.
84–7 *lines om* H.
84 saue] sauen M. art] are G. yholden] Iholde RF; holden Cr^{23}GY.
85 tresors arn] tresor ys F. tried] CG; Itryed OC^{2}; tried quod she WHmCrYLMF; tried q*uo*d he R. þe] *om* Cr^{1}.
86 deme] demen HmF; deme you G.
87 It] þat it RF. as(1)] all so Hm. dereworþe] derworþi C^{2}HmF. seluen] selue RCrC^{2}F.
88–97, 100 *from* telleþ *over erasure another hand and ink* Hm.
88 For who] Who WCr^{23}; whoso HmCr^{1}GYOC^{2}CLM; He R; he þat F; Q*uo*d sche he þat H. telleþ] and telleþ WHmCrGYOC^{2}CLMRF; ⁊ tellyd H.
89 Dooþ] And dooþ WHmCrYLMRFH; ⁊ do G; And dothy C; And OC^{2}. þe] goode H; *om* F. werkes] werke F. wilneþ] wylleth Cr; wyll GH. ille] no*n* yll H.
90 He is a] Ho is H.
91 *line om* FH. And ek] And WHmCrGYOC^{2}CLMR. ylik] lyke CrGC^{2}. Lukes] luke G.
92 The] *om* H. knowen] knowe CrGRFH; konweth Y. it(1)] H; þis WHmCrGYOC^{2}CLMRF. sholde] schulden HmO; xul H. kennen] kenne HmCrGYOC^{2}CLMFH.
93 *line om* H. cleymeþ it] cleyme heuene F.
94 sholde] schulden HmO. kepen] kepe CrGYC^{2}CLRFH.
95 Riden] Ryde H; and ryden GF. rappen] rappe GLRF; rapen CrC; rape H; repen Y. doun] adowne GOC^{2}R.
96 taken] take GOC^{2}H. *transgressores*] trangressores LCr^{23}; trespacers G. tyen] tye CrH.
97 hadde] haue H; *om* Cr. ytermyned] t*er*myned GHmCr; dete*r*myned F; termydyd H. hire] hys G. þe] *om* F.

[For Dauid in hise dayes dubbed kny3tes,
Dide hem sweren on hir swerd to s*er*uen truþe eu*er*e.
[That] is [þe] p*ro*fession apertli þat apendeþ to kny3tes,
And nau3t to fasten o friday in fyue score wynter,
But holden wiþ hym and w*ith* here þat [asken þe] truþe,
And neu*er*e leue hem for loue ne lacchynge of [yiftes];|
And whoso passe[þ] þat point [is] Apostata in [his] ordre.
[And] crist, kyngene kyng, kny3ted ten,
Cherubyn and Seraphyn, swiche seuene ⁊ [anoþer];
Yaf hem my3t in his maiestee, þe murier hem þou3te,
And ouer his meynee made hem Archangeles; |
Tau3te hem [þoru3] þe Trinitee [þe] treuþe to knowe: *fol. 7 a*
To be buxom at his biddyng, he bad hem nou3t ellis.
Lucifer wiþ legions lerned it in heuene
[And was þe louelokest of li3t after oure lord
Til] he brak buxomnesse; his blisse gan he tyne

98, 99 *copied after* 103 WHmCrGYOC^{2}CLMRFH; *see above*, p. 104.
98 dubbed] dobbes Y; doubbed the (the *same hand above cancelled* thy) G; thus dubbede his Hm.
99 Dide] And dide WHmCrGYOC^{2}CLMRFH. sweren] swere HmCrGYOC^{2}CLMRFH. hir] his HmGH; a F. swerd] swerdes R. to] *om* Y. seruen] s*er*ue HmCrGYOC^{2}CLMRFH.
100–3 *copied after* 97 WHmCrGYOC^{2}CLMRFH.
100 That is þe] ⁊ þat is þe HmCrYOC^{2}CLMRF; And þat is WG; þat H. apertli] ap*er*ly C; p*ro*perly F. þat] *om* H. to] for CLR. kny3tes] kyng*es* H.
101 to] *om* H. fasten] fast CrGH. wynter] wynters G.
102 But] And H. holden] hold CrGFH. and] or G; er F. þat...þe] ⁊ so wolde F. asken þe] asketh þe G; wolden alle WHmCrYOC^{2}CLMR; wold al H.
103 And] Ne RF. leue] leuen Hm. hem] *om* H. for] for to Hm. ne] G; ne for WHmCrYOC^{2}CLMRFH. lacchynge] lakkyng HmCrC^{2}H. yiftes] siluer WHmCrGYOC^{2}CLMRFH.
104 so] þ*at* F. passeþ] passed WHmCrGYOC^{2}CLMRFH. þat] þe OC^2. is] YOC^{2}M; was WHmCrGCLRH; *om* F. in...ordre] was holde F. his] hys H; þe WHmCr^{12}GYOC^{2}CLM; þ*at* Cr^3; þa:: R.
105 And] But WHmCrGYOC^{2}CLMRFH. kyngene kyng] kyng of kyngis CrG; kene kyng H; kny3ted kyng C^2. kny3ted] made knyghtes Cr. ten] ten oþere F.
106 *line om* F. swiche] ⁊ sweche H. ⁊] *om* H. anoþer] another Cr^{23}GYOC^{2}CLM (*same hand after cancelled* other G); oþere WHmCr^{1}RH.
107 Yaf] And yaf WHmCrGYOC^{2}CLMRFH. my3t] *om* H. in] of F. his] *om* C^2.
108 his] hys G; his meene WHmCrYOC^{2}CLMRFH. meynee] mey*nn*ge C. made] he made FH. hem] hem his Y; *om* H.
109 Tau3te] Thau3te YC; ⁊ tawhte FH. hem] *om* Cr. þoru3] by WHmCrGYOC^{2}CLMRH; of F. þe(2)] the G; *om* WHmCrYOC^{2}CLMRFH. to] for to GH.
110 *line om* H. To] And RF.
111 Lucifer] þan Lucyfer F. lerned] leryd H. heuene] helle F.
112 *not in* WHmCrGYOC^{2}CLMRFH.
113–40 *left margin cropped* R.
113 Til] RF; But for WHmCrGYOC^{2}CLMH. his] þa*n* F. gan] can CrG.

And fel fro þat felawshipe in a fendes liknesse
Into a deep derk helle to dwelle þ*ere* for eu*ere*;
And mo þousandes myd hym þan man kouþe nombre
Lopen out wiþ Lucifer in loþliche forme
For þei leueden vpon [Lucifer] þat lyed in þis man*ere*:
Ponam pedem in aquilone & similis ero altissimo.
And alle þ*at* hoped it myȝte be so, noon heuene myȝte hem holde,
But fellen out in fendes liknesse [ful] nyne dayes togideres
Til god of his goodnesse [garte þe heuene to stekie]
And [stable and stynte] and stonden in quiete.
Whan þise wikkede wenten out wonderwise þei fellen,
Som*me* in Eyr, som*me* in erþe, som*me* in helle depe.
Ac Lucifer lowest liþ of hem alle;
For pride þat he putte out his peyne haþ noon ende.
And alle þ*at* werchen w*ith* wrong wende þei shulle

114 þat] the HmF. in a] into a HmY; into þe F.
115 a] þe FH. deep derk] dyrk depe H; derke F. þ*ere*] þ*er*inne F.
116 þousandes] þowsende F. myd] wyth HmCrGYOC^{2}CLMRFH. man] ony man F; men GH. kouþe] can F.
117 *line om* H. out] dou*n* F. in] in a F; in or of *above line with caret main hand* C^{2}.
118 *line om* C. þei] these Cr. leueden] leued C^{2}; lyueden G; belevede F. vpon] on FH. Lucifer] lucyfer F; hym WHmCrGYOC^{2}LMRH. lyed...man*ere*] lord hym-selue made F. lyed] lyȝede hem Hm. in] on Cr. man*ere*] matyr H.
119 *line om* F. *pedem*] *pedem meum* GOC^{2}; *sedem meam* H. *in*] *ad* H. *&...altissimo*] *&c* R.
120 hoped] hopede*n* OH. noon] *om* F. myȝte] ne myghte F. hem holde] holdy*n* H.
121 fellen] fell CrGH. out] dou*n* H. in... liknesse] foule feendis F. ful nyne] nyne WHmCrGYOC^{2}CLMRFH. togideres] complet F.
122, 123 garte...stekie (122b), stable... stynte (123a) *transposed* WHmCrGYOC^{2}CLMRFH.
122 garte þe] made FH. to] be F; *om* C^{2}. stekie] stekþe C^{2}; steke ageyn F; spere H.
123 stable] gan stable CrGYOC^{2}CLRF; ga*n* stablen HM (n *suspension added to* stable *another ink* M); gan hem stable Hm; gan stablisse W. and(1)] he*m* to F. stonden] stonde HmCrH.
124 *line om* H. Whan] But whan F. þise] þo F; the Cr^{23}. wenten] went CrGYC^{2}CLMR. wonderwise] YOC^{2}CLMRF; in wonder wise WHmCr; wondrefullyche G. fellen] fell Cr.
125 Som*me*] But so*mme* fel H. Eyr] Hm CrGL; þe Eyr WCH; erthe YR; þe erþe OC^{2}MF. erþe] þe erthe C; eyre R; the eir YOC^{2}MF. so*mme*(2)] some G; and so*mme* WHmCrYOC^{2}CLMRFH. in(3)] i*n* þe F.
126 Ac] butt GF; And CrC^{2}CH. Lucifer ...liþ] in helle lyþ lucyfer lowest F. lowest liþ] lyth lowest there Hm. lowest] ȝet lowest H. liþ] lith YGOC^{2}CLMRH; liþ yet WCr.
127 he] he*m* H. putte] puttede OC^{2}; pult CrL; pelt R. out] forth Y. peyne] p*r*ide H. haþ] had Cr^{23}; hath ȝet H.
128 þ*at*] *om* C. werchen...wrong] after wrong wirchen F. werchen] worche L HmCrRH. wende] wenden HmYOCL MF. shulle] shullen M.

After hir deþ day and dwelle *with* þat sherewe.
[Ac] þo þ*at* werche wel as holy writ telleþ,
And enden, as I er seide, in truþe þat is þe beste,
Mowe be siker þ*at* hire soul[e] sh[a]l wende to heuene
Ther Treuþe is in Trinitee and troneþ hem alle.
Forþi I seye, as I seyde er, by si3te of þise textes:
Whan alle tresors arn tried truþe is þe beste.
Lereþ it þ[us] lewed men, for lettred it knoweþ,
That Treuþe is tresor þe trieste on erþe.'
'Yet haue I no kynde knowyng', quod I, 'ye mote kenne me bettre |
By what craft in my cors it comseþ, and where.' *fol. 7 b*
'Thow doted daffe!' quod she, 'dulle are þi wittes.
To litel latyn þow lernedest, leode, in þi youþe:
Heu michi quia sterilem duxi vitam Iuuenilem.
It is a kynde knowyng þat kenneþ in þyn herte

129 deþ day] dede day Y; day deth (*correct order noted*) O. and] thider and Hm; to RFH. dwelle] dwellen HmF.
130 *line om* H. Ac] HmYOLM; ::c R; butt G; And WCrC^{2}CF. werche wel] wel wirchen F. werche] worchen GHm OC^{2}CM. writ] chirche C^{2}. telleþ] hem techeþ F.
131 And] þey F; But þei þ*at* H. enden] end Cr. I] *om* F. er seide] seyde ere H. er] here G; oer R; erst OC^{2}. in] ⁊ C^{2}. þat is] for F. þe] *om* YOC^{2}MH.
132 Mowe] þey mowe F; man (*corrected to* may *another ink*) Hm. þat] of H. soule] YOC^{2}CLMRF (*final* s *added another ink* M); soules WHmCrGH. shal] CrGYOC^{2} CLMRF; shul WHm; to H. wende] wenden M; sty3en *in* F. heuene] blys H.
133 Treuþe] *om* Y. is] sytt Hm. in] *in* þe H; *with* þe F. and] for to R; þ*at* shal F; *om* G. troneþ] troweth Cr; trowyt H; coroned G; saue R; saven F. hem alle] full fayre G.
134 seye] sey3 3yt F; seyd G. er] *om* G. by] by þe Y. si3te of] *om* RF. þise] þe same F. textes] texte C.
135 *line om* OC^{2}. tried] ytried YCLR. truþe] than treuthe YM.
136 *line om* H. Lereþ] Lere F; Lerne CrG. it(1)] on HmCr; *om* GRF. þus] this Hm CrCLR; þise WYOC^{2}; thys ye GF; ye (*over erasure*) M. it(2)] men it WHmCr GYOC^{2}LMRF; men ne C. knoweþ] knowe YM.
137 *line om* H. is] ys þe fayrest F. þe ⁊ F; *om* GM. trieste] triedest Cr^{23}GM; tristest F. on] vpon Hm; In G.
138 Yet...I(1)] I haue CrF. I(1)] *om* R. quod I] *om* HmGH. ye mote] yet mot ye YGOC^{2}CLM; 3ette mote I R; y coueyte F; 3yt Hm. kenne me] me ke*n* Cr; lerne RF.
139 craft] *om* H. cors] crops Cr^{3}. comseþ] may come H.
140 Thow] A þou F. doted] dodid C^{2}; dotest CrF. daffe] dafte G; *om* F. dulle] to dulle F; full dull Hm.
I 141–II 40 defective R; *see above*, p. 12.
141 To] *om* G. litel] lyte Hm; tel Cr. lernedest] lernyst H; lerdiste C^{2}. leode] lewde C^{2}; lewyd (*over erasure another hand*) Hm; *om* H. youþe] thougthe C.
141α *line om* H. *quia*] *qui* Hm; *quod* F.
142 It] þat F. þat] quod she þat WHm GYOC^{2}FH; q*uod* he þat CCrLM (s *above line before* he M). kenneþ] knoweth Cr^{23}; comeþ FGH. þyn] þe Cr^{1}.

For to louen þi lord leuere þan þiselue.
No dedly synne to do, deye þeiȝ þow sholdest,
This I trowe be truþe; who kan teche þee bettre,
Loke þow suffre hym to seye and siþen lere it after.
[For þus witnesseþ his word; werche þow þerafter].
For truþe telleþ þ*at* loue is triacle of heuene:
May no synne be on hym seene þat vseþ þat spice,
And alle hise werkes he wrouȝte w*ith* loue as hym liste;
And lered it Moyses for þe leueste þyng and moost lik to heuene,
And [ek] þe pl[ante] of pees, moost p*re*cious of v*er*tues.
For heuene myȝte nat holden it, [so heuy it semed],
Til it hadde of þe erþe [y]eten [hitselue].
And whan it hadde of þis fold flessh and blood taken
Was neu*er*e leef vpon lynde lighter þerafter,
And portatif and persaunt as þe point of a nedle
That myȝte noon Armure it lette ne none heiȝe walles.
Forþi is loue ledere of þe lordes folk of heuene
And a meene, as þe Mair is, bitwene þe [commune] ⁊ þe [kyng];
Right so is loue a ledere and þe lawe shapeþ;

143 louen] loue CrGYOC^{2}CLMFH. þi(1)] the Cr^3. leuere] lerne Hm. selue] seluen YOCM.
144 No] ⁊ non F. to] that thow Y; *om* F.
145 *line om* H. be] by C; is good F. bettre] bette O.
146 *line om* H. lere] lerne HmCrC^{2}F (*over erasure* Hm); here C. after] soone F.
147 YOC^{2}CLMF; *line om* WHmCrGH; *here in the spelling of* W. werche] worcheth L.
148 þ*at*] þe H; to C^2. of] in YOC^2; for Cr. heuene] sinne Cr.
149 May no] þere may F. be on hym] on hy*m* be H. vseþ...spice] that spyce vseþ F.
150–8 *lines om* H.
150 And] *om* F. alle] *om* G. hise] this C. he] be F. as...liste] at his lykyng F.
151 lered] lerned HmCrOF; lerne C^2. it] it to F. þe] *om* OC^{2}F. leueste þyng] leve F. and...heuene] of all Cr. to] *in* OC^2.
152 ek] also WHmCrGYOC^{2}CLMF. þe] *om* CF. plante] plant Cr; plente HmGOC^{2}LF; plentee WC; pleente M; planetes Y. moost] ys moost F.
153 holden] hold CrOC^{2}F. so...semed] it was so heuy of hymself WHmCrGYOC^{2}CLM; so was it hevy hy*m*selue F.
154 yeten] LG; yoten Cr; yhetyn al F; eten WHmYOC^{2}M; heten C. hitselue] it selue Cr; his fille WGYOC^{2}CLMF; his fulle Hm.
155 it] he Y. þis fold] ma*n*hode F. þis] þe OC^2. fold] food Hm. taken] take F; *om* OC^2.
156 lynde] lende C^2.
157 *line om* F. persaunt] peysand Hm.
158 That] þer F. lette] lete C.
159 Forþi] for this Hm; þ*er*fore F; Þer H. is loue] loue is the Cr^{23}. is] his C^2. þe] our H. folk] loue Cr^{23}. of(2)] *in* H.
160 a...is] as þe Meyȝ*re* is meene F. þe(1)] a H. is] *om* G. commune...kyng] kyng ⁊ þe co*m*mune WHmGYCLMH; king ⁊ the co*m*mons CrOC^2; kyng ⁊ comonys F.
161 so] *om* C^2. is loue] loue ys G. a] *om* H.

Vpon man for hise mysdedes þe m*er*cyment he taxeþ.
And for to knowen it kyndely, it comseþ by myght,
And in þe herte þ*ere* is þe heed and þe heiȝe welle.
For in kynde knowynge in herte þer [comseþ a myȝt],
And þat falleþ to þe fader þat formed vs alle,
Loked on vs wiþ loue and leet his sone dye |
Mekely for oure mysdedes to amenden vs alle. *fol.* 8 *a*
And yet wolde he hem no wo þat wrouȝte hym þat peyne,
But mekely wiþ mouþe mercy [he] bisouȝte
To haue pite [on] þat peple þat peyned hym to deþe.
Here myȝtow sen ensample[s] in hymself oone
That he was myȝtful and meke and m*er*cy gan graunte
To hem þat hengen hym heiȝ and his herte þirled.
Forþi I rede [þe] riche, haueþ ruþe [on] þe pouere;
Thouȝ ye be myȝt[y] to mote beeþ meke [of] youre werkes,
For þe same mesur[e] þat ye mete, amys ouþ*er* ellis,

162 man] a man HmC. dedes] dede H. þe] ꝥ F; *om* H. m*er*cyment] amercyme*n*t Hm; m*er*cimentȝ M. taxeþ] askeþ FH.
163–70 *lines om* H.
163 And] *om* G. knowen] knowe Cr GYOC^{2}CLMF. it(1)] loue G. comseþ] cometh YCr. myght] nyght C.
164 þe(1)] þy*n* F. þ*ere*] *om* GF. þe(2, 3)] they G. heiȝe] hight Cr^{3}. welle] wyll Cr.
165 in(1)] of Cr. in(2)] off G. þer] *om* G. comseþ a myȝt] begynnyth a myght G; a myȝt bigynneþ WCrYOC^{2}CLM; myȝt bygynneth HmF.
166 vs] faire vs F; you Cr^{23}.
167 Loked] He looked CrF. and] whan he F.
168 Mekely] Mekel C. amenden] amende HmCrGYOC^{2}CLM.
169 And] *om* G. hem] *om* F. þat(1)] to þo þ*at* F. wrouȝte] wrouȝten HmOC^{2}. þat(2)] *om* F.
170 wiþ] bi OC^{2}. he] HmCrGYOC^{2} CLMF; *om* W.
171 To] ȝet loue mad cryst to H. on] HmCrGOC^{2}MFH; of WYCL. þat peple] he*m* H. þat(1)] the GF. peyned] pynyd HmMF.
172 myȝtow] myghtestow YGOC^{2}C; might you Cr. sen] se in Cr^{23}. ensamples] HmYOC^{2}LM; examples Cr^{12}; ensample WGCF; example Cr^{3}H. hym] þi*n* H; *om* Cr. self] seluen OC^{2}. oone] euene H.
173 myȝtful] myghty G; mercyful H. and(2)] þ*at* Cr. gan] can Cr.
174 hem þat] hy*m* qwa*n* he H. hengen] heng HCr^{1}. hym heiȝ] on height him Cr^{23}. hym] theym G; *om* H. heiȝ] heye G; on heiȝ WHmYOC^{2}CLMFH; on height Cr^{1}. and] þ*at* H. þirled] thyrleden G.
175 Forþi] Þ*er*fore H. þe(1)] F; yow WHmCrGYOC^{2}CLMH. riche] ryche men HmH. haueþ] haue CrGYOC^{2} CFH. ruþe] pety H; m*er*cy F. on] HmCrGC^{2}FH; of WYOCLM.
176 myȝty] myghty GCr; myȝtful WHm YOC^{2}CLMFH. beeþ] be ȝee F. of] G; in WHmCrYOC^{2}CLMFH. youre] *om* F. werkes] werk H; herte F; seluen G. *Here H copies line* 178α.
177 þe] be þe F. mesure] HmCrFH; mesures WGYOC^{2}CLM. þat] *om* GH. mete] meten HmGOC^{2}F. ouþ*er*] or G.

Ye shulle ben weyen þerwiþ whan ye wenden hennes:
Eadem mensura qua mensi fueritis remecietur vobis.
For þou3 ye be trewe of youre tonge and treweliche wynne,
And as chaste as a child þat in chirche wepeþ,
But if ye louen leelly and lene þe pouere,
[Of] swich good as god sent goodliche parteþ,
Ye ne haue na moore merite in masse n[e] in houres
Than Malkyn of hire maydenhede þat no man desireþ.
For Iames þe gentile [Ioyned] in hise bokes
That Feiþ wiþouten feet is [feblere þan nou3t],
And as deed as a dore[nail] but if þe ded[e] folwe:
Fides sine operibus mortua est &c.
Chastite wiþouten charite worþ cheyned in helle;
It is as lewed as a lampe þat no li3t is Inne.
Manye Chapeleyns arn chaste ac charite is aweye;
Are [none hardere] þan hij whan þei ben auaunced,

178 shulle] schullen HmYCLM. weyen] weye HmF. þer] *om* H. wenden] wende HmGYCLM.
178α *copied after line* 176 H. *remecietur*] *aliis remecietur* G.
179 ye] you G. youre] *om* F. wynne] wynnen OC^{2}M; selle F; worch Cr^{23}.
180 as(1)] all so Hm. a] þe F. child] chylyd H. in] in þe F. chirche] kerke C. wepeþ] lernyth G.
181 But if] But M; & but F. louen] loue CrGOC^{2}MFH. leelly] 3oure neyhebore F. lene] leue Cr^{13}; leene or gyve F; londe to H.
182 Of swich] Of swiche F; Swich WHmCrGYOC^{2}CLM; And scheche H. good] goodis FH. sent] hat sent H; yow sent WHmCrYOC^{2}CLMF; sendyth you G. goodliche] treuly H. parteþ] parte Cr; departeth HmG; do partyth H; with hem 3e parte F.
183 Ye] You Cr. ne(1)] *om* CrGMFH. moore] *om* C. merite] mede H. in(*both*)] of FH. ne(2)] HmGYOC^{2}CLMF; nor WCr; nyn H.
184 no man] alle men F. desireþ] desyren F; desyryd H. *Here* H *copies line* 187α.
185 þe gentile] þat Ientyl man F. Ioyned] Iugged WHmCrGYOC^{2}CLMFH. hise] *om* H.
186 outen] owte CrGCL. feet] fait Y; fewte F; þe feet WCrOC^{2}CLM (þe *above line* M); dede GH; the werk (werk *over erasure*) Hm. feblere...nou3t] wersse þan nouth H; ri3t noþyng worþi WHmYOC^{2}CLM; right nothing worth Cr; nothyng worthy GF.
187 And] But F. as(1)] all so H; *om* GH. as(2)] *om* C. a] *om* CrC^{2}F. nail] nayle GH; tree WHmCrYOC^{2}CLMF. but if] wythoute G. þe] *by correction* M; thy C; *om* FH. dede] G; dedes WHmCrYOC^{2}CLMFH. folwe] folewen OC^{2}; sewen F.
187α *copied after line* 184 H. &c] *apostolus Iacobus* H; *om* HmCr^{3}OC^{2}F.
188 Chastite] for chastyte GM; Forþi chastite WHmCrYOC^{2}CLF; Þerfore chastyte H. outen] oute YCr^{23}C^{2}CLM; ought Cr^{1}. worþ] worthi Cr; *in* H. cheyned] sheued G; chynyd H; cheines Cr.
189 It is] And H. as(1)] all so Hm; *om* F. a] þe F. lampe] lawpe C^{2}.
190 Manye] Fele F. Chapeleyns arn] chapeleyn is H. ac] but GFH; and CrC^{2}C; ne M.
191 Are] þere ben F. none] non GF; non men H; no men WHmCrOC^{2}LM; no man YC (e *above* a *another script* Y). hardere] herder G; Auarouser WHmYOC^{2}CLMH; averouserere F; auariciouser Cr. þan] *om* H. hij] they HmCrGOC^{2}F; *om* H. auaunced] auaumsed Hm.

Vnkynde to hire kyn and to alle cristene,
Chewen hire charite and chiden after moore.
Swich chastite wiþouten charite worþ cheyned in helle. |
[Ye] curatours [þat] kepen [yow] clene of [youre] bod[y], *fol.* 8 *b*
[Ye] ben acombred wiþ coueitise; [ye] konne noȝt [out crepe],
So harde haþ Auarice yhasped [yow] togideres.
[Th]at is no truþe of þe Trinite but tricherie of helle,
And lernynge to lewed men þe latter to deele.
Fo[r] þise [ben wordes] writen in þe [euaungelie]:
"*Date ⁊ dabitur vobis*, for I deele yow alle."
[Th]at is þe lok of loue [þat] leteþ out my gr*a*ce
To conforten þe carefulle acombred wiþ synne.
Loue is leche of lif and next oure lord selue,
And also þe graiþe gate þat goþ into heuene.

192 Vnkynde] ⁊ vnkyȝnde F. kyn] kynde Y. cristene] cr*i*stene peple F.
193 Chewen] they chewen GF; schewen Hm; And schewen C^{2}; þei schewe H.
194 *line om* Cr^{3}. outen] out Cr^{12}GC^{2}C. worþ] worthie Cr^{12}. cheyned] sheued G; chaynes Cr^{12}.
195 Ye] Manye WHmCrGYOC^{2}CLMH; Fele F. curatours] creaturs YH. þat kepen] kepen WHmGYOC^{2}CLM; kepe CrF; arn H. yow] hem WHmCrGYOC^{2}CLM; hemself F; *om* H. youre body] hire bodies WHmCrGYOC^{2}CLMFH.
196 Ye] ȝet H; Thei WCrGYOC^{2}CLM; But þey F; and Hm. ben] be þei H. acombred] acubrid F; encombred Hm. coueitise] couytous G. ye] þei WHmCrYOC^{2}CLMF; ⁊ GH. noȝt] *om* F. out crepe] F; crepe out H; crye ovte G; doon it from hem WCrYOC^{2}CLM; put it away Hm.
197 yhasped] haspede HmCr; happyd H. yow] hem WHmCrGYOC^{2}CLMFH.
198 That] And þat WHmCrGYOC^{2}CLMF; And H. no] not F; in OC^{2} (*above line main hand* O). tricherie] tresure H.
199 lernynge] lernyg H; lerned Y. to(2)] GFH; for to WHmCrYOC^{2}CLM. deele] delen G; leve synne F.
200 For] C^{2}; Forþi WHmCrGYOCLMF; Þerfore H. þise...wordes] ben þese wordys H; þise wordes ben WHmCrGYOC^{2}CLMF. writen] ywr*e*te weel F. þe] the holy Hm. euaungelie] gospel WHmCrGYOC^{2}CLMFH.
201 *as two lines divided after date* H. *vobis*] *vobis et quod gratys accepistis gratis date* ȝeuyth ⁊ I xal ȝeue ȝow H. deele] dele w*i*th F; ȝeue H.
202 That] Cr; And þat WHmYOC^{2}CLM; and ⁊ that G; For þat H; For *date* F. lok] look F; bok H. loue] lyf H. þat] that CrGMFH; and WHmYOC^{2}CL. leteþ] ledyt H.
203 conforten] conforte HmGYOC^{2}CLMFH. acombred] þ*a*t is acu*m*bred F; ⁊ comeryd H. wiþ] of H.
204 Loue] For love F. selue] seluen OC^{2}M; hymselue HmH; hymseluen GY; i*n* heuene F.
205 also] it ys F. graiþe] grette C^{2}; grete Hm; gr*a*cyous H; *om* Cr^{3}. goþ] good F. heuene] blysse F.

Forþi I seye as I seide er by [si3te of þise] textes:
Whan alle tresors ben tried treuþe is þe beste.
Now haue I told þee what truþe is, þ*a*t no tresor is bettre,
I may no lenger lenge; now loke þee oure lord.'

206 Forþi] Þ*er*fore H. er] here Hm; erst OC². si3te of] syght off GH; *om* WHmCr YOC²CLMF. þise] thes HmG; þe WCr YCLMFH; þe trewe OC².
207 tresors ben] tresor is F. tried] ytried YOC²CL. treuþe] 3yt trewþe F.
208 Now] So Cr. haue I] I haue G. þee] you Cr. þ*at*...bettre] tak it if þ*o*u lyke F. þ*a*t] & G; *om* H. is] *om* G.
209 lenge] lengþe C²; leue (ue *over erasure*) Hm; stonde H. now] þee wiþ now WCr YOC²CLM; the whyþ now Hm; þe w*ith* F; w*ith* þe H; but G. loke...lord] oure lord looke þe euere F. þee] ye Cr.

II

YEt [kneled I] on my knees and cried hire of gr*a*ce,
And seide 'm*er*cy, madame, for Marie loue of heuene
That bar þ[e] blis[sed] barn þat bouȝte vs on þe Rode,
Kenne me by som craft to knowe þe false'.
'Loke [o]n þi left half, and lo where he stondeþ,
Boþe Fals and Fauel and hi[s]e feeres manye.'
I loked on my left half as þe lady me tauȝte
And was war of a wo*m*man [wonder]liche ycloþed,
Purfiled wiþ Pelure, þe [pureste on] erþe,
Ycorouned [in] a coroune, þe kyng haþ noon bettre.
Fetisliche hire fyngres were fretted *with* gold wyr
And þ*er*on [riche] Rubies as rede as any gleede, |
And Diamaundes of derrest pris and double man*ere*
    Saphires, *fol. 9 a*
Orientals and Ewages enuenymes to destroye.

1 YEt...I] I Covrbet ȝyt F. kneled I] courbed I G; I courbed WHmCrYOC^{2} LM; I courred CH. cried] gradd F; pr*a*yd H.
2 seide m*er*cy] mercy seyd H. Marie] maris Cr; mercy G.
3 þe blissed] þ*at* blessed C^{2}; þe blisful Cr^{23}; þat blisful WHmCr^{1}GYOCLMFH. barn] barou*n* H. þe(2)] *om* GF.
4 Kenne] & kenne F; lerne Y. craft] craf H. to] for to GOC^{2}. knowe] knowen M; kenne G.
5 on] FH; vpon WHmCrGYOC^{2}CLM. half] hand H. and] q*uod* she & F; *om* GH. lo] loke H; se F. he] sche OC^{2}; þei H. stondeþ] stonde H.
6 Fals] fauel M. Fauel] fauinell G; fals M. hise...manye] many of her ferys H. hise] hire WHmCrGYOC^{2}CLMF.
7 half] hand H. me] *om* F. tauȝte] thaughte YC.
8 And] I H. wonderliche] wonderslyche G; was worcheply F; worþiliche WHmCrYOC^{2}CLMH. ycloþed] clothed HmCrGF; i*n* clothys H.
9 Purfiled] & purfylyd F. Pelure] plesure Cr^{12}. pureste on] purest on FH; fyneste vpon WHmCr^{13}GYOC^{2}CLM; fyuest vpon Cr^{2}.
10 Ycorouned] coroned GHmCrC^{2}H; & crowned she was F. in] wiþ WHmCrGYOC^{2}CLMFH. coroune] crowne of golde (e(2) *erased*) Hm. bettre] bitter Cr^{1}.
11 *line om* F. Fetisliche] Feytlyche G. were] weren HmOC^{2}M. fretted] fettred COC^{2}. gold wyr] rynge*s* G. gold] gol C; *om* Hm.
12 And...riche] & set abowhte *with* F. riche] rede WHmCrGYOC^{2}CLMH. Rubies] rebens C^{2}. as(1)] all so Hm.
13 And] & *with* F. Diamaundes] a dyamand Hm. of] þe F. pris] *om* F. man*ere*] man*er* of H; dyu*er*se F.
14 Ewages] ewage H; ewers Hm. enuenymes] venemis CrMH; enemyes F.

Hire Robe was ful riche, of reed scarlet engreyned,
Wiþ Ribanes of reed gold and of riche stones.
Hire array me rauysshed; swich richesse sauȝ I neu*ere*.
I hadde wonder what she was and whos wif she were.
'What is þis wo*m*man', quod I, 'so worþili atired?'
'That is Mede þe mayde, haþ noyed me ful ofte,
And ylakked my lemman þat leautee is hoten,
And bilowen h[ym] to lordes þat lawes han to kepe.
In þe popes Paleis she is pryuee as myselue,
But sooþnesse wolde noȝt so for she is a Bastard.
For Fals was hire fader þat haþ a fikel tonge
And neu*ere* sooþ seide siþen he com to erþe,
And Mede is man*er*ed after hym [as men of] kynde [carpeþ]:
Qualis pater talis filius: Bon[*a*] *arbor bonum fructum facit.*
I ouȝte ben hyer*e* þan she; I kam of a bettre.
My fader þe grete god is and ground of alle g*ra*ces,
Oo god wiþouten gynnyng, and I his goode douȝter;
And haþ yeuen me mercy to marie wiþ myselue,

15 ful] of C^2; *om* H. of] as H. engreyned] greynede YF.
16 Ribanes] rybane Hm; rubies Y. of(2)] ful of F.
18 what] that Hm. she(2)] it Hm. whos] *by correction* Y.
19 is...wo*m*man] wo*m*man ys þis F. worþili] wondurly M; rychely is H. atired] ytyred F.
20 That] She F. þe] þat H. mayde] mayden GOC^2MH. haþ] hath G; quod she haþ $WHmCrYOC^2CLMF$; q*uod* sche þat hat H. noyed] anoyed Y. ful ofte] most H.
21 And] ⁊ often F. ylakked] lakked GCrFH. leautee] leaut HmC (e(2) *added* Hm). hoten] hote Cr^1; ihote $Cr^{23}FH$.
22 bilowen] bilowe CrH; belyed (*altered to* alyed) G; she is lowly F. hym] hire $WHmCrGYOC^2CLMH$; *om* F. to(1)] *altered to* with G. lawes] lawe H. han] hathes C; har C^2. kepe] kepe*n* Cr^{23}.
23 In] ⁊ in F. she] *om* Y. is] is as F. selue] serue Y.
24 wolde] so wolde (so *cancelled*) Hm. noȝt] no F. is a] bor*e* F.
25 þat] ⁊ H. haþ] hadde YOC^2.
26 sooþ seide] seyd soth H. to] to þe M; til Y; on FHm.
27 man*er*ed] maried Cr. as...carpeþ] riȝt as kynde askeþ $WHmCrGYOC^2CLMF$; as kende askyth H.
27α *line om* H. *Bona*] $HmCrGYOC^2C$; *Bonus* WLM; *Iterum Bonus* F. *bonum...facit*] *bonus fructus habet Malus arbor malus fructus profert* F.
28 ben] to ben MH. hyer*e*] herre CL; herrer HmF. I(2)] for I H. kam] am F. a] the GH; *om* C. bettre] bettre roote F.
29 þe] *om* FH. and] *om* F. ground] groundre G. of] of vs H. g*ra*ces] grace $HmCr^{23}C^2C$ (*over erasure another ink* Hm); *om* H.
30 Oo] he is F. outen] oute CrGL. gynnyng] begynnyng $GCrC^2H$. I] y am F; *om* H. his] *om* C. goode] owne G; dere H.
31 haþ] haue H; he F. yeuen] yue Y; ȝoue LMH; geue C; gaf F. me] *om* GM (*corrector supplies* M). marie] maryen F. my] me OH. selue] seluen G.

And what man be m*er*ciful and leelly me loue
Shal be my lord and I his leef in þe heiȝe heuene.
And what man takeþ Mede, myn heed dar I legge,
That he shal lese for hire loue a l[i]ppe of *Caritatis*.
How construeþ David þe kyng of men þat [caccheþ] Mede,
And men of þis moolde þat mayntenep truþe,
And how ye shul saue yourself? þe Sauter bereþ witnesse: |
Domine quis habitabit in tabernaculo tuo &c. *fol. 9 b*
And now worþ þis Mede ymaried [t]o a mansed sherewe,
To oon fals fikel-tonge, a fendes biyete.
Fauel þoruȝ his faire speche haþ þis folk enchaunted,
And al is lieres ledynge þ*at* [lady] is þus ywedded.
Tomorwe worþ ymaked þe maydenes bridale;
[There] myȝtow witen if þow wilt whiche þei ben alle
That longen to þat lordshipe, þe lasse and þe moore.
Knowe hem þ*ere* if þow kanst and kepe [þee from hem alle],

32 me] *om* H. loue] loueþ HmCrOC^2 (þ *another ink* Hm); honowre F.
33 leef] life Cr; wyf H.
34 myn heed] my lif YOC^{2}M. dar] dary H.
35 hire] his C^2. a] his F. lippe] YCr; lappe WHmOC^{2}CLMFH; lomp G. of] of his Hm; of leall G; ful of F. *Caritatis*] *caritas* C^2; charyte GFH.
36 How] See how F. construeþ] construed GH; *om* F. Dauid þe kyng] kynge Dauyd (e *erased*) M; dauid meneþ F. þat] þe Cr^3. caccheþ Mede] Meede taken F. caccheþ] takeþ WHmYOC^{2}CL; take Cr GMH.
37 And] & of F. of] on Cr^{23}F. moolde] world H. mayntenep] mey*n*teyne GFH.
38 shul] should CrG; *om* H. your] ȝow HmYOC^{2}L. self] seluen OC^2. bereþ witnesse] ȝow techeþ F.
39 *habitabit*] *altered from habitauit* Hm; *tabernaculo*] *tabernaclo* L; taberuaculo Cr^2. &c] *aut quis stabit &c* H; *om* Hm.
40 And] *om* H. worþ þis] shal FH. ymaried] maried CrG; be Maried FH. to] GMFH (*after erasure* M); vnto WHmCr; al to YOC^{2}CL. a] *om* C^2. mansed] *glossed* cursid *main hand* O; manshid F; mased HmC; mauȝed Cr^3; cursid C^2; comeryd H; *om* G. sherewe] *om* OC^2.
41 **Here R resumes.** oon] a H. fikel] fikel of R; & Fykil of F; fykyk H. a] a foul F; and C; & of H. biyete] feere G.
42 þoruȝ] by Cr^{23}. his] hir C; *om* H. faire] fals HmF. haþ] full thyk hath Hm; *om* F. þis] hyr H; *om* Hm. enchaunted] ys enchauntyd F; enhau*n*cyd H.
43 is(1)] his Cr^{1}F. lieres ledynge] eyȝres eggynge F. lady] she WHmCrGYOC^{2}CLMRFH. is þus] shal be F. ywedded] wedded CrGH.
44 To] & to F; The Cr. morwe] morwen C. worþ] shall be C^{2}H; was Cr. ymaked] ymaad HmGYOCLMR; made CrC^{2}H; þe mariage & F. þe] that Hm. maydenes] meyden G; Maydes F; maydesnesse C. bridale] maryage Hm.
45 There] ther GH; And þere WHmCr YOC^{2}CLMRF. myȝtow] myghtest þou GOC^2; may þou F. witen] wite YCrG OC^{2}CLMRFH.
47 Knowe] knowen Hm. hem] hym Cr^{12}. kanst] can H. kepe] kepen R. þee...alle] þow þi tonge WHmCrGMH (þou þi *over erasure* M); wel þi tonge YOC^{2}F; thy tonge CLR.

And lakke hem noȝt but lat hem worþe til leaute be Iustice
And haue power to punysshe hem; þanne put forþ þi reson.
Now I bikenne þee crist', quod she, 'and his clene moder,
And lat no conscience acombre þee for coueitise of Mede.'
Thus lefte me þat lady liggynge aslepe,
And how Mede was ymaried in Metels me þouȝte;
That al þe riche retenaunce þat regneþ with [fals]
Were boden to þe bridale on boþe two sides,
Of alle manere of men, þe meene and þe riche.
To marien þis mayde [was] many m[a]n assembled,
As of knyȝtes and of clerkes and ooþer commune peple,
As Sisours and Somonours, Sherreues and hire clerkes,
Bedelles and baillifs and Brocours of chaffare,
Forgoers and vitaillers and [v]okettes of þe Arches;
I kan noȝt rekene þe route þat ran aboute Mede.
Ac Symonie and Cyuylle and Sisours of courtes
Were moost pryuee with Mede of any men me þouȝte.
Ac Fauel was þe firste þat fette hire out of boure

48 but] *om* H. worþe] worke Cr; do H. leaute] leaut HmC. be] were here Hm.
49 haue] *om* H. punysshe] punysshen YLR; punsche HmFH. þanne] & þan F; þat GC.
50 Now] For Cr. she] he R. clene] dere HmH.
51 lat] þat F; at R. acombre] combre HmG.
52 lefte me] leet mede (et *over erasure another ink*) Hm. liggynge aslepe] lyggen and slepe Hm.
53 how] *om* Hm. ymaried] maried CrG FH. Metels] metyng H.
54 That] And OC^{2}. al þe] al þe alle þe F. retenaunce] retenew F. regneþ] regned F; rennyth H. fals] HmC^{2}H; þe false WCr GYOCLMR; sire false F.
55 Were] Weren OC^{2}MRF. boden] byden G; bede RH; bounden Cr. þe] þis R; þat H; his F. on] faire on F. two] *om* F.
56 *line om* H. meene] men C.
57 marien] marye HmCrGOC^{2}CLMRFH; maryee Y. þis] þat FH; the Cr. mayde] maiden HmGYOC^{2}CLM. was] HmCr GYOC^{2}CLMRH; were W; wheryn F. many] manie a Cr; *om* F. man] HmCr GYOC^{2}CLMRH; men WF. assembled] ensembled R; ensemblyd þere F.
58 As] *om* F. of(2)] *om* YOC^{2}MH. clerkes] clekes H. ooþer] othe Y.
59 As] and Hm; Of FH. and(1)] of F. Sherreues] and scherreves HmFH.
60 Bedelles] Of Bedelis F; And bedelys H. baillifs] baylyfles Cr^{2}. and(2)] ad Y. Brocours] procures Hm. chaffare] chaffares M.
61 Forgoers] Forgowleres F. and(1)] *om* H. and(2)] *om* Cr^{2}G. vokettes] voketys HmYOC^{2}CLMRF; Aduokettes WCrGH. *Here* F *adds a spurious line; see above*, p. 222.
62 rekene] rekkenen M; redily rekne F.
63 Ac] but GFH; And CrC^{2}C. courtes] corut H; contres Hm.
64 Were] weren HmO. men] man H. me þouȝte] þere owte F. me] as me M; *om* R.
65 Ac] But FGH; And CrC^{2}C. fette] sett G. boure] chambre F.

And as a Brocour brouȝte hire to be wiþ fals enioyned.
Whan Symonye and Cyuylle seighe hir boþ*er* wille |
Thei assented for siluer to seye as boþe wolde. *fol.* 10 *a*
Thanne leep liere forþ and seide, 'lo! here a chartre
That Gile wiþ hise grete oþes gaf hem togidere',
And preide Cyuylle to see and Symonye to rede it.
Symonye and Cyuylle stonden forþ boþe
And vnfoldeþ þe feffement that Fals hath ymaked.
[Th]us bigynnen þ[e] gomes [and] greden [wel] heiȝe:
'*Sciant presentes & futuri &c.*
Witeþ and witnesseþ þat wonieþ vpon erþe
That Mede is ymaried moore for hire goodes
Than for any v*er*tue or fairnesse or any free kynde.
Falsnesse is fayn of hire for he woot hire riche;
And Fauel wiþ his fikel speche feffeþ by þis chartre
To be Princes in pride and pouerte to despise,

66 *line om* OC^{2}. as] *om* H. brouȝte] he browhte F. to...fals] *with* falshed to be H. wiþ] *with* þe Y; to Hm. enioyned] Ioynyd HHm.

67 Whan] & whan*n*e F. seighe] sey *cancelled for* seyd to *another hand* G; seyen FHm. hir] here (*altered from* there *another ink*) G. boþ*er*] botherys H; bothe Hm CrF; bethere R; beire CYL; both theire (theire *by corrector over another word*) G. wille] will*es* G.

68 Thei] And RF. assented] assenteden O. seye] seggen R; sei (i *cancelled*) L. wolde] wolden OC^{2}.

69 leep] come þ*er* a H. a] is a H; *om* Cr^{1}. chartre] chatere H.

70–99 *left margin cropped* R.

70 hise] *om* H. gaf] ȝaf HmH.

71 Cyuylle] symonye GH. to(1)] it to F. Symonye] cyuyll GH. to(2)...it] yt redde F.

72 Symonye] Thanne Symonye WHmCr GYOC^{2}CLMRFH. stonden] stond Cr^{1}; stoden YMF; stode H. boþe] both to-gyther Cr.

73 *line om* F. vnfoldeþ] vnfolde CrH; vnfoldeden Hm. þe] that Hm. hath] hadde HmGH. ymaked] maked Hm; ymade Cr; made GC^{2}.

74 *transposed with* 74α H. Thus] And þus WHmCrGYOC^{2}CLMRFH. bigynnen] bygonnen C^{2}; bygu*n*ne F. þe] þo F; þise WHmCrGYOC^{2}CLMRH. gomes] gromes CH (r *added above line* H); gemes Y. and] at R; to WHmCrGYOC^{2}CLM FH. greden] gedren Hm; rede H. wel] ful WHmCrGYOC^{2}CLMRFH. heiȝe] heyght Cr^{3}.

74α *& futuri*] *om* R. *&c*] *quod Ego falcitas &c* H.

75 Witeþ] weteþ wel F. witnesseþ] witnesse CH. þat] al þat Cr. vpon] GFH; vpon þis WCrYOC^{2}CLMR; on this Hm.

76 ymaried] maryed HmCrGOC^{2}CFH. hire] his C^{2}.

77 vertue] vertus C. or(1)] of HmGYOC^{2} CH. or(2)] or for YOC^{2}M; or of H; for Hm. any(2)] *om* H. kynde] kyne C.

78 he...riche] hyr grete ryches H. woot] wooteth Cr.

79 his] *om* H. fikel] Fylke G; fayr H. speche] felaw OC^{2}. by] him by Cr^{1}; hir by Cr^{23}; he*m* by F. þis] hys G.

80 be] be *with* (*with above line another hand*) M. Princes] prynce Cr^{1}; princesse OC^{2}H. in] of F. pouerte] pou*er*t H. to] *om* F.

To bakbite and to bosten and bere fals witnesse,
To scorne and to scolde and sclaundre to make;
Vnbuxome and bolde to breke þe ten hestes;
And þe Erldom of Enuye and [Ire] togideres,
Wiþ þe Chastilet of cheste and chaterynge out of reson,
The Countee of Coueitise and alle þe costes aboute,
That is vsure and Auarice; al I hem graunte
In bargaynes and brocages wiþ þe Burgh of þefte,
[Wiþ] al þe lordshipe of leccherie in lengþe and in brede,
As in werkes and in wordes and waityn[g] w*ith* eiȝes
And in we[n]es and in wisshynges and wiþ ydel þouȝtes
There as wil wolde and werkmanshipe fayleþ.'
Glotonye he [gyueþ] hem ek and grete oþes togidere, |
And al day to drynken at diu*er*se Tau*er*nes, *fol.* 10 *b*
And þ*er*e to Iangle and Iape and Iugge hir euenc*ri*sten,
And in fastynge dayes to frete er ful tyme were.

81 bakbite] bagbyten HmR; backbytours G. and(1)] *om* MH. to bosten] to boste OC[2]H; boste wel F. and(2)] and to HmCr F; to be H. bere] bere*n* CMF.
82 and(1)] *om* H. sclaundre] sklawndres F.
83 Vnbuxome...bolde] ::old and vnbuxu*m* R; ⁊ to be bold ⁊ vnbuxu*m* F. hestes] benfetys H.
84 And] To have F. Ire] wraþe WHmCr GYOC[2]CLMRFH.
85 Chastilet] castyl H. cheste] cleste C; gestes R; Ieestys F; theft H. chaterynge... reson] þe Iangelynge of synne F. reson] tyme R.
86 The] ⁊ al þe F; *cropped* R. Countee] cu*n*tre HCr[1]; Cu*n*tres F; comyte HmC[2]. Coueitise] couetous G. and] w*ith* F. alle] *om* H. þe] *om* Hm.
87 is] y Hm. al...graunte] I grau*n*te he*m* toged*er* H. I] *om* Cr[1]. graunte] gr*a*unted Hm.
88 bargaynes] bargayne Hm; bargany H. and] HmCr[23]GFH; and in WCr[1]YOC[2] CLMR. brocages] brocage HmH. þe] al þe WHmCrGYOC[2]CLMRH; þe bolde F. Burgh] bow H.
89 Wiþ] And WHmCrGYOC[2]CLMFH; ::d R. al] *om* H. in(*both*)] on H.
90 As] *om* HmF; *cropped* R. werkes] werkyngs H; werkynge F. and(1)] *om* FH. in(2)] *added main hand* Y. wordes] speche H. and(2)] YGOC[2]CLMR; and in WHmCr; in FH. waityng] waytyng Hm GF; waitynges WCrYOC[2]LMRH; wattynges C. w*ith*] of HmG. eiȝes] eyȝe H.
91 And in] *cropped* R. And] *om* HmF. wenes] wenyngis F; wendys H; wedes WHmCr[1]GYOC[2]CLM; weddes Cr[23]; wedynges R. and(1)] *om* F. in(2)] *om* Cr[23]YOC[2]MH. and(2)] *om* H. wiþ] in HmF. ydel] alle ydyl H; wast F.
92 *line om* H. wolde] ne wolde YCL (ne *in margin* L). and...fayleþ] werke ne were woo ⁊ drede F. and] ⁊ the Cr; *om* YOC[2] C; *cancelled* L. werkmanshipe] wermanship L.
93 *run together with* 94 Hm. Glotonye... hem] he ȝaf hem Glotonye F. gyueþ] gaf WCrGYOC[2]CLMR; ȝaf HmH. and... togidere] *om* Hm.
94 And...drynken] *om* Hm. drynken] drynke GCrYOC[2]CLMRFH. at] al fele F. diuerse] diu*er*ses Y.
95 Iape] to Iape YCrOC[2]CLMRF. Iugge] iuggen MF. euenc*ri*sten] emc*ri*stene (em *another ink*) Hm.
96 in] on HmG; with R.

And þanne to sitten and soupen til sleep hem assaille,
And breden as Burgh swyn, and bedden hem esily
Til Sleuþe and sleep sliken hise sydes;
And þanne wanhope to awaken h[y]m so wiþ no wil to amende
For he leueþ be lost, þis is [his] laste ende.
'And þei to haue and to holde, and hire heires after,
A dwellynge wiþ þe deuel and dampned be for eu*ere*
Wiþ alle þe [p]urtinaunces of Purgatorie into þe pyne of helle.
Yeldynge for þis þyng at one [yeres ende]
Hire soules to Sathan to suffre w*ith* hym peynes,
And w*ith* hym to wonye [in] wo while god is in heuene.'
In witnesse of which þyng wrong was þe firste,
And Piers þe P*ar*doner of Paulynes doctrine,
Bette þe Bedel of Bokynghamshire,
Reynald þe Reue of Rutland Sokene,
[Munde] þe Millere and many mo oþere:
'In þe date of þe deuel þ[e] dede [is asseled]

97 þanne to] softe F. sitten] sitte CrOC²H. soupen] soupe CrFH; to soupe OC². hem] gy*n* hy*m* F. assaille] afaylyd H.
98 breden] breede H; brede furth Cr; broode hy*m* F. as] as a RF; a Hm. and] *om* C². bedden] bedde FH. hem] hym RF. esily] on a bolstre F.
99 sleep] sleelp O; softe sleep F. sliken] slyke H. hise] her HmCrYMH (? r *over erasure* M).
100 þanne] þat H. to(1)] *om* FH. awaken] awake HmGYOC²CLMRF; wake H. hym] YOC²CLMRF; hem WHmCrGH. so] *om* GH. to(2)] it C. amende] amen*de* hy*m* F; *cropped* R.
101 he] thei HmCrH. leueþ] beleviþ F; beleue H; liuen Cr. be] he be OC²; to be HmGFH; by Cr. lost] yloste R; lust HCr. þis] that CrF. his] R; hir WHmCr GYOC²CLMH; þe F.
102 þei] *om* G. haue] haven F. holde] holden F; helde H. and(2)] & alle F. heires] heyre Cr².
103 A] A derk F; And H. dwellynge] dwelle H. dampned be] be da*m*pned F. dampned] damped Cr¹. be] *om* G. for] fo R.
104 alle] *om* G. þe(1)] *om* F. purtinaunces] purtenaunces LRF; appurtinaunces WCr G; purtynaunce HmYOC²CM; ap*er*ten-ans H. into] to G. pyne] paine CrGH; pyt Hm. of(2)] i*n* O.
105 *run together with* 106 H. Yeldynge... þyng] For þis þyng ȝeldynge F. for... ende] *om* H. for] *om* Hm. þyng] thyg G. yeres ende] YHmCrGOC²CLMRF; dayes tyme W.
106 to(1)] vnto G. Sathan] sathanas HmH. to(2)] and R. peynes] peyne H.
107 wonye] wonyen R. in] Cr²³YOC² CMRFH; w*ith* WHmCr¹GL. wo] peyne H.
108 which] þis RFH. was] is H; *om* C.
110 Bette] & Bette FH. Bokyngham] Bekyngh*a*m Y.
111 Reynald] And reynald HF. of] *om* C². Rutland] rokeland RF.
112 Munde] HmCr²³GOC²LMRH; & Munde F; Mand (? Maud) WYC; Maude Cr¹. and] wyth Cr.
113 þe(1)] *om* HmR. þe(3)] the Y; þis WHmCrGOC²CLMRFH. is asseled] ys aseled HmH; is yseled C; I assele YOL MRF; I ensele WCrG; we asele C².

By siȝte of sire Symonie and Cyuyles leeue.'
Thanne tened hym Theologie whan he þis tale herde,
And seide [to] Cyuyle, 'now sorwe [on þi bokes]
Swic[h] weddyng[e] to werche to wraþe wiþ truþe;
And er þis weddynge be wroȝt wo þee bitide!
For Mede is muliere of Amendes engendred
God *gra*unte[d] to gyue Mede to truþe,
And þow hast gyuen hire to a gilour, now god gyue þee sorwe! |
[The] text telleþ þee noȝt so, Truþe woot þe soþe, *fol.* 11 *a*
For *Dignus est operarius* his hire to haue,
And þow hast fest hire [wiþ] Fals; fy on þi lawe!
For al bi lesynges þow lyuest and lecherouse werkes;
Symonye and þiself shenden holi chirche;
The Notaries and ye noyen þe peple.
Ye shul abiggen boþe, by god þ*a*t me made!
Wel ye witen, wernardes, but if your*e* wit faille,

114 By] Be þe H. and] at R. Cyuyles] Cyuyle Hm.
115 tened] teneth R; was teenyd F; torned C. hym] *om* FH. herde] yherde R.
116 to] HmCrGYOC^{2}CLMRH; to sire F; vnto W. now] *om* HmH. on þi bokes] mote þow haue WHmGYOC^{2}CLMRFH; myght you haue Cr.
117 *line om* Hm. Swich weddynge] Swyche weddinge C^{2}G; Swiche weddynges WCrYOMRFH; Such wendynges LC. werche] make YH.
118 And] Ac O. er] he F. weddynge] weddyngs H. be] haþ F. wroȝt] ywroȝt R. wo...bitide] now god giue þe sorowe Cr^1. þee] hy*m* F.
119 is] ys a Hm; not a (not *above line another ink*) G. muliere] Mulirie O; moliree (*over erasure*) M. of] ⁊ off G. engendred] engendreth YCLR.
120 God] And god WHmCrGYOC^{2}CLMRF; And H. *gra*unted] YOC^{2}CF; grant H; *gra*unteþ WHmCrGLMR. to(2)] vnto G. truþe] a make H.
121 gyuen] gyue C^{2}RFH; ȝouen Hm. now...sorwe] wo the betyde Cr^1. now] *om* GH. god] lord G. gyue] ȝyue Hm; yeue (y *altered from* ȝ) M.
122 The] GYRFH; Thi WHmCrOC^{2}CLM. text] tixit R. þee] me Hm; *om* F. Truþe] god H.
123 *For this line* H *reads* **A** II 86α, 87. *est*] *twice* C. *operarius*] eperarius O. to] for to G.
124 fest] fastned HmCr; feffyd H. wiþ] wyth GF; to WHmCrYOC^{2}CLMRH.
125 al] ab Y. lesynges] leasynge Cr^3. lecherouse] lechores R. werkes] wordys H.
126 Symonye] þan Symonye F. þiself] Cyvyle F. shenden] schend H; scheden C; chydden F.
127 The] thees G; ⁊ seid þe F. noyen] noye Cr; noythis C; anoyȝeth Hm; noyȝe meche H; noyen offt G; foule noyȝhen F.
128 abiggen] abye CrC^{2}FH; byggen G. boþe] it boþe WHmCrGYOC^{2}CLMRFH (it *above line* H). god] hy*m* H. me made] made me CrC^2 (*correct order noted* C^2).
129 witen] wytte CrH. but if] þ*a*t F. wit] wyth H. faille] fayleþ F.

That Fals is fe[ynt]lees and fikel in hise werkes,
And [as] a Bastard ybore of Belsabubbes kynne.
And Mede is muliere, a maiden of goode;
[She] myȝte kisse þe kyng for cosyn and she wolde.
Wercheþ by wisdom and by wit [after];
Ledeþ hire to Londou*n* þ*er*e [lawe] is [yhandled],
If any [lewte] wol loke þei ligge togideres.
And [if þe] Iustic[e] Iugg[e] hire to be Ioyned [wiþ] Fals
Yet be war of [þe] weddynge; for witty is truþe,
[For] Conscience is of his counseil and knoweþ yow echone;
And if he fynde yow in defaute, and w*ith* [fals] holde,
It shal bisitte youre soules [wel] soure at þe laste.'
Herto assenteþ Cyuyle, ac Symonye ne wolde
Til he hadde siluer for his [seles] and [signes of] Notaries.
Thanne fette Fauel forþ floryns ynowe

130 feyntlees] feytles HC; feiþlees WHm CrGYOC^{2}LMRF. fikel] fals R. in] of HmH. hise] her Cr^2; *om* Hm.
131–60 *left margin cropped* R.
131 as] RF; was WHmCrGYOC^{2}CLM; *om* H. ybore] borne CrGH. Belsabubbes] belsabub his Hm; belsabuckis C^2.
132 is] is a CrG; *om* HmOC^2. muliere] moylerie Y. a] ⁊ a FH. maiden] mayde C^{2}FH. goode] god H.
133 She] sche Hm; And WCrGYOC^{2}CL MRFH. kisse] kyssen F. and] if CrH; yf that Hm. she] he RF. wolde] shuld G.
134 Wercheþ] Forþi wercheþ WHm GYOC^{2}CLMRF; Þ*er*fore werkyth H; Therefore worke Cr. wisdom] wyht H. by(2)] wytt by (wytt *cancelled*) G; *om* H. wit] my wyt Cr; witti OC^2; wysdam H. after] also WHmCrGYOC^{2}CLMRH; bothe F.
135 Ledeþ] And ledeþ WHmYOC^{2}CLM RF; And lede HCrG. lawe is] ys ytt G. lawe] YOC^{2}CLRF; þe lawe MH; it WHm Cr. yhandled] yshewed WHmGYOC^2 LRF; ychewed C; shewed CrMH.
136 lewte] lawe WHmCrGYOC^{2}CLM RFH. þei] that thei HmF. ligge] liggen Cr^{23}GMF.
137 if þe] yff G; þow þe H; þouȝ WHmCr YOC^{2}CLMRF. Iustice] iustice Cr^1; Iustices WHmCr^{23}GYOC^{2}CLMRF; Iuge ⁊ Iustyce H. Iugge] YCrCLMR; Iuggen WHmGOC^{2}F; *om* H. hire...Ioyned] Ionyȝe hyr H. to] *om* Hm. wiþ] w*ith* YOC^{2}CLMRF; to WHmCrGH. Fals] fase F.
138 þe] RGFH; *om* WHmCrYOC^{2}CLM.
139 For] And WHmCrGYOC^{2}CLMR FH. Conscience] coscyence G. is of] *om* F. of his] a G. counseil and] co*n*seylour*e* he F. one] *om* Cr^2.
140 fals] HmCr; þe false WGYOC^{2}CLM RH; sire false F.
141 *run together with* 142 H. It shal] he wil F. bisitte] bisette YCr; be set on H; beslo-t*er*e F. wel...laste] *om* H. wel] ful WHm CrGYOC^{2}CLMRF. soure] sore CrG. þe] *om* YC.
142 Her...Cyuyle] *om* H. assenteþ] assent Cr^{12}; assented Cr^{3}MF. ac] but FGH; and HmCrC^{2}C. Symonye] Cyvyle F. ne] not H.
143 Til...siluer] *over erasure* Hm. siluer] su*m* syluer*e* F; mony Cr^1. for...seles] *om* F. his] this R. seles] seruice WHmCr GYOC^{2}CLMRH. signes of] also þe WHmCrGYOC^{2}CLMR; also for H; all hise F.
144 floryns] florences CrG.

And bad gile '[go] gyu[e] gold al aboute,
And namely to þe Notaries þ*at* hem noon faille.
And feffe fal[s] witness[e] wiþ floryns ynowe,
For [he] may Mede amaistrye and maken at my wille'.
Tho þis gold was ygyue gret was þe þonkyng
To Fals and to Fauel for hire faire ȝiftes, |
And comen to conforten from care þe false *fol. 11 b*
And seiden, 'c*er*tes, cessen shul we neu*er*e
Til Mede be þi wedded wif þoruȝ wi[t] of vs alle,
For we haue Mede amaistried wiþ oure murie speche
That she graunteþ to goon wiþ a good wille
To london to loken if [þat] lawe wolde
Iuggen yow ioyntly in ioie for euere'.
Thanne was Fal[s] fayn and Fauel as bliþe,
And leten somone alle segges in shires aboute,
And alle be bown, beggers and oþere,
To wenden wiþ hem to westmynstre to witnesse þis dede.

145 go] HmCr^{3}GOC^{2}FH; to WCr^{12}YC LMR. gyue] YHmCrGOC^{2}CLMRFH; gyuen W. al] *om* Cr.
146 þe] þes G; *om* H. hem] thei HmF. noon] noone (? ne *another script*) O; nouȝt Hm. faille] fayle HmCrGOC^{2}MFH; ne faille WYCLR.
147 feffe] fastne Hm. fals witnesse] Y HmCrGOC^{2}CLRH; false witnesses WM; Fals be witnesse F. floryns] florence Cr^{1}; florences Cr^{23}G.
148 For] þat F. he] LRF; þei WHmCr GYOC^{2}CMH (*over erasure* M). amaistrye] maystrye Cr^{1}GC^{2}H; maystren Hm. maken] make Cr^{1}. my] her Hm.
149 Tho] whan FH; *cropped* R. ygyue] gyue HmGYOC^{2}CLM; geuen CrH. was þe] wyth was that (wyth *cancelled*) Hm.
150 to] *om* Hm. faire ȝiftes] gyftys fayre H. faire] great Cr^{23}.
151 ⁊ kestyn awey care ⁊ conforte sire false F. comen] come CrH; came G. conforten] conforte CHmYOC^{2}LMR.
152 seiden] seid C^{2}H; sithen saide Cr^{3}; sythen Cr^{12}. c*er*tes] c*er*tes sire WHmCr GYOC^{2}CLMRH; sire for soþe F. cessen] cesse C^{2}GYOCLMRFH.
153 be] bi C^{2}. þi wedded] weddid þi OCr^{23}C^{2}. þi] *om* Cr^{1}. wit] wytt GFH; wittes WHmCr^{23}YOC^{2}CLMR (es *over erasure* M); þe wits Cr^{1}.
154 Mede amaistried] maystryd mede H. amaistried] ymaystryed Hm; maistred Cr^{1}G. wiþ] thorȝ RFH. oure] *om* H.
155 graunteþ] grau*n*ted Cr^{23}. to] for to F; *om* R. a] *om* Hm.
156 *divided from* 157 *after* iuge R. loken] loke CrGYOC^{2}CLMRH. þat] R; that the YOC^{2}CLMF; þe WHmCrGH. wolde] wolle C^{2}F.
157 Iuggen] Iugge GHmCrYOC^{2}CLRH. yow] ::w R; it F. ioyntly] Iustelyche F. in ioie] togedyr H.
158 was Fals] Fals was F. Fals] fals Hm; Falsnesse WCrGYOC^{2}CLMRH. as] all so Hm; ful F. bliþe] blyue Hm.
159 And] to G. leten] lete HmGC^{2}F; dede H. somone] su*m*ne Hm. segges] the seggys GR; me*n* FH. shires] þe shyre GH.
160 And] And bade M; And bad hem WHmCrGYOC^{2}CLRFH. be] HmYOC^{2} CLMRFH; to be WCrG. oþere] otheres R; ellis Hm.
161 wenden] wende YHmCrGOC^{2}CMH. hem] him Cr^{23}RF. westmynstre] westmest*er* HmCr^{1}. þis] þe RF.

Ac þanne cared þei for caples to carien hem þider;
[Thanne fette Fauel] foles [of þe beste],
Sette Mede vpon a Sherreue shoed al newe,
And Fals sat on a Sisour þat softeli trotted,
And Fauel on [Fair Speche] fe[ynt]ly atired.
Tho hadde Notaries none; anoyed þei were
For Symonye and Cyuylle sholde on hire feet gange.
Ac þanne swoor Symonye and Cyuylle boþe
That Somonou*rs* sholde be Sadeled and s*er*uen hem echone,
'And late apparaille þise p*ro*uisours in palfreyes wise;
Sire Symonye hymself shal sitte vpon hir bakkes.
Denes and Southdenes, drawe yow togideres;
Erchedekenes and Officials and alle youre Registrers,
Lat sadle hem wiþ siluer oure synne to suffre,
As [de]uoutrye and diuorses and derne vsurie,
To bere Bisshopes aboute abrood in visitynge. |
Paulynes pryuees for pleintes in Consistorie *fol.* 12 *a*

162 Ac] but GF; and HmCrC^{2}C; *om* H. cared þei] þey cared C^2. cared] careden O; caried Cr. for] forth Cr. carien] carie C^{2}Cr; kairen LMR; kayre F. þider] to lu*n*den*n* F.
163 Thanne...Fauel] And fauel þa*n* forth fet H; And Fauel fette forþ þanne WHmCrYOC^{2}CLMR; ⁊ Favel fette furþ anoon fele F; and Fauinell fatt forth G. foles] felones H. of þe beste] of þe best H; ynowe WHmCrGYOC^{2}CLMR; sone F.
164 Sette] And sette WHmCrGYOC^{2}CLMRFH. vpon] vpp R; on GF; þe mayde on H. shoed] yshood FR. newe] a newe G.
166 on] sat on H. Fair Speche] a Flaterer*e* WHmCrGYOC^{2}CMRH; a flatere LF. feyntly] feytlyche G; feetely Cr; fetisly WHmYOC^{2}CLMR; ful fetyȝsly F; þ*at* freysly was H.
167 Tho] þan C^{2}FH. hadde Notaries] Notarijs hadde F. hadde] hadden HmO; had þe (*over erasure another ink*) M. anoyed] ⁊ anoyed F. þei were] therewyth G. were] weren OC^{2}F.
168 For] for then (then *above line*) G; þat F. sholde] schulden HmOR. hire feet] foote F. gange] gon HmH; renny*n* F.
169 Ac] But FH; and HmCrGC^{2}C.
170 sholde] schulde*n* OC^2. s*er*uen] serue CrGYOC^{2}CLRF.
171 late] propirly F. þise] þe R; *om* GFH.
172 Sire] ⁊ sire F. hym] hir Y. self] seluen YOC^{2}CLM. sitte] sytten HmRF. vpon] on CrGFH. bakkes] bak (*corrected*) H.
173 Denes] ⁊ denes F. drawe] let drawe F. yow] ȝe Hm; *om* F.
174 Officials] deknes officiales R. alle] *om* C. Registrers] regesters Cr.
175 Lat] and late Hm; ⁊ F. sadle] stoppe F. synne] synnes FG.
176 deuoutrye] deuoutrie R; voutrye Hm; Auoutrye WGYOC^{2}CLMH; aduoutrye Cr; devoos F. and(1)] *om* H. diuorses] vorsers Hm; devoutrye F.
177 aboute] abouty*n* H. abrood] i*n* brode H. in] to F; *om* H. visitynge] vysitacyou*n*s Hm; vysyte F.
178 Paulynes] ⁊ Pawlynes F; Paynles (*over erasure*) M. pryuees] *over erasure* M; prynces Hm; primus Cr^{23}; peple FG. for] and F. in] in the YOC^{2}LMRFH. Consistorie] constorye GFH.

Shul *ser*uen myself þat Cyuyle is nempned.
And [lat] Cartsadle þe Co*m*missarie; oure cart shal he [drawe]
And fecchen [oure] vitailles at *Fornicatores*.
And makeþ of lyer*e* a lang cart to leden alle þise oþere,
As [fobbes] and Faitours þat on hire feet [iotten].'
Fals and Fauel fareþ forþ togideres
And Mede in þe myddes and [al þis meynee] after.
I haue no tome to telle þe tail þ*at* [hem] folwe[þ]
[Of many maner man þat on þis molde libbeth],
Ac Gyle was Forgoer and gyed hem alle.
Sothnesse sei3 hem wel and seide but litel,
And priked [forþ on] his palfrey and passed hem alle
And com to þe kynges court and Conscience tolde,
And Conscience to þe kyng carped it after.
'By crist!' quod þe kyng, 'and I cacche my3te
Fals or Fauel or any of hise feeris
I wolde be wroken of þo wrecches þat wercheþ so ille,

179 Shul] schullen HmM; shuld G. *ser*uen] *ser*ue HmCrGYOC^{2}CLRH. self] seluen OC^{2}. nempned] inempned Cr^{23}; nemelyd H; neuened G; named Cr^{1}C^{2}; ynamed F.
180 And lat] And WHmCrGYOC^{2}CLMRFH. þe] oure YGOC^{2}MH. he] be H. drawe] lede WHmCrGYOC^{2}CLMRF; led H.
181 And] to F. fecchen] fecche RCrFH. oure] vs WHmCrGYOC^{2}CLMRFH. vitailles] vytayl H. *Fornicatores*] fornicatours HmG.
182 makeþ...a] lyere shal be F. makeþ] make GC^{2}CH. lyer*e*] lyers G. lang] long HmCrGYOC^{2}CLMFH. leden] lede YCrOC^{2}CL; cary*in* H. þise] þe F; *om* H.
183 fobbes] fobberes RF; Freres WHmCrGYOC^{2}CLMH. Faitours] fautouris O. iotten] rennen WHmCrGYOC^{2}CLMR; renne F; 3ede H.
184 Fals] And þus Fals WHmCrGYOC^{2}CLMRFH. forþ] *om* MH.
185 al...meynee] all thys meyny G; alle þise men WHmCrLR; alle thise other YOC^{2}CM; all þe oþ*er*e F; all oþ*er* H.
186 tome] tyme CrH. to] *om* H. telle] tell you G. hem] HmYOC^{2}CLMRFH; here Cr; hire WG. folweþ] folweth YHmCrGOC^{2}CLRF; folwed WMH (d *over erasure* M).
187 LCr^{23}YOC^{2}CMRFH; *line om* WHmCr^{1}G. many] many a F. man] men Cr^{23}C^{2}; of men MH. þis] þe F.
188 Ac] But FGH; And CrC^{2}C. gyed] gyded GCr; gylyd Hm.
189–221 *left margin cropped* R.
189 Sothnesse] þan Sothnesse F. sei3] seethe CrG. hem] hym HmYOCLM; *om* H. seide] sayth Cr. litel] a lytyl HmYOC^{2}CLRH; a lyte F.
190 And] But F. forþ on his] his WHmCrGYOC^{2}CLMRFH.
191 tolde] told G; it tolde WHmCrYOC^{2}CLMRFH.
193 By] Now by WHmCrGYOC^{2}CLMRFH. and] yff GH.
194 or(1)] other R; eyþ*er* F; ꝧ G; *altered another ink to* oþ*er* Hm. or(2)] other R. any...feeris] feerys of hise felachepe F. hise] here HCrG.
195 wroken] wroke YCLRFH; worken Cr^{23}. of] on HmGH; op Y. þo] þe YC. wercheþ] werche F. so] thys Cr.

And doon hem hange by þe hals and alle þ*at* hem mayntenеþ.
Shal neu*er*e man of þis molde meynprise þe leeste,
But riȝt as þe lawe [lokeþ] lat falle on hem alle.’
And comaunded a Constable þat com at þe firste
To attachen þo Tyrauntȝ ‘for any [tresor], I hote;
Fettreþ [Falsnesse faste] for any kynnes ȝiftes,
And girdeþ of Gyles heed; lat hym go no ferþer;
[And bryngeþ Mede to me maugree hem alle.
[Symonye and Cyuyle, I sende hem to warne
That holy chirche for hem worþ harmed for euere.]
And if ye lacche lyere lat hym noȝt ascapen
Er he be put on þe Pillory for any preyere I hote.’] |
Drede at þe dore stood and þe doom herde, *fol.* 12 *b*
And how þe kyng comaunded Constables and s*er*geauntȝ
Falsnesse and his felawship to fettren and to bynden.
Thanne Drede wente wyȝtliche and warned þe False
And bad hym fle for fere and hise [feeres] alle.
[Thanne] Falsnesse for fere fleiȝ to þe Freres;

196 hange] hongy*n* F. mayntenеþ] menteyne C^2; maytene H; meyghten F.
197 Shal] Sholde F. of] on Cr^{23}GOC^{2}FH; vpon Hm. þis] *above line another ink* M; *om* HmYOC^{2}CLRFH. leeste] beste H.
198 riȝt] righ Y. lokeþ] wol loke WHmCrGYOC^{2}CLMRH; will F.
199 And] Ano*n* he F. comaunded] co*m*maunde Cr^{1}G. þat] þat he G; to F; *om* Y. com] comen F; can Cr; *om* Y. þe] *om* C.
200 To] & goo F; ::oo R. attachen] attache CrGYOC^{2}CLMRH; tache HmF. þo] þe H. tresor] þyng WHmCrGYOC^{2}CLMRFH.
201 Fettreþ] And fettreþ WYOC^{2}CLMR; And fetter CrGFH; and fretteth Hm. Falsnesse faste] faste Falsnesse WCrGYOC^{2}CLMRH (fast *above line* H); fast fals HmF. kynnes] faire F. ȝiftes] ȝyfte H.
202 And] & loke þou F. girdeþ] gyrde CrHmGC^{2}FH; gideth (r *supplied another script*) Y. heed] heued R. lat] and lat WCrGYOC^{2}CLMRFH; and leteth Hm.
203 *copied after line* 207 WHmCrGOC^{2}CLMRFH; *line om* Y. And] & loke þou F. bryngeþ] bryngħt C; bringe CrGFH. to] vnto G. maugree] magre of H; in maugre Cr^{23}; in mauger Cr^1.
204, 205 *not in* WHmCrGYOC^{2}CLMRFH.
206 ye] thou CF; they G. lacche] lacchen (l *altered from* k) Hm; laccheth R; cache Cr^1. lat] leteth Hm. ascapen] askape FCrH; scape C^2.
207 þe] *om* YCF. preyere] prayers Cr; þing M. I hote] *om* G.
208 Drede...and] þan stood drede at þe dore & al F.
209 And] *om* HmCrGH. comaunded] demede R.
210 Falsnesse] fals Hm; þat False F. fettren] fetter CrFH. to(2)] *om* HmG. bynden] bynde HmYFH.
211 **Here collation of Hm^2 begins.** and warned] to warne H. þe] *om* HmHm^{2}F.
212 hym] hem YC^2. fere] ferd F. feeres] feerys F; felawes WHmHm^{2}CrGYOC^{2}CLMRH. alle] als H.
213 Thanne] whan Hm^2; & anon F; *om* WHmCrGYOC^{2}CLMH; *cropped* R. Falsnesse] Fals HmHm^{2}F. fere] HmHm^{2}GF; fere þanne WCrYOC^{2}CLMRH (þanne *above line* M). fleiȝ] fleiȝt R; fleis C; fledde CrGC^{2}MH. to] streyt to F.

And Gyle dooþ hym to go agast for to dye.
Ac Marchaunt3 metten w*ith* hym and made hym abyde
And bishetten hym in hire shoppes to shewen hire ware;
Apparailed hym as [a p]*re*ntice þe peple to serue.
Li3tliche Lyere leep awey þanne,
Lurkynge þoru3 lanes, tolugged of manye.
He was nowher welcome for his manye tales,
Ouer al yhonted and yhote trusse,
Til P*ar*doners hadde pite and pulled hym [to] house,
Wesshen hym & wiped hym & wounden hym in cloutes,
And senten hym [on Sondayes wiþ seles] to chirch[e],
And [gaf] pardoun for pens poundemele aboute.
Thanne lourede leches, and lettres þei sente
[For to] wonye w*ith* hem watres to loke.
Spycers speken w*ith* hym to spien hire ware

214 Gyle...to(1)] w*ith* hym Gyle gan F. to(1)] for to Hm. go] go & H; god Y. agast...to] for gast he sholde F.
215 Ac] but GFH; And CrC^{2}C; *cropped* R. metten] mette YGCLMRF; meten Cr; mete H. w*ith* hym] hym wyþ OC^{2} (hym *above line main hand* O). made] maden HmHm^{2}OC^{2}; byddy*n* H. abyde] to byde Cr^{23}.
216 bishetten] byschutte Hm^{2}; shitte Cr; settyn C^{2}FH; sett G. shoppes] shope Y OC^{2}CLMR. shewen] selly*n* H.
217 Apparailed] Apparayleden HmHm^{2}; And apparailled YC^{2}CLMRH; And apparayleden O; & paraylid F. as] ly3k F. a p*re*ntice] a Prentice CrHm^{2}GYOCLMR FH; App*re*ntice WHmC^{2}. serue] seruy*n* H.
218 Li3tliche Lyere] Lyere lytly H. Li3tliche] Full lyghtly HmHm^{2}F. leep] tho lepe HmHm^{2}. awey] and away Cr^{3}. þanne] þenne RF; thence GH; ranne Cr^{3}.
219 þoru3] be H. tolugged] lugged HmHm^{2}; to logge H; to be lugged (be *above line*) M; to be lodged Cr^{1}; to bugged Cr^{2}. of] w*ith* H.
220 nowher] naught where C; more G. tales] mery tales G.
221 Ouer] But ou*er* FH. yhonted] yhunted HmHm^{2}; hunted out Cr^{1}; hy*m* hunted H; ihouted Cr^{2}; Ihowted YOC^{2} CLMR; hy3e howted F; I omyted (?) G. yhote trusse] yhoote to trusse F; hoted to curse G; body*n* hy*m* go trus H.
222 Til] & F. hadde] hadden HmOC^{2}F. pite] pic H. pulled] pulleden Hm^{2}O; pulle*n* C^{2}. to] HmHm^{2}MFH; into WCr GYOC^{2}CLR.
223 Wesshen] They wesshen WHmHm^{2} GYC^{2}CLMR; þe wesschen O; Þei wesch HCr; & wasshed F. wiped] wypeden Hm^{2}O; wypten Hm; wypt H; wypen G; wipe Cr. wounden] wounde FG; woundem C. hym(3)] *om* YC. cloutes] clothes HmFH; cloth::: R.
224 senten] sente YCrOC^{2}CLR; senden G. on...seles] wiþ seles on Sondayes WHm Hm^{2}CrGYOC^{2}CLMRFH. chirche] YHm OC^{2}; chirches WHm^{2}CrGLMRFH; kyrkees C.
225 gaf] YGOC^{2}CLMRFH; 3af HmHm^{2}; yeuen W; gaue hym Cr.
226 lourede] loureden HmHm^{2}O. sente] senten OC^{2}F; to hy*m* sent H.
227 For to] That he sholde WHmCr GYOC^{2}CLMRH; thati*ne* (?) he schulde Hm^{2}; þ*at* he wolde F. watres] l*ett*res Y. loke] loken OC^{2}.
228 Spycers] Fele spyceris F. speken] spoke YCLMFH. w*ith*] to RF. hym] he*m* H. spien] spie Cr; aspyen HmHm^{2}C^{2}; aspy3e F.

For he kouþe [on] hir craft and knew manye go*m*mes.
A[c] Mynstrales and Messagers mette w*ith* hym ones
And [wiþ]helden hym an half yeer and elleuene dayes.
Freres wiþ fair speche fetten hym þennes;
For knowynge of comeres coped hym as a Frere.
Ac he haþ leue to lepen out as ofte as hym likeþ, |
And is welcome whan he wile and woneþ w*ith* hem
    ofte. *fol.* 13 *a*
Alle fledden for fere and flowen into hernes;
Saue Mede þe mayde na mo dorste abide.
Ac trewely to telle she trembled for [fere],
And ek wepte and wrong whan she was attached.

229 on] HmHm^{2}RF; of WCrGYOC^{2}CLMH. hir] þ*at* H. knew] know H. manye] fele F. go*m*mes] gomes OGC^2.
230 Ac] HmHm^{2}YOLMR; but GH; And WCrC^{2}C; þa*n*ne F. Mynstrales] mynstalles L. mette] metten HmHm^{2}OC^{2}RF; mete Cr^1. ones] o weye F.
231 wiþhelden] helden WHmHm^{2}GYOC^{2}CLMR; helde CrFH. hym] *om* G. an half] half a RCrFH.
232 Freres] But Freris F. fair] here fayre HmYC. fetten] fet CrG; fecched HmHm^{2}F. þennes] þenne F.
233 For] And for WHmHm^{2}CrGYOC^{2}CLMRFH. knowynge of comeres] komynge knowerys þey F. knowynge] knownis C^2. coped] copeden HmHm^2.
234 Ac] but GFH; And CrC^{2}C. he] *om* F. lepen] lepe GCrYOC^{2}CLMRH. ofte] ofty*n* FH. hym] hem Cr^{23}. likeþ] liked Y.
235 is] *om* Cr^3. and...ofte] w*ith*owty*n* ony daunger F. woneþ] went H. hem] hym Hm. ofte] eu*er* H.
236 Alle] all they rest (rest *above line*) G; & alle þe oþ*er*e F. fledden] fledde FH. flowen] flyen G; faste flown F. into] to F.
237 mayde] mayden HmHm^{2}OC^{2}M. na mo dorste] durst no mo G. na mo] no man R. dorste] dursten HmHm^{2}O.
238 Ac] butt GFH; And CrC^{2}C. trewely] trewþe F. fere] RF; drede WHmHm^{2}CrGYOC^{2}CLMH.
239 ek] also RF; *om* HmHm^{2}H. wepte] wepe C^2. wrong] weylede F. whan] for F; *om* R. she] heo R.

III

NOw is Mede þe mayde and na mo of hem alle
Wiþ Bedeles and baillies brouȝt [to] þe kyng.
The kyng called a clerk—[I kan] noȝt his name—
To take Mede þe maide and maken hire at ese.
'I [wol] assayen hire myself and sooþliche appose
What man of þis [world] þ*at* hire were leuest.
And if she werche bi wit and my wil folwe
I wol forgyuen hire þ[e] gilt, so me god helpe.'
Curteisly þe clerk þanne, as þe kyng hiȝte,
Took Mede bi þe myddel and broȝte hire into chambre.
A[c] þer was murþe ⁊ Mynstralcie Mede to plese;
[That] wonyeþ [at] westmynstre worshipeþ hire alle.

1 **Here collation of BmBoCot (B) begins.** mayde] mayd*y*n H. and] *om* B. na mo] nomen BoCot. hem] *om* C^{2}F.

2 Ibrowht byfor*e* þe kyng w*ith* bedel and bayly F. Bedeles] bedele H. and] Hm^{2}CrGOC^{2}BMH; and w*ith* WHmYCLR. brouȝt] ybrouȝt BR; brough Cr^3. to] B; bifore WHmHm^{2}CrGYOC^{2}CLMRH. kyng] *om* Y.

3 The] Ano*n* þe F. a] to hy*m* a B. I kan] y can BH; kan I WCrYOC^{2}CLMR; ne can y HmHm^2; I know GF. noȝt] not telle BH. name] *lost in sewing* Bm.

4 maide] maydyn C^{2}GBH. maken] make HmHm^{2}CrGYOC^{2}CBLMFH.

5 I...myself] But y will hire first asayȝe F. wol] wole B; shal WHmHm^{2}CrGYOC^{2}CLMRH. assayen] assaye HmHm^{2}CrGYOC^{2}CBLRH. sooþliche] softly H; couthliche R; sotilly hir*e* F. appose] apposen G.

6 man] wyȝe F. of þis] of C; vpon HmHm^{2}G. of] on C^{2}H. world] BRF; moolde WHmHm^{2}CrGYOC^{2}CLMH. hire] to hire B; she F. leuest] lyuest Bm.

7 *line om* B. she] sȝe Hm; heo R. bi] by my GYOC^{2}CLMRFH.

8 gyuen] gyue GCrYOC^{2}CLMRFH; ȝyue HmHm^{2}B. þe] BF; þis WHmHm^{2}CrGYOC^{2}CLMRH. gilt] gyltis FR.

9 Curteisly...þanne] þa*n*ne þe clerk curteysly dyde F. þanne] *om* C. hiȝte] hym hiȝt BF.

10–40 *left margin cropped* R.

10 Took] he took F. bi þe myddel] they meyde G. broȝte] mente F. into] *in* OC^2; to BFH. *Here* F *adds a spurious line*; *see above*, p. 222.

11 Ac] BmR; And WHmHm^{2}CrGYOC^{2}CBoCotLMF; *om* H. þer was] fette furþ F. ⁊] w*ith* F. Mynstralcie] minstrels Cr^2. to] for to GB; w*ith* to F.

12 That] þat B; They þ*at* WHmHm^{2}CrGYOC^{2}CLMRH; Su*m*me þ*at* F. wonyeþ] wone HCr. at] BGMRFH; in WHmHm^{2}CrYOC^{2}CL. worshipeþ] worchepe F; worshiped YCrCLR; worschipede*n* OHmHm^2; worcheþ H. hire alle] hem alle Hm^2; þey hir*e* make F.

Gentilliche wiþ ioye þe Iustices so*m*me
Busked hem to þe bour þer þe burde dwelle[þ],
Conforte[d] hire kyndely by clergies leue,
And seiden, 'mourne noȝt, Mede, ne make þow no sorwe,
For we wol wisse þe kyng and þi wey shape
To be wedded at þi wille and wher þee leef likeþ
For al Consciences cast [and] craft, as I trowe'.
Mildely Mede þanne m*er*ciede hem alle
Of hire grete goodnesse, and gaf hem echone |
Coupes of clene gold and coppes of siluer, *fol.* 13 *b*
Rynges wiþ Rubies and richesses manye,
The leeste man of hire meynee a moton of golde.
Thanne lauȝte þei leue, þise lordes, at Mede.
Wiþ þat comen clerkes to conforten hire þe same
And beden hire be bliþe: 'for we beþ þyne owene

13 Gentilliche] Ful gentili BF. þe] of þe F. Iustices] Iustyse H. so*m*me] some Hm^{2} Cr^{1}C; sone B; comen OC^{2}; came Cr^{23}G; þan H; manye F.
14 Busked] buskeden HmHm^{2}. hem] hym BoCotH. to þe] to H; boldly to hire F. þer] þer as B. burde] bride Cr; bred C^{2}. dwelleþ] dwellyth GBF; dwellede WHm Hm^{2}CrYOC^{2}CLMH; dwelte R.
15 Conforted] And comforthyd H; and conforteþ B; To conforten WHmHm^{2}G; To conforte CCrYOC^{2}LMRF. kyndely] kony*n*gly F.
16 And] þey F. seiden] sayde CrGYOC^{2} BFH. mourne] mo*ur*ne thow YHmHm^{2} OC^{2}M. Mede] *om* HmHm^{2}. make] *om* Y. þow] ye Cr; *om* H.
17 we] *om* Cot. wol] *by correction* M; willen B; *om* YOC^{2}CL. wisse] wissen OC^{2}; wyse R; kisse Cot. kyng] *altered from* kyndlye G. þi wey] the Cr^{1}. shape] schapen OC^{2}; make B.
18 *line om* B. be wedded] wedden G. þee] thy G. leef] levest F; loue Y; beste H.
19 Consciences] conscience CrHm^{2}GYO C^{2}CLMRH; co*n*syecys F. cast] crafte RF. and] CrBmR; a BoCot; or WHmHm^{2} GYOC^{2}CLMFH. craft] cast RF.
20 Mildely...þanne] þanne Myȝldely Meede F; Mildelich þa*n*ne Mede OC^{2}. þanne] *om* R. m*er*ciede] mercyde (cyde *over erasure*) Hm; mercie Hm^{2}; remercyed G. hem] *over erasure* Hm. alle] kryde Hm^{2}.
21 grete...echone] goodis and hire grete ȝiftis B. and] *om* M. gaf] ȝaf Hm^{2}H. hem] to hem F; he C^{2}.
22 Coupes] Copes Cr. and] w*ith* F. coppes] Copes Cr^{1}; cuppes HmHm^{2}Cr^{23} OMR; cupus C^{2}; coupys H; cases F; peces GB.
23 *copied after* 25 B. Rynges] wiþ ryngis B. richesses] ricchesse RF; Ryches CrCH. manye] ful thykke F.
24 *line om* H. The] For þe F. man] *om* F. meynee] mennge (*altered to* meynge) C; me*n* F. a] hadde a BF.
25 lauȝte] lauȝten O; lafte Cr^{1}; laugh Cr^{23}; toke C^{2}B. leue] her leue BF. þise] þo F. at] of B. Mede] Mete Hm^{2}.
26 Wiþ] ⁊ w*ith* F; Tho B. þat] *om* B. comen] come BH; comon Cr. clerkes] þise clerkis B. to conforten] to conforte CCrYOC^{2}BLR; ⁊ co*n*fortid F; and conforteden HmHm^{2}. hire þe same] *over erasure another ink* Hm. þe same] þanne B; sone Cr^{1}.
27–9 *lines om* Y.
27 beden] bodyn C^{2}; bad H; bydden CrGB; biden C. be bliþe] bliþe to be B.

For to werche þi wille [while þi lif lasteþ].'
Hendiliche heo þanne bihiȝte hem þe same,
To louen hem lelly and lordes [hem] make
And in Consistorie at court callen hire names.
'Shal no lewednesse [hym] lette, þe leode þat I louye,
That he ne worþ first auaunced, for I am biknowen
Ther konnynge clerkes shul clokke bihynde.'
Thanne cam *þer* a Confessour coped as a frere;
To Mede þe mayde [mekeliche he loutede]
And seide [wel] softely, in shrift as it were,
'Theiȝ [lered and lewed] hadde leyen by þee [echone],
And [þeiȝ] Fals[hede] hadde yfolwed þee alle þise fift[ene]
 wynter,
I shal assoille þee myself for a seem of whete,

28 to] *by correction* Bm. werche] werken B. while] BMH; þe while WHmHm^{2}CrGOC^{2}CLRF. þi lif] thy lyfe HmHm^{2}; oure lif B; we may GCr; þow myȝt WOC^{2}CLMR; þou mythyst H; þou may F. lasteþ] lasteth HmHm^{2}B; laste WCrGOC^{2}CLMRFH.
29 Hendiliche...þanne] Ful hendeli þanne she B; þanne she dede hendely ⁊ F. heo] sche HmHm^{2}CrGOC^{2}C; he*m* alle H. bihiȝte] hiȝte BH. hem] sche H.
30 louen] loue YOC^{2}CBLMRH. hem(1)] *over erasure* M; hym Bm; ȝow LR. hem(2)] he*m* H; hem to F; to WHmHm^{2}CrGYOC^{2}CBLMR. *Here* Cr *adds a line like* **C** III 33; *see above*, p. 221.
31 *line om* H. And] For F; *om* OC^{2}. in] CrG; in þe WHmHm^{2}YOC^{2}CBLMRF. Consistorie] constorie Hm^{2}GBmBoRF. at] HmHm^{2}CrOC^{2}R; at þe WGYCBLM; in þe F. callen] do callen WHmHm^{2}; do calle CrGYOC^{2}CBLMR; I shal do cowþe F. hire] youre COC^{2}BLMRF. names] name OC^{2}F.
32 hym lette] lette WHmHm^{2}CrGYOC^{2}CBLMRH; letty*n* F. þe] þo FH. leode] clerke Cr; clerkes RF; me*n* H.
33 *line om* H. ne] *om* RF. auaunced] vaunsed R. biknowen] byknowe R; wel beknowe F; well knoen G.
34 Ther] þere þat F. clerkes] clekis C^{2}. shul] shullen BCr. clokke] clokken G; knokke F.
35 cam] com*eth* H. coped] ycoped R was coped F.
36 þe] þis R; þat F. mayde] mayden HmHm^{2}GC^{2}BMH. mekeliche he] he melled CCrBLMRH; ⁊ meelyd F; he medled Y; he medelede OC^{2}; he mened WHmHm^{2}; he mouthed G. loutede] þise wordes WHmHm^{2}CrGYOC^{2}CBLMRFH.
37 *line om* H. wel] ful WHmHm^{2}CrGYOC^{2}CBLMRF. softely] sotely R. in] as in F; *om* BoCot. as] *om* F.
38 Theiȝ] Thewe C. lered...lewed] lered men ⁊ lewid men (*marked for transposition*) O; leernede me*n* ⁊ lewed me*n* F; lewed men and lered HmHm^{2}GH; lewed men and lered men WYC^{2}CBLMR; lewd me*n* ⁊ lerned me*n* Cr. hadde] hadden HmO; han BFH. echone] boþe WHmCrGYOC^{2}CBLMRFH; *om* Hm^{2}.
39 *line om* B. And þeiȝ] ⁊ þey F; And WHmHm^{2}CrGYOC^{2}CLMH; *cropped* R. Falshede] falsede R; Falsnesse WCrGYOC^{2}CLMH; fals HmHm^{2}F. hadde] have F; hat H. yfolwed] folwed YGM; yfouloed Cr^{2}; Ifoulid OCr^{3}C^{2}; fowled HmHm^{2}H; defoulyd F. alle] *om* GF. fiftene] fyftene F; fifty WHmHm^{2}Cr^{23}GYOC^{2}CLMRH; forti Cr^{1}.

And [ek] be þi [baudekyn] and bere wel þ[yn erende]
Amonges [clerkes] and [knyȝtes] Conscience to [felle]'.
Thanne Mede for hire mysdedes to þat man kneled
And shrof hire of hire sherewednesse, shamelees I trowe;
Tolde hym a tale and took hym a noble
For to ben hire Bedeman and hire [baude after].
Thanne he assoiled hire soone and siþen he seide,
'We haue a wyndow in werchynge wole [stonden] vs [wel] hye;
Woldestow glaȝe þ[e] gable ⁊ graue [þere] þy name
Syker sholde þi soule be heuene to haue'. |
'Wiste I þat', quod þ[e] wo*m*man, 'I wolde noȝt spare *fol.* 14 *a*
For to be youre frend, frere, and faile yow neuere
While ye loue lordes þat lecherie haunten
And lakkeþ noȝt ladies þ*at* louen wel þe same.
It is a freletee of flessh—ye fynden it in bokes—
And a cours of kynde wherof we comen alle;

41 ek...baudekyn] also be þi bedeman WCrGYOC^{2}CBLMRFH; be thy bedeman HmHm^{2}. bere] bery*n* H. þyn erende] þi*n* erdyn H; þy*n* name F; þi message WHmHm^{2}CrGYOC^{2}CBLMR.

42 clerkes...knyȝtes] Clerkys ⁊ knyghtys her*e* F; knyȝtes and clerkes WHmHm^{2}CrGYOC^{2}CBLMRH. felle] torne WHmCrGYOC^{2}CBLMRF; twyne H; serue Hm^{2}.

43 dedes] dede H. kneled] t*ur*nede F.

44 shrof] schref Hm^{2}; schorfe Hm. hire sherewednesse] his schrewnesse C^{2}. trowe] *rubbed* Hm^{2}.

45 Tolde...and] whan she hadde told hire tale she F.

46 hire(2)] *om* Cr^{1}. baude after] baud after G; on hand aft*er* H; brocour als WHmYOC^{2}CBLMRF; brokar also Cr; brocours als Hm^{2}.

47 Thanne] Anon F. assoiled] soyled HmHm^{2}. siþen he seide] seyde þese wordys aft*er* H. he] a R. seide] seiden Hm^{2}.

48 haue] hauen B. wyndow] wyndowne Bm; witdow Cr^{3}. in] a YCBLMR; *om* F. werchynge] glasyng G. stonden] stonde H; sitten WHmHm^{2}GOC^{2}CBoCotLMR; sytte F; setten Bm; set Cr; sithen Y. vs...hye] *rubbed* Hm^{2}. wel] L; ful WHmCr^{23}YOC^{2}CBMRFH; *om* Cr^{1}G. hye] heye (*cancelled for* in hie cost *another hand*) G.

49 Woldestow] wolde ȝe F. þe] þat WHmHm^{2}CrGYOC^{2}CBLMRFH. þere] þer*e* R; þ*er*Inne WHmCrGYOC^{2}CBLMFH; *om* Hm^{2}. þy] ȝoure F; *om* Hm^{2}. name] *om* Hm^{2}.

50 Syker] ful syker HmHm^{2}B; wol sekyr H; Sykirly F. þi] ȝoure F. be...haue] into hevene styȝe F; be of heueneryche blys H. haue] hauene C^{2}.

51–62 *lines om* RF; *in their place three lines resembling* **A** III 50, 51; *see above*, p. 221.

51 Wiste I] ȝyf I wyst H. þe] HCrM; þat WHmHm^{2}GYOC^{2}CBmBoL; *om* Cot. wo*m*man] mede Cot; mayde H. I wolde] ȝet wold I H.

53 ye] you Cr; þe B. loue] louen Hm^{2}OC^{2}; loue of B. þat] ⁊ H; *om* B. haunten] hauȝten C^{2}.

54 lakkeþ] lacke GCrH. noȝt] no G. louen] loue CrGH. wel] *om* H.

55 a] *om* Cr. freletee] frelede H; frailenes Cr. of] *twice, second erased* L; of the Cr C^{2}H (þe *added* C^{2}). ye] þei B. fynden] fynde CrGYC^{2}CBmBoLMH. in] in your Y.

56 And a] A comyn HmHm^{2}.

Who may scape [þe] sclaundre, þe scaþe is soone amended;
It is synne of þe seuene sonnest relessed.
Haue m*er*cy', quod Mede, 'of men þat it haunteþ
And I shal couere youre kirk, youre cloistre do maken,
Wowes do whiten and wyndowes glaȝen,
Do peynten and portraye [who] paie[d] for þe makynge
That [ech] segge shal [see] I am suster of youre house.'
Ac god alle good folk swich g*ra*uynge defendeþ,
To writen in wyndowes of hir wel dedes,
An auent*ure* pride be peynted þ*er*e and pomp of þe world;
For [god] knoweþ þi conscience and þi kynde wille
And þi cost and þi coueitise and who þe catel ouȝte.
Forþi I lere yow lordes, leueþ swic[h writynge],
To writen in wyndowes of youre wel dedes
Or to greden after goddes men whan ye [gyue] doles

57 Who] Whoso CrOC^2; scape] scapen HmHm^2; schape C^2; escape Cr. þe(1)] CrGYOC^{2}CBLMH; that HmHm^2; *om* W. scaþe] case H.
58 *line om* BH. is] ys a HmHm^2; is the (the *above line another ink*) M. þe] that Hm^2; *om* CLM. sonnest] þe sonest G; is sonnest OC^2. relessed] forgyuene C.
59 Haue] God haue HmHm^2. quod... haunteþ] on me q*uod* mede þ*at* I haue don H. of] on HmHm^{2}M. haunteþ] haunte YBoCotLM.
60 couere] do cure H. kirk] cherche Hm Hm^2; kike C. youre(2)] & ȝoure OHm^2 C^{2}H. do maken] do make OC^2; make HmHm^2; aboute H.
61 wyndowes do make & glase do wonys qwyte H. Wowes] Walles CrGC^2; and ȝoure wowes HmHm^2. do] *om* HmHm^2. and] *om* C^2. glaȝen] do glasen Cr^{23}.
62 Do] And B. peynten] paynte HmHm^2 B; purtreye C^{2}H. portraye] purtreie*n* M; portren G; peynten C^{2}H. who paied] and paie WHmHm^{2}CrGYOC^{2}CBLMH.
63 *Here* RF *resume.* ech] ech a FR; euery WHmHm^{2}CrGYOC^{2}CBLMH. segge] ma*n* C^{2}BH. shal] sholde F. see] F; Ise R; seye WHmHm^{2}CrGYOC^{2}CLMH; siegge B. am] am a Cot. of...house] to ȝow alle RF.
64 Ac] But HmGFH (*over erasure* Hm); and Hm^{2}CrC^{2}C. god] god to WHmHm^2 CrGYOC^{2}CBLMRF; to H. alle] *om* F. folk] men G. swich] qwech H. g*ra*uynge] wrytyng GH. defendeþ] defend Cr; god defendyth H.
65 To writen] To wryte CrH; & wrytynge F. wel] wille C^2; goode H.
66 Ne awht*er* do peynte for pompe of þe peple F. An] yn HmHm^{2}BH; And CR; for G. auent*ure*] *om* G. be] ys G; þ*er* be H. peynted] ypeynted R. þ*er*e and] i*n* H.
67 For] and G. god] R; crist WHmHm^2 CrGYOC^{2}CBLMFH.
68 And] Boþe F; *om* R. þi(1)] þe F. þi(2)] *om* H. þe] thy CrCot.
69–72 *lines om* FH.
69 Forþi] Therfore Cr. lere] lerne Cr; leren C^2. leueþ] leue MCr; leueht C; loueþ not (not *by corrector*) Bm. swich writynge] swiche werkes WHmHm^2 CrGYOC^{2}CBLMR.
70 wyndowes] wyndowe Cr^{12}.
71 greden] grede R; gedren Bm. ye] thei Cr^{1}B (*corrected* Cot). gyue] dele WG; delen HmHm^{2}CrYOC^{2}CBLMR.

On auent*ure* ye haue your*e* hire here and youre heuene als.
Nesciat sinistra quid faciat dextra:
Lat no3t þi left half, late ne raþe,
Wite what þow werchest wiþ þi ri3t syde,
For þus [bit god in] þe gospel goode men doon hir almesse.
Maires and Maceres þat menes ben bitwene
The kyng and þe comune to kepe þe lawes, |
[As] to punysshe on Pillories and [on] pynynge stooles *fol.* 14 *b*
Brew[e]rs and Bak[e]rs, Bochiers and Cokes;
For þise are men on þis molde þat moost harm wercheþ
To þe pouere peple þat *par*celmele buggen.
For þei [p]oisone þe peple pryueliche [wel] ofte
Thei richen þoru3 reg*ra*trie and rentes hem biggen
[Of] þat þe pou*er*e peple sholde putte in hire wo*m*be.
For toke þei on trewely þei tymbred nou3t so hei3e,
Ne bou3te none burgages, be ye [wel] certeyne.

72 On] yn HmHm[2]GB. ye] you Cr; þei B. haue] hauen Hm[2]Cot. youre(1)] here B. youre(2)] hire Cot. als] also Cr.
72α *copied after* 74 H. *sinistra*] *sinistra tua* Cr[3]H; *sinistra manus* HmHm[2]B. *faciat*] *facit* Cr[3]; *faciet* H. *dextra*] *dextra ⁊c* G; *dextera tua ⁊c* H. **Here Hm[2] ends.**
73 half] half ney*þer* F; hand H. ne] no OL; no*n* H.
74 Wyte] weety*n* F. þow werchest] ye worcheth G. wiþ] on H. þi] the G.
75 *line om* H. For] And OC[2]. þus] thys G. bit...in] bit YOC[2]CLR; byddeþ HmCr[23]GBM; biddis F; beddith Cr[1]; by W. doon] dos F; to do Bm. hir almesse] þerafter F.
76 and] wit*h* here F. Maceres] maces G; mercers (ercers *over erasure another ink*) Hm; maystres OCr[23]C[2]. þat] *om* C[2]. menes] meene H.
77 comune] comunes OGC[2]F. kepe] kepen MF. þe(2)] wel þe OC[2]F. lawes] lawe H.
78 As to] To WHmCrGYOC[2]CBLMRH; ⁊ F. punysshe] punysshen YCr[1]GOC[2]CLMF; punche BH. on(1)] vpon FR; on þe H. Pillories] pylory FH. on(2)] FH; *om* WHmCrGYOC[2]CBLMR.
79–108 *left margin cropped* R.
79 Brewers...Bakers] brousters ⁊ bakers C[2]; Brewesters and Baksters WHmCrGY OCBLMRH; Boþe websteres ⁊ bakesterys ⁊ F.
80 þise] þo F. on] vpon FR; of HmCB. þis] *om* FH. molde] erthe H. harm] hurte G. wercheþ] wirche F.
81 buggen] byghe CrH; beggen HmG.
82 *line om* Hm. For þei] And also R; ⁊ F. poisone] BCrGYCLMRFH; enpoisone W; punyschen OC[2]. wel] and WCrGY OC[2]CBLMRFH. ofte] ofty*n* H; softe F.
83 *line om* Hm. richen] rysen G. hem] hym Cot.
84 Of] Wiþ WHmCrGYOC[2]CBLMR FH. putte] putten Hm. wo*m*be] wombes CrGMH.
85 on] all Cr; not GH (*altered from* on *another script* G). trewely] vntreuly HG (vn *above line another script* G). tymbred nou3t] tymbreden not O; xuld not bygge H.
86 *line om* H. bou3te] bou3ten BmHm BoM. burgages] burgage R; bargayn F. be] by GB. ye] þe BF; they Cr[1]. wel] ful WHmCrYOC[2]CBLMRF; *om* G.

Ac Mede þe mayde þe Mair [she] bisouȝt[e]
Of alle swiche Selleris siluer to take,
Or *pre*sentȝ wiþouten pens as pieces of siluer,
Rynges or ooþer richesse þ[ise] Reg*ra*tiers to mayntene.
'For my loue', quod þat lady, 'loue hem echone,
And suffre hem to selle somdel ayeins reson.'
Salomon þe sage a s*er*mon he made
For to amenden Maires and men þ*at* kepen [þe] lawes,
And [took hym] þis teme þat I telle þynke:
Ignis deuorabit tabernacula eorum qui libenter accipiunt munera ⁊c.
Among þise lettrede l[or]des þis latyn [amounteþ]
That fir shal falle ⁊ [forbrenne at þe laste]
The hou[s] and [þe] ho[m] of hem þat desireþ
Yiftes or yeresyeues bycause of hire Offices.
The kyng fro conseil cam and called after Mede
And ofsente hire as swiþe; [sergeauntȝ hire fette]
And brouȝte hire to boure wiþ blisse and wiþ ioye.

87 Ac] but GFH; And CrC^{2}C. Mede þe mayde] now þe Maide meede F. mayde] maydyn C^{2}H. she bisouȝte] haþ bisouȝt WHmCrGYOC^{2}CBLMRH; haþ she p*ra*yed F.
88 take] taken F.
89 Or] and B. outen] oute CrGYOC^{2}CBLR (*above line* L). as] or Hm; ac Bm.
90 Rynges] or rynges F. or] other R. ooþer] *om* F. richesse] rycheses GBm. þise] þo C; þe WHmCrYOC^{2}BLMRFH; *om* G. mayntene] me*n*yghte F.
91 loue(1)] lord RF. loue(2)] loveþ F.
92 suffre] suffreþ F. selle] selly*n* H. som] sun Bm.
93 Salomon] kyng Salomo*n* F.
94 For to] For Cr; to GF. amenden] amende HmCrGYOC^{2}CBLMRFH. kep-en] kepe CrGRF. þe] FH; *om* WHmCr GYOC^{2}CBLMR. lawes] lawe H.
95 ⁊ þus he tolde his teeme þ*at* y shal telle ȝou aft*er* F. took hym] tolde hem WHm CrGYOC^{2}CBLMRH. teme] tyme C^2.
96 *deuorabit*] deuorbit OC^2; deuobit Bm. *accipiunt munera*] *om* RF. ⁊c] *om* HmCr GCotFH.
97 *line om* OC^{2}H. þise] *om* F. lordes] leodes WHmCrYCBLMF; lede R; men G. amounteþ] is to mene WHmCrGYCBL MRF.
98 That] þat is OC^2. forbrenne...laste] brenne al to bloo askes WHmCrGYOC^2 CBLMRFH.
99 hous...hom] houses and the homes YOC^{2}CBLMRFH; houses and homes WHmCrG. hem] men Cot. þat] *om* L.
100 Yiftes] Gyftes CrGCF; :::es R. yeresyeues] yeresgyues CrGF; ȝereȝiftes R; yeresyiftes C; ȝeregyftys H; resseyues C^2. Offices] office RFH.
101 The] þanne þe F. fro] OC^{2}CBLM; from YRF; fro þe WHmH; from the CrG. called] askyd H. Mede] *om* Y.
102 ofsente] of *erased* Bm; aft*er* sente C^2; sente aft*er* F; sent for CrH; dyd seeche G. as] also HmBoCot; a Cr; to se also Bm; *om* GFH. swiþe] blythe Hm. sergeauntȝ ...fette] wiþ sergeauntȝ manye WHmCr GYOC^{2}CLMRF; wiþ seruauntis manye B; sergantys many H.
103 And] that HmCrGYOC^{2}CBLMFH; *cropped* R. brouȝte] broughten YGOC^2 CBLMRF. hire] *om* FH.

Curteisly þe kyng comse[þ] to telle;
To Mede þe mayde [melleþ] þise wordes:
'Vnwittily, [wye], wroȝt hastow ofte, |
Ac worse wroȝtest [þ]ow neu*ere* þan þo þow Fals toke. *fol.* 15 *a*
But I forgyue þee þ[e] gilt and graunte þee my g*ra*ce;
Hennes to þi deeþ day do [þow] so na moore.
I haue a knyȝt, Conscience, cam late fro biyonde;
If he wilneþ þee to wif wiltow hym haue?'
'Ye, lord', quod þat lady, 'lord forbede ellis!
But I be holly at you*re* heste hange me [ellis].'
[Th]anne was Conscience called to come and appere
Bifore þe kyng and his conseil, clerkes and oþere.
Knelynge, Conscience to þe kyng louted,
What his wille were and what he do [sholde].
'Woltow wedde þis wo*m*man if I wole assente?

104 Curteisly þe kyng] Anon þe kyng curteysly F. Curteisly] Curteyly H. kyng] G; kyng þanne WHmCrYOC^{2}CBLMRH. comseþ] cumseth R; gynneth G; comsed WHmCrYOC^{2}CBLMF; bega*n* H. to] for to FH. telle] tell then G.

105 To] ⁊ to FH; *cropped* R. mayde] mayden HmMH. melleþ] OCrYC^{2}CBLMR; he meled F; mouthed G; he meneþ W; and meneth Hm; he menyd H.

106 Vnwittily wye] Vnwittily wo*m*man WHmCrGYOC^{2}CBLMRH; þou wom-man vnwittyly F.

107 Ac] but GFH; And CrC^{2}C; *cropped* R. worse...neu*ere*] wrouhtest thu neuere wurse Hm. wroȝtest þow] wroghtest þou GCrOBMFH; wroȝtestow WYCLR; wrout þou C^{2}. þo] whan HmGF; *om* H. Fals toke] took fals Y.

108 forgyue] furȝyue Hm. þee(1)] *above line main hand* W; þo CBmBo (*altered to* þe *another ink* Bm); *om* CotL. þe] þat WHmCrGYCBLMRFH; þis OC^{2} (*above line main hand* O). þee(2)] *om* Hm.

109 Hennes] Fram hens FG (from *in margin another hand* G). deeþ] ded H. do þow] do thow GH; yf þou do F; to do R; do WHmCrYOC^{2}CBLM.

110 I] But y F. a] *om* CrH. knyȝt] knyght hatte F; knyȝt hit (hit *by correction*) Bm.

111 wilneþ] willeth Cr; wilne F; wyll GH. hym haue] w*ith* hy*m* holde F.

112 þat] the HmF. lord(2)] ou*re* Lord F; God Cr; cryst H; lor C. forbede] OCr GC^{2}CLFH; forbede it WHmBM (it *added later* M); it me forbede R; forbode Y. ellis] *om* R.

113 holly] holely M. hange me ellis] lat hange me soone WHmCrGYOC^{2}CBLM RFH (lat] leteþ B; then G; hyȝe F; *om* Cr^{23}. me] *om* F).

114 Thanne] þa*n* HG (⁊ *before it in margin* G); And þanne WHmCrYOC^{2}CBLM RF. called] Icalled R; clepd F. come] comen RFH. and] and to B. appere] aperen F.

115 clerkes] GH; as clerkes WHmCrYOC^{2} CBLMRF.

116 Knelynge...to] þa*n*ne Consience knelynge vnto F. Knelynge] knelynge þoo B. Conscience...kyng] to the kynge conscyence Hm. to] ⁊ to (to *added main hand*) Y. louted] a lowtid B; he louted (he *another script*) G.

117 What] To wite what WCrGYOC^{2} CBLMRFH; to wyten what Hm. do sholde] xuld done H. sholde] GHmCr YOC^{2}CBLMRF; wolde W.

118 Woltow] Wolte Hm. wedde] weddy*n* F. if] yff G; quod þe kyng if WHmCrYOC^{2}CBLMRF; q*uod* þe kyng ⁊ H. I] sche HmBF. assente] assente*n* R.

For she is fayn of þi felaweshipe, for to be þi make.'
Quod Conscience to þe kyng, 'crist it me forbede!
Er I wedde swich a wif wo me bitide!
She is frele of hire feiþ, fikel of hire speche;
[She] makeþ men mysdo many score tymes.
[In] trust of hire tresor [she teneþ wel] manye.
Wyues and widewes wantoun[nesse] techeþ,
Lereþ hem lecherie þat loueþ hire ȝiftes.
Youre fader she felled þoruȝ false biheste,
[A]poisoned popes, [a]peired holy chirche.
Is noȝt a bettre baude, by hym þat me made,
Bitwene heuene and helle, [and] erþe þouȝ men souȝte.
She is tikel of hire tail, talewis of tonge,
As co*m*mune as [þe] Cartwey to [knaue and to alle],
To Monkes, to Mynstrales, to Meseles in hegges. |

119 For] *om* G. fayn...felaweshipe] of fair*e* shap F. fayn] *om* R. þi(1)] þe H.
120 þe] *om* R. kyng] kyng þo B. me] *om* HmH.
121 Er] ⁊ er F.
122 She] For she WHmCrGYOC²CBLMRFH. frele of hire] fykel of F. feiþ] flesch H. fikel] and fykel HmRH; ⁊ fals F. speche] dede H.
123 She] And WHmCrGYOC²CBLMRFH. men] *om* Cr¹. tymes] *main hand after cancelled* ways G; tyme HmYCB.
124 In...tresor] ⁊ þo þat tristne on trewþe F. In] G; *om* WHmCrYOC²CBLMRH. she teneþ] she treyȝeþ F; trayeþ HmYOCLMR; bitrayeþ WCrGC²B; dysseyuyt H. wel manye] ful manye WHmCrGYOC²CBLMRH; hem ofte F.
125 Wyues] Boþe wyvis F. widewes] wdydowes Cr¹. wantounnesse] wantou*n*nesse YHmOC²CBR; wantounes WCrGLMH; and wantowne wenchis F. techeþ] teychyth G; she techeþ WHmCrYOC²CBLMRH; *om* F.
126 Lereþ] And lereþ WHmYOC²CBLMRH; And lerneth CrGF. loueþ] loue Cr. ȝiftes] loore F.
127 *line om* H. Youre] Oure B (*altered to* ȝOure Bm). she] he R; *om* OC². false] hire false B; faire R; hir*e* fayr*e* F. biheste] heste F.
128 Apoisoned] And haþ apoisoned BYOC²CLMR; And haþ enpoisoned W; And hath poysoned CrHmG; Sche hat poysynd H; ⁊ she haþ ypoysoned F. popes] CBL; popes and WHmCrGYOC²MRFH (⁊ *another ink* M). apeired] appeyred HmF; appayreth R; peired WCrGYOC²CBLMH.
129 Is] Is þer B; þer is F. bettre] bytt*er*ere H. me] the G.
130 and(2)...men] þey me*n* al erthe F. and(2)] RH; in WHmCrGYOC²CBLM. souȝte] souȝten OC².
131 She] For she WHmCrGYOC²CBLMRFH. tikel] fikil OC². hire] *om* Y. talewis of] tale wise of R; ⁊ talewyȝs of FH; talewis of hir*e* BHmCrGYOC²CLM; and talewis of hire W.
132 As] ⁊ as F. þe] GH; a WCrYOC²CBLMR; *om* HmF. knaue] eche knaue HmGMF; ech a knaue WCrYOC²CBLR; euery knawe H. and to alle] þat walkeþ WHmCrGYOC²CBLMRH; of towhne F.
133 To Monkes] She takþ Masonys F. to(1)] ⁊ to CrYR; ⁊ F. Mynstrales] mynstalles L. to(2)] ⁊ F.

Sisours and Somonou*rs*, swiche men hire preiseþ; *fol.* 15 *b*
Sherreues of Shires were shent if she ne were.
She dooþ men lese hire lond and hire lif boþe;
[And] leteþ passe prisoners and paieþ for hem ofte,
And gyueþ þe Gailers gold and grotes togidres
To vnfettre þe fals, fle where hym likeþ.
[She] takeþ þe trewe bi þe top, tieþ h[y]m faste,
And hangeþ h[y]m for hatrede þat harm[e]de neu*ere*.
To be corsed in Consistorie she counteþ noȝt a [risshe];
For she copeþ þe Co*m*missarie and coteþ hise clerkes
She is assoiled as soone as hireself likeþ.
[She] may neiȝ as muche do in a Monþe one[s]
As youre secret seel in sixe score dayes.
She is pryuee wiþ þe pope, p*ro*uisours it knoweþ;
Sire Symonie and hirselue seleþ [þe] bulles.
She blesseþ þise Bisshopes [if] þei be lewed;

134 Sisours] Boþe sysoures F. men] shull F. preiseþ] p*re*yse F.
135 Sherreues] But sherevis F. of Shires] *om* GH. of] and Hm. were(1)] weren OBF. ne were] nere YOC^{2}CLMRF; were not Cr.
136 She] For she WHmCrGYOC^{2}CBLMRFH. lese] lesen MF; selle H. lif] lyues GH.
137 And] & she F; She WHmCrGYOC^{2}CBLMRH. leteþ] lat R. passe] passeþ Bm. prisoners] prisons R. paieþ...ofte] for hem ofte payeth Hm. paieþ] prayeth Cr^{1}Cot.
138 gyueþ] ȝyueþ Hm. þe] *om* M. Gailers] gailere FGH.
139–70 *left margin cropped* R.
139 To...fals] & vnfetreth fals to (*over erasure*) Hm. vnfettre] vnfettren Cr. fle] & flee F; *rubbed* H. hym] hem YCBmBoMH.
140 She] And WHmCrGYOC^{2}CBLMRFH. takeþ þe trewe] taketh trewthe RH; trewþe ys take F. top] top and WHmCrGYOC^{2}CBLMRFH. tieþ] teyȝed F. hym] HmCr^{1}OC^{2}CBLRH; hem WCr^{23}GYM; fyȝn F.
141 hangeþ] he hangyd F. hym] HmOC^{2}CBLRH; hem WCrGYM; *om* F. for] in H. harmede] harme dede HmC^{2}LR; harme dide CCrGM (e(1) *erased* M); harm dede CotH; harm dide WYOBmBoF.
142 be corsed] don curse F. in Consistorie] In constorye GBRF; *rubbed* H. she] he R. counteþ] acou*n*teþ F; settyth H. risshe] MYOC^{2}CBLRF; bene WHmCrGH.
143 she] he R. copeþ] coped CBm; rapyth H. and] *om* H. coteþ] klokiþ all F; cetes C.
144 She] & she F; he R. as(1)] also HmB; *om* F. self] seluen M.
145 She] F; And WHmCrGYOC^{2}CBLMRH. neiȝ as] nyȝ also B; almost also Hm. as...do] doon as myche F. ones] HmGYOC^{2}BRFH; one WCrCLM.
146 As] As maye Cr. youre] oure OC^2. secret] secre M. in] sire kyng in F. dayes] wynt*er* H.
147 She] For she WHmCrGYOC^{2}CBLMFH; For he R. prouisours] alle p*ro*visoures F. it] hyr H.
148 Sire] For Sire WHmCrGYOC^{2}CBLMRH; For Maist*er* F. selue] seluen M. seleþ] aseely*n* F; sellen G; selle H. þe] the HmCrGFH; hire WYOC^{2}CBLMR.
149 *run together with* 150 R. She] & she F. þise] the Cr^{23}; *om* FH. if...lewed] & beggerys she hateþ F; *om* R. if] þeiȝ WHmCrGYOC^{2}BLMH; thyo C. be] seme Hm.

Prouendre[s], p*er*sones and preestes [she] mayntenep
To [holde] lemmans and lotebies alle hire lifdaies,
And bryngeþ forþ barnes ayein forbode lawes.
Ther she is wel wiþ þe kyng wo is þe Reaume,
For she is fauo*ur*able to fals and [f]ouleþ truþe ofte.
By I*es*us! wiþ hire Ieweles youre Iustices she shendeþ
And liþ ayein þe lawe and letteþ hym þe gate
That feiþ may no3t haue his forþ, hire floryns go so þikke.
She ledeþ lawe as hire list and louedaies makeþ,
And doþ men lese þoru3 hire loue þat lawe my3te wynne;
The ma3e for a mene man þou3 he mote euere!
Lawe is so lordlich and looþ to maken ende;
Wiþouten p*re*sent3 or pens [he] pleseþ wel fewe.
Barons and Burgeises she bryngeþ in sorwe, |
And al þe comune in care þat coueiten lyue in truþe. *fol.* 16 *a*
Clergie and coueitise she coupleþ togidres.

150 Prouendres] P*r*ouendres C; Prouendreþ WHmCrGYOC^{2}BLMH; *om* RF. persones] *om* RF. she] F; a R; *om* WHmCrGYOC^{2}CBLMH. mayntenep] mayteynen Bo; meynteneþ w*it*h mennes wifes to deele F.
151 To] ⁊ to F. holde] haue WHmCrGYOC^{2}CBLMRFH. lemmans] lotebies R. and] *om* F. lotebies] lotobyes Hm; letebyes G; lemmanes R; *om* F. lif] lyues C; lief Cot.
152 bryngeþ] bryngen GYOC^{2}CLMR; so ben browht F. forbode] forboden OC^{2}M; forbyden G; fobode Y.
153 Ther] ⁊ þere F. she] he R. þe(2)] that Hm; to þ*a*t F.
154 she] he R. to] to the YOC^{2}CBLMR. fouleþ] HmCrGOC^{2}LMRH; defouleþ WF; folweþ CB; sowleth Y.
155 Iesus] ies*u* HmCBH. youre] þe RF. Iustices] iustice H. she] ofte sche Hm.
156 *line om* H. liþ] leiþ B. lawe] lawes Cr^{23}. letteþ] let R. hym] hem Cr^{23}; so F.
157 *line om* H. haue...forþ] be of force Cr. haue] hauen M. his] *altered to* her *another script* G. hire] for F; *om* G. floryns] floren3ys G. go] fli Cr. so] to Cr^{23}.
158 She] And H. ledeþ] let R. lawe] þe lawe WHmCrGYOC^{2}CBLMRFH. as] at H. hire] she F. and] ⁊ swiche F.
159 And doþ] þ*a*t F. lese] lesen M. þoru3] for HmH; be F. loue] iloue (il *smudged*) Hm. my3te wynne] wolde þey wonne F. wynne] wynnen YM.
160 The] 3ee þe F. ma3e] masse (s(2) *erased*) Bm. for] of Cr^{23}. mote] moote GF; mote hire WCBLMR (hire *erased* Bm); mote hure Hm; mote her Cr; mote here YOC^{2}; mote w*it*h hyr H.
161 Lawe] For þe Lawe F. so] to Cot. maken] make HmCrYOC^{2}CBLRFH. ende] an ende OC^{2}CotF.
162 outen] oute HmYC^{2}CBL. or] other R; of Cot. he] R; she WHmCrGYOC^{2}CBLMH; it F. wel] ful CrR; but FH. *Hereafter a spurious line* Cr^{23}; *see above*, p. 222.
163 Barons] Boþe Baronys F. Burgeises] burgeys HmYCBLMRH. in] into OC^{2}.
164 comune] comunes OC^{2}F. in(1)] i*n*to OC^{2}. coueiten lyue] lyue wolde Hm. coueiten] louyt H. lyue in] lyfe in Cr^{23}R; to lyue In GB; to leue*n* in C^{2}H; *om* F.
165 Clergie] For clergie WCrGYOC^{2}CBLMFH; for clergyse Hm; :::clergise R. she] he R. coupleþ] schappyt H.

This is þe lif of þat lady, now lord ȝyue hire sorwe,
And alle þ*a*t mayntenep hire men, meschaunce hem bitide!
For pou*er*e men may haue no power to pleyne þouȝ [hem] sm*er*te,
Swich a maister is Mede among men of goode.'
Thanne mournede Mede and mened hire to þe kynge
To haue space to speke, spede if she myȝte.
The kyng graunted hire g*ra*ce wiþ a good wille.
'Excuse þee if þow kanst; I kan na moore seggen,
For Conscience accuseþ þee to congeien þee for eu*er*e.'
'Nay lord', quod þat lady, 'leueþ hym þe werse
Whan ye witen witterly wher þe wrong liggeþ.
Ther þ*a*t meschief is [most] Mede may helpe.
And þow knowest, Conscience, I kam noȝt to chide,
Ne [to] dep*ra*ue þi p*er*sone wiþ a proud herte.
Wel þow woost, [Conscience], but if þow wolt [lie],
Thow hast hanged on myn half elleuene tymes,
And [ek] griped my gold [and] gyue it where þee liked.

166 This] that Hm; *cropped* R. now] oure FH; *om* Hm.
167 þ*a*t] hire F. mayntenep] maynteyne HmGC^2F (ynteyne *over erasure* Hm); maytene H. hire] & hire F. men] *om* H. meschaunce] mychance G; schame Hm.
168 *line om* H; *as two lines divided after* pleyne Hm. may] *om* F. haue no power] not G. to pleyne] FBoCotM; to pleyne hem WCrYOC^2CBmLR; hem to pleyne Hm; pleyne þem G. þouȝ...sm*er*te] tyl þey sore smerte and lowe adowne falle Hm. þouȝ] all thogh G; when Cr. hem] þei WCrGYOC^2CBLMRF. sm*er*te] smerten OC^2.
169 *line om* F. a] *om* Cr^{23}. goode] God Cr^1; gret good H.
170 mened...kynge] made mychil sorwe F. mened] meued Cr. hire] *om* H.
171 To...space] & *pra*yede þe kyng F. she] a R.
172 good] glad F.
173 kanst] can H. na...seggen] sey no more H. seggen] segge HmCrC^2; þis tyme F.
174 accuseþ] haþ accused F. congeien] congeye HmYOC^2CBLMRFH; conguere G. þee(2)] *om* H.
175 þat] þe H. leueþ] leue CrR; now leve F.
176 ye] ȝ Bo. witen] wytt GH. liggeþ] lyth C^2CrH.
177 Ther] For þere F. þ*a*t] the Hm. most] gret WHmCrGYOC^2CBLMRFH. helpe] *main hand after cancelled* spede C; helpen YM; it helpe F.
178 And] And þat RF. kam] can F. to] wi*th* þe F.
179 Ne] No*n* H. to] HmH; *om* WCrGYOC^2CBLMRF. dep*ra*ue] praue Hm. herte] wille Y.
180 Wel] But wel F. þow woost] wost thu Cot. woost] woteste Cr; wast G. Conscience] wernard WHmCrYOC^2CBLMRF; werward H; warned G. wolt] wyll Cr^1F; wold GCot; *om* Bm. lie] gabbe WHmCrGYOC^2CBLMRFH.
181 hast] *om* Y. myn] me Cr. half] hals HmH. tymes] tyme R; schor tymes H.
182 ek] also WHmCrGYOC^2CBLMRFH. griped] Igripe RF; grype H. and] BGF; *om* WHmCrYOC^2CLMRH. gyue] gyuen G; ȝyue Hm; ȝeuyth H; ȝaf B. it] *om* H. liked] lykyth H.

Whi þow wraþest þee now wonder me þynkeþ.
Yet I may, as I myȝte, menske þee wiþ ȝiftes,
And mayntene þi manhode moore þan þow knowest;
Ac þow hast famed me foule bifore þe kyng here.
For killed I neu*er*e no kyng, ne counseiled þ*er*after,
Ne dide as þow demest; I do it on þe kynge.
In Normandie was he noȝt noyed for my sake,
Ac þow þiself sooþly shamedest hym ofte;
Crope into a Cabane for cold of þi nayles;
Wendest þ*at* wynter wolde han ylasted euere; |
And dreddest to be ded for a dym cloude, *fol.* 16 *b*
And [hastedest þee] homward for hunger of þi wombe.
Wiþouten pite, Pilour, pou*er*e men þow robbedest
And bere hire bras at þi bak to Caleis to selle,
Ther I lafte wiþ my lord his lif for to saue.
I made his me[ynee] murye and mournynge lette;
I batred hem on þe bak and boldede hire hertes
And dide hem hoppe for hope to haue me at wille.
Hadde I ben Marchal of his men, by Marie of heuene!
I dorste haue leyd my lif and no lasse wedde

183 Whi] And whi WHmCrGYOC^{2}CB LMRH; But why F. þow] *om* Hm. þee] me H. þynkeþ] thynke G.
184 Yet] For ȝit F. menske] amende BH.
186 Ac] but GFH; And CrC^{2}C. famed] defamed HmF. me] *om* F.
187 killed I] t*ru*ly y kyllyd F. no] *om* Hm MFH. kyng] kyng ne pope H; kniȝt RF. ne] no*n* H. counseiled] co*n*seil Bm; co*ntri*vede F; coseled H. þ*er*after] therto Hm; þ*at* dede F.
188 þow] thu now Hm. I] me y F. it] me Y; *om* CLM. kynge] dede F.
189–94 *lines om* H.
189 In] For in F. was he] nas he Hm; þe ky*n*g was F. noyed] Inuyed R; anoied B.
190 Ac] but GF; And CrC^{2}C. shamedest] þou Shamedist F. ofte] often M.
191 Crope] and crope B; For crope F. into] in HmF. Cabane] capan C^2. of] on Hm.
192 Wendest] ⁊ wendist F; wenyst C^2. þ*at*] þou that G. ylasted] lasted CrGYCB LMF; laste HmR; durid OC^2.
193 And] ⁊ also þou F. be ded] haue be ded Hm; dyȝe F.
194 hastedest þee] hyedest þee OC^2; hyedest WHmCrGYBLMRF; hidest C. homward] vpward Cr.
195 Wiþ] ⁊ *with* F; But þou *with* H. outen] oute CrGYOC^{2}CLMR. Pilour] þou pylour F. pouere men] *in* norm*and*y H. robbedest] robbist C^{2}H.
196 at] on GH. to(1)] In F.
197 lafte] laste CrBm.
198 meynee] meene H; men WHmCrGY OC^{2}CBmBoLMRF; *om* Cot. and] ⁊ here F. mournynge] murnyge R. lette] letted YOC^{2}H; y lette F.
199 *line om* H. I] And I OC^2. hem] hym Bm. þe] here Cr.
200 *line om* H. And] I Cr. hem] *om* Cot. hoppe] hoppy*n* F; hope C^2. for] on F. at] atte Hm.
201 his] *om* OC^2. Marie of heuene] hy*m* þ*at* me made H.
202–28 *left margin cropped* R.
202 haue] a H. no] no*n* H. wedde] gage F.

He sholde haue be lord of þat lond in lengþe and in brede,
And [ek] kyng of þat kiþ his kyn for to helpe,
The leeste brol of his blood a Barones piere.
Cowardly þow, Conscience, conseiledest hym þennes
To leuen his lordshipe for a litel siluer,
That is þe richeste Reaume þat reyn ouerhoueþ.
It bicomeþ a kyng þat kepeþ a Reaume
To yeue [hise men mede] þat mekely hym *ser*ueþ,
To aliens, to alle men, to hono*ur*en hem *with* ȝiftes;
Mede makeþ hym biloued and for a man holden.
Emp*er*ours and Erles and alle man*ere* lordes
[Thoruȝ] ȝiftes han yonge men to [yerne] and to ryde.
The Pope [wiþ hise] p*re*lates p*re*sentȝ vnderfonge[þ],
And medeþ men h[y]mseluen to mayntene hir lawes.
Ser[u]auntȝ for hire *ser*uyce, we seeþ wel þe soþe,
Taken Mede of hir maistres as þei mowe acorde;

203 haue] a H. be] *om* F. þat] al þat B. in(1)] a YOC^{2}CLR; on H. in(2)] a YOC LR; on C^{2}H; *om* CrB. brede] bredth Cr.
204 ek] also WHmCrGYOC^{2}CBLMRFH. þat] al þat B. his] al his F. kyn] keen F; kynrede Hm. for] *om* HmF.
205 *line om* H. his] þis F. blood] lond RF; kynne CB.
206 Cowardly...Conscience] Cowardly co*n*cyens þou H; & þou Consience cowardly þou F. conseiledest] conseilled YCB; co*n*sellyst H. þennes] þenne F; thanne YOC^{2}M; ȝens H.
207 leuen] leue OC^{2}H; levyn so F.
208 *line om* H. Reaume] regne F. reyn ouerhoueþ] raygneth ouer heigh Cr^{1}. houeþ] oueth M.
209 bicomeþ] comeþ Bm; is co*n*uenyent H. a(1)] G; wel a F; to a WHmCrYOC^{2} CBLMRH. a(2)] the YOC^{2}CB.
210 hise...mede] mede to men WHmCr GYOC^{2}CBLMRFH. mekely] menskly F; myldelich OC^{2}. *ser*ueþ] *ser*ue F.
211 To] & F. to(1)] H; and to WHmCr GYOC^{2}CBLMR; & F. alle] oþ*ere* F. to(2)] þ*at* H; *om* M. hono*ur*en] honoure HmGYOC^{2}CBLRFH. hem] hym Bm CotH.
212 Mede] For Meede F. biloued] beloued CrG; be loued OCBmBoH; to be loued C^{2}. for] *om* F. holden] holde H; yholde F.
213 *line om* H. Erles] kynges (s *another ink*) Hm. alle] *om* Y. man*ere*] maner of Cr^{23}; erthely F.
214 *line om* H. Thoruȝ] þorghȝ F; :::urȝ R; For WHmCrGYOC^{2}CBLM. ȝiftes] gyftes CrG. yonge men] ȝoumen RF. yerne] ȝeerne F; ȝernen R; renne WHm Cr^{1}GYOC^{2}BL; rennen CM; go Cr^{23}.
215 wiþ hise] and and alle his Hm; and alle YOC^{2}CBmBoLMRH; and alle þe WCrGCot; also of F. vnderfongeþ] he vndirfongyþ F; vnderfongen WHmGYO C^{2}CBLMR; vndyrfonge H; vnderfoggen Cr.
216 medeþ] meden HmOC^{2}H; þey Meede F. hym] GBm; hem WHmCrYOC^{2}C BoCotLMRF; *om* H. seluen] selue MHmCotRF; selues Cr; *om* H. hir] hys G; þe F. lawes] lawe Hm.
217 Seruauntȝ] *Ser*uantȝ YCr^{23}OCBL; & seruau*n*tys F; ::::uantȝ R; Sergeauntȝ WHmCr^{1}GC^{2}MH (*over erasure* M). we... wel] who can seyȝ F.
218 Taken] take GFH. of] for Cr. maistres] mayster OC^{2}LF. as] and Cot. acorde] acordyn C^{2}.

Beggeres for hir biddynge bidden [of] men Mede; |
Mynstrales for hir myrþe Mede þei aske; *fol.* 17 *a*
The kyng haþ mede of his men to make pees in londe;
Men þ*a*t [kenne clerkes] crauen [of hem] Mede;
Preestes þat p*re*chen þe peple to goode
Asken Mede and massepens and hire mete [als];
Alle kynne craft[y] men crauen Mede for hir P*re*ntices;
[Mede and Marchaundiȝe] mote nede go togideres;
No wiȝt, as I wene, wiþouten Mede may libbe.'
Quod þe kyng to Conscience, 'by crist, as me þynkeþ,
Mede is worþi, [me þynkeþ], þe maistrie to haue'.
'Nay', quod Conscience to þe kyng and kneled to þe erþe.
'Ther are two manere of Medes, my lord, [bi] you*re* leue.
That oon god of his g*ra*ce [gyueþ] in his blisse
To [hem] þ*a*t [werchen wel] while þei ben here.
The p*ro*phete p*re*cheþ [it] and putte it in þe Sauter:

219 *line om* H. Beggeres] ⁊ beggerys F. biddynge] beddyng G; beggyng RF. bidden] asken Hm. of...Mede] mede men (*marked for transposition*) O. of men] for me*n* F; men WHmGYC^{2}CBLMR; me Cr.

220 Mynstrales] ⁊ Menstralis F. myrþe] merthes HmB. þei aske] me*n* hem p*ro*fre F. aske] asken HmOC^{2}M.

221 *line om* H. men] mene OC^2.

222 Men] ⁊ me*n* F; *cropped* R. kenne] teche WLH; techen HmCrGYOC^{2}CBMRF. clerkes] children WHmCrYOC^{2}CBLMRFH; chyldre G. crauen] craue GYCLM; asky*n* H. of hem] HmGYOC^{2}CBLMRFH; after WCr.

223 *divided from* 224 *after* Mede WHmCrGYOC^{2}CBLMRFH. p*re*chen] preche RF. to goode] to god R; of good H; of god HmF.

224 Asken] aske of hem Y; þey aske F; asked C^2. mete] meel F. als] at þe meel tymes WCr^{1}GYCBLM; at þe male tymes OC^2; at meal tymes R; at þe mel tyme HHmCr^{23}; at here mete tyȝme F.

225 kynne] man*er*e of FH; *om* G. crafty] HmYOC^{2}CBLMRFH; craftye*s* G; craftes WCr. crauen] crave F; aske H. for] of Y. P*re*ntices] p*re*ntys HmYCBLMFH.

226 Mede...Marchaundiȝe] Marchandyse ⁊ meede H; Marchauntȝ and Mede WHmCrGYOC^{2}CBLMR; ⁊ Marchauntys ⁊ meede F. mote...go] be*n* met H. mote] moten B. nede] nedes CrBMF.

227 outen] oute HmGYOC^{2}CBLR. Mede] me H. libbe] leffe C^2.

228 Quod] Than seyd F. þynkeþ] thynk H.

229 Mede is] Now ys Meede F. is] R; is wel WHmCrGYOC^{2}CBLMH. me...þe] þe WHmCrGYOC^{2}CBLMRFH.

230 to þe erþe] adou*n* H. to(2)] on CrF.

231 manere] man*er*es M. of] *om* G. bi] by R; be F; wiþ WHmCrGYOC^{2}CBLMH.

232 That oon] The on H; þe firste is þ*a*t F. oon] oon is BoCot; on his Bm. gyueþ] grau*n*teþ WHmCrGYOC^{2}CBLMRFH. in] to F. his(2)] *om* Cot.

233 hem] Cr; þo WHmGYOC^{2}CBLMRFH. werchen wel] wel werchen WHmCr^{23}GYOC^{2}BLMR; wel wirche F; wol worchen C; wyll worke Cr^1; wyl do wel H. while] while that Hm. ben] liuen Cr^{23}. here] on erthe F.

234 Þe p*ro*phece spekyth of þis i*n* þe sautyr book H. it(1)] þerof WHmCrGYOC^{2}CBLMRF. putte] puttiþ OC^2; is pyt F. it(2)] *om* F.

Domine, quis habitabit in tabernaculo tuo?
Lord, who shal wonye in þi wones wiþ þyne holy seintes,
Or resten in þyne holy hilles: þis askeþ Dauid.
And Dauid assoileþ it hymself as þe Sauter telleþ:
Qui ingreditur sine macula & operatur Iusticiam.
Tho þat entren of o colour and of one wille
And han ywroght werkes wiþ right and wiþ reson, |
And he þat vseþ noȝt þe lyf of vsurie, *fol.* 17 *b*
And enformeþ pouere [peple] and p*ur*sueþ truþe:
Qui pecuniam suam non dedit ad vsuram et munera super innocentem &c,
And alle þ*a*t helpen þe Innocent and holden w*ith* þe riȝtfulle,
Wiþouten Mede doþ hem good and þe truþe helpeþ,
Swiche maner*e* men, my lord, shul haue þis firste Mede
Of god at a gret nede whan þei gon hennes.
Ther is [a] Mede mesurelees þat maistres desireþ;
To mayntene mysdoers Mede þei take;
And þerof seiþ þe Sauter in a Salmes ende:
In quorum manibus iniquitates sunt; dextra eorum repleta est muneribus.

234α *Domine*] *om* Hm. *tuo*] *tuo &c* HmCr GOC^{2}R; *tuo atque quis requiescet in monte sancto eius imocens manibus et mundo corde* F.
235 Lord] he seyþ Lord F. shal wonye] so dwelleth G. wones] wone H; blysse G. wiþ] with RFH; and wiþ WHmCrGYO C^{2}CBLM (and *erased* Hm).
236 resten] reste H. in] on LMRF. hilles] hyl HHm. þis] þus FH. askeþ] asked RCotF.
237 assoileþ] asoyled FH. self] seluy*n* H. Sauter] book H.
237α *ingreditur*] *ingredietur* C. *macula*] maculo YC. *Iusticiam*] *iusticiam &c* Hm; *Iusticia* CBo.
238 Tho] They CrB. entren] entre H. and] he seiþ & also F. one] *om* Cot.
239 han] haven F; hath G. ywroght] wrought CrHmGYOC^{2}CBLMFH. wiþ (2)] *om* Hm.
240 he] þei H. þat...noȝt] wil nowht vse F. vseþ] vse H; ne vseth YOC^{2}CBLR.
241 *transposed with* 241α H. And] But F. peple] men WHmCrGYOC^{2}CBLMRFH. and p*ur*sueþ] & pursuyth aft*er* H; to pursue F; and preserueth Cr.
241α *line om* F. *vsuram*] vsuriam G. *&c*] *non accepit &c* G; *non accepit* HmCot; *non accipit* Cr; *non* H; *om* CBmBo.
242 alle] þo F. helpen] helpe CrF. þe Innocent] i*n*nocent*es* H. holden] hold CYOC^{2}LMRFH. riȝtfulle] treuthe H.
243 Wiþ] & *with* F. outen] oute OCrGC^2 CBLMR. hem] hym Bm. þe] *om* OC^{2}F. truþe] trewe RF. helpeþ] men helpe F.
244 men] of me*n* FGC^{2}H. my lord] *om* G. my] *om* H. þis] the HmCr^{23}YOC^{2}FH. firste] forseyd F.
245 a] þe B; here HmCrM (hir *over erasure* M); his F; *om* GOC^2. þei gon] he goth H.
246 Ther...Mede] þe seco*n*de Meede ys F. a] anoþ*er* WHmCrGYOC^{2}BLMRH; and other C. desireþ] desyre H.
247 mayntene] maytene RH. take] taken OC^{2}F.
248 And] *om* H. þerof] Þ*er*fore H; there HmB; of hem F. seiþ] speaketh Cr^{23}. a] þe H.
249 *sunt*] *om* CBmBo. *muneribus*] *muneribus &c* Hm; *om* H.

And he þat gripeþ hir [giftes], so me god helpe,
Shal abien it bittre or þe book lieþ.
Preestes and *per*sons þat plesynge desireþ,
That taken Mede and moneie for masses þ*at* þei syngeþ,
[Shul haue] Mede [on þis molde þat] Mathew [haþ graunted]:
Amen amen Rec[*eperu*]*nt mercedem suam.*
That laborers and lowe [lewede] folk taken of hire maistres
It is no manere Mede but a mesurable hire.
In marchaundise is no Mede, I may it wel auowe;
It is a *per*mutacion apertly, a penyworþ for anoþer.
Ac reddestow neu*er*e *Regum,* þow recrayed Mede,
Whi þ[at] vengeaunce fel on Saul and on his children?
God sente to Saul by Samuel þe *pro*phete |
That Agag of Amalec and al his peple after *fol.* 18 *a*
Sholden deye for a dede þat doon hadde hire eldres.
"Forþi", seide Samuel to Saul, "god hymself hoteþ [þ]ee
Be buxom at his biddynge his wil to fulfille.

250 And] *om* FH. he] Tho H. gripeþ] grypy*n* H. hir] þat (*cancelled for* her *main hand*) O; so F. giftes] gold WHmCrGY OC^{2}CBLMRFH. god] gold Cot.
251 Shal] he shal F. abien] abye CrYOC^2 CBoCotLRFH; abite Bm. it] it ful BRH. bittre] bittirli OGC^{2}BF; bettre Y; sore H. or] or ell*es* H; if F. book] bolk (*corrected*) Bm. lieþ] be trewe F.
252–4 *lines om* H.
252 Preestes] Boþe p*re*stys F. plesynge] pleasinges Cr; p*re*ysynge F.
253 That] þey F. taken] take HmGF; taked R. and] or HmM. masses] messe CBmBo. þ*at* þei] to F. syngeþ] synge HmCrF; songen R.
254 Shul...þat] ⁊ þerfor is he*re* Meede as sey*n*t F. Shul haue] Taken hire WCrGY OC^{2}CBLMR; take here Hm. on...þat] here as WHmCrGYOCBLMR; hire as C^2. haþ graunted] vs techeþ WCrGYCBL MR; vs telleth HmOC^{2}F.
254α *amen*] *amen dico vobis* HmG (*dico vobis over erasure another ink* Hm); *dico vobis* FH. *Receperunt*] HmOC^{2}FH (*over erasure another ink* Hm); *Recipiebant* WCr GYCBLMR.
255 That] But þ*at* F. laborers] laboris C^{2}F; laboren *above line main hand* G; lewde me*n* H. and] as G. lowe lewede] lowe WCr^1 GYOCBL; lewed HmC^{2}RFH; mene M; pore Cr^{23}. folk] men F. taken] take H.
256 is] nis R. manere] manere of HmH. mesurable] resonable BC.
257 In] Ne in F. is] it is M.
258 a(1)] *om* RF. apertly] *om* G. worþ] *om* HmG. anoþer] a peny H.
259 Ac] but GFH; And CrC^{2}C. neu*ere*] *supplied in margin* Cot.
260 Whi] Whe*n* Cr. þat] þe WHmCrG YOC^{2}CLMRFH; *om* B. on(2)] *om* GMF.
261 sente] seyde H.
262 That] to Hm. of] and Cr^{1}GOF (*corrected main hand* O). Amalec] annales G. al] *om* R. his] here F.
263 Sholden] schulde HmCrGYCLRH. deye] deyen Hm. a] þe F. hadde] hadde*n* O.
264 *divided from* 265 *after* hoteþ WHmCr GYOC^{2}CBLMRFH. Forþi] Therfore CrH; þus F. hymself] *om* G. hoteþ] þe hotethe GF; hothed H. þee] *spelled* Thee W; þou FH.
265 Be] to be HmOC^2. his(1)] my RF. his(2)] ⁊ his OC^{2}H. to] *om* OH.

Weend to Amalec w*ith* þyn oost & what þow fyndest þ*er*e sle it.
Burnes and beestes, bren hem to deþe;
Widwes and wyues, wo*m*men and children,
Moebles and vnmoebles, and al þow my3t fynde,
Bren it; bere it no3t awey be it neuer so riche;
For Mede ne for monee loke þow destruye it.
Spille it and spare it no3t, þow shalt spede þe bettre."
And for he coueited hir catel and þe kyng spared,
Forbar hym and his beestes boþe as þe bible witnesseþ
Ooþerwise þan he was warned of þe *pro*phete,
God seide to Samuel þ*a*t Saul sholde deye
And al his seed for þ*a*t synne shenfulliche ende.
Swich a meschief Mede made þe kyng to haue
That god hated hym for eu*er*e and alle hise heires after.
The *culorum* of þis cas kepe I no3t to [shewe];
On auenture it noyed m[e] noon ende wol I make,
For so is þis world went wiþ hem þ*a*t han power
That whoso seiþ hem soþe[s] is sonnest yblamed.

266 Weend] wynde C^2. to...oost] vnto amales G. what] þat G; al that Hm. fyndest] fynst RF. þere] *om* HmF; *erased* M. sle it] sle Hm; *om* H. it] *lost in sewing* Bm.
267 Burnes] & beernes F; Bren it bothe bernys H; barnes G; burwes Hm. bren] brennen Y; fel H. deþe] dethe (the *over erasure*) M; þe deth H; dede YOC^{2}CBLR.
268 Widwes] Wyuys H; Boþe wyvis F. wyues] wydewis FH. wommen] & wommen FH; womman Bm. and children] w*ith* chylde F.
269 Moebles (*both*)] Mevable FCr. vnmoebles] i*n*mobylys H. and(2)] *om* F. al] al that HmCrGYOC^{2}CBmLMRH. my3t] may G; may þere F.
270 *transposed with* 271 H. it(1)] it & H. it(2)] *om* Cr.
271 ne] nor HmCrYOC; no*n* H. loke... it] mak no þy*n* on lyve F. loke] but loke H.
272 Spille] But spille F. and] *om* Hm. þow] & þou F. spede] fare H; *om* Cr^1.
273 hir] the Hm. spared] he sparede F.
274 *line om* H. Forbar] & forbar F. boþe] *om* F. bible] book F. witnesseþ] wytnesse Bm; telliþ FG.
275 of] be H.
276 God seide] þan seyde god F.
277 al] *om* Cr^{23}. shenfulliche] shamfullyche GCr; xamely H; synfully þan F. ende] enden M; endede HmRF.
278 þe kyng] Saul þe kyng WHmCrGY OC^{2}CBLMRH; kyng saul F.
280 *culorum*] colour CrGH; co*n*struyng F. þis] the Y. kepe] ne kepe Cr. to shewe] YOC^{2}CBLMR; to telle WHmCrGH; expowne F.
281 *line om* H. On] yn HmGBm; For F; *om* R. auenture] hap if F. me] men WHmCrGYOC^{2}CBLMRF. noon] now Bm. wol] wolde OC^2.
282 *line om* H. went] wont Cr. han] hauen Hm.
283 That] But H. seiþ] seye Hm. hem] he*m* here F; hym here Hm; the G; *om* CrC^{2}H. soþes] OHmYC^{2}CBLMRF; sothe Cr; sonest soth H; soþest WG. is sonnest] sonest hys H. is] he ys F. yblamed] blamed GFH.

I, Conscience, knowe þis for kynde wit me tauȝte
That Reson shal regne and Reaumes gou*er*ne,
And riȝt as Agag hadde happe shul so*m*me.
Samuel shal sleen hym and Saul shal be blamed
And Dauid shal be diademed and daunten hem alle,
And oon cristene kyng kepen [vs echone].
Shal na moore Mede be maister [on erþe],
Ac loue and lowenesse and leautee togideres; |
Thise shul ben Maistres on moolde [trewe men] to saue. *fol.* 18 *b*
And whoso trespaseþ [to] truþe or takeþ ayein his wille,
Leaute shal don hym lawe and no lif ellis.
Shal no s*er*geant for [þat] s*er*uice were a silk howue,
Ne no pelure in his [panelon] for pledynge at þe barre;
Mede of mysdoeres makeþ manye lordes,
And ouer lordes lawes [ledeþ] þe Reaumes.
Ac kynde loue shal come ȝit and Conscience togideres

284 Conscience...þis] knowe it wel q*uod* co*n*sience F. knowe] *altered to* knew *another ink* Bm; knew BoCotH. þis] it H. kynde] *om* F. wit] *om* H. me tauȝte] me tauȝte it OC^2; me yt taughte $HmCr^{23}YC$ BLMRF (it *erased* M); it me tauȝte WCr^1 GH.
285 Reson] rosoun R.
286 hadde] hadde hap (hap *above line another hand*) M; hadde no harm F. happe] happen G; so happe F; happe ryth so H. shul] shullen B. so*m*me] come Cr.
287 Samuel] For samvel F. sleen] fle F. hym] hem Cr^1YH.
288 daunten] adawnty*n* F; daunted C^2; dimitty*n or* dunnty*n* H.
289 *line om* H. kepen] kepe Cr; shal kepen F. vs echone] hem echone MCrBm (echon *another ink* Bm); hem alle WHm $GYOC^2CBoCotLR$ (hem *above line by corrector* L); al þe frape F.
290 moore] *om* C^2. maister] maistry Cr. on] as she is $WHmCrGYOC^2CBoCotL$ MH; as he is R; as he she is Bm; so mychil as he ys F. erþe] nouþe WHmYOCBLM RF; now $GCrC^2H$.
291 Ac] But H; But boþe F; as G; And CrC^2C. lowenesse] lewednese CBoCot; lewinesse (i *over erasure*) Bm.
292 Thise] *om* Cr^{23}. shul] shullen B. on] of CB. trewe men] truþe WHmCrGY $OC^2CBLMRFH$. to] for to G.
293 so] *om* HmF. trespaseþ] trespas H. to] G; ayein $WHmCrYOC^2CBLMRFH$. takeþ] take H.
294 don] put G. lif] lief C.
295 s*er*geant] sergeantȝ YC^2. þat] his WCrGMH (is *over erasure* ? M); here $HmYOC^2CBLR$; no F. were] weren B. a] no Cr. silk] sylken $GHmOC^2H$. howue] howe C^2FH; howne Cr^{23}; hode Cr^1.
296 pelure] pylour G. panelon] cloke $WCrGYOC^2CBLMRFH$; clooth Hm.
297 But ofte Misdoeris þoru Meede ys Meyntened be lord*es* F.
298 & þoru þe Lordys be lawes for to rewle þe rewhme F. ouer] our H; oþer Bm. lordes] londis OC^2 (lordis *in margin* O). ledeþ] ruleþ $WHmCrGYOC^2CBL$ MRH (*over erasure* M). þe Reaumes] & þe rewme H.
299 Ac] but GF; And CrC^2CH. ȝit] *om* G. Conscience] kynde loue Y.

And make of lawe a laborer; swich loue shal arise
And swich pees among þe peple and a p*ar*fit truþe
That Iewes shul wene in hire wit, and wexen glade,
That Moyses or Messie be come into [myddel]erþe,
And haue wonder in hire hertes þ*a*t men beþ so trewe.
Alle þat beren baselard, brood swerd or launce,
Ax ouþ*er* hachet or any wepene ellis,
Shal be demed to þe deeþ but if he do it smyþye
Into sikel or to siþe, to Shaar or to kult*our*:
Conflabunt gladios suos in vomeres &c.
Ech man to pleye wi*th* a plow, Pykoise or spade,
Spynne or sprede donge or spille hymself wi*th* sleuþe.
Preestes and p*er*sons wiþ *Placebo* to hunte
And dyngen vpon Dauid eche day til eue;
Huntynge or haukynge if any of hem vse
His boost of his benefice worþ bynomen hym after.
Shal neiþ*er* kyng ne knyght, Constable ne Meir*e*
Ouer[carke] þe co*m*mune ne to þe Court sompne,

300 of] of the Hm. lawe a laborer] loue laborerys H. arise] ryse G.
301 *line om* H. And] And a C[2]. pees] RF; a pees WHmCrGYOC[2]CBLM. a] *om* F.
302 wexen] waxe CrGOC[2]BF. glade] Hm; wonder glade WCrGYOC[2]CBLM RFH.
303 That] Tat Bm. or] & Cr. Messie] messyas HmG. be come] be comen Hm GOFH; by comy*n* C[2]. into] to H. myddel] þis WHmCrYOC[2]CBLMR; the G; *om* FH.
304 hire] *om* F. beþ] be here F.
305 Alle] & all F. beren] bere H. baselard] baselardys H. brood] or brod F. swerd or launce] swerdys or lancys H.
306 Ax] Er ex F. ouþer] or CotFH; or yet Cr; orther L.
307 demed] da*m*pned F. þe] *om* CrG. if] *om* HmF. smyþye] smyþe OC[2]C; swythe H.
308 to(1)] into CrF; *om* HmH. to(2)] *om* H. to(3)] ell*es* H.
308α *line om* H. *Conflabunt*] *Et conflabunt* F. *&c*] *om* CrOC[2]F.
309 *line om* B. Ech] Euery Cr. to] shal F. a plow] þe plowh or F. Pykoise] pykeaxe Cr; pykes G. spade] spades G.
310 *line om* B. Spynne] Or spy*n*ne F. or(1)] other R. donge] du*n*k F. spille] lese RF. hym] þem G. wi*th*] for H.
311 and] or Cr. p*er*sons] p*er*osouns Bm. to] shull F.
312 dyngen] dynge HmCrOC[2]H; dyggen G. eche] eche a YOCLMR (a *above line* O); euery CrF. til eue] til euen CrYOC[2] H; to end G.
313 or] & H. haukynge] hawtyng Bm. vse] it vse FHm.
314 His] For his F; The Y. boost] best BmH. of] & H; *om* F. his] *om* Cr. worþ...after] xal be taky*n* hy*m* fro H. worþ] woll be Hm. bynomen] bynome CrGYOC[2]CBLMRF. hym] *om* Y.
315 neiþer] neuer*e* HmH. ne(1)] nor Hm; no*n* H. Constable ne Meire] ne Mey3r ne constable F. ne(2)] nor Cr[1]; no*n* H.
316 carke] lede WHmCrGYOC[2]CBLM RFH. ne] *om* Y. to] *om* Hm. þe(2)] her*e* F. sompne] he*m* somowne F; somonde G.

Ne putte hem in panel to doon hem pli3te hir truþe;
But after þe dede þat is doon oon doom shal rewarde |
Mercy or no m*er*cy as Truthe [may] acorde. *fol.* 19 *a*
Kynges Court and co*m*mune Court, Consistorie and Chapitle,
Al shal be but oon court, and oon [burn] be Iustice,
Tha[t] worþ Trewe-tonge, a tidy man þat tened me neu*er*e.
Batailles shul none be, ne no man bere wepene,
And what smyth þ*a*t any smyþeþ be smyte þ*er*wiþ to deþe:
Non leuabit gens contra gentem gladium &c.
And er þis fortune falle fynde men shul þe worste
By sixe sonnes and a ship and half a shef of Arwes;
And þe myddel of a Moone shal make þe Iewes torne,
And Sar3ynes for þat si3te shul synge *Gloria in excelsis &c*,
For Makometh and Mede myshappe shul þat tyme;
For *Melius est bonum nomen quam diuicie multe.*'
Also wroþ as þe wynd weex Mede in a while.
'I kan no latyn?' quod she, 'clerkes wite þe soþe!

317 putte] putten Hm. in] on H; *om* Cr^{1}. hem(2)] *om* F.
318 þat] *om* CrC^{2}H. oon] þe H. shal] *om* H.
319 Mercy or] Er wi*th* Mercy or wi*th* F. or no mercy] *twice* R. as] *om* G. may] wole WHmCrGYOC^{2}CBLMRFH. acorde] recorde G; asente F.
320 *run together with* 321 B. Kynges] Boþe kyngis F. and(1)] *om* Cr. Consistorie...Chapitle] *om* B. Consistorie] constorye GRF; co*n*strye H. Chapitle] chapter CrG; chapele H.
321 Al...court] *om* B. Al shal] Xal al H. burn] baron WHmCrGYOC^{2}BLMRFH; *om* C. be] by Cr; *om* HmH. *Here* H *copies* 324α.
322 *line om* H. That] *altered from* Thanne Bm; Thanne WHmCrGYOC^{2}CBoCotL MRF. worþ] wel worth Cr^{1}; wexe C^{2}. me neu*er*e] me*n* ofte F.
323 Batailles...none] Ne þa*n*ne shull no batailes F. no] *om* C^{2}H. bere] shal bere F.
324 smyth] smyte C^{2}; smytyth H. þat] *om* H. any smyþeþ] smythieth eny Hm. any] eny man B (man *cancelled* Bm). smyþeþ] *over erasure* M; smithie RF; smithed Cr; smythyng H; smyteth YC^{2}CBoCotL. be] he shal be F; *om* H. smyte] smyten HmCr GOC^{2}R. þerwith] *om* G. to deþe] to dede R; do deth H; to doþ Y; *om* F.
324α *copied after* 321 H. &c] *om* OC^{2}FH.
325 fynde...shul] men shulle fy3nde F. worste] werse F.
326 By] Bo H; For þer shul be F. sixe] þi H. half] *om* H.
327 torne] RGF; to torne WHmCrYOC^{2} CBLMH.
328 And] & þe F. for] of Cr^{1}. þat si3te] þe syghte þ*er*of FR. shul] shulle*n* Bm BoM. synge] sy*n*gyn F. &c] *deo &c* Cr^{1}Y; *deo* Cr^{23}; *om* HmGOC^{2}BmCotR FH.
329 For] þorgh3 F; And CB. myshappe shul] mysshapen shull þey F.
330 *transposed with* 331 H. For] *om* H. *bonum nomen*] *nomen bonum* H. *nomen*] *nomen habere* F. *multe*] *multe &c* HmG BmM.
331 Also] As Cr^{1}HmGMH; þo as F.
332 I...she] Q*uo*d she y can lytyl latyn F. no] *om* Cr^{3}R. wite] wyten BHm; wote CrGYCLMRH; woten OC^{2}; knowe F.

Se what Salomon seiþ in Sapience bokes!
That ȝyuen ȝiftes, [takeþ yeme], þe victorie wynneþ
And [muche] worshipe ha[þ] þerwiþ as holy writ telleþ:
Honorem adquiret qui dat munera &c.'
'I leue wel, lady', quod Conscience, 'þat þi latyn be trewe.
Ac þow art lik a lady þat radde a lesson ones
Was *omnia probate*, and þat plesed hire herte
For þat lyne was no lenger at þe leues ende.
Hadde she loked þat [left] half and þe leef torned
She sholde haue founden fel[l]e wordes folwynge þerafter:
Quod bonum est tenete; truþe þat text made.
And so [mys]ferde ye, madame; ye kouþe na moore fynde
Tho ye [souȝte] Sapience sittynge in youre studie. |
This text þat ye han told were [trewe] for lordes, *fol.* 19 *b*
Ac yow failed a konnynge clerk þat kouþe þe leef han torned.
And if ye seche Sapience eft fynde shul ye þat folweþ,

333 Se] But se H; Now see ȝee F. Sapience] sapiences R; *Sapientie* Cr^{1}. *Here* H *copies line* 336.

334 That] That þei þat WCr^{1}GB; That hij that YCLMR; That he that Cr^{23}OC^{2}; Þat þei H; Of hem þat F; they that Hm. ȝyuen] gyuen GCr^{23}F; gyue Cr^{1}H. ȝiftes...yeme] ȝiftes WHmYOC^{2}BLMR; gyftes CrGCFH.

335 And] þe H. muche] YOC^{2}CBLMR F; moost WHmCrGH. haþ] hath Cr^{23}; haue HmCr^{1}F; had GYC^{2}LH; haad R; hadde WOCBM (*over erasure* M). þerwith] he þerwith H; þerfore F.

336 *copied after* 333 H. *adquiret*] *adquirit* H. *&c*] *om* CrRFH.

337 wel] *om* G. lady] *om* GH. þi] þis H; the Cr^{12}; *om* Cr^{3}. trewe] trowe R.

338 Ac] But FGH; And CrC^{2}; An C. lik] *om* Hm. lady...lesson] Nunne Lady þat a lessoun redde F.

339 *as two lines divided after filo* H. Was] It was þus F; bas Cot; *om* H. *probate*] *autem probate* F; brobate G; *probate non plus in illo filo* And was asay all thyng H. herte] well CrG.

340–4 *lines om* H.

340 lyne] leefe G; *om* Cr. no] *om* OC^{2}. at] þan F. leues] lynes C^{2}.

341 she] *over erasure* M; ȝe BL. þat] on þat B; the G; on þe F. left] ooþer WHm Cr^{23}GYOC^{2}CBLMRF; ouer Cr^{1}. lef] lof Bm. torned] Iturned RF.

342 She] heo R; ȝe BL. haue] a R. founden] founde HmCr^{23}C^{2}RF; sound Cr^{1}. felle] fell G; fel Cr; fele WHmYOC^{2} CBLMRF. þer] *om* HmF.

343 *Quod*] þat seyde *quod* F.

344 mysferde] ferde WHmCrGYOC^{2}CB LMRF. ye...moore] no moore cowhde ȝee F.

345 Tho...souȝte] Of þat ȝee seyȝe in F. Tho] þouȝ C^{2}; to G; Qwan H. ye] you Cr^{23}; he H. souȝte] loked on WHmCr GYOC^{2}CBLMRH. studie] stede H.

346 This] But þis F. þat] *om* H. han] *om* M. told] Itolde R; told here H. were... lordes] ȝee takyn nout þe ende F. trewe] good WHmCrGYOC^{2}CBLMRH.

347 Ac] but GFH; And CrC^{2}C. yow] ȝe HmGF (*over erasure* Hm). failed] falyth H; faile F. konnynge] conyg H; good Cr^{1}. kouþe] can F. han torned] torne G; wel turne F.

348 And] for G. seche] sechyn Hm; seke in F. eft] oft Cr; *om* H. shul ye] ȝe schall HmCrH.

A ful teneful text to hem þat takeþ Mede:
Animam autem aufert accipientium &c.
And þat is þe tail of þe text of þat [teme ye] shewed,
That þeiȝ we wynne worship and wi*th* Mede haue victorie,
The soule þat þe soude takeþ by so muche is bounde.'

349 *line om* B; *run together with* 351 F. to... Mede] *om* F. takeþ] take Cr^{23}H.

350 *line om* F. *Animam*] H; And þat is *Animam* WHmCrGYOC^{2}CBLMR (And] *om* Hm). *autem*] *om* H. *accipientium*] *a bono munera* H. *&c*] *om* R.

351 And...text] *om* F. þat(1)] þis H. tail] tale Cr^{1}. teme] þ*at* WCrYOC^{2}CBoCot LMR; tale þ*a*t F; at H; *om* HmGBm. ye] Cr^{23}YOC^{2}CBLRF; she WHmCr^{1}GMH (*over erasure* M). shewed] scheweden O; schewyt H; schede R; to me pitte F.

352 That] & F. we] ȝe F. wynne] wynnen B. wi*th*] of F. Mede] me RF. haue] have þe F.

353 The] ȝit þe F. soule] send H. soude] souȝd R; sowed G; sonde Cr; syluer F; mede (*over erasure*) Bm. bounde] bounden OC^{2}; ybounde Cot; bonde H.

IV

'CEsseþ', sei[de] þe kyng, 'I suffre yow no lenger.
Ye shul sauȝtne, forsoþe, and serue me boþe.
Kis hire', quod þe kyng, 'Conscience, I hote!'
'Nay, by crist!' quod Conscience; 'congeye me [raþer]!
But Reson rede me þerto raþer wol I deye.'
'And I comaunde þee', quod þe kyng to Conscience þanne,
'Rape þee to ryde and Reson [þat] þow fecche.
Comaunde hym þat he come my counseil to here,
For he shal rule my Reaume and rede me þe beste
[Of Mede and of mo oþere, what man shal hire wedde],
And acounte wiþ þee, Conscience, so me crist helpe,
How þow lernest þe peple, þe lered and þe lewed.'
'I am fayn of þat foreward', seide þe freke þanne,
And [riȝt renneþ] to Reson and rouneþ in his ere;
[Seide hym] as þe kyng [sente] and siþen took his leue.

1 CEsseþ] CEce HmCr (ce *over erasure another ink* Hm); NOw sesiþ F. seide] seyde HmCr^{23}BmRFH; seiþ WCr^{1}GYOC^{2}CBoCotLM. kyng] kyng þo F; kyng þ*er* H. yow] ye G.
2 sauȝtne] sauȝtle HmGOC^{2}BF; sangtle Cr. for] for the G. serue] seruy*n* F.
3 quod] now q*uod* F. kyng] kyng to G; kyng þou F. hote] þe hote B; bydde þe H.
4 congeye] ere congeye Hm; conueye Cot; honge F. raþer] OCr^{23}GYC^{2}CBH; rather sone F; er for euere W; for euere HmCr^{1}LMR.
5 But] But if F. raþer] fryst H. wol I] y will F; wolde y Hm.
6 And] þanne F; *om* GH. þee] you Cr; *om* Y. quod] *om* Y. to] *om* F. þanne] he seyd F.
7 ryde] ryde anon F. and] *om* H. þat þow] þat þou F; þow WHmCr^{23}GYOC^{2}CBLMR; to Cr^{1}H.
8 Comaunde] & comawnde F. hym] *om* H. þat he] to Hm. come] come to me F. here] heren Y.
9 my] the Cr^{23}. þe] to þe F.
10 YCr^{23}OC^{2}; *line om* WHmCr^{1}GCBLMRFH; *here in the spelling of* W. mo] *om* Cr^{23}. what] and what Cr^{23}YOC^{2}. wedde] wedden Y.
11 And] *om* C^{2}. acounte] accou*n*ten Cr; acowntre F. þee] *om* H.
12 þow] þou *altered to* ȝou *another ink* Bm. lernest] leredyst H. þe(2)] boþe F; *om* R. lered] learned Cr. þe(3)] *om* R.
13 fayn of] redy to H. þat] þis F. foreward] forowarde Hm. þe] þat F.
14–16 *lines om* Hm.
14 riȝt...Reson] to resou*n* he rood ryght F. riȝt renneþ] ryt riȝt WCrYOCLMR; rydyth ryght GH; ridiþ B; riȝth C^{2}. rouneþ] rowned F.
15 Seide...sente] & tolde hy*m* as þe kyng seide F; And seide as þe kyng bad WCrGYOC^{2}CBLMRH. siþen] sytthe he F.

'I shal arraye me to ryde', quod Reson, 'reste þee a while',
And called Caton his knaue, curteis of speche,
And also Tomme trewe-tonge-tel-me-no-tales-
Ne-lesynge-to-lauȝen-of-for-I-loued-hem-neuere.
'Set my Sadel vpon suffre-til-I-se-my-tyme |
And lat warroke hym wel wiþ wit[ful] gerþes. *fol.* 20 *a*
Hange on hym þe heuy brydel to holde his heed lowe,
For he wol make wehee twies er [we] be þere.'
Thanne Conscience [o]n his capul [caireþ] forþ faste,
And Reson wiþ hym ryt, rownynge togideres
Whiche maistries Mede makeþ on þis erþe.
Oon waryn wisdom and witty his feere
Folwed h[e]m faste for þei hadde to doone
In [c]heker and in Chauncerye, to ben descharged of þynges.
And riden faste for Reson sholde rede hem þe beste
For to saue hem[seluen] from shame and from harmes.

16 shal] will go F. to ryde] *om* FH. quod Reson] *om* G. reste] go reste F. a] þ*er* F.
17 And...knaue] Ano*n* he klepede Catou*n* his knave ful F. called] callyt H.
18 tel me no] þ*at* tolde fewe F. tales] tale Hm.
19 Ne] no HmG. lesynge] lesyng*es* OC^{2}F. lauȝen] laughe CHmGYOC^{2}BLMRFH. of] at OC^{2}H. I] he F. loued] loue H. hem] hym Y.
20 Set] Sette M; And set WHmCrGYOC^{2}CBLRH; he bad go sette F. my] a F. vpon] vppe R; *om* H. suffre] Sufferau*n*ce Cr.
21 warroke] waroken Cr. hym] it Cr^{23} YOC^{2}CBLMR. wel] *om* F. witful gerþes] gyrtys þ*at* is w*ith* witty wordis F. witful] witty wordes WHmCrGYOC^{2}C BLMR; wyse wordys H. gerþes] gerte HmBm; gerd BoCot; *om* H.
22 Hange] And hange WHmCrGYOC^2 CBLMRFH. þe] an HmH. holde] helde R.
23 For] or Hm; And C^2. he wol] wille he C^2. wol...wehee] *in margin another script, erasure in text* O. make] makyn F; *om* C^2. twies] tweye LMR; to trewþe F; and wynche C^2. we] he WHmCrGYOC^{2}CB LMRFH. be] come CrGC^2; comyt H. þere] therde C.
24 on] GH; vpon WHmCrYOC^{2}CBLM RF. caireþ] kaireth YOCLMRF; carieþ WHmCr^{1}GC^{2}B; caried Cr^{23}; rydyth H.
25 wiþ...ryt] rydyth w*ith* hy*m* H. ryt] rydes CF; rith C^2; rygth Hm; riȝt Bm.
26 Whiche] Qwat H. maistries] maistres Cot. Mede...erþe] on eerth mede þe mayde maketh RF; þ*at* meede makyt on moolde H.
27 Oon] Ano*n* F; Tha*n* H. waryn] comy*n* H. and] & watte F.
28 Folwed] Foleweden O; And folwedy*n* H. hem] YOC^{2}CBmBoLMRFH; hym WHmCrGCot. for þei] *om* LR. þei] he M. hadde] hadden OC^{2}BF.
29 cheker] chekere H; þe checker GYOC^2 CBLMR; þe Chekkeryȝe F; thescheker W; the Eschequer HmCr. and] *om* R. in] yn Hm; in þe WCr^{1}YOC^{2}CB; at þe LCr^{23}R; þe G; *om* MFH. of þynges] þ*ere* F.
30 And...faste] Faste þey ryden F. And] Þei H. riden] ryde Hm. sholde] þ*at* he wolde F. hem] *om* OC^2. þe] for þe F; *om* Cr^{1}C^2.
31 saue hem] saven her*e* F. seluen] selue Y; syluer & he*m* F; fro siluer R; for siluer WHmCrGOC^{2}CBLMH. from(2)] *om* Cr^{1}F. harmes] schonde H.

A[c] Conscience knew hem wel, þei loued coueitise,
And bad Reson ryde faste and recche of hir neiþer.
'Ther are wiles in hire wordes, and *with* Mede þei dwelleþ;
Theras wraþe and wranglynge is þer wynne þei siluer,
Ac [þ]ere is loue and leautee [hem likeþ] noȝt come þere:
Contricio & infelicitas in viis eorum &c.
Thei ne [gy]ueþ noȝt of [good feiþ, woot god þe sooþe]:
Non est timor dei ante oculos eorum &c.
For [þei wolde do for a dyner or a doȝeyne capons
Moore þan for] loue of oure lord or alle hise leeue Seintes.
Forþi, Reson, lat hem ride þo riche by hemselue,
For Conscience know[e þei] noȝt, ne crist, as I trowe.'
And þanne Reson rood faste þe riȝte heiȝe gate
As Conscience hym kenned til þei come to þe kynge.
Curteisly þe kyng þanne com [in to] Reson,
And bitwene hymself and his sone sette hym on benche, |

32 Ac] And WHmCrGYOC^{2}CBLMRFH. hem] hym BmCot; *om* H. þei...coueitise] þ*at* koueytyse þey loveden F. loued] loueden HmO; louyd wel H.

33 *line om* CB. And] & he F. Reson] *om* R. faste] ȝarnere H. hir] hem CrGF.

34 Ther] For þere F; they GYOC^2. wiles] wily YOC^2. þei] þe C^2. dwelleþ] dwelle FCrH.

35 Ther] & þere F. as] *om* H. wraþe] wrothe G. wranglynge] wraglinge C^2; wranlyng H; wrastylyng G. wynne] wynnen OC^2; get Cr.

36 Ac] but G; And CrC^{2}CFH; *om* R. þere] LGYOC^{2}CBMR; where WHmCr FH. is...leautee] loue & lowte is H; þ*at* love & lewte ys F. hem likeþ] þey leete F; þei wol WHmCrGYC^{2}CBLMRH; þei wolen O. come] comy*n* H.

36α *transposed with* 37 F; *line om* H. &c] *om* CotF.

37 Thei ne] Thei H; For þey F. gyueþ] gyueth YOC^{2}CBLMR; gyue CrGFH; yeueþ WHm. of...sooþe] of god one goose wynge WHmCrGYOC^{2}CBLMR H; god nowht o goos feedre F.

37α *line om* H. dei] *Domini* CrYOC^{2}CB. &c] *om* CBoCotLMRF.

38 *as two lines divided after* chiknes WHm CrGYOC^{2}CBLMRFH. For] For woot god WGYOCLMR; For god woote Hm CrC^{2}BFH. wolde] wolden O; woll HmCrF. for...or] moore for WHmCr GYOC^{2}CBLMRF; more H. doȝeyne] doȝeyn of YM; dosey F. capons] chiknes Or as manye capons or for a Seem of Otes WHmCrGYOC^{2}CBLMRFH (chiknes Or] chykes Or for F. seem] comb H).

39 Moore...for] Than for CrYOC^{2}CBL MR; Than for þe WHmGFH. or] & GH. alle] a H; for F.

40 Forþi] Therfore CrFH; For þei Bm. Reson] *om* RF. þo] the CrG. riche] ryche me*n* F. selue] seluen GYOCL.

41 knowe þei] HF; knoweþ hem WHmCr GYOC^{2}CBLMR. ne] no G; no*n* H.

42 And] *om* F. Reson] *above line another hand* F. gate] weye M.

43 As] and HmCrG. hym kenned] him kenneth Cr^1; bykennyd H. þei] he GO C^2. come...kynge] to þe kyng keme F.

44 Curteisly] þan Curteysly F. þanne] ano*n* F. in to] ayeins WHmCrGYOC^2 CBLMRFH.

45 And] *om* G. self] *om* F. sette] he sette F. hym] hem Hm. on] on þe FH; on a Cot. benche] deyȝse F.

And wordeden [a gret while wel wisely] togideres. *fol.* 20 *b*
[Th]anne com pees into [þe] p*ar*lement and putte [vp] a bille
How wrong ayeins his wille hadde his wif taken,
And how he rauysshede Rose, Reignaldes looue,
And Margrete of hir maydenhede maugree hire chekes.
'Boþe my gees and my grys hise gadelynges fecchep.
I dar noȝt for fere of h[y]m fiȝte ne chide.
He borwed of me bayard [and] brouȝte hym [neuere ayein],
Ne no ferþyng þ*er*fore for [n]ouȝt I koude plede.
He mayntenep hise men to murþere myne hewen,
Forstallep my feires, fiȝtep in my Chepyng,
Brekep vp my bern[e] dore[s], berep awey my whete,
And takep me but a taille for ten quarters Otes;
And yet he betep me þ*er*to and lyþ by my mayde.
I am noȝt hardy for hym vnneþe to loke.'
The kyng knew he seide sooþ, for Conscience hym tolde

46 wordeden] worden C^{2}. a...wisely] wel wisely a gret while WHmCrGYOC^{2}CBLMRFH (wel] ful Hm; *om* H. a] at C; *om* Y. gret] long F).
47 Thanne] Tha*n* H; And þanne WHmCrGYOC^{2}CBLMRF. com pees] pes come H. into] in B; to F. þe] C^{2}H; þat F; *om* WHmCrGYOCBLMR. putte] puttede O; puttep C^{2}. vp] H; forþ WHmCrGYOC^{2}CBLMRF. bille] bulle Cot.
48 taken] take H; ytaken F.
49 *line om* H. how] *om* F. looue] loue HmCrGYOC^{2}CBmCotLMR; leve dowh*ter* F.
50 And] ⁊ berevede F. Margrete] margare H. of] *om* F. hede] hode HmGYOC^{2}CBLRH. hire] theyre G. chekes] wille F.
51 Boþe] ⁊ also F. grys] gryses GC^{2}. gadelynges] goodelyng*us* H.
52 *line om* H. I] ⁊ y F. fere] drede Hm. of] *om* F. hym] YCrOC^{2}CBLMR; hem WHmG; *om* F. fiȝte] fyghtyn F. ne] no C. chide] chyden F.
53 borwed...bayard] borwede*n* bayard of me (*correct order noted*) H. of me] oft my G; my Cr. and] HmCrRFH; he WGYOC^{2}CBLM. brouȝte] browty*n* H. hym] it R. neuere ayein] neu*ere* aȝen HmH; agey*n* neu*ere* F; neuer home Cr; hom neuere WYOC^{2}CBLMR; whom neu*er* G.
54 *line om* CBH. þerfore] for hym YOC^{2}. nouȝt] MLRF; ouȝt WHmCrGYOC^{2}. I] that I GOC^{2}.
55 He] Also he F. murþere] Murþere*n* C^{2}; moþere F. hewen] *altered to* heyen Bm; hennes RF.
56 Forstallep] He forstalleth R; ⁊ to forstalep F. feires] fayres Cr^{1}; feires and WCr^{23}GYOC^{2}CBLMRFH (⁊ *added later* Y); markett*es* and Hm. my(2)] þe F.
57 *line om* CB. Brekep] And brekep WHmCrGYOC^{2}LMRH; he brekiþ F. berne] OCrGYC^{2}MFH; bernes WHmLR. dores] Cr^{23}GYOC^{2}H; dore WHmCr^{1}LMRF. berep] and berep WHmGYOC^{2}LMRFH; ⁊ steleth Cr.
58 *line om* H. me] hym G. but] *om* C. for] for a CB; off G. quarters] quarter Cr; s *erased* M. Otes] otys HmCr^{12}GMF; of Otes WYOC^{2}CBLR; othes Cr^{3}.
59 And] *om* HmCrG. betep] bet YGOC^{2}CLR; thretiþ F. to] *om* G. lyþ] lyggeþ HmF; lay C^{2}.
60 *line om* H. am] nam CLM. hardy] so hardy Hm. vnneþe] vnees C. to] for to HmF.
61 knew] knew wel F. hym] so hy*m* F.

That wrong was a wikked luft and wroȝte muche sorwe.
Wrong was afered þ[o] and wisdom he souȝte
To maken [his] pees *with* hise pens and profred hym manye,
And seide, 'hadde I loue of my lord þe kyng litel wolde I
recche
Theiȝ pees and his power pleyned h[e]m euere'.
Tho [wan] Wisdom and sire waryn þe witty
For þ*a*t wrong hadde ywroȝt so wikked a dede,
And warnede wrong þo *with* swich a wis tale:
'Whoso wercheþ by wille wraþe makeþ ofte.
I seye it by myself, þow shalt it wel fynde,
But if Mede it make þi meschief is vppe,
For boþe þi lif and þi lond lyþ in his grace.'
Thanne wowede wrong wisdom ful yerne |
To maken [his] pees wiþ his pens, handy dandy payed. *fol. 21 a*
[Thanne Wisdom and wit] wenten togidres
And token Mede myd hem mercy to wynne.
Pees putte forþ his heed, and his panne blody:
'Wiþouten gilt, god woot, gat I þis scaþe.'

62 luft] lyft C; lust GBR; luske Cr; schrewe C^2; wyght F; gome H. wroȝte... sorwe] muche sorwe wrouȝte RH.
63 Wrong...þo] þanne wex wrong aferd F. afered] afraied Cr. þo] þanne WHm CrGYOC^{2}CBLMRH. and] *om* Cr^2.
64 maken his] maken W; make HmCrG YOC^{2}CBLMRFH. and] he MF. hym] *om* FH.
65 I(1)] *om* F. my lord] my Cot; *om* CrR FH. þe] *om* GC^{2}Cot. kyng] *om* G.
66 and] *with* F. his power] pou*er*t H. hem] HmCr^{23}GRH; hym WCr^{1}YOC^{2}C BLMF. euere] ofte F.
67–70 *lines om* F.
67 Tho] Thanne Y. wan] LR; whan CBo Cot; whant (t *another ink*?) Bm; wente WHmCr^{23}GYOC^{2}M (*over erasure of smaller word* M); wende Cr^1; *om* H. waryn] watkyn C^2.
68 þat] *om* H. ywroȝt] wrougth HmCrG; woruth H.
69 þo] *om* Hm. *with*] þat H. a] *om* C^2. wis] *om* Cr^3.
70 wercheþ] werke H. by] bi my OC^{2}M; my CB.
71 seye] seyȝ F; see Bm. it] *om* H. by] to F. my] m *over erasure* M; thy YOC^{2}LRF. þow shalt] you shal Cr.
72 But] For but F. if...it] mede if it (*correct order noted*) Bm. if] *om* C^2. þi... vppe] þou gost to gret myscheff H.
73 boþe] hoþe Bm. lyþ] lyeth bothe G. his] hyr CrGH.
74 Thanne] þo H. wowede] wewed Bm; worwyd H. ful] fur Y; *om* H.
75 maken his] make his HmCrGYOC^{2}Bo CotLMRF; make is CBm; maken W make H. wiþ] and Bm. his(2)] *om* C^{2}FH. handy...payed] ypayed handy dandy F; In hand payed G.
76 Thanne...wit] þanne wit & wisdom anon F; Wisdom and wit þanne WHmCr GYOC^{2}CBLMRH (wit] witty CB; Wytre Cr^1). wenten] went H; went bothe Cr.
77 token] toke CrGYOC^{2}CLH. Mede... hem] *with* hem meede H. myd] wyth HmGC^{2}CB.
78 panne] pate al F.
79 outen] owte GBR. god] HCr; god it WHmGYOC^{2}CBLMRF. gat] gett G; had H. scaþe] scape Cr^1.

Conscience and þe com*m*une kn[e]wen [wel] þe soþe,
Ac wisdom and wit were aboute faste
To ou*er*comen þe kyng wiþ catel if þei my3te.
The kyng swor by crist and by his crowne boþe
That wrong for hise werkes sholde wo þolie,
And comaundede a Constable to casten hym in Irens:
'[He shal] no3t þise seuen yer seen his feet ones!'
'God woot', quod wisdom, 'þat were no3t þe beste.
And he amendes mowe make lat maynprise hym haue,
And be bor3 for his bale and buggen hym boote,
Amenden þat [mysdede] and eu*er*emoore þe bettre.'
Wit acorde[þ] þ*er*wiþ and [witnessede] þe same:
'Bettre is þ*a*t boote bale adoun brynge
Than bale be ybet and boote neuer þe bettre.'
[Th]anne gan Mede to me[k]en hire, and m*er*cy bisou3te,
And p*ro*frede Pees a p*re*sent al of pure[d] golde.

80 Conscience] Boþe Concyense F. com*m*une] comones F; comune lawe Y. knewen wel] knowe wel F; knewen Hm BH; knowen WCrGYOC^{2}CLMR.
81 Ac] but GH; And CrC^{2}C; & þ*er*whilis F. wisdom] wit F. wit] witty M; wisdom F. were] weren HmCrOC^{2}BMH; wenty*n* F. aboute] abouten MFH.
82 comen] come HmCrGYOC^{2}CBLMRF H. catel] mede H. my3te] my3ten OC^{2}F.
84 sholde wo] woo sholde F. sholde] shulle*n* Bm. þolie] thorowly Cr; suffure H.
85 And] Ano*n* he F. comaundede] comande HC^2. casten] caste HmCrYOC^{2}CB MF; sette H. hym] hem Bm. Irens] stokkis F.
86 He shal] And lete hym WHmCrGYO C^{2}CBmBoLMRH; and lete Cot; & F. no3t] nowht aft*er* F. yer] yeres Cr. seen] he se F. feet] foot Cot.
87 God] A god F. þat] þo þat F.
88 And] But F. amendes] me*n*dys H. mowe] might Cr; mowe now F. lat] leteth Hm. maynprise hym] hym meynpris HmH (*over erasure* Hm). haue] holde F.
89 *line om* H. be...buggen] if he have borgh3 of his bale þey mowe bygge F. hym] hem C.
90 Amenden] And amende H; And so amenden WYCB; And so amende Hm Cr^{23}GOC^{2}LMRF; And so emende Cr^1. mysdede] is mysdo WHmCrGYOC^{2}CB LMRFH. eu*er*emoore] euer Cr^1; euer*e* be R; he shal do euer*e* F; so hy*m* H. þe] be H; do (*over erasure another script*) Bm. bettre] bote H.
91 Wit acordeþ] Ano*n* wit acordit F; Wit acorded WHmCrGYOC^{2}CBLMRH. þ*er*] here M. wiþ] to H. witnessede] seide WHmCrGYC^{2}CBLMRFH; seynde (n *cancelled*) O. þe] *om* Bm. same] same resou*n* F.
92 Bettre] þat bett*er*e RF. is...boote] it were þ*a*t boote sholde F. adoun] doun C^{2}F.
93 ybet] bett Cr^1; bety*n* H.
94 Thanne] Tha*n* CrH; And þanne WHm GYOC^{2}CBLMRF. gan] came Cr^1. to] *om* GH. meken] R; meke F; mengen WHmYOC^{2}CBL; mongen M; meue*n* Cr; meue G; medel H. bisou3te] BHm GCFH; she bisou3te WCrYOC^{2}LM; he bysou3te R.
95 p*ro*frede] p*ro*forys H. pured] pure WHmCrGYOC^{2}CBLMRFH. golde] syluer F.

'Haue þis [of me, man]', quod she, 'to amenden þi scaþe,
For I wol wage for wrong, he wol do so na moore.'
[Pees þanne pitously] preyde to þe kynge
To haue mercy on þat man þat mysdide hym ofte:
'For he haþ waged me wel as wisdom hym tau3te |
I forgyue hym þat gilt wiþ a good wille; *fol. 21 b*
So þ*a*t [ye] assente I kan seye no [moore],
For Mede haþ [maad myne amendes]; I may na moore axe.'
'Nay', quod þe kyng, 'so me crist helpe,
Wrong wendeþ no3t so awey [er] I wite moore.
Lope he so li3tly [awey], lau3en he wolde,
And [ofte] þe bolder*e* be to bete myne hewen.
But Reson haue ruþe on hym he shal reste in [þe] stokkes
As longe as [I lyue], but lowenesse hym borwe.'
Som[me] radde Reson to haue ruþe on þat shrewe;
And to counseille þe kyng and Conscience [boþe]

96 of me man] man of me WHmCrYOC^{2}CBLMRF; man G; of me H. amenden] amende HmCrGYOC^{2}CBLMRH. scaþe] state H.
97 wage] wagen Hm; wage me F. wol(2)] wel H.
98 Pees...pitously] þanne Pees pytously F; Petusly þ*a*n pees H; Pitously Pees þanne WHmCrGYOC^{2}CBLMR. to] for Cr^{1}. kynge] kyng þere F.
99 To] he wolde F. on] of OG. hym] *over erasure* M; *om* FH. ofte] MG; so ofte WHmCrYOC^{2}CBLRFH.
100 haþ] *om* M.
101 I] And I WHmCrGYOC^{2}CBLMRFH. forgyue] fur3iue Hm. þat] my F.
102 þat] *om* F. ye] the Cr^{1}; þe kyng WHmCr^{23}GYOC^{2}CBLMRFH. assente] asente þerto F. moore] bettre WHmCrGYOC^{2}CBLMRFH.
103 *line om* H. haþ] me hath Hm. maad ...amendes] made myn amendes RF; made me amendes YOC^{2}CBLM; me amendes maad WCrG; amendes maad Hm. may] can M. axe] axen M.
104 so] Hm; þo so WCrGYOC^{2}CBLMRFH. me crist] Christ me Cr; me cryste me (*corrected*) Hm; me god RFH.
105 no3t] no H. so] *om* Y. er I] H; or y G; erst I wil Cr; erst wole I WYOC^{2}CBLMR; furst y woll Hm; y will first F. wite] *om* C.
106 Lope] For lope WHmCrGYOC^{2}CBmLMRFH; For lepe BoCot. li3tly] lyghlye G; li3thi Bm. awey] F; *om* WHmCrGYOC^{2}CBLMRH. wolde] myghte F.
107 ofte] ofter G; eft WHmCrYOC^{2}CBLMRFH. þe...be] be the bolder Cr. þe] *om* HmG. boldere] badder Cot. be] to be F. bete] beten CotMRF. hewen] euen Cr^{1}; hynen M; hyne H; men G; *altered to* heyen Bm; *cancelled for* hynen Cot.
108 on] off G. hym] me Cot. reste] resty*n* H; sit Cr^{23}. þe] GH; my WHmCrYOC^{2}CBLMR; *om* F.
109 As] HG; And þat as WCrYOC^{2}CBLMRF; and that also Hm. I lyue] he lyueþ WHmCrGYOC^{2}CBLMRFH. lowenesse] mekenesse H. hym] hy R.
110 Somme] Summe HmH; Fele F; Som men WCrGYOC^{2}CBLMR. radde] radden OC^{2}B; redede H. to] MH; þo to WHmGYOC^{2}CBLRF; þo Cr. haue ruþe] ruwe M. on] off G. þat] þe GH.
111 *line om* H. And to] Cr; And for to WHmGYOC^{2}CBLMR; þ*a*t he myghte F. boþe] after WHmCrGYOC^{2}CBLMR; seyde aft*er* F.

That Mede moste be maynpernour Reson þei bisouȝte.
'Reed me noȝt', quod Reson, 'no ruþe to haue
Til lordes and ladies louen alle truþe
And haten alle harlotrie to heren or to mouþen it;
Til pernelles purfill be put in hire hucche,
And childrene cherissynge be chast[ised] wiþ yerdes,
And harlottes holynesse be holden for an [heþyng];
Til clerkene coueitise be to cloþe þe pouere and fede,
And Religiouse Romeris *Recordare* in hir cloistres
As Seynt Beneyt hem bad, Bernard and Fraunceis;
And til prechours prechynge be preued on hemselue;
Til þe kynges counseil be þe commune profit;
Til Bisshopes Bayardes ben beggeris Chaumbres,
Hire haukes and hire houndes help to pouere Religious;
And til Seint Iames be souȝt þere I shal assigne,
That no man go to Galis but if he go for euere. |
And alle Rome renneres, for Robberes [of] biyonde, *fol. 22 a*
Bere no siluer ouer see þat signe of kyng sheweþ,

112 That] And þat H. moste] might Cr GFH. maynpernour] maynperlour H; his paramour F. bisouȝte] besouȝten OC^2.
113 Reed] Now rede F. no] ony F; *om* G. to] for to G. haue] graunte F.
114 louen] loue Cr. alle] lovely F.
115 And haten] I hate H. heren] here HmCrG; heren it YCBLMRF (it *erased* M); here it OC^{2}H. or...it] of Mowthis F. to(2)] *om* H. mouþen] mowthe HmCr GMRH.
116 Til] & til F. pernelles] peronelle YC. purfill] pelure F. hucche] chiste F.
117 childrene] childernes Cr; Chydene F. cherissynge] chersyng CotF; cherynges H. be] by G. chastised] chastysed HmFH; chastising Cr^{23}GYOC^2; chastynge WCr^1 CBLMR. wiþ] by Hm. yerdes] ȝerde H.
118 *line om* H. holden] holde C^{2}F. an heþyng] vnhende YO; vnhynde C^2; an hyne WHmCr^{1}GCBLM; an hynde Cr^{23}; nauȝte R; vanyte F.
119 Til] and GF. clerkene] clerkes GCr^{23} YC^{2}BH. coueitise] coueytous H. be to] be H; *om* F. cloþe þe pouere] þe pore to clothe H. þe...fede] wel þe po F. þe] *om* HmM. and] & to YOC^{2}CBLR.
120 Romeris] romes H; rome renneris F. *Recordare*] recorde CotFH; Recordarie Cr^1; recordars Cr^{23}. cloistres] cloystre F.
121 Beneyt] Bernard M. Bernard] & Bernard F; Benet M.
122 And] *om* C. til] to G. on] off G. selue] seluen GYOCLMH.
123 Til] & tyl F. be] by Hm.
124 Til] & tyl þe F. Bayardes] barns Cr; barganoures F. beggeris] beggere R; beggerys in F.
125 Hire] & here F. hire] *om* F. houndes] hondis BmH. help] to helpe H; *om* Cr^1. to] þe CB; *om* FH. pouere] *om* F. Religious] religiouses R; relygyous howsys F.
126 And] *om* H. þere] as H.
127 Galis] Callice Cr^{1}CB; galylee H. if] *om* CotFH.
128 alle] also F. for Robberes] forbberes Y. of] Cr^{23}YOC^{2}CBmBoLMRH; *om* WHmCr^{1}GCotF.
129 see] shey G; the see HmFH. signe of] tokyn of þe H. sheweþ] beryth H.

Neiþ*er* [grotes ne gold ygraue wiþ kynges coyn]
V[p] forfeture of þat fee, wh[o] fynt [hym] at Douere,
But it be Marchaunt or his man or Messager wiþ l*ett*res,
P*ro*uysour or preest or penaunt for hise synnes.
And yet', quod Reson, 'by þe Rode! I shal no ruþe haue
While Mede haþ þe maistrie [to mote in þis] halle.
Ac I may shewe ensamples as I se ouþ[er].
I seye it by myself, and it so were
That I were kyng *with* coroune to kepen a Reaume,
Sholde neu*ere* wrong in þis world þ*at* I wite myȝte
Ben vnpunysshed [at] my power for p*er*il of my soule,
Ne gete my g*ra*ce [þoruȝ] giftes, so me god [helpe]!
Ne for no Mede haue m*er*cy but mekenesse it ma[de],
For *Nullum malum* þe man mette wiþ *inpunitum*
And bad *Nullum bonum* be *irremuneratum*.
Late [þi] Confess*our*, sire kyng, construe [it þee on englissh],

130 *line om* H. grotes...coyn] g*ra*ue ne vng*ra*ue gold neiþ*er* siluer WHmCrGYOC^{2}CBLMRF (g*ra*ue (*both*)] grauen CrOC^2. ne] nor HmCr).
131 Vp] H; Vpon WHmCrYOC^{2}CBLMRF; on G. þat] *om* F. who] GF; whoso WHmCrYOC^{2}CBLMRH. hym] GYOC^{2}CBLMRFH; it WHmCr. at] a H.
132 *run together with* 133 H. But] HmBMFH; But if WCrGYOC^{2}CLR. it] he CrGYOC^{2}CBF. Marchaunt...*lett*res] massagere or marchant H. Messager] messagers Y.
133 P*ro*uysour] Er p*ro*vysour F. preest... synnes] penant H. or(2)] ⁊ er (⁊ *added* ?) F.
134 Reson] rosou*n* H. no] *om* F. ruþe] rychesse H.
135 þe] *om* Y. to...þis] in þis moot WHmGYOC^{2}CBLMRH; in this mouth Cr; in þe moot F.
136 Ac] but GH; And CrC^{2}C; For F. may] shal F. ensamples] ensample F; ȝou ensample H. as] *om* CB. ouþer] ouþ*er*while WHmCrYOC^{2}CBLMF; otherwhyles G; othere otherwhile R; so*m*me tyme H.
137 *run together with* 138 B. it(1)] *om* H. self] selffe G; self quod he WHmCrYOC^{2}CBLMRFH. and...were] *om* B. and] ⁊ yff (⁊ *above line*) G; if F. so] so now F.
138 That...coroune] *om* B. were] were a Cr^3. kyng...coroune] crounyd H. kepen] kepe HmCrGC^{2}CBH. a] þe HmCr^{1}GF.
139 Sholde] Slolde Y; Xul H. þ*at*] ⁊ H. wite myȝte] mygth wyte Hm; wyte myste Bm.
140 vnpunysshed] vnpunsched HmBFH. at] in WHmCrGYOC^{2}CBLMRF; be H.
141 *line om* H. gete] getyn F. þoruȝ] RF; for WHmCrGYOC^{2}CBLM. giftes] ȝiftes HmC^2. me god] god me Hm. helpe] G; saue WHmCrYOC^{2}CBLMRF.
142 no] *om* Cr^1. but] but if Cr. made] HmCrRFH; make WGYOC^{2}CBLM.
143 *run together with* 144 H. *Nullum*] *multum* BoCot. þe man] *om* H. *impunitum*] inpugnitu*m* Hm.
144 bad] badde that Cr. *Nullum*] *ullum* (?) H.
145 þi] thy Cr; youre WHmGYOC^{2}CBLMRFH. Confess*our*] co*n*fessourys H. it þee] you thys G; þis WHmCrYOC^{2}CBLMRH; þis clause F. on englissh] englys H; englosid C^2; vnglosed WHmCrGYOCBLMRF.

And if [þow] werch[e] it in werk I wedde myne eris
That lawe shal ben a laborer and lede afeld donge,
And loue shal lede þi lond as þe leef likeþ.'
Clerkes þat were Confess*our*s coupled hem togideres
Al to construe þis clause for þe kynges p*ro*fit,
Ac no3t for confort of þe co*m*mune ne for þe kynges soule.
For I sei3 Mede in þe moot halle on men of lawe wynke
And þei lau3ynge lope to hire and lefte Reson manye.
Waryn wisdom wynked vpon Mede
And seide, 'madame, I am your*e* man what so my mouþ Iangle.
I falle in floryns', quod þat freke, 'and faile speche ofte.'
Alle ri3tfulle recordede þ*a*t Reson truþe tolde. |
[Kynde] wit acorded þ*er*wiþ and comendede hise wordes, *fol. 22 b*
And þe mooste peple in þe [moot] halle and manye of þe grete,
And leten Mekenesse a maister and Mede a mansed sherewe.
Loue leet of hire li3t and leaute yet lasse,
And seid[e] it so [loude] þ*a*t [soþnesse] it herde:

146 þow] you G; ye WHmCrYOC^{2}CLMRH; he BF. werche] werke FBH; werchen WHmCrGYOC^{2}CLMR. it] this HmH; that G. in] *om* HmG. wedde] dare wed Cr^{23}; ley H. myne] boþe myne OC^{2}H; þanne myne F.
147 a laborer] labourys H. afeld donge] dunk to feelde F.
148 þi] the Cr. þe leef] þe leevest F; þi*n* self H.
149 Clerkes...were] Ano*n* Clerkis ⁊ F. were] weren HmOBm. coupled] coupleden OH.
150 Al] *om* FH. þis] wel F. for] CrGYOC^{2}M; al for F; as for H; and for WHmCBLR.
151 Ac] but GFH; And CrC^{2}C. no3t] none H. for(1)] for þe Cr. confort of] p*ro*fyte of Hm; *om* H. þe(1)] the pore Cr. ne] no*n* H. for þe] *om* Cr.
152 moot] mouth Cr. on] of Y. wynke] wynken YOC^{2}MR.
153 And...hire] þei lepe to hyr laughyng H. lope] lopen OHmC^{2}B; lepe C. lefte ...manye] many lefte resou*n* C^{2}; leftyn aloone resou*n* F. lefte] laften B (en *erased* Bm).
154 Waryn] Sire wary3n F. wisdom] þe wytty H.
155 am] *om* C. man] owen GH. my mouþ] mi mony Cr^{1}; I H. Iangle] iangleth CrYOC^{2}CBLM; tellythe G.
156 *line om* H. falle in] fayle HmCrM (*over larger erasure* M, yle *over larger erasure* Hm); stumble at F. floryns] floren3ys G. þat] the Cr^{23}RF; *om* C^{2}. and] anf Cot; þ*a*t y F.
157 Alle] ⁊ ano*n* F. recordede] recordeden O; record H; recorden CrC^{2}.
158 Kynde] And WHmCrGYOC^{2}CBLMRF; I H. wit acorded] wyl acorde H. þ*er*] her M. comendede] come*n*de H; comendis BoCot; comaunded YC^{2}; comendyd wel F.
159 And þe mooste] Ano*n* all þe F. þe moot] þe WHmCrGYOC^{2}CBLMF; þis R; *om* H. þe(3)] þi H.
160 And] þey F; *om* YOC^{2}H. leten] lete C^{2}H; Lenten Y; helden F. a(1)] for a F. maister] maystrye G; maistresse B. a(2)] *om* Hm. mansed] mased CB; meche H.
161 Loue] *twice* R; þanne Love F. yet] well HmRF; meche H.
162 seide] YHmCrGOC^{2}CBLMRH; seiden W; cryeden F. it(1)] *om* F. loude... soþnesse] hei3e þ*a*t al þe halle WHmCrG YOC^{2}CBLMRFH (halle] *twice* Cr^{1}). it(2)] *twice* Cr^{1}; hem F; *om* H.

'Whoso wilneþ hire to wif for welþe of hire goodes,
But he be knowe for a Cokewold kut of my nose.'
Mede mornede þo and made heuy chere
For þe mooste co*m*mune of þat court called hire an hore.
Ac a Sisour and a Somono*ur* sued hire faste,
And [also] a Sherreues clerk bisherewed al þe route:
'For ofte haue I', quod he, 'holpen yow at þe barre,
And yet yeue ye me neu*er*e þe worþ of a risshe.'
The kyng callede Conscience and afterward Reson
And recordede þ*a*t Reson hadde riȝtfully shewed,
And modiliche vpon Mede wiþ myȝt þe kyng loked,
And gan wexe wroþ w*ith* lawe for Mede almoost hadde shent it,
And seide, 'þoruȝ [youre] lawe, as I leue, I lese manye eschetes;
Mede ouermaistreþ lawe and muche truþe letteþ.
Ac Reson shal rekene wiþ yow if I regne any while,
And deme yow, bi þis day, as ye han deserued.
Mede shal noȝt maynprise yow, by þe marie of heuene!

163 so] þat F. wilneþ] takyth H. hire(1)] Meede F. hire(2)] wordly F.
164 knowe] knowen Cr^{23}OC^{2}; knowne Cr^{1}. kut] bitte R. my nose] boþe oure erys F.
165 Mede...þo] þanne Meede M*ur*nede faste F. þo] þa*n* H; sore tho Cr.
166 þe mooste] all þe F. co*m*mune] comonys F; p*a*rt H; *om* Cot. þat] þe MFH. court] puple H. an] as F; *om* H.
167 Ac] but GH; and HmCrC^{2}C; Boþe F. a(2)] *om* GBm. sued] sueden OHm; þanne sewid F.
168 also] F; *om* WHmCrGYOC^{2}CBLMRH. bisherewed] byschrewyd (rewyd *over erasure*) Hm; yshrewe F. al] was all Hm.
169 For] Full GH; A F. he] she HmMFH *altered from* he HmM). holpen] holpe YCBLMFH; Ihulpe R.
170 yeue...neu*er*e] neuere ȝeve ȝee me F. yeue ye] ȝe ȝeue H. yeue] gaue CrGC; ȝyue O.
171 The...callede] þanne cleped þe kyng F. afterward] so he dede F.
172 recordede] recorde Cr^{1}. riȝtfully] reufulliche CB. shewed] yschewed R.
173 And] þanne F. Mede] Lawe F. wiþ... kyng] þat kyng w*ith* myth H. wiþ] *om* RF. þe] þat R. loked] loke RF.
174 gan] gand C; *om* CotF. wroþ] wþoþ Bm. almoost...it] had it nere she*n*t Cr; made hy*m* ashamed F. almoost hadde] had almost YM; had nyghe GH; hadde yt Hm. it] *om* HmC.
175 þoruȝ] by Cr^{23}; þow H. youre] YHm Cr^{23}GOC^{2}CBLMRFH; *om* WCr^{1}. as] *om* HmGH. I leue] *om* Hm. lese] lost Cr^{1}; leef Cot. manye] fele F; may Cr^{3}; myne BH. eschetes] chetes YGOC^{2}CLMRFH; enchetes Hm.
176 Mede] For Meede F. maistreþ] marryth H. lawe] so Lawe F. muche] mochul MF.
177 Ac] but GFH; And CrC^{2}C. I... while] eny while y reygne Hm. regne] leue H. any] a F; *om* Cr^{1}. while] stounde F.
178 yow] thou Cr^{1}. bi þis] by his Cot; on a OC^{2}.
179 Mede] Mee F. þe] *om* Cr^{23}GFH. of heuene] qween of glorie F.

I wole haue leaute in lawe, and lete be al youre ianglyng;
And as moost folk witnesseþ wel wrong shal be demed.'
Quod Conscience to þe kyng, 'but þe co*m*mune wole assente
It is [wel] hard, by myn heed, hert[o] to brynge it,
[And] alle youre lige leodes to lede þus euene'.
'By hym þat rauȝte on þe Rode!' quod Reson to þe kynge,
'But I rule þus youre Reaume rende out my guttes— |
If ye bidden buxomnesse be of myn assent.' *fol.* 23 *a*
'And I assente', seiþ þe kyng, 'by Seinte Marie my lady,
[Be] my counseil co[men] of clerkes and of Erles.
Ac redily, Reson, þow shalt noȝt [raike henne];
For as longe as I lyue lete þee I nelle.'
'I am redy', quod Reson, 'to reste wiþ yow eu*er*e;
So Conscience be of [y]oure counseil [kepe I] no bettre.'
'I graunte [gladly]', quod þe kyng, 'goddes forbode [he faile]!
Als longe as [I lyue] lyue we togideres.'

180 leaute] leaut C. in] for F. lete] leue HmF. be] *om* HmMF. al] *om* Cr^{23}GO C^{2}H.
181 moost] moste *twice* (*second cancelled*) Hm; alle RF. folk] wyȝes F; *om* OC^2. witnesseþ] wittenesse C^{2}CF. wel] wolle C^2; *om* CrGRFH. demed] ydemed R.
182 Quod] Sire q*uod* F. þe(2)] *om* C. co*m*mune] como*n*ys F. wole] *om* GF.
183 wel] ful WHmCrGYOC^{2}CBLMR FH. herto] CrGYOC^{2}CBMRF; hereto LH; hertoo W; here Hm.
184 And alle] Alle WHmCrGYOC^{2}CBL MRFH. lige] lyche HmH; londys F; *om* R. leodes] lordes Cr^{23}OC^{2}B. lede] leden Cr. þus] hem all F. euene] euer G.
185 rauȝte] reste Hm; rested (*over erasure*) Bm; was reed F. þe(1)] *om* F.
186 But] but HmBH; But if WCrGYOC^2 CLMRF. þus] this Cr^{3}G. rende] lete rende Hm.
187 bidden] bedde H; will bydde F. be... assent] to be assocyed to me F.
188 And] þerto F. seiþ] sayd Cr^{23}Bm; saye C; q*uod* HmGOC^{2}RFH. þe] the be Cot.
189 *line om* C. Be] YOC^{2}BoCotLMRH; By WHmCrGBm; To F. counseil comen] comen conseyl Hm. comen] GYOC^{2}BL; ycomen (y *another ink*?) M; Icome R; þ*at* ȝee kome F; co*m*mune WCr; *om* H. of(1)] amo*n*gys F. of(2)] *om* F. Erles] Lord*es* FH.
190 Ac] butt GFH; And CrC^{2}C. shalt... henne] ryde shalt not fro me F. raike henne] ryde hens H; ride fro me WHmCr YOC^{2}CBLMR; ryde me fro G.
191 as(1)] also Hm. lete] leaue CrGF.
192 redy] Cr; aredy YOC^{2}LMR; al redy WHmGCBFH. reste] resty*n* H.
193 *line om* F. youre] MC^2 (y *over erasure of* ȝ? M); oure WHmCrYOCBLR; my H; *om* G. kepe I] I kepe WHmCrGYOC^2 CBLMRH.
194 *line om* Hm. I...gladly] And I graunte WCrGYOC^{2}CBLMRFH. goddes] es *erased* Bm; god Cr^{23}GMFH. forbode] forbede MCr^{23}GFH. he faile] R; þou fayle F; it faile CrGYOC^{2}CBLMH; ellis W.
195 Als] also Hm. I lyue] oure lyf lasteþ WHmGYOC^{2}CBLM; oure lif last R; our lyues lasteth CrH; oure lyvis laste F lyue] leue RFH.

V

The kyng and hise kny3tes to þe kirke wente
To here matyns [and masse and to þe mete] after.
Thanne waked I of my wynkyng and wo was wi*th*alle
That I ne hadde slept sadder and ysei3en moore.
Ac er I hadde faren a furlong feyntise me hente
That I ne my3te ferþer a foot for defaute of slepynge.
[I] sat softely adoun and seide my bileue,
And so I bablede on my bedes þei brou3te me aslepe.
[Th]anne [mette me] muche moore þan I bifore tolde,
For I sei3 þe feld ful of folk þat I before [tolde],
And how Reson gan arayen hym al þe Reaume to p*re*che;
And wiþ a cros afore þe kyng comsede þus to techen.
He preued þ*at* þise pestilences were for pure synne,

1 The] Thanne þe F. and] w*ith* F. kirke] cherche Hm. wente] wenten OF.
2 here] heryn F. and(1)...mete] of þe day and þe masse WHmCrGYOC^{2}CBLMRFH (þe(2)] a F; *om* H).
3 Thanne...wynkyng] Off wynkynge I waked þo F. waked] awaked RB. my] *om* G. wynkyng] wynkyn H. was] was I C^{2}F; *om* C.
4–17 *over erasure* Hm.
4 slept] sleped YOC^{2}CBmBoLR. ysei3en] yseye HmOC^2; yseyn CotF; sighen Cr; sen HG.
5 Ac] But FH; And CrGC^{2}C. faren] fare H. feyntise] a feyntise OC^{2}F (a *above line main hand* O); a feyntnes G; fayntasy3e H.
6 ne my3te] myth nouth H; myght no G. ferþer a foot] a foote further*e* F; forther G. slepynge] slepe F.
7 I sat] þan sat y F; And sette me B. I] H; and y Hm; And WCrGYOC^{2}CLMR. softely] sothly Y. adoun] doun MH.
8 so I bablede] y bablede so F; babelyd I H; babeled R. on] vppon R; of OC^2. þei] til þei B. brou3te] brou3ten OHmC^2.
9 *line om* H. Thanne] And þanne WHmCrGYOC^{2}CBLMRF. mette me] sau3 I WHmGYOC^{2}CBLMR; I sawe Cr; y sey3 F. muche] mychil FC. bifore] beforehond F; fore Bm. tolde] HmGYOC^{2}CBLRF; of tolde WCrM (of *above line* M).
10 For] how C^2; and þa*n* H; *om* G. þe] a Hm. folk] for G. bifore] ere GH. tolde] of tolde H; of seide WHmCrGYOC^{2}CBLMRF.
11 And] *om* G. gan] can Cr^1; *om* F. arayen] araye HmH; arayed F.
12 wiþ a] at þe F; a OC^2. afore] byfore HmC^{2}CBRFH. comsede] he comsed F; come H. þus to techen] a teeme F. techen] teche HmOC^{2}H; p*re*chen Y.
13 He] And H. preued] preueþ OC^2; p*re*chede F. þise] þe F; theyre G; *om* H. pestilences] pestilence C. were] weren HmF; was OC^{2}CBmBoLR; was al YM.

And þe Southwestrene wynd on Saterday at euen
Was pertliche for pride and for no point ellis.
Pyries and Plumtrees were puffed to þe erþe
In ensample, [segges, þat ye] sholden do þe bettre;
Beches and brode okes were blowen to þe grounde |
[And] turned vpward hire tai[l] in tokenynge of drede *fol.* 23 *b*
That dedly synne er domesday shal fordoon hem alle.
Of þis matere I myȝte mamelen [wel] longe,
Ac I shal seye as I sauȝ, so me god helpe,
How pertly afore þe peple [preche gan Reson].
He bad wastour go werche what he best kouþe
And wynnen his wastyng wiþ som maner crafte.
[And] preide Pernele hir purfil to le[u]e
And kepe it in hire cofre for catel at nede.
Tomme Stowue he tauȝte to take two staues
And fecche Felice hom fro wyuen pyne.

14 þe] þat þe F; a H. westrene] west YOC^{2}CBLMRF; ward H. on] on a MFH; vppon a B. at] atte M. euen] eue CRF.
15 pertliche] apertly F; ap*er*ty H. pride] pryȝde FR; synne H; pure pride WHmCr GYOC^{2}CBLM.
16 *line om* H. Pyries] Boþe pyryes F. were] weren HmOBF.
17 *copied after line* 20 F; *line om* H. In] And in R; ⁊ al þese was F. segges...ye] þat ye segges WHm; ye segges ye YGOC^{2}CL MR; the segges ye Cr^1; tho segges ye Cr^{23}; ȝe segges BoCot; ȝe segge Bm; þ*at* we F. sholden] sholde GCrF; shull C^2.
18 Beches...okes] ⁊ broode okes ⁊ beechis F. Beches] Buschys H. brode] broke Bm. were] weren OM. blowen] blowe HmBRFH.
19 And] RF; *om* WHmCrGYOC^{2}CBL MH. turned] Turneden O. vpward] vpwar Bm. hire] the Cr^3. tail] tayl FR; tailes WHmCrGYOC^{2}CBLMH. in] *om* RF. tokenynge of] knowlechynge F. drede] drode Hm.
20 synne] *om* G. er] att *cancelled main hand for* ar G. shal] sholde F; wyl H. hem] vs FH. *Hereafter* F *copies line* 17.
21–3 *lines om* H.
21 Of] But of F; On Hm. myȝte] *om* F. mamelen] mamele GCrYOC^{2}CBLMRF. wel] ful WHmCrGYOC^{2}CBLMRF.
22 Ac] but GF; And CrC^{2}C. seye] seyȝn ȝow F.
23 pertly] ap*er*tly B; p*ro*pirly F. afore] bifore OCr^{23}C^{2}BoCotRF. preche... Reson] prechen gan resou*n* F; Reson gan to p*re*che YOC^{2}CLMR; Reson bigan to p*re*che WHmCrGB.
24 He] Resou*n* H. go] to R. what] that Cr^3.
25 wynnen] wynne CrH. crafte] of craft H; craftys R; of werkys F.
26 And] OHmC^{2}CBLMRH; He WCr GF; And after he Y. hir] þe proude hyr H. purfil] purple Cr^1; purfiles Cr^{23}. leue] lete WHmCrGYOC^{2}CBLMRFH.
27 it] þe coyn F. hire] catel i*n* H; *om* CB. for...at] tyl sche had H; to co*n*forte hire at F. nede] GFH; hire nede WHmCrYOC^2 CBLMR.
28 Tomme] Tomme of BH; ⁊ Thomme of F. Stowue] stowe HmOC^{2}FH; stouue (stoune ?) R; Stowne Cr; Trewe tonge Y. take] taken Cr. staues] stones R.
29 fecche] fecchen M. Felice] fylix H. hom] his wif hom F; hom fo Bm. wyuen] wyuene RF; þe wyuen WHmGYOC^{2}CB LM; the wynen Cr; þe wy*n* ⁊ fro þe H. pyne] pyȝe H.

He warnede watte his wif was to blame
[That] hire heed was worþ [a] marc & his hood no3t a grote.
[He] bad Bette kutte a bou3 ouþer tweye
And bete Beton þer*with* but if she wolde werche.
He chargede Chapmen to chasti3en hir children:
'Late no wynnyng [forwanye hem] while þei be yonge,
Ne for no poustee of pestilence plese hem no3t out of reson.
My sire seide to me, and so dide my dame,
"[Lo], þe leuer*e* child þe moore loore bihoueþ";
And Salomon seide þe same þat Sapience made,
Qui parcit virge odit filium:
Whoso spareþ þe spryng spilleþ hise children.'
And siþen he [preide] p*re*lates and preestes togideres,
'That ye p*re*chen þe peple, p*re*ue it yowselue, |

30 He] And he Cr; Also he F; And OC^2. watte] whtte C. his] þat his B; how hys F. was] þat was G.
31 That] CrYOC^{2}CBLMRFH; For W Hm; *om* G. a(1)] half a CrGYC^{2}CLMH (a *above line another ink* M); half WHmO BRF. marc] mare G. &] *om* GYOC^2 CLR; *added but erased* M. hood...grote] *over erasure another ink* Hm. hood] hede YC; hot H; *om* B. a(2)] HmGCotRH; worþ a WCrYOC^{2}CBmBoLMF.
32 He] F; And he Cr; And WHmGYOC^2 CBLMRH. bad] *om* R. Bette...tweye] his knave a bowh3 kytte komely to honde F. kutte] to cutte Hm; he cut H. ouþer] or Cr^{23}CBH; in Cr^1.
33 And...*with*] To beetyn þer*with* Betou*n* F. bete] betyn HmH. Beton] kytone G. if] *om* HmCBH. wolde] wol YCrC^{2}F. werche] swynk H.
34 He] And þanne he WHmCrGYOC^{2}C BLMRH; & namely he F. chasti3en] chastyse HmFH; chasten CrGCL; chaste R. children] chyldre G.
35 *line om* H. Late] & leete F. forwanye hem] forwayne hem F; hem forwanye WHmCrYOC^{2}CBLM; theym wanye G; forwanyen þe R.
36 Ne] And H. poustee] poust Cr^{23}; post G; ponste Cr^1; pyte F; *om* H. of(1)] ne Cot; *om* H. plese] ne pleese F. no3t] *om* GF.
37 to] CrC^2; so to WHmGYOCBLMRH; onys to F. so] also F. dide] seyde FH.
38 Lo] That WHmCrGYOC^{2}CBLMRH; How þat F. child] þe chyld is H. bihoueþ] hy*m* he houyth H.
39 Salomon] *sapiens* H. þe same] so H. Sapience] sapience book F; *Sapientie* Cr^1.
39α *parcit*] percit G. *filium*] *filium suum* M; *filium &c* HmGYBm. *Hereafter an additional line* WHmCrGYOC^{2}CBLMRF: The englissh of þis latyn is whoso wole it knowe (is] *om* HmCr. so] þat F. it] *om* Cr). *See above*, p. 193.
40 so] þat F. spryng] 3onge spryng F; 3erde B. spilleþ] he spilleth RF; spyllyd H. hise] the Cr^{1}H. children] child BHmH; barnes F.
41 And...and] Þanne p*ar*led he to p*er*sones & to F. preide] prayed HmCrGYOC^{2}C BLMH; p*re*chede W; p*re*ued R.
42 That] Looke F. ye] *after cancelled* they *main hand* G. prechen] p*re*che HmCrFH. þe] FH; to þe WHmCrGYOC^{2}CBLMR. preue] & preve F. it] H; it on WHmYOC^2 CBLMRF; on CrG. yow] 3oure OCrG YC^{2}CBLMFH. selue] seluen GYOC^{2}C LM.

And dooþ it in dede, it shal drawe yow to goode. *fol. 24 a*
[Lyue] as ye leren vs; we shul leue yow þe bettre.'
And siþen he radde Religion hir rule to holde
'Lest þe kyng and his conseil your*e* comunes apeire
And be Stywar[d] of your*e* sted[e] til ye be [stewed] bettre'.
And siþen he counseiled þe kyng his co*m*mune to louye:
'It is þi [tresor if treson ne were], and tryacle at þy nede.'
And siþen he preide þe pope haue pite on holy chirche,
And er he gyue any g*ra*ce gou*er*ne first hymselue.
'And ye þ*at* han lawes to [loke], lat truþe be your*e* coueitise
Moore þan gold ouþ*er* giftes if ye wol god plese;
For whoso cont*ra*rieþ truþe, he telleþ in þe gospel,
Amen dico vobis nescio vos.
And ye þat seke Seynt Iames and Seyntes [at] Rome,
Sekeþ Seynt Truþe, for he may saue yow alle

43 it(1)] it sadly F. it(2)] & ȝee F. drawe] driue Cr^{23}. yow] *om* F. *Hereafter a spurious line* F; *see above*, p. 222.
44 Lyue] If ye lyue CrF; If ye lyuen YHm OBLMR (y *altered from* o *or* e M); yff ye wole lyuen G; If ye leuen WC^{2}C; For & ye leue H. leren] lerne C^{2}CrRFH. shul] wyll G; *om* MF. leue] leuen M; byleue Cot.
45 And siþen] þanne aft*er* F. Religion... rule] Relygious here rewhlys F.
46 Lest] List C. and] by F. your*e* comunes] the co*m*mune G.
47 Styward] FHmCotH (e *erased at end* Hm); Stywardes WCrGYOC^{2}CBmBoL MR. stede] stedes WHmCrGYOC^{2}CBL MRFH. til] to G. be(2)] *om* Y. stewed] rewled HmGC^{2}RH; reulid BC; ruled WCrYOLM; *om* F. bettre] in bettre rewle F.
48 his...louye] to love þe comou*n* peple F. his] the GYOC^{2}CBLMR. co*m*mune] comunes HmCrOC^{2}H.
49 It is þi] For þat is F. tresor...were] tresore if treson ne were YCrGOC^{2}CBL MH; tresor yf tresou*n* ner*e* F; tresor if treson were R; tresoure ȝif resou*n* ne were Hm; trewe tresor W. þy] *om* FH.
50 haue] to haue GFH. pite] rewþe F. on] of C; off the G.
51 he] ye (y *over erasure*) M. gyue] gaue Cr^{23}; ȝyue Hm; grawnte F. gou*er*ne] to governe F; preue it H. first] *om* Hm. hym] yowre (y *over erasure*) M; *om* Cot. selue] seluen OC^{2}CBM.
52 lawes] þe lawe H. loke] kepe WHm CrGYOC^{2}CBLMRFH. lat] but H. truþe...coueitise] Coueytyse be *with* trewþe F.
53 ouþ*er*] or CrMH; or other YHmCBL RF; & oþ*er* OC^{2} (& *cancelled* O). giftes] ȝiftes HmB; sylu*er* H. ye] he OC^{2}. wol] willen B; wold G. god] trethe (god *in margin same hand*) H.
54 so] þat F; *om* B. cont*r*arieþ] cont*r*arie þe H; conr*a*rieth Cot. he] as F. in þe] þe trewe F. *Hereafter an additional line* WHm CrGYOC^{2}CBLMRFH: That god knoweþ hym noȝt ne no Seynt of heuene (god] he Hm. hym] hem Cr^{23}R. ne no] no*n* þe H. Seynt] seynt*es* H; coorseynt F. of] in CrGH). *See above*, p. 193.
55 *Amen*] *twice* HmCB. *nescio*] *quia nescio* G. *vos*] *vos &c* HmY.
56 seke] seketh Cr^{1}HmYOC^{2}CBF. and] or FH. Seyntes] ony sey*n*t F. at] CrG; atte Hm; of WYOC^{2}CBLMRFH.
57 Sekeþ] Seke CrFH. Seynt] first sey*nt* F. for...saue] fayre ȝow befalle for he xal sauy*n* H.

Qui cum patre & filio; þat faire hem bifalle
That seweþ my sermon;' and þus seyde Resou*n*.
Thanne ran Repentaunce and reherced his teme
And [made] wille to wepe water wiþ hise eiȝen.
Pernele proud-herte platte hire to þe erþe
And lay longe er she loked, and 'lord, m*er*cy!' cryde,
And bihiȝte to hym þat vs alle made
She sholde vnsowen hir serk and sette þ*er*e an heyre
To affaiten hire flessh þat fiers was to synne.
'Shal neu*er*e heiȝ herte me hente, but holde me lowe |
And suffre to be mysseyd, and so dide I neu*er*e. *fol.* 24 *b*
But now [wole I] meke me and m*er*cy biseche
[Of alle þat] I haue [had enuye] in myn herte.'
Lechour seide 'allas!' and [to] oure lady cryde
To maken m*er*cy for hi[s] mysded[e] bitwene god and [hym]
Wiþ þat he sholde þe Saterday, seuen yer þerafter,

58 *line om* (*but see* 57) H. þat] alle F.
59 *line om* H. Resou*n*] sire Resou*n* F; *om* Y.
60 Thanne] Nou F. and reherced] reherede OC^2. teme] tyme C^{2}CBoCot.
61 made] HmFH; garte WCrGOC^{2}CBLMR; gret Y. wille] welle Y. to] *om* Cr^{23}.
62 Pernele] & Peronyll F. proud] prout Cot; prou Bo. hire] *om* H. to] on F.
63 lay...loked] þere she lay longe F. longe] along Cr^{23}. she] he R. and] vp & our H; & oure F. cryde] he criede R.
64 bihiȝte] behyghe Cr^1; bisouȝte CB; besekyth H. to] vnto YOC^{2}M. þat] an hees þat F. made] formede F.
65 She] He R; þat she F. sholde] wolde F. vnsowen] vnsowe CrBFH. hir] hy F. serk] sylk H; scherte Hm; smok Cot. sette] setten RF. þ*er*e an] theron Cr.
66 *line om* Cr^1; *transposed with* 67 Cr^{23}. To] And Y. affaiten] afate H; affaynten Cr^{23}Cot; aflasshen F. fiers] frele HG.
67 neu*er*e] y neu*er*e have F. heiȝ] me hey H. me(1)] *om* FH. hente] *om* F. holde] holde*n* H. me(2)] HmCrGYOC^{2}CBLMRH; I wole me W; me eu*er*e F.
68 to be] me to be Cr; to F. so] so ȝit F.
69 now] *twice* BmBo (*second cancelled* Bm). wole I] woll y HmCrGYOC^{2}CBLMRFH; I wole W.
70 Of alle] For alle C^{2}BmBoM (e *erased* M); For al WHmCrGYOCCotLH; For RF. þat] þat F; þise B; þis WHmCrGYOC^{2}CLMRH. I haue] haue I H. had enuye] hated WHmCrGOC^{2}CLMFH; Ihated R; hated tofore Y; hauntid B. in ...herte] al my lyf tyme H. herte] herte longe F.
71 Lechour] Thanne lechour WCrGYOC^{2}CBLMR; Tha*n* letchery H; þe Lecchour F; Thanne seyde Hm. seide] seyde ofte F; lechour Hm. to] FH; on WHmCrGYOC^{2}CBLMR. cryde] cryed GHmOC^{2}H; he cryde WCrYCBLMRF.
72 *line om* Cr^1. maken] make HmCr^{23}GYOC^{2}CBLMR; make meke H; have F. his mysdede] hys mysdede H; hise mysdedes WHmCr^{23}GYOC^{2}CBLMRF. bitwene...hym] þat mychil he offendid F. hym] his soule WHmCr^{23}GYOC^{2}CBLMRH.
73 Wiþ þat] Be so F. þe Saterday] eu*er*y day F; on þe day R. seuen] þis sevene F; for seuen Cr. þer] *om* CrCFH.

Drynke but [wiþ] þe doke and dyne but ones.
Enuye wiþ heuy herte asked after shrifte,
And carefully [his coupe] he comse[þ] to shewe.
He was as pale as a pelet, in þe palsy he semed.
[He was] cloþed in a kaurymaury—I kouþe it nouȝt discryue—
[A] kirtel and [a] Courtepy, a knyf by his syde,
Of a Freres frokke were þe foresleues.
As a leek þat hadde yleye longe in þe sonne
So loked he wiþ lene chekes, lourynge foule.
His body was [b]ollen for wraþe þat he boot hise lippes,
And [wroþliche he wroþ his] fust, to wreke hym he þouȝte
With werkes or wiþ wordes whan he seyȝe his tyme.
Ech a word þat he warp was of a Neddres tonge;
Of chidynge and chalangynge was his chief liflode,
Wiþ bakbitynge and bismer*e* and berynge of fals witnesse;

74 but(1)] *om* F. wiþ] wyth HmC^{2}CRF; myd WCrGYOBLM; as H. doke] du*n*kele doke F; doke doth H; day Cr dyne] dyghnen F.
75 Enuye] þanne Envie F. asked] askiþ Bm. shrifte] chryfte H; Christe Cr^{1}.
76 his coupe] *mea culpa* WHmCrGYOC^{2}CBLMRH; wi*th* *mea culpa* F. he comseþ] he comsed WHmCrGYOC^{2}CBLMRF; bega*n* he H. shewe] schrewe R; shryve F; cryȝe H.
77 He] And Cr. as(1)] also HmB; *om* GH. pale] *om* Cot. pelet] pelote F; polet Hm; pylet H; pylour Cot. in] ⁊ in F. þe] *om* OC^{2}H. he] hym GH. semed] semyth H.
78 He was] F; And WHmCrGYOC^{2}CBLMRH. cloþed] cluted R. a] *om* CrF. kaurymaury] tawrymaury BmR. kouþe] can Cr. it nouȝt] nauȝt it R. it] hy*m* H. discryue] discryȝe FH; disceiue Cr^{3}.
79 A] In a BmBoRH; In WHmCrGYOC^{2}CCotLM (*corrector adds* a Cot); he hadde on F. a(1)] BH; in Y; *om* WHmCrGOC^{2}CLMRF. a(2)] and a WHmCrGYOC^{2}CBLMR; ⁊ a long FH.
80 Of] ⁊ of F. Freres] frere R. frokke] frogge H. were] weren OBF. þe] his RFH. fore] forme H.
81 *transposed with* 82 F. As] F; And as WHmCrGYOC^{2}CBLMRH. leek] clerk H. þat] *om* GYOC^{2}CBLMRF. hadde] hath Cr^{23}. yleye] yleyen C; yleyn F; leye Hm; lyed Cr; lyn H. in] ageyn F.
82 So] he F. he] *om* F. lene] lere OC^{2}. chekes] chekys ⁊ F. foule] brewys F.
83 body] bely Hm; ladye G. bollen] bolne H; bolle G; tobollen WOC^{2}CB; tobolle YCr^{23}LMR; al tobolne Hm; foule ybolned F; bowne Cr^{1}. for wraþe] ⁊ faste F. þat] *om* HmBF. lippes] lyppe H.
84 And] *om* G. wroþliche...fust] hise hondis he wrong F; wry*n*ga*n*de wi*th* hys fyst he ȝede H. wroþliche he wroþ] wryngynge he yede wi*th* WHmYOC^{2}CBLM; wryngyng he went wi*th* G; wringing wi*th* Cr; wryngyed with R. his] O C^{2}Cot; þe WHmCr^{12}GYCBmBoLMR; þat Cr^{3}. fust] first Cr^{23}. to] to ben F; *om* G. wreke] wreky*n* H; awreke F. hym] HmBH; hymself WCrGYOC^{2}CLMR; *om* F.
85 werkes] werk H. or] and HmG. wiþ] *om* GH.
86 Ech a] Ech CrGRH; ⁊ eu*er*y F. þat] *om* H. he] be Cr^{2}. warp] warped CrG; spak H. of] lyk F; *om* B. a Neddres] an addre HmRF; an andres Y.
87 and] YMFH; and of WHmCrGCBLR; of OC^{2}. chalangynge] ianglynge HmFH.
88 Wiþ] and Cot. and(1)] and with R. bismer*e*] bysmery H; bisme Cr^{1}. of] *om* Cr^{23}GF.

[This was al his curteisie where þat euere he shewed hym].
'I wolde ben yshryue', quod þis sherewe, 'and I for shame dorste.
I wolde be gladder, by god! þat Gybbe hadde meschaunce
Than þou3 I hadde þis wouke ywonne a weye of Essex chese.
I haue a ne3ebore [nei3] me, I haue anoyed hym ofte,
[And blamed hym bihynde his bak to brynge hym in fame;
To apeire hym bi my power pursued wel ofte],
And [bilowen] hym to lordes to doon hym lese siluer,
And [doon] his frendes be his foon þoru3 my false tonge.
His grace and his goode happes greuen me [wel] soore. |
Bitwene [meyne and meyne] I make debate ofte *fol.* 25 *a*
That boþe lif and lyme is lost þoru3 my speche.
Whan I met[t]e hym in Market þat I moost hate[de]
I hailse[d] hym hendely as I his frend were:
He is dou3tier þan I; I dar [noon harm doon hym],
Ac hadde I maistrie and my3t [I wolde murþere hym for euere].

89 HmCrGYOC^{2}CBLMRH; Swiche manerys he made to ech man he medled with F; *line om* W; *here in the spelling of* W. al] *om* G. þat euere] þat GC; euer H; so Hm. shewed hym] went H.
90 I...sherewe] þanne seyde þat shrewe y wolde be shryve F. wolde] woll Hm. ben] by M. yshryue] shryue GH; shryuen CrHmOC^{2}M. þis] that HmH. and] if CrF.
91 I] And I H; But 3it y F. by...þat] yf F.
92 *line om* F. þou3] if Cr; *om* GH. þis...ywonne] wonne this weke Cr. ywonne] Iwonnen OC^{2}; wonne HmGBmBoH. a weye] my wythe H.
93 nei3] CYLMRF (*final* e *erased* M); ny3 OC^{2}BmBo; nye HmCrGCot; by WH. anoyed hym] hym noyid H. anoyed] *over erasure* M; noy3ed HmCrF; ennuyed L; enuyed YOCBR; envied C^{2}. hym] hem C.
94, 95 *not in* WHmCrGYOC^{2}CBLMRFH.
96 And] By *over erasure another ink* M. bilowen] lowen on WHmCrGYOC^{2}CBLR; lowhe on F; lyid on H; lowen M. to...to] ful lowhde & F. doon] mad F; make Hm. lese] loost F; *om* H. siluer] BHm; his siluer WCrGYOC^{2}CLMRFH.
97 doon] maad WHmCr^{12}GYOC^{2}CBLMFH; make Cr^{3}; also R. frendes] frend CrHm (*final* e *erased* Hm). be] to ben BM; *om* HmGF. foon] foo HmCrBm.
98 *line om* H. His] For his F. his] *om* F. greuen] greve F; greued GC^{2}. wel] ful WHmCrGYOC^{2}CBLMRF.
99 meyne...meyne] mayne and mayne R; manye and manye WCrGYOC^{2}CBLMH; man and man Hm; hym & manye men F.
100 boþe] *om* H. lif...lyme] here lyvis & here lymes F. is] is bothe H; be F. þoru3] by Hm. speche] wykkyd speche H.
101 Whan I mette] and whan I mette C^{2}Bm; And whan I mete WHmCrGYOCBoCotLMRFH. hym] *om* H. hatede] hated C^{2}H; hate WHmCrGYOCBLMRF.
102 hailsed] haylsed G; halsyd H; hailse WYOCLMR; haile BF; halse HmCrC^{2}. hym] hym ful F.
103 He] For he WHmCrGYOC^{2}CBLMRFH. is] his YM; *om* F. noon...hym] do noon ooþer WHmCrGYOC^{2}CBLMRFH.
104 Ac] but GFH; And CrC^{2}C. hadde I] I hade C^{2}. and my3t] ouer hym F. I(2)...euere] god woot my wille WHmCrGYOC^{2}CBLMRFH (god] good C).

Whan I come to þe kirk and knele to þe Roode
[To] preye for þe peple as þe preest techeþ,
For Pilgrymes, for Palm*er*es, for al þe peple after,
Thanne I crye on my knees þ*at* crist ȝyue h[y]m sorwe
That [bar] awey my bolle and my broke shete.
Awey fro þe Auter turne I myne eiȝen
And biholde [how H]eyne haþ a newe cote;
[Thanne I wisshe] it were myn and al þe web after.
And of [his] lesynge I lauȝe, [it liȝteþ] myn herte;
[Ac of his] wynnynge I wepe and waille þe tyme.
[I] deme [men þere hij] doon ille, [and yet] I do werse;
Whoso vndernymeþ me herof, I hate hym dedly after.
I wolde þ*at* ech wight were my knaue.
[And] whoso haþ moore þan I, þat angreþ [myn herte].

105 Whan] And whan WHmCrGYOC^{2}CBLMRFH. þe(1)] *om* HmFH. kirk] cherche HmRF. and] ⁊ F; and sholde WHmCrGYOC^{2}CBLMRH. knele] p*ray* H. to(2)] tofor OC^{2}F.
106 *line om* H. To] And WHmCrGYOC^{2}CBLMR; ⁊ sholde F. preest] p*ar*shȝ p*re*st F.
107 for(1)] FH; and for WCrYOC^{2}CBmLR; and HmGBoCotM. for(2)] and for HmCr; ⁊ GF. al...after] penau*n*tys also F. þe] *om* Hm.
108 Thanne I crye] and þan I creed C^2. on my knees] for c*ri*stian F. þ*at*] þou Cr^3. hym] GCr; hem WHmYOC^{2}CBLMRH; hir*e* F.
109 bar] LHmCrGYCMRFH; baren OC^{2}B; beren W. broke] broken GHmOC^{2}B; brode H.
110 Auter] Auter þanne WHmCrGYOC^{2}CBLMRFH. turne] turned C^2. eiȝen] heye H; face Hm.
111 biholde] behelde C^{2}F. how] CrHmGYOC^{2}CBLMRFH; *om* W. Heyne] heleyne R; hervy F; Eleyne WHmCrGYOC^{2}CBLMH. haþ] hath on R; hadde on F. *Here* F *adds a spurious line; see above,* p. 222.
112 Thanne I wisshe] I wisshe þanne WYOCBLMR; I wisshed þan C^{2}Hm; I wyshe that CrGH; ⁊ wisshede ofte F. and] wit*h* Cr. þe] *om* C.
113 And] *om* G. of] for F; at CrH. his] R; mennes WHmCrGYOC^{2}CBLFH; many a (*over erasure, altered from* mennes ?) M. lesynge] lesyngis BC^{2}H; los (s *over erasure*) Hm. it] for it F; þat WHmCrGYOC^{2}CBLMRH. liȝteþ...herte] myn herte akeþ OCr^{23}YC^2. liȝteþ] likeþ WHmCr^{1}GLRH; lykeþ wel F; akeþ MB; werkes C.
114 Ac of his] Ac for his R; But for his F; And for his Y; And for hir WHmCrGOC^{2}CBLMH. wynnynge] wynnynges M. and] ⁊ ofte F. waille] wele Cr.
115 I] F; And WHmCrGYOC^{2}CBLMRH. men...hij] men þat hij R; þ*at* hij YCBLM; hem þ*at* F; þ*at* þei WHmCrGOC^{2}H. and yet] ⁊ F; þere WHmYOC^{2}CBmBoLMR; where G; qwa*n* H; thoughe Cr; the Cot. do] do wel WHmCrGYOC^{2}CBLMRH; do myselue wel F.
116 Whoso] ⁊ who þat F. nymeþ] mineth Cr; take H. herof] þereof MF; *om* G. hym] *om* Hm. dedly] euere FH.
117 *line om* H. I] And I OC^2. ech] ech a WHmCrGYOC^{2}CBLMR; euery F. were] man were become F. my] myn owne OC^2.
118 *line om* H. And] ⁊ F; For WHmCrGYOC^{2}CBLMR. so] þat F. þat] ȝee þat F. myn herte] me soore WHmCrGYOC^{2}CBLMRF.

[Th]us I lyue louelees lik a luþer dogge
That al my [brest] bolneþ for bitter of my galle.
I myȝte noȝt ete many yeres as a man ouȝte
For enuye and yuel wil is yuel to defie.
May no sugre ne swete þyng aswage my swellyng,
Ne no Diapenidion dryue it fro myn herte,
Ne neiþ*er* shrifte ne shame, but whoso shrape my mawe?'
'ȝis! redily', quod Repentaunce and radde hym to [goode]:
'Sorwe [for] synn[e] is sauacion of soules.' |
'I am sory', quod [enuye], 'I am but selde ooþer, *fol. 25 b*
And þat makeþ me [so mat], for I ne may me venge.
Amonges Burgeises haue I be, [bigg]yng at Londou*n*,
And gart bakbityng be a brocour to blame mennes ware.
Whan he solde and I nouȝt þanne was I redy
To lye and to loure on my neȝebore and to lakke his chaffare.
I wole amende þis if I may þoruȝ myȝt of god almyȝty.'

119 Thus] And þus WHmCrYOC^{2}CBLMRFH; ⁊ thys G. lyue] loue CB.
120 brest] body WHmCrGYOC^{2}CBLMRFH. for] so F. bitter] bitterhed B; byttyrnesse H. of] in R; ys F.
121 ete] eten CrHmF. ouȝte] xulde H.
122 yuel(2)] ylle H. defie] defyen GM.
123 May] þere may F. sugre] gyngere H. ne] no Hm; ne no Cr^{23}Cot; nor no Cr^{1}; ny*n* no H. aswage] swage Cr^{23}GH; abate Hm. my] the Cr^{23}. swellyng] wo*m*be F.
124 Ne] Non H; For B. Diapenidion] diapendion OCBF. dryue] may dryue B.
125 Ne] Non H; *om* CrB. neiþer] *om* HmH. shrifte] thrifte Cot. ne] no R; no*n* H; nether Cr. but] xal but H. whoso] who B; he wil F; *om* CrH. shrape] scrape H; sharpe G; shraping of Cr.
126 ȝis] þis OCr^{23}CB (*cancelled*, ȝis *in margin main hand* O). redily...Repentaunce] q*uod* Repentawnce redely F. redily] rede I OC^{2}; I reade Cr^{23}. and] haþ BC. radde] rede C^{2}; red Bo. hym to] me Hm. goode] þe beste WHmCrGYOC^{2}CBLMRFH.
127 Sorwe] Strong sorwe F. for] HmCrFH; of WGYOC^{2}CBLMR. synne] F; synnes WHmCrGYOC^{2}CBLMRH. is sauacion] saluation is Cr. of soules] to þe sowle F. **Here collation of H ceases**; *see above*, p. 9.
128 I(1)] Pet*er* y F. sory] euere sory RF. enuye] he F; the segge HmBoCot; þat segge WCrGYOC^{2}CBmLMR. but] *om* G. selde] selden OC^{2}F.
129 And] *om* G. so mat] þus megre WHmCrYOC^{2}CBLMRF; thys meygre G. for] þat Hm. ne] *om* G. may me] me may F; *om* Cot. venge] avenge HmOC^{2}F; not wenge G.
130 Amonges] I was among F. Burgeises] burgeys HmYCBRF. haue I] y haue Hm; *om* F. be...Londoun] þere me*n* bowhte ⁊ solde F. biggyng] dwellyng WHmCrGYOC^{2}CBLMR.
131 And] I F. gart] grete CB; dude Hm; made GF. bakbityng] bakbyter*e* F. be] by Hm; to Cot. a] *om* F. blame] lakke F.
132 Whan] ⁊ whan F. redy] aredy R; ful redy F.
133 and to loure] *om* G. to(1)] *om* Hm Cr^{23}. my neȝebore] hy*m* F. to(2)] *om* YOC^{2}CB. lakke] lakken RF; lakked C^{2}. chaffare] ware RF.
134 wole] wolde BC. þis] me F. þoruȝ] thrugh þe G; by YOC^{2}CB. myȝt of] migh of Cr^{2}; my of C; c*ri*stis myght i*n* F; dere B. god almyȝty] heue*n*ne F.

Now awakeþ Wraþe wiþ two white eiȝen,
And neuelynge wiþ þe nose and his nekke hangyng.
'I am wraþe', quod he, 'I was som tyme a frere,
And þe Couentes Gardyner for to graffen Impes.
On lymitours and listres lesynges I ymped
Til þei beere leues of lowe speche lordes to plese,
And siþen þei blosmede abrood in boure to here shriftes.
And now is fallen þ*er*of a fruyt þ*a*t folk han wel leuere
Shewen hire shriftes to hem þan shryue hem to hir p*er*sons.
And now p*er*sons han p*ar*ceyued þ*a*t freres parte wiþ hem
Thise possessioners p*re*che and depraue freres;
And freres fyndeþ hem in defaute, as folk bereþ witnesse,
That whan þei p*re*che þe peple in many places aboute
I, wraþe, walke wiþ hem and wisse hem of my bokes.
Thus þei speken of spiritualte þ*a*t eiþer despiseþ ooþ*er*
Til þei be boþe beggers and by my sp*irit*ualte libben,

135 Now...Wraþe] Hanne wratthe gan awake F. awakeþ Wraþe] waketh wrothe R.
136 And] al F. neuelynge] snevelynge HmGC^{2}CB; muelynge Cr^1; revelynge F. þe] his CYBF. and] wyth Hm. his] the GM.
137 wraþe] wrothe RF. quod...tyme] he seyde þo for su*m*tyme y was F. som tyme] continually Cr^1.
138 þe] *om* OC^2. Couentes] couent R. to] *om* G. graffen] graffe LCr^{1}MRF.
139 On lymitours] ⁊ on Lemetour F. and] and on HmF. listres] legistreris OCr^{23}C^2; lyȝstre F.
140 beere] beeryn Hm. lowe] louth Bm; smal Cr^1; smoth Cr^{23}.
141 blosmede] blosmeden OC^2; blomed F. abrood] so brode M; *om* RF. boure] bowres for F. here] her BmBo; huyre Cot; hire CCr^1; heeryn F. shriftes] shrift Cr^{23}.
142 fallen] falle RHmG. þer...fruyt] swich frut þ*er*of F. of] *om* G. han] had G. wel] *om* CB.
143 Shewen] To shewyn F; Shew CrG. shriftes] shrift YHmF. to(1)] til R. þan] that Hm; ⁊ F. shryue] shryuen CHmBm BoR; forsake F; *om* GYCotM. hem] *om* GYCCotMF. to(2)] til R; *om* F. persons] own p*er*sons Cot; p*er*soun F.
144 now] *om* Cr. persons han] *above line another ink* M; han p*er*sons YOC^{2}CBo CotRF; han p*er*souns it Bm. han] *om* L. parceyued] ap*er*ceyued R; yp*er*ceyvid F. freres...hem] here p*ar*sshenys love freris F. parte] p*ar*ten HmOC^{2}B.
145 Thise] ⁊ so F. possessioners] possessours HmCrC^2. preche] prechen OC^2 BRF. depraue] deprauen OC^{2}RF; depraue the G; dyspraue Hm; dempne C; demen B.
146 freres] *om* RF. fyndeþ] fynde HmF. defaute] faute G. bereþ] berth C; bere HmCrGF.
147 That] And Cr. preche] p*re*chen OC^2. many] fele F; any Y. places] place YCB LM.
148 walke] walkes C. hem(1)] hym R. of] on Hm.
149 Thus þei] ⁊ make hem so F. þei] the G. speken] speke YCBF. of] YOC^{2}CB LF; of my WHmCrGMR (my *above line another ink* M). þat] til MF; ⁊ Cr. eiþer] ech F; *om* Cr. despiseþ] despise CrF. ooþer] ech other Cr.
150 my] *om* HmRF. sp*irit*ualte] almesse F.

Or ellis al riche and ryden; I, wraþe, reste neu*er*e
[That] I ne moste folwe this folk, for swich is my g*ra*ce.
I haue an Aunte to Nonne and an Abbesse boþe;
Hir [were] leu*er*e swowe or swelte þan suffre any peyne. |
I haue be cook in hir kichene and þe Couent s*er*ued *fol. 26 a*
Manye Monþes wiþ hem, and wiþ Monkes boþe.
I was þe Prioresse potager and oþ*er*e pou*er*e ladies,
And maad hem Ioutes of Ianglyng þ*at* dame Iohane was a bastard,
And dame Clarice a kny3tes dou3ter ac a cokewold was hir sire,
And dame Pernele a preestes fyle; Prioresse worþ she neu*er*e
For she hadde child in chirietyme; al oure Chapitre it wiste.
Of wikkede wordes I, wraþe, hire wortes made
Til "þow lixt!" and "þow lixt!" lopen out at ones
And eiþ*er* hit[t]e ooþer vnder þe cheke.
Hadde þei had knyues, by crist! eiþ*er* hadde kild ooþer.
Seint Gregory was a good pope and hadde a good forwit:

151, 152 *so divided* Cr^{23}; *divided after* aboute Cr^{1}; *after* folwe B; *as three lines divided after* aboute, folwe WHmGYOC^{2}CLMRF.
151 Or...ryden] *om* B. al] boþe be F. ryden] ryden aboute WHmCrGYOC^{2}CLMR; ryally ryde abowte F. I] ⁊ y F. reste neu*er*e] haue such a fortune Cr^{1}.
152 That...moste] but renne aft*er* ⁊ F. That] *spelled* þat W. ne moste] *om* Cr^{1}. this] stil this Cr^{1}; This wikked WHmCr^{23}GYOC^{2}CBLMR; alle swiche wykkid F. for...g*ra*ce] *om* Cr^{1}.
153 to] to a F; a Cot. an(2)] eek an F; *om* OCot. boþe] *om* RF.
154 Hir] þey F. were] HmYOC^{2}CBLMR; wery*n* F; hadde WCrG. swowe] swowne CrGC^{2}C; *om* F. or swelte] to sweltre F. þan] þan to F; or OC^{2}. any peyne] awhyle F.
155 haue be] was F. hir] þe G. þe] her Cr.
156 Fele Moneþis of þe 3eer ⁊ Mawgre was my knave F. hem] hym Bm. boþe] alse R.
157 þe] *twice* Bm. Prioresse] pryoresses HmBLMR. potager] portager G.
158 And] I YCB. hem] hir CB; *om* Hm. Ioutes] wortes CB. of] with YOC^{2}CB. Iohane] Ione CrOC^{2}CotMRF; Iohan GC. a] *om* HmF.
159 Clarice] Clarence Cr. kny3tes] kyng*es* G. ac...sire] bu she knew not hire fadir F. ac] And Cr^{1}YOC^{2}CB; *om* HmCr^{23}G.
160 *line om* Hm. Pernele] Puel Cr^{1}. preestes] priest Cr^{1}. fyle] syst*er* F. worþ] worthes G; was Cr.
161 hadde child] childid F. oure] þe F. Chapitre] capitre Y.
162 I hakkede here wortis ech day *with* wordys ⁊ *with* spyes F. I] in Hm. hire...made] made here wortus M. hire] y here Hm. made] I made OC^{2}LR.
163 at] atte Hm.
164 eiþ*er*] ech F. hitte] OC^{2}BmBoLMR; hytt G; hyt CrYC; hutt Cot; hite W; redyly hytte Hm; cracchid F. vnder þe cheke] ⁊ hire kyrtlys rentyn F. vnder] vndreneythe G.
165 Hadde] Hadden O; Ha C. by crist] *om* G. eiþ*er*] eyþer HmCrGYOC^{2}CB; ech F; hir eiþ*er* WLMR. kild ooþer] a god forwytt Bm.
166 a...forwit] good resou*n* F.

That no Prioresse were preest, for þat he [purueiede];
They hadde þanne ben *Infamis*, þei kan so yuele hele co[unseil].
Among Monkes I myȝte be ac many tyme I shonye
For þ*ere* ben manye felle frekes my feeris to aspie,
Boþe Priour and Suppriour and oure *Pater Abbas*;
And if I telle any tales þei taken hem togideres,
And doon me faste frydayes to [þerf] breed and to watre;
And am chalanged in þe Chapitrehous as I a child were
And baleised on þe bare ers and no brech bitwene.
Forþi haue I no likyng, [leue me], wiþ þo leodes to wonye;
I ete þ*ere* unþende fissh and feble ale drynke.
Ac ouþ*er* while whan wyn comeþ, [whan] I drynke at eue,
[I] haue a flux of a foul mouþ wel fyue dayes after;
Al þe wikkednesse þ*at* I woot by any of oure breþ*er*en,

167 were] sholde be F. for þat] þ*at* lawe F. purueiede] prouided Cr; ordeyned WHmGYOC^{2}CBLMRF.
168 *as two lines divided after* daye Hm; *in its place two spurious lines* Cr; *see above*, p. 222. hadde] hadden OHmBR; *om* F. þanne ben] ben G; weryn F. *Infamis*] *infames* HmBmBo (*in over erasure* Hm); euell losed G. þei] YOC^{2}M; for þei G; þe firste day þei WHmCBLR; at þe firste so F. so... counseil] þei *con*seil close F. so] *om* GCB. yuele] ille CB; *om* G. hele] heyle no G; holde YOC^{2}CB. counseil] conseil YGOC^{2}CBLMR; conseyl whan they ben agreued Hm; co (*cropped*) W.
169 myȝte] mot G. ac] but GF; and CrC^{2}CR. many...shonye] ofte þanne y wonde F. tyme] tymes HmCr^{23}G. shonye] YHmGOC^{2}CBLMR; shonye it W; shame*n* Cr.
170 *line om* F. þere] they CrOC^{2}CB. felle] fele Y. feeris] Freris C^2. aspie] aspien M; spie Cr^1.
171 Boþe] Boþe of F. oure] ȝoure C^2; of F.
172 And] For F. taken] take YCBF.
173 faste] fasten M. to(1)] boþe F. þerf breed] breed WHmCrGYOC^{2}CBLMRF. to(2)] *om* HmF.
174 And] I Cr. am] ȝeet am R; y am F; *om* HmG. chalanged] chastysed F. in þe] in Cr^{23}GF; ⁊ chyde*n* in Cr^1. Chapitre] Champitre C^2. hous] *om* F. as...were] am y as yt were a childe Hm.
175 on] vppon B. þe] my F. ers] hers (*cancelled for* bak *another hand*) R; bak F. and...bitwene] þat my bely beendiþ F. and] *om* BoCot.
176 *line om* OC^2. Forþi] Therfore Cr; for Cot. haue I] I haue GCotF. leue me wiþ] wiþ WHmCrGYCBLMRF. þo] *om* BoCot. wonye] dwelle F.
177 I...þere] For þere y eet F. vnþende] vnhende HmCrYOC^2. feble...drynke] drank feble ale F. drynke] dronke Y.
178 Ac] but G; and C^{2}CF; *om* Cr. comeþ] come C. whan(2)] LGMR; þanne W; and HmCr^{23}YOC^{2}CB; *om* Cr^{1}F. I...eue] y at eue yt drynke Hm. at] wyn at WCr^{1}GLM; wel at RF; it at Cr^{23}YOC^{2}CB. eue] eue*n* CrYOC^{2}CBR.
179 I] CrHmGYOC^{2}CBLMR; þ*at* y F; And W. of] or GBm (*over erasure* Bm); ⁊ F. foul] fulle Y; ful CBoCot; fol (o *touched up*) Bm. mouþ] monethe Y. wel] *om* Hm.
180 Al] ⁊ al F. oure] your G; mi Cr^{1}F. breþeren] brether Cr^{1}YCBmBo.

I cou[ȝ]e it [vp] in oure Cloistre þ*at* al [þe] Couent woot it.'
'Now repente', quod Repentaunce, 'and reherce neu*ere*
Counseil þat þow knowest by contenaunce ne by [speche];
And drynk nat ouer delicatly, ne to depe neiþer, |
That þi wille [ne þi wit] to wraþe myȝte turne: *fol. 26 b*
Esto sobrius!' he seide and assoiled me after,
And bad me wilne to wepe my wikkednesse to amende.
[Th]anne cam Coueitise; [I kan] hym naȝt discryue,
So hungrily and holwe sire heruy hym loked.
He was bitelbrowed and baberlipped wiþ two blered eiȝen;
And [lik] a leþeren purs lolled hise chekes
Wel sidder þan his chyn; þei chyueled for elde;
And as a bondeman[nes] bacon his berd was [yshaue].
Wiþ an hood on his heed, a hat aboue,

181 couȝe it vp] couþe it WHmCr^{12}YOC LMRF; cowthe G; kiþe it B; make knowe it C^{2} (*so a marginal gloss main hand* O); knoth it Cr^{3}. oure] your G; þe F. þat] til F. þe] the HmYOC^{2}CBmBoF; th Cot; oure WCrLM; your G; *om* R. woot it] yt wote Hm; knowi*th* yt F.
182 Now] A F. quod] q*uo*d GF; þee quod WHmCr^{23}YOC^{2}CBLMR; you quod Cr^{1}. neu*ere*] þow neuere WHmCr^{23}GYOC^{2}C BLR; þou yt neu*ere* F; you neuer Cr^{1}; it neuere M.
183 Counseil] Of co*n*seyl F. by(2)] *om* Hm. speche] RF; sight Cr^{23}OC^{2}; riȝt WHmCr^{1}YCBLM; nyght G.
184 ouer] oþer Bm; to M.
185 þi(1)] þei Bm; *om* Hm. ne þi wit] by cause þ*er*of WHmCrGYOC^{2}CBLMRF. myȝte] myghe G; it þe F.
186 and] and so he R. me] me sone þ*ere* F; hym CrM (*over erasure another ink* M).
187 me] hym CrM (*by corrector* M). wilne] wyl Cr. my] his CrM (*by corrector* M).
188 Thanne] And þanne WHmCrGYO C^{2}CBLMR; Affter hy*m* F. I kan] I can OC^{2}RF; kan I WHmCrGYCBLM. hym naȝt] nouȝt hym CHmF (*correct order noted* C).
189 hungrily] hugerly F; hugely Hm. sire] So Cr. heruy] ru *over erasure another ink* M; henry GCLR; sternly Cr. hym] *twice* Bo; he Cr^{23}; *om* F.
190 *as two lines divided before* Wiþ WHm CrGYOC^{2}CBLMRF. bitel...lipped] baberlippud and bitelbrowed M. bitel] byttur HmB; brytyl F. baber] blabber G. wiþ] also Wiþ WHmCrGYOC^{2}LM; alse With RF; boþe With CB. blered] blere eyȝed *corrected another ink* Hm. eiȝen] eiȝen as a blynd hagge WHmCrGYOC^{2} CBLMRF.
191 lik] as WHmCrGYOC^{2}CBLMRF. lolled] lolleden OF; looked Hm.
192 sidder] synder C^{2}. þei] the G. chyueled] ryueleden (*in margin* chyueleden *main hand*) O; cheuerid B; clyueled Y; sheuered Cr; shyuede F. elde] olde Cr.
193 And] *om* G. mannes] man of his WHmCrGYOC^{2}CBLMR; ma*n* et F. his ...was] so was his berd F. yshaue] bidraueled WCrGYOC^{2}CBLMR; dravelyd F; bawdy Hm.
194 Wiþ an hood] His hood he hadde F. an] his R. a] & a Cr. hat] lousy hat WHm CrGYOC^{2}CBLMR; heyȝ hat F. aboue] abouen CM; þer vppe F.

In a [torn] tabard of twelf wynter age;
But if a lous couþe [lepe, I leue and I trowe],
She sholde noȝt [wandre] on þat wel[ch]e, so was it þredbare.
'I haue ben coueitous', quod þis caytif, 'I biknowe it here.
For som tyme I *ser*ued Symme atte [Nok]
And was his p*re*ntice ypliȝt his p*ro*fit to [loke].
First I lerned to lye a leef ouþ*er* tweyne;
Wikkedly to weye was my firste lesson.
To Wy and to Wynchestre I wente to þe Feyre
Wiþ many man*ere* marchaundise as my maister me hiȝte.
Ne hadde þe g*ra*ce of gyle ygo amonges my [ware]
It hadde ben vnsold þis seuen yer, so me god helpe.
Thanne drouȝ I me among drapiers my donet to lerne,
To drawe þe [list] along, þe lenger it semed;
Among þe riche Rayes I rendred a lesson;
[P]roche[d] hem wiþ a paknedle and playte hem togideres,

195 In] And in WHmCr^{23}GYOC^{2}CBLMR; And Cr^{1}; He hadde on F. torn] tawny WCrGYOC^{2}CLM; tawne R; tany F; tanne HmBoCot; Thanne Bm. twelf] ten F. wynter] ȝeer FM. age] of age YOC^{2}F. *Hereafter an additional line* WHmCrGYOC^{2}CBLMRF: Al totorn and baudy and ful of lys crepyng (Al] and all Hm. to] *twice* Bo. ful...crepyng] lappe syȝd it semede F). *See above*, p. 193.
196 But...lous] þ*a*t but if a lows were lyght ⁊ F. if] CotGR; if þ*a*t WCrYOC^{2}CBmBoLM; that Hm. lepe...trowe] lepe þe bett*ere* RF; han lopen þe bettre W; haue lopen the bettre YHmCrGOC^{2}CBL; þe bettre haue lopen M.
197 She] He F; He ne R. sholde] had Cr. noȝt] no F; *om* C^{2}. wandre] walke RF; walkt Cr; han walked W; haue walked YHmGOC^{2}CBLM. on...welche] LR; on þat welþe WCr^{1}M; on þe welte Cr^{23}; on þ*a*t web F; theron GYOC^{2}; there HmCB. so...bare] but his staf wer*e* pyked F.
198 coueitous] coueitise CB; couetyng G. þis] þat M. biknowe] knowe Y; am aknowe Hm; biknew Bm; knew BoCot. here] neuere BoCot.
199 Symme] synne C. atte] at CrCot. Nok] Style WHmCrGYOC^{2}CBLMRF.
200 his p*re*ntice] app*re*ntys Hm. ypliȝt] plight CrGC^{2}; aplyght F. loke] wayte WHmCrGYOC^{2}CBLMRF.
201 a] wel a F. ouþ*er*] or MRF; on ther Cr^{1}. tweyne] moore F.
202 Wikkedly] ⁊ skarsly F. weye] weyȝe þyngis F.
203 Wy] wyku*m*be F. þe Feyre] feyres F.
204 marchaundise] of marchaundyse Hm F; marchaundises OCB; marchaundes C^{2}.
205 ygo] go YGOC^{2}CBM; be þ*a*t gan gon F. ware] LMRF; chaffare WHmCr GYOC^{2}CB.
206 þis] *om* Hm. so...helpe] hereafter Hm.
207 drouȝ] drw (*corrector supplies* e) Cot; draue Cr. I] *om* Y. me among] to G. lerne] lere BoCot.
208 To] For to F. list] lyst G; lyȝste F; liser WHmCrCBLMR; leser YOC^{2}. þe(2)] þe cloþ þe F. it] *om* F.
209 Rayes] rayeres R. a] my HmF.
210 Proched] To broche WHmCrGYOC^{2} CBLMF; To brochen R. pak] *over erasure* M; bat LRF. playte] playted C^{2}Y OLR; plyte HmCr^{2}; plytid BCF; plitte Cr^{1}; plett G; splyt Cr^{3}. hem(2)] he*m* þan F.

Putte hem in a p*ress*[our] and pyn[ned] hem þ*er*Inne
Til ten yerdes or twelue tolled out þrittene. |
My wif was a [wynnestere] and wollen cloþ made, *fol. 27 a*
[And] spak to [þe] Spynnester[e] to spynnen it [softe].
[Th]e pound þ*at* she paied by peised a quartron moore
Than myn owene Auncer [whan I] weyed truþe.
I bouȝte hire barly; she brew it to selle.
Peny ale and puddyng ale she poured togideres;
For laborers and lowe folk þ*at* lay by hymselue.
The beste [in my bedchambre] lay [by þe walle],
And whoso bummed þ*er*of bouȝte it þerafter,
A galon for a grote, god woot no lesse,
[Whan] it cam In cuppemele, þis craft my wif vsed.
Rose þe Reg*ra*ter was hir riȝte name;
She haþ holden hukkerye [elleuene wynter].
Ac I swere now, so thee ik, þ*at* synne wol I lete

211 Putte...p*ress*our] And putte hem in a p*ress*e WHmCrGYOC^{2}CBLMRF (p*ress*e] prasse Y). pynned] Cr^{1}HmGYOC^{2}CBo CotM; penned Bm; pyned LRF; pynnen Cr^{23}; pyne W.
212 or] other Hm. tolled] LMRF; hadde tolled WCrGYC; hadden tollid B; hadde told OC^{2}; hadden tolde Hm.
213 wynnestere] webbster GCr; webber C^{2}; webbe WHmYOCBLMRF. cloþ] she F.
214 And] She WHmCrGYOBLMF; Sho C; Heo R; he C^{2}. to(1)] vnto (to *above line another ink*) M. þe Spynnestere] a spinnester RF; Spynnesteres WHmCrGYOC^{2}CBLM. spynnen] spynne C^{2}CotF. softe] oute WHmCrGYOC^{2}CBLMR; fair & klene F.
215 The] Ac þe WHmYOLMR; but the GF; Ac for þe B; And the CrC^{2}C. þat] *om* YOCB. by] be Cr^{1}; *om* B. peised] weyed HmYOC^{2}CM; al þouȝ it weied BmBo; thow hit weid Cot. quartron] quartou*n* Hm; quarter RF.
216 owene] *twice* C^{2}. whan I] whoso WHmCrGYOC^{2}CBLMR; who þat F.
217 I bouȝte] þan bowhte y F. bouȝte] brougth Hm. barly] R; barly malt WHmCrGYOC^{2}CBLMF. brew] brewed CrG. it] *om* G.
219 lowe] YCrOC^{2}CBMF; for lowe WHmGLR. þat lay] she leide it F. hym] it Cr; þe F; hem YGOC^{2}CBmBoM. selue] seluen OHmC^{2}.
220 The] & þe F. in...walle] ale lay in my bour or in my bedchambre WHmCrGYOC^{2}CBLMRF (ale] of alle R. lay] lye G. or] or els Cr. my(2)] *om* C. bed] *om* CrBm).
221 *line om* B. so] þat F. bummed] bu*m*meth R. bouȝte] he bouȝte OYC^{2}CRF; payde Hm. it] *om* Hm.
222 a] a grey (ey *touched up*) M. god] god yt Hm.
223 Whan] And yet WHmCrGYOC^{2}CBLMRF. it] *om* C. þis] swich F. my wif] she CrF. vsed] vseth RF.
224 þe] *om* F. was] is RF.
225 She] Heo R. holden] Iholde RF; holden in Bm. hukkerye] huksterye Cr^{3}HmF; hukkerth Cr^{1}. elleuene wynter] al hire lif tyme WHmCrGYOC^{2}CBLMRF.
226 Ac] but G; And CrC^{2}C; *om* F. swere] shrewe G. so...ik] sothelick Cr^{1}; sothelich Cr^{23}. so] also B. thee ik] theich R; þe ek C^{2}; theek (*final* e *erased*) Hm; þeech F; thyk Cot; thehi C. wol] wolde Cr. lete] leue Bm.

And neu*er*e wikkedly weye ne wikke chaffare vse,
But wenden to walsyngh*am*, and my wif als,
And bidde þe Roode of Bromholm brynge me out of dette.'
'Repentedestow eu*er*e', quod Repentaunce, 'or restitucion madest?'
'ȝis, ones I was yherberwed', quod he, 'wiþ an heep of chapmen;
I roos whan þei were areste and riflede hire males.'
'That was no restitucion', quod Repentaunce, 'but a robberis þefte;
Thow haddest be bettre worþi ben hanged þ*er*fore.'
'I wende riflynge were restitucion for I lerned neu*er*e rede on boke,
And I kan no frenssh in feiþ but of þe ferþest ende of Northfolk.'
'Vsedestow eu*er*e vsurie', quod Repentaunce, 'in al þi lif tyme?' |
'Nay, soþly', he seide, 'saue in my youþe. *fol. 27 b*
I lerned among lumbardes [a lesson and of Iewes],

227 wikkedly] wrongly F. wikke] wikked YHmCrOC^{2}CBRF; fals (*altered to* falce *another script*) G. chaffare] caffare O. **228** But] But y F; and G. wenden] wende HmCr^{23}. wif] *om* Bo. als] also Cr^{23}M; Alis Cr^{1}; w*ith* me F. **229** out of] out C; fr*am* F. **230** Repentedestow] Repentedest Hm; Repentestow YCrGOC^{2}CBLM; Repentist F. euere] the euere HmBmBoLMF. or] ne LMR; & F. madest] þou madist F; made G. **231** ȝis] ȝee q*uod* he F; *om* G. yherberwed] herberwed HmCrGYOC^{2}CLMRF; sobrid B. quod he] *om* F. wiþ] amonge Hm. **232** I...areste] & whan þei wery*n* in reste y roos F. I] and y Hm. roos] aros HmB. were] weren OB. areste] at reste BCrG; yn reste Hm. riflede] yrifled LR. **233** no] not Cr. restitucion] repentau*n*ce F. Repentaunce] he GF. a] *om* HmCr. þefte] dede F. **234** haddest] hadde Hm. be bettre] YHmCrGOC^{2}CBMF (be *above line* M); be þe bettre W; better LR. worþi] þ*er*fore F. ben] to be Cr^{3}YOC^{2}. hanged] anhanged Cot. þ*er*fore] be þe nekke F. *Hereafter an additional line* WHmCrGYOC^{2}CBLMRF: Than for al þat þat þow hast here shewed (þat] *om* HmCr^{23}YC^{2}CB; þe oþ*er* þyng F. hast] *om* Cot. here] here now YOC^{2}CB; herefoorth nowe Hm. shewed] yshewed CBM; shewed afore G). *See above*, p. 193. **235** wende] toke Cr. were] had byn G; for Cr. for] HmM; quod he for WCrL; quod heo for R; so F; quod he YOC^{2}CB; *om* G. I...neuere] kan y F. lerned] lerid B; *om* Cr. rede] to rede (to *over erasure*) M; *om* HmGYOC^{2}CB. on] *om* Cr. **236** And] Ne F; *om* Cr^{23}. I] *om* G. in feiþ] *om* G. þe...of] *om* F. þe] *om* C. ferþest] ferrest CCot; fer Cr. ende] *om* Hm. Northfolk] Norþfolk langage F. **237** Vsedestow] Vsed þou Cr. vsurie] any vsure Hm. Repentaunce] he G. **238** he seide] seyde he F. he] heo R. in my] su*m*tyme i*n* F. **239** among...of] a lessou*n* among lumbardis and Bm. a...Iewes] a lessou*n* and of iewes R; and Iewes a lesson WHmCrGYOC^{2}CBoCotLM; a lessou*n* be herte F.

To weye pens wiþ a peis and pare þe heuyeste
And lene it for loue of þe cros, to legge a wed and lese it.
Swiche dedes I dide write if he his day breke;
I haue mo Manoirs þoruȝ Rerages þan þoruȝ *Miseretur &*
    com[m]odat.
I haue lent lordes and ladies my chaffare
And ben hire brocour after and bouȝt it myselue.
Eschaunges and cheuysaunces, wiþ swich chaffare I dele,
And lene folk þat lese wole a lippe at euery noble.
And wiþ lumbardes lettres I ladde gold to Rome
And took it by tale here and tolde hem þere lasse.'
'Lentestow euere lordes for loue of hire mayntenaunce?'
'Ye, I haue lent lordes loued me neuere after,
And haue ymaad many a knyȝt boþe Mercer and draper
That payed neuere for his prentishode noȝt a peire gloues.'
'Hastow pite on pouere men þat [for pure nede] borwe?'
'I haue as muche pite of pouere men as pedlere haþ of cattes,

240 and] & þan to F. þe] awey þe M.
241 lene] to leene F; leue Cr^{1}; loue Y. it (1)] *om* F. þe cros] þe coris crois (coris *cancelled*) Bm; crese Cr^{23}. to legge] & if þey leyȝde F. a] *om* Hm. wed] weddes Y. and] *om* F. lese] lesen Cr; lesse G.
242 Swiche dedes] & doble dette F. dedes] dettys (ttys *over erasure another ink*) Hm. dide] dide do M. his] is HmM.
243 mo] no G. Manoirs] moneye Hm. þoruȝ(1)] of Hm; by Cr. Rerages] arerages Hm. þoruȝ(2)] by Hm. *miseretur*] *misereatur* Cr^{1}; Miseriatur Cr^{23}. *commodat*] CrCot; comodat WHmGYOC^{2}CBmBo LMR; *comedat* F.
244 lent] Ilente R. and...my] longe my lovely F.
245 hire] a F. and] *om* F. bouȝt] brought CotR. it] yt ageyn F; *om* Bm. selue] seluen M.
246 Eschaunges] & with changis F. swich] *om* F. chaffare] chaffares R. I dele] Idle Cr^{23}.
247 And] & y F; I Y. lippe at euery] shelyng in þe F.
248 ladde] hadde Hm.
249 *run together with* 250 G. by] here be F. tale] le *over erasure* M; taille YHmGOC^{2}CBLR (i *erased* Cot). here] þere R; *om* F. and...lasse] *om* G. hem] it F; *om* OC^{2}. þere] the Cot.
250 Lentestow...lordes] *om* G. Lentestow] lendestow CCr; Lenestow L; Lenedest þow R. lordes] to lordes Hm. for] quod he for F. hire] *om* F.
251 Ye I haue] yet haue I G. lent] CrHm GYOC^{2}CBLMRF; lent to W. loued] that loued CrC^{2}; þat loueden OHm; louede þei B; quod heo loued R; quod he þat lovede F.
252 And] & y F. haue] hath Cr^{23}. ymaad] maad HmCrGYOC^{2}CBMF (*erasure before it* M). a] *om* YOC^{2}CR. boþe] *om* G.
253 *line om* G. payed] paieden BmBo. neuere] not Cr. his] hir CB. noȝt] *om* HmCr. a] one Cr. gloues] of glouys HmCrC; clovis F.
254 Hastow] Haddestow Y. for pure] muste for F; mote WYC^{2}CLR; most GCr; moten OHmBM. nede] F; nedes WHmCrGYOC^{2}CBLMR.
255 as(1)] also B. muche] mikile C. of(1)] *altered to* on Bm; on HmCrGOC^{2} MF. pouere men] þe pore CrF; hem YOC^{2}CB. as(2)] as þe RF. haþ] *om* HmF. of(2)] on GC^{2}F.

That wolde kille hem if he cacche hem myȝte for coueitise of hir skynnes.'
'Artow manlich among þi neȝebores of þi mete and drynke?'
'I am holden', quod he, 'as hende as hound is in kichene;
Amonges my neȝebores namely swich a name ich haue.'
'Now [but þow repente þe raþer', quod Repentaunce,
'God lene þee neuere grace] þi good wel to bisette,
Ne þyne heires after þee haue ioie of þat þow wynnest,
Ne þyne executours wel bisette þe siluer þ*at* þow hem leuest; |
And þat was wonne wiþ wrong wiþ wikked men be despended. *fol.* 28 *a*
For were I frere of þat hous þer good feiþ and charite is
I nolde cope vs wiþ þi catel ne oure kirk amende
Ne haue a peny to my pitaunce, [for pyne of my soule],
For þe beste book in oure hous, þeiȝ brent gold were þe leues,
And I wiste witterly þow were swich as þow tellest.

256 *as two lines divided after* mygthe Hm. wolde] *om* Cr. kille] kyllyn F; kilth Cr. if he] and he R; all F. cacche hem] hem cacche Hm; ca*n* he*m* catch Cr; *om* GYO C^2CBF. myȝte] *om* CrF. coueitise of] coueytises of O; couet of Cr; to haue CB. skynnes] schynnes C; cotes as his praye asketh Hm.
257 among] to F. neȝebores] Neyȝhebo*ur* F. þi(2)] *om* GYOC^2CBF. mete] Metis F; me Y. and] & of YOC^2CB. drynke] drynkys F.
258 holden] holde HmF. quod...hende] as hende q*uod* he C^2YOCF; also hende q*uod* he HmB; as hende G. as(2)] as an B; as is Cr. hound] homyde (?) G. is] *om* CrGR. in] in the GF; in his R.
260 Now] *om* CrGOC^2. but...Repentaunce] god lene þee neu*er*e quod Repentaunce bu[t] þow repente þe raþ*er* WHm CrGYOC^2CBLMRF (god lene] lene god Bm. lene] leue Cr; gyve F. þee] *om* GY OC^2CBLMRF. neu*er*e] grace F; *om* CB. but] HmCrGYOC^2CBLMRF; bu W. þe] þe the Hm; þee O; *erased* M).
261 God...grace] The gr*a*ce on þis grounde WHmCrGYOC^2CBLMRF (The] Grawnte þe F; *om* HmCr. on] of BoGCot; of god (*corrected*) Bm). wel] wyl HmCr^1OC^2; so F. to] the Cr^2; þou F; *om* M.
262 Ne] þ*at* F. heires] *over erasure* M; ysue L; vssue R; houswif F.
263 Ne] and GF; To Cr^3. executours] seketoures RF. wel] wyll G; *om* YOC^2 CB. þe] þi GYOC^2. siluer] moneye Hm. hem] *om* GF. leuest] louest C^2.
264 And...was] For as it ys F. þat] *twice* BoCot. wonne] wo*n*nen OC^2BM. wiþ(1)] q*uod* Hm. wiþ(2)...be] it worþ w*ith* wastoures F. be] *om* GB. despended] spe*n*did F; dyspende ytt G.
265 I] I a C^2. þat] þe Cr^{12}; an F. good...is] feyþ is fownde þ*ere*Inne F.
266 nolde] wolde nouȝt RF. þi] thyer*e* G. catel] tatell C^2. kirk] cherche RF; brike Cr^1.
267 my(1)] *om* F. for...soule] so mote pyȝghne i*n* helle F. for...of] of þyne bi LYOC^2CBMR; so god WHmCrG. soule] BC; soule hele YOC^2LMR; soule helpe GHmCr; soule saue W.
268 þeiȝ...leues] bryght golde if it were Cr. brent] of brende Hm; *om* G.
269 I] *om* G. þow(1)] þat þou B. tellest] telleth L. *Hereafter a spurious line* Cr^{23}Y OC^2CB; *see above*, p. 224.

Seruus es alterius [cum] fercula pinguia queris;
Pane tuo pocius vescere: liber eris.
Thow art an vnkynde creature; I kan þee no3t assoille
Til þow make restitucion', [quod Repentaunce], 'and rekene wiþ hem alle;
And siþen þat Reson rolle it in þe Registre of heuene
That þow hast maad ech man good I may þee no3t assoille:
Non dimittitur peccatum donec restituatur [a]blatum.
For a[l] þat ha[þ] of þi good, haue god my trouþe,
[Is] holden at þe hei3e doom to helpe þee to restitue,
And whoso leueþ [þat I li3e] loke in þe Sauter glose,
In *Miserere mei deus*, wher I mene truþe:
Ecce enim veritatem dilexisti &c.
Cum sancto sanctus eris: construwe me þis on englissh.'
Thanne weex þ[e] sherewe in wanhope & wolde han hanged hym[self]
Ne hadde repentaunce þe raþer reconforted hym in þis manere:

269α *cum*] HmCrGYOC^{2}CBLMRF; *dum* W. *pinguia*] pinqua G.
269β *eris*] *eris &c* Hm.
270 an] *om* G. creature] creatour Cot. þee no3t] nou3t þe CB.
271 *line om* Y. quod Repentaunce] quod repentance R; *om* WHmCrGOC^{2}CBLMF. rekene] rekenyng Cr.
272 *line om* Y. siþen] þerto F. rolle] rollyd Hm. it] þe C; *om* B.
273 *line om* Y. That] tyll G; For til F. man] a man Hm; mande (*corrected by erasure* ?) C^2. þee no3t] nat the Cot. assoille] saue R.
273α *dimittitur*] dimittur M. *donec*] *nisi* CrRF. *restituatur*] *corrected from restituetur* G. *ablatum*] CrGCotRF; *ablatum &c* HmOC^{2}LM (*first* a *over erasure* Hm); *oblatum* WBmBo; *oblatum &c* YC.
274 al] CrGC; alle WHmYOC^{2}BLMRF. þat] þo þat HmF. haþ] hath LMR; han WHmOC^2; haue CrGYCF; hauen B. of] *om* F. haue god] as god have F.
275 He is holde to 3eelde it here if he may it qwyte F. Is] LMR; Ben WHmCrGYOC^{2}CB. holden] haldynge R. þee] *om* Hm. to] to þy Hm; *om* R. restitue] restitute Cr^{23}GB; restitucioun Hm.
276 *For this four spurious lines* F; *see above*, p. 222. And] *om* Cr. whoso] who M; he þat Hm. þat I li3e] no3t þis be sooþ WCrGYOC^{2}LMR; nat þat þys be soiþ Hm; this be nou3t soþ CB. þe] a R. glose] clause Cr; boke GM.
277 In] Or sey3 F. wher] wheþer HmCr; wich F. I] ys F; *om* B.
277α *line om and a spurious one in its place* F; *followed by that same line* R. *&c*] *&&c* Cr^{23}. *Hereafter an additional line* WHmCrGYOC^{2}CBLMRF: Shal neuere werkman in þis world þryue with þat þow wynnest (Shal] For schal RF. in...world] *om* G). *See above*, pp. 224, 193.
278 *eris*] *eris &c* YOC^{2}CBmBo. construwe...englissh] *om* C. me] þou me B; now wel F. þis] that HmCrGYOC^{2}BLR. on englissh] resoun F. on] yn HmCrG.
279 þe] RF; þat WHmCrGYOC^{2}CBLM. han hanged] an hongid F; hang CrG. self] CHmCrGYOC^{2}BLMRF; *cropped* W.
280 þe] *om* HmG. reconforted] conforted HmGR; reersyd F. hym...manere] þese wordis F. hym] *om* CB.

'Haue m*er*cy in þi mynde, and wiþ þi mouþ biseche it—
[*Misericordia eius super omnia opera eius ⁊c*]—
And al þe wikkednesse in þis world þat man myȝte werche or þynke
Nis na moore to þe m*er*cy of god þan [amyd] þe see a gleede:
Omnis iniquitas quantum ad misericordiam dei est quasi sintilla in medio m[*aris*]. |
Forþi haue m*er*cy in þy mynde, and marchaundise leue it, *fol.* 28 *b*
For þow hast no good ground to gete þee wiþ a wastel
But if it were wiþ þi tonge or ellis wiþ þi hondes.
For þe good þat þow hast geten bigan al wiþ falshede,
And as longe as þow lyuest þerw*ith* þow yeldest noȝt but borwest;
And if þow wite neu*er*e to [whom] ne [where] to restitue
Ber it to þe Bisshop, and bid hym of his g*ra*ce
Bisette it hymself as best [be] for þi soule.
For he shal answere for þee at þe heiȝe dome,
For þee and for many mo þat man shal yeue a rekenyng:
What he lerned yow in lente, leue þow noon ooþer,

281 mynde] Myȝnde ma*n* F. þi(2)] *om* Cr^{23}. biseche] god beseche F; biseh Cr^{1}. it] *om* HmF. *Hereafter an additional line* WHmCrGYOC^{2}CBLMRF: For goddes mercy is moore þan alle hise oþere werkes (alle] manye of F). *See above*, p. 193.

281α LYOC^{2}MR; line *om* WHmCrGCBF. *eius*(1)] *domini* R. ⁊*c*] *om* YOC^{2}.

282 þe] *om* CrOC^{2}. in] of OC^{2}; *om* F. þis] þe Cr; *om* CF. world] *om* F. man] ony man F. myȝte] may HmCr; may eyþ*er* F. werche] do YOC^{2}CB; *om* G. or] *om* G.

283 Nis] Is CrGF. mercy of god] godd*es* mercy F. amyd] in WHmCrGYOC^{2}CBLMRF.

283α *Omnis*] onnis G. *quasi*] *by corrector* M; *om* L. *maris*] HmCrGOC^{2}CLMRF; *maris* ⁊*c* YB; m (*cropped*) W.

284 Forþi] Therfore Cr. mercy...mynde] in þy mynde mercy F; þou merci in mind Cr. leue] þou leve F; loue G. it] *om* HmF.

285 to] go G. þee wiþ] þ*er*fore F. þee] ther Cr. a] *om* Cr.

286 if] *om* F. were] be F; *om* Bm. ellis] *om* M. þi(2)] thy GF; þi two WHmCrYOC^{2}CBLMR.

287 þe] al þe F. þow] *om* F. geten] gete RF. bigan al] it bigan al B; þe grownde bega*n* F. falshede] falsenesse MF.

288 as(2)] *om* F. þerwith] wit*h* it Cr^{23}; *om* G. yeldest] paist Cr.

289 wite] wost YOC^{2}CB. whom ne where] whiche ne whom WGYOC^{2}CBLMR; whiche ne to whom HmCr; wyche ne yt to whom F. to(2)] *om* HmF. restitue] restytute GR; make restitucio*un* B; restore CrF.

290 þe] te Bm; þy*n* F.

291 Bisette] þat he bysette Hm. be] Hm; is WCrGYOC^{2}CBLMRF. þi] þe HmYCot.

292 heiȝe] day of F.

293 for] *om* YOC^{2}CB. a] *om* MF.

294 What] ⁊ what F. lerned] lerede M; lene lerned (*corrected*) Bm. lente] lente*n* YOC^{2}CBoCotMF. leue] beleve F. þow] ȝe HmYOC^{2}M; you CrC.

And what he lente yow of oure lordes good to lette yow fro synne.'
Now bigynneþ Gloton for to go to shrifte
And [kaireþ] hym to kirkeward his coupe to shewe.
[Ac] Beton þe Brewester*e* bad hym good morwe
And [heo] asked [of hym] whiderward he wolde.
'To holy chirche', quod he, 'for to here masse,
And siþen I wole be shryuen and synne na moore.'
'I haue good Ale, gossib', quod she, 'Gloton, woltow assaye?'
'Hastow', quod he, 'any hote spices?'
'I haue pepir and pion[e] and a pound of garleek,
A ferþyngworþ of fenel seed for fastynge dayes.'
Thanne goþ Gloton In and grete oþes after.
Cesse þe [sowestere] sat on þe benche,
Watte þe warner and his wif boþe,
Tymme þe Tynker*e* and tweyne of his [knaues],

295 *line om* F. what he] þ*at* he Cr^{1}; *om* Cr^{23}G. yow(1)] 3 Bo. oure lordes] his YOC^{2}CB. lordes good] lord god Cr^{1}. lette] wite YOC^{2}CB; kepe Cr^{23}. *Hereafter a spurious line* YOC^{2}CB; *see above*, p. 224.
296 Now bigynneþ] HErly gan F. Gloton] glotonye Hm. for] *om* Cot. shrifte] cherche Hm.
297 kaireþ] kaireth YG; kaires OC^{2}CLMR; karieþ WCrB; caryes Hm; wendis F. hym] *om* Cot. to(1)] to the CrG. kirke] kyr Hm; cherche R. coupe] cope Cr^{2}; coppe Cr^{13}; synnes G.
298 Ac] YHmOBLMR; but G; An C; And WCrC^{2}; Ano*n* F.
299 And heo] And WHmCrGYOC^{2}CBLMRF. asked] freyned F. of] HmCr^{1}GYOC^{2}CBLR; at W; *om* Cr^{23}MF. hym] G; hym wiþ þat WHmCrYOC^{2}CBmLR; him with þat word (word *above line*) M; wiþ þat BoCot; hy*m* whens he cam ⁊ F. ward] þat F; *om* B.
300 quod] saide Cr^{23}. for] *om* CBF. here] heren amorwe F.
301 wole] woulde Cr. be] by Hm. shryuen] schryue HmBRF. synne] synnen (en *over erasure*) M.
302 I] ȝee y F. Ale] alle Bm. quod she] said he Cr^{23}; *om* G. she] he Cr^{1}. woltow] wold þou Cr.
303 Hastow] Hast þou in þy*n* purs F; Hastow ouȝt in þi purs WHmCrGYOC^{2}CBLMR. quod he] *om* HmCrGYOC^{2}CBLMR. hote spices] spyces fyȝne F.
304 pione] pioyne R; piones WHmCrGYOC^{2}CLMF; greynes B. and(2)] Hm; quod she and WOC^{2}MRF (s *another ink* M); quod he ⁊ CrYCBL; quod he G. garleek] gillofris F.
305 A] GHmYOCBLMR; And a WCrC^{2}F.
306 Thanne] Ano*n* F. In] in w*ith* hir*e* F.
307 Cesse] Sus Cr^{1}; ⁊ fond Symme F. þe(1)] *om* F. sowestere] BoBmCot; sowsteresse M; Souteresse WCrYOC^{2}CLR; sowt*er* Hm; sourseresse G; sowteres wif F. sat] sytty*ng*e F. on] vn C^{2}; vppon B.
308 Watte þe] ⁊ watte F. and] also ⁊ F. boþe] after OC^{2}.
309 Tymme] Tyme Cr^{12}; Tomme MGC^{2}; ⁊ Tomme F; Tume Bm; symme HmYCBoCotR. knaues] p*re*ntices WCrGOC; app*re*ntices Y; p*re*ntys HmC^{2}BLMRF.

Hikke þe hakeneyman and hugh þe Nedlere, |
Clarice of Cokkeslane and þe Clerk of þe chirche, *fol.* 29 *a*
[Sire Piers of Pridie and Pernele of Flaundres,
Dawe þe dykere and a doȝeyne oþere,]
A Ribibour, a Ratoner, a Rakiere of Chepe,
A Roper*e*, a Redyngkyng and Rose þe dyssher[e],
Godefray of Garlekhiþe and Griffyn þe walshe;
[Of] vpholderes an heep, erly by þe morwe,
Geue Gloton wiþ glad chere good ale to hanselle.
Clement þe Cobeler*e* caste of his cloke
And at þe newe feire nempned it to selle.
Hikke þe [Hostiler] hitte his hood after
And bad Bette þe Bocher ben on his syde.
Ther were chapmen ychose þis chaffare to preise:
Whoso hadde þe hood sholde han amendes of þe cloke.
T[h]o risen vp in Rape and rouned togideres
And preised þ[e] penyworþes apart by hemselue.

310 Hikke] ⁊ hikke F. Nedlere] medler Cr^{1}.
311 Clarice] ⁊ Clarys F. Cokkeslane] cockelane Cr^{23}. and] w*ith* F. þe(1)] *om* OC.
312, 313 *the order of* RF; *transposed* WHmCrGYOC^{2}CBLM.
312 Sire] And sire RF. Pridie] pryde GOC^{2}CBm. Pernele] puelle G.
313 Dawe] ⁊ Dawe F; Davy MCr^{23} (vy *over erasure* M). and] ⁊ wel F.
314 Ribibour] ribbo*ur* Cot. a(2)] and a C^{2}F. of] off þe GC^{2}. Chepe] chope Y.
315 a] ⁊ a F. Redyng] Rydyng YC^{2}C. þe] *om* F. dysshere] dyschere HmOC^{2}B; dyssheres WCrGYCL; disshers M; dissheres douȝter RF.
316 Godefray] ⁊ Godefrey F. Garlekhiþe] Garlyng heþe F. hiþe] hide M; hyue Cr. Griffyn] grifyth R; Geffrey F; gefferou*n* C^{2}. þe walshe] wasshere F.
317 Of] And WHmCrGYOC^{2}CBLMRF. vpholderes] vpholdesters Hm; vpholsters of cornhill C^{2}. an] a gret F; and Bm.
318 Geue] Geuen CrHmGYOC^{2}CLM; Goue*n* C^{2}; Ȝeuen to B; þey geve F. glad] good OC^{2}CB; *om* Y. good] a galou*n* F. ale] alle Bm. to] i*n* F; *om* Bm. hanselle] honde F.
319 Clement] Sone Clem*en*t F. caste of] of caste F.
320 at] to R; in F. feire] feyre R; feire he WHmCrGYOC^{2}CBLMF. nempned] nepnyd Hm; neuened G.
321 Hikke] Ano*n* hikke F. Hostiler] Hakeneyman WHmCrGYOC^{2}CBLMRF. hitte] cast G.
322 ben] to ben RF.
323 Ther] Tre Bm. were] weren OC^{2}BF; *om* R. ychose] ychosen M; chose G; chosen YOC^{2}CB. þis] þ*at* F. chaffare] ware Cr^{23}. preise] pryce G.
324 Whoso] CrHmGYOC^{2}CBLMR; That whoso W; which of hem sholde F. hadde] hath Cr; haue CBF; haueth GLMR. sholde] shul CGBMR; or who sholde F. amendes...cloke] þe boþe F.
325 Tho] BmR; Two WHmCrGYOC^{2}CBoCotLM; þan F. risen] ryse F. vp] þey F; *om* R. in] In þis G; ful F. Rape] rathely F. rouned] rounede*n* OF; rounen M; romed G.
326 preised] preyseden OHmBmMF. þe] RF; þise WHmCrGYOC^{2}CBLM. apart] ap*ar*tie C^{2}; and part Bm; ech p*ar*t F. hem] her C^{2}; hym HmRF; the Cr^{1}. selue] seluen M.

[There were oþes an heep, whoso it herde];
Thei kouþe no3t, by hir Conscience, acorden [togideres]
Til Robyn þe Ropere [arise þei bisou3te],
And nempned hym for a nounpere þat no debat nere.
Hikke þe hostiler [þanne] hadde þe cloke
In couenaunt þat Clement sholde þe cuppe fille,
And haue Hikkes hood [þe] hostiler and holden hym yserued,
And whoso repente[þ] raþest sholde aryse after
And greten sire Gloton wiþ a Galon ale.
There was lau3ynge and lourynge and 'lat go þe cuppe!'
[Bargaynes and beuerages bigonne to arise],
And seten so til euensong and songen vmwhile
Til Gloton hadde yglubbed a galon and a gille. |
Hise guttes bigonne to goþelen as two gredy sowes; *fol. 29 b*
He pissed a potel in a paternoster while,
And blew [þe] rounde ruwet at [þe] ruggebones ende

327 *not in* WHmCrGYOC^{2}CBLMRF; *see above*, p. 79.
328 Thei] But þei F. kouþe] couþen OC^{2}M. Conscience] consciences Bm. acorden] acorde F. togideres] in truþe WHmCrGYOC^{2}CBLMR; þat ty3me F.
329 *in margin another hand* Bm. arise... bisou3te] arise þe southe R; aroos by þe Southe WHmCrGYOC^{2}CBL; arose by þe sothe (þe *added above line*) M; was reysed fram his sete F.
330 nempned] nyuened G; nemp Hm. hym] *om* F. nounpere] nunpenere Bm. nere] were HmGBR; þere fylle F. *Hereafter a spurious line* Cr^{23}YOC^{2}CB; *see above*, p. 224.
331 Hikke] þanne Hikke F. þanne hadde] hadde WHmCrGYOC^{2}CBLMRF.
332 þat] *om* Y. sholde] shall G. þe] *om* F.
333 þe] Cr^{23}HmYBM; *om* WCr^{1}GOC^{2}CLRF. holden] holde HmOC^{2}BoCotLMRF; wold Bm. yserued] serued CrHmGYOC^{2}CB; apayed F.
334 so] þat YOC^{2}CBoCotF; *om* GBm. repenteþ] repentiþ OC^{2}B; repentes C; repente Hm; repented WCrGYLMRF. raþest] rather YOC^{2}CB. sholde] shul C. aryse] ryse HmF. after] sone F.
335 And] Ang Bo. greten] grete HmGYOC^{2}CBLMR. sire] wele sire YOC^{2}F; wel CB; *om* Hm. ale] of ale HmCrG.
336 was] were Cr^{12}.
337 *not in* WHmCrGYOC^{2}CBLMRF; *see above*, p. 79.
338 seten so] sytten so Cr^{1}GR; so seten O; so satten C^2; so seten they YC; so sytten they Cr^{23}; so þei setten B. so] þere F. til] stylle tyl Hm; to Cr^{23}. euen] eue HmCotR. song] songtyme C^2. songen] sunge F; syngen R. vmwhile] somewhyle Cr^{1}G; other while Cr^{23}OC^2; on wile Bm; merye songis F. *Here* Hm *copies line* 342.
339 yglubbed] glubbed OYC^{2}C; globred Hm; ygolped Cr; swelwid BoCot; shwelwid Bm. a galon] *twice* Y. a gille] more F.
340 Hise] þat hise F. bigonne] gonne HmLMRF; gunnen B. to] *om* C^2. goþelen] gothely YC; godly LMR; gowle GF; gurle (*corrected main hand*) O; grouly B; gotheli to grulle C^2. two] a F. gredy] gnedy R. sowes] sowe F.
341 He] I trowe he F. in] more in Bm; and more in BoCot.
342 *copied here and after* 338 Hm. And] He R. þe(1)] his WHmCrGYOC^{2}CBLMRF. rounde] *om* Hm(2). ruwet] reuet C^2; ryuet Cot. þe(2)] G; his WHmCrYOC^{2}CBLMRF. rugge] rigges CR. bones] bon LC.

That alle þat herde þat horn helde hir nos[e] after
And wisshed it hadde ben wexed wiþ a wispe of firses.
He [hadde no strengþe to] stonde er he his staf hadde,
And þanne gan he to go lik a glemannes bicche
Som tyme aside and som tyme arere,
As whoso leiþ lynes to lacche [wiþ] foweles.
A[c] whan he drouȝ to þe dore þanne dymmed hise eiȝen;
He [þr]umbled on þe þresshfold and þrew to þe erþe.
Clement þe Cobeler*e* kauȝte hym by þe myddel
For to liften hym o lofte and leyde hym on his knowes.
Ac Gloton was a gret cherl and grym in þe liftyng;
And kouȝed vp a cawdel in Clementes lappe.
Is noon so hungry hound in hertford shire
Dorste lape of þat leuynges, so vnlouely [it] smauȝte.
Wiþ al þe wo of þ[e] world his wif and his wenche

343 þat(1)...horn] þe folk i*n* þe hows F. herde] herden OHmC^{2}BoCot; *om* R. þat(2)] *om* R. helde] helden OHmBo CotF; holden Bm. hir] his Cr^1. nose] CrYOC^{2}CBmBoLRF; noses WHmGCot M (? es *over erasure* M).
344 wisshed] wissheden YHmOCBLMR. hadde ben] were F. wexed] wyped CrF. firses] Firris C^2; fryses G.
345 hadde...to] myȝte neiþ*er* steppe ne WHmCrGYOC^{2}CBLMRF (neiþ*er*] not F. ne] no C; nor Cr). er] tyll G; til *another hand* Bm. his] a CrF.
346 And] *om* G. to] *om* YCLMRF.
347 Som] and some G. aside] all asyde Hm; he ȝeede o syde F. som...arere] hidirward & þydirward F. arere] aderere Y.
348 As] and C^2. so] þ*at* F. lynes] liymȝerdis B. to...wiþ] for to lacche WCr YOC^{2}BLMR (l *altered to* k M); for to lacches C; for to cacche HmG; larkys to cacche F. foweles] *om* F.
349 Ac] R; And WHmCrGYOC^{2}CBL MF. to] *om* Cr^1. dore] doreward Hm. dymmed] dymmeden OM.
350 He] & F. þrumbled] stumbled WO C^2; stombled HmCrYCM (sto *over erasure* M); stomlid B; stomeled G; trembled L; tremled R; tr*i*pplid F. and] and ou*er* BoCotF; and oþ*er* Bm. þe erþe] grownde F.
351 Clement þe] Ano*n* Clem*en*t F. by þe myddel] in hise armes F.
352 For to] And B. liften] lifte OCrGY C^{2}CBLMRF. hym(1)] *om* C. on] vpon Cr^1; selfe on G.
353 Ac] but GF; And CrC^{2}C. cherl] karle G; gulch Cot. and] & GOC^{2}BF; and a WHmCrYCLMR. grym] heuy BmBo; groned Cot. in] for F. þe] to F; *om* HmCr^{3}C^2; *erased* M. liftyng] lyfte F.
354 vp a] a potel F. cawdel] candle Cr^{12}; galou*n* Hm.
355 Is] Is þer B; There is CrF; there nas Hm. so] *om* HmCot. hound] an hound C^2. in] in al F.
356 Dorste] þat leste F. lape] lapen M; haue lapped C^2. of] a F. þat] tho Hm CrM; þe GLR; lyte F. leuynges] leuyng R; leuenynges *in margin* O; þ*er*of F. vnlouely] loþly F. it] MHmBRF; þei WCrGYOC^{2}CL. smauȝte] smauȝten O; smakkyd HmC^2; smacchid Bo; smachetyd Bm; smellid F; were G.
357 Wiþ] þan wi*th* F. of] i*n* F. þe(2)] the HmMF; þis WCrGYOC^{2}CBLR. wenche] wence G.

Baren hym to his bed and brouȝte hym *þer*Inne,
And after al þis excesse he hadde an Accidie
That he sleep Saterday and Sonday til sonne yede to reste.
Thanne waked he of his wynkyng and wiped hise eiȝen;
The firste word þ*at* he [spak] was 'where is þe bolle?'
His wif [edwyted] hym þo [of wikkednesse and synne],
And Repentaunce riȝt so rebuked hym þat tyme:
'As þow wiþ wordes ⁊ werkes hast wroȝt yuele in þi lyue
Shryue þee and be shamed *þer*of and shewe it w*ith* þi mouþe.'
'I, Gloton', quod þe [gome], 'gilty me yelde
That I haue trespased w*ith* my tonge, I kan noȝt telle how ofte;
Sworen goddes soule [and his sydes] and "so me god helpe" |
There no nede was nyne hundred tymes; *fol.* 30 *a*
And ou*er*seyen me at my soper and som tyme at Nones
That I, Gloton, girte it vp er I hadde gon a myle,

358 Baren] Bare CrGYC; beryn *over erasure* Hm; þey beren F. to] RF; onto Bm; hom to WHmCrGYOC^{2}CBoCot LM. brouȝte] brouȝten OHmC^{2}BoCotM.
359 þis] his C^{2}Bm; þ*at* F. excesse] accesse HmYOC^{2}. an] swich an F. Accidie] axces G; attidie Bm.
360 sleep] shleppet Bm; sleep al F; slope Cr^{1}. Sonday] sonynday Hm. til] tyl the HmB. sonne...reste] eve F. yede to] wente to OCrGC^{2}; took YCB.
361 Thanne] ⁊ þ*an*ne F. waked] wakenede M; awaked F. of...wynkyng] wroþly F.
362 The] ⁊ þe F; *om* YOC^{2}C. spak] spake (e *erased*) Hm; warp WYOCBLM RF; warped CrG; warvp C^{2}. þe] þ*at* Cr^{2}.
363 His] ⁊ F. wif edwyted] wif gan edwyte WCr^{1}M (f *over erasure* M); wytte gan edwyte HmCr^{23}GYOC^{2}CBLRF (te(1) *erased* Hm). hym] *om* Cot. þo] *om* F. of ...synne] how wikkedly he lyuede WHm CrGYOC^{2}CBLMR; how wykkidly he wrouhte F.
364 Repentaunce...so] ryght so dede Repentance he F. so] þoo so OC^{2}; tho Cr^{23}G. hym] hem Cr^{2}.
365 As...hast] þou hast þourhȝ word ⁊ werk F. þow] *om* Cr. wiþ] In G. hast wroȝt] thou wroughst Cr. yuele] ille YCrOC^{2}CB. lyue] tyme Y.
366 Shryue] I rede þou shryve F. shamed] ashamed CrHmOC^{2}BRF. þerof] *om* GF. þi] *om* Cr^{23}YOC^{2}CB.
367 þan seyd þat gome Glotou*n* y have gyltyd god ofte F. þe] this Y; he G. gome] Cr^{23}YOC^{2}CBLMR; grom WHm Cr^{1}G. me] y me HmB.
368 *line om* F. That] Of þat R. my] *om* Cr^{23}. ofte] *om* Cr^{1}.
369 Sworen] sware G; ⁊ swor*e* F. goddes] god CM. and...sydes] R; ⁊ side F; *om* WHmCrGYOC^{2}CBLM. and(2)] *om* Cr^{3}. so...helpe] selpe me god and halydome M. me...helpe] god me helpe ⁊ holidome Cr^{23}GYOC^{2}CL; god me helpe ⁊ þe holidome Cr^{1}; help me god ⁊ holy dome RF; god me helpe at þe holy dom BoBmCot; god helpe me atte þe holy dome Hm.
370 no] þat no F. was] ne was OC^{2}CBL MR.
371 And] I have F. seyen] seyn FHm; seye YCrGOC^{2}CBoCotLR; sup Bm. my] þe BoYC; þo Bm; *om* OC^{2}CotF. soper] soupe Cr. tyme] tymes R. at(2)] atte HmBo. Nones] noon melis F; ones G.
372 Gloton] *om* F. it] *om* CrYOC^{2}CB MF. er] ageyn er F. hadde] gan F.

And yspilt þ*at* my3te be spared and spended on som hungry;
Ouer delicatly on [feeste] dayes dronken and eten boþe,
And sat som tyme so longe þ*ere* þ*at* I sleep and eet at ones.
For loue of tales in Tau*er*nes [to] drynke þe moore I [hyed;
Fedde me bifore] noon whan fastyng dayes were.'
'This shewynge shrift', quod Repentaunce, 'shal be meryt to þe.'
And þanne gan Gloton greete and gret doel to make
For his luþer lif þat he lyued hadde,
And auowed to faste for hunger or þurste:
'Shal neu*ere* fyssh on [þe] Fryday defyen in my wombe
Til Abstinence myn Aunte haue 3yue me leeue,
And yet haue I hated hire al my lif tyme.'
Thanne cam Sleuþe al bislabered wiþ two slymy ei3en.
'I moste sitte [to be shryuen] or ellis sholde I nappe;
I may no3t stonde ne stoupe ne wiþoute stool knele.

373 And] ⁊ ofte F; and so Hm. yspilt] spilt YHmOC^{2}CBM. be] a be C^2; han ben M; haue be B. spended] spe*n*t Cr; spend R; spend it F. on] vpo*n* B. som] þe GBoCot; *om* BmF. hungry] nedy F.
374 Ouer] ⁊ ouer F. feeste] fastyng WHmCrGYOC^{2}CBLMRF. dronken] dro*n*k Cr^{23}; ydru*n*ke F. eten] ete Hm. boþe] bothen C^2.
375 sat...tyme] su*m* tyme sat F. sat] saten B. som...*þere*] so longe þere somtyme M. þ*at* I] at y F; and R. sleep] sleped C; ete B. eet] ete boþe Hm; slepe Cot; sleep al BmBo.
376 For...of] To hery*n* F. to] HmCrGYOC^{2}CBLMRF; and for W. drynke] ete R. moore I hyed] su*n*nere y wente F. hyed] dyned WHmCrGYOC^{2}CBLR; dine M.
377 Fedde me bifore] And hyed to þe mete er WHmCrGYOC^{2}CBLMRF (And] ⁊ ofte F. to] me to B. þe] *om* F). were] weren OC^2; felle F.
378 This] Now þis F. shrift] of shrifte CotBmBo; furst G. meryt] m*er*cye YCB.
379 þanne] ano*n* F; *om* GC. greete] to grete HmBR; grede MCr^1 (de *over erasure* M); grety*n* F. gret] muche R. to] he F; *om* HmCr^{23}GYOC^2. make] maked G; made HmOC^{2}F.
380 luþer] loþ ly*þer* F; lewde Cr. he] he so F.
381 auowed] vowed CrOC^2; made his avowe B. to] *above line* M; *om* GLR. or] or for WHmGYOC^{2}CBLMR (for *above line* M); and for Cr; ⁊ F. þurste] þryst boþe F.
382 Shal] schal þere Hm; ⁊ seyd shal F; þat B. þe] BoCotLR; þo Bm; *om* WHmCrGYOC^{2}CMF. Fryday] frydayes HmG. defyen] diffie shal B. wombe] mawe Bm.
383 haue] hath R. 3yue] 3yuen OHmCrGC^{2}M; I3eue R. me] me good F.
384 haue] *om* Hm. hated hire] hyr hated G. al] In al F. lif] liue lif Bm.
385 Thanne] Hanne F. al] *om* BmF. bislabered] beslauered G; beslot*er*ed F; slabirt Bm. slymy] slymed RF; glemy C^2.
386 to be shryuen] seide þe segge WCrYOC^{2}CLMRF; sayd þat segge G; q*uo*d the segge Hm; I þe segge B. or ellis] or elles *twice* C. or] or y shal F. sholde I] I schulde OC^{2}BmBo; must I G; I most Cot; I must nedes Cr; *om* F.
387 no3t] neiþur B. ne(1)] ny Bm. ne(2)] *om* F. oute] outen OC^{2}Bm. stool] HmGRF; a stool WYOC^{2}CBLM; mi stole Cr.

Were I brouȝt abedde, but if my tailende it made,
Sholde no ryngynge do me ryse er I were ripe to dyne.'
He bigan *Benedicite* *with* a bolk and his brest knokked,
Raxed and [remed] and rutte at þe laste.
'What! awake, renk!' quod Repentaunce, 'and rape þee to shryfte!'
'If I sholde deye bi þis day [I drede me sore].
I kan noȝt parfitly my Paternoster as þe preest it syngeþ,
But I kan rymes of Robyn hood and Randolf Erl of Chestre,
Ac neiþ*er* of oure lord ne of oure lady þe leeste þat eu*er*e was maked. |
I haue maad auowes fourty and foryete hem on þe morwe; *fol.* 30 *b*
I p*ar*fournede neu*er*e penaunce as þe preest me hiȝte,
Ne riȝt sory for my synnes yet, [so þee I], was I neu*er*e.
And if I bidde any bedes, but if it be in wraþe,
That I telle wiþ my tonge is two myle fro myn herte.
I am ocupied eche day, halyday and ooþer,
Wiþ ydel tales at þe Ale and ouþ*er*while [in] chirche[s];

388 Were] But where F. a] *in* F. if] ȝif hit Bm; *om* F. tailende] talent G; bely F. it made] made ytt G. made] make Hm.
389 ryngynge] þyng BM (*over erasure another ink* M). er] til M.
390 bigan] gan F. w*ith*] on F. bolk] belke Cr; book F. his] on is B. knokked] he knokkyd F; kouȝkid Bm.
391 Raxed] And raxed W; and roxed GHmYOC^{2}CLR; And roskid B; And raskled CrM (*over erasure another ink* M); ⁊ rorede F. and(1)] w*ith* a F. remed] rored WHmCrGYOC^{2}CBLMR; raskeng F. rutte] rutted G; ritte C. at] al out at B.
392 What] *om* Cr^{23}GYOC^{2}CB. awake] wake Cr^1. renk] reuk Cr; and þenk B; *om* F.
393 If] Alþouȝ B; A þeyh F. I(1)] *om* Y. bi þis] *om* F. day] daye q*uod* he R; q*uod* he F. I(2)...sore] me list nouȝt to loke WHmCrGYOC^{2}CBLMR (list] lysse Cr^1); y may not now looke F.
394 parfitly] p*ar*tfully Hm; *om* F. it] me F; *om* YOC^{2}CB. syngeþ] siggeþ C^2; tawhte F.
395 kan rymes] Romau*n*ces F. and] and of BF. Randolf] Ra*n*dall Cr^{23}. Erl] *om* Cr^{23}OC^{2}F. of Chestre] þe Reve F.
396 Ac] But CrGF; and C^{2}C. neiþ*er*] no*n* F; *om* Cr. lord] lor R. ne] or Cr. of(2)] *om* CrGYOCMF. oure(2)] ourd C. þe... maked] I lerne nothyng at all Cr. þe leeste] þing G. euere was] is YOC^{2}CBF. maked] ymade Cot.
397 haue] *om* M. auowes] vowes CrGY OC^{2}CBLMR; fourty avowes F. fourty] fifty YOC^{2}CB; at eve F. foryete] forȝeten OCrC^{2}BF. hem] hem alle BC; *om* C^2. on] or R; at CBmBo; a Cot. þe] *erased* M; *om* OCBRF. morwe] morwen C^{2}Bo.
398 I] Ne y F. neuere] neuere my F. as] þat GF. hiȝte] Ioynede F.
399 Ne] *over erasure* Bm; For BoCot. riȝt] be F. synnes] synne CB. so þee I] soþly F; *om* WHmCrGYOC^{2}CBLMR.
400 any] my G. if(2)] *om* MF. in] of Cr^3; *om* Cr^{12}.
401 wiþ] it w*ith* C^2. is] it is F.
402 ocupied] ocuped RHm. eche] ech a HmR; euery CrF. day] day boþe F.
403 in chirches] YCr^{23}OC^{2}CBLM; yn cherche HmCr^{1}GRF; at chirche W.

Goddes peyne and his passion [pure] selde þenke I on.
I visited neu*ere* feble men ne fettred [men] in puttes.
I haue leuere here an harlotrye or a Somer game of Souters,
Or lesynge[s] to lauȝen [of] and bilye my neȝebores,
Than al þ*a*t euere Marc made, Mathew, Ioh*a*n and Lucas.
Vigilies and fastyng dayes, alle þise late I passe,
And ligge abedde in lenten and my lemman in myne armes
Til matyns and masse be do, and þanne [moste] to þe freres;
Come I to *Ite missa est* I holde me yserued.
I [a]m noȝt shryuen som tyme but if siknesse it make
Nouȝt twyes in two yer, and þanne [telle I vp gesse].
I haue be preest and p*er*son passynge þritty wynter,
Yet kan I neyþer solue ne synge ne seintes lyues rede;
But I kan fynden in a feld or in a furlang an hare
Bettre þan in *Beatus vir* or in *Beati omnes*

404 Goddes...and] On godd*es* peynys ne on F. pure] ful WHmCrYOC^{2}CBLM RF; *om* G. selde] selden OC^{2}. þenke I] y þy*n*ke F. on] OC^{2}C; on it WM (it *another ink* M); theron CrHmGYBLR; *om* F.

405 visited] vesite C^{2}. neu*ere*] seelde F. feble] seke R; syke F. ne] or F. men(2)] HmGM; folk WCrYOC^{2}CBLRF. puttes] p*r*isou*n* F.

406 haue] hadde RF. an] *om* GMF. a] seen a F; *om* C^{2}C. Somer] somers Cr. game] gamen BmHmBoM. of Souters] *om* CrF.

407 Or] And M. lesynges] HmCrGYO C^{2}CBLMRF; lesynge W. lawȝen] laughe HmCrGYOC^{2}CLRF. of] RF; at WHmCrGYOC^{2}CBLM. and] or GF. neȝebores] neighbore LMR; evync*r*istene F.

408 Than] [illegible] F; *om* R. Marc] Sey*n*t Mark F; marye G. Mathew] or Mattheu F; matwe C^{2}. Ioh*a*n] luke G. and] or GCot F. Lucas] luk B; Iohn G.

409 Vigilies] M; And vigilies WHmCrG YOC^{2}CBLRF. fastyng dayes] fastynges Hm. þise...I] þis I late R; y leet hem F.

410 And ligge] I lay F. abedde] in bedde CrGF. lenten] lente RCr. and] *om* G.

411 matyns] masse Hm. masse] Masses F; matyns Hm. and(2)] *om* C. þanne] *om* C^{2}F. moste] y muste F; go WHmGOC^{2} CBLR; go I CrYM.

412 Come] But come F. holde] am G. me] me wel F; well G. yserued] serued CrYOC^{2}CBmBo.

413 am] HmCrGYC^{2}RF; nam WOCB LM. shryuen...tyme] su*m* tyme shiruen Cot; shryve but selden F. shryuen] schriue R. if] ȝif yt Hm; *om* GYOC^{2}CB MF. it] *om* Hm.

414 two] þe F. yer] yeres G. telle... gesse] vp gesse I shryue me WHmCrGY OC^{2}CBLMR (vp] vpon G. gesse] gosse Cr^{1}. I] y me Hm. me] *om* HmC); me þynkþ to sone F. *Hereafter a Latin tag like* IV 36α *another hand* M.

415 passynge] xxxti G. þritty] twenty B; fourty F; wynters G. wynter] yere YOC^{2} CB; passyng G.

416 Yet] CrHmGYOC^{2}CBLMR; And yet WF. ne(1)] nor Hm. lyues] lyue G. rede] reden M.

417 But I kan] yet kan I G. fynden] fynde HmCrGYOC^{2}CBLMRF. a(1)] *om* Cr^{2}Bm. feld] fel C. or] of F. in(2)] *om* GF.

418 in(1)] a C^{2}.

Construe clause[m]el[e] and kenne it to my parisshens.
I kan holde louedayes and here a Reues rekenyng,
Ac in Canou*n* nor in decretals I kan no3t rede a lyne.
If I bigge and borwe au3t, but if it be ytailed,
I foryete it as yerne, and if men me it axe
Sixe siþes or seuene I forsake it wiþ oþes.
And þus tene I trewe men ten hundred tymes,
And my seruaunt3 som tyme: hir salarie is bihynde; |
Ruþe is to here rekenyng whan we shul rede acountes: *fol.* 31 *a*
So wiþ wikked wil and wraþe my werkmen I paye.
If any man dooþ me a bienfait or helpeþ me at nede
I am vnkynde ayeins [his] curteisie and kan nou3t vnderstonden it,
For I haue and haue had somdel haukes man*er*es;
I am no3t lured wiþ loue but *þer* ligge au3t vnder þe þombe.
The kyndenesse þat myn euenc*ri*stene kidde me fernyere,
Sixty siþes I, Sleuþe, haue foryete it siþþe

419 Construe] To construe F. clausemele] it clausemel RF; oon clause wel WHmCr^{1} GYOC^{2}CLM; me þis clause wel B; one clause Cr^{23}. kenne] lerne C^{2}. to] *om* F. my] mi *over erasure* Bm; þi C^{2}BoCot.
420 holde] holde wel F. and] or RF. here] heryn F; holde C^{2}.
421 *line om* CB. Ac] but GF; And CrC^{2}. nor] ne GYOC^{2}LMRF; or Cr^{1}; & Cr^{23}. in(2)] in þe GLMR; *om* OC^{2}.
422 If] & if F. bigge] biegge B; begge Cr^{1}GR. and] or GF. au3t] it YOC^{2}CBLMR; *om* F. if] *om* BF. be] be wel F. ytailed] tayled CrGYOC^{2}CBmBoM.
423 foryete] forget CrGC. as] also HmB. yerne] sone Cr^{23}OC^{2}; euene G. and] as Cr^{1}; *om* G. if] 3if HmLR; *om* M.
424 or] oþer BmHmBo. forsake it] forswere me F. wiþ] wit R.
425 þus] þ*er*with F. tene I] I tene BRF. I] I a Cr^{1}. men] man Cr^{1}. ten] te R.
426 som...salarie] salary somtimes Cr^{23}. tyme] tymes Cr^{1}.
427 Ruþe is] It is hard F. is] HmCrGYO C^{2}CLMR; it is WBoCot; it is so Bm. here] LMRF; here þe WHmCr^{12}GYOC^{2} CB; here þat Cr^{3}. shul] *om* GF. rede] 3elde Hm; make Cr. acountes] accou*n*t Cr^{23}.
428 So] & so F. and] and wi*th* Cr.
429 man] *om* Cr^{1}F. dooþ] do CrGYOC^{2} CB. a] *om* Cr^{23}G. or] & G. helpeþ] helpe CrGYOC^{2}CB. at] at my G.
430 I...curteisie] Ageyn hym y am vnky3nde F. vnkynde] vnhynde C^{2}; vnhende O. ayeins] to CB. his] HmCrG YOC^{2}CBoCotLMR; þis Bm; *om* W. vnderstonden it] vnderstonde it YHmCr GOC^{2}CBLMR; it knowe F.
431 del] of F.
432 I] For y F. am] nam OLM. lured] lered YGOC^{2}; leired C. loue] loice C. þer] if Cr^{23}OC^{2}; *om* HmCr^{1}GYCBF. ligge au3t] oght lygge GHmYOC^{2}; su*m*what lygge F; ought be CrCBoCot; au3t he Bm. þe] *om* RF.
433 The...kidde] My*n* kosy3nes gret ky3ndenesse kyddy*n* to F. The] That Cr. kidde] kydden OC^{2}. fernyere] fernere FCotL; ferther Cr.
434 Sixty] sixe HmCr. siþes] sithe R. I] for F. haue] y have F. foryete] for3eten OHmCrC^{2}B; fo3ete L.

In speche and in sparynge of speche; yspilt many a tyme
Boþe flessh and fissh and manye oþ*er*e vitailles;
Boþ[e] bred and ale, buttre, melk and chese
Forsleuþed in my seruice til it myȝte serue no man.
I [yarn] aboute in youþe and yaf me nauȝt to lerne,
And eu*er*e siþþe be beggere [by cause of my] sleuþe:
Heu michi quia sterilem vitam duxi Iuuenilem.'
'Repente[st]ow noȝt?' quod Repentaunce, & riȝt wiþ þat he swowned
Til *vigilate* þe veille fette water at hise eiȝen
And flatte it on his face and faste on hym cryde
And seide, 'ware þee, for wanhope wo[l] þee bitraye.
"I am sory for my synn[e]", seye to þiselue,
And beet þiself on þe brest and bidde hym of g*ra*ce,
For is no gilt here so gret þat his goodnesse [i]s moore.'
Thanne sat Sleuþe vp and seyned hym [faste]

435 In speche] In spence Cr[1]; *om* F. in] *om* G. of speche] of speches C; of spence Cr; *om* YOC[2]B. yspilt] I have spilt F; I spynte C[2]. many] fele F. a] *om* YOC[2]C BF. tyme] tymes CB; þy*n*gys F.
436 and(2)...vitailles] butter mylk & chese OYC[2]CB. manye] fele F; myn R.
437 Boþe] OHmYC[2]CBLMR; Boþ W CrG; As F. ale] alle Bm; beef & F. buttre...chese] mylk buttre and chese M; botere & bake metys manyȝe F; & many oþere vitaylis OYC[2]CB.
438 Forsleuþed] I have forslewthid F; For slewþenesse C[2]. til...man] so longe y haue kept yt F. myȝte] wold G. serue] s*er*uen M.
439 yarn] ran WHmCrGYOC[2]CBLMRF. yaf] gaf YCrGCB. lerne] lerning Cr.
440 And] þ*at* y am F. be] LR; haue be YCrCM (haue *above line* M); haue I be WHmOC[2]; I haue be GBmCot; I haue iben Bo; i am þe F. beggere] a begger Cr[23]; beggery Cr[1]; lewedere F. by...my] for my foule WHmCrGYOC[2]CBmBoL MR; for my soule Cot; þorghȝ my*n* grete F.
440α *michi*] *om* Hm. *quia*] *quod* BoCotRF. *vitam duxi*] *duxi vitam* HmCrGBoCotM. *Iuuenilem*] *Iuuenilem &c* Y.
441 Repentestow] CCrGOC[2]BLM; Repentest R; ȝee Repentest F; Repentedestow WHmY. noȝt] þe noȝt BLMRF; *om* Cr. riȝt] *om* HmG. wiþ þat] w*ith* Cr; þerwyþ Hm.
442 þe veille] & *orate* F. fette] set Cr[1].
443 *transposed with* 444 B. flatte] flappede F; fel flatt (fel *above line main hand*) G. it] water B; *om* GF. on(1)] vpon M; in B. faste] *om* R. on(2)] vpon M.
444 þee] þe now F. for] fro HmGCBL MRF. wol] wyl Cr; he wole F; wolde WHmGYOC[2]CLMR; he wolde B. þee] *om* (*corrector supplies*) L. bitraye] bitraien B.
445 synne] synnes WHmCrGYOC[2]CBL MRF. to] þou to B; so to LMR; now so F.
446 þe] þi CCotMF. and] *om* Cr[3]. hym] god CrBF.
447 is(1)] þer is BF; here is Hm. here] *om* Hm. þat] but þ*at* Cr; but G. his] is YC; goddis F. is(2)] HmCrGYOC[2]CBRF; nys WLM.
448 seyned] sygned F; blissid B; fayned Cr[1]. faste] swiþe WHmCrGYOC[2]CBL MR; on þe forhed F.

And made auow tofore god for his foule sleuþe:
'Shal no Sonday be þis seuen yer, but siknesse it [make],
That I ne shal do me er day to þe deere chirche
And here matyns and masse as I a monk were;
Shal noon ale after mete holde me þennes |
Til I haue euensong herd: I bihote to þe Roode. *fol.* 31 *b*
And yet wole I yelde ayein, if I so muche haue,
Al þat I wikkedly wan siþen I wit hadde,
And þouȝ my liflode lakke leten I nelle
That ech man shal haue his er I hennes wende;
And wiþ þe residue and þe remenaunt, bi þe Rode of Chestre,
I shal seken truþe er I se Rome.'
Roberd þe Robbere on *Reddite* loked,
And for þ*er* was noȝt wher[wiþ] he wepte swiþe soore.
Ac yet þe synfulle sherewe seide to hymselue:
'Crist, þat on Caluarie vpon þe cros deidest,
Tho Dysmas my bro*þer* bisouȝte [þee] of g*ra*ce
And haddest m*er*cy on þat man for *Memento* sake,
So rewe on þis Robber*e* þat *Reddere* ne haue

449 made] maked BoCot; makiþ Bm. tofore] before G; vnto F. for] for all G. foule] soule Cr^{1}Cot.
450 *line om* F. Shal] Shal þer BHm. Sonday] sonenday Hm. but] but ȝif HmMR. it] me R. make] lette WHm CrGYOC^{2}CBLMR.
451 ne] *om* HmBF. er] eu*er*y F. deere] derne F.
452 And] & þere F. here] heren LMR. matyns...masse] masse & mattyns (s *altered to* ce) G.
453 *line om* F. mete holde] metes holden M.
454 Til] til þat B. euen] eue CotHm. herd] yherd Cot. bihote] hoote G; hote now F.
455 And...I(1)] what I nam R; & what y haue take to F. ayein] agayne CrGF. I(2)] *om* C^{2}. muche haue] mychil welde F.
456 Al] Of al F. I(1)] y so F. wikkedly] wyckely Cr^{1}. wit] lyfe (e *erased*) Hm.
457 my] me R. lakke] lakken G. I] þerfore y F.
458 man] HmGOC^{2}BoCotRF; man ne WCrYCBmLM. hennes] heythen G.
459 þe(1)] *om* OC. residue...þe(2)] oþ*er* F; *om* G. þe(3)] *om* C.
460 seken] seke CrHmGYOC^{2}CBLMR. er] ere Hm; erst er WCrGYOC^{2}CBLMR; tryst er F. se] seke F.
461 Roberd] Anoon Rob*er*t F. on] vppon B. *Reddite*] *Reddere* Y.
462 And] *om* GF. þ*er* was] þer nas M; he hadde F. wiþ] of WHmCrGYOC^{2}CBL MRF. swiþe] wondir F. soore] *om* OC^{2}.
463 Ac] but GF; And CrC^{2}C. yet] *om* HmF. þe] th Cot; þ*at* F. seide] seyde þus F; ȝit seyde Hm. selue] seluen M.
464 Crist þat] whan þ*at* cryst F. on] vpon M; on þe OC^{2}. deidest] didest Cr; dyed GF.
465 *line om* B. Tho] þan F. Dysmas] bysmas R. þee] the (*over erasure another hand*) Hm; yow WCrGYOC^{2}CLMR; c*ri*st F.
466 haddest] he hadde F. on] of YOC. *Memento*] memeto is F.
467 þis] me HmF (*over erasure another hand* Hm). ne] he ne C^{2}; wil F. haue] haueth Cr^{23}M (th *added another ink* M); hath Cr^{1}OC^{2}; knowe F.

Ne neu*er*e wene to wynne wiþ craft þat I owe;
But for þi muchel mercy mitigacion I biseche:
Dampne me noȝt at domesday for þ*a*t I dide so ille.'
What bifel of þis feloun I kan noȝt faire shewe.
Wel I woot he wepte faste water wiþ hise eiȝen,
And knoweliched his [coupe] to crist yet eftsoones,
That *penitencia* his pik he sholde polshe newe
And lepe wiþ hym ou*er* lond al his lif tyme,
For he hadde leyen by *Latro*, luciferis Aunte.
[Th]anne hadde Repentaunce ruþe and redde hem alle to knele.
'I shal biseche for alle synfulle oure Saueo*ur* of g*ra*ce
To amenden vs of oure mysdedes: do m*er*cy to vs alle,
God, þat of þi goodnesse [g]onne þe world make,
And of nauȝt madest auȝt and man moost lik to þiselue,
And siþen suffredest [hym] to synne, a siknesse to vs alle, |
And for þe beste as I bileue whateu*er*e þe book telleþ: *fol.* 32 *a*
O felix culpa, o necessarium peccatum Ade &c.

468 wene] weneþ F; where (h *added main hand*) Bm. to] for to G. craft] craf F. owe] knowe CrRF; sewe (*altered to* sheewe) G; vse Hm.
469 But] *om* Hm. for] *om* C. þi] *om* F. muchel] muche HmG. mercy] m*er*cy su*m* F. I] me F; *om* OC^2. biseche] seende F.
470 *line om* F. Dampne] Ne dampne WHmCr^{23}GYOC^{2}CBLMR; Ne dapme Cr^1. at] a Cot; on HmG. þ*at*...so] my dedes G. so] *om* Cr^{23}OC^2.
471 of] on Cr^{1}G. feloun] felowe Cr; schrewe OC^2. noȝt] nouȝ Y. faire] fare R.
472 Wel] But wel F. hise] hyse FCrG; boþe hise WHmYOC^{2}CBLMR.
473 *line om* RF. coupe] gilt WHmCrGYOC^{2}CBLM. yet] *om* G. eft] efter O; after C^2.
474 his] ys F. pik] Pryck Cr^1. he] *om* F. newe] hy*m* newe F.
475 lif] *om* C.
476 For] & before F. hadde] hath R; *om* F. leyen] yleyn B; lay F; lyin (y *over erasure*) M; loyn C^2. by] *with* F.
477 Thanne] FG; And þanne WHmCrYOC^{2}CBLMR. hadde Repentaunce] Repentaunce hadde F. hadde] *om* Cr^1. hem] hym Cot. to] *om* G.
478 I] For I WHmCrGYOC^{2}CBLMR; & F. shal biseche] besechen F.
479 To] & þ*at* we F. amenden] amende HmCrGYOC^{2}CBLMRF. dedes] *om* F. do] and do WHmCr^{23}GYOC^{2}CBLMRF; and Cr^1. to] on F.
480 God] now god G; Now god quod he WHmCrYOC^{2}CBmLM; Now god quod R; Now quod he BoCot; & seid god F. þat] *om* YOC^{2}CBF. gonne] LHmCr^{23}GMR; þat gonne YOC^{2}CB; þou gu*n*ne F; bigonne W; coud Cr^1. þe] all the G; þis F. make] HmCrGYOC^{2}CBLMR; to make WF.
481 auȝt] alle þyng B. to] *om* CrGMF. selue] seluen M; lelf Cr^3.
482 suffredest] þou suffredist F; suffrest OC^{2}CBmBo. hym] RF; for WCrYOC^{2}CBLM; *om* HmG. to(1)] *cancelled* O; oure B; *om* CrC^{2}F. siknesse...alle] sekirnesse to ma*n*kynde F.
483 And] *om* G. for] al for WHmCrGYOC^{2}CBLMRF (al *above line* Y). bileue] leue Cr. euere] so G. þe book] bookys euere F. telleþ] telle CBF.
483α *repeated in another hand* W. *felix*] felex W^{2}G. *culpa*] calpa Cr^2. *peccatum Ade*] *ade peccatum* GOC^{2}CotM. *Ade*] *om* Cr^1. *&c*] *om* Cr^{23}GRF.

For þoruȝ þat synne þi sone sent was to erþe
And bicam man of a maide mankynde to saue,
And madest þiself wiþ þi sone vs synfulle yliche:
Faciamus hominem ad ymaginem [et similitudinem] nostram;
Et alibi, Qui manet in caritate in deo manet & deus in eo.
And siþþe wiþ þi selue sone in oure s[u]te deidest
On good fryday for mannes sake at ful tyme of þe daye;
Ther þiself ne þi sone no sorwe in deeþ feledest,
But in oure secte was þe sorwe and þi sone it ladde:
Captiuam duxit captiuitatem.
The sonne for sorwe þerof lees [s]iȝt [for] a tyme.
Aboute mydday, whan moost liȝt is and meel tyme of Seintes,
Feddest wiþ þi fresshe blood oure forefadres in derknesse:
Populus qui ambulabat in tenebris vidit lucem magnam.
[Th]e liȝt þat lepe out of þee, Lucifer [it] blent[e]
And blewe alle þi blessed into þe blisse of Paradys.
The þridde day [þer]after þow yedest in oure sute;
A synful Marie þe seiȝ er seynte Marie þi dame,

484 þoruȝ] *om* Cr^{1}. þat] *om* F. sent was] seynt was G; was sent doun F. to] into F; to þis WHmYOC^{2}BLR; to þe GCrM; to þs C.
485 maide] mayden B.
486 madest] makest Cr. sone] soun C^{2}. vs] and vs WHmCrGYOC^{2}CBLMRF. synfulle] silf B.
486α–9 *lines om* CB.
486α *et similitudinem*] CrHmGYOC^{2}LRF; & simlitudinem M; *om* W.
486β *&...eo*] *&c* YOC^{2}. *eo*] *eo &c* Hm.
487 þi] þe R. sute] HmCrGYOC^{2}LMR; sewht þou F; secte W. deidest] deieste C^{2}.
488 þe] *om* R.
489 Ther] Neyþer F. ne] nor Hm; & GR; in Cr^{1}. deeþ] dyȝeng F. feledest] feled Cr.
490 secte] selue F. þe] þat RF. sorwe] worwe Bm.
490α *duxit*] *duxi* CB. *captiuitatem*] *captiuitatem &c* HmYOC^{2}CB.
491 þer] her M. lees] he lees F; lees his C^{2}YOCotM (his *another ink* M). siȝt] Bo HmGCBmCotLRF; liȝt WCrYOC^{2}M (? l *altered from* s M). for] CrYOC^{2}CBL MRF; of W; at HmG. a] þat HmG.
492 Aboute] Abowhtyn F; At CrG. meel] mete (t *over erasure*) Bm; meke BoCot.
493 Feddest] þo feddyst þou F. wiþ] þo with R. fresshe] flessche & G; fleisch & þi B. fore] forme Hm; *om* BF.
493α *ambulabat*] *ambulat* Cr^{23}CBoF. *magnam*] *magnam &c* HmM.
494 The] And þoruȝ þe WGYOC^{2}CBL MR; And þorough þat HmF; And by þe Cr. lepe] cam G. out of] out M; of C^{2}G; fram F. þee] þe *altered to* þo M. it blente] it blent R; blente F; was blent WHmCr^{23}GYOC^{2}CBLM; was blind Cr^{1}.
495 And] For it F. in] þennes in R; þens boldely in F; *om* Y. þe...of] *om* F. þe] þy C.
496 The] & þe F. þerafter] after ȝit F; after WHmCrGYOC^{2}CBLMR. þow] *om* OC^{2}. yedest] yeldest Cr^{1}C^{2}; wendest G. in] forþ in F; into Cr.
497 A] Fyrst a F; And YOC^{2}CBM. þe] þow CB. seynte...dame] dede þy moodir dere F. dame] mother G.

And al to solace synfulle þow suffredest it so were:
Non veni vocare iustos set peccatores ad penitenciam.
And al þat Marc haþ ymaad, Mathew, Ioh*a*n and Lucas
Of þyne douȝt[iest] dedes was doon in oure armes: |
Verbum caro factum est & habitauit in nobis. *fol.* 32 *b*
And by so muche [it] semeþ þe sikerer we mowe
Bidde and biseche, if it be þi wille,
That art oure fader and oure broþ*er*, be m*er*ciable to vs,
And haue ruþe on þise Ribaudes þat repenten hem soore
That eu*er*e þei wraþed þee in þis world in word, þouȝt or dedes.'
Thanne hente hope an horn of *Deus tu conuersus viuificabis* [*nos*]
And blew it wiþ *Beati quorum remisse sunt iniquitates,*
That alle Seintes [for synful] songen at ones
'*Homines & iumenta saluabis quemadmodum multiplicasti misericordiam tuam, deus*'.
A þousand of men þo þrungen togideres,
Cride vpward to Crist and to his clene moder

498 And al] It was F. And] *om* CB. al] *above line main hand* W; *om* OC^{2}. solace] solace þe Hm. it] þat yt Hm. so were] so wele G; so falle F; soner Cr.

499 And] To BoCot. þat] þat euere Hm; of the F. Marc] marye G. haþ] *om* Cr. ymaad] maad HmCrG; maad & F. Ioh*a*n] luke G. Lucas] luc B; Iohan G.

500 douȝtiest] LMRF; douȝty WHmCrG YOC^{2}CB. was] were HmCrGYCLRF; weren OC^{2}M; þat were Cot; þat weren BmBo.

500α *Verbum*] *Quod uerbum* F. *habitauit*] habitauiu Cr^{2}. *nobis*] *nobis &c* Hm.

501 so] *om* G. it] RF; me WHmCrGYO C^{2}CBLM. sikerer] sykerloker R; sikere YF; siker Cr^{1}. we mowe] to styȝe to hevene F. mowe] wet::: Bm.

502 Bidde] we byddyn þe F. biseche] bysechyn F. if] if so F; it if YCB. be] *corrected from* bi M.

503 That...broþer] As þou fadir & brothir art F. m*er*ciable] merciful CrG. to] til YOC^{2}C; on F. vs] þy*n* peple F.

504 ruþe] mercy RF. on] off G. þise] thi Cot. repenten] repente CotCrGLM. hem] *om* G. soore] sore GCotRF; here soore WHmYOC^{2}CBmBoL; so sore M; selfs sore Cr.

505 þei] ȝit þey F; *om* Hm. wraþed] wraþþeden OC^{2}; wrathe C; wrattid Bm; warped Cr^{1}. in...world] *om* GRF. or] and Cr^{23}. dedes] dede HmCrGYOC^{2}CB MF.

506 hope] he vp (he *over erasure another hand*) Hm. of] was F. *conuersus*] conersis Bo. *nos*] CrGRF; *om* WHmYOC^{2}CB LM.

507 blew] he blew R.

508 That] then G; Til CB; & F. alle] alle the HmGYF. for synful] in heuene WHm CrGYOC^{2}CBLMRF. songen] ano*n* þus þey sungyn F; syngen Cot; sogen C.

509 &] *om* Hm. *saluabis*] *saluabis domine* F; *saluabit* BmBo. *deus*] *deus &c* HmGOC^{2}C BLM.

510 A] wel a F. of] *om* F. þrungen] þru*n*gyn alle F.

511 Cride] Criden CrOC^{2}; & cryden HmBF (*over erasure another hand* Hm). vp ...Crist] vp to cristwarde M. and] *om* G.

To haue *grace* to go [to] truþe, [God leue þat þei moten].
Ac þ*ere* was [wye] noon so wys þe wey þider kouþe,
But blustreden forþ as beestes ouer [baches] and hilles
Til late and longe, þ*at* þei a leode mette
Apparailled as a paynym in pilgrymes wise.
He bar a burdoun ybounde wiþ a brood liste,
In a wiþwynde[s] wise ywounden aboute.
A bolle and a bagge he bar by his syde.
An hundred of Ampulles on his hat seten,
Signes of Synay and shelles of Galice,
And many crouch on his cloke and keyes of Rome,
And þe vernycle bifore, for men sholde knowe
And se bi hise signes whom he souȝt hadde.
This folk frayned hym [faire] fro whennes he come.
'Fram Synay', he seide, 'and fram [þe Sepulcre]. |
[At] Bethlem, [at] Babiloyne, I haue ben in boþe, *fol.* 33 *a*

512 To haue] To graunte swich F; *om* R. to go] to god R; *om* F. to(2)] wiþ hem WHmCrGYOC^{2}CBLMR (wiþ *over erasure another hand,* e *touched up* Hm); *om* F. God ...moten] to seke WHmGOC^{2}CBLMR; to seken CrF; for to seke Y.
513 *line om* C. Ac] But F; And CrGC^{2} BoCot. was] ne was B. wye] wiȝt WHm GYOC^{2}LMR; *om* CrBF. þe] þat þe Hm. þider] þat þider (t *over erasure*) Bm; to hym F; *om* Hm.
514 *line om* Hm. blustreden] blustred C^{2}M; blusteren G; blustrenden C; blusterynge Cr. forþ] for C. baches] balkys F; bankes WCrGYOC^{2}CBLMR.
515 late] late was WHmCrGYOC^{2}CBL MR; it was late F. þat] til CB; ere Cr^{23}. a] wiþ a B. leode] lade Cr^{1}. mette] metten OC^{2}F.
516 Apparailled] Iparaylid F. paynym] palmere F. wise] wedys F.
517 ybounde] ybounden OC^{2}M; bounden Cr. brood] blod (*corrected another hand*) C^{2}.
518 a] *om* B. wiþwyndes] withwyndes M; wythewyndes HmGLR; wiþwynde W; wythe wandes Cr; swithe wyndes YOC^{2}C; wodebyndis B; whythyes F. ywounden] ywownde al F; wounden Cr^{3}; yboundyn Hm; bounden Cr^{1}; swounden Cr^{2}.
519 A] ⁊ a F. bolle] bulle RF. and] in F. syde] sydes G.
520 An] And an MF (an *above line another ink* M). of] *om* Cr. Ampulles] arpull*es* G. on] vpon F. seten] sete OCrC^{2}; syten G.
521 Signes] ⁊ fele sygnes F. Synay] seyntys F; asise R. of(2)] also of F. Galice] Calice Cr^{1}.
522 many] YCR; many a WHmCr^{12}GOC^{2} BLMF (a *above line* M); mady a Cr^{3}. cloke] croke C^{2}. and] and þe R; w*ith* þe F. Rome] *om* Y.
523 bifore] was byfore F. men] folk F. sholde] schulden OC^{2}. knowe] Iknowe R; hym knowe F.
524 signes] seynes R. he] he so Cr^{23}.
525 This] Thanne þis F. frayned] freyneden OBmBo. hym] hem Cot; *om* OC^{2}. faire] first WHmCrGYOC^{2}CBLMR; *om* F. fro] *om* HmF. he] þ*at* he F.
526 Synay] Snai Cr^{3}; þe sepulcre F. þe Sepulcre] oure lordes Sepulcre WHmCrG YOC^{2}CBLMR; synay hyȝe hill*es* F.
527 I have been boþe in Bedleem ⁊ in Babylonye also F. At] In WHmCrGYO C^{2}CBLMR. at] and in WHmCrGYOC^{2} CBLMR.

In Armonye, in Alisaundre, in manye oþ*er*e places.
Ye may se by my signes þat sitten on myn hatte
That I haue walked [wel] wide in weet and in drye
And sou3t goode Seintes for my soul[e] hel[e].'
'Knowestow au3t a corsaint', [quod þei], 'þat men calle truþe?
[Kanstow] wissen vs þe wey wher þat wye dwelleþ?'
'Nay, so [god glade me]', seide þe gome þanne.
'I [ne] sei3 neu*er*e Palmer*e* wiþ pyk ne wiþ scrippe
Asken after hym er now in þis place.'
'Peter!' quod a Plowman, and putte forþ his hed:
'I knowe hym as kyndely as clerc doþ hise bokes.
Conscience and kynde wit kenned me to his place
And diden me suren hym [siþþen] to s*er*uen hym for eu*er*e,
Boþe sowe and sette while I swynke my3te.
I haue ben his folwere al þis [fourty] wynter,
Boþe ysowen his seed and suwed hise beestes,

528 Armonye] heremonye Hm; Iermonye G. in(1)] and in R; and Cr. in(2)] and CrF.
529 sitten] sitte YC; be set Cr. on] in Cr^{23}. hatte] cloke F.
530 wel] ful WHmCrYOC^{2}CBLMR; *om* GF.
531 sou3t...Seintes] holy seyntis sowht F. goode] many good Cr. soule hele] soule helþe HmGCotMRF; soules helþe WYO C^{2}CBmBoL; soulis helpe Cr.
532 Knowestow] 3ee knowist þou F; knowest HmCot. au3t] not CrF. corsaint] crossent Cr^{23}. quod...þat] þat WHmCrGYOC^{2}CBLMRF. calle] callen OHmC^{2}BMR.
533 Kanstow] canst þou HmC^2 (*over erasure another hand* Hm); & canst þou F; Koudestow WCrGYOCBLMR. wissen] YGOC^{2}CB; wisshe F; au3t wissen WHm LMR (ougth *over erasure another hand* Hm); not wish Cr. þe] þat Cr^2. wey] ri3t way B. wher] þere R. wye] wight Cr^{13}R; he GYOC^{2}CB. dwelleþ] wonyeth MCr.
534 þ*anne* seyde þe goome nay so god me helpe F. so] so mote B. god...me] me god helpe WHmCrGYOC^{2}CBLMR. þe] that Cr. gome] gom *altered to* grom Cot.
535 ne(1)] B; *om* WHmCrGYOC^{2}CLM RF. neuere] neu*ere* þat F. pyk] a pike Y; poke Cr. ne(2)] nor HmCr. scrippe] scrippe wende OC^2.
536 Asken] aske HmCr; Ne man þat askyd F. er] YOC^{2}CB; er til WHmCr GLR; til MF.
537 a] Pers F; *om* G. hed] face F.
538 clerc] ony clerk F; clere G. doþ] *om* F. bokes] boke Cr^{23}YOC^{2}CB (s *added another ink* Cot).
540 diden] dide YHmCrGOC^{2}C; y haue F. me] *om* F. suren] sweren Cr^{23}; swere YOC^{2}CB; ensured F. hym(1)] he*m* RF; *om* Cr^{23}YOC^{2}CB. siþþen] sikerly WHm CrGYOC^{2}CBLMR; sewrly F. seruen] serue CrYOC^{2}CBLR.
541 sowe and] to sowe and to WHmCr GYOC^{2}CBLMRF. while] whyle GMF; þe while WHmCrYOC^{2}CBmLR; þer-while BoCot.
542 his] his foot F. fourty] LMRF; fifty WHmCrGYOC^{2}CB. wynter] wynters G.
543 ysowen] Isowe R; ysowed F; sowen CrHmGYCBM; sowe C^{2}O. seed] seedis F. suwed] suen G; swede Y; fedde OC^2 CCot; feed BmBo. hise] abowty*n* hise F.

Wiþ*I*nne and wiþouten waited his p*ro*fit,
Idyke[d] and Id[o]lue, Ido þat [he] hoteþ.
Som tyme I sowe and som tyme I þresshe,
In taillo*ur*s craft and tynkeris craft, what truþe kan deuyse,
I weue and I wynde and do what truþe hoteþ.
For þouȝ I seye it myself I serue hym to paye;
I haue myn hire [of hym] wel and ouþ*er*whiles moore.
He is þe p*re*steste paiere þ*at* pouer*e* men knoweþ;
He wiþhalt noon hewe his hire þ*at* he ne haþ it at euen.
He is as lowe as a lomb and louelich of speche.
And if ye wilneþ wite where þ*at* [wye] dwelleþ
I [wol] wisse yow [wel riȝt] to his place.'
'Ye! leue Piers', quod þise pilg*ri*mes and p*ro*fred hym huyre. |
'Nay, by [þe peril of] my soul[e]!' quod Piers and gan to swere: *fol.* 33 *b*
'I nolde fange a ferþyng for Seint Thomas Shryne;

544 WiþInne] ⁊ with*h*Inne boþe F. outen] oute CrGBR. waited] I wayted CrR; wated Y; waytou*n* Hm.
545 Idyked] I dyke WHmCrGYOC^{2}CBLMR; ⁊ boþe diggid F. Idolue] deluyd F; I delue WHmYOC^{2}LMR; delue CrGCB. Ido] I do WHmYCLMR; and do CrGOC^{2}B; ⁊ dyde F. he] RF; truþe WHmCrGYOC^{2}CBLM. hoteþ] me hoteþ B; me comau*n*did F.
546–8 *lines om* F.
547 craft(1)] crafte *above line* L; *om* Cr. and] in R. craft(2)] *om* GM. kan deuyse] deuyse can C^{2}.
548 weue] wene Cr^{1}; wynde B. I(2)] *om* B. wynde] wede BoCot; weve (v *touched up* ?) Bm. and(2)] and I C; I Y. hoteþ] me hotiþ B.
549 hym] hy R.
550 I] ⁊ y F. of hym] RF; *om* WHmCrGYOC^{2}CBLM. wel] *om* F.
551 þe] *om* Cr. men] man M. knoweþ] fynden G.
552 He] he GYOC^{2}CBRF; He ne WHmCrLM. wiþhalt] withholdeþ MG (oldeþ *another ink* M). hewe] hewen Bm; hyne HmG (? *over erasure* Hm); hynen BoCot; men R; ma*n* F; helk Cr. his] hire CotR. hire] hiren Bm. þat] but G. he] þei RF. ne] *om* GF. haþ] haue RF. at euen] at eue YOC; anone R; soone F.
553 He] ⁊ he F. is] *om* C. as(1)] also HmB. lowe] lowlich BmBoF; loulich Cot.
554 wilneþ] wyll Cr. wite] wytte Cr^{1}; wytt Cr^{23}; to wite WHmGYOC^{2}CBLRF; to witen M. þat] *om* Cr. wye] he WHmCrGYOC^{2}CBLMRF. dwelleþ] wonnith Cr.
555 wol...riȝt] shal wisse yow witterly þe wey WHmCrGYOC^{2}CBLMRF (þe] the hye Cr).
556 Ye] *om* G. þise] þo F. profred] profreden OBF. *Hereafter an additional line* WHmCrGYOC^{2}CBLMRF: For to wende wiþ hem to truþes dwellyng place (wende] wenden MF. to...place] þere trewþe gan dwelle F. truþes] treuthe YC). *See above*, p. 193.
557 þe...soule] my soule perel R; my soule helþe HmCr^{23}; my soules helþe WCr^{1}GLM; my soule YOC^{2}CBF. to] for to WHmCrGYOC^{2}CBLMR; *om* F. swere] sweren M; swere faste F.
558 fange] fongy*n* F. Seint...shryne] fyfty florey*n*s tolde F.

Truþe wolde loue me þe lasse a long tyme after.
Ac [ye þat] wilneþ to wende, þis is þe wey þider.
Ye moten go þoruȝ mekenesse, boþe men and wyues,
Til ye come into Conscience þ*at* crist wite þe soþe,
That ye louen oure lord god leuest of alle þynges.
And þanne your*e* neȝebores next in none wise apeire
Oþerwise þan þow woldest [men] wrouȝte to þiselue.
And so boweþ forþ by a brook, beþ/buxom/of/speche,
[Forto] ye fynden a ford, youre/fadres/honoureþ:
Honora patrem ⁊ matrem ⁊c;
Wadeþ in þat water and wasshe yow wel þ*er*
And ye shul lepe þe liȝtloker al youre lif tyme.
So shaltow se swere/noȝt/but/it/be/for/nede/
And/nameliche/on/ydel/þe/name/of/god/almyȝty.
Thanne shaltow come by a croft, [ac] come þow noȝt þ*er*Inne;
Th[e] croft hatte Coueite/noȝt/mennes/catel/ne/hire/wyues/
Ne/noon/of/hire/s*er*uauntȝ/þat/noyen/hem/myȝte;

559 Truþe] þan trewþe F. þe] *om* G. lasse] worse Cr^{1}. a] *om* CrYOC^{2}CB. tyme] wyle G. after] GYOC^{2}CBMF; þerafter WHmLR; therfor after Cr.
560 Ac] but GF; And CrC^{2}C. ye þat] ȝif ȝe HmCr^{23}GYOC^{2}CBLMRF; if yow WCr^{1}. wilneþ] wil Cr. to wende] wel to walke F. þis] F; wel þis WHmCrGYOC^{2}CBLMR. þider] þidirward F; þidiþ *corrected main hand* Bm. *Hereafter a spurious line* YOC^{2}CB; *see above*, p. 224.
561 Ye] you G. moten] mote GYCLRF; must Cr. go] *om* Cot. þoruȝ] be F.
562 ye] you Cr^{1}. come] comen BHm. in] *om* GYOC^{2}CBF. þat] *om* F. wite] woot MF (ot *over erasure* M).
563 That] ⁊ þat F. louen] loue OC^{2}. þynges] s *another ink* M; þynge F.
564 þanne] that Cr. neȝebores] neyhebore F. next] nxt Bm. in] ⁊ *in* F. apeire] appairen M; apeyre hy*m* F.
565 men] he WHmCrYOC^{2}CBLMRF; be G. þi] þe O. selue] seluen M.
566 so] *om* GF. boweþ] bowe CBR; beende F. forþ] for Hm. beþ] bet Bm. of] of þi RF.
567 Forto] Til WHmCrGYOC^{2}CBLMRF. ye] you Cr. fynden] fynde HmC^{2}MF. fadres] fadr*es* ȝee FCr^{23}OC^{2}. honoureþ] honoure OC^{2}F.
567α *in margin* O. ⁊c] *ut sis longeuus super terram* F; *om* R.
568 Wadeþ] Wade Cr. in] into BF. þat] *om* OC^{2}. wasshe] wascheth LHmBmBoR. yow] ye G. þer] there HmCrGYOC^{2}CBLR; þerInne WMF (Inne *another ink* M).
569 ye] you Cr. shul] shullen M. þe] *om* C. liȝtloker] lyghtlyer GOC^{2}B; lyghter CrC; lighlier Y. tyme] after Cr.
570 So] so G; And so WHmCrYOC^{2}CBoCotLMR; and also Bm; ⁊ sone F. se] *om* HmYOC^{2}. but] GBF; but if WHmCrYOC^{2}CLMR.
571 And...ydel] Ne ne*m*pe not i*n* ydelnesse F. on] yn HmGOC^{2}B.
572 Thanne] ⁊ þa*n*ne F. ac] but WHmCrGYOC^{2}CBLMRF. þow] *om* GYOC^{2}CB.
573 The] þe GRF; That WHmCrYOC^{2}CBLM. croft] name F. hatte] hatteth HmBm; ys F. Coueite] coueitise C^{2}Bm (*corrected* Bm). noȝt] þou nowht FHm. mennes] men YCR; neyþ*er* F. catel] maydi*ns* F; *om* R. ne] nor HmCr^{23}. hire] *om* F.
574 þat...myȝte] ne no þy*n*g to hy*m* longiþ F. noyen] anoien B. hem] *om* Y.

Loke [þow] breke no bowes þere but if it be [þyn] owene.
Two stokkes þer stondeþ, ac stynte [þow] no3t þere;
Thei hi3te Stele-no3t-[ne]-Sle-no3t; strik forþ by boþe;
Leue hem on þi lift half and loke no3t þerafter.
And hold wel þyn haliday heighe til euen.
Thanne shaltow blenche at a Bergh, bere-no-fals-witnesse;
He is fryþed In wiþ floryns and oþere fees manye;
Loke þow plukke no plaunte þere for peril of þi soule. |
Thanne [shalt þow] see seye-sooþ-so-it-be-to-doone- *fol.* 34 *a*
In-[no]-manere-ellis-no3t-for-no-mannes-biddyng.
Thanne shaltow come to a court, cler as þe sonne.
The moot is of mercy þe Manoir aboute;
And alle þe walles ben of wit to holden wil oute;
[The] kernele[s ben of] cristendom [þat] kynde to saue,
Botrased wiþ bileef-so-or-þow-beest-no3t-saued;
And alle þe houses ben hiled, halles and chambres,

575 Ne noyghe not hise bestis neyþer bollokys ne oþere F. þow] RCot; ye WHmCrGYOC^{2}CBmBoLM. breke] breken Cr^1. no] none BM. bowes] bowe Hm. it] thei CrG. be] be on R; *om* Bm. þyn] youre WHmCrGYOC^{2}CBLMR.
576 stondeþ] stonde YCBoCot. ac] but GF; and CrC^{2}C. stynte] stonde M. þow] þe C; you Cr; ye WHmGYOC^{2}BmBo LMRF; *om* Cot.
577 Thei] þat F. hi3te] hatten OHmC^2 BM; is F. Stele] stole Bm. ne] HmCr YOC^{2}CBLMRF; & WG. no3t(2)] not 3ee F; *om* Hm. forþ] for M. by boþe] bifore YOC^{2}CB (*corrected* Bm).
578 Leue] And leue WHmCrGYOC^{2}CB LMRF. on] vpon M. þi] the CrG. lift] ef Bm. half] hande CrF. þer] on hem F.
579 And] þat is F. heighe...euene] *with* holy *pr*ayeris F. til] tyl it be Hm. euen] heuene BmBo.
580 Bergh] burgh M; berch Cr; beru3 OR; berne3 C^2; beech F; brygge GCot. bere] þou bere F. *Hereafter a spurious line* F; *see above*, p. 222.
581 He] It F; *om* R. fryþed] Frendid C^2; florischid B. In] wiþ Inne B; *om* C^{2}F. wiþ] *om* Cr^1. fees] foos YCrOC^{2}LM.
582 þow] þow ne M; 3e RF. þere] þerof F. peril] perels Cr. þi soule] 3oure soules R; þe heyward F.
583 *line om* F. shalt þow] shall þou G; shul ye WHmCrYOC^{2}CBLMR. see] *om* HmR. seye] seiþ B. to] do OC^2. doone] done well (well *cancelled*) G.
584 *line om* F. no(1)] HmCrGYOC^{2}CCot LM; none BmBoR; good W. mannes] ma*n*ny C^2.
585 cler] as cler WHmCrGYOC^{2}CBLM RF. þe] *om* BoCot.
586 The] Þat BoCot. moot] moot it BmBo; moted Cot. is of] is O; þe C^2. þe] that Cr^{23}; *with* F. Manoir] Mary3s F. aboute] all abowte GF.
587 And] *om* YOC^{2}CB. walles ben] walle is Cot. holden] holde OC^{2}MF.
588 The...of] And kerneled wiþ WHmCr GYOC^{2}CBLM; And Icarneled with RF. þat] R; man WHmCrGYOC^{2}CBLMF.
589 Botrased] Ibuterased RF; Bitrased C; Bretaskid BmBo. wiþ] *with* good F. so] *om* CotF. no3t] nou3 Y. saued] ysaued YLMR; besauyd Hm.
590 And] *om* OC^2. hiled] Ihyled RF. halles] halle B (s *added another script* Bm); hy3e hall*es* F. chambres] chamberer C.

Wiþ no leed but wiþ loue and lowe[nesse] as breþeren [of o wombe].
The brugg[e] is of bidde/wel/þe/bet/may/þow/spede;
Ech piler is of penaunce, of preieres/to/Seyntes;
Of almesdedes are þe hokes þat þe gates hangen on.
Grace hatte þe gateward, a good man for soþe;
His man hatte amende/yow, for many m[a]n h[e] knoweþ.
Telleþ hym þis tokene: "[truþe woot] þe soþe;
I p*ar*fourned þe penaunce þe preest me enioyned
And am sory for my synnes and so [shal I] eu*er*e
Whan I þynke þeron, þeiȝ I were a Pope."
Biddeþ amende/yow meke hym til his maister ones
To wayuen vp þe wiket þat þe wo*m*man shette
Tho Adam and Eue eten apples vnrosted:
Per Euam cun[c]tis clausa est et per Mariam virginem [iterum] patefacta est;
For he haþ þe keye and þe cliket þouȝ þe kyng slepe.

591 Wiþ] wit CL. leed] leode C. and] & wit*h* F. lowenesse...wombe] lowe speche as breþ*er*en WHmCr^{23}GYOC^{2}CBLMR; louespech as bretherne Cr^{1}; lowly speche also F.
592 brugge] YLMR; brygge HmCrGOC^{2}CB; bregge F; brugg W. is] was G; *om* Y. of] *om* F. bidde] bide Cr. bet] better CrGCF. may] maist B.
593 Ech...of(1)] þe pilerys hatte F. Ech] eche a G; Euery Cr. of(2)] and of (and *above line another ink*) M; and HmF. preieres] preyer YOC^{2}CB. to] of CrG.
594 þe hokys ben almesdede þe gate god hy*m*selue F. dedes] dede YC. þe(1)] þo BmBo. þat] *om* YOC^{2}CB. gates] gate G. hangen] hange Hm; hangyth G.
595 Grace] & grace F. hatte] hatteth HmBo; hotith Cot; hatiþ Bm; hygh Cr^{12}.
596 His] & his F. hatte] hatteþ HmBo; hoteth Cot; hatiþ Bm. for] *om* RF. man he] man him LMRF; men hym WCrYOC^{2}CB; men hem HmG. knoweþ] knowen GOC^{2}.
597 Telleþ] Tell ȝee F; Tilliþ Bm. truþe woot] trewþe know*ith* F; þat truþe wite WHmCrGYOC^{2}CBoCotLMR; þat wyte Bm.
598 I] þ*at* y F. þe(2)] GHmYOC^{2}CBLMRF; þat þe WCr.
599 And] I G. am] F; am ful WHmCrGYOC^{2}CBLMR. for] of RF. shal I] CrHm; I shal WYOC^{2}CBLMRF; shall G. euere] ben euere F.
600 *line om* F. on] vppon B.
601 Biddeþ] & byddeþ F. meke] meke*n* CrR; mekely F. hym] *om* F. til] to GYOC^{2}MRF. ones] praye F.
602 wayuen] wayue HmGYOC^{2}CBLMRF; wayne Cr. wo*m*man] women Cr^{2}.
603 Tho] to HmYBm; After þ*at* F. apples] the apples Y; þe appil F. vnrosted] vnrostes C.
603α *line om* Y. *Per Euam*] *Paradisi porta per Euam* Cr^{23}; *Pena* Cr^{1}. *cunctis*] HmCrCBmBoMR; cuntis WGOC^{2}LF; *ianua paradisi* Cot. *est*(1)] *est &c* Hm. *Mariam virginem*] *virginem Mariam* Cr. *iterum*] RF; *om* WHmCrGOC^{2}CBLM. *patefacta est*] *&c* RF. *est*] *est &c* HmOC^{2}CB.
604 he] she BmCF (s *added* Bm). and] off G. þe(2)] *om* F. þe(3)] þat þe BmBo.

And if g*ra*ce g*ra*unte þee to go in [in] þis wise
Thow shalt see in þiselue truþe [sitte] in þyn herte
In a cheyne of charite as þow a child were,
To suffren hym and segge no3t ayein þi sires wille. |
A[c] be war þanne of Wraþe, þat wikked sherewe, *fol.* 34 *b*
[For] he haþ enuye to hym þat in þyn herte sitteþ
And pokeþ forþ pride to preise þiseluen;
The boldnesse of þi bienfe[et] makeþ þee blynd þanne,
And [so] worstow dryuen out as dew and þe dore closed,
Keyed and cliketted to kepe þee wiþouten
Happily an hundred wynter er þow eft entre.
Thus my3testow lesen his loue, to lete wel by þiselue,
And [gete it ayein þoru3] g*ra*ce [ac þoru3 no gifte ellis].
A[c] þ*er* are seuen sustren þat seruen truþe euere
And arn porters of þe Posternes þat to þe place longeþ.

605 *line om* F. þee] to the Cr. go] come Cr. in in] LM; in WHmCrGYOC^{2}CBR (after *added another script* G).
606 Thow shalt] þou shall C^{2}Bm; Þan shalt þou F. in(1)] *om* YF. selue] seluen M; selue where þat F; soule Hm. sitte] Y Cr^{23}OCBoCotLMR; sette C^{2}Bm; syttyþ F; *om* WHmCr^{1}G. in...herte] *om* F.
607 cheyne] cheyre Cr^{3}Bm (*partly over erasure* Bm); cheiere (ere *over erasure another ink*) M; chambre F. þow] he F. child] chlde L.
608 suffren] suffre HmCrGYOC^{2}CBLRF. hym...ayein] ony sey3eng ⁊ do F. and] ⁊ to GR. segge] se Cr^1. no3t] hym naught Cot; *om* R. sires] eires C; heiris B (*altered to* helris Bm).
609 Ac] HmYOBLMR; But F; And WCrC^{2}C; *om* G. þanne] thou Cr^1; *om* F. Wraþe] C^2; Wrath Cr; wratthe YCBMF; wraþþe O; wrath þe GL; wrathe þe R; Wraþe þee W; wratthe the Hm. þat] þat is a WHmCrGYOC^{2}CBLMR; he is a F.
610 For he] He WHmCrGYOC^{2}CBLM RF. to] til YOC^{2}CB.
611 pokeþ] prykketh G; paketh Cr^3; plukketh Y. forþ] for Cr^{1}C; *om* RF. to] p*ri*uyly to F. preise] praisen MC^2. þi] wel þy F. seluen] selue HmCrRF.
612 The] ⁊ þe F. þi] the Cr. feet] fetes WHmCrGYOC^{2}CBLMRF. makeþ] maken OC^2; make GYCBmBoF (þ *added by a corrector* Bm).
613 And] *om* G. so] þanne WHmCrGY CBLMR; *om* OC^{2}F. worstow] worþest þou OHmC^{2}M; worþ þou BmF (rþ *over erasure another ink* Bm); wast þou Cr; beest þou G. dryuen] dryve F; dryues C. as dew] *om* F. as] as a CB. closed] Iclosed RF.
614 Keyed] Icayed R; ⁊ key3ed F. cliketted] klykeded HmF; Iclycated R. kepe] kepyn F. outen] oute CrBM.
615 Happily] Haply YC. an] and Bm. wynter] wynters G. eft] eft in F.
616 my3testow] mi3t þow CYBLMRF. þi] the Cr^3. selue] seluen OHmC^{2}M.
617 gete...þoru3] neuere happily eft entre WHmCrGYOC^{2}CBLRF; neu*er*e aftur happiliche entre M. g*ra*ce] but g*ra*ce WHmCrYCBLMR; but his g*ra*ce F; but þou grace G; til grace OC^2. ac...ellis] þow haue WHmYOC^{2}CBLMRF; if thou haue Cr; haue G.
618 Ac] HmYOBLMR; but GF; And WCrC^{2}C. sustren] *ser*uau*n*tys F; 3iftes R.
619 And] þey F. porters] portes C. of] ouer R; at F; to Cr^{23}. Posternes] 3atys F. þe(2)] his F; *om* C. longeþ] bilo*n*g Cr.

That oon hatte Abstinence, and humilite anoþer;
Charite and Chastite ben hi[r]e chief maydenes;
Pacience and pees muche peple þei helpeþ;
Largenesse þe lady let in [wel] manye;
Heo haþ holpe a þousand out of þe deueles punfolde.
A[c] who is sib to þise [sustren], so me god helpe,
He is wonderly welcome and faire vnderfongen.
But if ye be sibbe to some of þise seuene
It is [wel] hard, by myn heed, any of yow alle
To geten ing[o]ng at any gate but *gr*ace be þe moore.'
'By Crist!' quod a kuttepurs, 'I haue no kyn þere.'
'Nor I', quod an Apeward, 'by auȝt þ*at* I knowe.'
'Wite god', quod a waf[erer], 'wiste I þis for soþe
Sholde I neu*er*e ferþer a foot for no freres *pr*echyng.'
'Ȝis!' quod Piers þe Plowman, and poked [hym] to goode,

620 That] the GF. oon] one of hem Cr; firste F. hatte] hattiþ Bm; ys F. and] *om* Cr. humilite] vmblete R. an] ys an F; þat M.

621 Charite] ⁊ Charite F. ben] þese been F. hire] hise WHmGYOC^{2}CBLMRF; the Cr. chief] chiel Y. maydenes] maydens there Cr; chyldry*n* F.

622 Pacience] ⁊ Pacience F. muche] mychil F; do muche Cr. þei] *om* Cr. helpeþ] helpe CrC.

623 Largenesse] ⁊ largenesse F. þe] þ*at* GF. lady] Ladye Cr; lady she WHmGY OC^{2}BMF (she *over erasure another ink* M); lady sho C; lady heo L; lady he R. let] leteþ BCrGMF. in] out OC^{2}F. wel] ful WHmCrGYOC^{2}CBLMRF.

624 Heo] Sho C; She CrHmGYOC^{2}B MF (*over erasure another ink* M). holpe] holpe*n* Cr^{23}HmGOC^{2}BM; delyueryd F. þousand] hundred Cr. punfolde] poustee Hm.

625 Ac who] And who WCrLMR; And who so YHmGOC^{2}CB; ⁊ she F. sib to þise] neyȝh by sibbe þe F. to] vnto Hm. sustren] seuene WHmCrGYOC^{2}CBLM RF.

626 ⁊ she will worchepely wolkome ȝow ⁊ wel ȝow vndirfonge F. He] heo R. fongen] fonge Cr^{1}; foggen Cr^{23}.

627 But] but G; And but WHmCrYOC^{2} CBLMRF. if] if þat R; *om* CrMF. ye] þe C; he B. to] q*uod* pers to F. þise] these systers Cr.

628 wel] ful WHmCrGYOC^{2}CBLMR; *om* F. heed] heed for FG; heed quod Piers for WHmCrYOC^{2}CBLMR.

629 geten] gete OCrGC^{2}B. ingong] OCr GYLMR; yngange HmC; ingoing WC^{2}B; in passage F. any] the YOC^{2}CB. but] F; þere but WCrGYOC^{2}CBLMR; there but ȝif Hm.

630 By] Now by WHmCrGYOC^{2}CBL MR; A by F. a] *om* GC^{2}. I] tha*n* I Cr.

631 Nor] Ne LMRF; Non O; Ne*n* C^{2}. I(2)] GOC^{2}CBLMRF; I kan WHmCrY.

632 Wite god] God wot B. Wite] Woot (ot *over erasure another ink*) M; wold G; A wolde F; wow to C^{2}. waferer] GOC^{2}BM; wafrestere WHmCrYCLR; Messag*er* F. wiste] þ*at* F. þis] þus G; wiste F. for] þe F; *om* R.

633 Sholde] Shul C. ferþer a foot] a fote ferther*e* F. no] ani CrY. freres] frere R.

634 Ȝis] *twice* F. þe] *om* MF. pokede] prycked G; pikked Y; pute C. hym] hem FG; hem alle WHmCrYBoCotLMR; he alle Bm; the alle C; alle OC^{2}.

'Mercy is a maiden þ*er*e haþ my3t ouer [hem] alle;
And she is sib to alle synfulle and hire sone also,
And þoru3 þe help of hem two, hope þow noon ooþer,
Thow my3t gete g*ra*ce þere so þow go bityme.' |
'Bi seint Poul!' quod a pardoner, 'p*ar*auent*ur*e I be no3t knowe
þ*er*e; *fol.* 35 *a*
I wol go fecche my box wiþ my breuettes ⁊ a bulle w*ith*
bisshopes l*ett*res.'
'By crist!' quod a co*mun*e wo*m*man, 'þi compaignie wol I folwe.
Thow shalt seye I am þi Suster.' I ne woot wher*e* þei bicome.

635 Mercy...þ*er*e] þere a Mayde þere Mercy she F. a] as C. maiden] mayde R. haþ] and hath HmB. hem] LCrMRF; *om* WHmGYOC^{2}CB.
636 And] *om* F. alle] *om* F. and] ⁊ so ys F.
637 two] two helpe (helpe *cancelled*) G. þow] ye Cr; *om* G.
638 my3t] my3tist OC^2. gete] gety*n* F. so] by soo HmCrYOC^{2}CBLF; be so R. tyme] tymes F.
639 p*ar*] on Cr; an *over erasure another ink* M; I G. auent*ur*e] trowe G. knowe þ*er*e] knowen þere MCr; welcome RF.
640 *as two lines divided after* al Cr. go] *om* YOC^{2}CB. fecche] fechy*n* F. box...my] *om* G. wiþ...bulle] *om* F. breuettes ⁊] breuets al And also Cr^3; brenets al And also Cr^{12}. bulle] bille Y. w*ith*] wyth a Cr; w*ith* þe F. bisshopes] bisshope C; *om* G. l*ett*res] lettre Cot; le::::: O.
641 þ^i] In þy*n* F. folwe] wende F.
642 Thow shalt] ⁊ F. shalt] shal C; meyst G; shat Cot. I(2)...bicome] in Cytes þ*er*e we wende F. ne woot] not GM. where] whether Cr. þei] þer Bm. bicome] bicomen OC^2; be gon Cr^1; begonne Cr^{23}.

VI

'This were a wikkede wey but whoso hadde a gyde
That [myȝte] folwen vs ech foot': þus þis folk hem mened.
Quod Perkyn þe Plowman, 'by Seint Peter of Rome!
I haue an half acre to erie by þe heiȝe weye;
Hadde I eryed þis half acre and sowen it after
I wolde wende wiþ yow and þe wey teche.'
'This were a long lettyng', quod a lady in a Scleyre.
'What sholde we wommen werche þe while?'
'So*m*me shul sowe þe sak for shedyng of þe Whete.
And ye louely ladies wiþ youre longe fyngres,
That ye haue silk and Sandel to sowe whan tyme is
Chesibles for Chapeleyns chirches to honoure.
Wyues and widewes wolle and flex spynneþ;
Makeþ cloþ, I counseille yow, and kenneþ so youre douȝtres.
The nedy and þe naked nymeþ hede how þei liggeþ;

1 whoso] if we Cr; we F.
2 myȝte folwen] wolde folwen WHmG LM; wolde folwe CYOC^{2}BRF; wold we*n*de wi*th* Cr. ech] eu*er*y F. foot] Cot GF; a foot WHmCrYOC^{2}CBmBoLMR. þus...mened] þ*at* no folk vs noyȝe F; ⁊ þ*at* wei tel Cr^{12}; ⁊ þe way tell Cr^3. þis] thilke Cot. hem] he G; hym M. mened] meneden O; monede M.
3 *line om* CB. Perkyn þe] Pers F. by] þo by F.
4 erie] erien M.
5 þis] þ*at* F. sowen] sowe C^2; ysowen MR; ysowe F.
6 wolde] wol YCLR. wende] wenden R Hm. and] ⁊ you G. teche] ȝow techen F.
7 in] wi*th* F.
8 *line om* CB. What] when G. sholde] schulden OC^{2}M; shull F. werche] worchen MF. þe] þ*ere* LMRF; to G; in the meane Cr. while] whiles HmGYOC^2 LMRF.
9 shul] shullen BmBo; shold G. sowe þe sak] sowe sakke L; sowen sakkus M. for] M; quod Piers for WHmCrYOC^{2}CBL RF; q*uo*d he for G. shedyng] schedynd O; spillinge M. þe(2)] *om* YCBF.
10 ye] you G; ye se Cr^{23}. ladies] lady B (s *added another hand* Bm). fyngres] fymgrys (g *altered from* b) Hm.
11 That] Loke F. sowe] sowen M; suwe Cot. tyme is] it ys tyme F.
12 Chesibles] To make Chesyplis F.
13 Wyues] ⁊ ȝee wyvis F. spynneþ] ȝee spy*n*ne F.
14 Makeþ] ⁊ Makeþ F; Make CrC. and] ad R. kenneþ] ken CrOC^2. so] *om* CB.
15 nymeþ] nyme O; takes C; take GC^2. þei] hij LM; a R. liggeþ] ligge CYB.

Casteþ hem cloþes [for cold] for so [wol] truþe.
For I shal lenen hem liflode but if þe lond faille
As longe as I lyue, for þe lordes loue of heuene.
And alle manere of men þ*at* [by þe] mete libbeþ,
Helpeþ hym werche wiȝtliche þat wynneþ youre foode.' |
'By crist!' quod a knyȝt þoo, '[þow] kenne[st] vs þe beste, *fol.* 35 *b*
Ac on þe teme trewely tauȝt was I neuere.
[Ac] kenne me', quod þe knyȝt, 'and [I wole konne erie].'
'By Seint Poul!' quod Perkyn, '[for þow profrest þee so lowe]
I shal swynke and swete and sowe for vs boþe,
And [ek] labour[e] for þi loue al my lif tyme,
In couenaunt þ*at* þow kepe holy kirke and myselue
Fro wastou*rs* and wikked men þat [wolde me destruye],
And go hunte hardiliche to hares and to foxes,
To bores and to [bukkes] þat breken myne hegges,

16 Casteþ] And casteþ WHmGYOC^{2}CB LMRF; And cast Cr. hem] on hem F; hym R. for(1)...wol] for so comaundeþ WHmCrYBLMR; for so comaunde C; for so co*m*maunded G; ⁊ so comau*n*diþ ȝow F; for so biddiþ OC^{2}.
17 lenen] lene Cr^{3}YOC^{2}CBLRF; leue Cr^{12}. þe] my*n* F. *Hereafter an additional line* WHmCrGYOC^{2}CBLMRF: Flessh and breed boþe to riche and to poore (Flessh] Boþe fleshȝ F; Breed B. breed] fleisch B. boþe] *om* F). *See above*, p. 193.
18 þe] oure OC^{2}M. of] in F.
19 of] *om* G. by] Hm; þoruȝ WCrGYO C^{2}CBLMR; wi*th* F. þe mete] mete and drynke WHmCrGYOC^{2}CBLMRF.
20 Helpeþ] Helpe CrG; Shull helpe F. hym] hym to WHmCrYOC^{2}CBmBoL MR; hem to CotG; to F. wiȝtliche] wyttiliche B. þat] and Hm; to F. wynneþ] wynnen G; wynne wi*th* F.
21 þow kennest] he kenneþ WHmCrGY OC^{2}CBLMRF.
22 Ac] but GF; And CrC^{2}C. on...trewely] trewly on þe teem F. teme] tyme Bm. tauȝt] caught C.
23 *supplied main hand, partly in text, partly at top margin* G. Ac] YHmOBLMR; But WGF; And CrC^{2}C. me] me it F. knyȝt] knygh Y. and...erie] *cropped* G. I ...erie] I wol assaye YOCB; wolle asaie C^{2}; by crist I wole assaye WHmCrLMRF.
24 quod] *om* C^{2}. for...lowe] ye p*ro*fre yow so faire WHmCrGYOC^{2}CBLMRF (p*ro*fre] p*ro*feren OC^{2}. yow so] ȝou sire so F; me Cr. faire] fairin C^{2}).
25 I] That I WHmCrGYOC^{2}CBLMRF. shal] will F; *om* Cot. swynke] sweyte G. swete] swety*n* F; swynke G.
26 And ek laboure] And oþere labours do WCrGYOC^{2}CBLM (labors *corrected from* laborour G); And other laboreres do R; ⁊ oþere laboreris shull F; as oþer laborers do (as oþer *over erasure another ink*) Hm. my] here F.
27 þow...and] holy chirche þou kepe as F. kepe] shalt kepe Cot. kirke] cherche Hm GCotR. my] þy CF. selue] seluen M.
28 and] YOC^{2}CBMF; and fro WHmCrG LR. wolde me destruye] þis world destruyeþ WCr; this world struyeth YHmG OC^{2}BLMRF; þis world struthes C.
29 go] goo þou F. hardiliche] hardlich Cot. to(*both*)] att G.
30 To...to] ⁊ to bawsynes ⁊ F. bukkes] R; brokkes WHmCrGYOC^{2}CBLM; boores F. þat] b*u*t F. breken] breke YCF. myne] doun myne W; adown myn Hm CrYOC^{2}CLMR; and don mi*n*e Bm; adou*n* men BoCot; downe menn*es* G; þou none F.

And [fette þee hoom] faucons foweles to kille
For [þise] comeþ to my croft and croppeþ my whete.'
Curteisly þe kny3t [conseyued] þise wordes:
'By my power, Piers, I pli3te þee my trouþe
To fulfille þis forward þou3 I fi3te sholde.
Als longe as I lyue I shal þee mayntene.'
'Ye, and yet a point', quod Piers, 'I preye [þee] of moore:
Loke [þow] tene no tenaunt but truþe wole assente,
And þou3 [þow] mowe am*er*cy hem lat m*er*cy be taxour
And mekenesse þi maister maugree Medes chekes;
And þou3 pou*ere* men p*ro*fre [þee] p*re*sentes and 3iftes
Nyme it no3t an auenture [þow] mowe it no3t deserue.
For þow shalt yelde it ayein at one yeres [ende]
In a [wel] p*er*ilous place [þat] Purgatorie hatte.
And mysbede no3t þi bondem[a]n, þe bettre [shalt] þow spede;
Thou3 he be þyn vnderlyng here wel may happe in heuene

31 fette...hoom] so affaite þi W; goo affayte thy HmOC^{2}CBMRF; go affayte the CrL; go assey þe G; to afaite thy Y. foweles] wilde foweles WHmCr^{23}YCBLMR; wyld foule GF; wild foles Cr^{1}; wylde bestis OC^{2}.
32 þise] þei F; swiche WHmCrGYOC^{2}CBLMR. comeþ to] come into F.
33 Curteisly þe kny3t] þanne þe knyght *cur*teysly F. þe] this Hm. conseyued] þanne comsed WHmCrGYOC^{2}CBLMR; comsede F. þise] hise OC^{2}.
34 I] quod he I WHmCrGYOC^{2}CBLMRF.
35 þis] þi R. forward] forowart Bm.
36 Als] Also B; & as F. I lyue] lyve i*n* londe F.
37 Ye] he G; But F. and yet] *om* F. a] a quod (*corrected*) Bm; *om* C. þee] þe F; yow WHmCrGYOC^{2}CBLMR.
38 Loke] Lokiþ þat B. þow] þou F; ye WHmCrGYOC^{2}CBoCotLMR; 3e ne (ne *erased*) Bm. tene] teme Cr^{1}.
39 þow] þou F; ye WHmCrGYOC^{2}CBoCotLMR; pore 3e Bm. mowe] mayst F. am*er*cy] amercyen Hm; angre F. hem] him Cr^{1}; men RF; *om* CB.
40 þi] þe CB; 3oure R. maugree] mauger Cr. Medes] mede R.
41 men] *om* G. p*ro*fre] proferen OC^{2}. þee] þe F; yow WHmCrGYOC^{2}CBLMR.
42 Nyme] Nemeþ B. it] hem MF (*altered from* him *another ink* M). an] yn HmGOC^{2}BF. þow] RF; ye WHmCrGYOC^{2}CBLM. mowe] maist F. it no3t] no3t hit BoCotF.
43 þow] 3e HmCr (*over erasure another ink* Hm); you G. shalt] shal CrHmG. yelde] yelden Cr^{3}. it] *om* Y. ayein] agayne CrG. ende] HmCrGYOC^{2}CBLMRF; tyme W.
44 In] Al in F. wel...þat] ful p*er*ilous place WHmCrYOC^{2}CBLMR; p*er*lyous place F; full perylyche place G. hatte] it hatte WHmGYOC^{2}CL; hit hatteþ BR; it hi3te MCr^{12}; it high Cr^{3}; me*n* name it F.
45 And] Ne F; *om* YOC^{2}CB. man] Hm RF (*altered from* men *another ink* Hm); men WCrGYOC^{2}CBLM. þe bettre] þo bittre Bm. shalt] F; may WHmGC^{2}CLMR; mayst OYB; migh Cr^{12}; might Cr^{3}. þow] the Hm.
46 þyn] here þy*n* F. here] re *erased* M; *om* GF. may] it may Cr. happe] happen Cr BmBo. in heuene] *om* Cr^{3}.

That he worþ worþier set and wiþ moore blisse:
Amice, ascende superius.
For in Charnel at chirche cherles ben yuel to knowe,
Or a knyȝt from a knaue; knowe þis in þyn herte. |
And þ*at* þow be trewe of þi tonge and tales þow hatie *fol.* 36 *a*
But if [it be] of wisdom or of wit þi werkmen to chaste;
Hold wiþ none harlotes ne here noȝt hir tales,
And namely at mete swiche men eschuwe,
For it ben þe deueles disours, I do þe to vnderstonde.'
'I assente, by Seint Iame', seide þe knyȝt þanne,
'For to werche by þi wor[d] while my lif dureþ.'
'And I shal apparaille me', quod Perkyn, 'in pilgrymes wise
And wende wiþ yow [þe wey] til we fynde truþe.'
[He] caste on [hise] cloþes, yclouted and hole,
[Hise] cokeres and [hise] coffes for cold of [hise] nailes,
And [heng his] hoper at [his] hals in stede of a Scryppe:

47 worþ] wortheþ M; were Cr; *om* HmGYOC^{2}CB. worþier] worthelier Cr^{23}. set] yset (set *over erasure*) M; sytte HmGOC^{2}C; sitteþ BoBmCot. and wiþ] þa*n* þou ⁊ in wel F. blisse] blis in heuen Cr^{3}. *Hereafter a spurious line* Cr^{23}; *see above*, p. 224.

47α *in margin* O. *superius*] *superius* ⁊c HmGY. *Hereafter a spurious line* YOC^{2}CB (*as one line with the Latin* B); *see above*, p. 224.

48 in] yn a HmRF; in þe Cr^{1}. Charnel] Charneles MG; chanel R; chapel F. at] atte HmLM; ⁊ in Cr^{23}YC^{2}CB; ⁊ O; or i*n* a F. chirche] churches G. cherles] clerkes R; a clerk F. ben] be ful Cr; is F. yuel] yll G.

49 Or] so is F. from] þere fra*m* F. knaue] GYOC^{2}CBF; knaue þ*ere* WHmCrLMR.

50 And þat] But loke F. þat þow] *om* GYOC^{2}CB. þi] *om* RF. tales þow] tales thowe G; tales þat þow WHmCrLMRF; loke thow tales YOC^{2}C; loke talis þat þow BoBmCot.

51 But...of(1)] ⁊ by F. if] *om* G. it be] YOC^{2}CB; þei ben WHmCrGLMR. of(1)] *om* GC. or] ⁊ F. of(2)] by F; *om* Cr^{23}GYOC^{2}CB. to] thow YF. chaste] chaste*n* Cr; chastise OC^{2}BF.

52 Hold] Holde nauȝt R; ⁊ holde not F.

53 at] GYOC^{2}; at þe WHmCr^{12}CLMR; at thy Cr^{3}BF. mete] mete bord F.

54 it] þei GCotF. ben] *om* G. þe(1)] þo BmBo.

55 seide þe knyȝt] the knyght said Cr^{23}YOC^{2}CB. seide] q*uo*d G.

56 For] *om* F. werche] worchen G. by] al aft*er* F. word] F; wordes G; wordes þe WHmCrYOC^{2}CBLMR. dureþ] endureth Cr.

57 And] *om* YOC^{2}CB. Perkyn] Piers MF. wise] wede B.

58 And] ⁊ y wyll F. wiþ yow] ȝou wi*th* C^{2}. þe wey] I wile WHmCrGYOC^{2}CBLMR; *om* F. we] þat we F.

59 He] And WHmCrGYOC^{2}CBLMR; I wil F. caste...cloþes] on my cloþis caste boþe B. caste] casty*n* F. hise] my WHmCrGYOC^{2}CMF; me my LR. yclouted] clouted CrGB. and hole] and Ihole R; and wole Bm; at þe fulle F.

60 Hise (*all*)] My WHmCrGYOC^{2}CBLMRF. of] on Cr.

61 heng] hange WHmCrGYOC^{2}CBLMR; y will hangy*n* F. his (*both*)] myn WHmCrGYOC^{2}CBLMRF. in...of] as i hadde F. a] þe B.

'A busshel of bredcorn brynge me þ*er*Inne,
For I wol sowe it myself, and siþenes wol I wende
To pilgrymage as palm*er*es doon pardon to haue.
And whoso helpeþ me to erie [or any þyng swynke]
Shal haue leue, by oure lord, to lese here in heruest
And make h[y]m murie þ*er*myd, maugree whoso bigruccheþ it.
And alle kynne crafty men þat konne lyuen in truþe,
I shal fynden hem fode þat feiþfulliche libbeþ,
Saue Ia[kk]e þe Iogelour and Ionette of þe Stuwes
And danyel þe dees pleyere and Denote þe baude
And frere faitour and folk of hi[s] ordre,
And Robyn þe Ribaudour for hise rusty wordes.
Truþe tolde me ones and bad me telle it [forþ]:
Deleantur de libro viuencium; I sholde noȝt dele wiþ hem,
For holy chirche is [holde] of hem no tiþe to [aske],
Quia cum iustis non scribantur.

62 A] ⁊ a F. of] *om* G. brynge me] brynke wiþ me (wiþ me *over erasure another ink*) Hm; y wil bere F.
63 wol(1)] wolde HmCr^{1}. sowe] sowen R. and] *om* B. siþenes] seten *corrected to* seþen *another ink* Bm. wol I] wi*th* ȝow F.
64 To] On BF. pilgrymage] pilgrimages MCrF; pylgrymes G. as] ⁊ G. to] GOC^{2}F; for to WHmCrYCBLMR.
65 And] Ac HmYOBmLMR; but GF. so] þat F. me] me for Cot; *om* G. erie] erien M. or] HmGYOC^{2}CBLMRF; and WCr. any...swynke] sowe er I wende OCrC^{2}CF; sowen er I wende GYB; sowen here er I wende WHmLMR.
66 Shal] He shal MF. lord] lord god Cr^{1}. lese] gle*n*e Cr; lacche YOC^{2}CB; large F. here in heruest] his heruest heere F. here] hire YOC^{2}Bo; hier (i *above line*) Bm; theyr G.
67 And] Ac B. make] make*n* CrR. hym] RF; hem WHmCrLM; þem G; *om* YOC^{2}CB. myd] wyth HmC; *om* Cr^{1}. maugree] mangre Cr^{3}. so] so it R; *om* F. bigruccheþ] begrucche RCr^{1}; gruccheth HmGYOC^{2}C; grucche BCr^{23}F. it] *om* HmGYOC^{2}CBRF.
68 alle kynne] as for (*by correction* ?) G. crafty] craftys G. konne] ku*n*nen OHmB. lyuen] lyue HmCrGYOC^{2}CCotF.
69 fynden] fynde HmCrGOC^{2}CCotRF. þat] for F. feiþfulliche] feyfullich Cot. libbeþ] þey lybbe F.
70 Iakke] YHmCrGOC^{2}CBLMRF; Iagge W. þe(1)] *om* F. Ionette] Ienet Cr^{23}C^{2}. of] at F. þe(2)] *om* Cot. Stuwes] styvis FR; styuehous B.
71 Denote] dyote G; Enote YOCBmBo (d *prefixed later* Bm); Emot C^{2}Cot; Benot Cr^{3}.
72 And] ⁊ also F. frere] frer*e* FCr; frere þe WHmGYOCLMR (*marked for transposition* O); þe Frere C^{2}B. and...his] wiþ al his hool B. and] ⁊ mo F. his] HmCrGYOC^{2}CLMRF; hire W.
73 þe] *om* F.
74 *line om* Hm. Truþe] For treuþe BF. me(1)] me it Cr^{23}. telle] tellen LR. it] *om* F. forþ] forþ after B; after WCrGYOC^{2}CLMRF.
75 I...hem] ⁊c B; *om* C. dele...hem] wi*th* hem deyle F. hem] hym Cr^{1}.
76 holde] F; hote WHmCrGYCBLMR; hoten OC^{2}. tiþe] tythes Cr^{23}G. to] *om* Cot. aske] R; take WHmCrGYOC^{2}CBLMF.
76α *iustis*] *istis* Y. *non*] *no* Bo. *scribantur*] *scribantur* ⁊*c* HmB; *scribantur* in þe registre in hevene F.

They ben ascaped good auenture, [now] god hem amende.'
Dame werch/whan/tyme/is Piers wif hiȝte; |
His douȝter hiȝte do/riȝt/so/or/þi/dame/shal/þee/bete; *fol.* 36 *b*
His sone hiȝte Suffre/þi/Sou*er*eyns/to/hauen/hir/wille/
Deme/hem/noȝt/for/if/þow/doost/þow/shalt/it/deere/abugge/
Lat/god/yworþe/wiþ/al/for/so/his/word/techeþ.
'For now I am old and hoor and haue of myn owene
To penaunce and to pilg*ri*mage I wol passe wiþ oþ*ere*;
Forþi I wole er I wende do write my biqueste.
In dei nomine, amen. I make it myselue.
He shal haue my soule þat best haþ des*er*ued,
And [defende it fro þe fend], for so I bileue,
Til I come to hise acountes as my [crede] me [techeþ]—
To haue relees and remission, on þat rental I leue.
The kirke shal haue my caroyne and kepe my bones
For of my corn and [my] catel [h]e craued þe tiþe;
I paide [hym] p*re*stly for p*er*il of my soule;

77 ascaped] skapid F. now] LMRF; but OC^2; *om* WHmCrGYCB.
78 whan] wel wan BF. Piers] Persis F; pieris his Cot.
79 His] ⁊ his F. hiȝte] *om* F. or] er F. þi] þe Cr^{12}. shal] wil F.
80 His] ⁊ his F. Suffre] wel F. þi] his Cot. to] *om* OC^{2}RF. hauen] haue HmCr GOC^{2}CBRF.
81 Deme] ⁊ deme F. for] *om* F. doost] do GYOC^{2}CB. shalt] schat Cot. it] ful OC^2; is C. abugge] bygge G.
82 *line om* CB. Lat] But lete F. yworþe] worþe OYC^{2}F; worche GCr. al] it al F. so] *om* YOC^2. word] word þe F.
83 I am] am I G. old] holde RF. of] good of F; *om* G. myn] mene Cr^3.
84 penaunce] pylg*ri*mage F. and to] ⁊ GYOC^{2}C; for F. pilg*ri*mage] penau*n*ce F. wiþ] wyth HmGYMF; wiþ þise WCrO C^{2}CBLR.
85 Forþi] Therefore Cr; For OC^2; But F. do] *om* G. write] wryty*n* F. biqueste] queste R; enqweste F.
86–8 *as two lines divided after* soule RF.
86 *dei*] *die* G. I...selue] *om* F. my] *om* Cot. selue] seluen GL.
87 He] god F. haþ des*er*ued] haþ des*er*ued it WHmCrC^2; hath it disserued (it *above line, the rest over erasure*) M; hath Iserued it YGOCBLR; ys worthy F.
88 defende...fend] fro þe fend it defende WHmCrGYOC^{2}CBLM; fro þe fende Ikeped it R; weyvid fram yt þe fendis F. for...bileue] *om* RF. for] and M.
89 to] til R. hise acountes] my counts Cr. my] *om* G. crede] HmCr^{3}C^{2}BRF; *Credo* WCr^{12}GYOCLM. me] *om* RF. techeþ] telleþ WHmCrGYOC^{2}CBLMR; spelliþ F.
90 *line om* F. haue] haue a WHmCrGYO C^{2}CBLMR. and] ⁊ GOC^{2}Cot; and a W HmCrYCBmBoLMR. leue] bileue CB.
91 The...haue] ⁊ þe kyrkeȝeerd shal kepe F. kepe] *om* F.
92 and my] and WHmCrGYOC^{2}CBLM RF. he] HmGYOC^{2}CBmLMR (s *prefixed another ink* Bm); she WCrBoCot; þe kirke F. þe] my Cr; *om* R. tiþe] tythes Cr^{23}.
93 I] ⁊ F. hym] it hym HmCrGYOC^{2}C LR; him ful M; it hem BmBo; hit hire Cot; it ful W; it F. p*re*stly] priestly Cr^2; trewly to þe preest F. for] for the Cr^{23}.

[He is] holden, I hope, to haue me in [mynde]
And mengen [me] in his memorie amonges alle c*ri*stene.
My wif shal haue of þat I wan wiþ truþe and na moore,
And dele among my [frendes] and my deere children.
For þouȝ I deye today my dettes are quyte;
I bar hom þat I borwed er I to bedde yede.
And wiþ þe residue and þe remenaunt, by þe Rode of Lukes!
I wol worshipe þ*er*wiþ truþe by my lyue,
And ben his pilgrym atte plow for pou*er*e mennes sake.
My plow[pote] shal be my pi[k] and [putte at] þe rotes,
And helpe my cultour to kerue and [close] þe furwes.'
Now is Perkyn and [þe] pilg*ri*mes to þe plow faren.
To erie þis half acre holpen hym manye;
Dikeres and Delu*er*es digged vp þe balkes; |
Therwiþ was Perkyn apayed and preised hem [yerne]. *fol.* 37 *a*
Oþere werkmen þ*er* were þat wroȝten ful [faste],
Ech man in his manere made hymself to doone,
And so*m*me to plese Perkyn piked vp þe wedes.

94 He is] Forþy he is FG; Forþi is he WYOC^{2}CBLMR; forþy is Hm; Therfore is he Cr. holden] beholdyn C^2; holde as F. haue] mind Cr. mynde] his masse WHmCrGYOC^{2}CBLMRF.
95 mengen] menge BF; megyn C^2. me] F; *om* WHmCrGYOC^{2}CBLMR. memorie] Meme*n*to F.
96 My] & my F.
97 dele] delen M; dele it F. my(1)] hir*e* F. frendes] douȝtres WHmCrGYOC^{2}CBLMRF. children] childres R.
98 For] For *truly* F. I] *om* F. deye] deyede RF. dettes] dette is R. are] ben all F; *om* R. quyte] Iquited R.
99 yede] wente F.
100 and] of CBF.
102 atte] at YGOC. mennes] men YCR; mo*n*nys BmBo. sake] *om* C^2.
103 plow] ploughwes B. pote] RF; foot WHmCrGYOC^{2}CBLM. shal be] ys F. pik] pikstaf WCrGYOC^{2}CLMRF; pyked staf HmB. and] þat F; to B. putte] pittyþ F; picche WCrGYOC^{2}CBLM; picchen R; plucche Hm. at] R; atwo WHmCrGYOC^{2}CBLM; awey F. þe] *om* B.
104 helpe] helpiþ F. and] & to F. close] clense WHmCrGYOC^{2}CBLMF; clenese R.
105 Perkyn] pers F. þe] F; þese R; hise WHmCrGYOC^{2}CBLM. faren] yfaren F.
106 erie] erien BF. þis] hys GF. acre] acre þer BF. holpen] helpen CrHmCB.
107 Dikeres] Boþe dykerys F. digged] diggeden OC^{2}BmBoMF; diggen CotC; dykyd Hm. balkes] bankis (? baukis) B.
108 Therwiþ...apayed] & *with* hem was Pers wel payed F. preised] preysydyn Hm. hem] hym Hm; hyn G. yerne] faste WHmCrGYOC^{2}CBLMRF.
109 *run together with* 110 Y. þ*er* were] þ*er* weren OC^{2}F; were there Cr^1. þat...faste] *om* Y. wroȝten] wrouȝte MCrC. faste] CM; yerne WHmCrGOC^{2}BLRF.
110 Ech...manere] *om* Y. Ech] Euery Cr. in] on F. hym] hem Y.
111 to] poore to F. Perkyn] Pers F. piked] pikeden OBm; þey pulliden F. wedes] rootys F.

At hei3 p*ri*me Piers leet þe plow3 stonde
To ou*er*sen hem hymself; whoso best wro3te
Sholde be hired þ*er*after whan heruest tyme come.
[Th]anne seten so*m*me and songen atte Nale
And holpen ere þ[e] half acre wiþ 'how trolly lolly'.
'Now by þe p*er*il of my soule!' quod Piers al in pure tene,
'But ye arise þe raþ*er* and rape yow to werche
Shal no greyn þ*at* [here] groweþ glade yow at nede;
And þou3 ye deye for doel þe deuel haue þ*at* recch[e]!'
Tho were faito*ur*s afered and feyned hem blynde;
So*m*me leide hir le[g] aliry as swiche lo[r]els konneþ
And made hir mone to Piers [how þei my3te no3t werche]:
'We haue no lymes to laboure *with*; lord, yg*ra*ced be [y]e!
Ac we preie for yow, Piers, and for youre plow3 boþe,
That god of his g*ra*ce your*e* greyn multiplie
And yelde yow [of] your*e* Almesse þat ye 3yue vs here;

112 At] Atte HmM; þ*an*ne at F. þe] his F. **113** To...best] ⁊ wente to seen hise werkme*n* how þ*at* þey F. To] And 3eed to R. who] B; and who WHmCrGYOC^{2}CLMR. **114** Sholde] He sholde WHmCrGYOC^{2}CLMR; For he sholde B; he wolde F. be hired] heren hem F. tyme] *om* G. **115** Thanne] Tha*n*ne HmF (*over erasure* Hm); And þanne WCrGYOC^{2}CBLMR. seten] sete R; fond he F. somme...songen] ⁊ songyn summe *partly over erasure* Hm. and] syttyn ⁊ F. songen] songe Cr; synge F; sogen C. Nale] alehous F. **116** And] And ho R. holpen] helpen GR. ere...acre] hym so to hery3e F. ere] erien M; to erye R; to erien BmBo. þe] þis W; his HmCrGYOC^{2}CBLMR. how] hoy F; hey CrOC^{2}. *Hereafter a spurious line* F; *see above*, p. 222. **117** Now] *om* G. þe...soule] my*n* sowlis pereyl F. þe] *om* Y. al] *om* F. tene] gret tene F. **118** arise] arisen B. **119** here] her (*above line ? main hand and ink*) M; *om* WHmCrGYOC^{2}CBLRF. groweþ glade] growen serue Cr^{1}. nede] 3our*e* neede F; ende Cr^{3}. **120** þou3] yff G. deye] deyen BF; deyede R. doel] defaute B (*over erasure another ink* Bm). haue] have hy*m* F; hym haue HmB; *om* G. þat] ytt G. recche] HmCrRF; reccheþ WGYOC^{2}CBLM. **121** Tho] Two C. were] weren OC^{2}BF. feyned] feyneden Bm. **122** leide] leyden OHmC^{2}BmBo. leg] legges WHmCrGYOC^{2}CBLMRF. aliry] swolle F. swiche] su*m* F. lorels] losels WHmCrGYOC^{2}CBLMRF. konneþ] kunne C^{2}; can CrG; knoues C; vsen F. **123** made] maden FHm; mane C^{2}. how ...werche] and preide hym of g*ra*ce WHmCrGYOC^{2}CBLMRF (preide] preyeden OB. hym] *om* Cr^{1}). **124** We] we G; For we WHmCrYOC^{2}CBLMR; ⁊ seyd we F. *with*] oure F. yg*ra*ced be] graced be CrGR; graceful be B; of grace bydde we Hm; do v*us* boote F. ye] CrGYOC^{2}CBLMR; þe WHm; *om* F. **125** Ac] But F; And CrGC^{2}C. we] *om* C. preie] preyen O; preied C^{2}. for(2)] *om* OC^{2}. plow3] plowh3me*n* F. **126** his] his grete F. **127** of] YOC^{2}CBLMR; for WHmCrG; *om* F. youre] *om* OC^{2}. þat] dede þat F. ye] you Cr^{23}. 3yue] 3yuen OHmC^{2}BMR; gyue CrGC.

For we may [neiþer] swynke ne swete, swich siknesse vs eyleþ.'
'If it be sooþ', quod Piers, 'þat ye seyn, I shal it soone aspie.
Ye ben wastours, I woot wel, and truþe woot þe soþe;
And I am his [h]olde hyne and [auȝte] hym to warne
Whiche þei were in þis world hise werkmen apeired.
Ye wasten þat men wynnen wiþ *tra*uaille and tene.
Ac truþe shal teche yow his teme to dryue,
Or ye shul eten barly breed and of þe broke drynke; |
But if he be blynd or brokelegged or bolted wiþ Irens, *fol.* 37 *b*
[Thei] shal ete [as good as I, so me god helpe],
Til god of his [grace gare hem to arise].
Ac ye myȝte *tra*uaille as truþe wolde and take mete and hyre
To kepe kyen in þe feld, þe corn fro þe beestes,
Diken or deluen or dyngen vpon sheues
Or helpe make morter or bere Muk afeld.
In lecherie and in losengerie ye lyuen, and in Sleuþe,
And al is þoruȝ suffraunce þ*at* vengeaunce yow ne takeþ.

128 *line om* Cot. may] ca*n* Cr. neiþer] BmBoCr; noȝt WHmYCLMR; not GO C^{2}F. ne swete] *om* F. ne] nor Hm. eyleþ] holdeþ F; *om* C.
129 it(1)] this YOC^{2}CB. quod Piers] þat ye sain M; *om* G. þat ye seyn] quod Piers M; *om* YOC^{2}CB. ye] you G.
130 Ye] þ*at* ȝee F; þo R. and] *om* R. woot(2)] wottethe G; wot wel R.
131 holde] olde WHmCrGYOC^{2}CBLMRF. auȝte] hiȝte WHmCrGYOC^{2}CBLMR; byhyȝhte F.
132 were] weren OC^{2}RF. hise] þat his B. men] wolde F. apeired] appeyreden O; apayreth R; apeyre F; ympeyren G.
133 Ye] For ȝee F. wasten] wast Cr. tene] YOC^{2}CB; wiþ tene WHmCrGLMRF.
134 Ac] but GF; And CrC^{2}C.
135 Or] for (? *over erasure*) Hm. shul] shullen B. eten] ete HmCrGYOC^{2}CBLMR.
136 if] *om* F. he] he þat F; ye Cr. be blynd] blynd be (be *above line main hand*) Cot. be] is F; *om* R. or(1)] *over erasure another ink* M; and L. broke] broke*n* CrGOC^{2}. bolted] boltild Cot.
137 Thei] He WHmGYOC^{2}CBLMRF; Ye Cr. shal] shalte C^{2}. ete] ety*n* F. as(1)...helpe] whete breed and drynke wiþ myselue WHmCrGYOC^{2}CBLMRF (whete] whyȝt F; swete OC^{2}. wiþ myselue] wyȝn or ale F).
138 grace...arise] goodnesse amendement hym sende WHmCrGYOC^{2}CBLMRF (hym] you Cr).
139 Ac] but GF; And CrC^{2}C. myȝte] þ*at* mygth (þ*at over erasure*) Hm; myȝten O. as...wolde] *tre*wly F.
140 kepe] kepen HmF. þe(2)] or F.
141 Diken] Or dyken F. or deluen] *twice* O. dyngen] dingine Cr^{3}; dyggy*n* F; picchen B. on] the G; *om* BF. sheues] rootys F.
142 helpe] helpy*n* F. make] maky*n* F; to make B. bere] leedy*n* F.
143 In...in(2)] & nowht to lyve in leccheryȝe ne in Losengryȝe & F. in(1)] *om* GYOC^{2}CB. losengerie] lustengerye Cr^{12}. ye] *om* R. lyuen] liue CrR.
144 And...þoruȝ] It is F. al] al this Cot. þat] of god þat F. ne] *om* F. takeþ] take OC^{2}.

Ac Ancres and heremites þat eten but at Nones
And na moore er morwe, myn almesse shul þei haue,
And catel to [cope] hem wiþ þat han Cloistres and chirches.
Ac Rob*ert* Renaboute shal [riȝt] noȝt haue of myne,
Ne Postles, but þei p*re*che konne and haue power of þe bisshop:
Thei shul haue payn and potage and [a pitaunce biside],
For it is an vnresonable Religion þat haþ riȝt noȝt of c*er*tein.'
[Th]anne gan wastour to wraþen hym and wolde haue yfouȝte;
To Piers þe Plowman he p*ro*frede his gloue.
A Bretoner, a braggere, [he b]osted Piers als
And bad hym go pissen w*ith* his plowȝ: '[pyuysshe] sherewe!
Wiltow, neltow, we wol haue oure wille
Of þi flour and þi flessh, fecche whanne vs likeþ,
And maken vs murye þ*er*[wiþ] maugree þi chekes.'
Thanne Piers þe Plowman pleyned hym to þe knyȝte
To kepen hym as couenaunt was fro cursede sherewes,

145 Ac] but GF; As C; And CrCot; Of C^2. eten] ete YCrC; eten ȝo (ȝo *cancelled*) Bm. but] CrLMRF; noȝt but WHmGY OC^{2}CB. at] *om* G. Nones] ones C^{2}G.
146 er] GCrYOC^{2}CBLMR; er þe W; til on F; tyl on the Hm. shul þei] þey shull F. þei] not they Cr; þe C^2.
147 And] Cr^{3}YOC^{2}CB; And of WHm Cr^{12}G; And of my LMRF. cope] YOC^2 CBLMR; kou*ere* F; kepe WHmCrG. han Cloistres] kepy*n* cloystre F. and] i*n* R. chirches] chirche F.
148 Ac] but G; And CrC^{2}C; But Daun F. riȝt noȝt] noȝt WHmCrGYOCBLMRF; no C^2. haue of myne] rewle my goodis F.
149 Postles] apostles Cr; preest F. þei] if þei C^2; he F. and] and ȝut R. power of þe] bishops Cr. bisshop] power Cr; *om* Y.
150 and(2)] w*ith* F. a...side] a pytawnce bysyde F; make hemself at ese WHmCr GYOC^{2}CBLMR (hem] hir Cr. self] *om* GYOC^{2}CB).
151 For...vnresonable] No reasonable Cr. For] *om* G. þat] hous þat F; *om* Cr. riȝt... of] noght off G; no þinge in YOC^{2}CB; re*n*tys none F. of] at Hm. c*er*tein] *om* F.
152 Thanne] YOC^{2}CBF; And þanne W HmCrGLMR. gan] gan a HmCrGYO C^{2}CBLMRF. to] *om* YCBF. wraþen] wrathe GHmCrYOC^{2}CBLMR; wexe wrothȝ F. hym] *om* F. haue] fayn a F. yfouȝte] yfouȝten OC^2; fought CrHm GCBF.
153 To] And to WHmCrGYOC^{2}CBLM RF. þe] *om* OC^{2}F. he] *om* OC^2.
154 A Bretoner] ⁊ w*ith* hy*m* cam F. he bosted] G; abosted WHmYOC^{2}CBLMR; ⁊ aboostide F; a bofted Cr^1; and bofeted Cr^{23}. als] also CrBF.
155 pissen] pysse CrGYOC^{2}CBMF. w*ith*] hym w*ith* GOC^2; on RF. pyuysshe] forpynede WHmCrGYOC^{2}CBLMRF.
156 Wiltow] Wiltow or WHmCrGYO C^{2}CBLM; wil þow or R; ⁊ seyd wilt þou Pers o F. neltow] nell þow R. wol] wolen B; wyln Hm.
157 Of] And of R; ⁊ F. and] ⁊ FCot M; and of WHmCrGYOC^{2}CBmBoLR. fecche] we fecche F; fette it BmBo; fet hit hit Cot.
158 maken] make YOC^{2}CBLMRF. wiþ] wyth HmGC^{2}CBM; myde WCrYOLRF. maugree] magr*e* of Cot.
159 þe(1)...knyȝte] wente kony*n*gly ⁊ to þe knyght pleyȝnede F. þe(1)] *om* OC^2. pleyned] plaiued Cr^2.
160 kepen] kepe CrGYOC^{2}CBLMR. was] *om* Cr^{12}.

'And fro þise wastours wolueskynnes þ*at* makeþ þe world deere,
For [þei] wasten and wynnen no3t and [þo] worþ neu*ere*
Plentee among þe peple þe while my plow3 liggeþ'. |
Curteisly þe kny3t þanne, as his kynde wolde, *fol.* 38 *a*
Warnede wastour and wissed hym bettre:
'Or þow shalt abigge by þe lawe, by þe ordre þ*at* I bere!'
'I was no3t wont to werche', quod Wasto*ur*, 'now wol I no3t bigynne!'
And leet li3t of þe lawe and lasse of þe kny3te,
And sette Piers at a pese and his plow3 boþe,
And manaced [hym] and his men if þei mette eftsoone.
'Now by þe p*er*il of my soule!' quod Piers, 'I shal apeire yow alle',
And houped after hunger þat herde hym at þe firste.
'Awreke me of wasto*urs*', quod he, 'þat þis world shendeþ.'
Hunger in haste þoo hente wastour by þe [mawe]
And wrong hym so by þe wo*m*be þ*at* [al watrede his ei3en].
He buffetted þe Bretoner aboute þe chekes

161 *line om* F. þise] þe G; *om* Hm. wolueskynnes] of wolues ky*nn*e B; off wolues kynd G. makeþ] make CrGY CB. þe] þis GR.

162 *divided from* 163 *after* while WHmCrG YOC^{2}CBLMR, *after* soþe F. þei] GMF; þo WHmCrYOC^{2}CBLR. wasten] waste LMR. wynnen] wynne GCrYCF; wynnnen M. and(2)] *om* C^2. þo] þat ilke while WHmCrGYOC^{2}CBmLMR; ilke while BoCot; wete wel for soþe F.

163 þe(1)] *om* R. þe(2)] þer CLM; *om* GF. liggeþ] lieþ B.

164 þanne] þo F. as] *om* C.

165 hym] him the Cr^{3}OC^2; to þe F.

166 shalt] shat Cot. by(1)] with R. by(2)] he seid be F. þat] *om* F.

167 was...werche] wroght neu*er* G. was] nas OC^2. wont] woned B; Iwont (*final* e *erased*) M; wone R. to...no3t] q*uod* he to wirche ne y wil not now F. now] and now WHmCrGYOC^{2}CBLMR. wol I no3t] I nill Cr^{3}GYOC^{2}CB.

168 li3t] li3tly RHmF. þe kny3te] his speche F.

169 Piers] also pers F.

170 manaced] þrette F. hym] Piers WHm CrGYOC^{2}CBLMRF. mette] metty*n* F; mete G. soone] sones GC^2.

171 Now by] by GR; Q*uod* pers be F. quod Piers] *om* F.

172 *line om* F. houped] called G.

173 Awreke] & awreke F. of] of þise WCrGYOC^{2}CBLRF; on these HmM. quod he] *om* GF. þis] the Hm. shendeþ] she*nd* F.

174 Hunger] Sone hu*n*gir F. þoo] þan B (*altered from* þou *another ink* Bm). mawe] HmCrGYOC^{2}CBLMRF; wombe W.

175 And] And he B. wo*m*be] wonbe Bm. al...ei3en] al watred his ey3es R; boþe hise ei3en watrede WHmCr^{3}YC^{2}CBLMF; boþe hise yen wattreden O; hys eyne watered GCr^{12}.

176 He] & he F. buffetted] boffette R; buffeteddin C^2. þe(1)] so þe F. Bretoner] breton Cr; braggere F. aboute] abowhty*n* F. þe(2)] bothe the (bothe *another script*) G; boþe hise F.

That he loked lik a lant*er*ne al his lif after.
He bette hem so boþe he brast ner hire [mawes].
Ne hadde Piers wiþ a pese loof preyed [hym bileue]
They hadde be [dede and] doluen, ne deme þow noon ooþ*er*.
'[Lat] hem lyue', he seide, 'and lat hem ete wiþ hogges,
Or ellis benes [and] bren ybaken togideres.'
Faito*ur*s for fere flowen into Bernes
And flapten on wiþ flailes fro morwe til euen
That hunger was noȝt hardy on hem for to loke.
For a pot[el] of peses þat Piers hadde ymaked
An heep of heremytes henten hem spades
And kitten hir copes and courtepies hem maked |
And wente as werkmen [to wedynge] and [mowynge] *fol.* 38 *b*
And doluen [drit] and [dung] to [ditte out] hunger.
Blynde and bedreden were bootned a þousand;

177 lik] liked (d *added, then cancelled*) Y. lant*er*ne] lant*er*ne horn F. after] tyme BoCot.
178 He] And Y. he] þat he B. brast] brake Cr. ner] nye G. mawes] guttes WHmCrGYOC^{2}CBLMRF.
179 preyed] Ipreyed Y. hym bileue] honger sese RF; hunger to cesse WHmCrGYOC^{2}CBLM.
180 hadde] hadden OC^{2}BM. dede... doluen] doluen WHmCrGYOC^{2}CBLM; dolue R; douy*n* F. ne] bothe ne YOC^{2}CLR; boþe BMF; depe *above line* (? *main hand*) G. deme] wilne B. þow noon] no man F.
181 *in top margin main hand but severely cropped* G. Lat] Suffre WHmCrGYOC^{2}CBLMRF. hem(1)] hem to BmBo; hym to Cot. he seide] seyd Pers F. and] *om* B. hem(2)] hym B. ete] eten MF.
182 and] HmCrGYOC^{2}CBLMRF; or W. ybaken] Ibake R; baken Cr^{12}GM; ybakyn boþe F; & bakon C^2. *Hereafter an additional line* WHmCrGYOC^{2}CBLMRF: Or ellis melk and mene ale þus preied Piers for hem (Or ellis] & drynke F. and] or CrF. mene] meny C^2; meyne OBRF; meynye C. ale] alle Bm. þus...hem] to mey*n*tene here lyvis F). *See above*, p. 193.
183 Faito*urs*] þanne Faytoures F; Fawtours O. fere] feer F; feere there G; fere herof WHmCr^{12}LMR; fere therof YCr^{3}OC^{2}CB. flowen] *after cancelled* fledde G; folwen BmBo. to] *om* R.
184 flapten] flappeden OB; flappen Cr^{12}; flattyn Hm. morwe] morwen OC^{2}BmBoR. til euen] to þe eve F.
185 hardy] RGF; so hardy WHmCrYOC^{2}CBLM. for to] onys to F; fort Bo.
186 potel] potful WHmCrGYOC^{2}CBLMRF. peses] pese CrYC. hadde] dide hem F. ymaked] makid BmBo; made G; make F.
187 An] Anon an F; And CBm (d *erased* Bm). henten] hente GCr^{12}R; in hande*s* henty*n* F. hem] *om* F.
188 kitten] kyt Cr; knetten Cot. maked] made HmCrGYOC^{2}CBLRF; maden M.
189 wente] wenten CrHmYOC^{2}CBLMRF. to...mowynge] to swynkyn abowtyn F; wiþ spades and wiþ shoueles WHmCrGLMR; with spades & shouelles YOC^{2}CB.
190 doluen] delueden OF. drit...out] and dikeden to dryue awey WHmCrGYOC^{2}CBLMRF (dikeden] dyggedyn Hm; diggen CrG; dykende*n* C^2).
191 Blynde] þa*n*ne blynde me*n* F. bedreden] bedrede HmOC^{2}B; beddredid F. were] weren OBmBo. bootned] botoned C. a þousand] and hundrid (d *of* and *erased*) Cot.

That seten to begge siluer soone were þei heeled,
For þat was bake for bayard was boote for many hungry;
And many a beggere for benes buxum was to swynke,
And ech a pouere man wel apaied to haue pesen for his hyre,
And what Piers preide hem to do as prest as a Sperhauk.
And [Piers was proud þerof] and putte hem [in office]
And yaf hem mete [and money as þei] my3te [asserue].
Thanne hadde Piers pite and preide hunger to wende
Hoom [in]to his owene [e]rd and holden hym þere [euere].
'I am wel awroke of wastours þoru3 þy my3te.
Ac I preie þee, er þow passe', quod Piers to hunger,
'Of beggeris and bidderis what best be to doone.
For I woot wel, be þow went þei wol werche ille;
Meschief it makeþ þei be so meke nouþe,
And for defaute of foode þis folk is at my wille.
[And it] are my blody breþeren for god bou3te vs alle;

192 That] And C. seten to] *twice* L; sytten to CrGC^{2}. were] weren OF. þei] *om* Cr^{12}.
193 þat was] þat at was (at *above line*) Bm; bread Cr. bake] baken CrOC^{2}MF. bayard] baierds Cr. for(2)] to R; *om* F. many] þe F.
194 *line om* Cr^{12}. a] *om* Cr^{3}YOC^{2}C. beggere] beggers Cr^{3}. buxum] ful buxom M; ful bown F; fayne R. was] were BCr^{3}.
195 a] *om* HmCrGMF. apaied] payed GYOC^{2}CMF. pesen] peyse G. for his] for her OC^{2}; to F.
196 to] for to R; *om* GF. as] also BmBo. a] *om* Cot. Sperhauk] hauke Cr; spark C^{2}.
197 Piers...þerof] þerof was Piers proud WHmCrGYOC^{2}CLMR; þerof was pieris so proud BmBo; þerfore wex pers prowd F; therof was so prowd Cot. in office] to werke WHmCrGYOC^{2}CBLMRF.
198 And] *om* G. mete] *om* F. and... asserue] as he my3te aforþe and mesurable hyre WHmCrGYOC^{2}CBLMRF (my3te] migh Cr^{23}. aforþe] forthe M; ford Cr; mete F. and] a G. mesurable] reasonable Cr^{3}OC^{2}).
199 Thanne] And þanne M. wende] wenden YCB.
200 into] OC^{2}CBLMR; yn tyl Hm; vnto WCr; to GYF. erd] LR; yerd WHmM (y *added* M); yard Cr^{12}; erthe YOC^{2}CB; yerthe G; yarth Cr^{3}; hold F. holden] holde F. þere euere] styll þere F; þere WHmCrGYOC^{2}CBLMR.
201 I] For I WHmCrGYOC^{2}CBLMRF. awroke] awroken OC^{2}B; Iwrooke G. of] now of YOC^{2}CBLMR; now on F. þoru3 þy my3te] by thi might nowe Cr; þis ty3me F.
202 Ac] but GF; And CrC^{2}C. to] vnto G, þo to RF.
203 and] CrYCBM; and of WHmGLRF; of OC^{2}. best be] is best F. be to] is to YR; to be Cr; be L; ben to Hm; to Cot.
204 wel] *om* M. þow] tho Cr^{2}. þei] thy Cr^{2}. wol] wolen OB; wyln Hm. werche] worchen M; don HmOC^{2}. ille] yll G; ful ille WHmCrYOC^{2}CBLMRF (ful *erased* M).
205 Meschief] For meschief WHmCrGYOC^{2}CBLMRF. nouþe] now CrGC^{2}C.
206 of] F; of hire WHmCrGYOC^{2}CBLMR.
207 And it] It R; & yet they YOC^{2}; Thei WHmCrGCBLMF. are] aren (*twice*) R. blody] bretheryn F; *om* G. breþeren] brether CrYC; of blood F. for] Y; quod Piers for WHmCrOC^{2}CBLMF; quod peres & R; quod pyers G. god] crist F.

Truþe tauȝte me ones to louen hem ech one,
And helpen hem of alle þyng [after þat] hem nedeþ.
Now wolde I wite, [if þow wistest], what were þe beste,
And how I myȝte amaistren hem and make hem to werche.'
'Here now', quod hunger, 'and hoold it for a wisdom:
Bolde beggeris and bigge þat mowe hir breed biswynke,
Wiþ houndes breed and horse breed hoold vp hir hertes,
[And] aba[u]e hem wiþ benes for bollynge of hir womb[e];
And if þe gomes grucche bidde hem go [and] swynke
And he shal soupe swetter whan he it haþ deserued. |
A[c] if þow fynde any freke þat Fortune haþ apeired *fol.* 39 *a*
[Wiþ fir or wiþ] false men, fonde swiche to knowe.
Conforte h[e]m wiþ þi catel for cristes loue of heuene;
Loue hem and lene hem [and] so [þe] lawe of [kynde wolde]:
Alter alterius onera portate.
And alle manere of men þat þow myȝt aspie
That nedy ben [or naked, and nouȝt han to spende,

208 louen] loue CrOC^{2}CBLRF.
209 And] CrG; And to WHmYOC^{2}CBLMRF. helpen] helpe YOC^{2}CBF. hem(1)] *om* G. after þat] ay as WHmCrGYOC^{2}CBLMRF. nedeþ] nedyd Hm.
210 Now] And now WHmCrGYOC^{2}CBLMRF. wite] wyten HmGLMR. if... wistest] of þee WHmCrYOC^{2}CBLMRF; *om* G. what] where G.
211 And] *om* F. amaistren] amastrie OC^{2}F; mastren Cr; maistrie YGCB. make] maken RF. to] *om* Cr.
212 Here] I here R; Now here F; Aeare Cr^1. now] me now B; wel me F. a] *om* Cr.
213 Bolde] þat bolde F. mowe] for F. biswynke] byswynken CotR; swinke CrM; mowe swynke F.
215 And abaue] & abate F; Abate WCrGYOC^{2}CBLMR; abayte Hm. hem] *om* G. bollynge] bowing Cr^{12}. wombe] CrGYOC^{2}CBLMR; wombes WF; herte Hm.
216 þe gomes] her gommes Cr^{12}; þe gromes M; they YOC^{2}CB. þe] þo F. bidde] thanne bidde YCr^{3}OC^{2}CB; bind Cr^{12}. hem] him Cr^2. go] to Cr^{12}C^2. and] RF; *om* WHmCrGYOC^{2}CBLM.
217 *line om* RF. it haþ] hath it Cr^{23}; hathe G. deserued] deserued ytt G; desedeserued Bo.
218 Ac] R; And WHmCrGYOC^{2}CBLMF. Fortune] falshed R; False F. apeired] asayȝed F.
219 *line om* CB. Wiþ...wiþ] Or any manere WHmCrGYOC^{2}LMRF. false] of false F; falty Cr^3; fawti OC^2; febul Hm. men] man Cr^{3}OC^2. swiche] þow swiche WHmCrGYOC^{2}LMRF. knowe] knowen Y.
220 *line om* CB. Conforte...catel] *with* þy catel knowe þou hem F. hem] Cr^{23}GYOC^{2}MR; hym WHmCr^{1}L. of] in F.
221 Loue] Hire B. hem(*both*)] hym CB. lene] leue Cr^{12}. and(2)...wolde] for so þe law of god techeth Y; for so þe lawe techiþ OCr^{3}C^{2}CB; so the law of God teacheth Cr^{12}G; so lawe of god techeþ WHmLMR; for godd*es* lawe so techiþ F.
221α *portate*] *portate &c* HmGOC^{2}B.
222 alle] alle oþere F. of] *om* BR. þat] *om* OC^{2}C. myȝt] myȝtist OC^2. aspie] aspien M.
223 or...spende] and nouȝty help hem wiþ þi goodes WHmCrGYOC^{2}CBLMRF (nouȝty] noȝt ha*n* B (ha*n* *over erasure another ink* Bm); noght G. wiþ] of Cr^3).

Wiþ mete or wiþ mone lat make hem fare þe bettre].
Loue hem and lakke hem noȝt; lat god take þe vengeaunce;
Theiȝ þei doon yuele lat [þow] god yworþe:
Michi vindictam ⁊ ego retribuam.
And if þow wilt be g*ra*cious to god do as þe gospel techeþ
And biloue þee amonges [lowe] men: so shaltow lacche g*ra*ce.'
Facite vo[bis] amicos de mammona iniquitatis.
'I wolde noȝt greue god', quod Piers, 'for al þe good on
    grounde!
Miȝte I synnelees do as þow seist?' seide Piers þanne.
'Ye I [h]ote þee', quod hunger, 'or ellis þe bible lieþ.
Go to Genesis þe geaunt, engendrour of vs alle:
In sudore and swynk þow shalt þi mete tilie
And laboure for þi liflode, and so oure lord hiȝte.
And Sapience seiþ þe same—I seiȝ it in þe bible:
Piger [propter frigus] no feeld [w]olde tilie;
He shal [go] begge and bidde and no man bete his hunger.
Mathew wiþ mannes face mouþe[þ] þise wordes:

224 *not in* WHmCrGYOC^{2}CBLMRF.
225 hem(1)] *om* Cr. lat] and lat HmM; lest Cr. þe] *om* F.
226 Theiȝ] ⁊ if F. yuele] evil agey*n* þe F. þow] LR; *om* WHmCrGYOC^{2}CBMF. god] god wit*h* hem F. yworþe] aworthe LMR; worthe OC^{2}CF; worche GCrYB.
226α *retribuam*] *retribuam ⁊c* HmG; *distribuam* Cr.
227 And] Ac O; *om* Cr. wilt] wil L; *om* R. be...to] gete g*ra*ce of F. god do] go do Cr^{3}OC^2; do good Cr^{12}.
228 And] þou F; *om* G. biloue] bilow LMR; loowe F. amonges] to F. lowe] BCrYOC^{2}CLMRF; lewed WHmG. so] ⁊ so F.
228α *vobis*] HmCrGYOC^{2}CBLMRF; *vos* W. *mammona*] *mammone* Cr. *iniquitatis*] *iniquitatis ⁊c* HmG.
229 I] For I Y. wolde noȝt] nolde CrG. quod Piers] pers seyde G. on] in Cot.
230 I] I do M. do] *om* M. seide...þanne] so me god helpe F.
231 Ye] I G; *om* F. hote þee] ye hoote G; hoote to god F; bihote þee WHmCrYOC^{2}CLM; þe bihote B; behote god R. hunger] Hongry Cr^{12}. or] ȝis or F.
232 Go] God Cr^{12}. geaunt] Geau*nt* F; geaunt þe WHmCrGYOC^{2}CBLMR.
233 *In sudore*] In sudour Cot; In swete G; He seyþ in swoot F. and] ⁊ in HmCr^{3}GOC^{2}MRF (*over erasure another ink* Hm). mete] brede M; foode F. tilie] wynne F.
234 þi] our Cr^{12}. and] for Cr^3. lord] lord þe F. hiȝte] hygh Cr^{12}.
235 Sapience] sapiense book F. I...bible] soþly to telle F. seiȝ] se CB. it] *om* R. bible] byll Cr^{12}.
236 *Piger*] þat *Piger* F; Piget Bo; Pige R. *propter frigus*] *pro frigore* WHmGYOC^{2}CBLMRF; *pre frigore* Cr. feeld] fildis F. wolde] HmCrMRF (*over erasure another ink* M); nolde WGYOC^{2}CBL. tilie] tylye in wynter (in wynter *another ink*) Hm.
237 He...go] And þerfore he shal WHmCrGLMRF; ⁊ therfore shal he YOC^{2}CB. begge] beggy*n* F. and bidde] *altered to* in somer *another ink* Hm; *om* F. bidde] bide C^2; bilde Y; bygge G. bete] beetyn F; bate Cr.
238 Mathew] Seynt Matthew F. mouþeþ] moutheth RF; mouþed WHmCrGYOC^{2}BLM; mouthe C.

Seruus nequam hadde a Mnam and for he [n]olde [it vse]
He hadde maugree of his maister eueremoore after,
And bynam hym his Mnam for he [n]olde werche
And yaf [it hym in haste þat hadde ten bifore];
And [siþen] he seide—[hise seruaunt3] it herde—
"He þat haþ shal haue and helpe þere [nede is] |
And he þat no3t haþ shal no3t haue and no man hym
    helpe, *fol.* 39 *b*
And þat he weneþ wel to haue I wole it hym bireue".
Kynde wit wolde þat ech wi3t wro3te,
Or [wiþ tech]ynge or [tell]ynge or trauaillynge [of hondes],
Contemplatif lif or Actif lif; crist wolde [it als].
The Sauter seiþ, in þe psalme of *Beati omnes*,
The freke þat fedeþ hymself wiþ his feiþful labour
He is blessed by þe book in body and in soule:
Labores manuum tuarum &c.'

239 *Seruus*] That *seruus* WHmCrGYOC^{2}CBLMRF. Mnam] man BoCotRF; besaunt Cr^{12}G; *glossed* besaunt WHmLM. and...he] þat F. nolde] Cr; nolde nougth HmYOC^{2}CB; wolde no3t WGLMRF. it vse] chaffare WHmCrGYOC^{2}CBLMRF.
240 He hadde] & he F. euere] for euere OCr^{3}C^{2}LMRF; & euer Cr^{12}.
241 And] & he F. hym] *above line another ink* M; *om* L. Mnam] nam Mnam (*corrected*) Bm; beysant G. nolde] CotGM; ne wolde WHmCr^{3}YOC^{2}BmBoLR; wold not Cr^{12}F; wolde C.
242 it...bifore] him þat mnam þat ten mnames hadde M; þat Mnam to hym þat ten Mnames hadde WHmCrYOC^{2}CBL; þat nam til hym þat ten napmes hadde R; þat besant to hym þat ten besantes hadde G; it to anoþer man þat ten napmes hadde F.
243 siþen...seruaunt3] wiþ þat he seide þat holy chirche WHmCrGYOC^{2}CBLMR; with þat dede he sey3de þat all men F. herde] had Cr^{12}.
244 haþ] had G. and] to F. þere] hym at F. nede is] it nedeþ WHmCrGYOC^{2}CBLR; with þat nedeth M; his neede F.
245 þat] *om* CBm. no3t haþ] hath not CrGCB. shal no3t] shal nou3 Y; noght shall GHmF. and] ne Cr. no] *om* C^2.
246 weneþ] hopeþ F. wel] for RF. I wole] men shull F. it] *om* Hm. bireue] reue M; beren C^2.
247 Kynde wit] For kende F. wit wolde] wolde witt Bm. ech] euery F. wi3t] wyght F; wygth wel Hm; a wi3t WCrGYOC^{2}CBLMR.
248 Or] other G; *om* F. wiþ techynge] in dikynge WHmCr^{1}GYOC^{2}CBLMF; in dichyng R; in digging Cr^{23}. tellynge] deluyng YCB; in deluynge WHmCrGOC^{2}LMRF. or(2)] or yn Hm. trauaillynge] trauayle HmCrG; doynge F. of hondes] of prayers HmCr^{23}; in preieres WCr^{1}GYOC^{2}CBLMRF.
249 Contemplatif] Eiþer Contemplatif F. or...lif] *om* Hm. lif(2)] *om* OC^{2}CBF. wolde] coueytyd F. it als] þei wro3te WHmCrGCB; þei wrou3ten OC^2; we wroughte F; men wroughte YLMR.
250 þe] a RF; *om* Cr^{12}. psalme] psalms Cr. of] In F.
251 þat] *om* BoCot. his] *om* GC.
252 *transposed with* 252α C^2. He is] Be Cr^{12}. in(2)] *om* Cr^{12}.
252α *in margin* O. &c] *quoniam manducabis* Cr^3; *quia manducabis &c* M; *quia manducabis batus es &c* F; *om* Y.

'Yet I preie [þee]', quod Piers, '*p[u]r charite*, and [þow] konne
Any leef of lechecraft lere it me, my deere;
For some of my seruaunt3 and myself boþe
Of al a wike werche no3t, so oure wombe akeþ.'
'I woot wel', quod hunger, 'what siknesse yow eyleþ.
Ye han manged ouer muche; þat makeþ yow grone.
Ac I hote þee', quod hunger, 'as þow þyn hele wilnest,
That þow drynke no day er þow dyne somwhat.
Ete no3t, I hote þee, er hunger þee take
And sende þee of his Sauce to sauore þi lippes,
And keep som til soper tyme and sitte no3t to longe;
[A]rys vp er Appetit haue eten his fille.
Lat no3t sire Surfet sitten at þi borde;
L[o]ue hym no3t for he is [a] lech[our] and likerous of tunge,
And after many maner metes his mawe is [alonged].
And if þow diete þee þus I dar legge myne [armes]
That Phisik shal hi[s] furred ho[od] for his fode selle,
And his cloke of Calabre [and] þe knappes of golde,

253 Yet] ye Y. þee] þe F; yow WHmCrGYOC^{2}CBLMR. *pur*] HmCr^{3}OC^{2}BF; *par* WGYCLMR; praye Cr^{12}. and] yff G. þow] þou F; ye WHmCrYOC^{2}CBLMR; you G.
254 Any] Of ony F. leef] *om* Cr^{12}. of] *om* Cr. lere] lerne Hm. me] *om* Cot. my deere] dere M; y *pra*ye F.
255 boþe] ben seke otherwhile YOC^2.
256 Of] And of Y. a] þe OC^{2}F. werche] worchen OC^{2}Cot. so] lord so Hm. wombe] s *added over erasure another ink* M.
257 I] A y F. yow] ye Cr^2; the Cr^3.
258 manged] yeyten G. ouer] to YOC^{2}CB. þat] B; and þat WHmCrGYOC^{2}CLMRF. grone] to grone YOC^{2}CB.
259 Ac] but GF; And CrYOC^{2}CB. hote] bihote Y. as] if F. þyn] *om* Cot. wilnest] willest Y; disyryst F.
260 þow] þow ne M. er...dyne] til þow haue dined M. somwhat] a mussel F.
261 Ete] Ne ete F. þee] *om* R. take] taketh Cr^3.
262 sende] bry*n*ge F. þi] þy MF; wiþ þi WCrGYOC^{2}CBLR; wyth 3oure Hm.
263 til] to YOC^{2}R; for CB. tyme] *om* MF. and] but F. no3t to] þou nowht F.
264 Arys] Arise LMR; And rys WHmCrGYOC^{2}CBmBo; And aryse Cot; But aryse F. haue] hathe G. eten] Iete R; loost F. his fille] al his strengþe F.
265 Lat] But lete F. sitten] syt Cr. at] on Cr^{12}. borde] table F.
266 Loue] MCot; Leue WHmCrGYOC^{2}CBmBoLRF. no3t] *om* F. for] *om* G. a lechour] lecherours Cr^1; lecherous WHmCr^{23}GYOC^{2}CotLMRF (leche *over erasure main hand* Cot); likerous CBmBo. likerous] lecherous CBmBo. of] of his YOC^{2}CB.
267 maner] maners CM; *om* F. metes his] of metys is Hm; of mete his MCr. alonged] alustyd F; afyngred WHmYOCBLMR; afygred C^2; ahu*n*gred CrG.
268 þee] *om* CCot. armes] eris WHmCrGYOC^{2}CBLMRF.
269 his...hood] OCrC^{2}BF; hise furred hodes WHmGYCLMR. for his] 3ee F. fode] lyflode Cot.
270 cloke] Clokes M. and] w*ith* F; wiþ alle WHmCrGYOC^{2}CBLMR. þe] his Cr^{12}G; *om* RF. gold] gold *þ*erone F.

And be fayn, by my feiþ, his Phisik to lete,
And lerne to laboure wiþ lond [lest] liflode [hym faille].
[Ther are mo lieres þan] leches; lord hem amende!
They do men deye þoruȝ hir drynkes er destynee it wolde.' |
'By Seint [Pernele]', quod Piers, 'þise arn *pro*fitable
    wordes! *fol.* 40 *a*
|[[Th]is is a louely lesson; lord it þee foryelde.
Wend now whan [þi wil is], þ*at* wel be þow eu*er*e.'|
'[I] bihote god', quod hunger, 'hennes [nil] I wende
[Er] I haue dyned bi þis day and ydronke boþe.'
'I haue no peny', quod Piers, 'pulettes to bugge,
Neiþer gees ne grys, but two grene cheses,
A fewe cruddes and creme and [a cake of otes],
[A lof] of benes and bran ybake for my fauntes.
And yet I seye, by my soule! I haue no salt bacon
Ne no cokeney, by crist! coloppes to maken.

271 his] *om* G. lete] leetyn F; leyue G; sulle Hm.
272 lerne] lere YOC^{2}C; to lere B. wiþ] on þe F. lond] hond Cr. lest...faille] for liflode is swete WHmCrGYOC^{2}CBLMRF.
273 Ther...þan] þer aren mo morareres þan R; Now are mo moraynerys þ*an* F; For m*ur*þereris are manye WHmCrGYOC^{2}CLM; For many lechys ben B. leches] morþereris BoCot; mortheries Bm. lord] our lord GF.
274 do] maken BmBo; mak Cot. deye] deien M; to dye GB. þoruȝ] wyþ Hm; by Cr. drynkes] drynkyngis BmBo. er] yer Cr; er here B. destynee] his tyme C^2. it] *om* GYOC^{2}CB.
275 Pernele] Poul WHmCrGYOC^{2}CBLMR; Pet*er* apostle F. Piers] Perkyn CB.
276 *transposed with* 277 WHmCrGYOC^{2}CBLMRF. This] For þis WHmCrGYOC^{2}CBLMRF. lord] the lord Cr^{23}; oure lord F. it] *om* YCB. þee] *om* Cr^2.
277 now] þou Cr^{12}. whan...is] hunger whan þow wolt WHmCrGYOC^{2}CBLMRF. þat] ⁊ F; *om* G. be] yow R; *om* F. þow] þe HmOC^{2}BmBoF; yow R. eu*er*e] betyȝde F.
278 I] GBF; *om* WHmCrYOC^{2}CLMR. bihote] hoote GF. god] the Cot. hunger] hongery Cr^2. nil I] ne wole I WHmCrLMR; ne wold I G; wol I nat YOC^{2}CBF.
279 Er] Til WHmCrGYOC^{2}CBLMRF. dyned bi] dyghne F. ydronke] y drynke G; dronken Cr; þ*er*to dru*n*ke F.
280 I] Peter y F. pulettes] peyȝneme*ns* F. to] for to CrYOC^{2}CBLR; þe to F.
281 *line om* CB. Neiþer] Nether Y; noþer Hm; Ne neiþer WCrGOC^{2}LMRF. gees] goos YCrOC^2; gryȝs F. grys] gryses G; gees F. but] but y have F.
282 A] ⁊ a F. and(2)] ⁊ þ*er*to F; *om* C^2. a...otes] an hauer cake WHmCrGYOC^{2}CBLMRF.
283 A lof] And two loues WHmCrGYOC^{2}CBLMRF. benes...bran] beene breed F. and] and of B. ybake] ybaken OC^2; bake CrG; y bok yt F; I take CB. fauntes] barnys F; folke Cr; fayntyse Cot.
284 yet] *om* M. seye] swere F.
285 no...crist] be *cr*ist no kokeney F. cokeney] kokeneys Hm. to] OC^2; for to WCrGYCBLMR; of to Hm; the to F. maken] make CrGYOC^{2}CBRF.

Ac I haue p*er*cile and pore[t] and manye [plaunte coles],
And ek a cow and a calf, and a cart mare
To drawe afeld my donge while þe droȝte lasteþ.
By þis liflode [I moot] lyue til lammesse tyme,
By þat I hope to haue heruest in my crofte;
[Th]anne may I diȝte þi dyner as [þee] deere likeþ.'
Al þe pou*er*e peple pescoddes fetten;
Benes and baken apples þei broȝte in hir lappes,
Chibolles and Cheruelles and ripe chiries manye;
And p*ro*frede Piers þis p*re*sent to plese wiþ hunger.
[Hunger eet þis] in haste and axed after moore.
Thanne pou*er*e folk for fere fedden hunger yerne
Grene poret and pesen; to [peisen] hym þei þoȝte.
By þat it neȝed neer heruest newe corn cam to chepyng.
Thanne was folk fayn and fedde hunger wiþ þe beste;

286 Ac] but GF; And CrC^{2}C. p*er*cile] perceley CrC^{2}B. poret] porete BR; porettes WHmCrGYOC^{2}CLMF. manye] fele F. plaunte coles] cole plauntes WHm CrGYOC^{2}CBLM; queynte herbes R; p*ro*pre herbys F.
287 ek] *om* G. and(2)] & eek F.
288 afeld my donge] dunk on felde F. while] whyle GBF; þe while WHmCrY OC^{2}CLMR. þe] *om* C. droȝte lasteþ] weder is drye YOC^{2}CB.
289 By] And by WHmCrGYOC^{2}CBLM RF. I moot] I must CrF; we mote WHm YCBLR; we moste G; we moten OC^{2}M. lyue] leue*n* C^2. til] to Cr^{23}YC. lammesse] herueste YOC^{2}CB. tyme] tyme come YOC^2.
290 By...hope] For y hope by þat F. By] Cr; And by WHmGYOC^{2}CBLMR. to] *om* G.
291 Thanne] And þanne WHmCrGYO C^{2}CBLMRF. may I] I may Cr. þi] þe C; my Cr^{12}. þee] þe F; me WHmCr^{3}YO C^{2}CBLMR; my Cr^{12}G. likeþ] lykete Bm; lykede BoCot.
292 Al] And al CrF. þe] þo Bm. peple] peple þo WHmCrYOC^{2}CBLMRF; poeple then G. fetten] fette HmCr^{12}Y; to fette B; fecchen GC^2; feccheden F.
293 *run together with* 294 CB. Benes] & beenys F. and...lappes] *om* CB. baken] bake F. broȝte] broughten YHmOC^{2}MR. lappes] lappe R.
294 Cheruelles] Cheruell *over erasure* M; chernell Cr; chirne mylk F. ripe...manye] many oþer herbes CB.
295 And p*ro*frede] & p*ro*feredy*n* F; To make YOC^{2}CB. þis] þ*a*t F; the Cr^{23}; a YOC^{2}CB. wiþ] wyth hys Cr^{3}OC^{2}CBm Bo.
296 Hunger...þis] Al hunger eet WHmCr GYOC^{2}LMR; & all þo hu*n*gir eet F; An hunger ete C; Ac hung*ur* ete B. axed] askiþ BmBo.
297 fedden] fedde CrGYCLMR. yerne] faste F.
298 Grene poret] Wiþ grene poret WHm CrGLMR; With grene poretts YOC^{2}C BF. and] and wiþ B. to peisen] to poisone WHmCrGYOC^{2}LMRF; *om* CB. hym] *over erasure* G; hunger YOC^{2}CBL MR. þoȝte] þouȝten OC^{2}F; souȝte Bo Cot; seuȝte Bm.
299 By] But by F; But Cr^2. it neȝed] neyȝhede it OC^2. it] *om* YC. neer] ney G; to Cr; *om* YOC^{2}CB. newe] HmCr GYOC^{2}LMR; & newe WF; and B; *om* C. cam to chepyng] ap*er*ede F.
300 *line om* B. Thanne was] & þ*er*of were F. fedde] fedden RHm. hunger wiþ] hem wit*h* F; hem of OC^{2}C.

Wiþ good Ale as Gloton taȝte [þei] garte [hym to] slepe.
And þo [n]olde Wastour noȝt werche, but wandre[d] aboute, |
Ne no beggere ete breed þat benes Inne [come], *fol.* 40 *b*
But Coket [or] clermatyn or of clene whete,
Ne noon halfpeny ale in none wise drynke,
But of þe beste and þe brunneste þat [brewesteres] selle.
Laborers þat haue no land to lyue on but hire handes
Deyne[þ] noȝt to dyne a day nyȝt olde wortes.
May no peny ale hem paie, ne no pece of bacou*n*,
But if it be fressh flessh ouþ*er* fissh [y]fryed,
And þat *chaud* and *plus chaud* for chillynge of hir mawe.
But he be heiȝliche hyred ellis wole he chide;
[That] he was werkman wroȝt [warie] þe tyme.
Ayeins Catons counseil comseþ he to Iangle:

301 *line om* CB. Wiþ] ⁊ wit*h* F. þei garte] and garte WHmCrGYOC^{2}LMR; þa*n* ga*n* F. hym] he F; hunger WHmCrGYOC^{2}LMR. to] HmCr^{3}GC^{2}; goo to F; a Cr^{12}; go WYOLMR.
302 And] But F; *om* G. þo] þo ne R; þa*n* F. nolde] wolde no RF; wolde WHmCrGYOC^{2}CLM; þey wolden B. Wastour] *om* CB. noȝt] no Cr; *om* RF. wandred] HmYOC^{2}CB; wandredid F; wandren WCrLMR; wandre G.
303 ete] eten M; eete no F. come] were WHmCrGYCBLMR; weren OC^{2}F.
304 *run together with* 306 CB. But] But of WHmCrGYOC^{2}CBLMRF. or(1)] HmOC^{2}LMF; or of R; and WCrGY; *om* CB. clermatyn] cleremeyne G; *om* CB. or(2)] CB; or ellis WHmCrGYOC^{2}LMRF. of] *om* C.
305 *line om* CB. Ne] And Y. noon] no man F.
306 But] and drynk CB. of] *om* G. þe(1)] *om* Cr^{23}. and...selle] ale CB. þe(2)] the GYOC^{2}M; of þe WHmCrLR; *om* F. þat] *om* F. brewesteres] in borewe is to R; in Burgh is to WCr^{3}OC^{2}LM; in burth is to Cr^{12}; yn the burgh is to Hm; yn brughe ys to G; in brugge is to Y; in borghȝ was to F.
307–9 *lines om* CB.
307 Laborers] ⁊ laboreris F. haue] hadde OC^{2}. to] but YOC^{2}F. lyue] lyuen HmMF. on but] with YOC^{2}F. hire] *om* Y.
308 *run together with* 309 YOC^{2}. Deyneþ ...day] wolde ete no Y; Wolden ete no OC^{2}. Deyneþ] deynen Hm; þey endeyȝhne F; Deyned WCrGLMR. noȝt] *om* Cr^{23}RF. a day] or suppe F; *om* M. nyȝt] wyth nyght Cr^{3}; *om* F.
309 May] Ne F; ne drynk no YOC^{2}. hem...bacou*n*] *om* YOC^{2}. hem] him Cr^{2}. ne] nor Cr^{1}; *om* G.
310 *run together with* 311 RF. if it be] it be MF; *om* YOC^{2}CB. fressh] hoot F. ouþer] or GM; ⁊ F. fissh] freshȝ F. yfryed] fryed ouþ*er* ybake WBo; fryed othur bake HmCr^{3}YCBmL; fryed oþ*er* baken O; Fried oþ*er* bakon C^{2}; fryed or bake GCot; fried ether or bake Cr^{12}; rosted or baken (*over erasure another ink*) M; *om* RF.
311 And...*chaud*(2)] *om* RF. *chaud*(1)] claude G. and] or CrYOC^{2}CBLM. chillynge] flasshy*n*g F. of] or Bm. hir] his R. mawe] mawes Hm.
312 But] But if Cr^{12}; and but HmYOC^{2}CBmMF; And but if WCr^{3}GBoCotLR. heiȝliche] hye OC^{2}. hyred] yhired Cot M.
313 *line om* YOC^{2}CB. That] And þat WHmCrGLMRF. was...wroȝt] cam swich werk to wirke he will F. wroȝt] ywrouȝt M. warie] waille WHmCrGLRF; waileþ he (eþ *over erasure another ink*) M. tyme] while M.
314 Catons] caton C.

Paupertatis onus pacienter ferre memento;
He greueþ hym ageyn god and grucccheþ ageyn Reson,
And þanne corseþ þe kyng and al [þe] counseil after
Swiche lawes to loke laborers to [chaste].
Ac whiles hunger was hir maister þ*er* wolde noon chide
Ne stryuen ayeins [þe] statut, so sterneliche he loked.
Ac I warne yow werkmen, wynneþ whil ye mowe
For hunger hiderward hasteþ hym faste.
He shal awake [þoruȝ] water wastours to chaste;
Er fyue [yer] be fulfilled swich famyn shal aryse.
Thoruȝ flo[od] and foule wedres fruytes shul faille,
And so sei[þ] Saturne and sente yow to warne.
Whan ye se þe [mone] amys and two monkes heddes,
And a mayde haue þe maistrie, and multiplie by eiȝte,
Thanne shal deeþ wiþdrawe and derþe be Iustice,
And Dawe þe dyker*e* deye for hunger
But [if] god of his goodnesse graunte vs a trewe. |

315 *copied after* 320 *but the correct order noted* Y. *memento*] *memento &c* Hm.
316 hym ageyn] grevously F. hym] *om* Cot. ageyn(*both*)] aȝeyn OHmYC^{2}CBLMR. and] for he F. grucccheþ] grucchede BoBm.
317 And] *om* R. þanne] þus F; *om* HmGYOC^{2}CB. corseþ] corseþ he WCrLMR; he curseth YOC^{2}CCotF; he cursed BmBo; curseth also (also *over erasure*) Hm; causethe he G. and] *om* G. al] *om* Hm. þe(2)] his WHmCrGYOC^{2}CBLMRF.
318 lawes] lawe C^2. chaste] greue WHmCrGYOC^{2}CBLMRF.
319 Ac] but GF; And YOC^{2}CB; *om* Cr. was...þer] gafe hem hier Cr. þer...noon] þa*n*ne wolde none F; þ*er* wolde noon of hem WHmLMR; non off þem wold G; not one of he*m* wold Cr; wolde they nat YC^{2}CB; wolden þei not O.
320 stryuen] stryue HmGYOC^{2}CBLMF; strue R. þe] BoCotF; *altered to* þis G; þo Bm; his WHmCrYOC^{2}CLMR. sterneliche] sterliche C^2. he] hu*n*ger F.
321 Ac] but GF; And CrC^{2}C. werk] yerk Y. wynneþ] wynne GCr; wurche M.
322 hiderward] hyȝeþ hidirward & F; hideward L. hasteþ] hyeth Hm. faste] ful faste RF; selfe Cr.
323 He shal] & he will F. þoruȝ] wiþ WHmCrGYOC^{2}CBLMR; su*m* F. water] wat R; what F. to chaste] to chastise OC^{2}BoCot; to chastiche Bm; dede F.
324 fyue] fewe B (ewe *over erasure* Bm). yer] ȝere HmCr^{3}YOC^{2}BRF (? *another hand* Y); *om* WCr^{12}GCLM. swich] *om* CB. aryse] rise M.
325 flood] flod R; flodes WHmCrGYOC^{2}CBLM; fowle wederys F. and] CrGYOC^{2}CBMRF; and þoruȝ WHmL. foule] foulis Bm; foolis BoCot; floodis F. wedres] weder Cr; werdis OC^{2}Bm; wordis BoCot; þat F. fruytes] fruite Cr; Fructus C^2. shul] shullen BoCotR; shelen Bm. faille] falle M.
326 þa*n*ne shal satu*r*ne sende to ȝow swich warny*ngger* serteyn F. seiþ] seide WHmCrGYOC^{2}CBLMR. and] þat G. sente] sent CrLR; sende B.
327 Whan] And whe*n* Cr. ye...mone] þe su*n*ne ȝee seen F. mone] sonne WHmCrGYOC^{2}CBLMR. and] wit*h* F.
328 *transposed with* 329 B. haue þe] þorghȝ F. and] be F. multiplie] multiplied LMRF (d *another ink* M). by] on F. eiȝte] heyght GF; hight Cr^{23}.
329 wiþdrawe] drawe to deyȝs F. be] by Bo; bye Cr^{12}.
330 And] & þa*n*ne F. Dawe] Dauie Cr^3. deye] shal die BCr; deye schal Hm.
331 But] nd R. if] CrHmGYOC^{2}CBLMR; *om* WF.

VII

TReuþe herde telle herof, and to Piers sente *fol.* 41 *a*
To [t]aken his teme and tilien þe erþe,
And p*ur*chaced hym a pardou*n* *a pena* ⁊ *a culpa*
For hym and for hise heires eueremoore after.
And bad hym holde hym at home and erien hise leyes,
And alle þat holpen to erye or to sowe,
Or any [maner] mestier þat my3te Piers [helpe],
Pardon wiþ Piers Plowman truþe haþ ygraunted.
Kynges and kny3tes þat kepen holy chirche
And ri3tfully in Rem[e] rulen þe peple
Han pardon þoru3 purgatorie to passen ful li3tly,
Wiþ Patriarkes and p*ro*phetes in paradis to be felawe.
Bysshopes yblessed, if þei ben as þei sholde
Legistres of boþe lawes þe lewed *þer*wiþ to p*re*che,

1 TReuþe] þa*n*ne Trewþe F. her] er F. sente] HmCrGOC^2; he sente WYCLMRF; he wente B.
2 To] ⁊ bad hy*m* F. taken] Cr^{3}HmYOC^{2}CBLMR; take F; maken WG; make Cr^{12}. and] ⁊ goo F. tilien] tylye GCr^{12}OC^{2}F. þe] his HmG. erþe] grownde F.
3 And] he G. p*ur*chaced] purchase C^2. hym] *om* CrM. *a*(2)] *om* Cr^{12}.
4 for] *om* G. euere] euer Hm; for euere WCrGYOC^{2}CBLMRF.
5 holde] holden RHm; to holde F. erien erye CrF.
6 holpen] holpe RYCLMF; helpen G; helpe Cr. to(1)] hym to WHmCrYOC^{2}CBLMRF; theym to *above line same hand* G. erye] erien YM. or] to sette or WHmGOC^{2}CBL; to setten or MR; to sette and Cr; or sette or Y; or to setty*n* or F. to(2)] *om* CCotMF. sowe] sowen M.
7 maner] ooþ*er* WHmCrGYOC^{2}CBLMRF. mestier] mistery Cr; mynysterye BoCot; master G. helpe] auaille WHmCrGYOC^{2}CBLRF; auaillen M.
8 Pardon] he haþ p*ar*dou*n* F. Plowman] þe plowman RB; *om* F. haþ] hath hem Hm; haþ it F. ygraunted] graunted CrHmGBmBoF.
9 Kynges] Boþe kynges F; Knyghtes Cr. kny3tes] kynges Cr. þat] þa Bo; thei Cot. chirche] cherches R.
10 And] þ*at* F. Reme] þe rewhme F; Remes WHmCrGYOC^{2}CBLMR. rulen] weel rewle F.
11 Han] Hath M; And R. þoru3] in M. passen] passe CrOC^{2}LRF. ful] þorh3 F. li3tly] lighte YOC^{2}CB.
12 Wiþ] ⁊ wi*th* F. and p*ro*phetes] *om* F. be] ben her*e* F. felawe] felawes LGMRF.
13 Bysshopes] ⁊ blessede F. yblessed] blessed Cr^{12}; Bisshopis F. if þei] þ*at* F. sholde] shulden YOC^{2}CLMR; mowe ame*n*de B.
14 Legistres] ⁊ legistris F. lawes] the lawes GYOC^{2}CLM. þe...wiþ] þerwi*th* þe lewide F. lewed] lewde men G.

And in as muche as þei mowe amenden alle synfulle,
Arn peres wiþ þe Apostles—þ[u]s pardon Piers sheweþ—
At þe day of dome at [hire] deys [to] sitte.
Marchaunt3 in þe margyne hadde manye yeres,
Ac noon *A pena & a culpa* þe pope [w]olde hem graunte
For þei holde no3t hir halidayes as holy chirche techeþ,
And for þei swere by hir soule and so god moste hem helpe
Ayein clene Conscience hir catel to selle.
Ac vnder his secret seel truþe sente hem a lettre,
[And bad hem] buggen boldely [what] hem best liked
And siþenes selle it ayein and saue þe wynnyng,
And [make] Mesondieux þ*er*[wiþ] myseise [to] helpe,
Wikkede weyes wightly amende
And [bynde] brugges [aboute] þat tobroke were,
Marien maydenes or maken hem Nonnes,

15 *line om* F. And] *om* OC^{2}. in] *om* Hm. muche] mechel Bm. amenden] amende HmCrOC^{2}CBLM.
16 Arn] þey are F. þe] *om* MF. Apostles] postell*es* G. þus] LMRF; þis WHmGYO C^{2}CB; such Cr. sheweþ] chewiþ Bm; *gr*aunteþ F.
17 At] And at WHmCrGYOC^{2}CBLM RF. at] MR; at þe WHmCrGYOC^{2}C BL; on F. hire] hi3e HmCrCCot; hye GOC^{2}; hie3e Bm; heie R; hei3e WYBo LMF. deys] dayes R. to] HmCrGYOC^{2} CBmBoLMRF; *om* WCot. sitte] sitten M.
18 Marchaunt3] þan Marchawntis F. hadde] hadden OHmC^{2}LM.
19 Ac] but GF; And CrC^{2}C. noon *A*] no RF. *a*] *om* CrO. wolde] GBR; wyll CrF; nolde WHmYOC^{2}CLM. hem] hem nau3t R; not F; *om* G.
20 holde] holden OHmC^{2}BoCotMF; held C; helden Bm. no3t hir] no*n* F. dayes] day RF; dy M. techeþ] telleth R.
21 swere] sweren OC^{2}F; sware G. by... and] ofte R; oftyn F. so] so grete F; als M; by G. moste] mote HmB; *om* GMRF. hem] hym G; me Cot. helpe] selue G.
22 hir] he F. catel] chaffare B.
23 Ac] but G; And CrYC^{2}CB; But trewþe F. his] her OC^{2}. truþe] he F. sente] send G. hem] him Cr^{2}.
24 And...hem(1)] That þei sholde WHm CrGYC^{2}CBLRF; þ*at* þei schulden OM. buggen] bugge HmCrGYOC^{2}CBLMR. what] B; þat WHmCrGYOC^{2}CLMRF. best liked] best liketh RF; likede best OC^{2}.
25 siþenes] sytthe to F. selle it] sellen it MF; sellen it vs R; it sulle Hm. saue] sauen RF. wynnyng] wynny*n*ges RF; wynnyge L.
26 And] *om* G. make] amende WHmCr GYOC^{2}CBLMF; amenden R. Mesondieux] mys endwayes G; meselis F. þer] her Cr^{12}. wiþ] wyth & GCBRF; myd and WHmYOC^{2}LM; mede & Cr. myseise] *followed by erasure* Hm; myseysed YCotM; mesylye G. to] folk WHmCr GYOC^{2}CBLMRF. helpe] also F.
27 *line om* CB. Wikkede] And wikkede WHmCrGYOC^{2}LMR; & also wykkede F. weyes] deyes Y. amende] hem amende HmYOC^{2}LMRF.
28 And] And to M; bynde...aboute] do boote to brugges WHmCrGYOC^{2}CBL MRF (to] do C; *om* G). tobroke] tobroken GHmOC^{2}CBM; broke abowte F. were] weren OC^{2}M.
29 Marien] & also marie F. maken] make C; to make B; helpe F. hem] he*m* make F.

Pouere peple [bedredene] and prisons [in stokkes]
Fynden [swiche] hir foode [for oure lordes loue of heuene], |
Sette Scolers to scole or to som [kynnes] craftes, *fol.* 41 *b*
Releue Religion and renten hem bettre.
'And I shal sende myselue Seint Michel myn [a]ngel
That no deuel shal yow dere ne [in youre deying fere yow],
And witen yow fro wanhope, if ye wol þus werche,
And sende youre soules in saufte to my Seintes in Ioye.'
Thanne were Marchaunt3 murie; manye wepten for ioye
And preiseden Piers þe Plowman þat purchaced þis bulle.
Men of lawe leest pardon hadde, [leue þow noon ooþer],
For þe Sauter saueþ hem no3t, swiche as take 3iftes,
And nameliche of Innocent3 þat noon yuel konneþ:
Super innocentem munera non accipies.
Pledours sholde peynen hem to plede for swiche and helpe;

30 *as one line with* 31 WHmCrGYOC^{2}CBLMRF. Pouere peple] & þe poore F. bedredene and] and WHmCrGYOC^{2}CBLMF; or R. prisons in stokkes] prisons WHmCr^{1}YOCBmLMR; prisoners Cr^{23}GC^{2}BoCotF.

31 Fynden] fynd GOC^{2}B. swiche] hem WHmCrGYOC^{2}CBLMRF. foode...heuene] foode WHmCrGLMRF; liflode YOC^{2}CB.

32 Sette] And sette WCrGYC^{2}CBLR; And setten OHmMF. or] or ell*es* to F; and M. to(2)] *om* M. som] *om* RF. kynnes] oþere WHmCrGYOC^{2}CBLRF; to o*þere* M.

33 Releue] Or to rewly*n* F. Religion] religious Y. and] or to F. renten] rente YGC^{2}M; reuten Cr^{1}. hem] hem yet M; hem þe F; hym HmCr^{1}. bettre] bette C.

34 sende] F; sende yow WHmCrGYOC^{2}CBLMR. myselue] seyd trewþe F; *om* Cr^{12}. myn] þe GF. angel] Aungel HmF; Archangel WCrGYOC^{2}CBLMR.

35 yow dere] derie yow M. in...yow] fere yow in you*re* deying WGLMRF; fere 3ow at 3owr dey3yng Hm; fere you in you*r* doynge YCrOC^{2}CB.

36 witen] wyte HmOC^{2}; whysshe F. ye] you G. wol] willen B. þus] this Cr^{3}.

37 sende] sente C. in(1)] into OC^{2}. saufte] safett G. to my] amo*n*g F.

38 were] weren OM; we*re* manye R; whe*re* þ*ere* manye F. murie] *om* RF. manye] and YOC^{2}M; þ*at* RF. wepten] wepte GCrCot.

39 preiseden] praysed CrGYC^{2}C. þe Plowman] ap*er*tly F. þe] *om* GM. þis] þe Cr.

40 *as two lines divided after* hadde RF. Men] But me*n* F. of] off þe G. leest...hadde] of p*ar*dou*n* þe leest p*ar*t þey haddyn F. leue...ooþer] þat pleteden for Mede WYOCBLM; pleteden for mede G; that pledyn for mede HmCr; þ*at* plesede*n* For mede C^{2}; þat pleteden for mede for þat craft is schrewed R; For þey for meede plety*n* moore þ*an* mychil for godd*es* helpe F.

41 For] Wherfore F. saueþ] savo*ure*þ F. take] take*n* CrHmYOC^{2}CBLMRF.

42 Innocent3] Innocens YC; Innocent Cr^{1}. yuel] YHmOC^{2}CBM; yuel ne WCrGLRF. konneþ] kan G; canneth Cr; know*ith* F.

42α *line om* RF. *munera*] munenera G. *accipies*] *accipies &c* Hm.

43 sholde] schulden O; shulle C^{2}Cot; shullen BmBo. peynen] peyne HmCrF; pynen B; pyne OC^{2}C. for] *om* G. and] in Cr; to G. helpe] helpe hem Hm; helth Cr.

Princes and p*re*lates sholde paie for hire t*ra*uaille:
A Regibus & principibus erit merces eorum.
Ac many a Iustice and Iurour wolde for Ioh*an* do moore
Than *pro dei pietate* [pleden at þe barre].
Ac he þat spendeþ his speche and spekeþ for þe pouere
That is Innocent and nedy and no man apeireþ,
Conforteþ hym in þat caas, [coueiteþ noȝt hise] ȝiftes,
[Ac] for oure lordes loue [lawe for hym sheweþ],
Shal no deuel at his deeþ day deren hym a myte
That he ne worþ saaf [sikerly]; þe Sauter bereþ witnesse:
Domine, quis habitabit in tabernaculo tuo.
Ac to bugge water ne wynd ne wit ne fir þe ferþe, |
Thise foure þe fader of heuene made to þis foold in
  co*m*mune; *fol. 42 a*
Thise ben truþes tresores trewe folk to helpe,
That neu*er*e shul wexe ne wanye wiþouten god hymselue.
Whan þei drawen on to [þe deþ] and Indulgences wolde haue,

44 Princes] & Pryncys F. sholde] schulden HmOB; shul C. paie] paien M.
44α &] *& a* Hm. *eorum*] *eorum &c* Hm.
45 Ac] but GF; And CrC^{2}C. a Iustice] Iustices YOC^{2}CB. and] & a G. Iurour] Iuroure*s* C^{2}BoCot; Iurrous Bm. wolde] wolden OC^{2}BmBo; wol M. Ioh*an*] Iakke F.
46 *pro*] *twice* BmBo; for Cr^{23}. pleden...barre] leue þow noon ooþer WHmYOC^{2}CBLMR; leue yow (? þow) no other CrG; beleve þou no*n* othir F.
47 Ac] but GF; And CrC^{2}C. spendeþ] speneth R.
48 apeireþ] can apeyȝre F.
49 Conforteþ] And conforteth RF; comforte G. in þat] in ony F; þat in B. coueiteþ...hise] wiþouten coueitise of WHmYOC^{2}CB (wiþ *twice* Bm); w*ith*out couetise of CrGLMR; w*ith*outy*n* coueytouse F.
50 Ac] And sheweþ lawe WHmYOC^{2}CB LMRF; and show lawe G; And spekith lawe Cr. lawe...sheweþ] as he it haþ ylerned WHmR; as he it hath lerned YGOC^{2}CBLM; as he haþ it leerned F; as he hath lernid Cr.
51 deeþ] deathes Cr; dede CGLR. deren] dere HmF; dearn Cr^3. a] worþ a F.
52 ne] no M; *om* F. sikerly] his soule C^2; and his soule WHmCrYOCBLMRF; *om* G. bereþ witnesse] wytnessythe G.
52α *tuo*] *tuo &c* HmGLMR; *tuo &cc* Y; *tuo &c ut supra* F.
53 Ac] but GF; And CrC^{2}C. to] no man sholde F. ne(1)] no R. wit...ferþe] fyȝr ne wit neyþ*er* F. þe] ne C^2.
54 Thise] For þese F. of] In G. made...co*m*mune] formede he*m* comou*n* on erthe F. þis] his HmYOC^{2}CB. foold] folk YG.
55 Thise] For þo F. truþes] trewest C. tresores] tresore C^2. helpe] helpyn F.
56 outen] oute BCrGLR; *om* OC^2. selue] seluen M.
57 þei] me*n* F. drawen] drawe HmYCBF. on to] vnto HmYOC^{2}CB; in to R; one to Cr^{12}; to GF. þe deþ] OYC^{2}BF; deth HmR; þe day C; deye WL; deiȝen M; die CrG. and] *om* C^2. Indulgences] indulge*n*ce Cr. wolde haue] wolden haue OC^{2}BmBo; wolden hauen M; dysire F.

Hi[s] pardon is [wel] petit at hi[s] partyng hennes
That any Mede of mene men for motyng takeþ.
Ye legistres and lawieres, [if I lye witeþ Mathew]:
Quodcumque vultis vt faciant vobis homines facite eis.
Alle libbynge laborers þat lyuen [by] hir hondes,
That treweliche taken and treweliche wynnen
And lyuen in loue and in lawe, for hir lowe hert[e]
Ha[dde] þe same absolucion þat sent was to Piers.
Beggeres [and] bidderes beþ noȝt in þe bulle
But if þe suggestion be sooþ þat shapeþ hem to begge,
For he þ*at* beggeþ or bit, but he haue nede,
He is fals wiþ þe feend and defraudeþ þe nedy,
And [ek g]ileþ þe gyuer*e* ageynes his wille.
For if he wiste he were noȝt nedy he wolde [it ȝyue]
Anoþ*er* that were moore nedy; so þe nedieste sholde be holpe.
Caton kenneþ me þus and þe clerc of stories.

58 His] YOC^{2}CBR; Hir WHmCrGLMF. pardon is] pardon*es* are G. wel] ful WHmCrGYOC^{2}CBLMRF. petit] pitit C^2. his] R; hir WHmCrGYOC^{2}CBLMF. partyng] dep*ar*ty*n*ge F. hennes] henne F; endis Cot.

59 That] For F. any] *om* R. mene] *om* Cot. for] for hir WHmCrGLMR; for his YOC^{2}CB; þ*at* for here F. takeþ] take Cr; toke F.

60 *as two lines divided after* truþe WHmCrGYOC^{2}CBLMRF. Ye] þe YCBmBoF. and] and ye R. if...Mathew] holdeþ þis for truþe That if þat I lye Mathew is to blame WHmCrGYOC^{2}CBLMRF (holdeþ] hold CrF; holden GOC^2. þis for] it a gret F. That] ⁊ F. þat] *om* CrBoCot. lye] lyȝe now sey*n*t F. is to] I B). *Hereafter an additional line* WHmCrGYOC^{2}CBLMR: For he bad me make yow þis and þis p*ro*uerbe me tolde (make] take OC^2; tel Cr; seyn M). *See above*, p. 193.

60α *vultis*] wltis R. *eis*] *eis ⁊c* HmM.

61 Alle libbynge] ⁊ also as F. lyuen] liuiden Cr^1. by] F; wiþ WHmCrGYOC^{2}CBLMR.

62 taken and] wirkyn as þey F.

63 lyuen] lyue Hm. for...lowe] w*ith* lowhe t*re*we F. herte] RF; hertes WHmCrGYOC^{2}CBLM.

64 Hadde] Haueþ WCrYLMR; haue HmG; þey have F; Has C; Han OC^2; Haþ B. þe] *om* F. sent] *om* F. Piers] Pers grau*n*tid F.

65 Beggeres] But beggeris F. and] MCr; ne WHmGYOC^{2}CBLRF. beþ] beth Hm; ben F; ne beþ WCrGYOC^{2}CBLMR. noȝt] nouȝ Y. bulle] bille YG.

66 sooþ] good G. shapeþ] shapma*n* F. hem] hym R. to] go G; *om* F. begge] bigge F.

67 or] one Cr. bit] biddeth Cot. but] but if WHmCrGYOC^{2}CBLMRF.

68 wiþ] as F.

69 ek gileþ] also begyliþ C^2; also he gyleth R; also he bigileþ WHmCrYOCBL; als he bigileþ M; begyleth GF. gyuer*e*] ȝyuer CotBo. ageynes] ayeins YHmOC^{2}CB. his] his goode F.

70 *divided from* 71 *after* anoþ*er* WHmCrGYOC^{2}CBLMRF. wiste he] *om* Cr. it ȝyue] it gyue YOC^{2}CB; gyue yt GF; ȝyue þatWHmLMR; giue þat to Cr.

71 nedy] nedyer RMF (ere *erased* M). so] þan he so WHmCrGYOC^{2}CBLM; þan he ⁊ so F; and nauȝtier so R. þe...be] þe nedyer*e* F. be] bi Bm. holpe] holpen CrOC^{2}M; helpe F.

72 me] men YCBLMRF. þus] þis M; so F. clerc] clere G; Myst*er* F. of] of þe LMRF.

Cui des videto is Catons techyng,
And in þe stories he techeþ to bistowe þyn almesse:
Sit elemosina tua in manu tua donec studes cui des.
Ac Gregory was a good man and bad vs gyuen alle
That askeþ for his loue þat vs al leneþ:
Non eligas cui miser[e]aris ne forte pretereas illum qui meretur accipere, |
Quia incertum est pro quo deo magis placeas. *fol.* 42 *b*
For wite ye neuere who is worþi, ac god woot who haþ nede.
In hym þat takeþ is þe trecherie if any treson walke,
For he þat yeueþ yeldeþ and yarkeþ hym to reste,
And he þat biddeþ borweþ and bryngeþ hymself in dette.
For beggeres borwen eueremo and hir borgh is god almyȝty
To yelden hem þat yeueþ hem and yet vsure moore:
Quare non dedisti pecuniam meam ad mensam vt ego veni[ens] cum vsuris ex[egissem illam]?
Forþi biddeþ noȝt, ye beggeres, but if ye haue nede;

73 *videto*] dideto Cr^{3}. is...techyng] *om* F. Catons] caton G.
74 And...bistowe] þe Mayster of stories techiþ the how þou shalt betake F. to] how to G. þyn] your Cr; þis C^{2}.
75 *Sit*] Siþ O. *tua*(1)] *om* LMRF. *tua*(2)] *om* G. *studes*] *studeas* GC^{2} (*a above line* C^{2}). *des*] *des* ⁊*c* Hm. *Hereafter a spurious line* F; *see above*, p. 222.
76 Ac] but GF; And CrC^{2}C. was a] is a R; þat F. and] he F. gyuen] ȝyuen OC^{2}. alle] to alle (to *above line another ink*) M.
77 his] oure lordes F. vs] leeneþ vs F. leneþ] leueth Cr^{12}; loueth Y; þynge F.
77α *Non*] *ne* G. *cui*] *twice* F. *miserearis*] CrGOC^{2}CotLMRF; miseriaris WHmYC BmBo. *pretereas*] preteras F; preterias GBmBo; pretereus Cr^{2}; preterearis Hm. *qui...accipere*] *om* F. *accipere*] *accipe* BoCot.
77β *deo*] *by correction* M; *deum* YOC^{2}CBm BoLRF. *placeas*] placias ⁊*c* Hm.
78 For] If F; *om* G. wite] wote HmG (e *erased* Hm); ye CrYOC^{2}CBF. ye] you G; wit Cr; wete F; woot YCB; woten OC^{2}. neuere] not CrF. ac] but GF; ⁊ CrC^{2}C. woot] knowth Cr^{1}. who... nede] the nedi Cr.
79 In...takeþ] For in þe takere F. In] Alle in R. þe] *om* RF. any] *om* C. walke] walkeþ F; wawe L.
80 he] *another ink* M; þe man F; *om* Cot. þat] *om* R. yeueþ] geueth CrGC; ȝift RF. yeldeþ and] ȝeviþ he F. hym to] his sowle F.
81 And] For B. he...biddeþ] þe takere F. biddeþ] bides C; bit R. and] yt ⁊ F. hymself] his sowle F.
82 For] Forthi RF. borwen] borwe FG. mo] *om* CrF. and] *om* G. borgh] brough YG; bowgh Cr^{1}.
83 yelden] ȝelde HmCr. yeueþ] geueth CrGC. and...moore] for here goode will F. moore] amore R.
83α *vt*] ⁊ Y. *ego*] ege O; *om* F. *veniens*] GYOC^{2}CBLMRF; *veniens meum* Cr^{23}; *veniam* WHm; *meum* Cr^{1}. *cum...illam*] *om* M. *exegissem*] Cot; ⁊ *exegissem* F; exigissem YCBmBo; ⁊ exigissem R; *exigerem* CrL; *exigere* WHmGOC^{2}. *illam*] *illam* ⁊*c* Cot; *vtique illam* F; ⁊*c* HmGOC^{2}CBmBo; *om* WCrYLR.
84 Forþi] Therfore Cr. biddeþ] bidde C^{2} Cr; beggiþ F. ye(1)] o ye Cr^{1}; as F. beggeres] neyȝbours Hm. if] *om* F. ye haue] it be Cr^{1}. nede] GYOC^{2}CBF; gret nede WHmCrLMR.

For whoso haþ to buggen hym breed, þe book bereþ witnesse,
He haþ ynouȝ þat haþ breed ynouȝ, þouȝ he haue noȝt ellis:
Satis diues est qui non indiget pane.
Lat vsage be your*e* solas of seintes lyues redyng.
The book banneþ beggerie and blameþ hem in þis manere:
Iunior fui etenim senui, & non vidi iustum derelictum ne[c] semen eius
[querens panem].
For [þei] lyue in no loue ne no lawe holde.
[Thei] wedde [no] wo*m*man þ*at* [þei] wiþ deele
But as wilde bestes *with* wehee worþen vppe and werchen,
And bryngen forþ barnes þ*at* bastardes men calleþ.
Or [his] bak or [his] boon [þei] brekeþ in his youþe
And goon [and] faiten *with* [hire] fauntes for eu*er*emoore after.
Ther is moore mysshapen amonges þise beggeres
Than of alle [oþere] manere men þat on þis moolde [wandreþ].

85 whoso] who þ*at* F; so C^2; he þ*at* Cr. haþ to] haþ *with* to F; may YOC^2CB; must nedis Cr^1. buggen] bugge $YCr^{23}OC^2CBRF$; bege*n* Cr^1. hym] *om* Cr^1.

86 haþ ynouȝ] *om* C^2. þat] *om* G. breed ynouȝ] but bred F; bred CrB. þouȝ] if C. haue] haþ F. noȝt] nouȝ Y; noþing G.

86α *non...pane*] *pane non indiget* F. *non*] *om* R. *indiget*] indeget M. *pane*] *pane &c* Hm.

87 be] by F. of] on M.

88 book] sawht*er* F. banneþ] blameþ MF. beggerie] beggers HmF. blameþ] banneth M; byddis F. hem] *om* $GYOC^2CBF$. in] on HmF.

89 *fui*] *fui &* F. *etenim*] *et iam* Cr^{23}. *vidi*] *om* F. *derelictum...panem*] *om* R. *nec... panem*] *&c* M. *nec*] $HmCrGYOC^2CBLF$; *ne* W. *querens panem*] CrYCF; *querens panem &c* $HmOC^2B$; *&c* WGL.

90 þei] begger*es* F; ye $WHmCrGYOC^2CBLMR$. lyue] lyuen $OHmC^2BM$. in] nouȝt in CB; nouȝ in Y. holde] holden YOC^2CB.

91 Thei] Many ma*n* F; Manye of yow $WHmCrGYOC^2CBLMR$. wedde] wed G; weddiþ F; ne wedde WHmYCBLMR; ne wedden OC^2; ye wed Cr. no] noȝt þe $WHmCrGYOC^2CBLMR$; nowht þ*at* F. wo*m*man] women $CrGC^2LMR$. þ*at*] *om* $GYOC^2C$. þei] he F; ye $WHmCrGYOC^2CBLMR$. wiþ] delen M. deele] delen $YHmOC^2CBLR$; delyþ F; with M.

92 as] as a F. bestes] beeste F; hors B. worþen] worth YCB; he worthiþ F; & worþ OC^2. werchen] werchiþ FB.

93 bryngen] bryng G; of hem come F. forþ] *om* F. þ*at* bastardes] bastardes that Hm. calleþ] callid BmBo.

94 Or] other G; & F. his(1)...þei] þe bak or þe bone þei R; here baak or su*m* boon þey F; þe bak or som boon he $WHmCrGYOC^2CLM$; þe bak or som bon ȝe B (ȝe *altered from* he Bm). brekeþ] breken R; breke CF. his(3)] hire CotRF; þe G. youþe] birthe F.

95 And] And siþþe WCrYCM; and syþþyn $HmGOC^2BR$; & so F; A sitthe L. and] þey F; *om* $WHmCrGYOC^2CBLMR$. hire] her OC^2RF; your*e* WHmCrGYCB LM. fauntes] seruaunts Cr^1. for] ful F; *om* G. euere] longe F. moore] *om* CrF.

96 Ther] For þere F. mysshapen] mys-schape HmGLRF; mishappe CrYC; myshappi B. amonges] peple amonges WOC^2MRF; peple amonge HmCrGY CBL. þise] a fewe F.

97 alle oþere] alle $WHmCrGYOC^2CBL MRF$. men] of men HmCrGF. þis] þe F. wandreþ] F; walkeþ $WCrGYOC^2CBL MR$; reignyn Hm.

[Tho] þat lyue þus hir lif mowe loþe þe tyme
That euere [he was man] wroȝt whan [he] shal hennes fare. |
Ac olde men and hore þat helplees ben of strengþe, *fol.* 43 *a*
And wo*m*men wiþ childe þat werche ne mowe,
Blynde and bedreden and broken hire membres
That taken þi[s] myschie[f] mekeliche as Mesels and oþ*ere*,
Han as pleyn pardon as þe Plowman hymselue;
For loue of hir lowe hert[e] oure lord haþ hem graunted
Hir penaunce and hir Purgatorie [vp]on þis [pure] erþe.
'Piers', quod a preest þoo, 'þi pardon moste I rede,
For I [shal] construe ech clause and kenne it þee on englissh.'
And Piers at his preiere þe pardon vnfoldeþ,
And I bihynde hem boþe biheld al þe bulle.
In two lynes it lay and noȝt a [lettre] moore,
And was writen riȝt þus in witnesse of truþe:
Et qui bona egerunt ibunt in vitam eternam;
Qui vero mala in ignem eternum.
'Peter!' quod þe preest þoo, 'I kan no pardon fynde
But do wel and haue wel, and god shal haue þi soule,

98 Tho] þo R; For þo F; And þei WHmCrGYOC^{2}CBLM. lyue] lyuen HmOC^{2}BMR; leede F. mowe] euere mowe þey F. loþe] lothen M. þe] theyre G.
99 That] þan C. he...man] GYOC^{2}CBLMR; was he man F; þei were men WHmCr. he(2)] Cr^{1}GYOC^{2}CBLMRF; þei WHmCr^{23}. fare] wende M; *om* C.
100 Ac] but GF; And CrC^{2}C.
101 wo*m*men] wo*m*man Bm. werche] werchen HmM.
102 *line om* F. bedreden] bedrede OHmGYC^{2}CBLMR. broken] broke Cr; broken in R.
103 & Meselis here myssese meekly it take F. þis myschief] LMR; þise myschiefs WHmYOC^{2}CB; the myscheues Cr^{13}; the mischenes Cr^2; meschefes G. mekeliche] *om* Hm.
104 Han] Haven F. as(1)] also B; a OC^{2}F. þe Plowman] pers haþ F. selue] seluen YHmOC^{2}CM.
105 herte] hertes WHmCrGYOC^{2}CBLMRF.
106 Hir] For here F. hir] *om* F. vpon...pure] here vpon þis R; here is open on F; here on þis WHmCrGYOC^{2}CBLM.
107 þoo] þen G.
108 For] & F; *om* G. shal] RF; wol WHmCrGYOC^{2}CBLM. ech] ech a Cr^{23}OC^{2}M; euery F. it þee] þi G. on] in CrG.
109 And] & sone F. þe] that Cr^1; his Cr^{23}MF. vnfoldeþ] he vnfoldeth R; vnfolded Cr^{23}F; vnffoldyn C^2.
110 I] y stood F. bihynde] behinden Cr. biheld] biholde YCBm; & behild F. þe] ouer þe F. bulle] bille YC (*corrected main hand* Y).
111 In] G; al yn HmCrYOC^{2}CBLMR; & al in F; And in W. lynes] leues BoCot. it] þe strengþe F. lettre] leef WHmCrGYOC^{2}CBLMRF.
112 writen] Iwriten R; ywryte F. in] *om* BF. witnesse] watinesse (*stained*) Bo.
113 *eternam*] *eternam &c* Hm.
114 *ignem*] ingnem G. *eternum*] *eternum &c* Hm; *eternam* CrBmBo.

And do yuel and haue yuel, [and] hope þow noon ooþer
[That] after þi deeþ day þe deuel shal haue þi soule.'
And Piers for pure tene pulled it [asonder]
And seide, '*Si ambulauero in medio vmbre mortis*
Non timebo mala quoniam tu mecum es.
I shal cessen of my sowyng', quod Piers, '⁊ swynke noȝt so harde,
Ne aboute my [bilyue] so bisy be na moore;
Of preieres and of penaunce my plouȝ shal ben herafter,
And wepen whan I sholde [werche] þouȝ whete breed me faille.
The prophete his payn eet in penaunce and in sorwe |
By þat þe Sauter [vs] seith, [and] so dide othere manye. *fol.* 43 *b*
That loueþ god lelly his liflode is ful esy:
Fuerunt michi lacrime mee panes die ac nocte.
And but if luc lye he lereþ vs [anoþer]
By foweles [þat are] noȝt bisy aboute þe [bely ioye];
Ne soliciti sitis he seiþ in þe gospel,

117–28 *over erasure another ink* Hm.
117 *line om* Cot. yuel (*both*)] yll Cr. and(2)] ⁊ F; *om* WHmCrGYOC^{2}CBmBo LMR. noon ooþer] after anothir F.
118 *line om* Cot. That] þat LMRF; But WHmCrGOC^{2}CBmBo; And Y. deeþ] deaths Cr; dede YGCL.
119 And] ⁊ anon F. it] þe bull F. asonder] atweyne WYOCBLMR; in twaine CrGF; atwynne HmC^2.
120 *Si*] þus *Si* F. *medio vmbre*] *umbra medio* G.
121 *mala*] *malum* Cr^{23}; *om* OC^2. *es*] *es domine* F; *es* ⁊*c* Hm.
122 shal] wil F. cessen] cesse MHmCrG C^{2}CotRF. of] now of F. quod Piers] *om* GF.
123 Ne] Ne be YOC^{2}CB. aboute] abouten BF. bilyue] bely ioye WHmCr GYOC^{2}CBLMRF. bisy be] bisily YOC^2 CB.
124 Of] But of F. of] *om* HmGYOC^{2}CB. penaunce] penaunces RF. her] *om* F.
125 wepen] wepe CrGOC^2. werche] slepe WCrGYOC^{2}CBLMRF; slepyn Hm. me] y F.
126 The] I fyȝnde þe F. his] *om* F. in(2)] *om* CrCot.
127 By] ⁊ after F. vs...and] seith WHm CrGYOC^{2}CBLMRF. dide] diden OHm C^{2}BF. othere manye] many other YO C^{2}CB.
128 That] he þat F. loueþ] louen HmCot. his] hire Cot. esy] redy F.
128α *nocte*] *nocte* ⁊*c* Hm.
129 *divided from* 130 *after* foweles WHmCr GYOC^{2}CBLMRF. And] *om* G. luc lye] seynt Luk lyȝeþ F. he] or RF; *om* Hm. lereþ] lerneþ FCr. vs anoþer] vs WHm CrGYOC^{2}CBLMRF.
130 By] be C^{2}RF. foweles] foles R; foolys F. þat are] We sholde WCrGYC^{2}LMRF; we schuldyn HmO; we shul CB. bisy] be busye Cr; be to bisy WHmGYOC^{2}CBL MRF. aboute] aboutyn HmF. þe] this Hm; *om* MF. bely ioye] worldes blisse WHmCrGOC^{2}CBLMRF; worldes Y.
131 he seyþ þus in his gospel *Ne solliciti scitis* F. *soliciti*] solicite Y. *sitis*] *scitis* Bo.

And sheweþ vs by ensampl[e] vs selue to wisse.
The foweles in þe [firmament], who fynt hem at wynter?
[Whan þe frost freseþ fode hem bihoueþ];
Haue þei no gerner to go to but god fynt hem alle.'
'What!' quod þe preest to Perkyn, 'Peter! as me þynkeþ
Thow art lettred a litel; who lerned þee on boke?'
'Abstynence þe Abbesse myn a b c me tauȝte,
And Conscience cam afte[r] and kenned me [bettre].'
'Were þow a preest, [Piers]', quod he, 'þow myȝtest p*re*che
    [whan þee liked]
As diuino*ur* in diuinite, wiþ *Dixit insipiens* to þi teme.'
'Lewed lorel!' quod Piers, 'litel lokestow on þe bible;
On Salomons sawes selden þow biholdest:
E[ji]ce derisores & iurgia cum eis ne crescant &c.'
The preest and Perkyn [a]pposeden eiþ*er* ooþ*er*,
And [þoruȝ hir wordes I wook] and waited aboute,

132 sheweþ...ensample] be swiche ensamplis he shewi*th* vs F. vs(1)] *om* Cr^{23}M. by] in Cr^{23}; *om* B. ensample] ensamples WHmGYOC^{2}CBLMR; examples Cr. vs(2)] our Cr^{23}OC^{2}BF. selue] seluen OCr^{23}GC^{2}MF. to] for to Hm. wisse] wissen F.
133 in] on LM; of R. firmament] feld WHmCrGYOC^{2}CBLMR; fylde F. fynt] findeth Cr^{31}GCF. hem] hem mete WHm CrGYOC^{2}CBLMRF. at] yn HmCrBF; & G. wynter] watre G.
134 *not in* WHmCrGYOC^{2}CBLMRF.
135 Haue þei] they haue GF. gerner] graner G. fynt] Fynde C^{2}; fyndeth GC; fedes Cr.
136 þe preest] prest þe C. Perkyn] Peers be F. þynkeþ] þynke C.
138 Abstynence] Mayster Abstynence F. þe Abbesse] *om* RF. myn] quod Piers myn WHmCrGYOC^{2}CBLMRF.
139 after] aftur M; afterward WHmCrG YOC^{2}CBLRF. kenned] teychyd G. bettre] better G; muche moore WHmCr YOC^{2}CBLMR; wil more F.
140 *at head of page main hand, but cropped* G. Were...he] Pers q*uod* he & þou were a preest F. Piers...he] coth he peris Cot. Piers] YHmOC^{2}CBmBoLMR; *om* WCr G. myȝtest] miȝte YHmCr^{23}CL. whan ...liked] wher*e* þou sholdest WHmYOC^{2} CBLM; wher þou shold Cr; where þow wold::: R; abowte F.
141 As] As a BF. diuino*ur*] Doctour F. in] of RGF. *Dixit*...teme] *om* F. *insipiens*] *incipiens* M. þi teme] the thyme Cot.
142 Lewed] A þou lewid F; Lew C. litel] þo ful litil B. lokestow] lokedest þou G. on] vpon B. þe] þi C^{2}CotR. bible] bille Y.
143 On] Vppon B; Or on OC^{2}; And on Y; And R; þere F. Salomons] salomon YC. sawes] sawis been F. selden] seld G; ful selde BF. þow] þou he*m* F.
143α *Ejice*] *Eice* OC^{2}BmCotMRF; *Ecce* WHmCrGYCBoL. *derisores*] *derisorem* F; *derisiones* Cr^{23}. *&...&c*] *& exibit cum eo iurgium cessabitque cause & contumelie* F; *om* R. *iurgia*] *iurga* C^{2}. *ne*] *non* Hm. *&c*] *om* CrGY.
144 The] & þus þe F. Perkyn] pers ech F. apposeden] LHmCotM; apposed CrG YOC^{2}RF; opposeden WBmBo; opposed C. eiþ*er*] *om* F.
145 And] That Y. þoruȝ...wook] þorgh here word*es* y awook F; thorough hire wordes awooke Y; I þoruȝ hir wordes awook WHmCrOC^{2}CBLMR; I thrugh theyre wordes arose G. waited] waytede al F; loked G.

And sei3 þe sonne [euene] South sitte þat tyme,
Metelees and moneilees on Maluerne hulles.
Musynge on þis metels [a myle] wey ich yede.
Many tyme þis metels haþ maked me to studie
Of þat I sei3 slepynge, if it so be my3te, |
And for Piers [loue] þe Plowman [wel] pencif in herte, *fol.* 44 *a*
And which a pardon Piers hadde þe peple to conforte,
And how þe preest inpugned it wiþ two propre wordes.
Ac I haue no sauour in songewarie for I se it ofte faille.
Caton and Canonistres counseillen vs to leue
To sette sadnesse in Songewarie for *sompnia ne cures*.
Ac for þe book bible bereþ witnesse
How Daniel diuined þe dre[mes] of a kyng
That Nabugodonosor nempne[þ þise] clerkes—
Daniel seide, 'sire kyng, þi [sweuene is to mene]
That vnkouþe kny3tes shul come þi kyngdom to cleyme;
Amonges lower lordes þi lond shal be departed.'

146 And] ⁊ y F. euene] in þe WHmCr GYOC^{2}CBLMRF. sitte] sitten M; satte YOC^{2}C; where it sat F; *om* B. þat] at þat BM.
147 I was Moneles ⁊ Meteles my Mawe gan groone F. moneilees] moueles Cr^{1}.
148 Musynge] But 3it y mewsed F. þis] thise YHmCr^{23}OC^{2}CB; thes G. a myle] a my R; on my M; as y my F; and my WHmCrOC^{2}CBL; my G; and many Y. ich] eche Cr^{1}; *om* F. yede] wente F.
149 Many] ⁊ many F. tyme] a tyme GF; tymes Cr. þis] thise YHmCr^{23}GOC^{2}CB; *om* F. haþ] It haþ F; han OC^{2}B; haue HmG. maked] made CrGOC^{2}F. to] *om* HmCrOC^{2}F.
150 it] that Cr. so be] be so GM; soþ be F.
151 for] G; also for WHmCrYOC^{2}CBL RF; als for M. loue þe] þe WHmCrGY OC^{2}CBLR; *om* MF. wel] ful WHmCr YOC^{2}CBLMRF; *om* G.
152 which] what Cr^{23}F; with Y. a] *om* F. þe] GF; al þe WHmCrYOC^{2}CBLMR.
154 Ac] but GF; And CrC^{2}C. sauour] sauery Cr. songewarie] sompnewarie OC^{2}F. for...faille] to sey*n* nout þerafter F. for] *om* G.
155 For Catou*n* co*n*seyliþ Catonistr*is* com*m*only it faylyþ F. Caton] Canou*n* Y. counseillen] counsel Cr; conseileden B.
156 To] ⁊ G. sette] settyn HmMF. sadnesse in] no soþnesse in no F. Songewarie] sompnewarie OC^{2}F. for...*cures*] *om* F. *cures*] *curis* Y.
157 Ac] but GF; And CrC^{2}C. for] for boldely F. book] book of the HmYOC^{2} CB; boke þe G; byble Cr^{23}F. bible] book FCr^{23}. bereþ] beriþ bettre F.
158 diuined] dimned Cr^{12}; demed Cr^{3}. þe...kyng] of a kyngys dremes F. dremes] GCrYOC^{2}CBLM; dreem WHmR. kyng] *om* Y.
159 That] That was WHmCrGYOC^{2}CB LMR; he was F. nempneþ þise] nempned of WHmYOCBLM; Inempned of RF; nemed of C^{2}; named of Cr; nyuyned off G.
160 Daniel...kyng] Sire kyng seyd Danyel F. sire] sure Hm; to þe G. sweuene] dremels WGYOLMR; dremes HmCrC^{2}CBF. is to mene] bitokneþ WHmYOCBLMRF; betoken CrGC^{2}.
161 vnkouþe] vnkowde G. shul] shullen M; shuld CBmBo. kyngdom to] corou*n* þe F. cleyme] cleue GOC^{2}LM; reue RF.
162 Amonges] ⁊ among F. lond] londes Y.

As Daniel diuined in dede it fel after:
The kyng lees his lordshipe and [lasse] men it hadde.
And Ioseph mette m*er*ueillously how þe moone and þe sonne
And þe elleuene sterres hailsed hym alle.
Thanne Iacob iugged Iosephes sweuene:
'*Beau fitʒ*', quod his fader, 'for defaute we shullen,
I myself and my sones, seche þee for nede.'
It bifel as his fader seide in Pharaoes tyme
That Ioseph was Iustice Egipte to loke;
It bifel as his fader tolde, hise frendes þ*er*e hym souȝte.
Al þis makeþ me on metels to þynke,
And how þe preest preued no pardon to dowel
And demed þ*a*t dowel Indulgences passe[þ],
Biennals and triennals and Bisshopes lettres.
Dowel at þe day of dome is digneliche vnderfongen;
[He] passeþ al þe pardon of Seint Petres cherche. |
Now haþ þe pope power pardon to graunte *fol.* 44 *b*
[Th]e peple wiþouten penaunce to passen [to ioye]?

163 As] And as WHmCrGYOC^{2}CBLMRF. diuined] dimned Cr^{12}; demed Cr^3. in] þe F. it] *om* F.
164 his] aftir his B. lasse] lower WHmCrGYOC^{2}CBLMRF. men] lord*es* F.
165 how] of F. þe(2)] *above line* M; *om* OC^{2}F.
166 And] ⁊ of F. þe] *om* Hm. elleuene] enleue BmBo. hailsed] halsed Cr; how þey heylid F; worschipede (*over erasure another ink*) Hm. hym] hem Cr^{1}OC^{2}C.
167 Thanne] Ano*n* F. sweuene] swevenys F.
168 we shullen] we shall Cr; after F.
169 I] *om* F. seche] sechen M; shull seeke F. þee] tho Hm.
170 bifel] fel F. Pharaoes] pharaones C^2.
171 Iustice] Iustices C. Egipte] al Egipte B; of Egypt F. loke] loken CrHmGYOC^{2}CBLM.
172 It bifel] and tho Hm; ⁊ F. as] al as B. frendes...souȝte] fawntys sowty*n* þere F. þ*er*e hym] hym þere R. souȝte] souȝten OC^{2}M.
173 Al] And al WHmCrGYOC^{2}CBLMRF. þis] this mat*er*e F. on] on þis WCrGCLMR; on thise YHmOC^{2}B; on my F. to] *om* F. þynke] þinken M.
174 preued] preiede (*glossed* praysed *another hand*) C^2.
175 demed] nempned R. Indulgences] all Indulgenses F; indulgence Cr^{23}YCBR; indulcences C^2. passeþ] passed WHmCrGYOC^{2}CBLMRF.
176 Biennals and] Or q*ui*nquenalis or F. and(2)] or þe F. lettres] seales Hm.
177 Dowel] And how dowel WHmCrGYOC^{2}CBLMRF. is] *om* C^2. digneliche] deyntely F. vnderfongen] vnderfonge RO; take F.
178 He] And WHmCrGYOC^{2}CBLMRF. passeþ] passed Cr^{3}GB. þe] *om* R. Petres] peter CB. cherche] of rome Hm.
179–86 *lines om* OC^2.
179 *so divided* F; *divided from* 180 *after* peple WHmCrGYCBLMR. Now...pope] þe pope haþ gret F.
180 The] *spelled* þe W; to þe GM; A F. peple] sowle F. outen] YCBF; outen any WHmLM; oute any GCrR. passen] passe HmCr. to ioye] into heuene WHmCrGYCBLMRF.

This is [a leef of] oure bileue, as lettred men vs techeþ:
Quodcumque ligaueris super terram erit ligatum & in celis &c.
And so I leue leelly, lor[d] forb[e]de ellis,
That pardon and penaunce and preieres doon saue
Soules þat haue synned seuen siþes dedly.
Ac to truste [on] þise triennals, trewely, me þynkeþ
[It] is no3t so siker for þe soule, certes, as is dowel.
Forþi I rede yow renkes þat riche ben on erþe
Vpon trust of youre tresor triennals to haue,
Be [þow] neuer þe bolder to breke þe x hestes,
And namely ye maistres, Meires and Iugges,
That haue þe welþe of þis world and wise men ben holden
To purchace pardon and þe popes bulles.
At þe dredful dome, whan dede shulle rise
And comen alle [bi]fore crist acountes to yelde,
How þow laddest þi lif here and hi[s] law[e] keptest,

181 is...of] is WHmCrGYCBLMF; *om* R. as...techeþ] þe gospel leyþ þe same F. vs techeþ] do vs teach Cr.
181α *line om* (*a space left for it*) F. *ligaueris*] *ligaueritis* Cr^{23}. *&c*] *om* CrCotR.
182 so] *om* F. I] *om* Cr. leue] beleve F. lord] oure lorde HmGF (de *followed by erasure* Hm); lordes WCrYCLMR; oure lordis B (is *erased* Cot). forbede] F; forbyd G; forbode WHmCrYCBLMR.
183 *divided from* 184 *after* sowlys F. That] then G. penaunce] prayers HmF. preieres] penaunce HmF. doon] *om* F. saue] saueth Hm; saven F; þe same YCB.
184 þat] þat þe bodijs F. haue] hauen B.
185 Ac] but GF; And CrC. truste] *crist* Cot. on] GF; to WHmCrYCBLMR. þise] this YMR; *om* F. triennals] triennale Y; trentals Cr^{23}. þynkeþ] thynke C.
186 It] RF; *om* WHmCrGYCBLM. for] to F. þe] *om* Hm. soule] soules HmCr^{1}G CB. certes] soþly F; *om* Cr. is(2)] to Cr.
187 Forþi] Therfore CrF. renkes] reuks Cr; thenke R; to þynk B; all F. ben on erþe] me*n* been heere F. on] on þis WHm CrGYOC^{2}CBLMR.
188 of] on GF; to M. youre] *om* Cr^{3}. triennals] trientales Cr^{23}. haue] p*ur*chase F.
189 þow] ye WHmCrGYOC^{2}CBLMRF. breke] breken M.
190 maistres] maires M. Meires] boþe Mey3hres F; maistres M. Iugges] althermen F.
191 haue] hauen B. þis] þe M. and] C^{2}G OCBRF; þ*a*t Y; and for WHmCrLM. men] me G. holden] holde F.
192 purchace] purchace yow WHmCrG YOC^{2}CBLMRF. pardon] pardo*n*s Cr. and] at OC^{2}; wit*h* F.
193 At] For at F; Ac Y. dede] the dede HmCrB; dede me*n* F. shulle] shullen BLR. rise] risen R; aryse HmCrGYOC^{2} CB; arisen M.
194 comen] come OC^{2}. bifore] YOC^{2} CBLMRF; tofore WHmCr; afore G. acountes] and acountes R; & 3our*e* acowntys F. to] for to Cr^{23}; *om* F. yelde] yelden M; yede Cr.
195 How] & how F. þow] 3e HmF. laddest] ladde Hm; ladden F; leadest Cr. þi] 3our HmF. here] there Hm; *om* GMF. his lawe] hise lawes WHmCrYOC^{2}CBL MR; here lawes G; 3our*e* lawis F. keptest] kepte Hm; kepyn F; kepest Cr.

[What] þow didest day by day þe doom wole reherce.
A pokeful of pardon þ*ere*, ne p*ro*uincials lettres,
Thei3 [þow] be founde in þe fraternite [among] þe foure ordres
And haue Indulgences doublefold, but dowel [þee] helpe
I sette youre patentes and your*e* pardon at one pies hele.
Forþi I counseille alle cristene to crie god mercy,
And Marie his moder be meene bitwene,
That god gyue vs g*ra*ce er we go hennes
Swiche werkes to werche, while we ben here,
That, after oure deeþ day, dowel reherce
At þe day of dome we dide as he hi3te. |

196 What] And how WHmCrGYOC^{2}C BLMRF. þow] 3e HmF. didest] dedyn Hm; dost R; don F. þe] þi G; this Y. wole] schall Hm.
197 poke] pouh3 R. ne] & G. p*ro*uincials] prouincial Cr.
198 Thei3...be] Be not F. þow] ye WHm CrGYOC^{2}CBLMR. founde] foun*den* CrHmOBM; *om* G. þe(1)] no F. among] of CrF; of alle WHmGYOC^{2}CBLMR. foure] fyue R.
199 *line om* Cr^1. And haue] Ne F. Indulgences] indulge*n*ce Cr^{23}GYCB. double] an .C. Cr^{23}. but] GRF; but if WHm Cr^{23}YOC^{2}CBLM. þee] yow WHm Cr^{23}GYOC^{2}CBLMF; wil 3ow R.
200 *line om* F. sette] beset Cr. pardon] pardoun3 LCr (3 *an addition* ? L). pies] pie M; pese Cr^{1}CB; pins Cr^2. hele] hule CCot; hoole BmBo.
201 Forþi] Therfore CrF; and G. to] for to Hm. crie] crien M. god] *crist* F.
202 And make Christ our meane that hath made eme*n*ds Cr. be] be oure WHmGY OC^{2}CLMRF; þat she be oure B. bitwene] bitwne Y; at neede F.
203 god] he F. gyue] 3yue HmC^{2}BM. er] er þ*at* F; here er WHmCrGYOC^2 CBLMR. we] *twice* Y. hennes] henne F.
204 werche] worchen M. while] þe while RF.
205 deeþ] deathes Cr; dede YGC. reherce] it reerse F.
206 dide] diden OC^2. as he] he *by correction* Cot; þat we hy*m* F.

VIII

Thus, yrobed in russet, I romed aboute *fol.* 45 *a*
Al a somer seson for to seke dowel,
And frayned ful ofte of folk þ*a*t I mette
If any wiȝt wiste wher dowel was at Inne;
And what man he myȝte be of many man I asked.
Was neu*er*e wiȝt as I wente þat me wisse kouþe
Where þis leode lenged, lasse ne moore,
Til it bifel on a Friday two freres I mette,
Maistres of þe Menours, men of grete witte.
I hailsed hem hendely as I hadde ylerned,
And preide hem, *p*[*u*]*r charite*, er þei passed ferþer
If þei knewe any contree or costes [aboute]
'Where þ*a*t dowel dwelleþ, dooþ me to witene.
For [ye] be men of þis moolde þ*a*t moost wide walken,
And knowen contrees and courtes and many kynnes places,

1 *before this two spurious lines* F; *see above*, p. 222. Thus] ⁊ F. yrobed] I robbed GBm; arobid C^{2}; robed HmCr^{23} (*over erasure of a longer word another hand and ink* Hm); throbed Cr^{1}; y Rob*er*t F. I] ga*n* F. romed] romed me B; rome F; runned Cr^{1}.
2 *line om* F. for] *om* G.
3 frayned] asked C. of] *om* F. mette] mete Cr^{1}.
4 wiȝt] wigh Y. wiste] knewe (*above line main hand*) G. was] were RF. at Inne] ostagid F.
5 man(2)] a ma*n* F; me*n* C^{2}BoCot; folk M.
6 Was] And was R; But þere was F. neu*er*e] nere Bm; *om* F. wiȝt...wente] in þis worlde R.
7 *line om* OC^{2}. þis] þat F. leode] ladde Cr. lenged] longud (o *touched up*) M; loogged was B. lasse] neyþ*er* lesse F. ne] or Cr; oþur B.
8 bifel] fel FM. on] vpon M. a] *om* Cot. two] wi*th* tweye F.
9 Maistres] And maistres R; ⁊ weryn Maystrys F. men...witte] ⁊ me*n* weel ylerned F.
10 *line om* F. hailsed] halsed CrB (hals *over erasure* Bm); halȝed Hm. ylerned] lerned HmCrGYOC^{2}CBLMR.
11 And] I F. *pur*] HmOC^{2}BF; *par* WGY LM; for CrCR. þei] y F. passed] passeden OB.
12 knewe] knewen OC^{2}BoCot; kewen Bm. any] In any GF. contree] contres Y; courte Cr^{23}RF. or] or in F. costes] cost HmCr^{1}; contrye Cr^{23}; toostes Y. aboute] as þei wente WHmCrGYCBLM; as þei wenten OC^{2}; þer þei wente R; þere þey wenty*n* F.
13 dooþ me to] y p*ra*ye ȝow ȝee me F. witene] wyt CrC^{2}B; witee Y; wisse F.
14–17 *lines om* RF.
14 ye] þei WHmCrGYOC^{2}CBLM. of] on Cr^{23}GLM. wide] wilde YOCB.
15 contrees...courtes] townes ⁊ contreijs B. kynnes] kings Cr^{1}.

Boþe p*ri*nces paleises and pou*er*e mennes cotes,
And dowel and do yuele, wher þei dwelle boþe.'
'[Marie]', quod þe [maistres, 'amonges vs he dwelleþ],
And euere haþ as I hope, and eu*er*e shal herafter.'
'*Contra!*' quod I as a clerc and comsed to disputen:
'*Sepcies in die cadit Iustus.*
Seuene siþes, seiþ þe book, synneþ þe rightfulle;
A[c] whoso synneþ, I sei[e, certes], me þynkeþ
[That] dowel and do yuele mowe noȝt dwelle togideres.
Ergo he nys noȝt alwey [at hoom] amonges yow freres;
He is ouþ*er*while elliswhere to wisse þe peple.'
'I shal seye þee, my sone', seide þe frere þanne,
'How seuen siþes þe sadde man [synneþ on þe day].
By a forbisne', quod þe frere, 'I shal þee faire shewe. |
Lat brynge a man in a boot amydde [a] bro[od] watre; *fol.* 45 *b*
The wynd and þe water and þe [waggyng of þe boot]
Makeþ þe man many tyme to falle and to stonde.

16 paleises] palays HmGYCB.
17 yuele] euell ⁊ G. dwelle] dwellen OC^{2}B.
18 Marie] Marye F; Amonges vs WHmCrGYOC^{2}CBLMR. quod þe maistres] þat mon is duellyng B. þe] þo F; a R. maistres] Menou*rs* WHmCrGYOC^{2}CLMRF. amonges...dwelleþ] amongys vs he dwellyþ F; þat man is dwellynge WHmCrGYOC^{2}CLMR; quod þe menouris Bo; quod þo menouris Bm; coth Mynours Cot.
19 *transposed with* 20 BmBo. euere] *om* B.
20 a] *om* YR. clerc] clere G; clek Bm; Clrec Y. comsed] bygane C. disputen] dispute OHmC^{2}R.
20α *line om* F. *Sepcies*] And seyde *sepcies* R; And seide sothli *sepcies* LM; And seide hem sooþly *Sepcies* WHmGYOC^{2}CB; And sayde hym sothlye *Septies* Cr.
21 Seuene] For sevene F. siþes] sithe YM; tymes as F. seiþ] on þe day seiþ BoBmCot; quod Hm. synneþ] slyȝdiþ F.
22 Ac] And WHmCrGYOC^{2}CBLMRF. so] þ*at* F. I seie] I say Cr; I seide WGYLMR; as y seyde Hm; he seyde OC^{2}C; seide he B; in doynge he F. certes] doþ evele F; dooþ yuele as WHmCrGYOC^{2}CBLMR. þynkeþ] thynke C.
23 *line om* OC^2. That] And WHmCrGYCBLMRF. wel] yuel CB. yuele] wel CB.
24 nys] is HmCrGYOC^{2}CBRF. at hoom] F; *om* WHmCrGYOC^{2}CBLMR. yow] ȝoure F.
25 He] But he F. is] *om* C. ouþ*er*while] *om* F. to] for to F. wisse] wyshen Cr.
26 shal] *om* B. þe] þe to F.
27 synneþ...day] synneþ on þe day tyȝde F; on þe day synneth LMR; on a day synneþ WHmCrGYOC^{2}CB.
28 a] *om* C^2. forbisne] ensample C^{2}Bo; example Cot; propre resou*n* F. quod þe frere] *om* F. faire] redyly F. shewe] shewen M.
29 a(2)] LR; þe WHmCrGYOC^{2}CBMF. brood] CHmGB; brode WCr^{23}YOC^{2}LRF; brodur M; broke Cr^1.
30 The] and þe Hm. waggyng...boot] boot waggyng WHmCrGYOC^{2}CBLMRF.
31 Makeþ] Make Cr. þe] a CrGYOC^2. tyme] CrOC^{2}R; a tyme WHmGYCBLMF. falle] meve F. and] þan BoCot; þa*n*ne (ne *over erasure*) Bm. stonde] stumble OC^2; stakere F.

For stonde he neuer so stif, he stumbleþ [in þe waggyng],
Ac yet is he saaf and sound, and so hym bihoueþ,
For if he ne arise þe raþ*er* and rauȝte þe steere
The wynd wolde wiþ þe water þe boot ouerþrowe.
[There] were [þe mannes] lif lost [for] lachesse of hymselue.
[Riȝt] þus it [fareþ]', quod þe frere, 'by folk here on erþe.
The water is likned to þe world þat wanyeþ and wexeþ;
The goodes of þis grounde arn like þe grete wawes,
That as wyndes and [watres] walkeþ aboute;
The boot is likned to [þe] body þat brotel is of kynde,
That þoruȝ þe fend and þe flessh and þe [false] worlde
Synneþ þe sadde man [seuen siþes a day].
Ac dedly synne doþ he noȝt for dowel hym [helpeþ],
[Th]at is charite þe champion, chief help ayein synne.
For he strengþeþ [þee] to stonde and steereþ [þi] soule
[That], þouȝ þ[i] body bowe as boot dooþ in þe watre,

32 stonde] stode Y. he(1)] *om* B. stumbleþ] tumbleþ BoCot. in þe waggyng] if he meue WHmCrCLMR; if he meueth YGOC^{2}BoCot; ȝef he meuy Bm; ⁊ falleþ F.
33 Ac] and HmCrGYC^{2}CBF. he] *om* Hm. and(2)] *om* G.
34 if] but F. ne arise] ryse F. þe] to þe WHmCrGYOC^{2}CBLMR; to hy*m* þe F. steere] sterne HmC^{2}RF.
35 wiþ] and R; on F. þrowe] terve F.
36 There] then G; And þanne WHmCrY OC^{2}CBLMRF. þe...for] his lif lost þoruȝ WHmCrGYOC^{2}CBLMRF. selue] seluen OM.
37 Riȝt...fareþ] Ryght þus fareþ it F; ⁊ þus ytt farethe G; And þus it falleþ WHmCr YOC^{2}CBLMR. þe] þ*at* C. here] er Bm; *om* F. on] on thys GF; in Y. erþe] grownd F.
38 is likned] y lykne F. þe] þo Bm; þis F. wanyeþ] wa*n*teþ B; waueth Cr^1.
39 The] ⁊ þe F. of] on F. grounde] world Cr. lik] lykned FCr. þe] F; to þe WHmCrGYOC^{2}CBLMR.
40 *line om* Hm. That] ⁊ F. as] as þe F; was Cr^3. wyndes] wynd BF. and] ⁊ þe F; as C. watres] wedres WCrGYOC^{2}C BLMR; wedir F. walkeþ] walweþ ML.
41 is likned] y lykne F. to] til Y. þe] oure WHmCrGYOC^{2}CBLMRF. body] bodies YCBF. is] ben Cot.
42 That] and B. fend...þe(2)] *om* Cr. fend] flessh M. and(1)] *om* G. þe(2)] þi LR; oure F. flessh] feende (*final* e *erased*) M. þe(3)] þis R. false] F; frele WHmCr GYOC^{2}CBLMR. worlde] world also F.
43 seuen siþes] a day WCrYOC^{2}CBLMR; ech day F; on the day Hm; on a day G. a day] seuen siþes WYOC^{2}CBLMRF; seuene tymes HmCrG.
44 Ac] but GF; And CrC^{2}C. noȝt] no*n* F. helpeþ] helpiþ F; kepeþ WHmCrGYOC^2 CBLMR.
45 That] And þat WHmCrGYOC^{2}CBL MRF. champion] chapman þe G. help] helper G; hop help Bm; *om* YF.
46 strengþeþ] strengthed YCr^{1}O; strengþ F; strenþe*n* C^2. þee] men W; man Hm CrGYOC^{2}CBLMRF. steereþ] stirreth Cr. þi] mannes WHmCrGYOC^{2}CBLM RF. soule] will F.
47 That] þat RF; And WHmCrYOC^{2}C BLM; *om* G. þouȝ] doiþ B. þi] OCr^{23} YCBLMRF; they Cr^{1}C^2; þe WHmG. body] *om* Cr^1. as] as þe F; as a (a *above line another ink*) M. boot] booth Bm. dooþ] *om* F. þe] *om* Cr^{23}C.

Ay is þi soule saaf but [þow þiselue wole
Folwe þi flesshes wille and þe fendes after,
And] do deedly synne and drenche þi[selue].
God wole suffre wel þi sleuþe if þiself likeþ,
For he yaf þee [to] yeresȝyue to yeme wel þiselue
Wit and free wil, to eu*er*y wiȝt a porcion,
To fleynge foweles, to fisshes and to beestes.
Ac man haþ moost þerof and moost is to blame
But if he werche wel *þer*wiþ as dowel hym techeþ.'
'I haue no kynde knowyng', quod I, 'to conceyuen [þi] wordes
Ac if I may lyue and loke I shal go lerne bettre.'
'I bikenne þee crist', quod he, 'þat on [þe] cros deyde.' |
And I seide 'þe same saue yow fro myschaunce, *fol. 46 a*
And ȝyue yow g*ra*ce on þis grounde goode men to worþe'.
[Th]us I wente widewher [dowel to seke,
And as I wente by a wode, walkyng myn one],
Blisse of þe briddes [abide me made],

48 Ay] Euere F. þi(1)] þe HmGM. but] LMR; but if WHmCrGYOC^{2}CBF. þow ...wole] þou þiseluen wole M; thiself woll HmGYOC^{2}CBLRF; þow wole þiselue W; thou wylt thyselfe Cr.
49 If þou folwe þy fowle fleshȝ & þe feend þereafter F; *line om* WHmCrGYOC^{2}CB LMR; *here in the spelling of* W.
50 And do] & doost F; Do C^2; Do a WHmCrGYOCBLMR. and] þou F. drenche] GYOC^{2}CB; drenche so WHm CrLMR; drenchist þ*an*ne F. þi] þe G. selue] R; soule WHmCrGYOC^{2}CBLMF.
51 God] But god F. suffre wel] þou save F. wel] *om* Hm. sleuþe] soule HmRF. if] þyf F. self] seluen M. likeþ] lyke F.
52 For] *om* F. yaf] gaue GCrC. to(1)] HmYOC^{2}CBLMR; two CrF; a WG. yeresȝyue] ȝeresgyue HmGC; ȝeresȝevis FCr^1; yeresgifts Cr^{23}. yeme] seme G; teme Cr. selue] seluen M.
53 Wit] And þat is wit WHmCrGYOC^2 CBLMR; & þo ben wit F. and] a LM. to] *om* Hm. wiȝt] man Hm.
54 fleynge] fleyge R; man & to F. and] & also GYOC^{2}CB.
55 Ac] But F; And CrGC^{2}C. man] þanne (þa *altered to* me *by erasure*) R. is] he is F.
56 if] *om* F. werche] worth Cr^3.
57 I(1)] Ȝee y F. conceyuen] conceyue HmCrGYOC^{2}CBLMRF. þi] þy F; alle þi R; alle youre WHmCrGYOC^{2}CBLM.
58 Ac] but GF; And CrC^{2}C; *om* Hm. lyue] leue R. go] *om* Y.
59 I] And I Y. quod he] *om* CrGYOC^{2}C BLM. he] þat on Hm; þei R. on] vppon B. þe] OHmCrYC^{2}CBLRF; *om* WGM.
60 same] same lord F. yow] þe F.
61 ȝyue] giue CrGOC; g*ra*unte F. yow] þe F. men] ende F. worþe] worthen M; make F.
62 Thus] And þus WHmCrGYOC^{2}CBL MR; & F. I wente] wente y F. dowel to seke] walkyng myn one WHmCrGYOC^2 CLR; walkynge bi myn one BMF (bi *above line another hand* M).
63 By a wilde wildernesse and by a wodes side WHmCrGYOC^{2}CBLMRF (By] In F. wilde] wyde HmCr. and] *om* F. wodes] wode HmOLMRF; brookes Cr^1).
64 Blisse] The blisse B; þanne blysse F. þe] tho HmLR. abide me made] abyde me made RF; brouȝte me aslepe WHmCrG YOC^{2}CBLM.

And vnder a lynde vpon a launde lened I a stounde
To [lerne] þe layes [þat] louely foweles made.
Murþe of hire mouþes made me to slep[e];
The m*er*ueillouseste metels mette me þanne
That euer dremed [driȝt] in [doute], as I wene.
A muche man me þouȝte, lik to myselue,
Cam and called me by my kynde name.
'What art [þ]ow', quod I þo, 'þ*at* my name knowest?'
'That þow woost wel', quod he, 'and no wiȝt bettre.'
'Woot I?' [quod I; 'who art þow]?' 'þouȝt', seide he þanne.
'I haue sued þee seuen yeer; seye þow me no raþer?'
'Artow þouȝt?' quod I þoo; 'þow koudest me [telle]
Where dowel dwelleþ, and do me [to wisse].'
'Dowel', [quod he], 'and dobet and dobest þe þridde
Arn þre faire v*er*tues, and ben noȝt fer to fynde.

65 a(1)] *om* BoCotR. vpon] vppo R; on CrGF; vnder B. lened] lay F. I] I me B.
66 lerne] heren B; lyþe WCrGYOC^{2}CL MR; lystne FHm. þat] þ*at* the CotR; þat þo BmBo; the HmCMF; þo WCrGYO C^{2}L. louely] *om* RF. foweles] foule G; Nytyngalis F. made] maden OHmC^{2}B MF.
67 Murþe] ⁊ þe merthe F. to slepe] there to slepe HmCrGYOC^{2}CBLR; þer to sleple W; aslepe MF.
68 The] ⁊ þe F; *om* R. merueillouseste] merueyluste Hm; Merueylokest RF; merueilous B. mette me] me mette B; mette I me YOC^2. me þanne] y þ*at* stownde F.
69 dremed...wene] wyȝght in þis world as y wene dremede F. dremed] *twice* L. driȝt] wiȝt WHmCrGYOC^{2}CBLMR. doute] world WHmCrGYOC^{2}CBLMR. wene] wente Cr^2.
70 *transposed with* 71 F. muche] mychil FC. me þouȝte] as me þouȝte and WHm CrGYOC^{2}CBmBoLM; a me thoughtte and Cot; as thouȝte and R; he was mychil F. to] *om* F. selue] selue*n* C^{2}M.
71 Cam] Me þowhte oon com F. kynde] ryght GMF.
72 art þow] RHmCrGOC^{2}BF; artow WYCLM. quod] quo Bo. þo] *om* R. þ*at*] þat M; þ*at* þow WHmGYOC^{2}CB LR; þ*at* þowhȝ F; thou þ*at* Cr.
73 That] *om* F. woost] wootest GCr. he] he þo F. wiȝt] man OC^2.
74 Woot I] I not neu*er*e F. quod...þow] who art þou F; what þow art WHmCrG YOC^{2}CBLMR. seide he þanne] y am he seyde F. he] *om* Y.
75 þee] þee þis WHmCrGYOC^{2}CBLM RF. yeer] yeres Cr. seye] ne seyȝe F.
76 *divided from* 77 *after* where R; *in head margin but cropped and illegible* G. Artow] art þou HmCrOC^{2}BLMRF. I] he Hm. þow koudest] canst þou F. koudest] kannes (a *altered from* o) C; knowest B. me telle] F; me wisse WHmCrYOC^{2}C BmLMR; ywysse BoCot.
77 Where] Where þ*at* WHmCrGYOC^2 CBLMRF. and] þou F; *om* G. to wisse] þat to knowe WCrGYOC^{2}CBLM; that knowe Hm; hym to knowe RF.
78 quod he] q*uo*d he F; *om* WHmCrGYO C^{2}CBLMR. bet] better CrG. þe] *om* OC^2. þridde] thrydde F; þridde quod he WHmCrGYOC^{2}CBLMR (quod *twice, the first cancelled* M).
79 vertues] felowis F. ben] dwell F. to fynde] to fecche M; o twynne F.

Whoso is [meke of his mouþ, milde of his speche],
Trewe of his tunge and of his two handes,
And þoru3 his labour or his land his liflode wynneþ,
Trusty of his tailende, takeþ but his owene,
And is no3t dronkelewe ne [d]eynous, dowel hym folweþ.
Dobet [þus dooþ], ac he dooþ muche moore.
He is as lowe as a lomb, louelich of speche; |
[Whiles he haþ ou3t of his owene he helpeþ þer nede is]; *fol.* 46 *b*
The bagges and þe bigirdles, he haþ [b]roke hem alle
That þe Erl Auarous [hadde, or] hise heires,
And wiþ Mammonaes moneie he haþ maad hym frendes;
And is ronne to Religion, and haþ rendred þe bible,
And precheþ þe peple Seint Poules wordes,
Libenter suffertis insipientes cum sitis ipsi sapientes:
[Ye wise] suffreþ þe vnwise wiþ yow to libbe,

80 *run together with* 81 WHmCrGYOC^{2}C BLMRF. Whoso] who Hm; For who F. meke...speche] ⁊ meeke in his herte ⁊ my3lde of his speche *as a separate line copied after* 81 F; *om* WHmCrGYOC^{2}CBLMR.
82 *transposed with* 83 F. his labour] labour his (*corrected*) Bm. his(1)] þe GF. or] Cr^{23}OC^{2}C; or þoru3 WHmLMR; and YCr^{1}B; of FG. land] londes YOC^{2}CB; hand F; handys G.
83 *line om* CB. Trusty] And is trusty WHmCrGYOC^{2}LMR; ⁊ trewe F. his(1)] *om* GOC^2. tailende] tayland Cr^1; taylyng Cr^{23}OC^2; taillying Y. takeþ] and taketh YGF.
84 is] *om* F. no3t] no Cr. deynous] BCF; dedeynous WYOC^{2}LMR (de- *cancelled* R); dysdeynous HmG; dedigyous Cr.
85 Dobet] And dobet F. þus dooþ] dooþ ri3t þus WHmCrGYOC^{2}CCotLMR; doþ ryght F; do ri3t þus BmBo (s *added to* do *another ink* Bm). ac] but F; ⁊ CrGYOC^2 CB. he] *om* BoCot. muche] michil F; ryght moche G; best moch Cot.
86 as(1)] also Hm; *om* B. lomb] lomb and WHmCrGYOC^{2}CBLMRF. louelich] lowhly F.
87 And helpeþ alle men after þat hem nedeþ WHmCrGYOC^{2}CBLMRF (after...nedeþ] ⁊ eseþ hem at neede F).
88 and þe bigirdles] bownde *with* brygerdlis F. broke] F; broken GHmB; tobroke WCr^{23}YOC^{2}C; tobroke*n* Cr^1 LMR.
89 þe] *om* B. Erl] Erl sire F. hadde or] heeld and WHmCrGYOC^{2}CBLMR; held for F.
90 And] RF; And þus WHmCrGYOC^{2}C BLM. wiþ] *om* Y. Mammonaes] Mamondes YC; mammomes B. haþ maad] hat3 ymade R; haad made B; makeþ M. hym frendes] freenschepis F.
91 ronne] ronnen BHmM. to] into LM RF. Religioun...rendred] religio*us* to rendre F. bible] bille R.
92 precheþ] preched YGOC^{2}CR. þe] F; to þe WHmCrGYOC^{2}CBLMR.
93 *insipientes*] *incipientes* RF. *sitis ipsi*] *scitis ipsi* BmBo; *ipsi sitis* R; *ipsi scitis* F. *sapientes*] *sapientes* ⁊*c* Hm.
94 *run together with* 95 CB. Ye wise] And WHmCrGYOC^{2}CBLMR; he seyþ 3ee sholde gladly F. suffreþ] suffer GF; suffren OC^2; *om* CB. þe] to þe CB. wiþ ...libbe] *om* CB. to] GF; for to WHmCr YOC^{2}LMR.

And wiþ glad wille dooþ hem good for so god hoteþ.
Dobest is aboue boþe and bereþ a bisshopes crosse;
Is hoked [at] þat oon ende to [holde men in good lif].
A pik is [in] þat potente to [punge] adown þe wikked
That waiten any wikkednesse dowel to tene.
And [as] dowel and dobet [dide] hem [to vnderstonde],
[Thei han] crowne[d a] kyng to [kepen] hem [alle],
That if dowel [and] dobet dide ayein dobest
[And were vnbuxum at his biddyng, and bold to don ille],
Thanne [sholde] þe kyng come and casten hem in [prison,
And putten hem þer in penaunce wiþoute pite or grace],
But dobest bede for hem [abide] þer for euere.
Thus dowel and dobet and dobest þe þridde

95 And...wille] *om* CB. dooþ] doon OC^{2}F; do GY; ȝe don B; ye do C. hem] *om* CB. so god] god so F. hoteþ] yow hoteþ WHmCrGYOC^{2}BLMRF; yow beddis C.
96 But dobest beriþ a bisshopis croos ⁊ is above hem boþe F. boþe] hem boþe OC^2.
97 Is] And is B; It is F. hoked] an hoke R. at] F; on WHmCrGYOC^{2}CBLMR. þat] þe GF. oon] *om* F. holde] halie WHmCrGYOC^{2}CBLRF; halen M. in... lif] fro helle WHmCrGYOC^{2}CBLMRF.
98 A...potente] ⁊ in þat potente ys a pyȝk F. A] and a B. is] *om* R. in] B; on WHmCrGYOC^{2}CLMR. þat] the Cr^{23}G YOC^{2}CB. potente] poyent B (y *over erasure* Bm). punge] pulte L; pelte R; pilte OC^2; pulle Y; pul Cr; putte WHm BM; pute C; put G; pytten F. adown] downe CrF. wikked] helle B.
99 any wikkednesse] eny wikenesse Bm; *with* wrong sire F. dowel] to do wel Bo Cot; to wel Bm.
100–11 *disordered with omissions thus*: 100, 101 *lines om*; 107–10; 102–5; 106 *line om*; 111 F.
100 *line om* F. And as] And WHmCrGO C^{2}CBLMR; *om* Y. and] haþ B. dide] amonges WHmCrGYOC^{2}CBLM; amoges R. to vnderstonde] han ordeyned WHm Cr; ordeyned YGC^{2}CLMR; ordeyneden O; ordeyneþ B.
101 *line om* F; *run together with* 108 R. Thei...a] To crowne oon to be WCrGY OC^{2}CBLM; to crownyn oon to be Hm; To croune and to be R. to...alle] *om* (*see* 108) R. kepen...alle] rulen hem boþe WHmGYOC^{2}CBM; reule hem bothe LCr.
102 *line om* R. That if] And þat if C^2; For if þat F. and] Cr; or WHmGYOC^{2}CBL MF. bet] better Cr^1. dide] deden BF; do GYM; doþ OC^2; arne Cr^{23}.
103 ⁊ weryn vnbuxum to don his byd-dyngge ⁊ bown to do Ille F; *line om* WHm CrGYOC^{2}CBLMR; *here in the spelling of* W.
104 *line om* R. sholde] F; shal WHmCr GYOC^{2}CBLM. come] comen M. casten] caste MCrG; comawnde F; put B (*above line another ink* Bm). hem] hym Hm. in] to F. prison] presoun F; Irens WHm CrGYOC^{2}CBLM.
105 ⁊ pitte hem þere in penawnce with-oute pite or grace F; *line om* WHmCrGY OC^{2}CBLMR; *here in the spelling of* W.
106 *line om* RF. But] And but if WHm CrGYOC^{2}CBLM. bede] bidde OC^{2}M; preye Hm; did CB. hem] hym HmCB. abide] þei to be WYCLM; they two be Hm; þei be GCrOC^2; þer to be B. þer] *om* B.
107 *line om* R. Thus] And þus F. bet] better G. dobest] best C. þe] *om* Y.

Crouned oon to be kyng, [and by hir counseil werchen],
And rule þe Reme by [rede of hem alle],
And ooþer wise [and ellis no3t] but as þei þre assent[e].'
I þonked þo3t þo þat he me [so] tau3te.
'Ac yet sauoreþ me no3t þi seying, [so me god helpe!
More kynde knowynge] I coueite to lerne,
How dowel, dobet and dobest doon among þe peple.'
'But wit konne wisse þee', quod þo3t, 'where þo þre dwelle
Ellis [n]oot [no man] þat now is alyue.' |
Tho3t and I þus þre daies we yeden, *fol.* 47 *a*
Disputyng [o]n dowel day after ooþ*er*,
A[c] er we [war were] wiþ wit gonne we mete.
He was long and lene, lik to noon ooþer;
Was no pride on his apparaill ne pouerte neiþer;
Sad of his semblaunt and of [a] softe [speche].

108 Crouned...kyng] *om* (*see* 101) R. Crouned] Crowneden O; haue crowne F. oon to] vnto them Cr^{1}. be] þe BoCot; a Cr^{1}. and...werchen] ⁊ be here co*n*seyl wirche F; to kepen hem alle WHmCr^{23}G YOC^{2}CLMR; to kepe hem all Cr^{1}; to help hem alle B.
109 And] And to WHmCrGYOC^{2}CBL MRF. rule] reulen M. þe] al þe F; þi OC^{2}. rede...alle] reed of hem alle F; hire þre wittes WHmCrGYOC^{2}CBLMR.
110 ooþer...no3t] noon ooþer wise WHm CrGYOC^{2}CLR; in non oþer wise BoCot M (non *and* o- *over erasure* M); be no*n* oþer wyse F; in oon oþur wise Bm. þre] ther G. assente] assenteþ B; assentes C; will assente F; assented WHmCrGYC^{2}LMR; assenteden O.
111 I þonked] þa*n*ne þankede y F. þo] *om* Hm. me so] so faire me F. so] þus WHm CrGYOC^{2}CLMR; *om* B.
112 *run together with* 113 WHmCrGYOC^{2} CBLMR. Ac...me] ⁊ seyde me savoureþ F. Ac] but G; And CrC^{2}CB. yet] ytt G; ri3t Bm; ari3t BoCot; *om* R. sauoreþ me] me sauoreth Cot; fauoreth me Cr^{1}. þi seying] 3yt wel F. seying] suging Cr^{23}; segge B. so...helpe] so me c*ri*st helpe F; *om* WHmCrGYOC^{2}CBLMR.
113 More...knowynge] For more ky3nde knowynge F; *om* WHmCrGYOC^{2}CBL MR. to] of 3ow to F. lerne] lere B.
114 How] wher*e* þat F. dobet] ⁊ dobet F; dobest Cr; *om* Y. best] better CrG. among þe peple] on þis molde F.
115 But] Trewly but F; *om* G. quod] *om* C. þo] þei BoCot; þat þey F; þe Bm. þre] *om* F. dwelle] dwellen OC^{2}CBM.
116 noot no man] woot I noon þat kan WHmCrGYOC^{2}CBLMRF (woot] knowe F. kan] can tell Cr^{23}; can þe telle B; can se Cr^{1}). is alyue] lyueþ B.
117 Tho3t...þus] þo þowht ⁊ y F. we] *om* GYOC^{2}CB. yeden] wentyn F; reden Bm.
118 on] F; vpon WHmCrGYOC^{2}CBL MR.
119 Ac] And WHmCrGYOC^{2}CBLMRF. we(1)] þat we F; y BoCot; *om* Bm. war were] R; were war WHmCrYC^{2}BoCot M; wery*n* war F; were ywar CGBmL (*correct order noted* Bm); weren ywar O. wiþ] wit Bm. we(2)] I OC^{2}. mete] meetyn F.
120 lik] ⁊ lyche GMF. to] *om* C^{2}.
121 on] vppon HmB; In GF. apparaill] paraile B. pouerte] pouert Cot.
122 Sad] But sad F. semblaunt] semulant Bm. of...speche] of softe chere WHmCr GYOC^{2}CBLMR; softe he was of chere F.

I dorste meue no matere to maken hym to Iangle,
But as I bad þoȝt þoo be mene bitwene,
[To] pute forþ som p*ur*pos to preuen hise wittes,
What was Dowel fro dobet and dobest from hem boþe.
Thanne þoȝt in þat tyme seide þise wordes:
'Wher dowel [and] dobet and dobest ben in londe
Here is wil wolde wite if wit koude [hym teche];
And wheiþ*er* he be man or [no man] þis man wolde aspie,
And werchen as þei þre wolde; th[i]s is his entente.'

123 dorste] durst not Cr. to(1)] for to F. maken] make HmCrGYOC^{2}CBLRF. to(2)] *om* F.
124 be] to be BoCotR.
125 To] F; And WHmCrGYOC^{2}CBLMR. som] his R. preuen] preue Cr^{1}B.
126 bet] bett*er* G.
128 Wher] Whether CrR; where dwellyþ F. and(1)] BF; *om* WHmCrGYOC^{2}CLMR. bet] better G. ben] was CB; *om* RF.
129 Here...wite] Fayn wolde y wete witt F. Here] there G. is] *om* R. wite] ywyte LMR. wit koude] þou cowdist F. hym teche] hym teyche G; teche hym WHmCrYOC^{2}CBLMR; me telle F.
130 And] *om* F. no man] RCB; noon F; man L; wo*m*man WHmCrGYOC^{2}M. þis man] y F. wolde] HmGYOC^{2}CB; wolde fayn F; fayn wolde WCrLMR (fayn *erased* M).
131 werchen] worche OCr^{23}C^2. þei] ȝee F. þre] þer G. wolde] wolden OC^2. this] Cr^{23}GYOC^{2}CBLMRF; thus WHmCr^1. is his] were my*n* F.

IX

'SIre Dowel dwelleþ', quod Wit, 'noȝt a day hennes
In a Castel þat kynde made of foure kynnes þynges.
Of erþe and Eyr [it is] maad, medled togideres,
Wiþ wynd and wiþ water witt[i]ly enioyned.
Kynde haþ closed þ*er*Inne, craftily wiþalle,
A lemman þat he loueþ lik to hymselue.
Anima she hatte; [to hir haþ enuye]
A proud prikere of Fraunce, *Princeps huius mundi*,
And wolde wynne hire awey wiþ wiles [if] he myȝte.
Ac kynde knoweþ þis wel and kepeþ hire þe bettre,
And [haþ] doo[n] hire wiþ sire dowel, duc of þise Marches.
Dobet is hire damyselle, sire doweles douȝter,
To seruen þis lady leelly, boþe late and raþe. |
Dobest is aboue boþe, a Bisshopes peere; *fol.* 47 *b*
That he bit moot be do; he [boldeþ] hem alle;

1 SIre] HEre Cr. Dowel dwelleþ] dowelleth (*second* l *erased*, eth *cancelled*, dwellis *above line another hand*) R. quod] wi*th* C^2. hennes] henne F.
2 kynnes] man*er* R; man*ere* of F.
3 and] HmCrGYOC^2CLMRF; and of WB. it is] HmOC^2F; is it WCrGYCBL MR. medled] & medlyd F; mi*n*gled Cr^{23}.
4 wittily] wittili OC^2; witterly WHmCr GYCBLMRF.
5 Kynde] Syre Keende F.
6 A] His F. he] hym Y. loueþ] loveþ wel F. lik] yliche R; she is lych F. to] *om* F. selue] seluen M.
7 hatte] hatteth HmBmR. to…enuye] ac enuye hir hateþ WHmYOBLMR; but enuye hyr hatethe GF; & envie hir hatiþ C^2CrC (s *erased before* hir C^2).
8 A] He is a F.
9 And] He F. wynne] wynnen M. wiles] wyle Hm. if] yff GF; and WHm CrYOC^2CBLMR.
10 Ac] but G; And CrC^2CRF. kynde… þis] þat knowi*th* kynde F. þis] hyr G.
11 And] As CB. haþ doon] OGYC^2LM; hath Ido R; dooþ WHmCrCBF. wiþ] dwelle wi*th* F. sire] *om* RF. duc] duke GYOC^2F; is duc WHmCrCBLMR. þise] þat F; þe R.
12 Dobet] dobett*er* G; & dobet F. hire] hys G. doweles] dowel YC.
13 To] She F. seruen] serue HmCrGYO C^2CBLMR; s*er*ueþ F. þis] þat F; the Hm; hyr G.
14 Dobest] & dobest F. aboue] abouen M; above hem F; aboute R. Bisshopes] bisshope C.
15 That] & þat F. bit] byddethe GC^2CF. he(2)] for he F. boldeþ] ruleþ WHmCr GYOC^2BLMRF; reule C.

[By his leryng is lad þat lady *Anima*].
Ac þe Constable of [þe] Castel þat kepeþ [hem alle]
Is a wis kny3t wiþalle, sire Inwit he hatte,
And haþ fyue faire sones bi his firste wyue:
Sire Se-wel, and Sey-wel, and here-wel þe hende,
Sire werch-wel-wiþ-þyn-hand, a wi3t man of strengþe,
And sire Godefray Go-wel, grete lordes [alle].
Thise [sixe] ben set to [saue] þis lady *anima*
Til kynde come or sende [and kepe] hire [hymselue].'
'What kynnes þyng is kynde?' quod I; 'kanstow me telle?'
'Kynde', quod [he], ' is creatour of alle kynnes [beestes],
Fader and formour, [þe first of alle þynges].
And þat is þe grete god þat gynnyng hadde neu*ere*,
Lord of lif and of li3t, of lisse and of peyne.
Aungeles and alle þyng arn at his wille
Ac man is hym moost lik of marc and of [shape].
For þoru3 þe word þ*at* he [warp] woxen forþ beestes,

16 By...leryng] *Anima* þat lady WHmCr GYOC^{2}CBLMR; ⁊ *Anima* þat lady F. þat...*Anima*] by his leryng WHmYOC BL (by *twice* C); by hys lernyng GCrC^2 RF; by hire lering M.

17 Ac] but GF; And CrC^{2}C. þe(2)] Cr^{23}F; þat WHmCr^{1}GYOC^{2}CBLMR. hem alle] al þe wacche WHmCrGYOC^2 CBLMRF.

18 hatte] hatteth HmBm.

19 sones] souls Cr^1. wyue] Lady F.

20 and(2)] and sire RF. hende] ende Hm Cr^{23}C^{2}BoCot.

21 Sire] ⁊ sire F; And CB.

22 Godefray Go wel] Goweel on grou*n*de F. grete lordes] a grete lord RF. alle] forsoþe WHmCrGYOC^{2}CBLMRF.

23 sixe] F; fyue WHmCrGYOC^{2}CBL MR. set] ysette B. saue] HmCrGYOC^2 CBLMRF; kepe W. þis] sown þys F. lady] *om* RF.

24 and kepe] to kepen F; to haue Hm; to saue CrLMR; to sauen WGYOC^{2}CB. hymselue] hy*m*selue F; for euere WHmCr GYOC^{2}CBLMR.

25 kynnes] *om* GYOC^{2}CB. quod I] *om* M.

26 Kynde...is] Q*u*od wit Kynde is a F. he is] wit is MR; wit is a WCrGYOC^{2}CBL; wytt a Hm. creatour] creature HmYOC^2 CBmBo (*corrected* C^2); cratour G. alle kynnes] alkynge C. beestes] þynges WHmCrGYOC^{2}CBLMRF.

27 þe...þynges] of alle þynge on erthe F; of al þ*at* euere was maked WHmCrGYO C^{2}CBLMR (was] were G. maked] made Cr^1).

28 And] *om* F. þat is] þis is M; He is F; *om* R. þe] *om* F. grete] get R. gynnyng] begynning Cr^{1}BoCotF.

29 *transposed with* 30 B. Lord] ⁊ lord F. li3t] lyth F. lisse] blisse BCrGMRF (? b *added later* BmM).

30 þyng] thynges G. arn] ben F.

31 Ac] but GF; And CrC^{2}C. hym moost] most hym RF. marc] makyng F. shape] CrC; shappe (*altered from* shapee) G; shafte WHmYOC^{2}BLMRF (*altered to* schape *another ink* C^2).

32 warp] spak WHmCrGYOC^{2}CBLM RF. woxen] wenty*n* F. *Hereafter two spurious lines* F; *see above*, p. 222.

[And al at his wil was wrou3t wiþ a speche],
Dixit ⁊ facta sunt,
[Saue man þat he made ymage] to hymself,
And Eue of his ryb bon wiþouten any mene.
For he was synguler hymself and seide *faciamus*
As who seiþ, "moore moot herto þan my word oone;
My my3t moot helpe forþ wiþ my speche".
Right as a lord sholde make l*ett*res; [if] hym lakked p*ar*chemyn,
Thou3 he [wiste to] write neu*er* so wel, [and] he hadde [a] penne,
The lettre, for al þe lordshipe, I leue, were neu*ere* ymaked.
And so it semeþ by hym [þere he seide in þe bible |
Faciamus hominem ad imaginem nostram];
He moste werche wiþ his word and his wit shewe. *fol.* 48 *a*
And in þis man*ere* was man maad þoru3 my3t of god almy3ty,
Wiþ his word and werkmanshipe and wiþ lif to laste.
And þus god gaf hym a goost [of] þe godhede of heuene
And of his grete grace graunted hym blisse,

33 ⁊ al was maad þorgh his word as his will wolde F; *line om* WHmCrGYOC^{2}CBLMR.

33α *in margin* OC^{2}; *line om* F. *Dixit*] *Et dixit* B. *sunt*] *sunt ⁊c* HmGYOC^{2}CB.

34 Saue...made] And made man WGYO C^{2}CBLMR (man] *above line another hand* R; *glossed* i. adam LM); And made Adam Cr; And made furst Adam man Hm; But he made Adam a man F. ymage] likkest WHmCrGYOC^{2}CBLMF; Ilikest R. to] *om* CotF. self] selue F; self one WHmCr GYOCBLR; selue*n* one C^{2}; one M.

35 of...bon] was maad of Adam is ryb F. outen] out Cr^{23}. mene] mede B.

36 For] ⁊ for F. synguler hymself] nowht syng*u*ler F. and] he F; *om* R.

37 As] And B. seiþ] sey GCrCR. herto] þerto GOC^{2}.

38 My] For my F. moot] myght G. forþ] now HmCrGYOC^{2}CBLMR.

39 Right] Eue*n* Cr. a] *om* GC. sholde] schul R. l*ett*res] a lettre F. if] and WHm CrGYOC^{2}CBLMRF. hym] he Cr; only F.

40 Though] Or þey3 F. wiste to] koude WHmCrGRF; kouþe YOC^{2}CBLM. and] ⁊ F; if WHmCrGYOC^{2}CBLMR. hadde] lakked F. a] CBF; no WHmCrGYOC^{2} LMR.

41 lettre] lettres OCr^{23}C^{2}. þe] his CrF. leue] lyue Cot. were] worth M; sholde F. neu*ere*] not be F. ymaked] maked Cr^{1} GF.

42 And] Ryght F; *om* G. semeþ] bisemeth M; semed R. hym] god F. þere...bible] as þe bible telleþ WHmCrLMRF; as þe boke tellethe GYOC^{2}CB.

43 þ*ere* god seyde þis sawe *faciamus hominem ad ymaginem ⁊c* F; There he seide *Dixit ⁊ facta sunt* WHmCrGYOC^{2}CBL MR (he] it CB. seide] seith YGOC^{2}CB. *sunt*] *sunt ⁊c* GYM).

44 moste werche] wroghte þus F. word] wordus M. and] ⁊ *with* F. shewe] gan shewe F.

45 was man] man was F. þoru3] by Cr. my3t...almy3ty] þre p*er*sones oone F.

46 and(1)...laste] he wroghte ma*n* ⁊ 3af hy*m* lyf after F. and(1)] ⁊ his Cr. lif] his lyf Hm.

47 þus] *om* F. gaf] yaf YC^{2}BmBo. of] HmCrGYOC^{2}CBLMRF; þoru3 W.

48 graunted] gr*a*unte Y; he grawntyd F.

Lif þat ay shal laste, [and] al his lynage after.
[Th]at is þe Castel þat kynde made; *caro* it hatte,
As muche to mene as man wiþ a Soule.
[Th]at he wroȝte wiþ werk and wiþ word boþe;
Thorgh myȝt of þe mageste man was ymaked.
Inwit and alle wittes [en]closed ben þ*er*Inne
For loue of þe lady *anima* þat lif is ynempned.
Ouer al in mannes body he[o] walkeþ and wandreþ,
A[c] in þe herte is hir hoom and hir mooste reste.
Ac Inwit is in þe heed and to þe herte he lokeþ
What *anima* is leef or looþ; he l[e]t hire at his wille,
For after þe grace of god þe gretteste is Inwit.
Muche wo worþ þat man þat mysruleþ his Inwit,
And þat ben glotons, glubberes; hir god is hire wombe:
Quorum deus venter est.
For þei seruen Sathan hir soules shal he haue;
That lyuen synful lif here hir soule is lich þe deuel.

49 Lif] And þat is lif WHmCrGYOC^{2}CBLMR; þere is F. ay] eu*er* GF. and] to WHmCrGYOC^{2}CBLMRF. his] our Cr; *om* HmGYOC^{2}CBLM. lynage] lynages GYOC^{2}C.
50 That] And þat WHmCrGYOC^{2}CBLMF; And þis R. is þe] *om* F. Castel] catel BR. hatte] hatteth HmB.
51 As] And is as WCrGYCBLMRF; and is also Hm; And þat is as OC^2. muche] mychel F.
52 That] And þat WHmCrGYOC^{2}CBLMRF. wroȝte] *om* Cr^1. wiþ(1)] it as F. word] his word F; his wordes R.
53 þe] his C^2. man was] þus was ma*n* F; in Ada*m* was Cr^1. ymaked] maked Cr^{1}G.
54 Inwit] Inwyttis B. enclosed] yclosed F; closed WHmCrGYOC^{2}CBLM; Iclothed R.
55 þe] þat HmF. ynempned] yneuened G; nempned Cr^3; named Cr^{12}; sprenklyd F.
56 *line om* CB. heo] ȝhe (*over erasure another ink*) Hm; she Cr; he WGYOC^{2}LMRF. walkeþ] walweþ F; waweth M.
57 Ac] YOBLR; but GF; And WHmCrC^{2}C; Ay (y *another ink*) M. hir(1)] his CBm; *om* BoCot. hir(2)] his CB.
58 Ac] but G; And CrC^{2}CF. Inwit] wytt BoCot. he] *om* CrR.
59 or] ⁊ OC^2. let] CGBmBo; ledyth CrCotF; lat WHmYOC^{2}LMR. his] hire R.
60 For] And Y. of] of grete F. þe(2)... Inwit] Inwit neest folwiþ F.
61 Muche] Mychil FC. þat(1)] tho (o *over erasure*) Hm; þe Cr^{23}. man] men (e *over erasure*) Hm; wiȝt RF. mysruleþ... Inwit] Inw*i*t may not rewle F. his] her (e *over erasure*) Hm.
62 þat] þo F; *om* Hm. glubberes] gluberous Hm; ⁊ gloseris F; clobberis BmBo. hir] þat F. is] is in F.
62α *in margin* OC^2. *est*] *est* ⁊*c* HmGY; *eorum est* BmBo; *eorum est* ⁊*c* Cot.
63 þei seruen] seruen they Cr. þei] swiche F. hir] ⁊ here F. soules] soule LMR. shal he haue] he shal welde F.
64 That] They Cr; For þey F. lyuen] liue in Cr. here] *om* HmF. soule] soules Cr^{23}C. deuel] deuelis OC^2; powke F.

And alle þat lyuen good lif are lik to god almyȝty:
Qui manet in caritate in deo manet &c.
Allas þat drynke shal fordo þat god deere bouȝte,
And dooþ god forsaken hem þat he shoop to his liknesse:
Amen dico vobis, nescio vos; Et alibi, Et dimisi eos secundum desideria eorum. |
[Fauntes and] fooles þat fauten Inwit, *fol.* 48 *b*
[Holy chirche is owynge to helpe hem and saue,
And] fynden hem þat hem fauted, and faderlese children,
And widewes þat han noȝt wherwith to wynnen hem hir foode,
Madde men and maydenes þat helplese were;
Alle þise lakken Inwit and loore [hem] bihoueþ.
Of þis matere I myȝte make a long tale
And fynde fele witnesses among þe foure doctours,
And þat I lye noȝt of þat I lere þee, luc bereþ witnesse.
Godfad[er] and godmod[er] þat seen hire godchildren
At myseise and at myschief and mowe hem amende
Shul [purchace] penaunce in purgatorie but þei hem helpe.

65 alle] þo F. are] *om* F. to] after F; *om* LR. god almyȝty] goddes techyng F.
65α *in margin* OC^2. *Qui*] Seynt Iohan seyþ *qui* F. *caritate*] chritate Bm. *&c*] *et deus in eo* F; *om* CrY.
66 fordo] forde G. bouȝte] aboughte GYOCB (a *erased* Bm).
67 dooþ] dothes C. forsaken] forsake Cr; forsakem Bm. hem] him Cr^{23}Cot. þat] *om* M. he shoop] shoop hem FR; he scoppe (*corrected another hand*) C^2. to] after F.
67α *line om* F. *Et*(1)...*eorum*] *om* R. *desideria*] *desiderata* Cr. *eorum*] *eorum ibunt &c* M; *eorum &c* HmOC^{2}Cot; *&c* GYCBmBo.
68–75 *very badly faded* O.
68, 69 Fooles þat fauten Inwit I fynde þat holy chirche WHmCrGYOC^{2}CBLMR (fauten] failen BHm); I fyȝnde þat holy chirche sholde neuere faylyn foolys F.
70 And...and] Ne knowe non defawhte of F. And] Sholde WHmCrGYOC^{2}CBLMR. fynden] fynde HmCr^{1}OC^{2}B. hem (2)] they (*over erasure another ink*) Hm; *om* CrR. fauted] fauteth YGOC^{2}BR; fauten Cr^{23}C; faute Cr^1; faylen Hm.
71 *line om* CB. And] Ne F. with] on G. wynnen] wynne OCrC^2. hem] *om* Hm GF.
72 Madde] And madde F; Mande Cr^3. were] weren OC^{2}F.
73 Alle] For alle F. lakken] lacke Cr. hem] F; *om* WHmCrGYOC^{2}CBLMR. bihoueþ] byhouen G.
74 Of] But of F. I myȝte] miȝte I M. make] maken FHm.
75 fynde] finden Cr^{23}Hm. fele] fell G. witnesses] witnesse YGOC^{2}CR. among] of F.
76 And] *om* Cr. of...þee] *in parentheses* G; *om* F. of þat] on þat Cr; *om* R. lere] lerne HmCr. luc] seynt Luk F.
77 God] þat boþe god F. fader...moder] YHmGOC^{2}CBLMRF; fadres and godmodres WCr.
78 At] In F; & G; þat is R. at] *om* GYOC^{2}CBMF. mowe] might Cr^1. hem] hem wel F.
79 Shul] þey shull F; Schullen B. purchace] haue WHmCrGYOC^{2}CBLMRF. þei] ȝif they HmYOC^{2}CBLMRF.

For moore bilongeþ to þe litel barn er he þe lawe knowe
Than nempnynge of a name and he neuer þe wiser.
Sholde no cristene creature cryen at þe yate
Ne faille payn ne potage and prelates dide as þei sholden.
A Iew wolde noȝt se a Iew go Ianglyng for defaute
For alle þe mebles on þis moolde and he amende it myȝte.
Allas þat a cristene creature shal be vnkynde til anoþer!
Syn Iewes, þat we Iugge Iudas felawes,
Eyþer of hem helpeþ ooþer of þat þat h[y]m nedeþ,
Whi [ne wol] we cristene of cristes good be as kynde?
[So] Iewes [shul] ben oure loresmen, shame to vs alle!
The commune for hir vnkyndenesse, I drede me, shul abye;
Bisshopes shul be blamed for beggeres sake.
He is [Iugged wiþ] Iudas þat ȝyueþ a Iaper siluer
And biddeþ þe beggere go for his broke cloþes:
Proditor est prelatus cum Iuda qui patrimonium christi minus distribuit; Et alibi, Perniciosus dispensator est qui res pauperum christi inutiliter consumit. |

80 bilongeþ] longiþ F; longer G. to þe] a F. knowe] conne Hm.
81 nempnynge] neuenyng G; nempned Cr^1; nempne F. of a] first his F. he] he be F; *om* CB.
82 Sholde] For þere shold F. cryen] crie CrOC^2. þe] þyn F.
83 Ne] And RF. faille] faylen HmF. ne] and HmGRF. dide] diden OHmC^{2}BF. as þei] here F. sholden] sholde GCrYC BR; devir F.
84 wolde] wol Cr. Ianglyng] Iangle G.
85 mebles] mouables CrG; nobles HmR; mone F. on] In G; of BR. þis] þe F. moolde] worlde G.
86 þat] þanne þat F. creature] man F. shal] sholde YF. be] be so YOC^{2}BM; so ben F. til anoþer] *om* F. til] to CrGYO C^{2}CBM.
87 Syn] Sytthyn þe F. Iugge] Iuggen GOC^{2}R; forIuggen to ben F. felawes] felawe F.
88 Eyþer] þat ayther R; Eche Cr; þat ech F. of hem] *om* RF. helpeþ] helpen Cot; helpe Cr^{23}. þat] hem RF. þat] of good þat F; *om* Hm. hym] YOC^{2}CBLMR; hem WHmCrGF.
89 ne wol] ne woll HmBR; nel WGYC^2 CLM; nylen O; wyl not Cr^{23}; wil Cr^{1}F. we] we not Cr^1. as] also HmBF. kynde] kynde willed (willed *another ink* M).
90 So...shul] As Iewes þat WHmCrGYO C^{2}CBLMRF. oure lores] forlore F. shame] *twice* (*second cancelled*) Y; to schame R; It is shame F. to] vnto M.
91 The] they G. commune] come G; ryche F. vnkyndenesse] wikkednesse CB. I...shul] shull yt ful sore F. abye] abide B.
92 shul] shullen BM.
93 is] *om* F. Iugged wiþ] wors þan WHm CrGYOC^{2}CBLMRF. a Iaper] Iapers Cr^{23}GYOC^{2}CB (*corrected main hand from* beggers G).
94 biddeþ] bit RG. beggere] beggers GB. go] go forþ B; gon awey F. broke] broken CrHmOC^{2}BM.
94α *Et...consumit*] *om* F. *est*(2)] *om* OC^2. *christi*(2)] *om* GYOC^{2}CB. *inutiliter*] *multipliciter* M.

He dooþ noȝt wel þat dooþ þus, ne drat noȝt god almyȝty, *fol.* 49 *a*
[Ne] loueþ noȝt Salomons sawes þat Sapience tauȝte:
Inicium sapiencie timor domini.
That dredeþ god, he dooþ wel; þat dredeþ hym for loue
And [dredeþ hym] noȝt for drede of vengeaunce dooþ þerfore þe bettre;
He dooþ best þat wiþdraweþ hym by daye and by nyȝte
To spille any speche or any space of tyme:
Qui offendit in vno in omnibus est reus.
[Tynynge] of tyme, truþe woot þe soþe,
Is moost yhated vpon erþe of hem þat ben in heuene;
And siþþe to spille speche þat [spire] is of grace
And goddes gleman and a game of heuene.
Wolde neu*ere* þe feiþful fader [h]is fiþele were vntempred
Ne his gleman a gedelyng, a goere to tau*er*nes.
To alle trewe tidy men þat trauaille desiren,

95 þus] so Cr. ne] & ne G; he F. drat] dredeþ HmCrGC^{2}F. noȝt(2)] *om* Cr. almyȝty] of might Cr.
96 Ne] YGOC^{2}CBLMR; He WHmCrF. loueþ] lokyþ F. tauȝte] telleþ M; made Hm; is named F.
96α *in margin* OC^{2}. *Inicium*] he seyþ *inicium* F. *domini*] *domini &c* HmY; *om* Bo.
97, 98 *as one line* YGOC^{2}CB: Drede god for loue & þou dost wel but noȝt for vengeance & þou dost bet (& þou(1)] *om* G. bet] bett*er* G).
97 That] For he þat F. dredeþ(1)] drad R. he] *om* F. þat] he F. dredeþ(2)] drad RM. hym...loue] god his makere F.
98 And...hym] And drad hym R; he dredyþ F; And WHmCrLM. drede] loue RF. dooþ þerfore] to do R; for to don F. bettre] bet Cr^{23}.
99 He...hym] thow doest best yff þou wi*th*drawe GYOC^{2}CB. He] But he F.
100 spille] spyllyn F.
100α *vno*] *-no over erasure* M; *verbo* LR; *vno verbo* F. *in*(2)] *est in* OCB; *est* C^{2}. *est*] *reus* HmF; *om* OC^{2}CB. *reus*] *reus &c* B; *est* F; *est &c* Hm.
101 Tynynge] Lesynge WHmCrGYOC^{2}CBLMR; Lesyngys F. of tyme] & ydilnesse F. woot] wootethe GCr.
102 yhated] hated CrHmGOC^{2}F. vpon] vp CLMR (on *above line* M); on G; *om* F. erþe] huttyrly F. þat ben] heyȝe F.
103, 104 *in lower margin another hand and ink* M.
103 siþþe] seche R; all swiche F. to spille] þat spillyn F. þat...of] here spiryȝt haþ no F. spire] YGOC^{2}CBLR; spicerie W; spicere Hm; enspired CrM (*over erasure another hand* M).
104 *run together with* 106 C. And] and a Hm; For þey seme*n* F. man...of] men to gamen he*m* in F; *om* C. game] gamyn Hm. heuene] *om* C.
105 *line om* C. þe] *rubbed* Hm. his] Cr HmGYOC^{2}BLMRF (h *over erasure* Hm); þis W. vntempred] vntymbred R.
106 Ne...gleman] *om* C. Ne his] now ys G. gedelyng] godelyng Y; galyng F. a(2)] & a G; *om* M. goere] goinge M. tauernes] tauerne CrF.
107 To] For to F. desiren] dysyre F.

Oure lord louep hem and lent, loude ouþer stille,
Grace to go to hem and ofgon hir liflode:
Inquirentes autem dominum non minuentur omni bono.
[Dowel in þis world is trewe wedded libbynge folk],
For þei mote werche and wynne and þe world sustene;
For of hir kynde þei come þat Confessours ben nempned,
Kynges and kny3tes, kaysers and [clerkes];
Maidenes and martires out of o man come.
The wif was maad þe w[y]e for to helpe werche,
And þus was wedlok ywro3t wiþ a mene persone,
First by þe fadres wille and þe frendes conseille,
And siþenes by assent of hemself as þei two my3te acorde;
And þus was wedlok ywro3t and god hymself it made. |
In erþe [þe] heuene [is]; hymself [was þe] witnesse. *fol. 49 b*
Ac fals folk, feiþlees, þeues and lyeres,
Wastours and wrecches out of wedlok, I trowe,
Conceyued ben in [cursed] tyme as Caym was on Eue
[After þat Adam and heo eten þe appul].

108 hem] *om* OC^{2}. and] or Y. lent] leneth hem Hm. loude] land to Cr^{1}.
109 to hem] to hem tille R; hem to F. and] to F. ofgon] agon HmCr^{23}GYOC^{2}CBLMR; getyn F.
109α *in margin* OC^{2}. *dominum*] *deum* G. *minuentur*] minientur G; *inuenientur* F. *bono*] *bono ⁊c* Hm.
110 Trewe wedded libbynge folk in þis world is dowel WHmCrGYOC^{2}CBLMRF.
111 mote] moten BF; most Cr^{1}; musten OC^{2}. werche] werchen M. and(1)] to F. wynne] wynnen M; wyne (*?* wyue) C.
112 hir] his Cr^{1}. þei] he RF. come] comen C^{2}BM; came *corrected from* camen O. Confessours] confessour Cr^{1}G. nempned] neuened G.
113 Kynges] ⁊ bothe kynggys F; kaysers B. kny3tes] knyghtys ⁊ F; kyngis B. kaysers] knyttis B. clerkes] CotBoF; cherles WHmCrGYOC^{2}CBmLMR.
114 Maidenes] ⁊ Maydenys F. o] *om* F. come] comen C^{2}; came G; kemen F.
115 The wif] ⁊ womman F. þe] a F. wye] wey3 F; weye WHmYOC^{2}CBLMR; way CrG. for] *om* CrCot. helpe] helpun M. werche] worchen M; to worche GCr.
116 *run together with* 119 RF. ywro3t] wrought Cr^{1}GF. wiþ...persone] *om* RF.
117, 118 *lines om* RF.
118 by] by the HmCrC^{2}. two] *om* Cr. my3te] my3ten OBmBoM.
119 And...ywro3t] *om* RF. ywro3t] wrought Cr^{1}G. and] *om* G.
120 In] þe C^{2}. þe(1)] GHmYOCBL; þere R; here F; in C^{2}; and in WCrM (and *above line* M). is] YHmGOC^{2}CBLMRF (*erased* M); *om* WCr. was þe] GHmCrYOC^{2}LMR; bereþ WCBF.
121 Ac] but GF; And CrC^{2}C. folk] folk and RF. þeues] boþe þevys F.
122 Wastours] ⁊ wastoures F.
123 Conceyued] Are conceyvid F. ben] *om* C^{2}F. in] *om* R. cursed] yuel WYOCLMR; euyl HmGC^{2}BF; ill Cr. Caym was] was chaym Cot. on] of Cr^{23}YOC^{2}F; and BoCot. Eue] heuene Y.
124 *not in* WHmCrGYOC^{2}CBLMRF.

Of swiche synfulle sherewes þe Sauter makeþ mynde:
Concepit dolore[m] & peperit iniquitatem.
And alle þat come of þat Caym come to yuel ende,
[For] god sente to Se[þ] and seide by an Aungel,
"Thyn issue in þyn issue, I wol þat þei be wedded,
And noȝt þi kynde wiþ Caymes ycoupled n[e] yspoused".
Yet [seþ], ayein þe sonde of oure Saueo*ur* of heuene,
Caymes kynde and his kynde coupled togideres,
Til god wraþed [wiþ] hir werkes and swich a word seide,
"That I [man makede now] it me forþynkeþ":
Penitet me fecisse hominem.
And com to Noe anon and bad hym noȝt lette:
"Swiþe go shape a ship of shides and of bordes;
Thyself and þi sones þre and siþen youre wyues,
Buskeþ yow to þat boot and bideþ þerInne
Til fourty daies be fulfild, *þat* flood haue ywasshen

125 makeþ mynde] seyþ þis sawe F.
125α *in margin* O. *dolorem*] HmRF (*over erasure another ink* Hm); *in dolore* WCrGY OC^{2}CBLM. *iniquitatem*] CrGBRF; *iniquitatem &c* WHmYOC^{2}CLM.
126 come (*both*)] comen BHmF. þat(2)] *om* F.
127 For] CrHmGYOCBLMRF; And W; *om* C^2. sente] -e *another ink* M; sent YLR; send G; hy*m* F. Seþ] seyn F; Sem CrOC^2 CBmBoR; Seem WHmGYCotLM. and] & þus F. by] *om* F. an] þe CBF.
128 in] wi*th* F. wol] wold Cot. wedded] ioyned Cr^{23}OC^2.
129 wiþ] in Cr. Caymes] caym R; Caines kind Cr; Cayn neyþir F. ycoupled] coupled CrGF. ne] GYOC^{2}CBLMRF; ner Hm; nor WCr. yspoused] spoused CrHmGYOC^{2}CBMF.
130 Yet seþ] But su*m*me ȝit F. seþ] Sem Cr; seem (*over erasure another ink*) M; some WGYCotL; so*m*me CR; summe HmOC^{2}BmBo. sonde] sou*n*d Cr; *by correction from* some Bm. Saueo*ur*] saviou*r*is F; lorde CB. of heuene] heeste F.
131 Caymes kynde] Cayn is keen F. his] her B. kynde(2)] kyn M. coupled] ycouplede OC^2; wery*n* cowpled F.
132 *run together with* 133 CB. god] god þey F. wraþed...seide] saide for wrathe CB. wraþed] wraþen C^2. wiþ] OGYC^2 MF; for WHmCrLR. werkes] werk F. swich a word] þis word he F.
133 I] y on moolde F. man...now] maked man now YGOC^{2}LMRF; made man now HmCr; makede man WCB. it me] me it YGOC^{2}M; me CB. forþynkeþ] athynketh YOC^{2}CBLM; þinketh R.
133α *in margin* OC^2. *fecisse hominem*] *hominem fecisse* F. *fecisse*] *fecisti* Cr^1. *hominem*] *hominem &c* HmGYB.
134 And] & þanne god F. com] so*m*me C; sente B. anon] *om* F. lette] lettyn F.
135 Swiþe] he seide F. a] þe a F. of(2)] *om* CB.
136 self] seluen M; folk B. sones þre] thre sones GYOC^{2}C; sones B.
137 Buskeþ] buske HmCrGYOC^{2}CBLM RF. to] into F. bideþ] byde CrC^{2}M; abydeth HmF. þer] þere F; ye þer WHm Cr^{1}GYOC^{2}CBLMR; you ther Cr^{23}.
138 þat] þat HmCr^{12}GOC^{2}CBoCotLR; *þat* þe WCr^{3}Y; þat þat (*second cancelled*) Bm; and M; & þe F. haue] haþ F. ywasshen] wayschen BCr^1; Iwasted RF.

Clene awey þe corsed blood þat Caym haþ ymaked.
Beestes þ*at* now ben shul banne þe tyme
That euere cursed Caym coom on þis erþe;
Alle shul deye for hise dedes by [dounes] and hulles,
And þe foweles þat fleen forþ wiþ oþ*ere* beestes,
Excepte oonliche of ech kynde a couple
That in [þe] shyngled ship shul ben ysaued."
Here abouȝte þe barn þe belsires giltes, |
And alle for hir [fore]fadres ferden þe werse. *fol.* 50 *a*
The gospel is hera[g]ein in o degre, I fynde:
Filius non portabit iniquitatem patris et pater non portabit iniquitatem filij.
Ac I fynde, if þe fader be fals and a sherewe,
That somdel þe sone shal haue þe sires tacches.
Impe on an Ell*ere*, and if þyn appul be swete
Muchel m*er*ueille me þynkeþ; and moore of a sherewe
That bryngeþ forþ any barn but if he be þe same
And haue a Sauo*ur* after þe sire; selde sestow ooþer:
Numquam collig[unt] de spinis vua[s] nec de tribulis ficus.
And þus þoruȝ cursed Caym cam care vpon erþe,

139 Clene] Al cleene F; al eue*n* C^2. awey] *om* F. ymaked] maked GCot; made Cr.
140 shul] shullen BM.
141 cursed] GHm; þat cursed WCrYOC^{2}CBLMRF. on] vpon F; in YC; to Hm.
142 *line om* F. shul] shullen B. dounes] dales WHmCrGYOC^{2}CBLMR. and] MR; and by WHmCrGYOC^{2}CBL. hulles] downes Cr.
143 þe] *om* C^2. fleen] flowe Cr. forþ] shull forþ F; for L. oþere] þe F.
144 ech] ech a YOC^2; euery CrF; on R. a] & a OC^2.
145 *line om* F. þe] þi WHmCrGYOC^{2}CBLM; þis R. shyngled] syngled GY. shul] shullen BM. ysaued] saued Cr^{1}Hm.
146 Here] ther G; þan dere F. abouȝte] boughte YCr^{23}GOC^2; abode Cr^1. þe(2)] his F. sires] syre GYC.
147 And alle] þat after F. hir] his B. fore-fadres] FHmCr^{23}YOC^{2}CLMR (*over erasure* Hm); fornefadres G; fadres WCr^1; sake B. ferden þe] fareden the Cr^3; fareden they Cr^2; fared they Cr^1; þei ferden þe WHmGYOC^{2}CBLMRF.
148 The] But þe F. her] þer GF. agein] agayn HmCrGYLRF; ayein WOC^{2}CBM. o] þis F.
149 *in margin* O. *patris*] *om* Cot. *et... portabit*] *nec pater* RF. *portabit*(2)...*filij*] *portabit &c* OC^2; *&c* GYCB. *filij*] RCrF; *filij &c* WHmL; *&c* M.
150 Ac] but GF; And CrC^{2}C. and] or YF.
151 þe(2)] of þe BmBo; of his F. sires] sire CR. tacches] tutches Cr.
152 Impe] For ympe F. on] vpon HmRF; in C; off G. Ellere] ellerne tre HmB. if] *om* B. þyn] the Hm. swete] soote F.
153 Muchel] muche HmCr^{23}GYOC^{2}CBMF. þynkeþ] thynk C. and] & ȝit F.
154 if] *om* Cr^{1}GF. he] it Cr.
155 haue a] *om* F. selde] selden OC^{2}B. sestow] sistow Bm.
155α *in margin* O. *colligunt*] coligunt F; *colligimus* GYOC^{2}CB; *colligitur* WHmCrLMR. *vuas*] GYOC^{2}CBLMRF (*s erased* M); *vua* WHmCr. *nec*] *ne* Bm. *ficus*] *ficus &c* Hm.
156 vpon] first on F.

And al for þei wroȝte wedlokes ayein [þe wille of god].
Forþi haue þei maugre of hir mariages þ*a*t marie so hir children.
For some, as I se now, sooþ for to telle,
For coueitise of catel vnkyndely ben [maried].
[A] careful concepcion comeþ of [swich weddynge]
As bifel of þe folk þat I bifore [shewed].
[For] goode sholde wedde goode, þouȝ þei no good hadde;
"I am *via & veritas*", seiþ crist, "I may auaunce alle."
It is an vncomly couple, by crist! as me þynkeþ,
To yeuen a yong wenche to [a yolde] feble,
Or wedden any wodewe for [wele] of hir goodes
That neu*er*e shal barn bere but it be in armes.
[In Ielousie, ioyelees, and ianglynge on bedde,
Many peire siþen þe pestilence han pliȝt hem togideres.

157 *line om* Cr^{1}. wroȝte] wrouȝten OC^{2}BRF. wedlokes] wedlok YCr^{23}GOC^{2}CB. þe...god] goddes wille WHmCr^{23}GYOC^{2}CBLMRF.

158 *as two lines divided after* vnkende F. Forþi] Therfore Cr^{1}. þi] þei B. haue...hir(1)] þey haddy*n* mawgrees for F. þei] þe Cr^{1}BoCot; þo Bm. of...mariages] *om* GYOC^{2}CB. of] for LMR. þat] & G; as me*n* R; vnkende & on þe same maner now me*n* F. marie so] so maryen GYOC^{2}C. marie] maryen HmBRF. so] now R; *om* BF.

159 as] me*n* as F. se] sey B. now] *om* F. sooþ for] the sothe Hm. telle] tellen M.

160 coueitise] couetous Cr^{1}. maried] wedded WHmCrGYOC^{2}CBLMRF.

161 A] a G; þan a F; As WCr^{1}LMR; Ac YOB; and HmCr^{23}C^{2}C. concepcion] Concepciouns M. of] to R. swich weddynge] swiche mariages WHmCrGYOC^{2}CBoCotLM; sheche mariagis Bm; þat mariages R; þat Maryage F.

162 As] As yt F. of] to G. þe] þat RF. þat] as G. bifore] *om* M. shewed] tolde Cr; of tolde WHmGYOC^{2}CBLMR; hond tolde F.

163 *line om* RF. For] CrHmGYOC^{2}CBLM; Therfore W. sholde] schulden O Hm; shul Y. þei no] her neyther Hm.

164 *line om* RF. I(1)] For I CB. seiþ crist] seid crist B; *om* OC^{2}. I(2)...alle] as me þynkeþ BoCot; as I me þynkiþe Bm. auaunce] auaunce*n* M. alle] HmCrGYOC^{2}CLM; yow alle W.

165 *transposed with* 166 B. an vncomly] *above line another ink* M; an oncomely (on *above line main hand*) L; an komely F; an vnkouþe C; a wond*ur* B. crist] Ihesus RF. þynkeþ] thynke C; semeþ F.

166 yeuen] yeue YOC^{2}BRF; geue CrC; gyuen G. a(1)] *om* F. wenche] Mayde F. a yolde] an olde HmCrYOC^{2}CLMR (e *erased* M); an old WGBF. feble] feble man HmB; baslard F.

167 Or...any] Er a ȝong ma*n* an old F. wedden] wedde Hm; weddyd C^{2}. wele] welþe WHmCrGYOC^{2}CBLMRF.

168 neu*er*e shal] shal neuer Cr. but] Hm GBMF; but if WCrYOC^{2}CLR. it be] *om* F. in] CrHmGOC^{2}CBLMR; in hir W; in two F; *om* Y.

169 *line om* RF; *copied after* 171 WHmCrGYOC^{2}CBLM. ioyelees] Ioyesles G; ioilisie Bm; geolous BoCot. and] *om* G. ianglynge] Ianglen CrBm. on] In G.

170 Many] Many a WHmCrGYOC^{2}CBLMRF. þe] *om* HmB. hem] hom L.

The fruyt þat [þei] brynge forþ arn [manye] foule wordes;
Haue þei no children but cheeste and [choppes] bitwene.
[Th]ouȝ þei do hem to Dunmowe, but if þe deuel helpe *fol. 50 b*
To folwen after þe flicche, fecche þei it neuere;
But þei boþe be forswore þat bacon þei tyne.
Forþi I counseille alle cristene coueite noȝt be wedded
For coueitise of catel ne of kynrede riche;
Ac maidenes and maydenes macche yow [ysamme];
[Wideweres and wodewes] wercheþ [riȝt also];
For no londes, but for loue, loke ye be wedded
And þanne gete ye *gra*ce of god and good ynouȝ to lyue wiþ.
And euery maner seculer [man] þat may noȝt continue
Wisely go wedde and ware [þee] fro synne,
Fo[r] lecherie in likynge is lymeyerd of helle.
Whiles þow art yong [and yeep] and þi wepene [yet] kene

171 þei] þey HmCrGYOC^{2}CBLMRF; *om* W. brynge] bryngen OBR; brngen C^{2}. manye] but F; *om* WHmCrGYOC^{2}CBLMR. *Here* WHmCrGYOC^{2}CBLM *copy line* 169.
172 Haue þei] þey have F. cheeste] chests Cr; chydes C; iangelynge R; *om* F. and] *om* F. choppes] choppyng GOC^{2}CBL; cloppyng Y; clappyng WCr; carpynge Hm; chidynge *over erasure another ink* M; gaying R; Ianglyng F. bitwene] hem bitwene WHmCrGYOC^{2}CBLMRF.
173–5 *lines om and three spurious lines in their place* RF; *see above*, p. 224.
173 Thouȝ] And þouȝ WHmCrGYOC^{2}CBLM. do hem] gone Cr^{1}. if] *om* G.
174 folwen] folwe BCrC.
175 But] B; And but WHmCrGYOC^{2}CLM. swore] sworen OC^{2}CB. þei tyne] get they neuyr (*a later hand*) M. tyne] tynen OC^{2}.
176 Forþi] Therfore Cr^{1}. counseille] conseleile Bm. cristene] crystyn men HmB; me*n* ȝee F. be] to be CrMR. wedded] weddyn C^{2}.
177 of (*both*)] of no B.
178 Ac] but GF; And CrC^{2}C. and] wi*th* F. macche] make R; marye F. ysamme] togideres WHmCrGYOC^{2}CBLMRF.
179 Wideweres] Wydeweres R; & wydewerys F; Wydwes HmCrGYOCBLM; Wodewes W; wedowes C^{2}. and] wi*th* F. Wodewes] wydewes RHmCrF; wideweres WGYOCBLM; wedowers C^{2}. wercheþ] werche FCrM. riȝt also] þe same WHmCrGYOC^{2}CBLR; ȝee þe same FM.
180 no] none HmB. londes] lond F. loke] lokiþ B. ye] þat ȝe R. be wedded] ne wedde F.
181 gete] geten O. ye] ȝe RF; ye þe WHmCrGYOC^{2}CBLM. lyue] liuen M; welde F. wiþ] *om* F.
182–8 *lines om* RF.
182 maner] man Cr. man þat] þat WHmCrGYOC^{2}CBLM. continue] conteynue Bm; conteyne HmCr^{23}OC^{2}BoCot.
183 go] to B. þee] þe G; hym WHmCrYOC^{2}CBLM.
184 For] CrHmGYOC^{2}CBLM; Fo W. likynge] lokyng Cr^{23}GYOC^{2}CB. is] ys a G.
185 and(1)...yet] and þi wepene WHmCrGYOC^{2}CBLM.

Wreke þee wiþ wyuyng if þow wolt ben excused:
Dum sis vir fortis ne des tua robora scortis;
Scribitur in portis, meretrix est ianua mortis.
Whan ye han wyued beþ war and wercheþ in tyme,
No3t as Adam and Eue whan Caym was engendred;
For in vntyme, trewely, bitwene man and womman
Sholde no [bedbourde] be; but þei boþe were clene
Of lif and of [loue] and [of lawe also]
That [dede derne] do no man ne sholde.
A[c] if þei leden þus hir lif it likeþ god almy3ty,
For he made wedlok first and [þus] hymself seide:
Bonum est vt vnusquisque vxorem suam habeat propter fornicacionem.
[That] oþergates ben geten for gedelynges arn holden,
As fals folk, fondlynges, faitours and lieres,
Vngracious to gete good or loue of þe peple; |
Wandren [as wolues] and wasten [if þei] mowe; *fol.* 51 *a*
Ayeins dowel þei doon yuel and þe deuel [plese],

186 Wreke] werke OC^{2}. wyuyng] wynnynge C^{2}B. wolt] wil L.
186α *as one line with* 187 O. *Dum*] *cum* GYOC^{2}CB. *sis*] *scis* Bm. *ne*] *non* Cot.
187 wercheþ] wurche HmCrG.
188 Caym] tyme Hm.
189 For] And R. in vntyme] in one tyme Cr; sum ty3me F; vnite CB.
190 Sholde] Ne sholde WHmCrGYOC^{2}CBLMRF (ne *corrected from* no Hm). no] not F. bedbourde] bourde on bedde WCrOC^{2}CBLM; bourde o bedde Y; berde a bedde R; bourde In bed G; berde in bedde Hm; lyggyn In bedde F. be] *om* F. but] F; but if WHmCrGYOC^{2}CBLMR. boþe were] were boþe Hm; were CB. were] weren O.
191 Of] R; Boþe of WHmCrGYOC^{2}CBLM; Boþe in F. of(1)...also] of soule and in parfit charite WHmCrGYOC^{2}CBLMR; in sowle ⁊ also in parfy3t charyte F.
192 dede derne] ilke derne dede WHmCrGYOC^{2}CBLMRF. do...sholde] shold non man don elles F. no man] *twice, first cancelled* M. ne] *om* R.
193 *transposed with* 194 Y. Ac] YO; but GCB; And WHmCrC^{2}LMR; ⁊ nou F. þei] men F. leden] lead Cr; ledden RC^{2}; ledde F. þus] þis G. likeþ] liked LR; wold lyke F. god] nat god Cot; *om* F. almy3ty] amy3ty C.
194 þus] F; *om* WHmCrGYOC^{2}CBLMR. self] seluen M. seide] seyde FCr^{23}; it seide WHmGYOC^{2}CBLMR; *om* Cr^{1}.
194α *vnus*] vuunus G. *propter*] *om* RF. *fornicacionem*] *fornicacionem* ⁊c Hm; *om* RF.
195 That] And þei þat WHmCrGYOC^{2}CBmBoLMRF; and thei Cot. ben] were Hm. holden] holde FCr.
196 As] and BRF. folk] folk ⁊ F. faitours] ⁊ faytoures F.
197 Vngracious] ⁊ vngracious F. gete] geten MF.
198 Wandren] But þey wandren F. as ...and] and WHmCrGYOC^{2}CBLMRF. wasten] waste YGC. if þei] what þei cacche WHmCrGYOC^{2}BLMR; what þe cacche C; what þey wynne F.
199 dowel] dewel R. þe] *by correction* Cot. plese] serue WHmCrGYCLMRF; seruen OC^{2}B.

And after hir deeþ day shul dwelle wiþ þe same
But god gyue hem grace here to amende.
Dowel, my [deere], is to doon as lawe techeþ:
To loue [and to lowe þee and no lif to greue;
Ac to loue and to lene], leue me, þat is dobet;
To ȝyuen and to yemen boþe yonge and olde,
To helen and to helpen, is dobest of alle.
[Thanne is dowel] to drede, and dobet to suffre,
And so comeþ dobest [aboute] and bryngeþ adoun mody,
And þat is wikked wille þat many werk shendeþ,
And dryueþ awey dowel þoruȝ dedliche synnes.'

200 deeþ] deathes Cr; dede CG. shul] shullen MR; þei shul F; soule C; þe soule Bm; þe soule shal BoCot. dwelle] dwellen M; dwelles C. þe] her*e* F. same] deuel R; Mayst*er* F.

201 god] go Bm. gyue] ȝeue BMR. hem] hym C. here] *om* Y. to] hemself to WHmGYOC^{2}LMR; hemseluen to CCrB; hemselue soone F.

202–6 *lines om* RF.

202 deere] frend WHmCrGYOC^{2}CBLM. to] *om* CB. as] as the GYOC^{2}CBM. lawe techeþ] lawes techen Cr.

203 *run together with* 204 WHmCrGYOC^{2}CBLM. and(1)...greue] *om* WHmCrGYOC^{2}CBLM.

204 Ac...lene] þi frend and þi foo WHmCrGYOC^{2}CBLM. bet] bett*er* G.

205 ȝyuen] gyuen GC; gyue Cr. and to yemen] vnto menne Cr. yemen] ȝeme B; ȝym*en* C^2.

206 helen] heele BoCot. helpen] holpen Bm.

207 Thanne] þus F; And þus R; And WHmCrYOC^{2}CBLM; *om* G. is dowel] RF; dowel is WHmCrGYOC^{2}CBLM. and] god and WHmCrGYOC^{2}CBLMRF. bet] bett*er* G. to(2)] ys to GYOC^{2}CB. suffre] suffre hy*m* F.

208 so] þa*n* F. comeþ] semeythe G. aboute] of boþe WHmCrGYOC^{2}CBLMRF. adoun] adoun þe WCrYOC^{2}CotLMF; adown þ C; adon þe BmBoR; dou*n* þe HmG.

209 wille] *om* Hm. werk] OHmCrGYC^{2}CBmBoLM; werkes RF; a werk WCot.

210 dryueþ] dryue C. þoruȝ] oonly þoru F; with CB. synnes] synne GYOC^{2}CBF.

X

Thanne hadde wit a wif was hote dame Studie,
That lene was of [liche] and of [lowe chere].
She was wonderly wroþ þat wit [so] tauȝte,
And al starynge dame Studie sterneliche [seide].
'Wel artow wis, [wit', quod she], 'any wisdomes to telle
To flatereres or to fooles þat frenetike ben of wittes',
And blamed hym and banned hym and bad hym be stille—
'Wiþ swiche wise wordes to wissen any sottes!'
And seide, '*noli*[*te*] *mittere*, man, margery perles
Among hogges þat han hawes at wille.
Thei doon but dr[a]uele þ*er*on; draf were hem leuere
Than al þe p*re*cious perree þat in paradis wexeþ.
I seye by [þo]', quod she, 'þat sheweþ by hir werkes
That hem were leu*er*e lond and lordshipe on erþe,
Or richesse or rentes, and reste at hir wille,

1 Thanne...wit] SIre wit hadde F. was] ⁊ was C^{2}; þat was BoCot; þ*at* wat Bm; *altered to* wych G. hote] hoten OHmC^{2}M; called R; klepid F.
2 lene] leue Cr; lefe (*final* e *erased*) Hm. of(1)] to Hm. liche] lire YCB; lere WHmCrGOLMRF; leree C^{2}. lowe chere] liche boþe WHmCrGYOC^{2}CBmBoLM; lichee bothe R; lith bothe (lith *by erasure another ink*) Cot; lycame boþe F.
3 wonderly] wondirful F. þat] *om* Cr. so] me so Cr; me þus WGYOC^{2}CBLMR; þus me Hm; me F. tauȝte] techid Cr.
4 al] al sterne F; *om* G. dame Studie] *om* F. sterneliche] sterliche C^{2}; ⁊ startlynge F; farnely Cr^{3}. seide] YHmCrOC^{2}CBLMR; she sayde GF; loked W.
5 wit...she] quod she to wit WHmCrGYOC^{2}CBLMR; q*uo*d she F. wisdomes] wisdom FG. telle] tellen M.
6 or to] ⁊ F. frenetike] feble F. wittes] witte B.
7 and banned hym] bustously F.
8 wissen] wysse GCrYOC^{2}C.
9 seide] seydyn Hm. *nolite*] *noli* WHmCrGYOC^{2}CBLMR; man *noli* F. man] *om* CBF. margery] Margarite Cr; magerye G.
10 Among] Byfore F. han] hety*n* F; hawes G. hawes] hewes Bm; haue G. at wille] at hoom at her*e* will F; Inowe G.
11 drauele] dravele FY; drauelen OC^{2}M; dryuele WCrGCL; dreuele BR; dreuelyn Hm. hem] hym Y. leuere] bettr*e* F.
12 Than] That Y. þe] *om* CrC. perree] Pearles Cr^{23}. þat] *om* M. wexeþ] þ*at* wexeþ M; wixiþ Bm; vexes C.
13 by þo] it by swiche WHmCrGYOC^{2}CBLMF; it be schuche R. sheweþ] shewe F; shew it Cr. hir] *om* M.
14 lordshipe] lorschipe C^{2}; wurschip Hm. on erþe] here RF.
15 *line om* F. Or] Other R; Of BoCot. richesse] richesses M; rychs Cr^{3}. or] other R; of Bm; and of BoCot. and] or Hm.

Than alle þe sooþ sawes þat Salomon seide euere. |
Wisdom and wit now is noȝt worþ a [risshe] *fol.* 51 *b*
But it be carded wiþ coueitise as cloþeres [don] hir wolle.
[That] kan con[strue] deceites and conspire wronges
And lede forþ a loueday to lette [þe] truþe,
[That] swiche craftes k[onne] to counseil [are] cleped;
Thei lede lordes wiþ lesynges and bilieþ truþe.
Iob þe gentile in hise gestes witnesseþ
That wikked men þei welden þe welþe of þis worlde,
And þat þei ben lordes of ech a lond þat out of lawe libbeþ:
Quare impij viuunt? bene est omnibus qui preuaricantur & inique agunt?
The Sauter seiþ þe same by swiche þat doon ille:
Ecce ipsi peccatores! habundantes in seculo obtinuerunt diuicias.
"Lo!" seiþ holy lettrure, "whiche [lordes] beþ þise sherewes";
Thilke þat god [moost gyueþ] leest good þei deleþ,

16 þe] *om* C.
17 Wisdom...now] For now wit & wisdom F. now is] is now M. worþ] *after cancelled* ak Bm. risshe] kirse Bm; kerse WHmCrGYOC^{2}CBoCotF; carse LMR.
18 But] MGF; But if WHmCrYOC^{2}CB LR. it be] he BoCot. carded] cartid C^2; garded Cr^1. wiþ] be with (be *above line another ink*) Cot. cloþeres] kembsters Hm; kytte F. don] kemben WHmGYOC^{2}C BLMR; kembeþ F; kemb Cr. hir] *om* GYOC^{2}CBRF.
19 That] Whoso WHmCrGYOC^{2}CBo CotLMR; whos Bm; who F. construe] contreue WHmOBLMR; contryue Cr GC^{2}F (y *altered from* e C^2); controue Y; troue C. conspire] conspiren MF.
20 lede] leden RF. to lette] and letten RF. þe] R; wiþ WHmCrGYOC^{2}CBLM; euere F.
21 *line om* F. That...konne] He þat swiche craftes kan WHmCrGYOC^{2}CBLMR. to ...cleped] is oft cleped to counsell Cr. are] is WHmGYOC^{2}CBLMR.
22 *line om* F. lede] leden OHmC^{2}BM. lordes] lordynges C. bilieþ] heliȝeth Cot.
23 þe] þat ys so F. gestes] geestes gretly YCr^{23}OC^{2}CB; gest greatly G. witnesseþ] tellyþ F.
24 þei] *om* HmCr^{23}GYOC^{2}CBF (? *erased* Hm). þe...worlde] welthys on moolde F.
25 þat þei] þey þat F; *om* G. of(1)] in HmR. ech...libbeþ] leedis as owtlawys þei lybbe F. a] *om* CrGYOC^{2}CB. lawe] *om* C. *Hereafter two spurious lines* F; *see above*, p. 222.
25α *Quare*] *Quare ergo* F. *impij*] impe Cr^3. *viuunt*] *viuunt* & M; viunt G. *bene... agunt*] *sulleuati sunt diuicijs* F. *omnibus*] *hominibus* GYOC^{2}CB. *agunt*] *agunt* &c Hm.
26 þat] as Cr. ille] euyl Cr.
26α *ipsi*] *impij* Hm. *peccatores*] *peccatores* & OC^2. *obtinuerunt*] *om* F. *diuicias*] *om* RF.
27 holy] þe holi OC^2. lettrure] lecture Cr Bo. whiche] suyche G. lordes] GCr^{23}Y OC^{2}CBLMRF; woordes Hm; *om* WCr^1. sherewes] *om* Hm.
28 Thilke] þo F. god] mooste goode (*final* e's *erased*) M. moost gyueþ] moost gyueth YGBL; gyueþ moost WHmCr; moost good gyueþ O; most good ȝeueþ C^2; most greueth CR; moost greve F; god yeueþ M. leest] mest F. þei] he hem F. deleþ] deleyne G.

And moost vnkynde to þe co*m*mune þat moost catel weldeþ:
Que perfecisti destruxerunt; iustus autem &c.
Harlotes for hir harlotrie may haue of hir goodes,
And Iaperis and Iogelo*urs* and Iangleris of gestes,
Ac he þat haþ holy writ ay in his mouþe
And kan telle of Tobye and of [þe] twelue Apostles
Or p*re*chen of þe penaunce þat Pilat wroȝte
To I*es*u þe gentile þat Iewes todrowe
[On cros vpon caluarye as clerkes vs techeþ],
Litel is he loued [or lete by] þat swich a lesson [techeþ],
Or daunted or drawe forþ; I do it on god hymselue.
But þoo þ*at* feynen hem foolis, and wiþ faityng libbeþ |
Ayein þe lawe of oure lord, and lyen on hemselue, *fol. 52 a*
Spitten and spuen and speke foule wordes,
Drynken and dreuelen and do men for to gape,
Likne men and lye on hem þat leneþ hem no ȝiftes,
Thei konne na moore mynstralcie ne Musik men to glade
Than Munde þe Millere of *Multa fecit deus*.
Ne [holpe hir] harlotrye, haue god my trouþe,

29 to] ben to MCr (ben *another ink* M). þat] be he*m* F. weldeþ] sendiþ F.
29α &c] *quid fecit* Cot; *om* Cr^{1}F.
30 may] shull F. haue] hauen M. of] *om* F.
31 And] As F. Iogelo*urs*] iu*n*golours Hm.
32 Ac] but GF; And CrC^{2}CB.
33 telle] telly*n* F. þe] HmCrGOC^{2}CBLMRF (*above line another ink* M); *om* WY.
34 þe] *om* GYOC^{2}CB. Pilat] YHmGOC^{2}CBLMR; Pilat wikkedly W; Pilate falsely Cr; Pilat to c*ri*st F.
35 To...gentile] Or of Ientil I*es*u F. todrowe] todrowen YGOC^{2}; dyde on roode F.
36 *not in* WHmCrGYOC^{2}CBLMRF.
37 Litel...loued] He is lytyl lovid now F. Litel] Ful litil B. or...techeþ] þat swich a lesson sheweþ WHmCrGYOC^{2}CBLMRF.
38 daunted] daunten Cr; daunteþ B; deyntely F. or] to G; *om* F. drawe] drawen OC^{2}M; draweþ B. god] ȝoure F; *om* B. hym] *om* F. selue] seluen M.
39 þoo] þei BoCot; *om* Bm. feynen] feyne FCr. libbeþ] lybbe F.
40 lord] *om* C. lyen] lyȝe F. hem] hym YC. selue] seluen M.
41 Spitten] þey spytty*n* F. speke] speken OHmC^{2}BMR.
42 Drynken] & drynkyn F; Drynkinge Cr^{1}. dreuelen] driuelen Cr^{23}GYCBmCotLM; drauelen OC^{2}F; driuelyng Cr^{1}. for] *om* HmGF. gape] gapen M; Iape B.
43 Likne] þey lykne F; likken YOMR; Lyken CrC^{2}C; kykne G. lye] lyen GYOC^{2}CBMRF (n *erased* M). on hem] *om* F. leneþ] leene F. no] none M. ȝiftes] gestis B.
44 konne] ku*n*nen OB.
45 Munde] Mundie Cr^{23}Cot; Maude Cr^{1}. Millere] mulier Cr^{1}. of...*deus*] on F.
46 holpe hir] were hir vile WHmCrGYOC^{2}CBLMRF.

[W]olde neu*ere* kyng ne kny3t ne [c]anon of Seint Poules
3yue hem to hir yeres3yue þe [value] of a grote.
Ac [mynstralcie and murþe] amonges men is nouþe
Lecherie, losengerye and losels tales;
Glotonye and grete oþes, þis[e arn games nowadaies].
Ac if þei carpen of crist, þise clerkes and þise lewed,
At mete in hir murþe whan Mynstrals beþ stille,
Than telleþ þei of þe Trinite [how two slowe þe þridde],
And bryngen forþ a balled reson, taken Bernard to witnesse,
And puten forþ p*re*sumpcion to preue þe soþe.
Thus þei dryuele at hir deys þe deitee to knowe,
And gnawen god [in] þe gorge whanne hir guttes fullen.
Ac þe carefulle may crie and carpen at þe yate
Boþe afyngred and afurst, and for chele quake;

47 Wolde] Sholde WHmCrGYOC^{2}BLM RF; Shul C. neu*ere*] neyþur MF. canon] CrR; Chanon WHmGYOC^{2}CBLM; þe comou*n* F. of...Poules] peple F. Seint] *om* Cr.

48 3yue] Gyue CrGC. yeres3yue] yeresgyfte Cr^{12}C; newyeres gyfte Cr^3; rewarde G. þe] 3ee the Hm; ne Cr^{12}; *om* Cr^3. value] YGOC^2; worth RF; 3ifte WHmBLM; gift CrC.

49 Ac] but GF; And CrC^{2}C. mynstralcie ...murþe] murþe and mynstralcie WHm CrGYOC^{2}CBLMRF (and] of Cr^1; *with* F). amonges] is amonge HmG. is] of C^2; nowt F; *om* HmG. nouþe] nowe G; nought CrB; ys F; qouthe C.

50 Lecherie] But leccherie BF. losengerye] and losengerye HmGYOC^{2}CBR; and loselrie M; be ley3d F. and] in F.

51 Glotonye] ⁊ gloteny3e F. þise arn] þese C^{2}O; þis WHmCr^{23}GYCBLMR; is Cr^1; þ*at* ys good F. games] glee M; myrþes OC^2; murþe WCrGYCBLRF; merthey Hm. nowadaies] þey louyeþ WHmCrGOC^{2}CBLM; louyeth YR; *om* F.

52 Ac] but GF; And CrC^{2}C. þei] 3ei R. carpen] harpen C. þise (*both*)] *om* G. and þise] to F.

53 At] at þe HmCr^{1}BLMR; And they Cr^{23}. mete] meet Cr^{23}. hir] *om* GYOC^2 CBF. murþe] murthes YGOC^{2}CBLM RF.

54 telleþ] telle YGC^{2}CB; talke F; *at end of line another ink* Hm. þei] *om* F. þe(1)] *om* Hm. how...þridde] a tale ouþer tweye WHmCrGYOC^{2}CBLMRF (ouþer] or CrF).

55 bryngen] bry*n*ge FG. forþ] *om* OC^{2}F. balled] ballen C^2; blade Cr^{23}. taken] and taken WHmCrGOC^{2}BLMR; ⁊ take YC; forþ ⁊ take F. to] *om* F.

56 puten] put CrF. forþ] forþ a WHm CrGYOC^{2}CBLMRF. p*re*sumpcion to] qwestiou*n* ⁊ F. preue] preuen M. þe] it for F.

57 dryuele] dryuelen OBmCotM; dreuell Cr; dreuelen C^{2}HmBo; dravele F. hir] þe F. deys] dayes R; dynn*ere* G. deitee] dyte F. knowe] scorne Cr^{23}.

58 gnawen] gnawe F. in] wiþ WHmCr GYOC^{2}CBLMRF. þe] hyr CrF. gorge] george Y. hir] þe Hm. guttes] gutte is YLR; guttis is C; guttes er G; guttes been OC^{2}B; guttes be MF (s *touched up*, be *above line* M). fullen] fulle YOC^{2}CBLM RF; fylled G; fallen Cr.

59 Ac] But FG; And CrC^{2}C. crie] cri3en F; carpe Hm. carpen] cry3en Hm; myskary3e F.

60 afyngred] anhungred HmOC^{2}Cot; ahungerd Cr^{1}GBmBo; for hu*n*ger F. afurst] aþurst HmGCotLMR; þurst F; athrust YOC^{2}CBmBo. chele] chelde C; chels Cr^1.

Is noon to nyme hym [in, ne] his [n]oy amende,
But [hunsen] hym as an hound and hoten hym go þennes.
Litel loueþ he þat lord þat lent hym al þat blisse
That þus parteþ wiþ þe pou*er*e a p*ar*cell whan hym nedeþ.
Ne were mercy in meene men moore þan in riche
Mendinaunt3 metelees my3te go to bedde.
God is muche in þe gorge of þise grete maistres,
Ac amonges meene men his mercy and hise werkes.
And so seiþ þe Sauter; [seke it in *memento*]:
Ecce audiuimus eam in effrata; inuenimus eam in campis silue. |
Clerkes and [kete] men carpen of god faste *fol. 52 b*
And haue hym muche in [hire] mouþ, ac meene men in herte.
Freres and faito*ur*s han founde [vp] swiche questions
To plese wiþ proude men syn þe pestilence tyme;
And p*re*chen at Seint Poules, for pure enuye of clerkes,
That folk is no3t fermed in þe feiþ ne free of hire goodes
Ne sory for hire synnes; so is pride woxen
In Religion and in al þe Reme amonges riche and pou*er*e

61 Is] CrHmGYOC^2CLMR; Is *þer* WB; þere ys F. nyme] nymen HmCrGYOC^2CBLMR; nempne F. hym] hem Cr^{23}GC^2Cot. in ne] in nor (in *above line*, nor *touched up*) M; neer WHmCrGYOC^2CBLRF. noy] nuye R; noy to CrHmGYOC^2CBLMF; anoy to W.
62 hunsen] hunten WHmCrM (*over erasure another ink* M); heon on GYCL; hoen on RF; howen on OC^2; howlen on B. as] as on Cot. hoten] hote F. hym(2)] þem G. þennes] hence Cr; his gate F.
63 lent] lente YOC^2CBMF. þat(3)] þe Cr^3.
64 þus parteþ] dep*art*eþ not F. parteþ] parten OC^2. hym] hem OGC^2F.
65 in(1)] wi*th* F.
66 Mendinaunt3] Manye me*n*dynau*n*tis F. my3te] myghten HmOC^2B.
67 muche] mychil F. þe] her*e* F. gorge] gorges RF; goorde C^2. þise] the GC^2. maistres] master G.
68 Ac] butt GF; And CrC^2CB. and] is ⁊ F.
69 so] þus G. seiþ] *twice* F. Sauter] sawt*er* book F. seke...*memento*] I haue sei3en it ofte WHmCrGOC^2CBMF; I haue yseye it ofte LR; I haue seyn ofte Y.
69α *eam* (*both*)] *eum* CrRF. *effrata*] *effrata* ⁊ CB. *inuenimus*] *inueniemus* CrBm. *silue*] *silue* ⁊*c* Hm.
70 kete] other GRF; oþer kyn Hm; oþere kynnes WCrYOC^2CBLM. god faste] godd*es* face F.
71 haue] hauen BHm. hym] *om* HmL. muche] mochil B. hire] her*e* FG; þe WHmCrYOC^2CLR; *om* BM. ac] but GMF; ⁊ CrC^2C. meene] *om* Y.
72 Freres and] But freris þo F. founde vp] founde WGYCLRF; founden Cr^{12}HmOC^2BM; fouden Cr^3. swiche] fair*e* F.
73 proude] the proud Cr. þe] *om* C. tyme] *om* RF.
74 Seint] *om* GF. Poules] poulis cros F. of] fo Cr^3.
75 is] nys M; been OC^2. no3t] *om* F. þe] *om* M. feiþ] fayit C. free] freer Cr^1.
76 for] of M. is pride] pruyde is R; p*r*i3de so hy3e is F. is] *om* Cr^1. woxen] waxe F.
77 in] *om* G. al] *om* CF. þe] þis F. amonges] bothe G.

That preieres haue no power þ[ise] pestilence[s] to lette.
[For god is def nowadayes and deyneþ [noȝt vs to here],
That girles for [oure] giltes he forgrynt hem alle].
And yet þe wrecches of þis world is noon ywar by ooþ*er*,
Ne for drede of þe deeþ wiþdrawe noȝt hir pride,
Ne beþ plenteuouse to þe pou*er*e as pure charite wolde,
But in gaynesse and glotonye forglutten hir good
And brekeþ noȝt to þe begger*e* as þe book techeþ:
Frange esurienti panem tuum &c.
And þe moore he wynneþ and welt welþes and richesse
And lordeþ in [ledes] þe lasse good he deleþ.
Tobye [techeþ] noȝt so; takeþ hede ye riche
How þe book bible of hym bereþ witnesse:
Si tibi sit copia habundanter tribue; si autem exiguum illud impertiri stude libenter.
Whoso haþ muche spende manliche, so [meneþ] Tobye,
And whoso litel weldeþ [wisse] hym þerafter,

78 haue] hauen B. power] pore Cr^{12}. þise] þis R; þese F; þe WHmCrGYOC^{2}CBLM. pestilences] RF; pestilence WHmCrGYOC^{2}CBLM.
79, 80 RF; *lines om* WHmCrGYOC^{2}CBLM; *here in the spelling of* W.
79 nowadayes] on þese dayes F. noȝt... here] not vs to her*e* F; his heres to opne R.
80 That girles] þe gystys F. oure] her*e* RF.
81 þe] þes G; no F. wrecches] wrecche F; wrocches Cot. of] in F. is] are Cr^{23}. noon] *om* F. ywar] war C^{2}HmCrF.
82 þe] *om* HmGM. drawe] drawen OHmC^{2}F. noȝt] *om* F. hir] of her B; he*m* fra*m* F.
83 beþ] *om* F. plenteuouse] plentuous Cr; plentous Cot; plentevo*u*sere F.
84 gaynesse] gaines CrG. and] & GYOC^{2}CBMF; and in WHmCrLR. forglutten] forglotte G; þei forglutte F; forgutten B. hir] *om* F. good] good hemselue WHmYOC^{2}CBLR; good hemseluen M; goods he*m*self Cr; goodes theyrselue G; he*m*-selue F.
85 brekeþ] breke F; bregen Y. noȝt] no breed F. book] book he*m* F.
85α *in margin* OC^2. &c] *om* C^{2}F.
86 welt] weldiþ BM (*over erasure another ink* M); wexeth Cr. welþes] of welthis F; welthy Cr. and] in Cr. richesse] richesses YOC^{2}BR.
87 And] Eu*er*e as he RF. lordeþ] lordes HmC; lord B; loondiþ F. in] of BF. ledes] leedis and londis B; londes WHmYOC^{2}CLMRF; landes CrG.
88 Tobye] But Thobye F. techeþ] techiþ F; techeth ȝow R; telleþ yow WHmCrGYOC^{2}CBLM. takeþ] takþ F; take CrGYOC^{2}CLM. hede] he C. ye] the GC.
89 book bible] byble boke CrF; book of þe byble HmGYOC^{2}CB. hym] hem CB.
89α *sit copia*] *copia sit* GYOC^{2}CB. *illud*] *om* GYOC^{2}CB. *impertiri*] *impertire* GC^{2}MRF; *impartiri* Cot. *stude*] *libenter* RF; *om* M. *libenter*] *libenter &c* Hm; *stude* RF.
90 haþ] haue Hm. muche] myche good F. spende] spene YCLMR; dispens B; spende it F. manliche] moche GYOC^{2}CB. so] *om* GBoCotF. meneþ] OHmCrGYC^{2}CLMR; meþ Bm; semeþ BoCot; seiþ WF.
91 And] *om* B. so] þat F. wisse] rule WHmCrGYOC^{2}CBLMRF.

For we haue no lettre of oure lif how longe it shal dure.
Swiche lessons lordes sholde louye to here,
And how he my3te moost meynee manliche fynde;
Nou3t to fare as a fiþeler*e* or a frere to seke festes,
Homliche at oþ*er*e mennes houses and hatien hir owene.
Elenge is þe halle, ech day in þe wike, |
Ther þe lord ne þe lady likeþ no3t to sitte. *fol.* 53 *a*
Now haþ ech riche a rule to eten by hymselue
In a pryuee parlour for pou*er*e mennes sake,
Or in a chambre wiþ a chymenee, and leue þe chief halle
That was maad for meles men to eten Inne,
And al to spare to [spille þat spende] shal anoþ*er*.
I haue yherd hei3e men etynge at þe table
Carpen as þei clerkes were of crist and of hise my3tes,
And leyden fautes vpon þe fader þat formede vs alle,
And carpen ayein cler[gie] crabbede wordes:
"Why wolde oure Saueo*ur* suffre swich a worm in his blisse
That bi[w]iled þe wo*m*man and þe [wye] after,

92 it shal] þ*a*t we F. dure] endure HmCr B.
93 lessons] lovely lessonys F. sholde] schuldyn HmOC^2. louye to] *om* F.
94 he] þey HmB; *om* G. my3te] my3ten B. meynee] meane G; meyn C.
95 Nou3t] Ac not O; And nou3t YGC^{2}C; And how no3t B. fare] faren F. fiþelere] vitelere Cot; Frere M. or a] or as a R; *om* F. frere] fytheler M; *om* F. to] HmCr GR; for to WYOC^{2}CBLMF. seke] fy3nde F.
96 Homliche] ⁊ ben hoomly F. oþere] her*e* F. mennes] men Cot; *om* F. houses] house LF. hir owene] his owe F.
97 Elenge] *altered to* Eyleng *and glossed* wobegon *another ink* C^2; Ful elenge F; elynge CotLR. þe(1)] þat B. ech] euery Cr. in] of F.
98 þe(1)] *above line* W. ne] ⁊ GYOC^{2}CB. likeþ] ne lykiþ F; liken OC^2. to] in to F; *om* O. sitte] sette Y.
99 riche] renke F; *om* Y. eten] ete OGC^2. hym] hem HmCr^{23}C. selue] seluen M.
100 parlour] paloure L. pouere] power G; pore *glossed* pure O; pure Y.
101 a(1)] *om* CrBmBo. wiþ] by R. a(2)] *om* F. þe] h*i*s F.
102 maad] *om* OC^2. meles men] men melys F. eten] eate Cr^{12}; teate Cr^3.
103 al] *om* OC^2. spare] sparen F. to(2)] and to CB; þe F. spille...spende] OHm GYC^{2}CBLM; spille þat spene R; spende þat spille WCr; pownd*es* þat spendy*n* F. shal] shulde M. an] on M.
104 yherd] herd HmCrGYOC^{2}CBMR; herd ry3t F. etynge...table] atte the table etynge Hm.
105 Carpen] Carpid F. were] weren OC^2. of(1)] by Hm. of(2)] *om* MF. my3tes] might Cr.
106 leyden] leyd MF (yd *over erasure another ink* M). fautes] faut Cr^{23}; defawte F. vpon] on GYOC^{2}CBF. formede] forme F.
107 carpen] carpedy*n* F. clergie] clerkes WHmCrGYOC^{2}CBLMR; clerkis swiche F.
108 his] *om* MF (in blisse *another ink* M).
109 biwiled] bigiled WHmCrGYOC^{2}CB LMRF. þe(1)] so the Hm. wye] man WHmCrGYOC^{2}CBLMRF.

Thoru3 whic[h werk and wil] þei wente to helle,
And al hir seed for hir synne þe same deeþ suffrede?
Here lyeþ youre lore", þise lordes gynneþ dispute,
"Of þat [ye] clerkes vs kenneþ of crist by þe gospel:
Filius non portabit iniquitatem patris &c.
Why sholde we þat now ben for þe werkes of Adam
Roten and torende? Reson wolde it neu*ere*!
Vnusquisque portabit onus suum &c."
Swiche motyues þei meue, þise maistres in hir glorie,
And maken men in mys bileue þ*at* muse on hire wordes.
Ymaginatif herafterward shal answere to [youre] purpos.
Austyn to swiche Argueres [he] telleþ þis teme:
Non plus sapere quam oportet.
Wilneþ neu*ere* to wite why þ*at* god wolde
Suffre Sathan his seed to bigile,
Ac bileueþ lelly in þe loore of holy chirche, |
And preie hym of pardon and penaunce in þi lyue, *fol.* 53 *b*

110 which...wil] whiche wiles and wordes WHmCrGYCBLMRF; whiche whyles & wordis OC^2 (wyles *above line another hand* C^2). wente] wenten YOC^{2}CBMR; wenty*n* boþe F.
111 synne] synnys Hm. suffrede] suffreden OF.
112 Here...youre] they lyen in here F. þise] þat þeise OC^{2}F; *om* Hm. lordes] word*es* F. gynneþ] gynne C^2; gonne HmG; beginneth Cr; *om* F. dispute] to dispute CrB; meven F.
113 Of þat] For F. ye] Cr^{23}YOC^{2}LMR; þe WHmCr^{1}GCBF. vs] þ*us* v*us* F; vn G. kenneþ] kenne G. of...by] by cryst of Hm; of cristes owne F.
114 *in margin* O. *patris*] *om* R. &c] *nec pater iniquitatem filij* F; *om* CrCot.
115 sholde] schulde*n* O. we] *om* F. Adam] *om* Y.
116 Roten and] Oure soulis Ragman F. Roten] be roten (*over erasure another hand and ink*) Hm; Botton (Be *before it another hand*) C^2. torende] rende GYCBMF; torente HmCr^{23} (*final* e *erased* Hm); renten OC^2; toreue R; to reade Cr^1.
116α *in margin* OC^2. *Vnus*] Vuus Cr^3. *portabit...suum*] *honus suum portabit* RF. *suum*] suun Bm. &c] *om* CrCotRF.
117 motyues] motynges Y; motyonys F. meue] meuen OC^{2}B. þise] þo F.
118 maken] make CrGYCMF. in] to Cr^3. muse] musen CrHmOC^{2}BF. on] Cr^{23}F; of Cr^1; muche on WGYOC^{2}CBLMR; mochyl on Hm.
119 ward] *om* CB. youre] CrHmGYOC^{2}CBLMRF; hir W.
120 Austyn] augustyne GLM; Sey*nt* Austyn F. he telleþ] he telleth Cr^1; he telleþ hem HmLMRF; telleþ WCr^{23}GYOC^{2}CB. þis] his OC^2. teme] tene Cr^1; tyme C^2.
121 *in margin* O. *Non*] Nou Cr^3. *oportet*] *oportet sapere* F; *oportet &c* HmGYOC^{2}CBR.
122 to] *om* OC^2.
123 Suffre] suffre so Hm; Suffre sory F; Suffered Cr^1.
124 Ac] but GF; And CrC^{2}CB. bileueþ] byleue HmCrLR. þe] *om* OC^{2}F. loore...chirche] holy chirche loore F. of] of al (al *above line main hand and ink*) M.
125 preie] preyede (de *cancelled*) O. hym] hem YGC; god F. and] & do F.

And for his muche mercy to amende [vs] here.
For alle þat wilneþ to wite þe [whyes] of god almyȝty,
I wolde his eiȝe were in his ers and his [hele] after,
That eu*ere* [eft] wilneþ to wite why þ*at* god wolde
Suffre Sathan his seed to bigile,
Or Iudas [þe Iew] I*es*u bitraye.
Al was as [he] wold[e]—lord, yworshiped be þ[ow],
And al worþ as þow wolt whatso we dispute—
And þo þat vseþ þise hauylons [for] to blende mennes wittes,
What is dowel fro dobet, [now] deef mote he worþe,
Siþþe he wilneþ to wite whiche þei ben [alle].
But he lyue in þe [leeste degre] þat longeþ to dowel
I dar ben his bolde borgh þ*at* dobet wole he neu*ere*,
Theiȝ dobest drawe on hym day after ooþer.'
And whan þ*at* wit was ywar [how his wif] tolde
He bicom so confus he kouþe noȝt [mele],

126 And for] þ*at* of F. muche] mochil BHmF. to] he F. vs] yow WHmCrGY OC^{2}CBLMRF.
127 *run together with* 129 CB. alle] who Cr. þat] þo þat F; þe Cr^3. þe...almyȝty] *om* CB. whyes] GYOM; weyes WHm CrC^{2}LRF. god] go Y; hevene F. almyȝty] almight Cr^{13}; *om* F.
128 *line om* CB. eiȝe] hond F. his(2)] *om* F. hele] fynger WHmCrGYOC^{2}LMR; elbowe F.
129 That...wite] *om* CB. eu*ere* eft] eu*ere* WHmCrGYOC^{2}LMRF.
130 Suffre] suffre so Hm; Suffre sory F.
131 þe Iew] RF; to þe Iewes WHmCrGY OC^{2}CBLM. bitraye] to betraye F.
132 Al] For al F. as] *om* G. he wolde] RF; þow wolde L; þow woldest WHmCrGY OC^{2}CBM. lord] be he F. yworshiped] worshyped GYOC^{2}CBF; worshyp Cr. be] *om* F. þow] OHmCrGYC^{2}CBLMR; þe W; eu*ere* F.
133 al] *om* HmC. þow] he F. wolt] will F; wold Cr. so] soeu*er* G; eu*ere* F. dispute] disputen OC^2.
134 þo...vseþ] þ*us* wit*h* F. vseþ] vse Cr^{23} YC. þise] swiche F; *om* G. hauylons] hanylones Cr^1; hanylowes Cr^{23}. for to] to WHmCrGYOC^{2}CBLMRF. blende] blynde GYOC^{2}CBF; blinde*n* Cr^{12}; blidde*n* Cr^3. mennes wittes] me*n* þey axe F.
135 now deef] deef now (*marked for transposition*) O. now] Cr^{23}GYC^{2}CBLMRF; þat W; ⁊ Cr^1; *erasure* (*of* and ?) Hm. mote] may G. he] þei F; be Cr^1; *om* Cr^2. worþe] worche G; woxe F.
136 Siþþe] siche B. he wilneþ] þei wilne F. alle] RF; boþe WHmCrGYOC^{2}CB LM.
137 But] but Hm; But if WCrGYOC^{2}CB LMR; If F. leeste degre] lif WHmCrGY OC^{2}LM; lyue CBR; lyȝne F.
138 I] F; For I WHmCrGYOC^{2}CBLMR (? for *erased* Cot). bolde] *om* RF. þ*at*] in F. bet] bett*er* G. wole] komeþ F. he neu*ere*] be nere R.
139 Theiȝ] for þouȝ Hm; þei B. dobest drawe] don best þat drawen B (þat] *om* Cot).
140 þ*at*] *om* F. ywar] war YCrGF. how... wif] how dame studie RF; what dame Studie WHmCrYOC^{2}CBLM; watt þ*at* dame stodie G.
141 He] s *prefixed* Bm. bicom] was B. confus] confused (d *added*) Hm; ysenfitid B (c *above* e Cot). kouþe] cu*n*neth Cr. noȝt] vneþes F. mele] loke WHmCrGYOC^{2}C BLMRF.

And as doumb as [a dore] drouȝ hym [aside].
A[c] for no carpyng I kouþe, ne knelyng to þe grounde,
I myȝte gete no greyn of his grete wittes,
But al lauȝynge he louted and loked vpon Studie
In signe þat I sholde bisechen hire of grace.
And whan I was war of his wille to his wif gan I [knele]
And seide, 'mercy, madame; youre man shal I worþe
As longe as I lyue, boþe late and raþe,
For to werche youre wille while my lif dureþ,
[To] kenne me kyndely to knowe what is dowel.'
'For þi mekenesse, man', quod she, 'and for þi mylde speche
I shal kenne þee to my Cosyn þat Clergie is hoten.
He haþ wedded a wif wiþInne þise [woukes sixe], |
Is sib to [þe] seuen artȝ, [þat] Scripture is [nempned]. *fol. 54 a*
They two, as I hope, after my [bis]echyng
Shullen wissen þee to dowel, I dar [wel] vndertake.'
Thanne was [I] also fayn as fowel of fair morwe,
Gladder þan þe gleman þat gold haþ to ȝifte,

142 as doumb] wex as deef F. as(2)] ⁊ G; a L. a dore] dore nail ⁊ F; deeþ and WHmCrYOC[2]CLMR (a dore nayle *above another hand* C[2]); deaffe ⁊ G; deef he B. hym] al B; *om* C. aside] on syȝde F; arere WHmCrGYOC[2]CBmBoLMR (asyde *above another hand* C[2]); aȝere Cot.
143 Ac] And WHmCrGYOC[2]CBLMRF. I] þat y (þat *above line another hand*) Hm; he Cot. ne] F; after ne WHmCrGYOC[2]CBLMR. to þe] on F. grounde] erth Cr.
144 gete] *om* CotF (*supplied after* greyn Cot).
145 vpon] on dame F.
146 bisechen] biseche YHmGOC[2]CBLMR; besekne F.
147 *line om* B. to his] *twice* C. gan] *om* Cr. knele] loute WHmGYOC[2]CLMRF; loutid Cr.
148 worþe] be C.
149 As] And as Cot; and Bo.
150 For] And for RF. to] y BoCot. werche] worchen Cr. while] whil HmF; þe while WCrGYOC[2]CCotLMR; þe wille BmBo. dureþ] endureth CrF; lastes C.
151 To] So ȝee F; so þat ȝe Hm; Wiþ þat ye WGYOC[2]CBLMR; With þat that ye Cr. kenne me] *om* R.
152 man] *om* G.
153 Clergie] clergise R. hoten] hote Cr[1]; yhotyn HmG; named F.
154 woukes sixe] sixe wykis F; sixe monþes WHmCrGYOC[2]CBLMR.
155 Is] þat is HmB; ⁊ she is F. to] *om* F. þe] HmCrGYOC[2]CBLMRF; *om* W. seuen] seued Cr[3]. þat...nempned] Scripture is hir name WHmCrGYOC[2]CBLMRF.
156 They] ⁊ þey F; Thew Cr[1]. after] ⁊ þou do after F. bisechyng] techyng WHmCrGYOC[2]CBLMRF (bysekynge *above another hand* C[2]).
157 Shullen] schull HmCrGYOC[2]C; þey wil F. wissen] wysse HmOC[2]BRF. to] *om* Cr. wel] R; it WHmGYOC[2]CBLMF; *om* Cr. take] taken R.
158 I] CrGYOC[2]CBMRF; he WHm; *om* (*corrector supplies*) L. also] as CrGMR; *om* F. of] on BF.
159 Gladder] And gladder WHmCrGYOC[2]CBLMRF. þe] a F. haþ to ȝifte] gadred at festis F.

And asked hire þe heighe wey where Clergie dwelte,
'And tel me som tokene [to hym], for tyme is þ*at* I wende'.
'Aske þe heighe wey', quod she, 'hennes to Suffre-
Boþe-wele-and-wo if þ*at* þow wolt lerne;
And ryd forþ by richesse, ac rest þow no3t þ*er*Inne,
For if þow coupl[e] þee [wiþ hym] to clergie comest [þow] neu*ere*;
And also þe [longe] launde þat lecherie hatte,
Leue [hym] on þi left half a large myle or moore
Til þow come to a court, kepe-wel-þi-tunge-
Fro-lesynges-and-liþer-speche-and-likerouse-drynkes.
Thanne shaltow se Sobretee and Sympletee-of-speche,
That ech wight be in wille his wit þee to shewe.
[So] shaltow come to Clergie þat kan manye [wittes].
Seye hym þis signe: I sette hym to Scole,
And þat I grete wel his wif, for I wroot hire [þe bible],
And sette hire to Sapience and to þe Sauter glose[d].
Logyk I lerned hire, and [al þe lawe after],

160 where] GF; where þ*at* WHmCrYO C²CBLMR. Clergie dwelte] glergye dwelleþ Hm.
161 And] *om* F. me] me by Hm. som... hym] q*uod* y su*m* tokne F. to hym] quod I WHmCrGYOC²CBLMR. I] we R.
162 heighe] *om* F. she] she þo F; stodye GYOC²CB. to] vnto F.
163 Boþe] Boþe in F; Beþ C. and] & in F; and eke Hm. if] & yff G. þat] *om* HmG. þow] þat BmBo. wolt] wold BmBo; wole Cot.
164 ryd] rayke F. by] þoru F. ac] but OC²F; and CrGYCB. þow] *om* GYOC² CBF.
165 couple] G; couplest WHmCrYOC²C BLMR; be cu*m*bred F. þee] *om* F. wiþ hym] þerwiþ WHmCrGYOC²CBLMRF. clergie] cherche R; c*r*ist F. comest þow] comest þou HmCrGOC²BmCotMRF; comestow WYCL; comeþ þou Bo.
166 And also] Be war of F. longe] likerouse WHmCrGYOC²CBLMRF. hatte] hatteth HmCB; is hote RF.
167 hym] HmLMR; it WCrGYOC²CBF. þi] þe M. half] hand Y. or] and CrGYO C²C.
168 Til] þan shalt F.
169 Fro] For C. lesynges] loselys F. liþer] luthers Cr¹.
170 Thanne] þer*e* F. Sobretee] Sobreite CrG; sobere C. and] ful F. Sympletee] simplicitie Cr; symplesse Hm; symplenes G; symple F. speche] berynge RF.
171 That ech] & eu*er*y F. be] ben R. in] in his Cr²³. þee] *om* Cr²³Cot.
172 So] þus G; And þus WHmCrYOC²C BLMRF. to] tome to (tome *erased*) Hm; *om* F. þat] þan BoBm. wittes] þynges WHmCrGYOC²CBLMRF.
173 Seye] Telle B; & telle F. signe] tokene BCF. I] þat I B; how y F.
174 þat I] also F. grete] grette OC²LMR. for] þat F; *om* G. þe bible] bokes MF (? *over erasure* M); manye bokes WHmCrG YOC²CBLR.
175 to(1)] *om* BF. to(2)] *om* Cot. glosed] BmHmBo; Iglosid Cot; ? iglosse G; glose WCrYOC²CLMRF.
176 Logyk] & Logy3k F. al...after] manye oþere lawes WHmCrGYOC²CB LMR; þe lawys manye F.

And alle [þe] Musons in Musik I made hire to knowe.
Plato þe poete, I putte [hym] first to boke;
Aristotle and oþ*ere* mo to argue I tauȝte;
Grammer for girles I garte first write,
And bette hem wiþ a baleys but if þei wolde lerne. |
Of alle kynne craftes I contreued tooles, *fol.* 54 *b*
Of Carpent[ers and] kerueres; [I kenned first] Masons
And lerned hem leuel and lyne þouȝ I loke dymme.
Ac Theologie haþ tened me ten score tymes;
The moore I muse þ*er*Inne þe mystier it semeþ,
And þe depper I deuyne[d] þe derker me [þouȝte].
It is no Science forsoþe for to sotile Inne;
[Ne were þe loue þat liþ þerinne a wel lewed þyng it were].
Ac for it leteþ best bi loue I loue it þe bettre,
For þ*ere* þ*at* loue is ledere lakke[þ] neu*ere* g*ra*ce.
Loke þow loue lelly if þee likeþ dowel,
For dobet and dobest ben [drawen] of loues [scole].

177 þe] HmCrGYOC^2CBLMRF; *om* W. Musons] vnisons Cr; mesours C^2. in] of HmOC^2. Musik] muke L. I] *om* R.
178 þe] þ*at* F. hym] HmCr^{13}GYOC^2CBLMRF; hem Cr^2; *om* W. first] *om* B.
179 Aristotle] & Aristotle F; Aristole Bm Bo. mo] *om* RF. to...tauȝte] I tauȝte to argue M; y taugth hem argue Hm. I] I hem B; hem y F.
180 Grammer] & g*ra*mere F. girles] cildire (c *altered from* g) C. write] YGOC^2CBLR; wrytyn F; to write WHmCrM.
181 baleys] wande C. if] *om* GF. wolde] wolden O.
182 Of] & to F. contreued] counturfetid CotF.
183 Carpenters and] carpenters & GF; carpenters of Cr^3; Carpentrie of WHmCr^{12}YOC^2CBLMR. I...first] and compased WHmCrGYOC^2CBLMR; & cu*m*pases to F.
184 And] I C^2F. lerned] ke*n*nede OC^2. leuel] to leuel HmF. and] be F.
185 Ac] But F; And Cr; *om* GOC^2CB. haþ] þ*at* F. tened] teneþ BoF; tene C. ten] seuen Cr^{23}.
187 deuyned] deuyne WHmCrGYOC^2C BLMR; delue F. þouȝte] þynkeþ F; it þynkeþ WHmCrGYOC^2CBLMR.
188 *line om* Cr. is] *om* C. Science] conscyence (con *erased*) Hm; sentens C. sotile] sauȝtele RF.
189 A ful leþi þyng it were if þ*at* loue nere WHmCrGYOC^2CBLMRF (A] And OC^2. leþi] lyght C; loþ B (þ *over erasure* Bm). nere] ne were F).
190 Ac] But F; And CrGYOC^2CB. leteþ] let OHmCrGYC^2CBLR; is led F; stant (*over erasure of smaller word*) M. best] *om* MF. þe] *om* C.
191 þere þat] þat þere R. þat] as CrM. ledere] ledere þer WG; ledere ne HmCrY OC^2CBLMRF. lakkeþ] OCrGYC^2CB (*altered from* lockiþ *another ink* Bm); lakked WHmLMRF. neu*ere*] no GYOC^2 CB.
192 Loke...lelly] þ*er*fore love þou leelly love F. Loke] loue R. þee] þow RF. likeþ] lyke Hm; leketh Cr^1; thenke R; þy*n*ke to F. dowel] dodwel Bm.
193 For] And OC^2F. dobet] dobett*er* G. ben] þey ben F. drawen...scole] of loues kynne WHmCrGYOC^2CBLMRF.

In ooþer Science it seiþ, I sei3 it in Catoun,
Qui simulat verbis [nec] corde est fidus amicus,
Tu quoque fac simile; sic ars deluditur arte.
Whoso gloseþ as gylours doon, go me to þe same,
And so shaltow fals folk and feiþlees bigile:
This is Catons kennyng to clerkes þat he lereþ.
Ac Theologie techeþ no3t so, whoso takeþ yeme;
He henneþ vs þe contrarie ayein Catons wordes,
[And] biddeþ vs be as breþeren and [blissen] oure enemys
And louen hem þat lyen on vs and lene hem [at hir nede]
And do good a[g]ein yuel; god hymself hoteþ:
Dum tempus [est] operemur bonum ad omnes, maxime autem ad domesticos fidei.
Poul preched þe peple, þat parfitnesse louede,
To do good for goddes loue and gyuen men þat asked,
And [souereynly] to swiche [þat] suwen oure bileue;

194 In...seiþ] ⁊ to þis same sentence F. Science] scienence Bo; sapyence G. it in Catoun] in Catoun onys F.
195, 196 *in margin* O.
195 *simulat*] *similat* Cr^{23}CotLRF. *nec...amicus*] *om* F. *nec*] HmCrGYOC^{2}CBM (*over erasure another ink* M); *vel* WLR. *corde*] *in corde* HmR.
196 *sic*] *cum* YOC^{2} (*altered from cur* Y). *deluditur*] diluditer Cr^{12}. *arte*] *arte* ⁊*c* Hm.
197 gloseþ] glosen G. go me to] do hem YGOC^{2}CBmBo; don hem Cot. me...same] fram here sawis F.
198 so] *om* C^{2}. shaltow] schalstow R. feiþlees] feyles CotBo (th *added another script* Cot).
199 is] is þe Hm; *om* C. Catons] catoun HmY. kennyng] kynnyng Bo. clerkes] clergonys F; folke (e *erased*) Hm. he] it Cr^{1}; *om* F. lereþ] lerneth Cr; leerne F; lerned G.
200 Ac] But F; And CrC^{2}C; *om* G. no3t] nou3 Y. so(2)] þat F. yeme] gome R; them Cr^{1}; hede Cr^{23}F.
201 He] ⁊ GYOC^{2}CB. vs] *om* Cr.
202 And] For he WHmCrGYOC^{2}CBLMRF. biddeþ] bit YHmGOCLMR. as] *om* BF. blissen] bidde for WHmCrGYOC^{2}CBLMRF.
203 louen] loue CrOC^{2}MF. lyen] lye Cr. on] *om* R. lene] lenen Bo. at...nede] whan hem nedeþ WHmGYOC^{2}CBLMRF; whan they nede Cr.
204 And] And also CB. agein] ageyn FCr; agaynst G; ayein WHm; ayeins YOC^{2}CLMR; a3enst B. god] for god (for *over erasure another ink*) Hm. self] selfe Cr; self it WHmGYOC^{2}CBLMR; selue so F. hoteþ] biddes C.
204α *tempus*] temptus Bo. *est*] RF; *habemus* WHmCr^{12}GYOC^{2}CBLM; *habemur* Cr^{3}. *operemur*] *operemus* Cr^{23}; *operiemur* BmBo. *ad omnes*] *om* R. *maxime*] *maximo* Y. *domesticos*] *domestico* BmBo. *fidei*] *fidei* ⁊*c* Hm; fidoi Cr^{3}.
205 þe] to the Y.
206 do] to (*corrected*) C. gyuen] gyue HmCrGOC^{2}RF; yeuen M. men] hem F. asked] asken Cr^{23}HmGOC^{2}BR; aske it F.
207 souereynly] namely WHmCrGYOC^{2}CBLMRF. swiche] swiche men F. þat] YHmCrOC^{2}CBLMRF; as WG. suwen] scheweth RF; showen G.

And alle *þat* lakkeþ vs or lyeþ oure lord techeþ vs to louye, |
And no3t to greuen hem *þat* greueþ vs; god [þat
forbedeþ]: *fol.* 55 *a*
Michi vindictam & ego retribuam.
Forþi loke þow louye as longe as þow durest,
For is no science vnder sonne so souereyn for þe soule.
Ac Astronomye is hard þyng and yuel for to knowe;
Geometrie and Geomesie [is] gynful of speche;
[That] þynkeþ werche *with* þo [þre] þryueþ [wel] late,
For sorcerie is þe Sou*er*eyn book *þat* to [þat] Scienc[e] [l]ongeþ.
Yet ar þer fibicches in [forelles] of fele mennes [wittes],
Exp*er*iment3 of Alkenamye [of Albertes makynge,
Nigromancie and perimancie þe pouke to raise];
If þow þynke to dowel deel þerwiþ neuere.
Alle þise Sciences I myself sotilede and ordeynede,
Founded hem formest folk to deceyue.

208 þat] þat vs Cr. lakkeþ] lakke FCr. vs(1)] *om* CrRF. or] and YOC^{2}CBM. lyeþ] lye Cr; lieth vs YOC^{2}CLR; leynd vs G; bilieþ vs B; lieþ on vs (on *above line*) M; ly3e on vs F. oure lord] god GYOC^{2}CB. techeþ...louye] bidd*es* vs love he*m* F.
209 to] *om* G. greuen] greue CrGYOC^{2}CBmBoF. greueþ] greue CrGYC. god] *om* F. þat forbedeþ] þ*at* forbedeth YGO C^{2}C; þat forbede B; hymself forbad it WHmCrLMR; It is not godd*es* will F.
209α *in margin* O. *retribuam*] *retribuam* god seid hy*m*selue F; *retribuam &c* HmGYC BmBo (*&c twice* Y); *distribuam* Cr^{23}.
210 Forþi] Therefor Cr. durest] lyuest M; lengyst heere F.
211 For] For þer BF. no] *om* F. science] co*n*scyence GYOC^{2}CBm (*corrected main hand* GBm); salue F. sonne] þe su*n*ne Cr. þe] thi CrGM.
212 Ac] but GF; And CrC^{2}C. Astronomye] *altered from* astromye C^2. is] RF; is an WHmYOC^{2}BLM; is a CrG; is and C. knowe] *om* C.
213 Geomesie] geomansye Cr. is] YGO C^{2}CBLMRF; so WHmCr. gynful] gylful CrG; gentyl Hm; synfull C^{2}B. speche] spechis F.
214 That] who F; Whoso WHmCrGYO C^{2}CBLMR. werche] to worche B. þre] two WHmCrGYOC^{2}CBLM; to R; two he F. wel] ful WHmGYOC^{2}CBLMRF; but Cr.
215 sorcerie] socerie Cot. Sou*er*eyn] souerenest Cr. book] bolk Bo; sekt F. þat] BG; þo WHmRF; þe YOC^{2}CLM; *om* Cr. Science] OCrGYC^{2}CBLMR; Sciences WHmF (s *added* Hm). longeþ] OHmCr^{1}GYC^{2}CBLMRF; bilongeþ W Cr^{23}.
216 fibicches] fibiche C; febichers Cr^{23}. in] *om* F. forelles] forceres WHmCr^{23}G YOC^{2}CBLMR; forseeris Cr^1; *om* F. fele] fel C; fell (? *originally* fele) M. mennes] men C; ma*n*nys BoCot; folkys F. wittes] makyng WHmCrGYOC^{2}CBLMRF.
217, 218 *run together* WHmCrGYOC^{2}CB LMRF: Experiment3 of Alkenamye þe peple to deceyue (of] & F. Alkenamye] alkamye L; alle kyn amye B. deceyue] deceiuen Cr^3).
219 þynke] þenkist B. þer] þou þer BF.
220 Alle] & all F. Sciences] science OC^2 CL. my] me Cr. sotilede] ysotild F.
221 Founded] And founded WHmCrGY OC^{2}CBLM; & fond F; And byfond R.

Tel Clergie þis[e] tokene[s], and [to] Scripture after,
To counseille þee kyndely to knowe what is dowel.'
I seide 'g*ra*nt m*er*cy, madame', and mekely hir grette,
And wente wightly [my w]ey wiþoute moore lettyng,
And [er] I com to clergie [koude I] neu*er*e stynte.
[I] grette þe goode man as [þe goode wif] me tauȝte,
And afterwardes [his] wif [I] worshiped boþe,
And tolde [hire] þe tokenes þat me tauȝt were.
Was neu*er*e gome vpon þis ground, siþ god made [heuene],
Fairer vnderfongen ne frendlier at ese
Than myself sooþly soone so he wiste
That I was of wittes hous and wiþ his wif dame Studie.
[Curteisly clergie collede me and kiste,
And askede how wit ferde and his wif studie].
I seide to h[y]m sooþly þat sent was I þider
Dowel and dobet and dobest to lerne. |
'It is a co*m*mune lyf', quod Clergie, 'on holy chirche to bileue *fol.* 55 *b*
Wiþ alle þe articles of þe feiþ þat falleþ to be knowe.

222 Tel] Now telle F; Tyl Cr^{1}. þise] OHm Cr^{23}YC^{2}BLMRF; thes G; þis WCr^{1}C. tokenes] HmCr^{23}GYOC^{2}CBLMRF; tokene WCr^{1}. to] RF; *om* WHmCrGYO C^{2}CBLM.
223 To] þat þey F; I GYOC^{2}CB. to] for to RF. knowe] knowen Cr. what is] *om* RF.
224 I...mercy] Grant mercy *quod* y F. hir] I here B. grette] grete Cr^{1}CB; grate Cr^{23}.
225 *line om* F. wightly] wiȝthi BmBo (? *touched up* Bm); miȝteliche R. my wey] R; awey WHmCrGYOC^{2}CBLM. oute] outen BHmM.
226 And] *om* F. er] til WHmCrGYOC^{2} CBLMF; *om* R. koude I] cowde y HmF; I koude WCrGYOC^{2}CBLMR.
227 I] R; And WHmCrGYOC^{2}CBLMF. grette] grete Cr^{1}CotLF; grate wel Cr^{23}. as] wel as OGC^{2}CB; ac Y. þe(2)...wif] þe gode wif R; þe Ientel lady F; Studie WHm CrGYOC^{2}CBLM. tauȝte] tolde Hm.
228 his...I] his wif y F; þe wif and WHm CrGYOC^{2}CBLMR. boþe] hem boþe WHmCrGYOC^{2}CBLMRF.
229 hire] hym Hm; hem WCrGYOC^{2}C BLMRF. were] weren OC^{2}.
230 Was] Was þere B. gome] *altered to* grome Cot; mane C. vpon] on HmCr. þis] *om* GF. made heuene] þis world made F; the world made *over erasure* M. made] makyd Hm. heuene] þe worlde WHmCr GYCBLR; þis world OC^{2}.
231 Fairer] Faire F. fongen] fonge R. frendlier] frendloker HmGYOC^{2}CBLM RF.
232 Than] As was F. my] me R. soone so] as soone as F.
233 was of] *om* F. wif] *om* C.
234, 235 *not in* WHmCrGYOC^{2}CBLM RF.
236 I] þanne y F. to] *om* F. hym] GYOC^{2} CBM; hem WHmCrLRF. sent...I] sent I was R; y was sent F.
237 Dowel] For Dowel F. bet] bett*er* G.
238 a] *om* CrGF. commune] com*en*lye G. lyf] *om* GF. to] *erasure* M; *om* F.
239 þe articles] þe articul O. falleþ] falle F. be] *above line another ink before* to M; by Hm. knowe] knowen CrOC^{2}.

And þat is to bileue lelly, boþe lered and lewed,
On þe grete god þat gynnyng hadde neu*er*e,
And on þe sooþfast sone þat saued mankynde
Fro þe dedly deeþ and [þe] deueles power
Thoruȝ þe help of þe holy goost þe which is of boþe;
Thre [propre] p*er*sones, ac noȝt in plurel nombre,
For al is but oon god and ech is god hymselue:
Deus pater, deus filius, deus spiritus sanctus:
God þe fader, god þe sone, god holy goost of boþe,
Makere of man [and his make] and of beestes boþe.
Austyn þe olde herof made bokes,
And hymself ordeyned to sadde vs in bileue.
Who was his Auctour? alle þe foure Eu*au*ngelistes.
And Crist cleped hymself so, þe [scripture] bereþ witnesse:
[*Ego in patre et pater in me est, et qui videt me videt et patrem meum*].
Alle þe clerkes vnder crist ne koude þis assoille,
But þus it bilongeþ to bileue to lewed þat willen dowel.
For hadde neu*er*e freke fyn wit þe feiþ to dispute,
Ne man hadde no merite myȝte it ben ypreued:
Fides non habet meritum vbi humana racio prebet experimentum.

240 And...to] þou must F. lered] lerned Cr; lewed me*n* F. lewed] lered F.
241 On] Vpon F. gynnyng] bygynnyng CotF.
243 þe(1)] *om* G. dedly deeþ] deeþ dedly (*transposition to* deeþ þe dedly *indicated*) Bm. þe(2)] HmCr^{1}GYOC^{2}CBLMRF; from the Cr^{23}; *om* W. deueles] fendys Hm.
244 þe(1 *and* 3)] *om* G. is] F; goost is WHmCrGYOC^{2}CBmBoLMR; holigost is Cot.
245 Thre] &c þey ben þre F. propre] propre R; *om* WHmCrGYOC^{2}CBLMF. ac] but GF; and CrC^{2}CR. in] In þe G.
246 ech] elkon C. hym] by his F. selue] seluen M; one F.
246α *in margin* O. *sanctus*] *sanctus &c* Hm. *Hereafter a Latin line* F; *see above*, p. 222.
247 þe(*both*)] is þe F. holy] þe holy CrG; ys þe holy F. of boþe] *om* F.
248 Makere] Makers C; Naþeles B (*cancelled for* maker *another hand* Bm). man... make] mankynde WHmCrGYOC^{2}CBLMRF. beestes] al þe Mounde F.
249 Austyn] augustyne G; Seyn*t* Austyn F. þe olde] þ*at* holy man F. made] he made LRF.
250 hymself ordeyned] ordeynede hy*m*selue F. to] it to CB. sadde] saue Cr^{13}.
251 Who] whoso Bo. alle] but F. þe] þese Hm.
252 And] How F. cleped] seyde F. hym] hem Hm. so] s Y; as G. scripture] wangelye F; eu*au*ngelieȝ R; euangelyst GYOC^{2}CB; Eu*au*ngelistes WHmCrLM.
252α YGOC^{2}CBLMRF; *line om* WHmCr. *est*] *om* RF. *videt*(1)] *om* RF. *videt et*] *vidit* R. *meum*] *meum &c* GBo; *meum videt* F.
253 koude] cowdyn HmO; cu*n* F.
254 þus] this CrG; *om* F. it] *om* CrGC. bilongeþ] longeþ OGC^{2}RF. lewed] men GYOC^{2}CB. willen] wole GYCF; wold Cr.
255 For] Ne B. neuere] neu*er*e ȝit F. fyn] so fien B; fyue Cr; *om* F. wit] wits Cr^{23}.
256 Ne] For OC^{2}. hadde] sholde have F. merite] mercy RF. it] sy*n*nys F. ypreued] y *erased* M; preued CrBRF.
256α *prebet*] *om* R. *experimentum*] *experimentum &c* Hm; *&c* R.

[So] is dobet to suffre for þ[i] soules helþe
Al þat þe book bit bi holi cherches techyng;
And þat is, man, bi þy myȝt, for mercies sake,
Loke þow werche it in werk þat þi word sheweþ;
Swich as þow semest in siȝte be in assay yfounde:
Appare quod es vel esto quod appares;
And lat no body be by þi beryng bigiled
But be swich in þi soule as þow semest wiþoute. |
Thanne is dobest to be boold to blame þe gilty, *fol. 56 a*
Syþenes þow seest þiself as in soule clene;
Ac blame þow neuere body and þow be blameworþy:
Si culpare velis culpabilis es[*se*] *cauebis;*
Dogma tuum sordet cum te tua culpa remordet.
God in þe gospel [grymly] repreueþ
Alle þat lakkeþ any lif and lakkes han hemselue:
Qui[*d*] *consideras festucam in oculo fratris tui, trabem in oculo tuo &c?*
Why meuestow þi mood for a mote in þi broþeres eiȝe,
Siþen a beem [is] in þyn owene ablyndeþ þiselue—
E[*j*]*ice primo trabem* [*de*] *oculo tuo &c*—

257 So] Thanne WHmCrGYOC^{2}CBLMRF. þi] OCr^{23}GYC^{2}CBLMRF; þe WHmCr^1. soules] soule CBRF. helþe] sake Cr^{23}GYOC^{2}CB.
258 Al] and HmGB. book] holy boke Cr^{23}. bit] byddethe GC^{2}C; biddes þe F. cherches] cherche GYOC^{2}CBLMRF.
259 man bi þy] mychil by goddes F.
260 it in] þy F. þat] as F. þi] þe F; þis R. word] werke CB (*corrected another hand* Bm).
261 *line om* F. yfounde] founde HmCrG; founden OC^2; yformde Bm.
261α *in margin* OC^2. *quod*(1)] qnoc Cr^3. *vel*] *aut* RF. *appares*] *appares &c* Hm.
262 by] *om* F. beryng] berynge be HmR; berynge here be F; lernynge CB.
263 be] be þou F; *om* GYOC^{2}CB (*corrector supplies* Bm). oute] outen R.
264 Thanne] & þanne F. dobest] dobet BoCot. to be] *om* F.
265 seest] semest Hm. as in] in þyn F.
266 Ac] but GF; And CrC^{2}C. body and] anoþer if F.
266α, 266β *in margin* O.
266α *Si*] *De corrected another hand* C^2. *culpabilis*] culbabilis G. *esse*] CrGYOC^{2}CBLMR; *te esse* F; *esto* WHm.
266β *tuum*] *tua* BmBo (*altered from tuum* Bm). *te*] *om* BmBo (*corrector supplies* Bm). *tua culpa*] *culpa tua* Bo. *remordet*] *remordet &c* Hm.
267 grymly] GYOC^{2}CBLMR; greuously WHmCrF.
268 Alle] þo F. lakkes] lackles Hm. selue] seluen M.
268α *Quid*] CrGYOC^{2}CBmBoLMRF; *Qui* WHmCot. *trabem*] *trabem autem* F. *in*(2)...*tuo*] *in* YCBm; *om* GOC^{2}BoCot. *&c*] *non vides* RF; *om* M.
269 in] ys yn G. broþeres] brother RF.
270 Siþen] whan F. is] F; *om* WHmCrGYOC^{2}CBLMR. owene] þat F. ablyndeþ] blyndeth CrOC^2; all blyndeth Hm.
270α *in margin* O; *transposed with* 271 F. *Ejice*] *Eiice* Cr; *Eice* WHmGYOC^{2}CBLMRF. *primo*] *primum* F. *de*] GYOC^{2}CBLMRF; *in* WHmCr. *&c*] *om* CrF.

Which letteþ þee to loke, lasse ouþer moore?
I rede ech a blynd bosard do boote to hymselue,
As persons and parissh preestes, þat preche sholde and teche,
Alle maner men to amenden bi hire myȝtes:
This text was told yow to ben ywar er ye tauȝte
That ye were swiche as ye sey[d]e to salue wiþ oþere.
For goddes word wolde noȝt be lost, for þat wercheþ euere;
[Thouȝ] it auailled noȝt þe commune it myȝte auaille yowselue.
Ac it semeþ now sooþly, to [siȝte of þe worlde],
That goddes word wercheþ noȝt on [wis] ne on lewed
But in swich manere as Marc meneþ in þe gospel:
Dum cecus ducit cecum ambo in foueam cadunt.
Lewed men may likne yow þus, þat þe beem liþ in youre eiȝen,
And þe festu is fallen for youre defaute |
In alle maner men þoruȝ mansede preestes. *fol. 56 b*
The bible bereþ witnesse þat al[le] þe [barnes] of Israel

271 Which] þe wiche F; witt R. ouþer] or Cr.
272 rede] consayle F. a] *om* HmGBF. boote] bett C^{2}M. to] on Hm. *Hereafter an additional line* WHmCrGYOC^{2}CBLMR: For Abbotes and for Priours and for alle manere prelates (for(*both*)] *om* GYOC^{2}CB. prelates] of prelates YOC^{2}CB); *likewise* F: Boþe prelatis & prioures sholde punshe here sogettis. *See above*, p. 193.
273 As] ac B; and HmCF. þat...sholde] sholde preche F. preche] prechen B. sholde] schulden O; schulle R.
274 men] of men HmYOC^{2}CBMF (of *above line another ink* M). to...myȝtes] be hem myghte amende F. amenden] amende HmCrGOC^{2}BR. myȝtes] myghte CrGYOC^{2}CBLMR.
275 This] the G. told] Itold RF. to] *om* MF. ywar] war HmCrGYOC^{2}CBLMRF. ye] you G. tauȝte] tauȝten OC^{2}; teche F.
276 ye(1)] *om* Cr^{1}. were] weren O. seyde] HmCrGYCBLMR; seyden OC^{2}; seye W; teche F. salue] saluen M; saue HmB. wiþ] wel F.
277 wolde] wole BmM. lost] boste R. þat] yt F.
278 Thouȝ] If WHmCrGYOC^{2}CBLMRF. auailled] availe C^{2}CotF. noȝt þe commune] þe commone not F. myȝte] may F. yow] your CrGC^{2}RF (r *added later* C^{2}). selue] seluen YOC^{2}LMR; *om* CB.
279 Ac] but GF; And CrC^{2}C. now] no R; not F; *om* G. siȝte...worlde] þe worldes siȝte WHmCr^{23}GYOC^{2}CCotLMF; worldes syght Cr^{1}R; þe wordis siȝte BmBo (worldes *in margin another hand* Bm).
280 word] wordes R; *om* F. noȝt] owt F. wis] lered WGYOC^{2}CBLMR; learned CrF; lewyd Hm. ne on] ne GYCB; nor yn Hm. lewed] leryd Hm.
281 swich] YCrGOC^{2}CBF; swich a WHmLMR. Marc] Mathew Cr^{23}. meneþ] meviþ F.
281α *in margin* OC^{2}. *cadunt*] *cadunt &c* Hm.
282 Lewed] A lewed F. men] man F; folke (e *erased*) Hm. þus] *om* GYOC^{2}CBF. þat] *erasure* M; *om* GF. eiȝen] eiȝe HmCr.
283 youre] ȝour owen Hm; ȝoure owe F.
284 In] Fram F. men] of men Cr^{23}G. mansede] mauȝed Cr; mased CBoCot (*erasure after* a Bo). preestes] prieste Cr^{1}.
285 *line om* F. bereþ] bers C. alle] OCotLMR; al WHmCrGYC^{2}CBmBo. barnes] folk WHmCrGYOC^{2}CBLMR.

Bittre abouȝte þe giltes of two badde preestes,
Offyn and Fynes; for hir coueitise
Archa dei myshapped and Ely brak his nekke.
Forþi, ye Correctours, claweþ heron and correcteþ first yowselue,
And þanne mowe ye [manly] seye, as Dauid made þe Sauter,
Existimasti inique quod ero tui similis; arguam te & statuam contra faciem tuam.
[Th]anne shul burel clerkes ben abasshed to blame yow or to greue,
And carpen noȝt as þei carpe now, [and] calle yow doumbe houndes:
Canes non valentes latrare,
And drede to wraþe yow in any word youre werkmanship to lette,
And be prester at youre preiere þan for a pound of nobles,
And al for youre holynesse; haue ye þis in herte.
[Amonges riȝtful religious þis rule sholde be holde.
Gregorie þe grete clerk and þe goode pope
Of religion þe rule reherseþ in hise morales,

286 *line om* F. Bittre] Bytterly Cr^{23}G; Ful bitterli B. abouȝte] abouȝtyn Hm; bouȝte OCr^{23}GYC^{2}C; bouȝten B. giltes of] gilt of þo B.
287 Offyn] Offny BHmC^{2}M (*altered from* Offyn C^{2}, *from* Offun BmM, y *over erasure* Hm); Looke Offyn F. Fynes] Finers Cr^{2}.
288 *Archa*] For *Archa* F. myshapped] mysshaped G; myschappid B; meskapud R. and] *om* F.
289 Forþi] For þei (*corrected later hand*) Bm; *om* F. ye] *om* Cr^{1}GYOC^{2}CBoCot; *by corrector* Bm. claweþ] claw Cr. her] þer G. on] *om* Cr^{23}. and] but F; *om* G. correcteþ] correct CrF. yow] your CrG YOC^{2}CBF. selue] seluen YOC^{2}CLMR.
290 ye] you G. manly] manliche R; soþly F; safly WHmCrGYOC^{2}CBLM. Dauid] Duid C. made] HmGYOC^{2}CBLMR; þat made Cr; made in W; seiþ in F.
291 *faciem tuam*] &c Cot; *om* Bm. *tuam*] *tuam* &c HmY; &c Bo.
292 Thanne] YCrGOC^{2}CB; And þanne WHmLMRF. shul] schullen R; sholde G. abasshed] bashid Cr; asshamed G. to... yow] you to blame CrF. or to greue] *om* RF. to] *om* HmCrGB.
293 carpen] carpe HmOC^{2}. carpe] carpen LMR; do GYOC^{2}CB. and] HmCrGYO C^{2}CBLMR; ne W; to F. doumbe houndes] cowardes F.
293α *in margin* C^{2}; *line om* F. *non*] *muti non* Cr^{23}. *valentes*] *volentes* B. *latrare*] *latrare* &c HmYB; *latrate* Cr^{2}.
294 drede] *om* Cr. wraþe] lacke Cr. in... word] *om* F. in any] with a Cr. werk] *om* F.
295 And] But Cr. prester] more preest B. preiere] preyeres R. for] *om* CB.
296 al] *om* B. ye] you CrG.
297–308 RF; *lines om* WHmCrGYOC^{2}C BLM. *Here in the spelling of* W.
298 Gregorie] Seynt Gregory F.
299 religion þe rule] Relygyonys rewle he F. morales] bookis F.

And seiþ it in ensample [þat] þei sholde do þerafter:
Whan fisshes faillen þe flood or þe fresshe water
Thei deyen for drouȝte, whan þei drie [lenge];
Riȝt so [by] religion, [it] ro[i]leþ [and] sterueþ
That out of couent and cloistre coueiten to libbe.
For if heuene be on þis erþe, and ese to any soule,
It is in cloistre or in scole, by manye skiles I fynde.
For in cloistre comeþ [no] man to [carpe] ne to fiȝte
But al is buxomnesse þere and bokes, to rede and to lerne].
In scole þere is scorn but if a clerk wol lerne,
And great loue and likyng for ech [loweþ hym to] ooþer.
Ac now is Religion a rydere, a [rennere by stretes],
A ledere of louedayes and a lond buggere,
A prikere on a palfrey fro [place] to Manere,
An heep of houndes at his ers as he a lord were,
And but if his knaue knele þat shal his coppe brynge
He loureþ on hym and [lakkeþ] hym: who [lered] hym curteisie?
Litel hadde lordes to doon to ȝyue lond from hire heires
To Religiouse þat han no rouþe þouȝ it reyne on hir Auters.

300 it] *om* F. þat] þat F; for R.
301 faillen] faile F. or] ⁊ F.
302 lenge] ligge RF.
303 *as two lines divided after* rolleth R, *after* trollyþ F. by...it] quod Grigori religioun RF. roileþ] rolleth R; trollyþ F. and steruеþ] Sterueth and stynketh and steleth lordes almesses R; It steruyþ ⁊ stynkþ ⁊ stelyþ lordes almess F.
305 on þis] in F. any] þe F.
306 manye] fele F.
307 no] F; *om* R. carpe] chide R; fyȝhte F. fiȝte] chyȝde F.
308 þere] *om* F.
309 þere...wol] is anoþer skyle for skorn but he F. is] ys a GYOC^{2}CB. scorn] skile and scorne R. a...wol] he R.
310 gret] a grete Y; *om* F. for] ys þere gret for F. loweþ...to] of hem loueþ WHmCrGYOC^{2}CBLMR; man loveþ F.
311 Ac] But F; And CrGYOC^{2}CB. is] *om* F. rennere] rennere F; Romere WHmCrGYOC^{2}CBLMR. by stretes] GHmYOC^{2}CBLMRF; by streate Cr; aboute W.
312 *transposed with* 313 *but the correct order shown* G. A] and Hm. a] *om* R. lond buggere] loude begger Cr.
313 on] of Cr^1. a palfrey] palfreys F. place] Manere WHmCrGYOC^{2}CBLMRF.
314 An] with an F; And CBo (d *cancelled* Bo). his] her Hm. he a lord] a lord he Hm.
315 if] *om* B. his(2)] hym GYC; hym þe OC^{2}B. coppe] cope Cr.
316 loureþ] loured Cr; lowryþ loþly F. lakkeþ...curteisie] lythirly hym thretyþ F. lakkeþ] lackeþ Hm; axeth YOC^{2}CBLMR; askeþ WG; asked Cr. hym(2)] *om* CrGYOC^{2}CB. lered] tauȝte WHmCrGYOC^{2}CBLMR.
317 hadde] hadden OC^{2}BR. lond] landes Cr; here londis F. hire heires] hem F.
318 han] hauen BmBo. rouþe] ryghte C. þouȝ] if Cr. hir Auters] þe awter F.

In many places þer þei [persons ben, be þei purely] at ese,
Of þe pouer*e* haue þei no pite, and þat is hir [pure chartre];
Ac þei leten hem as lordes, hire lon[d liþ] so brode. |
Ac þer shal come a kyng and confesse yow Religiouses, *fol.* 57 *a*
And bete yow, as þe bible telleþ, for brekynge of your*e* rule,
And amende Monyals, Monkes and Chanons,
And puten [hem] to hir penaunce, *Ad pristinum statum ire*;
And Barons wiþ Erles beten hem þoruȝ *Beatus vir*res techyng;
[Bynymen] that hir barnes claymen, and blame yow foule:
Hij in curribus & hij in equis ipsi obligati sunt &c.
And þanne Freres in hir fraytou*r* shul fynden a keye
Of Costantyns cofres [þer þe catel is Inne]
That Gregories godchildren [vngodly] despended.
And þanne shal þe Abbot of Abyngdou*n* and al his issue for eu*ere*
Haue a knok of a kyng, and incurable þe wounde.
That þis worþ sooþ, seke ye þat ofte ouerse þe bible:

319 many] *om* F. places] place YC. þer] where Cot; or Bo. þei(1)] the Cr^{1}; *om* G. persons ben] p*er*sou*n*s ben HmCrGYOC^{2}CBLMRF; ben p*er*sons W. be...purely] be hemself WOC^{2}CBLMRF; by hemselue YHmCrG.
320 Of] On F. þe] *om* OC^{2}F. hir] his C. pure chartre] pur*e* charite R; pur*e* charge F; charite WHmCrGYOC^{2}CBLM.
321 Ac] and HmCrGYOC^{2}CB; For F. leten] leden Cot. as] selue F. lond] GYOC^{2}CBLMR; londes WHmCrF. liþ] CGYOC^{2}BLMR; lyen WHmF; lye Cr.
322 Ac] but HmGF; And CrC^{2}C. come] come*n* F. and] a Bo. confesse yow] co*n*streyne þe F. Religiouses] relygyous HmCrGYOC^{2}CotF (s *over erasure another ink* Hm); religiou*n*s BmBo.
323 þe] *om* C. bible telleþ] book seyþ F.
324 amende] ame*n*dyn F. Monyals] Monyalis & F; ȝou monyals Cot.
325 puten] put CrGYOC^{2}CBF. hem] HmCrGYOC^{2}CBLMRF; *om* W. *Ad*] and (n *cancelled*) Bm; *om* BoCot. *pristinum*] prestinum G. *ire*] *om* HmG.
326 wiþ Erles] & erles GYOC^{2}CB; shull F. beten] bete OCrC^{2}; biten R; *om* G. hem] *om* G. *virres*] *vir* GYOC^{2}CF.
327 Bynymen that] That WHmCrGYOC^{2}CBLMR; & seyn F. barnes] baro*ns* Cr^{1}. claymen] cleyme of ȝow F. blame] blamen GHmOC^{2}.
327α *Hij*] *Hijs* C. &] *om* LM. &*c*] *et ceciderunt* F; *om* GYC^{2}Cot.
328 hir] *om* Cr^{1}. fraytour] freytou*r*s Hm. fynden] fynde HmCrOC^{2}B.
329 Costantyns] Constantynes CrGYOC^{2}CCot; Constanci*us* F. cofres] coffer G; tresore OC^{2}CB. þer...Inne] in which is þe catel WHmCrGYOC^{2}CBLMRF.
330 god] good HmGF; gode R. vngodly] han yuele WHmGYOC^{2}CBLMRF; had it Cr^{1}; had il Cr^{23}.
331 *as two lines divided after* abyndou*n* R. And] *om* GF. al] *om* G. his] *om* L.
332 of] *twice* Hm; wit*h* G. incurable] vncurable G. þe] ys the Hm.
333 þis] is Bo. worþ] is F. ouerse] haue seen F. þe] ȝour*e* B.

Quomodo cessauit exactor, quieuit tributum? contriuit dominus baculum impiorum, et virgam dominancium cedencium plaga insanabili.
Ac er þat kyng come Caym shal awake,
[Ac] dowel shal dyngen hym adoun and destruye his myȝte.'
'Thanne is dowel and dobet', quod I, '*dominus* and knyȝthode?'
'I nel noȝt scorne', quod Scripture; 'but scryueynes lye,
Kynghod [and] knyȝthod, [for auȝt] I kan awayte,
Helpeþ noȝt to heueneward [at] oone [y]eris ende,
Ne richesse [ne rentes] ne Reautee of lordes.
Poule preueþ it impossible, riche men [in] heuene;
Salomon seiþ also þat siluer is worst to louye:
Nichil iniquius quam amare pecuniam;
And Caton kenneþ vs to coueiten it nauȝt but as nede techeþ:
Dilige denarium set parce dilige formam. |
And patriarkes and prophetes and poetes boþe *fol. 57 b*
Writen to wissen vs to wilne no richesse,
And preiseden pouerte with pacience; þe Apostles bereþ witnesse

333α *Quomodo*] *Quando* HmBoCot. *impiorum*] imporum Hm; timpiorum Cr^3. *et*] *om* Cr^3. *cedencium*] *credencium* GYOC^{2}CBM; ⁊ (*erased*) Hm. *insanabili*] insabili CBmBo; *insanabili* ⁊c HmLM.
334 Ac] but G; But erst F; And CrC^{2}C.
335 Ac] HmLMR; But WF; And CrGYOC^{2}CB. dyngen] dynge HmCrGOC^{2}CotMF; dygen C. hym] hem Cr^3. adoun] doun HmCrGMF. destruye] destruyen HmLMR. myȝte] powher F.
336 quod I] *om* G. hode] yholde F; *om* Hm.
337 nel] woll HmCrF. but] F; but if WHmCrGYOC^{2}CBLMR. scryueynes] scriuiners CrGC^2. lye] lyȝen F.
338 Kynghod] knyȝthod B. and] BGYOC^{2}F; a C; ne WHmCrLMR. for...awayte] be not in þese dayes F. for auȝt] by aught Cr^{23}CotM; by noȝt WHmCr^{1}GYOC^{2}CBmBoLR. I] þat I Cot. awayte] wayte Hm.
339, 340 *run together* F: For þey helpe no man to heueneward so realte ouerrenneþ.
339 at...yeris] not a heyres G; oone heris WHmCrYOC^{2}CBLMR.
340 ne rentes] riȝt noȝt WHmCrGYOC^{2}CBLMR. Reautee] reute Y.
341 preueþ] prechith Hm. it] *om* OC^2. impossible] vnpossyble G. riche] þat ryche F. in] haue HmGYCLMR; haven F; to haue WCrOC^{2}B.
342 is...louye] god most hateþ F.
342α *in margin* C^2. *Nichil*] *Nil* Hm. *iniquius*] *impius* G. *pecuniam*] *pecuniam* ⁊c HmY.
343 And] *om* F. vs] *om* Cot. coueiten] coueyte OC^{2}BMF. it] *om* GYOC^{2}CB. as...techeþ] as it nedeth YOC^{2}CB; vs nedithe G; at pure nede R; in gret nede F.
343α *in margin* OC^2. *denarium*] *denarios* G. *dilige*] *diligere* F. *formam*] *formam* ⁊c HmY.
344 And] þese F. and(2)] ⁊ oþere F. boþe] manye F.
345 Writen] þey wrytyn F; wreten C^2. wissen] wyshe Cr. wilne] wyl CrCBoCot. no] to no F.
346 And] þey F. preiseden] preysed GCB; preysen Y; praise Cr; preyse wel F. pouerte] pouert BoCot. with pacience] *om* F. bereþ] bere HmCrF; *om* G. witnesse] wyttnessen G.

That þei han Eritage in heuene, and by trewe ri3te,
Ther riche men no ri3t may cleyme but of ruþe and g*ra*ce.'
'*Contra!*' quod I, 'by crist! þat kan I [wiþseye],
And preuen it by [þe pistel þat Peter is nempned]:
That is bapti3ed beþ saaf, be he riche or pou*er*e.'
'That is *in extremis*', quod Scripture, '[as] Sar3ens & Iewes
Mowen be saued so, and [so] is oure bileue;
That [arn] vncristene in þat caas may cristen an heþen,
And for his lele bileue, whan he þe lif tyneþ,
Haue heritage [in] heuene as [an hei3] cristene.
Ac cristene men wiþoute moore maye no3t come to heuene,
For þ*a*t crist for cristene men deide, and confermed þe lawe
That whoso wolde and wilneþ wiþ crist to arise,
Si cum christo sur[r]existis &c,
He sholde louye and lene and þe lawe fulfille.
That is, loue þi lord god leuest abouen alle,
And after alle cristene creatures, in co*m*mune ech man ooþ*er*;

347 in] of F. and...ri3te] by ry3t & be trewþe F.

348 Ther...no] For þ*er*e may no ma*n* F. Ther] Ther the Y. men] man R. no] no3t BmBo. may] *om* CBF. ruþe and] ruthe off G; ri3t and (ri3t *cancelled for* reuth *another hand*) R; godd*es* F.

349 þat] þ*a*t clause F. wiþseye] repreue WCrGYOC^{2}LMRF; reherce CB; preue Hm.

350 preuen] preue HmGYOC^{2}CBLMF. þe...nempned] Peter and by Poul boþe WHmCrGYOC^{2}CBLMRF (by] *om* CotF).

351 *line om* CB. That] þey þ*a*t F. is] ben Cr^{23}GYOC^{2}MF. beþ] be CrF; ben GYO C^{2}M; deth Hm. saaf] saued Cr^{23}GYOC^{2} M; saueth Hm. he] þei GYOC^{2}MF.

352 as] amonges WYOC^{2}LMR; among HmCrGCB; of F.

353 Mowen] They mowen WOLR; they mowe HmCr^{23}GYCM; They mown C^{2}BmBo; þey may F; They muste Cr^{1}; the mowen Cot. so(2)] þat WHmCrGY OC^{2}CBLMRF.

354 That] then G. arn] an WHmCrYO C^{2}CBLM (*altered to* arn C^{2}); on R; a GF. vncristene] vncristned Y; c*ri*stene ma*n* F. þat] this HmCB.

355 lele] lely HmCr. whan] whahan C. þe] his F.

356 Haue] Shal have F. heritage...hei3] þe heritage of heuene as any man WHmCrG YOC^{2}CBLMRF. cristene] yc*ri*stned F.

357 Ac] but GF; And CrC^{2}C. cristene men] to c*ri*stne a ma*n* F. oute] outen OC^{2} CBoCotMRF. maye] mowen OHm; he may F. come to] wy*n*ne F. heuene] hauen Cr^{3}.

358 þ*a*t] *om* F. men] man B. deide] dede C; dide B. confermed] confemed Bo.

359 wolde] wole Y. and] or G. wilneþ] willeth Cr; wilnede F. to] vp F. arise] arilse Cr^{23}.

359α *in margin* OC^{2}Cot; *line om* F. *surrexistis*] HmCrGYOC^{2}LR; surexistis WM; resurexistis C; resurexisti B.

360 and(1)] hy*m* F. lene] leynde G; leue Cr; leelly F.

361 *line om* F. þi...god] god þi lorde R. þi] þe BmBo. abouen] aboue CrGYOC^{2} LR; of CB. alle] al thyng CrGYOC^{2}; alle thynges CB.

362 man ooþ*er*] a lyche F.

And þus bilongeþ to louye þat leueþ [to] be saued.
And but we do þus in dede, [er] þe day of dome,
It shal bisitten vs ful soure þe siluer þ*at* we kepen,
And oure bakkes þ*at* moþeeten be and seen beggeris go naked,
Or delit in wyn and wildefowel and wite any in defaute.
For eu*er*y cristene creature sholde be kynde til ooþer,
And siþen heþen to helpe in hope of amendement.
God hoteþ heiȝe and lowe þ*at* no man hurte ooþ*er*,
And seiþ "slee noȝt þat semblable is to myn owene liknesse |
But if I sende þee som tokene", and seiþ *Non mecaberis*, *fol.* 58 *a*
Is slee noȝt but suffre and [so] for þe beste,
[For *michi vindictam et ego retribuam*]:
"I shal punysshe in p*ur*gatorie or in þe put of helle
Ech man for hi[s] mysded[e] but mercy it [make]." '
'This is a long lesson', quod I, 'and litel am I þe wiser;
Where dowel is or dobet derkliche ye shewen.
Manye tales ye tellen þ*at* Theologie lerneþ,

363 þus] thus him Cr^{23}; thys Cr^{1}B. bilongeþ] longeth Cr; it longiþ F. louye] love *crist* F. leueþ] beleven F; loueþ B. to(2)] HmCrGYOC^{2}CBLMRF; *om* W.
364 but...þus] þus but we doon F. þus] thys Cr^{1}G. er] HmCrOC^{2}MF; ar LR; or GYCB; at W. dome] dyȝeng F.
365 It] I L. bisitten] syttyn F. soure] sore CrGBoCot. kepen] kepe Cr.
366 And] For F. oure] *om* Y. bakkes] bakcloþis B; bak F; bocks Cr^{3}; *altered to* baggis *another hand* C^{2}; *cancelled for* bagges *another hand* G. þat] *om* F. moþeeten be] motthes etyn HmB; moghteyten beene G; mote eten ben R; mote be bety*n* F. and...go] we cloþe no begger*e* F. seen] son (?) Y.
367 Or] ⁊ F. delit] delytyn HmB. in(1)] vs in Cr^{23}GYOC^{2}CBF. wyn...fowel] wyȝnys stro*n*ge F. and(1)] ⁊ in R; or GCot. wite] wyten B; wote YHmCrGOCLMRF; wotte*n* C^{2}. any] he*m* F. in(2)] *om* Y.
368 til] to HmCrF; to an G.
369 *line om* CB. heþen] heypen G. helpe] helpen G.
370 *line om* B. hoteþ] bedes CF. heiȝe] bothe heigh YCrGOC^{2}CLMR. þat no man] no ma*n* sholde F.
371 *line om* F. seiþ] seyde GC. slee] sleeþ O. semblable is] is semblable YB; is sembland C. to] into Cr^{1}; *om* GY. myn] thyn Y.
372 if] *om* F. and] god F. seiþ] saye Cr; sayde C. *mecaberis*] *nechaberis* (*altered from mechaberis*) G; *necaberis* Cr^{23}YL (? *altered from mecaberis* L); *necabis* Cr^{1}OC^{2}; *occides* (*over erasure another hand and ink*) M.
373 Is] I Cr^{23}YOC^{2}CBM (? s *erased* M); God seiþ y F. so] al WHmCrGYOC^{2}CBLMR; al is F.
374 RF; *line om* WHmCrGYOC^{2}CBLM.
375 *run together with* 376 CB. I] y Hm; For I WCrGYOC^{2}CBLMRF. shal] *om* F. punysshe] punysshen LR; punsche BF. in(1)] RF; hem in WHmCrGYOC^{2}CBLM. or...helle] *om* CB.
376 Ech...dede] *om* CB. Ech] Iche a C^{2}; Euery Cr. his mysdede] hise mysdedes WHmCrGYOC^{2}LMRF. but] but if Cr; but my F. make] lette WHmCrGYOC^{2}CBLMRF.
377 am] y F; *om* Cr. I(2)] am F; *om* Cot.
378 dobet] dobetter G. shewen] me shewe F.
379 tellen] tell CrGF. lerneþ] it lerneth Hm; lyȝeþ F.

And þ*at* I man maad was, and my name yentred
In þe legende of lif longe er I were,
Or ellis vnwriten for wikkednesse as holy writ witnesseþ:
Nemo ascendit ad celum nisi qui de celo descendit.
I leue it wel by oure lord and on no lettrure bettre.
For Salomon þe sage þat Sapience [made],
God gaf hym g*ra*ce of wit and alle goodes after
[To rule þe reume and riche to make];
He demed wel and wisely as holy writ telleþ;
Aristotle and he, who wissed men bettre?
Maistres þat of goddes m*er*cy techen men and p*re*chen,
Of hir wordes þei wissen vs for wisest as in hir tyme,
And al holy chirche holdeþ hem boþe [in helle]!
And if I sh[al] werche by hir werkes to wynne me heuene,
That for hir werkes and wit now wonyeþ in pyne,
Thanne wrouȝte I vnwisly, whatsoeu*er*e ye p*re*che.
Ac of fele witty in feiþ litel ferly I haue
Thouȝ hir goost be vng*ra*cious god for to plese.

380 And] *om* F. man] *over erasure* Cot; am Bo. my] many Y. yentred] entred CrHmGY; is entryd F.
381 lif] seyntis OC^{2}. were] bore were F.
382 ellis] *om* G. vnwriten] ywrytyn F; wrytten Cr^{23}GOC^{2}M. for] GYOC^{2}C BF; for som WHmCrLMR. writ] *om* C. witnesseþ] witnesse C; telleth RF; manaceth Cr.
382α *ad*] *in* OC^{2}M. *de...descendit*] *descendit de celo* OC^{2}F (*the other order noted* O). *descendit*] *descendit &c* YCB; discendit *&c* Hm; decendit L.
383 I] And I R; For i F. leue it wel] beleve F. it] *om* OC^{2}. by...lord] be oure lorde R; on oure lord F; quod I by oure lord WHmCr^{1}L; bi our lord quod I Cr^{23} GYOC^{2}CB (I *main hand after cancelled* he G); quod I M. on] *om* CrG. lettrure] letture YC^{2}; letter Cr.
384 made] tauȝte WHmCrGYOC^{2}CBLM RF.
385 God] Good F. gaf] ȝaff C^{2}B. alle] R; of all F; alle hise WHmCrGYOC^{2}CBLM.
386 RF; *line om* WHmCrGYOC^{2}CBLM; *here in the spelling of* W. þe] his F. and] wel & hym F. to] *om* F.
387 wel] *om* C^{2}.
388 Aristotle] Boþe Arystotle F. wissed] wished CrF.
389 Maistres] & nou Maist*ris* F. þat of] of Hm; þoru F. mercy] m*er*cyes G. techen] teche F; preychen G. p*re*chen] p*re*che F; techen G.
390 þei] þey thay (þey *cancelled*) C. wissen] wish CrF. as] *om* GMRF.
391 al] as C. holdeþ] hold GYOC^{2}CBm BoF. boþe] *om* F. in helle] ydampned WHmGYOC^{2}CBLMR; dampned Cr; da*m*pned boþe F.
392 And] *om* F. shal] sholde WHmCrGY OC^{2}CBLMRF. hir] hys GCB. werkes] wekes C. wynne] wynnen MR.
393 and] and here RF. now wonyeþ] þey wone nou F. now] *om* Cr. wonyeþ] cometh Hm. pyne] payne CrGC^{2}B.
394 so] *om* BoCot. ye] you G; þe C. p*re*che] prechen OC^{2}.
395 Ac] But F; And CrGYOC^{2}CB. of] *om* OC^{2}. fele] fole C^{2}; here F. witty] wittis F.
396 hir] he Hm. vng*ra*cious] vngracyou*n*s BmBo; vnhappy G.

For many men on þis moolde moore setten hir hert[e]
In good þan in god; forþi hem g*ra*ce failleþ—
[Ac] at hir mooste meschief [mercy were þe beste],
Whan þei shal lif lete [a lippe of goddes grace]—
As Salomon dide and swiche oþ*er*e, þat shewed grete wittes
Ac hir werkes, as holy writ seiþ, [was] eu*er*e þe cont*ra*rie. |
Forþi wise witted men and wel ylettrede clerkes *fol. 58 b*
As þei seyen hemself selde doon þerafter:
Super cathedra[*m*] *Moysi &c.*
Ac I wene it worþ of manye as was in Noes tyme
Tho he shoop þat ship of shides and bordes:
Was neu*er*e wrighte saued þat wroȝte þ*er*on, ne ooþ*er* werkman ellis,
But briddes and beestes and þe blissed Noe
And his wif wiþ hise sones and also hire wyues;
Of w[r]ightes þat it wroȝte was noon of hem ysaued.
God lene it fare noȝt so bi folk þat þe feiþ techeþ
Of holi chirche þat herberwe is, and goddes hous to saue

397 many] *om* F. men] *by correction* M; man RF; beene G. on] of Cot. setten] sette YGCLMRF. hir] *by correction* C²; in F. herte] RF; hertes WHmCrGYOC² CBLM.
398 In] On erly F. in] on F. forþi] therfore Cr; sythe G. hem g*ra*ce] g*ra*ce he*m* F.
399, 400 *run together* WHmCrGYOC²CB LMRF: At hir mooste meschief whan þei shal lif lete (At] Ac YOB; but G; and C²C. hir] þe GYOC²CB. meschief] myscheef is OC² (is *added* O). þei...lif] lyf þei shull F. lif] þe lyf HmB).
401 dide...oþ*er*e] and other dede RF. shewed] scheweden OHmF. wittes] wisdom F.
402 Ac] but GF; And CrC²C. hir] hys G. werkes] wordes YCB (*corrected another ink* Cot). holy...seiþ] seyþ þe book F. seiþ] *om* R. was] GYOC²CBLMRF; were W HmCr.
403 Forþi] Therfore Cr; For þise B. and] ne R. ylettrede] lettred CrGC²F.
404 seyen] say Cr. self] syluen HmCr. selde] selden YHmOC²BLMR; ful selde F; senden C. doon] do þei F.
404α *in margin* OC²; *line om* F. *Super*] *Supra* Cr. *cathedram*] HmCrGOC²R; *cathedra* WYCBLM. *&c*] *om* C².
405 Ac] but GF; And CrC²C. it] I R. worþ] worthes Cr. in] of Hm.
406 he] þ*at* he F. þat] h*is* F. and] HmGY OC²CBLM; and of WCrRF.
407 Was...on] No wight þ*at* wroght thero*n* was salf Cr. neuere] no F. wrighte] wyghtte Cot. þat...on] aft*er* F. þeron] therynne Cot. ne ooþer] noþ*er* Cot; ne no*n* oþer F; ne any Cr. ellis] ell:: (*lost in sewing*) BmBo; *om* F.
408 But beestis & brydd*es* in bynnys yclosed F. þe] they G.
409 & Noe & his wif weryn þe ship *with*Inne / & here sones & here wyvis wery*n* all togydre F.
410 *line om* GYOC²CB. Of] And of M; But of F. wrightes] wriȝtes LRF; wryghtes (y *over erasure*) M; wightes WHmCr. wroȝte] wouȝte R. of hem] *om* F. ysaued] saued CrR.
411 lene] leue CrF. bi] nou be F; wyth Hm. þat] *om* F. þe] *om* Cot.
412 herberwe] heberwe L.

And shilden vs from shame þ*er*inne, as Noes ship dide beestes;
And men þat maden it amydde þe flood adreynten.
The *culorum* of þis clause curatours is to mene,
That ben Carpenters holy kirk to make for cristes owene beestes:
Homines & iumenta saluabis, domine &c.
[At domesday þe deluuye worþ of deþ and fir at ones;
Forþi I counseille yow clerkes, of holy [kirke] þe wri3tes,
Wercheþ ye as ye sen ywrite, lest ye worþe no3t þerInne].
On good Friday, I fynde, a felon was ysaued
That hadde lyued al his lif wiþ lesynges and þefte,
And for he bekne[w on] þe cros and to crist shrof hym
He was sonner ysaued þan seint Ioh*an* þe Baptist
Or Adam or Ysaye or any of þe p*ro*phetes
That hadde yleyen wiþ lucifer many longe yeres.
A Robber*e* was yraunsoned raþer þan þei alle,
Wiþouten penaunce of p*ur*gatorie, to p*er*petuel blisse.
Than Marie Maudeleyne [who my3te do] werse?
Or who [dide] worse þan Dauid þat vries deeþ conspired,

413 And] he F. shilden] shilde YGOC[2]C BMRF. Noes] Noe YC; þe F.
414 And] & all þe F. maden] made CrGF. adreynten] dreynten G; wery*n* dr*e*nklyd F; he drowned Cr; adrngend C.
415 *culorum*] Culor Cr; colour G; Conclusiou*n* F. clause] cause OC[2]. curatours is] is curatoures HmM. curatours] of curaturis F; in curatoures R; curates Cr[1]; curate Cr[23]. to mene] þe meny*n*g F.
416 That ben] þey be clepid F. holy kirk] holy cherche HmGYOCBR; of holy chyrch C[2]; *om* F. make] saven F. for... beestes] *om* Cot. for] *om* F. cristes] cryst G. owene] *om* F.
416α *in margin* O; *line om* F. &] *om* Y. &c] *om* CrG.
417–19 RF; *lines om* WHmCrGYOC[2]CB LM; *here in the spelling of* W.
417 deluuye] flood F. deþ] wat*er* F.
418 kirke] cherche RF. þe] *om* F.
419 Wercheþ] Werke F. ye(1)] 3ee F; 3e werkes R. ywrite] wrete o F. no3t þerInne] ydr*e*nklid F.
420 On] For on F; For a R. ysaued] saued CrGYOC[2].
421 lyued] ylyued CotMR. lesynges] leasinge Cr[23]. þefte] thefte HmF; *with* þefte WCrGYOC[2]CBLMR.
422 beknew on] Cr[23]GYOC[2]CBLMR; beknew it on F; beknede to WHm; bekened to Cr[1]. shrof] scrof L.
423 ysaued] saued CrHmGOC[2]CBLMF (*twice, second cancelled* Bm). þan] than was Cot. þe] *om* HmC[2]L.
424 Or] F; And or WCrL; and er HmG YOC[2]CBoCotM; and her Bm; And ar R. Adam] ysaak F. or(1)] & C[2]. þe] thes G.
425 hadde] hadden B; *om* F. yleyen] leyn HmCrG; ley3en lowe F.
426 A] þat F. yraunsoned] raunceoned YCrGOCB.
427 outen] outy*n* F; oute G; outen any WHmCrYOCBLMR; out ony C[2]. of] in F.
428 Than] & GYOC[2]CB; & also F. who ...do] what wo*m*man dide WHmCrGYO C[2]CBLMRF.
429 Or] & G. who] *om* F. dide worse] worse dede R; worse WHmCrGYOC[2]C BLM; *om* F. þan] þan dyde F.

Or Poul þe Apostle þat no pite hadde
Cristene kynde to kille to deþe?
And now ben [swiche] as Souereyns wiþ Seintes in heuene,
Tho þat wrouȝte wikkedlokest in world þo þei were; |
And þo þat wisely wordeden and writen manye bokes *fol.* 59 *a*
Of wit and of wisedom wiþ dampned soules wonye.
That Salomon seiþ I trowe be sooþ and certein of vs alle:
[*Sunt*] *iusti atque sapientes, & opera eorum in manu dei sunt &c.*
Ther are witty and wel libbynge ac hire werkes ben yhudde
In þe hondes of almyȝty god, and he woot þe soþe
Wher fo[r loue] a man worþ allowed þere and hise lele werkes,
Or ellis for his yuel wille and enuye of herte,
And be allowed as he lyued so; for by luþere men knoweþ þe goode.
And wherby wiste men which [is] whit if alle þyng blak were,
And who were a good man but if þer were som sherewe?
Forþi lyue we forþ wiþ [liþere] men; I leue fewe ben goode,

431 *line om* RF. Cristene] Muche cristene WHmCrGYOC^{2}CBLM. kille] put Cr. to(2)] to the G.
432 now ben] ben nou F. now] ȝit (*over erasure another ink*) Hm; *om* LR. swiche] þise WCrYOC^{2}CBLMR; *om* HmGF. as] *om* Cr^1. Souereyns] souereyne B. wiþ] & Cr^{23}GYOC^{2}C; *om* B.
433 Tho] & oþere F. wrouȝte] wrouȝten OHmC^{2}BMF. wikkedlokest] wickedlest CrM; wyckedest GYOC^{2}CB; werst F. in...were] here be heyest nou *in* hevene F. in] in þe B. þo] þe C. were] weren OC^2.
434 wordeden] wordede F; worde*n* Cr; wrouȝton B; werchedid C^2. writen] wrete F.
435 Of] & hadd F. of] *om* BF. wisedom] wisdames OC^2. wonye] wonyen OCrC^{2}CB; dwelle F.
436 *line om* F.
436α *in margin* O. *Sunt*] Cr^{23}RF; *Sint* B (t *erased* Bm); *Siue* (? *Sine*) WHmCr^{1}GYOC^{2}CLM. &c] *om* CrGOC^{2}CotRF.
437 Ther] Thay CB (a *altered from* e C); þat C^2; Summe F. are] were Hm; *om* Cot. witty] willy CB. libbynge] likyng B; learned Cr. ac] but F; & CrGYOC^{2}CB. yhudde] hudde HmCrGOC^{2}F.
438 almyȝty] *om* F. and] for F. woot] whot al F.
439 for...man] he F. for] OC^{2}LMR; **fore** WHmCrGYCB. loue] HmGYOC^{2}CBLMR; *om* WCr. a] of B. þere and] for love of F. and] in C^2. lele] leli Cr; *om* F.
440 yuel] yll Cr. and] YGOC^{2}CBMR; and for WHmCr; or L; þoruh F. of] of his F.
441 And be] He worþ F. as he lyued] of his lyf F. as] for R. lyued] leued C^{2}B. so] þere OC^2; *om* CrGF. for] fro F; as OC^2; *om* CB. by] HmCrGYLMR; by þe W; *om* OC^{2}CBF. luþere] lyþernesse F; yl Cr. men] is F. knoweþ] knowe CrGF. þe] *om* CrOC^{2}CB.
442 *line om* F. And wherby] For how Cr. wiste] -iste *over erasure* M; wist (ist *over erasure*) Bm; wite YC; witen OC^2; wete (*first* e *over erasure*) Hm; wote LR; wytty G. which] what Cr. is] HmCrGYOC^{2}CBLMR; were W.
443 And] Or R; For F. if] *om* F. þer] I G. were] wery*n* F. sherewe] wikke F.
444 Forþi] Therfore Cr. lyue] lyued Y. liþere] MGYOC^{2}CBLRF; oþere WHmCr. men] *om* M. I] thay C; hij B; & G. leue...ben] beþ fewe BC. ben] *om* OC^2.

For *quant oportet vient en place il nyad que pati.*
And he þat may al amende haue mercy on vs alle,
For soþest word þat eu*er* god seide was þo he seide *Nemo bonus.*
[And yet haue I forgete ferþer of fyue wittes techyng
That] Clergie of cristes mouþ comended was it [neuere],
For he seide to Seint Peter and to swiche as he louede,
"[*D*]*um steteritis ante Reges & presides* [*nolite cogitare*]*:*
Thou3 ye come bifore kynges and clerkes of þe lawe
Beþ no3t [afered of þat folk], for I shal [3yue yow tonge],
Konnyng [and clergie] to conclude hem alle".
Dauid makeþ mencion, he spak amonges kynges,
And my3te no kyng ou*er*comen hym as by konnynge of speche.
But wit [ne] wisedom wan neu*ere* þe maistrie
Whan man was at meschief wiþoute þe moore g*ra*ce.
The dou3tieste doctour and deuino*ur* of þe trinitee
Was Austyn þe olde, and hei3est of þe foure, |
Seide þus in a sermon—I seigh it writen ones— *fol. 59 b*

445 *quant*] quant3 RF; quan Bm; whan Bo Cot. *vient*] vyn RF; cometh YGOC^{2}CB. *en*] In GYOC^{2}CB; em Cr^{3}. *il...pati*] *om* BoCot. *nyad*] nad HmGYOC^{2}CBm. *que*] qe R; *qui* G. *pati*] *pati &c* Hm.
446 may al] alle may YM. on] of YOC^{2} CB. vs] *om* Cot.
447 For] For þe CrBoCotF; þe G. euer... seide] god euere spak F. was] *om* CB. þo he seide] *om* CrF. þo] þe Bm; þat Hm.
448 *not in* WHmCrGYOC^{2}CBLMRF.
449 That clergie] Clergie OC^{2}; Clergie þo WHmCrGYCBLMRF. comended] comend Bm. was] it Cr^{1}. it neuere] it litel WHmLMR; was litel Cr^{1}; litel Cr^{23} GYOC^{2}CB; þan lyte F.
450 swiche...louede] hise postlis alle F.
450α *in margin* OC^{2}; *transposed with* 451 B. *Dum*] YGOC^{2}CBLMRF; *Cum* WHmCr. *steteritis*] *steteris* Hm. &] *om* M. *presides*] *presipes* Cr^{2}; *om* M. *nolite cogitare*] F; *&c* WHmCrYOC^{2}CBLMR; *om* G.
451 come] comen Bm. clerkes] clarke Cr^{3}.
452, 453 *as three lines divided after* mouþes, conclude WHmCrGYOC^{2}CBLMRF: Beþ no3t abasshed for I shal be in youre mouþes And 3yue yow wit and wille and konnyng to conclude Hem alle þat ayeins yow of cristendom disputen (be] be buxum F. yow(1)] *om* B. and(1)] at LRF. and(2)] *om* R. konnyng] knonnyng Y. conclude] concluden RF. Hem alle] All hem F. of cristendom] goddes lawe F. of] *om* R. disputen] dispute F).
454 he...amonges] where he spekþ of F.
455 And] Al R; þere F. comen] come Hm CrGYOC^{2}CBLMRF. as] and C; *om* GBF. konnynge] kennyng G. of] *om* HmCr.
456 ne] GYOC^{2}CBLMR; and WHmCrF. wan] ne wan CGYBM. neuere] euere HmF. maistrie] maistre YCCot.
457 oute...grace] goddes grace plentyvous F. þe] *om* BoCot.
458 dou3tieste] douties Cr^{3}; dou3tiorokest R. and] ad Hm. þe trinitee] dyvinite FCr^{23}.
459 Austyn] Augustyne GLM; seynt Austy3n F. þe olde] yolde Bm; yholde BoCot. and] & þe G. þe(2)] hem R.
460 Seide] he seyþ F. þus] þou G. seigh] se Y.

"*Ecce ipsi ydiot[e] rapiunt celum vbi nos sapientes in inferno mergimur*".
And is to mene to [Englissh] men, moore ne lesse,
Arn none raþ*er* yrauysshed fro þe riȝte bileue
Than are þise [kete] clerkes þat konne manye bokes,
Ne none sonner saued, ne sadder of bileue,
Than Plowmen and pastours and [pouere] co*m*mune laborers,
Souteres and shepherdes; [swiche] lewed Iuttes
Percen wiþ a Paternost*er* þe paleys of heuene
And passen Purgatorie penauncelees at hir hennes partyng
Into þe [parfit] blisse of Paradis for hir pure bileue,
That inparfitly here knewe and ek lyuede.
Ye, men knowe clerkes þat han corsed þe tyme
That euere þe[i] kouþe [konne on book] moore þan *Credo in deum patrem*,
And p*ri*ncipally hir paternoster; many a p*er*sone haþ wisshed.
I se ensamples myself and so may manye oþ*ere*,

461 *in margin* O. *Ecce*] Eecce C; Ecci R. *ydiote*] CCrGYOC^{2}BF; ydioti WHmLMR. *nos*] *om* OC^2. *mergimur*] *mergimur* ⁊*c* Hm; *om* C.
462 And] þis F. is] *om* G. to(2)] In G; on YOC^{2}CB. Englissh] YHmCrGOC^{2}C BLMR; meene F; *om* W. men] me*n* neyþ*er* F; men to Cr^{23}; to GYOC^{2}CB. ne] no HmR; and to Cr^{23}GYOC^{2}CBmBo; and Cot. lesse] losse C.
463 *line om* Cot. Arn] þ*er*e are F. none] noon oþ*er*e OYC^{2}CBmBo. raþ*er*] su*n*nere F. yrauysshed] rauished CrGYOC^2 CBmBoMF. fro] for G.
464 *line om* G. kete] konnynge WHmCr YOC^{2}CBLMRF. konne] ku*n*ne*n* BM; knowe RF. manye] so many Hm; fele F.
465 *line om* G. sonner] souer Cr^3. saued] Isaued RF; sauer Cot.
466 Than] þa*n*ne trewe F. and(1)] ben F. pastours] pastorers Cr^1; postours Bm; portours BoCot; *om* F. pouere] pouer R; poore HmCrLMF; oþ*ere* WGYOC^{2}CB. laborers] peple F.
467 *line om* B. Souteres] As sowteres F. swiche] suche Cr^{1}LR; and suche HmCr^{23} GYOC^{2}CMF; and oþ*ere* W. Iuttes] Iottes YOC^{2}CLMR; Ioppis F; Ideotte*s* G.
468 Percen] That p*er*sen B; Swiche p*er*sen F; passen (ssen *over erasure another ink*) Hm. a] here F.
469 And] ⁊ þey F. passen] passen þurgh BF. penauncelees] *om* F. hennes partyng] lyvis dep*ar*tyn*g* F.
470 þe parfit] þe WHmCrGYOC^{2}CBLM RF. blisse of] pleyn F. for] þoruhȝ F.
471 That] þo þat F. inparfitly] vnperfitly Cr; *prefix erased* M; in p*ar*fit lif BF. here] *om* R. knewe...ek] ⁊ in clennesse F. knewe] knewen OHmC^2. ek] *om* R. lyuede] lyueden OHmC^{2}BM.
472 Ye] Yea Cr; *om* MF. knowe] knowen OC^2; haue knowen M; knowe su*m*me F. þat] þat þey F; *om* R. han] *om* CrR. corsed] cursen R.
473 þei] OHmCrYC^{2}CBLMRF; þe W; ye G. kouþe] couþen OC^2; *om* F. konne on book] on book Cot; on þe boke GYO C^{2}CBmBo; knowe (*after small erasure*) Hm; or knewe WCrLMR; knewe **F**. *patrem*] ⁊*c* YC; *om* HmCrGOC^{2}B.
474 hir] þe RF. a...wisshed] have þis dysyred F. a] *om* GC. haþ] haþ it Hm. wisshed] Iwisched R.
475 ensamples] exa*m*ples Cr; ensample G. my] by my Hm; many my OC^2. may] many Bm; *om* Hm. manye] many an HmCr^{1}LRF; may (*correct order noted*) Bm; *om* OC^2.

That *ser*uaunt3 þat seruen lordes selde fallen in arerage,
But þo þat kepen þe lordes catel, clerkes and Reues.
Right so lewed [laborers] and of litel knowyng
Selden falle so foule and so fer in synne
As clerkes of holy [k]ir[k]e þat kepen cristes tresor,
The which is mannes soule to saue, as god seiþ in þe gospel:
Ite vos in vineam meam.'

476 *ser*uaunt3] men F. selde fallen] fallyn selden F. selde] selden LHmCrM. fallen] falle HmCrGYOC²CBLMR. arerage] arerages HmCrYO; rerage R; reragys F; eragis C².

477 þo] *om* F. þat] *twice, second cancelled* Hm. kepen] kepe Cr. þe] my Hm; *om* RF. lordes] her*e* F. clerkes...Reues] by her*e* acou*n*tys þey fall F. Reues] rent*es* G.

478 laborers] men WHmCrGYOC²CBLMRF. and of] of a F. knowyng] kunnyng RF.

479 Selden] Selde CrGYOC²CBF. falle] fallen OMR. so(1)] RF; þei so WHmCrGYOC²CBLM.

480 kirke] YOC²CBmBoLMF; chirche WHmCrGCotR. kepen] kepe CrG.

481 to...þe] as seiþ godd*es* F.

481α *in margin* WL. *meam*] *meam &c* Hm GYCBMR; *meam et quod iustum fuerit dabitur vobis* F.

XI

Thanne Sc*ri*pture scorned me and a skile tolde,
And lakked me in latyn and li3t by me sette,
And seide '*Multi multa sciunt et seipsos nesciunt*'. |
Tho wepte I for wo and wraþe of hir speche *fol.* 60 *a*
And in a wynkynge [worþ til I weex] aslepe.
A m*er*ueillous metels mette me þanne,
[For] I was rauysshed ri3t þ*er*e; Fortune me fette
And into þe lond of longynge [and] loue she me brou3te
And in a Miro*ur* þat hi3te middelerþe she made me biholde.
[Siþen] she seide to me, 'here my3tow se wondres
And knowe þat þow coueitest and come þ*er*to p*ar*aunter'.
Thanne hadde Fortune folwynge hire two faire damyseles:
Concupiscencia carnis men called þe elder mayde
And Coueitise of ei3es [þat ooþer was ycalled].
Pride of parfit lyuynge pursued hem boþe

1 scorned] *illegible* (? serued) C. skile] skele me F. tolde] loked Cr.
2 And] For me F. me(1)] *om* F. in] a R; *om* F. and] *om* F. sette] YGOC^{2}CB; she sette WHmCrLM; he sette RF.
4 wepte...wraþe] for sorwe y wepte ⁊ was wroth3 F. wepte I] I weptte Cot. wo] sorwe R.
5 *For this line* F *reads six spurious lines; see above*, pp. 222, 223. a] *om* Hm. wynkynge] wyndyng YGOC^{2}CB. worþ] wraþe WHmCrGYOC^{2}CBLMR. til I weex] til I was R; weex I WHmGYOC^{2}CBLM; wexyd I Cr.
6 A] A ful B; Ano*n* a F; And Cr. metels] sweuene GYOC^{2}CBM. mette me þanne] me tydde to dreme RF. me] I me YOC^{2}.
7 For] RF; That WHmCrGYOC^{2}CBLM. ri3t þ*er*e] *om* F. Fortune] and Fortune WHmCrGYOC^{2}CBLMF; for fortune R.
8 And] *om* B. into] *altered from* and to Bm; in Y; to C. þe...of] *om* Hm. and loue] ⁊ loue R; alone B; allone WHmCrGYOC^{2}CLMF.
9 And] *om* CrOC^{2}. þat] *om* Cr. hi3te] is F. middelerþe] mydlerd YOC^{2}CBLMRF. me] GYOCB; me to WHmCrLMR; me in F; *om* C^{2}. biholde] loke Cr^{23}.
10 Siþen] OHmCrGYC^{2}CBLMR; ⁊ aft*er*ward F; Sone W. to] vnto OC^{2}. my3tow] myghtest thou Cr; meysthowe þou G; may þou F.
11 knowe] knowen F.
12 Thanne...two] þer*e* folwede Fortune four*e* F. hire] *om* G. damyseles] doghters G.
13 men] was F. called] calleden O. mayde] mayden M; *om* B.
14 ⁊ þe secu*n*de was Rycchesse Fu dey*n*tily arayed F. ei3es] heyghtes G. þat...ycalled] ycalled was þat ooþer WHmCrGYOC^{2}CBLMR (ycalled] called CrGYOC^{2}CB. þat] the Cr^{1}G).
15 Pride] þa*n*ne pri3de F.

And bad me for my contenaunce acounten Clergie li3te.
Concupiscencia carnis colled me aboute þe nekke
And seide, 'þow art yong and yeep and hast yeres ynowe
For to lyue longe and ladies to louye,
And in þis Mirour þow my3t se [myrþes] ful manye
That leden þee wole to likynge al þi lif tyme'.
The secounde seide þe same: 'I shal sewe þi wille;
Til þow be a lord and haue lond leten þee I nelle
That I ne shal folwe þi felawship, if Fortune it like.'
'He shal fynde me his frend', quod Fortune þerafter;
'The freke þat folwede my wille failled neu*ere* blisse.'
Thanne was þ*er* oon þat hi3te Elde, þat heuy was of chere;
'Man', quod he, 'if I mete wiþ þe, by Marie of heuene!
Thow shalt fynde Fortune þee faille at þi mooste nede
And *Concupiscencia carnis* clene þee forsake—
Bittrely shaltow banne þanne, boþe dayes and ny3tes,
Coueitise of ei3e, þat euere þow hir knewe—
And pride of parfit lyuynge to muche *per*il þee brynge.' |
'Ye? recche þee neu*ere*', quod Rechelesnesse, stood forþ in
    raggede cloþes; *fol. 60 b*

16 my] any OC^{2}F. acounten] acounte YCrGOC^{2}CBLMRF; counte Hm. li3te] ligthte (*corrected from* higth) Hm; lyte F.
17 *Concupiscencia*] conpuciscentia G. *carnis*] *caris* (*is above line*) Bm. colled] culled C^2.
18 yong] 3it 3ong F. and(1)] *om* G. yeep] yemp Cr; *om* G. yeres] 3eere F.
19 lyue] lyven F. and...louye] on londe ⁊ loven ladyes manye **F.**
20 in] *om* R. þis] þe G. þow] you Cr^1. my3t] myghtest GC^2; may F. myrþes] OCr^{23}GC^{2}CBL; murthes YMR; m*er*this F; my3tes WHmCr^1 (s *over erasure another ink* Hm). ful manye] ynowe F.
21 leden] lede YGOC^{2}CB; will leenge F. wole] wolen OB; wylie wyse Cr; wel R; *om* F. to] in F.
22 The secounde] þa*nn*e Ricchesse F. þe] þ C. same] same leue (leue *cancelled*) G. shal] wil F. sewe] shew G.
23 a] *om* YB. and haue] of F. leten] lete HmCrGYOC^{2}CBR; leve F.
24 That] but G. ne] *om* GF.
25 his] eu*ere* F. quod] tel F. þer] here G; þ*is* F. after] tale F.
26 folwede] folweþ CCr^{23}YBRF.
27 þat(1)] *om* GC^{2}F. hi3te] *om* F. of chere] *om* C.
28 mete] mette OBmBo (*corrected* O). by] be My3lde F.
29 þee] *om* F.
30 clene þee] loke clene þou F.
31 Bittrely] Ful bytt*er*ly F. banne] blame G. þanne] hem Cr; ell*es* F; *om* G. dayes] þe dayes C; day Cr. ny3tes] night Cr.
32 þ*at* euere in þis rewme rycchesse þou knewe F. ei3e] heght G; þe *corrected to* the eighe *another hand* C^2. euere...hir] þow hire eu*ere* M. hir] it YGOC^{2}CB. knewe] knowe Cot.
33 of] of þi R. to...peril] in p*er*eyl will F. brynge] brou3t CB.
34 Ye] 3it Hm. þee] þou Hm; *om* M. neu*ere*] not Cr^{23}. Rechelesnesse] recchelnesse Y; reccheles FCrG. stood] ⁊ stode Cr^{23}G; sta*n*d Cr^{1}B; was F. forþ] clad F; *om* G.

'Folwe forþ þat Fortune wole; þow hast wel fer til Elde.
A man may stoupe tyme ynoȝ whan he shal tyne þe crowne.'
'*Homo proponit*', quod a poete, and Plato he hiȝte,
'And *Deus disponit*', quod he; 'lat god doon his wille.
If truþe wol witnesse it be wel do Fortune to folwe
Concupiscencia carnis ne Coueitise of eiȝes
Ne shal noȝt greue þee [graiþly], ne bigile [þee], but þow wolt.'
'Ye! farewel, Phippe', quod Faunteltee, and forþ gan me drawe
Til *Concupiscencia carnis* acorded alle my werkes.
'Allas, eiȝe!' quod Elde and holynesse boþe,
'That wit shal torne to wrecchednesse for wil to haue his likyng!'
Coueitise of eiȝes conforted me anoon after
And folwed me fourty wynter and a fifte moore,
That of dowel ne dobet no deyntee me þouȝte;
I hadde no likyng, leue me, [þe leste] of hem to knowe.
Coueitise of eiȝes com ofter in mynde
Than dowel or dobet among my dedes alle.

35 þat] þe Cr^{3}; *om* F. Fortune wole] Fortunes wil F. wel] ful F; *om* G. fer] faire YO (*altered to* far O); Fare C^{2}C; for Cr^{1}. til] to HmGYOC^{2}CBMRF. Elde] *om* Y.

36 tyme] tymes HmLMR; by time Cr^{1}. he] Eld Cr^{23}; *om* Cr^{1}. tyne] lose G. þe] thy Cr^{3}; hys GF; *om* BoCot.

37 and] þo and R; þo Mayster F.

39 wol] do Cr. witnesse] þat F. be] is Cr^{23}. wel] *om* F.

40 Coueitise of eiȝes] Ricchesse of þis rewme F. eiȝes] eiȝe B; heghtes G.

41 Ne] þey F; *om* G. noȝt] non C^{2}; *om* Cr^{23}. graiþly] graythly RF; gretly WHm CrGYOC^{2}CBLM. bigile...wolt] but þou wilt begile the Cr. bigile] gyle F. þee(2)] OHmGYC^{2}CBLMRF; *om* W. but] Hm YOCBLRF; but if WC^{2}M; wit*h*owte G. wolt] YHmGOC^{2}CBLR; wolle M; wolt þi selue W; knowe F.

42 Faunteltee] Fauntele F. forþ] he Bm Bo; by Cot.

43 alle] til alle R; wiþ alle BoBmCot; *with* F.

44 eiȝe] heyghe G; þe *altered to* þo C^{2}; Ricchesse F.

45 to wrecchednesse] þis wrecche F. his] *om* F.

46–9 *lines om* RF.

46 eiȝes] heyghtes G. anoon] sone GYO C^{2}CB.

47 folwed] folow C. wynter] wy*n*ters G. and a fifte] or fifty and Cr^{23}YCB; or fifty or OGC^{2}.

48 bet] bett*er* G. þouȝte] ne þouȝte LM; thynke C.

49 leue me] *om* Cr^{23}GYOC^{2}CB. þe leste] if þe leste L;if þe lest M; if þee list W; ȝif thu list Hm; if ye list Cr^{1}; ne no luste Cr^{23}GYCB; ne luste C^{2}O. to] ouȝt to WHmCrGYOC^{2}CBLM.

50 *line om* F. Coueitise] for couetyse (for *added later*) Hm. eiȝes] eiȝe B; heyghtes G. ofter] o *over erasure* Bm; after Cr^{23}. in] in my Cr^{23}GOC^{2}R.

51 *line om* F. Than] And C. bet] bett*er* G.

Coueitise of ei3es [ofte me conforted];
'Haue no conscience', [quod she], 'how þow come to goode;
Go confesse þee to som frere and shewe hym þi synnes.
For whiles Fortune is þi frend freres wol þee louye,
And [festne] þee [in] hir Frat*er*nitee and for þe biseke
To hir Priour p*ro*uincial a pardon for to haue,
And preien for þee pol by pol if þow be *pecuniosus*.'
Pena pecuniaria non sufficit pro spiritualibus delictis.
By wissynge of þis wenche I [dide], hir wordes were so swete, |
Til I for[yede] youþe and yarn into Elde. *fol.* 61 *a*
And þanne was Fortune my foo for al hir faire [biheste],
And pou*er*te p*ur*sued me and putte me lowe.
And þo fond I þe frere afered and flittynge boþe
Ayeins oure firste forward, for I seide I nolde
Be buried at hire hous but at my parisshe chirche;
For I herde ones how Conscience it tolde,
[At kirke] þ*er*e a man were cristned by kynde he sholde be buryed.

52 *line om* CB. Coueitise of ei3es] þa*n* Coueytise & Ricchesse þei F. ei3es] heyghtes G. ofte me conforted] conforted me ofte WHmCrGYOC²LMRF.
53 Haue] And seide haue WHmCrGYOC²CBLMRF. no] thu no HmF. quod ...how] how WHmCrGYOC²CBLMRF. come to goode] good shal holde F.
54 þee] *om* LF. som] the Hm; a F.
55 freres] su*m* frere R. wol] woln Hm; wolen OB. louye] worchepe F.
56 festne] fette R; fecche WHmCrGYOC²CBLM; sette F. þee] *om* G. in] F; to WHmCrGYOC²CBLMR. for] faste for F. biseke] praye F.
57 Priour] provid F. a] *om* F. for] for þe F; *om* CrG.
58 preien] preye OCrGYC²CBF. be *pecuniosus*] *pecuniosus* be Hm. *pecuniosus*] pecunious RB; pecunyous holde F.
58α *in margin* OC². *Pena*] RF; *Set pena* WHmCrYOC²CBLM; *sed pecia* G. *pecuniaria*] *pecularia* R. *spiritualibus*] *spirituali* F. *delictis*] *delictis* &c Hm; *delicto* F.
59 By...dide] þa*n*ne wrowhte y after þat wenche F. dide] dede R; wrou3te WHmCrGYOC²CBLM. hir] theyr G. were] were*n* OBF. so] *om* G.
60 Til I foryede] & ty3htly fram F. foryede] foryat WHmBLMR; foryate YOC²; forgate CrGC (g *altered from* y C). and] y F. yarn] yerne YOC²; ran HmR; 3eede F; then G. in] streyght F.
61 was] fel F. for al] fro F. faire] *om* G. biheste] YHmCrGOC²CBLMRF; speche W.
62 pouerte] pouert Cot. and] *twice* Cr³. lowe] ful lowe F.
63 þo...I] I founde G. afered] vnstable BmBo; fals vnstable Cot. flittynge] flytyng to me F.
64 oure] our owen Cot; ouren BmBo.
65 buried] buriel BmBo.
67 That kind wold me*n* be biried ther thei were christe*n*id Cr. At kirke] That WHmGYOC²CBLMRF. were] was G. by...he] þ*er*e F. be] he be F. *Hereafter an additional line* WHmCrGYOC²CBLMRF: Or where he were parisshen ri3t þ*er*e he sholde be grauen (Or] *om* F. he(1)] þat he Cr. were] were a R; a F. ri3t] þat Cr; or noon 3it F; *om* G. þ*er*e...grauen] sholde he þere be grauyd F). *See above*, p. 193.

And for I seide þus to freres a fool þei me helden,
And loued me þe lasse for my lele speche.
Ac yet I cryde on my Confess*our* þat [so konnyng heeld hym]:
'By my feiþ! frere', quod I, 'ye faren lik þise woweris
That wedde none widwes but for to welden hir goodes.
Ri3t so, by þe roode! rou3te ye neuere
Where my body were buryed by so ye hadde my siluer.
Ich haue muche m*er*ueille of yow, and so haþ many anoþ*er*,
Whi youre Couent coueiteþ to confesse and to burye
Raþ*er* þan to bapti3e barnes þat ben Catecumelynges.
Bapti3ynge and buryinge boþe beþ ful nedefulle;
Ac muche moore meritorie, me þynkeþ, is to bapti3e,
For a bapti3ed man may, as maistres telleþ,
Thoru3 contricion [clene] come to þe hei3e heuene—
Sola contricio [delet peccatum]—
Ac [a] barn wiþouten bapteme may no3t be saued:
Nisi quis renatus fuerit.

68 seide] tolde F. to] þe F. helden] helde BF.
69 loued] loueden BHm. þe] *om* F. lele] lely Cr.
70 Ac] But F; And CrGYOC^{2}CB. yet] 3i3t Bm; *om* F. þat] þ*at* he G. so...hym] Cony*n*gge hyghte hy*m*selue F; heeld hymself so konnyng WHmGYOC^{2}CBLMR; helde himself cu*n*ni*n*g Cr.
71 faren] fare GF.
72 wedde] wedden OHmC^{2}BMRF. none] olde F. but] *om* F. for] *om* HmG. welden] welde HmCrGYOC^{2}CLMR; wedde*n* B. goodes] goed R.
73 Ri3t...ye] So it fareþ nou be 3ow for 3ee ne rowhte F. rou3te] rou3ten OC^2. ye] you Cr; þe C; þei B.
74 buryed] yburied BC^2. by] *om* GF; ? *by correction* M. hadde] hadden BHm. my (2)] þe GYOC^{2}CB.
75 muche] mochil B. haþ] han B. an] *om* CrGYOC^{2}CBR.
76 coueiteþ] coveyty*n* F. to(2)] *om* Cr.
77 Catecumelynges] cathecumynys OGC^2; cathecumys F; catekinlinges Cr^{1}CB; catechislinges Cr^{23}.
78 boþe beþ] and bothe Hm; hath ben CB. ful] *om* Cr. nedefulle] nedyful Hm.
79 Ac] but GF; And CrC^{2}C. muche] mychil F. meritorie] merytoryouse G. þynkeþ] þynke L. is] HmYOC^{2}C; it is WCrBLMRF; *om* G. bapti3e] *cri*stne F.
80 as] GYOC^{2}CLMR; as wel as B; as þise WHmCr; as *gre*te F.
81 *run together with* 81α WCr. Thoru3] þorgh3 gret F. clene come] come WHmCrGYOC^{2}CBLMRF. to] til R; into F. þe] *om* GF. hei3e heuene] heuenly blysse F.
81α *in margin* HmOC^{2}LM. *contricio*] *contricione* Cr. *delet peccatum*] HmGYOC^{2}CB; &c WLMR; *om* CrF. *peccatum*] *peccatum* &c GY.
82 Ac] but GF; And CrC^{2}C. a] HmGYOC^{2}CBLMRF; *om* WCr. barn] baren (barne *above it another hand*) C^2. outen] oute HmCrGYLM. be] CrGYOC^{2}CB; so be WHmLMR; so sone be F. saued] ysaued R.
82α *run together with* 83 WCrLMRF; *in margin* OC^2. *fuerit*] *fuerit* &c Hm; *fuerit ex aqua* C^2; *fuerit ex aqua* &c GYOCBmBo; *fuerit ex aqua & spiritu sancto* &c Cot.

Loke, ye lettred men, wheiþer I lye or noȝt.'
And lewte [louȝ] on me [for] I loured [on þe frere];
'Wherfore lourestow?' quod lewtee, and loked on me harde.
'If I dorste', quod I, 'amonges men þis metels auowe!' |
'ȝis, by Peter and by Poul!' quod he and took hem boþe to witnesse: *fol. 61 b*
Non oderis fratres secrete in corde tuo set publice argue illos.
'They wole aleggen also', quod I, 'and by þe gospel preuen:
Nolite iudicare quemquam.'
'And wherof serueþ lawe', q*uo*d lewtee, 'if no lif vndertoke it
Falsnesse ne faiterie? for somwhat þe Apostle seide
Non oderis fratrem.
And in þe Saut*er* also seiþ dauid þe p*ro*phete
Existimasti inique quod ero tui similis &c.
It is *licitum* for lewed men to [legge] þe soþe
If hem likeþ and lest; ech a lawe it graunteþ,
Excepte p*er*sons and preestes and p*re*lates of holy chirche.
It falleþ noȝt for þat folk no tales to telle

83 þis resou*n* y radde sone F. Loke] *om* R. wheiþ*er*] whet*ur* R; wher HmCrM; wheher C. lye] lye*n* Y. or] GYOC^2CB; or do WHmCrLR; or I do M.
84 louȝ] lok C; loked WHmCrGYOC^2B LM; þo loked RF. for] F; and WHmCrG YOC^2CBLMR. loured] gan so lowre F. on þe frere] after WHmCrGYOC^2CBL MR; *om* F.
86 If] Marye yf F. quod I] *om* G. þis] þes G; þise YCrOC^2B. auowe] to avowe F.
87 ȝis] ye GYOC^2LMRF; *om* CB. by(2)] *om* F. took] take GLMR. hem] þer (*cancelled*) Bm; *om* GYOC^2CBoCot. boþe] *om* M.
88 *in margin* O. *secrete...tuo*] *in corde tuo secrete* Cr. *secrete*] *secreto* F. *illos*] *illos &c* Hm.
89 wole] woln Hm; wolen OBM; *om* C^2. aleggen] alegge HmCrGYOC^2CB; ageyn F. also] *om* F. preuen] preue OGC^2; þ*us* preve F.
90 *in margin* OC^2. *Nolite*] How Iustly Iesu seyde *nolite* F. *quemquam*] *quemquam &c* HmGR.
91 And] *om* F. if] þa*n*ne if R. lif...it] man it wit*h*take F. it] *om* OC^2.
92 Falsnesse] For falsnesse F; falsheyde G. ne] & GCBF. faiterie] flatterye Cr. Apostle] gospel YCB. seide] it seid F.
93 *so divided from* 94 F; *run together with* 94 WHmCrGYOC^2CBLMR. *oderis*] *odoris* Cr^{23}.
94 also] *om* GCB. seiþ] seyde G. dauid þe prophete] *om* Y.
95 *quod ero*] *quid erit* Cr^1. *&c*] *arguam te & statuam* F; *om* Cr.
96 *licitum*] lefull $Cr^{23}C^2$; leueful O; lefsum BoCot; lifsu*m* Bm; *locutum* G. for] to G. men] me G. legge] segge GYOCBoLMR; seggyn F; seigge BmCot; sigge W; synge Hm; seie C^2; say Cr.
97 and] or OC^2. ech a] ech CGB; eu*er*y F. lawe] lawe euer*e* lawe F. it] that it Cr^1; *om* M.
98 prelates] me*n* F. chirche] cherches R.
99 for þat] to þis G. no] none BR; *om* G.

Thouȝ þe tale [were] trewe, and it touche[d] synne.
Þyng þat al þe world woot, wherfore sholdestow spare
To reden it in Retorik to arate dedly synne?
Ac be [þow] neueremoore þe firste [þe] defaute to blame;
Thouȝ þow se yuel seye it noȝt first; be sory it nere amended.
[Th]yng þat is pryue, publice þow it neuere;
Neiþer for loue [looue] it noȝt ne lakke it for enuye:
Parum lauda; vitupera parcius.'
'He seiþ sooþ', quod Scripture þo, and skipte an heiȝ and preched.
Ac þe matere þat she meued, if lewed men it knewe,
Þe lasse, as I leue, louyen þei wolde
[The bileue [of oure] lord þat lettred men techeþ].
This was hir teme and hir text—I took ful good hede—
'*Multi* to a mangerie and to þe mete were sompned,
And whan þe peple was plener comen þe porter vnpynned þe yate

100 were] HmCrGYOC^{2}CBLMRF; be W. touched] CrGYOC^{2}CBLMR; touche WHm; towche to F.
101 Þyng] Ac þinge R; A þyng F. þe] þis G.
102 To] And CrGYOC^{2}CBLMRF. it] *om* C^2. arate] araten RF.
103 Ac] but GF; And CrC^{2}C. be] *by correction* Bm. þow] thu HmF; *om* WCr GYOC^{2}CBLMR. moore] *om* HmCB. þe(1)] *om* Cr. þe(2)] HmCrGYOC^{2}CBL MRF; *om* W. defaute] fawty F.
104 Thouȝ] ⁊ þeyhȝ F. yuel] yll Cr. seye] ne seie Bo; tell F. it(1)] *om* G. first] *om* GF. be] but be F. nere] were F. amended] amend G; mendid F.
105 Thyng] a thyng GYB; And þing OC^{2}C; No þyng WHmCrLMR; ⁊ ony þyng F. þow] *om* HmG.
106 Neiþer] no neyþer Hm. loue...noȝt] leef ne for loþ F. loue] *om* Cot. looue] G; laude CrHmYOC^{2}CLM; labbe Cot; lab BmBo (*erasure after it* Bm); lakke R; preise W. ne] no G. it(2)] *om* F. for(2)] for no F; not for G; not For non C^2.
106α *in margin* O. *Parum*] *cancelled for Parce* C^2. *parcius*] *parcius* ⁊*c* HmGBm; *propicius* ⁊*c* BoCot.
107 sooþ] þe sothe R; *om* G. þo] *om* CBF. skipte] starte G; stey F. an heiȝ] vp Cr.
108 Ac] but GF; And CrC^{2}C. she] he GYOC^{2}CBF. meued] meaned Cr. if] *om* RF. it knewe] it knowe R; not knowe yt F.
109 Þe...louyen] ⁊ if þey knewe latyȝn leerne oþere F. louyen] loue G; lauyen Y. þei] þey F; it þei WHmCrGYOC^{2}CBL MR. wolde] wolden OC^2.
110 RF; *line om* WHmCrGYOC^{2}CBLM; *here in the spelling of* W. The bileue] But þei beleven F. of oure] on þe F; þat R. men] men hem F.
111–217, 218–424 *transposed and misplaced after* XII 81 Hm; *see above*, p. 10.
111 This...text] þus gan he his teeme F. hir(*both*)] theyre G. teme] tyme Bm. ful] þerto F.
112 *Multi*] þat *Multi* F. þe] a F. were] weren OBmBoF. sompned] sumpted Cr.
113 And] *om* Cr. peple] peole Cr^2. was] was al B; were Cr. plener] planere Hm Cot; *om* G. comen] come CrGCotRF. porter] *om* C.

And plukked in *Pauci* pryueliche and leet þe remenaunt go
rome.' |
Al for tene of hir text trembled myn herte, *fol. 62 a*
And in a weer gan I wexe, and wiþ myself to dispute
Wheiþ*er* I were chosen or no3t chosen; on holi chirche I þou3te
That vnderfonged me atte font for oon of goddes chosene.
For crist cleped vs alle, come if we wolde,
Sar3ens and scismatikes and so he dide þe Iewes:
O vos omnes sicientes venite &c,
And bad hem souke for synne [saufte] at his breste
And drynke boote for bale, brouke it whoso my3te.
'Thanne may alle cristene come', quod I, 'and cleyme þ*er*e entree
By þe blood þat he bou3te vs wiþ, and þoru3 bapteme after:
Qui crediderit & baptizatus fuerit &c.
For þou3 a cristen man coueited his cristendom to reneye,
Ri3tfully to reneye no reson it wolde.
For may no cherl chartre make ne his c[h]atel selle
Wiþouten leue of his lord; no lawe wol it graunte.
Ac he may renne in arerage and rome fro home,

114 plukked] pulled G. go] *om* G. rome] *om* Cr.
115 Al for] For al Y. Al] And Cr^{3}; & þ*a*nne F. hir] þ*a*t G; þis F. trembled] tre*m*breld F.
116 a] *om* C. weer] weyrye G. gan] þan F. to] *om* HmGYOC^{2}CBF. dispute] desputyd HmF; dispite C^{2}.
117 I(1)] þei G. were] was F. chosen(1)] chose CrRF. or no3t] *om* Y. chosen(2)] chose RF; *om* CrGYOC^{2}CB. chirche] kirke Cr.
118 fonged] fonge GHmOC^{2}CBLMRF; fengen Y. of] *om* F. chosene] closen Bm.
119 cleped] clepiþ F. wolde] wolden OC^{2}.
120 Sar3ens] Boþe sarsy3nes F.
120α *in margin* O; *line om* Y. *sicientes*] scicientes OC^{2}CBLMRF; *scientes* Cr^{2}G. *&c*] *ad aquas &c* HmG; *om* F.
121 souke] sonke Cr. saufte] safly WHm CrGYOC^{2}CBLM; saue RF. breste] brest bon F.
122 boote] but Cot; *om* G. brouke] dry*n*ke F. who] *om* C^{2}. so my3te] þ*a*t wolde F.
123 come] come*n* C^{2}; come yn F; men G. quod I] *om* Hm. and] *om* G. þere] her Cr; *om* F. entree] entre GC^{2}BLMR; enter Cr; to entre þ*er*e F.
124 By] þoru F. þat] *om* GRF. wiþ] *om* R. þoru3] þoru þe F.
124α *in margin* OC^{2}. *&c*] *saluus erit* F; *om* CrC^{2}M.
125 cristen] *om* F. coueited] coueyte G. cristendom] cristedom C. reneye] renewe Cot; forsake C; receyue RF.
126 Ri3tfully to] & vnryghtfully he F. reneye] renewe Cot; receyve it F. it wolde] shal save hy*m* F.
127 cherl] cherle a B; cherk a F; cherche C. ne] *om* F. chatel] catel WHmCrGYOC^{2} CBLMRF. selle] to selle F.
128 outen] out Cr^{3}G; oten Bo. leue] loue Y. no] ne R. lawe] leve F.
129 Ac] but GF; And CrC^{2}C. renne] rennen R. arerage] arerages CrGB; reragis F. rome] runne Cr; renne R; rayke F. fro] GR; fr*a*m F; so fro WYO CBL; so from HmCrC^{2}M. home] hys owne G.

As a reneyed caytif recchelesly rennen aboute.
A[c] reson shal rekene wiþ hym [and rebuken hym at þe laste,
And conscience acounte wiþ hym] and casten hym in arerage,
And putten hym after in prison in purgatorie to brenne;
For hise arerages rewarden hym þ*ere* [riȝt] to þe day of dome,
But if Contricion wol come and crye by his lyue
Mercy for hise mysdedes wiþ mouþe [or] wiþ herte.'
'That is sooþ', seide Scripture; 'may no synne lette
Mercy al to amende and Mekenesse hir folwe;
For þei beþ, as oure bokes telleþ, aboue goddes werkes:
Misericordia eius super omnia opera eius.'
'Ye? baw for bokes!' quod oon was broken out of helle.
'[I] Troianus, a trewe knyȝt, [take] witnesse at a pope
How [I] was ded and dampned to dwellen in pyne |
For an vncristene creature; clerkes wite þe soþe *fol. 62 b*

130 As] And as WHmCrGYOC^{2}CBLMR; & þey F. a] he RF. reneyed] renneth R; renne F. caytif] *om* F. recchelesly] recheles CrY; recchesly CMF. rennen] or romeþ F; *om* GYOC^{2}CBMLR (*corrector supplies* gon L).
131 *run together with* 132 WHmCrGYOC^{2}CBLM. Ac] YOBLMR; but G; ȝit F; And WHmCrC^{2}C. and...laste] RF; *om* WHmCrGYOC^{2}CBLM. rebuken] rebewke F.
132 And...hym(1)] RF; *om* WHmCrGYOC^{2}CBLM; *here in the spelling of* W. acounte] shal acou*n*te F. casten] caste YCrGOC^{2}CBMF. arerage] rerage F.
133 putten] putte OCrGC^2. hym] theym G; *om* YCLM. after] *om* F. in(1)] YGOC^{2}CCotR; in a WHmCrBmBoLM; in strong F.
134 For] And for R; & F. arerages] arerage GYOC^{2}CB; reragys F. rewarden] rewarde GYOC^{2}CBmBoMF; rewad Cot. riȝt] riȝte R; *om* WHmCrGYOC^{2}CBLMF. to] tyl CrBF. þe...dome] domes day Cr; oo day komy*n*ge F.
135 if] *om* G. wol] wel LR; *om* F. and] hy*m* to & m*ercy* F. lyue] leue R.
136 Mercy] & be sory F. or] CrGYOC^{2}CBmBoLMR; other Cot; and WHmF.
137 sooþ] *om* G. seide] saith M; quod HmGYOC^{2}CB. may] may þ*er*e F; þat may B. lette] be lettyd F.
138 Mercy] For m*er*cy F. al to] all Cr; may al RF. and] þat R; if F. hir] hy*m* F; he R; *om* G. folwe] folweþ HmR; felowe CrC^2.
139 oure] houre C; *om* GF. bokes] boke R. telleþ] tell F; *om* G. goddes] godes MR; all godd*es* F.
139α *in margin* OC^2. *eius*(1)] *domini eius* (*corrected*) G; *domini* F; *om* OC^2. *eius*(2)] *eius &c* HmY.
140 baw] baw waw F. quod] *om* G. broken] broke F.
141 I] Cr; Hiȝte WHmGYOC^{2}CLMR; That hiȝte B; he was F. Troianus] Tro*n*yans Cr^1. a(1)] Cr; þe F; hadde ben a WYOC^{2}CLMR; & hadde be*n* a B; that hadde ben a Hm; was a G. trewe] *om* F. take] Cr^1; toke Cr^{23}GOC^{2}LR; took WHmYCBM; he took F. at] of HmF. a(2)] the GYOC^{2}CBF.
142 I] Cr; he WHmGYOC^{2}CBLMRF. dwellen] dwelle HmCrR. pyne] paine CrGYOC^{2}CB; derk peyne F.
143 For] For he was F. creature] creatoure G. wite] witen OHmCrC^{2}CBLMR; woot Y; knowe F.

That al þe clergie vnder crist ne my3te me cracche fro helle,
But oonliche loue and leautee and my laweful domes.
Gregorie wiste þis wel, and wilned to my soule
Sauacion for sooþnesse þat he sei3 in my werkes.
And [for] he wepte and wilned [þat I] were [saued]
Graunted [me worþ] grace [þor3 his grete wille].
Wiþouten bede biddyng his boone was vnderfongen
And I saued as ye [may] see, wiþouten syngynge of masses,
By loue and by lernyng of my lyuynge in truþe;
Brou3te me fro bitter peyne þer no biddyng my3te.'
Lo! ye lordes, what leautee dide by an Emp*er*our of Rome
That was an vncristene creature, as clerkes fyndeþ in bokes:
Nou3t þoru3 preiere of a pope but for his pure truþe
Was þat Sarsen saued, as Seint Gregorie bereþ witnesse.
Wel ou3te ye lordes þat lawes kepe þis lesson haue in mynde
And on Troianus truþe to þenke, and do truþe to þe peple.
[This matere is merk for many, ac men of holy chirche,

144 þe] *om* C. clergie] clerkes M. ne] *om* GYOC^{2}CBLMRF. me] hym GBF; *om* C. cracche] crafthe Bm.
145 leautee] my leute R. and(2)] of RF. my] hys GF.
146, 147 *as three lines divided after* cause, helthe F.
146 Gregorie] Seynt Gregory F. þis wel] wel thys Cr^1; wel that Cr^{23}. and] what was his cause ⁊ F. wilned] wilneth YGO C^{2}CB. my] his F.
147 for...þat] ⁊ helthe For þe soþfastnesse F. for] for þe R. sei3] seith R. in] of RF; *om* CB. my] hise F.
148–50 *as two lines divided before* Grace WHmCrGYOC^{2}CBLMRF.
148, 149 And after þat he wepte and wilned me were graunted Grace WHmCr GYOC^{2}CBLMRF (wilned] wilneth Y; wisshed F. me] þat me M; hy*m* F. were graunted] graunted were (*the other order noted*) C).
150 outen] out CrGYC^2. bede] beyde G; any bede WHmCrYOC^{2}CBLMR; more F. boone] *altered to* loue *another hand* O. fongen] fonge GYCBR; foge*n* Cr.
151 I] was F. may] GYCBLMF; mowen O; mown C^2; now R; *om* WHmCr. outen] oute HmCrGOC^{2}BL. syngynge] syngen C; song F.
152 By] þoru F; *om* R. lernyng] leadynge Cr^{23}; leve F. of] ⁊ of C^2; ⁊ by G; ⁊ þoru F. my] *om* GF.
153 Brou3te me] It brouhte hy*m* F. biddyng] bede M; bede ne F.
154 what] þat Hm. leautee] leaut C. dide] doþ F; *om* R. an] þat F.
155 fyndeþ] finde CrGYCBoM; knowe F.
156 a] þe GF. for] of M.
157 Was] So was F. þat] þe Cr^{23}. as] *om* F. Seint] *om* G.
158 ou3te] oughte*n* CrOC^{2}F. ye] þe RF; þise B; *om* CrG. lordes] *om* F. þ*at*] the HmCr^3; *om* F. lawes] lawe CotF. kepe] kepe*n* Cr^{1}OC^{2}B; keperis F. þis] ⁊ þys Hm; þat Cr^{13}; þe Cr^2. haue] GYOC^{2}C BF; hold Cr; to haue WHmLMR.
159 truþe(1)] *om* F. and] ⁊ to G. truþe(2)] the trew (the *cancelled*) G.
160–170 RF; *lines om* WHmCrGYOC^{2}C BLM; *here in the spelling of* W.
160 ac] of 3ow ac R; save F.

The *legend*[*a*] *sanctorum* yow lereþ more largere þan I yow telle.
Ac þus leel loue and lyuyng in truþe
Pulte out of pyne a paynym of rome.
Yblissed be truþe þat so brak helle yates
And saued þe sarsyn from sathanas power
Ther no clergie ne kouþe, ne konnyng of lawes.
Loue and lewtee is a leel science,
For þat is þe book blissed of blisse and of ioye;
God wrouȝte it and wroot it wiþ his [owene] fynger,
And took it moises vpon þe mount alle men to lere].
'Lawe wiþouten loue', quod Troianus, 'ley þer a bene!'
Or any Science vnder sonne, þe seuene artȝ and alle—
But þei ben lerned for oure lordes loue, lost is al þe tyme,
For no cause to cacche siluer þ*er*by, ne to be called a maister,
But al for loue of oure lord and þe bet to loue þe peple.
For Seint Ioh*a*n seide it, and soþe arn hise wordes:
Qui non diligit manet in morte.
Whoso loueþ noȝt, leue me, he lyueþ in deeþ deyinge.
And þ*a*t alle manere men, enemyes and frendes,
Loue hir eyþer ooþer, and lene hem as hemselue.
Whoso leneþ noȝt he loueþ noȝt, [lord] woot þe soþe,

161 *legenda*] legende RF. yow lereþ] lerneþ ȝow F.
162 Ac] & F. lyuyng] leel lyvynge F.
163 Pulte] Pytten F. pyne] peyȝne F.
164 so brak] brak so F.
165 þe] þ*a*t F. sathanas] sathenases F; sathanas and his R.
167 Loue] þan is love F. is] ryght F.
168 *line om* F.
169 owene] owne F; on R.
170 vpon] on F. to] it to F.
171 Lawe] ȝee lawe F. outen] oute Hm CrGR; *om* F.
172 sonne] the sonne Cr. þe] of all þe F. and alle] *om* F.
173 *line om* B. But] But if (if *another hand*) L. oure lordes] godd*es* F. lost] Ilost R. al þe] thy Cr; her*e* F.
174 For] & for F. cacche siluer] siluer to kacche F. þerby] by Cr; *om* GF. ne to] or Cr.
175 for] for þe C^{2}. þe(1)] to Y; *om* G. bet] better GCF. peple] pope B.
176 seide it] seyþ þus F.
176α *in margin* OC^{2}. *non*] *non me* F. *morte*] *morte &c* YG.
177 so] soeuer Cr; *om* F. noȝt] me not Cr. leue] leueþ B; to love F; *om* HmCr. me] *om* Cr. he] *om* Cr^{3}M. lyueþ] leueth CBmBo. deeþ] deþis F; dede G. deyinge] drede F.
178 men] of men CrG; of men boþe F.
179 Loue] Louen YHmCBLMR; Shull loven F; leuen G. hir] here her Bo; *om* CrF. and] as F. lene] leynd G; leue Cr^{12}; loveþ F. hem(1)] hym GYCB; ma*n* F. as] att G; *om* F. hem(2)] hir YCBLMR; hys G; hym F. selue] seluen $YOC^{2}CB$; nede G.
180 Who] For ho RF. so] þ*a*t F. leneþ] *first* e *altered from* o Hm; leueth Cr^{12}; beleveþ F. he] *om* C^{2}. lord] oure lorde R; god $WHmCrGYOC^{2}CBLMF$.

[And] comaundeþ ech creature to conformen hym to louye
[Hir euencristene as hemself] and hir enemyes after.
For hem þat haten vs is oure merite to louye, |
And [souereynly] pou*er*e peple; hir preieres maye vs helpe. *fol.* 63 *a*
[For] oure Ioye and oure [Iuel], I*es*u crist of heuene,
In a pou*er*e mannes apparaille pursue[þ] vs euere,
And lokeþ on vs in hir liknesse and þat wiþ louely chere
To knowen vs by oure kynde herte and castynge of oure eiȝen,
Whei*þer* we loue þe lordes here bifore þe lord of blisse;
And exciteþ vs by þe Eu*au*ngelie þ*at*, whan we maken festes,
We sholde noȝt clepe oure kyn þ*er*to ne none kynnes riche:
Cum facitis conuiuia nolite inuitare amicos.
'Ac calleþ þe carefulle þ*er*to, þe croked and þe pou*er*e;
For youre frendes wol feden yow, and fonde yow to quyte
Youre festynge and youre faire ȝifte; ech frend quyteþ so oo*þer*.
Ac for þe pou*er*e I shal paie, and pure wel quyte hir *tra*uaille

181 And] CrHmGYOC^{2}CBLMR; he F; Crist W. comaundeþ] comaundede OC^{2}RF; comande C. ech] CrGYOC^{2}CBLMRF; ech a WHm. conformen] conforme HmCrOC^{2}CBLMRF; conferme YG. louye] love god F.
182 Hir...self] ⁊ his neyȝhebor*e* as hy*m*selue F; And souereynly þe pou*er*e peple WCr; and souereynly pore peple HmGYOC^{2}CBLMR. hir enemyes] hise enemyȝe F.
183 For] For fore F. oure] most F.
184 And souereynly] And WHmCrGYOC^{2}CBLMR; ⁊ to plese þe F. peple] F; peple to plese WHmCrGYOC^{2}CBLMR.
185 For] GYOC^{2}CBLMRF; And WHmCr. Iuel] euel R; hele HmYOC^{2}CBLM; heele W; heale G; helthe FCr. I*es*u] is I*es*u RF.
186 In] ⁊ in F. mannes] *om* F. pursueþ] OYC^{2}CBLMR; he p*ur*sueþ F; pursued WHmCrG. euere] after Cr.
187 *line om* B. lokeþ] loked Cr.
188 knowen] knowe GCrYOC^{2}CBF. oure(2)] *om* G. eiȝen] eyghe GYOC^{2}CB.
189 Whei*þer*] wherþer L; wher Hm; Whe R. loue] louen OC^2. lordes] loord F. þe(2)] oure YOC^{2}CBLMR. blisse] heyuen G.
190 And] he F. exciteþ] warneþ F; excited C. vs] *om* G. Eu*au*ngelie] eu*au*ngeliste B. þat] *om* GF. maken] make CrGF.
191 sholde] schulden OBmBo; shul CotC. clepe] clepen Cr; calle C^{2}CF. kynnes] kynne GOC^{2}BR; knowe me*n* F.
191α *in margin* OC^2; *transposed with* 192 F. *inuitare*] *imitare* BmBo. *amicos*] *amicos* ⁊*c* HmY.
192 Ac] but GF; And CrC^{2}C. calleþ] call CrG. pou*er*e] blyȝnde F.
193 youre] oure C. wol] wolen HmOBR. feden] fede HmOC^{2}BRF; fenden C. fonde] fonden R; fende C; w*ith* foode F. yow to] ageyn it F.
194 Youre] boþe F. festynge] festis F; fasty*n*g B. youre] *om* F. faire] *om* Y. ȝifte] yiftes YGOC^{2}CBRF. quyteþ] quit R; ȝeld*ith* F. so] *erasure* M; *om* G.
195 *line om* CB. Ac] but G; And CrC^{2}F. for] *om* F. I] *om* F. paie] p*r*ay for ȝow F. pure] *om* CrF. wel] *om* F. quyte] quiten R; aquyte F. hir] so ȝour*e* F.

That ȝyueþ hem mete or moneie [and] loueþ hem for my sake.'
[Alle myȝte god haue maad riche men if he wolde],
[Ac] for þe beste ben som riche and some beggeres and pouere.
For alle are we cristes creatures and of his cofres riche,
And breþeren as of oo blood, as wel beggeres as Erles.
For [at] Caluarie of cristes blood cristendom gan sprynge,
And blody breþeren we bicome þere of o body ywonne,
As *quasi modo geniti* gentil men echone,
No beggere ne boye amonges vs but if it synne made:
Qui facit peccatum seruus est peccati.
In þe olde lawe, as [þe] lettre telleþ, mennes sones men calle[d] vs
Of Adames issue and Eue ay til god man deide;
And after his resurexcion *Redemptor* was his name,
And we hise breþeren þoruȝ hym ybouȝt, boþe riche and pou*ere*.
Forþi loue we as leue [children shal], and ech man laughe of ooþer,

196 ȝyueþ] geue Cr. hem(1)] hym YCB. or] oþer BmBo. and] HmCrGYOC^{2}CBLMR; or WF. loueþ] loue Cr; leneth Y; amendiþ F. hem(2)] hym Cot.
197 RF; *line om* WHmCrGYOC^{2}CBLM; *here in the spelling of* W. Alle...riche] Almiȝty god hath made riche R; God myghte ryche a maad all F.
198 Ac] R; But F; *om* WHmCrGYOC^{2}CBLM. ben som] su*m*me be F. beggeres and] me*n* be F.
199 For] But F. alle...we] all we er G; we al ar Cr. cristes] hise F. his] *om* CB.
200 *run together with* 201 Cot. And] As R. breþeren] brether Cr^{1}. as(1)] ben F. oo] *om* GYOC^{2}CBF. as(2)...Erles] *om* Cot. as(2)] boþe F. wel] *om* OC^{2}F. beggeres] beggere F. as(3)] ⁊ OC^{2}F.
201 For...blood] *om* Cot. at] RF; on WHmCrGYOC^{2}CBmBoM; of (*cancelled for* on *another ink*) L. cristendom] cristene blood F.
202 blody] bodily F. þere] *om* GF. o] cristis F. ywonne] wonne GCrOC^{2}.
203 *quasi*] *quali* F. gentil] and gentil WHmCrGYOC^{2}CBLMRF.
204 No] Ne OC^{2}. ne] no Hm; ne no Cr^{1}; nor no Cr^{23}; is F. boye] *om* F. it synne] sinne it CrGF. made] make CrF.
204α *in margin* OC^{2}. *peccati*] CrOC^{2}CB RF; *peccati* ⁊*c* WHmGYLM.
205 *as two lines divided before* mennes WHm CrGYOC^{2}CBLMRF. þe(1)] *om* Cr^{1}. as] it seiþ as F. þe(2)] RF; holy WHmCrG YOC^{2}CBLM. telleþ] techiþ B. mennes ...men] þat þe sone of man we be F. men] vs Cot. called] CrHmGYOC^{2}CLMRF; callen W; calliþ B. vs] vs echone WHm CrGYOC^{2}CBmBoLMR; echone CotF.
206 Of...issue] þe issew is of Adam F. Of] and Hm. Adames] adamþis O. ay] *om* F. til] to G. man] mand C; ⁊ ma*n* F.
207 his name] he callyd F. his] *by correction* C^{2}.
208 þoruȝ] by Cr. ybouȝt] bought CrGY OC^{2}CBmBoF; broughtte Cot.
209 Forþi] and Forþi C^{2}; þerfore F. loue] lyue O; leue (*altered to* loue) C^{2}. leue] *om* G. children] childern RF; breþeren WHm Cr^{23}GYOC^{2}CBLM; brether Cr^{1}. shal] YHmGOCBLMR; shuld C^{2}; *om* WCrF. laughe] leue Cr^{1}; lene Cr^{23}. of] on GO C^{2}F; vpon YCB; vp LMR; *om* Cr.

And of þat ech man may forbere amende þere it nedeþ,
And euery man helpe ooþer for hennes shul we alle:
Alter alterius onera portate. |
And be we noȝt vnkynde of oure catel, ne of oure konnyng
neiþer, *fol. 63 b*
For woot no man how neiȝ it is to ben ynome fro boþe.
Forþi lakke no lif ooþer þouȝ he moore latyn knowe,
Ne vndernyme noȝt foule, for is noon wiþoute defaute.
For whateuere clerkes carpe of cristendom or ellis,
Crist to a commune womman seide, in [comen] at a feste,
That *Fides sua* sholde sauen hire and saluen hire of synnes.
Thanne is bileue a lele help, aboue logyk or lawe.
Of logyk [ne] of lawe in *legenda sanctorum*
Is litel alowaunce maad, but if bileue hem helpe;
For it is ouerlonge er logyk any lesson assoille,
And lawe is looþ to louye but if he lacche siluer.
Boþe logyk and lawe, þat loueþ noȝt to lye,
I conseille alle cristene clyue noȝt þeron to soore,

210 And] For OC^2. of] if YGOC^{2}CB. þat] *om* G. man] *om* Cot. þere] hym F. it] that Hm; þat is F. nedeþ] nedy F.
211 euery] ech F. for] here for RF. hennes] henne Hm.
211α *in margin* OC^2. *portate*] *portate &c* HmGYOC^{2}CB.
212 we] *om* Cot. oure(*both*)] *om* F. ne] nor Hm. of(2)] *om* G. konnyng] kinning Cr^1. neiþer] *om* Cr.
213 woot] noot YOC^{2}CLMR; no man BF. no man] not BmBo; wot CotF. neiȝ] *om* GYOC^{2}CB. it] he F. to ben] ne how sone he B. ynome] bynome CrC; take B.
214 *line om* Y. Forþi] Therfore CrF. lif ooþer] others life Cr. lif] leef F.
215 vndernyme noȝt] nyme no man oþer F. for] for þer B; *om* C. is noon] non is F; ys non *corrected from* ytt ys not G. oute] outen OHmC^{2}CMF. defaute] faute GCrYOCBLM.
216 carpe] carpen OC^2.
217 to] *om* C^2. comen] come G; commune WHmCrOC^{2}CBLMRF; conen Y. a(2)] þe HmCrGYCBF. *Hereafter* Hm *copies* XII 82 *ff*; *see apparatus at line* 111 *above.*
218 sauen] saue CrBF. hire(2)] *om* GYCB. of] of hyr GYCBM; of alle LHmCrR; *om* F.
219 Thanne] þat F. lele] lelly CrCot. aboue] abue R. or] & G.
220 Of] Neyþer F. ne] GYOC^{2}CBLMRF; or WHmCr. of] *om* Cr^{3}F. in *legenda*] ne legende of F.
221 Is] Been but F. alowaunce] alowed RF. maad] þei both R; *om* F. if] *om* GCotRF. hem] hym Cot.
222 is] us Hm. er] of F. assoille] tassoille (? t *another ink*) M.
223 to] *om* Hm. if] *om* F. lacche] take C; lacke Cr.
224 Boþe] But OC^2. þat...lye] love wel boþe to lyȝen F. loueþ] louen OC^2. to] for to R.
225 cristene] crystene men HmGOC^{2}C; cristen men to YB; cristene men ȝee F.

For some wordes I fynde writen, were of Feiþes techyng,
That saued synful men as Seint Iohan bereþ witnesse:
Eadem mensura qua mensi fueritis remecietur vobis.
Forþi lerne we þe lawe of loue as oure lord tau3te;
And as Seint Gregorie seide, for mannes soule helþe
Melius est scrutari scelera nostra quam naturas rerum.
Why I meue þis matere is moost for þe pouere;
For in hir liknesse oure lord [lome] haþ ben yknowe.
Witnesse in þe Pask wyke, whan he yede to Emaus;
Cleophas ne knew hym no3t þat he crist were
For his pouere apparaill and pilgrymes wedes
Til he blessede and brak þe breed þat þei eten.
So bi hise werkes þei wisten þat he was Iesus,
Ac by cloþyng þei knewe hym no3t, [so caitifliche he yede]. |
And al was ensample, [sooþliche], to vs synfulle here *fol.* 64 *a*
That we sholde be lowe and loueliche, [and lele ech man to oþer],
And [pacient as pilgrymes] for pilgrymes are we alle.

226 I] *om* F. writen] write CrR; ywryten L; y wrete F. were...techyng] wherof feiþ is rote F. were] HmCrYCLMR; weren O; þat were WGC^{2}BmCot (þat *added by main scribe* C^2); þa were Bo.
227 saued] saveþ F. men] man C^2. as] *om* Cr^{23}.
228 *in margin* O. *remecietur*] remencietur BM; remestietur R. *vobis*] *vobis &c* HmY.
229 Forþi] Therfore Cr. lerne] lere G. tau3te] techeþ F.
230 as] so seyþ F. seide] sayethe G; *om* F. mannes] mennys OC^2; synful F. soule] soules Cr^{23}; mannys F. helþe] helpe G.
231 *in margin* OC^2; *line om* F. *est*] *om* Cr^3. *scelera*] stelera C^2. *rerum*] *rerum &c* Hm.
232 meue] meane Cr. is] þat F. for] is to helpe F; *om* C.
233 hir] hys GYOC^{2}CB; pore F. oure lord] crist F. lome] ofte WCrGYOC^{2}C BLMF; of R; hath Hm. haþ] ofte Hm. yknowe] yknowen M; knowe HmG; knowen CrC.
234 in] of F. þe] *om* CrY. Pask] Passe C; Gospel F. wyke] *om* F. yede] wente M; *om* F. Emaus] Emaus wente F.
235 ne] *om* GYOC^{2}CBM.
236 apparaill] paraille LR. and] as G. wedes] wede B.
237 breed] breake Cr^1.
238 So] & so F. hise] these CrG. werkes þei] wordes the G. wisten] wyste CrG. þat...Iesus] þe soþe F. þat] *om* G.
239 Ac] but GF; And CrC^{2}C. by...no3t] þey knew hym not be cloþynge F. knewe] knewen OHmBmBo. so...yede] ne by carpynge of tunge WHmCrOC^{2}CBLM RF; ne by his carpyng of tonge Y; by carpyng off tong G.
240 al] al þat F. was] BMRF; was in WHmCrGYOC^{2}CL. ensample] example Cr. sooþliche] for sothe R; *om* WHmCr GYOC^{2}CBLMF.
241 sholde] schulden OC^2. and(2)...oþer] of speche WHmCrGC^{2}CBLMRF; of speches YO.
242 pacient as] apparaille vs no3t WHmCr GYOC^{2}CBLMF; apparailen vs nau3t R. pilgrymes(1)] proudly CrGOC^{2}F; ouer proudly WHmLMR; to proudely YCB. are we] we ben F.

And in þe apparaille of a pou*er*e man and pilgrymes liknesse
Many tyme god haþ ben met among nedy peple,
Ther neuere segge hym seiȝ in secte of þe riche.
Seint Ioh*a*n and oþ*er*e seintes were seyen in poore cloþyng,
And as pou*er*e pilgrymes preyed mennes goodes.
I*es*u crist on a Iewes doȝter liȝte, gentil wo*m*man þouȝ she were,
Was a pure pouere maide and to a pou*er*e man ywedded.
Martha on Marie Maudeleyne an huge pleynt made
And to oure Saueour self seide þise wordes:
Domine, non est tibi cure quod soror mea reliquit me solam ministrare?
And hastily god answerde, and eiþ*er*es wille [lowed],
Boþe Marthaes and Maries, as Mathew bereþ witnesse.
Ac pouerte god putte bifore and preised þe bettre:
Maria optimam partem elegit que non [*auferetur ab ea*].
And alle þe wise þ*a*t eu*er*e were, by auȝt I kan aspye,
Preise[n] pouerte for best lif if Pacience it folw[e],

243 *line om* F. in þe] In GC; *om* B. apparaille] paraile R.
244 Many...god] Ofte *cr*ist F. tyme] tymes HmCr. met] ymet FR; at þe mete B.
245 Ther] þat OC^2; they G. segge] segh G; *corrected from* mane *main hand* C. seiȝ] segge G. in] In þe G; wi*th* F. secte] sette Cr; syghtes F. of] lyk F.
246 were] weren OBmBoR. in] *om* C. poore] oþer B.
247 as] as a Y. preyed] prayden CrYO CB; preyude R; preysedyn Hm. mennes] men R; me*n* of here F. goodes] goddes C.
248 *line om* F. I*esu*] Iesus GBm. crist on] In G. liȝte] aliȝte OHmGYC^{2}CBLMR. womman] *om* Cr. she] a R.
249 *line om* F. Was] A was R; sche was Hm; Yet was she Y. pure pouere] pore pure B; pore Cr. maide] mayden BR. to] on Cr. ywedded] wedded GHmCr YOC^{2}CBL.
250 Marie...made] godd*es* modir made an huge tale F. an] and CR. made] she made CrHmGYOC^{2}CBmBoLMR.
251 And to] Vnto I*es*u F. self] syluen Hm; hymselue G; she F.
252 *in margin* O. *cure*] *cura* YCB. *quod... ministrare*] &c R. *reliquit*] reliquid FBmBo. *solam*] *sola* LMF. *ministrare*] *ministrare* &c HmLM; &c YOC^{2}CB; *om* G.
253 hastily] stilleliche B; *om* F. god] *cr*ist faire F. lowed] folwed WHmCrG YOC^{2}CBLMR; fulfylde F.
254 Boþe] bothe In GYOC^{2}CB. Marthaes] matha G. and] & In GYOC^{2}CB. Maries] marye G. as] and B.
255 Ac] but GF; And CrC^{2}C. pouerte] pouert Cot. god] he F; *om* Hm. bifore] tofore F. preised] preyseth Hm. þe] F; it þe YGOC^{2}CBLMR; þat þe WHm; that Cr.
255α *in margin* OC^2. *optimam*] obtimam Cr^1. *que...ea*] *om* R. *auferetur ab ea*] GY OC^{2}CBmBoF; *auferretur ab ea* &c Hm; *auferetur* &c Cot; &c WCrLM.
256 þe] *om* CB. wise] wise me*n* F; wyes Bo; weies Cot. were] were*n* OC^2. by auȝt] as F. I] þat y Hm.
257 Preisen] YHmCrGOC^{2}CBLR; Preyse F; Preiseden WM. pouerte] pouert Cot. for] for the CotM. it] *om* CrG. folwe] HmCrGYOC^{2}CBLM; folwed W; wolde R; welde F.

And boþe bettre and blesseder by many fold þan Richesse.
[Al]þouȝ it be sour to suffre, þe[r] comeþ swete [after].
As on a walnote wiþoute is a bitter barke,
And after þat bitter bark, be þe shelle aweye,
Is a kernel of confort kynde to restore.
So after pouerte or penaunce paciently ytake:
Makeþ a man to haue mynde in god and a gret wille |
To wepe and to wel bidde, wherof wexeþ Mercy *fol. 64 b*
Of which crist is a kernell to conforte þe soule.
And wel sikerer he slepeþ, þe [segge] þat is pouere,
And lasse he dredeþ deeþ and in derke to ben yrobbed
Than he þat is riȝt riche; Reson bereþ witnesse:
Pauper ego ludo dum tu diues meditaris.
Alþouȝ Salomon seide, as folk seeþ in þe bible,
Diuicias nec paupertates &c,
Wiser þan Salomon was bereþ witnesse and tauȝte
That parfit pouerte was no possession to haue,
And lif moost likynge to god as luc bereþ witnesse:
Si vis perfectus esse vade & vende [&c].

258 boþe...and] more F. many fold] skyle & bettre F.
259 Al] LMRF; and HmCrGYOC^{2}CB; For W. be] *om* Cot. þer] there GYOC^{2}CBLMRF; þerafter WHm; yet after Cr. after] GYOC^{2}CBLMRF (*another hand and ink* L); *om* WHmCr.
260 As] Ryght as F. on a] is a F; an G; a C^2. walnote] walshe note F. oute] outen YOC^{2}C. is a] ful F. bitter] bettre YBm. barke] ys þe ryȝnde F.
261 be] & F.
262 kynde] kyȝndely F; lyfe Cr.
263 So] CB; So is WHmCrGYOC^{2}LMRF. pouerte] pouert Cot. or] and Cr. penaunce] pacience OC^2. ytake] ytaken M; take Hm; taken CrG
264 Makeþ] Maketh RF; For it makeþ WHmCrGYOC^{2}CBLM. a(1)] *om* GYOC^{2}CB. to] *om* HmC^{2}F. in] on F. god] good Y. and] *om* G. a] in Cot. wille] whyle G.
266 *line om* OC^2. a] *om* F.
267 sikerer] syker Cr. slepeþ] slepe Y. segge] RF; man WHmCrGYOC^{2}CBLM.
268 he] *om* F. deeþ...derke] þe deþ ne dowhteþ F. deeþ] þe deth M. in] *om* Cr. yrobbed] robbed CrHmGYOC^{2}CBmCotLMRF; rubbid Bo.
269 riȝt] *om* F.
269α *in margin* O. *meditaris*] *meditaris &c* HmY.
270 Al] And OC^{2}BoCotF. seide] saith Cr. as] þus as F. folk] men RF. seeþ] seyne G; seith Cot; saide M. in] n Cr^3.
271 *in margin* OC^2. *nec*] *ne* Y; uec Cr^3. *paupertates*] *paupertas* BmBo. *&c*] *om* CrF.
272 Anoþer poete seyþ in his pure speche F.
273 parfit] propre F. pouerte] pouert CotR. was] *twice* C; ys F. haue] holde F.
274 And...moost] But lyve moost *in* F. to] of F. as] ac B; and C.
274α *in margin* O. *vende*] *vade* Y. *&c*] HmCrGYOC^{2}CBmBoLMR; *omnia* &c Cot; *omnia que habes &c* F; *om* W.

And is to mene to men þat on þis moolde lyuen,
Whoso wole be pure parfit moot possession forsake
Or selle it, as seiþ þe book, and þe siluer dele
To beggeris þat begge and bidden for goddes loue.
For failed neuere man mete þat myȝtful god serueþ;
As Dauid seiþ in þe Sauter: to swiche þat ben in wille
To serue god goodliche, ne greueþ hym no penaunce:
Nichil inpossibile volenti,
Ne lakkeþ neu*er*e liflode, lynnen ne wollen:
Inquirentes autem dominum non minuentur omni bono.
If preestes weren [wise] þei wolde no siluer take
For masses ne for matyns, noȝt hir mete of vsureres,
Ne neiþer kirtel ne cote, þeiȝ þei for cold sholde deye,
And þei hir deuoir dide as Dauid seiþ in þe Sauter:
Iudica me deus & discerne causam meam.
Spera in deo spekeþ of preestes þat haue no spendyng siluer,
That if þei trauaille truweliche, and truste in god almyȝty,

275 And] þis F. mene] many C. to(2)] *om* Cr^{1}; *erasure* M. þis] is Bm; *om* R. lyuen] dwelle F.
276 so] þat F. pure] pore B; pouere C. possession] possessio*n*s Cr.
277 dele] dely*n* þe nedy F.
278 begge] beggy*n* F; goon and begge WHmCrGYCBLMR; goon & beggen O C^{2}. bidden] byddyn F; bydde G; bidden good WCrOC^{2}LMR; bidde goode YCB; bydde syluer Hm. goddes] crystes Hm. loue] sake F.
279 serueþ] serued Cr^{23}GYOC^{2}CBLM. *Here* OC^{2} *add a Latin line like* VII 89; *see above*, p. 221.
280 *as two lines divided after* soþe F; *after* wille R. As] & F. seiþ] *om* C^{2}. to] & hise sawis ben soþe to F. swiche] whiche Hm. þat] as Cr^{23}GBF. wille] will to suffre wo for welthe F; wille With eny wel or wo R.
281 serue] seruen YCM. greueþ] greth Cr. hym] hem CrMRF; *om* Cot. no] noȝt no B; in Cr^{23}. penaunce] peyȝne F.
281α *in margin* OC^{2}. *inpossibile*] *difficile* RF. *volenti*] *volenti &c* HmGYR.
282 *line om* F. lakkeþ] taketh Hm. neu*er*e] noyther R. liflode] lilode Y; *om* C.
282α *in margin* OC^{2}; *line om* F. *minuentur*] munuentur R. *bono*] *bono &c* Hm.
283 weren] were HmCrGYC^{2}CM. wise] R; all wise me*n* F; parfite WHmCrGYO C^{2}CBLM. wolde] wolden OHmBmBo; sholde F.
284 ne] ner Hm. for] *om* F. noȝt] ne nougth Hm; ne Cr; but F. hir] þe G. mete] meates Cr^{23}. of vsureres] only F.
285 Ne] *om* F. ne] no C. þei] thi Cr^{3}. sholde] schulden OB. deye] pershe F.
286 And...deuoir] But seyn þus for here dygner F. dide] dedyn Hm; *om* RF. seiþ] seide R.
286α *in margin* O; *divided from* 287 *after* &c(2) GYOC^{2}CB. *discerne*] *decerne* Cr^{23}; deserne C^{2}. *meam*] *meam &c* HmGYCB; *&c* OC^{2}.
287 þey sholde speke of *spera in deo* whan spendy*n*ge wantiþ F. *deo*] *deo &c* YGOC^{2} CB. haue] haueþ B.
288 That] Tha*n* Cr; *om* F. if] of Y; *om* F. þei] & F. trauaille] trauaylen Hm. truste] truste*n* CrHmBLR. in] on F. almyȝty] of hevene F.

Hem sholde lakke no liflode, neyþer lynnen ne wollen. |
And þe title þat ye take ordres by telleþ ye ben auaunced: *fol. 65 a*
Thanne nedeþ yow no3t to [nyme] siluer for masses þat ye syngen,
For he þat took yow [a] title sholde take yow wages,
Or þe bisshop þat blessed yow [and embaumed youre fyngres].
For made neu*er*e kyng no kny3t but he hadde catel to spende
As bifel for a kny3t, or foond hym for his strengþe.
It is a careful kny3t, and of a caytif kynges makyng,
That haþ no lond ne lynage riche ne good loos of hise handes.
The same I segge for soþe by alle swiche preestes
That han nei*þer* konnynge ne kyn, but a crowne one
And a title, a tale of no3t, to his liflode at meschief.
He [ou3te no] bileue, as I leue, to lacche þoru3 his croune
[Moore þan cure] for konnyng or 'knowen for clene [of] berynge'.

289 Hem] þ*an* F. sholde] shall GC. lakke] þey lakke F. lynnen ne wollen] wollen ne lynnen GCrYOC^{2}CBLMRF (ne] nor Cr).

290 And...by] For 3our*e* tytle of 3o*ur* ordres F. þat] *om* CrGYOC^{2}CB. ye(1)] þey HmCrGYOC^{2}CBLM (? *over erasure* Hm). take] taken OHm; toke CrM (o *over erasure* M). ordres] *above line* M; ordre GYOC^2; her ordre B. telleþ] til CB. ye(2)] thei CrB.

291 nedeþ] nede Cr. yow no3t] nou3t yow YHmCrGOC^{2}CL; 3ou F. to nyme] to take WHmCrBLMR; take GYOC^{2}CF. siluer] no mone F. syngen] synge YHm CrGCBF.

292 yow(1)] ye Cr^1; *om* R. a] youre WHmCrGYOC^{2}CBLMR; þ*at* F. sholde] shall GC. take] þai Cr; *om* Y. yow wages] þ*at* 3e nede F. yow(2)] yow youre WHmCrGYOC^{2}CBLMR. wages] wage Cr^3; wags Cr^2.

293 Or] Of YGOC^{2}C. blessed] blesseþ HmGYOC^{2}CBLMRF. and...fyngres] if þ*at* ye ben worþi WHmCrGYOC^{2}CBL MRF.

294 kyng] no kyng HmL. no] ne HmY (*erased* Hm); a Cr. he...catel] catel he hadde F.

295 bifel...kny3t] fallyþ for his astat F. foond] fynde BF.

296 of] *om* F. a(2)] *om* GYOC^{2}C. caytif] Caytifis F; kayteuyd Hm. makyng] maky*n*ges C.

297 no] noþer R; neiþer BF. lond] londes M. ne(1)] nor Hm. lynage] lyflode F. riche] *om* RF. handes] hand B.

298 segge for] sette to sey þe F.

299 han] hauen BmBo. a] her*e* F. one] on hede B.

300 a(1)] her*e* F. tale] taile CB. his liflode] liue by Cr; take to F. at] GYOC^2 CBLMR; in F; at his WHmCr.

301 ou3te no] haþ moore WHmCrGYO C^{2}CBLMR; is moor*e* F. bileue] belevid F. as] *om* HmCr. leue] trowe F. lacche] lacchen R. þoru3] by Cr^{23}. his] *om* Cr^1.

302 Moore...cure] Cure þan WHmCrG OC^{2}CBLMR; A cure þan F; Cure þ*at* Y. konnyng] kennynge Cr. knowen] knowe F; knowing Cr^{23}GYOC^{2}CB. for(2)] or for Cr^{23}B; or G. of] HmGYOC^{2}CLMR; *om* WCrBF. *Hereafter two additional lines* WHmCrGYOC^{2}CBLMRF: I haue wonder for why and wherfore þe bisshop Makeþ swiche preestes þat lewed men bitrayen (for] and HmYOC^{2}CLMRF; þ*at* G; *om* CrB. Makeþ] Maken F. lewed] poore F). *See above*, p. 193.

A chartre is chalangeable bifore a chief Iustice;
If fals latyn be in þat lettre þe lawe it impugneþ,
Or peynted *par*entrelynarie, *par*celles ouerskipped.
The gome þat gloseþ so chartres for a goky is holden.
So is it a goky, by god! þat in his gospel failleþ,
Or in masse or in matyns makeþ any defaute:
Qui offendit in vno in omnibus est reus.
And also in þe Sauter seiþ Dauid to ouerskipperis,
Psallite deo nostro; psallite quoniam rex terre deus Israel; psallite sapien-
[*ter*].
The bisshop shal be blamed bifore god, as I leue,
That crouneþ swiche goddes kny3tes, þat konneþ no3t *sapienter*
Synge ne psalmes rede ne seye a masse of þe day.
A[c] neuer neiþer is blamelees, þe bisshop ne þe Chapeleyn; |
For hir eiþ*er* is endited, and that [of] '*Ignorancia* *fol. 65 b*
Non excusat episcopos nec ydiote*s* preestes'.
This lokynge on lewed preestes haþ doon me lepe from pou*er*te
The which I preise, þer pacience is, moore *par*fit þan richesse.

303 is] is a Cot. bifore] afore G.
304 þat] þa L; the Y. it] is Cr^{1}. impugneþ] impugne Cr^{1}; repugneþ F.
305 *par*entrelynarie] *par*auntre lynarye Hm; pentrelniarie Cr; þe lynyaryes F. *par*celles] GYOC^{2}CBLMR; or *par*celles WHmF; or percell Cr. skipped] kipped C.
306 þat] that so Hm; þat it F. so] *om* HmF. chartres] *om* F. holden] he holde F.
307 So] Ryght so F. is it] it is CrOC^{2}; is he F. his] þe G.
308 in(1)] in þe F; in a Cot. in(2)] *om* Cr GYOC^{2}CF.
309 *in margin* OC^{2}. *in*(2)...*reus*] *delitto reus est in omnibus* F. *est reus*] *&c* R. *reus*] *reus &c* HmGYCBLM.
310 And] *om* CrF. also...to] Dauid seyþ in þe sawter to swiche F. skipperis] skyppes Cr; kippers C.
311 *Psallite* (*all*)] Spallite F. *quoniam... Israel*] *om* F. *terre*] *omnis terre* (*over erasure another ink*) Hm. *Israel*] *om* HmM. *sapienter*] HmCrGYOC^{2}CBLMRF; sapien::: (*cropped*) W.
312 bifore] afore G. as] a C; *om* F.
313 crouneþ] crou*n*ed GCB; *om* OC^{2}. konneþ] kunne OCrC^{2}F; kannethe G. no3t *sapienter*] nat wysely G; lytil laty*n* F.
314 Synge] Neyþ*er* synge F. psalmes] psalme CrC^{2}. seye] synge B; syngy*n* of F. a...day] a feeste F.
315 Ac] YHmOBLMR; but G; And WCrC^{2}C; For F. neuer neiþer] neither nother Cot. ne] nor Hm; or Cr; and R. þe(2)] *om* C.
316 hir] her euer B; euer Cr^{23}GYOC^{2}; *om* F. eiþ*er* is] boþe been F. of] OGC^{2}CBL MR; is of Y; ys be F; is WHmCr. *Ignorancia*] ynorance F.
317 *excusat episcopos*] *episcopos excusat* G. ydiote*s*] idiotos Bo; *ydiote* F; ydiot:s (*letter before* s *blotted*) Cot. preestes] preestes *&c* Hm; crownid chapeleynys F.
318 This] Thus Hm; þe F. on] of OGC^{2}F. lewed] lewe Cr^{3}. haþ...me] I am Cr. haþ] han Hm. lepe] lope F; luppe R; leapt Cr.
319 The] *om* CrGYOC^{2}CB. þer] her CrB. is] *om* B. *par*fit þan] thanne *par*fit (ne *erased*) M. þan] þan is F.

Ac muche moore in metynge þus wiþ me gan oon dispute,
And slepynge I sei3 al þis, and siþen cam kynde
And nempned me by my name and bad me nymen hede,
And þoru3 þe wondres of þis world wit for to take.
And on a mountaigne þat myddelerþe hi3te, as me [þo] þou3te,
I was fet forþ by [forbisenes] to knowe
Thorugh ech a creature kynde my creatour to louye.
I sei3 þe sonne and þe see and þe sond after,
And where þ*at* briddes and beestes by hir mak[e þei] yeden,
Wilde wormes in wodes, and wonderful foweles
Wiþ fleckede feþeres and of fele colours.
Man and his make I my3te [se] boþe.
Pouerte and plentee, boþe pees and werre,
Blisse and bale boþe I sei3 at ones,
And how men token Mede and Mercy refused.
Reson I sei3 sooþly sewen alle beestes,
In etynge, in drynkynge and in engendrynge of kynde.
And after cours of concepcion noon took kepe of ooþer,

320 *line om and nine spurious lines in its place* F; *see above*, p. 223. Ac] ⁊ but (but *added main hand*) G; And CrC^{2}C.
321 And...siþen] I fel in a slu*m*bry*n*ge ⁊ sone to me F.
322 nempned] neuened G; named Cr; called C. my] *om* GYOC^{2}CB. bad] dude Hm. nymen] nyme OC^2.
323 And þoru3] Of F. wondres] wordis BR; worchynge F. of] yn Hm. þis] þe R. for] *om* Cr.
324 on a] vp on a (*over erasure another ink*) Hm; on hey3 F. erþe] erd YOC^{2}CBLMRF. as...þou3te] *om* F. þo] C^{2}GYOBmBoLMR; than C; *om* WHmCrCot. þou3te] though Cr^3.
325 was] was þidir F. by] *om* F. forbisenes] ensamples WHmCrGYOC^{2}BLMRF; ensampel C.
326 ech a] eu*er*y F. creature] creatures F; creature and WHmCrGYOC^{2}CBLMR. my] no Hm. creatour] creature HmC^2 (*corrected* C^2).
327 and þe(2)] *om* Y.
328 And] *om* B. where þat] *om* F. briddes ...beestes] bestys and bryddys Hm. make] HmYOC^{2}CBLMR; makes WCrGF. þei] BHmCrYCLMR; *om* WGOC^{2}F. yeden] wenty*n* F.
329 Wilde wormes] ⁊ wy3lde wlues F. in] and R. and] *om* G.
330 of fele] fele fair*e* F.
331 Man] Boþe ma*n* F. and] hadde OC^2. I my3te] ful manye F. se boþe] se bothe R; sey3 y þ*er*e F; boþe biholde WHmCrGYOC^{2}CBLM.
332 Pouerte] Pouert B; Boþe pou*er*te F. boþe] ⁊ eek F.
333 and] ⁊ also F. boþe] *om* F. at ones] YGOC^{2}CBLMR; al atones WHmCr; þere boþe atoonys F.
334 how] *om* OC^{2}F. token] toke CrGF. refused] refuseden O; forsoke F.
335 Thanne Resou*n* shewede me all man*er*e beestis F. sewen] schewen R.
336 in(1)] and HmCrGOC^{2}F. and] *om* GF. engendrynge] gendry*n*ge F. of kynde] *om* Y.
337 kepe] hep Cot. of(2)] *twice* Hm; to C^2; til R.

As whan þei hadde ryde in Rotey tyme anoon [reste þei] after;
Males drowen hem to males [al mornyng] by hemselue,
And [femelles to femelles ferded and drowe].
Ther ne was cow ne cowkynde þat conceyued hadde
That wolde [bere] after bol[e], ne boor after sowe;
Boþe hors and houndes and alle oþere beestes
Medled no3t wiþ hir makes, [saue man allone]. |
Briddes I biheld þat in buskes made nestes; *fol. 66 a*
Hadde neuere wye wit to werche þe leeste.
I hadde wonder at whom and wher þe pye
Lerned to legge þe stikkes in whiche she leyeþ and bredeþ.
Ther nys wri3te, as I wene, sholde werche hir nes[t] to paye;
If any Mason made a molde þer*to* muche wonder it were.
Ac yet me m*er*ueilled moore how many oþ*er*e briddes
Hidden and hileden hir egges ful derne

338–40 *lines om* F.
338 As] and HmGYOC^{2}CB. hadde] hadden OC^{2}BmBo. ryde] ryde*n* CrHm GOC^{2}. in] a C^{2}. Rotey] rotye G; rote CrCot. anoon] right anone Cr. reste þei] ri3t þer WHmGYOC^{2}CBLMR; *om* Cr.
339 drowen] draw Cr. al mornyng] all mornynge Hm; on morninge Cr^{3}; on morwnynge C^{2}; on mornings Cr^{2}; on mournes (on *altered to* In) G; on morwenynge*s* O; amornynges LCr^{1}; amorwenges YC; amorwynges Cot; amorwenynges WBmBoMR. selue] seluen O.
340 And] *om* OC^{2}. femelles(1)...drowe] in euenynges also þe males ben fro femelles WHmCrGYOC^{2}CBLMR (euenynges] euenynge C^{2}. þe] 3ede R; 3e L. ben] *om* GYOC^{2}CBLMR. fro] fro*m* the CrOC^{2}BM).
341 Ther] þe R. ne was] nas Hm; was non F; was GYOC^{2}CB. ne cowkynde] þoru ky3nde F; nor no female yn kynde Hm.
342 bere] belwe WHmCr^{1}GYOC^{2}CBL MF; belwen R; abellow Cr^{23}. bole] F; boles WHmCrGYOC^{2}CBLMR. sowe] a sowe M.
343 Boþe...alle] Ne grete hors ne hakeneys aft*er* F. oþere] schere B.
344 Medled] Medeleden OC^{2}; Ne þey medlid F. saue...allone] save ma*n* oone F; þat wiþ fole were WHmCrGCBLMR; þat wiþ foole weren OC^{2}; þ*at* with fooles were Y.
345 Briddes...þat] I beheld brydd*es* also F. made] maden OB; þey made F.
346 Hadde...wye] was neu*er*e 3it wy3e hadd F. Hadde] Hadden M. neuere] ner*e* R. wye] weye R; wi3th B; wryght Cr. wit] þe wyt Hm.
347 *divided from following after* lerned WHm CrGYOC^{2}CBLMRF. wonder] *om* (*in margin another hand*) R. at] of F.
348 to...stikkes] Stykkis to legge F. legge] lygge Cr. þe] *om* R. whiche... bredeþ] lengþe ⁊ in breede F. she] he GYOC^{2}CB; a R. leyeþ] lyethe G; lenth R.
349 Ther] *om* Cr. nys] is no RF. wri3te] wy3t OC^{2}; wit R. sholde] cold Cr; can F. werche] *om* Y. hir...to] to hir*e* F. nest] HmCr^{23}GYOC^{2}CBLMR; nestes W Cr^{1}. to] *om* Y.
350 If...made] Ne Mascou*n* to make F. a] *om* Cr^{2}. wonder] m*er*veyle F.
351 Ac] and HmCrGYOC^{2}CBLMR; *om* F. me m*er*ueilled] merveylid y F. how] of FG; *om* R.
352 Hidden] þey heledyn F. hileden] heddyn F. egges] eyren OC^{2}.

[For men sholde hem no3t fynde whan þei þerfro wente;
In Mareys and moores [manye] hidden hir egges]
For fere of oþ*ere* foweles and for wilde beestes.
And some troden, [I took kepe], and on trees bredden,
And brou3ten forþ hir briddes al aboue þe grounde.
And some briddes at þe bile þoru3 breþyng conceyued,
And some caukede; I took kepe how pecokkes bredden.
Muche m*er*ueilled me what maister [þei hadde],
And who tau3te hem on trees to tymbre so hei3e
Ther neiþ*er* burn ne beest may hir briddes rechen.
And siþen I loked on þe see and so forþ on þe sterres;
Manye selkouþes I sei3 ben no3t to seye nouþe.
I sei3 floures in þe fryth and hir faire colours
And how among þe grene gras growed so manye hewes,
And some soure and some swete; selkouþ me þou3te.
Of hir kynde and hir colour to carpe it were to longe.
Ac þat moost meued me and my mood chaunged,

353, 354 *arranged as follows*: 354a *combined with* 353a, 354b *with* 353b WHmCrGYO C^{2}CBLMR; 354a *and* 353a *as one line* F.
353 For] þat GF. men] men ne F. hem... fynde] not fynde hem M. hem] hym BmBo. no3t] *om* F. whan...wente] *om* F. wente] wenten OC^{2}R.
354 In...moores] with Moos in þe Mary3s F. moores] more Y. manye...egges] *om* F. manye] And WHmCrGYOC^{2}CBL MR. hidden] hidde B.
355 For] & F.
356 And] *om* F. troden] treden Cr^{23}RF. I...kepe] hir makes WHmCr^{12}GYOC^{2}C BLMRF; her markes Cr^3. bredden] bredde R; breden GCr^{23}F; bridden C^2.
357 brou3ten] brou3te CGYCot; brynge F; bredde R. al] FHm; so al WCrGOC^2 CBLMR; *om* Y.
358 *line om* CB. & summe blowe bele in bele & with here breeþ conseyve F. bile] bible O. breþyng] bredyng OC^2. conceyued] conceyueden O.
359 caukede] kakeled GYCB; kakeleden OC^2. kepe] hede R. how] as F. bredden] breden GCrR; wirche F.
360 Muche] Mychil F. me] me þan F. þei hadde] BHmCrGYCLMRF; þei hadden OC^2; hem made W.
361 tymbre] tymbren Cr.
362 Fram all beestys here bryddis to save F. Ther] that HmCrG. burn] barne Cr GYOC^{2}CB. may] ne may R; myght G. rechen] reche HmGYOC^{2}CB.
363 siþen] after F. loked] lokiþ Bm. on(1)] CrGYOC^{2}CBF; vpon WHmLMR. so] *om* F. forþ] *om* GYOC^{2}CBF. on(2)] GYOC^{2}CBF; yn Hm; vp on WCrLMR. sterres] sterris bryghte F.
364 Manye] & manye F. ben] þat ben BHm; y may F. no3t] no3 Bo. to] *om* F. seye] see Cr. nouþe] nowe CrGC.
365 in] of R. fryth...hir] fryth3 with ful F.
366 And how] þat F. growed] grewe GYOC^{2}CLMRF; growyn Hm. so... hewes] ful soote F.
367 And] *om* F. soure] soote F. swete] sowr gret F.
368 Of] But of F. kynde] kindes Cr. and] & of CrCotR; *om* F. hir] *om* F. colour] colours CrF. carpe] carpen Cr. it] *om* F. to(2)] *om* Cot.
369 Ac] but GF; And CrC^{2}C. meued] merveyled F. my] made my F; *om* (*corrector supplies*) R. chaunged] to change F.

That Reson rewarded and ruled alle beestes
Saue man and his make; many tyme [me þouȝte]
No Reson hem [ruled, neiþer riche ne pouere].
[Th]anne I rebukede Reson and riȝt til hym I seyde, |
'I haue wonder [in my wit], þat witty art holden, *fol. 66 b*
Why þow ne sewest man and his make þat no mysfeet hem folwe.'
And Reson arated me and seide, 'recche þee neu*ere*
Why I suffre or noȝt suffre; þiself hast noȝt to doone.
Amende þow, if þow myȝt, for my tyme is to abide.
Suffraunce is a souerayn v*er*tue, and a swift vengeaunce.
Who suffre[þ] moore þan god?' quod he; 'no gome, as I leeue.
He myȝte amende in a Minute while al þat mysstandeþ,
Ac he suffreþ for som mannes goode, and so is oure bettre.
[Holy writ', quod þat wye, 'wisseþ men to suffre:
Propter deum subiecti estote omni creature.
Frenche men and fre men affaiteþ þus hire children:
[*B*]*ele vertue est suffrance; mal dire est pet*[*ite*] *vengeance.*

370 rewarded] took reward F. ruled] rules Y.
371 *line om* CB. tyme] tymes RF. me þouȝte] and ofte WHmCrGYOC^{2}LMRF.
372 *divided from* 373 *after* rebukede WHmCrGYOC^{2}CBLMR; *after* þanne F. No] Ne no Y; Ne CB. hem...pouere] rewlyþ hem F; hem folwede WHmCrGYOC^{2}CBLMR.
373 Thanne...riȝt] ⁊ y rebewkyd hy*m* þanne ⁊ þus sadly F. Thanne] and þanne WHmCrYOC^{2}CBLMR; ⁊ þat G. til] to HmGOC^{2}F. hym] hymseluen WHmOCLMR; hymselue GCrYC^{2}B; hy*m* myseluen F. I(2)] *om* GYOC^{2}CBM.
374 haue] *om* M. in my wit] of þee quod I WHmCrGYOC^{2}CBLMRF. witty] Resou*n* F. holden] holde RF.
375 Why...ne] þou F. sewest] schewest R; makst F. and] of Y. þat] þat þem G; *om* F. misfeet] mysfaiþ BoCotR; mysfaut C; myschef F. hem] *om* G.
376 And] And þo B; þan F. þee] þou G.
377 þiself] þou F. hast] hath HmB. to] a G.
378 þow(1)] þou OGYC^{2}CBM; þow it WCrLR; it þou (þou *over erasure another ink*) Hm; it F. if] *om* F. for my] my G; not but F. tyme] tene B. is] y F. to] nouȝt to CB; *om* F.
379 a(1)] *om* GYOC^{2}CB. a swift] a swif Bm; vengable is F. a(2)] of OC^{2}.
380 Who...gome] Suffrance god suffrede to goomes F. suffreþ] HmCrGCBLMR; suffrede WYOC^{2}. gome] man (*glossed* gome *above line main hand*) C. leeue] wene Hm.
381 in] he*m* in F. Minute] litel C; *om* F. mysstandeþ] amise sta*n*deþ Cr; mys fonde F.
382 Ac] but G; And CrC^{2}C; ⁊ ȝit F. suffreþ] suffrede OC^{2}. so] HmCrGYOC^{2}CBLMRF; so it W. oure] vs Cot. bettre] bittre Y.
383–93 RF; *lines om* WHmCrGYOC^{2}CBLM; *here in the spelling of* W.
383 wye] weye RF. wisseþ] wyssheþ F.
384 *as two lines divided after* towne F. Frenche] Now will ȝe leere tale was told me in towne How Frensshe F. and...men] in France F. þus] *om* F.
385 *Bele*] *Beele* F; Vele R. *petite*] *pety* RF.

Bien dire et bien suffrir fait lui suffra[ble] a bien venir.
Forþi I rede', quod reson, '[þow] rule þi tonge bettre,
And er þow lakke my lif loke [þyn] be to preise.
For is no creature vnder crist can formen hymseluen,
And if a man myȝte make [laklees] hymself
Ech a lif wolde be laklees, leue þow noon oþer.
Ne þow shalt fynde but fewe fayne [wolde] heere
Of hire defautes foule bifore hem reherced].
The wise and þe witty wroot þus in þe bible:
De re que te non molestat noli certare.
For be a man fair or foul it falleþ noȝt to lakke
The shap ne þe shaft þat god shoop hymselue,
For al þat he [wrouȝt] was wel ydo, as holy writ witnesseþ:
Et vidit deus cuncta que fecerat & erant valde bona.
Euery creature in his kynde encreesse [he bad]
Al to murþe wiþ man þat moste wo þolie,
In fondynge of þe flessh and of þe fend boþe,
For man was maad of swich a matere he may noȝt wel asterte
That som tyme hym bitit to folwen his kynde;
Caton acordeþ þerwiþ: *Nemo sine crimine viuit.*'

386 *suffrir*] *soffrer* R; *suffre* F. *suffrable*] *soffrant* RF.
387 quod] þe F. þow] þou F; *om* R. þi... bettre] better þy tunge F.
388 lakke my lif] my lyf lakke F. þyn] þyn F; if þow R.
389 is] þere is F. seluen] selue F.
390 laklees hymself] lakles hymselue F; hymself goed to þe poeple R.
391 a lif] man F.
392 þow] *om* F. wolde] F; for to R.
393 defautes foule] fowle defawtys F. hem] here face F.
394 wise...witty] witty wyȝsman F. þe (1)] *om* YCBm. þus] þis G; wel F.
395 *in margin* O. *que te*] quiete R. *noli*] *nolite* R; *non* F; *certare*] *certare &c* HmG; *certaueris & in iudicio* F.
396 to] GOC^2; for to WHmCrYCBLMR; hym to F.
397 shap] schaft Hm; shampe Cr. þe] *om* C^2. shaft] schap HmCr. selue] seluen O.
398 þat he] þynges he F; þe (þat he *in margin another hand*) L. wrouȝt] RF; dide WHmCrGYOC^{2}CBLM. was] *om* F. ydo] do CrGOC^2; *om* F. holy] þe F. witnesseþ] witnesse CBmBo (? *loss in binding* Bm).
398α *in margin* O. *cuncta*] cunta GYCot LF. *erant*] erand Cot. *bona*] *bona &c* Hm.
399 Euery] And bad euery WHmCrGYO C^{2}CBLM; And bad to vch a R; God bad ech F. encreesse he bad] encreesse WHm CrGYOC^{2}CBLMRF.
400 Al] & al was F. moste] most CrGYO C^{2}CBoCotLRF. wo þolie] woo þolieþ OC^{2}RF; wa tholde C; woth holye Cr^{12}; worth holye Cr^3.
401 þe(1)] his F. of(2)] *om* G.
402 swich] *om* F. a] *om* HmCotF. wel asterte] fro it sterte F.
403 That] þat RF; That ne WHmCrGYO C^{2}CBLM. tyme] tymes LR. hym] it M. bitit] bitidiþ BHm; bited Cr; but (? bitt) suffre F. folwen] folwe COC^{2}BF.
404 þerwiþ] þerto F; herwiþ OC^2; with al R.

Tho cauȝte I colour anoon and comsed to ben ashamed
And awaked þerwiþ; wo was me þanne
That I in metels ne myȝte moore haue yknowen.
[Th]anne seide I to myself, '[slepyng hadde I grace]
[To wite] what dowel is, [ac wakyng neuere]'.
And as I caste vp myne eiȝen oon loked on me.
'[What is dowel?' quod þat wiȝt]; 'ywis, sire', I seide,
'To se muche and suffre moore, certes, is dowel.' |
'Haddestow suffred', he seide, 'slepynge þo þow were, *fol. 67 a*
Thow sholdest haue knowen þat clergie kan ⁊ [conceyued]
    moore þoruȝ Res[on],
For Reson wolde haue reherced þee riȝt as Clergie seide;
Ac for þyn entremetynge here artow forsake:
Philosophus esses si tacuisses.
Adam, whiles he spak noȝt, hadde paradis at wille,
Ac whan he mamelede about mete, and entremetede to knowe

405 Tho] And tho Hm. comsed] consed Bm. ashamed] shamed G.
406 And] And I YOC^{2}F. wo...me] ⁊ woo was y F.
407 in...myȝte] ne myghte in Metelys F. in] in my Cot. ne] *om* Hm. haue] hauen R; mater*e* F. yknowen] Iknowe BMRF, knowen Cr.
408 Thanne] YGOC^{2}CBF; And þanne WHmCrLMR. seide I to] chidd y F. slepyng...grace] and chidde þat tyme WHmGYOC^{2}CBLMR; and chyde that tyme Cr; ⁊ seyd þese woord*es* F.
409 To wite] Now I woot WHmGYOC^{2}CBLMR; Now do I ken Cr; Now F. what...is] dowel Cr. ac...neuere] quod I by deere god as me þynkeþ WHmCrGYOC^{2}CBLMRF (quod I] *om* G. deere] *om* CB. as me þynkeþ] as me think Cr; y knowe F).
410 And] *om* B. me] me and asked WHmCrGYOC^{2}CBLMRF.
411 What...wiȝt] Of me what þyng it were WHmCrGOC^{2}CBLMR; On me what thyng it were Y; what þyng þat Dowel ys F. ywis] I wysh Cr. I] y not y F.
412 *line om* F. To] Go C^2. certes] certes quod I WHmCrGYOC^{2}CBLMR (I *altered main hand to* he It G).
413 Haddestow...seide] þan seyd he haddist þou suffred F. Haddestow] haddist BoCot; Haste thu Hm. he seide] *om* G. slepynge...were] þo þou on slepe were F. slepynge] slepyn Bm.
414 Thow...knowen] The*n* hadst þou ke*n*de Cr. knowen] knowe BRF; Iknowe YOC^{2}C. þat] it of F. kan] came Cr^1; *om* F. conceyued] GYOC^{2}CBLMRF; co*n*treued WHm; kend Cr. moore] it F. þoruȝ] by HmCrGBF. Reson] resou*n* HmCrGYOC^{2}CBLMRF; Res (*cropped*) W.
415 þee] to the Hm.
416 *line om* F. Ac] And CrGYOC^{2}CB. þyn] þyng (g *erased*) Bm; thyne *altered to* theryne *main hand* G. entremetynge] entermentynge HmBm; ertirmetyng Bo. here] there G. forsake] forsaken OHmC^2.
416α *in margin* OC^2. *tacuisses*] *tacuisses ⁊c* HmCrG.
417 whiles] þe whiles R. spak noȝt] was heer*e* F. hadde] he had GF. at] at his C^{2}F.
418 Ac] But CrG; and C^{2}CF. aboute] on his F. and] he F. entremetede] entremette YGOC^{2}C; ent*er*mentyd Hm; menede F. to] hy*m* to GYOC^{2}CBM.

The wisedom and þe wit of god, he was put fram blisse.
And riȝt so ferde Reson bi þee; þow wiþ rude speche
Lakkedest and losedest þyng þat longed noȝt to doone;
Tho hadde he [litel] likyng for to lere þe moore.
Pryde now and *pre*sumpcion, *par*auent*ur*e, wol þee appele
That Clergie þi compaignye kepeþ noȝt to suwe.
Shal neu*er*e chalangynge ne chidynge chaste a man so soone
As shal shame, and shenden hym, and shape hym to amende.
For lat a dronken daffe in a dyk falle,
Lat hym ligge, loke noȝt on hym til hym liste aryse.
For þouȝ Reson rebuked hym þanne [reccheþ hym neuere;
Of clergie ne of his counseil he counteþ noȝt a risshe.
[To blame or] to bete hym þanne] it were but pure synne.
Ac whan nede nymeþ hym vp for [nede] lest he sterue,
And shame shrapeþ hise cloþes and hise shynes wassheþ,
Thanne woot þe dronken [wye] wherfore he is to blame.'

419 and...god] of his god ⁊ F. and] of YGOC^{2}CB. was] *om* C. blisse] þe blisse R.
420 bi] *with* Cr. þee...wiþ] þyn F. wiþ] OGYC^{2}LMR; wiþ þi WHmCrCB. rude] rusty Y.
421 Lakkedest] þou lakkedist F; Lokedst Cr^3. and] *om* F. losedest] lostest Cot; losest GYC; lordly F. longed] longeþ BG. noȝt] noght GHmCrYOC^{2}CBLMR; þe noȝt WF. to] to be HmCrGYCBLM; þe to R. doone] doute CB.
422 Tho...he] he hadde aft*er* F. litel] no WHmCrGYOC^{2}CBLMRF. lere] lerne OCrC^2.
423 Pryde now] ⁊ now wil p*r*iȝde F. now] *om* Hm. wol] wolen OB; *om* F. þee] me Cr.
424 þi] to thy Hm; in þi RF. kepeþ noȝt] nowht coueytyþ F. kepeþ] ne kepeþ OCrGYC^{2}CBLMR. to] efte to RF. suwe] shew Cr; sawe G; sitte RF. *Hereafter* Hm *copies lines* 111–217.
425 Shal] For schal RF. chalangynge] mor*e* F. ne] no HmF. chaste] chastyse HmOC^{2}F; caste B. a] *om* G. so soone] su*n*nere F.
426 As] he R; þan F. shal] *om* HmOC^2. shame...hym(1)] needful shame F. shenden] schende HmB. and(2)] if he F. shape] schape*n* R.
427 dronken] dru*n*ke F. a(2)] a deep F. dyk] dyche GOC^{2}B.
428 Lat] ⁊ lete F. loke...hym(2)] longe þer*e* F. aryse] to aryse Cr; ryse G; to ryse HmYOC^{2}CBLMRF.
429 *as one line with* 431b WHmCrGYOC^{2}CBLM. For] ⁊ F. rebuked] rebewke F. þanne] ȝit F. reccheþ...neuere] reccheth hym neuere R; rekkeþ he neuere F; *om* WHmCrGYOC^{2}CBLM.
430 RF; *line om* WHmCrGYOC^{2}CBLM; *here in the spelling of* W. counteþ] acownteþ F.
431 To...þanne] Or for to bete hym þanne R; For to betyn hy*m* þanne F; *om* WHmCrGYOC^{2}CBLM. were] nere Hm.
432 Ac] But F; And CrGYOC^{2}CB. nede(1)] nede is Hm. nymeþ...vp] hym vp nymeth Y. nymeþ] nyme BoCot; takes C. hym] *om* G. nede(2)] doute WHmCrGYOC^{2}CBLMRF.
433 *line om* F. shrapeþ] shaketh Cr^1; shraketh Cr^{23}. shynes] skyn Cr; hondis BoCot; hennis Bm. wassheþ] wasshede C.
434 woot] woteþ C^2. þe] that YF. dronken] dru*n*ke F; droken C. wye] daffe WHmCrGYOC^{2}CBLMRF.

'Ye siggen sooþ', quod I, 'ich haue yseyen it ofte.
Ther smyt no þyng so smerte, ne smelleþ so [foule]
As shame: þ*ere* he sheweþ hym, [hym shonyeþ euery man].
Why ye wisse me þus', quod I, 'was for I rebuked Reson.'
'Certes', quod he, 'þat is sooþ'; and shoop hym for to walken,
And I aroos vp ri3t wiþ þat and [reuerenced] hym [faire,
And if his wille were he wolde his name telle]. |

435 quod I] q*uod* y be my sowle F; by my soule q*uod* I R. yseyen] seen HmGB; sey3 F. it] þ*at* F.

436 smyt] smiteth Cr^{23}CB; smitte L. no þyng] nought Cr^{23}; non R; no ma*n* F. smelleþ] swellethe G; sku*m*fy3teþ non F; muilleth (s *prefixed another script and ink*) R. foule] R; soure WHmCrYOC^{2}CCot LM; sore GBmBoF.

437 þ*ere*] dooþ þ*ere* F. he] it Y. hym(2)...man] for euery man hym shonyeþ WHm YOC^{2}CBLM; for ech ma*n* him sho*n*ith Cr; for eu*er*y man hym shendethe G; no ma*n* loueth his felachipp RF.

438 ye wisse] 3e wissen OC^{2}; wy3sse 3ee F. was] *om* F. rebuked] rebewked so F.

439 he] I R. walken] walke HmCr^{3}GOC^{2} BF; wake*n* Cr^{1}R.

440 I...and] gan faren on hys wey3 & y F. I] *om* Hm. reuerenced] folwed WHmCr GYOC^{2}CBLMRF. hym] hem M; *om* GF. faire] after WHmCrGYOC^{2}CBLM RF.

441 And preyde hym of his curteisie to telle me his name WHmCrGYOC^{2}CBL MRF (of] for Hm).

XII

'I am ymaginatif', quod he; 'ydel was I neu*ere* *fol. 67 b*
Thouȝ I sitte by myself in siknesse n[e] in helþe.
I haue folwed þee, in feiþ, þise fyue and fourty wynter,
And manye tymes haue meued þee to [mynne] on þyn ende,
And how fele fernyeres are faren and so fewe to come;
And of þi wilde wantownesse [whiles] þow yong were
To amende it in þi myddel age, lest myȝt þe faill[e]
In þyn olde elde, þat yuele kan suffre
Pouerte or penaunce, or preyeres bidde:
Si non in prima vigilia nec in secunda &c.
Amende þee while þow myȝt; þow hast ben warned ofte
Wiþ poustees of pestilences, wiþ pou*er*te and w*ith* angres;
And wiþ þise bittre baleises god beteþ his deere children:
Quem diligo castigo.
And Dauid in þe Sauter seiþ, of swiche þat loueþ Ie*su*s,

1 was] am F.
2 ne] LMR; nor W; or F; and HmCrGY OC^{2}CB.
3 I] & y F. folwed] yfolwede M. þise] *om* F. wynter] wynters G.
4 manye] oft Cr. tymes] tyme F. haue] y haue Hm; haue I M; haued C. þee] *om* Y. mynne] þynke WCrGL; þy*n*kyn F; þenke HmYOC^{2}CMR; þenkyn B.
5 *line om* F. fernyeres] ferneres R; fernies Cr^{1}; fene*n*yeres G. are] an C. faren] fare Cot. come] come*n* CrYCBR.
6 of] on F; *om* BoCot. whiles] þo W HmCr^{23}GYOC^{2}CBLMRF; though Cr^{1}. yong] in ȝowthe F.
7 amende] amende*n* Cr^{1}R. it] þe HmG YF. þi myddel] mydde F. lest] a lest þy F. þe] *om* F. faille] YGOC^{2}CBMR; fayle aft*er* F; failled WHmCrL.
8 In] & in F. elde] age Hm. þat] that so YCB; þan F. yuele kan] canst evele F. kan] canst (*final* e *erased*) Hm.
9 Pouerte] pouert B; Ony pou*er*te F. preyeres] prayer HmCr. bidde] bydde HmCrGYOC^{2}CBLMR; to bidde W; to byddy*n* F.
9α *in margin* OC^{2}. *non*] *no* Y. *&c*] *om* CrGOC^{2}F.
10 þee] þe ye R. myȝt] myghteste G; may Cr.
11 poustees] poustee YC^{2}; postemes Cot; seeknesses F. of] and HmCBF. pestilences] pestilence YC; penances F; penaunce R. pou*er*te] pouert B; pou*er*tes F. w*ith*] *om* F.
12 And] For F. þise] þo F. deere] *om* F.
12α *in margin* OC^{2}. *castigo*] *castigo &c* HmY.
13 *line om* RF. And] for G. þat] as G. loueþ] loue GYC.

Virga tua ⁊ baculus tuus, ipsa me consolata sunt:
Alþouȝ þow strike me wiþ þi staf, wiþ stikke or wiþ yerde,
It is but murþe as for me to amende my soule.
And þow medlest þee wiþ makynges and myȝtest go seye þi sauter,
And bidde for hem þat ȝyueþ þee breed, for þer are bokes y[n]owe
To telle men what dowel is, dobet and dobest boþe,
And p*re*chours to preuen what it is of many a peire freres.'
I seiȝ wel he seide me sooþ, and somwhat me to excuse
Seide, 'Caton conforted his sone þat, clerk þouȝ he were,
To solacen hym som tyme; [so] I do whan I make:
Interpone tuis interdum gaudia curis.
And of holy men I her[e]', quod I, 'how þei ouþ*er*while
[In manye places pleyden þe parfiter to ben].
Ac if þer were any wight þat wolde me telle |
What were dowel and dobet and dobest at þe laste, *fol.* 68 *a*
Wolde I neu*ere* do werk, but wende to holi chirche

13α *line om* RF. *ipsa*] *ipse* C. *consolata*] *consolati* Cr^{23}. *sunt*] *sunt ⁊c* HmYCLM.
14 me] *om* Cr. þi] godd*es* F. staf] staffe or Cr^{1}. stikke...yerde] outy*n* stykkes sor*e* F. or] other YOC^{2}CB. wiþ(3)] *om* YOC^{2}C.
15 is] nys Hm. as for] to F.
16 And þow] Why F. þee] *om* Cr. makynges] makynge MRF; mastryes GY OC^{2}CB. and...sauter] þan þou myght bettr*e* go p*ra*ye F. myȝtest] myste Hm; myght G. þi] the G.
17 bidde] bidde*n* Cr^{1}Cot. ȝyueþ] ȝyue HmCrF. þee] þat Cr^{1}; me Bo. ynowe] HmCrGYCBLMRF; yknowe W; *om* OC^{2}.
18 To] And B. telle] tellyn F; telleþ B. men] me CrOC^{2}; *om* F. dowel...dobest] ys dobet ⁊ Dowel F. is] *om* CB. dobet and] dobett*er* ⁊ G; ⁊ dobet Cr^{3}.
19 preuen] p*re*ue HmGYOC^{2}CBLMRF. a] *om* GC.
20 I seiȝ] þan wiste y F. me] þe Cr^{23}; *om* F. and] ac R. somwhat] þouhte F.
21 Seide] And seide RF; I saide Cr^{23}. conforted] to conforte CB. his] YCr^{23}G OC^{2}CBLMRF; me his WHmCr^{1}. þat... were] ful konyngly y wene F. þat] *om* G.
22 Su*m* tyme to solace hy*m* selue ⁊ su*m* tyme sadly to stodie F. solacen] solace CrG. so] as WHmCrGYOC^{2}CBLM; and R.
22α *in margin* OC^{2}. *Inter*] nter F. *curis*] *curis ⁊c* HmYCLM.
23 And] ⁊ also F. of] *by correction* C; *om* HmR. I...I] quod I i herde M. I here] I here R; here y F; I herde WHmCrGYO C^{2}CBL. quod I] *om* GF. I(2)] *om* Cot. þei] þat þey F; *om* M.
24 Pleyden þe parfiter to ben in manye places WHmCrGYOC^{2}CBLMRF (Pleyden] þei *before it in margin another ink* M. manye places] her*e* p*ra*yer*es* aft*er* F. places] a place R).
25 Ac] butt G; And CrC^{2}C; Nou F; *om* R. if] if I Cot. wight] wit R; wryghtte (? r *erased*) Cot.
26 *line om and supplied at head of page but later cropped* G. and(1)] ad Bm. at þe laste] þe þrydde F.
27 do werk] wyrke C; worche B. wende] weendy*n* F.

And þ*er*e bidde my bedes but whan ich ete or slepe.
'Poul in his pistle', quod he, 'preueþ what is dowel:
Fides, spes, caritas, et maior horum &c.
Feiþ, hope and Charite, and alle ben goode,
And sauen men sondry tymes, ac noon so soone as Charite.
For he dooþ wel, wiþouten doute, þat dooþ as lewte techeþ.
That is, if þow be man maryed þi make þow louye
And lyue forþ as lawe wole while ye lyuen boþe.
Riȝt so if þow be Religious ren þow neu*er*e ferþer
To Rome ne to Rochemador, but as þi rule techeþ,
And hold þee vnder obedience þat heigh wey is to heuene.
And if þow be maiden to marye and myȝt wel continue,
Seke þow neuere Seint ferþer for no soule helþe.
[Lo]! what made lucifer to lese þe heiȝe heuene,
Or Salomon his sapience, or Sampson his strengþe?
Iob þe Iew his ioye deere abouȝte;
Aristotle and oþ*er*e mo, ypocras and virgile,
Alisaundre þat al wan, elengliche ended.
Catel and kynde wit was combraunce to hem alle.

28 þ*er*e] the Cot. bidde] byddy*n* F.
29 Poul in his] with poule in his R; See Poulis F. pistle] epystle G; pistles R. he] he he F.
29α *in margin* O; *another hand* Hm. *Fides spes*] *spes fides* G; *Nunc autem manent fides spes &* Hm. *Fides*] Ides F. *spes*] *spes &* Cot. *et...&c*] *caritas Maior autem horum est caritas* Hm. *et*] *om* Cr^{23}RF. *horum &c*] *horum est Karitas* F; *&c* R.
30 Feiþ] he seyþ feyþ F. and(2)] *om* RF.
31 sauen] saue G; saued C^{2}. ac] but GF; & $CrC^{2}C$. so] *om* F.
32 outen] oute HmGYBL. dooþ] douȝt Bm.
33 if] If þat F. þow(1)] he CB. man] *om* F. þi...louye] þou love þy make leelly F.
34 And] *om* R. lyue] lyueþ Hm. forþ] *om* F. as] as the Cot. while] þe while R; þe whilis F. ye] you Cr. lyuen] lyue R. boþe] here $GYOC^{2}CB$.
35 Riȝt] Al F. if] & G. ferþer] þe ferþer B; fram home F.
36 to] *om* Cr. techeþ] tellyþ F.
37 heigh...is] is þe heye wey F. heigh] þe hiȝe B; heighte Y.
38–40 *in margin main hand* G.
38 þow] ye G. maiden to] mayde & to R; a Mayde meeke F. marye] marien OC^{2}; *om* F. and] & þ*ou* F. myȝt] myghtest G. wel] wel þe F; *om* G. continue] contene OC^{2} (y *added after first* e C^{2}).
39 þow] ye G; *om* HmCr. neuere] neuere no HmCr. no] thi CrCBF. soule] soules Cr. helþe] heele B.
40 Lo] For $WHmCrGOC^{2}CBLMRF$; And Y. þe] his OC^{2}.
41 or] other R.
42 *line om* C. Iob þe Iew] Er Ioob al F. deere abouȝte] of hise Ientil childryn F. deere] dere he B; dere ytt G; dere he it HmCrYLMR; dere it he OC^{2}; ful deere W. abouȝte] bougth HmCr.
43 Aristotle] Er Arystotil F. and...mo] or Virgyle & F. ypocras] Hypocrates Cr. and(2)] þe F. virgile] virgilie Cot; wise F.
44 Alisaundre] Er Alysaundr*e* F. wan] wltnne C. elengliche] elengenlyche Hm; & alengely he F. ended] endeden O; endeth Cr^{1}.
45 Catel...to] Al was but catel & vnkende wit acu*m*bred F. was] was a B.

Felice hir fairnesse fel hire al to sclaundre,
And Rosamounde riȝt so reufulliche [bisette]
The beaute of hir body; in baddenesse she despended.
Of manye swiche I may rede, of men and of wommen,
That wise wordes wolde shewe and werche þe contrarie:
Sunt homines nequam, bene de virtute loquentes.
And riche renkes riȝt so gaderen and sparen
And þo men þat þei moost haten mynistren it at þe laste; |
And for þei suffren and see so manye nedy folkes *fol. 68 b*
And loue hem noȝt as oure lord bit, lesen hir soules:
Date & dabitur vobis.
[So catel and kynde wit acombreþ ful manye;
Wo is hym þat hem weldeþ but he hem [wel] despende:
Scient[es] et non facient[es] varijs flagellis vapulab[un]t.
Sapience, seiþ þe bok, swelleþ a mannes soule:
Sapiencia inflat &c];
And Richesse riȝt so but if þe roote be trewe.

46 Felice] Felicie Y; Er Felyce for F. fel] yt fel F. hire] hem Cr^{23}.
47 reufulliche] reufull B. bisette] OGYC^{2} CBLMR; she besette F; to bileue WHm Cr.
48 body] boy Y. baddenesse] badd vse RF; wikkidnesse B. she] *om* RF. despended] dispendiþ it C^{2}; spendyd Hm.
49 I may] may y F; men may I R; I myght GYOC^{2}CB. of(1)] bothe off GF. of(2)] *om* CrC^{2}F.
50 wolde shewe] wooldyn schewe Hm; can say GYOC^{2}CB. werche] werchen MR.
50α *in margin* OC^{2}. *Sunt*] unt F. *nequam*] *numquam* Cot. *bene de virtute*] *de virtute bene* GYOC^{2}CB. *loquentes*] *loquentes &c* Hm.
51 And] þere ben F. renkes] reukes Cr; men reken Cot; men þenken BmBo. riȝt] þat do F. so] so þat BF. gaderen] n *erased* M; gadderand C; gardyden G. sparen] sparden GY; sparyng C.
52 And...þat] Paraunter þem F. þo] to C. mynistren] minister CrF. it...laste] here goodys F. it] *om* G. laste] lest GC.
53 And] & þat ys F. suffren and] suffred & C^{2}; ofte F. manye] fele F.
54 loue] louen GHmOC^{2}CMF; lenen Cot. hem] *om* Cr^{23}. oure lord] god GYOC^{2} CBF. bit] biddeth CotC^{2}. lesen] GHm CrYOC^{2}CLMR; þei lesen W; þey lese F; and leesen B. hir] here owen F; ȝoure R. soules] soule F.
54α *in margin* OC^{2}. *Date*] God byddes ȝou do þus *date* F. *vobis*] *vobis &c* HmGYO CBLM.
55–7α RF; *lines om* WHmCrGYOC^{2}CB LM; *here in the spelling of* W.
55 so] & þerfore F. kynde] vnkynde F.
56 he] F; if he R. wel] F; wil R.
56α *Scientes*] *Scienti* R; cienti F. *et*] *bonum* & F. *facientes*] *facienti* RF. *vapulabunt*] *vapulabit* RF.
57 Sapience...bok] þe book seiþ þat sapyence F.
57α *Sapiencia*] apiencia F. *&c*] *om* F.
58 And] & also F. Richesse] riche C. riȝt] doþ ryȝt F.

Ac grace is a gras þ*er*[for] þo greuaunces to abate.
Ac grace ne groweþ no3t [til good wil yeue reyn];
Pacience and pouerte þe place [is] þer it groweþ,
And in lele lyuynge men and in lif holy,
And þoru3 þe gifte of þe holy goost as þe gospel telleþ:
Spiritus vbi vult spirat.
Clergie and kynde wit comeþ of si3te and techyng
As þe book bereþ witnesse to burnes þat kan rede:
Quod scimus loquimur, quod vidimus testamur.
Of *quod scimus* comeþ Clergie, [a] konnynge of heuene,
And of *quod vidimus* comeþ kynde wit, of si3te of diu*er*se peple.
Ac g*ra*ce is a gifte of god and of greet loue spryngeþ;
Knew neu*er*e clerk how it comeþ forþ, ne kynde wit þe weyes:
Nescit aliquis vnde venit aut quo vadit &c.
Ac yet is Clergie to comende and kynde wit boþe,
And namely Clergie for cristes loue, þat of Clergie is roote.
For Moyses witnesseþ þ*at* god wroot for to wisse þe peple
In þe olde lawe as þe lettre telleþ, þat was þe lawe of Iewes,

59 Ac] but GF; And CrC[2]C. a] as Cot; *om* F. gras] grace R; graffe Cr[23]; grate F. for] fore RF; of WHmCrGYOC[2]CBLM. þo] þe GYOC[2]CBM. greuaunces] greuau*n*ce Cr[1]GYOC[2]CB.
60 Ac] but GF; And CrC[2]C. ne] *om* BMF. groweþ] greueth R. no3t] nowher F. til...reyn] but amonges lowe WHmCrGYCBLMRF; but among þe lowe OC[2].
61 *line om* F. Pacience] Of pacience R. pouerte] pouert Cot. is] HmCrGYOC[2]CBLMR; hi3te W. þer] where G.
62 lele...men] me*n* in leele lyvynge F. men] *main hand after cancelled* place C. lele] lelly Cr.
63 þoru3] *om* F. þe(1)] þat F; *om* R. gifte of] gaf hem F; sy3t of B.
63α *in margin* OC[2]. *Spiritus*] piritus F. *spirat*] *spirat &c* HmGYCBLMR.
65 As] And CB. burnes] barnes CrHmY OC[2]CBR. kan] konnyn HmB.
65α *in margin* O. *Quod*] vod F. *scimus*] *simus* F; scimis M. *quod*] & *quod* HmF. *vidimus*] *videmus* G. *testamur*] *testamur &c* HmY.
66 *scimus* comeþ] *simus loquimur* komeþ F. Clergie a konnynge] connyng & clargye G. a] RF; and WHmCrYOC[2]CBLM.
67 And] *om* OC[2]. of(1)] *om* C. *quod*] *om* B. *vidimus*] *videmus* G. kynde] *om* F. of(2)] & G; þoru F. diu*er*se] dyuese L; oure F. peple] ey3es F.
68 Ac] But F; And CrGYOC[2]CB. is] *om* Cr[3]. gifte] 3ifte B. of(2)] *om* Cr[1].
69 Knew] 3it knew F; knoweþ C[2]; know C. it] he F. forþ] *om* CrF. ne] þe OC[2]; be F. wit þe] wit his R; witys F.
69α *Nescit*] escit F. *aut*] and G. *vadit*] *vadat* Hm. *&c*] *om* CrCBRF.
70 Ac] But F; And CrGC[2]C. yet] ri3t B.
71 þat...is] for he knowi*th* þe F. of] *om* B. Clergie is roote] clergies rote is Cot.
72 Moyses...to] god wroot to Moyses þ*at* he sholde F. witnesseþ] witnesse C. for... peple] þe puple to wish Cr.
73 In...as] After F. lettre] lettrure Hm. þat was] was GR; *om* F. of] off þe G; so was to þe F.

That what wo*m*man were in auoutrye taken, whe[r] riche or poore,
Wiþ stones men sholde hir strike and stone hire to deþe.
A wo*m*man, as [we] fynde[n], was gilty of þat dede,
Ac crist of his curteisie þoru3 clergie hir saued.
[For] þoru3 caractes þat crist wroot þe Iewes knewe hemselue
Giltier as afore god, and gretter in synne,
Than þe wo*m*man þat þ*ere* was, and wenten awey for shame. |
[Thus Clergie þere] conforted þe womman. *fol. 69 a*
Holy kirke knoweþ þis þat cristes writyng saued;
So clergie is confort to creatures þat repenten,
And to mansede men meschief at hire ende.
For goddes body my3te no3t ben of breed wiþouten clergie,
The which body is boþe boote to þe ri3tfulle
And deeþ and dampnacion to hem þat deyeþ yuele,
As cristes caracte[s] confortede, and boþe coupable shewed

74 That] *om* F. were] was F. in...taken] take*n* in auoutri Cr; take in avowtery F. in] *om* (*a corrector supplies*) L. auoutrye] deuoutrie R. wher] where she WF; were sche HmLM; were he R; *om* CrGYOC^{2}CB. or] other GYOC^{2}CBmBo.
75 men] she F. sholde] schulde*n* OHmB. hir strike] hire striken R; strike hir Cr; be stryken F. stone] stonen BR; stonye OC^{2}C; stoned F. hire] *om* F. deþe] dede R.
76 *line om* RF. we fynden] GHmCrYOC^{2}CBLM; I fynde W. gilty] gyltyffe G; gentil gilty (*corrected main hand*) Bm. of] *om* Cr^{23}. dede] death Cr.
77 Ac] but G; And CrC^{2}CF. þoru3] and þoru3 R; *om* F. clergie hir] o wo*m*man he F.
78 For] GYOC^{2}CBLMRF; And WHm Cr. caractes...wroot] cristes carectus RF. wroot] wrought Cr^{1}GOC^{2}C; *om* Y. knewe] knewen OC^{2}B. selue] seluen LMR.
79 Giltier] gyltyfere HmBm; more gyltye G; Gilty BoCot. as] *om* F. afore] tofore Hm; before G. and...in] ⁊ in gretter OC^2. in] was her*e* F.
80 was] stood F. wenten] we*n*t CrGYOC^{2}C.
81 Thus...þere] þus þoruh clergye þere F; The Clergie þat þ*ere* was WHmCrGYOC^{2}CBLMR. þe] was þe F. *Here* Hm *resumes the correct order*; *see apparatus at* XI 111 *above*.
82 kirke] cherche HmBRF. knoweþ] knew B. þis] wel F. saued] GYOC^{2}CBLR; saued hire WHmCrM; hir*e* savede F.
83 So...is] ⁊ so ys Clergye gret F. repenten] repentyn hem Hm; hem repe*n*ten B; will rep*en*te F.
84 And] ⁊ also F. mansede] manasid B; mased C. men] me*n* in F. hire] er C. ende] nede HmF.
85 For] For bread of Cr. of breed] *om* Cr. outen] out CrGOC^{2}R.
86 body] body in forme of breed F; bread Cr. boþe boote] boote F; bote to boþe B.
87 deyeþ] dye CrG. yuele] in vnklennesse F.
88 As] And Cr; Ac R; But F. caractes] GCrYOC^{2}CB; caracte WHmLMRF. confortede] counforteden O; comfortedid C^2. and boþe] hire ⁊ all þei wer*e* F. coupable] coupile C; couple B; coupled ⁊ C^2. shewed] scheweden O; sheweth M; *om* F.

The wo*m*man þat þe Iewes [iugged] þat Ie*s*us þou3te to saue:
Nolite iudicare & non iudicabimini.
Ri3t so goddes body, breþ*er*en, but it be worþili taken,
Dampneþ vs at þe day of dome as [dide þe caractes] þe Iewes.
Forþi I counseille þee for cristes sake clergie þat þow louye;
For kynde wit is of his kyn and nei3e Cosynes boþe
To oure lord, leue me; forþi loue hem, I rede.
For boþe ben as Mirours to amenden [by] defautes
And lederes for lewed men and for lettred boþe.
Forþi lakke þow neu*er*e logik, lawe ne hise custumes,
Ne countreplede clerkes, I counseille þee for euere.
For as a man may no3t see þat mysseþ hise ei3en,
Na moore kan no Clerk but if he cau3te it first þoru3 bokes.
Alþou3 men made bokes [þe maister was god]
And seint Spirit þe Samplarie, & seide what men sholde write.
[And ri3t as si3t serueþ a man to se þe hei3e strete]
Ri3t so [lereþ] lettrure lewed men to Reson.
And as a blynd man in bataille bereþ wepne to fi3te
And haþ noon hap wiþ his ax his enemy to hitte,

89 The] For þe F. þe] *om* YR. iugged] brou3te WHmCrGYCBLMF; brou3ten OC^2; bou3te R. þat] *om* F. Ie*s*us] Ie*s*u Hm; cryst F. to] *om* Cot.
89α *in margin* O. *Nolite*] olite F. *iudicare*] *indicare* Cr^1. *iudicabimini*] *iudicabimini &c* HmGYCBLMR.
90 body] dere body F; *om* B. breþeren] *om* GF. but] CrGYOCBLMRF; but if WHmC^2. taken] take CrF.
91 Dampneþ] Dampned YR. dide þe caractes] dede þe carecte RF; þe caractes dide WCrGYC^{2}CL; þe carectes dide*n* OHmB; carettes dide M. Iewes] Iwis Cr^1.
92 Forþi] Therfore Cr; For þe C^2. þ*at* þow] to GYOC^{2}CB.
93 nei3e] neer F. boþe] be boþe F.
94 me] þou me F. forþi...hem] loue þem forthy G. forþi] therfore Cr. hem] hym CCot.
95 amenden] amende HmCrGYOC^{2}CBF. by] oure WHmCrGYOC^{2}CBLMRF.
96 for(1)] to F.
97 Forþi] Therfore Cr. logik] logikis B. ne] nor Hm. hise] hise leve F; thes G.
98 clerkes] no clerkys F.
99 a] *om* F. ei3en] si3te RF.
100 no] a GOC^2. but] clergye but F. if] *om* GCCotF. cau3te] cacche OC^{2}F. first] *om* GF. þoru3] by Cr; of M; i*n* F.
101 Al] & al F. men] ma*n* F. made] maden OC^{2}B; make F. þe...god] god was þe maister WHmCrGYOC^{2}CBLMR; 3it god is Mayst*er* F.
102 þe] hys GYOC^{2}CB. &...what] to þe F. men] man OC^{2}R; ma*n* þat F. sholde] shulde*n* BmBo; *om* F. write] wryt yt F.
103 GYOC^{2}CBLMRF; *line om* WHmCr; *here in the spelling of* W. And] For F. si3t] wit F. þe hei3e] in þe F. strete] sterre (erre *over erasure*) M.
104 lereþ] lereth RF; ledeþ WHmCrGYO C^{2}CBLM. lettrure] letture CrG; clergie CB. lewed...to] ma*n* to knowe F.
105 bereþ] ber*e* R.
106 his(1)] *om* CF. enemy] enemyes OC^2.

Na moore kan a kynde witted man, but clerkes hym teche,
Come for al his kynde wit to cristendom and be saued;
Which is þe cofre of cristes tresor, and clerkes kepe þe keyes
To vnloken it at hir likyng, and to þe lewed peple |
ȝyue mercy for hire mysdedes, if men it wole aske *fol. 69 b*
Buxomliche and benigneliche and bidden it of g*ra*ce.
Archa dei, in þe olde lawe, leuytes it kepten;
Hadde neu*er*e lewed man leue to leggen hond on þat cheste
But he were preest or preestes sone, Patriark or p*ro*phete.
[Saul for he sacrificed sorwe hym bitidde,
And his sones also for þat synne myscheued,
And manye mo oþer men, þat were no leuites,
That wiþ *archa dei* [wenten] in [worship and reuerence]
And leiden hand þeron to liften it vp loren here lif after.
Forþi I conseille alle creatures no clergie to dispise
Ne sette short bi hir science, whatso þei don hemselue.
Take we hir wordes at worþ, for hir witnesse be trewe,
And medle noȝt muche wiþ hem to meuen any wraþe
Lest cheste cha[fe] vs to choppe ech man oþer:
Nolite tangere christos meos ⁊c.]
For Clergie is kepere vnder crist of heuene;

107 kynde] blynde C^{2}; *om* F. witted] witty Cr^{23}; wedded R; lewid F. but] but ȝif $HmYOC^{2}M$. clerkes] clergie CB.
108 Come] *om* F. cristendom...be] be c*ri*stnyd ⁊ F.
109 þe(1)] *om* F. kepe] ? *corrected from* kene R; kepen $OC^{2}B$. keyes] keyȝe F.
110 vnloken] vnloke FCr. and to] vnto F.
111 ȝyue] ȝeuen (ȝ *altered to* y) M; ⁊ g*ra*unteþ F; For R. hire] *om* F. mysdedes] mysdes C. it wole] it wolen B; wyll it CrF.
112 bidden] bydde F; biden C. of] as R.
113 kepten] kepen Cot.
114 man] *corrected from* men *main hand* CBm; men BoCot. leggen] legge YOCB; leyn HmF; ley GC^{2}. on...cheste] þereonne F. þat] þe $GYOC^{2}CBM$.
116–25α RF; *lines om* $WHmCrGYOC^{2}CBLM$; *here in the spelling of* W.
116 he sacrificed] his myssac*ri*fyse F.
117 myscheued] myschevedyn F.
118 were] wery*n* F.
119 wenten] wenty*n* F; ȝeden R. in...reuerence] w*ith* worchepeful *reuer*en*c*is F; in reu*er*ence and in worchipp R.
120 leiden...liften] leyde on hond ⁊ lyfte F. vp] vp and RF.
121 to] ȝee F.
122 sette short] settiþ lyght F.
123 we] *om* F. for] *om* F. witnesse] wytnesses F.
124 medle] F; ne medle we R. meuen any] meve he*m* to F.
125 cheste] Charyte F. chafe vs] chasen vs R; be chased owt F. to...man] þa*n* ech man choppi*th* F.
125α *Nolite*] olite F. ⁊*c*] *om* F.
126 For] *om* F. kepere] kepere þerof B; kynge and kepe*re* R; keye ⁊ kepere F. vnder] vnd F.

Was þ*er* neu*er*e [kyng ne] kny3t but clergie hym made.
Ac kynde wit comeþ of alle kynnes si3tes,
Of briddes and of beestes, [by] tastes of truþe.
[Dyuyneris] toforn vs [viseden and markeden]
[The] selkouþes þ*a*t þei sei3en, hir sones for to teche.
And helden it an hei3 science hir wittes to knowe;
Ac þoru3 hir science sooþly was neu*er*e soule ysaued
Ne bro3t by hir bokes to blisse ne to ioye,
For alle hir kynde knowyn[g] co[m] but of diu*er*se si3tes.
Patriarkes and p*ro*phetes repreueden hir science
And seiden hir wordes [ne] hir wisdomes [w]as but a folye;
A[s] to þe clergie of crist counted it but a trufle:
Sapiencia huius mundi stulticia est apud deum.
For þe hei3e holy goost heuene shal tocleue,
And loue shal lepen out after into þ[is] lowe erþe,
And clennesse shal cacchen it and clerkes shullen it fynde:

127 kyng ne] no kynge C^{2}; no WHmGY OCBLMRF; *om* Cr. kny3t] *om* C^{2}.
128 Ac] butt G; For F; A C; And CrC^{2}B. wit] *om* Cr^{1}. si3tes] syght Cr^{1}.
129 briddes] birde Cr^{3}; beestys F. and] *om* OC^{2}. beestes] brydd*es* F. by tastes] of tastes WHmCrGYOC^{2}LMR; *om* CBF. truþe] truþe and of deceites WHmCrGY OC^{2}CBLMRF.
130 Dyuyneris] Lyueris WHmCrGYO C^{2}CBLMRF. toforn] toformen Cot; aforne Cr; before GF. viseden] vsed-en WHmCrGYOC^{2}CBLM; vsede R; leerned bookys F. and markeden] to marke WHmYOC^{2}CBLM; to make Cr RF; the marke G.
131 The] YGOC^{2}CBLMRF; For WHm; *om* Cr. selkouþes] selcouthe YOC^{2}CB; Seldome Cr. sones] soules Hm. for] *by correction* L; *om* G.
132 helden] helde GYOC^{2}CBF. it] *om* G. an] and C.
133 Ac] But F; And CrC^{2}CCot; as G. science] scyencis F. sooþly] shortly B. soule] OGC^{2}CBF; soules Y; no soule WHmCrLMR. ysaued] saued CrGYO C^{2}CBRF.
134 bro3t] bou3te RF. ne] no Hm.
135 knowyng] GYOC^{2}CBF; knowynges WHmCrLMR. com] B; cam RF; come WHmCrYOC^{2}CLM; comethe G. but] *om* HmF.
136 Patriarkes] Boþe patr*ia*rchis F. re-preueden] repreued C^{2}HmGYCLM; re-preven FBR. science] scyences HmF; sightes CB.
137 seiden] seide RCr; seyn F. hir wordes] he word F. ne] CrGYOC^{2}CBL MRF; nor Hm; and W. wisdomes] wis-dome R; scyence F; cou*n*sell Cr. was] CrR; was al F; were not G; nas WHmY OC^{2}CBLM. a] *om* HmCrYF.
138 *transposed with* 138α C^{2}. As] HmCr YOC^{2}CBLMRF; ⁊ as G; And W. counted] acowntyd F; ys counted G. it] *om* GYOC^{2}CB. but] is F.
138α *in margin* O. *est*] *om* HmCr^{1}OC^{2}LR. *deum*] *deum ⁊c* HmGY; *⁊c* R.
139–47α *lines om* RF.
139 hei3e] hei3est Hm.
140 lepen] lepe HmGYOC^{2}CBLM. into] ⁊ to Y. þis] GHmCrYCBLM; his OC^{2}; þe W.
141 cacchen] cacche C^{2}Cr. shullen] schul OCrGYC^{2}CB. it] *om* C^{2}.

Pastores loquebantur ad inuicem.
He spekeþ þ*er*e of riche men ri3t no3t, ne of ri3t witty,
Ne of lordes þat were lewed men, but of þe hyeste lettred oute:
Ibant magi ab oriente.
If any frere were founde þ*er*e I 3yue þee fyue shillynges!
Ne in none [beggers] cote [n]as þat barn born, |
But in a Burgeises place, of Bethlem þe beste: *fol.* 70 *a*
Set non erat ei locus in diuersorio, et pauper non habet diuersorium.
To pastours and to poetes appered þe Aungel
And bad hem go to Bethlem goddes burþe to honoure
And songe a song of solas, *Gloria in excelsis deo.*
[Riche men rutte þo and in hir reste were
Tho it shon to shepherdes, a shewer of blisse].
Clerkes knewen it wel and comen wiþ hir p*re*sent3
And diden [hir] homage hon*ur*ably to hym þat was almy3ty.
Why I haue told [þee] al þis, I took ful good hede
How þow cont*ra*riedest clergie wiþ crabbede wordes,
How þ*a*t lewed men li3tloker þan lettrede were saued,
Than clerkes or kynde witted men of cristene peple.

142 *in margin* O. *inuicem*] *inuicem &c* Hm GYCBmBo.
143 þere...no3t] nought ther of rych me*n* Cr. ri3t(1)] *om* GYOC^{2}CB.
144 Ne] And Cr^{1}. were] were*n* OC^{2}. of þe] *om* G. hyeste] hexte LM. oute] *om* Cr^{23}.
144α *in margin* O. *oriente*] *oriente &c* Hm GYCBLM.
145 founde] founden OHmC^{2}BM. þee] you Cr. shillynges] fyngers G.
146 Ne] nor Hm. beggers] HmCrGYO C^{2}CBLM; burgeises W. nas] was WHm CrGYOC^{2}CBLM. born] corne Cr^{2}.
147 a] *om* Cr. Burgeises] burgeys HmCr GYC^{2}CBL. of] in Cr.
147α *in margin* O. *ei locus*] *locus* GYOC^{2} LM; *om* CB. *diuersorio*] *diuersio* Cr^{1}. *diuersorium*] *diuersorium &c* Hm.
148 To] Tho BmBo. poetes] pore men Hm. þe] þat LM; an RF.
149 goddes] cr*is*tis F. burþe] son B (*above line another hand* Bm). to] *om* F.
150 And] he F. songe] songen Cr^{13}HmO C^{2}; soogen Cr^{2}; syngen R. *Gloria...deo*] wich was F. *deo*] *deo &c* Y.
151 RF; *line om* WHmCrGYOC^{2}CBLM; *here in the spelling of* W. **rutte**] rowhted F. and] þat F. were] weryn F.
152 RF; *line om* WHmCrGYOC^{2}CBLM; *here in the spelling of* W. Tho...shepherdes] whan to shepperdis a sterre shon F.
153 Clerkes] And clerkes RF. knewen] knewe CrC^{2}CLR. comen] came G. hir] *om* F.
154 diden] dide YCrGCF. hir] YHmGO C^{2}CBLMR; *om* WCrF. hon*ur*ably] honou*r*ablely L; & honou*r* F. *Here* GYO C^{2}CB *add a spurious line; see above*, p. 223.
155 þee] OGYC^{2}CBR; *om* WHmCrL MF. al þis] þis tale F.
156 cont*ra*riedest] contraryest GYOC^{2}C; contriuedest Cr. wiþ] w*ith* þy F.
157 How] *om* F. li3tloker] li3tlier C^{2}G. lettrede] lettred men MF; lettreþ Bm. were] weren OBF. saued] Isaued R.
158 Than] & F. clerkes] clergie BoCot; clergis Bm. or kynde] þan cleer F. witted] witti C^{2}. of] of þe F.

And þow seidest sooþ of so*m*me, ac se in what manere.
Tak two stronge men and in Themese cast hem,
And boþe naked as a nedle, hir noon [sadder] þan ooþ*er*.
That oon [kan] konnynge and kan swymmen and dyuen;
That ooþer is lewed of þat labour, lerned neu*er*e swymme.
Which trowestow of þo two [in Themese] is in moost drede,
He þat neu*er*e ne dyued ne noȝt kan of swymmyng,
Or þe swymmer*e* þat is saaf by so hymself like,
Ther his felawe fleteþ forþ as þe flood likeþ
And is in drede to drenche, þat neuere dide swymme?'
'That swymme kan noȝt', I seide, 'it semeþ to my wittes.'
'Right so', quod þe renk, 'Reson it sheweþ
That he þat knoweþ clergie kan sonner arise
Out of synne and be saaf, þouȝ he synne ofte,
If hym likeþ and lest, þan any lewed [sooþly].
For if þe clerk be konnynge he knoweþ what is synne, |
And how contricion wiþoute confession confortep þe soule, *fol.* 70 *b*

159 þow] tho Cr^{1}. ac] but G; ⁊ CrC^{2}CF. se] se ytt GY; se ȝit OC^{2}CB. in...manere] in whanere R; an ensample F.
160 two] *twice* C; þou Y. and] *om* Cr^{12}. cast hem] hem caste OC^{2}F.
161 And boþe] bothe G; ⁊ looke boþe ben F. as...þan] noon be but as F. a] *om* M. hir] er YC; ar C^{2}; arn O; þat B (þat þoir (þoir *cancelled*) Bm); ther Cr; *om* G. sadder] sikerer WHmCrGYOC^{2}CB; syker LMR (er(2) *added another ink* M).
162 That] The CrG. kan(1)] can F; haþ WHmCrGYOC^{2}CBLMR. konnynge...and(2)] wel swymme ⁊ konynge to F. swymmen] swymme CrOC^{2}B. dyuen] dyue HmCrOC^{2}F (yue *over erasure* Hm); driuen R.
163 That] ⁊ þat F; þe GCr. of þat] to F. lerned] YHmCrOC^{2}CLMR; ⁊ lerned GB; þat lerned W; for he lerned it F. swymme] to swymme HmCrGYOC^{2}CBM (w *by correction another ink* C^{2}); *om* F.
164 þo] those Cr; þes G; this Y; þe OC^{2}; hem CBF. in Themese] LHmCrGYOC^{2}CBMRF; þat W. is...drede] shal drenche F. in moost] most in CrBM; inoost C.
165 He] But he F. ne(1)] *om* HmCrGCotMRF. noȝt kan] neu*er*e cowhde F.
166 Or] or ell*is* Cot; For F. þat] *om* F. by] be Cr; yf F; *om* G. like] likiþ B; yt lyke F.
167 *line om* CotF. Ther] thes *corrected main hand* G. fleteþ] flet OCrYC^{2}CLMR.
168 is] ⁊ þat oþ*er* ma*n* ys F. drenche...dide] dreche for he dyde neu*er*e F.
169 *line om* RF. I seide] *om* G. semeþ] comeþ BoCot. my] *om* C.
170 þe] that CB. renk] renke ryght F; reuk Cr; frek B. it] *om* CrF.
171 That] *om* F. sonner] sannore R.
172 and] to F. be] he be CrR. saaf] saued M. synne] senege R.
173 likeþ] likid B; lyke F. þan] þ*at* Y. sooþly] leelly WHmCrGYOC^{2}CBLMR; gooky F.
174 þe] a G. knoweþ] knowe C. what] *om* Y.
175 how] þorhu F. wiþoute] withouten MR; ⁊ F. conforteþ] co*n*fortyd ys F. þe] his F; mi Cr^{1}.

As þow seest in þe Sauter in Salmes oon or tweyne
How contricion is comended for it cacheþ awey synne:
Beati quorum remisse sunt iniquitates & quorum tecta sunt &c.
And þis co*n*forteþ ech a clerk and coue*re*þ fro wanhope,
In which flood þe fend fondeþ a man hardest.
Ther þe lewed liþ stille and lokeþ after lente,
And haþ no contricion er he come to shrifte; & þanne kan he litel telle
But as his loresman lereþ hym bileueþ and troweþ,
And þat is after p*er*son or parissh preest, [and] p*ar*auent*ur*e vnkonnynge
To lere lewed men as luc bereþ witnesse:
Dum cecus ducit cecum &c.
Wo was hym marked þat wade moot wiþ þe lewed!
Wel may þe barn blesse þ*at* hym to book sette,
That lyuynge after lettrure saue[d] hym lif and soule.
Dominus pars hereditatis mee is a murye v*er*set
That haþ take fro Tybo*ur*ne twenty stronge þeues,

176 As] and HmYOC^{2}CB; *om* G. þe] thy YOC^{2}CB. Salmes] psalme LR; a spalm F. oon or tweyne] it tellethȝ F.
177 for] *om* G. it cacheþ] he caste F.
177α *in margin* O. *tecta*] *om* G. *sunt*] *om* GYOC^{2}CB. *&c*] *peccata &c* Hm; *peccata* RF; *om* Y.
178 And þis] þis v*er*s F. ech a] eche G; eu*er*y F. coue*re*þ] kenneth RF. fro] hym fro WHmCrGYOC^{2}CBLMRF.
179 flood þe] þe foule F.
180 liþ] lyen G; ma*n* lyþ F. lokeþ... lente] aft*er* lewte lookeþ F. lokeþ] loken G. lente] lenten GYOC^2; leaut C; leaute B.
181 haþ...to] repenteth not before Cr. er ...to] ne F. er] er her C. come] go G. &] *om* G; for F. þanne] þereof ne F; *om* R. kan] ga*n* Hm. he(2)...telle] *om* C. litel] *om* F.
182 But] And CrGYOC^{2}CBLMR. man] me*n* F. lereþ] lerneth CrG; lerne F. hym] hy*m* so he F.
183 *divided from* 184 *before* vnkonnynge WHmCrGYOC^{2}CBLMRF. And...is] *om* F. after] aftir the Cot; Aft*er* his F; *om* Cr^3. or] & Cr. and] HmCrGYOC^{2}CB LMR; þe whiche ben W; *om* F. auent*ur*e] auenture he OCr^{2}C^2; adue*n*ture he is Cr^3; awnt*er* þey be F; auenter bothe R; aduerture BmBo. vnkonnynge] vnkony*n*g boþe F.
184 *line om* F. lere] lerne CrB. as] and Hm.
185 *in margin* O. *&c*] *ambo in foueam &c* OC^2; *om* F.
186 *line om* RF. þat] þ*at by correction* L.
187 þe barn] þat F. blesse] him blesse Cr^2; hem blesse Cr^3; blesse hy*m* F. þ*at*] GHm CrYOC^{2}CBLMRF; þat man þat W. hym...sette] hym sette to scole R; sette hy*m* fyrst to skole F.
188 That...lif] þ*at* þorhu his lettrure lerned his lyf is savid F. lettrure] letture CrY. saued] GHmYOC^{2}CBLMR; saueþ WCr. lif] both life Cr; silf Cot.
189 *Dominus*] *Dominis* C. *mee*] *mee &c* GOC^{2}CB. verset] verse Cr^{23}; versicle Cr^{1}F.
190 That] It F. take] taken CrGYOC^2 CBM. twenty] ten thowsend F. stronge] score C^2; *om* F.

Ther lewed þeues ben lolled vp; loke how þei be saued!
The þef þat hadde *gra*ce of god on good fryday, as þow spek[e],
Was for he yald hym creaunt to *cri*st & knewliched hym gilty,
And *gra*ce asked of god þat [graiþ is hem euere]
[Th]at buxomliche biddeþ it and ben in wille to ame*n*de*n* hem.
Ac þouȝ þat þeef hadde heuene he hadde noon heiȝ blisse,
As Seint Ioh*a*n and oþ*er*e Seintes þat des*er*ued hadde bettre.
Riȝt as som man yeue me mete and [sette me amydde þe floor];
[I] hadde mete moore þan ynouȝ, ac noȝt so muche worshipe
As þo þat seten at þe syde table or wiþ þe sou*er*eynes of þe halle,
But as a beggere bordlees by myself on þe grounde.
So it fareþ by þat felon þat a good friday was saued; |
He sit neiþ*er* wiþ Seint Ioh*a*n, Symond ne Iude, *fol.* 71 *a*

191 loke...saued] loo who haþ þe bettr*e* F. þei] tha C.
192 hadde] hath Y; hadde gret Hm. *gra*ce of god] gods grace Cr. as þow] as ȝe OC²; to F. speke] YBLMRF; spake CrGC; speken OC²; spekest WHm.
193 Was for] þat was for þat BmBo; þat was for Cot. yald] ȝeeldid F; knew Cr. hym(1)...to] *om* Cr. creaunt] recreaunt MR; *om* F. to *cri*st] *om* Hm. &] F; & vpon a cros R; on crosse & OC²; on þe cros & WHmCrGYCBLM. knewliched] knew GYOC²B; know C. hym(2)] his Cr; *om* R. gilty] sinne Cr.
194 *line om* RF. þat...euere] þat to graunten it is redy W; and he is eu*er*e redy HmCrGYOC²CBLM (to *added after* redy Cot).
195 & buxu*m* was in meende his M*er*cy was to crave F. That] HmCrGYOC²C BmLMR; þam BoCot; To hem þat W. biddeþ] bid YC. ben] *om* G. ame*n*de*n*] amende HmCrGYC²CBM. hem] hym GBmBo (? y *over erasure* Bo).
196 Ac] But F; And CrGYOC²CB. þat] þe Cr³. þeef hadde] *om* CB. noon] but not so B.
197 Ioh*a*n...Seintes] symou*n*d or stevene F. des*er*ued hadde] have disservid yt F. des*er*ued] asserued LR. hadde] hadde*n* O; alle Hm; ytt G.
198 as] as if CrB (? if *over erasure* Bm); so as Y. som man] a ma*n* Cr; Man F; summe men HmGYOC²CM; me*n* B. yeue] ȝyuen HmOC². and] *om* F. sette...floor] sette me amydde þe flore YCrCBLMR; setten me amydde þe flore OHmC²; sytt me amydde þe floore G; amydde þe floor sette me W; amyddis his hall F.
199 *marked for transposition with* 201 F. I] CrHmC²CBF; Ich YGOLMR; And W. hadde] haue HmCrGYOC²CBLMRF. moore þan] ryght F. þan] þa Bo. ac] but GF; & CrC²C.
200 þo] thei CrF. seten] sytten GYOC²C BMRF; sytte HmCr. þe(1)] *om* HmCr. syde] *om* GYOC²CBF. table] tables CrM (? s *added* M). or] *om* GF. þe(2)] *om* CrGYOC²CB. soureynes] souerey*n* F. of] yn G. halle] place F.
201 But...bordlees] & sytte boordles beggerely F. as] sete as W; settiþ as Bm Bo; sytte as HmCrGYOC²CLMR (e *over erasure* Hm); sitteth as Cot. a beggere] beggers GYOC²CB. bordlees] bredles G. þe] *om* F.
202 þat] þe Cr³.
203 sit] sytteþ HmCrGOC². neiþ*er*] not (*above line*) G. wiþ] by GYOC²CBM. Seint] *om* RF. Symond ne Iude] ne Iemes wit*h* Ierom ne wit*h* awsty*n* F. Symond] ne Symond R; nether symon G.

Ne wiþ maydenes ne wi*th* martires [ne wiþ mylde] wydewes,
But by hymself as a soleyn and serued on [þe] erþe.
For he þat is ones a þef is eu*er*emoore in daunger,
And as lawe likeþ to lyue or to deye:
De peccato propiciato noli esse sine metu.
And for to seruen a Seint and swich a þef togideres,
It were neiþ*er* reson ne riȝt to rewarde boþe yliche.
And riȝt as Troianus þe trewe knyȝt [tilde] noȝt depe in helle
That oure lord ne hadde hym liȝtly out, so leue I [by] þe þef
in heuene.
For he is in þe loweste of heuene, if oure bileue be trewe,
And wel lose[l]y he lolleþ þ*ere* by þe lawe of holy chirche:
Qui[a] reddit vnicuique iuxta opera sua.
A[c] why þat oon þeef on þe cros creaunt hym yald
Raþ*er* þan þat ooþ*er* þeef, þouȝ þow woldest appose,
Alle þe clerkes vnder crist ne kouþe þe skile assoille:
Quare placuit? quia voluit.
And so I seye by þee þat sekest after þe whyes

204 Ne wi*th* Martyres ne *con*fessoures ne wi*th* Maydenys clene F. with] *om* GYOC^{2}C. ne...mylde] ne confessoures ne R; Confesso*urs* ne WCrGYOC^{2}CBLM; confesso*ur* ne (n *of* ne *over erasure*) Hm.

205 But] *om* GCB. and] þat F; *om* Hm. on] vpon Cr^{23}; ys in F. þe] OGYC^{2}CBLMRF; *om* WHmCr. erþe] hall F.

206 is(2)] he is F. moore] aft*er* F.

207 likeþ to] will lyke to make hy*m* F. to(2)] *om* CrF. *Here* R *copies, then cancels* 213α.

207α *in margin* OC^2. *metu*] *metu &c* Hm GY.

208 And] But F. for] *om* C. seruen] serue GOC^2.

209 to] *om* C. rewarde] R; rewarde hem WCrGYOC^{2}CBoCotLMF; rewardyn hem Hm; rewarde hy*m* Bm. boþe] *om* MF. yliche] inlich C^2.

210 riȝt] *om* CrG. trewe] *om* F. tilde] YGCBLMR; tilte OC^{2}F; dwelte WHm Cr. depe in] so dep in Cr; into F.

211 *as two lines divided after* out B. That] But CrG. oure lord] *crist* F. ne] *om* Cr GF. by þe þef] þe theffe G; þe be R; it be F; þe þef be WHmCrYOC^{2}CLM; þat þe þief be B.

212 of] in F; *om* CrGYOC^{2}CBM. be] is Cr^{12}; *om* F.

213 wel] wol R. losely] loselich YOC^{2}BmBoLMRF; loselly WHmCrCot; lowselyche GC. þe] *om* Cr^{23}GF.

213α *in margin* O. *Quia*] YOC^{2}CL; *Qui* WHmCrBM (*followed by erasure* M); *omnia* G; And R; þere þe byble seyþ F. *reddit*] *reddite* RF. *sua*] CrOC^{2}CBRF; *sua &c* WHmGYLM.

214 Ac] R; But F; And WHmCrGYOC^{2}CBLM. þat] þe Cr^3. on] vpon R. hym yald] gan him yeld CrF. yald] yelded GM; gylty C.

215 þat] the Cr^{23}G. þouȝ] *om* F. woldest] wolde YGOC^{2}CBL; þynkst me to F. appose] oppose Cr^1.

216 kouþe] kouþen BmHmBo; cu*n*ne F. þe] þys Hm; *om* R. assoille] telle RF.

216α *in margin* OC^2. *voluit*] *voluit &c* Hm GY; *deus voluit* F.

217 I seye] seie I M. by] to F. þat] *om* Y. sekest] sikest CBmBo. þe] þo F; *om* HmBoCot. whyes] whaies C; wyes Bo; weyes CrC^{2}CotF.

And aresonedest Reson, a rebukynge as it were,
[And willest of briddes ⁊ beestes and of hir bredyng knowe,
Why some be alouȝ ⁊ some aloft, þi likyng it were;
And of þe floures in þe Fryth and of hire faire hewes,
Wherof þei cacche hir colours so clere and so briȝte,]
And of þe stones and of þe sterres; þow studiest, as I leue,
How euere beest ouþ*er* brid haþ so breme wittes.
Clergie ne kynde wit ne knew neu*ere* þe cause,
Ac kynde knoweþ þe cause hymself, no creature ellis.
He is þe pies patron and putteþ it in hir ere
[That þ]ere þe þorn is þikkest to buylden and brede;
And kynde kenned þe pecok to cauken in swich a [wise. |
Kynde] kenned Adam to knowe hise pryue membres, *fol.* 71 *b*
And tauȝte hym and Eue to helien hem wiþ leues.
Lewed men many tymes maistres þei apposen
Why Adam hiled noȝt first his mouþ þat eet þe Appul
Raþer þan his likame alogh; lewed asken þus clerkes.

218 aresonedest] reasonedest GCB; resonest Cr; hast yresoned F. Reson] aresou*n* C^2. a] *with* F. rebukynge] rebuke C^2.
219–22 *so ordered* RF; 219 *and* 220, 221 *and* 222 *transposed* WHmCrGYOC^{2}CBLM.
219 willest] wylnest HmMF. briddes... and] wyȝlde bryddys F. ⁊] GCrYOC^{2}C BL (of *above line another hand* L); ⁊ of WHmMR. of hir] here of Bm; hir Cr. knowe] HmGYOC^{2}CB; to knowe WCr LMRF.
220 be] so CB; *om* F. allouȝ] lowe CBRF. aloft] be a lofte G. likyng] likin Cr^1. it were] were to here F.
221 of] how F. þe(1)] *om* Cr^1. and of] have so F. hire] *om* Cr^{1}CF.
222 cacche] cacchen OC^{2}MF; caughte C; lauȝte BmBo; laughtten Cot. colours] colour RF. clere] faire Cr^{23}G.
223 þe(1)] *om* R. of þe(2)] þe F; *om* G. as I leue] as I wene G; in þy*n* meende F.
224 How þey may so styken ⁊ shynen fram þe walkene F. euere] euery CrGC^2 B. ouþ*er*] or HmGYOC^{2}CBLM; and Cr. so breme] so brenne Cr^1; sober Cr^{23}.
225 ne(2)] *om* GF. knew] knewen M.
226 Ac] but GF; And CrC^{2}C. þe cause] ytt G. hymself] *om* CBF. no] HmCrLM RF; and no WGYOC^{2}CB.
227 pies] pye R. putteþ] put Cr^{1}RF; putte HmCr^{23}. it] *om* GYOC^{2}CB. hir] hys GF.
228 That þere] MHmCrGYOC^{2}LRF; There W; That CB. þorn] thornes Cr; þornȝ *or* þoruȝ C^2. is] it Cr^3. to] þere to RF. buylden] builde CrHmR; byggen C; bygge F. and] in and B; and to HmC. brede] breden B.
229 kenned] kenneþ HmCrGYOC^{2}CBF. pecok] potok C^2. cauken] ca*n*ken Cr. in ...wise] *with* his make F. wise] kynde WHmCrGYOC^{2}CBLMR.
230 Kynde] And kende RF; And WHm CrGYOC^{2}CBLM. knowe] knowen R.
231 helien] hele FCr.
232 Lewed] But lewed F. þei] *om* GYOC^2 CBF. apposen] apose F.
233 Adam] HmGYOC^{2}CBF; Adam ne WCrLMR. first] *om* F. þat] whan he F; or þ*at* G.
234 alogh...clerkes] lowe þis is a lewid ma*n*nys mau*n*d F. lewed] þe lewid B; lewyd men Hm; lew C. asken] after Cr^1.

Kynde knoweþ whi he dide so, ac no clerk ellis.
Ac of briddes and of beestes men by olde tyme
Ensamples token and *ter*mes, as telleþ þ[ise] poetes,
And þ*at* þe faireste fowel foulest engendreþ,
And feblest fowel of fli3t is þat fleeþ or swymmeþ.
And þ*at* [is] þe pecok & þe Pehen [wiþ hir proude feþeres
Bitokneþ ri3t riche men þat reigne here on erþe.
For pursue a pecok or a pehen to cacche,
They may no3t flee fer ne ful hei3e neiþer];
For þe trailynge of his tail ouertaken is he soone.
And his flessh is foul flessh and his feet boþe,
And vnlouelich of ledene and looþ for to here.
Right so þe riche, if he his richesse kepe
And deleþ it no3t til his deeþ day, þe tail[le is al of] sorwe.
Ri3t as þe pennes of þe pecok peyneþ hym in his fli3t,
So is possession peyne of pens and of nobles
To alle hem þat it holdeþ til hir tail be plukked.
And þou3 þe riche repente þanne and birewe þe tyme

235 ac] but F; & CrGYOC^{2}CB. clerk] clarkes Cr.
236 Ac] but G; And CrC^{2}C; *om* F. of(2)] *om* M. by] off G. tyme] tymes F.
237 token] toke R. and] be F. þise] BGYCLMR; þe WHmCrOC^{2}F.
238 *before this a cancelled line containing elements of* 238 *and* 239 G. And þat] How F. fowel] sothely þe G. engendreþ] þey gendren F.
239 is] *om* F. fleeþ] fliest Y.
240–3 *as two lines divided after* bitokneþ WHmCrGYOC^{2}CBLMRF: And þat þe pecok & þe Pehen proude riche men bitokneþ For þe Pecok and men pursue hym may no3t flee hei3e (And] *om* GF. þat] that ys GYOC^{2}CBLMRF; *om* Cr. þe(1)...proude] þe prowhde Pookok & F. pecok(*both*)] potok C^{2}. þe(2)] *om* OC^{2}. proude] *om* CB. men(1)] men þei GCrY OC^{2}CBLMR; me*n* he F. bitokneþ] betokene GYC^{2}B; bitoknee C; tokenen M. þe(3)] *om* G. and] yff G. men(2)] he be F. pursue] pursuen HmOC^{2}R; p*ur*sued F. may] he may CrF; ne may R).
244 þe] *om* GF. trailynge] trauylyng G; trayle F. taken] take CrF. is he] he is B.
245 boþe] foule bothe F.
246 And] & he hath an F. of] on OC^{2}; *om* F. ledene] stevene F; cryeng C; hy dene (hy *over erasure*) Cot. looþ] loþli BF; layþ OGYC^{2}LMR; layeth Cr. for] *om* F.
247 riche] ryche man F. kepe] kepeth RF.
248 deleþ] deale G. deeþ] deths Cr. þe] þat Cr^{2}; hys G. taille] MLR (-le *erased* M); taile CrG; tail WHmYOC^{2}CBF. is al of] of alle is (-le *erased*) M; of alle WHm CrGYOC^{2}CBLRF.
249 as] HmCrGYOC^{2}LMRF; so as W Cot; so CBmBo. of] in Cr. pecok] potok C^{2}. peyneþ] peined GHmCLR. his fli3t] fleyng F.
250 of pens] to þe ryche of pens F; off peynnes (*second* e *cancelled*) G. and] or GYCB.
251 To] & to F. hem] men Hm. it] syluer F; *om* G. holdeþ] heldiþ B. til] to G. tail] taylles G.
252 repente] repente*n* M. þanne] hy*m* þ*an*ne OC^{2}. birewe] rewe G.

That euere he gadered so grete and gaf þ*er*of so litel,
Thouȝ he crye to crist þanne wiþ kene wil, I leue
His ledene be in oure lordes ere lik a pies chiteryng;
And whan his caroyne shal come in caue to be buryed
I leue it flawme ful foule þe fold al aboute,
And alle þe oþ*ere* þ*er* it lith enuenymeþ þoruȝ his attre.
By þe po feet is vnderstande, as I haue lerned in Auynet,
Execut*ours*, false frendes, þat fulfille noȝt his wille |
That was writen, and þei witnesse to werche as it wolde. *fol.* 72 *a*
Thus þe Poete preueþ þe pecok for hise feþeres;
So is þe riche [reuerenced] by reson of hise goodes.
The larke þat is a lasse fowel is moore louelich of ledene,
And wel awey of wynge swifter þan þe Pecock,
And of flessh by fele fold fatter and swetter;
To lowe libbynge men þe larke is resembled.
[Swiche tales telleþ Aristotle þe grete clerk];
Thus he likneþ in his logik þe leeste fowel oute.

254 crye...þanne] þanne *cri*ȝe to *cri*st F. þanne] *om* G. kene] clene BCF.
255 Ful lytil g*r*ace ys g*r*auntyd hy*m* for god may not hym heere F. ledene] lede (*erasure at end*) C^2. be] ys GYOCB; *om* C^2. ere] ere is (is *another hand*) C^2. lik] yliche OC^2; lyl R. pies] peyse G; piecok (cok *over erasure*) Cot. chiteryng] chatrynge Hm Cr; *om* GYOC^{2}CBLR.
256 And] But F. shal...be] ys kowchyd ⁊ in kave F. caue] graue C.
257 flawme ful] flawmeþ F. þe fold] *om* G. aboute] abowten F.
258 And] þat F; *om* CB. alle...enuenymeþ] yt envenymeþ þere it lyþ all oþ*ere* F. þe] *om* G. oþere] erþe OC^2; schere BmBo; shire Cot. þer] lere (*corrected another hand*) C^2. it] he G. enuenymeþ] enuenimed CrLR. attre] acter G; *om* Cr.
259 po] pocok Hm; pownes B; pro L. feet] sete Cr^1; *om* Hm. stande] stonden OC^{2}R. I] it F. haue] *om* GYOC^{2}CBF. lerned] seyþ F.
260 *run together with* 261 C. false] be þo false F. þat...wille] *om* C. fulfille] fulfille*n* OHmC^{2}B.
261 That...þei] Al is wrete to ber*e* F; *om* C. þei] þ*er* G. witnesse] witnesses R; *om* C. as] GYOC^{2}CBF; riȝt as WHmLMR; al þat Cr. it] he RF.
262 Thus] And thus Cr; þis G; Ryght as F. preueþ] preveþ FOC^2; preueþ þat WHm CrGYCBLMR. for hise] me*n* pulle hise F; *om* Cr^3. feþeres] fedr*e*s F; feþeres is reuerenced WHmCrGYOC^{2}CBLMR.
263 So] Riȝt so WHmCrGYOC^{2}CBLM RF. is] *om* Cr. riche] riche man BF. reuerenced by] by WHmCrYOC^{2}CBL MR; by þe G; bereeft F. reson of] hy*m* fram F.
264 ledene] stevene F.
265 wel] wyll Cr. awey] way C^2. swifter] ⁊ swyftere F.
266 by] *om* Hm. fatter] boþe fatter*e* F.
267 To] Ryght so to F. þe...resembled] is resembled the larke Cr; þe larke may be lykned F.
268 Aristotle þe grete clerk swiche tales he telleþ WHmCrGYOC^{2}CBLMRF (Aristotle] For aristotel RF; alyȝandre G. clerk] clere G. he] *om* GYOC^{2}CB. telleþ] tayleth Cr^1).
269 Thus] þe larke F. logik] glosing R; glose F. fowel] soghell G.

And wheiþ*er* he be saaf or no3t saaf, þe soþe woot no clergie,
Ne of Sortes ne of Salomon no scripture kan telle.
Ac god is so good, I hope þat siþþe he gaf hem wittes
To wissen vs [wyes] þerwiþ þat wiss[h]en to be saued—
And þe bettre for hir bokes to bidden we ben holden—
That god for his g*ra*ce gyue hir soules reste,
For lettred men were lewed yet ne were loore of hir bokes.'
'Alle þise clerkes', quod I þo, 'þat [o]n crist leuen
Seyen in hir Sermons þ*at* neiþ*er* Sarsens ne Iewes
Ne no creature of cristes liknesse *with*outen c*ri*stendom worþ
   saued.'
'*Contra!*' q*uo*d Ymaginatif þoo and comsed to loure,
And seide, '*Saluabitur vix Iustus in die Iudicij;*
Ergo saluabitur', quod he and seide na moore latyn.
'Troian*us* was a trewe knyght and took neu*ere* cristendom
And he is saaf, seiþ þe book, and his soule in heuene.
[Ac] þer is fullynge of Font and fullynge in blood shedyng
And þoru3 fir is fullyng, and þat is ferme bileue:
Aduenit ignis diuinus non comburens set illuminans &c.

270 *transposed with* 271 F. And] *om* F. wheiþ*er*] wher HmYOC^{2}CBLMR. no3t] no*n* F. saaf(2)] *om* CrGYOC^{2}CBF. woot no clergie] telliþ no byble F. no] þe GOC^{2}.
271 Ne...ne] & for soþe F. of(2)] *om* GYOC^{2}CB. no] ne Cr^{2}.
272 Ac] but GF; And CrC^{2}C. god] good C. hem] hym BF.
273 wissen] wishe*n* Cr^{3}F. vs] *om* F. wyes] wy3en F; weyes WHmYOBLR; waies CrGCM; wey C^{2}. þer] *om* G. wisshen] wishen vs Cr^{3}; wissen vs WHm Cr^{12}GYOC^{2}CBLMRF. to] *om* F.
274 hir] hise F. bidden] bydde GF. we] for hy*m* we F. holden] holde F.
275 for] of CrOC^{2}F. *grace*...hir] grete g*ra*ce grawnte his F. soules] soule RF.
276 lettred] lerned C. were] were*n* OBm BoF. lewed] YCr^{23}GOC^{2}CBF; lewed men WHmCr^{1}LMR. yet] *om* F. ne were] nere CGOC^{2}B; wern Y. hir] þe R; *om* F.
277 Alle] And Cr^{23}. þise] the Hm. on] HmCrGYOC^{2}CBLMRF; in W. leuen] beleven F.
278 Seyen] Sayand C; Seithe*n* Cr. neiþ*er*] no GYOC^{2}CB. Sarsens] sarasen YB (*erasure at end* Bm); Iewys F. Iewes] Iuwe Y; sarsy3nes F.
279 no] *om* Cr. of...liknesse] ly3k to c*ri*st F. *with*...saued] worth salf vn-christe*n*id Cr. outen] out HmGYBmR. c*ri*stendom] c*ri*stny*n*g F. worþ] beth **M**; worþe to be (to be *another hand*) C^{2}.
280 q*uo*d] q*uo*d I R. þoo] *om* G. comsed] bygane C. to] G; for to WHmCrYOC^{2}C BLMRF.
281 *Saluabitur vix*] *vix saluabitur* F. *vix*] *vir* Cr^{23}G.
283 was a] þ*at* F. and] *om* F. neu*ere*] neu*ere* no F.
284 is] *om* C^{2}R. saaf] seiþ C^{2}; *om* O. seiþ] saith Cr; so seiþ WHmGLMR; as seith YOC^{2}CBF. heuene] blysse F.
285 Ac] R; But F; For WHmCrGYOC^{2} CBLM. of] in Cr^{23}OC^{2}; in þe F. Font] fout Cr^{1}. fullynge(2)] also F. in] of Hm M.
286 fir] fier *in margin* Cot; þe holy goost F. and] *om* CrC^{2}.
286α *in margin* O. &*c*] *om* OC^{2}CotRF.

Ac truþe þat trespased neu*er*e ne *tra*uersed ayeins his lawe, |
But lyueþ as his lawe techeþ and leueþ þ*er* be no bettre, *fol.* 72 *b*
And if þ*er* were he wolde amende, and in swich wille deieþ—
Ne wolde neu*er*e trewe god but [trewe] truþe were allowed.
And wheiþ*er* it worþ [of truþe] or no3t, [þe] worþ [of] bileue
    is gret,
And an hope hangynge þ*er*Inne to haue a mede for his truþe;
For *Deus dicitur quasi dans* [*eternam vitam*] *suis, hoc est fidelibus;*
    Et alibi, si ambulauero in medio vmbre mortis.
The glose graunteþ vpon þat vers a greet mede to truþe.
And wit and wisdom', quod þat wye, 'was som tyme tresor
To kepe wiþ a co*m*mune; no catel was holde bettre,
And muche murþe and manhod;' and ri3t wiþ þat he
    vanysshed.

287 Ac] but GF; And CrC^{2}C. truþe] þe knyght F. þat] *om* RF. *tra*uersed] trauessid C^2; tra*n*suersed CrLR; *tra*nuersyd F.
288 But] and GF. lyueþ] lyued R; beleved F. his...be] was tawht hy*m* for he ne knew F. his lawe] þ*at* Cr. techeþ] tau3te R.
289 if] *om* B. þ*er* were] he were wykke F. and] *om* C^2. wille] a will F. deieþ] dye Cr.
290 trewe truþe] trewe treuthe R; truþe WHmCrGYOC^{2}CBLM; his wil F.
291 *line om* Y. wheiþ*er*] where C^{2}L; wher HmCr^1; were Cr^{23}GOCBMRF. worþ of truþe] worþ OCrGC^{2}CBLMRF; be worþ WHm. no3t...of] no3t worþ þe WF; worth nougth þe HmCr^{23}LMR; it worth not Cr^1; not þe OC^{2}CB; noght G. is] of it is Cr. gret] Cr; gret of truþe WHmGOC^{2}CBLMR; gret i*n* trewþe F.
292 *line om* Cot. to...truþe] þerfore meede to have F. a] *om* CrGYOC^{2}CBm BoM. for] *om* Bo.
293 For...*vitam*] *in margin* O. For] *quia* GYOC^{2}CB. *dicitur*] *dicit* G. *dans*] *om* G. *eternam vitam*] *vitam eternam* WHmCr GYOC^{2}CBLMRF. *hoc*] *id* F.
293α *mortis*] *mortis &c* HmGYOC^{2}CBR; *mortis non timebo mala quoniam tu mecum es domine* F.
294 vpon] vs on G. þat] þe Cr^3. to] of F. truþe] trewe R.
295 And] Boþe F. wye] vy3e G; weye R; wight Cr. was] wery*n* F. tresor] a tresor F; treysorye G.
296 wiþ a] hem fra*m* F. no] ne Cr^1. was] *om* G. holde] holden GOC^{2}CM; *om* F.
297 ri3t] *om* F. wiþ] myd R. þat] þat word F.

XIII

And I awaked þ*er*wiþ, witlees nerhande,
And as a freke þat [fey] were forþ gan I walke
In man*er*e of a mendynaunt many yer after.
And of þis metyng many tyme muche þou3t I hadde,
First how Fortune me failed at my mooste nede;
And how þ*at* Elde manaced me, my3te we eu*er*e mete;
And how þ*at* freres folwede folk þat was riche
And [peple] þat was pou*er*e at litel pris þei sette,
And no corps in hir kirk3erd n[e] in hir kirk was buryed
But quik he biqueþe [hem] au3t [or sholde helpe] quyte hir
    dettes;
And how þis Coueitise ouercom clerkes and preestes;
And how þ*at* lewed men ben lad, but oure lord hem helpe,
Thoru3 vnkonnynge curat*our*s to incurable peynes;
And how þ*at* Ymaginatif in dremels me tolde

1 And I awaked] AWake y gan F. awaked] wakede OC². **2** a] *om* C. þat] *om* F. fey] BmBo (ey *over erasure* Bm); faynt Cot; fere R; afeerd F; fre WHmCrGYOC²CLM. walke] walken R. **3** a mendynaunt] amendement BmBo. yer] yere YOC²CBMR; yeres G; a yer WHmCrLF. **4** þis metyng] þese metynges Hm. tyme] tymes HmGRF. muche] *om* F. þou3t] þou3 BmBo; had C²; Merveyle F. hadde] þou3te C². **5** me failed] faylede me F. **6** manaced] mansed R. my3te we eu*er*e] we myghte neu*er*e YGC²CB; we my3ten neu*er*e O. mete] mete*n* CrLRF. **7** þ*at*] the Cr. folwede] folweden CGYO C²BM. was] were HmG; weren OC²F. **8** peple] folk WHmCrGYOC²CBLMR; poor*e* folk F. was] were Hm; weren OC² F. pou*er*e at] *om* F. pris] of he*m* F. sette] setten OC²BMF. **9** ne] HmGYOC²CBLMR; nor WCr; *om* F. in hir(2)] in C; *om* CrF. kirk was buryed] wolde þei no*n* berye F. was] wer*e* R. **10** But] But þei B. he] he wolde F; *om* CB. hem] HmCrYOC²CCotLMRF; hym BmBo; *om* WG. au3t] *om* F. or... helpe] CHmYOC²BLMR; or helpe G; or CrF; to W. quyte] HmGYOC²CBLMR; quyte wiþ W; q*ui*te out F; quite part of Cr. **11** þis] þus R; that Cr; *om* GYOC²CBF. **12** þat] *om* Hm. **13** curat*our*s] creatures HmCr. in] vn F. peynes] peyne C. **14–20** *lines om* RF. **14** dremels] dremes HmCrC; dreme:es (*erasure*) C².

Of kynde and of his konnynge, and how curteis he is to bestes,
And how louynge he is to [ech lif] on londe and on watre— |
Leneþ he no lif lasse ne moore— *fol.* 73 *a*
[For alle] creatures þat crepen [or walken] of kynde ben engendred;
And siþen how ymaginatif seide '*vix saluabitur* [*iustus*]',
And whan he hadde seid so, how sodeynliche he passed.
I lay doun longe in þis þoȝt and at þe laste I slepte,
And as crist wolde þer com Conscience to conforte me þat tyme
And bad me come to his court, wiþ clergie sholde I dyne.
And for Conscience of Clergie spak I com wel þe raþer.
And þere I [mette] a maister, what man he was I nyste,
That lowe louted and loueliche to scripture.
Conscience knew hym wel and welcomed hym faire.
Thei wesshen and wipeden and wenten to þe dyner.
A[c] Pacience in þe Paleis stood in pilgrymes cloþes
And preyde mete '*p*[*u*]*r charite*, for a pouere heremyte'.
Conscience called hym In and curteisliche seide
'Welcome, wye, go and wassh; þow shalt sitte soone.'
This maister was maad sitte as for þe mooste worþi,

15 his] *om* GYOC^{2}CB.
16 ech lif] bestes GHmCrYOC^{2}CBLM; briddes W.
17 Leneþ] leynethe *altered to* leyvethe *another ink* G; Leueth Cr^1; Leaueth Cr^{23}. ne] nor Hm.
18 For alle] The WHmCrGYOC^{2}CBLM. creatures] creatouris C^2. or...of] of WHmCrGYOC^{2}CBLM. ben] they ben HmCr.
19 siþen] *om* OC^{2}CB. *vix*] *vix Iustus* GYCBLM. *iustus*] HmCr^{23}OC^2, *om* W Cr^{1}GYCBLM.
21 lay] lye G. doun] *om* CrCB. I(2)] *om* Hm. slepte] sleppe BmBo.
22 þer] *om* CrGF. com Conscience] *con*sc*ience* came Cr. to] and HmF. conforte] *con*forten M; conforted HmF. þat] i*n* þat R.
23 me] *om* Cr^{1}OC^2. to] in Cr^1. court] cu*n*tre F. sholde I] shul I C; y schulde Hm.
24 com wel] come wol (e *erased*) M; wyll G.
25 mette] seiȝ WHmCrGYOC^{2}CBLMRF.
26 That lowe] ⁊ lowe dou*n* y F. louted] he lowted Cr; a loutid B. to scripture] dyde hy*m* honoure F. to] vnto HmY.
27 Conscience] Conscien C; But Concyense F. hym(*both*)] me F. hym (1)] hem Cr^2. wel] *om* BoCot.
28 Thei] þan F. wesshen] wessheden YG OC^2; wesshenden C; washen Cr; wysshe þey F. wipeden] wypen Cr. wenten] wente YCrOC^{2}CR. to] aft*er* to F. þe] *om* GYOC^{2}CBF.
29 Ac] HmYOBLMR; but GF; And WCrC^{2}C. cloþes] wedys F.
30 *pur*] BF; por C^2; *par* WGYO; for HmCrCLMR.
31 Conscience] þan Concyense F. hym] hem M. seide] he seyȝde F.
32 wye go] wyel ȝe (*altered from* wy go) L. wye] wyght Cr; wysse G; *om* B. go and] and go M. þow] ⁊ þou F. sitte] sette BmBo. soone] i*n* haste F.
33 This] þe F. sitte] syttyn F. as] and HmGYOC^{2}CB. for þe mooste] moost of hem F.

And þanne clergie and Conscience and Pacience cam after.
Pacience and I [prestly] were put to be [mettes],
And seten bi oureselue at [a] side borde.
Conscience called after mete and þanne cam Scripture
And serued hem þus soone of sondry metes manye,
Of Austyn, of Ambrose, of [alle] þe foure Eu*aun*gelistes:
Edentes & bibentes que apud eos sunt.
Ac þis maister [of þise men] no maner flessh [eet],
Ac [he eet] mete of moore cost, mortrews and potages.
Of þat men myswonne þei made hem wel at ese, |
Ac hir sauce was ou*er* sour and vnsauo*ur*ly grounde *fol. 73 b*
In a morter, *Post mortem*, of many bitter peyne
But if þei synge for þo soules and wepe salte teris:
Vos qui peccata hominum comeditis, nisi pro eis lacrimas & oraciones eff[u]deritis, ea que in delicijs comeditis in tormentis euometis.
Conscience curteisly þo co*m*maunded Scripture
Bifore Pacience breed to brynge, [bitynge apart],

34 And] *om* GYOC^{2}CB.

35 prestly were] were WCrGYCLMR; weren HmOC^{2}BF. put] seet F. mettes] RF; macches WHmCrGYOC^{2}CBLM.

36 seten] sitten CrGC; sitte OC^{2}. selue] selues Cr^{23}. a] GOC^{2}CBLMRF; o Y; þe WHmCr. borde] table F.

37 Conscience] þan Concyense F. þanne] sone F.

38 hem] hym HmBR. of] wi*th* G.

39 of (1)] and HmGF. Ambrose] ambrosie Cot. of alle] YOC^{2}CBLMR; & of all G; and of WHmCr; & wi*th* F.

39α *in margin* O. *eos*] *illos* Cr^{23}. *sunt*] *sunt &c* Hm.

40 Ac] And CrGC^{2}C; *om* F. þis] þe F. of...men] ne his man HmGYOC^{2}CBLMR; nor his man W; and hys man Cr; ne no*n* oþ*er* ma*n* F. eet] eten WHmCrGYOC^{2}CBLMRF.

41 Ac] but G; And CrC^{2}C; For F. he] þei WHmCrGYOC^{2}CBLMRF. eet] ete YCr^{1}GCL; ate Cr^{23}; eten WHmOC^{2}BM; hadde RF. mete] metes RF. cost] cost as F. mortrews] mortrases G. and] *om* F. potages] potage Cr; powdred F.

42 men] man B. wonne] wonnen OHmC^{2}BRF. made] maden OHmC^{2}BmBoR. wel] *om* CB.

43 Ac] But F; And CrGC^{2}C. sauce] cause Bo. ouer] euer GYOC^{2}CB. vnsauo*ur*ly] vnsauorye YOC^{2}. grounde] groundyn Hm; ygrounde CB; ygrounden OC^{2}.

44 of] wi*th* F. many] HmCrGYOC^{2}CLR; many a WBMF (a *above line* M). peyne] paynes CrGOC^{2}.

45 But...synge] & shull sobbe F. þo] þe HmCr^{1}OC^{2}CBMF. and] with R; *om* F. wepe] wepte C^{2}; many RF.

45α *hominum*] *untranscribable* C^{2}. *lacrimas*] *lacrimis* C. *effuderitis*] GYOC^{2}CCot; *effunderitis* WHmCrBmBoLMRF (*n erased* HmM). *deliciis*] *delitus* Cr^{23}. *comeditis* (2)] *comedistis* F; *in comedis* R. *tormentis*] *r by corrector* C^{2}. *euometis*] euouometis Cot.

46 curteisly] YGOC^{2}CBF; ful curteisly W HmCrMR; for curteisly (? for *over erasure*) L. co*m*maunded] comended Y.

47, 48 *as one line* RFWHmCrGYOC^{2}CBLM; Byfore pacience brede to bringe and me þat was hys mete (mete] macche WHmCrLM; make GYOC^{2}CB).

And me þat was his [mette oþer mete boþe].
He sette a sour loof toforn vs and seide '*Agite penitenciam*',
And siþþe he [drouȝ] vs drynke, *Di*[*u*] *perseuerans*,
'As longe', quod [he], 'as [lif] and lycame may dure'.
'Here is p*ro*pre s*er*uice', quod Pacience, 'þer fareþ no Prince
 bettre.'
[And he brouȝte vs of *Beati quorum* of *Beatus vir*res makyng,
And þanne a mees of ooþ*er* mete of *Miserere mei deus*,]
Et quorum tecta sunt peccata
In a dissh of derne shrifte, *Dixi ⁊ confitebor tibi.*
'Bryng pacience som pitaunce pryueliche', quod Conscience,
And þanne hadde Pacience a pitaunce, *Pro hac orabit ad te omnis
 sanctus in tempore oportuno*;
And Conscience conforted vs and carped vs murye tales:
Cor contritum ⁊ humiliatum deus non despicies.
Pacience was proud of þat p*ro*pre seruice

49 a...vs] afore vs a soure loof F. toforn] before HmCr; afore G.
50 siþþe] aft*er* F. drouȝ] RGYOC^{2}CBLMF; brouȝte WHmCr. vs] vs a F. *Diu*] *diu* GOC^{2}BM (*u over erasure* BmM); was *diu* F; *Dia* WHmCrYCLR. *perseuerans*] perseueraunce Cr.
51 *in top margin main hand* G. As] also B. quod] as lyf q*uod* F; *om* Cot. he] OC^{2}RF; I WHmCrGYCBmBoLM; *om* Cot. as] *om* F. lif] R; I lyue WCrGYOC^{2}BLM; y leue HmC; *om* F. and...dure] *cropped* G. may] man Cr. dure] endure HmCr.
52 is] *om* Cr^{1}CF. propre] preti Cr. þer...Prince] no prince can fare Cr; no P*r*ince faret F. Prince] knyght G.
53 *transposed with* 54 WHmCrGYOC^{2}CBLMRF. ⁊ þerwit*h beati quorum tecta sunt* wit*h* blawnche poud*r*e stroued F. he...vs] *om* GYOC^{2}CB. vs] *om* R. of (1)] *om* G. *Beati*] beat C^{2}. of (2)] and of R. *Beatus*] Beatur Y. *virres*] *vir* his CotR; *vir* GYOC^{2}CBmBo.
54 And] *om* Cr. þanne] þanne he brouȝte vs forþ WLMR; than he brought forth YHmGOC^{2}CB (forth *over erasure* Hm); The*n* brought he forth Cr; þa*n* he browhte anoþ*er* F. a...*deus*] *over erasure* Hm. a...of] mees F; *om* HmGYOC^{2}CB. ooþ*er*] *om* CrF. mete] was F. *miserere*] miserrere L; miserre C^{2}. *deus*] *om* CrR.
54α ⁊ *beatus vir cui non imputauit F. Divided from* 55 *after* dissh WHmCrGYOC^{2}CBLMR; *after* loo F. *peccata*] *peccata ⁊c* Hm.
55 dissh of] plater a loo ⁊ F. derne] dernes Cr. ⁊] and HmCrGYOC^{2}CBLMR.
56 Bryng] And brynge CB. pitaunce] *om* CB. priueliche] *om* OC^{2}.
57 *as two lines divided before Pro* RF; *before* Of GYOC^{2}CB. And] *om* R. hadde] come to YGOC^{2}C; com þer to B; was brouht to F. a] þis F. *Pro*] ful soone *Pro* F; Ibroughte Of *pro* YGOCB; brouȝt Of *pro* C^{2}. *ad te*] *om* RF. *omnis sanctus*] *⁊c* Cr. *in...oportuno*] *om* HmCr.
58 And] ⁊ þan F. vs (1)] me F. vs (2)] þus Hm; *om* F. tales] wordis OC^{2}.
58α *in margin* O. *Cor*] Among was *cor* F. *despicies*] *despicies ⁊c* Hm; despecies *⁊c* Y.
59 Pacience was] þan was Pacyence F. was] tho was Hm.

And made hym murþe wiþ his mete, ac I mornede eu*ere*
For þis doctour on þe heiȝe dees drank wyn so faste:
Ve vobis qui potentes estis ad bibendum vinum.
He eet manye sondry metes, mortrews and puddynges,
Wombe cloutes and wilde brawen and egges yfryed wiþ grece.
Thanne seide I to myself so pacience it herde,
'It is noȝt foure dayes þat þis freke, bifore þe deen of Poules, |
Preched of penaunces þat Poul þe Apostle suffrede *fol. 74 a*
In fame & frigore and flappes of scourges:
Ter cesus sum & a iudeis quinquies quadragenas &c—
Ac o word þei ou*er*huppen at ech tyme þat þei p*re*che
That Poul in his Pistle to al þe peple tolde:
Periculum est in falsis fratribus.'
Holi writ bit men be war—I wol noȝt write it here
In englissh on auenture it sholde be reherced to ofte,
And greue þerwiþ [þat goode ben]—ac gramariens shul re[d]e:
Vnusquisque a fratre se custodiat quia vt dicitur periculum est in falsis fratribus.

60 hym] hem BM; *om* F. murþe] merye Cr. mete] mene R; mowht F. ac] but GF; & CrC^{2}C. mornede] moued G.

61 þis doctour] þe doctoures F. on] vpon R. þe] this HmR. heiȝe] *om* F. dees] benche Hm. drank] dru*n*ke F; drynk Y. so] *om* M.

61α *in margin* O. *vinum*] *vinum &c* HmGY; *om* CB.

62 He] þey F; And R. eet] etyn F. metes] metys & F. mortrews] mortreses G. and puddynges] ypowdred F.

63 why3lde braun & whombe clowtys & bacou*n* wit*h* eggys fryed F. yfryed] fryed HmCrGYOC^{2}CBR.

64 *line om* Y. to] *om* F. so] þat F.

65 is] *om* C. noȝt] not goo F. þat] go þat (go *above line*) M. þe...of] folk at F. of] of seynt R.

66 *run together with* 67 F. of...suffrede] *om* F. penaunces] penau*n*ce CrYCM. Apostle] postle BmBo.

67 *fame*] fam R. &] *et* CrBmBoR; and C; and in (and *cancelled for* &) Y. of] with Y.

67α *in margin* O. *Ter*] Ther Y. *quadragenas*] quadragintes Cr^{3}. *&c*] *added another ink* Cot; *om* CrOC^{2}RF.

68 Ac] but GF; And CrC^{2}C. huppen] hypped CrF. ech] CrHmGYOC^{2}CBF; ech a WLMR. þat] *om* F. preche] prechen YGOC^{2}CBMR.

69 his] hist C. Pistle] epistle O. al] *om* OC^{2}F.

70 *in margin* OC^{2}. *Periculum*] *Et in periculo* R. *est*] *om* RF. *in*] *om* OR. *fratribus*] *fratribus &c* HmYB; *fratribus* was neuere ȝit no teeme F.

71 bit] byddeþ HmGC^{2}CBMF. men] *om* F. wol] wolde BoCot. write] writen R.

72 In] on HmYOC^{2}CLMF. on] yn HmB; en F; If in (in *above line*) G. sholde be] were G. to] *om* G.

73 þat...ben] þat goode beene GYOC^{2}CBM; þat good men ben LRF; goode men WHmCr. ac] but GF; & CrC^{2}C. shul] schulde HmCrGCB; shul it F. rede] HmCrGYOC^{2}CBLMRF; redde W.

73α *Vnus...dicitur*] *over erasure late hand* L. *se custodiat*] *custodiat se* (*correct order noted*) OC^{2}. *se*] *suo se* Hm; *suo* (*cancelled, then marked stet*) G. *vt*] *om* F. *fratribus*] *fratribus &c* Hm.

Ac I wiste neu*er*e freke þ*a*t as a frere yede bifore men on englissh
Taken it for his teme and telle it wiþouten glosyng.
They p*re*chen þ*a*t penaunce is p*ro*fitable to þe soule,
And what meschief and maleese crist for man þolede,
'Ac þis goddes gloton', quod I, 'wiþ hise grete chekes
Haþ no pite on vs pou*er*e; he p*ar*fourn*e*þ yuele
That he p*re*cheþ [and] preueþ noȝt [com]pacience', I tolde.
And wisshed witterly, wiþ wille ful egre,
That disshes and doublers [þis doctour bifore]
Were molten leed in his mawe and Mahoun amyddes.
'I shal Iangle to þis Iurdan wiþ his Iuste wombe
[And appose hym] what penaunce is, of which he p*re*ched
    raþer.'
Pacience p*ar*ceyued what I þouȝte and [preynte] on me to be
    stille
And seide, 'þow shalt see þus soone, whan he may na moore,
He shal haue a penaunce in his paunche and puffe at ech a
    worde,

74 Ac] For Hm; And CrC^{2}C; *om* GRF. wiste] nyste F; sagh G. freke...a] ȝit F. as] *om* Hm. a] *om* R. yede] preche F. bifore...englissh] on englysshe byfore men G. on] in Cr.
75 Taken] Take CrGYOC^{2}CB; Took F. his] *over erasure another ink* M; her CrYO C^{2}CBLR. teme] tyme YC^{2}. telle] tellen MHmR; tolde F. it(2)] *om* Hm. outen] oute HmCrGYOC^{2}B. glosyng] glosyngs Cr^{1}; lesings Cr^{23}.
76 They] Ac þei R; But þey F. p*re*chen] preach Cr. þe] *om* F.
77 And] *om* F. and] or YOC^{2}CB. maleese] malasie Cot; malyce G.
78 Ac] but GF; And CrC^{2}C. þis] þus G.
79 Haþ] he haþ F. vs] þe F. he] men he GYOC^{2}CB. yuele] h*is* speche evele F.
80 and] R; *þus* ⁊ F; he WHmCrGYOC^{2} CBLM. preueþ] p*ro*uetes C; prueþ Bo. noȝt] yt F; *om* R. compacience] to Pacience WHmCrGYOC^{2}CBLMRF. I] p*ri*uyly y F.
81 wisshed] wyssed GC. witterly] wytterly GYOC^{2}CBLMRF; ful witterly WHm Cr. ful] of Y; for L; w*ith* woordys ful F.
82 and] a L. þis...bifore] byfor þis doctor R; bifore þis ilke doctour WHmCrGYO C^{2}CL; bifore þilke docto*ur* M; bifore þis ille doctour B; on dees befor*e* þe doctour F.
83 molten] molte R. leed] leded C. his] here R. and] a Y. amyddes] yn þe mydest G.
84 þis] þ*a*t F. Iurdan] yurdan Hm. Iuste] Iusty F; iuysty R; Iutte OC^{2}.
85 And...hym] To telle me WHmCrGY CBLMRF; To telle men OC^{2}. penaunce] pacyence Hm. he] *om* Cot. preched] prechiþ F. raþer] rathe Cr; eu*er*e F; þere aþ R.
86 p*ar*ceyued] p*ar*seyve F. what] þat Hm. þouȝte] seid F. preynte] wynked WHm CrGYOC^{2}CBLM; bad R; bad holde F. on] *om* RF. to] *om* CrCotRF. be] *om* CrF. stille] *om* Cr.
87 þow] þ Cr^{1}. shalt] schal BmBo; *by a corrector* L. þus] thys Cr^{23}G; aft*er* F. may] may etyn F.
88 a(1)] *om* CF. paunche] pau*n*ce Hm. ech] eu*er*y F. a(2)] *om* HmCrGYCBF. worde] speche F; *lost in sewing* Cot.

And þanne shullen hise guttes goþele and he shal galpen after.
For now he haþ dronken so depe he wole deuyne soone |
And preuen it by hir Pocalips and passion of Seint Auereys *fol. 74 b*
That neiþ*er* bacon ne braun, blancmanger ne mortrews,
Is neiþ*er* fissh n[e] flessh, but fode for a penaunt.
And þanne shal he testifie of [a] Trinite, and take his felawe to witnesse
What he fond in a [forel of] a freres lyuyng,
And but [þe] first [leef] be lesyng leue me neu*ere* after.
And þanne is tyme to take and to appose þis doctour
Of dowel and dobet, and if do[best] be any penaunce.'
And I sat stille as Pacience seide, and þus soone þis doctour,
As rody as a Rose [ruddede] hise chekes,
Coughed and carped, and Conscience hym herde
And tolde hym of a Trinite, and toward vs he loked.
'What is dowel, sire doctour?' quod I; 'is [dobest] any penaunce?'

89 shullen] schull HmCrGYOC^{2}CMF. goþele] gothelyn Hm; gottilen Cr; godele LR; grothele YGOC^2; gowle F; gruwe B. galpen] galpe B; gulp*en* Cr. after] *corrected from* ofte Y.
90 dronken] dronke CrGYCRF. deuyne] denye G; dynye BmBo; dyne Cot.
91 preuen] preue YGOC^{2}CBMF. by] byfor C; in F; *om* R. hir] his Cot; þe BmBoF. Pocalips] apokelyps FG; apocalipsis B. and] ⁊ in þe F. Auereys] Auarise Cr^{23}G; auereynes Hm; savoures F.
92 braun] braun ne RF. blancmanger] blamanc Hm; blameg*er*is F; blackemanger Cr. ne(2)] no Hm.
93 fissh] fleisch B. ne] CrGYOC^{2}CBo CotMRF; no L; nor WHm; neþer Bm. flessh] fisch B. a] þe R; *om* F. penaunt] penauntes RF; penaunce YC.
94 þanne...of] takþ testemonye on F. þanne] *om* C. of] it of Hm. a] GYOC^2 CBLMR; þe WHmCr^{23}F; *om* Cr^1. take] ek F. felawe] felawes YGOC^{2}CBmBo. witnesse] borwe F.
95 forel of] frayel after WHmCrGYOC^2 CBLMR; sell aft*er* F. a(2)] *om* GYOC^{2}CB. freres] fre*re* R. lyuyng] leuynge C^{2}GR; lyuyge C; dyȝeng F.
96 And] *om* GM. but] but if YGOC^{2}CBm BoLMR. þe] GYOC^{2}CBLMRF; he W HmCr. leef] OC^{2}Cot; leyeffe G; lif CBmBo; life Y; lyue Cr; lyue (? lyne) WHmLMR; lyȝne F. be] be in a F; by HmCr. lesyng] leasinges Cr; fals Y.
97 take] talke OC^{2}R; aposen F. to(2)] *om* OC^{2}CBF. appose þis] pyttyn to þe F.
98 Of] If F. and(1)] ⁊ of CrCBLMR. bet] better G. if] *om* F. best] HmCrGY OC^{2}CBLMRF; wel W. be] do B. any] *om* GF. penaunce] pennau*n*te C^2.
99 And] *om* F. as] an C. seide] bad F. þus] *om* GF. þis] þus G; þe F. doctour] Doctou*r* aft*er* F.
100 As] also HmB. a] þe F. ruddede] ruddud Hm; gan rodye F; rubbede WCr GYOC^{2}CBLMR.
101 Coughed] He Cowhede F; Comsed B.
102 hym] hem Cr^3; *om* F. a] þe Cr^{23}F. vs] vs al CB.
103 is] his C. doctour] *om* F. I] y ⁊ F. dobest] RF; dowel HmCrGYOC^{2}CBLM; it W. penaunce] penau*n*te C^2.

'Dowel', quod þis doctour and [drank after],
'Do noon yuel to þyn euencristen, nouȝt by þi power.'
'By þis day, sire doctour', quod I, 'þanne [in dowel be ye
nouȝt]!
For ye han harmed vs two in þat ye eten þe puddyng,
Mortrews and ooþer mete, and we no morsel hadde.
And if ye fare so in youre Fermerye, ferly me þynkeþ
But cheeste be þer charite sholde be, and yonge children dorste
pleyne.
I wolde permute my penaunce with youre, for I am in point
to dowel.'
Than Conscience curteisly a contenaunce made,
And preynte vpon pacience to preie me be stille,
And seide hymself, 'sire doctour, and it be youre wille,
What is dowel and dobet? ye dyuynours knoweþ.'
'Dowel', quod þis doctour, 'do as clerkes techeþ.
[That trauailleþ to teche oþere I holde it for a dobet].
And dobest doþ hymself so as he seiþ and precheþ: |
Qui facit & docuerit magnus vocabitur in regno celorum.' *fol. 75 a*

104 quod þis] is quod þe F. drank after] dronk after R; dronk anon þereafter F; took þe cuppe and drank WHmCrGYOC^{2}CBLM.

105 Do] GHmYOC^{2}CBLMRF; Is do WCr. nouȝt] nouȝ C. by] to Cr^{3}G.

106 day] *om* OC^2. doctour] *om* F. þanne] *om* CB. in...nouȝt] be ye nouȝt in dowel WHmCrGYOC^{2}CBLMRF (be ye] ye be Cr. in] nou in F).

107 han] *om* OC^2. eten] ete HmGOC^2; haue eaten Cr^3.

108 Mortrews] & Morterelis F. hadde] hadden OC^2.

109 And] *om* F. if] *om* R. ye] you G. fare] faren OC^{2}B.

110 *as two lines divided after* be(2) R. be(1)] with F; *om* GYOC^2. þer] þere as Hm; theyre G; *om* F. sholde] shol C; *om* F. and] *om* F. yonge] *om* CrGYOC^{2}CBF. children] chyldre GBmBo; y chyll F. dorste] dursten OC^2; sholde Y; on ȝow F.

111 wolde] wole YF. permute] permitte C^{2}F. youre] yours G; you Cr. for] *om* G. in] *om* F. dowel] spill F.

112 curteisly] ful curteislich RF. made] he made HmLMRF.

113 preynte] prentede R; prynkid B; plukkid F. pacience] penaunce B. to...me] & prayede hym F. be] GYOC^{2}CBF; to be WHmCrLMR.

114 and] & yff G.

115 and dobet] dobetter G. dyuynours] dyuynes Hm. knoweþ] knowe CrF. *Here* Y *copies line* 118α; *error noted by corrector.*

116 þis] þat F. do] is do Cr; ys to doon F; dos R. techeþ] teche FCr.

117 And dobet is he þat techeþ and trauailleþ to teche oþere WHmCrGYOC^{2}CBLMRF (bet] better G).

118 dobest] doiþ best Hm. doþ] doo C; *om* G. precheþ] preueþ Hm; techeþ FG.

118α *in margin* O; *copied after line* 115 Y. *facit*] *fecerit* OC^2. *docuerit*] *docuit* Y. *magnus*] *hic magnus* F. *regno*] *regum or* regus C^2. *celorum*] *celorum &c* HmYBmBo.

'Now þow, Clergie', quod Conscience, 'carp[e] what is dowel.'
'I haue seuene sones', he seide, '*ser*uen in a Castel
Ther þe lord of lif wonyeþ, to leren [hem] what is dowel.
Til I se þo seuene and myself acorde
I am vnhardy', quod he, 'to any wiȝt to preuen it.
For oon Piers þe Plowman haþ impugned vs alle,
And set alle sciences at a sop saue loue one;
And no text ne takeþ to mayntene his cause
But *Dilige deum* and *Domine quis habitabit*;
And [demeþ] þ*at* dowel and dobet arn two Infinites,
Whiche Infinites wiþ a feiþ fynden out dobest,
Which shal saue mannes soule; þus seiþ Piers þe Plowman.'
'I kan noȝt heron', quod Conscience, 'ac I knowe Piers.
He wol noȝt ayein holy writ speken, I dar vndertake.'
'Thanne passe we ouer til Piers come and preue þis in dede.
Pacience haþ be in many place, and *par*aunter [knoweþ]
That no clerk ne kan, as crist bereþ witnesse:
Pacientes vincunt &c.'

119 Now þow] A F. Clergie...Conscience] Conscience q*uo*d Cleargy Cr^{23}. quod] & Cr^{1}. carpe] carpe vs Cot; carpest WHmCrYOC^{2}BmBoLMR; þou carpist F; carpethe G; capest C.
120 seuene] *om* LR (*in margin by corrector* L). seide] seyd þ*at* F; seyth Hm. in] at YGOC^{2}CB.
121 leren] lerne HmCrGYOC^{2}CBF. hem] HmGYCBF; hym LMR; *om* WCrOC^{2}. what is] to YF.
122 Til I] I wolde F. þo] thos G; the Cr. and my] sones & ȝo*ure* F. acorde] acorden YHmCrGOC^{2}CBLMR.
123 he] he þ*an* F. to(2)] *om* RF. preuen] preue HmCrGYC^{2}CBLMRF.
124 oon] *om* F. þe] *om* F. haþ impugned] ap*er*tly haþ repugned F.
125 And] He F. sciences] science OC^{2}R. sop] Soupe Cr. one] onelye Cr; alone G.
126 *line om* CotM. text] tix R; oþ*er* tyxt F. ne takeþ] takþ he F.
127 *Dilige*] *diligo* Hm. *quis*] *quid* C. *habitabit*] *habitabit &c* GYOC^{2}CLMR.
128 And] He F. demeþ] seiþ WHmCrG OC^{2}BLMRF; seigh YC. þ*at*] *om* OC^{2}. bet] bett*er* G. Infinites] Infinytyes G; inffinitis C^{2}F.
129 Infinites] infinitis BmBoF. a] oo B; *om* Cr. fynden] fynde CrR. dobest] *om* F.
130 Which] þ*at* F. saue] haue G. þus] þys Hm. þe] *om* HmCrGYOC^{2}CBF.
131 heron] heyren G. ac] but G; and CrC^{2}C; & ȝit F. knowe] GYOC^{2}CBM; knowe wel WHmCrLRF. Piers] perkyn F; pyers plowman G.
132 ayein...speken] speke ageyn holy wryt F; gainesaie holi writ Cr. speken] speke GOC^{2}R. dar] YGOC^{2}; dar wel WHmCrLMR; dar wel wel F; *om* CB. take] taken R; stonde B.
133 Thanne] Now F. þis] we þus G; it Cr. dede] dide C.
134 place] a place R; places CrGYOC^{2} CBM. knoweþ] OGYC^{2}CBLMR; he know*ith* F; mootheþ Hm; mouþed WCr.
135 That no clerk] þere ben no Clerkis F. clerk] clere G. ne] *om* OC^{2}RF. kan] knoweþ OC^{2}; kone so meche F.
135α *in margin* OC^{2}. &c] *om* Cr^{23}C^{2}F.

'A[t] youre preiere', quod Pacience þo, 'so no man displese hym:
Disce', quod he, '*doce, dilige inimicos.*
Disce and dowel, *doce* and dobet, *dilige* and dobest:
[Th]us [lerede] me ones a lemman, loue was hir name.
"Wiþ wordes and werkes", quod she, "and wil of þyn herte
Thow loue leelly þi soule al þi lif tyme.
And so þow lere þe to louye, for [þe] lordes loue of heuene,
Thyn enemy in alle wise eueneforþ wiþ þiselue.
Cast coles on his heed of alle kynde speche;
Boþe wiþ wer[k] and *with* wor[d] fonde his loue to wynne;
And leye on hym þus *with* loue til he lau3e on þe. |
And but he bowe for þis betyng blynd mote he worþe!" *fol. 75 b*
Ac for to fare þus wiþ þi frend, folie it were;
For he þat loueþ þee leelly litel of þyne coueiteþ.
Kynde loue coueiteþ no3t no catel but speche.
Wiþ half a laumpe lyne in latyn, *Ex vi transicionis*,
I bere þ*er*, [in a bouste] faste ybounde, dowel,

136 At] YGOC^{2}CBmBoMRF; Ac WHm CotL; And Cr. þo] þen G. displese hym] be displesyd F. hym] hem R.
137 *doce*] *Doce* and CrGYCB; ⁊ *doce* ⁊ HmOC^{2}F. *dilige*] dilege G. *inimicos*] *inimicos tuos* F.
138, 139 *divided after* ones Hm, *after* dobette OC^{2}; *as three lines divided after* dobeste *and* once Cr, *after* dobet *and* ones WGYCBL MRF.
138 bet] bett*er* G. *dilige*...dobest] *om* OC^{2}. *dilige*] Dilege Cr^{1}.
139 Thus] *spelled* þus W; *om* OC^{2}. lerede...lemman] tau3te me ones A lemman þat I louede WHmCrGYCBLM R; was tawht me onis þanne a Lemman þat lovely spak F; A lemman þat I louede OC^{2}.
140 and(1)] YGOC^{2}CB; and wiþ WHm CrLMRF. and(2)] ⁊ good F. wil] loue G.
141 Thow...soule] þy sowle þowh love leely F. Thow] *om* R.
142 þow...þe] to lere and R; to leerne F. lere] lerne C^{2}Cr. louye] lowe the F. þe(2)] HmCrGYOC^{2}CBLMRF; oure W.
143 Thyn] ⁊ þyn F. enemy] enimies Cr. eueneforþ] love evene F. wiþ] as F; *om* Cot. selue] seluen GM.
144 of] and Cr^{23}GYOC^{2}CBL; þat ys F. kynde] kyn Hm. speche] of speache Cr; speches G.
145 werk...word] werk ⁊ word OGYC^{2} CB; werkes and *with* wordes WHmCrLM RF. fonde...wynne] to wynne his love þou fonde F.
146 leye] lye C; beie B.
147 þis] his Hm; thy Y. mote] might Cr. worþe] be Cr.
148 Ac] but GF; And CrC^{2}C. for] *om* G. folie] a folye Y; greet folye F.
149 litel] lyte LR. coueiteþ] desireth R; he desyreþ F.
150 Kynde] For kende F.
151 Wiþ] wh wiþ Bm. laumpe] lampe Cr^{23}F; launpe Hm; lumpe Cr^{1}; lounge (ge *apparently an alteration by main scribe*) G. lyne] lyfe (e *erased*) Hm; lyite Y; *om* Cr.^{1} in] of F. *transicionis*] *transgressionis* OC^{2}.
152 I bere] I bare Cr^{23}; ⁊ beryþ F. in] Cr; Inne WHmGYOC^{2}CBLMRF. a bouste] aboute WCrLMRF; abounte HmY (nte *over erasure another ink* Hm); a bewte OC^{2}; a beaute GB; a beaut C. ybounde] bounde Cr.

In a signe of þe Saterday þat sette first þe kalender,
And al þe wit of þe wodnesday of þe nexte wike after;
The myddel of þe Moone [i]s þe [m]yght of boþe.
And herw*ith* am I welcome þer I haue it wiþ me.
Vndo it; lat þis doctour deme if dowel be þ*er*Inne.
For, by hym þat me made, myȝte neu*ere* pouerte,
Misese ne meschief ne man wiþ his tonge,
Coold ne care ne compaignye of þeues,
Ne neiþ*er* hete ne hayl ne noon helle pouke,
Ne [neiþer] fuyr ne flood ne feere of þyn enemy
Tene þee any tyme, and þow take it wiþ þe:
Caritas nichil timet.
[And ek, haue god my soule, and þow wilt it craue
There nys neiþer emperour ne emperesse, erl ne baroun,
Pope ne patriark, þat pure reson ne shal [þee] make
Maister of alle þo men þoruȝ myȝt of þis redels,
Nouȝt þoruȝ wicchecraft but þoruȝ wit; and þow wilt þiselue
Do kyng and quene and alle þe comune after
Yeue þee al þat þei may yeue, as þee for best yemere;
And as þow demest wil þei do alle hir dayes after:
Pacientes vincunt].'
'It is but a dido', quod þis doctour, 'a disours tale.

153 In] I Cot. sette] syt F. þe(2)] in þe F.
154 And] In OC^{2}. þe(1)] *om* CM. of(2)] ⁊ F.
155 is] Cr^{23}GYOC^{2}CBLMRF; as WHm Cr^{1}. myght] CrGYOC^{2}LMRF; nyght WHmCB
156 her] ther CrGF. *with*] fore F. am I] I am Cr.
157 Vndo] Vnder Cr^{3}. it] it and RF; þis M. þis] þe MF. deme if] *corrected from* sen if L; se where R; se it wher F. þ*er*] her*e* R.
158 pouerte] pouert B.
159 meschief] myschell C^{2}. ne(2)] HmCr GYOC^{2}CBLMRF; ne no W.
160 Coold] Ne Catel F.
161 Ne] *om* F.
162 neiþer] BHmCrGYOC^{2}CLMRF; *om* W. enemy] enemyes OC^{2}.
163 any] att any G.
163α *in margin* OC^{2}. *timet*] CrOC^{2}CLM RF; *timet ⁊c* WHmGYB.
164–71α RF; *lines om* WHmCrGYOC^{2}CB LM; *here in the spelling of* W.
164 ek] eek so F. it] love F.
165 neiþer] *om* F. erl] neyþ*er* Erl F; erl kyng*e* R.
166 ne(2)] *om* F. þee] the F; *om* R.
167 Maister] Mayst*er* F; þe meyster R. þo] *om* F. þis redels] his reede F.
168 wicche] no ryche F. and...þi] of he*m* F.
169 *line om* F.
170 Yeue] To ȝeve F. þee(2)] þ*o*u F. best] beest F.
171 *line om* F.
171α *vincunt*] F; *vincunt ⁊c* R.
172 a(1)] as a BoCot; as CBm. þis] þe F. a(2)] ⁊ a F. disours] disertes Cr; diners Cot.

Al þe wit of þis world and wiȝt mennes strengþe
Kan noȝt [parfournen] a pees bitwene [þe pope] and hise enemys,
Ne bitwene two cristene kynges kan no wiȝt pees make
Profitable to eiþ*er* peple;' and putte þe table fro hym,
And took Clergie and Conscience to conseil as it were
That Pacience þ[o] most passe, 'for pilgrymes konne wel lye'.
Ac Conscience carped loude and curteisliche seide,
'Frendes, fareþ wel', and faire spak to clergie,
'For I wol go wiþ þis gome, if god wol yeue me g*ra*ce,
And be Pilgrym wiþ pacience til I haue preued moore.' |
'What!' quod Clergie to Conscience, 'ar ye coueitous nouþe *fol. 76 a*
After yeresȝeues or ȝiftes, or yernen to rede redels?
I shal brynge yow a bible, a book of þe olde lawe,
And lere yow if yow like þe leeste point to knowe
That Pacience þe pilgrym parfitly knew neu*ere*.'
'Nay, by crist!' quod Conscience to Clergie, 'god þee foryelde;
For al þat Pacience me p*ro*freþ proud am I litel.
Ac þe wil of þe wye and þe wil of folk here

173 Al þe wit] For all wyttys F. and] ne RF. wiȝt] *with* C^{2}Cot; wiþ O; waytyng of F. mennes] ma*nn*ys F.
174 parfournen] conformen WHmYOC^{2}CLMR; confourme B; co*n*firme CrGF. a] *om* F. bitwene] twixe F. þe pope] HmCr^{12}GYOC^{2}CBLMRF; þat pope Cr^3; *om* (*no gap*) W. enemys] enemye CB.
175 bitwene] twene F. two] no M. kan no wiȝt] þei cu*nn*e no F.
176 eiþer] euery F. and] ⁊ þ*erwith* he F.
178 That] ⁊ leet F. Pacience] pacien C. þo] GHmCr^{23}YOC^{2}CBLR (*over erasure another ink* Hm); þow WCr^{1}M (*over erasure another ink* M); *om* F. most] forþ F. pilgrymes] pilg*ri*me F. konne] connyn HmBmBo. wel] *om* G. lye] l C.
179 Ac] but G; And HmCrC^{2}C; þan F. loude] aloude R; len*n*de C^2; wyde Hm.
180 fareþ] fare Cr. wel] all wel F.
181 yeue] gyue HmCrGOC^{2}CRF. me] the CBmBo.
182 pacience] Patient Cr^1.
183 Clergie to Conscience] Conscyense to Clergye F. ar] ⁊ C^2. ye] you G. nouþe] nowe CrG.
184 yeresȝeues] yersgyfftes G; yeresegyft Cr. or(1)] and GOC^{2}CBF. ȝiftes] gyftes CrGC. or(2)] other R. yernen] yerne GB. to] ye to CB. rede] reedy*n* F.
185 a(2)] þe best a (þe best *cancelled*) Bm.
186 And] To Y. lere] lerne GCrBF. yow like] ȝe liken RF. leeste] best GOC^{2}CB. point] lyȝne F.
187 That] *om* R. þe] þ*at* F. neuere] euere HmR.
188 to Clergie] *om* CBF. god] cryst F. foryelde] forbeede F.
189 þat] *om* F. litel] but lytle GCBmBo; but lyte F; but lithe Y; ful litil OC^2.
190 Ac] but GF; And CrC^{2}C. þe(2)] that CB; *om* M. wye] weie CotR; weyȝ F. þe(3)] ye YOC^{2}CB; *om* F. wil(2)] wille CHmBmBoLM; wull C^2; wol YCot; wolen O. of(2)] *above line* M; *om* CBLR.

Haþ meued my mood to moorne for my synnes.
The goode wil of a wight was neu*ere* bouȝt to þe fulle,
For þer [is] no tresour [þerto] to a trewe wille.
Hadde noȝt [Marie] Maudeleyne moore for a box of salue
Than ȝacheus for he seide "*dimidium bonorum meorum do pauperibus*",
And þe poore widewe [purely] for a peire of mytes
Than alle þo þat offrede into *Gaȝophilacium*?'
Thus curteisliche Conscience congeyed first þe frere,
And siþen softeliche he seide in clergies ere,
'Me were leuere, by oure lord, and I lyue sholde,
Haue pacience p*ar*fitliche þan half þi pak of bokes.'
Clergie of Conscience no congie wolde take,
But seide ful sobreliche, 'þow shalt se þe tyme
Whan þow art wery [for]walked; wille me to counseille'.
'That is sooþ', [seide] Conscience, 'so me god helpe.
If Pacience be oure partyng felawe and pryue *with* vs boþe
Ther nys wo in þis world þ*at* we ne sholde amende;
And conformen kynges to pees; and alle kynnes londes,
Sarsens and Surre, and so forþ alle þe Iewes,
Turne into þe trewe feiþ and intil oon bileue.' |
'That is sooþ', [seide] Clergie, 'I se what þow menest. *fol. 76 b*

191 Haþ] Have F. moorne] mowne G.
192 The] For þe F. a] vch a R; eu*ery* F; þe C^2. neu*ere*] nere R. þe fulle] der*e* F.
193 is] HmCrGYOC^{2}CBMF; nys WLR. þerto] BHmCrGYOC^{2}CLMRF; forsoþe W. to] vnto Hm; as to F.
194 Marie] FGR; *om* WHmCrYOC^{2}CB LM.
195 for he seide] hadde for F. *do pauperibus*] *om* Y. *do*] *da* C. *pauperibus*] *&c* M.
196 purely for] for WHmCrGYOC^{2}CB LMRF. of] *om* M.
197 offrede] offreden YHmOC^{2}CBLMRF. into] in M; gold in F.
198 curteisliche] curtessye Cr^1. congeyed] concludid F. first] *om* GOC^{2}MF. frere] Mayst*er* F.
199 softeliche] sotlyche (f *added*) Y; sothelyche GCB.
200 were] wolde F. leuere] leuer*er*e F. and] & longe F.
201 þi] this CB. pak] bak C^{2}O.
202 of] *over erasure another ink* M; to HmYOC^{2}CBL; and R; ne F.
203 seide] þei seiden F. shalt] schal B.
204 forwalked] GHmYOC^{2}CBoCotLM RF; forwalkiþ Bm; for walking Cr; of walked W. wille] wylne GYOC^{2}CBL MRF.
205 That] thys G. seide] seyde HmCrLM R; quod WGYOC^{2}CBF.
206 felawe] feere F. pryue] p*r*eue CotF.
207 nys] ne is R; is no HmGYOC^{2}CBF. wo] wrong F. ne sholde] shull yt F.
208 conformen] co*n*forme F; confirmen CrGCB. kynges] kyng C^2. and] of RF.
209 Sarsens] And sarasynes RF. and(1)] and al B; of F. Surre] surres Hm. and(2)] *om* C^2. þe] *om* R.
210 Turne] Turnen R; & turnen F. into] he*m* to F. þe] *om* CotF. til] to HmCrG MF. oon] oure BoCot; trewe F.
211 seide] quod WHmCrGYOC^{2}CBLM RF. I] *om* Hm. what] wel what F.

I shal dwelle as I do my deuoir to shewe,
And confermen fauntekyns ooþ*er* folk ylered
Til Pacience haue preued þee and parfit þee maked.'
Conscience þo wiþ Pacience passed, pilgrymes as it were.
Thanne hadde Pacience, as pilgrymes han, in his poke vitailles:
Sobretee and symple speche and sooþfast bileue,
To conforte hym and Conscience if þei come in place
There vnkyndenesse and coueitise is, hungry contrees boþe.
And as þe[i] wente by þe weye—of dowel þei carped—
Thei mette wiþ a Mynstral, as me þo þou3te.
Pacience apposed hym and preyde he sholde telle
To Conscience what craft he kouþe, and to what contree he wolde.
'I am a Mynstrall', quod þat man, 'my name is *Actiua vita.*
Al yde[l] ich hatie for of Actif is my name.
A wafrer, wol ye wite, and s*er*ue manye lordes,
[Ac] fewe robes I fonge or furrede gownes.
Couþe I lye [and] do men lau3e, þanne lacchen I sholde

212 dwelle] dwelly*n* F; do well G. shewe] shewen CrHmYOCBLMR.
213 confermen] conferme Hm; co*n*fourme*n* GR; enformen F. ooþ*er*] and ooþ*er* WHmCrGYOC^{2}CBLMRF. ylered] lered G; learned Cr; to leerne F.
214 haue] *twice* Cot; haþ HmF. preued] p*ri*ued Y; s*er*ued OC^{2}. parfit] p*ar*fy3tly F. maked] made C^{2}.
215 þo] *om* F. passed] passeden F; passiþ B. pilgrymes] pylg*ri*mage*s* Hm. it] þei GF.
216 as...poke] in his pooke pylg*ri*mes F. vitailles] vitail Cr.
217 Sobrete] Sobrietie Cr. symple] simplite (te *cancelled for* e *another script*) Y.
218 conforte] conforten MHm. hym] hem M. and] in C^{2}. if] where F. come] come*n* C^{2}F.
219 There] For F. coueitise] couetous Cr^{1}. is] be F; arn Hm; þes are G. hungry] honger R.
220 þei(1)] GHmCrYOC^{2}CBLMRF; þe W. wente] wenten OHmC^{2}RF. of] and of RF. þei(2)] þe C^{2}; *om* RF. carped] carpeden OC^{2}F.
221 mette] metten OHmC^{2}RF. as me] a mychil ma*n* he*m* F. þo] *om* BF.
222 apposed] posed Cr. hym] hy*m* F; hym þoo OC^{2}; hym first WHmCrGYCBLMR. he] hym he LMR; hy*m* F. sholde] to F. telle] tel Cr; tellen F; hem telle WGYOC BmBoLR; hym telle HmC^{2}CotM (hym *erased* M).
223 to...contree] whither Cr. to] *om* G.
224 a] *om* Cr^{1}. *Actiua*] *om* Y. *vita*] *om* HmY.
225 Al] Al maner F; And alle OC^{2}. ydel] YCrGOC^{2}CBLMR; ydelnesse WHmF. of] all Cr^{1}; *om* YOC^{2}F.
226 A] I am a F. wol] well Cr^{12}R. s*er*ue] worshepe F.
227 Ac] But F; A B; And WHmCrGYO C^{2}LMR; I C. fonge] song Cr^{1}. or] or onye F.
228 Couþe] Can Cr^{1}. and] RF; to WHm CrGYOC^{2}CBLM. lacchen] lacche CF. I(2)] su*m* y F; I ne Cr^{3}C^{2} (ne *another hand* C^{2}). sholde] wolde F.

Ouþ*er* mantel or moneie amonges lordes Mynstrals.
Ac for I kan neiþ*er* taboure ne trompe ne telle no gestes,
Farten ne fiþelen at festes ne harpen,
Iape ne Iogele ne gentilliche pipe,
Ne neiþ*er* saille ne [sautrie] ne synge wiþ þe gyt*er*ne,
I haue no goode giftes of þise grete lordes
For no breed þ*at* I brynge forþ, saue a benyson on þe sonday
Whan þe preest preieþ þe peple hir Pat*er*noster to bidde
For Piers þe Plowman and þ*at* hym p*ro*fit waiten.
And þat am I, Actif, þat ydelnesse hatie,
For alle trewe t*ra*uaill*ou*rs and tiliers of þe erþe
Fro Mighelmesse to Mighelmesse I fynde hem wiþ wafres. |
Beggeris and bidderis of my breed crauen, *fol. 77 a*
Faitours and freres and folk wiþ brode crounes.
I fynde payn for þe pope and p*ro*uendre for his palfrey,
And I hadde neu*er*e of hym, haue god my trouþe,
Neiþ*er* p*ro*uendre ne p*er*sonage yet of [þe] popes ȝifte,
Saue a pardon wiþ a peis of leed and two polles amyddes.

229 mantel] metell C^{2}. or] oþ*er* Hm. lordes] GHmCr^{23}OC^{2}CBLMR; lordes or WCr^{1}; oþere F; *om* Y.
230 Ac] but GF; And CrC^{2}C. I kan] þ*at* I am G. neiþ*er*] nougth noþ*er* Hm. ne trompe] *om* F. telle] telly*n* F. no] none MR.
231 Farten] Ne fayten F. ne(1)] nor Hm. fiþelen] fyslen Cr^{12}; fisten Cr^{3}. at] and atte Hm; at none faire F. ne(2)] *om* HmF. harpen] iapyn Hm; *om* F.
232 *line om* CB. Iape] Ne Iapen F; harpyn Hm. ne(1)] nor Hm. Iogele] iogolou*n* Hm; iangele R; Ianglyn F. pipe] pipyn Hm.
233 Ne] *om* Hm. neiþ*er*] *om* F. saille] saylen CrHm; sawtrye F. sautrie] sautre C; saute WCrGYOC^{2}BLMR; sauten Hm; saylen F. wiþ] to Cr. gyt*er*ne] harpe F. *Here* F *adds a spurious line*; *see above*, p. 223.
234 goode] *om* Cot. giftes] ieftys Hm; geestis Cot.
235 no] *om* Hm. þat] *om* F. brynge] brouȝt RF. forþ] hem F. benyson on þe] bu*nn*e a F. sonday] sonynday Hm.
236 preieþ] p*re*chiþ BC. hir] þe theyr G; þe CrF. bidde] saie Cr.
237 Piers] pier C. þ*at*] þo þat B; all F.
238 þat(1)] for F. am I] I am GYOC^{2}CBR; me F. þat(2)] ⁊ G; also þat F. ydelnesse hatie] haate al ydelnesse F. hatie] hateth HmC^{2}.
239 For] ⁊ for F; Of R. t*ra*uaill*ou*rs... tiliers] tylyeris ⁊ t*ra*uayloures F. of] on MF. þe] *om* HmGYOC^{2}CBF.
240 Fro] for GY. to] tyl F. I... wafres] þo me*n* t*ra*uaile sore F. hem] hym BmBo. wiþ] BHmGYCLR; wiþ my WCrM (*above line another ink* M); *om* OC^{2}.
241 Beggeris] Boþe beggerys F; Bieggeris Bm. bidderis] bilderis B.
242 Faitours... freres] ⁊ Freris ⁊ Faytoures F.
243 p*ro*uendre] p*ro*uende BmBo.
244 I hadde] ȝit hadde I F.
245 p*ro*uendre] p*re*bendre Y; prebend G; p*er*sonage F. p*er*sonage] p*ro*vendre F. yet] *om* F. þe] HmCrYOC^{2}CBLMRF; *om* WG. ȝifte] yiftes YR.
246 a(2)] *om* C^{2}. peis] piece Cr; pece G; plu*m* F. amyddes] In þe myddes G.

Hadde ich a clerc þat couþe write I wolde caste hym a bille
That he sente me vnder his seel a salue for þe pestilence,
And þat his blessynge and hise bulles bocches myȝte destruye:
In nomine meo demonia e[j]icient & super egros manus imponent & bene habebunt.
And þanne wolde I be prest to þe peple paast for to make,
And buxom and busy aboute breed and drynke
For hym and for alle hise, founde I þat his pardoun
Miȝte lechen a man as [me þynkeþ] it sholde.
For siþ he haþ þe power þat Peter hadde he haþ þe pot wiþ þe salue:
Argentum & aurum non est michi; quod autem habeo tibi do; in nomine domini surge et amb[ula].
Ac if myȝt of myracle hym faille it is for men ben noȝt worþi
To haue þe grace of god, and no gilt of [þe] pope.
For may no blessynge doon vs boote but if we wile amende,
Ne mannes masse make pees among cristene peple
Til pride be pureliche fordo, and [þat] þoruȝ payn defaute.

247 Hadde] hade *corrected from* hate G; I wolde F. ich a] iche a O; eche a GC; euery F. clerc] clere G. I wolde] I wol Y; hadd F. caste] castyn Hm. bille] bulle M.
248 That...vnder] þat þe Pope wolde seendyn F. sente] sent Cr^{12}CLR; sende B; send G.
249 And] *om* RF. þat] *om* B. his] *om* C^{2}. blessynge] blessinges M. bocches myȝte] myȝte bocches OC^{2}. myȝte] myghten Hm Bm; mȝte R. destruye] distroyen F.
249α *demonia*] *demonis* Y. *ejicient*] *eiicient* Cr; *eicient* WHmGYOC^{2}CBMRF; *eiciunt* L. &(1)] *om* HmM. *habebunt*] *habebunt &c* GYC; ? *cropped* W.
250 And] *om* F. be] *om* F. prest] priest Cr^{1}; prs F. to þe peple] *om* Cot. þe] *om* HmL. for] *om* Cr^{23}.
251 aboute] also abowtyn F; be aboute B. and(2)] or Cot.
252 for] *om* HmC^{2}. founde...his] to fyȝnden swich a F.
253 Miȝte] Miȝten B; þat myghte F. lechen] leche Cot. me þynkeþ] I bileue WHmCrGYOC^{2}CCotLMRF; bileue Bm Bo. it] he F; *om* OC^{2}.
254 *as two lines divided after* hadde WHm Cr^{1}GYOC^{2}CBLMRF, *after* selfe Cr^{23}. he(1)] þe Pope F. haþ(1)] hadde M. þe(1)] *om* F. þat Peter] as seynt F. hadde] F; hymself hadde WHmCr^{1}GYOC^{2}CBLM R; had hymselfe Cr^{23}. salue] salue sooþly as me þynkeþ WHmCr^{1}GYOC^{2}CBLM RF; truly as me thinketh Cr^{23}.
254α *Argentum & aurum*] *aurum & argentum* Cot. *autem*] *om* Cr^{23}. *tibi*] *hoc tibi* OC^{2} CotRF. *in...domini*] *om* OC^{2}. *ambula*] CrGYOC^{2}CLMRF; *ambula &c* HmB; amb (*cropped*) W.
255 Ac] but GF; And CrC^{2}C. myȝt of] I myghtte of a Cot; *om* F. hym] *om* G. it ...men] to men þat F. worþi] worth Cr.
256 þe(1)] no RF; *om* Cr. and no gilt] to gete gryþ F. þe(2)] YHmCrGOC^{2}CBL MRF; *om* W.
257 For] þere F; *om* R. doon] dos C. if] *om* F. wile] wolen OC^{2}B. amende] amende vs F.
258 Ne...masse] Ther may no man Cr; Ne no myscheef F.
259 pureliche] puirlicle Bm; priueliche RF. and] *om* F. þat] HmGYOC^{2}CBL; alle R; *om* WCrMF. payn] paynes F.

For er I haue breed of mele ofte moot I swete,
And er þe co*mm*une haue corn ynouȝ many a cold morwenyng;
So er my wafres be ywroȝt muche wo I þolye.
Al londou*n*, I leue, likeþ wel my wafres,
And louren whan þei lakken hem; it is noȝt longe ypassed
There was a careful co*mm*une whan no cart com to towne
Wiþ [bake] breed fro Stratford; þo gonnen beggeris wepe |
And werkmen were agast a lite; þis wole be þouȝt
  longe: *fol.* 77 *b*
In þe date of oure driȝte, in a drye Aprill,
A thousand and þre hundred, twies [þritty] and ten,
My wafres were gesene whan Chichestre was Mair*e*.'
I took [greet] kepe, by crist! and Conscience boþe,
Of haukyn þe Actif man and how he was ycloþed.
He hadde a cote of cristendom as holy kirke bileueþ.
Ac it was moled in many places wiþ manye sondry plottes,
Of pride here a plot, and þ*ere* a plot of vnbuxom speche,

260 *line om* B. For] *om* Hm. of] a Cr; or G. ofte] of Cr; efte Hm; erst GYOC^{2}C; mychil F. moot] most GF.
261 þe] þei G. co*mm*une] com*m*onnys F; come G. corn ynouȝ] hoom here corn is F. a] *om* CrGYOC^{2}CB. morwenyng] morwe F; mornynges G.
262 So] *om* F. wafres] wafreres F. ywroȝt] wrought CrGYOC^{2}CBF. muche] mychel F.
263 Al] Ac Hm. I] as y F.
264 *as two lines divided after* wantyn F; *line om* CB. And...hem] & þey þat lakke hem lowren for largyte þey wanty*n* F. louren] loure Cr. lakken] lacke Cr. hem] it Hm GYLM; *om* OC^2. is] was F. ypassed] passed CrHmGYOC^2; ypassed lewed me*n* wery*n* needy F.
265 was] is Cot. co*mm*une] comou*n*te F.
266 bake] RF; *om* WHmCrGYOC^{2}CBL M. Stratford] stretforth L; statforde R. þo] then G. gonnen] gan Cr^{23}HmGLRF.
267 were] weren OBmBo; were so F. a lite] a litel YHmCrGOC^{2}CBLMR; *om* F. þis] it F. wole] wel R; *om* F. longe] on longe B; on longe aft*er* F.
268 þe] *om* Cr. driȝte] dryȝtne Hm; dryghten F. Aprill] apparel Cot.
269 twies...ten] syxty and nyne (*over erasure another hand and ink*) Hm. twies] thries (hri *over erasure another ink*) M; ȝeer & two & F. þritty] thretty LR; twenty WCrGYOC^{2}CBMF.
270 were] GC; weren YOC^{2}B; were þ*ere* HmF; þ*ere* were WCrLMR. gesene] gefene Bo; gyue Cot. Chichestre... Mair*e*] *our* meyȝr Chychest*re* F. was] were R.
271 greet kepe] keep good Hm. greet] grete RF; good WCrGYOC^{2}CBLM. by crist] of pacyense be *cri* F. and] & of F.
272 Of] how F. haukyn] Hankyn Cr. he] þ*at* he G. ycloþed] clothed CrGYOC^2 CB.
273 a] on a F. cote] cyte GCBmBo; syȝt Cot. kirke] chirche YHmGOC^{2}CBF.
274 Ac] but GF; And CrYC^{2}C. places] place R. wiþ manye] fele F. plottes] spottys HmF (sp *over erasure* Hm).
275 here] he R; was þ*ere* F. plot...plot] spoot & F. plot(*both*)] spot (sp *over erasure*) Hm.

Of scornyng and of scoffyng and of vnskilful berynge;
As in apparaill and in porte proud amonges þe peple;
Ooþerwise þan he haþ wiþ herte or siȝte shewynge hym;
Willyng þat alle men wende he were þat he is noȝt,
Forwhy he bosteþ and braggeþ wiþ manye bolde oþes;
And inobedient to ben vndernome of any lif lyuynge;
And so singuler by hymself [as to siȝte of þe peple
Was noon swich as hymself], ne [noon] so po[pe] holy;
Yhabited as an heremyte, an ordre by hymselue,
Religion saunȝ rule [and] resonable obedience;
Lakkynge lettrede men and lewed men boþe;
In likynge of lele lif and a liere in soule;
Wiþ Inwit and wiþ outwit ymagynen and studie
As best for his body be to haue a [bold] name;
And entremetten hym ouer al þer he haþ noȝt to doone;

276 scornyng] schorning Cr^1; skorny*nges* F. and(1)] *om* F. of(1)] of of Hm. scoffyng] schoffinge Cr^1; skoffyngis F. vnskilful] vnskeful Cot.

277 in(1)] of F. and in porte] peyntyd ⁊ F. porte] power Cr^1.

278, 279 *divided after* shewynge WHmCrGYOC^{2}CBLMRF.

278 wise] wayes G. he] HmCrGYOC^{2}CBLMRF; he hym W. wiþ] wit Bm; wytt BoCot; *om* F. herte] herd F. or] and R; *om* F. siȝte] seyd F; eyghe GYOC^{2}CB. shewynge] shewings Cr^1; m*er*veyles F.

279 Willyng] wilnynge R; weny*ng*e F. wende] wenden OC^2. þat...noȝt] most myghty F. he(2)] *om* Cr^1.

280 why] thy G. bosteþ...braggeþ] bosted and bragged C. manye] fele F. bolde] greate G.

281 And] And is Cr. inobedient] vnobedie*nt* Cr; looþ F. ben] *om* G.

282 *run together with* 283 WHmCrGYOC^{2}CBM. so] HmGYOC^{2}CBLMR; noon so WCr; goo F. hym] my Cot. as... peple] as to syȝte of þe poeple LRF; *om* WHmCrGYOC^{2}CBM. as to] in F.

283 Was...self] Was none suche as hymself LRF; *om* WHmCrGYOC^{2}CBM. Was] þat þere is F. hymself] he ys F. ne] nor Cr; *om* Hm. noon] HmGYOC^{2}CBLMRF; *om* WCr. pope] CrGR; poppe OYC^{2}CBF; poup (p(2) *over erasure another ink*) M; pomp WHmL.

284 Yhabited] habytyd G; In habite Cr^{23}OC^{2}BoCot; For he is enhabyȝtid F; Hated Cr^1. as] lyȝk F. an(2)] and CF. ordre] ordred F. hym] hem HmM. selue] seluen M.

285 Religion saunȝ] But religiou*n* is saved be F. and] HmCrGYOC^{2}CBLMR; ⁊ be F; or W. resonable] vnreasonable Cr. obedience] obediente Y.

286 Lakkynge] Lacked CrCot; It is lakky*ng* to F. lettrede] lewid F. lewed] to lered F.

287 likynge] liknyng OC^2; lyknesse F. of] it is a F. lele] lely Cr^{23}. in] to his F.

288 Wiþ] Boþe w*ith* F; *om* B. wiþ] *om* CrRF. ymagynen] ymagyne B; ymageny*n*g G; he ymageneþ F. studie] studien OC^{2}M; stodyeþ F.

289 haue] ber*e* F. bold] FR; badde WHmCrGYOC^{2}CBLM.

290 And] ⁊ to F. entremetten] entermete OC^{2}F; entermentyn HmBm; entremetyng Y. hym] *om* Hm. noȝt] nouȝ C; nothyng G. to] do Bo; a G.

Willynge þat men wende his wit were þe beste,
[Or for his crafty konnynge or of clerkes þe wisest,
Or strengest on stede, or styuest vnder girdel,
And louelokest to loken on and lelest of werkes,
And noon so holy as he ne of lif clennere,
Or feirest of feitures of forme and of shafte,
And most sotil of song oþer sleyest of hondes,
And large to lene, [loos] þerby to cacche].
And if he gyueþ ou3t to pouere gomes, telle what he deleþ;
Pouere of possession in purs and in cofre;
And as a lyoun on to loke and lordlich of speche;
Boldest of beggeris; a bostere þat no3t haþ,
In towne and in Tauernes tales to telle
And segge þyng þat he neuere sei3 and for soþe sweren it;
Of dedes þat he neuere dide demen and bosten;
And of werkes þat he wel dide witnesse and siggen,
'Lo! if ye leue me no3t, or þat I lye wenen, |
Askeþ at hym or at hym and he yow kan telle *fol.* 78 *a*
What I suffrede and sei3 and somtymes hadde,
And what I kouþe and knew and what kyn I com of'.

291 Willynge] wylnynge HmCrGOC^{2}LM R. wende] wendy*n* F; wolde Hm.
292–8 RF; *lines om* WHmCrGYOC^{2}CBL M; *here in the spelling of* W.
292 or] *om* F. þe] he were þe F.
293 vnder] gyrt *with* F.
294 louelokest] lowlyest F.
295 ne] ne non F.
296 forme...shafte] face ne of forme F.
297 And] Or F. oþer] or F.
298 Or looþ for to leene & large for to cacche F. loos] losse R.
299 gyueþ] giue CrOC^2; 3yueþ Hm; yeue MF (y *over erasure* M). ou3t] *om* F. to] to þe G; the CB; *om* LR. gomes] me*n* to F. telle] telleþ OC^{2}B; til C. deleþ] delte F.
300 *line om* F. of] yn GCot. in(2)] *om* B. cofre] coffre LR; cofre boþe WHmCrM; cofers bothe GYOC^{2}CB.
301 on] vppon B; *om* RF. loke] looken on F. lordlich] loueliche Y.
302 Boldest] & boldest F. a...haþ] boostynge at þe nale F. a] as a B.
303 towne] townes G. in] *om* Cot. telle] tellyn F.
304 segge] saies C. þyng] thynge*s* G. þat] *om* F. neuere sei3] sygh neuer G. sei3] ysey3 F; er sawe C. for] for a HmM (a *above line another ink* M). sweren] swere CrGF.
305 *run together with* 306 M. þat] *om* F. demen...bosten] *om* M. demen] to demen F; demeþ B (þ *over erasure* Bm). bosten] boste R; posteþ B.
306 And...dide] *om* M. þat] *om* F. witnesse] seggen G. siggen] segge OC^2; syngyn Hm; tellyn F; wyttnessen G.
307 ye] þou GYOC^{2}CB. me] *om* F. or] *om* F. wenen] wene OC^2; 3e wenen HmB; 3ee wene F; wenest G.
308 Askeþ] Aske CrG; Goo aske F. at(*both*)] *om* F. hym(2)] hire F. yow] the Cr.
309 What] whan C. and...and] or seyde or what y F. tymes] tyme HmCF.
310 *in margin main hand* G. And(1 *and* 2)] Or F. knew] knowe C. and(3)] or of F.

Al he wolde þat men wiste of werkes and wordes
Which myȝte plese þe peple and preisen hymselue:
Si hominibus placerem christi seruus non essem; Et alibi, Nemo potest duobus dominis seruire.
'By crist!' quod Conscience þo, 'þi beste cote, Haukyn,
Haþ manye moles and spottes; it moste ben ywasshe.'
'Ye, whoso toke hede', quod haukyn, 'bihynde and bifore,
What on bak, and what on body half, and by þe two sides
Men sholde fynde manye frounces and manye foule plottes.'
And he torned hym as tyd and þanne took I hede;
It was fouler bi fele fold þan it first semed.
It was bidropped wiþ wraþe and wikkede wille,
Wiþ enuye and yuel speche entisynge to fighte,
Lyinge and la[kk]ynge and leue tonge to chide;
Al þat he wiste wikked by any wight tellen it,
And blame men bihynde hir bak and bidden hem meschaunce;
And þat he wiste by wille [to watte tellen it],
And þat [by] watte [he] wiste wille wiste it after,

311 wiste] wisten OC^{2}. and] RF; and of WHmCrGYOC^{2}CBLM.
312 Which] Swiche F. myȝte] mygthen Hm; talis F. and] wan he F. preisen] prayse Cr; preyseþ F. hym] hem OC^{2}CR. selue] seluen YOC^{2}CLMR.
312α *in margin* O. *essem*] *essem &c* Y. *seruire*] *seruire &c* OC^{2}CBmBo.
313 beste cote] corteby F. Haukyn] Hankyn Cr.
314 it] and B. moste] wold G. ywasshe] ywasshen GYOC^{2}CB; waschen RCr.
315 Ye...toke] who takþ F. toke] take Cr^{2}. hede] kepe G. haukyn] Hankyn Cr.
316 and(1)] *om* CM. what] *om* GOC^{2}RF. half] *om* GYOC^{2}CB. by þe two] on bothe F.
317 sholde] schulden OHmC^{2}. manye (*both*)] fele F. frounces] fowle sides Cr^{1}. plottes] plettes Y; spottys F.
318 And] & þerwith F. as] all so HmB. took I] y took F.
319 *in margin main hand* G. It] þat yt F. bi] *om* Hm. þan] that G.
320 bidropped] bitropped Y. and] & with F.
321 enuye...entisynge] evil speche & envye & excitynge F. enuye] enenye R. yuel] yuel wicked OC^{2} (yuel *above line main hand* O). speche] wyll G.
322 Lyinge] with lyenge F; lyuyng Y. and(1)] or R. lakkynge] FR; laughynge WHmCrGYOC^{2}CBLM. and(2)] a R; & with a F; and a (a *above line main ink*) G. chide] chiden BmBo; chidyng Cot.
323 Al] & al F; Al the C. wikked] *om* F. tellen it] tell ytt G; it telle Hm; to tellen it BM; wykkydly out it telle F.
324 blame] blamen Hm. men] me Y. bihynde] byende G. bak] backes G. bidden] bidde OGYC^{2}CBF. hem] hym BmBo.
325 wiste by] *om* (*corrected to* wiste of) Cot. wille] willyem F. to...it] tellyn it to watte HmCrBmBoR; telle it to watte OC^{2}Cot; tellen it watte WGYCLM; to tellyn yt to walter F.
326 þat] al þat F. by...he] he of walter F; watte WHmCrGYOC^{2}CBLMR. wille] willyem F. after] soone F.

And made of frendes foes þoruȝ a fals tonge.
'Or wiþ myȝt [of] mouþ or þoruȝ m[a]nnes strengþe
Auenge me fele tymes, oþer frete myselue wiþInne;
As a shepsteres shere ysherewed [myn euencristen]:
Cuius malediccione os plenum est ⁊ amaritudine; sub lingua eius labor et dol[or]; Et alibi, Filij hominum dentes eorum arma ⁊ sagitte et lingua eorum gladius a[cutus].
Ther is no lif þat me loueþ lastynge any while. |
For tales þat I telle no man trusteþ to me. *fol. 78 b*
And whan I may noȝt haue þe maistrie [wiþ] malencolie Itake,
That I cacche þe crampe, þe Cardiacle som tyme,
Or an Ague in swich an Angre and som tyme a Feu*ere*
That takeþ me al a tweluemonþe, til þat I despise
Lechecraft of oure lord and leue on a wicche,
And seye þat no clerc ne kan, ne crist as I leue,
To þe Sout*ere* of Southwerk or of Shordych dame Emme;
[For] goddes word [ne grace] gaf me neu*ere* boote,

327 And] Also he F. of] *om* BF. a] his F.
328 wiþ] with (h *erased*) Y; þoru F. myȝt] *om* Y. of] HmCrYOC^{2}CBLMRF; or G; or wit*h* W. þoruȝ] wit*h* G. mannes] GCrYOC^{2}CBLMRF; mennes WHm.
329 *divided from* 330 *after* selue WHmCr GYOC^{2}CBLMRF. Auenge] Auenged R; ⁊ but y avenge F. oþer] or G; evele y F. wiþInne] *om* F.
330 As] As dooþ F. a] *om* Cot. shepsteres] shepster GYCLR; shepperis F. ysherewed] in sherwid Cot; In shrewid Bo; so shrewidly F. myn euencristen] me*n* ⁊ cursed CrGYOC^{2}CBLMR; men and cursyd hem Hm; man and cursed W; y grynte F.
330α ⁊(1)] *om* R. *amaritudine*] *amaritudo* G. *sub*] ⁊ *dolo sub* F. *labor et dolor*] ⁊*c* GYOC^{2}CB. *dolor*] HmCrLMRF; dol (*cropped*) W. *Et...acutus*] *om* RF. *et*(2)... *acutus*] ⁊*c* OC^2. *acutus*] CrGYCBLM; *acutus* ⁊*c* Hm; a (*cropped*) W.
331 þat] *om* F. me loueþ] y loue HmGY OC^{2}CBLMR; y leve F. lastynge] will leste me F.
332 trusteþ] trust Y; t*r*istneþ F.
333 may...haue] have not F. wiþ] OGYC^{2}CBL; which R; swich WHmCrMF (*over erasure another ink* HmM).
334 That] ⁊ þat sone F. crampe] crappe C^2. þe(2)] the HmCrGYOC^{2}CLMR; and þe WBF. Cardiacle] cardiache Bm. som tyme] aft*er* F.
335 Ague] angue HmY. in...an] for F. an Angre] a manere Hm. som...a] þ*er*with an hoot F.
336 That] and G. takeþ] heldeþ Hm; it holdiþ B. al] *om* F.
337 of] be F; or LR. leue] beleve F; take me G. on] of Cr; to G.
338 And] þat F. seye] seyþ F; seggeþ OC^2. ne(1)] *om* GF. ne(2)] by F. leue] beleve F.
339 To þe] As doþ F. Soutere] sortry Cr. or] ⁊ OC^2; *om* G. Shordych] short dytch Cr; sordich OC^{2}F; shrodiche Cot. Emme] enuye Cot.
340 For] þey seyn þat F; and sugge that Hm; And seye þat no WCrGYCLMR; And seggeþ þat no OC^2; And seie þat none of B. goddes] goodis C^{2}C (*corrected* C). word] wordes YCot (*above line another hand* Cot); *om* BmBo. ne...gaf] gaf WHmCrGYOC^{2}CLMRF; ȝauen B. me] *om* B.

But þoruȝ a charme hadde I chaunce and my chief heele.'
I waitede wisloker and þanne was it soilled
Wiþ likynge of lecherie as by lokynge of his eiȝe.
For ech a maide þ*a*t he mette he made hire a signe
Semynge to synneward, and som he gan taste
Aboute þe mouþ, or byneþe bigynneþ to grope,
Til eiþ*er*es wille wexeþ kene and to þe werke yeden,
As wel fastyng dayes [as] Fridaies [and] forboden nyȝtes,
And as [lef] in lente as out of lente, alle tymes yliche.
Swiche werkes *with* hem were neu*er*e out of seson
Til þei myȝte na moore; and þanne [hadde] murye tales,
And how þ*a*t lecchours louye laughen and Iapen,
And of hir harlotrye and horedom in hir elde tellen.
Thanne Pacience p*ar*ceyued of pointes [his] cote
[Was] colomy þoruȝ coueitise and vnkynde desiryng.

341 hadde I] he hadde F. chaunce...heele] hele ⁊ of þe feue*re* bote (bote *over erasure another ink*) Hm. my] many Cr; his F.
342 wisloker] wislykor*e* F; bisiloker YOC^{2}CB; more busyly G. and] on hy*m* ⁊ F; aboute ⁊ Y. þanne] that C. was] what Cot; *om* C. it] I R; he F; *om* Cot.
343 likynge...as] lykyngeryȝe F. as] and HmGYOC^{2}CBR. by] *with* F; *om* GBo Cot. lokynge] lokyngis F. of] *with* F. his] myn RF. eiȝe] eighen MF; eyght Cr^{3}.
344 ech] eu*er*y F. a(1)] *om* GF. maide] mayden OC^{2}. he(*both*)] y F. hire] swich F. a(2)] to Cr; *om* F. signe] syghnes F.
345 som] su*m*me F; som tyme WHmCr GYOC^{2}CBLMR. he] y F. taste] ataste F.
346 Aboute þe] Mowþ *with* F. bigynneþ] he gynneth Y; p*ri*uyly ga*n* hire F. to] *om* F. grope] croppe Cr^{1}.
347 eiþ*er*es] either YGOC^{2}C. wexeþ] wexet C^{2}; wexe FG. to þe] þan to F. yeden] ȝede Hm; wenty*n* F.
348 wel] RF; wel in WCr^{23}GYOC^{2}CBL; well on HmCr^{1}; woll in M. fastyng] fastynges Cr^{1}. dayes] day F; *om* Cr^{1}. as] GYOC^{2}CB; and WHmCrLMRF. Fridaies] fryday F. and] ⁊ HmCrYOC^{2} CBLMRF; ⁊ other G; as W. forboden] forbode YHmRF.
349 And] *om* GYF. as(1)] also B. lef] RF; wel WHmCrGYOC^{2}CBLM. lente(1)] lenten CBmBoF. of lente] of lenten CBmBo; ⁊ F.
350 hem] hym C; me ⁊ he*m* F. were] weren O; was L.
351 myȝte] myȝten OHmC^{2}B. and þanne] do but F. hadde] GYC^{2}CLMR; hadde*n* OB; helde it F; *om* WHmCr. tales] talky*n*g F.
352 And] *om* F. lecchours] lechoure Cr^{12}; lecherous GYC^{2}CBmCot; leccherous me*n* F. louye] louyen HmCrGYOCBLMR; leue*n* C^{2}; love wel *with* F. laughen] laughtyn Hm; lawynge F. Iapen] Iapeng C; Iapis F.
353 And of] Or R. hir(1)] *om* RF. and] ⁊ of F. in] and in R. hir(2)] *om* F. elde] age Cr. tellen] þey have burde F.
354 of] þe F. his] LR; off hys GYOC^{2}CB MF (of *above line* M); of þis WHmCr.
355 Was] HmCrGYOC^{2}CBLRF; were (ere *over erasure*) M; That were W. colomy] colmy C^{2}Cr^{23}OBLR; comely Hm; cru*m*plyd F. coueitise] couetouse Cr^{23}. and] *with* F. vnkynde] vkynde L. desiryng] desyre G.

Moore to good þan to god þe gome his loue caste,
And ymagynede how he it myȝte haue
[Thoruȝ] false mesures and met, and wiþ fals witnesse;
Lened for loue of þe wed and looþ to do truþe;
And awaited þoruȝ [wittes wyes] to bigile;
And menged his marchaundise and made a good moustre:
'The worste *with*Inne was; a greet wit I let it.
And if my Neghebore hadde a[n] hyne or any beest ellis |
Moore p*ro*fitable þan myn, manye sleiȝtes I made. *fol.* 79 *a*
How I myȝte haue it al my wit I caste,
And but I hadde by ooþ*er* wey at þe laste I stale it,
Or pryueliche his purs shook, vnpikede hise lokes.
Or by nyȝte or by daye aboute was ich eu*ere*
Thoruȝ gile to gaderen þe good þat ich haue.
If I yede to þe Plowȝ I pynched so narwe
That a foot lond or a forow fecchen I wolde
Of my nexte Neghebore, nymen of his erþe;
And if I r[o]pe ouerreche, or yaf hem reed þat ropen

357 how] nyght ⁊ day how F. it myȝte] myghte it F. it] it beste Y.
358 Thoruȝ] Wiþ WHmCrGYOC^{2}CBLMRF. mesures] mesure OC^{2}. and (1)] ⁊ false F. wiþ] eek *with* F. witnesse] wyghtes Cr^{1}; weights Cr^{23}.
359 Lened] ⁊ leenede F; Leued Cr^{3}; louede C^{2}. for] it for YOC^{2}.
360 And] And I OC^{2}. awaited] awayte Cr; waytid BF. þoruȝ] yn Hm; bi Cr. wittes] whit*us* R; his wit F; wyche GC^{2}; which WHmCrYOCBLM. wyes] fele wyȝes F; wey*us* R; weye HmOC^{2}BM; wey WYL; waye Cr^{13}; way Cr^{2}GC. to] his neyhbo*urs* to Hm; he myght CrM (*over erasure another ink* M); he myȝte best B.
361 marchaundise] merchadyȝes G. made] make BmBo (*corrected* Bm). good] fayr F. moustre] maistry Cr.
362 The] ⁊ þe F. worste] wors OC^{2}. a] ystuffyd a Hm; *om* OC^{2}. I let] he held F.
363 if] *om* GYOC^{2}C. hadde] have F. an] RF; any WHmCrGYOC^{2}CBLM. hyne] hynde CrG. any...ellis] ell*es* eny beest Hm.
364 manye] *om* Cot. made] maake F.
365 haue] wynne F. al] and all Hm.
366 but] but if CrR. hadde] GCrOC^{2}CBR; it hadde WLM; hadde it HmY; gete yt F. ooþer] anoþer B; ony F. at...it] y geete it be stelthe F. þe] *om* Cr^{3}. laste] lest Cr^{12}C.
367 shook] y shook F; scoke C^{2}. vnpikede] OHmCrGYC^{2}CBLMR; or y vnpykede F; and vnpikede W.
368 Or] Other R; Eyþ*er* F. or] other R. aboute] aboutyn Hm. was] harm was F. euere] neuere (*corrected another hand*) C^{2}.
369 gile] gele Cr^{2}. gaderen] geddre G. good] goodes Cr^{3}F. haue] welde F.
370 If] For if F. pynched] picched C; pikid BoCot; pichik Bm.
371 or] ou*er* F. fecchen] fetche Cr^{1}R.
372 *run together with* 373 RF. nymen... erþe] *om* RF. nymen] GHmCrYOC^{2}CBLM; and nymen W.
373 And...reche] *om* RF. I] *om* L. rope] CLM; repe WHmCrGYOC^{2}; repie Bm; ripye BoCot. ouer] y ou*er* HmB. reche] rechen Cr. or...þat] whan y sholde F. or] ⁊ GOC^{2}. yaf] ȝeue *over erasure another ink* Hm. ropen] rope OC^{2}; repen CrYBoCotR; repen it F.

To seise to me wiþ hir sikel þat I sew neu*er*e.
And [what body] borwed of me abouȝte þe tyme
Wiþ p*re*sentes pryuely, or paide som c*er*teyn;
So, [wolde he] or noȝt wolde, wynnen I wolde.
And boþe to kiþ and to kyn vnkynde of þat ich hadde;
And whoso cheped my chaffare, chiden I wolde
But he p*ro*frede to paie a peny or tweyne
Moore þan it was worþ, and yet wolde I swere
That it coste me muche moore; swoor manye oþes.
[I]n haly daies at holy chirche whan ich herde masse
Hadde I neu*er*e wille, woot god, witterly to biseche
Mercy for my mysdedes, þ*at* I ne moorned moore
For losse of good, leue me, þan for likames giltes;
As if I hadde dedly synne doon I dredde noȝt þat so soore
As whan I lened and leued it lost or longe er it were paied.
So if I kidde any kyndenesse myn euencristen to helpe
Vpon a cruwel coueitise m[y conscience] gan hange.

374 To] And CrGYOC^{2}CBM. seise] seysed B. to] *om* HmF (? *erased* Hm). hir] my GYOC^{2}CB. þat] þe wiche F. I] CrGOC^{2}BoCotF; I ne WHmYCBmLMR (ne *cancelled* Bm). sew] sewed Cr.
375 what body] whoso WHmCrYOC^{2}CB LMR; who wolde F; wo G. borwed] borweþ HmGYOC^{2}CBL; borwe F. of me] at me M; Monee F. abouȝte] aboute GCr^{3}LR; he bouȝte B (he *and* ȝ *added later* Bm); tyl a serte*yn* F. þe] *om* F.
376 he muste legge pleggys of heuyere peyȝs ⁊ p*ri*uy presentis F. presentes] p*re*sent CB. paide] paye Cr^3.
377 wolde he] HmCrGYOC^{2}CBLMR; he wolde W; wheyþ*er* he wolde F. noȝt wolde] nouht wolde he HmCr^{1}LM; would he not Cr^{23}; he nolde YGOC^{2}CBmBoF; nolde he Cot. wynnen] wynne GYCB. wolde(2)] nolde (*corrected in margin another hand*) Y.
379 so] þ*at* F. cheped] cheypythe G; cleped Y. my] of my C^2. wolde] wolden B.
380 to] me to HmGYOC^{2}CB. paie] peyȝen F.
381 swere] swer*e* faste F.
382 coste] costid Cot. me] *om* RF. muche] mychil F. swoor] swore CrGYCLR; y swoor HmF; swor I (I *over erasure of final* e) M; ⁊ swore OC^{2}B; and so swoor W.
383 In] HmCrGYOC^{2}CBLMR; ⁊ in F; On W. haly] *om* Y. at] yn GOC^{2}F; and YCB. herde] here OC^2; shold her*e* F.
384 Hadde I] I had G; Hadde LR. woot god] god wote HmBF. to biseche] god bysechen F.
385 Mercy] Ne aske m*er*cy F. for] of Cr. mysdedes] myse F. I] *om* Y. moore] sore Cr^3.
386 losse] loste Cr^{1}Cot; leesynge F. good ...me] my*n* goodys F. me] thu me Hm. for] fore R; for my WHmCrGYOC^{2}CBL MF. likames] likam Cr; Foule C^2. giltes] gylte GYCBF.
387 As] And Cr^{23}GCB. if] whan F. dedly...doon] do dedly sy*n*ne F. dredde] drede HmCrGYOC^{2}CB; dred L. noȝt þat] þat noȝt BoCot.
388 As] And Cr^{1}G. lened] haue lent it B; *om* Y. and] good ⁊ F; I G; *om* YOC^{2}C. leued it lost] lost it F; is lost BmBo; his lost Cot. were] be B.
389 So] ⁊ F.
390 a] *om* OC^2. my conscience] my consience RF; myn herte WHmCrGYOC^{2}CB LM. gan] bygan to Hm. hange] hangen MF.

And if I sente ouer see my seruaunt3 to Brugges,
Or into Prucelond my Prentis my p*ro*fit to waiten, |
To marchaunden wiþ [my] moneie and maken [here] eschaunges, *fol. 79 b*
Mi3te neu*ere* me conforte in þe mene [tyme]
Neiþ*er* masse ne matynes, ne none maner si3tes;
Ne neu*ere* penaunce p*ar*fou*r*nede ne Pat*er*noster seide
That my mynde ne was moore on my good in a doute
Than in þe g*ra*ce of god and hise grete helpes:
Vbi thesaurus tuus ibi & cor tuum.'
[Yet glotoun wiþ grete oþes his [garnement] hadde soiled
And foule beflobered it, as wiþ fals speche,
As þere no nede was goddes name an Idel;
Swoor þerby swiþe ofte and al biswatte his cote;
And moore mete eet and dronk þan kynde my3te defie,
'And kau3te siknesse somtyme for my [surfetes] ofte
And þanne I dradde to deye in dedlich synne',
That into wanhope he [worþ] and wende nau3t to be saued.
The whiche is sleuþe so slow þat may no slei3tes helpe it,

391 if] *om* OC^{2}. see] þe see HmGF. my] ony F. seruaunt3] seruaunt BF. Brugges] burduwes Cot.
392 Prucelond] spruce land GCCot; sprws F. waiten] wayte HmRF; awayte G.
393 marchaunden] Marchaunte F; m*er*chandye G; marchaunde in Cr^{1}; marchaundisen B. wiþ] *om* F. my] F; *om* WHmCrGY OC^{2}CBLMR. and] or to F. maken] make HmCrGYOC^{2}CB. here] BmBoR; her HmCrOC^{2}L; hire WCotM; hir YC; þ*er* G; *om* F. eschaunges] chaunges RF.
394 neu*ere*] nere R. me conforte] thyng conforte me HmF (*over erasure* Hm). me] man me G. conforte] conforten Cr. tyme] GYOC^{2}CBLMRF; while WHmCr.
395 masse] messis F. maner] nother G. si3tes] shytes R.
396 neu*ere*] neither Cr^{23}; *om* F. *parfour*-nede] *par*forme F. seide] byddyn F.
397 That] Tha C. ne was] was Cr^{1}F; nas M. on] in R; In a dowte on (In a dowte *cancelled*) G. a] *om* GOC^{2}F.
398 and] and yn HmCrG; or in F. grete] goode F. helpes] helpe Cr; halwis F.
398α *in margin* OC^{2}. *Vbi*] *Vbi est* CotR. &] *est &* Cot; *om* Cr^{1}. *tuum*] *tuum &c* HmGB; *tuum est* F.
399–408 RF; *lines om* WHmCrGYOC^{2}CB LM; *here in the spelling of* W.
399 glotoun] þat goome F. garnement] garnem*en*t F; granement R. hadde] was F.
400 as] al F.
401 As] & F. was] F; ne was R. goddes... Idel] ne*m*pnede god ydellyche F.
402 Swoor] & swoor F. and...cote] abowte þe ale cuppe F.
403 And] & ofte F. mete] *om* F.
404 kau3te...tyme] su*m*tyme kawte seknesse F. for my surfetes] þoruh surfetys F; for my forfetes R.
405 and þanne] þat for dowhte F. deye] dy3en F.
406 That] & F. he] y F. worþ] wrathe R; wente F. and] y F. nau3t] neuere F.
407 is sleuþe] slewþe is F. þat] þere F. slei3tes] sleyghte F; slithes R. helpe it] it helpe F.

Ne no mercy amenden þe man þat so deieþ].
[Ac] whiche ben þe braunches þat bryngen a man to sleuþe?
[Is whan men] moorneþ no3t for hise mysdedes, ne makeþ no sorwe;
[Ac] penaunce þat þe preest enioyneþ *par*four*n*eþ yuele;
Dooþ noon almes[dede]; dred hym of no synne;
Lyueþ ayein þe bileue and no lawe holdeþ.
Ech day is halyday *with* hym or an hei3 ferye,
And if he au3t wole here it is an harlotes tonge.
Whan men carpen of crist or clennesse of soul[e]
He wexeþ wroþ, and wol no3t here but wordes of murþe;
Penaunce [and] pou*er*e men and þe passion of Seintes,
He hateþ to here þ*er*of and alle þat it telleþ.
Thise ben þe braunches, beþ war, þat bryngen a man to wanhope.
Ye lordes and ladies and legates of holy chirche
That fedeþ fooles sages, flatereris and lieris,
And han likynge to liþen hem [in hope] to do yow lau3e—

408 amenden] amende it F. so deieþ] dy3eþ þ*er*eInne F.
409 Ac] R; þe Hm; *om* WCrGYOC^{2}CBLMF. whiche] þese F. bryngen] brynge CrGY. to] in F.
410 Is...men] Is qwa*n* man B (qwa*n* *over erasure* Bm); Is wha*n*ne a man OC^{2}; hys woma*n* GYCLR; He þat WHmCrM (*over large erasure another ink* M); þat F. mysdedes] myssis F; mysse Cr; dedis OC^{2}. ne] *om* G. no] for he*m* F.
411 Ac] YOBL; but G; And WHmCrC^{2}CR; And þe (nd *over erasure*, þe *above line*) M; Ne F. penaunce] pacience Y. enioyneþ] enioyned BC; enyoigneth Y; hy*m* took he F. parfourneþ] parfourned CF; p*ar*forme B. yuele] it euele Hm; ill Cr; hij nylleþ B; neu*er*e F.
412 Dooþ noon] Ne neyþ*er* doþ F. almesdede] YHmGOC^{2}CBLRF (dede *cancelled, then added main hand* G); almesdedes CrM (dedes *over erasure another ink* M); almesse W. dred] dredeth HmOC^{2}; ne dred*i*þ F. hym of no] neuere F.
413 Lyueþ] ⁊ he þat ly3eþ F. þe] *om* F.
414 Ech] For ech F. is] is an YGOC^{2}M; or eche BC. *with* hym] *om* OC^{2}. or] os is F; as B; ⁊ OC^{2}. an] *om* Cot. ferye] feire M; feste F; as the ferye Cot.
415 And] *om* M. au3t wole] wil owt F.
416 Whan] And wha*n*ne OC^{2}; For whan F. or] GYOC^{2}CBF; or of WHmCrLMR. soule] HmGYOC^{2}CBLMRF; soules WCr.
417 He wexeþ] þa*n*ne wexeþ he F. wol...but] wolde her*e* F.
418 Penaunce] ⁊ þe penau*n*ce F. and(1)] HmCrGYOC^{2}CBLMR; of WF. þe] *om* OC^{2}. passion] possessiou*n* C; passessioun (ess *cancelled*) Bm.
419 here þerof] heery*n* of hem F. þat] þo F. it] he Cr.
420 þe] *om* Cr^{3}. beþ war] *om* F. bryngen] brynge YGF. a...to] me*n* in F.
421 Ye lordes] *twice* R. Ye] The CrG; I co*n*seyle F. and(1)] ⁊ the Cr. chirche] cherches R.
422 That] Tha C. fedeþ] Fynden C^{2}; fynde F; *om* (feden *in margin another hand*) O. fooles] fole R. sages] sage OC^{2}; sage ⁊ F. and] ben ⁊ F.
423 likynge] liken Cr^{1}; lyst F. liþen] lystne F; listem C; leyen G; heren BmBo; hiren Cot. hem] *om* G. in...yow] to do you GR; to do yow to WHmCrYOC^{2}CBLMF.

Ve vobis qui ridetis &c—
And ȝyueþ hem mete and mede, and pouere men refuse,
In youre deeþ deyinge I drede me soore
Lest þo þre maner men to muche sorwe yow brynge:
Consencientes & agentes pari pena punientur.
Patriarkes and prophetes, prechours of goddes wordes,
Sauen þoruȝ hir sermo[n] mannes soule fro helle;
Riȝt so flatereris and fooles arn þe fendes disciples
To entice men þoruȝ hir tales to synne and harlotrie. |
Ac clerkes þat knowen holy writ sholde kenne lordes *fol.* 80 *a*
What Dauid seiþ of swiche men as þe Sauter telleþ:
Non habitabit in medio domus mee qui facit superbiam & qui loquitur iniqua.
Sholde noon harlot haue audience in halle n[e] in Chambre
Ther wise men were, witnesseþ goddes wordes,
Ne no mysproud man amonges lordes ben allowed.
[Clerkes and kniȝtes welcomeþ kynges minstrales,
And for loue of [hir] lorde liþeþ hem at festes;
Muche moore, me þynkeþ, riche men sholde

423α *in margin* OC^{2}. *ridetis*] *ridens* Y. *&c*] *om* Cr^{1}RF.
424 ȝyueþ] ȝeve FCr. hem] hym C; swiche F; *om* G. men] me Y. refuse] refusen OC^{2}; to refuse Cr.
425 In] I G; Syker in F. deeþ] *om* F. deyinge] doynge BmBo. I] ȝee may F. drede] feare Cr. me] R; me ful WHmCr GYOC^{2}CBLM; *om* F.
426 Lest] laste Hm. þo þre] swiche F; þe thre GYOC^{2}C. men] of men CrCF (of *cancelled* C). muche] muche to mykil C. yow] þou Y; *om* R.
426α *punientur*] *punientur &c* Hm; *puniendi sunt* RF.
427 prophetes] prophetes and WHmCrGY OC^{2}CBLMRF. goddes] god F. wordes] woord HmCr^{23}; *in* hevene F.
428 Sauen] saue G. sermon] BGYOC^{2} CLMRF; sermons WHmCr. mannes] manne C.
429 flatereris] flateres LF. fooles] foulis BmBo. arn] & GYOC^{2}C.
430 entice] tempte F; eten C. and] HmCr YOC^{2}CBLRF; and to WGM (to *above line* M).
431 Ac] but GF; And CrC; As OC^{2}. knowen] knowe GF. holy] woly G. sholde] schulden OHmC^{2}. kenne] kennen MR; kennyn so F.
432 seiþ] said Cr^{23}.
432α *&...iniqua*] *om* F. *&*] *om* HmR. *qui*(2)] *om* Cot. *iniqua*] *iniqua &c* HmY.
433 harlot] harlotes CB; *om* Hm. haue] haue non F. ne] HmCrGYOC^{2}CBLMRF; nor W. Chambre] chaumbres HmYO C^{2}CLMR.
434 Ther] þere þat F. were] weren OC^{2}F. witnesseþ] witnesse OC^{2}C; witnesse on F. wordes] woord Hm.
435 ben] *om* F. allowed] alewid Bm.
436–53 RF; *lines om* WHmCrGYOC^{2}CB LM; *here in the spelling of* W.
436 Clerkes...kniȝtes] Boþe knyghtis & clerkis F. welcomeþ] wolkome F.
437 for] for þe F. hir] here F; þe R. liþeþ] þey lyghten F.
438 Muche] Mychil F. riche] þan ryche F.

Haue beggeres bifore hem þe whiche ben goddes minstrales
As he seiþ hymself; seynt Iohan bereþ witnesse:
Qui vos spernit me spernit.
Forþi I rede yow riche, reueles whan ye makeþ,
For to solace youre soules swiche minstrales to haue:
The pouere for a fool sage sittyng at þ[i] table,
And a lered man to lere þee what our lord suffred
For to saue þi soule from sathan þyn enemy,
And fiþele þee wiþoute flaterynge of good friday þe [geste],
And a blynd man for a bourdeour, or a bedrede womman
To crie a largesse bifore oure lord, youre good loos to shewe.
Thise þre maner minstrales makeþ a man to lauȝe,
And in his deeþ deyinge þei don hym gret confort
That bi his lyue liþed hem and loued hem to here.
Thise solaceþ þe soule til hymself be falle
In a welhope, [for he wrouȝte so], amonges worþi seyntes],
[There] flateres and fooles þoruȝ hir foule wordes
Leden þo þat [liþed] hem to Luciferis feste
Wiþ *turpiloquio*, a l[a]y of sorwe, and luciferis fiþele.
Thus haukyn þe Actif man hadde ysoiled his cote
Til conscience acouped hym þerof in a curteis manere,
Why he ne hadde [w]asshen it or wiped it wiþ a brusshe.

439 þe] *om* F.
441 Forþi] þerfore F. riche] riche at R; ryche men at F. makeþ] make F.
442 to(2)] ȝee F.
443 sittyng] ȝee sette F. þi] þe F; þe heyȝ R.
444 lered] leerned F. lere] leerne F.
446 fiþele...flaterynge] withowtyn flaterynge fythele F. friday þe] frydaes F. geste] storye RF.
447 And] & tak F. for a] þy F.
448 bifore] to F. youre] þyn F.
449 maner] manere of F. makeþ a man] make men F.
451 liþed] he lystned F.
452 Thise...þe] þey solace þy F. hym] þy F. falle] fallyn F.
453 wel] wol good F. hope...so] hope RF. worþi] goode F.
454 There] þere RF; Ac WHmYOBLM; but G; And CrC^{2}C. flateres] flaterers HmCrGYOCB. þoruȝ] with F. foule] lewde Cr.
455 þo] þem G. liþed] loued R; lovedyn F; louen WHmGYOC^{2}CBLM; loue Cr. feste] Festis C^{2}.
456 lay] HmCrGYOC^{2}CBLMRF; lady W. and] in F. luciferes] lucifere C.
457 Thus] thys G. haukyn] Hankyn Cr. þe] *om* F. ysoiled] soyled CrHmGR.
458 acouped] couped G. þerof] *om* F.
459 ne hadde] had ne Cr^{23}; had Cr^{1}. wasshen] YOC^{2}CLM; waschyn Hm; waischen B; whasshen WG; washed CrR; wasshe F. or...brusshe] er with a brushȝ rubbid it F. it(2)] *om* OC^{2}.

XIV

'I haue but oon hool hater', quod haukyn, 'I am þe lasse to blame
Thouȝ it be soiled and selde clene: I slepe *þer*Inne o nyȝtes;
And also I haue an houswif, hewen and children—
Vxorem duxi & ideo non possum venire—
That wollen bymolen it many tyme maugree my chekes.
It haþ be laued in lente and out of lente boþe
Wiþ þe sope of siknesse þat sekeþ wonder depe,
And [laþered] wiþ þe losse of catel [forto me] looþ [were]
To agulte god or good man by aught *þat* I wiste,
And [siþþe] shryuen of þe preest, þat [for my synnes gaf me]
To penaunce pacience and pou*er*e men to fede,
Al for coueitise of my cristendom in clennesse to kepen it.
And kouþe I neu*er*e, by crist! kepen it clene an houre
That I ne soiled it wiþ siȝte or som ydel speche,

1 hool] *om* LRF. haukyn] Ha*n*kin Cr.
2 selde clene] fowle GYOC^{2}CB. selde] selden MHm. I] for y F.
3 And] *om* G. an houswif] a wif YGOC^{2}C; a wif and B. hewen] & hewen F; hynen Cot. and] boþe & F.
3α *in margin* OC^{2}. venire] *venire &c* Hm G; *&c* R.
4 wollen] wellyn (? *touched up*) Hm; will F; wolden YOC^{2}CB; wold G. bymolen] bemoole F; bemoulled G; bifoule C; defoule B. it] *om* G. tyme] tymes Cr^{23}GR F; adayes Cr^{1}. chekes] clekis C^{2}.
5 laued] laueþ B; laven F. lente(*both*)] lenten OC^{2}RF; lewte HmB. lente(1)] lenten C.
6 þe] *om* F. sekeþ] sekest CBmBo. wonder] wonders Cr^{23}. depe] dede C^{2}.
7 *divided from* 8 *after* leese F; *after* agulte WHmCr^{1}GYOC^{2}CBLMR; *after* agyle Cr^{23}. laþered wiþ] wiþ WHmCrGYO C^{2}CBLMRF. þe] *om* F. losse] lost Cot. forto...were] *þat* looþ me was to leese F; looþ for WHmCrGOC^{2}LMR; bothe for YCB.
8 & grucched ageyn god whan grevis he me sente F. agulte] agyle Cr^{23}. or] or any WHmCrGYOC^{2}CBLM; ar any R.
9 siþþe] was WHmCrGYOC^{2}CBLMRF. shryuen] shryve F. þe] a Cr. þat] he G. for...me] gaf me for my synnes WHmCr GYOC^{2}CBLMRF.
10 To...pacience] Pacyense to penau*n*ce F. pacience and] or pacience as Y. men] me Y. fede] feeden F.
11 Al] & G; *om* F. kepen] kepe CrGYOC^{2} CBF. it] *om* C^{2}.
12 And...I] But y cowhde F. neu*er*e] nouȝt RF. by...clene] kepen it bi *cr*ist clene B; kepe it be *cr*iȝst not F. kepen] kepe CrGOC^{2}. it] *om* G. houre] hour togydre F.
13 ne] *om* F. soiled] fouled C. or] or wit*h* CrF. ydel] yuell C^{2}.

Or þoruȝ werk or þoruȝ word or wille of myn herte
That I ne flobre it foule fro morwe til euen.' |
'And I shal kenne þee', quod Conscience, 'of Contricion to make *fol. 80 b*
That shal clawe þi cote of alle kynnes filþe:
Cordis contricio &c.
Dowel shal wasshen it and wryngen it þoruȝ a wis confessour:
Oris confessio &c.
Dobet shal beten it and bouken it as bright as any scarlet
And engreynen it wiþ good wille and goddes *gra*ce to amende þe,
And siþen sende þee to Satisfaccion for to [sonnen] it after:
Satisfaccio.
Dobest [shal kepe it clene from vnkynde werkes].
Shal neu*ere* [myx] bymolen it, ne moþe after biten it,
Ne fend ne fals man defoulen it in þi lyue.
Shal noon heraud ne harp*our* haue a fairer garnement

14 or(1)] off G. þoruȝ word] thouȝt R; ell*es* þowht F. þoruȝ(2)] *om* Cr^{3}GYOC^{2}CB. or(2)] or þoruh F; and other R. myn] *om* F.

15 That] but GYOC^{2}C. I ne] y F; *om* Cr^2. flobre] flobered F; slober Cr; slobered G. it] ful F. morwe] morwen OC^2. til] to G. euen] eue HmGCBLR; þe eve F.

16 And] *om* F. I] *om* C. kenne] telle B. to] a brushȝ to F.

17 That] that he Hm. clawe] *om* CB. þi ...of] of þy coote F. cote] cote make clene B. kynnes] kinds of Cr; vnclene F. filþe] fylthys F; synnes OC^2.

17α *in margin* OC^2; *line om* F.

18 shal] *above line* M; *om* GYCBLRF. wasshen] wasshe FCrG. wryngen] wrynge BoCrGCotF. þoruȝ] *with* F.

18α *in margin* OC^2; *line om* F. &c] *om* Cr^{13}.

19 bet] bett*er* G. shal] þat schal R; *om* F. beten] beat Cr; bowke F. it(1)] *om* R. bouken] bouke GC; bo*n*ke Cr; beete F. any] ys F.

20 engreynen] engreyne HmC^{2}F; engraue*n* Cr. it] *om* C. and...þe] *with* helpe of godd*es* grace F.

21 *copied before* 23 F. siþen] *om* GF. sende þee] goo F. to(1)] *om* GYOC^{2}CB. for] sone for F. sonnen] R; su*n*ne F; sowen WHmCr^{1}GYCBLM; sowne Cr^{23}; sewe OC^2. it] þe F; *om* OC^2.

21α *in margin* OC^2; *as one line with* 22 WHmCrLMR; *line om* F. *Satisfaccio*] *Satisfaccio &c* YGOC^{2}CB.

22 *as one line with* 23 GYOC^{2}CBL. Dobest] & Dobest F; Dobet B. shal... werkes] & keep þe cleene fram vnkyȝnde werkis F; *om* WHmCrGYOC^{2}CBLMR. *Hereafter a spurious line* (*see above*, p. 223) *followed by* 21 F.

23 Shal] & þa*n* shal F. myx] myst GYOC^{2}CBLMRF; chiste Hm; cheeste WCr. bymolen] bymole R; moole F; bynolnen CB. it(1)] *om* GY. moþe] moche BoCot. after...it] do it skaþe F. biten] byte CrC^2; bete*n* B.

24 Ne] Ne neyþ*er* F. fend] fynde Y. defoulen] defoule F. in] *om* Y.

25 Shal] þere shal F. haue] *om* Y. a fairer] an hender*e* F. garnement] garment GCrCotR.

Than Haukyn þe Actif man, and þow do by my techyng,
Ne no Mynstrall be moore worþ amonges pouere and riche
Than Hauky[n] wi[l] þe wafrer, [which is] *Actiua vita.*'
'And I shal purueie þee paast', quod Pacience, 'þou3 no plou3 erye,
And flour to fede folk wiþ as best be for þe soule;
Thou3 neuere greyn growed, ne grape vpon vyne,
All þat lyueþ and lokeþ liflode wolde I fynde
And þat ynogh; shal noon faille of þyng þat hem nedeþ:
Ne soliciti sitis &c; Volucres celi deus pascit &c; pacientes vincunt &c.'
Thanne laughed haukyn a litel and lightly gan swerye;
'Whoso leueþ yow, by oure lord! I leue no3t he be blessed.'
'No?' quod Pacience paciently, and out of his poke hente
Vitailles of grete vertues for alle manere beestes
And seide, 'lo! here liflode ynogh, if oure bileue be trewe. |
For lent neuere was lif but liflode were shapen, *fol.* 81 *a*
Wherof or wherfore or wherby to libbe:
First þe wilde worm vnder weet erþe,
Fissh to lyue in þe flood and in þe fir þe Criket,

26 Haukyn] Hankin Cr. and] & yff G. þow] þo BmBo. by] *om* CF.
27 and] ne Hm.
28 Haukyn] F; Haukyns WHmGYOC^{2}CBLMR; Hankyns Cr. wil] wif WHmCrGYOC^{2}CBLMR; *om* F. þe] *om* G. which is] RF; with his WHmCrGYOC^{2}CBLM.
29 quod] & Cr. no] þow no RF. erye] holde F.
30 And] Of F. folk] þy folk Hm. wiþ] withal Cr. þe] þi GOC^{2}CBF.
31 greyn] grene Cr^{12}; greue Cr^{3}. growed] growe HmB; growe on grownde F. ne] nor Cr^{1}. vyne] þe vyne B.
32 All] CrGCBmBo; alle HmYOC^{2}CotLMR; To all W; For all F. lyueþ] liued Cr^{23}. lokeþ] loked Cr^{23}; lackethe G. wolde] wol CF.
33 ynogh] I nought C; y HmB. faille] failled Y. of] o C^{2}; *om* G. þyng þat] swich as F. *Hereafter an additional line* WHmCrGYOC^{2}CBLMRF: We sholde no3t be to bisy abouten oure liflode (We...to] No man shal be F. sholde] schulden OC^{2}. abouten] aboute HmCrGYCBM. oure] his F).
33α *Ne*] *Dum* B. &c(1)...&c(3)] *om* F. *Volucres*] volecres G. *pascit*] *pascit eos* Y; *om* Cot. &c(3)] *om* CrG.
34 laughed] low3 OC^{2}. haukyn] Hankyn Cr. litel...swerye] lyte & a lytil ooþ he made F.
35 leueþ] loueþ C^{2}B; trowith eyþer of F. by...lord] *om* F. by] noþer be R. I] & G. leue no3t] trowe F. blessed] vnblessid F.
36 Pacience] Conscience Cr. hente] he hente F.
37 of] *om* F. for] of F. beestes] goodnesse F.
38 here] here is F. oure] 3our Hm. bileue] feyþ F.
39 lent] lewte F. neuere was] was neuer CotF; nere was þere R. lif but] so ryf as F. were] is F. shapen] shape GR; yshape F.
40 *line om* F. Wher] her Hm. or(2)] & OC^{2}R.
41 wilde] wide Y. weet] þe wete BF.
42 Fissh...flood] & in þe flodis fysshis F.

The Corlew by kynde of þe Eyr, moost clennest flessh of
briddes,
And bestes by gras and by greyn and by grene rootes,
In menynge þ*at* alle men myȝte þe same
Lyue þoruȝ leel bileue, [as oure lord] witnesseþ:
*Quodcumque pecieritis a patre in nomine meo &c; Et alibi, Non in solo pane
viuit homo set in omni verbo quod procedit de ore dei.'*
But I [listnede and] lokede what liflode it was
[Th]at pacience so preisede, [and of his poke hente]
A pece of þe Pate*r*noster [and profrede vs alle];
And þanne was it *fiat voluntas tua* [sholde fynde vs alle].
'Haue, haukyn', quod Pacience, 'and et þis whan þe hungreþ
Or whan þow clomsest for cold or clyngest for drye.
Shul neu*ere* gyues þee greue ne gret lordes wraþe,
Prison ne peyne, for *pacientes vincunt.*
By so þ*at* þow be sobre of siȝte and of tonge,
In [ondynge] and in handlynge and in alle þi fyue wittes,
Darstow neu*ere* care for corn ne cloþ ne for drynke,

43 of þe Eyr] of hem are Cr; *om* F. moost] *om* Cr. clennest] cleane G. flessh of briddes] is of foulis F.
44 bestes] best BmBo. gras...greyn] gr*a*sees þey lyve F. by(2)] *om* GYOC^{2}CB. greyn] grene Cr. grene] grete M.
45 myȝte] myȝten OHmC^2; sholde F. þe] do the GYOC^{2}MF; see þe B; se C. same] same do Cr.
46 Lyue] Lif R; & lyve F. leel] lelly Cr^{23}. as...lord] as goode god F; and loue as god WHmCrGYOC^{2}CBLMR.
46α *a patre*] *om* RF. *in*(1)] *meo in* Cr^1. &c] *dabitur vobis* F. *Et alibi*] *om* C^2. *in*(2)] *om* Cr. *de...dei*] &c GYCB. *dei*] *dei* &c Hm; *meo* Cr^1.
47–50 *as two lines divided after* preisede WHmCrGYOC^{2}CBLMRF: But I lokede what liflode it was þat pacience so preisede And þanne was it a pece of þe Paternoster *fiat voluntas tua* (But] And Cr; þ*a*n F. liflode it] þat liflode RF. so] *om* F. And] *om* F. þanne] that Hm; þ*er*e F; it Cr. it(2)] *above line* OM; *om* HmCrRF).
51 haukyn] Hanken Cr. þe hungreþ] thou hu*n*grest Cr^{23}.
52 whan] than Cr^2. clyngest] chillist OC^2. drye] drouȝthe R; drowhtys F.
53 Shul] Shulde C^{2}B; Schulden O; And schal R; þ*er*e shal F. gyues] gyue Bm; gomes OC^2; feytoures R; fayto*ur* F; synne BoCot. lordes] lord þe F.
54 Prison ne] Ne p*r*isou*n* þe F. for] fo R; whil F. *pacientes*] pacience C^2. *vincunt*] vicunt G.
55 By] *om* G. þat] *om* F. of(1)] boþe of F. of(2)] *om* F.
56 ondynge] etynge WHmCrGYOC^{2}CB LMRF. in(1)] *om* F. in(2)] *om* GYOC^{2}CB. þi] the Cot.
57 *divided from* 58 *after* wollen WHmCrG YOC^{2}CBLMRF. Darstow neu*ere*] Neu*ere* tharst þou F. Darstow] tharst thu HmO C^{2}BmBoR; Tharthow Y; Thardestow C; there the G. cloþ] lynnen cloþ ne wollen WHmCrGYOC^{2}CBLMR; lyne*n* ne wollene F.

Ne deeþ drede [ne deuel], but deye as god likeþ
Or þoru3 hunger or þoru3 hete, at his wille be it;
For if þow lyue after his loore, þe shorter lif þe bettre:
Si quis amat christum mundum non diligit istum.
For þoru3 his breeþ beestes woxen and abrood yeden:
Dixit & facta sunt &c;
Ergo þoru3 his breeþ [boþe] men and beestes lyuen,
As holy writ witnesseþ whan men seye hir graces:
Aperis tu manum tuam & imples omne animal benediccione. |
It is founden þat fourty wynter folk lyuede withouten tulying, *fol.* 81 *b*
And out of þe flynt sprong þe flood þat folk and beestes dronken.
And in Elyes tyme heuene was yclosed
That no reyn ne roon; þus rede men in bokes,
That manye wyntres men lyueden and no mete ne tulieden.
Seuene slepe, as seiþ þe book, seuene hundred wynter
And lyueden wiþouten liflode and at þe laste þei woken.

58 Ne] *om* GF. deeþ drede] dreede no dethe G; for breed Hm. deeþ] deaths Cr^{23}. ne...but] but WHmCrGYOC^{2}CBLMRF. as] wan F. likeþ] will F.
59 Or þoru3] Ne for F. or þoru3] ne F. at...it] for no þyng shal þe greve F.
60 For] *om* F. lyue] lyuest HmYOC^{2}CBLMR. shorter] shotter L; scort*er* C^{2}. bettre] leuere RF.
60α *in margin* O. *istum*] *istum &c* HmBmBo.
61 þoru3] *om* G. beestes] mowen men and beestis B. woxen] wexeth R; were*n* F. and] & wy3de F. yeden] wenty*n* F.
61α *in margin* OC^{2}; *line om* F. *Dixit*] *dixi* C. *&c*] *om* CrOC^{2}.
62 boþe] mowen WHmYOCBLMR; mown C^{2}; mowe we F; may CrG. men ...beestes] men and beast Cr^{1}; beestis & me*n* F. lyuen] lyue OC^{2}.
63 witnesseþ] witnesse C. whan...graces] & dauid in þe sawter F. whan] yt when G. seye] se in Cr^{3}; songo*n* in C^{2}. graces] grace R.
63α *in margin* O. *benediccione*] *benediccione &c* Hm.
64 founden] founde FCr. wynter] wynters G. lyuede] lyuede*n* OHmC^{2}B. outen] oute HmCrGYC^{2}CBMR. tulying] tilthe F.
65 beestes] best BmBo. dronken] dronke HmCrGYCLRF.
66 And] & also F. yclosed] closed Cr.
67 ne] *om* HmMF. roon] reynd GHmCF. rede men] men rede MF. rede] reden OC^{2}; rett R. in] on R.
68 That] & 3it F. manye] *om* F. wyntres] wynter CrR; *om* F. lyueden] lyuede BCrR. no] *om* F. mete] mete & drynk F; me*n* Y. ne] *om* GF. tulieden] tylied C; hadden F.
69 Seuene] & seue*n* me*n* F. slepe] slepen OHmC^{2}BRF. seuene] seue Hm. hundred] hundre CM. wynter] wy*n*ters G; 3ere Cot.
70 lyueden] lyued Cr. outen] oute HmCrGYCotLM. liflode] loflode C^{2}. at] *om* C. woken] awoken F.

And if men lyuede as mesure wolde sholde neu*ere* moore be defaute
Amonges cristene creatures, if cristes wordes ben trewe.
Ac vnkyndenesse *caristiam* makeþ amonges cristen peple,
[Oþer] plentee makeþ pryde amonges poore and riche.
[Ac] mesure is [so] muche worþ it may noȝt be to deere.
For þe meschief and þe meschaunce amonges men of Sodome
Weex þoruȝ plentee of payn and of pure sleuþe:
Ociositas & habundancia panis peccatum turpissimum nutriuit;
For [men] mesured noȝt hemself of [mete] and dr[y]nke,
Diden dedly synne þat þe deuel liked,
Vengeaunce fil vpon hem for hir vile synnes;
[So] thei sonken into helle, þe Citees echone.
Forþi mesure we vs wel and make [we] feiþ oure sheltrom;
And þoruȝ feiþ comeþ contricion, conscience woot wel,
Which dryueþ awey dedly synne and dooþ it to be venial.

71 And] *om* Cr. lyuede] lyueden OHm C^{2}M. as] be F. wolde] þere F. neu*ere*] no Cr^{23}; *om* F. moore] *om* GYOC^{2}CBF. be] be no F; *om* BoCot. defaute] defaute be B.

72 Amonges] Amoges R. creatures] creatoures R. cristes] criste R. wordes] word O. ben trewe] þei take F.

73 Ac...makeþ] But welthe is so mych a maist*er* F. Ac] but G; And CrC^2 C. *caristiam*] *caristia* HmGYOC^{2}CBLM R. cristen] *cri*stes R.

74 Oþer] And oþer B; And ouer WHm CrGYOC^{2}CLMR; þ*at* ou*er* F. pryde] *om* CB.

75 Ac] YOBLMR; but G; and HmC^{2}CF; Therfore WCr. so] HmCrGYOC^{2}CBL MRF; *om* W. muche] mychil F. may] ca*n* Cr^{23}.

76 þe(2)] *om* OC^{2}F.

77 Weex] was GF. payn] foode G.

77α *in margin* O; *line om* F. *peccatum... nutriuit*] *om* R. *nutriuit*] *nutriuit &c* Hm; *incitauit* (?) C^2.

78 men] þei WHmCrGYOC^{2}CBLMRF. mesured] mesurede*n* OB. hem] hym BmBo. of] neyþ*er* F. mete] meete F; þat þei ete WHmCrGYCBL; þ*at* þei eten OC^{2}MR. and] ne F. drynke] GF; dronke WHmYBLMR; dranke CCr; drunken OC^2.

79 Diden] YHmGOC^{2}CBLR; Diden i*n* (i*n above line another ink*) M; Thei diden W; They dyd Cr; & dyden swich F. dedly] dely O. synne] synnes F. deuel] devil he*m* F.

80 Vengeaunce] So vengeaunce WHmCr GYOC^{2}CLMR; and vengeaunce B; & swich vengau*n*ce F. vpon] on F. vile] foule FG. synnes] synne B.

81 So thei] þat þei F; Thei WHmCrGYO C^{2}CBLMR. þe] tho Cr^{2}YLMF. echone] bothe F.

82 Forþi] Therfore CrF. we(1)] wel Cot; wy C^2; þe F; *om* G. vs] *om* F. wel] silue Cot. we(2)] oure WHmGYOC^{2}CBLMR; þy F; *om* Cr. oure] þy F. sheltrom] shyltren G; feltron Cr.

83 And] For F. woot] wot yt HmOC^2; heer whoot F.

84 Which] the whiche Hm. synne] sy*n*nes F. dooþ] maketh M. it to] he*m* F. be] be as F; *om* Cr.

And þouȝ a man myȝte noȝt speke contricion myȝte hym saue
And brynge his soule to blisse, so þ*at* feiþ bere witnesse
That whiles he lyuede he bileuede in þe loore of holy chirche.
Ergo contricion, feiþ and conscience is kyndeliche dowel,
And surgiens for dedly synnes whan shrift of mouþe failleþ.
Ac shrift of mouþ moore worþi is if man be y[n]liche contrit,
For shrift of mouþe sleeþ synne be it neu*er* so dedly—
Per confessionem to a preest *peccata occiduntur*— |
Ther contricion dooþ but dryueþ it doun into a venial synne *fol.* 82 *a*
As Dauid seiþ in þe Sauter: *et quorum tecta sunt peccata.*
Ac satisfaccion sekeþ out þe roote, and boþe sleeþ and voideþ,
And as it neu*ere* [n]adde ybe to noȝte bryngeþ dedly synne
That it neu*ere* eft is sene ne soor, but semeþ a wounde yheeled.'
'Where wonyeþ Charite?' quod Haukyn; 'I wiste neu*ere* in my lyue
[Wye] þat wiþ hym spak, as wide as I haue passed.'
'Ther parfit truþe and poore herte is, and pacience of tonge,

85 *line om* CB. þouȝ] if F. myȝte (*both*)] may F. speke] speke ȝit F. hym] *om* Cr. **86** brynge] bryngyn Hm; bryngeþ B. soule] *om* F. blisse] blish Cr^{3}. so] HmGY OC^{2}CB; be so CrLRF; for so WM. bere] bereþ HmMF (th *erased* M); here C^{2}O; were Cr. **87** lyuede he] *om* F. he bileuede] *om* HmG. in] *om* GYOC^{2}CB. þe] *om* F. loore] law Cr^{23}. chirche] cherche he beleued G; chirche he leevede F. **88** *Ergo* contricion] Concyense *ergo* F. and] *om* Y. conscience] co*n*triciou*n* F. is] be G; *om* F. dowel] is to Dowel F. **89** And] *om* F. surgiens] surgien OC^{2}; Sorwe F. synnes] synne HmCrBR; senne ys F. failleþ] faylede OC^{2}. **90** Ac] but GF; And CrC^{2}C. is] *om* C. be] *om* CR. ynliche] Inlich YOMR; yliche WHmC^{2}CBL; lik Cr^{1}; verylyche G; wi*th* F; *om* Cr^{23}. **91** synne] synnes CB. be it] ben þei B. **92** *Per*] For bi (bi *above line*) Cot; For BmBo. *confessionem*] *confessione* C; con-fessiou*n* B; *passionem* G. **93** dooþ] ne doþ F. but] *om* Cr. dryueþ] driue CrGCot. it] *om* CrM. doun] *om* GCB. in] *om* G. to] *om* F. a] *om* Cr. **94** As] And Cr^{23}GYOC^{2}CB. *et*] *om* F. *tecta...peccata*] *sunt peccata tecta* Bm. *tecta*] *secta* Cr^{1}. **95** Ac] but GF; And CrC^{2}C. sekeþ] sekest C. and] *om* C^{2}. boþe sleeþ] sleeþ boþe F. sleeþ] slepe Cr^{1}. **96** nadde] hadde WHmCrGYOC^{2}CBLM RF. ybe] be OCrC^{2}RF. to...bryngeþ] ys þan þ*at* F. dedly] dealy Cr^{1}. **97** That it] Ne F. it...is] ytt ys neu*er* efte GOC^{2}CB; is neuere eft Y; eft it is not Cr. eft...soor] aft*er* þat soor is seene F. ne] no Cr^{23}; *om* CB. semeþ] *om* B. a] as a B; as Y. yheeled] heled YCrGOC^{2}CBF. **98** Where] Ȝe where RF. Haukyn] Ha*n*kin Cr. I wiste] ȝit wiste y F. neuere] nere R. in my lyue] *om* F. **99** Wye] Man WHmCrGYOC^{2}CBLMR; Ony ma*n* F. passed] wandred F. **100** Ther] Q*uo*d hee þ*er*e F; That Cr. truþe] lyf F. and(2)] & þa*n*ne OC^{2}. pacience] Patient Cr^{23}; pacyet F.

There is Charite þe chief, chaumbrer*e* for god hymselue.'
'Wheiþer paciente pou*er*te', quod Haukyn, 'be moore plesaunt
to oure d[ri3te]
Than richesse ri3tfulliche wonne and resonably despended?'
'Ye? *quis est ille*?' quod Pacience; 'quik, *laudabimus eum*!
Thou3 men rede of richesse ri3t to þe worldes ende,
I wiste neu*er*e renk þat riche was, þat whan he rekene sholde,
Whan he drogh to his deeþ day þ*a*t he ne dredde hym soore,
And þ*a*t at þe rekenyng in Arrerage fel raþ*er* þan out of dette.
Ther þe poore dar plede and preue by pure reson
To haue allowaunce of his lord; by þe lawe he it cleymeþ.
Ioye þat neu*er*e ioye hadde of ri3tful Iugge he askeþ,
And seiþ, "lo! briddes and beestes þat no blisse ne knoweþ
And wilde wormes in wodes, þoru3 wyntres þow hem greuest
And makest hem wel nei3 meke and mylde for defaute,
And after þow sendest hem somer þat is hir sou*er*eyn ioye
And blisse to alle þat ben, boþe wilde and tame."
Thanne may beggeris, as beestes, after boote waiten
That al hir lif han lyued in langour and defaute.

101 Charite þe chief] charytees F. þe] of þe (of *erased*) M; *om* B. chaumbrere] chambre HmGCBMRF. for] for he is F. selue] seluyn Hm.
102 Wheiþer] Wher Cr. paciente] pacyence GYC^{2}C; pacyence or HmB (or *above line main hand* Hm); pacience and RF. pou*er*te] porti Cr. Haukyn] Ha*n*ki*n* Cr. moore] *om* F. oure dri3te] god more F. dri3te] LHmCrYM; dri3ten O; d (*cropped*) W; sight CB; lorde GR; saueoure C^2.
103 wonne] wonnen OHmC^2; ywonne LMR. resonably] resonable G. despended] yspended LMR; spendid OC^{2}BF; spente GYC.
104 quik] quyk *et* G. *eum*] *eum* &c Hm.
105 rede] reden F; redde Y; redde*n* OC^2.
106 I wiste] Fond F. renk] reuke Cr; freik B. þat] þan BoCotF.
107 Whan] *om* F. he(1)] it LR; & F. drogh] droue C. deeþ] deyd G; dethes Cr. dredde] drede C^2; dred CL.
108 And] *om* F. þat] *om* GMR. at þe] his F. Arrerage] rerage F.
109 plede] nat plede Y. by] it be F.
110 þe] *om* GF. allowaunce] a louaunce R; aloau3ce C^2.
111 Ioye] A wy3e F. ioye hadde] hadde Ioye Cot. ri3tful] a F. askeþ] axid Cot.
112 seiþ lo] seeth so Cr. knoweþ] knowe F; couthe GYOC^{2}CB.
113 þoru3] by Cr; wi*th* F. þow hem] yow Cr^1; hem Cr^{23}. hem] hy*m* BmBo. greuest] greuith Cr.
114 *line om* G. makest] maketh Cr. nei3] *om* F.
115 hem] hym CBmBo. hir] *om* B.
116 And] & gret F. blisse] blyshe Cr^3. alle] hem Cr^{23}; *om* Cr^1.
117 as] and HmGYOC^{2}CBRF. beestes] breddis C^2; bidders O. boote] bothe C; hoote Y; heate G. waiten] wayte B.
118 langour] hungur B. and] BG; and in WHmCrYOC^{2}CLMRF.

But god sente hem som tyme som man*er*e Ioye
Ouþ*er* here or elliswhere, kynde wolde it neuere;
For to wroþerhele was he wroȝt þat neu*er*e was Ioye shapen. |
Aungeles þat in helle now ben hadden ioye som tyme, *fol.* 82 *b*
And diues in deyntees lyuede and in *douce vie*;
Right so reson sheweþ þ*a*t [þo renkes] þat were [lordes]
And hir [ladies] also lyuede hir lif in murþe.
Ac god is of [a] wonder wille, by þat kynde wit sheweþ,
To ȝyue many m[e]n his [mercymonye] er he it haue deserued.
Riȝt so fareþ god by som riche; ruþe me it þynkeþ,
For þei han hir hire heer and heuene as it were,
And greet likynge to lyue wiþouten labour of bodye,
And whan he dyeþ ben disalowed, as Dauid seiþ in þe Sauter:
Dormierunt & nichil inuenerunt; [*et alibi*], *velud sompn*[*i*]*um surgencium domine in Ciuitate tua, et ad nichilum rediges &c.*
Allas þ*a*t richesse shal reue and robbe mannes soule

119 sente] sent HmCrYCCotLR; send G; wold sende F. hem] hym YCBmBo. som(1)] *om* Y. Ioye] of Ioie MF.
120 *line om* G. Ouþ*er*] or HmCrCot. kynde] god F. wolde] woll Hm. it neuere] it nere R; so be keende F.
121 to] *om* Hm. wroþerhele] wrothele F; wo other wel CBmBo; woo or wel Cot; ouermuch wo Cr^{23}GYOC^{2}. he] *om* F. was Ioye] Ioie was YHmRF. shapen] shape F.
122 hadden] had CrG. ioye...tyme] som tyme Ioie Y.
123 deyntees] deytees C; deutis Cr^{1}. *douce vie*] doute vrrie B.
124 sheweþ] redyþ F. þat] *om* CotF. þo renkes] þo men GOC^{2}CBmBoLMRF; þe men WHmCr; þo þ*a*t men Cot; no men Y. þat] shull F; *om* CotR. were] weren OC^{2}B; redyly F; *om* R. lordes] riche WHmCrGYOC^{2}CBLM; acou*n*te F; *om* R.
125 ladies] makes WHmCrGYOC^{2}CBLMRF. lyuede] lyueden OHm; þ*a*t ledden F. hir lif] her lyues Cr; *om* G. in] in moche G.
126 Ac] but GF; And CrC^{2}C. a] HmCrGYOC^{2}CBLMRF; *om* W. wonder] wonderous Cr. wille by] but G.
127 many] *om* F. men] HmYOC^{2}CBLMR; man WCrGF. his] *om* Cr. mercymonye] LHmCrGYOC^{2}CBMR; mercyme*n*t F; mede W. it haue] have it F; it hath Cr.
128 fareþ] doþ F. som] suyche G. riche] ryche ma*n* F. it] *om* F.
129 hir...and] here her huyre and Hm; here her *salarium* her B. it] is Cr^{1}.
130 And] And ek YOC^{2}; and ys GCBmLR; And his BoCot. to lyue] to þe lif R; of lyf F. outen] oute GCrYOC^{2}CBLMR. labour of bodye] body t*r*auayle F. of] of the Cr.
131 whan he dyeþ] in her*e* dyȝenge F. ben] he Cr^{1}; is Cr^{23}. disalowed] dislowed F. seiþ...Sauter] in þe sawt*er* tell*ith* F. seiþ] said Cr.
131α *inuenerunt*] *inuenerunt &c* R; inuenierunt Cr^{1}. *et alibi*] F; And in anoþer stede also WCrGYOC^{2}CBLMR; & also yn annoþer stede (*with preceding line*) Hm. *velud*] Velunt Cr^{3}. *sompnium*] F; sompnum WHmCrGYOC^{2}CBLMR. *surgencium*] *insurgentium* Cot. *et*] *om* OC^{2}RF. *rediges*] *eorum rediges* R. *&c*] *ymaginem* F; *c* Hm; *om* CrGYOC^{2}CLMR.

Fram þe loue of oure lord at his laste ende!
Hewen þ*at* han hir hire afore arn eu*er*emoore nedy,
And selden deyeþ he out of dette þat dyneþ er he dese*r*ue it,
And til he haue doon his deuoir and his dayes iournee.
For whan a werkman haþ wro3t, þan may men se þe soþe,
What he were worþi for his werk and what he haþ dese*r*ued,
And no3t to fonge bifore for drede of disalowyng.
So I seye by yow riche, it semeþ no3t þ*at* ye shulle
Haue heuene in your*e* her[berw]yng and heuene þ*er*after
Ri3t as a se*r*uaunt takeþ his salarie bifore, & siþþe wolde clayme moore
As he þat noon hadde and haþ hire at þe laste.
It may no3t be, ye riche men, or Mathew on god lyeþ:
De delicijs ad delicias difficile est transire.
Ac if ye riche haue ruþe and rewarde wel þe poore, |
And lyuen as lawe techeþ, doon leaute to hem alle, *fol.* 83 *a*
Crist of his curteisie shal conforte yow at þe laste,

134 Hewen] þay BoCot; For F. þ*at*] þei G. afore] before Cr^{3}G; tofore RF; after C. arn...moore] been heer*e* moost F. nedy] nedys F; redy C^{2}.
135 And] For F; *om* G. selden] selde BCr RF. deyeþ] þei suppe F. he(*both*)] *altered from* þei G. he(1)] *om* RF. þat dyneþ] & dy3hgne F. er] her Bm. he(2)] þei RF. dese*r*ue] aserue F; diuerse (*corrected another hand*) Cot.
136 And] *om* F. haue] hath Hm. his(1)] hir C^{2}. deuoir] dyner Cot. dayes] *om* C.
137 For] & G. may men] mowe*n* me*n* OC^{2}; men may HmBoCotF; men Cr. se] say Cr.
138 he were] were he B. for...werk] *om* F.
139 fonge] fongen F; fing Cr^{23}; si*n*g Cr^{1}. disalowyng] dislowy*ng* F; disanulli*ng* Cr.
140 So...it] Be ryche me*n* þ*at* F. no3t] ryght soo þe same F; *om* R. shulle] schulde HmCr.
141 Cleyme two hevenys oon here & anoþ*er* heereaft*er* F. Haue...in] haue to heuenes for R. in...herberwyng] here yn 3our berynge HmG. herberwyng] her*e* beryng YCr^{1}; hee beryng C; hi3e beryng B; heer beyng OCr^{23}LMR; here byinge C^{2}; here dwellyng W. þ*er*] ther GR; also þ*er* W; her HmCrYOC^{2}CBLM.
142 *as two lines divided after* before HmR; *after* terme F. as] HmCrGYOC^{2}CBLMR F; so as W. salarie] hire C. &] his t*er*me & F. siþþe] after CF. moore] more 3if he mygth Hm; huir*e* R; his heere eft soones F.
143 noon] non ne R; no*n* hevene F; *om* G. hire] heuene RF.
144 no3t] not so F. ye] the Cr^{1}. or] if F. on...lyeþ] be t*r*ewe F. god] yow CB.
144α *in margin* O. *transire*] *transire &c* HmB; *ascendere* RF.
145 Ac] And CrGYC^{2}C; *om* F. ye] the Cr^{1}GLMF. riche] riche me*n* OC^{2}; Ryche man F. haue] hauen B. wel] *om* F.
146 lyuen] lyue HmCr^{1}F; lyke Cr^{23}. as] as þe CB. techeþ] tellyþ F. doon] YHm CrGOC^{2}CLMR; and doon WB; & dooþ F. hem alle] his brothir F. hem] hy*m* Bm; *om* LR.
147 Crist] þan c*r*ist F. at þe laste] alle Y. þe] *om* G.

And rewarden alle double richesse þat rewful hertes habbeþ.
And as an hyne þat hadde his hire er he bigonne,
And whan he haþ doon his deuoir wel men dooþ hym ooþ*er* bountee,
3yueþ hym a cote aboue his couenaunt, ri3t so crist 3yueþ heuene
Boþe to riche and to no3t riche þat rewfulliche libbeþ;
And alle þat doon hir deuoir wel han double hire for hir tr*a*uaille,
Here for3ifnesse of hir synnes, and heuene blisse after.
Ac it is but selde yseien, as by holy seintes bokes,
That god rewarded double reste to any riche wye.
For muche murþe is amonges riche, as in mete and cloþyng,
And muche murþe in May is amonges wilde beestes;
And so forþ while somer lasteþ hir solace dureþ.
Ac beggeris aboute Midsomer bredlees þei [soupe],
And yet is wynter for hem worse, for weetshoed þei [gange],
Afurst soore and afyngred, and foule yrebuked
And arated of riche men þat ruþe is to here.
Now, lord, sende hem somer, and som maner ioye,

148 rewarden] rewarde OCrGYC^{2}CBLM RF. alle] you al CrM (yow *above line* M); *om* F. hertes] hert Cr. habbeþ] haue Cr G; hases C; haddyn C^{2}F.

149 þat] *om* OC^{2}F. hadde] haþ F. bigonne] bygonne to wurche Hm; to worche beganne G; h*is* werk bygy*n*ne F.

150 & he dooþ wel his devir he is ou*er* þat rewardyd F. And] *om* Cr. hym] þem G. ooþ*er* bountee] ouir bou*nt* Cr.

151 3yueþ] Giue CrC; *om* F. hym] *om* F. cote] Cite CB. aboue] aboue*n* C^{2}HmBm Bo; ouer F.

152 Boþe] Bot C. to (2)] *om* HmCrB. no3t] no F; no3t to BHm. rewfulliche] ri3tfullich R; ryghtfully heer*e* F.

153 alle] þo F. deuoir] connande C. han] and B. hire] *om* BF.

154 Here] Of F; *om* GCB. of] for Cr.

155–9 *lines om* RF.

155 Ac] but G; And CrC^{2}C. it is] it nys HmYOC^{2}CBLM (*twice* Y). selde] selden OHmC^{2}B. yseien] seyn HmCrGOC^2; so yseie Cot; so seyn CBmBo. holy] *om* Cr. bokes] lyues YOC^{2}M.

156 double] doublid BmBo. wye] weye Y; wyght G; man Cr; gome C^2.

157 riche] þe ryche G. in] *om* G. cloþyng] clothes Cr.

158 muche] mykyl C.

159 while] the while Cr. dureþ] endureþ HmG.

160 Ac] but GF; And CrC^{2}C; *om* R. aboute] abowty*n* F. bredlees] and bredles Y. soupe] HmCrGYCBLMRF; soupen OC^2; slepe W.

161 gange] HmCrGYCBLMR; gangen OC^2; gone W; wandr*e* F.

162 Afurst soore] Sore afrust B; & afyrst F. Afurst] athurst HmGC^2. afyngred] anhungryd HmB; ahongered G; afryngrid F. foule] fouliche OGYC^{2}CB; foule ofte F. yrebuked] rebuked CrHmGYOC^{2}CBF.

163 arated] rated Cr. men] *om* OC^2. is] ytt is GF.

164 hem] to hem F. maner] man*er* of F; *om* C^2.

Heuene after hir hennes goyng þat here han swich defaute.
For alle myȝtestow haue maad noon mener þan ooþer
And yliche witty and wise, if þee wel hadde liked.
[And] haue ruþe on þise riche men þat rewarde noȝt þi prisoners;
Of þe good þat þow hem gyuest *ingrati* ben manye;
Ac god, of þi goodnesse gyue hem grace to amende.
For may no derþe hem deere, droghte ne weet,
Ne neiþer hete ne Hayll, haue þei hir heele;
Of þat þei wilne and wolde wanteþ hem noȝt here.
Ac poore peple, þi prisoners, lord, in þe put of meschief,
Conforte þo creatures þat muche care suffren
Thoruȝ derþe, þoruȝ droghte, alle hir dayes here, |
Wo in wynter tymes for wantynge of cloþes, *fol.* 83 *b*
And in somer tyme selde soupen to þe fulle.
Conforte þi carefulle, crist, in þi rich[e],
For how þow confortest alle creatures clerkes bereþ witnesse:
Conuertimini ad me & salui eritis.
Thus *in genere* of gentries I*es*u crist seide

166 noon] & noon F.
167 yliche] liche BCr. þee wel] thy wyll GOC^{2}CBMF. liked] ylyked CotHm.
168 And] HmCrGYOC^{2}CBLMR; But lord W; *om* F. haue] saue Cr. on] of CrGOC^{2}CB; ȝee F. þise] *om* F. rewarde] rewarde*n* OHmC^{2}B. noȝt] no F. þi] *om* HmF. prisoners] prisones R; porayle F.
169 of...gyuest] & ȝeve hem of þy*n* good for F. Of] and of Hm. þe] thy G. gyuest] yauest (y *altered from* ȝ) M. *ingrati*] vnkynde OC^2.
170 Ac] but GF; And CrC^{2}C. hem] vs OC^2. to amende] of me*n*deme*n*t F.
171 hem] OCr^{23}C^2; be hem WHmCr^{1}GY CBLMR; ben F. deere] to deere neyþ*er* F. droghte] drie C^2. weet] LHmGYOC^2 CBMRF; weet hem greue WCr.
172 Ne] *om* GBF. ne] ner Y; nor C. haue þei] if þey haven F. heele] helth Cr^{23}.
173 Of] For al F. wilne] wilnen OC^{2}R; wyl Cr. wolde] wolden OC^2; wolde have F. wanteþ hem] þem wantethe G. hem] *om* Cot. noȝt] no*n* F.
174 Ac] ac þe Hm; but G; But þe F; And CrC^{2}C. peple] *om* F. þi] þei BmBo; & G; in F. prisoners] p*r*isones R; p*r*isou*n* F. lord] lore R; lyȝn F. þe] þy HmC^2. put] pete C^2; pyte C.
175 Conforte] þou co*n*forte F. þo] the Cr. muche] mychil F. care] woo G.
176 derþe] death Cr^1; drighte Y. þoruȝ] & through Cr^3; & GYOC^{2}CBm; of Bo Cot.
177 Wo] þey have woo F. wynter] wyntres RF. tymes] tyme RF. for] & F.
178 in...selde] seelden in þe som*er* tyme F. selde] selden OC^{2}C. soupen] soupe G; suppe þey F.
179 Conforte...crist] Now c*r*ist conforte þo careful kyng F. þi(2)] *om* B. riche] YGOC^{2}CBLRF; richesse WHmCrM (esse *over erasure* M).
180 For] *om* F. how] *om* G. confortest] confortedest Hm. bereþ witnesse] bere wytnes Hm; knowen all F.
180α *in margin* OC^2. *eritis*] *eritis &c* HmY.
181 *genere*] general Cr^{23}. gentries] his genitrice L; alle his genitrice R; alle Ientylis F.

To robberis and to Reueris, to riche and to poore,
[To hores, to harlotes, to alle maner peple].
Thou tauȝtest hem in þe Trinite to taken bapteme
And be clene þoruȝ þat cristnyng of alle kynnes synne.
And if vs fille þoruȝ folie to falle in synne after
Confession and knowlichynge [and] crauynge þi mercy
Shulde amenden vs as manye siþes as man wolde desire.
A[c] if þe [pouke] wolde plede herayein, and punysshe vs in conscience,
[We] sholde take þe Acquitaunce as quyk and to þe queed shewen it:
Pateat &c: Per passionem domini,
And putten of so þe pouke, and preuen vs vnder borwe.
Ac þe parchemyn of þis patente of pouerte be moste,
And of pure pacience and parfit bileue.
Of pompe and of pride þe parchemyn decourreþ,
And principalliche of al[l]e peple but þei be poore of herte.
Ellis is al on ydel, al þat euere [we diden],

182 and(1)] *om* R. to(1)] *om* Y.
183 RF; *line om* WHmCrGYOC^{2}CBLM; *here in the spelling of* W. hores...maner] harlotys & to hoorys & to all oþer F.
184 in] of F. þe] thy Cr^1. taken] take HmCrGYOC^{2}CBLMR.
185 And] *om* F. be] HmCrGYOC^{2}CBLMR; to be WF. þat] *om* F. synne] sinnes CrHmGYOC^{2}CMRF; *om* L.
186 if] *om* HmGYOC^{2}CBLM. vs] *om* G. fille þoruȝ] befelle be F. falle] fally*n* F. synne] synnes Y; som C; somer B.
187 Confession...knowlichynge] knowlechyng and confession R; & beknowleche it In co*n*fessiou*n* F. and(2)] HmCrGYOC^{2}CBLMRF; in W. crauynge] cr*a*ue F.
188 Shulde] Shal Cr^1; we shold F. amenden] amende HmCrGYOC^{2}CBLMRF. as(1)] *om* B. manye siþes] ofte F. man] we F.
189 Ac] YOBLM; but G; And WHmCrC^{2}CRF. pouke] RF; pope WHmCrGYOC^{2}CBLM. wolde] *om* F. her] there GRF. and] to F. punysshe] punissh*en* MR. vs] on vs R.
190 *divided from* 190α *after* quycke Cr^1; *run together with* 190α Cr^{23}. We] F; He WHmCrGYOC^{2}CBLM; Ho R. þe(1)] *om* F. Acquitaunce] quyttance G; acquietaunce Hm. as quyk] *om* F. to] do R. shewen] shewe YHmCrOC^{2}CBLMR; shewed G; it F. it] shewe F.
190α *in margin* OC^2. *Pateat &c*] *Pateant vniuersi* F. *Per*] *quod ad* Hm. *domini*] *domini &c* HmGYOC^{2}CB; *domini nostri iesu christi* F.
191 And...so] & so pytte of F. putten] put Cr. so] *om* GYOC^{2}CB. preuen] preve F; pynnen G.
192 Ac] but GF; And CrC^{2}C. þis] the CrM. of...moste] muste be*n* of pouerte F.
193 pure] pou*er*e YC; pore B (*corrected* Cot). pacience] paciente Cr^1. and] & of F.
194 Of] & if F. and of] or F. þe] doþ þe F. decourreþ] decorreth YOC^{2}CBLM; cowre F; declareth Cr.
195 principalliche] principalitie Cr. alle] HmCrGYOC^{2}CBLR; alle þe M; al þe W; þe F. of (2)] In G.
196 on] yn HmG; *om* CrF. ydel] ydelnesse F. al(2)] and all Cr; *om* YCot. we diden] we wryten CrGYOC^{2}BLMR; we wryte Hm; we written C; þey wryten F; writen W.

Paternost[er] and penaunce and Pilgrymag[e] to Rome,
But oure spences and spendynge sprynge of a trewe w[e]lle;
Ellis is al oure labour lost—lo, how men writeþ
In fenestres at þe freres—if fals be þe foundement.
Forþi c*ris*tene sholde be in co*m*mune riche, noon coueitous for hymselue.
For seuene synnes þer ben assaillen vs eu*er*e;
The fend folweþ hem alle and fondeþ hem to helpe,
Ac wiþ richesse þ[o] Ribaud[es] raþest men bigileþ.
For þer þ*at* richesse regneþ reuerence[s] folweþ,
And þat is plesaunt to pride in poore and in riche. |
[Ac] þe riche is reu*er*enced by reson of his richesse *fol.* 84 *a*
Ther þe poore is put bihynde, and p*ar*auent*ur*e kan moore
Of wit and of wisdom, þat fer awey is bettre
Than richesse or reautee, and raþer yherd in heuene.
For þe riche haþ muche to rekene, and [riȝt softe] walkeþ;

197 noster] CrGYOC^{2}CBR; nostres WHm LMF. penaunce] penaunces HmR; penau*n*tis F. Pilgrymage] pilgrymage HmY OC^{2}CBLMR; Pilgrymages WCrG; pilg*r*imes F.
198 But] And R; w*ith* F. spences] spence C; spendyng F. and] and oure BR; of F. spendynge] spekynge F. sprynge] spryngen Hm. a] *om* Cr. welle] HmGYBLM RF (well *corrected from* wyll G); wille WCr OC^{2}C.
199, 200 *as three lines divided after* trowe, freris F.
199 is] *om* F. lost lo] is laweles y trowe looke F. writeþ] writtyn C^2.
200 þe(1)] *om* G. þe(2)] *om* Cot. foundement] fowndeme*nt* it fawseþ al atoonys F.
201 *line om* F; *as two lines divided after* ryche Hm. Forþi] for þe G; Therfore Cr. sholde] schulden B; men schulde Hm. be] *om* OC^2. coueitous] couetise Cr; coueyte GYOC^{2}CB. selue] sylue yn harmyng of his neyhbour Hm.
202 For] For þe Hm; *om* F. þer ben] þer ben C^{2}YOC; þer ben þat WGBF; þat þ*er*e ben HmCrLMR. assaillen] asayle F. vs] þee OC^2; man G.
203 The] ⁊ þe F. helpe] helpen F.
204 Ac] but GF; And CrC^{2}C. þo Ribaudes] þo ribaudes RF; þ*at* ribaude YHmG OC^{2}CBmBoLM; þat Ribaud he WCr^1; that rybaunde he Cr^{23}; the ribawde Cot. raþest] rachest Bm. men] theym G. bigileþ] bygyle F.
205 reuerences] R; reu*er*ences it F; reuerence WHmCrGYOC^{2}CBLM.
206 is] *om* F. in...in] to poore ⁊ eek to F. poore] pouerte C; pouert B.
207 Ac] R; But F; And WHmCrGYOC^2 CBLM. reuerenced] yreu*er*enced C. by] by þe G.
208 Ther] And Cr; That C. put] put him C^2.
209 *line om* F. fer] *om* B. awey] wei R; alwey Cot.
210 richesse or] þe ryche ma*n* so F. reautee] ryal F; reute (? rente) B. yherd] herd HmCrGYOC^{2}CBF.
211 haþ] haue G. muche] mychel F. and] off and G. riȝt softe] OHmGYC^{2}CBLM RF (softe *over erasure another ink* Hm); right ofte him þat Cr; many tyme hym þ*at* W. walkeþ] walken G.

The heiȝe wey to heueneward [ofte] Richesse letteþ:
Ita inpossibile diuiti &c,
Ther þe poore preesseþ bifore wiþ a pak at his rugge:
Opera enim illorum sequ[u]ntur illos,
Batauntliche as beggeris doon, and boldeliche he craueþ
For his pouerte and pacience a perpetuel blisse:
Beati pauperes quoniam ipsorum est regnum celorum.
A[c] pride in richesse regneþ raþer þan in pouerte;
[Or] in þe maister [or] in þe man som mansion he haueþ.
Ac in pouerte þer pacience is pride haþ no myȝte,
Ne none of þe seuene synnes sitten ne mowe þer longe,
Ne haue power in pouerte, if pacience [it] folwe.
For þe poore is ay prest to plese þe riche
And buxom at hi[s] biddyn[g] for his broke loues,
And buxomnesse and boost [ben] eueremoore at werre,
And eiþer hateþ ooþer in alle maner werkes.
If wraþe wrastle wiþ þe poore he haþ þe worse ende
[For] if þei pleyne [þe feblere is þe poore];

212 heiȝe] ryght GRF; *om* C^{2}. ofte] HmGYCBLMR; often OC^{2}; but ofte þe F; *om* WCr. Richesse] riche RF. letteþ] OHmGYC^{2}CBLMR; hym letteþ WCr; is lettyd F.
212α *in margin* O; *line om* F. *inpossibile*] *possibile* HmCrGYOC^{2}CBmBoLR.
213 Ther] *om* Hm. preesseþ] praiseth Cr^{1}; preiseth Cr^{23}Bo; precheth R; procheþ F. bifore] tofoore F. wiþ] *with* F; þe riche wiþ WHmCrGYOC^{2}CBLMR. pak] poke Hm. at...rugge] ycharged F.
213α–15 *lines om* F.
213α *in margin* O. *sequuntur*] C^{2}; sequntur WHmCrGYOCBLMR. *illos*] *illos &c* HmYC^{2}; *eos* G.
214 Batauntliche] Batanliche C; bantalyche G.
215 pouerte] pouert B. and] YGOC^{2}CBM; and his WHmCrLR. perpetuel] pertual Cr^{23}.
215α *in margin* O. *pauperes*] *pauperis* Cr^{3}; *pauperes spiritu* GF. *est*] *est enim* F. *regnum celorum*] *celorum regnum &c* Hm.
216 Ac] R; But F; And WHmCrGYOC^{2}CBLM. þan] þam R. pouerte] pouert BR.
217 Or] RF; Arst WHmCrGYOC^{2}CBLM. or] CrRF; þan WHmGYOC^{2}CBLM. þe(2)] his F; *om* O. he] *om* R.
218 Ac] but GF; And CrC^{2}C. pouerte] pouert B. myȝte] strengthe F.
219 sitten] sitte OCrGC^{2}F. ne] *om* GCot.
220 *line om* Cr^{3}. pouerte] pouert B. it] Cr^{12}HmGYOC^{2}CBLMR; hem F; *om* W.
221 to plese] for to pleesen F.
222 his biddyng] YHmCrGOC^{2}CBoCotLMRF; is biddynd Bm; hise biddynges W. broke] broken GHmOC^{2}; broode F. loues] noblis F.
223 ben] þey been F; arn WHmYOCB; aren LMR; are CrGC^{2}. moore] *om* CBF.
224 werkes] of werkes MF.
225 If] & if F. wrastle] wrestelethe G; wrystel C. þe(2)] *om* Cot.
226 For] YGOC^{2}CBLMRF; And WHmCr. pleyne...poore] boþe pleyne þe poore is but feble WHmCrGYOC^{2}CBLMRF (but] to F).

And if he chide or chatre hym cheueþ þe worse,
[For lowliche he lokeþ, and louelich is his speche
That mete or money of oþere men moot asken.
And if glotonie greue pouerte he gadereþ þe lasse
For his rentes ne wol nauȝt reche no riche metes to bigge;
And þouȝ his glotonye be to good ale he goþ to cold beddyng
And his heued vnheled, vnesiliche ywrye
For whan he streyneþ hym to strecche þe strawe is his shetes.
So for his glotonie and his greete sleuþe he haþ a greuous
penaunce,
That is welawo whan he wakeþ and wepeþ for colde,
And som tyme for his synnes; so he is neuere murie
Wiþoute mournynge amonge, and meschief to bote].
And if Coueitise cacche þe poore þei may noȝt come togideres,
And by þe nekke namely hir noon may hente ooþer;
For men knowen wel þ*at* Coueitise is of [a] kene wille
And haþ hondes and armes of [a long] lengþe,
And Pouerte nys but a petit þyng, apereþ noȝt to his nauele,
And louely layk was it neu*ere* bitwene þe longe and þe shorte. |
And þouȝ Auarice wolde angre þe poore he haþ but litel
myȝte, *fol.* 84 *b*
For pouerte haþ but pokes to putten in hise goodes
Ther Auarice haþ Almaries and yren bounden cofres.

227 he] the riche Cot.
228–38 RF; *lines om* WHmCrGYOC^{2}CBLM; *here in the spelling* of W.
229 mete] ony meete F.
231 ne] *om* F.
232 glotonye be to] glut be in F. to(2)... beddyng] acold to bedde F.
233 vnheled] euele yhelyd & F.
234 shetes] schete F.
235 his(1)] his grete F. and...sleuþe] *om* F.
236 wepeþ] wepiþ sor*e* F.
238 oute] outy*n* F. meschief] myche myschef F.
239 if] þouȝ RF. cacche] wolde cacche LRF. come togideres] come*n* same F.
240 And] *om* F. þe] ne G. hir] þer FCr; for BoCot; *om* G. hente] henten R; henden F.
241 knowen] knowe GYF. wel] *om* HmOC^2. Coueitise] couetouse Cr. a] HmGYOC^{2}CBLMRF; *om* WCr.
242 haþ] haveþ F. hondes] hedes Y. armes] harmes Bm. a long] GHmCrYOC^{2}CBLM; longe R; an huge F; ful greet W.
243 And] *om* Cr. Pouerte] pouert B. nys] ne is R; is CrGYOC^{2}F. a] *om* OC^2. petit] pety F. apereþ] & aperiþ F; ytt perethe G. nauele] novele F; name BoCot.
244 And] A F. louely layk] louelike Cr. was] ys F. it] yet Cr; *om* GYOC^{2}CB. þe (2)] *om* GF. shorte] scorte C^2.
245 And] *om* Cr. wolde] wole Cr^{23}. angre] angry Cr; *om* C. but] but a BmBo. myȝte] migh Cr^2; strengþe F.
246 pouerte] pouert Cot; poreti Cr. putten] put Cr. goodes] good Cr^3; soddes CB.
247 Ther] That Y. bounden] bounde YCrCLF; bond G.

And wheiþ*er* be liȝter to breke? lasse boost [it] makeþ
A beggeris bagge þan an yren bounde cofre.
Lecherie loueþ hym noȝt for he ȝyueþ but litel siluer
Ne dooþ hym noȝt dyne delicatly ne drynke wyn ofte.
A straw for þe stuwes! [it] stoode noȝt, I trowe,
Hadde þei no[on haunt] but of poore men; hir houses stoode vntyled.
And þouȝ Sleuþe suwe pou*er*te, and s*er*ue noȝt god to paie,
Meschief is [ay a mene] and makeþ hym to þynke
That god is his grettest help and no gome ellis,
And he his seruaunt, as he seiþ, and of his sute boþe.
And wheiþ*er* he be or be noȝt, he bereþ þe signe of pouerte
And in þat secte oure saueour saued al mankynde.
Forþi [al] poore þat pacient is [of pure riȝt] may cleymen,
After hir endynge here, heueneriche blisse.
Muche hardier may he asken þat here myȝte haue his wille
In lond and in lordshipe and likynge of bodie
And for goddes loue leueþ al and lyueþ as a beggere.

248 wheiþ*er*] wheter Y. lasse] HmGYO C^{2}CBLRF; and lasse WCrM (& *above line another ink* M). it] HmGYOC^{2}CBLMR (*erased* M); he F; *om* WCr.
249 beggeris] begger C. þan an yren] or a F. bounde] bounde*n* GYOC^{2}CBMF. cofre] coffires C.
250 hym] hem Cot. for] but Cr^1; *om* G. he...siluer] lytyl syluer he delyþ F.
251 Ne dooþ] To doon F. Ne] No Bm Cot. noȝt] *om* BoCotF. ne] ne to F.
252 *line om* RF. stuwes] styuehous B. it] CrHmGYOC^{2}CLM; it ne B; þei W.
253 *line om* RF. Hadde] Hadden O. noon haunt] none L; no þyng WHmCrYOC^2 CBM; noght G. of] of a B; *om* OC^2. men] man B. houses] house Cr^3. stoode] stode*n* OHmC^{2}Bm; stonden Bo; were L. vntyled] vnhiled OC^2.
254 And] *om* G. pou*er*te] pouert B. god] *om* C.
255 is...mene] his mayster is Hm. ay a mene] his maister WCrGYOC^{2}CBLMRF. hym] hem Cr^{1}M. þynke] þy*n*ken F.
256 his] *om* BRF. help] his helpe F. gome] ma*n* C^{2}C (*glossed* gome *main hand* C).
257 *transposed with* 258 B. he(1)] *above line* M; *om* HmGYOC^{2}CBL. his(1)] is CBR. as] *om* C^2. sute] seutes (s *added later*) G. boþe] bethe C.
258 wheiþ*er*] where LR. be noȝt] noght be G. be(2)] *om* Cr^{3}C. pouerte] pou*er*t Cot.
259 secte] sewte is F. saued] þat saueþ F. man] men Y.
260 Forþi] Therfore Cr. al] YHmCrGO C^{2}CBLMRF; euery W. poore] pou*er*te GCrYOC^{2}CB. pacient] paciens C. is] ben Hm. of...cleymen] may cleymen and asken WHmCrGYOC^{2}CBLMRF (cleymen] claime CrCot).
261 here] day F. heueneriche] heuenlyche Cr^{23}; enlyche Cr^1.
262 Muche] Michel YOC^{2}CBF. may] myghtte Cot. asken] aske CrF. here...his] haþ heere myght & F. haue] has Y. his] her Hm; *om* Y.
263 In...in] As a lord of F. lond] lorde R. and(2)] and in Cr; & haþ F. likynge] lackinge C^2. of] ob C. bodie] bodily helþe F.
264 loue] *in margin another hand* Cot.

And as a mayde for mannes loue hire moder forsakeþ,
Hir fader and alle hire frendes, and folweþ hir make—
Muche is [þat maide] to loue of [a man] þat swich oon takeþ,
[Moore] þan [a maiden is] þat is maried þoruȝ brocage
As by assent of sondry parties and siluer to boote,
Moore for coueitise of [catel] þan kynde loue of boþe—
So it [preueþ] by ech a persone þat possession forsakeþ
And put hym to be pacient and pouerte weddeþ,
The which is sib to god hymself, [so neiȝ is pouerte].'
'Haue god my trouþe', quod Haukyn, '[I here yow] preise
    faste pouerte. |
What is Pouerte, pacience', quod he, 'properly to mene?' *fol.* 85 *a*
'*Paupertas,*' quod Pacience, '*est odibile bonum, Remocio curarum,*
    possessio sine calumpnia, donum dei, sanit[*atis*] *mater, absque*
    sollicitudine semita, sapiencie temperatrix, negocium sine dampno,
    Incerta fortuna, absque sollicitudine felicitas.'
'I kan noȝt construe', quod haukyn; 'ye moste kenne me þis
    on englissh.'
'[Al þis] in englissh', quod Pacience, 'it is wel hard to expounen,

265 for] for a R.
266 Hir] ⁊ hire F; his Hm; And OC^{2}Cot (*altered from* hir Cot). alle hire] hire al (*correct order noted*) Bm; hire M. folweþ] folwed R. hir] forþ hire F.
267 Muche] YHmGOC^{2}CBLMRF; Muche moore WCr. þat maide] þat mayde RF; suche a mayde HmYC^{2}CBL; swich a mayden OM; a meyde G; *om* WCr. to] the Cr. a man] hym WHmCrGOC^{2}CBLMRF; *om* Y.
268 Moore] FHmGYOC^{2}CBLMR; *om* WCr. a...is(1)] CHmCrGYOBLMR; a mayde is C^2; þat mayden ys F; is þat maiden W. is(2)] *om* C.
269 As] and GYOC^{2}CB. and] ⁊ peyȝe F.
270 coueitise] couetous Cr. catel] good WHmCrGYOC^{2}CBLMRF.
271 preueþ] fareþ WHmCrGYOC^{2}CBLMRF. ech] euery F; *om* G. a] *om* CrF.
272 put] putteþ HmGYOC^{2}CB. weddeþ] wyddeþ Hm.
273 The which] which R; Such Cr. so...pouerte] and so neyȝ is pouerte R; ⁊ so neer is þat persone F; and so to hise seintes WHmCrGYOC^{2}CBLM.
274 Haukyn] Hankyn Cr. I...yow] y heere F; þat huyre R; ye WHmCrGYOC^{2}CBLM. preise faste] preysen fast OC^{2}M; faste preyse R; preyse F. pouerte] pouert BmBo.
275 pacience] R; wiþ pacience WHmCrGYOC^{2}CBLM; *om* F. quod he] *om* OC^2.
276 *Remocio*] *Remoue* Y. *curarum*] *curatum* Cr^1. *possessio*] pessessio C^2. *donum*] *domum* C. *sanitatis*] HmCr^{23}GOC^{2}LMF; *sanitas* WCr^{1}YCB; *semita* R. *sollicitudine*(1)] *solitudine* Cr^{2}OC^{2}BRF. *sollicitudine*(2)] sollittudine B. *felicitas*] *felicitas* ⁊*c* Hm.
277 *as two lines divided before* ye R. construe] construe þys HmGYOC^{2}CB; construe al þis WCrLMRF. haukyn] Hankyn Cr. ye] þou F. moste] musten OBmBo; *om* F. kenne] telle Hm; seyn YGOC^{2}CB. me þis] þis HmCrLM; it OC^{2}BF; *om* GYC. on] yn HmCr.
278 Al...Pacience] Quod pacience in englyȝs F. Al...in] In WHmCrGOC^{2}CBLMR; On Y. wel] full HmB; *om* F. to] HmCrGF; wel to WYOC^{2}CBLMR. expounen] expowne HmCrGOC^{2}Cot; expowne it to soþe F.

Ac somdeel I shal seyen it, by so þow vnderstonde.
Pouerte is þe firste point þat pride moost hateþ;
Thanne is it good by good skile, al þat agasteþ pride.
Riȝt as contricion is confortable þyng, conscience woot wel,
And a sorwe of hymself and solace to þe soule,
So pouerte p*ro*preliche penaunce [is to þe body,
And Ioye to pacient pouere], pure spiritual helþe,
[And Contricion confort and *cura animarum*;
Ergo paupertas est odibile bonum.]
Selde sit pouerte þe soþe to declare,
[O]r as Iustice to Iugge men enioyned is no poore,
Ne to be Mair aboue men ne Mynystre vnder kynges;
Selde is any poore yput to punysshen any peple.
[*Ergo* pouerte and poore men p*ar*fou*r*nen þe comaundement
Nolite iudicare quemquam:
Remocio curarum.]
Selde is poore [riȝt] riche but of riȝtful heritage.

279 Ac] but GF; And CrC^{2}CR. by] *om* G. þow] ye YC^{2}CB. stonde] stonde it F.
280 moost] mode Bm.
281 is it] it is Cr; is C. al...agasteþ] þat it agaste F.
282 as] ⁊ Cr. is] is a Cr. þyng] *om* G. woot] it woot OC^2; wot it Cr.
283 And a] And Cr; þey it be F. of] to GF; for Y. and] ⁊ CrGYOC^{2}CB; and a WHmLMR; it is F. þe] his F.
284 So] Ryght so F. pouerte] pouert B. propreliche] properly ys F. is...body] and Ioye WHmCrGYOC^{2}CBLMRF.
285 And...pouere] Is to þe body WHmCr^1 GYOC^{2}CBLMR; Is the bodyes Cr^{23}; ⁊ to þe body ys F. spiritual] perpetuel OC^2. helþe] helpe F; leche Cr.
286 *transposed with* 287 WHmCrGYC^{2}CBL MRF. And Contricion] And *Contricio* M; *Contricio* is F. confort] conforteth Cr. *animarum*] *animarum* þe second GYOC^{2}C B; *anima animarum* þe seconde Cr^{23}.
287 *in margin opposite* 285 O. *bonum*] *bonum* ⁊*c* HmY.
288 Selde] For selden F. sit] sytteth Cr^{23} GB. pouerte] pouert B; the pure Y.
289 Or] Cr^{23}GYOC^{2}CBLR; hor Hm; For WCr^{1}M (ff *over erasure* M); As sytt a F. as] a BoCot. Iustice] iusticie Hm. enioyned...poore] of gyltys F; *om* R.
290 to] for to R; as F. be] be a YOCBL MR; a F. aboue] abouen YOCB; ouere R; on F. kynges] kyng OC^2.
291 Selde] Selden OHmC^{2}LMF. any(1)] þe F; enemye R. yput] put CrGYOC^{2}C BmBoM. punysshen] punysch HmCrGY OC^2; punschen BF. any(2)] the GF. *Here* WHmCrGYOC^{2}CBLMR *copy line* 293α (*in margin* OC^2).
292 pouerte] pouert B. þe] godd*es* F. comaundement] commaundementes Cr^{23} GC^2.
293 *quemquam*] Cot; *quemquam* þe þridde WHmCrGYOC^{2}CBmBoLMRF.
293α *line om* F; *copied after* 291 WHmCrG YOC^{2}CBLMR. *curarum*] *curarum* ⁊ *cetera* Hm; *ergo curarum* Cot.
294 Selde] Selden OC^{2}F. poore riȝt] pore riȝt RF; any poore WHmYOC^{2}CBLM; any pore men Cr^1; any pore man Cr^{23}; any pouerte G. but of] but of his R; but it be of F; of Cr; of any G. riȝtful] ryghful Cr^1; vnrightfull Cr^{23}.

Wynneþ he no3t wiþ wi3tes false ne wiþ vnseled mesures,
Ne borweþ of hise neighebores but þat he may wel paie:
Possessio sine calumpnia.
The ferþe is a fortune þat florissheþ þe soule |
Wiþ sobretee fram alle synne and also 3it moore; *fol.* 85 *b*
It afaiteþ þe flessh fram folies ful manye,
A collateral confort, cristes owene 3ifte:
Donum dei.
The fifte is moder of [my3t and of mannes] helþe,
A frend in alle fondynges, [of foule yueles leche],
And for þe [lewde] euere [yliche] a lemman of alle clennesse:
Sani[*tatis*] *mater.*
The sixte is a path of pees; ye! þoru3 þe paas of Aultou*n*
Pouerte my3te passe wiþouten p*er*il of robbyng.
For þer þ*at* Pou*er*te passeþ pees folweþ after,
And euer þe lasse þ*at* he [lede], þe [li3ter] he is of herte:
[*Cantabit paupertas coram latrone viato*[*r*],
And an hardy man of herte among an heep of þeues;

295 Wynneþ he] he wynneþ F. he] *om* OC^{2}. wi3tes false] falce weyghtes G; false weight Cr^{23}; hise wy3les F. wi3tes] weight Cr^{1}; wittes R. false] *om* B. wiþ(2)] *om* GYOC^{2}CB.
296 neighebores] neyheboure F. paie] payen F.
296α *in margin* OC^{2}. *calumpnia*] *calumpnia &c* HmY.
297 is a] it is a R; is B. florissheþ] florcheþ F.
298 sobretee] sobrietie Cr. synne] synnes YOC^{2}.
299 folies] foles CrF.
300 cristes owene] criste owene BmBo; comeþ of c*ri*stis F. 3ifte] 3iftis C^{2}; gyfe Cr^{3}.
300α *in margin* HmOC^{2} (*another hand and ink* Hm). *dei*] *igitur dei* Cot.
301 *run together with* 302 WHmCrGYOC^{2}CBLMRF. is] is þe F; it is þe R. of(1)... mannes] of WHmCrGYOC^{2}CBLMRF. helþe] hele RF.
302 A] and F. fondynges...leche] fondynges WHmCrGYOC^{2}CBLMR; fondy*nge* F.
303 lewde] GOC^{2}B; lawde YCR; land WHmCrLM; lawe F. yliche] ylyche F; a liche R; a leche WHmCrGYOC^{2}CBLM. alle] *om* GF.
303α *in margin* OC^{2}. *Sanitatis*] HmCr^{23} GOC^{2}LMRF; *Sanitas* WCr^{1}YCB. *mater*] *mater & cetera* Hm.
304 The] The þe C^{2}. is] it is R. ye...Aultou*n*] platou*n* beryþ witnesse F. þe] *om* G. paas] pa R. of(2)] to G; *om* R.
305 Pouerte] Pouert B. outen] oute Hm CrGYOC^{2}CBLMR.
306 þat] *om* M. Pouerte] pouert B.
307 *line om* F. þat] *om* OC^{2}. lede] bereþ WHmCrGYOC^{2}CBLMR. li3ter] hardier WHmCr^{23}YOBLMR; harder Cr^{1}GC^{2}C (*corrected* C^{2}). he(2)] *om* R.
307α *transposed with* 309 WHmCrGYOC^{2}CBLMRF (*in margin by* 308 OC^{2}). *Cantabit*] *Cantabat* CrCotR. *paupertas*] *pauper* OC^{2}Cot. *viator*] GOC^{2}CBLRF; *viator &c* Hm; *viatore* WCrM; *&c* Y.
308 And] and in Cot; he is F.

Forþi seiþ Seneca *Paupertas est absque sollicitudine semita.*|
The seuenþe is welle of wisedom and fewe wordes sheweþ
[For] lordes alloweþ hym litel or listneþ to his reson;
He tempreþ þe tonge to truþeward [þat] no tresor coueiteþ:
Sapiencie temperatrix.
The eighteþe is a lele labour and looþ to take moore
Than he may [soþly] deserue, in somer or in wynter;
And [þou3] he chaffareþ he chargeþ no losse, mowe he charite wynne:
Negocium sine dampno.
The nynþe is swete to þe soule, no sugre swetter,
For pacience is payn for pouerte hymselue,
And sobretee swete drynke and good leche in siknesse.
Thus lered me a lettred man for oure lordes loue, Seint Austyn:
A blessed lif wiþouten bisynesse for body and soule:
Absque sollicitudine felicitas.
Now god þat alle good gyueþ graunte his soule reste |

309 *transposed with* 307α WHmCrGYCBLMRF; *copied before* 308 OC^2. Forþi] Therfore Cr. Seneca] senecta R. *sollicitudine*] *ci cancelled* O; *solitudine* C^{2}BRF. *semita*] *om* Cr.
310 is] it is R. welle] wille CB. wordes] wordis he F.
311 For] GHmYOC^{2}CBLMRF; Therfore WCr. alloweþ] alow Cr. litel] lite R.
312 He] YHmGOC^{2}CBLMRF; For he WCr. þe] his CrF. þat] þat RF; and WHmCrGYOC^{2}CBLM. tresor] tresoun F.
312α *in margin* OC^2; *line om* RF. *Sapiencie*] *Sapiencia* BmBo. *temperatrix*] *temperatrix &c* HmY.
313 The eighteþe] Theght Cr^1. eighteþe] eight Cr^{23}GCB; eyte C^2. is] it is R; *om* G. a] *om* B. lele] lely Cr. labour] labourer CrLRF. take] taken F.
314 he] she G. may] *om* Cr. soþly] wel WHmCrGYOC^{2}CBLMRF. deserue] deserueth Cr.
315 þou3] if WHmCrGYOC^{2}CBLMRF. he(1)] *om* L. chaffareþ] chaffare HmGYOC^{2}CBmBoM. losse] loste Cot. mowe] if F. wynne] wynte R.
315α *in margin* OC^2. *dampno*] *dampno &c* Hm.
316 nynþe is] nythe it is R. to] for OC^2. no] & no G. swetter] GYOC^{2}CB; is swetter WHmCrLMRF.
317 pouerte] pouert B. hym] he is hym F. selue] seluen M.
318 sobretee] sobryete G. swete] is sweete F. and] & a F. siknesse] swetenesse Cot.
319–20α *divided after* loue, bysynesse HmGYOC^{2}CBLR; *after* loue, ladde M; *after* heuene, ladde WCr; *after* heuene, bisinesse F.
319 Thus] thys G. lered] lerned CrF. lettred] lered RF. loue] HmGYOC^{2}CBLMR; loue of heuene WCrF. Austyn] Augustyn C^2; austyn ledde Hm; Austyn seyþ it ys F; augustyne had had (had(2) *cancelled*) G.
320 A] *om* CB. outen] oute HmCrGC^{2}B; outyn ony F. bisynesse] YHmGOC^{2}CBLRF; bisynesse ladde WCrM (ladde *another ink* M). soule] GYOC^{2}CB; for soule WHmCrLMRF.
320α *Absque*] *om* R. *sollicitudine*] *solitudine* BoCot; solittudine Bm.
321 gyueþ] 3eueth (3 *altered to* y) M.

That þ[u]s first wroot to wissen men what Pouerte was to
mene.' *fol.* 86 *a*
'Allas', quod Haukyn þe Actif man þo, 'þ*at* after my cristendom
I ne hadde be deed and doluen for dowelis sake!
So hard it is', quod haukyn, 'to lyue and to do synne.
Synne seweþ vs euere', quod he and sory gan wexe,
And wepte water wiþ hise eighen and weyled þe tyme
That [euere he] dide dede þat deere god displesed;
Swouned and sobbed and siked ful ofte
That euere he hadde lond ouþ*er* lordshipe lasse oþ*er* moore,
Or maistrie ouer any man mo þan of hymselue.
'I were noȝt worþi, woot god', quod haukyn, 'to werien any
cloþes,
Ne neiþ*er* sherte ne shoon, saue for shame one
To couere my careyne', quod he, and cride mercy faste
And wepte and wailede, and þerwiþ I awakede.

322 þus] GYOC^{2}CBLMRF; þis WHmCr. wissen] wysse GMRF. Pouerte] pouert B. was] is Y. to mene] *om* Cr.
323 Haukyn] Ha*n*kin Cr. þe...þo] þanne F; *om* R. þo] þen G.
324 I] þat y Hm. ne] *om* F. doluen] deluen C; doluell Cr. dowelis] dowell GC; de wel Y.
325 it is] is yt Hm. quod haukyn] *om* F. quod] for Cr^3. haukyn] Hankyn Cr. lyue] lyuen Hm; lyven heere & F. do] do no Cr; lyȝn longe in F; *om* Hm. synne] *cancelled for* well *main hand* G.
326 seweþ] scheweth RF. euere...he] good se*m*blau*n*t F. wexe] he wexen F; wepe Cr.
327 weyled] weyles Hm.
328 euere he] YHmCrGOC^{2}CBLMRF; he euere W. dede] ony dede F. þat] þ*at* he G. displesed] displeside*n* C^2; dispeased Cr^3.
329 Swouned] Swowede OLMR; he swowned BF. sobbed] snobbed Cot.
330 ouþ*er*] or HmGYOC^{2}CBLMRF; *om* Cr. lordshipe] larde OC^2. oþ*er*] of CrG Cot.
331 maistrie] maistre C. of] ou*er* F. selue] seluen M.
332 were] werere O. woot god] wite god R; *om* GYOC^{2}CBF. haukyn] Ha*n*kyn Cr. werien] werie CCrGYOC^{2}BLMR.
333 Ne] *om* BF. shoon] shoo Cr^3; show Cr^{12}. one] only Cr.
334 couere] coue*r*en C^2. quod] wiþ quod B. cride] crien Cr^1. mercy faste] fast me*r*cye GYOC^{2}CB.
335 awakede] waked CrGC.

XV

AC after my wakynge it was wonder longe
Er I koude kyndely knowe what was dowel,
And so my wit weex and wanyed til I a fool weere.
And some lakkede my lif—allowed it fewe—
And lete me for a lorel and looþ to reu*er*encen
Lordes or ladies or any lif ellis,
As p*er*sons in pelure wiþ pendaunt3 of siluer;
To sergeaunt3 ne to swiche seide no3t ones,
'God loke yow, lordes', ne loutede faire,
That folk helden me a fool; and in þat folie I raued
Til reson hadde ruþe on me and rokked me aslepe,
Til I sei3, as it sorcerie were, a sotil þyng wiþ alle.
Oon wiþouten tonge and teeþ tolde me whider I sholde
And wherof I cam & of what kynde. I coniured hym at þe laste
If he were cristes creature [for cristes loue] me to tellen. |

1 Ac] But G; ANd CrC^{2}C; As B; *om* F. wakynge] walkyng BmBoR. wonder] *om* CF. longe] longe after F.
2 was] is M.
3 weex] wexed C. wanyed] waued Cr^{1}. a fool] ful Cot.
4 my lif] me self Cr. allowed] aloweden O; & alowed G; þ*er*e alowed F. it] it but M.
5 lete] leten HmCrGYOC^{2}CBLMRF. me] *above line* M; *om* HmGYOC^{2}CL. reu*er*encen] reu*er*ence YCB; don me worchepe F.
6 Lordes] Eyþ*er* lordis F. or(1)] and Hm C^{2}.
7 As] And Cr^{1}. in] wi*th* F. wiþ] and with YOC^{2}CB. of] *twice* Y.
8 sergeaunt3] sergeau*n*t Hm. ne] and RF. swiche] none such Hm; swiche me*n* F; suche and R. seide] YGOC^{2}CBLRF; seide I WHmCrM (I *above line* M).
9 ne] ne y F; & G. faire] to he*m* fayre F.
10 helden] helde GYCBF. me] *om* C. þat] my F. I] *om* F. raued] reued C^{2}; reygned Cr.
12 Til...were] þan sey3 y a syght of sorsery3e F. it] it of R. a] & OC^{2}.
13 Oon] *om* Cot. outen] oute GR. and] or HmCr^{23} MF. whider] wonder R.
14 *as two lines divided after* schulde R. I(1)] he Cr. &] *om* F. of(2)] *om* GYOC^{2}CBRF. what kynde] what kynne Cr^{3}; kendely F; whider I schulde R. I(2)...laste] þan co*n*iowred y hy*m* in haste F. coniured] conyouryd Hm. þe] *om* Cr^{1}.
15 creature] creature quod he B. for... loue] MGYOC^{2}CBLRF; leue Hm; anoon WCr. tellen] telle HmGYOC^{2}CBF.

'I am cristes creature', quod he, 'and [of his kyn a party], *fol. 86 b*
In cristes court yknowe wel and of [cristene in many a place].
Is neiþer Peter þe Porter ne Poul wiþ [þe] fauchon
That wole defende me þe dore, dynge I neuer so late.
At mydnyght, at mydday, my vois so is knowe
That ech a creature of his court welcomeþ me faire.'
'What are ye called', quod I, 'in þat court among cristes peple?'
'The whiles I quykne þe cors', quod he, 'called am I *anima*;
And whan I wilne and wolde *animus* ich hatte;
And for þat I kan [and] knowe called am I *mens*;
And whan I make mone to god *memoria* is my name;
And whan I deme domes and do as truþe techeþ
Thanne is *Racio* my riȝte name, reson on englissh;
And whan I feele þat folk telleþ my firste name is *sensus*,
And þat is wit and wisdom, þe welle of alle craftes;
And whan I chalange or chalange noȝt, chepe or refuse,
Thanne am I Conscience ycalled, goddes clerk and his Notarie;
And whan I loue leelly oure lord and alle oþere
Thanne is lele loue my name, and in latyn *Amor*;

16 cristes] criste C. creature] creatures Y. of...party] cristene in many a place WHmCrGYOC^{2}CBLMRF (a] *om* GCotR. place] places G).
17 cristes] crist C. cristene...place] his kyn a party WHmCrGYOC^{2}CBLMRF (his] *cristis* F; *om* CB. party] *parte* G).
18 Is] þer is (þer *over erasure another script*) Hm. þe Porter] *om* Y. þe(1)] ne Hm. þe(2)] R; his WHmCrGYOC^{2}CBLMF.
19 That] þa L.
20 so is] is so HmCrYRF; ys G. knowe] knowen OC^2; yknowe HmBLMR; y-knawen C; well Iknowe GF.
21 ech] euery F. a] *om* GF. welcomeþ] welcome BmBo.
22 What] But what F. ye] *om* F. quod...court] yn þat court *quod* y HmGYOC^{2}CBM. among] amogest G.
23 The] Ther Hm; *om* G. quykne] quicke*n* Cr; quykke LMR; qwyke in F; quyk was yn HmGYOC^{2}CB. cors] body C. quod he] *om* F. called] Icald R. am I] y am HmF.
24 whan] whand C. wilne] wylle HmCr. and] or OC^2. *animus*] *anima* B.
25 *copied after* 28 F. And...þat] for G. and] HmCrGYOC^{2}CBLMR; y F; *om* W. am I *mens*] *mens* y am ofte F. *mens*] *mens* thouȝte R.
26 *memoria*...name] my name is Memorye F.
27 whan] wh Y. domes] on dees F.
28 is...name] *racio* my*n* name is ryght (is *above line*) F. name] name and GYOC^2. on] in Cr^{23}G. englissh] englyssh tunge F. *Here* F *copies line* 25.
29 my] me my G. firste] *om* GCB.
31 I] *om* OC^2. chalange (2)] calange Bm. noȝt] nouȝ C. chepe] clepe YOC^2.
32 Conscience] *om* C. ycalled] called Cr GYOC^{2}CB. goddes...his] *cristis* clerkis F.
34 lele] Leli Cr. loue] *om* Cot. and] *om* C.

And whan I flee fro þe flessh and forsake þe careyne
Thanne am I spirit spechelees; *Spiritus* þanne ich hatte.
Austyn and Ysodorus, eiþer of hem boþe
Nempnede me þus to name; now þow myȝt chese
How þow coueitest to calle me, now þow knowest [alle] my names.
Anima pro diuersis accionibus diuersa nomina sortitur: dum viuificat corpus anima est; dum vult animus est; dum scit mens est; dum recolit memoria est; dum iudicat racio est; dum sentit sensus est; dum amat Amor est; dum negat vel consentit consciencia est; dum spirat spiritus est.' |
'Ye ben as a bisshop', quod I, al bourdynge þat tyme, *fol.* 87 *a*
'For bisshopes yblessed bereþ manye names,
Presul and *Pontifex* and *Metropolitanus*,
And oþere names an heep, *Episcopus* and *Pastor*.'
'That is sooþ', seide he; 'now I se þi wille.
Thow woldest knowe and konne þe cause of alle [hire] names,
And of [myne] if þow myȝtest, me þynkeþ by þi speche.'
'Ye, sire!' I seide, 'by so no man were greued
Alle þe sciences vnder sonne and alle þe sotile craftes
I wolde I knewe and kouþe kyndely in myn herte.'

35 flee] flye YOCBL. fro þe flessh] fleschly lust F. þe(1)] ⁊ Cr^{2}; þat Cr^{3}. þe(2)] *om* F.

36 spirit] CrHmGYOC^{2}CBLMR; a spirit WF. *Spiritus*] and *Spiritus* LRF.

37 Austyn] augustyne G. Ysodorus... boþe] ambrose have brevid on here bookis F. eiþer] ⁊ eyther G; oþer B. hem] hym Bm.

38 Nempnede] Named Cr; neuened G; þey nempned F. to] be F. now] HmCrGYOC^{2}CBLMRF; and now W. myȝt] myȝtist OC^{2}; may G.

39 coueitest to] wilt F. calle] cally*n* F; knowe Y. now] HmCrGYOC^{2}CBLMR; for now W; *om* F. þow knowest] knowest þou OGYCB; knowest C^{2}. alle] HmCrYOC^{2}CBLMRF; *om* WG.

39α *scit*] *sit* R; *discernit* Cot; *om* BmBo. *est*(4)] *om* G. *est*(9)] *est* ⁊*c* HmY.

40 Ye] what ȝee F. as] *om* BoCot. al bourdynge] ⁊ gan burde F.

41 yblessed] blessed Cr^{1}; þ*at* ben yblessid F. bereþ] bereth MYOC^{2}CB; beyre G; þei bereþ WHmLRF; they beare Cr.

42 *Metropolitanus*] metropolanus RF.

43 heep] heape as G. and] *et* F.

44 seide] þan seyde F; quod Y. now] for now F.

45 konne] ken Cr. hire] MHmCrGYOC^{2}CBLR (here *over erasure another ink* Hm); my WF.

46 myne] GHmCrYOC^{2}CBLMRF; me W. þinkeþ] thinke CrG. þi] my*n* F.

47 I] he G; þan F. by] y F; *om* G. so] so þ*at* GB. greued] agreued YOC^{2}MF.

48 Alle] and alle Hm. sciences] science YOC^{2}CBR. craftes] crafte Cr^{3}.

49 I knewe] knowe GOC^{2}CB. kouþe] konne GOC^{2}; knew F. kyndely] parfytelyche G.

'Thanne artow inparfit', quod he, 'and oon of prides kny3tes.
For swich a lust and likyng Lucifer fel from heuene:
Ponam pedem meum in aquilone ⁊ similis ero altissimo.
It were ayeins kynde', quod he, 'and alle kynnes reson
That any creature sholde konne al except crist oone.
Ayein swiche Salomon spekeþ and despiseþ hir wittes
And seiþ, *Sicut qui mel comedit multum non est ei bonum, Sic qui scrutator est maiestatis opprimitur a gloria.*
To englisshe men þis is to mene, þat mowen speke and here,
The man þat muche hony eteþ his mawe it engleymeþ,
And þe moore þat a man of good matere hereþ,
But he do þerafter, it dooþ hym double scaþe.
"*Beatus est*", seiþ Seint Bernard, "*qui scripturas legit*
Et verba vertit in opera fulliche to his power."
Coueitise to konne and to knowe scienc[e]
[Adam and Eue putte out of Paradis]:
Sciencie appetitus hominem inmortalitatis gloria[m] spoliauit.
And ri3t as hony is yuel to defie and engleymeþ þe mawe, |
Right so þat þoru3 reson wolde þe roote knowe *fol.* 87 *b*
Of god and of hise grete my3tes, hise g*ra*ces it letteþ.

50 inparfit] vnp*ar*fytt GYOC^{2}CB. prides] pride C.
51 *hereafter an additional line* F: *see above*, p. 223.
51α *meum*] *om* Cr. *altissimo*] *altissimo ⁊c* Hm.
52 and] of Hm; *om* C^{2}. alle] *om* Cr.
53 konne] kenne CrRF. oone] alone G; hy*m* oone F; *om* R.
54 *divided from* 55 *after mel* C^{2}. despiseþ] disputiþ F. wittes] wis Cr^{3}.
55 And] he F. *Sicut qui*] *si quis* F. *comedit*] *comedet* Cr. *ei bonum*] *bonum ei* F. *maiestatis*] *maiestas* Y. *opprimitur*] *opprimatur* R; *opprimetur* F. *gloria*] *gloria ⁊c* Hm.
56 To...mene] That is to mean to english me*n* Cr^{23}. men] *om* Cr^{1}. mene] men C. mowen speke] men spekyn Hm. here] heeren F.
57 The] þ*at* C^{2}. muche] mychel F. eteþ] eet RF. it engleymeþ] is engleymed BCr^{23}R; mote be engleymed F.
58 And] Ryght so F. hereþ] etith Cot.
59 after] fore Cr. it] he Hm. double] mychil F.
60 *est*] *vir* G; *qui* Bm; *om* BoCot. Seint] *om* M. *scripturas*] *scripturam* Cr; *scriptura* C.
61 *verba vertit*] *vertit verba* HmRF. fulliche] holly F.
62 *line om* C. Coueitise] he þat Coueytiþ F. konne] ken Cr. science] CrHmGY OC^{2}BLMR; sciences WF.
63 Putte out of Paradis Adam and Eue WHmCrGYOC^{2}BLMRF (Putte] Pulte LMR (*altered to* Putte M); Pullede OC^{2}; was pyt F. Adam] as adam F); *line om* C.
63α *in margin* O. *Sciencie*] *Sciencia* B. *gloriam*] GYOC^{2}CBLMRF (*m cancelled* O); *gloria* WHmCr. *spoliauit*] *spoliauit ⁊c* Hm.
64 And] but G. ri3t] 3et R. and] *om* C^{2}. engleymeþ] engleyme F.
65 so] HmGYOC^{2}CBLMRF; so he WCr. þat] *om* F. wolde] he wolde F.
66 of] *om* C^{2}CB. grete] *om* GYOC^{2}CB. g*ra*ces] grace HmGYOC^{2}CBF. it] is Y; gan it F. letteþ] lette F.

For in þe likynge liþ a pride and licames coueitise
Ayein cristes counseil and alle clerkes techynge,
That is *Non plus sapere quam oportet sapere.*
Freres and fele oþ*ere* maistres þat to [þe] lewed [folk] p*re*chen,
Ye moeuen materes vnmesurable to tellen of þe Trinite
That [lome] þe lewed peple of hir bileue doute.
Bettre it were [by] manye doctours to [bi]leuen swich techyng
And tellen men of þe ten comaundementȝ, and touchen þe seuene synnes,
And of þe braunches þ*at* burioneþ of hem and bryngen men to helle,
And how þ*at* folk in folies [hir fyue wittes mysspenden],
As wel freres as ooþ*er* folk, foliliche spenden
In housynge, in haterynge, [in] heigh clergie shewynge
Moore for pompe þan for pure charite; þe peple woot þe soþe.
That I lye noȝt, loo! for lordes ye plesen
And reuerencen þe riche þe raþer for hir siluer:

67 þe] þat B; *om* F. liþ] lyges C. a] gret F. and] ⁊ a OC^{2}LMR; ⁊ in Cot; ⁊ In a GYCBmBo. licames] likinge C^{2}.
69 *in margin* OC^{2}. *sapere*(1)] sapire G. *sapere*(2)] *om* Cr^{23}.
70 fele] *om* GRF. þe] HmCrGYCBmBo LMR; *om* WOC^{2}CotF. folk] men WHm CrGYOC^{2}CBLMRF.
71 Ye] *om* Cr^{23}GYOC^{2}CB. moeuen materes] meve mateer F. vnmesurable] inmesurable CrYCot; vnmesurables RG; ynmesurables HmOC^{2}CBmBoLM. tellen] tel Cr.
72 *line om* RF. That] And OC^{2}. lome] ofte tymes WHmCrGYOC^{2}CBL M. doute] douten CrHmGYOC^{2}CBLM.
73 were...bileuen] *over erasure another hand and ink* M. it were] were M; byleue were L; beleue were (e(1) *over erasure*) Hm; beleue where Cr^{1}; to leue were YCr^{23}GC Cot; to leue weren BmBo; to bileue were OC^{2}; byleue R. by] R; to WF; *om* Hm CrGYOC^{2}CBLM. manye] mone R; beleve on as F. to bileuen] bileue (bi *erased*) M; to leuen W; *om* HmCrGYOC^{2} CBLRF. swich] *om* RF. techyng] vs techeþ F.
74 And] To C. tellen] telle YCrGOC^{2} CR. men] *om* F. of] *om* GR. þe(1)] *om* CrYC. touchen] touche GYOC^{2}CBF; techen M.
75 *line om* GCB. of(1)] *om* F. burioneþ] bourgeleth R; budde Cr. bryngen] brynge Hm.
76 in] in hire M; *with* F. hir...mysspenden] mysspenden hir fyue wittes WHm CrGYOC^{2}CBLMRF (mysspenden] mispend Cr. fyue] *om* Hm).
77 folk] me*n* F. foliliche] folysshlyche G; folich YC^{2}; folish Cr^{3}. spenden] they spenden YOC^{2}M; spenen CrCLR; speken B.
78 in(1)] and yn Hm. in(2)] yn G; into RF; and into WHmCrLM; and YOC^{2}CB.
79 pure] *om* CotF.
80 I] I ne YOC^{2}. noȝt] no woord F. loo] so Cr. ye] they Cr.
81 reuerencen] reue*r*ence YBF. þe riche] *om* Cr^{1}. þe(2)] me*n* þe F; *om* R. siluer] goodis OC^{2}.

Confundantur omnes qui adorant sculptilia; Et alibi, Vt quid diligitis vanitatem ⁊ queritis mendacium?
Gooþ to þe glose of þ[e] vers, ye grete clerkes;
If I lye on yow to my lewed wit, ledeþ me to brennyng!
For as [me þynkeþ] ye forsakeþ no mannes almesse,
Of vsurers, of hoores, of Auarouse chapmen,
And louten to þise lordes þat mowen lene yow nobles
Ayein youre rule and Religion; I take record at I*es*us
That seide to hise disciples, "*Ne sitis personarum acceptores*".
Of þis matere I myȝte make a long bible,
Ac of curatours of cristen peple, as clerkes bereþ witnesse,
I shal tellen it for truþes sake; take hede whoso likeþ.
As holynesse and honeste out of holy chirche [spryngeþ] |
Thoruȝ lele libbynge men þat goddes lawe techen, *fol.* 88 *a*
Right so out of holi chirche alle yueles [spredeþ]
There inparfit preesthode is, p*re*chours and techeris.
[And] se it by ensaumple in somer tyme on trowes:
Ther some bowes ben leued and some bereþ none
Ther is a meschief in þe more of swiche man*ere* [stokkes].

81α *sculptilia*] *sculptilia ⁊c* YGOC^{2}CB; scultilia L. *alibi*] *alibi dicitur* F. *diligitis*] *diligis* G. *mendacium*] *mendacium ⁊c* Hm; *⁊c* R.
82 Gooþ] go ye G. þe(2)] YCrGOC^{2}CB LMRF; þise WHm. ye] the Cr^1. grete] þat been F.
83 If] ⁊ yff G. ledeþ] leade CrF.
84 me þynkeþ] it semeþ WHmCrGYO C^{2}CBLMRF. forsakeþ] forsake CrGCF. mannes] me*n*nys F.
85 of(2)] ⁊ of F; and R.
86 And] ⁊ ȝee F. þise] þe F.
87 rule...Religion] religions rewle F. and] ⁊ ȝoure R. at] of YGOC^{2}CB.
88 *sitis*] *scitis* BmBoF. *personarum acceptores*] *acceptores personarum* RF.
89 make] *twice* C; maken F. long] grete R; mychil F.
90 Ac] but GF; And CrC^{2}C. curatours] curats Cr. of] ouer R. cristen] þe F. as clerkes] ac clergie Y. bereþ] bear Cr.
91 tellen] telle HmGC^{2}F. truþes] treuth LGRF. hede] he C; *om* Cot. whoso] wh it F. likeþ] lokethe GC.
92 As] and B. honeste] honestete L. out of] in F. spryngeþ] spryngeth (*over erasure another ink*) M; spredeþ WHmCr GYOC^{2}CBLRF.
93 lele] lelly Cr. libbynge] leuing Cr^{23}. lawe] lawes RF.
94 yueles] euell GYB (*erasure after it* Bm). spredeþ] spredeth HmCrGYOC^{2}CBLM RF; spryngeþ W.
95 inparfit] vnp*ar*fit B. is] is and RF.
96 And] YGOC^{2}CBLMR; I WHmCr; *om* F. in...trowes] on trees in som*er* tyme F. in] on Y.
97 Ther] *om* F. bereþ] bere CrG.
98 Ther is] For F. in] is in F. more... man*ere*] maist*er* roote þat is ca*m* of þe F. stokkes] bowes WHmCrGYOC^{2}CBLM RF.

Right so p*er*sons and preestes and p*re*chours of holi chirche
[Is þe] roote of þe right feiþ to rule þe peple;
A[c] þer þe roote is roten, reson woot þe soþe,
Shal neuere flour ne fruyt [wexe] ne fair leef be grene.
Forþi wolde ye lettrede leue þe lecherie of cloþyng,
And be kynde as bifel for clerkes and curteise of cristes goodes,
Trewe of youre tonge and of youre tail boþe,
And hatien to here harlotrie, and [au]ȝt to vnderfonge
Tiþes [of vn]trewe þyng ytilied or chaffared,
Loþe were lewed men but þei youre loore folwede
And amende[n] hem þat [þei] mysdoon moore for youre ensaumples
Than for to prechen and preuen it noȝt—ypocrisie it semeþ.
[For ypocrisie] in latyn is likned to a [loþly] dongehill
That were bisnewed wiþ snow and snakes wiþInne,
Or to a wal þat were whitlymed and were foul wiþInne;

99 Right...and(1)] So yt fareþ be F. so] HmGYOC^{2}CBLMR; so bi (bi *above line main hand*) W; so of Cr. preestes] prestoes C. p*re*chours] men M. of] in F. chirche] cherches R.
100 Is þe] R; That aren WHmCrGYOC^{2}CBLM; þey sholde been F. roote] rootes G. right] *om* GF.
101 Ac] HmYOBLMR; but GF; And WCrC^{2}C. þer þe] þe mayst*er* F. roten] rote F.
102 Shal...ne(1)] Shal it neu*er*e bery*n* F. fruyt wexe] fruyt WHmCrGYOC^{2}CBLMRF. fair...grene] branche of grene levis F.
103 Forþi] Therfore Cr. wolde] wolden O. ye] þe BRF. leue] leven F; men leue OCrC^2. þe] *om* F. of] ⁊ F.
104 bifel...clerkes] clerkis sholde F. bifel] fell GOC^2.
105 Trewe] ⁊ trewe F. youre(*both*)] here F. tonge] tonges G. tail] tales G. boþe] ende F.
106 hatien] hate CrGOC^2; hauen C. to here] al Y. here] heeren F. and] ytilied and (ytilied *cancelled*) C. auȝt] R; noȝt WHmYCBLM; not CrGOC^2; looþ wrong F. to(2)] *om* HmF.
107 Tiþes] the tythes (the *cancelled*) G; Of tythis F. of vntrewe] YHmOC^{2}CBLM; off trewe GRF; but of trewe WCr. þyng] þy*ng*is F. ytilied] tilyed CrG. or] ⁊ G. chaffared] ychaffaryd HmRF; chaffare Y.
108 Loþe] Both Cr^1. were] weren OF. loore] rule G. folwede] foleweden OC^2.
109 amenden] YCrOCLMR; amende GC^2; amendyd HmBF (-d *over erasure* Hm); amendeden W. þei] R; *om* WHmCrGYOC^{2}CBLMF. moore] þe moore F. for] thrugh G. youre] yuel Y.
110 for] *om* Cr. prechen] p*re*che OCrGC^{2}BF. preuen] preue YCrGCBLRF.
111 For ypocrisie] CHmCrGYOC^{2}BLMRF; The which W. is likned] likned is CB. is] *om* Y. a loþly] a WHmCr^{23}GYOC^{2}CBLMRF; *om* Cr^1. dongehill] dongou*n* RF.
112 snow] oute F. wiþ(2)] been *þere* F.
113 *line om* HmGCB. þat were] were Cr^1; *om* F. lymed] timed Cr^1. and were] wi*th*out ⁊ Cr^{23}YOC^2; withouten and were (withouten *over erasure another ink*) M. foule] dunk F.

Right so [preestes, prechours and prelates manye],
Ye aren enblaunched wiþ *bele paroles* and wiþ [*bele* cloþes]
Ac your*e* werkes and wordes þervnder aren ful [wol]ueliche.
Ioh*an*nes Crisostomus of clerkes [carpeþ] and preestes:
Sicut de templo omne bonum progreditur, sic de templo omne malum procedit. Si sacerdocium integrum fuerit tota floret ecclesia; Si autem corruptum fuerit omnium fides marcida est. Si sacerdocium fuerit in peccatis totus populus conuertitur ad peccandum. Sicut cum videris arborem pallidam & marcidam intelligis quod vicium |
habet in radice, Ita cum videris populum indisciplinatum & *fol.* 88 *b*
irreligiosum, sine dubio sacerdocium eius non est sanum.
If lewed [ledes] wiste what þis latyn meneþ,
And who was myn Auctour, muche wonder me þinkeþ
But if many preest [forbeere] hir baselardes and hir broches
[And beere] bedes in hir hand and a book vnder hir arme.
Sir Ioh*a*n and sire Geffrey haþ [of siluer a girdel],

114 preestes...manye] manye preestes prechours and p*re*lates WHmCrGYOC^{2}CBLMR; manye p*re*latis p*re*choures & preestis F.
115 Ye] *om* Cr^{23}GYOC^{2}CBF. aren] were Cr^{1}. enblaunched] blaunched MF. *bele paroles*] Belopolis Cr^{1}; Belperopis Cr^{3}. wiþ...cloþes] blewe burnet cloþis F; with clothes R; wiþ cloþes also WHmCrGYO C^{2}CBLM.
116 Ac] but G; And CrC^{2}CRF. and] YGOC^{2}CB; and youre WHmCrLMRF. þer] þat YC; *om* B. ful] al F; *om* GYBo Cot. wolueliche] wlueliche R; foxly F; vnloueliche WHmCrYOC^{2}CBLM; vnlyche G.
117 Ioh*an*nes] Iohanne OC^{2}; Iohn Cr^{23}. Crisostomus] Chrisostome Cr^{23}; criostomus R. carpeþ] spekeþ WHmCrGYOC^{2} CBLMR; he spekiþ F. preestes] prechiþ F.
118 *progreditur*] *egreditur* GYOC^{2}CB; *procedit* RF. *procedit*] *procedet* Cr^{2}. *integrum*] *incorruptum* Cr. *floret*] *floreret* OC^{2}. *corruptum*] *corupta* RF. *sacerdocium*(2)] *sacerdos* RF. *conuertitur*] *conuertetur* Cr; couertitur L. *peccandum*] *peccatum* Cr^{23}RF. *Sicut*(2)] *si* G. *cum*(1)] *si* CB; *om* F. *pallidam & marcidam*] *marcidam & pallidam* OGC^{2}CB. *intelligis*] *inteliges* Cr; Intellis R. *Ita...sanum*] *om* F. *videris*(2)] *dideris* Cr^{1}. *sanum*] *sanum &c* Hm.
119 ledes] men WHmCrGYOC^{2}CBLMR F. wiste] wysten HmOC^{2}F. meneþ] moueth Y.
120 who] *om* BoCot. was] were F. muche] gret F. me þinkeþ] me thynke Cr; wolde þey haven F.
121 if many] euery F. preest] MRF; prists Cr; a preest WHmGYOC^{2}CBL. forbeere] beere for WHmCrGYCBLMR; sholde ber*e* for F; heer for OC^{2}. hir(1)] hys G. baselardes] baselard G; broches R; broode F. and hir] and for her*e* R; & hys G; & B; *om* F. broches] baselardes RF.
122 Schulden go synge *ser*uyseles wiþ sire philip þe sparwe OC^{2}. And beere] A peire YGCBLR; A peire of WHmCrMF. hir(*both*)] hys G. hand] ha*n*ds Cr. and] or RF. vnder...arme] to bydde on F. vnder] in M.
123 haþ] haven F. of...girdel] a girdel of siluer WHmCrGYCBLMR; gyrdeles of siluer OC^{2}F.

A baselard or a ballokknyf wiþ botons ouergilte,
Ac a Porthors þat sholde be his Plow, *Placebo* to sigge—
Hadde he neu*ere* [saued] siluer þerto [for spendyng at ale];
[He syngeþ seruice bokelees], seiþ it w*ith* ydel wille.
Allas, ye lewed men, muche lese ye on preestes!
Ac þing þat wikkedly is wonne, and wiþ false sleightes,
Wolde neu*ere* þe wit of witty god but wikkede men it hadde,
The whiche arn preestes inparfite and p*re*chours after siluer,
Executours and Sodenes, Somono*urs* and hir lemmannes.
[This] þ*at* wiþ gile was geten vngr*a*ciousliche is [s]pended.
So harlotes and hores arn holpe wiþ swiche goodes
A[c] goddes folk for defaute *þer*of forfaren and spillen.
Curato*urs* of holy kirke, as clerkes þat ben auarouse,
Lightliche þat þei leuen losels it habbeþ,
Or [endeþ] intestate and þanne [entreþ þe bisshop]
And makeþ murþe þer[wiþ] and hise me[yne] boþe;

124 A] & a F. or a] & a GYC^{2}CB; & O. wiþ] & OC^{2}F. botons] barres OC^{2}. gilte] gilt bryghte F.
125 Ac] but GF; And CrC^{2}C. a] his F. þat] *om* G. sholde] shul Y; *om* F. be] is F. to] on to F. sigge] seggen F; synge Cr. *Hereafter an additional line* F; *see above*, p. 223.
126, 127 *as one line* WHmCrGYOC^{2}CBLMRF: Hadde he neu*ere* seruice to saue siluer þerto seiþ it w*ith* ydel wille (Hadde] If F. neu*ere*] hadd no F. to saue] to haue R; ne F. þerto] *om* F. seiþ...wille] w*ith* evil will he will sy*n*ge F; for spendyng at ale OC^{2}. it] *om* BoCot. ydel] yvel LR).
128 muche] mychil F; full muche Hm. lese] lesen OC^{2}. ye] they G; *om* Cot.
129 Ac] but G; For F; and C^{2}C; And a Cr. þing...and] wikkidly þey wynnen gold & F. wikkedly is] is wikkedliche M. wonne] wonnen OC^{2}; ywonnen M. false] slyȝe F.
130 þe...god] of witty god the wit YGOC^{2}CB. þe] *om* CrLMRF. wit] wylle Hm. wikkede] vnwitty F. it] he*m* F. hadde] hadden M; maked R; made F.
131 The] þ*at* F; *om* G. whiche arn] swiche F. and...after] lyve & p*re*chen for F.
132 *transposed with* 133 Cr^{23}. Executours] sectours GYOC^{2}CCotLR; Sectorous Bm Bo; & ben seketoures F. and Sodenes] of sowlis good & F. Sodenes] sodekenes B; sodemes Cr. Somono*urs*] samoners Cr. and...lemmannes] w*ith* here feeris F.
133 This] HmGYOC^{2}CBLMR; That WCr; Al F. þ*at*] *om* Cr^{23}. was] is Cr^{23}; þey F. geten] gete R. spended] CrHmG YOC^{2}CBLMF; despended W; spened R.
134 arn] have F. holpe] holpen HmCrG YOC^{2}CBLMR. wiþ] þoruȝ OC^{2}; owt F. goodes] godeth R.
135 Ac] R; But F; And WHmCrGYOC^{2} CBLM. folk] folks Cr. defaute] defatue Cr^{2}. þerof] herof Hm; *om* F. spillen] spille Cr^{23}.
136 Curato*urs*] Of curatoures F. of] and Hm. kirke] chirche YHmGOC^{2}CBoCot RF; che Bm. as] and RF. auarouse] warous Cr^{1}.
137 Lightliche...leuen] þ*at* þey sparen lyghtly F. habbeþ] haþ BC.
138 endeþ] deieþ WMR; dyeth CrGYCB L; dyen HmOC^{2}; þey deye F. þanne] þer B; *om* Cr. entreþ þe bisshop] þe bisshop entreþ WHmCrGYOC^{2}CBLMR F.
139 murþe] *om* Cot. wiþ] OHmGYC^{2}C BmBoLMRF; w*ith* mery (mery *another hand*) Cot; myd WCr. meyne] HmF; men WCrGYOC^{2}CBLMR.

And [nempneþ hym] a nygard þat no good myȝte aspare
To frend ne to fremmed: "þe fend haue his soule!
For a wrecchede hous [he held] al his lif tyme,
And þat he spared and bisperede [s]pende we in murþe."
By lered, by lewed, þat looþ is to [s]pende
Thus goon hire goodes, be þe goost faren.
Ac for goode men, god woot, greet doel men maken,
And bymeneþ goode meteȝyueres and in mynde haueþ
In preieres and in penaunces, and in parfit charite.' |
'What is charite?' quod I þo; 'a childissh þyng', he seide: *fol.* 89 *a*
'*Nisi efficiamini sicut paruuli non intrabitis in regnum celorum.*
Wiþouten fauntelte or folie a fre liberal wille.'
'Where sholde men fynde swich a frend wiþ so fre an herte?
I haue lyued in londe', quod [I], 'my name is longe wille,
And fond I neuere ful charite, bifore ne bihynde.
Men beþ merciable to mendinauntȝ and to poore,
And wollen lene þer þei leue lelly to ben paied.

140 nempneþ hym] seyen he was WHmC^{2}BF; say he was GC; sigg*en* he was CrOLMR; segge he was Y. þat] & Y. aspare] spare HmCrGOC^{2}MF.

141 fre*m*med] frem B; Frende C^{2}. fend] *om* C^{2}. his] nou his F.

142 hous] housholde Hm. he held] CHmGYOC^{2}BLMR; held he W; he healed Cr^{1}; he hyled Cr^{23}; he hild F.

143 and] he F. bisperede] sperede MF; byspared GCB; disperid Cr^{1}. spende] HmCrGYOC^{2}CBF; spene LMR; dispende W. we] we yt HmB; we now F; *om* C.

144 By] Boþe after F; Be it HmM (*over erasure* M); Be þei OC^{2}; Be he B. lered] learned Cr; lewid BF. by] and by CrG; & F; be it HmM (*over erasure* M); be þei OC^{2}; be he B. lewed] lerid BF. is] are G; ben F. spende] HmCrGYOC^{2}CBLMF; spene R; despende W.

145 Thus] thys G. be] away be Hm; by GYC. faren] yfaren F.

146 Ac] but GF; And CrC^{2}C. doel] dowel Cr^{1}.

147 And bymeneþ] & þey bemeene F. in] *om* C. haueþ] he*m* haueþ BR; he*m* have F.

148 In preieres] ye prears G. in(1)] *om* G. penaunces] penance CrGYOC^{2}CB. *Here* Y *adds a Latin tag; see above*, p. 224.

149 What] A what F. childissh] childist B (*corrected* Cot).

149α *in margin* OC^{2}. *paruuli*] *om* Y. *in...celorum*] *&c* OC^{2}. *in*] *om* Cr. *celorum*] *celorum &c* Hm.

150 outen] oute GCrR. fauntelte] fauteltie Cr; fau*n*tee OC^{2}. a] er a F; *om* Cr.

151 sholde] schulde*n* O. fynde] *om* GCB.

152 I(1)] *om* B. lyued] *om* CB. londe] longe Cr^{1}. I(2)] Cr^{23}GYOC^{2}CBLMRF; he WHmCr^{1}. my...wille] & longe will is my name F. longe wille] *om* Y.

153 fond...charite] ful charyte fond y neu*er*e F. ne] me ne F.

154 Men beþ] For me*n* be not F. and] ne F; *om* R. poore] þe pore OC^{2}; pou*er*e bothe G.

155 And] But þey F. wollen] wolle C^{2}GYCR; *om* F. lene] lenen M. leue] leuen OC^{2}; beleven F; loue CCot. lelly to ben] to been lelly F. paied] ypeyed F; apayed R.

Ac charite þat Poul preiseþ best, and moost plesaunt to oure
    [Saueour]—
Non inflatur, non est ambiciosa, non querit que sua sunt—
I sei3 neuere swich a man, so me god helpe,
That he ne wolde aske after his, and ouþerwhile coueite
Thyng þat neded hym no3t and nyme it if he my3te.
Clerkes kenne me þat crist is in alle places
Ac I sei3 hym neuere sooþly but as myself in a Mirour:
[*Hic*] *in enigmate, tunc facie ad faciem.*
And so I trowe trewely, by þat men telleþ of [it,
Charite] is no3t chaumpions fight ne chaffare as I trowe.'
'Charite', quod he, 'ne chaffareþ no3t, ne chalangeþ, ne craueþ.
As proud of a peny as of a pound of golde,
And is as glad of a gowne of a gray russet
As of a tunycle of tarse or of trie scarlet.
He is glad wiþ alle glade and good til alle wikkede
And leneþ and loueþ alle þat oure lord made.
Corseþ he no creature ne he kan bere no wraþe,
Ne no likynge haþ to lye ne laughe men to scorne.

156 Ac] but G; and C[2]C; But not for F; *om* Cr. preiseþ] precheþ OC[2]. best... moost] It F. and] *om* Cr. plesaunt] plesing Cr; pleseþ YGOC[2]CBF. to] is to (is *above line*) Hm; *om* GYOC[2]CBF. oure] *om* RF. Saueour] MHmGYOC[2]C BL; lord WCr[1]; God Cr[23]R; god in heuene F.
157 *Non*] CGB; As *non* YOC[2]LRF; Is *Non* WHmCrM (is *over erasure* M). *inflatur*] *inflatus* L. *est*] *above line* M; *om* L. *sunt*] HmCrGYOC[2]CBLMRF; *sunt* ⁊*c* W.
158 me god] god me Cr.
159 ne] *om* F. wolde] wole Y. aske] asken F. coueite] more coueyten F.
160 Thyng] Of þyng F. neded hym] hym neded RF; nedeþ hym YGOC[2]CB. nyme] take C. it] *om* Hm. if he my3te] f Y. he] thay C.
161 Clerkes] Crerkis F. kenne] kennen BHmMR; knne Y; tellen OC[2]. me] me soþly F. alle] al his C[2].
162 Ac] but GF; And CrC[2]C. neuere] *om* OC[2]. self] lyf Cot. a] *om* RF.
162α *in margin* OC[2]. *Hic*] FMR; *Ita* GYO C[2]CB; *It* L; *om* WHmCr. *faciem*] *faciem* ⁊*c* Hm.
163 And] Al B. by] be he F. telleþ] tell CrG. of] *om* F. it] charite WHmCrGYO C[2]CBLMRF.
164 Charite] It WHmCrGYOC[2]CBLMR; he F. no3t] no HmGF (*over large erasure* Hm). chaumpions] champioun with to F.
165 quod...no3t] chaffareþ not quod he F. ne(1)] *om* Cr. ne(2)] noþer R.
166 As] he is as F. of(1)] as of (of *another hand*) Cot; as CBmBo.
167 as] also HmB. a(2)] *om* CrCot.
168 of (2)] of of a Y. tarse] Carse C; say B. or] ⁊ F. trie] tried CrGOC[2]C; fyn B. scarlet] veluet F.
169 wiþ] to G. til] to CrGC[2]BF; ty L.
170 And] He YRF. leneþ] leueth Cr; beleviþ F. þat] þo þat F. lord] lord god F.
171 Corseþ he] he curseþ F. he(1)] *om* Cr. ne] *twice* C. he(2)] *om* HmOC[2].
172 no...haþ] he haþ lykynge F. haþ to] haue R. ne] ne to F. men] me R; non F.

Al þat men seyn, he leet it sooþ and in solace takeþ,
And alle manere meschiefs in myldenesse he suffreþ.
Coueiteþ he noon erþely good, but heueneriche blisse.' |
'Haþ he anye rentes or richesse or any riche frendes?' *fol. 89 b*
'Of rentes n[e] of richesse rekkeþ he neuere,
For a frend þat fyndeþ hym failed hym neuere at nede:
Fiat voluntas tua fynt hym eueremoore,
And if he soupeþ eteþ but a sop of *Spera in deo.*
He kan portreye wel þe Paternoster and peynte it with Aues
And ouþerwhile he is woned to wenden on pilgrymages
Ther poore men and prisons liggeþ, hir pardon to haue;
Thouȝ he bere hem no breed he bereþ hem swetter liflode;
Loueþ hem as oure lord biddeþ and lokeþ how þei fare.
And whan he is wery of þat werk þan wole he som tyme
Labouren in [a] lauendrye wel þe lengþe of a Mile,
And yerne into youþe and yepeliche [seche]
Pride wiþ al þe appurtenaunces, and pakken hem togideres,

173 Al] & all G. leet it] letethe G. and] & it F.
174 meschiefs] of myscheuys F; mischiefe Cr. myldenesse] mydenesse Y.
175 Coueitiþ he] he coueytiþ F. erþely] erly F; yerly G. good] godes RF. heueneriche] heuenlych Cr; heuynly hyȝe F.
176 *run together with* 177 Cr. rentes or] *om* F. richesse] richesses M. or(2)... frendes] *om* Cr. or(2)] quod he er F. riche] *om* G.
177 Of...richesse] *om* Cr. ne] HmGYOC^{2}CBLMRF; nor W. richesse] richesses M. rekkeþ] reckeþ C^{2}HmGYOCB; ne rekkeþ WCrLMR; quod he ne reccheþ F. he] hym Y.
178 a] þe F. fyndeþ] fynt R; dyndeth Y. failed] fayleth CrYCB. hym] hy R.
179 *Fiat*] For *fiat* F. fynt] fyndeþ HmCr^{23}OC^{2}CB; feedyþ F.
180 if] þerto F. soupeþ] soupe Cr^{23}GOC^{2}CM; souped Cr^1. eteþ] he eteþ HmCr^{23}GOC^{2}B; eet R; ette L; he ete YC; *om* F. but] *om* F. sop] soupe Cr.
181 wel] *om* OC^2. peynte] peynten R. Aues] aue RF; Pitie Cr; *om* C.
182 while] wille Y; *om* C^2. he is] he G; is R; is his HmLM. woned] wont GCF; wone HmYOC^{2}BmLMR; wonne Cr. wenden] wende YCrGOC^{2}CBLR. on] *in* BLM; *om* GYC. pilgrymages] pylgrymage HmCrOC^{2}LMR.
183 Ther] The Y. prisons] prisoners Cr GYOC^{2}CBF. liggeþ] lygge F; ligged Cr^1; been OC^2. hir] ther GF.
184 hem(1)] hym C. bereþ] bear Cr^1. hem(2)] *om* CrGMF. swetter] sotere F; bettre Hm. liflode] fode Cr^{23}; *om* OC^2.
185 Loueþ] For he loveþ F. hem] him Cr^1; *om* G. oure lord] god F. biddeþ] bit RF; bade Cr. fare] faren OC^{2}F.
186 wole] wold Cr^1. tyme] *om* B.
187 Labouren] Laboure CrLR; Sore laboure F. a] LR; *om* WHmCrGYOC^{2}CB MF. wel] *om* OC^{2}F.
188 yerne] ȝeernen F. youþe] þout B; trought G. seche] R; þere seken F; speke WHmCrGYOC^{2}CBLM.
189 þe] *per* G; hise F. appurtenaunces] appurtenaunce LHmYOC^{2}CBmBo; pertynaunces F; purtenaunce RCot. and] *om* Cr^3. pakken] pakke FCr.

And bouken hem at his brest and beten hem clene,
And leggen on longe wiþ *Laboraui in gemitu meo,*
And wiþ warm water at hise eiȝen wasshen hem after.
[Th]anne he syngeþ whan he doþ so, and som tyme wepynge,
Cor contritum & humiliatum deus non despicies.'
'By crist! I wolde I knewe hym', quod I, 'no creature leu*ere*.'
'Wiþouten help of Piers Plowman', quod he, 'his p*er*sone sestow neu*ere*.'
'Wheiþ*er* clerkes knowen hym', quod I, 'þat kepen holi kirke?'
'Clerkes haue no knowyng', quod he, 'but by werkes and wordes.
Ac Piers þe Plowman parceyueþ moore depper
What is þe wille and wherfore þ*a*t many wight suffreþ:
Et vidit deus cogitaciones eorum.
For þer are [pure] proude herted men, pacient of tonge
And buxome as of berynge to burgeises and to lordes, |
And to poore peple han pepir in þe nose, *fol.* 90 *a*
And as a lyoun he lokeþ þer men lakken hise werkes.
For þ*er* are beggeris and bidderis, bedemen as it were,

190 bouken] bonden Cr^{1}. beten] beate Cr; bowken G.
191 leggen] lieggen B; liggen CrGC.
192 warm] warne Cr^{3}. at] of F.
193 Thanne] þanne RF; And þanne WHmCrGYOC^{2}CBLM. tyme] tyme seiþ WHmCrGYOC^{2}CBLMRF.
194 *in margin* OC^{2}. *deus*] *om* OC^{2}F. *despicies*] *despicies &c* Hm; *despicies domine* F; *despicias* (*as over erasure*) M.
195 By] but G. I(2)] CrGYF; þ*a*t I WHmOC^{2}CBLMR. quod I] *om* GYOC^{2}CB.
196 *as two lines divided after* he R. outen] oute GMF; out the Cr. Plowman] þe plowman MR; *om* F.
197 Wheiþ*er*] Where CrGYOC^{2}CBmBoLMRF. clerkes] clergie CB. knowen] knowe CrGYF; knew CB. þat] þa R.
198 haue] hauen BmBo. knowyng] knowlechynge R. but] *om* Cr^{1}. wordes] GCr^{2}YOC^{2}CBF; word Cr^{3}; by wordes WHmCr^{1}LMR.
199 Ac] but GF; And CrC^{2}C. þe] *om* F. parceyueþ] p*a*rceyuede OC^{2}C. depper] depelye Cr.
200 What] wh *over erasure* M; þat LRF; where GYOC^{2}CB. þe] *om* RF. wille] welle CB; why F. þat] for F. wight] a wyght GOC^{2} (a *above line* C^{2}); wit R. suffreþ] yknoweþ F.
200α *in margin* OC^{2}. *Et*] And R. *vidit*] vidis C. *deus*] *om* Cr^{3}. *eorum*] *eorum &c* Hm.
201 are] is B. pure] ful WHmCrGYOC^{2}CBLMRF. herted] herte R; *om* C^{2}. men] men & ben F.
202 buxome as] buxu*m* F; buxomest Hm. burgeises] burgeis Cr^{1}HmYOC^{2}CBLMR.
203 And to] But to þe F. han] *om* F. in þe nose] is in her*e* noseþerlys F. þe] her HmCot.
204 a] *om* Y. he] they *over erasure* Hm. lakken] lakke FCr. hise] her *over erasure* Hm. werkes] werdis F.
205 For] And Hm; *om* F. beggeris] bugeysys G. it] þei C^{2}F. were] weren F.

Loken as lambren and semen [lif]holy,
Ac it is moore to haue hir mete [on] swich an esy manere
Than for penaunce and *par*fitnesse, þe pouerte þat swiche takeþ.
Therfore by colour ne by clergie knowe shaltow [hym] neu*ere*,
Neiþ*er* þoruȝ wordes ne werkes, but þoruȝ wil oone,
And þat knoweþ no clerk ne creature on erþe
But Piers þe Plowman, *Petrus id est christus.*
For he [lyueþ] noȝt in lolleris ne in londleperis heremytes
Ne at Ancres þ*ere* a box hangeþ; alle swiche þei faiten.
Fy on faitours and *in fautores suos*!
For charite is goddes champion, and as a good child hende,
And þe murieste of mouþ at mete where he sitteþ.
The loue þat liþ in his herte makeþ hym liȝt of speche,
And is compaignable and confortatif as crist bit hymselue:
Nolite fieri sicut ypocrite tristes &c.
For I haue seyen hym in silk and som tyme in russet,
Boþe in grey and in grys and in gilt harneis,
And as gladliche he it gaf to gomes þat it neded.
Edmond and Edward, [eiþer] were kynges

206 Loken] þat lokyn Hm; & þey looken F. semen] seme of F; semed R. lif] YHmCr GOC^{2}CBLMRF; ful W.
207 Ac] but GF; And CrC^{2}C. on] RF; yn HmGYOC^{2}CB; wiþ WCrLM. an] *om* GYOC^{2}CBF. esy] *om* G.
208 and] or CrGYOC^{2}CB. þe] swich F. pouerte] pou*ere* Y; penau*n*ce Cr^1. þat... takeþ] is vnholy F.
209 colour] colou BoCot (*corrected* Cot); clergye Hm. ne by] of F. clergie] colour Hm. shaltow] schal þow R. hym neuere] neu*er* hym Cot. hym] HmGYOC^{2}BmBo LMRF; he*m* C; *om* WCr.
210 wordes ne werkes] works nor words Cr^1; works or words Cr^{23}; word ne þorghȝ werk F. oone] alone G.
211 *line om* Hm. ne] in C. on] in YGOC^2 CBLM.
212 *Petrus*] properly pers F. *id est*] it is B.
213 lyueþ] loveþ F; is CrGYOC^{2}CB; nys WHmR; ne is LM. noȝt] noone F. in(*both*)] wit*h* Cr^{23}; *om* F. lolleris] losels Cr^{2}OC^2; lesels Cr^3; freris B. lond] lewde G. leperis] lepynge HmB. heremytes] neyþir F.
214 at] in Cr^{1}OC^{2}B; wit*h* Cr^{23}; *om* F. a] any F. alle] for all F. þei faiten] fayte F.
215 on] vpon G; on þo F; on a B. faitours] faytour B. *in*] on GYCF; *om* B. *fautores*] *factores* F.
216 is] to G. a] *om* Hm.
217 murieste] merieþ Bm; merþe BoCot. at] atte Hm. where] wherso Hm. sitteþ] setteth Cr.
218 *line om* F. The] To R.
219 And] & he F. confortatif] confortif YGC; co*n*fort F. bit] bydiþ C^2. selue] seluen M.
219α *in margin* OC^2. *fieri...&c*] *tristes fieri sicut ypocrite* R. *&c*] *om* CrGYOC^{2}F.
221 Boþe] & furrid F. in(1,2)] wit*h* F. in(3)] in a Cr^{23}; goon in F.
222 as] also B.
223 Edmond and] Seyn*t* Edmu*nd* & seyn*t* F. eiþer] eyther CrGYOC^{2}CBLMRF; boþe WHm. were] weren F; of hem were BoCot; of hym were Bm.

And seintes yset; [stille] charite hem folwede.
I haue yseyen charite also syngen and reden,
Riden and rennen in raggede wedes,
Ac biddynge as beggeris biheld I hym neu*ere*.
Ac in riche robes raþest he walkeþ,
Ycalled and ycrymyled and his crowne yshaue.
And in a freres frokke he was yfounden ones,
Ac it is fern [and fele yeer in] Fraunceis tyme; |
In þat secte siþþe to selde haþ he ben [knowe]. *fol. 90 b*
Riche men he recomendeþ, and of hir robes takeþ
That wiþouten wiles ledeþ [wel] hir lyues:
Beatus est diues qui &c.
In kynges court he comeþ ofte þer þe counseil is trewe,
Ac if coueitise be of þe counseil he wol no3t come þ*er*Inne.
In court amonges [þe commune] he comeþ but selde
For braulynge and bakbitynge and berynge of fals witnesse.
In þe Consistorie bifore þe Co*m*missarie he comeþ no3t ful ofte

224 And] And be (be *above line*) M; & now be þey F. yset] sette CrF. stille] til YGOC^{2}CBL; so RF; for WHmCrM (*over erasure* Hm). hem] hym BmBo; he F.
225 yseyen] seien BHmCrGYOC^{2}CLMF. syngen] synging Cr^{23}. reden] redand (*altered main hand from* redend) C; reding Cr^{23}.
226 Riden] Ryding Cr^{23}; bydden G. rennen] runnyng Cr^{23}.
227 Ac] But F; And CrC^{2}C; for G. biddynge] bydden Cr. beggeris] beggers doone G; a begger BMF (*small erasure at end* Bm; a *above line*, beggere *altered from* beggers M). biheld I] biholde CB.
228 Ac] but GF; And CrC^{2}C. walkeþ] walkest Y.
229 Ycalled] Called Cr. and(1)] *om* OC^2. ycrymyled] crymayled YGC; Crimised Cr. yshaue] shaue Cr^{1}GYCBLM; shau*en* Cr^{23}OC^2. *Hereafter a spurious line* GYOC^{2}CB; *see above*, p. 223.
230 freres] frere R. yfounden] yfounde YCBLR; founden OHmC^{2}M; founde GCr.
231 Ac] but GF; And CrC^{2}C. fern] fer OGYC^{2}CBLMR. and...in] ago in Seint WHmCrGYOC^{2}CBLMRF.
232 In] and In GYOC^{2}CBF. secte...to] seut sytthen F. selde] selden OC^{2}F. he] *om* OC^2. knowe] Cr^{1}MRF; knowen GHmCr^{23}YOC^{2}CBL; founde W.
233 of] *om* GB.
234 That] Of þoo F. outen] oute R. ledeþ] heere lowly ledyn F. wel hir] hir WHmCrGYOC^{2}CBLMRF.
234α *in margin* OC^2. *est*] *om* B. &*c*] *om* F.
235 In] yn þe GF. he comeþ] *om* F. ofte] often OC^2. þe] his F.
236 Ac] but G; And CrC^{2}CF. if] *om* F. of þe] of CrG; in his F. no3t] not (*by corrector*) Bm; *om* C.
237 þe commune] Iaperis WHmCrGYOC^{2}CBLMRF. he comeþ] cometh he M. he] charite F. but] GLMR; no3t but WHmCrYOC^{2}B; nou3t be C; *om* F. selde] selden M.
238 braulynge] braggyng B. berynge] kepyng Y. of] *om* Cr. witnesse] hede F.
239 þe(1)] *om* GBF. Consistorie] constorye HmBLRF. bifore] afore F. ful] *om* F.

For hir lawe dureþ ouerlonge but if þei lacchen siluer,
And matrimoyne for moneie maken and vnmaken,
And þat Conscience and crist haþ yknyt faste
Thei vndoon it vn[digne]ly, þo doctours of lawe.
[Amonges erchebisshopes and bisshopes, [for beggeres sake],
For to wonye wiþ hem his wone was som tyme,
And cristes patrymonye to þe poore parcelmele dele;
Ac auarice haþ þe keyes now and kepeþ for his kynnesmen
And for his seketoures & his seruaunt3, & som for hir children].
Ac I ne lakke no lif, but lord amende vs alle,
And gyue vs g*ra*ce, goode god, charite to folwe.
For whoso my3te meete [wiþ] hym swiche man*er*es hym eileþ:
Neiþ*er* he blameþ ne banneþ, bosteþ ne preiseþ,
Lakkeþ ne loseþ ne lokeþ vp sterne,
Craueþ ne coueiteþ ne crieþ after moore:
In pace in idipsum dormiam &c.
The mooste liflode he lyueþ by is loue in goddes passion;
Neiþer he biddeþ ne beggeþ ne borweþ to yelde.
Misdooþ he no man ne wiþ his mouþ greueþ.
Amonges cristene men þis myldenesse sholde laste

240 hir] *om* Y. ouer] *om* F. lacchen] lacche GF.
241 *line om* F. maken] þei maken M.
242 And] & þo F. yknyt] knytt $GCr^{23}CF$; knilte Cr^1. faste] togydre F.
243 Thei] þat C. it] *om* Cot. vndignely] vnworþily $WHmCrGYOC^2CBLMRF$. þo] þe HmCrC; þes G; thise Y; *om* F. of] of þe F.
244–8 RF; *lines om* $WHmCrGYOC^2CBL$ M; *here in the spelling of* W.
244 *as two lines divided after* bisshopes(2) R. Amonges...bisshopes] wit*h* Bisshopis & abbotys F. and] and oþer R. for...sake] And prelates of holy cherche RF.
246 patrymonye] parsymonye F. dele] þey deltyn F.
247 Ac] But F. now] *om* F.
248 his(2)] *om* F. hir] hise F.
249 *line om* CB. Ac] but GF; And CrC^2. ne] *om* MF. but] but oure F.
250 And...god] & god graunte vs grace þat F. And gyue] But 3eue B. god] *om* C. to] may vs F.
251 For] And Y. so] *om* G. wiþ] OHm $CrGYC^2CBLMRF$; myd W. eileþ] *om* C.
252 Neiþer] *om* F. blameþ] blanneþ Bo; blamneþ (*one minim cancelled*) Bm; banneth $YGOC^2CCot$ (*erasure after* b Cot). ne(1)] ne he M; neyþer ne F. banneþ] blameþ OC^2B; blamed C; blameth ne YGF.
253 *transposed with* 254 $GYOC^2CB$. Lakkeþ] Ne lakkeþ F. ne(1)] he ne Cr. loseþ] lesseþ F. vp sterne] no þy*n*g sternyþ F.
254 Craueþ] Ne c*r*aueþ F.
254α *line om* RF; *in margin* OC^2. &c] *et requiescam* CrG; & *requiescam* &c Hm.
255 he] $CrGYOC^2CBMF$; þat he WHm LR. by] *om* R. loue in] *om* F.
256 he] he ne R. ne(1)] ne he HmC. to] but he it F.
257 Misdooþ he] he mysdoþ F. his] *om* Y. greueþ] hy*m* greveþ F.

In alle manere angres, haue þis at herte
That þeiȝ þei suffrede al þis, god suffrede for vs moore
In ensample we sholde do so, and take no vengeaunce |
Of oure foes þat dooþ vs falsnesse; þat is oure fadres wille. *fol.* 91 *a*
For wel may euery man wite, if god hadde wold hymselue,
Sholde neuere Iudas ne Iew haue I*es*u doon on roode,
Ne han martired Peter ne Poul, ne in prison holden.
Ac he suffrede in ensample þ*at* we sholde suffren also,
And seide to swiche þ*at* suffre wolde,
Pacientes Vincunt verbi gracia, and [verred] ensamples manye.
[Lo]! in *legenda sanctorum*, þe lif of holy Seintes,
What penaunce and pouerte and passion þei suffrede,
In hunger, in hete, in alle manere angres.
Antony and Egidie and oþ*er*e holy fadres
Woneden in wildernesse among wilde beestes,
Monkes and mendinauntȝ, men by hemselue
In spekes and spelonkes; selde speken togideres.
Ac neiþ*er* Antony ne Egidie ne heremyte þat tyme

259 at] atte HmR; in CrG; euer*e* at F.
260 þei] þow F; he Cr. suffrede(1)] suffreden OC^{2}; suffre MF. þis] þese F. god] go R. suffrede(2)] suffreth M.
261 sholde] schulden O; schul C. take] take*n* CrF. no] *om* R.
262 Of] On F. þat(1)] þe Cr^{3}. þat(2)] þis F. oure] out Cr^{2}; þe F; *om* OC^{2}.
263 wel...man] euery man may wel RF. hadde] *om* GRF. selue] seluen M.
264 Sholde] Shul C. neuere] ner*e* R. ne] þe BR; þ*at* F. I*es*u] Iesus Cr^{1}.
265 Ne] No Y. martired] martires Y. ne(1)] and Hm. ne(2)] *above line* M; *om* G. holden] holde R; he*m* holden F.
266 Ac] but GF; And CrC^{2}C. ensample] example Cr. þat] & þat C^{2}. sholde] schulden OC^{2}; *om* GCB. suffren] suffre HmCrGYOC^{2}CBLMRF.
267 *divided from* 268 *after Vincunt* WHmCrGYOC^{2}CLMRF; *after viuunt* B. seide] seyden O. suffre] suffren B. wolde] wolde*n* OC^{2}BmBoM.
268 *Pacientes...gracia*] þat *Pacientes Vincunt Verbi gracia* quod he WHmCrGYOC^{2}CBLMRF (*Vincunt*] *viuunt* B). verred] F; verray WHmCrGYOCBLMR; verri C^{2}. ensamples] examples Cr.
269 Lo in] In WHmCrGYOC^{2}CBLMR; In þe F. þe] ys þe F.
270 *transposed with* 271 Y. þei] the G. suffrede] suffreden OC^{2}.
271 In] & F. in(1)] & yn GYOC^{2}CB; & F. in(2)] & C^{2}F. alle] manye F. manere] maneres C; oþer*e* F.
272 Antony] Seyn*t* Antonye F. fadres] farders C.
273 Woneden] þey woneden F; Wending Cr. wildernesse] wildernesses R.
274 Monkes] & also mukys F. hem] hym Bm. selue] seluen OC^{2}M.
275 spekes] Caues F. and] CCrGOC^{2}BMR; and in WHmYLF. spelonkes] spekelonkes YGCB (*corrected* Cot); spelu*n*ses & F. selde] selden CrHmYOC^{2}CBLM. speken] speke HmGO; spoke F.
276 Ac] but GF; And CrC^{2}C. neiþ*er*] neu*er* G. ne(1)] nor Cr. ne(2)] ne no*n* F. heremyte] herymytes G.

Of leons ne of leopardes no liflode ne toke,
But of foweles þat fleeþ; þus fyndeþ men in bokes.
Except þ*at* Egidie after an hynde cride,
And þoruȝ þe mylk of þat mylde beest þe man was sustened;
And day bi day hadde he hire noȝt his hunger for to slake,
But selden and sondry tymes, as seiþ þe book and techeþ.
Antony adayes aboute noon tyme
Hadde a brid þat brouȝte hym breed þat he by lyuede,
And þouȝ þe gome hadde a gest god fond hem boþe.
Poul *primus heremita* hadde parroked hymselue
That no man myȝte hym se for mosse and for leues.
Foweles hym fedde, fele wyntres wiþ alle,
Til he foundede freres of Austynes ordre, [or ellis freres lyen]. |
Poul after his p*re*chyng paniers he made *fol.* 91 *b*
And wan wiþ hise hondes þat his wombe neded.
Peter fisshed for his foode and his felawe Andrew;
Som þei solde and som þei soden, and so þei lyued boþe.
And also Marie Maudeleyne by mores lyuede and dewes,
Ac moost þoruȝ [meditacion] and mynde of god almyghty.

277 of] *om* GF. no] ne Cr^{1}. ne(2)] þei BF; to Cr. toke] token OC^{2}F; take Cr.
278 of] of þe RF; as of Y. foweles] foloughes C. fleeþ] flyen O; flyghen G; fleigh YCBF. þus] this Cr; þat B. fyndeþ] fynde HmGYB; fynt LR; is fownde F. men] *om* F.
279 an] and M. cride] called F.
280 þoruȝ] be F. mylk of þat] *om* Hm. þat] þe F. mylde] meke R; hynde B; *om* F. sustened] ysusteyned R.
281 And...he] he hadde F. And] Ac R. he hire] neuer Cr. his] euery day his F; *om* C^{2}. for] *om* Cr.
282 selden] selde GCrYC. tymes] tyme RF.
283 Antony] Seynt Antonye F. adayes] on a day RF; ech a daye Cr^{23}. aboute] abowt the HmOC^{2}. noon] nones M.
284 Hadde] he hadde F. a brid] bred C^{2}. hym] hym to F; hym his R. þat(2)... lyuede] to his lyfloode F.
285 þe] þat F. fond] fedde RF. hem] hym Bm.
286 hadde] and C. parroked] parroke C; proroked Cr. hym] in hym RF. selue] seluen M.
288 Foweles] & fowlis F. fedde] fedden OC^{2}.
289 he foundede] þat he was fowndour of F. Austynes] austyn C^{2}; augustynes G; fraunces F. or...lyen] or ellis frerys lyen B (*another hand and ink* Bm); *om* WHmCr GYOC^{2}CLMRF.
290 Poul] Anoþer poule OC^{2}. his *pre*chyng] *cris*tis pynynge F.
291 hise] *om* CR. neded] nedethe G.
293 Som] & summe F. solde] solden OC^{2}F; sothyn Hm; shalde C. þei(2)] *om* Hm. soden] soþe BmCrGLM; seþ BoCot; sothey Y; soldyn Hm; eeten RF. þei(3)] *om* F. lyued] lyueden OC^{2}F.
294 lyuede and] and by RF. mores] *erasure before* m M.
295 Ac] but GF; And CrC^{2}C. þoruȝ] by F. meditacion] deuocion WHmCrGYO C^{2}CBLMRF. of] on F.

I sholde noȝt þise seuen daies siggen hem alle
That lyueden þus for oure lordes loue many longe yeres.
Ac þer ne was leou*n* ne leopard þat on laundes wenten,
Neiþer bere ne boor ne ooþ*er* beest wilde,
That ne fil to hir feet and fawned wiþ þe tailles;
And if þei kouþe han ycarped, by crist! as I trowe,
Thei wolde haue yfed þat folk bifore wilde foweles;
[For al þe curteisie þat beestes konne þei kidde þat folk ofte,
In likkyng and in lowynge, þer þei on laundes yede].
Ac god sente hem foode by foweles and by no fierse beestes
In menynge þ*a*t meke þyng mylde þyng sholde fede.
[Riȝt so] Religiouses rightfulle men sholde [fynde],
And lawefulle men to lif holy men liflode brynge;
And þanne wolde lordes and ladies be looþ to agulte,
And to taken of hir tenauntȝ moore þan trouþe wolde,
Founde þei þ*a*t freres wolde forsake hir almesses
And bidden hem bere it þere it [yborwed was].

296 sholde] shol C. siggen] seyn ȝow F; tellen C.
297 lyueden] liued CrC^{2}. þus] thys G. many...yeres] amonges wilde bestes RF.
298 Ac] but G; For F; And CrC^{2}C. ne(1)] *om* F. leopard] leopartȝ R. laundes] landes CrGB; londe F. wenten] wente RCrF.
299 Neiþer bere] Ne beer*e* neyþ*er* F; nether G. beest] beestis FCr.
300 ne] it ne B; þey F. fil] felly*n* F. fawned] faunede*n* O; fawneþ B. wiþ] hem wit*h* F. þe] her HmCrGBF. tailles] taile R.
301 kouþe han] hadde cowd F. kouþe] couþen O. ycarped] carped HmCrG.
302 wolde] wolden OHmF. yfed] fed HmCrGL. þat] þo C^{2}.
303, 304 RF; *lines om* WHmCrGYOC^{2}CBLM; *here in the spelling of* W.
303 curteisie...konne] kyȝndenesse þ*a*t þey cowde F. þat(2)] to F.
304 in lowynge] lovynge F. laundes yede] londis wentyn F.
305 Ac] but GF; And CrC^{2}C. sente] send G. hem] hym Bm. foweles] fowle C; folis F. fierse] wylde GF.
306 menynge] mevinge C^{2}. sholde] schul C. fede] serue Hm.
307 Riȝt so] As whoso seith MF; As who seiþ WHmGOC^{2}CBLR; As who say Cr; And who seith Y. Religiouses] religious CrGYOC^{2}CBLMRF; relygiou*ns* Hm. sholde] schol C. fynde] HmCrGYOC^{2}CBLMR; fede WF.
308 to] *om* F. brynge] HmCrGYOC^{2}CBLMR; sholde brynge W; sholde bryngen F.
309 wolde] wolden O. be] by R.
310 to] *om* F. taken] take HmCr^{23}GYOC^{2}CBLMR. moore] no more (no *cancelled*) O.
311 Founde] Founden OC^{2}; & fonde F. þei þat] þei þa Bo; thei than Cot; if þ*a*t ony F. wolde] wolden OC^{2}M. forsake] forsaken OC^{2}. hir] *om* Hm. almesses] almesse OCrGYC^{2}CBMRF.
312 bidden] bidde B. hem] hym BmBo. bere] beren RF. it(2)] þ*a*t it F. yborwed was] was yborwed WHmGOC^{2}CBLM; was borwed YCrRF.

For we [by] goddes [behestes] abiden alwey
Til briddes brynge vs [wherby] we sholde lyue.
For hadde ye potage and payn ynogh and penyale to drynke,
And a mees þermyd of o maner kynde,
Ye hadde riȝt ynoȝ, ye Religiouse, and so you*re* rule me tolde.
Num[quid], dicit Iob, rugi[e]t onager cum herbam habuerit aut mugiet
bos cum ante plenum presepe steterit? brutorum animalium natura
te condempnat, quia cum eis pabulum | commune sufficiat; ex adipe
prodijt iniquitas tua. *fol. 92 a*
If lewed men knewe þis latyn þei wolde loke whom þei yeue,
And auisen hem bifore a fyue dayes or sixe
Er þei amortisede to monkes or [monyales] hir rente[s].
Allas, lordes and ladies, lewed counseil haue ye
To ȝyue from you*re* heires þat you*re* Aiels yow lefte,
And [bisette] to bidde for yow to swiche þat ben riche,
And ben founded and feffed ek to bidde for oþere.
Who p*ar*fou*r*neþ þis p*ro*phecie of þe peple þat now libbeþ,
Dispersit, dedit pauperibus?

313 For] ⁊ sey*n* F. by] be GOCB; ben WHmCrYC^{2}LMF; beth R. behestes] foweles and WHmCr^{1}GYOC^{2}CBLMRF; foles and Cr^{23}. abiden] abide OC^{2}. alwey] awey YC^{2}.
314 Til] Tyl þat F. brynge] bryngen Bo HmBmRF. wherby] þat WHmCrLMR F; mete þat YGOC^{2}CB. sholde] schulden OC^{2}F. lyue] lyue by WHmCrGYOC^{2} CBLMR; lyven by F.
315 hadde] han Y; haue OC^{2}. potage... payn] payn ⁊ potage F. ynogh] *om* GOC^{2}F. to drynke] ynoghe G.
316 þer] þe BoCot; to ȝore F. myd] amyde Cr; wyþ HmOC^{2}C; meete F. o] any GYOC^{2}CB. kynde] of kyȝnde F.
317 hadde] hadden MHm; han OC^{2}. and] *om* CrG. rule] ordre RF. me tolde] techiþ F.
318 *Numquid*] FCr^{23}; *Numquam* WHmCr^{1} GYOC^{2}CBLMR. *rugiet*] RF; *rugit* WHm CrGOC^{2}CBLM; *om* Y. *onager*] onerger L. *herbam habuerit*] *habuerit herbam* ORF. *cum*(2)] *tum* BmBo. *ante*] *ante se* G. *brutorum...sufficiat*] *om* RF. *quia*] *om* OC^{2}. *sufficiat*] *sufficit* Cr. *tua*] *tua ⁊c* HmY (? *⁊c added by rubricator* W).
319 lewed] *om* F. knewe] knewe*n* O. wolde] wolde*n* OC^{2}. whom þei] to G. þei] the C. yeue] ȝyuen OC^{2}.
320 auisen] auyse HmCrGYOC^{2}CBLMR. hem] hym BmBo. bifore] afore Cr^{1}G. a] *om* GOC^{2}RF.
321 amortisede] amortiseden YC; mortiseden OC^{2}; enmorteisid BHm. to] sikirly vnto F. or] ⁊ G; *om* F. monyales] Chanons WHmCrGYOC^{2}CBLMR; *om* F. rentes] CrHmGYOC^{2}CBLMRF; rente W.
323 ȝyue] ȝevyn F; giue CrG. youre(2)] *om* C. Aiels] elders Cr^{23}C^{2}. yow] *om* GCB. lefte] laften OF; lesten C^{2}; had GCB.
324 bisette] ȝyueþ HmYOC^{2}CLMR; gyuethe G; ȝyueþ it WBF; giue it Cr. þat] as CrMRF. ben] ar Hm.
325 founded] Ifounded RF; founden CrC^{2}. feffed] fed Cr; feasted G. bidde] bydden RF.
326 þis] þe OC^{2}CB. þe] *om* OC^{2}.
327 *in margin* OC^{2}. *dedit*] *Deus* BmBo. *pauperibus*] *pauperibus ⁊c* HmYBLMR; *pauperibus Iusticia eius manet in seculum seculi* F.

If any peple p*ar*fou*r*ne þat text it are þise poore freres,
For þat þei beggen aboute in buyldynge þei spende,
And on hemself som, and swiche as ben hir laborers;
And of hem þat habbeþ þei taken and ȝyueþ hem þat [ne] habbeþ.
Ac clerkes and knyȝtes and co*m*muners þat ben riche,
Fele of yow fareþ as if I a forest hadde
That were ful of faire trees, and I fondede and caste
How I myȝte mo þ*er*Inne amonges hem sette.
Right so ye riche, ye robeþ þat ben riche
And helpeþ hem þat helpeþ yow and ȝyueþ þer no nede is,
As whoso filled a tonne [ful] of a fressh ryuer
And wente forþ wiþ þat water to woke wiþ Temese.
Right so ye riche, ye robeþ and fedeþ
Hem þat han as ye han; hem ye make at ese.
Ac Religiouse þat riche ben sholde raþer feeste beggeris
Than burgeises þat riche ben as þe book techeþ,

328 peple] pe*n*ple Cr[1]. p*ar*fou*r*ne] perfome G. þat] þis GYOC[2]CBF; þe Cr[23]. þise] þe GYOC[2]CB.

329 beggen] begge CrB. aboute] abouten LF. buyldynge] biggynge F. spende] GBR; spendyn C[2]; spene YLM; spenen O; it spende HmF; spende it WCrC.

330 And] ⁊ su*m* F; *om* G. hem] theyre G; hym B. som] *om* F. and] ⁊ on GBF. swiche] hem Cot; hym BmBo. as] þat BF; *om* R.

331 hem(1)] *om* GCB. habbeþ...and] þei habben Itake B. habbeþ(1)] haue GC[2]F; haueth not Cr[1]; haue not Cr[23]. taken] take CrF. ȝyueþ] ȝyue HmGYL. ne] GYOC[2]LMR; na C; nede BF; *om* WHm Cr. habbeþ(2)] hath Cr[23]C[2]C.

332 Ac] but GF; And CrC[2]C; as B. co*m*muners] commers Bo; comonys F.

333 Fele of] feele how G. as] ⁊ G. a... hadde] hadde a Forest M.

334 That] ⁊ it F. I] *om* B. fondede] foondd C; found Cr; fond B; as a fonne F. and(2)] a Cr; *om* F.

336 ye(1)] þe B; *om* G. ye(2)] that Hm. robeþ] robbeþ HmBR; robben OC[2]; robbe CrGF. þat] þem þ*at* GF. ben] be not F.

337 helpeþ(2)] helpe Cr[3]; helpiþ not F.

338 As] And Cr[1]. filled] fylleth CrF. ful] RF; *om* WHmCrGYOC[2]CBLM. a(2)] *om* Y. fressh] ful R; *om* F.

339 þat] þe Y. woke] wokyn Hm; awoke G; eeke *over erasure* Cot. wiþ] wiþ þe OC[2]F.

340 ye(1)] the Cr[1]. ye(2)] me*n* ȝee F; that Hm; *om* G. robeþ] robbeth YGBR; robben OHmC[2]F; robbe Cr. fedeþ] fede Cr[23]; fedde Cr[1].

341 hem] *om* GY. make] maken OHmC[2].

342 Ac] butt GF; And CrC[2]C. sholde] schulden OC[2]BmBo. feeste] fede RF.

343 burgeises] burgeys YHmOC[2]CBLM RF. riche ben] ben ryche Hm. techeþ] telleth CrOC[2].

Quia sacrilegium est res pauperum non pauperibus dare. Item, peccatoribus dare est demonibus immolare. | Item, monache, si indiges & accipis pocius das quam accipis; Si autem non eges & accipis rapis. Porro non indiget monachus si habeat quod nature sufficit. *fol.* 92 *b*
Forþi I counseille alle cristene to conformen hem to charite,
For charite wiþouten chalangynge vnchargeþ þe soule,
And many a prison fram p*ur*gatorie þoruȝ hise preieres deliu*er*eþ.
Ac þer is a defaute in þe folk þat þe feiþ kepeþ,
Wherfore folk is þe febler and noȝt ferm of bileue.
As in lussheburwes is a luþer alay, and yet lokeþ he lik a sterlyng;
The merk of þat monee is good ac þe metal is feble;
And so it fareþ by som folk now; þei han a fair speche,
Crowne and cristendom, þe kynges mark of heuene,
Ac þe metal, þat is mannes soule, [myd] synne is foule alayed.
Boþe lettred and lewed beþ alayed now wiþ synne
That no lif loueþ ooþer, ne oure lord as it semeþ.
For þoruȝ werre and wikkede werkes and wederes vn[s]esonable

343α *Item*(1)] *Item idem* RF. *immolare*] Imulare Y. *Item*(2)...*rapis*] *om* RF. *eges*] *indiges* Cr. *sufficit*] *sufficit &c* YHm.
344 Forþi] Therfore CrF. conformen] conforme HmCr^{12}GYOC^{2}CCotF; *con*firme Cr^{3}; conforte BmBo. hem] vs Hm; ȝow F.
345 outen] oute GHmCrLR. vnchargeþ] vnclargeþ Y. þe soule] *om* R.
346 a] *om* Cr. prison] prisoner Cr^{1}GC^{2}CotF; prisoners Cr^{23}. fram...deliuereþ] by his praier he pulith from paine Cr. hise] hir Y; *om* F. preieres] prayere CF. deliuereþ] C^{2}GYOCB; he deliu*er*eþ WHmLM; is deliuered R; ben dylyu*er*ed F.
347 Ac] but GF; And CrC^{2}C. feiþ kepeþ] lawe kepe G.
348 fore] *om* CotR. is] been OC^{2}. of] in F.
349 As] Ryght as F; and GOC^{2}CB; *om* Y. in] þe F. lussheburwes] lussheburwe YCr^{1}F; Lushburth Cr^{23}. is] *om* G. a(1)] *om* F. alay] of lay F. and] a G; *om* Cr. lokeþ he] lokith Cr; it lookeþ F. lik a sterlyng] fayre F. a(2)] *om* Cr.
350 The] For þe F. þat] þe F. ac] but GF; & CrC^{2}C. is(2)] *om* Cr^{23}.
351 And...fareþ] So farith it Cr.
352 Crowne] & crowne F. þe kynges] *twice, the first cancelled* Bm.
353 Ac] but GF; And CrC^{2}C. þe] þ*at* C. þat] *om* Cot. mannes] man YC. myd] wiþ WHmCrGYOC^{2}CBLMRF. foule] ful OC^{2}; so F.
354 *line om* GCBF. alayed now] now alayed YOC^{2}M; arayed now Cr^{23}.
355 loueþ] ne louethe G; beleviþ F. it semeþ] I leue OC^{2}.
356 For] For what RF. þoruȝ] by Cr; þough BmBo. wikkede werkes] wikydnesses F. vnsesonable] vnseasonable Cr^{23}; vnstable F; vnresonable WHmCr^{1}GYOC^{2}CBLMR.

Wederwise shipmen and witty clerkes also
Han no bileue to þe lifte ne to þe [lodesterre].
Astronomiens alday in hir Art faillen
That whilom warned bifore what sholde falle after.
Shipmen and shepherdes þat wiþ [shipe] wenten
Wisten by þe walkne what sholde bitide;
As of wedres and wyndes þei warned men ofte.
Tilieris þat tiled þe erþe tolden hir maistres
By þe seed þat þei sewe what þei sel[l]e myȝte,
And what to leue and to lyue by; þe lond was so trewe.
Now faileþ þe folk of þe flood and of þe lond boþe,
Shepherdes and shipmen, and so do þise tilieris. |
Neiþ*er* þei konneþ ne knoweþ oon cours bifore anoþ*er*. *fol.* 93 *a*
Astronomyens also aren at hir wittes ende;
Of þat was calculed of þe element þe cont*ra*rie þei fynde.
Grammer, þe ground of al, bigileþ now children,

357 Weder] þ*at* wedir F; whedir CBmBo; whethir Cot; wyther G. wise shipmen] wysheppers Cr^{12}; wishyppers Cr^{3}. witty] *om* OC^{2}.
358 Han] þey have F. þe(1)] ye (*over erasure another hand and ink*) M; *om* YF. lifte] lif B; list Cr^{23}G; clyfte C^{2}; *cr*ist F. lodesterre] loore of Philosofres WHmCr GYOC^{2}CBmBoLMRF; lor*e* of philosophie Cot.
359 Astronomiens] Astronomers Cr; Astr*i*nomyes F; astromyens OC^{2}BLR. alday] also alday Y. Art] artes G; herte Cr^{1}. faillen] þey fayle F.
360 warned] warneden O. bifore] tofor*e* F. falle] fally*n* F; byfalle R.
361 Shipmen] Shipman Y; Chapmen CB. and...þat] *with* schippis ⁊ schepp*er*des *with* F. shepherdes] heerdis OC^{2}. shipe] ship and sheep WHmCrGOC^{2}LMR; ship ⁊ shepen Y; ship and shipmen C; scheep F; schep ⁊ schipme*n* B. wenten] wente HmB.
362 Wisten] þey wisten F; Wyshen Cr. bitide] after bytyȝde F.
363 As] and B; *om* F. and] and of BRF; *om* G. þei] þ*at* Cot. warned] warneden O. ofte] ofte*n* C^{2}.
364 þat tiled] of F. tiled] tileden MYOC^{2} Cot; tilien BmBo. tolden] tolde Cr; þey tolden F. maistres] maystryes Hm.
365 By] whi B. þat] *om* F. sewe] sewe*n* OC^{2}F; shewe G. selle] YHmCrGOC^{2}C BLMR; selly*n* F; selde W. myȝte] myȝten OC^{2}.
366 to(1)] *om* F. leue] leau Cr^{2}. to(2)] LMRF; what to WHmCrGYOC^{2}CB.
367 Now] ⁊ now F. faileþ] faylen OC^{2}. þe(2)] *om* OC^{2}. þe(3)] *om* C^{2}.
368 Shepherdes] Boþe schepp*er*dis F; Sepeheardes Cr^{3}.
369 þei] *om* G. konneþ] konne GC^{2}CF; canneth Cr. knoweþ] knowe C^{2}F. oon] no F. bifore] afore G; tofor*e* F.
370 Astronomyens] Astronomers Cr; Astromyens C^{2}BLR; ⁊ astronomyes F.
371 calculed] calclede G. þe(1)] *om* RF. element] elymente*s* GYOC^{2}CB; clement RF. þei] nou þey F. fynde] fynden OC^{2}.
372 Grammer] For gram*er*e F. þe] þ*at* is þe F; that is Hm. al] all it F. now] now the Cr.

For is noon of þise newe clerkes, whoso nymeþ hede,
[That kan versifie faire ne formaliche enditen],
[Ne] nauȝt oon among an hundred þat an Auctour kan construwe,
Ne rede a lettre in any langage but in latyn or englissh.
Go now to any degree, and but if gile be maister,
[And as vsher vnder hym to fourmen vs alle
Flaterere his felawe, ferly me þynkeþ].
Doctours of decrees and of diuinite maistres,
That sholde konne and knowe alle kynnes clergie
And answere to Argumentȝ and [assoile] a *Quodlibet*—
I dar noȝt siggen it for shame—if swiche were apposed
Thei sholde faillen of hir Philosophie and in Phisik boþe.
Wherfore I am afered of folk of holy kirke,
Lest þei ou*er*huppen as ooþ*er*e doon in office and in houres.
[Ac] if þei ou*er*huppe, as I hope noȝt, oure bileue suffiseþ,
As clerkes in *Corpus Christi* feeste syngen and reden
That *sola fides sufficit* to saue wiþ lewed peple.
And so may Sarȝens be saued, Scribes and [Grekes].

373 is] þ*ere* is F; it is Cr. noon] now F. þise] *om* F. newe] now CB. clerkes] clerke R. so] þ*at* F. nymeþ] takeþ FC.
374 GYOC^{2}CBLMRF; *line om* WHmCr; *here in the spelling* of W. versifie] versifien M. ne] or G. enditen] endyte G; endenten R.
375 Ne] YGCBLMRF; no Hm; Is OC^{2}; *om* WCr. nauȝt oon] *om* F. þat] *om* GF. an] on B. Auctour] auter Cr; Anteme (*touched up*) F.
376 in(2)] *om* GYOC^{2}CB. or] Cr^{3}F; or in WHmCr^{12}LMR; & GYOC^{2}CB.
377 and] *om* G. if] *om* BF. be] be the Y; me C.
378, 379 And Flaterere his felawe vnder hym to fourmen / Muche wonder me þynkeþ amonges vs alle WHmCrGYOC^{2}CBLMRF (Flaterere] flatre R; flatterers Cr^{1}. vnder...fourmen] to formen his speche & F. fourmen] fourme G. Muche] And muche R. þynkeþ] thynke C).
380 Doctours] Of doct*our*is F. decrees] degrees CrF. maistres] þe Maystr*is* F.
381 sholde] schulden HmOC^{2}BMF. konne] kenne CrYF; fynde Hm. knowe] knowen F. alle] a Cot.
382 assoile] also to WHmCrGYOC^{2}CBLMRF. *Quodlibet*] quodibet Y.
383 siggen] sygge HmCrGYOC^{2}CBF. were] weren YOC^{2}CBmBoLMRF.
384 Thei] That M. sholde] schulden OHmC^{2}B. faillen] faille YHmCrGOC^{2}CBMRF. of] yn GLMRF. hir] *om* F. and] *om* C^{2}. in] in her OGC^{2}M; *om* Cr^{3}BoCot.
385 Wher] Ther Cr. afered] afrayed Cr.
386 huppen] hippe OC^{2}. office] offyces HmCrYOC^{2}CBLR.
387 Ac] YOBLMR; but GF; And WCrC^{2}C; *om* Hm. if] þouȝ R; *om* F. ouer] oon F. huppe] hippen OHmC^{2}. hope] hoppe C; hope do (do *above line main hand*) F. suffiseþ] suffise C; *sufficit* RF; suffreth Cr^{3}.
388 syngen...reden] reedyn & syngyn F; syngynge and redynge C.
389 wiþ] þe F; suche G.
390 may] many YB. Scribes] boþe scr*i*bis F; sribes Y. Grekes] Iewes WHmCrGYOC^{2}CBLMRF.

Allas, þanne, but oure looresmen lyue as þei leren vs,
And for hir lyuynge þ*at* lewed men be þe loþer god agulten.
For Sarȝens han somwhat semynge to oure bileue,
For þei loue and bileue in o [lord] almyghty
And we lered and lewed [bileueþ in oon god;
Cristene and vncristene on oon god bileueþ].
A[c] oon Makometh, a man, in mysbileue
Brouȝte Sarȝens of Surree, and see in what manere.
This Makometh was cristene [man], and for he moste noȝt
ben pope |
Into Surrie he souȝte, and þoruȝ hise sotile wittes *fol.* 93 *b*
Daunted a dowue and day and nyȝt hire fedde.
The corn þat she croppede he caste it in his ere,
And if he among þe peple p*re*ched, or in places come,
Thanne wolde þe colu*ere* come to þe clerkes ere
Menynge as after mete; þus Makometh hire enchauntede,
And dide folk þanne falle on knees; for he swoor in his
p*re*chyng
That þe coluere þat com so com from god of heuene
As messager to Makometh, men for to teche.
And þus þoruȝ wiles of his wit and a whit Dowue

391 þanne] *om* YF. loores] lordys Hm. lyue] lyuen HmGYOC^{2}LMRF; lyued Cr; leuen CB. leren] lerne CrF; teyche G.
392 And] þat G. þ*at*] *om* G. men] *om* F. þe] *om* G. agulten] agulte HmCrC; to agulten O; to agylte G; to gulten C^2; þey gilte F.
394 loue] louen O; belouen C^2. bileue] bileuen OC^2. in] on F; *om* Cr. lord] god Cr; persone WHmGYOC^{2}CBLMRF.
395 lered] lerned Cr. bileueþ...god] yn o god byleueþ HmYOC^{2}CBmBoLMRF; in one god beleue CrG; in oon god almyȝty WCot.
396 RF; *line om* WHmCrGYOC^{2}CBLM; *here in the spelling of* W. cristene] ⁊ so cristene F. bileueþ] ben leven F.
397 *divided from* 398 *after* brouȝte WCr. Ac] BLR; But F; And WHmCrGYOC^{2}CM. Makometh] Machabeus F. in] of YOC^{2}F.
398 and] þerein F.
399 This Makometh] At the first he Cr. was] CrGYOC^{2}CBRF; was a WHmLM. cristene] cristend C. man] LRF; *om* WHm CrGYOC^{2}CBM. and] but F. moste noȝt] might not CrG; ne myght F. pope] HmCrGCotMF (? *over erasure* Hm); a pope WYOC^{2}CBmBoLR.
401 Daunted] CrYOC^{2}CBLMR; He daunted WHmGF. day...nyȝt] aday ⁊ anyghtte Cot; day be day F.
402 The] ⁊ þe F. it] *om* Cr.
403 *line om* RF. places] place GYOC^{2}CB. come] co*m*mne Bo; comune BmCot.
404 *line om* RF. þe(1)] *om* C. to] Into GOC^2.
405 as] *om* B. hire] is Y. enchauntede] chaunted R; chawnteþ F.
406 And] A L; Tha*n* Cr. þanne] *above line* O; *om* CrGYF. falle] fally*n* F.
407 of] in C^2.
408 As] And RF. teche] techen MF.
409 wiles] willes C. a] of a F; *om* B.

Makometh in mysbileue men and wo*m*men brouȝte,
That [lered] þere and [lewed] ȝit leeuen on hise lawes.
And siþþe oure Saueour suffred þe Sarȝens so bigiled
Thoruȝ a cristene clerk acorsed in his soule—
[Ac] for drede of þe deeþ I dar noȝt telle truþe,
How englisshe clerkes a colu*ere* fede þat coueitise hiȝte,
And ben manered after Makometh þat no man vseþ trouþe.
Ancres and heremytes and Monkes and freres
Peeren to Apostles þoruȝ hire parfit lyuynge.
Wolde neu*ere* þe feiþful fader þ*a*t [þ]ise Ministres sholde
Of tirauntȝ þat teneþ trewe men taken any almesse,
But doon as Antony dide, dominyk and Fraunceys,
[Boþe] Beneit and Bernard, þe whiche hem first tauȝte
To lyue by litel and in lowe houses by lele mennes almesse.
Grace sholde growe and be grene þoruȝ hir goode lyuynge,
And folkes sholden [fynde], þat ben in diuerse siknesse,
The bettre for hir biddynges in body and in soule.
Hir preieres and hir penaunces to pees sholde brynge

410 brouȝte] browhte he*m* F.
411 lered] GYOC^{2}CBLR; leernede me*n* F; lewyd Hm; lyued þo WCrM (lyued *over erasure*, þo *above line* M). þere] *om* GYOC^{2}CBF. lewed] YGOC^{2}CBLRF; lered (ered *over erasure*) Hm; lyue W; liue*n* CrM (*over erasure* M). leeuen] beleven þere F; leuing Cr; lyuen L. on] in Y.
412 þe] so þe F; þo M; thise Cot. so] þus B; to F.
413 cristene] cursed G. clerk] Clerk ⁊ F.
414 Ac] LR; But F; and HmGYOC^{2}CB M; *om* WCr. drede] dreþe C^2. þe] *om* CrGY. telle] tellen HmF. truþe] þe trewthe GM; þe soþe F.
415 englisshe] Crysten F. fede] feden Hm GYOC^{2}CBLMR. coueitise] couetouse G. hiȝte] hatteþ HmB.
416 manered] manere YCr^1. after] of Cr. þat] for F. vseþ] vsed C.
417 Ancres] Bothe Ankres F. and(2)] *om* CrGM.
418 Peeren] Peres R; Been peeris F. to] HmCrGYOC^{2}CBLMR; to þe WF. lyuynge] louyng Bm.
419 neu*ere*] ner*e* R; neuet Cr^2. fader] fadiþ Bo. þise] hise WHmCrGYOC^{2}C CotLMRF; is BmBo. sholde] schulden OC^{2}MF.
420 teneþ] tene FG. taken] take CrOC^2.
421 Antony] seynt Antonye F; domynyk OC^2. dide] dyde or F. dominyk] antony OC^2. and] or RF.
422 Boþe Beneit] Beneit WHmCrGYOC^2 CBLMR; Or benyȝt F. and] or RF. þe] *om* G.
423 and] *om* OC^{2}F. houses] house R. lele] lely Cr. almesse] fyndyng*e* RF.
424 Grace] tha*n*ne g*r*ace (tha*n*ne *over erasure another ink*) Hm; Grasse CrR. goode] lele RF.
425 folkes] folk HmCCotRF. sholden] sholde GHmCrYC^{2}CBLMRF. fynde] G CrYOC^{2}CBLMRF; fare W; faren (aren *over erasure another ink*) Hm. diuerse] greate G.
426 biddynges] byddyng G. body] bodyes G. in(2)] *om* Cot. soule] soules G.
427 Hir] ⁊ here F. hir] *om* M. penaunces] penaunce Y. brynge] hem bringe RF.

Alle þat ben at debaat and bedemen were trewe:
Petite & accipietis &c.
"Salt saueþ catel", siggen þise wyues:
Vos estis sal terre &c. |
The heuedes of holy chirche, and þei holy were, *fol. 94 a*
Crist calleþ hem salt for cristene soules,
Et si sal euanuerit in quo salietur?
[Ac] fressh flessh ouþer fissh, whan it salt failleþ,
It is vnsauory, forsoþe, ysoden or ybake;
So is mannes soule, sooþly, þat seeþ no goo[d] ensampl[e]
Of hem of holi chirche þat þe heighe wey sholde teche
And be gide and go bifore as a good Banyer,
And hardie hem þat bihynde ben, and ȝyue hem good euidence.
Elleuene holy men al þe world tornede
Into lele bileue; þe lightloker me þinkeþ
Sholde alle maner men; we han so manye maistres,
Preestes and prechours and a pope aboue,
That goddes salt sholde be to saue mannes soule.
Al was hethynesse som tyme Engelond and Walis

428 debaat] þe bate Hm. and] if F. bedemen] redemen G. were] wer*en* BmBoF; been G.
428α *in margin* OC^2. &c] *querite & inuenietis pulsate* F.
429 saueþ] saue Cr^1. catel] OCr^{23}GC^{2}CLMR; þe catel WHmYBF; thy catel Cr^1. siggen] as seyn F; saynge C. þise] the Cr^1; wyse Cot; sadde F.
429α–92 lines *om* F.
429α *in margin* OC^2. &c] *om* Cr.
430 heuedes] henedes Cr^1; bedis C^2; beydes G. were] weren OC^2.
431 calleþ] called R. cristene] cristned B; cristynes C.
431α *in margin* OC^2. *euanuerit*] euanerit G. *salietur*] CrGOC^{2}CBmLMR; *salietur &c* WHmYBoCot.
432 Ac] HmYOBLMR; but G; and C^{2}C; For WCr. ouþer] or M. failleþ] falliþ BmBo.
433 It] *om* OC^2. vnsauory] vnsanery Cr^2. ysoden] ysode CotGYOCLM; sothen R; sodde CrC^2. or] oþer BmBo. ybake] ybaken BmBo; bake G; baken RCr.
434 seeþ] soeþ Bo; sayes C. good ensample] GHmYOC^{2}CBLM; gode saumple R; good exemple Cr; goode ensamples W.
435 sholde] shuld*en* BmBo. teche] techen Cot.
436 a] *om* R. Banyer] banerour Cot; rauenour Cr.
437 hardie] hardien M; hard*en* Cr. bihynde ben] ben behynde C^{2}GO. ȝyue] yeuen (y *altered from* ȝ) M. euidence] euidences Y.
438 Elleuene] Elleue Y; Ale*n*uen Cr^1.
439 lele] lelly Cr. lightloker] lyghtlyer GC^2. þinkeþ] thynke C.
440 Sholde] Schulden OC^2. men] of men HmCr^{2}M. so] to Hm.
441 aboue] abouen C.
442 sholde] schulden OB.
443 hethynesse] hethen M. Engelond] Englong BmBo.

Til Gregory garte clerkes to go here and preche.
Austyn [þe kyng cristnede at Caunterbury],
And þoruȝ miracles, as men mow rede, al þat marche he tornede
To crist and to cristendom and cros to honoure,
And follede folk faste, and þe feiþ tauȝte
Moore þoruȝ miracles þan þoruȝ muche p*re*chyng;
As wel þoruȝ hise werkes as wiþ hise holy wordes
[Enformed] hem what fullynge and feiþ was to mene.
Clooþ þat comeþ fro þe weuyng is noȝt comly to were
Til it be fulled vnder foot or in fullyng stokkes,
Wasshen wel wiþ water and wiþ taseles cracched,
Ytouked and yteynted and vnder taill*ours* hande.
[And] so it fareþ by a barn þat born is of wombe;
Til it be cristned in cristes name and confermed of þe bisshop
It is heþene as to heueneward and helplees to þe soule. |
Heþen is to mene after heeþ and vntiled erþe, *fol.* 94 *b*
As in wildernesse wexeþ wilde beestes
Rude and vnresonable, rennynge wiþouten [keperes].
Ye mynnen wel how Mathew seiþ, how a man made a feste.
He fedde hem wiþ no venyson ne fesauntȝ ybake

444 garte] made G; and grete BR. to] gu*nn*en B. here] hyder Hm; *om* GYOC^{2}CBR. and] ⁊ to GYOC^{2}CR.
445 Austyn] augustyne G. þe...Caunterbury] at Caunterbury cristnede þe kyng WHmCrGYOC^{2}CBLMR (kyng] kynge þer*e* R).
446 þoruȝ] bi Cr. as] þat Hm. mow] *om* M. rede] reden C^2. marche] marsh Cr. he] *om* G.
447 and(2)] þe G.
448 faste] *om* R. and] that Y.
450 hise(1)] *om* Cr. wiþ] þurgh HmCrM. holy] woly G. wordes] werkis (*corrected another hand*) Bm.
451 Enformed] And seide WHmCrGYO C^{2}CBLR; And seiden M. what] what þe Hm; wat was B. and] was ⁊ Hm.
452 þe weuyng] wetyng G. þe] þ C.
453 be] is LMR. fulled] foulled C. stokkes] stocke B.
454 Wasshen] Iwaschen R. water] watres M.
455 Ytouked] Touked Cr; ywalked C. yteynted] teynted CrR. hande] handes HmR.
456 And] CrHmGYOC^{2}CBLMR; Right W. barn] baron C^2. of] YGOC^{2}CBLR; of a WHmCrM.
457 it] he Hm. and] *om* Cr. þe] *om* Hm Cr^{23}G.
460 in] in wilde WHmCrGYOC^{2}CBLM R. wildernesse] wirdernesse Bo.
461 outen] oute YHmCrGOC^{2}CBLMR. keperes] R; creperes LYO; crepres GC^2; cropers HmCrCBM; cropiers W.
462 mynnen wel] take wel hede R. mynnen] mennen Cot; menen CrHmOC^2; nymmen L; nymen Y; ny*m*methe G; neme*n* BmBo; take C. how(1)] what GR. seiþ] seyde OC^2. how(2)] *om* M.
463 hem] *om* Y. ybake] baked Cr.

But wiþ foweles þat fram hym nolde but folwede his whistlyng:
Ecce altilia mea & omnia parata sunt;
And wiþ calues flessh he fedde þe folk þat he louede.
The calf bitokneþ clennesse in hem þat kepeþ lawes,
For as þe Cow þoruȝ kynde mylk þe calf norisseþ til an Oxe,
So loue and leaute lele men susteneþ.
And maidenes and mylde men mercy desiren
Right as þe cow calf coueiteþ [swete melk];
So [menen] riȝtfulle men [after] mercy and truþe.
[And by þe hond fedde foules [i]s folk vnderstonde
That loþ ben to louye wiþouten lernyng of ensaumples.
Riȝt as capons in a court comeþ to mennes whistlyng,
In menyng after mete folweþ men þat whistlen;
Riȝt so rude men þat litel reson konneþ
Louen and bileuen by lettred mennes doynges,
And by hire wordes and werkes wenen and trowen;
And as þo foules to fynde fode after whistlyng
So hope þei to haue heuene þoruȝ hir whistlyng.
And by þe man þat made þe feste þe mageste bymeneþ
That is god of his grace, gyueþ alle men blisse.
Wiþ wederes and wiþ wondres he warneþ vs wiþ a whistlere
Where þat his wille is to worshipen vs alle,
And feden vs and festen vs for eueremoore at oones].
Ac who beþ þat excuseþ hem þat [arn] persons and preestes,
That heuedes of holy chirche ben, þat han hir wil here,
Wiþouten trauaille þe tiþe deel þat trewe men biswynken?

464 folwede] folewede*n* O; folowen C; folwe B. his] hym Hm.
464α *in margin* OC^2. *altilia*] *volatilia* B. *sunt*] *sunt &c* HmGOC^{2}CBoCotLMR.
465 And] *om* OC^2. he(1)] *om* C^2. þe] *om* M.
466 kepeþ] kepe þe G.
467 norisseþ] norisshe C. til] to GC^2.
468 So] So doth R. and] & and L. lele] lely Cr; and lele R; lewde G. susteneþ] sustened CB; systeyane G.
470 as] so OC^2. swete melk] swete melke RHmCrGYOC^{2}CBLM; melk swete W.
471 menen...after] doon riȝtfulle men WHmCrGYOC^{2}CBLMR.
472–85 R; *lines om* WHmCrGYOC^{2}CBLM; *here in the spelling of* W.
472 is] his R.
486 Ac] but G; And CrC^{2}C. who] whoso HmCr^{23}. beþ] be tho M; *om* Cr^{23}. þ*at*(2)] *om* R. arn] HmYOC^{2}BM; aren CLR; are G; ar Cr; ben W.
487 heuedes] heneds Cr. chirche] cherches R.
488 outen] oute GCrYOC^{2}BLR. deel] dole G.

They wol be wrooþ for I write þus, ac to witnesse I take
Boþe Mathew and Marc and *Memento domine* dauid:
[*Ecce audiuimus e*[*a*]*m in effrata &c*].
What pope or prelat now parfourneþ þat crist highte,
Ite in vniuersum mundum & predicate &c?
Allas, þat men so longe [sholde bileue on Makometh]!
So manye prelates to preche as þe Pope makeþ,
Of Naȝareth, of Nynyue, of Neptalym and Damaske,
That þei ne wente as crist wisseþ, siþen þei wille haue name,
To be pastours and preche þe passion of Iesus,
And as hymself seide [so] to lyue and dye:
Bonus pastor animam suam ponit &c.
And seide it in saluacion of Sarȝens and oþere; |
For cristene and vncristene crist seide to prechours *fol. 95 a*
Ite vos in vineam meam &c.
And siþ þat þise Sarȝens, Scribes and [Grekes]
Han a lippe of oure bileue, þe lightlier me þynkeþ
Thei sholde turne, whoso trauail[e wolde] to teche hem of
þe Trinite.

489 wol] wolen O; wold Cr. be] *om* Cr. for I write] þat I wroote G. þus] this CrG. ac] but G; & CrC^{2}C. to] *om* OC^{2}CB. I(2)] *om* Cr.
490α R; *line om* WHmCrGYOC^{2}CBLM. *eam*] *eum* R.
491α *in margin* OC^2. *&c*] *euangelium* Cr; *om* OC^{2}B.
492 Allas] Alls R. men] *om* C^2. sholde... Makometh] on Makometh sholde bileue WHmCrGYOC^{2}CBLMR (on] yn Hm. sholde] shulden C^2; schulden so O; schullen R).
493 *Here* F *resumes.* to] ben to F. Pope makeþ] peple makþ meende F.
494 and] and of Cot; of FG. Damaske] Damasco Cr^{23}.
495 wente] wenten RF. wisseþ] hem wisseþ F; wissed C; wysheth Cr. wille] wolen OBmBo; wilne RF. haue] þe F; a LR.
496 pastours] pastour Cr.
497 *line om* Hm. hym] hem Cr^3. self] seluen M. so] CrOC^{2}CBmBoLMR; go Cot; *om* WGYF. dye] CrGYOC^{2}CBLMR; dyȝe for oþere F; to dye W.
497α *in margin* OC^2; *line om* F. *ponit &c*] *dat pro omnibus suis* Cot; popnit *&c* Y; *&c* BmBo.
498 And] he F. it] it is B; so F. in] of Hm; for F. of] to Cr. oþere] Iewes G.
499 For] To R; & to F. and] and to RF. to prechours] on þis wyse F.
500 *in margin* OC^2. *vos*] & *vos* F. *vineam*] veneam YC^2 (*altered from veniam* Y). *&c*] *om* CrCotLRF.
501 Sarȝens] sarasyng Bo. Scribes and] & scribis & eek F. Grekes] Iewes WHmCrGYOC^{2}CBLMRF.
502 Han] haven F; hand C. a] *om* C^2. lightlier] lyȝtloker HmYBLMRF (*corrected from* liȝtlokeþ Bm, liȝthlokeþ Bo); liȝtliker O; lyghlier Cr^3. me þynkeþ] me thynke C; it semeth RF.
503 sholde] schulden OC^2. turne] turnen F. so] *om* GF. trauaile wolde] BGYOC^{2}CLRF; trauailed WHmCr^{23}M (d *over erasure* M); traueled Cr^1. to teche] & techen R.

Querite & inuenietis &c. |
[For alle paynymes preieþ and parfitly bileueþ fol. 95 b
In [o] gre[et] god, and his grace asken,
And make hir mone to Makometh hir message to shewe.
Thus in a feiþ leue þat folk, and in a fals mene,
And þat is rouþe for riȝtful men þat in þe Reawme wonyen,
And a peril to þe pope and prelates þat he makeþ
That bere bisshopes names of Bethleem and Babiloigne.
[Whan þe hye kyng of heuene sente his sone to erþe
Many myracles he wrouȝte m[e]n for to turne,
In ensaumple þat men sholde se by sadde reson
Men myȝte noȝt be saued but þoruȝ mercy and grace,
And þoruȝ penaunce and passion and parfit bile[ue].
And bicam man of a maide and *metropolitanus*,
And baptised and bishined wiþ þe blode of his herte
Alle þat wilned and wolde wiþ Inwit bileue it.
Many a seint syþen haþ suffred to deye
Al for to enforme þe faith; in fele contrees deyeden,
In ynde, in alisaundre, in ermonye and spayne,
In dolful deþ deyeden for hir faith.
In sauacion of [mannes soule] seint [Thomas] was ymartired;

503α *in margin* OC^2. &c] *om* F.
504–10, 529–32 *copied after lines* 533–69 (*which* RF *omit*) WHmCrGYOC^{2}CBLM: *see above*, pp. 176–9.
504 alle paynymes] al paynym L. preieþ] preire Bo; preiere BmCot. and...bileueþ] to on persone to helpe R; to oon persone of helpe F. parfitly] parfithi BmBo.
505 In] On R; & on F. o greet] o RF; þe holy grete WHmCrGYOC^{2}CBLM. god] god þei greden RF. grace] RF; grace þei WHmCrGYOCBLM; grace þe C^2.
506 make] maken OHmC^{2}RF; makiþ B. mone] meene F; monoye Y.
507 a(1)] *om* CrC^2. leue] leueþ HmOC^2 (eueþ *over erasure* Hm); liue Cr; lyueth LRF. in(2)] *om* BmBo. a(2)] *om* F.
508 for] for þe R; of Cr. þe] *om* Cr. wonyen] dwell F.
509 *line om* F. a] in a YCB; yn GOC^2. peril] parel Cot. to] of Cr; for G. and] and to R.
510 That] And OC^2. bere] beren OHmC^{2}BRF. names] name Y. of] in Y. and] and of HmCrGOC^{2}CBRF.
511–28 RF; *lines om* WHmCrGYOC^{2}CBLM; *here in the spelling of* W.
512 men] man RF.
513 men] *om* F. by] þat by RF.
515 bileue] beleve F; byle R.
516 man] *om* F. *metropolitanus*] *metropolitanus* after F.
517 And] & was F. bishined] ysygned F.
518 Inwit] inne wit R; wit F.
519 haþ] haven F. deye] dyȝen F.
520 enforme] ferme F. deyeden] dyȝen F.
521 in(1)] F; and in R. and] and in R; in F.
522 In] & in F. deyeden] þey dyeden F. faith] faith sake R; feyþis sake F.
523 mannes soule] þe fayth RF. Thomas] F; *erasure* R.

Amonges vnkynde cristene for cristes loue he deyede,
And for þe riȝt of al þis reume and alle reumes cristene.
Holy chirche is honoured heiȝliche þoruȝ his deying;
He is a forbisene to alle bisshopes and a briȝt myrour,
And souereynliche to swiche þat of surrye bereþ þe name],
[And nauȝt to] huppe aboute in Engelond to halwe mennes
    Auteres
And crepe [in] amonges curatours, confessen ageyn þe lawe:
Nolite mittere falsem in messem alienam.
Many man for cristes loue was martired [amonges] Romayne[s] |
Er cristendom [were] knowe þere, or any cros
    honoured. *fol. 96 a* |
It is ruþe to rede how riȝtwise men lyuede, *fol. 95 a*
How þei defouled hir flessh, forsoke hir owene wille,
Fer fro kyth and fro kyn yuele ycloþed yeden,
Baddely ybedded, no book but conscience,
Ne no richesse but þe roode to reioisse hem Inne:
Absit nobis gloriari nisi in cruce domini nostri &c.
And þo was plentee and pees amonges poore and riche,
And now is rouþe to rede how þe rede noble

524 Amonges] And among F. loue] *om* F.
527 a forbisene] beleve F.
529 And...to] RF; That WHmCrGYOC^{2}CBLM. huppe] hippen OHmC^{2}B. aboute...to] here & þeere for F. in] here in R; *om* OC^2. Engelond] Englong BmBo. to] for to R. halwe] halwen CHmC^{2}BmBoF. mennes] *om* HmRF.
530 crepe] crepen CrHmOBF; cropen C^2. in] RF; *om* WHmCrGYOC^{2}CBLM. curatours] HmCrGYOC^{2}CBmLM; creatouris BoCot; curatours and WRF. confessen] confesse F; confesse men R; confessyon GC^{2}B.
530α *in margin* OC^2; *copied after* 532 Y. *alienam*] CrGYOC^{2}BmBoF; *alienam &c* WHmCCotLM; *&c* R.
531 man] a man CrCotRF. amonges] R; in WHmCrGYOC^{2}CBLMF. Romaynes] romaynes R; Romayne WHmGYOC^{2}CBmBoM; Romanye L; Rome CrCot; grete roome F.
532 Er] F; Ar R; er þan Hm; Er any WCrGM; Er þat eny B; Er þan any OC^2; Er ar any YCL. were] were RF; was WHmCrGYOC^{2}CBLM. knowe] knowen OC^2. or] er BmBo. cros] cros þere R. *Here* Y *copies* 530α.
533–69 *lines om* RF; *copied after line* 503α *and followed by lines* 504–10, 529–32 WHmCrGYOC^{2}CBLM.
533 lyuede] lyueden YGOC^{2}CB.
534 defouled] defouleden O. forsoke forsoken OHmC^2; & forsoken B.
535 Fer] fir Bo. kyth] kid kiþ (kid *cancelled*) Bo. fro(2)] fer fro Hm; *om* M. yuele] ill Cr. ycloþed] clothed CrGYM.
536 Baddely] Ful baddeli B. ybedded] bedded Cr; clade G.
537 reioisse] reioycen OC^2. Inne] therin Cr.
537α *in margin* OC^2. *nobis*] *mihi* OC^2; *vos* Cr.
539 *as one line with* 540 *over erasure another hand* Hm. And] Ac Hm.

Is reuerenced er þe Roode, receyued for [þe] worþier
Than cristes cros þat ouercam deeþ and dedly synne.
And now is werre and wo, and whoso why askeþ:
For coueitise after cros; þe croune stant in golde.
Boþe riche and Religious, þat roode þei honoure
That in grotes is ygraue and in gold nobles.
For coueitise of þat cros [clerkes] of holy kirke
Shul [ouer]torne as templers dide; þe tyme approcheþ faste.
[Mynne] ye noȝt, wise men, how þo men honoured
Moore tresor þan trouþe? I dar noȝt telle þe soþe;
Reson and rightful doom þ[o] Religiouse d[ampn]ede.
Right so, ye clerkes, for youre coueitise er [come auȝt] longe
Shal þei demen *dos ecclesie*, and [depose yow for youre pride]:
Deposuit potentes de sede &c. |
If knyghthod and kynde wit and þe commune [and]
conscience *fol. 95 b*
Togideres loue leelly, leueþ it wel, ye bisshopes,
The lordshipe of londes [lese ye shul for euere],
And lyuen as *Leuitici* as oure lord [yow] techeþ:

540 receyued] GHmYOC^{2}CLM; and receyued WCrB. þe] HmCrGYOC^{2}CBLM; *om* W.
541 synne] synnes G.
542 askeþ] aske Hm.
543 stant] standes CrC.
544 honoure] honouren OGC^2.
545 in grotes] yn þe grote G. ygraue] ygrauen MG; grauen CrHmOC^2. in(2)] yn þe G; *om* C. gold] golden OC^2; *om* Cr^3.
546 coueitise] couetous Cr. clerkes] men WHmCrGYOC^{2}CBLM. kirke] cherche HmOC^{2}B.
547 ouertorne] ouerturne B (ouer *another ink* Bm); torne WHmCrGYOC^{2}CLM. dide] diden OC^{2}M. faste] nere Cr.
548 Mynne] Wite WHmCrYOC^{2}CBLM; wote G. wise] YOC^{2}CBLM; ye wise WHmCrG. honoured] honoureden OC^2.
549 telle] sey M.
550 þo] GYOC^{2}CBLM; þe WHmCr. dampnede] damneden BmBo (*over erasure another ink* Bm); demede WHmCrGYCLM; demeden OC^2.
551 ye] you Cr. er...auȝt] er WHmCrGYOC^{2}CBLM.
552 demen] deme CrOC^2. depose...pride] youre pride depose WHmCrGYOC^{2}CBLM (depose] deso depose B).
552α *in margin* OC^2.
553 knyghthod] knyȝhode C^2; knyghode Cr^1. þe] *om* HmCrGYOC^{2}CBLM. and(3)] & B (*above line* Bm); by WCrM (*above line* M); *om* HmGYOC^{2}CL.
554 loue] louen *altered to* loued Bo; loued louen (louen *cancelled*) Bm; loued Cot. leueþ] leue *twice* C. it] *om* Cot.
555 lordshipe] lordshyps CrCB. of] HmCrGYOC^{2}CBLM; of youre W. londes] lande G. lese...euere] for euere shul ye lese WHmCrGYOC^{2}CBLM (shul ye] ye shul YGOC^{2}C; ȝee shullen B).
556 lyuen] lyue CrOC^{2}B. *Leuitici*] leuatici BmBo; leuytes G. yow] YHmCrGOC^{2}CBLM; *om* W.

Per primicias & decimas &c.
Whan Costantyn of curteisie holy kirke dowed
Wiþ londes and ledes, lordshipes and rentes,
An Aungel men herden an heigh at Rome crye,
"*Dos ecclesie* þis day haþ ydronke venym
And þo þat han Petres power arn apoisoned alle."
A medicyne moot þerto þat may amende p*re*lates.
That sholden preie for þe pees, possession hem letteþ;
Takeþ hire landes, ye lordes, and leteþ hem lyue by dymes.
If possession be poison and inparfite hem make
[Charite] were to deschargen hem for holy chirches sake,
And purgen hem of poison er moore p*er*il falle.
If preesthode were parfit þe peple sholde amende
That cont*ra*rien cristes lawe and cristendom dispise.]
Euery bisshop þat bereþ cros, by þat he is holden *fol. 96 a*
Thoruȝ his p*ro*uince to passe and to his peple shewe hym,
Tellen hem and techen hem on þe Trinite to bileue,
And feden hem wiþ goostly foode and [nedy folk to fynden.

556α *in margin* OC^2. &] *om* Hm. *decimas*] *diuicias* YGCB (*corrected* G). &c] *om* YL.
557 kirke] chirche YHmGOC^{2}CB. dowed] endewed YCot.
559 An] And BmBo. herden] herde LG. *Hereafter a Latin line* OC^2; *see above*, p. 224.
560 ydronke] ydronken BOM; dronke GCr; dronkyn HmC^2.
561 þo] they Cr. apoisoned] enpoisoned MG; poysoned Cr.
562 moot] mo Bo.
563 That sholden] thanne schuldyn they Hm. sholden] shold GCr; shul C. preie] praien M. þe] *om* Cr. possession] possessiou*n*s Hm.
564 Takeþ] take CrGCL. leteþ] let CrGO C^{2}L. hem] hym CBmBo. dymes] þeir dymes G; demes Cr^1; *decimis* Cr^2; *decimus* Cr^3.
565 inparfite] vnp*ar*fit Hm. make] makeþ Hm.
566 Charite] Good WHmCrGYOC^{2}CL M; Good it B. were] *twice, the first cancelled* Y. to] it to Cr; *om* Hm. deschargen] discharge CrCot; dyschare G. chirches] chirche YCBL; kyrkes Cr^1; kyrke Cr^{23}.
567 purgen] purge Cr. of] of þat B (þat *above line* Bm).
568 preesthode] prested C. sholde] schul C; wold G; solde L.
569 dispise] dispisen C^{2}O. *Hereafter* WHm CrGYOC^{2}CBLM *copy lines* 504–10, 529–532.
570 *Here* RF *resume*. cros] a croos F. he] *om* R. holden] holde RF.
571 *transposed with* 572 F. Thoruȝ] & þorgh F. shewe] GYOC^{2}CBF; schewyn Hm; to shewe WCrLMR. hym] *om* Cr.
572 Tellen] Telle OC^{2}B; To telly*n* F. hem(*both*)] *om* F. techen] teche OC^{2}B; schewen RF. on] of OC^{2}BoCot.
573b–6a RF; *om* WHmCrGYOC^{2}CBLM *which read* 573a *and* 576b *as one line*; *here in the spelling of* W.
573 And] & To B (& *added by main scribe* Bm). feden] fede OC^{2}B. hem] hym Bm Bo. fynden] feeden F.

Ac ysaie of yow spekeþ and oȝias boþe,
That no man sholde be bisshop but if he hadde boþe
Bodily foode and goostly foode to] gyue þere it nedeþ:
In domo mea non est panis neque vestimentum et ideo nolite constituere me Regem.
Oȝias seiþ for swiche þat sike ben and feble,
Inferte omnes [decimas] in orreum meum vt cibus in domo mea.
Ac we cristene creatures þat on þe cros bileuen
Arn ferme as in þe feiþ, goddes forbode ellis,
And han clerkes to kepen vs þerInne & hem þat shul come after.
And Iewes lyuen in lele lawe; oure lord wroot it hymselue
In stoon for it stedefast was and stonde sholde euere.
Dilige deum & proximum is parfit Iewen lawe;
And took it Moyses to teche men til Messie coome,
And on þat lawe þei l[e]ue and leten it þe beste.
And ȝit knewe þei crist þat cristendom tauȝte,
[And] for a parfit prophete þat muche peple sauede
Of selkouþe sores; þei seiȝen it ofte,

574 Ac] But F. of...spekeþ] as how þou spekist F.
576 foode(2)] *om* F. gyue] gyuen HmF. nedeþ] nedede R.
576α *me*] *me in* GYOC^{2}CB. *Regem*] *regem &c* HmYB; *regem* ysa. 3 F; *regem* y 3 LR.
577 *transposed with* 578 C^2. Oȝias] Malachias Cr^{23}. for] þat for G. þat] as Cr^{3}G. ben] men Y.
578 *in margin* O. *decimas*] HmCrGYOC^{2}CBLMRF; *om* W. *vt*] *vt sit* CrOC^2. *mea*] *mea &c* HmR; *&c* GYOC^{2}CB.
579 Ac] but GF; And CrC^{2}C.
580 ferme] for me R; formed F. as] *om* Cr^{23}G. goddes] god HmCr^{23}GM (*erasure at end* M). forbode] forbede HmGCot.
581 kepen] kepe HmCrGOC^{2}F; kepepen C. shul] *om* CrG. come] comen F; comethe G. after] GHmCrYOC^{2}CBF; after vs WLMR.
582 And] Þe F. lyuen] *corrected from* leuen G; leuen C^2; beleven F. lele lawe] lelli loue Cr. it] *om* GYOC^{2}CB. selue] seluen M.
583 was] is YGOC^{2}CB. sholde] shal Cr YOC^2; shall for G.
584 *Dilige*] *Diligite* B. &] *tuum &* F. is] *tuum* is OC^{2}F; *et cetera* is BmBo. Iewen] þe Iewis F.
585 And] And he C; ac he B. it] it to Cr. Moyses] Moyse F. teche] techen BoCotR. men] it hem RF.
586 on] *om* OC^2. leue] CrR; leuen Hm GYOC^{2}CBmBoM; beleeve F; lyue W; lyuen L; lyeuen Cot. and] RF; ȝit and WHmCr^{13}GYOC^{2}CBLM; it and Cr^2. it] it for F.
587 ȝit] *om* M. knewe] knowe GYCB; knowen OC^2. þei] þey after F.
588 And] RF; *om* WHmCrGYOC^{2}CBLM. muche] mychil F.
589 þei] tha C. it ofte] hym heele manye F.

Boþe of miracles and m*er*ueilles, and how he men festede,
Wiþ two fisshes and fyue loues fyue þousand peple,
And by þat mangerie [þei] myȝte wel se þ*at* Messie he semede;
And whan he lifte vp Laȝar þat leid was in graue
And vnder stoon deed and stank; wiþ stif vois hym callede:
Laȝare veni foras;
Dide hym rise and rome riȝt bifore þe Iewes.
Ac þei seiden and sworen wiþ sorcerie he wrouȝte,
And studieden to struyen hym and struyden hemselue, |
And þoruȝ his pacience hir power to pure noȝt he brouȝte: *fol. 96 b*
Pacientes vincunt.
Daniel of hire vndoynge deuyned and seide
Cum sanctus sanctorum veniat cessabit vnxio vestra.
And [ȝit] wenen þo wrecches þ*at* he were *pseudopropheta*
And þ*at* his loore be lesynges, and lakken it alle,
And hopen þ*at* he be to come þ*at* shal hem releue;
Moyses eft or Messie hir maistres deuyneþ.
Ac pharisees and Sarȝens, Scribes and [Grekes]

590 of] *om* G. miracles...merueilles] merveylis ⁊ myraklis F; miruaille and miracles (*correct order noted*) C. and(1)] and of B. and how] whan þat F. he] *om* R.
591 fisshes] syshes Cr^1. loues] leues C.
592 þei] RF; men WHmCrGYOC^{2}CBL M. myȝte] myȝten O. wel] *om* CrGOC^2 F. semede] were F.
593 And] *om* F. vp] vs Cr^2. in] in þe F.
594 stoon] stoune G; stond Cot. deed... stank] stanke and dede R; he stank ded F. deed] deyde G; *om* Cr. stif] stil Y. hym] he hy*m* F; he YOC^{2}CB; ⁊ G.
594α *in margin* OC^2. *foras*] *foras ⁊c* Hm YB.
595 Dide] he dyde F. hym] hem BmBo. riȝt] ȝut Cot.
596 Ac] but GF; And CrC^{2}C. seiden] seyde OCrR. sworen] swore CrG. he] þ*at* he F.
597 studieden] studied Cr^{23}C^2; studed Cr^1; stoded C. to...hym] hym to stroye G. struyen] struye OC^2; destruyen Cot; destruye HmCr. hym] hem Bo; *om* C. struyden] stroyed Cr; struyde*n*d C^2. hem] hym BmBo. selue] seluen MCr.
598 his] *om* G. pure] *om* Cr. he] *above line main hand* W.
598α *in margin* OC^2. *Vincunt patientes* Cr. *vincunt*] *vincunt ⁊c* HmYCB; *vincunt Maliciam* F.
599 Daniel] But Danyel F. vndoynge] doynge CrMF; vndirstondyng B.
600 *in margin* OC^2. *Cum*] *Cum veniat* RF. *veniat...vestra*] *⁊c* R; *om* F. *vestra*] *vestra ⁊c* HmBmBo.
601 ȝit] OHmGYC^{2}CBLMRF; *om* WCr. þo] the CBoCot. wrecches] Iewis Cot. *pseudo*] speudo F; seudo R; pheudo G.
602 *line om* CB. his] ys GC^2. and] ⁊ þey F.
603 hopen] hoope G. he] *om* Cr^{1}F. come] comen HmC^2.
604 Moyses] Or Moyses F. hir] ȝet here RF. maistres] maystryes OR. deuyneþ] dyuineth R; dyuyne F; ȝit deuyneþ WHm CrYOC^{2}CBLM; þei dyuyne G.
605 Ac] but GF; And CrOC^{2}C. pharisees] saraȝens YGOC^{2}CB. and(1)] *om* G. Sarȝens] pharisees YGOC^{2}CB. Scribes] ⁊ scribis F. Grekes] CrGYOC^{2}CBLMR F; Iewes WHm.

Arn folk of oon feiþ; þe fader god þei honouren.
And siþen þat þe Sarȝens and also þe Iewes
Konne þe firste clause of oure bileue, *Credo in deum patrem omnipotentem*,
Prelates of cristene prouinces sholde preue if þei myȝte
Lere hem litlum and litlum *et in Iesum Christum filium*,
Til þei kouþe speke and spelle *et in Spiritum sanctum*,
[Recorden it and rendren] it wiþ *remissionem peccatorum*
Carnis resurreccionem et vitam eternam amen.'

606 of] *above line* Cot; *om* BmBo.
608 *as two lines divided after* beleeve F. Konne] kunnen HmBR. *patrem*] *om* Cr. *omnipotentem*] *omnipotentem &c* HmR; *&c* OC^2; *om* CrGYCB.
609 of] and G. cristene] crystes Hm. *pro*uinces] prouince R. sholde] schulden OC^2; slulde (*touched up*) Bm. preue] preven F. myȝte] myȝten OC^2.
610 Lere] YGOC^{2}CLR; leren HmM (To *in margin before it* M); To lere WB; To learne Cr; ⁊ lerne F. hem] þem by G. litlum(*both*)] lytle CrG; lytsom Hm. *filium*] *filium eius* Cot; *filium eius &c* GYOC^{2}CBmBo.
611 *line om* Cot. kouþe] couþen OC^{2}F. speke...spelle] speken ⁊ spellyn F. *et*] and R; *Credo* F. *sanctum*] *sanctum &c* GYCBmBo.
612 Recorden...rendren] And rendren it ⁊ recorden L; And reden it and recorden WHmCrGYOC^{2}CBMRF (reden] rede OCrC^2. it] *om* G. recorden] recorde OCrC^{2}F).
613 *in margin* OC^2. *Carnis*] ⁊ þerwith *Carnis* F. *amen*] *amen &c* Hm.

XVI

'NOw faire falle yow', quod I þo, 'for your*e* faire shewyng!
For Haukyns loue þe Actif man euere I shal yow louye.
Ac 3it I am in a weer what charite is to mene.'
'It is a ful trie tree', quod he, 'trewely to telle.
Mercy is þe more þerof; þe myddul stok is ruþe;
The leues ben lele wordes, þe lawe of holy chirche;
The blosmes beþ buxom speche and benigne lokynge.
Pacience hatte þe pure tree and [pouere] symple of herte,
And so þoru3 god and goode men groweþ þe fruyt Charite.'
'I wolde t*ra*uaille', quod I, 'þis tree to se twenty hundred myle, |
And to haue my fulle of þat fruyt forsake a[l] oþ[er] saule[e]. *fol.* 97 *a*
Lord!' quod I, 'if any wight wite whiderout it groweþ?'
'It groweþ in a gardyn', quod he, 'þat god made hymselue
Amyddes mannes body; þe more is of þat stokke.
Herte highte þe herber þat it Inne groweþ,
And *liberum arbitrium* haþ þe lond [to] ferme,

1 *Befreo this two additional lines* F; *see above*, p. 223.
2 Haukyns] Haukyne F; Ha*n*ke*n*s Cr. þe] that Y. yow] þe M.
3 Ac] but GF; And CrC^{2}C. in] *om* C^2. what] wha C; þ*a*t Cr^1.
4 trie] tried CrGOC^2; drye Cot. trewely] treuthe R; good trewþe F.
5 more] moste F. is ruþe] is rycthe C; aboute Hm.
6 lele] lelly Cr.
7 speche] speches HmF. lokynge] lokyngys F.
8 hatte] hattith Cot; hatiþ BmBo; haþe C^2. pure] pouere Y. and] *om* B. pouere] pouere CM; pore LRF; pore and B; pure WHmCrGYOC^2.
9 and] YCrGOC^{2}CBRF; and þoru3 WLM; and pure Hm. þe] þat B; *om* F. fruyt] fruy Y. Charite] *caritas* B; of charyte HmF.
10 wolde] wole B. quod I] *om* F. se] seen q*uo*d y F. myle] myles G.
11 And] *om* F. to] Cr^{23}GYOC^{2}CBRF; for to WHmCr^{1}LM. fulle] wyll G; self Cot. fruyt] frut & F. al...saulee] al other saulee LHmYOC^{2}CBmBoMF; alle oþere saulees WG; al other salue Cr; al other soule CotR.
12 whider] where HmF. out] out þat R; *om* HmF. it groweþ] þat tre spryngiþ F.
13 a] *om* L. selue] seluen LMF.
14 is] *om* G. stokke] tree Hm.
15 highte] hatteþ Hm; hatiþ (iþ *erased*) Bm; hath Cot. þe] þ*a*t F. herber] herbergh B. þat] þa C. it Inne] yn ytt G; þe tree in F.
16 to] HmCrGYOC^{2}CBLMRF; þe W.

Vnder Piers þe Plowman to piken it and weden it.'
'Piers þe Plowman!' quod I þo, and al for pure Ioye
That I herde nempne his name anoon I swowned after,
And lay longe in a louedreem; and at þe laste me þou3te
That Piers þe Plowman al þe place me shewed
And bad me toten on þe tree, on top and on roote.
Wiþ þre piles was it vnderpight; I *par*ceyued it soone.
'Piers', quod I, 'I preie þee, whi stonde þise piles here?'
'For wyndes, wiltow wite', quod he, 'to witen it fro fallyng:
Cum ceciderit iustus non collidetur quia dominus supponit ma[num suam];
And in blowyng tyme abite þe floures but if þise piles helpe.
The world is a wikked wynd to hem þat willen truþe.
Coueitise comþ of þat wynd and crepeþ among þe leues
And forfreteþ nei3 þe fruyt þoru3 manye faire sightes.
Thanne *with* þe firste pil I palle hym doun, *potencia de[i patris]*.
The flessh is a fel wynd, and in flouryng tyme,
Thoru3 likynge and lustes so loude he gynneþ blowe

17 Vnder] And vnder RF. Piers] is pers F. Plowman] powman Y. piken] pyke CrM. and] OGYC^{2}CBF; and to WHm CrLMR. weden] wede CrM. it(2)] *om* Hm.
18 I] he B.
19 nempne] nyuyne G; nempe Cr. swowned] showned Y.
20 lay longe] longe lay F. loue] lone Cr^1. dreem] derne C. þe] *om* Cr.
21 al] anon al F.
22 me] GOC^{2}LMRF; me to WHmCrYC B. toten] totren Cot; totre Cr. þe] þat Hm. on(2, 3)] oon Hm; one Cr^1. top] crop HmCr^1; trop Cr^2.
23 Wiþ] ⁊ *with* F. piles...it] pyleris it was F. vnderpight] pyght vndre (vndre *above line*) G.
24 I(2)] *om* MR. stonde] stonden HmOC^2 MRF. piles] pileris F; pykes GC.
25 wyndes] wydis C^2. wite] weten Hm. witen] weten BmBo; kepen R; kepe F. it] in Cr^2.
25α *line om* F. *manum suam*] CrGOC^{2}CL MR; *manum suam ⁊c* Hm; *manum suum* Y; ma (*cropped*) W; *misericordiam suam* B.
26 And] that *over erasure* Hm; *om* CrF. blowyng] blomynge F. abite] byte Hm Cr; abid F. þe] no F. if] *om* CotF. piles] pileris F; floures CB. helpe] helpen F.
27 *run together with following* RF. to... truþe] *om* RF. hem] hym C. willen] wilneþ C^2; wyl Cr; wolden L.
28 Coueitise...wynd] *om* RF. and] a Bo. crepeþ] cryeþ Hm; wend*ith* F.
29 forfreteþ] forfrete Y; forfret LMRF; fofrete C. manye] fele F.
30 Thanne] That CB; And R; *om* F. *with*] *om* F. pil] pyler F. I] *om* Cot. palle] pale Cr; pulle HmGOC^{2}CBmBo; call F; *om* Cot. hym doun] *om* F. *potencia*] G; þat is *potencia* WHmCrYOC^{2}CBLMR; ys *potencia* F. *dei patris*] HmCrGYOC^{2}CB LMR; *dei* F; de (*cropped*) W.
31 fel] feble B. and] þat fleeþ F; *om* Hm. in] in þe C^2.
32 likynge] libyng C. and] of OC^2; þorgh3 F. loude] lowe B. he] yt Hm; be BmBo (*altered from* he Bm); by Cot; *om* CrY. blowe] to blowe HmCrC^2.

That it norisseþ nyce sightes and [anoþer] tyme wordes
And wikkede werkes þerof, wormes of synne,
And forbiteþ þe blosmes riȝt to þe bare leues.
Thanne sette I to þe secounde pil, *sapiencia dei patris*, |
That is þe passion and þe power of oure prince I*es*u. *fol.* 97 *b*
Thoruȝ preieres and penaunces and goddes passion in mynde
I saue it til I se it ripen and somdel yfruyted.
And þanne fondeþ þe fend my fruyt to destruye
Wiþ alle þe wiles þat he kan, and waggeþ þe roote
And casteþ vp to þe crop vnkynde Neighebores,
Bakbiteris [brewe]cheste, brawleris and chideris,
And leiþ a laddre þerto, of lesynges are þe ronges,
And feccheþ awey my floures som tyme afore boþe myne eighen.
Ac *liberum arbitrium* letteþ hym som tyme,
That is lieutenaunt to loken it wel bi leue of myselue:
Videatis qui peccat in spiritum sanctum numquam remittetur ⁊c; Hoc est idem qui peccat per liberum arbitrium non repugnat.
Ac whan þe fend and þe flessh forþ wiþ þe world

33 That] and þat Hm. it norisseþ] norysshyng G. nyce] nye Cr. anoþer] som WHmCrGYOC^2CBLMRF. tyme] tyme nyse F.

34 And] ⁊ þerof come*n* F. þerof] ⁊ F. wormes] worme C^2.

35 forbiteþ] forbetes C. riȝt] euen Cr. to] so to Y.

36 pil] piler þat is F. *dei*] *om* F. *patris*] *cancelled for filij another hand* G.

37 þe(1)] *om* F. Iesu] I*es*us OC^2CB.

38 Thoruȝ] with RF. and(1)] YGOC^2C BF; and þoruȝ WHmCrLMR. penaunces] penau*n*ce CrOC^2M. and(2)] *om* Cr^3Y. goddes] *cri*stis F.

39 I saue] þus save y F. I se] *om* Y. ripen] rype GOC^2F. yfruyted] fruted Cr; wel yfruted F.

40 And] ⁊ *above line* Y. þanne] *om* F. þe] *om* R. fend] fynde C.

41 þe(1)] *om* F. and] he F. waggeþ] waggede OC^2C; wacchethe G.

42 to] ynto G; *om* Cr. crop] crompe Cr. Neighebores] conseyl ofte F.

43 brewe] R; brokke (*over erasure*) M; breke YGOC^2CBL; breke þe WHmCr; ⁊ boosteris F. cheste] chestes C; ⁊ F. brawleris] blawreris F. chideris] childris Cot.

44 and] He he F. ronges] longes GB; roundes Cr; rybbis F. *Hereafter an additional line* F; *see above*, p. 223.

45 And] he F. feccheþ] fecche CCr^{23}. my] the Cot. som tyme] bytyme Hm; *om* GF. afore] before GCCotRF; tofore BmBo.

46 Ac] but GF; And CrC^2C. letteþ] lacchiþ BC. hym] hem $HmCr^{23}$R.

47 is] ys his F; *om* Hm. loken] loke GF. wel] *om* F. selue] seluen M; sowle Hm.

47α *numquam*] *above cancelled non* O. *Videatis*] Vidiatis Cr^{23}. *remittetur*] *remittitur* BoCot; *re ⁊c* R; *om* F. *⁊c*] *ei ⁊c* Hm; *om* CrF. *non*] *om* Hm. *repugnat*] *repurgatur* Cr; *om* Hm.

48 Ac] but GF; And CrC^2C. whan] what RF. forþ] ⁊ forth G.

Manacen bihynde me, my fruyt for to fecche,
Thanne *liberum arbitrium* lacchep þe [þridde] plan[k]e
And pallep adoun þe pouke pureliche þoruȝ *gr*ace
And help of þe holy goost, and þus haue I þe maistrie.'
'Now faire falle yow, Piers', quod I, 'so faire ye discryuen
The power of þise postes and hire *pro*pre myȝt[e].
Ac I haue þouȝtes a þreve of þise þre piles,
In what wode þei woxen and where þ*at* þei growed,
For alle are þei aliche longe, noon lasse þan ooþer,
And to my mynde, as me þinkeþ, on o more þei growed;
And of o greetnesse and grene of greyn þei semen.'
'That is sooþ', [seide] Piers, 'so it may bifalle.
I shal telle þee as tid what þis tree highte.
The ground þere it groweþ, goodnesse it hatte;
And I haue told þee what hiȝte þe tree; þe Trinite it meneþ.' |
And egreliche he loked on me and þerfore I spared *fol.* 98 *a*
To asken hym any moore þ*er*of, and bad hym ful faire
'To [dyuyse] þe fruyt þat so faire hangeþ'.
'Heer now byneþe', quod he þo, 'if I nede hadde,

49 Manacen] Manasse C; þey manace F.
50 lacchep] takes C. þridde] thridde LRF; firste WHmCrGYOC^{2}CBM. planke] RF; plante WHmCr^{23}GYOC^{2}CBLM; polante Cr^1.
51 pallep] pullip C^2; puttyþ F; fallep HmB. adoun] downe G. pureliche] puriliche OC^2; priueliche RF.
52 And] ⁊ *with* F.
53 yow] ȝee F. ye] you G. discryuen] dyscryue GYCB.
54 postes] postles C. myȝte] OCrGYC^{2}CBLMR; myȝtes WHmF.
55 Ac] But F; And CrGYOC^{2}CB. þouȝtes] thought CrF; toughes B. þreve] threwe CrBm; þrowe HmF; theeve (*altered to* feve *another ink*) G; trewe BoCot. piles] poles Cr^{23}; pyleris F; pilours Cot.
56–91 *lines om* CB.
56 þei(1)] þe G. woxen] wexen GYM; waxen HmOC^2; wope*n* Cr. þat] *om* Y. growed] groweden O; groweþ M; growded C^2.
57 are þei] *om* GYOC^2. aliche] ylyche HmGYOC^2. longe] longe þei ben Y; been þei longe OC^2. noon] no Cr^1.
58 on] in F. more] manere Hm. growed] growe G; grewe F; groweth Y; growen OC^2.
59 *in margin main hand* G. of(1)] al of F; *om* R. o] *om* Cr^1. of(2)] of oo OC^2.
60 seide] LRF; quod WHmCrGYOC^{2}M. so it may] it may so F; it myght so Y. it] *om* GR. may] myght GOC^2. bifalle] bifallen YMF; Falle C^2.
61 telle] telly*n* F. tid] stit Y. highte] hatteþ Hm.
62 groweþ] grow*ith* on F. it hatte] me*n* it call F.
63 And] *om* G. haue] *om* F. þee] þe erst F. hiȝte þe tree] ytt hyght G.
64 And] ⁊ þ*a*nne F.
65 asken] aske CrGF. of] fore Cr. and bad] but p*re*yede F. faire] ȝare Hm.
66 dyuyse] discryue WHmCrGYOC^{2}LMRF. þe] me þe F. hangeþ] hangede F.
67 now] *om* G. he] y HmG.

Matrimoyne I may nyme, a moiste fruyt wiþalle.
Thanne Continence is neer þe crop as kaylewey bastard.
Thanne bereþ þe crop kynde fruyt and clennest of alle,
Maidenhode, Aungeles peeris, and [erst] wole be ripe
And swete wiþouten swellyng; sour worþ it neu*ere*.'
I preide Piers to pulle adoun an Appul and he wolde,
And suffre me to assaien what sauour it hadde.
And Piers caste to þe crop and þanne comsed it to crye;
And waggede widwehode and it wepte after;
And whan [he] meued matrimoyne it made a foul noise.
I hadde ruþe whan Piers rogged, it gradde so rufulliche;
For euere as þei dropped adoun þe deuel was redy
And gadrede hem alle togideres, boþe grete and smale,
Adam and Abraham and Ysaye þe p*ro*phete,
Sampson and Samuel and Seint Ioh*an* þe Baptist,
Bar hem forþ bo[lde]ly—no body hym letted—
And made of holy men his hoord *In limbo Inferni*,
There is derknesse and drede and þe deuel maister.
And Piers for pure tene þat a pil he [l]auȝte;
He hitte after hym, [happe] how it myȝte,

68 Matrimoyne] ⁊ matrymoygne G. may] myȝte Y. nyme] neuen Y; name Cr^{12}; nome Cr^{3}.
69 Thanne] þ*at* GYOC^{2}; And M. Continence] continuance Y; co*n*scyence G. neer] nerre L; here Cr^{3}. as] as a OC^{2}.
70 kynde] kendest F. clennest] cleynnes G.
71 peeris] pere HmCr. and] ⁊ þo F. erst] raþest WHmCrGLMRF; rapest YO C^{2}. wole] wolde OC^{2}.
72 outen] oute GHmCrLRF. sour] sore G; sorwe F. neu*ere*] euere F.
73 I preide] In priede (e(1) *added another hand*) R. Piers] YHmCrGOC^{2}LMRF; Piers þo W. pulle] pully*n* F. adoun] downe CrGC^{2}F. and] ȝif HmCr^{3}F.
74 assaien] assaye HmCrGYOC^{2}LMRF.
75 it] *om* C^{2}. crye] cri*ȝ*en F.
76 And] ⁊ anoon F; A R. waggede] waged Cr^{1}. it] sore F. wepte] wepe Cr^{2}.
77 he] RF; it WHmCrGYOC^{2}LM. meued] meue*n* C^{2}. foul] full Cr; myche F. noise] nose Y.
78 I hadde] þan had y F. I] Cr; And I WHm; that y GYOC^{2}LM; þat R. rogged] ragged Cr; rused R; rusched F. so] of Cr^{23}. rufulliche] ruthfully Cr.
79 dropped] droppeden O. adoun] downe CrG. was] was þer*e* F.
81 Adam] Boþe Adam F. Abraham] eue GYOC^{2}. Ysaye] ysaac OC^{2}.
82 Sampson] ⁊ Sampson F. and(1)] *om* Cr. þe] *om* Cr^{3}.
83 Bar] ⁊ bar F. boldely] LHmCrGOC^{2} MRF; bodily WY. hym] wolde hy*m* F; hem YGOC^{2}R. letted] lette RCrF.
84 men] *om* OC^{2}. his] myne G.
85 is] as Y. derknesse] dernesse R. and(2)] is ⁊ Y.
86 for] of Cr. þat] HmGYOC^{2}LMR; þo F; of þat WCr. a pil] oo pyler F; appull HmCr. he] *om* Cr^{23}. lauȝte] HmGYOC^{2} LMRF; rauȝte W; caught Cr.
87 He] ⁊ GYOC^{2}LMRF. hitte] hent G. after] oft at Cr. happe] HmGYOC^{2}LM RF (*corrected from* hente (?) *another ink* G, *over erasure* M); hitte WCr. how] if Cr. it] he Cr^{23}OC^{2}; happe Y.

Filius by þe fader wille and frenesse of *spiritus sancti*
To go robbe þat Rageman and reue þe fruyt fro hym.
And þanne spak *spiritus sanctus* in Gabrielis mouþe
To a maide þat hi3te Marie, a meke þyng wiþalle,
That oon I*esu*s a Iustices sone moste Iouke in hir chambre |
Til *plenitudo temporis* [tyme] comen were *fol. 98 b*
That Piers fruyt floured and felle to be rype.
And þanne sholde I*esu*s Iuste þerfore bi Iuggement of armes
Wheiþ*er* sholde fonge þe fruyt, þe fend or hymselue.
The maide myldeliche þo þe messager graunted
And seide hendeliche to hym, 'lo me his handmaiden
For to werchen his wille wiþouten any synne:
Ecce ancilla domini; fiat michi [*secundum verbum tuum*]'.
And in þe wombe of þat wenche was he fourty woukes
Til he weex a faunt þoru3 hir flessh and of fightyng kouþe
To haue yfou3te wiþ þe fend er ful tyme come.
And Piers þe Plowman p*ar*ceyued plener tyme
And lered hym lechecraft his lif for to saue
That, þou3 he were wounded w*ith* his enemy, to warisshen
    hymselue;

88 fader] faders CrRF. *spiritus sancti*] *spiritus sanctus* (?) G; *om* Y.
89 reue] bereve F; reuend R. hym] his place F.
90 And] *om* F. þanne] *om* Cr. Gabrielis] gabriel R.
91 maide] maiden YHmOC^{2}M.
92 *Here* CB *resume*. Iesus] Iesu Cr^{23}; *om* F. Iustices] Iustice CrGYCBmBoLMR. Iouke] iouken RHmF; io*n*ke*n* Cr; Ioyuke G. chambre] wo*m*be Cr.
93 tyme] RF; fully WHmCrGOC^{2}CBL M; fullen Y. comen] come GC^2; Icome R; come it F.
94 Piers] Peersis F. fruyt] *twice* C. to be] to Cr; whan it was F. *Hereafter a Latin line* OC^2: *see above*, p. 224.
95 þanne] *om* Cr. sholde Ies*us*] Iesus shold Cr^3. sholde] schul COC^2. Ies*us* Iuste] I*es*u Iustne F. bi] ⁊ by R.
96 fonge] fonde CYBLR; song Cr^1. þe fend] to fynde B. selue] seluen M.
97 maide] mayden HmGOC^{2}M. graunted] she grauntyd F; grawnteþ B; grated Cr^1; greted Cr^{23}.
98 hendeliche] myldelyche Hm. maiden] maide YF.
99 werchen] worke CrC. outen] out CrG.
99α *in margin* OC^2. *secundum...tuum*] GBmCotF; *secundum verbum tuum* ⁊*c* HmBo; ⁊*c* WCrYOC^{2}CLMR.
100 þe] þat OC^2. þat] þe Cr^3.
101 faunt] fainct Cr^1. hir] hys GC^2. of] on F; *om* Cot. fightyng] fyt3 he F.
102 yfou3te] foughte CCrG; fou3ten OHmC^{2}B.
103 þe Plowman] *om* F. p*ar*ceyued] parseyued þe R; y p*ar*seyuede in þat F.
104 lered] lerned FCr. hym] hym a CB; hem Y. saue] saven F.
105 That] ⁊ Y. þou3 he were] *om* Cr. wounded w*ith*] of F. his] *om* HmCB. enemy] enuye Cot. to] he might Cr; hurt to F. warisshen] warisshe YHmCr GOC^{2}CBmBoLMF; waysche Cot. selue] seluen M; sone F.

And dide hym assaie his surgenrie on hem þat sike were
Til he was parfit praktisour if any peril fille.
And souȝte out þe sike and [saluede blynde and crokede,
And commune wommen conuertede and clensed of synne,
And sike and synfulle boþe so] to goode turnede:
Non est sanis opus medicus set in[firmis].
Boþe meseles and mute and in þe menyson blody,
Ofte [he] heeled swiche; he held it for no maistrie
Saue þo he leched laȝar þat hadde yleye in graue;
Quatriduanus quelt quyk dide hym walke.
Ac [er] he made þe maistrie *mestus cepit esse*
And wepte water with hise eiȝen; þer seiȝen it manye.
Some þat þe sighte seiȝen seiden þat tyme
That he was leche of lif and lord of heigh heuene.
Iewes iangled þerayein [þat] Iuggede lawes,
And seide he wroȝte þoruȝ wichecraft & with þe deueles myȝte:
Demonium habe[s] &c. |

106 hym] hem M. his] *om* F. surgenrie] surgery CrGYOC^{2}CCotLMRF. hem] hym BmBo. were] weren OC^{2}F.
107 was] were G. if] of L. peril] pereylis F; daunger Cr^3. fille] fellen F.
108–10 And souȝte out þe sike and synfulle boþe And saluede sike and synfulle boþe blynde and crokede And commune wommen conuertede and to goode turnede WHmCrGYOC^{2}CBLMRF (þe] of the CB. and(1)] & þe OMF. boþe(1)...synfulle(2)] *om* C^2. And(2)] he F. saluede] saued G. sike(2)] þe syke F. And(3)] *om* R. conuertede] he conuertyd F. goode] god C^2; crist F. turnede] turned hem F).
110α *in margin* OC^2. *sanis*] *sanus* C^2; *suauis* Y. *medicus*] *medico* CrOC^{2}CotM; *medici* R; *medicine* G. *set*] *om* Cr^3. *infirmis*] *infirmis &c* OC^2; *in &c* WHmGYCBL; *male habentibus* F; *m h &c* R; *&c* CrM.
111 mute] dombe GC; mysseses F. and in] þat of F. blody] weren F.
112 Ofte] Of C. he(1)] HmCrGYOC^{2}CB LMRF; *om* W. heeled] heliþ B. he(2)] HmOC^{2}MF; he ne WCrGYBLR; he nowth C. held] helid Cot. it] *om* YCLM. for no] no G; lytil F.
113 þo he] þo þat he had G; than he C. leched] heled Cr. yleye] leyn HmCrGB; loyn C^2.
114 *Quatriduanus*] *Quatriduanas* Cr^3; *Quatriduanis* C^2; *Quadriduanus* Y; *Quatridianus* Cr^1. quelt quyk] boþe quert & quik he F. hym] hem Cr^2. walke] wake Cr; ryse F.
115 Ac] but GF; And CrC^{2}C. er] as W HmCrGYOC^{2}CBLMRF. þe] þat RF.
116 seiȝen] seien *altered from* seiden Bm.
117 Some] And som CBF. þe] he Cr^1. seiȝen] seye RF. seiden] seide YCr^{23}GCL MR; ayde Cr^1. þat] in þat F.
118 was] was a F.
119 Iewes] þe Iewis F. iangled] iangleden O; iangle Cr^{12}. þat] R; þo þat F; and WHmCrGYOC^{2}CBLM. Iuggede] iuggeden O; Iugged þe F.
120 seide] seiden BHmM. þoruȝ] wyþ HmGYOCB; with his C^2.
120α *in margin* OC^2. *habes*] HmCrGYOC^2 CBLMRF; *habet* W. *&c*] þe domesmen seyden F; *om* CrG.

'Thanne are ye cherles', [chidde Iesus], 'and youre children
boþe, *fol. 99 a*
And Sathan youre Saueour; [youre]self now ye witnessen.
For I haue saued yowself and youre sones after,
Youre bodies, youre beestes, and blynde men holpen,
And fed yow wiþ two fisshes and wiþ fyue loues,
And lefte baskettes ful of broke mete, bere awey whoso wolde.'
And mysseide þe Iewes manliche and manaced hem to bete
And knokked on hem wiþ a corde, and caste adoun hir stalles
That in chirche chaffareden or chaungeden any moneie;
And seide it in sighte of hem alle so þat alle herden:
'I shal ouerturne þis temple and adoun þrowe,
And in þre daies after edifie it newe,
And maken it as muche ouþer moore in alle manere poyntes
As euere it was and as wid; wherfore I hote yow
Of preieres and of parfitnesse þis place þat ye callen:
Domus mea domus oracionis vocabitur.'
Enuye and yuel wil [arne] in þe Iewes.

121 cherles] clerkes HmYC^{2}BoCot. chidde Iesus] quod iesus R; quod crist F; quod ich WYOC^{2}CLM; quod I CrHm GBmCot; quod *followed by erasure* Bo. children] chyldre GR.
122 youre] CHmCrGOC^{2}BF; yow YLM R; ye W. now] may F. ye] ben Cot; *om* OC^{2}MF (*erased* M). witnessen] witnesse CotCrGF.
123 haue] *om* Hm. saued] salued F. yow] your CrGYOC^{2}CF. self] selue RF; self seiþ crist WCrGYOC^{2}CLM; seyþ cryst HmB.
124 bodies] bodies & F. holpen] holpe Hm; yholpe F.
125 two] ij *above line* M; om GYOC^{2}CB LR. wiþ(2)] *om* C.
126 *run together with* 128 C^{2}. ful] *om* F. broke mete] breed broken O. broke] broken HmCrC; *om* C^{2}. mete] brede YGC^{2}CB. bere...wolde] *om* C^{2}. whoso] who F; þat Cr.
127 *line om* C^{2}. And] he F. and] þus & F. hem] hym BmBo.
128 And...corde] *om* C^{2}. hem] hym B. adoun] down Cr^{13}GF; dowe Cr^{2}.
129 That] And C. or] and Y. chaungeden] chaungid C^{2}RF; chalenged G.
130 seide] seide seid BmBo. it] þus F; *om* GOC^{2}. hem] hym BmBo. herden] it herde F.
131 turne] terve F. þis] þe M. adoun] downe Cr^{23}. þrowe] OHmCrGYC^{2}CB LMR; þrowe it W; it þrowe F.
132 *line om* CB. edifie] edifien OC^{2}; edified M. it] *om* M.
133 maken] make CrGYCBLMRF. it] it moke (*corrected*) Bo; *om* G. as] also Hm. ouþer] or CrGBMF.
134 wher] & ther Cr. yow] ȝow heere F.
135 preieres] praiere M. of] *om* GOC^{2}. þis] the C. þat] *om* F. callen] calle OCr GC^{2}; callyn after F.
135α *in margin* OC^{2}. *vocabitur*] *vocabitur &c* HmYCBoCot.
136 Enuye] Boþe Envie F. wil] *om* Cot. arne] aren R; was WHmCrGYOC^{2}CBL MF. in] among F.

Thei casten and contreueden to kulle hym whan þei myȝte;
Eche day after ooþ*er* hir tyme þei awaiteden
Til it bifel on a friday, a litel bifore Pasqe.
The þursday bifore, þere he made his [cene],
Sittynge at þe soper he seide þise wordes:
'I am sold þoruȝ [som] of yow; he shal þe tyme rewe
That euere he his Saueour solde for siluer or ellis.'
Iudas iangled þerayein, ac I*es*us hym tolde
It was hymself sooþly and seide '*tu dicis*'.
Thanne wente forþ þat wikked man and wiþ þe Iewes mette
And tolde hem a tokne to knowe wiþ I*es*us;
And which tokne to þis day to muche is yvsed,
That is kissynge and fair contenaunce and vnkynde wille. |
And [þus] was wiþ Iudas þo þat I*es*us bitrayed: *fol. 99 b*
'*Aue, raby*', quod þat Ribaud, and riȝt to hym he yede
And kiste hym to be caught þerby and kulled of þe Iewes.
Thanne I*es*us to Iudas and to þe Iewes seide,
'Falsnesse I fynde in þi faire speche
And gile in þi glad chere and galle is in þi laughyng.
Thow shalt be myrour to many men to deceyue,

137 casten] cast G; casteden OC^{2}. contreueden] controueden Y. kulle] kullen R. myȝte] myȝten OC^{2}.
138 hir] *om* OC^{2}. þei] þey þan F. awaiteden] awaytede HmCrYC^{2}LMR; wayted GCBF.
139 it] *om* C. bifel] fel M. a...Pasqe] byfore pask a lytel F. litel] lite R; littie Cr^{12}. Pasqe] þe pasq*ue* GCB.
140 The] On F. bifore] þerebifore M. þere] þat þan F. cene] RF; maundee WHmCrGYOC^{2}CBLM.
141 Sittynge] Sittande R; & syttende F. þe] þ*at* F; hys G. he] and R; hy*m*selue F.
142 som] su*m*me RF; oon WHmCrGYOC^{2}CBLM. he] ye Y. þe] þ*at* F; *om* G.
143 euere he] he eu*ere* (*marked for transposition*) O. he] *om* R. his...ellis] solde his sauyour for siluerene plates F.
144 ac] but G; and CrC^{2}CF. I*es*us] Ientil I*es*u F.
145 self] *above line* M; *om* L.
146 þe] *om* C. Iewes] Iewis he F.
147 hem] hym C. a] be what F. to] G; how to WHmCrYOC^{2}CBLMR; þey sholde F. knowe] *om* C. wiþ] *om* HmCrMF. I*es*us] his mayst*er* F.
148 And] þe RF. to(1)] into F. to(2)...is] ys to moche GOC^{2}; ys here mychil F. muche] muchil Hm. yvsed] vsed CrHmGYOC^{2}CotRF.
149 is] *om* F. and(1)] *with* F. and(2)] & *with* F.
150 And þus] And so WHmCrGYOC^{2}LMRF; As B; And C. Iudas] Iewes Y. þat] he GOC^{2}CB.
151 yede] wente F.
152 be] by F. and] *om* Cr^{23}. of] þoruȝ RF.
153 þe] all þe F.
154 faire] false F.
155 þi(*both*)] the Cr^{12}. is] *om* CrGOC^{2}.
156 shalt] shal BmBo. be] be a YOC^{2}M; *om* F. to(1)] after to F. men] man B. to(2)] hem to B; the poeple to G.

Ac [to] þe [worldes ende] þi wikkednesse shal worþe vpon þiselue:
Necesse est vt veniant scandala; ve homini illi per quem scandalum venit.
Thouȝ I bi treson be take [to] youre [iewene] wille
Suffreþ myne Apostles in [pays] and in [pees] gange.'
On a þursday in þesternesse þus was he taken;
Thoruȝ Iudas and Iewes Ie*s*us was [ynome]
That on þe friday folwynge for mankyndes sake
Iusted in Iher*usal*em, a ioye to vs alle.
On cros vpon Caluarie crist took þe bataille
Ayeins deeþ and þe deuel; destruyed hir boþ*er*es myȝtes,
Deide and dee[þ] fordide, and day of nyȝt made.
And I awaked þerwiþ and wiped myne eiȝen
And after Piers þe Plowman pried and stared.
Estward and westward I waited after faste
And yede forþ as an ydiot in contree to aspie

157 Ac] but GF; And CrC^{2}C. to...ende] thy wordes & Cot; þe work & Cr^1; thy worcke & Cr^{23}; þe worse and WYOC^{2}CBmBoLMRF; þe wurste and Hm; þe wors for G. þi(1)] þe HmOC^{2}MRF; *om* Cr^{23}. vp] *om* GOC^{2}F.
157α *in margin* OC^2. *veniant*] *venient* Bm Bo; *veniat* CF. *scandala*] *scandalum* F; scandula G; sandala Y. *ve*] *ve tamen* Cr^{23}. *homini*] *illi* Bo; *om* Cot. *per...venit*] *&c* G. *scandalum venit*] *&c* YOC^{2}CB. *venit*] *venit &c* Hm.
158 bi...be] be þorghȝ tresou*n* F. take] taken OC^{2}C; ytake LM; *om* Cr^3. to] at WHmCrGYOC^{2}CBLM; and R; & þorgh F. iewene] owene WHmCrGYOC^{2}CB LMRF.
159 Suffreþ] Suffre Cr. Apostles] postles LR. pays] HmYOC^{2}BLMR; pees WCr GCF (peas *altered to* peace G). and in pees] p*ri*uyly forþ to F. pees] HmGYOC^2 CBLMR (peas *altered to* peace G); pays WCr.
160 On] vpon Hm; In RF. in] in þe OC^2. þesternesse] the sterns Cr; þerknesse F; Mirkenesse C. he] y F; *om* Cot. taken] take Cr.
161 Iewes] þe Iewis F. Ie*s*us] Ie*s*u F. ynome] þan taken F; his name WHmCr GYOC^{2}CBLMR.
162 That on þe] & on F. man...sake] cause of ma*n*kende F. kyndes] kynde YCr^{12}GCBLMR.
163 Iusted] he Iustned F; In stede Cr^1. a] gret F. to] for G.
164 On] On a CB; & on a F. vp] *om* F.
165 *run together with* 166 F. deeþ] þe deþ OC^2. destruyed...myȝtes] *om* F. destruyed] to dystroye G. hir boþeres] hir bother YOC^{2}CBmBo; hire bothe Cot; þere beire R; both her CrGM.
166 Deide...fordide] *om* F. deeþ] HmCr GYOC^{2}CBLMR; deed W. and(2)] þe F. of] & G; for þe F. made] he made F.
167 And] þan F; *om* M. awaked] wakid BoCot; waknede F. myne] boþe my*n* F. *Hereafter three additional lines* F; *see above*, p. 223.
168 þe] *om* GYOC^{2}CBF. pried] y pryȝede F.
169 Estward] Estware Cr^2. I] and CB. waited] awayted L. after] hy*m* ful F.
170 forþ] *om* F. contree] cu*n*trees F.

After Piers þe Plowman; many a place I souȝte.
And þanne mette I wiþ a man, a mydlenten sonday,
As hoor as an haweþorn and Abraham he highte.
I frayned hym first fram whennes he come
And of whennes he were and whider þat he [þ]ouȝte.
'I am feiþ', quod þat freke, 'it falleþ noȝt to lye,
And of Abrahames hous an heraud of armes; |
[I] seke after a segge þat I seiȝ ones, *fol.* 100 *a*
A ful bold bacheler; I knew hym by his blasen.'
'What berþ þat buyrn', quod I þo, 'so blisse þee bitide?'
'Thre leodes in oon lyth, noon lenger þan ooþer,
Of oon muchel and myght in mesure and lengþe.
That oon dooþ alle dooþ and ech dooþ bi his one.
The firste haþ myȝt and maiestee, makere of alle þynges;
Pater is his propre name, a persone by hymselue.
The secounde of þa[t] sire is Sothfastnesse *filius*,
Wardeyn of þat wit haþ; was euere wiþouten gynnyng.
The þridde highte þe holi goost, a persone by hymselue,

171 *line om* OC^2. þe] *om* F. many a place] fele places F. I] y *corrected from* he G.
172 a(2)] on Cr^{23}GYOC^{2}MF. lenten] lent HmOC^{2}B. sonday] sonenday BmHmBo.
173 an] any CB. and] *om* HmF.
174 frayned] fraymed Y; frain C. he] þat he F.
175 of] from Cr. þat] ward M; *om* GYOC^2. þouȝte] OHmCrGYC^{2}CBLMRF; souȝte W.
176 þat] þis GYOC^{2}CB. noȝt] nauȝt me R; me nowht F.
177 Abrahames] abrahame C. an] and CBoCot.
178 I(1)] CrHmGYOC^{2}CBLMRF; And W. segge] man C. þat I seiȝ] y sey hym but F.
179 knew] knowe Cr^{23}GOC^{2}C.
180 buyrn] barn YGOC^{2}CB. þo] tho tho C. þee] ȝe C^2.
181 leodes] leode Hm. in] on Cr^{23}GYOC^{2}CB. oon] a Cr^{23}. lyth] *over erasure* M; lithe YC; lyȝth C^{2}F; lyethe G; liche B. ooþer] another M.
182 and(1)] and oon YCr^{23}OC^{2}CB; ⁊ of oon F. myght] mageste OC^2. in] ⁊ majeste yn GYCB. mesure] lengthe F. and(2)] ⁊ GYCBF; and in WHmCrOC^{2}LMR. lengþe] mesure F.
183 That] ⁊ þat F. ech] ichon M. his] hym GYF. one] owne CrG; selue F.
184 and] in F. makere] make Bo. þynges] thyng YOC^{2}CBR.
185 is his] his is BmBo. propre] *om* GYOC^{2}CB. selue] seluen M. *Here* 189 *copied, then cancelled* O.
186–8 *lines om* F.
186 of...is] ys off that syre GYOC^{2}CB. þat] HmCrLMR; þa W. Sothfastnesse] soþeffaste C^2; stedfastnesse C; stedfast Cot; stefast BmBo.
187 of] of al OC^2. haþ] hat R; *om* G. outen] owt HmCrGYOCBmBoL. gynnyng] bygynnyng Cot.
188 highte] haþ OBmBo (*corrected to* hatte O); has C. þe] he þe (*corrected*) Bo. selue] seluen MR.

The light of al þat lif haþ a londe and a watre,
Confortour of creatures; of hym comeþ alle blisse.
So þre bilongeþ for a lord þat lordshipe cleymeþ:
Might and [a] mene [his owene myȝte to knowe],
Of hym[self] and of his seruaunt, and what [suffreþ hem] boþe.
So god, þat gynnyng hadde neuere but þo hym good þouȝte,
Sente forþ his sone as for seruaunt þat tyme
To ocupie hym here til issue were spronge,
That is children of charite, and holi chirche þe moder.
Patriarkes and prophetes and Apostles were þe children,
And Crist and cristendom and cristene holy chirche.
In menynge þat man moste on o god bileue,
And þere hym likede and [he] louede, in þre persones hym shewede.
And þat it may be so and sooþ [sheweþ it manhode]:
Wedlok and widwehode wiþ virginite ynempned,
In tokenynge of þe Trinite, was [taken out of a man], |
Adam, oure aller fader. Eue was of hymselue, *fol.* 100 *b*

189 The...haþ] þat alle þe liȝt of þe lif R; þat al þe lyght & þe lyf F. al] *above line* Bo; hal C. lif] lygth Hm. haþ] haue G; han Cot.

190 Confortour] he is confortour F. creatures] creatouris C[2]R. blisse] blyshe Cr[3].

191 þre] ther CB. for] to Cr[1]. a] *om* F. lord þat] *om* Y. cleymeþ] laymes C.

192 a] CrGYBLMR; eek a F; *om* WHm OC[2]C. mene] meyne (? *altered from* meene) F. his...knowe] to knowe his owene myȝte WHmGYOC[2]CBLM; to know his might Cr; to his owene miȝte R; to his myght owiþ F.

193 self] selue RF; *om* WHmCrGYOC[2] CBLM. of] *om* F. seruaunt] seruauntys Hm. and(2)] & sum F. suffreþ hem] suffreþ hem FR; þei suffre WHmCrGYCB LM; þei suffren O; þei suffred C[2].

194 god] go C. gynnyng] bigynnyng OC[2]Cot. neuere] nere R. good] god B.

195 Sente] he sente F. for] for his F; a Hm. þat] a þat (a *cancelled*) Bo.

196 ocupie] ocupyen GYOC[2]CCotLRF; ocupiem BmBo. til] ty F. spronge] sprungen OC[2]; ysprunge F; ysprongen M.

197 children] childur F. chirche] kirke Cr.

198 Patriarkes] & patriarchis F. were] weren OM. þe] þo F. children] barnes RF.

199 Crist and] cristys F. and] and alle RF.

200 man] a man F. on] in CrRF. o] *om* Hm.

201 and he] and WHmCrGYOC[2]CBLM RF. þre persones] one person Cr[1]. hym(2)] he hym F.

202 *line om* Cr[23]OC[2]. þat] *twice* G. sheweþ...manhode] manhode it sheweþ WHmCr[1]GYCBLMRF.

203 Wedlok] As wedloke F. wiþ] & OC[2]F. ynempned] Ineuened G; nempned Cr; first nempned F.

204 In] and C[2]. tokenynge] tokne Y. þe] *om* Cr[1]. taken...man] YHmOC[2]CBL; take out of o man R; taken owte off man GM; take out of mankynde F; out of man taken WCr.

205 Adam] HmCrGYOC[2]CBLMR; Adam was WF. aller] aldre Hm; alþer OC[2]B; olde Cr; forme F. Eue] CrHmGYOC[2]C BLMR; and Eue WF.

And þe issue þat þei hadde it was of hem boþe,
And eiþer is oþeres ioye in þre sondry persones,
And in heuene and here oon singuler name.
And þus is mankynde and manhede of matrimoyne yspronge
And bitokneþ þe Trinite and trewe bileue.
Migh[t] is [in] matrimoyne þat multiplieþ þe erþe
And bitokneþ trewely, telle if I dorste,
Hym þat first formed al, þe fader of heuene.
The sone, if I dorste seye, resembleþ wel þe widewe:
Deus meus, Deus meus, vt quid dereliquisti me?
That is, creatour weex creature to knowe what was boþe.
As widewe wiþouten wedlok was neuere ȝit yseyȝe,
Na moore myȝte god be man but if he moder hadde.
So widewe withouten wedlok may noȝt wel stande,
Ne matrimoyne withouten Mul[eri]e is noȝt muche to preise:
Maledictus homo qui non reliquit semen in Israel.
Thus in þre persones is parfitliche [pure] manhede,
That is man and his make and mulliere children;

206 þei] he GYOC^{2}CBmBo; *om* Cot.
207 oþeres] other GC^2.
208 here] in earth CrOC^2.
209 And] *om* F. þus] þis L; þat RF. is] his BmBo; *om* F. and] or CrGYOC^{2}CB LMRF. matrimoyne] manhod F. ysponge] ysprungen O; spronge BCrR; sprongyn C^2; *om* C.
210 *line om* GYOC^{2}CB. And] & it F. and trewe] þat trewe is to oure F.
211 Might] YHmGOC^{2}CBLMRF; Mighty WCr. in] RF; *om* WHmCrGYOC^{2}CB LM. þat] and Cr. þe] on F.
212 And] & it F. bitokneþ] bitoneþ C^2. if] it if YGOC^{2}CB; ȝow if F.
213 Hym] he GYOC^{2}CBLMR. formed al] all formede F. þe] *om* Cr^3.
214 The] & þe F. if] is if YGOC^{2}C. I] CrHmGYOC^{2}CBMF; I it WLR. seye] it say F. resembleþ] resemblant YGOC^2 CBmBo; in semblaunt Cot; ensample F. wel] to GYOC^{2}CBF. þe] *om* OCBF. widewe] widuwes B.
214α *in margin* OC^2. *meus*(1)] *om* Hm. *quid*] *quid me* R. *me*] *me &c* HmC^{2}B; *om* R.
215 is] his F. creatour] creature Y. weex] was CrGF. creature] creatoure C^2.
216 As] a G. outen] oute YHmCrGCBL MR. yseyȝe] yseyȝen HmF; seye YCr.
217 Na moore] Ne namore R. myȝte] *om* C^2. he] he a Hm. moder] mder Y.
218 So] Ne F. outen] oute YCrGOLMR; *om* C.
219 with] *twice* C^2. outen] oute GCrYC^2 CBLR. Mulerie] mulerie OCr^{23}YBLM; Muliere WHmGC^{2}RF; mulier Cr^1.
219α *in margin* OC^2. *reliquit*] *reliquet* CB; reliquid F. *Israel*] CrGYOC^{2}CBF; *Israel &c* WHmLMR.
220 in] been F. is] if BmBo (*corrected* Bm); oon F. pure] puir R; þorghȝ F; *om* WHm CrGYOC^{2}CBLM.
221 is] ys a GYCB. mulliere] moillerie Y; moilre B; mulerer O. children] her children LRF.

And is noȝt but gendre of a gen*er*acion bifore Ie*s*u c*ri*st in heuene:
So is þe fader forþ *with* þe sone and fre wille of boþe,
Spiritus procedens a patre & filio &c,
Which is þe holy goost of alle, and alle is but o god.
Thus in a somer I hym seiȝ as I sat in my porche;
I roos vp and reu*er*enced hym and riȝt faire hym grette.
Thre men, to my siȝte, I made wel at ese,
Wessh hir feet and wiped hem, and afterward þei eten
Calues flessh and Cakebreed; and knewe what I þouȝte.
Ful trewe toknes bitwene vs is to telle whan me likeþ. |
First he fonded me if I, [feiþ], louede bettre *fol.* 101 *a*
Hym or Ysaak myn heir, þe which he hiȝte me kulle.
He wiste my wille bi hym; he wol me it allowe.
I am ful siker in soule þerof, and my sone boþe.
I circumscised my sone siþen for his sake,
Myself and my meynee; and alle þat male weere
Bledden blood for þat lordes loue and hope to blisse þe tyme.
Myn affiaunce and my feiþ is ferme in þis bileue
For hymself bihiȝte to me and to myn issue boþe
Lond and lordshipe and lif wiþouten ende.

222 And] ytt G. gendre] gendred GC. of] yn Hm; for F. a] *om* HmCrGYOC^{2}BMF. Iesu] Ie*s*us G; *om* B. *crist*] *om* GF. in heuene] *om* Cr.
223 So] Ryght so F. forþ] *om* F. of] of he*m* CrM.
223α *in margin* OC^{2}. *a*] & OC^{2}. *&c*] *om* CrOC^{2}CBmLRF.
224 holy] *om* OC^{2}. of] *om* F. alle(2)] *om* Cr^{1}. but o god] god oone F.
225 a] *om* HmGYOC^{2}. porche] perche Cr^{1}.
226 roos] aroos OC^{2}B. vp] *om* C^{2}. hym(2)] *om* F.
227 to] yn Hm; at Cr^{1}.
228 Wessh] & weschȝ F. and(1)] in R. hem] hes R. ward] *om* Cr^{1}M.
229 *line om* Hm. and(2)] þey F. knewe] knewen ORF; knowen C^{2}.
230 is] are G; be*n* CrOC^{2}. telle] telly*n* F. me] we BoCot.
231 if] whether CrM. I feiþ] I WHmCrGYOC^{2}CBLMRF. bettre] hym bettre Hm.
232 Hym] *om* Hm. þe] *om* Cr. he] *om* B. hiȝte] high Cr^{12}; het B; bad G. kulle] to kill Cr.
233 he] a R. me it] it me Hm; ytt G.
234 in...of] my sowle is þer*e* F. sone] sones F; soule GY.
235 circumscised] circu*m*sidid BmBo; circuncyded M.
236 male] males GF. weere] weren OC^{2}F.
237 Bledden] Bledde MCr; bleden GYC^{2}. þat] þe Cr^{3}. loue] sake OC^{2}. and] in F. hope] hopen HmOC^{2}. to...tyme] blysse to wy*n*ne F. þe] þ*a*t Cr^{23}.
238 þis] my*n* F; his CB.
239 self] seluy*n* F. to(1)] *om* F.
240 Lond] Beþe lond F. outen] out Cr.

To me and to myn issue moore yet he [me] grauntede,
Mercy for oure mysdedes as many tyme as we asken:
Quam olim Abrahe promisisti & semini eius.
And siþþe he sente me to seye I sholde do sacrifise
And doon hym worship wi*th* breed and wiþ wyn boþe,
And called me foot of his feiþ, his folk for to saue
And defende hem fro þe fend, folk þat on me leneden.
Thus haue I ben his heraud here and in helle
And conforted many a careful þat after his comynge waite[n],
And þus I seke hym', he seide, 'for I herde seyn late
Of a [buyrn] þat baptised hym—Ioh*a*n Baptist was his name—
That to patriarkes & pr*o*phetes and ooþer peple in derknesse
Seide þ*a*t he seiȝ here þat sholde saue vs alle:
Ecce agnus dei &c.'
I hadde wonder of hise wordes and of hise wide cloþes
For in his bosom he bar a þyng þat he blissed euere.
And I loked in his lappe; a laȝar lay þerInne
Amonges patriarkes and pr*o*phetes pleyinge togideres.

241 To] & to F. moore yet] ȝit moore F. yet] ȝif B; *om* C^2. me] HmCrGYOC^{2}CLMRF; i*n*ne (? *for* men) BmBo; me*n* Cot; *om* W.
242 Mercy] More CB. for] of CrCot. mysdedes] mysdede F. as(1)] *om* Cr^{23}. tyme] tymes CrGBM. asken] aske CrOC^{2}F.
242α *in margin* OC^2. *Quam*] *Omnia* B. *promisisti*] promisti G. *eius*] *eius &c* HmYB.
243 sente] send G. seye] see Cr^1.
244 worship] worschpe R.
245 And] & he F. me] CrGYOC^{2}CBMF; me þe WHmLR. foot] forþ OC^2; stot YGCB. folk for] poeple G.
246 defende] defendede OHmGC^{2}F; defenden M. hem] him Cr^{1}C. folk þat] þe folk F. leneden] lened GHmR; leueden Cr^1; leued Cr^{23}; bileueden B; beleveþ F.
247 in] eek in F.
248 *line om* F. a] *om* GYOC^{2}CB. comynge] comyn Bo. waiten] CrHmGOC^{2}CBLMR; waiteden WY.
249 *line om* F. hym] hem B. herde] heare Cr^{23}; *om* L.
250 buyrn] R; burne F; barn WHmCrGYOCBLM; barm C^2. baptised] bapsid Cr^3. his] hir Y.
251 to] *om* G. &] GYOC^{2}CBF; & to WHmCrLMR. and] YGOC^{2}CB; and to WHmCrLMRF.
252 Seide...he] Seyden as y F. seiȝ] seyde RF. here] eer F; hir C; hym GOC^2. sholde] shul CR; he schal F. saue] sauen R; have F. vs] hem RF.
252α *in margin* OC^2. *&c*] *qui tollit peccata mundi &c* Hm; *ecce qui tollit peccata mundi* F.
253 I hadde] þan hadde y F. hadde wonder] hadder B.
254 For] And RF. bosom] bosonn Bo. þat] & þat RF.
255 in] on GYOC^{2}CBLMR. lay] lay þan F; lye G.
256 *line om* CB. pleyinge] pleyande L; pleyende F; pleyede R; pleyeng there G.

'What awaitestow?' quod he, 'and what woldestow haue?' |
'I wolde wite', quod I þo, 'what is in youre lappe.' *fol.* 101 *b*
'Loo!' quod he and leet me see; 'lord, mercy!' I seide,
'This is a p*re*sent of muche pris; what prynce shal it haue?'
'It is a p*re*cious p*re*sent', quod he, 'ac þe pouke it haþ attached,
And me þer[wiþ]', quod þat [wye]; 'may no wed vs quyte,
Ne no buyrn be oure borgh, ne brynge vs fram his daunger—
Out of þe poukes pondfold no maynprise may vs fecche—
Til he come *þat* I carpe of; crist is his name
That shal deliu*ere* vs som day out of þe deueles power
And bettre wed for us [wage] þan we ben alle worþi,
That is lif for lif; or ligge þus euere
Lollynge in my lappe til swich a lord vs fecche.'
'Allas!' I seide, '*þat* synne so longe shal lette
The myght of goddes mercy þat my3te vs alle amende.'
I wepte for hise wordes; wiþ þat sau3 I anoþer
Rapeliche renne forþ þe ri3te wey [we] wente.
I affrayned hym first fram whennes he come,
What he highte ⁊ whider he wolde, and wightly he tolde.

257 awaitestow] waytest þou HmGC^{2}; art þou B. quod he] *om* Cot. he] he þoo OC^{2}. what] wote G. woldestow] wildestow R.
258 is] is þis OC^{2}.
259 lord] þan Lord F. I] he Y.
260 This is] Is þis F. a] *om* L. muche] mychil F. prynce] pryce G; pris Y.
261 p*re*cious p*re*sent] p*re*sent p*re*ciouse Hm. ac] but GF; ⁊ CrC^{2}C. it haþ] hath it CrMF. attached] tachid F. *Here* 265 *copied, then cancelled* G.
262 wiþ] wyþ HmGCRF; myde WCrYO C^{2}BLM. wye] wy3e F; weye R; man WHmCrGYOC^{2}CBLM. may] ther may Cr. vs] me Cr. quyte] qwyten F.
263 buyrn] barne CrGOC^{2}CBF.
264 *line om* RF. no] ne no GYOC^{2}CB. may] *om* OC^{2}.
265 carpe] carped F.
266 deliu*ere*] delieuren M. som day] *om* OC^{2}.
267 And] ⁊ a F. wage] legge WHmYO C^{2}CBLMRF; ligge CrG. we] *above cancelled* he Bo.
268 ligge...euere] eu*ere* to lygge þus stylle Hm. ligge] lyggen F; leigge Cot; leegge BmBo. þus] shull we þus F.
269 Lollynge] ⁊ þus shal y loll F. lord] lorod Bo.
270–3 *in place of these three spurious lines* RF; *see above*, p. 224.
270 shal] sholde G.
271 alle] wel Cr.
272 for hise] wi*th* thes G. sau3 I] I saw CrGM.
273 we] he WHmCrGYOC^{2}CBLM.
274 I] and y G; þan y F. affrayned] frayned HmCrGOC^{2}MF. whennes] whens *þat* F.
275 What] RF; And what WHmCrGYO C^{2}CBLM. and] *om* Y. wightly] wighly Cr^{1}; wyttelyche G.

XVII

'I am *Spes*, [a spie', quod he], 'and spire after a Knyght
That took me a maundement vpon þe mount of Synay
To rule alle Reames wiþ; I bere þe writ [riȝt] here.'
'Is it enseled?' I seide; 'may men see þ[e] lettres?'
'Nay', he seide, '[I] seke hym þat haþ þe seel to kepe,
And þat is cros and cristendom and crist þeron to honge;
And whan it is enseled [þerwiþ] I woot wel þe soþe
That Luciferis lordshipe laste shal no lenger. |
[And þus my lettre meneþ; [ye] mowe knowe it al].'
'Lat se þi lettres', quod I, 'we myghte þe lawe knowe.' *fol.* 102 *a*
[He plukkede] forþ a patente, a pece of an hard roche
Wheron [was] writen two wordes on þis wise yglosed.
Dilige deum ⁊ proximum tuum,
This was the tixte, trewely; I took ful good yeme.
The glose was gloriously writen wiþ a gilt penne:

1 a...he] a spie q*uod* he RF; quod he A spie WHmGYC^{2}CBL; quo he a spye O; quod þat spye M; q*uod* he Cr. and] *om* R. spire] spere HmC^{2}BRF; spure G; spye Cr. a Knyght] þat knyght kowþe F.
2 That...me] Me was taken F. of] *om* HmCrB.
3 wiþ] þerewith RF. þe] it YOC^2. writ riȝt] writ WHmGCBR; writte LM; write YCr; writen OC^2; rolle F.
4 Is it] It is CrC^{2}Cot. enseled] asseled HmYOC^{2}CBLMRF. I seide] seyd y F; he sayde G. may] many Cr^1. þe] GCrYOC^{2}CBMF; þi WHmLR. lettres] lettre F.
5 seide] sayethe G. I] CrHmGYOC^{2}CBLMRF; *om* W. þe seel] þeal C. þe] *om* Bo.
6 is] is þe HmF. þeron] *twice* Bm.
7 *line om* Cot; *as one line with* 8 RF. enseled þerwiþ] enseled so WCrG; asseled so HmYOC^{2}CBmBoLMRF. I...soþe] *om* RF.
8 sathenas haþ lost his power F. That...lordshipe] sathanas power R. That] Than Cr. laste shal] shall last CrGR.
9 FR; *line om* WHmCrGYOC^{2}CBLM; *here in the spelling of* W. ye...al] *om* R. ye] men F.
10 Lat] Let vs CrG. þi] the CrG; þat RF. lettres] l*ett*re RF. lawe] lawes F.
11 He plukkede] A plucked R; ⁊ he plukkede F; Thanne plukkede he WHmGYOC^{2}CBLM; Than pulled he Cr. a patente] a pauntelet B; *om* Cr^{23}.
12 on(1)] in Cr. was] LRF; were WHmCrGYC^{2}CBoCotM; weren OBm. writen] wryte Hm; weten *corrected to* wreten Bm. two] these Cr. yglosed] glosed GC^2; vnglosid F.
13 *in margin* O. *tuum*] *tuum ⁊c* HmCr^{1}GYCBLMR; *⁊c* Cr^{23}OC^2.
14 was] *om* Cr^{23}. ful] þerto F. yeme] gome R; keepe F.
15 The] ⁊ þe F. gloriously] glorious Cr. writen] wrete F; Iwrite R.

In hijs duobus mandatis tota lex pendet ⁊ prophet[*e*].
'[Is] here alle þi lordes lawes?' quod I; 'ye, leue me', he seide.
'Whoso wercheþ after þis writ, I wol vndertaken,
Shal neu*er*e deuel hym dere ne deeþ in soule greue;
For, þouȝ I seye it myself, I haue saued w*ith* þis charme
Of men and of wo*m*men many score þousand.'
'[He seiþ] sooþ', seide þis heraud; 'I haue [founded] it ofte.
Lo! here in my lappe þat leeued on þat charme,
Iosue and Iudith and Iudas Macabeus,
Ye! and sixti þousand biside forþ þat ben noȝt seyen here.'
'Youre wordes arn wonderfulle', quod I, 'which of yow is trewest
And lelest to leue [on] for lif and for soule?
Abraham seiþ þat he seiȝ hoolly þe Trinite,
Thre p*er*sones in p*ar*celles departable fro ooþer
And alle þre but o god; þus Abraham me tauȝte;
And haþ saued þat bileued so and sory for hir synnes,
He kan noȝt siggen þe so*m*me, and some arn in his lappe.
What neded it [now] a newe lawe to [brynge]

16 *in margin* OC^{2}. *In*] *De* Y. *mandatis... pendet*] *pendet tota lex* R. *prophete*] CrGYO CBmBoMF; *prophete ⁊c* C^{2}Cot; *prophetia* WLR; *prophecia ⁊c* Hm.
17 Is] LRF; Ben WHmCrGYOC^{2}CBM. here] þ*er* G. alle þi lordes] in þese two alle þe Hm. þi] the Cr^{23}. lawes] lawe F. me] CrGRF; me wel WHmYOC^{2}BLM; me wille C.
18 Whoso] YGOC^{2}CB; And whoso W HmCrLMR; ⁊ who þ*at* F. þis writ] my wit R. taken] take CrGOC^{2}.
19 deuel] do *followed by erasure* F. hym] you Cr^{12}. deeþ] deet Y; dette OC^{2}CB; deuel F. in] his F.
20 self] seluen M.
21 of] *om* CrYCBM. þousand] thowsandys HmCrGYOC^{2}CBLMRF.
22 He seiþ] OCrGYC^{2}CBLMRF; Ye seien WHm. sooþ] *om* Y. seide] seiþ OC^{2}M; q*uod* Hm. þis] þe GYOC^{2}CBF. founded it] YCB; founden it HmGOC^{2}; fownde it F; yfounde it WLR; it found CrM.
23 leeued] belevedy*n* F. on] of R.
24 Iosue] Boþe Iosue F.
25 Ye] *om* RF. and] ⁊ and G. sixti] vi Cr. forþ] *om* F.
26 I] YGOC^{2}CBF; I þo WHmCrLMR.
27 leue] beleve F; lyue Hm. on] CrGYO C^{2}CBLMRF; so WHm. for...for] to þe lyf or to F.
28 hoolly] holy YGCBmBoLR.
29 p*ar*celles] percels ech Cr; p*ar*celle C. departable] dispartable Cot.
30 god] *om* F.
31 haþ] þey been F. þat] þ*at* I CBmBo. bileued] byleeue GC^{2}F; bileueth R. synnes] synne YOC^{2}CB.
32 He] I Cr^{23}OC^{2}. noȝt] *om* F. siggen] sygge HmCr^{23}GYOC^{2}CBLMR; seyȝ F; se Cr^{1}. so*m*me] commune Cr^{1}. and some] of þo þat B (þo *above line* Bo). his] mi Cr^{23}OC^{2}.
33 neded] nedeþ YGOC^{2}CBF. it] þee OC^{2}. now] þanne WHmCrGYOC^{2}CB LMRF. brynge] FR; bigynne WHmCr GYOC^{2}CBLM.

Siþ þe firste suffiseþ to sauacion and to blisse?
And now com[s]eþ *Spes* and spekeþ, þat [haþ] aspied þe lawe,
And telleþ noȝt of þe Trinite þat took hym hise lettres,
To bileeue and louye in o lord almyghty
And siþþe riȝt as myself so louye alle peple. |
The gome þat gooþ wiþ o staf, he semeþ in gretter heele *fol.* 102 *b*
Than he þat gooþ wiþ two staues to sighte of vs alle;
And riȝt so, bi þe roode, Reson me sheweþ
It is lighter to lewed men o lesson to knowe
Than for to techen hem two, and to hard to lerne þe leeste!
It is ful hard for any man on Abraham bileue
And wel awey worse ȝit for to loue a sherewe.
It is lighter to leeue in þre louely p*er*sones
Than for to louye and lene as wel lorels as lele.
Go þi gate!' quod I to *Spes*, 'so me god helpe,
Tho þat lernen þi lawe wol litel while vsen it.'
And as we wenten þus in þe wey wordynge togideres
Thanne seiȝe we a Samaritan sittynge on a Mule,
Ridynge ful rapely þe righte wey we yeden,
Comynge from a contree þat men called Ierico;
To a Iustes in Ier*usal*em he [I]aced awey faste.

34 þe] þat þe F. suffiseþ] *sufficit* C^2; suffise C; ys sufficiau*nt* F. to(1)] to a Cr^3. sauacion and] save vs F. to(2)] *om* Cr.
35 now] þan F. comseþ] comeþ WHmCrGLMRF; bigynneth YOC^2; bicometh CB. haþ] HmCrYOC^2CBLMRF; *om* WG.
36 hise] þes G.
37 bileeue] beleven F. louye] lovyen F. o] our Cr. lord] god F.
38 riȝt] righ Y. my] þi G. louye] to loven F. alle] all the CrYMF.
39–49 *lines om* RF.
39 gome] mane C. in] in a B. gretter] gret C^2Cr^1.
40 wiþ] *om* Cot.
42 It] HmCrGYOC^2CBLM; That it W. knowe] lere B.
43 techen] teche BCr. to(2)] *om* G. to(3)] *om* Hm. lerne] lere GYOC^2CBm; here BoCot.
44 bileue] to byleeue HmG.
45 wel awey] weylawey YCBmBo.
46 lighter] lyghlyer G. leeue in] byleeue on Hm.
47 lene] leue Cr. lorels] loselles Hm. lele] lelly Cr; leles YGOC^2CB.
48 I] *om* Cot; *erased* Bo. to] *om* GYOC^2CB. so] for so CrM.
49 lernen] learne Cr; leren OC^2; loueth Cot. wol] wel HmCrYBM; *om* GOC^2.
50 *Here* RF *resume.* we] *om* Cot. wenten] went GYCB. þus] vs þus BoCot; *om* CrF. in] by G; *om* M. wey] way thus CrF.
51 sittynge] sittende LRF; ryding Cr^1.
52 Ridynge] ⸫ Rydende F; Ryden R. ful] well CrM. we] þat we Hm; he C^2. yeden] ȝede C^2.
53 Comynge] Comynde R; Com CB. þat] *om* Cr. called] calleden O; callyn HmC^2F; call Cr.
54 Iustes] Iustice Cr^1GB. in] at Cr. he] and he Hm. Iaced] chaced WHmGYOC^2CBLMRF; chaseth Cr.

Boþe þe heraud and hope and he mette atones
Where a man was wounded and wiþ þeues taken.
He my3te neiþ*er* steppe ne stande ne stere foot ne handes
Ne helpe hymself sooþly, for semyvif he semed,
And as naked as a nedle and noon help aboute.
Feiþ hadde first si3te of hym, ac he flei3 aside
And nolde no3t neghen hym by nyne londes lengþe.
Hope cam hippynge after þat hadde so ybosted
How he wiþ Moyses maundement hadde many men yholpe,
Ac whan he hadde sighte of þat segge aside he gan hym drawe
Dredfully, bi þis day! as doke dooþ fram þe faucon.
Ac so soone so þe Samaritan hadde si3te of þis leode
He lighte adown of Lyard and ladde hym in his hande, |
And to þe wye he wente hise woundes to biholde, *fol.* 103 *a*
And p*ar*ceyued bi his pous he was in p*er*il to dye
And but he hadde recou*er*er þe ra[þ]er þ*at* rise sholde he neu*ere*.
[And breide to hise boteles and boþe he atamede]; 71
Wiþ wyn and w*ith* oille hise woundes he wasshed,

55 þe] *om* CB. hope] *spes* F. and(2)] & me F; *om* B.
56 a] þat a F. wounded] Iwounded R. taken] take YCB; ytake G; *om* C^2.
57 He] A R. steppe] steppen F. stande] stonden F. handes] ha*nd* CrB.
58 helpe] helpen F.
59 a] þe F. aboute] R; abowten F; aboute hym WHmCrGOC^{2}CBLM; but hymselue Y.
60 of] on RF. ac] but GF; and CrC^{2}C. flei3] fled C.
61 nolde] wolde FCrGC. no3t] no Cr^1. neghen] neighe CGOC^{2}BF. by] neer be F; *om* BoCot.
62 þat] & GYOC^2. ybosted] bosted Cr Hm.
63 many] *om* F. men] man GR. yholpe] yholpen OC^{2}M; holpe HmYCot; holpe*n* Cr.
64 Ac] but GF; And CrC^{2}C. þat] þe Cr^{23}. segge] grome C. he(2)...drawe] *om* Y. hym] *om* G.
65 Dredfully] Dredful BmBo. as] as a BF. þe] *om* CrM.
66 Ac] but GF; And CrC^{2}C. so(2)] as HmF; *om* Cr. þe] this CrM. þis] þ*at* F.
67 adown] downe CrGF. of] of his B. and] *om* Cr^3. ladde] *om* CBM (led *above line another ink* Cot, held *above line* M). hande] handes RF.
68 to þe] with þat R. wye] weye C^{2}BR; wey3 F; way G.
69 And] & he F. bi] in R.
70 but] but 3if HmYOC^{2}CLMR. he(1)] *om* C^2. recouerer þe raþer] þe rathere recure F. recou*er*er] recourere LR; recouer Cr^{23}GC^2; recouered Cr^{1}B; socur C. raþer] BHmCrGYOC^{2}CLMR; rapelier W. þat] *om* GF.
71 RF; *line om* WHmCrGYOC^{2}CBLM; *here in the spelling of* W. And breide] he breyded F. atamede] hem tamede F.
72 wyn and] wynene (*corrected*) C^2. wasshed] weisch Hm.

Enbawmed hym and bond his heed and in his [barm] hym leide,
And ladde hym so forþ on Lyard to *lex Christi*, a graunge
Wel sixe Mile or seuene biside þe newe Market;
Herberwed hym at an hostrie and þe hostiler called:
'Haue, kepe þis man', [quod he], 'til I come fro þe Iustes.
And lo, here siluer', he seide, 'for salue to hise woundes.'
And he took hym two pens to liflode and seide,
'What he spendeþ moore [for medicyne] I make þee good herafter,
For I may noȝt lette', quod þat Leode and lyard he bistrideþ
And raped hym to [ryde þe riȝte wey to Ierusalem].
Feiþ folwede after faste and fondede to mete hym,
And *Spes* spakliche hym spedde, spede if he myȝte,
To ouertaken hym and talke to hym er þei to towne coome.
And whan I seiȝ þis I soio*ur*ned noȝt but shoop me to renne
And suwed þat Samaritan þat was so ful of pite,
And graunted hym to ben his [gome]; 'graunt m*er*cy', he seide;
'Ac þi frend and þi felawe þow fyndest me at nede.'

73 Enbawmed] ⁊ Enbawmed F. hym(1)] hem Cot. barm] lappe WHmCrGYOC^{2}CBLMRF. hym(2)] he CB.
74 on] to G.
75 Mile] miles Cr. biside] bysyden F; fro G. þe] *om* F.
76 Herberwed] ⁊ herberwid F. þe] RF; to þe WHmCrGOC^{2}CBLM; to Y.
77 Haue...he] And seide haue kepe þis man WHmCrGYOC^{2}CBLMRF (þis] þou þis F). þe] *om* F. Iustes] Iustyse CotG.
78 here] heere is F; hire C^{2}M. to] for Cr.
79 *divided from* 80 *after* weere WHmCrGYOC^{2}CBLMRF. to] for CrF. liflode] liflode as it weere WHmCrGYOC^{2}CBLMRF.
80 What he] whatso he M; whoso Cr. spendeþ] spe*n*d Cr; spendid F; speneth YOLR. for...I] I WHmCrGYOC^{2}CBLMRF. þee] it CrM.
81 For] *om* F. noȝt] nouȝ C; no lenger*e* F. lette] letty*n* F; *om* OC^{2}. lyard] hard Y. bistrideþ] bistrode YGOC^{2}CB.
82 raped] rapeþ F. ryde...Ierusalem] Ier*usal*emward þe riȝte wey to ryde WHmCrGYOC^{2}CBLMRF (ward] *om* Cr.)
83 Feiþ] þan fayth F. folwede] folweth LR. after] hy*m* F. to...hym] hym to meete F. mete] meten Cr. hym] wiþ hym OC^{2}.
84 spakliche] sparkliche RF; sparliche C^{2}; scharpli B; specially Hm. spede] speden F.
85 To] and Hm. taken] take Cr^{3}GYOC^{2}CBLMRF; takeþ Hm. talke] talkeþ Hm. to(1)] til YOC^{2}CB. þei] he CrF.
86 to] *om* Cr^{1}C.
87 þat(1)] þe RF.
88 And] ⁊ he F. hym] me y F. gome] goome GBmRF (*altered to* grome Bm); groom WHmCrYOC^{2}CBoCotLM. he] y F.
89 Ac] but G; and HmCrC^{2}CF. þi(2)] *om* GYO. þow] thou CrGOC^{2}M; quod he þow WHmLRF; he seide thow YCB.

And I þanked hym þo and siþþe [þus] I hym tolde
How þ*at* feiþ fleiȝ awey and *Spes* his felawe boþe
For sighte of þ[e] sorweful [segge] þ*at* robbed was w*ith* þeues.
'Haue hem excused', quod he; 'hir help may litel auaille.
May no medicyne [vnder mone] þe man to heele brynge,
Neiþer Feiþ ne fyn hope, so festred be hise woundes,
Wiþouten þe blood of a barn born of a mayde.
And [he be] baþed in þat blood, baptised as it were,
And þanne plastred wiþ penaunce and passion of þat baby, |
He sholde stonde and steppe; ac stalworþe worþ he
neu*ere* *fol.* 103 *b*
Til he haue eten al þe barn and his blood ydronke.
For wente neu*ere* wye in þis world þoruȝ þat wildernesse
That he ne was robbed or rifled, rood he þere or yede,
Saue feiþ and [myselue and] *Spes* [his felawe],
And þiself now and swiche as suwen oure werkes.
For [an] Outlaw[e is] in þe wode and vnder bank lotieþ,
And [may] ech man see and good mark take
Who is bihynde and who bifore and who ben on horse;

90 And] ⁊ þanne F. þanked] thank Cot. and] *om* Hm. þus] F; *om* WHmCrGYO C^{2}CBLMR. I hym] he me G.
91 his] ⁊ his Cr^{1}M.
92 þe] HmCr^{1}GYOC^{2}CBLMRF; þat W Cr^{23}. segge] man WHmCrGYOC^{2}CBL MRF.
94 May] þere may F. vnder mone] vnder molde RF; on molde WHmCrGYOC^{2}C BLM. þe] þ*at* F. heele] helthe F.
96 outen] oute GHmCrBLMR; *om and twice supplied* Y. born] þ*at* shal be born F. mayde] mayden CrOC^{2}M.
97 he be] Cr^{12}GYOC^{2}CBM; he Cr^{3}; be he WHmL; be R; been F. þat] the C; his F. it] he F.
98 And] *om* Cr. þanne] make a F. plastred] plastre F; pastrid B. wiþ] w*ith* the Cot. and] and þe R; w*ith* þe F. baby] babe F; body GY.
99–346 defective (three leaves wanting) O.
99 He sholde] ⁊ þan shal he F. steppe] steppen F. ac] but GF; ⁊ CrC^{2}C. worþ] *om* Cr^{3}.
100 haue] haþ F. þe] þe al (*corrected*) Bo. blood] blold Bo. ydronke] ydronken CMR; dronken CrHmC^{2}.
101 wye] weyȝ F; wiȝt BR.
102 That] Thad C. ne] was ne C; *om* F. or(1)] ne R; ⁊ F. rood] wode Cr^{1}. þere] eyþir F; *om* Cr. or(2)] other R.
103 my...felawe] his felawe *Spes* and myselue WHmCrGYC^{2}CBLMRF (my] y my G. selue] seluen M).
104 now] nowthe F. and] as BoCot. as] þ*at* C^{2}R. suwen] sewe F.
105 an...is] an owtlawe is F; an outlaw Cr^{23}; outlawe is R; Outlawes WHmCr^{1} GYC^{2}CBLM. bank] bankes (es *over erasure*) M; balkis F. lotieþ] lotien C^{2}; loutith CrG; lowted C.
106 And] ⁊ he F. may] CrLRF; mowe GYCM; mowen WCot; mown HmC^{2} BmBo. ech] eu*er*y F. take] taketh RF.
107 who(1)] who ys GB; *om* F. ben] so be*n* Cr; is F.

For he halt hym hardier on horse þan he þat is [on] foote.
For he seigh me þat am Samaritan suwen Feiþ & his felawe
On my Capul þat highte *caro*—of mankynde I took it—
He was vnhardy, þat harlot, and hidde hym *in Inferno*.
Ac er þis day þre daies I dar vndertaken
That he worþ fettred, þat feloun, faste wiþ Cheynes,
And neuere eft greue gome þat gooþ þis ilke gate:
[O *mors ero mors tua &c*].
And þanne shal Feiþ be forster here and in þis Fryth walke,
And kennen outcom[en] men þat knowen no3t þe contree
Which is þe wey þat I wente and wher forþ to Ierusalem;
And Hope þe Hostile[r] shal be þer [an helyng þe man lith];
And alle þat feble and feynte be, þat Feiþ may no3t teche,
Hope shal lede hem forþ with loue as his lettre telleþ,
And hostele hem and heele þoru3 holy chirche bileue
Til I haue salue for alle sike; and þanne shal I turne
And come ayein bi þis contree and conforten alle sike
That craueþ it [or] coueiteþ it [and] crieþ þerafter.

108 halt] haldes C; þat holdethe G. hardier] harde there Cot. þan] þat B (*corrected* BmBo). he(2)] him Cr. on(2)] HmCrGY C^{2}BMF; a LR; at C; *om* W.
109 seigh] seeth Cr^{23}; seiþ C^{2}GRF. þat am] a G; *om* F. suwen] sue Cr^{23}G; & sewyn Hm; þat F. Feiþ] forth Y. felawe] felawe sewen F.
110 highte] hatteþ HmB; hate C^2. took it] it tooke F.
111 vnhardy...harlot] but an harlot F; vnharlot R. hidde] had Cr^1. *in Inferno*] *om* Y.
112 Ac] but GF; and HmCrC^{2}C. þis] thise CB. day] dayes CB; *om* F. daies] *om* B. taken] take GC^{2}CBF.
113 Cheynes] stronge cheynes F.
114 gome] grome YCBL. þis ilke] þulke Hm; by thys G.
114α RF; *line om* WHmCrGYC^{2}CBLM. &c] *morsus tuus ero inferne* F.
115–26 *lines om* RF.
115 shal] shalt BmBo. forster] fostred Cot. here] *om* Hm. walke] *om* C.
116 kennen] kenne GC^{2}C. outcomen] outcommen Cr^{23}; out common Cr^1; owt comoun Hm; out comune WLM; comune GYC^{2}C; vnkummande (? *altered to* vnkunnande) Bo; vnkunnande Bm; vnken Cot. knowen] knowe G. no3t] no3 Hm.
117 forþ] fore HmCr^1.
118 Hostiler] Hostilers man WHmCrGC^{2}CBLM; hestilers man Y. an...lith] þe man lith anhelyng WHmCrGYC^{2}CBLM. (an] in CrY; at M; to GC^{2}CB. helyng] heale G).
119 þat(2)] þe G.
120 lede] leden B. hem] hym C. forþ with] for Cr^{1}M. lettre] lore Cr. telleþ] hem telliþ BmCBo; hym tellith Cot; teacheth Cr^1; teache Cr^{23}.
121 *run together with* 122 G. hostele] hostelen Cr^{1}M; herber C. hem] hym Cot. heele] heele hem BmGCBo; hele hym Cot. þoru3...bileue] *om* G. chirche] chirchis BCrM.
122 Til...sike] *in margin main hand* G. shal I] I shall G. turne] returne CrGYC^{2}CBL M.
123 conforten] conforte HmGYC^{2}CBLM.
124 it(1)] *om* C^2. or] HmCrGYC^{2}CBLM; and W. and] HmCrGYC^{2}CBLM; or W.

For þe barn was born in Bethleem þat w*ith* his blood shal saue
Alle þat lyuen in Feiþ and folwen his felawes techynge.'
'A, swete sire', I seide þo, 'wher I shal bileue,
As Feiþ and his felawe enformed me boþe,
In þre p*er*sones departable þat p*er*petuele were euere, |
And alle þre but o god? þus Abraham me tauȝte; *fol.* 104 *a*
And Hope afterward he bad me to louye
O god wiþ al my good, and alle gomes after
Louye hem lik myselue, ac oure lord abouen alle.'
'After Abraham', quod he, 'þat heraud of armes,
Sette [faste] þi feiþ and ferme bileue;
And as hope highte þee I hote þ*at* þow louye
Thyn euenecristene eu*er*emoore eueneforþ w*ith* þiselue.
And if Conscience carpe þerayein, or kynde wit eyþer,
Or Eretikes wiþ argumentȝ, þyn hond þow hem shewe.
For god is after an hand; yheer now and knowe it.
The fader was first as a fust wiþ o fynger foldynge
Til hym [likede] and liste to vnlosen his fynger,
And p*ro*fre[d] it forþ as w*ith* a pawme to what place it sholde.

125, 126 *as three lines divided after* mayde, feith YGC^{2}CB.
125 born] *om* C. þat...shal] of a clene mayde That shal with his blood YGC^{2}CB (of] on G. mayde] maydyn C^2. his] *om* C^2).
126 Feiþ] truþe C^2. folwen] folowe Cr^1. his...techynge] þe techinge of hope þ*at* is his Felaw C^{2}GYCB (hope] holpe Y. his] *om* C).
127 *Here* RF *resume.* I seide] seyde y Hm CrGBF. wher] whether CrR; wheyþ*er* of ȝow F. I shal] shal I CrHmGYC^{2}CB MF. bileue] leve F.
128 As] and G; For F. enformed] enformeden Hm; enformen YGC^{2}CB. me boþe] bothe me (*correct order noted*) C.
129 In] Of F; and C^2. departable] dep*art*ables G. þat] ꝥ F. were] were*n* C^{2}B; ben F.
130 *run together with* 132 F. þre] this C; þis is B. þus...tauȝte] *om* F.
131 *line om* F. he] *om* G. bad] bab Y.
132 *line om* C^2. O...good] *om* F. alle] alle my HmG.
133 selue] suluen R. ac] but GF; and Cr C^{2}C. abouen] aboue CrGYC^{2}BLRF.
134 quod] seid q*uo*d (seid *above line main hand*) F.
135 Sette] he settte F. faste] GCrYC^{2}CB LMRF; fully WHm. bileue] þy beleve F.
136 highte] hyghe Cr; bihiȝt RF. hote] hope B. þ*at*] the that CrMF.
137 selue] seluen M.
138 þerayein] cherysshym G. eyþer] other CrGCotR.
139 hem] hym GCrYC^{2}CBLM.
140 yheer] here Cr; þou here it F.
141 as] *om* GYC^{2}CB. foldynge] folden RF; holdyng Cr^1.
142–51α *over erasure another hand and ink* Hm.
142 hym] he F. likede] lykede Hm; louede WCrGYC^{2}CBLM; leued R; lyþed F. vnlosen] vnlose HmC^{2}F; vnclosen B.
143 p*ro*fred] profered RF; p*ro*fre WGYC^2 CBLM; p*ro*feryn Hm; put Cr. it(1)] *om* G. as] *om* F. a] þe F. pawme] pawne Hm.

The pawme is [þe piþ of] þe hand, and profreþ forþ þe fyngres
To ministren and to make þat my3t of hand knoweþ;
And bitokneþ trewely, telle whoso likeþ,
The holy goost of heuene: he is as þe pawme.
The fyngres þat fre ben to folde and to serue
Bitoknen sooþly þe sone þat sent was til erþe,
That touched and tastede at techynge of þe pawme
Seinte Marie, a mayde, and mankynde lau3te:
Qui conceptus est de spiritu sancto &c.
The fader is [þanne] as a fust wiþ fynger to touche—
Omnia traham ad me ipsum &c—
Al þat þe pawme parceyueþ profitable to feele.
Thus are þei alle but oon, as it an hand weere, |
And þre sondry sightes [shewynge in oon], *fol.* 104 *b*
The paume for [he] putteþ forþ fyngres and þe fust boþe.
Right so, redily, Reson it sheweth
How he þat is holy goost sire and sone preueþ.
And as þe hand halt harde and alle þyng faste
Thoru3 foure fyngres and a thombe forþ *with* þe pawme,
Right so þe fader and þe sone and Seint Spirit þe þridde

144 þe...of] of F; purely WHmCrGYC^{2}CBLMR. profreþ] profer C. fyngres] fynger G.
145 ministren] mynystre HmCrYC^{2}CBLMRF; mynyste (?) G. to] *om* Hm. þat] þe Cr^{23}. hand] man F. knoweþ] knowen Cr^{23}; knowe Hm.
146 And] It F. telle] telle it Hm; to tellen F. so] so it HmYCB. likeþ] liked CBmBo; lydyd Cot.
147 he] *om* C^{2}. as] lykned F. þe] a Hm.
148–50 *lines om* CB.
148 The] & þe F.
149 sooþly] sotly M. til] to HmC^{2}F; to the CrG.
150 That...tastede] & þorgh3 towchyng & tastyng F. at] at þe C^{2}L; all þe G; and RF.
151 a] þat F. mayde] mayden R. and] *om* F. lau3te] sche lawhte F; kaght G.
151α *in margin* C^{2}. est] *twice* Bo. &c] *natus &c* GYCB; *ex maria virgine* Hm; *om* CrC^{2}F.
152 þanne] HmCrGYC^{2}CBLMR (*over erasure another hand and ink* Hm); pawme W; *om* F. as] a C; *om* Cot. a] *om* R. fynger] fyngers Cr^{3}. touche] chouche R.
152α *in margin* C^{2}. Omnia] Quia omnia WHmCrGYC^{2}CBLMRF. &c] *om* CrF.
153 Al] & al F. þe] *om* Cr^{1}CotF.
154 Thus] & þus F; Than Cr. an hand] a fust RF.
155 shewynge in oon] in oon shewynge WHmCrGYC^{2}CBLMF; in oen in schewynge R.
156 he] HmCrGYC^{2}CBLM; þe paume R; it WF. putteþ] put RF. forþ] out Cr^{3}. þe] *om* CrMF.
157 redily] ful redyly Hm; redely good F. it] me G. sheweth] sweweþ (h *above* s) C^{2}.
158 How] That Cr^{1}M (*in margin* M). preueþ] ypreve F.
159 halt] holdeth GCrC. and] *om* F. þyng] thinges Cr; þyngis & F.
160 a] *om* BoCot. forþ] for Cot.
161 þe(2)] *om* F.

[Halt] al þe wide world wiþInne hem þre,
Boþe wolkne and þe wynd, water and erþe,
Heuene and helle and al þat is þerInne.
Thus it is—nedeþ no man trowe noon ooþer—
That þre þynges bilongeþ in oure [fader] of heuene
And aren serel[e]pes by hemself; asondry were þei neuere;
Na moore [may an hand] meue wiþoute fyngres.
And as my fust is ful hand y[f]olden togideres
So is þe fader a ful god, formour and shappere:
Tu fabricator omnium &c.
Al þe myȝt myd hym is in makynge of þynges.
The fyngres formen a ful hand to portreye or peynten;
Keruynge and compasynge [i]s craft of þe fyngres.
Right so is þe sone þe Science of þe fader
And ful god as is þe fader, no febler ne no bettre.
The pawme is pureliche þe hand, haþ power by hymselue
Oþerwise þan þe wriþen fust or werkmanshipe of fyngres.

162 Wythin hem thre the wyde worlde holden CrM (*over erasure another hand* M). Halt] YHmC^{2}BLR; Haldes C; holdethe G; holden F; *om* W. wide] wyld Cot. Inne] *om* RF. hem] hym BmBo. þre] C^{2}HmGYCBLR; þre holden W; þre togydres F.
163 Boþe] boþe þe HmCrGBF. water and] þe water & þe F.
164 is þerInne] therin is CrGYC^{2}CBM; þere is Inne LRF.
165 Thus] thys G. is] is it C^2; *om* HmGC BRF. no] euery F. trowe] to trowe C^{2}YL; to trowen RF. noon] on no*n* F.
166 bilongeþ] longen to F. in] on Cot. fader] lord WHmCrGYC^{2}CBLMRF.
167 serelepes] LM; surleps R; serelopes WCr^1; sereples HmGYC^{2}CB (*over erasure another ink* Hm); Serples Cr^{23}; sunderlepis F. hem] hym BmBo. a] & a F; *om* G. sondry] sundre C^{2}YF; so*n*der Cr. were] weren F. þei] *om* LRF.
168 may an hand] þan may an hand RF; þan myn hand may WHmCrGYC^{2}CBL M (hand *above line* G). oute] oute*n* YC^{2}L RF. fyngres] HmLRF; my fyngres WCr GYC^{2}CBM.
169 And] *om* B. fust is] neef if C. yfolden] yffolden C^2; yfolde YCBLMR; folden CrG; & yfolde F; yholden W; yholde Hm.
170 shappere] chappere BoCot (s *added later* Cot); maker Cr.
170α *in margin* C^{2}B. &c] *om* BF.
171 Al] YGC^{2}CB; And al WHmCrLMR F. þe] that Cr^{1}M; thy Y. myd] w*ith* GC. of] of al Cr^{23}GYC^{2}CB. þynges] thyng Y.
172 formen] frame*n* Cr^{23}. or] or to C^2 CBMF; & to Cr. peynten] peynte Hm Cr^{1}GC^{2}CotMF.
173 Keruynge] To keruy*n*ge F. and] or RF. is] CrR; þat is F; as WHmGYC^{2}CB LM. craft] crist C.
175 And] & he F. is] *om* Cot. ne] nor Cr.
176 pawme] plawme (w *above* m) C^2. is] þat is CrM (þat *above line* M). pureliche] pur lych F. haþ] HmCrGYCBLM R; and haþ WC^2; but he F. selue] seluen M.
177–97 *over erasure another hand and ink* Hm.
177 þan] þat F. þe wriþen] he wriþeþ þe BmBoC; he wryeth the Cot; þe writen YR (*corrected* Y); wryty*n*ge F. of] of þe F.

For [þe pawme] haþ power to putte out þe ioyntes
And to vnfolde þe fust, [for hym it bilongeþ,
And receyue þat þe fyngres recheþ and refuse boþe
Whan he feleþ þe fust and] þe fyngres wille;
So is þe holy goost god, neiþer gretter ne lasse |
Than is þe sire [or] þe sone and in þe same myghte, *fol.* 105 *a*
And alle [þre] but o god as is myn hand and my fyngres.
Vnfolden or folden, my fust and my pawme
Al is but an hand, [howso I turne it.
Ac who is hurte in þe hand], euene in þe myddes,
He may receyue riȝt noȝt; reson it sheweþ.
For þe fyngres þat folde sholde and þe fust make,
For peyne of þe pawme power hem failleþ
To clucche or to clawe, to clippe or to holde.
Were þe myddel of myn hand ymaymed or yp*er*issed
I sholde receyue riȝt noȝt of þat I reche myghte;
Ac þouȝ my þombe and my fyngres boþe were toshullen

178 þe pawme] C[2]CrGYCBLMRF; he WHm. putte] pitty*n* F; pult R. þe] RF; alle þe WHmCrGYC[2]CBLM. *Hereafter an additional line* B; *see above*, p. 221.
179 *run together with* 181 WHmCrGYC[2]CBLM. vnfolde] vnfolden GC[2]B. þe] RF; þe folden WCrGYC[2]CLM; þe folde BmBo; þe ful Cot; *om* Hm. fust] Neue C. for...bilongeþ] R; for it to hym longeþ F; *om* WHmCrGYC[2]CBLM; *here in the spelling of* W.
180 RF; *line om* WHmCrGYC[2]CBLM; *here in the spelling of* W. And(*both*)] & to F. recheþ] reche F.
181 Whan...fust] RF; *om* WHmCrGYC[2]CBLM; *here in the spelling of* W. and] RF; as GYCB; at WHmCrC[2]LM. þe(2)] *om* BoCot. wille] willen B.
182 So] To C.
183 or] RF; and WHmCrGYC[2]CBLM. and] *om* Cot. in] of F; *om* Cr[1]. myghte] strengþe F.
184 þre] thre Cr[23]; they are GF; are þei WHmCr[1]YC[2]CBLMR. is] *om* HmGYC[2]. myn] *om* F. my] *om* CF.
185 or] and Cr[1]M. my...and] *twice* Y. and] er F.
186 *run together with* 187 WHmGYC[2]CB. is] ys it F. how...it] RCrLMF (*over erasure another hand* M); *om* WHmGYC[2]CB. so] soeuer Cr.
187 *in margin by corrector of* 186 M. Ac... hand] RCrLMF; *om* WHmGYC[2]CB; *here in the spelling of* W. Ac] But F; And Cr. who] whoso CrM. in(1)] on Cr. in þe(2)] a M.
188 *line om* GYC[2]CB; *run together with* 193 F. reson it sheweþ] *om* F.
189–92 *lines om* F.
189 sholde] shulden C[2]; shulle Cot. fust] Neeue C.
190 pawme] loofe C. hem] hym Cot.
191 clucche] clenche CB; cratche Cr. or(1)] & C[2]. to(2)] or CB.
192 ymaymed] ymayheymed C; maymed Cr. or] other R. yperissed] ypersed R; Iperisshed Y; ypersshed L; perisched Hm Cr[1]GC[2]BM; pershed Cr[23].
193 I...noȝt] *om* F. of] and of CB. I] he F. reche] reche my Cot.
194 Ac] but GF; And CrC[2]; As C. my(2)] *om* Cot. were] were*n* C[2]F. shullen] schirnerd C; swollen (swo *over erasure*) M; swolle HmR; swoll F; swolen Cr[23].

And þe myddel of myn hand wiþoute maleese,
In many kynnes maneres I myghte myself helpe,
Boþe meue and amende, þou3 alle my fyngres oke.
By þis skile', [he seide], 'I se an euidence
That whoso synneþ in þe Seint Spirit assoilled worþ he neu*ere*,
Neiþ*er* here ne elliswhere, as I herde telle:
Qui peccat in spiritu[m] sanct[um] &c,
For he prikeþ god as in þe pawme þat *peccat in spiritu[m]*
    sanct[um].
For god þe fader is as a fust; þe sone is as a fynger;
The holy goost of heuene [he] is as þe pawme.
So whoso synneþ in þe Seint Spirit, it semeþ þat he greueþ
God þat he grypeþ wiþ, and wolde his *gra*ce quenche.
[For] to a torche or a tapur þe Trinite is likned,
As wex and a weke were twyned togideres,
And þanne a fir flawmynge forþ out of boþe.
And as wex and weke and [warm] fir togideres
Fostren forþ a flawmbe and a fair leye
[That serueþ þise swynkeres to se by ani3tes],
So dooþ þe Sire and þe sone and also *spiritus sanctus*

195 myddel] myddis F. hand] hond wer*e* F. oute] outen MF. maleese] malasie Cot.
196 In] 3it in F. maneres] man*er* G.
197 and amende] me in manere F. oke] oken C^{2}F.
198 skile] kile R. he seide] he seyde RF; me þynkeþ WHmCrGYC^{2}BM; me þynke L; my thynketh C. I] þou F. an euidence] an euident Cr^1; anidence C.
199 þe] *om* HmGYC^{2}CB. Seint] holy F.
200 herde] here CrC^{2}M; have herd F.
200α *line om* F; *in margin* C^2. *peccat*] *pectat* M. *spiritum sanctum*] CrC^2; *spiritu sancto* WHmGYCBLMR. &c] *numquam &c* R.
201 *run together with* 202 C. he] he þat Cr. as] *cancelled* C; *om* GC^{2}F. in...*sanctum*] *om* C. þat] *Qui* CrM. *spiritum sanctum*] *spiritu sancto* WHmGYC^{2}BLMRF; spi Cr.
202 For...fader] *om* C. as(1)] *om* Cr^{1}F. a(1)] þe G. is(2)] *om* G. as(2)] *om* HmF. a(2)] þe YC^{2}CB.
203 he is as] is as it were WHmCrGYC^{2}CBLMR; is as he wer*e* F. þe] a Hm; *om* C^2.
204 So] And CrGY. so] þat F; *om* GC^2. in] a3eynes RF. þe] *om* HmCrGYC^{2}CotL. Seint] holy F. it] *om* Hm. semeþ] seme F.
205 God] his hond F. wolde...quenche] his owene *gra*ce he qwenchiþ F.
206 For] RF; And WHmCrGYC^{2}CBLM. to a] *twice* F. or] or to CRF. is] he G. likned] ylikned YCB.
207 As] & þat is but F. a] *om* HmF. were twyned] wroght boþe F.
208 þanne a] a fayr F. flawmynge] flaumende LR; flawmeþ F. out of] ou3t of R; of hem F.
209 warm] FR; woote G; hoot WHmCrYC^{2}CBLM. togideres] is togydres (is *above line main hand*) F.
210 a(2)] *om* B. leye] lowe C; lyght GC^2.
211 *not in* WHmCrGYC^{2}CBLMRF.
212 also...*sanctus*] *sanctus spiritus* also F.

[Fostren forþ amonges folk loue and bileue]
That alle kynne cristene clenseþ of synnes. |
And as þow seest som tyme sodeynliche a torche, *fol.* 105 *b*
The blase þerof yblowe out, yet brenneþ þe weke—
Wiþouten leye or light [liþ fir in þe macche]—
So is [þe] holy goost god and *gr*ace wiþoute m*er*cy
To alle vnkynde creatures þat coueite to destruye
Lele loue or lif þat oure lord shapte.
And as glowynge gledes gladeþ noȝt þise werkmen
That werchen and waken in wyntres nyȝtes
As dooþ a kex or a candle þat caught haþ fir and blaseþ,
Na moore dooþ sire ne sone ne seint spirit togidres
Graunte no grace ne for[g]ifnesse of synnes
Til þe holy goost gynne to glowe and to blase,
So þ*at* þe holy goost gloweþ but as a [glede vn]glade
Til þ*at* lele loue ligge on hym and blowe.
And þanne flawmeþ he as fir on fader and on *filius*
And melteþ hire myȝt into mercy, as men may se in wyntre
Ysekeles in euesynges þoruȝ hete of þe sonne
Melte in a Mynut while to myst and to watre.

213 CrGYC^2CBLMRF; *line om* WHm; *here in the spelling of* W. Fostren] Brynges C. loue] boþe love F. bileue] leele byleue GC^2.
214 That] And Cr; *om* C^2. kynne cristene] c*ri*stene kynde it F. clenseþ] clensede R. synnes] synne Y.
216 The] þer BmBo. yblowe] yblowen MHm; blowe C^2; blowen CrG. yet] ⁊ ȝit F.
217 outen] oute GCrYC^2CBLMR. leye] lowe C. liþ...macche] þ*at* þe macche brenneþ WHmCrGYC^2CBLMRF (þat] eu*er*e F. macche] smacche YGC^2. brenneþ] swellith C^2G).
218 þe] HmCrGYC^2CBLMRF; *om* W. goost] *om* C^2. oute] oute*n* BC; greet F.
219 coueite] coueyten BG.
220 Lele] Lelly Cr. or] oþ*er* HmGYC^2CB LMR; to þe F. shapte] gave GC^2.
221–47 *lines om* RF.
221 as] as a GYC^2CB. glowynge] glowande L. gledes] gleden Cr^{23}; glede ne YGC^2CB. gladeþ noȝt] gladen G.
222 werchen] waken Cr. waken] walken G; worken Cr. wyntres] winter Cr.
223 kex] kyse C^2; lix Cot. caught] kauȝt hauȝt (*corrected*) Bo. blaseþ] blasid BoCot.
225 Graunte] Graunteth L. forgifnesse] forgyvenes GCrC; forȝifnesse WHmYC^2 BLM.
226 gynne] gynnyþ (yþ *added*) Hm. to(2)] *om* B.
227 þ*at*] doth C^2. gloweþ] glowede G; glowe B. glede vnglade] glede HmCr GYC^2CBLM; glade W.
228 lele] lelly Cr.
229 he] *om* Cot. on(*both*)] one Cr^1. fader] *pater* GYC^2. on(2)] *om* Cot.
230 into] to GYC^2B; o C.
231 in] ⁊ Cr. euesynges] eueses HmCr^{12} YLM; eues Cr^3. þe] *om* CB.
232 Melte] Melteth YCr^1GC^2CBLM. a] *om* Cr^1. Mynut] mynute*n* BmBo.

So g*ra*ce of þe holy goost þe grete myȝt of þe Trinite
Melteþ to mercy, to merciable and to [noon] oþere.
And as wex wiþouten moore on a warm glede
Wol brennen and blasen, be þei togideres,
And solacen hem þat mowe [noȝt] se, þat sitten in derknesse,
So wol þe fader forȝyue folk of mylde hertes
That rufully repenten and restitucion make,
In as muche as þei mowen amenden and paien;
And if it suffise noȝt for assetȝ, þat in swich a wille deyeþ,
Mercy for his mekenesse wol maken good þe remenaunt.
And as þe weke and fir wol maken a warm flaumbe
For to murþen men [wiþ] þat in [m]erke sitten, |
So wole crist of his curteisie, and men crye hym m*er*cy, *fol.* 106 *a*
Boþe forȝyue and foryete, and ȝit bidde for vs
[Fro] þe fader of heuene forȝifnesse to haue.
Ac hewe fir at a flynt foure hundred wynter;
But þow haue tow to take it wiþ, tonder or broches,
Al þi labour is lost and al þi long trauaille;
For may no fir flaumbe make, faille it [h]is kynde.
So is þe holi goost god and grace wiþouten m*er*cy

234 to(1)] into L; *om* Cr^{23}. noon] MGY C^{2}CBL; no Cr; *om* WHm.
235 outen] oute GCrYC^{2}. on] and Cr.
236 brennen] brenne HmG. blasen] blase HmCr^{1}G. be þei] all CrM.
237 noȝt se] se WHmCrGYC^{2}CBLM. sitten] sytte Cr^{3}; syte Cr^{2}; setten B; sate Cr^{1}.
238 wol] wold Cot; *om* Cr. fader] *om* C^{2}. forȝyue] forgeueth Cr. of] þ*at* be of Cr^{2}; that haue Cr^{3}.
239 make] maken BM.
240 In] þi Bo; *om* Cot. amenden] amende Cr. paien] paye Cr.
241 And] for G. suffise] suffiseth YCB. for] for to BmBo; to Cot. assetȝ] a seght G. þat] *om* Y. a] *om* Cr^{23}GYC^{2}CB.
242 wol] wold Cr^{1}; ꝯ Y. maken] make CrGYC^{2}CBLM.
243 and] and þe (þe *above line*) M. maken] make CrGYC^{2}CBLM. warm] faire Y.
244 murþen] murthe YCrGC^{2}CLM; norische B. wiþ] BHmCr^{23}GYC^{2}CLM; myd WCr^{1}. in] YHmCr^{3}GC^{2}CBLM; in þe WCr^{12}. merke] CrHmGYC^{2}CBL M; derke W. sitten] setten BoCot.
245 and] yff G. crye] crien M. hym] hem Cr^{2}.
246 forȝyue] forgyue GCrC. foryete] forget CrG; Forȝeue C^{2}.
247 Fro] To WHmCrGYC^{2}CBLM.
248 *Here* RF *resume.* Ac] but GC^{2}F; And CrC. hewe] hewe þou F; smyt Hm. at] on F; and R. a] the CrM; *om* R. foure] forure C. wynter] wynters G.
249 tow] towne (n *cancelled*) Bo; tonder Hm; tacche RF. tonder] tudir F; towe Hm. or] oþ*er* Hm.
250 al] *om* CrM.
251 no] *om* F. flaumbe] ne flaumbe Hm. faille it] and it fayle Hm. his] HmCrGY C^{2}BmCotLMRF; is WCBo.
252 is] *om* Hm. outen] oute YHmCrGR; gret F.

To alle vnkynde creatures; crist hymself witnesseþ:
Amen dico vobis, nescio vos &c.
Be vnkynde to þyn euenecristene and al þat þow kanst bidde,
Delen and do penaunce day and nyght euere,
And purchace al þe pardon of Pampilon and Rome,
And Indulgences ynowe, and be *ingratus* to þi kynde,
The holy goost hereþ þee no3t ne helpe may þee by reson.
For vnkyndenesse quencheþ hym þat he kan no3t shyne
Ne brenne ne blase clere, fo[r] blowynge of vnkyndenesse.
Poul þe Apostel preueþ wheiþer I lye:
Si linguis hominum loquar &c.
Forþi beþ war, ye wise men þat wiþ þe world deleþ;
That riche ben and reson knoweþ ruleþ wel youre soule;
Beþ no3t vnkynde, I conseille yow, to youre euenecristene.
For manye of yow riche men, by my soule, men telleþ,
Ye brenne but ye blase no3t; þat is a blynd bekene:
Non omnis qui dicit domine, domine, intrabit &c.
[Mynne ye no3t, riche men, to whiche a myschaunce
That] Diues deyde, dampned for his vnkyndenesse
Of his mete and moneie to men þat it nedede?

253α *Amen*] *twice* Hm. *&c*] *Vigilate itaque quia nescitis diem neque horam* F; *om* CrYC Bm.
254 þat þow] þou C^2; þan BmBo (*corrected to* þou Bm). bidde] bidden YC^{2}CBLRF.
255 Delen] Deale Cr; Er deele F. and(1)] or GYC^{2}CBF. and(2)] or BoCotF. euere] and othere Hm.
256 And] Er F. purchace] purchasen Hm; *om* Cot. of] purchace of Cot. Pampilon] þe pope F. and] of CotF.
257 And] Add Cr^3. Indulgences] indulgence Cr^{12}; Indulges F. *ingratus*] *ingratis* YCBmBo; ingrat RF; vngrateful Cr^3. kynde] kynne Cr^{3}RF.
259 quencheþ] qwenche R. hym] hem R. kan no3t] may not F; ne cane G.
260 brenne] *twice* Y. ne] no Cr^1. blase] blasen F. for] HmCrGC^{2}CBLMRF; fo W; but Y. blowynge] brennyng Cr^{1}M. vnkyndenesse] vnkynde F.
261 Poul] Seynt Powl F. wheiþer] where GYC^{2}CBLMR; þat y not F.
261α *linguis*] *lingua* B. *&c*] *& angelorum &c* Cot; *& angelorum caritatem non habuero nichil mihi prodest* F; *om* R.
262 Forþi] For Cr^1; wherfore (wher *in margin another hand*) M. beþ] *om* C. world] wolde L. deleþ] dele Cr.
263 knoweþ] knowe F. ruleþ] rule CrCF. soule] soules Cr^{1}BoCot; selue FC^2; selues Cr^{23}.
265 yow] 3ow 3e Hm. telleþ] telle F.
266 brenne] brenneth R. blase] blaseth LCMR. þat] & þat RF. a blynd] an vnkynde CB.
266α *dicit*] *dicit mihi* F. *intrabit*] *om* GYC^{2}CBmBo. *&c*] *in regnum celorum* Cot; *in regnum celorum set qui facit voluntatem* F.
267 *not in* WHmCrGYC^{2}CBLMRF.
268 That] For F; *om* WHmCrGYC^{2}CBLMR. dampned] Idampned R; & dampned F.
269 Of his] he 3af no F. and] YR; and his CLM; and of his WHmCrGC^{2}B; ne F. nedede] nediþ BoCCot.

Ech a riche, I rede, reward at hym take
And gyueþ youre good to þat god þat grace of ariseþ. |
For þat ben vnkynde to hise, hope I noon ooþer *fol.* 106 *b*
But þei dwelle þer Diues is dayes wiþouten ende.
Thus is vnkyndenesse þe contr*ar*ie þat quencheþ, as it were,
The g*ra*ce of þe holy goost, goddes owene kynde.
For þat kynde dooþ vnkynde fordooþ, as þise corsede þeues,
Vnkynde cristene men, for coueitise and enuye
Sleeþ a man for hise moebles wiþ mouþ or w*ith* handes.
For þat þe holy goost haþ to kepe þ[o] harlotes destruyeþ,
The which is lif and loue, þe leye of mannes body.
For eu*er*y manere good [man may] be likned
To a torche or a tapur to reuerence þe Trinite,
And who[so] morþereþ a good man, me þynkeþ, by myn Inwit,
He fordooþ þe leuest light þat oure lord louyeþ.
A[c] yet in mo maneres men offenden þe holy goost;
Ac þis is þe worste wise þat any wight myghte
Synnen ayein þe Seint Spirit, assenten to destruye
For coueitise of any kynnes þyng þat crist deere bouȝte.

270 Ech] Euery F. a] *om* GBF. riche] riche ma*n* BF. rede] redde G. take] ȝee take F.

271 gyueþ] gyue HmCr; yiueth YC^{2}B; yif (y *altered from* ȝ) M. þat(1)] your Cr^{1}M. þat(2)] þat alle B; þere F. ariseþ] riseth CrB.

272 þat] LCr^{1}MR; þei þat WHmCr^{23}GY C^{2}CB; þo þat F. I] þou F.

273 But] þat F. þei] þei shall GYC^{2}CF; þat þei shal B. dayes] daye Cr. outen] oute CotCr. ende] ende*n* Bo.

274 is] *om* F. vnkyndenesse] kyndenesse BF (*erasure before it* F). þe] is his (his *above line*) F. þat] for it F. as it were] hys g*ra*ce F.

275 goddes] is goddys F.

276 kynde dooþ] kendeness F. vnkynde] vnkindnes Cr^{1}MF. as] as done CrM; as ben (ben *above line*) F. þise] these*n* Cr^{1}.

277 and] of C^{2}G (*corrected to* ⁊ G.)

278 Sleeþ] Sleue Cr^{1}. moebles] mouables Cr. mouþ] mowuþ mouþe (mowuþ *cancelled*) Bo. or] ⁊ G.

279 þo] BCrYCLMRF; þe WHmGC^{2}. destruyeþ] distroye F.

280 lif] þe lif CB. þe] ⁊ F. leye] leþe C^{2}; lyght G.

281 *divided from* 282 *after* torche WHmCr GYC^{2}CBLMRF. manere] *om* HmF. man may] HmCrGYC^{2}CBLMRF; may b W. be] heere by F.

282 or] Or ellis to WCrGYC^{2}CBLMRF; or elles ynto Hm.

283 so] HmGYC^{2}CBRF; þat CrM; *om* WL. me] ne C. myn Inwit] my wytte G; good resou*n* F.

285 Ac] HmYBLMR; but C^{2}F; And W CrC; for G. in] in manye WHmCrGY C^{2}CBLMRF. offenden...goost] þe holy goost offende F. offenden] offe*n*d CrGY C^{2}CB.

286 Ac] but GC^{2}F; And CrC. wise] wisse C; wayes G.

287 Synnen] Sinne Cr. þe] *om* HmCrGY C^{2}CB. assenten] assente R. destruye] destruyen MCr.

288 of] *om* Cr. kynnes] *om* GYC^{2}CBF. þat] off that G; þe Cr^{3}. deere] so deer*e* F.

[How myȝte he aske mercy, or any mercy hym helpe],
That wikkedliche and wilfulliche wolde *mercy* aniente?
Innocence is next god and nyght and day it crieþ
"Vengeaunce, vengeaunce! forȝyue be it neuere
That shente vs and shedde oure blood, forshapte vs as it [semed]:
Vindica sanguinem iustorum."
Thus "vengeaunce, vengeaunce!" verrey charite askeþ.
And siþ holy chirche and charite chargeþ þis so soore
Leue I neu*ere* þ*at* oure lord [at þe laste ende]
Wol loue [þat lif] þat [lakkeþ charite],
Ne haue pite for any preiere þer þat he pleyneþ.'
'I pose I hadde synned so and sholde [nouþe] deye,
And now am sory þ*at* I so þe Seint Spirit agulte,
Confesse me and crye his g*ra*ce, [crist] þat al made, |
And myldeliche his m*er*cy aske; myghte I noȝt be
saued?' *fol.* 107 *a*
'Ȝis', seide þe Samaritan, 'so þow myght repente
That rightwisnesse þoruȝ repentaunce to ruþe myȝte turne.
Ac it is but selden yseiȝe, þer sooþnesse bereþ witnesse,
Any creature [be] coupable afore a kynges Iustice

289 CrLMRF; *line om* WHmGYC^{2}CB; *here in the spelling of* W. myȝte he] may F. aske] axen M.
290 wikkedliche] wicked Cr; wyllfullyche G. wilfulliche] wyldfullyche Hm; wyckedlyche G. wolde] woole F. aniente] anynte LMR; anyentyce HmGYC^{2}B; amentyce Cr^{23}; amitte F.
291 Innocence] For innocense F; *Innocentes* B. next] nex C. it] *om* HmCr.
292 forȝyue] forgyuen Cr^{23}C. be] *om* Cr^1.
293 vs(1)] *om* RF. forshapte] ⁊ forschop F. semed] R; semeþ F; were WHmCrGYC^{2}CBLM.
293α *Vindica*] *Vindica domine* Cr^{23}; *Vindicta* CBmBo. *iustorum*] *iustorum ⁊c* HmGC^{2}CB; *nostrum* Cr^{23}.
295 chirche] kyrke Cr. so] *om* HmF.
296, 297 *as one line* WHmCrGYC^{2}CBLMRF: Leue I neu*ere* þ*at* oure lord wol loue þat charite lakkeþ (Leue I] I beleeve F. lakkeþ] hatiþ B; hattes C).
299 pose] suppose CotC^2. synned] ysynned Cot. nouþe] now WCrYLMF; nouȝ R; nougth HmC^2; nouȝt C; noȝt BmBo; not (*cancelled*) G; nat Cot.
300 And] *om* M. now] nouȝt RF; *om* Cr. am] GCrYC^{2}CBLRF; am I WHmM. I] *om* LR. so] dude so HmCr^{23}. þe] *om* HmCot. agulte] agulted F; I agulte R; þus agylte Hm.
301 Confesse] But co*n*fesse F. g*ra*ce] mercy C^2. crist] god WHmCrGYC^{2}CBLMRF.
302 m*er*cy] grace C^2. myghte] mygh Y. saued] Isaued R.
303 Ȝis] Thus HmGCB. so] RF; so wel WHmCrGYC^{2}CBLM. myght] miȝtest RF.
304 þoruȝ] by Cr; to RF. to] ⁊ to F.
305 Ac] but GF; but ȝet C^2; And CrC. it is] is it Bo. selden] seelde F. yseiȝe] seye YHmCrGC^{2}CB. þer] her Cr^1; the Cr^{23}CB; that Y. sooþnesse] soth Cot. bereþ] wiþ beriþ (wiþ *cancelled*) Bo.
306 be] RF; þat is WHmCrGYC^{2}CBLM. coupable] coupble R. afore] before CrMRF. Iustice] Iustices C.

Be raunsoned for his repentaunce þer alle reson hym dampneþ.
For þer þat partie pursueþ þe [peel] is so huge
That þe kyng may do no mercy til boþe men acorde
And eyþer haue equyte, as holy writ telleþ:
Numquam dimittitur peccatum &c.
Thus it fareþ by swich folk þat [folwen] al hire [wille],
Yuele lyuen and leten noȝt til lif hem forsake.
[Drede of desperacion [þanne] dryueþ awey grace
That mercy in hir mynde may noȝt þanne falle];
Good hope, þat helpe sholde, to wanhope torneþ.
Noght of þe nounpower of god, þat he ne is myghtful
To amende al þat amys is, and his mercy gretter
Than alle oure wikkede werkes as holy writ telleþ—
Misericordia eius super omnia opera eius—
Ac er his rightwisnesse to ruþe torne som restitucion bihoueþ;
His sorwe is satisfaccion for [swich] þat may noȝt paie.
Thre þynges þer ben þat doon a man by strengþe
For to fleen his owene [hous] as holy writ sheweþ.
That oon is a wikkede wif þat wol noȝt be chastised;

307 for] before Cr. repentaunce] gilt F; *om* R. dampneþ] dampned Y.
308 þer] *om* Hm. þat] þat þe F; þe Cr^3. partie] pity Cr^1. peel] RLF; plee CrM; peple WHmGYC^2CB.
309 til] to G. acorde] acoorden F.
310 eyþer] neither CBm (n *erased* Bm). haue] haþ oþir F. equyte] aquyte Cot; yqwit F.
310α &c] *donec &c* YCot; *nisi restituatur ablatum* F.
311 it fareþ] fareþ it Hm. folwen...wille] falsly al hire lyues WHmCrGYC^2CBLM RF (lyues] lyue RF).
312 Yuele] I wull C^2. lyuen] lyue Cr. leten] lete C^2G; lyueth Cr^1. noȝt] *om* Cr^1. lif hem] hem lyf F; þe lyf hem Hm; lif hym BmBo; hymsilf Cot. forsake] forsakeþ Hm.
313, 314 RF; *lines om* WHmCrGYC^2CB LM; *here in the spelling of* W.
313 Drede] & drede F. þanne...awey] F; dryueth aweye þanne R.
315 Good] & good F. þat helpe] *om* CB. þat] & þat (þat *above line main hand*) G. wanhope] wanhopope C; wanpe (*corrected*) Bo. torneþ] it turneþ F; turne B.
316 þe] *om* Y. power] per R; pere F. ne is] is Cr^1; is euere F.
317 *run together with* 318 Cot. amys] mys F. and...gretter] *om* Cot. mercy] mercy is F.
318 Than...werkes] *om* Cot. alle] *om* C^2.
318α *eius*(1)] *domini* RF. *eius*(2)] *eius &c* HmGYBmBoM.
319 Ac] but GC^2F; And CrC. his] is Bo; þis GCot; *om* Cr. rightwisnesse] ryghtfulnes GYC^2CB. bihoueþ] biho C.
320 *line om* RF. is] his BmBo. swich] hym WHmCrGYC^2CBLM.
321 þer] that C. a man] *twice, second cancelled* Hm.
322 For to] *om* GC^2. fleen] flye Cr. hous] HmCrGYC^2CBLMRF; *om* W.
323 is] his BmBo. chastised] chasted LYC CotR.

Hir feere fleeþ hire for feere of hir tonge.
And if his hous be vnhiled and reyne on his bedde
He sekeþ and sekeþ til he slepe drye.
And whan smoke and smolder smyt in his sighte
It dooþ hym worse þan his wif or wete to slepe;
For smoke and smolder [smerteþ] hise eighen |
Til he be blereighed or blynd and [þe borre] in þe þrote; *fol.* 107 *b*
Cogheþ and curseþ þat crist gyue h[y]m sorwe
That sholde brynge in bettre wode or blowe it til it brende.
Thise þre þat I telle of ben þus to vnderstonde:
The wif is oure wikked flessh þat wol no3t be chastised
For kynde clyueþ on hym eu*er*e to cont*ra*rie þe soule;
And þou3 it falle it fynt skiles þ*at* "frelete it made",
And "þat is lightly for3yuen and for3eten boþe
To man þat mercy askeþ and amende þenkeþ".
The reyn þat reyneþ þer we reste sholde
Ben siknesse and sorwes þat we suffren o[u3]te,

324 Hir] þere hire F. fleeþ] flyeth CrGYC; flien BmBo. hire] hire RF; fro hire WHm CrGYC^{2}CBLM.
325 his] *om* C. vnhiled] vntiled Cr^{1}. and] ⁊ it F. on] in YCB. bedde] head Cr.
326 He] Sokoure he F. and sekeþ] þa*nne* F; al aboute Cr^{23}GYC^{2}CB. slepe] mowe sleepe F; lygge GYCB; liggith C^{2}.
327 *run together with* 329 Y. and] or GY C^{2}CB. smoke] smolke Cr^{3}. smolder] smodre G. smyt...sighte] *om* Y. smyt] smytethe G; smyten F. sighte] ey3en F.
328 *line om* Y. or...slepe] er þe wat*ur* eyþir F.
329 For...smolder] *om* Y. smoke] smolke Cr. smolder] smolder so F; smother Hm. smerteþ] FR; smytethe GCL; smyteþ in WCrYC^{2}BM (in *above line* M); smyt in Hm.
330 be] *om* BmR (*corrector supplies* Bm). blereighed] blerenyed LR; blerid BoCrCot. and] or Cr^{3}. þe borre] cow3he R; a bold cowhe F; hoos GCr^{1}YC^{2}CB; hoors WHm Cr^{23}LM. in þe þrote] after F. þe] his B.
331 Cogheþ] he coghethe GR (he *in margin* G); Than Cougheth he C^{2}; Coughed Y; þan kenely he F. and] *om* F. curseþ] rou3theþ Hm. þat] and byt HmB. hym] GYC^{2}CBMRF; hem WHmCrL.
332 sholde] schul C. or] ⁊ F. blowe] blowen R. it(1)] *om* HmGB. brende] brenne HmCrC^{2}B.
333 ben þus] þus ben RF; beene þis G. to] *om* CR.
334 The] þþe Bm; þre Bo. þat] *om* R. nou3t] nou3 C. chastised] chasted CrYC LMR.
335 clyueþ] cleymi*th* F. cont*ra*rie] constrarie (s *cancelled*) C^{2}.
336 falle it] *om* Cot. fynt] fyndethe G. þ*at*] þe HmL; for Cot. frelete] froltee Y. it(2)] is Cr^{23}GYC^{2}C.
337 for3yuen] for3yue R; fo3yve F. for-3eten] for3ete RF.
338 To] to a G. and] and to C^{2}BF. þenkeþ] hym þynkiþ B; hym he þynkeþ F.
339 reste sholde] restyn scholden F.
340 Ben] By Cr^{23}. siknesse] syknesses HmBLMRF. and] and other R. ou3te] R; awhten F; ofte WHmCrGYC^{2}CBLM.

As Poul þe Apostle to þe peple tauȝte:
Virtus in infirmitate perficitur.
And þouȝ þat men make muche doel in hir angre
And ben inpacient in hir penaunce, pure reson knoweþ
That þei han cause to contrarie by kynde of hir siknesse;
And lightliche oure lord at hir lyues ende
Haþ mercy on swiche men þat so yuele may suffre.
Ac þe smoke and þe smolder þat smyt in oure eighen,
That is coueitise and vnkyndenesse þat quencheþ goddes mercy;
For vnkyndenesse is þe contrarie of alle kynnes reson.
For þer nys sik ne sory, ne noon so muche wrecche
That he ne may louye, and hym like, and lene of his herte
Good wille, good word [boþe], wisshen and willen
Alle manere men mercy and forȝifnesse,
And louye hem lik hymself, and his lif amende.
I may no lenger lette', quod he, and lyard he prikede
And wente awey as wynd and þerwiþ I awakede. |

341 As] As seynt F.
341α *in*] *om* Cr^3. *perficitur*] CrBmRF; *perficitur &c* WHmGYC^{2}BoCotLM; *&c* C.
342 make] maken F. hir] *om* C. angre] angris F.
343 ben] *om* GYC^{2}CBLM. inpacient] vnpacient B; ympacyentȝ G; pacient F.
344 cause] resoun RF. to] to þe (þe *added*) G. contrarie] contrarien M.
345 And] and ful B. lightliche] liȝthi *corrected to* liȝtly Bm. lord] lord god F. hir] our G.
346 Haþ] he haþ F; Haue C. so] *om* CB.
347 **Here O resumes.** Ac] but GC^{2}F; And CrC. smoke] smolke Cr.
348 That] *om* GYOC^{2}CB. is] *om* R. þat] þey F; *om* R. quencheþ] qwenche F.
349 þe] *om* Hm. of] to F.
350 þer] þere *above line another ink* L. nys] nys neyþer Hm. muche] mychel a F; yuele a O. wrecche] werche C; wroiche Cot.
351 ne] *om* HmF. and(1)] if Cr. lene] leue Cr.
352 good] FR; and good WHmCrGYO C^{2}CBLM. boþe] HmCrGYOC^{2}CBLM RF (þe *over erasure* Hm); and W. wisshen] wissen Y. willen] wilnen RF.
353 Alle] to alle Hm; & to all F. men] of men boþe F; of CrM. and] and of Cr.
354 louye] louethe G. hem] him Cr^{1}M. hym] my O.
355 lette] lettyn F. lyard he] harde GYO C^{2}CB. prikede] prikede forþ O.
356 awey] *om* O. as] as þe GC^{2}F. awakede] waked CrGMR; waknede F; awakiþ BmBo.

XVIII

fol. 108 *a*

Wolleward and weetshoed wente I forþ after
As a recchelees renk þat [reccheþ of no wo],
And yede forþ lik a lorel al my lif tyme
Til I weex wery of þe world and wilned eft to slepe
And lened me to a lenten, and longe tyme I slepte;
[Reste me þere and rutte faste til *Ramis palmarum*.
Of gerlis and of *Gloria laus* gretly me dremed,
And how Osanna by Organye olde folk songen,
And of cristes passion and penaunce, þe peple þat ofrauȝte.]
Oon semblable to þe Samaritan and somdeel to Piers þe Plow[man]
Barefoot on an Asse bak bootles cam prikye
Wiþouten spores oþer spere; spakliche he lokede
As is þe kynde of a knyght þat comeþ to be dubbed,
To geten hym gilte spores [and] galoches ycouped.

1 Wolleward] AN wellowerd F. wente I] y wente F. after] þanne F.
2 As] ⁊ as GYOC^{2}CB. a] *om* O. renk] reuke Cr; freek B. reccheþ] of no wo WHmCrGYOC^{2}BLMRF; of no C. of no wo] reccheþ OHmCrYC^{2}CLMRF; recched G; roughte WB.
3 And] Bot F. forþ] *om* F.
4 weex] were G. wilned] willed Cr; wilnes C. eft] oft BmBo. to] *om* R.
5 a] *om* G. and] a Hm. slepte] slepe B.
6–8 *copied after* 9 WHmCrGYOC^{2}CBLMRF.
6 Reste] Rested LR; I reste BoCot; y restyd HmBmF. þere] *om* F.
7 Of] ⁊ of F. and] *om* O. gretly] grealye Cr^{3}. me] y F.
8 by] wi*th* F. Organye] orgene HmR; organ B; orgenes F. folk] folkes CB; men OF (folk *above line main hand* O).
9 *copied after* 5 WHmCrGYOC^{2}CBLMRF. And of] me þowhte þat (þat *altered from* þe) F. and penaunce] *om* F. þe] þ*er* B (? *corrected* Bm). þat] þ*er* GBF; *om* Cr^{23}O. of] ofte O. rauȝte] taughte Y Cr^{23}GOC^{2}CB.
10 Oon...to(1)] ⁊ oon lyȝk F. to þe] þe to (*correct order indicated*) Bo; to þat Cr^{23}. to(2)] *om* G. Piers] *petrus* C^{2}. þe(2)] *om* HmGOC^{2}CBF. man] HmCrGYOC^{2}CB LMRF; *cropped* W.
11 on] vpon Hm; and on YOC^{2}CB. Asse...bootles] asses bak al bootewles F. cam] gan GYOC^{2}CB. prikye] prickynge CrR; spr*inge* F.
12 outen] oute YCrGC^{2}LR. spores] spore Cr. oþer] or CrOCotM; eyþ*er* F. spakliche] spracliche RF; sharpliche B; meliche C^{2}; apertlyche (apert *over erasure another ink*) Hm.
13 *line om* B. is] *om* Hm. þe] *om* F. a] *om* Y. be] *om* C.
14 geten] gete OCrG; gente B. hym] hem L. and] CrGYOC^{2}CBoCot; and scharpliche (scharpliche *cancelled*) Bm; or WHmLMR; on F. ycouped] couped Cr.

Thanne was feiþ in a fenestre and cryde 'a! *fili dauid!*'
As dooþ an heraud of armes whan Auentrous comeþ to Iustes.
Olde Iewes of Ierusalem for ioye þei songen,
Benedictus qui venit in nomine domini.
Thanne I frayned at Feiþ what al þat fare bymente,
And who sholde Iuste in Ierusalem. 'Iesus', he seide,
'And fecche þat þe fend claymeþ, Piers fruyt þe Plowman.'
'Is Piers in þis place?' quod I, and he preynte on me.
'This Iesus of his gentries wol Iuste in Piers armes,
In his helm and in his haubergeon, *humana natura*;
That crist be noȝt [y]knowe here for *consummatus deus*
In Piers paltok þe Plowman þis prikiere shal ryde,
For no dynt shal hym dere as *in deitate patris*.'
'Who shal Iuste wiþ Iesus', quod I, 'Iewes or Scrybes?' |
'Nay', quod [feiþ, 'but] þe fend and fals doom [to deye]. *fol.* 108 *b*
Deeþ seiþ he shal fordo and adoun brynge
Al þat lyueþ [or] lokeþ in londe [or] in watre.
Lif seiþ þat he lieþ and leieþ his lif to wedde
That, for al þat deeþ kan do, wiþInne þre daies to walke

15 in] a in G. cryde] crie C. a(2)] O Cr; *om* GBF. *fili dauid*] *om* F.
16 Auentrous] auntres Hm; aunterers G; an awntrous F. Iustes] iustice Cr[1].
17 Olde] & olde F. for] for gre F. songen] songe GR.
17α *in margin* O. *domini*] *domini &c* Hm GYOC[2]CBmBo; demini Cr[3].
18 Thanne] That C. I frayned] freynede y F. bymente] mente FG.
19 And] *om* Cr. sholde] *om* R. Iesus] Ientil Iesu F.
20 fecche] feccheth R; fettyn F. þat] out þat B. þe(*both*)] *om* F. Piers] *petrus* C[2]. fruyt] fruye Y.
21 Piers] petris C[2]. þis] þat B. I] *om* C. and] & þanne F. preynte] twynclid B.
22 This] þis is F; þus B. of] In G. gentries] gentrye HmCrBRF. Piers] peersis F.
23 in] *om* GOCBM. his(2)] *om* O. haubergeon] herbergeon Cr. *humana*] þat is *humana* F.
24 *transposed with* 25 B. yknowe] GC[2] CBm; yknowen O; knowe YBoCot; knowen HmCrM; biknowe WLRF. *consummatus*] *consummatum* C[2]B. *deus*] *est* GYOC[2]CB.
25 In Piers] he is in perses F. paltok] palcot C[2]. þe] *om* F. shal] þat shal F. ryde] aride Y.
26 no] þere is no F. shal] þat shal F. as] *om* F.
27 Iuste] Iustne F. quod I] *om* G. I] y eyþir F. or] and Y.
28 feiþ...þe] faith but þe R; feythȝ non but þe F; he þe foule WHmCr[1]GYOC[2] CBLM; he the fould Cr[23]. fals] also G. to deye] RF; and deeþ WHmCrGYOC[2] CBLM (and] ad Bo).
29 seiþ] seethe G. adoun] adom B; downe GC[2]. brynge] bryngen F.
30 or(1)] HmCrGYOC[2]CBLM; and WR F. in(*both*)] on F. or(2)] HmCrGYOC[2] CBLMR; eyþer F; and W.
31 he] *om* C. lieþ] liȝeþ B; likthe LRF; liueth Cr[23].
32 *divided from* 33 *after* daies WHmCrGYO C[2]CBLMRF. Inne] Innen F. to walke] *om* F.

And fecche fro þe fend Piers fruyt þe Plowman
And legge it þer hym likeþ, and Lucifer bynde,
And forbete and adoun brynge bale deeþ for euere:
O mors ero mors tua.'
Thanne cam *Pilatus with* muche peple, *sedens pro tribunali*,
To se how doghtiliche deeþ sholde do and deme hir boþeres
    right.
The Iewes and þe Iustice ayeins I*esu* þei weere,
And al þe court on hym cryde '*crucifige*!' sharpe.
Tho putte hym forþ a p[e]lour bifore Pilat and seide,
'This I*es*us of oure Iewes temple Iaped and despised,
To fordoon it on o day, and in þre dayes after
Edifie it eft newe—here he stant þat seide it—
And ȝit maken it as muche in alle manere poyntes,
Boþe as long and as large bi lofte and by grounde.'
'*Crucifige*!' quod a Cachepol, '[he kan of wicchecraft]!'
'*Tolle, tolle*!' quod anoþer, and took of kene þornes
And bigan of [grene] þorn a garland to make,
And sette it sore on his heed and seide in enuye;

33 And] ⁊ to G; ando to Hm; he shal F. fecche] fetty*n* F. Piers] peersis F. þe(2)] *om* YF.
34 And] and to C^2; to G. legge] lede BF. it] hym G. þer] where Hm.
35 forbete] forbite R; for to bete YCr^{23}G OC^{2}CB. adoun] adon BmBo; doun Hm CrGMRF. bale] bale and HmGYOC^2; bale of B. deeþ] det C.
35α *in margin* O. *ero...tua*] *ero tua mors ⁊c* Cot; *mors tua ero* R. *tua*] *tua ⁊c* Hm GYOC^{2}CBmBo; *tua morsus tuus ero* F.
36 *Pilatus*] Pilate Cr. muche] gret F; *om* GYOC^{2}CB.
37 doghtiliche] doughty Cr. deeþ] *om* F. sholde] schol C. deme hir] deme*n* F. boþeres] boþes MCr^1; boþe F; beither R; brothers Cr^{23}GCB; brethers C^2. right] ryghtys F; myȝt O.
38 þe] *om* CrBoCotM. Iustice] iustices Cr^{23}YOCBF. I*esu*] i*esus* HmC^2. þei] *om* G. weere] weren OF.
39 þe] her LR. on] vpon M; vp Cr^1; of YCot. hym] iesu R; hem Cot; and Cr^1. sharpe] ful sharpe F; ful scharply Hm.
40 Tho] to BoCot. pelour] pilour WHm CrGYOC^{2}CBLMRF. bifore] tofore Hm; *om* G.
41 This] þus B. of] apon Cr; wi*th* F. oure] *om* Cr. Iewes] *om* RF. temple] peple CB. Iaped] GHmCrYOC^{2}CBLM R; haþ Iaped W; he Iapede F. *Hereafter an additional line* B; *see above*, p. 222.
42 To] and B; he will F. on] in BGM RF.
43 Edifie] Edifien R. it eft] ift Y. he] stant Y. stant] standes CrC; standethe G; he Y. seide it] it seide B.
44 maken] to maken B; make Cr. it] *om* G. as] also HmB. manere] maner of CrGF.
45 as(*both*)] also B. bi] on BF; a R.
46 *copied twice* F. *Crucifige*] Crufige L. he...craft] I warante hym a wicche WHm CrGYOC^{2}CBLMRF (a] *om* C^2).
47 *line om* F. of] o L. kene] kenne C.
48 grene] kene WHmCrGYOC^{2}CBLMR; þ*at* F. þorn] thornes Cr. to] for to M.
49 sette...heed] on his heed sette it sore F. in] wi*th* F.

'*Aue, raby*', quod þat rybaud and þrew reedes at hym.
Nailed hym w*ith* þre nailes naked on [a] roode;
And poison on a poole þei putte vp to hise lippes
And beden hym drynken his deeþ [to lette and] hise daies [lengþe],
And [seide], 'if þ*at* þow sotil be [þiselue] now [þow help].
If þow be crist and kynges sone com down of þe roode; |
Thanne shul we leue þ*at* lif þee loueþ and wol noȝt lete þee deye.' *fol.* 109 *a*
'*Consummatum est*', quod crist and comsede for to swoune.
Pitousliche and pale, as a prison þat deieþ,
The lord of lif and of light þo leide hise eighen togideres.
The day for drede wiþdrouȝ and derk bicam þe sonne;
The wal waggede and cleef and al þe world quaued.
Dede men for þat dene come out of depe graues
And tolde why þat tempeste so longe tyme durede:
'For a bitter bataille', þe dede body seide;
'Lif and deeþ, in þis derknesse hir oon fordooþ hir ooþer.
Shal no wight wite witterly who shal haue þe maistrie

50 quod] saide Cr. þat] þe R; þo F. rybaud] ribaudes RF. reedes] rides C; redelys F.
51 Nailed] ⁊ nayled F; þei nailid B. þre] fowre F. on] vpon R. a] þe WHmCrGYOC^{2}CBLMRF.
52 ⁊ to hise lyppis þey pyttyn poysou*n* on a poole F. on] vppon B. putte] putten BHmC^{2}. vp] *om* R.
53 beden] bede YGC^{2}CCotLR; bidde*n* Cr. drynken] drynke HmCrGYOC^{2}CBLRF. deeþ...and] deeþ yuel WHmGYOC^{2}CLMRF; dethes euil Cr; euyl deeþ B. hise] for hise F. lengþe] were ydone WLMR; wer don HmCrGYC^{2}CCotF; weren done OBmBo.
54 seide if] if WHmCrGYOC^{2}CBLMRF. þat] *om* CB. sotil] so sotyl F. þi...help] help now þiselue WHmCrGYOC^{2}CBLMRF (help] save F. now] thu Hm. selue] seluen GYOC^{2}CBLMR).
55 þe] *om* M.
56 shul] schulde BmCrBo. leue] beleeve F.
57 *est*] *by correction* Bm. comsede] comseth Cr; bigan C^{2}. swoune] swowe HmYOBLM; swowen C.
58 Pitousliche] Ful pitousliche BF. as] and as Hm. prison] prisoner CrGC^{2}F. þat] doth that CrM.
59 The] Tyl þe F; Til R. lord] lore R. þo] þer G; *om* F.
60 The] þan þe F. bicam] bigan YOF.
61 wal] wall*es* F; wallis of þe temple B. waggede] waggeden F. world] wer (ld *above line*) O. quaued] quaked HmBF.
62 Dede] ⁊ deede F. dene] dymme G; deeþ B. come] comen OHmB. depe] dede Cot; here RF; her dede Hm; *om* G.
63 tolde] tolden OHmBF. tempeste] temple Hm. durede] endured Cr.
64 body seide] bodyes seyden HmBF.
65 Lif] þat lyf F. hir(1)] þer F; *om* G. hir(2)] þe CrF; an G. ooþer] toþer F.
66 wite] wety*n* F. þe] *om* Cr.

Er sonday aboute sonne risyng'; and sank wiþ þat til erþe.
Some seide þat he was goddes sone þat so faire deide:
Vere filius dei erat iste.
And some seide he was a wicche; 'good is þat we assaye
Wher he be deed or noȝt deed doun er he be taken.'
Two þeues [þat tyme] þoled deeþ [also]
Vpon a croos bisides crist; so was þe comune lawe.
A Cachepol cam forþ and craked boþe hir legges
And [hir] armes after of eiþer of þo þeues.
Ac was no bo[y] so boold goddes body to touche;
For he was knyȝt and kynges sone kynde foryaf þat [þrowe]
That noon harlot were so hardy to leyen hond vpon hym.
Ac þer cam forþ a knyȝt wiþ a kene spere ygrounde,
Highte Longeus as þe lettre telleþ, and longe hadde lore his sight;
Bifore Pilat and ooþer peple in þe place he houed.
Maugree his manye teeþ he was maad þat tyme
To [Iusten wiþ Iesus, þis blynde Iew Longeus].
For alle þei were vnhardy þat houed [þer] or stode

67 sonday] sonenday HmBmBo. aboute] aboute þe OB; at þe F. sank...þat] *with* þat he sank F. til] to Cr^{1}C^2; into BF. erþe] the erþe CotCr^1.

68 Some] and some Cot. seide] seyden OHmBmBoF. þat(1)] *om* F.

68α *in margin* O. iste] *iste ⁊c* HmGYOC^{2}CBmBoLM.

69 seide] seyden HmOBF. þat] *om* RF. we] *om* R. assaye] assaie*n* Cr^{1}MF.

70 Wher] Whether CrC^2. he(1)] *altered to* be Bm; *om* Bo. be(1)] *om* Cot; *erasure* Bm. deed(1)] deyed Cot. or] ar R. deed doun] adoun B. taken] take GF.

71 Two] ⁊ two F. þat tyme] also WHmCrGYOC^{2}CBLMRF. þoled] þoleden OHmBF. also] þat tyme WHmCrGYOC^{2}CBLMRF.

72 Vpon...crist] Besides Christe apon a crosse CrM. a] *om* HmBF. croos] croyses HmF. crist] *om* Hm.

73 A] Ac a R; But a F; And Y. Cachepol] chacchepol BmBo. craked] cragged Cr. hir] hise Y; the Cr.

74 hir] YHmGOC^{2}CBLMRF; þe WCr. of(1)] for Y. eiþer of] *om* B. þo] tho two HmB; þe C^{2}CF.

75 Ac] ac þer B; But GC^2; But *þere* F; And CrC. boy] HmCrYOC^{2}CBmBoLMRF; body WGCot. goddes] crystis F.

76 foryaf] forȝaft B. þrowe] FR (r *above line another script* R); tyme WHmCrGYOC^{2}CBLM.

77 leyen] leynd F. hond] an hand RBo (*corrected* Bo); hondys F. vpon] on F.

78 Ac] but GC^{2}F; And CrC. ygrounde] ygrounden O; grounde BCrF.

79 Highte] he hyȝghte F; þat hiȝte B. Longeus] Longeys F; Lo*n*gis Cr.

80 Bifore] ⁊ byfore F.

81 Maugree] ⁊ mawgre FB. his manye] manye of his F; hys GBmCot; he Bo.

82 To take þe spere in his hond and Iusten wiþ I*es*us WHmCrGYOC^{2}CBLMRF (take] taken M. þe] þat Hm; his Cr. Iusten] iuste OC^{2}R. I*es*us] Iesu G; I*es*us þere F).

83 were] weren HmGOBmBoF. houed] houede*n* OHm. þer or] on horse or WHmCrLMRF; on hors ⁊ GYOC^{2}CB. stode] stoden O; stede RF.

To touchen hym or to tasten hym or taken doun of roode, |
But þis blynde bacheler baar hym þoruȝ þe herte. *fol.* 109 *b*
The blood sprong doun by þe spere and vnspered [his] eiȝen.
Thanne fil þe knyȝt vpon knees and cryde [Iesu] m*er*cy:
'Ayein my wille it was, lord, to wownde yow so soore.'
He sighed and seide, 'soore it me aþynkeþ!
For þe dede þ*a*t I haue doon I do me in youre g*r*ace.
Haue on me ruþe, riȝtful I*es*u;' and riȝt wiþ þat he wepte.
Thanne gan Feiþ felly þe false Iewes despise;
Callede hem caytyues, acorsed for euere.
'For þis foule vileynye vengeaunce to yow falle!
To do þe blynde bete [þe dede], it was a boyes counseille.
Cursede cayt[yues]! knyghthood was it neu*er*e
To [bete a body ybounde wiþ any briȝt wepene].
The gree ȝit haþ he geten for al his grete wounde,
For youre champion chiualer, chief knyȝt of yow alle,
ȝilt hym recreaunt re[m]yng, riȝt at I*es*us wille.
For be þis derknesse ydo deeþ worþ [yvenquisshed];

84 touchen] touche OCrLRF. hym(1)] *om* CrRF. to] *om* GYOC^{2}CBM. tasten] taste CrOLRF. taken] take HmGOLRF. doun] hym downe GYOC^{2}CBLRF. of] of þe BF; on C.

85 baar] þat bare RF; þanne bar HmGYOC^{2}CBL.

86 The] þat BoCot. sprong] span F; ran B. vnspered] opned RF. his] CrGYOC^{2}CB; þe knyȝtes WHmLMRF.

87 fil] falle C^{2}. knees] his knees HmCr^{23}C^{2}B. Iesu] i*es*u R; c*ri*st F; hym WHmCrGYOC^{2}CBLM.

88 Ayein] For ageyn F. lord] *om* F.

89 He] How he C; and he B; full sore he Hm. and] ofte ⁊ F. soore] ful sore B; and ful sore Hm. it me] me it Hm. aþynkeþ] forthinketh Cr.

90 do] putte Hm.

91 Iesu] I*esus* G; c*ri*st F.

92 felly] ful felly F. þe] ⁊ the G.

93 Callede] and kallid B; he callyd F. hem] hem all F. acorsed] ycursed G; cursid Hm; ⁊ he cursede F. for] hem for RF.

94 vileynye] vilenyȝe shal be F. falle] alle YCrOCBLMRF.

95 do] do d Bo. bete] beety*n* F. þe dede] hym ybounde WHmGYC^{2}CBLMR; him bou*n*d Cr; hym bounden O; ⁊ bynde F.

96 Cursede] foule cursyd Hm; A ȝee *curse* F. caytyues] OHmCrBRF; caytif WGYC^{2}CLM. knyghthood] knighode Cr^{1}; castyng knyȝthood O.

97 To mysdo a deed body by daye or by nyȝte WHmCrGYOC^{2}CBLMRF (or] nor Cr; ne M).

98 The] ⁊ þe F; þre B. gree] grythe C. ȝit...he] hath he ȝit F. ȝit] ye C. geten] genten BmBo. wounde] wounbe BmBo; wombe Cot.

99 youre] *om* Hm. chief] ⁊ chef F.

100 ȝilt] ȝeldeþ F. remyng] rennyng WCr^{3}YOC^{2}CBLMRF; rynnyng G; runnyng Cr^{12}; renegat Hm. at] as G; a F.

101 For] *om* Y. be] by Cr^{12}. þis] *om* C. ydo] do Cr^{1}. deeþ] FR; his deeþ WHmCrGYOC^{2}CBLM. yvenquisshed] Ivenkesched RF; avenged WHmCrGYOC^{2}CBLM.

And ye, lurdaynes, han ylost for lif shal haue þe maistrye;
And youre fraunchise þat fre was fallen is in þraldom;
And ye, cherles, and youre children cheue shulle [ye] neuere,
[Ne] haue lordshipe in londe ne no lond tilye,
But [as] barayne be and [by] vsurie [libben],
Which is lif þat oure lord in alle lawes acurseþ.
Now youre goode dayes arn doon as daniel prophecied;
Whan crist cam hir kyngdom þe crowne sholde [lese]:
Cum veniat sanctus sanctorum cessabit vnxio vestra.'
What for feere of þis ferly and of þe false Iewes
I drow me in þat derknesse to *descendit ad inferna*
And þere I sauȝ sooþly, *secundum scripturas*,
[Where] out of þe west coste a wenche as me þouȝte |
Cam walkynge in þe wey; to helleward she loked. *fol.* 110 *a*
Mercy highte þat mayde, a meke þyng wiþ alle,
A ful benigne burde and Buxom of speche.
Hir suster, as it semed, cam so[fte]ly walkynge
Euene out of þe Est and westward she lokede,
A comely creature [and a clene]; truþe she highte.
For þe vertue þat hire folwede afered was she neuere.

102 ye] þe C^2; *om* CB. han] arn Hm. ylost] lost HmCr.
103 is] it BmBo; *om* CotM. in] into C^{2}Cot; in his M.
104 ye] þe C^2. cherles] clerkes YCB. and] and alle Hm. children] chydrene G. cheue] cheven FCr. shulle] shullen M. ye] GHmYOC^{2}CBLMRF; you Cr; *om* W.
105 Ne] CrGYOC^{2}CBLMRF; To WHm. londe] honde YOC^{2}C. lond tilye] londys tylthe F.
106 as] al WHmCrGYOC^{2}CBLMR; al shal F. be] schall ȝe be Hm. by] Hm; ȝee F; *om* WCrGYOC^{2}CBLMR. libben] ȝowr lyf lede Hm; vsen WCrYOC^{2}CBLMR; to vsen G; shull vse F.
107 is] is þe HmB. þat] of F. acurseþ] acursyd HmB.
108 arn doon] erun doun Y.
109 crist cam] cam crist (*correct order noted*) Bm. hir] YCr^{23}OC^{2}CBL; þier G; þe R; of hir WHmCr^{1}M (of *above line* M); to his F. þe] ⁊ Cr^{23}GYOC^{2}CB; his F. sholde] he shuld F. lese] RF; cesse WHmCrGYOC^{2}BM; iesse C; *om* L.
109α *in margin* O. *veniat*] *venerit* CrM. *cessabit...vestra*] *om* RF. *cessabit*] *tunc cessabit* CrM. *vestra*] *vestra* ⁊*c* Hm.
110 þis] the Cr. þe] þo R.
111 in] to F. þat] a F; *om* Y. to] þat to F.
113 Where out] Out WHmCrGYOC^{2}CBLMRF. me] me son Bo.
114 walkynge] wandrynge B. in] by G. þe] þat R. to helleward] ⁊ to hell F.
116 of] *twice* Bo.
117 softely] BHmGOCLF; sofly R; sooþly WYC^{2}M; worthely Cr. walkynge] hire after F.
118 Euene] Eve F.
119 A] A ful WHmCrGYOC^{2}CBLMRF. comely] manli B; many C. and...truþe] truþe WHmCrGYOC^{2}CLMRF; treute Bm; treuli BoCot.
120 folwede] folweþ Hm; folwe F.

Whan þise maydenes mette, mercy and truþe,
Eiþer asked ooþer of þis grete wonder,
Of þe dyn and þe derknesse and how þe day rowed,
And which a light and a leme lay bifore helle.
'Ich haue ferly of þis fare, in feiþ', seide truþe,
'And am wendynge to wite what þis wonder meneþ.'
'Haue no m*er*ueille', quod m*er*cy; 'murþe it bitokneþ.
A maiden þat highte Marie, and moder wiþouten felyng
Of any kynnes creature, conceyued þoruȝ speche
And grace of þe holy goost; weex greet wiþ childe;
Wiþouten [wommene] wem into þis world broȝte hym.
And þ*a*t my tale be trewe I take god to witnesse.
Siþ þis barn was ybore ben xxx^{ti} wynter passed
Which deide and deeþ þoled þis day aboute mydday,
And þat is cause of þis clips þat closeþ now þe sonne,
In menynge þ*a*t man shal fro merknesse be drawe
The while þis light and þis leme shal Lucifer ablende.

121 Whan] And whan RF. mette] metten OBF. truþe] trowe (*corrected*) Bm.
122 wonder] m*er*ueille MCr (*over erasure* M).
123 Of] And of Y. dyn] dymme Hm. þe(2)] GYC^{2}CBmBoF; of þe WCrOCot LMR; of þe grete Hm. how] why F. rowed] raued Cr^1; renned Cr^{23}; so lowred F.
124 which] what Cr^3; swich RF. a(2)] *om* Hm.
125 fare in] *om* Cr^1. in feiþ] forsoþe Hm.
126 am...to] *þus* y wende for to F. wendynge] wyndinge C^{2}Y. þis] þ*a*t F. wonder] wonde R.
127 murþe] for m*er*the F; trewþe Hm. bitokneþ] bitokne C.
128 maiden] maide C^{2}CrGRF. highte] hattiþ BmBo. outen] oute GHmCrYC^2 LMR.
129 any] mannys B. kynnes] kyn Hm; kende RF; skynnes BmBo. creature] creature she F.
130 And] ⁊ þorghȝ F; þoro B (*altered from* þe Bm). weex] wexed G; she wex BF.
131 outen] oute GCrYC^2; outem C. wommene wem] we*m*me of ma*n* C^2; we*m*me GOBm; wembe CrY (be *cancelled* Y); wem WHmCLMRF; he*m*me BoCot. to] *om* GY. broȝte] she broȝte WCrGYOC^{2}CBLMR; sche hym brouhte Hm; a kaue child she broghte F. hym] hym forþ O; *om* HmF.
133 Siþ] Sit C; Siþee Bm; ⁊ sytthe F. ybore] born HmCrGYOC^{2}CBLMRF. ben] ys F. xxx^{ti}] xx^{ti} F. wynter] wynters G; *om* F. passed] ypassed F.
134 deeþ] *om* YOCB. aboute] abowty*n* F.
135 clips] enclypse Hm. closeþ] closed Cr. þe] so þe F.
136 fro] for BoCot. merknesse] merk- *over erasure* Hm; derknesse F; mekenesse B. be] is BmBo; *om* Cot. drawe] drawe*n* CrM.
137 while] whiche HmCrMF (? *over erasure* M). þis(*both*)] *om* F. þis(1)] þe BoCot. shal Lucifer] lucyfer shal F. ablende] bleenden F; ablynd GCr^3; blynde Y.

For patriarkes and prophetes han preched herof ofte
That man shal man saue þoruȝ a maydenes helpe,
And þat was tynt þoruȝ tree, tree shal it wynne.
And þat deeþ adown brouȝte, deeþ shal releue.'
'That þow tellest', quod Truþe, 'is but a tale of waltrot! |
For Adam and Eue and Abraham wiþ oþere *fol.* 110 *b*
Patriarkes and prophetes þat in peyne liggen,
Leue þow neuere þat yon light hem alofte brynge
Ne haue hem out of helle; hold þi tonge, mercy!
It is trufle þat þow tellest; I, truþe, woot þe soþe,
For þat is ones in helle out comeþ [it] neuere.
Iob þe [parfit] patriark repreueþ þi sawes:
Quia in Inferno nulla est redempcio.'
Thanne Mercy ful myldely mouþed þise wordes,
'Thoruȝ experience', quod [heo], 'I hope þei shul be saued;
For venym fordooþ venym, [þer fecche I euydence
That Adam and Eue haue shul bote].
For of alle venymes foulest is þe scorpion;

138 han] hand C. preched] prechen C^{2}. her] þ*er* G; it Cr^{23}. of] on O; *om* CrB. ofte] often CrGYOC^{2}CBLMRF.

139 man shal] a man sholde F. maydenes] maiden BmBo; maydes Cot; womans Cr^{1}.

140 was] ther was Hm. tynt] tyne Cr^{23}. tree(*both*)] a tree F. shal] sholde F. it] *om* Hm.

141 adown] doun HmCrGYOC^{2}CBLM RF. shal] sholde F.

142 That] Al þis F. Truþe] *om* C. is] it is HmYC^{2}CBmBo. tale of] *twice* C; taile BmBo. waltrot] walter hod F; *om* C.

143 and(2)] *om* CrM. wiþ] and CrGMF.

144 þat] yet Cr^{1}.

145 Leue] Beleeve F. þow] *om* O. yon] yonder G; you Cr^{1}; þou C^{2}. hem] shal hem F; them may Cr; *om* GYOC^{2}CB. alofte] alofte shall GYC^{2}CB; alofte schal hem O.

146 haue] heue Y. hem] hym BoCot; *om* O. hold] helde L. þi...mercy] styll mercy þyn tunge F.

147 is] ys a G; is but R; is but a WHmCr YOC^{2}CBLM; yt but F. trufle] trewfelis F. I] *om* RF.

148 For] CrGYOC^{2}CBLMR; For he W HmF. is ones] oones is F. it] YGOC BLMR; he WHmCrC^{2}F.

149 parfit] prophete WHmCrGYOC^{2}CB LMRF. patriark] and patriark CotF; and patriak Bo; and propatriak Bm; patriarkes Cr^{1}. repreueþ] repugneth Cr. þi] þi thy M; þise B. sawes] lawes Hm.

149α *in margin* O. *redempcio*] redem *redempcio* Y; *redempcio &c* HmBoCot.

150 myldely] mekelye Cr.

151 quod] qud quod (*corrected*) Bo. heo] he Cr^{1}RF; she WHmCr^{23}GYOC^{2}CBLM. þei] þow R; I Cr^{3}F. shul] schalt R.

152 þer...euydence] and that y preue by resoun HmCrGYOC^{2}CBmLMRF; and þat preue I by reson WCot; and þat proue be resoun Bo.

153 *not in* WHmCrGYOC^{2}CBLMRF.

154 venymes] venym YOCB. scorpion] scorpiom BmBo.

May no medicyne [amende] þe place þer he styngeþ
Til he be deed and do *per*to; þe yuel he destruyeþ,
The first venymouste, þoruȝ [vertu] of hymselue.
So shal þis deeþ fordo, I dar my lif legge,
Al þat deeþ [d]ide first þoruȝ þe deueles entisyng,
And riȝt as [þe gilour] þoruȝ gile [bigiled man formest]
So shal gr*ac*e that bigan [al] make a good [ende
And bigile þe gilour, and þat is good] sleighte:
Ars vt artem falleret.'
'Now suffre we', seide Truþe; 'I se, as me þynkeþ,
Out of þe nyppe of þe North noȝt ful fer hennes
Rightwisnesse come rennynge; reste we þe while,
For he[o] woot moore þan we; he[o] was er we boþe.'
'That is sooþ', seide Mercy, 'and I se here by Sowþe
Where pees comeþ pleyinge in pacience ycloþed.
Loue haþ coueited hire longe; leue I noon ooþer
But [loue] sente hire som lettre what þis light bymeneþ
That ouerhoueþ helle þus; she vs shal telle.' |
Whan Pees in Pacience ycloþed app*ro*ched ner hem
tweyne *fol.* 111 *a*

155 May] For þ*er*e may F. amende] helpe WHmCrGYOC^{2}CBLMRF. þer] þ*a*t Y. he] it O; *om* F.
156 he(1)] *om* G. deed] dey Y. to] do Y. he(2)] þ*an* he F.
157 The] Of þe F. venymouste] wenomythe G; venemeth C^{2}; venym CotF; venym most Y; venym is moost O; venime moyst Cr^{23}. vertu] v*er*tue RF; venym WHmCrGYOC^{2}CBLM.
158 deeþ] *om* Cr^{1}M. fordo] do RF. my] y Bo. legge] liegge Cot; ligge CrG.
159 dide] YCrGOCBLMF; dede C^{2}R; fordide W; fordede Hm. deueles] deuel Y; devely F. entisyng] te*m*ptyng F.
160 riȝt] *om* Cr^{3}. þe...formest] þoruȝ gile man was bigiled WHmCrGYOC^{2}CBLM RF.
161, 162 So shal gr*ac*e þat bigan make a good sleighte WHmCrGYOC^{2}CBLMRF (bigan] all bigan C^{2}; he gan F. make] maken F. sleighte] sighte CB; seeþ (sighte *in margin*) O; ende YGC^{2}).
162α *in margin* O. *falleret*] *falleret &c* Hm GB; fallereth R.
163 we] me G. seide] q*uo*d F.
164 ful fer] farre from G.
165 come] cam YCr^{1}OC. þe] a HmB.
166 heo(*both*)] he WHmCrGYOC^{2}CBL MR; she F. woot] wotteth Cr.
167 seide] q*uo*d G. here] hir*e* Bo.
168 pees comeþ] cometh pes R. ycloþed] clothed CrC^{2}M.
169 leue] leege Bo; leigge Cot.
170 loue] he WHmCrGYOC^{2}CBLMRF. bymeneþ] bement C^{2}; meneth Cot.
171 That] What Cr^{1}. she] he RF. vs shal] shall vs GCot; shal vs all F.
172 ycloþed] clothed GOC^{2}RF; clothed thus Cr; is cloþid Hm; is ycloþid BmBo. app*ro*ched] app*ro*ochethe (*second* h *altered to* d) G. ner] neigh YCr^{23}GOC^{2}CB; *om* F. hem] hy*m* Bo. tweyne] two Hm.

Rightwisnesse hire reu*er*enced by hir riche cloþyng
And preide pees to telle hire to what place she wolde,
And in hire gaye garnement3 whom she grete þou3te.
'My wil is to wende', quod she, 'and welcome hem alle
That many day my3te I no3t se for merknesse of synne,
Adam and Eue and oþere mo in helle.
Moyses and many mo mer[ye] shul [synge];
[Thanne] I shal daunce þerto; do þow so suster.
For Ie*s*us Iustede wel Ioye bigynneþ dawe:
Ad vesperum demorabitur fletus & ad matutinum leticia.
Loue þat is my lemman swiche lettres me sente
That mercy, my suster, and I mankynde sholde saue,
And þat god haþ forgyuen and graunted me, pees, & m*er*cy
To be mannes meynp*ernour* for eueremoore after.
Lo! here þe patente', quod Pees, '*In pace in idipsum*,
And þ*at* þis dede shal dure *dormiam & requiescam*.'
'What, rauestow?' quod Rightwisnesse, 'or þow art right
dronke?
Leuestow þ*at* yond light vnlouke my3te helle
And saue mannes soule? suster, wene it neu*er*e.

173 Rightwisnesse] Rightfulnes Cr. hire] hy*m* C^2; hem YOCB. by] for CrGYOC^{2}CBLMRF. cloþyng] cloþis F.
174 telle] tellen Hm. she] he GRF (*corrected to* she *another ink* G).
175 garnement3] garment*es* GYR; germent Cr. she] he R; to F; so Cot. þou3te] he þowhte F.
176 is] his C; q*uod* he to F. wende] wynde C^2; wonde Y. quod she] *om* F. quod] quo C. she] he R. and] and to Cr. welcome] welcomyn Hm; welcomede O.
177 day] a day CrGC^{2}F. my3te] ny3te Bo. I] *om* CrYMF.
178 Adam] As Adam F. oþere] manye F. in] þat weren yn Hm.
179 Moyses] & Moyses F. many] oþ*er*e F. merye...synge] mercy shul haue WHmCr GYOC^{2}CBLMRF (shul] schullen HmB; shull þey F).
180 *line om* RF. Thanne] And WHmCr LM; *om* GYOC^{2}CB. þow] *om* G. so] also B.
181 *line om* GC^2. Iustede] haþ Iusted F; iusteth Cr. dawe] to dawe Cr^{3}OB.
181α *in margin* O; *line om* F. &] *om* Cr^1. *leticia*] *leticia &c* Hm; liticia C; *&c* Cot; *om* BmBo.
182 me] he me R.
183 my] *om* ORF. suster] *om* RF. sholde] schude C; shul Y. saue] saven F.
184 And] & how F. forgyuen] forgyue RF; foryeuen YHmC^{2}M.
185 meynp*ernour*] meynp*erour* C.
186 *idipsum*] *idipsum &c* Hm.
187 þis] þes G; is Cot; *om* Cr^{1}MF. dede] dedes G. dure] eu*er*e dure F; endure HmB.
188 Rightwisnesse] repentance G. þow art] art þou HmF. right] halfe G; y F. dronke] dronkyn HmO.
189 Leuestow] Beleevist þou F. þat] ***om*** GC^2. yond] 3onder HmGOB.
190 it] þow it RF.

[At] þe bigynn[yng god] gaf þe doom hymselue
That Adam and Eue and alle þat hem suwede
Sholden deye downrighte and dwelle in pyne after
If þ*at* þei touchede a tree and þe [trees] fruyt eten.
Adam afterward, ayeins his defence,
Freet of þat fruyt and forsook, as it weere,
The loue of oure lord and his loore boþe,
And folwede þat þe fend tauȝte and his [flesshes] wille
Ayeins Reson. [I], rightwisnesse, recorde þus wiþ truþe
That hir peyne be p*er*petuel and no preiere hem helpe. |
Forþi lat hem chewe as þei chosen and chide we noȝt,
sustres, *fol.* 111 *b*
For it is botelees bale, þe byte þat þei eten.'
'And I shal preue', quod Pees, 'hir peyne moot haue ende,
And wo into wele mowe wenden at þe laste.
For hadde þei wist of no wo, wele hadde þei noȝt knowen;
For no wight woot what wele is þat neu*er*e wo suffrede,
Ne what is hoot hunger þat hadde neu*er*e defaute.
If no nyȝt ne weere, no man as I leeue

191 At þe] OCrGYBLMR; Atte C; Ac atte þe Hm; at C^{2}; For at þe fyrste F; For god þe W. bigynnyng god] YHmCrOC^{2}CBLMRF; gynnyng god G; bigynner*e* W. gaf] yaf CC^{2}BM. þe(2)] *om* F.
192 suwede] sueden O; sulked C.
193 Sholden] sholde GCrYC^{2}LMR; Shul C. deye] dyȝen F. pyne] payne Cr^{3}C^{2}CBRF.
194 þat] *om* G. touchede] toucheden O. þe] of þe F. trees] Hm; *om* WCrGYOC^{2}CBLMRF. eten] eyte G.
195 Adam] and adam BF.
196 Freet] he freet F; Freted C^{2}. as it weere] goddis forboode F.
197 The] ⁊ þe F. of] *om* F. oure] your G.
198 tauȝte] hy*m* tolde F. flesshes] felawes WHmCrGYOC^{2}CBLMR; feerys F.
199 *line om* RF. I] L; and WHmCrGYOC^{2}CBM. rightwisnesse] riȝtfulnesse B. þus] þis G.
200 hem] may he*m* F; hym Cot.
201 Forþi] Therfore Cr. chewe] cheue Cr. chosen] chose HmCrYC^{2}CBmBoLMRF; choyse Cot; chase G. sustres] sustre GYOC^{2}CBF.
202 þe] they Cr^{1}. byte] bittes F. eten] byten Hm.
203 And] *om* F. I] *om* YLR. preue] preue it Y; preie RF. moot] schall Hm. ende] an ende CHmC^{2}BF.
204 wo] GYOC^{2}CBLMRF; from wo WHm; we Cr. mowe] mot MF; must Cr; shal B; mowyn Hm. wenden] wende HmCrGYOCBLMR; wedde C^{2}. þe] *om* Cr.
205 hadde þei] þey hadd (hadd *above line*) F; þei R. wele...noȝt] hadde þey no weele F. knowen] knowe HmCrRF.
206 woot] wotes Cr.
207 hoot] hot B; hote YCLR; whote Cr; wootte G. hadde neuere] neuer had CrGM.
208 If] For if F. nyȝt] might Cr^{1}. ne weere] nere CrMF; were Cot. as] is as CB. I] *cancelled* Y. leeue] *after cancelled* wene *main hand* G; beleve F; wene B; a lyue Y.

Sholde wite witterly what day is to meene.
Sholde neu*ere* riȝt riche man þat lyueþ in reste and ese
Wite what wo is, ne were þe deeþ of kynde.
So god þat bigan al of his goode wille
Bicam man of a mayde mankynde to saue
And suffrede to be sold to se þe sorwe of deying,
The which vnknytteþ alle care and comsynge is of reste.
For til *modicum* mete wi*th* vs, I may it wel auowe,
Woot no wight, as I wene, what [is ynogh] to mene.
Forþi god, of his goodnesse, þe firste gome Adam,
Sette hym in solace and in souereyn murþe,
And siþþe he suffred hym synne sorwe to feele,
To wite what wele was, kyndeliche [to] knowe it.
And after god Auntrede hymself and took Adames kynd[e]
To [se] what he haþ suffred in þre sondry places,
Boþe in heuene and in erþe, and now til helle he þenkeþ
To wite what alle wo is [þat woot of] alle ioye.
So it shal fare by þis folk: hir folie and hir synne
Shal lere hem what langour is and lisse wiþouten ende.
Woot no wight what werre is þer þat pees regneþ,

209 wite] YCrGOC^{2}CBLMR; weten F; neu*ere* wite WHm.
210 man] *om* Hm. lyueþ] lyve F. and] and yn Hm; *om* C^{2}.
211 Wite] Wety*n* F. what] where G. is] is ne wele BC.
212 goode] godde Bo.
213 Bicam] and bicam B. mayde] mayden OC.
214 And] ⁊ he F. suffrede] suffer Cr^{23}R. to(2)] and RF. se] *om* Cr^{1}M.
215 comsynge] bigynny*n*ge C^{2}.
216 mete] mette HmGYOBRF; met CrC. wi*th*] mid Cr^{1}. vs] hym Cr^{23}O.
217 is ynogh] is ynowȝ C^{2}CrGOCBLM; ynogh is WHm; is ynought Y; is nouȝte R; it is F. mene] name G.
218 Forþi] Therfore Cr. of his] his of (*correct order noted*) BmBo.
219 Sette] he sette F. in(2)] in a F. murþe] ioye RF.
220 he] *om* C^{2}. hym] hem Hm. synne] synnen F. sorwe] sorowes G.
221 To] ⁊ GC^{2}. was] was ⁊ G; is R; ys ⁊ F. to] HmCrYOCBLMRF; and W; *om* GC^{2}. knowe] knowen C. it] *om* CB.
222 Auntred] graunted GYOC^{2}CB. kynde] HmYOC^{2}CBLMRF; kynd WG Cr (? *cropped* W).
223 se] wite WHmCrGYOC^{2}CBLMRF. haþ] had Cr^{23}; *om* F. þre] þe GYC; *om* B. places] place Y.
224 and(2)] *om* Y. now] *om* Cr. til] to CrOC^{2}MF.
225 þat...of] OCrYC^{2}CBLMRF; þ*at* woote what G; and what is WHm. ioye] Ioy ys G.
226 So] *om* Hm. hir(1)] þ*at* her C^{2}.
227 *run together with* 228 F. lere] leeren G; lerne CrF. hem] hym BmBo. and... ende] *om* F. lisse] lyfe Cr; blysse GYR. outen] out Cr.
228 Woot...is] *om* F. Woot] whatt G.

Ne what is witterly wele til weylawey hym teche.' |
Thanne was þer a wight wiþ two brode eiȝen; *fol.* 112 *a*
Book highte þat beaupeere, a bold man of speche.
'By goddes body', quod þis book, 'I wol bere witnesse
That þo þis barn was ybore þer blased a sterre
That alle þe wise of þis world in o wit acor[de]den
That swich a barn was ybore in Bethleem þe Citee
That mannes soule sholde saue and synne destroye.
And alle þe elementȝ', quod þe book, 'herof beren witnesse.
That he was god þat al wroȝte þe wolkne first shewed:
[The oostes] in heuene token *stella com*[*a*]*ta*
And tendeden [hire] as a torche to reuerencen his burþe;
The light folwede þe lord into þe lowe erþe.
The water witnesse[þ] þ*a*t he was god for he wente on it;
Peter þe Apostel parceyued his gate,
And as he wente on þe water wel hym knew and seide,
"*Iube me venire ad te super aquas.*"
And lo! how þe sonne gan louke hire light in hirselue
Whan she seiȝ hym suffre þat sonne and see made.
The Erþe for heuynesse þ*a*t he wolde suffre

229 Ne] & F. til] *om* F. hym teche] shal hy*m* techen F.
230 two] tweyn F.
231 bold] bol Cot.
232 goddes body] my Fethe C^2.
233 ybore] born OCrGYC^2.
234 wise] wise me*n* Cr; men RF. of] in RF. þis] þe Hm. acordeden] OLR; acorded Hm; acorden WCrGYC^2CBMF.
235 ybore] born HmCrGYOC^2CBL. Bethleem] Bethlems Cr. þe] *om* HmCr GYOC^2CBLMF.
236 That] and þat C^2. and] & sori F.
237 *line om* C. quod] saith Cr. beren] bere C^2; iberiþ F.
238 was] is F. first] first he F. shewed] schewyn C^2.
239 The oostes] Tho þat weren WHmCr GYOC^2CBLMRF (Tho] & þo F. þat] ther Cr^1. weren] were CrG). *comata*] Cr^1YOC^2CBLMRF (*at over erasure* M); *cometa* WHmCr^{23}G.
240 tendeden] tendid CotF. hire] HmCr GYOC^2CBLMRF; it W. as] *om* O. reuerencen] reu*er*ence HmCrGYOC^2CCot LF. his] hyr G.
241 The] & þ*a*t F. þe(1)] our*e* F.
242 The] that þe GC^2; that HmYCBLM. witnesseþ] YGOC^2BRF; witnessed WHm CrLM; witnesse C. þat] *om* Cr^3. for] for þat Cr^3; þat G. it] *om* G.
243 Peter] Sey*n*t Peet*er* F. parceyued] aparceyuede F; parceyue B.
244 as] whan F; *om* C. he] hey Bo. wente] seyȝ F. þe] þat R. water] wate C. wel...knew] he knew hy*m* wel F. hym knew] he hym knew HmBmBo; knewe him C^2; knewe he hym G.
244α *in margin* O. *venire ad te*] *ad te venire* Hm. *aquas*] *aquas &c* HmB.
245 And] *om* C^2. sonne] lyght G. louke] loke RF; lacke Cr. hire] þe G. light] lygh C^2. hir] hym G.
246 she] he G. see] mone RF.
247 heuynesse] buxomnesse CB.

Quaked as quyk þyng and al biquasshed þe roche.
Lo! helle my3te nat holde, but opnede þo god þolede,
And leet out Symondes sone[s] to seen hym hange on roode.
And now shal Lucifer leue it, þou3 hym looþ þynke.
For [Iesus as a] geaunt wiþ a gyn [comeþ yonde]
To breke and to bete adoun [alle] þat ben ayeins [hym],
[And to haue out of helle alle þat hym likeþ].
And I, book, wole be brent but I*es*us rise to lyue
In alle my3tes of man and his moder gladie,
And conforte al his kyn and out of care brynge,
And al þe Iewene Ioye vnioynen and vnlouken; |
And but þei reu*er*[en]sen his roode and his Resurexion *fol.* 112 *b*
And bileue on a newe lawe be lost, lif and soule.'
'Suffre we', seide truþe; 'I here and see boþe
A spirit spekeþ to helle and biddeþ vnspere þe yates:
Attollite portas.
A vois loude in þat light to lucifer crieþ,
"Prynces of þis place, vnpynneþ and vnloukeþ,

248 as] as a CotF. biquasshed] biquasche RF; besquate C^{2}; byquassethe G; toquassed Cr; to clief B.
249 helle] heue*n* Cr^{1}. my3te] ne mygth Hm. nat] not hy*m* F. þo] þ*er* GC^{2}. god] c*r*ist F.
250 leet] leety*n* F. sones] OCrGC^{2}CLM RF; sone WHmB; *om* Y.
251 leue] leyue leaue (leaue *cancelled*) G; leese F; *om* R. hym] hyn G.
252 *line om* RF. For] *om* BoCot. Iesus as a] *gigas* þe WHmCrGYOC^{2}CBmLM; fi gigas þe Bo; figigat the Cot. gyn] synne Hm. comeþ yonde] engyned HmCrGY OC^{2}CBLM; haþ engyned W.
253 *line om* RF. adoun] downe CrGL. alle...hym] þat ben ayeins I*es*us WHmCr GYOC^{2}CBLM.
254 *not in* WHmCrGYOC^{2}CBLMRF.
256 alle] al þe F. of] of a RF. gladie] gladen C^{2}.
257 conforte] conforten CrHmM. his] *om* Y. care] car*e* hem F.
258 vnioynen] vnioyne CrO; vnloken GC^{2}; to Ioyneen F. vnlouken] vnlowke HmO; vnbynden GC^{2}; to lowke F.
259 but] but if CrMF. þei] þe G. reuer*e*nsen] MHmYLR (*over erasure* M); reuer*e*nce Cr^{23}GOC^{2}CBF; reu*er*sen W; reuerse Cr^{1}.
260 bileue] leue O; leuen GYC^{2}CB. a] the Cot. newe] knewe Bo. be] þey been F. *Hereafter an additional line* GYOC^{2}CB; *see above*, p. 223.
261 we] *om* F. see] I se Cr.
262 A] RF; How a WHmCrGYOC^{2}CB LM. spekeþ] speked Cr^{23}. biddeþ] byt HmCrGYOC^{2}BLMR. vnspere] vspere Bo.
262α *in margin* O; *as one line with* 263 RF. *Attollite*] *Tollite* F. *portas*] RF; *portas &c* WCr^{1}YOC^{2}CBLM; *porta &c* Cr^{23}; *portas principes vestras &c* HmG.
263 loude] ful lowde Hm; *om* F. crieþ] cryed GOC; sayd Cr^{23}.
264 Prynces] 3ee p*r*inces F. of] in Cr. þis] þe Hm. vnpynneþ] oppeneþ O; vnbyndeth C^{2}. vnloukeþ] vnlouken C.

For here comeþ wiþ crowne þat kyng is of glorie." '
Thanne sikede Sathan and seide to he[l]le,
'Swich a light, ayeins oure leue laȝar [i]t fette.
Care and [c]ombraunce is comen to vs alle.
If þis kyng come In mankynde wole he fecche
And lede it þer [laȝar is] and lightliche me bynde.
Patriarkes and *pro*phetes han parled herof longe
That swich a lord and [a] light sholde lede hem alle hennes.'
'Listneþ!' quod lucifer, 'for I þis lord knowe;
Boþe þis lord and þis light, is longe ago I knew hym.
May no deeþ [þis lord] dere, ne no deueles queyntise,
And where he wole is his wey; ac ware hym of þe *per*ils:
If he reu[e] me my riȝt he robbeþ me by maistrie.
For by right and by reson þe renkes þat ben here
Body and soule beþ myne, boþe goode and ille.
For hymself seide, þat Sire is of heuene,
If Adam ete þe Appul alle sholde deye
And dwelle wiþ vs deueles; þis þretynge [driȝten] made.
And [siþen] he þat Sooþnesse is seide þise wordes,

265 here] he G. þat] the HmF. is] þ*at* is F; *om* Hm.
266 sikede] seyde F. and] soone & F. to] þus to F. helle] RF; hem alle WHmCr GYOC^{2}CBLM.
267 leue] loue BoCot. it] HmGYOC^{2}C LMRF; out WCr; is B.
268 combraunce] HmCrGYOC^{2}CLMRF; encombraunce WB. comen] come GYC^2 CR.
270 lede] do O. it] hem RF. laȝar is] R F; hym likeþ WHmCrGYOC^{2}CCotLM; hym lif likiþ (lif *cancelled*) Bm; hy likiþ Bo. me] vs GC^2. bynde] bynde*n* C^{2}F.
271 han] þan F; har C^2. parled] proled Cr^1. her] þ*er* G. longe] *corrected from* loude L; loude Bo.
272 a(2)] CrGYOCBLMRF; *om* WHmC^2. light] lighe Cr^2. sholde] schal RF; shol C. hem] hym BmBo. alle hennes] fra*m* þese woones F.
273 quod] now quod B.
274 þis(*both*)] þe F. is] it is BF. hym] hem CotF; it HmCr; *om* Y.
275 þis lord] þis lorde RF; hym WHmCr GYOC^{2}CBLM. deueles] fendes Cr^{1}M.
276 And] ac Hm. wole] wolde Bo. is his] his is Bo; is R. ac] but GC^{2}F; & CrC. ware] warne Cr. *per*ils] *per*eyl F.
277 reue] HmCrGOBLMRF; reueþ WY C^2; reuees C. me(1)] me of CrRF; *om* C. he robbeþ] & robbe RF. by] wi*th* G.
278 For] *om* GC^2. by(2)] *om* YOC^{2}CBF. þe] tho GYOC^{2}LM. renkes] reukes Cr; freikis B. ben here] ich haue O.
279 and(1)] *twice* Bo. beþ] þey ben F. ille] euil Cr.
280 *line om* GYOC^{2}CB. þat Sire] so þat syre þat F.
281 If] þat ȝif RF. þe Appul] *om* R. alle] ap*er*tly he F. sholde] schulden O; shull C^2.
282 dwelle] dwelly*n* heer*e* F. deueles] *om* F. þretynge] þreteny*n*ge FCrB. driȝten] he WHmCrGYOC^{2}CBLMRF.
283 siþen he] he WHmCrGYOC^{2}CBL MF; *om* R. þise] to hy*m* þese F.

And siþen I [was] seised seuene [þousand] wynter
I leeue þ*at* lawe nyl no3t lete hym þe leeste.'
'That is sooþ', seide Sathan, 'but I me soore drede, |
For þow gete hem wiþ gile and his Gardyn breke, *fol.* 113 *a*
And in semblaunce of a serpent sete vpon þe Appultree
And eggedest hem to ete, Eue by hirselue,
And toldest hire a tale, of treson were þe wordes;
And so þow haddest hem out and hider at þe laste.'
'It is no3t graiþly geten þer gile is þe roote,
For god wol no3t be bigiled', quod Gobelyn, 'ne byiaped.
We haue no trewe title to hem, for þoru3 treson were þei
    dampned.'
'Certes I drede me', quod þe deuel, 'lest truþe [do] hem fecche.
Thise þritty wynter, as I wene, [he wente aboute] and p*re*ched.
I haue assailled hym *with* synne and som tyme yasked
Wheiþ*er* he were god or goddes sone; he [g]af me short
    answer*e*;
And þus haþ he trolled forþ [lik a tidy man] þise two and
    þritty wynter.

284 And] And I R; *om* F. I was] y was F; I WHmLMR; is YGOC^{2}; he CrCB. seised] sesed F; seased Cr; sessed R; ysesid O; yseisd Y; ysayde G. seuene] þis seuene F; þise seue R; many YO. þousand] hundred WHmCrOC^{2}BF; hundreþ YGCLR; hundre M. wynter] wynters G.
285 þat] *twice* GC^{2}. nyl] wil BGOF. lete] leten C^{2}G; leaue Cr; leuen M.
286 seide] quod Cr. me] *om* F.
287 gete hem] hem gete (hem *above line*) M. gete] gatist B. hem] *by correction* Hm; him C^{2}CBo. Gardyn] graden Cr^{2}. breke] brakest G.
288 semblaunce] semblant GC^{2}BF; semulaunt O; liknees C. serpent] Nedder C. sete] þou seete FHm; sattest G. vpon] on HmGYOC^{2}CBLRF.
289 eggedest] eggest GYC. hem] him C^{2}Cot. ete] ete þerof B; eyte and G. hir] hym F. selue] name Cr.
290 were] weren O. þe] thy Cr.
291 so] al so RF. hem] hym B. þe] *om* G.
292 graiþly] trewly C^{2}. geten] gete RF; gayten Cr. gile] gele BmBo.
293 be bigiled] gyled bee F. be] be nou3t (*corrected*) C. byiaped] be iapyd HmCr^{12}C^{2}CotMRF; Iaped Cr^{3}.
294 title] tilyle R. for] *om* GF. þoru3] bi Cr; *with* B. treson] resou*n* F. were] were*n* OM.
295 drede me] me dred Cr^{1}; dread Cr^{23}. þe] this Cr^{23}GYOC^{2}. do] wol WHmCrGYOC^{2}CBLMRF. hem] hy*m* B. *Hereafter an additional line* Cr^{23}GYOC^{2}CB; *see above*, p. 224.
296 wene] leue BmBo; lyue Cot. he...aboute] RF; haþ he gon WHmGYOC^{2}CBL; he hath gone CrM. and] *om* Cr^{1}.
297 assailled] asayed F; assoiled YC. tyme] *om* RF. yasked] asked CrGC^{2}B; y have hy*m* asked F.
298 Wheiþ*er*] Wher HmCrGYOC^{2}CBLMRF. goddes] goodes C. gaf] HmCrGYCLR; yaf WOC^{2}BMF. short] scorte C^{2}; scorth Bo.
299 haþ he] he hath CrRF; hathe G. trolled] tollid BoCot. forþ...man] forþ WHmCrGYOC^{2}CBLMRF. wynter] wynters G.

And whan I sei3 it was so, [s]lepynge I wente
To warne Pilates wif what done man was I*es*us,
For Iewes hateden hym and han doon hym to deþe.
I wolde haue lengþed his lif, for I leued if he deide
That his soule wolde suffre no synne in his sighte;
For þe body, while it on bones yede, aboute was eu*ere*
To saue men from synne if hemself wolde.
And now I se wher a soule comeþ [silynge hiderward]
Wiþ glorie and w*ith* gret light; god it is, I woot wel.
I rede we fle', quod [þe fend], 'faste alle hennes,
For vs were bettre no3t be þan biden his sighte.
For þi lesynges, Lucifer, lost is al oure praye.
First þoru3 þe we fellen fro heuene so hei3e:
For we leued þi lesynges [we lopen out alle;
And now for þi laste lesynge] ylorn we haue Adam,
And al oure lordshipe, I leue, a londe and [in helle]:
Nunc princeps huius mundi e[i]icietur foras.'
Eft þe light bad vnlouke and Lucifer answerde

300 slepynge] OCr^{23}GYC^{2}CBmCotLM RF (s *erased* M); lepynge WHmCr^{1}; sepynge Bo.
301 warne] wrne C. done...I*es*us] was w*ith* *crist* to doone F. done] doones GOL (n *altered to* m *another ink* G); doynge C^{2}; dene B.
302 For] for þe GF. hateden] hated Cr^{23} CF; haten Cr^{1}.
303 I(1)] And I RF. lengþed] lenged YC^{2} CCot. leued] leue RF.
304 soule] soulde Cr^{2}. wolde] shuld Cr; nolde Hm. suffre] nau3t suffre RF.
305 while...bones] þ*at* above F. aboute] abouten OF.
306 saue] saven F. men] man Cr. hem] him Cr. self] selfien(?) (ien *cancelled*) O. wolde] wolden O.
307 silynge hiderward] hiderward seillynge WHmGCBLMF; hitherward saili*ng* Cr YOC^{2}R.
308 glorie] *gloria* F; Ioie C. w*ith*] *om* ORF. light] lygh C^{2}. god...wel] y knowe *crist* is his name F.
309 we] HmCrGYOC^{2}CLMRF; þ*at* we WB. þe fend] he WHmCrGYOC^{2}CBL MRF. alle] away G.
310 vs] we F. no3t] her*e* not F. biden] abyde Cr; to abiden B. his] in his F.
311 praye] tr*a*uayle F.
312 þoru3...fellen] we fylle þorgh3 þe F. fellen] felle RCr; fallen Bo.
313 *run together with* 314 WHmCrGYOC^{2} CBLM. we] þ*at* we (þ*at above line*) G. leued] leueden O; beleued Cr; belevedyn F; lyuyden Hm; loueden B. þi] GHmY OC^{2}CBmLMRF; þise BoCot; on þi WCr. we(2)...alle] we loopen out all F; we loupen oute alle with þe R; *om* WHm CrGYOC^{2}CBLM.
314 And...lesynge] And now for thi last lesynge RF; *om* WHmCrGYOC^{2}CBLM. ylorn] lore C^{2}. we haue] haue we RF.
315 lordshipe] lordships Cr^{12}; lordche F. in helle] on watre HmCrGOC^{2}BMF; a watre WYCLR.
315α *in margin* O. *huius mundi*] *mundi huius* R. *eiicietur*] Cr; *eicietur* WHmGOC^{2} CLMF; *eicitur* YBR. *foras*] &c Hm; *om* BoCot.
316 light] lygh C^{2}. vnlouke] vnlouken Y.

[‘*Quis est iste?*
What lord artow?’ quod Lucifer; | þe light soone seide *fol.* 113 *b*
‘*Rex glorie*,]
[The] lord of myght and of ma[y]n and alle manere vertues,
Dominus virtutum.
Dukes of þis dymme place, anoon vndo þise yates
That crist may come In, þe kynges sone of heuene!’
And wiþ þat breeþ helle brak with Belialles barres;
For any wye or warde wide opned þe yates.
Patriarkes and prophetes, *populus in tenebris*,
Songen seint Iohanes song, *Ecce agnus dei*.
Lucifer loke ne myȝte, so light hym ablente.
And þo þat oure lord louede into his light he laughte,
And seide to Sathan, ‘lo! here my soule to amendes
For alle synfulle soules, to saue þo þat ben worþi.
Myne þei ben and of me; I may þe bet hem cleyme.
[Al]þouȝ Reson recorde, and riȝt of myselue,
That if [þei] ete þe Appul alle sholde deye,
I bihiȝte hem noȝt here helle for euere.

316α–18 *as two lines divided after iste* RF.
316α–17α *as two lines divided after* iste WHmCrGYOC^{2}CBLM. What lord artow quod Lucifer *Quis est iste Rex glorie* þe light soone seide WHmCrGYOC^{2}CBLMRF (*Rex*...seide] þe Lyght seyde *Rex eterne* F. light] lygh C^{2}. soone] *om* R).
318 *as one line with* 318α WOC^{2}CBmBoL. The] þe RF; And WHmCrGYOC^{2}CLM; and a B. myght...and(2)] *om* F. of(2)] *om* O. mayn] HmCrGYOC^{2}CCotLM; man WR; mani BmBo (n *altered to* y Bm).
318α *line om* YF; *as one line with* 319 R. *virtutum*] *virtutum &c* G; *fortis & potens dominus virtutum ipse est rex glorie &c* Hm.
319 Dukes] Duk R; þou dewk F. þise] the Cr^{1}M; ȝeise O.
320–2 *lines om and supplied by correction*: 320 *in paragraph space after* 319; 321, 322 *at foot of page after* 331 M.
320 þe] *om* R. *Hereafter two Latin lines* Hm; *see above*, p. 224.
321 brak] braste RF. with] & F. Belialles] belial YOC. barres] berres Y.
322 wye] wey C^{2}; weey F; wysse G. opned] openeden F; open CrGYOC^{2}CBLM.
323 *populus*] and *populus* F.
324 Songen] Singing Cr^{1}. Iohanes] Iohan YBmBo; Iesus Cr^{1}.
325 Lucifer] þan Lucifer F. loke] lokene C^{2}. ablente] ablyndyde C; ablynde BoCot.
326 lord] *om* L. he] *om* Cr^{1}. laughte] tooke C.
327 soule] soulis BoCot. amendes] amende C^{2}G.
328 saue] saven F. þo] hem F; *om* Cr^{1}CotM. þat...worþi] fram peyȝne F.
329 bet] better CrGC^{2}CB.
330 Al] CrGOC^{2}BLMF; Alle YCR; And WHm. recorde] recor BmBo. riȝt] myght Cr^{23}. selue] seluen O.
331 That if þei] If þey þat F. þei] GCrYOC^{2}CBLMR; he WHm. ete] eeten OBF. sholde] schulden OB. deye] dyȝen F.
332 hem] hym BmBo; *om* Cot.

For þe dede þat þei dide, þi deceite it made;
Wiþ gile þow hem gete ageyn alle reson.
For in my paleis, Paradis, in p*er*sone of an Addre
Falsliche þow fettest þyng þat I louede.
Thus ylik a Lusard wiþ a lady visage
Thefliche þow me robbedest; þe olde lawe graunteþ
That gilours be bigiled and þat is good reson:
Dentem pro dente & oculum pro oculo.
Ergo soule shal soule quyte and synne to synne wende,
And al þat man haþ mysdo I man wole amende.
Membre for membre [was amendes by þe olde lawe],
And lif for lif also, and by þat lawe I clayme
Adam and al his issue at my wille herafter;
And þat deeþ in hem fordide my deeþ shal releue |
And boþe quykne and quyte þat queynt was þoruȝ synne; *fol.* 114 *a*
And þat gr*ac*e gile destruye good feiþ it askeþ.
So leue [it] noȝt, lucifer, ayein þe lawe I fecche hem,
But by right and by reson raunsone here my liges:
Non veni soluere legem set adimplere.

333 þe] þei Bo. dede] dyede C. dide] diden OF.

334 gete] gatteste G. ageyn] aȝeyn OC^{2}CBM.

335 my] *om* O. paleis] paleys of F; place Cr^{1}GYOB. p*er*sone] likenesse C^{2}G. of] as F.

336 fettest] fecchedest M; fecchest R. þyng] there thyng HmCrGC^{2}CBLMRF.

337 Thus] þou F. ylik] lyke CrG; lyknest þe to F. lady] ladyes CrGF.

338 Thefliche] & þefly F. robbedest] robbest Cr. þe] HmCrGYOC^{2}CBLMRF; and þe W. lawe] lawe it B.

339 *line om* Y. be] þat ben B; *om* C^2.

339α *in margin* O. *oculum*] ? ocul*am* F. *oculo*] *oculo &c* HmB.

340 soule(2)] *om* B. to synne] *om* C.

341 man wole] may wel OCr^{23}; may it wel F. amende] amende it R.

342 was...lawe] by þe olde lawe was amendes WHmCrGYOC^{2}CBLMRF (by] in Cr. amendes] amendid B).

343 þat] the YO. clayme] RF; clayme it WHmCrGYOC^{2}CBLM.

344 al] *om* B. wille...after] wel craftere F.

345 þat] at R.

346 quykne] quyke YGOC^{2}CCotLR; quykye BmBo; qwyt F. queynt...þoruȝ] þou qwenchist w*ith* F. queynt] queynthe C.

347 gile] *om* F. destruye] destroyeth CrRF; distroyed CB.

348 So leue] Beleve F; So loue Y. it] LRF; I WHmCrGYOC^{2}CB (y *altered to* þou *another ink* G); thow (*above line another ink*) M. noȝt] nougth quod Hm; neuere RF. ayein] þat aȝen HmB; þat y ageyn F. I] *om* F. fecche] fecched Hm.

349 But] And O. right] reson YC^2. by(2)] *om* GYOC^{2}BRF. reson] resou*n* y HmF; right YC^2. here] *above line* M; *om* GC^2.

349α *in margin* O. *soluere*] soluare BmBo. *legem*] *legem atque prophecias* F. *adimplere*] *adimplere &c* Hm; *implere* R.

Thow fettest myne in my place [maugree] alle resoun,
Falsliche and felonliche; good feiþ me it tauȝte
To recouere hem þoruȝ raunsoun and by no reson ellis,
So þat þoruȝ gile þow gete þoruȝ grace it is ywonne.
Thow, lucifer, in liknesse of a luþer Addere
Getest bi gile þo þat god louede;
And I in liknesse of a leode, þat lord am of heuene,
Graciousliche þi gile haue quyt: go gile ayein gile!
And as Adam and alle þoruȝ a tree deyden,
Adam and alle þoruȝ a tree shul turne to lyue,
And gile is bigiled and in his gile fallen:
Et cecidit in foueam quam fecit.
Now bigynneþ þi gile ageyn þee to turne
And my grace to growe ay gretter and widder.
[Þe bitternesse þat þow hast browe, now brouke it þiselue];
That art doctour of deeþ drynk þat þow madest.
For I þat am lord of lif, loue is my drynke,
And for þat drynke today I deide vpon erþe.
I fauȝt so me þursteþ ȝit for mannes soule sake;

350 fettest] fettedste Cr^3; foched C. myne] hem BmCot; hym Bo. maugree] ayeins WYOC^{2}CLMR; aȝenst HmB; agaynst CrG; ageyn F. alle] ryght & F; *om* R.
351 felonliche] felonouslyche HmG; felously Cr^1; Fouliche C^2. me it] it me C^{2}BoCot.
352 recouere] recorue O. þoruȝ] by CrM.
353 þoruȝ(1)] with RF. þow] thu hem Hm. þoruȝ(2)] with F. it is] it is it (*first* it *cancelled*) C; is it O; ys G; it was RF; þey ben Hm. ywonne] ywonnen M; wonne HmCrGYOC^{2}CB.
354 Thow] þat B; & þey F. in] þoruȝ O.
355 Getest] gettedest GCr^{1}Y; Gettistdest C^2; Gete RB; Geetyn F. þo] þing RF. *Hereafter* Y *copies* 360α.
356 I] *om* CrGYOC^{2}CB. þat] & F. of] y of F; In G.
357 þi] *om* F. haue] haue I YBoCot; haþ þe F. gile(2)] riȝt B.
358 *run together with* 359 Cr^1. And] as and (as *cancelled*) Bm. alle] alle other CB; all men F. deyden] deied C^{2}Cr^{23}F; *om* Cr^1.
359 Adam...tree] *om* Cr^1. Adam] So Adam F. shul] shulde Cr. turne] RF; turne ayein WHmCrGYOC^{2}CBLM. to lyue] *om* Cr^1.
360 bigiled] gyled Cr. gile(2)] ge gile (*corrected*) Bo.
360α *in margin* O; *copied after* 355 Y. *fecit*] *fecit &c* HmG.
361 ageyn] ayein YOC^{2}CB. þee to] the C; to the G; þy gyle to F. turne] turnen R.
362 to] *om* Cr^{1}M. growe] growen R. ay] euere F; *om* G. widder] grettere RF.
363 RHmCrGYOC^{2}CBLMF; *line om* W. Þe] & þe F. þat] *om* C^{2}F. hast] *om* GYOC^{2}CB. browe] brewed Cr. now] *om* HmCrGYOC^{2}CBLM. it] it in O. selue] seluen YCLM.
364 That] Thou Cr. þat] of þat F.
366 drynke] I drynk Bo. deide] dye Cr^1. erþe] the erthe Cot.
367 *transposed with* 368 B. þursteþ] thryste C; thrusted G. ȝit] *om* G. soule] soulis C^{2}Cr^3; sole Hm.

May no drynke me moiste, ne my þurst slake,
Til þe vendage falle in þe vale of Iosaphat,
That I drynke ri3t ripe Must, *Resureccio mortuorum.*
And þanne shal I come as a kyng, crouned, wiþ Aungeles,
And haue out of helle alle mennes soules.
Fendes and f[e]ndekynes bifore me shul stande |
And be at my biddyng wherso [best] me likeþ. *fol.* 114 *b*
A[c] to be merciable to man þanne my kynde [it] askeþ
For we beþ breþeren of blood, [ac] no3t in baptisme alle.
Ac alle þat beþ myne hole breþeren, in blood and in baptisme,
Shul no3t be dampned to þe deeþ þat [dureþ] wiþouten ende:
Tibi soli peccaui &c.
It is no3t vsed in erþe to hangen a feloun
Ofter þan ones þou3 he were a tretour.
And if þe kyng of þat kyngdom come in þat tyme
There [a] feloun þole sholde deeþ ooþer Iuwise
Lawe wolde he yeue hym lif if he loked on hym.
And I þat am kyng of kynges shal come swich a tyme
Ther doom to þe deeþ dampneþ alle wikked,

368 *line om* F.
369 þe(1)] *om* B. vendage] vengeaunce BF. Iosaphat] Psaphat Cr^1.
370 ri3t] *om* F.
371 And] *om* G. a] *om* Y.
372 out] now out F. mennes] my*n* me*n*nys F; mannes YOC^2; manere CB.
373 fendekynes] LCr^{23}C^{2}BRF; fendkyns HmCr^{1}GYOM; fyndekynes WC. shul] shullen B.
374 biddyng] byddynge*s* G. best] eu*ere* WHmCrGYOC^{2}CBLMRF.
375 Ac] R; But F; And WHmCrGYOC^{2}CBLM. to be] not so F; *om* R. þanne] that Cr^{23}; *om* YRF. it] HmCrGYC^{2}CBLM; þanne it R; may not F; *om* WO. askeþ] aske F.
376 ac] but WHmCrGYOC^{2}CBLMR; & F. no3t] *om* F. in] of CrM.
377 Ac] but HmGC^{2}F; And CrC. þat] *om* F. in(2)] *om* Cr.
378 Shul] Shullen B. no3t] nou3 C. þe] *om* Cr. dureþ] is WHmCrGYOC^{2}CBLMRF. outen] out Cr.
378α *line om* F; *in margin* O. &c] *om* R.
379 in] on R.
380 Ofter] Oftener O. ones] oþes Bo.
381 of] *twice (corrected)* C; in Y.
382 a] þe HmCrGYOC^{2}CBLMRF; *om* W. þole] tholed G; schulde O. sholde] þole O. deeþ] þeeþ deeþ (þeeþ *cancelled*) Bm. ooþer] other CrM; or ooþer WHmGYC^{2}CBLRF; ouþ*er* oþer O. Iuwise] Iouesse? (*blotted*) G; wise YOCBLRF; els CrM.
383–5 *in margin main hand* M.
383 Lawe] The law Cr^{23}O. he(1)] haue Cr. yeue] 3af C^{2}GOMR. if] and RF. on] vpon GC^2.
384 þat] *om* F. shal] & shal F. come] on Cr. tyme] tyme come Cr^{23}.
385 Ther] & þeyre F; where GYOC^{2}CB. doom] þe doom O; deedis deme F. dampneþ] & da*m*pne F.

And if lawe wole I loke on hem it liþ in my g*ra*ce
Wheiþ*er* þei deye or deye no3t for þat þei diden ille.
Be it any þyng abou3t, þe boldnesse of hir synnes,
I [may] do mercy þoru3 [my] rightwisnesse and alle my
wordes trewe;
And þou3 holy writ wole þat I be wroke of hem þat diden ille—
Nullum malum impunitum &c—
They shul be clensed clerliche and [keuered] of hir synnes
In my prisone Purgatorie til *parce* it hote.
And my mercy shal be shewed to manye of my [halue]breþeren,
For blood may suffre blood boþe hungry and acale
Ac blood may no3t se blood blede but hym rewe:
Audiui archana verba que non licet homini loqui.
Ac my rightwisnesse and right shul rulen al helle,
And mercy al mankynde bifore me in heuene.
For I were an vnkynde kyng but I my kynde helpe,
And nameliche at swich a nede þer nedes help bihoueþ:
Non intres in Iudicium cum seruo tuo.
Thus by lawe', quod oure lord, 'lede I wole fro hennes |

386 loke on hem] on hym loke O. hem] hym Cot. liþ] lyght Cot.

387 þei(1)] he O. deye or] deie or *twice* Bm. deye(*both*)] dey3en F. diden] dyd Cr^{23}; done Cr^{1}.

388–90 *lines om* CB.

388 it] *om* O. abou3t] aboute MCr; abowten F; *om* GYOC^{2}.

389 may] LRF; *om* WHmCrGYOC^{2}M. þoru3...trewe] many fold with*ou*tyn ryghtwisnesse F. þoru3 my] þoru3 WHm CrGYOC^{2}LMR. trewe] been trewe OC^{2}.

390 wole] wolde F. þat I] I GR; *om* F. wroke] wroke*n* O. hem] þoo Hm. diden] did CrG. ille] euyll Cr.

390α *in margin* O. *Nullum*] For *nullum* O; *Nullum peccatum* B (*peccatum cancelled* Bm). *malum*] *om* Cot. *&c*] *et nullum bonum* irremuneritum (*another ink*) Bo; *om* Bm CotRF.

391 shul] shullen B; shuld Cr. clensed] wasshen G. keuered] wasshen WHmCr YOC^{2}CBLMRF; clensed G.

392 *parce*] parcye G. it hote] y seende F.

393 my halue] my WHmCrGYOC^{2}CBL MRF.

394 blood(2)] his blood F. hungry] hung*er* C^{2}Cr^{3}GC; onhu*n*gred FCot; and hungred BmBo. acale] acalde C; acold B; colde Cr^{23}GC^{2}.

395 *in margin main hand* Bm. Ac] but GC^{2}F; And CrC. se] se his RF. hym] 3if hym HmY; it CB.

395α *in margin* O. *Audiui*] *Audiuit* F. *que*] *qui* Cr^{3}. *licet*] *licent* G. *loqui*] *loqui &c* HmGYC^{2}.

396 Ac] but GC^{2}F; And CrC. my] *om* F. rightwisnesse] ri3tfulnesse B. rulen] rule CrHmGCBF.

398 kynde] kyn RF. helpe] holpe GC^{2}B LRF.

399 nameliche] mandlich C; manliche Bm; maliche Bo. nedes] nede BmBo; *om* Cot. bihoueþ] bhouees C.

399α *in margin* O. *tuo*] *tuo &c* HmGB; *tuo domine* OF.

400 Thus] thys G. oure] this CrM. lede... hennes] ledyn fram hennes y will F. fro] *om* G.

Tho [ledes] þat [I] lou[e], and leued in my comynge; *fol.* 115 *a*
And for þi lesynge, lucifer, þat þow leighe til Eue
Thow shalt abyen it bittre!' and bond hym wiþ cheynes.
Astroth and al þe route hidden hem in hernes;
They dorste noȝt loke on oure lord, þe [leeste] of hem alle,
But leten hym lede forþ [what] hym liked and lete [what] hym liste.
Manye hundred of Aungeles harpeden and songen,
Culpat caro, purgat caro, regnat deus dei caro.
Thanne pipede pees of Poesie a note:
Clarior est solito post maxima nebula phebus;
Post inimicicias [*clarior est et amor*].
'After sharpe shoures', quod pees, 'moost shene is þe sonne;
Is no weder warmer þan after watry cloudes;
Ne no loue leuere, ne leuer frendes,
Than after werre and wo whan loue and pees ben maistres.
Was neuere werre in þis world ne wikkednesse so kene
That loue, and hym liste, to laughynge ne brouȝte;
And Pees þoruȝ pacience alle perils stoppeþ.'

401 ledes...I] þat I RF; þat me WHmCr GYOC^{2}CBLM. loue] louede WHmCr GYOC^{2}CBLMRF. leued in] þei me beleveden on F. comynge] connyng Y.
402 And] *om* C^{2}. lesynge] lesyngis C^{2}F. leighe] liest Cr^{2}; liedst Cr^{3}. til] to Cr^{23}G C^{2}RF.
403 abyen] abye HmCrGYOC^{2}CBLM RF. it] *om* F. bittre] bytterly GOF; better CrB. and] and a Bo; ⁊ anon he F. hym] hym fast G. cheynes] a cheyne Hm.
404 Astroth] ⁊ astarot F. þe] þi G. hidden] hyd Cr. in] sone in F.
405 dorste] dursten OHmB. loke] loken Cr. leeste] boldeste WHmCrGYOC^{2}CB LMRF.
406 But...lede] þan ledde F. leten] lete YGOC^{2}C. forþ] forth with hym CB; with hym F. what(1)] HmCrGYOC^{2}LM RF; whom W; who C; alle þat B. lete] leue Hm; lefte CBF. what(2)] HmCrGY OC^{2}CBLMRF; whom W.
407 Manye] ⁊ Manye F. harpeden] harped Cr^{1}C^{2}; harpen Cr^{23}. songen] sange Cr.
407α *in margin* O. *regnat*] *regna* Cr^{1}.
408 of] off a G.
408α, β *in margin* O.
408α *as one line with* 408β WHmCrOBm BoLM. *solito*] *solitus* R.
408β *inimicicias*] *inimicicia* C. *clarior... amor*] GYOC^{2}CBRF; ⁊*c* HmLM; ⁊ (*cropped*) W; *om* Cr.
409 sharpe] scharpest RF. moost] *om* G. shene] clene B (cl *over erasure another ink* Bm); clere G.
410 Is] þer is F. þan] that Hm. watry] water Y.
411–XX 26 defective R: *see above*, p. 12.
411 ne] no Cr^{23}. leuer] leuerere to F; better Cr^{23}; more better O.
412 maistres] mais C; oned F.
413 wikkednesse] wikkenesse C.
414 That] Cr^{1}CBMF (*erasure after it* M); That ne WHmCr^{23}GYOC^{2}L. laughynge] laught Cr^{1}. ne] he F; it Hm.
415 perils] pereylis he F; perell Cr. stoppeþ] stopped CrHmGYOC^{2}CBLM (-de *over erasure* Hm; -d *altered to* þ M).

'Trewes', quod Truþe, 'þow tellest vs sooþ, by I*es*us!
Clippe we in couenaunt, and ech of vs [kisse] ooþer,
And leteþ no peple', quod pees, 'p*ar*ceyue þ*at* we chidde;
For inpossible is no þyng to hym þat is almyghty.'
'Thow seist sooþ', [seyde] Rightwisnesse, and reu*er*entliche
hire kiste:
Pees, and pees h[i]re, *per secula seculorum*:
Misericordia & veritas obuiauerunt sibi; Iusticia & pax osculate su[*nt*].
Truþe trumpede þo and song *Te deum laudamus*,
And þanne lutede [loue] in a loud note:
Ecce quam bonum & quam iocundum &c. |
Til þe day dawed þise damyseles [carolden] *fol.* 115 *b*
That men rongen to þe resurexion, and riȝt wiþ þat I wakede
And callede kytte my wif and Calote my doghter:
'[Ariseþ] and reu*er*ence[þ] goddes resurexion,
And crepe[þ] to þe cros on knees and kisse[þ] it for a Iuwel
For goddes blissede body it bar for oure boote;
And it afereþ þe fend, for swich is þe myȝte
May no grisly goost glide þere it [shadweþ].'

416 þow] þo þou F. by] of F.
417 in] in þis F. kisse] CrHmGYOC²CB LMF; clippe W.
418 And] ȝee F. leteþ] lete HmCrGYO C²CBLMF. þ*at*] what Cot. chidde] chyd Cr; chide HmGYC²CBM; chiden OF.
419 þat] *om* Cot. is al] al is F.
420 Thow] Tow Y. seyde] LM; quod WHmCrGYOC²CBF. hire] him Cr; he*m* F.
421 *line om* F. hire] here WHmCrYOC² CBLM; there G. *per*] *per omnia* CrG.
421α *in margin* O. *Iusticia...sunt*] *om* F. *osculate*] *osculat* Bo; oculate Y. *sunt*] CrBo CotLM; *sunt &c* HmGYOC²C; su (*cropped*) W; *om* Bm.
422 Truþe] þa*n*ne trewþe F. and] a Cot. song] treblide F. *laudamus*] *laudamus &c* GC²CBm.
423 þanne...loue] love lawhte of hym F. loue] GCrYOC²CBLM; *om* WHm. in] into B. loud] luddere F; lowe C.
423α *in margin* OBmBo. *iocundum*] *iocundum habitare fratres in vnum* HmCot. *&c*] *om* BF.
424 carolden] F; dauncede WHmCrGYC² CBLM; daunceden O.
425 rongen] ronge YCrGCB. wiþ þat] þer*with* F. wakede] awakid B.
426 And] and I B; I F.
427 Ariseþ] OHmYC²BLMF; Arises C; Arise CrG; And bad hem rise W. reu*er*enceþ] HmYOC²BLM; goo reuerensiþ F; reuerence WCrGC. goddes] q*uod* I godes (q*uod* I *above line another ink*) M; cristis B; þe F. resurexion] ressurecciou*n* at kyrke F.
428 crepeþ] HmYOC²CBLMF; crepe WCrG. to...knees] on knees to þe cros F. kisseþ] YHmOC²BLM; kisses C; kisse WCrGF.
429 goddes] cristis BF. blissede] owen B. it bar] bar it F.
430 myȝte] strengþe F.
431 May] þ*at* þ*er*e may F. shadweþ] shadweth YCrGOC²CBLMF; schawyþ Hm; walkeþ W.

XIX

Thus I awaked and wroot what I hadde ydremed,
And dighte me derely and dide me to chirche
To here holly þe masse and to be housled after.
In myddes of þe masse þo men yede to offryng
I fel eftsoones aslepe, and sodeynly me mette
That Piers þe Plowman was peynted al blody
And com in wiþ a cros bifore þe comune peple,
And riȝt lik in alle [lymes] to oure lord I*es*[u].
And þanne called I Conscience to kenne me þe soþe:
'Is þis I*es*us þe Iust*ere*', quod I, 'þ*at* Iewes dide to deþe?
Or it is Piers þe Plowman? who peynted hym so rede?'
Quod Conscience and kneled þo, 'þise arn Piers armes,
Hise colours and his cote Armure; ac he þat comeþ so blody
Is crist wiþ his cros, conquerour of cristene.'
'Why calle [ye] hym crist, siþen Iewes calle[d] hym I*es*us?

1 Thus] ANon F. awaked] waked Cr^{3}; wakned F; walked Cr^{12}M. and] ⁊ þa*n* y F. I hadde] þ*at* y F. ydremed] dremed YHmCrGOC^{2}BLMF.

3 *run together with* 4 GYOC^{2}CB. here] heeren F. holly þe] wholy þe Cr^{1}; holy þe HmCr^{23}GYC^{2}CL (y *over erasure* Hm); holyly þe F; þe holi B. and...after] *om* GYOC^{2}CB.

4 In...masse] *om* GYOC^{2}CB. In] ⁊ F. þo] whan (*over erasure another ink*) Hm; *om* CrF. yede] ȝeden OB; wente CrM; wenty*n* F. to] to þe M. offryng] offre F.

5 *line om* GYOC^{2}CB. I] ⁊ y F. eftsoones] *om* F. me mette] y dre*m*pte F.

6 That] þanne O. was] cam F. al blody] a reede F.

7 com in wiþ] browhte w*ith* hy*m* F. a] *om* C^{2}. þe] *om* C^{2}.

8 lymes] YHmCrGOC^{2}CBLMF; þynges W. I*es*u] HmGYOC^{2}CBLM; I*es*us WCr; hy*m*selue F.

9 And] *om* CrGYOC^{2}CBMF. þanne...I] Ano*n* y clepid F.

10 Is þis] wheyþ*er* he were F. I*es*us] Iesu Cr^{23}F. quod I þ*at*] þ*at* þe F. dide] diden OHmBF. to] hy*m* to O.

11 it is] is it Cr^{23}GC^{2}; it Cr^{1}; ys he F. þe] *om* Cr^{3}F. who] þat is F. hym] *om* F.

12 þo] dou*n* F. Piers] cr*ist*is F.

13 colours] colour Cr. and] of F. his] *om* Cr^{3}. ac] but GC^{2}; ⁊ CrC; *om* F. þat] *om* F. so blody] fram þe Iustis F.

14 Is] he ys F; wiþ Bo. conquerour of] he haþ co*n*qwere all F. cristene] cr*ist*ene sowlis F; christendome Cr.

15 ye] CrHmGYOC^{2}CBLMF; *om* W. crist] crist quod I WHmCrGYOC^{2}CB LM; cr*ist* q*uod* he F. called] HmGYCB; calleden O; calle WCrC^{2}L; callen M: named F.

Patriarkes and pr*o*phetes pr*o*phecied bifore
That alle kynne creatures sholden knelen and bowen
Anoon as men nempned þe name of god I*es*u;
Ergo is no name to þe name of I*es*us, |
Ne noon so nedeful to nempne by ny3te ne by daye. *fol.* 116 *a*
For alle derke deueles arn adrad to heren it,
And synfulle aren solaced and saued by þat name,
And ye callen hym crist; for what cause, telleþ me.
Is crist moore of my3t and moore worþi name
Than I*es*u or I*es*us þat al oure Ioye com of?'
'Thow knowest wel', quod Conscience, 'and þow konne reson,
That knyght, kyng, conquerour may be o persone.
To be called a knyght is fair for men shul knele to hym.
To be called a kyng is fairer for he may knyghtes make.
Ac to be conquerour called, þat comeþ of special gr*a*ce,
And of hardynesse of herte and of hendenesse,
To make lordes of laddes of lond þat he wynneþ
And fre men foule þralles þat folwen no3t hise lawes.
The Iewes þat were gentil men, I*es*[u] þei despised,

16 Patriarkes] ⁊ patr*ia*rkis F. pr*o*phecied] pr*o*phecieden BHm; þey pr*o*fecyden F.
17 sholden] sholde C^{2}CrGYCBF; schull Hm. knelen...bowen] knele and bowe HmCr.
18 men] me Cot. nempned] nempneden O; named Cr; nyuyned G; nepned C. þe] þe hei3e M; this highe Cr^{13}; this hight Cr^2. god] þ*a*t Ientyl F; *om* CrM. I*es*u] ie*s*us HmCr. *Hereafter an additional line like* 80α F; *see above*, p. 223.
19 is] there ys GBF. þe] þat B. of] tof Hm; *om* YCB.
20 so] name so F. nempne] neuene G; name Cr. ny3te] nyghtis F; nygh Cr^2. ne] nor Cr; and M. daye] dayes F.
21 alle] all the CrF. adrad] dradde G. heren] here CrGYOC^{2}CBM. it] ynem*p*-ned F.
22 aren] soul*es* ben F.
23 Why calle 3ee hy*m* þanne cr*ist* what cause 3ee me tell F. ye] thay C. callen] call Cr; kallid B. telleþ] tel Cr^{13}; tyl Cr^2.
24 Is crist] For cr*ist* is F. and] ⁊ of F. worþi] worthier*e* F.
25 com of] comeþ of BmBo; of spryngeþ F.
26 Thow knowest] knowest þou F. konne] canst O; knowest G; kone good F.
27 That] þ*a*t a F. knyght kyng] kyng kny3t O. kyng] kyng and B; ⁊ a kyng ⁊ F. be] be of Y; ben al F.
28 called] clepd F. shul] schulde Hm. to] til F.
29 To] And to O. a] *om* Cr. is] *om* O. he] a kyng F. may] many Y.
30 Ac] And CrGYOC^{2}CB; For F. be] be a Hm. called] clepyd Hm. comeþ] come O. of] of godd*es* F.
31 hardynesse] hardenesse C^2. of(2)] also of F. hendenesse] heendenesse bothe YCr^{23}OCB.
32 make] maken HmF. of(1)] and Hm GF; or Cr. laddes] ladyes HmCrF; lydyes G. of...wynneþ] in londys þ*a*t þey wynne F. wynneþ] y *altered to* o G.
33 folwen] folwe FCrG. no3t] *om* G.
34 The] For þe F. were] weren OBF. I*es*u] GCrYOCBLMF; I*es*us WHmC^2. despised] dispiseden O.

Boþe his loore and his lawe; now are þei lowe cherles.
As wide as þe world is [wonyeþ þer noon]
But vnder tribut and taillage as tikes and cherles.
And þo þat bicome cristene bi counseil of þe baptis[t]e
Aren frankeleyns, free men þoruȝ fullynge þat þei toke
And gentil men wiþ Ie*s*u, for Ie*s*u[s] was yfulled
And vpon Caluarie on cros ycrouned kyng of Iewes.
It bicomeþ to a kyng to kepe and to defende,
And conquerour of [his] conquest hise lawes and his large.
And so dide Ie*s*us þe Iewes; he Iustified and tauȝte hem
The lawe of lif þat laste shal euere,
And defended from foule yueles, feu*er*es and Fluxes,
And from fendes þat in hem [was] and false bileue.
Tho was he Ie*s*us of Iewes called, gentile p*ro*phete,
And kyng of hir kyngdom and croune bar of þornes. |
And þo conquered he on cros as conquerour noble; *fol.* 116 *b*
Mighte no deeþ hym fordo ne adoun brynge
That he naroos and regnede and rauysshed helle.
And þo was he conquerour called of quyke and of dede,

35 now] & now F.
36 As] also B. þe] this HmGF. wonyeþ...noon] HmGYOC^{2}CBLMF (therInne *added main hand over erasure* M); wonneth none therin Cr; noon of hem þer wonyeþ W.
37 and(1)] or HmCr^3.
38 *run together with* 39 Hm. And] al and (al *cancelled*) Bm. bicome] bicoomen O; became Cr. bi...baptiste] *om* Hm. þe] *om* F. baptiste] L; baptisme WCrGYOC^{2}CBMF.
39 Aren...men] *om* Hm. free] & free OF. fullynge] þe fullyng B; fully G. toke] token O; take F.
40 And] are (e *over erasure*) Hm. Ie*s*us] CrGYOCBLM; Ie*s*u WHmC^{2}F. yfulled] fulled Cr^{1}C^2.
41 And] *om* F. on] on a Hm; on þe F. ycrouned] crowned CrGC^2; & korouned F.
42 bicomeþ] cometh Y. to(1)] wel to F. kepe] kepen his lond F. to(3)] *om* HmOCot. defende] defende it F.
43 And] And a CBm; As Cr. his(1)] F; *om* WHmCrGYOC^{2}CBLM. lawes...his] lordis to ȝeve he*m* F. large] charge (c *over erasure*) Cot.
44 þe] to the CotF. Iustified] Iusted F.
45 of] of longe O. laste] lasten F. euere] euere more F.
46 defended] fended LBmCotMF; fendod (*corrected*) C; defende Cr; fende OGC^2; fenden Y; fendist Bo. from] hem from OHm; fram he*m* F; it From C^{2}G. yueles] evelis boþe F. feueres] feners Cr^{23}. and] & eek F.
47 from] *om* OF. in] *om* O. was] LF; were WHmCrGYC^{2}CBM; werren O. and] & al O; & eek F.
48 he] *om* C^2. Ie*s*us] Ie*s*u F. of...called] called of iewys Hm. gentile] & þe Ientil F.
49 hir] *om* Cr^{1}MF. bar] he bar F.
50 he] *om* YCot. on] on þe BF. as] a F.
51 hym] hem BmBo. adoun] noþy*n*g dou*n* F.
52 naroos] ne ros HmGO; aros CBF.
53 called] calle C; *om* BoCot. of(1)] *om* C^2.

For he yaf Adam and Eue and oþere mo blisse
That longe hadde yleyen bifore as Luciferis cherles,
[And took [Lucifer þe loþely] þat lord was of helle
And bond [hym] as [he is bounde] wiþ bondes of yrene.
Who was hardiere þan he? his herte blood he shadde
To maken alle folk free þat folwen his lawe].
And siþ [alle hise lele liges largely he yeueþ]
Places in Paradis at hir partynge hennes
He may [be wel] called conquerour, and þat is crist to mene.
Ac þe cause þat he comeþ þus wiþ cros of his passion
Is to wissen vs þe*r*wiþ, þ*a*t whan we ben tempted,
Ther*with* to fiȝte and [f]enden vs fro fallynge in[to] synne,
And se bi his sorwe þ*a*t whoso loueþ ioye
To penaunce and to pou*er*te he moste puten hymseluen,
And muche wo in þis world willen and suffren.
Ac to carpe moore of crist and how he com to þat name,
Faithly for to speke, his firste name was I*es*us.
Tho he was born in Bethleem, as þe book telleþ,
And cam to take mankynde kynges and Aungeles
Reu*er*enced hym [riȝt] faire wiþ richesses of erþe.

54 blisse] blyssed Cr^{23}.
55 hadde] hadden OHmBM. yleyen] leyn HmCrGYOC^{2}CBLMF. as] at G. Luciferis] lucifer Y.
56–9 F; *lines om* WHmCrGYOC^{2}CBLM; *here in the spelling of* W.
56 took] þanne took he F. Lucifer þe loþely] lotthly lucifer F.
57 hym] his F. he is bounde] his bondema*n* F.
58 he(1)] he þ*a*t F.
59 lawe] lawes F.
60 alle...yeueþ] he ȝeveþ largely all hise leele lygis F; he yaf largely alle hise lele liges WHmCrGYOC^{2}CBLM (alle] to alle B. lele] lelly Cr; trewe C^{2}).
61 partynge] dep*ar*tynge F.
62 be wel] wel be WHmCrYOC^{2}CBLMF; be G. called] callid a C^{2}F.
63 Ac] but GC^{2}F; And CrC. he] *om* C. cros] his cros F. his] þe Cr^{1}M; *om* HmCr^{23}GYC^{2}CB.
64 þ*a*t] *om* F. we] YBoCotF; þ*a*t we W HmCrGOC^{2}CBmLM. tempted] yte*mp*tyd F.
65 and] and to Hm; *om* C^{2}. fenden] GYC^{2}LM; fende OCrCBmBo; defenden W; defende CotHmF. into] YHmCrGOC^{2}CBLMF; to W. synne] *om* C.
66 se] to seen F. so] *om* GYOC^{2}CB.
67 puten] putte HmCrGYOC^{2}CBM. seluen] selue GHmCrYOC^{2}CBF.
68 muche] mychel F. wo] *om* O. willen] YHmCrGOC^{2}CBLM; wylnen F; to willen W.
69 Ac] but GC^{2}F; As CB; And Cr. to(1)] for to CrM. moore] *om* BoCot. name] *om* C.
70 Faithly] Feiþfulli BmGBo (ful *above line another ink* G); feyfuly Cot. for] *om* Cr^{23}.
71 þe...telleþ] bookys boldly telly*n* F.
72 take] make G. kynges] boþe kyngys F.
73 Reu*er*enced] Reuerenseden BmBo. riȝt] ryght F; *om* WHmCrGYOC^{2}CBLM. richesses] rychesse HmCrGYOC^{2}CBLMF. of] of thys CrM (th *over erasure* M).

Aungeles out of heuene come knelynge and songe,
Gloria in excelsis deo ⁊c.
Kynges come after, knelede and offrede [sense],
Mirre and muche gold wiþouten merc[ede] askynge
Or any kynnes catel; but knowelich[ede] hym souereyn
Boþe of [s]ond, sonne and see, and siþenes þei wente
Into hir kyngene kiþ by counseil of Aungeles.
And þere was þat word fulfilled þe which þow of speke,
Omnia celestia terrestria flectantur in hoc nomine Iesu; |
For alle þe Aungeles of heuene at his burþe knelede, *fol.* 117 *a*
And al þe wit of þe world was in þo þre kynges.
Reson and Rightwisnesse and Ruþe þei offrede;
Wherfore and why wise men þat tyme,
Maistres and lettred men, *Magi* hem callede.
That o kyng cam wiþ Reson couered vnder sense.
The seconde kyng siþþe sooþliche offrede
Rightwisnesse vnder reed gold, Resones felawe;

74 out] *om* B. come] comen BmBoM. songe] songen BHmOF.
74α *in margin* O. ⁊c] *Et in terra pax hominibus ⁊c* Hm; *om* CrOF.
75 *divided from* 76 *before* Ensens F. Kynges] HmCrGYOC^{2}CBLMF; Kynges þat W. come] comyn HmCrOC^{2}BMF. after] aftir and BF. knelede] kneliden B; knellinge Cr^{23}YO. and] to hym ⁊ F. offrede] offreden OCotF. sense] (? *added another hand*) Cot; Ensens F; *om* WHmCr GYOC^{2}CBmBoLM.
76 Mirre] ⁊ myrre F. muche] mylkyle C. outen] oute YCrGC^2; myche F. mercede] mercede (ede *over erasure another ink*) Cot; mede CrM (*over larger erasure* M); mercy WHmGYOC^{2}CBmBoLF. askynge] asked F.
77 Or] Er of F. but] þey F. knowelichede] knowlechid FG; knoweliche M Cr^1; knowelichynge WHmCr^{23}YOC^{2}C BL. hym] him For C^2; hym here F.
78 sond] GCr^{23}YOC^{2}CLM; lond WHm Cr^1; sunne F; soule B. sonne] of sunne BmBo; ⁊ sonne YO; and of sonne C; of sond F. siþenes] syþis hoom F. wente] wenten CrOMF.
79 hir] erþe BmBo. kyngene kiþ] kingdome kyth Cr; kyngdomes G; kyngenelich C; kyngnelith (e *added*) O; kyngenlith Y; kyngelich C^2; kyngriche B. counseil] kennynge F. Aungeles] a aungeles C; an angel BF.
80 þere] þerwith F. þat] þe F. word] world Y. þow of] first þou F.
80α *in margin* O. *celestia*] *celestia ⁊* (⁊ *above line*) Hm. *Iesu*] *iesu ⁊c* Hm.
81 knelede] kneleden O; þey kneliden F.
82 of] in F. þe] thys GF. in þo] þoo in F. kynges] þynges F.
83 Rightwisnesse] rightfulnesse CBL. Ruþe] Truthe Cr^1. offrede] offreden OF.
85 Boþe Maistris ⁊ men yleerned Magy hem nameden F.
86 o] of Y. couered] ykouered F; offerryd G. sense] ensense F.
87 seconde] toþer F. kyng] *om* Hm. siþþe] sothly CrM; eke GC^{2}CB; ech Y. sooþliche] sithens CrM. offrede] he offered CrBMF (*over erasure* M).
88 *run together with* 89 F. Rightwisnesse] Riȝtfulnesse B. reed] *om* B. Resones felawe] *om* F.

Gold is likned to leautee þat laste shal eu*ere*
[For it shal turne tresoun to ri3t and to truþe].
The þridde kyng þo kam knelynge to I*es*u
And p*re*sented hym wiþ pitee apperynge by Mirre;
For Mirre is mercy to mene and mylde speche of tonge.
[Erþeliche] honeste þynges w[as] offred þus at ones
Thoru3 þre kynne kynges knelynge to I*es*u.
Ac for alle þise p*re*ciouse p*re*sent3 oure lord [prynce] I*es*us
Was neiþ*er* kyng ne conquerour til he [comsed] wexe
In þe manere of a man and þat by muchel sleighte,
As it bicomeþ a conquerour to konne manye sleightes,
And manye wiles and wit þat wole ben a ledere.
And so dide I*es*u in hise dayes, whoso [dorste] telle it.
Som tyme he suffrede, and som tyme he hidde hym,
And som tyme he fau3t faste and flei3 ouþer while,
And som tyme he gaf good and grauntede heele boþe.
Lif and lyme as hym liste he wro3te.
As kynde is of a Conquerour, so comsede I*es*u
Til he hadde alle hem þ*at* he for bledde.

89 Gold...leautee] *om* F. Gold] YHmCrGOC^{2}CBLM; For gold W. leautee] beaute B. laste] lasten F; fast Y.
90 FHmCrGYOC^{2}CBLM; *line om* W; *here in the spelling of* W. For...tresoun] F; and resou*n* to ryche gold HmCrGYOC^{2}CBLM. truþe] trewe GC^2.
91 kyng] *om* O. þo] *om* CB. kam] can G. knelynge] ⁊ knelid F; knekyng Cot. I*es*u] Iesu lowe F.
92 p*re*sented] p*re*sente C. apperynge] appaieryng Y; a pilgrym B. by] to CrCM.
94 *run together with* 95 CB. Erþeliche] Erthely F; Thre yliche WHmGYOC^{2}CLM; Thre in like Cr; þise þree ylikne B. was...ones] *om* CB. was] LF; were WHmCrGYC^{2}M; weren O. þus] vp G.
95 Thoru3...kynges] *om* CB. I*es*u] Iesus CrM.
96 Ac] but GC^2; And CrC; *om* F. alle] *om* F. prynce] HmCrGYOC^{2}CBLMF; kyng W.
97 comsed] gan to WHmCrGYOC^{2}CBLMF. wexe] wepe Cr^1.
98 þe] þise B. þat] *om* Y. by] þorgh3 F. muchel] muche YCrGOC^{2}CBLMF.
99 it] *om* Cr. konne] knowe F. sleightes] wilis B.
100 wiles...wit] sotile wytis B.
101 I*es*u] Iesus CrOC^{2}M; Iohan B. hise] those Cr. so] *om* GF. dorste] hadde tyme to WHmCrGYOC^{2}CLMF; holdiþ tyme B. it] *om* F.
102 Som] So þat B. hym] hy*m*selve F.
103 he] *om* G. fau3t faste] Fast Fau3te C^2. and] ⁊ he F. flei3] fledde HmC; pleieþ B.
104 gaf] 3af BC^2. good] gold B. heele] hile BmBo; hilthe Cot.
105 Lif] ⁊ also ly3f F. hym] hymsilf Cot; he CrF. he] so he Hm.
106 a] *om* BoCot. so] ⁊ so GYC^2. comsede] began C^2. I*es*u] ie*s*us Hm.
107 hadde] badde C. alle hem] hem alle Bm. þat he for] for whome þ*at* he G. for] forþ Bm. bledde] blede C^2.

In his Iuuentee þis Ie*s*us at Iewene feeste |
Water into wyn turnede, as holy writ telleþ. *fol.* 117 *b*
And þ*er*e bigan god of his grace to do wel:
For wyn is likned to lawe and lif holynesse,
And lawe lakkede þo for men louede no3t hir enemys,
And crist counseileþ þus and comaundeþ boþe,
[Boþe] to lered and to lewede, to louyen oure enemys.
So at þat feeste first as I bifore tolde
Bigan god of his g*ra*ce and goodnesse to dowel,
And þanne was he [cleped and] called no3t [oonly] crist but Ie*s*u,
A faunt[ek]yn ful of wit, *filius Marie.*
For bifore his moder Marie made he þat wonder
That she first and formest ferme sholde bileue
That he þoru3 g*ra*ce was gete and of no gome ellis.
He wro3te þat by no wit but þoru3 word one,
After þe kynde þat he cam of; þere comsede he do wel.
And whan he [was woxen] moore, in his moder absence,
He made lame to lepe and yaf light to blynde
And fedde wiþ two fisshes and *with* fyue loues

108 *divided from* 109 *after* turnede F. Iuuentee] inuente Cr; innocence HmGC^{2}CB. at] at the Cr^{23}YOL.
109 Water] he t*ur*nede water F. turnede] he turned C^{2}G; *om* F.
110 to] *om* GYOCBF.
111 is...to] y lykne to þe F. and] or F. lif] lyf of HmCrGYOC^{2}CBLMF.
112 louede] loueden OM; loueþ BoCot.
113 *line om* C^2. And] Ans BmBo; as Cot; But F. counseileþ] counselde C. þus] þus vs F; vs GYOCB. comaundeþ] comaunde C. boþe] vs boþe F; also Cr.
114 *line om* C^2. Boþe] YCrGOCBLM; *om* WHmF. to(1)] *om* Cot. lered] learned Cr. to(3)] for to F. louyen] louye YHmCrGOCBLMF. oure] her Hm.
115 at] þat B. þat] the CrGYOC^{2}CBLMF. I] *om* Cot. tolde] sayde CrM.
116 and] and his Cr^1; ⁊ of his Cr^{23}F.
117 þanne] tho CrGYOC^{2}CBLMF. he] *om* Cot. cleped and] cleped ⁊ CrHmGYOC^{2}CBLMF; *om* W. oonly] MCrF (oo *over erasure* M); holy WHmGYOC^{2}CBL. crist] chirche CB. Ie*s*u] Iesus GC^2.
118 fauntekyn] fantekyn F; faunt fyn WHmCrGYOC^{2}CBLM.
119 For] ⁊ F; *om* CrM.
120 and formest] *twice but corrected* C. ferme sholde] scholde ferme þe F.
121 gete] geten O; begete F. of] *om* Cr^{23}GYOC^{2}CB.
122 wit] wi3t B. þoru3] by CrM. one] alone G; onely Cr.
123 þat] *om* Hm. þere] the Y. comsede] comisid Bm; bigan C^{2}C. he(2)] he to CrC^{2}M.
124 was woxen] BCrGYOC^{2}CLM (was *above line* O); was waxe F; woxen was WHm. moder] modres HmCrGC^2. absence] absent HmY; p*re*sense F.
125 to(1)] men to HmB. and] ⁊ he F. light] syght G.
126 And] ⁊ he F. two] twey*n* F. loues] loes Cr^1.

Sore afyngred folk, mo þan fyue þousand.
Thus he confortede carefulle and caughte a gretter name
The which was dobet, where *þat* he wente.
For deue þoruȝ hise doynges and dombe speke [and herde],
And alle he heeled and halp þat hym of g*ra*ce askede;
And þo was he called in contre of þe comune peple,
For þe dedes þat he dide, *Fili dauid, Iesus.*
For dauid was doghtiest of dedes in his tyme;
The burdes þo songe, *Saul interfecit mille et dauid decem milia.*
Forþi þe contree þer Ie*s*u cam called hym *fili dauid,*
And nempned hym of Naȝareth; and no man so worþi
To be kaiser or kyng of þe kyngdom of Iuda,
Ne ouer Iewes Iustice, as Ie*s*us was, hem þouȝte. |
[Her]of Cayphas hadde enuye and oþ*er*e Iewes, *fol.* 118 *a*
And for to doon hym to deþe day and nyȝt þei casten.
Killeden hym on cros wise at Caluarie on Friday,
And siþen buriede his body, and beden *þat* men sholde
Kepen it fro nyghtcomeris wiþ knyghtes yarmed

127 Sore...folk] Folk soore anhu*n*grid F. afyngred] afho*n*gered G; ahungerd CBm; anhungryd HmCot; and hungrid Bo. mo...þousand] fyue þowsan and mo B. fyue] a YC. þousand] thowsandes G.
128 carefulle] the carefull CrBF. a] *om* Y. gretter] gret BCrF.
129 bet] bett*er* G. he] we Cr^{3}.
130 þoruȝ...doynges] men he made B. doynges] doynge F. and(1)] ⁊ F; to here and WHmCrGYOC^{2}CBLM. speke] to speke BCrM. and herde] ⁊ herde F; he made WHmCrGYOC^{2}LM; made C; *om* B.
131 he] *om* BoCot. heeled] lehelid (*corrected*) Bm.
132 he] *om* Cot. contre] cowrt F.
133 þe] tho G. dedes] drdes C. *Fili...Iesus*] *Iesu fili dauid* GYOC^{2}CBF. *Iesus*] *erasure* Hm.
134 was] was þe FCot. of] for G. his] *om* BoCot.
135 The] þerfor*e* F; *om* C^{2}. burdes] berdes LO; breddis C^{2}; burges BoCot; me*n* F. þo] þat GYOCB; þan C^{2}; *om* F. songe] songen MHmOBF. *Saul*] *sal* CB (u *added* Cot).
136 Forþi] Therfore Cr; For B. Ie*s*u] Iesus Cr^{1}. cam] cam þey F. *fili dauid*] *om* F.
137 nempned] nempneden Bo; menpneden Bm; nyuened G; named CrF.
138 kaiser] cesare G. kyngdom] kyndom BmBo. Iuda] Iude C; Iudee B.
139 Ne] And be BmBo; and he Cot. Iewes] þe iewes Hm. Iustice] Iustices C. Ie*s*us] Iesu Cr^{23}; *om* BoCot. hem] hym Cot.
140 Her...hadde] þerfor*e* hadde kayphas F. Her] Wher WHmCrGYOC^{2}CBLM. Iewes] kony*n*ge Iewis F; of þe Iewes WHmCrGYOC^{2}CBLM.
141 And] *om* HmF. casten] cast G; castid C^{2}.
142 Killeden] Killed CrGYC^{2}C; And killiden B; ⁊ kulled F. cros...at] þe cros on F. on(2)] on a HmCrC^{2}F; on þe B.
143 siþen] aft*er* F. buriede] buryeden HmOBLM; beried þey F. beden] badde G. sholde] schulden O.
144 Kepen] Kepe CrO. knyghtes] knyght Cr^{3}. yarmed] armed Cr^{13}Y.

For no fren[d] sholde [it] fecche; for p*ro*phetes hem tolde
That þat blissede body of burieles [sholde risen]
And goon into Galilee and gladen hise Apostles
And his moder Marie; þus men bifore de[uyn]ede.
The knyghtes þat kepten it biknewe hemseluen
That Aungeles and Archaungeles, er þe day sponge,
Come knelynge to þe corps and songen
Christus [*rex*] *resurgens*, [and it aroos after],
Verray m[a]n bifore hem alle and forþ wiþ hem yede.
The Iewes preide hem pees, and [preide] þe knyghtes
Telle þe comune þ*at* þer cam a compaignie of hise Apostles
And biwicched hem as þei woke and awey stolen it.
Ac Marie Maudeleyne mette hym by þe weye
Goynge toward Galilee in godhede and manhede
And lyues and lokynge and aloud cride

145 frend] freend F; frendes WHmCrGY OC^2CBLM. sholde] schulde*n* OHm. it] F; hym WHmCrGYOC^2CBLM. hem] him Cr^1; beforen F. tolde] tolde*n* OCot.
146 That] how Hm. þat] cr*is*tis F. blissede] blisful C; blesful Cot; bisseful Bm Bo. of] fro G. sholde] YCrGOC^2CBL MF; risen W; ryse Hm. risen] ryse GYO C^2CBmBoL; vp ryse F; arise CrCotM; sholde WHm.
147 and] to G.
148 men] þei B. bifore] byforehond F. deuynede] demede WHmCrGYC^2CBLM F; demeden O.
149 The] þan þe F. knyghtes] kynȝtis Bm. kepten] kept Cr^{23}G; kepe Cr^1. it] hym HmGYOC^2CB (*over erasure another ink* Hm). biknewe] beknewen F; biknewe it WCrGYC^2CLM; byknewen it HmOB. hem] hym CBmBo. seluen] selue GHm YC^2CBF.
150 sponge] spornge Y; gan spr*i*nge F.
151, 152 *so divided* CotF; *as one line* WHm CrGYOC^2CBmBoLM.
151 Come] comen HmCr^{12}OBMF. knelynge] kynlyn knelynge B (kynlyn *cancelled* Bm). þe] þat F. corps] corees C. songen] song Cr^3G; konyngly su*n*ge F.
152 *Christus resurgens a mortuis* ⁊ anoon he roos after F; *christus resurgens a mortuis* ⁊c Cot; *Christus resurgens* WHmCrGYOC^2C BmBoLM.
153 man] HmCrGYOC^2CBLMF (*over erasure* Hm); men W. wiþ...yede] before he*m* wente F. yede] he yede WHm CrGYOC^2CBLM.
154 preide(1)] prayeden HmCrOM. hem] HmGYOC^2CBL (e *over erasure* Hm); hem be W; hem of F; *om* CrM. and...þe] al þo p*ro*pre F. preide(2)] bisouȝte WCrG YC^2CBL; bisoughten HmOM. þe] þo Cot.
155 Telle] to telle HmB; ⁊ telly*n* F. þe comune] þe to*m*men Cr^1; *om* O. cam] coomen O. Apostles] postlis F.
156 And] had C^2. biwicched] biwiccheden M. hem] hym Cot. as] ar BmBo (r *over erasure* Bm); er Cot; or C^2; þ*at* F. þei] þere F. woke] woken CrHmO. stolen] stole C^2F. it] hym HmCrB; þe body F.
157 Ac] but GC^2; But sone F; And CrC. by] in F.
158 in] boþe in F. godhede...manhede] manhede ⁊ godhide C^2. and] ⁊ in F.
159 And] *om* Cr. lyues] Alyue CrGYOC^2; lyvynge F; lymes CB. and(2)] and she WHmCrGOC^2LM; and so YCB; ⁊ *with* F. aloud] lowhde voyȝs he F.

In ech a compaignie þer she cam, *Christus resurgens.*
Thus cam it out þat crist ouercoom, recouerede and lyuede:
Sic oportet Christum pati & intrare &c;
For þat womm[a]n witeþ may noȝt wel be counseille.
Peter parceyued al þis and pursued after,
Boþe Iames and Iohan, Iesu to seke,
Thaddee and ten mo wiþ Thomas of Inde.
And as alle þise wise wyes weren togideres
In an hous al bishet and hir dore ybarred
Crist cam In, and al closed boþe dore and yates, |
To Peter and to [h]ise Apostles and seide *pax vobis*; *fol.* 118 *b*
And took Thomas by þe hand and tauȝte hym to grope
And feele wiþ hise fyngres his flesshliche herte.
Thomas touched it and wiþ his tonge seide:
"[*Dominus*] *meus & [deus] meus.*
Thow art my lord, I bileue, god lord Iesu;
Deidest and deeþ þoledest and deme shalt vs alle,
And now art lyuynge and lokynge and laste shalt euere."

160 *copied twice* CB. In] and in B^2. ech] euery F. a] *above line* O; *om* GF. þer] wer B^1. she] he F. *Christus resurgens*] and so aloude criede C^1; ful lowde sche gradde B^1.

161 Thus] thys G. recouerede] & recurede F. lyuede] leuede BmC^{2}BoF.

161α *line om* F; *in margin* O. *oportet*] *oportebat* O. *pati*] *om* C. *&c*] *om* Cr.

162 *line om* F. þat] LCrG; þat þat WHm YOC^{2}CBM. womman] Y; wommen WHmCrGOC^{2}CBLM. witeþ] wyten HmOC^2; wootethe G; witethes C.

163 parceyued] parceyues C. al] *above line main hand* L; *om* CrM.

164 Boþe] & eek F. to] for to WHmCr GYOC^{2}CBLMF. seke] seken F.

165 Thaddee] & Thadeus F. Inde] Indye G.

166 as] *above line* C^2; *om* GB. alle] *om* Cr. wyes] weyes YC^{2}F; wyghtes G; men B.

167 al] & G. bishet] bysett GYC^{2}C. hir dore] the dores Cr. ybarred] barred Cr; Isperred YGOCB; spered C^2.

168 and(1)] *om* GYOC^{2}CB. closed] cloþid C^2. dore] dores Cr^{3}GF.

169 To...and(1)] & apertly F. to] *om* YC^2. hise] OCrGYC^{2}CLMF; þise WHm; þe B. and(2)] he F; *om* Cr. *pax vobis*] *erasure* F.

170 And] he F.

171 feele] felen F. flesshliche] fleshy Cr.

172 *line om* G. Thomas] þan Thomas F. seide] he seyde F.

172α *in margin* O. *Dominus*] CrCotF; *Deus* WHmGYOC^{2}CBmBoLM. *deus*] CrBF; *dominus* WHmGYOC^{2}CLM. *meus*(2)] *meus &c* HmGBmBo; *meus* & doun he fel to grownde F.

173 god...Iesu] & greet love þou schewist F. god] HmCrGYOC^{2}CLM; my god W; my lord B. lord] god B.

174 Deidest] Thow deidest WHmCr^{23}G YOC^{2}CBLMF; Thou diest Cr^1. deeþ þoledest] þoledyst deeþ F. þoledest] tholest Cr^{12}G. deme] dome G. shalt] þou shalt F; shall CrGBmBo.

175 art...lokynge] þou lyvist & lokist F. shalt] þou shalt F; schalt þou O; shall Cr^{12}BmBo.

Crist carpede þanne and curteisliche seide,
"Thomas, for þow trowest þis and treweliche bileuest it
Blessed mote þow be, and be shalt for euere.
And blessed mote þei be, in body and in soule,
That neu*ere* shul se me in sighte as þow [seest] nowþe,
And lelliche bileue al þis; I loue hem and blesse hem:
Beati qui non viderunt [⁊ *crediderunt*]."
And whan þis dede was doon do best he [þouȝte],
And yaf Piers [pardon, and power] he grauntede hym,
[Myght [men] to assoille of alle manere synne[s],
To alle maner men mercy and forȝifnesse]
In couenaunt þ*at* þei come and knewelich[e] to paie
To Piers pardon þe Plowman *redde quod debes*.
Thus haþ Piers power, b[e] his pardon paied,
To bynde and vnbynde boþe here and elli[s],
And assoille men of alle synnes saue of dette one.
Anoon after an heigh vp into heuene

176 curteisliche] curteliche C. seide] he seyde F.
177 þis] thus G; it Cr. bileuest it] leuest it O; it belevist F.
178 mote] might Cr. shalt] schal BmBo. for] *om* G.
179 mote] moten O; might Cr. be] GC^{2}F; alle be WHmCrYOCBLM. in(2)] *om* Cot.
180 shul se] seye Hm; seien B. sighte] seȝte BmBo. seest] O; doost WHmCr^{23} GYC^{2}CBLMF; hast Cr^{1}. nowþe] now CrGC^{2}CB.
181 lelliche] trewlich C^{2}. bileue] bileuen BHmLMF. hem(1)] hym B. hem(2)] hem all (all *another ink*) M; hym Cot.
181α *in margin* O. *non...crediderunt*] *crediderunt ⁊ non viderunt* (*corrected above line another hand*) O. *⁊ crediderunt*] F; *⁊ crediderunt ⁊c* HmGYC^{2}CB; *⁊c* WCr LM.
182 And] *by correction* Bm. doon] Idoon M. þouȝte] tauȝte WHmCrGYOC^{2}CB LM; took sone F.
183 *divided from* 185 *after* grauntede WHm CrGYOC^{2}CBLM; *after* graunte F. pardon...power] power and pardon WHm CrGYOC^{2}CBLMF. he] hym B; to F. grauntede] graunte F. hym] hys GYC^{2}; he HmB; *om* F.
184 *copied after* 185 WHmCrGYOC^{2}CBL MF. Myght] myght may G; myȝth mowe C^{2}; power myȝte Y; ⁊ power F. men] HmGYC^{2}CBL; *erased* M; *om* WCrOF. to] *om* HmGYC^{2}B. assoille] assoillen M. of] men of Cr^{23}O; he*m* of F; *om* C^{2}. synnes] OYC^{2}CBLM; of sinnes CrGF; synne WHm.
185 men] of men CrCF.
186 þat] *om* GC^{2}. knewelich*e*] MCrGYO C^{2}CBLF; knewelich*ed* WHm.
187 Piers] Pierces Cr^{23}; piere*s* his Cot. pardon þe Plowman] plowhman p*ar*doner F.
188 Thus] thys G. haþ] *om* OF. power] plowhman F. be] HmCrGYOCBmLM (e *over erasure* M); by WC^{2}BoCot; for F. paied] yp*ai*ed M; p*ra*yede F.
189 bynde] byȝnden F. and(1)] and to C^{2}L. ellis] elles LF; elliswhere WHmCr GYOC^{2}CBM.
190 assoille] assoylen Cr; assoyled G; soilled C. alle] here F; *om* CB. of(2)] *om* Cr^{2}. one] onelye Cr; alone G.
191 Anoon] þanne ano*n* F. an] in F. vp] *om* Cr^{23}. into] into þe Y; to þe GC^{2}CB.

He wente, and wonyeþ þere, and wol come at þe laste
And rewarde hym right wel þat *reddit quod debet*,
Paieþ parfitly as pure truþe wolde.
And what persone paieþ it nouȝt punysshen he þenkeþ, |
And demen hem at domesday, boþe quyke and dede, *fol.* 119 *a*
The goode to godhede and to greet Ioye,
And wikkede to wonye in wo wiþouten ende.'
Thus Conscience of crist and of þe cros carpede
And counseiled me to knele þerto; and þanne cam, me pouȝte,
Oon *Spiritus paraclitus* to Piers and to hise felawes.
In liknesse of a lightnynge he lighte on hem alle
And made hem konne and knowe alle kynne langages.
I wondred what þat was and waggede Conscience,
And was afered [for] þe light, for in fires [lik]nesse
Spiritus paraclitus ouerspradde hem alle.
Quod Conscience and knelede, 'þis is cristes messager
And comeþ fro þe grete god; grace is his name.
Knele now', quod Conscience, 'and if þow kanst synge
Welcome hym and worshipe hym wiþ *Veni creator Spiritus*.'
Thanne song I þat song; so dide manye hundred,
And cride wiþ Conscience, 'help vs, [crist], of grace!'
[Th]anne bigan grace to go wiþ Piers Plowman

192 wol] wo Bo. þe] *om* CrYC.
193 And] and wyll GL. rewarde] rewardyn Hm. *reddit*] rat *redde* F. *debet*] *debes* F.
194 Paieþ] And payeth Cr^{23}GOC^{2}F.
195 it...þenkeþ] not pers þynkeþ hym to punche F. punysshen] punish Cr; to punnysshe G; pumisshem C.
196 demen] domen G. hem] him Cr^{1}OC^{2}CB. at] a YC^{2}C; on G. boþe...dede] eyþer to deþ or lyve F.
197 The] ⁊ þe F. to(1)] to þe WHmCrGYOC^{2}CBLMF. and] gon F. to(2)] to þe C^{2}Cot; into þe F. greet] good Cr^{1}.
198 And] ⁊ þe F; The Cr. wikkede] wikke L. wonye] wonnen C^{2}. outen] out Cr.
199 Thus] þus þe F. þe] *om* O. cros] cros he F.
200 þer] here Cr^{1}; *om* Cr^{23}. to(2)] *om* Cr^{23}GC^{2}. me(2)] to me Hm; as me Cr^{23}.
201 to(2)] *om* F.
202 liknesse] lyghtnesse F. he] ⁊ F. on] vpon Cr.
203–6 *lines om* F.
203 kynne] maner G.
204 waggede] wegged BoCot; waged Hm.
205 for þe] of þe WHmCrLM; off þat GYOC^{2}CB. liknesse] YHmCrGOC^{2}CBLM; lightnesse W.
208 god] F; god and WHmCrGYOC^{2}CBLM.
210 wiþ] *om* Cr^{1}. *Veni...Spiritus*] *om* F.
211 *line om* F. so] and so CrGYOC^{2}CBLM. dide] dyden B; *om* Cr^{2}.
212 *line om* F. cride] cryden GHmYOCBLM. crist] god WHmCrGYOC^{2}CBLM.
213 Thanne] Than Cr; And þanne WHmYOCBLM; ⁊ tho GC^{2}; ⁊ F. go] god G. Piers] peers þe O.

And counseillede hym and Conscience þe comune to sompne:
'For I wole dele today and [dyuyde] grace
To alle kynne creatures þat [k]an hi[se] fyue wittes,
Tresour to lyue by to hir lyues ende,
And wepne to fighte wiþ þat wole neu*er*e faille.
For Antecrist and hise al þe world shul greue
And acombre þee, Conscience, but if crist þee helpe.
And false p*ro*phetes fele, flatereris and gloseris,
Shullen come and be curatours ouer kynges and Erles;
And Pride shal be Pope, Prynce of holy chirche,
Coueitise and vnkyndenesse Cardinals hym to lede. |
Forþi', quod g*ra*ce, 'er I go I wol gyue yow tresor *fol.* 119 *b*
And wepne to fighte wiþ whan Antecrist yow assailleþ.'
And gaf ech man a g*ra*ce to gide wiþ hymseluen
That ydelnesse encombre hym no3t, enuye ne pride:
Diuisiones graciarum sunt &c.
Some [wyes] he yaf wit with wordes to shewe,
[To wynne wiþ truþe þat] þe world askeþ,
As p*re*chours and preestes and Prentices of lawe:
They lelly to lyue by labour of tonge,

215 wole] wolde C^{2}. dele...and] today doon F. dyuyde] OCrGYC^{2}CBLM; dyviden F; 3yue diuine WHm.
216 To] Of Y. kan] LF; han WHmCr^{23} Y OC^{2}BM; haue Cr^{1}GC. hise] F; hir WHmCrGYOC^{2}CBLM.
217 Tresour] A tresor F. lyue] leve F.
218 *as one line with* 226 GYOC^{2}CB. And] & a F. þat...faille] *om* GYOC^{2}CB. wole] shal Cr^{23}.
219–25 *lines om* GYOC^{2}CB.
220 þee(2)] *om* CrM.
221 And] For F. fele] & fele F.
222 Shullen] schull HmCrF. come] comen F. Erles] knyghtis F.
223 Pride shal] þa*n* shal Pry3de F. Prynce] and prynce Cr^{23}F.
224 Cardinals] shul ben cardinal*es* F. hym] hem Cr.
225 Forþi] Therfore Cr. gyue] yeue (y *over erasure*) M.
226 And...wiþ] *om* GYOC^{2}CB. And] & a F. Antecrist] any cristyne CB.
227 gaf] 3af OYC^{2}BM; giue Cr. ech] *om* O. a] *om* Cr^{3}F. gide] gye HmLMF; go GYOC^{2}CB. seluen] selue GHmCrYO C^{2}CBF.
228 encombre] acu*m*bre F. enuye] ne envy3e F. ne] nor Cr^{3}.
228α *in margin* O. &c] *om* CrF.
229 Some] To some Cr; So Y. wyes he] he WHmCrGYOC^{2}CBLMF. with] wiþ is BmBo; wi*th* his Cot; & F.
230 To...þat] Wit to wynne hir liflode wiþ as WHmCrGYOC^{2}CBLMF (Wit] & wit F; wi*th* GBmBo; *om* Cot. hir] his Y. wiþ] *om* F). world] werk O; lond F.
231 Prentices] prentys HmC^{2}LF; p*r*incis B. of] of þe FG. lawe] lawes O.
232 lelly] trewly C^{2}. lyue] lyven F; leue C^{2}C. by] bi a B; þoru3 O. of] of her C^{2}GF.

And by wit to wissen oþere as g*ra*ce hem wolde teche.
And some he kennede craft and konnynge of sighte,
[By] sellynge and buggynge hir bilyue to wynne.
And some he lered to laboure [on lond and on watre
And lyue, by þat labour], a lele lif and a trewe.
And some he tauȝte to tilie, to [coke] and to thecche,
To wynne wiþ hir liflode bi loore of his techynge;
And some to deuyne and diuide, [figures] to kenne;
And some to [kerue and compace], and colours to make;
And some to se and to seye what sholde bifalle,
Boþe of wele and of wo [and be ware bifore],
As Astronomyens þoruȝ Astronomye, and Philosofres wise.
And some to ryde and to recou*ere* þat [vnriȝt]fully was wonne:
He wissed hem wynne it ayein þoruȝ wightnesse of handes
And fecchen it fro false men wiþ Foluyles lawes.
And some he lered to lyue in longynge to ben hennes,
In pou*er*te and in [pacience] to preie for alle cristene.

233 by] by he*re* F. as] and B. hem wolde] wolde he*m* F. hem] hym BmBo.
234 he] by Hm; *om* B. kennede] kynde Hm. craft] crafftis C^{2}CB.
235 By] Wiþ WHmCrGYOC^{2}CBLMF. buggynge] beggynge F; beynge C^2. bilyue] lyflode HmCr^{12}BMF (*over erasure* Hm); liuelodes Cr^3.
236 *run together with* 237 WHmCrGYOC^{2}CBLM. some he] *om* Cr. lered] lerned Cr^{1}F; lerned some Cr^{23}. to] *om* GC^2. on(1)...watre] F; *om* WHmCrGYOC^{2}CBLM; *here in the spelling of* W.
237 And...labour] F; *om* WHmCrGYOC^{2}CBLM; *here in the spelling of* W. lele] lelly Cr. a(2)] *om* GYOC^{2}CBmBoF.
238 to(2)] *om* Cr^{23}. coke] dyke HmCot; dyche WCrGYOC^{2}CBmBoLMF. thecche] þresche F; hegge Cr^{23}GYOC^{2}CB.
240 And] *om* CrM. to(1)] *om* YB. and] and to M. diuide] dyuyded Hm. figures] noumbres WHmCrGYOC^{2}LMF; membres CB. kenne] knowe F.
241 *line om* Cr. kerue...compace] compace craftily WHmGYOC^{2}CBLMF.
242 to(2)] some to GOC^{2}CB. sholde] shulle BoCot; slode Y.
243 and(2)...bifore] telle it er it felle WHmCrGYOC^{2}CBLMF (telle] to tell F; tyll Cr^3. felle] falle Cot).
244 Astronomyens] astronomers Cr; astrymyens G; astronomyes C^{2}B. þoruȝ] by Cr; of F. Astronomye] astromye BmBo. and] on O. wise] wyȝsdom F.
245 And] *om* Hm. ryde] rekne F. to(2)] some to GHmYOC^{2}CB; *om* Cr^{23}F. recouere] recoueren M; recoeure LF. vnriȝtfully] LCrGYOC^{2}CBMF; ryȝtfully Hm; wrongfully W. wonne] wonnen OM.
246 *line om* F. wissed] wissen Cot; wissem Bo. hem] HmCrGYC^{2}CLM; hem to WOB (to *above line* O). wynne] wynnen M. wightnesse] wytnesse HmCBmBo; wightwisnesse Y; rithwyssnese C^2; ryghtyousnes G; *om* (myȝt *above line another hand*) Cot. handes] ha*n*d Cr.
247 fecchen] fecche OCr. Foluyles] folwyles G; forluylis B; foule iuels Cr^{12}; foule euyll Cr^3. lawes] lawe BF.
248 lered] lerned CrHmGF. lyue] leue C^2.
249 In] As in F. pou*er*te] pouert BmBo. pacience] FHm; penaunce WCrGYOC^{2}CBLM. for alle] fol C.

And alle he lered to be lele, and ech a craft loue ooþer,
[Ne no boost ne] debat [be] among hem [alle].
'Thouȝ some be clenner þan some, ye se wel', quod Grace, |
'[That al craft and konnyng come] of my ȝifte. *fol.* 120 *a*
Lokeþ þat no[on] lakke ooþer, but loueþ as breþeren;
And who þat moost maistries kan be myldest of berynge.
And crouneþ Conscience kyng and makeþ craft youre Stiward,
And after craftes conseil cloþeþ yow and fede.
For I make Piers þe Plowman my procuratour and my reue,
And Registrer to receyue *redde quod debes*.
My prowor and my Plowman Piers shal ben on erþe,
And for to tilie truþe a teeme shal he haue.'
Grace gaf Piers a teeme, foure grete Oxen.
That oon was Luk, a large beest and a lowe chered,
And Mark, and Mathew þe þridde, myghty beestes boþe;
And Ioyned to hem oon Iohan, moost gentil of alle,
The pris neet of Piers plow, passynge alle oþere.
And Grace gaf Piers of his goodnesse foure stottes,

250 he] *om* F. lered] lerned CrF. lele] lelli Cr; lee BmBo; trewe C[2]. a] *om* GBF. loue] to loue BF.
251 And forbad hem alle debat þat noon were among hem WHmCrGYOC[2]CBLMF (alle] *om* F. debat] debatis B. were] weren BmBo).
252 se] seyn Bm. *Hereafter an additional line* WHmCrGYOC[2]CBLMF: That he þat vseþ þe faireste craft to þe fouleste I kouþe haue put hym (he...vseþ] men of Cr. þe faireste] fayr F. I] *om* B. hym] *om* Cr). *See above*, p. 193; *then a further four lines* F; *see above*, p. 223.
253 *line om* GYOC[2]CB. That...come] Thynkeþ alle quod Grace þat grace comeþ WHmCrLMF (Thynkeþ] Think Cr. quod] now quod F).
254 Lokeþ] Loke CrGYOC[2]CBLM; & looke F. þat] *om* F. noon] OHmCrGC[2]CBLM; non ne F; no Y; no man W. loueþ] loue CrGC; *om* Y. as] alle as WHmCrYOC[2]CBLMF; togeddre as G.
255 who] þo C[2]; þei B. þat] *om* (*corrector supplies*) Cot. kan] konne C. be] þe Cr. myldest] mylde B.
256 crouneþ] crowne CrGO; crowned Y CB. makeþ] make CrO; maked CBmBo.
257 *line om* C. cloþeþ] cloþe HmCrG C[2]B; ȝee clothe F. fede] fedeþ O.
258 þe] *om* Cr[3]GF. procuratour] procour F.
259 Registrer] register CrGYC[2]BoCot.
260 prowor] purveour C[2]G; procour F; prouisor Cr[23]; power Cr[1]; plowght C; plough B.
261 tilie] tell Cr. truþe] trewly F. teeme] tyme G.
262 Grace] þan grace F. gaf] ȝaf C[2]B. foure] YHmCrGOC[2]CBLMF; of foure W.
263 That] the GF. oon] firste F. a(2)] a ful F; of B. lowe] ? loue C[2]. chered] chere BF.
264 And] *om* Hm. beestes] blasts Cr[3].
265 And] he F. moost] þe most YOC[2]CB. of] of hem F.
266 The pris] & prysest F. neet] of þe neyte (of þe *above line*) G; *om* F. Piers] Pierces Cr[23]. plow] plow and CrF.
267 And] & ȝit F. gaf...goodnesse] of his goodnesse gaf peers F. gaf] ȝaf C[2]B. of...goodnesse] also goode (also *over erasure*; *erasure after* goode) M. foure] foure grete CB.

Al þat hise oxen eriede þei to harewen after.
Oon highte Austyn and Ambrose anoþer,
Gregori þe grete clerk and [þe goode Ierom];
Thise foure, þe feiþ to teche, folwe[de] Piers teme
And harewede in an handwhile al holy Scripture
Wiþ two [aiþes] þat þei hadde, an oold and a newe:
Id est vetus testamentum & nouum.
And Grace gaf [Piers] greynes, Cardynal[es] vertues,
And sew [it] in mannes soule and siþen tolde hir names.
Spiritus prudencie þe firste seed highte,
And whoso ete þat ymagynen he sholde,
Er he [dide] any [dede] deuyse wel þe ende;
And lerned men a ladel bugge wiþ a long stele
[That] caste for to ke[l]e a crokke to saue þe fatte aboue. |
The seconde seed highte *Spiritus temperancie.* *fol.* 120 *b*
He þat ete of þat seed hadde swich a kynde:
Sholde neuere mete ne [meschief] make hym to swelle;

268 Al þat] that all G. eriede] eriedem O; ereden F. þei] hem O. to] *om* G. harewen] harewe YCrC^{2}CLMF; harrowed G. after] it after CrBMF.
269 Oon] þe firste F. Austyn] augustyne G. and] *om* Cot. Ambrose anoþer] anoþer ambrose B. anoþer] is anoþir F.
270 Gregori] & Gregorie F. þe...Ierom] Ierom þe goode WCrGOC^{2}CBLM; ieromye þe goode HmY; Ieroom þe fowrthe F.
271 Thise] & þese F. to teche] techen & F. folwede] folweþ WCrYBLM; folwen HmGOC^{2}F; folowes C. Piers] Pierces Cr^{23}F. teme] tyme (*corrected main hand*) C.
272 harewede] hareweden OB; harewen C^{2}F. in] it in Cr^1. an] *om* YF. while] wihile C.
273 two] tweye F. aiþes] hayȝtes F; harewes WHmCrGYOC^{2}CBLM. hadde] hadden OBF. an] and CB (*corrected* C); þe F. oold] olde lawe F. a] þe F; *om* Cot.
273α *in margin* O. *Id est*] *om* GYOC^{2}CB. *nouum*] *nouum testamentum* F; *nouum &c* HmBo.
274 gaf] ȝaf C^{2}B. Piers greynes] peers greynes F; greynes þe WHmCrGYOC^{2}CBLM. Cardynales] GYOC^{2}CBLMF; Cardynal WHmCr.
275 And] & he F. sew] sewen YM; swee C. it in] yn ytt (yn *above line*) G. it] Cr YOCBLMF; hem WHmC^2. tolde] Hm Cr^{23}GYOC^{2}CB; he tolde WCr^{1}LMF.
277 And...þat] þat who eetyþ of þat frut F. ete] eateth CrM. ymagynen] ymagyne GHmCrYOC^{2}CBLF.
278 dide...dede] YHmCrGOC^{2}CBLMF; deide any deeþ W. deuyse] avyse GB. wel] hym wel of B; he sholde F.
279 lerned] lered HmG; lerneth C^2. men] hym F. a(*both*)] *om* Cr^1. ladel] ladel to OF; lady Y. bugge] be Cr^1.
280 That] CrGC^{2}CBLM; To O; And WHmY; For he F. for] *om* F. kele] kepe WHmCrGYOC^{2}CBLMF. to saue] & keepe F. aboue] abouen CLM.
281–358 defective O: *see above*, p. 12.
281 seed] heed C^2. highte] þat he sew was F.
282 ete] eteþ HmF. hadde] it had C^2; he shal have F.
283 Sholde] ne schulde Hm. mete] *om* Y. meschief] myschef F; muchel drynke WYCLM; moche drynke HmCrGC^{2}B. make] maken F.

Ne [sholde] no scorner*e* out of skile hym brynge;
Ne wynnynge ne wele of worldliche richesse,
Waste word of ydelnesse ne wikked speche moeue;
Sholde no curious cloop comen on his rugge,
Ne no mete in his mouþ þ*at* maister Ioh*an* Spicede.
The þridde seed þat Piers sew was *Spiritus fortitudinis*,
And who[so] ete [of] þat seed hardy was euere
To suffren al þat god sente, siknesse and Angres.
Mighte no [lyere wiþ lesynges] ne los of worldly catel
Maken hym, for any mournynge, þat he nas murie in soule,
And bold and abidynge bismares to suffre;
And pleieþ al wiþ pacience and *Parce michi domine*;
And cou*er*ed hym vnder conseille of Caton þe wise:
Esto forti animo cum sis dampnatus inique.
The ferþe seed þat Piers sew was *Spiritus Iusticie*,
And he þ*at* ete of þat seed sholde be [euene] trewe
Wiþ god, and nau3t agast but of gile one.
For gile gooþ so pryuely þat good feiþ ouþer while
[Shal] nou3t ben espied [þoru3] *Spiritus Iusticie*.
Spiritus Iusticie spareþ no3t to spille [þe] gilty,

284 sholde] YCrGC^{2}CBLMF; *om* WHm. out] F; ne scolde out WHmCrYC^{2}CB LM; ne skolde hym oute G. hym] *om* G.
285 *line om* GYC^{2}CB. wele] welþe Hm CrLMF. of] of no F.
286 Waste] Ne wast F; Waste a (a *above line*) M; what B. ne] ne no GYCB. speche] speches F.
287 Sholde] & also sholde F. comen] come Cr.
288 þat] but G. Spicede] it spyede F.
289 was] ys G.
290 so...of] YHmCrGC^{2}CBmCotLMF; so se ete of (se *cancelled*) Bo; ete W. was] CrGYC^{2}CLM; was he WHm; he was BF.
291 suffren] suffre HmCrGYC^{2}CBLMF. sente] sent & Y. siknesse] seeknessis F. and] or CrM.
292 Mighte] þer myghte F. lyere] lesynge L; lesynges WHmCrGYC^{2}CBMF. wiþ] ne WHmCrGYC^{2}LM; no C; hym B; of F. lesynges] lyere WCrGYC^{2}LMF; lyers Hm; ber C; dere B. los] loste Cot. worldly] eny Cot; no BmBo.
293 Maken] Make CrGB. þat he nas] but euer G. nas] ne was B; was F.
294 bismares] busynece (ce *altered from* s) G.
295 pleieþ al] he pleted eu*er*e F. and] & *with* Y.
296 And] & he F. cou*er*ed] coue*r*eþ BCrF (þ *corrected from* n Bm); coueren YC^{2}C; couer G.
296α *inique*] *inique &c* Hm.
297 *Iusticie*] *iusticie &c* Hm.
298 ete] eateth Cr. sholde] shal Cr. euene] euere WHmCrGYC^{2}CBmCotL MF; neuere Bo.
299 Wiþ...and] & of god F. one] alone G.
300 good feiþ] good Cot; god sayth Cr[1].
301 Shal] May WHmCrGYC^{2}CBLMF. nou3t] nou3 C. þoru3] for WHmGYC^2 CBLMF; fro Cr.
302, 303 *as three lines divided after* spille, correcte WHmCrGYC^{2}CBLMF.
302 þe] Hem þat ben WHmCrGYC^{2}CB LMF.

And to correcte [þ]e kyng if [þe kyng] falle in gilt.
For counteþ he no kynges wraþe whan he in Court sitteþ;
To demen as a domesman adrad was he neu*ere*
Neiþ*er* of duc ne of deeþ, þ*at* he ne dide lawe
For p*re*sent or for preiere or any Prynces lettres.
He dide equyte to alle eueneforþ his [knowynge]. |
Thise foure sedes Piers sew, and siþþe he dide hem harewe *fol.* 121 *a*
Wiþ olde lawe and newe lawe þat loue myȝte wexe
Among þ[e] foure v*er*tues and vices destruye.
'For comunliche in contrees cammokes and wedes
Foulen þe fruyt in þe feld þer þei growen togideres,
And so doon vices vertues; [f]orþi', quod Piers,
'Hareweþ alle þat konneþ kynde wit by conseil of þise docto[urs],
And tilieþ [to] hir techynge þe Cardynale v*er*tues.'
'Ayeins þi greynes', quod Grace, 'bigynneþ for to ripe,
Ordeigne þee an hous, Piers, to herberwe Inne þi cornes.'

303 and for to correcte The kyng if he falle in gilt or in trespas WHmCrGYC^{2}CBLMF (The...falle] þey me*n* falle ageyn þe kyng F. he] þ*at* he G. in(2)] in ony C^{2}G).
304 For...kynges] He coueyȝteþ no keene F. counteþ] acounteþ HmB. in] *om* Cr.
305 as] ryght as F. adrad] dradde G. was] is F. he] *twice* Bo.
306 ne(1)] nor Hm. þat...dide] if he doo F. lawe] þe lawe LF.
307 p*re*sent or] presentes ne Cr. preiere] prayers CrM. or(2)] er for F.
308 He] and B. equyte] qwite F. to] for Cr^{1}. alle] alle me*n* F. his] to his Cr^{3}G (to *above line* G). knowynge] power W HmCrGYC^{2}CBLMF.
310 Wiþ] wit*h* þe FCr^{23}. and] ⁊ þe F. lawe(2)] *om* Cr.
311 þe] the CrGYC^{2}CBLM; þo WHm; þese F. vices] vices to CrF.
312 For] ⁊ F; Fo Y. comunliche] comunes Y. in] growit*h* in F. cammokes] calokes B (r *inserted after* a BmCot); came monks Cr^{1}.
313 Foulen] þey fowle F. þe feld] feeldis F. growen] growe HmCrGYC^{2}CBLM.
314 *divided from* 315 *after* worþi WHmCr GYC^{2}CBLM; *after* vertues F. And] Ryght F; *om* G. vertues forþi] worthy fayre vertues F. forþi] worþi WHmCrG YC^{2}CBLM. quod] And Cr^{3}.
315 *as two lines divided after* wytt HmCr. Hareweþ] harwen C^{2}. konneþ] konne YGC^{2}CB; knowen F. kynde] kyndly YGC^{2}CB; *om* F. by] by rede and by Hm. þise] þese fowr Hm; *om* G. doctours] HmCrGYC^{2}CBLMF; docto (*cropped*) W.
316 And] And after Y. tilieþ] telles C. to] after WHmCrGC^{2}CBLMF; *om* Y. hir] hys GC; þis C^{2}. þe] þese F; *om* Bo Cot.
317 þi] þe HmCr^{1}F; these Cr^{23}; þei þi (þei *cancelled*) Bm. greynes] tyme F. Grace] *gr*ace to Piers YGC^{2}C; grace to Peris þat þi B; grace þ*at* þy frut F. bigynneþ] gynneth CrMF; greyneþ B. for to] to GY; *om* BF.
318 Ordeigne] Peers ordeyne F. Piers] q*uo*d piers LCr^{12}M; *om* GYC^{2}CBF. þi] þe Cr. cornes] corne CrGYC^{2}C.

'By god! Grace', quod Piers, 'ye moten gyue tymber,
And ordeyne þat hous er ye hennes wende.'
And Grace gaf hym þe cros, wiþ þe [garland] of þornes,
That crist vpon Caluarie for mankynde on pyned.
And of his baptisme and blood þat he bledde on roode
He made a manere morter, and mercy it highte.
And þerwiþ Grace bigan to make a good foundement,
And watlede it and walled it wiþ his[e] peyne[s] and his
    passion;
And of al holy writ he made a roof after;
And called þat hous vnitee, holy chirche on englissh.
And whan þis dede was doon Grace deuysede
A cart highte cristendom to carie [home] Piers sheues,
And gaf hym caples to his carte, contricion and confession;
And made preesthod hayward þe while hymself wente
As wide as þe world is wiþ Piers to tilie truþe
[And þe [lond] of bileue, þe lawe of holy chirche].
Now is Piers to þe plow; pride it aspide
And gadered hym a greet Oost; greuen he þynkeþ
Conscience and alle cristene and Cardinale vertues, |
Blowe hem doun and breke hem and bite atwo þe mores. *fol.* 121 *b*

319 god] goddis BF. moten] moote Cr^{23}YC^{2}F; most CGB; might Cr^1. gyue] yeue YC^{2}BM. tymber] me tymbir CotF.
320 þat] & caste þat F. hennes] henne Hm. wende] wenden F; wente Bo.
321 gaf] ȝaf C^{2}BM. wiþ] & F. garland] croune WHmCrGYC^{2}CBLMF.
322 on pyned] on peyned Cot; kawhte F.
323 his] this Cr^1. and] & of þe F.
324 and] *om* F.
326 And...it(2)] & he peyntyde þe wallis F. watlede] watrid B; walled CrM. walled] watled CrM. hise...and] þe woundis of F. hise peynes] YHmCrGC^{2}CBLM; his peyne W. his] *above line* M; *om* Hm.
327 al] *om* C^2. made a] wroghte þe F.
328 on] in CrC^2.
329 dede] dide C. Grace] grace anon GC^2.
330 highte] high C^2; þat hette F. carie] carien M. home Piers] hoom F; Piers WHmGYC^{2}CBLM; Pierces Cr. sheues] theues Cr^1.
331 hym] peers F. contricion...confession] *om* F.
332 And] & he F. þe] þer Hm; *om* CrGYM.
333 As] also B.
334 F; *line om* WHmCrGYC^{2}CBLM; *here in the spelling of* W. lond] loore F. þe(2)] & þe F.
335 plow] plow and WHmCrGYC^{2}CBLMF. it] is B. aspide] spied Cr.
336 And gadered] & he gadreþ F. Oost] ost F; host to CrGYC^{2}CLM; oost for Hm; Oost for to W; ost hym to B. greuen] greue CrGCot. he] him he CrGC^{2}F.
337 *line om* GYC^{2}CB. Conscience...cristene] & Conscience & *cri*stendom F.
338 Blowe] blew GCBF. hem(1)] hym B. breke] breeken F; brak B. hem(2)] hym Cot. bite...mores] beetyn doun here maneres F. bite] bot B.

And sente forþ Surquidous, his sergeaunt of Armes,
And his Spye Spille/loue, oon Spek/yuel/bihynde.
Thise two coome to Conscience and to cristen peple
And tolde hem tidynges, þ*at* tyne þei sholde
[Th]e sedes [þat sire] Piers [sew], þe Cardynale ve*r*tues.
'And Piers bern worþ ybroke; and þei þat ben in vnitee
Shulle come out, Conscience; and your*e* [caples two],
Confession and Contricion, and your*e* carte þe bileeue
Shal be coloured so queyntely and cou*er*ed vnder [oure] Sophistrie
That Conscience shal noȝt knowe who is cristene or heþene,
Ne no manere marchaunt þat wiþ moneye deleþ
Wheiþ*er* he wynne wiþ right, wiþ wrong or wiþ vsure.'
Wiþ swiche colours and queyntise comeþ pride yarmed
Wiþ þe lord þat lyueþ after þe lust of his body,
'To wasten on welfare and in wikked [kepyng]
Al þe world in a while þoruȝ oure wit', quod Pryde.
Quod Conscience to alle cristene þo, 'my counseil is to wende

339 sente] senty*n* F. Surquidous...sergeaunt] surq*ui*doures were *ser*gawntys F. Surquidous] Sarquidons Cr^{1}.
340 Spye] spyȝes F. oon] ⁊ F; *om* Hm.
341 coome] comen HmCrBMF.
342 *divided from* 343 *after* sedes WHmCr GYC^{2}CBLMF. tolde] tolden BHmMF. hem] hym CM. tidynges] tythynge*s* GY; tiynges C. tyne...sholde] þey wolde stroye F. tyne] tene C^{2}; tyme Y.
343 The] *spelled* þe W. þat sire] That WHmCrGYC^{2}CBLMF. sew] plowhman seew all F; þere hadde ysowen WGYCB LM; þere hadde sowyn HmCrC^{2}.
344 Piers bern] peersis doore F. worþ] wroþ BmBo; were Cr; with C. ybroke] broke GYCL; broken CrC^{2}. ben] been *above cancelled* were *main hand* G.
345 Shulle] Shulde BoCrYCot. out] oute of (of *cancelled*) Y; out on B; out and WHmCrGC^{2}CLM; to vs F. caples two] two caples WHmCrGYC^{2}CBLMF.
346 Confession] Boþe Co*n*fessiou*n* F. your*e*] þe F. þe] of F.
347 oure] YHmCr^{23}GC^{2}CBmBoLM; your Cr^{1}Cot; *om* WF.
348 *as two lines divided after* contricion WHmCrGYC^{2}CBLM; *after* knowe F. Conscience] consciou*n* L. shal noȝt] ne cont*r*iciou*n* shal not ben F. who] Ne be co*n*fessiou*n* who F; by contricion Ne by Confession who WHmCrGYC^{2}CBLM. or] ne CrM.
349 manere] *om* F.
350 Wheiþ*er*] where GYC^{2}CBmBoLM. wynne] wynneþ F. wiþ(2)] or w*ith* CrF.
351 colours] colour Cr. and] of and (of *cancelled*) C; *om* F. queyntise] couetise Cr^{1}M; ypey*n*tid F. pride] *om* F. yarmed] armed CrC^{2}CB.
352 þe(2)] *om* G. lust] lustys F. body] herte F.
353 wasten on welfare] waaste ⁊ wel faren F. in] on HmCrYCBLM; *om* GC^{2}F. wikked] wikkednesse F. kepyng] CHm CrGYC^{2}BLM; lyuyng W; he meyntiþ F.
354 quod] off G.
355 alle] *om* F. my] y F. is] þe F.

Hastiliche into vnitee and holde we vs þere.
Praye we þ*at* a pees weere in Piers berne þe Plowman.
For witterly, I woot wel, we beþ noȝt of strengþe
To goon agayn Pride but Grace weere wiþ vs.'
And þanne kam Kynde wit Conscience to teche,
And cryde and comaundede alle cristene peple
To deluen a dych depe aboute vnitee
That holy chirche stode in [holynesse] as it a Pyl weere.
Conscience comaundede þo alle cristene to delue,
And make a muche moot þat myghte ben a strengþe |
To helpe holy chirche and hem þ*at* it kepeþ. *fol.* 122 *a*
Thanne alle kynne cristene saue comune wo*m*men
Repenteden and [forsoke] synne, saue þei one,
And [a sisour and a somonour] þat were forsworen ofte;
Witynge and wilfully wiþ þe false helden,
And for siluer were forswore—sooþly þei wiste it.
Ther nas no cristene creature þat kynde wit hadde
Saue sherewes one swiche as I spak of,
That he ne halp a quantite holynesse to wexe,

356 into] to F. holde we] wee shull holde F. we vs] vs well GC^2. þere] heere F.
357 Praye] And praye WHmCrGYC^{2}CB LMF. a] *om* CF. Piers] Pierces CrF. þe] *om* F.
358 we] þ*at* we Cr.
359 Here O resumes. agayn] ayein YBM.
360 And] *om* GYOC^{2}CB.
361 alle] to all Cr.
362 To] For to WHmCrGYOC^{2}CBLMF. deluen] delue HmCr^{1}BF. a] and HmCr YOC^{2}CBF. dych] dichen O; dyke Hm BF; digge Cr. depe] depe all F.
363 stode] stonde C^2. in holynesse] in vnitee WHmCrGYOC^{2}CBLM; strong F. Pyl] piler (*over erasure*) Cot. weere] *om* L.
364 delue] doluе*n* Cr^{23}.
365 make] maken CrHmF. muche] mychil F. moot] mute (oo *above* u) Y. a(2)] off g (g *cancelled*) G; of F.
366 helpe] helpyn HmF. hem] he CB.
367 Thanne] that GC^2. saue] creaturis saue C^2. wo*m*men] wo*m*man B (e *above* a Bm).
368 Repenteden] Repented CrF. forsoke] refused WCrGLF; refuseden YHmOC^2 CBM. one] onely Cr; alone GF.
369 *as two lines divided* after þeues WHm CrGYOC^{2}CBLMF. a(1)...somonour] false men flatereris vsurers and þeues Lyeris and questemong*er*es WHmCrGY OC^{2}CBLMF (flatereris] flateres YC^{2}L; ⁊ flateris ⁊ F). were] weren OBmBoM; ben F. sworen] swore GYC^{2}CF. ofte] often O.
370 Witynge] Wyttingely CrGOC^2. wilfully] wilful ⁊ F. helden] helde F; holden Cr.
371 were] weren O; ben F. swore] sworen OB. sooþly...it] ⁊ soþly knowe þe co*n*tr*ar*ie F. wiste] wysten HmOB.
372 nas] was F.
373 Saue] saue þo C^2. one] onely Cr; oone and Y; oonly ⁊ F; ⁊ GO. as] *om* F. spak] speake Cr^{23}. of] of toforehond F.
374 halp] hape Y. to] make to F.

Some þoruȝ bedes biddynge and some [by] pilgrymag[e]
And oþ[er] pryue penaunc[e], and so*m*me þoruȝ penyes delynge.
And þanne wellede water for wikkede werkes
Egreliche ernynge out of mennes eighen.
Clennesse [of þe] comune and clerkes clene lyuynge
Made vnitee holy chirche in holynesse stonde.
'I care noȝt', quod Conscience, 'þouȝ pride come nouþe.
The lord of lust shal be letted al þis lente, I hope.
'Comeþ', quod Conscience, 'ye cristene, and dyneþ,
That han laboured lelly al þis lenten tyme.
Here is breed yblessed, and goddes body þervnder.
Grace, þoruȝ goddes word, [g]af Piers power,
[Myȝt] to maken it and men to ete it after
In help of hir heele ones in a Monþe,
Or as ofte as þei hadde nede, þo þat hadde ypaied
To Piers pardon þe Plowman *redde quod debes*.'
'How?' quod al þe comune; 'þow conseillest vs to yelde
Al þat we owen any wight er we go to housel?' |

375 þoruȝ] by Cr. some] *om* F. by] Cr; þoruȝ WHmGYOC^{2}CBLMF. pilgrymage] YHmCrGOC^{2}CBLMF; pilgrymages W.

376 Su*m*me þorghȝ pens dely*ng* & su*m*me þorghȝ pr*i*ue penau*n*ces F. oþer] HmCrG YC^{2}CBLM; oþ*ere* WO. penaunce] Hm GYOC^{2}CBL; penaunces W; paines CrM. penyes] pens Cr^{23}YOB; paines Cr^1; pennau*n*ce GC^2.

377 wellede] walmede F; willid Bo; walkyd C^2. water] weter Y. for] with C; þurgh B.

378 Egreliche] Ful eg*r*ily F. ernynge] ȝernynge HmB; rennyng GCr^{23}OC^2. of mennes] of menys *twice* C^2.

379 of þe] OCrGYC^{2}CBLMF; out of WHm.

380 Made] madyn Hm. vnitee] vnite in F. in holynesse] holylyche F. stonde] YF; to stonde WHmCrGOC^{2}CBLM.

381 þouȝ...come] þey keme F. þouȝ] if O. nouþe] now CrG.

382 The] & þe F. lente] lentene F; leaute Y. hope] tr*o*we F.

383 Comeþ] Come Cr. quod] wi*th* me q*uo*d F; *om* B. ye] þe B; y Y; iche O. dyneþ] dyne Cr.

384 lelly] trewly C^2. lenten] lente CrHm GYC^{2}CBL.

385 Here] hiree C. yblessed] blessed CrG. vnder] Inne F.

386 Grace] þan Grace F. gaf] HmCrGY OCLMF; yaf WC^{2}B. Piers] pers his F.

387 Myȝt] Mighte C; Myȝtes LGYOC^2 BM; And might CrF; And myȝtes WHm. to(1)] for to F. maken] make CrB. it(*both*)] *om* Y. men] mete G. ete] eten YHmBM.

388 Monþe] twelfmoneþ F.

389 hadde(1)] hadden OLM. þo] they GY. hadde(2)] hadden M; *om* O. ypaied] payed YCrBF.

390 Piers] Pierces Cr. pardon þe Plowman] plowhma*n*nys p*ar*dou*n* F.

391 How] Ow F. conseillest] counseilis C^2; comandist F. yelde] ȝeldyn F.

392 owen] owe Cr. we(2)...housel] þat we come to husly*ng* F.

'That is my conseil', quod Conscience, 'and Cardinale vertues; *fol.* 122 *b*
[Or] ech man forȝyue ooþer, and þat wole þe Paternost*er*:
Et dimitte nobis debita nostra &c,
And so to ben assoilled and siþþen ben houseled.'
'Ye? baw!' quod a Brewer*e*, 'I wol noȝt be ruled,
By I*esu*! for al your*e* Ianglynge, wiþ *Spiritus Iusticie*,
Ne after Conscience, by crist! while I kan selle
Boþe dregges and draf and drawe at oon hole
Thikke ale and þynne ale; þat is my kynde,
And noȝt hakke after holynesse; hold þi tonge, Conscience!
Of *Spiritus Iusticie* þow spekest muche on ydel.'
'Caytif!' quod Conscience, 'cursede wrecche!
Vnblessed artow, Brewer*e*, but if þee god helpe.
But þow lyue by loore of *Spiritus Iusticie*,
The chief seed þat Piers sew, ysaued worstow neu*ere*.
But Conscience [be þi] comune[s] and Cardinale v*er*tues
Leue it wel [þow art] lost, boþe lif and soule.'
'Thanne is many a [lif] lost', quod a lewed vicory.

393 Cardinale] cardynales M; cardial Cr^1.
394 Or] F; That WHmCrGYOC^{2}CBLM. ech] *om* F. man] a man HmM (a *over erasure* M); ony F. and] *om* G.
394α *in margin* O. &c] *om* YOF.
395 ben(2)] to ben YGOC^{2}CBF; *om* CrM. houseled] yhouseled MF.
396 baw] bow YC (*altered to* how C); how GC^{2}B; baw wawh F. wol] wolde Cot. noȝt] *om* C^2. be] so be F.
397 By Iesu] By I*es*us YCr; Ne Iustefied by I*es*u so F. al] *om* CrC. wiþ...*Iusticie*] here F.
398 after] after þe F. by...kan] but I can wel F. while] wille Bo.
399 at] O; it Hm; out an F; it at YCrGC^{2}CBLM; it out at W. oon] an HmCr^{1}YC^{2}Cot; *om* C. hole] hole tappe F.
400 Thikke] Boþe þykke F; Thilke C. ale(1)] alle Bo; *om* Cot. ale(2)] alle BoCot; *om* F. þat] þat F; for þat WHmCrGYOC^{2}CLM; boþe for þat B. kynde] craft cleene F.
401 hold...Conscience] now hold co*n*sciense þy*n* tu*n*ge F.
402 spekest] spyllyst F. muche] *om* CBF. on] yn HmG; *om* F. ydel] ydel speche F.
403 Caytif] A Caytyf F. cursede] þou art a cursyd F.
404 þee god] god þe F; god M.
405 But] But if Cr; and but C^{2}F. lyue] leue C^2. by] bi þe BF.
406 sew] soweth Cot. ysaued] saued Cr C^{2}F. worstow] worþest þou OG; worth Cr^{23}.
407 But] & but F; and C^2. be þi] be þy*n* F; be C^2; þe WHmCrGYOCBLM. comunes] comune Fode C^{2}F; comune fede WCr^{23}YCBLM; commune fedde Cr^1; comyn fede Hm; comune seed O; come seede G. Cardinale] cardynales M.
408 *line om* Y. Leue] lyue Cot. it] me F; *om* Cr. þow art] þou art F; þei ben WHm CrGOC^{2}CBLM. lif] litil lif (litil *cancelled*) Bm.
409 a(1)] *om* L. lif] man WHmCrGYOC^2 CBLMF. lost] ylost HmC^{2}LM.

'I am a Curatour of holy kirke, and cam neu*er*e in my tyme
Man to me þat me kouþe telle of Cardinale v*er*tues,
Or þ*a*t acountede Conscience at a cokkes feþere.
I knew neu*er*e Cardynal þat he ne cam fro þe pope.
And we clerkes, whan þei come, for hir comunes paieþ,
For hir pelure and palfreyes mete and pilours þat hem folweþ.
The comune *clamat cotidie*, ech a man til ooþer,
"The contree is þe corseder þat Cardinals come Inne,
And þer þei ligge and lenge moost lecherie þere regneþ".
Forþi', quod þis vicory, 'by verray god I wolde
That no Cardynal coome among þe comune peple, |
But in hir holynesse helden hem stille *fol.* 123 *a*
At Auynou*n* among Iewes—*Cum sancto sanctus eris &c*—
Or in Rome as hir rule wole þe relikes to kepe;
And þow Conscience in kynges court, and sholdest neu*er*e come þennes;
And Grace þat þow gr[e]dest so of, gyour of alle clerkes;
And Piers [þe Plowman] wiþ his newe plow and [þe] olde

410 I] That Cr^{1}. kirke] chirche C^{2}BF. neu*er*e] meuer*e* Bo.
411 Man] Men Cr. to me] *om* F. þat] *om* Cr^{1}. me(2)] *om* CrGYC^{2}; cowde F. kouþe] me F. Cardinale] cardynales M.
412 Or þat] þ*a*t euer*e* F. acountede] cou*n*ted CrGYOC^{2}C. at a] oon F. feþere] fedre F; feþere or an hennes WHmCr GYOC^{2}CBLM.
413 I] I ne Cr. þat] v*er*tues þ*a*t B. he ne] *om* F.
414 And...clerkes] For we vykeres F. come] comen OM; came G. paieþ] paye F; payed C; payden C^{2}.
415 For] & for F. pelure] pelures CrM; *om* F. and(1)] & Cr; and hir WHmGYO C^{2}CBLM; *om* F. and(2)] & for F. folweþ] folwe BoCrCot; folowed C.
416 The comune] & þe comewnys F. *clamat*] *clamant* HmGF. a] of Y; *om* GOF. man] hem Y. til] to CrGYOC^{2}CBLM.
417 The] þat þe F. þat] þer*e* F. come] comen HmCrOBF.
418 þei] þat þey F. ligge] liggen OF. and] *om* F. lenge] lengen OC^{2}; *om* F.
419 Forþi] Therfore CrF. þis] þ*a*t F; the CB.
420 no] neuer*e* F. coome] ne come Cr^{23}. þe] *om* Y.
421 But] But been at hoom F. hir] her owne O. helden] holden YHmLM; holde O; & þere holde F; helidem Bm Bo; holidem Cot. stille] stille at home O.
422 Auynou*n*] auyou*n* HmCr^{3}GYOCF; Anyon Cr^{12}; avision (*corrected*) C^{2}. Iewes] Iewis F; þe Iewes WHmCrGYOC^{2}CB LM. *eris*] *erit* Cr^{1}. *&c*] *om* HmCrYC^{2}F.
423 in] at Y. as] at Cot. hir] they Cr^{1}. wole] wolde Hm; well Cr^{1}. þe] *om* G. relikes] Iewis B. to kepe] keepen F.
424 sholdest...þennes] come þens sholdist þou neuer*e* F. þennes] þenne Hm.
425 gredest] HmCrGYOC^{2}CBLMF; graddest W. gyour] gidar CrG; sholde be gyȝere F. of(2)] off vs G.
426 And] & also F. þe Plowman] plowman F; *om* WHmCrGYOC^{2}CBLM. his] *om* B. þe(2)] F; ek wiþ his WHmCrGY OC^{2}BLM; als w*it*h his C.

Emp*er*our of al þe world, þat alle men were cristene.
Inparfit is þat pope þat al [peple] sholde helpe
And [soudeþ hem] þ*at* sleeþ [swiche as] he sholde saue.
A[c] wel worþe Piers þe plowman þat p*ur*sueþ god in doynge,
Qui pluit super Iustos & iniustos at ones
And sent þe sonne to saue a cursed mannes tilþe
As brighte as to þe beste man or to þe beste wo*m*man.
Right so Piers þe Plowman peyneþ hym to tilye
As wel for a wastour and wenches of þe stewes
As for hymself and hise s*er*uaunt3, saue he is first yserued.
[So blessed be Piers þe Plowman þat peyneþ hym to tilye],
And trauailleþ and tilieþ for a tretour also soore
As for a trewe tidy man alle tymes ylike.
And worshiped be he þat wro3te al, boþe good and wikke,
And suffreþ þ*at* synfulle be [til som tyme þat þei repente].
And [Piers] amende þe pope, þat pileþ holy kirke
And cleymeþ bifore þe kyng to be kepere ouer cristene,
And counteþ no3t þou3 cristene ben killed and robbed,
And fynt folk to fi3te and cristen blood to spille

427 Emp*er*our of] Sholde be Emp*er*our ou*er* F. þat] & F. were] weren OBF.
428 Inparfit] For Inp*ar*fy3t F. þat(1)] the Cr^{23}YOCBF. peple] BL; þe peple HmGYOC^{2}CMF; þe world WCr.
429 And] For he F. soudeþ hem] sendeþ hem HmCrGYOC^{2}CBLMF; sendeþ swiche W. swiche as] OHmCrGYC^{2}CBLMF; hem þat W. saue] haue Cr^{23}.
430 Ac] But F; And WHmCrGYOC^{2}CBLM. þe] *om* Cr^{3}GC^{2}F. p*ur*sueþ] p*ur* *erased* L. doynge] dede F.
431 at] boþe at BF.
432 And] For he F. sent] sente HmOC^{2}B. þe] thy Y; is C^{2}. sonne] sone YBmBo. saue] shy3ne on F. mannes] ma*n*ne F.
433 As] & as F. to(1)] *om* Y. or] and HmGYOC^{2}CBLM. to(2)] *om* HmCr^{23}.
434 þe] *om* F.
435 *line om* F. As] *twice* G; Also B. for] to (*above cancelled* as) G. stewes] styuehous B.
436 *line om* F. self] seluen C. and] or G. is] *om* C. yserued] serued CrHmGYOC^{2}CB.
437 *not in* WHmCrGYOC^{2}CBLMF.
438 tilieþ] toyleþ F. also] as F.
439 a] the Cr; *om* Cot. tidy] lyue*n*g C. man] men CrCot. ylike] in lyke F.
440 worshiped be he] worchepeþ hy*m* F. wro3te al] all wrou3te C^{2}G. wikke] wikked CCr^{1}; ille OCr^{23}GC^{2}.
441 And] & he F. suffreþ] suffer G. þ*at*] þo þat BF; þe Cr^{2}. til...repente] MHmCrGYOC^{2}CBLF (som] *a final* e *erased* M; *om* F. þat] *om* G); *erasure* W.
442 And] Grete F. Piers] god WHmCrGYOC^{2}CBLMF. holy] so holy F. kirke] chiche Bm.
443 kepere] kepe Cr^{12}; kept Cr^{3}; *om* O. ouer] our C; of Cr; on Y.
444 counteþ] acownteþ F. no3t] at nou3t O; *om* Y. and] or GC^{2}.
445 fynt] fyndethe GCF. blood] folke Cr.

Ayein þe olde lawe and newe lawe, as Luc [bereþ] witness[e]:
Non occides: michi vindictam &c.
It semeþ bi so hymself hadde his wille
He reccheþ ri3t no3t of þe remenaunt.
And crist of his curteisie þe Cardinals saue
And torne hir wit to wisdom and to welþe of soule. |
For þe comune', quod þis Curatour, 'counten ful litel *fol.* 123 *b*
The counseil of Conscience or Cardinale *ver*tues
But [it soune], as by sighte, somwhat to wynnyng.
Of gile ne of gabbyng gyue þei neu*ere* tale,
For *Spiritus prudencie* among þe peple is gyle,
And alle þo faire *ver*tues as vices þei semeþ.
Ech man subtileþ a slei3te synne to hide
And coloureþ it for a konnynge and a clene lyuynge.'
Thanne lou3 þer a lord and, 'by þis light!' seide,
'I holde it ri3t and reson of my Reue to take
Al þat myn Auditour or ellis my Styward

446 and] & þe F. lawe(2)] *om* BF. Luc] Paule Cr^{23}. bereþ witnesse] beriþ witness F; þerof witnesse C; þerof witnesseþ WHmCrGYOC^{2}BLM.

446α *in margin* O. *michi*] *Iterum Michi* F; *&c michi* GOC^{2}. *vindictam*] *vindiciam* Cr^{1}. *&c*] & *ego retribuam* F.

447 bi so] bi so þat B; so by (*corrected main hand, altered to* so he *another*) G. self] seluen OC. his] his owne OF; he hys (he *above line and cancelled*) G.

448 He] he ne CotF; That he WHm; That he ne CrGYOC^{2}CBmBoLM. reccheþ] retche Cr^{1}; rowhte F. ri3t] *om* G. of] of al WHmCrGYOC^{2}CBLM; how F. þe] þe toþer O. remenaunt] renaunt BmBo; remnau*n*t fareþ F.

449 And] But F. his] *om* F. þe] mend the Cr^{3}; þo F. saue] frame Cr.

450 wit] wyttis B; willfull wytt (willfull *above line and cancelled*) G. to(2)] here F; *om* Cr. welþe] wele HmCrGYOC^{2}CBmBoLM; hele Cot. of] of her Cr; to F. soule] sowle helpe F.

451 For] *om* BoCot. comune quod] comeunes of F. þis] the3 (3 *added*) Y. counten] acownten F; accounteþ it B. ful] but F.

452 Conscience] Consciene Cr^{1}. or] or of (or *above line*) M; of F. Cardinale] cardynals BmBo.

453 it] if þei WHmCrGYOC^{2}CBLMF. soune] sowne F; sowe L; sei3e WHm; sei3 C^{2}C; seie BM; see CrG; seen O; sight Y. by] to F.

454 Of] Ne of F. of] *om* F. gyue] gyuen O; 3eue C^{2}; gil Y. þei] thou Cr. neu*ere*] no GC^{2}.

456 *line om* B. þo] the CrGYOC^{2}C. faire...vices] foule vices as vertues CrM (foule *over erasure*: ? *original ink* M). semeþ] semed HmCr^{1}GYC^{2}CM.

457 Ech] eche a Hm; For eu*ery* F. subtileþ] suttelde C; subtiliche C^{2}. to] F; for to WHmCrGYOC^{2}CBLM.

458 coloureþ] coloure C^{2}; colourd C; keuereþ B. for] *with* Cr^{23}GYOC^{2}CB. a(1)] *om* Cr^{23}GC^{2}F. a(2)] *om* BoCot.

459 lou3] lowrede F. þis] the Cr; *om* C. light] lygh C^{2}. seide] he tolde F.

460–5 *lines om* Hm.

460 Reue] reme (? reiue) B.

461 myn] men myn (*corrected*) Bm. Auditour] auditours Cr^{3}; endentou*r* C^{2}. or] haþ herd or F.

Counseilleþ me bi hir acounte and my clerkes writynge.
Wiþ *Spiritus Intellectus* þei [toke] þe reues rolles
And wiþ *Spiritus fortitudinis* fecche it, [wole he, nel he].'
And þanne cam þer a kyng and by his croune seide,
'I am kyng wiþ croune þe comune to rule,
And holy kirke and clergie fro cursed men to [de]fende.
And if me lakkeþ to lyue by þe lawe wole I take it
Ther I may hastilokest it haue, for I am heed of lawe;
Ye ben but membres and I aboue alle.
And siþ I am your*e* aller heed I am your*e* aller heele
And holy chirches chief help and Chieftayn of þe comune,
And what I take of yow two, I take it at þe techynge
Of *Spiritus Iusticie* for I Iugge yow alle.
So I may boldely be housled for I borwe neu*ere*,
Ne craue of my comune but as my kynde askeþ.'
'In condicion', quod Conscience, 'þ*at* þow [þe comune] defende
And rule þi reaume in reson [as right wol and] truþe

462 Counseilleþ] ⁊ co*n*seyleþ F; Conseille C^2. acounte] acowntes F. my] be my C^2F; by Cr.

463 Wiþ] þat F. þei] to $GYOC^2CB$. toke] tooken F; seke $WCrGYOC^2CBLM$. reues] rewes Bm; Iewes BoCot. rolles] rollers Cr^{12}.

464 fecche] fetchen CrO; þey fecchid F. it] hym F; *om* L. wole...he(2)] I wole $LCr^{23}GOC^2CBM$; I wole after W; wole Y; whole Cr^1; to p*re*sou*n* F.

465 þanne] *om* O. seide] he seyde F.

466 am] am a CrGM. comune] co*m*mones F.

467 kirke] chirche OGC^2CB (*above line main hand* G). fro] fram þe F. men] *om* F. to] *om* OF. defende] $YCrGOC^2CBL$ MF; fende W; fonde Hm.

468 me] y F. lakkeþ] lakke C^2F. by] *twice* GF (*second above line* G). þe] *om* F. I] þ*at* I C^2.

469 may] may it Hm. hastilokest] hastlokest OCotLM; hastlyest C; hastlyer*e* F; hastylyche G; moost hastely Cr. it haue] have it FG; haue Hm.

470 Ye] for ȝe $HmCrYOC^2CLMF$; And ye W; for þei GB. I] y am F. aboue] aboven GOM; abowe (w *cancelled*) Bo. alle] ȝow alle HmF.

471 siþ] seiþ Bo; seye Cot. aller(1)] alþer OF; alder C^2; eldir B. heed] hord Hm. aller(2)] alþer OBF; alder C^2.

472 chirches] chirche $YCr^{12}GC^2CBLF$; kyrkes Cr^3. Chieftayn] chyuentayn Hm BF; chefest am Cr. comune] comon*is* F.

473 I(1)] þat I O. two] me to F. at] of CrM. þe] þe te Bm.

474 Of] O Y.

475 I may] may I CrM. be] bi Bo. borwe] borowed G; borowed it C^2.

476 craue] care B. comune] co*mm*onys F.

477 þe comune] konne $WHmGYOC^2CB$ LM; can Cr; kunne he*m* F.

478 in] by HmCrOM (? *over erasure* M); ⁊ YC. as...and] as right wyll ⁊ Cr; in ryght ⁊ in FHm; right wel and in WGY OC^2CBLM.

[Haue] þow mayst [þyn askyng] as þi lawe askeþ:
Omnia tua sunt ad defendendum set non ad deprehendendum.'
The viker hadde fer hoom and faire took his leeue
And I awakned þerwiþ and wroot as me mette. |

479 Haue] Take WHmCrGYOC^{2}CBLM; þ*at* F. mayst] may YOC^{2}CBLM; might CrHm; *om* F. þyn askyng] þy*n* lykyng have F; in reson WHmCrGYOC^{2}CBLM. þi] the CrOF. lawe askeþ] lawes asken F. **479α** *in margin* O. *tua sunt*] *sunt tua* F. *set*] *set* a Bo. *deprehendendum*] deprehendum F; deprehendam *altered to* depredendum C^{2}; *depredandum* CrOLM; *deprecandum* YCB; *opprimendum* G.
480 viker] vicorie O. took] he took FCr^{12}.
481 awakned] awaked CrHmGC^{2}BmCot M; awakiþ Bo. and] ⁊ y F. wroot] wroth Cr^{2}; wrought Cr^{3}OBoCot. me] y F.

XX

Thanne as I wente by þe wey, whan I was thus awaked, *fol.* 124 *a*
Heuy chered I yede and elenge in herte.
I ne wiste wher to ete ne at what place,
And it neghed neiȝ þe noon and wiþ nede I mette
That afrounted me foule and faitour me called.
'[Coudes]tow noȝt excuse þee as dide þe kyng and oþ*ere*:
That þow toke to þi bilyue, to cloþes and to sustenaunce,
[Was] by techynge and by tellynge of *Spiritus temperancie*,
And þow nome na moore þan nede þee tauȝte?
And nede haþ no lawe ne neuere shal falle in dette
For þre þynges he takeþ his lif for to saue.
That is mete whan men hym werneþ and he no moneye weldeþ,
Ne wight noon wol ben his boruȝ, ne wed haþ noon to legge;
And he [cacche] in þat caas and come þerto by sleighte
He synneþ noȝt, sooþliche, þat so wynneþ his foode.
And þouȝ he come so to a cloop and kan no bettre cheuyssaunce

1 ANd wan y was wakned y wente forþ aloone F. as] *om* Cr. thus] *om* B.
2 Heuy...yede] Syȝghenge ⁊ evycheryd F. chered] chere C.
3 I] For y F. at] in C^2G.
4 neiȝ] ner HmGYOC^2CBmF; ne Bo. þe] *om* F. and] ⁊ þan F.
5 That] Tha C; ⁊ he F. afrounted] frountede O; afrowned Cr^3. me(1)] me wel YC^2CB; me ful O. and] and a Bo Cot. faitour] factour Bm; saytour G.
6 Coudestow] L; ⁊ seyd coudist þou F; Kanstow WHmCrGYOCBmM; kansþou C^2; kant þou Bo; kan þou Cot. dide] *om* F.
7 þi...to(2)] lyve by but F. bilyue] bileue Cr^{12}HmGYC^2CB; beleue Cr^3. to(3)] *om* F.
8 Was] ⁊ þat was F; As CrLM; And WHmGYOC^2CB. by(2)] *om* GYOC^2C BF. tellynge] telle Hm. *Spiritus temperancie*] *om* F.
9 And] ⁊ þat F. nome] take C. moore] mere Bm. þan] þan y F.
10 And] For F. haþ] YCrOC^2MF; ne haþ WHmGCBL. ne] ⁊ G.
11 þynges] kyngis B. he] þat he F.
12 hym] yt G. werneþ] warne Cr. weldeþ] welde Cr^1.
13 Ne] ne no G; No BmCot. noon(1)] ne BmBo; þat CrF; *om* GCot. wol] wald C. ne...noon] ⁊ hath no wed Cr. ne] ne no F. haþ] haþ ne BmBo; hath he Cot. noon(2)] *om* F. legge] ligge CrG.
14 And] ⁊ if F. he] he be GC^2. cacche] cauȝte WHmCrGYOC^2CBLM; caste F. come] came Cr. sleighte] sleyghtes CrM.
16 come] comeþ BmBo; ca*m* CrM. so] *om* G. a] *om* B. no...cheuyssaunce] ne better che C.

Nede anoon righte nymeþ hym vnder maynprise.
And if hym list for to lape þe lawe of kynde wolde
That he dronke at ech dych er he [deye for þurst].
So nede at gret nede may nymen as for his owene
Wiþouten conseil of Conscience or Cardynale vertues,
So þat he sewe and saue *Spiritus temperancie*.
For is no vertue bi fer to *Spiritus temperancie*,
Ne[iþer] *Spiritus Iusticie* ne *Spiritus fortitudinis*.
For *Spiritus fortitudinis* forfeteþ [wel] ofte;
He shal do moore þan mesure many tyme and ofte,
And bete men ouer bittre, and so[m body] to litel,
And greue men gretter þan good feiþ it wolde.
And *Spiritus Iusticie* shal Iuggen, wole he, nel he, |
After þe kynges counseil and þe comune like. *fol.* 124 *b*
And *Spiritus prudencie* in many a point shal faille
Of þat he weneþ wolde falle if his wit ne weere;
Wenynge is no wysdom, ne wys ymaginacion:
Homo proponit ⁊ deus disponit;
[God] gouerneþ alle goode vertues.

17 righte] *om* F. nymeþ] takes C; winneth Cr.
18 if] gif BmBo (g *added* Bm); gyue Cot; ȝeueþ (*over erasure*) Hm. hym] he F. list] lif BmBo; leue HmCot (*over erasure* Hm). for] *om* GYOC^{2}CB. lape] lapen F; laye Cr^1.
19 ech] ech a YC^{2}M (a *over erasure* M); euery F. deye...þurst] for þurst deide WHmCrGYOC^{2}CBLMF (þurst] first Cot).
20 nymen] nyme OF.
21 outen] owte HmCrGBmL. conseil] *om* F. or] er of F; and G.
22 sewe] sawe F. saue] serue Cr^3.
23 For] For þer BF. fer to] fore F.
24 Neiþer] BHmCrGYOC^{2}CLMF; Ne W. *Spiritus*(1)] *om* F. *Iusticie*] *fortitudinis* G. *fortitudinis*] *Iustitie* G.
25 For] But F. forfeteþ] sufferethe G. wel] ful WHmCrGYOC^{2}CBLMF. ofte] often F.
26 *line om* C. He...do] For he dooþ F. do] do no GB (no *cancelled* GBmCot). many...ofte] ofte and many tyme Hm. tyme] a tyme Cr; tymes GF.
27 **Here R resumes.** bete] bette C; beetyþ F. ouer] ful O. bittre] bytterly HmGOCotF; betterly BmBo. som body] sum body R; summe bodijs F; some of hem WHmCrGYOC^{2}CBLM.
28 And] ⁊ he F. greue] greueth Cr^{1}MF. men] men ofte F. gretter] gretly more Hm. it] *om* HmGYOC^{2}CB.
29 Iuggen] Iugge CCrGC^{2}B; Iugge hym F. wole] wol wyl C. he(1)] he or OC^2; or G.
30 and] *om* F. like] ⁊ he asente F.
31 a] *om* CrCF. point] pointes CrF.
32 wolde] woldeþ Y. falle] faile CrG.
33 Wenynge] For wenyng F. ne] ne non F.
33α–5 *as two lines divided after* vertues W HmCrGYOC^{2}CBLM; *after* alle RF.
33α ⁊] *om* CrYCotM.
34 God] and WHmCrGYOC^{2}CCotLM RF; *etc* and BmBo. goode] To goode F.

Ac nede is next hym for anoon he mekeþ
And as lowe as a lomb for lakkyng þat hym nedeþ;
[For nede makeþ nede fele nedes lowe herted].
[Philosophres] forsoke wele for þei wolde be nedy
And woneden [wel elengely] and wolde noȝt be riche.
And god al his grete Ioye goostliche he lefte
And cam and took mankynde and bicam nedy.
So [he was nedy], as seiþ þe book in manye sondry places,
That he seide in his sorwe on þe selue roode:
"Boþe fox and fowel may fle to hole and crepe
And þe fissh haþ fyn to flete wiþ to reste;
Ther nede haþ ynome me þ*a*t I moot nede abide
And suffre sorwes ful soure, þat shal to Ioye torne."
Forþi be noȝt abasshed to bide and to be nedy
Siþ he þat wroȝte al þe world was wilfulliche nedy,
Ne neu*er*e noon so nedy ne pou*er*er deide.'
Whan nede ha[dde] vndernome me þus anoon I fil aslepe
And mette ful m*er*ueillously þat in mannes forme
Antecrist cam þanne, and al þe crop of truþe

35 Ac] but C^2; And CrGR; *om* F. mekeþ] meketh hym MCr^{12} (hym *another ink* M); maketh him Cr^3.
36 as(1)] also B; is as Hm. lakkyng] lacke GC^2. þat] RF; of þat $WHmCrGYOC^2CBLM$. nedeþ] endeth Cr^3.
37 RF; *line om* $WHmCrGYOC^2CBLM$; *here in the spelling of* W. nede fele] fele for F. herted] of herte F.
38 *copied twice* C. Philosophres] FR; Wise men $WHmCrGYOC^2CBLM$. forsoke] forsoken OC^2B. wele] welthe C^2GRF. wolde] wolden OBmBo.
39 woneden] woned C^2; weneden Cr. wel] R; wol F; in $WHmCrGYOC^2CBm$ BoLM; *om* Cot. elengely] FR; wildernesse $WHmCrGYOC^2CBLM$. wolde] wolden OHmBMR. noȝt] neu*er*e F.
40 god] þo god B. al] of BoCot. his] thes G. Ioye] Ioyes GC^2; Ioye of F.
41 nedy] heere al needy F.
42 So...nedy] R; he was so needy F; So nedy he was $WHmCrGYOC^2CBLM$.
44 fowel] gray B. fle] flee and CrM; fle ⁊ go G; go B. and(2)] *om* CrM.
45 to(1)] it C; þat it B. flete] fletiþ B. to(2)] or to RF; ⁊ to G.
46 Ther] where C^2. ynome] ynomen O; innomed Cr. nede(2)] nedes Cr.
47 sorwes] sorowe C^2. soure] sore Hm GB. þat] to Bo; þo Cot.
48 Forþi] Therfore Cr. be(1)] be þou F. bide] bid Y; bydde GOCBR; bowe F.
49 *line om* Cr^1. was] ys G.
50 ne] ne noon F; ne also O; ne so HmG (*over erasure* Hm). pouerer] porer OF; pore HmCrG (*over erasure* Hm); pouer (o *above* u *main hand*) C.
51 hadde] $HmCrGYOC^2CBLMRF$; haþ W. vndernome] vndirnomen O; nome F; vndone Cr. me] *above line* M; *om* OR. I] a BoCot.
52 ful] *om* G. merueillously] m*er*uyouslyche G; m*er*ueilysch Cot. þat] tat C; *om* $HmCr^{23}$. in] yn a HmCrF.
53 þe] *om* CBR. crop] croppis F.

Torned it [tid] vp so doun and ouertilte þe roote,
And [made] fals sprynge and sprede and spede mennes nedes.
In ech a contree þer he cam he kutte awey truþe
And gerte gile growe þere as he a god weere.
Freres folwede þat fend for he gaf hem copes,
And Religiouse reuerenced hym and rongen hir belles,
And al þe Couent cam to welcome [a] tyraunt
And alle hise as wel as hym, saue oonly fooles; |
Whiche foolis were wel [gladdere] to deye *fol.* 125 *a*
[Th]an to lyue lenger siþ [Leute] was so rebuked
And a fals fend Antecrist ouer alle folk regnede.
[And] þat were mylde men and holye þat no meschief dradden;
Defyed alle falsnesse and folk þat it vsede;
And what kyng þat hem conforted, knowynge [hir gile],
They cursed and hir conseil, were it clerk or lewed.
Antecrist hadde þus soone hundredes at his baner,

54 Torned] Anon he turnede F. it tid] it WHmYOC^{2}BLMR; *om* CrGCF. ouer] vp F. tilte] tilth R.
55 made] RF; *om* WHmCrGYOC^{2}CBLM. sprynge] spryngiþ B; sprang Cr^{23}GOC^{2}. sprede] sprediþ B; spredde GOC^{2}. spede] spedde GOC^{2}CB; sped Cr; speddes Y; schende F.
56 ech] euery F. a] *om* HmGF. contree] Court CB. he(2)] ⁊ G.
57 gerte] dede C^{2}; gert (er *over erasure*) Bm; syet Bo; sitthe Cot. growe] grew B. a] of Cr^{1}.
58 folwede] folwiden BO. gaf] fond F. hem] hym BmBo.
59 And] ⁊ fele F. Religiouse] religiouses R; religiouns Hm. reuerenced] reuerensiden BmBo. rongen] rong GCrF; ragen (a *altered from* o) C. hir] ageyn hym F.
60 cam] RF; forþ cam WHmCrGYOC^{2}CBLM. to] holly to F. a] R; þat WHmCrGYOC^{2}CBLMF.
61 hise] þe hise (þe *cancelled*) Bm; thes G. as(1)] also BmBo. as(2)] *above line* W. hym] thes G.
62 *divided from* 63 *after* lyue WHmCrGYOC^{2}CBLMRF. foolis] *om* F. were] weren HmOB. wel] *om* GRF. gladdere] FR; leuere WHmCrGYOC^{2}CBLM.
63 Than] *spelled* þan W; and than (*corrected*) C. to] to gon on F. lenger] ⁊ langoured so F. siþ] with F; than YCr^{23}OC^{2}. Leute] leute RHmCr^{1}BF (*by correction* HmBm); Lenten WGYOC^{2}CLM; Leten Cr^{23}. was] to be Cr^{23}YOC^{2}; ⁊ weren F. so] so sore (sore *above line*) G; sore F. rebuked] robbid and reued B.
64 And] Of F. a] HmCrGYOC^{2}CBLMRF; as a W. fend] frend GYOC^{2}. ouer] þat ouer F.
65 And] CrHmGYOC^{2}CBLMRF; Saue W. þat(1)] þo þat C^{2}. were] weren O; wee F; we R. men and] *om* F. holye] holy men CrF. meschief] mesch of Bo. dradden] dredde HmF; dreden GC^{2}; drede Cr.
66 Defyed] Defieden CrHmOBMF. and] ⁊ þe F. vsede] vsiþ BoCot.
67 hem] hym CCotF. conforted] contrefeted Y. hir] hem WHmCrGYOC^{2}CBLMR; hym F. gile] gyle RF; any while WHmCrGYOC^{2}CBLM.
68 cursed] curseden O. and] hem ⁊ F; all G. it] it to Hm; he F. clerk] clarkes Cr. lewed] oþer F.
69 þus] *om* F. soone] some Cr^{1}. hundredes] hundriste C^{2}.

And pride [bar it bare] boldely aboute
Wiþ a lord þat lyueþ after likyng of body,
That kam ayein conscience þat kepere was and gyour
Ouer kynde cristene and Cardynale *ver*tues.
'I conseille', quod Conscience þo, 'comeþ wiþ me, ye fooles,
Into vnite holy chirche and holde we vs þere.
And crye we to kynde þ*a*t he come and defende vs
Fooles fro þise fendes lymes, for Piers loue þe Plowman.
And crye we [on] al þe comune þ*a*t þei come to vnitee
And þ*er*e abide and bikere ayeins Beliales children.'
Kynde Conscience þo herde and cam out of þe planetes
And sente forþ his forreyours, Feu*er*es and Fluxes,
Coughes and Cardiacles, Crampes and tooþaches,
Rewmes and Radegundes and roynouse sca[ll]es,
Biles and bocches and brennynge Agues,
Frenesies and foule yueles; forageres of kynde
Hadde ypriked and prayed polles of peple;
Largeliche a legion loste [þe] lif soone.
There was 'harrow!' and 'help! here comeþ kynde

70 bar it bare] bar yt bare F; bar þe baner Y; it bar WCrGOC^{2}CLMR; it bar ful B; it bar vp ful hiȝe Hm. boldely] buldly BmBo; loldelich Y. aboute] abouten O; about where he yede Cr.
71 after] after the CrM; aft*er* lust & þe (lust & *above line main hand*, þe *cancelled*) O; w*ith* F. of] of his CrGC^{2}M.
72 That...ayein] þan cam F. gyour] gydour CrG.
73 kynde] alkynne Y. Cardynale] cardinales R.
74 þo] ye G; *om* CrM. comeþ] come CrG. wiþ] *twice* Bo. ye] you G; *om* CrM. fooles] foulis BmBo.
75 holy] of holy F.
76 kynde þ*a*t] keene kyng F. come] comeþ Bo. and] to G.
77 þise] þis YLR; þe HmGOC^{2}F. fendes] feend C. loue þe] þe loue Y. þe Plowman] *om* F.
78 on] RF; to WHmCrGYOC^{2}CBLM. comune] co*m*munes G. come] comen F.
79 abide] abyden F. bikere] abyker*e* F.
80 þo herde] herde þo F.
81 sente] sende R. forþ] afor*e* F. forreyours] forru*n*ners G. Feu*er*es] feuerer*es* Cot; boþe feveris F.
82 Coughes] & kowhes F. aches] ache Hm.
83 roynouse] ruyouse Y. scalles] HmCrGYOC^{2}CBLMRF; scabbes W.
84 Biles] & beelis F. Agues] angwes C; a*n*gwise Y; anguyshis C^2.
85 Frenesies] & frenesis F; Freneges Cr^1; feuers G. yueles] euill Cr. forageres] forgoers G; all weren Forayneris F.
86 Hadde] Hadden Cr; þey hadde F. ypriked] pricked CrO; pyked F; yprayed Hm. prayed] pr*o*ued C^2; ypryked Hm. of] of the CrGYOC^{2}CBMF.
87 Largeliche] RF; That largeliche WHmCrGYOC^{2}CBLM. loste] losten HmCrGF; lese L; lose R; loren YOC^{2}CM; lorn B. þe] hir WHmCrGYOC^{2}CBLMRF. lif] liues Cr^{3}C^2.
88 There] Ter Bm. here comeþ] how þere cam F.

Wiþ deeþ þ*at* is dredful to vndo vs alle!'
The lord þat lyued after lust þo aloud cryde |
After Confort a knyght to come and bere his baner: *fol.* 125 *b*
'Alarme! alarme!' quod þat lord, 'ech lif kepe his owene!'
[Th]anne mette þise men, er Mynstrals myȝte pipe,
And er heraudes of Armes hadden discryued lordes,
Elde þe hoore; [he] was in þe vauntwarde
And bar þe baner bifore deeþ; bi riȝt he it cleymede.
Kynde cam after wiþ many kene soores
As pokkes and pestilences, and muche peple shente;
So kynde þoruȝ corrupcions kilde ful manye.
Deeþ cam dryuynge after and al to duste passhed
Kynges and knyghtes, kaysers and popes.
Lered [ne] lewed he leet no man stonde,
That he hitte euene, þ*at* eu*er*e stired after.
Manye a louely lady and [hir] lemmans knyȝtes
Swowned and swelted for sorwe of [deþes] dyntes.
Conscience of his curteisie [þo] kynde he bisouȝte

89 vs] hem F.
90 lyued] lyueth Cr^{23}. þo] to Hm. aloud] lowde B; lowde he F.
91 Confort] *om* RF. a] a komely F; *om* R. come] come*n* F.
92 lif] a lyf Hm; man GF.
93 Thanne] þanne RF; And þanne WHm CrGYOC^{2}CBLM. mette] metten OF. er] their Cr. myȝte] myghten HmOB.
94 er] hire (*corrected main hand*) Cot; their Cr. hadden] had CrGYC^{2}CMF.
95 *line om* GYOC^{2}CB. Elde] þan Elde F; Age Cr. hoore] horel RF (? l *added* R). he] HmCrLMRF; þat W. was in] hild F. þe(2)] *om* R.
96 *line om* GYOC^{2}CB. bar þe] *twice* F.
97 Kynde] & keende F. after] after hym RF. kene] kenne F. soores] sorowes G.
98 pestilences] pestylence GC^{2}. and(2)] þat O. peple] peple he F; pepe Bm.
99 þoruȝ] w*ith* F. corrupcions] corru*m*pcioun C^{2}.
100 Deeþ cam] þan ca*m* deeþ F. dryuynge] dryuende LRF; aft*er* C^{2}. after] dryuy*n*nge C^{2}; *om* F. al] *om* Cr^{1}. to] *om* C^{2}. passhed] paschte (*altered to* daschte) R; passid B; he daschede he*m* F.
101 Kynges] Boþe kyngis F. knyghtes] knyghtis & F; Kaysers CrM. kaysers] knightes CrM.
102 Lered] Learned Cr; Neyþ*er* lewede F. ne] HmCr^{3}GYOC^{2}CBLMRF; and W Cr^{12}. lewed] lered F. he] he ne CrM (ne *erased* M). leet] left RF. no man] non F.
103 That] þo þ*at* F. he] he ne YOC^{2}Cot. hitte] ? *altered to* hurte Cot. þat] *altered to* þay Bm; they Cot; he Cr; *om* HmG; *illegible* Bo. eu*er*e stired] stired neuere YHmGC^{2}CB (*over erasure* Hm). eu*er*e] euere he F; neuer CrO. stired] stode CrM.
104 Manye] þan many F. lady] *om* R. and...knyȝtes] for hire levis sake F. hir lemmans] lemmans of WHmCrGYOC^{2} CBLM; lemmanes R.
105 Swowned] Swownede*n* OCr^{1}M; swowed BoCot. swelted] swelt*e*de*n* O; swelten Cr^{1}M; sweltrid F. deþes] Hm CrGYOC^{2}BLMR; dethe C; dentis F; hise W.
106 Conscience] þa*nne* Conscience F. þo] to WHmCrGYOC^{2}CBLMRF. he] *om* C^{2}.

To cesse and suffre, and see wher þei wolde
Leue pride pryuely and be parfite cristene.
And kynde cessede [sone] to se þe peple amende.
Fortune gan flatere þanne þo fewe þ*a*t were alyue
And bihighte hem long lif, and lecherie he sente
Amonges alle manere men, wedded and vnwedded,
And gaderede a greet hoost al agayn Conscience.
This lecherie leide on wiþ [laughynge] chiere
And wiþ pryuee speche and peyntede wordes,
And armede hym in ydelnesse and in heigh berynge.
He bar a bowe in his hand and manye brode arewes,
Weren feþered wiþ fair biheste and many a fals truþe. |
Wiþ vntidy tales he tened ful ofte *fol.* 126 *a*
Conscience and his compaignye, of holy [kirke] þe techeris.
Thanne cam Coueitise and caste how he myȝte
Ouercome Conscience and Cardinale v*er*tues;
And armed hym in Auarice and hungriliche lyuede.
His wepne was al wiles, to wynnen and to hiden;
Wiþ glosynges and gabbynges he giled þe peple.
Symonye hym [suede] to assaille Conscience,

107 cesse] se CB. and(1)] and to C. wher] whether CotHmF (*by correction* Hm). wolde] wolden O.
108 Leue] Leven F. be parfite] p*ar*fyȝtly lyve as F.
109 sone] F; þo WHmCrGYOC^{2}CBLMR.
110 Fortune...þanne] ⁊ þ*an*ne gan Fortune flatr*e* F. flatere] flatteren CrGYC^{2}CBLMR. þo] to C^2. were] weren HmMRF.
111 bihighte] hight Cr. he] hem F; she Cr.
112 men] of men Cr^{3}F.
113 al] ano*n* F. agayn] ayeins Y.
114 This] thus G. wiþ] with RF; wiþ a WHmCrGYOC^{2}CBLM. laughynge] CrGYOC^{2}CBLMRF; Ianglynge WHm.
115 And] as G. wiþ] with a CrM. pryuee] p*r*ide p*r*iue (p*r*ide *cancelled*) Bm. and] ⁊ p*ro*pre F.
116 hym] hem HmC^2.
117 brode] blody YCrGOC^{2}CBLMR.
118 Weren] Were CrYC; þ*a*t were F; *om* GC^2. biheste] speche GC^{2}F. many a] fele F. truþe] behestis F.
119 Wiþ] with R; ⁊ wit*h* F; Wiþ hise WHmCrGOC^{2}CBM; Wit his L; For with hise Y. ful] me full G. ofte] often Cr.
120 kirke] CrRF; chirche WHmGYOC^{2}CBLM. þe] *om* F. techeris] techer Hm.
122 Cardinale] cardinales R. v*er*tues] grace C^2.
123 And] ⁊ he F; *om* B. hungriliche] vngreliche C; vngryly F; honglelich Y; vng*r*iseliche R. lyuede] he lyued YC^{2}F.
124 His...al] ⁊ his wepnes were F. wepne] wepned C. al] all of Hm. wynnen] wynne OF; wynnyng BoCot. to(2)] *om* G. hiden] hyde O; holde*n* B; holde F.
125 and] C^{2}GYOCBR; and wiþ WHmCrLMF. gabbynges] glabbinges Cr^1. he giled] he bigiled Hm; to bigyle O.
126 Symonye hym] ⁊ symonye he F. suede] seude R; soughte Hm; sente WCrGYOC^{2}CBLMF. assaille] assailen BmBo; assoille YF.

And [pressed on] þe [pope] and p*re*lates þei maden
To holden wiþ Antecrist, hir temporaltees to saue.
And cam to þe kynges counseille as a kene baroun
And [knokked] Conscience in Court afore hem alle;
And garte good feiþ flee and fals to abide,
And boldeliche bar adoun wiþ many a bright Noble
Muche of þe wit and wisdom of westmynstre halle.
He Iogged to a Iustice and Iusted in his eere
And ouertilte al his truþe wiþ 'tak þis vp amendement'.
An[d] to þe Arches in haste he yede anoon after
And tornede Cyuyle into Symonye, and siþþe he took þe Official.
For a [Meneuer Mantel he] made lele matrymoyne
Departen er deeþ cam and deuors shapte.
'Allas!' quod Conscience and cryde, 'wolde crist of his g*ra*ce
That Coueitise were cristene þat is so kene [to fighte],
And boold and bidynge while his bagge lasteþ.'
And þanne lough lyf and leet daggen hise cloþes,
And armed hym [in] haste [in] harlotes wordes,

127 pressed...pope] p*re*ched to þe peple WHmCrGYC^{2}CBLMRF; p*re*cheden to þe peple O. þei] they CrM; þei hem WHmGYOC^{2}LRF; hem CB. maden] made GBF.
128 holden] holde RCrF. saue] sauen M.
129 cam] comen HmO. þe] *om* Cr.
130 knokked] kneled to WHmCrGYC^{2}C BLMRF; kneleden to O. in] at Y. afore] aforen Hm; before Cr^{3}GCBRF.
131 garte] dede C^{2}; maden F. flee] to flee F.
132 adoun] dou*n* FCr^{1}. a] *om* YC^{2}CB. bright] rede RF. Noble] noblis B.
134 He] H C. Iogged] Iugged GYOC^{2}C BmBoLMR; iuged HmCot; iustled Cr; Iusted F. to] til YCr^{12}GOC^{2}CBLMR; ageyn F. a Iustice] Iustises F. Iusted] Iangled F; rouned Cot.
135 his] *om* GF. wiþ] will Cr^{12}; wel Cr^{3}; *om* B. vp] vpon BCr^{12}; on Cr^{3}; to G.
136 And] HmCrGYOC^{2}CBLMRF; An W. to] ynto HmR; þa*n*ne into F. in haste] *om* Cr^{3}. yede anoon] wente F.
137 Cyuyle] Ci (*cancelled*) Bm; *om* BoCot. into] to GC^{2}F; *om* B. he] *om* HmG.
138 For] & for F. Meneuer Mantel] menyuer*e* ma*n*tel RF; Mantel of Meneuer WHmCrGYOC^{2}CBLM. he] HmCrGY OC^{2}CBLMRF; and W. lele] lelly Cr; a lele C; an vnleele B; trewe C^{2}.
139 Departen] Departe O; Departed Cr^{3} C^{2}; departeden Cot; To dep*ar*ty*n* F; be dep*ar*tid Hm. and] and a RF. shapte] shapen G; he schapede F.
140 and cryde] *om* CrM. wolde] F; þo wolde WHmCrGYOC^{2}CBLMR. crist] god G. his] *om* R.
141 were] were a CrM. kene] kine Cr^{12}. to fighte] to fiȝte RF; a fightere WHmCr YOC^{2}CBL; fyghter GM.
142 bidynge] abidynge HmCrOBRF; byddyng G. while] þe while RF. bagge] baggis F; bake C. lasteþ] laste Y; lasten F.
143 And] *om* Hm. and] lyghtly & F. daggen] dagge HmCrGYOC^{2}CBLMR.
144 in...in] YHmCrGOC^{2}CBLMRF; an haste wiþ W. harlotes] harlot*rie* F. wordes] wedes Y.

And heeld holynesse a Iape and hendenesse a wastour,
And leet leautee a cherl and lyere a fre man.
Conscience and counseil, he counted [it] f[o]lye. |
Thus relyede lif for a litel fortune *fol.* 126 *b*
And prike[d] forþ wiþ pride; preiseþ he no v*er*tue,
Ne careþ noȝt how Kynde slow and shal come at þe laste
And kille a[l] erþely creatur[e] saue conscience oone.
Lyf lepte aside and lauȝte hym a lemman.
'Heele and I', quod he, 'and heighnesse of herte
Shal do þee noȝt drede, neiþ*er* deeþ ne elde,
And [so] forȝyte sorwe and [of synne ȝyue noȝt].'
This likede lif and his lemman fortune
And geten in hir glorie a gadelyng at þe laste,
Oon þat muche wo wroȝte, Sleuþe was his name.
Sleuþe wax wonder yerne and soone was of age
And wedded oon wanhope, a wenche of þe Stuwes.
Hir sire was a Sysour þat neu*er*e swoor truþe,
Oon Tomme two-tonge, atteynt at ech [a q]ueste.
This Sleuþe [wex sleiȝ] of werre and a slynge made,

145 And] ⁊ he F. holynesse] holy Y.
146 And] he F. leautee] lenten Hm.
147 Conscience] ⁊ boþe Co*n*science F. and] HmCrGYOC^{2}CBLMRF; and his (his *above line*) W. counted] accountyd Hm. it folye] YCr^{23}GOC^{2}CBR; it a folye HmLM; at foly Cr^1; it but folye F; at a flye W.
148 relyede] relyued B; releved F; reuellid C^2; rayled Cr^{3}G; leled Cr^1. lif] lyff long C^2. for] wi*th* F.
149 priked] CrHmGYOC^{2}CBLMRF; prikeþ W. preiseþ] preysed GCrYM; ⁊ preysy*n*g F. he] of F. v*er*tue] vertues F.
150 Ne] Ne he F; He CrGYOC^{2}CM; and HmB; A L. how] þ*at* F. slow...come] shal come and sle hy*m* B. slow] slouth Cr^1; fleyȝ F. and] *om* Cr^1. þe] *om* CrYC.
151 kille] calle RF. all Cr^3; all Cr^{12}GYF; alle WHmOC^{2}CBLMR. erþely] erly F. creature] YLR; creatures WHmCrGOC^{2}CBMF. oone] onely Cr; alone G.
152 lepte] seith R; seyde F. aside] asede Cr^1; *occide* RF. lauȝte] caught Cr^{1}M. a] *om* C^2.
153 Heele] Health Cr. heighnesse] heuynesse CotCr.
154 noȝt drede] drede naught Cot. noȝt] no Cr.
155 And] But OF. so] to WHmCrGYOC^{2}CBLMRF. ȝyte] get CrGC. sorwe] deþ MCr^1. of...noȝt] ȝyue noȝt of synne WHmYC^{2}BLMRF; gyue nought of synne CrGOC.
156 This] thus G; þis lessou*n* F.
157 geten] gat Cr. þe] *om* Cr^{1}Y.
158 muche] mys F. wo] *om* RF.
159 soone was] was soone F. soone] swyþe Hm.
160 Stuwes] stif hous B.
162 two] þe F. tonge] tou*n*gis B; tonged G. atteynt] ytaint Y. at] of CrM; in F. ech] eu*er*y F. a queste] HmCrGYOC^{2}CBLMR; enqueste W; qwestis F.
163 This] þus BoCotR; *om* F. wex] YOC^{2}CB; wexed (d *added*) G; was WHmCrLMRF. sleiȝ] war WHmCrYC^{2}CBLMRF; werre GO. of] of þis F; ⁊ O. made] he made F.

And threw drede of dispair a doȝeyne myle aboute.
For care Conscience þo cryde vpon Elde
And bad hym fonde to fighte and afere wanhope.
And Elde hente good hope and hastiliche he shifte hym
And wayued awey wanhope and wiþ lif he fighteþ.
And lif fleiȝ for feere to phisik after helpe
And bisouȝte hym of socour and of his salue hadde;
[And] gaf hym gold good woon þat gladede his herte,
And þei gyuen hym ageyn a glaȝene howue.
Lyf leeued þat lechecraft lette sholde Elde
And dryuen awey deeþ wiþ Dyas and drogges.
And Elde auntred hym on lyf, and at þe laste he hitte |
A Phisicien wiþ a furred hood þat he fel in a palsie, *fol.* 127 *a*
And þere dyed þat doctour er þre dayes after.
'Now I se', seide lif, 'þat Surgerie ne phisik
May noȝt a myte auaille to med[l]e ayein Elde.'
And in hope of his heele good herte he hente
And rood [so to] reuel, a ryche place and a murye,
The compaignye of confort men cleped it som tyme.

164 threw] þrow Bm; drow Bo; drw Cot; trewe Y. of] in F; ꝧ O. myle] myles Cr.
165 cryde] crieden R. Elde] age Cr.
166 hym] *om* RF. fonde to fighte] fend a sight Cr^{1}. afere] affor (a *above line main hand*) C^{2}.
167 Elde] helde Bm; helpe BoCot; age Cr. he] *om* O. shifte] chifte BmBo; shyftes Cr^{1}; shapte Y; hyȝed F.
168 wayued] wained Cr. fighteþ] fyghted GYC^{2}CB; faught Hm.
169 And] *om* C^{2}. fleiȝ] fleeth CrGC^{2}; flieth Y; flee C; fly Cot.
170 of(1)] of his CrCotM. socour] socerye Cot. salue] sabae Cot. hadde] HmCrG YOC^{2}CBLMR; he hadde WF.
171 And] HmCrGYOC^{2}CBLMRF; He W. gaf] ȝaff C^{2}B. gold] goel R. gladede] gladdes Y. his herte] here hertes R.
172 þei] he F. gyuen] gyue C; ȝyuen OC^{2}; gafen BmBo; gaue CrCotF. ageyn] ayein YOC^{2}CB. howue] houe R; howe F; howne Cr.
173 leeued] beleevede F. lette] letty*n* F. sholde] shlud Cr^{2}.
174 dryuen] dryue OCr^{23}CB; to driue RF. Dyas] dayes RF; diapenidion G; diagragmator B. and] þo F; *om* G. drogges] dragges CrOC^{2}CBLMRF; drages Hm; dragmas Y; *om* G.
175 auntred] auentred CrB. þe] *om* Cr. he] hy*m* F.
176 A] On a F. Phisicien] phicien YC. a(2)] the CrYC^{2}CBM (*above line* M); *om* O.
177 þat] þe G.
178 I] *erasure* F. Surgerie] surgenry HmM; surgiens YGC^{2}CB.
179 a...auaille] avayle a myte F. medle] HmCrGOC^{2}CBLMF; medelen R; meldle Y; mede W.
180 in] I C^{2}. herte] hope O. he] *om* BoCotR.
181 so to] HmCrGYOC^{2}CBLMRF; forþ to a W. a(1)] to a GC^{2}; ryght a F. place ...murye] myryȝe place F.
182 The] that was þe GC^{2}. confort] courte Cr^{23}GYOC^{2}CB. men] of BoCot. cleped] clepede*n* OBR. it] *om* GC^{2}.

And Elde after [hym]; and ouer myn heed yede
And made me balled bifore and bare on þe croune;
So harde he yede ouer myn heed it wole be sene *euere*.
'Sire yuele ytauȝt Elde!' quod I, 'vnhende go wiþ þe!
Siþ whanne was þe wey ouer mennes heddes?
Haddestow be hende', quod I, 'þow woldest haue asked leeue.'
'Ye, leue, lurdeyn?' quod he, and leyde on me wiþ Age,
And hitte me vnder þe ere; vnneþe [may] ich here.
He buffetted me aboute þe mouþ [and bette out my wangteeþ];
And gyued me in goutes: I may noȝt goon at large.
And of þe wo þ*at* I was Inne my wif hadde ruþe
And wisshed ful witterly þ*at* I were in heuene.
For þe lyme þ*at* she loued me fore and leef was to feele
On nyghtes namely, whan we naked weere,
I ne myghte in no manere maken it at hir wille,
So Elde and [heo] hadden it forbeten.
And as I seet in þis sorwe I sauȝ how kynde passede
And deeþ drogh neiȝ me; for drede gan I quake,
And cryde to kynde: 'out of care me brynge!

183 after] anoon after WHmCrGYOC^{2}CBLMRF. hym] RF; me WHmGYOC^{2}CBLM; *om* Cr. and] *om* F. myn] mynd C. heed] hed he OCr^{23}; head she Cr^1. yede] wente F.
184 on] vppon B. þe] my Cr.
185 it] þ*at* it Cr. be] by Cot. sene] seue Cr^1. euere] euene Bo.
186 ytauȝt] taught CrG.
187 þe] þe wyde F; thy GOC^2. mennes] men L.
188 woldest] wolde Cr^{23}. haue] *om* Hm.
189 leue] leef YC. lurdeyn] lordynge YOCBoCot.
190 ere] eere þ*at* F. vnneþe] vnnees C. may] HmCrGYOC^{2}CBLMRF; myȝte W.
191 He buffetted] & beet F. me] HmCrGYOC^{2}CBLMRF; me so W. and...my] and bet out my CrLMR; & bett me on þe GYOC^{2}CB; & buscht out my*n* F; and my Hm; þ*at* out my W. wangteeþ] FR; teth CrGYOC^{2}CBLM; teeþ he bette W; teeþ owt beet Hm.
192 gyued] gyede OC^2; guyded G; he begyled F. in goutes] w*ith* þe gowte F.
193 wif] lyf Cot.
194 wisshed] wisshen C^2; wissed Y. ful] wel R; often F. þ*at* I were] y hadde ben F. þ*at*] þa Bo.
195 þ*at*] *om* F. and] þ*at* F. was to] she was F.
196 On] off G. we] sche O. weere] weren F.
197 maken] make CrGOF. at] *om* BoCot.
198 heo] hee R; she sooþly WHmCrGOC^{2}BLM; she soth Y; so sothly C; þe gowte & she F. hadden it] hadde yt F; it hadde R; had Cr. beten] beyten *main hand after cancelled* byden G; bete RF; beaten it Cr; boden B.
199 And...þis] þus was y set w*ith* F. as] was R. how] *om* CrMF. kynde] my*n* stat F.
200 neiȝ] nere CrMF. gan I] y gan F. quake] quake*n* RF.
201 And] & y F. me] thu me Hm.

Lo! Elde þe hoore haþ me biseye.
Awreke me if youre wille be for I wolde ben hennes.' |
'If þow wolt be wroken wend into vnitee *fol.* 127 *b*
And hold þee þere euere til I sende for þee.
And loke þow konne som craft er þow come þennes.'
'Counseille me, kynde', quod I, 'what craft is best to lerne?'
'Lerne to loue', quod kynde, 'and leef alle oþere.'
'How shal I come to catel so to cloþe me and to feede?'
'And þow loue lelly lakke shal þee neu*ere*
[Weede] ne worldly [mete] while þi lif lasteþ.'
And [I] by conseil of kynde comsed to rome
Thoruȝ Contricion and Confession til I cam to vnitee.
And þ*er*e was Conscience Conestable, cristene to saue,
And bisegede [sikerly] wiþ seuene grete geauntȝ
That wiþ Antecrist helden harde ayein Conscience.
Sleuþe wiþ his slynge an hard [s]aut he made.
Proude preestes coome *with* hym; [passynge an hundred]
In paltokes and pyked shoes, [purses and] longe knyues,
Coomen ayein Conscience; wiþ Coueitise þei helden.

202 Lo] & seyde loo F. me] my lif RF. biseye] seye R; byseged G; besette Cr^{23}; byfeye Cr^{1}.
203 Awreke] wreke G. youre] thye G. I ...hennes] wendy*n* hens y wolde F.
204 wolt] wold Cr. wroken] wroke B; ywroken OLM; ywroke $GYC^{2}RF$. wend into] q*uo*d he wende vnto F.
206 come þennes] come hens C^{2}; thennes go Y.
207 Counseille] Conseileth R. kynde] *om* F. I] y þo F. is...to] y myȝhte F. is] be R. lerne] lere G.
208 leef] leue $RCr^{1}F$; leef of WC; leue of $HmCr^{23}GOC^{2}BLM$; loue of Y. oþere] oþ*ere craftys* F.
209 to(3)] *erased* M; *om* HmGF. feede] fete Y; fode Cr^{23}.
210 lelly] trewly C^{2}. lakke] RF; quod he lakke $WHmCrGYOC^{2}CBmLM$; quod I lacke BoCot. shal] shalt F. þee] þou FCr^{23}.
211 Weede] Wede RF; Mete $WHmCrGYOC^{2}CBLM$. mete] RF; mede Hm; weede $WCrGYOC^{2}CBLM$.
212 I] þ*er*e $WHmCrGYOC^{2}CBLMRF$. kynde] kende R; kynde I $WHmCrGYOC^{2}CBLM$; kende he F. comsed] began C^{2}. rome] runne Cr; reme (? *rubbed*) Cot.
213 til] to G. to] til BmBo.
214 was Conscience] was R; he was mad a F. to] for to O. saue] saven F.
215 And] he was F. sikerly] sooþly $WHmCrGYOC^{2}CBLMRF$. seuene] *om* Y.
216 helden] holden Cr.
217 Sleuþe] þan slewthe F. wiþ] was CrM. an] and $Cr^{13}YCBoR$; and an (an *above line*) M. saut] $LHmC^{2}RF$; assaut WCrGYOCBM. he] *om* $CrGYOC^{2}CBM$.
218 coome] comen HmOBmBo. passynge an hundred] passyng an hundreth RF; mo þan a þousand $WHmCrGYOC^{2}CBLM$.
219 purses and] and gypsers GC^{2}; and pisseris $WHmCr^{23}YOCBLMRF$; and pisfers Cr^{1}. longe knyues] ful longe F.
220 Coomen] þey keme*n* F. wiþ] & *with* F. Coueitise] coueitous Y. helden] helde YBmCot; holde Bo.

'By [þe] Marie!' quod a mansed preest, [was] of þe March of
[Irlonde],
'I counte na moore Conscience by so I cacche siluer
Than I do to drynke a drauȝte of good ale.'
And so seiden sixty of þe same contree,
And shotten ayein wiþ shot, many a sheef of oþes,
And brode hoked arwes, goddes herte and hise nayles,
And hadden almoost vnitee and holynesse adown.
Conscience cryede, 'help, Clergie or I falle
Thoruȝ inparfite preestes and *pre*lates of holy chirche.' |
Freres herden hym crye and comen hym to helpe, *fol.* 128 *a*
Ac for þei kouþe noȝt wel hir craft Conscience forsook hem.
Nede neghede þo neer and Conscience he tolde
That þei come for coueitise, to haue cure of soules.
'And for þei are pou*er*e, *par*auenture, for patrymoyne [hem]
faille[þ],
They wol flatere [to] fare wel folk þ*at* ben riche.
And siþen þei chosen chele and cheitiftee
Lat hem chewe as þei chose and charge hem *wiþ* no cure.

221 þe(1)] R; *om* WHmCrGYOC^{2}CBLMF. mansed] mased CBoCot. was] RF; *om* WHmCrGYOC^{2}CBLM. Irlonde] C^{2}HmCrGYOCBLMRF; walys W.
222 counte] acownte F; count hitt (hitt *another hand*) G. moore] more bi OB. by] *om* G. so] so þat B.
223 ale] stale ale F; alle Bm.
224 so...sixty] *with* hy*m* swooren syxty moo F. seiden] sayde GCrC^{2}LR. same] sane Bo; seyd G.
225 & gu*n*ne for scheete faste þykke scheef oþis F. wiþ] hym *with* YOCB. many] *with* many GYOCB (ny *by correction main hand* G). a] *om* HmGYOCB. of oþes] arwes B.
226 arwes] arwes *with* FG. hise] *om* F. nayles] bones B.
227 hadden] hadde BCr. adown] vndone G.
228 help] help to F. or] or ellis WHmCrGYOC^{2}CBLMRF. I] y now F.
229 inparfite] vnp*ar*fit B. preestes] preest Y.
230 Freres] Fryes Cr^{23}. herden] harde Cr. hym crye] criȝen F. and] *om* BoCot. comen] came Cr. helpe] helpen M.
231 Ac] But F; And CrGYOC^{2}CB. kouþe] couþen O. forsook hem] hem forsoke Cr.
232 Nede] þa*n*ne neede F. þo] to C; hem F. neer] þere BoCot.
233 come] coomen O; came CrG; keme F. for] for no RF. soules] soule Cr.
234 are] *om* F. *par*auenture for] & F. patrymoyne] patrymones G. hem failleþ] he*m* failith CrGYOC^{2}CBLRF; hem failled M; þei faille WHm.
235 wol] wollen HmO; *om* CrM. to] CrGYOC^{2}CBLMRF; and WHm. folk] HmCrGYOC^{2}CBLMR; wiþ folk W; of folk F.
236 siþen] seyen GO; seyn YC^{2}CB. cheitiftee] cheitiftee pouerte WLR; chaytyf pouerte HmCrGYOCM; caitiff pou*er*te C^{2}; pore cheytifte BmBo; chastite & pouert F; pur*e* chastite Cot.
237 Lat] they G. chewe] chewen B; cheve F. chose] chose*n* CrYOC^{2}CBM; haue chosen G.

For lomer*e* he lyeþ þat liflode moot begge
Than he þat laboureþ for liflode and leneþ it beggeris.
And siþen freres forsoke þe felicite of erþe
Lat hem be as beggeris or lyue by Aungeles foode.'
Conscience of þis counseil þo comsede for to laughe,
And curteisliche conforted hem and called in alle freres,
And seide, 'sires, sooþly welcome be ye alle
To vnitee and holy chirche; ac o þyng I yow preye:
Holdeþ yow in vnitee, and haueþ noon enuye
To lered ne to lewed, but lyueþ after your*e* reule.
And I wol be your*e* boruȝ: ye shal haue breed and cloþes
And oþere necessaries ynowe; yow shal no þyng [lakke]
Wiþ þat ye leue logik and lerneþ for to louye.
For loue lafte þei lordshipe, boþe lond and scole,
Frere Fraunceys and Domynyk, for loue to be holye.
And if ye coueite cure, kynde wol yow [telle]
That in mesure god made alle maner*e* þynges,
And sette [it] at a *cer*tain and [at] a siker nombre.
And nempnede [hem names], and noumbrede þe sterres:

238 *line om* RF. lomere] *altered to* longere *another ink* G; lymer Hm; lowder C^{2}. lyeþ] lith Y. moot] muste Cr^{23}; might Cr^{1}. begge] bygge GO; beige Cot.
239 *line om* RF. þat] tha C. it] it to O.
240 And] For RF. forsoke] forsoken O. þe] *om* GRF. of] of the CrGM (þe *erased* M). erþe] herte erthe (herte *cancelled*) C.
241 or] & G. foode] fodie (i *cancelled*) Bo.
242 Conscience of] þan Conscience for F. þo] *om* RF. comsede] began C^{2}. for] *om* CrGC^{2}M. laughe] lauȝte Bo.
243 curteisliche] curteysly he F; curteilich L. hem] hym HmCrB. in] *om* Hm.
244 ye] you Cr.
245 and] and to CF; *om* O. ac] but GC^{2}F; and C; *om* Cr.
246 Holdeþ] Hold Cr. in] w*ith* F. and] *om* F. haueþ] haue Cr; haþ F.
247 lered] lerned men Cr; lewed F. lewed] lerede F. lyueþ] lyue Cr.
248 shal] shullen BmBo. cloþes] cloth Cr.
249 oþere] otheris Bo. yow] ye CrO; for ȝee F; þow R. shal] schalt R. lakke] RF; faille WHmCrGYOC^{2}CBLM.
250 Wiþ] So F. ye] he Y. leue] leeuen B. lerneþ] lerne OCrCot. for] *om* CrM.
251 & þan leefte for love lond lordchepe & skole F. lafte] laften O; þerof lofte Bo; þerof loste BmCot; lost Cr; þei GC^{2}. þei] the Cr; lafte GC^{2}. lond...scole] lowde and stille C^{2}.
252 Frere] Freres YOCB; Boþe F. for] fo R.
253 coueite] coueyten HmGYC^{2}CBLM. cure] kures F. kynde] kynd wytt GC^{2}. telle] R; tellyn F; teche WHmCrGYOC^{2}CBLM.
254 þynges] of þyngys F; þynge B.
255 it] HmGYOC^{2}CBLMR; hem WCrF. at(1)] in C^{2}GF. at(2)] HmYOC^{2}CBLMR; yn GF; *om* WCr. a(2)] *om* GC. nombre] mombre Cr^{2}.
256 nempnede] neuened G. hem...and] hem names and newe RF; names newe and WHmCrGOC^{2}CBLM; names ynowe and Y. noumbrede] nombre R. sterres] preestes GYOCB; prestes sterreȝ C^{2}.

Qui numerat multitudinem stellarum et omnibus eis [*nomina vocat*].
Kynges and knyghtes þat kepen and defenden |
Han Officers vnder hem, and ech of hem a *cer*tein. *fol.* 128 *b*
And if þei wage men to werre þei write hem in noumbre;
⌈Wol no [tresorer take] hem [wages], *tra*uaille þei neu*er* so soore,
[But þei ben nempned in þe noumbre of hem þat ben ywaged].
Alle oþ*er*e in bataille ben yholde Brybours,
Pylours and Pykeharneys, in ech a [parisshe] ycursed.⌋
Monkes and Moniales and alle men of Religion,
Hir ordre and hir reule wole to han a *cer*tein noumbre
Of lewed and of lered; þe lawe wole and askeþ
A *cer*tein for a *cer*tein, saue oonliche of freres.
Forþi', quod Conscience, 'by crist! kynde wit me telleþ
It is wikked to wage yow; ye wexen out of noumbre.
Heuene haþ euene noumbre and helle is wiþoute noumbre.
Forþi I wolde witterly þat ye were in þe Registre

256α *in margin* O. *Qui*] *Quis* R. *et...eis*] *om* OR. *omnibus*] *omnia* F. *eis*] *om* Cr. *nomina vocat*] Cot; *nomina &c* YC^{2}CBm Bo; *&c* WHmCrGOLM; *om* RF.
257 kepen] kepten R. and defenden] me*n* to defende hem F.
258 hem(1)] hym BmBoR. and] & of O; of F. hem(2)] hym BmBo. a] *above line* M; *om* CrGYC^{2}CLR.
259 wage] wagen C^{2}B. to] *om* G. write] wryten HmYOBRF.
260 *copied here* CrGYOC^{2}CLMRF; *after* 263 WHmB. Wol] Or they wil CrM (wil *above line* M); Ellys will F; And þer-fore wolen B. no tresorer] HmGYOC^{2} LRF; no tresore CCrM; no man tresore W; men no tresor B. take...wages] take he*m* wages F; taken hym wages R; wages hem paie C^{2}; hem paie WHmCrGYOC BLM. *tra*uaille] taille C^{2}. neu*er*] ner F. so soore] so long G; *om* C.
261 *not in* WHmCrGYOCBLMRF; but he kunne rekene ariȝt her names in his rollis C^{2}.
262 Alle] For all Cr. oþ*er*e] oþeris Bo; other þat Cot. bataille] batailis BmBo. yholde] I holde Cot; yholden GO; holden CrM. Brybours] but brybouris bysyȝde F; brokouris O.
263 Pylours] As piloures F. harneys] harneyses Hm. ech] eu*er*y F. a] *om* GYC BF. parisshe] parische RF; place WHm CrGYOC^{2}CBLM. ycursed] accursed CrGYOC^{2}CBMRF. *Here* WHmB *copy line* 260.
264 Monkes] Boþe mu*n*kes F.
265 Hir...and] þer is in F; heraude R. wole] wolde MCr; wel F. a] *om* Cot.
266 lewed] lered MF; learned Cr. lered] lewed MCrF. wole] it wole OHm. and(2)] it F. askeþ] aske F; asked Cr^{3}.
267 a] *om* F. oonliche] holiche BmBo. of] þe F; *om* Cot.
268 Forþi] Therfore Cr.
269 wikked] wikke F. ye] you G. wexen] wexe CrGM. out of] of on R; *ouer* ony F; without Cr^{3}. noumbre] noubre Bm.
270 *line om* Y. Heuene] Euene O. wiþ-oute] owt of F; outyn C^{2}. noumbre] serteyn F.
271 Forþi] Therfore Cr. þat] *om* F. were] weren OBF. þe] *erased* M; þat F; *om* O. Registre] registres CrM (*final* s *erased* M).

And your*e* noumbre vnder Notaries signe and neiþ*er* mo ne lasse.'
Enuye herde þis and heet freres go to scole
And lerne logyk and lawe and ek contemplacion,
And p*re*che men of Plato, and preue it by Seneca
That alle þynges vnder heuene ouȝte to ben in comune.
He lyeþ, as I leue, þat to þe lewed so p*re*cheþ,
For god made to men a lawe and Moyses it tauȝte:
Non concupisces rem proximi tui.
And yuele is þis yholde in parisshes of Engelonde,
For p*er*sons and parissh preestes þat sholde þe peple shryue
Ben Curatours called to knowe and to hele,
Alle þ*a*t ben hir parisshens penaunce enioigne,
And [be] ashamed in hir shrift; ac shame makeþ hem wende
And fleen to þe freres, as fals folk to westmynstre
That borweþ and bereþ it þider and þanne biddeþ frendes
Yerne of forȝifnesse or lenger yeres loone. |
Ac while he is in westmynstre he wol be bifore *fol.* 129 *a*
And maken hym murie wiþ ooþer mennes goodes.

272 noumbre] nounbre Bm. Notaries] notarye HmGLRF. signe] signes YCB. and] *om* GF.
273 Enuye] þ*a*nne Envie F. heet] leete O; bad CrM (*above line* M). go] HmCrGYO C^2BMRF; to go WCL.
274 lerne] lerned G. ek] leeve F. contemplacion] constellaci*oun* O.
275 preue] p*re*uen RHmF; priue Cr^{23}.
276 alle] *om* CB. ouȝte] ouȝten OHmY C^2CBM. to] *om* OF. in] *om* Cot.
277 He] RF; And yet he WHmCrGYOC^2 CBLM. p*re*cheþ] prechen F.
278 god made] made god BmBo. to] *om* CrM. it] hem F.
279 *in margin* O. *concupisces*] comcupisses BmBo. *tui*] *tui &c* HmGYOCBR.
280 þis] his Cr^1. yholde] yholden O; holde Cr; to hold G; ȝolden B. parisshes] Innes F. of] in C^2G.
281 sholde] sholden CotO; shullen Bm Bo.
282 to(2)] *om* BF.
283 Alle] & all F; To all Cr^1. penaunce] penaunces RF. enioigne] enioynen R; to enioigne WHmCrGYOC^2LM; to enIoynen F; and enioigne C; hem to enIoyne B.
284 be] been F; beth R; sholde be YCr GC^2C; sholden ben MHmOL; shullen be B; sholden W. ashamed] shamed G. in] to tell F. shrift] schriff C^2. ac...wende] þ*a*t hem wend maketh Cr^{23}. ac] but GC^2; and CCr^1F. shame makeþ] þ*er*fore F. hem] hy*m* Bo; þey F; *om* Cr^1. wende] *om* Cr^1.
285 And] To CB. as] and B. to(2)] doon to F.
286 That] & F. bereþ] bere C^2G. it] *om* CrGYOC^2CBM. þider] thyer Cr^2. biddeþ] he bydd*es* F.
287 Yerne of] Ful ȝeerne F; yeres off G. forȝifnesse] forgyuenesse CCrG. yeres] yere R; þey F. loone] of loone B; lene (? leue) LR; bleve þere F.
288 Ac] but GC^2; Bu F; And CrC. in] *corrected from* at Bm.
289 maken] make HmCrOBoCotL; makeþ RF. hym] them *altered to* ther G. mennes] men R.

And so it farep *with* muche folk þat to freres shryueþ,
As sisours and executours; þei [shul] ȝyue þe freres
A parcel to preye for hem and [pleye] wiþ þe remenaunt,
And suffre þe dede in dette to þe day of doome.
Enuye herfore hatede Conscience,
And freres to philosophie he fond [hem] to scole,
The while coueitise and vnkyndenesse Conscience assaillede.
In vnitee holy chirche Conscience held hym
And made pees porter to pynne þe yates
Of alle taletelleris and titeleris in ydel.
Ypocrisie and h[ij] an hard assaut þei [ȝeuen].
[Ypocrisie at þe yate harde gan fighte]
And woundede wel wikkedly many a wys techer*e*
That wiþ Conscience acordede and Cardynal*e* v*er*tues.
Conscience called a leche þat koude wel shryue:
'Go salue þo þat sike ben and þoruȝ synne ywounded.'
Shrift shoop sharp salue and made men do penaunce

290 it] *om* G. fareþ] falliþ F. *with*] by HmYO. to] CrRF; to þe WHmGYOC^{2}CBLM. freres] HmCrGYC^{2}CBLMR; freres hem WOF.
291 shul] schul RF; wol WHmCrGYC^{2}CBLM; wolen O. ȝyue þe] þe (ue *added above another script*) L.
292 *as two lines divided after* murye WHmCrGYOC^{2}CBLMRF. hem] hym Bo. pleye...remenaunt] *with* þe remnau*n*t make meryȝe Of þe residue of þe good þ*at* oþ*er*e men byswonken F; make hemself murye Wiþ þe residue and þe remenaunt þat oþ*er*e men biswonke WHmCrGYOC^{2}CBLMR (hem] hym BmBo. self] selue*n* O; *om* R. þe(*both*)] *om* R. biswonke] biswonken OCr; byswonge Hm).
293 suffre] suffren Hm. dede] dead CrG. dette] hell lyȝn F. to] tyl F; byfore G.
294 Enuye] þanne Envie F. her] ther CrG.
295 philosophie] philosophires C. hem] HmCrGYC^{2}CBLMRF; þanne W; *om* O.
296 The] *om* F. Conscience] *om* B. assaillede] assayleden O.
297 Conscience] & holy chirche F. held] hold Bo; *with*held F; hylde C^{2}; healed Cr^{1}.
298 pees] pees the Y. pynne] vnpynne GC^{2}. þe] wel þe F.
299 Of] For O; To Cr. titeleris] tutelers CrC; totelerys F; titerers YHmOC^{2}BmBoLMR; tyter*es* Cot; tycyrers G. in] an R; of F; to G; *om* Cr^{23}. ydel] ydeltie F.
300 *line om* F. hij] he WHmCrGYOC^{2}CBLMR. an] and B; *om* G. hard] h::: Cot. assaut] sawt HmOLR; asent Cot. þei] *om* Cot. ȝeuen] made WCrGYC^{2}CBLMR; maden HmO.
301 HmCrGYOC^{2}CBLMRF; *line om* W; *here in the spelling of* W. Ypocrisie] þan ypoc*r*isie F. þe] *om* Cr^{1}. gan] gan to CrOBM.
302 wel] full G. a] *om* HmCr^{23}GYOC^{2}CLM. techere] techers HmCr^{23}GOC^{2}M.
303 wiþ] wit C. Cardynale] cardinales R.
304 Conscience] þan Conscience F. koude wel] wel kouthe YGOC^{2}CB.
305 Go] HmCrGYOLMR; To go W; To C^{2}CBF. þo] þou G. ben] wer*e* R; weren F. and] *above line* M; *om* GYOC^{2}CBL. ywounded] wounded Cr; & woundid O.
306 men] hem HmCr; *om* BoCot. do] to do C^{2}.

For hir mys[fetes] þat þei wroȝt hadde,
And þ*at* Piers [pardon] were ypayed, *redde quod debes.*
Some liked noȝt þis leche and lettres þei sente
If any surgien were [in] þe seg[e] þ*at* softer koude plastre.
Sire leef-to-lyue-in-lecherie lay þ*ere* and gronede;
For fastynge of a fryday he ferde as he wolde deye.
'Ther is a Surgien in þ[e] sege þat softe kan handle,
And moore of phisik bi fer, and fairer he plastreþ;
Oon frere Flaterer*e* is phisicien and surgien.' |
Quod Contricion to Conscience, 'do hym come to vnitee, *fol.* 129 *b*
For here is many a man hurt þoruȝ ypocrisye.'
'We han no nede', quod Conscience; 'I woot no bettre leche
Than p*er*son or parisshe preest, penitauncer or bisshop,
Saue Piers þe Plowman þat haþ power ouer alle
And Indulgence may do but if dette lette it.
I may wel suffre', seide Conscience, 'syn ye desiren,
That frere flaterer*e* be fet and phisike yow sike.'
The frere herof herde and hiede faste
To a lord for a lettre leue to haue
To curen as a Curatour; and cam w*ith* hi[s] l*ett*r[e]
Boldely to þe bisshop and his brief hadde

307 mysfetes] mysdedes WHmCrGYOC BLMRF; myssedis C^{2}. wroȝt] wrouȝten O. hadde] hadden Cr^{1}HmYC^{2}CBLMRF.
308 pardon] þe ploughma*n* B; þe C; *om* WHmCrGYOC^{2}LMRF. ypayed] payed HmCrGYOC^{2}CBLMRF.
309 liked] lykeden HmO; lickid Bo. sente] senten YOC^{2}CBM.
310 in þe sege] RCrF; þe segge HmGYO C^{2}CLM (*second* g *cancelled another ink* L); þe segg W; *om* B. softer] softe Y.
311 leef] lyf HmCrRF. lay] lye G.
312 For] For þe B; *illegible* O. he(2)] *om* F.
313 þe] þis WHmCrGYOC^{2}CBLMRF (*twice* O). sege] segge HmM (*over erasure* M).
314 And] and can B. bi fer] he ca*n* be feer F; he can CrM; beffore C^{2}.
315 is] ys boþe F. phisicien] phicien Y.
316 Conscience] co*n*fessyon GC^{2}. come] to come Hm.
317 is] *om* F. a] *om* GC^{2}Cot.
318 woot] not F.
319 penitauncer] pentaunc*er* HmF; pen-auncer R.
320 haþ power] power haþ F. alle] RGF; hem alle WHmCrYOC^{2}CBLM.
321 Indulgence] Indulgences Y. if] if that Cr. lette it] it lette F.
322 seide] quod HmCrF. syn] seinge Cr. desiren] disyre F.
323 and] a Cr^{1}.
324 her] ther G. hiede] lyed Y. faste] hym faste OC^{2}B; full faste CrMF.
325 *divided from* 326 *after* curen WHmCr GYOC^{2}CBLMRF.
326 To] *om* HmCrGYOC^{2}CB. curen] cure HmOC^{2}B; cures G. as] and as GYOC^{2}CBF. and] he were and WHm CrGYOCBLMR; he were he C^{2}F. his lettre] his lett*er*e RF; hise l*ett*res WHmCr GYOC^{2}BLM; lis letters C.
327 brief] breef he F; breues G.

In contrees þer he coome confessions to here;
And cam þ*ere* Conscience was and knokked at þe yate.
Pees vnpynned it, was Porter of vnitee,
And in haste askede what his wille were.
'In faiþ', quod þis frere, 'for p*ro*fit and for helþe
Carpe I wolde wiþ contricion, and þ*er*fore cam I hider.'
'He is sik', seide Pees, 'and so are manye oþ*ere*.
Ypocrisie haþ hurt hem; ful hard is if þei keuere.'
'I am a Surgien', seide þe [frere], 'and salues kan make.
Conscience knoweþ me wel and what I kan boþe.'
'I praye þee', quod Pees þo, 'er þow passe ferþer,
What hattestow, I praye þee? hele noȝt þi name.'
'Certes', seide his felawe, 'sire *Penetrans domos*.' |
'Ye? go þi gate!' quod Pees, 'by god! for al þi phisik, *fol.* 130 *a*
But þow konne [any] craft þow comest nouȝt herInne.
I knew swich oon ones, noȝt eighte wynter [passed],
Coom in þus ycoped at a Court þ*ere* I dwelde,
And was my lordes leche and my ladies boþe.
And at þe laste þis lymyto*ur*, þo my lord was oute,

328 coome] coome inne OHmCrGYC^{2}C BLM. confessions] confession CrO. to here] *om* R.
329 And] ⁊ he F.
330 Pees] ⁊ pees F; Piers B. vnpynned] vnpinnen Cr^{23}; oppened C^2. was] þ*at* was GF (þat *added main hand* G).
331 askede] he askede F. his] þ*at* his F.
332 þis] these Cot. frere] freris B (s *cancelled* Bm). helþe] hele O; herthe Y.
333 Carpe] Carpen F. wolde] wyll G. þ*er*...hider] þis is my cawse F. cam I] I cam C^{2}Cr; come I L.
334 seide] q*uo*d Y. are] is CrM. oþ*ere*] another CrM.
335 hurt] *om* G. hem] him CrGC^{2}MF. ful] *om* F. is] it is HmB. if] *om* Cr. þei] he C^{2}MF; he of Cr^1; he to Cr^{23}.
336 a] *om* Cr^1. seide] quod Hm; y B. frere] FR; segge WHmCrGYOC^{2}CBLM. and] *om* F. kan] kan I YF.
337 kan] kan do WHmCrGYOC^{2}CBLM RF.
338 ferþer] fortherer G.
339 hattestow] hightest thou CrM. I... þee] hyghtly ⁊ F.
340 Certes] *sir* certes G; Sire B; þe Frere F. seide] he sayde GC^2; felaw seyde O. his] thys CrCot; he YOC; *om* GC^{2}F. felawe] properly F; *om* O.
341 Ye] *om* Cr. gate] gates Cr. Pees] piers CB. þi(2)] *om* B.
342 konne] kenne Cr. any] R; more F; sum HmCrGYOC^{2}CBLM; som ooþ*er* W. her] ther YCB; he R.
343 knew] knowe Y. eighte] oo F. wynter] winters CrG; ȝeer F. passed] HmCrYOC^{2}CBLMR; ypassid F; hennes WG.
344 Coom] and cam B. in þus] þus In F. ycoped] coped Cr. þ*ere*] þere þat BmBo; wher CrCotM. dwelde] dede dwelle C^2; wiste F.
345 lordes] ladyes GYC^{2}CB; lady O. ladies] lordes GYOC^{2}CB.
346 þe] *om* Cr. þis] þat F.

He saluede so oure wo*m*men til some were wiþ childe.'
Hende speche heet pees, 'opene þe yates.
Lat in þe frere and his felawe, and make hem fair cheere.
He may se and here [here, so] may bifalle,
That lif þoruȝ his loore shal leue coueitise
And be adrad of deeþ and wiþdrawe hym fram pryde
And acorde wiþ Conscience and kisse hir ei*þer* ooþer.'
Thus þoruȝ hende speche [þe frere entred]
And cam to Conscience and curteisly hym grette.
'Thow art welcome', quod Conscience; 'kanstow heele sike?
Here is Contricion', quod Conscience, 'my cosyn, ywounded.
Conforte hym', quod Conscience, 'and tak kepe to hise soores.
The plastres of þe *per*son and poudres biten to soore;
[And] lat hem ligge ouerlonge and looþ is to chaunge;
Fro lenten to lenten he lat hise plastres bite.'
'That is ouerlonge', quod þis Lymyto*ur*, 'I leue. I shal amende it!'
And gooþ gropeþ Contricion and gaf hym a plastre
Of 'a pryuee paiement and I shal praye for yow
[And] for [hem] þat ye ben holden to al my lif tyme,

347 wo*m*men] wo*m*man C^{2}Cot. some] sixe or seuene F. were] weren HmM. wiþ childe] grete F.
348 heet] bad F. pees] pees to YCrO; Pees þoo to F; pees þo R. opene] vppon BmBo.
349 Lat] ⁊ lete F. þe] *om* R. hem] him CrBo.
350 and here] his sykenesse F. here so] her so R; er so F; so it WHmCrGYOC^{2}CBLM.
351 leue] leven F.
353 kisse] kissen F. hir] *om* CrGC^{2}BF.
354 þe...entred] entred þe frere WHmCrGYOC^{2}CBLMR; in entrid þo frerys F.
355–86 defective Bm; *see above*, p. 1.
355 cam] kemen F; *om* Y. to] Cr; in to WHmGYOC^{2}CBoCotLMRF.
356 sike] syke RF; þe sike WHmCrGYOC^{2}CBoCotLM.
357 ywounded] wou*n*ded Cr.
358 quod...and] wi*th* conseyl F. to] off G.
359 plastres] plastre BoCot. and] ⁊ þe F. biten] byte F; bitten C; ben R; beate*n* Cr. to] *above line* W; so C^{2}F; *om* HmG.
360 And] R; He WHmCrGYOC^{2}CBoCotLMF. lat] letteth Cr. hem] hym C. ligge] liggen RF. chaunge] chaunge hem WHmCrGYOC^{2}CBoCotLRF; chaunge*n* hem M.
361 lenten(*both*)] lente R. to] tyl F. he] *om* Cr^{23}. lat] letiþ BoCot; *om* Cr^{23}. bite] byten CrM; bitte R.
362 That] This C. ouer] to Hm. amende] ame*n*de*n* M.
363 And] ⁊ he F. gooþ] goth R; gooþ and WHmCrGYOC^{2}CBoCotLMF. gropeþ] grypeth Cot. gaf] ȝaff C^2; gyuethe G.
364 a] *om* C^2. paiement and] pyneme*n*t F.
365 And...hem] And for all CrGYOC^{2}CBoCotF; For al WHmLMR. ye] *om* F. holden] holde YGC^{2}CLRF. tyme] longe Cr.

And make [of] yow [*memoria*] in masse and in matyns
As frere[s] of oure Frat*er*nytee, for a litel siluer'.
Thus he gooþ and gadereþ and gloseþ þ*er*e he shryueþ
Til Contricion hadde clene foryeten to crye and to wepe |
And wake for hise wikked werkes as he was wont to
doone. *fol.* 130 *b*
For confort of his confessour Contricion he lafte,
That is þe souerayn[e] salue for alle [synnes of kynde].
Sleuþe seigh þat and so dide pryde,
And comen wiþ a kene wille Conscience to assaille.
Conscience cryed eft [Clergie to helpe],
And [bad] Contricion [come] to kepe þe yate.
'He lyþ [adreynt] and dremeþ', seide Pees, 'and so do manye
oþere.
The frere wiþ his phisyk þis folk haþ enchaunted,
And [doþ men drynke dwale]; þei drede no synne.'
'By crist!' quod Conscience þo, 'I wole bicome a pilgrym,
And [wenden] as wide as þe world [renneþ]
To seken Piers þe Plowman, þat pryde [myȝte] destruye,

366 of...*memoria*] of ȝow memory F; yow my lady WHmCrGYOC^{2}CBoCotLMR. masse] masses CrM.

367 As] All þe F. freres] GCrC^{2}CBoCot LMRF; frere WHmO; sust*er* Y. Frat*er*nytee] frateritie Cr^2.

368 and(2)] gold ⁊ F.

369 hadde] haue F. clene] *om* G. foryeten] forȝeete F. to(1)...wepe] for cr*i*ȝeng ⁊ for wepynge F. to(2)] *om* Hm.

370 wake] awake C; awakid BoCot; for wakyng F. hise] *om* C. wikked] *om* CrM. as] þ*at* F. was] *om* R.

371 Contricion] conscyence Hm. lafte] lost CrCotM.

372 souerayne] souerayneste WHmCrGY OC^{2}CBoCotLMRF. for] of O. alle] as Y. synnes of kynde] kynne synnes WHm YOC^{2}CBoCotLMRF; kinnes synnes CrG.

373 Sleuþe...and] þ*at* seeyȝ slewthe wel ⁊ ryght F. seigh] seithe C^2; seethe G; þ*an*ne saw O. so] also O.

374 comen] come LGYOC^{2}CBoCotM RF.

375 Conscience] ⁊ Conscience F. eft] out Cr. Clergie to helpe] and bad clergie helpe YGOC^{2}CBoCot; and bad Clergie helpe hym WHmCrLMRF.

376 bad...come] also Contricion for W HmCrGYOC^{2}CBoCotLMRF.

377 lyþ] lyght Cot. adreynt...dremeþ] adreynt Cot; and dremt Bo; and dremeþ WHmCrGYOC^{2}CLMRF. do] doth Cr RF; did Y. oþere] anoþ*er* F.

378 þis] þise YOC^2; þus BoCot; *om* G. haþ] hath so RF.

379 doþ...dwale] plastred hem so esily WHmCrGYOC^{2}CBoCotLMRF (hem] it C^2). drede] dreden OF; dradde Cot. synne] syȝknesse F.

381 wenden] walken WHmCrGYOC^{2}C LMRF; walke BoCot. as(1)] also HmBo Cot. as(2)] as al YHmGC^{2}CBoCotLMR. renneþ] lasteþ WHmCrGYOC^{2}CBoCot LMR; askeþ F.

382 seken] seke HmCrGYOC^{2}CBoCotL MRF. þe] *om* F. myȝte] R; he myȝhte F; may WHmCrGYOC^{2}CBoCotLM. destruye] stroyȝe F.

And þat freres hadde a fyndyng þat for nede flateren
And countrepledeþ me, Conscience; now kynde me avenge,
And sende me hap and heele til I haue Piers þe Plowman.'
And siþþe he gradde after Grace til I gan awake.

383 *line om* F. And] *om* BoCot. hadde] hadden HmOBoCot. for] for no Cr.
384 And] For he F.
385 þe] *om* F.
386 And siþþe] So sore F; *illegible* R. til I gan] þat he began (he *erased*) F.

THE MMA ENCYCLOPEDIA

JONATHAN SNOWDEN & KENDALL SHIELDS

PHOTOGRAPHS BY PETER LOCKLEY

ECW Press

Published by ECW Press
2120 Queen Street East, Suite 200, Toronto, Ontario, Canada M4E 1E2
416-694-3348 info@ecwpress.com

LIBRARY AND ARCHIVES CANADA CATALOGUING IN PUBLICATION

Snowden, Jonathan, 1975-
The MMA encyclopedia / Jonathan Snowden and Kendall Shields.

Includes bibliographical references.
ISBN 978-1-55022-923-3

1. Mixed martial arts--Encyclopedias. I. Shields, Kendall II. Title.

GV1102.7.M59S65 2010 796.81503 C2010-901256-9

Developing Editor: Michael Holmes
Cover Design: Dave Gee
Text Design: Tania Craan
Color Section Design: Rachel Ironstone
Typesetting: Gail Nina
Photos copyright © Peter Lockley, 2010
Printing: Solisco Tri-Graphic 1 2 3 4 5

The publication of *The MMA Encyclopedia* has been generously supported by the Government of Ontario through Ontario Book Publishing Tax Credit, by the OMDC Book Fund, an initiative of the Ontario Media Development Corporation, and by the Government of Canada through the Canada Book Fund.

Canadä

PRINTED AND BOUND IN CANADA

ECW PRESS
ecwpress.com

Contents

Introduction

On its surface, mixed martial arts is a simple game. There's something universal about fighting, after all. And when two combatants square off inside a cage in a brutal contest that leaves one man standing and the other unwilling or unable to continue, audiences connect on a visceral, primal level, not an intellectual one. So why, you might ask, is this book necessary?

Because, as simple as the concept of mixed martial arts may be, the execution is infinitely complex. Take the fistic repertoire of traditional western boxing and add to that the precise savagery of Muay Thai kickboxing, the explosive athleticism of collegiate and international wrestling, the dynamic grappling techniques of judo and sambo, and the methodical submission fighting of the world's top Brazilian Jiu-jitsu stylists. These diverse disciplines, each one complex enough to warrant a lifetime of study on its own, now regularly collide, with fascinating results, at MMA events the world over.

With *The MMA Encyclopedia* we hope to provide some insight into the techniques, styles, and tactics on display in the cage, as well as shed light upon the fighters and promotions that have helped make MMA one of the fastest growing sports in the world. Along the way, many of the sport's luminaries tell their own stories under the heading "In Their Own Words." The entries are arranged alphabetically, and when we make reference to a topic addressed elsewhere in the encyclopedia, the subject appears in bold type. As you'll see, the world of mixed martial arts is deeply interconnected.

Peter Lockley has provided some of his top notch photography to illustrate the book, and Chris "Mookie" Harrington helped put together the appendices: a complete look at the results from every major fight show in both America and Japan as well as a collection of interesting miscellany. We hope you'll agree that these combined efforts have yielded the best overall picture of the mixed martial arts industry ever put to press.

Abbott, David

Nickname: Tank
Height: 6′
Weight: 285 lbs
Born: 4/16/65
Debut: UFC 6 (7/14/95)
Career Record: 10-14
Notable Wins: Paul Varelans (UFC 6); Yoji Anjo (UFC 15.5); Wesley "Cabbage" Correira (ROTR 7)
Notable Losses: Oleg Taktarov (UFC 6); Dan Severn (Ultimate Ultimate 95); Don Frye (Ultimate Ultimate 96); Pedro Rizzo (UFC 17.5); Kevin "Kimbo Slice" Ferguson (EliteXC: Street Certified)

It wasn't the brutal knockout of the 400-pound **John Matua** that made David "Tank" Abbott stand out in a crowded MMA landscape. It was the dance — just a little shimmy mimicking Matua's scary convulsions as he lay unconscious on the mat — that immediately made Abbott one of the **UFC**'s biggest stars.

Before Abbott burst onto the scene in 1995 at UFC 6, the UFC was filled with respectful athletes, martial artists who conducted themselves with class and dignity. With his crass interviews, often mocking his opponents and making light of the trauma he had just inflicted on their brains with his hammering fists, Abbott was a breath of fresh air. He was the anti–martial artist, a welcoming and familiar figure for fans who still weren't sure what to make of **Gracie Jiu-jitsu** and the ground game. This was a fighter they could feel comfortable with: a bar fighter with a bald head, barrel chest, and long beard. This was what a fighter was supposed to look like.

"I just got out of jail for beating somebody up — in fact, a cop's son," Abbott said. His background gave UFC promoters reason to worry. But Abbott had a solid case for his inclusion in the event. "Isn't this supposed to be about fighting? And they said, 'Yeah, but you've got to have some kind of a black belt or something.' And I said, 'That's not what I'm about. I'm about fighting in the streets.' They called me a couple days later and said, 'We came up with this thing called Tank Abbott. It's from the *Every Which Way But Loose* movie from Clint Eastwood.' That's where the Tank came from."

It was a brilliant marketing ploy, not just by Semaphore Entertainment Group, but by Abbott himself. The Tank may have looked like an ignorant thug, but that was for show. He was a legitimately tough guy, but he was also a college graduate and a junior college wrestling star. This wasn't part of the UFC's pitch, though. Fans preferred to think of Abbott as a menacing street fighter and that was what SEG gave them.

Unfortunately for Abbott, the martial artists he professed to hate so much were more than a match for him. Abbott's career is filled with devastating knockouts of journeymen and tomato cans, but every time he stood in the cage with a legitimate martial artist, he lost and lost convincingly. Even in defeat, Tank was still able to convince fans he was the tougher guy. He was famous for heading to the bar while his conqueror headed to the hospital.

It was an act that seemed to age poorly. If tapping out to a sneering **Frank Mir**'s **toe hold** didn't kill the Abbott myth, a first round knockout in just 43 seconds at the hands of street fighter **Kimbo Slice** surely did. Despite these convincing losses, Abbott will continue to fight on. As long as there are promoters who are willing to pay big bucks for the nostalgia of having Tank Abbott on their cards, the Tank will be there, lacing up his gloves and ready to fall down for old time's sake.

■ Tank Abbott: Wrestling Star

During his UFC run, Tank Abbott's biggest nemesis was the promotion's pretty boy **Ken Shamrock**. One SEG insider thought of Shamrock's **Lion's Den** and Abbott's crew as the Sharks and the Jets. Like the gangs in *West Side Story*, the two crews seemed destined to rumble. Instead, the fireworks were all verbal, especially after Shamrock left fighting for **professional wrestling**. Abbott mocked him mercilessly, but as the UFC paychecks got smaller, Abbott's opposition to pro wrestling shrank as well. In 1999, Abbott took the leap with Time Warner's World Championship Wrestling.

He joined the promotion in a tumultuous time. WCW had peaked with an evil Hulk Hogan leading his New World Order stable against aging good guys like Sting and Ric Flair. They were desperate for the next big thing and were tossing ideas against the wall with reckless abandon. Abbott was far from the only experiment; WCW also brought in KISS to help christen a KISS Demon character and signed the rapper Master P to headline a rap versus country music feud.

In this creative chasm, Abbott's wrestling persona changed by the day. He was a tough guy with one-punch-knockout power during a "Colors on a Pole" match with Big Al at one pay-per-view and the goofy dancing bodyguard for the boy-band knockoff "3 Count" at another show.

"The powers that be in WCW were changing every day; you never knew who was in charge. They just came up with new ideas and things for me to do. I think they were hoping it wouldn't go well for me," Abbott said. "I thought it was actually kind of funny to go out and dance with those guys. What the hell – let's go have some fun."

Achilles hold: see **Leg locks**

ADCC

The Abu Dhabi Combat Club Submission Wrestling World Championship — more often referred to as ADCC, or simply Abu Dhabi — is the most prestigious competition in the world of no-**gi** submission grappling. Founded by MMA enthusiast Sheik Tahnoon Bin Zayed Al Nahyan and his **Brazilian Jiu-jitsu** instructor Nelson Monteiro in 1998, the ADCC's mandate is to bring grapplers from various disciplines together to compete under rules agreeable to competitors from all styles — though ADCC rules resemble those of Brazilian Jiu-jitsu more closely than those of any other art or sport. And indeed, Brazilian Jiu-jitsu practitioners have enjoyed far more success at ADCC than representatives of **sambo**, **judo**, or **wrestling**. Aside from **Mark Kerr** and **Sanae Kikuta**, representing wrestling and judo respectively, all ADCC champions have been top Brazilian Jiu-jitsu exponents. This is no doubt due to at least two factors: the undeniable, inherent quality of Brazilian Jiu-jitsu as the premier submission discipline of its era, and the fact that the ADCC is simply not on the radar of active elite wrestlers and judo players. Perhaps one day Sheik Tahnoon's dream of top athletes from every major grappling discipline competing under a common rule set will be fully realized. Until then, it is

In Their Own Words: Matt Hume on ADCC

"Sheik Tahnoon saw me defeat Kenny Monday in the first world submission wrestling championship called 'The Contenders.' At the time, he was training in Brazilian Jiu-jitsu with Nelson Montero. He had seen Gracie Jiu-jitsu defeat all comers in the early **UFC**s, but started to see wrestlers come in and have success over some of the good jiu-jitsu practitioners. Then he saw me defeat the most decorated wrestler in only 45 seconds! He had his assistant contact me and I went to Abu Dhabi to train him and his combat team. Shortly after I taught him, he decided to hold the first Abu Dhabi submission championships and the rest is history.

"Training Sheik Tahnoon and his combat team was a great experience. He is a true martial artist and always seeks to improve his technique and ability. Everyone that I met in Abu Dhabi was very nice and had a true interest in learning what I taught them. I went back on several occasions and it was always like a reunion with good friends and family. I feel very fortunate to have had that opportunity and to have them as friends today."

what it is: a slightly dry but intriguing tournament featuring many of the biggest names in Brazilian Jiu-jitsu and MMA.

Affliction

It might be best to think of the Affliction clothing company's foray into the world of mixed martial arts as a noble failure. Backed, at least nominally, by Donald Trump, and partnered with Oscar De La Hoya's powerhouse Golden Boy Promotions, Affliction Entertainment put together two stacked, genuinely entertaining shows before falling apart days before their much anticipated Trilogy event in the summer of 2009. The premise was simple, and almost irresistible: take the Affliction brand, which enjoyed enormous success among the demographic that underpinned the popularity of mixed martial arts, partner it with the best heavyweight fighter on the planet, **Fedor Emelianenko**, and watch the money pile up. It didn't quite work out that way, in part because of a lack of proven draws on the top of the card and in part because of the hefty salaries paid out to the likes of **Tim Sylvia**, **Josh Barnett**, **Andrei Arlovski**, **Matt Lindland**, and **Vitor Belfort** — all admirable and accomplished fighters, but none of them capable of pulling in the kind of pay-per-view numbers needed to keep things viable.

By the summer of 2009, there were rumors and rumblings that the end might be in sight, and once Barnett failed a pre-fight drug test — the third positive test for a banned steroid of his career — Affliction's third event collapsed, and the promotion itself followed suit not long thereafter. A partnership with **Strikeforce** was considered but never consolidated, forcing Affliction to turn to **Dana White**. The **UFC**, which had banned Affliction clothing when word first began to spread that the company was considering running its own events, absorbed several fighters' contracts and welcomed the clothing company back as a sponsor. In the end, the Affliction affair showed that while there are some intriguing synergies between mixed martial arts and elaborately goony sportswear, success in one doesn't necessarily guarantee success in the other.

Akebono

Real Name: Chad Rowan **Height:** 6'8"
Weight: 500 lbs **Born:** 5/8/69
Debut: Dynamite!! (12/31/04) **Career Record:** 0-4
Notable Losses: Royce Gracie (Dynamite!! 2004); Don Frye (Hero's 5)

The Japanese sumo fans were more disappointed than angry when it turned out Chad Rowan just didn't get it. They had embraced Rowan as "Akebono," the first foreigner ever promoted to the exalted rank of yokozuna. He was among the most successful sumo of his era, winning 11 top division championships, and the notoriously xenophobic Japanese adopted him as one of their own. He even represented his new homeland at the 1998 Winter Olympics opening ceremonies in Nagano.

Then came retirement. Although he was given a job training the next generation of wrestlers, it wasn't easy navigating the extremely political world of the sumo. It seems strange to many foreigners, but in Japan, a long-term position of authority in sumo isn't earned — it's bought and paid for by the athletes and their wealthy fans and sponsors. Akebono was on that path, an apprentice stable-master vying for one of a very few positions as head of a stable. The cost of that position, because of its scarcity, could exceed $2 million and Akebono had lost all his financial backing. In Japan, sumo are held to higher standards than other athletes, and Akebono had disappointed his richest backers by dumping his long-time Japanese girlfriend and marrying a Japanese-American only after he had impregnated her.

Despite their status in the country, top sumo were more wealthy than rich. They did well, earning as much as $500,000 a year, but Akebono had expensive tastes and was struggling. He hadn't made enough to live comfortably in retirement and he had lost his opportunity to make a lifelong living in sumo. When the restaurant he purchased failed, he felt he had little choice but

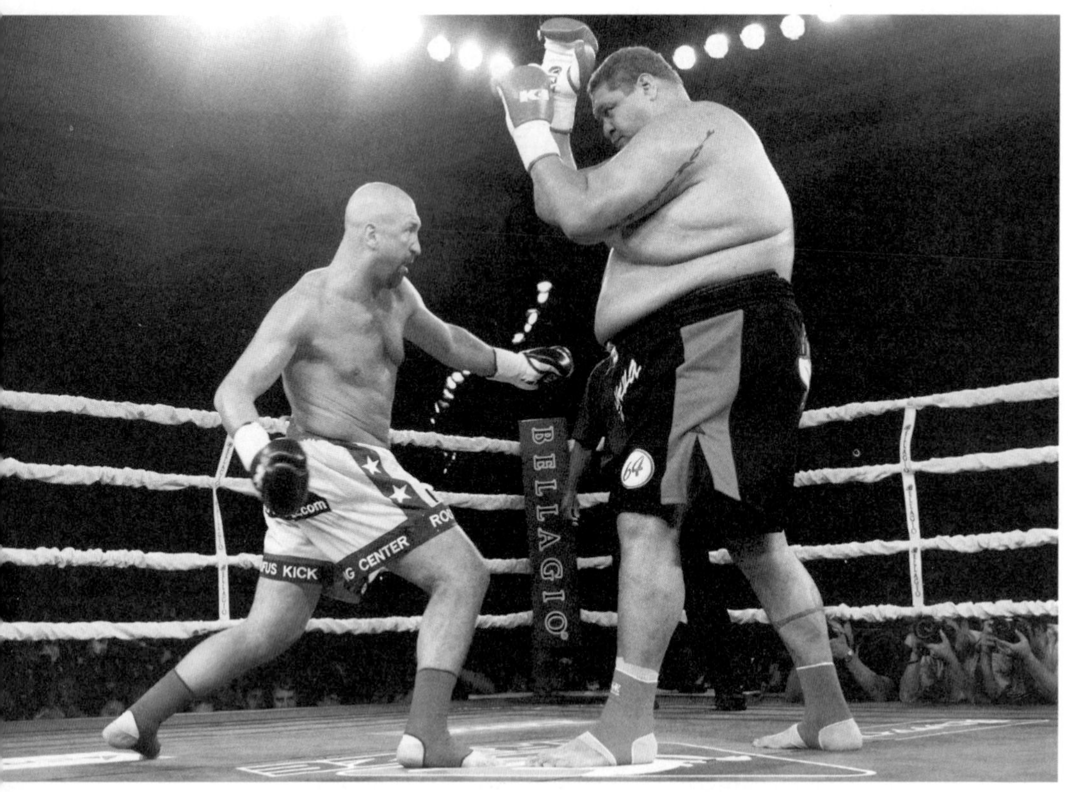

to go out on his own. Consequently, one of the top men in a very traditional sport joined the loud and flashy K-1 kickboxing show. He may have abandoned years of tradition, but he didn't come cheap: Akebono's salary for a K-1 fight was more than $1 million.

In the ring, whether it was kickboxing or MMA, watching Akebono fight was a little like watching Michael Jordan play baseball. It was sad to watch a true great struggle at a new game, every embarrassing loss destroying his legacy a little more. Although he never found success at this new sport, fans were more than happy to tune in and watch the spectacle. His 2003 fight with fellow giant **Bob Sapp** attracted more than 50 million television viewers in a country of just over 120 million people. Almost half the country tuned in to see the former giant become just a little smaller, if not in size then in stature.

Akiyama, Yoshihiro

Nickname: Sexiyama
Height: 5'10"
Weight: 185 lbs
Born: 7/29/75
Debut: Dynamite!! 2004 (12/31/04)
Career Record: 13-2-2

Notable Wins: Melvin Manhoef (Hero's 7); Denis Kang (Hero's 2007)

Notable No Contests: Kazushi Sakuraba (Dynamite!! 2006); Kazuo Misaki (Yarennoka)

Notable Loss: Chris Leben (UFC 116)

Top middleweight Yoshihiro Akiyama's notoriety as a fighter is surpassed only by his reputation as a cheater.

Akiyama's reputation for foul play began during his international **judo** career, where his World Championship trials win in 2002 and fifth-place finish at the 2003 Osaka World Championships were clouded by credible allegations and formal protests over the slipperiness of his **gi**. The reputation was cemented when Akiyama was disqualified and a no contest was declared in his high-profile New Year's Eve bout against MMA legend **Kazushi Sakuraba**. Sakuraba, unable to secure a grip, complained vociferously to the referee throughout the brief, lopsided fight, but was ignored.

A subsequent investigation by K-1 officials revealed that Akiyama had entered the ring covered in a layer of Olay Body Quench lotion. He pleaded ignorance of the foul, and although it's possible that Akiyama was using the lotion to replenish moisture for naturally radiant skin, it seems far more likely that this was a deliberate if unnecessary act aimed at improving his already excellent chances against the fading Sakuraba.

Before the Sakuraba scandal, Akiyama was a Japanese crowd favorite. Afterward, he was a disgraced, hated villain — but also the **Hero's/Dream** organization's biggest television ratings draw. While the Japanese fans love to hate him, Koreans, it seems, simply love him. Though Japanese-born and naturalized, Akiyama (Choi Sung-Ho) is ethnically Korean and a mainstream celebrity in that country, where audiences focus less on his questionable sportsmanship and more on his dandyish fashion sense and smooth pop crooning.

Akiyama's last significant fight in Japan was his heated New Year's Eve 2007 contest against **Kazuo Misaki** in front of an uncommonly energized Saitama crowd. What looked like a decisive KO loss for Akiyama — the first since an early bout with heavyweight kickboxer Jerome LeBanner — was later ruled a no contest when Misaki's head kick was shown to have landed while Akiyama was on all fours. No longer content to play the villain at home, Akiyama made a solid American debut at **UFC** 100, taking Fight of the Night honors for his split decision win over Alan Belcher and becoming something of a cult hero as the irresistible "Sexiyama."

Aldo, Jose

Nickname: Junior **Height:** 5'7"

Weight: 145 lbs **Born:** 9/9/86
Debut: EcoFight 1 (8/10/04) **Career Record:** 17-1
Notable Wins: Alexandre Nogueira (WEC 34); Mike Brown (WEC 44); Urijah Faber (WEC 48)
Notable Loss: Luciano Azevedo (Jungle Fight 5)

WEC featherweight champion Jose Aldo exploded from obscurity to become, at just 23 years of age, one of the youngest men ever to win a major MMA championship.

The dynamic young striker looks up to boxer Mike Tyson and there is something Tyson-esque about the Amazonian warrior. Boxing fans in the '80s could never forget the young heavyweight from Queens who won his first 17 fights by knockout. Aldo has been on a similar streak since joining the WEC. Starting with former **Shooto** standout **Alexandre Nogueira**, he's dispatched of six consecutive opponents, the last being champion **Mike Brown**.

When confined to the world of MMA, the fighter Aldo most resembles is the young **Vitor Belfort**. "The Phenom" entered the **UFC** Octagon in the early days with blazing hands and furious power. It was only later that opponents and fans would find out his heart would often wilt when the going got tough. So far no one has been able to put Aldo to the test. More than half of his fights have ended in the first round. How well he is prepared to go into the championship rounds could be the difference in whether he is a flash in the pan or a future legend.

Alessio, John

Nickname: The Natural **Height:** 5'9"
Weight: 170 lbs **Born:** 7/5/79
Debut: Ulimate Battle (5/17/98) **Career Record:** 28-13
Notable Wins: Chris Brennan (KOTC 15); Ronald Jhun (KOTC 29); War Machine (TPF 5)
Notable Losses: Pat Miletich (UFC 26); Jason Black (UCC 12); Diego Sanchez (UFC 60); Thiago Alves (UFC: The Final Chapter)

John Alessio picks things up quickly. Whether it's a backward steamroller on his BMX bike, or an **arm bar** from guard, Alessio is a fast learner. He was good enough on his bike to win the Nationals for trick biking twice, but he set his sights on MMA competition instead. He decided early that he wanted to be a pro fighter, moving from Vancouver, BC, in Canada to California so he could train at the infamous Shark Tank with Eddy Millis. He was just 19.

When it came to the ground game, Alessio really was a natural. His ground game steadily improved and he won a four-man tournament at

SuperBrawl 16 to earn a shot at the **UFC**. When he fought **Pat Miletich** in the semi-main event at UFC 26 for the UFC lightweight title, he was just 20 years old. Miletich submitted him in the second round, but the scrappy Alessio put up a solid fight.

It became the story of his career. Alessio dispatched lesser opponents with relative ease. But when he stood across the cage from bigger name fighters, he was never able to reach inside for that will to win. He lost fights to **Diego Sanchez**, **Thiago Alves**, Joe Doerkson, Jason Black, Jonathan Goulet, Carlos Condit, Paul Daley, and Brock Larson. It will be his legacy: too good for average fighters and just good enough to make a good fighter look bad.

Alvarez, Eddie

Nickname: The Silent Assassin **Height:** 5'8"

Weight: 155 lbs **Born:** 1/11/84

Debut: Ring of Combat 5 (12/14/03) **Career Record:** 20-2

Notable Wins: Joachim Hansen (Dream 3); Tatsuya Kawajiri (Dream 4)

Notable Losses: Nick Thompson (BodogFight: Clash of the Nations); Shinya Aoki (Dynamite!! 2008)

Taking fights for assorted minor promotions in the U.S., Canada, Japan, and Russia, Eddie Alvarez built a reputation as a tough up-and-coming welterweight and amassed an impressive 13–1 record to start his career. But it was as a lightweight fighting in **Dream**, Japan's foremost organization, that Alvarez made the MMA world take notice. After putting on a fight of the year–caliber bout against the fierce **Joachim Hansen** in the quarter-final of the Dream Lightweight Grand Prix, Alvarez proved his first win over first-rate competition was no fluke by stopping the heavy-handed **Tatsuya Kawajiri** in the next round. Although an eye injury kept him from the tournament final, it was clear that Eddie Alvarez had arrived. A much-anticipated New Year's Eve bout with top Dream star **Shinya Aoki** for the WAMMA lightweight title fell short of expectations, however, when Alvarez was caught in a **heel hook** early in the first round. After his success in Dream's Grand Prix, Alvarez tried his luck in the upstart **Bellator** promotion's lightweight tournament. Unsurprisingly, Alvarez breezed through the competition to become Bellator's first lightweight champion. It wasn't Alvarez's first title — he'd held the Maximum Fighting Challenge/BodogFight welterweight championship before dropping down — and given his proven ability to hang with the best in the world at 155 pounds, it's unlikely that it will be his last.

Alves, Thiago

Nickname: The Pit Bull
Height: 5'9"
Weight: 170 lbs
Born: 10/3/83
Debut: Champions Night 2 (6/30/01)
Career Record: 17-6
Notable Wins: Karo Parisyan (*Ultimate Fight Night* 13); Matt Hughes (UFC 85); Josh Koscheck (UFC 90)
Notable Losses: Spencer Fisher (*Ultimate Fight Night* 2); Jon Fitch (*Ultimate Fight Night* 5); Georges St. Pierre (UFC 100); John Fitch (UFC 117)

Today the fight world knows Thiago Alves as a powerful striker who can finish his opponents with dynamic blows. He throws **Muay Thai** knees, punches, and kicks with equal aplomb. In 2006, however, Thiago Alves was on his way to being cut by the **UFC**. He had lost two of his first four fights, including two decisive losses to Spencer Fisher and **Jon Fitch**. Then Alves got big. Real big. Going in to welterweight fights at 200 pounds is a significant advantage and Alves routinely had ten pounds on his opponents going into the fight. While everyone cut weight, no one did it quite as well as Alves. Coincidentally, Alves hasn't lost since, running together a seven-fight win string.

In Their Own Words: Thiago Alves on cutting weight

"Usually I'm waking up around 191, 192; you know that's normal for me right now, it's always – actually that's pretty good for me right now but I think on the day of the fight I'll be around 190, 195, something like that.

"The cutting weight thing, it's never an easy thing to do. . . . Nobody likes to lose weight, especially like drain yourself, you know, dehydrate yourself, but it's part of the game. You know you have to do it. . . . It's not a mystery and it's not a thing that you never done before. You know every time you fight it has to go through those things. You know, so you know if you do it right you're going to perform as well. You know if you don't, it's your fault; it's your mistake. You're not going to perform very well. So it is what it is.

"I mean, we're going to weigh in the same way. You know we're both going to have to weigh 170. . . . I don't think the size advantage at this point, at this level, is going to count much. I'm not counting on that, you know; I'm just counting on my training and everything that I know and everything that I've been through, you know, all the struggle that I've been through in my life and I'm just going to let it go."

Cutting that much weight isn't always easy. At UFC 66 Alves was caught doping, busted by the Nevada State Athletic Commission for using a diuretic, Spironolactone. He was suspended for eight months and paid a $5,500 fine. Upon his return, Alves continued to shine. He impressed hard-core fans with his strong standup, out-striking the free-swinging Chris Lytle and the judoka **Karo Parisyan.**

The Parisyan win proclaimed Alves a legitimate prospect. His next fight provided a chance to climb yet another rung on the ladder. After several fights fell through, Alves and **Matt Hughes** agreed to fight in the main event of UFC 85 on short notice. For Hughes, the tables were turning. Just two years earlier he had been the young gun making his name off the legendary **Royce Gracie.** Now he was the veteran legend that the young prospect, Alves, was looking to put out to pasture.

Alves came into the fight much bigger than Hughes. Unfortunately, he also came into the fight four pounds heavier than the 170-pound weight limit. No one can say for certain if the additional weight helped, but Alves manhandled the legend. Hughes couldn't take him down and Alves dropped him with a thunderous left knee.

Alves's takedown defense was no fluke. He outwrestled former NCAA **wrestling** champion **Josh Koscheck** in his next fight and destroyed him with powerful leg kicks. The Koscheck win took Alves to the top of the pecking order. He was ready to step into the cage with world champion **Georges St. Pierre.** He wasn't ready, however, for the Canadian's unstoppable takedowns. Alves spent much of the fight on his back, looking up at the man who entered the Octagon as champion that night and left it the same way.

Americana: See **Kimura and Americana**

American Top Team

Coconut Creek, Florida's American Top Team (ATT) was founded in 2003 by two prominent members of **Brazilian Top Team,** Ricardo Liborio and **Marcus Silveira.** Since then, it has produced or become home to a truly remarkable roster of champions and contenders: **Thiago Alves, Gesias Cavalcante,** Thiago Silva, **Jeff Monson, Antonio Silva, Denis Kang,** and **Brazilian Jiu-jitsu** living legend **Marcelo Garcia** are but the tip of the iceberg. Recently, however, ATT has drawn criticism for its promotional alliance with the Martial Arts Industry Association. ATT franchises out its respected name through the MAIA to "Certified Level 1 American Top Team Instructors," who participate in a $3,500 three-day seminar followed by monthly payments totaling $4,200 in the first year. Andre

Benkei, a respected coach, left ATT over the scheme in 2008, and told *Tatame* magazine the gym had turned into "a big McDonald's." He criticized team leaders for "selling our work to people that take advantage of our name and never went to ATT — owners of **karate** gyms that simply do a seminar and now have a right to teach MMA with ATT's name." Only time will tell whether this controversial program will dilute the name of one of the top fight teams in the country. In the meantime, expect American Top Team fighters to either hold or challenge for the sport's top titles on a regular basis.

Anaconda choke: see **Arm triangle**

Anjo, Yoji

Nickname: Mr. 200 Percent **Height:** 5'10"

Weight: 200 lbs **Born:** 12/31/69

Debut: U-Japan (11/17/96) **Career Record:** 0-5-1

Notable Losses: Tank Abbott (UFC 15.5); Matt Lindland (UFC 29); Ryan Gracie (Pride Shockwave 2004)

As a fighter, Yoji Anjo was completely forgettable. Like other Japanese pro wrestlers before and since, he got by on a combination of heart and chutzpah. Anjo was undeniably tough: even the routinely disrespectful **Tank Abbott** made a point of noting Anjo's never-quit fighting spirit. Still, his MMA career was completely unremarkable, except for an incident in 1994 that helped make **Rickson Gracie** a star in Japan.

Anjo was the toughest wrestler in the shoot-style UWFi. The promotion had drawn huge crowds to see the toughest of the tough. Despite the group's great success, UWFi booker Yuki Miyato could feel that the game was almost up. His pro wrestlers had convinced a nation that they were the baddest men on the planet, but the advent of **Pancrase**, the **UFC**, and now **Vale Tudo** Japan was starting to make that illusion a tougher sell to the Japanese populace.

After failing to sign Rickson to a pro **wrestling** match, he sent his toughest guy, mid-carder Yoji Anjo, to challenge Rickson to a fight on December 7, 1994 — Pearl Harbor Day. They expected that Rickson would decline the impromptu fight, or that Anjo would beat him. Either way, they would return to Japan with a public relations victory. They didn't know Rickson.

He got the call that a Japanese wrestler was at his Los Angeles dojo with the media in tow when he was home with his family. They all went to see what was happening and Anjo called Rickson a coward in front of his entire family and his students. The fight was on. It started quickly. Asked if he needed time to get ready, Rickson replied, "I was born ready, motherfucker." Instead of a gentle demonstration of jiu-jitsu, Gracie brutalized Anjo. The fight took place behind closed doors at the dojo, but witnesses say Gracie got the **mount** position and rained down punch after punch on the helpless wrestler's face. The pictures that surfaced in the Japanese papers showed a man who looked like he had been in a car accident, his face turned to hamburger by Gracie's vicious assault.

The public humiliation helped speed shoot-style wrestling's inevitable demise. Anjo's failure to protect the business left his mentor **Nobuhiko Takada** no choice but to fight Gracie. The resulting match propelled MMA from a niche sport in Japan into a mainstream spectacle, making Anjo's ill-fated trip to the Gracie dojo one of the most important butt kickings of the decade.

Ankle lock: see **Leg locks**

Aoki, Shinya

Nickname: Tobikan Judan | **Height:** 5'11"

Weight: 161 lbs | **Born:** 5/9/83

Debut: Deep 15th Impact (7/3/04) **Career Record:** 24-5 (1 No Contest)

Notable Wins: Akira Kikuchi (Shooto: The Victory of the Truth); Joachim Hansen (Pride Shockwave 2006); Gesias Cavalcante (Dream 2); Caol Uno (Dream 5); Eddie Alvarez (Dynamite!! 2008)

Notable Losses: Hayato Sakurai (Shooto: Alive Road); Joachim Hansen (Dream 5); Hayato Sakurai (Dream 8)

Nicknamed "Tobikan Judan" ("tenth degree master of flying locks") for his propensity for spectacular submissions, Shinya Aoki became the centerpiece of Japan's **Dream** promotion following successful stints in **Shooto** and **Pride FC**, and was recognized December 31, 2008, as the first WAMMA Undisputed World Lightweight Champion. At a time when mixed martial arts came to be defined by the balanced, versatile fighter skilled in all aspects of the game, Aoki managed to succeed on the strength of his submission grappling alone.

A ne waza (ground fighting)–focused collegiate **judo** player turned **Brazilian Jiu-jitsu** exponent, Aoki opened his MMA career with an unremarkable two-fight stint in **Deep**, but began turning heads immediately upon arrival in Shooto, winning his debut bout with a devastating standing arm lock rarely seen in MMA: a controversial wakigatame that broke Keith Wisniewski's arm at the elbow in an instant. A competitive loss to **Hayato Sakurai** and a solid decision win over **Akira Kikuchi** to claim Shooto's middleweight (167 pounds) championship solidified Aoki's reputation among hard-core fans, but it was in his Pride Bushido debut that Aoki truly began to make his mark. The quick submission win by triangle choke over Jason Black answered any questions about Aoki's ability to perform on a bigger stage, but left us with a more burning question: where did Aoki get those remarkable pants? Aoki's colorful compression tights, which improve grip as well as fabulousness, quickly became as important to the Aoki package as his inescapable rubber guard and dynamic "Baka Survivor" ring entrance.

A win using the rare **gogoplata** over perennial contender **Joachim Hansen** at Pride's 2006 Shockwave event positioned Aoki as the sport's premier submission fighter and helped raise his profile to the point that, on New Year's Eve, 2007, his bout against Korean Olympic medalist Jung Bu-Kyung closed the one-off Yarennoka! event. In 2008, Aoki signed on as one of the key players in Fighting Entertainment Group's nascent Dream promotion, but his reputation suffered following his Dream 1 main event against **Gesias "JZ" Cavalcante.** In that bout Aoki chose not to continue, following elbow strikes to the back of the neck, which were ruled illegal but did not appear to be a serious foul to most observers. A dominant performance against Cavalcante in a rematch, as well as subsequent wins over **Caol Uno** and **Eddie Alvarez**, helped to cement Aoki's status among the premier lightweight fighters in the world, but ground-and-pound TKO losses in rematches with Joachim Hansen and Hayato Sakurai kept him from a legitimate claim to **B.J. Penn**'s top spot.

■ Shinya Aoki's Spectacular Submissions

For many fans, the definition of a great fight is two men standing and trading blows, setting their feet and unloading bombs worthy of a Rocky movie, come what may. By that definition, Shinya Aoki has never had a great fight. He's never even had a good one. Aoki seems to dislike throwing punches almost as much as he dislikes receiving them – which is plenty. But for aficionados of the submission game, there's nobody quite like him. Every time Aoki steps into the ring, there's a very real chance you're going to see something you've never seen before, something you might not even have thought possible. From a career filled with memorable submission finishes, here are his five best.

5. vs. David Gardner (4/5/09), **rear naked choke**

Journeyman David Gardner came to Saitama, Japan, with only the slimmest chance at victory, and everybody knew it – even, apparently, Gardner himself, who couldn't bring himself to take the fight seriously. As expected, Aoki was dominant and completely controlled the fight on the ground. When Gardner found himself on the wrong end of yet another back **mount**, he decided to try a novel escape: waving to the crowd, he shouted out, "Hello, Japan!" Aoki wasted no time sinking the rear naked choke for the win in one of the strangest finishes in MMA history.

4. vs. Katsuhiko Nagata (6/15/08), mounted gogoplata

An Olympic silver medalist in Greco-Roman wrestling, Katsuhiko Nagata didn't come short on credentials. He did, however, come short on submission defense, which made him easy prey for the Tobikan Judan. Aoki took Nagata down with ease (no mean feat), mounted, and wound his right leg around Nagata's left arm, forcing his shin across Nagata's throat to earn the tap out and the win with a technique few had seen before. After some initial confusion concerning nomenclature (an **omoplata** from the top? a locoplata?), a consensus emerged. Aoki had finished with a mounted gogoplata, of all things.

3. vs. **Eddie Alvarez** (12/31/08), **heel hook**

Gardner and Nagata were ready-made opponents, blank canvases for a submission artist like Aoki. But the hard-hitting and versatile Eddie Alvarez came into his bout with Aoki as one of the most dangerous lightweight fighters on the planet. Consecutive wins over the rock-solid **Tatsuya Kawajiri** and **Joachim Hansen**, and a 15-1 record over all meant Alvarez was for real. Aoki looked like he was in trouble when his game plan of butt scooting followed by even more butt scooting failed to yield early returns, but no matter. After an impressive hip throw from Alvarez and a deft scramble from Aoki, the match ended in a mere 1:38, with Alavarez screaming in obvious pain from a notoriously dangerous hold.

2. vs. Joachim Hansen (12/31/06), gogoplata
It's one thing to pull off a picture-perfect gogoplata finish on a network-televised New Year's Eve card, the biggest stage in the Japanese fight game. It's another to do so against the tough and savvy Joachim Hansen. But Aoki dominated their brief contest from start to finish, taking the Norwegian down at will, wrapping Hansen up in an inescapable rubber **guard**, and driving his shin forcefully across Hansen's throat for the textbook submission. Although Hansen would even the score in their eventual rematch, Aoki's dissection of Hansen on the ground in their first encounter remains some of the slickest guard work ever seen in MMA.

1. vs. Keith Wisniewski (1/29/05), waki gatame
This is a fight that's hard to watch twice. Once you know that the bout is going to end with Wisniewski's arm audibly snapped at the elbow from a standing side arm lock applied so suddenly that surrender is completely impossible, you can't unknow it. And you can't help but cringe as the moment approaches. Aoki's application of this technique to the point of swift and nauseating fracture was controversial, but Aoki reminded us of an important point: fundamentally, joint locks aren't about compelling your opponent to tap; they're about breaking the joint. If your opponent taps out before this happens, so much the better for him. But if he lacks either the time or the inclination, the results can be devastating – especially when Shinya Aoki is involved.

Arlovski, Andrei

Height: 6'4" **Weight:** 244 lbs
Born: 2/4/79 **Debut:** M-1 MFC: World Championship 1999 (4/9/99)
Career Record: 15-8
Notable Wins: Vladimir Matyushenko (UFC 44); Tim Sylvia (UFC 51); Paul Buentello (UFC 55); Fabricio Werdum (UFC 70); Roy Nelson (EliteXC: Heat)
Notable Losses: Ricco Rodriguez (UFC 32); Pedro Rizzo (UFC 36); Tim Sylvia (UFC 59, UFC 61); Fedor Emelianenko (Affliction: Day of Reckoning)

Twice in his career, perennial top-ten heavyweight Andrei Arlovski has seemed on the cusp of greatness. And twice, he's fallen short.

In 2005, as the sport exploded in popularity following the success of the first season of ***The Ultimate Fighter***, and with **Frank Mir** on the sidelines following a devastating motorcycle accident, Arlovski was poised atop the heavyweight division, having just won the UFC interim heavyweight title over **Tim Sylvia** by Achilles lock in less than a minute. A young, charismatic fighter with fast hands, quick feet, and slick **leg locks**, Arlovski could have become the face of the heavyweight division as the sport reached new heights. But, after quick wins over Justin Eilers and the tragicomic **Paul Buentello**, and an upgrade from interim to undisputed heavyweight champion, Arlovski and Sylvia met again in another match that didn't get out of the first round. This time, though, it was Arlovski staring at the ceiling, TKO'd only moments after he'd tagged Sylvia and gone in for the kill. An immediate rematch saw Arlovski on the losing end of a dull, plodding fight that went the distance. Although Arlovski rattled off three subsequent UFC wins against quality opposition, another title shot did not materialize.

And so it was off to the greener pastures of **Affliction**, where Arlovski found another opportunity for greatness. With solid wins over two true heavyweights, Ben Rothwell and **Roy Nelson**, Arlovksi earned a shot at **Fedor Emelianenko**, the consensus top heavyweight in the world. Under Freddie Roach, who has trained such boxing greats as Oscar De La Hoya, Manny Pacquiao, and Bernard Hopkins among many others, Arlovski's boxing had supposedly reached new heights. There was much pre-fight talk of Arlovski's crisp, technical boxing being too much for the unorthodox Emelianenko to handle. Indeed, Arlovki's reach, head movement, and footwork gave Emelianenko all kinds of problems — until Fedor knocked a leaping Arlovski out cold with a massive right hand 3:14 into the first round.

Following the Emelianenko loss, and a subsequent lightning-fast beating at the hands of up-and-comer **Brett Rogers**, Arlovski's career seemed at a crossroads. Plans to pursue a future in pro boxing seem shaky given Arlovski's now very questionable chin.

Arm bar

An arm lock, usually but not exclusively applied on the ground, in which the attacker manipulates his opponent's arm such that the elbow joint is hyperextended. Although there exists a variety of techniques that are properly classified as arm bars, the term is generally used in mixed martial arts to refer specifically to the technique known to practitioners of **judo** and **Brazilian Jiu-jitsu** as juji gatame (cross mark hold). While there are many ways of entering the technique, the end result is the same: the attacker, perpendicular to his opponent (hence "cross mark"), controls his opponent's wrist, sits low against his opponent's shoulder, controlling his opponent's arm between his thighs. With one leg over his opponent's head, and the other either across the chest or tucked into his opponent's side, the attacker extends his opponent's arm and raises his hips to apply pressure to the elbow.

This technique can be executed with the attacker and opponent facing either up or down, and can be applied from any number of grappling positions, top or bottom. The most spectacular variation, rarely seen in modern mixed martial arts, is the flying arm bar, in which the attacker, usually gripping the arm at the bicep, leaps and throws a leg across his opponent's face, often finishing the technique face down as both fall to the mat. And surely the most spectacular flying arm bar in MMA history belongs to **Rumina Sato**, who dashed across the **Shooto** ring and finished poor Charles Taylor only six seconds into the first fight of Taylor's career. It remains perhaps the most amazing submission finish ever seen in MMA — and given the look on Taylor's face as he turned to his corner, maybe the most demoralizing career debut, too.

Arm triangle

A chokehold often, though not exclusively, executed from top position, in which the attacker positions his arms such that he traps his opponent's head and a single arm. In the most basic application, the traditional kata gatame (shoulder hold) found in both **judo** and **Brazilian Jiu-jitsu**, the attacker generally begins in **mount** or **side control**, secures the hold either by clasping his hands together or by gripping the bicep of his supporting arm with the hand of the strangling arm, and completes the technique by shifting his body to the side of the opponent's trapped arm. The effect is similar to the **triangle choke** performed with the legs, in that the opponent is strangled, in part, against his own shoulder.

This basic application of the arm triangle can still be seen at the sport's highest level. **Lyoto Machida** finished **Sokoudjou** at **UFC** 74 with a textbook example of the technique, and Marcus Aurellio ended **Takanori Gomi**'s ten-fight **Pride** winning streak with another at Bushido 10. **Kimo Leopoldo** finished **Tank Abbott** with a slow, deliberate application of the hold at UFC 43 as the crowd booed what they saw as a lack of action. Closely related to this basic application is a standing variation, which Japanese pro wrestler **Kazuyuki Fujita** has used with some success.

When the arm triangle is performed from a front head lock position with a rolling finish to tighten the hold, it is referred to as the anaconda choke or gator roll. **Antonio Rodrigo Nogueira** was the first to successfully apply this variation in MMA with his Pride wins over Hirotoka Yokoi and **Heath Herring**; **Randy Couture** debuted the technique in the UFC against Mike Van Arsdale a year later.

A popular, recent arm triangle variation seen is the brabo or D'Arce (after innovative **Renzo Gracie** black belt Joe D'Arce). Some controversy exists as to whether the brabo and D'Arce are best understood as distinct techniques or merely different grips for the same basic hold, but regardless, the fundamentals remain the same: the attacker, often from inside his opponent's half **guard**, performs an arm triangle such that the opponent's raised arm is trapped against the attacker's body as the strangling arm applies pressure from underneath the opponent's neck. Kendall Grove's finish of Alan Belcher at UFC 69 shows the possibilities for this particular application.

Arona, Ricardo

Height: 5'11" **Weight:** 205 lbs

Born: 7/17/78 **Debut:** Rings: Millennium Combine 1 (4/20/00)

Career Record: 14-5

Notable Wins: Dan Henderson (Pride 20); Kazushi Sakuraba (Pride Critical Countdown 2005); Wanderlei Silva (Pride Final Conflict 2005)

Notable Losses: Fedor Emelianenko (Rings: King of Kings 2000); Quinton Jackson (Pride Critical Countdown 2004); Mauricio Rua (Pride Final Conflict 2005); Rameau Thierry Sokoudjou (Pride 34)

When a referee fails in his duty to protect the fighters, and a bout is allowed to go on too long, the match risks turning into the kind of bloody spectacle we saw when Ricardo Arona overwhelmed **Kazushi Sakuraba** and pummeled him literally beyond recognition. By the time they met in 2005, the once great Sakuraba was already very much on the decline, and the bigger, stronger, younger Arona looked like the future of **Pride**'s stacked middleweight (205 pounds) division.

There was every reason to believe Arona, an aggressive **Brazilian Jiu-jitsu** black belt with solid takedowns and a suffocating top game, would be a major player in the sport for years to come. He began his career with an impressive run in **Rings** that looks all the more impressive in hindsight: Arona, in his third pro fight, came as close as anyone has come to besting **Fedor Emelianenko**, losing a close decision many think he should have won. Granted, Rings' rules took away Emelianenko's most dangerous weapon, his relentless **ground and pound**, but Arona held his own with the best heavyweight in the history of the sport.

Once in Pride, Arona collected a series of decision wins that some would call tactical, others boring, over the likes of **Guy Mezger**, **Dan Henderson**, **Murilo Rua**, and even **Wanderlei Silva** at a time when "The Axe Murderer" was all but unstoppable at 205 pounds. The only blemish on Arona's Pride record was a questionable TKO off a highlight-reel slam by **Quinton Jackson** that, on closer inspection, clearly resulted from a head butt to the jaw. Five years and 14 bouts into a career fought against extraordinarily tough competition, Arona had yet to be beaten decisively.

Everything went right for Ricardo Arona until everything went wrong. On the same night he smothered Silva, Arona was outwitted, outworked, and finally stomped by Silva's **Chute Boxe** teammate **Mauricio Rua** in the finals of the 2005 middleweight Grand Prix. Defeat in a New Year's Eve rematch with Silva followed. After he looked to be back on track with solid first round win over **Alistair Overeem**, Arona suffered a shocking KO loss to **Rameau Thierry Sokoudjou** in less than two minutes while reportedly suffering the effects of Dengue fever. Inexplicably, this is the last we've seen of Arona, with the UFC showing no apparent interest in the former Pride star.

Bader, Ryan

Nickname: Darth **Height:** 6'2"

Weight: 205 lbs **Born:** 6/7/83

Debut: WFC: Desert Storm (3/31/07) **Career Record:** 11-0

Notable Wins: Vinicius Magalhaes (*The Ultimate Fighter* 8 Finale); Keith Jardine (UFC 110)

Ryan Bader is a pretty ordinary guy. That's a good thing sometimes. For every **Brock Lesnar**, complete with wild and out of control **pro wrestling** antics, you also need a **Rich Franklin**, a quiet and unassuming regular guy. Bader fits that bill perfectly. He looks like the tight end or fullback from everyone's high school football team — if that tight end was also a two-time Division I Wrestling All-American.

In Their Own Words: Ryan Bader on transitioning from wrestling to MMA

"The hardest for me was probably starting off on my back. In the beginning I'd rather turn my back than pull guard, you know? The other hard part for me was the stance. It's been hard to stay loose so you can do standup when you're used to being so compact. You have to loosen up or you're going to get beat up. So those are probably two of the hardest things.

"The beneficial thing I've taken from wrestling is hard work. I was in wrestling for a lot of seasons. It's grueling. I've been around hard work; I know how to work. I know how to push through things. When other people say, 'Oh my God I'm tired,' I've been there a million times before. You get through it. You know you'll feel better in a couple of minutes. Hard work, the mentality, and just the competition. So many big matches. I've been in the Pac-10 Finals four years in college; I wrestled on ESPN. I've been around the competition and the crowd."

Bader comes to the Octagon with a willingness to learn and one superlative skill. He has a hard-nosed wrestler's mentality, a work ethic that guided him through ***The Ultimate Fighter*** house on his way to winning the eighth season of the seminal reality show. Bader showed his growth as a fighter in the season finale, knocking out the dangerous ground fighter Vinicius Magalhaes with an overhand right. Training with the up-and-coming Arizona Combat Sports team under Todd Lally, Bader was poised to become the first *Ultimate Fighter* winner in years to make a run at championship gold.

Barnett, Josh

Nickname: The Baby-Faced Assassin **Height:** 6'3"

Weight: 255 lbs **Born:** 11/10/77

Debut: UFCF: Clash of the Titans (1/11/97)

Career Record: 26–5

Notable Wins: Dan Severn (SuperBrawl 16); Semmy Schilt (UFC 32, Inoki Bom-Ba-Ye 2003); Randy Couture (UFC 36); Yuki Kondo (Pancrase: 10th Anniversary Show); Antonio Rodrigo Nogueira (Pride Final Conflict Absolute); Pedro Rizzo (Affliction: Banned)

Notable Losses: Pedro Rizzo (UFC 30); Mirko Cro Cop (Pride 28, Pride 30, Pride Final Conflict Absolute); Antonio Rodrigo Nogueira (Pride Shockwave 2006)

Josh Barnett is an exceptional fighter, but in the annals of MMA, all his in-ring accomplishments will be lost in a cloud of controversy, deceit, and deception. Bluntly put, Barnett dopes.

He wants us to believe otherwise. After his first public positive test for **steroids**, following the greatest victory of his career over **Randy Couture** at **UFC** 36, Barnett and trainer **Matt Hume** cried wolf, telling the world that Barnett was not guilty. That he would be vindicated. They even hinted that it might have all been part of a grand conspiracy. Hume and Barnett wanted people to believe that the positive test was part of the UFC's dirty negotiating techniques. Immediately after the Couture win, Barnett and **Zuffa** entered into intense negotiating sessions. Barnett claimed this was why the test had come back positive. It was a shocking claim, one many people believed because of the sheer audacity of the charge. Barnett had nothing to lose. His UFC 36 title victory over Couture was tainted, his UFC career in shambles, his title reign like it never happened.

What few knew at the time was that Barnett had actually failed a previous test in 2001 after a UFC 28 fight with Bobby Hoffman. This was before the sport had an organized drug program and the Nevada Commission was essentially surveying the fighters to see if they might have a problem on their hands. Barnett had a chance to clean himself up, but it appeared that he hadn't. Fans might have believed Barnett was innocent; those in the know suspected otherwise.

Barnett moved his career east, to a place he believed he belonged all along. In Japan he could follow his childhood dream of being a professional wrestler. He signed with the legendary **Antonio Inoki** and wrestled for New Japan Pro Wrestling, clowned around trying to pull off elaborate wrestling throws on men 70 pounds lighter in **Pancrase**, and eventually fought some of the world's best in **Pride**.

Barnett acquitted himself well in the land of the rising sun, a place that — despite its strict drug laws for regular citizens — was like the wild west for MMA fighters. Barnett and — to be fair — all his opponents too could put anything they wanted into their bodies. In this free-for-all he excelled against every fighter he faced, even taking a win off the great **Antonio Rodrigo Nogueira**. He beat everyone he faced bar one: **Mirko Cro Cop**. Cro Cop handed Barnett three losses, preventing him from ever earning a title shot at Pride champion **Fedor Emelianenko**.

After Pride was bought by a UFC promotion still holding a grudge for Barnett's post–UFC 36 behavior, Josh was stuck in limbo. He could find fights in Japan in an increasingly dim spotlight, but, now past 30, he wanted to face the best in the world. With all of Pride's significant fighters heading to the UFC, Barnett's long-desired match with Emelianenko seemed all but impossible. And then, as if he had been kissed by the gods, the fates began to align. UFC President **Dana White** tried to verbally bully Emelianenko into signing. White didn't count on the Russian's pride preventing him from working with a man he didn't respect, a man who had insulted him.

Fedor was a free agent, a fighter in desperate need of feature opponents. He made short work of former UFC champions **Tim Sylvia** and **Andrei Arlovski** for **Affliction**. As a former UFC champion himself, Barnett was walking around with a giant bull's-eye on his back. He was targeted for Affliction's third pay-per-view spectacular, a matchup between the men considered by many to be the two best heavyweights in the sport. Despite the slim odds of the fight ever taking place after the UFC became the dominant power in the MMA world, Barnett had exactly what he wanted: a main event fight with the world's best.

Then disaster struck. Barnett's license to fight in California had expired. When he applied to renew it, he was required to take a spot drug test. Most steroid users are fine with drug tests . . . when they know to expect them. This test, however, was several weeks before Barnett expected to pee in a bottle. He casually acquiesced and took the test, never hinting there might be a problem. Then, when the results came in, chaos reigned.

Barnett was out, and with such short notice no acceptable replacement could be found. Not only was the Affliction show canceled, but the entire fight promotion soon folded. No matter what else happens in his career, no matter the mountains he moves or champions he conquers, this is Barnett's legacy: a drug cheat and a promotion killer. Who could trust him to headline a major show again? His history was too damning to invest millions in promoting an event with his face on the poster. To American MMA promotions, Barnett was untouchable. It was a bed he made; now he has to lie in it: a potential all-time great remembered for the needles he allegedly stuck in his butt rather than for all the butt he kicked.

Baroni, Phil

Nickname: New York Bad Ass
Height: 5'9"
Weight: 170–185 lbs
Born: 4/16/76
Debut: VATV 9 (8/5/00)
Career Record: 13–12
Notable Wins: Dave Menne (UFC 39); Ikuhisa Minowa (Pride Bushido 7); Ryo Chonan (Pride Bushido 8); Yuki Kondo (Pride Bushido 10)
Notable Losses: Matt Lindland (UFC 34, UFC 41); Evan Tanner (UFC 45, UFC 48); Ikuhisa Minowa (Pride Bushido 9); Frank Shamrock (Strikeforce: Shamrock vs. Baroni)

Phil Baroni figured out on his own what it took many professional wrestlers years to determine: the best way to create a memorable character is to take your natural personality and amplify it by ten. For Baroni, that worked wonders. In all fairness, a fighter with Baroni's credentials should be long forgotten. His win–loss record teeters right around .500. This means he's as likely to lose as he is to win. For most fighters, this level of achievement earns a ticket right out of the major leagues. Phil Baroni should have punched that ticket years ago. But because of the "New York Bad Ass" character he created, his brash and boastful alter ego, he keeps getting chance after chance.

Like **Tito Ortiz**, Baroni came into a **UFC** desperate for some personality and for a villain. With his sunglasses, his fancy robes, and his trash talk, Baroni stood out. In a world of the similar, this was a good thing. UFC fighters had previously been cut from the same cloth: respectful and bland Midwestern wrestlers and quiet Brazilian killers. Baroni, for the first time since **Tank Abbott**, broke that mold. He was loud when others were soft-spoken. He was in your face when others showed respect. And he was absolutely among the most entertaining fighters of the early **Zuffa** era.

The most memorable feud of Baroni's career was a study in contrasts. **Matt Lindland** was an Olympic silver medalist and the picture of red state values. He was Baroni's polar opposite and the two men clashed wills as well as cultures. Lindland beat Baroni twice, but they were the kind of fights no one loses. The fights were so exciting and the storyline so compelling that both fighters came out of the confrontations bigger stars and better fighters.

Baroni had solid **wrestling** and heavy hands, but his style was very predictable. Like his training partners **Mark Coleman** and **Kevin Randleman** at the **Hammer House**, Baroni never developed his game. While other fighters continued to grow, Baroni stood still. Soon opponents were figuring him out. After four consecutive losses, Baroni was on his way out of the UFC.

Like his Hammer House brethren, Baroni rediscovered himself in the land of the rising sun. He made his **Pride** debut at Bushido 7, taking on one of Japan's most popular fighters, **Ikuhisa "The Punk" Minowa**. Before the fight, fans saw a glimpse of Baroni at his best. "I know he's a punk," Baroni said. "I know he's got a mullet, I know he wears Speedos — and I don't want him touching me."

Minowa was a grappler, but he had a flair for the dramatic. He fancied himself a pro wrestler, and his goal was always to entertain the crowd, even at the expense of winning. He stood toe-to-toe with Baroni in an epic slugfest. After a back-and-forth first round, including some surprisingly deft ground exchanges where Baroni more than held his own, both men were exhausted in their respective corners. It was only a matter of time until one of the fighters could stand no longer, and that man was Minowa. After some huge right hands, Minowa went down in the corner and, utilizing the more lenient Pride rules, Baroni used soccer kicks and stomps to finish him off. The New York Bad Ass was back.

In Their Own Words: Phil Baroni explains his disdain for Frank Shamrock

"He was armchair quarterbacking, when I was fighting the best fighters around the world, and he was sitting at home, ridiculing and talking about everybody. The guy had a lot to say. I never thought he would back it up, and I still will not believe it until we get to the ring and they lock the cage door. I thought that he was looking for a way out of this fight. I do not believe he is going to back it up. I issued a challenge. Everybody wants to fight that punk. It is not just me. He, being the so-called legend, got to pick his opponent, and he picked the wrong cat. He is getting knocked out.

"I think he is a scumbag. I am not going to hold any punches. The guy is a hypocrite. I think he is a fraud, and everyone that has ever dealt with him does not like him. I mean Javier Mendez, who was his old trainer, all the guys at AKA that I have trained with over the years, **Dana White**, UFC president, who is a personal friend of mine. Everyone I know that has dealt with the guy thinks he is a asshole. . . . Wait till he steps in with the real deal. I am the real deal, and I am going to throw punches with bad intentions at his fucking head and put him to sleep."

Now established as a serious player in Pride, Baroni took on Japan's best at 185 pounds. He beat **Ryo Chonan**, at the time the hottest fighter in Japan with consecutive wins over **Anderson Silva** and **Carlos Newton**, with a devastating combination of punches to further cement his place as a top shelf fighter. After losing a rematch to Minowa, Baroni rebounded with a quick knockout of **Pancrase** stalwart Yuki Kondo. He traded wins and losses throughout his Pride tenure, but his position seemed secure, since a Phil Baroni fight was guaranteed to be a barnburner.

Then Pride self-destructed and, like many of the other Americans, Baroni was a fighter without a home. His return to the United States was an enormous failure. Something about being on U.S. soil just didn't seem to work for him. Some speculated it was simply age, others that more rigid drug laws made it harder for Phil and others to train the way they were used to.

Whatever the reason, Baroni lost three consecutive fights — four if you include the war of words with **Frank Shamrock** before their June 2007 fight. He seemed to be simply overwhelmed by even mid-level fighters. Like a power pitcher who has lost his fastball, Baroni without a knockout punch was a sad sight indeed. He will finish out his career in the UFC, an opponent for their rising stars, bringing plenty of sizzle but very little steak to some of their preliminary bouts.

Belfort, Vitor

Nickname: The Phenom **Height:** 6′

Weight: 205 lbs **Born:** 1/4/77

Debut: SuperBrawl 2 (10/11/96) **Career Record:** 19-8

Notable Wins: Tank Abbott (UFC 13); Wanderlei Silva (UFC 17.5); Heath Herring (Pride 14); Randy Couture (UFC 46); Matt Lindland (Affliction: Day of Reckoning); Rich Franklin (UFC 103)

Notable Losses: Randy Couture (UFC 15, UFC 49); Kazushi Sakuraba (Pride 5); Chuck Liddell (UFC 37.5); Tito Ortiz (UFC 51); Dan Henderson (Pride 32)

Most MMA nicknames are silly, but everyone in the **UFC** seems to be required to have one. Sometimes, in rare cases, the names really fit. **Randy Couture** really was "Captain America" and "Tank" fit **David Abbott** to a tee. It was the same way with Vitor Belfort. "The Phenom" just felt right. It was just who he was and what he was. At the age of 19, he thrust himself into the MMA scene and didn't pause until he was at the precipice of greatness.

Belfort had the entire package the UFC had been missing before his debut. He had the looks — the kind of muscled action figure body SEG executives had longed for since they saw **Ken Shamrock** at UFC 1. And unlike Shamrock, he could also really fight. Better than that, he didn't rely on the slower ground fighting popular with most Brazilians. He had the fastest and most powerful hands of anyone in the sport. So fast that he ended the nights of the sport's two toughest street fighters, Tank Abbott and Scott Ferrozzo, in less than two minutes combined.

The UFC placed one more live body in front of him, to help build him up for a planned title shot against champion **Maurice Smith** at UFC Japan. Instead, Randy Couture shocked everyone by outboxing and outworking the young prodigy. Couture took Belfort down, and despite being a titular **Carlson Gracie** jiu-jitsu black belt, Belfort seemed to possess little in the way of submissions off his back. Couture beat him up standing as well, until Belfort was too tired to take anymore.

The bubble of infallibility had burst, but Belfort made a quick recovery. He blasted **Wanderlei Silva** across the cage in less than 45 seconds, landing more than 25 punches in the blink of the eye. It was his last fight in the UFC for almost four years. Like so many of the top fighters of the era, Belfort traveled

to Japan to compete for the big money in **Pride**. He did well there, winning four of five, but losing the only one that mattered: a decision to **Kazushi Sakuraba**.

When **Zuffa** bought the UFC in 2001, and more importantly, the money returned, Belfort was back. It was none too soon for the UFC. Belfort was still a hot property, because fans remembered his exciting fights inside the Octagon. Belfort was supposed to come back for the main event of the UFC's return to pay-per-view at UFC 33 against **Tito Ortiz**. When he was sidelined by an injury, Vladimir Matyushenko had to fill in, an unknown in one of the biggest fights of all time.

When Belfort was ready to fight, the UFC used him for an equally big card. ***The Ultimate Fighter*** was not the UFC's first opportunity to make a splash on television. They were featured prominently on Fox Sport's *Best Damn Sports Show Period*. The event was created at the last minute, with the **Robbie Lawler** and Steve Berger fight becoming the first MMA contest ever aired on cable television.

Belfort and **Chuck Liddell** were in the main event, in a number one contenders fight for the light heavyweight title. The Vitor that returned to the

UFC was a very different fighter than the one who left in 1998. He no longer seemed to have the mental ability to explode or to attack aggressively. He was cautious, more likely to wait for his moment, even using his **wrestling** ability to hold fighters down for a decision. He went the distance with Liddell, losing in a unanimous decision.

Despite a loss to Liddell, Belfort needed just one fight, a win over Marvin Eastman, to earn himself a title shot. It was a rematch with Randy Couture at UFC 46 and a chance to avenge the first loss of his career. In a bizarre finish, Belfort's glove cut Couture's eyelid in the first exchange of the fight. The fight was stopped and Belfort became the UFC light heavyweight champion.

It was a strange time for Belfort. What should have been a crowning moment was eclipsed by events in his private life. His sister Priscilla had disappeared and would later be found dead. When Belfort faced Couture in a rubber match at UFC 49, he was staring down demons. He was also staring across the cage at one of the best and smartest fighters in UFC history.

The loss sent Belfort's career into a downward spiral. He lost four of his next six fights, including a close decision to Tito Ortiz and one of the most boring fights imaginable to **Alistair Overeem**. Just when Belfort seemed finished, he found redemption with his old rival. He dropped to 185 pounds and began training with Randy Couture at Xtreme Couture in Las Vegas. Belfort found new life as a middleweight, and knocked off the highly regarded **Matt Lindland** before returning to the UFC after a four-year absence to stop **Rich Franklin** in the very first round. A career that began with such enormous promise, only to be marred by personal tragedy, looks set to end in triumph.

Bellator

Bjorn Rebney joined Gary Shaw and hosts of other boxing promoters nationwide, both big and small, by placing his bet on the future of combat sports being MMA. Rebney was one of the architects of the defunct Sugar Ray Leonard Promotions, a boxing enterprise that lost millions and ran into trouble with the law in the 1990s.

His MMA project, Bellator (the Latin word for warrior), seemed to be off to a better start. The promotion targeted a niche market in the MMA game: the Hispanic fight fan. A dominant force in boxing, the audience that made Oscar De La Hoya, Julio Cesar Chavez, and many others megastars in two countries has yet to embrace MMA. Bellator, starting with a prime spot on the Spanish language ESPN Deportes, was poised to capitalize if the market ever stood up and took notice. Hispanic stars like **Eddie Alvarez** headlined surprisingly good cards, featuring top to bottom action reminiscent of **Zuffa**'s **WEC**.

In Their Own Words: Bjorn Rebney on how Bellator will stand out in the marketplace

"I think it's the format, the structure of the organization. We've taken the suit, the matchmaker in his shiny suit sitting behind his desk, and eliminated him from the equation. In Bellator, you will never see a guy fight his heart out, bloody and covered in sweat, [and then] have to drop to his knees and beg me for a title shot. In Bellator you win three fights in a tournament and you are either the champion or the number one ranked challenger. And every time you fight you make more money. The top contenders at 45, 55, 70, and 85 – each guy will walk away with six figures and a shot at the world title. It boils down to what fighters want. They like to fight, they like to make money, they want to be on TV, and they want a chance at a world title. And they want to be able to control it. Fighters want to control their own destiny."

After delighting fans and cash-hungry fighters with four tournaments to crown champions (with a $100,000 cash prize to go along with the title) the promotion seemed poised for big things. Instead, they went immediately on hiatus. The company intends to promote two new seasons in 2010, on bigger and more inclusive networks, hoping to expand Bellator's audience beyond the hard-core MMA fans who happen to have a high-end cable package.

Beneteau, Dave

Nickname: Dangerous | **Height:** 6'2"
Weight: 250 lbs | **Born:** 7/16/68
Debut: UFC 5 (4/7/95) | **Career Record:** 6-5-1
Notable Wins: Patrick Smith (U-Japan); Carlos Baretto (UFC 15)
Notable Losses: Dan Severn (UFC 5); Oleg Taktarov (UFC 6, Ultimate Ultimate 95)

Dave Beneteau works in construction. Before that, he was briefly a criminal defense lawyer after graduating from York University's Osgoode Hall Law School in 2002. But before *that*, he slugged it out in the (almost) anything-goes era of the Ultimate Fighting Championship. Beneteau, a big, powerful wrestler, was the UFC 5 runner-up, steamrolling his opposition in the first two rounds before running into **Dan Severn** in the tournament finals. He later dropped a pair of quick bouts to **sambo** submission ace **Oleg Taktarov**, and managed wins over tough Brazilian Carlos Baretta and UFC 1 veteran **Patrick Smith**, but Beneteau never really equaled the success of his debut performance. More recently, Beneteau has become a vocal critic of the sport, and in a 2008 appearance on Canadian sports network TSN, he argued that MMA is held back from further growth by the fighters' tattoos and use of phrases such as "yo, bro." Aside from **Randy Couture** and a handful of others, Beneteau has no regard for any current MMA competitor: "everything underneath that — trash." Beneteau thinks the overall classlessness of the sport is exemplified by **Dana White**'s language, and that it's this classlessness that will keep mixed martial arts from ever truly capturing the boxing audience. And what's more, Beneteau argued, "They don't deserve it."

Bisping, Michael

Nickname: The Count
Height: 6'2"
Weight: 185-205 lbs
Born: 2/28/79
Debut: P & G 2 (4/10/04)
Career Record: 19-3
Notable Wins: Josh Haynes (*The Ultimate Fighter* 3 Finale); Matt Hamill (UFC 75); Chris Leben (UFC 89); Wanderlei Silva (UFC 110)
Notable Losses: Rashad Evans (UFC 78); Dan Henderson (UFC 100)

Michael Bisping was like a gift from the heavens for the **UFC**. Just as they were planning an expansion into the United Kingdom, a native Briton, a superstar, appeared out of nowhere. Bisping was the European star they desperately needed, the perfect man to sell the sport on a new continent.

In Their Own Words: Michael Bisping on advice for *Ultimate Fighter* winners

"They are all going to get a lot of attention after this and you know just to take it. Try and maximize the potential and make the most out of it. I told them all to get themselves a good manager. I think that's very important, especially in this game now. Especially, you know, this show is business, the bulk of it now.

"I was on *The Ultimate Fighter* and when I won it, that was great. It was fantastic. It was a massive opportunity. But it was one thing winning the ultimate fighter and the prize of the contract with the UFC. That's all well and good. Now, you've got to go out and you've got to be competitive and ultimately you've got to win your fights in the UFC. And you know if you don't do that then the prize is worth nothing really at the end of the day. You know no one wants to go out, win the ultimate fighter, and then lose your fights. The easy part for me was winning the ultimate fighter. Now, the hard part is to win your fights in the UFC."

Bisping was the winner of the third season of **The Ultimate Fighter**, but he wasn't thought to be the same level of prospect the UFC had found in the first two seasons. He was a striker with a weak **wrestling** game, a dangerously limited combination for a fighter seeking success in the Octagon. In the season finale, Bisping struggled to defeat journeyman Josh Haynes, an undersized yet somehow overweight fighter from Oregon's **Team Quest**.

When he made it to the UFC proper, Bisping showed remarkable improvement, winning three fights in a row (one a controversial decision win over *Ultimate Fighter* nemesis **Matt Hamill**) before making his first appearance in a main event against fellow *Ultimate Fighter* winner **Rashad Evans** at UFC 78. Evans out-pointed Bisping to win a split decision and the fight made one thing abundantly clear: Bisping was too small to fight at 205 pounds.

His move to middleweight was another tremendous success. Bisping won three in a row at the new weight, making a strong case for a possible title shot. He almost earned that opportunity, being cast as a coach opposite **Dan Henderson** on *The Ultimate Fighter* 9. Britain's top MMA star fronted a team of his countrymen against Henderson's Team USA. Bisping's team was victorious, but Henderson got the ultimate revenge, knocking out the charismatic Brit in the first round at UFC 100.

But Bisping soldiers on. Whether dismantling **Denis Kang**, going the distance with the great **Wanderlei Silva**, or grinding it out against Dan Miller, Bisping unquestionably gives his all, much to the delight of his legions of loyal British fans.

Blatnick, Jeff

When Jeff Blatnick flew into Tulsa, Oklahoma, for **UFC** 4, he didn't know what to expect. Blatnick, a 1984 Olympic gold medalist in Greco-Roman **wrestling**, knew only his old friend **Dan Severn**. The other fighters on the card were a mystery to him, as were the techniques and strategies. In the finals, Severn faced the previously unbeatable **Royce Gracie**. As Gracie snuck his legs up for a fight-ending **triangle choke**, Blatnick assured the audience that there was no danger to Severn. When Severn tapped the mat (and a joyous **Jim Brown** taunted Blatnick), the wrestler realized he had a lot to learn.

To his credit, learn it he did. Blatnick has long been interested in the idea of mixed matches. Years earlier, in his Olympic heyday, he would argue with friends that feared heavyweight boxer Mike Tyson would be unable to stop his wrestling technique. Once exposed to the UFC, he wanted to know more. He rolled on the mat with champions like **Frank Shamrock** so he could understand the strategy on the ground. As the color commentator for more than seven years' worth of UFC cards, Blatnick became a keen observer of the sport. His Olympic credentials also allowed him to become a powerful advocate, addressing state athletic commissions and legislatures about the sport's safety record and well-established rules.

In 1998, Blatnick became the UFC's commissioner. He was also put in charge of establishing the sport's rules. Contrary to a myth perpetrated in the media by the UFC's new owners at **Zuffa**, the sport had already established most of the rules used today before **Dana White** was ever involved in the company. Blatnick, with the help of current UFC vice president **Joe Silva** and referee **John McCarthy**, created the Mixed Martial Arts Council (MMAC). The MMAC created a rulebook that was the foundation of the **Unified Rules** still used today across the nation.

In Their Own Words: Jeff Blatnick on coining the term "mixed martial arts"

"When I first started with the UFC, at UFC 4, we didn't really have a good name for all of this. Some people called it NHB, for no-holds-barred, but I just called it fighting. But then Joe Silva reminded me of something I had said when I was broadcasting the UWF 1 events from Japan. They were like the UFC, but a work. My broadcast partner was Al Rosen and he asked me what we would be seeing in the ring. I said all they were doing was mixing the martial arts. They were doing nothing illegal; everything was allowed under the rules of a martial arts discipline. That was even more true of the UFC. No one had ever combined the martial arts like this. I coined the phrase mixed martial arts and it stuck. I grabbed it, used it, and that was how we sold it. It wasn't NHB, which had a stigma. It was MMA."

After UFC 32, Zuffa retired Blatnick as an announcer, bringing in comedian **Joe Rogan** to fill his role as color commentator. Today, Blatnick continues to be an advocate for the sport of MMA in his native New York and serves as a judge and referee in the state of New Jersey.

Bohlander, Jerry

Height: 5'11" **Weight:** 200 lbs

Born: 2/12/74 **Debut:** UFCF 2 (11/9/95)

Career Record: 11-4

Notable Wins: Scott Ferrozzo (UFC 8); Kevin Jackson (UFC 16)

Notable Losses: Gary Goodridge (UFC 8); Murilo Bustamante (Pentagon Combat); Tito Ortiz (UFC 18)

Among **Ken Shamrock**'s many great students, Jerry Bohlander stood out from the very start. As a teenager he was hooked from the first moment he saw Shamrock and **Royce Gracie** lock horns at **UFC** 1. He and his high school buddy **Pete Williams** drove an hour from their homes to train with the legend. Bohlander beat one of Ken's experienced fighters that night and Shamrock invited him to try out for his pro team, the **Lion's Den**.

Bohlander and Williams moved into the fighters' house, where they lived with **Frank Shamrock**, Mikey Burnette, and Jason DeLucia. The Lion's Den was designed to test fighters mentally and physically. Many others came through the fighters' house. Very few lasted long; Bohlander was a survivor.

When Shamrock had to choose a student to compete in the UFC, Bohlander had a chance to earn his shot at the big time. Nothing was given in the Den. Bohlander had to fight his buddy Williams for the opportunity. Despite giving up 40 pounds, he tapped out his friend with a **heel hook**.

The larger Williams ended up being an appropriate test. UFC 8 was a David versus Goliath event, pitting lighter weight fighters against a bevy of monsters. Across the cage from Bohlander was the 350-pound Scott Ferrozzo. Incredibly, Bohlander was able to outlast Ferrozzo, finishing him off with a **guillotine choke** after more than nine minutes of fighting. He fell short in his second fight against arm wrestler **Gary Goodridge**, but had proven he belonged. Bohlander had earned another shot.

At UFC 12 he was pitted against men his own size and made short work of them, taking the first lightweight tournament after only two minutes in the cage. It ended up being one of his career highlights. The other was an **arm bar** win over Olympic gold medalist Kevin Jackson at UFC 16. It was a whirlwind few weeks. After being pulled from the fight in favor of Fabio Gurgel (whom

Bohlander had beaten at UFC 11) Bohlander was offered the fight a second time after Gurgel pulled out with less than four weeks left to train. Even though he knew he would be out of shape, Bohlander thought it was too good an opportunity to pass up. He submitted Jackson, the last time he would earn a victory at the highest level of the sport.

Bohlander's defeat at the hands of **Tito Ortiz** at UFC 18 was one of the early shots fired in the war between the Lion's Den and Ortiz. Bohlander was burned out and losing interest in the sport. There simply didn't seem to be a way to make a living in those days, the dark era when the sport had no cable deal and didn't even release the shows on home video. After 9/11, Bohlander's future seemed clear to him. He joined the police force in Napa, California, where he serves as a SWAT team member while occasionally teaching MMA at a local school. At 35, he is still young enough to have the occasional itch to take it up again. Then he thinks about his wife and the family they want to start and holds fast to the stability, health insurance, and other benefits of his new life.

Bonnar, Stephan

Nickname: American Psycho | **Height:** 6'4"

Weight: 205 lbs | **Born:** 4/4/77

Debut: IHC 3 (11/10/01) | **Career Record:** 12-7

Notable Win: Keith Jardine (*Ultimate Fight Night* 4)

Notable Losses: Forrest Griffin (*The Ultimate Fighter* 1 Finale, UFC 62); Rashad Evans (*Ultimate Fight Night* 5); Mark Coleman (UFC 100)

With the rise of **Forrest Griffin** from reality show contestant to champion, it's easy to forget that the man on the cover of the UFC video game could have just as easily been Stephan Bonnar. Bonnar and Griffin went toe-to-toe and punch for punch to conclude the first season of *The Ultimate Fighter*. It's a fight that has been widely credited with saving the entire sport. The two men showed the kind of guts that made many viewers fans for life. The blood, sweat, and sheer drama of it all helped Spike TV decide to renew the show.

Griffin and Bonnar seemed to be mirror images, but in the ensuing two years differences emerged. While Griffin trained like a maniac and devoted himself to becoming the best fighter in the sport, Bonnar was more likely to be seen in the clubs and hanging out with porn stars. When the two had their inevitable rematch, their skill levels had diverged dramatically. Griffin simply outclassed Bonnar the second time around, a victory for hard work and dedication in a world that often rewards taking the easy route.

To make matters worse, after the fight Bonnar tested positive for the **steroid** Boldenone, a drug used by veterinarians to rehabilitate injured horses. It seems Bonnar couldn't even put in the effort to cheat right. Athletes and body builders almost never use Boldenone because it can stay in your system for months. Bonnar, to his credit, was honest about his use with the Nevada State Athletic Commission, simply admitting to using the drug and apologizing. This helped minimize his fine and resulted in just a nine-month suspension.

Bonnar seemed to be getting his career back on track after two undercard wins when a serious knee injury caused him to miss all of 2008. When he returned he looked like the same fighter he had been in 2005, losing handily to rising prospect **Jon Jones**. Because of his important role in laying the foundation for the company's success, Bonnar's place in the UFC seems secure. But it appears it will be as an undercard attraction. Bonnar will have a cageside view from that position, watching Forrest Griffin in the main events and wondering what might have been.

Bowles, Brian

Height: 5'7" **Weight:** 135 lbs

Born: 6/22/80 **Debut:** Wild Bill's Fight Night 2 (5/12/06)

Career Record: 8-1

Notable Wins: Damacio Page (WEC 35); Will Ribeiro (WEC 37); Miguel Torres (WEC 42)

Notable Loss: Dominic Cruz (WEC 47)

It's pretty wild to have your name mentioned among the sport's pound-for-pound best before your tenth professional fight, but that's exactly what happened for Brian Bowles after he came apparently out of nowhere to stop the unbeatable **Miguel Torres** and claim the **WEC** bantamweight (135 pounds) championship. It all happened pretty quickly for a man who only a couple of years before was fighting out of a promotion called Wild Bill's Fight Night in Duluth, Georgia. A product of The Hardcore Gym in Athens, the same team that produced future light heavyweight champion **Forrest Griffin**, Bowles is a solid wrestler with serious natural punching power. Just ask Torres, whom Bowles staggered with his first punch of their title bout. Minutes later, Torres thought he had Bowles hurt with a solid right hand of his own, and chased his backpedaling opponent behind a wild flurry of looping punches. But Bowles kept his composure, and connected with a short hook that put the champ on his back. Referee Josh Rosenthal came in late with the stoppage as Bowles rained down blows, but you can understand his moment of hesitation. Nobody thought they were going to see anything but another routine title defense from a fighter who hadn't been stopped in almost 40 professional bouts. But Brian Bowles changed all that in an instant, claiming the most prestigious bantamweight title in the MMA world, and inscribing his name alongside those of the best in the game.

Boxing

For years, boxing set the standard when it came to combat sports worldwide. The Asian martial arts had some cachet, with their exotic styles and infamous death touches, but the consensus was that the world heavyweight boxing champion was the toughest man on the planet. That's why establishing MMA's primacy, placing it atop the sweet science, has been such an obsession for martial artists and promoters in both **professional wrestling** and MMA.

Almost every heavyweight boxing champion, from Jack Dempsey forward, got involved in the world of professional wrestling when they retired. Their role was a simple one: the boxer would serve as a special referee. When the bad guy went too far, the boxer would knock his lights out, earning a healthy paycheck and sending the crowd home happy. The boxers were never in-ring participants. There was talk of putting together a big match between Dempsey

and Ed "Strangler" Lewis, but Dempsey knew enough to realize he would be out of his element when Lewis took him to the mat.

Helio Gracie never got a major boxer involved in **Vale Tudo**, despite years of trying. Unlike the wrestling promoters, Gracie wasn't offering an easy buck; he wanted a fight. He challenged the legendary Joe Louis, but the Brown Bomber was likely unaware of Gracie's existence. The world's top boxers became a Holy Grail for the Gracie family. **Rorion Gracie** challenged Mike Tyson and **Ralph Gracie** challenged Roy Jones when both boxers were in their prime. Neither boxer answered the challenge. And why would they? A top professional boxer made millions for every fight. It made no sense to risk their health and take a significant pay cut to accept the Gracie Challenge. It was this obsession with top boxers that made Rorion insist that **Royce Gracie**'s first opponent at **UFC** 1 be the one-gloved Art Jimmerson. A fringe contender, Jimmerson was no Tyson. But he was as close as a Gracie would come to beating a top contender until **Renzo Gracie** beat former cruiserweight champion James Warring.

Martial artists had better luck getting boxers into the ring in Japan. Muhammad Ali helped create the shoot-style **wrestling** movement with his famous match against **Antonio Inoki** in 1976. Others followed Ali's lead. Probably because they figured no one would ever hear about it back in the States, champion boxers were willing to step into the ring with the Japanese stars. The "Hands of Stone" Roberto Duran squared off with **Masakatsu Funaki** in a surprisingly good wrestling match. Former heavyweight champion Trevor Berbick got a rude surprise in his match with **Nobuhiko Takada**. Assuming that no kicks were allowed below the waist, like many of the kickboxing matches that aired on American television, Berbick was brutalized by Takada's hard leg kicks. He complained after each kick. After the third kick he was through, hopping out of the ring and limping to the back, complaining all the way.

Eventually, the top MMA fighters realized they had plenty to learn from boxing. With bare knuckles, fighters weren't able to effectively utilize many boxing techniques. The UFC's adoption of gloves allowed fighters to use modified modern boxing techniques, including blocking incoming punches with the hands. Among the first fighters to show that boxing could be applied intelligently among the many mixed techniques of an MMA fight was **Randy Couture**. Couture, relying on basic boxing techniques he learned in the Army, was able to use foot movement and dirty boxing to befuddle the younger and quicker **Vitor Belfort**. Today, there are few successful fighters in MMA who haven't studied boxing. Among fighters who want to maintain their balance and avoid fighting on the ground, boxing has surpassed **Muay Thai** as the standup art of choice.

Brabo: see **Arm triangle**

Bravo, Eddie

Unfortunately, it can be hard to take no-**gi** **Brazilian Jiu-jitsu** innovator Eddie Bravo seriously sometimes. It's obviously not his competition record — a stunning win by **triangle choke** over **Royler Gracie** at the 2003 **ADCC** Submission Wrestling Championships is no mean feat. It's definitely not the 10th Planet jiu-jitsu style he founded — the complex and physically demanding rubber **guard** system Bravo pioneered has proven itself a valuable grappling tool. You might think it's his enthusiastic online support of conspiracy theories, his choice to include an atrocious blackface comedy bit on his instructional DVD, or his baffling introductory essay to *Mastering the Rubber Guard*, in which he expounds on such key fighting topics as marijuana (Eddie likes), his relationship with his father (Eddie does not like), and his various musical projects (dude, Blackened Kill Symphony found the Linkin Park sound before Linkin Park!). But it's not any of that, really. What makes Eddie Bravo the butt of so many jokes is simple: it's the names. The *names*.

"Sometimes my students come up with the names," Bravo explains. "More often it's just myself, depending on how stoned I am." The Drowning Wizard, Zombie, Night of the Living Dead, Exhumer, Mission Control, Crack Head Control, Jiu-Claw, East Coast Croc, Rescue Dog, Chill Dog, Mad Dog Control, Drowning Jiu, The Carni, The Snitch . . . this is but the tip of the iceberg. These arbitrary names for techniques and positions are often laughable — which, one assumes, is at least partly the point: say what you will, Eddie Bravo is obviously a man with a sense of humor. But they also serve as a kind of secret language available only to insiders. If you're on the mat and you hear your opponent's coach calling for a **Kimura**, you know what to look out for. But what if you hear him asking for Retard Control? What on earth do you do with that?

The cat is out of the bag, however, now that Bravo has published much of his system, and his friend and student **UFC** announcer **Joe Rogan** enthusiastically calls out 10th Planet positional names whenever a fighter so much as approximates rubber guard — an open guard variation in which a fighter holds one leg very high on his opponent's back with the opposite arm, breaking down posture and creating increased opportunities for a variety of submissions (including the otherwise very rare **omoplata** and **gogoplata**). There's no doubt Bravo is on to something, and something genuinely effective. It would be a shame if his considerable contributions to jiu-jitsu were overshadowed by his eccentricities.

Brazilian Jiu-jitsu

It seems as though every martial art has its share of tall tales about its early days, oft-repeated exaggerations or half-truths that don't bear scrutiny but somehow survive all the same. Brazilian Jiu-jitsu — "Gracie Jiu-jitsu" is a narrower term, in effect a brand name closely guarded by **Rorion Gracie** — is no exception. There's no question that **Carlos Gracie** studied briefly under Kodokan **judo** fourth-degree black belt **Mitsuyo Maeda** and, alongside brother **Helio Gracie**, laid the foundation for one of the world's most celebrated grappling arts. That much is certain. But what, exactly, Maeda taught the young Gracie is the subject of some dispute. Despite a lack of evidence that Maeda ever studied traditional koryu jiu-jitsu — or any other martial art besides sumo before entering the Kodokan — members of the Gracie family stubbornly maintain otherwise. Crosley Gracie is perhaps the worst offender, offering an account of Maeda using his classical jiu-jitsu skills to overmatch his first five opponents at the Kodokan en route to being awarded his purple belt — never mind that colored belts beyond white, brown, and black to indicate rank were not introduced until decades later by Mikonosuke Kawaishi teaching in France. Even **Renzo Gracie**, who, with his co-author John Danaher, quite reasonably suggests that Brazilian Jiu-jitsu resembles early Kodokan judo much more closely than any branch of koryu jiu-jitsu, maintains that Maeda was "a highly regarded student of classical jiu-jitsu [who] eventually switched to Kodokan judo." In every telling of the tale, there's the suggestion that the Gracies, through Maeda, represent a link to the mysterious jiu-jitsu of the past, to ancient principles and techniques that would otherwise be lost to the modern world. It's been an important part of the Gracie myth.

It's a shame, because the truth, while less exotic, is far more impressive. The jiu-jitsu (simply an older transliteration of the same kanji that give us "jujitsu" or "jujutsu") that the Gracies developed out of Carlos's brief, four-year study under Maeda is an incredible achievement, one born of constant technical refinement and the Gracies' willingness to test themselves against exponents of all styles. Maeda's teachings were by all accounts influenced by his own long career of challenge matches and prizefights, and the Gracies put that knowledge to good use. By emphasizing the importance of ground fighting and articulating their own view of **positional hierarchy** with perfect clarity, the Gracies turned the absolute basics of judo into arguably the finest submission fighting system in the world. The family's success in the earliest days of mixed martial arts — most notably in the **Ultimate Fighting Championship**, an event designed for this express purpose — proved the effectiveness of their then little-known style to a broad audience. The slow, incremental improvements on the ground led inevitably to chokes, arm locks, and the occasional **leg lock**; audiences were transfixed, and the Gracie empire was born.

Those jiu-jitsu practitioners who have stayed closest to the original Gracie lineage continue to emphasize their system as a method of self-defense, first and foremost. The further one branches out from the many-limbed Gracie family tree, however, the more one veers towards sport Brazilian Jiu-jitsu, with its emphasis on point-based competition strategies. But jiu-jitsu practitioners of either variety continue to demonstrate the undeniable effectiveness of their discipline at the highest levels of MMA, where no fighter is truly prepared to enter the ring or the cage without a solid grounding in the principles Maeda imparted to the Gracie family almost a century ago.

Brazilian Top Team (BTT)

You could say that Brazilian Top Team isn't what it used to be. But that's only because BTT used to be the best mixed martial arts fight team in the world, home to **Antonio Rodrigo Nogueira**, **Antonio Rogerio Nogueira**, **Ricardo Arona**, **Vitor Belfort**, and **Paulo Filho**, alongside founders **Murilo Bustamante** and **Mario Sperry**. The team took shape under Bustamante, Sperry, Luis Roberto Duarte,

and Ricardo Loborio in April 2000, after an acrimonious split with **Carlson Gracie**, and quickly earned its reputation by producing champions in both **Pride** and the **UFC**. A protracted feud between Rio's BTT and Curitiba's **Chute Boxe Academy** reached its climax at Pride's Final Conflict 2005, where Arona defeated Chute Boxe standard-bearer **Wanderlei Silva** before being KO'd on the same night by **Mauricio Rua**. Loborio left to found **American Top Team** in 2003, and BTT was further diminished by the departures of **Mario Sperry** and the Nogueira brothers after the death of Pride changed the economics of the sport. But BTT soldiers on under the leadership of Bustamante, and has established satellite schools in America, Canada, England, Australia, Hong Kong, and Belgium.

Brown, Jim

In 1993, the **UFC** was looking to establish an identity, to tell people and sportswriters what they were all about. They needed an announcer and advocate who impressed older sports media, one who also had a passing familiarity with violence. Jim Brown was perfect. To football fans in the baby boomer generation, Brown was simply the greatest. Not only was he the NFL's all-time leading rusher, he accomplished that goal while never taking a step back and never stepping out of bounds to avoid a hit.

Brown also had a street edge that worked well with the UFC's underground vibe. He worked with gangs, had been an outspoken activist, and looked like a man who wouldn't be afraid to sock you in the mouth. Brown had also been accused of violence against women and beating people up on the street.

In Their Own Words: Jim Brown on violence

"I have never touched my wife, and since 1988, I have not said a loud word to anyone based upon the work and the people that I am dealing with, because I deal with violent people every day and I must set an example and I must have them believe I'm not a hypocrite or a phony . . . have been an independent man in our society. I have been an activist. I have been a community person. I have been outspoken. I have been around Malcolm. I have been around the Nation of Islam. I have been in what you might call volatile situations. I have fought all of my life for freedom, equality, and justice when there was racism up to here in this country. I am 63 years old. I have not ever succumbed to the authorities. I have always been known as an outspoken, independent individual."

He was edgy, but he didn't have any real martial arts background. Producers were savvy enough not to try to pigeonhole him in that role. Instead, he was the everyman and his presence was integral as the voice of the fan. Brown watched the fights and said aloud the things fans were thinking, asked the questions many were asking at home about jiu-jitsu and grappling. And when Jim Brown said someone was a tough guy, well, that meant something.

Brown, Mike

Height: 5'6"
Weight: 145 lbs
Born: 9/8/75
Debut: Mass Destruction 1 (4/1/01)
Career Record: 23-6
Notable Wins: Yves Edwards (BodogFight: St. Petersburg); Jeff Curran (WEC 34); Urijah Faber (WEC 36, WEC 41)
Notable Losses: Hermes Franca (HOOKnSHOOT: Kings 1); Genki Sudo (UFC 47); Joe Lauzon (Combat Zone 8); Masakazu Imanari (Deep 22nd Impact); Jose Aldo (WEC 44)

If you knew about Mike Brown before he made his **WEC** debut in 2008, it was probably because you'd seen **Genki Sudo** style on him years before in the **UFC**. Or maybe you'd watched a YouTube clip of **Masakazu Imanari** dislocating Brown's knee with a truly horrific **heel hook**. It didn't matter that Brown had amassed a record of 18 wins against only four losses by the time he stepped into the cage to face Jeff Curran; the man was thoroughly obscure. But with his solid performance in a decision win over Curran, Brown earned a shot at **Urijah Faber**'s featherweight title. It looked like it was going to be just another routine defense for "The California Kid," who'd been making it look easy. But after getting a little too fancy, and trying out an admittedly very cool-looking reverse elbow, Faber found himself staring up at the ceiling after a Mike Brown right hook. Brown silenced any critics who considered his upset title win a fluke when he went the distance against Faber in the rematch, controlling the pace of the fight and doing enough damage to easily take the decision in a first-rate fight. It's a shame Brown had to wait so late in his career to finally achieve some measure of acclaim, but such has been the fate of fighters competing anywhere below lightweight. By putting on the kinds of bouts he has with Faber and with **Jose Aldo** — Brown is helping to change that.

Browning, Junie

Nickname: The Lunatik
Height: 5'9"
Weight: 155 lbs
Born: 5/12/85

Debut: Freestyle Cage Fighting (1/19/08) **Career Record:** 4-3
Notable Win: Dave Kaplan (*The Ultimate Fighter* 8 Finale)
Notable Loss: Cole Miller (*Ultimate Fight Night* 18)

There are, broadly speaking, two approaches a fighter can take to appearing on ***The Ultimate Fighter*** reality show. He can recognize the singularity of the opportunity before him, embrace the challenge, and use the six weeks of secluded training to better himself as an athlete and take an important step forward in both his technical development and his professional career. Or he can tell racist jokes, engage in drunken sob stories and self-pity, throw glasses and coffee mugs at people, ignore the advice of world-class coaches and trainers, and denounce even the most routine civilities as "gay as hell." Junie Browning, an absurd, pathetic, tiny man, chose the second course. And, in so doing, Browning became by far the most interesting part of the otherwise completely forgettable eighth season of *TUF*. Unfortunately, it turned out Browning couldn't fight a lick, which kept his stated plan of becoming the new **Chris Leben** from becoming a reality. He left us, though, with one of the most memorable exchanges in *TUF* history when confronted by **Dana White** about his self-destructive behavior. "Junie," White asked, "what the fuck is wrong with you?" Junie's single-word answer said it all: "Drinkin'." In the fall of 2009, just when it seemed like we were done with Junie, he put himself in the headlines after freaking out nurses treating him for a drug overdose by screaming, "Do you know who I am? I will kill you and rape your family." Nice, Junie. Real nice.

Buentello, Paul

Nickname: The Headhunter **Height:** 6'2"
Weight: 245 lbs **Born:** 1/16/74
Debut: USWF 4 (4/12/97) **Career Record:** 28-12
Notable Wins: Justin Eilers (UFC 51); David "Tank" Abbott (Strikeforce: Tank vs. Buentello); Gary Goodridge (Affliction: Banned)
Notable Losses: Ricco Rodriguez (KOTC 7); Andrei Arlovski (UFC 55); Alistair Overeem (Strikeforce: Four Men Enter, One Man Survives)

When Paul Buentello yells, "Don't fear me" in a post-fight interview, he's *really* hoping you'll yell back "Fear the consequences." But it doesn't always work out that way.

The chubby, doe-eyed Buentello, a kickboxer capable of highlight-reel knockouts against B- and C-level opponents, has cut a swath through the second tier of American MMA organizations. He also posted a solid 3–1 record during a **UFC** tenure, which, unfortunately for him, was defined by two inglorious moments: his goofy, failed catchphrase, and a 15-second loss to **Andrei Arlovski** in a heavyweight title bout.

Blink and you'll miss it: a mere eight seconds into round one, Arlovski and Buentello both throw right hands. Arlovski's connects with Buentello's chin, and Buentello slumps over Arlovski's back, falling to the mat. **John McCarthy** rushes in to stop the fight, much to the confusion of the booing crowd and commentator **Joe Rogan**: "Arlovski takes him down — what happened? What happened?" Only upon replay could anyone but Big John see the blow that ended the fight.

And so it was on to the **Tank Abbott**s, **Gary Goodridge**s and Ruben Villareals of the world for Paul Buentello, lesser opponents on lesser shows. Given the power Buentello packs in his right hand, a return to the bright lights of the UFC doesn't seem out of the question. He's still capable of lighting up most pro heavyweights on any given night.

Okay now, all together this time: *don't fear him . . .*

Buffer, Bruce

Michael Buffer is the premier ring announcer in the world. If there is a major fight in boxing, or a big match in **professional wrestling**, it's likely Buffer will be there with his trademark phrase "Let's get ready to rumble." Contrary to popular belief, Michael Buffer was also the ring announcer for several early **UFC** events, but had to step back when his primary employer, the WCW wrestling group, decided that the UFC was competition. His stepbrother Bruce Buffer stepped in for him and never looked back.

Bruce was one of several ring announcers the UFC used after that, but none wanted it more than he did. Buffer maneuvered his way onto the popular television show *Friends* when **Tank Abbott** made his appearance in

1997 and used the attention to secure the position for good, starting with UFC 13. Buffer has been the "Voice of the Octagon" ever since, popularizing catch-phrases of his own, like "It's time."

One of the highlights of seeing the UFC live is experiencing the "Buffer 180." When Buffer is introducing a fighter, he will often look to the opposite corner before making a dramatic 180 degree turn towards the fighter whose name he's calling. It's hilarious and theatrical and one of the things that make the UFC a great live experience.

Bustamante, Murilo

Height: 6'2" **Weight:** 185 lbs

Born: 7/30/66 **Debut:** Desafio: Jiu-jitsu vs. Luta Livre (9/26/91)

Career Record: 22-7-1

Notable Wins: Yoji Anjo (UFC 25); Jerry Bohlander (Pentagon Combat); Sanae Kikuta (UFC 33); Dave Menne (UFC 35); Matt Lindland (UFC 37)

Notable Losses: Chuck Liddell (UFC 33); Quinton Jackson (Pride Total Elimination 2003); Dan Henderson (Pride Final Conflict 2003, Pride Shockwave 2005); Kazuhiro Nakamura (Pride Final Conflict 2004)

If it wasn't for bad luck, Murilo Bustamante would have none at all. The **Brazilian Top Team** founder and **Carlson Gracie** black belt was in more than his fair share of tight, back-and-forth battles over the course of his fine career, and he always seemed to come out on the wrong end of the judges' decision. It's true that Bustamante holds a record of three wins and six losses in fights that have gone the distance. But a number of those decision losses have been so questionable that it's difficult to see Bustamante as anything but hard done by.

Bustamante began his career undefeated in eight fights, picking up wins over slick grapplers **Jerry Bohlander** and **Sanae Kikuta**, and fighting the enormous **Tom Erikson** to a draw. Bustamante then went the distance with **Chuck Liddell** in an extremely close fight at a time when Liddell was streaking towards his first shot at the light heavyweight title. After that loss, Bustamante decided a change to middleweight was in order. He knocked out **Dave Menne** to become the **UFC**'s second middleweight champion, which set the stage for his title defense against the then-undefeated **Matt Lindland** in one of the weirdest fights you'll ever see.

In the first round, Bustamante put on a clinic. He clinched with the Olympic Greco-Roman **wrestling** silver medalist, took him down with an outside trip, and systematically worked his way from **guard** to **half-guard** to **mount**.

As Lindland bridged and rolled to escape, Bustamante seized hold of Lindland's arm and straightened it out into a textbook **arm bar**. Lindland made several ambiguous movements with his free hand that looked enough like tapping for referee **John McCarthy** to step in. Bustamante, a sportsman, relinquished the hold immediately, but McCarthy had second thoughts. Lindland insisted he hadn't tapped, and McCarthy, in a rare instance of poor judgment, sent the fighters back to their corners and restarted the bout. This could happen to no one but Murilo Bustamante. Ultimately, it wouldn't matter, as Bustamante handled Lindland the rest of the way, dropping him with a straight right hand in the third round and finishing with a **guillotine choke** in the ensuing scramble.

Bustamante departed for the greener pastures in **Pride** while still holding the UFC middleweight title, but his strange luck followed him there, as he dropped a decision to **Quinton Jackson** after doing what probably should have been enough to win — in a fight he took on only five days' notice, no less. Bustamante would never again claim championship gold, but came tantalizingly close after fighting his way through Pride's welterweight (183 pounds) tournament to meet **Dan Henderson** at the 2005 Shockwave New Year's Eve show. True to form for both fighters, Henderson squeaked through with a split decision in a fight that could easily have gone the other way, and Bustamante was left wondering what he had to do to catch a break.

Cage Force

Cage Force, the most recent series of events promoted by the longstanding Greater Common Multiple organization, is marked by two distinctions. First, it runs under the most generic possible name, seemingly a product of a random MMA promotion generator. Second, it's the only Japanese organization to run in a cage rather than a ring. This makes it well positioned as a proving ground for Japanese fighters with an eye towards competition abroad. **UFC** middleweight contender **Yushin Okami** — the last man to defeat **Anderson Silva**, albeit by DQ — and welterweight **Yoshiyuki Yoshida** are two Greater Common Multiple alumni who have taken that path. Expect to see more fighters follow their lead. With eight to ten events a year, and annual tournaments separating the wheat from the chaff, Greater Common Multiple's Cage Force events could become a significant source of Japanese talent for the UFC.

Cage Rage

As the story goes, Alex Jones and Tom Bell had no grand design, no master plan behind the first fight show they put on together. They were just trying to get enough money together to buy some new mats for their club. They succeeded beyond all expectations, and slowly built Cage Rage into the U.K.'s premier mixed martial arts organization. Naturally, they showcased native U.K. talent like **Michael Bisping**, Ian Freeman, and **James Thompson**, but they also brought in top international fighters like **Vitor Ribeiro**, **Anderson Silva**, and **Vitor Belfort**. Any promotion that has featured both Butterbean *and* **Herb Dean** — not in the same bout, unfortunately — clearly deserves the support and respect of the discerning MMA fan. In September 2007, Cage Rage was acquired by **EliteXC**, a ridiculous company that ingloriously crashed out of the MMA business altogether a year later, spelling the end for the venerable U.K. promotion. No worries, though: former Cage Rage executives Dave O'Donnell and Andy Geer quickly changed the name of the previously announced Cage Rage 29 event on just a few weeks' notice, formed a new group called

Ultimate Challenge U.K., and continue to run regularly out of The Troxy in London.

Canseco, Jose

Height: 6'4" **Weight:** 253 lbs
Born: 6/2/64 **Debut:** Dream 9 (5/26/09)
Career Record: 0-1
Notable Loss: Hong-Man Choi (Dream 9)

If MMA is the new boxing, is the corollary that celebrity MMA is the new celebrity boxing? If the career death spiral of former big league slugger and current D-list personality Jose Canseco is any indication, then maybe. Never one to shy away from a camera (or a paycheck), the 1988 American League MVP made his MMA debut at the age of 44 against a diminished Hong-Man Choi as part of the **Dream** organization's boldly named Super Hulk Grand Prix. The results were about what you'd expect: less entertaining than the fly ball that famously ricocheted off Canseco's head for a home run, but more entertaining than Canseco's accounts of his erotic near miss with Madonna. A Tae Kwan Do black belt, Canseco managed an offense of a few jerky punches and hopeful kicks to the body of the listless giant, but a bum knee had Canseco on the mat tapping to strikes in only 77 seconds. Worryingly, Canseco did not announce his retirement from the sport immediately following the bout.

Carano, Gina

Nickname: Conviction **Height:** 5'8"
Weight: 140–145 lbs **Born:** 4/16/82
Debut: WEF: Orleans Arena (6/10/06) **Career Record:** 7-1
Notable Win: Kelly Kobald (EliteXC: Heat)
Notable Loss: Cris "Cyborg" Santos (Strikeforce: Carano vs. Cyborg)

Gina Carano, whether deserving or not, is the face of women's MMA. Busty, pretty, and goofily charming, Carano made as many waves with her *Maxim* magazine photo shoot as she did with wins over Kaitlyn Young, Julie Kedzie, or Kelly Kobald. Carano's sex appeal may actually transcend the fight game. She's on the path to bigger things: television and video games already leading up to movie cameos, leading in turn to bigger movie roles.

Carano looms over the entire women's sport. While much of that does come down to her good looks, Carano is also a heck of a fighter. Starting as

In Their Own Words: Carano on her problems making weight

"My first couple of fights I didn't have the right people around me. I did everything wrong you could possibly do. Afterward, you realize that could be a lot easier than you made it. I've got a nutritionist and she's a body builder chick so she knows. Because being female is different. We have to deal with the time of the month, and for some reason that time always pops up when you have to fight. For me at least. It's such a bitch, really, what that does to you that week and the week before. For pretty much two weeks out of the month, and I don't know if other females are like this, I feel like an insane person because my body is just all over the place. It really blows, because emotionally, it messes with your training. You don't have the drive and you feel weak. And on top of that, you're five pounds heavier because you're bloating.

"So it sucks cutting weight as a female. Everyone has their downfalls; mine's definitely been the weight issue. I'm getting more balanced. I've got the people around me now who are giving me the correct information. So I'm relying on them instead of myself. I know I'm going to freak out about everything and it's nice to have people there who are going to say 'Hey, everything's going to be okay. You're going to be fine.' I've got much more balancing to do, and I want to keep this up after the fight and not balloon up like I usually do. But I say that every fight. I'm just trying to do the best I can."

a **Muay Thai** kickboxer, Carano got interested in fighting to be closer to her then-boyfriend, fighter Kevin Ross. Her personal magnetism brought cameras into her orbit from the very beginning. Carano's earliest training escapades were filmed for the documentary *Ring Girls*.

"When we did *Ring Girls* it was still all just for fun," Carano said. "It was like, 'Yeah of course I'll go to Thailand! You're going to pay for us to go to Thailand and fight? Of course I'm going to do it! You want to film us while we're training and make some little story about it? Fine.'"

Thai boxing led to mixed martial arts, where Carano was an immediate sensation. Her standup striking was more technical than any of the girls she fought and she was a good enough athlete to survive the ground game while she learned how to grapple. Her appearances on Showtime for **EliteXC** made her a bona fide star and made her picture a popular internet search. When EliteXC ran the first MMA show in network television history, Carano was a feature performer.

After a second starring role on CBS, Carano was ready to main event. For the first time in the sport's 16-year history, two women main evented a major MMA card. She and her opponent, the fearsome Brazilian **Cris "Cyborg" Santos** were an unqualified success. They drew almost 14,000 fans to the HP Pavilion in San Jose, California, and set a Showtime record for MMA television.

It was a high point for women's MMA, but many critics expressed concern for the future of women's fighting. Carano was badly beaten in the first round and immediately departed the cage, and then the sport, taking on a starring role in the Steven Soderbergh spy thriller *Haywire*.

Carter, Shonie

Nickname: Mr. International **Height:** 5'10"
Weight: 170-185 lbs **Born:** 5/3/72
Debut: Extreme Challenge 3 (2/15/97) **Career Record:** 49-23-7
Notable Wins: Dave Menne (Extreme Challenge 5); Chris Lytle (Pancrase: 2000 Anniversary); Matt Serra (UFC 31)
Notable Losses: Pat Miletich (Extreme Challenge 27, UFC 32); Nathan Quarry (UFC 53); Marcus Davis (UFC Fight Night: Sanchez vs. Riggs)

Shonie Carter is a real life ronin. Like the rogue samurai of ancient times, Shonie has no master. He journeys through the world, learning martial techniques and fighting skills, and then learning some more. He's studied **wrestling** at Carson Newman College, **karate**, **judo** at the Kodokan, and **boxing** at some of the toughest gyms in the country. It's this variety of skills that makes Shonie Carter a dangerous fighter and his extensive travel that makes him such an interesting man.

Carter has earned his nickname "Mr. International" the hard way — by traveling all over the world. Carter has fought in Japan, Germany, Ireland, Canada, Poland, and Mexico. Along the way he's amassed 46 wins to go with 18 losses, but it's his style more than his skill that makes Carter stand out. Carter is one of MMA's first prominent African American fighters, and he brings a street edge to shows that are all too often filled with similar haircuts, bad tattoos, and **Affliction** T-shirts. Into this sea of sameness appears Carter, resplendent in a top hat, pimp suit, and cane.

He carries this style into the cage as well. His fights often feature high-amplitude and high-velocity judo throws and outrageous karate style strikes, including his most famous moment, a desperation spinning backfist that ended the night for **Matt Serra** at UFC 31.

For all his success, Carter had amassed only a 3–2 record in the **UFC**. Looking for another opportunity, he auditioned for the fourth season of ***The Ultimate Fighter***, a show designed to give seasoned veterans a second shot. Carter was born for reality television, livening up the worst season the show had ever had. Carter was a walking sound-bite and, stuck in a house with 16 other guys, went out of his way to annoy them with his trash talk and art projects. His best work was his sequined hat and he made an offer to everyone in the house: "If you bring it, I will bling it."

In Their Own Words: Shonie Carter's Wild Day (as posted on The Underground Forum)

Ok, last time I was in California when it all started, but this time I have really messed up! I was out one night partying up and before I knew it, I am on a private jet. I laughed at first and passed out on the plane. I woke up in Istanbul, Turkey. The reason I know because I am looking at the Black Sea! WTF!

Later that day:
I got a ride to Bulgarian/Turkish border looking for American Embassy. Does anybody have any ideas on how to get back? The one time I leave my friggin' passport at home I need the damned thing! Somebody let bodybag76 and Immaculata know to message me here please! I am in hotel business center and my two cell phones don't work. I forgot all about that! Help me. Mr. International.

Later:
I am gonna try getting to Greece it is only an hour away. Just get me help! Send messages here [and] not MySpace – it has been phished! I just found out and don't know how to fix it yet. Gotta go, I will be back on in an about an hour! I gotta get a ride to Greece.

Final Update:
Wow, ok I made it [through] Turkey. I am in Sofia, Bulgaria, as I found out now. I got a ride from the Bulgarian girl. The truth of the matter is she was a diplomat's daughter and she was with him at the UFC. I didn't think they were serious about all of this. I am headed to an authority office of visitors since I can't find the damned U.S. embassy. Fellas this is the type of shit I go [through] in my life. I gotta get back and pay the mortgage and see my kids! I gotta train for my world middleweight title fight in the Shidokan World Championships and black belt test [on] November 22 & 23. I know you guys don't have a reason to believe me right now, but shit happens to me like [everyone] else but on a much larger scale. I have made it to a hotel business center here in Sofia, Bulgaria.

Carter was so wildly entertaining he seemed to affect the people around him. Even the fights he refereed ended up being amazing spectacles. At a Legends of Fighting event Carter was the third man in the cage when two first-time pros knocked each other out simultaneously. It was an almost unheard of double knockout, made all the better by Carter's hamming it up in amazement. It was a great moment, one of many made better by Shonie Carter.

Carwin, Shane

Nickname: The Engineer
Height: 6'1"
Weight: 260 lbs
Born: 1/4/75
Debut: WEC 17 (9/21/93)
Career Record: 21-1
Notable Wins: Christian Wellisch (UFC 84); Gabriel Gonzaga (UFC 96); Frank Mir (UFC 111)
Notable Loss: Brock Lesnar (UFC 116)

Shane Carwin is an outlier, standing apart from almost every other competitor in the sport of MMA. While the other top fighters train full-time, waking up late and lounging between their workouts, Carwin packs up his lunch pail and rolls into work as a mechanical engineer.

Carwin is a former NCAA Division II national champion wrestler, but has made his mark in MMA with his powerful punching. It's hard for his punches not to hurt — along with **Brock Lesnar**, he's one of only two fighters in the **UFC** who wear 4XL gloves.

For all of his talent, it took some time for Carwin to catch on in the UFC. His first two fights were on the untelevised undercard. Most fans had only seen his UFC 96 win over former contender **Gabriel Gonzaga** when the promotion made the surprise announcement that Carwin had earned a shot at the UFC heavyweight champion Lesnar.

In Their Own Words: Shane Carwin on coming up through the ranks in MMA

"I know I wasn't walked through the front door of the UFC with people holding the door for me. I wasn't fed fights that sell pay-per-views. I was matched up by promoters and took whatever they put in front of me.

"One of those fights was the former enforcer for the Mongols Motorcycle Club. His previous fight ended when Mongols in the crowd started fighting and stabbing people.

"For Brock [Lesnar] to say that I have hand-picked my fights is just stupid.

"I got my start in the **WEC** and I have fought everyone the UFC put in front of me. I have fought three times as many people [as] Brock has. If he wants to disrespect the opponents I have fought, that is his choice. I say any man or woman that enters that cage to face an opponent is worthy of my respect. They have trained hard, and to disrespect MMA fighters is disrespecting the sport of MMA."

Interview by Jeremy Botter, Heavy.com

Carwin, normally even-tempered and mild-mannered, had put himself into the mix in the heavyweight division with his nationally publicized comments after Lesnar's second fight with **Frank Mir** at UFC 100. Like many fans, Carwin was disappointed in Lesnar's disrespectful post-fight antics and called him out online. Lesnar responded, and the war of words caught fans' attention. Carwin would be Lesnar's biggest challenge; with strong wrestling and true knockout power, "The Engineer" has the ability to drop any man on the planet — even the mighty Lesnar.

The two squared off at UFC 116, after Carwin had battled and defeated **Frank Mir** and Lesnar had faced down an even tougher opponent — an illness initially diagnosed as mononucleosis and then later determined to be diverticulitis. Carwin caught Lesnar with one of his giant hamhocks and had the champion reeling. Lesnar seemed on the brink of defeat, but Carwin's gas tank was empty quickly. At the halfway point of the very first round, Carwin started to slow, eventually allowing Lesnar, who was all but beaten moments before, to not just survive, but end the round on his feet and on the attack. In the second, Carwin had nothing left. In postfight interviews he would describe feeling like he was in the midst of a full body cramp. He was helpless and Lesnar quickly took him down, passed his guard, and submitted him with an arm triangle. As Lesnar locked the submission in tighter, it's possible Carwin was having second thoughts — about his training routine and his decision to be a part-time fighter.

Castillo, Gil

Height: 5'9" **Weight:** 170–185 lbs

Born: 10/21/65 **Debut:** IFC WC 6 (3/25/00)

Career Record: 19–5

Notable Wins: Vernon White (Stockton Extreme Fighting); Nate Marquardt (IFC WC 14); Chris Brennan (UFC 35)

Notable Losses: Dave Menne (UFC 33); Matt Hughes (UFC 40); Renato Verissimo (ROTR 4)

Gil Castillo was just another frustrated ex-jock when the sport of MMA exploded into the American consciousness in 1993. He had been a star wrestler at Cal State Long Beach, even making a run at the 1988 Olympic team at 147 pounds. Those days were well behind him; Castillo was behind a desk working as a stockbroker when he got curious about **Gracie Jiu-jitsu** and just how a wrestler like **Dan Severn** could lose to a man 80 pounds lighter.

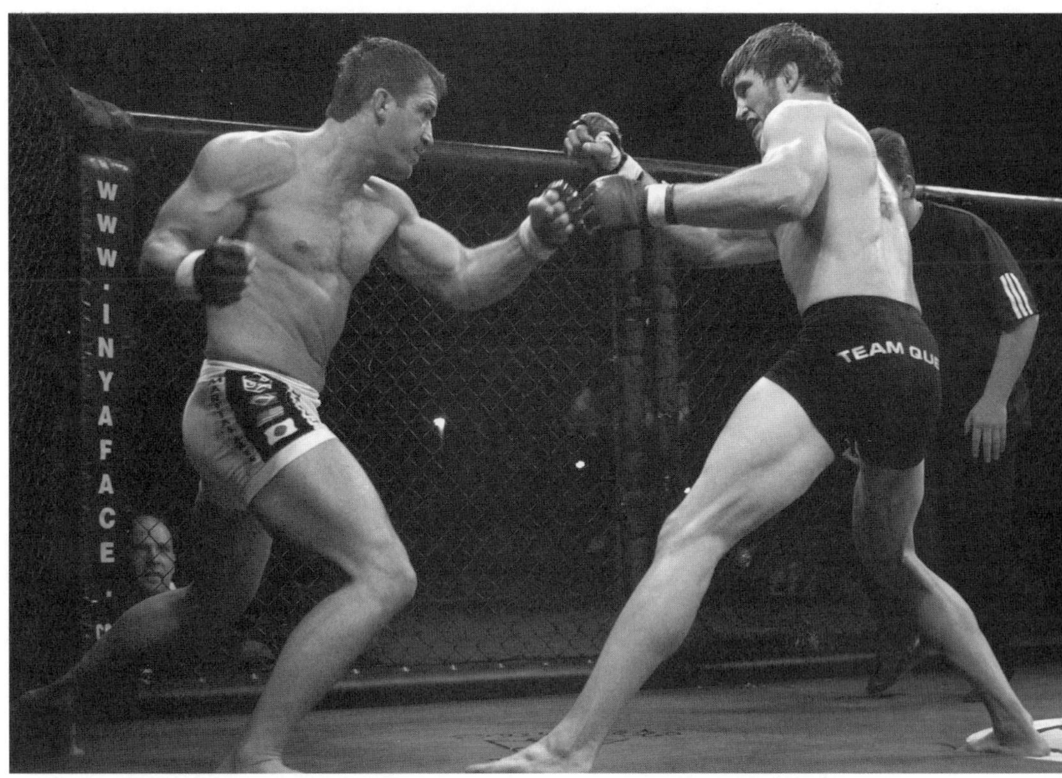

He started training with **Ralph Gracie** in 1995, and just over two years later he was making his fighting debut. Fourteen wins later, he had officially caught the MMA bug and was looking to get the attention of scouts for the **UFC** and **Pride.** Castillo won the **King of the Cage** welterweight championship from **Lion's Den** prospect Joey Hurley, but that wasn't enough to earn a shot in a crowded UFC landscape.

Instead, Castillo got the UFC's attention when **Joe Silva** and **Dana White** came to an IFC card to scout **Pancrase** star **Nate Marquardt**. Castillo and Marquardt put on a great show, with Castillo getting the best of their exchanges to win the IFC welterweight title. White and Silva tracked Castillo down at a restaurant after the fight to offer him a title shot at UFC 33, the promotion's big return to pay-per-view in 2001. The problem: it was a shot at the middleweight title.

Castillo was beaten soundly by **Dave Menne** but was impressive enough to get a second shot at his natural welterweight class. He won his next UFC fight against Chris Brennan before losing to **Matt Hughes** after being cut by an illegal head butt. Already 37 years old, Castillo was past his athletic prime. After losing three of his next five fights, Castillo hung up his wrestling shoes again, this time for good.

Catch wrestling

In the 19th and early 20th century, the world was a very different place. That may seem obvious, but bears consideration. There were no televisions, no radio, and no internet. You couldn't lose yourself in video games — not even Pong. You could either read or, if you weren't of an intellectual bent, you could amuse yourself through athletics.

Needless to say, Americans were considerably more physically active then than they are today. And while team sports were often expensive, requiring equipment and the proper locale, all you needed to wrestle were two men and a bit of space. **Wrestling** and **boxing** were much more prevalent than they are today, and traveling carnivals, which endeavored to provide the entertainment people were desperate for, often included an athletic show as part of the fun.

It was there that local toughs could test themselves against seasoned professionals, often with money up for grabs. The wrestlers at these carnivals had to be tough. With his pride on the line, in front of his family and best girl, a local wrestling prodigy might stoop to dirty tactics to win a match. To prevail, the professional wrestler had to be better — and often had to be dirtier.

They developed techniques, called hooks, that could disable an opponent, causing him to cry uncle and end a match before it could become dangerous. It was called "catch as catch can" and borrowed heavily from the Lancashire style popular in Great Britain, with an American twist. In the wild and wooly West, wrestlers could often be identified by their missing eyes — gouging was not an unknown or unusual technique when the grappling got serious.

At the same time as baseball and boxing were becoming America's favorite spectator sports, wrestling was coming into its own as an attraction. Men like Frank Gotch, who had once traveled the carnival circuit — even going into lumberjack camps to find a match — were becoming popular enough to charge a paying audience eager to see them ply their trade. Instead of him coming to the fans, fans would come to him. These early **professional wrestling** contests would often last for hours. Soon everyone involved understood that it would be easier, more entertaining, and more profitable simply to give the crowd a good show. Professional wrestling didn't maintain its innocence for long, if it ever had any.

While catch wrestling with its hooks and submission holds did fall out of favor, as professionals turned to faked bouts and amateurs turned to a folk style that scored wins via pinfall only, it never died completely. Kept alive by a few die-hards like Karl Gotch and Billy Robinson, a generation of Japanese pro wrestlers learned all the hooks and holds they needed to know to be devastating on the mat. When **Pancrase** made wrestling real again in 1993, the catch style was back in a big way.

Cavalcante, Gesias

Nickname: JZ **Height:** 5'8"

Weight: 155 lbs **Born:** 7/6/83

Debut: Absolute Fighting Championships 7 (2/27/04)

Career Record: 15-3-1 (1 No Contest)

Notable Wins: Rani Yahya (Hero's 7); Caol Uno (Hero's 7); Vitor Ribeiro (Hero's 10)

Notable Losses: Joachim Hansen (Shooto 2004: 7/16 in Korakuen Hall); Shinya Aoki (Dream 2); Tatsuya Kawajiri (Dream 9)

American Top Team's Gesias Cavalcante is arguably the best fighter nobody in North America really talks about. But those who follow the Japanese fight game with any interest at all know that the fighter billed there as "JZ Calvan" is without question one of the best lightweights in the sport. A slick **Brazilian Jiu-jitsu** stylist and an aggressive striker, Cavalcante put together a 13-fight unbeaten streak that saw him claim both the 2006 and 2007 **Hero's** middleweight (155 pounds) Grand Prix, stopping most of his opponents not just in the first round, but in the first minute.

JZ seemed all but unstoppable as he entered the ring to face Japanese lightweight star **Shinya Aoki** in the main event of the nascent **Dream** promotion's debut show. The much-anticipated fight ended as anticlimactically as could be imagined, though, as Cavalcante landed a number of questionable elbows to the back of Aoki's neck that were judged illegal. Aoki was either unwilling or unable to continue after the unintentional fouls, and the bout was ruled no contest. There were many who questioned the legitimacy of Aoki's injuries, thinking he took the easy way out in a fight where he looked overmatched against an equally skilled but much stronger and more aggressive opponent. In those few minutes they spent in the ring together, JZ looked like the top lightweight in Japan. All he needed was one more opportunity to prove it.

But when the rematch came, the crafty Aoki controlled Cavalcante with his sophisticated **guard** work en route to a unanimous decision victory, and JZ hasn't quite managed to get back on track since. He looked to avenge an early career loss to **Joachim Hansen** on K-1 Dynamite!! 2008 New Year's Eve show, but Hansen's late withdrawal due to medical problems left Cavalcante without an opponent. After a somewhat surprising loss to the dangerous **Tatsuya Kawajiri** at Dream 9, injury trouble kept Cavalcante out of action for much of 2009. But even though he hasn't actually won a match since taking the 2007 Hero's tournament title, there can be little doubt that JZ Calvan — with his tools and his talents at only 26 years of age — will be a presence at or near the top of the lightweight division as soon as he returns.

Cheating

It's commonly believed that the earliest **UFC** contests had no rules. That's not exactly true. There were three rules in place at UFC 1 — no groin strikes, no biting, and no eye gouging — they just weren't rules that could be enforced. Punishment entailed a small fine, paid to your opponent after the fight. You could foul your way to victory, and the meager $1,000 fine would be easily offset by the $50,000 in prize money. Luckily for decent people, MMA fighters couldn't do the math and no foul-fests occurred. Although no fighter paid a price after that first show, the dirty Dutchman Gerard Gordeau did bite **Royce Gracie**'s ear in the evening's final fight. The long and glorious history of MMA cheating had begun.

The discussions in the martial arts media (most prominently in *Black Belt* magazine) after the show were interesting. Instead of complaining about the brutality and lack of rules, many martial artists were insisting there were too *many* rules. After all, a number of fighting disciplines used eye gouges, and strikes to the groin were a common technique of many karateka. The UFC decided eye gouging was too dangerous and beyond the pale to ever legalize, and Gordeau showed they made the right decision by nearly blinding Yuki Nakai at **Vale Tudo** Japan 1994.

The UFC did bow to the pressure from traditional martial artists and allowed strikes to the groin. It made little difference to most karate and kung fu types, but **Keith Hackney** made it work to his advantage at UFC 4 against Joe Son. In a clip replayed thousands — perhaps millions — of times on YouTube, Hackney brutalized Son with six hard punches to the testicles. Viewers cringed, but considering that Son was later charged with a horrific rape, it seems a fitting punishment in retrospect.

Over the years, many of the sport's most blatant rule breakers have been from Holland, perhaps following in Gordeau's treacherous footsteps. "Dirty" **Bob Schrijber** seemed to be capable of anything in the ring but was a gentleman outside the confines of combat. **Gilbert Yvel** was unable to confine his illegal attacks to his opponents. When a referee attempted to separate the fighters, Gilbert punched the official. To make it clear it was no accident, he kicked him while he was down for good measure.

In the UFC, the most controversial cheater of the **Zuffa** era is clearly "The Iceman" **Chuck Liddell**. Liddell has thumbed multiple opponents in the eye. Commentators **Mike Goldberg** and **Joe Rogan** have been careful to always proclaim the attacks "inadvertent," even if they were blatant, or fail to mention them all together. Liddell was the company's most famous fighter and it didn't pay to call his achievements into question. It is worth discussing, however, how inadvertent Liddell's repeated eye gouges actually were. Liddell's original art is Kempo Karate, a fighting style that includes plenty of eye strikes and gouges. Liddell used eye gouges to his advantage in some of his biggest career victories, including wins over **Randy Couture** and **Tito Ortiz**.

Following the lead of its professional sports brethren, the most controversial form of cheating in MMA doesn't happen in the ring or cage. **Steroid** abuse has become a significant issue for the sport. Significantly more MMA competitors than boxers test positive for illegal drugs in the state of California. And UFC fighters are not immune; despite being able to afford more sophisticated mechanisms for hiding their steroid use, UFC stars continue to get caught doping. Three active UFC champions have tested positive and were stripped of their titles: **Josh Barnett**, **Tim Sylvia**, and **Sean Sherk**. Legendary former champions, including **Kevin Randleman**, Royce Gracie, and **Ken Shamrock** have also tested positive and been suspended.

Chonan, Ryo

Nickname: Piranha **Height:** 5'9"

Weight: 170 lbs **Born:** 10/8/76

Debut: Pancrase: Neo-Blood Tournament Elimination 1 (5/5/01)

Career Record: 17–11

Notable Wins: Hayato Sakurai (Deep 12th Impact); Carlos Newton (Pride Bushido 5); Anderson Silva (Pride Shockwave 2004)

Notable Losses: Dan Henderson (Pride Bushido 9); Paulo Filho (Pride Bushido 12); Karo Parisyan (UFC 78)

"That was beautiful. You can only see this in demonstrations — this guy just did it for real." That was how **Bas Rutten**, a man who has seen it all, described the single greatest submission finish in the history of mixed martial arts, Ryo Chonan's flying scissors entry into a **heel hook** against **Anderson Silva**.

When the two met in the **Pride** ring on New Year's Eve 2004, Anderson Silva was not yet what Anderson Silva would become: the **UFC**'s middleweight champion, and a perennial contender for the mythical title of top pound-for-pound fighter in the world. He was, however, a 12–2 fighter with clean, technical striking, a slick submission game, and tremendous conditioning whose previous loss (an embarrassing upset via **triangle choke** to journeyman **Daiju Takase**) was a year and a half behind him.

Ryo Chonan, a Kyokushin **karate** and **Muay Thai** exponent with no previous submission success to speak of, had hardly set the world on fire in an up-and-down run in **Deep**. His wins over **Hayato Sakurai** and **Carlos Newton** came at a time when neither of those fighters was near the top of his game. Coming in against Silva, Chonan seemed seriously overmatched, and in the early going, he was: Silva landed a quick combination and took Chonan's back on the ground, looking to finish with a **rear naked choke**. Chonan settled in, however, generally maintaining a solid top position when the fight was on the ground, and keeping Silva at bay with a barrage of leg kicks when they returned to their feet.

Then, with Chonan less than two minutes away from an almost certain decision win, it happened. Chonan leapt at the southpaw Silva's lead right leg, entangled it, and transitioned to a heel hook as they fell to the mat. Wisely, Silva tapped immediately to the dangerous hold. Three seconds earlier, Silva had been trying desperately to land the knockout shot he needed to steal the fight. But Chonan shut the door on that possibility with his singular submission finish.

And that was by far the brightest moment for the bleached blond, creepily dead-eyed Chonan. He was unable to move up the Pride ranks after the Silva upset, dropping quick, decisive bouts to **Phil Baroni**, **Dan Henderson**, and **Paulo Filho**. A move to welterweight for his UFC debut seemed as though it might reinvigorate his flagging career, but Chonan lost three of four, and was cut from the UFC roster after a split decision loss to up-and-comer T.J. Grant. A return to the minor Japanese scene seems likely.

Chute Boxe

Curitiba, Brazil's Chute Boxe Academy, is perhaps best known now as the home of women's MMA phenom **Cristiane Santos**, her husband Evangelista, and **Strikeforce** heavyweight contender **Fabricio Werdum**. But it wasn't long ago that Rudimar Fedrigo's fight team was home to some of the most fearsome **Muay Thai** strikers in all of mixed martial arts, men who terrorized **Pride** and went toe-to-toe with their great rivals, **Brazilian Top Team**. Before a series of departures accelerated by the death of Pride and the shakeup throughout the MMA world that followed, Chute Boxe once claimed a roster that included **Wanderlei Silva**, **Mauricio** and **Murilo Rua**, **Anderson Silva**, **Gabriel Gonzaga**, and Thiago Silva. Even **Kazushi Sakuraba**, three times bested by Wanderlei Silva, once traveled across the Pacific to sharpen his striking game alongside the men who had engineered his downfall. The result? A flash knockout of **Ken Shamrock** in his first fight back. If Chute Boxe could turn a broken-down Sakuraba into a threat on his feet, it's no wonder they could turn men like Wanderlei Silva and Mauricio Rua into the kings of Pride's incredibly deep middleweight (205 pounds) division.

Clinch

The clinch is where grappling and striking meet, a phase of fighting as technically complex and nuanced as any ground fighting position (see **positional hierarchy**) and just as important. When two fighters are locked together standing — whether in a collar-and-elbow tie-up, a **Muay Thai** neck clinch, a rear clinch, or in some configuration of overhooked and underhooked arms — the live crowd's attention sometimes tends to drift, and unless you're listening to a first-rate announce team, it can be difficult to discern what, exactly, each fighter is working for by slipping an arm here, turning his hips there.

Broadly speaking, strikers might be looking for powerful knees to the head or body — think **Anderson Silva** mauling poor **Rich Franklin** — or the kind of short hooks and uppercuts from a single-collar tie that **Randy Couture** has made a career out of. Grapplers are likely to look for trip takedowns (Couture again), hip or shoulder throws (**Hayato Sakurai, Karo Parisyan**), or to initiate submissions (**Rumina Sato**'s flying **arm bar, Renzo Gracie**'s **guillotine** on **Pat Miletich**). A well-rounded mixed martial artist, of course, looks for all of these opportunities the clinch provides at once. Think **Fedor Emelianenko** tying up **Mirko Cro Cop**, turning in for a hip throw, which Cro Cop blocks only for Fedor to land a powerful hook as he re-squares his hips. Or, again, the great Randy Couture, arguably the best clinch fighter in the game, whose dirty boxing sets up his outside leg trips beautifully.

The clinch can be used defensively by a grappler looking to buy some time against a better striker, or a striker looking to avoid a superior grappler's takedowns. It can be used offensively by a grappler who wants to take the fight to ground, or a striker who wants to get close and stay close while he works his man over. It's perhaps the least appreciated aspect of the fight game — by fans, not by fighters who understand that fights can be won or lost in the clinch.

Coleman, Mark

Nickname: The Hammer
Height: 6'1"
Weight: 205–245
Born: 12/20/64
Debut: UFC 10 (7/12/96)
Career Record: 16–10

Notable Wins: Don Frye (UFC 10, Pride 26); Dan Severn (UFC 12); Igor Vovchanchyn (Pride Grand Prix 2000 Finals); Mauricio Rua (Pride 31)

Notable Losses: Maurice Smith (UFC 14); Pete Williams (UFC 17); Pedro Rizzo (UFC 18); Antonio Rodrigo Nogueira (Pride 16); Fedor Emelianenko (Pride Total Elimination 2004, Pride 32); Mirko Cro Cop (Pride 29); Randy Couture (UFC 109)

1992 **Olympian** Mark "The Hammer" Coleman revolutionized MMA and helped usher in the era of the wrestler. Before Coleman, amateur **wrestling** had been represented by **Dan Severn**. Severn was an excellent wrestler in his day, but by the time he fought **Royce Gracie** at **UFC** 4 he was already in his mid-thirties. With his baggy black trunks and his old-school mustache, Severn looked more like your favorite uncle than a killing machine.

Coleman was different. He was 250 pounds of muscle and while Severn was clearly uncomfortable dealing damage after a takedown, Coleman had no such compunctions. When he took a man down, the attack that followed was savage and brutal. Writers needed a new term to describe what Coleman did; they settled on **"ground and pound."**

Coleman looked unstoppable. For the first time since Gracie, a fighter appeared to have found a magic formula for success. Over the course of two UFC tournaments and a Super Fight to win the UFC heavyweight title against Severn, Coleman rewrote the book on what it took to succeed in the Octagon.

When Coleman faced **Extreme Fighting** champion **Maurice Smith** at UFC 15, he was beyond a heavy favorite. Smith was a kickboxer with limited takedown defense. Conventional wisdom said Coleman would hardly break a sweat. But Smith had identified a weakness. If you could survive the initial storm, Coleman would tire quickly and be nearly helpless. Smith won a decision, a loss that sent Coleman's career into a tailspin. Even the most famous head kick of all time, a knockout blow delivered by the **Lion's Den**'s **Pete Williams**, failed to wake Coleman up. A subsequent loss to Pedro Rizzo sent Coleman searching for answers.

Coleman found himself in Japan, regaining his spot at the top of the sport. But first, he had to hit rock bottom. Coleman allegedly agreed to lose a match to **Pride** star **Nobuhiko Takada** in exchange for money he needed to make ends meet. Coleman was a family man by then and wasn't making it with the UFC's paltry paydays. The money allowed him to concentrate on getting his career back on track and he made the most of his new lease on life.

The win over Coleman wasn't enough to propel Takada back into prominence. He was done as a main event draw. To replace him, Pride looked to have one man run through a gauntlet of the best fighters in the world. They called their tournament the Pride 2000 Grand Prix and it was an all-star gathering of the greats: Coleman, **Mark Kerr**, Takada, **Royce Gracie**, **Kazushi Sakuraba**, and **Igor Vovchanchyn**. When the dust settled, Coleman was kneeing Vovchanchyn over and over again in the head, on his way to being crowned the top fighter in the world. Three years after losing his UFC title, Coleman had scratched and pulled his way back to the top.

His stay at the top didn't last long. A new generation of heavyweights had come along, too skilled on the ground for Coleman to utilize his patented

In Their Own Words: Mark Coleman on changing the rules of the game

"I think eventually the head butt would have been taken out anyway, but the way I used it so effectively definitely sped up the process. I think I had a say in how fast it was eliminated in the way I used it. But it was obviously going to be eliminated eventually and I agree that it had to be eliminated eventually for the sport to get where it's at. The knees on the ground and the head butt had to go. Everything was new to me and I was just excited the sport had started up. I was relatively naive. I was content with the weapons that I had. I didn't feel I needed to add any weapons, but all of a sudden when they did eliminate the head butt, I was way behind in the game. I had a lot of catching up to do. I hadn't improved my game at all because I felt what I had was enough to win just about any fight. When the head butt was gone, it became a completely different sport. I definitely prefer the older rules and feel I am a better fighter with no rules. But I'm glad they added them or the sport wouldn't even be around today."

ground and pound without falling victim to a submission. **Antonio Rodrigo Nogueira** and **Fedor Emelianenko**, the two most dominant heavyweights in history, both finished Coleman with an **arm bar**. As a serious contender, Coleman was finished. There were several more memorable moments, including a win over **Chute Boxe**'s **Mauricio Rua,** followed by a post fight donnybrook, and an emotional embrace with his daughters after a second loss to Emelianenko.

In 2008, Coleman was inducted into the UFC Hall of Fame. It was a fitting tribute for a fighter who revolutionized the sport. But it was just a prelude to Coleman's return to the Octagon. Coleman was scheduled to fight **Brock Lesnar** at UFC 87, but a knee injury forced him to pull out of the match. Preparing for Lesnar helped Coleman realize that he was no longer able to handle a giant wrestler of Lesnar's caliber. The former dominant heavyweight, now 44 years old, decided to drop 30 pounds and compete as a light heavyweight for the first time in his career.

Coleman impressed the UFC brass with a spirited loss to Rua in his 205-pound debut, winning Fight of the Night and plenty of respect. He won his next fight against **Stephan Bonnar** and appears to be ready to fight into his late forties. Despite his diminished physical presence, Coleman is still a good enough wrestler to give anyone pause. In a stacked division, Coleman won't lack willing opponents, fighters looking to challenge themselves by taking out a legend. These young lions will find The Hammer waiting and willing, ready to knock them down a peg on his own path back to championship glory.

Correira, Wesley

Nickname: Cabbage | **Height:** 6'3"
Weight: 260 lbs | **Born:** 11/11/78
Debut: Rings: USA (7/22/00) | **Career Record:** 19-14
Notable Win: Tank Abbott (UFC 45)
Notable Losses: Tim Sylvia (UFC 39); Andrei Arlovski (UFC 47); Tank Abbott (ROTR 7)

Hawaiian Wesley "Cabbage" Correira was once considered the toughest man in the sport, the proud owner of a chin that made him impossible to knockout. But, this never made Correira a great fighter. **Tim Sylvia** beat him to a pulp at **UFC** 39, but he never hit the mat, no matter how many times he got hit.

Correira's top feud was with the famous street fighter **Tank Abbott**. During Abbott's woefully dismal return to the cage early in the **Zuffa** era, he was fed to a number of rising prospects. When he fell to Correira at UFC 45, the Hawaiian did his trademark cabbage patch dance. Abbott's entourage was incensed and a near riot ensued in the cage.

Abbott had his revenge almost two years later on Correira's home turf in Hawaii's Blaisdell Arena. This time a huge Abbott right hand knocked Correira cold. After five years of taking punishment, Cabbage's chin had taken all it could handle. He's still a staple on the local scene, but after losing a bout with **Antonio Silva** for **EliteXC** in 2007, Cabbage's days as a national level performer may be over.

Côté, Patrick

Nickname: The Predator **Height:** 5'11"

Weight: 185 lbs **Born:** 2/29/80

Debut: UCC Proving Ground 8 (11/3/02)

Career Record: 13-6

Notable Wins: Kendall Grove (UFC 74); Ricardo Almeida (UFC 86)

Notable Losses: Tito Ortiz (UFC 50); Travis Lutter (*The Ultimate Fighter* 4 Finale); Anderson Silva (UFC 90)

A five-year Canadian Army veteran who served in Bosnia, Patrick Côté has a little bit of everything in his fighting background. **Judo**, **boxing**, **Muay Thai**,

wrestling, **Brazilian Jiu-jitsu** — Côté has done it all. But his success as a mixed martial artist boils down to two factors: his toughness and his big right hand.

Côté stepped into the cage on a mere four days' notice to make his **UFC** debut against **Tito Ortiz**, who was just two fights removed from a three-and-a-half-year light heavyweight title reign. To say Côté was out of his depth in only his sixth professional fight would be an understatement, but to his immense credit Côté kept coming forward and went the distance in a match he had no business even being a part of. Despite this promising first showing, success at the UFC level eluded Côté, who seemed more at home in second-tier organizations against more modest opposition.

Côté was selected as a competitor on "The Comeback" fourth season of ***The Ultimate Fighter***. Although he dropped the tournament final to submission expert Travis Lutter, Côté earned a spot in the UFC with his strong showing throughout the series, and a four-fight winning streak saw Côté emerge as a title contender in the company's slightly thin middleweight division. Côté managed to take a listless **Anderson Silva** into the third round for the first time in Silva's UFC career, but Côté's night ended early when he blew out his right knee throwing a kick. The fight was an unmitigated disaster. Was Silva bored, uninterested in the bout? Or was he overly cautious of the power in Côté's right hand? Côté, of course, likes his chances in a rematch, should it ever happen. But who would watch it?

Couture, Randy

Nickname: The Natural, Captain America **Height:** 6'1"
Weight: 205–225 lbs **Born:** 6/22/63
Debut: UFC 13 (5/30/97) **Career Record:** 18–10
Notable Wins: Vitor Belfort (UFC 15, UFC 49); Maurice Smith (UFC 15.5); Pedro Rizzo (UFC 31, UFC 34); Chuck Liddell (UFC 43); Tito Ortiz (UFC 44); Tim Sylvia (UFC 68); Mark Coleman (UFC 109)
Notable Losses: Enson Inoue (Vale Tudo Japan 98); Josh Barnett (UFC 36); Ricco Rodriguez (UFC 39); Vitor Belfort (UFC 46); Chuck Liddell (UFC 52, UFC 57); Brock Lesnar (UFC 91); Antonio Rodrigo Nogueira (UFC 102)

Randy Couture is MMA's living legend. He's defied size, strength, and the ravages of time to inspire fans and fellow fighters alike. Even a cynical comedian like **UFC** color commentator **Joe Rogan** can't help but look on in wonder, a tear in his eye, and say, "That man is my hero."

Couture is the perpetual underdog. At every step of his UFC career he's been expected to lose. At every opportunity he defies those expectations. It started at UFC 15. After winning the UFC 13 tournament, Couture was brought back specifically to be fed to the sharks, in this case, "The Phenom" **Vitor Belfort.**

Belfort was the UFC's darling, a young, handsome, and outrageously muscular fighter who ended his fights with lightning fast punches. He was their dream UFC champion and the promotion expected him to easily run through the 34-year-old wrestler on his way to a title shot.

Instead, Couture used what had just been a few weeks' worth of Army **boxing** training he had at Fort Rucker, Alabama, to confuse and disorient Belfort. Combining his Greco-Roman **wrestling clinch** with his short rabbit punches, Couture took advantage of what would become his trademark style: dirty boxing.

A two-time NCAA wrestling runner-up at Oklahoma State and twice an Olympic alternate, Couture could control almost any man alive in the clinch position. It turns out adding punches into the mix only made his wrestling more effective. In his next bout, just the fourth of his MMA career, Couture became the UFC heavyweight champion, defeating kickboxer **Maurice Smith** — who would later become Couture's standup trainer — in a grueling decision win at UFC Japan.

Couture was rising in stature as the UFC was sinking nearer and nearer bankruptcy. The company simply couldn't afford to pay Couture the $80,000 they had promised him. Rather than take a drastic pay cut and defend his newly won title, Couture walked away. He had a surprisingly unsuccessful tenure in Japan, losing three times by submission and never really impressing in his three decision wins.

Three years after being stripped of the title, Couture received a call from then–UFC matchmaker **John Perretti**, offering him an opportunity to come back and fight for the title against fellow wrestler **Kevin Randleman.** For a purse of $85,000, Couture agreed to step into the Octagon once again. His next contract dispute would be for much higher stakes.

Couture's win over Randleman was a turning point in many ways for the entire sport. UFC 28 was the first UFC event sanctioned by the state of New Jersey and the sport was still very much on provisional status. When the Commissioner of the New Jersey State Athletic Control Board Larry Hazzard saw Randleman and Couture, two NCAA All-Americans and world-class athletes, it did more than anyone had imagined to convince him that MMA was a real sport and much more than a bar room scuffle. As always, Couture was the perfect ambassador for the sport of MMA.

This time, Couture stuck around long enough to defend his title. After two great fights (and two wins) over perennial contender Pedro Rizzo, Couture ran into a big problem — literally. He had wrestled in college at 190 pounds and was succeeding in MMA's heavyweight division at a relatively lithe 220 pounds. This was fine against kickboxers like Smith and Rizzo or even a wrestler like Randleman who was starting from an even smaller base than he was. Against giants like **Josh Barnett** and **Ricco Rodriguez**, it was a major problem. Couture held his own against both men, but when the lesser (with the exception of girth) fighters got on top of him, there was little he could do. He lost his heavyweight crown to Barnett, regained it when Barnett subsequently tested positive for **steroids**, and then immediately lost it again to Rodriguez.

At a crossroads, Couture made the decision to drop down to 205 pounds where **Tito Ortiz** was the longtime kingpin of a talent-stacked division. Because of Tito's refusal to fight his former training partner **Chuck Liddell** (actually an extended contract renegotiation between Ortiz and the UFC) Couture's first fight at light heavyweight would be against Liddell and would be for the interim title. Liddell was close friends with UFC President **Dana White**, who saw Couture as simply a stepping-stone to get the title into Liddell's hands.

"The Iceman" Liddell had the mega-star entrance, complete with a light show, unheard of in a promotion that had been pinching pennies for years, a

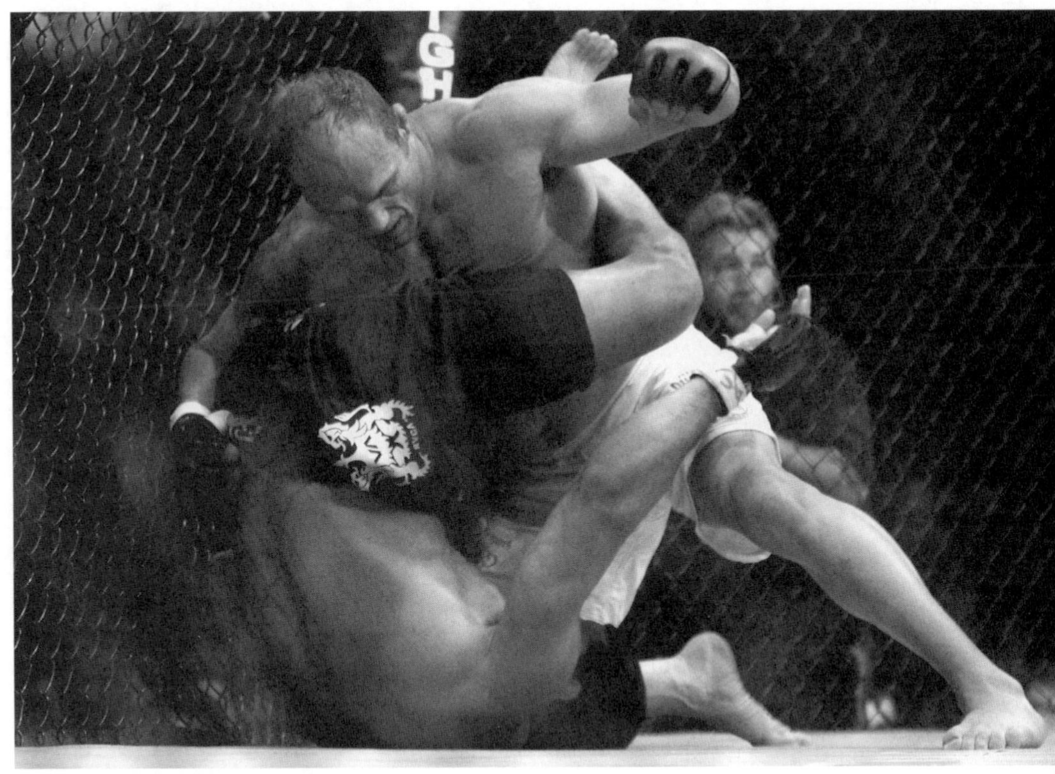

spectacle straight out of pro wrestling that included a special remixed version of Vanilla Ice's "Ice, Ice Baby." Then Couture beat him at his own game, keeping the dangerous knockout puncher off balance with his own standup attack before taking him down and forcing a stoppage in the third round. Just weeks before his fortieth birthday, Couture was again the champion of the world. Or at least the interim champion; he solidified his claim against a returning Ortiz, literally spanking MMA's bad boy on his way to a five-round decision.

After trading the title with his old nemesis Vitor Belfort, Couture was part of another seismic shift in the MMA landscape. UFC landed a spot on cable television, a reality television show called ***The Ultimate Fighter.*** Couture and Liddell were the coaches. Not only would the show offer two lucky fighters a six-figure UFC contract, but it would also build up a huge rematch between Couture and Liddell. **Zuffa** officials were confident that weeks of television would leave viewers hungry to see the two coaches square off. It was a brilliant concept and brilliant execution. The rematch at UFC 52 was the promotion's most lucrative show ever, both at the box office and on pay-per-view. This time Liddell came out on top with a first round knockout. He won

In Their Own Words: Randy Couture on why losing can be a good thing

"If the worst thing that happens to you is you lose a fight, you're doing pretty damn good. I don't see that as a negative. It's all part of a learning and growing process. I think the adversity of losing that fight is going to be very important in your development as a fighter. I know from my own experience that the fights that I've lost were very important to me. If I could go back and change them, I don't think I would. I think I learned more and became a better person and a better athlete for having experienced those things."

the rubber match at UFC 57 as well, again by knockout, and Couture announced his retirement in the cage.

Like many retirements in combat sports, it didn't stick. One year later, Couture was back in the cage and back in the heavyweight division. Months after the release of *Rocky Balboa*, a movie that saw a middle-aged Sylvester Stallone come back to challenge the heavyweight champion, Couture lived out the film's plotline in his real life. Even the fictional movie didn't want to strain credibility with the viewers — the writers just had Rocky surviving the fight, hanging in valiantly and losing a decision. The 43-year-old Couture wasn't limited by what would seem plausible. He went out and took the title from **Tim Sylvia**, winning all five rounds, the fans standing and cheering voraciously throughout.

It *was* the perfect ending to a storybook career. Or should have been. Instead, after winning a title defense against **Gabriel Gonzaga**, Couture entered into an extended contract dispute with the UFC. When the company couldn't come to terms with **Fedor Emelianenko**, Couture's heavyweight counterpart in the defunct **Pride** promotion, Couture wanted out. His time as a fighter was coming to an end and he wanted Fedor before he retired. A vicious battle took place, with dueling press conferences, unprecedented financial information leaked, and insults flying right and left.

Realizing the dispute could linger in the legal system for years, Couture went slinking back to the UFC. Now 45 years old, he didn't seem like the same fighter. He lost to **Brock Lesnar** at UFC 92 and dropped a decision at UFC 102 to **Antonio Rodrigo Nogueira** in his adopted hometown of Portland, Oregon. Again feeling outgunned as a heavyweight, he made the drop back down to 205 pounds. At 46, Couture shows no signs of slowing down. After UFC 102 he announced he had signed a new six-fight contract. The eternal warrior will continue to fight until he is 48 years old — and perhaps beyond.

Cox, Monte

Monte Cox is a man of many hats. Working as a newspaper editor in the Quad Cities, Cox saw dollar signs when he went to his first MMA show. Soon he was promoting his own events, the popular **Extreme Challenge** shows where, in his own words, he "made out like a motherfucking bandit." Before long, he left the newspaper business behind to make his living in the fight game.

Cox was more than the promoter of local events. He was also an agent, starting with local star **Pat Miletich** and expanding his business exponentially as a better and better class of athlete came to train with the **UFC** welterweight champion in Bettendorf, Iowa. Cox's multiple roles were handy for him and the fighters he had handshake deals with. (There were no contracts with Cox. If you didn't like how he was conducting business, you were free to leave.) As a promoter, he always had plenty of fighters to fill out his shows. Conversely, as a manager, he could always find his guys plenty of fights. Some would call this a conflict of interest — including the federal government, had the fights Cox was promoting been boxing instead of MMA — but his fighters never seem to complain about the arrangement.

Like everyone in the business, Cox suffered through the dark ages, as politicians and cable companies declared war on the sport. He weathered the storm very well. With his carny charm and connections in the state's boxing community, Cox was able to get MMA legalized in Iowa — Extreme Challenge was safe. He also had a special relationship with UFC matchmaker **John Perretti**, making sure his fighters always had a spot on the UFC cards. Cox has made a mint in the sport of MMA. He is a millionaire but maintains the loyalty of his cadre of fighters, who are generally not making big money, by being extremely generous. When **Jens Pulver** came to Iowa to train with Miletich, he lived for months with Cox at his home. A lot of Cox fighters have similar stories. Cox doesn't just sign existing stars; he builds them, helping their careers from the very beginning. Because of these relationships, Cox became MMA's first mega-agent. He controlled many of the sport's very best, including almost every fighter from the Midwest, like **Matt Hughes**, Pulver, and **Tim Sylvia**. In all, Cox has managed seven UFC champions.

In 2008, after years of being self-employed, Cox became the CEO of M-1 Global. Despite his wearing a suit for the first time in his life, the venture was an abject failure. Designed to promote M-1 fighter **Fedor Emelianenko**, the promotion fizzled when Fedor chose to fight with **EliteXC** instead. Like a cat, Cox landed smoothly on his feet. He quickly switched gears to promoting his own Adrenaline MMA, a slightly larger scale version of Extreme Challenge. And, of course, he still has his massive roster of fighters, making sure Cox will be involved in every promotion worldwide for the foreseeable future.

Cro Cop, Mirko

Real name: Mirko Filipovic | **Height:** 6'2"

Weight: 226 lbs | **Born:** 9/10/74

Debut: K-1 Andy Hug Memorial (8/19/01) | **Career Record:** 37-7-2 (1 No Contest)

Notable Wins: Kazushi Sakuraba (Pride Shockwave 2002); Igor Vovchanchyn (Pride Final Conflict 2003); Josh Barnett (Pride 28, Pride 30, Pride Final Conflict Absolute); Kevin Randleman (Pride Shockwave 2004); Mark Coleman (Pride 29); Hidehiko Yoshida (Pride Critical Countdown Absolute); Wanderlei Silva (Pride Final Conflict 2009)

Notable Losses: Antonio Rodrigo Nogueira (Pride Final Conflict 2003); Kevin Randleman (Pride Total Elimination 2004); Fedor Emelianenko (Pride Final Conflict 2005); Mark Hunt (Pride Shockwave 2005); Gabriel Gonzaga (UFC 70)

"Right kick hospital, left kick cemetery." That's how former Croatian anti-terrorist police officer (hence "Cro Cop") Mirko Filipovic once described his game, and for a large portion of his career spent as the heavyweight division's most feared striker, it was bang-on. But championship gold eluded Cro Cop throughout much of his **Pride** tenure, and disaster struck in the **UFC** stint that followed it. As his career winds down, Mirko Cro Cop's legacy is largely one of unrealized potential — that, and a highlight reel filled with stomach-turning head kick knockouts.

Although far too many mixed martial artists are described as having "K-1-level striking," it's no exaggeration in the case of Mirko Cro Cop, who competed for Japan's premier kickboxing organization for years, earning wins over the likes of Jérôme Le Banner, Mike Bernardo, Peter Aerts, **Mark Hunt**, **Bob Sapp**, and Japanese star Akio "Musashi" Mori. Late in his K-1 run, however, Cro Cop began to transition to MMA, and debuted with a quick cut-stoppage win over iron-headed wrestler **Kazuyuki Fujita**. Professional wrestlers were common opponents for Cro Cop in the early days: add **Nobuhiko Takada**, Yuji Nagata, **Dos Caras Jr.**, and Yoshihisa Yamamoto to the list of cannon fodder Pride ran out there to help build their new star.

There was more serious competition, too. Stopping a luchador on strikes early in the first round is one thing; managing the same against the likes of **Heath Herring** and **Igor Vovchanchyn** is quite another. But Cro Cop made it all

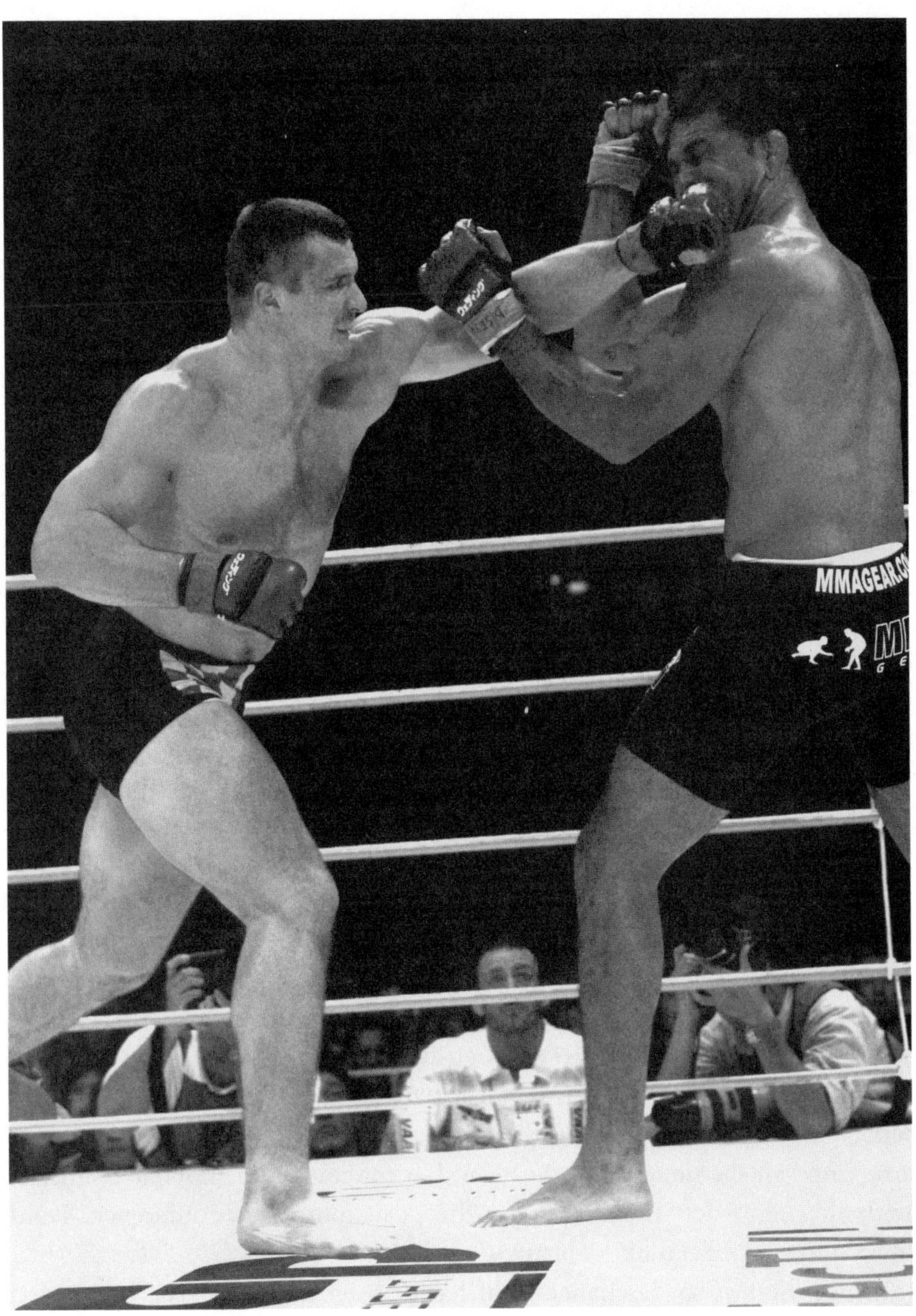

look easy with his thunderous kicks and top-notch takedown defense, a combination that set the standard for heavyweight **sprawl and brawl**. It proved too much for the always game but badly undersized **Kazushi Sakuraba**, who took on Cro Cop in a headlining match at Tokyo's massive National Stadium. Cro Cop left with the win. Sakuraba left with a fractured orbital bone.

When Cro Cop met the great **Antonio Rodrigo Nogueira** for the Pride interim heavyweight championship in 2003, it was yet another instance of the classic striker versus grappler matchup. Cro Cop easily evaded Nogueira's takedown attempts throughout the first round, and landed some horrific kicks to the body, all setting up a left head kick that connected an instant before the bell. Nogueira looked understandably dazed as he slowly rose to his feet and stumbled towards his corner. But Nogueira put Cro Cop on his back with his first takedown attempt of round two, and the striker looked like a fish out of water. Quickly mounted by the finest heavyweight submission artist the sport has ever seen, Cro Cop was caught in an **arm bar** as he turned to avoid a barrage of punches, and he signaled his submission in his first championship bout.

It was a setback, but there could be no shame or embarrassment in being tapped out by Antonio Rodrigo Nogueira. It was all part of the learning process, the slow transformation from kickboxer to true mixed martial artist. Under the tutelage of **Brazilian Jiu-jitsu** ace **Fabricio Werdum**, a refocused Cro Cop worked to improve his ground defense, to ready himself for his next title shot — which was surely just around the corner. A stunning upset loss to the wildly inconsistent **Kevin Randleman** in Pride's 2004 Grand Prix, however, put his title dreams on hold once again. Cro Cop would avenge that loss (by submission, if you can believe it) before the end of 2004 — a year in which he fought an impressive eight times. But the knockout loss to Randleman created doubts about Cro Cop's chin, which had previously been unassailable.

Cro Cop was deemed sufficiently rehabilitated for a second title shot after rattling off seven consecutive wins against opposition of varying quality. Pride put such promotional effort into their heavyweight knockout king that by the time he stepped into the ring to face **Fedor Emelianenko**, the unstoppable Russian almost seemed the underdog. But Emelianenko pressured Cro Cop throughout their three-round contest, backing him up, unloading with his wild, looping punches, and engaging in sporadic but effective **ground and pound**. Cro Cop lost the unanimous decision, but the few good shots he connected with that night left their mark: at the post-fight press conference, Fedor looked like he'd been hit by a truck.

Since the loss to Emelianenko, it hasn't been the same. The build-up to that second title challenge was exhilarating, but Cro Cop has never managed that kind of momentum since. He finally earned his first major mixed martial arts title with a victory in Pride's 2006 Open Weight Grand Prix, and while that is hardly an achievement to be scoffed at, you can't help but look at his road to the title with a slightly raised eyebrow. First, there was **Ikuhisa Minowa**, an entertaining but middling middleweight. Then, the ancient and *really* fat **Hidehiko Yoshida**, whose famously awful knees couldn't withstand the barrage of leg kicks Cro Cop had in store. In the same night, Cro Cop put away the smaller but, of course, ferocious **Wanderlei Silva** with a devastating head kick, and **Josh Barnett**, who had just gone the distance with Nogueira. Cro Cop had decided to retire if he came up short in the Open Weight Grand Prix, and his tournament win has to be counted as a victory over self if nothing else, but surely it was cold consolation after coming up short against Emelianenko for the real prize.

After the demise of Pride, the UFC unsurprisingly came calling. But Cro Cop's UFC career has been nothing short of disastrous. After a tune-up fight against poor Eddie Sanchez, Cro Cop was knocked out — by a head kick, no less — by **Gabriel Gonzaga** in a fight that destroyed his mystique permanently. Bouncing back and forth between the UFC and **Dream**, Cro Cop now wins some and loses some. But the time when the most feared heavyweight striker on the planet was, incongruously, the same man who came to the ring to the strains of Duran Duran is long gone.

Cruz, Dominick

Nickname: Dominator
Height: 5'8"
Weight: 135 lbs
Born: 9/3/85
Debut: Rage in the Cage 67 (1/29/05)
Career Record: 15-1
Notable Wins: Joseph Benavidez (WEC 42); Brian Bowles (WEC 47)
Notable Loss: Urijah Faber (WEC 26)

The reigning WEC bantamweight champion is one of the most unique fighters in the sport. He's perhaps the fastest fighter in the game, and in a sport filled with guys content to swing wildly, Cruz focuses on not getting hit. He isn't

In Their Own Words: Dominick Cruz on his fighting style

"I always wanted to have a style that would catch someone's eye. There's so many good fighters and you have to stand out some way. My outlook on this is that we're wearing four-ounce gloves, and four ounce gloves aren't very forgiving. So my mindset is to get hit as little as possible.

I thought if I don't get hit at all in a fight, how can I lose? I decided to make my feet as fast as I could and make my footwork ridiculous because Muhammad Ali always preached about it, so it's got to work."

afraid to move backward, feint, and pitter-patter his way to victory with lots of fast and accurate punches.

The title win over Bowles was textbook Cruz. He faked kicks, teased Bowles by sticking his head forward, then cracked counter punches when Bowles came forward swinging wildly. Cruz's footwork is unique, a combination of meth head's herky-jerkiness and Bruce Lee's kung fu wizardry. It was enough to confuse Bowles and will likely cause Cruz opponents fits for years to come.

Cummo, Luke

Nickname: The Silent Assassin
Height: 6′
Weight: 170 lbs
Born: 4/27/80
Debut: Ring of Combat 1 (10/12/02)
Career Record: 6-6

In Their Own Words: Luke Cummo on the *Ultimate Fighter* experience

"I won't lie and say it was peaches and cream the whole time we were there. Six weeks with no outside contact got pretty rough at times and I missed my friends and family a lot. I'm the type of person that thrives under a strict regimen. The times when I get into trouble are after fights when I have nothing to do except play video games and eat junk food. The public got a glimpse of this after my bout against Anthony Torres when I ate myself into a food coma.

"On the show we trained twice a day almost every day. We were there for one reason and that was to fight. As a fighter, that was the best environment for me to practice and get better. I really improved mentally and physically while training on *TUF* 2. All we did was sleep, train, and eat. When people go to Thailand to train [in] **boxing** or Brazil for jiu-jitsu, that is what they do. You can get a lot of experience in a condensed amount of time. We also had some great coaches like Ganyao Fairtex, Peter Welch, Mark Laimon, and Matt Hughes brought in **Jeremy Horn** who is amazing.

"As for being picked last, I didn't need any more motivation than having to fight. I know that someone somewhere is training with every ounce of energy that they have, and their ultimate goal is to kick my ass. That is my motivation and it's something that comes from the deepest region of my brain. It's similar to 'fight or flight,' except that strategy comes into play when competing in sport."

Notable Win: Josh Haynes (UFC 69)

Notable Loss: Joe Stevenson (*The Ultimate Fighter* 2 Finale)

Luke Cummo dresses like a ninja before his fights. Luke Cummo reads comic books, wears glasses, and looks like a bully's wet dream. Luke Cummo also kicks plenty of ass.

Cummo, a **Matt Serra** student, was the last fighter picked during the second season of ***The Ultimate Fighter*** reality show. That ended up being a huge mistake for coaches **Matt Hughes** and **Rich Franklin**, as Cummo proved everyone wrong, making it to the *TUF* 2 finale. He did more than just show up for that fight too; he gave the favored **Joe Stevenson** all he could handle.

His post-*TUF* career is significant mostly because of the revelation that he drinks his own urine. Cummo believes that recycling his urine allows hormones and minerals a second chance to arrive at their destination in the body. This unusual diet hasn't helped Cummo achieve a winning record in the Octagon, but has secured his place as one of MMA's world-class weirdos.

Danzig, Mac

Height: 5'8"
Weight: 155 lbs
Born: 1/2/80
Debut: Extreme Challenge Trials (10/7/01)
Career Record: 19-8-1
Notable Win: Tommy Speer (*The Ultimate Fighter* 6 Finale)
Notable Loss: Hayato Sakurai (Pride 33)

When the sixth season of ***The Ultimate Fighter*** began, it looked as though the field consisted of former **King of the Cage** lightweight champ Mac Danzig . . . and then everybody else. Sure, Danzig hadn't looked great losing his title to Clay French (albeit by split decision), and he looked worse getting tossed around the **Pride** ring by the bigger, better, and more experienced **Hayato Sakurai**, but he didn't need to be better than Sakurai to win a **UFC** contract. He needed to be better than such luminaries as Richie "The Dirty Samurai" Hightower and the man who would come to be known simply, if inexplicably, as **War Machine**. Danzig kept his distance from the usual *TUF* shenanigans and pranks, and seemed to approach the competition with an air of confidence that bordered on a sense of superiority. And Danzig did indeed prove superior, living up to his reputation as a stand-out grappler by breezing through the tournament with four first-round submission wins. He has found little success in the UFC since, however, with only a win over Marc Bocek to show against tough losses to **Clay Guida** and Josh Neer. An outspoken vegan, Danzig became the first professional mixed martial artist to appear in a PETA print ad.

D'Arce: see **Arm triangle**

Davie, Art

Art Davie is the man behind XARM, a hybrid combat sport that he describes as a combination of "the best of hard-core arm wrestling, kickboxing, and jiu-jitsu." Nuts and gum, together at last! Fortunately for everybody, Davie

dogged — largely unfairly — by a reputation for stopping fights prematurely. In a sport that carries with it the risk of serious, life-altering injury, it's obviously better to err on the side of caution, and take the chance of stopping fights a little too early rather than too late (see **Mazzagatti, Steve**). But it's a fine line.

Dean came under fire for his role in the **UFC** 61 meeting between **Tito Ortiz** and **Ken Shamrock**. The enormously successful third season of ***The Ultimate Fighter*** built up the rematch between these old rivals for months, and many were understandably disappointed to see the fight stopped only 1:18 into the first round. Ortiz delivered five unanswered, unopposed elbows from inside Shamrock's **guard**, and Dean decided he had seen enough of the obvious mismatch. But Shamrock jumped to his feet immediately, insisting he hadn't been in any real trouble, the fans felt cheated, and Dean was widely criticized for stepping in when he did.

Dean, however, defended his decision. "I believe he was unconscious," he later told **Sherdog**. "I think he was out with the first one. At that critical time, he was unable to defend himself. I was certain of that. I can't think of another reason to take five elbows without doing anything else." The Nevada State Athletic Commission supported the call, but the UFC responded to Shamrock's complaints and to general fan sentiment, airing a third and final Shamrock/Ortiz bout live on Spike TV. This result was virtually identical, with referee **John McCarthy** calling a stop to the match after a half-dozen unanswered punches from Shamrock's guard in 2:23. You can take that as vindication of Dean's stoppage in their second fight, or you can consider it completely unrelated. Either way, Dean is unconcerned. "I'm going to have to make calls that people aren't going to be happy about," he told Sherdog. "That's my job. I can't do what everyone else wants. It's my conscience."

Dean's finest moment in the Octagon came in another bout that appeared, at least at first glance, to be stopped too soon. When **Frank Mir** started working an **arm bar** on **Tim Sylvia** in their UFC 41 title fight, something didn't quite look right. Sylvia's arm wasn't completely extended, and his elbow wasn't quite past Mir's hips — the usual fulcrum over which an arm is extended in an arm bar — but Herb Dean rushed in to stop the match as the fighters continued to struggle. "Oh, shit!" Dean exclaimed, "Stop! Stop! Stop! The fight is over!" Sylvia, in apparent disbelief, couldn't understand why the fight had been stopped. "It's fucking *broken*," Dean explained. "Your arm is broken." Dean was right: Sylvia had suffered a serious injury. But Sylvia initially denied it, and until the replays ran, no one in the arena beside the three men in the ring had any idea what had happened. The crowd was livid.

But regardless of what the crowd wants to see, a good referee is going to stop the fight when he sees what he needs to see. And when it's Herb Dean in the cage, it's almost always going to be the right call.

Deep/ZST

At first glance, the partnership between second-tier Japanese promotions Deep and ZST ("Zest") might not seem particularly significant. On the surface, it's two tiny organizations that run tiny shows in tiny halls — usually with tiny fighters — agreeing to share their talent and their modest promotional resources in a move with minimal impact on the broader world of MMA. But look a little closer, and you see that the Deep/ZST alliance has a lot to say about the state of the sport in Japan given the history of each promotion. And the history of each promotion is bound up in their respective in-ring rules.

ZST follows a unique set of rules focused on fast-paced action. To that end, it prohibits the closed **guard**, forcing bottom players to work a much more active open guard, and promotes tag team bouts, which, while intriguing in theory, are somewhat less so in practice. Just as strangely — ok, *almost* as strangely — ZST makes gloves optional and bans strikes to the head on the ground. It's this last rule that helps tell the tale. ZST operates largely in the tradition of **Akira Maeda**'s pioneering **Rings**, and serves as a kind of proving ground for fighters on their way to the high-profile K-1 organization's **Hero's** brand, which operated under Maeda's direction.

Deep, on the other hand, with its more aggressive rules calling for soccer kicks and stomps to a downed opponent, had an intimate relationship with **Pride**. The companies were in fact deeply intertwined: Deep President Shigeru Saeki also served as a public relations officer for Pride parent company Dream Stage Entertainment.

The partnership between Deep and ZST, then, mirrors the partnership between K-1 and former Pride executives that took shape in after the sale (or death, if you prefer) of Pride led to the formation of **Dream**. While MMA in North America continues to grow at a breakneck pace, the sport has fallen on hard times in Japan, and consolidation, rather than competition, has sometimes become an increasingly attractive option for the parties involved. And that appears to be as true of the Deeps and ZSTs of the world as it is on the level of the big-time players.

DeLaGrotte, Mark

Mark DeLaGrotte did more than walk down the street to his local **karate** dojo in his pursuit of martial arts perfection. He traveled all the way to Thailand and lived among the people, learning Thai fighting directly from the masters of the art. He studied under Kru Yodtong at the Sityodtong Boxing Camp. Not only did he learn the fight game, but the language as well, allowing him a deeper understanding of the Thais and their culture.

Returning home, DeLaGrotte opened up a satellite Sityodtong school in Boston where he helps bring the art of Thai boxing to the American people. Along the way, his ability to break down opposing fighters (and build up his own students) has attracted some top talent to his gym. Complete with his trademark hats and loud Boston accent, DeLaGrotte can be found in the corner of many New Englanders, dispensing advice, at times penetrating and keen, but often merely obscene. He was the kickboxing instructor for ***The Ultimate Fighter*** 4, but is probably best known for cornering top **UFC** fighters **Kenny Florian** and **Marcus Davis**.

DeSouza, Tony

Nickname: The Peruvian Savage **Height:** 6′

Weight: 170 lbs **Born:** 7/26/74

Debut: CFF: Cobra Classic 2000 (8/26/00)

Career Record: 10–4

Notable Wins: Luiz Azeredo (Meca World Vale Tudo 11); Dustin Hazelett (UFC: The Final Chapter)

Notable Losses: Jutaro Nakao (UFC 33); Thiago Alves (UFC 66)

Peruvian Tony DeSouza combines black-belt level **Brazilian Jiu-jitsu** with excellent **wrestling** and an even better beard. Viewers of ***The Ultimate Fighter*** will remember him as Team Penn's wrestling coach from the show's fifth season. When contestant Noah Thomas seemed to be taking his training too lightly, it was DeSouza's job to straighten him out on the mat. DeSouza's career as an active fighter seems to have come to a close following knockout losses to dangerous striker **Thiago Alves** and fellow grappler Roan Carneiro, but his influence is seen whenever a fighter employs the Peruvian necktie, a modified **guillotine choke** of DeSouza's invention. Tony DeSouza is *that* Peruvian.

Diabate, Cyrille

Nickname: Snake | **Height:** 6′6″
Weight: 205 lbs | **Born:** 6/10/73
Debut: Golden Trophy 1999 (3/20/99) | **Career Record:** 16-6-1
Notable Wins: Bob Schrijber (2H2H 5); James Zikic (EF 1)
Notable Losses: Renato Sobral (Cage Rage 9); Mauricio Rua (Pride Final Conflict Absolute)

Cyrille Diabate is perhaps the toughest man in all of France. Although that may sound like damning him with faint praise, Diabate is plenty tough. He has the perfect kickboxer's frame. He's tall and wiry and his elbows seem unusually sharp. When the fight remains standing, he's a threat to anyone in the world at 205 pounds. It's when the fight goes to the ground that things get a little dicey.

Diabate had his highest profile fight for Pride in 2006, when he was stomped out by an in-his-prime **Mauricio Rua**. Since then it's been smaller fish on smaller shows, but a stint as **Dan Henderson**'s striking coach on ***The Ultimate Fighter*** 9 got Diabate thinking about making his first appearance in the Octagon. At 36, it's now or never for the flashy Frenchman to make his mark at the highest level of the game.

Diaz, Nate

Height: 6′ | **Weight:** 155 lbs
Born: 4/16/85 | **Debut:** WEC 12 (10/21/04)
Career Record: 12-5
Notable Wins: Joe Hurley (WEC 21); Manvel Gamburyan (*The Ultimate Fighter* 5 Finale)
Notable Losses: Hermes Franca (WEC 24); Clay Guida (UFC 94); Joe Stevenson (*The Ultimate Fighter* 9 Finale)

In Their Own Words: Nate Diaz on his confrontation with Karo Parisyan during _The Ultimate Fighter_ 5

"I didn't like his attitude when he was on the show, man. He wasn't being very respectful. He kept touching me, grabbing my shoulder and fucking slapping my back and shit. I was cool with him at first because I knew his cousin. But he doesn't know me. You just don't start touching people you don't know. He ain't my boy. So I was like, 'Bro, what the fuck are you doing? Don't fucking touch me.' And he said, 'Are you serious?' And I said, 'Hell yeah, I'm fucking serious.'

"That's when he tried to act all hard. On TV they didn't even show it all. Before that he was being disrespectful to **Jens** [**Pulver**]. He was clowning Jens a little bit when Jens is the coach. It's his thing. I know your cousin is there and he's fighting but you don't just walk in like you own the place."

Diaz was the winner of ***The Ultimate Fighter*** 5, but kind of by default. He was actually being controlled by judoka Manny Gamburyan until Gamburyan separated a previously injured shoulder and had to quit. It was not the strongest start to his **UFC** career, but Diaz made the best of it, winning his first four fights on his way towards fringe contender status.

Nate, like his brother **Nick Diaz**, brings a certain edge to the UFC that is often missing in shows filled with homogenous MMA fighters showing respect and expecting heated feuds to end in the cage with a smile and a handshake. To Diaz, things that happen in the cage are real. He doesn't believe in contrived feuds and fake smiles.

Diaz is just as willing to settle differences outside the cage, and what you see from him is always real, never put on for effect. Fans saw this attitude put into action when Diaz got into a shouting match with UFC welterweight star **Karo Parisyan** during the filming of *The Ultimate Fighter* 5. Parisyan was the established star, but Diaz refused to back down, ready and willing to fight him in front of the cameras and the world at the UFC Training Center. Combine this attitude with an exciting style that earned him three Fight of the Night bonuses and you have a fighter that **Zuffa** can count on to provide an exciting fight on any card.

After his early win streak that made many in the industry consider him a potential future champion, Diaz has settled towards the middle of the pack in the lightweight division. Consecutive losses to **Clay Guida** and **Joe Stevenson**, bigger wrestlers who held him down, moved Diaz from pay-per-view broadcasts back to Spike TV.

Diaz, Nick

Nickname: Bad Boy　　**Height:** 6′

Weight: 155-185 lbs　　**Born:** 8/2/83

Debut: IFC WC 15 (8/31/01)　　**Career Record:** 22-7-1

Notable Wins: Robbie Lawler (UFC 47); Frank Shamrock (Strikeforce: Shamrock vs. Diaz) Hayato Sakurai (Dream 14)

Notable Losses: Karo Parisyan (UFC 49); Diego Sanchez (*The Ultimate Fighter* 2 Finale); K.J. Noons (EliteXC: Renegade)

Nick Diaz is certifiable. Every fighter is a little crazy; it takes a certain kind of person just to step into the cage. Diaz, however, takes it to a new level. He was so upset by his loss to Joe Riggs at **UFC** 57 that he actually fought his opponent after the show just to set things straight. The catch? Both men had been taken to the hospital to recover from the grueling battle. The rematch went down in hospital gowns.

For any other fighter, that's a career defining moment. For Nick Diaz, it was just another fight. He once threw a shoe at **Diego Sanchez** prior to a fight, he taunted K.J. Noons and his family mercilessly during their feud, and he fought one of the world's best lightweights, **Takanori Gomi**, while stoned out of his mind on marijuana. Nothing Diaz could do would surprise MMA fans. He's unpredictable and that's a big part of his charm.

Diaz is more than just a goofy character. He's also a very good fighter. Diaz is a Cesar Gracie black belt who is competitive with anyone on the ground, but he uses those skills primarily as a deterrent from being taken down to the ground. Diaz prefers to stay standing, using his **boxing** prowess to win fights. It's an unusual style, especially for MMA, where many fighters try to take advantage of the smaller four-ounce gloves to throw nothing but

> ***In Their Own Words:* Joe Riggs on his hospital fight with Nick Diaz**
>
> "It wasn't too much of a fight inside the hospital. He actually did hit me, and I dropped to my knees in the hospital. But then I got up, and we were running around. We were like over and under hooks, and we were rabbit punching each other in the back of the head. He was . . . toe-stomping me, trying to bite me, and I was worried more about my IV coming out, to be honest with you. It was weird, but it turned out all right."
>
> Interview courtesy of Insidefights.com

haymakers. Diaz takes a different route, throwing punches in volume and pitter-pattering away with a lot of jabs and short shots. He almost never puts everything into a single punch, instead counting on sheer numbers to overwhelm his opponents.

The result is often a compelling, fan-friendly fight. Diaz has been in some of the most exciting fights in MMA history, including action-packed contests with Sanchez, **Karo Parisyan**, and Gomi.

Diaz is also a regular and vocal marijuana advocate. He has a medical marijuana card and legally smokes weed in California. What is legal in a court of law, however, is not legal in a prizefight. Diaz had his biggest career win, over Gomi, turned into a no contest after testing positive for marijuana. He also had to remove himself from an August 2009 **Strikeforce** fight with Jay Hieron for the company's welterweight title when the state of California demanded he take a drug test on short notice. Soon after, Diaz announced his intention to box professionally, to test his standup skills against a better breed of striker.

Dos Caras Jr.

Real name: Alberto Rodriguez II **Height:** 6′4″
Weight: 220 lbs **Born:** 5/25/77
Debut: Deep 2nd Impact (8/18/01) **Career Record:** 7-4
Notable Win: Kengo Watanabe (Deep 2nd Impact)
Notable Loss: Mirko Cro Cop (Pride Bushido 1)

Alberto Rodriguez II was born to be a wrestler. It runs in his blood. His father and uncle are two of Mexico's all-time best and he was guaranteed success based on his pedigree alone. Of course, his father and uncle were never Olympic standouts or NCAA champions. They are professional wrestlers, better known to **wrestling** fans on three continents as Dos Caras and Mil Mascaras. Rodriguez is wrestling royalty, but before he turned pro and joined the family business, he wanted to test himself on the amateur circuit.

Success quickly followed. At 6'4" and a chiseled 215 pounds, Rodriguez was good enough to join the Mexican national wrestling team and do well in international competition. The main American competition in his weight class was future **UFC** champion **Randy Couture**. Rodriguez was a shoo-in for the Olympic team in the 2000 Sydney Olympic Games, but Mexico decided not to field a team. Instead, Rodriguez turned pro, becoming the masked sensation Dos Caras Jr.

Despite his legendary family, Dos Caras Jr. didn't immediately click as a pro wrestler, lacking that innate charisma possessed by the great ones. His name did open some doors in Japan where promoters wanted him to try his hand at MMA, fast surpassing **pro wrestling** as a spectator event in that country. Dos Caras Jr. (wearing a modified lucha libre mask) made his MMA debut for **Deep** in 2001, beating highly touted **Pancrase** prospect Kengo Watanabe with a suplex that broke the Japanese fighter's arm.

Caras Jr. continued against a comical collection of pro wrestling castoffs in Deep before being thrown to the wolves in his **Pride** debut. With two weeks' notice he fought the most feared heavyweight in the world — knockout artist **Mirko Cro Cop**. He wanted to take his mask off for this fight, but promoters thought it would be a better visual to leave it on. His impaired vision cost him. Cro Cop's legendary left leg ended Dos Caras Jr.'s night in less than a minute.

Dos Caras Jr.'s career as a serious martial artist was over after a subsequent loss to journeyman **Kazuhiro Nakumura**. He still dabbles in the occasional MMA match, but his day job as a pro wrestling main eventer keeps him plenty busy.

dos Santos, Junior

Nickname: Cigano | **Height:** 6'4"

Weight: 235 lbs | **Born:** 9/12/84

Debut: 7/16/06 | **Career Record:** 11-1

Notable Wins: Fabrico Werdum (UFC 90); Mirko Filopovic (UFC 103); Gilbert Yvel (UFC 108); Gabriel Gonzaga (UFC Live: Vera vs. Jones)

Notable Loss: Joaquim Ferreira (MTL-Final)

While explosive wrestlers like **Cain Velasquez** and **Shane Carwin** get all the attention, Junior dos Santos quietly lurks, waiting for his opportunity at the **UFC** heavyweight title. It's interesting that dos Santos has been able to fly under the radar. After all, heavyweights with knockout power tend to attract

> **_In Their Own Words:_ Dana White on Junior dos Santos**
>
> "Dos Santos came bursting onto the scene. He's done some big things. He's an exciting fighter. He trains with Nogueira. He could have gone in their and shot and tried to take (fights) to the ground. He didn't. He stood toe-to-toe with **Mirko Cro Cop** and tried to knock him out. And eventually he did. He's an exciting fighter and I'm really excited about our heavyweight division right now."

the eye. But dos Santos is as quiet and as mild mannered as a church mouse, so despite five knockouts in five UFC fights, he hasn't yet developed a significant fan following. That will no doubt change as he adds bigger and bigger names to his hit list.

A student of **Antonio Rodrigo Nogueira**, dos Santos is alleged to have outstanding skills on the ground. No one has seen them in the Octagon yet though, as a powerful jab and a steady diet of strikers have allowed him to keep the fights standing. That won't be the case when he faces some of the division's top wrestlers. For all his boxing prowess, Cigano's career arc will depend on how well he defends takedowns and how well he defends off his back. In a real sense, dos Santos will be only as good as his grappling allows him to be.

Double wrist lock: see **Kimura and Americana**

Dream

The death of **Pride** was a serious disappointment for fans of Japanese MMA, especially the way it just sort of fizzled out with the lackluster Pride 34: Kamikaze card headlined by **Jeff Monson** and **Kazuyuki Fujita**. It hardly seemed a fitting end to a promotion that had staged many of the most spectacular events the sport had seen. Fortunately, a proper send-off was just around the corner, as former Pride executives collaborated with Fighting Entertainment Group (FEG), the company behind K-1 and **Hero's**, to promote Yarennoka!!, a New Year's Eve 2007 card in the best tradition of Japanese year-end blowouts. Pride's welterweight Grand Prix champion **Kazuo Misaki** took on Hero's villain **Yoshihiro Akiyama** in an incredibly heated contest, submission ace **Shinya Aoki** faced debuting Korean **judo Olympian** Jung Bu-Kyung, and **Fedor Emelianenko** squared off against Hong-Man Choi in a meaningless freak show match. *This* was more like it.

Six weeks later, FEG announced that Hero's was finished, and "the great dream alliance" that produced Yarennoka!! would continue its collaboration under the name Dream. The optimism was palpable at a press conference that featured every significant Japanese fighter who had been a part of either Hero's or Pride. But Dream has had a hard time maintaining their early momentum, and shaky television ratings have left Tokyo Broadcasting System executives unimpressed. Through their first two years of existence, Dream has been touch and go.

The promotion has embraced links with American organizations, first **EliteXC** and then **Strikeforce**. They've maintained the Japanese mania for the Grand Prix, whether featherweight, lightweight, welterweight, middleweight, or Super Hulk (see: **Canseco, Jose**). Their first 11 events all featured tournament bouts of one kind or another. And then things got weird. As though conceding that the **UFC**'s vision of the sport was the only viable way forward, Dream abandoned years of Pride and Hero's tradition by discarding the ring in favor of a hexagonal cage, and moved to a system of three five-minute rounds, rather than the ten-five-five split familiar from Pride. What's next, a ban on soccer kicks?

Despite Dream's best efforts, Japanese interest in the sport has cooled considerably from Pride's peak, and it doesn't look set to rebound any time soon. Although Dream looked destined to emerge as a power to rival the UFC at the time of its formation, just two years later that seems impossible.

Edgar, Frankie

Nickname: The Answer **Height:** 5'6"

Weight: 155 lbs **Born:** 10/16/81

Debut: Ring of Combat 9 (10/29/05) **Career Record:** 12-1

Notable Wins: Sean Sherk (UFC 98); B.J. Penn (UFC 112)

Notable Loss: Gray Maynard (UFC Fight Night 13)

It was one of the biggest upsets in **UFC** history. Frankie Edgar was small, often encouraged by the UFC brass to cut down to 145 pounds and try his hand at competing in the **WEC**'s featherweight division. He lacked one-punch knockout power. And there was no way he was going to take down and submit the legendary **B.J. Penn**. In short, Edgar winning the UFC lightweight title was next to impossible. Odds makers agreed; Edgar was a +600 underdog. That means a $100 bet on Edgar would have scored a brave soul $600 if they had the courage to wager on Edgar in his UFC 112 title challenge. Of course, fights aren't won or lost in the sportsbook. That only happens in the Octagon, where Edgar out-hustled, out-boxed, and out-worked Penn on his way to a unanimous decision.

Frankie Edgar may be the UFC's most improbable champion ever. He wasn't even considered a good enough prospect to make it onto ***The Ultimate Fighter*** reality show. **Dana White** and UFC Vice President **Joe Silva** auditioned him, but he didn't make the cut, though other natural 155-pound fighters like **Kenny Florian** and **Diego Sanchez** appeared on the show. Silva saw enough in him to bring him into the fold, but it was no easy path to the title. In his first Octagon appearance, Edgar survived a deep and dangerous **Tyson Griffin knee bar** on his way to a decision win.

It was one of three Fight of the Night performances for Edgar, who combined an expanding striking game with his collegiate-level **wrestling**. His only setback was a decision loss to Gray Maynard in 2008, but Edgar rebounded with convincing wins over **Hermes Franca** and **Sean Sherk** on his way to a title

> ***In Their Own Words:* Frankie Edgar on refusing to tap to Tyson Griffin**
>
> "I didn't think about it then. I felt I was up on the judge's score cards and knew there wasn't a lot of time left. That isn't to say I would never tap, but I was willing to let him pop my knee out, to give that up, to get the 'W.'
>
> "Would I ever tap? I don't know, man. Right now I can say yes. For sure I would. But in the middle of a fight with all the adrenaline? I'm a pretty competitive person. I guess we'd have to find out. Hopefully we never will."

shot. Clean-cut and personable, Edgar became the second fighter signed by **Georges St. Pierre**'s agent Shari Spencer. With a championship reign to his credit, Edgar is now on his way to GSP-level success. With Spencer at his side, he could be on his way to GSP-level endorsement opportunities as well.

Edwards, Yves

Nickname: The Texas Gunslinger **Height:** 5'10"

Weight: 155 lbs **Born:** 8/30/76

Debut: WPC 1 (10/26/97) **Career Record:** 37-16-1

Notable Wins: Aaron Riley (HOOKnSHOOT: Showdown); Hermes Franca (UFC 47); Josh Thomson (UFC 49)

Notable Losses: Rumina Sato (SuperBrawl 17); Caol Uno (UFC 37); Joachim Hansen (Pride Bushido 9); K.J. Noons (EliteXC: Return of the King)

The inventor of Thugjitsu, Houston's Yves Edwards is one of the fastest and most fluid strikers in MMA history. His early career included an amazing pair of fights with Aaron Riley for HOOKnSHOOT, fights so good they earned both men a shot at the **UFC**. He was the uncrowned UFC lightweight champion when the promotion had dropped the title, beating a series of tough opponents and culminating his run with one of the most memorable knockouts the sport had ever seen.

Holding Josh Thomson in a waist lock, Edwards shoved him forward. As Thomson spun around to face his opponent, Edwards's shin was right there waiting for him. It was a once in a lifetime knockout.

While his striking made him dangerous, it was his submissions that made him world-class. Early in his career, Japan's **Rumina Sato** submitted Edwards in just 18 seconds. This loss convinced Edwards to focus harder on his mat game, and by the time he was in his prime he was as likely to finish a fight with an **arm bar** as he was with a punch. In fact, of his 27 decisive wins, only 13 were by knockout. Fourteen were by submission, making Edwards a remarkably well-rounded fighter.

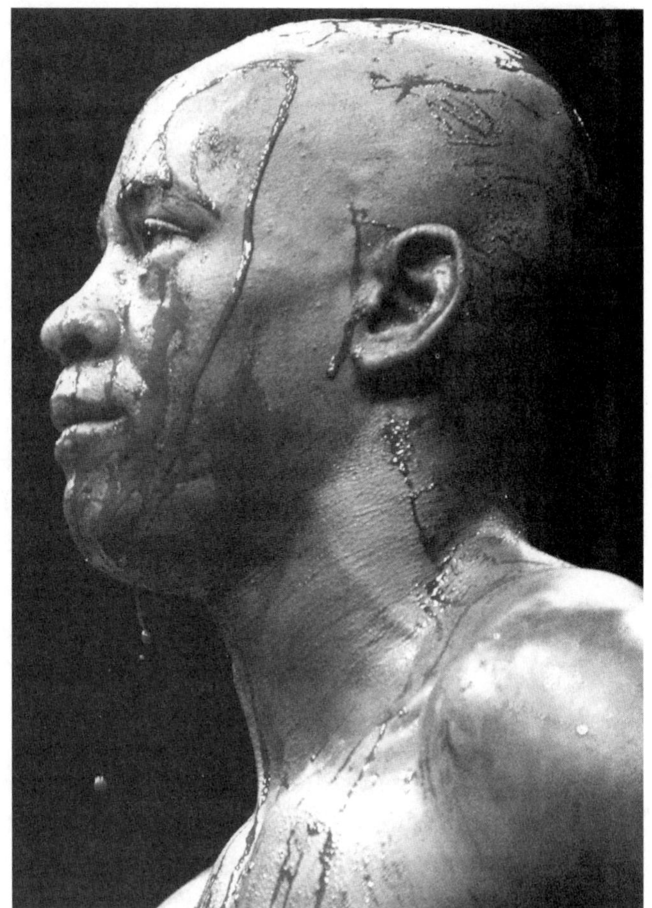

After so many grueling battles early in his career, Edwards struggled just as the sport started to grow. His fights were still entertaining, but more and more he was on the losing side of the docket. His fight with Norwegian juggernaut **Joachim Hansen** at **Pride** Bushido 9 seemed to drain him. Edwards lost six of his next ten and never again appeared to be a title contender.

Einemo, Jon Olav

Height: 6′6″ **Weight:** 225 lbs

Born: 12/10/75 **Debut:** Focus Fight Night 4 (10/6/00)

Career Record: 6–1

Notable Win: James Thompson (2H2H: Pride & Honor)

Notable Loss: Fabricio Werdum (Pride 31)

Jon Olav Einemo is one of Europe's top heavyweights, but he has never made a firm commitment to MMA. He's one of the very best grapplers in the world, winning the prestigious Abu Dhabi Combat Club grappling championship in 2003. However, that success hasn't translated to the top levels of MMA competition.

With Einemo, there are constant rumors. He is always about to sign with **UFC, Pride, Dream,** you name it. If there's a major promotion in the world, Einemo has been rumored to appear there. It almost never comes to fruition.

Injuries and a regular job have kept him from pursuing MMA as a vocation. As he approaches his mid-thirties, the time for Einemo is now or never. With the expansion of MMA in Europe just beginning, it seems likely that Einemo will find another opportunity to make a run at making fighting a career and not just a hobby.

EliteXC

In short, EliteXC was a disaster. Despite drawing more viewers for their top matches than any other promotion in U.S. television history, the company went out of business within two years of its founding, after piling up $55 million in losses. Start anywhere you'd like: the terrible deal with Showtime that meant the company lost money on every show it ever aired on the cable channel; the acquisition spree that saw them mindlessly snatch up four promotions and invest in a fifth (losing $18 million dollars on **Cage Rage** alone); the decision to build around a 30-something backyard brawler with no chin; or the allegations of fight fixing that helped to bring it all crashing down in the end. Any way you approach EliteXC, any angle you take, it all comes back to that single word: disaster.

The coup de grace came days after Heat, EliteXC's third and final Saturday night CBS event. After the wobbly eared **James Thompson** almost proved too much for EliteXC meal ticket **Kimbo Slice** in the company's network debut, a safer foe was needed. **Ken Shamrock** — a big name from the sport's early days who hadn't won in over four years — fit the bill perfectly. But at the eleventh hour, Shamrock decided to hold out for more money. When he was rebuffed, the famously short-fused Shamrock erupted and went too hard in a sparring session trying to blow off steam. He was cut and couldn't be medically cleared to fight. Kimbo needed an opponent, and the best EliteXC could come up with on such short notice was the workman-like **Seth Petruzelli**, a light heavyweight scheduled to compete on the undercard. In a video posted later that night on YouTube, **UFC** color man **Joe Rogan** called the fight as it happened, hanging out backstage at a comedy club in Atlanta. "Seth Petruzelli is fighting Kimbo Slice. This is a last-minute replacement. I gotta think Seth Petruzelli is gonna fuck him up. If I'm wrong, you'll never see this."

But we saw it, all right. Kimbo came dashing in and was floored by a weak jab thrown off one leg and pounded out in 14 seconds. As if this wasn't enough of a disaster for EliteXC, Petruzelli gave a radio interview two days later where things started to sound more than a little fishy: "The promoters kind of hinted to me and they gave me the money to stand and trade with him. They didn't want me to take him down. Let's just put it that way. It was worth my while to try and stand up and punch with him." If that was true, it was illegal. Although a Florida Department of Business and Professional Regulations investigation made no finding of wrongdoing, Petruzelli and EliteXC executives Jeremy Lappen, Gary Shaw, and Jared Shaw (a.k.a. rapper $kala on MySpace) couldn't seem to get their stories straight about what exactly was offered and why. In the end, it didn't matter. If EliteXC had tried to fix the fight, it hadn't worked anyway.

EliteXC died days later. **Strikeforce** scooped up a few worthwhile assets, including **Gina Carano**, the sport's biggest (and only) female star, and soon thereafter announced their own deal with both Showtime and CBS. You've got to think they'll have a better network run than EliteXC — if for no other reason than that things couldn't possibly go any worse.

Emelianenko, Aleksander

Nickname: The Grim Reaper
Height: 6'6"
Weight: 258 lbs
Born: 8/2/81
Debut: Pride Bushido 1 (10/5/03)
Career Record: 17-3
Notable Wins: Pawel Nastula (Pride Shockwave 2005); Sergei Kharitonov (Pride Final Conflict Absolute)
Notable Losses: Mirko Cro Cop (Pride Final Conflict 2004); Josh Barnett (Pride Total Elimination Absolute); Fabricio Werdum (2H2H: Pride & Honor)

Although he's not without his detractors, heavyweight legend **Fedor Emelianenko** is widely regarded as one of the classiest fighters in the game. His younger brother Aleksander, however, served the better part of a five-year sentence for armed robbery — he has the prison tattoos to prove it — and it's rumored that he was forced to withdraw from a scheduled **Affliction** bout against **Paul Buentello** after testing positive for hepatitis B in his pre-fight medical. None of that is particularly classy.

The hepatitis story is a strange one. While it has never been officially substantiated or confirmed by the California State Athletic Commission, Emelianenko has curiously confined himself — or been confined — to fighting in Russia ever since his Anaheim fight was called off only moments before the competitors were about to weigh in. Although the hepatitis story was widely reported, the CSAC would only say that Emelianenko failed to meet the medical standards for licensing. Emelianenko, for his part, denies that there was any problem at all with his test results, and claims that his removal from the Affliction card was simply a question of mishandled paperwork.

Since then, this heavy-handed **sambo** player has continued to hover just outside the heavyweight top ten. But with seemingly no one and nowhere to fight aside from second-rate opposition in second-tier promotions, it's hard to know what kind of future Emelianenko has in the sport. It's an unfortunate turn of events for a fighter who showed such promise from the moment he made his MMA debut in the **Pride** ring. Emelianenko is a finisher, with only two decisions in over 20 professional fights, and only three losses, all against absolutely first-rate competition. There's got to be a market for a heavyweight like that — if he's clean.

Emelianenko, Fedor

Nickname: The Last Emperor **Height:** 6′

Weight: 231 lbs **Born:** 9/28/76

Debut: Rings: Russia vs. Bulgaria (5/21/00)

Career Record: 32-2 (1 No Contest)

Notable Wins: Ricardo Arona (Rings: King of Kings 2000 Block B); Renato Sobral (Rings: 10th Anniversary); Heath Herring (Pride 23); Antonio Rodrigo Nogueira (Pride 25, Pride Shockwave 2004); Mark Coleman (Pride Total Elimination 2004, Pride 32); Kevin Randleman (Pride Critical Countdown 2004); Mirko Cro Cop (Pride Final Conflict 2005); Tim Sylvia (Affliction: Banned); Andrei Arlovski (Affliction: Day of Reckoning)

Notable Losses: Tsuyoshi Kohsaka (Rings: King of Kings 2000 Block B); Fabrico Werdum (Strikeforce: Fedor vs. Werdum)

Ask other professional mixed martial artists who they see as the top fighter in their sport, and Fedor Emelianenko's name comes up more often than any other. Dangerous from any position, in any phase of the fight, Emelianenko has dominated his division like none before him. With only one legitimate loss in over 30 fights, two frighteningly dominant performances against the great **Antonio Rodrigo Nogueira**, and decisive wins over five former **UFC** champions, there's no question the humble and soft-spoken Emelianenko is MMA's most accomplished heavyweight. Some, like UFC legend **Randy Couture**, have gone so far as to praise Emelianenko as the top pound-for-pound fighter in the world. But while Couture and Nogueira — both of whom join Emelianenko on the short list of the greatest heavyweight fighters to ever step into the ring or cage — continue to test themselves against top competition in the twilight of their careers, Emelianenko has chosen a different path. It's a path that has frustrated fans, potential opponents, and, not least of all, UFC President **Dana White**, who has tried and failed to land the biggest free-agent prize in the game on more than one occasion. Despite the millions of dollars White has put on

the table, Emelianenko has proven he has different priorities.

When he began his career, however, it was all about the money. After his stint in the Russian army, Emelianenko was broke and fought out of sheer necessity. He'd completed the requirements for the International Master of Sports distinctions in both **judo** and its uniquely Russian offshoot **sambo**, and had medaled in the Russian national judo championships and a pair of prestigious world cup events. Earning a spot on the Russian national team was the realization of a long-held dream, but it didn't provide Emelianenko with enough to support his young family. **Akira Maeda**'s **Rings** promotion did.

Emelianenko enjoyed considerable success in Rings, including wins over **Ricardo Arona** and **Renato Sobral**, despite competing under rules that limited his most dangerous offensive weapon — his unrivaled **ground and pound**. Emelianenko's time in Rings is most notable now, though, not for the ten matches he won, but for the lone match he lost. Seventeen seconds into the first round of his King of Kings tournament bout with rugged journeyman **Tsuyoshi Kohsaka**, Emelianenko was sliced open by an inadvertent but illegal elbow. The fight was stopped, and under a tournament format that precluded draws and no contests, "TK" was awarded the match. It would be ten years before Emelianenko would taste defeat again.

Two fights into his Pride career, Emelianenko made his presence felt. Although it can be difficult to recall a time when **Heath Herring** would be favored in a bout with Fedor Emelianenko, that's how it was when the two met to determine the number-one contender for Antonio Rodrigo Nogueira's **Pride** heavyweight title. Ten brutal minutes later, when the doctors stopped the fight, play-by-play man **Stephen Quadros** spoke for many of us when he said, "I don't know that I've ever seen a more destructive fighter on the ground." Emelianenko offered further evidence to support this claim when he pounded Pride's great champion from inside the **guard** for almost the entirety of their three-round fight. Nogueira, the sport's most skilled heavyweight submission artist, managed sweeps late in rounds one and two, and half-threatened with **triangle choke** and **omoplata** attempts. But Emelianenko, who holds no rank in **Brazilian Jiu-jitsu**, was never in any real danger as he teed off again and again, leaving a battered and disconsolate Nogueira in the arms of teammate **Mario Sperry** as they awaited the inevitable decision. A rematch ended disappointingly in a no contest on an accidental head butt, but their third encounter was as decisive as their first — and once again it fell in Fedor's favor.

Over the course of 16 Pride fights, Emelianenko was only in trouble a handful of times. There was the enormous right hand from **Kazuyuki Fujita** that had Emelianenko wobbling around the ring, his arms flailing — that match ended less than two minutes later with Fujita on the wrong end of a **rear naked choke**. There was the **Kevin Randleman** suplex, perhaps the most spectacular throw ever seen in mixed martial arts, that dumped Emelianenko on his head early in the first round. A minute later, Emelianenko swept and finished with a **Kimura**. There was the strange sight of Emelianenko underneath **Mark Hunt** and nearly arm locked, but that match too ended in a first-round Kimura for the champion. But that was as close to defeat as Emelianenko came. Not even the dangerous **Mirko Cro Cop** at the height of his powers proved to be much of an obstacle. If anyone was going to stop Emelianenko, the feared striker with top-notch takedown defense seemed most likely to do it. But Emelianenko pressured Cro Cop constantly, never allowing him to set himself and land one of his trademark head kicks. It was just one more dominant performance to add to the list.

It was only after Pride that things got weird. First, there was the **Matt Lindland** bout, contested while Emelianenko was still technically under contract to Pride, but permitted to fight in Russia for whomever he chose. He chose billionaire Calvin Ayre's upstart BodogFight, and fought in front of Russian president (and judo black belt) Vladimir Putin and action star Jean-Claude Van Damme, who sat side by side and enjoyed a night at the fights while Moscow police cracked down on a group of pro-democracy protestors led by chess champion Gary Kasparov. After Emelianenko finished the undersized Lindland with an **arm bar** in the first round, he passed the remainder of the evening with Putin — and Van Damme, naturally — at the Presidential Palace.

After the death of Pride, Dana White was determined to bring Emelianenko on board for a heavyweight title unification match with then-champion Randy Couture. The deal proved impossible, however, when Emelianenko's management team, headed by M-1 Global's Vadim Finkelstein, made a series of unusual demands, including the construction of a stadium in Russia and co-promotion of any events in which Emelianenko was to appear. Another sticking point was Emelianenko's desire to continue to compete in combat sambo — a slightly more obscure, full-contact variant of the Russian grappling art. Negotiations broke down, and ultimately Emelianenko signed a contract with his management's own M-1 Global organization, and rather than facing Randy Couture in a dream fight, he took on the Korean giant Hong-Man Choi in a Japanese sideshow.

This was disappointing, to say the least. Fans and analysts began to grumble, some at Dana White for not getting the deal done, some at Emelianenko for choosing to fight the non-competition that remained in Japan rather than take on the UFC's best. The level of competition stepped up sharply, however, when Emelianenko agreed to headline **Affliction**'s first foray into MMA against **Tim Sylvia**, who had fought eight times with some version of the UFC heavyweight title on the line over the previous five years. Emelianenko had already defeated former champs Kevin Randleman and **Mark Coleman**, but they were both very much on the down slope of their careers. The Affliction bout was our first look at Emelianenko in the ring against a former UFC champion who was still in his prime, or at least not that far removed from it. But the fight was over almost before it began: Sylvia was laid out and choked out in a mere 36 seconds. Sylvia's old rival, **Andrei Arlovski**, at least managed to put Emelianenko on his heels for a minute or so on the next Affliction card before he leaped into an Emelianenko overhand right to end the match just over three minutes into the first round.

Emelianenko accepted a fight against catch wrestler **Josh Barnett** in what should have been in his biggest challenge in years, but their fight — and ultimately the entire Affliction promotion — was sunk by Barnett's pre-fight positive test for anabolic **steroids**. Emelianenko's contract status again became the hottest story in mixed martial arts, and the UFC made every attempt to finally reel in the biggest fish in the pond. This time, minor details like whether

In Their Own Words: Fedor Emelianenko on fighting Antonio Rodrigo Nogueira

"Me and my team studied him (we watched all his fights) and I trained a lot on the ground before the fight. I trained a lot with lighter quicker fighters but I don't change my training regime for any fighter. For Nogueira I will train more on the ground, for Cro Cop more standup for instance, but the routine stays the same. I have great respect for him. I think he still is one of the best fighters in the world. He has a big fighter's heart!"

or not Emelianenko would be permitted to compete in combat sambo were not going to stand in the way of an Emelianenko/**Brock Lesnar** contest to determine the true number one heavyweight in the world. "He can go fight in sambo every fucking Thursday night if he wants to," Dana White told the press. But again Finkelstein would not back down from their demands for co-promotion, and left millions on the table.

Finkelstein and M-1 Global found the comparatively small-time **Strikeforce** much more amenable to the demands for co-promotion. And so Emelianenko found a new home with an organization that lacks the competitive depth and promotional muscle of the UFC, but that, through its CBS network television deal, can quite possibly expose him to an even wider audience. Millions of viewers were no doubt surprised to turn their dials to the Tiffany Network to find out that the baddest man on the planet was an affable, slightly chubby yet undersized Russian heavyweight with a sly smile clubbing his way out of danger against the enormous **Brett Rogers**. But that surprise was soon dwarfed by the utter shock MMA fans felt when they saw their greatest champion baited into a **Fabricio Werdum** triangle choke only moments into their Strikeforce contest. Emelianenko was forced to concede defeat for the first time in his career. True to form, the enigmatic Russian reacted to his first real loss with the same stoicism he had always shown in victory. "The one who doesn't fall," Fedor said through his interpreter, "doesn't stand up."

Erikson, Tom

Nickname: The Big Cat | **Height:** 6'3"
Weight: 285 lbs | **Born:** 7/6/64
Debut: MARS (11/22/96) | **Career Record:** 9-4-1
Notable Wins: Kevin Randleman (Brazil Open 97); Gary Goodridge (Pride 8)
Notable Losses: Heath Herring (Pride 11); Antonio Silva (Hero's 5)

Tom Erikson, a two-time junior college national champion and two-time NCAA All-American, was long considered the most fearsome fighter in MMA's heavyweight division. He beat **Kevin Randleman** and everyone else put in front of him and waited for a phone call from the **UFC** that never came.

Erikson was big and strong as an ox, but he also had a reputation for being dull. His fight with **Murilo Bustamante** was a 40-minute stall fest and the UFC was a little scared about putting him in front of a national audience. The promotion had a rule limiting the number of fighters they had from any particular style and had plenty of wrestlers already on the roster.

Instead, Erikson journeyed to Japan where he took exactly one fight a year. He beat **Gary Goodridge** at **Pride** 8 and was expected to dispatch with **Heath Herring** just as easily at Pride 11. But by then Erikson was 36 years old and a little past his sell-by date. Herring outworked him, survived on the bottom, and finished Erikson with a **rear naked choke.**

It was the Big Cat's last significant fight. His only other moment of note was a Pride 17 fight that saw him finish future boxing champion Matt Skelton with a big ham hock around the neck, squeezing his neck with a single fist, what the boys in the back laughingly called the "bitch choke." The move was banned before the next show, Erikson's contribution to the development of the MMA rulebook.

Evans, Rashad

Nickname: Sugar **Height:** 5'11"

Weight: 205 lbs **Born:** 9/25/79

Debut: Dangerzone: Cage Fighting (4/10/04)

Career Record: 15-1-1

Notable Wins: Brad Imes (*The Ultimate Fighter* 2 Finale); Chuck Liddell (UFC 88); Forrest Griffin (UFC 92); Quinton Jackson (UFC 114)

Notable Loss: Lyoto Machida (UFC 98)

The fan perception of Rashad Evans was formed from a single comment on ***The Ultimate Fighter*** 2. Coach **Matt Hughes** took exception to Rashad having a bit of fun in the cage during Evans's fight with an overmatched Tom Murphy. Hughes accused Rashad of showboating, a label that has stuck to the Michigan-based wrestler ever since. Instead of seeing Evans as a rising star, fans view him as a cocky jerk, an unwelcome encroachment by a big-time, trash-talking modern athlete into their world of budo and "respecting the sport."

Evans won the six-figure contract that season by beating the gargantuan 6'7" Brad Imes in a closely contested final. A drop down to light heayweight

and four straight wins followed before matchmaker **Joe Silva** decided Rashad was ready for stiffer competition. The former Michigan State Spartan wrestler had trouble taking down **UFC** legend **Tito Ortiz**. Ortiz outwrestled Evans and was on his way until he was penalized a point for grabbing the fence during an Evans takedown attempt. The fight was declared a draw, but everyone watching knew Ortiz had been the better man.

A rematch was scheduled to main event UFC 78, but Ortiz pulled out to film a season of *Celebrity Apprentice* with Donald Trump. Evans instead faced *Ultimate Fighter* 3 winner **Michael Bisping**. It was a fight that many in the media and online didn't think was worthy of a UFC main event. Fans disagreed. The *TUF* winners were big stars to the fans who had seen them on Spike TV and the show drew surprisingly well on pay-per-view.

Evans won a closely fought split decision and the win earned him the biggest fight of his career. The UFC traveled to Atlanta for the first time for UFC 88 where Evans fought **Chuck Liddell**. Liddell was the favorite, especially with the southern fans who let Evans know about their displeasure. When he knocked the former champion out with an overhand right that sounded like a gunshot, the arena fell into an eerie silence.

Liddell was the UFC's most popular fighter. Already disliked, beating Chuck didn't do much to make Evans any more popular. Winning the UFC

In Their Own Words: Rashad Evans on knocking out a legend

"I didn't really mind the boos that much, because that's what I expected. If I hadn't expected it, I might have gotten my feelings hurt. But I knew they would all be rooting for Chuck. I like Chuck, too. I was clapping and dancing to his music when he came out. I was going to have fun with it. I wasn't going to be like, 'Oh no! This is my death.' Being relaxed allowed me to fight the way I'm capable of fighting.

"My boxing coach Mike Winklejohn had me work on that overhand right over and over again. He's the best coach in the business. I was ready to hit it and hit it hard. It happened just like he said it would. I was trying to catch him. I was trying to get him to come out of his comfort zone. Usually he lets you chase him, but I had him frustrated by the end of the first round. He started to stalk me and catch me on the fence and that's when I thought I might catch him.

"It's good, man, but the thing about a highlight reel knockout is that one day you could be on the other end of that highlight. That's the reality of the situation."

light heavyweight title from the promotion's second most popular fighter, **Forrest Griffin**, didn't help the cause either.

Evans was being booed before fights at the weigh-ins, in the introductions, and after his victory celebrations. Pre-match nipple tweaking and in-cage dance displays furthered his image as an abrasive jerk. He wasn't. Backstage he was intelligent and affable, but that didn't stop fans from making him the least popular fighter since **Tim Sylvia**. Evans was so despised that even **Lyoto Machida**, a foreign fighter with a reputation for being a boring decision artist, was cheered for finally putting a check in the loss column, ending Evans's undefeated streak and taking his title.

Evans returned to action with a matchup fans were eagerly anticipating — a battle with fellow African American star **Quinton Jackson**. The fight would mark the first time two black fighters main evented a pay-per-view in the **Zuffa** era, and the UFC pulled out all the stops. The battle was promoted with a season of *The Ultimate Fighter* and later by the UFC's cutting edge *Primetime* specials on Spike. Labeled "black on black crime" by the personable Jackson, the fight sold more than one million pay-per-views, a tremendous success that should permanently kill the myth that black fighters don't sell tickets to MMA fans. Evans, resplendent in Tom Ford suits and designer shades, is fast becoming an MMA fashion icon, and with a dominating win over Jackson, he's become the top African American star in the sport as well.

Extreme Challenge

While the **UFC** struggled in the mid to late 1990s, battling with politicians and the cable companies, the sport of MMA was thriving on the grassroots level. It was most popular in the Midwest, in places like Iowa where **wrestling** was a religion. While **Pat Miletich** was the fighting face of the Iowa scene, the man pulling all the strings was **Monte Cox.**

Cox was the sports editor of the *Quad City Times*. He covered the local champion, Miletich, as he challenged all comers at an event in Chicago called the Battle of the Masters. Cox liked what he saw.

A boxer and promoter as well as a newspaperman, Cox took a chance on this new sport. Using Miletich as his main drawing card he held his first show on January 20, 1996. Called the Quad City Ultimate, the show drew almost 10,000 fans. Cox would later change the name of the event to Extreme Challenge.

Extreme Challenge is the longest running MMA promotion in America besides the UFC. Cox has promoted more than 500 shows on the local and regional level. Because of his role as a fight manager as well as a promoter, many of the top fighters in the world got their start in Extreme Challenge. Former Extreme Fighter competitors included future world champions like Miletich, **Matt Hughes**, and **Jens Pulver.**

Extreme Fighting

While the UFC was still struggling with developing time limits, still very much a promotion built on spectacle rather than sport, an early competitor was demonstrating what the future of mixed martial arts would look like. Extreme Fighting was ahead of its time; when the UFC was still booking freakshow fights and tons of mismatches, Extreme Challenge matchmaker **John Perretti** had a show that resembled modern MMA. The difference in quality was apparent. Perretti brought in some of the world's best, like **Ralph Gracie**, Igor Zinoviev, **Mario Sperry**, **Pat Miletich**, and **Maurice Smith.**

Many of the safety precautions and sporting aspects that are credited to **Zuffa** and **Dana White** were actually Perretti innovations. The sporting atmosphere, weight classes, rounds (which Perretti hilariously insisted be called "phases"), and rules we associate with today's UFC were mostly in place all the way back in 1995.

Like the UFC, Extreme Fighting struggled with political pressure. Their very first show in November 1995 had to be moved at the last minute from New York to North Carolina after threats to shut them down. Things got much worse. Extreme Fighting's second show was scheduled for Kahnawake,

In Their Own Words: John Perretti on the chaos in Montreal

"I turned myself in. I left my pregnant wife at home and turned myself in. I flew back to Montreal. Those were my boys. People who were fighting for me. I also will say a lot of people crapped out and got paid off not to come. They're a bunch of scumbags. I have physical fights with people over what happened in Montreal. [Former UFC owner] **Bob Meyrowitz** can laugh with me all day long. I like Bob a lot and consider him a friend. But he paid off fighters so they wouldn't show up to fight for me. One minute I have eight guys signed and the next minute I have eight who don't want to show. As soon as we announced who was fighting, the Ultimate came and paid them off.

"We were on a shoestring budget as it was. We were fighting all of Montreal. Customs stopped guys. Immigration wouldn't let guys in. I lost three quarters of my fighters. They confiscated our satellite. Donald Zuckerman in a last-ditch effort had another satellite brought in that they didn't know about. We hid it from them and they didn't know we had hooked it up."

a Mohawk Indian reservation in Quebec, Canada. Indian reservations would be an MMA mainstay for years, able to circumvent the law because of their special status and unique sovereignty. But in this case, the Canadian government was seemingly obsessed with shutting the show down. They couln't stop the fights themselves, but they could prevent fighters from getting to the reservation and filed an injunction to stop the promotion from broadcasting via satellite.

As these MMA evangelists always seemed to do, Extreme Fighting found a way. Zuckerman, driving like a bat out of hell, got a new satellite truck on site. The event made the air, making Canadian government officials furious. Eight fighters were arrested. Eventually charges were dropped, but it was becoming clear that finding a place to stage these fights was only going to get harder. If you couldn't even fight on an Indian reservation in Canada, where could you fight?

As the promotion started to bleed red, Extreme Fighting continued to be a trendsetter, doing everything just a little bit better than the UFC. While **Dan Severn** and **Mark Coleman** were undeniably great wrestlers, Perretti scored a coup for his fourth card. For the first time two Olympic Gold Medalists would compete. Kenny Monday and Kevin Jackson were both victorious, lending their prestige and Olympic status to the continuing PR battle between no holds barred fighting and the government. It was too little, too late.

Just days after their fourth event, culminating with **Maurice Smith** knocking out Kazunari Murakami with a vicious right hand, Extreme Fighting was out of business.

They had run circles around the politicians, moving the show to places like Oklahoma that didn't have any rules preventing the fights from taking place. But they couldn't outwit the cable companies. The show was being removed from much of the pay per view universe, and without that income, the event just wasn't viable. Perretti was hired by the UFC as their main matchmaker, bringing with him most of Extreme Fighting's best fighters.

Ezequiel choke

A chokehold often, though not exclusively, executed from the mount, in which the attacker wraps one arm around his opponent's neck, places the opposite forearm across the throat, and scissors his opponent's neck between his forearms. Depending on the angle of attack, the Ezequiel can act on either the trachea or the carotid arteries. Although there are a variety of no-**gi** adaptations, the technique is far more common in gi grappling, where one of the attacker's hands can be inserted into or otherwise grasp the opening of the opposite sleeve for increased leverage. Known in **judo** as sode guruma jime ("sleeve wheel choke") or simply sode jime ("sleeve choke"), **Brazilian Jiu-jitsu** players renamed the technique in honor of Ezequiel Paraguassu, a former Brazilian judo international, respected in both styles for his proficiency with his signature ne waza ("ground fighting") technique.

Because the gi plays an important role in most applications of the Ezequiel choke, it is rarely seen in MMA outside of Japan, where the traditional gi still maintains a presence in competition. The most famous — or perhaps infamous — Ezequiel choke in mixed martial arts came in **Hidehiko Yoshida**'s much disputed win over **Royce Gracie** in a special rules match at **Pride**'s massive Shockwave 2002 event. As Yoshida worked his way through Gracie's **guard** and into **mount**, he slipped his left arm around Gracie's head and grabbed the inside of his right sleeve with this left hand. Forcing his right arm across Gracie's throat, Yoshida leaned forward, tightening the hold — and obscuring the referee's view. As Gracie briefly lay motionless beneath him, Yoshida looked up at the referee and asked, "Did he pass out?" The match was stopped, and the livid Gracie sprang to his feet and protested immediately that he had neither passed out nor had he tapped. In the years since, every application of the technique calls to mind that moment in Tokyo National Stadium where the protests of one irate Brazilian were drowned out by the celebration of tens of thousands of rapturous Japanese.

Faber, Urijah

Nickname: The California Kid **Height:** 5′6″
Weight: 145 lbs **Born:** 10/14/79
Debut: Gladiator Challenge 20 (11/12/03) **Career Record:** 23-4
Notable Wins: Dominick Cruz (WEC 26); Jeff Curran (WEC 31); Jens Pulver (WEC 34, WEC 38)
Notable Losses: Tyson Griffin (Gladiator Challenge 42); Mike Brown (WEC 36, WEC 41); Jose Aldo (WEC 48)

If Urijah Faber were a few inches taller and ten or twenty pounds heavier, he might very well have become one of the biggest names in the sport. A UC Davis **wrestling** standout with solid kickboxing and an ever-improving submission game, the easygoing "California Kid" has the kind of dynamic fighting style and natural charisma that stars are made of. But for much of his career, it didn't matter how many thrilling fights he was involved in or how many tough opponents he stopped in what seemed like no time at all, nobody outside of the MMA hard-core had any idea who he was. Such is the life of a featherweight. When **UFC** parent company **Zuffa** bought **World Extreme Cagefighting** (WEC) in December 2006 and turned it into a showcase for the lighter weight classes, that changed — at least a little. It's not like Urijah Faber became a household name all of a sudden, but at least he'd stopped toiling in *complete* obscurity.

After a fifth successful defense of his WEC title — a hard-fought decision win against the tough veteran **Jens Pulver** in one of the best matches of 2008 — it seemed like Faber would reign atop the featherweight division indefinitely. A dream match against Japanese superstar **Kid Yamamoto** was a long shot, but it was also one of the few fights that fans seemed to think might offer Faber a real challenge. Despite Faber's wishes, that fight unsurprisingly never materialized, but a legitimate challenger soon appeared: **Mike Brown**. The heavily favored champion got caught with a right hook that sent him crashing to the mat after attempting a flashy but risky reverse elbow. Unable to regroup, the champion was pounded out mid-way through the first round. Faber got back on track with a quick **guillotine choke** win in a return match against Pulver, and no doubt approached his much-anticipated rematch with Brown more seriously than he did their first encounter.

In the biggest fight in the history of the featherweight division, Faber and Brown put on an absolute classic, a back-and-forth battle that went the full five rounds and still left the crowd wanting more. Faber, who broke his right hand in the early going and later sustained an injury to his left, basically ran out of bullets, but fought on regardless. Although Brown deservedly won the match on all three judges' score cards, this was one of those relatively rare instances where there was a winner but no real losers. Faber came up short, but his reputation as one of the most exciting fighters in the sport grew even stronger. A poor showing in a subsequent title challenge against the seemingly unstoppable **Jose Aldo** spelled the end for Faber in the featherweight division, as he has chosen to ply his trade among the even more frenetic bantamweights.

Fertitta brothers

The Fertitta brothers, Frank Fertitta III and his younger sibling Lorenzo, were an MMA fan's dream come true. Heirs to the Station Casino business, the two brothers had aggressively turned their father's modest Las Vegas casino into a billion-dollar real estate and gambling enterprise. They were young, ambitious, and very, very rich. They also had a love for the sport of MMA, as well as close ties to the Nevada State Athletic Commission. If you were creating the perfect **UFC** owners from scratch, men who could see the UFC through tough times, get the sport approved in Las Vegas (and back on pay-per-view) they would look a lot like Lorenzo and Frank.

Although the MMA business is now a thriving international industry, things weren't quite as easy for the UFC's perfect owners as many imagined they might be. After buying the UFC from **SEG** for just $2 million, they had a long road back to prosperity. The UFC, even the entire sport of MMA, was damaged goods. But the underlying premise, men testing themselves in the cage, was so promising that there was reason for confidence.

They met their goals early, getting the sport into Nevada and back on pay-per-view. But it had been half a decade since the UFC had been in the public limelight. The fans who stuck with the sport were passionate and loyal, but many others had forgotten all about MMA. Getting them to shell out $30 for a pay-per-view turned out to be an enormous challenge.

After losing more than $30 million, the Fertittas were ready to tap out in 2005. They had done all they could. They built their existing stars like **Tito Ortiz**, created a new star in **Chuck Liddell**, and brought back the legends of the past like **Ken Shamrock** and **Tank Abbott**. Nothing seemed to work.

When ***The Ultimate Fighter*** aired on Spike, it was a last-ditch effort by desperate men. They funded the show themselves, confident it would change things forever. The success was almost immediate. Pay-per-view records that had stood the test of time since the **Royce Gracie** era were falling monthly. Soon shows that had once drawn only 30–40,000 buys were bringing in ten times as many fans. The money-losing company of 2005 was estimated to be worth more than $1 billion in 2008.

In the struggling economy, the UFC was soon outperforming the Fertittas' real estate and casino business. To keep up with the demands placed on an increasingly busy UFC President **Dana White**, Lorenzo Fertitta left Station Casinos to work full-time with the promotion in 2008. Confident that White had the United States under control, Fertitta turned his attention to the international market. The UFC has charged head first into the United Kingdom, Germany, and Canada, and has its eye on a number of other foreign locales. Expect Fertitta to lead the company to fertile new ground like China, Brazil, Mexico, and even India. The promotion that had once been relegated to Indian casinos and the deep south is now going worldwide.

Figure four: see **Kimura and Americana**

Filho, Paulo

Nickname: Ely
Height: 5'8"
Weight: 185 lbs
Born: 5/24/78
Debut: Heroes 1 (7/24/00)
Career Record: 20-1
Notable Wins: Yuki Kondo (Deep 2nd Impact); Amar Suloev (Pride Bushido 6); Kazuo Misaki (Pride Bushido 13); Chael Sonnen (WEC 31)
Notable Loss: Chael Sonnen (WEC 36)

Brazilian Top Team fighter Paulo Filho went from shining star to burnout with alarming speed. A **judo** and **Carlson Gracie Brazilian Jiu-jitsu** black belt, Filho was a smothering, dominant grappler in an undefeated run through **Pride** that saw him emerge as one of the top middleweights in the world. Had he not suffered a knee injury in a submission win over eventual tournament champion **Kazuo Misaki**, there's every reason to believe Filho would have claimed Pride's 2006 welterweight (183 pounds) Grand Prix title.

After the demise of Pride, and a nine-month layoff, Filho made his American debut in **Zuffa**'s **WEC**, fighting for the vacant middleweight title against Canadian grappler Joe Doerksen. Although Filho exhibited solid takedown defense and knocked the tough Doerkson out in the first round, something didn't seem right: Filho appeared smaller, less aggressive. It was easy to chalk the Doerksen fight up to ring rust, but a pair of bizarre matches against **Team Quest**'s **Chael Sonnen** would fully expose how far Filho had fallen.

In their first bout, a passive Filho looked largely helpless through two rounds before catching a careless Sonnen in a well-executed **arm bar** from **guard**. Sonnen screamed in pain, yelling "Tap!" in an obvious verbal submission. Sonnen immediately denied that he'd submitted, however, and berated referee Josh Rosenthal for stopping the fight.

A rematch was signed, but delayed when Filho entered rehabilitation for a substance abuse problem. After nearly a year, the two met again, but in a non-title contest after Filho failed to make weight, missing by an astounding seven pounds. After a passable first round, Filho fought the rest of the match in a strange state of mind, glancing around the cage in nervous distraction as he ate a steady diet of jabs en route to a unanimous decision loss. Although it was Filho's first loss in a career filled with solid wins over serious competition, it looked an awful lot like the end of the line.

Fitch, Jon

Height: 6'
Weight: 170 lbs
Born: 2/24/78
Debut: RFC 1 (7/13/02)

Career Record: 23-3 (1 No Contest)

Notable Wins: Shonie Carter (Shooto USA); Thiago Alves (*Ultimate Fight Night* 5); Diego Sanchez (UFC 76); Thiago Alves (UFC 117)

Notable Losses: Wilson Gouveia (HOOKnSHOOT: Absolute Fighting Championship 1); Georges St. Pierre (UFC 87)

In another sport, Jon Fitch might be called a "grinder." He's never going to be the prettiest, the most athletic, or the smoothest. But he might be the hardest working, the toughest, and the best prepared.

Fitch will never be mistaken for a dynamic action fighter. A former Purdue wrestler, Fitch is the epitome of the "Big 10 style." He grinds his opponents into the fence, takes them down, makes them work. It was an effective style, leading to eight consecutive wins in the Octagon, but it was also a style that fans and the **UFC** brass considered a little dull.

While Fitch was making an undeniable case for a title shot with win after win, he was doing it primarily outside of the public spotlight. His fights were often on the untelevised undercard and he just didn't seem television-friendly. Fitch was scheduled for the first season of ***The Ultimate Fighter***, but was pulled from the show as he was on his way to the airport for the flight to Las Vegas. Spike television officials didn't think he had what it took to entertain.

In Their Own Words: Jon Fitch on confidence despite anonymity

"I think it's a key factor in any career. For someone to be successful, if you don't have the confidence in yourself to achieve the things that lay in front of you, then you're always going to be a failure. I think I struggled early in my **wrestling** career at Purdue because I lacked confidence. But ever since I've started fighting, I've put myself on the same playing field mentally as all my opponents, and my confidence is through the roof. I'm just as much of an athlete or just as much of a man as anybody else I'm facing.

"Because of the way I came up through the UFC, a lot of people didn't see a lot of my fights. People develop an attachment to fighters that they see fight live. When they see you in a pay-per-view or they see you in a live event and they watch you fight, they develop a real attachment to you. So yeah, I think a lot of fans still don't know who I am, really. They haven't developed that kind of attachment or an appreciation for me. But it's not really their fault, I guess; it's just the way things go. We had a stacked weight division, and I just kind of slipped through the cracks."

Through it all, Fitch has remained remarkably patient. He called out the UFC once, before UFC 68, when his fight with Luigi Fioravanti was scheduled for the untelevised portion of the show. He quickly recanted. For the most part, Fitch's solution was to go back to the gym and work harder. Eventually, his wins could not be denied. Beating top contenders **Thiago Alves** and **Diego Sanchez** earned Fitch his shot at the welterweight title.

Georges St. Pierre was too much for Fitch, but he earned respect from fans for a display of heart and guts. He took a beating from St. Pierre, but he took it like a man. Unfortunately for Fitch, his moment in the sun was short. He challenged the UFC brass over their insistence that he and others sign away lifetime license rights for the new UFC video game and was briefly released from the promotion. He caved in to the UFC's strong-arm tactics the very same day, but was punished for his temerity. For his next fight, with his profile at an all-time high after a main event title shot, Fitch was back on the undercard. It appears Fitch will have to fight his way back towards contendership. He wouldn't have it any other way.

Florian, Kenny

Nickname: Ken Flo **Height:** 5'10"

Weight: 155 lbs **Born:** 5/26/76

Debut: Mass Destruction 10 (1/25/03) **Career Record:** 14-4

Notable Wins: Chris Leben (*The Ultimate Fighter* 1); Din Thomas (UFC Fight Night 11); Roger Huerta (UFC 87); Joe Stevenson (UFC 91); Takanori Gomi (UFC Fight Night 21)

Notable Losses: Diego Sanchez (*The Ultimate Fighter* 1 Finale); Sean Sherk (UFC 64); B.J. Penn (UFC 101)

Kenny Florian is the ultimate underdog. He wasn't just an afterthought during the filming of ***The Ultimate Fighter***; he wasn't even supposed to be there. Florian was extremely fortunate to set foot in a house stocked with prime prospects. He was a virtual unknown when **UFC** executives journeyed to Massachusetts to scout Drew Fickett. At the end of the night, Fickett was victorious, but it was Florian who was on his way to Las Vegas for the reality television show. He just had "something" — that intangible feature that made the UFC suspect he would be a game opponent.

Even in the house, he was underestimated time and again. He ended up fighting in the UFC at 155 pounds, but during *The Ultimate Fighter* he was competing at middleweight, clearly the runt of the litter. He was known as a solid ground fighter, but during that first season fans and opponents discovered his secret weapon: his razor sharp elbows. He cut the prohibitive favorite

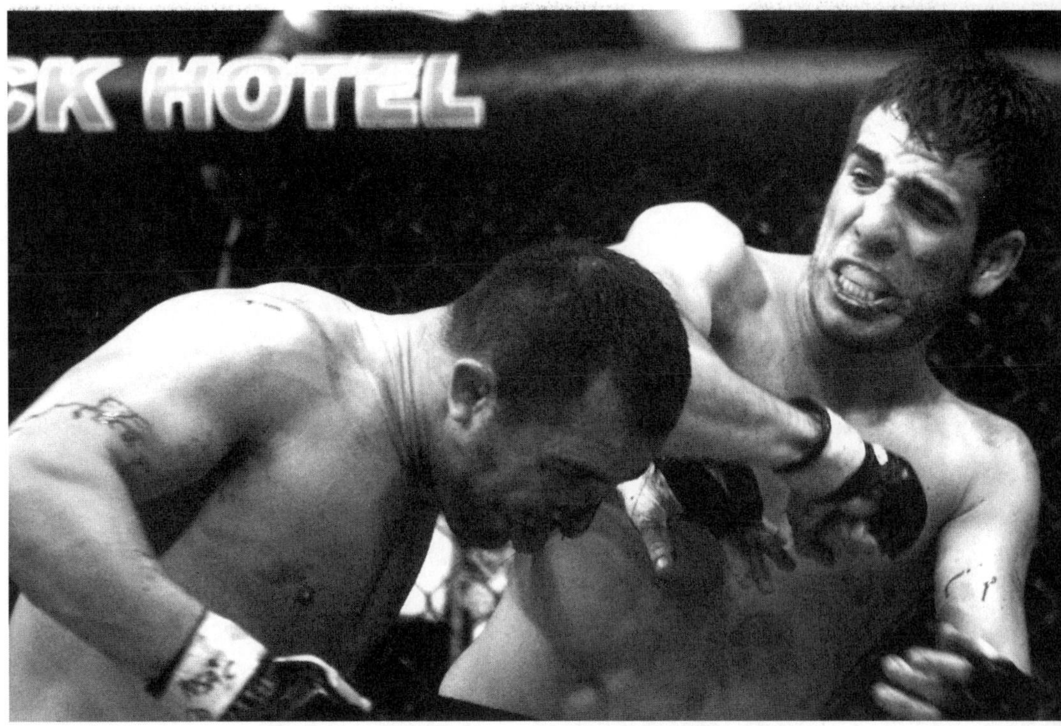

Chris Leben with elbows and advanced to the finals where he lost convincingly to **Diego Sanchez** in the first round.

Many *TUF* runner-ups eventually disappear into near obscurity. It's almost a curse at this point to be the *TUF* runner-up: **Stephan Bonnar**, Brad Imes, **Luke Cummo**, Josh Haynes, and **Ed Herman** have all struggled since coming up just short. Florian is the lone exception. He's grown remarkably as a fighter since being manhandled by Sanchez, gaining confidence and building his body into a vessel that allows him to compete with the best in the world.

Florian improved so fast that he became the first *Ultimate Fighter* alumnus to earn a UFC title shot. At UFC 64, he and **Sean Sherk** battled for the vacant UFC lightweight championship, the first lightweight title bout since **B.J. Penn** fought **Caol Uno** to a draw at UFC 41 in 2003. Florian lasted all five rounds with Sherk, even cutting him with one of his patented elbows, but clearly had room to grow.

Since that loss, Florian has been undefeated. He rolled through Japanese sensation Dokojanuse Mishima and worked his way back into contention. Progressively better fighters felt Florian's wrath, including rising stars Joe Lauzon and **Roger Huerta**. Not only was Florian winning fights, he was finishing them, winning four in a row decisively by submission or knockout. When Florian got a second chance at the lightweight title against B.J. Penn, he was ready and the fans were ready for him as a legitimate challenger. He fell to Penn, but established himself as the real deal. Florian has become a star, not just in the cage, but outside it. As the co-host of ESPN's *MMA Live* he's preparing for a life beyond fighting. It seems whether he wins a title or not, Florian will be around the sport for years to come.

Franca, Hermes

Height: 5'6" **Weight:** 155 lbs

Born: 8/26/74 **Debut:** HOOKnSHOOT: Kings 1 (11/17/01)

Career Record: 19–9

Notable Wins: Caol Uno (UFC 44); Spencer Fisher (UFC Fight Night 8); Marcus Aurelio (UFC 90)

Notable Losses: Josh Thomson (UFC 46); Yves Edwards (UFC 47); Sean Sherk (UFC 73); Frank Edgar (UFC Fight Night: Silva vs. Irvin)

With more than ten fights in the **UFC**, an appearance in the 2003 K-1 **Hero's** Grand Prix, and impressive wins and competitive losses against some of the best lightweight fighters in the world, Hermes Franca has had a respectable career by almost any measure. In more than 25 appearances in the ring and the

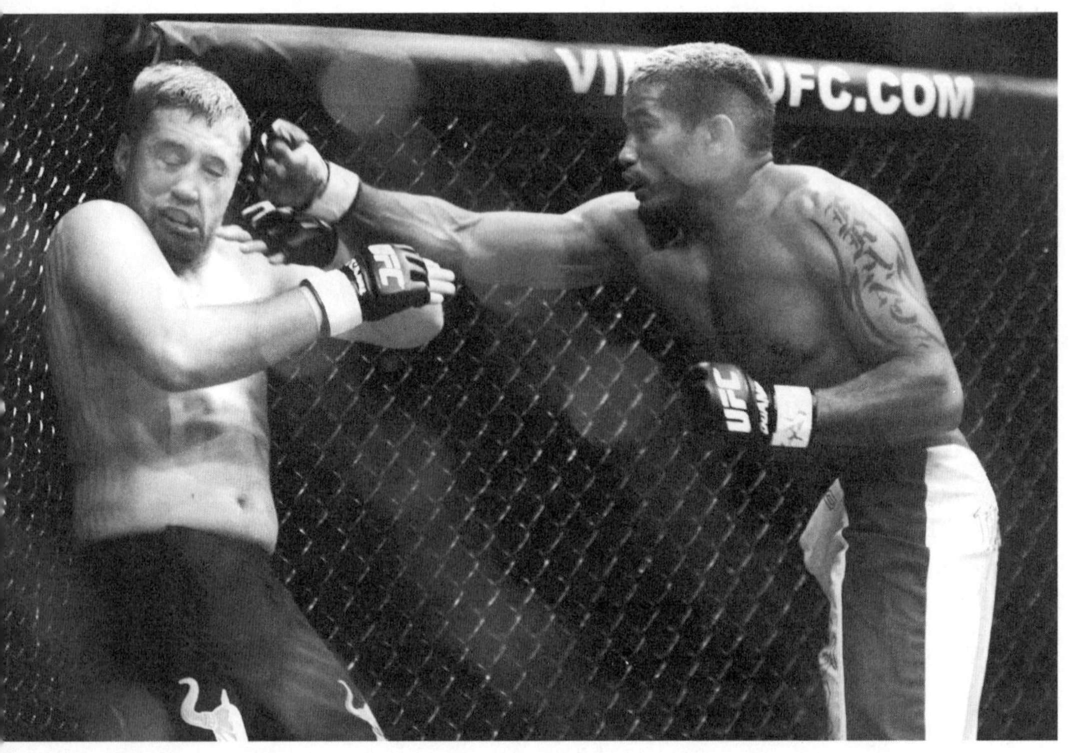

cage matched up against top competition, he's been stopped only once — a remarkable achievement. It's a shame, then, that Hermes Franca will be best remembered for his part in one of the sport's most embarrassing episodes.

Franca challenged **Sean Sherk** for his lightweight title at the unwittingly appropriately titled UFC 73: Stacked. After a sleeper of a fight, in which Sherk blanketed Franca for the better part of five rounds to take a unanimous decision, both champion and challenger tested positive for banned substances: Sherk for Nandrolone, which he denied, and Franca for Drostanolone, which he admitted. Franca released a statement in which he reminded us that fighting is how he makes a living, and explained that he chose to take **steroids** only after an ankle injury threatened to keep food from his family's table. Franca joined the long list of busted fighters who took steroids only once, to rehab an injury, rather than to gain a competitive edge by being bigger, stronger, and faster than their opponents.

Franklin, Rich

Nickname: Ace | **Height:** 6'1"

Weight: 185-205 lbs | **Born:** 10/5/74

Debut: WEF 6 (6/19/99) | **Career Record:** 28-5 (1 No Contest)

Notable Wins: Marvin Eastman (WFA 1); Evan Tanner (UFC 42, UFC 53); Ken Shamrock (*The Ultimate Fighter* 1 Finale); Yushin Okami (UFC 72); Matt Hamill (UFC 88); Wanderlei Silva (UFC 99); Chuck Liddell (UFC 115)

Notable Losses: Lyoto Machida (Inoki Bom-Ba-Ye 2003); Anderson Silva (UFC 64, UFC 77); Dan Henderson (UFC 93); Vitor Belfort (UFC 103)

When the **UFC** first began its major expansion in 2005, one of the poster boys for the sport was middleweight Rich Franklin. Franklin was the perfect fighter to trot out in front of critics and media looking to portray the Octagon as the arena of bloodthirsty barbarians. Franklin was as clean-cut as you could imagine: a former school teacher and a devout, well-spoken Christian.

While many people remember the famous **Forrest Griffin/Stephan Bonnar** fight, the actual main event of the UFC's first live fight show on Spike TV was in fact Franklin taking on "The World's Most Dangerous Man" **Ken Shamrock**. Shamrock had long since ceased to be a great fighter and was no longer in prime fighting shape. But to most fans, he was a name synonymous with the early UFC. Franklin's decisive win did exactly what matchmakers expected it to do: it catapulted their hand-picked new star into the stratosphere.

Franklin proved worthy of the promotion's confidence, winning several tough fights and taking the UFC middleweight title from **Evan Tanner** at UFC 53.

In Their Own Words: Rich Franklin on moving to 205 pounds

"I think that for me these are going to be tough matchups just for the simple fact that I'm not a big 205-pound fighter. And so a lot of these guys are taller than me, wider than me, longer than me. I'm going to deal with weight issues and strength issues, probably. So a lot of the matchups are going to be tough, but I'm willing to try to tackle them.

"At this point in time I'm not in the title hunt at 205. Perhaps I will be at some point in time as long as I keep winning fights. But until then, you know, if the UFC has exciting fights for me at 195 pounds and fights that the fans want to see than I'm willing to drop and do what I need to do just to pull in good fights.

"Honestly, it really doesn't matter to me. I think at this point in time, I'm interested in putting on exciting fights for the fans. So if in the process of that whole thing if I continue doing the things that I need to do and winning fights and stuff like that, eventually I'll make my way back to a title run. And, you know, if I can get back to the title run that would be a great Cinderella story for me before I retire."

Despite this success Franklin didn't catch on with the audience the way **Chuck Liddell**, **Randy Couture**, or even **Matt Hughes** did. Perhaps all the traits that made him the perfect corporate spokesman didn't help him win over the harder edged UFC audience that preferred the mohawked party boy Liddell to the creationist Christian. For whatever reason, Franklin's pay-per-view main events were routinely among the least purchased UFCs of any given year.

Inside the cage, after two successful title defenses, Franklin ran head first into a brick wall known as **Anderson Silva**. The spindly "Spider" was a silky smooth striker as well as a dangerous ground fighter. He dismantled Franklin not once, but twice, pummeling him in the **clinch** and stopping him twice with knees to the head. The second loss, in his home state of Ohio, seemed to deflate Franklin's fighting spirit. The two losses had left him in an awkward predicament. He was too big a star and too good a fighter to simply fill a role as the middleweight gatekeeper, but at the same time, no one could imagine a third fight with Silva.

Instead, Franklin moved up to 205 pounds, looking to reinvent himself as a light heavyweight. Just a bit too small for the division, Franklin was in kind of a netherworld. The UFC exacerbated the problem by booking him in two catchweight bouts at 195 pounds, one a win over **Wanderlei Silva**, the other a dramatic knockout loss to **Vitor Belfort**. Stuck between two weight classes, Franklin was wasting precious time he needed to bulk himself up so he could be a legitimate light heavyweight. He took a step forward with a dramatic knockout of the fading legend Liddell at UFC 115, but lagging pay-per-view sales indicated it would take more than that to reestablish Franklin as a top name. Already 35, his window of opportunity in this new division is closing quickly.

Frye, Don

Nickname: The Predator **Height:** 6'1"

Weight: 219 lbs **Born:** 11/23/65

Debut: UFC 8 (2/15/96) **Career Record:** 20-8-1 (1 No Contest)

Notable Wins: Gary Goodridge (UFC 8); Tank Abbott (Ultimate Ultimate 96); Ken Shamrock (Pride 19); Yoshiro Takayama (Pride 21)

Notable Losses: Mark Coleman (UFC 10, Pride 26); Hidehiko Yoshida (Pride 23)

Don Frye is a walking stereotype, the prototypical American tough guy. He's a gravelly voiced, mustachioed firefighter who's not afraid to stand toe-to-toe with any man on the planet. Frye's sly sense of humor and his refusal to quit under any circumstances have made him a main event star on two continents.

Fans have watched him morph from a handsome Tom Selleck look-alike into a craggy, used-up cowboy. But we understand — we've seen him age years from brutal battles inside the cage.

Like many of the most successful fighters in the early years of the **UFC**, Frye was a wrestler by trade, coached by **Dan Severn** at Arizona State and a teammate of **Randy Couture** at Oklahoma State. When Frye saw Severn at UFC 4 he knew MMA was the perfect fit for him. He joined Severn's entourage and, after a couple of underground fights, got his shot at UFC 8 in Puerto Rico. He was never really listed as a wrestler in the UFC, preferring to claim **judo** and **boxing** as his arts. There was an unofficial quota on wrestlers in the Octagon, so it was important for Frye not to be stuck in that mold. It didn't matter much. No matter what you called him, he was tremendously effective.

UFC 8 was **SEG** executive Campbell McLaren's brainchild, a last and desperate attempt to keep the UFC from becoming boring. The idea was simple: take the **Keith Hackney**/Emmanuel Yarborough fight from UFC 3 and try to replicate it several times in one night. The tournament was called David and Goliath and was divided between monsters and mere men. It ended just as McLaren imagined, with a David battling a Goliath for the title of Ultimate Fighting Champion. Frye, the David at just over 200 pounds, made short work of the fake **Kuk Soon Wol** black belt **Gary Goodridge** to claim the championship and immediately became a crowd favorite.

After beating jiu-jitsu wizard Amaury Bitetti at UFC 9, Frye advanced to the finals of UFC 10 where he ran into a juggernaut named **Mark Coleman**. Coleman, like Frye, was a wrestler. But while Frye was a good wrestler, Coleman was exceptional, a former **Olympian** who looked unstoppable. Coleman gave Frye a merciless beating, and fans saw Frye's heart displayed for the first time. He refused to quit and after 11 minutes the fight was finally stopped.

Frye took advantage of a second chance to win another UFC tournament, beating **Tank Abbott** in the finals of Ultimate Ultimate 96. Abbott, a bar room brawler with an amazing bench press and hands of stone, almost had Frye beaten early, rocking him with a strong punch that sent the smaller man stumbling. Abbott fell over his own feet when he swooped in for the kill and Frye took his back for the win. It was his final UFC fight.

The UFC was struggling with politicians and cable companies and the money just wasn't there. Like **Ken Shamrock**, Frye had the looks and charisma to escape the sinking ship and join the wacky world of **professional wrestling**. Frye went to New Japan Pro Wrestling where his tough guy reputation and subtle bad guy tactics, like refusing to break a hold when his opponent was

In Their Own Words: Don Frye on painkillers

"Painkillers are real easy to get addicted to, mostly because you only start taking them because you really need them. Then one day you're howling at the moon and telling yourself that you're not the kind of person who does drugs, even if you're spending most of your day high on pharmaceutical-grade opiates.

"Here's the hard truth: life is pain. Most mornings I feel like I got shot out of a cannon. Other mornings it's really bad. You just have to learn to live with it. Try easing off from Vicodin to Advil. Tequila don't hurt, either."

in the ropes, made him a huge star. Frye was selected to face **Antonio Inoki** in the Japanese legend's final professional wrestling match, a rare honor for a foreigner new to the sport.

When Inoki wanted to push his wrestlers into real fights in an ill-fated attempt to remake them in his own image, Frye was a natural choice to return to the ring. Five years after his retirement from the sport, he returned against **Gilbert Yvel** in an ugly, foul-plagued fight at **Pride** 16 that saw Yvel stick his fingers into Frye's eyes on multiple occasions.

Pride was at the height of its popularity in Japan and was finally making an effort to conquer the U.S. market as well. The biggest fight they had available for the American fans was Frye against long-time rival Ken Shamrock. The two were among the biggest names in UFC history and had legitimate bad blood.

Frye had become close to Shamrock's adopted father Bob, who had indicated he would support Frye rather than Ken in the fight. It was one of the greatest fights in Pride history. Frye won all the standup collisions and the decision. But his refusal to tap out to Shamrock's vicious **leg locks** left him in near constant pain and eventually led to a crippling addiction to pain pills. It also ended Frye's career as a serious and legitimate contender to the best fighters in the sport.

Frye was still capable of crowd-pleasing slugfests, like his legendary fight with professional wrestler **Yoshihiro Takayama**. But against top stars, like Mark Coleman and **Hidehiko Yoshida**, he was all but helpless. Today, Frye is best known for his comedy stylings, including a popular interview segment on the **IFL** shows called "Dear Don." At 43, he is still active and when you see him fight you know just what to expect: he's going to give all he has until somebody falls down.

Fujita, Kazuyuki

Nickname: Ironhead
Height: 6′
Weight: 240 lbs
Born: 10/16/70
Debut: Pride Grand Prix 2000 Opening Round (1/30/00)
Career Record: 15–9
Notable Wins: Mark Kerr (Pride Grand Prix 2000 Finals); Ken Shamrock (Pride 10); Bob Sapp (K-1 MMA Romanex)
Notable Losses: Mark Coleman (Pride Grand Prix 2000 Finals); Mirko Cro Cop (K-1 Andy Hug Memorial, Inoki Bom-Ba-Ye 2002); Fedor Emelianenko (Pride 26); Wanderlei Silva (Pride Critical Countdown Absolute); Jeff Monson (Pride 34); Alistair Overeem (Dynamite!! 2009)

Iron-headed, heavy-handed Japanese Greco-Roman **wrestling** champion Kazuyuki Fujita has held his own against some of the biggest names in all of mixed martial arts, from early greats like **Ken Shamrock**, **Mark Coleman**, and **Mark Kerr** to current stars like **Fedor Emelianenko**, **Mirko Cro Cop**, **Wanderlei Silva**, and **Brock Lesnar**. The Lesnar match was a little different from the others, though, in that it was less an MMA contest, and more a three-way International Wrestling Grand Prix title match with both Lesnar and Masahiro Chono in the main event of a New Japan Pro Wrestling Tokyo Dome show.

Don't let Fujita's parallel career as a professional wrestler (under the guidance of wrestling legend and MMA pioneer **Antonio Inoki**) fool you: his MMA accomplishments are completely legitimate. Fujita came as close as anyone to stopping Fedor Emelianenko when he staggered the undisputed heavyweight king with an enormous, clubbing right hand. For a few brief seconds, a woozy Emelianenko swayed from side to side, flailing his arms overhead as he tried to maintain his balance. Fedor instinctively worked his way into a **clinch**, only to have Fujita plant the Russian on his back as the frenzied Yokohama crowd chanted, "FU-JI-TA! FU-JI-TA!"

But Fedor, being Fedor, managed to escape to his feet. Although still wobbly, Fedor sent Fujita tumbling to the mat seconds later with a liver kick and a right-left combination, took the back, and ended the fight with a **rear naked choke** only 90 seconds after Fujita had put him in the most trouble he'd ever seen. Fujita has never again looked as dangerous as he did against Emeliankeno — how could he? — but between that tremendous bout, and his part in the infamous **Petey, My Heart!** episode, there can be no doubt that Kazuyuki Fujita has left his mark.

Full Contact Fighter

Joel Gold's monthly newspaper *Full Contact Fighter* was the semi-official chronicle of the sport in its darkest days. Gold was a boxer who got interested in the **UFC** and began learning submissions. A neck injury kept him from pursuing a career in the Octagon, but Gold still wanted to be close to the unique world of MMA.

Starting with UFC 13, Gold covered every UFC event until the paper was stripped of its credentials in October 2005. Along the way, *Full Contact Fighter* became the bible of MMA. The paper covered events large and small and featured interviews with the biggest names in the sport.

Before the internet MMA scene exploded at the end of the '90s, fans often waited for their monthly issue of *Full Contact Fighter* to see who had won fights around the world. The writers Gold brought in to assist him became a who's who of MMA reporters, including Jim Genia, Eddie Goldman, Josh Gross, and Loretta Hunt.

When sites like **Sherdog** and **The Underground** made MMA information available more quickly, and for free, *Full Contact Fighter* had a hard time competing. The coverage they offered didn't change to reflect the new reality of online news. To succeed, *Full Contact Fighter* needed to focus on their interviews and expert analysis. Instead, they continued to approach their paper as a medium to provide event results, results that were weeks old by the time *Full Contact Fighter* arrived in the mailbox.

Today, the bible of MMA is an afterthought. Many fans don't even know it still exists. But during the dark days of MMA, when the UFC wasn't even available to cable customers on pay-per-view, *Full Contact Fighter* was the absolute best source for MMA news on the planet.

Funaki, Masakatsu

Height: 6' **Weight:** 190 lbs

Born: 3/13/69

Debut: Pancrase: Yes, We Are Hybrid Wrestlers 1 (19/21/93)

Career Record: 39-13-1 (1 No Contest)

Notable Wins: Bas Rutten (Pancrase: Pancrash! 1); Ken Shamrock (Pancrase: Road to the Championship 4); Minoru Suzuki (Pancrase: Road to the Championship 5); Frank Shamrock (Pancrase: Eyes of Beast 2); Guy Mezger (Pancrase: 1995 Anniversary Show, Pancrase: 1997 Anniversary Show); Yuki Kondo (Pancrase: Truth 9, Pancrase: Alive 11); Semmy Schilt (Pancrase: Alive 2, Pancrase: Advance 4); Ikuhisa Minowa (Dream 6)

Notable Losses: Ken Shamrock (Pancrase: Yes, We Are Hybrid Wrestlers 1); Jason DeLucia (Pancrase: Road to the Championship 2); Frank Shamrock (Pancrase: Eyes of Beast 6); Bas Rutten (Pancrase: 1996 Anniversary Show); Yuki Kondo (Pancrase: Alive 4); Guy Mezger (Pancrase: Advance 5); Semmy Schilt (Pancrase: 1998 Anniversary

Show); Rickson Gracie (Colosseum 2000); Kazushi Sakuraba (Dynamite!! 2007); Kiyoshi Tamura (Dream 2)

Masakatsu Funaki was expected to be a **professional wrestling** megastar. He was a protégé of **Antonio Inoki** and had the looks and skill in the ring to become a wrestling legend. In a training class that included future stars Jushin Liger, Chris Benoit, and Shinya Hashimoto, Funaki was the standout. His future was assured, but he was prepared to give it all up to live out a dream: real professional wrestling.

Funaki's **Pancrase** promotion brought professional wrestling full circle. What had started as legitimate matches between tough guys at the turn of the 20th century had become a sideshow spectacle with flamboyant characters and over-the-top antics. Funaki wanted to take wrestling back to an earlier time. Instead of copying the latest American tomfoolery, he was prepared to embrace the ethos of an earlier time. His wrestling matches would use standard rules fans were familiar with, but would also be legitimate contests.

Trained by Yoshiaki Fujiwara and Karl Gotch, Funaki was the best and most technically proficient of the Pancrase fighters. While others, like **Ken Shamrock** and **Bas Rutten**, focused their energies primarily on becoming better fighters, Funaki had bigger challenges. Because he was the promoter as well as the star, his personal training was often compromised, as he spent much of his time teaching his own competitors. Funaki was the chief trainer in Japan for both Shamrock and Rutten, two fighters who both beat him in the ring.

Funaki was often involved in Pancrase's most controversial fights. As the promoter, it was frequently more important for him to keep an eye towards developing new stars than it was to worry about his own win–loss record. Sometimes that meant losing to fighters he should have (and could have) beaten like Jason DeLucia, Yuki Kondo, and Rutten. Funaki was already an established star thanks to his wrestling pedigree, good looks, and personal charisma; he could afford to lose and remain strong with his fan base. His pro wrestling mentality gave him no compunctions about throwing fights. The goal each time was simple-building more star fighters for Pancrase.

As the promotion felt the pressure from the larger and better funded **Pride** group, Funaki was finally ready to take the lead role instead of propping up others on his broad shoulders. He beat his protégé, Yuki Kondo, for the King of Pancrase title in December 1997, but it was too little, too late. His best fighting days were behind him and he was unable to hold off **Guy Mezger** in his first defense. In Pancrase, Funaki and the other main stars fought once a month, every month, for years. It was a crazy schedule, guaranteed to break down bodies and shorten careers. By the time he had his retirement match with **Rickson Gracie** at Colosseum 2000, Funaki was a shadow of his former self. He was dispatched quickly, yet another pro wrestler victimized by the most brutal Gracie.

Funaki stayed in the spotlight in retirement, taking several starring movie roles including playing **Masahiko Kimura** in a movie about wrestling legend Rikidozan. He shocked the world in December 2007 by making a brief return to MMA for K-1. The extra rest and relaxation may have helped his body heal, but it didn't make him a better fighter. Funaki fought fellow legends **Kazushi Sakuraba** and **Kiyoshi Tamura**, but was beaten badly in both matches, barely putting up a fight.

The crowds lost interest quickly, as Funaki didn't carry himself like a fighting legend. He was always a stoic fighter, but in his return he seemed disinterested, lacking any of the fighting spirit so important to Japanese fans. In the final fight of his short-lived comeback, Funaki made amends. Against former Pancrase undercarder **Ikuhisa Minowa**, Funaki had one last magical moment. Sporting gray hair and an unbelievably cut body for a 40-year-old man, Funaki was able to turn back the clock to upset his former student. Minowa wore wrestling boots, a mistake against a **leg lock** specialist like Funaki. The legend made him pay, securing a **heel hook** in less than a minute. Funaki broke into tears as the crowd went wild one last time.

He shocked Japan again with a surprise announcement. The man who revolutionized professional wrestling and helped pave the way for legitimate fighting in Japan was making a return to the business he had rejected years ago. Funaki was returning to traditional professional wrestling.

Garcia, Marcelo

Nickname: Marcelinho **Height:** 5'7"

Weight: 181 lbs **Born:** 1983

Debut: Hero's 2007 in Korea (10/28/07)

Career Record: 0-1

Notable Loss: Dae Won Kim (Hero's 2007 in Korea)

Although he's far from a household name, any fan who watched Travis Lutter's non-title bout with **UFC** middleweight champ **Anderson Silva** has at least heard of Marcelo Garcia. When play-by-play man **Mike Goldberg**, in his enthusiasm, repeated a comment by matchmaker **Joe Silva** suggesting that Travis Lutter was in possession of not merely average black-belt level **Brazilian Jiu-jitsu** skills, but in fact "Michael Jordanesque" abilities relative to his peers, **Joe Rogan** was having none of it. "No," Rogan said flatly, "No, he's not. He's not that good. Marcelo Garcia is more like Michael Jordan."

Rogan was right. While Lutter is an accomplished black belt, Marcelo Garcia is a four-time Brazilian Jiu-jitsu world champion and three-time **ADCC** champion, widely recognized as the most technically adept submission artist of his era in both **gi** and no-gi grappling. Like Jordan, Garcia is simply on his own level. So, understandably, when Garcia signed with K-1 to make his MMA debut at their 2007 **Hero's** in Korea event, expectations were high.

Garcia's opponent was the journeyman Dae Won Kim, a Korean **judo** player whose most notable fight was a **Pride** Bushido contest against **Akihiro Gono** in which an aggressive Kim managed a few impressive throws before being caught in an **arm bar** late in the ten-minute first round. Few gave Kim much of a chance against the great Garcia — and no chance at all, naturally, if Garcia was able to take the fight to the ground. Which he was, almost immediately: Garcia worked doggedly to secure a single-leg takedown, and then passed from **guard** to **half-guard** to **mount** in a beautiful display of the ground skills that made his reputation. When Garcia took Kim's back with just over three minutes remaining in the round, a **rear naked choke** finish seemed inevitable.

But it never came. Kim survived Garcia's attacks from back mount, ultimately reversing into Garcia's guard as the round expired. Clearly wanting no part of Garcia on the ground in round two, Kim came out firing, landing a right hand that had Garcia backpedaling. As a visibly shaken Garcia desperately attempted a takedown, Kim caught him with a hard knee that opened a fight-ending cut.

Kim came away with the biggest win of his career. Garcia was left with a hugely disappointing loss, and no burning desire to try his luck at the sport again any time soon. And we were all reminded that in modern mixed martial arts, even Michael Jordanesque ability in a single discipline is not nearly enough to guarantee success.

Gator roll: see **Arm triangle**

Gholar, Darrel

Height: 5'10" **Weight:** 210 lbs

Born: 7/16/64 **Debut:** IVC 5 (4/26/98)

Career Record: 5-6

Notable Win: Amar Suloev (M-1 MFC: European Championship 2000)

Notable Loss: Evan Tanner (UFC 18)

Gholar, a former Pan American Championship silver medalist in Greco-Roman **wrestling**, was an unexceptional fighter. He had once placed fourth at the World Cup, but couldn't find a way to translate his talents into MMA success. With the number of highly successful wrestlers among the short list of MMA legends, it's important to remember that wrestling pedigree isn't an automatic ticket to fighting immortality. For every **Randy Couture**, there is a Royce Alger. For every **Kevin Randleman**, there is a, well, Darrel Gholar.

Where Gholar excelled was as a coach. He journeyed to Brazil to train **Vitor Belfort** and didn't come back home for almost three years. Gholar was the official wrestling trainer for the **Brazilian Top Team**, one of the most successful MMA teams of all time. His work was evident immediately. Jiu-jitsu fighters who normally fought off their backs were now completing takedowns against seasoned wrestlers. Among the stars Gholar trained include **Murilo Bustamante**, **Ricardo Arona**, **Mario Sperry**, and the **Nogueira** brothers.

Gholar is also a bit of a Renaissance man. He graduated from the University of Minnesota with a degree in world literature. He has written screenplays, stage plays, and was named one of the world's 200 best living poets in 2003.

Gi

The traditional martial arts keikogi (literally "practice dress") has all but disappeared from contemporary MMA competition. Although the **UFC** was built on the strength of a skinny Brazilian in a gi taking on all comers, the gi is not permitted under the **Unified Rules of Mixed Martial Arts** that have been followed in North America since 2000. It survives in Japanese MMA, but it's only worn by a handful of fighters, and only under specific circumstances where the gi might prove strategically useful. If a **judo** fighter — **Hidehiko Yoshida**, for example, or **Yoshihiro Akiyama** — wants to increase traction in the **clinch**, work a few gi-specific chokes on the ground, or simply provide a bigger billboard for his sponsors, he might well compete in his gi. But that's about it.

Throughout this decline, the gi has maintained its importance as a training tool — depending on whom you ask, at least. There are those, like the innovator **Eddie Bravo**, who believe that the best way to develop MMA-specific grappling skill is to discard the gi from the outset. But many top competitors

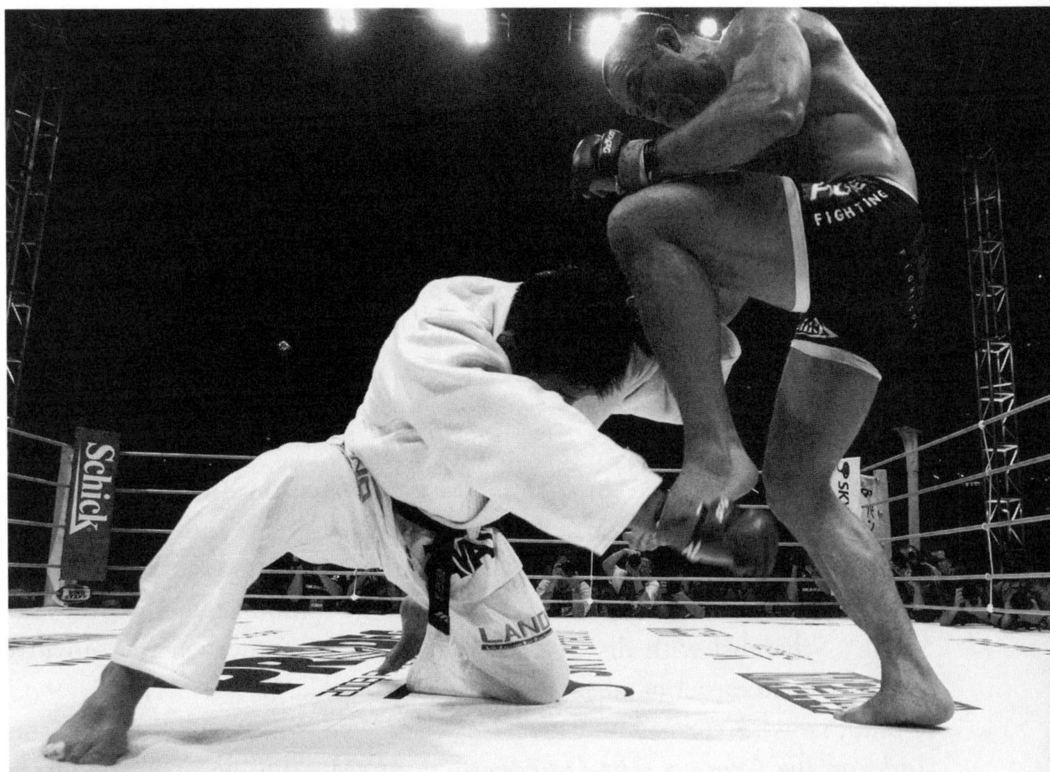

— **B.J. Penn** and **Georges St. Pierre** among them — still elect to train in the gi, choosing the deliberate pace of gi grappling to supplement and complement the more explosive, dynamic movements of no gi. It's an ongoing debate within the **Brazilian Jiu-jitsu** world: traditionalists argue that no-gi grappling should be built upon a solid gi grappling base, iconoclasts contend that the gi is a vestige.

You can question the direct relevance of the gi to modern mixed martial arts, but there's no denying the importance of the gi to any number of modern mixed martial artists. There's no small number of fighters who continue to proudly wear their keikogi as they make their way to the ring or the cage, choosing to represent their traditional roots as martial artists — as jiu-jitsuka, judoka, samboists, and karateka — even while competing in a very untraditional sport.

Gibson, Lance

Nickname: Fearless **Height:** 5'10"
Weight: 185 lbs **Born:** 11/20/70
Debut: SuperBrawl 4 (4/9/97) **Career Record:** 4-5
Notable Wins: Akihiro Gono (SuperBrawl 13); Masanori Suda (Shooto: R.E.A.D. 6)
Notable Losses: Dan Severn (SuperBrawl 5); Evan Tanner (UFC 29); Masanori Suda (Shooto: Treasure Hunt 1)

Lance Gibson is a Canadian fighter best remembered for insisting that the **UFC** announcers refer to him as Lance Gibson Senior during a pay-per-view broadcast. Gibson made an early splash on the international scene, beating top Japanese fighters **Akihiro Gono** and Masanori Suda for **Shooto**. Then he ran into a freight train named **Evan Tanner** at UFC 29 and was absolutely brutalized by the future UFC middleweight champion. Following a loss to Masanori Suda in a rematch, Gibson retired from the sport. He teaches fighters at Gibson's MMA in Port Moody, British Columbia.

Gogoplata

A chokehold, usually executed from **guard**, in which the attacker winds his leg around the opponent's arm and forces the lower shin and instep against the opponent's throat. **Brazilian Jiu-jitsu** innovator **Eddie Bravo**, whose rubber guard system has facilitated and popularized the technique, credits Antonio "Nino" Schembri with discovering the gogoplata; however, the move is recorded much earlier in the **judo** texts of Mikonosuke Kawaishi (*My Method of Judo*, 1955), Kyuzo Mifune (*The Canon of Judo*, 1960), and E.J. Harrison (*Judo on the Ground: The Oda Method*, 1954). Although the gogoplata lurked in the darker corners of the judo ne waza syllabus for decades as kakato (or kagato) jime (literally "heel strangle"), the technique rose to prominence in the context of mixed martial arts through the efforts of a single judoka turned Brazilian Jiu-jitsu player, **Shinya Aoki**. Ryusuke "Jack" Uemura probably holds the distinction of being the first to win a match via gogoplata in mixed martial arts (vs. Isao Terada, ZST: Grand Prix 2 — Finals, January 23, 2005). But it was Aoki who first managed the feat at the highest level of the sport (vs. **Joachim Hansen**, **Pride**: Shockwave 2006, December 31, 2006). Other successful applications of the gogoplata in mixed martial arts include **Nick Diaz**'s overturned submission win over **Takanori Gomi** (Pride: Second Coming, February 24, 2007), Aoki's mounted gogoplata over Katsuhiko Nagata (**Dream** 4, June 15, 2008), and heavyweight Brad Imes' improbable two wins by the same technique in two months (vs. Zak Jensen, WFC: Downtown Throwdown, September 14, 2007; vs. Bo Cantrell, King of the Cage: Arch Rivals, October 27, 2007).

Goldberg, Mike

Professional wrestling has Jim Ross. Basketball has Dick Vitale and Marv Albert. Football had John Madden. MMA's iconic announcer is the **UFC**'s Mike Goldberg.

Goldberg took over for the competent Bruce Beck at Ultimate Japan in 1997 and has called almost every UFC fight since. His first partner was Olympic gold medalist **Jeff Blatnick** who did his best to teach him the sport. Goldberg was an unemployed hockey announcer who knew nothing about the world of MMA. In the beginning, when the fights hit the ground Goldberg was lost at sea. Relying on Blatnick to call the action there, he made a strong effort to figure out the sport by getting down on the mats himself. He turned out to be a quick learner. Goldberg was so good that he was one of only a handful of employees who remained with the company long-term when **SEG** sold the UFC to **Zuffa.**

Working primarily with comedian **Joe Rogan**, Goldberg has the difficult task of calling the action while finding a time to plug the UFC's various sponsors. Some hard-core fans dislike their often bombastic commentary and Goldberg's catch phrase of "It's all over." For casual fans, the two do an amazing job of making every fight seem important and special.

It appeared for a time in 2005 that Goldberg would leave the UFC for **professional wrestling.** Vince McMahon was on his yearly quest to replace lead announcer Ross on WWE RAW. The UFC had caught fire among mainstream media outlets, making Goldberg a hot commodity. The WWE offered him a reported $1.5 million over three years. Ultimately, Goldberg chose to stay and was well rewarded by the **Fertittas** and **Dana White**. It's almost impossible to imagine a UFC broadcast without Goldberg and Rogan. They've become as iconic as the Octagon itself: two future Hall of Famers who help make the sport such an enjoyable television spectacle.

Gomi, Takanori

Nickname: Fireball Kid **Height:** 5'8"

Weight: 160 lbs **Born:** 9/22/78

Debut: Shooto: Las Grandes Viajes 6 (11/27/99) **Career Record:** 31-6 (1 No Contest)

Notable Wins: Rumina Sato (Shooto: To the Top Final Act); Tatsuya Kawajiri (Pride Bushido 9); Hayato Sakurai (Pride Shockwave 2005)

Notable Losses: B.J. Penn (ROTR 4); Marcus Aurelio (Pride Bushido 10); Nick Diaz (Pride 33); Kenny Florian (UFC Fight Night 21)

Pride's Bushido series was essentially **Shooto** for the masses. It took the top ranks of Japan's premier organization for lightweight fighters, and presented them to a broader audience than the venerable International Shooting Commission was ever able to reach. And Bushido's ace, the man Pride built the series around, was Takanori Gomi.

A strong, heavy-handed wrestler who was big for his weight class, Gomi was not the archetypal Japanese lightweight fighter. But he was among the most popular, and, during a remarkable two-year, ten-fight undefeated run in Bushido, he was also the best.

Gomi began his pro career undefeated through his 14 Shooto bouts, earning the Shooto world welterweight championship (154 pounds) from submission expert **Rumina Sato** along the way. After a razor-thin decision loss to **Joachim Hansen** cost him the title, and a one-sided **rear naked choke** loss to the great **B.J. Penn** followed in Hawaii, Gomi returned to Japan and began the streak that made him a star. It began unremarkably enough, with a win over **Chute Boxe** lesser light Jadson Costa, but culminated with title tournament wins over **Tatsuya Kawajiri**, Luiz Azeredo, and **Hayato Sakurai**, making Gomi Pride's first Japanese champion.

The biggest hole in Gomi's game, an inability to work from his back, cost him dearly in his first fight as champion, a non-title embarrassment against Marcus Aurelio. Aurelio, who has done little of note since, persistently and methodically worked towards an **arm triangle** that everyone seemed to see coming except for Gomi, who refused to tap and was choked into unconsciousness. A narrow, split-decision win over Aurelio later in 2006 did little to convince anyone that Gomi was back on track, nor did his debut on American soil, a **gogoplata** loss to **Nick Diaz** in which an out-of-shape Gomi looked exhausted only minutes in. (The fight was later ruled a no contest when Diaz tested positive for marijuana.) Since the demise of Pride, Gomi has been given every opportunity to get back on track, first in **Sengoku** and subsequently in the **UFC**, but the fighting form that took him to the top of the ever competitive lightweight division has proved elusive.

Gono, Akihiro

Nickname: The Japanese Sensation **Height:** 5'9"

Weight: 170 lbs **Born:** 10/7/74

Debut: Lumax Cup Tournament of J '94 (4/23/94) **Career Record:** 32-15-7

Notable Wins: Hector Lombard (Pride Bushido 11); Gegard Mousasi (Pride Bushido 12); Yuki Kondo (Pride Shockwave 2006); Hayato Sakurai (Dynamite!! 2009)

Notable Losses: Matt Hughes (Shooto: 10th Anniversary Event); Yuki Kondo (Pancrase: Proof 7); Mauricio Rua (Pride Bushido 2); Dan Henderson (Pride Bushido 9); Jon Fitch (UFC 94)

An Afro wig, a leisure suit, dancing cornermen, and the occasional sequined gown: these are the trademarks of Akihiro Gono. Or, more specifically, the trademarks of his ring entrance alter ego "DJ Gozma," a parody of Japanese pop star DJ Ozma. Gono's elaborate entrances made him a hit with fans, but his opponents are more likely to have been impressed with his tenacity, his unorthodox strikes thrown from strange, unpredictable angles, and his solid submission game. Or maybe his zebra-print trunks.

Like **Grabaka** teammate **Sanae Kikuta**, Gono made his debut in the proto-MMA Lumax Cup. Gono then spent the better part of a decade fighting his way through the **Shooto** and **Pancrase** ranks before becoming a fixture in **Pride**'s Bushido series, where he took on such top competition as **Mauricio Rua**, **Dan Henderson**, and **Gegard Mousasi**. Gono handed the dangerous Mousasi what was only his second career loss with a slick **arm bar** in the dying seconds of their 2006 bout in a display of submission skills Gono would repeat in his **UFC** debut against Tamdan McCrory. Despite earning a Submission of the Night bonus for that finish, Gono was bounced from the UFC two fights later after dropping consecutive decisions to Dan Hardy and top-ranked welterweight contender **Jon Fitch**. After his mediocre UFC stint, Gono joined teammates Kikuta and **Kazuo Misaki** in the **Sengoku** organization, Japan's unofficial home for fighters over 30.

Gonzaga, Gabriel

Nickname: Napao
Height: 6'2"
Weight: 256 lbs
Born: 10/18/79
Debut: Brazilian Gladiators 2 (4/2/03)
Career Record: 11-5
Notable Win: Mirko Cro Cop (UFC 70)
Notable Losses: Fabricio Werdum (Jungle Fight 1, UFC 80); Randy Couture (UFC 74); Shane Carwin (UFC 96)

It looked like Gabriel Gonzaga was going to be just another heavyweight. Despite his distinguished **Brazilian Jiu-jitsu** competition record, the best Gonzaga had to show for himself after eight professional MMA fights was a win over the undistinguished Carmelo Marrero. So when he entered the cage against **Mirko Cro Cop** soon after the Croatian's **Pride** Open Weight Grand Prix championship, the five-to-one odds against Gonzaga seemed almost generous.

That Gonzaga versus Cro Cop ended with one of the most spectacular head kick knockouts the sport had ever seen was not surprising in and of itself. But that it was Gonzaga who threw the kick, and Cro Cop who was left lying in a twisted heap on the mat . . . now *that* took more than a few people by surprise. Gonzaga thoroughly dominated the few short minutes the fight lasted, taking Cro Cop down and cutting him with powerful elbows. After a curious standup late in the round, a visibly stunned Cro Cop dropped his hands as Gonzaga landed the single blow that would define his career.

That extraordinary victory earned Gonzaga a heavyweight title fight against **Randy Couture**. Although Gonzaga managed to break Couture's arm with a blocked head kick, it was far from enough, as MMA's ageless wonder grounded Gonzaga and pounded him out in the third. Stopped by **Fabricio Werdum** (for the second time) in his next fight, Gonzaga was clearly on his way back down the **UFC**'s heavyweight rankings. Dramatic first-round KO losses to rising stars **Shane Carwin** and **Junior dos Santos** furthered that slide, perhaps irrevocably.

Goodridge, Gary

Nickname: Big Daddy
Height: 6'1"
Weight: 250 lbs
Born: 1/17/66
Debut: UFC 8 (2/16/96)
Career Record: 23-22-1
Notable Wins: Oleg Taktarov (Pride 1); Don Frye (Pride Shockwave 2003)
Notable Losses: Don Frye (UFC 8, Ultimate Ultimate 96); Mark Coleman (UFC 10); Marco Ruas (Pride 2); Igor Vovchanchyn (Pride 4, Pride Grand Prix 2000 Finals); Naoya Ogawa (Pride 6); Ricco Rodriguez (Pride 9); Gilbert Yvel (Pride 10); Antonio Rodrigo Nogueira (Pride 15); Fedor Emelianenko (Pride Total Elimination 2003)

Gary Goodridge is an opponent. Over the course of a long career that started all the way back at **UFC** 8, he's been in the ring and the cage with an absolute who's who of heavyweight greats spanning the eras. From **Don Frye** and **Mark Coleman** in the mid-'90s UFC to **Antonio Rodrigo Nogueira** and **Fedor Emelianenko** in the glory days of **Pride**, Goodridge has faced them all — and gone down in the first, more often than not. He has played much the same role in the world of kickboxing, although there he tends to stay upright a little longer. Goodridge might not be equipped to seriously challenge any top-tier heavyweight, but he's tough enough to have earned steady, high-profile work for more than a decade. The respected veteran has given us some memorable moments, beginning with the barrage of elbows he delivered from the crucifix position against the undersized and overmatched Paul Herrera in his UFC debut. Then there are the head kicks: the one that Goodridge threw at Pride's 2003 New Year's Eve show that put Don Frye out of commission, and the one Gilbert Yvel landed on Goodridge seconds into their Pride 10 contest in one of the most spectacular knockouts the sport has ever seen. He's never been afraid to trade, and he's never been afraid of taking fights on short notice, either: in 2008, after **Aleksander Emelianenko** failed to get medical clearance to face **Paul Buentello**, Goodridge stepped in on only 22 hours notice. He lost, of course. But he went the distance.

Grabaka

Sanae Kikuta — **ADCC** submission **wrestling** champion, national high school **judo** champion, and former King of **Pancrase** — founded the Grabaka (literally "grappling fool") gym and fight team in central Tokyo in June 2000. The initial team roster consisted of Hiroo Matsunaga, Eiji Ishikawa, and the charismatic **Genki Sudo**. Sudo would leave not long thereafter, but Kikuta would be joined by **Akihiro Gono** and **Kazuo Misaki**. Grabaka fighters were under exclusive contract with Pancrase before that relationship ended in 2005, and a Grabaka versus Pancrase-ism rivalry flourished, but the team's biggest win came with Misaki's 2006 **Pride** welterweight (183 pounds) Grand Prix title. The gym has also served as a training ground for the kind of gimmick celebrity fighters, like Bobby Ologun and Koji Imada, who flourished in Japan's MMA boom. In the horrific world of MMA fashion, Grabaka stands alone with its boldly skull- and dragon-free "Vote for Grabaka" and "Grappling Party" T-shirt designs.

Gracie, Carlos

It all started in 1917. **Mitsuya Maeda**, a Japanese judoka turned pro wrestler, was performing in Brazil when a 14-year-old Carlos Gracie saw him at the Teatro Paz in Belem, Brazil, a theater normally reserved for classical musicians and the opera. Gracie was mesmerized by what he saw, a demonstration of the techniques and power of Jigoro Kano's **judo**. Soon, through his father's connections in the business and political sphere, Gracie was taking lessons in the sport — lessons that would eventually change combat sports forever.

No other instructor on the planet would have been better suited to help Gracie develop what would eventually become **Gracie Jiu-jitsu**. For the most part, martial artists competed against others in their own discipline. Maeda had fought everyone, across disciplines, for years. While other judo instructors taught with words, Maeda liked to prove the sport's effectiveness in a fight. He had competed with **karate** men, wrestlers, savate fighters literally all over the world. This gave Maeda's students a firm grounding in the practical application of judo as a combat art.

After four years studying under Maeda, Gracie moved with his family to Rio de Janeiro, where he later opened the first **Brazilian Jiu-jitsu** academy. When his father became ill, Carlos took in his younger brother **Helio**, a sickly child who watched his older brothers train but was unable to participate. Eventually Helio began teaching classes and, because of his physical weakness and frailty, made some changes that helped create the jiu-jitsu we know today.

As Helio surpassed Carlos as a fighter and trainer, Gracie moved towards managing the academy and focused on his true love: the Gracie Diet. Carlos, who suffered from crippling migraines, was fascinated by what he saw as an unimpeachable connection between his diet and his physical well-being. Soon Carlos was a neighborhood guru, helping people with their health problems and encouraging a diet that focused on keeping "the blood neutral."

Gracie, Carlson

When **Helio Gracie** retired from fighting in 1955, the Gracies were in danger of losing their status as Brazil's first family of fighting. Helio was over 40 and had just lost decisively to former student Waldemar Santana. The family had lost prestige and was losing business as well. The draw to studying with the family had always been their impeccable reputations as the toughest men in Rio. Santana had become the top dog by defeating Helio and was leaching students away from his former instructor.

Helio was the youngest of the five Gracie brothers. None of his siblings could possibly avenge the family against Santana. Instead, a young man from the next generation was forced to take a large step forward and represent his family name. Carlson was Carlos Gracie's eldest son, all of 19 years old when he faced off with his former friend Santana in August of 1956. It was one of the best fights of all time: a back-and-forth affair that went more than 30 minutes before the two men toppled out of the ring and only Gracie returned.

Gracie became the king of Brazilian **Vale Tudo**, fighting 19 times, including five more fights with Santana, with Carlson winning three more and going to a draw twice. His only loss was in 1968, when at the age of 36 he lost to **Luta Livre** fighter Euclides Pereira, a controversial fight that Gracie claimed involved a crooked referee.

His fighting career was integral in maintaining the Gracie name, but it was his work in developing and spreading **Gracie Jiu-jitsu** that was the most important part of his legacy. Carlson eventually split with his uncle Helio and opened his own school across town in Copacabana.

With him went Rolls Gracie, the family's top fighter of the 1970s. This move helped keep jiu-jitsu vibrant. Instead of comfortably training with no real competitors, the family created its own internal rivalries. It wasn't enough anymore to be better than the other fighters in Brazil; now the Gracies had to be better than each other, pushing each other to new heights. Carlson also opened up jiu-jitsu to the masses. While Helio taught all students the most basic techniques, the more advanced jiu-jitsu was reserved for select students and family. Carlson taught everyone, opening up the closed world of Gracie Jiu-jitsu to all of Brazil.

In the battle of the Gracies, Carlson usually came out on top. He taught a very aggressive style of jiu-jitsu, befitting his voluble personality and quick temper, and his students included some of the very best jiu-jitsu and Vale Tudo fighters of the 1970s forward, including Sérgio Iris, Ricardo de la Riva, **Murilo Bustamante**, **Mario Sperry**, and Wallid Ismail. While Helio believed that size and strength mattered less than technique and skill, Carlson disagreed. A truly great fighter needed the entire package. His students were top performers in the sport of Brazilian Jiu-jitsu, but also prepared for Vale Tudo competition. In 1991, before the MMA boom had begun, Gracie led a team of jiu-jitsu players against a team of Luta Livre fighters, with jiu-jitsu winning all three contests.

When his cousin **Rorion Gracie** brought Vale Tudo to America with the **Ultimate Fighting Championship**, the rivalry began anew. Carlson created his own fight team, **Brazilian Top Team**, dominating fighting competitions the world over. **Vitor Belfort** was a standout in the UFC, while **Antonio Rodrigo Nogueira** and Mario Sperry starred in Japan. In 2000, Carlson was shocked when most of his top students left the gym to go out on their own. Although many of them had gotten their first opportunities because they trained under the legendary Gracie, once they established their own reputations and the money started coming in, they felt Gracie was taking too big a share.

Gracie was shattered by the desertion. The anger burned in him until his dying day. Even at the age of 70, Carlson wasn't too old to try to start a fight with his former student Belfort after his fight with **Tito Ortiz** at UFC 51. Training fighters — fighters who eventually turned on him — cost Gracie everything. He lost his thriving gym in West Hollywood while focusing on Belfort and his other fighters. When he had no more team to train, the Brazilian, who loved the heat, moved to the blustery and cold Midwest to start over. While he trained new students in Chicago, including future stars **Miguel Torres** and **Stephan Bonnar**, he always felt the sting of betrayal. Carlson Gracie passed away in 2006 at the age of 72.

Gracie, Helio

Helio Gracie is one of the most influential men in the history of MMA. Without him, the **UFC** and MMA as we know it would not exist. His creation, **Gracie Jiu-jitsu**, became one of the most important new martial arts in a century. He introduced the art to Brazil; his sons took it worldwide. Even today it is impossible to compete at the highest level of MMA without learning jiu-jitsu, or at least learning how to defend against it.

It's true that Gracie Jiu-jitsu was not created in a vacuum. **Carlos Gracie** unquestionably introduced many of the techniques of Gracie Jiu-jitsu to his brothers and to the nation of Brazil. But Carlos was simply passing on the **judo** instruction he had received from **Mitsuyo Maeda**. It was his younger brother Helio who developed the art into one of the most effective fighting systems in the world. Carlos was essentially teaching judo. He was strong and quick; his brother Jorge was an even better natural athlete and they could perform the moves Jigoro Kano had perfected in Japan.

Helio was different. He was sickly and weak. There were many techniques he simply could not execute, making refining the art necessary. Like many geniuses, he adapted what he found and made it better. The art Gracie created was focused more on ground fighting and less on explosive throws.

Gracie was committed to making sure his brand of jiu-jitsu worked, not just in cooperative demonstrations, but in real confrontations. He tested himself on the streets (once he even had to be pardoned by Brazil's president after he seriously injured a man in a street fight) and in the ring. His opponents included local martial artists, but also American pro wrestlers working in Brazil. Gracie acquitted himself well, either winning with ease or holding much larger men to a stalemate.

His most famous battles came later in his life, and despite his numerous conquests, his best known fights were both losses. He fought the legendary Japanese judo ace **Masahiko Kimura** in 1951 at the Maracanã Stadium in Rio de Janeiro, Brazil. The Maracanã was brand new, one of the biggest stadiums in the world with a standing room capacity of almost 200,000 people. Gracie didn't fill it, but he did bring in 20,000 people for what was more than a battle of wills. Gracie was striving to prove his art's superiority to judo. Kimura was fighting for his livelihood: his **pro wrestling** shows were struggling in the wake of Gracie choking out his countryman Kato months earlier.

Although the Gracie public relations team has since declared that Kimura was a 220-pound giant, he was actually a well-proportioned 180 pounds for the contest, outweighing Helio by just 25 pounds. The show was quite a spectacle. There was a growing Japanese immigrant population in Brazil and the fight became a jingoistic battle of nations. Even Brazil's future president Café Fihlo was in attendance. Before the fight, Kimura was amused to see a coffin at ringside. He was told Helio had brought it for him.

Instead of finishing Kimura, it was Helio who was beaten soundly. Kimura was considered quite possibly the best judoka of all time. He threw Gracie like a rag doll, choking him out (Gracie admitted to being out cold before Kimura released the hold), and finally breaking his arm with a shoulder lock called the ude-garami. Helio refused to tap out, but his brother Carlos threw in the towel. In honor of his conqueror, the hold he beat Gracie with was known as the "**Kimura**" from then on.

Gracie's second most famous fight was against former student Waldemar Santana. Gracie had retired from professional fighting when Santana began taking pro wrestling bookings to earn much needed cash. Gracie was against pro wrestling and forbid it. Soon a reporter was playing the two men off each other, and the 42-year-old Gracie came out of retirement to teach Santana a lesson. Unlike the Kimura fight, this was a private affair, held at a local YMCA out of the public eye. The fight was a marathon. Both men were bathed in sweat, but after nearly four hours, Gracie was exhausted. He was caught with kick to the head and was knocked out, ending his 23-year career.

Gracie was an interesting man. He gave all of his nine children names beginning with the letter R. He also taught those children jiu-jitsu, and through them, took his life's work around the globe. His son **Rorion Gracie** was one of the early owners of the UFC and brought Gracie Jiu-jitsu to America, slowly but surely building a national following. His younger sons, **Rickson** and **Royce**, became legends — Royce in America with the UFC, and Rickson in Japan with **Vale Tudo** Japan and later **Pride**.

It was the culmination of everything Gracie had worked for. His ideas and his art form were being taught worldwide and even into his nineties he was thinking about jiu-jitsu daily, still training and teaching students all over the planet.

Gracie Jiu-jitsu: see **Brazilian Jiu-jitsu**

Gracie, Ralph

Nickname: The Pit Bull | **Height:** 5'9"
Weight: 155 lbs | **Born:** 1971
Debut: Desafio: Gracie Vale Tudo (1/1/92) | **Career Record:** 6-1
Notable Win: Dokojanuse Mishima (Pride Bushido 1)
Notable Loss: Takanori Gomi (Pride Bushido 3)

There was something about the descendants of the founder of **Gracie Jiu-jitsu**, Carlos Gracie Sr. They were a little on the wild side, and you can tell that is true in particular of Ralph Gracie just by looking at him. He has crazy eyes, wild eyes, and his approach to jiu-jitsu reflects it.

When Ralph made his American MMA debut at **Extreme Fighting** 1 in November 1995, fans were used to a different style of Gracie Jiu-jitsu. They had seen **Royce Gracie** in action — by this point 12 times in the **UFC** — and thought they had a feel for what Gracie Jiu-jitsu was all about. Royce, more often than not, was on the bottom. He would bide his time, like in his fight with **Dan Severn**, before finally finishing his opponent. Ralph threw that all out the window. Nicknamed "The Pit Bull," his style was aggressive and brutal. He didn't believe in waiting for an opening to finish the fight; he was going to create his own opening by coming forward as hard and fast as he could. Even his uncle, the legendary **Rickson Gracie**, looked passive compared to the infamous pit bull.

In Extreme Fighting this approach worked wonders. Ralph won three fights in the short-lived but innovative promotion, all of them in less than two minutes. His most famous fight of the era was against former national **sambo** champion and United States Shoot Wrestling Federation founder Steve Nelson. Ralph thought Nelson had been cavalier in expressing his desire to fight a member of the Gracie clan. Instead of using a joint lock or a choke, he punished Nelson with strikes for his perceived disrespect.

For Ralph, this kind of vendetta was a way of life. His father Robson encouraged the boys to settle problems with their fists. When they would throw down, Robson wouldn't admonish them, only tell them how they could have fought more effectively. Ralph once shot at his brother **Renzo Gracie** with a crossbow ("Just to scare him," he says now with a grin) and the brothers and cousins fought constantly. Even when his adult son, Ralph's late brother **Ryan Gracie**, attacked Wallid Ismail in a nightclub, his father justified it because Wallid had been bragging about beating three Gracies (Renzo, Ralph, and Royce). To Robson, the claim was a lie, because Royce didn't really count. "He is just the seller of T-shirts," he said dismissively. Besides, said Robson, Wallid "had homosexual tendencies."

With this kind of upbringing, there was little chance of escaping a life of violence. For the most part, Ralph was able to keep it contained to competition. There was an occasional flare-up, like his 2002 dust-up with Bobby Southworth at a grappling tournament. But Ralph was generally able to sate his need to inflict and receive pain by teaching at his jiu-jitsu schools, warrior academies where he created a generation of tough jiu-jitsu players in his mold. His best student was future UFC champion **B.J. Penn**, but the two had a falling out after B.J. challenged Ralph's brother Renzo Gracie to a fight. Ralph was, by all reckoning, a very good instructor. This was enough, and for five years he sat out of MMA competition.

In Their Own Words: Ralph Gracie on Extreme Fighting 2

"[Steve] Nelson said he had a dream to fight the Gracie family. I made that dream come true. Before the fight he had a lot of big words. After the fight, none. This was the fight when many of the fighters were arrested in Canada. The government was against the fight, but they were not able to go onto the Indian reservation to stop it. We had word that they were coming to the hotel after to arrest everybody. My friend called me and quickly I left my room to go to Nino Schembri's room. We stayed there for three days until the problem was solved. Nino was going crazy in the room and tried to tie all the sheets together so he could climb out of the window. It was very different than the fights today."

In 2003, he made his return and immediately showed he was still among the very best lightweights on the planet. Ralph beat the very tough Dokojanuse Mishima at **Pride** Bushido 1 before facing the Bushido ace **Takanori Gomi** at Bushido 3. Gomi had quickly established himself as a world-class competitor. He beat **Rumina Sato** to win the **Shooto** title and, like Gracie, he had beaten Mishima. His combination of punching prowess and charisma earned him the call up from Pride.

It was a tradition for Japanese Pride stars to make their name against the Gracies, and Gomi was no exception. Ralph charged forward, Gomi threw the knee, and Ralph ran right into it. The fight, and Gracie's MMA career, was over in less than ten seconds.

Gracie, Renzo

Height: 5'10" **Weight:** 185 lbs

Born: 3/11/67 **Debut:** Desafio: Gracie Vale Tudo (1/1/92)

Career Record: 13-7-1

Notable Wins: Oleg Taktorov (MARS); Maurice Smith (Rings: King of Kings 1999); Pat Miletich (IFL: Gracie vs. Miletich); Frank Shamrock (EliteXC: Destiny)

Notable Losses: Kiyoshi Tamura (Rings: King of Kings 1999); Kazushi Sakuraba (Pride 10); Dan Henderson (Pride 13); Carlos Newton (Pride Bushido 1); Matt Hughes (UFC 112)

There was a time growing up when Renzo was much like his brother **Ryan Gracie**. He fought on the streets and generally terrorized Rio de Janeiro. Today, Renzo Gracie is by far the most likeable of the fighting Gracies. His brothers **Ralph** and the late Ryan Gracie were quick-tempered and at times just plain

mean. Renzo is different. He's quick to laugh, friendly, and an indefatigable bundle of energy.

Renzo is not as good a grappler as **Royler**. He's not as physically gifted as **Rickson**. He doesn't have **Royce**'s resume. But Renzo was probably the best all-around fighter in the Gracie family. While the other Gracies believed jiu-jitsu alone was enough to beat the world's best, Renzo followed the example of his mentor and uncle, Rolls Gracie. He wanted to learn it all. Grappling, kickboxing, **wrestling**, and **boxing** — Renzo took them all up with his customary enthusiasm. The end product was the most well-rounded of all the Gracies.

Gracie was part of some of the most memorable finishes in the history of MMA. Against the Russian **Oleg Taktarov**, Renzo finished the fight with a huge up-kick from the **guard**, quickly jumping to his feet to land some extra punches to seal the deal. Taktarov was one of the most feared fighters of his generation. Renzo finished him in just one minute.

When he fought **Luta Livre** artist **Eugenio Tadeu**, the end of the fight was even more explosive. Tadeu had once fought Renzo's cousin Royler Gracie to an hour-long draw and the rivalry between his camp and the Gracies was fierce. Renzo and Tadeu had engaged in a titanic back-and-forth when, after more than 15 minutes, fans rushed the cage. A full-scale riot ensued, the lights went out, shots were fired, and people were fighting all over the building. The fight between Gracie and Tadeu, as epic as it was, paled in comparison. It was declared a no contest.

Renzo was the third Gracie to fight Japanese sensation **Kazushi Sakuraba**. Sakuraba had talked trash to the others in the family, but he respected Renzo too much to do so to him. Sakuraba saw Renzo as a very similar fighter to himself, equally skilled in all facets of the game. The fight was an all-time great. It was an amazing display of striking and grappling, with Renzo winning the striking exchanges and the two going back and forth on the mat, including an amazing cartwheel guard pass by Sakuraba. At the end of the round, Sakuraba secured a **Kimura** lock. Like his cousin Royler, he refused to tap. Unlike with Royler, the referee let the fight continue until Renzo's arm was dislocated at the elbow. From Renzo there were no complaints. "Many people make excuses when they lose," Gracie told the fans. "I have only one. He was better than me tonight."

Renzo's last unbelievable finish was in the final fight of his career. The Gracies and Shamrocks began fighting at **UFC** 1. Fifteen years later, they were still squabbling. **Frank Shamrock**, like Renzo, had become the best fighter in his family. The two seemed evenly matched, but from the start, Renzo imposed his will. Renzo was able to take Shamrock down whenever he wanted and a frustrated Frank delivered several illegal knees to the back of the head.

Renzo suffered a concussion and headed to the hospital with a bruised brain, but also as the victor. It was the final fight of his great career — or so it seemed. Three years later Gracie made a surprise return and his UFC debut. Gracie had helped the UFC broker a deal with his jiu-jitsu student Sheikh Mohammed bin Zayed Al Nahyan and the Abu Dhabi-government-owned Flash Entertainment. The group bought a 10 percent stake in **Zuffa** and Renzo walked away with a six-fight UFC contract. The first, and possibly only, fight was against wrestler **Matt Hughes.**

Hughes had beaten Renzo's cousin **Royce Gracie** and engaged in a bitter rivalry with Renzo's top American student, **Matt Serra.** What could have been a grudge match turned into a plodding affair that saw Hughes easily outwork the 43-year-old Gracie. Renzo, true to form, was still smiling at the end, but his legendary career had likely come to a close.

Gracie, Rickson

Height: 5'10" **Weight:** 185 lbs

Born: 11/20/58 **Debut:** 4/25/80

Career Record: 11-0

Notable Wins: Zulu (Maracanã Stadium); Yuki Nakai (Vale Tudo Japan 95); Nobuhiko Takada (Pride 1, Pride 4); Masakatsu Funaki (Colosseum 2000)

When he was just 15 years old and a jiu-jitsu purple belt, black belts ran in terror from the aggressive young teenager called Rickson Gracie. He was a monster, more than even a grown man could handle. By his early twenties, Rickson was traveling to every jiu-jitsu school in Rio de Janeiro, Brazil, and submitting all their black belts. To compound the embarrassment, Rickson would tell each man how he was going to tap him out. Then he would go out and execute it. Each sport has a limited number of prodigies — young men so gifted at such an early age that they far outpace their contemporaries, existing on a different level. Rickson Gracie was one such man.

Rickson was the third son of the legendary **Helio Gracie** and inherited the mantle of "family champion" passed on from Helio to his cousin **Carlson Gracie**, and then to his half-brother Rolls Gracie. Rickson was unquestionably the greatest Gracie of the 1980s. He made his **Vale Tudo** debut at the turn of the decade, twice beating the monstrous Zulu in front of large crowds. Rickson also dominated **Brazilian Jiu-jitsu** competition. He had the advantage of soaking in knowledge from his brother **Rorion Gracie** and his father during half the week and journeying across town to the Copacabana to train with Carlson on the remaining days. The result was an artist with Helio's keen eye for maximizing leverage and technique and Carlson's emphasis on aggression and physical strength.

Lacking the organized MMA competitions we see today, Rickson sought to prove himself where many young hotheads do: on the streets. There was an intense rivalry between jiu-jitsu, a rich man's game, and **Luta Livre**, the ghetto equivalent. Rickson and his gang would often settle their differences with the Luta Livre crew on the beaches of Brazil and occasionally in the gym or arena. Some of the fights were legendary and iconic. No one who was present could forget Rickson walking up to Hugo Duarte on the beach, slapping him in the face, and eventually mounting him and making him say, "Rickson is the king."

Like his younger brother **Royce Gracie**, Rickson joined Rorion in America to help teach **Gracie Jiu-jitsu** to Hollywood and the world. In 1989, they taught classes out of Rorion's garage, eventually moving on to the world-famous Gracie Academy. When Rorion realized his dream and the **Ultimate Fighting Championship** went from concept to the cage, many assumed Rickson would represent the family. Rorion, to his credit, went with Royce. Rickson was, simply, too good for the UFC. The focus would be on him, a well-muscled superlative athlete who would aggressively dismantle his opponents. The focus would not be on the art of jiu-jitsu. When the frail Royce ran through the competition, it exhibited how well even a limited athlete could defend himself with the right tools.

Still, the slight didn't sit well with Rickson. When his father and cousin had been family champion, they had represented the clan in the ring against all comers. Rickson too wanted to show the world what he could do. With Rorion's stranglehold on America nearly complete, Rickson left the comfort of his brother's shadow and journeyed to Japan to help bring Gracie Jiu-jitsu back to the land where it all began.

Winning Vale Tudo Japan 1994 was the easy part. Rickson sliced through the overwhelmed competition, winning three matches in just over six minutes. The real challenge was the next day, when he held a seminar for many of the top grapplers in the country. One after another, more than 60 of Japan's best challenged him, with Rickson tapping them all out in rapid succession. What happened next changed MMA in Japan forever.

UWFi 1 mid-carder **Yoji Anjo**, looking to maintain the lie that his form of shoot-style **professional wrestling** was real, came to Los Angeles with a large group of Japanese media to challenge Rickson to a fight. They expected Gracie to decline the last-minute impromptu matchup. Instead, feeling slighted by insults flung in front of his family and students, Gracie proceeded to beat the hell out of Anjo in a closed-door dojo challenge.

As the senior man in the promotion, **Nobuhiko Takada** was bound to defend the promotion's — and the whole nation's — honor against the Gracies. The

In Their Own Words: Rickson Gracie on the power of jiu-jitsu

"I see too many mixed martial artists today trying to mix all the styles with cross training. This is very difficult to do. Most people cannot do this perfectly. It is very rare for someone to take up **boxing** and immediately become an expert in this area. It is hard for someone to start **wrestling** and immediately become great.

"The best way for jiu-jitsu athletes to win isn't by confronting an opponent in the other person's strongest art. Yes, you have to understand the other arts so you can solve them. And the solution is jiu-jitsu. Neutralize their game and bring the match to your area of expertise. This is where you have a much better chance to win.

"The main goal of jiu-jitsu is not winning a match. It is to survive, to use leverage and technique to survive when you are put under pressure. It's the defensive concept that makes jiu-jitsu unbeatable. This is why jiu-jitsu is growing all over the world. It is the techniques and the confidence that is the most valuable thing jiu-jitsu offers."

resulting fight between Takada and Rickson took Japanese MMA to a whole new level. The two fought in the Tokyo Dome in front of tens of thousands of fans. When Gracie defeated Takada, the era of shoot-style wrestling was over, and the era of MMA had begun.

Unlike some of his brothers and cousins, Rickson didn't actively pursue the top fighters in the world. He was not shy about the reason he was competing: money. Already 40 years old, Rickson wanted the easiest matchups for the most cash. It was as simple as that. A year to the day after the Takada fight, he won a rematch at **Pride** 4. Almost two years later, he had the final fight of his career against **Pancrase** founder **Masakatsu Funaki**. Occasionally, even though he is over 50, Rickson's name will still come up in a fantasy booked dream scenario. He still believes he could defeat top champions like **Brock Lesnar** and **Fedor Emelianenko** — and a subset of his biggest fans believe it too. Though his career has long been dead and gone, the legend of Rickson Gracie lives on.

Gracie, Roger

Height: 6'4"
Weight: 220 lbs
Born: 9/26/81
Debut: BodogFight: USA vs. Russia (12/2/06)
Career Record: 3-0

Notable Wins: Ron Waterman (BodogFight: USA vs. Russia); Yuki Kondo (Sengoku 2); Kevin Randleman (Strikeforce: Heavy Artillery)

Roger Gracie (née Gomes — a Gracie on his mother's side) is a unique prospect, a fighter with only two professional bouts who could nevertheless pose considerable problems for even the most seasoned and battle-tested competitors. An eight-time world champion in his family's art of **Brazilian Jiu-jitsu**, Gracie added two prestigious **ADCC** titles to his resume in 2005, taking gold in both the 99 kg and open-weight categories, finishing all seven of his opponents — including such familiar names as Ronaldo Souza, **Fabricio Werdum**, and **Shinya Aoki** — by submission. Gracie is simply the finest heavyweight Brazilian Jiu-jitsu competitor in the world today. And while that isn't enough to guarantee success in modern MMA competition, that credential coupled with his humility and willingness to learn — British writer Mark Law describes this "charming and most modest of men" taking his place among the beginners as he trained **judo** at the London Budokwai to improve his standing work — is enough to make you wonder. A solid light-heavyweight debut against **Kevin Randleman**, which ended, inevitably, by **rear naked choke**, only served to further the intrigue surrounding the Gracie clan's young champion.

Gracie, Rorion

When Rorion Gracie came to America in 1978 to attempt to spread his family's art to the world, he wasn't even the first Gracie teaching in the United States. His cousin Carley Gracie had been instructing students in their modified version of **judo** since 1972. Carley was teaching without incident, without challenges, without street fights, and without success . . . or at least without the kind of success Rorion envisioned for his family's greatest creation. Rorion didn't want to eke out a living or become the most popular grappling instructor in Los Angeles. He wanted success on a global scale.

It's important to consider what a bold move this was on Rorion's part. He could easily have stayed in Brazil, like most of his family, and made a living off his father **Helio**'s name. In Rio de Janeiro at least, the Gracie name was well known and there was no shortage of students looking to train with the first family of Brazilian martial arts. But Rorion's ambition shouldn't be underestimated. He enjoyed the adventure and the idea of building something on his own, with only his hard work and his smarts as his weapons.

That's not entirely true. His other weapon, of course, was **Gracie Jiu-jitsu**: a martial arts system that was undeniably effective. To Rorion, it was clearly the best martial art in the world. Gracie Jiu-jitsu, despite what are now obvious merits, took ten years to catch America's attention. That was almost ten years of flipping burgers and working as a gardener for Rorion, but his confidence never seemed to waver. To try and convince people that Gracie Jiu-jitsu — so different from the kind of high-flying, explosive martial arts people had seen in Bruce Lee movies — was actually effective, Rorion took a page out of the earlier generation's playbook.

He instituted his own Gracie Challenge. He and his younger brothers (**Rickson**, **Royler**, and **Royce** eventually joined him in America) would accept challenges from any and all comers. Rorion often filmed the competition, confrontations in dojos that were dominated by the Gracies who invariably befuddled the traditional martial artists on the ground.

Eventually, like many good-looking men in Hollywood, Rorion caught the eye of a television producer (or, more accurately, his future wife) and began to get bit roles in movies and TV shows. Now the students in his classes, taught out of his garage in southern California, were likely to be in the entertainment industry. In 1989, when they had more than 180 students and a large waiting list, Rorion was able to move the classes from the garage to a real training facility, the Gracie Jiu-jitsu Academy in Torrance, California.

1989 was also the year the Gracies were discovered. It wasn't *Black Belt* or *Inside Kung Fu* that came calling on the men wiping the mats with every other martial artist in California; it was *Playboy* magazine in a feature article called "Bad." The article brought Rorion to the attention of **Art Davie**, an energetic advertising executive looking for unconventional pitchmen. Together, the two marketed *Gracie in Action* tapes, showing the Gracie family, well, in action over the years, complete with Rorion's classic broken English descriptions of the action.

To further spread the art of Gracie Jiu-jitsu, Rorion turned to another of his father's oldest tricks. **Vale Tudo**, anything goes fighting, had been big in Brazil during Helio's prime. Rorion thought they could sell in America as well and Davie agreed. They formed a company called WOW (War of the Worlds) and the two used all their contacts in the television industry, but came away empty-handed. HBO and Showtime both turned them down flat. They called pay-per-view companies as well, finally hitting paydirt with the struggling **Semaphore Entertainment Group**. The **Ultimate Fighting Championship** was born.

For Gracie, the goal never changed. The UFC, like his other projects, was just a way to bring Gracie Jiu-jitsu to the world. On November 12, 1993, the world of martial arts was forever changed. The UFC didn't just pit athlete versus athlete; it pitted style versus style. Soon it became obvious which martial art was the most successful. Just as Rorion expected, Gracie Jiu-jitsu proved itself to be the most effective martial art on the planet. And in the blink of an eye, Gracie Jiu-jitsu became a worldwide phenomenon.

The show, despite having no television programming or institutional support, was an immediate hit. The first UFC attracted 86,000 pay-per-view buyers, and by UFC 5 that number had more than tripled. Gracie sold his share of the company at that point. The rules were changing, instituting time limits and other constraints that would make his style less effective. Besides, Rorion had already proven his point and accomplished his goal. The Gracie name is now the most famous name in martial arts, not just in Brazil, but the world over.

Gracie, Royce

Height: 6′ **Weight:** 175 lbs

Born: 12/12/66 **Debut:** UFC 1 (11/12/93)

Career Record: 14-2-3

Notable Wins: Ken Shamrock (UFC 1); Kimo Leopoldo (UFC 3); Dan Severn (UFC 4); Akebono (Dynamite!! 2004); Kazushi Sakuraba (Hero's Dynamite!! USA)

Notable Losses: Kazushi Sakuraba (Pride Grand Prix 2000 Finals); Matt Hughes (UFC 60)

Royce Gracie is not just the most important fighter in the history of the **UFC**; he is one of the most important martial artists of the 20th century. Gracie changed the way the world thought about the martial arts. Ever since Bruce Lee exploded into America's cultural conscience in the 1970s, people thought of the martial arts as an esoteric collection of spinning and flying kicks, death touches, and the one-inch punch. Gracie changed all of that, showing the world what worked in a real fight and what didn't.

The Gracie family had been refining their ground-focused version of **judo** for almost 70 years when Royce made his MMA debut against boxer Art Jimmerson at UFC 1 on November 12, 1993. Gracie was a brilliant choice to represent the family in this no-holds-barred fighting competition. He was skinny and awkward-looking, 175 pounds dripping wet in a loose-fitting white **gi**, but he beat the boxer in just over two minutes. Even after he defeated Jimmerson, fans were trained to expect an easy **Ken Shamrock** victory in Royce's second round fight. Shamrock was impressively muscled with a body builder's physique, and looked like an action movie star. When Gracie choked him out and then dispatched Gerard Gordeau in the final fight of the evening, it was a victory not just for an athlete but for an art.

Gracie showed that technique can overcome size and strength, making **Gracie Jiu-jitsu** the most intriguing new martial art in the world almost overnight. The UFC was part of a brilliant plan to market the Gracie's system worldwide, but it only worked because the jiu-jitsu itself really worked. There was some criticism that the event, co-owned by Royce's brother **Rorion Gracie**, was providing easy fodder for the jiu-jitsu fighter. Nothing could be further from the case. They actually brought in Shamrock, a man who knew more about submission fighting than 95 percent of martial artists, and later brought in a big bruising wrestler named **Dan Severn**, to push Royce to his limits. No one could beat him, because his art was too good, too effective at equalizing the odds between a big strong man and a small weak one. It was the way Royce's father **Helio** had designed it to work.

Today, every successful MMA fighter has to know about **Brazilian Jiu-jitsu**, either how to use it as an offensive weapon or how to defend against its techniques. Even more than **wrestling** or striking, an inability to defend against submissions spells certain doom for even the most dominant athletes. Without it, you cannot be successful long-term in the sport. Even when Gracie lost in later years, it was to opponents well schooled in his family's techniques — the ultimate victory for the evangelical martial arts family.

All told, Gracie went undefeated in his first UFC tenure, winning three of the first four tournaments. His only recorded "defeat" was a fight with Canadian **Harold Howard** that saw Gracie's corner throw in the towel before the fight began at UFC 3. He beat fighters in a variety of disciplines, including kung fu, **karate**, wrestling, kickboxing, street fighting, and judo. He beat opponents both big and small. When he and his brother Rorion departed the company after fighting Ken Shamrock to a draw at UFC 5, he left behind an incomparable record of accomplishment.

For five years, it seemed like Royce's MMA story had been told in its entirety. But he had an urge to fight, to test himself against the best of the fighters he had inspired. And also, of course, to collect some of the mega paydays Japanese promotions were paying for fighters with the Gracie name. He made his return as part of the greatest tournament the sport of MMA had ever seen. Sixteen men did battle to claim the **Pride** Fighting Championship World Grand Prix. The best of the best were there, including **Igor Vovchanchyn**, **Mark Kerr**, **Mark Coleman**, and **Kazushi Sakuraba**. Royce beat wrestling legend **Nobuhiko Takada** in a lackluster return to the ring, but it set up the match fans were dying to see: Gracie versus the man the media was calling "the Gracie killer."

Because of his brother **Royler**'s controversial loss to Sakuraba, Royce insisted on special rules for the match. There would be no time limit, the referee could not stop the fight for any reason, and only the corner or the fighter himself could call an end to the match. The bout would be contested in 15-minute rounds to a finish. It was an epic battle, and Royce more than held his own against the Japanese sensation. After 90 minutes of fighting, Royce's legs were beaten and battered and he told his corner he didn't think he could walk. Rorion threw in the towel and, for the first time in his MMA career, Royce Gracie was a loser.

Gracie continued his career in Japan, fighting for both Pride and K-1. He was a main event star, continuing the old school tradition of art versus art by taking on judo gold medalist **Hidehiko Yoshida** and Sumo Yokozuna **Akebono**.

Despite the loss to Sakuraba, to most fans in America Gracie was still a legend, the ultimate fighter who had never been defeated. They had never seen the Sakuraba fight, so to them, it was as if it never existed.

With a newly created television audience, most of whom were familiar with the legend of Royce Gracie, **Zuffa** took an interest in bringing Royce and the other early stars of the UFC back to the Octagon. Royce had been approached before, but the UFC could never afford him. This time he asked for a $400,000 guarantee and a cut of the pay-per-view profits. Zuffa agreed and like that, the Gracie train was on the move to the UFC.

Gracie's opponent was long-time welterweight champion **Matt Hughes**. Hughes had been as big a failure at the box office as he'd been a success in the cage. He was considered a great, but boring, fighter. The second season of ***The Ultimate Fighter*** changed all that. He came into the Gracie fight as one of the UFC's biggest villains, the perfect foil for the legendary Brazilian. The pre-fight interviews were amazing. Gracie put it into terms everyone could understand: "This is my house. I built it."

The fight resonated with fans like none other that preceded it. More people bought this show on pay-per-view (620,000) than had purchased any other UFC in history. In the cage, the fight wasn't a classic. Hughes dismantled Gracie in the first round. But it wasn't all for naught — to beat the legend, Hughes employed the techniques the Gracies had shared with the world. It was a loss for Royce Gracie, but a win for Gracie Jiu-jitsu.

The Hughes fight would have been the perfect ending to a storybook career. The older fighter could have departed with his head held high, content that the younger man had to play his own game in order to best him. Instead, he fought one more time. Although he avenged his loss to Sakuraba, the win came with a heavy price. Gracie tested positive for the **steroid** Nandrolone in a post-fight screening. He protests his innocence, but MMA's all-time greatest fighter left the sport with a black cloud hanging over a glorious career.

Gracie, Royler

Height: 5′8″ **Weight:** 155 lbs
Born: 12/6/65 **Debut:** UVF 2 (6/24/96)
Career Record: 11-5
Notable Win: Noboru Asahi (Vale Tudo Japan 96)
Notable Losses: Kazushi Sakuraba (Pride 8); Genki Sudo (K-1 MMA Romanex); Norifumi Yamamoto (Hero's 3)

Royler Gracie's 1999 **Pride** fight with **Kazushi Sakuraba** must have felt an awful lot like déjà vu for his father, **Helio Gracie**. Royler was fighting the best Japanese technician in the world, he was giving up 30 pounds, and then he got caught in a **Kimura** lock. It was like a flashback to Helio's own 1951 fight with **Masahiko Kimura** himself. In that contest, Helio's brother **Carlos** threw in the towel. At the Tokyo Dome, Royler's cornermen were willing to let him see it through until the end.

Instead, the referee stepped in to stop the fight. The Gracie contingent was furious. The rules of the fight dictated that only the fighters and their corners could stop the fight, but concerned for Royler's arm, the official put a stop to things with less than two minutes remaining. The Gracies were unconcerned, sure that the exceptionally flexible Royler would have survived the hold, or — like his cousin **Renzo** in a later match — allowed Sakuraba to rip his arm to shreds. For Royler it was a matter of honor. Once a fight started, he only wanted it to end with his arm raised or leaving on a stretcher.

It was a typical match for Royler during his MMA career. He was the most accomplished Gracie on the jiu-jitsu mats, winning the World jiu-jitsu title four times and winning the prestigious Abu Dhabi Combat Club (**ADCC**) Submission Wrestling Championship title three times in a row. But he never developed the overall skills he needed to succeed in the new era of cross-trained MMA.

Gracie, Ryan

Nickname: The Bulldog **Height:** 5′9″
Weight: 185 lbs **Born:** 8/14/74
Debut: Pride 10 (8/27/00) **Career Record:** 5-2
Notable Wins: Tokimitsu Ishizawa (Pride 10); Ikuhisa Minowa (Pride Bushido 3)
Notable Losses: Kazushi Sakuraba (Pride 12); Tokimitsu Ishizawa (Pride 15)

The Gracie bad boy, Ryan stayed true to the family's long-standing tradition of street fights and grandstand challenges. He was a solid professional fighter, with wins over **Ikuhisa Minowa** and **pro wrestling**'s Kendo Kashin (Tokimitsu Ishizawa) but his fights in **Pride** were always overshadowed by his life outside the ring.

Ryan was, simply put, a wild man. He got in a number of street fights, was shot in the leg under questionable conditions, and died in prison after a crime spree in Rio de Janeiro. Even during his most stable days, when he was building his fighting career, Ryan was more famous for his fights that occurred on the street.

Ryan's most famous feud, albeit one that never ended in an officially sanctioned fight, was with fellow Brazilian grappler Wallid Ismail. The two were signed to fight several times but the fights always fell through . . . unless you mean in a nightclub or on the beach; then it was on. Ryan punched Wallid at a club and was rendered unconscious with a **guillotine choke**. The two had words on Pepino Beach where Ryan, in his own words, "spit in his face and called him a fag. I was trying to start a fight."

Much of the back-and-forth between the two men may have been for show. Both spent years trying to turn their war of words into a megafight. But other confrontations were all too real. A fight between the two was canceled when Gracie was arrested for stabbing a man in a bar fight.

His demons proved too much for him in the end. On December 14, 2007, Gracie went on a rampage, stealing a car, crashing it, and then attempting to steal a motorcycle. The cyclist hit him over the head with his helmet and a group of bystanders helped restrain him until police could arrive. Tests show Gracie was high on a cocktail of prescription and recreational drugs. A doctor prescribed some medication to calm Gracie, but the result was tragic. The next morning, Ryan Gracie was found dead in his cell. He was 33 years old. Ryan Gracie is survived by his wife Andrea and son Rayron.

Griffin, Forrest

Height: 6'3" **Weight:** 205 lbs

Born: 7/1/79 **Debut:** RSF 5 (10/27/01)

Career Record: 17-6

Notable Wins: Jeff Monsen (WEFC 1); Stephan Bonnar (*The Ultimate Fighter* 1 Finale); Mauricio Rua (UFC 76); Quinton Jackson (UFC 86); Tito Ortiz (UFC 106)

Notable Losses: Jeremy Horn (IFC: Global Domination); Tito Ortiz (UFC 59); Keith Jardine (UFC 66); Rashad Evans (UFC 92); Anderson Silva (UFC 101)

Forrest Griffin is a little bit crazy. That needs to be noted up front. He is a man who enjoys pain, yet has had to learn to avoid punishment to be successful in the cage. He is smart and self-deprecating, yet will chase a rude driver to his

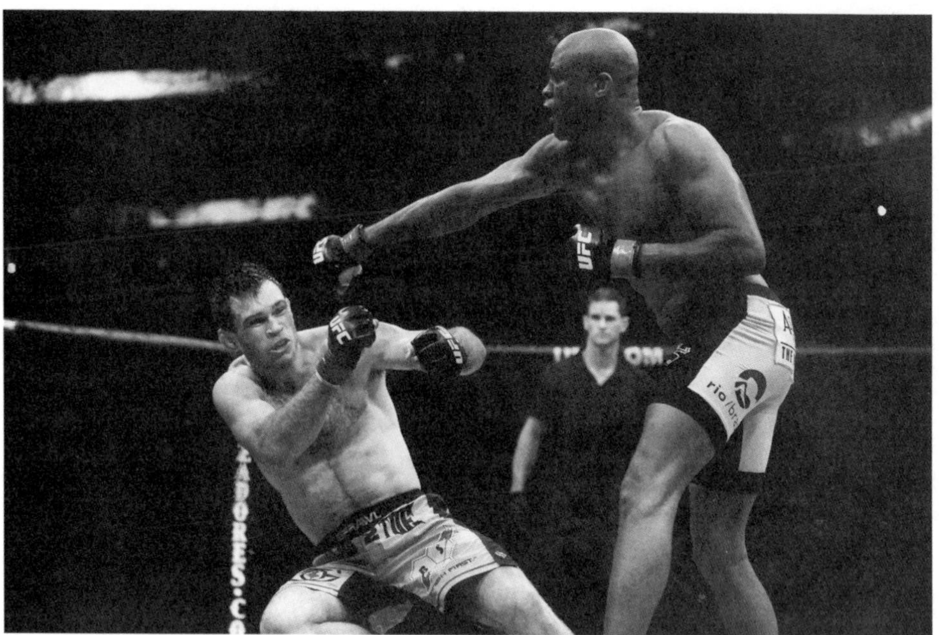

destination looking for a street fight. He's rich and famous, yet lives well below his means and drives a beat-up Scion. His friends all love him, yet to strangers and reporters he is often rude and standoffish. He's a walking conundrum. He may also be the most important fighter in **UFC** history.

Griffin loves to fight — always has. Growing up in Georgia, he took plenty of beatings, always coming back to look for more. A football player without the athletic talent to pursue sports as a career, Griffin was lucky enough to meet Rory and Adam Singer at the University of Georgia, where he quickly became obsessed with MMA. Griffin had an affinity for fighting and a rare toughness that allowed him to keep going long after others have given up. This wasn't enough for him to make it; making it big in MMA is hard and is often as much about good luck as about talent. Griffin was almost ready to fall back on Plan B, a job as a police officer, when he got the offer to join the cast of a new reality show called ***The Ultimate Fighter***.

The rest is history. Griffin narrowly beat **Stephan Bonnar** to win the light heavyweight prize. It was one of the best fights in UFC history, a display of willpower and balls that made many people fans for life. It was a fight that helped display for Spike TV executives exactly what MMA was all about. The UFC quickly signed a new television contract and the company's subsequent growth was nothing short of phenomenal.

After winning the title of "Ultimate Fighter," Griffin quickly announced his presence as a fighter to be reckoned with. Fighters in the gym were amazed

In Their Own Words: Griffin on validating *TUF*

"You know, obviously I think it's a good form of validation; two guys from the show fighting for the title is pretty impressive. And I think now they make the guys on the show fight like ten times before they're ever done with the show. So if you win that or you even come out of that and do well, you've got to think this guy has been fighting every other week . . . he's had four or five fights the way they're doing the show now. So I think they're earning it now. The guys watch the show. And each time you kind of want to top the guys that came before you. So I think it's almost a sense of pushing the envelope or trying to raise the bar."

by his work ethic and his refusal to give anything less than his best. Still, greatness seemed beyond his grasp. He lost to a past-his-prime **Tito Ortiz** and to **Keith Jardine.** The way he handled those losses, with humor and a shrug of his shoulders, helped Griffin remain a fan favorite. But he seemed miles away from a title shot.

The loss to Jardine seemed to flip a switch in Griffin's brain. He had already developed his skills significantly since the first fight with Bonnar. The Jardine fight made him even smarter. Now, when Griffin stepped in the cage, he was ready for whatever his opponent might do. Success followed. He beat the heavily favored **Mauricio Rua** to earn his first title shot. Griffin had come full circle. He had made his name on *The Ultimate Fighter*; now he was coming back to the show — as a coach. Griffin went on to upset **Quinton "Rampage" Jackson** over five grueling rounds to win the light heavyweight title. The people's champion was now the actual champion.

Success, hard to come by, was fleeting. Griffin lost his title in his very first defense. It was a proud moment for the *Ultimate Fighter* franchise, as the champion fell to fellow *TUF* alumnus **Rashad Evans**, but a low for Griffin. In a crowded light heavyweight picture, Griffin was suddenly shuffled back into the pack.

Griffin, Tyson

Height: 5'6" **Weight:** 155

Born: 4/20/84 **Debut:** Gladiator Challenge 32 (11/18/04)

Career Record: 14-3

Notable Wins: Urijah Faber (Gladiator Challenge 42); Duane Ludwig (Strikeforce: Revenge); Clay Guida (UFC 72); Hermes Franca (UFC 103)

Notable Losses: Frank Edgar (UFC 67); Sean Sherk (UFC 90)

In many ways, Tyson Griffin is a 155-pound **Randy Couture**. Like his mentor, Griffin is a very good wrestler with surprisingly good hands. Like Couture, Griffin is also notorious for his lack of finishing prowess, with seven fights in a row going to the judges' score card. Combine those elements with a work ethic in the cage second to none and the result is a series of exceptional fights. This was both a good and a bad thing. Fans were treated to some all-time classics, including five bouts that won the coveted Fight of the Night honors from the **UFC** brass. But it also meant Griffin never had an easy night, putting his body through the rigors that can only be dished out in a 15-minute war.

Griffin ended the string of judges' decisions by knocking out **Hermes Franca** at UFC 103, becoming the first fighter ever to stop the super-tough veteran. Together with previous wins over a diverse set of fighters like Thiago Tavares and **Clay Guida**, the victory pointed towards Griffin being an enduring force in the UFC's lightweight division. Just don't count on him fighting for another 20 years like his coach Couture. The similarities have to end somewhere.

Ground and pound

A fundamental ground fighting tactic in which a grappler secures a stable and relatively safe top position (see: **positional hierarchy**) and delivers punches, elbows, and knees to his opponent. Relentless ground and pound limits the effectiveness of submission attacks from the bottom fighter's **guard**, and creates

opportunities for the fighter on top to improve his position further, attempt a submission attempt of his own, or finish the fight with strikes. Pioneered by **Mark Coleman**, a dominant wrestler with limited submission skills, ground and pound has grown from one man's unique approach to a ubiquitous staple of the sport. Its greatest contemporary exponent is the peerless **Fedor Emelianenko**, who complements his smooth takedowns and fine positional grappling with the most ferocious ground and pound attack seen in ring or cage since "The Hammer" first showed the martial arts world just how important it was to get on top — and stay there.

Guard

A grappling position in which a fighter, on his back, uses his legs and hips to control his opponent's movements and prevent him from gaining a dominant pinning position. Although the list of guard variations is long and ever-expanding — take the rubber guard, spider guard, butterfly guard, half-butterfly guard, leg hook guard, high guard, X-guard, and De la Riva guard, for starters — we can simplify matters somewhat by distinguishing broadly between two categories. If the fighter has wrapped his legs tightly around his opponent's body, and locked them together, he's playing a closed guard; if his legs are not closed, but are used in such a way that his opponent is nevertheless kept in front of him, unable to pass, it's an open guard. There is a commonly held misconception that an open guard is offensive while a closed guard is necessarily defensive, but in truth there are a wide variety of sweeps and submissions available in each variation, making every guard position simultaneously a tool for both offense and defense. There are virtually no submission holds in MMA that can't be either executed or initiated from guard, whereas, in terms of submission attempts, the top player has only **leg locks** at his disposal — low percentage attacks in modern MMA that tend to sacrifice position.

This is not to suggest that the guard is an inherently advantageous position. Given roughly comparable grappling abilities, the guard is at best neutral for the fighter on his back. The top fighter can attempt to pass his opponent's guard and move into a dominant **side control** or **mount**, or he can choose to posture up and strike. The familiar saying that you can turn a black belt into a brown belt (and on down the line) with a solid shot to the head is never truer than in the guard position, with a strong top player maintaining his upright posture and dropping elbows.

See also **positional hierarchy**

Guida, Clay

Nicknames: The Carpenter, The Caveman **Height:** 5'7"
Weight: 155 lbs **Born:** 12/8/81
Debut: Silverback Classic 17 (7/26/03) **Career Record:** 27-11
Notable Wins: Josh Thomson (Strikeforce: Shamrock vs. Gracie); Nate Diaz (UFC 94)
Notable Losses: Gilbert Melendez (Strikeforce: Revenge); Tyson Griffin (UFC 72); Roger Huerta (*The Ultimate Fighter* 6 Finale); Kenny Florian (UFC 107)

When Clay Guida is having a bad day at the gym — when he just doesn't feel like doing that extra rep, when he wants to quit and go home — he sucks it up. Because as hard as most fighters train, Guida knows what real work is.

When he was 21 years old Guida spent months on the Bering Sea, fishing in deep cold waters for crab. Life for Guida was like scenes from the television show *The Deadliest Catch*. He broke up ice to find the living treasure beneath, bringing up hundreds of pounds of ocean life while the 200-foot boat sat precariously in the windy and deadly ocean. Crews often worked for 20 hours a day. Nothing again will ever seem hard.

It's that work ethic that has made Guida a MMA star. The Chicago native burst onto the scene with an amazing win over Josh Thomson for **Strikeforce**. The hype on that card was for **Frank Shamrock** taking on Cesar Gracie. Afterward, no one could stop talking about the relentless wrestler who refused to lose against a bigger, stronger, and more athletic opponent. Guida has become a **UFC** fan favorite, fighting furiously with his trademark flowing hair flying into his eyes, while he tries to close his opponent's. His record is just 5–4 in the Octagon, and he may never win a UFC title, but it's not his success that makes fans love him — it's his ability to fight hard and fast for the entirety of three rounds. Guida may not win, but fans will always know they've been watching a fight.

Guillotine choke

A chokehold in which the attacker, either standing in front of his opponent or in **guard**, encircles the opponent's neck and restricts the flow of either blood or oxygen to the brain, depending on which variation of the technique is employed. The attacker wraps his strangling arm around the opponent's neck, and grips the wrist of the strangling arm with his free hand. Pulling the strangling arm high towards the sternum while keeping the shoulder of the strangling arm low, the attacker applies pressure to either the trachea or the carotid arteries, depending on the precise placement of the forearm. Relatively simple to apply, but difficult to master, the guillotine is among the most common submission holds in MMA. Any time a fighter leaves his head low in the **clinch** or in a failed takedown attempt, the opportunity is there.

Strangely, the most widely viewed guillotine choke in the history of the sport came in a match initially seen by a very small audience. When venerable CBS news magazine *60 Minutes* ran a piece in late 2006 on the incredible growth of MMA, correspondent Scott Pelley spent time with **Pat Miletich** and **Renzo Gracie** as they prepared to face off in the now defunct **International Fight League**. Pelley's piece ended with Gracie securing an arm-in, flying guillotine (one of many possible variations) to finish Miletich in fine fashion in front of what turned out to be an audience of nearly 16 million.

Hackney, Keith

Nickname: The Giant Killer
Height: 5'11"
Weight: 200 lbs
Born: 1960
Debut: UFC 3 (9/9/94)
Career Record: 2-2
Notable Wins: Emmanuel Yarborough (UFC 3); Joe Son (UFC 4)
Notable Losses: Royce Gracie (UFC 4); Marco Ruas (Ultimate Ultimate 95)

Of the many early **UFC** competitors who took a handful of fights and then disappeared from the sport almost completely, Keith Hackney is perhaps the most fondly remembered. A tough-as-nails Kenpo **karate** practitioner with B-movie action star looks, Hackney seemed as though he'd leapt straight out of the pages of *Black Belt* magazine: black tank top; baggy, tapered-leg black pants with "Kenpo" emblazoned down one side; even full-on karate *hair*. Keith Hackney had The Look.

His short career was distinguished by two memorable wins, both by full-on pummeling. The first came against the enormous Emmanuel Yarborough, whom Hackney dropped with a big right before breaking his own hand delivering a series of unanswered punches to the back of Yarborough's head. It was ugly, but not as ugly as Hackney's next UFC appearance, in which he rained down blows upon the (later indicted) groin of *Austin Powers* henchman and alleged rapist Joe Son. Like many competitors of his era, Hackney was simply out of his depth when faced with skilled grapplers like **Royce Gracie** and **Marco Ruas**, but Hackney made his mark. He currently teaches in Roselle, Illinois.

Half-guard (Half-mount)

A grappling position in which the fighter on bottom traps one of his opponent's legs, preventing him from gaining the more dominant **mount** or **side control** positions. Sport **Brazilian Jiu-jitsu** practitioners in particular have developed what was once a principally defensive position into a potentially dangerous place for the top fighter to be. The fighter on bottom works to stay on his side, rather than flat on his back, so that he can threaten his opponent with a variety of sweeps, escapes to **rear mount**, and submission holds, including the **Kimura**, **knee bar**, **omoplata**, **triangle choke**, and **guillotine**. And for the fighter on bottom looking to scramble back to his feet, half-guard can actually be a much better position than full **guard**.

But despite the ever-increasing technical sophistication of the half-guard game, in modern MMA it's almost always more desirable to be on top, and half-guard — or half-mount, from the perspective of the top player — is no exception. There's no small number of submissions available from the top, such as the Kimura and Americana entangled arm locks, advanced **arm triangle** chokes like the D'Arce and brabo, and, for the fighter who is willing to risk position for submission, **leg locks**. The top fighter can work to continue his progress towards side control or mount, or he can choose to settle in and deliver short elbows and punches from a relatively stable position.

See also **positional hierarchy**

Hallman, Dennis

Nickname: Superman **Height:** 5′9″

Weight: 170 lbs **Born:** 12/2/75

Debut: UFCF: Clash of the Titans (1/11/97)

Career Record: 42-13-2 (1 No Contest)

Notable Wins: Matt Hughes (Extreme Challenge 21, UFC 29)

Notable Losses: Dave Menne (Shooto: 10th Anniversary Event); Caol Uno (Shooto R.E.A.D. 3); Jens Pulver (UFC 33); Frank Trigg (WFA 3, UFC 48)

Here is a complete list of fighters who have managed the Herculean task of defeating **Matt Hughes**, the **UFC**'s greatest welterweight champion, not once, but twice: (i) **Georges St. Pierre**, who is arguably the most complete fighter in the history of the sport, and who looks set to dominate the division as Hughes himself once did; and (ii) Dennis Hallman, who is . . . Dennis Hallman. While there can be no doubt Hallman is a fine wrestler and a competent submission artist, he's also the very definition of a journeyman — which makes this all very strange. With over 50 verifiable fights (and 20-odd more, Hallman claims, that don't appear on any database) in an alphabet soup of MMA promotions, Hallman has bounced around the world, grinding out a living the hard way, while a man he tapped twice, first to a **guillotine choke**, then to an **arm bar** — both times in *under twenty seconds* — went on to fame and fortune as a main event fighter cashing enormous checks.

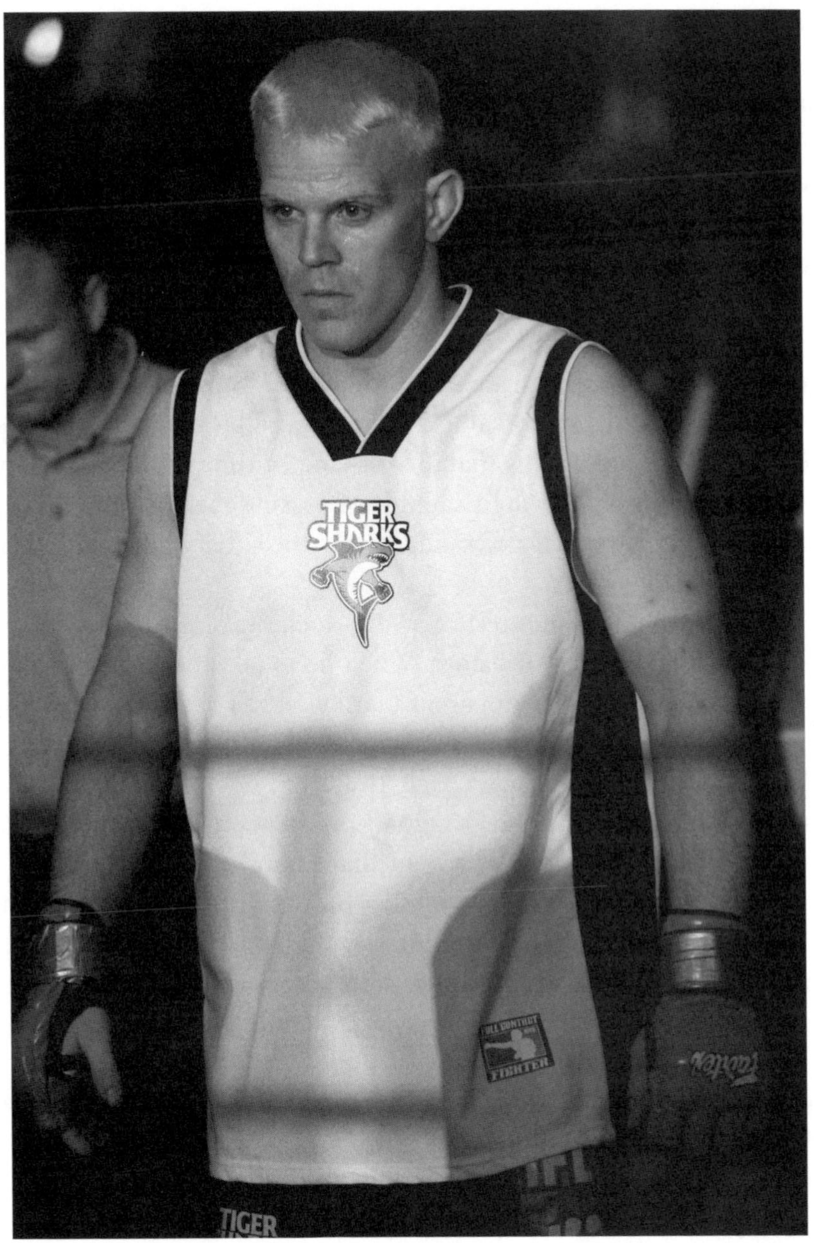

Hallman has been consistently active throughout his now long career, fighting as often as nine times a year, with the notable exception of 2008, when he served a year-long suspension after testing positive for both Drostanolone and Nandrolone following a **Strikeforce** bout against Jeremiah Metcalf. With that behind him, and a few more trademark first-round submission wins under his belt, Hallman signed a four-fight UFC deal in the summer of 2009. If Matt Hughes isn't nervous, he should be.

Hamill, Matt

Nickname: The Hammer
Height: 6'1"
Weight: 205 lbs
Born: 10/5/76
Debut: XFO 7 (6/24/06)
Career Record: 9–2
Notable Wins: Tim Boetsch (UFC Fight Night 13); Keith Jardine (*The Ultimate Fighter* 2 Finale)
Notable Losses: Michael Bisping (UFC 75); Rich Franklin (UFC 88)

Matt Hamill is an Olympic television producer's dream. He would be the perfect feature for one of those pieces they love so much, the ones that humanize the otherwise unknowable athletes. Hamill is the **UFC**'s first disabled athlete. Deaf since birth, his inability to sing in tune didn't stop him from growing into a hoss more than capable of tossing men around on the mat. He was good at it, even if he couldn't hear the satisfying grunt when they hit the ground.

Hamill was a standout wrestler at the Rochester Institute of Technology and is a Division III Hall of Famer. When he joined the cast of ***The Ultimate Fighter*** 3, it quickly became apparent that he wasn't there as a nod to political correctness. Hamill wasn't just going to be competitive, he was the odds-on favorite to win. Even coach **Tito Ortiz**, one of the most dominant wrestlers to ever appear in the Octagon, couldn't control Hamill on the mat.

It just as quickly became apparent that Hamill was not a loveable and cuddly teddy bear. He was a bully and a bit of a jerk, so cocky that he was essentially a hearing-impaired **Matt Hughes**. In this at least, Hamill did more than almost anyone to break down stereotypes. Deaf athletes could not only compete with the best in the world; they could also be domineering frat boy jerks.

Amazingly, the other fighters in the house were so repellant that they managed to make the swaggering Hamill into a sympathetic figure. **Michael Bisping** was transparently jealous of Hamill's skills and conspired with Kendall Grove to take a sparring session to the next level, intentionally trying to hurt and embarrass Hamill. The season was building towards a climatic finale of Hamill versus Bisping, but it wasn't to be. Hamill was injured during his fight with Mike Nickels and couldn't continue. Bisping and Grove, Hamill's on-screen nemeses, went on to earn six-figure contracts with the UFC. Hamill would have to wait for his revenge.

After three wins in his first three UFC preliminary fights, Hamill earned his shot at Bisping. Fighting in Bisping's home country of England, Hamill gave Bisping all he could handle at UFC 75. He battered the Brit standing and controlled him on the ground. Even Bisping's countrymen were shocked when he was announced as the winner. As the British fans booed the decision, Hamill's transformation from villain to hero was complete.

Since that fight — one of the most controversial decisions in UFC history — Hamill has established that he is more than a journeyman, but has yet to establish that he is a legitimate contender for UFC gold. A loss to former middleweight champion **Rich Franklin** at UFC 88 seemed to cement Hamill's standing as a fighter who fell just short of championship potential. Hamill will be just good enough to beat most everyone the UFC puts in front of him, while remaining just limited enough never to beat the best. His most important role will be one at which he's already excelled: shattering stereotypes and proving that a disability should never prevent you from pursuing a dream.

Hammer House

The Hammer House was different from some of the other famous fight teams in MMA's early years. **Ken Shamrock** moved his **Lion's Den** to progressively nicer digs as they got more and more successful. **Pat Miletich** did the same with his Miletich Fighting Systems team. And even when the team trained on the racquetball court of a local gym, they at least had a regular place to go work out.

Mark Coleman was a simpler man, one who took going back to basics to a whole different level. When his team (including **Kevin Randleman**, **Wes Sims**, and **Phil Baroni**) trained, they did it in Coleman's house. In the basement.

In Their Own Words: Wes Sims on the Hammer House

"In Columbus there is nothing. The Hammer House is Mark's basement. It was much like Stu Hart's Dungeon. There was a lot of blood spilled. We trained pretty hard. There were a lot of injuries in those early days. Broken nose. Broken fingers. Broken toes. Nothing severe, thank God, but there were a lot of injuries.

"I was a basketball player, but I always wanted to be a pro wrestler. My doctor was Mark's doctor and he hooked me up with Mark. I had seen the UFC, like the first five, and I was like, 'Wow. That's some crazy shit there.' When I met Mark [I] thought, 'Fuck it, I'll give it a swing.' He was getting ready to fight Ricardo Morais so he was ready to give me a shot. He needed a big boy in the gym with him. I went over and worked out and it was crazy. We just hit it off and we trained together ever since."

It was hard-core training, concentrating mostly on the **wrestling** base that made Coleman and Randleman NCAA champions. The two men would throw each other around the basement, banging into walls, dripping blood, and hugging when it was all over. The two became **UFC** heavyweight champion and Coleman ascended to the top of the sport in Japan as well. At the same time, Baroni became one of the most entertaining fighters in the sport.

Eventually, the members of the Hammer House all fell from the top of the game. While the sport moved towards cross-trained and well-rounded fighters, the Hammer House seemed trapped in a time warp where Coleman's patented **ground and pound** style was still unbeatable. Their games never moved to the next level, but their toughness, athleticism, and wrestling prowess made them a threat in any fight, as some of MMA's best — including **Mirko Cro Cop** and **Fedor Emelianenko** — learned to their dismay.

Hansen, Joachim

Nickname: Hellboy | **Height:** 5'9"
Weight: 155 lbs | **Born:** 5/26/79
Debut: FinnFight 3 (11/6/99) | **Career Record:** 19-10-1

Notable Wins: Rumina Sato (Shooto 2003: 3/18 in Korakuen Hall); Takanori Gomi (Shooto 2003: 8/10 in Yokohama Gymnasium); Gesias Cavalcante (Shooto 2004: 7/16 in Korakuen Hall); Caol Uno (K-1 Hero's 1); Shinya Aoki (Dream 5)

Notable Losses: Vitor Ribeiro (Shooto 2003: Year-End Show); Hayato Sakurai (Pride Bushido 9); Shinya Aoki (Pride Shockwave 2006)

"I would rather have bleeding hemorrhoids than fight for the **UFC**," Joachim Hansen once said. This colorful image helps explain why Hansen remains a virtual unknown to North American MMA fans, despite being one of the premier lightweight fighters in the world. A slick grappler and dangerous striker with some of the best knees in the business, Hansen has consistently fought top competition in Japan, putting together a resume unlike any other in his weight class.

Hansen built his reputation as an aggressive attacking fighter in the **Shooto** organization, earning early career wins over legendary submission artist **Rumina Sato** and the heavy-handed **Takanori Gomi**, taking Gomi's Shooto welterweight title in the process. In his first title defense, however, Hansen tapped to an **arm triangle** by **Vitor "Shaolin" Ribeiro** in an outstanding grappling contest. Surprisingly, it was the last championship Hansen would hold for five years.

Hansen earned a tough decision win over a young **Gesias Cavalcante**, and knocked out both **Caol Uno** and **Masakazu Iminari** with devastating knees before ruining a second shot at Shooto gold against **Tatsuya Kawajiri** a mere eight seconds into that fight when he connected with a match-ending kick to the groin. It was not until the **Dream** Lightweight Grand Prix 2008 that Hansen truly took center stage, dropping a grueling first round match to **Eddie Alvarez** before earning his way into the tournament finals with a reserve bout submission win over Kultar Gill. In the tournament final, Hansen avenged his 2006 **Pride** loss to **Shinya Aoki**, finishing the "Tobikan Judan" with punches on the ground to become the first Dream lightweight champion. It was a fitting reward: no one in the sport has put on better fights against better competition than Joachim Hansen.

Han, Volk

Real name: Magomedhan Amanulajevich Gamzathanov **Height:** 6'3"
Weight: 230 lbs **Born:** 4/15/61
Debut: 5/20/00 **Career Record:** 7-1
Notable Wins: Bobby Hoffman (Rings: King of Kings 2000 Block B); Andrei Kopylov (Rings: Russia vs. Bulgaria)
Notable Loss: Antonio Rodrigo Nogueria (Rings: King of Kings 2000 Final)

Han is, in the opinion of many experts, the single best professional wrestler in the history of that sport. His gift was an ability to make his scripted contests look real, fluidly moving into and out of holds and building the drama for an explosive finish.

His skill quickly made him the top foreign foil for **Rings** frontman **Akira Maeda**. The two were great opponents, as Han's flashy submissions were pitted against Maeda's hard kicks and devastating suplexes.

In 2000, upon Maeda's retirement, Rings went from fake fights to legitimate contests. Han was 39 years old and many expected him to fade into the background with his old rival. Instead, he established that everything he had pretended to be for the past decade was real. Han really was a **sambo** expert. He really was a tough submission fighter. And he could look just as tough when the fights were real as he did when they were fake. His only career loss came to the man who would soon establish himself as the world's best heavyweight, **Antonio Rodrigo Nogueira**.

Not only did Han establish his bona fides, he was also the man responsible for helping **Fedor Emelianenko** prepare for Rings competition. The two, together with Andrei Kopylov, **Sergei Kharitonov**, and Mikhail Iliokhine, pushed each other to new heights and made the Russian Top Team one of the best training camps in the sport. Although Fedor left the team to join Red Devil after a dispute, he has said he retains much respect for Han.

"I regard Han very well. He is one of trailblazers in Rings," Emelianenko said. "And though Rings is fairly far from **Pride**, personally my experiences of fights in this organization were very useful to me."

Hazelett, Dustin

Nickname: McLovin'
Height: 6'1"
Weight: 170 lbs
Born: 4/29/86
Debut: KOTC: Dayton (10/23/04)
Career Record: 12-5
Notable Wins: Rhalan Gracie (Gracie Fighting Challenge: Team Gracie vs. Team Hammer House); Josh Burkman (*The Ultimate Fighter* 7 Finale); Tamdan McCrory (UFC 91)
Notable Loss: Tony DeSouza (UFC: The Final Chapter)

In an era where every fighter who steps into the ring or the Octagon at the sport's highest level has trained extensively in submission fighting, nobody should be able to do the things Dustin Hazelett has been able to do. Only fighters of **Demian Maia**'s or **Shinya Aoki**'s caliber have put on the kinds of grappling clinics Hazelett managed against Josh Burkman and Tamdan McCrory in back-to-back **UFC** appearances in 2008. When Hazelett climbed up Josh Burkman's back after a half-successful whizzer takedown/uchi mata **judo** throw and transitioned seamlessly into an **arm bar**, it wasn't just the Submission of the Night; it was one of the most amazing submission finishes anyone had ever seen in mixed martial arts.

Clearly, Hazelett developed a taste for the kind of bonus money that comes along with displays like that, because he was right back at it a few months later against "The Barn Cat," Tamdan McCrory. From **guard**, Hazelett attacked with an **omoplata**, which is generally used as a transitional move in contemporary MMA. It's exceedingly hard to finish even the tightest omoplata without your opponent rolling to relieve the pressure or simply slipping out of the hold. But Hazelett was attacking early in the fight, before the sweat would be thick enough to facilitate an escape. Hazelett stuck with the hold for over a minute, slowly breaking down McCrory's posture until he could contort the arm at a truly unnatural angle for another spectacular arm bar.

At only 24 years of age, there's still a lot we don't know about what kind of fighter Dustin Hazelett is going to be. The long, lean Hazelett might not turn out to have the athleticism or the chin to hang with fighters at the top of the UFC's deep welterweight division. But for now, at least, we'll just sit back and enjoy the astounding finishes this young **Brazilian Jiu-jitsu** black belt has already proven himself capable of.

HDNet

Mark Cuban, the brash billionaire owner of the National Basketball Association's Dallas Mavericks, wasn't the first entrepreneur to see dollar signs in the burgeoning success of the **UFC**. Before Calvin Ayre went belly up, he wasn't even the wealthiest. But he might be the savviest competitor the UFC could face. Savvy enough to realize that he would need some promotional muscle to battle the **Fertitta brothers** on their own turf. Savvy enough to seek out the very best money could buy: Vince and Linda McMahon, the brains behind the legendary World Wrestling Entertainment juggernaut.

That potentially devastating (and undoubtedly wildly entertaining) pairing never happened. The McMahons decided to stick with what they were best at — promoting wrestling — fearing another network partnership after the XFL debacle. Cuban, after just two events, took a step back from promoting MMA. Instead, HDNet became the station of choice for any independent promoter with a fight card and a high definition camera.

The station, struggling to establish a foothold in the suddenly crowded high definition television market it had helped pioneer, featured fights big and small, all designed to attract the coveted 18–34 male demographic. HDNet showed everything from the big budget Japanese **Dream** and K-1 cards, featuring the best non-UFC talent in the world, to glorified independent shows like Ring of Fire and Ring of Combat, in which the fighters were virtual unknowns.

Although Cuban remains a vocal MMA supporter, he seems to have decided not to put his money where his mouth is. He's content to let others challenge the **Zuffa** empire, becoming simply the medium to present those challengers to those viewers who want their carnage in the cage at 1080i. The dueling press conferences between Cuban and the equally boisterous UFC President **Dana White** will remain just a figment of our imaginations . . . for now. With Cuban anything is possible.

Heel hook: see **Leg locks**

Henderson, Dan

Nicknames: Hollywood, Hendo | **Height:** 6′

Weight: 185-205 lbs | **Born:** 8/24/70

Debut: Brazil Open 1997 (6/15/97) | **Career Record:** 25-8

Notable Wins: Carlos Newton (UFC 17); Antonio Rodrigo Nogueira (Rings: King of Kings 99); Murilo Bustamante (Pride Final Conflict 2003); Wanderlei Silva (Pride 33); Rich Franklin (UFC 93)

Notable Losses: Wanderlei Silva (Pride 12); Antonio Rodrigo Nogueira (Pride 24); Quinton Jackson (UFC 75); Anderson Silva (UFC 82); Jake Shields (Strikeforce: Nashville)

There is a lot of talk in the MMA world from guys who claim they just plain love to fight. Dan Henderson is more candid and more open than most fighters. He got into it for the money. Henderson was an **Olympian** in both 1992 and 1996 but never medaled, finishing 10th and 12th respectively. He was looking for one more chance, but with a wife and later a new baby on the way, the $650 stipend he got monthly to train wasn't going to cut it.

Henderson was days away from letting his dream die and becoming a chiropractor when he got a call from two old **wrestling** buddies, Rico Chiapparelli and **Randy Couture**. They wanted him to join their new fight team, the Real American Wrestlers (RAW), and supplement his income in the new sport of MMA. Henderson's wrestling career got new life and MMA got one of the sport's all-time greats.

For his first several MMA contests, Henderson had almost no experience or training. He hadn't worked on submissions much or done any **boxing** training outside of pounding a heavy bag. But he was a quick study. He had to be, be-

cause he was thrown in with the lions from the very beginning. After winning an open-weight tournament in Brazil in 1997, he won the first **UFC** lightweight tournament by beating the tough Alan Goes and future champion **Carlos Newton** all in one night. His bank account got a boost when he won the inaugural **Rings** King of Kings tournament in early 2000, earning plenty of respect to go along with the then unheard-of purse of $200,000.

Henderson stands out just as much for his level of competition as he does for his four tournament victories and multiple championships. He's taken on a who's who of MMA: Carlos Newton, both **Nogueira** brothers, **Wanderlei Silva,**

In Their Own Words: Dan Henderson on getting started in MMA

"When I started MMA, I was still trying to make the 2000 Olympic team and I was fighting to support myself. There is zero money in wrestling, so I was just doing MMA for the money. I didn't know a lot and had never even sparred before. Going into UFC 17, I knew Carlos Newton was a jiu-jitsu guy, but he came out kicking my leg. I had done very little training and no sparring and I didn't know how to stop the kicks. It was a great night, despite a little bit of a sore leg, but I wish I had known a little more MMA then. It would have been a lot easier night.

"Even with Rings, I was still just in it for the money. It was important because it allowed me to train for wrestling full-time. They offered me an appearance fee just to show up and compete. It was a 32-man open weight class tournament. I didn't expect to win; I was just looking to bring back some appearance money for my wrestling training. I did almost no MMA training going into Rings.

"I won my first two fights in that tournament against a Russian wrestler and a tough Japanese fighter, Kanehara. I expected trouble from the Russian, who had took second in the world in Greco-Roman wrestling at 220 pounds, but he was a complete wuss. Some guys just didn't like getting hit and I kneed him in the body and he collapsed to the mat and tapped out.

"On the final night of the tournament I fought **Gilbert Yvel**, Antonio Rodrigo Nogueira, and Babalu, all on the same night. That was probably my toughest night of fighting. I only had a half hour between my last two fights and Nogueira had hurt my knee pretty bad when he jumped to pull **guard**. I almost didn't fight at all.

"That was just a few months before the Olympic trials. When I didn't make the team, I still went to Sydney as a training alternate. That was when I was contacted by Pride. I was going to fight **Vitor Belfort**, but then he hurt his hand and they told me I was fighting a guy I hadn't heard of. Some guy named Wanderlei Silva."

Murilo Bustamante, **Quinton Jackson**, **Anderson Silva**, and **Rich Franklin**, among others. Despite wrestling at just 181 pounds, the bulk of Henderson's MMA career happened at 205 pounds, even competing in open weight and heavyweight bouts.

No matter who it was that Henderson stepped into the ring or cage to fight, he was guaranteed to get a heck of a battle. Despite his wrestling pedigree, Henderson discovered he had a hard right hand. He actually preferred going toe-to-toe with the hardest hitters in the sport.

Like his friend Couture (with whom he left RAW to form **Team Quest** in 2000), Henderson peaked late. He beat former UFC middleweight champion Murilo Bustamante to become **Pride**'s first champion at 183 pounds. Because Bustamante had left the UFC over a contract dispute and never lost his title in the ring, Henderson was considered by most to be the true champion in that weight class.

Despite this success, Henderson hated fighting as a middleweight. Cutting weight was hard, especially as he got older, and he felt he was more than competitive at 205 pounds. It was at that weigh that he fought Pride legend Wanderlei Silva in 2007, avenging his first career loss and winning the Pride Championship in a second weight class.

When **Zuffa** bought Pride, Henderson's status as champion earned him main event title unification bouts at both light heavyweight and middleweight levels — bouts he lost to the UFC's reigning champions Quinton Jackson and Anderson Silva. Just as Henderson, now in his late thirties, seemed destined to fade from the limelight, he was given a second chance to make his name in the UFC, where fans had never seen him at his best. He earned a prestigious coaching role on ***The Ultimate Fighter*** 9 by beating Rich Franklin at UFC 93. His fellow coach was British star **Michael Bisping**, who Henderson both called a douche *and* knocked out in memorable fashion at UFC 100. Bisping was knocked cold and Henderson got an extra shot in for good measure, perhaps punishing the Brit for all the reality television trash talk.

His biggest win inside the Octagon was also his last UFC appearance. Upset about likeness rights and sponsorship issues, Henderson left Zuffa to sign with **Strikeforce**, preferring the bigger stage on CBS television. His first fight with his new organization was a huge disaster, however, for all concerned. Henderson lost to **Jake Shields** who almost immediately signed with the UFC. It was an ignomious debut for Strikeforce's new star, who vowed, at the age of 39, that cutting to middleweight was too hard. From now on, Dan Henderson will compete at light heavyweight only.

Herman, Ed

Nickname: Short Fuse **Height:** 6'2"

Weight: 185 lbs **Born:** 10/2/80

Debut: Xtreme Ring Wars 2 (5/10/03) **Career Record:** 19-7

Notable Wins: Nick Thompson (Hand2Hand Combat); Dave Menne (Extreme Challenge 63); Joe Doerkson (UFC 78)

Notable Losses: Joe Doerkson (SF 7); Kendall Grove (*The Ultimate Fighter* 3 Finale); Demian Maia (UFC 83)

"Short Fuse" Ed Herman was the **Stephan Bonnar** of ***The Ultimate Fighter*** 3. Like Bonnar, he put up a spirited battle in the finals, losing to Kendall Grove by unanimous decision. As with Bonnar, **UFC** President **Dana White** was so impressed with his moxie that he offered Herman a UFC contract in the face of his upset loss. And like Bonnar, Herman has failed to thrive in the UFC, working his way squarely into the middle of the pack with a 4–4 record in his first eight fights.

As similar as they were, in some ways Herman was the anti-Bonnar. While Stephan was laid back and funny, Herman was intense, living up to his nickname of Short Fuse. A student of **Randy Couture** and **Matt Lindland**, Herman felt he should have been one of the favorites to win the reality show. Then it was time for coaches **Tito Ortiz** and **Ken Shamrock** to select their teams. Pick after pick went by and Herman seethed on the sidelines. When Shamrock selected him as his last pick, Herman was ready to explode.

His anger drove him to the finals of the show, but it sometimes gets him into trouble. His losses in the UFC have often been the result of his inability to keep control of his emotions and keep to his game plan. Yet, despite his meagre record, there have been enough flashes of brilliance, a demonstrated ability standing and on the ground, to make many think that the entire Ed Herman story hasn't been told.

Hero's

Dream isn't the first foray into mixed martial arts for Fighting Entertainment Group (FEG), the parent corporation behind kickboxing giant K-1. Before there was Dream, there was Hero's, with its elaborate television productions, its strange weight classes, and its even stranger punctuation. Before that, there was K-1 Romanex (a name meant to evoke the gladiatorial combat of the ancients), and there was no shortage of MMA on year-end K-1 Premium Dynamite!! cards, either. But it was Hero's, launched March 26, 2005, under the direction of **Rings** pioneer **Akira Maeda**, that marked FEG's commitment to mixed martial arts with a steady, ongoing series of events.

Hero's was an instant ratings hit, offering **Pride** serious competition from the very beginning. They built fighters like **Kid Yamamoto** and **Yoshihiro Akiyama** into major native draws, and brought in foreign stars like **Royce Gracie**, K-1 regular **Bob Sapp**, and even reigning **UFC** welterweight champion **B.J. Penn** in a stunt that cost Penn his title. Hero's was the first major MMA organization to tap directly into the Korean market, running in Seoul in 2005, and even ventured into America in 2007 with K-1 Hero's Dynamite!! USA, an event that saw NFL veteran Johnnie Morton knocked out by a comedian, Royce Gracie test positive for **steroids**, and the debuting **Brock Lesnar**'s scheduled opponent fail his medical basically for being a giant. It didn't go well.

Network television ratings — the be-all and end-all for Japanese promotions — declined significantly throughout 2007, and the switch to the Pride-styled Dream in 2008 did nothing to end the slide for FEG and their Tokyo Broadcasting System partners. As evidenced by the numbers, the glory years of Japanese mixed martial arts now seem firmly a part of the past.

Herring, Heath

Nickname: Texas Crazy Horse **Height:** 6'4"

Weight: 250 lbs **Born:** 3/2/78

Debut: USWF 4 (4/12/97)

Career Record: 28-14 (1 No Contest)

Notable Wins: Mark Kerr (Pride 15); Igor Vovchanchyn (Pride 19)

Notable Losses: Antonio Rodrigo Nogueira (Pride 17, Pride Critical Countdown 2004, UFC 73); Fedor Emelianenko (Pride 23); Mirko Cro Cop (Pride 26); Brock Lesnar (UFC 87)

Heath Herring is more than just an also-ran with intricately styled, outrageously bad hair. A dangerous, **sambo**-based grappler with solid kickboxing and powerful knees, Herring spent much of his career among the sport's top heavyweights before settling into his now-familiar gatekeeper role.

Herring first came to prominence in his second **Pride** fight, where he used an impressively active **guard** to weather the storm against the enormous **Tom Erikson**. After stalling Erikson out enough to earn a standup, a visibly fired-up Herring landed two quick high kicks, spun to Erikson's back with the quickness of a middleweight, and sunk in a **rear naked choke** for a huge upset win. Impressive TKO finishes against **Enson Inoue** and a still marginally relevant **Mark Kerr** landed Herring in Pride's first heavyweight title fight. In his first and only shot at championship gold, Herring came up just short, dropping a

decision to the great **Antonio Rodrigo Nogueira**.

Herring soon found himself across the ring from another legend in the making. Underdog **Fedor Emelianenko** absolutely pounded Herring to a doctor's stoppage in a contest to determine the number one contender to Nogueira's title. And things didn't get any easier from there: Herring's very next fight after the Emelianenko drubbing came against **Mirko Cro Cop**, who finished Herring early in the first. Five years later, when Herring was steamrolled by another future heavyweight champion, **Brock Lesnar** (who broke Herring's orbital bone seconds into a fight that went the distance), it seemed in keeping with a well-established pattern.

Between his Pride and **UFC** runs, Herring had a brief but controversial stint in K-1. At the 2005 K-1 Dynamite!! New Year's Eve show, Herring was scheduled to face Yoshihiro Nakao, but the fight was over before it began. Literally. During the referee's instructions in the center of the ring, Nakao decided to spice up the stare-down by leaning forward and kissing Herring. Herring reacted with a tight right hook to the chin that put Nakao to the floor, and left him in no condition to actually fight. "He tried to kiss me on the lips like a homosexual," Herring yelled from his corner, "I'm not gay! I'm *not* gay." Although the fight was originally ruled a disqualification, K-1 officials ultimately concluded that both fighters had committed fouls, and changed the ruling to an unusually fabulous no contest.

Horn, Jeremy

Nickname: Gumby **Height:** 6'1"
Weight: 185-205 lbs **Born:** 8/25/75
Debut: Atlanta Fights (3/1/96) **Career Record:** 85-19-5

Notable Wins: Chuck Liddell (UFC 19); Gilbert Yvel (Pride 21); Vernon White (KOTC 23); Forrest Griffin (IFC: Global Domination)

Notable Losses: Frank Shamrock (UFC 17); Antonio Rodrigo Nogueira (WEF 8); Kiyoshi Tamura (Colosseum 2000); Randy Couture (Rings: King of Kings 2000); Anderson Silva (Gladiator FC Day 2); Chuck Liddell (UFC 54); Nate Marquardt (UFC 81)

Jeremy Horn is not a great athlete. It's important to get that out of the way immediately. He doesn't look like a fighter; he's more like a dumpy, balding assistant manager at your local Office Depot. That's what makes his accomplishments so impressive, even more than at first glance. He's our greatest cerebral fighter, winning 82 fights with his big brain and his impeccable technical skills.

Horn has been a fighting fanatic as long as he can remember. The Dog Brothers would be proud of Horn — he and his brothers started stick fighting almost as soon as they could walk. Later he became a black belt under Robert Bussey, making him a certified ninja. Martial arts were fun, but it was only after seeing his first **UFC** at 19 that Horn devoted his life to them.

His first fight was in a warehouse in Atlanta. Many more followed throughout the Midwest. Horn met **Pat Miletich** through their mutual friend and manager **Monte Cox** and soon after moved to Bettendorf, Iowa, to train with what would become the top fight team in the world. By the time he fought UFC middleweight (now called light heavyweight) champion **Frank Shamrock** at UFC 17 in 1998, Horn was a grizzled veteran of 14 professional fights, including a draw with UFC legend **Dan Severn**, who outweighed him by 50 pounds.

Horn more than held his own with Shamrock, who was the very best fighter in the world. It opened his eyes to his own abilities and soon Horn was fighting all the time. He fought 21 times in 1999 alone, his only setback a questionable decision loss to hometown favorite Hiromitsu Kanehara in **Rings.** That included three wins in the UFC, one over future champion **Chuck Liddell.**

Horn never fought that many times again in a single calendar year, but stayed plenty active. His 106 fights include battles with some of the very best competitors in the world including **Antonio Rodrigo Nogueira**, **Randy Couture**, **Anderson Silva**, and **Forrest Griffin**. All told, Horn fought seven current or future world champions.

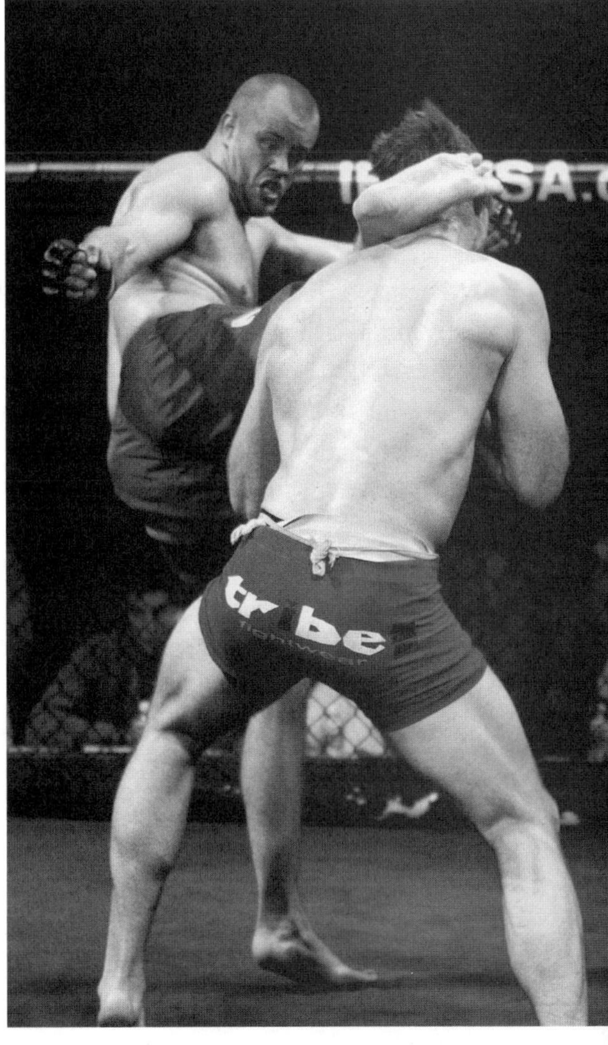

All that fighting may have worn on Horn. He lost several times in 2001, including an upset submission loss to Elvis Sinosic at UFC 30. With that, Horn was gone from the UFC, but hardly done with fighting. He fought regularly in Japan, for Rings and then for **Pride**, and helped break in the Canadian market with several appearances for UCC.

In 2005, the UFC, desperate for contenders to take on Liddell — by then the dominant light heavyweight champion — brought Horn back for an immediate title shot. Liddell had grown immensely as a fighter, while Horn had reached his peak years earlier. This time Liddell dominated, beating Horn to a pulp over four long and excruciating rounds. He was knocked down several times and the fight was mercifully stopped when Horn told the referee he couldn't see.

Already outgunned athletically, Horn was now also routinely outsized by opponents at 205 pounds. He made a long overdue drop down to middleweight and won his next two UFC fights. After a stint with the **IFL**, including a loss to **Matt Lindland**, Horn was back in the UFC. This time it was clear that Horn, despite his prowess on the mat, was no match for the younger, hungrier, and more athletic fighters in the modern UFC. He lost three in a row and was released from his UFC contract. But with several fights on the independent circuit since his departure from the UFC, it seems clear his fighting career is far from done.

Howard, Harold

Height: 6'2" **Weight:** 240 lbs
Born: 1958 **Debut:** UFC 3 (9/9/94)
Career Record: 2–3
Notable Win: Royce Gracie (UFC 3)
Notable Loss: Steve Jennum (UFC 3)

"My name is Harold Clarence Howard. I'm representing Canada and Niagara Falls in the Ultimate Fighting Challenge. We have a saying back home that if you're comin' on . . . *come on*." These are the immortal words Howard spoke before his **UFC** debut against Roland Payne. It wasn't what he said so much as how he said it — tearing off his wraparound shades to reveal the man in all his crazy-eyed, mulleted glory — that has made Howard so fondly remembered by fans who watched those strange early events.

A **karate** man and a Japanese jiu-jutsu practitioner, Howard made short work of Payne in his first tournament bout, knocking him out in under a minute to earn a shot at then two-time champion **Royce Gracie**. But Gracie, exhausted from a grueling back-and-forth contest against **Kimo Leopoldo**, wasn't able to fight. Rather than forfeit the match backstage, Gracie entered the Octagon only to have his corner throw in the towel before the match could begin. Howard was devastated, as he would explain to **Sherdog**'s Jason Probst years later. "When I won the first fight, all we were saying was 'We got to Gracie.' That was the only thing we wanted to do; that was the biggest disappointment." But the disappointment didn't end there. "I remember saying, 'At least we got [**Ken**] **Shamrock**.' Shamrock's entourage was behind me when we got into the ring. I bowed to him, and I thought he was gonna get in. We got [**Steve**] **Jennum** in there instead."

Howard didn't last long against Jennum, but long enough to attempt a forward flip kick that remains, to this day, a truly astounding sight. If you wanted to reduce everything we thought we knew about martial arts before MMA into a single image, you couldn't do much better than a gap-toothed, mulleted, tough-as-nails dude in **gi** pants, a tank top, and a well-worn black belt aerial somersaulting towards his opponent. If you'd ever wondered how Ken from *Street Fighter II* would fare in the Octagon — and naturally, many of us did — here was your answer. "I told you, if it worked, it worked," Howard said when it was all over. "And it didn't — I didn't. So in the end it didn't."

Huerta, Roger

Nickname: El Matador **Height:** 5'9"

Weight: 155 lbs **Born:** 5/20/83

Debut: EC: Best of the Best 2 (8/2/03) **Career Record:** 21-4-1 (1 No Contest)

Notable Win: Clay Guida (*The Ultimate Fighter* 6 Finale)

Notable Loss: Kenny Florian (UFC 87)

In 2007 the **UFC** got a slew of good publicity. Article after article appeared in mainstream magazines, newspapers, and on Web sites. They all told the same story: the sport was growing at a tremendous rate. The **Fertitta brothers** had bought the company for a mere $3 million. Now it was estimated to be worth $1 billion.

It was great news on its face, but to Roger Huerta it was infuriating. Huerta had come up hard — surviving abuse, living in foster homes or on the street. He was sleeping on rooftops when no better place could be found to rest his head. After a wild trip from America to El Salvador, he even weathered a civil war. Huerta had survived the worst life was likely to throw at him. He became comfortable, even wealthy. But he wondered, increasingly aloud, if the UFC is doing so well, why was he touring the country promoting **Zuffa** on a $50 per day per diem? He was featured on the cover of *Sports Illustrated* and was the company's lone hope of reaching the dormant Hispanic audience. If the UFC was making millions, why was he being paid just $17,000 to fight and $17,000 to win?

While Huerta continued to thrive in the cage, winning six in a row, including a come from behind classic over **Clay Guida**, he was growing

In Their Own Words: Roger Huerta on taking it to the next level

"It really took a different level of toughness, a mentality which I didn't think I'd have to reach until I was fighting for the title. In that third round I was a different fighter. I was willing to die in there with Guida, basically. I was out for several seconds when he knocked me down. Everything went red for me. But it never even crossed my mind that I was going to lose the fight. Even when he rocked me, I knew. Never – not even after I got rocked. I was going to find a way to win, some way or form.

"It never crosses my mind that I'm going to lose. No matter what is happening, my mentality is that I'm going to win. I'm going to win every time. I'll do whatever it takes; it doesn't matter what it takes. Anything within the rules, of course. I'll find a way to win."

increasingly disgruntled. After his first Octagon loss to **Kenny Florian** at UFC 87, Huerta announced he would not be signing a new contract with the UFC. He was leaving Zuffa to pursue success on his own terms, in the movie business. The final fight on his UFC contract was with Gray Maynard at UFC Fight Night 19, where Huerta dropped a split decision to the rising contender.

Hughes, Matt

Height: 5'8"

Weight: 170 lbs

Born: 10/13/73

Debut: JKD Challenge (1/1/98)

Career Record: 45-7

Notable Wins: Dave Menne (Extreme Challenge 21); Carlos Newton (UFC 34, UFC 38); Hayato Sakurai (UFC 36); Sean Sherk (UFC 42); Frank Trigg (UFC 45, UFC 52); Georges St. Pierre (UFC 50); Royce Gracie (UFC 60); B.J. Penn (UFC 63); Matt Serra (UFC 98)

Notable Losses: Dennis Hallman (Extreme Challenge 21, UFC 29); Jose Landi-Jons (Warriors War 1); B.J. Penn (UFC 46); Georges St. Pierre (UFC 65, UFC 79); Thiago Alves (UFC 85)

Believe it or not, once upon a time Matt Hughes was considered a boring fighter. The **UFC** painted him with the same brush as the milquetoast **Rich Franklin**, portraying him as a generic, respectful Midwesterner. While Hughes was enormously successful in the cage, once winning 13 fights in a row against top competition, at the box office he was a complete bust. It was only

after his appearance on the second season of ***The Ultimate Fighter*** that Hughes realized his potential as one of the UFC's premier villains.

Additional time in the spotlight only added fuel to Hughes' fire. Whether it was his cocky pre-fight interview before his bout with the legendary **Royce Gracie** in 2006, his comparing himself with the biblical Queen Esther, or his autobiographical admission that he and his twin brother Mark once beat up their own father, Hughes was the gift that kept on giving.

His grating personality shouldn't diminish his obvious excellence in the cage. Hughes is undoubtedly one of the very best fighters of all time, as dominant a champion as the UFC has ever seen. Hughes took the **ground and pound** style of **Mark Coleman** forward a generation. He was more than an excellent wrestler; with the help of great coaches like **Jeremy Horn** and **Pat Miletich**, he was able to develop an adequate submission and striking game as well. Hughes used these tools to beat a who's who of the best fighters in the world. Conquests included **Carlos Newton**, **Frank Trigg**, **Sean Sherk**, **B.J. Penn**, Royce Gracie, and **Georges St. Pierre.**

By the time he was dethroned by St. Pierre at UFC 65, Hughes was relieved to relinquish the title. Except for a brief hiccup when he lost the belt to Penn at UFC 46, Hughes had been the top fighter in the division for five years. The nonstop pressure got to him, and the years of training had taken their toll on a fighter who would rather be anywhere else than the training room. Hughes

In Their Own Words: Matt Hughes on his fight with the legendary Royce Gracie

"I had no idea it was going to be that easy. When it hit the ground I thought, 'Royce Gracie is going to pull out a magical Gracie submission that I've never heard of and he's gonna submit me.' So as soon as I take him down you can tell that I'm just relaxing and not really doing anything, trying to stay tight so he doesn't submit me. It doesn't take very long before I figure out he doesn't have any submission moves whatsoever. For the rest of the fight, I never felt threatened one bit. I never felt threatened by a submission hold or any type of a strike from the bottom. It took me about 30 to 45 seconds to figure out he's not going to be able to do anything. I went for the straight **arm bar** and finally gave up on that because I didn't want to waste all my energy and so I thought I'd go to another submission. I do think I'm more of an athlete than anyone he's faced but I think this sport has passed Royce Gracie by. It's evolved and Royce has not evolved. He just hasn't kept up with the sport."

simply needed a break from the mental and physical pressures of being the best in the world.

In his post-title run, Hughes maintained a visible position in the sport. He and **Matt Serra** set the standard as coaches on *The Ultimate Fighter* during the show's sixth season, building up a grudge that was still fiery hot months later when the two finally met in the cage. Hughes beat Serra by decision, but that fight, and a previous loss to **Thiago Alves**, showed a fighter who had lost a step or three. Hughes had gotten by for years by being stronger and quicker than the other guy in the cage. That didn't seem to be the case anymore. While Hughes was a big enough star to maintain fan interest, it seemed apparent that he would never again fight at the championship level.

Hume, Matt

Nickname: The Wizard **Height:** 5'10"
Weight: 170 lbs **Born:** 7/14/66
Debut: Pancrase: Pancrash! 3 (4/21/94) **Career Record:** 5-0
Notable Wins: Eric Paulson (Extreme Fighting 3); Pat Miletich (Extreme Fighting 4)

It was July 6, 1994, and **Pancrase** was the most talked-about new wrestling promotion in Japan. Called "hybrid wrestling," Pancrase was **professional wrestling** with standard professional wrestling rules. The caveat? Pancrase was real. Or at least it was supposed to be. Many people had their suspicions and on this night in the Amagasaki Gym those suspicions were confirmed. Not all Pancrase matches were on the up and up.

Hume was taking on **Ken Shamrock**, Pancrase's top foreign fighter and their representative in the new **Ultimate Fighting Championship**. Throughout the fight Hume tossed Shamrock with some serious high amplitude throws, despite Shamrock's 50-pound weight advantage and his strong wrestling skill. This was questionable, but it was possible Hume was just that good a wrestler. The finish of the fight was the final straw: Shamrock launched Hume with a pro wrestling throw called the Northern Lights Suplex and finished him off with a **Kimura** lock. The whole sequence was obviously phony — what pro wrestlers call a work. To those who knew what they were watching, the cat was out of the bag.

Of course, his involvement in the development of Japanese MMA, warts and all, shouldn't prevent anyone from recognizing what a great martial artist Hume was and would become. "The Wizard" would make the short list of the most influential trainers of all time and his influence on Sheik Tahnoon bin Zayed Al Nahyan, son of Sultan Zayed of Abu Dhabi in the United Arab Emirates, helped lead to the formation of the **ADCC**'s World Submission

> ***In Their Own Words:* Hume on his training philosophy**
>
> "Teaching a student to be a martial artist instead of a fighter is the most important thing to me. Anyone can be a fighter – I do not respect or admire someone because they fight. I respect and admire those who make a lifetime commitment to being the best martial artist they can be. Studying all aspect of martial arts: technique in all areas, conditioning, mental strength, respect, ethics, loyalty, and the other important things that make a person a unique martial artist instead of a random fighter.
>
> "I have been teaching and competing in Pankration, **Muay Thai**, **boxing**, and submission **wrestling** all my life. I trained, taught, and competed before UFC or the term MMA existed. My goals are as a martial artist and have nothing to do with MMA or UFC or any other organization. If they all disappeared today, I would still be doing the same thing that I was doing before their existence that helped put them on the map when they arrived. If you have the right mindset, you will always evolve your technique regardless of what goes on around you with other schools, promotions, people, et cetera."

Wrestling tournaments.

While many UFC fighters were still focused on a single discipline, Hume was engaging in all-time great fights with Eric Paulson and **Pat Miletich**. He also helped end the debate about how a submission fighter would handle a world-class wrestler when he submitted Olympic gold medalist Kenny Monday months before **Frank Shamrock** caught **Kevin Jackson** at UFC Japan.

A severe tear of his Achilles tendon ended Hume's active fighting career, but he remained one of the sport's top trainers. Hume also joined the **Pride** organization in Japan, becoming one of the most powerful and important Americans in the promotion's upper management. Starting as a judge, Hume became the rule director and later the official trainer.

With Pride's demise, Hume has filled a similar role in the new **Dream** promotion in Japan. He also continues to train fighters from all over the world, including UFC standout **Rich Franklin**.

Hunt, Mark

Nickname: The Super Samoan | **Height:** 5'10"

Weight: 280 lbs | **Born:** 3/23/74

Debut: Pride Critical Countdown 2004 (6/20/04) | **Career Record:** 5-6

Notable Wins: Wanderlei Silva (Pride Shockwave 2004); Mirko Cro Cop (Pride Shockwave 2005); Tsuyoshi Kohsaka (Pride Total Elimination Absolute)
Notable Losses: Hidehiko Yoshida (Pride Critical Countdown 2004); Josh Barnett (Pride Critical Countdown Absolute); Fedor Emelianenko (Pride Shockwave 2006); Melvin Manhoef (Dynamite!! 2008)

For a moment in time, Mark Hunt looked to be a future world champion. But five consecutive losses have demonstrated just how quickly things can turn. Hunt was a kickboxer who got by on his amazing chin and natural toughness. He was never, frankly, much of a technical fighter. His reputation was built on winning the 2001 K-1 World Grand Prix. Hunt was far from the favorite, but on that single night, the dominos fell in his favor. By beating Jerome LeBanner, Stefan Leko, and Francisco Fihlo in a single night, Hunt laid claim, for at least one year, to being the top kickboxer in the world.

In reality, Hunt was a journeyman contender who had one great night. His overall career kickboxing record was just 30–13. In the months leading up to his glorious achievement he had lost three of four. In Japan, however, winning the K-1 World Grand Prix is monumental, and Hunt was made for life as a main event fighter. When he reverted back to form as a kickboxer, struggling to maintain even a .500 record, his newfound fame offered him a second life in MMA.

His first fight, against **judo** gold medalist **Hidehiko Yoshida**, came too quickly. He lost early by **arm bar**, but showed enough of a spark in that fight and a subsequent tune up bout with Dan Bobish to be an intriguing prospect. What came next shocked the world. Hunt became the first fighter in almost five years to beat "The Axe Murderer," **Wanderlei Silva**. Silva had run over everyone he'd faced in **Pride** in 19 fights, but the neophyte Hunt shrugged off his powerful punches and decked him throughout the fight.

When Hunt followed up that upset with a win over fellow K-1 refugee **Mirko Cro Cop**, a title shot seemed imminent. After two more easy wins, Hunt ended up across the ring from former **UFC** champion **Josh Barnett**. Barnett was the worst possible opponent for Hunt: a big, strong grappler who could take advantage of the kickboxer's weakness on the ground.

Only in Japan would a loss lead directly to a title shot. Hunt did surprisingly well against the world's best fighter, **Fedor Emelianenko**, and despite two losses in a row, his status as a future star seemed secure. Then the losing continued. Hunt lost three in a row, two to fighters almost 100 pounds lighter. None lasted as long as two minutes. As quickly as he burst onto the scene, he became a laughingstock. At 35, a return to form seems unlikely. Now a journeyman in two sports, Hunt is the kickboxing equivalent to "Butterbean" Eric Esch. He once seemed to hold the world in the palm of his hand; now he's been relegated to freak shows and spectacles.

IFL: see **International Fight League**

Imanari, Masakazu

Nickname: Ashikan Judan | **Height:** 5'5"

Weight: 143 lbs | **Born:** 2/10/76

Debut: Premium Challenge (5/6/02) | **Career Record:** 19-7-1

Notable Wins: Jorge Gurgel (ZST: Grand Prix Opening Round); Mike Brown (Deep 22nd Impact); Yoshiro Maeda (Deep 22nd Impact)

Notable Losses: Dokonjonosuke Mishima (Deep 11th Impact, Deep 35th Impact); Joachim Hansen (Pride Bushido 8)

No fighter is more closely associated with a single class of techniques than Masakazu Imanari is with **leg locks**. He is without question the most dangerous leg lock man in the entire sport, once stopping both **Mike Brown** and Yoshiro Maeda in the same night — the former with a **heel hook**, the latter with a toe hold — to become the **Deep** featherweight champion. If you've ever wondered why the use of leg locks is restricted in most prominent grappling arts and even some MMA organizations, look no further than the notorious flying heel hook that finished Brown, the one of that left him screaming with a thoroughly dislocated knee in one of the grossest in-ring injuries you're ever going to see. Lest you think the "Ashikan Judan" (literally "tenth-degree master of leg locks") is completely one-dimensional, it should be noted that he mixes in the occasional **arm bar** — none more impressive than the flying entry with which he finished a baffled Robbie Oliver only 27 seconds into the first round. Although Imanari hasn't enjoyed the same level of success as his high-profile teammate **Shinya Aoki** — his striking is nothing to write home about, and he can be controlled on the ground by grapplers with strong top games — there are few who want anything to do with the man once he gets in position to employ his favorite techniques. The mind boggles at the thought of Imanari in early **Pancrase**, where stylish boots were mandatory and leg locks were plentiful.

Inoki, Antonio

The most interesting thing about Antonio Inoki's prototypical MMA fight with **boxing** legend Muhammad Ali is that it was never intended to be a legitimate contest. Ali, a long-time **professional wrestling** fan, was supposed to have a plain old wrestling match with Inoki. Inoki would be beaten up throughout, cut his forehead to draw blood, and collapse into the corner. Ali would encourage the referee to stop the fight. As he turned to insist the fight should be called, Inoki would "Pearl Harbor" him by kicking him in the back of the head. Ali would lose, but it would be obvious he was the better man. He would collect $6 million and Inoki would go on to worldwide wrestling fame.

It didn't quite work out that way. Somewhere along the way, some of Ali's advisors convinced him that going through with the fake match would soil his legacy. Just days before the fight, Ali insisted it would have to be a real fight. There were no mixed martial arts. No one in either camp knew exactly what to expect or how to legislate a match like this. The rules were in a constant state of flux right up until the evening of the fight.

The eventual rules of the bout overwhelmingly favored Ali. He had all of the power in the negotiations. The Japanese had so much invested in the show that they capitulated to all of Ali's demands. No takedowns were allowed below the waist. No back suplexes were permitted because they had seen Inoki use the move in professional wrestling bouts. Inoki was not allowed to throw a punch with his bare-knuckled fist, nor throw kicks to the head or body. If he secured a takedown with an upper body throw, strikes on the ground were illegal. Essentially, Inoki was nearly helpless. Faced with the fight of his life, a battle with the best heavyweight boxer of all-time, he had a single weapon: the leg kick.

Over 15 long rounds, Inoki used his one weapon over and over again. He brutalized Ali's left leg, fighting from his back and chasing Ali around the ring like a crab. Although fans at the time blamed Inoki for not standing and trading like a real man, in truth the heavyweight champion of the world was helpless to prevent this continued assault. The official decision was a draw, but in retrospect, Inoki clearly won an easy decision. Ali landed just five punches in 45 minutes of fighting. Inoki landed more than 50 leg kicks, dropping Ali several times and sending him to the hospital.

What started as a fun show designed to help both men turned into a disaster for both. Ali was never the same. Many of his trainers blamed the leg kicks for hobbling him for the remaining fights of his career. Inoki, intended to become a worldwide star, was a laughingstock in the United States and a huge disappointment to his fans in Japan.

A genius promoter, Inoki was able to turn this to his advantage. He took on all comers from a variety of martial arts disciplines. Full contact karateka Everett Eddy, Kyokushin karateka Willie Williams, boxer Chuck Wepner, and wrestler Akrum Pelwan all fell to his hand. In 1978, Inoki was declared the World Martial Arts Champion. Inoki's emphasis on the martial arts and legitimate holds like the **arm bar** influenced a whole generation of young wrestlers. They grew up idolizing Inoki and all he had done in the 1970s to legitimize wrestling as the strongest martial art. When they came of age, these burgeoning stars like **Akira Maeda** took Inoki's style to a whole new level of realism with the creation of the UWF. Then Inoki protégé **Masakatsu Funaki** blew things wide open by founding **Pancrase**, professional wrestling that was (for the most part) not predetermined.

As Pancrase gave way to **Pride** and MMA surpassed pro wrestling in popularity in Japan, Inoki's Ali debacle was reinvented. Instead of being a complete disaster, Inoki was now looked on as a man ahead of his time. Trying to capitalize on MMA's emergence, Inoki sent many of his star wrestlers to compete in real fights, while at the same time making sure the wrestlers he devoted the most promotional energy to were also adequate fighters.

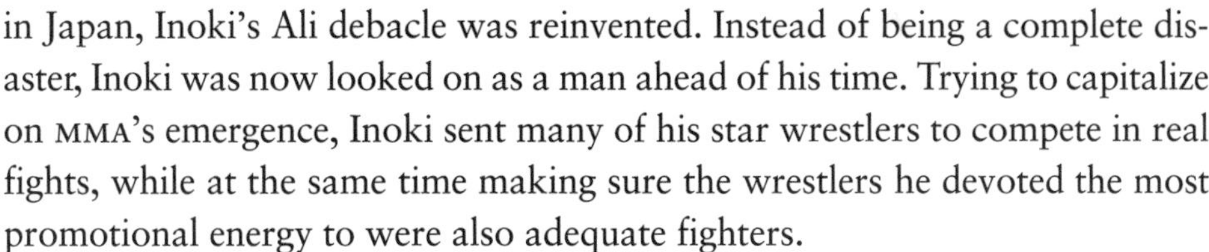

The strategy was catastrophic. The professional wrestlers were typically embarrassed in real fights, while the shooters he brought in to headline the wrestling shows lacked the charisma or presence to adequately entertain pro wrestling's demanding fans. Wrestling hit an all-time low in Japan. Unlike Inoki, it hasn't been able to recover from its ruinous first foray into MMA.

Inoue, Enson

Nickname: Yamato Damashi
Height: 5'10"
Weight: 215 lbs
Born: 4/15/67
Debut: Shooto: Vale Tudo Access 3 (1/21/95)
Career Record: 12-8
Notable Win: Randy Couture (Vale Tudo Japan 98)

Notable Losses: Frank Shamrock (Vale Tudo Japan 97); Mark Kerr (Pride Grand Prix 2000); Igor Vovchanchyn (Pride 10); Antonio Rodrigo Nogueira (Pride 19)

Sitting around a table with members of the Japanese mafia, smoking, joking, and drinking, Enson Inoue commands respect. Although he was born in Hawaii, Inoue is Japanese to the core. Japan's criminal class, men who respect traditional warrior values, seem to hold Inoue in high esteem despite his status as a foreigner. That's because Inoue lives by a code as old as the island nation he has adopted as his home: "Yamato Damashi."

It means no fear. It means never giving up. It's the spirit of the samurai. And Inoue personifies it. It's a code that demands courage beyond reason. Inoue fights for more than just money or glory. He fights to test himself, to see if he really has the spirit inside of him to look death in the eye and still come forward. It's a pursuit of perfection and Inoue has come closer than anyone else in MMA history to living up to those high standards.

Of course, fighting to test your manhood isn't the best way to pad a record and may not be the best strategy for long-term success as a professional fighter. Inoue battled the best on their terms, going to toe-to-toe with feared striker **Igor Vovchanchyn** and refusing to quit while taking a horrendous beating from wrestler **Mark Kerr**. All told, Inoue fought many of the top athletes of his era. He gave his all, but with the lone exception of an **arm bar** win over **Randy Couture**, always came out on the losing end of things.

For new fans, he's nearly forgotten, a man with an unimpressive 11–8 record, a mere footnote in the career of Randy Couture or that guy from David Mamet's ***Redbelt***. For anyone who saw him fight in his prime, he's a legend, a transcendent warrior whose courage will stand in their memory for years to come.

In Their Own Words: Enson Inoue on why he fights

"You know, for me, winning and losing isn't about the W or the L. You can win a fight and not learn anything and get nothing from the fight. Like when I fought Igor [Vovchanchyn], I lost the battle but I won because I learned so much about myself in that fight. If I had opened his cut and I hit him again and I won the fight, I would have won . . . record-wise, but as far as for me as a person, I wouldn't have won what I won that night. As far as the experience of seeing what was inside me."

Interview by Tom Hackett, Total-MMA.com

International Fight League

While many competitors tried to copy the successful tactics of the **Ultimate Fighting Championship,** the International Fight League took an entirely different approach in 2006. Founded by real estate mogul Kurt Otto and *Wizard* magazine creator Gareb Shamus, the promotion had major plans to shake up the entire industry.

Everything was different in the IFL. For starters, it was a team sport. Organized into teams divided by city (later by MMA camps) the events were designed like a college **wrestling** meet. Each team, coached by MMA legends like **Ken Shamrock** and **Pat Miletich**, fielded squads of five fighters from five weight classes. The winner was the first squad with three victories.

The financial approach was also markedly different. The IFL offered fighters a regular salary, including health benefits. Used to the boom and bust cycle of the typical pro fighter, living large immediately after a fight but struggling after a couple of months with no cash coming in, many competitors enjoyed the new stability.

Otto and Shamus did well selling the IFL to sponsors, investors, and television networks — everyone but the fans. After surviving a UFC lawsuit, it turned out that the IFL's biggest problem was an inability to connect with their audience. It was the first time that UFC owner Lorenzo **Fertitta**'s words seemed prophetic. There wasn't an MMA boom. There was a UFC boom.

Despite television deals with Fox Sports and MyNetwork TV, the league struggled to survive. They raised $24 million with a public offering, but with an average cost of $1.2 million per show (and a television contract paying only $50,000 per show) the promotion wasn't long for this world. After losing $21.7 million in 2007, the company went under in 2008.

■ **IFL Team Champions**

2006 (Season 1): Quad City Silverbacks (Coach Pat Miletich)

2006 (Season 2): Quad City Silverbacks (Coach Pat Miletich)

2007: New York Pit Bulls (Coach **Renzo Gracie**)

International Vale Tudo Championship

In 1993, martial arts fans were shocked at the blood and brutality of the **Ultimate Fighting Championship**. By 1997, though, the UFC seemed downright tame compared to the newly formed IVC. The IVC was not "mixed martial arts." It was unabashed no-holds-barred Brazilian **Vale Tudo** and proud of it. Almost anything was allowed: head butts, elbows, stomps on the ground, knees to the head on the ground, and bare-knuckle **boxing** were all within the rules.

The IVC's promoter was Sergio Batarelli, no stranger to the world of Vale Tudo. Batarelli had studied kung fu and later helped bring full contact **karate** to Brazil. He had even stepped in the ring against Vale Tudo legend Zulu. Batarelli was helping promote Frederico Lapenda's World Vale Tudo Championship when the two had a disagreement. Soon after, Batarelli was gone from the WVC and the IVC was formed.

The fights were outrageously violent. Although many critics found the UFC's Octagon uncouth, these contests in a ring were as gruesome as anything fans had ever seen. Between the bottom rope and the middle ring rope there was canvas netting surrounding the entire ring. When a fighter got taken down in the ropes he often found himself trapped in the net, helpless against the head butts and elbows that were soon to follow.

The first event featured UFC icons **Gary Goodridge** and **Dan Severn**. Goodridge took full advantage of the looser rule set to attack his opponent Pedro Otavio's groin with his feet, putting his toes inside Otavio's trunks and applying an unusual submission attempt. Goodridge one-upped **Keith Hackney**'s brutal testicular assault and took home a win.

Some of the sport's legendary figures made their name in the ring of the IVC. "The Iceman" **Chuck Liddell** traveled to São Paulo to test himself against the best, defeating the smaller Jose "Pele" Landi-Johns over 30 grueling minutes. On the same show (IVC 6), future Liddell opponent **Wanderlei Silva** announced his presence to the world, decimating top wrestler Mike Van Arsdale in just four minutes. While Van Arsdale would later complain that Silva was greased up like a pig and hard to takedown because of it, the win established Silva as a force to be reckoned with in MMA. His next fight would be in the UFC Octagon against fellow phenom **Vitor Belfort.**

Eventually the propensity for spontaneous violence and the inability of Brazilian martial artists to separate the personal from the professional led to the ban of MMA in São Paulo, Brazil. São Paulo is Brazil's largest city and one of the most populous urban areas in the entire world. For the IVC, this was the end of the line. Batarelli tried three shows outside Brazil, in Venezuela, Yugoslavia, and Portugal, but they weren't able to draw as well as he hoped. The IVC wasn't able to compete for the top talent anymore. With most Brazilian and American stars taking bigger money deals with **Pride** in Japan, Batarelli called it quits.

Jackson, Greg

Camp Name: Jackson's MMA

Significant Fighters: Diego Sanchez, Rashad Evans, Georges St. Pierre, Keith Jardine, Joey Villesenor, Nathan Marquardt

No one has benefited more from ***The Ultimate Fighter*** reality television show than New Mexico–based trainer Greg Jackson. Two of Jackson's students, **Diego Sanchez** and **Rashad Evans**, won the grand prize in the show's first two seasons. This opened up better and more high profile fight cards for Jackson's students.

Before Sanchez, Jackson had coached fighters mostly on local and regional shows. After the show, he was responsible for preparing his fighters for the sport's elite. Jackson proved up to the task. He was able to find a way to motivate the fighters who migrated to his gym. His fighters would never lose a fight because they were out of shape, and he prided himself in never being out-thought by a competing trainer. He led both Evans and **Keith Jardine** to wins over legendary light heavyweight **Chuck Liddell**. With Jackson in his corner, welterweight star **Georges St. Pierre** was able to conquer the formidable **Matt Hughes**.

New Mexico now hosts a bevy of the world's best fighters, and with Jackson leading the training, that looks to be true for a long time. What makes Jackson's gym special is the sense of family there. Many fighters train together for fights, but they aren't a family. There is always a fear that they might eventually have to fight their training partners. They hold back their best.

It's different with Greg Jackson. None of his fighters will fight each other. Period. This has created tension between Jackson fighters and **Dana White** when White suggested a Jardine/Evans matchup. The fighters refused to do it. That kind of fight would fracture the trust and camaraderie Jackson has worked so hard to create.

In Their Own Words: Greg Jackson on the legends of the sport

"A fighter is a fighter to me. I'm never a fan of these guys. That doesn't mean I don't respect them; I think they're amazing athletes. But I'm never like, 'Wow, this is a legendary fighter.' All they are is math problems in front of me. If it's Chuck Liddell or it's Joe Six-Pack, it's all the same to me. It's a problem in front of me and I've got to figure out the best way to get around that.

"These legendary fighters are amazing, but everybody, even my guys, has holes in their games. It's just a matter of identifying comfort zones and taking them out of them and understanding the angles and the psychology of your fighters. Getting a good game plan early so it becomes second nature to them. All of these are variables that you can control. I'm never worried that that's Chuck Liddell in the opposite corner. I'm thinking, 'This guy's an amazing striker, he's got good this and good that' and I've got to make sure we get around it.

"That's where their teammates come in, because they're really competitive guys. Their teammates will really push them. Instead of sitting back on their laurels, a guy like Georges St. Pierre comes down and they train and their teammates can really push them. Hold them down, tap them out, rock them with punches, or whatever it takes. The team is a real key element at that point, because you're able to say, 'You're this great guy but so-and-so just whacked you in the head. You can't have that happening and it's because you're doing this or that.' I just try to keep them improving, keep them focused on constantly getting better, constantly looking for a new challenge. Even if it's outside the cage. Trying to keep them interested – that's my job."

Jackson, Quinton

Nickname: Rampage **Height:** 6'1"

Weight: 205 lbs **Born:** 6/20/78

Debut: International Sport Combat Federation: Memphis (11/13/99)

Career Record: 30-8

Notable Wins: Igor Vovchanchyn (Pride 22); Kevin Randleman (Pride 25); Murilo Bustamante (Pride Total Elimination 2003); Chuck Liddell (Pride Final Conflict 2003, UFC 71); Ricardo Arona (Pride Critical Countdown 2004); Matt Lindland (World Fighting Alliance: King of the Streets); Dan Henderson (UFC 75); Wanderlei Silva (UFC 92)

Notable Losses: Kazushi Sakuraba (Pride 15); Wanderlei Silva (Pride Final Conflict 2003, Pride 28); Mauricio Rua (Pride Total Elimination 2005); Forrest Griffin (UFC 86); Rashad Evans (UFC 114)

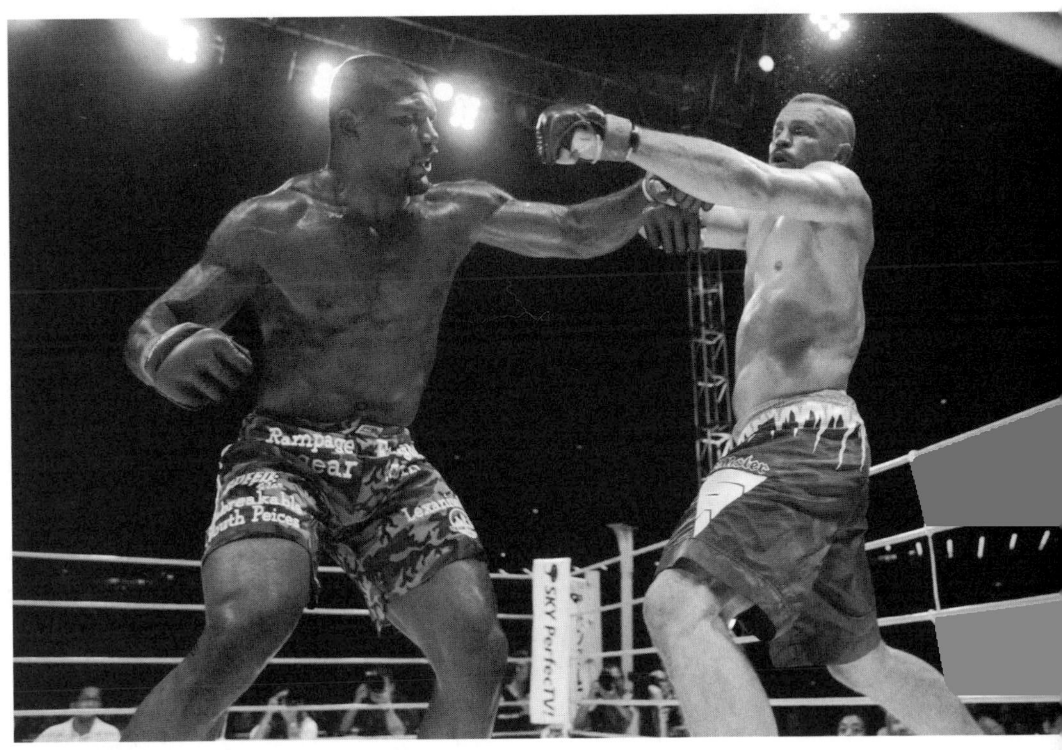

Quinton "Rampage" Jackson is a character — one of the sport's most colorful ones. With his howling ring entrances, trademark chain, and overall showman's flair, you could be forgiven for mistaking Rampage for a **professional wrestling** character, and a pretty good one. He's funny, engaging, and charismatic. But Jackson's controversial shtick — heavy on racial humor, sometimes at the expense of other black men — has been derided by up-and-comer **Mo Lawal** as "a minstrel show," and there have been more than a few episodes of bizarre behavior and the occasional run-in with the law. There's often more than enough going on in Jackson's life to make his in-ring accomplishments seem secondary. But once the bell rings, there's no mistaking Quinton Jackson for anything but a first-rate competitor, and one of the top light heavyweights in the world.

An All-State wrestler at Ralley-Egypt High School in Memphis, Tennessee, Jackson broke into mixed martial arts in the Gladiator Challenge and King of the Cage promotions, where his propensity for the big slam and the exciting finish brought him to the attention of **Pride** officials. Given the Japanese public's strange relationship with black athletes — look no further than **Kevin Randleman**'s "Ultimate Donkey Kong" entrance, or **Bob Sapp** mashing bananas into his mouth while mimicking a gorilla — who knows what Pride had in mind when they brought Jackson in to face their number one native draw, **Kazushi Sakuraba**. One thing is for certain, however: they didn't want him to win. "They told me, 'If you win this fight, you get $10,000,'" Jackson revealed to *MMA Today* years later. "I don't know if the president of Pride knew about it, but they told me, 'If you lose by knockout or submission, but don't tap, you get $12,000.'" Jackson tossed Sakuraba around the ring in spectacular fashion before being caught in a **rear naked choke** by the great submission fighter. To Jackson's credit, he tapped — for the first time in his career, and also the last.

After rattling off seven wins in his next eight fights, including victories over Kevin Randleman and the once-mighty **Igor Vovchanchyn** (the only bump along the road was a richly deserved DQ loss for kneeing **Daijiro Matsui** *unbelievably* squarely in the groin), Jackson was awarded a berth in Pride's stacked 2003 middleweight Grand Prix. Jackson squeaked by the hard-luck **Murilo Bustamante** to earn his way into the final four, where, remarkably, he faced **Chuck Liddell** and **Wanderlei Silva** in the same night. Jackson dominated Liddell, proving himself both the better striker and the superior grappler, pounding on The Iceman until his corner wisely decided to throw in the towel. As much as any other single fight, Jackson's one-sided drubbing of one of the **UFC**'s best helped perpetuate the notion that Pride was home to the top light heavyweights in the world. It was never as simple as that, and the caveat that styles make fights most definitely applies, but seeing the ease with which Jackson overwhelmed Liddell, and then watching Silva destroy Jackson with knees from the **clinch** later that night, it's understandable that many would come to that conclusion.

Silva had Jackson's number. After Jackson rebounded from his tournament loss with wins over crowd-pleaser **Ikuhisa Minowa** and **Brazilian Top Team** standout **Ricardo Arona** — the former by way of a solid knee, the latter with a dramatic power-bomb knockout slam that *may* have included an illegal head butt — he faced Silva again, this time with the Pride middleweight (205 pounds) title on the line. The result was the same: Silva ruined Jackson's night with knees from the **Muay Thai** clinch. Jackson fared no better against **Mauricio Rua**, Silva's **Chute Boxe** teammate, who stopped him with a punishing barrage of soccer kicks. Again, styles make fights, and Jackson had no answer to Chute Boxe's all-out brawling Muay Thai.

It was around this time that the fairly un-Christian Jackson was "born again," renewing his faith after both he and his son awoke from eerily similar nightmares. His newfound religious conviction had a direct impact on his in-ring performance at least once: with less than a week to go before the second Silva fight, Jackson decided to fast for three days to help "fend off the devil." No wonder, then, that he seemed to tire so early, to have so little in reserve. Some also perceived less aggression, less of an edge in the reborn fighter.

In May 2006, Jackson left Pride for the **World Fighting Alliance**, an on-again-off-again promotion that took one shot at the big time with its King of the Streets card. Jackson squared off against high-profile middleweight **Matt Lindland** in the main event, and earned a split decision win in a fight that could easily have gone either way. When the WFA folded, the UFC scooped up the contracts of both Jackson and **Lyoto Machida** in a move that would have lasting effects on the light heavyweight division.

After avenging an early career loss against Marvin Eastman in his UFC debut, Jackson was offered a title shot against Liddell, who was undefeated in the three and a half years since they'd last met. Jackson, who had tightened up his **boxing** considerably under the tutelage of trainer Juanito Ibarra, countered a terribly sloppy left to the body with a tight right hook that put the champion on the mat less than two minutes into the first round. Soon thereafter, Jackson unified the UFC light heavyweight and Pride middleweight titles by besting **Dan Henderson** in a brilliant bout that went the full five. The newly unified title wouldn't be defended for almost ten months, however, as Jackson accepted a coaching role on ***The Ultimate Fighter*** to build towards **Forrest Griffin**'s title challenge.

At times in the Griffin bout, especially in the first round, Jackson looked like he was clearly the better fighter. At others, he looked oddly hesitant. Jackson took the loss by unanimous decision in a fight many thought he won. And then he freaked out completely. After four sleepless nights — and *again* with the fasting — Jackson was in and out of a mental institution for observation. He was also charged with two felonies and three misdemeanors after bombing around careening into cars in the camo Ford F-350 he had had custom painted with his likeness. It was a rough week. One of the victims whose car was struck was a pregnant woman whose baby was later stillborn. Predictably, a civil suit followed.

The UFC stood by their fighter throughout this ordeal, and through the subsequent embarrassment of Jackson sexually harassing a female reporter on camera. After a bad break with Ibarra, Rampage began to train at London's Wolfslair gym, and the change of scenery seemed to help him straighten himself out. Jackson finally earned a win over Wanderlei Silva — third time's a charm — stopping him in the first round of their UFC 92 meeting, and he followed that effort with a decision win in a tough, competitive fight against **Keith Jardine**. He took another coaching assignment on *The Ultimate Fighter*, building towards a hometown battle against **Rashad Evans**. He even landed a potential career-making acting role, cast as B.A. Baracus in the *A-Team* remake. Everything seemed to be going his way.

But a falling out with **Dana White** led to Jackson's abrupt announcement of his retirement in the fall of 2009, citing White's open mockery of his acting ambitions, the UFC's failure to promote him as a unified world champion following the Henderson fight, and a handful of other accumulated slights. While few believed this retirement would prove permanent, Jackson's move changed the landscape of the light heavyweight division considerably — until, that is, Jackson returned to the sport in May of 2010, dropping a hard-fought unanimous decision to Rashad Evans in their much-anticipated bout. It was a solid effort from a man who hadn't fought in over a year, but only time will tell whether Jackson's future lies in the cage or on the silver screen.

Jardine, Keith

Nickname: The Dean of Mean **Height:** 6'2"

Weight: 205 lbs **Born:** 10/31/75

Debut: Gladiator Challenge 5 (8/19/01) **Career Record:** 15-8-1

Notable Wins: Forrest Griffin (UFC 66); Chuck Liddell (UFC 76); Brandon Vera (UFC 89)

Notable Losses: Rashad Evans (*The Ultimate Fighter* 2); Stephan Bonnar (*Ultimate Fight Night* 2); Wanderlei Silva (UFC 84); Quinton Jackson (UFC 96); Thiago Silva (UFC 102)

Keith Jardine is at heart a man of the coffeehouse: an avid reader and independent cinema enthusiast. He's also a former bounty hunter who bombs around Albuquerque in a sweet-ass 1996 Ford Bronco. No one thing defines him.

A key member of **Greg Jackson**'s team, Jardine inserted himself into the **UFC**'s light heavyweight title picture with an upset win over **Chuck Liddell** in The Iceman's first fight after dropping the belt to **Quinton Jackson**. Jardine controlled the pace of the fight from start to finish, picking the former champ apart with kicks en route to a split decision victory. It was, and remains, the finest performance of Jardine's UFC career, a career that began two years earlier with a decision loss to future Jackson's Submission Fighting teammate **Rashad Evans** on the second season of ***The Ultimate Fighter***. Jardine rebounded from that disappointing debut with five solid performances in the Octagon, collecting four wins — including a career-making KO of **Forrest Griffin** — against only one loss, a controversial decision against *TUF* 1 runner-up **Stephan Bonnar**.

A stunning first round — indeed, first minute — loss to the unheralded and ultimately unsuccessful Houston Alexander caused Jardine's stock to drop significantly, which is what made his fine showing against Liddell in his next bout all the more surprising. He was supposed to be a relatively easy win for Liddell, allowing the former champ to get back on track. Jardine, of course, had other ideas. But he hasn't fared well in the upper echelons of the light heavyweight division since, dropping three of four fights. While there's obviously no shame in going the distance in a losing effort against Quinton Jackson, or in getting caught early by the still terrifying **Wanderlei Silva**, it's increasingly clear that Jardine has found his level: as a gatekeeper, not a legitimate title threat.

Jennum, Steve

Height: 5'10" | **Weight:** 210 lbs
Born: 1961 | **Debut:** UFC 3 (9/9/94)
Career Record: 2–3 | **Notable Win:** Harold Howard (UFC 3)
Notable Losses: Tank Abbott (Ultimate Ultimate 95); Marco Ruas (World Vale Tudo Championships 1)

Like a good ninja (he was an instructor for Robert Bussey's Warrior International), Jennum appeared out of nowhere at **UFC** 3 to win the $60,000 in prize money. Jennum had a significant advantage: unlike past winners, he didn't have to win several fights to claim the title of "Ultimate Fighter." It was a tournament filled with injuries and bizarre behavior. Both favorites, **Ken Shamrock** and **Royce Gracie**, withdrew due to injuries. Gracie's decision to quit came only after he marched down to the cage with his entire entourage, only to throw in the towel against Canadian **Harold Howard**. Gracie's exit from the competition enraged and discouraged Shamrock, who had focused obsessively on the Brazilian champion since being choked out at UFC 1.

Shamrock's decision not to fight Howard opened the door for Jennum, a Nebraskan policeman, to essentially steal the title. Howard disrespected him by starting the fight with a dismissive front flip. Jennum made him pay by mounting him and punching him until not one but two towels came flying into the cage to signal Howard's surrender.

Jennum's win changed the way the UFC's tournaments would work going forward. From then on, an alternate would have to earn his place in the tournament by winning a fight. This would place him on equal ground with fighters in the main draw. No one would go in, as Jennum had, completely fresh. New rules in place, Jennum returned for UFC 4 and beat the second prominent boxer to try his hand at the UFC, former IBF champion Melton Bowen. After taking some hard punches, the Nebraskan ninja took the boxer down and submitted him with an **arm bar**. Unfortunately, the champion broke his hand in the scuffle and was, somewhat ironically, replaced by an alternate.

Jennum was a tough guy, a cop who later fended off multiple attackers in a robbery attempt. But he wasn't an elite fighter. Against stiffer competition, like **Tank Abbott**, **Marco Ruas**, and **Lion's Den** student Jason Godsey, Jennum wasn't up to the challenge. His name is in the history books, but it is a hollow achievement. Jennum may have been crowned the UFC 3 tournament champion, but the best fighters that night were backstage nursing their wounds, not in the cage.

Jewels: see **Smackgirl**

Johnson, Anthony

Nickname: Rumble
Height: 6'2"
Weight: 170 lbs
Born: 3/6/84
Debut: PF 2 (8/16/06)
Career Record: 8-3
Notable Wins: Kevin Burns (*The Ultimate Fighter* 8 Finale); Yoshiyuki Yoshida (UFC 104)
Notable Losses: Rich Clementi (UFC 76); Kevin Burns (UFC Fight Night 14); Josh Koscheck (UFC 106)

For such a soft-spoken and unassuming guy, Anthony Johnson's **UFC** fights sure seem to be awfully controversial and chaotic. First there was his fight with Kevin Burns on Spike TV. Johnson was poked in the eye repeatedly, but when controversial referee **Steve Mazzagatti** finally stepped in to stop the carnage, it wasn't to disqualify the dastardly Burns (who UFC announcers **Joe Rogan** and **Mike Goldberg** insisted wasn't gouging John intentionally, despite repeated evidence to the contrary): it was to award him the fight when Johnson couldn't continue. Johnson avenged the loss with a tremendous head kick in his next fight and, despite the setback, seemed on his way to being a force in the division.

Johnson was an enormous welterweight. After making an extreme weight cut down to 170 pounds, he would spring back up overnight, entering the cage at nearly 200 pounds. It was a dangerous game, and against **Yoshiyuki Yoshida** at UFC 104, it cost him dearly. Johnson missed the 170-pound limit by a whole six pounds. He forfeited 20 percent of his purse to Yoshida, and after knocking him out with a booming right hand, had to forfeit a $60,000 Knockout of the Night bonus as well.

It was a stiff financial lesson for Johnson who has two choices: either make weight, every time, or move up a class. He still has potential to be a world

In Their Own Words: Anthony Johnson on missing weight

"I was working with this trainer, a friend of my agent. He wanted me to try barely eating anything but getting a lot of fluids in me. So we did that, and I was 192 on Monday and I should have been less than 185 on Wednesday, and I wouldn't need to make the hard cut on Friday. The trainer told me, 'Drink a lot of water and don't eat too much.' So I did that, and then on Thursday I did a three-hour workout and dropped from 198 to 183. I was 192, and I drank all of this water that he wanted me to drink and got back up to 198. Doing his thing – it was cool but I think the process got started too late. If I'd done things the way I always did, I would have been fine, but trying this new method, this new way of doing things, really jacked my body up.

"You know, I haven't missed weight in two years. I always try my best, and when I don't succeed, it irritates me and I get bummed out. It pisses me off, it pisses off the UFC, and it pisses off my fans. It makes everybody mad, you know?

"After this, though, I told my coaches, my agent, everybody that hangs out with me or that will ever be in my corner that we all have to sit down and get everything situated. Because I can't be losing weight like that. And the type of training I did for this fight, certain things weren't right, some things were. But we have to get everything in order, you know? I can't have that, especially when we are trying to make a run for the title. I want everything organized and complete."

Interview by Jeremy Botter for Heavy.com

champion, but the title he wins may end up being in the middleweight, and not the welterweight, weight class.

Johnston, Brian

Nickname: Fury **Height:** 6'4"
Weight: 225 lbs **Born:** 1/1/70
Debut: UFC 10 (7/12/96) **Career Record:** 5-5
Notable Losses: Don Frye (UFC 10); Mark Coleman (UFC 11); Ken Shamrock (Ultimate Ultimate 96)

For **SEG**'s **UFC**, the key to success was finding stars. They had eschewed selling sport; instead they were selling personalities. Brian Johnston seemed like the perfect find. He was young, ripped, and good-looking. He even displayed his patriotism right on his American flag Speedos. Unfortunately, he just wasn't a very good fighter. He lost to **Don Frye** at UFC 10, **Mark Coleman** at UFC 11, and **Ken Shamrock** at Ultimate Ultimate 96. It was a who's who of MMA at the time and clearly demonstrated that Johnston didn't belong at the top of the sport.

Johnston was smart, though. When Frye jumped to New Japan Pro Wrestling in search of greener pastures, Johnston jumped with him. Although he was never a great pro wrestler, Johnston found his niche training the Japanese wrestlers for MMA fights. **Antonio Inoki** was busy pushing the fighters into real contests and there was no shortage of business coming Johnston's way.

Then, in August 2001, tragedy struck. Johnston was simply grabbed in a neck crank in training. This had happened thousands of times before, but this time it went tragically awry. Johnston popped a blood vessel in his neck and suffered a stroke. He almost died and could communicate only by blinking his eyes. Eventually, to the surprise of his doctors, Johnston not only lived but was able to walk again.

Jones, Jon

Nickname: Bones **Height:** 6'4"
Weight: 205 lbs **Born:** 7/19/87
Debut: 4/12/08 **Career Record:** 10-1
Notable Wins: Stephan Bonnar (UFC 94); Brandon Vera (UFC Live: Vera vs. Jones)
Notable Losses: Matt Hamill (*The Ultimate Fighter* Finale 10)

When his legacy is written years from now, Jones may be labeled the **UFC**'s first fighter from the digital age. For Jones, the internet isn't just a source of entertainment and information — it's a bona fide training tool. Before he made the move to **Greg Jackson**'s all-star camp in New Mexico, much of Jones's training came from watching YouTube videos and endlessly perfecting the techniques he saw there. And not just the conventional ones. Jones believes any technique can work effectively, as long as the fighter drills it endlessly and believes in it completely.

The result of this belief is a hodgepodge of weird moves and throws that makes Jones stand out even in the diverse world of professional MMA. He's borrowed striking from video game characters, throws from professional wrestlers, and taught himself **judo** by watching YouTube videos. His signature move is a lightning-fast spinning elbowsmash — a clubbing blow he has used effectively against multiple foes. So far, the unpredictable Jones has been a mystery opponents have had no answer for. His only loss was by way of disqualification in a fight he was dominating against wrestler **Matt Hamill**. After stunning Hamill with a takedown, Jones dropped elbow after elbow, wrecking his opponent's face. Unfortunately, they were illegal "12-6" downward elbows, moves banned in a simpler time when scared politicians believed the tip of the elbow was somehow more dangerous coming directly up and down.

Jones rebounded nicely with a win over failed prospect **Brandon Vera** and seems on his way to becoming a future champion. But the fight with Vera could be seen as an object lesson for Jones. Vera himself was once seen as similarly destined for greatness. For Jones to continue on a path to the top he can't be content to stay static. But if past is prelude, Jones is probably on the internet right now, finding the next wild and weird move to spring on an unsuspecting opponent.

Judo

When Jigoro Kano synthesized the teachings of Kitōryū and Tenjin Shin'yōryū jiu-jitsu, and further expanded their syllabi by incorporating new techniques guided by the principle of maximum efficiency, he called his new art judo rather than jiu-jitsu. "Ju" — gentleness, flexibility, yielding — remained, but the shift from "jitsu" (technique) to "do" (way) was significant, signaling a movement away from the pure battlefield utility of the techniques inherited from the samurai past and towards a training method that encouraged personal growth and moral development. The martial element remained vital — without it, Kano could not have proven the benefits of his Kodokan (literally "a place to study the way") over the competing jiu-jitsu schools of the day — but judo aspired to be more than a martial art: it took as its aim the harmonious development and eventual perfection of human character.

The philosophical underpinnings of judo did not emerge fully formed out of the mind of a mere 22-year-old — Kano's age at the founding of the Kodokan at Eishoji Temple in 1882. They would take shape over the course of long career in education, one influenced by the philosophical and pedagogic writings of John Dewey, John Stuart Mill, Herbert Spencer, and Jeremy Bentham. But the principles that guided the training methods at the Kodokan — seiryoku zenyo (maximum efficiency) and jita kyoei (mutual welfare) — had immediate impact. First, Kano's belief in the maximum efficient use of energy put great emphasis on kuzushi, unbalancing the opponent, so that he could be thrown using comparatively little strength. ("To oversimplify it, **wrestling** is pushing, while judo is pulling," says **Don Frye**, who's done both.) Second, the principle of mutual welfare and benefit entailed a concern for the safety of your training partner, and a focus on techniques that could be trained safely at full resistance rather than theoretically effective moves that are too potentially injurious to drill meaningfully.

The result of these guiding principles wasn't only that Kano was turning out better people — he was turning out better fighters. Kano's judo (sometimes referred to as "Kano Jiu-jitsu" in early texts) proved the victor over rival schools in an 1886 contest sponsored by the Tokyo Metropolitan Police, and quickly rose to prominence as Japan's foremost martial art. Challenges that it won with ease confirmed its training methods; schools that offered greater difficulty were asked to instruct at the Kodokan so that techniques could be further refined. The jiu-jitsu schools of Kano's youth had risked complete collapse under the weight of their thuggish reputations. By cleaning up jiu-jitsu's rough image through his Kodokan, Kano ensured that their knowledge accumulated over centuries would not be lost.

The internationalization of judo began in earnest in the earliest years of the 20th century, with instructors fanning out across the globe. Kano, an internationalist, believed the principle of maximum efficient use of physical and mental energy inherent in judo training could benefit people the world over. This spirit of internationalism led not only to the firm establishment of judo throughout the globe — there are 192 members states in the United Nations, and 187 in the International Judo Federation — but also to the development of closely related disciplines. **Mitsuyo Maeda**'s travels took him to Brazil, where a young **Carlos Gracie**, alongside his frail young brother **Helio**, transformed a brief, basic instruction in judo into the now-thriving art of **Brazilian Jiu-jitsu** by placing unprecedented emphasis on ne waza (ground technique) and constantly testing their art against all comers. The Russian Vasaly Oshchepkov trained in judo as an orphan boy attending Vladivostok's Tokyo Christian school and was integral in the development of **sambo** (cambo), a fusion of judo and the folk wrestling traditions of the Soviet lands.

Despite this internationalization, and Kano's standing as the first Asian representative to the International Olympic Committee, judo's founder was surprisingly ambivalent about the sport's inclusion in the Olympic Games. "If it be the desire of other member countries," he wrote in a 1936 letter, "I have no objection. But I do not feel inclined to take any initiative. For one thing, judo in reality is not a mere sport or game. I regard it as a principle of life, art, and science. In fact, it is a means for personal cultural attainment." Writing on the eve of the Berlin Olympics, it's understandable that Kano would worry that "the Olympic Games are so strongly flavored with nationalism that it is possible to be influenced by it and to develop contest judo as a retrograde form, as jiu-jitsu was before the Kodokan was founded."

All the same, Olympic judo has flourished since its inclusion at the 1964 Tokyo Games, and, in an outcome that would perhaps give Kano little comfort, contest judo broadly speaking has produced no small number of professional mixed martial artists. Olympic champion **Hidehiko Yoshida**, Asian Champion **Yoshihiro Akiyama**, former Russian national team member **Fedor Emelianenko**, and American junior champion **Karo Parisyan** have all translated their dynamic throwing skills and strong groundwork into successful MMA careers, exposing new audiences to the techniques and principles of judo. From its humble beginnings with nine students on twelve mats more than a century ago, Jigoro Kano's judo continues to grow, and helps its practitioners do the same.

Just Bleed Guy

If you didn't quite know what to make of ***TUF*** alumnus "Filthy" Tom Lawlor's strange appearance at the **UFC** 100 weigh-in, it's probably because you'd never had the privilege of watching **Mark Kerr**'s 17-second manhandling of Greg "Ranger" Stott way back at UFC 15. That match, brief though it was, has become something of a cult classic. There are a number of reasons for this.

First, there's the general goofiness of Greg Stott, who delivered perhaps the finest pre-fight interview in the history of the sport, which we proudly present here in its entirety: "My name's Greg 'Ranger' Stott. I'm a former airborne ranger and combat veteran. Currently I'm a hand-to-hand instructor and a founder of my own style, which we call 'RIP.' RIP stands for Ranger International Performance, and it's the most expeditious and effective form of hand-to-hand combat in the world. That's why the RIP team is here at UFC 15: to prove why RIP rules — and all others rest in peace."

Next, there's the fact that Ranger International Performance turned out to be *awful*. Stott managed no more offense than a baffling simultaneous stomp kick/punch combination before being kneed into unconsciousness by a Mark Kerr very much in his drug-fueled, squeaky-voiced prime.

Both of these things were truly wonderful. But the highlight of the bout, for all who saw it then and all who have seen it since, had nothing to do with the action inside the Octagon. No, it was the action in the stands. Specifically, it was a five-second clip of the single greatest fan to ever grace the sport of mixed martial arts: Just Bleed Guy.

For years, little was known about Just Bleed Guy. But this much we could say with certainty: sometime before the Stott/Kerr showdown, he had anointed his forehead with the letters "UFC" in neon green body paint, and, more importantly, the words "JUST BLEED" on his chest in white above a poor but discernible Nike swoosh. He then found his way to Casino Magic Bay in beautiful Bay St. Louis, Missouri. He took his seat, one row in front of and slightly to the right of a bearded man smoking a joint with a fierce lean on. At some point over the course of the evening, Just Bleed Guy purchased or otherwise obtained at least one beer. Then, just as ring announcer **Bruce Buffer** finished his stirring introduction of the proud Grenada veteran Stott, it happened: Just Bleed Guy, shirtless, magnificent, plastic beer cup in hand, scowled and flexed in an angry, unyielding "most muscular" pose. Those of us watching at home didn't really know what we were seeing. But we knew instantly that it was something we'd needed to see all along.

All too soon, it ended. The camera senselessly cut back to the cage. But Just Bleed Guy left his mark in those five short seconds, and over the next decade his legend grew and the mystery deepened. Just who was the man behind the paint? What led him to that singular moment, and what had happened to him since? As with virtually anything actually worth knowing, the answer ultimately came from **The Underground** Forum. In late 2008, poster and professional fighter Joe Nameth (a scrappy 3–20, but currently on a 12-fight slide) offered photographs of and with Just Bleed Guy from a subsequent UFC card in New Orleans. "I have known 'Just Bleed' since we were kids," Nameth revealed. "That's me in the green shirt and hat." Unfortunately, it also turned out that Just Bleed Guy — known to some, including the authorities, as James Ladner — was serving time in a Mississippi prison, convicted on a charge of receiving stolen property, specifically farming equipment. If the world was ever going to see a man stripped to the waist at an MMA event with an all-caps call for blood scrawled on his chest, it looked like it would have to wait until at least 2012.

Enter "Filthy" Tom Lawlor: fighter, showman, genius. Realizing, perhaps, that there could be no greater stage in mixed martial arts than that provided by UFC 100, Lawlor seized the opportunity to bring this unrivaled moment in the history of the sport he loves to the attention of the broadest possible audience. As he approached the scales to weigh in at Mandalay Bay Event Center the day before the event, his forehead ("UFC") and chest ("JUST BLEED") screaming out in body paint the two things that most needed to be said, there could be no doubt whose star shone brightest that day. It wasn't **Brock Lesnar**'s. It certainly wasn't **Georges St. Pierre**'s. It wasn't even Tom Lawlor's. No, that day belonged to one man and one man only. It belonged to James Ladner. It belonged to Just Bleed Guy.

Kang, Denis

Height: 5'11" **Weight:** 185 lbs

Born: 9/17/77 **Debut:** Ultimate Warrior Challenge 1 (8/2/98)

Career Record: 32-12-1 (2 No Contests)

Notable Wins: Murilo Rua (Pride Bushido 11); Amar Suloev (Pride Bushido 12); Akihiro Gono (Pride Bushido 13)

Notable Losses: Kazuo Misaki (Pride Bushido 13); Yoshihiro Akiyama (Hero's 2007 in Korea); Gegard Mousasi (Dream 2); Alan Belcher (UFC 93)

Depending on where he's fighting, Denis Kang is introduced to the crowd as either Korean or Canadian. That might seem slightly confusing, but it's actually the simple version: raised in Vancouver, Kang was born to Korean and French parents in the tiny French colony of St. Pierre and Miquelon, off the coast of Newfoundland. After an indifferent beginning in a collection of minor North American promotions and a brief, unsuccessful run in **Pancrase**, Kang's career came to life in Seoul's Spirit MC, where his heavy hands and dynamic, explosive style made him a crowd favorite.

His success in Korea earned him a spot in **Pride**'s Bushido series, and a berth in the 2006 Bushido welterweight (185 pounds) tournament. After convincing wins over **Murilo Rua**, Amar Suloev, and **Akihiro Gono**, Kang dropped a closely contested final by split decision to **Kazuo Misaki**. Kang was impressive in defeat, battling through a torn biceps muscle, and competing not long after the death of his longtime girlfriend and fellow **American Top Team** member Shelby Walker, who took her own life in the fall of 2006.

Kang was undefeated in 23 fights prior to the Misaki loss, but since, he hasn't looked the same. First came a surprising knockout loss to **Yoshihiro Akiyama**, a top competitor at 185 pounds, but not a fighter known for his hands. Then there was the baffling submission loss to **Gegard Mousasi**, in which Kang — a Marcus Soares black belt in **Brazilian Jiu-jitsu** — fell into an easy **triangle choke**. Another loss, this time by **guillotine choke** to Alan Belcher in Kang's

UFC debut, created further doubts still. Once considered among the world's top middleweights, Denis Kang is no longer part of that discussion.

Karate

Before there were MMA schools on every corner in America, there were karate dojos. Plenty of them. Karate came back west with American soldiers after World War II and became a favorite after-school activity and babysitter for American suburban kids across the country. Along the way karate, once designed to allow samurai to kill with their bare hands in Okinawa, lost its edge.

By the time the **Ultimate Fighting Championship** was created in 1993, a karate master was ill equipped to fight a martial artist with skills grounded in reality combat like **Brazilian Jiu-jitsu**'s **Royce Gracie**. Karate and other traditional martial arts became laughingstocks in the mixed martial arts community.

Some successful fighters came from a karate background, including **Bas Rutten**, **Georges St. Pierre**, and the late K-1 standout Andy Hug. These fighters may have come from a karate background, but by the time they were finished products, you could barely see the karate base beneath the submission grappling and kickboxing techniques. It wasn't until **Lyoto Machida** won the UFC light heavyweight title that karate began to fulfill its promise as a legitimate fighting style.

Like Rutten and St. Pierre, Machida had to learn Brazilian Jiu-jitsu, Thai boxing, and **wrestling** to be successful. But unlike the other two karateka who went on to MMA glory, karate remains Machida's main style. His unusual stance, fluid movement, and pinpoint striking have given opponents fits and brought much pride to an art form that needed a pick-me-up.

■ Kyokushin versus Shotokan

Karate is represented in MMA competition by two major styles: Shotokan and Kyokushin. Until recently, Kyokushin karate has been the dominant form of karate seen in MMA cages and kickboxing rings worldwide. That makes sense in light of the mentality of its founder, Masatatsu Oyama. Oyama was a man who enjoyed fighting and violence. Kyokushin instructors helped spread the art around Japan with their fists. Oyama himself would impress crowds wherever he traveled by killing bulls with his bare hands. He was called "God Hand" because on multiple occasions he killed a bull with a single strike.

Oyama's style of karate was hard and aggressive. Fighters suffered grueling physical punishment in training to toughen them up and their fighting approach allowed no step backwards. You can see this mentality in Rutten and St. Pierre, aggressive fighters who were always coming forward. Kyokushin karate focuses heavily on full contact sparring and fighting. Oyama allowed no protective equipment; his only protection for students was a ban on punches to the face in training.

Shotokan, perhaps reflecting the values of its founder Gichin Funakoshi, took a less outwardly aggressive and reckless approach. Funakoshi was a poet and a scholar, and his style of karate focused on the mental aspect of fighting. He still remembered when karate was a legitimate form of self-defense, designed to evade the long swords of a samurai and strike quickly with a killing blow. Although he didn't advocate sport karate, Funakoshi's Shotokan has developed a point fighting system of karate. Although competitors are often in extensive padding, it remains true to its roots by placing a premium on elusiveness. Some of the ethos of true karate remains, including a "one strike, one kill" mentality. No Shotokan fighter had ever achieved success in MMA until Lyoto Machida used the best of karate to dominate more traditional strikers inside the UFC Octagon.

Kasteel, Joop

Height: 6'3" **Weight:** 265 lbs

Born: 8/27/64 **Debut:** Fight Gala: Mix Fight Night (6/15/96)

Career Record: 19–13

Notable Wins: Roman Zentsov (MilleniumSports: Veni, Vidi, Vici); Dan Severn (Rings Holland: Men of Honor)

Notable Losses: Kiyoshi Tamura (Rings: Rise 5th); Gilbert Yvel (Rings Holland: There Can Only Be One); Cheick Kongo (Rings Holland: World's Greatest)

Early on, the **UFC** was obsessed with finding a marketable fighter. They wanted someone who looked like a fighter people would see on late night television martial arts movies. That desire wasn't limited to American fight promotions. The Japanese were always on the lookout for great-looking guys as well, men to wear what the fighters in Japan called "banana hammocks," the tiny Speedos that helped draw in the female fans.

Pancrase had the **Lion's Den** guys and **Bas Rutten**, but **Rings**, frankly, had too many big, hairy, and ugly foreign fighters. Chris Doleman, **Volk Han**, and Andrei Kopilov were great pioneers of the sport, but not much to look at. Enter Joop Kasteel.

A body builder from the Rhino Gym in Holland, Kasteel had the look that Doleman needed for the Japanese shows. He had almost no fighting experience, but he was big and he was strong. He was also a fast learner, developing the skills he needed to compete with experienced fighters in Japan. He was good enough to earn two title shots in Rings, losing to both **Kiyoshi Tamura** and

Gilbert Yvel. In his final fight, Kasteel earned gold for the first time, beating the ubiquitous **Dan Severn** for a now forgotten European heavyweight title.

Kawajiri, Tatsuya

Nickname: Crusher
Height: 5'7"
Weight: 154 lbs
Born: 5/8/78
Debut: Shooto: R.E.A.D. 4 (4/12/00)
Career Record: 26-6-2
Notable Wins: Yves Edwards (Shooto 2003: 8/10 in Yokohama); Vitor Ribeiro (Shooto 2004 Year-End Show); Joachim Hansen (Shooto: The Victory of the Truth); Gesias Cavalcante (Dream 9)
Notable Losses: Vitor Ribeiro (Shooto 2002: Year-End Show); Takanori Gomi (Pride Bushido 9); Gilbert Malendez (Pride Shockwave 2006); Eddie Alvarez (Dream 5); Shinya Aoisi (Dream 15)

If you can remember a time before Tatsuya "Crusher" Kawajiri was undoubtedly among the top lightweight fighters in the world, you've been following Japanese MMA for quite a while now. After only two years of martial arts training, Kawajiri made his **Shooto** debut with a quick **rear naked choke** loss in 2000. Immediately thereafter, he began to show the world what he was made of — and it's tough, tough stuff. His heavy hands, solid **wrestling**, and thunderous **ground and pound** propelled him past a host of young Shooto hopefuls, and serious opposition like **Yves Edwards** and **Vitor "Shaolin" Ribeiro**. Kawajiri claimed Shooto's welterweight (154 pounds) title when he stopped Ribeiro at the 2004 year-end show, avenging a decision loss two years to the day prior.

When **Pride** scooped up much of Shooto's top talent for their lightweight-focused Bushido series, Kawajiri met fellow Shooto alumni **Takanori Gomi** in a hotly anticipated match later selected by Pride fans as the best of 2005. Gomi got the better of Kawajiri standing in a wide-open affair, and finished him with a choke after knocking him to the canvas, handing Crusher his first loss in almost three years. It must have been disheartening for the Shooto faithful to see this great bout among two of their top fighters occur under the banner of another promotion, but Kawajiri returned to the Shooto ring to defend his title against **Joachim Hansen** — in a match that ended in eight seconds on a groin kick. If you, like **Joe Rogan**, are strangely fascinated by kicks to the groin, Kawajiri/Hansen is an all-time classic. Anyone else would have been badly disappointed.

Kawajiri has fought only rarely in Shooto since, and now calls **Dream**'s lightweight division home. Although he was upset by **Eddie Alvarez** in the semifinal of the Dream Lightweight Grand Prix, Kawajiri has since rebounded, picking up a particularly impressive decision win over **Gesias Cavalcante**, a top fighter five years his junior. That match confirmed what we've all known for years now: that the Crusher is a man with staying power.

Kennedy, Tim

Height: 5'11"
Weight: 185 lbs
Born: 9/1/79
Debut: IFC WC 15 (8/31/01)
Career Record: 12-2
Notable Wins: Jason Miller (Extreme Challenge 50); Nick Thompson (Strikeforce: Challenge 2); Trevor Prangley (Strikeforce: Los Angeles)
Notable Loss: Jason Miller (HDNet Fights: Reckless Abandon)

For some fighters, going to the resort town of Big Bear, California, for a few weeks before a fight helps toughen them up and get them focused. Army Staff Sergeant Tim Kennedy is not that brand of tough. Before the Army Combatives tournament in 2005, Kennedy wasn't roughing it in cabin with his boys. He was completing one of the Army's most difficult courses. SERE stands for Survival, Evasion, Resistance, and Escape. You start in the woods of Fort Bragg, on your own, with some of the Army's top Special Forces soldiers trying to track you down. That's the easy part.

When you are captured — and you will be — you are taken prisoner. Then they will break you — however they can. Remember all of the atrocities at the Abu Ghraib prison in Iraq? Forced nudity, stress positions, endless physical training, even water boarding? The Army does this to its own soldiers at SERE

In Their Own Words: Tim Kennedy on being a soldier and a fighter

"Days are long. I start my days real early when I do my conditioning and my strength training and my day ends real late when I get off work and then go to the gym and work on my boxing and jiu-jitsu. The military has been good to me, and I don't have any complaints there. I know that even when I'm talking with companies about when my fights are coming up, I'm still in the military. When something comes up I'm going to have to press pause on my fighting and take care of my first commitment and keep my word and do whatever it is the Army has asked me to do.

"Am I giving enough to my fighting? Am I giving enough to my country? Am I doing everything I possibly can to be a good soldier? That's something I have other people keeping me accountable on, to make sure I'm doing the right thing all the time."

school to prepare them for the worst-case scenario. One week before his fights in 2005, the Army tried to break Tim Kennedy. Instead, he won the tournament. Tim Kennedy is that kind of tough.

When Arizona Cardinals football star Pat Tillman left fame and fortune behind to serve his country in the Army Rangers, it was national news. More quietly, a fledgling professional fighter from San Luis Obispo, California, made the same leap. Tim Kennedy was a Columbia graduate, so it's no surprise that the attacks of September 11th affected him profoundly. He had a successful career just taking off in MMA, beating Cruz Chacon and **Jason Miller** at Extreme Challenge 50. He seemed on the path to **UFC** stardom, but instead didn't fight again for three years. At least not professionally. Instead he joined the Army, went to Iraq, went to Ranger School, and became one of the most elite soldiers in the world when he moved to the Special Forces. Instead of UFC champion, Kennedy became an honest-to-goodness war hero.

Kerr, Mark

Nicknames: The Specimen, The Smashing Machine **Height:** 6'3"

Weight: 255 lbs **Born:** 12/21/68

Debut: World Vale Tudo Championship 3 (1/19/97)

Career Record: 15-11 (1 No Contest)

Notable Wins: Paul Varelans (World Vale Tudo Championship 3); Pedro Otavio (Pride 3); Enson Inoue (Pride Grand Prix 2000)

Notable Losses: Kazuyuki Fujita (Pride Grand Prix 2000 Finals); Igor Vovchanchyn (Pride 12); Heath Herring (Pride 15); Oleg Taktarov (Yamma Pit Fighting)

Former **UFC** tournament champion Mark Kerr has been immersed in the world of MMA since his freshman year in high school, even if he didn't know it at the time. That was in 1983, ten years before the first UFC. Kerr spent that freshman year working out with a grizzled senior by the name of **Pat Miletich**, another future UFC champ.

College was like another UFC all-star team. Kerr faced off with the now legendary **Randy Couture** in the finals of the 1992 NCAA tournament. Couture was a great collegiate wrestler, but Kerr made him look like a chump, winning the NCAA title by a score of 12–4. It was a tremendous victory, one that helped propel Kerr onto the national stage. Before he could make a run at the Olympic Games, however, Kerr had to find the right weight class. Cutting down to 190 pounds, like he did in college, just wasn't an option anymore.

"In that last year of college, for me to get down to 190 pounds, I had to cut 46 pounds from my preseason physical," Kerr said. "Imagine that. So when the floodgates opened and I was able to eat all year long, my body just filled out. I had forgotten how comforting food is."

Kerr fell short of his Olympic dream, losing to future gold medalist Kurt Angle in the qualifying tournament. Like many former **wrestling** standouts, Kerr followed a coach, Richard Hamilton, into the world of MMA. Kerr quickly established himself as one of the most dominating fighters on the face of the planet. While Kerr enjoyed the monetary compensation, he found out right away that the fight game was far from glamorous. His first fight tournament was in Brazil, hidden away in the basement of a hotel. From there he moved immediately into the UFC where he won consecutive tournaments at UFC 14 and 15.

Then trouble started. Kerr's contract called for one more tournament, but the UFC wanted to go another direction and book single bouts. Kerr saw an opening and looked to escape his UFC contract for greener pastures in Japan with the newly formed **Pride Fighting Championships**.

"They sued me in federal court and put me through every circumstance you could imagine," Kerr said. "I'd get a phone call that would say you have to be in New York City to be deposed tomorrow. I'd pay $1,000 on airline tickets and then they'd ask me three questions and send me home. It was ugly."

In the end, Kerr bought the contract out and became an immediate icon in Japan for Pride. Most people in the sport considered him the best heavyweight in the world. Looking back, it's hard to see that in retrospect. Kerr was an amazing wrestler and a solid all-around fighter. Unfortunately, he never faced the level of competition that would have allowed him to prove his worth. His first 11 opponents had a combined record of 60–51–2. More than half of the wins came courtesy of Pedro Otavio and Dan Bobish.

In Their Own Words: Kerr on working with Nobuhiko Takada in Pride

"I made it perfectly clear that it was my reputation and my integrity on the line. I made it clear to them that there was no way I would ever compromise it for financial gain. It would be too hard for me to carry that to bed every night.

"This is the way the Japanese do business. They pulled me aside and said, 'Hey Mark, we want to talk to you about something you maybe don't understand. The Japanese fans, they love technique. They really know this sport and are familiar with it and the techniques.' That being said to me, well, you can kind of fill in the lines. Meaning, they don't want to see me get on top of him and pound the crap out of him. That's what I took out of the conversation. It was a whole conversation with the promoters talking about how they appreciated technical things. And they just left it at that. I left the meeting kind of chuckling. If I needed to go out there and punch him in the face until his nose fell [off] I would have done it. But he gave up the submission, and that was easier for me."

While kickboxing champion Branko Cikatic and **Luta Livre** ace Hugo Duarte ended up being MMA busts, Kerr did face the best of the best in grappling competition. While many wrestlers stuck with the skills that brought them to the game, Kerr branched out into submission grappling and was nigh unbeatable. The same thing couldn't be said in the ring. **Igor Vovchanchyn** knocked Kerr out, a loss later changed to a no contest due to illegal knees. Knees to the head of a grounded opponent were illegal on that night, one of many rules shifts that made fighting in Pride such an adventure. Even though the fight was not officially a loss, it ruined Kerr's reputation for invincibility, and sent his life spiraling out of control. The fall from grace due to drug abuse was made thoroughly public in the documentary film *The Smashing Machine*.

Kerr took three years off before coming back to the ring, only to knock himself out with a powerful takedown against Japanese fighter Yoshisha Yamamoto. Kerr dropped Yamamoto so hard to the mat that his own head struck the ground and knocked him unconscious. He stayed out of MMA for almost three more years after that, but has returned to fight several times a year, losing seven of his last nine and five in a row. It's apparent that while he is healthier and happier, Kerr will never be the same athlete again.

Keylock: see **Kimura and Americana**

Kharitonov, Sergei

Height: 6'4" **Weight:** 242 lbs
Born: 8/18/80 **Debut:** Brilliant 2 (8/11/00)
Career Record: 16-4
Notable Wins: Murilo Rua (Pride Total Elimination 2004); Semmy Schilt (Pride Critical Countdown 2004); Pedro Rizzo (Pride Critical Countdown 2005); Fabricio Werdum (Pride 30); Alistair Overeem (Hero's 10)
Notable Losses: Antonio Rodrigo Nogueira (Pride Final Conflict 2004); Alistair Overeem (Pride 31); Aleksander Emelianenko (Pride Final Conflict Absolute); Jeff Monson (Dream 8)

It's easy to forget that not long ago, Sergei Kharitonov was a top-ten heavyweight on virtually everyone's list. And rightly so: the heavy-handed Russian soldier with technically sound **boxing** and an aggressive **sambo** grappling game made quite an impression as he demolished **Chute Boxe**'s **Murilo Rua** and sliced up kickboxing giant Semmy Schilt in **Pride**'s 2004 heavyweight Grand Prix tournament. Although his tournament run ended when he dropped a unanimous decision to **Antonio Rodrigo Nogueira**, his reputation hardly took a hit by going the distance with one of the greatest heavyweight fighters the sport has seen. After that most minor setback, Kharitonov continued to roll, stopping the inconsistent but dangerous **Pedro Rizzo** early and earning a tough split-decision win over **Brazilian Jiu-jitsu** standout **Fabricio Werdum**.

Then, 2006 happened. Ugly first round TKO losses to both **Alistair Overeem** and **Aleksander Emelianenko**, fighters Kharitonov was expected to handle, ended any speculation about the specific problems Kharitonov might pose for **Fedor Emelianenko**. If those losses, coupled with the emergence of what would turn out to be chronic back trouble, signaled the beginning of the end of Kharitonov's run as a serious heavyweight contender, an embarrassing submission loss to **Jeff Monson** in less than two minutes in **Dream** signaled the end, full stop.

Kikuchi, Akira

Height: 5'8" **Weight:** 167 lbs
Born: 7/23/78 **Debut:** Shooto: Treasure Hunt 2 (1/25/02)
Career Record: 16-4
Notable Wins: Jake Shields (Shooto 2004: Year End Show); Katsuya Inoue (Hero's 2)
Notable Losses: Jake Shields (Shooto 2003: 8/10 in Yokohama Gymnasium); Shinya Aoki (Shooto: Victory of the Truth, Shooto: Back to Our Roots 1); Yoshiyuki Yoshida (GCM: Cage Force 4)

Shooto stalwart Akira Kikuchi was a **judo** and **wrestling** stylist with competent standup, neatly efficient takedowns, and an aggressive, submission-oriented top game. He was also, for a time, Japan's top welterweight fighter.

Kikuchi's crowning moment came in late 2004, when he took a unanimous decision in a one-sided drubbing of **Jake Shields** to claim the Shooto middleweight (167 pounds) title and avenge his only career loss to that point. Over the course of three dominant rounds, Kikuchi schooled Shields in all phases of the ground game, making him look slow and confused — the last words one would usually use to describe Shields' grappling. That match stands as Jake Shields' only loss over the course of seven years and eighteen fights.

In his only appearances in the big leagues of Japanese MMA, Kikuchi picked up two **Hero's** wins over the next year, including a devastating first round **ground and pound** stoppage over interim King of **Pancrase** Katsuya Inoue. Kikuchi was riding high, and entered his Shooto title defense against a young **Shinya Aoki** as the prohibitive favorite. But after two competitive rounds, Kikuchi spent virtually the entire third and final round of the championship bout with Aoki clinging to his back while Aoki landed headshots that made up in quantity what they lacked in quality. Despite his best efforts, including an improvised forward rolling head spike maneuver, a bloodied Kikuchi was unable to shake the young grappler, and his title reign was over.

The match cost him more than his title: Kikuchi and indeed the entire Killer Bee fight team was banned from both amateur and professional Shooto for six months after a bizarre incident during the Aoki fight, in which the hotheaded **Norifumi "Kid" Yamamoto** kicked and berated a fight doctor for not agreeing that Kikuchi had been cut by an illegal elbow.

An improved showing against Aoki a year to the day later wasn't enough to reclaim his Shooto title, but Kikuchi nevertheless entered the 2007 **Cage Force** welterweight tournament as the man to beat. A positional slip up on the ground in the semi-final against **Yoshiyuki Yoshida** saw Kikuchi beaten with a barrage of elbows — ending the fight, Kikuchi's shot at a **UFC** contract, and his career. Kikuchi unexpectedly announced his retirement at the age of 29.

Kikuta, Sanae

Nickname: Newaza King **Height:** 5'9"

Weight: 200 lbs **Born:** 9/10/71

Debut: Lumax Cup Tournament of J '96 (3/30/96)

Career Record: 28-6-3 (1 No Contest)

Notable Wins: Ikuhisa Minowa (Pancrase: 2001 Anniversary Show); Minoru Suzuki (Pancrase: Breakthrough 11); Hidehiko Yoshida (Sengoku: No Ran 2009)

Notable Losses: Renzo Gracie (Pride 2); Murilo Bustamante (Pancrase: Trans 6); Antonio Rodrigo Nogueira (UFO: Legend); Yuki Kondo (Pancrase: Hybrid 10)

Founder of the **Grabaka** ("grappling fool") gym and fight team, and a former light heavyweight King of **Pancrase**, Sanae Kikuta is also one of the few non–**Brazilian Jiu-jitsu** based competitors to win his division at the **ADCC** submission **wrestling** championships.

As a young **judo** player, Kikuta won the prestigious National Athletic High School Meeting, and studied under judo legend Toshihiko Koga at Nippon College of Physical Education. After leaving both college and competitive judo behind, Kikuta made his MMA debut in the now largely forgotten Lumax Cup, an event contested on an open mat surface (rather than in a ring or cage) that required its competitors to wear open-fingered gloves and a **gi** jacket (but not gi pants). Kikuta's Tournament of J '96 and heavyweight Tournament of J '97 Lumax Cup titles earned him a place in **Pride**'s second ever event, where the submission expert proceeded to lay in **Renzo Gracie**'s **guard** for the better part of an hour before falling prey to a **guillotine choke** in a bout even duller than one would expect given that description.

Although Kikuta had his moments in Pride, **Shooto**, **Deep**, and even the **UFC**, it was in Pancrase that Kikuta found the most success, claiming that organization's light heavyweight title in 2001 with a cut-stoppage win over the entertaining **Ikuhisa Minowa**, and holding it until a KO loss two years later to fellow Pancrase stalwart Yuki Kondo as part of the ongoing rivalry between Kikuta's Grabaka and Kondo's Pancrase-ism fight teams. Although the aging Kikuta's MMA appearances have become increasingly rare in recent years, he has found a home in **Sengoku**, where, most notably, he earned a narrow, split-decision victory over fellow ancient judoka **Hidehiko Yoshida** in a match that saw only marginally more action than Kikuta's Gracie bout years before.

Kim, Dong Hyun

Nickname: Stun Gun
Height: 6'1"
Weight: 170 lbs
Born: 11/17/81
Debut: Spirit MC 3 (4/10/04)
Career Record: 13-0-1 (1 No Contest)
Notable Wins: Jason Tan (UFC 84); Matt Brown (UFC 88); T.J. Grant (UFC 100)

Dong Hyun "Stun Gun" Kim might seem like just another welterweight prospect. Young, undefeated, but largely untested, the slim **judo** player shows promise but hardly stands out from the crowd — unless you happen to be

Korean. Then he's actually kind of a big deal. Kim's **UFC** debut against Jason Tan was the subject of a one-hour, prime time hype special in Korea, and that preliminary match — which Kim won with hard elbows after a spectacular harai goshi judo throw — was aired three times on Korean TV before the regular broadcast got underway.

Perhaps surprisingly, Kim is only the second Korean to fight inside the Octagon (the first was the notorious Joe Son all the way back at UFC 4), and the martial-arts-mad nation has embraced Kim as their champion. Kim's early success in the **Spirit MC** and **Deep** promotions earned him a **Pride** contract just as the once great Japanese organization was crumbling. Although Kim was offered a contract with **World Extreme Cagefighting** by the new owners, it was ultimately decided that a deal with the UFC, with its existing television presence in Korea, had a bigger upside for both parties.

His much-hyped debut against Jason Tan was followed by a split decision win over Matt Brown, a cult hero from ***The Ultimate Fighter***'s seventh season, and a decision loss to **Karo Parisyan** that was later overturned when post-fight drug tests revealed Parisyan to be a walking pharmacy. Kim was given the opportunity to fight in the prelims of the historic UFC 100 card, and earned a solid decision win over Cole Harbour, Nova Scotia's T.J. Grant, a promising young **Brazilian Jiu-jitsu** fighter with a fine **wrestling** base. If Kim can maintain his winning ways, he'll soon find himself not just in prelims but on the main card, maybe someday with a title shot. But in his native Korea, he's a headliner already.

Kim, Min-Soo

Height: 6'1" **Weight:** 254 lbs

Born: 1/22/75 **Debut:** Hero's 1 (3/26/05)

Career Record: 3-6

Notable Win: Ikuhisa Minowa (Hero's Korea 2007)

Notable Losses: Bob Sapp (Hero's 1); Semmy Schilt (Hero's 6); Don Frye (Hero's 7); Brock Lesnar (Dynamite!! USA)

Min-Soo Kim can't fight. But that hasn't kept him from trying. And, for whatever reason, it hasn't kept K-1 from running him out there.

In the first minute of his MMA debut against **Bob Sapp**, Kim looked unpolished but legitimately dangerous, stopping Sapp's headlong charge with a flurry of punches that sent "The Beast" to a neutral corner to have his bloodied face checked over by officials. That's Kim's career highlight — it's been downhill ever since. Seconds after the match was restarted, the Min-Soo Kim we would come to know emerged: he caught a lead right hand directly on the chin, and the match was stopped at 1:12 of the first.

There are the wins — over professional wrestlers Sean O'Haire and Yoshihisa Yamamoto, and the much, much smaller **Ikuhisa Minowa** — and there are the KO losses — to kickboxers Ray Sefo and Mighty Mo, and hero-to-all **Don Frye**. But above all, there is the *awfulness*. Despite taking a silver medal in **judo** at the 1996 Olympics, Kim hasn't shown even minimal grappling skill in MMA (witness, if you dare, his submission loss by **triangle choke** to Dutch kickboxer Semmy Schilt).

Kim is best known to North American fans as a footnote, the first man to face **Brock Lesnar** in an MMA bout. A late substitution for Korean giant Hong-Man Choi, who failed a pre-fight medical, Kim was utterly overmatched and overwhelmed against the future **UFC** heavyweight champ. Kim was the first to be taken down and ingloriously pounded out by Lesnar, but he wouldn't be the last.

Kimura and Americana

Closely related arm locks, usually though not exclusively applied on the ground, in which the attacker controls his opponent's wrist, and grasps the wrist of his own controlling arm with his free hand such that the opponent's arm is isolated and entangled. Maintaining a 90-degree angle in the opponent's elbow, the attacker twists the arm, applying pressure to the elbow, shoulder, or both. If the opponent's trapped arm is configured such that his hand begins near his head, the hold is referred to in **Brazilian Jiu-jitsu** as an Americana; if the trapped hand begins near his hip, it's known as the Kimura. In **judo**, both techniques are classified as ude garami, literally "arm entanglement," although occasionally the Kimura variation is referred to as gyaku ude garami, "reverse arm entanglement." **Catch wrestlers** sometimes favor the terms key lock, figure four, or double wristlock. Different disciplines, different nomenclature, but in the context of mixed martial arts, it's the clear and useful Brazilian Jiu-jitsu terminology that dominates.

But it's fitting that the terms now widely used to describe these techniques — techniques important to several styles — originated in encounters between the Gracie family and practitioners of those other arts. The American after whom the Americana is named is wrestling legend Bob Anderson, who trained with Rolls Gracie in the 1970s. "I didn't come down there and go, 'Okay, I'm going to show you the Americana **arm bar** and I'm the guy that invented it,'" Anderson recalled. "It just grew out of what I knew and what he [Rolls] liked . . . he later — I didn't even know — he called it the Americana because

I was the American wrestler that came down and showed him the move and that's how the Americana arm bar got started." The Kimura is named in tribute to **Masahiko Kimura**, the Japanese judo legend who broke **Helio Gracie**'s arm with the technique in their famous 1955 bout in Rio's Estádio do Maracanã, forcing Gracie's corner to concede the match.

While the Americana is a proven, effective technique from **side control**, **north-south**, **mount**, and for the top fighter in **half-guard**, the Kimura is a vastly more versatile technique. The Kimura can be applied in any of those same positions, often with less risk of escape. Additionally, the Kimura can be used to initiate a variety of sweeps from **guard** or half-guard, and is a much more effective fight ender from the bottom than the Americana (although finishing from the bottom with either technique is difficult against a skilled top player). Successful standing applications of the Kimura are less common, but **Karo Parisyan**'s Kimura grip sumi-gaeshi sacrifice throw and finish against Dave Strasser at **UFC** 44, Mitsuhiro Ishida's similar Kimura grip sumi-gaeshi transition to arm bar against Justin Wilcox in **Strikeforce**, and the great **Kazushi Sakuraba**'s Kimura counter after **Renzo Gracie** took his back standing at **Pride** 10 are suggestive of the possibilities. Watching that Pride match, those who knew their history recognized that it wasn't the first time a member of the famed Gracie family fell prey to this hold against a top Japanese grappler, nor was it the first time his arm snapped under the strain. It wasn't the first time a Gracie refused to quit, either.

Kimura, Masahiko

No one before Kimura, they say, and no one after. A four-time All-Japan **judo** champion with only four documented losses over the course of his long competitive career, Masahiko Kimura is universally regarded as one of the finest judo players of all time and one of the greatest grapplers of the 20th century. His expertise in ne waza (ground fighting) was surpassed only by his mastery of osoto gari, an outside trip he would practice by slamming his body against a tree — and cruelly slamming his unlucky training partners off the mat. Kimura fell out of favor with the Japanese judo establishment when, after his final All-Japan title, he turned down the position of chief instructor for the Tokyo Metropolitan Police and instead took up with a short-lived professional judo circuit before falling in with the world of **professional wrestling**. For this betrayal of judo's longstanding spirit of amateurism, Kimura's rank was frozen, and he never progressed past the schihidan (seventh-degree black belt) he had been awarded in 1947 at the age of 30.

But Kimura, whose wife was in hospital with tuberculosis, needed money much more urgently than he needed rank. He took a three-month contract to

In Their Own Words: Masahiko Kimura on his contest against Helio Gracie (from _My Judo_)

"The gong rang. Helio grabbed me in both lapels, and attacked me with O-soto-gari and Kouchi-gari. But they did not move me at all. Now it's my turn. I blew him away up in the air by O-uchi-gari, Harai-goshi, Uchimata, Ippon-seoi. At about ten-minute mark, I threw him by O-soto-gari. I intended to cause a concussion. But since the mat was so soft . . . it did not have much impact on him. While continuing to throw him, I was thinking of a finishing method. I threw him by O-soto-gari again. As soon as Helio fell, I pinned him by Kuzure-kami-shiho-gatame. I held still for two or three minutes, and then tried to smother him by belly. Helio shook his head trying to breathe. He could not take it any longer, and tried to push up my body extending his left arm. That moment, I grabbed his left wrist with my right hand, and twisted up his arm. I applied Udegarami. I thought he would surrender immediately. But Helio would not tap the mat. I had no choice but keep on twisting the arm. The stadium became quiet. The bone of his arm was coming close to the breaking point. Finally, the sound of bone breaking echoed throughout the stadium. Helio still did not surrender. His left arm was already powerless. Under this rule, I had no choice but twist the arm again. There was plenty of time left. I twisted the left arm again. Another bone was broken. Helio still did not tap. When I tried to twist the arm once more, a white towel was thrown in. I won by TKO. My hand was raised high. Japanese Brazilians rushed into the ring and tossed me up in the air. On the other hand, Helio let his left arm hang and looked very sad withstanding the pain."

give judo exhibitions and take on local challengers in the Hawaiian Islands, and agreed to a four-month stint in Brazil for a Japanese newspaper promoting professional wrestling events. Kimura came to Brazil to perform, not to fight, but once there he felt compelled to answer the repeated challenges of **Helio Gracie** — especially after Gracie defeated Kato, another Japanese judoka on the tour, choking him into unconsciousness. Gracie, who had refined the judo basics his older brother Carlos had learned under the tutelage of **Mitsuyo Maeda** into his own Gracie Jiu-jitsu, would reveal years later that he knew the challenge was hopeless from the beginning. "I myself thought that nobody in the world could defeat Kimura," he told Yoshinori Nishi in 1994.

He was right. In front of thousands in Rio's Estádio do Maracanã, Kimura tossed Gracie around effortlessly, thoroughly controlled him on the mat, and ultimately finished the fight with ude garami, the entangled arm lock that has since been known in jiu-jitsu and mixed martial arts circles by the great judoka's name. Kimura never knew it, but it wasn't the first hold that had incapacitated Gracie that night: in that same remarkable 1994 interview, Gracie admitted that he had been caught in a chokehold earlier in the bout, and lapsed into unconsciousness while trying to decide whether or not he should submit. "But since I didn't give up," he remembered, "Kimura let go of the choke and went into the next technique. Being released from the choke and the pain from the next technique revived me and I continued to fight. Kimura went to his grave without ever knowing the fact that I was finished."

After his years as a traveling showman, Kimura took up a teaching position at Tokushoku University in 1960, where he trained Kaneo Iwatsuri to an All-Japan title and Canadian Doug Rogers to a silver medal at the 1964 Tokyo Olympics. After a life lived as one of Japan's most celebrated judo heroes, Kimura's legend has only grown since his death in 1993 at the age of 75.

King of the Cage

No one can accuse King of the Cage (KOTC) owner Terry Trebilcock of jumping on the MMA bandwagon. When he started his California-based promotion in 1998, MMA was close to extinction in North America. The sport was banned in many states, including California, and Trebilcock and other promoters spent much of their time traipsing through Indian casinos, looking for an arena to host their shows.

Despite the MMA-unfriendly atmosphere, King of the Cage did very well, eventually becoming the second biggest promotion in the country. Many of the best fighters in the world got their start in Trebilcock's cage, most notably former **UFC** light heavyweight champion **Quinton Jackson** and ***The Ultimate Fighter*** season 1 winner **Diego Sanchez**.

Although King of the Cage never passed the UFC as the top promotion in the world, their fights were certainly available to more fans. An amazing DVD distribution deal saw KOTC DVDs on the shelf at Best Buy and FYE at a time when the UFC didn't even have a video deal. Many KOTC video packages included up to ten full fight cards on a five-DVD set. Affordably priced, the sets were popular with hard-core fans searching for hidden gems on cards featuring mainly local talent.

In 2007, Trebilcock sold the promotion to **EliteXC**, but continued running it as if nothing had changed. When EliteXC failed, he bought KOTC back and continued going strong. Always looking to break new ground, Trebilcock entered into partnership with reality TV guru Mark Burnett of *Survivor* fame.

Together, they created *Bully Beatdown*, the popular MTV show starring **Jason "Mayhem" Miller**.

Today the company is no longer a major feeder system to the UFC or the main Japanese promotions. Most of the cards are produced with a local and not a national audience in mind. While this may make the shows unpalatable to many fans, it ensures they do well in the local market in tough economic times.

Knee bar: see **Leg locks**

Kohsaka, Tsuyoshi

Nickname: TK **Height:** 5'11"
Weight: 225 lbs **Born:** 3/6/70
Debut: Rings: Budokan Hall 1995 (1/25/95)
Career Record: 26-18-2 (1 No Contest)
Notable Wins: Pete Williams (UFC 17.5); Fedor Emelianenko (Rings: King of Kings 2000 Block B); Ron Waterman (Pancrase: Brave 10); Mario Sperry (Pride 31)
Notable Losses: Bas Rutten (UFC 18); Pedro Rizzo (UFC 23); Randy Couture (Rings: King of Kings 2000 Final); Renato Sobral (Rings: Worth Title Series 2); Ricco Rodriguez (UFC 37); Fedor Emelianenko (Pride Bushido 6); Mark Hunt (Pride Total Elimination Absolute)

Tsuyoshi Kohsaka's name survives as a footnote: the first and, for years, only man to defeat the great **Fedor Emelianenko**. There is, however, a footnote to that footnote: it was an inadvertent, illegal elbow thrown only seconds into the first round that ended that bout. The right call would have been a no contest, but, as part of **Rings**' King of Kings tournament, the match needed a winner. And so it was the veteran Kohsaka who advanced and the newcomer Emelianenko who was saddled with the loss.

That brief fight with its lucky finish has kept Kohsaka's name in the sport years after his retirement. It is, in a sense, his legacy. But it was the kind of heart and determination a battered and bruised TK showed in a second match with Emelianenko years later — a fighting spirit he'd shown throughout his long career — that made him one of the best loved fighters of the sport's early years among hard-core fans. TK was a cult classic.

A fourth degree black belt and member of Toray Corporation's **judo** team (big Japanese companies often "employ" promising athletes), it was a serious knee injury that ended Kohsaka's career in his first sport in 1993. A year later, he debuted in **Akira Maeda**'s shoot-style Rings promotion, a proto-MMA organization that offered both worked and legitimate matches alongside each other on the same cards. Although Rings consisted of nothing but legitimate contests by the end of the decade (and featured many future top **Pride** and **UFC** fighters), it's hard to know exactly what to make of the early years of Kohsaka's career. While all of the familiar MMA databases list Kohsaka's June 27, 1998, draw against **Kiyoshi Tamura** as a legitimate fight, **professional wrestling** fans refer to the bout as one of the top shoot-style works of the decade. Take TK's win–loss record with a grain of salt.

What can we say with certainty, then? What do we *know* was real? His tournament win in the open-mat, **gi**-mandatory Lumax Cup, his decision win over **Pete Williams** and dramatic overtime KO loss to **Bas Rutten** in the UFC's heavyweight title tournament, and his late Rings bouts against the likes of **Antonio Rodrigo Nogueira** and **Randy Couture** certainly all check out. As does his pioneering cross training with **Maurice Smith** and **Frank Shamrock** as part of the Alliance (the "TK Guard" was, at one time, much discussed). So too does his **Pancrase** super heavyweight title win over the enormous **Ron Waterman**, his stoppage of **Brazilian Top Team** co-founder **Mario Sperry**, and his tragically heroic effort against **Mark Hunt** in what would turn out to be his farewell bout. When the referee stepped between Hunt and a thoroughly pounded Kohsaka to stop the fight with less than a minute to go, TK was devastated. No doubt he wanted it to end like his famous "contest" against Tamura years before, nobly holding on as the seconds wound down, going the distance.

Koppenhaver, Jon: see **War Machine**

Koscheck, Josh

Nickname: Kos **Height:** 5'10"

Weight: 170 lbs **Born:** 11/30/71

Debut: King of the Rockies (1/3/04) **Career Record:** 15-4

Notable Wins: Chris Leben (*The Ultimate Fighter* 1); Diego Sanchez (UFC 69); Dustin Hazelett (UFC 82); Yoshiyuki Yoshida (UFC: Fight for the Troops); Frank Trigg (UFC 103)

Notable Losses: Georges St. Pierre (UFC 74); Thiago Alves (UFC 90); Paulo Thiago (UFC 95)

The grudge match between Josh Koscheck and **Chris Leben** on the first season of ***The Ultimate Fighter*** was, at the time, the most watched mixed martial arts contest in U.S. television history. An audience of more than two million viewers watched Leben, an alcoholic with serious abandonment issues, try to exact his revenge against a man who had the *audacity* to spray him with a hose after a night of drinking. It was pretty lame. And the fight itself wasn't much: Koscheck, a 2001 NCAA Division I **wrestling** champion, blanketed the overmatched Leben in a classic display of **lay and pray** en route to a one-sided decision win. But the Leben/Koscheck feud helped make the early episodes of *The Ultimate Fighter* a ratings success, and it's no secret that the success of *The Ultimate Fighter* was instrumental in transforming the failing **UFC** into the juggernaut we know today, taking the sport from relative obscurity into the mainstream. You can thank Josh Koscheck the next time you see him.

Koscheck's reputation as a blanket — a wrestler content to take his opponent down and then do exactly nothing — started with the Leben fight and dogged him throughout the early bouts of his UFC career. But after falling in with the American Kickboxing Academy, Koscheck transformed from a highly accomplished but one-dimensional wrestler into a well-rounded mixed martial artist. He avenged his *TUF* loss to the previously undefeated **Diego Sanchez**, proudly announcing Sanchez's record after their fight as "Nineteen and one! Nineteen and *one!*" All of a sudden Koscheck was putting together slick combinations, even throwing head kicks — just ask **Dustin Hazelett**, who found himself on the wrong end of both.

But there have been bumps along the road. At UFC 74, Koscheck had the misfortune of running into **Georges St. Pierre** in his first fight back after he shockingly dropped his title to **Matt Serra**. There's never a good time to face GSP, but this was arguably the worst. It was no surprise that St. Pierre emerged the victor; what was surprising was that Koscheck was outwrestled. That hadn't happened before, and it hasn't happened since. He dropped a fight to the dangerous and enormous **Thiago Alves**, a bout he took on only two weeks' notice, and was stopped by Paulo Thiago in his UFC debut. For all the ups and downs, though, there can be no doubt that Josh Koscheck's name belongs among the top ten welterweights in the world.

Kuk Sool Won

In the early days of the **UFC**, when a fighter didn't practice a martial art, it became necessary to manufacture a fighting background. Streetfighter **Tank Abbott** famously became a "pit fighter." Like Abbott, **Gary Goodridge**'s fighting credentials essentially involved being an extremely large man.

In 1996, a lot of extremely large men wanted to get into the UFC. Goodridge needed a gimmick and pretended to be an expert in Kuk Sool Won. Kuk Sool Won is modern Korea's favorite martial art, but it may not have been the best choice for Goodridge's fake fighting art. It incorporates a jumble of dazzling high kicks, animal movements, and spinning techniques — the exact opposite of Goodridge's straightforward steamroller approach.

Kuk Sool Won practitioners, martial artists who place a premium on physical conditioning and flexibility, may have been embarrassed by their faux comrade when he proved to have less than stellar cardio. But they were surely happy to claim him when he nearly caved in Paul Herrera's skull with a series of brutal elbows. A true Kuk Sool Won artist could have helped heal Herrera with acupuncture and herbs. Unfortunately for Paul, Goodridge was only good for flexing his muscles and yelling.

Kung fu

The famous Shaolin monastery sits in at the base of the Songshan Mountain in China. Its monks, clad in orange robes, seemed like easy targets for bandits when they approached in 725 AD. The robbers were in for a rude surprise. These monks not only studied the teachings of the Buddha, they also perfected their physical strength and mastered the art of kung fu. The bandits were defeated and the Shaolin monks secured a lasting legacy.

Their techniques and strategies formed the basis of hundreds of martial systems. In fact, kung fu doesn't describe any single art form. It's a generic term that refers to a practitioner's skill level, not any particular martial system. The term, and the modern equivalent Wushu, are essentially shorthand for "Chinese martial arts."

For practical purposes, in the cage, any and all forms of kung fu have been dismal failures. Many Chinese martial artists focus more on show than combat. For the warriors who do train for real fighting, much of the technique involves the use of weapons. MMA may be extreme, but it doesn't allow bo staffs or broadswords.

The Chinese government may have encouraged kung fu's current emphasis on showmanship, but kung fu was at one point more than a Cirque du Soleil act. Until the practice was banned in 1928, kung fu fighters tested their mettle on the Lei Tai. The Lei Tai was a raised platform. Two men went up, but on many occasions only one came down. Or, at least, came down alive. If only modern kung fu fighters were as strong, fierce, or as fast as lightning.

■ Emin Boztepe: Chicken?

When **Royce Gracie** ran through a bevy of traditional martial artists in the first several **Ultimate Fighting Championship**s, many people who made their living selling kung fu and karate panicked. And rightfully so: Gracie was talking the talk and then backing up his words in the cage. The Asian arts were looking more than a little silly and it was threatening to cost them money.

The martial arts magazines and the emerging internet forums were filled with traditional martial artists arguing and explaining to any who would listen that their style was perfectly suited to defeat the Gracies. Others, like Wing Tsun master Emin Boztepe, seemed above the fray. That is, above the fray until a poster on a message board forum called Boztepe a chicken. Then it was on. Well, almost on. Boztepe wrote a scathing letter to Cinturon Negro in Europe, claiming the UFC was fake, that he himself was undefeated after more than 300 bare-knuckle fights, and that he would bring five Wing Tsun masters to challenge the Gracies.

The feud escalated as UFC matchmaker **Art Davie** called his bluff, offering him a coveted spot in the UFC. Boztepe's lawyer and UFC frontmen **Rorion Gracie** and Davie exchanged a series of increasingly funny letters and faxes, trying to negotiate a time and a place for a Gracie/Boztepe superfight. Davie even offered Boztepe a one-on-one fight with Gracie, allowing the Wing Tsun man to avoid the customary UFC tournament.

No arrangement suited Boztepe, but the UFC matchmakers agreed that the idea of matching up Royce with an elite star, instead of putting him in a tournament for a fifth time, had plenty of promise. The Superfight was born, with **Ken Shamrock** assuming Boztepe's place as Gracie's challenger. It was a match the UFC had wanted badly to culminate UFC 3, but had fallen apart when both men were injured. The crowd was dying to see Shamrock and Gracie square off again – their Superfight held the distinction of being the most successful UFC show on pay-per-view for more than ten years.

Lashley, Bobby

Nickname: The Dominator　　**Height:** 6'3"

Weight: 250 lbs　　**Born:** 7/16/76

Debut: Mixed Fighting Alliance: There Will Be Blood (12/13/08)

Career Record: 5-0

Notable Wins: Jason Guida (SRP: March Badness); Bob Sapp (Ultimate Chaos); Wes Sims (Strikeforce: Miami)

Like fellow World Wrestling Entertainment refugee **Brock Lesnar**, Bobby Lashley is much more than a body builder who sees big dollar signs attached

In Their Own Words: Bobby Lashley on getting started as a pro wrestler

"Well, Kurt Angle was in the WWE at the time and he came to Colorado Springs to the Olympic Training Center. He was doing a little vignette, a promo, and they were talking about his amateur days. That was the first time I met Kurt. And Kurt said, 'Have you thought about it? You have a great look for the WWE.' At the time I was still wrestling, but I had watched it as a kid. I enjoyed it, but I had never seen myself doing it. We exchanged numbers and talked from time to time. Then I got a call from [WWE executive] Gerald Brisco because they were discussing me again. This time when they said, 'Come out and we'll have a look at you,' I did.

"It was probably the most fun I've had in my whole life. Professional wrestlers aren't actors, so we can't really play a character. Very, very few are good enough actors to play a character. Vince would say, 'We just want you to be yourself, but with the volume turned up. Think about who you are, and then turn the volume up.' It was actually a fun transition, because you get to find out who you are."

to the three letters M, M, and A. He was a world class wrestler, guiding Missouri Valley to its first two NAIA championships while winning three individual national titles of his own at 177 pounds. From college, it was on to the Army, where Lashley continued to excel on the mat, winning the Armed Forces Championship and earning a silver medal in the prestigious World Military Games in 2002.

Of course, it isn't this sterling record that attracts MMA promoters by the bucketful. His WWE experience does that. Three years of national television exposure, as well as a Wrestlemania 23 main event where he helped Donald Trump shave Vince McMahon bald, made Lashley, if not a household name, at the very least a recognizable face. With pay-per-view draws in short supply, Lashley will find no shortage of callers. In 2008, the **UFC** wasn't interested. **Dana White** even pretended not to know who Lashley was when asked about him in the media flurry over Lesnar's MMA ascendance. But it is a relative certainty that if Lashley can keep winning, his face will show up on Spike TV or on pay-per-view, sooner rather than later.

Lawal, Muhammed

Nickname: King Mo **Height:** 6′

Weight: 205 lbs **Born:** 1/11/81

Debut: Sengoku: Fifth Battle (9/28/08) **Career Record:** 7-0

Notable Wins: Mark Kerr (M-I: Global:Breakthrough); Gegard Mousasi (Strikeforce: Nashville)

In the world of amateur wrestling, "King Mo" Lawal came as close as you can to the ultimate goal of every young wrestler: Olympic glory. After beating Andy Hrovat at the 2008 U.S. nationals, Lawal fell to Hrovat at the Olympic trials by a razor-thin margin. Lawal won match one; Hrovat match two. In the rubber match, the two men actually tied a thrilling battle that saw both score final-second points. Hrovat went on to the Olympic team by virtue of having the higher scoring individual technique.

It was a bitter pill for Lawal to swallow and at 27 he turned his attention to MMA. The Olympic trials were in June — by September he was making his fighting debut for **World Victory Road: Sengoku.**

Success has come quickly for Lawal in the mixed martial arts. He travels the world to find the best training partners and continues to refine his techniques. Mo is a self-described student of the game, often watching hours of film to get a feel for how the most successful fighters are able to impose their will. Lawal also has a naturally engaging personality, making his interviews

> **In Their Own Words: King Mo on the difference between collegiate and international wrestling**
>
> "The thing is, NCAA champions come a dime a dozen. To me NCAA champion is a joke. I don't care about that. It's a different level when you hit the world scene. International wrestling. That's where you become a man. **Mark Kerr** was good, but he hasn't wrestled in so long. After five years, once you stop competing and working out with world class athletes, your skills deteriorate. Look at **Dan Henderson**, **Matt Lindland**, and **Randy Couture**. Those guys get taken down by guys that have never wrestled before. If you haven't trained wrestling in a while, your skills deteriorate. Same thing with jiu-jitsu and boxing."

and ring entrances stand out in a sport that features many fighters that might be politely described as "bland." At times his pre-fight antics are more exciting than his conservative fighting style — like dozens of world class wrestlers, King Mo hasn't been afraid to **ground and pound** his way to victory, often drawing boos from bloodthirsty crowds. The jeering can rain down; Lawal intends to do what it takes to win, even if it isn't popular with the crowd. Just 19 months into his career he defeated **Gegard Mousasi** to become the **Strikeforce** light heavyweight champion, solidifying his status as one of MMA's top prospects.

Lawler, Robbie

Nickname: Ruthless
Height: 5'11"
Weight: 170–185 lbs
Born: 3/20/82
Debut: Extreme Challenge 39 (4/7/01)
Career Record: 19-6 (1 No Contest)
Notable Wins: Joey Villasenor (Pride 32); Frank Trigg (Icon: Epic); Scott Smith (EliteXC: Unfinished Business)
Notable Losses: Nick Diaz (UFC 47); Evan Tanner (UFC 50); Jason Miller (Icon: Mayhem vs. Lawler); Jake Shields (Strikeforce: Lawler vs. Shields)

Robbie Lawler was the **UFC**'s top prospect when **Zuffa** bought the company in 2001. Just 19 years old and a bit of a prodigy, he was one of the first fighters to literally grow up with the sport of MMA. **Pat Miletich** discovered him when he was still in high school and he's been fighting ever since.

Things came easily to Lawler. He was a good natural athlete, a **wrestling** standout with natural power in his hands, and he had that itch to fight that you can't teach. He won his first six fights before getting the call to come to

Bossier City, Louisiana, for UFC 37. Lawler opened the show with Midwest tough guy Aaron Riley, a punching bag quickly becoming famous for his grit and heart. It was a 15-minute war that saw Lawler get the win, and, more importantly, establish his reputation as a dangerous young fighter. More victories followed and Lawler got confident, bordering on cocky.

Cocky is the most dangerous thing to be in the sport of MMA, where every fighter is capable of hurting you in a dozen ways and it's incredibly easy to make a fight-changing mistake. Lawler's inability to control his emotions cost him again and again. He and Chris Lytle slung punches back and forth at UFC 45, with Lawler earning a decision and a place on the UFC highlight reel when he dropped his hands and yelled out in the middle of the fight, caught up in the moment.

Lawler, it seemed, was always caught up in the moment. His fights were wars but there was very little strategy involved. He simply attacked, as hard and as fast as he could. Lesser opponents were overwhelmed. Better fighters like **Nick Diaz** and **Evan Tanner** simply waited him out, eventually using his own aggression against him.

After losing three of four, he was sent on his way. The UFC brass wanted him to improve his skills. Everyone at Zuffa loved his attitude and his warrior spirit; they just wanted to see it combined with the tools that could make him a champion. Instead, Robbie Lawler has continued to be Robbie Lawler. He won two titles, for Icon Sport in Hawaii and for **EliteXC**, by exploding on people who made the mistake of standing and trading with him. Against slick grapplers, he was still vulnerable, losing by submission to **Jason "Mayhem"**

Miller and **Jake Shields** in high profile matchups. Now 27 years old, and almost a decade into his professional career, Lawler seems likely to remain the fighter he is today. The potential that seemed destined to make him a world champion will go unrealized. He may have the best fight on the card, but Robbie Lawler will never be the best fighter.

Lay and pray

For whatever reason, the mixed martial arts world loves its rhyming jargon. You've got **sprawl and brawl**, where a fighter uses their **wrestling** skills defensively in order to stand up and bang. You've got **ground and pound**, where fighters put their opponents on their back and rain down blows from the top. Those are both terms that fighters embrace to describe their strategies. There's nothing pejorative about either of them; they're purely descriptive. The same cannot be said of lay and pray, which is more like a charge leveled against a fighter than an openly discussed strategy. When a grappler establishes a strong top position but does nothing to finish the fight by improving position (see **positional hierarchy**), striking, or working towards a submission, that's lay and pray: lying on top of your opponent, and praying the judges' decision goes your way. If MMA were pure sport, it would be a perfectly sound strategy. But paying fans demand entertainment, and nothing brings on a chorus of boos faster than one man lying in another's **guard** with no action. **Sean Sherk** has been accused of lay and pray on more than one occasion — sometimes fairly, sometimes not — as have Gray Maynard, **Ricardo Arona**, and **Josh Koscheck** early in his career. But probably the most notorious lay and pray the sport has ever seen was **Ken Shamrock**'s rematch against **Royce Gracie** at **UFC** 5, where Shamrock spent nearly all of the fight's 35 minutes inside Gracie's guard, doing absolutely nothing. The fight was not judged, and was declared a draw once the five-minute overtime had expired. You can't really pray for a judges' decision in an unjudged fight, so you could say Shamrock/Gracie II doesn't really count if you wanted to split hairs. But Shamrock did more than enough laying that night, and you've got think at least one prayer was uttered somewhere along the line.

Leah, Rachelle

Most of the time, ring card girls are nearly anonymous. They only have a single job to do: entertaining 10,000 bloodthirsty men during the one minute between rounds they aren't being actively amused by man-on-man action. Rachelle Leah transcended that role, making the leap from cageside eye candy to television eye candy.

In Their Own Words: Rachelle Leah on hosting *UFC All Access*

"I've had a lot of great moments hosting *All Access*. The most memorable was with **Anderson Silva**. He is hysterical. He's a goofball and you'd never expect it. As intense as he is in the Octagon, he's completely the opposite outside of it. He just started singing Michael Jackson. He was breaking it down and he got me to break it down on camera in his house. I took off my shoes and everything. Those kinds of moments, just be able to relax and be yourself, those are my favorite moments.

"If you met most of our guys, you wouldn't guess they were fighters. Some of them were teachers and have degrees. You go to their homes and see them in the gym and they're just perfectly normal."

Leah became the host of ***UFC** All Access*, a Spike TV show designed to make the UFC's valiant warriors seem a little more human. Leah traveled to their homes, to the gym, and checked out their cars in UFC's homage to MTV's seminal *Cribs*.

Just as the UFC seemed to replace pro wrestling as the sport of choice for young men, Leah and fellow Octagon Girl Ariany Celeste took over for the WWE Divas as cultural icons. Leah was just the first to go mainstream, posing for the cover of *Playboy* and making the move into acting. Gone but not forgotten, Leah has opened the door for future Octagon beauties to go as far as their talent and determination can take them.

LeBell, Gene

The much-loved "**Judo**" Gene LeBell has done a little bit of everything over the course of his long and storied career. He's been an actor, a stuntman, a professional wrestler, and a two-time AAU national judo champion. He was the referee in the infamous proto-MMA debacle between Muhammad Ali and **Antonio Inoki**. He trained with both Bruce Lee and Chuck Norris. He took a vicious beating at the hands of Steve Martin in *The Jerk*. And depending on who you ask — long-time *Sports Illustrated* writer Jon Wertheim is the most credible to have gone on record with the story, though it has circulated in various forms for years — LeBell may very well have strangled pony-tailed action star Steven Seagal until he soiled himself on the set of *Under Siege*. In short, if it's incredibly cool, there's a pretty good chance Gene LeBell has done it, probably while wearing his signature pink **gi** and hamming it up for any cameras that happen to be nearby.

LeBell was an early advocate of cross-training in an era where that was hardly common practice, and competed in a bout closely resembling mixed martial arts decades before the sport really took shape. Billed as a "judo/karate" fighter, LeBell took on Milo Savage, a credible middleweight boxer, in a 1963 challenge match in Salt Lake City, and choked him out in the fourth three-minute round. LeBell later claimed that he passed up several opportunities to finish the fight earlier by **arm bar**, as he had no interest in breaking the arm in the likely event that Savage wouldn't surrender. LeBell wanted to show that judo could be effective without causing serious injury.

"I was grappling before grappling was cool," LeBell once said. And he's still on the mats as he approaches his 80th birthday. He continues to teach every Monday night alongside his top student Gokor Chivichyan at the Hayastan Academy in North Hollywood, the gym that turned out **UFC** competitors **Karo Parisyan** and Manny Gamburyan. Should you have the good fortune to attend one of his seminars, and you're willing to let LeBell put you all the way out, you'll be rewarded with a little patch that reads, "I was choked out by Gene LeBell." Just try to keep it together a little better than Seagal.

Leben, Chris

Nicknames: The Crippler, The Cat Smasher **Height:** 5'11"

Weight: 185 lbs **Born:** 7/21/80

Debut: Full Contact Fighting Federation: Rumble at The Rose Garden 4 (8/10/02)

Career Record: 21-6

Notable Wins: Jason Thacker (*The Ultimate Fighter* 1 Finale); Patrick Côté (*Ultimate Fight Night* 1); Yoshihiro Akiyama (UFC 116)

Notable Losses: Josh Koscheck (*The Ultimate Fighter* 1); Kenny Florian (*The Ultimate Fighter* 1); Anderson Silva (*Ultimate Fight Night* 5); Michael Bisping (UFC 89)

In the debut episode of the very first season of ***The Ultimate Fighter*** (*TUF*), Chris Leben got ruinously drunk, pissed on Jason Thacker's bed, and tore up the house after Bobby Southworth and **Josh Koscheck** sprayed him with a hose. It made him a star. Leben immediately set the tone for the series and modeled behavior for every subsequent marginal fighter looking for a few minutes of fame before they crashed out of the competition. In later seasons, it was not uncommon for fighters to invoke Chris Leben's name when describing the kinds of shenanigans they got up to in the house (see **Browning, Junie**).

Leben's *TUF* feud with Koscheck, however, ended not with a bang but a whimper when Leben couldn't do anything at all with the vastly superior wrestler, and the vastly superior wrestler couldn't do anything at all with his vastly superior position. Koscheck took the decision, but after an injury put Nate Quarry out of the tournament, Leben got another chance to "put the stamp on kids." He came up against **Kenny Florian**, who sliced Leben open with elbows and stopped him in the second round, but it wouldn't be the last we'd see of "The Cat Smasher," not by a long shot.

After *The Ultimate Fighter*, Leben became a staple of Spike TV's Ultimate Fight Night cards, picking up wins against mid-level competition in each of the first four events. Things began to unravel pretty quickly, however, after Leben followed a completely understandable first-minute loss to **Anderson Silva** with poor showings against the likes of Jason MacDonald and Kalib Starnes. Leben was still a crowd-pleaser with his heavy hands and wide open style, and he managed to get the best of Jorge Santiago, Terry Martin, and Alessio Sakara — all solid professionals, but not exactly contenders.

A probation violation and jail sentence stemming from a DUI cost Leben a high-profile **UFC** 85 bout against **Michael Bisping**. After they finally met at UFC 89, Leben tested positive for Stanozolol, a banned **steroid**, and got hit with a one-year suspension only a week after a Spike TV special detailed Leben's triumph over his longstanding substance abuse issues. In 2010, with those troubles behind him, Leben proved himself a genuine middleweight contender when he managed to stay on his feet and finish Aaron Simpson, a well-credentialed wrestler, then surprised **Yoshihiro Akiyama** with a last-minute **triangle choke** only two weeks later. Leben had spent much of that bout being **judo** tossed and slugged in the face, and admitted afterwards that he didn't even know which round he was in — he had no idea just how dramatic his come-from-behind win had been. But drama is what we've all come to expect from Chris Leben, the kind of drama that has pulled audiences in since that first assault on Jason Thacker's bed — which, for the record, Leben maintains was only a spritzing.

Le, Cung

Height: 5'10" **Weight:** 185 lbs

Born: 5/25/72 **Debut:** Strikeforce: Shamrock vs. Gracie (3/10/06)

Career Record: 7-1

Notable Wins: Tony Fryklund (Strikeforce: Shamrock vs. Baroni); Frank Shamrock (Strikeforce: Shamrock vs. Le); Scott Smith (Strikeforce: Fedor vs. Werdum)

Notable Loss: Scott Smith (Strikeforce: Evolution)

In all of martial arts, there are plenty of great showmen and plenty of great fighters. There are few who are both. Most martial artists are either all for show — actors in the Wushu tradition like Jackie Chan or Jet Li — or they eschew that kind of style and flair to focus on practical techniques.

Cung Le is both, an actor and showman (even in the cage), and also one of the most skilled technicians in the world. When Le fights, it's like a real life movie fight scene. Graceful spinning kicks, powerful spinning backfists, hard throws, and amazing suplexes: Le can do it all and combines the techniques into a beautiful ballet of violence.

Le was an All-American in **wrestling** at California's West Valley Junior College. He also studied tae kwon do and other striking arts, and found the opportunity to combine the two with the Chinese fighting art called san shou. Le's International Sport Karate Association san shou fights scored punches, kicks, and throws equally. With his quickness and high level wrestling, Le was almost unbeatable in this style, racking up a 17–0 professional record.

Le was not only developing his techniques, like a lightning fast high kick and an impressive array of slams and suplexes; he was also becoming a star. In his hometown of San Jose, the Vietnamese-American was an icon to the huge immigrant population. When he began fighting MMA in 2006, a matchup with fellow hometown boy **Frank Shamrock** seemed inevitable.

Before he could count his money from a Shamrock matchup, Le had to earn it. San shou and MMA were similar, but there was one important difference.

In Their Own Words: Le on getting started in MMA and fighting a legend

"Actually it was Frank Shamrock's old trainer, and now my trainer, Javier Mendez. He talked me into doing MMA. Back in 2006 he said, 'The time is now, MMA's about to explode.' I said, 'Okay, I'll give it a shot.'

"Frank and I were on the same card in March two years ago and it was a sell-out. I guess there were over 18,000 that showed up. We're expecting another big show. Two years later, I'm just fortunate to have the chance to compete for a title and fight someone like Frank. It's only been two years for me in the MMA game, and I just feel like I came in at the right time. I was at the right place at the right time and have been blessed. Frank gave me the shot, and I'm grateful."

When the fight hit the ground in san shou, it was stood right back up. In MMA, Le would have to defend against submissions as well.

It was never an issue. Before the Shamrock fight, Le was carefully matched with fighters unlikely to challenge him on the ground. He either fought fellow strikers who were planning to fight him on their feet, or guys who wouldn't be able to take Le to the mat. He won five fights in a row and was ready to face the former **UFC** champion.

The two hometown boys drew a crowd of more than 13,000 and a gate of over $1.1 million to San Jose's HP Pavilion. The fight was an explosive affair, fought almost entirely standing. Le defeated the legend when Shamrock had to quit after a series of Le high kicks broke his right wrist. Le was the **Strikeforce** middleweight champion and a legitimate start. He was also outgrowing MMA.

The star-making performance was Le's last MMA fight for some time. Already in his mid-30s, Le decided he would be better off focusing on acting opportunities. There his physical decline would be less noticeable and he would only be getting punched in the face if a stuntman made a mistake. Le was set to star in the upcoming *Tekken* movie as well as films with David Carradine and Dennis Quaid. It seems likely that Le's fights will now take place almost exclusively on the silver screen, as he looks close to becoming MMA's first breakout film star.

Leg locks

It's been a long, hard road back to respectability for leg locks. Although present in the koryu jiu-jitsu schools of feudal Japan, leg locks all but disappeared

from the day-to-day, living culture of **judo** when they were excluded from sparring and tournament competition over safety concerns, and instead confined to formal, rehearsed kata. **Brazilian Jiu-jitsu** practitioners banned some particularly dangerous leg locks from all but the highest levels of competition, and even when permitted, a kind of gentleman's agreement discouraged their use, seeing them as cheap. There's a pedagogical reason jiu-jitsu players have often discouraged techniques that sacrificed position and could be attempted without working one's way methodically towards a superior position, given their rigorous belief in **positional hierarchy**, but however justified, the net result was a hole in the otherwise unassailable jiu-jitsu submission game. As **catch wrestling** disappeared, the only remaining discipline that both allowed and encouraged at least certain varieties of leg locks was **sambo**, an art that remains fairly obscure outside of Russia and the former Soviet Republic.

But the no-holds-barred ethos of early mixed martial arts brought about a renewed interest in this broad and versatile class of techniques. The influence of catch stylists Karl Gotch and Billy Robinson over young Japanese grapplers like **Masakatsu Funaki** and Satoru Sayama led to the extensive use of leg locks in both **Shooto** and **Pancrase**. Think of early Pancrase, and surely one of the first images to come to mind is a pair of fighters fumbling with each other's brightly colored boots, struggling to twist or extend the knee or the ankle just so.

Maybe they were looking for the heel hook, a dangerous twisting hold banned from sambo and much Brazilian Jiu-jitsu that can feel like nothing special one moment and leave you with a wrenched ankle, a ruined knee, or even on rare occasion a fractured shin the next. Or maybe it was an Achilles lock they were after: a straight ankle lock that exerts serious pressure as the Achilles tendon is stretched over the attacker's forearm. Maybe a toe hold, a twisting ankle lock that uses the double-wrist or figure-four grip, like a **Kimura** or **Americana**. The knee bar was a popular option, too, hyperextending the knee with the same basic principles that underlie the jujigatame **arm bar**.

In both Pancrase and the early **UFC**, **Ken Shamrock** did as much as anyone to demonstrate the effectiveness of the leg lock. Heel hook, knee bar, Achilles lock — Shamrock could do it all, leaving some particularly hopeful old fans liking Shamrock's chances against any modern fighter we haven't yet seen defend against the leg lock. Such is the aura Shamrock created around these techniques that had all but faded away. It's no surprise, then, that when Shamrock left MMA for an extended stay in the World Wrestling Federation, his signature submission move was an ankle lock — a toe hold, to be exact.

Leopoldo, Kimo

Height: 6'3" **Weight:** 235 lbs

Born: 1/4/68 **Debut:** UFC 3 (9/9/94)

Career Record: 10-7-1

Notable Wins: Patrick Smith (K-1 Legend 94, UFCF 1); Kazushi Sakuraba (Shoot Boxing S Cup 96); Tank Abbott (UFC 43)

Notable Losses: Royce Gracie (UFC 3); Ken Shamrock (UFC 8, UFC 48); Wes Sims (Extreme Wars 5)

Rumors of Kimo's demise have been greatly exaggerated. Or so Kimo claimed at a July 2009 press conference after a thread started by Beau "OMA" Taylor as a prank on **The Underground** spiraled out of control. All of a sudden, legitimate media sources were claiming that the **UFC** veteran had indeed passed away of heart attack at the age of 41 while vacationing in Costa Rica. His friends and family, who tried but failed to contact him, were understandably shocked and concerned. As was Kimo himself, who, as it turned out, was not so much dead as sleeping one off at a friend's place in Orange County.

It was a strange return to the spotlight for the man we first met at UFC 3 as the odd protégé of man-of-faith/alleged-rapist Joe Son. Kimo, known by that name alone, carried a giant wooden cross to the ring as part of their tandem gimmick as religious warriors. He gave two-time defending tournament champion **Royce Gracie** all he could handle in their brief match. Although Gracie got the win by **arm bar** in fewer than five minutes, the physically imposing Kimo bullied Gracie around the ring in a way we hadn't seen before, and left Gracie exhausted and unable to continue into the next round.

Although Kimo stayed relatively active over the course of his 12-year career, he never really equaled the excitement of that first performance. Sure, there were wins over **Patrick Smith** and **Paul Varelans**, an **arm triangle** that stopped **Tank Abbott**, and another that apparently got the best of **Kazushi Sakuraba** in a match that may not have been entirely on the up-and-up. There were losses to **Ken Shamrock**, the entertaining **Ikuhisa Minowa**, and the game **Tsuyoshi Kohsaka**. And then there was the draw — *that* draw — against **Dan Severn** in an incredibly uneventful match even by the low standards of early **Pride**. But for Kimo, for his place in the memory of the sport, it's all about that first night, that first fight. Kimo was the first fighter to make Royce Gracie seem almost beatable.

Lesnar, Brock

Nickname: The Next Big Thing
Height: 6'3"
Weight: 280 lbs
Born: 7/12/77
Debut: Dynamite!! USA (6/2/07)
Career Record: 5-1
Notable Wins: Heath Herring (UFC 87); Randy Couture (UFC 91); Frank Mir (UFC 100); Shane Carwin (UFC 116)
Notable Loss: Frank Mir (UFC 81)

Pro wrestlng fans knew Brock Lesnar was tough long before he ever entered the Octagon to wreak havoc in the **UFC**. Sure, he looked tough, but it was more than that. A lot of wrestlers look like a million bucks but can't pull the tough guy act off when it matters. Lesnar though, he was tough. No one who had seen Wrestlemania XIX could ever doubt that.

Lesnar was wrestling Kurt Angle — like Brock a former amateur standout — in the biggest match of either man's career. To make it special, Lesnar was going to attempt a move that he hadn't tried since he was first breaking into the wrestling business, a move he had never done on WWE television. He dragged his massive body, all six feet three inches, every one of his 300 pounds to the top rope. And then he jumped, or rather did an inverted flip, a move wrestling fans know as the shooting star press.

It's normally the domain of the cruiserweights, little guys known more for their acrobatics than their musculature. That's what was going to make it so impressive when Lesnar pulled it off to steal the show on the biggest card of the year. Only there was a problem. Lesnar didn't make it all the way around to land safely on Angle. In fact, he didn't even come close. He landed square on his face, all 300 pounds supported by only his head and neck. And he lived. Not only lived, but he got up in a concussed state and finished the match. Now that's tough.

Brock Lesnar has always been tough. He grew up in Webster, South Dakota, home to fewer than 2,000 people. Lesnar worked on his family's dairy farm, struggling to make ends meet in a dead-end town on the Minnesota border. In a state full of farm boy wrestlers, Brock was one of the very best. But he never won a high school championship, a failure that drove him to continue **wrestling**, to continue working hard. At Bismarck College in North Dakota, Lesnar became a star, winning the Junior College National Championship in 1998. He finished his two years there with a 56–3 record. Coaches from every Big Ten school called, but in the end, there was only one choice that made sense: the University of Minnesota.

It was obvious by this point that Lesnar had presence, that special kind of charisma that only the rare athlete possesses. When Brock Lesnar walked into a NCAA wrestling meet, heads turned. The man is just a physical freak — especially in the world of college wrestling, where bodies are more functional than sculpted. He was big, strong, cocky, and damn good. Lesnar won the Big Ten title and was the runner-up at Nationals, losing to Cal-State Bakersfield's Stephen Neal, the best wrestler in the country, 3–2.

Lesnar's loss burned inside all summer long. He didn't just lose the national championship for himself; his loss cost the team a title, too. That wasn't something that sat well with the ultra-competitive Lesnar. He wouldn't be denied the second time around, winning the national championship in 2000, finishing his NCAA career with a record of 106–5.

At 23, Lesnar had a lot of choices. He could stick around the amateur wrestling game, taking a stab at the 2004 Olympics. He could try his hand at MMA, a sport that suited his skills, but was struggling to survive political and social pressures that had driven the entire industry underground. Or, he could take a guaranteed six-figure contract to join Vince McMahon's traveling professional wrestling circus. To a poor kid from South Dakota, that choice seemed easy.

As with almost everything else in his life, Lesnar was a natural at pro wrestling. He became not just a good wrestler, but a great one. He had the size the WWE loved, the physical skills to pick up the complicated match routines, and a cocky persona that made him the perfect villain. But the wrestler's life isn't for everyone. It is a long grind, filled with constant travel and stress. To Lesnar, even the million-dollar salary couldn't make up for the quality of life. Lesnar hated the dysfunctional atmosphere, hated seeing the zombie-like wrestlers and what they had to do to get ready for matches night after night. And he didn't want to get older and wonder if he could have made it as a professional athlete.

He tried out for the NFL's Minnesota Vikings, showing the athletic talent but not the football skill to make it. Only after trying professional football did Lesnar turn his attention to the sport of MMA.

As good as he was in the professional wrestling ring, Lesnar was even better in the cage. He seemed born to be a fighter. Like some of the most successful amateurs to make the jump from college to MMA, Lesnar wasn't a great technician. Like former UFC champion **Mark Coleman**, Lesnar was a power wrestler, a bruiser with a real mean streak.

"I'm an amateur wrestler first of all, pro wrestler second. There was a little pressure, but my amateur wrestling is who I am and I'm going to evolve into a fighter," Lesnar said. "Unfortunately I have this black cloud over my head because I was a pro wrestler. It just goes to show that even though pro wrestling is a scripted sport it is entertainment; this is entertainment, but it's real when I get in the ring."

After beating a warm-up opponent name **Min-Soo Kim** at K-1's Dynamite show at the L.A. Coliseum, Lesnar was ready for the big time. **Dana White** announced his coup to the world at UFC 77. Brock would be thrown immediately into the deep end, to either sink or swim amongst the world's best. His first opponent would be a former world champion, the equally brash **Frank Mir.**

Among MMA fans, Lesnar was immediately a divisive figure. Wrestling fans were excited by his signing, knowing that his amateur skills, physical superiority, and pro wrestling persona would combine to provide plenty of entertainment in the cage. Hard-core MMA fans were furious, uncomfortable with the idea of a "fake" wrestler bringing his goofy antics into their pristine sport.

His debut was all you could ask for. Lesnar exploded across the cage like an angry gorilla, dropping Mir with a punch and nearly finishing him on the ground. Lesnar was a giant and scarily fast. Everything about him was big, from his oversized personality to the giant phallic sword tattooed on his chest. Even his hands were big, so big the UFC had to create a 4XL glove just to protect them.

Lesnar was bigger, possibly more skilled, and much meaner than Mir. In the end it wasn't Mir; it was Brock's own enthusiasm that got the best of him. Mir caught him with a **leg lock** and Lesnar was forced to tap. Even in defeat, even with a fight that was barely a minute long, Lesnar was clearly a future star in the sport.

White and the UFC could smell money and wanted to be sure Lesnar didn't lose two in a row. His second opponent was supposed to be the ancient Coleman, an older, smaller version of Lesnar who was well past his fighting prime. When Coleman dropped out, they went instead with "Texas Crazy Horse" **Heath Herring.** Herring was a tough veteran fighter, but one whose weaknesses corresponded nicely with Lesnar's strengths. As expected, Lesnar took him down and rode him like a bucking bronco for three rounds.

With just one win to his name in the UFC, Lesnar was immediately fast-tracked into a title shot. Brock overwhelmed a returning **Randy Couture** to win the UFC title in just his fourth professional fight. Couture, twice a heavyweight champion and a three-time light heavyweight titleholder, was simply outsized. The monstrous new champion dwarfed Couture, and there was only so much Couture could do to combat Lesnar's 60 extra pounds. "Those are some big-ass ham hocks coming at you," Couture said after the fight.

The win established Lesnar as the promotion's biggest star. For the third time in a row, a show he headlined topped 600,000 pay-per-view buys, with the Couture fight approaching a million purchases. Lesnar was now the champion, but not an undisputed one. Couture had been involved in a contract dispute for almost a year and the company had crowned an interim champion, a title that was held by Lesnar's old nemesis, Frank Mir.

Mir had been very vocal about his win, refusing to give Brock credit and dismissing his chances in a rematch, scheduled for the biggest show in the company's history, UFC 100. The heat between the two men simmered for months, exploding in the cage at UFC 100. This time, with another year and a half of submission defense under his belt, Lesnar controlled his opponent, refusing to lose his composure or his cool. He saved that until after his win in the second round.

An angry Lesnar stood over his vanquished opponent, not to offer a hug or a word of encouragement like most fighters, but to talk trash. He flipped the bird to the booing crowd, insulted one of the UFC's biggest corporate sponsors, and told the world he was going home to have sex with his wife. Depending on your point of view, the display was either repulsive and repugnant or amazingly awesome. There was no middle ground.

That's exactly what the UFC is counting on. Love him or hate him, people can't take their eyes off Brock Lesnar. The UFC 100 buyrate was the biggest in MMA history, topping 1.6 million buys. It was a record-setting performance, one the UFC hoped Lesnar could duplicate for years to come.

In October, 2009, disaster struck. Lesnar, feeling ill while training to meet **Shane Carwin** at UFC 106, was forced to pull out of the fight. Looking to unwind and recover, he journeyed to Canada for a relaxing weekend of hunting and hanging out. Then his body collapsed. Stuck in a Canadian hospital he referred to as "third world," Lesnar's wife, Rena, drove like a bandit for the United States and eventually Brock checked into Med Center One in Bismark, South Dakota. UFC officials sent the company jet to fly him to the Mayo Clinic.

From there, speculation ran wild: Lesnar was said to have everything from mononucleosis to cancer. Dana White would only confirm that he didn't have "AIDS or anything like that." Eventually the champion was diagnosed with a potentially career-ending ailment called diverticulitis. Surgery was scheduled and it looked like Lesnar's hiatus could become retirement. But, in what Lesnar described as a "medical miracle," surgery wasn't necessary. His body actually healed itself and the UFC heavyweight champion was ready to hit both the gym and the cage.

His first opponent would be Carwin, who, while waiting for Brock to recover, beat Lesnar's nemesis Frank Mir to become the interim heavyweight champion. Carwin was almost as big as Brock and had a respectable, if somewhat less distinguished, wrestling pedigree. The two argued back and forth about who was the best wrestler, but the point was moot.

Carwin, known for his punching power, didn't have to wrestle Brock to the ground — he knocked him down instead with battering blows. On top, Carwin landed dozens of hard punches. It seemed Lesnar was finished, but every time referee Josh Rosenthal asked Lesnar to defend himself, the champion responded. He weathered the storm and at the midway point of the first round Carwin was spent.

As the second round opened, Carwin was practically immobile. Lesnar immediately took him to the mat, passed his guard, and submitted him with an **arm triangle**. Lesnar, for the first time, looked human. After the fight, there were none of his usual hysterics. Instead, Lesnar took the microphone to reflect on the most trying year of his life.

"I am blessed by God," he said.

Lewis, John

Height: 6′ **Weight:** 155 lbs

Born: 7/16/69 **Debut:** UFCF 1 (9/8/95)

Career Record: 3-4-3

Notable Losses: Kenny Monday (EF 4); Rumina Sato (Vale Tudo Japan 97); Jens Pulver (UFC 28)

John Lewis has just three wins in ten career fights, but that's a little deceptive. From 1995 to 1997, Lewis would have been on plenty of people's top ten pound-for-pound fighter lists. His wins aren't really very impressive. He beat Jim Treachout and other fighters forgotten to history. But his draws — now that was where he shined.

Lewis was the first fighter in modern MMA to shatter the Gracie myth. He didn't just take Carlson Gracie Jr. to a draw over 20 minutes at the first **Extreme Fighting** show in 1995 — if there had been judges, he would have won the fight. The same applies to Japanese legend **Rumina Sato**. Sato was already more myth than man when the two fought at **Vale Tudo** Japan 1996, but Lewis was too much for him that night. It is a draw in the record book, but sometimes the record book lies.

Of course, even if Lewis had never fought, his presence would still have forever altered the course of MMA history. Lewis has done it all in his 14 years in the sport. He's been a fighter, a trainer, a promoter (**World Fighting Alliance**), and an agent. Lewis's name comes up everywhere you turn. He's like the MMA Kevin Bacon: anyone can be connected to him in just a few moves. Extreme Fighting founder **John Perretti**? Lewis trained with him under "Judo" **Gene LeBell**. **UFC** President **Dana White**? Lewis introduced him to his best MMA clients, **Chuck Liddell** and **Tito Ortiz**, when White was still a manager. UFC own-

In Their Own Words: John Lewis on fighting to a draw

"I loved fighting in Japan because the fans were very loyal. They just want to see a good fighter who's willing to fight hard. That's all they care about. Rumina was the man over there and I wasn't sure I was good enough. I was not too confident; I was just a young kid at the time. I was honored to fight him, because he was my favorite fighter. Even afterward, he was one of my favorite fighters forever because he is such a free-willed fighter. He did whatever he wanted to do. I beat him, but it was called a draw. If you look at my record, people think you were a certain kind of fighter because of all the draws. In those days they didn't have judges. You either knocked him out, submitted him, or they called it a draw – no matter how clearly you were winning. The Carlson Gracie Jr. fight, I dominated that fight. The Sato fight, the Johil de Oliveira fight, those were all considered draws. But I dominated those fights."

ers Frank and Lorenzo **Fertitta**? Lewis taught the competitive brothers jiu-jitsu for years after they took an interest in the fledging sport of MMA.

Everywhere you look, Lewis is there. And the sport is better for it.

Liddell, Chuck

Nickname: The Iceman **Height:** 6'2"

Weight: 205 lbs **Born:** 12/17/69

Debut: UFC 17 (5/15/98) **Career Record:** 21-8

Notable Wins: Jeff Monson (UFC 29); Kevin Randleman (UFC 31); Guy Mezger (Pride 14); Murilo Bustamante (UFC 33); Vitor Belfort (UFC 37.5); Renato Sobral (UFC 40, UFC 62); Tito Ortiz (UFC 47, UFC 66); Randy Couture (UFC 52, UFC 57); Jeremy Horn (UFC 54); Wanderlei Silva (UFC 79)

Notable Losses: Jeremy Horn (UFC 19); Randy Couture (UFC 43); Quinton Jackson (Pride Final Conflict 2003, UFC 71); Keith Jardine (UFC 76); Rashad Evans (UFC 78); Mauricio Rua (UFC 97); Rich Franklin (UFC 115)

With appearances on *Dancing with the Stars* and *The Simpsons* to add to his *ESPN: The Magazine* cover story and *Entourage* cameo, **UFC** Hall of Fame member Chuck Liddell remains the most visible athlete in the sport even as he lingers in a company-mandated state of pseudo-retirement. The stars aligned for "The Iceman," who finally captured his long-overdue UFC light heavyweight championship just as the company entered an unprecedented level of popularity on the strength of the massive success of ***The Ultimate Fighter***

reality series. It couldn't have happened to a more deserving fighter. Ever since his debut in an unaired alternate bout way back at UFC 17 at the Mobile, Alabama, Civic Center, Liddell has taken on all comers with his wide open, crowd-pleasing style.

It takes the edge off Liddell's tattooed skull, at least a little, to learn that the kanji running down the left side of his head reads, "place of peace and prosperity." That's the literal translation of the **karate** style he began training in as a child, Koei-Kan. But the mohawk — that's something he did with some buddies before taking in a Slayer concert. These two seemingly trivial details actually give you the broad outline of Chuck Liddell, a soft-spoken, easy-going man drawn to what can seem like extraordinary violence.

Before embarking on his pro career, Liddell wrestled at Division I California Polytechnic State University while he earned a degree in business and accounting. Then, in a scene that sounds like something out of the movies, Liddell presented himself at the age of 21 at The Pit, John Hackleman's Hawaiian Kempo school, to see if the master would train him. The master and the would-be student boxed for 19 minutes, and Hackleman asked if Liddell would be back the next day. Liddell, who had driven out on a 250cc Honda motorcycle in the rain, said he would. Hackleman tossed him the keys to his truck. It was the beginning of a partnership that has lasted to this day. From Liddell's curtain-jerking bout before a scattered crowd in Mobile to his main event fights in Vegas, John Hackleman has been a fixture in his man's corner.

Liddell came out of the gate strong, with only a single loss — by **triangle choke** to submission expert **Jeremy Horn** — against wins over such solid competition as **Jeff Monson**, former UFC heavyweight champion **Kevin Randleman**, **Guy Mezger**, **Murilo Bustamante**, **Vitor Belfort**, and **Renato Sobral**. It was more than enough to merit a light heavyweight title shot against reigning champion **Tito Ortiz**, but Ortiz wouldn't take the fight, arguing that fighting a friend wasn't worth what little the UFC was offering for the match. Liddell's position was that they were never that close, and the money was fine. An interim championship bout was announced, with Liddell taking on **Randy Couture**, who'd been stopped in his last two fights at heavyweight and was willing to move down to light heavyweight to help the company out of a fix. In a fight Liddell was supposed to win easily, Couture out-boxed the great knockout artist, and took him down almost at will. Once Couture established a dominant position on the ground, Liddell was out of options. He didn't make it out of the second round.

Coming off that loss, Liddell was entered in the 2003 **Pride** middleweight (205 pounds) Grand Prix as a representative of the UFC. In the opening moments of his quarter-final bout against **Alistair Overeem**, Liddell took full advantage of the more liberal Pride rules, and delivered repeated knees to the head of his downed opponent. When Overeem regained his feet, he put Liddell on his heels until the counter-puncher could find his rhythm. Once he found it, it was all over, as Liddell connected with his trademark overhand right, and finished Overeem with a flurry of wide looping hooks. Liddell secured himself a spot in the stacked tournament's final four alongside **Wanderlei Silva**, **Hidehiko Yoshida**, and his semi-final opponent, **Quinton Jackson**. Jackson, much like Couture, got the best of Liddell with straight punches and strong takedowns. All of a sudden Liddell, who had lost only once in his first four years in the sport, had been pounded out twice in four months.

Clearly, he'd had enough of it. When he returned to the UFC to finally face Ortiz — they had apparently decided they weren't such dear friends after all — Liddell fought like a man possessed. With first-rate takedown defense and his strange, looping punches thrown from all kinds of unusual angles, he stopped Ortiz in the second. **Vernon White** didn't last a round. And then, after a season-long build on *The Ultimate Fighter*, the UFC's Hail Mary shot at cultural relevance and profitability, Liddell met Couture in an enormously anticipated rematch for the title. This time, everything went according to plan. Liddell knocked the veteran grappler out in minutes to finally become UFC light heavyweight champion just as the company reached a new high. The outcome, decisive as it was, was not entirely without controversy: before he put Couture on his back, he'd clearly poked him in the eye. Although the eye-poke was ruled inadvertent, it's undeniable that it influenced the outcome of the fight — and it wasn't the last time Liddell would be seen pawing at his opponent's eyes.

In his first title defense, Liddell looked to avenge his loss to the workmanlike Jeremy Horn, a man with over 90 professional fights at the time. Although Horn had been out of the spotlight for years, competing in smaller organizations, he fought constantly. A battle-tested submission artist, Horn boldly declared that he was willing to stand and trade punches with Liddell this time around. Although this sounded foolhardy, it was also his only real option: there was no way Horn, with his indifferent takedowns, was going to be able to take the fight to the mat against the greatest **sprawl and brawl** fighter in the sport. Horn was game as always, and lasted longer than many expected, but couldn't continue past the fourth round when he admitted to the referee that he couldn't see.

The fight everyone wanted to see was next: the rubber match with Randy Couture. The first round was a classic that left Liddell cut over the eye and Couture with a broken nose. With two takedowns late, it looked like Couture might be able to implement the strategy that earned him the upset in their first meeting. But early in the second, Couture threw an awkward right hand that left him exposed, and Liddell countered with a right of his own that signaled the beginning of the end. Immediately after the bout, Couture announced a retirement that would last a little more than a year.

Liddell defended next against the streaking Sobral, looking to avenge a previous loss that ended with a highlight-reel head kick KO, the most impressive of Liddell's long career. This time Sobral fared no better: he was caught rushing in, and that was that. Tito Ortiz, a hot commodity again after drawing big audiences for two blowout wins over **Ken Shamrock**, presented no real threat to Liddell's title reign, but produced record-setting business when the two met for a second time. Ortiz was able to hang tough before ultimately succumbing to strikes late in the third. Liddell's first four title defenses couldn't have gone much more smoothly for the champ.

That would be the end of the line, however. When the UFC purchased the assets of the defunct **World Fighting Alliance**, it was a move designed to get Quinton Jackson into the UFC as soon as possible. After a tune-up fight against Marvin Eastman, Jackson was thrust into a title shot even earlier than he would have preferred. But less than two minutes into the contest, Liddell threw the kind of sloppy body shot he's thrown countless times and gotten away with; this time, though, Jackson countered with a big right that ended the champ's night, his title reign, and, as it turned, his long run as a top-tier light heavyweight.

Regardless of what happened when they first met in the 2003 Grand Prix, Liddell's loss to Jackson the second time around was an upset. His loss to the tough but otherwise unremarkable **Keith Jardine**, though, was a *stunning* upset. Liddell had no answer for Jardine's awkward punches and steady stream of leg kicks. Something seemed wrong, and a solid performance in a long anticipated and genuinely thrilling bout against Wanderlei Silva wasn't enough to completely dispel that notion. Back-to-back knockouts at the hands of **Rashad Evans** and **Mauricio Rua** weren't just surprising; they were worrying.

After the Rua loss, **Dana White** insisted that Liddell was done. He wasn't willing to watch his personal friend and his company's once great champion put his health on the line against younger, faster competition once it was clear Liddell had lost a step at the age of 39. The worry is that it's more than just a step: go to YouTube and call up a Chuck Liddell interview from early in his career. Compare it with a clip from the last few years. The deterioration in Liddell's speech is noticeable. Given the ease with which he's been knocked out in his most recent fights, you can't help but wonder how much damage has been done over the course of a career spent fighting exactly the style fans want to see: wide open, full tilt. Then there's the infamous *Good Morning Texas* interview, where Liddell appeared on a morning talk show almost completely incoherent. The official story is that Liddle was exhausted, sick with pneumonia, and under the influence of sedatives he'd taken only hours before to help him sleep. Given Liddell's reputation as a man who enjoys the nightlife more than most, and the many pitfalls that await retired fighters looking for ways to replace the highs of competition, let's hope Lidell finds a place of peace and prosperity in a long, healthy retirement.

Lindland, Matt

Nickname: The Law
Height: 6′
Weight: 185 lbs
Born: 5/17/70
Debut: WFF (2/14/97)
Career Record: 22-7
Notable Wins: Ricardo Almeida (UFC 31); Phil Baroni (UFC 34, UFC 41); Pat Miletich (UFC 36); Jeremy Horn (IFL: Portland); Carlos Newton (IFL: Houston)

Notable Losses: Murilo Bustamante (UFC 37); David Terrell (UFC 49); Quinton Jackson (WFA: King of the Streets); Fedor Emelianenko (BodogFight: Clash of Nations); Vitor Belfort (Affliction: Day of Reckoning); Ronaldo de Souza (Strikeforce: Evolution)

"The Law." It's a pretty good nickname. The story behind it is even better. Matt Lindland was one of the best Greco-Roman wrestlers in the world when he was upset by Keith Sieracki at the 2000 U.S. Olympic trials. After winning three consecutive U.S. championships, Lindland had seemingly lost his opportunity to represent America in the Olympic Games. But not so fast: Lindland protested the loss, saying Sieracki had tripped him illegally to earn the victory. A rematch was ordered and Lindland dominated, winning 8–0. And then the battle, previously played out on the mats, was suddenly being contested in the courts. The case went all the way to the United States Supreme Court. Less than a month before the Games began, the case was being combated in court. In the end, Lindland was on the team, earning a silver medal in Sydney. Sieracki was the first to fight the Law; the Law won.

Lindland, like many collegiate wrestlers, had flirted with MMA a little before the Olympic Games. Silver medal in hand, he was ready to move directly into the big time, making his **UFC** debut in Japan at UFC 29, beating pro wrestler **Yoji Anjo** in the first round. Lindland formed one of the most respected and successful fight teams of all time, **Team Quest**, with fellow Greco-Roman **wrestling** stars **Randy Couture** and **Dan Henderson**.

He was a quick learner, soaking in information from his more experienced teammates, enough to run through the UFC's middleweight division. He wasn't given any easy marks either, taking on submission ace Ricardo Almeida, brawler **Phil Baroni**, and the legendary **Pat Miletich**. Although this wouldn't always be the case, the UFC loved Lindland in these early years of his career. The promotion was looking to prove to critics that it was more than a collection of bikers and bar-room brawlers. Lindland's college education and Olympic pedigree lent the promotion immediate credibility.

He won his first seven fights to earn a title shot against jiu-jitsu standout **Murilo Bustamante**. Bustamante beat Lindland not once, but twice. Early in the fight he caught the **Olympian** in an **arm bar**. It looked like Lindland tapped and referee "Big" **John McCarthy** called a halt to the fight. Lindland insisted he hadn't tapped, despite what seemed to be compelling visual evidence, and McCarthy inexplicably restarted the fight. It made little difference as Bustamante submitted him with a **guillotine choke** in the third round. Even in the UFC, Lindland couldn't escape controversy.

He was never again able to earn a UFC title shot, despite six more wins in the promotion. Just when things seemed to heading in that direction, the train would fall off the tracks. Against tough Hawaiian Falaniko Vitale, Lindland knocked himself out with an errant Greco-Roman throw. When he got back on track with two wins, David Terrell upset him at UFC 49 with a blistering left hand. And then, after two more wins, he was gone.

After a win against journeyman Joe Doerkson at UFC 54, Lindland was unexpectedly bounced from the promotion. Prior to the weigh-ins, Lindland and the other fighters were told that several controversial sponsors had been banned from the show. Lindland wore a T-shirt for Sportsbook.com that was specifically prohibited. He and Team Quest partner Randy Couture had just signed a six-figure deal with the bookmaker and thought they could get away with wearing the shirt anyway. Couture might have been able to. Lindland was not Couture — he was fired.

Conspiracy theorists don't believe that the number one contender for the UFC's middleweight crown was let go over a T-shirt dispute. "They had invested hundreds of thousands of dollars in [UFC champion] **Rich Franklin**, bringing in **Ken Shamrock** to fight him," Lindland said. "They knew I would beat Franklin. Do you think I was fired over a T-shirt?"

It was his final fight for the UFC. They were never able to reconcile their differences and Lindland began his tour of the world's second-rate promotions. His next nine fights were contested for seven different organizations, and finding big fights against fellow 185-pound fighters was difficult, making it necessary for Lindland to step up against bigger men. He lost to future UFC light heavyweight champion **Quinton Jackson** in a great fight for the WFA and gave the best heavyweight in the world, **Fedor Emelianenko**, a scare before losing to an arm bar for BodogFight.

His luck was little better in politics. Lindland failed in his bid to win a seat in the Oregon State House of Representatives, losing to Democrat Suzanne VanOrman. His career in MMA became a campaign issue. VanOrman ran attack ads criticizing Lindland's "brutal fights" that stated, "I'll stay focused on the fights that really matter for our families."

With a UFC return as far away as ever, Lindland signed a three-fight contract with **Strikeforce** in April 2009. With potential opponents like **Jason Miller**, **Jake Shields**, and **Robbie Lawler**, the end of Lindland's career is stacking up to be just as interesting as the beginning.

Lion's Den

Ken Shamrock's Lion's Den was famous for its grueling physical initiation. Fighting was a tough business; fighting daily through the hard-core training at the Den even tougher. Shamrock was looking for people who wouldn't quit, who would persevere through the pain, reach their limits, then keep going.

Candidates for the elite team would start with 500 hindu squats, 200 pushups, and 200 sit-ups. Then it got interesting. There were runs with a man on your back, both sprints and for distance. You hit the bleachers, running steps in the hot California sun. When you were as exhausted as you've ever been in your life, they took you to the gym. Barely able to move, prospective students would spar with Shamrock or one of his protégés for up to an hour.

It was no easy thing, joining the Lion's Den. And yet, after going through this ordeal, most quit soon after. People who were tough enough to meet this challenge would give up on their dream and slink away in the middle of the night. Because the real challenge of the Lion's Den was mental, never physical.

"It was all mental," Lion's Den lightweight Mikey Burnett said. "He would come in in the morning, sometimes 4:30 or 5:00, and wake you up by whispering, 'I'm going to kill you tonight.' And sometimes he would show up that night and tear into you and sometimes he would show up and not even look at you. He just totally screwed with your head until you got to the point [where] there was no fear of death."

The actual training in the Lion's Den was somewhat primitive. The fighters were ahead of the curve thanks to Shamrock's submission training in **Pancrase,** but Shamrock had trouble explaining what he learned. Most often the instruction consisted of Ken telling guys to "hook it up," followed by hard-core sparring for a half an hour. No one did anything at half speed. They sparred like they fought: bare-knuckled and hard.

As tough as the gym was, the Fighter's House was often an even harder road for fighters to walk. New members started as "young boys." Like the Japanese system Shamrock had been trained in, these were whipping boys. They cleaned the gym, cleaned the house, did the dishes, and prepared the meals. They were also victims of physical and mental abuse. Established fighters like **Frank Shamrock** or **Jerry Bohlander** would sneak up on a victim, choke him into unconsciousness, and then wake him up with a gun in his face, threatening death if he let himself be taken unawares again.

It was hazing, pure and simple, and for many it was too much. Plenty of fighters snuck out of the house, never to return. The fighters that remained, after all this, were the cream of the crop. It was an MMA all-star team, the first world-class fight team, leading the way for future superstar teams like **Team Quest**, Miletich Fighting Systems, and Jackson's Mixed Martial Arts. Shamrock himself was the King of Pancrase and **UFC** Superfight Champion. Bohlander was the UFC 12 tournament winner. **Guy Mezger** was the UFC 13 winner and King of Pancrase. Ken's adopted brother Frank Shamrock was the King of Pancrase and the UFC middleweight (now light heavyweight) champion.

In Their Own Words: **Scott Bessac on training at the Lion's Den**

"Back then, Ken didn't know any better and I certainly didn't know any better. I was just a fighter out on the streets. We did sparring with no pads. With just kempo gloves and no shin protection. It wasn't until **Maurice Smith** talked to us one day in Japan. 'What do you mean you don't spar with equipment?' I said, 'No, we spar shin to shin.' And that was like two years later, after we'd been doing it for years. We used to kick shin to shin. It was basically just Ken beating the hell out of us. One, we were all young and stupid. And two, he had been trained by the Japanese in submission. And they whooped the hell out of him. They worked him hard and beat the heck out of him. They would lock him in submissions until he was black and blue. That was the only way he knew to pass that on. So that's what he did to me. And it's what I did to everyone else. And when **Vernon White** came in, that's what he did to Vernon. So, that's what Vernon did to everyone else. It just went down the line that way."

Despite this success, by the end of the 1990s, the Lion's Den had all but collapsed. The energy once focused on feuding with **Tito Ortiz** or **Tank Abbott** was turned inward on each other. Ken Shamrock left MMA for the world of **professional wrestling**. His relationship with Pancrase had fallen apart and the UFC simply couldn't afford to pay him anymore. That left Frank Shamrock in charge, and the two men didn't see eye to eye. Frank wanted to focus on technique and cardiovascular training, while Ken continued to see toughness as the key to fighter success. One blowup between the two ended with a computer monitor flying through the air at Frank, who left, never to return.

Today the Lion's Den continues to churn out fighters at several locations throughout California and the southwest. It's no longer an elite team, having burned bright and burned out.

"You can sprint for a certain amount of time," Burnett said. "But you can't sprint forever."

Lombard, Hector

Nickname: Shango
Height: 5'9"
Weight: 185 lbs
Born: 2/2/78
Debut: Spartan Reality Fight 11 (9/26/04)
Career Record: 26-2-1
Notable Win: Jared Hess (Bellator 12)
Notable Losses: Akihiro Gono (Pride Bushido 11); Gegard Mousasi (Pride Bushido 13)

Cuban **judo** champion and 2000 **Olympian** Hector Lombard was about to make his American MMA debut against fellow judo player **Karo Parisyan** at **UFC** 78. There was just one hitch: Lombard, though training and fighting out of Melbourne, Australia, held only a Cuban passport and was denied a P1 visa to work in the U.S. He'd made appearances in **Pride**, gassing out and coming up short in Bushido bouts against **Akihiro Gono** and Gegard Mousasi, but this was Lombard's real shot at the big time: a fight against a perennial welterweight contender in the sport's premier organization. But the match was scrapped, and the explosive Lombard went back to grinding it out in Sydney's unimaginatively named Cage Fighting Championship. In 2008, with his papers in order, Lombard joined **American Top Team** in Coconut Creek, Florida, and was crowned the nascent **Bellator** promotion's middleweight champion a year later with three dominant TKO tournament wins. Another UFC opportunity seems inevitable.

Luta Livre

Every great hero needs a foil. For **Brazilian Jiu-jitsu** masters, that foil was Luta Livre, translated from Portuguese as "free fighting." Although many people incorrectly suggest Luta Livre is simply a jiu-jitsu offshoot without the **gi**, its origin is actually in freestyle and **catch wrestling**.

The identity of the wrestler who brought this grappling art to Brazil has been lost to history, but what we now call submission wrestling began cropping up in Brazil in the late 1920s. The local leader of the movement was Euclydes "Tatu" Hatem, a prototypical wrestler: short and thick and deadly on the mat. He is credited with turning a martial art into a sport, much the way the Gracies created a sporting version of jiu-jitsu years later. Hatem called these grappling competitions Luta Livre Esportivo.

Hatem and his students and training partners were excellent grapplers. Although many of the holds were the same techniques found in **judo** (and thus in the judo offshoot known as **Gracie Jiu-jitsu**) there was one important difference. Luta Livre did not use the gi, believing that reliance on an instrument like that would make a fighter less effective in real life situations and confrontations.

For many years, Gracie Jiu-jitsu was a closed art, a carefully guarded set of techniques passed on only to those willing to pay. Luta Livre didn't have these associated costs. While jiu-jitsu attracted the wealthy and elite, many of Brazil's working class poor gravitated to Luta Livre where they didn't have to pay for lessons or a gi.

Hatem did more than teach and train. He put his teaching to the test, winning many challenge matches including a fight in the 1940s with George Gracie, believed by many to be the most physically dominant of the Gracie brothers. Just as they refused to meet Brazil's top judoka Robert Mehdi, the Gracies never again challenged Hatem, perhaps fearing the potential effect of a loss on their burgeoning reputation.

Luta Livre continued developing side by side with jiu-jitsu over the years in Brazil. There were many challenges and plenty of dojo fights, with jiu-jitsu generally getting the better of things. Luta Livre did earn one enormous victory when Euclides Pereira beat **Carlson Gracie** in 1968 in an extremely controversial fight. To his dying day, Carlson was furious about what he felt was a victory stolen from him by corrupt judges. Others who were there say Pereira was the better man that day. It was Gracie's only loss and established Pereira as a legend in his own time. He and Roberto Leitao, a university professor who wrote copiously about the martial arts and grappling, led the way for Luta Livre in the 1970s.

Only in the 1980s did the rivalry between Luta Livre and jiu-jitsu become a full-blown feud. A new generation of ultra-aggressive Gracie men was on the scene, led first by Rolls Gracie and later by **Rickson Gracie**. They were met head-on by the toughest Luta Livre fighters — men like **Eugenio Tadeu** and Hugo Duarte, who refused to back down from any challenge. The fights between the two factions couldn't be contained in a dojo or gym. They spread from the gym to the street, and in several memorable cases, to the beach.

The feud culminated, it seemed, at Desafio 91, a team challenge pitting three jiu-jitsu players against three of Luta Livre's best (Tadeu, Denilson Maia, and Marcelo Mendes). Carlson Gracie led the way for jiu-jitsu, bringing in some of his best students, including Wallid Ismail, Fabio Gurgel, and **Murilo Bustamante**. Jiu-jitsu carried the day, taking three of three challenge matches.

Soon after, many of the Gracies moved to America and the MMA boom began in 1993 with the creation of the **Ultimate Fighting Championship**. Where jiu-jitsu traveled, it seemed Luta Livre soon followed. Luta Livre star **Marco Ruas** won the tournament at UFC 7 and dazzled the world with his exciting combination of striking technique and submission grappling. Tadeu, Duarte, and other top Luta Livre stars soon made their way into modern MMA, with varying degrees of success.

The final curtain for the Luta Livre/jiu-jitsu feud fell at the ill-fated Pentagon Combat show in 1997. **Renzo Gracie** represented jiu-jitsu in the main event, while Tadeu flew the banner for Luta Livre. The two had a remarkable back-and-forth fight with a raucous crowd edging ever closer to the cage. Soon, the lights went out in the building and all hell broke loose. The riot set MMA in Brazil back years, and the feud between the two arts seemed to die along with the sport they had worked so hard to build.

Today, Luta Livre artists train jiu-jitsu. And jiu-jitsu players, who once refused to grapple without a gi, now practice no-gi grappling. The most common grappling tournaments in the world, including the famous Abu Dhabi Submission Grappling Championships (**ADCC**), are essentially the progeny of Luta Livre and jiu-jitsu, gi-less grappling borrowing heavily from sport jiu-jitsu scoring and rules. Like jiu-jitsu, Luta Livre has also spread worldwide, making notable headway in Germany, where no-gi grappling is widespread and growing.

Machida, Lyoto

Nickname: The Dragon **Height:** 6'1"

Weight: 205 lbs **Born:** 5/30/78

Debut: New Japan Pro Wrestling: Ultimate Crush (5/2/03)

Career Record: 16–1

Notable Wins: Stephan Bonnar (Jungle Fight 1); Rich Franklin (Inoki Bom-Ba-Ye 2003); B.J. Penn (Hero's 1); Vernon White (WFA: King of the Streets); Kazuhiro Nakamura (UFC 76); Rameau Thierry Sokoudjou (UFC 79); Tito Ortiz (UFC 84); Thiago Silva (UFC 94); Rashad Evans (UFC 98)

Notable Loss: Maurico Rua (UFC 113)

"**Karate** is back," Lyoto Machida announced after he knocked **Rashad Evans** out cold in the second round of their **UFC** title fight. As he strapped the light heavyweight championship belt over his paper-thin **gi**, there could be no doubt. Machida, trained by his father Yoshizo in shotokan karate since the age of three, had overturned everything we thought we knew about mixed martial arts. "Ladies and gentlemen," **Joe Rogan** said in an awed tone as the new champion fell to his knees in celebration, "Welcome to the Machida era."

Karate, in short, wasn't supposed to work. Not in 2009. The failure of traditional karate stylists in the early days of the UFC was seen by many in the martial arts community as the end of the art as a relevant fighting system. The karate club might still be a good place to drop the kids off after school, let them burn off some energy and improve their fitness in an environment that emphasized focus, discipline, and self-control. For most practitioners, those have always been the real benefits of the martial arts anyway, and a good karate dojo still holds to those values. But traditional karate was thought to be incapable of turning out fighters that could compete in the full-contact free-for-all of modern mixed martial arts.

Enter "The Dragon." Machida was by no means the first prominent mixed martial artist to hold rank in a traditional karate discipline, but he was the first to look like a karate fighter in the cage, to move like one. Leaping in and out of striking range with his head back in an uncommonly upright posture, throwing kicks from unpredictable angles, and disguising foot sweeps behind straight punches, Machida is a Sonny Chiba movie brought to life. Although he began training in both sumo and **Brazilian Jiu-jitsu** as a teen, his study of other styles has always been in the service of implementing his family's art. When Japanese **professional wrestling** legend **Antonio Inoki** took him under his wing, Machida added **Muay Thai** and **wrestling** to his repertoire. The end result of this extensive cross-training is a fighter who is versed in everything his opponents might throw at him — while his opponents have never seen anyone like Machida before.

The knock on Machida has always been his lack of aggression, his caution, his unwillingness to take a punch in order to land one. If you subscribe to the "stand and bang" ethos that dominates the sport, Lyoto Machida doesn't have anything to offer you. He's not going to plant his feet and throw power shots in the middle of the cage; he's going to move, and a lot of that movement is going to be backwards, slipping just out of range. You can call his conservative, counterstriking style elusive and intelligent or you can call it dull and cowardly — it's been called all of the above — but at this point there's no denying its effectiveness.

Machida has recently silenced many of his critics by winning the biggest fights of his career with huge knockouts rather than earning the methodical decision victorious that had become his trademark. When he knocked out Thiago Silva at UFC 94, it was Machida's first stoppage due to strikes since overwhelming **Rich Franklin** five years and ten fights earlier. In between, there was never any shortage of solid wins over the likes of **Kazuhiro Nakamura**, **Tito Ortiz**, and a 191-pound version of **B.J. Penn** — but finishes were few and far between. After his dramatic KO of the previously undefeated Rashad Evans to become light heavyweight champion, however, few people were talking about Machida's supposedly overcautious, timid approach. Instead, they wondered who, if anyone, had the stylistic answer for the unique problems Machida presented. They wondered just how long this karate fighter who had yet to lose a single round in seven UFC fights would stay on top.

The answer, when it came, came quickly: **Mauricio Rua**, after dropping a controversial decision to the karateka, threw caution to the wind in his next attempt on Machida's light-heavyweight title, and ended their second contest with a thunderous first-round knockout. The Machida problem, for one fighter, for one night, at least, had been solved. But there's every reason to believe Machida isn't done showing us that what we thought we knew about mixed martial arts, about what works and what doesn't, is very much a work in progress.

Maeda, Akira

Akira Maeda is one of the most important men in the history of Japanese MMA, but it isn't for his accomplishments in the cage or ring. Although Web site **Sherdog**'s Fight Finder lists Maeda as having a 7–5 pro record, he's never actually been in an MMA fight. Sherdog can breathe a sigh of relief: many Japanese wrestling fans were also fooled by Maeda's shoot style of pro wrestling. It was designed to look real, using real submission holds and throws from **judo** and wrestling, and it helped make Maeda one of the biggest stars in **professional wrestling**.

Maeda was discovered by New Japan pro wrestling executive Hisashi Shinma at a **karate** tournament in 1977. The young Maeda only cared about two things: motorcycles and fighting. New Japan was a natural fit and Maeda had the look and — at 6'3" and 240 pounds — the size to be a top star. Shinma was grooming him to fill the very big shoes of Japan's top wrestling star, **Antonio Inoki**.

But in the mid-1980s professional wrestling was going through a seismic upheaval in the United States: a shift towards entertainment and wacky gimmicks that was slowly invading Japan as well. Maeda hated the American style and his frustration often boiled over in the ring, where he soon had a reputation for working too stiffly, sometimes forgetting to take some of the steam off his kicks and slaps. The American wrestlers convinced the legendary Andre the Giant to do something about it.

During a match in 1986, the mammoth Giant refused to cooperate with Maeda. It was then and there that Maeda made his reputation as one of wrestling's legitimate tough guys. Maeda brutalized Andre's legs with hard kicks and took him down to the mat several times. Despite giving up eight inches in height and hundreds of pounds, Maeda more than held his own. Inoki himself eventually had to come into the ring to break up the chaos.

Maeda's temper often seemed to get the better of him. He punched out Keiji Muto, better known to American fans as the Great Muta, in a street fight and lost his job with New Japan when he kicked star Riki Choshu for real, breaking the orbital bones in Choshu's eye. Choshu, who had once been an Olympic wrestler, never even fell to the ground and was ready to fight. Maeda, wisely, bailed out of the ring before a legitimate tough guy shattered his reputation.

Maeda's cheap shot opened the door for the shoot-style wrestling revolution. Refusing to accept his punishment for blindsiding Choshu, Maeda and his cohorts left New Japan to form the Universal Wrestling Federation. The UWF quickly became the hottest ticket in Japan's urban centers like Tokyo, drawing primarily young men who loved the wrestlers' tough guy personas.

Although the UWF splintered into several competing groups after three years, it's helped to make the growth of MMA in Japan possible. Many of the most successful and important fighters in MMA history came from this talent pool. Fighters like **Ken Shamrock, Nobuhiko Takada, Kazushi Sakuraba, Dan Severn, Masakatsu Funaki,** and **Kiyoshi Tamura** all spent time in the UWF or one of its offshoots.

As big as those stars were, Maeda was bigger than them all. His splinter group **Rings**, didn't have the same highs as Takada's UWFi, but it did consistently big business for half a decade before injuries sidelined Maeda. He used his celebrity and drawing power to help try to establish MMA culture in Japan and around the world. He and his partners successfully promoted events not just in Japan, but around the world. Rings events took place in Japan, Holland, Russia, Australia, and the United States.

As a promoter, Maeda had an eye for talent. He brought future stars like **Dan Henderson, Antonio Rodrigo Nogueira, Gilbert Yvel**, and **Fedor Emelianenko** to the Japanese fans for the first time, only to see them poached by Takada's **Pride Fighting Championships.** It frustrated Maeda, who felt he was doing all the work, while reaping little of the reward. In 2000, he snapped.

Pride had recently stolen Rings champion Yvel, and Maeda was furious. When he saw **Pancrase** President Masami Ozuki eating lunch with Rings fighter **Jeremy Horn**, he was sure Ozuki was looking to take away another of his fighters. Rings and Pancrase were working together at the time to co-promote Colisseum 2000, a major show headlined by Pancrase founder Funaki taking on **Rickson Gracie.** This made the betrayal far worse in Maeda's eyes. Later that night, the enormous Maeda slapped the smaller Ozuki backstage and injured his neck and back. Ozuki eventually won a $12,000 settlement.

In 2002, Rings finally collapsed for good. After having their lucrative deal with the cable station WOWOW cut in half, the group was unable to compete for top-flight talent. The much better funded Pride Fighting Championships won the war for Japanese MMA.

After years on the sidelines, Maeda was hired in 2005 to be a consultant for K-1's new MMA show called **Hero's**. When the group joined forces to work with the former executives from Dream Stage Entertainment, whose Pride promotion had run Rings into the ground, the proud Maeda quit. Today, Maeda runs an amateur MMA contest called The Outsider.

Maeda, Mitsuyo

The Gracie family's purported dislike of **professional wrestling** is a bit ironic when you consider the fact that the man who taught **judo** to **Carlos Gracie** was himself a wrestler. Mitsuyo Maeda traveled the world, not only teaching judo, but also making his living inside the ring in a variety of wrestling troupes. America, Cuba, England, Belgium, Spain, Mexico, and the Caribbean: Maeda was everywhere, using all of his 140 pounds to throw larger men to the mat with deceptive ease.

It was in Spain that Maeda earned the nickname that would follow him for the rest of his days. He became known as Conde Koma, the Count of Combat. After ten years on the road — wrestling, competing in countless challenge matches where spectators were offered $250 if they could throw the judo master, and spreading Kano's judo to the world — Maeda finally settled down in Brazil. There, by the purest of chance, Maeda taught a student who would change the world of martial arts forever.

In 1917, Carlos Gracie was a rambunctious 14-year-old who happened upon one of Maeda's demonstrations at the Teatro de Paz in Belem, Brazil. Gracie was hooked and became Maeda's student until the Gracie family moved to Rio de Janeiro in 1920. Three years was hardly enough to learn all the intricacies of judo, but Gracie had the basics down. He taught his brothers, who taught their children, one of whom (**Rorion Gracie**) founded the **Ultimate Fighting Championship** in 1993.

Maeda was an excellent fighter in his own right, but how good remains a mystery. Because of his years as a professional wrestler, many of his fights are rightfully viewed with an air of skepticism. He certainly defeated hundreds of people in challenge matches all over the world. He also competed against dozens of western wrestlers, **karate** men, and even a capoeirista with a knife in one memorable Brazilian encounter. It was this eye for what techniques work and which don't, honed against local martial artists from across the globe, that made Maeda the perfect man to help spawn a modern combat art crafted to defeat all comers.

Maia, Demian

Height: 6′
Weight: 185 lbs
Born: 11/6/77
Debut: The Cage: Volume 4 (12/3/05)
Career Record: 12-2
Notable Wins: Ed Herman (UFC 83); Nate Quarry (UFC 91); Chael Sonnen (UFC 95)
Notable Losses: Nate Marquardt (UFC 102); Anderson Silva (UFC 112)

UFC middleweight contender Demian Maia is a lifelong martial artist, trained variously in **judo**, **kung fu**, and **karate** from an early age. But he's made his mark as a mixed martial artist based almost entirely on his mastery of a single discipline: **Brazilian Jiu-jitsu**. At a time when versatility has become the hallmark of the successful fighter, Maia is unusually one-dimensional. But his skill in that single dimension, the submission game, so far outstrips that of his competition that he has rocketed up the middleweight ranks.

An **ADCC** submission wrestling champion, Maia made his UFC debut after three impressive submission wins in his first five professional fights, all victories. His winning ways continued in the Octagon as he put together a string of five consecutive submission wins, each of them absolute grappling clinics. For the most part, neither Maia nor his opponents looked like they'd even been in a fight as they left the cage. "That's what I want to do," he told **Joe Rogan** after finishing **Chael Sonnen** with a picture-perfect **triangle choke** after a smooth ankle-block takedown. "I want to show the jiu-jitsu to the world, and show the people that you can win the fight without hurting your opponent."

Former **Pancrase** champion **Nate Marquardt** showed the people something else when he decked Maia with a huge straight right hand, ending their UFC 102 contest in only 21 seconds and handing the Brazilian his first career loss. Regardless, Maia has established himself as one of the top submission artists in all of mixed martial arts, an analytical and expert grappler whose technical elegance serves as a counterpoint to the now all-too-familiar stand-and-bang ethos of ***TUF***-era MMA.

Manhoef, Melvin

Nickname: Marvelous | **Height:** 5'8"
Weight: 185 lbs | **Born:** 5/11/76
Debut: Battle of Amstelveen (12/2/95) | **Career Record:** 24-8-1
Notable Wins: Kazushi Sakuraba (Dream 4); Mark Hunt (Dynamite!! 2008)
Notable Losses: Bob Schreiber (2H2H 11); Yoshihiro Akiyama (Hero's 7); Dong Sik Yoon (Dynamite!! USA); Gegard Mousasi (Dream 6); Paulo Filho (Dream 10)

Melvin Manhoef is a monster. A true K-1-level striker with serious knockout power and unparalleled aggression, Manhoef is without question one of the scariest men in the sport — until you get him on the ground. Then, it's all of a sudden a very different story.

Manhoef is first and foremost a **Muay Thai** fighter, a kickboxer willing to throw down under mixed martial arts rules, but not a true mixed martial artist. Although his complete lack of a ground game obviously limits how far he can go in the sport, it didn't stop him from capturing the **Cage Rage** light heavyweight title and defending it for nearly two years. It didn't stop him from blitzing the legendary **Kazushi Sakuraba** and stopping him in the first round, or from taking out the iron-headed heavyweight **Mark Hunt** in only 18 seconds.

It did mean, though, that he had no answer for **Yoshihiro Akiyama**, who caught him in a beautiful **arm bar** transition in the first round of their **Hero's** title fight after the **judo** competitor managed to weather an early storm so fierce that Akiyama's mother was in tears at ringside. It also meant that he was thoroughly controlled throughout his bout with Yoon Dong Sik before succumbing once again to an arm bar (or "Dongbar," as it has come to be known in Yoon's particular case). Add **Gegard Mousasi** and **Paulo Filho** to the list of fighters who've made Manhoef look silly on the ground. It would be wrong to say that they exposed him — there's nothing to expose. Everybody already knows Manhoef has nothing to offer once the fight hits the mat. Until it gets there, though, look out.

Marquardt, Nathan

Nickname: Nate the Great
Height: 6′
Weight: 185 lbs
Born: 4/20/79
Debut: WVF: Durango (4/17/99)
Career Record: 29-9-2
Notable Wins: Yves Edwards (Bas Rutten Invitational 4); Shonie Carter (Pancrase: Anniversary Show 2000); Kiuma Kunioku (Pancrase: Spirit 9); Jeremy Horn (UFC 81); Demian Maia (UFC 102)

Notable Losses: Genki Sudo (Pancrase: Breakthrough 11); Ricardo Almeida (Pancrase: Hybrid 10); Anderson Silva (UFC 73); Chael Sonnen (UFC 109)

Nate Marquardt is one of the friendliest guys you'll ever meet. Soft-spoken with an infectious smile, Nate always seems to be in good spirits. It's his hands that give him away as a professional fighter. The middle knuckle on both hands is swollen all the time. On his left hand, one of the knuckles is missing, pushed up into his hand courtesy of long-ago bare-knuckle fights early in his career. Make no mistake: Marquardt is a great guy, a religious family man from Colorado. But he can and will throw down with the best of them.

Occasionally the two sides of Nate Marquardt will intersect, although he tries to keep the fighter separate from his family. In his **UFC** 102 fight with fellow contender **Demian Maia**, Marquardt sent his opponent flying with a brutal knockout in just 21 seconds. Many fighters, like Marquardt's fellow middleweight contender **Dan Henderson** or even his teammate **Rashad Evans**, would have used that split second between punch and ref stoppage to gleefully rain

In Their Own Words: Nate Marquardt on fighting Anderson Silva again

"He's done so well for himself and he's made some of the fights look easy. When people make fights look easy, especially against top opponents, people start to fear them. But I train with some of the best in the world. Not even necessarily the best MMA fighters in the world, but the best boxers and the best grapplers. I have confidence that I can beat him. Against a guy like Anderson, confidence is huge. If you don't have confidence going in, you don't even have a chance. Because you are going to hold back and he's going to attack all day. When you look at someone and see fear, that's normal. It's how they react to that fear. All fighters have fear; it's how they react to it. If they are going to focus in and go harder, go for the knockout or push back, that's different than someone who's going to get hurt and turn away. And you can see that in their eyes sometimes. I won't back away.

"I have an idea how that fight would go. I wouldn't want to reveal my strategy, but I can tell you I'm a completely different fighter than I was the first time I fought him. I'm a lot better technically. I'm faster and stronger. And the main thing is that mentally going into the fight, I'm a totally different fighter. It would look a lot different than the first time."

down a few extra and unnecessary blows. Not Marquardt. He saw Maia was out and held his blow at the last moment, a gentleman to the end.

Before he was a top contender for the UFC, Marquardt was earning the respect of the hard-core fans in Japan. He never appeared in one of the big promotions there, sticking instead to **Pancrase**, a blue-collar promotion closer to his own roots. There he established himself as the middleweight King of Pancrase and one of the best fighters in the world.

His first UFC fight was a disaster. He was known as an exciting well-rounded fighter and was signed to battle another dynamic fighter, Ivan Salaverry, in the main event of the first *Ultimate Fight Night* on Spike TV. It was one of the worst fights of all time, and to make matters worse, despite winning a lackluster decision, Marquardt was the true loser after testing positive for the steroid Nandrolone after the fight.

Marquardt recovered smartly, winning three in a row before falling victim to middleweight champion **Anderson Silva** at UFC 73. Since then, Nate the Great has been on a journey to regain the opportunity to challenge for the UFC gold. Along the way he's shed his reputation as a boring fighter, winning three in a row by spectacular knockout. At 30 years of age, Marquardt is just entering his physical prime. Combine that with an ever-expanding skill set that started with **karate** as a kid, skills honed to perfection by famed trainer **Greg Jackson**, and a UFC title seems likely to attach itself to Marquardt's resume before his career is over.

MARS

The **Extreme Fighting** Championship wasn't the **UFC**'s only big money competition. Despite rising controversy and a very shaky future, the sport continued to attract eager promoters. One such, Atlanta surgeon John Keating, was the ultimate money mark. He had been the ringside doctor at UFC 7 and was dying to get involved in the MMA business. Keating paid $10,000 for private jiu-jitsu lessons from **Royce Gracie**, but that just whetted his growing appetite. After staging some fights in dojos and warehouses, including a fight with future UFC standout **Jeremy Horn**, Keating was ready to take the leap with a full-blown extravaganza.

Martial Arts Reality Superfighting, better known as MARS, had plenty of potential. The concept was "Russia versus Brazil," which could have been entertaining. Instead, Keating was unable to secure any of the standout Russian fighters he wanted, and Brazil swept three less-than-super superfights. A 16-man tournament somehow ended in a draw when **Murilo Bustamante** stalemated the gigantic wrestler **Tom Erickson** in a tepid 40-minute starefest, and MARS was starting to look like a disaster. It was up to two of the world's best to save the show. **Oleg Taktarov** was scheduled to fight **Renzo Gracie** in the main event.

Taktarov was the one superstar Russian MARS had managed to bring in, but he had Keating pulling out his hair from the moment the papers were signed. First, Taktarov allegedly demanded $50,000 to cancel a fight with **Marco Ruas** that was scheduled just two weeks before MARS. Keating refused, and the fight went forward and resulted in an injury to Taktarov's hand. Then, moments before he was supposed to hit the ring, he asked for more money again, threatening to walk out if he didn't get his way. He was persuaded to honor his obligations and, in a display of the power of karma, was knocked out by a prone Gracie with an up-kick, an unusual ending for an unusual and disastrous show.

Matsui, Daijiro

Height: 5'9" **Weight:** 199 lbs

Born: 12/05/72 **Debut:** Pride 3 (6/24/98)

Career Record: 11-23-4

Notable Wins: Bob Schrijber (Pride 7); Jose Landi-Jons (Pride 14); Quinton Jackson (Pride 18)

Notable Losses: Carlos Newton (Pride 6); Wanderlei Silva (Pride 8); Igor Vovchanchyn (Pride 9); Vitor Belfort (Pride 10); Ryo Chonan (Deep 13th Impact); Paulo Filho (Gladiator FC Day 2); Yuki Kondo (Pancrase: Blow 6)

Strangely enough, as Daijiro Matsui collapsed in a writhing heap only 14 seconds into his **Pride** 18 bout against **Quinton Jackson**, it was actually a career highlight of sorts. Taking a solid knee to the groin from one of the world's top light heavyweight fighters is a tough way to make a living, but that DQ win was about as good as it ever got for the game but perpetually overmatched Japanese **catch wrestler**. Matsui managed to go the distance with an impressive list of top competitors, but only took the decision over one: Jose "Pele" Landi-Jons, a dangerous **Chute Boxe** striker who put Matsui down, but not out. A Pride staple, and a fixture in the corner of longtime training partner **Kazushi Sakuraba**, Matsui continued to compete in smaller Japanese organizations like **Deep** and **Pancrase** after his time in the big leagues had passed, and found a small measure of success in England's **Cage Rage**.

Matua, John

Height: 6'2" **Weight:** 400 lbs

Debut: UFC 6 (7/14/95) **Career Record:** 1-4

Notable Loss: Tank Abbott (UFC 6)

John Matua was a central part of one of the most iconic moments in MMA history. Unfortunately for the big Hawaiian, his star turn came when he was knocked unconscious by a giant **Tank Abbott** right hand. As Matua convulsed on the mat, arms locked straight like Frankenstein, he was mercilessly mocked by his conqueror. At that moment, Tank Abbott became a star, and the ultimate spectacle that was **SEG**'s **UFC** had its ultimate highlight.

Mazzagatti, Steve

In the build to his rematch with **Frank Mir** at **UFC** 100, **Brock Lesnar** argued that the only reason he hadn't finished Mir the first time around was an unfair standup and point deduction administered by referee Steve Mazzagatti when Mir was down and almost out. Mazzagatti thought he saw punches land to the back of Mir's head and intervened immediately — which was particularly surprising given Mazzagatti's reputation for sometimes letting beatings go on dangerously long. Lesnar also complained that Mazzagatti was inexplicably slow in breaking Mir's hold as Lesnar tapped again and again to the match-ending **knee bar**. Looking at the tape, it's hard to argue with either of those points. Lesnar, never one to mince words, puts his feelings towards Mazzagatti this way: "I'd like to punch his fucking moustache right off his face. *Man*, I hate the fucking guy."

He's not alone. Mazzagatti has faced an enormous amount of criticism for his work inside the cage, and not just from aggrieved fighters trying to explain away a loss, analysts dissecting split-second decisions with the benefit of replay, or message board posters quick to jump on any perceived slip-up. No, Mazzagatti has taken heat from the most powerful man in the sport. Soon after the Lesnar/Mir rematch — which, unsurprisingly, saw **Herb Dean** as the third man in the Octagon this time around — UFC President **Dana White** appeared on *The Opie & Anthony Show*, where he was asked, among other things, for his thoughts on Mazzagatti. "Mazzagatti, as a referee? This fucking guy shouldn't even be watching MMA on TV, let alone refereeing it," White answered. "I think he's the worst ref in the history of any fight business, ever. He's horrible."

"It's not that I don't like him," White took pains to clarify. "He's a nice guy. He's an absolute nice guy, [but] he has no business whatsoever being anywhere near mixed martial arts." The hosts were confused and wondered how it was that Mazzagatti was able to referee UFC events despite White's complete disdain for his work. "We don't pick the refs," White explained. "The athletic commission does. Those guys are picked by the government."

And somehow, Mazzagatti keeps on getting picked. It might be easier to make sense of this had Mazzagatti once been a top-notch referee who had since fallen off, but was still getting by on the strength of his reputation. But Mazzagatti has been questionable almost since his UFC debut — and not questionable in a niggling, nit-picking sort of way, but in a way that makes you wonder how poor Jay Hieron survived the seemingly endless beating **Georges St. Pierre** was forced to put on him before Mazzagatti would end the fight. An underground compilation of "Mazzagatti Moments" of this kind has been circulating around the internet for some time now, and while it's not for the faint of heart, it's definitely illuminating. At the very least, it helps you understand where Brock Lesnar is coming from.

McCarthy, John

How many times have you been watching an MMA show and had not the slightest clue who was fighting? Two bald, tattooed, anonymous dudes, one in red shorts and one in black. Characters in an old-school video game were easier to distinguish than most of these guys. But you always knew the referee. It was "Big" John McCarthy, and you could count on him to do the right thing. Has he made a mistake or two? Did he once break **Brian Johnston**'s nose trying to pull him off a finished opponent? Sure. Did he try to say **Kazushi Sakuraba** was down and out when he was clearly just looking for a takedown at **UFC** Japan? Well, yes. No one is perfect, but Big John is close.

McCarthy's ubiquitous "Are you ready? Are you ready? Let's get it on!" is as synonymous with MMA as referee Ed Hochuli's sculpted physique and skin-tight shirt is with the NFL. John McCarthy is *the* UFC referee. The former police officer makes the shows seem bigger by his very presence. And, let's be honest, most of the new guys are horrible. They either want to stop a fight the first time a blow lands (I'm looking at you, Yves Lavigne) or they seem to be hoping and praying someone is beaten to death (I'm looking at you, **Steve Mazzagatti**).

McCarthy, on the other hand, has perfect timing. Just as you think to yourself, 'Man, they probably should stop this, I think that one guy's eyeball is about to pop out of his head,' *bam*. There he is: Big John to save the day and some chump's eyeball.

He's unquestionably a great referee, one who seems bulletproof to the controversies that perhaps should have become bigger issues. When he joined the promotion after UFC 2, it was at the invitation of **Rorion Gracie**. McCarthy was friends with the family and trained with them at their Torrance, California, Gracie Academy. It was an obvious conflict of interest, yet McCarthy seemed to fly under the radar. There was no real media coverage of the new sport and what coverage there was focused on whether the fighting should be legal at all. No one discussed the nuances, like whether or not it was appropriate for a Gracie student to make important decisions about a Gracie's fights.

Of course, we know now McCarthy was beyond reproach. In a judgment call business, his decision making was unparalleled. He left refereeing behind to join the Fight Network in 2007, providing coverage and commentary of the fight game, including criticism of fellow officials and commissions that would come back to haunt him. He also did commentary for the **Affliction** promotion, earning himself a spot on the infamous **Zuffa** enemies list, making a return to the UFC unlikely.

In 2009, he applied for a referee's license in the state of Nevada, looking to make a return to the Octagon. Athletic Commissioner Keith Kizer, rumored to be upset about McCarthy's public criticisms when he was a member of the media, rebuffed the legend. McCarthy saw his application placed in the slush pile, joining more than a dozen other applicants for a rare opening in the state. McCarthy continues to officiate events in California for **Strikeforce** and runs Big John McCarthy's Ultimate Training Academy in Los Angeles.

Melendez, Gilbert

Nickname: El Niño
Height: 5'9"
Weight: 155 lbs
Born: 4/12/82
Debut: WEC 5 (10/18/02)
Career Record: 18-2

Notable Wins: Rumina Sato (Shooto: Alive Road); Clay Guida (Strikeforce: Revenge); Tatsuya Kawajiri (Pride Shockwave 2006); Shinya Aoki (Strikeforce: Nashville)

Notable Losses: Mitsuhiro Ishida (Yarennoka); Josh Thomson (Strikeforce: Melendez vs. Thomson)

Gilbert Melendez seemed like an unstoppable force. He came charging forward and nothing stopped him until the bell rang or his opponent was finished. Melendez did the impossible, even dropping Naoya Uematsu with a **professional wrestling** move called the Death Valley Driver, picking him up over his shoulders and dropping him on his head. The press came up with the perfect nickname for this wrecking ball: "El Niño." Like the deadly storm, Melendez wiped out everything in his path, even **Shooto** legend **Rumina Sato**.

Melendez's path to the top of the lightweight division continued: after beating **Clay Guida** to win the **Strikeforce** lightweight championship, he moved from Shooto to **Pride** to compete with some of Japan's top little men. He upset **Tatsuya Kawajiri** and was suddenly at or near the top of most top ten lists. Then the train seemed to come off the tracks. Melendez was outwrestled and outworked by Mitsuhiro Ishida in a high profile fight in Japan and then lost his Strikeforce title to **UFC** washout Josh Thomson. After trying, and failing twice, to get a rematch with Thomson, the two finally met in one of 2009's best fights. For the second time, Melendez avenged a loss and moved on to fight Japanese sensation **Shinya Aoki**. Many in the media speculated that Aoki might actually be the best lightweight in the world. Melendez put that speculation to rest with a dominating five-round decision, establishing himself as one of the division's very best.

Menne, Dave

Height: 5'10" **Weight:** 185 lbs

Born: 7/29/74 **Debut:** HOOKnSHOOT: Lightweight Championship (4/4/97)

Career Record: 43-16-2

Notable Wins: Dennis Hallman (Shooto: 10th Anniversary); Fabiano Iha (UFC 24); Jose Landi-Jons (WEF 9); Carlos Newton (Warriors War 1); Gil Castillo (UFC 33)

Notable Losses: Shonie Carter (Extreme Challenge 5); Matt Hughes (Extreme Challenge 21); Kiyoshi Tamura (Rings: King of Kings 99); Murilo Bustamante (UFC 35); Phil Baroni (UFC 39); Hayato Sakurai (Deep 10th Impact); Josh Koscheck (*Ultimate Fight Night* 5)

Dave Menne has seen the highs and lows of the MMA business, fought in the biggest shows on the glitzy Las Vegas strip and in the most humble circumstances imaginable. His first MMA bout was supposed to be for a small promotion in Wisconsin, in a respectable gym in front of a thousand or so fans. Unfortunately for Menne, the show was scheduled during the peak of the anti-**UFC** backlash, when local and state governments were shutting shows down right and left. The show had to be held on the down low, and instead

In Their Own Words: Dave Menne on his near-death experience

"I was diagnosed with Lyme disease. It was a weird kind of hell. It's something that's impossible to explain to somebody. I had heart palpitations and various other things. Every other odd and crazy thing that could possibly happen to a human being. There was a lack of neural sensation on the outside of my body. As I started to come back, my body would react differently. I don't entirely know what to say. After two months, I was wonderful. But that was after two months of being as bad off as you could imagine. Everything after that felt great. I've been in the building stages since then, working on my striking, working on my grappling, working on my strength. Now it's a matter of getting everything down, tightening up the strings, and playing a pretty song."

of an arena, it ended up going down in an abandoned house, with no heat, in the middle of the freezing cold Wisconsin winter.

From that humble beginning, Menne rose all the way to the very top: he was the first UFC middleweight champion, winning the title at UFC 33. It was a hollow victory for a fighter who had beaten some of the sport's very best. His opponent for the inaugural middleweight title was a welterweight in his first bout at 185 pounds: former wrestler **Gil Castillo**. Castillo showed heart, but wasn't able to keep up with Menne's quick transitions on the ground and his steady clinch attack on his feet. Menne's five-round decision win was the highlight of one of the UFC's very worst cards. It was their first time in Las Vegas and the first time on pay-per-view, and the fighters up and down the card turned in dreadful performances.

It was the peak for Menne. He lost his title in his first defense, outgunned by the superlative **Murilo Bustamante**, the **Brazilian Jiu-jitsu** specialist who was at the top of his game. His comeback fight, at UFC 39, saw Menne on the wrong end of a highlight still seen on UFC broadcasts today, a victim of the fast and furious fists of **Phil Baroni**.

Menne was never the same after the Baroni fight. He did well on independent shows against low-level competition, but every time he stepped up in class against UFC-caliber opposition, Menne came up short.

Mercer, Ray

Nickname: Merciless
Height: 6'1"
Weight: 256 lbs
Born: 4/4/61
Debut: 6/23/07
Career Record: 1-1

Notable Win: Tim Sylvia (Adrenaline III)

Notable Loss: Kimbo Slice (Cage Fury Fighting Championship 5)

Ray Mercer was a former Olympic gold medalist and WBO heavyweight **boxing** champion fallen on hard times. At 46, he was quickly running out of dough, and ex-boxers aren't blessed with a ton of other workplace opportunities. That meant Mercer had to do the only thing he knew how to do: fight.

Like many in the world of boxing, Mercer saw a quick buck in the growing sport of MMA. He fought internet sensation **Kimbo Slice** in 2007 but was completely unprepared to handle Slice on the ground, losing quickly via submission.

His second chance in MMA was actually intended to be a boxing match. Former **UFC** champion **Tim Sylvia** was at a crossroads in his MMA career and wanted to try his hand at boxing. Mercer seemed like a safe choice. He had a big name but was 48 years old. A boxing match in a cage with a washed-up old has-been seemed like a winnable fight for Sylvia. New Jersey disagreed. Sylvia had no career boxing matches; Mercer had 44 professional fights.

Because New Jersey wouldn't sanction the fight, promoter **Monte Cox** moved it to the anything-goes state of Alabama. That kind of thing may work in the freewheeling world of MMA, but a new federal law made it illegal in boxing. The fight would have to be MMA to continue forward. Mercer was game and it seemed to make little difference to him. He hit Sylvia with the first punch he threw, a right hand that knocked the big man cold. With Sylvia shaking on the mat, Mercer celebrated in the cage. Like Kimbo Slice, he would now live forever on the internet, a YouTube legend in an increasingly digital world.

In Their Own Words: Ray Mercer on fighting Tim Sylvia in MMA

"I got to feel like this is the best day of his life, because I've got to come over to his world and do his thing. But I'm willing to do that. Because I am who I am. But if MMA isn't getting him anywhere, he should box me. Be a man and do what we said we were going to do and that's box. So it's going to boil down to who's a real man and who's going to do what he said he was going to do. We can get in there and kick and all that. I'm not going to be kicking or nothing. I'm going to do boxing. If he wants to box, we'll box. If he wants to kick and get down there and rassle, we'll do that shit too. I'll do MMA, MCI, AT&T, I'll do all of it. Anything he wants to do, I'm ready."

Although mixed martial arts is contested around the world in rings and cages of all kinds, it's the UFC's Octagon that has become the most powerful symbol of the sport.

Another powerful symbol of the sport.

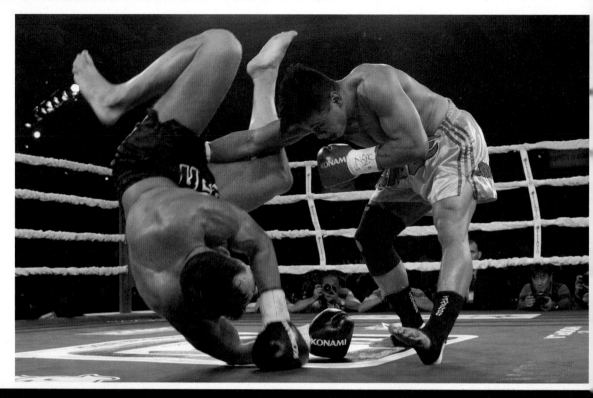

With dynamic strikes and unconventional throws, Cung Le fights like a kung fu movie come to life.

Wanderlei Silva batters Quinton Jackson with a barrage of knees in the final moments of Pride's epic 2003 Middleweight Grand Prix.

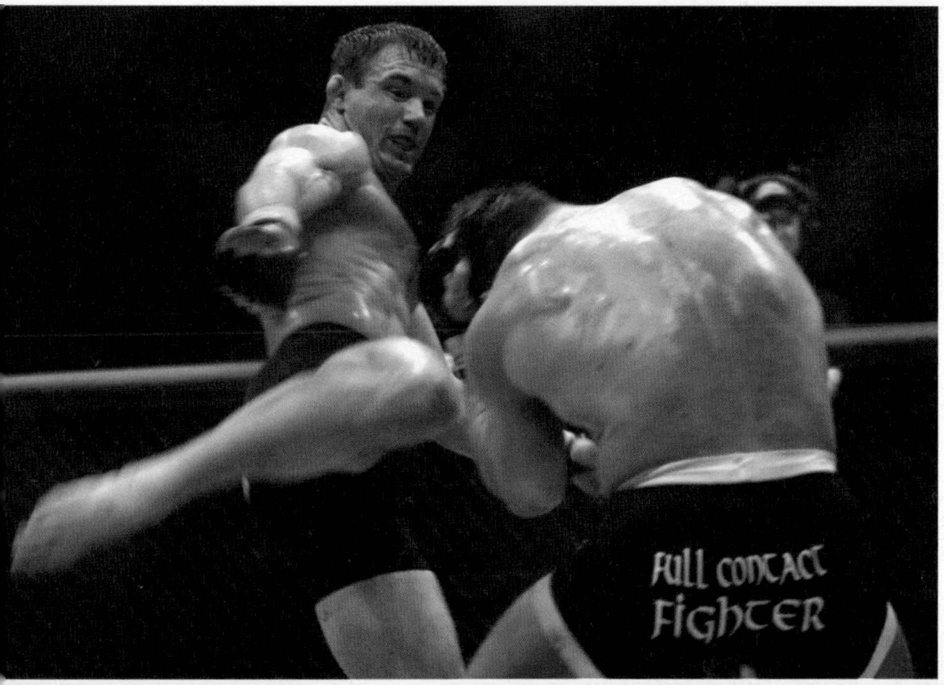

Few fighters have reigned over their divisions with the kind of dominance Matt Hughes displayed as UFC welterweight champion.

Former high school math teacher Rich Franklin takes the fight to Evan Tanner, a wandering spirit who met his untimely end in 2008.

The iron-jawed Wesley "Cabbage" Correira was famed for his ability to take a beating, like the one handed out here by future UFC heavyweight champion Andrei Arlovski.

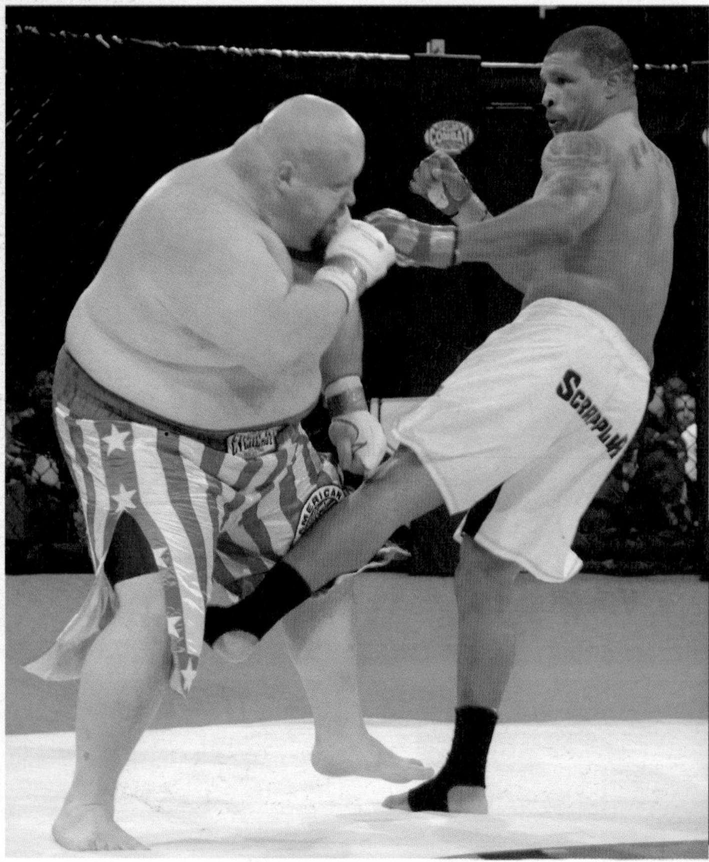

A thoroughly nasty veteran of the sport's outlaw era, Patrick Smith took on Eric "Butterbean" Esch at the disastrous Yamma Pit Fighting event.

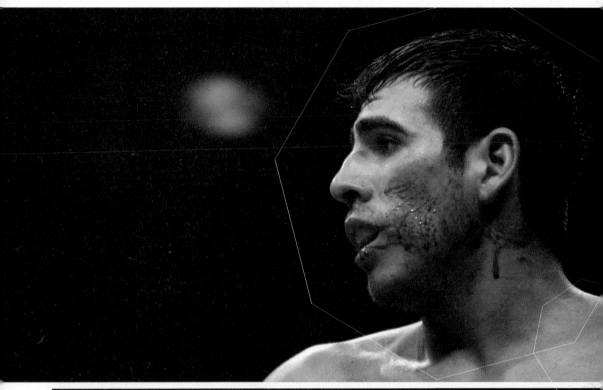

Often bloodied but rarely beaten, Kenny Florian has made his reputation on his ability to finish fights.

True to form, the great Antonio Rodrigo Nogueira emerged victorious from his UFC 73 bout against Heath Herring despite being knocked silly in the early going.

In only his second UFC fight, Georges St. Pierre aims a high kick at Jay Hieron, showing the form that would eventually propel him to the pinnacle of his sport.

Brazilian Jiu-jitsu black belt Renato Verissimo works to maintain his dominant position over Canadian grappler Carlos Newton.

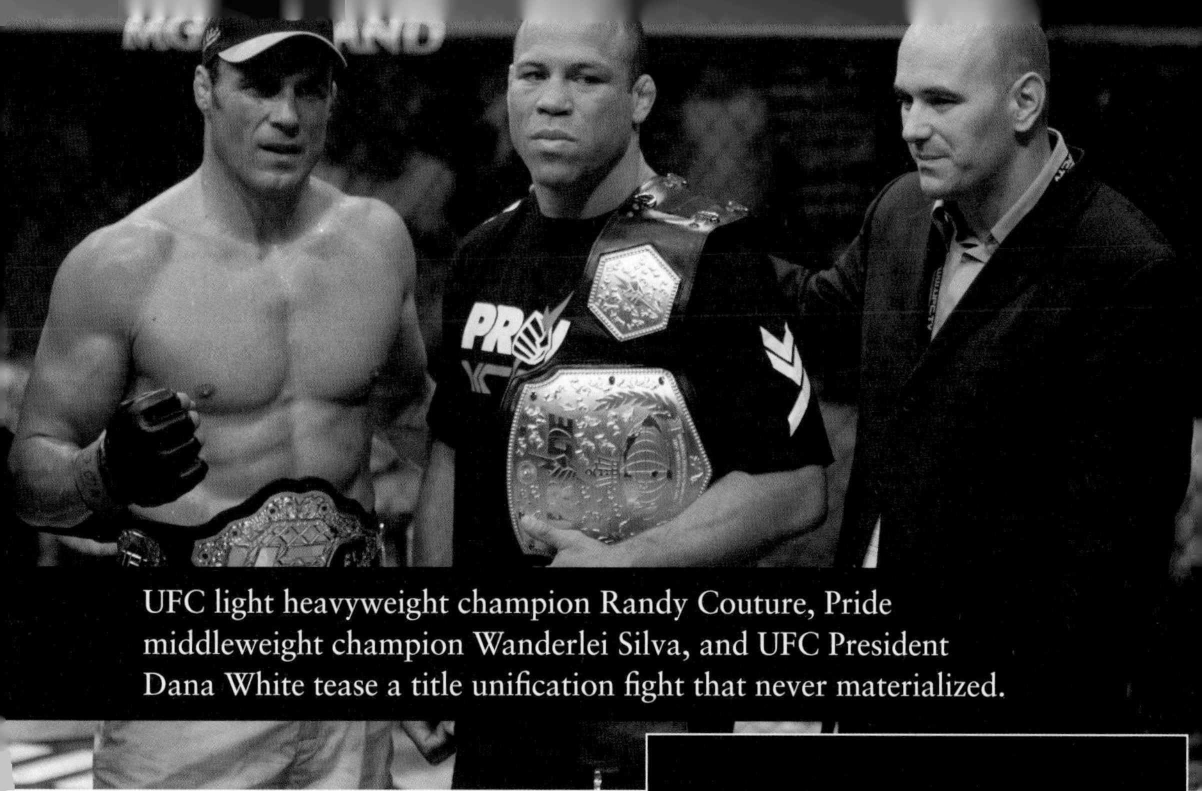

UFC light heavyweight champion Randy Couture, Pride middleweight champion Wanderlei Silva, and UFC President Dana White tease a title unification fight that never materialized.

Nick Diaz and Karo Parisyan, fiery and colorful students of Cesar Gracie and "Judo" Gene Lebell respectively, going the distance at UFC 49.

Nate Marquardt, King of Pancrase, on the streets of Tokyo.

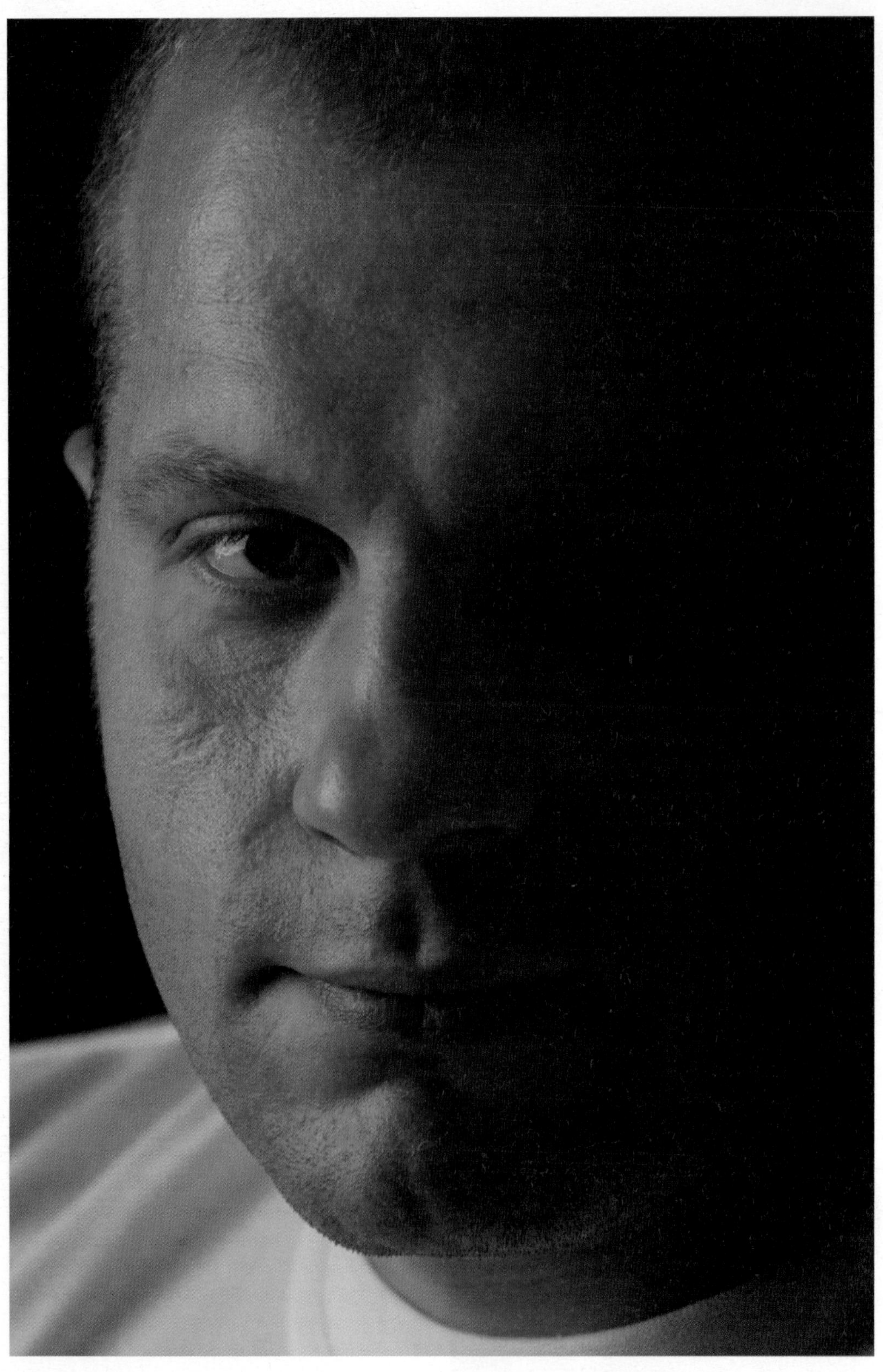

The most dangerous fighter in the history of mixed martial arts, Fedor Emelianenko.

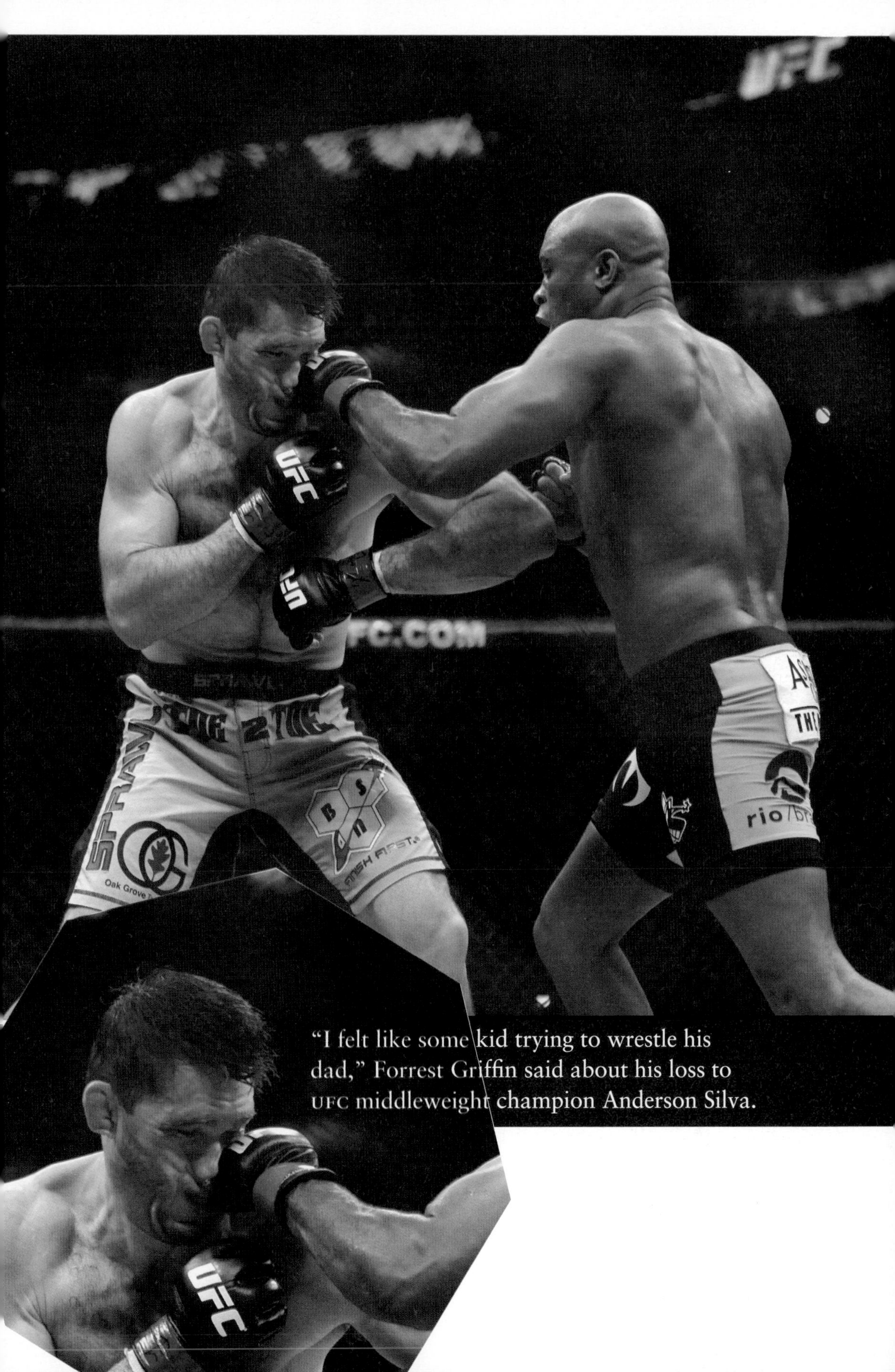

"I felt like some kid trying to wrestle his dad," Forrest Griffin said about his loss to UFC middleweight champion Anderson Silva.

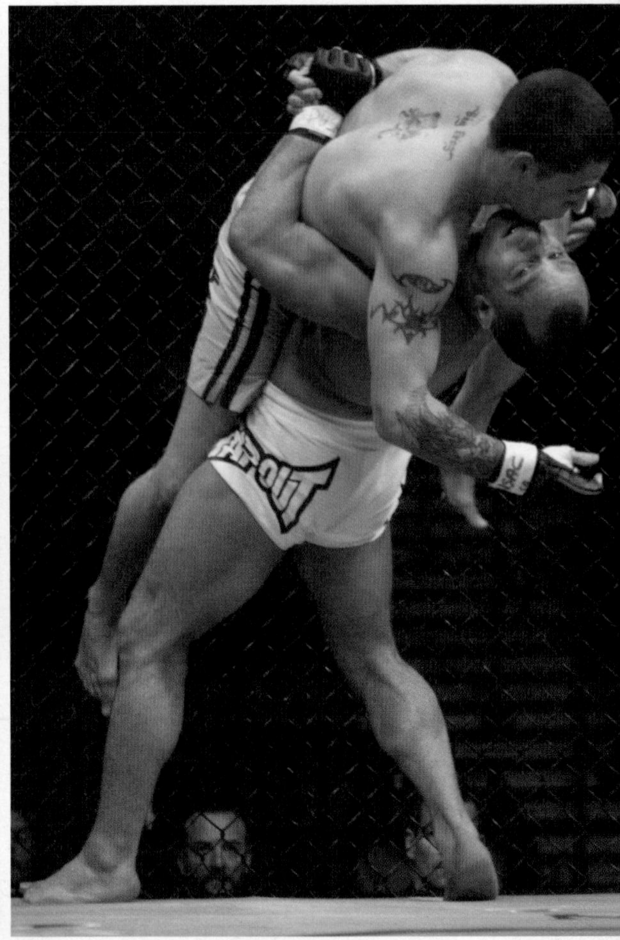

Chuck Liddell's iconic victory celebration.

Future UFC welterweight champion Matt Serra launches Jeff Curran with a spectacular throw at UFC 46.

In a clash of Brazilian grapplers, Renato "Babalu" Sobral takes Mauricio "Shogun" Rua to the mat.

Eddie Alvarez loses the fashion battle to Daisuke Hanazawa in early career action for both men.

Despite the fireworks, tough but plodding UFC heavyweight champion Tim Sylvia failed to truly connect with fans.

Bob Sapp styled his incredibly popular fighting persona after the professional wrestling greats. His ring entrance is pure Ric Flair.

David "Tank" Abbott was the original street-fighting MMA star, a forerunner to the Kimbo Slice experiment.

Japanese legend Kazushi Sakuraba hunts for a submission against the powerful Kevin Randleman.

Nick Diaz has used his pawing jab to great effect throughout his career, even against such heavy hitters as "Ruthless" Robbie Lawler.

A clash of two of Pride's top heavyweight stars, Antonio Rodrigo Nogueira and Mirko Cro Cop.

Despite the one-sided bouts it produced, the Tito Ortiz/Ken Shamrock feud did big business when the UFC needed it most.

Randy Couture forced a doctor's stoppage in his title fight against Vitor Belfort with the help of ferocious elbows from guard.

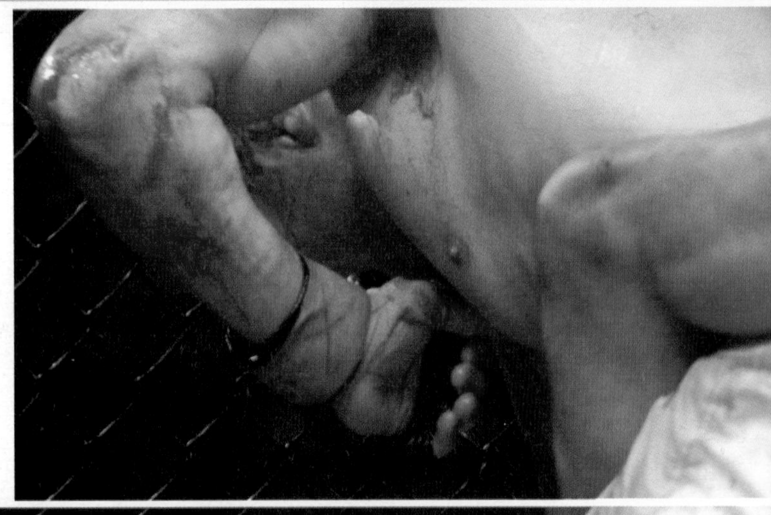

Meyrowitz, Bob: see **Semaphore Entertainment Group**

Mezger, Guy

Height: 6'1" **Weight:** 205 lbs

Born: 1/1/68 **Debut:** UFC 4 (12/16/94)

Career Record: 31-13-2

Notable Wins: Yuki Kondo (Pancrase: Truth 10); Tito Ortiz (UFC 13); Masakatsu Funaki (Pancrase: Advance 5)

Notable Losses: Bas Rutten (Pancrase: Truth 10); Tito Ortiz (UFC 19); Chuck Liddell (Pride 14)

Guy Mezger was an MMA pioneer, the King of **Pancrase** when that title still meant something, and able to hold his own with some of the best fighters the sport has ever seen. He fought competitively with **Chuck Liddell** and **Wanderlei**

In Their Own Words: Guy Mezger on old-school versus new-school MMA

"I really enjoyed my time as a combat athlete. It's always been my dream since I was a kid to be somebody special, especially in athletics. For me to have gotten the opportunities I've had, I have to realize how blessed I've been. To have been a part of the original thing has been kind of fun, because I'm sure when I get a lot older and I'm half senile, I'll be 80 years old saying, 'You think you've got it tough, kid? When I fought they didn't have rules! No rules and no weight classes. You guys are wimps today!'

"I had to learn the submission game and we learned the **catch wrestling** style of submission, which is a very fast moving style. It was something new to me at the time. Fighters today don't really have to go through what we did. I was a wrestler and a **karate** fighter and then a **judo** player and then I learned kickboxing. I learned the whole gamut of stuff I didn't need to learn. Today we take a little bit from here and a little bit from there and we make ourselves an MMA fighter. Now we've got guys who've never wrestled competitively who have great takedowns. We have guys that are technically white belts in judo or jiu-jitsu that know how to do very good **arm bars** and chokes. Really what's happened now, is that it's gone from this individual style into its own sport. Not only is it a sport, but it's a style of fighting now. So they cut to the chase, cut through a lot of the crap to what's really going to work. And that's really kind of the biggest difference between today and yesterday."

Silva, and beat top stars like Yuki Kondo, **Masakatsu Funaki**, and **Tito Ortiz**. Unfortunately, Mezger will likely be remembered not for his fights, but for his part in one of MMA's must vicious feuds.

At **UFC** 13, Mezger won the UFC lightweight tournament. He was the favorite coming in, but his win was not without controversy. In the finals he met an alternate named Tito Ortiz, a future champion who was just starting his MMA career. Ortiz had Mezger in trouble, raining knees down on his head, when referee **John McCarthy** inexplicably stood them up to check on a cut. When the action started again, Ortiz had lost his dominant position and was caught in a Mezger **guillotine choke** to end the fight. After the fight, Ortiz felt Mezger and his camp, the **Lion's Den**, were disrespectful and cocky. It was the beginning of a long feud between Tito and the Den.

After beating Mezger's training partner **Jerry Bohlander**, Ortiz got a chance at revenge. This time he made the most of it, beating Mezger mercilessly in a one-sided fight. When McCarthy stopped this fight, it was to declare Oritz the winner. Tito shot two birds at the Lion's Den corner and put on a custom-made T-shirt that said, "Gay Mezger Is My Bitch." In Mezger's corner, Lion's Den founder **Ken Shamrock** went ballistic. The Shamrock/Ortiz feud had begun, leaving Guy Mezger in the shadows, a forgotten fighter.

Miletich, Pat

Nickname: Croatian Sensation **Height:** 5'10"

Weight: 170 lbs **Born:** 3/9/68

Debut: BOTM 1 (10/28/95) **Career Record:** 29-7-2

Notable Wins: Mikey Burnett (UFC 17.5); Shonie Carter (Extreme Challenge 27, UFC 32)

Notable Losses: Matt Hume (EF 4); Jose Landi-Jons (WEF 8); Kiyoshi Tamura (Rings: Millenium Combine 3); Carlos Newton (UFC 31); Matt Lindland (UFC 36); Renzo Gracie (IFL: Gracie vs. Miletich)

Pat Miletich was a fine fighter and a brilliant trainer. Pat Miletich, despite revisionist history courtesy of L. Jon Wertheim's *Blood in the Cage*, was not the top fighter of his generation. In fact, he was never even close. He preyed on local fighters for promoter **Monte Cox**'s **Extreme Challenge** and beat some pretty good fighters in the **UFC**. But every time Miletich fought a world-class opponent, he failed.

Growing up without a father, the youngest of five children, Pat Miletich was a born fighter. Older brothers toughen you up, and being a little guy in a big man's world tends to leave a chip on your shoulder. Unlike almost everyone in

Iowa, Miletich didn't grow up with **wrestling** on his mind. It was just something he did between football seasons. Miletich was a tough, scrappy football player, but there is little future in the sport for a 165-pound nose guard. Wrestling, on the other hand, came naturally to him. Instead of being outweighed by 100 pounds, his opponent was the same size he was. He had a real shot of pursuing the sport after high school, with plans to go to Sioux Empire Junior College, but he just couldn't bring himself to care about school. Instead, he drifted.

With no college education and no connections, Miletich struggled to make ends meet. He poured concrete and even dug in dumpsters when money was tight. Under no circumstances would he ask anyone for help, no matter how desperate the times. Simply put, he was heading nowhere, just drifting through life, working dead-end jobs and brawling in the street. Eventually he found focus in the martial arts, studying **karate**, kickboxing, and eventually finding his way to a **Renzo Gracie** grappling seminar in Chicago in 1992.

Miletich became obsessed with **Brazilian Jiu-jitsu**, studying Gracie's instructional videos and sparring with friends in the basement of their karate dojo. When he had the opportunity to test himself in the sport then called "No Holds Barred," Miletich was ready. He had all the tools: standup skills from karate and **boxing**, high school wrestling, and some rudimentary jiu-jitsu. It was enough. At the Battle of the Masters, the 170-pound Miletich beat all comers to take home $5,000. He had finally found his calling.

Among fighters in the Midwest, Miletich quickly became a legend. He beat everyone at local shows. Soon the region's other top fighters, like grappling wizard **Jeremy Horn**, were moving to Bettendorf, Iowa, to work with Miletich in a racquetball court he rented from a local gym. Miletich was obsessed with the UFC, waiting for a phone call that never came. When he did get the call up to the big time, it was for **John Perretti**'s **Extreme Fighting**.

Perretti was ahead of his time. Unlike the UFC, still pitting the little guys against giants in freak show contests, Extreme Fighting instituted weight classes and rounds. In short, it treated fighting as a sport and was the perfect fit for the hard-nosed Miletich. Unfortunately, for Miletich at least, his opponent was a more experienced and more skilled fighter from **Pancrase** named **Matt Hume**.

Like Miletich, Hume would go on to become one of MMA's top trainers, but that was some time ahead for both men. On this night, the two went back and forth in a bout that looked like it had been brought back in time from the next decade. The two were both complete fighters, well-tuned fighting machines trading blows, holds, and takedowns. After one furious round of action, the doctor stopped the fight because of a Miletich broken nose. For the tough guy from Iowa, who once chased a man down in a street fight after having his teeth knocked out of his mouth, having a professional fight stopped because of a broken nose burned.

It was the story of Miletich's career. Against middling fighters, Miletich was a monster. Against the best of the best, like Jose "Pele" Landi-Jons, **Carlos Newton**, and Renzo Gracie, Miletich always came out of the fray with an "L" on his record. That doesn't entirely dismiss Miletich's greatness. He was a solid, smart, and skilled fighter. When he finally got his shot in the UFC, he made the most of it. He won seven in a row inside the Octagon, winning a lightweight tournament and the welterweight title. Wertheim and others confused this success with a dominant run as one of the sport's best. The problem with that theory? Miletich lost three times outside the UFC during his "undefeated" run as champion. He was a good but not great fighter, and Carlos Newton proved it at UFC 31.

While Miletich was the type of fighter that might bring a lunch pail into the cage, a blue-collar hard-nosed Midwesterner who took no prisoners, Newton was his polar opposite. Newton was an explosive athlete and charismatic performer. He entered the cage with aplomb and celebrated his wins like he was a *Street Fighter* video game character. Newton submitted Miletich with a bulldog choke, ending his three-year run as UFC welterweight champion.

Many have forgotten just how unpopular Miletich was with the UFC's fans and their brass. Few had forgotten the horrifying sight of Miletich grabbing Mikey Burnett's shorts for 21 sleep-inducing minutes at UFC Brazil. Miletich cemented a reputation as a boring fighter that night, one he never completely escaped. Once he lost the title, the UFC was intent that he wouldn't regain it. A young welterweight stud was lurking at Miletich's camp, a stud named **Matt Hughes**. When **Zuffa** took over the UFC, they were looking for Hughes to represent his camp in a title shot with Newton. After a three-year reign as champion, there would be no rematch.

A demoralized Miletich tried to take things in stride. He moved up to 185 pounds, but was never given a chance to develop slowly at this new weight. He was immediately thrown in with Olympic silver medalist **Matt Lindland**, who used his size and wrestling prowess to overwhelm Pat on the ground. Miletich was physically beaten up; 34 years old and convinced his opportunities to compete at the top of his natural weight class were long gone, Pat called it quits. It wasn't worth sticking around for a paycheck in those days — the paychecks just weren't that good. It was Miletich's last fight for the UFC, a sad end for a great champion.

> ***In Their Own Words:* Jens Pulver on Pat Miletich's ability as a trainer**
>
> "People always ask for Pat's secret ingredient. There wasn't no secret ingredient. That's why I made that comment about our 'supposed leader.' There was no one leader, man. We all did it together. Jeremy Horn was the leader when it comes down to it. We all ran after that guy. We all said, 'Teach us coach.' Everyone always thought Pat had a magical touch and was teaching us all these magical things. No, he wasn't. No. Never. Never ever. It was a great combination of things that left. Jeremy left, Matt [Hughes] left, Robbie [Lawler] left. Matt Pena left. Everybody grew up more or less. We weren't there anymore. And that's why the great experiment is over."

To make things worse, even Miletich's past exploits have essentially been erased from UFC history. Miletich joined up with the fledgling **International Fight League** where he coached two teams to championships and made an ill-fated return to the ring against Renzo Gracie. Doing so was tantamount to declaring war on **Dana White** and the UFC, a situation that only escalated when Miletich gave a scathing anti-UFC deposition in a lawsuit between the two promotions.

Today, Miletich continues to train fighters at his gym in Bettendorf. No longer the home of champions, the camp still produces a number of UFC-caliber fighters, insuring Miletich will be seen, but never mentioned, in the corner during UFC broadcasts for years to come.

Miller, Jason

Nickname: Mayhem
Height: 6'1"
Weight: 185 lbs
Born: 12/24/80
Debut: Rage in the Cage 27 (4/28/01)
Career Record: 23-7 (1 No Contest)
Notable Wins: Denis Kang (Extreme Challenge 50); Egan Inoue (SuperBrawl 32); Robbie Lawler (Icon Sport: Mayhem vs. Lawler); Tim Kennedy (HDNet Fights: Reckless Abandon)
Notable Losses: Tim Kennedy (Extreme Challenge 50); Georges St. Pierre (UFC 52); Frank Trigg (Icon Sport: Mayhem vs. Trigg); Ronaldo de Souza (Dream 4); Jake Shields (Strikeforce: Fedor vs. Rogers)

By his own assertion, Jason Miller is a pro wrestler. Not according to the usual definition — there are no worked matches, no flying elbows off the top of the cage. But to the extent that virtually everything Jason Miller says or does is calculated to entertain fans and create a persona, there's really no other way to describe what he does. The masked, machete-wielding entrances, the in-ring antics, the goofy mugging: that's **pro wrestling** all over.

Although Miller claims to have been competing in 1997 (note that he also claims "Parts Unknown" as his hometown), there's no record of him in action before 2001. His big break came two years later in a fight he was supposed to lose. Miller was invited to Honolulu to be an easy win for Egan Inoue, a Hawaiian star who'd just dropped his SuperBrawl title and needed to get back on track. In the first round, Inoue nearly ended the fight with a deep **Kimura**, but Miller escaped after an incredible sequence of four forward rolls to relieve the pressure. By the end of the first, though, Miller controlled Inoue in **rear mount**, and literally spanked him, which didn't exactly endear him to the Honolulu crowd. A round later, when an obviously injured Inoue was unable to continue, a smiling, strutting, and *break-dancing* Miller instantly became the SuperBrawl (later Icon) promotion's most hated man. That is, until several headlining bouts later, when the crowd slowly caught on to Miller's act. He wasn't a bad guy — he was an entertainer playing the role of the pro wrestling heel.

Miller had the misfortune of making his lone **UFC** appearance against **Georges St. Pierre** in the French Canadian's first fight after his loss to **Matt Hughes**. St. Pierre's pre-fight comments were on the mark: nobody *could* handle his rhythm. Despite his corner's exhortations ("Retard strength, Jason! Retard strength!"), Miller took a hellacious beating from the future welterweight champ. It's a testament to his toughness that he was able to go the distance against the clearly superior athlete.

Although his colorful act seemed perfect for Japan, where style is worth at least as much as substance, it wasn't until 2008 that Miller made his Japanese debut. In the opening round of the **Dream** middleweight (185 pounds) Grand Prix, Miller made short work of Katsuyori Shibata, an actual, honest-to-goodness, fake-fights-and-everything pro wrestler, and earned a date with "Jacaré" — **Brazilian Jiu-jitsu** world champion Ronaldo de Souza. Although Miller is no slouch on the ground, Jacaré is almost without peer, and the Brazilian pressured Mayhem constantly en route to a unanimous decision win. Their heated rematch at Dream 9 ended in controversy, as an illegal kick to the downed de Souza opened a nasty cut and ended the bout in a no contest. Mayhem/Jacaré III seems an inevitability, but

In Their Own Words: Mayhem Miller on his illegal kick to Ronaldo de Souza

"It was a mistake. Jacaré calls me a clown and disrespects me all the time, head butted me and opened a cut on my eye. If he could've done it to me, he would have. I'll beat the shit out of him legally next time. What's he gonna do? Submit me? LOL Kayo me? LMMFAO.

"Brazilian nuthuggers can suck my mother fuckin dick that gets more pussy than any one of you could imagine, due to my MTV show, my good looks, and my tons of money.

"How is that for classy? Oh, you know what, I don't give a fuck what you think, I'm the fucking man. Hey [Underground poster] CRE, what was your down syndrome Brazilian gonna break? NOTHING. Bitch ass had me on the ground for 3 seconds.

"Let me get my bread for fucking him up in a rematch, and watch you all cry about how I 'don't respect the sport.' In the words of **Dana White**, 'Fuck you you fucking cunt.'

"Go jerk off to ***TUF***."

(from **The Underground**)

there's no telling how long fans might have to wait. Miller is a busy man, splitting his time between his fighting career, his hosting duties on MTV's reality series *Bully Beatdown*, and trolling MMA message boards with his absolutely first-rate puerile rants.

Minowa, Ikuhisa

Nickname: Minowaman (formerly The Punk) **Height:** 5'9"

Weight: 181 lbs **Born:** 1/12/72

Debut: Lumax Cup Tournament of J '96 (3/30/96) **Career Record:** 46-30-8

Notable Wins: Phil Baroni (Pride Bushido 9); Eric "Butterbean" Esch (Pride Bushido 12); Don Frye (Deep: Gladiator); Bob Sapp (Dream 9); Rameau Thierry Sokoudjou (Dynamite!! 2009)

Notable Losses: Phil Baroni (Pride Bushido 7); Kazushi Sakuraba (Pride Shockwave 2005); Mirko Cro Cop (Pride Total Elimination Absolute)

Ikuhisa Minowa, better known these days as "Minowaman," identified his fighting style as **professional wrestling** long before ever having worked a professional wrestling match as most of us would understand the term. This tells you almost everything you need to know about the red-trunked, intensely mulleted Ikuhisa Minowa's approach to MMA.

An entertainer first and a competitor second, Minowa became a Japanese crowd favorite with his flair for the dramatic, his use of pro wrestling–style dropkicks in legitimate fights, and his willingness to fight opponents twice his size. While his back-and-forth Bushido battles against **Phil Baroni** showed Minowa at his fighting best, it was his freak show bouts against the likes of **Giant Silva**, Butterbean, Zuluzinho, and **Bob Sapp** that made his reputation. Minowa has clearly gotten the most out of a career that began somewhat ingloriously: he won only twice in his first 13 contests for **Pancrase**, his home for six years and an incredible 41 fights.

A Minowaman of diverse talents, Minowa delivered a lecture at the Kanezawa Hakkei Campus of Kanto Gakuin University in 2006 titled, "About Real — Ultramodern — New Style — Superhuman." "If you think about the time from the big bang until now," Minowa suggested, "the very moment we are living in is, without a doubt, Ultramodern." That much seems irrefutable. He went on to explain that "if you want to be Superhuman, you have to completely exceed your genetics. I'm still testing it, but if I can make my genes 100 percent complete, I will start a revolution in, and outside of, my brain." A hopeful world awaits.

Mir, Frank

Height: 6'3"
Weight: 245 lbs
Born: 5/24/79
Debut: HOOKnSHOOT: Showdown (7/14/01)
Career Record: 13-5
Notable Wins: Pete Williams (UFC 36); Tank Abbott (UFC 41); Tim Sylvia (UFC 48); Brock Lesnar (UFC 81); Antonio Rodrigo Nogueira (UFC 92)
Notable Losses: Ian Freeman (UFC 38); Brandon Vera (UFC 65); Brock Lesnar (UFC 100); Shane Carwin (UFC 109)

For Frank Mir, fighting is a family affair. His first teacher was his father, a Kenpo **karate** instructor who taught him how to punch and kick. The Mirs thought they knew how to fight. It wasn't until father and son saw the first **UFC** that they realized how little they understood about a real fight. **Royce Gracie** had made it clear that standup striking alone wasn't enough to be successful against the world's toughest men.

Mir turned his attention to grappling, winning a high school **wrestling** championship and becoming a black belt in **Brazilian Jiu-jitsu**. This superlative grappling skill, combined with his years of karate, formed a potent combination, a fast track to success.

Mir was pushed to the top of the sport with a shocking speed. UFC matchmaker **Joe Silva** saw him train and encouraged him to take up the sport as a professional. After just two tune-up fights, Mir was in the UFC, amazing the world with a submission win over highly touted jiu-jitsu artist Roberto Traven.

Mir had the look the UFC was pushing at the time, a clean-cut all-American boyishness that also led the promotion to get behind **Rich Franklin** and **Matt Hughes**. The sport was still under attack by fierce critics. The UFC thought it was important to be able to counter attacks with clean-cut, articulate fighters explaining what the sport was all about.

Mir got a plum spot, opposite returning legend **Tank Abbott**. Abbott was a great personality, but one who talked better than he fought. It was a foregone conclusion, at least for people who followed the sport closely, that Mir would walk away victorious. He tapped the Tank with a **toe hold** and a star was born.

After a bizarre feud with **Wes Sims** that saw Sims disqualified for illegally stomping a prone Mir in the head, Mir was fighting for the UFC title after just eight professional fights. Across the cage at UFC 48 was the mammoth champion, **Pat Miletich**–trained **Tim Sylvia**. Sylvia was a 6'8" giant who used his long reach to keep opponents at bay with a jab and a careful style that minimized risk. Mir's only hope was getting the champ down and tapping him out. Minutes into the bout, Mir trapped Sylvia's right arm and looked to finish the fight. Sylvia was defending when referee **Herb Dean** jumped in to stop the contest. Sylia, the crowd, and UFC President **Dana White** were all furious. Then they

In Their Own Words: Frank Mir on the motorcycle accident that changed his life

"I had enjoyed being an athlete my whole life. After the accident I was hobbling around and I lost a lot of my identity. I went from being one of the top martial artists in the world to being a guy who might not ever be able to fight again. It took me four years to get back to where I was before the wreck. There were several times I was in the UFC front office begging not to be cut. I was one decision, one breath, away from never having my career again.

"A lot of times, when people get hurt, it's because they don't fear something. Fear is a very healthy thing. I'm afraid every time I step in the cage. All my losses occurred when I got a certain level of arrogance and wasn't afraid anymore. When I got hit by the car, I was so comfortable on my bike that I literally had my forearm on the gas tank and was just chilling. Being comfortable in the situation allowed me to be hurt. I haven't forgotten that lesson."

saw the replay. Instead of an early stoppage, Dean was right on time. Mir had actually broken Sylvia's arm. The adrenaline coursing through his brain hadn't let his body tell his mind yet. Mir was the new heavyweight champion.

Then, disaster struck. Cruising on his motorcycle down Sahara Avenue in his hometown of Las Vegas, Nevada, Mir was on top of the world. He was on his way to work, still providing security at the Spearmint Rhino strip club, thinking about his upcoming wedding. He never saw the car coming. Mir went flying more than 70 feet, snapping his leg in half.

It looked, for a time, like Mir would never recover. His return was sad to see. After 18 months of rest and rehab, Mir was still not the fighter he had been. He lost his return fight with Marcio Cruz at UFC 57, struggled with the unheralded Dan Christison, and was embarrassed by prospect **Brandon Vera**. There were whispers he wouldn't be able to get medical clearance to fight anymore. The old Frank Mir was gone, buried under a layer of blubber and self-doubt.

It was this past-his-prime Mir that was selected to be the first opponent for UFC megastar **Brock Lesnar** at UFC 81. Lesnar was a former professional wrestler who had strong amateur credentials but almost no experience. Mir, a talented grappler, caught Lesnar at exactly the right time in his career. Lesnar was dominating the fight, tossing Mir around and pounding him, when the wily veteran caught him in a **knee bar** out of nowhere.

The Lesnar fight reinvigorated Mir's career. He and **Pride** legend **Antonio Rodrigo Nogueira** were opposing coaches on the eighth season of ***The Ultimate***

Fighter. After the season they fought for the interim UFC heavyweight championship, vacated by **Randy Couture** during a contract dispute. Mir knocked out the legend in the second round, just the second knockout of his career.

The stars had aligned for the UFC. Mir was the interim champion, while Lesnar dispatched of a returning Couture to win the heavyweight crown. Two titles demanded a title unification bout, a rematch between two men who legitimately disliked each other. Mir was a martial artist who didn't appreciate Lesnar's pro wrestling theatrics and what he thought was an undeserved opportunity.

It was the biggest fight in UFC history. UFC 100 sold out before tickets ever hit the street. Its 1.6 million pay-per-view buys were the most ever, by a significant margin. Lesnar was the biggest star the sport had seen and Mir was a great foil. The difference was the additional year and a half Lesnar had to study the submission game. This time he blitzed Mir, easily beating him in the second round to become the undisputed champion.

Misaki, Kazuo

Nickname: Grabaka Hitman **Height:** 5'10"

Weight: 183 lbs **Born:** 4/25/76

Debut: Pancrase Neo-Blood Tournament (5/5/01)

Career Record: 22-10-2 (1 No Contest)

Notable Wins: Phil Baroni (Pride Bushido 11); Dan Henderson (Pride Bushido 12); Denis Kang (Pride Bushido 13); Joe Riggs (Strikeforce: At the Mansion II)

Notable Losses: Nate Marquardt (Pancrase: Spirit 3, Pancrase: Brave 10); Dan Henderson (Pride Bushido 10); Paulo Filho (Pride Bushido 13); Frank Trigg (Pride Bushido 33)

There are the wins, over the likes of one-time middleweight stand-out **Denis Kang** and the great **Dan Henderson**. There are the losses, against top competition like **Nate Marquardt** and the enigmatic **Paulo Filho**. There are the strange twists of fate, like a **Pride** welterweight (183 pounds) Grand Prix championship that came on the same night Misaki was eliminated from the tournament. And there's scandal: a conviction and three-year suspended sentence for a hit-and-run on a Tokyo police officer. But for **Grabaka** fighter Kazuo Misaki, for all the ups and downs, there's really only one night: New Year's Eve 2007.

It was as much a morality play as it was a fight. **Yoshihiro Akiyama** was the most hated man in Japanese MMA, loathed by the fans for cheating **Kazushi Sakuraba** a year to the day earlier, when he illegally greased himself to avoid the grappler's takedowns. For one night, Kazuo Misaki was the avenger, the man who was going to punish Akiyama for his misdeed. Although their bout didn't go on last, this fight was the true main event of Yarennoka!, an unofficial farewell to **Pride**. The Saitama fans jeered like never before as Akiyama and his cornermen kneeled and bowed on their way to the ring to the familiar strains of "Con Te Partiro"; they exploded when Misaki bounced down the aisle to the pounding beat of The Mad Capsule Markets.

The bout between two expert grapplers turned into a heated kickboxing contest, the crowd hanging on every blow. When Akiyama floored Misaki with a quick one-two midway through the long first round, it looked like the villain might prevail, but Misaki fought to his feet, and soon thereafter landed a solid left hook that staggered Akiyama. When Misaki connected with a vicious kick to the scrambling Akiyama's head and the referee dove between them to stop the fight, the crowd was rapturous.

"You betrayed the trust of many fans and children, and it is something that I cannot overlook," Misaki lectured a woozy Akiyama in a strange scene at the center of the ring. "But you fought well tonight and you showed heart. From this point forth, I want to see you put your sincerity and a feeling of apology into fighting for the fans and the children."

Misaki's kick was later judged to have connected while Akiyama was still technically in the four-points, grounded position, and the bout was rightly ruled a no contest. But that night in Saitama, it seemed like something akin to justice.

M-1 Global

When **Fedor Emelianenko** was negotiating a contract with the **UFC** in 2009, the deal killer was an unusual request: Fedor wanted his fights to be co-promoted by M-1 Global. This was ridiculed in the MMA media. After all, what could M-1 offer the UFC behemoth? It was assumed that they had little promotional experience; that couldn't have been further from the truth. M-1 has been promoting events worldwide for over a decade. Although they haven't yet become a global powerhouse, the group has done a tremendous job laying the groundwork for the coming MMA explosion in Europe and particularly in Russia. They have also co-promoted major events with **Affliction** and **Strikeforce** featuring Emelianenko in a starring role.

M-1 Global's flagship event is its M-1 Challenge series. The competition is similar to the **International Fight League**'s approach, picking up where that defunct promotion left off. It's a team-based competition featuring athletes from around the world. Instead of dividing the fighters into teams based on the camps they train out of, the M-1 Challenge is more like the MMA Olympics (actually billed as the "World Cup" of MMA). The teams feature fighters from 13 countries. Each team has fighters in five weight classes, competing in best of five meets, with the winner being the first team to reach three victories. It's a great promotion for some of the very best young fighters in the world to get their feet wet in international competition, building fighters and a new generation of stars with television contracts in almost 100 countries worldwide.

Monson, Jeff

Nickname: The Snowman **Height:** 5'9"

Weight: 247 lbs **Born:** 1/18/71

Debut: UFCF: Night of Champions (3/14/98) **Career Record:** 31-8

Notable Wins: Kazuyuki Fujita (Pride 34); Ricco Rodriguez (Mixed Fighting Alliance: There Will Be Blood); Roy Nelson (SRP: March Badness); Sergei Kharitonov (Dream 8)

Notable Losses: Chuck Liddell (UFC 29); Ricco Rodriguez (UFC 35); Forrest Griffin (WEFC 1); Tim Sylvia (UFC 65); Pedro Rizzo (Art of War 3); Josh Barnett (Sengoku 2)

Jeff Monson is a fierce competitor inside the cage. But that's where he thinks the competition should end. "We walk out of the ring, or the cage; the fight should be over," Monson told Wisconsin Combat Sports. "When it comes to living, we shouldn't have to compete with each other." Ask him about his politics, and he'll tell you he's a libertarian communist, an anarchist, opposed to any and all social institutions that promote or maintain class divisions. Ask him if he feels his radical politics set him apart from his fellow fighters, and he'll tell you no, fundamentally they're all just wage slaves in this thing together. But there's a sense in which the MMA world doesn't quite know what to make of Monson. Consider longtime **UFC** commentator **Mike Goldberg**. As Jeff Monson stepped into the cage to challenge **Tim Sylvia**'s heavyweight title at UFC 65, here's the best the well-meaning Goldberg could manage: "He's a very political, socio-economic dude, who comes from a middle-class background, and wants to make a statement inside the Octagon here tonight." Not Goldberg's finest moment.

Monson's politics are by their nature controversial. But whether or not you respect the tenets of Jeff Monson's anarchism or his strident pacifism, you've got to respect his honesty. Unlike many athletes who deny the use of performance enhancing drugs even after multiple positive tests, Monson, who has never failed a drug test, readily admits to past use of performance enhancing drugs, and, in a position consistent with his politics, argues that they should be legalized. In the current **steroid**-mad cultural climate, that borders on sedition.

Monson wrestled at the University of Illinois, earning a bachelor's degree in psychology; graduate work and a master's degree from the University of Minnesota at Duluth followed. After four years of working in mental health services and fighting part time, Monson took the plunge and committed himself fully to MMA as a career. An **ADCC** submission **wrestling** champion and **Brazilian Jiu-jitsu** black belt, Monson put together an impressive string of 16 consecutive wins — many by way of his signature **north-south** choke — that included UFC triumphs over Branden Lee Hinkle, Anthony Perosh, and his rival from the world of submission grappling, Marcio "Pe de Pano" Cruz.

And so a shot at the ever unpopular Tim Sylvia, an enormous, lumbering, sad sack heavyweight champion whose cautious style and woe-is-me demeanor made him singularly unlikable among UFC headliners. But the biggest fight of Monson's career turned out to be something of a dud. An 11-inch height difference proved too much for Monson to overcome — he was comically unable to reach Sylvia's head while punching from **guard** in the third round (the only round Monson won). The fight ground to such a standstill that referee **John McCarthy** stopped the action (such as it was) in the fifth round to remind them, "This is a fight, and you guys gotta *fight*."

Upon his own request, Monson was released from his UFC contract after he came up short in his title challenge, and has stayed busy since, taking fights in both high profile Japanese promotions (**Pride**, **Dream**, and **Sengoku**) and obscure American organizations. He's quietly put together the kind of winning streak that earned him his last shot in the UFC, and could very well land him there again. That is, if he can stay out of jail: after an *ESPN: The Magazine* profile included a photograph of Monson spray-painting an anarchist symbol and scrawling the words "no war" and "no poverty" on the Washington State Capitol, he pled guilty to a charge of malicious mischief and entered an Alford plea on a charge of graffiti. No stranger to the importance of a judge's decision, this one ultimately fell his way: Monson avoided jail time for what his lawyer characterized as "an act of conscience."

Mount

A dominant ground fighting position in which the attacker straddles his opponent's torso, anywhere from the hips to the chest, with knees tight against his opponent's sides. The widely used term "mount" comes to us from **Brazilian Jiu-jitsu** and the Portuguese montada; the position is classically known as tate-shiho gatame (upright four-quarters hold) in **judo**. As ne-waza (ground technique) expert Katsuhiko Kashiwazaki notes, "The intrinsic quality of the technique is very high, though it is quite difficult to master."

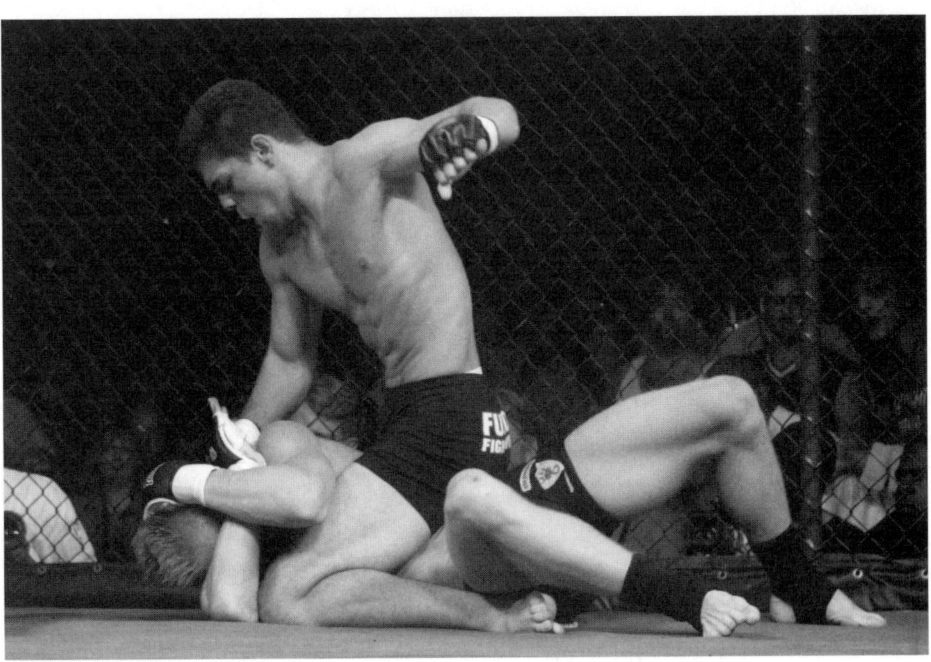

Broadly speaking, the attacker has three options from the mounted position: (i) he can stay low and tight to his opponent for maximum control; (ii) he can work towards a variety of arm locks (**arm bar, Kimura/Americana**) or chokes (**arm triangle, Ezequiel, triangle, gogoplata**); or (iii) he can posture up and deliver punches and elbows to which his supine opponent can offer only minimal defense. Strikes from the mount often cause the opponent to turn to the prone position, allowing the attacker to secure **rear mount**, another dominant position.

There are a number of escapes available to the mounted fighter. He can attempt to bridge and roll into the mounting fighter's **guard**, or twist and shrimp onto his side such that he can reestablish his own **half-guard** and, eventually, guard. If the attacker is sitting high on the mounted fighter's chest and his balance is poor, the mounted fighter can buck up and scramble out the back door (between the attacker's legs). But every escape is complicated by the steady stream of shots to the head that tends to come along with being on the wrong end of the mount. The mounted fighter absolutely must improve his position — and quickly.

See also **positional hierarchy**

Mousasi, Gegard

Nickname: The Dreamcatcher **Height:** 6'1"

Weight: 205 lbs **Born:** 8/1/85

Debut: 2H2H: 1st Open Team Mixfight Championships (4/27/03)

Career Record: 29-3-1

Notable Wins: Hector Lombard (Pride Bushido 13); Denis Kang (Dream 2); Melvin Manhoef (Dream 6); Ronaldo Souza (Dream 6); Mark Hunt (Dream 9); Renato Sobral (Strikeforce: Carono vs. Cyborg)

Notable Losses: Akihiro Gono (Pride Bushido 12); Muhammed Lawal (Strikeforce: Nashville)

After running into trouble against tough veteran **Akihiro Gono** in his first real test, Gegard Mousasi ran off 15 wins in a row against some of the world's best. The young Armenian star became one of the sport's top prospects, winning the **Dream** Middleweight Grand Prix and then stepping up in weight and making his mark on the light heavyweight division as well.

Mousasi, highly coveted by the **UFC**, signed with **Strikeforce** instead and won the promotion's light heavyweight title over former UFC star **Renato Sobral**. Many fans were putting him in the same class as the sport's very best,

In Their Own Words: Gegard Mousasi on MMA's prospects in Europe

"A celebrity? I don't think I am one. In the Netherlands they like sports like cycling, darts, and ice skating – there isn't any interest in MMA. There is a big difference with countries like the USA and Japan. It won't be big in Europe. Maybe in countries like Great Britain and Germany because the combat sport is popular there, like boxing."

but **"King Mo" Lawal** put an end to that talk with a smothering win to take Mousasi's title. If the Netherlands-based fighter is going to regain his title, or make his mark in the UFC down the road, it's clear that he had better learn some wrestling first.

Muay Thai

There's no substitute for good old-fashioned western **boxing** for training the hands, but no single striking art has proven itself more valuable in the context of mixed martial arts than Muay Thai. The Art of Eight Limbs — hands, shins, elbows, knees — has a storied Thai history stretching from the era of Muay Boran (literally "ancient boxing") to the modern heroes of Bangkok's sweltering Lumpinee Boxing Stadium who take to the ring every Tuesday, Friday, and Saturday evening. But the Muay Thai fighters who have made their mark most indelibly in MMA thus far have fought out of Brazil. Curitiba, Brazil, to be precise, and Master Rudimar Fedrigo's **Chute Boxe** Academy, which has produced many of the most dangerous strikers in the history of the sport, **Wanderlei Silva**, **Mauricio Rua**, and **Anderson Silva** foremost among them. Watch them turn their hips powerfully into the low kicks that chip away at their opponents' mobility, the body kicks that punish the ribs and bring their opponents hands down to their side, readying them for the thunderous head kicks that lay them out. Witness Anderson Silva's outrageous reverse elbow knockout of Tony Fryklund, catching him with a technique that would seem at home in Tony Jaa's *Ong Bak: Muay Thai Warrior*. See Wanderlei work **Quinton Jackson** over with knees from the clinch, or Anderson do the same to **Rich Franklin**, rearranging his facial features with a single blow. Or take a look at Rua's classic Muay Thai stance — left arm high, right hand at his cheek, chin low, light lead leg springing off the mat — as it contrasts to **Lyoto Machida**'s upright **karate** stance in their light heavyweight title bout at **UFC** 104. It might not be Lumpinee, but it's not half bad.

Nakamura, Kazuhiro

Height: 5'11" **Weight:** 205 lbs

Born: 7/16/79 **Debut:** Pride 25 (3/16/03)

Career Record: 15-10

Notable Wins: Murilo Bustamante (Pride Final Conflict 2004); Kevin Randleman (Pride Total Elimination 2005); Igor Vovchanchyn (Pride Final Conflict 2005); Yuki Kondo (Pride Shockwave 2005); Hidehiko Yoshida (Astra)

Notable Losses: Wanderlei Silva (Pride Critical Countdown 2005); Josh Barnett (Pride 31); Mauricio Rua (Pride Shockwave 2006); Lyoto Machida (UFC 76); Kazuo Misaki (Sengoku 9)

When Kazuhiro Nakamura tested positive for marijuana after his **UFC** 76 loss to the elusive **Lyoto Machida**, it confirmed something many of us had suspected for quite some time: Kazuhiro Nakamura is a guy wants to do **judo** and get high, and not necessarily in that order. The giant blue penguins that accompanied Nakamura to the ring in his **Pride** days were one hint. The ornate kimonos, umbrellas, and traditional jingasa hats coupled with respiratory masks and hitched-up floral print shorts that defined his UFC-era fashion sense were another. Now there could be no doubt. It should be noted that Nakamura protested the results of the drug test, but — well, come on.

A Yoshida Dojo fighter, Nakamura began competing in MMA after a successful judo career that saw him win a handful of minor international tournaments and place as high as an impressive third in the Japanese national championships (100 kg). He entered the Pride ring still very much in his athletic prime at age 24, and, perhaps because of this, Nakamura managed to adapt his judo throwing techniques to MMA much more fluidly than his mentor **Hidehiko Yoshida**, the vastly more accomplished judo player. Nakamura succeeded not just with inside and outside trips, but the dramatic hip and shoulder throws that one most associates with judo. Combine that ability with the smooth, calm groundwork he showed in his early bouts, and it seemed like the sky was the limit.

Except it totally wasn't. After an impressive debut in a losing effort to submission expert **Antonio Rogerio Nogueira**, Nakamura picked up solid wins over former UFC champions **Murilo Bustamante** and **Kevin Randleman** before facing **Wanderlei Silva** in what is in many ways the defining bout of Nakamura's career. Five minutes into a competitive fight, in which Nakamura was, shockingly, holding his own on his feet against one of the most feared strikers in the sport, Nakamura decided to undress, to remove his strange, short-sleeved **gi** jacket — *while the match continued*. This was, of course, an absolutely terrible idea. Nakamura was promptly floored, mounted, and pounded out.

The best one can say about the baffling ordeal that is Kazuhiro Nakamura's career is that he has fought some of the best in world at 205 pounds, often quite competitively. But he is without question on the outside of that group looking in. Cut from the UFC following back-to-back losses, Nakamura has found a home in the middleweight (190 pounds) division of **Sengoku.**

Nastula, Pawel

Height: 6′ **Weight:** 235 lbs

Born: 6/26/70 **Debut:** Pride Critical Countdown 2005 (6/26/05)

Career Record: 1-4

Notable Losses: Antonio Rodrigo Nogueira (Pride Critical Countdown 2005); Aleksander Emelianenko (Pride Shockwave 2005); Josh Barnett (Pride 32)

When Pawel Nastula stepped into the **Pride** ring on his 35th birthday to face heavyweight legend **Antonio Rodrigo Nogueira**, it marked the debut of the most accomplished international **judo** player to try his hand at mixed martial arts. The 1995 and 1997 world and 1996 Olympic judo champion in the 95-kilogram division, Nastula amassed an astounding streak of 312 consecutive wins over nearly four years, all the while battling top international competition. And so there was no slow build to Nastula's MMA career: he was immediately thrust into the sport's highest level.

He didn't fare well. An inexperienced and overmatched Nastula was stopped by Nogueira, and he was finished in subsequent fights by heavyweight contenders **Aleksander Emelianenko** and **Josh Barnett** as well. His only professional win came over one-dimensional striker Edson Draggo. While there's no shame in any of that, there's at least a little in this: following the Barnett fight, notably the only time Nastula has fought under the auspices of a state athletic commission, Nastula tested positive not only for **steroids** but for three banned stimulants as well. The usual denials followed.

After the demise of Pride, Nastula found his way to **Sengoku**, where he faced undefeated Korean fighter Dong Yi Yang in a bout that saw one of the sport's all-time baffling finishes. Yang, who was penalized for a series of blows to the groin in the first round, was nearly caught in a Nastula **arm bar** in the second. Yang escaped and scrambled back to his feet, while Nastula was slow to rise. Nastula indicated some problem with his protective cup to the referee. To Nastula's protests, the fight was stopped and awarded to Yang. Although officially recorded as a TKO, Nastula seems to be the first fighter to have lost a bout due to an arm bar *escape*, the lone distinction in Nastula's disappointing foray into mixed martial arts.

Nelson, Roy

Nickname: Big Country **Height:** 6′

Weight: 264 lbs **Born:** 6/20/76

Debut: Rage on the River (4/17/04) **Career Record:** 15-5

Notable Wins: Antoine Jaoude (IFL: World Grand Prix Finals); Brad Imes (IFL: Connecticut); Kimbo Slice (*The Ultimate Fighter* 10)

Notable Losses: Ben Rothwell (IFL: Moline); Andrei Arlovski (EliteXC: Heat); Jeff Monson (SRP: March Badness); Junior dos Santos (UFC 117)

Roy Nelson wants you to know that he's kind of a big deal. After his appearance on the tenth season of ***The Ultimate Fighter*** — in particular his first-round drubbing of **Kimbo Slice** in the fourth most-watched MMA fight in U.S. history — you're probably already aware of how much game Nelson manages to pack into that enormous, frowning, pendulous belly. Somehow, neither **Quinton**

In Their Own Words: Roy Nelson on what he learned from Ken Shamrock

"The one thing you have to respect about Ken is that he gets the whole entertainment side of the MMA business. That's one thing he showed me. You don't have to be the greatest fighter out there to make money in this sport. Myself, I've got a double bonus. I can fight and I can also entertain. I just try to be myself. Normally I'm a shy person, so I just try to put myself out there a little bit more. And a lot of times there are things that need to be said and nobody will say it. I don't mind being the mouthpiece."

Jackson nor **Rashad Evans** seemed to know much about Nelson's past as an IFL champion when they were selecting their teams. Maybe they just didn't care. But either way, the **Renzo Gracie** black belt somehow ended up the ninth pick out of an undistinguished group of 16 despite having gone the distance with the likes of **Jeff Monson** and "Big" Ben Rothwell.

With his decent hands, technical grappling, and surprising quickness, agility, and cardio for a man of his truly remarkable girth, Nelson is a tough night for anyone in the heavyweight division — even former **UFC** champion **Andrei Arlovski**. Nelson put Arlovski on his back in the first round of their **EliteXC** contest, and thoroughly outmaneuvered him on the ground before the fighters were inexplicably stood up despite Nelson threatening with a **Kimura** from well-established **side control**. It was an absurd call that cost him dearly, as he was tagged in the second and stopped for the first time in his career.

Nelson's entry into the UFC's heavyweight division was long overdue, and his win over the notorious Kimbo in front of an audience of millions helped prove that he's for real. Still, no matter how often you see Nelson perform, no matter how much skill he shows every time out there, you can't help but think about that belly. "That's a big belly," Quinton Jackson once said, with an air of almost philosophical consideration. "The biggest belly I ever seen."

Newton, Carlos

Nickname: The Ronin | **Height:** 5'9"

Weight: 170 lbs | **Born:** 8/17/76

Debut: EF 2 (4/26/96) | **Career Record:** 15-14

Notable Wins: Erik Paulson (Vale Tudo Japan 97); Pat Miletich (UFC 31); Jose Landi-Jons (Pride 19); Renzo Gracie (Pride Bushido 1); Shonie Carter (Warrior 1)

Notable Losses: Dan Henderson (UFC 17); Kazushi Sakuraba (Pride 3); Dave Menne (Warriors War 1); Matt Hughes (UFC 34, UFC 38); Renzo Gracie (IFL: Championship Final); Matt Lindland (IFL: Houston)

First and foremost, Carlos Newton fought beautifully. Both in victory — a back-from-the-brink submission win over Jose Landi-Jons, a title-fight upset over the great tactician **Pat Miletech** — and in defeat — slammed unconscious by a choked-out **Matt Hughes**, back and forth on the mat with a prime **Kazushi Sakuraba** — Newton was part of some of the greatest contests in the history of mixed martial arts. But Newton, who started young and peaked early, saw considerable decline after a brief fling with the **UFC** welterweight title, and

In Their Own Words: Carlos Newton on his UFC 34 match with Matt Hughes

"I won that fight. I know I did. Because Matt told me, pretty much, 'Yeah, I was out.' He made it pretty clear to me that he thought it was a lucky break. That fight was a great fight and it shows why this sport is so appealing. It's so unpredictable. You have to consider so many variables. At the end of the day, when a guy really does dominate in this sport, he isn't just the better man. He's the guy that has the wind to his back, making it happen."

never regained the form that saw him rise to the top of the MMA world before his 25th birthday.

Fittingly known as "The Ronin," Newton had no particular fight camp or even primary discipline with which he was associated throughout his career. As a teenager he began his study of traditional Japanese jiu-jitsu, **judo**, and general submission fighting that would form the basis of his self-styled "Dragon Ball Jiu-jitsu" at Moni Aizik's Samurai Club in Richmond Hill, Ontario. It would be easy to look at the slightly goofy name Newton gave his fighting style, the kame hame ha anime theatrics that followed each win, or the spectacularly ill-advised Afro-wigged "Bootylicious" entrance at **UFC** 34, and think Newton was, if not a joke, something less than completely serious. But that notion would be easily dispelled by watching any of his early fights. His 41-second dismantling of Erik Paulson — double-leg takedown, **side control**, **mount**, **arm bar** — in what was only Newton's second career bout would be as good a place to start as any.

Newton made his debut in the big time, such as it was in 1998, at UFC 17 in Mobile, Alabama, as part of a one-night middleweight (205 pounds) tournament that saw the first UFC appearances of both **Dan Henderson** and, in a reserve bout, **Chuck Liddell**. In his opening round bout, the undersized but technically superior Newton made short work of Bob Gilstrap, catching him in a **triangle choke** in the first minute. A narrow, split decision loss to Henderson in a barnburner of a tournament final took nothing away from the seemingly unlimited potential on display from the 22-year-old that night.

Newton followed that performance with an absolute classic in his next fight. His **Pride** 3 bout against Kazushi Sakuraba was a wide open, fluid grappling contest that has yet to be equaled in the decade since. Both fighters slipped into and out of submission attempt after attempt until Sakuraba threatened with a **toe hold**, setting up the tight **knee bar** that ended the fight.

Success in Pride and **Shooto** led to a UFC welterweight title shot against Pat Miletich, who was undefeated in the Octagon in seven fights, four of them title defenses. In the third round, Newton seized on an uncharacteristic, momentary lapse on Miletich's part, and secured the rarely seen bulldog or schoolyard choke to become the UFC's youngest champion. His reign would be brief, however, and it would end in controversy.

In the second round of Newton's first title defense at UFC 34, it looked like Newton had Matt Hughes where he wanted him. Newton threw up his legs in a triangle choke attempt, trapping Hughes' head and one of his arms, but the choke wasn't fully applied — Newton's leg wasn't *quite* in the right position across the back of Hughes' neck. Hughes knew he was in trouble, and although he wasn't able to break the hold, he managed to stand and lift Newton over his head, backed up against the cage, as Newton made the final adjustments to the triangle. What followed looked more like a **pro wrestling** powerbomb than anything else. Newton was out, but so was Hughes — he'd been choked out standing. Understandably, referee **John McCarthy** awarded the match — and the title — to the fighter who *wasn't* flat on his back, the victim of a massive slam. When Hughes regained himself, moments later, he seemed as surprised as anyone to learn that he'd won.

A rematch naturally followed, but this time the finish was far more decisive: Hughes established side control, trapped one of Newton's arms between his legs, and pounded his way to a stoppage in the fourth round. Between those two Hughes fights, Newton managed to squeeze in another classic, a Pride bout against Jose "Pele" Landi-Jons. The grappler overcame the fearsome striker to finish with a beautiful arm bar.

Aside from two fine technical matches with fellow **International Fight League** coach **Renzo Gracie** — a split decision win in 2003, a split decision loss in 2006 — things have not gone well for Carlos Newton in either the ring or the cage. The fighter who seemed so promising in his mid-twenties looked washed-up by 30. Granted, Newton has pursued other avenues and interests to a much greater extent than most professional athletes: plans to undertake a career in medicine eventually yielded to the study of architecture, his current passion and pursuit, and he's found financial security outside the fight game. It's impossible to find fault with a fighter taking steps to prepare for a time when the bright lights have faded. Still, you can't help but wonder what kind of fighter Carlos Newton could have been had the soft-spoken Ronin found a first-rate group of training partners in his prime, and dedicated himself to the sport full-time. You can't help but wonder how many more classics we might have seen.

Nogueira, Antonio Rodrigo

Nicknames: Minotauro, Big Nog | **Height:** 6'3"
Weight: 235 lbs | **Born:** 6/2/76
Debut: WEF 5 (6/12/99) | **Career Record:** 32-6-1 (1 No Contest)

Notable Wins: Jeremy Horn (WEF 8); Mark Coleman (Pride 16); Heath Herring (Pride 17, Pride Critical Countdown 2004, UFC 73); Bob Sapp (Pride Shockwave); Dan Henderson (Pride 24); Mirko Cro Cop (Pride Final Conflict 2003); Josh Barnett (Pride Shockwave 2006); Tim Sylvia (UFC 81); Randy Couture (UFC 102)

Notable Losses: Dan Henderson (Rings: King of Kings 1999); Fedor Emelianenko (Pride 25, Pride Shockwave 2004); Josh Barnett (Pride Final Conflict Absolute); Frank Mir (UFC 92)

One of a pair of twins born in the city of Vitoria da Conquista, Brazil, Antonio Rodrigo Nogueira's life is defined by the one thing he didn't share with his twin (confusingly, a professional fighter named **Antonio Rogerio Nogueira**). When he was ten years old, Nogueira was hit by a truck. He was in a coma for days, but he lived, apparently coming out of the experience with a drive and lack of fear that defines who he is as a fighter. He has a mentality, and a large scar on his back, that helps distinguish him from his twin brother — a fine fighter, but not a transcendent one like Rodrigo.

A judoka almost since birth, Nogueira took up **boxing** in his teens. More importantly, he met Ricardo De La Riva, a revolutionary student of **Carlson Gracie** who was redefining the sport of **Brazilian Jiu-jitsu**. Nogueira got his black belt in April 1999. Like many BJJ schools at the time, only black belts were allowed to fight professionally. Just two months later, Nogueira would take the plunge into MMA competition, beating **UFC** veteran David Dodd at WEF 6.

In Their Own Words: Antonio Rodrigo Nogueira on fighting Randy Couture in his hometown

"I had a mental picture of the fight, starting two weeks before. I knew I would go into the Octagon and the people would boo me. My heartbeat was going more and more. But my breathing made my heart rate go down. I came here and I made a good show for them. People are going to appreciate that. I come from another country to make a show for them."

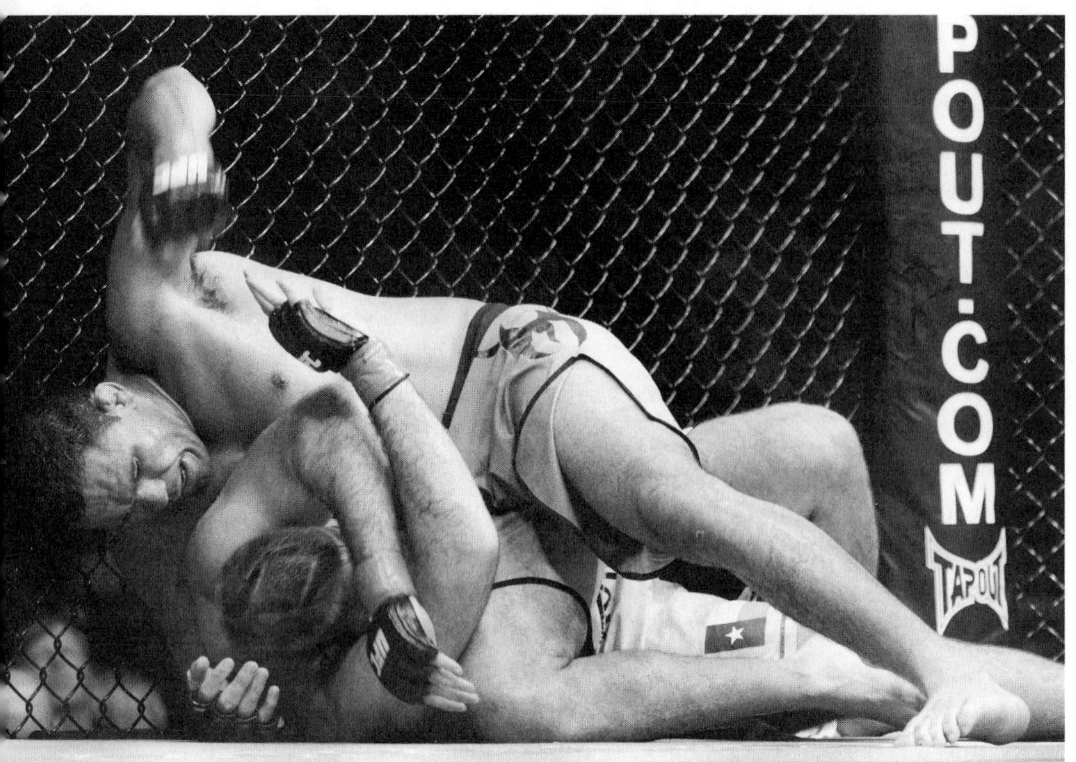

Nogueira immediately showed he was a prospect to be reckoned with, both in America and in Japan for **Rings**. He was beaten in a controversial decision by **Dan Henderson** in the first Rings King of Kings tournament in 1999, but came back to win the tournament (which featured top fighters like **Fedor Emelianenko**, **Jeremy Horn**, **Randy Couture**, **Kiyoshi Tamura**, and **Renato Sobral**) the next year, winning five fights and the $250,000 prize.

The victory put Nogueira on the map in Japan, and soon the biggest company in the world came calling. **Pride** was poaching all of the top stars in Rings, treating the smaller company like a glorified minor league feeder system. It was in Pride that fans saw a fighter with the potential to be special. He beat the best wrestler in MMA history, **Mark Coleman** with a **triangle choke/arm bar** combination to show he had what it took on the ground, then stood toe-to-toe with a banger like **Heath Herring** on the very next show to prove he could hang in there with a tough brawler.

The win over Herring made Nogueira the Pride heavyweight champion, a title he defended for almost two years. He submitted **Enson Inoue**, **Pancrase** standout Semmy Schilt, and his old nemesis Dan Henderson in that period, all great wins over top class opponents. But it was another fight that made him a legend.

Bob Sapp was a neophyte, but that inexperience came in a 360-pound package of pure muscle. Sapp would go on to become a mainstream celebrity in Japan. He would be so busy with his outside commitments that there would be little time for things like training and learning the fight game. But that would come later. This version of Bob Sapp was in the best shape he would ever be in and knew just enough to be incredibly dangerous. He overwhelmed Nogueira with pure size, slamming him like a rag doll, once even spiking him head first with a **pro wrestling** powerbomb.

Sapp may have hit like a truck, but as we know, Nogueira had been hit by a truck before. He survived Sapp the same way he survived as a child. When the moment was right, he struck, submitting Sapp with a textbook arm bar. It was an amazing moment, a real life David versus Goliath.

Eventually, Nogueira would run into a goliath he couldn't simply pop in the head with a slingshot and then arm bar. The goliath was 230 pounds, pale, and slightly doughy. His name was Fedor Emelianenko and he was the best fighter in the short history of MMA. The two men fought three times. Once, in the first contest, Nogueira could barely stand up straight, collapsing in the streets of Tokyo because of a pre-existing back issue on the way to the arena. In the second fight, Nogueira was doing well before an inadvertent head butt forced a no contest. It was the third battle that showed once and for all who was the better man.

Fedor brushed aside every Nogueira submission attempt, showing the world a new level of speed, power, and technical prowess. He won a unanimous decision and from that point forward, Nogueira, once the best heavyweight in history, had to settle for being second best.

Besides Fedor, only one other man beat Antonio during his 21-fight career in Pride: former UFC champion **Josh Barnett**. In his final fight with the promotion, Nogueira avenged that loss. He joined many of Pride's best in the **UFC** with a big win in his pocket and the UFC title on his mind. Before he could earn a title shot though, he first had to reacquaint himself with an old friend.

Nogueira and Heath Herring had one of the most action-packed heavyweight fights in MMA history. The rematch inside the UFC Octagon had a lot to live up to, but it did not disappoint. Herring hit Nogueira as hard as a man can hit another man at UFC 73. The tough champion has few memories of this epic back-and-forth; he went through much of it in a daze after a Herring kick rocked him. Somehow Nogueira survived, winning a three round decision on instinct alone.

The Herring fight showed clearly what many had suspected for some time. The once-great man's reflexes had slowed dramatically. Although he was surviving thanks to his legendary toughness, Nogueira was taking beating after beating, and they were taking a toll on his physical well-being.

He survived another shellacking, coming from behind once again to beat the gargantuan **Tim Sylvia** for the UFC interim heavyweight title. The UFC had a problem. They could tell fans Nogueira was a great fighter until they were blue in the face. Hard-core fans were comfortable with him and other Pride mainstays in the main event. But to the bulk of American MMA fans, he and fellow Pride refugee **Quinton Jackson** were virtual unknowns.

The UFC fixed that problem with the best weapon in the promotion's considerable marketing arsenal: a coaching appearance on ***The Ultimate Fighter***. Nogueira's opposite number was **Frank Mir**, a former UFC champion coming off a huge win over **Brock Lesnar**, the closest thing to Nogueira/Sapp the sport had ever seen. The two were a study in contrasts, Nogueira coming off as a loveable guru and Mir as the cocky and brash golden boy. Unfortunately, the fight between the coaches that culminated the season at UFC 92 wasn't a coming out party for the good guy. Nogueira suffered from a bad staph infection that prevented him from training properly. He looked lethargic and was stopped standing by Mir, a fighter not known for his striking prowess.

Against fellow legend Randy Couture, however, it was a different story. This was the Nogueira of old — or at least it resembled a slightly slower version of him. He and Couture put on an epic performance in front of Randy's hometown Portland, Oregon, crowd at UFC 102. It was a fight for the ages, and one that propelled Nogueira back into title contention. Now a known commodity, the aging legend is looking for one more magical moment to cap a memorable career.

Nogueira, Antonio Rogerio

Nicknames: Minotoro, Little Nog **Height:** 6'2"

Weight: 205 lbs **Born:** 6/2/76

Debut: Deep 2nd Impact (3/18/01) **Career Record:** 19–3

Notable Wins: Tsuyoshi Kohsaka (Deep 6th Impact); Guy Mezger (Pride 24); Kazuhiro Nakamura (Pride 25, Pride Bushido 4); Kazushi Sakuraba (Pride Shockwave 2003); Alistair Overeem (Pride 29, Pride Critical Countdown Absolute); Dan Henderson (Pride Total Elimination 2005); Vladimir Matyushenko (Affliction: Day of Reckoning)

Notable Losses: Vladimir Matyushenko (UFO: Legend); Mauricio Rua (Pride Critical Countdown 2005); Rameau Thierry Sokoudjou (Pride 33)

It's got to be tough to be a **Brazilian Jiu-jitsu** black belt, a Brazilian and South American Games super heavyweight **boxing** champion, and a Pan American

Games bronze medalist, and *still* be seen as the second best fighter in your own immediate family. Such is the fate of Antonio Rogerio Nogueira. When your identical twin brother is **Antonio Rodrigo Nogueira** — an absolute legend in the sport, the top heavyweight submission artist in the game, admired in equal measure for his technical prowess, toughness, and incredible heart — that's just how it's going to be.

But Rogerio — "Minotoro" rather than "Minotauro," but more often referred to as "Little Nog" by MMA fans to avoid confusion — has spent virtually all his fighting career as a legitimate top ten fighter in his own right. Competing in **Pride**'s stacked middleweight (205 pounds) division, Nogueira amassed an impressive record of 8–2. The first of his Pride losses is easy to overlook: clearly there's no shame in dropping a decision to **Mauricio Rua** at a time when the dangerous "Shogun" was at his absolute peak. In Pride's 2005 middleweight Grand Prix, Rua tore through **Quinton Jackson**, Alistair Overeem, and **Ricardo Arona** in less than 15 total minutes. Rogerio lasted longer than those three top contenders combined.

It was Nogueira's other Pride loss that raised more than a few eyebrows. When the unheralded judoka **Rameau Thierry Sokoudjou**, in only his fourth professional fight, knocked the accomplished boxer Nogueira out in only 23 seconds, it was hard to know what to make of it. When Sokoudjou went on to do much the same against Ricardo Arona, it seemed as though Nogueira had been the first victim of the division's new star. As Sokoudjou has fallen back down the light heavyweight ladder, though, it seems Nogueira simply got caught with something of a lucky punch. Since that enormous upset, Nogueira has fought and won in a variety of promotions — **Sengoku**, **Affliction**, Hardcore Fighting Championships, Jungle Fight — before the welcome news broke in the summer of 2009 that Nogueira would be joining his brother in the **UFC** by year's end.

North-south

A dominant ground fighting position in which the attacker, kneeling above his opponent's head, pins his opponent chest to chest. **Judo** players know the position as kami-shiho gatame (upper four-quarters hold) and consider it a distinct pinning technique, whereas **Brazilian Jiu-jitsu** practitioners often classify the position as a variation of **side control**. Under the widely observed **Unified Rules of Mixed Martial Arts**, in which knees to the head of a downed opponent are illegal, the north-south position is far less dangerous for the pinned opponent than it is under the more relaxed rule sets followed in the Japanese **Pride**, **Dream**, and **Sengoku** organizations. Nevertheless, under any rules, the pinned fighter must work to improve his position. He can turn to his knees, incrementally work his way towards the **half-guard** and **guard** positions, or attempt a more dramatic escape, like throwing his legs up over his own head in an attempt at **rear mount**, or a sweep into either side control or a north-south pin of his own. The fighter on top has a variety of possibilities for submissions, most prominently the **Kimura**, **arm bar**, **arm triangle** choke, or the aptly named north-south choke, in which the attacker encircles his opponent's neck (sometimes trapping an arm) and constricts blood flow with his biceps.

See also **positional hierarchy**

Ogawa, Naoya

Height: 6′4″ **Weight:** 253 lbs
Born: 3/31/68 **Debut:** Red Devil Free Fight (9/27/97)
Career Record: 7–2
Notable Win: Gary Goodridge (Pride 6)
Notable Losses: Hidehiko Yoshida (Pride Shockwave 2005), Fedor Emelianenko (Pride Final Conflict 2004)

What might Naoya Ogawa have been? A four-time world **judo** champion, seven-time All-Japan judo champion, and Olympic silver medalist, Ogawa could have entered MMA as one of the world's most decorated grapplers. Instead, he entered the sport as a professional wrestler looking to add credibility to his fake fighting persona. From the world of **professional wrestling**, **Antonio Inoki**'s golden boy brought with him a showman's sense of style and flair, a loyal following of Japanese fans who had been captivated by Ogawa's era-defining bouts with Shinya Hashimoto, and, unfortunately, matches with fixed outcomes. It's difficult to say anything conclusive about thrown or worked fights, but if Ogawa's **Pride** fights against **Gary Goodridge**, Masaaki Satake, and Stefan Leko look a little strange to you, you're definitely not alone. Ogawa's legitimate MMA contest experience could well be limited to his one-minute mauling at the hands of **Fedor Emelianenko**, and a New Year's Eve loss to judo rival **Hidehiko Yoshida** that was, at the time, the richest payout in MMA history. None of this detracts from the splendor of "Hustle March," Ogawa's self-performed wrestling theme song, or the awkward hip thrusting that so often accompanies it.

Okami, Yushin

Nickname: Thunder **Height:** 6′2″
Weight: 185 lbs **Born:** 7/21/81
Debut: GCM: Demolition 1 (9/8/02) **Career Record:** 24–5

Notable Wins: Anderson Silva (ROTR 8); Evan Tanner (UFC 82); Dean Lister (UFC 92)

Notable Losses: Jake Shields (ROTR 9); Rich Franklin (UFC 72); Chael Sonnen (UFC 104)

Although it resulted from a disqualification, Yushin Okami holds the distinction of being the last man to defeat **UFC** middleweight champion **Anderson Silva.** With no particularly threatening challengers to Silva's throne on the horizon, and with Silva's continued talk of an imminent retirement from mixed martial arts in order to test his skills in the sport of **boxing**, that's a distinction Okami might hold permanently. And while a DQ win — in a match where he was actually on the run almost from the moment the opening bell sounded — might not necessarily seem like much for Okami to hang his hat on, it might have to do. Because no matter what he does, who he beats, Yushin Okami can't seem to catch a break in the UFC.

A big middleweight with strong **wrestling** and **judo** as well as a dangerous **ground and pound** game, Okami comes to MMA by way of the Wajyutsu Keisyukai gym in Tokyo, best known as the home of lightweight submission stylist **Caol Uno**. After fighting his way through the ranks of Japan's second tier promotions, and making one-fight appearances in both **Pride**'s Bushido series and K-1, Okami competed in **Rumble on the Rock**'s 2006 welterweight tournament, where he earned his DQ win over Silva before dropping a decision to **Jake Shields** in a close contest.

Later that same year, Okami made his UFC debut, and impressively fought three times in just over four months, earning a decision win over Alan Belcher and stopping both Rory Singer and Kalib Starnes with strikes. These impressive prelim performances earned Okami a main card bout against the popular Mike Swick, and a solid decision win over the former ***TUF*** contestant earned him an opponent with some real name value: former middleweight champion **Rich Franklin**. After two close rounds, Okami nearly finished Franklin with a **Kimura** in the third, only to lose in a unanimous decision. Although far from a robbery, as it was not difficult to make the case that Franklin narrowly won rounds one and two, the decision was controversial, as clearly Okami came closest to ending a very even fight.

You'd think this would have cemented Okami's status as a legitimate contender in the middleweight division. At the very least, you'd think this would have positioned Okami as a main card fighter, rather than an up-and-comer relegated to the preliminaries. But in a promotion that understandably values entertainment value above all else, Okami was hampered by a reputation as a fighter content to grind out a decision rather than throw caution to the wind and push desperately for a finish.

It's this reputation, more than any hole in his game or weakness his opponents have been able to identify, that has held Okami back and kept him out of the limelight. More recently, injuries have taken their toll too: a broken hand put a rematch and title challenge against Anderson Silva on ice. When he returned from injury, Okami was once again relegated to the preliminaries. In the UFC, it's not enough to win. You've got to win the right way to make it to the top.

Olympians

They are the best athletes in the world in their respective sports, sacrificing their time, bodies, their youth to the country they love. They represent what is best about athletics, a purity that transcends the big-money business sports (and even the Olympics themselves) have become. Is there any question about why MMA would want to have some of these true blue American Olympians in their back pocket?

In the early days of no-holds-barred fighting (now called mixed martial arts or MMA) the events were often unregulated and unbelievably violent. Many of the fighters, frankly, were not great athletes. They were exactly what they appeared to be: local tough guy martial artists and bar fighters, waiting in a long line to be humbled by one of the Gracie brothers or another skilled grappler. The sport evolved quickly. Fighters saw what was working and soon the contests were filled with highly skilled, well trained athletes. But the reputation as human cockfighting, the reputation of being a sport for thugs and bar room fatsos was harder to shed. You could argue about whether **Royce Gracie** was an athlete or a street fighter. But no one could argue with an Olympic medal.

While there were many superlative athletes involved in MMA from the beginning, the first bona fide Olympian to make his mark in the Octagon was heavyweight Mark Schultz. Schultz was interested in MMA, working out with **Rickson Gracie** and giving the jiu-jitsu ace plenty of trouble before eventually tapping out to a **triangle choke**. Schultz didn't come to **UFC** 9 in Detroit intending to fight; he was cornering Canadian **Dave Beneteau**. When Beneteau had to withdraw, UFC matchmaker **Art Davie** spent hours convincing Schultz to fight. He was in good shape for a bout, but hadn't really prepared, physically or mentally, for a fight. He was inclined to say no, but the promotion, desperate not to lose a fight in the midst of a distracting legal battle, gave him 50,000 reasons to say yes.

Schultz — in borrowed gear — outwrestled **Gary Goodridge** in his first and only MMA fight, bloodying the big man's face and forcing "Big" **John McCarthy** to stop the fight. Schultz might have been the best UFC heavyweight of all time, but we'll never know. Schultz was the head **wrestling** coach at Brigham Young University, a conservative school in Utah, and the UFC, regularly lambasted in the media, was quickly becoming a hot button issue in Republican circles thanks to the efforts of Arizona Senator John McCain. He was told he could fight or he could coach, but he couldn't do both. He kept his day job, leaving MMA with a great "what if."

Two other Olympic gold medalists, Kenny Monday and Kevin Jackson, also gave MMA a try, in **John Perretti**'s **Extreme Fighting**. But the wrestler that really left his mark on the sport never appeared on the medal stand. **Mark Coleman** had finished seventh as a freestyle wrestler in the 1992 Olympics and immediately established himself as a transcendent force in MMA, developing a brutal **ground and pound** style that was hard to stop.

While Coleman was a freestyle wrestler, focused on explosive double leg takedowns at the expense of almost everything else, two other Olympians who specialized in Greco-Roman wrestling took a different approach. **Dan Henderson** (10th place 1992, 12th place 1996), **Matt Lindland** (2000 silver medalist), and teammate **Randy Couture** (himself an Olympic alternate) all made ends meet in MMA while continuing to pursue their Olympic dreams.

The three formed **Team Quest** in Portland, Oregon, and developed a new approach for wrestlers in MMA. The Greco style, one that doesn't allow holds below the waist, ended up being particularly well suited to MMA. The wrestler could control his opponent against the cage, scoring points with short punches, or taking the action to the mat on a whim. Henderson was arguably the most successful Olympian (or wrestler) of all, winning two world titles in **Pride**, ironically on the strength of his right hand more than any wrestling techniques.

Other Olympic gold medalists have moonlighted in the fight game, including boxer **Ray Mercer**, wrestler Rulon Garner, and the **judo** triumvirate of **Pawel Nastula**, **Hidehiko Yoshida**, and Makoto Takimoto. While Yoshida became a star in Pride, the other judokas saw limited success. In Henderson and Coleman's day, pure grapplers could excel based on their one extraordinary skill. By the time the judoka entered the sport, fighters needed to be ready to battle in all areas at a very high level — at least they did against top competition.

The most interesting one-time wonder was Egyptian Karam Ibrahim Gaber. Gaber had dominated the 2004 Olympic Games in Athens, Greece. Even against the best in the world he proved to be on an entirely different plane, winning the semi-finals 11–0 and taking the gold medal by a score of 12–1. Perhaps such success demanded a dose of humility.

Karam, who wrestled at 211 pounds, was booked in a match with 240-pound Pride stand-out **Kazayuki Fujita** for New Year's Eve 2004. Gaber was confident in the limited **boxing** he had worked on in the gym, and like many wrestlers before him and many to follow, forgot what brought him to the dance. He stood and traded with Fujita, more than holding his own, but only for a minute. At 1:07 of the first round, Fujita shellacked him with a punch that almost resembled a **pro wrestling** clothesline. It was another lesson that fighters needed to learn: once the cage door shuts, MMA recognizes no pedigree, only performance.

Omoplata

An arm lock, often though not exclusively executed from **guard**, in which the attacker traps the opponent's arm between his legs and attacks the elbow, shoulder, or both in a manner similar to the **Kimura** or ude garami. As the Japanese term for this technique sankaku garami ("triangular entanglement") implies, the attacker's legs are often locked into a triangular configuration to secure the hold. A vastly more common attack in **Brazilian Jiu-jitsu** than **judo**, the technique is almost universally known by its Portuguese name, literally "shoulder blade."

Although a staple of **gi**-grappling, the omoplata ends few matches in the slipperier no-gi context of mixed martial arts. Hidetaka Monma, Alberto Crane, Gil Castillo, and **Mac Danzig** are among the handful of fighters who have managed to finish fights with the technique. The omoplata has proven effective, however, as a transitional move setting up the **arm bar**, **triangle choke**, and a variety of sweeps.

Dustin Hazelett's spectacular submission win over Tamdan McCrory at **UFC** 91 is a prime example. From guard, Hazelett triangled his legs around McCrory's right arm, contorting it such that McCrory was forced to somersault to relieve the pressure. A single-minded Hazelett secured the hold once again, straightened McCrory's arm, and applied a twisting, inverted arm bar that was either a sickening sight or a thing of beauty, depending on your disposition. While a win by omoplata remains a rare sight, and is unknown at the sport's highest level, there are countless ways the technique can lead to victory, however indirectly.

Ortiz, Tito

Nickname: The Huntington Beach Bad Boy
Height: 6'2"
Weight: 205 lbs
Born: 1/23/75
Debut: UFC 13 (5/30/97)
Career Record: 15-7-1

Notable Wins: Jerry Bohlander (UFC 18); Guy Mezger (UFC 19); Wanderlei Silva (UFC 25); Yuki Kondo (UFC 29); Ken Shamrock (UFC 40, UFC 61, UFC: The Final Chapter); Vitor Belfort (UFC 51); Forrest Griffin (UFC 59)

Notable Losses: Guy Mezger (UFC 13); Frank Shamrock (UFC 22); Randy Couture (UFC 44); Chuck Liddell (UFC 47, UFC 66); Lyoto Machida (UFC 84); Forrest Griffin (UFC 106)

It was a simple T-shirt, plain black cotton, adorned with none of the flourishes and elaborate script that have come to define MMA couture. Tito Ortiz slipped it on after beating the **Lion's Den**'s **Jerry Bohlander** at **UFC** 18. The predecessor of the "Condom Depot" ad on the fighter's trunks, it read simply, "I Just F**cked Your Ass." It was crude, socially unacceptable, and pure bad boy. Tito Ortiz, who had been one of many hard-nosed wrestlers looking to make it in the UFC, was suddenly a cartoon character. The Huntington Beach Bad Boy was born.

Much has been lost in the wake of Tito Ortiz's epic feud with UFC President **Dana White**. "You know I hate Tito," White once said. "Why are you asking about him?" That answer is easy. Tito Ortiz, whether you whitewash him out of the official UFC history or not, is the most dominating and important champion of the UFC's dark ages and early rise to prominence. He won the light heavyweight title in a match with **Wanderlei Silva** and never looked back. He defended the belt five times, something **Randy Couture**, **Chuck Liddell**, and even **Frank Shamrock** can't match. Along the way, Ortiz became the UFC's signature villain, understanding that colorful and cocky characters sell fights. Ortiz, much to White's chagrin, always understood that in the end, fighting was a business.

It all started with **Tank Abbott**. The UFC's original bad boy needed a wrestler to train with and Ortiz was a willing victim. Like so many wrestlers, Ortiz had a real affinity for the sport, picking things up quickly and enjoying it more than a little. But Ortiz wasn't a professional yet. He was still dreaming of wrestling success, enrolling at Cal State Bakersfield, and looking to follow in the footsteps of NCAA champion Stephen Neal. It wasn't meant to be. An argument with a hard-nosed coach sent Ortiz scurrying. It was the best thing that could have possibly happened to the struggling UFC promotion.

Ortiz's feud with **Ken Shamrock**'s Lion's Den lit a fire beneath an entire sport. After the T-shirt gimmick at UFC 18, Ortiz took it up a notch at the next show against Bohlander's teammate **Guy Mezger**. Mezger had beaten Ortiz at UFC 13, when Tito had very little MMA training, and Ortiz felt he was disrespecting him in the pre-fight buildup. The T-shirt he put on after dismantling Mezger was

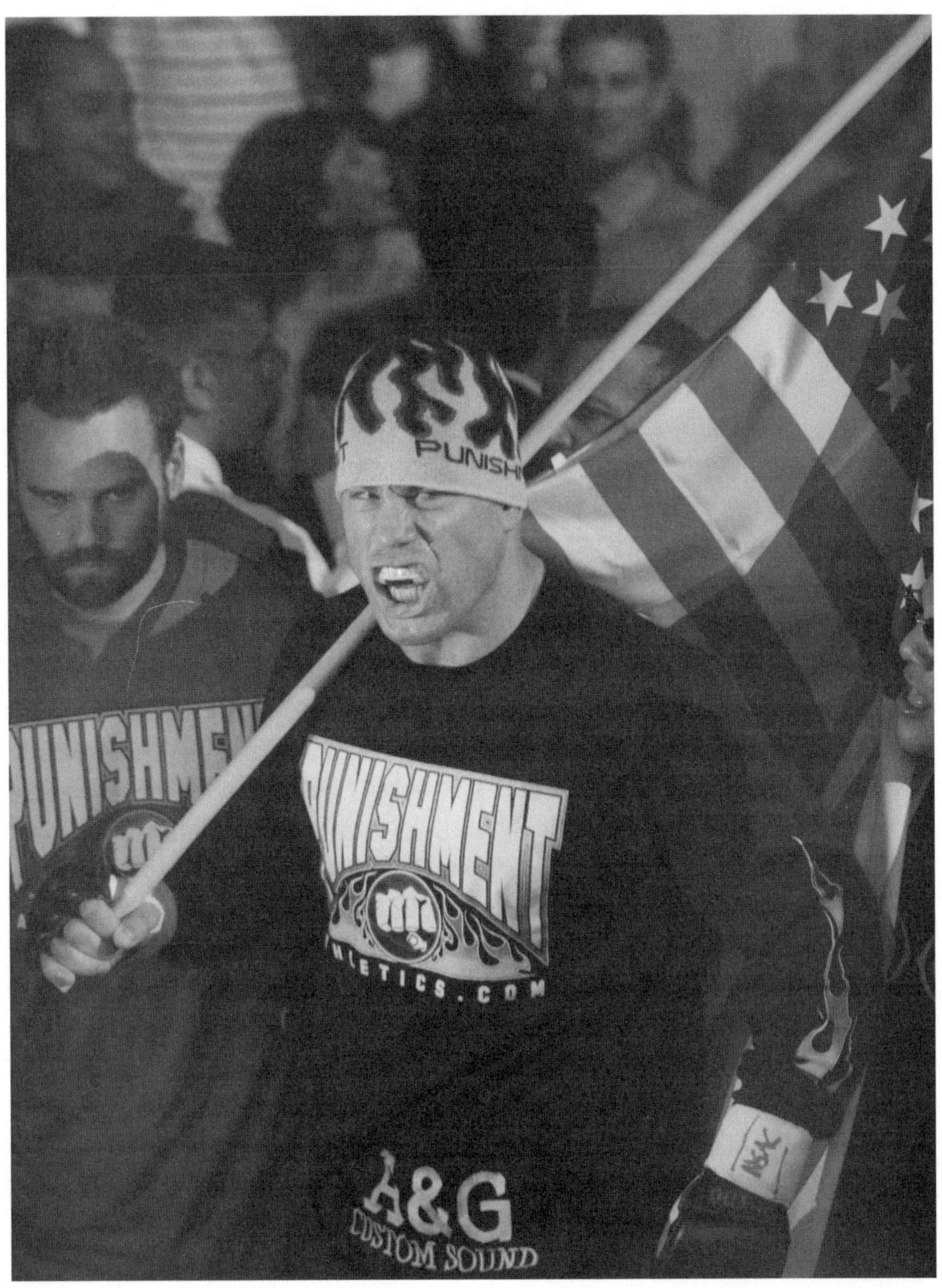

more to the point: “Gay Mezger Is My Bitch.” Shamrock was furious, leaning over the top of the cage, pointing and screaming. “Tito,” the legendary fighter said. “Don’t let me catch you wearing that T-shirt.”

It was the start of something special. Unfortunately, Shamrock was under contract with the WWE. The fight between Ken and Ortiz would have to wait more than two and a half years. Luckily, the UFC had an ace up their sleeves,

Ken's adopted brother Frank. Frank Shamrock had established himself as the best fighter in the world. He and Ken were estranged, not even on speaking terms, but a good story is a good story.

In the storyline, Frank was looking to avenge Ortiz's victories over the Lion's Den, and that's just what he did. It was the performance of a lifetime, a display of physical endurance unparalleled in MMA history. Shamrock simply outlasted Ortiz, as strong in the fourth round as he was in the first. Ortiz learned important lessons that night in 1999. He was the better fighter, he was confident of that. But he wasn't the best prepared, and it cost him; he vowed not to let it happen again.

Ortiz perfected his art and his theatrics over the next three years. He won the title in a fight with Wanderlei Silva, giving the UFC bragging rights when Silva went on to become the top fighter in Japan's **Pride** promotion. Once he had the title, Ortiz worked hard to keep it. He beat all comers, becoming the UFC's best fighter and best draw at the gate. After his wins, Ortiz would pretend to dig a grave, symbolically burying the opponent he had just defeated.

At UFC 40, he finally got his shot at Ken Shamrock. Shamrock was game, but out of his league. It was the biggest pay-per-view since **Zuffa** had gotten the UFC back on cable networks, finally proving to fans that the new generation of fighters like Ortiz were a notch ahead of the old guard. It was his fifth consecutive defense, and afterward Ortiz was as cocky as ever. The UFC had their villain. Now they needed a hero, and they found one in Randy Couture.

While Ortiz held out for more money, going back and forth in the media with his former manager White, Couture beat Chuck Liddell to win the interim title. Fans and critics had suggested Ortiz was afraid of Liddell, rumors he lent credence to by immediately returning to fight Couture. Ortiz was confident that the older Couture, a fighter who had lost twice in a row in the heavyweight division, wouldn't be much of a challenge. Instead, Couture proved he was as good as ever, just a little undersized against the mammoth heavyweights. He took Ortiz, who had always won the **wrestling** phase of any fight, down to the mat with ease. To punctuate the storyline, Couture spanked the bad boy as the fifth round came to an end. With tears in his eyes, Ortiz put his UFC title around Couture's waist. He would never taste gold again.

Next for Tito was the long awaited showdown with Liddell. The two had trained together briefly when White managed both men. Ortiz used their friendship as a reason not to give Liddell a well earned title shot. Liddell thought Ortiz was ducking him. The resulting war of words captivated UFC fans, who for the most part sided with the likeable Liddell. When he knocked Ortiz out in the second round at UFC 47, Liddell became a bona fide star.

After consecutive losses, Ortiz desperately needed to get his career back on track. He was able to do that, beating **Patrick Côté** and **Vitor Belfort**. But by this point Ortiz's most compelling feud was with White and UFC management. Anything happening in the cage seemed secondary to this bigger battle. After the Belfort fight, Ortiz left the promotion, teasing a move to Pride or a jump to **pro wrestling**. Because of his problems with White, a return to the UFC appeared unlikely.

As they say, appearances can be deceiving. Ortiz made a dramatic UFC return more than a year later to coach against his hated rival Ken Shamrock in the third season of ***The Ultimate Fighter***. It was the best season of the show, both in terms of drama and in the ratings. Ortiz, the ultimate bad boy, became the crowd favorite, showing an effortless ability to coach and motivate his fighters. Shamrock, by contrast, seemed angry and out of touch. It was a shocking role reversal.

After the show, the two men stepped into the Octagon; 12 weeks of compelling television drama had built up a heated grudge match. UFC 61 set pay-per-view records for the company thanks to the two men, inexplicably put second from the top behind a **Tim Sylvia/Andrei Arlovski** fight for the heavyweight crown. In front of a pro-Ortiz crowd, Tito pounded Shamrock out in less than two minutes. The end was nigh when referee **Herb Dean** jumped in to stop the fight, a tad early for the final fight in that monumental feud.

The crowd was livid, Shamrock was livid, and Dana White had a hard choice. Instead of a profitable fight on pay-per-view, White booked a rematch that he showed free on Spike TV to make things right for the fans who felt cheated by the unsatisfactory ending. The third fight was almost a carbon copy of the second. Shamrock could no longer back up his tough talk. He could promote a fight as well as anyone; he just couldn't hold up his end anymore.

Two high profile wins put Ortiz in line for a title shot against his old nemesis Liddell. Since they last met, "The Iceman" had taken over for Ortiz as the face of the company. The bad blood had only gotten worse over the years and Tito convinced many that this time he had a real shot. It was a tough matchup for Ortiz, no matter how much trash he talked. Liddell was a good enough wrestler to stay on his feet. And while he had made a great deal of progress with his **Muay Thai** boxing, Ortiz just wasn't able to compete with the heavy-handed champion. He couldn't win, but he did a good job of convincing fans he might. UFC 66 set a record for pay-per-view buys that stood for almost three years.

Ortiz was still a huge star, but physically he was falling apart. A bad back hobbled him, to the point that he could barely walk at times, let alone train.

His fought two future champions, battling **Rashad Evans** to a draw and falling victim to **Lyoto Machida** in the final fight of his contract. He pushed those both to the brink, but seemed more interested in a proposed **boxing** match with White that never happened. Every confrontation with White seemed to distract him from the real mission at hand: returning to the top of the sport.

In the year and a half he was out of the promotion, Ortiz was busy. Just before the Machida fight, he starred in Donald Trump's *Celebrity Apprentice*. In 2009 Ortiz and porn star girlfriend Jenna Jameson had twin boys. More importantly for his fighting career, Ortiz had surgery to repair his damaged back. Ortiz was ready to make a serious comeback. He teased going to **Strikeforce**, **Affliction**, and **EliteXC**. When the news dropped that he had made a decision, it came from his old nemesis White and it came on Twitter: "welcome back tito :)"

Osborne, Jeff

In his 15 years in the sport, former pro wrestler Jeff Osborne has literally done it all. He's been a fighter, an event promoter in his home state of Indiana with HOOKnSHOOT, an announcer for the **Ultimate Fighting Championship**, the commissioner of BodogFight, and one of the biggest proponents of women's fighting on the planet.

Osborne has never been flashy. As an announcer, he was best known for his robotic mannerisms, monotone voice, and encyclopedic knowledge of the sport. The events he promotes reflect these same values. Osborne never attempted to promote a major pay-per-view, never tried to bring in major name fighters he couldn't afford, and always seemed to make money.

In the early days of MMA, Osborne's HOOKnSHOOT often featured fighters who were UFC-bound. **Yves Edwards**, Aaron Riley, Steve Berger, and Chris Lytle all made their mark with Osborne before becoming UFC mainstays. Today, that's no longer the case. Osborne tends to sell local fighters to a local audience. But he did remain a step ahead of others in the sport by being the first promoter to fully embrace women's MMA.

Osborne promoted his first women's fight all the way back in March of 2001, between Judy Neff and Jessica Ross, years before anyone outside of her family had high hopes for one **Gina Carano**. In 2002, Osborne took it to another level, promoting North America's first all women's card.

HOOKnSHOOT Revolution, held in April 2002, was a huge challenge for Osborne. He matched up 14 women in seven fights out of an entire field of about 30 legitimate female fighters. Many of the fights were blowouts, but the women proved to doubters that they could entertain just as well as the men. Osborne found a diamond in the rough Tara LaRosa on this card, and Angela Restad and Mayra Conde put on a fight that would make any male fighter proud.

The event was a success at the box office and later on DVD, and women became a staple of Osborne's Indiana-based promotion. He remains a huge supporter of women in the sport and runs the popular GFIGHT.TV Web site.

Overeem, Alistair

Nickname: Demolition Man **Height:** 6'5"

Weight: 255 lbs **Born:** 5/17/80

Debut: 10/24/99 **Career Record:** 33-11 (1 No Contest)

Notable Wins: Vitor Belfort (Pride Total Elimination 2005, Strikeforce: Revenge); Igor Vovchancyn (Pride Critical Countdown 2005); Mark Hunt (Dream 5); Kazayuki Fujita (Dynamite!! 2009); Brett Rogers (Strikeforce: Heavy Artillery)

Notable Losses: Chuck Liddell (Pride Total Elimination 2003); Antonio Rogerio Nogueira (Pride 29, Pride Critical Countdown Absolute); Mauricio Rua (Pride Final Conflict 2005, Pride 33); Fabricio Werdum (Pride: Total Elimination Absolute); Ricardo Arona (Pride Final Conflict Absolute); Sergei Kharitonov (Hero's Tournament Final)

For most of his up and down career, Alistair Overeem was a perfectly serviceable fighter. He had the solid kickboxing you'd expect from a Dutchman and a surprisingly effective **guillotine choke** that was his go-to submission hold. Against lesser lights, he shined. But when up against the best in the light heavyweight division, it was no contest (and not the kind of no contest he earned by smashing **Mirko Cro Cop** in the groin over and over again). Against **Chuck Liddell, Ricardo Arona,** and **Mauricio Rua,** Overeem showed that he was somewhere just below a top tier fighter.

Then he grew. And grew. Then he grew some more. By the time he was done, the new Overeem looked like the Hulk, the old Overeem the scrawny and weak Bruce Banner by comparison. Almost overnight he was sporting 50 pounds of solid muscle and was suddenly the hottest prospect in the heavyweight division. The new Overeem, called Ubereem by his fans, went on a rampage through the weakened Japanese scene that was unprecedented in MMA history. He looked like the muscle-bound cult favortie **Bob Sapp,** but a Bob Sapp who could fight. Like Sapp, Overeem was a multisport hit in Japan; along with his MMA wins, he had a solid showing in K-1, including a knockout win over Badr Hari and a close decision loss to Remy Bojansky.

This success in Japan was great for Overeem's career. It was less great for San Jose, California, based **Strikeforce.** In 2007, Overeem quietly won the

Strikeforce heavyweight title from **Paul Buentello.** It would be his last fight on American soil for almost three years. As Overeem grew in stature in Japan, Strikeforce went through its own transformation from regional promotion to national powerhouse. Eventually Strikeforce President Scott Coker made an offer Overeem couldn't refuse and he was back in the fold, demolishing prospect **Brett Rogers** in a scary display of power and skill.

Coker was building to Strikeforce's first pay-per-view spectacular. The plan was for Overeem to clash with the immortal **Fedor Emelianenko** in the main event. But it's always dangerous to make long-term plans in MMA. **Fabricio Werdum**, who had beaten Overeem in **Pride** as well, threw a wrench in the works by upsetting Emelianenko in less than two minutes. If Overeem was going to lock horns with the Russian legend, it wouldn't have quite the shine it did months before. Fedor or no Fedor, after his impressive national television debut against Rogers, the world awaits Overeem's next move with baited breath.

P

Pancrase

Many people assume that modern MMA started with **UFC** 1 at the McNichols Arena in Denver, Colorado, in November 1993. In fact, the first mixed fights had taken place months earlier at the Tokyo NK Hall in Japan, where a small troupe of maverick pro wrestlers had taken the wrestling business back to its roots.

Masakatsu Funaki and **Minoru Suzuki** had tons of potential in traditional **professional wrestling.** Funaki had a real shot at succeeding **Antonio Inoki** as the biggest star on the Japanese circuit, and Suzuki had an amateur pedigree that could take him far. But the students of Yoshiaki Fujiwara and Karl Gotch weren't looking to take pratfalls for giant American steroid machines like the Road Warriors. They wanted to take wrestling back to a simpler time, when the matches were real and the showmanship was in the context of actual competition.

The idea wasn't exactly new. Inoki had wrestled a variety of martial artists in matches billed as the real deal back in the 1970s. In the 1980s the UWF and its offspring presented the public with "shoot-style" wrestling, predetermined matches using real techniques and real holds and designed to be realistic enough to pass for an actual fight.

It was Funaki and Suzuki who wanted to take it a step further. They wanted a match, contested under modified pro wrestling rules (break when you get into the ropes, no punches to the face), that was a legitimate shoot. The concept was unheard of, failure the predicted result. With straight matches up and down the card, the first event featured just 13 minutes and five seconds of action spread over six fights. Something would have to change.

The skill of the Japanese fighters and the exceptional American **Ken Shamrock** far exceeded their game but untrained opponents. They had learned an important lesson, deciding from then on to make sure the crowd got a show before they disposed of their hapless foes.

"You didn't want to go out there and just destroy them," Shamrock said. "You want to go out there and maybe give some encouragement to try harder next time."

Funaki realized quickly that the key to the promotion's survival was the creation of new stars. As a pro wrestler, he understood that it took a star to make a star. With that philosophy is mind, Funaki and other stalwarts like Shamrock and Suzuki would sometimes intentionally lose matches to lesser opponents in an attempt to make them big-time players.

Soon a new generation of fighters was catching up with the original trio of greats. **Bas Rutten**, a Dutch kickboxer who lost two early matches to Shamrock, was able to master the mat game and become the best fighter in the promotion, going on a 19-fight win streak, unheard of in Pancrase history.

"It was the loss to Ken. I really had it," Rutten said. "I'm a very sore loser and I knew what the problem was. It was because I didn't train any ground. That decided it for me. . . . So I start concentrating on grappling twice a day, seven days a week. I really took it to the next level."

Rutten's match with Funaki in September 1996 was the promotion's high point and its last grasp at relevance in a rapidly changing fight game. Rutten dismantled the legend standing, bloodying the man who had taken the time to teach him the submission game, in order to create the opponents for himself that he couldn't otherwise acquire.

The Pancrase game was maybe a little too refined, lacking the violence fans saw from the UFC and the newly created **Pride** organization in Japan. Funaki attempted to adjust course, going to more traditional **Vale Tudo** rules in 1998, including the legalization of punches to the head. But it was too lit-

In Their Own Words: Ken Shamrock on Pancrase rules

"Pancrase was, in the standup, open hand palm strikes. You could kick, but you wore shin guards and knee pads. You could knee when you were standing too and punch to the body. On the ground, pretty much everybody went for submissions. There wasn't a lot of striking. It was definitely a lot more technical with submissions when you were on the ground. And the standup had more of a combination of punching and kicking than early UFC. In the UFC it was closed fist, bare-knuckle. And no rules. It was a huge difference from Pancrase, where you could grab a rope and escape and start over again standing up. But you lost points when you did that. You lose five points and the fight's over. That's a whole lot of chances to escape out of a submission hold. It was a lot more strategic and you had to be a lot more skilled in your submission game. The UFC was less skilled, but a lot more dangerous than Pancrase."

tle, too late. Most of the top foreign talent had left for greener pastures in the UFC and Pride. To make matter worse, the established Japanese stars were wearing down. Years of grueling training sessions and a fight every single month had taken their toll on the Pancrase founders.

Today, the promotion continues to put on a monthly show. But it isn't an important player, even on a diminished Japanese scene. It is now firmly an independent promotion, and only the most die-hard of fans can remember a time when the best fighters in the world wore the famous Pancrase banana hammock trunks and shin guard combination.

Parisyan, Karo

Nickname: The Heat
Height: 5'10"
Weight: 170 lbs
Born: 8/28/82
Debut: Kage Kombat 12 (2/1/99)
Career Record: 19-5-1
Notable Wins: Nick Diaz (UFC 49); Matt Serra (UFC 53)
Notable Losses: Georges St. Pierre (UFC 46); Diego Sanchez (UFC Fight Night 6)

Over the course of his **UFC** tenure, Karo Parisyan has proven to be both one of the sport's most exciting fighters and one of its most frustrating. A junior national **judo** champion trained under Gokor Chivichyan and "Judo" **Gene LeBell**, Parisyan was the first American fighter to consistently employ the throwing techniques of judo (usually dependent on the **gi**) in the no-gi context of **The Unified Rules of MMA**. Parisyan's highlight reel includes spectacular examples of harai goshi, seoi otoshi, and sumi gaeshi, but it also includes an infamous and bizarre appearance on season five of ***The Ultimate Fighter*** in which a cocky Parisyan confronts an unsuspecting **Nate Diaz**, asking, "Do you even know me? Do you know who I am?" Parisyan earned a title shot against **Matt Hughes** with a hard-fought decision win over **Matt Serra**, but a hamstring injury kept him from entering the Octagon against the welterweight champ. Decision victories over mid-level opposition have followed, but Parisyan's career has never truly gotten back on track after his loss to **Diego Sanchez** in a fight-of-the-year contender in 2006. Held back by diagnosed anxiety issues, indifferent training, and, most recently, banned prescription painkiller use, this fading welterweight contender has proven to be his own worst enemy.

Penn, B.J.

Nickname: The Prodigy
Height: 5'9"
Weight: 155–170 lbs
Born: 12/13/78
Debut: UFC (5/4/01)
Career Record: 15-6-1
Notable Wins: Caol Uno (UFC 34); Takanori Gomi (ROTR 4); Matt Hughes (UFC 46); Renzo Gracie (K-1 World Grand Prix Hawaii); Sean Sherk (UFC 84); Diego Sanchez (UFC 107)
Notable Losses: Jens Pulver (UFC 35); Lyoto Machida (Hero's 1); Georges St. Pierre (UFC 58, UFC 94); Matt Hughes (UFC 63); Frankie Edgar (UFC 112)

Prodigies are very rare, but very real. In music there was Wolfgang Amadeus Mozart, composing by the age of five and entertaining royalty with his intricate work. The Brontë sisters took it upon themselves to write a novel each and the results changed English literature forever. Mike Tyson won the heavy-

weight boxing title at just 19 years of age. And B.J. Penn conquered the Mundials, **Brazilian Jiu-jitsu**'s Super Bowl, after training in the sport for just three years.

It wasn't just that Penn almost immediately became one of the best mixed martial artists on the planet. It wasn't just that he was winning; it was the way he was winning. Penn did things no one had seen before. He blitzed the super-tough **Caol Uno** and knocked him out in less than ten seconds. Then — and this is what made the moment — instead of waiting around for the interminably long series of announcements, Penn climbed out of the cage and sprinted to the back. The message was simple and endeared Penn to the fans: he had done what he came to do. All the rest of the pomp was nonsense. He was there to fight and that part of the evening was over. He was ready to go home.

Penn had a knack for the dramatic. After failing to win the **UFC** lightweight title, losing in a shocker to **Jens Pulver** and fighting Uno to a draw in a rematch, Penn didn't wait around for another shot. Instead he moved up a weight class and dismantled the best fighter on the planet, welterweight champion **Matt Hughes**.

The Hughes fight was Penn's last in the UFC for almost two years. This was before ***The Ultimate Fighter*** and the UFC simply wasn't the biggest game in town. Penn was happy to continue fighting in the Octagon; he just wanted to be able to cash in on paydays in Japan too. The UFC held firm, stripped Penn of the title, and watched the best fighter in the world take on middleweights and even heavyweights, like future UFC light heavyweight champion **Lyoto Machida**, for K-1 in Japan.

The Penn that made his return to the UFC was not the young and energetic star who left the promotion in 2004. He insisted on fighting at 170 pounds and looked a little chunky at that weight, like a Hawaiian Buddha. Never one to shy away from controversy, Penn came to the cage carrying the welterweight title belt he had won from Hughes and never lost in competition. His bravado was tremendous, but it was his lack of commitment to training, not his lack of chutzpah, that cost him big. In a fight for the number one contender's slot against the young Canadian star **Georges St. Pierre**, Penn looked amazing through one round. He busted St. Pierre up with a pinpoint left jab, clearly taking the round. Then the wheels came off. An exhausted Penn couldn't keep up with the hungrier fighter and dropped a split decision. The difference, perhaps, was a huge slam from St. Pierre that was the most memorable moment of the third round.

One judge, Penn, and many fans thought he had won the fight. And perhaps he did — otherwise why would karma work in his favor? St. Pierre was

In Their Own Words: B.J. Penn on controversy surrounding his fights

"It's kind of a catch-22. You know, you try to build up the fights and pump up the fights, but you never know how you're going to be portrayed. But you know for me, where my head is right now, it's just all about fighting.

"The Sean Sherk one, I just really didn't like the fact that Sean Sherk was cheating. So, you know, I was just kind of irritated about that. The whole GSP thing got started with hyping up the fight and then prime time where they wanted to portray me as an asshole instead of some guy, you know, passionate about winning his dream fight. Then Dana starts speaking, the stuff he doesn't even know about, saying I am surrounded by yes men. And then back and forth, and that just blew out of proportion. I'm just trying to go out and defend my title and walk out of the cage the 155-pound champion, and that's the only thing that's on my mind right now."

injured and unable to cash in on the title shot he had earned against Penn. B.J. was happy to step up and take on Hughes again. It was a fight fans had looked forward to for years and the arena was crazy for both men. Hughes was coming off his win over **Royce Gracie** and had never been a bigger star. Penn knew how to drive the audience into a frenzy. The atmosphere was electric. "I can't believe this is my job," exclaimed UFC color man **Joe Rogan**. Again, Penn dominated the early going, nearly finishing Hughes with a **triangle choke** to end the second round. Then, the engine died. Penn was exhausted and Hughes was able to take him down and pound him out. It seemed evident that the better fighter hadn't won the bout, merely the better conditioned one.

The consecutive losses sent Penn back where he belonged: the lightweight division. He reestablished himself as the best fighter in the world at 155 pounds, winning the UFC title against **Joe Stevenson** and defending that belt against former champion **Sean Sherk** at UFC 84. B.J also continued his knack for controversy, calling out Sherk for his steroid use and licking his opponent's blood from his hands in both bouts. After a disastrous superfight with St. Pierre at UFC 94, Penn was back defending his title.

Many thought Penn would reign well into the new decade. He was training hard for the first time in years and seemed committed to establishing his legacy as one of the sport's all-time greats. A devoted, well conditioned, and focused Penn was a scary sight — to everyone but unheralded challenger **Frankie Edgar**.

At UFC 112, the promotion's debut in the Middle East, Edgar outworked and outhustled Penn on his way to a five-round decision. The king was unceremoniously tossed from his throne, but the legend of B.J. Penn lived on. When the two meet again, the challenger will be favored instead of the champion. It's never smart to bet against B.J. Penn.

Pentagon Combat

Renzo Gracie wanted the fight, wanted it really badly. As the sport of MMA continued to grow worldwide, the long feud between **Luta Livre** and **Brazilian Jiu-jitsu** was beginning to fade away. But **Eugenio Tadeu** was different. Ever since he fought Renzo's cousin **Royler Gracie** all the way back in 1984, he had been a thorn in the Gracies' side.

Even though his big money Japanese debut at **Pride** 1 against **Akira Shoji** was just two weeks away on October 11, 1997, Gracie was willing to risk injury and defeat for this fight. It wasn't just a chance to create an emphatic ending for the decades-long feud between the two styles; it was also an opportunity to bring big-time **Vale Tudo** back to its spiritual home in Rio de Janeiro, Brazil.

Sheik Tahnoon Bin Zayed Al Nahyan was more than just one of thousands of neophyte jiu-jitsu students in California, interested in the art after the success of **Royce Gracie** in the **UFC**. He was also the son of the Sheik Zayed bin Sultan Al Nahyan, the former leader of the United Arab Emirates in the Middle East. His late father's wealth was estimated to top $24 billion. The family lived a life of leisure and Sheik Tahnoon wanted to continue studying jiu-jitsu. Instead of staying near his teacher to continue his instruction, Sheik Tahnoon simply brought jiu-jitsu instructor Nelson Monteiro with him back to the United Arab Emirates.

Monteiro had an amazing opportunity. For years Vale Tudo had been all but illegal in Rio de Janeiro and constant fights in the street between martial artists left the sport with a bad reputation among locals and politicians. The fight game had slowly been creeping back into Brazil, with the **International Vale Tudo Championship** (IVC) and World Vale Tudo Championship (WVC) both running shows in the country. These shows featured top fighters but were poorly produced and distinctly minor league. American fighter **Mark Kerr** was shocked when he was snuck into the basement of a hotel for his WVC fight.

Monteiro was proposing something altogether different for an event called Pentagon Combat. With Tahnoon's enormous fortune and, as a huge fan of the sport, his complete support, Monteiro wanted a world-class event for

Brazil. He brought in a nice cage rather than a dilapidated old boxing ring, planning on making this an enjoyable evening for fight fans and young couples out on the town.

Monteiro and event organizers made one fatal mistake: they skimped on security. Hundreds of fighters and street kids invaded the Tijuca Gymnasium hours early, staking a claim on cageside seats and refusing to budge (or to pay admission). What could have been the potential tipping point for MMA in Brazil was instead its death knell.

It was a startlingly hot day in Brazil, and as the temperatures rose, so did the tempers. **Oleg Taktarov** beat Sean Alvarez and **Murilo Bustamante** beat UFC 12 champion **Jerry Bohlander** in the other top fights. But in Brazil, the only fight that mattered was coming on last. By the time the main event began, the arena was a powder keg, ready to explode at any moment. Tadeu and Gracie had a spirited back-and-forth battle. Gracie claimed after the fight that Tadeu had oiled himself up before the fight and then rubbed himself dry. When the sweat began to pour, however, he became too slippery to control. The only way to control him was to push him up against the fence.

While the two men did battle, a more interesting contest was taking place cage side. The two camps, Luta Livre and jiu-jitsu, were fighting over coaching territory, arguing, screaming, and shoving. Ten minutes into the fight, the entire cage was packed with people, screaming and hanging on for dear life.

The fighters too were just looking to survive. Both men were exhausted, with Tadeu throwing lackluster leg kicks and Renzo too tired to do anything but watch them connect. As he toppled to the ground next to the cage and refused to stand, daring the Luta Livre ace to join him on the mat, Renzo sent the crowd into a fever pitch. They were screaming, shaking the cage, even kicking him through the mesh.

Then the lights went out, a man was tossed from the cage, and a full scale riot began. Chairs were flying, gun shots were heard from a distance, and a potential classic ended with no winner. No contests are fairly common. No contests because of a riot? Only in Brazil.

What could have been a major MMA promotion in Brazil was finished before it started. The riots confirmed the poor reputation of the MMA community in the country. Sheik Tahnoon wanted no more to do with MMA. He turned his energies and money in another direction. The death of Pentagon Combat led to the creation of the Abu Dhabi Combat Club and the world's top grappling contest. From death comes life: MMA in Brazil, busy confirming the basic principles of the universe.

Perretti, John

Before there was an **Ultimate Fighting Championship**, John Perretti says he had a vision in his mind of a battle between the martial arts to see who the best fighter in the world was — and to see which styles were real, and which were more show than go. If only Woodstock 2 hadn't been such a huge disaster, **Extreme Fighting** might still be around, thriving, the top promotion in the world instead of forgotten to history. John Perretti might have been the acerbic and foul-mouthed president, in place of **Dana White.**

"We were booked for Madison Square Garden before the first Ultimate," Perretti said. "They didn't even exist. We were backed by Polygram Records. We were ready to go on. I had all my fighters lined up."

But when Woodstock went up in smoke, the executive who had cut a deal to bring Extreme Fighting to the air lost his job. "They lost $28 million in one day," Perretti said. "They put us on hold. We had to go out and refinance the whole show." By the time Perretti and his partner Donald Zuckerman put all the pieces back together, they had missed their window. Extreme Fighting, fairly or not, would be seen as a UFC copycat.

Despite following in the UFC's very large footsteps, Extreme Fighting was able to carve out an audience by bringing together a collection of world-class athletes. Perretti traveled around the world looking for fighters. Unlike the UFC's **Art Davies**, who often looked at a resume or an old training tape, Perretti wanted to see what each man could do personally. "I wrestled with everybody, he said. "I did standup with everybody. I was their proving ground."

To critics, and there are many, this is typical Perretti hyperbole. There is a famous story in MMA circles about Perretti's claims to personally test the sport's athletes. After Extreme Fighting went under, Perretti was scooped up to be the UFC's new matchmaker. He was bragging to others in **SEG** about rolling on the mat with wrestling stalwart **Randy Couture**, impressed with how well Couture handled himself. When asked about the encounter, Couture was confused. "I've never even met John Perretti," the future UFC legend revealed.

Besides being a matchmaker and a martial artist, Perretti was also the color commentator for Extreme Fighting and his own grappling competition, The Contenders. Good-looking and smart, Perretti had trouble hiding his disdain for fighters, other announcers, and even legendary wrestler Dan Gable. He spent much of his time on the air, especially when he had guest shots on UFC broadcasts, critiquing fighter's body types and disparaging their techniques. The greatest Perretti announcing moment was his complete dismissal of former UFC champion **Dan Severn.** Asked by announcer **Mike Goldberg** what Severn had left to offer, Perretti replied, "Did he ever have anything to offer?" The problem with this honest assessment? Severn was about to come out for a main event fans had paid good money to see.

Perretti was never afraid to say what he was thinking. The world seemed to be split into two factions, those in his camp and his bitter enemies. Opinions of his UFC matchmaking exemplify this divide. Some, including Perretti, say he was revolutionizing the promotion. Others suggest that he sent out a booking sheet to two agents. One would go to super-agent **Monte Cox**. Once Cox filled in his fighters, the sheet would be sent to agent Phyllis Lee to fill in their opponents.

When **Zuffa** bought the company in 2001, Perretti lost a struggle with long-time UFC consultant **Joe Silva**. Silva was a veteran martial artist like Perretti, and had the advantage of following the sport and its fighters as closely as anyone on the planet. Silva became the UFC matchmaker; Perretti cut the sport out of his life entirely. He continued his work as a Hollywood stuntman and coordinator, only occasionally appearing on Eddie Goldman's *No Holds Barred* podcast. He made his return to the broadcast booth in 2008 for **Yamma Pit Fighting**. The show was like an SEG reunion, bringing together former UFC owner **Bob Meyrowitz**, announcers Bruce Beck and **Jeff Blatnick**, and Perretti. The show was an epic disaster. With no follow-up in site, it appears Perretti's mixed martial arts contributions are all in the past. And while many have forgotten his role in the sport's creation, he will be sure to remind anyone who will listen.

"They [Zuffa] were born on third base," Perretti said. "And they think they hit a triple."

Petey, My Heart!

MMA's most infamous verbal submission, or urban myth? Two fights into his return to mixed martial arts after a four-year stint in **professional wrestling**, **Ken Shamrock** was absolutely tearing it up against iron-jawed wrestler **Kazuyuki Fujita** at **Pride** 10. Miraculously, Shamrock was able to keep the fight standing, and consistently landed clean head shots that would have finished virtually anyone else. But late in the first round, pressed into the corner by the relentless Fujita, Shamrock ran out of steam. Then it happened: an exhausted Shamrock said *something* to his cornerman **Pete Williams** that caused him to throw in the towel. But what? Did he really exclaim, "Petey, my heart!" as internet legend has it? "I remember my heart was coming through my chest and I was seeing white spots," Shamrock told radio host Bob Carson. "I don't remember exactly what I said. It was a long time ago."

In Their Own Words: Ken Shamrock on training for Kazuyuki Fujita

"I had some issues that were really weighing on me heavy. I was going through a divorce and my kids were basically dropped off on me two or three weeks before the fight. I had a two-bedroom apartment and suddenly four children living there. They just got dropped off and left there. I was scrambling to try and provide for them. I completely lost focus on everything I was doing. I had some health issues, like high blood pressure and everything that comes along with that. It was a bad time for me. But you know what, man? It was a learning experience. I was able to get in there and do the best I could. It happened the way it happened, and that's the way it is. I would not sacrifice my family to win that fight."

Petruzelli, Seth

Nickname: The Silverback
Height: 6′
Weight: 205 lbs
Born: 12/3/79
Debut: WVF: Battlejax (8/26/00)
Career Record: 12-5
Notable Wins: Dan Severn (KOTC 32); Kimbo Slice (EliteXC: Heat)
Notable Losses: Matt Hamill (UFC: The Final Chapter); Wilson Gouveia (UFC Fight Night 9)

As far as we know, Seth Petruzelli is the only Smoothie King franchisee to hold a win over **Dan Severn**. He also managed both to shatter the myth of **Kimbo Slice** and to kill an entire MMA organization over the course of a mere three days. Seth Petruzelli, in short, is a hero.

After he crashed out of the second season of ***The Ultimate Fighter*** with a tough split decision loss to Brad Imes, and then out of the **UFC** altogether after back-to-back losses to **Matt Hamill** and Wilson Gouveia, there was every reason to think that was the last we'd see of Seth Petruzelli under the bright lights of the sport's biggest stage. But **EliteXC**, with its prime-time CBS network television deal, and a main event that fell apart at the last minute, made an offer Seth Petruzelli couldn't refuse.

EliteXC was in a bad way. **Ken Shamrock**, one day after holding up CBS for more money, was medically disqualified from taking part in his bout with YouTube sensation Kimbo Slice after a light, pre-fight workout session ended with a nasty cut over Shamrock's left eye. The promoters turned to Petruzelli, scheduled to face light heavyweight Aaron Rosa on the undercard, and offered him a spot against the man *Rolling Stone* magazine dubbed "The King of The Web Brawlers."

In Their Own Words: Seth Petruzelli on fighting Kimbo Slice

"I was warming up for my undercard fight and I was about 45 minutes from going out for my match. They told me Ken Shamrock was hurt and offered me the Kimbo fight and I accepted right away. I thought it would be awesome. The nerves actually kind of went away when they offered me that fight. I was nervous about my undercard fight, but the pressure kind of went away because there was nothing to lose. It was a win-win situation. I was taking it on short notice so if I went out there and lost, well, I did my best. If I won, obviously all this would happen.

"All I remember is him rushing me. And I saw his chin stick out. I was trying to throw a push kick and his chin stuck out and I threw kind of like a jab hook and caught him right on his chin. He went down to his knees and all I remember was seeing the blood on the ground and following up. I kept going and going and going. I knew if I just kept punching him the ref was going to have to jump in."

Proving definitively that the web is not the cage, Petruzelli, standing on one leg, dropped Slice with what looked like a nothing right hand seconds into the fight. Slice never recovered, and Petruzelli pounded him out for a TKO win 14 seconds into the first round. EliteXC's Jared Shaw, horrified, berated the referee for allowing supposedly illegal strikes to the back of Slice's head. Excitable CBS announcer Gus Johnson called it "the most remarkable victory in the history of mixed martial arts." Not exactly: Petruzelli was a legitimate, if undistinguished, MMA fighter, whereas Slice was one promotion's fantasy of what an MMA fighter might be.

Slice was finished, but Petruzelli wasn't. Two days later, talking to a Florida radio show about the strange, last-minute circumstances that led up to the fight, Petruzelli had this to say: "The promoters kinda hinted to me and they gave me the money to stand and throw with him; they didn't want me to take him down. Let's just put it that way. It was worth my while to try and stand up punch him." Although Petruzelli would later claim to have been misunderstood, and the Florida Department of Business and Professional Regulation investigated and found no wrongdoing, the mere suggestion of this kind of impropriety took its toll. EliteXC went from the UFC's most credible rival to a laughingstock overnight. Less than a month after Petruzelli's right hand shut down Kimbo Slice, his loose lips helped shut the doors of EliteXC for good.

Positional hierarchy

Once lightweight champion **B.J. Penn** had challenger **Kenny Florian** where he wanted him in the main event of **UFC** 101 — tired, on his back, holding fast — the Philadelphia crowd snapped to attention. Although Florian is a legitimate **Brazilian Jiu-jitsu** black belt, he was out of his depth against "The Prodigy," and the Philly fans knew it. Florian managed to entangle one of Penn's legs between both of his, offering him some measure of defense, but it was clear Penn wasn't content to settle into Florian's **half-guard:** he wanted to pass to **mount** and finish the fight. As Penn pushed down on Florian's thigh, trying to create enough space to swing his trapped leg clear, the crowd responded as though someone had landed a solid one-two combination. They weren't responding to a successful transition from half-guard to a dominant, potentially fight-ending position — that would come a little later, when Florian's defenses were broken down even further. At that moment, the Philadelphia fans were responding to Penn's mere attempt to pass the half-guard. "The audience *cheers* for that," color commentator **Joe Rogan** said with a hint of surprise, "which shows you how educated mixed martial arts fans are now."

It wasn't that long ago that any action on the ground more subtle than an elbow to the face or a match-ending choke or joint lock would be met with impatience or, at best, indifference from the live audience. The ground game is at once the heart of mixed martial arts and the most difficult facet of the sport for newcomers to grasp. The first-time viewer sees two fighters entangled on the mat, working tactically, methodically — and, at times, desperately — towards *something*, but what, exactly? Why, under a torrent of blows, expend so much energy and effort to change slightly the position of a leg, the angle of the hips? Because, in short, it makes all the difference. One minute, with just one of B.J. Penn's legs held between his ankles, Kenny Florian was in a position of relative safety. The next, with that leg freed, the end was in sight, and inevitable. Position is everything.

Although there can be (and often is) disagreement among martial artists about the finer points and relative merits of one ground position versus another, usually based on stylistic or personal preference, there are certain general, accepted truths about the hierarchy of positions in modern mixed martial arts competition that seem — for now, at least — fixed.

First off, all else being equal, it's better to be on top than on bottom. Although this sounds obvious, it was not apparent in early MMA, where Brazilian Jiu-jitsu practitioners were able to win from their backs with regularity against hapless fighters unfamiliar with the realities of submission grappling. But as the sport has evolved, submission defense has improved markedly among even non-grapplers. As submissions from bottom positions have become rarer, the intuitive advantages of fighting from the top have reasserted themselves. Better to strike an opponent who is beneath you, his head inches from the mat, than to work uphill.

That said, the **guard**, in which the bottom fighter controls his opponent's movements with his legs and hips, remains a fundamentally neutral position, or as near neutral as exists on the ground. If the bottom fighter is a far more advanced submission grappler than his opponent, it's entirely possible that the guard will prove to be to his advantage. If the top fighter is a particularly dangerous **ground and pound** specialist, then the advantage in the guard will in all likelihood be his. But given comparable levels of skill, the wide array of sweeps and submissions available to the bottom fighter and the striking advantage and opportunities for positional improvement open to the top fighter are, roughly, a wash.

As the fighter on top frees a leg and progresses to top half-guard (half-mount), the striking advantage he enjoyed in guard increases, particularly if he's able to keep his opponent flat on his back, rather than on his side, and he can begin to work towards a variety of chokes and arm locks. The bottom fighter from this position will look to set up a half-guard sweep, escape to his feet, or take something of a long shot on a submission attempt — but principally he'll look to reestablish his full guard, knowing that things are not, from his perspective, moving in the right direction. In **gi** grappling, there are circumstances in which the bottom player can be extremely dangerous from half-guard, but this is far less often the case in mixed martial arts.

Once the top fighter has passed the guard completely, both legs freed from the bottom fighter's entanglements, he has established a clearly dominant position. Whether the top fighter favors the mount or one of the many variations of **side control**, either way he seriously constrains his opponent's movements, threatens with a wide assortment of submissions, and enjoys a distinct striking advantage. Needless to say, the bottom fighter will do whatever he can to sweep his opponent from this position, in a best case scenario, or, failing that, to work his way back to the much safer half-guard. From underneath mount or side control, submission possibilities are minimal, striking options are poor — this is, in short, not the place to be.

The only worse place to be is **rear mount**, a position that affords virtually no offensive possibilities to the defending fighter. This is where the overmatched Kenny Florian found himself once B.J. Penn passed his half-guard in front of that keen Philadelphia crowd. Penn mounted and forced Florian to turn and expose his back with a flurry of blows to the head. Penn took the back, sunk his hooks deep to establish rear mount, and began hunting for the **rear naked choke**. Florian, ever game, did his best to roll and escape, but Penn seamlessly transitioned from rear mount to mount and back again — from dominance to dominance to dominance — until he slipped his arm across the challenger's throat, and forced the grimacing Florian to concede the bout. Position is everything.

See also **guard**, **half-guard**, **mount**, **rear mount**, **north-south**, and **side control**

Pride Fighting Championships

Tokyo's Pride Fighting Championships began with a single premise: could **professional wrestling** star **Nobuhiko Takada** fight for real? That question was quickly answered in the negative, but it didn't stop parent companies Kakutougi Revolution Spirits and later Dream Stage Entertainment from turning what was intended as a one-off event built around Takada and **Brazilian Jiu-jitsu** legend **Rickson Gracie** into Japan's most successful mixed martial arts promotion. Before it collapsed under the weight of a yakuza scandal, Pride set the standard with its top-notch production values and a roster of international talent second to none.

Early Pride, however, was borderline unwatchable — unless you happen to be a fan of listless 30-minute draws with the occasional worked match thrown into the mix. After Takada's quick submission loss to Gracie in the main event of the inaugural show, the company's priority was to rehabilitate their star and promote a rematch, and Pride was not above staging fights rather than risk his drawing power. There can be little doubt Takada's Pride 3 win over Kyle Sturgeon was a sham, but if it helped pack the Tokyo Dome for the Gracie rematch that followed a few months later, it was good business as far as Pride officials were concerned. After Takada's second loss to Gracie, **Mark Coleman** was the next American paid to do the honors in Pride's ongoing efforts to legitimate their pro wrestling hero.

Although Takada was never able to translate his gift for impressively realistic fake fighting into competitive success in Pride, one of his pro wrestling understudies, **Kazushi Sakuraba**, went on to become one of the most accomplished fighters in all of mixed martial arts. He began turning heads with a grappling classic against **Carlos Newton** at Pride 3 and a strong showing against **Vitor Belfort**, and then came the Gracies: **Royler**, **Royce**, **Renzo**, **Ryan**, each falling in turn. Sakuraba combined the showman flair of professional wrestling with submission grappling skills of the highest order and succeeded where Takada had failed. In the process, Sakuraba became the face of Pride to the tens of thousands who attended live events and the prime time audience of millions watching at home on Fuji TV.

Sakuraba's winning ways ended abruptly when he ran into **Wanderlei Silva**, who stopped Pride's great hero three times in just over two years to establish himself as the king of Pride's middleweight (205 pounds) division. Silva claimed his middleweight title in November 2001 at Pride 17, the same event that saw **Antonio Rodrigo Nogueira** become Pride's first heavyweight champion with a win over **Heath Herring**. Silva would hold his title until Pride's second last show, six years later; Nogueira's reign would be comparatively short-lived as the unstoppable **Fedor Emelianenko** soon emerged as the greatest heavyweight in the history of the sport. Pride would award lightweight (160 pounds) and welterweight (183 pounds) titles after a 2005 tournament largely contested in their secondary Bushido series, with **Takanori Gomi** and **Dan Henderson** emerging as the respective champions.

Throughout the Pride era, its Grand Prix tournaments were the organization's crowning glory. The 2000 Grand Prix is best remembered as the site of Sakuraba's epic 90-minute battle against Royce Gracie, but it also featured Mark Coleman's return to championship form after falling on hard times. The 2003 middleweight Grand Prix brought **Chuck Liddell** to Japan to try his luck against the best collection of 205-pound fighters in the world, and come up short to **Quinton Jackson**, who in turn was blown out by Wanderlei Silva, still on top of his game. Silva's closely contested semi-final bout against **Hidehiko Yoshida** helped turn the Japanese **judo** legend into Pride's top native star as Sakuraba's long fade continued. In 2004, the heavyweights had their turn, and to no one's surprise Emelianenko and Nogueira met in the finals, with Emelianenko again emerging the victor. The 2005 edition of the middleweight Grand Prix signaled the end of Silva's unquestioned dominance over the division, but **Mauricio Rua** kept the tournament title within the **Chute Boxe** camp with a devastating knockout of **Ricardo Arona**. A somewhat anticlimactic 2006 openweight tournament marked **Mirko Cro Cop**'s first major championship, but at that point the writing was already on the wall.

On June 5, 2006, Fuji TV canceled its television contract with Dream Stage Entertainment, Pride's parent company, citing breach of contract after prominent Japanese weekly *Shukan Gendai* ran a series of articles alleging strong yakuza ties. Seia Kawamata, promoter of a New Year's Eve 2003 fight card called Inoki Bom-Ba-Ye, stated in an interview with the magazine that he was the victim of yakuza intimidation after he signed Pride champion Fedor

Emelianenko to fight on his show. According to Kawamata, not only was Pride head Nobuhiko Sakakibara aware of this intimidation — he was in the room when yakuza directly threatened Kawamata's life. Without the support of network television, the promotion was doomed.

After a few last gasps, including a pair of brilliant Las Vegas shows, Pride closed its doors. **Lorenzo and Frank Fertitta**, the men behind the **UFC**, bought Pride's assets and intended to run events in Japan indefinitely. But Japanese networks did not receive the new American owners with any enthusiasm whatsoever, and a return to television proved impossible. The Fertittas closed Pride's Japanese office October 4, 2007, and Dream Stage Entertainment employees took up with K-1 to form **Dream**, the successor to both Pride and K-1's **Hero's** series. Most of Pride's top talent went to the UFC — with the notable exception of the elusive Emelianenko, much to UFC President **Dana White**'s frustration.

Pride's death signaled the end of any real international competition. Dream and **Sengoku** have their Japanese niche, and American challengers will no doubt continue to emerge so long as MMA remains a hot commodity, but with Pride gone it's clear that the true future of the sport both in America and abroad rests with the UFC.

Professional wrestling

Pro wrestling and MMA are like peas in a pod. Although many MMA fans don't like to hear that, the fact remains that MMA and wrestling have a long-running historical connection, both in Japan and in the Americas.

The sport in the Americas traces its path back to Japanese judoka **Mitsuya Maeda**. Maeda was one of the Kodokan's top fighters; his mission was to spread the art of **judo** far and wide, all around the world. His round trip ticket as a judo emissary was essentially paid for by his nascent pro wrestling career.

Maeda liked testing himself, and in the United States the men most likely to give him a contest were **catch wrestlers** on the professional circuit. Wrestling may have been a show, but its roots were in real contests. While the shows for the fans were staged, plenty of hard sparring went on in the gym before the matches. Soon Maeda joined their traveling sideshow and found himself traveling to Europe, Mexico, and finally Brazil.

It was in Brazil that Maeda, the professional wrestler, taught the basics of judo to a young Brazilian named **Carlos Gracie**. Gracie's nephew **Rorion Gracie** took these teachings, after a generation of practicing and perfecting the care-

fully crafted ground techniques, and created the **Ultimate Fighting Championship** to showcase them. In a very real sense, the UFC would not exist without professional wrestling. Not only did a pro wrestler help create **Gracie Jiu-jitsu**, but the leading stars of the early UFC were either pro wrestlers (**Ken Shamrock** and **Dan Severn**) or pro wrestling–style characters (**Tank Abbott** and **Kimo Leopoldo**).

In Japan, the connections between MMA and pro wrestling were more overt. The spiritual founder of MMA there was pro wrestler **Antonio Inoki**, who fought Muhammad Ali in an early proto-MMA match all the way back in 1976. Inoki later took on a variety of martial artists, proclaiming himself the World Martial Arts Champion.

Many of Inoki's successors took his example and went a step further than he ever imagined. Star wrestlers like **Nobuhiko Takada** and **Akira Maeda** popularized "shoot-style" wrestling promotions, presenting professional wrestling matches designed to look real. **Masakatsu Funaki** and **Minoru Suzuki** brought professional wrestling full circle; their **Pancrase** promotion was legitimate pro wrestling. The rules were the same as traditional pro wrestling. The only difference was a major one: the action was real.

In addition to Pancrase, the other major MMA promotions in the country all had wrestling roots. **Shooto** was the brainchild of Satoru Sayama, the legendary wrestler called Tiger Mask. Akira Maeda ran **Rings**, a combination of shoot-style pro wrestling and, later, legitimate fighting. The biggest promotion of all, the **Pride Fighting Championship**, was built to showcase Takada. When he failed twice against **Rickson Gracie**, his successor, **Kazushi Sakuraba**, was also a former professional wrestler.

Today the professional wrestling connection in the UFC is as strong as ever. The promotion's biggest star is former WWE wrestler **Brock Lesnar**. Matchmakers have also found that wrestling-style antics, combative interviews, and manufactured feuds between fighters sell better than pure sport. While UFC officials bristle when compared to wrestling, the connections have never been more apparent. More than sixty pro wrestlers have entered the Octagon and of the six men inducted into the UFC Hall of Fame, half have been professional wrestlers.

Pulver, Jens

Nickname: Little Evil | **Height:** 5'7"

Weight: 145–155 lbs | **Born:** 12/6/75

Debut: Bas Rutten Invitational 2 (4/24/99) | **Career Record:** 22-13-1

Notable Wins: Joe Stevenson (Bas Rutten Invitational 3); John Lewis (UFC 28); Caol Uno (UFC 30); B.J. Penn (UFC 35)

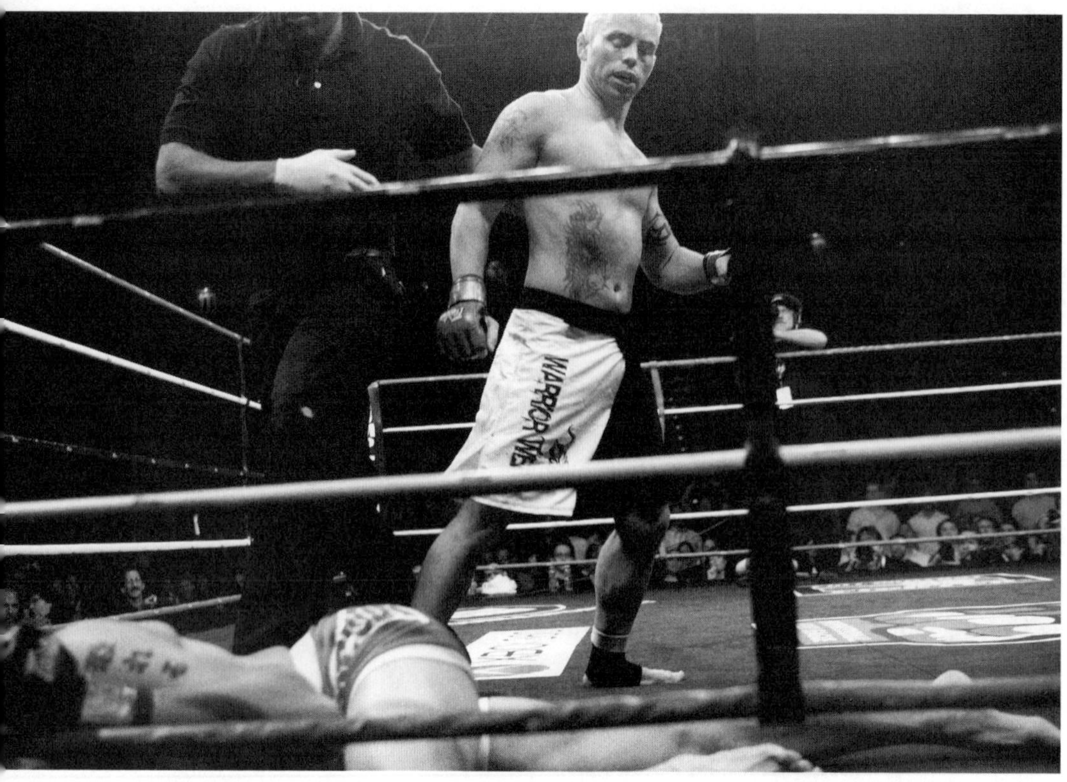

Notable Losses: Din Thomas (WEF: New Blood Conflict); Duane Ludwig (UCC 12); Takanori Gomi (Pride Shockwave 2004); Hayato Sakurai (Pride Bushido 9); B.J. Penn (*The Ultimate Fighter* 5 Finale); Urijah Faber (WEC 34, WEC 38)

You realize right away that Jens Pulver is a little different the first time you meet him. He has an intense, penetrating gaze that captivates. Pulver's right eye is blue and his left eye is brown. They are eyes have seen things they never should have.

Pulver was abused as a child, beaten and ridiculed by his father, a semi-professional horse jockey with a grudge against the world. He once held a gun in seven-year-old Jens' mouth and told him he was only alive because "he wasn't worth the bullets."

Many fighters come from similar backgrounds. They've been hardened, perhaps allowing them the strength to put their bodies and minds through the torment it takes to become a professional pugilist. Pulver became a solid wrestler, a junior college star and a starter at Boise State before he injured his wrists so badly that he called it a career.

It was in college that Pulver discovered MMA and found out he had a knack for throwing down in underground matches. He was discovered by **UFC**

In Their Own Words: Jens Pulver on fighting at his ideal weight

"A lot of people say, 'You got demoted, you got dropped down.' No way. I asked to go to 145. I wanted to go to the WEC. At the end of the day, I am a pioneer. I helped pioneer the 155-pound weight class and I want to help do the same thing here. At 145 I've got nine fights: eight by knockout and one by submission. At 145 pounds or any other weight, my signature move is my left hand. I hit like a ton of bricks. Everybody understands that. One thing you know about me is that I am going to bite down on my mouthpiece and throw down until the fight is over. For a little guy I've got a lot of pop."

matchmaker **John Perretti** at the **Bas Rutten** Invitational in 1999. Perretti was looking to form a lighter weight division in the UFC, similar to the one found in Japan's **Shooto**. The action there was fast-paced and non-stop and Perretti, a long-time proponent of smaller fighters dating back to his days with **Extreme Fighting**, thought Pulver could be one of the showcase fighters in this new division.

Artistically, the smaller fighters were a great success, and Pulver stood at the front of the pack as the best in the division. He earned a title shot with a stunning win over longtime standout **John Lewis** at UFC 28. Lewis had starred in both Shooto and Extreme Fighting, but lasted just seconds with Pulver before a wicked left hook dropped him. Pulver proceeded to beat **Caol Uno**, the Shooto star who was widely considered the best fighter in the weight class, in a five-round classic to win what was then called the UFC bantamweight title.

Now training with the legendary **Pat Miletich**, Pulver was part of a team that included four current or future world champions (Pulver, Miletich, **Matt Hughes**, and **Tim Sylvia**). His fighting skills were at a peak, and he proved it by avenging his teammate Hughes' two losses to **Dennis Hallman**. Then Pulver faced the challenge of his career: a young fighter named **B.J. Penn**.

Penn was special. Known as "The Prodigy," he was a jiu-jitsu expert who also had power in his hands. While Pulver employed the cautious **sprawl and brawl** approach to fighting, using his **wrestling** base to keep the fight standing where he had confidence in his big left hand, Penn was explosive and unpredictable. While Jens had struggled over five long rounds with Uno, Penn had destroyed the Japanese fighter in seconds. Despite his success in the division, Pulver went into the fight an underdog. For a temperamental and sensitive young man, this was just the fuel he needed to find the edge necessary to tame

Penn. He won a majority decision and was in tears after the fight. "Sometimes hype isn't enough," the champion proclaimed. "This is my fucking cage."

The words had a ring of truth to them at the time but are ironic now, considering Pulver would never again win a fight in the famed Octagon. A contract dispute in 2002 cost him four years in the middle of his fighting prime. He traveled the world, fighting in Canada, Japan, and Hawaii. While Pulver found some success at his natural weight of 145 pounds, there simply weren't money fights there.

When he moved up to lightweight to take on the best fighters in Japan, **Takanori Gomi** and **Hayato Sakurai**, he was too small and, perhaps, too limited to win. Pulver had become predictable. He had eschewed wrestling entirely, and even his standup attack was easy to combat once you knew that the left hand would be his primary weapon.

In 2006 Pulver was ready to return to the **Zuffa** empire. The idea was to reintroduce him with a tune-up fight and then have him coach ***The Ultimate Fighter*** 5 opposite old rival B.J. Penn. Little-known Joe Lauzon threw a wrench into these carefully laid plans by knocking Pulver out in just 47 seconds. Pulver went on to coach the show despite the embarrassing loss. This was particularly awkward, as Lauzon was also on the show, as a cast member looking for a shot at the big time. It was the first time one of the superstar coaches had actually lost a fight to one of the show's inexperienced contenders.

Penn was fired up for the rematch. For years Pulver had talked and talked about the fight, which had become his career's singular achievement. Penn was ready to silence him and choked Pulver out in the second round. It was

In Their Own Words: Jens Pulver on leaving the UFC

"I just wanted to be the highest paid lightweight. I was the champ. I beat everybody they put in front of me. I felt I deserved it. Looking back? Sure, I regret it now. If I had that opportunity to do over again, knowing what I know now, I wouldn't have left. But you don't know. I love the guys, but I don't know if it will ever be like it was. Me and Dana – I don't know if it will be patched up. We'll probably never be friends again because of it.

"I don't get to talk to Dana like I used to be able to. I can't even leave a message for him. I've talked to him twice in the last four years. I used to fly on his plane and hang out with him every day. It is what it is, man. That's how small I've gotten, that's how big he's gotten. It's cool. It doesn't mean I love him any less. We just don't talk."

obvious that Jens had no future at lightweight. But Zuffa thought he still had value, using him to help make stars out of their crop of talented but unknown 145-pounders in the **WEC**.

Even against these fledgling fighters, Pulver looked out of his league. He lost four of five WEC fights, but he served his purpose. Two back-and-forth encounters with Pulver helped make **Urijah Faber** a superstar in the eyes of the fans. Now, in his mid-thirties and on the losing end of four fights in a row, Pulver doesn't even have the stature to make a name for a young contender. After losing eight of his last eleven, an emotional Pulver called it quits after being choked out by Josh Grispi at WEC 41.

Of course, retirements in MMA never seem to stick. Most of the fighters who paved the way for the sport's success never made the huge paydays that could support a fighter into retirement. Soon enough, Pulver was back in the cage. But after one too many losses, WEC officials decided enough was enough. Like his contemporary **Chuck Liddell**, if Jens Pulver fights again, it won't be inside the Octagon.

Q

Quadros, Stephen

Stephen Quadros is a lifelong martial artist who segued a stint as a judge at **UFC** 8 into a career as an MMA announcer. Quadros doesn't have any experience in the cage, but that hasn't made him shy about offering his opinion about, well, everything. This has been controversial, because those kinds of critiques are usually reserved for other fighters, who presumably have the bona fides to criticize their peers. Quadros doesn't always call the action, as much as announce what he thinks should be happening and what he thinks the fighters should be doing at any given moment. Although this is grating to some of the fighters he criticizes, Quadros does have a rare gift for breaking down the action in the cage and explaining to a novice fan what is happening and why.

In Their Own Words: Stephen Quadros on teaming with Bas Rutten

"One of my fondest memories about when Bas Rutten and I worked together with the old Pride shows is when we were going to introduce two dolls that were available for purchase on the Pride Web site. One doll was of **Wanderlei Silva** and the other was of **Don Frye**. Now, I do a dead-on Frye impersonation. But this put Bas at a bit of a loss for what to say that would match my Don vocal caricature, because Wanderlei in real life did not speak English during any of our interviews with him. So I told Bas to just say three things over and over again: 'Rudimar,' '**Muay Thai**,' and '**Vale Tudo**.'

"So we're doing the recap and it's time for me to go to the dolls and I do my Don voice and Bas says his little bit and then I get set to toss it to the next fight, figuring we're done with the dolls. But then suddenly Bas, in a complete improvisation, said to me, 'Hey, let's do a little staredown.' Fortunately the cameraman, who was Japanese and probably didn't understand a single word that we were saying, had the instinct to zoom in on the dolls. So while the dolls are facing off we are doing this completely ridiculous voice over, like we are two little boys playing army or something: [in Don Frye voice] 'Hey, Wanderlei, I'm not scared of you, et cetera.' and Bas started saying in a broken Portuguese/Dutch accent, 'Rudimar, Vale Tuuuuudo, Rudimar. . . . Then I turned my Don Frye doll in a way and had it slug the Wanderlei doll in the face, all the while making a **kung fu** movie whoosh-thud-type sound effect. Bas returned fire with his doll. Then suddenly the dolls are duking it out in a camera closeup, à la *Team America, World Police*. It was us totally reverting back to childhood. Priceless and hysterical!"

Quadros, along with his partner **Bas Rutten**, was part of what many considered the best broadcast team in the sport. The two called the fights for the Japanese promotion **Pride** and were best known for the goofy pre-fight skits and their rare ability to fill the dead air during deadly boring fights. When Jerry Millen became Pride producer, Quadros was let go. He landed on his feet, announcing for a variety of promotions, and can currently be heard on **Strikeforce** Challengers shows on Showtime with his partners Mauro Ranallo and **Pat Miletich.**

Randleman, Kevin

Nickname: The Monster | **Height:** 5'10"
Weight: 205–225 lbs | **Born:** 8/10/71
Debut: UVF 4 (10/22/96) | **Career Record:** 17–15
Notable Wins: Maurice Smith (UFC 19); Pete Williams (UFC 23); Pedro Rizzo (UFC 26); Mirko Cro Cop (Pride Total Elimination 2004)
Notable Losses: Bas Rutten (UFC 20); Randy Couture (UFC 28); Fedor Emelianenko (Pride Critical Countdown 2004)

Kevin Randleman is one of MMA's greatest enigmas. He is capable of defeating the sport's very best, as he showed by dismantling Pedro Rizzo and shocking **Mirko Cro Cop**. At the same time, he is also capable of losing to the most ordinary journeyman like **Ron Waterman** and **Kazuhiro Nakamura**. Despite winning the **UFC** heavyweight championship, his career has to be considered a disappointment, if only because of glimpses of the brilliance that could have been.

Simply put, Randleman is one of the best athletes ever to step into the cage. He was a two-time national champion wrestler at Ohio State and joined former coach **Mark Coleman** in the "**Hammer House**" (one of early MMA's most dominant fighting teams). His rise to the top was explosive. Even though he wrestled in college at 167 and then 177 pounds, when he made his MMA debut he was a ripped 220 pounds, lending fuel to the fire that the influx of American wrestlers into the sport were powered by a mix of anger and **steroids**, a charge Randleman has repeatedly and strenuously denied.

Like many of his fellow wrestlers, Randleman learned his trade in the rough world of Brazilian **Vale Tudo**. By the time he reached the UFC in 1999, he was ready to compete with the very best in the world. He beat former champion **Maurice Smith** to earn a shot at the heavyweight championship. With the title on the line, Randleman lost one of the most controversial fights in UFC history to **Bas Rutten**. Despite Randleman being on top almost

the entire contest, the judges went with the charismatic Dutchman, crowning him the new heavyweight champion.

Rutten almost immediately retired and Randleman got a second chance at glory. This time he wasn't going to be denied, running over **Lion's Den** standout **Pete Williams** to win the title.

His first defense was emblematic of his entire career. There were high hopes for the new champion and his challenger Pedro Rizzo at UFC 24. It was a bout that would have to wait three months. Warming up backstage, Randleman slipped while doing his patented high leaps and cracked his head on the cement floor. He was taken to the hospital and the highly touted main event was off. Although Randleman went on to beat Rizzo at UFC 26, his career never completely recovered from the debacle.

After losing the title to **Randy Couture** in a tremendous contest at UFC 28, Randleman tried to reinvent himself as a light heavyweight, but was immediately knocked down the rankings in that division by a **Chuck Liddell** left hook. Soon Randleman was on his way to join his mentor Mark Coleman in Japan's **Pride Fighting Championships**, and the rest of his career was to be a mixture of the bizarre and the sublime.

Randleman made short work of opponents meant to build his status in the eyes of the Japanese fans, before losing six of his next seven fights. His only respite from steadily mounting losses was the flash knockout of Filipovic, at the time one of the most feared fighters in the world. Randleman caught the Croatian with a fast right hand and knocked him cold. He bristled at the idea that the win was a fluke, but Cro Cop set matters straight with a quick submission win in the inevitable rematch.

Even in defeat, Randleman often amazed. At Pride Critical Countdown 2004, Randleman launched **Fedor Emelianenko** — widely considered to be the best fighter in the world — with a devastating suplex. The Russian recovered quickly to win via submission, but Randleman's throw took a deserving place among the greatest highlights in MMA history. It was Randleman in a nutshell: a teasing glance at potential greatness, followed by a disastrous loss.

Ratner, Marc

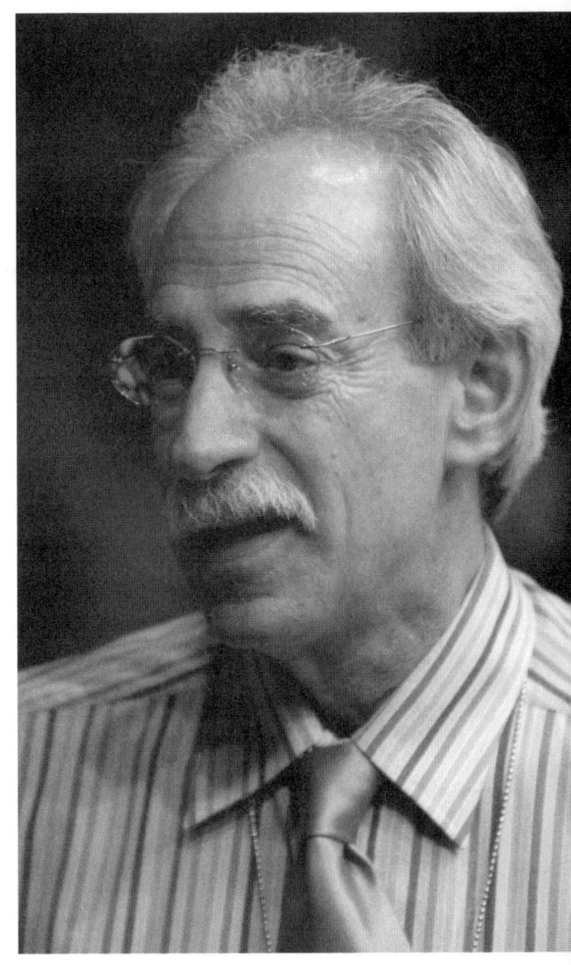

Marc Ratner's support for the sport of mixed martial arts has been all over the map. As the Executive Director of the Nevada State Athletic Commission, he was one of the **UFC**'s biggest enemies. He once testified in front of Congress that MMA had no future with no rules. Later, he joined Senator John McCain to badmouth the sport on *Larry King Live*, debating against **Ken Shamrock** and UFC owner **Bob Meyrowitz**.

Ratner, to his credit, was open-minded enough to give the sport a second chance. As the UFC strived to clean up its own act, with the **Jeff Blatnick**–led Mixed Martial Arts Council forming a set of comprehensive rules, Ratner recognized that it was a sport that could be safe for participants with the right kind of regulation. He helped create the **Unified Rules of Mixed Martial Arts**, and brought the sport to Nevada in 2001.

In Their Own Words: Ratner on his initial thoughts on MMA

"When I first became aware of it, they advertised no-holds-barred, no rules, anything goes. I knew as a regulator it would never be in Nevada. I went on *Larry King*, Senator McCain and myself, arguing against MMA. The former owner, Bob Meyrowitz and Ken Shamrock, a fighter you might have heard of, were on the other side. I said then, to the world, that we would never have it in Nevada. As long as there were no rules, it wasn't a sport you could regulate.

"In 2000, the state of New Jersey under director Larry Hazzard worked with promoters and other regulators to create what we called the Unified Rules. I was on the phone with them for four hours working out the details. Once there were rules, it became a sport that could become regulated. The state of Nevada approved the sport and we had our first fight card in September 2001."

As executive director, Ratner was widely considered to be the most respected man in combat sports. He was well liked and held in high esteem in a business where everyone has enemies. Ratner didn't just direct officials and referees; he was one. On Saturdays in the fall, Ratner could be found on the football field, a line judge for the Mountain West Conference who was good enough to work three bowl games.

In 2006, the best regulator in the game went to work for the UFC, joining **Zuffa** as the vice president of Government and Regulatory Affairs. Today his job is far removed from his time as a prominent UFC critic. He travels around the country and the world, working to get the sport of MMA approved throughout the nation and working with commissions internationally to make sure the shows go off without a hitch. The former ferocious detractor has now become the sport's most powerful advocate.

Rear mount (Back mount)

A dominant ground fighting position — perhaps the most dominant ground fighting position — in which the attacker straddles his opponent from behind, hooking his feet inside his opponent's thighs to control the hips. Alternatively, the attacker may choose to triangle his legs around his opponent's torso, increasing control and restricting his opponent's breathing. The rear mount can be achieved with the opponent face down and the attacker on top, or with the opponent face up and the attacker beneath. In either case, the attacker is able to threaten with strikes, the **rear naked choke**, and, if he is willing to sacrifice position to attempt a submission, the **arm bar**, while his opponent is effectively unable to attack. The defending fighter must work to improve his position, creating enough space to roll into the attacker's **guard** or **half-guard**. Direct escapes to **side control** are possible, though far more difficult to execute against skilled grapplers.

See also **positional hierarchy**

Rear naked choke

A chokehold in which the attacker, from behind, encircles the opponent's neck with his arms and restricts the flow of either blood or oxygen, depending on which variation of the technique is employed. The choke is "naked" in the sense that it is performed without the aid of a **gi**. Known as the mata leão ("lion killer") in **Brazilian Jiu-jitsu** and hadaka jime ("naked choke") in **judo**, the rear naked choke is among the most frequently applied holds in mixed martial arts. When properly applied, it simply ends fights — by submission, or, failing that, unconsciousness.

The variation most commonly seen in MMA restricts blood flow. The attacker wraps his strangling arm around the opponent's neck such that the elbow of the strangling arm is tucked beneath the opponent's chin. The hand of the strangling arm is placed palm down against the biceps of the supporting arm, which, in turn, reaches behind the opponent's head or neck to secure the hold. Think **Matt Hughes** glued to **Frank Trigg**'s back at **UFC** 45 in a rare standing application of the technique. As Hughes locked his arms into position and the effects of the choke took hold, Trigg dramatically tapped out as he fell backwards to the mat, seconds from unconsciousness.

When applied as a blood choke, the rear naked choke is painless and nearly instant. This is not true of the variation that attacks the trachea. With hands clasped, the attacker brings the inner edge of his wrist forcefully against the opponent's windpipe, restricting airflow, causing pain and inducing panic. Although this variation is seen rarely in MMA, it's the preferred method of heavyweight great **Fedor Emelianenko**, who used the technique to finish both iron-headed Japanese wrestler **Kazuyuki Fujita** and former UFC champion **Tim Sylvia**. Sylvia, asked to talk about the rarely seen choke in the post-fight press conference, answered, "I think it was on my windpipe. Because it hurt like hell."

Redbelt

Redbelt is, of all things, a 2008 mixed martial arts movie written and directed by celebrated playwright and filmmaker David Mamet. "In a lot ways," Mamet said, "it's an American Samurai film. I think it's a script Kurosawa would have liked." But — and this is to say the *very* least — Kurosawa it ain't.

Chiwetel Ejiofor plays Mike Terry, a down-on-his-luck **Brazilian Jiu-jitsu** instructor who speaks almost entirely in maxims. Terry's inability to make ends meet without relying on his wife's income or her family's business connections is supposed to signal the purity of his martial way (rather than, say, a stubborn inability to handle his business). Against his higher principles, and through a series of increasingly labored plot contrivances, Terry finds himself compelled to enter an MMA tournament in order to settle the debts of a former student's widow. But the competition is crooked, a prestidigitator from Act One reappears, and nothing is as it seems!

Mamet, a BJJ purple belt under Renato Magno, cast prominent figures from MMA and elsewhere in the martial arts world wherever possible, including **Enson Inoue**, **Frank Trigg**, John Machado, Dan Inosanto, **Mike Goldberg**, and **Randy Couture** as television analyst Dylan Flinn, who gets off such zingers as, "I think boxing is as dead as Woodrow Wilson." Nothing hangs together, and the film's message about honor drifts from muddled to incoherent. But all of this awfulness was nearly redeemed by a strange but real sign of the sport's cultural arrival: the remarkably incongruous sight of Randy Couture standing beside David Mamet on the red carpet.

Ribeiro, Vitor

Nickname: Shaolin
Height: 5'8"
Weight: 155 lbs
Born: 2/24/79
Debut: WFA 1 (11/3/01)
Career Record: 20-4
Notable Wins: Tatsuya Kawajiri (Shooto: Year End Show 2002); Joachim Hansen (Shooto: Year End Show 2003); Mitsuhiro Ishida (Shooto Hawaii: Soljah Fight Night)
Notable Losses: Tatsuya Kawajiri (Shooto: Year End Show 2004); Gesias Cavalcante (Hero's: Tournament Final); Shinya Aoki (Dream 10)

A **Brazilian Jiu-jitsu** world champion several times over, "Shaolin" Ribeiro is one of the lightweight division's top submission artists. In 2003, Ribeiro claimed **Shooto**'s welterweight (154 pounds) title with a win over the dangerous **Joachim Hansen**, finishing the fight by way of **arm triangle** choke — a technique that has become Shaolin's signature, accounting for fully one third of his career victories. His title reign ended a year to the day later when Japanese slugger **Tatsuya Kawajiri** avenged an early decision loss, stopping Ribeiro in the second round with a flurry of punches. Ribeiro went on to a successful stint in **Cage Rage**, where he captured the English promotion's lightweight championship in a bout with fellow Brazilian Jean Silva.

All of this earned Ribeiro a berth in K-1 **Hero's** 2007 middleweight (155 pounds) tournament, where he ran into **Gesias Cavalcante**, better known to Japanese fans as "JZ Calvan," in a bout that cost Shaolin more than a shot at the tournament title — it cost him a year. In a violent, one-sided beating that lasted only 35 seconds, Ribeiro suffered an eye injury that required retinal surgery and threatened his career. Making the most of his year away from the sport, Ribeiro opened a New York academy, and returned in 2009 to stop Olympic Greco-Roman **wrestling** medalist Katsuhiko Nagata in the first round, and to drop a disappointing decision to fellow grappling ace **Shinya Aoki**. As is often the case when two top submission fighters face each other under MMA rules, the fight turned into a middling kickboxing bout rather than the kind of grappling chess match fans had hoped for. Still, it speaks volumes that not even the great Aoki wanted anything to do with Vitor Ribeiro on the ground.

Rings

In 1989, the Universal Wrestling Federation was flying high, announcing a November 29 date at Japan's Tokyo Dome. They sold out the front row in less than five minutes. By the end of the first day, there were more than 40,000 tickets sold. The final tally was 60,000 in the building, a Japanese wrestling record. The group was formed by some of Japanese **pro wrestling**'s biggest stars to present a new style of wrestling to the fans. Their leader, **Akira Maeda**, was very vocal about how phony traditional wrestling was. All the outlandish moves, leaps from the turnbuckles, and devastating strikes with steel chairs were obviously staged. This style of wrestling, they promised, was the real thing. And in a world before the **UFC** and **Pride**, many fans believed.

The contests were unmistakably fake, the results scripted and shared with both performers before the bout. But the action in the ring was based on reality. Kicks and open hand blows were hard and fast and on the ground the wrestlers used submission holds from **catch wrestling** and **judo**. It was no wonder that the wrestlers knew exactly how to mimic a real contest; their main instructor was Karl Gotch, the hooker known as the "God of Wrestling" in Japan.

The UWF had many of the same stars that would go on to build the MMA industry in Japan. Joining Maeda were **Nobuhiko Takada**, Yoshiaki Fujiwara, **Yoji Anjo**, **Masakatsu Funaki**, and **Minoru Suzuki**. There were, perhaps, too many stars, a collection of chiefs with no Indians. In 1991, this powder keg exploded. The stars all went a different direction. Takada formed the UWFi, a showier and more traditional form of professional wrestling. Funaki and Suzuki, after a pit stop in a UWF-style promotion led by Fujiwara, formed the first MMA promotion in Japan, called **Pancrase**, in 1993. And the biggest star of them all, Maeda, formed Rings.

To Maeda, Rings was more than a promotion or an organization of wrestlers. Maeda was thinking bigger than that. Like **Dana White** and **Lorenzo Fertitta**, Maeda saw what we would soon call MMA as a global sport, as big as soccer or baseball. He pursued this vision with a passion, forming a network of Rings promotions throughout the world, most importantly in Holland and Russia.

While Maeda saw the fighters of Rings as a network and collaboration, the cable television channel WOWOW that promoted his cards saw things differently. Like the fans, they saw Rings as a one-man show. So much so that the contract they signed with Rings included a unique stipulation: if Maeda did not fight, Rings did not get paid.

This created a tough situation for Maeda the promoter and Rings the promotion. Maeda had a vision to move towards real fights. The Rings undercard frequently had competitive bouts, while the more important matches at the top of the card were all scripted wrestling matches. They had to stay that way, despite a number of tough fighters available from Chris Doleman's gym in Holland and **Volk Han**'s Russian Top Team.

This was a vision that couldn't be carried out because Maeda was not ready for real fights. He was in his thirties and his body had been destroyed by years of hard sparring and professional wrestling. The WOWOW contract made things worse. He tore a ligament in his right knee, but worked through it. Rings needed him too much. Eventually the knee got so bad he could barely walk. Maeda waited until he could sign a new contract with the television network, working through the pain to protect his investment in Rings. In 1993, he had no choice but to get surgery.

It was a time of change for the sport in Japan. Many of the kickboxers Maeda brought to Japan through Rings, like Peter Aerts, joined with promoter Kaz Ishii to form K-1. At the same time, Funaki and Suzuki's Pancrase promotion revolutionized shoot-style wrestling by putting on fights up and down the card that were real. And then the UFC made its debut that November. Suddenly the brutal Rings matches were seen by the fans to be clearly just as fake as the matches Maeda mocked in the traditional wrestling organizations.

While Rings could no longer claim to be the leading promotion in Japan, they were still breaking new ground worldwide. Maeda helped create a burgeoning MMA revolution in Holland and Russia, not only bringing in fighters to compete in Japan, but also helping entrepreneurs to promote Rings events in Europe. In Japan the promotion was making the awkward transition from professional wrestling to MMA.

Maeda had a second knee surgery in 1996 and when he returned he was fat and out of shape — a shell of his former self, clearly on his way out. Rings brought in **Kiyoshi Tamura**, Takada's understudy in UWFi, to be the heir apparent. Tamura was both a legitimate fighter and one of the best professional wrestlers in the world: the perfect man to bridge the gap between real and fake in Rings.

Tamura took a rare win from Maeda in 1997 on his way to becoming the Rings champion. He was expected to do it all; like Rings he would mix wrestling matches and real fights in his contests. It went wrong almost immediately. Tamura was talented, but only 180 pounds. His first fight as champion was against the lightly regarded Valentijn Overeem. Overeem had 50 pounds on Tamura and dominated him, making the champion and the promotion look bad. Tamura never recovered from the embarrassment; his opportunity to replace Maeda was lost, with his credibility, in a single bout. Tamura lost the title in his next fight, a worked wrestling match with Tariel Bitsadze.

Rings had one final show where the promotion mattered, where it was as big as any other in Japan, if only for a night. Maeda's retirement match was expected to be with **Rickson Gracie**. The storyline had even been built. Gracie had beaten Maeda's UWF rival Nobuhiko Takada and it was up to Maeda, as the senior man, to avenge wrestling's reputation. But Rings had the same trouble negotiating with Gracie that Takada's UWFi did. The Brazilian star was adamantly opposed to doing a pro wrestling match, even if he was supposed to win in the end.

The replacement for Gracie was another legend. Russian Greco-Roman wrestler Alexander Karelin was considered by many to be the best wrestler in modern Olympic history. Karelin won three gold medals and was undefeated in international competition for 13 years before falling victim to American Rulon Gardner in his final match.

He was a credible opponent for a star like Maeda's closing match and Rings packed more than 17,000 fans into the Yokohama Arena to say goodbye to the legend. Karelin won the match and even used his famous Karelin Lift on Maeda. Unlike **Antonio Inoki**, Maeda didn't insist on winning his final match.

The company used the big platform and all of the nationwide media to try and rehabilitate Tamura. He beat Overeem in a rematch; wisely, this time Rings asked for a worked match. The crowd, however, refused to accept

Tamura on top. Attendance dwindled below 5,000 fans for all of Tamura's bouts as the headliner and the promotion was forced to make the change to legitimate MMA.

Before Rings made this monumental change, Maeda wanted to be sure he had a fighter who could compete with the world's very best. Tamura had been their candidate, but he was simply too small for the role. They found their man in Rings veteran **Tsuyoshi Kohsaka.** Kohsaka had been on the undercard of Rings' fights for years, but never made it far because of his lack of charisma. It turned out, however, that Kohsaka could fight. His breakout wins in the UFC convinced Maeda that he had his man. The King of Kings tournament was then created, bringing in fighters like **Renzo Gracie** and **Randy Couture** to headline a new era of Rings matches.

With what eventually became two King of Kings Tournaments, Rings was able to bring in some of the very best martial artists in the world, this time for legitimate competition. **Dan Henderson** won the tournament in 1999 and **Antonio Rodrigo Nogueira** took the top prize in 2000. Rings introduced many of the world's best fighters to the Japanese audience, including Henderson, Nogueira, **Ricardo Arona**, **Alistair Overeem**, and **Fedor Emelianenko.**

A pattern was soon apparent. No sooner would Rings develop a star than Pride Fighting Championships would sign them away. Takada's group treated Rings like it was a minor league training ground. Rings went out of business in February 2002 after more than a decade of revolutionizing the sport of MMA in Japan.

Rodriguez, Ricco

Nickname: Suave | **Height:** 6'4"

Weight: 250 lbs | **Born:** 8/19/77

Debut: Extreme Cage (3/25/99) | **Career Record:** 42-11

Notable Wins: Gary Goodridge (Pride 9); Tsuyoshi Kohsaka (UFC 37); Randy Couture (UFC 39)

Notable Losses: Tim Sylvia (UFC 41); Antonio Rodrigo Nogueira (Pride Total Elimination 2003); Antonio Silva (EliteXC: Street Certified); Travis Wiuff (Yamma Pit Fighting)

It's not often that a fighter comes into the cage for the first time as a heavy favorite, but when you are the first American heavyweight to win the **Brazilian Jiu-jitsu** world championship much is expected of you. Ricco Rodriguez had not only won a bevy of jiu-jitsu championships; he was also the 1998 **ADCC** Submission Wrestling World Championship absolute champion. The potential was there to be one of the sport's all-time greats and he was well on his way. Then it all fell apart.

Rodriguez rose up the ranks quickly, winning seven fights in a row in **Pride** and the **UFC** (MMA's two major leagues at the time) to earn a title shot against the legendary **Randy Couture**. At UFC 39, Rodriguez achieved a dream, using his size and grappling acumen to overwhelm Couture in the fifth and final round. At 25, Rodriguez was the world champion and the sky was the limit. But behind the scenes, Rodriguez was falling apart.

Rodriguez had grown up in what he called "the ghetto of ghettos" in Patterson, New Jersey. He had never had any money, and the sudden celebrity and wealth was overwhelming. Living in Las Vegas, there was plenty of trouble to be found and Rodriguez managed to locate most of it. Training became an afterthought and soon drugs were a big part of his lifestyle.

Rodriguez lost his title in his next fight, to Miletich Fighting Systems fighter **Tim Sylvia**, and lost twice more before being cut from the UFC. Amazingly enough, Rodriguez never again beat a world-class opponent. As his glory days were further and further in the rearview mirror, his weight ballooned until he was a laughingstock. The former world champion regularly topped 350 pounds.

In 2008, Rodriguez made an effort to get his life under control, if not for himself then for his two children. He appeared on the first season of VH-1's *Celebrity Rehab* and has reportedly maintained his sobriety. Although he has returned to the fight game, it's safe to say that beating drugs was the toughest and most satisfying battle of his life.

Rogan, Joe

Joe Rogan has made a career of exploring the extremes of human behavior. On Tuesday nights he watched people challenge themselves to overcome their

greatest fears (and also eat lots of gross stuff) on NBC's hit reality show *Fear Factor*. One Saturday night a month, he'd also watch men face their fears and pursue excellence in the cage as the longtime color man for the **Ultimate Fighting Championship.**

Rogan, at first glance, seems like a very unlikely choice as the UFC expert in a two-man booth with **Mike Goldberg**. He was a standup comedian best known for his role as Joe Garrelli in the sitcom *NewsRadio*. Could you imagine Carrot Top or Jimmy Kimmel in that position?

A former U.S. tae kwon do champion, Rogan has been studying **Brazilian Jiu-jitsu** for more than a decade. He loves MMA, what he calls "developing your human potential." His interest is obvious and infectious. As an announcer, Rogan is absolutely fearless. Sure, he's never fought professionally and mainstream sports have taught fans to expect an ex-pro in the color man's chair. Rogan has defied the odds to excel in his position; it's his passion for the sport that makes it all work.

In Their Own Words: Joe Rogan-isms

Joe Rogan is a fluid and entertaining announcer, but online fans have noticed some phrases or crutches he comes back to again and again. Favorite Rogan-isms:

"He's got heavy hands."

"He's rocked!"

"His jiu-jitsu skills are world-class."

"[Fighter A] is in [Fighter B's] world now."

"He is in deep trouble. That's tight."

Rogan comes back to these phrases early and often. Play the Joe Rogan Drinking Game at your own peril.

Rogers, Brett

Nickname: The Grim
Height: 6'5"
Weight: 265 lbs
Born: 2/17/81
Debut: EFX: Fury (5/3/06)
Career Record: 10-2
Notable Win: Andrei Arlovski (Strikeforce: Lawler vs. Shields)
Notable Losses: Fedor Emelianenko (Strikeforce: Fedor vs. Rogers); Alistair Overeem (Strikeforce: Heavy Artillery)

Just weeks before his **Strikeforce** fight with former **UFC** heavyweight champion **Andrei Arlovski** in June 2009, Brett Rogers was still working in Sam's Club, changing tires. It's been a whirlwind ride for the Minnesotan struggling to put food on the table for his three children while keeping his fighting dream alive.

Rogers, with only a dozen career fights, is relatively inexperienced. But he's been lucky in a way — almost all the formative fights of his career were on national television for either **EliteXC** or Strikeforce. Millions of fans have seen him develop, knocking out every single opponent he faced on the national stage. It's his heavy hands that make Rogers a threat to any man he faces. Even the mighty **Fedor Emelianenko**, the greatest fighter in the sport's history, knew better than to take Rogers lightly. "His heavy hitting is a big strength," the Russian said.

And sure enough, Rogers had his moments in their unlikely encounter, cutting the thin-skinned Emelianenko above the nose in the opening exchange, and briefly unloading with some **ground and pound** after a successful sweep from **half guard**. Sure, Fedor ended the fight in the next round with an incredibly powerful overhand right, but by any reasonable standard, Rogers impressed. In his next bout, not so much: **Alistair Overeem**, "Ubereem" version, unceremoniously pounded him out in the first. He might never acquire the all-around skills necessary to be a true top-notch heavyweight contender, but as long as he's in possession of that "heavy hitting" that rightly had Fedor worried, Brett Rogers will remain a dangerous man.

Rua, Mauricio

Nickname: Shogun
Height: 6'1"
Weight: 205 lbs
Born: 11/25/81
Debut: Meca World Vale Tudo 7 (11/8/2002)
Career Record: 19-4
Notable Wins: Quinton Jackson (Pride Critical Countdown 2005); Antonio Rogerio Nogueira (Pride Total Elimination 2005); Alistair Overeem (Pride Final Conflict 2005, Pride 33); Ricardo Arona (Pride Final Conflict 2005); Kevin Randleman (Pride 32);

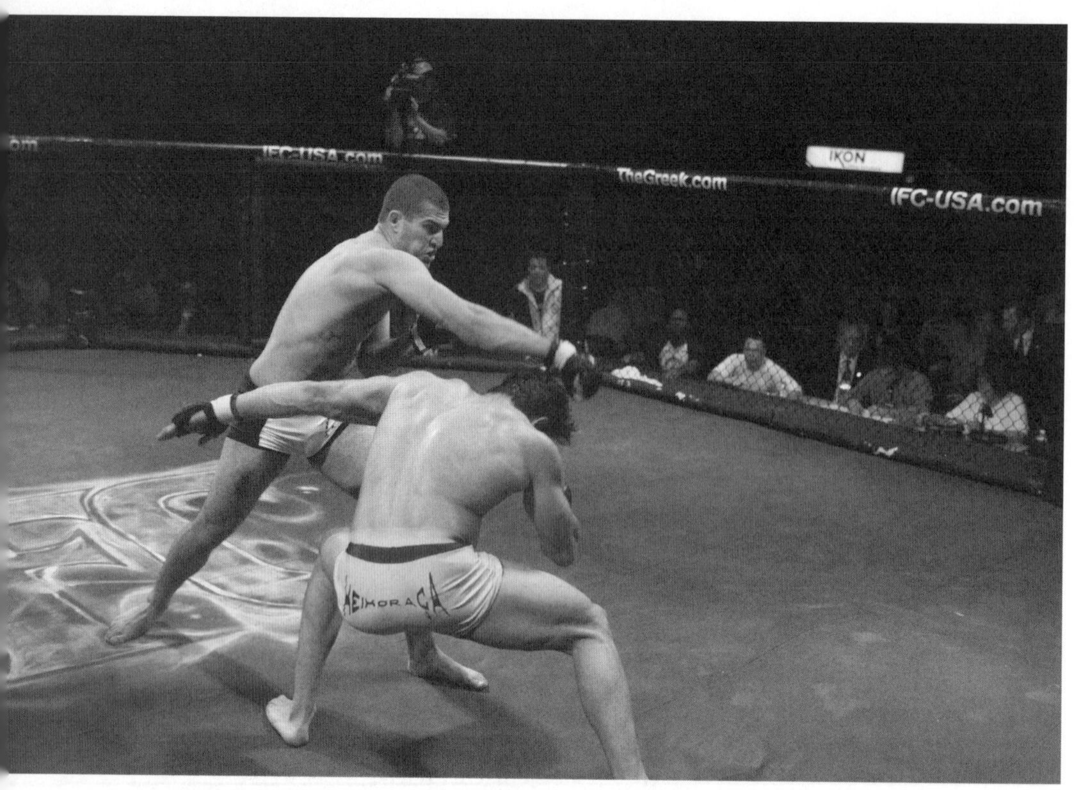

Kazuhiro Nakamura (Pride Shockwave 2006); Mark Coleman (UFC 93); Chuck Liddell (UFC 97); Lyoto Machida (UFC 113)

Notable Losses: Renato Sobral (IFC: Global Domination); Mark Coleman (Pride 31); Forrest Griffin (UFC 76)

You could say it's been up and down for the past few years for **Chute Boxe** product Mauricio "Shogun" Rua. In 2005, Rua took his place among the best 205-pound fighters in the world by completely overwhelming his considerable competition in **Pride**'s middleweight Grand Prix. By the end of 2006, he was widely if not universally regarded as the sport's top light heavyweight fighter. But after an inglorious 2007 **UFC** debut, he was supposedly washed-up, or worse, exposed as a product of a half-crooked Japanese promotion who couldn't stand up to the rigors of legitimate, drug-tested, unified-rules MMA. Two fights later, he knocked out a legend and became the number one contender to the undefeated **Lyoto Machida**'s UFC light heavyweight title. In the world of mixed martial arts, things can change pretty quickly.

A devastating **Muay Thai** striker with a hint of Capoeira flair, Rua lost only once in his first 13 professional fights, caught in a **guillotine choke** by the vastly more experienced **Renato Sobral**. Aside from a freak injury, a broken arm suffered on a **Mark Coleman** takedown seconds into their first bout, Shogun wouldn't lose again in Pride as he cut a swath through the promotion's deep middleweight (205 pounds) division. When faced with journeymen like **Akira Shoji** or Hiromitsu Kanehara, Rua would stomp or soccer kick them to the point of incapacity within minutes; when he found himself standing across the ring from legitimate title contenders like **Quinton Jackson, Ricardo Arona**, or **Alistair Overeem**, the results were much the same. Over the course of his career-defining Pride run, only two fighters managed to go the distance with Shogun: the sure and steady **Antonio Rogerio Nogueira** and the largely inexplicable **Kazuhiro Nakamura.** Those rare Rua fights that went longer than a couple of minutes allowed him to show that he was more than a Muay Thai specialist; he was also a smooth grappler with dangerous **leg locks** and a slick **omoplata.** In the same year that he claimed Pride's middleweight Grand Prix title, Shogun was awarded his **Brazilian Jiu-jitsu** black belt after only four years of training.

And so expectations were understandably high when Rua made his UFC debut against fan favorite **Forrest Griffin.** Rua was arguably the best in the world, and Griffin had just followed a surprising knockout loss to the then unheralded **Keith Jardine** with a less than impressive performance against Hector Ramirez in a gimme fight. But Griffin, in a thrilling performance, maybe the best of his career, not only managed to hang with Rua but grind him down, outlast him. An exhausted Rua was forced to tap to a **rear naked choke** with only 15 seconds left in the third and final round.

As stunning as that upset was, it could be explained away in part by Rua's choice to fight on a bad knee less than two weeks after his wedding day. But there was no real accounting for how bad he looked in his next fight. After two major knee surgeries put him out of action for more than a year, Shogun returned to the Octagon to avenge his freak loss to Mark Coleman, a once dominant but broken down fighter coming off an even longer layoff than the Brazilian 17 years his junior. Rua managed to stop Coleman late in the third, but don't be fooled by the UFC's Fight of the Night award: both were exhausted early in what turned out to be a terrible fight. Although he took the win, it was a disastrous showing, perhaps the worst of Rua's career.

But at UFC 97, Shogun put himself right back into the mix at the top of the light heavyweight division with an impressive first round KO of **Chuck Liddell**, attacking with hard leg kicks before landing the left hook to put "The Iceman" on his back. With other top contenders **Rashad Evans** and Quinton Jackson tied up in coaching assignments on ***The Ultimate Fighter***, Shogun's win over the fading Liddell was enough to earn him the first shot at Lyoto Machida's light heavyweight title. Although it appeared to most observers that Shogun did enough to win no less than four of five rounds against the champ, all three judges inexplicably saw it the other way. In their rematch, however, Rua left no room for disagreement, blitzing the champion and laying him out in the first round to claim the UFC light heavyweight title and cement his status among the greatest fighters to compete on either side of the Pacific.

Rua, Murilo

Nickname: Ninja **Height:** 5'11"

Weight: 185 lbs **Born:** 10/22/80

Debut: Meca World Vale Tudo 1 (5/27/00) **Career Record:** 19-10-1

Notable Wins: Mario Sperry (Pride 20); Joey Villasenor (Strikeforce: Shamrock vs. Baroni)

Notable Losses: Dan Henderson (Pride 17); Ricardo Arona (Pride 23); Quinton Jackson (Pride 29); Paulo Filho (Pride Bushido 10); Robbie Lawlor (EliteXC: Uprising)

Over the course of his career, former **Chute Boxe** mainstay Murilo "Ninja" Rua has stepped into the ring against some of the best middleweights, light heavyweights, and heavyweights in the sport. Unfortunately for **Mauricio Rua**'s older, stylistically similar but less accomplished brother, he hasn't beaten any of them. After earning a tough win over **Brazilian Top Team** co-founder **Mario Sperry** in **Pride**, Rua dropped decisions to both **Ricardo Arona** and **Paulo Filho** as the rivalry between the two great Brazilian fight teams intensified. An ill-advised jump to heavyweight for Pride's 2004 Grand Prix pitted a plump Rua against then undefeated heavyweight up-and-comer **Sergei Kharitonov**, who tossed Rua around the ring and promptly knocked him out.

The best showing of Rua's career came in his strange decision loss to **Quinton Jackson** in a 2005 bout so poorly judged that an embarrassed Jackson tried to award his victor's trophy to Rua in the ring after the fight. Since then, it's been a steady stream of disappointing performances. Even the lone post-Pride bright spot, Rua's **EliteXC** middleweight championship, was short-lived: less than three months after stopping Joey Villasenor to win the belt, an exhausted Rua was knocked out in the third round of his first title defense by **Robbie Lawler**. Maybe it was the Chute Boxe name, or maybe it was his own surname, but Murilo Rua was never able to live up to expectations, fair or not.

Ruas, Marco

Nickname: The King of the Streets **Height:** 6'1"

Weight: 215 lbs **Born:** 1/23/61

Debut: JJ vs. MM (10/31/84) **Career Record:** 8-4-2

Notable Win: Gary Goodridge (Pride 2)

Notable Losses: Oleg Taktarov (Ultimate Ultimate 95); Maurice Smith (UFC 21, IFL: Chicago)

Royce Gracie showed the world the power of **Brazilian Jiu-jitsu, Dan Severn** demonstrated the power of amateur **wrestling**, and at **UFC** 7, Marco Ruas illustrated just how devastating **Muay Thai** kickboxing could be. Before Ruas, it was assumed that only grapplers could succeed at the highest levels of MMA. Ruas and kickboxing star **Maurice Smith** changed those perceptions, one leg kick at a time.

Ruas was a legendary street fighter from Rio de Janeiro, Brazil. A **Luta Livre** fighter and a rival to the powerful **Gracie Jiu-jitsu** faction, Ruas was a well-known competitor a decade before the UFC was created. By the time he made his Octagon debut, Ruas was already in his mid-thirties. But a past-his-prime Ruas was more than enough to handle almost anyone the UFC had to throw at him.

He won the UFC 7 tournament by chopping down the "Polar Bear," **Paul Varelans.** After conditioning his legs by kicking coconut trees over and over again, attacking the fleshy limbs of the gigantic Varelans seemed like child's play. It was the first time fans and commentators had seen how effective a good Thai attack could be.

Ruas was much more than just a standup striker. He was among the first cross-trained fighters in the sport, combining his stellar kickboxing with a solid ground game. Although Ruas was part of an intense rivalry with the Gracie family, he wasn't ignorant of the ground game like so many who challenged them. How could he be? He was preparing to beat them.

UFC 7 was the high point of Ruas's MMA career. He had two horrible fights with **Oleg Taktarov**, dreadfully dull contests that sent fans into a stupor and had promoters pulling their hair out. By the time he made his way to Japan to fight for **Pride**, Ruas was already 37 years old and his body was failing him. He suffered an embarrassing loss to pro wrestler Alexander Otsuka when an anti-inflammatory he was taking for a busted knee made him too lethargic to perform at his best. His knee went out again in his comeback fight against Smith, essentially ending his career as a competitive fighter.

Ruas excelled as a trainer, coaching a new generation of athletes to the top of the sport, most notably former UFC contender **Pedro Rizzo**. Training with Ruas was no walk in the park. Fighters carried Ruas on their back while they ran stairs. He toughened their legs up by whacking them with broomsticks. It might not work for everyone, but fighters knew that when they stepped into the cage with a Ruas **Vale Tudo** student, you were stepping in with a legitimate tough guy.

Rubber guard: see **Bravo, Eddie**

Rumble on the Rock

Rumble on the Rock was essentially a Hawaiian promotion, like so many others trying to draw a crowd to see the local tough guys go at it. MMA had been big on the islands since the very beginnings of the sport, with T.J. Thompson bringing in plenty of big stars from the mainland for his **SuperBrawl** shows. Rumble on the Rock was a little more relaxed, a show for and starring Hawaiians. At least it was until **B.J. Penn** was available. Then the show exploded into international prominence before things died down again when Penn returned to the **UFC**.

B.J.'s brother J.D. Penn was the president of Rumble on the Rock and excited about the opportunity to build an international brand. The Penns didn't think small and Rumble on the Rock 4 was no exception. They went all out. This was no little show in a high school gym with an old boxing ring. They had their own custom built cage, large screens for the fans to watch the action once it hit the ground, and media coverage that blanketed the island. They also had a dream match: the number one and number two lightweight fighters in the world were set to square off. B.J. Penn, the top fighter in the weight class in America, was taking on the top lightweight in Japan, **Takanori Gomi.**

Penn on that night proved he was in another class, humbling the Japanese star and laying claim to the coveted title of best pound-for-pound fighter in the world. It was a big night and the whole sport was watching. Even UFC President **Dana White** was there to watch the action. This was before ***The Ultimate Fighter*** put **Zuffa** and the UFC on a different playing field, and Penn wanted more than just the UFC. After winning the welterweight title from **Matt Hughes** at UFC 46, he signed a contract with K-1 to help build their new MMA productions. Penn still wanted to defend the UFC title; he just wanted to earn big paydays in Japan and Hawaii at the same time.

Zuffa had been through this before. **Carlos Newton** had actually signed to fight for Pride when he was still the UFC champion, but lost the title to Hughes at UFC 34 before he was able to journey to Japan as champion. Zuffa didn't want Penn, the welterweight champion, to fight for other promotions. When he announced his intention to fight for K-1, they stripped him of the UFC title. Penn lost the ensuing legal struggle and was out of the UFC.

This opened him up to fight full-time for K-1, which had signed a promotional agreement with Rumble on the Rock. He headlined another show in Hawaii, in a packed Blaisdell Arena, where nearly 9,000 fans saw him dispatch Rodrigo Gracie at Rumble in the Rock 6. It was Penn's last fight for the promotion.

The explosion in pay-per-view business after *The Ultimate Fighter* reignited his interest in the UFC. In 2006 Penn was back, losing two in a row for the first time ever, to welterweights Hughes and **Georges St. Pierre**, before beginning a dominant run in the lightweight class where his career started.

Rumble on the Rock had one final hurrah, a co-promotion with **EliteXC** and former rival Hawaiian promotion Icon Sports. The show featured **Robbie Lawler**, **Nick Diaz**, and **Gina Carano** and was broadcast on Showtime. Future events were in the works when EliteXC collapsed under colossal mismanagement.

Today Rumble on the Rock is right back where it started, developing local talent and putting on small shows for a local audience. That looks to remain the case until B.J. Penn has another falling out with the UFC. Then it's anybody's guess, but a Rumble on the Rock return to prominence is only a signing away.

Rutten, Bas

Nickname: El Guapo　　**Height:** 6'1"

Weight: 220 lbs　　**Born:** 2/24/65

Debut: Pancrase: Yes, We Are Hybrid Wrestlers 1 (9/21/93)

Career Record: 28-4-1

Notable Wins: Minoru Suzuki (Pancrase: Road to the Championship 2, Pancrase: 1995 Anniversary Show); Frank Shamrock (Pancrase: 1995 Neo-Blood Tournament Round 2, Pancrase: Truth 5); Masakatsu Funaki (Pancrase: 1996 Anniversary Show); Guy Mezger (Pancrase: Truth 2); Tsuyoshi Kohsaka (UFC 18); Kevin Randleman (UFC 20)

Notable Losses: Masakatsu Funaki (Pancrase: Pancrash! 1); Ken Shamrock (Pancrase: Road to the Championship 3, Pancrase: Eyes of Beast 2); Frank Shamrock (Pancrase: King of Pancrase Tournament: Round 1)

If you're new to mixed martial arts, you might only know Bas Rutten as the wacky Dutch co-host of *Inside MMA*, HDNet's weekly round-up of news and notes. If you go back a little further, you might remember him as the longtime color commentator for **Pride**'s English-language broadcasts, extolling the virtues of the liver kick, and offering every grounded fighter the same advice: "He needs to *explode* right here." Or maybe you know him from his truly insane self-defense video, *Bas Rutten's Lethal Street Fighting*, clips of which can and must be seen on YouTube. Immediately.

But if you've been with the sport since the very beginning, or close to it, you know Bas Rutten as a King of **Pancrase** and the **UFC**'s fourth heavyweight champion. A Dutch kickboxer who soaked up the submission game like a sponge once he came to Japan, Rutten learned from his early Pancrase losses to grapplers **Masakatsu Funaki** and **Ken** and **Frank Shamrock**, and was never caught in a finishing hold again. In fact, after his March, 1995, loss by **knee bar** to Ken Shamrock, Rutten never lost again, period. He remained undefeated in his final 19 Pancrase bouts, earning championship titles and combining with Masakatsu Funaki to put on what is widely regarded as the finest match in the organization's history. Funaki was as dangerous as ever on the ground, and almost finished the fight in the early going when he secured a heel hook and twisted Rutten's leg to a shockingly unnatural angle. "I can still not believe that I escaped that situation," Rutten reflected a decade later. The canny Rutten escaped, though, and over the course of a 17-minute classic, battered the courageous Funaki with a seemingly endless barrage of kicks, elbows, and the open-handed palm strikes synonymous with Pancrase.

Rutten's winning ways followed him to the UFC, where he was immediately thrust into the heavyweight title picture. A dramatic knockout win in a back-and-forth battle against the always tough **Tsuyoshi Kohsaka** earned Rutten a date with **Kevin Randleman** to crown a new heavyweight champion after **Randy Couture** vacated the title. Rutten, famously unable to defend the takedown, spent much of the fight beneath the powerful wrestler, but was awarded the match in a decision still hotly debated by fans more than a decade later.

That was the last time we'd see Rutten in action for years. After dealing with Randleman's power, Rutten wisely decided to move down a weight division, but a string of serious training injuries forced his retirement in 1999. He transitioned into acting and broadcasting, worked the occasional **professional wrestling** match, and published a series of instructional books and DVDs, including the impressively comprehensive *Bas Rutten's Big Book of Combat* in addition to his aforementioned masterpiece, *Lethal Street Fighting*.

It wasn't until 2006 that Rutten would fight again, taking on the professional opponent Ruben "Warpath" Villareal after **Kimo Leopoldo** failed a pre-fight **steroid** test. Rutten pounded Warpath with leg kicks and stopped him in the first round, but was in such rough shape from the rigors of training that he was unable to perform his trademark split-legged jump to celebrate the win. There can be little doubt now that Rutten has indeed fought for the last time, but he remains a much loved fixture on the mixed martial arts scene

all the same with his infectious enthusiasm, goofy charm, and vast knowledge of the sport.

In Their Own Words: Bas Rutten on how Ken Shamrock inspired him to be great

"It was the loss against Ken. I really had it. I'm a very sore loser and I knew what the problem was. It was because I didn't train any ground. That decided it for me. Forget about striking, nobody's going to strike with me anyway, even **Maurice Smith** took me down in a fight. So I start concentrating on grappling two times a day, seven days a week. I really took it ot the next level in training. I always told Ken, 'Thank you for that, buddy, because that actually made me very good.' I never lost again."

Sakuraba, Kazushi

Nicknames: Saku, The Gracie Hunter, The IQ Wrestler **Height:** 5'11"

Weight: 183 lbs **Born:** 7/14/69

Debut: Shoot Boxing S Cup 1996 (7/14/96)

Career Record: 26-13-1 (2 No Contests)

Notable Wins: Marcus Silveira (UFC 15.5); Carlos Newton (Pride 3); Vitor Belfort (Pride 5); Royler Gracie (Pride 8); Royce Gracie (Pride 2000 Grand Prix Finals); Renzo Gracie (Pride 10); Ryan Gracie (Pride 12); Quinton Jackson (Pride 15); Kevin Randleman (Pride Final Conflict 2003); Ken Shamrock (Pride 30)

Notable Losses: Igor Vovchanchyn (Pride 2000 Grand Prix Finals); Wanderlei Silva (Pride 13, Pride 17, Pride Total Elimination 2003); Mirko Cro Cop (Pride Shockwave 2002); Antonio Schembri (Pride 25); Antonio Rogerio Nogueira (Pride Shockwave 2003); Ricardo Arona (Pride Critical Countdown 2005); Kiyoshi Tamura (Dynamite!! 2008)

The once-great Kazushi Sakuraba has spent so much of his career as just that — the *once-great* Kazushi Sakuraba — that it's easy to lose sight of his singular place in the history of mixed martial arts. Every time he takes another lopsided beating, every time he squeaks by some trivial opponent by the narrowest of margins, the images of Sakuraba doing the impossible against the best in the world are pushed a little farther back in the mind. We used to approach every new Sakuraba bout with a sense of anticipation, a feeling that we were about to see things we'd never seen before and might never see again. But that anticipation has turned to dread, a sense that each new battle brings the much loved Sakuraba not just closer to retirement, but ever nearer to real, lasting harm. And it's been this way for years.

Sakuraba's long road began with his decision to enter the world of **professional wrestling** after his amateur days at Chuo University, where he had captained the **wrestling** team. He joined the red-hot UWFi, a shoot-style organization that did its best to present the most realistic-looking grappling contests possible while still scripting the outcomes. Sakuraba slowly worked his way up the card, but by the

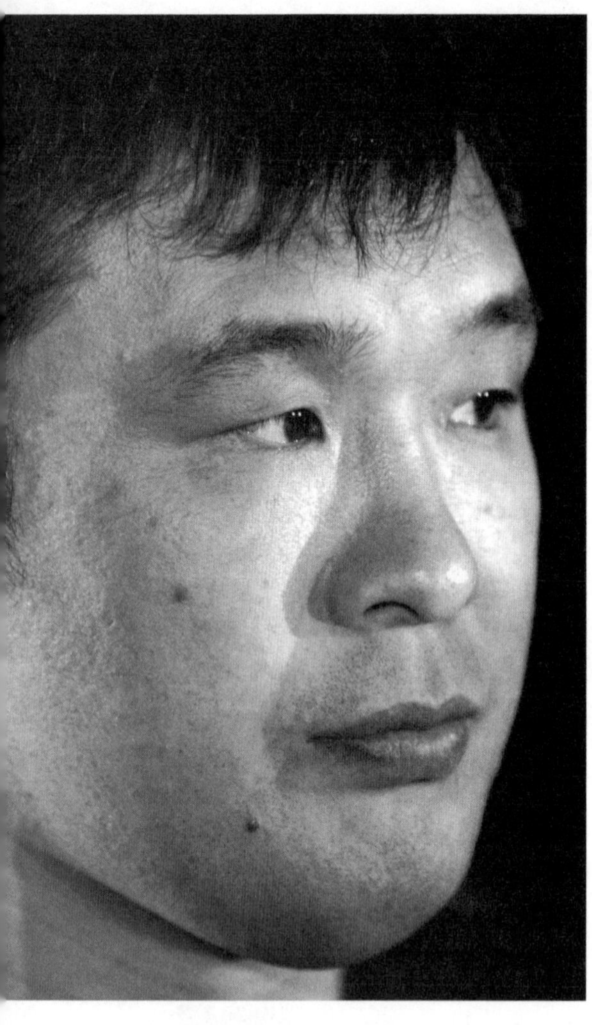

time he made it to the top, the business was collapsing around him: Sakuraba's first headlining match came on the promotion's final show. He maintained his main event status in **Nobuhiko Takada**'s Kingdom Pro Wrestling after the demise of the UWFi, but the Japanese public's appetite for extremely realistic professional wrestling dwindled as their exposure to legitimate mixed martial arts increased. When Takada stepped into the ring to face **Rickson Gracie** in a legitimate contest at the inaugural **Pride** event, it was clear that an era was coming to a close.

It was the best thing that could have happened to Kazushi Sakuraba. With a style informed by professional wrestling's spirit of showmanship and the **catch wrestling** he studied under the legendary Billy Robinson in his UWFi days, Sakuraba became Pride's top draw, and, for a time, a legitimate national sports hero.

His beginnings in mixed martial arts had been humble enough, with a submission loss to **Kimo Leopoldo** by **arm triangle** at the 1996 Shoot Boxing S Cup in a bout that many maintain was less a legitimate fight than an extension of Sakuraba's professional wrestling career. We can be a little surer of the legitimacy of his appearance in the heavyweight tournament at **UFC** Japan, but it was thoroughly weird all the same. First of all, there's the matter of Sakuraba's weight, which couldn't have been anywhere near the 203 pounds he listed in order to compete as a heavyweight. Then, there was the first-round debacle against **Marcus Silveira**. Minutes in, Sakuraba was under fire and dropped low to attempt an ankle pick takedown. Referee **John McCarthy** immediately stopped the fight under the mistaken impression that Sakuraba had been knocked out. Sakuraba didn't take it well, to say the least, and protested immediately. After some back-room deliberations, it was ruled that Sakuraba could re-enter the tournament in place of the injured **Tank Abbott**, and faced Silviera a second time, quickly winning by **arm bar** and announcing, "In fact, pro wrestling is strong."

The relative ease with which he put away Silveira, a black belt under **Carlson Gracie**, meant Sakuraba's submission skills were for real. But no one could have anticipated all that followed. In his Pride debut, he put away journeyman **Vernon White** with an arm bar after what seemed like an eternity. It was nothing special. His next bout, against Canadian grappler **Carlos Newton**, on the other hand, most definitely was. In a fluid, back-and-forth grappling clinic that still stands as one of the greatest ground battles in MMA history more than a decade later, Sakuraba emerged the victor when he found his way to a **knee bar** midway through the second ten-minute round. Then came the Brazilians: a draw against Allan Goes, and wins over **Vitor Belfort** and Ebenezer Fontes Braga. The Japanese fans were eager to see their wrestling heroes hold their own against the Brazilian **Vale Tudo** fighters who had thus far bested them, and Sakuraba gave them just what they were looking for. Sakuraba was succeeding where his stablemate Takada had famously failed.

A series of matches against the legendary Gracie family took Sakuraba from a promising up-and-comer to the pinnacle of his sport over the course of just 13 months. First, there was **Royler**, the smallest but most technically proficient of the Gracie clan. Sakuraba punished him with leg kicks throughout their match, and trapped Royler in a trademark **Kimura** with less than two minutes to go. With Royler's arm contorted at an unnatural angle, the referee stepped in and controversially ended the bout against the Gracies' wishes. They protested passionately, insisting they'd been cheated. When Sakuraba met **Royce** in the second round of the Pride 2000 Grand Prix, it was under rules modified to deal with the Gracie family's concerns: there would be no time limits and no referee stoppages. But the hotly anticipated meeting between Japan's top native star and the hero of the UFC's first tournaments almost didn't happen. It took an absolute gift of a judges' decision to keep Sakuraba alive after an indifferent showing against Pancrase veteran **Guy Mezger**.

With that taken care of, however unjustly, the stage was set for an unforgettable classic. Every serious MMA fan needs to see Sakuraba's 90-minute battle against Royce Gracie at least once. Not because of any particularly spectacular exchanges, not because of any sudden, dramatic twists or turns, but simply because of the sheer madness of a 90-minute mixed martial arts contest. Sakuraba came close to finishing early with a knee bar, and Gracie had his chance with a **guillotine choke**, but it was Sakuraba's leg kicks that would once again prove the difference over the long haul, forcing Gracie's corner to throw in the towel rather than watch their fighter take any more abuse. As if Sakuraba hadn't given the ecstatic Tokyo Dome crowd enough, he came back later that night to face **Igor Vovchanchyn**, the most feared heavyweight striker on the planet. Sakuraba somehow managed to hold his own against the stout Ukrainian despite weighing in at only a scant 173 pounds that night — and despite having already fought for *an hour and a half* against Royce Gracie. Sakuraba's corner wisely stopped the Vovchanchyn bout after the first round. Their man had nothing more to prove.

This is the Kazushi Sakuraba we want to remember: the best show in all of mixed martial arts, equal parts peerless submission grappler and brilliant physical comedian. The one who paid tribute to his pro wrestling heroes with elaborate ring entrances, delivered exaggerated "Mongolian" chops, cartwheeled around the **guard**, and dragged his butt-flopping **Brazilian Jiu-jitsu** opponents around the ring by their ankles. The one who could hit match-ending submissions from seemingly any position against any fighter, regardless of size or skill. There was no one like *that* Kazushi Sakuraba before, and there's been no one like him since.

The point of inflection might have been Sakuraba's bout against the game **Renzo Gracie** at Pride 10. An almost perfectly even contest ended abruptly with less than a minute remaining in the second ten-minute round, when Sakuraba seized Gracie's arm in a Kimura grip and spun to the ground. The arm was broken, the match was over, and the two great fighters embraced. Although Sakuraba would later defeat **Ryan Gracie**, and rumors of a showdown with Rickson Gracie would persist for years, his victory over Renzo was truly the culmination of Sakuraba's rivalry with the Gracie family, a rivalry that elevated both Sakuraba and the sport itself to unprecedented levels of popularity in Japan.

In the many years since, however, it's been a long way down. There were the three devastating losses to **Wanderlei Silva**, and the broken orbital bone suffered in a senseless but strangely compelling bout against **Mirko Cro Cop** that helped fill Tokyo National Stadium. Those losses were dispiriting, but there could be no shame in losing to bigger, stronger, ferocious strikers. The real turning point, the first definitive sign that Kazushi Sakuraba wasn't what he used to be, came in a loss to the otherwise completely unremarkable Antonio Schembri, who found no real success in the sport beyond his first-round knockout of the Japanese legend. Sakuraba avenged the loss a year later, but it seemed like too little, too late. We couldn't fool ourselves any longer. Kazushi Sakuraba hadn't just lost a step — he was washed-up.

As if to hammer that point home, Sakuraba was ludicrously booked in a 2005 middleweight Grand Prix bout against the powerful young **Ricardo Arona**, who beat Sakuraba beyond recognition. Since then, Sakuraba has been handled with kid gloves, treated to fights against beatable opposition rather than the sport's elite. There was a flash knockout over **Ken Shamrock**, a grappling duel with the entertaining but ineffectual **Ikuhisa Minowa**, and, as the tears poured out from behind Sakuraba's Tiger Mask getup, a shocking departure from the dying Pride to longtime rival K-1. As part of **Hero's**, and later **Dream**, Sakuraba's fights alternated between winnable matches against newcomers to the sport and a kind of MMA legends circuit. It's unclear what a win over **Masakatsu Funaki** means in 2007, or a loss to **Kiyoshi Tamura** in 2008. But at least they're relatively safe outings for a man who has already been hospitalized once for restricted blood flow to his brain, no doubt the result of years of brutal in-ring punishment.

Sakuraba's last bout of real significance came on New Year's Eve 2006 against rising star **Yoshihiro Akiyama**. Try as he might, Sakuraba was unable to secure a grip on the **judo** player, and complained loudly to the referee both during and after the fight that something wasn't right. As it turned out, Akiyama had illegally greased his body to avoid the great grappler's takedowns. The revelation that he had cheated one of mixed martial arts' great legends — perhaps its greatest legend — was nothing short of scandalous. In the world of professional wrestling that gave Sakuraba his start and formed his sensibility, this was a heel turn, one that manipulated the audience's love for the fading hero into hatred for the villain who tried to cheat him, and rocketed the newly loathed Akiyama to top-draw status. Sakuraba was rightly furious: there was no question he'd been wronged, and he couldn't be expected to see any upside to what had transpired. But seen in a certain light, it was a fitting end — of relevance, at least — for the man who once fought to prove that "in fact, pro wrestling is strong."

Sakurai, Hayato

Nickname: Mach
Height: 5'9"
Weight: 168 lbs
Born: 8/24/75
Debut: Shooto: Let's Get Lost (10/4/96)
Career Record: 35-11-2
Notable Wins: Caol Uno (Shooto: Let's Get Lost); Frank Trigg (Shooto: R.E.A.D. Final); Shinya Aoki (Shooto: Alive Road, Dream 8); Jens Pulver (Pride Bushido 9); Joachim Hansen (Pride Bushido 9)
Notable Losses: Anderson Silva (Shooto: To the Top 7); Matt Hughes (UFC 36); Jake Shields (Shooto: Year End Show 2002); Dave Menne (Deep 10th Impact); Takanori Gomi (Pride Shockwave 2005); Nick Diaz (Dream 14)

When Hayato Sakurai was at his best — like the 20-fight undefeated run that opened his career, or his road to **Pride**'s lightweight tournament final — he could do it all. From any position, in any situation, he was dangerous. Whether hanging back and landing those punishing leg kicks, or clinching up to deliver knees to the body or launch into a huge hip throw, Sakurai was always more than most could handle on their feet. And once the fight got to the ground, his opponents had to contend with a man who finished second in the open-weight absolute category in the 1999 **ADCC** submission **wrestling** championship — as a welterweight.

For a recent example of the breadth of what Sakurai had to offer as a fighter, look no farther than his 2007 Pride bout against ***The Ultimate Fighter*** season six winner **Mac Danzig**. No, Danzig was never quite first-tier competition, skilled and tough as he is, and by 2007 Sakurai was a little past his prime, but if you want to see the full range of technique, if you want to see it all in one place, it's all here. Sakurai lands heavy, straight punches to the body, short hooks on his way into and out of the clinch, **Muay Thai** knees, a spinning back fist, cringe-inducing leg kicks, huge ippon seoi-nage and o-goshi **judo** throws, and a near **arm bar** submission. And that's just the first round. In the second, Sakurai bullied Danzig with left hook, right leg kick combos before knocking him out with a spectacular, whirling overhand right.

This was nothing new to Sakurai, who'd been doing much the same to all comers for more than a decade before he outclassed Mac Danzig. He first stepped into the ring in 1996 against another debuting future **Shooto** legend, **Caol Uno**. Sakurai beat Uno with an arm bar in the first round, and never looked back. It would be five years, 20 fights, and seven successful defenses of his 168-pound Shooto title before Sakurai first tasted defeat, dropping a unanimous decision to **Anderson Silva**. Sakurai followed his loss to the man who would become the **UFC**'s greatest middleweight champion with a dream match against the UFC's most accomplished welterweight champion, **Matt Hughes**. Hughes, in his first defense of the welterweight title he'd claimed with a controversial win over **Carlos Newton**, was at the height of his powers, and stopped Sakurai in the fourth.

For years, it looked as though that was the end of Hayato Sakurai as a top contender. He seemed unable to get back on track after a serious car accident between the title loss to Silva and the title challenge to Hughes. Maybe it was the crash, maybe not, but for whatever reason, Sakurai went from one of the most consistent fighters in the game to an unpredictable mess in the ring. The unshakeable calmness that characterized him at his best drifted into something closer to indifference. He dropped fights to Gracies you've probably never heard of, and even in victory fell short of the "Mach" we'd come to expect.

But he found new life on a new stage: Pride Fighting Championship's Bushido series. In an effort to finally crown a Japanese champion, Pride put together a 160-pound lightweight tournament built around their dynamic, heavy-handed star, **Takanori Gomi**. Although Gomi was clearly the centerpiece, the eight-man tournament was stacked with legitimate lightweight contenders, like **Yves Edwards**, **Chute Boxe**'s Luiz Azeredo, the UFC's first lightweight champion **Jens Pulver**, and former Shooto champs **Joachim Hansen** and **Tatsuya Kawajiri**. Sakurai advanced to the New Year's Eve finals on the strength of two impressive wins on the same night, a first round knockout of Pulver and a beautiful back-and-forth battle with Joachim Hansen in the best fight on one of the best cards in MMA history.

Sakurai fell short in the championship final. He opened strong against the dangerous Gomi, but after attempting a hip throw too close to the ring ropes, Sakurai was caught badly out of position, and the opportunistic Gomi pounded him out before he could regroup. Still, the 2005 Bushido tournament marked the return of the Sakurai everyone hoped to see again, the Sakurai who could do it all.

Now well into his thirties, Sakurai has settled into a role just below title contention. Although he still drops the occasional bout you'd never expect him to (David Baron? *Really?*), he can still surprise you in the other direction too. Was anyone counting on him picking up a second career win over top lightweight **Shinya Aoki**? The organizers of the **Dream** welterweight tournament who matched them up in the first round probably had other ideas. But while Sakurai might not be championship material any longer, he brings more than enough to the table to be one hell of a spoiler.

Salaverry, Ivan

Height: 6' **Weight:** 185 lbs

Born: 1/11/71 **Debut:** PPKA: Wenatchee (8/22/99)

Career Record: 12-7

Notable Wins: Andrei Semenov (UFC 37); Tony Fryklund (UFC 50); Joe Riggs (UFC 52)

Notable Losses: Akihiro Gono (Shooto: To the Top 1); Matt Lindland (UFC 39); Nate Marquardt (*Ultimate Fight Night* 1)

Ivan Salaverry was a dynamic fighter, but one damned by history to be remembered more for his biggest failure than his many successes. In 2005 the **UFC** had finally realized **Dana White**'s dream: his own version of boxing's old *Tuesday Night Fights*, a live fight program to showcase his UFC talent to a large cable television audience on Spike TV. This was an opportunity to help

In Their Own Words: Ivan Salaverry on Rooster Budo and his cockfighting tattoo

"Over here [in Chile], it's in somebody's ranch and there's a bunch of guys surrounding a cage. There, they have auditoriums where they have cockfighting. A whole scene people get into. You have the older gentlemen in the front rows betting. You have a young crowd. You have music playing. It's just a different culture. And if you ever see a fighting cock, the gymnastic level these little guys have is incredible. I've seen them get cut up and still go.

"I'm not even really a proponent of cockfighting, but what I saw made an impression. I'll give you an example. There was this one cockfight. One of the cocks was jabbing down on the other, and basically was winning. The injured cock's beak is about to hit the sand, and once the beak hits the sand, you lose. This cock was pecking, pecking away at him. And then the other cock jumps up, and whoom, cuts his head off. It was this beautiful jump, and the blade hit just the right place, and the head comes off. The crowd went wild. Both cocks died, but the winner, the one who beheaded the other, they lifted him up and they walked around with him. And the crowd just loved it, went crazy. Adored that chicken! After that I was like, wow.

"That's the one thing that I can tell you about it is that I want people to love me in that capacity. You know what I mean? When you're out there in a cage and you fight hard you want to know the people are loving you for what you brought to them. It stuck with me. This is the kind of spirit I would like to have."

Interview by Tommy Hackett, Total-MMA.com

establish not just stars for future pay-per-view bouts, but to establish for a new audience just what ultimate fighting was all about. The main event needed to provide a mix of action-packed fighting on the ground and on the feet. And Ivan Salaverry was entrusted with that responsibility.

Salaverry was exciting. His last two UFC wins had come by way of submission, both ending in the first round. After the fights he would do a cartwheel or blow a kiss to the crowd. His opponent was **Nate Marquardt**, another exciting and multi-faceted fighter the UFC had high hopes for. Instead of fireworks, the crowd was treated to one of the worst fights of all time. The fight was so bad that Salaverry was let go from his UFC contract. It was a tough call for the UFC. Salaverry was very popular personally with almost everyone in the industry. But the only thing worse than losing a fight is losing one of the most boring fights ever.

His career never recovered from the *Fight Night* debacle, but Salaverry continues to stay active in the business, training fighters at his Seattle gym.

Sambo

For most fans of mixed martial arts, sambo is the grappling art most closely associated with names like **Fedor Emelianenko**, **Andrei Arlovski**, **Sergei Kharitonov**, or, for those who have been watching since the sport's earliest days, **Oleg Taktarov**. Understandably, few would recognize the names Vasily Sergeevich Oshchepkov or Viktor Afanasievich Spiridonov. But these are the two most important names of all, the founding fathers of the discipline.

Vasily Oshchepkov grew up an orphan in the Pacific port city Vladivostok. Supported by a local charity, Oshchepkov attended Vladivostok's Tokyo Christian school, where he was first exposed to **judo**. Oshchepkov earned his black belt, founded a club of his own, and, in 1917, invited a Japanese team to Vladivostok to compete against his own students in one of the earliest instances of international competition in the sport. Oshchepkov, who had visited Japan twice to grade as a young man, maintained close ties with the country throughout his professional life, and worked in Tokyo for several years as a military interpreter — or, if Russian judo expert Andrew Moshanov is correct, as an intelligence agent. All the while, Oshchepkov kept up his studies at the Kodokan, and became a proficient second-degree black belt in the art.

In 1923, Oshchepkov was charged with the task of improving upon the Red Army's existing self-defense program. He was joined by Viktor Spiridonov, a veteran of the Russo-Japanese War whom Russian statesman and sportsman Vladimir Putin describes as "a top expert in applied military gymnastics, a strong and nimble man who quickly appreciated jujitsu's merits." Judo historian Mark Law offers this outline of their efforts:

> In a programme of "creative sessions" at four main sports centers in Moscow, including the Red Army's Central Club, [Oshchepkov and Spiridonov] brought together people from all over the USSR to meet in a succession of exploratory confrontations. The techniques of the Tajiks were assessed against those of the Khazaks; Georgians, who never fought on the ground, were pitted against Turkmen; Uzbek throws were tested against the pickups and leg grabs of the Azerbaijanis.

The sambo (literally "self-defense without weapons") that emerged from this crucible was at first confined to the Spetsnaz Soviet special forces, but later spread to the population at large under sport rules similar to those of judo, but with several important differences, beginning with the uniform. The red or blue jackets, called kurtka, are worn tighter than the judogi, shorts take the place of **gi** pants, and competitors take to the mat in **wrestling** shoes rather than bare feet. **Leg locks** are prominent, strangulations are banned, and throws are only scored if the attacker manages to stay on his feet. Less restrictive gripping regulations — reminiscent of judo rules in the 1920s, when sambo began to take shape — lead to a variety of throws executed while holding the belt. Those differences aside, there is an enormous amount of crossover between the techniques and strategies of both sports.

And between competitors, too: with judo's inclusion in the 1964 Tokyo Olympics, the Soviets combed their sambo ranks to identify those who might flourish under the closely related rules of modern competitive judo. Top Soviet sambo players and top Soviet judo players were one and the same. The uniquely Soviet judo that grew out of Oschepkov and Spiridonov's sambo was characterized by the leg grabs and pickups of the traditional wrestling styles of the Soviet lands, expert **arm bars** executed from all angles, and an athleticism that brought a quickened pace to the sport. The Soviets enjoyed immediate and lasting success, and Russia remains a robust judo power to this day.

Oschepkov, however, didn't live long enough to see the fruits of his labor. His close ties with Japan, which formed the basis of his life's work, would ultimately prove to be his undoing as Stalin's distrust of all things foreign deepened throughout the 1930s. As one of the millions undone by The Great Purge of 1937, Oschepkov was arrested under accusations of espionage and died soon after his imprisonment at the age of 44. His name was effectively wiped out of the official history of the martial art he fathered, as was the word "judo" for many years — both were tainted by their association with a foreign power, and had no place in the Republics.

Sambo today is practiced around the world, though its organizational structure beyond Russia and its former satellites is loose at best. In addition to the grappling-sport sambo described above, there exists a more obscure variant known as combat sambo, which allows chokes and a variety of strikes in addition to the throws, leg locks, and arm locks permissible under sport sambo. Combat sambo thus closely resembles a jacketed version of MMA, and indeed heavyweight MMA legend Fedor Emelianenko is a four-time world champion in the sport. It should be noted, however, just how minor a sport combat sambo is at present: en route to his 2007 world championship, two of Emelianenko's opponents failed to even show up, which is inconceivable in any truly credible world-class event. The grappling-only sport sambo, though perhaps of less immediate interest to fans of mixed martial arts, is vastly more competitive than its more rugged offshoot.

Sanchez, Diego

Nickname: Nightmare **Height:** 5'11"

Weight: 155–170 lbs **Born:** 12/31/81

Debut: Ring of Fire 5 (5/21/02) **Career Record:** 21-4

Notable Wins: Kenny Florian (*The Ultimate Fighter* 1 Finale); Nick Diaz (*The Ultimate Fighter* 2 Finale); Karo Parisyan (UFC Fight Night 6); Clay Guida (*The Ultimate Fighter* 9 Finale)

Notable Losses: Josh Koscheck (UFC 69); Jon Fitch (UFC 76); B.J. Penn (UFC 107)

Fans first learned Diego Sanchez was a little different during the first season of ***The Ultimate Fighter***. While others drank and made mischief, Sanchez explained some of his interesting philosophies to the world. Sanchez was incredibly intense, a devotee of self-help guru Tony Robbins, but also a bit of a mystic. He warmed up outside in the rain, convinced the storm brought him energy, and practiced yoga in the sauna to cut weight. Of all the fighters in that first season, none wanted it more than Sanchez. He dominated the competition, including future **UFC** stalwarts **Chris Leben**, **Kenny Florian**, and **Josh Koscheck**, on his way to winning the six-figure contract.

In the UFC proper, Sanchez looked better than ever before. His skills were solid, but nothing was better than good: he was a good striker, a good grappler, and a good wrestler. But he wasn't great at anything. What separated Sanchez from the pack was his insatiable desire. He simply went out and fought harder than his opponent. It was a virtual guarantee that Sanchez would go full-out for 15 minutes. Not many fighters could match his pace, and he took advantage of opponents who tired.

On his way to what seemed an inevitable title shot, Sanchez beat some of the UFC's very best welterweights, including **Nick Diaz** and **Karo Parisyan**, in fights that were among the best ever in the Octagon. Many of his fights main evented Spike television specials and he became one of the UFC's most recognizable fighters. Yet a title shot eluded him.

He had momentum on his side and with his television notoriety, he seemed a likely candidate to face the legendary **Matt Hughes**. Then he ran into a roadblock constructed by "Crazy" Bob Cook and the American Kickboxing Academy. Sanchez lost an atypical fight with former *Ultimate Fighter* teammate Josh Koscheck, who made huge strides expanding his repertoire at AKA. The two men had been friendly on the show, but in ensuing years had developed into bitter rivals. Koscheck got into Sanchez's head and Diego was so afraid of his opponent's takedown prowess that he refused to engage. It was later revealed that Sanchez had been ill and had a staph infection, explaining why the usually swarming Sanchez offensive attack was replaced with a defensive shell. Sanchez lost for the first time in his professional career, a bitter pill to have to swallow during a difficult time.

After spending his entire career with trainer **Greg Jackson** in New Mexico, Sanchez was moving on. Jackson had brought in **Georges St. Pierre**, a former champion, to train with his all-star team. Sanchez saw this as a sign that Jackson didn't think Sanchez would ever be a champion; after all, if St. Pierre were to become champion again, Jackson would never allow Diego to fight a teammate.

Leaving his friends and family for the first time, Sanchez relocated to California, where he trained with legendary jiu-jitsu instructor Saulo Ribeiro. His first fight outside the Jackson family was a bitter disappointment. He lost to Koscheck's ATT teammate **Jon Fitch**, a victim of Fitch's superior size more than his superior techniques.

In Their Own Words: Diego Sanchez on getting down to 155 pounds

"Man, I've been an experiment. I've been a human science experiment since the day that I got in this game. I started supplementing when I was a junior in high school, the Rip Fuel. Name it, man. I've been addicted to ephedrine. I've done creatine and O2s. I've done it all. And then the nutrition part, really, started to excel for me. You know when I was on *The Ultimate Fighter*, man, I was eating a box of Rice Krispies every night. I used to eat meat because I heard that fighters should eat meat, red meat, and I'd eat red meat super-well done, like a piece of rubber.

"But then I actually hired Rob Garcia, Oscar de la Hoya's strength and conditioning and nutritionist coach. And he coached me for two and a half years, taught me how to cook, taught me a lot of stuff. You know I used to be on a big-time brown rice, egg whites, a lot of spinach, healthy fats like olive oil, and that diet was good for me at 170 but I had to make some adjustments to dropping to 155. I had to cut more fats out. Cut more carbs out. It's really hard. I don't know, man, right now my calories, I'm probably maybe at about 1,100. So yes, my meals are real small and real precise."

Eventually, Sanchez bowed to pressure and moved down a weight class to lightweight. It was an immediate success. Sanchez had always been smaller than his opponents at 170 pounds. Now he was like-sized and just as dangerous. He beat top contenders **Joe Stevenson** and **Clay Guida**, not only securing important wins, but also earning Fight of the Night honors. The old Sanchez was back, and at 155 pounds, seemed likely to earn the title shot he never managed to secure at welterweight.

Santos, Cristiane

Nickname: Cyborg | **Height:** 5′8″
Weight: 145 lbs | **Born:** 7/9/85
Debut: Show Fight 2 (5/17/05) | **Career Record:** 10-1
Notable Wins: Shanya Baszler (EliteXC: Unfinished Business); Hitomi Akano (Strikeforce: Shamrock vs. Diaz); Gina Carano (Strikeforce: Carano vs. Cyborg)
Notable Loss: Erica Paes (Show Fight 2)

As you would expect from a woman nicknamed "Cyborg," Cris Santos is like a machine — one that goes in a single direction: forward. She plows ahead methodically, stalking her victims across the cage, waiting for the moment to unleash the kind of fury rarely seen in women's MMA.

Like many Brazilian MMA fighters, Santos was born in Curibata. Like many champions, including **Wanderlei Silva**, **Mauricio Rua**, and **Anderson Silva**, her devastating attack was honed in the gyms of Rafael Cordeiro. The head of **Chute Boxe** saw her compete in a high school handball tournament. One year later, she was making her MMA debut.

Santos uses her strength advantage to push her opponents into the cage and wear them down with a constant barrage of strikes. She has yet to meet her physical equal, having run over a series of overmatched opponents. Some opponents were simply not good enough to beat her. Others, like Japanese submission star Hitomi Akano, were tremendously outsized, in Akano's case a disadvantage compounded by Santos missing the contracted weight by almost six pounds.

EliteXC and, when they went out of business, **Strikeforce** almost immediately saw what they had in Santos. She was the perfect foil for the face of women's MMA, **Gina Carano**. The two were polar opposites. Carano was centerfold pretty and a media darling. Santos looked like exactly what she was: a female body builder.

It was a compelling contrast and in 2009 the two women became the first female fighters to headline a major MMA card in America. More than 13,500 fans packed the HP Pavilion in San Jose, California, to cheer on Carano.

There wasn't much to celebrate though; Cyborg overwhelmed the fan favorite to become the first Strikeforce women's champion.

Sapp, Bob

Nickname: The Beast
Height: 6′5″
Weight: 350 lbs
Born: 9/22/72
Debut: Pride 20 (4/28/02)
Career Record: 11-6-1
Notable Wins: Kiyoshi Tamura (Pride 20); Yoshiro Takayama (Inoki Bom-Ba-Ye 2002)
Notable Losses: Antonio Rodrigo Nogueira (Pride Shockwave); Kazayuki Fujita (K-1 MMA Romanex)

Bob Sapp is a ridiculously large man. There have been plenty of big men in the world of MMA, some even bigger than Sapp. But no one had ever packed quite so much muscle onto quite so large a frame. Sapp wasn't just 350 pounds — he was a ripped and cut 350 pounds. Before he found fighting, Sapp struggled to find a use for his amazing genetics. After failing in football and failing in **professional wrestling**, the former Washington Husky was moving furniture and preparing for a life of manual labor. Then he was discovered by the Japanese promotion K-1 and his life would never be the same.

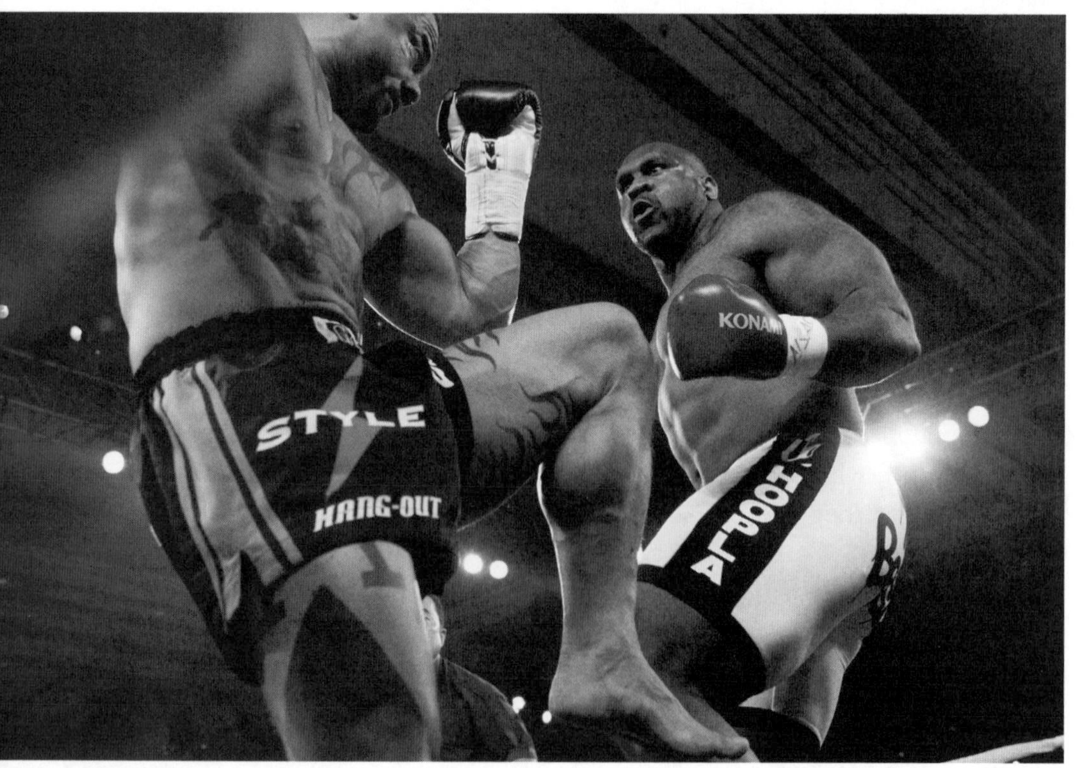

Sapp's success story is one you hear often, but it's normally attached to teen idols like the Jonas Brothers or Britney Spears. Sapp became more than a fighter in Japan. He is a cultural icon. The combination of his unusual size and bigger-than-life personality resonated with fans in Japan. He exploded onto the scene at the same time the sport was reaching the peak of its popularity. Sapp became the face of MMA in Japan. His fights set ratings records on network television. Sapp's fight with sumo star **Akebono** in 2003 attracted 54 million fans. He also starred on talk shows and pitched products from washing machines to televisions.

Sapp is unusual, because he peaked in the first year of his fighting career. In an amazing eight-month run in 2002, Sapp came close to defeating the world's best heavyweight MMA fighter **Antonio Rodrigo Nogueira**. He used a pro wrestling–style powerbomb to rattle Nogueira, but the champion had too much heart to lose. He secured an **arm bar** when Sapp got tired. It was an epic fight and Sapp's ascension to the top of the sport would soon follow.

Just a month later he beat the world's best kickboxer, Ernesto Hoost. Then he beat him again. Using his size to bully the smaller champion, Sapp looked nearly unbeatable, but the eight fights in eight months may have been too much. He's never been the same. As the outside distractions mounted, Sapp's

In Their Own Words: Bob Sapp on racism

"I get asked about the banana thing and everything else. Bottom line is the 'Beast' not only had bananas, I had raw meat and all kinds of crazy stuff going on. It wasn't anything that had to do with racism. What happens, and this is very common, we in America assume that the rest of the world has all our same views. Sometimes I've been criticized for my Panasonic commercial, they say, 'You look like a pimp.' I start laughing and say, 'That's not the way the Japanese are going to look at it.' That's how Americans look at it. They don't have pimps over here, they have mama-sans. It's a female, the mama, who is in charge of the prostitutes. Not a male. Not a pimp. So they had no idea. But it's very common that it happens.

"They aren't in the streets hollering negro this, nigger this, they're out there saying, 'Bob Sapp, Bob Sapp' and everyone is going nuts. Would you say it's racism because I've also got the number one selling women's sex toy in Japan? The Bob Sapp Wild Sapp Dildo. The closest thing that compares to it is a horse. I don't think it has anything to do with a gorilla. I think what's occurring is that things are going so well people say, 'Why don't we knock him down a peg?'"

training time and devotion to being a great fighter waned. He struggled with ordinary fighters like **Kimo Leopoldo** and **Seth Petruzelli** and lost to terrible fighters like Jan Nortje. Seven years after his stunning debut, the idea of Sapp beating a world champion is laughable.

Today he is a familiar face to fans worldwide, guaranteed to get a fight card some extra media attention. What he's not is a champion. Sapp loves the limelight, but he doesn't love fighting. It's just something he does in between television appearances — just another of his many engagements.

Sato, Rumina

Nickname: Tsukiokami ("Moon Wolf") **Height:** 5'6"

Weight: 143 lbs **Born:** 12/29/73

Debut: Shooto: Vale Tudo Access 2 (11/7/94) **Career Record:** 20-14-2

Notable Wins: John Lewis (Vale Tudo Japan 97); Charles Diaz (Shooto: Devilock Fighters); Yves Edwards (SuperBrawl 17); Bao Quach (Shooto Hawaii: Soljah Fight Night)

Notable Losses: Joel Gerson (Shooto: Las Grand Viajes 2); Caol Uno (Shooto: 10th Anniversary Event, Shooto: R.E.A.D. Final); Takanori Gomi (Shooto: To the Top Final Act); Joachim Hansen (Shooto: 2003 3/18 in Korakuen Hall); Takeshi Inoue (Shooto: Tradition Final)

Had he been born a little later, had he began his mixed martial arts career when lightweight fighters were front and center in Japan, submission ace Rumina Sato could have been a star. Instead, he'll be remembered as a cult hero only by the small but devoted **Shooto** audience that has stuck by his side during a 15-year (and counting) odyssey that has seen Sato come up just short of championship gold time and time again.

Sato burst onto the professional Shooto circuit in 1994, and captured the imagination of the Shooto faithful with the extraordinary range of his submission fighting skills. It's not just that he was finishing people, and finishing them early — it's that he was finishing them with calf slicers and flying reverse **triangle chokes** in addition to your garden variety **arm bars, Kimuras, rear naked chokes**, and **heel hooks**. In the early years, only the tough **John Lewis** gave him any trouble, and probably got the better of Sato in a match that went the distance at **Vale Tudo** Japan 1996. But without judges to render a decision, the match was declared a draw, and Sato ultimately ran his unbeaten streak to a dozen bouts with a decisive arm bar win over Lewis a year later.

Then came Canadian Joel Gerson, whom few outside of Ontario **judo** and jiu-jitsu circles, or Moni Aizik's Samurai Club in Richmond Hill (the same

> ***In Their Own Words:* UFC star Joe Lauzon on Rumina Sato's influence**
>
> "Sato was one of my favorite guys to watch. He is probably to blame for me being so reckless with submissions. I used to watch his highlight reels all day long. I learned so many things just from watching highlight videos. Crazy, low percentage, off the wall moves. But he'd just go for it. And that's influenced what I do so much. That guy never had a boring fight. Maybe he didn't win every fight, but he was always worth watching. He might not submit someone, but the possibility is always there. It's like a **Chuck Liddell** fight. He's got all that power in his right hand and the knockout can come anytime. So, you watch."

gym that turned out **Carlos Newton**), had every really heard of. In a stunning upset, Gerson threw Sato at will, and handed him his first career loss when he applied a picture-perfect arm bar late in the first round. "Commentators in the first row stood, their mouths open in utter disbelief," Toronto sports reporter Beverly Smith wrote in the *Globe and Mail*. "One woman looked as if she wanted to cry."

Many of Sato's best moments were yet to come, like a dazzling, six-second win by flying arm bar over Charles Taylor, and an all-time classic battle with **Caol Uno** at Shooto's 10th Anniversary Event, his first bid for championship gold. But it was never quite the same after that first loss. Sato vowed that he would not leave the organization before he'd earned a Shooto world title, and the short version of the Rumina Sato story is that more than a decade later, he's still there. His most recent title challenge came against Takeshi Inoue in commemoration of Shooto's 20th anniversary — and fittingly, Sato came up short. It was hardly a surprise: Sato hadn't won since 2007, and hasn't finished anyone by way of submission since 2004. But the much-loved Shooto stalwart soldiers on, no longer as a legitimate title contender but as the visible soul of the organization he's always called home.

Schrijber, Bob

Nickname: Dirty Bob
Height: 6′
Weight: 235 lbs
Born: 3/3/65
Debut: CFT 1 (1/1/95)
Career Record: 20-17-1
Notable Wins: Gilbert Yvel (IMA: Knockout Power); Hugo Duarte (2H2H 1); Ian Freeman (It's Showtime: Christmas Edition); Melvin Manhoef (2H2H 6)

Notable Losses: Gilbert Yvel (Rings Holland: The Final Challenge); Daijiro Matsui (Pride 7); Heath Herring (World Vale Tudo Championship 9); Wanderlei Silva (Pride Grand Prix 2000); Semmy Schilt (It's Showtime: Exclusive); Gary Goodridge (2H2H 2); Igor Vovchanchyn (It's Showtime: Amsterdam Arena 2003); Melvin Manhoef (It's Showtime: Amsterdam Arena 2005)

At the pre-fight rules conference before **Pride** 7, the camera panned to catch Holland's Bob Schrijber listening intently. He need not have bothered. The next night, during his fight with **Daijiro Matsui**, Schrijber was disqualified. He illegally held the ropes, while illegally stomping Matsui with illegal blows to the back of the head, all after the bell to end the first round had rung. Matsui learned the hard way why they call him "Dirty Bob."

Make no mistake: Schrijber was a dirty fighter, but he was also dangerous. He was a bouncer who had been in hundreds of street fights. His kickboxing matched up with anyone in the world. He knocked out two of the best strikers in the sport, **Gilbert Yvel** and **Melvin Manhoef**, and went toe-to-toe with **Igor Vovchanchyn** and **Wanderlei Silva** before the veterans took the easy way out, taking it to the mat and tapping Schrijber out. For all of his standing prowess, the ground remains Schrijber's Achilles heel. Ten of his 17 losses came by way of submission.

Dirty Bob was also one of the fight game's great showmen. During his 2000 fight with fellow Dutchman Semmy Schilt, Schrijber brought a ladder into the ring so he could look the seven-foot Schilt in the eye during the introductions. The rest was vintage Schrijber. He took a horrific beating from the better fighter, but he refused to quit. Eventually it was a submission hold that ended his night.

Today, Schrijber doesn't just train fighters like **UFC** veteran Stefan Struve. He's also been a referee for several MMA fights in Europe. After all, if anyone knows how to spot a dirty fighter, it's Bob Schrijber.

Semaphore Entertainment Group (SEG)

Semaphore Entertainment Group (SEG) was struggling before the **Ultimate Fighting Championship** became an overnight success in September 1993. The pay-per-view industry was still in its formative years, and SEG was among a handful of companies trying to find a product Americans were willing to watch at a premium. SEG had tried everything: concerts with bands like Iron Maiden, a comedy show with a past-his-prime Andrew Dice Clay, even a kid's show with the developers of Thomas the Tank Engine. Nothing stood out. It seemed America was only willing to pay for three things: **boxing, professional**

wrestling, and porn. With that in mind, SEG executive Campbell McLaren began searching for visceral entertainment along those lines, programming that would feel like a slap in the face. McLaren was considering green-lighting a demolition derby or Mexican professional wrestling when a proposal for "War of the Worlds" came across his desk.

McLaren immediately took the idea to his boss, former radio maverick Bob Meyrowitz. **Rorion Gracie**, ad-man **Art Davie**, and Hollywood heavyweight John Milius had the inkling of an idea that could be refined into something special. The proposal was for a multi-show tournament to crown the "World's Hand-to-Hand Combat Champion." Bouts would be contested in a pit with Greek columns and statues surrounding it, a nod to the original Olympic pankration. That wouldn't work, the producers agreed, but neither would a simple boxing ring. Gracie was adamant that a ring could not contain a real fight. Soon, ideas were flying around fast and furious, including fighters surrounded by a moat filled with piranhas and fights enclosed by a Plexiglas cage. In the end, a Hollywood set designer created the now-famous Octagon.

The UFC was a huge hit from the very beginning, drawing an unbelievable 86,000 pay-per-view buys with no television or media support. The event included an eight-man tournament for a prize of $50,000, won by Rorion's brother **Royce Gracie** with relative ease, including a victory over future hall of famer **Ken Shamrock** in the semi-finals. On their first attempt, SEG had struck gold, finding two stars in Shamrock and Gracie, both compelling and memorable characters.

The second event was expected to feature a rematch between the two, a match that was postponed when Shamrock broke his arm training with **Vernon White**. After the first show ran short, matchmaker Art Davie booked a whopping 16 men for the second one-night tournament. The prize money was bumped to $60,000. The extra $10,000 may have come from money saved on expenses — the fighters and their entourages were housed in a scary hotel normally occupied by hookers and drug dealers. Gracie survived four men, and the hotel, to win his second tournament. The most notable addition to the UFC crew was referee "Big" **John McCarthy**. McCarthy was the third man in the cage, but not empowered to stop the fights. He insisted on that authority going forward and became as recognizable as any fighter and a powerful behind-the-scenes influence.

UFC 3 was a disaster, albeit an entertaining one that ended up making the promotion more popular than ever. The UFC was counting on Shamrock and Gracie finally meeting, even creating a poster that featured the two in an intense staredown. Still thinking they could control the outcome, promoters put the two men in opposite brackets, figuring a meeting in the finals would be more dramatic than a first-round encounter. **Kimo Leopoldo**, a street fighter turned missionary from Hawaii, was more than happy to play the role of spoiler. Kimo came to the cage carrying a giant cross on his back. He had enough strength afterwards to take the fight to Gracie, battering him badly before finally falling victim to an **arm bar**. An exhausted Gracie couldn't return and an injured Shamrock didn't have the spirit to continue on against anyone but Gracie. The finals featured the mulleted **Harold Howard** taking on alternate **Steve Jennum.** Jennum, facing competition for the first time in the finals, took home the title of Ultimate Fighting Champion, the first non-Gracie to do so.

The pro wrestling–esque spectacle of the third event made the promotion bigger than ever. At UFC 4, they more than doubled the pay-per-view sales of their first event and sold out the arena in Tulsa, Oklahoma. Unfortunately, the backlash had begun. Senator John McCain sent a letter to the Oklahoma Attorney General and tried to get the event canceled. Pressure was also placed on pay-per-view carriers, but the event was selling well enough that they refused to give in. **Dan Severn** made his MMA debut, but only after another competitor bowed out after an injury. Severn had failed to impress matchmaker Art Davie, but wowed the world with two amazing back suplexes on an out-sized Anthony Macias. Severn advanced to the finals to take on Gracie, and controlled him for 15 minutes before succumbing to a **triangle choke**. It was an amazing finish, but one most around the country didn't see. The UFC had been allotted just two hours for their show. When the Severn/Gracie match went past that mark, it was cut off in thousands of homes nationwide. The UFC's most dramatic come-from-behind victory went unseen by the masses, and what should have been their biggest payday to date was lost when cable companies refunded millions to unhappy customers.

By UFC 5, SEG had learned their lesson. Shamrock and Gracie were removed from the tournament altogether, instead clashing in the UFC's first Superfight. Fans were anticipating something epic; instead, Shamrock and Gracie turned in the worst performances in MMA history. Neither was willing to engage and the fight was a 36-minute dud. Luckily Severn returned to liven things up in a dominant performance, winning three bouts in just nine minutes on his way to the tournament championship. The event was the last for Rorion and Royce Gracie. Unhappy with new time limits, in place to prevent another UFC 4 disaster, Gracie and Art Davie sold their share of the UFC to Bob Meyrowitz. It was the end of an era.

It was also the high point for business under SEG. More than 260,000 homes bought the event on pay-per-view, a record that stood well into the

Zuffa era. The UFC had captured an audience, but couldn't out-fight John McCain. At every event McCain placed incredible pressure on local politicians. The UFC hoped to escape mounting political pressure in the continental United States with UFC 8, but inadvertently walked into a minefield in Puerto Rico. McCain continued to attack the event, encouraging the Puerto Rican government to ban the show. His ally across the aisle, Democrat Joe Lieberman from Connecticut, successfully lobbied pay-per-view giant Cablevision to pull the show from their network. A negative piece on ABC's *20/20* did little to help. The UFC's David Isaacs was in court just the day before the event when he finally secured permission for the show to go on. Inside the cage, it was SEG executive Campbell McLaren's finest moment. He had loved the **Keith Hackney**/Emmanuel Yarborough fight from UFC 3, a battle between a small **karate** man and a gargantuan sumo, and devised a "David versus Goliath" format for the UFC 8 tournament. It was a tremendous success, as former collegiate wrestler **Don Frye** won a thrilling eight-man contest. In the main event, Ken Shamrock successfully defended his title over Kimo Leopoldo, locking in a **knee bar** and making the big Hawaiian tap out.

Things went from bad to worse at UFC 9 as enemies mounted. The American Medical Association may have been against boxing and mixed martial arts, but they sure weren't afraid to kick the UFC while it was down. The group's president, Lonnie Bristow, issued a scathing indictment of "human cockfighting," and continuing pressure from McCain and other advocates of media censorship nearly saw the event canceled. The fiercest battle of the day was in court where a judge allowed the event to continue, but with two important rule changes: no head butts and no closed-fist punches to the head. The UFC devised a perfect work-around; punches were technically illegal, but the punishment would be a fine of just $50. The main event was the worst fight in UFC history, a 30-minute dance between Severn and Shamrock. Shamrock had almost decided not to fight at all. He saw himself as a role model and didn't want to knowingly break the law. He also feared pre-fight injuries, including a broken nose and injured ribs, would slow him down. Pressure from Isaacs, Bob Meyrowitz, and his father, Bob Shamrock, convinced him to show up — he didn't do much fighting, but he at least went into the Octagon. Before the event, pay-per-view outlets in Canada decided not to carry the UFC. Since Canada accounted for up to a quarter of the UFC's pay-per-view income on some shows, this was another major blow to the company's bottom line. The ship, it seemed, was sinking.

By UFC 12 it was clear that McCain had won. This show was a logistics triumph for Isaacs. At the last minute, the UFC had to move the show from

Niagara Falls, New York, to Dothan, Alabama. The New York legislature, despite approving the sport overwhelmingly, backtracked after negative press in the *New York Times*. Because state law didn't allow the legislature to change the law so quickly, the athletic commission came up with a new set of rules to govern no-holds-barred fighting. New rules would require a gigantic 40-foot cage, mandate headgear, and allow no submission holds. With just three days to comply with these ridiculous new restrictions, the UFC was confident it would win the legal battle — they had won everywhere else. Shockingly, the New York courts sided with the government. The UFC chartered two planes to carry everyone and everything associated with the event (even the Octagon itself) to Alabama. Dog-tired fighters arrived at the hotel at 5 a.m. The promoters and television crew didn't have that luxury. They went to the Waffle House, loaded up on coffee, and got ready to set up a live pay-per-view event, something that usually took days, in just hours. It was another costly night for the UFC. The move cost more than a quarter of

In Their Own Words: SEG Vice President David Isaacs on SEG's role in creating the UFC fans see today

"I think Dana White has done a lot of really good things. I really, really do. But I also think he's kind of propagated this myth of the old UFC – that we had no rules, we were outlaws and not trying to get it regulated, and that they changed so many things. Eh. You know I hired **Joe Silva**. What's he doing now? John McCarthy we hired through Rorion. **Joe Rogan**, Campbell found. **Mike Goldberg**? I found. The producer? I found. The director? I found. Dana is telling a story that isn't entirely true based on the facts, but I think it's a good story for the media. This is the new UFC. The mainstream press doesn't understand it so they are looking for the headline version. Human cockfighting was that headline. Today it's 'Fastest Growing Sport in the World.' That's the story. They just don't have the time or the interest to really understand the details. We got into this because we thought there was something there that was very compelling. We as a company had been looking for new types of programming for pay-per-view but as we fought through this we just thought we were right. It was safer than boxing. And we had the facts to prove it. It was a struggle, but we did believe at the end of the day that the truth and the work and the money we're putting into it would win out. But for a couple of things that happened, I think we would have been there. "

a million dollars and there was no paid attendance. With no time to advertise or sell tickets, the seats were given away to locals and to soldiers from nearby Fort Rucker. Amazingly, the event went off without a hitch. **Mark Coleman** wrecked Dan Severn to become the UFC champion and young Brazilian **Vitor Belfort** announced his presence as a future contender by dropping Scott Ferrozzo in the finals of a heavyweight tournament. **Lion's Den** standout **Jerry Bohlander** won the lightweight tournament for fighters under 200 pounds. Since there were no actual weigh-ins, the fighters just had to appear to be less than 200 pounds. The UFC had a long way to go to become a big league promotion. Soon after the show TCI Cable, Time Warner, and most cable providers dropped UFC pay-per-views. Senator McCain, the new chair of the powerful Commerce Committee, looked like he had finally won his long battle with cage fighting.

The UFC under SEG continued on, promoting events mostly in the deep south, waiting for the day that the sport would find its way back onto pay-per-view television and back in some of the country's major markets. Considerable effort went into cleaning up a reputation that they themselves had played a major part in slandering. Once, SEG was proud to play up the chance of a death in the Octagon, happy to tell the world they were banned across America. Now they were adding weight classes and creating their own rules under the guiding hand of former Olympic gold medalist **Jeff Blatnick**. Bob Meyrowitz was sure that the UFC was still an event that Americans would support and get behind and he held out hope for as long as he could. In 2000, after failing to see the sport approved by the powerful Nevada State Athletic Commision, Meyrowitz and SEG began looking to sell the UFC. Matchmaker **John Perretti** found funding and many within SEG were terrified the unpopular Perretti would be their new boss. Instead, Meyrowitz sold the show to the billionaire **Fertitta brothers** and their partner **Dana White**.

Sengoku Raiden Championships: see **World Victory Road: Sengoku**

Serra, Matt

Nickname: The Terra
Height: 5'6"
Weight: 170 lbs
Born: 6/2/74
Debut: VATV 3 (4/1/98)
Career Record: 11-6
Notable Wins: Yves Edwards (UFC 33); Jeff Curran (UFC 46); Georges St. Pierre (UFC 69)
Notable Losses: Shonie Carter (UFC 31); B.J. Penn (UFC 39); Karo Parisyan (UFC 53); Georges St. Pierre (UFC 83); Matt Hughes (UFC 98)

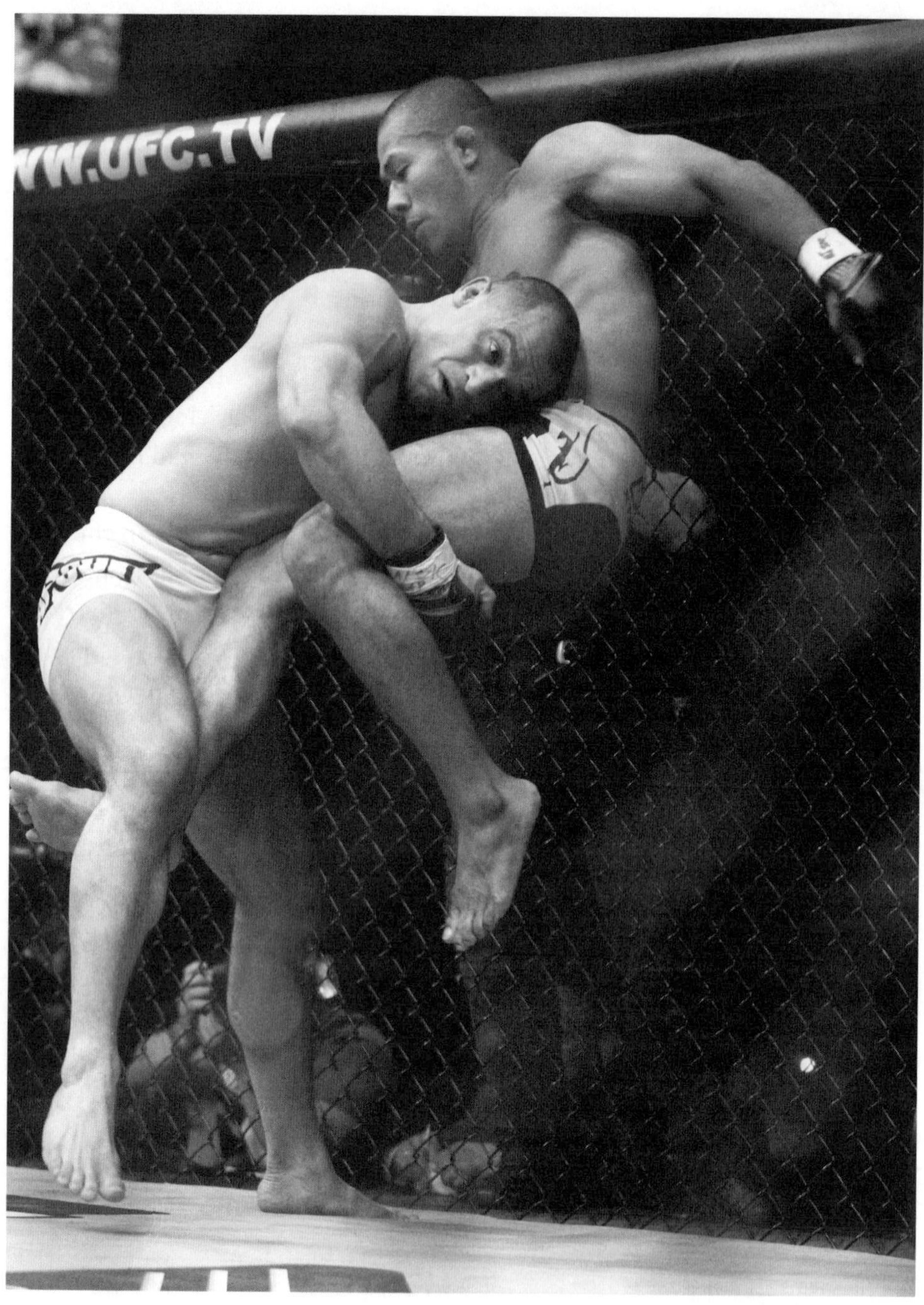

"It's crazy," a slighted agitated Matt Serra told Setanta Sports as his second bout against **Georges St. Pierre** drew near. "Last year may have been an upset but, believe me, it was no fluke. What is a 'lucky punch'? Who do these people think I was trying to punch in the face if not Georges? Seriously, you tell me, if you aim at something, and then hit it time and time again, was it luck or did you just do what you were trying to do?" Serra definitely had a point. But how else to make sense of an eleven-to-one underdog overwhelming the young champion who everyone agreed was the future of the sport? How did a journeyman like Serra even find himself standing across the cage from St. Pierre, a man who looked like he was not just in another league, but of a different species?

Dana White likes to say that ***The Ultimate Fighter*** (*TUF*) reality series can change lives, and Matt Serra is a prime example of that possibility. The fourth season of *The Ultimate Fighter* was billed as The Comeback, an opportunity for fighters who had already enjoyed an opportunity in the **UFC**, but had either crashed out or drifted away, to get back to that level of competition. Serra, an experienced and accomplished **Brazilian Jiu-jitsu** stylist and **ADCC** medalist who had split his eight UFC fights, was probably best known to UFC fans as the fighter on the wrong end of **Shonie Carter**'s amazing spinning backfist KO. His other UFC losses had come by tough, hard-fought decisions against opponents who ranged from good (**Din Thomas**, **Karo Parisyan**) to great (**B.J. Penn**), but that one big win had always eluded him.

But *TUF* tournament wins over Pete Spratt, Shonie Carter, and Chris Lytle earned Serra — who had fought most of his career at lightweight — a welterweight title shot. The first shot, in fact, was at new champion Georges St. Pierre, who demolished the great **Matt Hughes** to take the title. Much has been made of Serra's big right hand, the "lucky punch" that caught St. Pierre behind the ear and sent him staggering three minutes into the fight, but not enough has been said about the impressive body work that set it up. Changing levels, throwing hard shots to the body, and getting out of harm's way against a fighter with a six-inch reach advantage — that looked an awful lot like sound, well-executed strategy. Once Serra had the champ hurt, he was relentless, and forced GSP to tap to strikes from the **mount** at 3:25 of the first round.

To say that Matt Serra never again equaled that moment is true, but hardly the point. How do you top perhaps the greatest upset in MMA history? In his second bout with St. Pierre, Serra was taken down and dominated for the better part of two lopsided rounds before the referee stepped in. A year later, Serra dropped a long delayed and ultimately anticlimactic grudge match against Matt Hughes, almost certainly ending Serra's run at or near the top of the card. There can be no doubt, though, that Serra realized his potential, and got the most out of his unimposing physique. Asked about performance enhancing drugs in the sport, the stocky Serra once answered, "Dude, if you test me, I'll test positive for marinara sauce. That's about it." Given the standout coaching and cornering he showed on *The Ultimate Fighter*, and his two successful Brazilian Jiu-jitsu academies in New York, it would surprise no one to someday see Serra cageside, convincing a new generation of fighters that "small hammer fists are fine."

Severn, Dan

Nickname: The Beast | **Height:** 6'2"
Weight: 250 lbs | **Born:** 6/8/58
Debut: UFC 4 (12/16/94) | **Career Record:** 93-16-7

Notable Wins: Oleg Taktarov (UFC 5, Ultimate Ultimate 95); Tank Abbott (Ultimate Ultimate 95); Ken Shamrock (UFC 9); Paul Buentello (USWF 6); Marcus Silveira (WEF 9); Wes Sims (RSF 2); Forrest Griffin (RSF 5)

Notable Losses: Royce Gracie (UFC 4); Ken Shamrock (UFC 6); Mark Coleman (UFC 12); Josh Barnett (SuperBrawl 16); Pedro Rizzo (UFC 27)

Dan Severn started his MMA career as an object lesson. In his late thirties, sporting a wicked mustache and extra baggy black trunks, Severn looked like he had been transported from a 1920s magazine ad for athletic equipment directly to the Octagon. He was a big wrestler, a legitimate amateur who had qualified for the 1980 Olympic team. To a man like **Royce Gracie**, Severn was something else entirely: he was prey.

With just four days of training, Severn came into **UFC** 4 with no submission experience, no striking experience, and no chance. He just didn't know it yet. If he had been a killing machine like **Mark Coleman** was to be, it might have been a different story. But Severn was just a little too cerebral, even perhaps a little too decent, to do what it took to defeat Gracie. Instead, the smaller man wrapped his legs around Severn's head and neck and squeezed. If Severn was like announcer **Jeff Blatnick**, a fellow amateur star and a 1984 Olympic gold medalist, he probably thought it was nothing . . . until he saw black and had to tap out. Severn had fallen victim to a **triangle choke** and MMA had just had its first classic fight.

The Severn that returned for UFC 5 was a different man. A pro wrestler, he had developed a persona that he thought would fit this new sport. Dan Severn was no longer. In his place was "The Beast." The new Severn was much more aggressive, winning three fights in just nine minutes on his way to the tournament championship.

He wanted a rematch with Gracie, but Royce had fought his final bout in the UFC on that same show. His brother **Rorion Gracie** sold his share of the company to **Semaphore Entertainment Group** and he and Royce departed the group with their heads held high. Instead, Severn would be matched up against the super-popular **Ken Shamrock**. Although Shamrock had yet to win an important UFC fight, he was a crowd favorite. His muscular sculpted frame made him stand out and fans had been trained by movies and **pro wrestling** to associate large muscles with toughness. Severn and Shamrock were both pro wrestlers and were able to bring a little pizzazz to the UFC's drab pre-fight presentation. They had a spat at the press conference and fans were buzzing. The UFC had their first grudge match, which Shamrock won in the first round with a **guillotine choke**.

Severn would get his rematch, but first he would have to run the gauntlet of some of the best fighters in UFC history. The event was called The Ultimate Ultimate, and Severn conquered a field that included **Oleg Taktarov**, **Tank Abbott**, and **Marco Ruas**. It was the most stacked tournament MMA had ever seen and Severn had to fight for almost 50 minutes to win the $150,000 purse.

The Shamrock rematch at UFC 9 in Detroit, Michigan, was one of the very worst fights, worst sporting events, and worst entertainment experiences in world history. The UFC was under intense political pressure and a court banned closed fist strikes for the bout. The result was a timid affair, 30 minutes of staring at each other and about one minute of actual fighting. The fans turned on both men, even the home state favorite Severn, booing the fighters and chanting, "Let's go Red Wings." Even referee "Big" **John McCarthy** got into the act, imploring them to get busy. Severn won a decision that neither man deserved.

It was the last win of Severn's UFC career. His next bout was against fellow wrestler Mark Coleman, a bigger and better version of Severn himself. Coleman was younger, more aggressive, and a strong favorite. He demolished Severn in the first round to become the first UFC heavyweight champion.

Severn had eight fights on the independent circuit before getting another shot

In Their Own Words: SEG executive Campbell McLaren on Dan Severn

"I brought Dan in because he had legitimate credentials and would start to make us look like a real organization. Dan is a real wrestler, but he's not a real fighter. And there's a difference. Dan couldn't end a fight; he wasn't a puncher. Dan is a very nice man, but he reminds me of the horses on the Budweiser commercial. The Clydesdales? They can pull a wagon but they're not going to win any races. Everyone wanted him to be better and wanted to see what would happen next time. No one went, 'Bullshit, I'm never watching this again.' We still were presenting a more interesting thing than anyone else had."

in the UFC. He was unpopular with the UFC brass, who saw him as a boring wrestler, but the promotion needed his star power. Ken Shamrock and **Don Frye** had both left for professional wrestling and the UFC needed a popular name to challenge new champion **Maurice Smith.** Then Severn made a decision that would cost him. Just one week before UFC 15, Severn fought on the first **Pride** card in Japan. He beat **Kimo Leopoldo** in another horrible fight, but was banged up enough over the course of 30 minutes that he was in no shape to fight for the UFC. Tank Abbott filled in at the last minute, famously getting up off the bar stool to step into the Octagon, and Severn was blacklisted. He didn't make another appearance in the UFC for more than three years.

Realistically Severn was done as a meaningful MMA fighter. As he entered his forties, Severn just wasn't able to compete with the very best inside the cage. But his strong wrestling and ring experience served him well against dozens and dozens of young fighters around the world. Severn fought anyone he could, as often as he could. Along the way he's lost to rising prospects like **Josh Barnett** and come out ahead against future champions like **Forrest Griffin.**

Severn continues to fight, even as he enters his sixth decade on the planet. While **Randy Couture** gets all the attention as MMA's honorary old man, Severn grinds away, looking for that landmark 100th win. As amazing as his early exploits were, his success well into middle age may be the greatest achievement of Severn's athletic career.

Shamrock, Frank

Nickname: The Legend **Height:** 5'10"

Weight: 185–205 lbs **Born:** 12/8/72

Debut: Pancrase: King of Pancrase Tournament (12/16/94)

Career Record: 23-10-2

Notable Wins: Bas Rutten (Pancrase: King of Pancrase Tournament); Masakatsu Funaki (Pancrase: Eyes of Beast 6); Enson Inoue (Vale Tudo Japan 97); Kevin Jackson (UFC 15.5); Igor Zinoviev (UFC 16); Jeremy Horn (UFC 17); Tito Ortiz (UFC 22); Phil Baroni (Strikeforce: Shamrock vs. Baroni)

Notable Losses: Masakatsu Funaki (Pancrase: Eyes of Beast 2); Bas Rutten (Pancrase: 1995 Neo-Blood Tournament, Pancrase: Truth 5); John Lober (SuperBrawl 3); Renzo Gracie (EliteXC: Destiny); Cung Le (Strikeforce: Shamrock vs. Le)

When Frank Juarez stepped out of prison, his first stop was **Ken Shamrock**'s gym. The infamous **Lion's Den** was like a little military camp, filled with clean-cut fighters with short hair and an all-American look. Into their midst came Frank, a long-haired scrapper who, like Ken, came from Bob Shamrock's

Boys' Ranch. He took a horrible beating. Everyone wanted to be the one to initiate the cocky new guy, but Ken wanted to do it himself. If Frank was going to train with his team, he was going to earn it.

From those humble beginnings sprang forth the world's top fighter. Frank Shamrock was the very best fighter of his generation. Starting with his adopted brother Ken in Japan, Frank was the first **Pancrase** fighter to successfully adapt his technical grappling style to life inside the unforgiving cage. Before he could become the sport's best, however, Shamrock had to leave behind the only family he had ever known. He had to blow up a system that seemed to be working in order to develop one that could take him to unknown heights.

Shamrock was an amazingly fast learner. From the beginning of his fighting career he was able to hang with the best grapplers on the planet. He got a little help along the way. Ken was Pancrase's biggest foreign star. His good-looking "brother," a young fighter with serious potential, was carefully protected. Pancrase stars **Masakatsu Funaki** and **Minoru Suzuki** were both former pro wrestlers. They understood the value of building new stars and both men were willing to help Shamrock's career by taking it easy on him in early fights.

By 1996, Shamrock was thriving. He won the interim King of Pancrase title in a fight with Suzuki before losing it to his rival **Bas Rutten**. Rutten had started as a neophyte grappler and lost early fights to both Shamrock brothers. He continued to develop though, adding strong grappling to his amazing standup. Soon he had pushed past the Lion's Den fighters to become the best technical fighter in the promotion.

After losing twice to Rutten, and then losing a brutal fight to John Lober in Hawaii, Frank started questioning the way he had been preparing for his fights. Some of the problems he saw were easy to fix, like the fact he was smoking and drinking in Japan before the fights. Other problems were larger in scope. **Maurice Smith**, a professional kickboxer who came to the Den to work on his grappling skill, was appalled by the way they went about business. Guys were sparring bare-knuckle and there was no focus on cardiovascular conditioning at all; it was a primitive approach.

When Ken Shamrock left MMA for the wild world of **professional wrestling**, Frank took an opportunity to change some of the ways the Den operated. Ken was not used to being challenged. He was the leader, no questions asked, and Frank was supposed to follow direction. After a frenzied argument, that included Ken throwing a computer monitor at Frank, there was no turning back. Frank Shamrock was on his own.

Together with Maurice Smith and Japanese judoka **Tsuyoshi Kohsaka** (TK),

Shamrock created the Alliance. The three men exchanged techniques and strategy with unprecedented honesty. Instead of just "getting in there and scrapping" — the traditional instruction in the Lion's Den — Shamrock was learning to fight on his feet and to develop his body to its maximum potential. His first fight with Smith and TK in his corner was an amazing battle with **Enson Inoue** at **Vale Tudo** Japan 1997. Shamrock showed off his newly improved standup by knocking out Inoue with a knee to the jaw. There was almost a second fight that evening, when Inoue's brother Egan charged the ring to tackle Shamrock.

Order was restored and the win propelled Shamrock into a match for the first **UFC** middleweight (now called light heavyweight) title against former Olympic gold medalist Kevin Jackson. Fourteen seconds into the fight, Jackson was tapping and a new star was born. A subsequent 22-second win over Igor Zinoviev saw Shamrock effortlessly slam the **Extreme Fighting** standout to the mat, ending his evening and his career with a broken collarbone.

The two dominant wins over top fighters made him an immediate star. His win over **Tito Ortiz** at UFC 22 made him a legend. Ortiz had run through two of Frank's former Lion's Den teammates, **Jerry Bohlander** and **Guy Mezger**, and had an intense shouting match with Ken. Even though Frank had left the Den years earlier, the UFC played the event up as Frank getting revenge for his friends and family. Backstage while preparing for a photo shoot, Frank and Tito shared a laugh while the UFC prepared to advertise their fight as a blood feud.

It was an epic fight, one of the very best in the UFC's history. Ortiz outweighed Shamrock by close to 30 pounds and dominated the early going. But Shamrock's intense focus on conditioning paid off. He survived the best Tito had to offer, and when Ortiz tired, Shamrock pounced. At the end of the fourth round, Ortiz could take no more. Shamrock had conquered his greatest foe and after the fight announced his retirement in the Octagon.

The UFC was nearing bankruptcy and owner **Bob Meyrowitz** was honest with Frank: he simply could not afford to pay him what they had agreed to. Shamrock actually had to take a pay cut to fight Ortiz. Not willing to risk his health or his reputation for paltry paydays, Shamrock left the UFC behind him. Leaving martial arts behind wasn't so easy.

After fighting twice for K-1 in Japan, and after an aborted 2003 comeback, Shamrock was back as a full-time fighter in 2006. He had stayed involved in the sport, as an announcer and a trainer, keeping his name out there with a new generation of fans. More importantly, he had carefully studied successful promotional techniques. When he came back for **Strikeforce** and **EliteXC**, he was ready to make money, for himself and the promoters he worked with. The new Frank Shamrock wasn't nearly as good in the cage, but he was much better at selling the Frank Shamrock brand. Every Shamrock fight, no matter the opponent, became an entertaining war of words. He beat journeyman **Phil Baroni** and an inexperienced Cesar Gracie, but looked badly out of his depth against **Renzo Gracie** and **Nick Diaz.**

The best fight of Shamrock's third act was a titanic struggle with san shou (and movie) star **Cung Le.** The two were the most popular fighters in their hometown of San Jose, California, and the crowd was on edge for the entire fight. Shamrock chose to stand and exchange with Le, landing the more solid punches, but also falling victim to several unorthodox kicks. One kick broke Shamrock's forearm. Although he finished the third round, the fight was called and Le became the Strikeforce middleweight champion. It was one of the best fights of 2008, and proof that while Shamrock may no longer be a great fighter, he is still an entertaining one.

Shamrock, Ken

Nickname: The World's Most Dangerous Man **Height:** 6′

Weight: 205–220 lbs **Born:** 2/11/64

Debut: Pancrase: Yes, We Are Hybrid Wrestlers 1 (9/21/93)

Career Record: 27-13-2

Notable Wins: Masakatsu Funaki (Pancrase: Yes, We Are Hybrid Wrestlers 1); Bas Rutten (Pancrase: Road to the Championship 3, Pancrase: Eyes of Beast 2); Dan Severn (UFC 6); Kimo Leopoldo (UFC 8, UFC 48)

Notable Losses: Royce Gracie (UFC 1); Minoru Suzuki (Pancrase: Eyes of Beast 4); Dan Severn (UFC 9); Don Frye (Pride 19); Tito Ortiz (UFC 40, UFC 61, UFC: The Final Chapter); Rich Franklin (*The Ultimate Fighter* 1 Finale); Kazushi Sakuraba (Pride 30)

It was one of the most memorable moments in **UFC** history. After a dull as dirt fight between **Tito Ortiz** and **Guy Mezger**, Ken Shamrock took it upon himself to liven things up. Still in the midst of his **pro wrestling** run in the WWE, Shamrock brought a little pro wrestling flavor into the Octagon. The crowd, the announcers, fellow fighters — everyone was loving it. As Ortiz celebrated in the cage, putting on an obscene T-shirt and shooting the bird towards Shamrock and his corner, the "World's Most Dangerous Man" flipped out. Hanging over the cage, yelling and pointing, Shamrock looked deadly serious as he told Ortiz, "Tito, don't let me catch you wearing that T-shirt."

It was pure Ken Shamrock. Some of it was no doubt for show, but enough of the hysterics were real to make the situation seem a little dangerous. UFC officials were scared to death that Ken and Tito would soon be fighting backstage. It was a compelling moment, one that helped make the struggle between Ortiz and Shamrock's **Lion's Den** the most successful blood feud in UFC history. This is what Ken Shamrock brought to the Octagon. What he lacked in skill, he more than made up for in charisma and the ability to sell a fight. It's why Shamrock, despite a pedestrian 7–6–2 record in the UFC, is still the biggest star in MMA history.

Ken Wayne Shamrock has been at the forefront of the sport since the very beginning. He won the main event at the very first **Pancrase** card in Japan, beating his mentor **Masakatsu Funaki** with an **arm triangle**, and also wowed fans with his muscular physique and submission skills at the very first UFC a month later. Even though he lost to eventual champion **Royce Gracie** in the semi-finals, Shamrock still came out of the event looking like a million bucks.

Ken Shamrock's story is the story of MMA. Like the sport itself, Shamrock started strong. He won the King of Pancrase title in Japan and was the UFC's first Superfight champion, beating **Dan Severn** at UFC 6. As the UFC took fire from politicians and cable companies, Shamrock himself was criticized for a series of boring performances. Thirty minute–plus deadly draws at UFC 5 with Royce Gracie and UFC 7 with **Oleg Taktarov** earned Shamrock a reputation as a cautious and dull fighter. His performance at UFC 9, now affectionately called the "Dance in Detroit," confirmed it. Shamrock and Severn refused to engage at all, as the crowd booed and chanted, "Let's go Red Wings."

And then, the UFC disappeared from public view, banned in many states and pulled from pay-per-view. Shamrock left for greener pastures, returning to his original career in professional wrestling. Unlike fellow UFC stars, like Severn and **Tank Abbott**, who followed Shamrock into big-time American wrestling, the World's Most Dangerous Man thrived in the WWE ring. His charisma and ability to work a crowd translated into wrestling, although his lack of in-ring presence seemed to hold him back from reaching the very top.

While Shamrock excelled professionally, his personal life and relationship with his MMA team, the Lion's Den, was falling apart. The wrestling lifestyle, tiresome hours on the road, and rampant drug abuse were wearing on him. His adopted brother **Frank Shamrock** left the team and the former home of champions was struggling in the ring.

It was time for Shamrock himself to return, to set things right. It's no coincidence that Shamrock's MMA homecoming happened as the sport was taking off in Japan. Shamrock was a true professional, fighting for money, and the money was in Japan's **Pride**.

Shamrock's MMA second act was a mixed bag. His skills actually looked better than ever. While he had always been a super submission artist, he

had worked hard to add a respectable standup game to his arsenal. He beat up Japanese pro wrestler Alexander Otsuka on his feet and then dominated **Kazayuki Fujita**, fresh off a win over megastar **Mark Kerr**, until things got weird. Still in the first round, Shamrock seemed to suddenly tire. He called to his cornerman **Pete Williams**, "**Petey, my heart**!" The fight was soon stopped, and despite an impressive performance, Shamrock walked away as the loser.

The final fight on his Pride contract was the shining moment of Shamrock's career. He and fellow pro wrestling refugee **Don Frye** were asked to help promote their Pride 19 fight in America, hoping to challenge the UFC's dominance of the pay-per-view market. What followed was one of the greatest feuds in MMA history. Sometimes this kind of verbal sparring, highlighted by Frye's below the belt attacks on Shamrock's personal struggles, ends with a timid fight. Not this time. These two MMA pioneers gave all they had. Despite crippling Frye with his devastating **leg locks**, Shamrock ended up on the losing end of a split decision. Even in defeat, Shamrock had proven to Frye and his other critics that he was still a great fighter and on any given night was capable of amazing things.

While Shamrock was in Pride, the MMA landscape changed right under his nose. The UFC, his original home, had been sold to the mega-rich **Fertitta brothers** and was now being run by the ultra-aggressive **Dana White.** White and the new UFC were willing to commit the resources to finally bring fans the fight they had been craving for three and a half years: Ken Shamrock would finally get his shot at Tito Ortiz.

The UFC had struggled under the new ownership. They expected that getting the sport approved in Nevada and back on cable pay-per-view would solve all the ills from the **SEG** days. Instead, the sport failed to thrive. Part of the problem was the absence of a changing of the guard. The UFC was presenting a new generation of fighters, like Ortiz, as among the best in the world. Fans weren't buying it, in part because they had never seen this new group compete against the legends of old. That's what drove this fight and made it the most successful UFC pay-per-view since Shamrock's early days with the company.

Shamrock and Ortiz played up their feud to the hilt, throwing chairs during press conferences and talking trash back and forth. It seemed like phony pro wrestling theatrics, but Shamrock had worked himself into a legitimate frothing at the mouth frenzy. He had thought about the disrespect and thought about the T-shirt for three years. Now he was ready to make Ortiz pay. Unfortunately, a knee injury hurt Shamrock's training. Instead of making a natural cut to 205 pounds, an inability to do cardio work on his bum wheel forced Shamrock into a crash diet. By fight time he was exhausted and far from his best. Ortiz took advantage, battering the 38-year-old veteran for three rounds before Ken's student Tra Telligman threw in the towel.

The win established Ortiz as the top fighter in the business, but without Shamrock, the company still struggled to draw money with their pay-per-view shows. Something about Shamrock just made people want to watch him; he had that "it" factor you hear so much about but can't ever quite seem to be able to put your finger on.

In 2005, the UFC struck gold with the reality television show ***The Ultimate Fighter***. The show had been a qualified ratings success, drawing some big numbers early but losing momentum when the **Chris Leben–Josh Koscheck** grudge match turned into a snoozefest. **Zuffa** needed a strong final show to put themselves in the best possible negotiating position. Needing to attract interest, Dana White knew just who to call: Ken Shamrock. While everyone remembers the fight between **Forrest Griffin** and **Stephan Bonnar**, it was Shamrock and rising star **Rich Franklin** who drew the television ratings in the main event.

It was clear that the old-school stars were still money in the bank for the UFC. Royce Gracie, the jiu-jitsu star who fought Shamrock twice in the early days of MMA, had come back to draw more pay-per-view buys that anyone in history against **Matt Hughes** at UFC 60. White and his matchmaker **Joe Silva** knew of one main event that could top even that mega-event: the rematch between Tito Ortiz and Shamrock.

The two built towards what everyone expected would be the culminating fight of their long feud as competing coaches on the third season of *The Ultimate Fighter*. It was the best rated season of the show in history (until the recent debut of internet sensation **Kimbo Slice**) and the focus was on the squabbling coaches. Shamrock had a hair trigger temper. It was part of his wrestling character in the WWE, but he was like that in real life too. His televised arguments with Ortiz seemed like they would break down into physical violence at a moment's notice. By the time the two were scheduled to meet in the Octagon, the fight was red hot.

Unfortunately, the fight couldn't possibly live up to this electric build-up. Shamrock just wasn't the fighter he used to be and was quickly taken off his feet, slammed to the mat, and elbowed into oblivion. He was clearly seconds away from being finished, when referee **Herb Dean** stopped the fight after just 1:18. Shamrock hopped immediately to his feet, furious about the early stop. The fans were incensed, and the show's 775,000 pay-per-view buys seemed

In Their Own Words: Ken Shamrock on coaching *The Ultimate Fighter 3*

"Anytime you're put into a situation where the fighter [and] the trainer have to work with each other whether they mesh or not, it always becomes a problem. Then, when there are one or two guys you don't really mesh with, then it trickles down to the rest of the team. Unfortunately for me, not that the fighters were bad or anything, I just got a bunch of guys on the team that I didn't see eye to eye with. Me being a coach and running my own team for a long time, being able to call all the shots, it didn't work very well for me to have guys telling me what they wanted to do.

"It's a tough thing for a coach, especially for me. For so long I've been able to control things and bring these guys up and nurture them and mold them into great fighters. I was very successful at that early on. But when I was thrown into that situation, I knew the score. I knew there could be problems and there were. I had a hard time with that. Other guys, like Tito and Randy, really had some success with it. But for me it was difficult."

less important than brewing fan discontent.

A third match was announced, not for pay-per-view, but as a television special on Spike TV. To apologize for the second fight, the UFC was literally giving away a fight between its two biggest stars. Little had changed between July and October. This time Shamrock lasted two minutes instead of one. In the post-fight chaos, Shamrock tracked Ortiz down. "It was all business," Shamrock told Ortiz, who was trying to pull away from his bitter enemy. "You and me made a lot of money together. It was all business."

It would have been a great ending to a magnificent career. But fighters rarely go so quietly into that good night. Shamrock, in his forties, still thought he had more to give. He also needed the money. He had lost everything he made in his lucrative wrestling days and needed to fight to put food on the table. The results, as they often are for older fighters hanging on, were embarrassing for the proud Shamrock.

Journeyman Robert Berry knocked him out in his ProElite debut for **Cage Rage**, but Shamrock's star had seemingly not dimmed. He was tapped to fight Kimbo Slice for **EliteXC**, main eventing their second card on CBS. It would end up being the highest rated MMA show ever in North America; unfortunately for everyone involved, Ken Shamrock didn't end up fighting.

Hours before the fight, Shamrock confronted EliteXC management about his pay. He was furious that it was lower than Slice's, but officials insisted he stick with their signed agreement. Shortly after that blow-up, executives were shocked to find out Shamrock had cut himself during some last-minute training. Instead of using the old fighter's trick of super-gluing the cut shut, Shamrock had chosen to go and get stitches, knowing that meant he wouldn't be able to fight.

As if he hadn't tainted his reputation enough, things went from bad to worse. After the EliteXC debacle, no major promoter would touch Shamrock. Instead, he promoted his own fight, a win over Ross Clifton, a nondescript fighter with a losing record. Things were looking up. Shamrock was scheduled to fight fellow WWE alumnus **Bobby Lashley** in March 2009 when the California State Athletic Commission made an announcement many had expected to hear for years. Shamrock had tested positive for three illegal anabolic **steroids** — Norandrosterone, Noretiocholanolone, and Stanozolol.

Suspended for a year, Shamrock would be almost 46 when eligible to make a return to the ring. It seemed likely that his fighting career would continue, as longtime fans would continue to pretend anything that happened post-UFC was all part of one horrible extended nightmare.

Sherdog

The world's biggest MMA Web site, Sherdog has top-notch podcasts, exclusive content, and the amazing Fight Finder, an online database that chronicles the fight records of everyone from **Chuck Liddell** to the local fighter next door.

"Sherodogian" has not become an adjective because of these great features, but instead because Sherdog also has a very active message board, home to the best and worst of MMA discourse. Many of the forum posters are amazingly knowledgeable. Others are a step behind on the evolutionary scale. The stereotypical Sherdog poster trashes "noobs" and "nut huggers" and considers every fighter in the world overrated — except his favorite.

Sherdog has also become the home of MMA's rogue journalists. The site went to war with **UFC** President **Dana White**, who was furious when Sherdog covered Japanese promotions K-1 and **Pride** as if they were the equals of the UFC. White demanded that the site keep the focus on the UFC, even sending Sherdog owner Jeff Sherwood obscene text messages when the site covered one of K-1's failed American adventures.

White ended up pulling the media credentials from the whole organization. Urban legend says Sherdog lost their credentials because then editor Josh Gross (now with *Sports Illustrated*) spoiled the fourth season of ***The Ultimate Fighter*** on his radio show, revealing the results of the pre-taped reality program. The credentials were actually pulled months earlier, primarily because of the coverage of competing promotions.

From there, the relationship with the UFC went from bad to worse. Gross wrote an open letter critical of UFC's response to rampant **steroid** use in the sport. White was furious.

You might have expected the relationship between the top Web site and the top promotion to improve when the hypercritical Gross moved on, but instead the powder keg exploded. New editor Loretta Hunt's seemingly innocuous story about managers losing their backstage passes to UFC fights sent White into an embarrassing rampage where he insulted homosexuals and called Hunt "a dumb bitch."

The controversy propelled Hunt and Sherdog into the national media spotlight. The end result was Sherdog's triumphant return to UFC events. The sport's chronicle of record is back in business with the sport's biggest promotion — but just for a handful of events. Soon a disagreement (and an appearance by Sherwood and Hunt in Matt Lindland's *Fighting Politics* documentary) left Sherdog once again on the outside looking in. Of course, that didn't stop Sherdog from continuing to provide the most diverse and in-depth coverage of the sport available anywhere online.

Sherk, Sean

Nickname: Muscle Shark **Height:** 5'6"

Weight: 155 lbs **Born:** 8/5/73

Debut: Dangerzone: Mahnomen (6/19/99) **Career Record:** 33-4-1

Notable Wins: Karo Parisyan (RSF 1, RSF 2); Nick Diaz (UFC 59); Kenny Florian (UFC 64)

Notable Losses: Matt Hughes (UFC 42); Georges St. Pierre (UFC 56); B.J. Penn (UFC 84)

"I've probably eaten more baby food in my lifetime than any baby out there," Sean Sherk once told **Sherdog** writer T.J. De Santis. Take that, babies.

The *UFC: All Access* episode that aired prior to Sherk's **UFC** 73 lightweight title defense revealed, however, that baby food and hard work alone aren't necessarily enough to reach the highest levels of the sport: Sherk was also fanatical about nutritional supplements, ingesting dozens a day. And, if you believe Sherk's version of things, it was a tainted supplement that caused him to test positive for Nandrolone. Or maybe it was laboratory error, "carryover" from previous urinalyses? Whichever Sherk explanation you favor, the end result was a fine and suspension from the California State Athletic Commission, and an end to Sherk's lightweight title reign. (In an embarrassing turn, challenger **Hermes Franca** tested positive for Drostanolone at the same event.)

The **steroid** suspension was by far the biggest setback in Sherk's otherwise exceptional career. Often maligned as a one-dimensional, **lay and pray** wrestler, Sherk so excelled in that single aspect of the game that his limitations as a fighter were rarely exposed. Despite his diminutive stature, Sherk competed most of his career as a welterweight and was undefeated in 18 fights before running into a prime **Matt Hughes**. Sherk managed to go the distance with the champ and even win rounds at a time when Hughes seemed all but unbeatable. Fighting anywhere and everywhere, Sherk

amassed 12 more wins before his next loss, a TKO at the hands of a physically overwhelming **Georges St. Pierre**.

Soon thereafter, Sherk opted to move down to the UFC's rebooted lightweight division, winning a convincing decision over a game **Kenny Florian** to become the organization's first champion at 155 pounds in four years. Stripped of the title after his first defense, Sherk returned from suspension only to be knocked out by a spectacular flying knee from **B.J. Penn**, who openly taunted Sherk about his steroid suspension in the build-up to their championship fight.

Sherk's only career defeats had come against true legends in the sport until a baffling loss at the hands of heavy underdog **Frankie Edgar** at UFC 98. Sherk, once a dominating wrestler who gutted out methodical wins over some of MMA's best, has gradually drifted towards a **boxing**-heavy style that suits neither his talents nor his frame, and does not bode well for his future at the elite level.

Shields, Jake

Height: 5'11" **Weight:** 170 lbs

Born: 1/9/79 **Debut:** CFF: The Cobra Qualifier (10/23/99)

Career Record: 25-4-1

Notable Wins: Hayato Sakurai (Shooto: 2002 Year End Show); Yushin Okami (ROTR 9); Nick Thompson (EliteXC: Unfinished Business); Robbie Lawler (Strikeforce: Lawler vs. Shields); Dan Henderson (Strikeforce: Nashville)

Notable Loss: Akira Kikuchi (Shooto: 2004 Year End Show)

For years, Jake Shields was the best fighter in the world who had never made it. He never appeared on ***The Ultimate Fighter*** or on **UFC** pay-per-view. He's never been on Spike TV and never fought in Japan for **Pride**. And for a long time there was a good reason for that. The phrase "boring **lay and pray** fighter" was coined with Jake Shields in mind.

There was a stretch from 2001 to 2006 when 11 of Shields' 12 fights went to a decision. This probably seems completely foreign to many new fans of the sport. To them Shields is an exciting finisher, a man who has ended seven fights in a row decisively, all seven on national television or pay-per-view. But in the beginning it was a very different story.

Shields exploded onto the MMA scene with a huge win over **Hayato "Mach" Sakurai** for **Shooto** in Japan. At the time, Sakurai was considered a top three fighter at 170 pounds and Shields was immediately on the map as a big time player at welterweight. Although getting the win was a huge thrill, there was plenty of criticism as well. Many hard-core fans thought Shields did little more than hold Sakurai down and his corner was literally yelling at him to do nothing at all and let the clock run out.

That Shields is long gone. In his place is a confident professional, one of the very best ground fighters in the world, who is slowly but surely improving his striking game as well. Shields became the first and only **EliteXC** welterweight champion, but a lack of quality opponents at that weight outside of the UFC forced his hand. Shields made the move up to middleweight and quickly dispatched the EliteXC champion in that weight class (**Robbie Lawler**) as well.

Shields may be the last world-class fighter to never step into the Octagon or Pride ring, but he's not an unknown anymore. Shields was selected as **Dan Henderson**'s first opponent when the former Pride and UFC star made his **Strikeforce** debut. The fight was supposed to propel Henderson to national television stardom. Instead, millions watching CBC saw Shields win easily. Instead of making a star, Strikeforce lost one: it was the last fight on Jake's

In Their Own Words: Shields on his life-altering fight with Hayato Sakurai

"It was great to get a shot at the number one guy. I only got 13 days notice, so obviously they were bringing me in to lose. They fly you over two or three days before the fight. It's a 12-hour flight, going forward 17 hours. Once you get there, they have you scheduled for an hour of training time at 10 p.m., it's hard to find saunas, and things like that. But it was a good experience overall and helped bring me up in the MMA rankings. I did start with some top fighters early on, with short notice. It makes a difference when you get to train for six or eight weeks and have the necessary cardio going into the fight."

contract. Soon after, Shields was on his way to the UFC, finally getting his shot in the world's biggest promotion.

Shoji, Akira

Height: 5'8" **Weight:** 194 lbs

Born: 1/31/74 **Debut:** KP vs. WK: Koppo vs. Keisyukai (11/30/96)

Career Record: 14-16-5

Notable Wins: Wallid Ismail (Pride 4); Guy Mezger (Pride 6)

Notable Losses: Igor Vovchanchyn (Pride 5); Mark Coleman (Pride 2000 Grand Prix Finals); Dan Henderson (Pride 14); Semmy Schilt (Pride 16); Paulo Filho (Pride 22, Pride Bushido 4); Mauricio Rua (Pride Bushido 1); Kazuo Misaki (Deep 23rd Impact); Gilbert Yvel (Pride 34)

Stout in build and in spirit, Akira Shoji has fought a who's who of fighters nobody should ever even consider fighting at only 5'8" and 194 pounds. Consider the madness, if you will, of a man Shoji's size stepping into the ring against **Mark Coleman** or **Igor Vovchanchyn** at or very near their dominant, destructive peaks. And consider the significance of taking both men the distance, albeit in a losing battle. Akira Shoji never racked up the kinds of wins you might expect of a 23-fight **Pride** veteran, and his best wins came early in his career: a questionable split decision win over the hapless **Guy Mezger**, and a second-round stoppage of fiery **Brazilian Jiu-jitsu** fighter Wallid Ismail. But Shoji became a fan favorite on sheer guts and fighting spirit. And a bit of showmanship: although his wins were few and far between, Shoji always made the most of them, shouting wildly to the crowd in celebration. Shoji's best work remains his draw with **Renzo Gracie** at the inaugural Pride show, where he managed to hang on the ground with the Gracie family's best all-around fighter.

Shooto

Definitions of Shooto vary. To some, it's a slightly obscure Japanese mixed martial arts promotion — the very first mixed martial arts promotion, in fact, organizing amateur events as early as 1986 and staging professional fights in 1989, four years before either **Pancrase** or the **UFC** got off the ground. To others, including those who run it and many who compete under its banner, Shooto is not just another MMA promotion, but instead its own distinct sport, indeed its own distinct martial art. **Caol Uno**, when recently asked by a fashion publication to introduce himself, answered in part, "My life revolves around training and the mastery of techniques, more specifically Shooto, a form of martial art that continues to evolve." Shooto isn't a company he competed for; it's the discipline he trains in. Note, also, that Uno had competed in Shooto a grand total of once in the nine years before that interview, and yet Shooto defined him as a martial artist still. It's an integral aspect of his identity.

Regardless of your perspective on that academic point, whether you understand Shooto to be a style unto itself or a proto–mixed martial arts organization ahead of its time, there is one thing both sides of the question can invariably agree on: Shooto is really, *really* awesome.

It began in 1986, when Satoru Sayama, formerly New Japan Pro Wrestling's original Tiger Mask, grew weary of the world of **professional wrestling**. The shoot-style UWF was tantalizingly close to real, but still not real enough to satisfy Sayama. And so Shooto. The name, derived from the English word "shoot" — to wrestle for real, rather than follow a predetermined script — is represented by Japanese characters that can be translated back into English as "learn combat." That's fitting, since there is a kind of pedagogy at work in Shooto's well-developed amateur system, which every aspiring Shooto fighter must successfully navigate before earning professional status.

Professional Shooto status hardly guarantees a life of fame and fortune. Despite the passion and loyalty Shooto inspires among both fighters and fans, it has only ever attracted a small audience. But that audience has been witness to some of the greatest fights and the greatest fighters Japan has produced. **Hayato Sakurai**, Caol Uno, **Rumina Sato**, **Takanori Gomi**, **Shinya Aoki**, **Kid Yamamoto**, and **Akiri Kikuchi** are but a few of the many who've come up through the ranks; **Matt Hughes**, **Anderson Silva**, **Joachim Hansen**, and **Carlos**

Newton a handful of the top fighters from around the world who have competed in the Shooto ring. All have taken in part in something quite unlike anything else in mixed martial arts.

Side control (Side mount)

A dominant grappling position in which the attacker lays across his opponent's body and pins him chest to chest. This elastic term encompasses an unusually broad range of techniques, from a solid, knees-down, square-hipped side pin, through the assorted spread-legged kesa gatame (scarf hold) variations of **judo** and the powerful, transitional uki gatame (floating hold) or knee-on-belly position prized by **Brazilian Jiu-jitsu** stylists, to modern no-**gi** refinements like the iconoclastic **Eddie Bravo**'s twister side control. The term sometimes stretches so far as include a side control that isn't really a *side* control at all — the **north-south** position.

What unites this disparate group of holds and positions is the incredible range of offensive possibilities available to the fighter on top: knees, elbows, punches, hammer fists, and a seemingly endless assortment of submissions attacking either the upper or lower body. The fighter on bottom is limited largely to positional work, compelled to look either for incremental improvements to **half-guard** and **guard**, or for sweeps to assume a top position of his own. Although it's possible for a fighter held in side control to secure and even finish with a **Kimura** or **triangle choke** from this disadvantageous position, it's far from likely against even a moderately skilled top player.

See also **positional hierarchy**

Silva, Anderson

Nickname: The Spider **Height:** 6'2"

Weight: 185 lbs **Born:** 4/14/75

Debut: Meca World Vale Tudo 1 (5/27/00) **Career Record:** 27-4

Notable Wins: Hayato Sakurai (Shooto: To the Top 7); Carlos Newton (Pride 25); Jeremy Horn (Gladiator FC Day 2); Rich Franklin (UFC 64, UFC 77); Dan Henderson (UFC 82); Forrest Griffin (UFC 101); Chael Sonnen (UFC 117)

Notable Losses: Daiju Takase (Pride 26); Ryo Chonan (Pride Shockwave 2004)

It was easy to be skeptical when **Dana White** began trumpeting Anderson Silva as the best pound-for-pound fighter in the world. It seemed a strange distinction for a fighter who sat atop a notoriously weak division. The **UFC**'s middleweight ranks have always been thin to the point of meagerness when compared with the depth

the company has historically had to offer at both light heavyweight and welterweight, and pointing to Silva as the pound-for-pound best seemed more like a way to rebut talk of the unattainable **Fedor Emelianenko**'s greatness than anything else. But as time wore on, and the wins continued to roll in — against credible light heavyweight opposition, in addition to an ever-increasing list of middleweight contenders — it became a lot easier to buy what White had been selling all along. Although Anderson Silva has never been a consensus selection as MMA's all-around best, he's undeniably a necessary part of that conversation.

Before he hit the UFC, Silva was nowhere near that level. A former **Shooto** and **Cage Rage** title holder, Silva had no doubt had his moments: he'd handed **Hayato Sakurai** his first career loss; he'd stopped **Carlos Newton** at a time when that still mattered; and he'd knocked out the hapless Tony Fryklund with a ridiculous reverse elbow that commentator **Stephen Quadros** rightly described as something out of Tony Jaa's *Ong Bak*. But he'd also looked clueless on the ground, trapped in a methodical **triangle choke** applied by the unremarkable **Daiju Takase**. He'd also found himself on the wrong end of one of the most spectacular submissions ever seen, **Ryo Chonan**'s flying scissor heel hook. **Chris Leben**, just before he stepped into the cage to meet Silva in his Octagon debut, had it right when he told Spike TV's *Ultimate Fight Night* audience, "I've seen Anderson Silva beat some very tough guys. On the flip side of that, the guys that beat Anderson Silva haven't exactly been the best. They've been the guys that refuse to play into his game plan." But what he said next — "After he gets in there with me and I knock him out, he may want to go back to Japan or somewhere where the competition's a little easier" — didn't hit the mark in quite the same way.

The long, lean Silva lit Leben up with precision striking the likes of which is rarely seen in mixed martial arts. Given the limited pool of middleweight challengers, Silva was rewarded for his efforts with an immediate title shot at **Rich Franklin** — whom Silva utterly dominated in the **clinch**, delivering a barrage of knees to the body to set up the knee to the face that would spell the end for the defending champion. It was a thoroughly impressive, one-sided drubbing of one of the UFC's middleweight poster boys. **Brazilian Jiu-jitsu** black belt Travis Lutter, fresh off his tournament win on the fourth season of ***The Ultimate Fighter***, was next in line for a title shot, but blew his chance by missing weight, and then blew the fight despite having Silva pinned beneath him in **mount**. Silva, a Brazilian Jiu-jitsu black belt himself, whose ground skills have come an awful long way since Takase got the best of him, ultimately got the better of Lutter on the ground, finishing with a triangle choke of his own while simultaneously raining down elbows on Lutter's trapped head. Silva's ground game had started to catch up with his perhaps unparalleled striking.

Former King of **Pancrase Nate Marquardt** fared no better, nor did a returning Rich Franklin. The only real challenge he's faced as middleweight champion was the cagey veteran **Dan Henderson**, **Pride**'s first and only welterweight (183 pounds) title holder. Henderson managed to control Silva on the ground in the first round of their UFC 82 title unification bout, but Silva had his way with him in the second, landing some serious blows standing before outmaneuvering Henderson on the ground to secure the **rear naked choke**.

Seemingly and justifiably bored at middleweight, and with a desire to fight as often as possible, Silva took a fight against light heavyweight journeyman James Irvin. "There's no reason I can't knock him out or catch him with something," Irvin reasoned. "He's *much* smaller than me." Irvin, it turned out, was wrong on both counts. Silva hardly looked undersized standing across the Octagon from the regular light heavyweight competitor — and Silva put him on his back with a huge right hand a minute into the first round, ending the bout seconds later. Not that James Irvin was a world beater — far from it — but Silva's clear demonstration that he was a legitimate presence in a weight class 20 pounds above his best weight was convincing proof that he belonged at or near the top of everyone's pound-for-pound ranking.

But that kind of status can be a curse. Expectations and anticipation for Silva's bouts grew to the point that winning wasn't enough — if Silva wasn't styling on his opponents, bobbing and weaving and landing precision strikes at will like he did in his second fight with Rich Franklin, he was underperforming. Silva was well on his way to outscoring **Patrick Côté** when the French-Canadian slugger blew out his knee, and Dana White publicly derided the performance. Silva controlled fellow Brazilian Thales Leites for five rounds en route to a record ninth consecutive win in the UFC, but he was chastized for playing it safe. It wasn't until Silva moved up once again, this time to face fan favorite and former light heavyweight champion **Forrest Griffin**, that Silva would silence his critics, and have the MMA world universally singing his praises once again. Silva made poor Griffin look like a rank amateur, knocking him down three times in the first round, and finishing him with a jab thrown off his back foot. Griffin, humbled, ran from the cage once he collected his bearings.

Silva's that good. There's no one in sight at middleweight who can touch him, and he's proven himself championship-level at light heavyweight as well. **Yushin Okami**, the last man to defeat Silva — albeit by a controversial disqualification — seems nowhere near Silva's level at this point, and his slow, deliberate pace has kept him from moving up the card despite win after win. A potentially huge fight against welterweight champion **Georges St. Pierre** has been discussed, but seems unlikely given the considerable size difference between the two. It's hard to know what the future has in store for Anderson Silva, who has spoken more than once about an imminent retirement from the sport, and a long cherished dream to face the great Roy Jones Jr., not in the Octagon but in the **boxing** ring. That might be the one fight Anderson Silva can't win. But at this stage of the game, given the absolute dominance he's shown since first making his presence felt on American soil, you can't blame him for seeking out new challenges.

Silva, Antonio

Nicknames: Junior, Big Foot **Height:** 6'4"

Weight: 265 lbs **Born:** 9/14/79

Debut: UK Mixed Martial Arts Championship 10 (3/6/05)

Career Record: 14-2

Notable Wins: Tom Erikson (Hero's 5); Wesley Correira (EliteXC: Destiny); Ricco Rodriguez (EliteXC: Street Certified); Justin Eilers (EliteXC: Unfinished Business); Andrei Arlovski (Strikeforce: Heavy Artillery)

Notable Losses: Eric Pele (BodogFight: USA vs. Russia); Dan Henderson (Strikeforce: Nashville)

You could be forgiven for confusing Antonio Silva with Paulo César da Silva, better known by *nom de guerre* **Giant Silva**. Both are enormous Brazilian heavyweight/super heavyweight mixed martial artists, legitimate acromegalic giants, but the similarities end there. Giant Silva is a gimmick, not a fighter

— Antonio Silva is the real deal, a comparatively quick and athletic heavyweight hovering just outside the division's top ten. The first and only **EliteXC** heavyweight champion before the company imploded, Silva has built his fearsome reputation with impressive wins over real competition, like former **UFC** heavyweight champion **Ricco Rodriguez**, and solid pros like **Tom Erikson**, the limited but hard-headed **Wesley Correira**, and the late Justin Eilers. The only real bump in the road for Silva so far was a positive test for the banned steroid Boldenone, a result that earned him a one-year suspension from the California State Athletic Commission. Japanese promotions have never let little things like that get in the way, though, and **Sengoku** welcomed "Junior" with open arms for two 2009 bouts. With that episode behind him, Silva joined **Strikeforce**'s suddenly intriguing heavyweight division, where he could soon find himself squaring off against the great **Fedor Emelianenko**.

Silva, Giant

Real name: Paulo César da Silva **Height:** 7'2"
Weight: 385 lbs **Born:** 7/21/63
Debut: Pride Shockwave 2003 (12/31/2003) **Career Record:** 2-6
Notable Win: Chad "Akebono" Rowan (Dynamite!! 2006)
Notable Losses: Heath Herring (Pride Shockwave 2003); Naoya Ogawa (Pride Critical Countdown 2004); Ikuhisa Minowa (Pride Bushido 10)

Paulo César da Silva was a basketball player who competed for the Brazilian national team. He was also a professional wrestler, who worked, for a time, in a minor role for the World Wrestling Federation. Paulo César da Silva may have been any number of things to any number of people, but he was never a fighter. However, that didn't stop **Pride** from parading him out to the ring semi-regularly to make a spectacle of himself.

Silva had no martial arts background to speak of, excluding a crash course in **Brazilian Jiu-jitsu** from Ricardo and Ralek Gracie, but his sheer size made him problem enough for **Heath Herring**, at least, who needed three rounds to finish the debuting giant. None of Silva's other bouts — neither the **Kimura** wins over two largely clueless former sumo wrestlers, Henry Miller and **Akebono**, nor the losses to fighters upwards of 200 pounds smaller than him — made it out of the first round.

But even watching Silva flail around the ring for a minute or two was painful. Not just because it was embarrassingly unskilled and just plain bad, though it certainly was both of those things, but because the gentle giant was clearly a man with no inclination whatsoever towards the sport of mixed martial arts — or any other physical activity the least bit rugged, for that matter. Silva showed no interest in the competition, in either hitting or being hit, only in earning a paycheck for his family. And while that is itself a respectable aim, you don't have to respect the spectacle that deprives a man of his dignity in pursuit of that end.

Silva, Joe

Joe Silva, the **UFC**'s vice president of Talent Relations, has been searching for the perfect fighting style all his life. He tried a variety of martial arts, but none seemed to work exactly as advertised. To make matters worse, when he questioned sensei about real world application of their carefully crafted kata, he was often rudely rebuffed.

The closest thing to a fighting style that actually worked were the **professional wrestling**–rules matches he put on with other kids in his neighborhood growing up. Before there was such a thing as **Pancrase**, Silva was engaging in real wrestling matches with his buddies, and learning quickly what worked and what didn't.

When Silva saw the first UFC, it was like winning the lottery. Here is what he had been looking for all along. Before the advent of the internet, he was the ultimate superfan, sending in suggestions to the UFC brass. His well thought out and well crafted missives got plenty of attention, and he was soon brought in as a consultant.

While others in the **SEG** hierarchy had a variety of business skills and creative ideas for promoting the company, only Silva knew the fight game. As fight promotions popped up worldwide, he followed them all with a fan's passion and, thanks to years of experimentation, as a seasoned martial artist as well.

After the fall of **Extreme Fighting**, the UFC hired matchmaker **John Perretti**, but never fully let him in. The controlling Perretti was one of the least popular figures on the fighting circuit, an intelligent and verbose micromanager who wasn't afraid to tell you exactly what he thought. The UFC management used Silva to help rein Perretti in: when he told them something about a fighter, they would often double-check it with Silva before running with the idea.

When **Zuffa** purchased the UFC in 2001, Silva was one of the few employees from the SEG era to join the new team, where he quickly became a member of the inner circle. UFC President **Dana White** and owner **Lorenzo Fertitta** are both aggressive and impulsive decision makers. It's Silva's role to play devil's advocate, offering advice as needed. While White and Fertitta focus on the big

In Their Own Words: Lorenzo Fertitta on hiring Joe Silva

"The UFC literally only had two or three employees. And they had a matchmaker – his name was John Perretti. He did a good job and the prior owner, **Bob Meyrowitz**, used to use Perretti to put on the fights. He also had this other guy, stashed away, that nobody really knew about. His name was Joe Silva. He would bounce things off Joe Silva to kind of get a second opinion . . .

"When we took over the company John Perretti left to do something else. We were left hanging out there without a matchmaker. Dana actually had a conversation with **Tito Ortiz** and Tito said, 'You know who you should talk to? There's this kid that nobody really knows about – his name is Joe Silva. He's smarter than anybody in the business and he's kind of the go-to guy to provide information for Bob Meyrowitz. You should talk to him.'

"We flew Joe Silva out and had an instant connection. We couldn't believe how smart he was. He was like a walking encyclopedia of the history of the UFC. He's a very strategic thinker and he puts on great fights."

picture, Silva runs the day-to-day operations of talent relations from his home in Richmond, Virginia.

He books most of the bouts on every UFC fight card, carefully matching up opponents and building fighters for a run at UFC gold. Exceptionally well organized, with a keen mathematical mind, Silva manages a roster of more than 200 fighters with skill and aplomb, helping make every UFC card among the more competitive and entertaining in the industry.

Silva, Wanderlei

Nickname: The Axe Murderer **Height:** 5'11"

Weight: 205 lbs **Born:** 7/3/76

Debut: Brazilian Vale Tudo 6 (11/01/96) **Career Record:** 33-10-1 (1 No Contest)

Notable Wins: Dan Henderson (Pride 12); Kazushi Sakuraba (Pride 13, Pride 17, Pride Total Elimination 2003); Hidehiko Yoshida (Pride Final Conflict 2003, Pride Total Elimination 2005); Quinton Jackson (Pride Final Conflict 2003); Kazuhiro Nakamura (Pride Critical Countdown 2005); Ricardo Arona (Pride Shockwave 2005); Kazuyuki Fujita (Pride Critical Countdown Absolute); Keith Jardine (UFC 84)

Notable Losses: Vitor Belfort (UFC 17.5); Tito Ortiz (UFC 25); Ricardo Arona (Pride Final Conflict 2005); Mirko Cro Cop (Pride Final Conflict Absolute); Dan Henderson (Pride 33); Chuck Liddell (UFC 79); Quinton Jackson (UFC 92); Rich Franklin (UFC 99)

Wanderlei Silva is terrifying. With his tattooed head shaved bare, his dead-eyed stare, and his mouth hanging ever so slightly agape, his presence in the corner before a fight is so threatening that even the most routine movement — his trademark wrist-roll warm-up, for instance — takes on an air of menace. And that's *before* the bell rings, before the wild-man rush across the ring, the thunderous looping punches, the head kicks, the knees, the soccer kicks, the stomps. Before any of that has even started, Wanderlei Silva is the scariest man in a scary, scary sport.

Silva made a pair of **UFC** appearances early on — blitzed in under a minute by a prime **Vitor Belfort**, laid on for three rounds by **Tito Ortiz** — but it was in **Pride** that Silva made his mark. Despite his wide open, almost feral style, his complete willingness to take a shot in order to land one, it took seven years and 27 fights for anyone to put Silva away inside the Pride ring. And over that period, few in the history of the sport have been so devastating: the three brutal beatings of **Kazushi Sakuraba**, Pride's great hero, and the total domination

In Their Own Words: Wanderlei Silva on giving the fans what they want to see

"I know what the fans like. I know what the fans want to see. I give them a show. I lose sometimes, because I take chances. But I have more respect from my fans and the fighters. My fans know I give everything I have. Win or lose, that's just one part of the fight. A good show. I want to give fans a good show. This is entertainment, not just a fight."

of **Quinton Jackson** in the **clinch** not once but twice stand out among Silva's many conquests. There were impressive wins in less one-sided affairs, too, like his pair of hard-fought decisions he took over **Hidehiko Yoshida**, Pride's top Japanese draw once Sakuraba's star began to fade, and his narrow decision win in a title defense against **Ricardo Arona**, in which Silva gained a measure of revenge against the man who had ended his long middleweight (205 pounds) unbeaten streak by controlling the fearsome striker on the ground in Pride's 2005 tournament. Through it all, Silva was standing in the middle of the ring, feet planted, swinging for the fences.

When it started to come apart, though, it came apart in a hurry. Silva had a tough road in Pride's 2006 open weight Grand Prix, facing **Mirko Cro Cop** two months after going toe-to-toe with **Kazuyuki Fujita.** He'd stopped the iron-headed Fujita with a barrage of soccer kicks, but Cro Cop — whom Silva had impressively fought to a draw four years before — was a different kind of problem, a precise heavyweight striker at the top of his game. There are two lasting images from their 2006 contest. The first is Silva standing in a neutral corner, pleading with the ringside doctors to leave him be and let him continue to fight before the eye they were examining swelled completely shut, blinding him. Silva knew he didn't have much time left, and he was desperate to get back to the middle of the ring and take his chances for as long as could. The second is Silva wilting to the canvas minutes later, the victim of a Cro Cop head kick he couldn't have seen coming.

A knockout loss to **Dan Henderson** cost Silva his long-held middleweight title in his final Pride bout, and the demise of the promotion set the stage for what had been the most anticipated fight in the sport for years: Wanderlei Silva versus **Chuck Liddell.** One can only imagine what this fight might have been had it happened in 2003, when the UFC entered Liddell in Pride's middleweight Grand Prix. Liddell's loss to Quinton Jackson kept that from happening. What we were left with in late 2007 was a battle between two legends, but two fighters who had clearly lost a step, and whose chins weren't quite what they once were. It was, nevertheless, thrilling. Liddell, the counter puncher, got the better of most of the exchanges, but Silva got his licks in. Silva did what few fighters have ever managed: worry Liddell enough standing that Liddell felt compelled to take his opponent down. The unanimous decision rightly went to Liddell, but Silva acquitted himself well enough to win over the American audience, few of whom had seen "The Axe Murderer" in action before.

The showdown with Liddell was really the first step of a transformation Silva has undertaken, an entrance into a new phase of his career. He's no longer a championship-level fighter or serious contender. Now, he's a much-loved veteran whose role is to entertain his fans — who are there to celebrate what he's already done more than anticipate what he might yet do. A lightning fast win over **Keith Jardine** briefly offered hope that the old Wanderlei might be back, but a first-round loss to Jackson, whom Silva had destroyed twice before, confirmed that the present was not the past. Silva's gradual move down to the UFC's 185-pound middleweight division saw him meet **Rich Franklin** at a catchweight of 195 pounds in a bout that went the distance but didn't fall Silva's way.

He's not the same fighter. There's no question the heart is still there, but the power isn't and the quickness isn't either. The years of fierce battles have taken their toll, and there can be no doubt that Silva's best is behind him. But every time he enters the Octagon, there's still that aura about him, still that presence, still that possibility that something unforgettable — and *extraordinarily* violent — is about to happen.

Silveira, Marcus

Nickname: Conan
Height: 6'3"
Weight: 242 lbs
Born: 12/17/64
Debut: EF 1 (11/18/95)
Career Record: 6-4
Notable Win: Maurice Smith (WEF 7)
Notable Losses: Maurice Smith (EF 3); Kazushi Sakuraba (UFC 15.5); Dan Severn (WEF 9)

Carlson Gracie gave him the nickname when he was still just a kid. Even then, Marcus Silveira was big, strong, fast, and super-aggressive. He was "Conan," a barbarian in the ring.

Like Carlson's other top young prospect, **Vitor Belfort**, you'd have been hard pressed to tell Silveira was an accomplished grappler. He preferred to stand and bang with his opponents, contesting most of his fights on his feet. That strategy worked well until he ran into kickboxing legend **Maurice Smith**.

The two met in the first round of a four-man tournament to crown the first **Extreme Fighting** heavyweight champion. Silveira was supposed to run over Smith on his way to the finals, where he was expected to meet Bart Vale. Instead, Silveira was knocked out by a Smith head kick and Vale fell to unheralded judoka Kazunari Murakami.

Silveira was just the first upset victim on Smith's road to the **UFC** title. But that memorable knockout loss wasn't the most remarkable fight of Conan's career. In the first UFC show in Japan, Conan was matched with young Japanese pro wrestler **Kazushi Sakuraba** as part of a four-man tournament.

Silveira won quickly, rocking Sakuraba with a punch. When Sakuraba dropped down for a takedown, referee "Big" **John McCarthy** thought he had been knocked out. It was one of Big John's rare mistakes, but Sakuraba wasn't content to let the bad decision stand.

He protested in the ring for almost an hour. Behind the scenes, the Japanese yakuza were also upset. Eventually, the decision was made that Sakuraba, and not alternate Tra Telligman, would replace the injured **Tank Abbott** in the tournament final against Silveira. In their second Fight of the Night, a dispirited and disinterested Silveira lost by **arm bar** in under four minutes.

Already past his prime before the sport hit big in the United States, Silveira left active competition to pass on his knowledge to a new generation of fighters. Silveira was one of the co-founders of the **American Top Team**, home of some of the world's best fighters like **Mike Brown** and **Thiago Alves**.

Sims, Wes

Nickname: The Project
Height: 6'10"
Weight: 260 lbs
Born: 10/12/79
Debut: RSF 2 (6/23/01)
Career Record: 22-13-1 (2 No Contests)
Notable Wins: Marcus Silveira (Absolute Fighting Championships 1); Kimo Leopoldo (Extreme Wars 5)
Notable Losses: Frank Mir (UFC 43, UFC 46); Tim Sylvia (SuperBrawl 38); Daniel Gracie (IFL: Championship 2006)

Wes Sims is one of MMA's most colorful characters. When there is legitimate debate about whether you are the nuttiest member of a team like **Hammer House**, you must be spectacularly interesting. Whether illegally stomping **Frank Mir** into the canvas, raising hell in Japan with his friends, or power bombing random MMA tomato cans, Sims is anything but boring.

At 6'10", he's one of the tallest men in the business. Unlike other giants, like K-1 and **Pancrase** champion Semmy Schilt, Sims has never quite figured out how to use that height to his advantage. His career has included plenty of setbacks. Even his most glorious night, the **UFC** 43 shellacking of the favored Frank Mir, ended with a check in the loss column. Sims was inadvertently gouged in the eye during a Mir choke attempt. When he got back to his feet, he snapped. Instead of punching Mir, as the rules allowed, Sims put the boots to him. He was disqualified, but left the cage as the clear winner of the fight, if not the contest. Mir, however, settled any questions about who was truly the better fighter in a rematch at UFC 46.

Sims was soon on his way out of the UFC. He made a good living fighting on the independent circuit, but a series of injuries and the accompanying medical bills, along with the loss of income, left him in a precarious position. Soon Sims was actually living on the street, joining the millions of homeless people in a hidden America few pay much attention to. After years of struggle, Sims started putting his life back together.

Sims was offered a chance at redemption, joining the cast of ***The Ultimate Fighter*** for the show's tenth season. Most of the contestants on the reality show complain about living for several months in the posh Las Vegas mansion. Sims was just the opposite. He was just happy to be out of the rain. Sims was getting a second chance, but he was not prepared to forget where he came from. He was working to draw attention to the plight of the homeless, at least as hard as he was working on his resurgent fight career.

In Their Own Words: Wes Sims on his famous fight with Frank Mir

"I watch it myself sometimes and just laugh. If it was **Pride** rules, I beat the shit out of him. Nobody likes somebody who thinks they're smarter than everybody else. Those kind of kids in school got the shit kicked out of them on a daily basis. They're probably rich now, designing the most elegant things in the world. But they're not very popular. I made a big mistake that night. I could sit here and dwell on it, go back and tell everybody how sorry I am . . . No. It's not my style. I made a mistake that night. I shouldn't have stomped him. I should have dropped down and punched the shit out of him. Beat his lights out. But he gouged me in the eye. I've forgiven Mir since then. It wasn't something he tried to do maliciously. He was trying to put a **rear naked choke** in and couldn't get it, so he grabbed my eyes to lift my head up. So when I got free, I stomped the dude. Like I said back then: it happened, it's over, bring it on."

Slice, Kimbo

Real name: Kevin Ferguson **Height:** 6'2"

Weight: 235 lbs **Born:** 2/8/74

Debut: Cage Fury Fighting Championships 5 (6/23/07)

Career Record: 4-2

Notable Wins: Ray Mercer (Cage Fury Fighting Championship 5); Tank Abbott (EliteXC: Street Certified); Houston Alexander (*The Ultimate Fighter* 10 Finale)

Notable Losses: Seth Petruzelli (EliteXC: Heat); Roy Nelson (*The Ultimate Fighter* 10)

Things have changed pretty dramatically for Rosemary Clarke's baby boy, Kevin Ferguson, since Hurricane Andrew hit in 1992, destroying his house and his life. For a time he lived in his car, a 1987 Nissan Pathfinder. But the man now known as Kimbo Slice never gave up hope. Today he's the most recognizable mixed martial artist on the planet, making hundreds of thousands of dollars, and seeing how long his 15 minutes of fame can extend. The shelf life of an internet YouTube sensation is short; yet Kimbo remains at the forefront of the public consciousness, like the scariest LOLcat or dancing baby imaginable.

Not long ago, Kimbo Slice was working as a bouncer at a strip club. This was the height of his ambition at the time — but opportunities seem to find Kimbo Slice, whether he's looking for them or not. One day an old high school friend named Mike "Icey Mike" Ember walked into Kimbo's joint and left with the big man in tow. Kimbo became a limousine driver, a bodyguard, and finally part of a family. Ember was, not to mince words, a pornographer, one of the men behind the Reality Kings franchise of films and short clips.

The short videos weren't all hard-core action. Some were classic "ball in the groin" films one notch removed from *America's Funniest Home Videos*. In these, a sexy host would pay unsuspecting marks to let her friend tackle them or punch them in the arm as hard as he could. They would agree, trying to look tough in front of the hot young girl. And then out would come Kimbo Slice, a 240-pound bushy-bearded African American who was as intimidating a presence as you could imagine.

Other videos featured Kimbo throwing down in the streets. No one knew exactly where these videos were going, but they became the talk of the internet. More importantly they helped Kimbo Slice find his path in life.

"The very first fight, when I got a couple hundred dollars — that was big," Slice said. "That's when I decided to do this for a living. This is another way. I could start robbing, start selling dope or some shit like that. I didn't want to do that. My old girl, my mother, she wasn't with that. I couldn't get caught stealing something from somebody's house. Not with a mother like mine. This was an opportunity. I could take my ass to work and do it the honest way . . . What we did was raw. There was no training. It was just straight war. I'm coming right into your backyard. I'm gonna knock a nigga's ass out, leave his blood on the ground. And I'm dippin'."

Fortune 500 companies have trouble monetizing the internet; they're still looking for that magic application that turns clicks into cash. Kimbo Slice found it. People around the world were emailing each other links to Slice's street fights. He fought in backyards, South Beach alleys, and most comically, in a boatyard. Even **UFC** officials caught Kimbo fever, eventually bringing one of his opponents, police officer Sean Gannon, into the Octagon. Kimbo and Icey Mike started to attach dollar signs to Slice's enormous hands. He was cracking heads in the streets for next to nothing. But why give Kimbo away for free, especially when America was so willing to buy?

The rise was astronomical. He went from fighting a washed-up boxer named Ray Mercer on the Atlantic City boardwalk to main eventing the first MMA show ever held on network television in less than a year. **EliteXC** President Gary Shaw immediately saw Slice's potential. While the UFC had gone after Gannon, the white police officer, Shaw realized that fight fans found the dangerous street fighters more compelling.

Slice was immediately catapulted into main event fights. He was sent to the legendary **Bas Rutten** and **boxing** coach Randy Khatami to sculpt the rough

In Their Own Words: Kimbo Slice on street fights versus sport fights

"In a street fight, first of all you've got to have that respect from your homeboys and everybody in the street. They've got to know and understand what's about to happen here. If I knock your boy out, his crew got to know this nigga just got knocked out. You can't be pulling out pistols and talking about 'He need another chance' and this and all that. That has to be established before the two guys even engage in combat. There's no comparison though between a street fight and where I am right now as a professional fighter. A street fight is one-dimensional. All you have to worry about is a guy throwing punches. You don't have to worry about nothing except getting knocked the fuck out. In mixed martial arts, you have to train and be prepared. These guys have skills and these guys are professionals. And you can be hurt."

edges, but EliteXC didn't have time to wait on a finished product. They were millions in debt from the get-go and, despite his lack of experience, Kimbo was their most marketable and most popular fighter. He couldn't be built slowly on the undercard; in fact, Slice was the headliner for two fights on Showtime and for the first show ever on network television, EliteXC: Primetime on CBS.

Opponents were carefully selected for the new superstar. EliteXC would only consider fellow strikers, men who would keep the fight standing and allow Slice to do what he did best: punch people in the face. Kimbo was street certified, but there was little doubt that his fame had exceeded his skill level. Professional fighting at the highest levels is a tricky game. Fighters have to be able to navigate dangerous ground both standing and on the mat. There are dozens of techniques that Kimbo needed to be able to execute and, more importantly, defend against.

EliteXC was trying to buy Slice time, but then disaster struck. On CBS's third MMA card, the legendary, but now immobile and slightly punchy, **Ken Shamrock** suffered a late cut in training. With just hours to go before the fight was scheduled to begin, Slice had no opponent. Ken's adopted brother **Frank Shamrock** was briefly considered for the slot, but eventually EliteXC settled on journeyman **Seth Petruzelli**. When Petruzelli, a Smoothie King franchiser with dyed pink hair, knocked Slice out in just 14 seconds with an off-balance jab, Kimbo's tough guy aura was dented, if not outright destroyed.

Despite years of mocking Kimbo — par for the course if you were a fighter for the UFC's opposition — **Dana White** and the UFC were quick to sign Slice.

Strikeforce made an offer as well, but it was a pay cut when compared to his purses in EliteXC. There was more potential in the UFC, even if Slice had to start at the beginning. Some considered the offer to appear on ***The Ultimate Fighter***, a reality television show used to create new UFC stars, an insult. After all, Kimbo had drawn more television viewers than anyone on the UFC roster. But as a fighter, Kimbo Slice was right where he needed to be, learning the fight game from the bottom up.

The Ultimate Fighter season 10, centered around Slice and a selection of ex-NFL stars, set UFC television records, proving once again that Slice was a tremendous ratings draw if not yet a tremendous fighter. Kimbo Slice was now where he belonged all along: another cog in the UFC machine, co-existing with Dana White, the man who was once his most vocal critic.

"It's not like we sit down together for tea and toast, but we're businessmen," Kimbo said. "He's a promoter and I'm a fighter. We do what we do."

Smackgirl

While fans in the west didn't discover the excitement of women's MMA until breakout star **Gina Carano** put the sport on the map in 2008, Japanese fans — the hard-cores, at least — had been watching the likes of Yuka Tsuji and Megumi Fuji light it up in Smackgirl for years. As the name implies, Smackgirl featured women's mixed martial arts exclusively. Running from 2000 through 2008, the promotion staged as many as 12 shows a year, mostly in small Tokyo venues like Korakuen Hall, Differ Ariake, and, in the earliest days, the hopping Club Atom in Shibuya. Smackgirl rules called for no strikes to the head of a downed opponent and a scant 30-second limit for ground fighting, which meant a breakneck pace. But women's MMA is a tough sell, a niche sport within a niche sport, and after a bad 2008 financially, the company was sold and reintroduced as Jewels, positioned as "Smackgirl's daughter" by the Japanese fight press. Jewels has started strong, putting on solid shows in front of small but devoted audiences in Shinjuku Face, a 500-seat hall. Hardly Carano/**Santos** numbers, to be sure, but the action is top-notch.

Smith, Maurice

Nickname: Mo
Height: 6'2"
Weight: 220 lbs
Born: 12/13/61
Debut: Pancrase: Yes, We Are Hybrid Wrestlers 3 (11/08/93)
Career Record: 12-13

Notable Wins: Minoru Suzuki (Pancrase: Yes, We Are Hybrid Wrestlers 3); Marcus Silveira (EF 3); Mark Coleman (UFC 14); Tank Abbott (UFC 15); Marco Ruas (UFC 21, IFL: Chicago)

Notable Losses: Minoru Suzuki (Pancrase: Road to the Championship 1); Ken Shamrock (Pancrase: King of Pancrase Tournament Round 1); Bas Rutten (Pancrase: Eyes of Beast 4, Pancrase: Eyes of Beast 6); Tsuyoshi Kohsaka (Rings: Budokan Hall 1996); Kiyoshi Tamura (Rings: Maelstrom 6); Randy Couture (UFC 15.5); Kevin Randleman (UFC 19); Renzo Gracie (Rings: King of Kings 1999 Block B); Renato Sobral (UFC 28); Hidehiko Yoshida (Sengoku 3)

"He doesn't know how to punch," Maurice Smith said about **Mark Coleman** before their title fight at **UFC** 14. "He punches like, well, he punches like a girl, okay? He may punch hard, but it's not like a solid punch. It's more like scratching than hitting me." Smith sounded awfully confident for an over-the-hill kickboxer who was about to step into the Octagon against the unstoppable Coleman. Smith had no doubt picked up a thing or two from his stints in **Pancrase** and **Extreme Fighting**, and his cross-training with **Frank Shamrock** at the **Lion's Den** had to be worth something, but there was no question Maurice Smith stepped into the cage as a huge underdog. Grapplers had completely dominated the UFC to that point, and nobody expected this bout to go any differently.

But after Smith weathered the storm early — a quick takedown and a steady stream of head-butts from the champion — the fight went entirely his way. Coleman was gassed only two minutes into the fight, and Smith scored with countless elbows from the bottom. Once Smith finally escaped to his feet, the fight was effectively over. An exhausted Coleman had no answer for Smith standing. "The striker beats the grappler," Greco-Roman **wrestling** Olympic gold medalist **Jeff Blatnick** said on commentary. "It's the first time in the UFC that has really happened." That's Maurice Smith's legacy.

Smith dropped his heavyweight title to **Randy Couture** only five months later. He stayed active for another three years, sensibly retired at the age of 38, and then resurfaced as an **International Fight League** coach and competitor after a seven-year absence from the sport. He even turned up in **Sengoku**, of all places, as a safe opponent for Japanese favorite **Hidehiko Yoshida**. Smith has won a few and he's lost a few in the years since he claimed the UFC heavyweight title, but needless to say he's never again equaled that game-changing night at UFC 14.

Smith, Patrick

Height: 6'2" **Weight:** 225 lbs

Born: 8/28/63 **Debut:** UFC 1 (11/12/93)

Career Record: 18–14

Notable Wins: Scott Morris (UFC 2); Eric Esch (Yamma Pit Fighting)

Notable Losses: Ken Shamrock (UFC 1); Royce Gracie (UFC 2); Kimo Leopoldo (K-1 Legend 94); Kiyoshi Tamura (K-1 Hercules 95); Dave Beneteau (U-Japan); Marco Ruas (World Vale Tudo Championship 4)

Like many of the earliest **UFC** competitors, Patrick Smith wasn't a skilled mixed martial artist by today's standards, but he was a scary, scary man all the same. After losing to **Ken Shamrock** by **heel hook** less than two minutes into their UFC 1 contest, the kickboxer Smith devoted himself to the submission game, and took two matches by **guillotine choke** at UFC 2. But the most memorable moment of his career came in a knockout — a gruesome, frightening knockout of ninjitsu stylist Scott Morris, with huge elbows from the **mount** that left a bloodied Morris stumbling around the cage as he tried to regain his feet. It was a key image from the early days of the sport, proving beyond all doubt that what the audience was watching was real, and not some kind of particularly convincing **professional wrestling** ruse. An already scary Patrick Smith seemed even scarier when it emerged in 2008 that he'd been arrested for failing to register following a 1999 conviction for a

sexual assault on a child. Still an active fighter, his most high-profile bout in recent years came against Eric "Butterbean" Esch at the unbelievably awful **Yamma Pit Fighting** event, where Smith won again with a barrage of punches and elbows on the ground.

Sobral, Renato

Nickname: Babalu | **Height:** 6'1"

Weight: 205 lbs | **Born:** 9/7/75

Debut: Desafio: Rio vs. Sao Pauls (9/27/97) | **Career Record:** 36-8

Notable Wins: Kiyoshi Tamura (Rings: King of Kings Final 1999, Rings: King of Kings Final 2000); Mauricio Rua (IFC: Global Domination); Jeremy Horn (IFC: Global Domination); Robbie Lawler (Strikeforce: Los Angeles)

Notable Losses: Dan Henderson (Rings: King of Kings Final 1999); Fedor Emelianenko (Rings: 10th Anniversary); Chuck Liddell (UFC 40, UFC 62); Gegard Mousasi (Strikeforce: Carano vs. Cyborg)

Renato Sobral plays a key role in every **Chuck Liddell** highlight package you've ever seen. "Babalu" throws a low kick, backs away from a counter right hand,

and starts to shoot in for the takedown. It's at this exact moment that Babalu ends up on the wrong end of a Liddell head kick in what might be the most impressive KO of Liddell's storied career. Not Babalu at his best.

He *was* at his best, however, when he rattled off ten consecutive wins over the next three and a half years, including wins over **Mauricio Rua**, Trevor Prangley, and **Jeremy Horn** — all in the same night. Or, years before, when he competed in **Akira Maeda**'s **Rings** promotion when it featured many of the best in the world, twice getting the best of **Kiyoshi Tamura** at a time when that meant something.

But despite his strong **wrestling** base, and submission skills befitting a **Brazilian Jiu-jitsu** black belt under Carlos Gracie Jr., Babalu was never able to break through to the major championship level. He fared no better in a second bout against Liddell than he did in the first, knocked out less than two minutes into the first round. Only two fights later, Sobral was out of the **UFC**, apparently for good, after a bizarre finish against David Heath. Sobral choked a badly bloodied Heath into unconsciousness despite Heath's obvious attempts to submit and referee **Steve Mazzagatti**'s instructions to break the hold. "He called me 'motherfucker,'" Sobral explained, sort of. "He has to learn respect. He deserved that shit."

Be that as it may, Babalu has since had to ply his trade in **Affliction** and **Strikeforce**, rather than the UFC. In his first Strikeforce fight, he won that organization's light heavyweight title, the most prestigious championship that can be awarded for a bout against Bobby Southworth. This will probably have to be enough for Babalu, as another shot at elusive UFC gold seems unlikely.

Sokoudjou, Rameau Thierry

Nickname: The African Assassin **Height:** 6′

Weight: 205 lbs **Born:** 4/18/85

Debut: Total Combat 15 (6/15/06) **Career Record:** 9-6

Notable Wins: Antonio Rogerio Nogueira (Pride 33); Ricardo Arona (Pride 34); Kazuhiro Nakamura (UFC 84); Bob Sapp (Dream 11)

Notable Losses: Lyoto Machida (UFC 79); Renato Sobral (Affliction: Day of Reckoning); Gegard Mousasi (Strikeforce: Fedor vs. Rogers); Ikuhisa Minowa (Dynamite!! 2009)

Rameau Thierry Sokoudjou looked like a world-beater — until he didn't. Sokoudjou burst onto the scene with an absolutely stunning first-round knockout of upper-echelon light heavyweight **Antonio Rogerio Nogueira** that had everybody wondering whether the Cameroonian **judo** player was the next big thing, or a heavy-handed fighter who got lucky. When he followed that performance with another first-round KO, this time over an even more highly regarded **Pride** star, **Ricardo Arona**, there was every reason to believe he was the real deal. And so as Sokoudjou walked to the cage to make his **UFC** debut, looking slightly ridiculous in his enormous Predator mask, expectations were understandably high. But after being tooled on the ground and tapped out by **Lyoto Machida**, and knocked out by Luiz Cane, Sokoudjou's disappointing UFC tenure came to a quick end. After an equally ineffectual showing against **Renato Sobral** in **Affliction**, Sokoudjou found himself back in Japan, competing in **Dream**'s Super Hulk Grand Prix alongside fellow tournament entrants Hong-Man Choi, **Bob Sapp**, and, yes, **Jose Canseco**. It was a long way down for a fighter who seemed near the top of the sport at age 23 only to appear washed-up at 25.

Sonnen, Chael

Height: 6′1″ **Weight:** 185 lbs

Born: 4/3/77

Debut: HFP 1: Rumble on the Reservation (3/30/02)

Career Record: 24-11-1

Notable Wins: Trevor Prangley (*Ultimate Fight Night* 4); Paulo Filho (WEC 36); Yushin Okami (UFC 104); Nate Marquardt (UFC 109)

Notable Losses: Forrest Griffin (IFC: Global Domination); Jeremy Horn (EC 57, SF 6, UFC 60); Renato Sobral (UFC 55); Paulo Filho (WEC 31); Demian Maia (UFC 95); Anderson Silva (UFC 117)

Chael Sonnen's dominant performance against **UFC** middleweight champion **Anderson Silva** at UFC 117 could serve as a microcosm of his entire career.

Sonnen controlled Silva for 23 minutes, clobbering him with almost 300 punches. Not only did he put Silva on his back in all five rounds, he even managed to knock down the sport's best striker with an improved **boxing** attack. And then, moments away from walking out of the cage with title gold and the biggest upset in UFC history, Sonnen blew it. Silva capitalized on a careless moment and caught Sonnen in a fight-ending **triangle choke**. Silva pulled victory from the jaws of defeat — or so it seemed. To those familiar with Sonnen's career, the opposite was true — Sonnen had once again found a way to lose when winning seemed the only option.

A former all-American at Oregon and an Olympic alternate, Sonnen is a tremendous wrestler. There hasn't been an opponent yet that he couldn't take to the mat with disturbing ease. Once he has the fight where he wants it, Sonnen is relentless. Cardio is no issue: once he has you down he never stops attacking. It's a recipe for success, but Sonnen seems to be missing one key ingredient and it separates him from the greats — mental toughness. When he feels threatened, especially by a submission hold, his instinct is to quit. It's natural: most fighters feel uneasy when a limb is threatened or they risk unconsciousness from a chokehold. But the best fight through it. A survival instinct kicks in and they do whatever they can to escape. Sonnen taps. He lost eight fights by submission, most by way of triangle choke or **arm bar** — holds locked in while Sonnen was in a dominant position.

Against average fighters it hardly matters. Sonnen is so good he's rarely threatened. He earned his shot at Silva by dispatching two super tough opponents, **Yushin Okami** and **Nate Marquardt**, with shocking ease. Despite these big wins, critics didn't give the **Team Quest** star much of a chance against the Spider. It was looking like just another ho-hum Silva title defense when Sonnen turned up the intensity. He went after the champ with a starling ver-

In Their Own Words: Chael Sonnen talks trash at the UFC 115 fan Q & A

"Yeah, when you get [Anderson Silva] down you're not out of the woods yet. But he has a black belt from the Nogueira brothers, which is like getting a toy in your happy meal if you ask me. One of them is a punching bag and the other is really just irrelevant. . . . This is a one-sided dance. I saved Anderson's job. Uncle Dana was going to give him his walking papers, and I begged him, 'Keep him around. Keep him around for one more fight. I will retire this guy.'"

bal attack. For months, Sonnen was everywhere, looking to get under Silva's skin with a series of increasingly insulting tirades that touched on nationality, race, and even Silva's status as one of the sport's best fighters. Chael Sonnen promised to do what many of Silva's previous opponents had been too frightened to do — bring the fight to the champion. He was as good as his word, coming forward, attacking *and* winning. But in the end, all the talk in the world couldn't prevent the inevitable: as Sonnen tapped with less than two minutes left, his fans no doubt felt a familiar pang. A submission loss after a superior performance? That was Sonnen being Sonnen.

Soszynski, Krzysztof

Nickname: The Polish Experiment **Height:** 6'1"

Weight: 205–235 lbs **Born:** 8/2/77

Debut: 4/17/99 **Career Record:** 21-10-1

Notable Wins: Alex Andrade (Rinf of Combat 18); Brian Stann (UFC 97); Andre Gusmao (UFC 98); Stephan Bonnar (UFC 110)

Notable Losses: Matt Horwich (Freedom Fight: Canada vs. USA); Ben Rothwell (IFL: 2007 Semi-Finals); Brandon Vera (UFC 102); Stephan Bonnar (UFC 116)

Krzysztof Soszynski started his grappling career in a very different industry. Although **Brock Lesnar** gets all the attention from fans and the media, Soszynski was also a wrestler in another life. Discovered as a massive 318-pound body builder, he was soon hopping around the ring and taking pratfalls all over Canada.

His career path seemed set when he encountered wrestling legend "Bad News" Allen Coage. Bad News Allen was more than a professional wrestler. He was also the 1976 Olympic bronze medalist in **judo**. Coage was the toughest man in a tough man's business. As a black man in a notoriously racist industry, Bad News was continually forced to defend himself from insensitive and downright insulting remarks. Many black wrestlers were content to pretend not to hear the horrible slights on their person and their race. That wasn't Bad News Allen.

In one famous incident, the monstrous Andre the Giant was making racist comments on a bus ride in front of all the other wrestlers. When Coage confronted him, Andre refused to stop. Allen walked to the front of the bus and asked the driver to stop. He stepped outside and challenged the 6'10", 500-pound Giant to step outside with him. Andre refused. The next day at the hotel, Bad News renewed his challenge. Finally, the Giant backed down and apologized. Even a monster wanted no part of Allen Coage.

***In Their Own Words:* Soszynski on his wrestling mentor Bad News Allen Coage**

"I met him after he had two hip replacement surgeries. He was still on the floor in his fifties, still grappling with the kids he was teaching. I could definitely imagine how tough he was back then and how well he would have done if the sport had been around. He traveled extensively to Japan as well, learning aikido and jiu-jitsu. I had the privilege of meeting him during one of my circuits across Canada. He invited me out for a two-week camp at his place in Calgary and that's where he showed me a **Kimura** and an **arm bar**. I was hooked. Immediately after that two-week training camp, I came back to Winnipeg, quit wrestling, and took up **Brazilian Jiu-jitsu**. Six months later I had my first fight. So, he was very instrumental to me turning into a mixed martial arts fighter. If it weren't for him, I wouldn't be here. I'd be doing something else."

The fans certainly seem happy about Soszynski's chance encounter with Coage. He's quickly become a favorite because of his aggressive style and his lead role in ***Ultimate Fighter*** shenanigans in the reality show's eighth season. After falling short on the show, Soszynski continued his training under former champion **Dan Henderson** at **Team Quest** in California. He was looking to refine some skills, but Henderson and coaches like Heath Sims have taught him more than wrestling and striking. They've also shown him how to conduct himself outside the cage and helped hone an already keen work ethic.

Sperry, Mario

Nickname: Zen Machine
Height: 6'2"
Weight: 210 lbs
Born: 9/28/66
Debut: Duela De Titas (9/1/95)
Career Record: 13–4
Notable Wins: Vernon White (Caged Combat 1); Igor Vovchanchyn (Pride 17)
Notable Losses: Murilo Rua (Pride 20); Yuki Kondo (Pride Shockwave 2003); Tsuyoshi Kohsaka (Pride 31)

Growing up in Leblon, one of the wealthiest neighborhoods in all of Brazil, fighting was by no means the only career path open to Mario Sperry. His father was an air force officer, and Sperry earned a degree in economics. But like so many of Rio's best **Brazilian Jiu-jitsu** practitioners, Sperry eschewed the usual comforts of his class and chose to fight for a living. A **Carlson Gracie** black belt since 1995, Sperry is an **ADCC** and BJJ world champion, but most notable as a co-founder and leader of **Brazilian Top Team** (BTT) alongside **Murilo Bustamante.** Sperry was never able to match his sport grappling success in the full contact world of MMA, but he definitely had his moments — a first-round win by **arm triangle** choke over the dangerous **Igor Vovchanchyn** in Sperry's **Pride** debut foremost among them. Although the title fights and championships that many of his BTT teammates earned over the years may have eluded Sperry himself, his aggressive attacking, fast-paced approach to ground fighting, and singular work ethic have made Sperry an equally respected figure in the sport.

Spirit MC

From 2003 through 2008, Seoul's Spirit MC was a kind of extremely minor Korean **UFC**. They built their stars with a reality show, the superbly titled *Go! Super-Korean*. They showcased future UFC fighters like **Denis Kang** and **Dong Hyun Kim** on more than one occasion. And they even featured the best referee in the business, **Herb Dean**, albeit in a role North American fans might not immediately recognize him in: professional mixed martial artist (he lost an October 2006 bout by submission to Jungyu Choi). The analogy ends there, though, as Spirit MC bouts were contested not inside the Octagon but in a ring, under rules much more similar to **Pride:** stomps and soccer kicks to the head of a downed opponent were a staple. With no word from the organization on either its immediate or long-term future since its brief association with the now defunct **EliteXC,** there's no telling if or when Spirit MC will again fill

Jang Chung Gymnasium. There's no doubt that the burgeoning Korean MMA scene is poorer for its absence.

Sprawl and brawl

"Sprawl and brawl" is like the twisted cousin of **Mark Coleman**'s patented "**ground and pound.**" Both are styles employed by former collegiate and amateur wrestlers, but that's where the comparisons end. Sprawl and brawl is like the Bizarro version of ground and pound. Instead of trying to take an opponent to the mat, these fighters use the skills they've worked so hard on in the **wrestling** room to stay on their feet. The idea was to combat strong grapplers, primarily jiu-jitsu artists with strong submissions, by simply staying away from the floor. Since it was the only place the submission artists could ply their trade, the advantage shifted to the wrestler.

It's a style that only works for a select few grapplers. The men who created the concept and utilized it to win **UFC** gold were both wrestlers who had dynamite in their hands: **Chuck Liddell** and **Jens Pulver**. The two would spend the entire fight doing everything in their ability to stay on their feet — and since both were Division I-A wrestlers this ability was considerable — biding their time and hoping to land that one knockout punch.

It is the combination of two skills (takedown defense and power punching) that make sprawl and brawl work. It's not for everyone — in fact only Pulver, Liddell, and **Dan Henderson** have used it regularly to great success at the highest levels. Other wrestlers have tried this strategy, most notably **Josh Koscheck**, but without power punching the fight becomes a roll of the dice. Without that fight ending power, the bouts become kickboxing contests between two inexperienced grapplers not used to slugging it out — complete crapshoots.

Stand and Wang

B.J. Penn received mixed reviews for his coaching stint on the fifth season of ***The Ultimate Fighter***. Who knows what was real and what was the product of reality show editing, but Penn seemed at times aloof, disengaged. He was never more engaged, though, than when he cornered **Brazilian Jiu-jitsu** black belt Andy Wang in a preliminary-round fight against Brandon Melendez. The plan was for Wang to take Melendez to the ground, where he would enjoy a clear advantage over the lanky striker with limited grappling skills. But Wang wasn't there to follow the plan. He was there to "stand and Wang."

"Take him *down*, Wang! Go for the takedown, Wang, let's go!"

"Get that single, Andy!"

"Andy, let's go with the shot! Set up a shot, Andy!"

"Overhand right, single!"

"I want shots!"

"Why are we punching? Wang?"

"Take him down, Andy!"

"Get that *single*, Andy!"

"Take him down, and then you start to fight. Take him down. Promise?"

Wang promised, but he couldn't help himself. To Penn's utter exasperation, Wang never made a genuine effort at taking the fight to the ground, seemingly content to stand firmly on both feet and bang out a unanimous decision loss. And so a term was born: whenever a fighter with superior grappling ability elects to stay on his feet and engage in a kickboxing contest he's bound to lose, that's stand and Wang.

"I would like to be remembered for something better," Wang told internet radio host Bob Carson when asked about his unwitting gift to the mixed martial arts lexicon. "That's why I'm back now," he said after a two-year absence from the sport, "so the 'stand and Wang' thing will become an asterisk instead of the main footnote beside my name." Alas, it was not to be. In his very next fight, Wang faced skilled striker Atsuhiro Tsuboi at an Art of War card in Macau, and ProMMA.com was there with the call: "As the fight went into the second round Wang was picked apart with strikes. With his corner yelling to take the fight to the ground, Wang chose to remain standing, taking the fight the distance, and thereby ending the main event in an anti-climactic draw." Next time, take him down, Wang. Promise.

Stann, Brian

Nickname: All-American | **Height:** 6'1"

Weight: 205 lbs | **Born:** 9/24/80

Debut: SF 14 (1/6/06) | **Career Record:** 8-3

Notable Wins: Steve Cantwell (WEC 26); Doug Marshall (WEC 33)

Notable Losses: Steve Cantwell (WEC 35); Krzysztof Soszynski (UFC 97)

Brian Stann is a promoter's dream come true. He is a legitimate American hero, everything the WWE wanted Hulk Hogan to be. His service in the Marine Corps was bona fide — he wasn't simply an athlete like **Randy Couture** or **Bobby Lashley**. He was a warrior, holding his ground during an intense battle in Karabilah, Iraq, earning a Silver Star for valor.

A former linebacker at the U.S. Naval Academy, Stann had the complete package. He had athleticism, rugged good looks, and innate toughness. What he didn't seem to have was submission or takedown defense. After winning six in a row against carefully selected opponents who were likely to keep it standing with the strong striker, he lost two straight. Yet, if anyone can forge victory out of defeat, mount a comeback, and save a floundering career, it will be Brian Stann. As the Marines say: Oorah!

Steroids

Steroid scandals have consumed even sports like baseball, known mostly for slightly overweight men chewing tobacco and scratching themselves, occasionally exerting the effort to swing a stick at a ball. If steroids worked in a sport like that — and there is no question that steroids work — was there any doubt that performance enhancing drugs (PEDs) would also engulf a sport where men bludgeon each other for minutes at a time?

We know MMA has a drug problem. When the state of California began testing every fighter on the card in 2007 they found more abuse in MMA than in **boxing**. During the last eight months of 2007, there were 15 positive steroid tests in 54 MMA cards held in the state. During the same time frame, only two boxers tested positive with a much larger sample size.

It was K-1's mega-event at the Los Angeles Memorial Coliseum that brought the problem into a stark spotlight. **UFC** pioneer **Royce Gracie** tested positive for Nandrolone, Tim Persey was caught with methamphetamines, and former Detroit Lions star football player Johnnie Morton had Chris Benoit levels of testosterone flowing through his veins.

While baseball and football can survive a drug scandal, MMA is still new enough to be hurt badly by any negative stereotyping. The sport is only recently recovered from a long-term smear campaign headed by politicians looking for an easy target. Painting fighters with broad brushstrokes as steroid-raging meatheads doesn't do anyone any favors, but fighters are still using, consequences be damned. Some in the MMA community estimate that more than half of the world's top fighters are secretly using PEDs, an astounding number that could result in real trouble down the road for a growing sport.

The UFC has been relatively lucky, with a surprisingly low number of positive steroid tests. Since Nevada began testing regularly in 2002 the promotion has, however, seen three of its world champions (**Josh Barnett**, **Tim Sylvia**, and **Sean Sherk**) test positive for steroids, forcing them to be stripped of their titles. Other high profile busts include Gracie, **Kimo Leopoldo**, **Ken Shamrock**, **Vitor Belfort**, and **Nate Marquardt**.

Keep in mind that these drug failures are coming in droves despite a flawed testing system that is relatively easy to beat. The testing programs vary from state to state, but are almost exclusively relegated to post-event pee tests and possibly a urinalysis when a fighter gets his or her license in the state. That means a fighter knows exactly when a test is coming, allowing them to cycle off the drugs they are using, in plenty of time to beat the test. Additionally, in many states, only a few fighters are tested on each card because of the costs of such tests. The system is merely window dressing. Any real effort to stop drug use in the sport will have to include random year-round testing. And while there has been noise about such rigorous testing from Nevada and California, fighters are safe to use drugs year-round, right up until a couple of weeks before their fight.

Stevenson, Joe

Nickname: Daddy
Height: 5'7"
Weight: 155 lbs
Born: 6/15/82
Debut: ESF: Empire 1 (5/15/99)
Career Record: 31-11
Notable Wins: Luke Cummo (*The Ultimate Fighter* 2 Finale); Yves Edwards (UFC 61); Nate Diaz (*The Ultimate Fighter* 9 Finale)

In Their Own Words: Joe Stevenson on starting young

"I feel like I'm 47. But honestly, with the correct training and stuff, there's no reason a 47-year-old can't fight. My camps are about peak performance and not killing my body every day. It's about being the best person on that day and . . . being able to rise to the occasion.

"Other than that, yes, it hurts when I wake up sometimes and when it's cold. But most people that are working a nine to five, like when I was doing concrete, you know, back in the day, or when I was running the forklift, I felt the same pain. They're just pains that happen and now that I've learned nutrition a little bit better, it's helped me a lot.

"I'm going to ride this car until the wheels come off. Honestly, it will be a decision that happens when my family wants me home more, and luckily I've been blessed with a great wife and great kids that are very supportive and help me tremendously in my life."

Notable Losses: Jens Pulver (Bas Rutten Invitational 2); Josh Neer (*Ultimate Fight Night* 4); B.J. Penn (UFC 80); Kenny Florian (UFC 91); Diego Sanchez (UFC 95)

If you wonder how Joe Stevenson has more than 40 fights at the tender age of 27, it's because he's been doing this for a long time. For 11 long years he's been fighting in the cage. Do the math; Stevenson got his start when he was just 16. Sixteen. With the consent of his parents, so protective that they wouldn't allow him to play high school football, he was fighting on Indian reservations in California before he graduated from high school. And he was winning.

By the time Stevenson worked free from the **King of the Cage** breeding grounds, where **UFC** fighters often learned their profession before joining the big leagues, he was just 23. Stevenson already had a fully formed game when he was invited to join the second season of ***The Ultimate Fighter***. He was the favorite and lived up to that billing, winning the UFC contract by beating an overmatched Jason Von Flue and a game **Luke Cummo**.

After a slow start, losing to the tough Josh Neer, Stevenson dropped down to lightweight and ran off four wins in a row. His win streak, combined with his *TUF* notoriety, earned Stevenson a title shot. At UFC 80, Stevenson finally learned what it felt like to be Luke Cummo or Von Flue. He was overmatched and decimated by an unusually motivated **B.J. Penn**. Penn was looking for the title that had eluded him throughout his storied career: the UFC lightweight title. Penn had failed in two previous attempts, losing to **Jens Pulver** at UFC 35 and fighting to a draw with **Caol Uno** at UFC 41.

The fight was a bloodbath. Stevenson was dropped in the first exchange with a right hand and struggled to survive. Stevenson relied on his vast experience to hold on, but at the end of the round Penn opened up a giant cut with an elbow. He choked Joe out in the second round, both men slippery from Stevenson's blood. It was Stevenson at his peak: good but, as Penn demonstrated, not world-class.

St. Pierre, Georges

Nicknames: GSP, Rush **Height:** 5'10"

Weight: 170 lbs **Born:** 5/19/81

Debut: UCC 7 (1/25/02) **Career Record:** 20-2

Notable Wins: Karo Parisyan (UFC 46); Frank Trigg (UFC 54); Sean Sherk (UFC 56); B.J. Penn (UFC 58, UFC 94); Matt Hughes (UFC 65, UFC 79); Matt Serra (UFC 83); Jon Fitch (UFC 87); Thiago Alves (UFC 100)

Notable Losses: Matt Hughes (UFC 50); Matt Serra (UFC 69)

Georges St. Pierre is on top, and there's no telling how long he might stay there. The dominant champion of the deepest division in the sport's premier organization, St. Pierre has achieved unparalleled success; no one has faced the level of competition he has over the course of his career and won with the same kind of regularity. He's done it with a combination of top-notch athleticism; crisp, efficient striking; black-belt level **Brazilian Jiu-jitsu**; and MMA-specific **wrestling** skills that put NCAA Division I All-Americans to shame. At only 28 years old, with no unavenged losses, and no credible threats to his welterweight title either inside or outside the **UFC**, all that remains for St. Pierre is to cement his status among the legends of the sport, the true all-time greats.

It all started for St. Pierre as a boy hoping to defend himself against neighborhood bullies by studying the rugged Kyokushin style of **karate** under Jean Couture in the small community of Saint-Isidore, Quebec. After the death of his instructor in 1997, St. Pierre broadened his training to include wrestling, **boxing**, and, inspired by the exploits of **Royce Gracie** in the early days of the UFC, Brazilian Jiu-jitsu. He made his professional debut at the age of 20 for the promotion that would become Montreal's **TKO Major League MMA**, and became a local champion after only the second fight of his career.

A shot in the true major leagues of the sport soon followed. When the 22-year-old St. Pierre stepped into the cage against the 21-year-old **Karo Parisyan** at UFC 46, it was a glimpse of the future of the welterweight division, two fighters who would become UFC fixtures. St. Pierre proved both the better striker and the better wrestler, and took the unanimous decision in their preliminary bout. Later that same night, two fighters who would figure prominently in St. Pierre's career faced off when lightweight **B.J. Penn** challenged **Matt Hughes** for the welterweight title. Penn floored the champion with a right hand and finished him with a **rear naked choke** while Hughes was still dazed, ending Hughes' title reign of more than two years. Penn was stripped of the welterweight championship soon thereafter for fighting in a rival organization in Japan. The UFC needed an opponent for Matt Hughes to fight for the vacant title. Georges St. Pierre, only two fights into his UFC career, got the call.

He was in way over his head. Although St. Pierre clearly had the technical ability and athleticism to hang with Hughes at that time, he didn't have the composure. St. Pierre was in such awe of his opponent that he couldn't so much as look him in the eye during referee **John McCarthy**'s pre-fight instructions. The two traded takedowns in the opening minutes in an impressive showcase of St. Pierre's wrestling skills. Despite a lack of any serious amateur background, St. Pierre's wrestling had been — as it would be for several years to come — honed by training with the Canadian national team. After fighting his way back to his feet, GSP put Hughes on his heels with a spinning back kick to the ribs that appeared to have the veteran hurt, but Hughes put St. Pierre on his back as the round wound down. It looked like we were in for a long, competitive fight, until St. Pierre attempted a sloppy **Kimura** from **half-guard** with only ten seconds to go, which Hughes expertly turned into an **arm bar** to force the submission with only a single second remaining in the first round.

The road back to title contention a second time around would prove an awful lot tougher. First, there was the madman **Jason Miller**, who smiled and laughed his way through a one-sided beating that lasted the full three rounds. Next **Frank Trigg**, a tough two-time challenger to Hughes' welterweight title, whom St. Pierre blasted through and strangled in the first. From there, it was **Sean Sherk**, who had never been stopped in 30 professional bouts — until St. Pierre pounded him out in the second. Finally, the biggest test of them all: the man who had defeated Hughes and then vanished, B.J. Penn. St. Pierre's meeting with Penn at UFC 58 was not the main event, but it was by far the most anticipated fight of the night. It didn't disappoint, going the distance in a back-and-forth affair that ultimately saw St. Pierre emerge the victor in a split decision that could have just as easily gone the other way. The stage was set for Hughes/St. Pierre II.

This time, with the hero worship and awe completely behind him — "I'm not impressed by your performance," he famously told Hughes after a pretty damn impressive win over Penn — St. Pierre stepped into the Octagon fo-

In Their Own Words: GSP on his training philosophy

"Philosophy helped me with my fighting. I can show you many examples. It's like war. We've seen it in the past: the country or civilization with the most advanced weapons win the war. Genghis Khan dominated the world during his time because he had a weapon nobody else had. America won World War II with the atomic bomb. Same thing in MMA. I want to have a weapon that nobody else has. That's why I've been traveling a lot. I want to have some techniques, some weapons, so I can win and dominate my sport. That's what I need to have to stay ahead of the game. . . .

"Before I lost to Serra, I was lifting weights by myself because I study kinesiology at the university. I was training by myself pretty much. I thought I knew everything already. After I lost, I decided to work with a specialist, a sports conditioning guy. It's helped me improve dramatically. I became way more explosive and he helps me peak at the right time. Periodization of the training. It's changed everything. It helps me a lot."

cused, resolute. And he lit Matt Hughes up. Hughes was unable to take St. Pierre down, and had no answer for St. Pierre's long jabs and high inside leg kicks — two of which John McCarthy saw as unintentional groin shots, although Hughes later admitted the second kick in particular actually struck nerves in his thigh. In the closing seconds of the opening round, St. Pierre connected with a superman punch (a leaping cross following a feinted rear-leg kick) that put Hughes down and nearly out. Hughes was clearly dazed as he stumbled back to his corner, and wasn't doing much better after a minute's rest. Early in the second, St. Pierre floored Hughes with a head kick and followed up with undefended punches and elbows from **guard** that forced McCarthy to call the match at 1:25 of the second round. **Mike Goldberg** captured the moment perfectly: "Tonight, the future has become the present — Georges St. Pierre is the new welterweight champion."

There was every reason to think the young champion was set to reign over the division for years to come. His first title defense, at any rate, was going to be a walk in the park: **Matt Serra** was next in line for a title shot that few felt he truly deserved. The journeyman Serra had fought only sporadically over the previous few years, and only barely squeaked through a tournament of also-rans on ***The Ultimate Fighter*** 4: The Comeback, yet here he was, challenging the man who had just effortlessly dispatched the great Matt

Hughes. Serra stepped into the Octagon an 11-to-one underdog. He left it the new welterweight champion of the world. In the three and a half minutes in between, he'd overcome his serious reach disadvantage to send St. Pierre reeling from a heavy, looping shot that connected just behind the ear and set him staggering. Serra pounced and forced St. Pierre to tap to strikes in one of the most stunning upsets in the history of the sport.

It turns out it was just what St. Pierre needed. "In my career, there have been two great turning points," St. Pierre would later reflect. "The first is when I lost to Matt Hughes and the second is when I lost to Serra. After those losses, I made a lot of changes in my training, my entourage, and everything in my life. I become better after every fight, but after these two losses I became way better. It gave me a little push up." The refocused and re-energized St. Pierre who emerged after the loss to Serra has proven even more impressive than the one who first streaked to the title. He outwrestled four-time NCAA Division I All-American **Josh Koscheck** for three rounds. He tossed Matt Hughes around like a rag doll before forcing him to verbally submit to an arm bar. He put on a positional clinic against Brazilian Jiu-jitsu expert Serra to reclaim his title. And he battered the face of legitimate number-one contender **Jon Fitch** into something out of a horror movie.

The stage was set for a hotly anticipated rematch with B.J. Penn. Although their first match was a back-and-forth affair that ended in a much-discussed split decision, the result this time around was far less ambiguous. St. Pierre wore Penn out in the **clinch** in the early rounds, to the point that the visibly exhausted Penn could do nothing to stop St. Pierre's takedowns as the fight progressed. Penn's usually dangerous guard game was completely nullified by St. Pierre's excellent positional work — and the steady stream of blows he landed to the head of the quickly fading lightweight champ. Penn's corner stopped the one-sided fight after the fourth round. Controversy erupted soon after, when Penn's camp filed a formal complaint to the Nevada State Athletic Commission that Phil Nurse, one of St. Pierre's cornermen, had illegally applied petroleum jelly to St. Pierre's chest and back between rounds. Penn wanted licenses revoked, fines imposed, and the bout ruled no contest, but the NSAC didn't see it that way. The controversy quickly died down, and UFC President **Dana White** expressed no enthusiasm at the prospect of a third fight between the two great champions. The last word in the Georges St. Pierre/B.J. Penn story seems to have been written.

The welterweight division has historically been the sport's deepest, but St. Pierre's dominance is such that it's getting harder for the UFC to generate credible challengers to his title. **Thiago Alves**, a **Muay Thai** striker fighting out of the highly regarded **American Top Team**, was perhaps the last real threat we'll see for some time. If anyone in the division was going to get the better of St. Pierre standing, it was the dangerous "Pit Bull," whose size and ferocity had earned him eight stoppages in 11 UFC fights. But St. Pierre took him down and dominated him for five rounds — despite tearing his groin in the fourth. It was another incredible performance from a fighter who makes incredible performances seem routine.

St. Pierre continues to split his training time between **Greg Jackson**'s Albuquerque, New Mexico, camp and Tristar Gym in Montreal. Rumors of a 2010 contest against UFC middleweight ace **Anderson Silva** persist, although it's unclear whether or not that fight would make sense for either competitor. St. Pierre could move up a weight division and take a run at that title. Or he could continue to clean out the division he has so clearly established as his and his alone. Either way, every fight, every win brings him closer to the title he wants most. "I don't want to fight to be champion anymore because I'm already champion," St. Pierre told the press in late 2008. "I want to fight to become a legend in the sport."

Strikeforce

Even though Strikeforce promoted its first MMA event in 2006, the promotion has years of experience in creating compelling and successful fight shows in President Scott Coker's home state of California. The official U.S. partner of K-1 kickboxing, they've been putting on kickboxing shows since 1985. It's these 25 years of learning the tricks of the trade, figuring out what works in the market, that made Strikeforce the envy of regional promoters everywhere.

Unlike other fledgling groups, Coker's K-1 had no intention of competing with the **UFC** on a national level. They were strictly a regional group, like an old-time **pro wrestling** territory, running shows in San Jose, California, with local talent they knew would draw. The events were spectacular successes, outdrawing even UFC events in California, and included a **Frank Shamrock** and Cesar Gracie grudge match that set the North American attendance record, bringing in 17,465 paying fans in March 2006. Even UFC President **Dana White** was impressed.

"Have you ever heard me say a bad word about Strikeforce?" White asked in 2008. "I wish them all the luck in the world. Strikeforce is a good show. They've been putting on great fights for a long time. That's good. It's a positive thing. Those guys run a real promotion. They don't try to tamper with fights. They don't have fucking goofballs from backyard barbecues trying to fight. It's a good thing."

Today, you'd be hard pressed to hear such kind words from White. When **EliteXC** collapsed in a whirlwind of horrible decisions and controversy, Coker and his partners at Silicon Valley Sports and Entertainment were there to pick up the pieces. The little engine that could, the textbook example of a successful local promoter, was ready to go national. The same day, they announced a deal with Showtime for 16 shows a year, with the option for four more on CBS.

Coker and Strikeforce immediately looked to distinguish themselves from the UFC. The one area the UFC had completely ignored was the flourishing women's MMA scene, and Coker snapped up the hottest star in the game, **Gina Carano**. Coker wasn't going to make women a sideshow; in fact, in a historic first for women's MMA, Carano and **Cristiane "Cyborg" Santos** headlined the Strikeforce card at the HP Pavilion in August 2009. The two women became the first female fighters to be featured in the main event of a major MMA show, and they more than delivered. After being built for more than a year, first by the now defunct EliteXC and then by Strikeforce, the fight was a hot commodity, drawing 13,524 fans, the vast majority of them cheering wildly for Carano.

It was the high point of Strikeforce's run in the national spotlight. Santos beat Carano handily in the first round and Carano left MMA, perhaps permanently, to pursue opportunities in the movie business. But Coker had shown the ability to attract international interest in his shows. Earlier that month, Strikeforce shocked the entire MMA community, swooping in during a failed negotiation between the UFC and the world's top heavyweight fighter, **Fedor Emelianenko**, and signing the Russian to a three-fight deal.

It was enough to get CBS — on the fence after the EliteXC debacle — to commit to airing Strikeforce events on national television. The first event, with Fedor in the main event against undefeated prospect **Brett Rogers**, was scheduled for November 7, 2009, in Chicago, Illinois. Fedor defeated Rogers in a spirited bout. The show was a ratings success, but not a smash hit, peaking at 5.46 million viewers for the main event.

Sudo, Genki

Nickname: Neo Samurai **Height:** 5'9"

Weight: 155 lbs **Born:** 3/8/78

Debut: Extreme Shoot 2 (6/6/98) **Career Record:** 16-4-1

Notable Wins: Nate Marquardt (Pancrase: Breakthrough 11); Eric Esch (Dynamite!! 2003); Mike Brown (UFC 47); Royler Gracie (K-1 MMA Romanex)

Notable Losses: Duane Ludwig (UFC 42); Kid Yamamoto (Dynamite!! 2005)

Genki Sudo was a showman. Regardless of what happened in the ring, Sudo always made his biggest impression either before or after the fight. Before the fight, there were elaborately staged entrances, whether he took up Charlie Sheen's "Wild Thing" character from the baseball comedy *Major League* (and did the robot), donned a shiny silver spaceman suit (and did the robot), or paraded out in African tribal garb (and did the robot). There was seemingly no end to the variety and inventiveness of his entrances (minus the robot). Post-fight, the observant Buddhist would do his best to communicate his message of universal peace and love, and insist that "We Are All One." Even during the fight, he'd adopt weird stances and even turn away from his opponents, a strange tactic that never really seemed to cost him like you might think. Genki Sudo was, in short, a character.

He was a fighter, too. With his dynamic submission skills and wins over **Royler Gracie**, **Mike Brown**, and the much bigger **Nate Marquardt**, there was never any doubt about that. After stints in **Pancrase**, the **UFC**, **Rings** and K-1, Sudo retired young after a New Year's Eve 2006 win over future **WEC** bantamweight regular Damacio Page. But his last real bout of consequence came a year earlier when he was stopped by **Kid Yamamoto** in their **Hero's** tournament final. Many thought the match was stopped early, but at the post-fight press conference, the always chill Sudo didn't particularly seem to mind. Since then, Genki has just kept on being Genki. He's been acting, recording ("Love and Everything" and "World Order" are his standout tracks to date), and every now and then he turns up at **Dream** events as a color commentator.

SuperBrawl

Hawaii's leading MMA show started in 1995, as far removed from the 8,800-seat Blaisdell Arena it would later call home as one could possibly imagine. Former Chippendales dancer T. Jay Thompson originally called the event FutureBrawl, and the fights in the crowd were often more compelling than the ones in the ring. The shows were held at the legendarily violent Gussie L'Amour's in Honolulu, a club where soldiers from the local military base would often clash heads with local tough guys. The smarter fans in the audience had an empty beer bottle at the ready and their chair in hand, ready to throw if it came time to throw down.

Just a year later the show, renamed SuperBrawl, was a top breeding ground for MMA's larger promotions worldwide. In the days before six-figure contracts, Thompson could get many of the sport's rising stars on his shows with the simple promise of a Hawaiian vacation. **Pat Miletich**, **Frank Shamrock**, **Pete Williams**, **Vitor Belfort**, **Rumina Sato**, and **Matt Hughes** all had fights with SuperBrawl, and top Hawaiian prospects like **Wesley Correira** and Ronald Jhun also cut their teeth there. In 2005 the promotion was rechristened Icon Sport and continued to combine established international-level talents like **Robbie Lawler** and **Jason Miller** with native prospects like Kala Hose. After 12 years of promoting MMA on the islands, Thompson sold Icon Sport to Pro Elite in September 2007. As part of the sale, Thompson took a position with the doomed **EliteXC** promotion as a consultant. When EliteXC folded, Thompson re-emerged on the Hawaiian scene with Kingdom MMA.

Suzuki, Minoru

Height: 5'10" **Weight:** 195 lbs

Born: 6/17/68 **Debut:** Pancrase: Yes, We Are Hybrid Wrestlers 1 (9/21/93)

Career Record: 28-20-1

Notable Wins: Ken Shamrock (Pancrase: Pancrash! 1, Pancrase: Eyes of Beast 4); Maurice Smith (Pancrase: Road to the Championship 1); Matt Hume (Pancrase: King of Pancrase Tournament); Guy Mezger (Pancrase: Eyes of Beast 7); Jushin Liger (Pancrase: Spirit 8)

Notable Losses: Maurice Smith (Pancrase: Yes, We Are Hybrid Wrestlers 3); Bas Rutten (Pancrase: Road to the Championships 2, Pancrase: 1995 Anniversary Show); Masakatsu Funaki (Pancrase: Road to the Championships 5); Frank Shamrock (Pancrase: Eyes of Beast 3); Yuki Kondo (Pancrase: Truth 6); Semmy Schilt (Pancrase: Advance 1); Sanae Kikuta (Pancrase: Breakthrough 11); Denis Kang (Pancrase: 2000 Anniversary Show)

Minoru Suzuki was **Pancrase**'s bad boy. He dressed in black, wore a black towel over his head, and walked to the ring with a purpose. Behind the scenes, he brutalized students and was notoriously distant from the foreign talent. Inside the ring he went all-out too, mixing aggressive standup and great amateur **wrestling**. Trained by Yoshiaki Fujiwara, Suzuki also had excellent submissions, making him one of the first cross-trained fighters in the history of the sport.

Suzuki was the first fighter to beat **UFC** Hall of Famer **Ken Shamrock** under Pancrase rules. It was a fight rumored to be fixed, a bout between two pro wrestlers who understood business. Shamrock had lost to **Royce Gracie** at UFC 1 and the Japanese promotion was afraid of their best fighter losing again in the Octagon. Shamrock tapped out to a **knee bar** and Suzuki was immediately propelled into the main event stratosphere. If Shamrock was losing, it was going to be to someone in their own promotion.

It happened again more than a year later. Shamrock, who had become the King of Pancrase, was facing fellow pro wrestler **Dan Severn** at UFC 6. Severn was an opening match wrestler for a competing promotion in Japan. There was a good chance that he would beat Shamrock, a potentially embarrassing turn of events for Pancrase. Shamrock agreed to drop his championship to Suzuki, again tapping out to a knee bar.

Just two years into his MMA career, Suzuki had already begun a steep decline. He fought 22 times, almost monthly, and trained almost constantly between bouts. Suzuki and the other Pancrase founders pushed themselves too hard, fighting too often, and their bodies couldn't handle the strain. In the next two years Suzuki, who had been winning regularly, lost eight of 11 matches.

By 1998, Suzuki was simply a shell of the fighter who had once inspired terror. He was knocked out so regularly that he was unable to stand up to the force of even mild blows to the head. Soon Pancrase was pushing Suzuki into grappling only matches, homages to the **catch wrestling** that had inspired the promotion's creation.

In 2003, Suzuki returned to traditional **pro wrestling**, becoming one of the hottest wrestlers in the business. He eventually became the All Japan Triple

Crown Champion and remains one of the top performers in Japan, excelling at the sport of excess he had eschewed ten years before.

Sylvia, Tim

Nickname: The Maine-iac **Height:** 6'8"
Weight: 265 lbs **Born:** 3/5/76
Debut: IFC: Battleground 2001 (1/19/01) **Career Record:** 26-6
Notable Wins: Ricco Rodriguez (UFC 41); Andrei Arlovski (UFC 59, UFC 61)
Notable Losses: Frank Mir (UFC 46); Andrei Arlovski (UFC 51); Randy Couture (UFC 68); Antonio Rodrigo Nogueira (UFC 81); Fedor Emelianenko (Affliction: Banned)

Poor Tim Sylvia. He just wants to be loved, adored by fans, and respected by his peers. Instead, he's MMA's least popular fighter. Sylvia didn't have the prototypical jock's life growing up. He was awkward, clumsy, and picked on by his classmates. The result was a man desperate to make it, and then tell everyone about it.

Sylvia is his own worst enemy. Once, his agent **Monte Cox** secured him a big sponsorship, Sylvia, Cox, and the sponsor went out to celebrate. At the end of the evening, the sponsors rescinded their offer. Sylvia couldn't rein in his attitude long enough to impress someone interested in giving him money. "I can't do it," the sponsor said. "This guy is an asshole."

It's a shame that Sylvia has such a large chip on his shoulder, because his story should inspire. He overcame poor genetics and limited athleticism to become the **UFC** heavyweight champion. When he first arrived at **Pat Miletich**'s gym in Iowa he was almost useless. No one thought he would make it. Through hard work, and his sheer size, he continued to develop and win.

After 13 victories in a row, he made his UFC debut against **Wesley "Cabbage" Correira.** Cabbage had the reputation of being unstoppable, so granite-chinned that he would never be out of a fight. Sylvia became the first to punch his ticket and, in turn, earned a shot at **Ricco Rodriguez**'s heavyweight title. Rodriguez's life and fighting career were spiraling out of control, and Sylvia dispatched him in the first round.

The new champion's first title defense was a fiasco. He beat challenger Gan McGee handily, but after the fight he tested positive for the **steroid** Stanozolol and was forced to vacate his title. Sylvia claimed the drug use wasn't to achieve an athletic advantage, but rather to improve his doughy physique. With any other fighter, fans and the media would be skeptical of that claim. From Sylvia, however, it seemed plausible. He was that anxious to impress.

Upon his return from a six-month suspension, Sylvia fought **Frank Mir** to regain his title. Mir handed him his first professional loss with a gruesome **arm bar** finisher. Initially fans didn't understand why the fight had been stopped. Even UFC President **Dana White** was up in arms about what he thought was a poor decision by referee **Herb Dean.** Then they showed the replay on the big screen and the crowd was silent. It was clear that Mir had broken Sylvia's arm with the hold.

Sylvia got a third chance at the championship at UFC 51 against the sensational **Andrei Arlovski.** Arlovski dropped Sylvia with a punch and finished him with an Achilles lock in the first 50 seconds. Even though he went on to regain the title from Arlovski at UFC 59, Sylvia was never the same fighter after this loss. The aggressive warrior who once finished 16 of his first 18 fights became a cautious jabber, using his reach to do just enough to win. Five of his next seven UFC contests went to the judges' score cards, causing Sylvia to gain a reputation for boring fights.

It was this reputation for lackluster performances that made the UFC decide it no longer needed his services following a loss to **Antonio Rodrigo Nogueira** at UFC 81. The fans hated Sylvia and his constant backroom bickering over money was growing tiresome in the **Zuffa** front office.

In Their Own Words: Tim Sylvia on not getting respect

"I think . . . the true fans and the people that are knowledgeable about the sport respect me. You got your average bozos that don't know anything about the sport, who see **Brock Lesnar** coming in or see these superstars like **Kimbo Slice**, who really haven't done anything, and they think they are studs. I don't know; I'm always so big and a lot of people don't like me because I'm the biggest guy in the division. So they are always pulling for the underdog.

"I always perform best when I'm in the underdog role. When I'm favored, I usually end up losing. So it's a good spot for me to be in. I like it. I have this thing where I like proving people wrong my whole life. This is just another opportunity I get to do that and basically I get to stick it to the man."

Sylvia landed on his feet, thanks to Cox's connections in the industry, securing a title shot for the newly created WAMMA heavyweight title. His fight with the legendary **Fedor Emelianenko** was the main event of the T-shirt company **Affliction**'s first pay-per-view show. Fedor was fighting for the first time in front of a significant American audience and wasted little time impressing them. He knocked down Sylvia with a punch — recalling shades of the Arlovski fight — and then choked him out in just 36 seconds.

The quick loss badly damaged Sylvia's stock and made finding a fight for the money he demanded unlikely. He took a **boxing** match with 48-year-old Olympic gold medalist **Ray Mercer** that had to be converted to an MMA fight at the zero hour after the Association of Boxing Commissions put a stop to it. It was a black eye for MMA when the inexperienced Mercer knocked Sylvia out in just ten seconds. When Sylvia toppled like a giant redwood tree, his entire career seemed down for the count.

Tadeu, Eugenio

Height: 5'8"

Weight: 160 lbs

Born: 1965

Debut: JJ vs. MA (11/30/84)

Career Record: 3-3-1 (1 No Contest)

Notable Loss: Mikey Burnett (UFC 16)

Before **Kazushi Sakuraba** came around, Eugenio Tadeu was the Gracie family's greatest modern rival. Unchallenged for years as the toughest men in Rio de Janeiro, no one quite knew what to do when Tadeu and a new generation of **Luta Livre** artists refused to cede ground. Tadeu wanted nothing more than to test himself against the best. When there was trouble between the two camps, whether it be a street fight or a dojo challenge, you could count on Tadeu to be right in the middle of it.

Every official or semi-official fight between Tadeu and a Gracie fighter seemed to end in an unsatisfying manner. Against **Royler Gracie** in a gym challenge, the fight was declared a draw after both men had given their all. No winner was chosen, although it seemed to many onlookers that Tadeu had carried the day. In 1991, during the famous Desafio Challenge, Tadeu fought **Carlson Gracie** student Wallid Ismail. Ismail was attempting some **ground and pound** next to the ropes and the two men tumbled dangerously to the floor. Fans immediately surrounded them and Ismail took the opportunity to throw a couple of cheap shots on the floor. In a moment straight out of **pro wrestling**, Tadeu was counted out of the ring and given a very questionable loss.

Of course the most famous and bizarre finish in Tadeu (or anyone's) career was at **Pentagon Combat** in 1997. After 15 grueling minutes, Tadeu and **Renzo Gracie** were both exhausted, hoping against hope that the other would finally give in to fatigue. Then the lights went out, the crowd rioted, and the fight was called a no contest. When it was called, it seemed Tadeu had finally gotten the upper hand.

All of this served to make Eugenio Tadeu a legendary figure in the early years of MMA. When he finally got a chance at the Octagon, five years after the debut of the **Ultimate Fighting Championship**, Tadeu proved to be worth the wait. He and the **Lion's Den**'s Mikey Burnett went toe-to-toe for almost ten minutes before the referee called a stop to the fight. UFC matchmaker **John Perretti** called it the best fight he had seen in the UFC, a fitting tribute to one of the sport's pre–MMA legends.

Takada, Nobuhiko

Height: 6'1" **Weight:** 225 lbs
Born: 4/12/62 **Debut:** Pride 1 (10/11/97)
Career Record: 2-6-2 **Notable Win:** Mark Coleman (Pride 5)
Notable Losses: Rickson Gracie (Pride 1, Pride 4); Mark Kerr (Pride 6); Royce Gracie (Pride Grand Prix 2000); Igor Vovchanchyn (Pride 11); Kiyoshi Tamura (Pride 23)

Nobuhiko Takada wanted a fight with **Rickson Gracie**, but he didn't want it like that. Alone in the ring at **Pride** 1, Takada was where he had no intention of being just two years earlier. As the top wrestler in the shoot-style UWFi wrestling promotion, Takada was always looking for opponents to give his brand of realistic wrestling an edge. Amateur wrestling stars like Gary Albright and Duane Koslowski, ultimate fighters like **Dan Severn**, and judoka like "Bad News" Allen Coage gave the promotion credibility. And after his star turn at **Vale Tudo** Japan 1994, Takada wanted to add Rickson Gracie to the list.

MMA was taking off in Japan. The fans had seen **Pancrase**, the UFC, and real Brazilian-style Vale Tudo. The whispers were beginning to start: the UWFi wasn't all it was cracked up to be. Looking to head that off at the pass, the company made a huge offer to Gracie to come in and split a pair of matches with Takada. The proud fighter declined.

If Gracie wouldn't come to them, they would come to Gracie. Takada and UWFi matchmaker Yukoh Miyato sent their toughest guy, **Yoji Anjo**, to embarrass Gracie in his California dojo. Instead Gracie beat Anjo bloody. The UWFi was shell-shocked, and shoot-style wrestling's demise came a little faster than it otherwise might have.

After a crushing series of inter-promotional matches with wrestlers from New Japan Pro Wrestling, traditional wrestling showmen, Takada was at a career crossroads. He could either return to **pro wrestling** as a diminished star or try his hand at this new sport that in a very real sense his wrestling had inspired.

Pride was built specifically to showcase Takada. There was little doubt who his first opponent would be. Japanese culture dictated that Takada had a responsibility to stand up for his protégé Anjo. It was necessary for him to challenge Rickson Gracie.

When the fight finally happened on October 11, 1997, Takada's remarkably poor performance shocked fans. He had been built for years as the toughest man in professional wrestling. Where were his kicks that allegedly struck blows more powerful than a man swinging a baseball bat? Where were his vaunted submissions? Gracie submitted him easily with an **arm bar** in less than five minutes.

Takada's reputation died that night at the Tokyo Dome. He came back in a worked match against Kyle Sturgeon, but showed little improvement in a rematch with Gracie at Pride 4. By this point, Takada was a shell of the athlete who had dominated pro wrestling in the 1990s. He had been wrestling professionally for 17 years and his body simply wouldn't work with him anymore. He seemed perpetually stiff, almost as if he was unable to move, a malady that hurt his performance in the ring.

After the second loss to Gracie, Pride allegedly paid off former UFC champion **Mark Coleman** to take a dive. Coleman needed the money and, after a losing streak had ended his UFC career, was looking for a new fighting home. Even this win did little to rehabilitate Takada's reputation. Yet, despite his limited skills, you can't say the man didn't have courage. He fought the best guys of his generation, from uber-wrestler **Mark Kerr**, to the ground wizard **Royce Gracie**, to the fearsome Russian wrecking ball **Igor Vovchanchyn**.

He lost them all, but it never seemed to faze him. He'd be back again and again, realizing that even though the fights were hopeless, the promotion needed his presence on the card to sell tickets. Finally, at the age of 40, Takada was ready to call it quits.

His last match was with one of his students, the amazing **Kiyoshi Tamura**. Tamura was a professional wrestling savant but, unlike Takada, one who had taken well to real fighting. He knocked Takada out in the second round. With tears in his eyes, he embraced his teacher and with that, Nobuhiko Takada's MMA career had as memorable an end as it did a beginning.

Takahashi, Yoshiki

Real Name: Kazuo Takahashi **Height:** 5'10"

Weight: 205–225 lbs **Born:** 3/13/69

Debut: Pancrase: Yes, We Are Hybrid Wrestlers 1 (9/21/93)

Career Record: 28-24-4

Notable Wins: Wallid Ismail (UFC 12); Minoru Suzuki (Pancrase Anniversary Show 1998)

Notable Losses: Ken Shamrock (Pancrase: Yes, We Are Hybrid Wrestlers 2); Bas Rutten (Pancrase: Road to the Championship 1); Josh Barnett (New Japan Pro Wrestling: Ultimate Crush 2003)

Yoshiki Takahashi was a stranger in a strange land. Among the Japanese wrestlers who formed the **Pancrase** promotion in 1993, Takahashi was the only one who wasn't a slick and technical grappler. Takahashi was a straight up bar brawler, plowing forward until someone fell down. Usually it was him, but fans didn't seem to mind. He quickly became a crowd favorite (and one of **Ken Shamrock**'s preferred training partners) because of his courage and fighting spirit.

Takahashi was able to get almost everyone in the early years of Pancrase to engage with him in his fight — at least for a while, before they usually finished him off. Even the stoic **Masakatsu Funaki**, the Pancrase founder who preferred to do his work on the mat, went toe-to-toe with Takahashi in a memorable slugfest in 1994. Funaki won handily, one of many big name opponents to run over the Japanese punching bag in his 15-year career. Takahashi's list of opponents reads like a who's who of MMA (including Ken Shamrock, **Bas Rutten**, **Guy Mezger**, Semmy Schilt, **Josh Barnett**, **Heath Herring**, and **Igor Vovchanchyn**). They all beat him, but that's okay. The world of sports needs noble and valiant losers too. They help the heroes shine brighter.

Takase, Daiju

Height: 6'0" **Weight:** 183 lbs

Born: 4/20/78 **Debut:** Pride 3 (6/24/98)

Career Record: 7-13-1

Notable Wins: Anderson Silva (Pride 26); Carlos Newton (Pride Bushido 3)

Notable Losses: Jeremy Horn (UFC 21); Nate Marquardt (Pancrase: Trans 4); Hayato Sakurai (Pride Shockwave 2003)

Daiju Takase bears the ignoble distinction of having been awarded the first yellow card for inactivity in the history of **Pride**. In his MMA debut, Takase found himself in the unenviable position of being outweighed by over 400 pounds by his opponent Emmanuel Yarborough, whom early **UFC** fans best remember as the poor soul on the wrong end of **Keith Hackney**'s White Tiger Kenpo fury. Whereas Hackney's approach to Yarborough had been to come right at the big man, Takase's was subtly but importantly different: he ran away. An historic yellow card and minutes that felt like years later, Takase attempted a takedown, and in the ensuing scramble, an overwhelmed Yarborough tapped to strikes.

Revisiting that match years later, it's strange to think that Daiju Takase, running and somersaulting away from an exhausted morbidly obese man, would go on to be one of only two fighters to finish top pound-for-pounder **Anderson Silva**. Silva's flying scissors **heel hook** loss to **Ryo Chonan** is often dismissed as a fluke (despite the fact that Chonan was more than holding his own against "The Spider"), but there's no way around the fact that Takase schooled Silva from the moment their fight hit the ground. Takase came out tentative, but managed an ugly takedown after several poor attempts. Once on the mat, Takase pressured his opponent relentlessly, and threatened submissions consistently for the better part of eight minutes. A reverse **triangle choke** looked dangerous; a **Kimura** looked worse. When Takase finally secured a triangle from the top and rolled on to his back to finish the choke, he seemed as surprised as anyone to have beaten the heavily favored Silva. Never before and never since has Silva looked so out of his league.

And this to the journeyman Takase, who trained with quality fighters throughout his career — **Kazushi Sakuraba, Genki Sudo, Hidehiko Yoshida, Tsuyoshi Kohsaka** — but never had another notable win to speak of, aside from besting a **Carlos Newton** who had long since seen better days. MMA is strange like that, and it's never been stranger than when Daiju Takase, of all people, dominated Anderson Silva.

Takayama, Yoshihiro

Height: 6'5" **Weight:** 253 lbs

Born: 9/19/66 **Debut:** Pride 14 (5/27/01)

Career Record: 0-4

Notable Losses: Kazuyuki Fujita (Pride 14); Semmy Schilt (Pride 18); Don Frye (Pride 21); Bob Sapp (Inoki Bom-Ba-Ye 2002)

Yoshihiro Takayama is awful, but that never stopped him from being awesome — not for a single moment of his gloriously inglorious MMA career.

Takayama got his start in the shoot-style **professional wrestling** outfit Union of Wrestling Forces International (UWFi) alongside such key figures in the development of Japanese mixed martial arts as **Nobuhiko Takada**, **Kazushi Sakuraba**, and **Kiyoshi Tamura**. The UWFi claimed to present legitimate contests, and, at its best, it almost looked that way. But being skilled in convincingly pretending to fight is no substitute for the real thing, as Takayama learned while being pounded and choked into unconsciousness by **Kazuyuki Fujita**, knocked out in the first round by Semmy Schilt, and somehow managing to lose by **arm bar** to **Bob Sapp**. Unlike some of his UWFi peers, he never amounted to much of a legitimate fighter, but Takayama could take a beating. Never was this more apparent than when Takayama faced off with **Don Frye** at **Pride** 21 in the fiercest brawl in the history of the sport. Yoshihiro Takayama was never pretty, but by the end of an ugly MMA career, he was a hell of a lot uglier.

Taktarov, Oleg

Nickname: The Russian Bear | **Height:** 6′
Weight: 215 lbs | **Born:** 8/26/67
Debut: White Dragon (10/22/93) | **Career Record:** 16-5-2
Notable Wins: Tank Abbott (UFC 6); Marco Ruas (Ultimate Ultimate 95); Mark Kerr (Yamma Pit Fighting)
Notable Losses: Dan Severn (UFC 5, Ultimate Ultimate 95); Renzo Gracie (Martial Arts Reality Superfight); Gary Goodridge (Pride 1)

If Oleg Taktarov is ever forgotten — and with only a handful of major wins in his brief career he just may be — one hopes his rolling **knee bar** stands the test of time. We saw it first at Ultimate Ultimate 1995 against greased-up Canadian wrestler **Dave Beneteau**. Taktarov was looking for a **judo** throw but couldn't get a good grasp on the slippery Canadian. Instead, he dropped to the ground, positioning one of Beneteau's legs between his own and executing a nifty forward roll. After that, his body was a fulcrum and his opponent's a lever. It was just pure science. Although the wrestler managed to escape the knee bar, Taktarov segued beautifully to the Achilles lock for the win. It was, at the time, the most advanced grappling technique ever seen in the **UFC** Octagon.

Oleg Taktarov was a blue-eyed assassin, a counter-terrorist instructor from the mountains of Russia. A **sambo** champion, Taktarov thought the UFC would be right up his alley. He traveled across the world, to the Russian section of Los Angeles where his lack of English would be less of a detriment. Near starving, he was given a chance by UFC matchmaker **Art Davie**, in part Davie says because **Rorion Gracie** was so adamant they not use him. Smelling a rat,

Davie thought Taktarov must be pretty good indeed if he was intimidating even the Gracie brothers.

He got a shot at UFC 5 where **Dan Severn** mercilessly beat him, opening a gaping wound on the Russian's head. Trainer Gokor Chivichyan threw in the towel. Taktarov looked good enough to earn a second chance. This time **Ken Shamrock**'s **Lion's Den** adopted him. He and Ken had some legendarily brutal sessions, fighting bare-knuckle right up until a week before UFC 6 where Shamrock had a superfight with Severn.

While the win over Beneteau was an artistic masterpiece, his win in the finals of the eight-man tournament at UFC 6 over **Tank Abbott** was a display of grit and heart for the ages. The show was in Casper, Wyoming, in the thin mountain air. After two fights, both men were already tired. Almost 18 minutes later, they were the walking dead. But Taktarov, the expressionless Russian soldier, had just a little bit more will to win than Abbott, securing a **rear naked choke** in the UFC's most dramatic match ever. Post-fight, Taktarov was administered oxygen, but what he really needed was fluids. He was eventually hospitalized and given an IV. Abbott would brag that he was at the after-party while his opponent was in the hospital. That might have been true, but Taktarov still took home the winner's purse.

Taktarov drew Shamrock in a lackluster superfight and lost a rematch to Severn in the finals of the Ultimate Ultimate. He tried his rolling **leg lock** again, but Severn was strong enough to pull away, eventually winning an unanimous decision. Other high profile knockout losses, to **Renzo Gracie** and **Gary Goodridge**, sent Taktarov looking for a new path.

He found a niche onscreen, playing a Russian villain in a variety of Hollywood movies and television shows. His most critically acclaimed performance was in the Robert De Niro vehicle *15 Minutes*, where Taktarov starred as the lead villain, Oleg Razgul.

In 2007, ten years after his last major fight in **Pride**, Taktarov returned to the ring for BodogFight. That fight was just a warm-up for his "Master's Fight" with another aging superstar, fellow UFC tournament champion **Mark Kerr**. Taktarov dismantled Kerr in the main event of the debut (and final) **Yamma Pit Fighting** card. With his movie career going strong in his native Russia, and his age creeping past 40, Taktarov's MMA career is likely over. One can only hope Taktarov joins the early pioneers he spilled blood with, Severn and Shamrock, in the UFC Hall of Fame.

Tamura, Kiyoshi

Height: 5'11" **Weight:** 185–205 lbs

Born: 12/17/69 **Debut:** K-1 Hercules 95 (12/9/95)

Career Record: 17–11–1

Notable Wins: Patrick Smith (K-1 Hercules 95); Dave Menne (Rings: King of Kings 99 Block B); Renzo Gracie (Rings: King of Kings 99 Finals); Pat Miletich (Rings: Millennium Combine 3); Nobuhiko Takada (Pride 23); Masakatsu Funaki (Dream 2); Kazushi Sakuraba (Dynamite!! 2008)

Notable Losses: Renato Sobral (Rings: King of Kings 99 Finals); Antonio Rodrigo Nogueira (Rings: King of Kings 2000 Block A); Wanderlei Silva (Pride 19); Bob Sapp (Pride 21); Hidehiko Yoshida (Pride: Total Elimination 2003)

Kiyoshi Tamura is, in many people's estimation, the best shoot-style professional wrestler of all time. His bouts with **Volk Han** and **Tsuyoshi Kohsaka** set a new standard of excellence and he walked closer to the line between real and fake than any man before or since.

With his good looks, perhaps amplified by his trademark skin-tight banana hammock red Speedos, Tamura was a favorite of female fans. He was perfect as a supporting player, the man who came on just before the main event. In the UWFi, he set the stage for **Nobuhiko Takada** on top. When the UWFi folded, he moved to **Rings** to fill the same role for **Akira Maeda.**

Unlike many of his contemporaries, Tamura was actually an excellent shooter. He had fast and powerful kicks (**Frank Shamrock** called them the hardest he had ever felt) to go along with solid grappling skills. He was a good fighter, not a great one, but decision makers in Rings weren't able to tell the difference. When the company made the decision to go to all legitimate bouts in 1999 after Maeda's retirement, Tamura was chosen to be the new leading man. He wasn't up to the challenge.

His first legitimate match in Rings was an upset loss to Valentijn Overeem. While Tamura rebounded to win several big fights in his Rings career, including decisions over **Renzo Gracie** and former **UFC** champions **Pat Miletich** and **Dave Menne,** he never recovered from his loss of stature in the eyes of the fans.

In 2001 Tamura jumped to **Pride** for several mega-matchups. He was knocked out by the vicious **Wanderlei Silva** and was a fed to the monstrous **Bob Sapp,** a fighter who outweighed Tamura by almost 200 pounds. Then Pride gave the fans what they really wanted.

In Japan, bouts were often between foreigners (called gaijin) and native Japanese. For the most part, the top Japanese fighters didn't compete with each other. This had been the pattern for many years within Japanese **professional wrestling** and the school of thought had dominated MMA match-making as well. But fans were demanding the answer to a question they had been thinking about for years: who was really the toughest wrestler in the UWF?

To answer that question, Pride convinced Tamura to step into the ring with his mentor Takada in the legend's final match. Fans crowded the Tokyo Dome to see the two wrestlers do battle. The fight was actually left off the American pay-per-view broadcast, but in Japan, it was the match that packed the building. Tamura, to the surprise of no one, knocked Takada out with right hook, then dropped to his knees as the emotion overcame him.

It was a great moment and with it, Tamura had found his role in the company. The major matches in his career from that point forward were with other high profile Japanese. He split a pair of matches with Olympic gold medalist judoka **Hidehiko Yoshida** and Makoto Takimoto. Those fights set the stage for two final dream matches.

He beat fellow UWF alumnus **Masakatsu Funaki** at **Dream** 2, overwhelming him with a series of right hands before finishing with a flurry of **ground and pound**. Then came the fight fans had been demanding for nearly a decade. **Kazushi Sakuraba** had undoubtedly been the best of the former shoot-style wrestlers. In his prime, he was widely considered the best fighter in the world. Hard-core fans badly wanted to see him in the ring against Tamura, generally considered the second-best Japanese fighter of that era — but Tamura resisted.

It was rumored that when Tamura was an established star in the UWFi, he mistreated a young Sakuraba. Such abuse was fairly common practice in the Japanese wrestling industry, but the victims rarely had an opportunity to settle matters in the ring. When the fight finally happened, it was a huge disappointment. Sakuraba was a shell of himself and the promised grudge match fireworks fizzled when Tamura employed a defensive strategy to win a boring decision. Now 40 years old, it may have been the final fight of a long career. Age and injuries wear on any man, and Tamura has been involved in the industry for 20 years. No doubt he will be back, though, waiting for a young Japanese star to dethrone him as the king of the professional wrestlers.

Tanner, Evan

Height: 6′ **Weight:** 185 lbs

Born: 2/11/71 **Debut:** USWF 4 (4/12/97)

Career Record: 32–8

Notable Wins: Paul Buentello (USWF 4); Heath Herring (USWF 7); Ikuhisa Minowa (Pancrase: 1998 Neo-Blood Tournament Round 1); Phil Baroni (UFC 45, UFC 48); David Terrell (UFC 51)

Notable Losses: Heath Herring (PSDA); Tito Ortiz (UFC 30); Rich Franklin (UFC 42, UFC 53); David Loiseau (*Ultimate Fight Night* 2); Yushin Okami (UFC 82); Kendall Grove (*Ultimate Fight Night* 7)

"I always thought of myself as the poet, the writer, or the philosopher — I never thought of myself as a fighter," Evan Tanner once said. "But here I am." Tanner was a traveler by nature, an adventurer, and his mixed martial arts career wasn't the realization of a long-held dream; it was just another experience to add to the collection. A two-time Texas state champion wrestler, Tanner taught himself the basics of **Brazilian Jiu-jitsu** working from old Gracie family instructional tapes, and found success on the local level working with those rudiments. That success followed him all the way to Japan, where he won the **Pancrase** Neo-Blood tournament in 1998. On the strength of that showing, Tanner earned an appearance at **UFC** 18, and over the course of 17 fights in the organization, he would challenge for both the light heavyweight and middleweight titles. He became middleweight champion when he stopped David Terrell in the first round at UFC 51, only to lose it in a grueling contest against **Rich Franklin** in his next fight.

A year later, Tanner was gone from the UFC, not because he was no longer competitive, but because of chaos in his personal life. Tanner's very public problems with alcohol got the best of him throughout 2007, when fans became accustomed to reading revealing and often uncomfortably personal posts on Tanner's blog detailing his struggles and his strange aborted plan to set up his house as a training camp for underprivileged young men from difficult circumstances. But Tanner's own personal circumstances were bad and getting worse, as he lost much of what he had to the bottle. He returned to the UFC in 2008 but was knocked out by a **Yushin Okami** knee, and dropped a close decision to Kendall Grove in what would turn out to be his last fight.

***In Their Own Words:* from Evan Tanner's blog, August 27, 2008**

"It seems some MMA Web sites have reported on the story, posting up that I might die out in the desert, or that it might be my greatest opponent yet, etc. Come on, guys. It's really common down in southern California to go out to the off-road recreation areas in the desert about an hour away from L.A. and San Diego. So my plan is to go out to the desert, do some camping, ride the motorcycle, and shoot some guns. Sounds like a lot of fun to me. A lot of people do it. This isn't a version of *Into the Wild*."

In the summer of 2008, Tanner began writing with great anticipation about a desert camping trip he was planning. The harsh conditions he was setting out to face alone caused no small degree of worry among his readers but Tanner, ever independent, dismissed their concerns and embarked on what would turn out to be his last adventure. Tanner was found dead of heat exposure September 8.

Tapout

It's easy to deride the truly hideous Tapout clothing aesthetic, or make light of the goofy public personas of Charles "Mask" Lewis, Timothy "Skyscrape" Katz, or Dan "Punkass" Caldwell. Recall, if you dare, Lewis's profoundly embarrassing **Chuck Liddell** introduction at **UFC** 43, in which he perplexing referred to the light heavyweight contender as "intolerant." But love it or hate it, the company Lewis and Caldwell founded in 1997 has grown from a couple of guys selling T-shirts out of the trunk of their car to a global brand, complete with a reality television series, a monthly magazine, and annual sales

***In Their Own Words:* Charles "Mask" Lewis's UFC 43 introduction for Chuck Liddell**

"Ladies and gentlemen, good evening. I'm Mask, from the notorious Tapout crew. Is it me, or is it getting cold in here? [giggles] Who's in the house? The Iceman's in the house. I'm talking about Chuck Liddell. A professional killer. An assassin. Aggressive. Intolerant. Unrelenting. Tenacious. Can ya feel me? *Can . . . ya feel . . . me?* You wanna step to the Iceman? You're gonna get knocked out [maniacal laughter]."

in excess of $100 million. Along the way, the Tapout crew stayed unfailingly true to the grassroots of the sport, sponsoring fighters, offering vital financial support, and maintaining their legitimacy with the hard-core MMA fan base while going lucratively mainstream at the same time. Tragedy struck the team in March 2009, however, when Lewis was killed by a driver later charged with gross vehicular manslaughter while intoxicated. Lewis was posthumously inducted into the UFC Hall of Fame later that year.

Team Quest

The legendary fight team from Gresham, Oregon, started with three old wrestling buddies looking for a place to train. **Matt Lindland**, **Dan Henderson**, and **Randy Couture** were all on the same U.S. Greco-Roman wrestling team in 1997, forging a bond that lasts to this day. When the three all ended up in cage fighting, a partnership seemed natural and the Team Quest Fight Club was born in 1999. Joining the three champion wrestlers was coach Robert Follis. Team Quest started in the back of a car dealership Lindland bought after returning from the 1996 Olympic Games. The wrestlers didn't see the ramshackle training grounds as a place for potential profit. Follis thought otherwise and was soon helping run the business, creating a gym with more than 100 members. He also found he had a knack for training fighters. With just a year and a half head start on his pupils, Follis became their jiu-jitsu and grappling coach, as well as a strategist and corner man. Follis believed too many fighters concentrated on what their opponents did well. He focused his fighters instead on how to disrupt an opponent's game plan and make him fight on their turf.

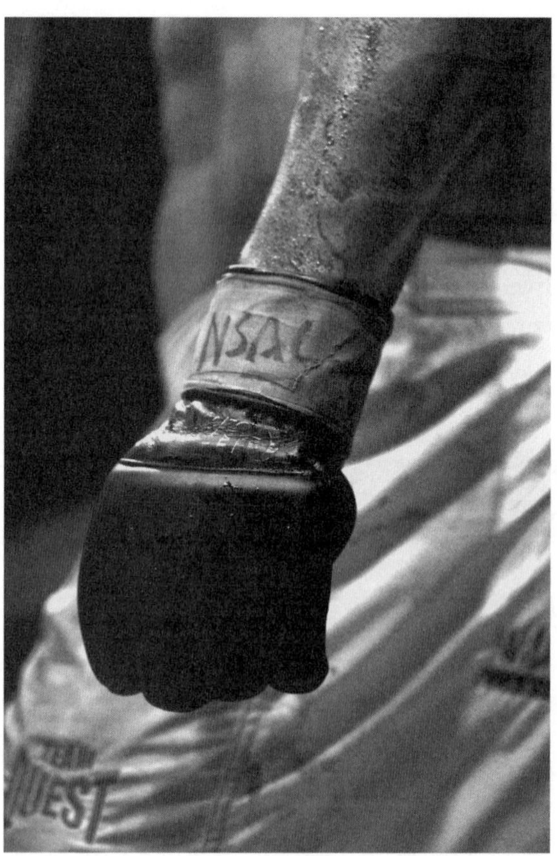

The team's success is unquestionable. Couture and

In Their Own Words: Matt Lindland on Team Quest

"There's a lot of speculation about guys leaving. Dan's always lived in California. That's where he wants to be, where his home is. He lives by his family. Randy moved to Vegas, where the UFC is based. That's his career, you know? That was his focus. It had nothing to do with him leaving the gym. His ex-wife lived here and he wanted to move away. I think there's a lot of speculation around all this stuff. These guys are doing their own thing and living their own lives. It doesn't mean we don't still care about them. I love these guys; we're family. Team Quest doesn't stop because you started your own gym or you moved out of state."

Henderson both reached the top of the sport, in the **UFC** and **Pride** respectively, and Lindland was a major player in the UFC's middleweight division. The ride came to an end, not because of anything inside the cage, but because of turmoil outside it. While filming the first season of ***The Ultimate Fighter***, Couture met Kim Borrego at a party thrown by **John Lewis**. Couture would leave his wife Trish soon after, sparking tension in the camp that was more like a family than a business partnership. When Couture appeared with Kim on television at UFC 51, members of Team Quest were furious over Trish's public embarrassment. Couture ended up leaving the team, moving to Las Vegas where he opened up a new gym, Xtreme Couture, and married Kim in 2006.

Henderson would soon part ways with his buddies in Oregon as well, leaving to open his own branch of Team Quest in 2006 near Temecula, California. While Henderson and his California-based team often train with Lindland and Follis in Oregon, and Couture even returned to the gym in the weeks before his UFC 102 fight in Portland against **Antonio Rodrigo Nogueira**, the team that dominated the sport for much of the early 2000s is functionally no more.

The Ultimate Fighter

The **UFC** was floundering. Despite the best efforts of the **Fertitta brothers** and President **Dana White**, the company had lost more than $40 million in four years. They had tried everything: pyro-rific ring entrances straight out of **professional wrestling**, Carmen Electra as their spokeswoman, the return of washed-up legends like **Ken Shamrock** and **Tank Abbott**. Nothing was capturing America's attention.

For years people in the sport were sure that all the UFC needed to succeed was television. America, they said, would immediately embrace the sport. Lukewarm success on Fox Sports cured UFC executives of that delusion. The television had to reach the right fans, at the right time, with the right platform. They needed the right concept. White wanted to re-do the old *Thursday Night Fights* boxing show he had grown up on as a kid, but putting the live shows on the air was a hard sell. Despite a ten-year history with no deaths on a major sanctioned show, executives feared that someone would die in the cage. They needed something else, but ideas were tough to come by.

Then the Fertittas starred in a little-seen television reality show called *American Casino*. Reality television was taking the entire industry in a new and exciting direction. There were shows set in the kitchen, at the beach, in the professional wrestling business: why not a reality show centered on the world of MMA? The original idea was a spinoff of *American Casino*, called *American Promoter*. Dana White would star and it would take fans into the world of big-time fighting. White was personable and a natural on-camera talent. But then someone had a company altering idea. Why not focus the show on the fighters themselves? White could still have a major role, but in the end, there would be no UFC without the fighters in the Octagon. This was their story: it was called *The Ultimate Fighter*.

The show was a ratings success, brilliantly serving two purposes. First, it was a breeding ground for new talent. Fans could learn to love a new batch of young stars every season, and then follow their careers in the UFC. The undercards, at the very least, would be stocked with recognizable (and cheap) talent for years to come. The show also served to promote the UFC's veteran fighters, who would serve as coaches for the young up-and-comers. Not only would fans get to know them better, but the two coaches would also square off in a pay-per-view main event right after the season ended. The show would create stars, while also functioning as a 12-week commercial for UFC pay-per-view.

It was a brilliant concept, one that was executed to perfection. Pay-per-view business exploded, fans got to know the fighters, and a new generation of stars was created. *Ultimate Fighter* winners like **Forrest Griffin**, **Matt Serra**, and **Rashad Evans** became world champions while others like **Joe Stevenson**, **Michael Bisping**, and **Diego Sanchez** became headliners and legitimate contenders.

After nine star-making seasons, as the show seemed to be losing steam, both critically and in the ratings, **Zuffa** changed the equation. Internet sensation and **EliteXC** headliner **Kimbo Slice** was brought in, setting record ratings early and breathing new life into an old favorite. While Kimbo wasn't the prototypical struggling young fighter (in fact, sources say he was paid $300,000 for his time) he was, despite his headline status, a fighter trying to figure out his place in the sport. Slice was portrayed as a famous fighter in over his head, humble in defeat and happy to learn what it took to make it in the UFC. It was a dramatic change in public persona, peeling away the street thug to show the family man with a heart of gold. Slice was like *The Ultimate Fighter* itself in a way — after years in the spotlight, both were still able to surprise and delight.

Thomas, Din

Nickname: Dinyero **Height:** 5′9″

Weight: 155 lbs **Born:** 9/28/76

Debut: WVF: Jacksonville Vale Tudo 1 (10/28/98)

Career Record: 24-8

Notable Wins: Jens Pulver (WEF: New Blood Conflict); Matt Serra (UFC 41)

Notable Losses: Caol Uno (Shooto: Renaxis 4, UFC 39); B.J. Penn (UFC 32); Kenny Florian (*Ultimate Fight Night* 11)

Din Thomas was a player in the **UFC**'s first, abortive foray into the lightweight division, the one that ended when title-holder **Jens Pulver** left the company over a contract dispute and **B.J. Penn** and **Caol Uno** fought to a draw in the anticlimax of a four-man tournament to crown a new champion. Thomas, who entered the UFC already holding a win over Pulver in a smaller promotion, dropped his UFC debut to B.J. Penn, and fell to Caol Uno before earning a narrow decision win over **Matt Serra**. With his sharp striking and black belt–level **Brazilian Jiu-jitsu**, Thomas was able to hang with some of the best in the world.

This was almost as true four years later, when Thomas got another shot at the big time as a cast member of ***The Ultimate Fighter***. Billed as "The Comeback," the fourth season of the reality series featured fighters who, like Thomas, had already had at least one prior UFC appearance, but had either crashed out or faded away. Unfortunately, the most memorable exchange Thomas was involved in on the show didn't come inside the Octagon; it came in a sushi restaurant, when he was on the receiving end of what was either light-hearted ribbing or racial taunting, depending on your ear. **Matt Hughes**, seeing Thomas whispering conspiratorially to **Georges St. Pierre**, shouted across the room, "It's not like you got really tiny lips! I can see those lips movin' around!" It was uncomfortable to say the least.

Thomas failed to get by Chris Lytle in the tournament semi-final, but managed to stay with the company for five fights after the show ran its course.

Thomas picked up a decision win over **Clay Guida**, but dropped his highest-profile bout against **Kenny Florian** after he blew out his knee in the first round. A loss to Josh Neer spelled the end for his second UFC stint, and it was back to grinding it out on the independent circuit as an **American Top Team** fighter. In a strange 2007 incident, Thomas was arrested on charges of illegally staging fights out of his academies in front of surprisingly large paying crowds. The charges were dismissed only a month later — there's no question everything was on the up-and-up. But a move into fight promotion might not be a bad idea.

Thompson, James

Nickname: The Colossus **Height:** 6′4″

Weight: 257 lbs **Born:** 12/16/78

Debut: Ground & Pound 2 (1/25/03) **Career Record:** 15–13 (1 No Contest)

Notable Wins: Dan Severn (Ultimate Combat 11); Hidehiko Yoshida (Pride Shockwave 2006); Don Frye (Pride 34)

Notable Losses: Kazuyuki Fujita (Pride Total Elimination Absolute); Kimbo Slice (EliteXC: Primetime)

Has there ever been a more sickening sight in mixed martial arts than James Thompson's wobbly, exploding cauliflower ear? As the ear bobbed and weaved its way to the cage in front of a CBS audience of over seven million viewers tuned in to see **Kimbo Slice**, you knew there was going to be trouble. The official outside the cage lingered over the ear as he checked Thompson over, even going so far as to *touch* that thing, but what was he going to do, call off the main event minutes before it was set to begin? No, it was full speed ahead for James Thompson and the bizarre fetus hanging off the side of his head.

The aftershocks of every decent shot Kimbo landed over the course of their three-round debacle could be seen in that ear, which swayed about in transfixing recoil. It was really, really gross. And then it blew up. Early in the third, Kimbo landed a hard right hook to the side of the head, and it popped. Color commentator **Frank Shamrock** fixed in words what we all felt: "That ear popped! That ear popped! It . . . popped!" As blood and *whatever* ran down his neck, a dazed Thompson ate a few more solid shots against the cage before the fight was stopped on a TKO.

It was awful. It was also by far the most interesting moment in the career of James Thompson, an enormous former body builder who was sometimes able to overwhelm smaller opponents with his size and aggression, but who largely got by on his look. He was a gimmick, with a monstrous, inflated physique that made him appear to be a much more credible opponent than he ever actually was. James Thompson, the fighter, was largely forgettable. But that *ear* — that's going to be hard to forget.

TKO Major League MMA

Enter the name of former TKO President and CEO Stéphane Patry into a Google search, and your top result will be a **Sherdog** thread titled "Stéphane Patry is a Weasel." That's got to hurt. As the manager of prominent Canadian mixed martial artists like **Georges St. Pierre** (since departing to join Shari Spencer), **Patrick Côté**, and David Loiseau, Patry has drawn probably more than his fair share of criticism for his handling of business issues and contract disputes surrounding some of his fighters. The fight game is greasy, and whether or not Stéphane Patry is a particularly greasy, greasy weasel is a point that can be argued either way. But what is indisputable is that Patry was instrumental in building Montreal into one of the best MMA markets in North America through TKO Major League MMA. While the "Major League" tag was always more aspirational than actual, especially in the beginning, by the end the promotion's eight-year run TKO had staged eight shows in the cavernous Bell Centre, home of the Canadiens — and in Montreal, that's as major league as it gets. Patry moved on in late 2008, and the promotion was shuttered soon thereafter, but in its heyday it was without question the most important MMA organization in Canada. "I honestly don't think there are too many places we could go and sell 22,000 tickets as fast as we did here," **Dana White** said about Montreal. "Canada is the mecca of mixed martial arts right now and I didn't see that one coming." Maybe Stéphane Patry did.

Toe hold: see **Leg locks**

Tokoro, Hideo

Height: 5'7" **Weight:** 139 lbs
Born: 8/22/77 **Debut:** Titan Fighting Championship 1 (9/29/00)
Career Record: 26-22-1
Notable Wins: Royler Gracie (Dynamite!! 2006); Abel Cullum (Dream 9)
Notable Losses: Caol Uno (Hero's 3); Kiyoshi Tamura (Dynamite!! 2007)

The way he was marketed by K-1, it was always tempting to dismiss Hideo Tokoro as a gimmick. A good-looking Japanese kid who worked as a janitor, lived in a tiny apartment, and bathed in a sink while fighting to make it as mixed martial artist for the tiny **ZST** promotion, there's no doubt Tokoro was a compelling story. K-1 took him out of obscurity and made him a star, and he gave the broad audience that he reached some genuinely compelling moments. Foremost among them: a draw against the legendary **Royce Gracie**, where Gracie was only saved the embarrassment of a loss to a much smaller man by his insistence no judges score the fight. There can be no doubt that Tokoro gives his all every time out, fighting at a breakneck pace and often showing excellent positional work on the ground, but he's also proven to be wildly inconsistent. Never a world-beater, Tokoro has looked particularly bad since the emergence of the **Dream** promotion in early 2008. Tokoro was an unlikely star to begin with, and his time in the public eye looks to be running out.

Torres, Miguel

Height: 5'9" **Weight:** 135 lbs

Born: 1/18/81 **Debut:** Finke's Full Contact Challenge (3/27/00)

Career Record: 37-3

Notable Wins: Chase Beebe (WEC 32); Yoshiro Maeda (WEC 34); Manny Tapia (WEC 37); Takeya Mizugaki (WEC 40)

Notable Loss: Brian Bowles (WEC 42)

Like a handful of other richly deserving fighters — **Urijah Faber**, **Mike Brown**, and **Brian Bowles** among them — Miguel Torres was rescued from virtual anonymity when the **UFC**'s parent company **Zuffa** purchased the **WEC** in late 2006 and brought the excitement of the bantamweight and featherweight divisions to a broader audience. Before he made his WEC debut in 2007, it didn't matter that Torres had fought more than 30 professional fights — and who knows how many unofficial, unsanctioned contests — with only a single decision loss to show for it, or that **Carlson Gracie** thought he was the best fighter in the world at 135 pounds. Torres was never going to receive the respect (or the paydays) a man of his talents deserved fighting exclusively out of small shows close to home in Indiana. The WEC changed that.

The **Brazilian Jiu-jitsu** black belt and dangerous **Muay Thai** striker with the best mullet in the game showed such well-rounded skills in his first five WEC fights that he was universally acclaimed as one of the top ten pound-for-pound fighters in the world. The submission skills he demonstrated against Jeff Bedard and Chase Beebe, the quick hands against Manny Tapia, and the toughness on display in his bouts with Yoshiro Maeda and Takeya Mizugaki proved Torres to be on par names like **Anderson Silva**, **Georges St. Pierre**, and **Fedor Emelianenko** — the kind of company he began to keep. And so it was legitimately shocking

In Their Own Words: Miguel Torres on the early days

"When I first started fighting, it was kind of crazy, man. Back then it was banned in Chicago, so a lot of the fights were here in Indiana. I started fighting at bars. They had clubs that put up a little ring in the middle of the dance floor in the bar and put tables around it. You go to the pre-fight meetings and there wasn't arranged fights. There was a room of like 20 guys, they say, 'How much do you weigh? How much do you weigh?' There were no scales, it was on the honor system, no blood tests. They let us in, and that's how you fought. I fought bikers, Marines, boxers. I fought a barrage of different guys. . . . Those fights taught me how to handle pressure, how to fight in an environment where, you know, I'm not from that place. I was the only . . . well, it was me and my corner man going into a redneck bar, it was like a bunch of bikers. It gave me all my experience."

to see Torres caught rushing in against Brian Bowles at their WEC 42 contest, dropped by a short right hook and pounded out to lose the world title that looked to be his for as long as he wanted to keep it. But given Torres's relative youth, his well-balanced attacked, and his uncommon focus and desire, few think it will be his last run atop the bantamweight division.

Triangle choke

A chokehold, often though not exclusively executed from **guard**, in which the attacker traps the opponent's neck and one of his arms between his legs. The foot of the attacker's strangling leg is locked into position underneath the opposite knee, creating a constricting triangular configuration.

Brazilian Jiu-jitsu great Jean Jacques Machado once strangely claimed that the triangle choke was "invented" in the 1970s by Sergio Dorileo, who "had been studying a Japanese book of positions and invented the Triangle." Romero "Jacare" Cavalcanti clarified this somewhat when he told *Martial Arts Illustrated* that Dorileo, training at Rolls Gracie's academy, "showed everyone what he had learned from some old **judo** book and since then everyone has known the triangle. I mean, all the jiu-jitsu guys." It's remarkable that one of MMA's most successful submission holds entered the diverse Brazilian Jiu-jitsu syllabus so late. But the triangle choke is a relatively modern innovation.

Sankaku jime (sometimes transliterated as sangaku jime) was not a part of the early judo that **Mitsuyo Maeda** brought with him to Brazil in 1914 which formed the basis of the Gracie family's art. Nor was it part of the traditional koryu ("old school") battlefield Japanese jujutsu teachings out of which judo emerged. The reason for this is obvious enough: as judo world champion Katsuhiko Kashiwazaki writes, "In a combat with no rules, it is inadvisable — to say the least — for a man to wrap his legs around an opponent's neck, putting his groin area within biting reach." Sport, however, is another matter entirely, and it was in the era of intercollegiate kosen judo competition that ground fighting legend Tsunetane Oda is credited with developing the versatile technique, which can be applied from the front or side against a turtled (on all fours) opponent, or from the back, in addition to the familiar attack from guard. In the decades since, the triangle has become an integral component of judo ground fighting or ne waza.

For MMA fans, the triangle choke begins with **Royce Gracie** catching **Dan Severn** in the hold at **UFC** 4 after a grueling 15 minutes underneath the powerful wrestler. Finally seeing the kind of opening he'd been waiting for all along, Gracie methodically secured Severn's right arm as he wrapped his legs around Severn's neck and locked his right foot behind his left knee. Severn began to go limp as the choke took hold, while color commentator and Greco-Roman Olympic champion **Jeff Blatnick** assured the viewers at home that there was nothing there. Severn tapped, most of the audience was left wondering what they'd just seen, and Gracie took his last UFC title — thanks in no small part to an old judo book.

Trigg, Frank

Nickname: Twinkle Toes
Height: 5'9"
Weight: 170 lbs
Born: 5/7/72
Debut: USWF 7 (10/18/97)
Career Record: 19-8
Notable Wins: Jean Jacques Machado (Vale Tudo Japan 98); Dennis Hallman (WFA 3, UFC 48); Jason Miller (Icon Sport: Mayhem vs. Trigg); Kazuo Misaki (Pride 33)
Notable Losses: Hayato Sakurai (Shooto: R.E.A.D. Final); Matt Hughes (UFC 45, UFC 52); Georges St. Pierre (UFC 54); Robbie Lawler (Icon Sport: Epic); Josh Koscheck (UFC 103); Matt Serra (UFC 109)

"I did a lot of nude modeling when I first started coming through to kinda make ends meet when I first moved out to L.A., and so there's a lot of nude modeling pictures out there of me. . . . You know, it's not that I'm against nudity; it's just that I think that portion of my career, as far as modeling goes, is over." These are not the words of a Hollywood actress trying to explain away some newly surfaced, slightly embarrassing photos from a time before she caught her big break. No, these, unfortunately, are the words of welterweight contender Frank Trigg. Google him if you dare.

Trigg has often seemed almost desperate to be famous. How else to explain the modeling, the acting, the **professional wrestling**, and a stint on forgotten VH-1 reality series *Kept*, in which Jerry Hall — model, actress, former Mrs. Mick Jagger, and current boner-pill spokeswoman — searched for a kept man? He was eliminated early, finishing tenth out of 12 contestants, in what was perhaps his biggest career loss that did not come by way of **rear naked choke**.

None of this silliness takes away from the considerable talents of Frank Trigg, the fighter. After **wrestling** his way as far as the 2000 Olympic trials, Trigg turned his attention (most of it, anyway) to an MMA career that saw him rise quickly through the welterweight ranks. With only one loss (to **Shooto** champ **Hayato Sakurai**) in his first 11 fights, Trigg challenged the great **Matt Hughes** for his welterweight title at **UFC** 45. Trigg, always a talker, had gotten under Hughes' skin with his pre-fight comments, but it was Hughes that got under Trigg's chin for the dramatic, standing rear naked choke finish to a great fight. Trigg followed his unsuccessful title challenge with two 2004 UFC wins and found himself across the cage from Hughes once again, but that bout ended much like the first: rear naked choke, round one.

Bounced from the UFC following another first round, rear naked choke loss — this time to a then-rising star, **Georges St. Pierre** — Trigg had his ups and downs fighting in Japan and Hawaii, picking up solid wins over **Jason Miller** and **Kazuo Misaki**, and dropping bouts to Carlos Condit and "Ruthless" **Robbie Lawler**. He also took on the impossible job of replacing the irreplaceable **Bas Rutten** as **Pride**'s English language color commentator. But Trigg proved that he's still serious about competition, rather than just calling the action, by signing a four-fight UFC deal in 2009.

TUF: see ***The Ultimate Fighter***

Ultimate Fighting Championship (UFC)

It began with a belch — a unique introduction to a unique combat sports concept, courtesy of the highly caffeinated announcer "Superfoot" Bill Wallace. It was plenty funny, but the comical mood didn't last long. It was obvious right away that the UFC was very serious business.

Gerard Gordeau kicked a tooth out of a sumo wrestler's mouth, **Ken Shamrock** twisted **Patrick Smith**'s foot until the man who claimed he felt no pain screamed out loud. Then Shamrock "tapped the mat three times," submitting to a **Royce Gracie** choke. To those raised on **kung fu** movies and **boxing** — basically every fight fan in America — it was a confusing whirlwind of new techniques and strategies.

Brazilian Jiu-jitsu, proven effective by the skinny and unimposing Gracie, had suddenly relegated most other traditional martial arts to a secondary status. And that, after all, was the entire point of the exercise.

They say success has many fathers, while failure is an orphan. That may be a cynical take, but in the case of the Ultimate Fighting Championship, it certainly took a real team effort to transport an updated version of the old Gracie Challenge from **Rorion Gracie**'s imagination to America's television screens. Gracie had a clear mission in mind: spreading his family's martial art, a **judo** variant they called **Gracie Jiu-jitsu**.

Teaming with ad man **Art Davie**, Gracie struck out all over town. No one was interested in their quasi-legal street fighting. No takers for a battle of the martial arts champions. It looked like just another good idea destined to fail; until Campbell McLaren was intrigued enough to take it to his boss Bob Meyrowitz at **Semaphore Entertainment Group**. Meyrowitz, though he didn't attend the first event, deserves credit for taking a chance on a product no one else was willing to try.

There was no recognition, in the beginning, that they were creating a new sport. McLaren, in fact, wanted nothing to do with sport. This was, to borrow a term from its critics, a freak show. Davie mixed experienced martial

artists in with street brawlers, fat sumo, and a collection of pro wrestlers (and **pro wrestling** wannabes) to create a show that was sure to shock and awe. But as UFC 1 gave way to UFC 10, it became clear that this contest of wills and skills was here to stay. The American public had embraced what announcer **Jeff Blatnick** called MMA: mixed martial arts. Politicians, pundits, and cable programmers had very different opinions — and in the end theirs meant more.

They were under pressure for the enormous quantity of sex and violence on the airwaves. Instead of recognizing this as a pervasive problem, one that was spread across the culture, they were on the lookout for scapegoats. And the best targets available were rap music and what they called "human cockfighting," a sport that claimed in its own advertising to be lawless and potentially lethal.

Led by future U.S. presidential hopeful John McCain, an Arizona Republican who sent letters to the governors of all 50 states encouraging them to ban the sport, the UFC faced a hard battle against regulators everywhere they went, men and women devoted to putting the promotion out of business. It came to a head in New York, where a last-minute push by Mayor Rudy Giuliani sent the UFC scrambling to Dothan, Alabama, just a day before UFC 12. Soon the only home for UFC shows was on a satellite dish. Even though fans had to choose with their wallets to buy pay-per-view shows, cable companies under pressure from McCain — now head of the powerful Senate Commerce Committee — wouldn't allow adults to choose their own method of entertainment.

It was a dark time for the UFC. Great fighters like **Frank Shamrock**, **Bas Rutten**, **Tito Ortiz**, and **Kevin Randleman** were as good as anyone who ever stepped in the Octagon, but almost no one saw them ply their trade. To make matters worse, no end was in sight. As the promotion trudged from town to town, primarily in Alabama, Mississippi, and Louisiana, SEG officials led by David Isaacs, Blatnick, and **Joe Silva** tried desperately to get the show regulated across the country. They spearheaded the sport's legalization in New Jersey, but the state that mattered more than any other, that led the way in the fight game, was Nevada. When the UFC's overtures were rejected there, Meyrowitz made a tough call: it was time, after giving almost seven years and so much heart and energy, to sell.

Dana White, a former small-scale boxing promoter and manager of fighters like **Tito Ortiz** and **Chuck Liddell**, was the frontman for the new organization called **Zuffa**, Italian for "scrap." White's backers were the **Fertitta brothers**, ultra-wealthy casino owners with the connections to get the sport onto the glittery Las Vegas strip.

The show was almost immediately back on pay-per-view and legal in Las Vegas. Success, thought sure to follow, was hard earned. The UFC lost more than $40 million in their first few years, trying to find a formula that worked. Their first show widely available on pay-per-view, UFC 33, was an unmitigated disaster. The fights went to dull decisions and the show went long, cutting off the main event and costing the promotion millions.

A business venture that had started with such promise seemed to have run its course. The Fertittas asked White to find a buyer for their struggling sports franchise. They had an offer for three times what they had paid. They wouldn't get rich, but everyone would see a tidy return on their investment. But the Fertittas refused to give in. Having hundreds of millions of dollars and tremendous confidence in your project made that decision possible. They knew success was in the cards and were just waiting for the ace in the hole.

The Ultimate Fighter reality show was that opportunity they had been waiting for, but one that almost passed them by. White and the Fertittas almost went with a show that would have focused on Dana, called *American Promoter*. Had that happened, the UFC as we know it would likely not exist today. It was *The Ultimate Fighter* that saved the company. Reality TV was the right medium to attract younger fans who weren't ready to jump right into the deep end of pay-per-view. These new fans got to sample the product, got introduced to the sport's nuances, and got to know a new generation of stars.

The company that just one year before had lost tens of millions of dollars was making a mint. Old stars like Ken Shamrock and Royce Gracie were brought back into the fold, lending their names and hard earned credibility to younger fighters like Ortiz and **Matt Hughes** in front of record-setting audiences. And with that, the UFC was off and running.

Ortiz's blood feud with "The Iceman" Chuck Liddell drew more than a million pay-per-view buys, and with his knockout win Liddell became the UFC's first breakout star. He made the television talk-show rounds, made the cover of *ESPN: The Magazine*, and appeared on the HBO show *Entourage*. And, oh yeah, he also won seven fights in a row, all by devastating knockout.

Just as business seemed to be settling into a comfortable (and very profitable) rut, there was another massive influx of fans. This time they were from the world of pro wrestling, following the massive muscle-bound **Brock Lesnar** into the sport of MMA. Lesnar was a physical specimen, 280 pounds of muscle and a former NCAA champion wrestler. From his WWE days he knew instinctively how to sell a fight, but he also had a fierce competitive streak that drove him to excel. After losing his first fight in the UFC, falling victim to a **Frank Mir knee bar** despite running over Mir like a freight train for the first minute, Lesnar won three in a row. He took the UFC title from **Randy Couture**

In Their Own Words: Dana White on the UFC's success

"Since the first season of *The Ultimate Fighter*, this thing has continued to grow. Part of the reason the UFC is doing so great is a lot of the athletes we have. These guys always deliver. It's very rare to see a bad UFC fight. You don't come to one of our events and have everything suck. That just doesn't happen. These guys come to fight and the athletes deliver time and time again. People ask me all the time about how much this thing has grown since 2001. It's great, believe me, and it's been a fun ride. I couldn't wait for us to be on the cover of *Sports Illustrated* and we got that. We got our TV show. We got sanctioned in all these states, had our first fight overseas. There have been so many milestones and so many great things that have happened since the beginning of the business. And there are a lot more to come. We haven't even scratched the surface on how big this business is going to be. We're just getting started as far as I'm concerned."

at UFC 91 and avenged his loss to Mir at UFC 100, setting the UFC record with 1.6 million pay-per-view buys in the process.

The UFC had conquered the American market. They surpassed both pro wrestling and boxing as the leading combat sport in the niche pay-per-view market. White and the Fertittas weren't satisfied with that — they were the kind of men who would never be satisfied, always wanting more. They had their eye on international expansion and a groundbreaking network television deal. And with their track record there can be little doubt that wherever the UFC leads, success will follow.

Ultimate Ultimate

The **UFC**'s version of the "All Star" game was held in Colorado on December 16, 1995. The event, known as UU95 to fight nerds and tape collectors, was missing the UFC's two biggest stars. **SEG** offered **Royce Gracie** a multi-fight contract and a new car, but his brother **Rorion** wanted no part of it. They wanted Royce to be able to negotiate a new deal after every event. Many thought the influx of bigger and better fighters into the promotion had as much to do with Royce's decision as money. Gracie proved doubters wrong by returning in a tournament featuring the world's best fighters years later in **Pride. Ken Shamrock** was also unavailable — he had a fight two days earlier in Japan for **Pancrase** and was wary of fighting such tough competition so quickly after what could potentially be a grueling bout. Their absence left the door open for **Dan Severn**, who dispatched all competition thanks in part to the introduction of the judge's decision. Severn decisioned **David Abbott** and **Oleg Taktarov** on his way to winning $150,000 in prize money.

The UFC's second "All Star" tournament — December 7, 1996 in Birmingham, Alabama — was once again missing the sport's best fighter. **Mark Coleman**, the man who dominated the previous two UFC tournaments (UFC 10 and UFC 11) was too ill to compete. With no Coleman, the tournament was built to showcase a single fight: Ken Shamrock versus David "Tank" Abbott. The two had been itching to fight for some time and the two entourages had gotten into scraps on more than one occasion. The fight seemed set after Shamrock beat **Brian Johnston**, but with Shamrock there was always a catastrophe lurking around the corner. He broke his hand on Johnston's head and couldn't face Abbott in the semi-finals. It would be his last fight in the Octagon for six years. Instead, it was up to **Don Frye** to derail the Tank. Allegedly he had some help. Frye was set to face Mark Hall in the semi-finals and attorney Robert DePersia managed both men. Frye beat Hall in seconds, in a fight many considered fishy, winning with a **leg lock** he had never used before and has never used since. Frye, who had been ill prior to the show, was going in against Abbott feeling fresh. Abbott pounded Frye, bloodying the smaller man and looked on his way to the tournament championship. Losing a standup exchange, Frye somehow managed to floor Abbott by stepping on his foot. That was all it took. He was able to secure a **rear naked choke** and an exhausted Abbott tapped immediately. It was one of the most exciting back-and-forth fights of all time. It was also Frye's swan song in the UFC. Like Shamrock, he turned to the more lucrative **professional wrestling** industry, leaving fighting for New Japan Pro Wrestling.

Underground, The

For the most part, it's a locker room. At its worst, it's a sewer. But at its best, Kirik Jenness' Underground Forum (at www.MixedMartialArts.com) takes the pulse of the sport, offers posters a chance to interact with a considerable number of pro fighters, and produces truly weird stuff that you will simply never find anywhere else. A multi-page thread devoted to **Brock Lesnar**'s theoretical Dungeons & Dragons stats? First-person reports of **Shonie Carter**'s latest intercontinental mishaps, complete with pleas for help? **Sean Gannon** and **Kimbo Slice**'s people laying the groundwork for the infamous dojo brawl that helped both men fight their way to the big time? **Tito Ortiz** defending the honor of his porn star significant other? **Jason Miller** describing *with precision* the kinds of sexual acts "Brazillian nuthuggers" might want to consider? **Eddie Bravo** and **Joe Rogan** spreading the internet conspiracy theory du jour, and living out their epic bromance for all to see? There's only one place to find it. At the time of this writing, the top thread at the Underground reads, "BAM! Brock Lesnar smacks your GF. What do you do?" The Underground, ladies and gentlemen. ***TUF*** noobs beware.

Unified Rules of Mixed Martial Arts

The **UFC** began in Colorado in 1993, billed as fights with no rules. That was never the case — although in the early UFC shows the rules were more like suggestions. At UFC 1, there were prohibitions only against biting and eye gouging. Rule violations would result in the offender being fined $1,000; they would not affect the outcome of the fights. **Semaphore Entertainment Group**'s Campbell McLaren, the man who first made the call to give the UFC a chance on pay-per-view, thought that the sport was best promoted as a brutal spectacle.

Eventually, promoters realized some rules were necessary for the sport to survive the fierce political battle waged by Arizona senator John McCain.

SEG officials were also, rightfully, concerned about fighter well-being and safety. Color commentator **Jeff Blatnick** was put in charge of creating formal rules for the UFC, and to that end he created the Mixed Martial Arts Council to bring together the sport's most ardent supporters.

For Blatnick, necessity was the mother of invention. As fighters found new and increasingly creative ways to take advantage of the rules, Blatnick and the council would respond with new and better rules. Changes came slowly. Time limits were enforced for all fights at UFC 7, judges could render a decision when a fight went to a draw at **Ultimate Ultimate** 1995, weight classes were established at UFC 12, and gloves (first used in Japan's **Shooto** promotion) became mandatory for all fighters at UFC 14.

When the UFC began looking for official sanctioning from state athletic commissions in 1999, they were prepared. Over the years, their own rulebook had become a substantial document. It was adapted, almost word for word, in both California and New Jersey in 2000 as the sport began its phoenix-like return from obscurity. While the California State Athletic Commission approved a set of rules that became the foundation for all rules to follow, they couldn't get approval to run fight shows in the state until 2005. New Jersey would take the lead.

In Their Own Words: Jeff Blatnick on the MMAC manual, which became the Unified Rules

"The UFC created a manual. We covered everything from conflicts of interest for the judges and referees to the basics of how to regulate the sport. The job was given to me, but I had a lot of help from **John McCarthy**, **Joe Silva**, and many of the fighters themselves. I wanted to get a handle on what people thought the right way to do things was. What is the right length of a round? How could we balance the rules to be fair to both grapplers and strikers? It all came together cleanly and we formed the Mixed Martial Arts Council. From there we had to change things as fighters pushed the envelope. When **Tank Abbott** tried to throw Cal Worsham over the fence. When a Japanese fighter grabbed his opponent's glove and almost turned it inside out. When **Mikey Burnett** grabbed **Pat Miletich**'s shorts for almost an entire 15 minutes. Anything that popped up, we had to address. Things you never thought of, like **Phil Baroni** licking **Matt Lindland**'s face. Finger in an orifice. As fighters pushed the envelope, we had to respond."

Interestingly, it was not the UFC that promoted the first officially sanctioned event in New Jersey, where New Jersey State Athletic Control Board Executive Director Larry Hazzard was at the forefront of the movement to bring MMA into the mainstream. Paul Smith, who had once worked with **Ken Shamrock** in an ill-fated attempt at running his own shows in California, joined the International Fighting Championship promotion to spearhead the legalization of MMA in both California and New Jersey. The IFC held the first sanctioned event in September 2000, headlined by **Vernon "Tiger" White**. The UFC followed in November with UFC 28.

The events were almost like a tryout for the new sport. Hazard liked what he saw, and in April 2001, he got serious. A number of promoters, including the new UFC owners **Zuffa**, met with Hazard at his Trenton, New Jersey, offices. **Marc Ratner**, then executive director of the prestigious Nevada State Athletic Commission, joined them via conference call. They established what are now called the Unified Rules of Mixed Martial Arts. The rules were nearly identical to Blatnick's MMAC manual, with several important differences. The iconic **gi**, made famous in MMA by **Royce Gracie**, was no longer allowed. Wrestling shoes were also banned, not for any safety reasons, but because of a bizarre concern about hygiene. Fighters would be barefoot to prevent debris from outside being brought into the cage by their shoes. No one could explain why fighters' shoes would be any dirtier than the ring announcer's or the referee's, who would still be allowed to wear their shoes.

The other major change was to weight classes. The Unified Rules established the same weight classes used in MMA today, from flyweights (under 125 pounds) to super heavyweights (above 265 pounds). Today, the Unified Rules are re-examined yearly by the Association of Boxing Commissions. The MMA committee is headed by New Jersey's Nick Lembo and includes Nevada's Keith Kizer and other important regulators from across the nation.

Uno, Caol

Nickname: Uno Shoten

Height: 5'7"

Weight: 154 lbs

Born: 5/8/72

Debut: Shooto: Let's Get Lost (10/4/96)

Career Record: 27-13-5

Notable Wins: Rumina Sato (Shooto: 10th Anniversary Event); Din Thomas (Shooto: Renaxis 4, UFC 39); Yves Edwards (UFC 37); Hideo Tokoro (Hero's 3)

Notable Losses: Hayato Sakurai (Shooto: Let's Get Lost); Jens Pulver (UFC 30); B.J. Penn (UFC 34); Joachim Hansen (Hero's 1); Kid Yamamoto (Hero's 3); Gesias Cavalcante (Hero's 7); Shinya Aoki (Dream 5); Spencer Fisher (UFC 99)

Outside the ring, Caol Uno doesn't necessarily look like a fighter. Once inside, though, something changes. He flips a switch, and all of a sudden the man who only moments before looked like an uncommonly fashionable Keebler elf is suddenly transformed into a highly skilled, first-rate submission wrestler and dynamic mixed martial artist — who still kind of looks like a Keebler elf.

Uno's solid win–loss record becomes all the more impressive when you consider the level of competition he's faced throughout his long career. When the best lightweight fighters were in **Shooto**, so was he, making his debut in 1996 alongside another future Japanese great, **Hayato Sakurai**. Three years later, Uno had fought his way to the top of the card, and took the Shooto welterweight (154 pounds) title in a classic bout against **Rumina Sato** that remains one of the sport's all-time best. Soon thereafter he was part of the **UFC**'s first foray into the lightweight division, going the distance against the likes of **Jens Pulver** and **B.J. Penn**. When K-1 helped raise the profile of lightweights with its **Hero's** series, there he was, putting on arguably the best match of 2004 against **Joachim Hansen** in the promotion's very first show. After the landscape of Japanese MMA changed, **Dream** hosted many of the best lightweight matches in the world in its 2008 Grand Prix, and Uno fought his way to the semi-finals, ultimately coming up short against top-star **Shinya Aoki**. With that behind him, it was back to the UFC in what was seen as the time as a surprise move. But we should have expected it. Caol Uno constantly seeks out new challenges, new opportunities to test himself against the best in the world, wherever they may be.

Between bouts, Uno somehow finds time to juggle four fashion labels, an activity which he sees as complementary to the world of martial arts. "Since I started competing Shooto in high school," Uno told fashion Web site Freshness in 2009, "fashion was always an integral part of the sport. My role model, Shooto veteran Rumina Sato, was not only skillful and strong, but fashionable too." On both fronts, you can definitely make the case that the student has surpassed the master.

Vale Tudo

The original Brazilian Vale Tudo (Portuguese for "anything goes") was born in the traveling carnival. A part of the show, together with the bearded lady and other sideshow attractions, was the **boxing** booth. The booth was a large tent inside which the fighters who were part of the show would accept challengers from the crowd. Often these challengers were ringers — part of the act masquerading as an audience member to make the show more interesting. These shows didn't always feature boxers: many great **catch wrestlers** made their living on the carnival circuit as well, easily beating local toughs.

It wasn't until the late 1950s that a new meaning took shape for the words Vale Tudo. Years after the original Gracie brothers' challenge matches pitted discipline versus discipline, Brazilian Vale Tudo came to television in Rio de Janeiro. The show was called the *Heróis do Ringue*, and featured many of the Gracies' top students and even the occasional family member. Like in the original **UFC** events, jiu-jitsu often proved superior to all other arts; also like the early UFCs, the Gracie family was controlling the matchmaking. But, as fights tend to do, things spun out of control. Joao Alberto Barreto, later known as the incompetent referee at UFC 1, broke an opponent's arm with an arm lock when he refused to tap out. That brutal display spelled the end for *Heróis do Ringue* and for Vale Tudo as a major spectator sport in Brazil. It was replaced on television by **professional wrestling.**

It wasn't until MMA exploded in popularity worldwide that the kind of fights that influenced **Rorion Gracie** the most made their triumphant return to Brazil. Like the early UFC shows, Vale Tudo fights barely resemble modern MMA fights. Rules were very limited when Vale Tudo reappeared on the scene in São Paulo, Brazil, in the form of the World Vale Tudo Championship and the **International Vale Tudo Championship**. Head butts, elbows, stomps to the head, knees to a downed opponent: they were not just legal, but encouraged. The fights were bloody spectacles, often wars of attrition fought bare-knuckle until the last man was standing.

Like they had in the 1960s, the fights proved too controversial to last for long. São Paulo banned Vale Tudo events and the sport of MMA was forced underground in its spiritual homeland of Brazil. There is hope on the horizon. The UFC is airing shows in the country and hopes to promote events in Brazil. The Brazilian economy is booming and the kinds of middle-class consumers who can purchase UFC events are being rapidly created by increased energy independence.

It's the circle — or perhaps the Octagon — of life. The UFC sprang from old-school Brazilian Vale Tudo. Perhaps a Brazilian MMA renaissance will come from the UFC's promotional efforts in MMA's homeland?

Varelans, Paul

Nickname: The Polar Bear
Height: 6'8"
Weight: 300 lbs
Born: 1969
Debut: UFC 6 (7/14/95)
Career Record: 9-9
Notable Losses: Tank Abbott (UFC 6); Marco Ruas (UFC 7); Dan Severn (Ultimate Ultimate 95); Igor Vovchanchyn (IFC 1); Kimo Leopoldo (Ultimate Ultimate 96); Mark Kerr (World Vale Tudo Championship 3)

As far as we know, Paul Varelans is the only professional mixed martial artist to represent the art of trap fighting — whatever that is. Varelans fought 18 pro bouts over the course of his career, so we had plenty of opportunities to figure it out, but it was never clear what exactly was supposed to be trapped. As best as anybody could tell, trap fighting involved being absolutely enormous, and getting pasted by any and every name fighter you come up against. Varelans' size and his ability to take a beating were his calling cards, and while that didn't exactly translate into MMA success, it did earn him a relatively high-profile shoot-style **professional wrestling** bout against Peter "Taz" Senerchia, who worked a pseudo–MMA gimmick. According to the incredibly lurid autobiography of wrestling personality Missy Hyatt, Varelans was induced to lose the bout when Hyatt promised him a blow job. Afterward, in an impressive bit of wordplay, she then informed him that she didn't blow *jobbers*, the losers of pro wrestling matches. Varelans then apparently went berserk and trap fought the backstage area into complete disarray.

Vazquez, Javier

Nickname: Showtime
Height: 5'7"
Weight: 145–155 lbs
Born: 7/16/77

Debut: Neutral Grounds 5 (6/28/98) **Career Record:** 14-4

Notable Wins: Rumina Sato (Shooto: Treasure Hunt 7); Jens Pulver (WEC 47)

Notable Loss: Alberto Crane (KOTC 21)

Sometimes a fighter proves more in a loss than he ever could in a winning performance. That was never truer than during Javier Vazquez's dropped decision to Alberto Crane at **King of the Cage** 21. In the first 15 seconds, Vazquez's knee was ripped to shreds. It was a fluke injury, one of those strange things that happen occasionally in competitive sports. Vazquez's body was conditioned for war, his limbs ready to be twisted, punched, and kicked. Instead, his knee fell apart just by taking a hard step forward.

That's not the amazing part. The next 15 minutes were the miracle. Vazquez fought valiantly on a torn anterior cruciate ligament. His ACL was ripped, his knee virtually useless. Almost anyone else would have quit. Vazquez is a different kind of warrior. He decided to come forward and take the fight to Crane. Vazquez didn't just look to survive: he was actively pursuing submissions and even kneed Crane with his injured leg!

One of the top prospects in the world, Vazquez seemed to be on the path to recovery. He was training for his **UFC** debut against **Matt Serra** at UFC 46 when his ACL again betrayed him. He retired from the sport, but competitive grappling wasn't enough to quench his desire for combat.

In 2007, Vazquez returned to MMA. He looked ready to pick up right where he left off, winning his first three fights and finally having an opportunity to compete at his natural weight class of 145 pounds. "Showtime" is again poised on the brink of big things.

In Their Own Words: Javier Vazquez on his retirement

"When I stopped, when I retired, I had just had my second daughter. She was a newborn and I also had her sister who was a year and a half old at the time. It was overwhelming and I had no time. But when I stopped fighting I missed it. I said, 'I am going to stop fighting, but I don't have to stop training.' But the more I trained, the more I wanted to fight again. Physically, this is the healthiest I've been in years. I'm ready to fight anybody. I think I can hang with the best guys in the world. All my fights have been at 155 pounds, and I'm finally getting a chance to fight in my weight class. Look out."

In Their Own Words: Ryan Bader on Cain's "Brown Pride"

"He's a great guy. You look at him and he's a big Mexican dude with 'Brown Pride' tattooed across his chest; he looks like he's a gangster. But he's a great guy. He's a family man now, just had a baby a little while ago. He's also one of the hardest working guys I've ever seen. Once he gets his mind set on something, he goes after it. He was at his first MMA fight just a week after [NCAA] Nationals. He's just one of those intense guys that says, 'When it's time to work, it's time to work.' But when you're just hanging out with him he's just a sweet guy."

Velasquez, Cain

Height: 6'1" **Weight:** 240 lbs

Born: 7/28/82 **Debut:** Strikeforce: Tank vs. Buentello (10/7/06)

Career Record: 8-0

Notable Wins: Cheick Kongo (UFC 99); Ben Rothwell (UFC 104); Antonio Rodrigo Nogueira (UFC 110)

Before he had ever stepped in the **UFC** Octagon, Cain Velasquez was already a legend in the insular MMA community. The kid was the ultimate gym warrior. Training at the American Kickboxing Academy, a camp filled to the brim with some of the best fighters in the world like **Josh Koscheck** and **Jon Fitch**, the two-time collegiate All-American still stood out. Manager Bob Cook couldn't find anyone willing to fight his young heavyweight. In his first two years, champing at the bit, Velasquez only had two fights, both first-round TKOs.

Cook and the team at AKA had wanted to develop the potential champion slowly, but not this slowly. They had wanted to wait on the UFC until Velasquez was ready to contend for a title, but instead had to sign him up to learn on the job; it was the only way to find him a fight.

UFC fans immediately understood what the buzz was all about. Velasquez showed a combination of slick striking and devastating **ground and pound** en route to convincing wins against an ever increasing caliber of opposition. First it was workmanlike fighters like Brad Morris, Jake O'Brien, and Denis Stojnic. Then it was fringe contenders like Cheick Kongo and Ben Rothwell. By the time Velasquez got his hands on the great **Antonio Rodrigo Nogueira**, knocking him out cleanly in the first round, a consensus began to form: if anyone has the tools to knock **Brock Lesnar** off his perch atop the UFC heavyweight division, it's got to be Cain Velasquez.

Vera, Brandon

Nickname: The Truth **Height:** 6'3"

Weight: 205 lbs **Born:** 10/10/77

Debut: Excalibur Extreme Fight Challenge 11 (7/6/02)

Career Record: 11-5

Notable Wins: Frank Mir (UFC 65); Krzysztof Soszynski (UFC 102)

Notable Losses: Tim Sylvia (UFC 77); Fabricio Werdum (UFC 85); Keith Jardine (UFC 89); Randy Couture (UFC 105); Jon Jones (UFC Live: Vera vs. Jones)

It wasn't that long ago that Brandon Vera talked about becoming the first man to simultaneously hold the **UFC** heavyweight and light heavyweight titles. But after missing almost a year in the prime of his career due to a contract dispute, and dropping three of his first four fights upon his return to the UFC, Vera's prospects looked awfully different than they did when he rocketed up the heavyweight rankings with four straight finishes over tough competition — including former heavyweight champ **Frank Mir**.

A skilled striker and dangerous submission fighter, Vera wrestled at Old Dominion University and in the Air Force before being medically discharged after a serious elbow injury. His balanced, well-rounded game and his knack for the big finish, whether by knockout or submission, made him one of the hottest prospects in the sport — and he knew it. With only one fight left on his contract, Vera put himself in line for a heavyweight title shot with his first-round stoppage over Mir. But, understandably, the UFC has a policy of not offering title shots to fighters who have not committed to the company long-term. Vera didn't help his chances any by meeting with **EliteXC**'s Gary Shaw, reportedly fielding offers from **Pride**, and publicly stating that the next contract he signed would be with "whoever wants to take care of [him] the best."

And so he sat. Until, soon after the MMA landscape changed with the UFC's acquisition of Pride, Vera fired his management and signed an extension that would see him back in action and keep him in the UFC. The time away from the cage didn't do him any favors, though, as the previously dynamic fighter was stalled out in an awful bout against former heavyweight champ **Tim Sylvia**, losing by unanimous decision. Vera dropped his next fight to **Fabricio Werdum**, although he was adamant that while he had been mounted and Werdum's shots were landing, the fight was stopped early. That may well be, but the Werdum fight was enough to convince Vera to finally make the much-discussed move down to 205 pounds. After a win over journeyman Reese Andy, Vera took a tough loss by split decision to **Keith Jardine**, whose awkward style kept Vera guessing much of the match. Subsequent wins over Mike Patt and

Krzysztof Soszynski put Vera back on track, but after a narrow loss to the legendary but ancient **Randy Couture** and a devastating defeat at the hands of rising star **Jon Jones**, it seems increasingly unlikely that "The Truth" will ever attain the level of success many observers once thought possible — and certainly that Vera predicted for himself.

Vitale, Falaniko

Nickname: Niko **Height:** 5'10"
Weight: 185 lbs **Born:** 1975
Debut: Rumble in the Cage 2 (10/15/99) **Career Record:** 26-9
Notable Wins: Matt Lindland (UFC 43); Dave Menne (SuperBrawl 33); Yushin Okami (SuperBrawl 36); Masanori Suda (SuperBrawl 39)
Notable Losses: Matt Lindland (UFC 45); Robbie Lawler (SuperBrawl: Icon, Icon Sport: Lawler vs. Niko 2); Jason Miller (Icon Sport: Opposites Attract); Jeremy Horn (IFL: Oakland); Frank Trigg (Strikeforce: Payback)

Falaniko Vitale is probably best known for a fluke win over Olympic silver medalist **Matt Lindland** at **UFC** 43. Lindland was looking to throw Vitale and accidentally dropped himself on his own head. It was a knockout win for "Niko," but not one he could be super-proud of. Lindland settled the score five months later, but it took him three rounds to do it. Vitale may have won the first fight in a comical fashion, but he was no joke.

A mixture of four nationalities (Samoan, Chinese, German, and Portuguese), Vitale is a tough former football player who learned the fight game from Hawaiian journeyman Ronald Jhun. Vitale came up before the fight game exploded into prominence with ***The Ultimate Fighter*** and was never able to make fighting his vocation. Despite a backbreaking job working construction and demolition, he trained hours every day and fought frequently. His crowning achievement was beating **Shooto** champion Masanori Suda in 2005, avenging his teacher Jhun's loss and reestablishing himself as an international level fighter.

Since then, Vitale has fought some of the world's best, including **Robbie Lawler** twice, always coming up short in his biggest fights. One thing is for certain: Vitale never leaves anything in the ring. That's what makes him one of Hawaii's most popular fighters. He may not beat the best, but they'll know they've been in a fight.

Vovchanchyn, Igor

Nickname: Ice Cold **Height:** 5'8"

Weight: 229 lbs **Born:** 8/6/73

Debut: International Absolute Fighting Championship 1 (9/25/95)

Career Record: 47-9-1 (1 No Contest)

Notable Wins: Kazushi Sakuraba (Pride Grand Prix 2000 Finals); Enson Inoue (Pride 10); Mark Kerr (Pride 12)

Notable Losses: Mark Coleman (Pride Grand Prix 2000 Finals); Heath Herring (Pride 19); Mirko Cro Cop (Pride Total Elimination 2003)

A short, stocky power puncher with an absolutely devastating overhand right, Igor Vovchanchyn was, for a time, the most dangerous heavyweight in the sport. Before making his **Pride** debut against **Gary Goodridge**, Vovchanchyn amassed a staggering 23–1–1 record fighting in Russia, Brazil, Israel, and his native Ukraine, ending all but one of his winning efforts with strikes (his only loss in this period came by one of the strangest submissions recorded in MMA: a chin to the eye).

Once in Pride, Vovchanchyn continued his feverish pace, running through Goodridge, **Akira Shoji**, and Carlos Bareto before finishing a prime **Mark Kerr** with knees to the head on the ground — a tactic that had been legal previously, and would be again, but had been specifically forbidden for Pride 7. The match was rightly ruled a no contest, but it was clear from Vovchanchyn's domination of the highly touted wrestler and **UFC** tournament champion that Igor was the man to beat heading into the Pride 2000 Grand Prix. Wins over Alexander Otsuka, Goodridge once more, and a valiant but exhausted **Kazushi Sakuraba** put Vovchanchyn in the tournament finals, but a legitimately shocking upset loss to **Mark Coleman** cost him the title.

Following the loss to Coleman, Vovchanchyn never truly regained his form. Over the later years of his career, Vovchanchyn managed a respectable 14–7 record and sensibly began to compete in Pride's middleweight (205 pounds) division rather than take on all comers as a heavyweight. But ultimately injury — especially an inability to properly open and close that once awesome right hand — took its toll and forced his retirement in 2005.

War Machine

Real name: Jon Koppenhaver
Height: 5'11"
Weight: 170 lbs
Born: 11/30/81
Debut: Total Combat 2 (2/29/04)
Career Record: 11-4
Notable Win: Jared Rollins (*The Ultimate Fighter* 6 Finale)
Notable Loss: Yoshiyuki Yoshida (UFC 84)

Oh, War Machine. Will you ever learn?

Jon Koppenhaver's first contribution to modern culture came late in the sixth season of ***The Ultimate Fighter*** (*TUF*), when he helped introduce the audience to the fecal prank euphemistically known as "The Upper Decker." But this was only the beginning for the man who would legally change his name to War Machine after a copyright dispute with a **professional wrestling** company threatened to rob him of his cherished nickname. War Machine, you see, was no ordinary *TUF* mook. No, War Machine turned out to be the greatest *TUF* mook of them all.

Only two fights into a not particularly promising **UFC** career — an *Ultimate Fighter* finale win over Jared Rollins was followed by a first-minute loss to **Yoshiyuki Yoshida** — Koppenhaver somehow got the notion that he was in a position to pick his opponents. A dispute with matchmaker **Joe Silva** spelled the end for War Machine's UFC tenure. Well, that, and the MySpace post in which War Machine argued that **Evan Tanner**'s then-recent, tragic death was in fact a suicide directly stemming from the UFC's neglect of its former fighters. That didn't help.

Astoundingly, War Machine managed to outdo himself. In what has to be a first, the fighter (and wordsmith) was cut from the **Bellator** promotion before they ran a single show, after War Machine unleashed a subhuman, homophobic tirade against the newly inaugurated President Obama, going so far as to advocate not only *his* assassination, but the assassination of all future presidents. He later issued an apology, but the damage was done as far ESPN's nascent promotion was concerned.

> ***In Their Own Words:* War Machine's MySpace post on Obama**
>
> Jan 20, 2009 10:32 PM
> Subject: Fuck an Obama
>
> I could care less about the mother fucker . . . everywhere I turn I have to see his face or hear his fuckin' name . . . wtf? And the liberals and the blacks are so happy because of "change"?? Ain't shit gonna change. All he is a rich white guy with a dark tan . . . lol Shittt. Fuck any president that was RICH before he came into office. How is some rich faggot gonna represent "the people" when he can't understand what it's like to struggle? I hope someone smokes that fucker and every president to come until they can actually give us a candidate that is truly one of THE PEOPLE.
>
> WM

This is to say nothing of War Machine's legal troubles, the assault charges, the dustups at gay bars, the aborted foray into the world of pornography. No single thing defines him. War Machine is vast; he contains multitudes. But we get a glimpse of the mind inside the Machine in his MySpace entry on who he'd like to meet. In addition to bisexual women, War Machine would "like to meet the person who invented 'civilization' and then kill all of his descendants." That comes close to saying it all.

Waterman, Ron

Nickname: H_2O
Height: 6'2"
Weight: 280 lbs
Born: 11/23/68
Debut: Bas Rutten Invitational 1 (2/6/99)
Career Record: 16-6-2
Notable Wins: Valentijn Overeem (Pride 24); Kevin Randleman (Pride Final Conflict 2004); Ricco Rodriguez (WEC 16)
Notable Losses: Mirko Cro Cop (Pride 27); Tsuyoshi Kohsaka (Pancrase: Brave 10); Ricco Rodriguez (WFA: King of the Streets)

"I absolutely see myself as a warrior for God," Ron Waterman will tell you with the utmost sincerity. As part of the evangelical Team Impact ministry, which spreads the word through feats of strength and athleticism, the enormous Waterman will gladly tear a phone book in half or roll up a frying pan in His name. Waterman has that showman mentality that comes with being a

professional wrestler as well as an MMA fighter. He also has the cartoonish, body builder physique, but Waterman is hardly all show, no go. He possesses at least *some* go, as he demonstrated with submission wins over Valentijn Overeem and **Kevin Randleman** in **Pride**, and a decision win over **Ricco Rodriguez** (fat version). He holds the distinction of being the physically strongest man **Mirko Cro Cop** has ever faced, by Cro Cop's own admission — but he also holds the more dubious distinction of being on the wrong end of one of Cro Cop's most grisly soccer kick TKOs. It's a mixed bag, being Ron Waterman.

WEC: see **World Extreme Cagefighting**

Weir, Mark

Nickname: The Wizard **Height:** 6'2"

Weight: 185 lbs **Born:** 9/19/67

Debut: 1996 **Career Record:** 20-16-1

Notable Wins: Eugene Jackson (UFC 38); Johil De Oliveira (Cage Rage 8); Akira Shoji (Cage Rage 14)

Notable Losses: David Loiseau (UFC 42); Jorge Rivera (Cage Rage 7); Matt Lindland (Cage Rage 7); Denis Kang (Pride Bushido 10); Nick Thompson (BodogFight: Vancouver); Paul Daley (Cage Rage 23)

One of the few martial artists to migrate from point tae kwon do competition to MMA with some degree of success, Mark Weir was Britain's top prospect before **Michael Bisping**. Growing up as a black kid in England, Weir was often outnumbered and beaten bloody by his white neighbors. Then he learned to fight. After one explosive confrontation, he realized that fighting might not just be something he needed to survive — he might actually be good at it.

Tae kwon do championships followed, but Weir also focused on the practical application of martial arts techniques. When he saw the **UFC** and **Royce Gracie**, he wasn't too proud to admit that he might have something to learn from the Brazilian's ground technique.

Already almost 30, there was only so much catching up Weir could do. **Wrestling** and jiu-jitsu were hardly commonplace when he started fighting in 1996. By the time he was fighting full-time, Weir's standup game was as strong as his wrestling was weak. When the UFC held a card in London's Royal Albert Hall in 2002, Weir was one of the Brits tapped to add some local flavor to the show. Few expected him to beat Eugene Jackson, and no one would have predicted a knockout in just ten seconds.

The win earned Weir a spot in the UFC's middleweight division, but his next two fights made his weaknesses apparent to all. Weir was a match for anyone in a striking match. On the ground, however, he was vulnerable. What followed was an up-and-down career. Weir was a solid middle of the card attraction for Britain's **Cage Rage**, but wasn't able to beat the international level competition promoters brought in for him to face. As age diminished the strong skills standing he had possessed, Weir began a slide down the card. Still competing at 40-plus, Weir will be remembered as one of the earliest British fighters able to hold his own against the world's best, a necessary building block that made the rise of Michael Bisping and other British stars like Paul Daley and Dan Hardy possible.

Werdum, Fabricio

Nickname: Vai Cavalo **Height:** 6'4"

Weight: 256 lbs **Born:** 7/30/77

Debut: Millennium Brawl 7 (6/16/02) **Career Record:** 14-4-1

Notable Wins: Gabriel Gonzaga (Jungle Fight 1, UFC 80); Alistair Overeem (Pride Total Elimination Absolute); Aleksander Emelianenko (2H2H: Pride & Honor); Brandon Vera (UFC 85); Fedor Emelianenko (Strikeforce: Fedor vs. Werdum)

Notable Losses: Sergei Kharitonov (Pride 30); Antonio Rodrigo Nogueira (Pride Critical Countdown Absolute); Andrei Arlovski (UFC 70); Junior dos Santos (UFC 90)

When **Pride** first introduced us to Fabricio Werdum, it was in his role as **Mirko Cro Cop**'s **Brazilian Jiu-jitsu** coach. While that might not necessarily sound like the most impressive grappling credential, Werdum is not exactly hard up for those: a three-time Pan-American Brazilian Jiu-jitsu, three-time World Brazilian Jiu-jitsu, and **ADCC** weight class champion, Werdum is among the best submission heavyweight fighters in the sport.

His slick submission wins over the likes of **Alistair Overeem** and **Aleksander Emelianenko** whetted fans' appetite for Werdum's **UFC** debut against former champion **Andrei Arlovski**. Unfortunately, the two combined for one of the dullest, least engaging high-profile UFC bouts in memory as both fighters did little but circle after the first round. It got so bad, in fact, that referee **Herb Dean** threatened both fighters with single-point deductions for passivity.

Werdum atoned for his listless debut loss with impressive TKO wins over both **Brandon Vera** and **Gabriel Gonzaga**, and seemed well on his way up the rankings of the somewhat thin UFC heavyweight division when disaster struck: a devastating, first-round upset KO at the hands of Junior Dos Santos left Werdum flat on his back and bounced from the UFC. He found new life in **Strikeforce**, however, with wins over Mike Kyle and the imposing **Antonio Silva**, setting the stage for his career-defining bout with the great **Fedor Emelianenko**, who had not been legitimately defeated in his near decade-long run atop the sport.

Seconds into their contest, Werdum stumbled and fell to his back, either reeling from Emelianenko's attack or baiting the Russian into his guard, depending on how you choose to read the exchange. As Emelianenko dove in to pursue his **ground and pound** attack, Werdum immediately began to hunt for a submission, locking a tight **triangle choke**, threatening all the while with an **arm bar**. For the first time in his MMA career, Fedor was forced to concede defeat. Werdum, widely respected in the sport not only for his technical abilities but for his class and dignity as well, was characteristically humble in victory: "Thank you, Fedor, for the opportunity. Fedor is the best in the world. This night, I beat Fedor, but Fedor is the best." Maybe Werdum is right. Maybe Fedor still is the best in the world despite what happened in that brief, thrilling encounter. Certainly, Werdum will enter their inevitable rematch as the underdog once again. But regardless of what happens then, or anywhere else down the line, for that matter, Werdum will forever be remembered as the man who finally proved that in this sport, anyone — yes, *anyone* — can be defeated.

White, Dana

Dana White is the best, most successful, and most important promoter in the history of MMA. No one else is even close. He took a sport that was floundering and made it a worldwide sensation. He took a company that was bleeding red, and turned it into a billion-dollar behemoth.

When White and childhood friends **Lorenzo and Frank Fertitta** took over the reins of the **Ultimate Fighting Championship**, it was a company in a very bad place. They were giving away tickets in New Jersey, struggling to fill even modest arenas. The once popular pay-per-view spectaculars were available only to fans with satellite television. Cable wouldn't touch them. Las Vegas, home of every fight that mattered, wouldn't touch them. It was a long road to respectability, let alone profitability. White helped them walk that road, struggling along the way and almost turning back, but eventually finding a way to bring cage fighting to the masses.

Dana White is a man who works hard for everything he has. Behind the scenes at a UFC event, White manages every aspect of the show, from the television production to the choice of music. Everything has to be perfect, and White has devoted his life to making sure that it is. Today White rolls around Las Vegas in a bad-ass Bentley, enjoying the spoils of his success. But it is his roots — the single mother who raised him, the crappy jobs as a doorman and in construction — that really drive him.

Less than a decade ago, White was a struggling **boxing** manager, looking for a break and teaching boxercise classes in his gym to make a living. He dreamed about being a famous boxing promoter like Don King or Bob Arum — ironic considering his long-running feud with the sport of boxing and everyone involved in it — and now he's living that dream. It's just been altered a bit: sped up and amped up violence for a new generation of fight fans.

For White, the pieces seemed to fall into place. He was reacquainted with the Fertitta brothers, thanks to Lorenzo's work with the Nevada State Athletic Commission. The three became interested in MMA after a chance meeting with jiu-jitsu ace **John Lewis** at a nightclub. White took on some of the MMA fighters he met, most notably **Tito Ortiz** and **Chuck Liddell**, as clients. During a particularly rough contract negotiation with UFC owner Bob Meyrowitz, White learned the company might be for sale. A few phone calls to the billionaire Fertittas later, the UFC had brand new owners. The company, valued at more than a billion dollars today, was purchased at the cut-rate price of $3 million. White was given a ten percent ownership stake, at the time virtually worthless. That ten percent has made him a multimillionaire, but those millions were hard earned. And success was no guarantee as the new company, called **Zuffa**, would soon find out.

In the beginning, White struggled to find his way. The two primary goals were to get back on pay-per-view nationwide and to become regulated and approved to run shows in Nevada. Las Vegas was the fighter's mecca. Without Vegas the promotion would never seem like a big deal. Without pay-per-view, the promotion would never count big bills.

Amazingly, they achieved these goals in the first year; everyone in the company expected these triumphs to be a license to print money. Instead, the show continued to flounder. The first UFC to play to a wide audience, live on pay-per-view and emanating from the Mandalay Bay Events Center, was a colossal disaster. The action wasn't compelling, many fans didn't recognize the new generation of fighters, and the show went over on time, causing many to miss the end of the final match and costing the promotion millions. It was clear that White had a lot to learn.

The big break that made the UFC a financial and pop culture juggernaut almost slipped right through White's grasp. No one disputes that ***The Ultimate Fighter*** reality show saved the promotion that until that point was hemorrhaging money. But what many don't know is that the television breakthrough was almost an opportunity missed. Some in the promotion wanted to run a different reality series, one called *American Promoter*, that would focus on the charismatic UFC boss and the day-to-day operations of running the UFC. While it would have no doubt been a great showcase for White, it wouldn't have produced a new generation of young superstars and wouldn't have created the perfect platform for promoting the pay-per-view fights. White had an important decision to make: which show would he choose? The one that would make him an icon, or the one that was better for business? He went with the one better for the industry, and the rest was history.

White really came into his own once the promotion started to thrive. It had taken more than four years for White and Zuffa to rise to the top of the sport. Once he was there, he solidified his hold on the American market with a ruthless streak and an iron grip. There was never any doubt that White was the boss. He responded to any challenges with a brutality that was unprecedented in the sport. White didn't have competitors; he had enemies.

White didn't just vanquish all comers — he demolished them, then rubbed it in their faces. A rogue's gallery of promoters, including Gary Shaw, Jay Larkin, Calvin Ayre, and Tom Atencio were not just humbled; they were verbally lambasted by the foul-mouthed UFC frontman. To White, these other men were simply trying to cash in on what he created. This was his life. No one else seemed to have his level of commitment. He beat them in court, in the ratings, on pay-per-view, everywhere he could.

His unquestioned passion was a key component in building the UFC to heights unimagined in the **SEG** era. Once the company was negotiating with Fortune 500 partners and in the public limelight, White's hard charging manner became a liability. In 2009 White, a man normally so good at controlling the story, became the story. He attacked **Sherdog** reporter Loretta Hunt in a video posted on YouTube, at the same time slandering homosexuals and generally coming off as a thug.

White had a fine line to walk. Fans enjoyed his profane and over-the-top act, but there had to be limits. Going forward, White would be dealing with bigger fish than "scumbag Hollywood agents" and recalcitrant fighters. He would be dealing with television executives, major media pundits, and big-time advertisers. It was a whole new game . . . but few who knew him had any doubts that Dana White would find all the angles, taking himself and the UFC straight into the American mainstream and, from there, to the world.

White, Vernon

Nickname: Tiger **Height:** 6'

Weight: 205 lbs **Born:** 12/3/71

Debut: Pancrase: Yes, We Are Hybrid Wrestlers 1 (9/21/93)

Career Record: 26-34-10

Notable Wins: Yoshiki Takahashi (Pancrase: Truth 3); Vladimir Matyushenko (IFC: Montreal Caged Combat)

Notable Losses: Bas Rutten (Pancrase: Pancrash! 3); Pedro Rizzo (World Vale Tudo Championship 2); Kazushi Sakuraba (Pride 2); Chuck Liddell (UFC 49); Lyoto Machida (WFA: King of the Streets)

Vernon White is a product of the old school. Before there was even a **Lion's Den**, White trained with **Ken Shamrock** inside a racquetball court at a local gym. The training was rudimentary. Students took a beating from Shamrock, either learning to defend themselves or leaving. There was no third option. White learned, enough that Shamrock was comfortable bringing him with him to Japan for the debut of **Pancrase**.

The Japanese ring announcers made love to his name, even in an era that predated Lenny Hardt's memorable and seemingly minute-long odes to the warriors of **Pride**. It was an introduction that exceeded what was sure to follow in the ring or cage. "Vereeeenon 'Tiger' White-o" was fun to say, but less fun to watch in his early matches.

White struggled in his early matches, losing seven of his first eight. He came from a tae kwon do background and had a hard time when the fight went to the ground. He learned quickly though, eventually defeating one of Pancrase's founders **Minoru Suzuki** and earning a shot at the newly formed Pride Fighting Championship. He fell to a rising star named **Kazushi Sakuraba**.

It's been the pattern White's career has followed everywhere he's gone. He's capable of defeating other journeyman and occasionally a mid-level fighter like Vladimir Matyushenko, but he's always lost to world-class competition. White is essentially an MMA nomad, the ultimate journeyman. He was there for the very first show in Japan and seems to show no signs of slowing down.

Whatever else he might be, White is an exceedingly loyal friend, as Ken Shamrock found with the Lion's Den. When every member of the team had long ago moved on, to new careers or new fight teams, White remained. He's always there, watching Ken's back and grooming the next generation of fighters.

Williams, Pete

Nickname: El Duro **Height:** 6'3"

Weight: 237 lbs **Born:** 7/10/75

Debut: Pancrase: 1996 Neo-Blood Tournament (7/23/96)

Career Record: 11-6

Notable Win: Mark Coleman (UFC 17)

Notable Losses: Yuki Kondo (Pancrase: 1996 Neo-Blood Tournament Round 2); Tsuyoshi Kohsaka (UFC 17.5); Kevin Randleman (UFC 23); Frank Mir (UFC 36)

Pete Williams was a grappler, which is what made the ridiculous so sublime. When he kicked former **Olympian Mark Coleman** right in the grill, it was truly surprising. Who could have predicted that MMA's signature knockout would come from Pete Williams, better known for his **knee bar** than his high kick?

Once the biggest knockout in the history of MMA, it has now been replaced on highlight reels by **Gabriel Gonzaga**'s decapitation of **Mirko Cro Cop** or **Rashad Evans**' colossal kick to the dome of Sean Salmon. Now Williams, and even his shining moment in the spotlight, has been largely forgotten.

Williams was a high school teammate of **Jerry Bohlander** and followed his friend to **Ken Shamrock**'s **Lion's Den.** Together they joined Jason DeLucia and **Frank Shamrock** as part of a clique that terrorized new fighters with the temerity to try to join the legendary team.

Like his teammates, Williams had immediate success in the new sport of MMA. He won the second **SuperBrawl** tournament in Hawaii and shocked the world with his knockout of Coleman, one of the most dominating wrestlers of the era. It was his single marquee win. Every other fight with a legitimate opponent ended in defeat. He lost to **Tsuyoshi Kohsaka** in a match to crown a number one contender for the heavyweight title and later dropped a boring decision to **Kevin Randleman** in a match for the vacant **UFC** belt.

After a brief foray to **King of the Cage**, where he dominated two overmatched opponents, Williams made a final run at UFC glory. He lost three in a row, all decisively, and left the business for good. Like many of the products of the Lion's Den, Williams had trained too hard, pushing himself physically and mentally further than could possibly be healthy. At the age of 27, he was exhausted. Williams left the sport, never to return. Today he makes his living as a chef, presumably in a restaurant where no one ever has the courage to send anything back to the kitchen.

World Extreme Cagefighting

The furiously fast back-and-forth action between **Urijah Faber** and Jeff Curran was one thing. It was an exciting fight, but we'd seen fast-paced fights in the **UFC**'s lightweight division too. It was the jumping knee by Faber, while Curran was holding his other leg looking for a takedown, that really made fans sit up and take notice. These guys were on a whole different level, fighting with a swiftness and ferocity that would put Usain Bolt to shame.

Although the WEC made its live television debut in June 2007, the promotion has actually been around since 2001. Before they showcased the very best in the world at 135 and 145 pounds, the WEC was just another respectable California-based independent promotion. They held almost every one of their 24 events at the Tachi Palace Hotel and Casino in Lemoore, California, and were best known for hosting **Frank Shamrock**'s return to MMA action in 2003.

In Their Own Words: WEC President Reed Harris on changing focus

"When we decided to focus on the lighter weights we knew we had our work cut out for us. But if you look at boxing for example, it took many years, but now the lightweight guys are the guys everybody is interested in. If you look at the time frame, I only started really focusing on the lightweights about eight months ago. Now look where we are at. Everyone in the MMA industry says the best lightweights in the world fight for WEC. I get calls from across the world, from Japan, from Korea, from Brazil, with coaches saying, 'I've got lightweight fighters we want to bring into the WEC, because these guys want to fight the best.' It used to be the other way around. We used to have to chase after them."

The WEC was purchased in 2006 by **Zuffa**, parent company of the UFC. It was an interesting move, during a period in MMA history full of intrigue and backroom dealings. The Japanese promotion **Pride** had lost their network television deal, victims of a magazine exposé that revealed ties to organized crime. The promotion was for sale, and although Pride had struggled to gain a foothold in the American market, Zuffa didn't want to take any chances with a competitor acquiring Pride's legendary fighters and securing a national television deal. They made a pre-emptive strike, buying the WEC from Reed Harris and Scott Adams and signing the group to a long-term contract with the Versus network, preventing anyone who bought Pride from making the same deal.

It was all moot. The UFC actually ended up buying Pride, folding the group into their existing organization. Pride was out of the picture, but Zuffa found themselves the proud owners of a second active MMA promotion after all their defensive maneuvering: the WEC.

It took some time for the revamped company to find its identity and make its mark. They knew they didn't want to be UFC Lite, a breeding ground or minor league for talent that eventually "graduated" to the UFC. Although they were resistant to the idea at first, WEC officials eventually agreed to focus only on the lighter weight classes, dropping the 205-, 185-, and 170-pound divisions. Instead of featuring second-rate champions in these divisions, the WEC became an American **Shooto**, a promotion that showcased the top lighter-weight fighters in the world.

The star of the early shows was Faber, a bronzed surfer type from southern California who happened to be one of the most exciting fighters in all of MMA. The WEC was blessed with the chance to match Faber with a UFC star, former lightweight champion **Jens Pulver**. Pulver was way past his expiration date, but had an established name. Faber's five round dismantling of the aging veteran immediately gave him credibility with fans. It was a true star-making performance, one that has made Faber as a legitimate television draw.

Other astounding performances soon followed. **Miguel Torres**, Jose Aldo, **Mike Brown**, **Brian Bowles**, and Donald Cerrone helped make sure no WEC was without its magical moments. The promotion, however, had seemingly peaked early. The show was getting solid ratings and putting on great fights. There was only one way to move forward, to push the WEC to the next level: promoting on pay-per-view, something Harris pulled the trigger on in 2010.

The first pay-per-view, promoted heavily by **Dana White** and the whole Zuffa team, didn't bear the promotion's name so it could be sold on both the Versus and Spike television networks. It may not have been labeled "WEC" but there was no mistaking the action in the cage. The show, main evented by Urijah Faber and **Jose Aldo**, was a typical WEC barnburner — all action, all the time. Well received by the media and the fans, it seemed a follow up was likely.

World Fighting Alliance

It's best to think of the World Fighting Alliance (WFA) as two completely distinct organizations that just happened to promote MMA events under the same name. The first incarnation of the WFA was operated by John Lewis and John Huntington, and billed itself as "Where the fight club meets the nightclub." With laser light shows, go-go dancers, extra-sleazy ring girls — even Ice-T one time! — WFA put on three shows at The Joint in Las Vegas's Hard Rock Hotel starting in November 2001. After their disastrous third show a year later, where accredited photographers were inexplicably displaced from ringside and, in some cases, ejected from the building entirely, the WFA ruined its relationship with the MMA media, and a fourth show never materialized. The company returned in name only in 2006 under the direction of Ross Goodman and Louis Palazzo, and dove headlong into the free-agent market, coming away with **Quinton Jackson**, **Lyoto Machida**, and **Matt Lindland**; they even had **Bas Rutten** on board for a comeback fight. After a solid but sparsely attended first show bombed on pay-per-view, that was pretty much it for the second incarnation of the World Fighting Alliance, which sold off a number of its assets to the **UFC** — including the contracts of Jackson and Machida, both future light heavyweight champions. Ice-T's future in the sport remains uncertain.

World Victory Road: Sengoku

The demise of **Pride** in late 2007 permanently altered the landscape of Japanese mixed martial arts. The longstanding Pride and K-1 rivalry was over, and the consolidation of top Pride fighters and executives under K-1's **Dream** banner in early 2008 seemed to indicate the direction of the sport in the land of the rising sun. Dream had the fighters, they had the promotional muscle, and, perhaps most importantly, they had the prime time network TV contract with TBS (Tokyo Broadcast System). The upstart World Victory Road organization managed to snag three significant native Japanese stars: **Kazuo Misaki**, just as his feud with **Yoshihiro Akiyama** made him a hero; **Takanori Gomi**, around whom Pride had built its Bushido series of events; and **Hidehiko Yoshida**, a battered and ancient **judo** hero who nevertheless remained a solid draw and a major player. But with their only exposure coming through a 30-minute block on the relatively minor TV Tokyo, it didn't seem like they'd be anything but small-time.

But while K-1 has struggled to satisfy TBS with its Dream ratings, World Victory Road has made their Sengoku series work on a smaller scale. They've been canny and clever every step of the way. Take the "Sengoku" name to begin with; the word literally translates to something akin to "fighting mastery," but is simultaneously a homophonic reference to the feudal Japanese period of warring states. That's hardly the reason for their success, but given the general mindlessness of MMA promotion names and event titles, Sengoku borders on genius. Just as clever, but much more significant, was World Victory Road's decision to differentiate themselves from the kind of freak show matchups that Dream promoted, and focus on a more straight-ahead sport product. This meant, in addition to promoting its stars from the Pride era, rounding out their cards with as many elite amateur combat athletes as they could muster — **Olympians** wherever possible.

They landed the biggest catch of all when Beijing heavyweight judo gold medalist and All-Japan champion Satoshi Ishii ended his flirtations with the much higher profile **UFC** and Dream and surprisingly opted for the slow-but-steady World Victory Road instead. After announcing his retirement from competitive judo at age 22, Ishii became the hottest Japanese free agent in the sport. After Ishii agreed to a New Year's Eve match with Hidehiko Yoshida, rumors that had already been swirling for months began to gain more momentum still. Will TBS drop Dream and replace them with Sengoku? Or is Fuji TV, which hasn't carried mixed martial since its profound embarrassment over the Pride yakuza scandal, at last interested in returning to that kind of programming in prime time? Only time will tell. But as Dream stumbles, World Victory Road rolls on.

Wrestling

Although Brazilian **Vale Tudo** rightly receives much of the credit, it certainly wasn't the only influence on modern mixed martial arts. Thousands of years earlier, during the Roman occupation of Britain, men were wrestling, using submission locks and chokes in brutal competitions very similar to modern grappling tournaments. The art was called Lancashire wrestling, and it was a bit too rough for the Roman invaders, who preferred their tamer style with its emphasis on throws and pins, today called Greco-Roman wrestling.

Lancashire wrestling was the founding father of **catch wrestling**, which, in turn, spawned American folkstyle wrestling. When you think about wrestling in mixed martial arts, it's this style that predominates. Called "scholastic wrestling" because it is primarily practiced in high schools and colleges, this form of wrestling is catch wrestling with most of the dangerous elements removed. Throws are less violent and submissions are illegal, making control the primary aim of the art. Folkstyle wrestlers seek to control their opponent on the mat, winning either by pinfall or by scoring points for manoeuvres that showed dominance or helped put them in position to secure a victory.

While this kind of wrestling couldn't help a competitor finish a fight, it could certainly help put him in a position to do so. From almost the very beginning, wrestlers found a happy home in MMA competition. While **Dan Severn**, an NCAA All-American, lost to **Royce Gracie** at **UFC** 4, he showed exactly how dominant his art form could be in the future. For much of their 15-minute fight, Severn was in complete control, holding Gracie on the mat and restraining his every action. It was only Severn's lack of killer instinct that allowed Gracie the time to secure the fight-ending **triangle choke** from the bottom, much to announcer **Jeff Blatnick**'s chagrin and **Jim Brown**'s delight.

It was **Mark Coleman**, a 1992 **Olympian**, who really showed just how dominating a truly outstanding wrestler could be. Coleman was walking testosterone. Unlike Severn, when he took an opponent to the mat, he made them pay. Coleman originated the **ground and pound** technique, taking an opponent to the mat and then simply pounding him until he broke. With head butts being legal at the time, Coleman was unstoppable, even in the vaunted **Brazilian Jiu-jitsu guard** (see **positional hierarchy**). Rule changes and a failure to adapt prevented Coleman from reaching his full potential (although winning a UFC title and the 2000 **Pride** Grand Prix is nothing to be ashamed of), but he opened the door for countless wrestlers to follow.

The most important advantage excellent wrestling gives a fighter in MMA is the ability to dictate where the fight takes place. Some wrestlers, like Coleman, Severn, **Mark Kerr**, and **Kevin Randleman**, prefer the fight to take place on the mat. Despite the chance of falling victim to a submission lock, they feel in control there and are happy to risk the lock in exchange for the opportunity to ground and pound. Others, like **Chuck Liddell**, prefer to use their wrestling skills to prevent opponents from taking them to the mat. Liddell, **Jens Pulver**, and **Dan Henderson** are just a few of the many wrestlers preferring to employ **sprawl and brawl**. These heavy-handed wrestlers like to keep things standing, feeling they are better able to deal with submission experts on their feet with developing striking games.

Whichever style they prefer, it's their wrestling skills that make it possible for these fighters to impose their will on an opponent. It's this ability to dictate where the fight takes place that makes wrestling one of the most important, and undervalued, skills in all of mixed martial arts.

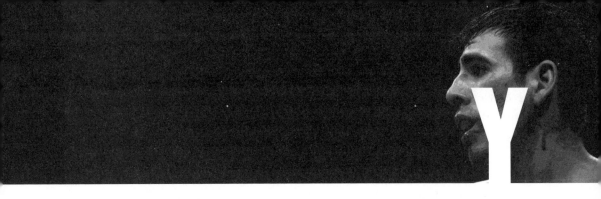

Yamada, Keiichi

Nickname: Jushin "Thunder" Liger **Height:** 5'7"
Weight: 208 lbs **Born:** 11/10/64
Debut: Pancrase: Spirit 8 (11/30/02) **Career Record:** 0-1
Notable Loss: Minoru Suzuki (Pancrase Spirit 8)

In 1989, pro wrestler Keiichi Yamada ceased to exist; he was replaced by the extravagantly masked Jushin "Thunder" Liger. The original Liger was a cartoon character with remarkable powers. Liger the professional wrestler was almost as impressive, flying around the ring and taking the inherent risks of **professional wrestling** to unfathomable heights.

None of those powers seemed present when Liger made his MMA debut in **Pancrase**. He tried his trademark rolling koppa kick, a technique many Japanese pro wrestlers use to start fights, just to, you know, show the world they are pro wrestlers. For Liger this went horribly awry. He missed badly and never recovered. **Minoru Suzuki** mounted him and eventually choked him out. It was the first and final fight for Liger, but also the last legitimate fight of Suzuki's career. The Pancrase legend hung up his boots, only to put on identical boots when he joined the pro wrestling world just days later.

Yamamoto, Kid

Real name: Norifumi Yamamoto **Height:** 5'4"
Weight: 143 lbs **Born:** 3/15/77
Debut: Shooto: To the Top 2 (3/2/01) **Career Record:** 18-3 (1 No Contest)
Notable Wins: Royler Gracie (Hero's 3); Caol Uno (Hero's 3); Genki Sudo (Dynamite!! 2005)
Notable Loss: Joe Warren (Dream 9)

Norifumi "Kid" Yamamoto is one of the biggest stars in Japanese MMA. Figuratively speaking, that is — at only 5'4" he's quite literally the smallest.

But before he ill-advisedly left the sport in his prime to chase an Olympic freestyle **wrestling** dream, Yamamoto's name would often come up in discussions of the best pound-for-pound fighters in the sport. With serious wrestling credentials, sound submission fighting, and an ability to hang with the best in the world in straight kickboxing, that kind of talk was well founded.

Yamamoto's skills couldn't be criticized. His arrogance and hostility, on the other hand, definitely could. On more than one occasion, Yamamoto showed dangerous disregard for the protocols of the sport and complete disdain for his opponents by continuing to pound away on his hapless foes despite the referee's attempts to intervene. Kid was a problem — and the Japanese audience couldn't get enough of him. A New Year's Eve 2004 kickboxing match against Masato, Japan's best, drew a 31.6 rating. Despite giving up over ten pounds and fighting under his opponent's rules, Yamamoto went the distance and even scored a knockdown in the first round. Two years later, an easy win in an MMA match against Hungarian Olympic gold medalist Istvan Majoros produced a 25.0 rating. Both matches remain among the most watched in Japanese television history.

Kid's crowning achievement was the **Hero's** 2005 middleweight (154 pounds) Grand Prix, a tournament he breezed through despite coming into the ring significantly lighter than all three of his highly regarded opponents: **Royler Gracie**, **Caol Uno**, and **Genki Sudo**. None of them made it out of the second round against the ferocious Yamamoto, although it's worth noting that the Sudo stoppage in the first round of the tournament final seemed somewhat premature.

Since then, everything with Yamamoto has seemed a little off. First came his decision in late 2006 to take a leave of absence from mixed martial arts to follow in the footsteps of his father, a 1972 **Olympian** in freestyle wrestling. The timing seemed very strange: Yamamoto was at the peak of his popularity, and hadn't competed in freestyle in the eight years since a bizarre incident involving the yakuza and a pellet gun ultimately led to his expulsion from university and the end of his amateur career. Predictably, his return to the sport didn't go well: an arm-whip takedown dislocated his right elbow only seconds into his semi-final match in the 132-pound division of The Emperor's Cup event in Tokyo.

Then came scandal. In 2008, *Shukan Gendai*, the news magazine that essentially took down **Pride**, published a report detailing alleged "marijuana parties" hosted by Yamamoto. Neighbors complained to police about "sweet herbal smells" and "cars in the driveway playing reggae music." Although police searches failed to turn anything up, the allegations alone were a real problem for Yamamoto, given Japanese cultural attitudes towards marijuana use.

Slowed by injury, Yamamoto has fought only sporadically since his return to the sport. In mid-2009, Kid suffered his first MMA loss in seven years when Joe Warren — an American Greco-Roman wrestling world champion whose Olympic dreams were derailed by a positive test for THC — controlled the Japanese star en route to a split decision win. It's hard to say where Yamamoto goes from here. When Japanese MMA was at its peak, Kid Yamamoto was at his. Now both have fallen on comparatively hard times.

Yamma Pit Fighting

The brainchild of the original **UFC** owner **Bob Meyrowitz**, Yamma Pit Fighting was one of the most disastrous shows in the long, proud lineage of terrible MMA events. It all started with the name. "Yamma" roughly translates from Russian as "pit." That made the name of the event "Pit Pit Fighting."

True to their word, promoters did indeed put the fighters in a pit. Instead of a mere cage, the Yamma was a mat with a sloped orange ring leading up several feet to a cage. Intended to keep the action moving and avoid fighters leaning up against the cage, the new structure instead assured every fight would feature combatants awkwardly grappling on an incline. The slope made preventing the takedown impossible. Instead of creating a more exciting brand of fighting, the pit guaranteed fights decided by timid takedowns and careful positioning. It's not clear if that is the revolution designers had in mind when they created the Yamma.

An event like Yamma Pit Fighting wouldn't be complete without an announcing team worthy of its stature. In this case, it was a reunion of past UFC playcallers, bringing together a slightly embarrassed Bruce Beck, a clueless **Jeff Blatnick**, and the amazing **John Perretti**. Perhaps the least popular personality in MMA history, Perretti always called it like he saw it. On this night he seemed only to see glutes and amazing calves. He seemed to be willing **Kevin Randleman** to appear, but it never happened. In the history of creepy performances, this may have outcreeped them all.

It was as if the whole promotion had been transported in time from a decade gone by. The main event was **Oleg Taktarov** versus **Mark Kerr** — a great fight in 1998, but an embarrassing spectacle in 2008. At least it was better than the other "Masters" fight, a contest between a 400-plus-pound Eric "Butterbean" Esch and UFC 1 veteran **Pat Smith**. Even the tournament, designed to crown a new young star, ended with Travis Wiuff as the winner. Wiuff was hardly a rising star. He was a 30-year-old journeyman with 11 losses in a nondescript career. He, needless to say, failed to impress with his awful **lay and pray** wins.

The shining light eclipsing this dismal display, was ring announcer Scott Ferrall. Ferrall is apparently a radio personality, despite sounding like he swallowed glass. His performance was among the worst things MMA ever thrust upon the world — worse than all the tattoos and horrible T-shirts combined. Even the referees weren't spared his aural assault. "Kevin Mulhall will be our referee for this beautiful matchup of warriors and freaks ready to pound and dance," Ferrall exclaimed.

A second Yamma show, announced for June 2008, never took place.

Yoon, Dong Sik

Height: 6′ **Weight:** 198 lbs

Born: 8/24/72 **Debut:** Pride Total Elimination 2005 (4/23/05)

Career Record: 5–7

Notable Win: Melvin Manhoef (Dynamite!! USA)

Notable Losses: Kazushi Sakuraba (Pride Total Elimination 2005); Quinton Jackson (Pride 31); Murilo Bustamante (Pride Bushido 13); Gegard Mousasi (Dream 4)

At first it seemed like Dong Sik Yoon was a victim of bad timing, a fighter who had what it took to succeed but who was never able to put it all together when it counted most. It's a reputation that followed him from an international **judo** career that saw him earn victories over some of the biggest names in the sport, and win some of the most prestigious and competitive tournaments in the world, but never put everything together when it counted to earn an Olympic berth.

When he made his MMA debut against the legendary but fading **Kazushi Sakuraba** and was knocked out early, it was easy to write it off as a learning experience. When he went the distance in his next fight, against Olympic judo champion Makoto Takimoto, it seemed as though he was starting to learn the ropes. And after dropping competitive decisions to first-rate, championship-caliber mixed martial artists like **Quinton Jackson** and **Murilo Bustamante**, more than one observer noted that Yoon Dong Sik had to be the best 0–4 fighter in the history of the sport.

Yoon evened out his record by rattling off four straight wins, most notably over the ferocious Dutch kickboxer **Melvin Manhoef**. Three of these wins came by came by way of **arm bar**, completely run-of-the-mill applications of the technique that were nevertheless taken up by posters at **The Underground** and quickly celebrated as "The Dongbar." Urbandictionary.com defines the

Dongbar as "an arm bar applied by Dong Sik Yoon and rumored to have been taught to him by God who, momentarily, found himself caught in one and was obliged to tap." Although the sources of these rumors are undisclosed, they seem credible.

But before Dongbar-mania could truly take hold, Yoon was back to old form, going the distance against rising star **Gegard Mousasi** in a losing effort. Subsequent losses to the undistinguished Andrews Nakahara and ***TUF*** alum Jesse "JT Money" Taylor suggested that Yoon, at 37 years of age, might soon be finished. The Dongbar, glorious while it lasted, might not be ours to gaze upon much longer. Cherish it today.

Yoshida, Hidehiko

Height: 5'11" **Weight:** 225 lbs

Born: 9/3/69 **Debut:** Pride 23 (11/24/02)

Career Record: 9-8-1

Notable Wins: Don Frye (Pride 23); Kiyoshi Tamura (Pride Total Elimination 2003); Mark Hunt (Pride Critical Countdown 2004); Naoya Ogawa (Pride Shockwave 2005); Satoshi Ishii (Dynamite!! 2009)

Notable Losses: Wanderlei Silva (Pride Final Conflict 2003, Pride Total Elimination 2005); Rulon Gardner (Pride Shockwave 2004); Josh Barnett (Sengoku 1); Kazuhiro Nakamura (ASTRA)

As **Nobuhiko Takada**'s contests against **Rickson Gracie** mercifully receded into memory, and **Kazushi Sakuraba**'s willingness to fight much larger opponents began to catch up with him, Hidehiko Yoshida emerged as **Pride**'s top Japanese star. Unlike his predecessors in that role, who came from the world of **professional wrestling**, Yoshida entered MMA as a decorated **judo** player. A 1992 Olympic gold medalist in Barcelona (-78 kg) and world judo champion in 1999 (-90 kg), a slightly battered Yoshida reached the end of a long and distinguished international career at the age of 32 and took to the ring against MMA pioneer **Royce Gracie** in front of over 90,000 fans at Shockwave 2002.

Yoshida and Gracie fought under rules modified to commemorate the 50th anniversary of Royce's father **Helio Gracie**'s grappling match against judo legend **Masahiko Kimura.** Strikes to the head were forbidden, but, perhaps more importantly, the rules Gracie requested specified that the referee had no power to stop the match. However, when Gracie appeared to fall limp under Yoshida's sode guruma jime or **Ezequiel choke,** the referee intervened and awarded the match to Yoshida. The Tokyo fans were ecstatic; the Gracies were irate; and more than a few observers thought Pride was protecting their new star.

That Yoshida was the beneficiary of either fixed or worked fights was never substantiated, and seems dubious in hindsight, but the notion plagued the early part of his career. Submission wins over **Don Frye** and **Kiyoshi Tamura** — seriously accomplished legitimate fighters, but also professional wrestlers — weren't enough to convince skeptics that Yoshida was for real. But a stirring loss to **Wanderlei Silva**, in which Yoshida went toe-to-toe with the dominant Pride middleweight (205 pounds) champion in one of the best fights of 2003, seemed to do the trick. Less than two months after that punishing decision loss, Yoshida was again paired with Gracie, this time fighting to a draw that would have been a Gracie win but for Gracie's insistence that no judges score the bout.

Yoshida went the distance with Silva one more time, losing a split decision in their 2005 rematch. Impressively, Yoshida was again unafraid to stand and trade with one of the most feared strikers in the sport. Over the course of four dominant years, Silva finished 13 consecutive fights at 205 pounds by knockout or TKO, with the exception of the Yoshida bouts that went the distance, making this pair of losses Yoshida's greatest achievement in his second career.

That, and getting seriously paid: Yoshida received $2 million for his New Year's Eve bout against judo rival and fellow ratings draw **Naoya Ogawa** in one of the most watched fights in Japanese history, and Yoshida's decision loss to 2000 Olympic Greco-Roman **wrestling** gold medalist Rulon Gardner found an even bigger audience.

In the dying days of Pride, a battered Yoshida perhaps foolishly tried his hand against a streaking **Mirko Cro Cop** and paid the price, while the first **Sengoku** card saw him drop an entertaining contest to the bigger, younger, and much better **Josh Barnett**. Although his skills had seriously declined with advancing age and an ever-expanding waistline, old man Yoshida had just enough left in the tank to get the best of debuting Olympic judo champ Satoshi Ishii in a high profile New Year's Eve 2009 contest. In April 2010, Yoshida announced his retirement after a loss to longtime student **Kazuhiro Nakamura** contested at the celebrated Nippon Budokan — a fitting place for the venerable judoka to take his final bow.

Yoshida, Yoshiyuki

Nickname: Zenko **Height:** 5'11"

Weight: 170 lbs **Born:** 5/10/74

Debut: Shooto 2005 in Kitazawa Town Hall (2/6/05)

Career Record: 11-5

Notable Wins: Satoru Kitaoka (Pancrase: Brave 10); Akira Kikuchi (GCM: Cage Force 4)

Notable Losses: Josh Koscheck (UFC: Fight for the Troops); Anthony Johnson (UFC 104)

Twice in his career, **judo** fighter Yoshiyuki Yoshida has been carried out of the cage on a stretcher. Oddly enough, the first time was in victory: a brutal **ground and pound** win over former **Shooto** champion **Akira Kikuchi** earned Yoshida a bout with Dan Hardy in the finals of the 2007 **Cage Force** welterweight tournament, a match Yoshida won by disqualification when Hardy inadvertently landed a truly epic kick to the groin.

On the strength of that tournament win, Yoshida made his **UFC** debut against Jon Koppenhaver (or **War Machine**, if you prefer) at the relatively advanced age of 34. Yoshida made short work of the controversial ***TUF*** also-ran, tossing him with a huge harai goshi hip throw and choking him into unconsciousness with a deft anaconda choke (see **arm triangle**), all inside the fight's first minute.

Karo Parisyan's eleventh-hour withdrawal from a scheduled match amid various physical (and perhaps psychological) ailments cost Yoshida a shot against a perennial welterweight contender, but Yoshida found another such opportunity soon thereafter, matched against **Josh Koscheck**. And that would lead to stretcher number two. Midway through the first round, Koscheck landed two big right hands, the first of which staggered Yoshida, the second of which turned out the lights.

A subsequent **guillotine choke** win over former Navy SEAL Brandon Wolff suggests that Yoshida may have found his level: he's capable of finishing second-tier fighters with relative ease, but probably out of his depth against the best in the world.

Yvel, Gilbert

Nickname: The Hurricane **Height:** 6'2"

Weight: 235 lbs **Born:** 6/30/76

Debut: Rings Holland: The Final Challenge (2/2/97)

Career Record: 36–15–1 (1 No Contest)

Notable Wins: Tsuyoshi Kohsaka (Rings: Rise 2); Semmy Schilt (Rings Holland: The Kings of the Magic Ring); Kiyoshi Tamura (Rings: Millennium Combine 1); Gary Goodridge (Pride 10); Cheick Kongo (It's Showtime: Amsterdam)

Notable Losses: Dan Henderson (Rings: King of Kings 99); Vitor Belfort (Pride 9); Igor Vovchanchyn (Pride 14); Don Frye (Pride 16); Jeremy Horn (Pride 21); Josh Barnett (Affliction: Day of Reckoning)

Gilbert Yvel was one of the most exciting fighters on the planet for most of the last ten years. Unfortunately, his career, filled with amazing moments and explosive knockouts, will likely be reduced to caricature. Yvel will be

In Their Own Words: Gilbert Yvel on gouging Don Frye

"There was no way I was going to win that fight. He came out to the national anthem of America, the 'Terrorists Suck' T-shirt, and a flak vest. It was like I was the terrorist and he was the fucking army. I made some mistakes. I got all fucked up and mad because he didn't want to fight with me and only wanted to take me to the ground. It was stupid. I was just stupid.

"In Pride the people were just scared. No one wanted to stand up with me. They would just put me on the ground and didn't want to fight with me. I got frustrated with all those fighters in Pride who didn't want to stand up and trade with me. They just wanted to lie on the ground."

remembered as the world's dirtiest fighter, the key evidence being a legendary YouTube clip from a 2004 fight in Finland against Atte Backman.

A frustrated Yvel punched the referee in that fight. For good measure, he kicked him when he was down. Sure, there were extenuating circumstances. The referee was also the trainer of his opponent. And maybe he wasn't enforcing the rules the way Yvel would have liked. But assaulting the referee was inexcusable and, combined with a pattern of behavior, colored Yvel's reputation and helped deny him a license to fight in the state of Nevada.

Yvel's bad behavior is legendary. He's bitten an opponent (Karim Barkalaev); blatantly used illegal elbows (**Dan Henderson**); repeatedly gouged an opponent's eye (**Don Frye**); and, yes, punched out the referee. His opponents aren't the only ones who suffer; Yvel is also a victim of these transgressions. The culprit is not the affable Yvel who charms everyone he meets. It's the Mr. Hyde version, the one who can't control his temper.

It's this uncontrollable anger that's kept Yvel from meeting his true potential as a fighter. No game plan can stick with him. It's all thrown out the window when the bell rings. A switch flips then, and Yvel goes on the attack.

In the beginning, this style served Yvel well. He had great success using his superior standup against the grapplers in Japan's **Rings** promotion. If his rush to glory resulted in a takedown, the rules allowed him to grab the ropes to force a standup, in turn losing a point. With these rules in place, Yvel usually had five chances to finish the fight before he ran out of points. This was normally not a problem, and Yvel burst into international prominence by beating top Japanese stars like **Tsuyoshi Kohsaka** and **Kiyoshi Tamura**.

As Rings struggled financially, Yvel made a controversial jump to **Pride**. This infuriated Rings' president **Akira Maeda**, who had an agreement with Yvel's manager that he would stay in exchange for a big fight with Tamura. Instead, his manager had already committed to Pride, increasing his paycheck fourfold. It was good for the pocketbook, but a poor move for his fighting career. In Pride, fighters like **Vitor Belfort** could take Yvel down and there were no rope escapes to rescue him. He turned into an ordinary fighter, albeit one capable of astounding feats like his spectacular knockout of **Gary Goodridge**. Yvel remains a fringe contender in the heavyweight division, remains an explosive striker, but remains vulnerable when the fight hits the ground.

Z

ZST: see **Deep/ZST**

Zuffa

By 2000, years of turmoil and dozens of battles with politicians and cable executives had worn **Bob Meyrowitz** down. After almost a decade of fighting the machine, he was ready to sell. The **UFC** had secured sanctioning from Larry Hazzard and the New Jersey Athletic Control Board. Profitability seemed possible and there were plenty of interested parties. When he heard the promotion might be for sale **Dana White**, the manager of top UFC fighters **Chuck Liddell** and **Tito Ortiz**, acted quickly. White got in touch with his old friend Lorenzo **Fertitta**, a former member of the Nevada State Athletic Commission — and a billionaire casino mogul to boot. When the UFC attempted to get MMA sanctioned in Nevada, Fertitta was unsure whether it was a good fit for his state. A year later, everything had changed. He had even begun training with jiu-jitsu wizard **John Lewis**. Lorenzo was now a fan — one with the connections and money to help the UFC grow. He and his brother Frank Fertitta III bought the company for $2 million in January 2001. They formed Zuffa, Italian for "scrap," to become the UFC's parent company and put millions into developing the brand and the sport. Today, the consensus value of Zuffa at is over a billion dollars.

The Fertittas have steadfastly avoided taking Zuffa public and have turned down numerous offers to buy the company, including one reportedly of $1.2 billion. In 2010 they sold a 10 percent share of Zuffa to Flash Entertainment, an entertainment company run by the government in Abu Dhabi, the capital of the United Arab Emirates. With the sale, 40.5 percent of Zuffa is now held by Lorenzo, the company's CEO and chairman; 40.5 percent by his older brother, Frank; and, 10 percent by Flash Entertainment. Dana White personally holds the remaining 9 percent.

Appendix I

Ultimate Fighting Championship Results

UFC 1

11/12/93

McNichols Sports Arena (Denver, Colorado)

Main Event: Royce Gracie defeated Gerard Gordeau (rear naked choke, won UFC 1 Tournament)

Other Fights:

- Royce Gracie defeated Ken Shamrock (gi choke)
- Gerard Gordeau defeated Kevin Rosier (TKO)
- Ken Shamrock defeated Pat Smith (heel hook)
- Royce Gracie defeated Art Jimmerson (submission to position)
- Kevin Rosier defeated Zane Frazier (corner stoppage)
- Gerard Gordeau defeated Teila Tuli (TKO)
- Jason DeLucia defeated Trent Jenkins (rear naked choke)

UFC 2

3/11/94

Mammoth Gardens (Denver, Colorado)

Main Event: Royce Gracie defeated Patrick Smith (submission to strikes, won UFC 2 Tournament)

Other Fights:

- Royce Gracie defeated Remco Pardoel (gi choke)
- Patrick Smith defeated Johnny Rhodes (guillotine choke)
- Royce Gracie defeated Jason DeLucia (arm bar)
- Remco Pardoel defeated Orlando Weit (elbows)
- Johnny Rhodes defeated Fred Ettish (side choke)
- Patrick Smith defeated Scott Morris (KO)
- Royce Gracie defeated Minoki Ichihara (gi choke)
- Jason DeLucia defeated Scott Baker (submission to strikes)
- Remco Pardoel defeated Alberto Cerra Leon (arm bar)
- Orlando Weit defeated Robert Lucarelli (TKO)
- Frank Hamaker defeated Thaddeus Luster (submission)
- Johnny Rhodes defeated David Levicki (submission to strikes)
- Patrick Smith defeated Ray Wizard (guillotine choke)
- Scott Morris defeated Sean Daugherty (guillotine choke)

UFC 3

9/9/94

Grady Cole Center (Charlotte, North Carolina)

Main Event: Steve Jennum defeated Harold Howard (submission to strikes, won UFC 3 Tournament)

Other Fights:

- Harold Howard defeated Royce Gracie (forfeit)
- Ken Shamrock defeated Felix Lee Mitchell (rear naked choke)
- Royce Gracie defeated Kimo Leopoldo (arm bar)
- Harold Howard defeated Roland Payne (KO)
- Ken Shamrock defeated Christophe Leninger (submission to strikes)
- Keith Hackney defeated Emmanuel Yarborough (submission to strikes)

UFC 4

12/16/94

Expo Square Pavilion (Tulsa, Oklahoma)

Main Event: Royce Gracie defeated Dan Severn (triangle choke, won UFC 4 Tournament)

Other Fights:

- Dan Severn defeated Marcus Bossett (rear naked choke)
- Royce Gracie defeated Keith Hackney (arm bar)
- Dan Severn defeated Anthony Macias (rear naked choke)
- Steve Jennum defeated Melton Bowen (arm bar)
- Keith Hackney defeated Joe Son (submission to strikes)

Royce Gracie defeated Ron van Clief (rear naked choke)

Guy Mezger defeated Jason Fairn (corner stoppage)

Marcus Bossett defeated Eldo Diax Xavier (KO)

Joe Charles defeated Kevin Rosier (arm bar)

UFC 5

4/7/95

Independence Arena (Charlotte, North Carolina)

Main Event: Dan Severn defeated Dave Beneteau (key lock, won UFC 5 Tournament)

Other Fights:

Royce Gracie vs. Ken Shamrock (draw)

Dan Severn defeated Oleg Taktarov (TKO)

Dave Beneteau defeated Todd Medina (TKO)

Dan Severn defeated Joe Charles (rear naked choke)

Oleg Taktarov defeated Ernie Verdicia (choke)

Todd Medina defeated Larry Cureton (choke)

Jon Hess defeated Andy Anderson (TKO)

Guy Mezger defeated John Dowdy (TKO)

Dave Beneteau defeated Asbel Cancio (TKO)

UFC 6

6/14/95

Casper Events Center (Casper, Wyoming)

Main Event: Oleg Taktarov defeated David Abbott (rear naked choke, won UFC 6 Tournament)

Other Fights:

Ken Shamrock defeated Dan Severn (guillotine choke, won UFC Superfight Championship)

Oleg Taktarov defeated Anthony Macias (guillotine choke)

David Abbott defeated Paul Varelans (TKO)

Oleg Taktarov defeated Dave Beneteau (guillotine choke)

Pat Smith defeated Rudyard Moncayo (rear naked choke)

Paul Varelans defeated Cal Worsham (TKO)

David Abbott defeat John Matua (KO)

Anthony Macias defeated He-Man Gipson (submission to strikes)

Joel Sutton defeated Jack McGlaughlin (submission to strikes)

UFC 7

9/8/95

Memorial Auditorium (Buffalo, New York)

Main Event: Marco Ruas defeated Paul Varelans (TKO, won UFC 7 Tournament)

Other Fights:

Ken Shamrock vs. Oleg Taktarov (draw)

Paul Varelans defeated Mark Hall (key lock)

Marco Ruas defeated Remco Pardoel (submission to position)

Marco Ruas defeated Larry Cureton (heel hook)

Remco Pardoel defeated Ryan Parker (choke)

Mark Hall defeated Harold Howard (submission to strikes)

Paul Varelans defeated Gerry Harris (submission to strikes)

Joel Sutton defeated Geza Kalman (TKO)

Scott Bessac defeated David Hood (guillotine choke)

Onassis Parungo defeated Francesco Maturi (submission to strikes)

The Ultimate Ultimate 1

12/16/95

Mammoth Gardens (Denver, Colorado)

Main Event: Dan Severn defeated Oleg Taktarov (decision, won Ultimate Ultimate Tournament)

Other Fights:

Oleg Taktarov defeated Marco Ruas (decision)

Dan Severn defeated David Abbott (decision)

Marco Ruas defeated Keith Hackney (rear naked choke)

Oleg Taktarov defeated Dave Beneteau (ankle lock)

David Abbott defeated Steve Jennum (neck crank)

Dan Severn defeated Paul Varelans (arm triangle)

Mark Hall defeated Trent Jenkins (arm bar)

Joe Charles defeated Scott Bessac (arm bar)

UFC 8

2/16/96

Ruben Rodriguez Coliseum (San Juan, Puerto Rico)

Main Event: Don Frye defeated Gary Goodridge (submission to strikes, won UFC 8 Tournament)

Other Fights:

Ken Shamrock defeated Kimo Leopoldo (knee bar)

Gary Goodridge defeated Jerry Bohlander (TKO)
Don Frye defeated Sam Adkins (doctor stoppage)
Gary Goodridge defeated Paul Herrera (KO)
Jerry Bohlander defeated Scott Ferrozzo (guillotine choke)
Paul Varelans defeated Joe Moreira (decision)
Don Frye defeated Thomas Ramirez (KO)
Sam Adkins defeated Keith Mielke (submission to strikes)

UFC 9

5/17/96

Cobo Arena (Detroit, Michigan)

Main Event: Dan Severn defeated Ken Shamrock (decision, won UFC Superfight Championship)

Other Fights:

Don Frye defeated Amaury Bitetti (TKO)
Mark Hall defeated Koji Kitao (TKO)
Mark Schultz defeated Gary Goodridge (TKO)
Rafael Carino defeated Matt Andersen (submission to strikes)
Cal Worsham defeated Zane Frazier (submission to strikes)
Steve Nelmark defeated Tai Bowden (TKO)

UFC 10

6/12/96

Fairgrounds Arena (Birmingham, Alabama)

Main Event: Mark Coleman defeated Don Frye (TKO, won UFC 10 Tournament)

Other Fights:

Mark Coleman defeated Gary Goodridge (submission to exhaustion)
Don Frye defeated Brian Johnston (submission to strikes)
Gary Goodridge defeated John Campetella (KO)
Mark Coleman defeated Moti Horenstein (TKO)
Brian Johnston defeated Scott Fielder (TKO)
Don Frye defeated Mark Hall (submission to strikes)
Geza Kalman defeated Dieusel Berto (TKO)
Sam Adkins defeated Felix Lee Mitchell (decision)

UFC 11

9/20/96

Augusta Civic Center (Augusta, Georgia)

Main Event: Mark Coleman won UFC 11 Tournament by default

Other Fights:

Scott Ferrozzo defeated David Abbott (decision)
Mark Coleman defeated Brian Johnston (submission to strikes)
Jerry Bohlander defeated Fabio Gurgel (decision)
David Abbott defeated Sam Adkins (neck crank)
Brian Johnston defeated Reza Nasri (TKO)
Mark Coleman defeated Julian Sanchez (choke)
Roberto Tavern defeated Dave Berry (TKO)
Scott Ferrozzo defeated Sam Fulton (TKO)

The Ultimate Ultimate 2

12/7/96

Fair Park Arena (Birmingham, Alabama)

Main Event: Don Frye defeated David Abbott (rear naked choke, won Ultimate Ultimate 2 Tournament)

Other Fights:

Don Frye defeated Mark Hall (Achilles hold)
David Abbott defeated Steve Nelmark (KO)
Kimo Leopoldo defeated Paul Varelans (TKO)
David Abbott defeated Cal Worsham (submission to strikes)
Don Frye defeated Gary Goodridge (submission to exhaustion)
Ken Shamrock defeated Brian Johnston (choke)
Steve Nelmark defeated Marcus Bossett (choke)
Mark Hall defeated Felix Lee Mitchell (TKO)

UFC 12

2/7/97

Dothan Civic Center (Dothan, Alabama)

Main Event: Mark Coleman defeated Dan Severn (choke, won UFC Heavyweight Championship)

Other Fights:

Vitor Belfort defeated Scott Ferrozzo (TKO, won UFC 12 Heavyweight Tournament)
Jerry Bohlander defeated Nick Sanzo (choke, won UFC 12 Lightweight Tournament)
Vitor Belfort defeated Tra Telligman (TKO)
Scott Ferrozzo defeated Jim Mullen (TKO)
Kazuo Takahashi defeated Wallid Ismail (decision)
Jerry Bohlander defeated Rainy Martinez (choke)

Justin Martin defeated Eric Martin (heel hook)
Nick Sanzo defeated Jackie Lee (TKO)

UFC 13

5/30/97

Augusta Civic Center (Augusta, Georgia)

Main Event: Vitor Belfort defeated David Abbott (TKO)

Other Fights:

- Randy Couture defeated Steven Graham (TKO, won UFC 13 Heavyweight Tournament)
- Guy Mezger defeated Tito Ortiz (guillotine choke, won UFC 13 Lightweight Tournament)
- Randy Couture defeated Tony Halme (rear naked choke)
- Steven Graham defeated Dmitri Stepanov (Americana)
- Enson Inoue defeated Royce Alger (arm bar)
- Guy Mezger defeated Christophe Leninger (decision)
- Jack Nilson defeated Saeed Hosseini (TKO)
- Tito Ortiz defeated Wes Albritton (TKO)

UFC 14

7/27/97

Boutwell Auditorium (Birmingham, Alabama)

Main Event: Maurice Smith defeated Mark Coleman (decision, won UFC Heavyweight Championship)

Other Fights:

- Mark Kerr defeated Dan Bobish (submission to chin in the eye, won UFC 14 Heavyweight Tournament)
- Kevin Jackson defeated Tony Fryklund (rear naked choke, won UFC 14 Middleweight Tournament)
- Dan Bobish defeated Brian Johnston (TKO)
- Mark Kerr defeated Moti Horenstein (TKO)
- Kevin Jackson defeated Todd Butler (TKO)
- Joe Moreira defeated Yuri Vaulin (decision)
- Alex Hunter defeated Sam Fulton (TKO)
- Tony Fryklund defeated Donnie Chappell (choke)

UFC 15

10/17/97

Casino Magic (Bay St. Louis, Mississippi)

Main Event: Maurice Smith defeated David Abbott (submission to strikes)

Other Fights:

- Mark Kerr defeated Dwayne Carson (rear naked choke, won UFC 15 Heavyweight Tournament)
- Randy Couture defeated Vitor Belfort (TKO)
- Dave Beneteau defeated Carlos Barreto (decision)
- Mark Kerr defeated Greg Stott (KO)
- Dwayne Carson defeated Houston Dorr (TKO)
- Alex Hunter defeated Harry Moskowitz (decision)

UFC 15.5: Ultimate Japan

12/21/97

Yokohama Arena (Yokohama, Japan)

Main Event: Randy Couture defeated Maurice Smith (decision, won UFC Heavyweight Championship)

Other Fights:

- Kazushi Sakuraba defeated Marcus Silveira (arm bar, won Ultimate Japan Heavyweight Tournament)
- Vitor Belfort defeated Joe Charles (arm bar)
- Frank Shamrock defeated Kevin Jackson (arm bar, won UFC Middleweight Championship)
- Kazushi Sakuraba vs. Marcus Silveira (no contest)
- David Abbott defeated Yoji Anjo (decision)
- Tra Telligman defeated Brad Kohler (arm bar)

UFC 16

3/13/98

Pontchartrain Center (New Orleans, Louisana)

Main Event: Frank Shamrock defeated Igor Zinoviev (KO)

Other Fights:

- Tsuyoshi Kosaka defeated Kimo Leopoldo (decision)
- Pat Miletich defeated Chris Brennan (choke, won UFC 16 Lightweight Championship)
- Jerry Bohlander defeated Kevin Jackson (arm bar)
- Pat Miletich defeated Townsend Saunders (arm bar)
- Mikey Burnett defeated Eugenio Tadeu (TKO)
- Chris Brennan defeated Courtney Turner (arm bar)
- LaVerne Clark defeated Josh Stuart (TKO)

UFC 17

5/15/98

Mobile Civic Center (Mobile, Alabama)

Main Event: Frank Shamrock defeated Jeremy Horn (knee bar)

Other Fights:

Pete William defeated Mark Coleman (KO)

Dan Henderson defeated Carlos Newton (decision, won UFC 17 Middleweight Tournament)

David Abbott defeated Hugo Duarte (TKO)

Mike Van Arsdale defeated Joe Pardo (Kimura)

Carlos Newton defeated Bob Gilstrap (triangle choke)

Dan Henderson defeated Allan Goes (decision)

Andre Roberts defeated Harry Moskowitz (decision)

Chuck Liddell defeated Noe Hernandez (decision)

UFC 17.5: Ultimate Brazil

10/16/98

Ginasio da Portuguesa (Sao Paulo, Brazil)

Main Event: Frank Shamrock defeated John Lober (submission to strikes)

Other Fights:

Vitor Belfort defeated Wanderlei Silva (TKO)

Pedro Rizzo defeated David Abbott (KO)

Pat Miletich defeated Mikey Burnett (decision)

Tsuyoshi Kohsaka defeated Pete Williams (decision)

Ebenezer Fontes Braga defeated Jeremey Horn (guillotine choke)

Cesar Marsucci defeated Paulo Santos (TKO)

Tulio Palhares defeated Adriano Santos (TKO)

UFC 18

1/8/99

Pontchartrain Center (New Orleans, Louisiana)

Main Event: Pat Miletich defeated Jorge Patino (decision)

Other Fights:

Pedro Rizzo defeated Mark Coleman (decision)

Bas Rutten defeated Tsuyoshi Kohsaka (TKO)

Tito Ortiz defeated Jerry Bohlander (doctor stoppage)

Mikey Burnett defeated Townsend Saunders (decision)

Evan Tanner defeated Darrel Gholar (rear naked choke)

Laverne Clark defeated Frank Caracci (submission to strikes)

UFC 19

3/5/99

Casino Magic (Bay St. Louis, Mississippi)

Main Event: Tito Ortiz defeated Vitor Belfort (TKO)

Other Fights:

Gary Goodridge defeated Andre Roberts (submission to strikes)

Jeremy Horn defeated Chuck Liddell (arm triangle)

Kevin Randleman defeated Maurice Smith (decision)

Evan Tanner defeated Valeri Ignatov (TKO)

Pete Williams defeated Jason Godsey (submissin to knee bar)

UFC 20

5/7/99

Boutwell Auditorium (Birmingham, Alabama)

Main Event: Bas Rutten defeated Kevin Randleman (decision, won UFC Heavyweight Championship)

Other Fights:

Pedro Rizzo defeated Tra Telligman (KO)

Pete Williams defeated Travis Fulton (arm bar)

Wanderlei Silva defeated Tony Petarra (KO)

Marcelo Mello defeated David Roberts (TKO)

Laverne Clark defeated Fabiano Iha (doctor stoppage)

Ron Waterman defeated Chris Condo (submission to strikes)

UFC 21

7/16/99

Five Seasons Events Center (Cedar Rapids, Iowa)

Main Event: Maurice Smith defeated Marco Ruas (corner stoppage)

Other Fights:

Pat Miletich defeated Andre Pederneiras (doctor stoppage)

Jeremy Horn defeated Daiju Takase (TKO)

Paul Jones defeated Flavio Luiz Moura (rear naked choke)

Tsuyoshi Kohsaka defeated Tim Lajcik (doctor stoppage)
Eugene Jackson defeated Royce Alger (KO)
Andre Roberts defeated Ron Waterman (KO)
Travis Fulton defeated David Dodd (decision)

UFC 22

9/24/99
Lake Charles Civic Center (Lake Charles, Louisiana)
Main Event: Frank Shamrock defeated Tito Ortiz (submission to strikes)
Other Fights:
Tim Lajcik vs. Ron Waterman (draw)
Jeremy Horn defeated Jason Godsey (arm bar)
Brad Kohler defeated Steve Judson (KO)
Chuck Liddell defeated Paul Jones (TKO)
Matt Hughes defeated Valeri Ignatov (decision)
John Lewis defeated Lowell Anderson (TKO)
Jens Pulver vs. Alfonso Alcarez (draw)

UFC 23: Ultimate Japan 2

11/19/99
Tokyo Bay NK Hall (Tokyo, Japan)
Main Event: Kevin Randleman defeated Pete Williams (decision, won UFC Heavyweight Championship)
Other Fights:
Pedro Rizzo defeated Tsuyoshi Kohsaka (TKO)
Kenichi Yamamoto defeated Katsuhisa Fujii (knee bar, won Ultimate Japan 2 Tournament)
Joe Slick defeated Jason DeLucia (TKO)
Eugene Jackson defeated Keiichiro Yamamiya (KO)
Kenichi Yamamoto defeated Daiju Takase (decision)
Katsuhisa Fujii defeated Masutatsu Yano (TKO)

UFC 24

3/10/00
Lake Charles Civic Center (Lake Charles, Louisiana)
Main Event: Tedd Williams defeated Steve Judson (TKO)
Other Fights:
Lance Gibson defeated Jermaine Andre (KO)
Dave Menne defeated Fabiano Iha (decision)
Bob Cook defeated Tiki Ghosn (rear naked choke)
Jens Pulver defeated David Velasquez (TKO)
Shonie Carter defeated Brad Gumm (decision)
Scott Adams defeated Ian Freeman (heel hook)

UFC 25: Ultimate Japan 3

4/14/00
Yoyogi National Gymnasium (Tokyo, Japan)
Main Event: Tito Ortiz defeated Wanderlei Silva (decision, won UFC Middleweight Championship)
Other Fights:
Murilo Bustamante defeated Yoji Anjo (arm triangle)
Sanae Kikuta defeated Eugene Jackson (arm bar)
Ron Waterman defeated Satoshi Honma (decision)
Ikuhisa Minowa defeated Joe Slick (TKO)
LaVerne Clark defeated Koji Oishi (decision)

UFC 26

6/9/00
Five Seasons Events Center (Cedar Rapids, Iowa)
Main Event: Kevin Randleman defeated Pedro Rizzo (decision)
Other Fights:
Tyrone Roberts defeated David Dodd (decision)
Pat Miletich defeated John Alessio (arm bar)
Amaury Bitetti defeated Alex Andrade (DQ)
Matt Hughes defeated Marcelo Aguiar (doctor stoppage)
Jens Pulver defeated Joao Roque (decision)
Ian Freeman defeated Nate Schroeder (submission to strikes)
Shonie Carter defeated Adrian Serrano (decision)

UFC 27

9/22/00
Lake Front Arena (New Orleans, Louisiana)
Main Event: Pedro Rizzo defeated Dan Severn (submission to strikes)
Other Fights:
Maurice Smith defeated Bobby Hoffman (decision)
Jeremy Horn defeated Eugene Jackson (arm bar)
Fabiano Iha defeated LaVerne Clark (arm bar)
Yuki Kondo defeated Alexandre Dantas (TKO)
Ian Freeman defeated Tedd Williams (decision)
Brad Gumm vs. C.J. Fernandes (draw)
Jeff Monson defeated Tim Lajcik (decision)

UFC 28

11/17/00

Trump Taj Mahal (Atlantic City, New Jersey)

Main Event: Randy Couture defeated Kevin Randleman (TKO, won UFC Heavyweight Championship)

Other Fights:

Renato Sobral defeated Maurice Smith (decision)
Josh Barnett defeated Gan McGee (TKO)
Andrei Arlovski defeated Aaron Brink (arm bar)
John Lewis defeated Jens Pulver (KO)
Mark Hughes defeated Alex Stiebling (decision)
Ben Earwood defeated Chris Lytle (decision)

UFC 29

12/16/00

Differ Ariake (Tokyo, Japan)

Main Event: Tito Ortiz defeated Yuki Kondo (neck crank)

Other Fights:

Pat Miletich defeated Kenichi Yamamoto (guillotine choke)
Matt Lindland defeated Yoji Anjo (TKO)
Fabiano Iha defeated Daiju Takase (TKO)
Even Tanner defeated Lance Gibson (TKO)
Dennis Hallman defeated Matt Hughes (arm bar)
Chuck Liddell defeated Jeff Monson (decision)

UFC 30

2/23/01

Trump Taj Mahal (Atlantic City, New Jersey)

Main Event: Tito Ortiz defeated Evan Tanner (KO)

Other Fights:

Jens Pulver defeated Caol Uno (decision, won UFC Bantamweight Championship)
Phil Baroni defeated Curtis Stout (decision)
Sean Sherk defeated Tiki Ghosn (submission)
Fabiano Iha defeated Phil Johns (arm bar)
Pedro Rizzo defeated Josh Barnett (KO)
Elvis Sinosic defeated Jeremy Horn (arm bar)
Bobby Hoffman defeated Mark Robinson (KO)

UFC 31

5/4/01

Trump Taj Mahal (Atlantic City, New Jersey)

Main Event: Randy Couture defeated Pedro Rizzo (decision)

Other Fights:

Carlos Newton defeated Pat Miletich (side choke, won UFC Welterweight Championship)
Chuck Liddell defeated Kevin Randleman (KO)
Shonie Carter defeated Matt Serra (KO)
Semmy Schilt defeated Pete Williams (TKO)
Matt Lindland defeated Ricardo Almeida (DQ)
B.J. Penn defeated Joey Gilbert (TKO)
Tony DeSouza defeated Steve Berger (decision)

UFC 32

6/29/01

Continental Airlines Arena (East Rutherford, New Jersey)

Main Event: Tito Ortiz defeated Elvis Sinosic (TKO)

Other Fights:

B.J. Penn defeated Din Thomas (TKO)
Josh Barnett defeated Semmy Schilt (arm bar)
Pat Miletich defeated Shonie Carter (KO)
Caol Uno defeated Fabiano Iha (TKO)
Vladimir Matyushenko defeated Yuki Kondo (decision)
Ricco Rodriguez defeated Andrei Arlovski (TKO)
Tony DeSouza defeated Paul Rodriguez (guillotine choke)

UFC 33

9/22/01

Mandalay Bay Events Center (Las Vegas, Nevada)

Main Event: Tito Ortiz defeated Vladimir Matyushenko (decision)

Other Fights:

Jens Pulver defeated Dennis Hallman (decision)
Chuck Liddell defeated Murilo Bustamante (decision)
Matt Serra defeated Yves Edwards (decision)
Dave Menne defeated Gil Castillo (decision)
Jutaro Nakao defeated Tony DeSouza (KO)
Ricardo Almeida defeated Eugene Jackson (triangle choke)
Din Thomas defeated Fabiano Iha (decision)

UFC 34

11/2/01

MGM Grand (Las Vegas, Nevada)

Main Event: Randy Couture defeated Pedro Rizzo (TKO)

Other Fights:

Ricco Rodriguez defeated Pete Williams (TKO)

Matt Hughes defeated Carlos Newton (KO, won UFC Welterweight Championship)

B.J. Penn defeated Caol Uno (KO)

Josh Barnett defeated Bobby Hoffman (submission to strikes)

Evan Tanner defeated Homer Moore (arm bar)

Matt Lindland defeated Phil Baroni (decision)

Frank Mir defeated Roberto Traven (arm bar)

UFC 35

1/11/02

Mohegan Sun Arena (Uncasville, Connecticut)

Main Event: Jens Pulver defeated B.J. Penn (decision)

Other Fights:

Ricco Rodriguez defeated Jeff Monson (TKO)

Murilo Bustamante defeated Dave Menne (KO, won UFC Middleweight Championship)

Chuck Liddell defeated Amar Suloev (decision)

Andrei Semenov defeated Ricardo Almeida (KO)

Kevin Randleman defeated Renato Sobral (decision)

Gil Castillo defeated Chris Brennan (decision)

Eugene Jackson defeated Keith Rockel (guillotine choke)

UFC 36

3/22/02

MGM Grand (Las Vegas, Nevada)

Main Event: Josh Barnett defeated Randy Couture (TKO, won UFC Heavyweight Championship)

Other Fights:

Pedro Rizzo defeated Andrei Arlovski (KO)

Matt Hughes defeated Hayato Sakurai (TKO)

Matt Lindland defeated Pat Miletich (TKO)

Evan Tanner defeated Elvis Sinosic (doctor stoppage)

Frank Mir defeated Pete Williams (shoulder lock)

Matt Serra defeated Kelly Dullanty (triangle choke)

Sean Sherk defeated Jutaro Nakao (decision)

UFC 37

5/10/02

CenturyTel Center (Bossier City, Louisiana)

Main Event: Murilo Bustamante defeated Matt Lindland (guillotine choke)

Other Fights:

Ricco Rodridguez defeated Tsuyoshi Kosaka (TKO)

B.J. Penn defeated Paul Creighton (TKO)

Phil Baroni defeated Amar Suloev (KO)

Caol Uno defeated Yves Edwards (decision)

Ivan Salaverry defeated Andrei Semenov (TKO)

Benji Radach defeated Steve Barger (TKO)

Robbie Lawler defeated Aaron Riley (decision)

UFC 37.5

6/22/02

Bellagio Hotel and Casino (Las Vegas, Nevada)

Main Event: Chuck Liddell defeated Vitor Belfort (decision)

Other Fights:

Benji Radach defeated Nick Serra (decision)

Pete Spratt defeated Zach Light (arm bar)

Robbie Lawler defeated Steve Berger (TKO)

Tony Fryklund defeated Rodrigo Ruas (TKO)

Yves Edwards defeated Joao Marcos Pierini (TKO)

UFC 38

7/12/02

Royal Albert Hall (London, England)

Main Event: Matt Hughes defeated Carlos Newton (TKO)

Other Fights:

Ian Freeman defeated Frank Mir (TKO)

Mark Weir defeated Eugene Jackson (KO)

Elvis Sinosic defeated Renato Sobral (decision)

Genki Sudo defeated Leigh Remedios (rear naked choke)

Phillip Miller defeated James Zikic (decision)

Evan Tanner defeated Chris Haseman (decision)

UFC 39

9/27/02

Mohegan Sun Arena (Uncasville, Connecticut)

Main Event: Ricco Rodriguez defeated Randy Couture (submission to strikes, won UFC Heavyweight Championship)

Other Fights:

- Tim Sylvia defeated Wesley Correira (corner stoppage)
- B.J. Penn defeated Matt Serra (decision)
- Caol Uno defeated Din Thomas (decision)
- Gan McGee defeated Pedro Rizzo (corner stoppage)
- Phil Baroni defeated Dave Menne (KO)
- Matt Lindland defeated Ivan Salaverry (decision)
- Sean Sherk defeated Benji Radach (TKO)

UFC 40

11/22/02

MGM Grand (Las Vegas, Nevada)

Main Event: Tito Ortz defeated Ken Shamrock (corner stoppage)

Other Fights:

- Chuck Liddell defeated Renato Sobral (TKO)
- Matt Hughes defeated Gil Castillo (TKO)
- Carlos Newton defeated Pete Spratt (Kimura)
- Robbie Lawler defeated Tiki Ghosn (TKO)
- Andrei Arlovski defeated Ian Freeman (TKO)
- Vladimir Matyushenko defeated Travis Wiuff (submission to strikes)
- Phillip Miller defeated Mark Weir (rear naked choke)

UFC 41

2/28/03

Boardwalk Hall (Atlantic City, New Jersey)

Main Event: Tim Sylvia defeated Ricco Rodriguez (KO, won UFC Heavyweight Championship)

Other Fights:

- Frank Mir defeated David Abbott (toe hold)
- B.J. Penn vs. Caol Uno (draw)
- Matt Lindland defeated Phil Baroni (decision)
- Vladimir Matyushenko defeated Pedro Rizzo (decision)
- Din Thomas defeated Matt Serra (decision)
- Gan McGee defeated Alexandre Dantas (TKO)
- Yves Edwards defeated Rich Clementi (rear naked choke)

UFC 42

4/25/03

American Airlines Arena (Miami, Florida)

Main Event: Matt Hughes defeated Sean Sherk (decision)

Other Fights:

- Pete Spratt defeated Robbie Lawler (submission)
- Wesley Correira defeated Sean Alvarez (TKO)
- Rich Franklin defeated Evan Tanner (TKO)
- Duane Ludwig defeated Genki Sudo (decision)
- Dave Strasser defeated Romie Aram (decision)
- Hermes Franca defeated Richard Crunkilton (decision)
- David Loiseau defeated Mark Weir (KO)

UFC 43

6/6/03

Thomas and Mack Center (Las Vegas, Nevada)

Main Event: Randy Couture defeated Chuck Liddell (TKO, won UFC Interim Light Heavyweight Championship)

Other Fights:

- Kimo Leopoldo defeated David Abbott (arm triangle)
- Vitor Belfort defeated Marvin Eastman (TKO)
- Ian Freeman vs. Vernon White (draw)
- Frank Mir defeated Wes Sims (DQ)
- Yves Edwards defeated Eddie Ruiz (decision)
- Falaniko Vitale defeated Matt Lindland (TKO)
- Pedro Rizzo defeated Tra Telligman (doctor stoppage)

UFC 44

9/26/03

Red Rock Resort Spa and Casino (Las Vegas, Nevada)

Main Event: Randy Couture defeated Tito Ortiz (decision, unifies UFC Interim Light Heavyweight Championship and UFC Light Heavyweight Championship)

Other Fights:

- Andrei Arlovski defeated Vladimir Matyushenko (KO)
- Tim Sylvia defeated Gan McGee (KO)
- Jorge Rivera defeated David Loiseau (decision)
- Rich Franklin defeated Edwin DeWees (TKO)

Karo Parisyan defeated Dave Strasser (Kimura)
Josh Thomson defeated Gerald Strebendt (KO)
Nick Diaz defeated Jeremy Jackson (arm bar)
Hermes Franca defeated Caol Uno (KO)

UFC 45

11/21/03

Mohegan Sun Arena (Uncasville, Connecticut)

Main Event: Matt Hughes defeated Frank Trigg (rear naked choke)

Other Fights:

Matt Lindland defeated Falinko Vitale (submission to strikes)
Wesley Correira defeated David Abbott (doctor stoppage)
Robbie Lawler defeated Chris Lytle (decision)
Evan Tanner defeated Phil Baroni (TKO)
Pedro Rizzo defeated Ricco Rodriguez (decision)
Keith Rockel defeated Chris Liguori (guillotine choke)
Yves Edwards defeated Nick Agallar (TKO)

UFC 46

1/31/04

Mandalay Bay Events Center (Las Vegas, Nevada)

Main Event: Vitor Belfor defeated Randy Couture (doctor stoppage, won UFC Light Heavyweight Championship)

Other Fights:

Renato Verissimo defeated Carlos Newton (decision)
B.J. Penn defeated Matt Hughes (rear naked choke, won UFC Welterweight Championship)
Frank Mir defeated Wes Sims (KO)
Lee Murray defeated Jorge Rivera (triangle arm bar)
Georges St. Pierre defeated Karo Parisyan (decision)
Josh Thomson defeated Hermes Franca (decision)
Matt Serra defeated Jeff Curaan (decision)

UFC 47

4/2/04

Mandalay Bay Events Center (Las Vegas, Nevada)

Main Event: Chuck Liddell defeated Tito Ortiz (KO)

Other Fights:

Chris Lytle defeated Tiki Ghosn (side choke)
Yves Edwards defeated Hermes Franca (decision)
Andrei Arlovski defeated Wesley Correira (TKO)
Nick Diaz defeated Robbie Lawler (KO)
Mike Kyle defeated Wes Sims (KO)
Jonathan Wiezorek defeated Wade Shipp (TKO)
Genki Sudo defeated Mike Brown (arm bar)

UFC 48

6/19/04

Mandalay Bay Arena (Las Vegas, Nevada)

Main Event: Ken Shamrock defeated Kimo Leopoldo (TKO)

Other Fights:

Frank Trigg defeated Dennis Hallman (TKO)
Frank Mir defeated Tim Sylvia (arm bar, won UFC Heavyweight Championship)
Matt Hughes defeated Renato Verissimo (decision)
Evan Tanner defeated Phil Baroni (decision)
Matt Serra defeated Ivan Menjivar (decision)
Georges St. Pierre defeated Jay Hieron (TKO)
Trevor Prangley defeated Curtis Stout (neck crank)

UFC 49

8/21/04

MGM Grand (Las Vegas, Nevada)

Main Event: Randy Couture defeated Vitor Belfort (doctor stoppage, won UFC Light Heavyweight Championship)

Other Fights:

Joe Riggs defeated Joe Doerkson (submission to strikes)
Chuck Liddell defeated Vernon White (KO)
David Terrell defeated Matt Lindland (KO)
Justin Eilers defeated Mike Kyle (KO)
Chris Lytle defeated Ronald Jhun (guillotine choke)
Karo Parisyan defeated Nick Diaz (decision)
Yves Edwards defeated Josh Thomson (KO)

UFC 50

10/22/04

Trump Plaza (Atlantic City, New Jersey)

Main Event: Tito Ortiz defeated Patrick Côté (decision)

Other Fights:

Rich Franklin defeated Jorge Rivera (arm bar)
Matt Hughes defeated Georges St. Pierre (arm bar, won UFC Welterweight Championship)
Frank Trigg defeated Renato Verissimo (TKO)
Evan Tanner defeated Robbie Lawler (triangle choke)
Ivan Salaverry defeated Tony Fryklund (body triangle)
Travis Lutter defeated Marvin Eastman (KO)

UFC 51

2/5/05
Mandalay Bay Arena (Las Vegas, Nevada)
Main Event: Tito Ortiz defeated Vitor Belfort (decision)
Other Fights:

Pete Sell defeated Phil Baroni (guillotine)
Andrei Arlovski defeated Tim Sylvia (Achilles lock, won UFC Interim Heavyweight Championship)
Evan Tanner defeated David Terrell (TKO, won UFC Middleweight Championship)
Paul Buentello defeated Justin Eilers (KO)
Mike Kyle defeated James Irvin (KO)
David Loiseau defeated Gideon Ray (TKO)
Karo Parisyan defeated Chris Lytle (decision)
Nick Diaz defeated Drew Fickett (TKO)

The Ultimate Fighter 1 Finale

4/9/05
Cox Pavillion (Las Vegas, Nevada)
Main Event: Rich Franklin defeated Ken Shamrock (TKO)
Other Fights:

Forrest Griffin defeated Stephan Bonnar (decision, won Light Heavyweight *TUF* Tournament)
Diego Sanchez defeated Kenny Florian (TKO, won Middleweight *TUF* Tournament)
Sam Hoger defeated Bobby Southworth (decision)
Chris Leben defeated Jason Thacker (TKO)
Josh Koscheck defeated Chris Sanford (KO)
Nate Quarry defeated Lodune Sincaid (TKO)
Mike Swick defeated Alex Schoenauer (KO)
Alex Karalexis defeated Josh Rafferty (TKO)

UFC 52

4/16/05
MGM Grand (Las Vegas, Nevada)
Main Event: Chuck Liddell defeated Randy Couture (KO, won UFC Light Heavyweight Champion)
Other Fights:

Renato Sobral defeated Travis Wiuff (arm bar)
Matt Hughes defeated Frank Trigg (rear naked choke)
Matt Lindland defeated Travis Lutter (guillotine choke)
Georges St. Pierre defeated Jason Miller (decision)
Ivan Salaverry defeated Joe Riggs (triangle choke)
Joe Doerksen defeated Patrick Côté (rear naked choke)
Mike Van Arsdale defeated John Marsh (decision)

UFC 53

6/4/05
Boardwalk Hall (Atlantic City, New Jersey)
Main Event: Andrei Arlovski defeated Justin Eilers (TKO)
Other Fights:

Karo Parisyan defeated Matt Serra (decision)
Rich Franklin defeated Evan Tanner (doctor stoppage, won UFC Middleweight Championship)
Forrest Griffin defeated Bill Mahood (rear naked choke)
Paul Buentello defeated Kevin Jordan (guillotine choke)
Nathan Quarry defeated Shonie Carter (TKO)
David Loiseau defeated Charles McCarthy (TKO)
Nick Diaz defeated Koji Oishi (TKO)

Ultimate Fight Night

8/6/05
Cox Pavillion (Las Vegas, Nevada)
Main Event:

Nate Marquardt defeated Ivan Salaverry (decision)
Chris Leben defeated Patrick Côté (decision)
Stephan Bonar defeated Sam Hoger (decision)
Nate Quarry defeated Pete Sell (KO)
Josh Koscheck defeated Pete Spratt (rear naked choke)

Mike Swick defeated Gideon Ray (KO)
Kenny Florian defeated Alex Karalexis (doctor stoppage)
Drew Fickett defeated Josh Neer (rear naked choke)

UFC 54

8/20/05
MGM Grand (Las Vegas, Nevada)
Main Event: Chuck Liddell defeated Jeremy Horn (doctor stoppage)
Other Fights:

Tim Sylvia defeated Tra Telligman (KO)
Randy Couture defeated Mike Van Arsdale (anaconda choke)
Diego Sanchez defeated Brian Gassaway (submission to strikes)
Georges St. Pierre defeated Frank Trigg (rear naked choke)
Matt Lindland defeated Joe Doerksen (decision)
Trevor Prangley defeated Travis Lutter (decision)
James Irvin defeated Terry Martin (KO)

Ultimate Fight Night 2

10/3/05
Hard Rock Hotel and Casino (Las Vegas, Nevada)
Main Event: David Loiseau defeated Evan Tanner (TKO)
Other Fights:

Chris Leben defeated Edwin DeWees (arm bar)
Brandon Vera defeated Fabiano Scherner (TKO)
Drew Fickett defeated Josh Koscheck (rear naked choke)
Spencer Fisher defeated Thiago Alves (triangle choke)
Jon Fitch defeated Brock Larson (decision)
Jonathan Goulet defeated Jay Hieron (TKO)

UFC 55

10/7/05
Mohegan Sun Arena (Uncasville, Connecticut)
Main Event: Andrei Arlovski defeated Paul Buentello (KO, won UFC Heavyweight Championship)
Other Fights:

Forrest Griffin defeated Elvis Sinosic (TKO)
Branden Lee Hinkle defeated Sean Gannon (TKO)
Renato Sobral defeated Chael Sonnen (triangle choke)
Joe Riggs defeated Chris Lytle (doctor stoppage)
Jorge Rivera defeated Dennis Hallman (decision)
Marcio Cruz defeated Keigo Kunihara (rear naked choke)
Alessio Sakara vs. Ron Faircloth (no contest)

The Ultimate Fighter 2 Finale

11/5/05
Hard Rock Hotel and Casino (Las Vegas, Nevada)
Main Event: Diego Sanchez defeated Nick Diaz (decision)
Other Fights:

Rashad Evans defeated Brad Imes (decision, won Heavyweight *TUF* Tournament)
Joe Stevenson defeated Luke Cummo (decision, won Welterweight *TUF* Tournament)
Kenny Florian defeated Kit Cope (rear naked choke)
Josh Burkman defeated Sammy Morgan (KO)
Melvin Guillard defeated Marcus Davis (TKO)
Keith Jardine defeated Kerry Schall (TKO)

UFC 56

11/19/05
MGM Grand (Las Vegas, Nevada)
Main Event: Rich Franklin defeated Nathan Quarry (KO)
Other Fights:

Gabriel Gonzaga defeated Kevin Jordan (KO)
Matt Hughes defeated Joe Riggs (Kimura)
Georges St. Pierre defeated Sean Sherk (TKO)
Jeremy Horn defeated Trevor Prangley (decision)
Sam Hoger defeated Jeff Newton (rear naked choke)
Thiago Alves defeated Ansar Chalangov (TKO)
Nick Thompson defeated Keith Wisniewski (decision)

Ultimate Fight Night 3

11/16/06
Hard Rock Hotel and Casino (Las Vegas, Nevada)
Main Event: Tim Sylvia defeated Assuerio Silva (decision)

Other Fights:

Stephan Bonnar defeated James Irvin (Kimura)
Chris Leben defeated Jorge Rivera (TKO)
Josh Burkman defeated Drew Fickett (guillotine choke)
Josh Neer defeated Melvin Guillard (triangle choke)
Duane Ludwig defeated Jonathan Goulet (TKO)
Spencer Fisher defeated Aaron Riley (doctor stoppage)
Jason Von Flue defeated Alex Karalexis (arm triangle)

UFC 57

2/4/06
Mandalay Bay Events Center (Las Vegas, Nevada)
Main Event: Chuck Liddell defeated Randy Couture (KO)
Other Fights:

Marcio Cruz defeated Frank Mir (TKO)
Brandon Vera defeated Justin Eilers (KO)
Renato Sobral defeated Mike Van Arsdale (rear naked choke)
Joe Riggs defeated Nick Diaz (decision)
Alessio Sakara defeated Elvis Sinosic (decision)
Paul Buentello defeated Gilbert Aldana (TKO)
Jeff Monson defeated Branden Lee Hinkle (north-south choke)
Keith Jardine defeated Mike Whitehead (decision)

UFC 58

3/4/06
Mandalay Bay Events Center (Las Vegas, Nevada)
Main Event: Rich Franklin defeated David Loiseau (decision)
Other Fights:

Georges St. Pierre defeated B.J. Penn (decision)
Mike Swick defeated Steve Vigneault (guillotine choke)
Nathan Marquardt defeated Joe Doerksen (decision)
Mark Hominick defeated Yves Edwards (triangle arm bar)
Sam Stout defeated Spencer Fisher (decision)
Jason Lambert defeated Rob MacDonald (Kimura)
Tom Murphy defeated Icho Larenas (TKO)

Ultimate Fight Night 4

4/6/06
Hard Rock Hotel and Casino (Las Vegas, Nevada)
Main Event: Stephan Bonnar defeated Keith Jardine (decision)
Other Fights:

Rashad Evans defeated Sam Hoger (decision)
Josh Neer defeated Joe Stevenson (decision)
Chris Leben defeated Luigi Fioravanti (decision)
Luke Cummo defeated Jason Von Flue (decision)
Jon Fitch defeated Josh Burkman (rear naked choke)
Dan Christison defeated Brad Imes (arm bar)
Josh Koscheck defeated Ansar Chalangov (rear naked choke)
Chael Sonnen defeated Trevor Prangley (decision)

UFC 59

4/15/06
Arrowhead Pond (Anaheim, California)
Main Event: Tim Sylvia defeated Andrei Arlovski defeated (TKO, won UFC Heavyweight Championship)
Other Fights:

Tito Ortiz defeated Forrest Griffin (decision)
Sean Sherk defeated Nick Diaz (decision)
Evan Tanner defeated Justin Levens (triangle choke)
Jeff Monson defeated Marcio Cruz (decision)
Karo Parisyan defeated Nick Thompson (submission to strikes)
David Terrell defeated Scott Smith (rear naked choke)
Jason Lambert defeated Terry Martin (TKO)
Thiago Alves defeated Derrick Noble (TKO)

UFC 60

5/27/06
Staples Center (Los Angeles, California)
Main Event: Matt Hughes defeated Royce Gracie (TKO)
Other Fights:

Diego Sanchez defeated John Alessio (decision)
Brandon Vera defeated Assuerio Silva (guillotine choke)

Mike Swick defeated Joe Riggs (guillotine choke)
Dean Lister defeated Alessio Sakara (triangle choke)
Jeremy Horn defeated Chael Sonnen (arm bar)
Spencer Fisher defeated Matt Wiman (KO)
Gabriel Gonzaga defeated Fabiano Scherner (TKO)
Melvin Guillard defeated Rick Davis (KO)

The Ultimate Fighter 3 Finale

6/24/06

Hard Rock Hotel and Casino (Las Vegas, Nevada)

Main Event: Kenny Florian defeated Sam Stout (rear naked choke)

Other Fights:

Michael Bisping defeated Josh Haynes (TKO, won *TUF* Light Heavyweight Tournament)
Kendall Grove defeated Ed Herman (decision, won *TUF* Middleweight Tournament)
Keith Jardine defeated Wilson Gouveia (decision)
Rory Singer defeated Ross Pointon (triangle choke)
Kalib Starnes defeated Danny Abbadi (rear naked choke)
Luigi Fioravanti defeated Solomon Hutcherson (KO)
Matt Hamill defeated Jesse Forbes (TKO)
Mike Nickels defeated Wes Combs (rear naked choke)

Ultimate Fight Night 5

6/28/06

Hard Rock Hotel and Casino (Las Vegas, Nevada)

Main Event: Anderson Silva defeated Chris Leben (KO)

Other Fights:

Jonathan Goulet defeated Luke Cummo (decision)
Rashad Evans defeated Stephan Bonnar (decision)
Mark Hominick defeated Jorge Gurgel (decision)
Josh Koscheck defeated Dave Menne (decision)
Jason Lambert defeated Branden Lee Hinkle (TKO)
Jon Fitch defeated Thiago Alves (TKO)
Rob MacDonald defeated Kristian Rothaermel (arm bar)
Jorge Santiago defeated Justin Levens (KO)

UFC 61

7/8/06

Mandalay Bay Events Center (Las Vegas, Nevada)

Main Event: Tim Sylvia defeated Andrei Arlovski (decision)

Other Fights:

Tito Ortiz defeated Ken Shamrock (TKO)
Josh Burkman defeated Josh Neer (decision)
Frank Mir defeated Dan Christison (decision)
Joe Stevenson defeated Yves Edwards (TKO)
Hermes Franca defeated Joe Jordan (triangle choke)
Jeff Monson defeated Anthony Perosh (TKO)
Cheick Kongo defeated Gilbert Aldana (TKO)
Drew Fickett defeated Kurt Pellegrino (rear naked choke)

Ultimate Fight Night 6

8/17/06

Red Rock Resort Spa and Casino (Las Vegas, Nevada)

Main Event: Diego Sanchez defeated Karo Parisyan (decision)

Other Fights:

Chris Leben defeated Jorge Santiago (KO)
Dean Lister defeated Yuki Sasaki (decision)
Josh Koscheck defeated Jonathan Goulet (submission to strikes)
Martin Kampmann defeated Crafton Wallace (rear naked choke)
Joe Riggs defeated Jason Von Flue (triangle choke)
Jake O'Brien defeated Kristof Midoux (TKO)
Forrest Petz defeated Sammy Morgan (decision)
Anthony Torres defeated Pay Healy (rear naked choke)

UFC 62

8/26/06

Mandalay Bay Events Center (Las Vegas, Nevada)

Main Event: Chuck Liddell defeated Renato Sobral (TKO)

Other Fights:

Forrest Griffin defeated Stephan Bonnar (decision)
Hermes Franca defeated Jamie Varner (arm bar)
Nick Diaz defeated Josh Neer (Kimura)

Cheick Kongo defeated Christian Wellisch (KO)
Eric Schafer defeated Rob MacDonald (arm triangle)
Wilson Gouveia defeated Wes Combs (rear naked choke)
David Heath defeated Cory Walmsley (rear naked choke)
Yushi Okami defeated Alan Belcher (decision)

UFC 63

9/23/06
Arrowhead Pond (Anaheim, California)
Main Event: Matt Hughes defeated B.J. Penn (TKO)
Other Fights:
Mick Swick defeated David Loiseau (decision)
Rashad Evans defeated Jason Lambert (KO)
Joe Lauzon defeated Jens Pulver (KO)
Melvin Guillard defeated Gabe Ruediger (TKO)
Roger Huerta defeated Jason Dent (decision)
Eddie Sanchez defeated Mario Neto (KO)
Jorge Gurgel defeated Danny Abbadi (decision)
Tyson Griffin defeated David Lee (rear naked choke)

Ortiz vs. Shamrock 3

10/10/06
Seminole Hard Rock Hotel and Casino (Hollywood, Florida)
Main Event: Tito Ortiz defeated Ken Shamrock (KO)
Other Fights:
Kendall Grove defeated Chris Price (submission to strikes)
Jason MacDonald defeated Ed Herman (triangle choke)
Matt Hamill defeated Seth Petruzelli (decision)
Nate Marquardt defeated Crafton Wallace (rear naked choke)
Tony DeSouza defeated Dustin Hazelett (Kimura)
Rory Singer defeated Josh Haynes (decision)
Thiago Alves defeated John Alessio (decision)
Marcus Davis defeated Forrest Petz (guillotine choke)

UFC 64

10/14/06
Mandalay Bay Events Center (Las Vegas, Nevada)
Main Event: Anderson Silva defeated Rich Franlkin (TKO, won UFC Middleweight Championship)
Other Fights:
Sean Sherk defeated Kenny Florian (decision, won UFC Lightweight Championship)
Carmelo Marrero defeated Cheick Kongo (decision)
Jon Fitch defeated Kuniyoshi Hironaka (decision)
Spencer Fisher defeated Dan Lauzon (TKO)
Yushin Okami defeated Kalib Starnes (TKO)
Clay Guida defeated Justin James (rear naked choke)
Kurt Pellegrino defeated Junior Assuncao (rear naked choke)

The Ultimate Fighter 4 Finale

11/11/06
Hard Rock Hotel and Casino (Las Vegas, Nevada)
Main Event: Matt Serra defeated Chris Lytle (decision, won *TUF* Welterweight Tournament)
Other Fights:
Travis Lutter defeated Patrick Côté (arm bar, won *TUF* Middleweight Tournament)
Din Thomas defeated Rich Clementi (rear naked choke)
Pete Spratt defeated Jeremy Jackson (submission, neck injury)
Scott Smith defeated Pete Sell (KO)
Charles McCarthy defeated Gideon Ray (arm bar)
Martin Kampmann defeated Thales Leites (decision)

UFC 65

11/18/06
ARCO Arena (Sacramento, California)
Main Event: Georges St. Pierre defeated Matt Hughes (TKO, won UFC Welterweight Championship)
Other Fights:
Tim Sylvia defeated Jeff Monson (decision)
Drew McFedries defeated Alessio Sakara (TKO)
Brandon Vera defeated Frank Mir (TKO)
Joe Stevenson defeated Dokonjonosuke Mishima (guillotine choke)
Nick Diaz defeated Gleison Tibau (TKO)

Antoni Hardonk defeated Sherman Pendergrast (KO)
James Irvin defeated Hector Ramirez (TKO)
Jake O'Brien defeated Josh Schockman (decision)

UFC Fight Night 7

12/13/06
MCAS Miramar (San Diego, California)
Main Event: Diego Sanchez defeated Joe Riggs (KO)
Other Fights:

Josh Koscheck defeated Jeff Joslin (decision)
Karo Parisyan defeated Drew Fickett (decision)
Marcus Davis defeated Shonie Carter (decision)
Alan Belcher defeated Jorge Santiago (KO)
Luigi Fioravanti defeated Dave Menne (TKO)
David Heath defeated Victor Valimaki (decision)
Brock Larson defeated Keita Nakamura (decision)
Logan Clark defeated Steve Byrnes (decision)

UFC 66

12/30/06
MGM Grand (Las Vegas, Nevada)
Main Event: Chuck Liddell defeated Tito Ortiz (TKO)
Other Fights:

Keith Jardine defeated Forrest Griffin (TKO)
Jason MacDonald defeated Chris Leben (guillotine choke)
Andrei Arlovski defeated Marcio Cruz (KO)
Michael Bisping defeated Eric Schafer (TKO)
Thiago Alves defeated Tony DeSouza (KO)
Gabriel Gonzaga defeated Carmelo Marrero (arm bar)
Yushin Okami defeated Rory Singer (submission to strikes)
Christian Wellish defeated Anthony Perosh (decision)

UFC Fight Night 8

1/25/07
Seminole Hard Rock Hotel and Casino (Hollywood, Florida)
Main Event: Rashad Evans defeated Sean Salmon (KO)
Other Fights:

Jake O'Brien defeated Heath Herring (decision)
Hermes Franca defeated Spencer Fisher (TKO)
Nate Marquardt defeated Dean Lister (decision)
Josh Burkman defeated Chad Reiner (decision)
Ed Herman defeated Chris Prince (arm bar)
Din Thomas defeated Clay Guida (decision)
Rich Clementi defeated Ross Pointon (rear naked choke)

UFC 67

2/3/07
Mandalay Bay Events Center (Las Vegas, Nevada)
Main Event: Anderson Silva defeated Travis Lutter (triangle choke)
Other Fights:

Quinton Jackson defeated Marvin Eastman (KO)
Mirko Filipovic defeated Eddie Sanchez (TKO)
Roger Huerta defeated John Halverson (TKO)
Patrick Côté defeated Scott Smith (decision)
Frank Edgar defeated Tyson Griffin (decision)
Terry Martin defeated Jorge Rivera (KO)
Lyoto Machida defeated Sam Hoger (decision)
Dustin Hazelett defeated Diego Saraiva (decision)

UFC 68

3/3/07
Nationwide Arena (Columbus, Ohio)
Main Event: Randy Couture defeated Tim Sylvia (decision, won UFC Heavyweight Championship)
Other Fights:

Rich Franklin defeated Jason MacDonald (corner stoppage)
Matt Hughes defeated Chris Lytle (decision)
Martin Kampmann defeated Drew McFedries (arm triangle)
Jason Lambert defeated Renato Sobral (KO)
Matt Hamill defeated Rex Holman (TKO)
Jon Fitch defeated Luigi Fioravanti (rear naked choke)
Gleison Tibau defeated Jason Dent (decision)
Jamie Varner defeated Jason Gilliam (rear naked choke)

UFC Fight Night 9

4/5/07
The Palms Casino Resort (Las Vegas, Nevada)

Main Event: Joe Stevenson defeated Melvin Guillard (guillotine choke)

Other Fights:

Justin McCully defeated Antoni Hardonk (decision)

Kenny Florian defeated Dokonjonosuke Mishima (rear naked choke)

Kuniyoshi Hironaka defeated Forrest Petz (decision)

Wilson Gouveia defeated Seth Petruzelli (guillotine choke)

Drew Fickett defeated Keita Nakamura (decision)

Kurt Pellegrino defeated Nate Mohr (ankle lock)

Roan Carneiro defeated Rich Clementi (decision)

Thiago Tavares defeated Naoyuki Kotani (decision)

UFC 69

4/7/07

Toyota Center (Houston, Texas)

Main Event: Matt Serra defeated Georges St. Pierre (TKO, won UFC Welterweight Championship)

Other Fights:

Josh Koscheck defeated Diego Sanchez (decision)

Roger Huerta defeated Leonard Garcia (decision)

Yushin Okami defeated Mike Swick (decision)

Kendall Grove defeated Alan Belcher (D'Arce choke)

Heath Herring defeated Brad Imes (decision)

Thales Leites defeated Pete Sell (decision)

Marcus Davis defeated Pete Spratt (Achilles lock)

Luke Cummo defeated Josh Haynes (KO)

UFC 70

4/21/07

Manchester Evening News Arena (Manchester, England)

Main Event: Gabriel Gonzaga defeated Mirko Filipovic (KO)

Other Fights:

Andrei Arlovski defeated Fabricio Werdum (decision)

Michael Bisping defeated Elvis Sinosic (TKO)

Lyoto Machida defeated David Heath (decision)

Cheick Kongo defeated Assuerio Silva (decision)

Terry Etim defeated Matt Grice (guillotine choke)

Junior Assuncao defeated David Lee (rear naked choke)

Alessio Sakara defeated Victor Valimaki (TKO)

Jess Liaudin defeated Dennis Siver (arm bar)

Paul Taylor defeated Edilberto de Oliveira (TKO)

UFC 71

5/26/07

MGM Grand (Las Vegas, Nevada)

Main Event: Quinton Jackson defeated Chuck Liddell (TKO, won UFC Light Heavyweight Championship)

Other Fights:

Karo Parisyan defeated Josh Burkman (decision)

Terry Martin defeated Ivan Salaverry (TKO)

Houston Alexander defeated Keith Jardine (KO)

Kalib Starnes defeated Chris Leben (decision)

Thiago Silva defeated James Irvin (TKO)

Alan Belcher defeated Sean Salmon (guillotine choke)

Jeremy Stephens defeated Din Thomas (arm bar)

Wilson Gouveia defeated Carmelo Marrero (guillotine choke)

UFC Fight Night 10

6/12/07

Seminole Hard Rock Hotel and Casino (Hollywood, Florida)

Main Event: Spencer Fisher defeated Sam Stout (decision)

Other Fights:

Jon Fitch defeated Roan Carneiro (rear naked choke)

Drew McFedries defeated Jordan Radev (KO)

Thiago Tavares defeated Jason Black (triangle choke)

Forrest Petz defeated Luigi Fioravanti (decision)

Tamdan McCrory defeated Pete Spratt (triangle choke)

Gleison Tibau defeated Jeff Cox (arm triangle)

Anthony Johnson defeated Chad Reiner (KO)

Nate Mohr defeated Luke Caudillo (decision)

UFC 72

6/16/07

The Odyssey (Belfast, Northern Ireland)

Main Event: Rich Franklin defeated Yushin Okami (decision)

Other Fights:

Forrest Griffin defeated Hector Ramirez (decision)
Tyson Griffin defeated Clay Guida (decision)
Ed Herman defeated Scott Smith (rear naked choke)
Jason MacDonald defeated Rory Singer (TKO)
Eddie Sanchez defeated Colin Robinson (TKO)
Dustin Hazelett defeated Stevie Lynch (anaconda choke)
Marcus Davis defeated Jason Tan (KO)

The Ultimate Fighter 5 Finale

6/23/07

Palms Hotel and Casino (Las Vegas, Nevada)

Main Event: B.J. Penn defeated Jens Pulver (rear naked choke)

Other Fights:

Nate Diaz defeated Manvel Gambaryan (injury, dislocated shoulder, won *TUF* Lightweight Tournament)
Thales Leites defeated Floyd Sword (arm triangle)
Roger Huerta defeated Doug Evans (TKO)
Joe Lauzon defeated Brandon Melendez (triangle choke)
Cole Miller defeated Andy Wang (TKO)
Rob Emerson vs. Gray Maynard (no contest)
Leonard Garcia defeated Allen Berube (rear naked choke)
Matt Wiman defeated Brian Geraghty (TKO)

UFC 73

7/7/07

ARCO Arena (Sacramento, California)

Main Event: Anderson Silva defeated Nate Marquardt (TKO)

Other Fights:

Tito Ortiz vs. Rashad Evans (draw)
Sean Sherk defeated Hermes Franca
Antonio Rodrigo Nogueira defeated Heath Herring (decision)
Kenny Florian defeated Alvin Robinson (TKO)
Stephan Bonnar defeated Mike Nickels (rear naked choke)
Jorge Gurgel defeated Diego Saraiva (decision)
Chris Lytle defeated Jason Gilliam (Kimura)
Frankie Edgar defeated Mark Bocek (TKO)

UFC 74

8/25/07

Mandalay Bay Events Center (Las Vegas, Nevada)

Main Event: Randy Couture defeated Gabriel Gonzaga (TKO)

Other Fights:

Georges St. Pierre defeated Josh Koscheck (decision)
Roger Huerta defeated Alberto Crane (TKO)
Joe Stevenson defeated Kurt Pellegrino (decision)
Patrick Côté defeated Kendall Grove (KO)
Renato Sobral defeated David Heath (anaconda choke)
Frank Mir defeated Antoni Hardonk (Kimura)
Thales Leites defeated Ryan Jensen (arm bar)
Clay Guida defeated Marcus Aurelio (decision)

UFC 75

9/8/07

The O_2 Arena (London, England)

Main Event: Quinton Jackson defeated Dan Henderson (decision, unifies Pride Middleweight Championship and UFC Light Heavyweight Championship)

Other Fights:

Michael Bisping defeated Matt Hamill (decision)
Cheick Kongo defeated Mirko Filipovic (decision)
Houston Alexander defeated Alessio Sakara (TKO)
Marcus Davis defeated Paul Taylor (arm bar)
Gleison Tibau defeated Terry Etim (decision)
Thiago Silva defeated Tomasz Drwal (KO)
Dennis Siver defeated Naoyuki Kotani (KO)
Jess Liaudin defeated Anthony Torres (TKO)

UFC Fight Night 11

9/19/07

The Palms Casino Resort (Las Vegas, Nevada)

Main Event: Kenny Florian defeated Din Thomas (rear naked choke)

Other Fights:

Chris Leben defeated Terry Martin (KO)

Nate Diaz defeated Junior Assuncao (guillotine choke)
Nate Quarry defeated Pete Sell (KO)
Dustin Hazelett defeated Jonathan Goulet (arm bar)
Thiago Alves defeated Kuniyoshi Hironaka (submission to strikes)
Cole Miller defeated Leonard Garcia (decision)
Luke Cummo defeated Edilberto de Oliveira (TKO)
Gray Maynard defeated Joe Veres (KO)

UFC 76

9/22/07
Honda Center (Anaheim, California)
Main Event: Keith Jardine defeated Chuck Liddell (decision)
Other Fights:

Forrest Griffin defeated Mauricio Rua (rear naked choke)
Jon Fitch defeated Diego Sanchez (decision)
Lyoto Machida defeated Kazuhiro Nakamura (decision)
Tyson Griffin defeated Thiago Tavares (decision)
Rich Clementi defeated Anthony Johnson (rear naked choke)
Jeremy Stephens defeated Diego Saraiva (decision)
Christian Wellisch defeated Scott Junk (heel hook)
Matt Wiman defeated Michihiro Omigawa (decision)

UFC 77

10/20/97
U.S. Bank Arena (Cincinnati, Ohio)
Main Event: Anderson Silva defeated Rich Franklin (TKO)
Other Fights:

Tim Sylvia defeated Brandon Vera (decision)
Alvin Robinson defeated Jorge Gurgel (decision)
Stephan Bonnar defeated Eric Schafer (TKO)
Alan Belcher defeated Kalib Starnes (TKO)
Yushin Okami defeated Jason MacDonald (decision)
Demian Maia defeated Ryan Jensen (rear naked choke)
Josh Burkman defeated Forest Petz (decision)
Matt Grice defeated Jason Black (decision)

UFC 78

11/17/07
Prudential Center (Newark, New Jersey)
Main Event: Rashad Evans defeated Michael Bisping (split decision)
Other Fights:

Thiago Silva defeated Houston Alexander (KO)
Ed Herman defeated Joe Doerkson (KO)
Karo Parisyan defeated Ryo Chonan (decision)
Frank Edgar defeated Spencer Fisher (decision)
Thiago Alves defeated Chris Lytle (doctor stoppage)
Joe Lauzon defeated Jason Reinhardt (rear naked choke)
Marcus Aurelio defeated Luke Caudillo (TKO)
Akihiro Gono defeated Tamdan McCrory (arm bar)

The Ultimate Fighter 6 Finale

12/8/07
The Pearl at The Palms (Las Vegas, Nevada)
Main Event: Roger Huerta defeated Clay Guida (rear naked choke)
Other Fights:

Mac Danzig defeated Tommy Speer (rear naked choke, won *TUF* Welterweight Tournament)
Jon Koppenhaver defeated Jared Rollins (TKO)
George Sotiropoulos defeated Billy Miles (rear naked choke)
Ben Saunders defeated Dan Barrera (decision)
Matt Arroyo defeated John Kolosci (arm bar)
Jonathan Goulet defeated Paul Georgieff (rear naked choke)
Roman Mitichyan defeated Dorian Price (ankle lock)
Troy Mandaloniz defeated Richie Hightower (TKO)

UFC 79

12/29/07
Mandalay Bay Events Center (Las Vegas, Nevada)
Main Event: Georges St. Pierre defeated Matt Hughes (arm bar, won UFC Interim Welterweight Championship)
Other Fights:

Chuck Liddell defeated Wanderlei Silva (decision)
Rich Clementi defeated Melvin Guillard (rear naked choke)
Eddie Sanchez defeated Soa Palelei (TKO)
Lyoto Machida defeated Rameau Thierry Sokoudjou (arm triangle)
Manvel Gamuryan defeated Nate Mohr (Achilles lock)
Dean Lister defeated Jordan Radev (decision)
Roan Carneiro defeated Tony DeSouza (TKO)
James Irvin defeated Luiz Cane (DQ)
Mark Bocek defeated Doug Evans (decision)

UFC 80

1/19/08

Metro Radio Arena (Newcastle, England)

Main Event: B.J. Penn defeated Joe Stevenson (rear naked choke)

Other Fights:

Fabricio Werdum defeated Gabriel Gonzaga (TKO)
Wilson Gouveia defeated Jason Lambert (KO)
Jorge Rivera defeated Kendall Grove (TKO)
Marcus Davis defeated Jess Liaudin (KO)
Sam Stout defeated Per Eklund (decision)
Alessio Sakara defeated James Lee (TKO)
Antoni Hardonk defeated Colin Robinson (TKO)
Paul Kelly defeated Paul Taylor (decision)

UFC Fight Night 12

1/23/08

The Palms Casino Resort (Las Vegas, Nevada)

Main Event: Mike Swick defeated Josh Burkman (decision)

Other Fights:

Patrick Côté defeated Drew McFedries (TKO)
Thiago Tavares defeated Michihiro Omigawa (decision)
Nate Diaz defeated Alvin Robinson (triangle choke)
Kurt Pellegrino defeated Alberto Crane (TKO)
Gray Maynard defeated Dennis Siver (decision)
Jeremy Stephens defeated Cole Miller (TKO)
Corey Hill defeated Joe Veres (TKO)
Matt Wiman defeated Justin Bucholz (rear naked choke)

UFC 81

2/2/08

Mandalay Bay Events Center (Las Vegas, Nevada)

Main Event: Antonio Rodrigo Nogueira defeated Tim Sylvia (guillotine choke, won UFC Interim Heavyweight Championship)

Other Fights:

Frank Mir defeated Brock Lesnar (knee bar)
Nate Marquardt defeated Jeremy Horn (guillotine choke)
Ricardo Almeida defeated Rob Yundt (guillotine choke)
Tyson Griffin defeated Gleison Tibau (decision)
Chris Lytle defeated Kyle Bradley (TKO)
Marvin Eastman defeated Terry Martin (decision)
Tim Boetsch defeated David Heath (TKO)
Rob Emerson defeated Keita Nakamura (decision)

UFC 82

3/1/08

Nationwide Arena (Columbus, Ohio)

Main Event: Anderson Silva defeated Dan Henderson (rear naked choke, unifies Pride Welterweight Championship and UFC Middleweight Championship)

Other Fights:

Heath Herring defeated Cheick Kongo (decision)
Yushin Okami defeated Evan Tanner (KO)
Chris Leben defeated Alessio Sakara (TKO)
Jon Fitch defeated Chris Wilson (decision)
Andrei Arlovski defeated Jake O'Brien (TKO)
Josh Koscheck defeated Dustin Hazelett (KO)
Diego Sanchez defeated David Bielkheden (submission to strikes)
Luigi Fioravanti defeated Luke Cummo (decision)
Jorge Gurgel defeated John Halverson (decision)

UFC Fight Night 13

4/2/08

Broomfield Event Center (Broomfield, Colorado)

Main Event: Kenny Florian defeated Joe Lauzon (TKO)

Other Fights:

Gray Maynard defeated Frank Edgar (decision)
Thiago Alves defeated Karo Parisyan (TKO)
Matt Hamill defeated Tim Boetsch (TKO)

Nate Diaz defeated Kurt Pellegrino (triangle choke)
James Irvin defeated Houston Alexander (TKO)
Josh Neer defeated Din Thomas (decision)
Marcus Aurelio defeated Ryan Roberts (arm bar)
Manvel Gamburyan defeated Jeff Cox (guillotine choke)
Clay Guida defeated Samy Schiavo (TKO)
George Sotiropoulos defeated Romany Mitichyan (TKO)
Anthony Johnson defeated Tommy Speer (KO)

UFC 83

4/19/08

Bell Centre (Montreal, Quebec, Canada)

Main Event: Georges St. Pierre defeated Matt Serra (TKO, won UFC Welterweight Championship)

Other Fights:

Rich Franklin defeated Travis Lutter (TKO)
Michael Bisping defeated Charles McCarthy (TKO)
Nate Quarry defeated Kalib Starnes (decision)
Mac Danzig defeated Mark Bocek (rear naked choke)
Jason Day defeated Alan Belcher (TKO)
Demian Maia defeated Ed Herman (triangle choke)
Jason MacDonald defeated Joe Doerkson (TKO)
Rich Clementi defeated Sam Stout (decision)
Cain Velasquez defeated Brad Morris (TKO)
Jonathan Goulet defeated Kuniyoshi Hironaka (TKO)

UFC 84

5/24/08

MGM Grand (Las Vegas, Nevada)

Main Event: B.J. Penn defeated Sean Sherk (TKO)

Other Fights

Wanderlei Silva defeated Keith Jardine (KO)
Goran Reljic defeated Wilson Gouveia (TKO)
Lyoto Machida defeated Tito Ortiz (decision)
Thiago Silva defeated Antonio Mendes (submission to strikes)
Rousimar Palhares defeated Ivan Salaverry (arm bar)
Rameau Thierry Sokoudjou defeated Kazuhiro Nakamura (TKO)
Rich Clementi defeated Terry Etim (decision)
Yoshiyuki Yoshida defeated Jon Koppenhaver (anaconda choke)
Dong-Hyun Kim defeated Jason Tan (TKO)
Shane Carwin defeated Christian Wellisch (KO)

UFC 85

6/7/08

O_2 Arena (London, England)

Main Event: Thiago Alves defeated Matt Hughes (TKO)

Other Fights:

Michael Bisping defeated Jason Day (TKO)
Mike Swick defeated Marcus Davis (decision)
Thales Leites defeated Nate Marquardt (decision)
Fabricio Werdum defeated Brandon Vera (TKO)
Martin Kampmann defeated Jorge Rivera (guillotine choke)
Matt Wiman defeated Thiago Tavares (KO)
Kevin Burns defeated Roan Carneiro (triangle choke)
Luiz Cane defeated Jason Lambert (TKO)
Antoni Hardonk defeated Eddie Sanchez (KO)
Paul Taylor defeated Jess Liaudin (decision)

The Ultimate Fighter 7 Finale

6/21/08

The Pearl at The Palms (Las Vegas, Nevada)

Main Event: Kendall Grove defeated Evan Tanner (decision)

Other Fights:

Amir Sadollah defeated C.B. Dolloway (arm bar, won *TUF* Middleweight Tournament)
Diego Sanchez defeated Luigi Fioravanti (TKO)
Spencer Fisher defeated Jeremy Stephens (decision)
Matthew Riddle defeated Dante Rivera (decision)
Dustin Hazelett defeated Josh Burkman (arm bar)
Drew McFedries defeated Marvin Eastman (KO)
Matt Brown defeated Matt Arroyo (TKO)
Dean Lister defeated Jeremy Horn (guillotine choke)
Rob Kimmons defeated Rob Yundt (guillotine choke)

UFC 86

7/5/08

Mandalay Bay Events Center (Las Vegas, Nevada)

Main Event: Forrest Griffin defeated Quinton Jackson (decision, won UFC Light Heavyweight Championship)

Other Fights:

- Patrick Côté defeats Ricardo Almeida (decision)
- Joe Stevenson defeated Gleison Tibau (guillotine choke)
- Josh Koscheck defeated Chris Lytle (decision)
- Tyson Griffin defeated Marcus Aurelio (decision)
- Gabriel Gonzaga defeated Justin McCully (Americana)
- Justin Buchholz defeated Corey Hill (rear naked choke)
- Melvin Guillard defeated Dennis Siver (KO)
- Cole Miller defeated Jorge Gurgel (triangle choke)

UFC Fight Night 14

7/19/08

Palms Casino Resort (Las Vegas, Nevada)

Main Event: Anderson Silva defeated James Irvin (KO)

Other Fights:

- Brandon Vera defeated Reese Andy (decision)
- Frank Edgar defeated Hermes Franca (decision)
- Cain Velasquez defeated Jake O'Brien (TKO)
- Kevin Burns defeated Anthony Johnson (TKO)
- C.B. Dollaway defeated Jesse Taylor (Peruvian necktie)
- Tim Credeur defeated Cale Yarbrough (TKO)
- Nate Loughran defeated Johnny Rees (triangle choke)
- Shannon Gugerty defeated Dale Hartt (rear naked choke)
- Rory Markham defeated Brodie Farber (KO)
- Brad Blackburn defeated James Giboo (TKO)

UFC 87

8/9/08

Target Center (Minneapolis, Minnesota)

Main Event: Georges St. Pierre defeated Jon Fitch (decision)

Other Fights:

- Brock Lesnar defeated Heath Herring (decision)
- Rob Emerson defeated Manny Gamburyan (KO)
- Kenny Florian defeated Roger Huerta (decision)
- Demian Maia defeated Jason MacDonald (rear naked choke)
- Tamdan McCrory defeated Luke Cummo (decision)
- Cheick Kongo defeated Dan Evensen (TKO)
- Jon Jones defeated Andre Gusmao (decision)
- Chris Wilson defeated Steve Bruno (decision)
- Ben Saunders defeated Ryan Thomas (arm bar)

UFC 88

9/6/08

Phillips Arena (Atlanta, Georgia)

Main Event: Rashad Evans defeated Chuck Liddell (KO)

Other Fights:

- Rich Franklin defeated Matt Hamill (TKO)
- Dan Henderson defeated Rousimar Palhares (decision)
- Nate Marquardt defeated Martin Kampmann (TKO)
- Dong-Hyung Kim defeated Matt Brown (decision)
- Kurt Pellegrino defeated Thiago Tavares (decision)
- Ryo Chonan defeated Roan Carneiro (decision)
- Tim Boetsch defeated Mike Patt (TKO)
- Jason MacDonald defeated Jason Lambert (rear naked choke)

UFC Fight Night 15

9/17/08

Omaha Civic Auditorium (Omaha, Nebraska)

Main Event: Nate Diaz defeated Josh Neer (decision)

Other Fights:

- Clay Guida defeated Mac Danzig (decision)
- Alan Belcher defeated Ed Herman (decision)
- Eric Schafer defeated Houston Alexander (arm triangle)
- Alessio Sakara defeated Joe Vedepo (KO)
- Wilson Gouveia defeated Ryan Jensen (arm bar)
- Joe Lauzon defeated Kyle Bradley (TKO)
- Jason Brilz defeated Brad Morris (TKO)
- Mike Massenzio defeated Drew McFedries (Kimura)
- Dan Miller defeated Rob Kimmons (rear naked choke)

UFC 89

10/18/08

National Indoor Arena (Birmingham, England)
Main Event: Michael Bisping defeated Chris Leben (decision)
Other Fights:
- Keith Jardine defeated Brandon Vera (decision)
- Luiz Cane defeated Rameau Thierry Sokoudjou (TKO)
- Chris Lytle defeated Paul Taylor (decision)
- Marcus Davis defeated Paul Kelly (guillotine choke)
- Shane Carwin defeated Neil Wain (TKO)
- Dan Hardy defeated Akihiro Gono (decision)
- Terry Etim defeated Sam Stout (decision)
- David Bielkheden defeated Jess Liaudin (decision)
- Jim Miller defeated David Baron (rear naked choke)
- Per Eklund defeated Samy Schiavo (rear naked choke)

UFC 90

10/25/08
Allstate Arena (Rosemont, Illinois)
Main Event: Anderson Silva defeated Patrick Côté (TKO, knee injury)
Other Fights:
- Thiago Alves defeated Josh Koscheck (decision)
- Gray Maynard defeated Rich Clementi (decision)
- Junior Dos Santos defeated Fabricio Werdum (KO)
- Sean Sherk defeated Tyson Griffin (decision)
- Thales Leites defeated Drew McFedries (rear naked choke)
- Spencer Fisher defeated Shannon Gugerty (triangle choke)
- Dan Miller defeated Matt Horwich (decision)
- Hermes Franca defeated Marcus Aurelio (decision)
- Pete Sell defeated Josh Burkman (decision)

UFC 91

11/15/08
MGM Grand (Las Vegas, Nevada)
Main Event: Brock Lesnar defeated Randy Couture (TKO, won UFC Heavyweight Championship)
Other Fights:
- Kenny Florian defeated Joe Stevenson (rear naked choke)
- Dustin Hazelett defeated Tamdan McCrory (arm bar)
- Gabriel Gonzaga defeated Josh Hendricks (TKO)
- Demian Maia defeated Nate Quarry (rear naked choke)
- Aaron Riley defeated Jorge Gurgel (decision)
- Jeremy Stephens defeated Rafael dos Anjos (KO)
- Mark Bocek defeated Alvin Robinson (rear naked choke)
- Matt Brown defeated Ryan Thomas (arm bar)

UFC: Fight for the Troops (Fight Night 16)

12/10/08
Crown Coliseum (Fayetteville, North Carolina)
Main Event: Josh Koscheck defeated Yoshiyuki Yoshida (KO)
Other Fights:
- Mike Swick defeated Jonathan Goulet (KO)
- Steve Cantwell defeated Razak Al-Hussan (arm bar)
- Tim Credeur defeated Nate Loughran (TKO)
- Matt Wiman defeated Jim Miller (decision)
- Luigi Fioravanti defeated Brodie Farber (decision)
- Steve Bruno defeated Johnny Rees (rear naked choke)
- Ben Saunders defeated Brandon Wolff (TKO)
- Dale Hart defeated Corey Hill (TKO, leg injury)
- Justin McCully defeated Eddie Sanchez (decision)

The Ultimate Fighter 8 Finale

12/13/08
The Pearl at The Palms (Las Vegas, Nevada)
Main Event: Efrain Escudero defeated Phillipe Nover (decision, won *TUF* Lightweight Tournament)
Other Fights:
- Ryan Bader defeated Vinicius Magalhaes (TKO, won *TUF* light heavyweight champion)
- Anthony Johnson defeated Kevin Burns (KO)
- Wilson Gouveia defeated Jason MacDonald (submission to strikes)
- Junie Browning defeated Dave Kaplan (arm bar)
- Krzysztof Soszynski defeated Shane Primm (Kimura)

Eliot Marshall defeated Jules Bruchez (rear naked choke)
Tom Lawlor defeated Kyle Kingsbury (decision)
Shane Nelson defeated George Roop (decision)
Rolando Delgado defeated John Polakowski (guillotine choke)

UFC 92

12/27/08

MGM Grand (Las Vegas, Nevada)

Main Event: Rashad Evans defeated Forrest Griffin (TKO, won UFC Light Heavyweight Championship)

Other Fights:

Frank Mir defeated Antonio Rodrigo Nogueira (TKO, won UFC Interim Heavyweight Championship)
C.B. Dollaway defeated Mike Massenzio (TKO)
Quinton Jackson defeated Wanderlei Silva (KO)
Cheick Kongo defeated Mostapaha Al Turk (TKO)
Yushin Okami defeated Dean Lister (decision)
Antoni Hardonk defeated Mike Wessel (TKO)
Matt Hamill defeated Reese Andy (TKO)
Brad Blackburn defeated Ryo Chonan (decision)
Patrick Barry defeated Dan Evensen (TKO)

UFC 93

1/17/09

The O_2 Dublin (Dublin, Ireland)

Main Event: Dan Henderson defeated Rich Franklin (decision)

Other Fights:

Mauricio Rua defeated Mark Coleman (TKO)
Rousimar Palhares defeated Jeremy Horn (decision)
Alan Belcher defeated Denis Kang (guillotine choke)
Marcus Davis defeated Chris Lytle (decision)
John Hathaway defeated Thomas Egan (TKO)
Martin Kampmann defeated Alexandre Barros (TKO)
Eric Schafer defeated Antonio Mendes (TKO)
Tomasz Drwal defeated Ivan Serati (KO)
Dennis Siver defeated Nate Mohr (TKO)

UFC 94

1/31/09

MGM Grand (Las Vegas, Nevada)

Main Event: Georges St. Pierre defeated B.J. Penn (corner stoppage)

Other Fights:

Lyoto Machida defeated Thiago Silva (KO)
Jon Jones defeated Stephan Bonnar (decision)
Karo Pariysan vs. Dong-Hyun Kim (no contest)
Clay Guida defeated Nate Diaz (decision)
Jon Fitch defeated Akihiro Gono (decision)
Thiago Tavares defeated Manvel Gamburyan (decision)
John Howard defeated Chris Wilson (decision)
Jake O'Brien defeated Christian Wellisch (decision)
Dan Cramer defeated Matt Arroyo (decision)

UFC Fight Night 17

2/7/09

USF Sun Dome (Tampa, Florida)

Main Event: Joe Lauzon defeated Jeremy Stephens (arm bar)

Other Fights:

Josh Neer defeated Mac Danzig (triangle choke)
Cain Velasquez defeated Denis Stojnic (TKO)
Anthony Johnson defeated Luigi Fioravanti (TKO)
Kurt Pellegrino defeated Rob Emerson (rear naked choke)
Dan Miller defeated Jake Rosholt (guillotine choke)
Matt Veach defeated Matt Grice (TKO)
Gleison Tibau defeated Rich Clementi (guillotine choke)
Nick Catone defeated Derek Downey (key lock)
Matthew Riddle defeated Steve Bruno (decision)

UFC 95

2/21/09

O_2 Arena (London, England)

Main Event: Diego Sanchez defeated Joe Stevenson (decision)

Other Fights:

Dan Hardy defeated Rory Markham (KO)
Nate Marquardt defeated Wilson Gouveia (TKO)

Demian Maia defeated Chael Sonnen (triangle choke)
Paulo Thiago defeated Josh Koscheck (KO)
Terry Etim defeated Brian Cobb (TKO)
Junior Dos Santos defeated Stefan Struve (TKO)
Evan Dunham defeated Per Eklund (TKO)
Mike Ciesnolevicz defeated Neil Grove (heel hook)
Paul Kelly defeated Troy Mandaloniz (decision)

UFC 96

3/7/09

Nationwide Arena (Columbus, Ohio)

Main Event: Quinton Jackson defeated Keith Jardine (decision)

Other Fights:

Shane Carwin defeated Gabriel Gonzaga (KO)
Matt Brown defeated Pete Sell (TKO)
Matt Hamill defeated Mark Munoz (KO)
Gray Maynard defeated Jim Miller (decision)
Tamdan McCrory defeated Ryan Madigan (submission to strikes)
Kendall Grove defeated Jason Day (TKO)
Jason Brilz defeated Tim Boetsch (decision)
Brandon Vera defeated Mike Patt (TKO)
Shane Nelson defeated Aaron Riley (TKO)

UFC Fight Night 18

4/1/09

Sommet Center (Nashville, Tennessee)

Main Event: Martin Kampmann defeated Carlos Condit (decision)

Other Fights:

Ryan Bader defeated Carmelo Marrero (decision)
Tyson Griffin defeated Rafael dos Anjos (decision)
Cole Miller defeated Junie Browning (guillotine choke)
Gleison Tibau defeated Jeremy Stephens (decision)
Ricardo Almeida defeated Matt Horwich (decision)
Brock Larson defeated Jesse Sanders (rear naked choke)
Tim Credeur defeated Nick Catone (guillotine choke)
Jorge Rivera defeated Nissen Osterneck (decision)
Rob Kimmons defeated Joe Vedepo (guillotine choke)
Aaron Simpson defeated Tim McKenzie (TKO)

UFC 97

4/18/09

Bell Centre (Montreal, Quebec, Canada)

Main Event: Anderson Silva defeated Thales Leites (decision)

Other Fights:

Sam Stout defeated Matt Wiman (decision)
Mauricio Rua defeated Chuck Liddell (TKO)
Krzysztof Soszynski defeated Brian Stann (Kimura)
Cheick Kongo defeated Antoni Hardonk (TKO)
Luiz Cane defeated Steve Cantwell (decision)
Denis Kang defeated Xavier Foupa-Pokam (decision)
Nate Quarry defeated Jason MacDonald (TKO)
Ed Herman defeated David Loiseau (decision)
Mark Bocek defeated David Bielkheden (rear naked choke)
T.J. Grant defeated Ryo Chonan (decision)
Eliot Marshall defeated Vinicius Magalhaes (decision)

UFC 98

5/23/09

MGM Grand (Las Vegas, Nevada)

Main Event: Lyoto Machida defeated Rashad Evans (KO, won UFC Light Heavyweight Championship)

Other Fights:

Matt Hughes defeated Matt Serra (decision)
Drew McFedries defeated Xavier Foup-Pokam (TKO)
Chael Sonnen defeated Dan Miller (decision)
Frank Edgar defeated Sean Sherk (decision)
Brock Larson defeated Mike Pyle (arm triangle)
Tim Hague defeated Patrick Barry (guillotine choke)
Kyle Bradley defeated Phillipe Nover (TKO)
Krzysztof Soszynski defeated Andre Gusmao (KO)
Yoshiyuki Yoshida defeated Brandon Wolff (guillotine choke)
George Roop defeated Daved Kaplan (decision)

UFC 99

6/13/09

Lanxess Arena (Cologne, Germany)

Main Event: Rich Franklin defeated Wanderlei Silva (decision)

Other Fights:

Cain Velasquez defeated Cheick Kongo (decision)
Mirko Filipovic defeated Mostapha Al Turk (TKO)
Mike Swick defeated Ben Saunders (TKO)
Spencer Fisher defeated Caol Uno (decision)
Dan Hardy defeated Marcus Davis (decision)
Terry Etim defeated Justin Buchholz (D'Arce choke)
Dennis Siver defeated Dale Hartt (rear naked choke)
Paul Taylor defeated Peter Sobotta (decision)
Paul Kelly defeated Rolando Delgado (decision)
Stefan Struve defeated Denis Stojnic (rear naked choke)
John Hathaway defeated Rick Story (decision)

The Ultimate Fighter 9 Finale

6/20/09

The Pearl at The Palms (Las Vegas, Nevada)

Main Event: Diego Sanchez defeated Clay Guida (decision)

Other Fights:

James Wilks defeated DaMarques Johnson (rear naked choke, won *TUF* Welterweight Tournament)
Chris Lytle defeated Kevin Burns (decision)
Ross Pearson defeated Andre Winner (decision, won *TUF* Lightweight Tournament)
Joe Stevenson defeated Nate Diaz (decision)
Melvin Guillard defeated Gleison Tibau (decision)
Brad Blackburn defeated Edgar Garcia (decision)
Tomasz Drwal defeated Mike Ciesnolevicz (TKO)
Nick Osipczak defeated Frank Lester (rear naked choke)
Jason Dent defeated Cameron Dollar (anaconda choke)

UFC 100

7/11/09

Mandalay Bay Events Center (Las Vegas, Nevada)

Main Event: Brock Lesnar defeated Frank Mir (TKO, unified UFC Heavyweight Championship and UFC Interim Heavyweight Championship)

Other Fights:

Georges St. Pierre defeated Thiago Alves (decision)
Dan Henderson defeated Michael Bisping (KO)
Yoshihiro Akiyama defeated Alan Belcher (decision)
Jon Fitch defeated Paulo Thiago (decision)
Mark Coleman defeated Stephan Bonnar (decision)
Jon Jones defeated Jake O'Brien (guillotine choke)
Jim Miller defeated Mac Danzig (decision)
Dong-Hyun Kim defeated T.J. Grant (decision)
Tom Lawlor defeated C.B. Dollaway (guillotine choke)
Shannon Gugerty defeated Matt Grice (guillotine choke)

UFC 101

8/8/09

Wachovia Center (Philadelphia, Pennsylvania)

Main Event: B.J. Penn defeated Kenny Florian (rear naked choke)

Other Fights:

Anderson Silva defeated Forrest Griffin (KO)
Aaron Riley defeated Shane Nelson (decision)
Johnny Hendricks defeated Amir Sadollah (TKO)
Ricardo Almeida defeated Kendall Grove (decision)
Kurt Pellegrino defeated Josh Neer (decision)
John Howard defeated Tamdan McCrory (decision)
Alessio Sakara defeated Thales Leites (decision)
Matt Riddle defeated Dan Cramer (decision)
George Sotiropoulos defeated George Roop (Kimura)
Jesse Lennox defeated Danillo Villefort (TKO)

UFC 102

8/29/09

Rose Garden (Portland, Oregon)

Main Event: Antonio Rodrigo Nogueira defeated Randy Couture (decision)

Other Fights:

Thiago Silva defeated Keith Jardine (KO)

Jake Rosholt defeated Chris Leben (arm triangle)
Nate Marquardt defeated Demian Maia (KO)
Brandon Vera defeated Krzysztof Soszynski (decision)
Gabriel Gonzaga defeated Chris Tuchscherer (TKO)
Mike Russow defeated Justin McCully (decision)
Aaron Simpson defeated Ed Herman (TKO)
Todd Duffee defeated Tim Hague (KO)
Mark Munoz defeated Nick Catone (decision)
Evan Dunham defeated Marcus Aurelio (decision)

UFC Fight Night 19

9/16/09
Cox Convention Center (Oklahoma City, Oklahoma)
Main Event: Nate Diaz defeated Melvin Guillard (guillotine choke)
Other Fights:

Gray Maynard defeated Roger Huerta (decision)
Carlos Condit defeated Jake Ellenberger (decision)
Nate Quarry defeated Tim Credeur (decision)
Brian Stann defeated Steve Cantwell (decision)
Mike Pyle defeated Chris Wilson (guillotine choke)
C.B. Dollaway defeated Jay Silva (decision)
Jeremy Stephens defeated Justin Buchholz (TKO)
Mike Pierce defeated Brock Larson (decision)
Ryan Jensen defeated Steve Steinbeiss (guillotine choke)

UFC 103

9/19/09
American Airlines Center (Dallas, Texas)
Main Event: Vitor Belfort defeated Rich Franklin (KO)
Other Fights:

Junior Dos Santos defeated Mirko Filipovic (submission)
Paul Daley defeated Martin Kampmann (TKO)
Josh Koscheck defeated Frank Trigg (TKO)
Tyson Griffin defeated Hermes Franca (TKO)
Efrain Escudero defeated Cole Miller (KO)
Tomasz Drwal defeated Drew McFedries (rear naked choke)
Jim Miller defeated Steve Lopez (TKO)
Nik Lentz defeated Rafaello Oliveira (decision)
Ricky Story defeated Brian Foster (arm triangle)
Eliot Marshal defeated Jason Brilz (decision)
Vladimir Matyushenko defeated Igor Pokrajac (decision)
Rafael dos Anjos defeated Rob Emerson (decision)

UFC 104

10/28/09
Staples Center (Los Angeles, California)
Main Event: Lyoto Machida defeated Mauricio Rua (decision)
Other Fights:

Cain Velasquez defeated Ben Rothwell (TKO)
Gleison Tibau defeated Josh Neer (decision)
Joe Stevenson defeated Spencer Fisher (submission to strikes)
Anthony Johnson defeated Yoshiyuki Yoshidas (TKO)
Ryan Bader defeated Eric Schafer (decision)
Patrick Barry defeated Antoni Hardonk (TKO)
Chael Sonnen defeated Yushin Okami (decision)
Jorge Rivera defeated Rob Kimmons (TKO)
Kyle Kingsbury defeated Razak Al-Hassan (decision)
Stefan Struve defeated Chase Gormley (triangle choke)

UFC 105

11/14/09
Manchester Evening News Arena (Manchester, England)
Main Event: Randy Couture defeated Brandon Vera (decision)
Other Fights:

Dan Hardy defeated Mike Swick (decision)
Michael Bisping defeated Denis Kang (TKO)
Matt Brown defeated James Wilks (TKO)
Ross Pearson defeated Aaron Riley (doctor stoppage)
John Hathaway defeated Paul Taylor (decision)
Terry Etim defeated Shannon Gugerty (guillotine choke)
Nick Osipczak defeated Matthew Riddle (TKO)
Dennis Siver defeated Paul Kelly (TKO)
Alexander Gustafsson defeated Jared Hamman (KO)
Andre Winner defeated Rolando Delgado (KO)

UFC 106

11/21/09

Mandalay Bay Events Center (Las Vegas, Nevada)

Main Event: Forrest Griffin defeated Tito Ortiz (decision)

Other Fights:

- Josh Koscheck defeated Anthony Johnson (rear naked choke)
- Paulo Thiago defeated Jacob Volkman (decision)
- Antonio Rogerio Nogueira defeated Luiz Cane (TKO)
- Amir Sadollah defeated Phil Baroni (decision)
- Ben Saunders defeated Marcus Davis (KO)
- Kendall Grove defeated Jake Rosholt (triangle choke)
- Brian Foster defeated Brock Larson (TKO)
- Caol Uno defeated Fabricio Camoes (draw)
- George Sotiropoulos defeated Jason Dent (arm bar)

The Ultimate Fighter 10 Finale

12/5/09

The Pearl at The Palms (Las Vegas, Nevada)

Main Event: Roy Nelson defeated Brendan Schaub (KO, won *TUF* Heavyweight Tournament)

Other Fights:

- Mat Hamill defeated Jon Jones (DQ)
- Kimbo Slice defeated Houston Alexander (decision)
- Frank Edgar defeated Matt Veach (rear naked choke)
- Matt Mitrione defeated Marcus Jones (KO)
- James McSweeney defeated Darrill Schoonover (TKO)
- Jon Madsen defeated Justin Wren (decision)
- Brian Stann defeated Rodney Wallace (decision)
- John Howard defeated Dennis Hallman (KO)
- Mark Bocek defeated Joe Brammar (rear naked choke)

UFC 107

12/12/09

FedExForum (Memphis, Tennessee)

Main Event: B.J. Penn defeated Diego Sanchez (TKO)

Other Fights:

- Frank Mir defeated Cheick Kongo (guillotine choke)
- Jon Fitch defeated Mike Pierce (decision)
- Kenny Florian defeated Clay Guida (rear naked choke)
- Stefan Struve defeated Paul Buentello (decision)
- Alan Belcher defeated Wilson Gouveia (TKO)
- Matt Wiman defeated Shane Nelson (decision)
- Johnny Hendricks defeated Ricardo Funch (decision)
- Rousimar Palhares defeated Lucio Linhares (heel hook)
- DaMarques Johnson defeated Edgar Garcia (triangle choke)
- T.J. Grant defeated Kevin Burns (TKO)

MOST CUMULATIVE TIME FIGHTING IN A UFC RING (THROUGH 2009)

1. Randy Couture: 264 minutes in 21 fights
2. Tito Ortiz: 256 minutes in 22 fights
3. B.J. Penn: 208 minutes in 16 fights
4. Matt Hughes: 199 minutes in 21 fights
5. Chuck Liddell: 199 minutes in 22 fights
6. Georges St. Pierre: 178 minutes in 15 fights
7. Sean Sherk: 171 minutes in 11 fights
8. Pedro Rizzo: 167 minutes in 14 fights
9. Jon Fitch: 163 minutes in 12 fights
10. Chris Lytle: 163 minutes in 15 fights
11. Diego Sanchez: 157 minutes in 13 fights
12. Rich Franklin: 155 minutes in 16 fights
13. Matt Serra: 150 minutes in 12 fights
14. Hermes Franca: 149 minutes in 11 fights
15. Karo Parisyan: 149 minutes in 12 fights
16. Ken Shamrock: 146 minutes in 15 fights
17. Josh Koscheck: 141 minutes in 16 fights
18. Forrest Griffin: 141 minutes in 12 fights
19. Tim Sylvia: 137 minutes in 13 fights
20. Spencer Fisher: 133 minutes in 12 fights

MOST FIGHTS IN A UFC RING (THROUGH 2009)

Tito Ortiz: 22 fights (16-6)

Chuck Liddell: 22 fights (14-7-1)

Randy Couture: 21 fights (14-7)

Matt Hughes: 21 fights (16-5)

David Abbott: 18 fights (8-10)
Evan Tanner: 17 fights (11-6)
Rich Franklin: 16 fights (12-4)
Josh Koscheck: 16 fights (12-4)
B.J. Penn: 16 fights (11-4-1)
Ken Shamrock: 15 fights (7-6-2)
Georges St. Pierre: 15 fights (13-2)
Frank Mir: 15 fights (11-4)
Chris Lytle: 15 fights (6-9)
Royce Gracie: 14 fights (11-2-1)
Pedro Rizzo: 14 fights (9-5)
Andrei Arlovski: 14 fights (10-4)
Tim Sylvia: 13 fights (9-4)
Kenny Florian: 13 fights (10-3)
Jeremy Horn: 13 fights (6-7)
Diego Sanchez: 13 fights (10-3)
Dan Severn: 13 fights (9-4)
Chris Leben: 13 fights (8-5)
Vitor Belfort: 12 fights (8-4)
Thiago Alves: 12 fights (9-3)
Spencer Fisher: 12 fights (8-4)
Matt Serra: 12 fights (6-6)
Matt Lindland: 12 fights (9-3)
Marcus Davis: 12 fights (8-4)
Karo Parisyan: 12 fights (9-3)
Jon Fitch: 12 fights (11-1)
Joe Stevenson: 12 fights (8-4)
Forrest Griffin: 12 fights (8-4)

MOST DAYS BETWEEN FIGHTS IN UFC

Royce Gracie: 4,068 days (UFC 5, 4/7/95: DRAW Ken Shamrock – UFC 60, 5/27/06: LOST Matt Hughes)

Mark Coleman: 3,662 days (UFC 18, 1/8/99: LOST Pedro Rizzo – UFC 93, 1/17/09: LOST Mauricio Rua)

Dan Henderson: 3,403 days (UFC 17, 5/15/98: WON Carlos Newton – UFC 75, 9/8/07: LOST Quinton Jackson)

Wanderlei Silva: 2,815 days (UFC 25, 4/14/00: LOST Tito Ortiz – UFC 79, 12/29/07: LOST Chuck Liddell)

Mike Van Arsdale: 2,528 days (UFC 17, 5/15/98: WON Joe Pardo – UFC 52, 4/16/05 WON John Marsh)

Ricardo Almeida: 2,213 days (UFC 35, 1/11/02: LOST Andrei Semenov – UFC 81, 2/2/08 WON Rob Yundt)

John Alessio: 2,178 days (UFC 26, 6/9/00: LOST Pat Miletich – UFC 60, 5/27/06: LOST Diego Sanchez)

Ken Shamrock: 2,176 days (Ultimate Ultimate 96, 12/7/96: WON Brian Johnston – UFC 40, 11/22/02: LOST Tito Ortiz)

Caol Uno: 2,087 days (UFC 44, 9/26/03: LOST Hermes Franca – UFC 99, 6/13/09: LOST Spencer Fisher)

Jason Delucia: 2,079 days (UFC 2, 3/11/94: LOST Royce Gracie – UFC 23, 11/19/99: LOST Joe Slick)

FEWEST DAYS BETWEEN FIGHTS IN UFC

Same-day fights:

UFC 1: Gerard Gordeau, Ken Shamrock, Kevin Rosier, Royce Gracie

UFC 2: Jason Delucia, Johnny Rhodes, Orlando Weit, Patrick Smith, Remco Pardoel, Royce Gracie, Scott Morris

UFC 3: Harold Howard, Ken Shamrock, Royce Gracie

UFC 4: Dan Severn, Keith Hackney, Marcus Bossett, Royce Gracie

UFC 5: Dan Severn, Dave Beneteau, Oleg Taktarov, Todd Medina

UFC 6: Anthony Macias, David Abbott, Oleg Taktarov, Paul Varelans

UFC 7: Marco Ruas, Mark Hall, Paul Varelans, Remco Pardoel

Ultimate Ultimate 1: Dan Severn, David Abbott, Marco Ruas, Oleg Taktarov

UFC 8: Don Frye, Gary Goodridge, Jerry Bohlander, Sam Adkins

UFC 10: Brian Johnston, Don Frye, Gary Goodridge, Mark Coleman

UFC 11: Brian Johnston, David Abbott, Mark Coleman, Scott Ferrozzo

Ultimate Ultimate 2: David Abbott, Don Frye, Mark Hall, Steve Nelmark

UFC 12: Jerry Bohlander, Nick Sanzo, Scott Ferrozzo, Vitor Belfort

UFC 13: Guy Mezger, Randy Couture, Steven Graham, Tito Ortiz

UFC 14: Dan Bobish, Kevin Jackson, Mark Kerr, Tony Fryklund

UFC 15: Dwayne Cason, Mark Kerr

UFC 15.5: Kazushi Sakuraba, Marcus Silveira

UFC 16: Chris Brennan, Pat Miletich

UFC 17: Carlos Newton, Dan Henderson

Multiple fights in one day totals

Royce Gracie: 12 fights in 4 events
David Abbott: 10 fights in 4 events
Don Frye: 9 fights in 3 events
Dan Severn: 9 fights in 3 events
Oleg Taktarov: 8 fights in 3 events
Remco Pardoel, Paul Varelans, Mark Coleman, Marco Ruas, Gary Goodridge: 5 fights in 2 events
Scott Ferrozzo, Patrick Smith, Mark Kerr, Mark Hall, Brian Johnston, Ken Shamrock, Jerry Bohlander, Patrick Smith: 4 fights in 1 event (UFC 2)
Gerard Gordeau, Johnny Rhodes, Dave Beneteau, Harold Howard: 3 fights in 1 event
Vitor Belfort, Kevin Jackson, Kevin Rosier, Jason Delucia, Marcus Bossett, Marcus Silveira, Keith Hackney, Guy Mezger, Kazushi Sakuraba, Nick Sanzo, Dan Bobish, Orlando Weit, Pat Miletich, Carlos Newton, Chris Brennan, Randy Couture, Dan Henderson, Anthony Macias, Sam Adkins, Dwayne Cason, Scott Morris, Steve Nelmark, Steven Graham, Tito Ortiz, Todd Medina, Tony Fryklund: 2 fights in 1 event

(Harold Howard actually threw in the towel at the start of the Gracie match at UFC 3, so you could deduct a fight from each of their totals.)

Jason MacDonald: 28 days later
UFC 87 (8/9/08): lost to submission to Demian Maia
UFC 88 (9/6/08): won via submission over Jason Lambert

C.B. Dollaway: 28 days later
The Ultimate Fighter 7 Finale (6/21/08): lost to submission to Amir Sadollah
UFC Fight Night 14 (7/19/08): won via submission over Jesse Taylor

Krzysztof Soszynski: 35 days later
UFC 97 (4/18/09): won via submission over Brian Stann
UFC 98 (5/23/09): won via KO over Andre Gusmao

Xavier Foupa-Pokam: 35 days later
UFC 97 (4/18/09): lost via unanimous decision to Denis Kang
UFC 98 (5/23/09): lost via TKO to Drew McFedries

Rich Clementi: 35 days later
UFC 83 (4/19/08): won via decision over Sam Stout
UFC 84 (5/24/08): won via unanimous decision over Terry Etim

Dan Miller: 38 days later
UFC Fight Night 15 (9/17/08): won via submission over Rob Kimmons
UFC 90 (10/25/08): won via decision over Matt Horwich

Drew McFedries: 38 days later
UFC Fight Night 15 (9/17/08): lost via submission to Mike Massenzio
UFC 90 (10/25/08): lost via submission to Thales Leites

Brandon Vera: 42 days later
UFC 85 (6/7/08): lost via TKO to Fabricio Werdum
UFC Fight Night 14 (7/19/08): won via decision over Reese Andy

Kevin Burns: 42 days later
UFC 85 (6/7/08): won via submission over Roan Carneiro
UFC Fight Night 14 (7/19/08): won via TKO over Anthony Johnson

Jason Lambert: 42 days later
UFC 58 (3/4/06): won via submission over Rob MacDonald
UFC 59 (4/15/06): won via TKO over Terry Martin

Alessio Sakara: 42 days later
UFC 80 (1/19/08): won via TKO over James Lee
UFC 82 (3/1/08): lost via TKO to Chris Leben

Benji Radach: 43 days later
UFC 37 (5/10/02): no contest – overturned by State Commission vs. Steve Berger
UFC 37.5 (6/22/02): won via decision over Nick Serra

Robbie Lawler: 43 days later
UFC 37 (5/10/02): won via decision over Aaron Riley
UFC 37.5 (6/22/02): won via TKO over Steve Berger

Steve Berger: 43 days later
UFC 37 (5/10/02): no contest - overturned by State Commission vs. Benji Radach
UFC 37.5 (6/22/02): lost via TKO to Robbie Lawler

Yves Edwards: 43 days later
UFC 37 (5/10/02): lost via decision to Caol Uno
UFC 37.5 (6/22/02): won via TKO over Joao Marcos Pierini

Joe Riggs: 43 days later
UFC 55 (10/7/05): won via TKO over Chris Lytle
UFC 56 (11/19/05): lost via submission to Matt Hughes

MOST WINS / LOSSES / DRAWS

Wins

Chuck Liddell: 16 wins
Matt Hughes: 16 wins
Tito Ortiz: 14 wins
Randy Couture: 13 wins
Georges St. Pierre: 13 wins
Rich Franklin: 12 wins

Losses

David Abbott: 10 losses
Chris Lytle: 9 losses
Jeremy Horn: 7 losses
Chuck Liddell, Tito Ortiz, Randy Couture, Evan Tanner, Ken Shamrock, Matt Serra, Elvis Sinosic: 6 losses

Draws

Ken Shamrock: 2

LONGEST STREAKS

Anderson Silva: 10 wins in a row
BEGIN: *Ultimate Fight Night* 5 (6/28/06)
END: (ongoing) UFC 101 (8/8/2009)

Jon Fitch: 8 wins in a row
BEGIN: *Ultimate Fight Night* 2 (10/3/05)
END: UFC 82 (3/1/08)
(lost at UFC 87)

Chuck Liddell: 7 wins in a row
BEGIN: UFC 22 (9/24/99)
END: UFC 40 (11/22/02)
(lost at UFC 43)

Chuck Liddell: 7 wins in a row
BEGIN: UFC 47 (4/2/04)
END: UFC 66 (12/30/06)
(lost at UFC 71)

Lyoto Machida: 7 wins in a row
BEGIN: UFC 67 (2/3/07)
END: (ongoing) UFC 98 (5/23/09)

Pat Miletich: 7 wins in a row
BEGIN: UFC 16 (3/13/98)
END: UFC 29 (12/16/00)
(lost at UFC 31)

Randy Couture: 7 wins in a row
BEGIN: UFC 13 (5/30/97)
END: UFC 34 (11/2/01)
(lost at UFC 36)

Rich Franklin: 7 wins in a row
BEGIN: UFC 42 (4/25/03)
END: UFC 58 (3/4/06)
(lost at UFC 64)

Royce Gracie: 8 wins in a row
BEGIN: UFC 1 (11/12/93)
END: UFC 3 (9/9/94)
(threw in the towel at UFC 3 finals – went on to win three more matches at UFC 4 and then fight to a draw at UFC 5)

Thiago Alves: 7 wins in a row
BEGIN: UFC: The Final Chapter (10/10/06)
END: UFC 90 (10/25/08)
(lost at UFC 100)

Georges St. Pierre: 6 wins in a row
BEGIN: UFC 74 (8/25/07)

END: UFC 100 (7/11/09)

Gray Maynard: 6 wins in a row
BEGIN: UFC Fight Night 11 (9/19/07)
END: UFC Fight Night 19 (9/16/09)
(Gray actually went to a no contest with Robert Emerson at *The Ultimate Fighter* 5 Finale so you could say his undefeated streak is at 7.)

Those who have won five in a row:

Anderson Silva, Andrei Arlovski, Chuck Liddell (twice), Chuck Liddell, Diego Sanchez, Don Frye, Georges St. Pierre, Jens Pulver, Jon Fitch, Kenny Florian, Lyoto Machida, Marcus Davis, Mark Coleman, Matt Hughes (twice), Pat Miletich, Randy Couture, Rich Franklin, Roger Huerta, Royce Gracie, Thiago Alves, Tito Ortiz, Yves Edwards

Elvis Sinosic: 6 losses in a row
BEGIN: UFC 32 (6/29/01)
END: UFC 70 (4/21/07)
(did debut with a win at UFC 30; hasn't appeared since UFC 70)

Those who have lost four in a row:

Chris Lytle, Dave Menne, David Abbott, Elvis Sinosic (obviously), Joe Doerksen, Mark Coleman, Patrick Côté, Pete Sell, Pete Williams, Phil Baroni, and Tiki Ghosn

FIGHTERS' FIVE FASTEST FIGHTS

Vitor Belfort: 4 minutes and 15 seconds
UFC 12: vs. Scott Ferrozzo, win via TKO, 0:43
UFC 17.5: Ultimate Brazil: vs. Wanderlei Silva, win via TKO, 0:44
UFC 46: vs. Randy Couture, win via TKO, 0:49
UFC 13: vs. David Abbott, win via TKO, 0:52
UFC 43: vs. Marvin Eastman, win via TKO, 1:07

Frank Mir: 4 min and 44 seconds
UFC 36: vs. Pete Williams, win via submission, 0:46
UFC 41: vs. David Abbott, win via submission, 0:46
UFC 48: vs. Tim Sylvia, win via arm bar, 0:50
UFC 34: vs. Roberto Traven, win via arm bar, 1:05
UFC 74: vs. Antoni Hardonk, win via Kimura, 1:17

Don Frye: 4 min and 52 seconds
UFC 8: vs. Thomas Ramirez, win via KO, 0:08
Ultimate Ultimate 1996: vs. Mark Hall, win via achilles hold, 0:20
UFC 8: vs. Sam Adkins, win via TKO, 0:48
Ultimate Ultimate 1996: vs. David Abbott, win via rear naked choke), 1:22
UFC 8: vs. Gary Goodridge, win via submission, 2:14

David Abbott: 5 min and 13 seconds
UFC 6: vs. John Matua, win via KO, 0:20
UFC 17: vs. Hugo Duarte, win via TKO, 0:43
Ultimate Ultimate 1996: vs. Steve Nelmark, win via KO, 1:03
Ultimate Ultimate: vs. Steve Jennum, win via submission, 1:14
UFC 6: vs. Paul Varelans, win via TKO, 1:53

Mike Swick: 5 min and 43 seconds
The Ultimate Fighter Finale: vs. Alex Schoenauer, win via KO, 0:20
Ultimate Fight Night: vs. Gideon Ray, win via TKO, 0:22
UFC: Fight for the Troops: vs. Jonathan Goulet, win via TKO, 0:33
UFC 58: vs. Steve Vigneault, win via guillotine choke, 2:08
UFC 60: vs. Joe Riggs, win via guillotine choke, 2:19

Royce Gracie: 6 min and 36 seconds
UFC 1: vs. Ken Shamrock, win via rear naked choke, 0:57
UFC 2: vs. Jason Delucia, win via arm lock, 1:07
UFC 2: vs. Patrick Smith, win via submission, 1:17
UFC 2: vs. Remco Pardoel, win via submission, 1:31
UFC 1: vs. Gerard Gordeau, win via rear naked choke, 1:44

Tito Ortiz: 6 min and 36 seconds
UFC 13: vs. Wes Albritton, win via TKO, 0:31
UFC 30: vs. Evan Tanner, win via KO, 0:32
UFC 61: vs. Ken Shamrock, win via TKO, 1:18
UFC 29: vs. Yuki Kondo, win via neck crank, 1:52
UFC: The Final Chapter: vs. Ken Shamrock, win via TKO, 2:23

Dan Severn: 8 min and 56 seconds

UFC 4: vs. Marcus Bossett, win via rear naked choke, 0:52

UFC 5: vs. Joe Charles, win via rear naked choke, 1:38

Ultimate Ultimate: vs. Paul Varelans, win via arm triangle choke, 1:40

UFC 4: vs. Anthony Macias, win via rear naked choke, 1:45

UFC 5: vs. Dave Beneteau, win via submission, 3:00

Andrei Arlovski: 9 min and 36 seconds

UFC 55: vs. Paul Buentello, win via KO, 0:15

UFC 51: vs. Tim Sylvia, win via achilles lock, 0:47

UFC 28: vs. Aaron Brink, win via arm bar, 0:55

UFC 40: vs. Ian Freeman, win via TKO, 1:25

UFC 44: vs. Vladimir Matyushenko, win via KO, 1:59

Ken Shamrock: 14 min and 27 seconds

UFC 48: vs. Kimo Leopoldo, win via KO, 1:26

UFC 1: vs. Patrick Smith, win via heel hook, 1:49

UFC 6: vs. Dan Severn, win via guillotine choke, 2:14

UFC 8: vs. Kimo Leopoldo, win via knee bar, 4:24

UFC 3: vs. Felix Mitchell, win via rear naked choke, 4:34

Chris Leben: 15 min and 36 seconds

The Ultimate Fighter Finale: vs. Jason Thacker, win via TKO, 1:35

Ultimate Fight Night 3: vs. Jorge Rivera, win via TKO, 1:44

UFC 82: vs. Alessio Sakara, win via TKO, 3:16

Ultimate Fight Night 2: vs. Edwin Dewees, win via arm bar, 3:26

UFC Fight Night 6: vs. Jorge Santiago, win via KO, 5:35

Evan Tanner: 16 min and 35 seconds

UFC 36: vs. Elvis Sinosic, win via TKO, 2:06

UFC 50: vs. Robbie Lawler, win via triangle choke, 2:22

UFC 19: vs. Valeri Ignatov, win via TKO, 2:58

UFC 59: vs. Justin Levens, win via triangle choke, 3:14

UFC 51: vs. David Terrell, win via TKO, 4:35

Chuck Liddell: 17 min and 4 seconds

UFC 31: vs. Kevin Randleman, win via KO, 1:18

UFC 62: vs. Renato Sobral, win via TKO, 1:35

UFC 52: vs. Randy Couture, win via KO, 2:06

UFC 40: vs. Renato Sobral, win via KO, 2:55

UFC 22: vs. Paul Jones, win via TKO, 3:53

Josh Koscheck: 18 min and 11 seconds

Ultimate Fight Night: vs. Pete Spratt, win via rear naked choke, 1:53

UFC Fight for the Troops: vs. Yoshiyuki Yoshida, win via KO, 2:15

Ultimate Fight Night 4: vs. Ansar Chalangov, win via rear naked choke, 3:29

UFC Fight Night 6: vs. Jonathan Goulet, win via submission, 4:10

The Ultimate Fighter Finale: vs. Chris Sanford, win via KO, 4:21

Tim Sylvia: 19 min and 28 seconds

UFC 44: vs. Gan McGee, win via TKO, 1:54

UFC 59: vs. Andrei Arlovski, win via TKO, 2:43

UFC 41: vs. Ricco Rodriguez, win via TKO, 3:08

UFC 54: vs. Tra Telligman, win via KO, 4:59

UFC 39: vs. Wesley Correira, win via corner stoppage, 6:43

There have been only *five* feuds which have had three matches in UFC:

Randy Couture/Vitor Belfort (UFC 15/46/49): Randy leads 2-1 (all TKOs)

Ken Shamrock/Tito Ortiz (UFC 40/61/Final Chapter): Tito leads 3-0 (all TKOs)

Georges St. Pierre/Matt Hughes (UFC 50/65/79): GSP leads 2-1 (submission/TKO/submission)

Chuck Liddell/Randy Couture (UFC 43/52/57): Chuck leads 2-1 (all KO/TKOs)

Andrei Arlovski/Tim Sylvia (UFC 51/59/61): Tim leads 2-1 (submission/TKO/decision)

Additionally, only *35* pairs have fought twice in UFC:

Aaron Riley vs. Shane Nelson (UFC 96 and 101): Tied 1-1

Anderson Silva vs. Rich Franklin (UFC 64 and 77): Anderson Silva leads 2-0

Anthony Johnson vs. Kevin Burns (UFC Fight Night 14 and *The Ultimate Fighter* 8 Finale): Tied 1-1

B.J. Penn vs. Caol Uno (UFC 34 and 41): B.J. Penn won the first match, draw in second

B.J. Penn vs. Georges St. Pierre (UFC 94 and 58): Georges St. Pierre leads 2-0

B.J. Penn vs. Jens Pulver (UFC 35 and *The Ultimate Fighter* 5 Finale): Tied 1-1

B.J. Penn vs. Matt Hughes (UFC 63 and 46): Tied 1-1

Brock Lesnar vs. Frank Mir (UFC 81 and 100): Tied 1-1

Carlos Newton vs. Matt Hughes (UFC 34 and 38): Matt Hughes leads 2-0

Chuck Liddell vs. Jeremy Horn (UFC 19 and 54): Tied 1-1

Chuck Liddell vs. Renato Sobral (UFC 40 and 62): Chuck Liddell leads 2-0

Chuck Liddell vs. Tito Ortiz (UFC 47 and 66): Chuck Liddell leads 2-0

Dan Severn vs. Ken Shamrock (UFC 9 and 6): Tied 1-1

Dan Severn vs. Oleg Taktarov (UFC 5 and Ultimate Ultimate 1): Dan Severn leads 2-0

Dave Beneteau vs. Oleg Taktarov (UFC 6 and Ultimate Ultimate 2): Oleg Taktarov leads 2-0

Don Frye vs. Gary Goodridge (Ultimate Ultimate 2 and UFC 8): Don Frye leads 2-0

Don Frye vs. Mark Hall (UFC 10 and Ultimate Ultimate 2): Don Frye leads 2-0

Evan Tanner vs. Phil Baroni (UFC 48 and 45): Evan Tanner leads 2-0

Evan Tanner vs. Rich Franklin (UFC 42 and 53): Rich Franklin leads 2-0

Fabiano Iha vs. LaVerne Clark (UFC 20 and 27): Tied 1-1

Falaniko Vitale vs. Matt Lindland (UFC 43 and 45): Tied 1-1

Forrest Griffin vs. Stephan Bonnar (*The Ultimate Fighter* 1 Finale and UFC 62): Forrest Griffin leads 2-0

Forrest Griffin vs. Tito Ortiz (UFC 59 and 106): Tied 1-1

Frank Mir vs. Wes Sims (UFC 46 and 43): Wes Sims was DQed in the first match, Frank won the second

Frank Trigg vs. Matt Hughes (UFC 52 and 45): Matt Hughes leads 2-0

Georges St. Pierre vs. Matt Serra (UFC 69 and 83): Tied 1-1

Guy Mezger vs. Tito Ortiz (UFC 19 and 13): Tied 1-1

Kazushi Sakuraba vs. Marcus Silveira (UFC 15.5 Ultimate Japan 1): Match was prematurely stopped at first, rematch was later on the card and Sakaruba won

Ken Shamrock vs. Kimo Leopoldo (UFC 8 and 48): Ken Shamrock leads 2-0

Ken Shamrock vs. Royce Gracie (UFC 1 and 5): Gracie submitted Ken in the first match, second match was a draw

Matt Lindland vs. Phil Baroni (UFC 34 and 41): Matt Lindland leads 2-0

Nate Quarry vs. Pete Sell (*Ultimate Fight Night* and *Fight Nigh*t 11): Nate Quarry leads 2-0

Pedro Rizzo vs. Randy Couture (UFC 31 and 34): Randy Couture leads 2-0

Pedro Rizzo vs. Tra Telligman (UFC 43 and 20): Pedro Rizzo leads 2-0

Sam Stout vs. Spencer Fisher (UFC 58 and Fight Night 10): Tied 1-1

There have been 681 fighters in the UFC over the last 134 events.

That's 1,187 matches.

Of those 681 fighters:

- 249 fought once (37%)
- 144 fought twice (21%)
- 76 fought three times (11%)
- 43 fought four times (6%); includes Brock Lesnar
- 29 fought five times (4%); includes Frank Shamrock
- 24 fought six times (4%)
- 31 fought seven times (5%)
- 19 fought eight times (3%)
- 15 fought nine times (2%)
- 17 fought ten times (2%)
- 34 fought more than ten times (5%)

Those fighting more than ten times

8 fought 11 times (Forrest Griffin, Joe Stevenson, Jon Fitch, Marcus Davis, Mark Coleman, Sean Sherk, Spencer Fisher, Vitor Belfort)

7 fought 12 times (Chris Leben, Diego Sanchez, Karo Parisyan, Kenny Florian, Matt Lindland, Matt Serra, Thiago Alves)

3 fought 13 times (Dan Severn, Jeremy Horn, Tim Sylvia)
5 fought 14 times (Andrei Arlovski, Frank Mir, Josh Koscheck, Pedro Rizzo, Royce Gracie)
5 fought 15 times (B.J. Penn, Chris Lytle, Georges St. Pierre, Ken Shamrock, Rich Franklin)
1 person fought 17 times (Evan Tanner)
1 person fought 18 times (David Abbott)
1 person fought 19 times (Randy Couture)
2 people fought 21 times (Matt Hughes and Tito Ortiz)
1 person fought 22 times (Chuck Liddell)

At UFC 21, the five-round structure was installed

Heavyweight: 21 Championship Fights
Light Heavyweight: 18 Championship Fights
Middleweight: 17 Championship Fights
Welterweight: 18 Championship Fights
Lightweight: 11 Championship Fights
Bantamweight: 1 Championship Fight (UFC 30: Jens Pulver/Caol Uno – quickly renamed Lightweight)

Of the 86 five-round championship fights:

27% of championship fights ended in Round 1 (average fight 2:42)
20% of championship fights ended in Round 2 (average fight 7:42)
20% of championship fights ended in Round 3 (average fight 13:22)
8% of championship fights ended in Round 4 (average fight 18:45)
26% of championship fights ended in Round 5 (average fight 24:54); includes fights that went the distance

Fight Endings by Weight Division:

Round 1: 0 light, 6 welter, 6 middle, 5 light heavy, 6 heavy
Round 2: 4 light, 4 welter, 3 middle, 2 light heavy, 4 heavy
Round 3: 1 light, 3 welter, 3 middle, 6 light heavy, 4 heavy
Round 4: 1 light, 3 welter, 2 middle, 1 light heavy, 0 heavy
Round 5: 6 light, 2 welter, 3 middle, 4 light heavy, 7 heavy

Average Fight Length by Weight Division:

Lightweight: 99-04 avg = 19 min, 05-09 avg = 20 min
Welterweight: 01-04 avg = 8.5 min, 05-09 avg = 12 min
Middleweight: 99-04 avg = 12.5 min, 05-09 avg = 12.5 min
Light heavy: 01-04 avg = 14 min, 05-09 avg = 12 min
Heavyweight: 99-04 avg = 16 min, 05-09 avg = 10.5 min
Total: 99-04 avg = 13 min, 05-09 avg = 12.5 min

Eleven other championship fights prior to UFC 21:

UFC 12: Mark Coleman vs. Dan Severn, 2:57 (heavyweight title)
UFC 14: Maurice Smith vs. Mark Coleman, 21:00 (heavyweight title)
UFC 15: Maurice Smith vs. David Abbott, 8:08 (heavyweight title)
UFC 17.5 Ultimate Japan 1: Frank Shamrock vs. Kevin Jackson, 0:16 (middleweight title)
UFC 17.5 Ultimate Japan 1: Randy Couture vs. Maurice Smith, 21:00 (heavyweight title)
UFC 16: Frank Shamrock vs. Igor Zinoviev, 0:22 (middleweight title)
UFC 17: Frank Shamrock vs. Jeremy Horn, 16:28 (middleweight title)
UFC 17.5: Ultimate Brazil: Pat Miletich vs. Mikey Burnett, 21:00 (lightweight title)
UFC 17.5: Ultimate Brazil: Frank Shamrock vs. John Lober, 7:40 (middleweight title)
UFC 18: Pat Miletich vs. Jorge Patino, 21:00 (lightweight title)
UFC 20: Bas Rutten vs. Kevin Randleman, 21:00 (heavyweight title)

6 of 11 fights (55%) went less than 21 minutes prior to UFC 21. Since then, 65 of 86 fights have gone less than 21 minutes (76%). About 73% of all UFC fights have gone less than 21 minutes. Only one fight has ended after the 21-minute mark, prior to a decision: Ricco Rodriguez/Randy Couture at UFC 39 (submission).

Fights/Year

1994 to 2004 average of 40 UFC fights/year.
2005 was a big year where they doubled to 80 fights.
2006 doubled that again to 158 fights.
2007 had 171 fights.
2008 had 201 fights.
2009 had 215 fights.

2006 to 2009 averages by weight divisions

46 lightweight fights
47 welterweight fights
38 middleweight fights
33 light heavyweight fights
23 heavyweight fights

There is an average of 2 championship bouts per weight class each year.

Average fight lengths are remarkably similar in all of the weight categories (across 745 fights from 2006-2009)

Lightweight: 9:25 (drops to 8:59 without championship bouts)
Welterweight: 9:38 (drops to 9:27 without championship bouts)
Middleweight: 8:36 (drops to 8:27 without championship bouts)
Light Heavyweight: 8:49 (drops to 8:24 without championship bouts)
Heavyweight: 8:24 (drops to 7:47 without championship bouts)
Average: 9:04 (drops to 8:46 without championship bouts)

Appendix II

Other Major MMA Results

PRIDE FIGHTING CHAMPIONSHIPS

Pride 1

10/11/97

Tokyo Dome (Tokyo, Japan)

Main Event: Rickson Gracie defeated Nobuhiko Takada (arm bar)

Other Fights:

- Kimo Leopoldo vs. Dan Severn (draw)
- Nathan Jones defeated Koji Katao (key lock)
- Renzo Gracie vs. Akira Shoji (draw)
- Gary Goodridge defeated Oleg Taktarov (KO)
- Kazunari Murakami defeated John Dixon (arm bar)
- Branko Cikatic vs. Ralph White (no contest, kickboxing rules)

Pride 2

3/15/98

Yokohama Arena (Yokohama, Japan)

Main Event: Mark Kerr defeated Branko Cikatic (DQ)

Other Fights:

- Marco Ruas defeated Gary Goodridge (heel hook)
- Renzo Gracie defeated Sanae Kikuta (guillotine choke)
- Kazushi Sakuraba defeated Vernon White (arm bar)
- Akira Shoji defeated Juan Mott (rear naked choke)
- Royler Gracie defeated Yuhi Sano (arm bar)
- William Roosmalen defeated Ralph White (KO, kickboxing rules)
- Tasis Petridis defeated George Randolph (decision, kickboxing rules)

Pride 3

6/24/98

Nippon Budokan (Tokyo, Japan)

Main Event: Nobuhiko Takada defeated Kyle Sturgeon (heel hook)

Other Fights:

- Mark Kerr defeated Pedro Otavio (Kimura)
- Gary Goodrige defeated Amir Rahnavardi (KO)
- Kazushi Sakuraba defeated Carlos Newtson (knee bar)
- Daiju Takase defeated Emmanuel Yarborough (submission to strikes)
- Dijiro Matsui vs. Akira Shoji (draw)

Pride 4

10/11/98

Tokyo Dome (Tokyo, Japan)

Main Event: Rickson Gracie defeated Nobuhiko Takada (arm bar)

Other Fights:

- Mark Kerr defeated Hugo Duarte (TKO)
- Alexander Otsuka defeated Marco Ruas (TKO)
- Satoshi Honma defeated Yuhi Sano (TKO)
- Kazushi Sakuraba vs. Allan Goes (draw)
- Sanae Kikuta vs. Daijiro Matsui (draw)
- Akira Shoji defeated Wallid Ismail (TKO)
- Igor Vovchanchyn defeated Gary Goodridge (TKO)

Pride 5

4/29/99

Nagoya Rainbow Hall (Nagoya, Japan)

Main Event: Nobuhiko Takada defeated Mark Coleman (heel hook)

Other Fights:

- Kazushi Sakuraba defeated Vitor Belfort (decision)
- Enson Inoue defeated Soichi Nishida (rear naked choke)
- Igor Vovchanchyn defeated Akira Shoji (decision)

Francisco Bueno defeated Satoshi Honma (TKO)
Egan Inoue defeated Minoru Toyonaga (TKO)

Pride 6

7/4/99
Yokohama Arena (Yokohama, Japan)
Main Event: Mark Kerr defeated Nobuhiko Takada (Kimura)
Other Fights:

- Kazushi Sakuraba defeated Ebenezer Fontes Braga (arm bar)
- Naoya Ogawa defeated Gary Goodridge (Americana)
- Akira Shoji defeated Guy Mezger (decision)
- Igor Vovchanchyn defeated Carlos Barreto (decision)
- Carlos Newton defeated Daijiro Matsui (decision)
- Carl Malenko defeated Egan Inoue (decision)

Pride 7

9/12/99
Yokohama Arena (Yokohama, Japan)
Main Event: Mark Kerr vs. Igor Vovchanchyn (no contest)
Other Fights:

- Kazushi Sakuraba defeated Anthony Macias (arm bar)
- Akira Shoji defeated Larry Parker (decision)
- Maurice Smith defeated Branko Cikatic (forearm choke)
- Wanderlei Silva defeated Carl Malenko (decision)
- Daijiro Matsui defeated Bob Schrijber (DQ)
- Enson Inoue defeated Tully Kulihaapai (arm bar, grappling rules)
- Nobuhiko Takada defeated Alexander Otsuka (TKO, professional wrestling exhibition)

Pride 8

11/21/99
Ariake Coliseum (Tokyo, Japan)
Main Event: Kazushi Sakuraba defeated Royler Gracie (Kimura)
Other Fights:

- Renzo Gracie defeated Alexander Otsuka (decision)
- Igor Vovchanchyn defeated Francisco Bueno (KO)
- Tom Erikson defeated Gary Goodridge (decision)
- Mark Coleman defeated Ricardo Morais (decision)
- Allen Goes defeated Carl Malenko (arm triangle)
- Frank Trigg defeated Fabiano Iha (TKO)
- Wanderlei Silva defeated Daijiro Matsui (decision)

Pride Grand Prix 2000 Opening Round

1/30/00
Tokyo Dome (Tokyo, Japan)
Main Event: Royce Gracie defeated Nobuhiko Takada (decision)
Other Fights:

- Mark Kerr defeated Enson Inoue (decision)
- Igor Vovchanchyn defeated Alexander Otsuka (decision)
- Mark Coleman defeated Masaaki Satake (neck crank)
- Kazushi Sakuraba defeated Guy Mezger (forfeit)
- Kazuyuki Fujita defeated Hans Nijman (decision)
- Akira Shoji defeated Ebenezer Fontes Braga (decision)
- Gary Goodridge defeated Osamu Tachihikari (forearm choke)
- Wanderlei Silva defeated Bob Schrijber (rear naked choke)

Pride Grand Prix 2000 Finals

5/1/00
Tokyo Dome (Tokyo, Japan)
Main Event: Mark Coleman defeated Igor Vovchanchyn (submission to knee strikes, won Pride Grand Prix Championship)
Other Fights:

- Ken Shamrock defeated Alexander Otsuka (TKO)
- Mark Coleman defeated Kazuyuki Fujita (corner stoppage)
- Igor Vovchanchyn defeated Kazushi Sakuraba (corner stoppage)
- Guy Mezger defeated Masaaki Satake (decision)
- Kazuyuki Fujita defeated Mark Kerr (decision)
- Mark Coleman defeated Akira Shoji (decision)
- Kazushi Sakuraba defeated Royce Gracie (corner stoppage)
- Igor Vovchanchyn defeated Gary Goodridge (TKO)

Pride 9

6/4/00

Nagoya Rainbow Hall (Nagoya, Japan)

Main Event: Vitor Belfort defeated Gilbert Yvel (decision)

Other Fights:

Igor Vovchanchyn defeated Daijiro Matsui (TKO)
Ricco Rodriguez defeated Gary Goodridge (decision)
Akira Shoji defeated John Renken (arm bar)
Carlos Newton defeated Yuhi Sano (arm bar)
Allan Goes defeated Vernon White (decision)
Carlos Barreto defeated Tra Telligman (decision)
Heath Herring defeated Willie Peeters (rear naked choke)

Pride 10

8/27/00

Seibu Dome (Tokorozawa, Japan)

Main Event: Kazushi Sakuraba defeated Renzo Gracie (Kimura)

Other Fights:

Ryan Gracie defeated Tokimitsu Ishizawa (TKO)
Kazuyuki Fujita defeated Ken Shamrock (corner stoppage)
Masaaki Satake defeated Kazunari Murakami (TKO)
Igor Vovchanchyn defeated Enson Inoue (TKO)
Mark Kerr defeated Igor Borisov (neck crank)
Gilbert Yvel defeated Gary Goodridge (KO)
Ricco Rodriguez defeated Takayuki Okada (north-south choke)
Wanderlei Silva defeated Guy Mezger (KO)
Vitor Belfor defeated Daijiro Matsui (decision)

Pride 11

11/31/00

Osaka Castle Hall (Osaka, Japan)

Main Event: Kazushi Sakuraba defeated Shannon Ritch (Achilles lock)

Other Fights:

Naoya Ogawa defeated Masaaki Satake (rear naked choke)
Igor Vovchanchyn defeated Nobuhiko Takada (submission to strikes)
Akira Shoji defeated Herman Renting (arm bar)
Alexander Otsuka defeated Mike Bourne (arm bar)
Gary Goodridge defeated Yoshiaki Yatsu (TKO)
Wanderlei Silva vs. Gilbert Yvel (no contest)
Heath Herring defeated Tom Erikson (rear naked choke)

Pride 12

12/9/00

Saitama Super Arena (Saitama, Japan)

Main Event: Kazushi Sakuraba defeated Ryan Gracie (decision)

Other Fights:

Igor Vovchanchyn defeated Mark Kerr (decision)
Kazuyuki Fujita defeated Gilbert Yvel (decision)
Wanderlei Silva defeated Dan Handerson (decision)
Heath Herring defeated Enson Inoue (TKO)
Ricardo Almeida defeated Akira Shoji (decision)
Ricco Rodriguez defeated John Marsh (decision)
Carlos Newton defeated Johil de Oliveira (decision)
Guy Mezger defeated Alexander Otsuka (TKO)

Pride 13

3/25/01

Saitama Super Arena (Saitama, Japan)

Main Event: Wanderlei Silva defeated Kazushi Sakuraba (TKO)

Other Fights:

Tra Telligman defeated Igor Vovchanchyn (decision)
Tadao Yasuda defeated Masaaki Satake (decision)
Mark Coleman defeated Allan Goes (TKO)
Dan Henderson defeated Renzo Gracie (KO)
Heath Herring defeated Denis Sobolev (key lock)
Guy Mezger defeated Egan Inoue (KO)
Vitor Belfort defeated Bobby Southworth (rear naked choke)

Pride 14

5/27/01

Yokohama Arena (Yokohama, Japan)

Main Event: Kazuyuki Fujita defeated Yoshihiro Takayama (arm triangle)

Other Fights:

Igor Vovchanchyn defeated Gilbert Yvel (rear naked choke)
Wanderlei Silva defeated Shungo Oyama (TKO)
Dan Henderson defeated Akira Shoji (TKO)
Vitor Belfort defeated Heath Herring (decision)
Gary Goodridge defeated Valentijn Overeem (submission to strikes)
Chuck Liddell defeated Guy Mezger (KO)
Dajiro Matsui defeated Jose Landi-Jons (decision)
Nino Schembri defeated Johil de Oliveira (arm bar)

Pride 15

7/29/01

Saitama Super Arena (Saitama, Japan)

Main Event: Tokimitsu Ishizawa defeated Ryan Gracie (TKO)

Other Fights:

Kazushi Sakuraba defeated Quinton Jackson (rear naked choke)
Antonio Rodrigo Nogueira defeated Gary Goodridge (triangle choke)
Heath Herring defeated Mark Kerr (TKO)
Igor Vovchanchyn defeated Masaaki Satake (decision)
Daijiro Matsui defeated Ebenezer Fontes Braga (decision)
Wallid Ismail defeated Shungo Oyama (arm triangle)
Assuerio Silva defeated Valentijn Overeem (heel hook)

Pride 16

9/24/01

Osaka Castle Hall (Osaka, Japan)

Main Event: Antonio Rodrigo Noguiera defeated Mark Coleman (triangle arm bar)

Other Fights:

Don Frye defeated Gilbert Yvel (DQ)
Semmy Schilt defeated Akira Shoji (KO)
Ricardo Arona defeated Guy Mezger (decision)
Murilo Rua defeated Daijiro Matsui (KO)
Assuerio Silva defeated Yoshihisa Yamamoto (KO)
Gary Goodridge defeated Yoshiaki Yatsu (TKO)

Pride 17

11/3/01

Tokyo Dome (Tokyo, Japan)

Main Event: Wanderlei Silva defeated Kazushi Sakuraba (doctor stoppage, won Pride Middleweight Championship)

Other Fights:

Antonio Rodrigo Nogueira defeated Heath Herring (decision, won Pride Heavyweight Championship)
Mirko Cro Cop vs. Nobuhiko Takada (draw)
Tom Erikson defeated Matt Skelton (front choke)
Mario Sperry defeated Igor Vovchanchyn (arm triangle)
Semmy Schilt defeated Masaaki Satake (TKO)
Dan Henderson defeated Murilo Rua (decision)
Quinton Jackson defeated Yuki Ishikawa (KO)
Renzo Gracie defeated Michiyoshi Ohara (decision)

Pride 18

12/23/01

Marine Messe Fukuoka (Fukuoka, Japan)

Main Event: Semmy Schilt defeated Yoshihiro Takayama (KO)

Other Fights:

Wanderlei Silva defeated Alexander Otsuka (doctor stoppage)
Jeremy Horn defeated Akira Shoji (decision)
Igor Vovchanchyn defeated Valentijn Overeem (heel hook)
Yoshihisa Yamamoto defeated Jan Nortje (arm bar)
Murilo Rua defeated Alex Andrade (decision)
Alex Stiebling defeated Allan Goes (TKO)
Daijiro Matsui defeated Quinton Jackson (DQ)

Pride 19

2/24/02

Saitama Super Arena (Saitama, Japan)

Main Event: Wanderlei Silva defeated Kiyoshi Tamura (KO)

Other Fights:

Don Frye defeated Ken Shamrock (decision)
Antonio Rodrigo Nogueira defeated Enson Inoue (triangle choke)

Heath Herring defeated Igor Vovchanchyn (decision)
Carlos Newton defeated Jose Landi-Jons (arm bar)
Rodrigo Gracie defeated Daijiro Matsui (guillotine choke)
Alex Stiebling defeated Wallid Ismail (decision)
Tom Erikson defeated Tim Catalfo (rear naked choke)

Pride 20

4/28/02
Yokohama Arena (Yokohama, Japan)
Main Event: Mirko Cro Cop vs. Wanderlei Silva (draw)
Other Fights:

Sanae Kikuta defeated Alexander Otsuka (decision)
Murilo Rua defeated Mario Sperry (decision)
Ricardo Arona defeated Dan Henderson (decision)
Antonio Rogerio Nogueira defeated Yusuke Imamura (guillotine choke)
Quinton Jackson defeated Masaaki Satake (TKO)
Bob Sapp defeated Yoshihisa Yamamoto (TKO)

Pride 21

6/23/02
Saitama Super Arena (Saitama, Japan)
Main Event: Don Frye defeated Yoshihiro Takayama (TKO)
Other Fights:

Fedor Emelianenko defeated Semmy Schilt (decision)
Daniel Gracie defeated Takashi Sugiura (decision)
Shungo Oyama defeated Renzo Gracie (decision)
Jeremy Horn defeated Gilbert Yvel (decision)
Anderson Silva defeated Alex Stiebling (TKO)
Gary Goodridge defeated Achmed Labasanov (decision)
Bob Sapp defeated Kiyoshi Tamura (TKO)

Pride Shockwave 2002

8/28/02
Tokyo National Stadium (Tokyo, Japan)
Main Event: Mirko Cro Cop defeated Kazushi Sakuraba (doctor stoppage)
Other Fights:

Hidehiko Yoshida defeated Royce Gracie (Ezekiel choke, modified rules)
Antonio Rodrigo Nogueira defeated Bob Sapp (arm bar)
Jerome Le Banner defeated Don Frye (KO, K-1 kickboxing rules)
Ernesto Hoost vs. Semmy Schilt (draw, K-1 kickboxing rules)
Gary Goodridge defeated Lloyd Van Dams (TKO)
Jerrol Venetiaan defeated Daijiro Matsui (decision)
Wanderlei Silva defeated Tatsuya Iwasaki (TKO)

Pride 22

9/29/02
Nagoya Rainbow Hall (Nagoya, Japan)
Main Event: Ryan Gracie defeated Shungo Oyama (arm bar)
Other Fights:

Quinton Jackson defeated Igor Vovchanchyn (TKO)
Mario Sperry defeated Andrei Kopylov (TKO)
Heath Herring defeated Iouri Kotchkine (TKO)
Paulo Filho defeated Akira Shoji (arm bar)
Anderson Silva defeated Alexander Otsuka (decision)
Guy Mezger defeated Yoshihisa Yamamoto (decision)
Kevin Randleman defeated Michiyoshi Ohara (decision)

Pride 23

11/24/02
Tokyo Dome (Tokyo, Japan)
Main Event: Wanderlei Silva defeated Hiromitsu Kanehara (corner stoppage)
Other Fights:

Kazushi Sakuraba defeated Gilles Arsene (arm bar)
Kiyoshi Tamura defeated Nobuhiko Takada (KO)
Hidehiko Yoshida defeated Don Frye (arm bar)
Antonio Rodrigo Nogueira defeated Semmy Schilt (triangle choke)
Fedor Emelianenko defeated Heath Herring (doctor stoppage)

Ricardo Arona defeated Murilo Rua (decision)
Kevin Randleman defeated Kenichi Yamamoto (TKO)
Hirotaka Yokoi defeated Jerrel Venetiaan (arm bar)

Pride 24

12/23/02

Marine Messe Fukuoka (Fukuoka, Japan)

Main Event: Antonio Rodrigo Nogueira defeated Dan Henderson (arm bar)

Other Fights:

Kevin Randleman defeated Murilo Rua (TKO)
Alistair Overeem defeated Bazigit Atajev (TKO)
Yoshihisa Yamamoto defeated Alexander Otsuka (TKO)
Rodrigo Gracie defeated Yuki Sasaki (decision)
Ron Waterman defeated Valentijn Overeem (Americana)
Antonio Rogerio Nogueira defeated Guy Mezger (decision)
Daijiro Matsui defeated Kazuki Okubo (decision)

Pride 25

3/16/03

Yokohama Arena (Yokohama, Japan)

Main Event: Fedor Emelianenko defeated Antonio Rodrigo Nogueira (decision, won Pride Heavyweight Championship)

Other Fights:

Quinton Jackson defeated Kevin Randleman (TKO)
Antonio Schembri defeated Kazushi Sakuraba (TKO)
Dan Henderson defeated Shungo Oyama (TKO)
Anderson Silva defeated Carlos Newton (KO)
Alexander Otsuka defeated Kenichi Yamamoto (decision)
Akira Shoji defeated Alex Stiebling (decision)
Antonio Rogerio Nogueira defeated Kazuhiro Nakamura (arm bar)

Pride 26

6/8/03

Yokohama Arena (Yokohama, Japan)

Main Event: Fedor Emelianenko defeated Kazuyuki Fujita (rear naked choke)

Other Fights:

Mirko Cro Cop defeated Heath Herring (TKO)
Mark Coleman defeated Don Frye (decision)
Quinton Jackson defeated Mikhail Illoukhine (submission to knee strikes)
Alistair Overeem defeated Mike Bencic (submission to strikes)
Daiju Takase defeated Anderson Silva (triangle choke)
Kazuhiro Hamanaka defeated Antonio Schembri (decision)

Pride Total Elimination 2003

8/10/03

Saitama Super Arena (Saitama, Japan)

Main Event: Wanderlei Silva defeated Kazushi Sakuraba (KO)

Other Fights:

Hidehiko Yoshida defeated Kiyoshi Tamura (Ezekiel choke)
Mirko Cro Cop defeated Igor Vovchanchyn (KO)
Antonio Rodrigo Nogueira defeated Ricco Rodriguez (decision)
Quinton Jackson defeated Murilo Bustamante (decision)
Chuck Liddell defeated Alistair Overeem (KO)
Fedor Emelianenko defeated Gary Goodridge (TKO)

Pride Bushido 1

10/05/03

Saitama Super Arena (Saitama, Japan)

Main Event: Mirko Cro Cop defeated Dos Caras Jr. (KO)

Other Fights:

Aleksander Emelianenko defeated Assuerio Silva (decision)
Mauricio Rua defeated Akira Shoji (KO)
Ryan Gracie defeated Kazuhiro Hamanaka (TKO)
Rodrigo Gracie defeated Daiju Takase (decision)
Kazuhiro Nakamura defeated Daniel Gracie (decision)
Ralph Gracie defeated Dokonjonosuke Mishima (decision)

Carlos Newton defeated Renzo Gracie (decision)
Sergei Kharitonov defeated Jason Suttie (arm bar)
Chalid Arrab defeated Rodney Faverus (decision)

Pride Final Conflict 2003

11/9/03

Tokyo Dome (Tokyo, Japan)

Main Event: Wanderlei Silva defeated Quinton Jackson (TKO, won Pride Middleweight Grand Prix)

Other Fights:

Antonio Rodrigo Nogueira defeated Mirko Cro Cop (arm bar)
Kazushi Sakuraba defeated Kevin Randleman (arm bar)
Heath Herring defeated Yoshihisa Yamamoto (rear naked choke)
Dan Henderson defeated Murilo Bustamante (TKO)
Wanderlei Silva defeated Hidehiko Yoshida (decision)
Quinton Jackson defeated Chuck Liddell (TKO)
Gary Goodridge defeated Dan Bobish (TKO)

Pride Shockwave 2003

12/31/03

Saitama Super Arena (Saitama, Japan)

Main Event: Antonio Rogerio Nogueira defeated Kazushi Sakuraba (decision)

Other Fights:

Kiyoshi Tamura defeated Rony Sefo (arm bar)
Yuki Kondo defeated Mario Sperry (doctor stoppage)
Daniel Gracie defeated Wataru Sakata (arm bar)
Gary Goodridge defeated Don Frye (KO)
Royce Gracie vs. Hidehiko Yoshida (draw)
Murilo Rua defeated Akira Shoji (KO)
Hayato Sakurai defeated Daiju Takase (decision)
Heath Herring defeated Giant Silva (rear naked choke)
Quinton Jackson defeated Ikuhisa Minowa (TKO)

Pride 27

2/1/04

Osaka Castle Hall (Osaka, Japan)

Main Event: Mirko Cro Cop defeated Ron Waterman (TKO)

Other Fights:

Heath Herring defeated Gan McGee (decision)
Yoshihisa Yamamoto defeated Mark Kerr (TKO)
Kazuhiro Nakamura defeated Dos Caras Jr. (decision)
Murilo Rua defeated Alexander Otsuka (arm triangle)
Sergei Kharitonov defeated Cory Peterson (arm bar)
Igor Vovchanchyn defeated Dan Bobish (TKO)

Pride Bushido 2

2/15/04

Yokohama Arena (Yokohama, Japan)

Main Event: Wanderlei Silva defeated Ikuhisa Minowa (KO)

Other Fights:

Mauricio Rua defeated Akihiro Gono (TKO)
Takanori Gomi defeated Jadson Costa (TKO)
Mirko Cro Cop defeated Yoshihisa Yamamoto (TKO)
Rodrigo Gracie defeated Hayato Sakurai (decision)
Daiju Takase defeated Chris Brennan (decision)
Mario Sperry defeated Mike Bencic (KO)
Sean Sherk defeated Ryuki Ueyama (decision)
Yasuhito Namekawa defeated Egidijus Valavicius (guillotine)
Yushin Okami defeated Ryuta Sakurai (decision)
Mu Bae Choi defeated Yusuke Imamura (rear naked choke)

Pride Total Elimination 2004

4/25/04

Saitama Super Arena (Saitama, Japan)

Main Event: Fedor Emelianenko defeated Mark Coleman (arm bar)

Other Fights:

Antonio Rodrigo Nogueira defeated Hirotaka Yokoi (anaconda choke)
Kevin Randleman defeated Mirko Cro Cop (KO)
Naoya Ogawa defeated Stefan Leko (arm triangle)
Semmy Schilt defeated Gan McGee (arm bar)
Giant Silva defeated Henry Miller (Kimura)
Sergei Kharitonov defeated Murilo Rua (KO)

Heath Herring defeated Yoshiki Takahasi (TKO)

Pride Bushido 3

5/23/04

Yokohama Arena (Yokohama, Japan)

Main Event: Ryan Gracie defeated Ikuhisa Minowa (decision)

Other Fights:

Takanori Gomi defeated Ralph Gracie (TKO)
Ricardo Almeida defeated Ryo Chonan (decision)
Mirko Cro Cop defeated Hiromitsu Kanehara (decision)
Kazuhiro Nakamura defeated Chalid Arrab (arm bar)
Akira Shoji defeated Tsuyoshi Tamakairiki (TKO)
Daiju Takase defeated Carlos Newton (decision)
Kazuo Misaki defeated Jorge Patino (decision)
Mu Bae Choi defeated Yoshihisa Yamamoto (decision)
Aleksander Emelianenko defeated Matt Foki (rear naked choke)
Shamoji Fujii defeated Kim Jin Oh (rear naked choke)
Bertrand Amoussou defeated Rao Rao (KO)

Pride Critical Countdown 2004

6/20/04

Saitama Super Arena (Saitama, Japan)

Main Event: Fedor Emelianenko defeated Kevin Randleman (Kimura)

Other Fights:

Antonio Rodrigo Nogueira defeated Heath Herring (anaconda choke)
Hidehiko Yoshida defeated Mark Hunt (arm bar)
Naoya Ogawa defeated Giant Silva (TKO)
Sergei Kharitonov defeated Semmy Schilt (TKO)
Quinton Jackson defeated Ricardo Arona (KO)
Kazushi Sakuraba defeated Antonio Schembri (decision)

Pride Bushido 4

7/19/04

Nagoya Rainbow Hall (Nagoya, Japan)

Main Event: Antonio Rogerio Nogueira defeated Kazuhiro Nakamura (decision)

Other Fights:

Takanori Gomi defeated Fabio Mello (TKO)
Paulo Filho defeated Akira Shoji (decision)
Mirko Cro Cop defeated Shungo Oyama (TKO)
Takashi Sugiura defeated Giant Silva (TKO)
Ikuhisa Minowa defeated Kenichi Yamamoto (TKO)
Hayato Sakurai defeated Brady Fink (guillotine choke)
Amar Suloev defeated Dean Lister (decision)
Dokonjonosuke Mishima defeated Marcus Aurelio (decision)
Luiz Firmino defeated Hiroyuki Abe (arm triangle)
Kyosuke Sasaki vs. Eiji Mitsukoa (draw)

Pride Final Conflict 2004

8/15/04

Saitama Super Arena (Saitama, Japan)

Main Event: Fedor Emelianenko vs. Antonio Rodrigo Nogueira (no contest)

Other Fights:

Wanderlei Silva defeated Yuki Kondo (KO)
Mirko Cro Cop defeated Aleksander Emelianenko (KO)
Ron Waterman defeated Kevin Randleman (key lock)
Fedor Emelianenko defeated Naoya Ogawa (arm bar)
Antonio Rodrigo Nogueira defeated Sergei Kharitonov (decision)
Kazuhiro Nakamura defeated Murilo Bustamante (decision)

Pride Bushido 5

10/14/04

Osaka Castle Hall (Osaka, Japan)

Main Event: Takanori Gomi defeated Charles Bennett (Kimura)

Other Fights:

Crosley Gracie defeated Hayato Sakurai (arm bar)
Ryo Chonan defeated Carlos Newton (decision)
Igor Vovchanchyn defeated Shamoji Fujii (KO)
Ikuhisa Minowa defeated Ryuki Ueyama (decision)
Luiz Firmino defeated Masakazu Imanari (decision)

Henry Miller defeated Mal Foki (KO)
Mauricio Rua defeated Yasuhito Namekawa (TKO)

Pride 28

10/31/04
Saitama Super Arena (Saitama, Japan)
Main Event: Wanderlei Silva defeated Quinton Jackson (KO)
Other Fights:
Mirko Cro Cop defeated Josh Barnett (TKO)
Dan Henderson defeated Kazuhiro Nakamura (TKO)
Mark Hunt defeated Dan Bobish (TKO)
Alistair Overeem defeated Hiromitsu Kanehara (TKO)
Aleksander Emelianenko defeated James Thompson (KO)
Ricardo Arona defeated Sergey Ignatov (rear naked choke)
Mu Bae Choi defeated Soa Palalei (rear naked choke)
Heath Herring defeated Hirotaka Yokoi (KO)

Pride Shockwave 2004

12/31/04
Saitama Super Arena, (Saitama, Japan)
Main Event: Fedor Emelianenko defeated Antonio Rodrigo Nogueira (decision, won Pride Heavyweight Grand Prix)
Other Fights:
Mark Hunt defeated Wanderlei Silva (decision)
Takanori Gomi defeated Jens Pulver (KO)
Dan Henderson defeated Yuki Kondo (decision)
Mirko Cro Cop defeated Kevin Randleman (guillotine choke)
Rulan Gardner defeated Hidehiko Yoshida (decision)
Makoto Takimoto defeated Henry Miller (decision)
Ryo Chonan defeated Anderson Silva (heel hook)
Ryan Gracie defeated Yoji Anjo (arm bar)
Mu Bae Choi defeated Giant Silva (arm triangle)
Ikuhisa Minowa defeated Stefan Leko (heel hook)

Pride 29

2/20/05
Saitama Super Arena (Saitama, Japan)
Main Event: Mirko Cro Cop defeated Mark Coleman (KO)
Other Fights:
Quinton Jackson defeated Murilo Rua (decision)
Antonio Rogerio Nogueira defeated Alistair Overeem (decision)
Kiyoshi Tamura defeated Aliev Makhmud (TKO)
Sergei Kharitonov defeated Mu Bae Choi (KO)
Kazuhiro Nakamura defeated Stefan Leko (TKO)
Igor Vovchanchyn defeated Yoshiki Takahasi (KO)
Mauricio Rua defeated Hiromitsu Kanehara (TKO)
Fabricio Werdum defeated Tom Erikson (rear naked choke)
Mario Sperry defeated Hirotaka Yokoi (TKO)

Pride Bushido 6

4/3/05
Yokohama Arena (Yokohama, Japan)
Main Event: Fedor Emelianenko defeated Tsuyoshi Kohsaka (TKO)
Other Fights:
Ikuhisa Minowa defeated Gilbert Yvel (toe hold)
Murilo Bustamante defeated Ruta Sakurai (decision)
Aleksander Emelianenko defeated Ricardo Morais (KO)
Daniel Acacio defeated Daiju Takase (TKO)
Luiz Azeredo defeated Luiz Firmino (decision)
Marcus Aurelio defeated Daisuke Nakamura (decision)
Dean Lister defeated Akira Shoji (triangle choke)
Paulo Filho defeated Amar Suloev (arm bar)
Denis Kang defeated Takahiro Oba (arm bar)

Pride Total Elimination 2005

4/23/05
Osaka Dome (Osaka, Japan)
Main Event: Wanderlei Silva defeated Hidehiko Yoshida (decision)
Other Fights:
Murilo Rua defeated Quinton Jackson (KO)
Kazushi Sakuraba defeated Yoon Dong-Sik (KO)

Antonio Rogerio Nogueira defeated Dan Henderson (arm bar)
Alistair Overeem defeated Vitor Belfort (guillotine choke)
Igor Vovchanchyn defeated Yuki Kondo (decision)
Ricardo Arona defeated Dean Lister (decision)
Kazuhiro Nakamura defeated Kevin Randleman (decision)

Pride Bushido 7

5/22/05

Differ Ariake (Tokyo, Japan)

Main Event: Takanori Gomi defeated Luiz Azeredo (KO)

Other Fights:

Phil Baroni defeated Ikuhisa Minowa (TKO)
Ryo Chonan defeated Antonio Schembri (decision)
Tatsuya Kawajiri defeated Kim In Seok (corner stoppage)
Akihiro Gono defeated Crosley Gracie (decision)
Hayato Sakurai defeated Miltion Vieira (decision)
Aaron Riley defeated Michihiro Omigawa (KO)
Yves Edwards defeated Dokonjonosuke Mishima (arm bar)
Jens Pulver defeated Tomomi Iwama (KO)
Charles Bennett defeated Yoshiro Maeda (KO)

Pride Critical Countdown 2005

6/26/05

Saitama Super Arena (Saitama, Japan)

Main Event: Wanderlei Silva defeated Kazuhiro Nakamura (TKO)

Other Fights:

Ricardo Arona defeated Kazushi Sakuraba (corner stoppage)
Antonio Rodrigo Nogueira defeated Pawel Nastula (TKO)
Kiyoshi Tamura defeated Makato Takimoto (decision)
Mirko Cro Cop defeated Ibragim Magomedov (KO)
Alistair Overeem defeated Igor Vovchanchyn (guillotine choke)
Mauricio Rua defeated Antonio Rogerio Nogueira (decision)
Sergei Kharitonov defeated Pedro Rizzo (TKO)

Pride Bushido 8

6/17/05

Nagoya Rainbow Hall (Nagoya, Japan)

Main Event: Takanori Gomi defeated Jean Silva (decision)

Other Fights:

Phil Baroni defeated Ryo Chonan (KO)
Ikuhisa Minowa defeated Kimo Leopoldo (Achilles lock)
Tatsuya Kawajiri defeated Luiz Firmino (decision)
Daniel Acacio defeated Kazuo Misaki (decision)
Joachim Hansen defeated Masakazu Imanari (KO)
James Thompson defeated Henry Miller (KO)
Kazuki Okubo defeated Kazuki Okubo (arm bar)
Marcus Aurelio defeated Jutaro Nakao (decision)
Denis Kang defeated Andrei Semenov (decision)
Josh Thomson defeated Daisuke Sugie (knee bar)

Pride Final Conflict 2005

8/28/05

Saitama Super Arena (Saitama, Japan)

Main Event: Mauricio Rua defeated Ricardo Arona (KO, won Pride Middleweight Grand Prix)

Other Fights:

Fedor Emelianenko defeated Mirko Cro Cop (decision)
Hidehiko Yoshida defeated David Abbott (kata ha jime)
Fabricio Wedrum defeated Roman Zentsov (triangle arm bar)
Mauricio Rua defeated Alistair Overeem (TKO)
Ricardo Arona defeated Wanderlei Silva (decision)
Kazuhiro Nakamura defeated Igor Vovchanchyn (decision)

Pride Bushido 9

9/25/05

Ariake Coliseum (Tokyo, Japan)

Main Event: Takanori Gomi defeated Luiz Azeredo (decision)

Other Fights:

Hayato Sakurai defeated Joachim Hansen (decision)
Murilo Bustamante defeated Ikuhisa Minowa (TKO)
Dan Henderson defeated Akihiro Gono (KO)

Luiz Azeredo defeated Naoyuki Kotani (KO)
Takanori Gomi defeated Tatsuya Kawajiri (rear naked choke)
Joachim Hansen defeated Yves Edwards (decision)
Hayato Sakurai defeated Jens Pulver (TKO)
Dokonjonosuke Mishima defeated Charles Bennett (ankle lock)
Murilo Bustamante defeated Masanori Suda (arm bar)
Ikuhisa Minowa defeated Phil Baroni (decision)
Dan Henderson defeated Ryo Chonan (KO)
Akihiro Gono defeated Daniel Acacio (decision)
Paulo Filho defeated Ryuta Sakurai (arm bar)

Pride 30

10/23/05
Saitama Super Arena (Saitama, Japan)
Main Event: Mirko Cro Cop defeated Josh Barnett (decision)
Other Fights:

Kazushi Sakuraba defeated Ken Shamrock (TKO)
Makato Takimoto defeated Yoon Dong Sik (decision)
Sergei Kharitonov defeated Fabricio Werdum (decision)
Quinton Jackson defeated Hirotaka Yokoi (TKO)
James Thompson defeated Alexander Lungru (TKO)
Murilo Rua defeated Murad Chunkaiev (heel hook)
Zuluzinho defeated Henry Miller (TKO)

Pride Shockwave 2005

12/31/05
Saitama Super Arena (Saitama, Japan)
Main Event: Hidehiko Yoshida defeated Naoya Ogawa (arm bar)
Other Fights:

Wanderlei Silva defeated Ricardo Arona (decision)
Mark Hunt defeated Mirko Cro Cop (decision)
Kazushi Sakuraba defeated Ikuhisa Minowa (Kimura)
Takanori Gomi defeated Hayato Sakurai (KO, won Pride Lightweight Championship)
Dan Henderson defeated Murilo Bustamante (decision, won Pride Welterweight Championship)
Fedor Emelianenko defeated Zuluzinho (submission to strikes)
Aleksander Emelianenko defeated Pawel Nastula (rear naked choke)
Sanae Kikuta defeated Makoto Takimoto (decision)
James Thompson defeated Giant Silva (TKO)
Kazuhiro Nakamura defeated Yuki Kondo (decision)
Charles Bennett defeats Ken Kaneko (arm bar)

Pride 31

2/26/06
Saitama Super Arena (Saitama, Japan)
Main Event: Mark Hunt defeated Yosuke Nishijima (KO)
Other Fights:

Mark Coleman defeated Mauricio Rua (TKO)
Antonio Rodrigo Nogueira defeated Kiyoshi Tamura (arm bar)
Josh Barnett defeated Kazuhiro Nakamura (rear naked choke)
Alistair Overeem defeated Sergei Kharitonov (TKO)
Tsuyoshi Kohsaka defeated Mario Sperry (TKO)
Fabricio Werdum defeated Jon Olav Einemo (decision)
Quinton Jackon defeated Yoon Dong Sik (decision)
Roman Zentsov defeated Pedro Rizzo (KO)

Pride Bushido 10

4/2/06
Differ Ariake (Tokyo, Japan)
Main Event: Marcus Aurelio defeated Takanori Gomi (arm triangle)
Other Fights:

Dan Henderson defeated Kazuo Misaki (decision)
Ikuhisa Minowa defeated Giant Silva (TKO)
Phil Baroni defeated Yuki Kondo (KO)
Akihiro Gono defeated Dae Won Kim (arm bar)
Paulo Filho defeated Murilo Rua (decision)
Joachim Hansen defeated Luiz Azeredo (KO)
Denis Kang defeated Mark Weir (submission to knee strikes)

Jens Pulver defeated Kenji Arai (KO)
Mitsuhiro Ishida defeated Paul Rodriguez (guillotine choke)
Yves Edwards defeats Seichi Ikemoto (decision)

Pride Total Elimination Absolute

5/5/06
Osaka Dome (Osaka, Japan)
Main Event: Hidehiko Yoshidsa defeated Yosuke Nishijima (triangle choke)
Other Fights:

Antonio Rodrigo Nogueira defeated Zuluzinho (arm bar)
Mirko Filipovic defeated Ikuhisa Minowa (TKO)
Kazuyuki Fujita defeated James Thompson (KO)
Josh Barnett defeated Aleksander Emelianenko (key lock)
Mark Hunt defeated Tsuyoshi Kohsaka (TKO)
Fabricio Werdum defeated Alistair Overeem (KO)
Roman Zentsov defeated Gilbert Yvel (Kimura)

Pride Bushido 11

6/4/06
Saitama Super Arena (Saitama, Japan)
Main Event: Kazuo Misaki defeated Phil Baroni (decision)
Other Fights:

Denis Kang defeated Murilo Rua (KO)
Akihiro Gono defeated Hector Lombard (decision)
Hayato Sakurai defeated Olaf Alfonso (KO)
Tatsuya Kawajiri defeated Charles Bennett (knee bar)
Mitsuhiro Ishida defeated Marcus Aurelio (decision)
Gegard Mousasi defeated Makoto Takimoto (TKO)
Ryo Chonan defeated Joey Villasenor (decision)
Paulo Filho defeated Gregory Bouchelaghem (decision)
Amar Suloev defeated Murilo Bustamante (decision)
Jason Black defeated Won Jin Eoh (corner stoppage)

Pride Critical Countdown Absolute

7/1/06
Saitama Super Arena (Saitama, Japan)
Main Event: Mirko Cro Cop defeated Hidehiko Yoshida (TKO)
Other Fights:

Josh Barnett defeated Mark Hunt (Kimura)
Wanderlei Silva defeated Kazuyuki Fujita (TKO)
Antonio Rodrigo Nogueira defeated Fabricio Werdum (decision)
Kazuhiro Nakamura defeated Evangelisa Santos (key lock)
Antonio Rogerio Nogueira defeated Alistair Overeem (TKO)
Vitor Belfort defeated Kazuo Takahasi (KO)
Yoshihiro Nakao defeated Eun Soo Lee (doctor stoppage)
Pawel Nastula defeated Edson Draggo (arm bar)

Pride Bushido 12

8/26/06
Nagoya Rainbow Hall (Nagoya, Japan)
Main Event: Takanori Gomi defeated David Baron (rear naked choke)
Other Fights:

Kazuo Misaki defeated Dan Henderson (decision)
Akihiro Gono defeated Gegard Mousasi (arm bar)
Paulo Filho defeated Ryo Chonan (arm bar)
Denis Kang defeated Amar Suloev (rear naked choke)
Ikuhisa Minowa defeated Eric Esch (arm bar)
Hayato Sakurai defeated Luciano Azevedo (TKO)
Mitsuhiro Ishida defeated Christiano Marcello (decision)
Tatsuya Kawajiri defeated Chris Brennan (TKO)
Gilbert Melendez defeated Nobuhiro Obiya (decision)
Shinya Aoki defeated Jason Black (triangle choke)
Hatsu Hioki defeated Jeff Curran (decision)
Hiroyuki Abe defeated Naoki Matsushita (draw)
Daisuke Nakamura defeated Seichi Ikemoto (arm bar)

Pride Final Conflict Absolute

9/10/06
Saitama Super Arena (Saitama, Japan)

Main Event: Mirko Cro Cop defeated Josh Barnett (submission to strikes, won Pride Absolute Grand Prix)

Other Fights:

Ricardo Arona defeated Alistair Overeem (submission to strikes)

Mauricio Rua defeated Cyrille Diabate (TKO)

Kazuhiro Nakamura defeated Yoshihiro Nakao (decision)

Ricardo Morais defeated Tae Hyun Lee (corner stoppage)

Aleksander Emelianenko defeated Sergei Kharitonov (TKO)

Josh Barnett defeated Antonio Rodrigo Nogueira (decision)

Mirko Cro Cop defeated Wanderlei Silva (KO)

Evangelista Santos defeated Yosuke Nishijima (rear naked choke)

Pride 32

10/21/06

Thomas & Mack Center (Las Vegas, Nevada)

Main Event: Fedor Emelianenko defeated Mark Coleman (arm bar)

Other Fights:

Mauricio Rua defeated Kevin Randleman (knee bar)

Josh Barnett defeated Pawel Nastula (toe hole)

Eric Esch defeated Sean O'Haire (TKO)

Dan Henderson defeated Vitor Belfort (decision)

Phil Baroni defeated Yosuke Nishijima (Kimura)

Kazuhiro Nakamura defeated Travis Galbraith (TKO)

Robbie Lawler defeated Joey Villasenor (KO)

Pride Bushido 13

11/5/06

Yokohama Arena (Yokohama, Japan)

Main Event: Kazuo Misaki defeated Denis Kang (decision, won Pride Welterweight Grand Prix)

Other Fights:

Takanori Gomi defeated Marcus Aurelio (decision)

Shinya Aoki defeated Clay French (triangle choke)

Mitsuhiro Ishida defeated David Bielkheden (decision)

Ikuhisa Minowa defeated Mike Plotcheck (decision)

Sanae Kikuta defeated Jean-Francois Lenogue (decision)

Joe Pearson defeated Yoshiro Maeda (guillotine choke)

Luiz Firmino defeated Nobuhiro Obiya (decision)

Murilo Bustamante defeated Yoon Dong Sik (decision)

Denis Kang defeated Akihiro Gono (decision)

Paulo Filho defeated Kazuo Misaki (arm bar)

Gegard Mousasi defeated Hector Lombard (decision)

Pride Shockwave 2006

12/31/06

Saitama Super Arena (Saitama, Japan)

Main Event: Fedor Emelianenko defeated Mark Hunt (Kimura)

Other Fights:

Antonio Rodrigo Nogueira defeated Josh Barnett (decision)

James Thompson defeated Hidehiko Yoshida (TKO)

Takanori Gomi defeated Mitsuhiro Ishida (TKO)

Kazuyuki Fujita defeated Eldar Kurtanidze (submission to strikes)

Gilbert Melendez defeated Tatsuya Kawajiri (decision)

Mauricio Rua defeated Kazuhiro Nakamura (decision)

Akihiro Gono defeated Yuki Kondo (decision)

Shinya Aoki defeated Joachim Hansen (gogoplata)

Kiyoshi Tamura defeated Ikuhisa Minowa (KO)

Pride 33

2/24/07

Thomas & Mack Center (Las Vegas, Nevada)

Main Event: Dan Henderson defeats Wanderlei Silva (KO, won Pride Middleweight Championship)

Other Fights:

Nick Diaz vs. Takanori Gomi (no contest)

Mauricio Rua defeated Alistair Overeem (KO)

Sergei Kharitonov defeated Mike Russow (arm bar)

Hayato Sakurai defeated Mac Danzig (KO)

Rameau Thierry Sokoudjou defeated Antonio Rogerio Nogueira (KO)

James Lee defeated Travis Wiuff (guillotine choke)
Frank Trigg defeated Kazuo Misaki (decision)
Joachim Hansen defeated Jason Ireland (arm bar)

Pride 34

4/8/07
Saitama Super Arena (Saitama, Japan)
Main Event: Jeff Monson defeated Kazuyuki Fujita (rear naked choke)
Other Fights:

Rameau Thierry Sokoudjou defeated Ricardo Arona (KO)
Shinya Aoki defeated Brian Lo-An-Joe (arm bar)
James Thompson defeated Don Frye (TKO)
Gilbert Yvel defeated Akira Shoji (TKO)
Makoto Takimoto defeated Zelg Galesic (arm bar)
Eric Esch defeated Zuluzinho (key lock)
Yoshihiro Nakao defeated Edson Drago (neck crank)

YARENNOKA

Yarennoka

12/31/07
Saitama Super Arena (Saitama, Japan)
Main Event: Shinya Aoki defeated Jung Bu-Kyung (decision)
Other Fights:

Hayato Sakurai defeated Hidehiko Hasegawa (decision)
Fedor Emelianenko defeated Hong-Man Choi (arm bar)
Kazuo Misaki vs. Yoshihiro Akiyama (no contest)
Mitsuhiro Ishida defeated Gilbert Melendez (decision)
Makoto Takimoto defeated Murilo Bustamante (decision)
Tatsuya Kawajiri defeated Luiz Azeredo (decision)
Mike Russow defeated Roman Zentsov (north-south choke)

DREAM

Dream 1

3/15/08
Saitama Super Arena (Saitama, Japan)
Main Event: Shinya Aoki vs. Gesias Cavalcante (no contest)
Other Fights:

Tatsuya Kawajiri defeated Kultar Gill (decision)
Eddie Alvarez defeated Andre Amade (TKO)
Mirko Cro Cop defeated Tatsuya Mizuno (TKO)
Mitsuhiro Ishida defeated Jung Bu-Kyung (decision)
Katsuhiko Nagata defeated Artur Oumakhanov (decision)
Luis Firmino defeated Kazuyuki Miyata (rear naked choke)
Joachim Hansen defeated Kotetsu Boku (decision)
Hayato Sakurai defeated Hidetaka Monma (TKO)
Ikuhisa Minowa defeated Lee Kwan Bum (knee bar)

Dream 2

4/29/08
Saitama Super Arena (Saitama, Japan)
Main Event: Kazushi Sakuraba defeated Andrews Nakahara (neck crank)
Other Fights:

Gegard Mousasi defeated Denis Kang (triangle choke)
Kiyoshi Tamura defeated Masakatsu Funaki (TKO)
Ronaldo de Souza defeated Ian Murphy (rear naked choke)
Zelg Galesic defeated Magomed Sultanakhmedov (arm bar)
Yoon Dong Sik defeated Sungo Oyama (decision)
Taiei Kin defeated Ikuhisa Minowa (decision)
Shinya Aoki defeated Gesias Cavalcante (decision)

Dream 3

5/11/08
Saitama Super Arena (Saitama, Japan)
Main Event: Caol Uno defeated Mitsuhiro Ishida (rear naked choke)
Other Fights:

Eddie Alvarez defeated Joachim Hansen (decision)
Tatsuya Kawajiri defeated Luiz Firmino (decision)
Nick Diaz defeated Katsuya Inoue (TKO)
Daisuke Nakamura defeated Jung Bu-Kyung (KO)
Melvin Manhoef defeated Dae Won Kim (TKO)
Jason Miller defeated Katsuyori Shibata (TKO)

Takeshi Yamazaki defeated Shoji Maruyama (decision)

Dream 4

6/15/08

Yokohama Arena (Yokohama, Japan)

Main Event: Melvin Manhoef defeated Kazushi Sakuraba (KO)

Other Fights:

Ronaldo de Souza defeated Jason Miller (decision)
Zelg Galesic defeated Taiei Kin (TKO)
Gegard Mousasi defeated Yoon Dong Sik (decision)
Hideo Tokoro defeated Darren Uyenoyama (decision)
Ralek Gracie defeated Alavutdin Gadzhiyev (arm bar)
Alistair Overeem defeated Lee Tae-Hyun (KO)
Shinya Aoki defeated Katsuhiko Nagata (gogoplata)

Dream 5

7/21/08

Osaka-jo Hall (Osaka, Japan)

Main Event: Joachim Hansen defeated Shinya Aoki (TKO, won Dream Lightweight Grand Prix and Dream Lightweight Championship)

Other Fights:

Alistair Overeem defeated Mark Hunt (key lock)
Yoshihiro Akiyama defeated Katsuyori Shibata (Ezekiel choke)
Hideo Tokoro defeated Takeshi Yamazaki (decision)
Kuniyoshi Hironaka defeated Motoki Miyazawa (doctor stoppage)
Joseph Benavidez defeated Junya Kudo (guillotine choke)
Joachim Hansen defeated Kultar Gil (arm bar)
Eddie Alvarez defeated Tatsuya Kawajiri (TKO)
Shinya Aoki defeated Caol Uno (decision)
Daisuke Nakamura defeated Andy Ologun (arm bar)

Dream 6

9/23/08

Saitama Super Arena (Saitama, Japan)

Main Event: Gegard Mousasi defeated Ronaldo de Souza (KO, won Dream Middleweight Grand Prix and Dream Middleweight Championship)

Other Fights:

Mirko Cro Cop vs. Alistair Overeem (no contest)
Shinya Aoki defeated Todd Moore (neck crank)
Yoshihiro Akiyama defeated Masanori Tonooka (arm bar)
Hayato Sakurai defeated Kuniyoshi Hironaka (decision)
Masakatsu Funaki defeated Ikuhisa Minowa (heel hook)
Atsushi Yamamoto defeated Hideo Tokoro (decision)
Sergei Kharitonov defeated Jimmy Ambriz (KO)
Keita Nakamura defeated Adriano Martins (decision)
Ronaldo de Souza defeated Zelg Galesic (arm bar)
Gegard Mousasi defeated Melvin Manhoef (triangle choke)
Andrews Nakahara defeated Yoon Dong Sik (TKO)

Dream 7

3/8/09

Saitama Super Arena (Saitama, Japan)

Main Event: Masakazu Imanari defeated Atsushi Yamamoto (decision)

Other Fights:

Hiroyuki Takaya defeated Jong Won Kim (TKO)
Yoshiro Maeda defeated Micah Miller (decision)
Tatsuya Kawajiri defeated Ross Ebanez (rear naked choke)
Shinya Aoki defeated David Gardner (rear naked choke)
Mitsuhiro Ishida defeated Daisuke Nakamura (decision)
Abel Cullum defeated Akiyo Nishiura (decision)
Joe Warren defeated Chase Beebe (doctor stoppage)
Bibiano Fernandes defeated Takafumi Otsuka (decision)

Dream 8

4/5/09

Nippon Gaishi Hall (Nagoya, Japan)

Main Event: Hayato Sakurai defeated Shinya Aoki (TKO)

Other Fights:

Jason High defeated Yuya Shirai (rear naked choke)

Marius Zaromskis defeated Seichi Ikemoto (decision)

Andre Galvao defeated John Alessio (arm bar)

Daiki Hata defeated Hideo Tokoro (decision)

Jeff Monson defeated Sergei Kharitonov (north-south choke)

Riki Fukuda defeated Murilo Rua (decision)

Vitor Ribeiro defeated Katsuhiko Nagata (doctor stoppage)

Andrews Nakahara defeated Shungo Oyama (TKO)

Katsuyori Shibata defeated Ikuhisa Minowa (decision)

Dream 9

5/26/09

Yokohama Arena (Yokohama, Japan)

Main Event: Jason Miller vs. Ronaldo de Souza (no contest)

Other Fights:

Joe Warren defeated Norifumi Yamamoto (decision)

Bibiano Fernandes defeated Masakazu Imanari (decision)

Hiroyuki Takaya defeated Yoshiro Maeda (TKO)

Hideo Tokoro defeated Abel Cullum (rear naked choke)

Tatsuya Kawajiri defeated Gesias Cavalcante (decision)

Gegard Mousasi defeated Mark Hunt (Kimura)

Rameau Thierry Sokoudjou defeated Jan Nortje (TKO)

Hong-Man Choi defeated Jose Canseco (submission to strikes)

Ikuhisa Minowa defeated Bob Sapp (Achilles lock)

Dream 10

7/20/09

Saitama Super Arena (Saitama, Japan)

Main Event: Marius Zaromskis defeated Jason High (KO, won Dream Welterweight Grand Prix)

Other Fights:

Shinya Aoki defeated Vitor Ribeiro (decision)

Jesse Taylor defeated Yoon Dong Sik (TKO)

Paulo Filho defeated Melvin Manhoef (arm bar)

Katsunori Kikuno defeated Andre Dido (TKO)

Jason High defeated Andre Galvao (decision)

Marius Zaromskis defeated Hayato Sakurai (TKO)

Tarec Saffiedine defeated Seichi Ikemoto (decision)

Dream 11

10/6/09

Yokohama Arena (Yokohama, Japan)

Main Event: Hiroyuki Takaya defeated Bibiano Fernandes (decision, won Dream Featherweight Grand Prix and Dream Featherweight Championship)

Other Fights:

Shinya Aoki defeated Joachim Hansen (arm bar, won Dream Lightweight Championship)

Kazushi Sakuraba defeated Rubin Williams (Kimura)

Tatsuya Kawajiri defeated Melchor Manibusan (TKO)

Rameau Thierry Sokoudjou defeated Bob Sapp (TKO)

Ikuhisa Minowa defeated Hong-Man Choi (heel hook)

Bibiano Fernandes defeated Joe Warren (arm bar)

Hiroyuki Takaya defeated Hideo Tokoro (TKO)

Kazuyuki Miyata defeated D.J. Taiki (decision)

Dream 12

10/25/09

Osaka-jo Hall (Osaka, Japan)

Main Event: Alistair Overeem defeated James Thompson (guillotine choke)

Other Fights:

Eddie Alvarez defeated Katsunori Kikuno (arm triangle)

Marius Zaromskis defeated Myeon Ho Bae (KO)

Kazushi Sakuraba defeated Zelg Galesic (knee bar)

Yoon Dong Sik defeated Tarec Saffiedine (decision)

Yoshiro Maeda defeated Chase Beebe (rear naked choke)
Kuniyoshi Hironaka defeated Won Sik Park (corner stoppage)
Tomoya Miyashita defeated Keisuke Fujiwara (decision)

DYNAMITE!!

Dynamite!! 2008

(combined kickboxing/MMA event)
12/31/08
Saitama Super Arena (Saitama, Japan)
MMA Main Event: Kiyoshi Tamura defeated Kazushi Sakuraba (decision)
Other MMA Fights:

Shinya Aoki defeated Eddie Alvarez (heel hook, won WAMMA Lightweight Championship)
Melvin Manhoef defeated Mark Hunt (KO)
Mirko Cro Cop defeated Hong-Man Choi (TKO)
Hayato Sakurai defeated Katsuyori Shibata (TKO)
Semmy Schilt defeated Mighty Mo (triangle choke)
Bob Sapp defeated Akihito Tanaka (TKO)
Andy Ologun defeated Yukio Sakaguchi (KO)
Daisuke Nakamura defeated Hideo Tokoro (arm bar)
Ikuhisa Minowa defeated Errol Zimmerman (toe hold)

Dynamite!! 2009

(combined kickboxing/MMA event)
12/31/09
Saitama Super Arena (Saitama, Japan)
MMA Main Event: Hidehiko Yoshida defeated Satoshi Ishii (decision)
Other MMA Fights:

Shinya Aoki defeated Mizuto Hirota (hammer lock)
Gegard Mousasi defeated Gary Goodridge (TKO)
Alistair Overeem defeated Kazuyuki Fujita (KO)
Masanori Kanehara defeated Norifumi Yamamoto (decision)
Tatsuya Kawajiri defeated Kazunori Yokota (decision)
Hideo Tokoro defeated Jong Man Kim (decision)
Melvin Manhoef defeated Kazuo Misaki (TKO)
Akihiro Gono defeated Hayato Sakurai (arm bar)
Michihiro Omigawa defeated Hiroyuki Takaya (TKO)
Hiroshi Izumi defeated Katsuyori Shibata (decision)
Ikuhisa Minowa defeated Rameau Thierry Sokoudjou (TKO)

SENGOKU

Sengoku 1

Sengoku Vanguard
3/5/08
Yoyogi National Gymnasium (Tokyo, Japan)
Main Event: Josh Barnett defeated Hidehiko Yoshida (heel hook)
Other Fights:

Takanori Gomi defeated Duane Ludwig (TKO)
Kazuo Misaki defeated Siyar Bahadurzada (guillotine choke)
Kazuyuki Fujita defeated Peter Graham (north-south choke)
Evangelista Santos defeated Makoto Takimoto (Achilles lock)
Ryo Kawamura defeated Antonio Braga Neto (decision)
Nick Thompson defeated Fabricio Monteiro (decision)

Sengoku 2

5/18/08
Ariake Coliseum (Tokyo, Japan)
Main Event: Josh Barnett defeated Jeff Monson (decision)
Other Fights:

Roger Gracie defeated Yuki Kondo (rear naked choke)
Kevin Randleman defeated Ryo Kawamura (decision)
Yoshihiro Nakao defeated Jim York (TKO)
Jorge Santiago defeated Yuki Sasaki (arm bar)
Eiji Mitsuoka defeated Kwang Hee Lee (rear naked choke)
Mike Pyle defeated Dan Hornbuckle (triangle choke)
Satoru Kitaoka defeated Ian James Schaffa (guillotine choke)

Sengoku 3

6/8/08

Saitama Super Arena (Saitama, Japan)

Main Event: Hidehiko Yoshida defeated Maurice Smith (scarf hold)

Other Fights:

- Travis Wiuff defeated Kazuyuki Fujita (TKO)
- Kazuo Misaki defeated Logan Clark (decision)
- Nick Thompson defeated Michael Costa (Kimura)
- Sanae Kikuta defeated Chris Rice (arm bar)
- Marcio Cruz defeated Choi Mu Bae (triangle arm bar)
- Rodrigo Damm defeated Jorge Masvidal (TKO)
- Fabio Silva defeated Yoshiki Takahashi (KO)

Sengoku 4

8/24/08

Saitama Super Arena (Saitama, Japan)

Main Event: Takanori Gomi defeated Bang Seung Hwan (decision)

Other Fights:

- Frank Trigg defeated Makoto Takimoto (decision)
- Satoru Kitaoka defeated Clay French (Achilles lock)
- Eiji Mitsuoka defeated Rodrigo Damm (rear naked choke)
- Kazunori Yokota defeated Bojan Kosednar (decision)
- Mizuto Hirota defeated Ryan Schultz (KO)
- Dong Yi Yang defeated Pawel Nastula (TKO)
- Moise Rimbon defeated Peter Graham (rear naked choke)
- Valentijn Overeem defeated Kazuo Takahasi (KO)

Sengoku 5

9/28/08

Yoyogi National Gymnasium (Tokyo, Japan)

Main Event: Alexandre Ribeiro defeated Takashi Sugiura (TKO)

Other Fights:

- Muhammed Lawal defeated Travis Wiuff (TKO)
- Yuki Sasaki defeated Yuki Kondo (rear naked choke)
- Kazuhiro Nakamura defeated Paul Cahoon (decision)
- Jorge Santiago defeated Logan Clark (arm triangle)
- Siyar Bahadurzada defeated Evangelista Santos (TKO)
- Kiuma Kunioku defeated A Sol Kwon (decision)
- Jorge Masvidal defeated Ryan Schultz (TKO)

Sengoku 6

11/1/08

Saitama Super Arena (Saitama, Japan)

Main Event: Satoru Kitaoka defeated Kazunori Yokota (decision, won Sengoku Lightweight Grand Prix)

Other Fights:

- Jorge Santiago defeated Kazuhiro Nakamura (TKO)
- Sergey Golyaev defeated Takanori Gomi (decision)
- Muhammed Lawal defeated Fabio Silva (TKO)
- Antonio Rogerio Nogueira defeated Moise Rimbon (decision)
- Jorge Masvidal defeated Bang Seung Hwan (decision)
- Joe Doerkson defeated Izuru Takeuchi (TKO)
- Satoru Kitaoka defeated Eiji Mitsuoka (heel hook)
- Kazunori Yokota defeated Mizuto Hirota (decision)
- Kazuhiro Nakamura defeated Yuki Sasaki (decision)
- Jorge Santiago defeated Siyar Bahadurzada (heel hook)

Sengoku Rebellion 2009

1/4/09

Saitama Super Arena (Saitama, Japan)

Main Event: Satoru Kitaoka defeated Takanori Gomi (Achilles lock, won Sengoku Lightweight Championship)

Other Fights:

- Jorge Santiago defeated Kazuo Misaki (rear naked choke, won Sengoku Middleweight Championship)
- Sanae Kikuta defeated Hidehiko Yoshida (decision)
- Muhammed Lawal defeated Yukiya Naito (TKO)
- Antonio Silva defeated Yoshihiro Nakao (TKO)
- Eiji Mitsuoka defeated Sergey Golyaev (arm bar)
- Choi Mu Bae defeated Dave Herman (TKO)
- Maximo Blanco defeated Seigo Inoue (KO)

Hidetade Irie defeated Minoru Kato (TKO)

Sengoku 7

3/20/09

Yoyogi National Gymnasium (Tokyo, Japan)

Main Event: Muhammed Lawal defeated Ryo Kawamura (decision)

Other Fights:

- Hatsu Hioki defeated Chris Manuel (triangle arm bar)
- Nam Phan defeated Hideki Kadowaki (TKO)
- Jim York defeated James Thompson (KO)
- Michihiro Omigawa defeated L.C. Davis (decision)
- Marlon Sandro defeated Matt Jaggers (arm triangle)
- Masanori Kanehara defeated Jong Man Kim (decision)
- Chan Sung Jung defeated Shintaro Ishiwatari (rear naked choke)
- Ronnie Mann defeated Tetsuya Yamada (decision)
- Nick Denis defeated Seiya Kawahara (TKO)

Sengoku 8

5/2/09

Yoyogi National Gymnasium (Tokyo, Japan)

Main Event: Hatsu Hioki defeated Ronnie Mann (triangle choke)

Other Fight:

- Michihiro Omigawa defeated Nam Phan (TKO)
- Kazunori Yokota defeated Leonardo Santos (decision)
- Alexandre Ribeiro defeated Kei Yamamiya (KO)
- Masanori Kanehara defeated Chan Sung Jung (decision)
- Marlon Sandro defeated Nick Denis (KO)
- Makoto Takimoto defeated Michael Costa (heel hook)
- Stanislav Nedkov defeated Travis Wiuff (KO)
- Akihiko Mori defeated Maximo Blanco (DQ)
- Shigeki Osawa defeated Kota Ishibashi (decision)
- Hirotoshi Saito defeated Yoshitaka Abe (arm bar)

Sengoku 9

8/2/09

Saitama Super Arena (Saitama, Japan)

Main Event: Mizuto Hirota defeated Satoru Kitaoka (TKO, won Sengoku Lightweight Championship)

Other Fights:

- Masanori Kanehara defeated Michihiro Omigawa (decision, won Sengoku Featherweight Grand Prix)
- Kazuo Misaki defeated Kazuhiro Nakamura (guillotine choke)
- Blagoi Ivanov defeated Kazuyuki Fujita (decision)
- Dan Hornbuckle defeated Akihiro Gono (KO)
- Eiji Mitsuoka defeated Clay French (guillotine choke)
- Chan Sung Jung defeated Matt Jaggers (triangle choke)
- Michihiro Omigawa defeated Marlon Sandro (decision)
- Hatsu Hioki defeated Masanori Kanehara (decision)
- Yoshihiro Nakao defeated Mu Bae Choi (decision)
- Ikuo Usuda defeated Koji Ando (decision)
- Shigeki Osawa defeated Toru Harai (TKO)
- Ryosuke Komori defeated Takeshi Numajiri (TKO)

Sengoku 10

9/23/09

Saitama Super Arena (Saitama, Japan)

Main Event: Antz Nansen defeated Hiroshi Izumi (TKO)

Other Fights:

- Antonio Silva defeated Jim York (arm triangle)
- Makoto Takimoto defeated Jae Sun Lee (decision)
- Kazunori Yokota defeated Ryan Schultz (KO)
- Fabio Silva defeated Ryo Kawamura (corner stoppage)
- Dan Hornbuckle defeated Nick Thompson (TKO)
- Joe Doerkson defeated Takanori Sato (TKO)
- Maximo Blanco defeated Tetsuya Yamada (TKO)
- Ikuo Usuda defeated Woo Hyon Baek (TKO)
- Shigeki Osawa defeated Ki Hyun Kim (decision)
- Jae Hyun So defeated Ryosuke Komori (decision)

Sengoku 11

11/7/09

Ryogoku Kokugikan (Tokyo, Japan)

Main Event: Michihiro Omigawa defeated Hatsu Hioki (decision)

Other Fights:

Mamed Khalidov defeated Jorge Santiago (TKO)
Jorge Masvidal defeated Satoru Kitaoka (KO)
Tomoaki Ueyama defeated Hirokazu Konno (rear naked choke)
Kazunori Yokota defeated Eiji Mitsuoka (decision)
Stanislav Nedkov defeated Kevin Randleman (decision)
Akihiro Gono defeated Yoon Young Kim (decision)
Marlon Sandro defeated Yuji Hoshino (KO)
Dave Herman defeated Jim York (KO)
Ronnie Mann defeated Shigeki Osawa (decision)
Ryota Uozomi defeated Yuichiro Yajima (arm bar)

MOST CUMULATIVE TIME FIGHTING IN A PRIDE FC RING

1. Kazushi Sakuraba: 435 minutes in 27 fights
2. Akira Shoji: 298 minutes in 23 fights
3. Igor Vovchanchyn: 295 minutes in 27 fights
4. Wanderlei Silva: 280 minutes in 28 fights
5. Daijiro Matsui: 272 minutes in 15 fights
6. Antonio Rodrigo Nogueira: 253 minutes in 21 fights
7. Dan Henderson: 211 minutes in 18 fights
8. Kazuhiro Nakamura: 210 minutes in 17 fights
9. Heath Herring: 178 minutes in 17 fights
10. Mirko Cro Cop : 175 minutes in 24 fights
11. Alexander Otsuka: 163 minutes in 12 fights
12. Murilo Rua: 158 minutes in 13 fights
13. Quinton Jackson: 156 minutes in 17 fights
14. Ricardo Arona: 156 minutes in 12 fights
15. Renzo Gracie: 152 minutes in 8 fights
16. Daiju Takase: 135 minutes in 9 fights
17. Gary Goodridge: 133 minutes in 19 fights
18. Guy Mezger: 130 minutes in 10 fights
19. Antonio Rogerio Nogueira: 130 minutes in 10 fights
20. Fedor Emelianenko: 129 minutes in 15 fights
21. Royce Gracie: 125 minutes in 3 fights
22. Hidehiko Yoshida: 123 minutes in 12 fights
23. Ikuhisa Minowa: 122 minutes in 17 fights
24. Akihiro Gono: 115 minutes in 9 fights
25. Kazuo Misaki: 115 minutes in 8 fights

MOST FIGHTS IN A PRIDE FC RING

Wanderlei Silva: 28 fights (22-4-2)
Kazushi Sakuraba: 27 fights (18-8-1)
Igor Vovchanchyn: 27 fights (18-8-1)
Mirko Cro Cop: 24 fights (18-4-2)
Akira Shoji: 23 fights (9-12-2)
Antonio Rodrigo Nogueira: 21 fights (17-3-1)
Gary Goodridge: 19 fights (10-9-0)
Dan Henderson: 18 fights (13-5-0)
Quinton Jackson: 17 fights (12-5-0)
Kazuhiro Nakamura: 17 fights (11-6-0)
Ikuhisa Minowa: 17 fights (9-8-0)
Heath Herring: 17 fights (12-5-0)
Takanori Gomi: 15 fights (13-1-1)
Fedor Emelianenko: 15 fights (14-0-1)
Daijiro Matsui: 15 fights (5-8-2)
Alistair Overeem: 14 fights (7-7-0)

LONGEVITY IN PRIDE FC

Akira Shoji: 10 years = 2.3 fights/year
Wanderlei Silva: 9 years = 3.1 fights/year
Kazushi Sakuraba: 8 years = 3.4 fights/year
Igor Vovchanchyn: 8 years = 3.4 fights/year
Dan Henderson: 8 years = 2.3 fights/year
Gary Goodridge: 7 years = 2.7 fights/year
Mark Coleman: 7 years = 1.9 fights/year
Alexander Otsuka: 7 years = 1.7 fights/year
Renzo Gracie: 7 years = 1.1 fights/year
Mirko Cro Cop: 6 years = 4 fights/year
Antonio Rodrigo Nogueira: 6 years = 3.5 fights/year
Quinton Jackson: 6 years = 2.8 fights/year
Alistair Overeem: 6 years = 2.3 fights/year
Murilo Rua: 6 years = 2.2 fights/year
Ricardo Arona: 6 years = 2 fights/year
Antonio Rogerio Nogueira: 6 years = 1.7 fights/year
Gilbert Yvel: 6 years = 1.7 fights/year
Nobuhiko Takada: 6 years = 1.5 fights/year
Carlos Newton: 6 years = 1.5 fights/year
Mario Sperry: 6 years = 1.2 fights/year

LONGEST STREAK

Fedor Emelianenko: 8 wins, no contest, 6 wins
BEGIN: Pride 21 (6/23/02)
END: Pride Final Conflict 2004 (8/15/04)

Fedor won 8 matches in a row at Pride before finally going to a no contest with Antonio Rodrigo Nogueira at Pride Final Conflict 2004 due to "No Contest – Accidental Cut." You could consider his streak 14 wins at Pride.

In Pride, he defeated Semmy Schilt, Heath Herring, Antonio Rodrigo Nogueira, Kazuyuki Fujita, Gary Goodridge, Mark Coleman, Kevin Randleman, Naoya Ogawa, Antonio Rodrigo Nogueira, Tsuyoshi Kohsaka, Mirko Cro Cop, Wagner da Conceicao Martins (Son of Zulu), Mark Coleman, and Mark Hunt.

Wanderlei Silva: 4 wins, draw, 6 wins, draw, 8 wins
BEGIN: Pride 7 (9/12/99)
END: Pride 28 (10/31/04)

Between 9/12/99 (Pride 7) and 10/31/04 (Pride 28), Silva never lost a match.

He had two draws with Gilbert Yvel and Mirko Cro Cop but defeated Carl Greco, Daijiro Matsui, Bob Schrijber, Guy Mezger, Dan Henderson, Kazushi Sakuraba (twice), Shungo Oyama, Kazushi Sakuraba, Alexander Otsuka, Kiyoshi Tamura, Tatsuya Iwasaki, Hiromitsu Kanehara, Hidehiko Yoshida, Quinton Jackson (twice), Ikuhisa Minowa, and Yuki Kondo.

Finally, he was stopped by Mark Hunt via split decision at Pride Shockwave 2004.

Takanori Gomi: 10 wins
BEGIN: Pride Bushido 2 (2/15/04)
END: Pride Shockwave 2005 (12/31/05)

Paulo Filho: 8 wins
BEGIN: Pride 22 (9/29/02)
END: Pride Bushido 13 (11/5/06)

Mauricio Rua: 8 wins
BEGIN: Pride Bushido 1 (10/5/03)
END: Pride Final Conflict 2005 (8/28/05)

Antonio Rodrigo Nogueira: 7 wins
BEGIN: Pride 15 (7/29/01)
END: Pride 24 (12/23/02)

Antonio Rogerio Nogueira: 7 wins
BEGIN: Pride 20 (4/28/02)
END: Pride Total Elimination 2005 (4/23/05)

Mirko Cro Cop: 7 wins
BEGIN: Pride Bushido 3 (5/23/04)
END: Pride Critical Countdown 2005 (6/26/05)

Gilbert Yvel: 6 losses
BEGIN: Pride 12 (12/9/00)
END: Pride Total Elimination Absolute (5/5/06)

Yuki Kondo: 6 losses
BEGIN: Pride Final Conflict 2004 (8/15/04)
END: Pride Shockwave 2006 (12/31/06)

MOST DAYS BETWEEN FIGHTS IN PRIDE

Kimo Leopoldo: 2,805 days (Pride 1, 11/11/97: DRAW Dan Severn – Pride Bushido 8, 7/17/05: LOST Ikuhisa Minowa)

Frank Trigg: 2,652 days (Pride 8, 11/21/99: WON Fabiano Iha – Pride 33, 2/24/07: WON Kazuo Misaki)

Ricardo Morais: 1,960 days (Pride 8, 11/21/99: LOST Mark Coleman – Pride Bushido 6, 4/3/05: LOST Aleksander Emelianenko)

MOST MATCHES ENDING IN A KO/TKO

Wanderlei Silva: 17 matches (15 wins + 2 losses)
Mirko Cro Cop: 14 matches (13 wins + 1 loss)
Kazushi Sakuraba: 11 matches (4 wins + 7 losses)
Gary Goodridge: 11 matches (7 wins + 4 losses)
Quinton Jackson: 10 matches (7 wins + 3 losses)
Mauricio Rua: 10 matches (9 wins + 1 loss)
Igor Vovchanchyn: 10 matches (9 wins + 1 loss)
Ikuhisa Minowa: 8 matches (2 wins + 6 losses)
Dan Henderson: 8 matches (8 wins)
Alistair Overeem: 8 matches (4 wins + 4 losses)
Takanori Gomi: 7 matches (7 wins)
Akira Shoji: 7 matches (2 wins + 5 losses)
James Thompson: 7 matches (5 wins + 2 losses)
Heath Herring: 7 matches (5 wins + 2 losses)

MOST MATCHES ENDING IN A SUBMISSION

Kazushi Sakuraba: 11 matches (11 wins)
Antonio Rodrigo Nogueira: 11 matches (11 wins)
Igor Vovchanchyn: 7 matches (3 wins + 4 losses)
Fedor Emelianenko: 7 matches (7 wins)
Nobuhiko Takada: 6 matches (2 wins + 4 losses)
Mark Coleman: 6 matches (2 wins + 4 losses)
Josh Barnett: 6 matches (4 wins + 2 losses)
Hidehiko Yoshida: 6 matches (6 wins)
Heath Herring: 6 matches (5 wins + 1 loss)

MOST MATCHES ENDING IN A DECISION

Kazuhiro Nakamura: 9 matches (7 wins + 2 losses)
Igor Vovchanchyn: 9 matches (6 wins + 3 losses)
Akira Shoji: 9 matches (4 wins + 5 losses)
Wanderlei Silva: 8 matches (6 wins + 2 losses)
Dan Henderson: 8 matches (5 wins + 3 losses)
Daijiro Matsui: 8 matches (3 wins + 5 losses)
Antonio Rodrigo Nogueira: 8 matches (5 wins + 3 losses)
Kazuo Misaki: 7 matches (4 wins + 3 losses)
Ricardo Arona: 6 matches (5 wins + 1 loss)
Murilo Rua: 6 matches (2 wins + 4 losses)
Murilo Bustamante: 6 matches (2 wins + 4 losses)
Daiju Takase: 6 matches (3 wins + 3 losses)

MOST MATCHES ENDING IN A DQ, DRAW, OR NO CONTEST

Daijiro Matsui: 4 matches (2 DQs, 2 draws)
Wanderlei Silva: 2 matches (1 draw, 1 no contest)
Mirko Cro Cop: 2 matches (2 draws)
Mark Kerr: 2 matches (1 DQ, 1 no contest)
Gilbert Yvel: 2 matches (1 DQ, 1 no contest)
Akira Shoji: 2 matches (2 draws)

AVERAGE FIGHTS PER FIGHTER

312 people fought in Pride over the 68 events: an average of 3.8 fights/person. If you look at the fighters who appeared more than once, the average is 6 fights/person.

THE WINLESS

Sadly, these fellas could not even buy a win:

0-4

Yosuke Nishijima, Valentijn Overeem, Ryuta Sakurai, Hiromitsu Kanehara, Dong Sik Yoon

0-3

Yuhi Sano, Yoshihiro Takayama, Bob Schrijber, Takahiro Oba, Stefan Leko, Ryuta Sakurai, Dan Bobish, Kenichi Yamamoto, Kazuo Takahashi, Johil de Oliveira

THEY NEVER LOST (. . . IN PRIDE!)

Fedor Emelianenko: 14-0-1
Paulo Filho: 8-0-0
Shinya Aoki: 4-0-0
Rodrigo Gracie: 4-0-0
Yushin Okami: 3-0-0
Jeremy Horn, Sokun Koh, Frank Trigg, Rickson Gracie, Ricardo Almeida, Rameau Thierry Sokoudjou, Kyosuke Sasaki, Gilbert Melendez: 2-0-0

PRIDE FEUDS

4-match feud

Gracie vs. Sakuraba: Kazushi Sakuraba 4-0
Pride 8: Kazushi Sakuraba d. Royler Gracie (Kimura)
Pride 10: Kazushi Sakuraba d. Renzo Gracie (Kimura)
Pride 12: Kazushi Sakuraba d. Ryan Gracie (decision)
Pride Grand Prix 2000 Finals: Kazushi Sakuraba d. Royce Gracie (TKO)

3-match feuds

Josh Barnett vs. Mirko Cro Cop: Mirko Cro Cop 3-0 (2 submissions, 1 decision)

Antonio Rodrigo Nogueira vs. Fedor Emelianenko: Fedor Emelianenko 2-0 (2 decisions) and one fight went no contest.

Kazushi Sakuraba vs. Wanderlei Silva: Wanderlei Silva 3-1 (via TKO/KO)

Gracie vs. Takada: Gracies 3-0
Pride 1: Rickson Gracie d. Nobuhiko Takada (submission)
Pride 4: Rickson Gracie d. Nobuhiko Takada (submission)
Pride Grand Prix 2000 Opening Round: Royce Gracie d. Nobuhiko Takada (decision)

Notes on the Photos

Page 1: Tank Abbott
Page 6: Akebono (with Rick Roufus)
Page 12: Jeff Monson of the American Top Team
Page 17: Andre Arlovski
Page 25: Phil Baroni
Page 28: Vitor Belfort
Page 33: Jeff Blatnick interviewing Travis Wiuff
Page 37: Tito Ortiz (right) boxing
Page 41: Murilo Bustamante of the Brazilian Top Team weighing in
Page 45: Bruce Buffer
Page 47: Murilo Bustamante
Page 53: Shonie Carter makes an entrance
Page 57: Gil Castillo (left) in the WEC
Page 64: Mark Coleman
Page 67: Wesley Correira
Page 68: Patrick Côté (right) and Tito Ortiz
Page 71: Randy Couture (top) and Vitor Belfort
Page 75: Mirko Cro Cop (left) and Antonio Rodrigo Nogueira
Page 84: Herb Dean
Page 89: Nick Diaz
Page 97: Yves Edwards
Page 101: Fedor Emelianenko
Page 106: Rashad Evans (right) and Tito Ortiz
Page 113: Lorenzo Fertitta
Page 117: Kenny Florian in action
Page 118: Hermes Franca (right) at UFC 61
Page 120: Rich Franklin
Page 131: Wanderlei Silva delivering a knee
Page 137: Gary Goodridge
Page 145: Renzo Gracie
Page 157: Forrest Griffin (left) battles Anderson Silva
Page 159: Ground and pound from Reality Combat
Page 165: Dennis Hallman
Page 172: Dan Henderson celebrates
Page 177: Heath Herring (right)
Page 179: Jeremy Horn (left)
Page 182: Matt Hughes
Page 191: Antonio Inoki
Page 193: Teams from the IFL
Page 199: Quinton Jackson (left) and Chuck Liddell
Page 203: Keith Jardine (right)
Page 219: Mark Kerr
Page 238: Robbie Lawler
Page 243: Kung Le
Page 245: Renato Sobral (bottom) and Trevor Prangley
Page 247: Kimo Leopoldo
Page 254: Chuck Liddell
Page 258: Matt Lindland
Page 261: Ken Shamrock
Page 273: Nathan Marquardt kicking
Page 278: "Big" John McCarthy
Page 291: Frank Mir
Page 296: Jeff Monson
Page 297: Nick Diaz in the mount position
Page 308: Antonio Rodrigo Nogueira punishes Heath Herring
Page 319: Tito Ortiz
Page 327: Karo Parisyan
Page 328: B.J. Penn
Page 341: Wanderlei Silva with the Pride belt
Page 342: WWE's The Undertaker with Matt Hughes and team
Page 344: Jens Pulver
Page 349: Stephen Quadros (right)
Page 352: Kevin Randleman takes down Kazushi Sakuraba
Page 353: Marc Ratner
Page 361: Ricco Rodriguez
Page 362: Joe Rogan interviews Ken Shamrock
Page 364: Mauricio Rua punching
Page 371: Bas Rutten holding Pride Dolls
Page 374: Kazushi Sakuraba

Acknowledgments

Jonathan Snowden would like to thank:

Kristina, Sean, and Eli for their patience while I watched a huge number of fights and talked for hours on the phone. Professionally, I couldn't have done this without Dave Meltzer, Jeremy Botter, Nate Wilcox, Alan Conceicao, and everyone else who made things happen. Thanks to the crew at ECW Press who are such a pleasure to work with, especially Michael Holmes for his guidance and support. And a special thanks to Kendall Shields. Kendall made so many great suggestions for *Total MMA* that I had to bring him on board for this one and I'm glad I did. He made me look good. Again.

Kendall Shields would like to thank:

The instructors who inspired my love of the martial arts — Jorge Comrie, Bill Anderson, Jimmie Warren — and the training partners and students who help sustain it. Thanks to Jonathan for bringing me on board as a partner in this project, and to Michael Holmes and everyone at ECW Press for their enthusiasm from the outset. Thanks above all to my wife, Gillian, for her unfailing patience, love, and support.